D1609548

Department of Economic
and Social Affairs
Statistics Division

Département des affaires
économiques et sociales
Division de statistique

Statistical Yearbook
Fiftieth issue
Data available as of March 2006

Annuaire statistique
Cinquantième édition
Données disponibles en mars 2006

United Nations | Nations Unies
New York, 2006

Department of Economic and Social Affairs

The Department of Economic and Social Affairs of the United Nations Secretariat is a vital interface between global policies in the economic, social and environmental spheres and national action. The Department works in three main interlinked areas: (i) it compiles, generates and analyses a wide range of economic, social and environmental data and information on which States Members of the United Nations draw to review common problems and to take stock of policy options; (ii) it facilitates the negotiations of Member States in many intergovernmental bodies on joint courses of action to address ongoing or emerging global challenges; and (iii) it advises interested Governments on the ways and means of translating policy frameworks developed in United Nations conferences and summits into programmes at the country level and, through technical assistance, helps build national capacities.

Note

ST/ESA/STAT/SER.S/26

UNITED NATIONS PUBLICATION
Sales No. E/F.06.XVII.1

ISBN 92-1-061220-5
ISSN 0082-8459

Département des affaires économiques et sociales

Le Département des affaires économiques et sociales du Secrétariat de l'Organisation des Nations Unies assure le lien essentiel entre les politiques adoptées au plan international dans les domaines économique, social et écologique et les mesures prises au plan national. Il mène ses activités dans trois grands domaines interdépendants : i) il compile, produit et analyse une grande variété de données et d'informations économiques, sociales et écologiques dont les États Membres de l'ONU tirent parti pour examiner les problèmes communs et faire le point sur les possibilités d'action; ii) il facilite les négociations que les États Membres mènent dans un grand nombre d'organes intergouvernementaux sur les moyens d'action à employer conjointement pour faire face aux problèmes mondiaux existants ou naissants; et iii) il aide les gouvernements intéressés à traduire les orientations politiques établies lors des conférences et sommets de l'ONU en programmes nationaux et contribue à renforcer les capacités des pays en leur apportant une assistance technique.

Note

ST/ESA/STAT/SER.S/26

PUBLICATION DES NATIONS UNIES
Numéro de vente : E/F.06.XVII.1

ISBN 92-1-061220-5
ISSN 0082-8459

Preface

This is the fiftieth issue of the United Nations *Statistical Yearbook*, prepared by the Statistics Division of the Department of Economic and Social Affairs. Ever since the compilation of data for the *Statistical Yearbook* series was initiated in 1948, it has consistently provided a wide range of internationally available statistics on social and economic conditions and activities at the national, regional and world levels.

The fiftieth edition continues that tradition, this time with a new look. The *Yearbook* has undergone a facelift and has been printed in colour for the first time, which has significantly improved its readability and, we hope, its appeal to our users.

The tables include series covering from two to ten years, depending upon data availability and space constraints. The ten-year tables generally cover the years 1994 to 2003 or 1995 to 2004. For the most part, the statistics presented are those which were available to the Statistics Division as of March 2006.

The *Yearbook* tables are based on data which have been compiled by the Statistics Division mainly from official national and international sources as these are more authoritative and comprehensive, more generally available as time series and more comparable among countries than other sources. These sources include the United Nations Statistics Division in the fields of national accounts, industry, energy, transport and international trade, the United Nations Statistics Division and Population Division in the field of demographic statistics, and over 20 offices of the United Nations system and international organizations in other specialized fields. In a few cases, official sources have been supplemented by other sources and estimates, where these have been subjected to professional scrutiny and debate and are consistent with other independent sources.

The United Nations agencies and other international, national and specialized organizations which furnished data are listed under "Statistical sources and references" at the end of the *Yearbook*. Acknowledgement is gratefully made for their generous and valuable cooperation in continually providing data.

The 76 tables of the *Yearbook* are organized in four parts. The first part presents key world and regional aggregates and totals. In the other three parts, the subject matter is generally presented by countries or areas, with world and regional aggregates shown in some cases only. Parts two, three and four cover, respectively, population and social topics, national economic activity and international economic relations. Each chapter ends with brief technical notes on statistical sources and methods for the tables it includes.

Préface

La présente édition de l'*Annuaire statistique* des Nations Unies est la cinquantième, préparée par la Division de statistique du Département des affaires économiques et sociales. Depuis son instauration en 1948 comme outil de compilation des données statistiques internationales, l'*Annuaire statistique* s'efforce de constamment diffuser un large éventail de statistiques disponibles sur les activités et conditions économiques et sociales, aux niveaux national, régional et mondial.

La cinquantième édition ne rompt pas avec cette tradition, même si elle se dote d'un nouveau visuel. L'*Annuaire* a fait peau neuve et a, pour la première fois, été imprimé en couleurs, ce qui a assurément amélioré sa lisibilité et, nous l'espérons, son attrait aux yeux des utilisateurs.

Les tableaux présentent des séries qui couvrent de deux à dix ans, en fonction de la disponibilité des données et des contraintes d'espace. Les tableaux décennaux couvrent généralement les années 1994 à 2003 ou 1995 à 2004. La majeure partie des statistiques présentées ici sont celles dont disposait la Division de statistique en mars 2006.

Les tableaux de l'*Annuaire* sont construits essentiellement à partir des données compilées par la Division de statistique et provenant de sources officielles, nationales et internationales; c'est en effet la meilleure source si l'on veut des données fiables, complètes et comparables, et si l'on a besoin de séries chronologiques. Ces sources sont: la Division de statistique des Nations Unies pour ce qui concerne la comptabilité nationale, l'industrie, l'énergie, les transports et le commerce extérieur, la Division de statistique et la Division de la population des Nations Unies pour les statistiques démographiques; et plus de 20 bureaux du système des Nations Unies et d'organisations internationales pour les autres domaines spécialisés. Dans quelques cas, les données officielles sont complétées par des informations et des estimations provenant d'autres sources qui ont été examinées par des spécialistes et confirmées par des sources indépendantes.

Les institutions spécialisées des Nations Unies et les autres organisations internationales, nationales et spécialisées qui ont fourni des données sont énumérées dans la section "Sources statistiques et références" figurant à la fin de l'ouvrage. Les auteurs de l'*Annuaire* statistique les remercient de leur précieuse et généreuse collaboration.

Les 76 tableaux de l'*Annuaire* sont regroupés en quatre parties. La première partie présente les principaux agrégats et totaux aux niveaux mondial et régional. Dans les trois parties suivantes, les thèmes sont généralement présentés par pays ou régions. Les agrégats mondiaux ou régionaux ne son indiqués que dans certains cas seulement. Ces trois parties sont consacrées à la population et aux questions sociales (deuxième partie), à l'activité économique nationale (troisième partie) et aux relations économiques internationales (quatrième partie). Chaque

The three annexes contain information on country and area nomenclature and the conversion coefficients and factors used in the various tables, and list those tables which were added to or omitted from the last issue of the *Yearbook*.

* * *

The *Statistical Yearbook* is prepared by the Statistical Dissemination Section, Statistical Services Branch of the Statistics Division, Department of Economic and Social Affairs of the United Nations Secretariat. The programme manager is Mary Jane Holupka and the chief editor is Keping Yao. They are assisted by Anna Marie Scherning and Maria Jakosalem. Juni Sairin, Thataw Batun, Sibylle Marxgut, Jacob Assa, Leah McDavid, Naoko Mishima and Xiomara Fiallo-Hernandez also contributed to the production of this *Yearbook*. Bogdan Dragovic developed the software and Alain Gaugris helped with the French translation of the Introduction. Diego Aragon and Rachel Babruskinas of the Copy Preparation and Proofreading Section deserve special thanks for greatly enhancing the *Yearbook*'s presentation by formatting the tables and texts in colour.

Comments on the present *Yearbook* and its future evolution are welcome. They may be sent via e-mail to statistics@un.org or to the Director, United Nations Statistics Division, New York, NY 10017, USA.

chapitre termine par une brève note technique sur les sources et les méthodes statistiques utilisées pour les tableaux présentés.

Les trois annexes donnent des renseignements sur la nomenclature des pays et des zones, ainsi que sur les coefficients et facteurs de conversion employés dans les différents tableaux. Une liste des tableaux ajoutés et supprimés depuis la dernière édition de l'*Annuaire* y est également disponible.

* * *

L'*Annuaire statistique* est préparé par la Section de la diffusion des statistiques, Service des statistiques de services de la Division de statistique, Département des affaires économiques et sociales du Secrétariat de l'Organisation des Nations Unies. La responsable du programme est Mary Jane Holupka, et le rédacteur en chef est Keping Yao. Ils sont secondés par Anna Marie Scherning et Maria Jakosalem. Juni Sairin, Thataw Batun, Sibylle Marxgut, Jacob Assa, Leah McDavid, Naoko Mishima et Xiomara Fiallo-Hernandez contribuent également à la publication de cet *Annuaire*. Bogdan Dragovic est chargé des logiciels. Alain Gaugris s'est chargé de la traduction en français de l'Introduction. Diego Aragon et Rachel Babruskinas, de la Section de la préparation de copie et de la correction d'épreuves, méritent un remerciement particulier pour avoir fortement amélioré le visuel de l'*Annuaire* en intégrant des couleurs aux tableaux et au texte.

Les observations sur la présente édition de l'*Annuaire* et les suggestions de modification pour l'avenir seront reçues avec intérêt. Elles peuvent être envoyées par message électronique à statistics@un.org, ou adressées au Directeur de la Division de statistique des Nations Unies, New York, N.Y. 10017 (États Unis d'Amérique).

Contents

Table des matières

Contents (*continued*)

Table des matières (*suite*)

Contents (*continued*)

Table des matières (*suite*)

Contents (*continued*)

Table des matières (*suite*)

** Asterisks preceding table names identify tables that were presented in previous issues of the *Statistical Yearbook* which are not contained in the present issue. These tables will be updated in future issues of the *Yearbook* when new data become available.

** Ce symbole indique les tableaux publiés dans les éditions précédentes de l'*Annuaire statistique* mais qui n'ont pas été repris dans la présente édition. Ces tableaux seront actualisés dans les futures livraisons de l'*Annuaire* à mesure que des données nouvelles deviendront disponibles.

Explanatory notes

In general, the statistics presented in the present publication are based on information available to the Statistics Division of the United Nations Secretariat as of March 2006.

Units of measurement

The metric system of weights and measures has been employed throughout the *Statistical Yearbook*. For conversion coefficients and factors, see annex II.

Country notes and nomenclature

As a general rule, the data presented in the *Yearbook* relate to a given country or area within its present de facto boundaries. A complete list of countries and territories is presented in Annex I.

It should be noted that unless otherwise indicated, for statistical purposes, the data for China exclude those for Hong Kong Special Administrative Region of China, Macao Special Administrative Region of China and Taiwan province of China.

Symbols and conventions used in the tables

.	A point is used to indicate decimals.
-	A hyphen between years, e.g., 1998-1999, indicates the full period involved, including the beginning and end years.
/	A slash between years indicates a financial year, school year or crop year, e.g., 1998/99.
...	Data not available or not applicable.
0 or 0.0	Less than half of the unit used.
*	Provisional or estimated figure.
#	Marked break in series.

Details and percentages in the tables do not necessarily add to totals because of rounding.

Numbers in square brackets ([ ]) in the text refer to the numbered entries in the section "Statistical sources and references" at the end of the *Yearbook*.

Notes explicatives

En général, les statistiques qui figurent dans la présente publication sont fondées sur les informations dont disposait la Division de statistique du Secrétariat de l'ONU en mars 2006.

Unités de mesure

Le système métrique de poids et mesures a été utilisé dans tout l'*Annuaire statistique*. On trouvera à l'annexe II les coefficients et facteurs de conversion.

Notes sur les pays et nomenclature

En règle générale, les données renvoient au pays ou zone en question dans ses frontières actuelles effectives. Une liste complete des pays et territoires figure à l'annexe I.

Il convient de noter que sauf indication contraire, les données statistiques relatives à la Chine ne comprennent pas celles qui concernent la région administrative spéciale de Hong Kong, la région administrative spéciale de Macao et la province chinoise de Taiwan.

Signes et conventions employés dans les tableaux

.	Les décimales sont précédées d'un point.
-	Un tiret entre des années, par exemple "1998-1999", indique que la période est embrassée dans sa totalité, y compris la première et la dernière année.
/	Une barre oblique entre des années renvoie à un exercice financier, à une année scolaire ou à une campagne agricole, par exemple "1998/99".
...	Données non disponibles ou non applicables.
0 ou 0.0	Quantité inférieure à la moitié de l'unité utilisée.
*	Chiffre provisoire ou estimatif.
#	Discontinuité notable dans la série.

Les chiffres étant arrondis, les totaux ne correspondent pas toujours à l a somme exacte des éléments ou pourcentages figurant dans les tableaux.

Les chiffres figurant entre crochets ([ ]) se réfèrent aux entrées numérotées dans la liste des sources et références statistiques à la fin de l'ouvrage.

Introduction

Introduction

Celebrating over 50 years of global data service

This is the fiftieth issue of the United Nations *Statistical Yearbook*, prepared by the Statistics Division of the Department of Economic and Social Affairs. When such milestones are reached, often the natural tendency is to look ahead by looking back and to make a retrospective assessment of the event or product being commemorated. The United Nations Statistics Division feels a sense of pride in drawing the readers' attention to the fact that this compendium has been updated and released for publication consistently fifty times so far. This is an opportunity to take stock of the *Statistical Yearbook*'s success in providing an overall portrait of the evolving socio-economic situation of the world and to appraise how well it has stood the test of time as a useful vehicle which summarizes, in a comprehensive and convenient way, a great variety of important international statistics. At the same time, a reflection is warranted as to how to meet the challenges that lie ahead for the global statistical system, and for such a print publication in this electronic era.

Objective and content of the *Statistical Yearbook*

The main purpose of the *Statistical Yearbook* is to provide in a single volume a comprehensive compilation of internationally available statistics on social and economic conditions and activities, at world, regional and national levels, covering a ten-year period to the extent possible.

Most of the statistics presented in the *Yearbook* are extracted from more detailed, specialized databases prepared by the Statistics Division and by many other international statistical services. Thus, while the specialized databases concentrate on monitoring topics and trends in particular social and economic fields, the *Statistical Yearbook* tables aim to provide data for a more comprehensive, overall description of social and economic structures, conditions, changes and activities. The objective has been to collect, systematize, coordinate and present in a consistent way the most essential components of comparable statistical information which can give a broad picture of social and economic processes.

The content of the *Statistical Yearbook* is planned to serve a general readership. The *Yearbook* endeavours to provide information for various bodies of the United Nations system as well as for other international organizations, governments and non-governmental organizations, national statistical, economic and social policy bodies, scientific and educational institutions, libraries and the public. Data published in the *Statistical Yearbook* may also be of interest to companies and enterprises and to agencies engaged in market research. The *Statistical Yearbook* thus provides information on a wide range of social and economic

Célébration de plus de 50 ans de fourniture de données mondiales

La présente édition de l'*Annuaire statistique* des Nations Unies, préparée par la Division de statistique du Département des affaires économiques et sociales, est la cinquantième. Lorsqu'un tel cap est franchi, une tendance naturelle est d'envisager l'avenir en se tournant vers le passé et en effectuant une évaluation rétrospective de l'évènement ou du produit que l'on commémore. La Division de statistique des Nations Unies est fière d'attirer l'attention du lecteur sur le fait que cet annuaire a, sur une base régulière, été jusqu'à présent actualisé et publié cinquante fois. Une opportunité lui est ici offerte de faire le point sur le succès de l'*Annuaire statistique*, en brossant un portrait général de l'évolution de la situation socioéconomique mondiale, et en évaluant sa persistance à travers les années à constituer un instrument utile qui résume, de façon à la fois pratique et exhaustive, des statistiques internationales importantes et variées. Dans le même temps, une réflexion est engagée pour relever les défis qui s'annoncent, concernant d'abord le système statistique mondial, mais aussi l'existence même, à l'ère du numérique, d'une telle publication en format papier.

Objectif et contenu de l'*Annuaire statistique*

Le principal objectif de l'*Annuaire statistique* est de fournir en un seul volume un inventaire complet de statistiques internationales concernant la situation et les activités sociales et économiques aux niveaux mondial, régional et national, sur une période s'étalant, dans la mesure du possible, sur dix ans.

La plupart des données qui figurent dans l'*Annuaire statistique* proviennent de bases de données spécialisées davantage détaillées, préparées par la Division de statistique et par bien d'autres services statistiques internationaux. Tandis que les bases de données spécialisées se concentrent sur le suivi de domaines socioéconomiques particuliers, les données de l'*Annuaire* sont présentées de telle sorte qu'elles fournissent une description globale et exhaustive des structures, conditions, transformations et activités socioéconomiques. On a cherché à recueillir, systématiser, coordonner et présenter de manière cohérente les principales informations statistiques comparables, de manière à dresser un tableau général des processus socioéconomiques.

Le contenu de l'*Annuaire statistique* a été élaboré en vue d'un lectorat large. Les renseignements fournis devraient ainsi pouvoir être utilisés par les divers organismes du système des Nations Unies, mais aussi par d'autres organisations internationales, les gouvernements et les organisations non gouvernementales, les organismes nationaux de statistique et de politique économique et sociale, les institutions scientifiques et les établissements

Figure 1
A sample of various facts published in the 50th issue of the *Statistical Yearbook*

Figure 1
Echantillon de différents faits publiés dans la 50ème édition de l'*Annuaire statistique*

International tourism	Aid to developing countries
· From 2000 to 2004, 100% of the tourists visiting Andorra were Europeans. · In 2004, the number of tourists visiting the United States had almost recovered to the level in 2001 after two consecutive declines in 2002 and 2003.	By 2000, net official development assistance to developing countries from Denmark, Luxembourg, the Netherlands, Norway and Sweden met the United Nations aid target of 0.7% of gross national income.
Source of the data: United Nations World Tourism Organization.	Source of the data: Organisation for Economic Co-operation and Development.
Civil aviation	**Population**
In 2003, 26,264 million kilometres were flown and 1,691,233,000 passengers were carried on scheduled airline services.	Macao Special Administrative Region of China had the highest population density in 2003 —17,118 people per square kilometre of surface area.
Source of the data: International Civil Aviation Organization.	Source of the data: United Nations Statistics Division.
Beer	**Education**
Of all countries reporting to the UN Statistics Division, Germany was the biggest beer producer in 2003 with 98,933 thousand hectolitres.	In 2004, six students were enrolled in tertiary education in the Turks and Caicos Islands. All of them were female.
Source of the data: United Nations Statistics Division.	Source of the data: UNESCO Institute for Statistics.

Tourisme international	Aide aux pays en développement
· De 2000 à 2004, 100% des touristes visitant Andorre étaient Européens. · En 2004, le nombre de touristes visitant les Etats-Unis était quasiment identique à 2001, après deux années consécutives de déclin, en 2002 and 2003.	En 2000, l'assistance officielle nette aux pays en développement du Danemark, du Luxembourg, des Pays-Bas, de la Norvège et de la Suède atteignait la cible d'aide des Nations Unies établie à 0,7% du revenu national brut.
Source : Organisation mondiale du tourisme.	Source : Organisation de coopération et de développement économiques.
Aviation civile	**Population**
En 2003, 26 264 000 000 de kilomètres ont été parcourus et 1 691 233 000 passagers ont été transportés par les compagnies aériennes commerciales.	La région administrative spéciale de Macao de la Chine avait en 2003 la plus forte densité de population —17 118 habitants au kilomètre carré.
Source : Organisation de l'aviation civile internationale.	Source : Division de statistique des Nations Unies.
Bière	**Instruction**
De tous les pays rendant compte à la Division de statistique de l'ONU, l'Allemagne était le premier producteur de bière en 2003, avec 98 933 000 hectolitres.	En 2004, six étudiantes ont entamé des études supérieures dans les îles Turques-et-Caïques.
Source : Division de statistique des Nations Unies.	Source : Institut de statistiques de l'UNESCO.

issues which are of concern in the United Nations system and among the governments and peoples of the world. A particular value of the *Yearbook* is that it facilitates meaningful analysis of issues by systematizing and coordinating the data across many fields and shedding light on such interrelated issues as:

- General economic growth and related economic conditions;
- Progress towards the Millennium Development Goals;
- Population and urbanization, and their growth and impact;
- Employment, inflation and wages;
- Energy production and consumption and the development of new energy sources;
- Expansion of trade;
- Supply of food and alleviation of hunger;
- The financial situation of countries and external payments and receipts;
- Education, training and eradication of illiteracy;
- Improvement in general living conditions;
- Pollution and protection of the environment;
- Assistance provided to developing countries for social and economic development purposes.

d'enseignement, les bibliothèques et les particuliers. Les données publiées dans l'*Annuaire* peuvent également intéresser les sociétés et entreprises, et les organismes spécialisés dans les études de marché. L'*Annuaire* présente des informations sur un large éventail de questions socioéconomiques liées aux préoccupations actuelles du système des Nations Unies, des gouvernements et des peuples du monde entier. Une qualité particulière de l'*Annuaire* est de faciliter une analyse approfondie de ces questions en systématisant et en articulant les données d'un domaine/secteur à l'autre, et en apportant un éclairage sur des sujets interdépendants, tels que :

- La croissance économique générale, et les conditions économiques qui lui sont liées;
- Les progrès accomplis dans la réalisation des Objectifs du Millénaire pour le Développement;
- La population et l'urbanisation, leur croissance et leur impact;
- L'emploi, l'inflation et les salaires;
- La production et la consommation d'énergie et le développement de nouvelles sources d'énergie;
- L'expansion des échanges;

Historical background of the *Statistical Yearbook*

The first issue of the United Nations *Statistical Yearbook* was released in 1949 - only four years after the establishment of the United Nations itself. The *Yearbook* was prepared by the Statistical Office of the United Nations, which was located at that time in Lake Success, New York. The new *Statistical Yearbook* was a continuation as well as a considerable expansion of the work begun in Geneva in 1926 by the League of Nations, which published 17 issues of its *International Statistical Year-Book* from 1927 to 1945. The first United Nations *Statistical Yearbook* in 1949 included 158 statistical tables and contained 482 pages. Today's *Yearbook* contains almost twice the amount of pages, reflecting a considerable expansion both in terms of topics and country coverage. This is also testimony to the advancements of the global statistical system and the strengthening of statistical capacity in many countries of the world.

Table 1
Comparison of *Statistical Yearbook* prices
and US wages – then and now

Statistical Yearbook issue	Purchase price of the *Statistical Yearbook* (US dollars)	Wages in manufacturing: wage earners in the United States (US dollars)
1st issue, published 1949[1]	6	1.40 per hour (in 1949)
50th issue, published 2006[1]	145	16.14 per hour (in 2004)

Source of wage data: International Labour Organization.
[1] Since several issues were released biennially, the 50 issues of the *Yearbook* have been published over a period of more than 50 years.

Evolution of the *Statistical Yearbook*

Thematic coverage

A review of the topics covered in the *Statistical Yearbook* reveals continuity and change at the same time. Some of the statistical series presented today are in fact very similar or even identical to those in the first issues. The "classic" statistical series, such as population (see figure 2), agriculture, industrial production and international trade, will always continue to be relevant and of interest. One of the great values of the *Statistical Yearbook* has in fact been the continuity and stability of its contents. Since official statistics are most valuable when they can be used as a reference point to measure change and gauge whether progress has been made or not, data which have been measured consistently over an extended period of time are essential if meaningful comparisons are to be made.

On the other hand, the selection of topics covered by the *Statistical Yearbook* during the past several decades has also reflected the changing panorama of world economic and social

- L'approvisionnement alimentaire et la lutte contre la faim;
- La situation financière, les paiements et recettes extérieurs des pays;
- L'éducation, la formation et l'élimination de l'analphabétisme;
- L'amélioration des conditions de vie;
- La pollution et la protection de l'environnement;
- L'assistance aux pays en développement à des fins socioéconomiques.

Petite histoire de l'*Annuaire statistique*

La première édition de l'*Annuaire statistique* date de 1949 – quatre ans seulement après la création des Nations Unies elles-mêmes. L'*Annuaire* fut préparé par l'Office statistique des Nations Unies, situé à l'époque à Lake Success, dans l'État de New York. Le nouvel *Annuaire statistique* constitua la continuation, mais aussi un considérable élargissement, du travail initié à Genève en 1926 par la Ligue des Nations, qui elle-même avait publié 17 éditions de son *Annuaire statistique international* entre 1927 et 1945. La première édition de l'*Annuaire statistique* de 1949 comportait 482 pages et 158 tableaux statistiques. Aujourd'hui, l'*Annuaire* a à peu près doublé de volume, ce qui reflète une considérable expansion, à la fois en termes de sujets et de pays couverts. C'est aussi un témoignage des avancées du système statistique global et du renforcement de la capacité statistique dans nombre de pays de par le monde.

Tableau 1
Comparaison du prix de l'*Annuaire statistique* et des salaires
américains – à l'époque et aujourd'hui

Edition de l'*Annuaire statistique*	Prix à l'achat de l'*Annuaire statistique* ($ E.U.)	Salaires dans le secteur manufacturier américain ($ E.U.)
1ère édition, publiée en 1949[1]	6	1,40 de l'heure (en 1949)
50ème édition, publiée en 2006[1]	145	16,14 de l'heure (en 2004)

Source : Bureau International du Travail
[1] Dans la mesure où plusieurs éditions ont été publiées sur une base biannuelle, les 50 éditions de l'*Annuaire* couvrent une période supérieure à 50 ans.

Evolution de l'*Annuaire statistique*

Couverture thématique

Un examen des sujets abordés par l'*Annuaire statistique* révèle une continuité et un changement tout à la fois. Certaines des séries statistiques présentées aujourd'hui sont en fait très similaires, voire identiques, à celles des premières éditions. Les séries statistiques classiques, telles que la population (cf. Figure 2),

Figure 2
World population by region, 1950-2003 (percentages)

Figure 2
Population mondiale par région, 1950-2003 (pourcentages)

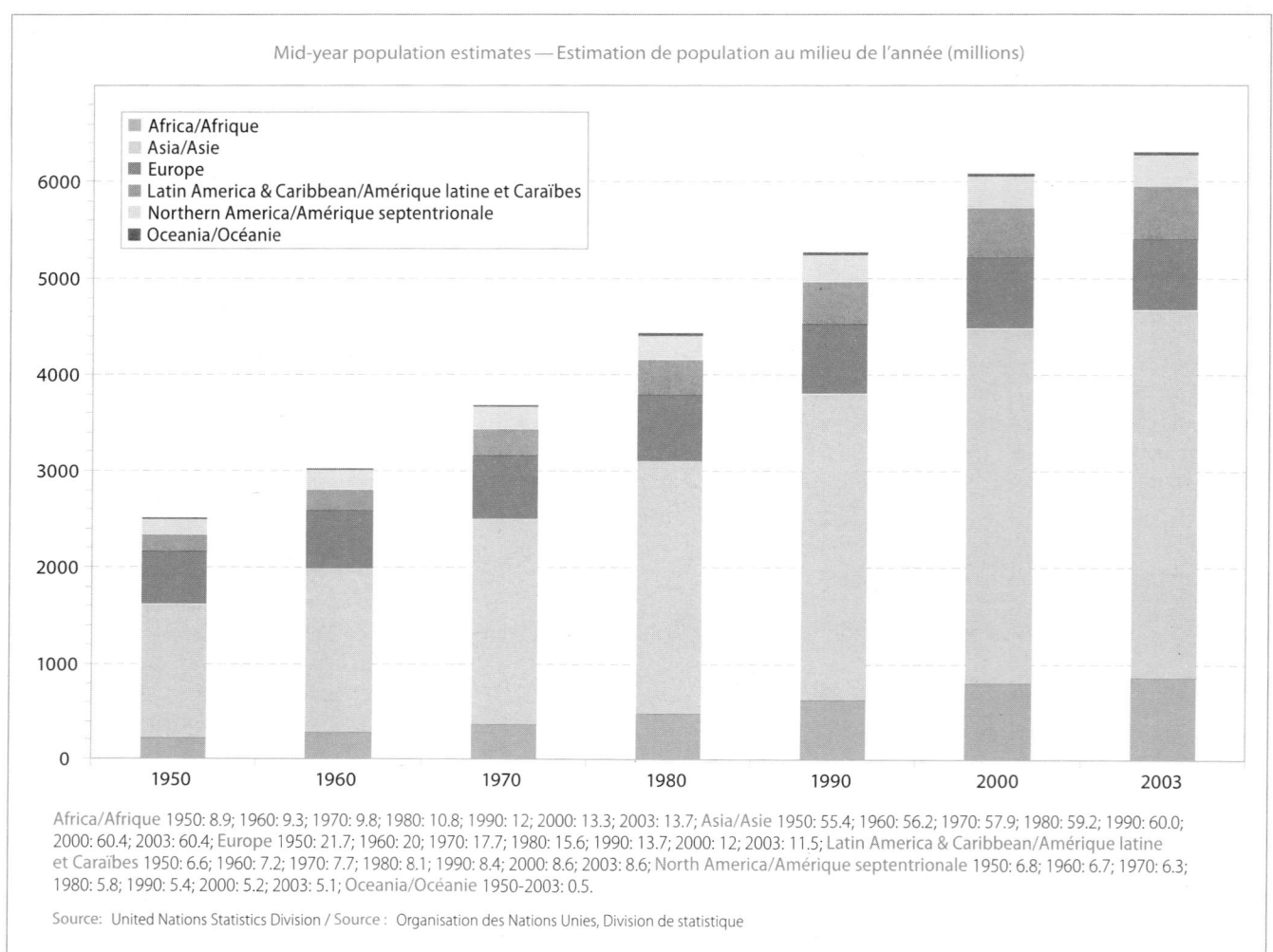

Mid-year population estimates — Estimation de population au milieu de l'année (millions)

- Africa/Afrique
- Asia/Asie
- Europe
- Latin America & Caribbean/Amérique latine et Caraïbes
- Northern America/Amérique septentrionale
- Oceania/Océanie

Africa/Afrique 1950: 8.9; 1960: 9.3; 1970: 9.8; 1980: 10.8; 1990: 12; 2000: 13.3; 2003: 13.7; Asia/Asie 1950: 55.4; 1960: 56.2; 1970: 57.9; 1980: 59.2; 1990: 60.0; 2000: 60.4; 2003: 60.4; Europe 1950: 21.7; 1960: 20; 1970: 17.7; 1980: 15.6; 1990: 13.7; 2000: 12; 2003: 11.5; Latin America & Caribbean/Amérique latine et Caraïbes 1950: 6.6; 1960: 7.2; 1970: 7.7; 1980: 8.1; 1990: 8.4; 2000: 8.6; 2003: 8.6; North America/Amérique septentrionale 1950: 6.8; 1960: 6.7; 1970: 6.3; 1980: 5.8; 1990: 5.4; 2000: 5.2; 2003: 5.1; Oceania/Océanie 1950-2003: 0.5.

Source: United Nations Statistics Division / Source : Organisation des Nations Unies, Division de statistique

development. In addition to the above-mentioned long-standing statistical series, data on additional topics addressing new economic and emerging social and environmental concerns have been introduced in the *Statistical Yearbook* at appropriate intervals.

In the economic sphere, the expansion of topics has reflected the fact that the focus of human activities has shifted over time from the traditional manufacturing and agricultural activities to other industries, especially those in the service industry. For example, data series on science and technology (e.g. gross domestic expenditure on research and development by source of funds), were added in the early 1970s, and several series on telecommunication were added in the early 1990s and 2000s. The field of communication is of course a particularly illustrative and fascinating example of rapid changes (see table 2). In

l'agriculture, la production industrielle et le commerce extérieur, seront toujours pertinentes et susciterons toujours l'intérêt. Une des grandes qualités de l'*Annuaire* a sans doute été la continuité et la stabilité de ses contenus. Etant donné que les statistiques officielles gagnent en valeur lorsqu'elles peuvent êtres utilisées comme point de référence pour mesurer le changement et évaluer le progrès, des données mesurées régulièrement sur une longue période s'avèrent essentielles dès que des comparaisons sérieuses doivent être entreprises.

D'un autre côté, la sélection des sujets abordés par l'*Annuaire* durant les dernières décennies a suivi l'évolution du panorama du développement socioéconomique mondial. A côté des séries statistiques classiques mentionnées plus haut, des données concernant des sujets additionnels liés à la nouvelle économie et aux nouvelles préoccupations sociales et environ-

Table 2
Increase in new Internet users from 2003 to 2004

Tableau 2
Croissance des nouveaux utilisateurs d'Internet, de 2003 à 2004

Country Pays	Number of new Internet users Nombre d'usagers nouveaux d'Internet 2003-2004	Percentage increase Pourcentag de croissance	Country Pays	Number of new Internet users Nombre d'usagers nouveaux d'Internet 2003-2004	Percentage increase Pourcentage de croissance
United States / Etats-Unis	23,367,600	14%	Eritrea / Erythrée	40,500	426%
India / Inde	16,518,956	89%	Morocco / Maroc	2,500,000	250%
China / Chine	14,500,000	18%	Haiti / Haïti	350,000	233%
Japan / Japon	13,400,000	22%	Albania / Albanie	45,000	150%
Germany / Allemagne	8,263,000	25%	Congo / Congo	21,000	140%
Indonesia / Indonésie	6,428,000	80%	Nigeria / Nigéria	1,019,661	136%

contrast to early editions of the *Statistical Yearbook* which presented data on letter mail, telegraph service and telephones, the more recent editions focus on internet use and cellular mobile phones.

In the area of social development, since the late-1980s, themes such as maternal mortality, unemployment by sex and the number of women engaged in research and development were added, reflecting a broadening concern with human development, including, in particular, the welfare and status of women.

Another important topic, namely environment, has been included in the *Statistical Yearbook* since the early-1990s as the policy issue of sustainable development has enjoyed increasing public attention. Data series, such as carbon dioxide (CO_2) emissions, consumption of ozone-depleting chlorofluorocarbons (CFCs) and water supply and sanitation coverage have been presented in the *Statistical Yearbook* since 1993.

As shown in the previous paragraphs and in the table below, the *Statistical Yearbook* has responded to the general

nementales ont été, lorsque cela a été jugé approprié, introduites dans l'*Annuaire*.

Au niveau économique, le développement des sujets a suivi l'évolution de la concentration des activités humaines, qui est passée au cours du temps des activités agricoles et manufacturières, traditionnelles, à d'autres types d'industries, notamment les industries de services. Par exemple, des séries de données concernant la science et la technologie (comme par exemple la dépense domestique brute en recherche et développement par type de financement), ont été introduites au début des années 1970, et plusieurs séries sur les télécommunications ont été ajoutées au début des années 1990 et 2000. Le domaine de la communication est bien entendu un particulièrement illustratif et fascinant exemple de changement rapide (voir Tableau 2). Alors que les premières éditions de l'*Annuaire* présentaient des données sur le courrier postal, le service télégraphique et les téléphones, les plus récentes éditions mettent l'accent sur l'utilisation d'Internet et les téléphones mobiles.

Dans le domaine du développement social, depuis la fin des années 1980, des thèmes comme la mortalité maternelle,

Table 3
Introduction of new series
in the past 20 years — chronology

Tableau 3
Introduction de nouvelles séries
au cours des 20 dernières années — chronologie

Selected examples of new series included in the *Statistical Yearbook* Sélection d'exemples de nouvelles séries dans l'*Annuaire statistique*	Issue in which new series first appeared Edition dans laquelle les nouvelles séries sont apparues pour la première fois
Food supply / Disponibilités alimentaires	34th — 34ème
Maternal mortality / Mortalité maternelle	37th — 37ème
Research and development personnel / Personnel employé dans la recherche et le développement	37th — 37ème
Unemployment (by sex) / Chômage (par sexe)	37th — 37ème
Consumption of chlorofluorocarbons (CFCs) / Consommation de chlorofluorocarbones	38th — 38ème
CO_2 emissions estimates / Estimations des émissions de CO_2	38th — 38ème
Water supply and sanitation coverage / Accès à l'eau et à l'assainissement	38th — 38ème
Cellular mobile telephone subscribers / Abonnés au téléphone mobile	39th — 39ème
Threatened species / Espèces menacées	44th — 44ème
Internet users / Usagers d'Internet	45th — 45ème

United Nations development policy debate by expanding its social and environment data coverage over the years, providing, thus, a more comprehensive description of human welfare.

Country coverage

The *Statistical Yearbook* has of course mirrored the geopolitical changes in the world during the past half-century. In 1949, the year in which the first Statistical Yearbook was issued, the United Nations had 59 Member States. Many countries or areas had not yet gained independence at that time, so data on areas such as French and Portuguese India, Spanish Guinea and British and French Somaliland, which no longer exist today, can be found in the early *Statistical Yearbooks*.

Over the past several decades, as the United Nations membership continued to expand (growing to 192 by mid-2006), the country coverage of the *Statistical Yearbook* has also significantly increased, mainly as a result of two important developments. The first important wave of change was in the 1960s and early 1970s when many previously-colonized areas gained independence, especially in Africa. A second group of new countries began emerging in the early 1990s with the dissolution of the former Soviet Union as well as Yugoslavia, from which newly-independent countries have come into existence as recently as 2006.

These geo-political changes have posed many challenges for statisticians. In many of the newly-established countries, statistical capacity had to be built or strengthened in order to enable them to produce and report reliable data in line with international standards and practices. Furthermore, changes in country coverage inevitably leads to difficulties regarding the inter-temporal comparability of national data. Often regional data are affected as well when a change at the country level affects a geographical or economic country grouping. Since backward revisions of historical data are not always possible, data breaks in the time series may result, complicating consistent policy analysis.

Coverage, in terms of series and countries, improves over time, mainly due to two factors: (i) statistical capacity, especially in developing countries, is strengthened continuously and (ii) international standards, reflecting agreed-upon concepts and methodologies, are further refined. A good example in this context is the area of national accounting. The first issue of the *Statistical Yearbook* contained just one basic national income table with data on about 40 countries. In recent issues of the *Yearbook*, national accounting tables have become more detailed and complete, as the 1993 System of National Accounts has now been adopted by countries which together contribute more than 90 per cent of world

le chômage selon le sexe et le nombre de femmes engagées dans la recherche et développement ont été ajoutés, de façon à rendre compte des préoccupations grandissantes quant au développement humain, en particulier le bien-être et le statut des femmes.

Un autre thème important, l'environnement, a fait son apparition dans l'*Annuaire statistique* au début des années 1990, la question des politiques de développement durable attirant de plus en plus l'attention du public. Des séries de données, à l'instar des émissions de dioxyde de carbone (CO_2), de la consommation de chlorofluorocarbones (CFC) qui appauvrissent la couche d'ozone, et de l'approvisionnement en eau et de son assainissement, sont présentes dans l'*Annuaire* depuis 1993.

Comme indiqué dans les paragraphes précédents ainsi que dans le tableau ci-dessus, l'*Annuaire* a répondu au débat général des Nations Unies sur la politique de développement par l'élargissement de son offre de données sociales et environnementales au fil des années, fournissant, ainsi, une description plus détaillée du bien-être humain.

Couverture géographique

L'*Annuaire statistique* a bien entendu reflété les changements géopolitiques intervenus dans le monde au cours du dernier demi-siècle. En 1949, année de la première publication de l'*Annuaire statistique*, les Nations Unies ne comprenaient que 59 Etats Membres. Nombre de pays ou de régions du monde n'avaient à l'époque pas encore accédé à l'indépendance. Ainsi, des données sur des zones telles que les Indes françaises ou portugaises, la Guinée espagnole, la Somalie française ou britannique, qui n'existent plus de nos jours, peuvent être trouvées dans les premiers *Annuaires*.

Tout au long des dernières décennies, tandis que le nombre des membres des Nations Unies ne cessait de croître (jusqu'à 192 à la mi-2006), le nombre de pays couverts par l'*Annuaire statistique* augmentait également significativement; principalement porté par deux importants développements. La première vague de changement s'est déroulée des années 1960 au début des années 1970, lorsque beaucoup de pays colonisés acquirent l'indépendance, notamment en Afrique. Un second groupe de nouveaux pays commença à émerger au début des années 1990, avec la dissolution de l'ancienne Union soviétique et de la Yougoslavie. De cette dissolution, des pays nouvellement indépendants sont nés, jusqu'à pas plus tard que 2006.

Ces évolutions géopolitiques ont été autant de défis pour les statisticiens. Dans beaucoup des nouveaux pays ainsi constitués, la capacité statistique a dû être créée ou renforcée, afin de leur permettre de produire et de déclarer des données fiables, en ligne avec les standards et pratiques internationales.

output. The national accounting tables of the *Yearbook*, thus, now provide a more comprehensive description of global economic development.

User groups and data communication

Since its inception, the *Statistical Yearbook* has aimed to serve a broad range of user groups from within the United Nations and its agencies, other international organizations, governmental and non-governmental organizations, national statistical, economic and social policy bodies, scientific and educational institutions, libraries and the public. With the recently increased focus on evidence-based policy decision making, especially with respect to development policies, the general public has become more interested in understanding the global situation. The *Statistical Yearbook* is of course one key element in the strategy of the United Nations Statistics Division to make relevant national and global data more accessible in order to meet the ever-increasing user demand for statistical information.

As the topics and geographical coverage have increased over the years, the sheer volume of data contained in the *Statistical Yearbook* has increased substantially as compared to the early issues. Thanks to the internet and to communication technology, the data collection and transfer processes have improved significantly, which has made it possible to transmit large amounts of statistical data from individual countries or from partner international agencies to the United Nations Statistics Division. In the early years, most of the statistical information was transmitted to the Statistics Division via mail or fax in paper format, and a good deal of manual labour was then required to process the statistical information. Nowadays, only a small portion of the data for the *Statistical Yearbook* is still transmitted from the sources in paper format. In most cases, the Statistics Division either receives the statistical information electronically or downloads the data from the websites of respective specialized agencies or individual countries. The advances in communication technology have also contributed to improving the data quality, as the Statistics Division can now more easily and quickly double-check with the data providers to clarify any queries that may arise.

Advances in information technology have naturally also had a positive impact on the data dissemination side. Eleven issues of the *Statistical Yearbook* were produced in both print and electronic formats, beginning with the thirty-eighth issue and ending with the forty-eighth. The *Statistical Yearbook CD-ROM* contained the complete time series data from 1980 to the most recent year available, and included the historical data of those series not shown in the print versions due to space limitations. In 2005, it was decided to discontinue the production of the CD-ROM and to instead make the data available

En outre, les changements dans la couverture des pays mènent inévitablement à des difficultés dans la comparabilité intertemporelle des données nationales. Souvent, les données régionales sont également affectées lorsqu'une modification au niveau du pays affecte un groupe géographique ou économique de pays. Puisque les révisions rétrogrades de données historiques ne sont pas toujours possibles, les séries chronologiques peuvent présenter une discontinuité notable, ce qui peut compliquer une analyse cohérente des politiques.

La couverture, en termes de séries et de pays, s'améliore au cours du temps, principalement grâce à deux facteurs : (i) la capacité statistique, spécialement dans les pays en développement, connaît un renforcement continu, et (ii) les standards internationaux, reflétant les concepts et méthodologies sur lesquels un accord a été trouvé, sont en train d'être raffinés. Un bon exemple dans ce contexte est le domaine de la comptabilité nationale. La première édition de l'*Annuaire* contenait seulement un tableau basique de revenu national, avec des données sur environ 40 pays. Les tableaux de comptabilité nationale des dernières éditions de l'*Annuaire* sont davantage détaillées et exhaustives, suite à l'adoption du Système de comptabilité nationale de 1993 par nombre de pays, représentant ensemble 90 pour cent de la production mondiale. Ainsi, les tableaux de comptabilité nationale de l'*Annuaire* fournissent désormais une description bien plus détaillée du développement économique global.

Groupes d'utilisateurs et communication des données

Depuis sa création, l'*Annuaire statistique* s'est donné pour objectif de servir un large éventail de groupes d'utilisateurs, depuis les divers organismes du système des Nations Unies lui-même, jusqu'aux autres organisations internationales, les gouvernements et les organisations non gouvernementales, en passant par les organismes nationaux de statistique et de politique économique et sociale, les institutions scientifiques et les établissements d'enseignement, les bibliothèques et les particuliers. La récente attention portée sur les prises de décisions de politique basées sur des preuves, notamment en ce qui concerne les politiques de développement, a aiguisé l'intérêt du grand public à comprendre la situation mondiale. L'*Annuaire* est bien sûr un élément clé dans la stratégie de la Division de statistique des Nations Unies de rendre les données nationales et mondiales davantage accessibles, afin de satisfaire la demande sans cesse croissante des utilisateurs en information statistique.

Suivant la croissance, au cours des ans, de la couverture géographique et thématique, le volume même des données contenues dans l'*Annuaire statistique* a substantiellement augmenté, comparé aux premières éditions. Grâce à l'Internet et aux technologies de l'information, la collecte des données et

in electronic format to users faster by including the data in the United Nations Common Database (UNCDB). The United Nations Statistics Division is presently working on a project "Statistics as a Public Good", which will increase the volume of web-accessible data and make the current UNCDB interface even more user-friendly. Information on the UNCDB is available at http://unstats.un.org/unsd/cdb.

The Statistics Division also produces the *Monthly Bulletin of Statistics* and the *Monthly Bulletin of Statistics Online,* which provide a valuable complement to the *Statistical Yearbook* by covering current international economic and social statistics for most countries and areas of the world. Further information on these products is available at http://unstats. un.org/unsd/mbs/.

Challenges for the way ahead

The major challenge continuously facing the *Statistical Yearbook* is to present series which are as nearly comparable across countries as the available statistics permit. Considerable efforts have already been made among the international suppliers of data and by the staff of the *Statistical Yearbook* to ensure the compatibility of various series by coordinating time periods, base years, prices chosen for valuation, and so on. This is indispensable in relating various bodies of data to each other and in facilitating analysis across different sectors. Thus, for example, relating data on short-term interest rates to those on prices makes it possible to arrive at a general understanding about the inflation environment, and relating a country's data on tourism expenditure in other countries to those on its per capita GDP provides a gauge on that country's wealth status. In general, the data presented reflect the methodological recommendations of the United Nations Statistical Commission issued in various United Nations publications, and of other international bodies concerned with statistics. Publications containing these recommendations and guidelines are listed in the section "Statistical sources and references" at the end of the *Yearbook.* The use of international recommendations not only promotes international comparability of the data but also ensures a degree of compatibility regarding the underlying concepts, definitions and classifications relating to different series. However, much work remains to be done in this area and, for this reason, some tables can serve only as a first source of data, which require further adjustment before being used for more in-depth analytical studies. While on the whole, a significant degree of comparability has been achieved in international statistics, there will remain some limitations, for a variety of reasons.

One common cause of non-comparability of economic data is different valuations of statistical aggregates such as national income, wages and salaries, output of industries and so forth.

les processus de transfert se sont significativement améliorés, ce qui a permis aux pays et aux agences internationales partenaires de transmettre un grand nombre de données statistiques à la Division de statistique des Nations Unies. Tandis que, les premières années, la majeure partie de l'information statistique était transmise à la Division de statistique via courrier ou fax en format papier, et qu'un travail manuel laborieux était alors requis pour traiter l'information statistique, seule une faible part des données destinées à l'*Annuaire* est encore transmise en format papier aujourd'hui. Dans la plupart des cas, la Division de statistique soit reçoit l'information statistique par voie électronique, soit télécharge les données depuis les sites Internet des pays ou des agences spécialisées respectives. Les avancées dans les technologies de la communication ont aussi contribué à améliorer la qualité des données, dans le sens où la Division de statistique peut désormais facilement et rapidement revérifier avec les fournisseurs de données lorsque des points à éclaircir apparaissent.

Les avancées qu'ont connues les technologies de l'information ont naturellement aussi eu un impact positif sur la diffusion des données. Onze numéros de l'*Annuaire statistique* ont été publiés en format à la fois papier et électronique, des numéros 38 à 48. Le CD-ROM de l'*Annuaire* contenait les séries chronologiques complètes depuis 1980 jusqu'aux séries les plus récentes disponibles, ainsi que les statistiques passées de séries qui n'avaient pas été incluses, faute de place, dans les versions papier. En 2005, il a été décidé de ne plus produire le CD-ROM et, en contrepartie, de mettre plus rapidement les données à la disposition des utilisateurs, sous forme électronique, en les insérant dans la Base de données Commune des Nations Unies (UNCDB). La Division de statistique travaille actuellement sur le projet « Statistique comme bien public », qui à terme augmentera le volume de données accessibles sur le Web, et rendra l'interface d'UNCDB plus conviviale. Pour tout renseignement sur cette base de données commune, consulter l'adresse suivante: http://unstats.un.org/unsd/cdb.

La Division de statistique publie également le *Bulletin Mensuel de Statistiques* et le *Bulletin Mensuel de Statistiques* en ligne, qui constituent un complément précieux à l'*Annuaire Statistique*, puisqu'ils couvrent les statistiques économiques courantes pour la plupart des pays et régions du monde. Pour toute information supplémentaire sur ces produits, visiter http://unstats.un.org/unsd/mbs/.

Les prochains défis à relever

Le défi majeur auquel l'*Annuaire Statistique* fait continuellement face est de présenter des séries aussi comparables entre les pays que la disponibilité des statistiques le permettent. Les sources internationales de données et les auteurs de l'*Annuaire* ont réalisé des efforts considérables pour faire en sorte que

Conversion of these and similar series originally expressed in national prices into a common currency, for example into United States dollars, through the use of exchange rates, is not always satisfactory owing to frequent wide fluctuations in market rates and differences between official rates and rates which would be indicated by unofficial markets or purchasing power parities. The use of different kinds of sources for obtaining data is another cause of incomparability. This is true, for example, in the case of employment and unemployment, where data are obtained from different sources, namely household and labour force sample surveys, establishment censuses or surveys, official estimates, social insurance statistics and employment office statistics, which are not fully comparable in many cases. Non-comparability of data may also result from differences in the institutional patterns of countries. Certain variations in social and economic organization and institutions may have an impact on the comparability of the data even if the underlying concepts and definitions are identical. These and other causes of non-comparability of the data are briefly explained in the technical notes to each chapter.

A further set of challenges relate to timeliness, quality and relevance of the data contained in the *Yearbook*. Users generally demand the most up-to-date statistics. However, due to the different development stages of statistical capacity in different countries, data for the most recent years may only be available for a small number of countries. For a global print publication, therefore, a balance has to be struck between presenting the most updated information and satisfactory country coverage. Of course the UN Statistics Division's website offers greater flexibility in presenting continuously updated information and is therefore a useful complement to the annual print publication. Furthermore, as most of the information presented in this *Yearbook* is collected through specialized United Nations agencies and partners, the timeliness is continuously enhanced by improving the communication and data flow between countries and the specialized agencies on the one hand, and between the UN Statistics Division and the specialized agencies on the other. The development of new XML-based data transfer protocols will address this issue and is expected to make international data flows more efficient in the future.

Data quality at the international level is a function of the data quality at the national level. The UN Statistics Division in close cooperation with its partners in the UN agencies and the international statistical system continues to support countries' efforts to improve both the coverage and the quality of their data. Extensive metadata, as for example reflected in the footnotes and technical notes of this publication, are an important service to the user to allow an informed assessment of the quality of the data. Given the wide variety of sources for

diverses séries soient compatibles, en harmonisant les périodes de référence, les années de base, les prix utilisés pour les évaluations, etc. Cette démarche est indispensable si l'on veut rapprocher divers ensembles de données, et faciliter l'analyse intersectorielle de l'économie. Ainsi, lier les données concernant les taux d'intérêt à court terme à celles des prix permet d'arriver à une compréhension globale de l'environnement de l'inflation; lier les données de dépenses touristiques d'un pays dans d'autres pays à celles de son PIB par tête fournit un indicateur de la richesse de ce pays. De façon générale, les données sont présentées selon les recommandations méthodologiques formulées par la Commission de statistique des Nations Unies, et par les autres entités internationales impliquées dans les statistiques. Les titres des publications contenant ces recommandations et leurs lignes directrices figurent à la fin de l'*Annuaire*, dans la section "Sources et références statistiques". Le respect des recommandations internationales tend non seulement à promouvoir la comparabilité internationale des données, mais elle assure également une certaine comparabilité entre les concepts, les définitions et classifications utilisés. Mais comme il reste encore beaucoup à faire dans ce domaine, les données présentées dans certains tableaux n'ont qu'une valeur indicative, et nécessiteront des ajustements plus poussés avant de pouvoir servir à des analyses approfondies. Bien que l'on soit parvenu, dans l'ensemble, à un degré de comparabilité appréciable en matière de statistiques internationales, diverses raisons expliquent que subsistent encore de nombreuses limitations.

Une cause commune de non comparabilité des données économiques réside dans la diversité des méthodes d'évaluation employées pour comptabiliser des agrégats tels que le revenu national, les salaires et traitements, la production des différentes branches d'activité industrielle, etc. Il n'est pas toujours satisfaisant de ramener la valeur des séries de ce type—exprimée à l'origine en prix nationaux—à une monnaie commune (par exemple le dollar des États-Unis) car les taux de change du marché connaissent fréquemment de fortes fluctuations, et parce que les taux officiels ne coïncident pas avec ceux des marchés officieux ni avec les parités réelles de pouvoir d'achat. Le recours à des sources diverses pour la collecte des données est un autre facteur qui limite la comparabilité. C'est le cas, par exemple, des données d'emploi et de chômage, obtenues par des moyens aussi peu comparables que les sondages, le dépouillement des registres d'assurances sociales et les enquêtes auprès des entreprises. Dans certains cas, les données ne sont pas comparables en raison de différences entre les structures institutionnelles des pays. Des changements dans l'organisation et les institutions économiques et sociales peuvent affecter la comparabilité des données, même si les concepts et définitions sont fondamentalement identiques. Ces causes, et

the *Yearbook*, there is of course an equally wide variety of data formats and accompanying metadata. An important challenge for the UN Statistics Division and its partners for the future is to work further towards the standardization, or at least harmonization, of metadata.

The final challenge relates to maintaining the relevance of the series included in the Yearbook. As new policy concerns enter the developmental debate, the UN Statistics Division will need to introduce new series that describe concerns that have gained prominence as well as to prune outdated data and continue to update the recurrent Yearbook series that still address those issues which are most pertinent. Often choosing the appropriate moment when the statistical information on new topics has matured sufficiently so as to be able to disseminate meaningful global data can be challenging. Furthermore, a balance has to continuously be found between the ever-increasing amount of information available for dissemination and the space limitations of the print version of the Statistical Yearbook. International comparability, data availability and data quality will remain the key criteria to guide the UN Statistics Division in its selection.

Needless to say, more can always be done to improve the *Statistical Yearbook's* scope, coverage, design, metadata and timeliness. The *Yearbook* team continually strives to improve upon each of these aspects and to make its publication as responsive as possible to its users' needs and expectations, while at the same time focusing on a manageable body of data and metadata. Since data disseminated in digital form have clear advantages over those in print, as much of the *Yearbook* information as possible will continue to be included in the UN Common Database. Still, due to its history, the *Statistical Yearbook* will continue to claim its rightful place among the products of the Statistics Division as long as there continues to be a strong user/customer base.

d'autres, de non comparabilité des données sont brièvement expliquées dans les notes techniques de chaque chapitre.

Un autre ensemble de défis à relever concerne la fraîcheur, la qualité et la pertinence des données présentées dans l'*Annuaire*. Les utilisateurs exigent généralement des données les plus récentes possibles. Toutefois, selon le niveau de développement de la capacité statistique des pays, les données pour les dernières années peuvent n'être disponibles que pour un nombre limité de pays. Dans le cadre d'une publication mondiale, un équilibre doit être trouvé entre la présentation de l'information la plus récente et une couverture géographique satisfaisante. Bien entendu, le site Internet de la Division de statistique des Nations Unies offre une plus grande flexibilité, puisqu'il propose une information actualisée au fil de l'eau, et constitue ainsi un complément utile à la publication papier annuelle. Par ailleurs, étant donné que la plupart des informations présentées dans cet *Annuaire* sont collectées parmi les agences spécialisées des Nations Unies et autres partenaires, la fraîcheur des données est continuellement améliorée, grâce à une meilleure communication et un meilleur échange de données entre les pays et les agences spécialisées d'une part, et entre la Division de statistique des Nations Unies et les agences spécialisées d'autre part. Le développement de nouveaux protocoles de transfert de données basés sur le langage XML devrait contribuer à rendre, à l'avenir, les échanges de données internationales encore plus efficaces.

La qualité des données au niveau international est fonction de la qualité des données au niveau national. La Division de statistique des Nations Unies, en étroite collaboration avec ses partenaires dans les agences de l'ONU et dans le système statistique international, continue de soutenir les efforts des pays pour améliorer à la fois la couverture et la qualité de leurs données. Des métadonnées détaillées, comme l'illustrent les notes de bas de page et les notes techniques de cette publication, constituent un important service fourni à l'utilisateur pour lui permettre d'évaluer de manière avisée la qualité des données. Etant donné la grande variété des sources de l'*Annuaire*, il y a bien entendu une non moins grande variété de formats de données et de métadonnées associées. Un important défi que la Division de statistique des Nations Unies et ses partenaires doivent relever dans le futur est d'aboutir à la standardisation, ou au moins l'harmonisation, des métadonnées.

Le dernier défi concerne la constance de la pertinence des séries présentées dans l'*Annuaire*. Au fur et à mesure que de nouvelles préoccupations politiques pénètrent le débat lié au développement, la Division de statistique des Nations Unies doit introduire dans l'*Annuaire* de nouvelles séries qui leur sont liées, et, ce faisant, effectuer une coupe sombre parmi les données qui lui semblent dépassées, tout en s'assurant de continuer à actualiser les séries récurrentes de qui paraissent

encore pertinentes. Souvent, choisir le moment idoine auquel les données statistiques sur de nouveaux thèmes sont suffisamment matures pour qu'elles puissent, au niveau mondial, être diffusées sans hésitation, est un défi en soi. Par ailleurs, un équilibre doit continuellement être trouvé entre le volume toujours croissant d'informations disponibles à la diffusion, et les contraintes d'espace de la version papier de l'*Annuaire statistique*. La comparabilité internationale, la disponibilité des données et leur qualité devront rester le principal critère à considérer par la Division de statistique des Nations Unies dans sa sélection.

Inutile de dire qu'il est toujours possible d'améliorer l'*Annuaire statistique* en ce qui concerne son champ, sa couverture, sa conception générale, ses métadonnées et sa mise à jour. L'équipe en charge de l'*Annuaire* s'évertue en permanence à améliorer chacun de ces aspects, et de faire en sorte que cette publication réponde au plus près aux besoins et aux attentes de ses utilisateurs, sans toutefois oublier de mettre l'accent sur un corpus gérable de données et de métadonnées. Puisqu'il est avéré que les données diffusées de manière digitale ont des avantages comparés à celles diffusées sur papier, autant d'informations de l'*Annuaire* que possible continueront d'être inclues dans la Base de données Commune des Nations Unies. L'*Annuaire statistique* garde toujours, en vertu de son histoire, une place de choix parmi les produits de la Division de statistique, légitimée par une solide base d'utilisateurs/clients.

## PART ONE

World and region summary

Aperçu mondial et régional

Chapter I   World and region summary (tables 1-7)

Chapitre I   Aperçu mondial et régional (tableaux 1 à 7)

This part of the *Statistical Yearbook* presents selected aggregate series on principal economic and social topics for the world as a whole and for the major regions. The topics include population and surface area, agricultural and industrial production, motor vehicles in use, external trade, government financial reserves, and energy production and consumption. More detailed data on individual countries and areas are provided in the subsequent parts of the present *Yearbook*. These comprise Part Two: Population and Social Statistics; Part Three: Economic Activity; and Part Four: International Economic Relations.

Regional totals between series may be incomparable owing to differences in definitions of regions and lack of data for particular regional components. General information on regional groupings is provided in annex I of the *Yearbook*. Supplementary information on regional groupings used in specific series is provided, as necessary, in table footnotes and in the technical notes at the end of chapter I.

Cette partie de l'*Annuaire statistique* présente, pour le monde entier et ses principales subdivisions, un choix d'agrégats ayant trait à des questions économiques et sociales essentielles: population et superficie, production agricole et industrielle, véhicules automobiles en circulation, commerce extérieur, réserves financières publiques, et la production et la consommation d'énergie. Des statistiques plus détaillées pour divers pays ou zones figurent dans les parties ultérieures de l'*Annuaire*, c'est-à-dire dans les deuxième, troisième et quatrième parties intitulées respectivement: population et statistiques sociales, activités économiques et relations économiques internationales.

Les totaux régionaux peuvent être incomparables entre les séries en raison de différences dans la définition des régions et de l'absence de données sur tel ou tel élément régional. A l'annexe I de l'*Annuaire*, on trouvera des renseignements généraux sur les groupements régionaux. Des informations complémentaires sur les groupements régionaux pour certaines séries bien précises sont fournies, lorsqu'il y a lieu, dans les notes figurant au bas des tableaux et dans les notes techniques à la fin du chapitre I.

1

Selected series of world statistics
Population, production, transport, external trade and finance

Séries principales de statistiques mondiales
Population, production, transports, commerce extérieur et finances

Series Séries	Unit or base Unité ou base	1995	1996	1997	1998	1999	2000	2001	2002	2003	2004
Population — Population											
World population [1] Population mondial [1]	million	5 692	5 772	5 852	5 930	6 008	6 086	6 162	6 238	6 314	6 389
Output / production — Production											
Gross domestic product — Produit intérieur brut											
GDP at current prices PIB aux prix courants	billion US $ milliard $ E.–U.	29 486	30 109	29 963	29 746	30 850	31 654	31 398	32 616	36 572	40 998
GDP per capita PIB par habitant	US $ $ E.–U.	5 180	5 220	5 120	5 020	5 140	5 200	5 100	5 230	5 790	6 420
GDP real rates of growth Taux de l'accroissement réels	%	2.9	3.3	3.7	2.5	3.2	4.0	1.6	1.9	2.7	4.0
Agriculture, forestry and fishing production — Production agricole, forestière et de la pêche											
Index numbers — Indices											
All commodities Tous produits	1999–01 = 100	88	91	94	95	98	100	102	103	106	111
Food Produits alimentaires	1999–01 = 100	87	91	93	95	98	100	102	104	107	110
Crops Cultures	1999–01 = 100	87	93	94	95	98	100	102	102	105	111
Cereals Céréales	1999–01 = 100	90	98	100	99	100	99	101	97	99	108
Livestock products Produits de l'élevage	1999–01 = 100	90	91	93	96	98	100	102	105	107	110
Quantities — Quantités											
Oil crops Cultures d'huile	million t.	92	93	98	103	109	110	112	114	124	134
Meat Viande	million t.	148	147	152	157	160	161	163	168	172	176
Roundwood Bois rond	million m³	3 251	3 234	3 304	3 224	3 292	3 357	3 284	3 301	3 348	3 402
Fish production Production halieutique	million t.	117	120	123	118	127	131	131	134	133	141
Industrial production — Production industrielle											
Index numbers [2] — Indices [2]											
All commodities Tous produits	1995 = 100	100	103	108	111	115	123	121	122	126	133
Mining Mines	1995 = 100	100	103	105	106	104	108	107	107	110	112
Manufacturing Manufactures	1995 = 100	100	103	109	111	117	125	123	124	128	137
Quantities — Quantités											
Coal Houille	million t.	3 730	3 794	3 825	3 703	3 470	3 391	3 670	3 887	4 218	...
Lignite and brown coal Lignite et charbon brun	million t.	937	943	925	915	882	898	901	897	905	...
Crude petroleum Pétrole brut	million t.	3 097	3 151	3 252	3 288	3 210	3 347	3 325	3 282	3 416	...
Natural gas Gaz naturel	petajoules pétajoules	84 913	89 661	89 335	91 660	92 777	97 921	99 653	101 874	104 404	...

1 Selected series of world statistics — Population, production, transport, external trade and finance (*continued*)

1 Séries principales de statistiques mondiales — Population, production, transports, commerce, extérieur et finances (*suite*)

Series / Séries	Unit or base / Unité ou base	1995	1996	1997	1998	1999	2000	2001	2002	2003	2004
Pig-iron and ferro-alloys / Fonte et ferro-alliages	million t.	547	539	566	557	562	598	606	638	695	...
Leather footwear / Chaussures de cuir	million pairs / million paires	2 089	2 063	1 977	1 952	1 760	1 710	1 685	1 641	1 720	...
Sulphuric acid / Acide sulfurique	million t.	87	88	91	94	89	89	90	97	101	...
Refrigerators / Réfrigérateurs	million	64	64	69	67	70	73	74	78	84	...
Washing machines / Machines à laver	million	47	49	54	53	56	59	59	65	68	...
Machine tools — Machines outils											
Drilling and boring machines / Perceuses	thousands / milliers	90	71	67	55	50	55	50	40	44	...
Lathes / Tours	thousands / milliers	74	71	68	67	63	80	92	63	53	...
Lorries — Camions											
Assembled / Assemblés	thousands / milliers	609	646	680	608	598	675	634	683	722	...
Produced / Fabriqués	thousands / milliers	5 430	5 655	5 815	5 482	5 374	5 581	5 315	5 226	5 471	...
Aluminium / Aluminium	thousand t. / millier t.	25 637	27 123	28 050	29 699	30 914	32 116	31 531	31 785	35 607	...
Cement / Ciment	thousand t. / millier t.	1 424	1 471	1 510	1 517	1 574	1 641	1 703	1 811	1 979	...
Electricity [3] / Electricité [3]	billion kWh / milliard kWh	13 376	13 805	14 111	14 296	14 764	15 475	15 578	16 175	16 770	...
Fertilizers [4] / Engrais [4]	million t.	143	147	146	147	148	144	147	148	...	...
Sugar, raw / Sucre, brut	million t.	118	125	125	126	135	130	131	142	148	148
Woodpulp / Pâte de bois	million t.	162	157	163	160	164	172	166	168	171	175
Sawnwood / Sciages	million m³	392	387	394	378	386	388	379	393	399	416
Motor vehicles / Véhicules automobiles											
Passenger cars / Voitures de tourisme	million	34.50	35.95	36.88	36.23	37.66	39.27	36.94	37.75	38.23	...
Commercial vehicles / Véhicules utilitaires	million	6.66	6.78	6.99	6.72	6.87	6.90	6.69	6.62	6.86	...
Transport — Transports											
Motor vehicles in use [5] — Véhicules automobiles en circulation [5]											
Passenger cars / Voitures de tourisme	thousands / milliers	457 763	470 587	452 101	475 450	489 697	504 408	507 569	528 965	...	...
Commercial vehicles / Véhicules utilitaires	thousands / milliers	165 368	186 867	176 943	184 862	187 750	199 117	210 791	214 525	...	...
External trade — Commerce extérieur											
Value — Valeur											
Import, c.i.f. / Importations c.a.f.	billion US$ / milliard $E.-U.	4 940	5 170	5 350	5 295	5 514	6 228	5 997	6 213	7 236	8 787
Exports, f.o.b. / Exportations f.o.b.	billion US$ / milliard $E.-U.	4 909	5 101	5 291	5 217	5 410	6 067	5 829	6 101	7 074	8 567

1
Selected series of world statistics — Population, production, transport, external trade and finance (*continued*)

Séries principales de statistiques mondiales — Population, production, transports, commerce, extérieur et finances (*suite*)

Series / Séries	Unit or base / Unité ou base	1995	1996	1997	1998	1999	2000	2001	2002	2003	2004
Volume: index of exports — Volume : indice des exportations											
All commodities / Tous produits	2000 = 100	70	73	81	85	90	100	99	103	108	122
Manufactures / Produits manufacturés	2000 = 100	66	71	80	82	89	100	101	105	113	...
Unit value: index of exports [6] — Valeur unitaire : indice des exportations [6]											
All commodities / Tous produits	2000 = 100	116	116	108	102	100	100	97	97	107	113
Manufactures / Produits manufacturés	2000 = 100	122	117	110	108	103	100	98	98	104	...
Primary commodities: price indexes [6,7,9] — Produits de base : indices des prix [6,7,9]											
All commodities / Tous produits	1990 = 100	72	76	71	56	63	81	73	...	...	...
Food / Produits alimentaires	1990 = 100	92	90	87	80	74	69	69	...	...	...
Non–food: of agricultural origin / Non alim. : d'origine agricole	1990 = 100	106	98	90	81	73	72	66	...	...	...
Minerals / Minéraux	1990 = 100	58	67	62	43	57	87	76	...	...	...
Finance — Finances											
International reserves minus gold, billion SDR [8] — Réserves internationals moins l'or, milliard de DTS [8]											
All countries / Tous les pays	billion SDR / milliard DTS	991.3	1145.7	1265.4	1248.5	1372.6	1556.1	1709.4	1856.6	2123.9	2489.1
Position in IMF / Disponibilité au FMI	billion SDR / milliard DTS	36.7	38.0	47.1	60.6	54.8	47.4	56.9	66.1	66.5	55.8
Foreign exchange / Devises	billion SDR / milliard DTS	934.9	1089.1	1197.8	1167.5	1299.4	1490.2	1633.0	1770.9	2037.4	2413.0
SDR (special drawing rights) / DTS (droits de triage spéc.)	billion SDR / milliard DTS	19.8	18.5	20.5	20.4	18.5	18.5	19.6	19.7	19.9	20.3

Source

Databases of the Food and Agriculture Organization of the United Nations (FAO), Rome; the International Monetary Fund (IMF), Washington, D.C.; and the United Nations Statistics Division, New York.

Source

Les bases de données de l'Organisation des Nations Unies pour l'alimentation et l'agriculture (FAO), Rome ; du Fonds Monétaire International (FMI), Washington, D.C. ; et de la Division de statistique de l'Organisation de Nations Unies, New York.

Notes

[1] Annual data: mid–year estimates.
[2] Excluding China and the countries of the former USSR (except Russian Federation and Ukraine).
[3] Electricity generated by establishments for public or private use.
[4] Year beginning 1 July.
[5] Source: *World Automotive market Report*, Auto and Truck International (Illinois).
[6] Indices computed in US dollars.
[7] Export price indices.
[8] End of period.
[9] Series discontinued.

Notes

[1] Données annuelles : estimations au milieu de l'année.
[2] Non compris la Chine et les pays de l'ancienne URSS (sauf la Fédération de Russie et Ukraine).
[3] L'électricité produite par des enterprises d'utilisation publique ou privée.
[4] L'année commençant le 1er juillet.
[5] Source : *World Automotive Market Report*, Auto and Truck Internationl: (Illinois).
[6] Indice calculé en dollars des Etats–Unis.
[7] Indices des prix à l'exportation.
[8] Fin de la période.
[9] Séries discontinuées.

2

Population, rate of increase, birth and death rates, surface area and density

Population, taux d'accroissement, taux de natalité, taux de mortalité, superficie et densité

Major areas and regions Grandes régions	Mid–year population estimates (millions) Estimations de population au milieu de l'année (millions)							Annual rate of increase Taux d'accrois-sement annuel %	Crude birth rate Taux bruts de natalité (p.1 000)	Crude death rate Taux bruts de mortalité (p.1 000)	Surface area Superficie (km²) (000)	Density[1] Densité[1]
	1950	1960	1970	1980	1990	2000	2003	2000–2005			2003	2003
World — Monde	2 520	3 024	3 697	4 442	5 280	6 086	6 314	1.2	21	9	136 056	46
Africa — Afrique	224	282	364	479	636	812	868	2.2	38	15	30 250	29
Eastern Africa Afrique orientale	65	82	109	146	198	256	275	2.4	41	17	6 300	44
Middle Africa — Afrique centrale	26	32	41	54	73	96	104	2.6	46	20	6 613	16
Northern Africa Afrique du Nord	53	67	86	112	144	175	184	1.7	26	7	8 525	22
Southern Africa Afrique australe	16	20	26	33	42	52	54	0.7	24	17	2 675	20
Western Africa — Afrique occidentale	64	80	102	134	178	234	252	2.4	42	18	6 138	41
Northern America [2] Amérique septentrionale [2]	172	204	232	256	283	315	324	1.0	14	8	21 776	15
Latin America and the Caribbean Amérique latine et Caraïbes	167	219	285	362	444	523	546	1.4	22	6	20 546	27
Caribbean — Caraïbes	17	20	25	29	34	38	38	0.9	20	8	234	165
Central America Amérique centrale	37	50	68	91	113	136	143	1.6	24	5	2 480	58
South America Amérique du sud	113	148	192	242	297	349	365	1.4	21	6	17 832	20
Asia [3] — Asie [3]	1 396	1 699	2 140	2 630	3 169	3 676	3 815	1.2	20	8	31 870	120
Eastern Asia — Asie orientale	671	792	987	1 178	1 350	1 479	1 507	0.6	13	7	11 763	128
South–central Asia Asie centrale et du Sud	496	617	780	978	1 226	1 485	1 560	1.6	26	9	10 791	145
South–eastern Asia Asie du Sud–Est	178	223	286	358	440	519	541	1.4	21	7	4 495	120
Western Asia — Asie occidentale	51	67	88	116	154	193	206	2.1	26	6	4 822	43
Europe [3] — Europe [3]	547	604	656	692	721	728	729	0.0	10	12	22 050	33
Eastern Europe Europe orientale	220	254	276	295	311	305	300	−0.5	10	14	18 814	16
Northern Europe Europe septentrionale	77	81	86	89	92	94	95	0.3	11	10	1 748	54
Southern Europe Europe méridionale	109	118	127	138	143	146	148	0.4	10	10	1 317	112
Western Europe Europe occidentale	141	152	166	170	176	184	185	0.2	10	10	1 108	167
Oceania [2] — Océanie [2]	13	16	20	23	27	31	32	1.3	17	7	8 564	4
Australia and New Zealand Australie et Nouvelle–Zélande	10	13	16	18	20	23	24	1.1	13	7	8 012	3
Melanesia — Mélanésie	2	3	3	4	6	7	7	2.0	31	10	541	14
Micronesia — Micronésie	0	0	0	0	0	1	1	1.9	26	5	3	167
Polynesia — Polynésie	0	0	0	1	1	1	1	1.2	24	5	8	75

2 Population, rate of increase, birth and death rates, surface area and density (*continued*)
Population, taux d'accroissement, taux de natalité, taux de mortalité, superficie et densité (*suite*)

Source

United Nations Statistics Division, New York, *Demographic Yearbook 2003* and the demographic statistics database.

Notes

[1] Population per square kilometre of surface area. Figures are merely the quotients of population divided by surface area and are not to be considered either as reflecting density in the urban sense or as indicating the supporting power of a territory's land and resources.

[2] Hawaii, a state of the United States of America, is included in Northern America rather than Oceania.

[3] The European portion of Turkey is included in Western Asia rather than Europe.

Source

Organisation des Nations Unies, Division de statistique, New York, *Annuaire démographique 2003* et la base de données pour les statistiques démographiques.

Notes

[1] Nombre d'habitants au kilomètre carré. Il s'agit simplement du quotient du chiffre de la population divisé par celui de la superficie: il ne faut pas y voir d'indication de la densité au sens urbain du terme ni de l'effectif de population que les terres et les ressources du territoire sont capables de nourrir.

[2] Hawaii, un Etat des Etats–Unis d'Amérique, est compris en Amérique septentrionale plutôt qu'en Océanie.

[3] La partie européenne de la Turquie est comprise en Asie Occidentale plutôt qu'en Europe.

3

Index numbers of total agricultural and food production
1999 – 2001 = 100

Indices de la production agricole totale et de la production alimentaire
1999 – 2001 = 100

Country or area — Pays ou zone	1995	1996	1997	1998	1999	2000	2001	2002	2003	2004
World — Monde										
Total agricultural production — Production agricole totale	88	91	94	95	98	100	102	103	106	110
Food production — Production alimentaire	87	91	93	95	98	100	102	103	106	110
Africa — Afrique										
Total agricultural production — Production agricole totale	84	93	92	96	99	100	102	103	107	108
Food production — Production alimentaire	84	92	91	95	99	100	101	103	107	109
America, North — Amérique du Nord										
Total agricultural production — Production agricole totale	90	94	97	97	99	101	100	98	101	107
Food production — Production alimentaire	89	93	96	97	99	101	99	99	102	107
America, South — Amérique du Sud										
Total agricultural production — Production agricole totale	86	87	90	92	98	100	103	107	112	116
Food production — Production alimentaire	86	87	91	92	98	100	102	106	113	116
Asia — Asie										
Total agricultural production — Production agricole totale	84	88	91	94	97	100	103	105	110	113
Food production — Production alimentaire	83	87	90	94	97	100	103	106	110	112
Europe — Europe										
Total agricultural production — Production agricole totale	98	101	101	99	100	100	100	102	98	104
Food production — Production alimentaire	98	101	101	99	100	100	100	102	98	104
Oceania — Océanie										
Total agricultural production — Production agricole totale	83	91	92	96	99	99	103	90	99	97
Food production — Production alimentaire	83	90	91	95	98	99	103	91	103	99

Source

Food and Agriculture Organization of the United Nations (FAO), Rome, FAOSTAT data, 2005, last accessed August 2005, and the *FAO Production Yearbook*.

Source

Organisation des Nations Unies pour l'alimentation et l'agriculture (FAO), Rome, données FAOSTAT, 2005, dernier accès août 2005, et l'*Annuaire FAO de la production*.

Index numbers of per capita agricultural and food production
1999 – 2001 = 100

Indices de la production agricole et de la production alimentaire par habitant
1999 – 2001 = 100

Region — Région	1995	1996	1997	1998	1999	2000	2001	2002	2003	2004
World — Monde										
Per capita agricultural prod. — Prod. agricole par habitant	95	102	98	100	101	100	99	98	100	99
Per capita food production — Prod. alimentaire par habitant	93	96	97	98	100	100	100	101	102	105
Africa — Afrique										
Per capita agricultural prod. — Prod. agricole par habitant	91	93	95	96	99	100	101	103	105	107
Per capita food production — Prod. alimentaire par habitant	94	101	98	100	101	100	99	99	100	99
America, North — Amérique du Nord										
Per capita agricultural prod. — Prod. agricole par habitant	89	96	95	98	100	99	101	87	96	92
Per capita food production — Prod. alimentaire par habitant	95	98	100	100	101	101	98	96	98	102
America, South — Amérique du Sud										
Per capita agricultural prod. — Prod. agricole par habitant	94	96	97	98	100	100	100	101	102	105
Per capita food production — Prod. alimentaire par habitant	93	92	95	95	99	100	101	103	108	109
Asia — Asie										
Per capita agricultural prod. — Prod. agricole par habitant	98	101	101	99	100	100	100	102	98	105
Per capita food production — Prod. alimentaire par habitant	90	92	94	96	99	100	101	103	106	107
Europe — Europe										
Per capita agricultural prod. — Prod. agricole par habitant	96	98	100	99	101	101	98	96	98	102
Per capita food production — Prod. alimentaire par habitant	98	101	101	99	100	100	100	102	98	105
Oceania — Océanie										
Per capita agricultural prod. — Prod. agricole par habitant	93	93	94	95	99	100	101	104	108	110
Per capita food production — Prod. alimentaire par habitant	89	96	95	98	100	99	102	89	99	94

Source

Food and Agriculture Organization of the United Nations (FAO), Rome, FAOSTAT data, 2005, last accessed August 2005, and the *FAO Production Yearbook*.

Source

Organisation des Nations Unies pour l'alimentation et l'agriculture (FAO), Rome, données FAOSTAT, 2005, dernier accès août 2005, et l'*Annuaire FAO de la production*.

5

Index numbers of industrial production: world and regions
1995 = 100

Indices de la production industrielle : monde et régions
1995 = 100

Region and industry [ISIC Rev. 3] Régions et industrie [CITI Rév. 3]	Weight(%) Pond.(%)	1998	1999	2000	2001	2002	2003	2004
World — Monde								
Total industry [CDE] — Total, industrie [CDE]	100.0	110.5	115.2	122.5	121.4	122.0	125.7	133.4
Total mining [C] — Total, industries extractives [C]	7.4	106.0	103.8	107.7	107.3	107.4	109.6	111.9
Coal — Houille	0.7	99.5	100.3	99.7	101.6	102.3	104.2	108.1
Crude petroleum and natural gas Pétrole brut et gaz naturel	5.0	104.9	101.4	105.6	104.8	104.4	106.6	108.4
Metal ores — Minerais métalliques	0.7	115.8	117.5	123.3	122.2	124.1	125.8	130.2
Total manufacturing [D] Total, industries manufacturières [D]	82.6	111.2	116.8	124.8	123.3	123.8	127.7	136.5
Food, beverages, tobacco Industries alimentaires, boissons, tabac	10.3	103.6	104.7	106.1	106.8	108.0	109.4	111.4
Textiles — Textiles	2.4	97.8	96.1	97.1	92.0	89.8	86.2	85.1
Wearing apparel, leather and footwear Articles d'habillement, cuir et chaussures	2.7	89.9	85.3	83.6	77.4	70.4	66.0	63.6
Wood and wood products — Bois et articles en bois	1.9	102.8	104.9	106.6	101.2	102.2	102.8	106.7
Paper, printing, publishing and recorded media Papier, imprimerie, édition et supports enregistré	7.1	104.9	106.9	108.3	104.7	103.9	103.5	105.7
Chemicals and related products Produits chimiques et alliés	14.0	110.0	113.4	116.6	116.2	119.1	121.4	125.4
Non-metallic mineral products Produits minéraux non métalliques	3.4	102.0	103.3	105.8	104.2	103.6	104.1	106.5
Basic metals — Métallurgie de base	4.7	102.9	103.3	108.6	105.9	107.6	109.8	114.1
Fabricated metal products Fabrications d'ouvrages en métaux	11.7	104.6	104.1	110.9	106.9	104.5	103.9	110.7
Office and related electrical products Machines de bureau et autres appareils élect.	12.7	143.8	174.0	210.7	213.1	213.6	237.4	274.5
Transport equipment — Equipement de transports	8.0	115.0	120.5	124.3	124.7	129.4	132.7	141.9
Electricity, gas, water [E] — Electricité, gaz et eau [E]	10.0	107.8	111.1	114.9	115.8	118.0	120.4	123.6
Developed regions [1] — Régions développées [1]								
Total industry [CDE] — Total, industrie [CDE]	100.0	110.8	115.6	122.5	121.3	120.7	123.7	130.3
Total mining [C] — Total, industries extractives [C]	4.6	102.7	100.7	101.9	101.8	100.4	100.2	99.9
Coal — Houille	0.6	94.7	93.2	90.8	91.0	89.0	87.3	87.9
Crude petroleum and natural gas Pétrole brut et gaz naturel	2.7	103.3	100.2	102.4	102.5	100.6	100.3	98.9
Metal ores — Minerais métalliques	0.4	105.3	100.5	102.8	99.9	96.6	94.8	94.9
Total manufacturing [D] Total, industries manufacturières [D]	84.9	111.9	117.3	124.9	123.4	122.7	125.9	133.4
Food, beverages, tobacco Industries alimentaires, boissons, tabac	9.5	103.0	103.7	104.8	105.4	106.1	106.4	107.1
Textiles — Textiles	1.8	97.7	94.5	93.9	88.3	84.2	79.4	75.9
Wearing apparel, leather and footwear Articles d'habillement, cuir et chaussures	2.4	88.0	82.5	78.1	71.4	62.9	57.2	53.3

Region and industry [ISIC Rev. 3] Régions et industrie [CITI Rév. 3]	Weight(%) Pond.(%)	1998	1999	2000	2001	2002	2003	2004
Wood and wood products Bois et articles en bois	2.0	104.2	106.8	108.4	102.5	103.4	103.2	106.6
Paper, printing, publishing and recorded media Papier, imprimerie, édition et supports enregistré	8.1	105.1	107.0	108.2	104.7	103.5	102.8	104.6
Chemicals and related products Produits chimiques et alliés	13.7	108.6	111.6	114.6	114.1	117.3	118.5	121.0
Non–metallic mineral products Produits minéraux non métalliques	3.2	101.1	101.6	104.1	101.7	99.4	98.9	100.6
Basic metals — Métallurgie de base	4.7	101.5	100.5	105.8	102.4	102.9	103.2	106.5
Fabricated metal products Fabrications d'ouvrages en métaux	12.7	105.9	104.7	110.4	106.1	102.8	101.7	101.7
Office and related electrical products Machines de bureau et autres appareils élect.	14.0	145.1	174.7	209.9	213.6	209.8	232.8	266.3
Transport equipment — Equipement de transports	8.7	115.6	120.2	122.3	121.6	125.2	126.8	132.8
Electricity, gas, water [E] — Electricité, gaz et eau [E]	10.5	105.9	108.5	111.8	112.4	114.1	115.9	118.6
Developing economies [2] — Econ. en dévelop. [2]								
Total industry [CDE] — Total, industrie [CDE]	**100.0**	**109.1**	**113.9**	**122.6**	**121.8**	**126.9**	**133.6**	**145.6**
Total mining [C] — Total, industries extractives [C]	18.3	109.2	106.8	113.5	112.7	114.4	118.8	123.8
Coal — Houille	1.2	108.2	113.4	116.3	121.4	127.0	135.6	145.7
Crude petroleum and natural gas Pétrole brut et gaz naturel	14.3	106.1	102.2	108.0	106.5	107.4	111.4	115.6
Metal ores — Minerais métalliques	1.7	126.5	134.6	144.1	144.7	152.0	157.1	166.0
Total manufacturing [D] Total, industries manufacturières [D]	73.7	108.1	114.5	123.9	122.9	128.8	136.1	150.6
Food, beverages, tobacco Industries alimentaires, boissons, tabac	13.3	105.5	107.5	110.1	110.7	113.4	118.2	123.4
Textiles — Textiles	4.8	97.8	98.5	102.1	97.9	98.4	96.7	99.3
Wearing apparel, leather and footwear Articles d'habillement, cuir et chaussures	3.6	94.9	92.9	98.2	93.6	90.9	89.7	91.4
Wood and wood products — Bois et articles en bois	1.5	94.6	94.4	96.3	94.1	95.7	100.5	106.8
Paper, printing, publishing and recorded media Papier, imprimerie, édition et supports enregistré	3.2	103.3	105.8	108.7	104.7	107.1	110.6	115.9
Chemicals and related products Produits chimiques et alliés	15.0	115.0	120.0	124.2	123.8	125.7	132.2	141.5
Non–metallic mineral products Produits minéraux non métalliques	4.2	104.8	108.5	111.2	112.0	116.6	120.2	124.8
Basic metals — Métallurgie de base	4.7	108.3	114.2	119.6	119.4	125.9	136.0	144.4
Fabricated metal products Fabrications d'ouvrages en métaux	7.9	96.3	100.3	114.1	111.6	115.3	118.5	133.7
Office and related electrical products Machines de bureau et autres appareils élect.	7.3	134.0	168.9	216.5	209.4	242.5	272.4	337.5
Transport equipment — Equipement de transports	5.2	110.8	122.8	138.3	145.4	157.8	172.0	202.7
Electricity, gas, water [E] — Electricité, gaz et eau [E]	8.0	117.8	124.5	131.2	133.4	138.6	143.7	149.7
Northern America [3] — Amérique septentrionale [3]								
Total industry [CDE] — Total, industrie [CDE]	**100.0**	**122.7**	**133.7**	**143.9**	**144.8**	**144.8**	**151.3**	**164.8**
Total mining [C] — Total, industries extractives [C]	6.6	102.6	98.5	100.9	101.4	97.8	98.9	99.3

Region and industry [ISIC Rev. 3] Régions et industrie [CITI Rév. 3]	Weight(%) Pond.(%)	1998	1999	2000	2001	2002	2003	2004
Coal — Houille	0.6	107.3	104.5	103.2	108.7	103.7	100.6	105.1
Crude petroleum and natural gas Pétrole brut et gaz naturel	4.8	100.8	95.7	98.8	99.4	95.9	97.9	97.0
Metal ores — Minerais métalliques	0.6	105.9	99.0	101.7	95.2	88.3	82.1	82.9
Total manufacturing [D] Total, industries manufacturières [D]	81.6	126.9	140.3	152.3	153.4	153.3	161.1	177.2
Food, beverages, tobacco Industries alimentaires, boissons, tabac	8.1	104.9	104.2	106.0	106.5	107.0	107.0	109.7
Textiles — Textiles	1.6	104.3	104.0	103.1	93.1	91.4	83.7	80.7
Wearing apparel, leather and footwear Articles d'habillement, cuir et chaussures	2.1	91.7	87.9	85.5	73.5	62.3	54.3	50.9
Wood and wood products — Bois et articles en bois	2.9	112.9	117.9	118.2	110.8	114.3	113.4	118.2
Paper, printing, publishing and recorded media Papier, imprimerie, édition et supports enregistré	9.1	106.0	108.1	108.9	103.2	100.5	99.4	101.3
Chemicals and related products Produits chimiques et alliés	14.2	111.5	113.3	115.1	111.9	116.7	115.9	120.2
Non–metallic mineral products Produits minéraux non métalliques	2.0	117.4	118.3	119.2	115.8	116.5	116.4	121.7
Basic metals — Métallurgie de base	3.5	109.2	109.5	107.5	98.4	100.4	97.6	102.5
Fabricated metal products Fabrications d'ouvrages en métaux	12.1	112.2	111.5	117.6	107.0	103.4	100.3	107.7
Office and related electrical products Machines de bureau et autres appareils élect.	13.7	206.5	277.1	342.5	377.2	371.9	425.0	500.4
Transport equipment — Equipement de transports	9.5	119.8	127.9	122.9	117.3	122.3	124.3	129.3
Electricity, gas, water [E] — Electricité, gaz et eau [E]	11.8	104.7	107.4	110.2	109.5	112.8	113.0	115.5
Latin America and the Caribbean — Amérique latine et Caraïbes								
Total industry [CDE] — Total, industrie [CDE]	**100.0**	**112.3**	**113.2**	**119.1**	**118.4**	**119.8**	**122.8**	**131.3**
Total mining [C] — Total, industries extractives [C]	10.2	124.5	126.7	135.9	137.0	136.7	141.0	149.9
Coal — Houille	0.3	104.4	111.1	106.2	96.1	97.1	99.3	97.2
Crude petroleum and natural gas Pétrole brut et gaz naturel	5.6	118.7	115.7	120.5	121.4	118.6	118.7	125.4
Metal ores — Minerais métalliques	2.7	125.1	141.0	147.2	147.2	151.1	163.0	178.9
Total manufacturing [D] Total, industries manufacturières [D]	81.2	110.4	110.5	116.2	115.6	117.0	119.8	129.0
Food, beverages, tobacco Industries alimentaires, boissons, tabac	18.4	107.6	110.5	111.4	113.1	115.2	117.8	123.7
Textiles — Textiles	3.3	95.6	90.8	96.6	89.7	85.3	86.5	94.2
Wearing apparel, leather and footwear Articles d'habillement, cuir et chaussures	3.4	100.2	92.6	97.7	90.0	87.7	85.9	89.6
Wood and wood products — Bois et articles en bois	2.0	102.5	107.1	110.2	108.8	114.6	121.1	130.4
Paper, printing, publishing and recorded media Papier, imprimerie, édition et supports enregistré	3.7	108.4	107.9	113.0	109.2	111.0	115.6	121.8
Chemicals and related products Produits chimiques et alliés	19.5	113.6	115.0	117.8	115.8	115.6	118.4	126.2
Non–metallic mineral products Produits minéraux non métalliques	4.0	114.9	111.1	114.2	112.8	114.0	114.2	120.7

Region and industry [ISIC Rev. 3] Régions et industrie [CITI Rév. 3]	Weight(%) Pond.(%)	1998	1999	2000	2001	2002	2003	2004
Basic metals — Métallurgie de base	4.1	116.6	115.3	118.7	116.6	120.5	130.6	141.8
Fabricated metal products Fabrications d'ouvrages en métaux	8.8	104.3	102.1	112.2	112.5	113.5	114.1	126.9
Office and related electrical products Machines de bureau et autres appareils élect.	4.9	122.8	119.8	135.5	134.8	128.9	127.3	137.9
Transport equipment — Equipement de transports	5.5	123.1	125.2	146.4	152.3	162.1	166.6	187.3
Electricity, gas, water [E] — Electricité, gaz et eau [E]	8.6	116.2	122.0	126.6	123.5	125.9	128.9	130.8
Asia — Asie								
Total industry [CDE] — Total, industrie [CDE]	**100.0**	**102.1**	**105.0**	**111.9**	**107.1**	**109.0**	**113.5**	**121.0**
Total mining [C] — Total, industries extractives [C]	7.9	105.7	102.4	107.9	106.2	108.4	110.6	113.7
Coal — Houille	0.7	105.3	110.4	113.6	121.0	124.5	133.6	145.0
Crude petroleum and natural gas Pétrole brut et gaz naturel	5.8	104.2	99.9	106.2	103.5	104.2	106.5	109.1
Metal ores — Minerais métalliques	0.3	141.1	140.9	157.8	157.7	184.8	168.1	158.1
Total manufacturing [D] Total, industries manufacturières [D]	82.8	100.7	104.1	111.4	105.5	107.2	112.0	120.2
Food, beverages, tobacco Industries alimentaires, boissons, tabac	10.3	99.1	100.0	101.7	101.3	101.9	104.7	104.9
Textiles — Textiles	2.8	93.5	93.6	94.0	90.1	89.4	86.0	85.6
Wearing apparel, leather and footwear Articles d'habillement, cuir et chaussures	2.9	82.4	79.2	75.8	69.2	63.2	59.9	57.0
Wood and wood products — Bois et articles en bois	1.2	81.0	76.9	75.2	69.1	64.8	64.8	65.5
Paper, printing, publishing and recorded media Papier, imprimerie, édition et supports enregistré	5.7	100.2	100.6	100.1	97.6	97.0	96.6	97.0
Chemicals and related products Produits chimiques et alliés	13.1	105.4	109.6	112.2	111.8	112.6	116.5	120.5
Non–metallic mineral products Produits minéraux non métalliques	3.7	91.3	91.7	93.4	89.9	89.1	89.5	88.9
Basic metals — Métallurgie de base	5.9	94.2	95.8	104.0	101.8	104.5	109.0	112.9
Fabricated metal products Fabrications d'ouvrages en métaux	9.0	91.6	91.5	99.0	91.4	87.9	90.6	99.8
Office and related electrical products Machines de bureau et autres appareils élect.	16.4	113.9	127.9	154.3	134.8	144.1	161.6	188.2
Transport equipment — Equipement de transports	7.3	102.0	106.0	111.2	112.8	121.3	125.6	139.9
Electricity, gas, water [E] — Electricité, gaz et eau [E]	9.3	111.2	114.9	120.3	122.4	125.5	128.8	134.4
Asia excluding Israel and Japan — Asie à l'exception de l'Israël et du Japon								
Total industry [CDE] — Total, industrie [CDE]	**100.0**	**106.8**	**114.9**	**126.2**	**125.2**	**133.1**	**142.1**	**157.5**
Total mining [C] — Total, industries extractives [C]	19.1	105.6	102.1	108.3	106.3	108.1	110.3	113.2
Coal — Houille	1.8	109.3	114.4	119.0	126.9	133.3	143.1	155.5
Crude petroleum and natural gas Pétrole brut et gaz naturel	15.7	104.2	99.9	106.2	103.4	104.2	106.4	109.0
Metal ores — Minerais métalliques	0.7	143.2	142.8	160.8	161.0	188.9	171.7	161.4
Total manufacturing [D] Total, industries manufacturières [D]	73.2	105.8	116.9	129.9	128.5	138.0	149.1	168.4
Food, beverages, tobacco Industries alimentaires, boissons, tabac	11.0	101.7	102.7	106.8	107.1	111.2	119.1	123.4
Textiles — Textiles	5.6	98.2	101.4	104.4	101.2	104.1	101.3	102.1

Region and industry [ISIC Rev. 3] / Régions et industrie [CITI Rév. 3]	Weight(%) Pond.(%)	1998	1999	2000	2001	2002	2003	2004
Wearing apparel, leather and footwear / Articles d'habillement, cuir et chaussures	3.7	85.9	88.1	94.0	90.5	88.0	87.9	88.8
Wood and wood products — Bois et articles en bois	1.2	86.2	81.7	82.4	78.6	76.8	79.9	83.3
Paper, printing, publishing and recorded media / Papier, imprimerie, édition et supports enregistré	3.1	98.3	102.7	103.5	98.7	101.4	103.5	107.5
Chemicals and related products / Produits chimiques et alliés	13.6	116.4	124.5	130.5	130.9	134.5	143.9	155.2
Non–metallic mineral products / Produits minéraux non métalliques	4.3	95.9	104.0	108.2	110.2	117.7	123.6	126.9
Basic metals — Métallurgie de base	5.4	102.8	112.5	119.2	120.6	128.1	137.0	145.3
Fabricated metal products / Fabrications d'ouvrages en métaux	7.9	88.4	97.4	114.9	110.4	115.9	121.7	139.2
Office and related electrical products / Machines de bureau et autres appareils élect.	9.0	136.5	180.3	235.4	226.9	269.0	306.1	384.0
Transport equipment — Equipement de transports	5.4	102.0	121.4	133.2	141.5	156.2	178.1	216.8
Electricity, gas, water [E] — Electricité, gaz et eau [E]	7.7	119.5	126.9	135.8	141.3	148.8	155.3	164.2
Europe — Europe								
Total industry [CDE] — Total, industrie [CDE]	**100.0**	**107.9**	**110.2**	**116.1**	**116.6**	**115.8**	**116.8**	**120.0**
Total mining [C] — Total, industries extractives [C]	5.1	99.3	100.4	100.4	99.5	100.3	100.0	100.5
Coal — Houille	1.1	83.6	80.2	76.2	73.0	70.7	70.1	69.4
Crude petroleum and natural gas / Pétrole brut et gaz naturel	3.1	105.0	106.0	105.7	106.2	108.2	107.6	108.5
Metal ores — Minerais métalliques	0.2	90.6	93.6	99.2	98.3	105.1	108.6	111.0
Total manufacturing [D] / Total, industries manufacturières [D]	85.0	108.6	111.0	117.4	117.9	116.8	117.6	121.1
Food, beverages, tobacco / Industries alimentaires, boissons, tabac	10.4	103.7	105.5	106.7	108.3	110.9	112.0	113.2
Textiles — Textiles	2.5	98.0	94.0	95.7	92.4	88.3	85.4	81.6
Wearing apparel, leather and footwear / Articles d'habillement, cuir et chaussures	2.7	90.9	84.3	81.4	79.5	72.2	68.0	63.7
Wood and wood products — Bois et articles en bois	1.9	104.2	107.0	112.6	108.8	109.0	110.6	115.0
Paper, printing, publishing and recorded media / Papier, imprimerie, édition et supports enregistré	7.4	107.8	111.3	114.6	112.6	113.0	113.4	116.7
Chemicals and related products / Produits chimiques et alliés	13.9	111.0	115.1	120.8	123.0	127.0	130.0	132.8
Non–metallic mineral products / Produits minéraux non métalliques	4.2	100.3	103.1	107.6	107.6	105.4	106.0	108.8
Basic metals — Métallurgie de base	4.6	104.5	102.0	110.4	110.1	108.5	108.7	112.6
Fabricated metal products / Fabrications d'ouvrages en métaux	15.5	107.0	106.2	112.5	114.5	112.6	112.3	116.8
Office and related electrical products / Machines de bureau et autres appareils élect.	9.7	117.1	126.1	145.5	143.3	134.2	136.0	143.6
Transport equipment — Equipement de transports	8.1	122.0	126.8	134.9	137.4	137.0	140.0	146.6
Electricity, gas, water [E] — Electricité, gaz et eau [E]	9.8	106.2	109.0	112.8	114.8	115.3	118.6	120.7
Oceania — Océanie								
Total industry [CDE] — Total, industrie [CDE]	**100.0**	**108.0**	**108.3**	**111.4**	**114.2**	**119.2**	**119.2**	**119.1**
Total mining [C] — Total, industries extractives [C]	18.3	112.1	109.6	121.0	123.6	116.3	124.7	121.2
Coal — Houille	4.2	108.5	116.6	126.5	134.3	142.5	144.6	148.5

Region and industry [ISIC Rev. 3] Régions et industrie [CITI Rév. 3]	Weight(%) Pond.(%)	1998	1999	2000	2001	2002	2003	2004
Crude petroleum and natural gas Pétrole brut et gaz naturel	6.0	107.9	94.9	116.4	119.4	114.3	109.3	97.5
Metal ores — Minerais métalliques	6.7	120.6	122.8	131.6	134.3	131.4	135.1	136.8
Total manufacturing [D] Total, industries manufacturières [D]	69.4	107.3	108.5	109.9	112.6	115.1	118.7	119.7
Food, beverages, tobacco Industries alimentaires, boissons, tabac	15.0	112.6	115.2	116.9	121.7	121.0	123.4	123.3
Textiles — Textiles	1.9	96.5	96.4	93.9	87.8	78.9	72.2	68.7
Wearing apparel, leather and footwear Articles d'habillement, cuir et chaussures	2.2	96.4	96.3	93.8	87.6	78.7	72.1	68.5
Wood and wood products — Bois et articles en bois	2.8	99.2	97.9	107.0	105.7	109.1	113.4	114.3
Paper, printing, publishing and recorded media Papier, imprimerie, édition et supports enregistré	7.3	104.0	104.2	107.9	110.7	113.3	110.9	112.3
Chemicals and related products Produits chimiques et alliés	10.0	109.0	110.1	113.7	116.7	120.2	129.9	125.6
Non–metallic mineral products Produits minéraux non métalliques	3.7	98.6	103.9	110.0	112.5	120.8	130.4	135.2
Basic metals — Métallurgie de base	8.5	105.7	107.9	104.0	103.6	109.8	110.7	113.1
Fabricated metal products Fabrications d'ouvrages en métaux	5.6	107.8	108.0	107.9	111.0	115.4	119.4	123.6
Office and related electrical products Machines de bureau et autres appareils élect.	4.8	110.7	110.3	109.9	115.8	118.4	124.7	128.8
Transport equipment — Equipement de transports	5.8	110.9	110.6	110.1	115.9	118.5	124.8	128.9
Electricity, gas, water [E] — Electricité, gaz et eau [E]	12.3	106.0	105.3	105.9	109.5	111.1	114.1	113.2

Source

United Nations Statistics Division, New York, the index numbers of industrial production database.

Notes

[1] Northern America (Canada and the United States), Europe, Australia, Israel, Japan, New Zealand and South Africa.
[2] Latin America and the Caribbean, Africa (excluding South Africa), Asia (excluding Israel and Japan), Oceania (excluding Australia and New Zealand).
[3] Canada and the United States.

Source

Organisation des Nations Unies, Division de statistique, New York, la base de données pour les indices de la production industrielle.

Notes

[1] Amérique septentrionale (le Canada et les Etats–Unis), Europe, l'Australie, l'Israël, la Nouvelle–Zélande et l'Afrique du Sud.
[2] Amérique latine et Caraïbes, Afrique (non compris l'Afrique du Sud), Asie (non compris l'Israël et le Japon), Océanie (non compris l'Australie et la Nouvelle–Zélande).
[3] Le Canada et les Etats–Unis.

Production, trade and consumption of commercial energy
Thousand metric tons of oil equivalent and kilograms per capita

Production, commerce et consommation d'énergie commerciale
Milliers de tonnes d'équivalent pétrole et kilogrammes par habitant

Region	Year Année	Primary energy production – Production d'énergie primaire					Changes in stocks Variations des stocks	Imports Importations	Exports Exportations
		Total Totale	Solids Solides	Liquids Liquides	Gas Gaz	Electricity Electricité			
World	1997	9 034 564	2 371 334	3 640 375	2 143 177	879 678	15 999	3 338 900	3 335 339
	1998	9 073 261	2 263 074	3 697 192	2 207 493	905 502	54 547	3 391 782	3 429 555
	1999	8 972 774	2 146 650	3 629 488	2 264 912	931 725	−58 530	3 421 236	3 412 249
	2000	9 202 839	2 139 262	3 768 449	2 340 310	954 817	−50 294	3 652 215	3 628 613
	2001	9 386 609	2 289 458	3 755 240	2 381 696	960 215	54 727	3 713 279	3 662 696
	2002	9 528 831	2 397 209	3 721 932	2 434 779	974 911	9 683	3 760 255	3 619 959
	2003	9 890 057	2 568 362	3 855 277	2 495 245	971 174	9 286	3 918 771	3 855 051
Africa	1997	655 930	158 053	389 221	99 269	9 388	6 367	68 019	410 703
	1998	685 286	160 341	410 899	104 188	9 859	16 929	76 089	401 472
	1999	686 295	160 891	402 991	112 230	10 183	9 932	77 889	407 898
	2000	712 635	161 388	421 358	119 475	10 414	829	76 745	435 669
	2001	718 547	162 261	424 677	121 555	10 054	4 322	76 771	433 551
	2002	720 329	162 863	420 116	126 168	11 181	−1 697	81 306	429 124
	2003	761 999	171 748	445 309	133 592	11 350	263	83 517	466 588
America, North	1997	2 342 755	605 265	770 928	694 299	272 263	408	712 599	363 757
	1998	2 350 922	613 243	732 616	718 655	286 409	36 641	748 948	372 317
	1999	2 335 538	601 645	711 602	718 986	303 305	−8 845	769 134	358 648
	2000	2 348 852	586 670	721 290	732 503	308 389	−54 113	821 190	378 555
	2001	2 387 758	616 079	723 694	748 360	299 625	62 158	852 778	382 392
	2002	2 373 765	595 410	730 281	736 649	311 425	−21 724	836 166	385 459
	2003	2 353 218	579 708	740 136	725 741	307 633	−10 476	881 229	406 834
America, South	1997	491 891	28 191	340 738	77 422	45 540	163	86 381	251 142
	1998	513 641	30 206	350 223	86 744	46 468	217	89 120	259 115
	1999	510 940	29 242	344 666	90 674	46 357	−4 349	80 714	245 581
	2000	528 096	33 755	350 811	94 216	49 313	495	80 828	253 179
	2001	525 128	36 594	346 114	93 663	48 756	2 290	81 948	254 844
	2002	515 090	36 322	331 201	97 259	50 308	13 830	80 805	239 919
	2003	505 690	39 812	317 831	95 443	52 604	4 144	78 393	234 659
Asia	1997	3 109 730	1 030 760	1 464 660	432 734	181 576	7 554	1 129 546	1 245 499
	1998	3 102 003	932 629	1 532 708	445 247	191 419	87	1 104 128	1 310 199
	1999	3 006 027	831 294	1 498 791	483 858	192 084	−37 811	1 139 467	1 301 849
	2000	3 134 114	830 966	1 571 941	533 016	198 191	−5 460	1 248 043	1 397 390
	2001	3 227 120	930 843	1 540 899	553 508	201 870	−9 830	1 243 982	1 395 801
	2002	3 341 047	1 058 032	1 491 775	589 711	201 528	5 036	1 285 331	1 304 244
	2003	3 628 487	1 221 610	1 580 234	629 730	196 913	5 832	1 350 186	1 430 277
Europe	1997	2 215 285	403 964	640 220	805 809	365 292	−560	1 311 596	941 751
	1998	2 187 709	370 800	632 972	818 416	365 521	146	1 342 871	952 351
	1999	2 202 904	365 724	639 805	823 638	373 738	−13 242	1 316 631	960 320
	2000	2 226 586	358 502	662 129	823 712	382 243	6 966	1 392 058	1 015 667
	2001	2 258 834	360 561	678 043	826 242	393 988	−3 739	1 423 329	1 034 065
	2002	2 304 806	354 660	710 338	845 556	394 251	10 399	1 442 339	1 095 098
	2003	2 368 782	364 400	736 195	871 557	396 630	7 622	1 489 624	1 149 236
Oceania	1997	218 973	145 102	34 608	33 644	5 619	2 067	30 759	122 487
	1998	233 699	155 856	37 773	34 244	5 826	526	30 627	134 102
	1999	231 071	157 854	31 632	35 526	6 059	−4 216	37 401	137 953
	2000	252 556	167 982	40 920	37 388	6 267	989	33 352	148 152
	2001	269 221	183 118	41 813	38 368	5 922	−475	34 472	162 043
	2002	273 795	189 921	38 220	39 436	6 218	3 839	34 308	166 115
	2003	271 880	191 084	35 571	39 182	6 043	1 901	35 822	167 457

Source

United Nations Statistics Division, New York, *Energy Statistics Yearbook 2003* and the energy statistics database.

6 Production, trade and consumption of commercial energy — Thousand metric tons of oil equivalent and kilograms per capita (*continued*)

Production, commerce et consommation d'énergie commerciale — Milliers de tonnes d'équivalent pétrole et kilogrammes par habitant (*suite*)

Bunkers – Soutes			Consumption – Consommation							
Air Avion	Sea Maritime	Unallocated Nondistribué	Per capita Par habitant	Total Totale	Solids Solides	Liquids Liquides	Gas Gaz	Electricity Electricité	Year Année	Région
90 618	131 881	476 429	1 387	8 323 197	2 382 011	2 914 522	2 147 601	879 063	1997	Monde
98 119	136 840	489 494	1 356	8 256 487	2 268 068	2 900 507	2 182 547	905 366	1998	
101 056	146 190	476 874	1 347	8 316 173	2 183 952	2 936 404	2 263 917	931 900	1999	
105 358	148 448	529 107	1 356	8 493 823	2 227 119	2 959 357	2 352 676	954 671	2000	
103 407	140 792	529 447	1 357	8 608 818	2 291 228	2 993 416	2 363 382	960 792	2001	
104 009	145 705	538 871	1 381	8 870 857	2 425 844	3 020 338	2 448 748	975 927	2002	
106 106	142 248	577 765	1 398	9 118 372	2 608 885	3 044 205	2 494 279	971 003	2003	
2 775	7 369	30 087	365	266 649	115 109	95 108	47 219	9 213	1997	Afrique
3 231	7 023	55 529	371	277 191	113 470	98 833	55 111	9 777	1998	
3 483	8 078	48 117	374	286 674	117 591	102 432	56 143	10 508	1999	
4 106	7 468	55 758	363	285 549	117 430	102 192	55 472	10 456	2000	
3 769	7 581	53 177	364	292 919	118 210	104 341	60 091	10 277	2001	
3 647	6 733	54 676	376	309 152	122 668	111 081	64 112	11 291	2002	
3 630	7 803	50 699	376	316 532	127 011	111 627	66 682	11 212	2003	
21 011	27 263	155 293	5 380	2 487 622	559 501	961 772	694 089	272 259	1997	Amérique du Nord
22 037	27 433	139 534	5 348	2 501 909	555 945	959 266	700 191	286 508	1998	
23 496	31 283	131 086	5 431	2 569 005	561 100	985 704	718 839	303 362	1999	
23 612	33 499	136 261	5 541	2 652 228	582 467	999 948	761 492	308 320	2000	
21 840	24 462	141 265	5 302	2 608 419	577 500	1 009 831	721 544	299 543	2001	
21 223	28 308	137 801	5 333	2 658 863	582 315	1 011 268	753 598	311 683	2002	
20 659	24 137	148 742	5 245	2 644 551	587 154	1 026 015	723 845	307 537	2003	
2 353	3 640	27 972	897	293 003	21 829	148 053	77 564	45 555	1997	Amérique du Sud
2 399	3 607	30 956	925	306 466	22 113	151 211	86 668	46 474	1998	
2 235	4 486	36 906	908	306 796	21 140	149 673	89 640	46 344	1999	
1 992	5 127	36 725	908	311 405	21 057	147 075	94 074	49 199	2000	
1 959	5 632	32 633	882	309 718	19 694	148 207	93 140	48 677	2001	
1 936	5 755	23 521	873	310 934	19 148	144 163	97 449	50 175	2002	
2 145	5 490	30 118	846	307 528	19 730	139 311	96 199	52 287	2003	
20 723	47 999	198 323	766	2 719 178	1 141 602	946 311	449 435	181 830	1997	Asie
24 826	52 746	200 321	726	2 617 952	1 047 188	921 126	457 722	191 916	1998	
23 269	57 910	187 347	714	2 612 930	974 247	949 040	497 172	192 471	1999	
24 069	55 504	230 005	722	2 680 650	984 182	972 880	524 684	198 904	2000	
24 721	54 900	233 598	738	2 771 912	1 047 457	972 458	549 417	202 581	2001	
27 204	55 740	259 474	781	2 974 680	1 183 674	998 771	590 034	202 201	2002	
28 173	55 329	277 148	822	3 181 915	1 342 623	1 016 133	626 219	196 940	2003	
40 930	44 380	62 624	2 850	2 437 755	493 865	724 064	855 240	364 586	1997	Europe
42 580	44 910	60 744	2 840	2 429 849	476 526	730 002	858 456	364 865	1998	
45 434	43 264	70 214	2 819	2 413 545	455 738	708 203	876 448	373 156	1999	
48 722	45 622	67 452	2 837	2 434 215	467 757	695 137	889 796	381 524	2000	
47 717	47 091	67 569	2 906	2 489 460	466 621	718 435	910 611	393 793	2001	
47 145	48 019	63 438	2 900	2 483 045	461 638	713 047	914 001	394 359	2002	
48 424	48 433	70 519	2 960	2 534 173	476 338	708 525	952 327	396 983	2003	
2 827	1 231	2 131	4 118	118 990	50 104	39 214	24 053	5 619	1997	Océanie
3 046	1 121	2 410	4 165	123 120	52 827	40 069	24 399	5 826	1998	
3 139	1 168	3 205	4 251	127 223	54 137	41 353	25 674	6 059	1999	
2 858	1 228	2 906	4 281	129 777	54 227	42 125	27 158	6 267	2000	
3 403	1 127	1 206	4 441	136 389	61 746	40 144	28 578	5 922	2001	
2 854	1 151	−40	4 302	134 183	56 402	42 008	29 555	6 218	2002	
3 075	1 057	540	4 168	133 672	56 028	42 593	29 007	6 043	2003	

Source

Organisation des Nations Unies, Division de statistique, New York, *Annuaire des statistiques de l'énergie 2003* et la base de données pour les statistiques énergétiques.

Total imports and exports: index numbers
Volume and unit value indices and terms of trade (2000 = 100)

Importations et exportations : indices
Indices du volume et de la valeur unitaire et termes de l'échange (2000 = 100)

Region [&]	1996	1997	1998	1999	2001	2002	2003	2004	Région [&]
Total									**Total**
Exports: Volume [1]	73	81	85	90	99	103	108	122	Exp. : Volume [1]
Exports: Unit value indices US $ [2]	116	108	102	100	97	97	107	113	Exp. : Indices de la val. unit. en $ E.–U. [2]
Imports: Volume [1]	74	80	84	90	99	103	110	122	Imp. : Volume [1]
Imports: Unit value indices US $ [2]	113	107	101	99	97	96	104	114	Imp : Indices de la val. unit en $ E.–U. [2]
Developed economies [3]									**Economies développées [3]**
Exports: Volume [1]	75	83	86	90	98	100	102	112	Exp. : Volume [1]
Exports: Unit value indices US $ [2]	119	110	107	104	98	100	112	119	Exp. : Indices de la val. unit. en $ E.–U. [2]
Imports: Volume [1]	71	78	84	91	99	101	106	116	Imp. : Volume [1]
Imports: Unit value indices US $ [2]	116	109	103	100	96	97	107	116	Imp : Indices de la val. unit en $ E.–U. [2]
Terms of trade [4]	102	102	104	104	102	103	105	102	Termes de l'echange [4]
Africa [5]									*Afrique [5]*
Exports: Volume [1]	84	91	83	88	103	102	98	...	Exp. : Volume [1]
Exports: Unit value indices US $ [2]	114	113	104	100	95	96	123	...	Exp. : Indices de la val. unit. en $ E.–U. [2]
Imports: Volume [1]	94	103	99	91	100	104	119	...	Imp. : Volume [1]
Imports: Unit value indices US $ [2]	107	107	99	98	94	94	115	...	Imp : Indices de la val. unit en $ E.–U. [2]
Terms of trade [4]	106	106	105	102	100	103	107	...	Termes de l'echange [4]
North America									*Amérique du Nord*
Exports: Volume [1]	77	85	87	89	94	91	92	98	Exp. : Volume [1]
Exports: Unit value indices US $ [2]	103	102	99	100	99	97	101	106	Exp. : Indices de la val. unit. en $ E.–U. [2]
Imports: Volume [1]	65	74	82	91	96	100	105	116	Imp. : Volume [1]
Imports: Unit value indices US $ [2]	102	99	93	94	97	95	98	103	Imp : Indices de la val. unit en $ E.–U. [2]
Terms of trade [4]	102	102	106	106	102	103	104	103	Termes de l'echange [4]
Asia									*Asie*
Exports: Volume [1]	81	90	88	90	89	95	99	109	Exp. : Volume [1]
Exports: Unit value indices US $ [2]	106	97	91	96	94	90	97	105	Exp. : Indices de la val. unit. en $ E.–U. [2]
Imports: Volume [1]	85	86	81	89	104	100	105	111	Imp. : Volume [1]
Imports: Unit value indices US $ [2]	108	103	91	91	88	87	92	102	Imp : Indices de la val. unit en $ E.–U. [2]
Terms of trade [4]	98	94	100	105	107	103	105	102	Termes de l'echange [4]
Europe									*Europe*
Exports: Volume [1]	73	80	85	90	102	104	106	119	Exp. : Volume [1]
Exports: Unit value indices US $ [2]	129	117	114	107	99	102	119	126	Exp. : Indices de la val. unit. en $ E.–U. [2]
Imports: Volume [1]	71	78	85	91	100	102	106	115	Imp. : Volume [1]
Imports: Unit value indices US $ [2]	126	115	111	104	98	100	115	127	Imp : Indices de la val. unit en $ E.–U. [2]
Terms of trade [4]	102	102	103	103	101	103	104	99	Termes de l'echange [4]
Oceania									*Océanie*
Exports: Volume [1]	82	88	87	92	101	101	100	103	Exp. : Volume [1]
Exports: Unit value indices US $ [2]	119	114	101	97	99	100	111	129	Exp. : Indices de la val. unit. en $ E.–U. [2]
Imports: Volume [1]	80	84	89	96	95	106	118	135	Imp. : Volume [1]
Imports: Unit value indices US $ [2]	118	112	101	102	94	95	105	112	Imp : Indices de la val. unit en $ E.–U. [2]
Terms of trade [4]	101	102	99	95	105	105	105	115	Termes de l'echange [4]
Developing economies [3]									**Econ. en dévelop. [3]**
Exports: Volume [1]	68	77	84	91	100	109	123	148	Exp. : Volume [1]
Exports: Unit value indices US $ [2]	108	103	88	90	94	92	96	101	Exp. : Indices de la val. unit. en $ E.–U. [2]
Imports: Volume [1]	81	86	84	87	98	107	120	139	Imp. : Volume [1]
Imports: Unit value indices US $ [2,6]	104	103	95	96	97	94	98	107	Imp : Indices de la val. unit en $ E.–U. [2,6]
Terms of trade [4,6]	104	99	93	93	97	98	98	94	Termes de l'echange [4,6]

7 Total imports and exports: index numbers — Volume and unit value indices and terms of trade (2000 = 100) *(continued)*

Importations et exportations : indices — Indices du volume et de la valeur unitaire et termes de l'échange (2000 = 100) *(suite)*

Region &	1996	1997	1998	1999	2001	2002	2003	2004	Région &
Africa									Afrique
Exports: Volume [1]	90	96	102	97	100	109	134	152	Exp. : Volume [1]
Exports: Unit value indices US $ [2]	89	82	68	83	93	88	86	93	Exp. : Indices de la val. unit. en $ E.–U. [2]
Americas									Amériques
Exports: Volume [1]	71	78	87	90	99	101	106	124	Exp. : Volume [1]
Exports: Unit value indices US $ [2]	101	102	90	93	97	96	100	104	Exp. : Indices de la val. unit. en $ E.–U. [2]
Imports: Volume [1]	81	77	87	88	99	100	103	109	Imp. : Volume [1]
Imports: Unit value indices US $ [2]	91	111	103	98	99	91	92	105	Imp : Indices de la val. unit en $ E.–U. [2]
Terms of trade [4]	110	92	88	95	97	105	109	100	Termes de l'echange [4]
Asia									Asia
Exports: Volume [1]	66	75	82	90	100	111	127	153	Exp. : Volume [1]
Exports: Unit value indices US $ [2]	112	104	89	89	93	92	95	101	Exp. : Indices de la val. unit. en $ E.–U. [2]
Imports: Volume [1]	82	88	81	84	98	108	125	149	Imp. : Volume [1]
Imports: Unit value indices US $ [2]	106	101	91	95	96	95	99	108	Imp : Indices de la val. unit en $ E.–U. [2]
Terms of trade [4]	106	103	98	94	97	97	96	94	Termes de l'echange [4]
Asia Middle East									Moyen–Orient d'Asie
Exports: Volume [1]	87	98	117	104	99	115	125	143	Exp. : Volume [1]
Exports: Unit value indices US $ [2]	75	71	50	70	93	85	95	106	Exp. : Indices de la val. unit. en $ E.–U. [2]
Imports: Volume [1]	76	86	89	88	96	105	117	129	Imp. : Volume [1]
Imports: Unit value indices US $ [2]	113	108	100	98	102	105	115	130	Imp : Indices de la val. unit en $ E.–U. [2]
Terms of trade [4]	66	66	50	72	91	81	82	82	Termes de l'echange [4]
Other Asia									Autre Asie
Exports: Volume [1]	61	70	73	87	99	110	128	156	Exp. : Volume [1]
Exports: Unit value indices US $ [2]	124	116	104	95	93	93	96	99	Exp. : Indices de la val. unit. en $ E.–U. [2]
Imports: Volume [1]	82	88	80	84	98	109	127	153	Imp. : Volume [1]
Imports: Unit value indices US $ [2]	105	100	90	94	95	93	96	104	Imp : Indices de la val. unit en $ E.–U. [2]
Terms of trade [4]	118	116	116	101	98	101	99	96	Termes de l'echange [4]

Source

United Nations Statistics Division, New York, trade statistics database.

Notes

& The regional analysis in this table is in accordance with the groupings of countries or areas specified in Table 65.

[1] Volume indices are derived from value data and unit value indices. They are base period weighted.

[2] Regional aggregates are current period weighted.

[3] This classification is intended for statistical convenience and does not, necessarily, express a judgement about the stage reached by a particular country in the development process.

[4] Unit value index of exports divided by unit value index of imports.

[5] Beginning January 1998, data refer to South Africa only. Prior to January 1998, data refer to Southern African Common Customs Area.

[6] Indices, except those for Europe, are based on estimates prepared by the International Monetary Fund.

Source

Organisation des Nations Unies, Division de statistique, New York, la base de données pour les statistiques du commerce extérieur.

Notes

& L'analyse régionale dans ce tableau est conforme aux groupes des pays ou zones paraissant dans tableau 65.

[1] Les indices du quantum sont calculés à partir des chiffres de la valeur et des indices de valeur unitaire. Ils sont àcoéfficients de pondération correspondant à la périod en base.

[2] Les totaux régionaux sont à coéfficients de pondération correspondant à la période en cours.

[3] Cette classification est utilisée pour plus de commodité dans la presentation des statistique et n'implique pas nécessairement un jugement quant au stage de développement auquel est parvenu un pays donné.

[4] Indices de la valeur unitaire des exportations divisé par l'indice de la valeur unitaire des importations.

[5] A compter de janvier 1998, les données se rapportent qu'à l'Afrique du Sud. Avant janvier 1998, le données se rapportent à l'Union Douanière de l'Afrique.

[6] Le calcul des indices, sauf ceux pour l'Europe, sont basés sur les estimations préparées par le Fonds monétaire.

Table 1: The series of world aggregates on population, output, production, transport, external trade and finance have been compiled from statistical publications and databases of the United Nations and the specialized agencies and other institutions [5, 6, 7, 8, 14, 18, 22, 23, 24, 25]. The sources should be consulted for detailed information on compilation and coverage.

Table 2 presents estimates of population size, rates of population increase, crude birth and death rates, surface area and population density for the world and regions. Unless otherwise specified, all figures are estimates of the order of magnitude and are subject to a substantial margin of error.

The population estimates and rates presented in this table were prepared by the Population Division of the United Nations Secretariat and published in *World Population Prospects: The 2004 Revision* [28].

The average annual percentage rates of population growth were calculated by the Population Division of the United Nations Secretariat, using an exponential rate of increase formula.

Crude birth and crude death rates are expressed in terms of the average annual number of births and deaths respectively, per 1,000 mid-year population. These rates are estimated.

Surface area totals were obtained by summing the figures for the individual countries or areas.

Density is the number of persons in the 2003 total population per square kilometre of total surface area.

The scheme of regionalization used for the purpose of making these estimates is presented in annex I. Although some continental totals are given, and all can be derived, the basic scheme presents macro regions that are so drawn as to obtain greater homogeneity in sizes of population, types of demographic circumstances and accuracy of demographic statistics.

Tables 3-4: The index numbers in table 3 refer to agricultural production, which is defined to include both crop and livestock products. Seeds and feed are excluded. The index numbers of food refer to commodities which are considered edible and contain nutrients. Coffee, tea and other inedible commodities are excluded.

The index numbers of total agricultural and food production in table 3 are calculated by the Laspeyres formula with the base year period 1999-2001. The latter is provided in order to diminish the impact of annual fluctuations in agricultural output during base years on the indices for the period. Production quantities of each commodity are weighted by 1999-2001 average national producer prices and summed for each year. The index numbers are based on production data for a calendar year. As in the past, the series include a large

Tableau 1 : Les séries d'agrégats mondiaux sur la population, la production, les transports, le commerce extérieur et les finances ont été établies à partir de publications statistiques et bases de données des Nations Unies et les institutions spécialisées et autres organismes [5, 6, 7, 8, 14, 18, 22, 23, 24, 25]. On doit se référer aux sources pour tous renseignements détaillés sur les méthodes de calcul et la portée des statistiques.

Le *Tableau 2* présente les estimations mondiales et régionales de la population, des taux d'accroissement de la population, des taux bruts de natalité et de mortalité, de la superficie et de la densité de population. Sauf indication contraire, tous les chiffres sont des estimations de l'ordre de grandeur et comportent une assez grande marge d'erreur.

Les estimations de la population et tous les taux pré-sentés dans ce tableau ont été établis par la Division de la population du Secrétariat des Nations Unies et publiés dans *World Population Prospects: The 2004 Revision* [28].

Les pourcentages annuels moyens de l'accroissement de la population ont été calculés par la Division de la population du Secrétariat des Nations Unies, sur la base d'une formule de taux d'accroissement exponentiel.

Les taux bruts de natalité et de mortalité sont exprimés, respectivement, sur la base du nombre annuel moyen de naissances et de décès par tranche de 1.000 habitants au milieu de l'année. Ces taux sont estimatifs.

On a déterminé les superficies totales en additionnant les chiffres correspondant aux différents pays ou régions.

La densité est le nombre de personnes de la population totale de 2003 par kilomètre carré de la superficie totale.

Le schéma de régionalisation utilisé aux fins de l'établissement de ces estimations est présenté dans l'annexe I. Bien que les totaux de certains continents soient donnés et que tous puissent être déterminés, le schéma de base présente les grandes régions qui sont établies de manière à obtenir une plus grande homogénéité en ce qui concerne l'ampleur des populations, les types de conditions démographiques et la précision des statistiques démographiques.

Tableaux 3 et 4 : Les indices du tableau 3 se rapportent à la production agricole, qui est définie comme comprenant à la fois les produits de l'agriculture et de l'élevage. Les semences et les aliments pour les animaux sont exclus de cette définition. Les indices de la production alimentaire se rapportent aux produits considérés comme comestibles et contenant des éléments nutritifs. Le café, le thé et les produits non comestibles sont exclus.

Les indices de la production agricole et de la production alimentaire présentés au tableau 3 sont calculés selon la formule de Laspeyres avec les années 1999-2001 comme période de référence, cela afin de limiter l'incidence, sur les indices cor-

number of estimates made by FAO in cases where figures are not available from official country sources.

Index numbers for the world and regions are computed in a similar way to the country index numbers except that instead of using different commodity prices for each country group, "international commodity prices" derived from the Gheary-Khamis formula are used for all country groupings. This method assigns a single "price" to each commodity.

The indexes in table 4 are calculated as a ratio between the index numbers of total agricultural and food production in table 3 described above and the corresponding index numbers of population.

For further information on the series presented in these tables, see the *FAO Production Yearbook* [5] and http://faostat.fao.org.

Table 5: The index numbers of industrial production are classified according to tabulation categories, divisions and combinations of divisions of the *International Standard Industrial Classification of All Economic Activities, Revision 3*, (ISIC Rev. 3) [50] for mining (category C), manufacturing (category D), and electricity, gas and water (category E).

The indices indicate trends in value added at constant prices. The measure of value added used is the national accounts concept, which is defined as gross output less the cost of materials, supplies, fuel and electricity consumed and services received.

Each series is compiled using the Laspeyres formula, that is, the indices are base-weighted arithmetic means. The weight base year is 1995 and value added, generally at factor cost, is used in weighting.

For most countries the estimates of value added used as weights are derived from the results of national industrial censuses or similar inquiries relating to 1995. These data, in national currency, are adjusted to the ISIC where necessary and are subsequently converted into US dollars.

Within each of the ISIC categories (tabulation categories, divisions and combinations of divisions) shown in the tables, the indices for the country aggregations (regions or economic groupings) are calculated directly from the country data. The indices for the World, however, are calculated from the aggregated indices for the groupings of developed and developing countries.

China and the countries of the former USSR (except Russian Federation and Ukraine) are excluded from their respective regions.

Table 6: For a description of the series in table 6, see the technical notes to chapter XIII.

Table 7: For a description of the series in table 7, see the technical notes to chapter XVI. The composition of the regions is presented in table 65.

respondant à la période considérée, des fluctuations annuelles de la production agricole enregistrée pendant les années de référence. Les chiffres de production de chaque produit sont pondérés par les prix nationaux moyens à la production pour la période 1999-2001 et additionnés pour chaque année. Les indices sont fondés sur les données de production de l'année civile. Comme dans le passé, les séries comprennent un grand nombre d'estimations établies par la FAO lorsqu'elle n'avait pu obtenir de chiffres de sources officielles dans les pays eux-mêmes.

Les indices pour le monde et les régions sont calculés de la même façon que les indices par pays, mais au lieu d'appliquer des prix différents aux produits de base pour chaque groupe de pays, on a utilisé des "prix internationaux" établis d'après la formule de Gheary-Khamis pour tous les groupes de pays. Cette méthode attribue un seul "prix" à chaque produit de base.

Les indices du tableau 4 sont calculés comme ratio entre les indices de la production alimentaire et de la production agricole totale du tableau 3 décrits ci-dessus et les indices de population correspondants.

Pour tout renseignement complémentaire sur les séries présentées dans ces tableaux, voir l'*Annuaire de la production de la FAO* [5] et http ://faostat.fao.org.

Tableau 5 : Les indices de la production industrielle sont classés selon les catégories de classement, les divisions ou des combinaisons des divisions de la *Classification internationale type, par industrie, de toutes les branches d'activité économique, Révision 3* (CITI Rev. 3) [50] qui concernent les industries extractives (la catégorie C) et les industries manufacturières (la catégorie D), ainsi que l'électricité, le gaz et l'eau (la catégorie E).

Ces indices représentent les tendances de la valeur ajoutée aux prix constants. La mesure utilisée pour la valeur ajoutée correspond à celle qui est appliquée aux fins de la comptabilité nationale, c'est-à-dire égale à la valeur de la production brute diminuée des coûts des matériaux, des fournitures, de la consommation de carburant et d'électricité ainsi que des services reçus.

Chaque série a été établie au moyen de la formule de Laspeyres, ce qui signifie que les indices sont des moyennes arithmétiques affectées de coefficients de pondération. L'année de base de pondération est l'année 1995 et on utilise généralement pour la pondération la valeur ajoutée au coût des facteurs.

Pour la plupart des pays, les estimations de la valeur ajoutée qui sont utilisées comme coefficients de pondération sont tirées des résultats des recensements industriels nationaux ou enquêtes analogues concernant l'année 1995. Ces données, en monnaie nationale, sont ajustées s'il y a lieu aux normes de la CITI et ultérieurement converties en dollars des Etats-Unis.

A l'intérieur de chacune des subdivisions de la CITI (catégories de classement, divisions et combinaisons des divisions) indiquées dans les tableaux, les indices relatifs aux assemblages de pays (régions géographiques ou groupements économiques) sont calculés directement à partir des données des pays. Toutefois, les indices concernant le *Monde* sont calculés à partir des indices agrégés applicable aux groupements de pays développés et de pays en développement.

La Chine et les pays de l'ancienne URSS (sauf la Fédération de Russie et Ukraine) sont exclus de leurs régions respectives.

Tableau 6 : On trouvera une description de la série de statistiques du tableau 6 dans les notes techniques du chapitre XIII.

Tableau 7 : On trouvera une description de la série de statistiques du tableau 7 dans les notes techniques du chapitre XVI. La composition des régions est présentée au tableau 65.

Part Two of the *Yearbook* presents statistical series on a wide range of population and social topics for all countries or areas of the world for which data have been made available. The topics include population and population growth, surface area and density; education; food supply; life expectancy, childbearing and mortality; newspapers; telephones and Internet users.

La deuxième partie de l'*Annuaire* présente, pour tous les pays ou zones du monde pour lesquels des données sont disponibles, des séries statistiques concernant une large gamme de questions démographiques et sociales: population et croissance démographique, superficie et densité; instruction; disponibilités alimentaires; l'espérance de vie, la maternité et la mortalité; journaux; téléphones et usagers d'Internet.

8

Population by sex, rate of population increase, surface area and density

Population selon le sexe, taux d'accroissement de la population, superficie et densité

Country or area Pays ou zone	Date	Latest census Dernier recensement			Mid-year estimates (thousands) Estimations au milieu de l'année (milliers)		Annual rate of increase (%) Taux d'accroisse-ment annuel (%)	Surface area (km²) Superficie (km²)	Density Densité
		Both sexes Les deux sexes	Men Hommes	Women Femmes	2000	2003	2000-03	2003	2003+
Africa **Afrique**									
Algeria [1] Algérie [1]	25 VI 1998	29 100 867	14 698 589	14 402 278	30 416	31 848	1.5	2 381 741	13
Angola [2,3] Angola [2,3]	15 XII 1970	5 646 166	2 943 974	2 702 192	...	...	...	1 246 700	...
Benin Bénin	11 II 2002	6 769 914	3 284 119[1]	3 485 795[1]	6 169[3]	...	...	112 622	...
Botswana [3] Botswana [3]	17 VIII 2001	*1 680 863	*813 488	*867 375	1 653	...	...	581 730	...
Burkina Faso [3] Burkina Faso [3]	10 XII 1996	10 312 609	4 970 882	5 341 727	...	...	...	274 000	...
Burundi [3] Burundi [3]	16 VIII 1990	5 139 073	2 473 599	2 665 474	...	...	...	27 834	...
Cameroon [3] Cameroun [3]	10 IV 1987	10 493 655	...	...	...	...	...	475 442	...
Cape Verde [3] Cap-Vert [3]	16 VI 2000	436 863	211 479	225 384	435	461	2.0	4 033	114
Central African Rep. [3] Rép. centrafricaine [3]	8 XII 2003	3 151 072	1 569 446	1 581 626	...	3 151	...	622 984	5
Chad [3,4] Tchad [3,4]	8 IV 1993	6 279 931	...	...	...	...	...	1 284 000	...
Comoros [3,5] Comores [3,5]	15 IX 1991	446 817	221 152	225 665	...	...	...	2 235	...
Congo [3] Congo [3]	22 XII 1984	1 843 421	...	...	2 893	...	...	342 000	...
Côte d'Ivoire [3] Côte d'Ivoire [3]	1 III 1988	10 815 694	5 527 343	5 288 351	16 402	18 001	3.1	322 463	56
Dem. Rep. of the Congo [3] Rép. dém. du Congo [3]	1 VII 1984	29 916 800	14 543 800	15 373 000	...	...	...	2 344 858	...
Djibouti [3] Djibouti [3]	11 XII 1960	81 200	...	...	...	...	...	23 200	...
Egypt [3] Egypte [3]	19 XI 1996	59 312 914	30 351 390	28 961 524	63 976	67 976	2.0	1 001 449	68
Equatorial Guinea [3,6] Guinée équatoriale [3,6]	4 VII 1994	406 151	...	...	...	...	...	28 051	...
Eritrea [3] Erythrée [3]	9 V 1984	2 748 304	1 374 452	1 373 852	...	...	...	117 600	...
Ethiopia [3] Ethiopie [3]	11 X 1994	53 477 265	26 910 698	26 566 567	63 495	...	...	1 104 300	...
Gabon [3] Gabon [3]	31 VII 1993	1 014 976	501 784	513 192	1 206	...	...	267 668	...
Gambia [3] Gambie [3]	15 IV 2003	*1 364 507	*676 726	*687 781	1 393	...	...	11 295	...
Ghana [3] Ghana [3]	26 III 2000	18 912 079	9 357 382	9 554 697	*18 412	...	...	238 533	...
Guinea [3] Guinée [3]	1 XII 1996	*7 156 406	*3 497 979	*3 658 427	...	...	...	245 857	...

Country or area		Latest census Dernier recensement			Mid-year estimates (thousands) Estimations au milieu de l'année (milliers)		Annual rate of increase (%) Taux d'accroisse-ment annuel (%)	Surface area (km²) Superficie (km²)	Density Densité
Pays ou zone	Date	Both sexes Les deux sexes	Men Hommes	Women Femmes	2000	2003	2000-03	2003	2003+
Guinea-Bissau [3] Guinée-Bissau [3]	1 XII 1991	983 367	476 210	507 157	...	1 267	...	36 125	35
Kenya [3] Kenya [3]	24 VIII 1999	28 686 607	14 205 589	14 481 018	30 208	32 692	2.6	580 367	56
Lesotho Lesotho	14 IV 1996	1 960 069	964 346 [1]	995 723 [1]	2 144 [3]	...	...	30 355	...
Liberia [3] Libéria [3]	1 II 1984	2 101 628	1 063 127	1 038 501	...	...	...	111 369	...
Libyan Arab Jamah. [3,7] Jamah. arabe libyenne [3,7]	11 VIII 1995	4 404 986	2 236 943	2 168 043	5 125	...	...	1 759 540	...
Madagascar [3] Madagascar [3]	1 VIII 1993	12 238 914	6 088 116	6 150 798	15 085	...	...	587 041	...
Malawi [3,8] Malawi [3,8]	1 IX 1998	9 933 868	4 867 563	5 066 305	*10 475	*11 549	3.3	118 484	97
Mali [1] Mali [1]	1 IV 1998	9 790 492	4 847 436	4 943 056	10 243	...	...	1 240 192	...
Mauritania [3] Mauritanie [3]	1 XI 2000	2 548 157	1 240 414	1 307 743	2 645	...	...	1 025 520	...
Mauritius [1] Maurice [1]	2 VII 2000	1 178 848	583 756	595 092	1 187	1 223	1.0	2 040	599
Morocco [3] Maroc [3]	1 IX 2004	*29 891 708	...	...	28 705	30 088	1.6	446 550	67
Mozambique [3,9,10] Mozambique [3,9,10]	1 VIII 1997	16 099 246	7 714 306	8 384 940	17 691	...	...	801 590	...
Namibia [3,11] Namibie [3,11]	27 VIII 2001	1 830 330	887 721	942 572	*1 817	...	...	824 292	...
Niger [3] Niger [3]	20 V 1988	7 248 100	3 590 070	3 658 030	...	...	...	1 267 000	...
Nigeria [3,8] Nigéria [3,8]	26 XI 1991	88 992 220	44 529 608	44 462 612	115 224	126 153	3.0	923 768	137
Réunion Réunion	8 III 1999	706 180	347 076 [1]	359 104 [1]	722 [3]	764 [3]	1.9	2 510	304
Rwanda [1] Rwanda [1]	16 VIII 2002	8 128 553	3 879 448	4 249 105	...	...	...	26 338	...
Saint Helena ex. dep. [3] Sainte-Hélène sans dép. [3]	8 III 1998	5 157	2 612	2 545	...	...	...	122	...
Ascension [3] Ascension [3]	31 XII 1978	849	608	241	...	...	...	88	...
Tristan da Cunha [3] Tristan da Cunha [3]	31 XII 1988	296	139	157	...	...	...	...	...
Sao Tome and Principe [3] Sao Tomé-et-Principe [3]	4 VIII 1991	116 998	57 837	59 161	140	...	...	964	...
Senegal [1] Sénégal [1]	27 V 1988	6 896 808	3 353 599	3 543 209	9 427	10 165	2.5	196 722	52
Seychelles [3] Seychelles [3]	29 VIII 1997	75 876	37 589	38 287	81	83	0.7	455	182
Sierra Leone [3] Sierra Leone [3]	4 XII 2004	*4 963 298	*2 412 860	*2 550 438	4 944	5 280	2.2	71 740	74
Somalia [3] Somalie [3]	15 II 1987	7 114 431	3 741 664	3 372 767	...	...	...	637 657	...
South Africa [3,10] Afrique du Sud [3,10]	10 X 2001	*44 819 778	*21 434 041	*23 385 737	43 686	46 430	2.0	1 221 037	38
Sudan [3] Soudan [3]	15 IV 1993	24 940 683	12 518 638	12 422 045	31 081	33 334	2.3	2 505 813	13

8 Population by sex, rate of population increase, surface area and density (*continued*)

8 Population selon le sexe, taux d'accroissement de la population, superficie et densité (*suite*)

| Country or area | | Latest census | | | Mid-year estimates (thousands) | | Annual rate of increase (%) | Surface area (km²) | Density |
| Pays ou zone | | Dernier recensement | | | Estimations au milieu de l'année (milliers) | | Taux d'accroissement annuel (%) | Superficie (km²) | Densité |
	Date	Both sexes Les deux sexes	Men Hommes	Women Femmes	2000	2003	2000-03	2003	2003+
Swaziland [3] Swaziland [3]	11 V 1997	929 718	440 154	489 564	...	...	...	17 364	...
Togo [3] Togo [3]	22 XI 1981	2 719 567	1 325 641	1 393 926	4 629	...	...	56 785	...
Tunisia [3] Tunisie [3]	20 IV 1994	8 785 711	4 439 289	4 346 422	9 564	*9 840	0.9	163 610	60
Uganda [3] Ouganda [3]	12 IX 2002	24 442 084	11 929 803	12 512 281	22 972	...	...	241 038	...
United Rep. of Tanzania [3] Rép.-Unie de Tanzanie [3]	24 VIII 2002	*34 443 603	*16 829 861	*17 613 742	...	...	...	945 087	...
Western Sahara [3] Sahara occidental [3]	31 XII 1970	76 425	43 981	32 444	...	...	...	266 000	...
Zambia [3] Zambie [3]	25 X 2000	9 885 591	4 946 298	4 939 293	9 337	10 744	4.7	752 618	14
Zimbabwe [3] Zimbabwe [3]	17 VIII 2002	11 631 657	...	...	...	...	...	390 757	...
America, North Amérique du Nord									
Anguilla [3] Anguilla [3]	9 V 2001	11 430	5 628	5 802	11	12	2.7	91	134
Antigua and Barbuda [3] Antigua-et-Barbuda [3]	28 V 2001	77 426	37 002	40 424	...	...	...	442	...
Aruba [1] Aruba [1]	14 X 2000	90 508	43 435	47 073	91	*96	1.9	180	534
Bahamas [3] Bahamas [3]	1 V 2000	303 611	147 715	155 896	*303	*317	1.5	13 878	23
Barbados [3] Barbade [3]	1 V 2000	250 010	119 926	130 084	*267	...	...	430	...
Belize [3] Belize [3]	12 V 2000	240 204	121 278	118 926	250	*274	3.0	22 966	12
Bermuda [1,12] Bermudes [1,12]	20 V 2000	62 059	29 802	32 257	63	62	-0.4	53	1 177
British Virgin Islands [3] Iles Vierges britanniques [3]	21 V 2001	*20 647	*10 627	*10 020	...	*22	...	151	144
Canada [1,13] Canada [1,13]	15 V 2001	30 007 095	14 706 850	15 300 245	30 770	31 660	1.0	9 970 610	3
Cayman Islands Iles Caïmanes	10 X 1999	39 410	...	...	40[1]	...	...	264	...
Costa Rica [1] Costa Rica [1]	26 VI 2000	3 810 179	1 902 614	1 907 565	3 486	4 089	5.3	51 100	80
Cuba Cuba	6 IX 2002	11 177 743	5 597 233[1]	5 580 510[1]	11 130[3]	11 215[3]	0.3	110 861	101
Dominica [3] Dominique [3]	12 V 2001	69 625	35 073	34 552	72	...	...	751	...
Dominican Republic Rép. dominicaine	20 X 2002	8 562 541	4 265 215[1]	4 297 326[1]	8 552[3]	8 715[3]	0.6	48 671	179
El Salvador [3] El Salvador [3]	27 IX 1992	5 118 599	2 485 613	2 632 986	6 276	6 638	1.9	21 041	315
Greenland [1,14] Groenland [1,14]	1 VII 2000	56 124	29 989	26 135	...	57	...	2 175 600	...
Grenada [3,15] Grenade [3,15]	25 V 2001	102 632	50 481	52 151	101	...	...	344	...

Country or area Pays ou zone	Date	Latest census Dernier recensement			Mid-year estimates (thousands) Estimations au milieu de l'année (milliers)		Annual rate of increase (%) Taux d'accroisse-ment annuel (%)	Surface area (km²) Superficie (km²)	Density Densité
		Both sexes Les deux sexes	Men Hommes	Women Femmes	2000	2003	2000-03	2003	2003+
Guadeloupe [1,16] Guadeloupe [1,16]	8 III 1999	422 222	203 146	219 076	428	439	0.8	1 705	257
Guatemala [10] Guatemala [10]	24 XI 2002	11 237 196	...	...	11 385[3]	12 084[3]	2.0	108 889	111
Haiti [1] Haïti [1]	30 VIII 1982	5 053 792	2 448 370	2 605 422	7 959	...	...	27 750	...
Honduras [3] Honduras [3]	28 VII 2001	*6 071 200	*3 000 530	*3 070 670	6 369	6 861	2.5	112 088	61
Jamaica [1] Jamaïque [1]	10 IX 2001	2 607 632	1 283 547	1 324 085	2 589	2 630	0.5	10 991	239
Martinique [1] Martinique [1]	8 III 1999	381 325	180 910	200 415	385	*391	0.5	1 102	354
Mexico [1] Mexique [1]	14 II 2000	97 483 412	47 592 253	49 891 159	100 569	104 214	1.2	1 958 201	53
Montserrat [3] Montserrat [3]	12 V 2001	4 491	2 418	2 073	*5	...	...	102	...
Netherlands Antilles [1,17] Antilles néerlandaises [1,17]	29 I 2001	175 653	82 521	93 132	179	179	-0.1	800	223
Nicaragua [1] Nicaragua [1]	25 IV 1995	4 357 099	2 147 105	2 209 994	4 957	5 268	2.0	130 000	41
Panama [3] Panama [3]	14 V 2000	2 839 177	1 432 566	1 406 611	2 856	3 116	2.9	75 517	41
Puerto Rico [1,18] Porto Rico [1,18]	1 IV 2000	3 808 610	1 833 577	1 975 033	3 818	3 879	0.5	8 875	437
Saint Kitts and Nevis [3] Saint-Kitts-et-Nevis [3]	14 V 2001	45 841	22 784	23 057	40	...	...	261	...
Saint Lucia [3] Sainte-Lucie [3]	22 V 2001	157 164	76 741	80 423	156	161	1.0	539	298
Saint Pierre and Miquelon [3] Saint-Pierre-et-Miquelon [3]	8 III 1999	6 316	3 147	3 169	...	...	...	242	...
St. Vincent-Grenadines [3,19] St. Vincent-Grenadines [3,19]	14 V 2001	*109 202	...	...	112	...	...	388	...
Trinidad and Tobago [3] Trinité-et-Tobago [3]	15 V 2000	1 262 366	633 051	629 315	1 290	1 282	-0.2	5 130	250
Turks and Caicos Islands Iles Turques et Caïques	20 VIII 2001	19 886	9 896[3]	9 990[3]	18[1]	22[1]	5.9	417	53
United States [1,20] Etats-Unis [1,20]	1 IV 2000	281 421 906	138 053 563	143 368 343	275 265	*290 811	1.8	9 629 091	30
United States Virgin Is. [1,18] Iles Vierges américaines [1,18]	1 IV 2000	108 612	51 864	56 748	109	*109	0.1	347	314
America, South **Amérique du Sud**									
Argentina [3] Argentine [3]	18 XI 2001	36 260 130	17 659 072	18 601 058	37 032	37 870	0.7	2 780 400	14
Bolivia [3] Bolivie [3]	5 IX 2001	8 280 184	4 130 342	4 149 842	8 428	9 025	2.3	1 098 581	8
Brazil [21] Brésil [21]	1 VIII 2000	169 799 170	83 576 015[1]	86 223 155[1]	167 724[3]	178 985[3]	2.2	8 514 877	21
Chile [3] Chili [3]	24 IV 2002	15 116 435	7 447 695	7 668 740	15 398	15 919	1.1	756 096	21
Colombia [3] Colombie [3]	24 X 1993	33 109 840	16 296 539	16 813 301	42 299	44 531	1.7	1 138 914	39

Country or area Pays ou zone	Latest census Dernier recensement				Mid-year estimates (thousands) Estimations au milieu de l'année (milliers)		Annual rate of increase (%) Taux d'accroissement annuel (%)	Surface area (km²) Superficie (km²)	Density Densité
	Date	Both sexes Les deux sexes	Men Hommes	Women Femmes	2000	2003	2000-03	2003	2003+
Ecuador [3,22] Equateur [3,22]	25 XI 2001	12 156 608	6 018 353	6 138 255	12 299	12 843	1.4	283 561	45
Falkland Is. (Malvinas) [3,23,24] Iles Falkland (Malvinas) [3,23,24]	8 IV 2001	2 913	1 598	1 315	...	...	...	12 173	...
French Guiana [1] Guyane française [1]	8 III 1999	156 790	78 963	77 827	164	181	3.3	90 000	2
Guyana [3] Guyana [3]	12 V 1991	701 704	344 928	356 776	742	746	0.2	214 969	3
Paraguay [3] Paraguay [3]	28 VIII 2002	5 163 198	2 603 242	2 559 956	...	...	...	406 752	...
Peru [3,10,25] Pérou [3,10,25]	11 VII 1993	22 048 356	10 956 375	11 091 981	25 939	27 148	1.5	1 285 216	21
Suriname [1,26,27] Suriname [1,26,27]	2 VIII 2004	*487 024	*244 931	*241 084	464	481	1.2	163 820	3
Uruguay [3,10] Uruguay [3,10]	22 V 1996	3 163 763	1 532 288	1 631 475	3 301	3 304	...	175 016	19
Venezuela (Bolivarian Rep. of) [3,25] Venezuela (Rép. Bolivar. du) [3,25]	30 X 2001	23 054 210	11 402 869	11 651 341	24 311	...	...	912 050	...
Asia **Asie**									
Afghanistan [3,28] Afghanistan [3,28]	23 VI 1979	13 051 358	6 712 377	6 338 981	21 770	...	...	652 090	
Armenia [29] Arménie [29]	10 X 2001	3 002 594	1 407 220 [3]	1 595 374 [3]	3 221 [1]	3 211 [1]	-0.1	29 800	108
Azerbaijan Azerbaïdjan	27 I 1999	7 953 438	3 883 155 [1]	4 070 283 [1]	8 049 [3]	8 234 [3]	0.8	86 600	95
Bahrain [3] Bahreïn [3]	7 IV 2001	650 604	373 649	276 955	638	689	2.6	694	993
Bangladesh [3] Bangladesh [3]	22 I 2001	*123 151 246	*62 735 988	*60 415 258	...	...	...	143 998	...
Bhutan [3] Bhoutan [3]	11 XI 1969	1 034 774	...	...	678	...	...	47 000	...
Brunei Darussalam [3] Brunéi Darussalam [3]	21 VIII 2001	*332 844	*168 974	*163 870	325	350	2.5	5 765	61
Cambodia [3,30] Cambodge [3,30]	3 III 1998	11 437 656	5 511 408	5 926 248	12 688	13 415	1.9	181 035	74
China [31,32,33,34] Chine [31,32,33,34]	1 XI 2000	1 242 612 226	640 275 969 [1]	602 336 257 [1]	1 262 645 [3]	1 288 400 [3]	0.7	9 596 961	134
China, Hong Kong SAR [1,35] Chine, Hong Kong RAS [1,35]	14 III 2001	6 708 389	3 285 344	3 423 045	6 665	6 803	0.7	1 099	6 190
China, Macao SAR [1] Chine, Macao RAS [1]	23 VIII 2001	435 235	208 865	226 370	431	445	1.1	26	17 118
Cyprus [1,36] Chypre [1,36]	1 X 2001	689 565	338 497	351 068	694	721	1.3	9 251	78
Georgia Géorgie	17 I 2002	4 371 535	2 061 753 [1]	2 309 782 [1]	4 418 [3]	4 329 [3]	-0.7	69 700	62
India [3,37,38] Inde [3,37,38]	1 III 2001	1 028 610 328	532 156 772	496 453 556	1 014 825	1 068 214	1.7	3 287 263	325
Indonesia [39] Indonésie [39]	30 VI 2000	206 264 595	103 417 180 [3]	102 847 415 [3]	...	214 251 [1]	...	1 904 569	112
Iran (Islamic Rep. of) [1] Iran (Rép. islamique d') [1]	23 X 1996	60 055 488	30 515 159	29 540 329	63 664	66 480	1.4	1 648 195	40

Population by sex, rate of population increase, surface area and density (*continued*)

Population selon le sexe, taux d'accroissement de la population, superficie et densité (*suite*)

Country or area Pays ou zone	Date	Latest census Dernier recensement Both sexes Les deux sexes	Men Hommes	Women Femmes	Mid-year estimates (thousands) Estimations au milieu de l'année (milliers) 2000	2003	Annual rate of increase (%) Taux d'accroisse- ment annuel (%) 2000-03	Surface area (km²) Superficie (km²) 2003	Density Densité 2003+
Iraq [3,40] Iraq [3,40]	16 X 1997	19 184 543	9 536 570	9 647 973	23 577	...	...	438 317	...
Israel [1,41] Israël [1,41]	4 XI 1995	5 548 523	2 738 175	2 810 348	6 289	6 690	2.1	22 145	302
Japan [3,42] Japon [3,42]	1 X 2000	126 925 843	62 110 764	64 815 079	126 843	127 649	0.2	377 873	338
Jordan [3,43] Jordanie [3,43]	10 XII 1994	4 139 458	2 160 725	1 978 733	4 970	5 404	2.8	89 342	60
Kazakhstan Kazakhstan	26 II 1999	14 953 126	7 201 785 [1]	7 751 341 [1]	14 884 [3]	14 909 [3]	0.1	2 724 900	5
Korea, Dem. P. R. [3] Corée, R. p. dém. de [3]	31 XII 1993	21 213 378	10 329 699	10 883 679	...	...	...	120 538	...
Korea, Republic of [3,44] Corée, République de [3,44]	1 XI 2000	46 136 101	23 158 582	22 977 519	47 008	47 925	0.6	99 538	481
Kuwait [3] Koweït [3]	20 IV 1995	1 575 570	913 402	662 168	2 190	2 325	2.0	17 818	131
Kyrgyzstan Kirghizistan	24 III 1999	4 822 938	2 380 465 [1]	2 442 473 [1]	4 915 [3]	5 039 [3]	0.8	199 900	25
Lao People's Dem. Rep. [3] Rép. dém. pop. lao [3]	1 III 1995	4 574 848	2 260 986	2 313 862	5 218	...	...	236 800	...
Lebanon [45,46] Liban [45,46]	15 X 1970	2 126 325	1 080 015	1 046 310	...	...	...	10 400	...
Malaysia [47,48] Malaisie [47,48]	5 VII 2000	23 274 690	11 853 432 [1]	11 421 258 [1]	23 495 [3]	*25 048 [3]	2.1	329 847	76
Maldives [3] Maldives [3]	31 III 2000	270 101	137 200	132 901	271	285	1.6	298	957
Mongolia [3] Mongolie [3]	5 I 2000	2 373 493	1 177 981	1 195 512	2 407	2 504	1.3	1 564 116	2
Myanmar [3] Myanmar [3]	31 III 1983	35 307 913	17 518 255	17 789 658	...	...	...	676 578	...
Nepal [1,49] Népal [1,49]	22 VI 2001	23 151 423	11 563 921	11 587 502	*22 904	...	...	147 181	...
Occupied Palestinian Terr. [3,50] Terr. palestinien occupé [3,50]	9 XII 1997	2 601 669	1 322 264	1 279 405	3 149	3 515	3.7	6 020	584
Oman [3] Oman [3]	7 XII 2003	2 340 815	1 313 239	1 027 576	2 401	...	...	309 500	...
Pakistan [3,51] Pakistan [3,51]	2 III 1998	130 579 571	67 840 137	62 739 434	137 510	147 662	2.4	796 095	185
Philippines [1] Philippines [1]	1 V 2000	76 504 077	38 524 267	37 979 810	76 348	81 081	2.0	300 000	270
Qatar [3] Qatar [3]	16 III 2004	744 029	496 382	247 647	616	719	5.1	11 000	65
Saudi Arabia [3] Arabie saoudite [3]	15 IX 2004	*22 673 538	*12 557 260	*10 116 278	20 474	22 019	2.4	2 149 690	10
Singapore [3,52] Singapour [3,52]	30 VI 2000	4 017 700	2 061 800	1 955 900	4 018	4 185	1.4	683	6 128
Sri Lanka [3,53] Sri Lanka [3,53]	17 VII 2001	*16 864 544	*8 343 964	*8 520 580	19 359	...	...	65 610	...
Syrian Arab Republic [3,54] Rép. arabe syrienne [3,54]	3 IX 1994	13 782 315	7 048 906	6 733 409	16 320	17 550	2.4	185 180	95
Tajikistan [3] Tadjikistan [3]	20 I 2000	*6 127 000	*3 082 000	*3 045 000	6 188	6 573	2.0	143 100	46

8 Population by sex, rate of population increase, surface area and density (*continued*)
8 Population selon le sexe, taux d'accroissement de la population, superficie et densité (*suite*)

Country or area Pays ou zone	Date	Latest census Dernier recensement Both sexes Les deux sexes	Men Hommes	Women Femmes	Mid-year estimates (thousands) Estimations au milieu de l'année (milliers) 2000	2003	Annual rate of increase (%) Taux d'accroisse- ment annuel (%) 2000-03	Surface area (km²) Superficie (km²) 2003	Density Densité 2003+
Thailand [1] Thaïlande [1]	1 IV 2000	60 617 200	29 850 100	30 767 100	61 770	...	...	513 115	...
Timor-Leste [3] Timor-Leste [3]	11 VII 2004	*924 642	*467 757	*456 885	...	...	...	14 874	...
Turkey [3] Turquie [3]	22 X 2000	67 803 927	34 346 735	33 457 192	67 420	70 713	1.6	783 562	90
Turkmenistan [3] Turkménistan [3]	10 I 1995	4 483 251	2 225 331	2 257 920	...	...	...	488 100	...
United Arab Emirates [3,55] Emirats arabes unis [3,55]	17 XII 1995	2 411 041	1 606 804	804 237	...	4 041	...	83 600	48
Uzbekistan Ouzbékistan	12 I 1989	19 810 077	9 784 156[1]	10 025 921[1]	24 650[3]	...	...	447 400	...
Viet Nam [3] Viet Nam [3]	1 IV 1999	76 323 173	37 469 117	38 854 056	77 686	80 670	1.3	331 689	243
Yemen [3] Yémen [3]	16 XII 1994	14 587 807	7 473 540	7 114 267	18 261	...	...	527 968	...
Europe **Europe**									
Albania [3] Albanie [3]	1 IV 2001	*3 069 275	*1 530 443	*1 538 832	3 061	3 111	0.5	28 748	108
Andorra [3] Andorre [3]	12 VII 1989	46 166	...	...	66	70	1.8	468	149
Austria [1] Autriche [1]	15 V 2001	8 032 926	3 889 189	4 143 737	8 012	8 118	0.4	83 858	97
Belarus Bélarus	16 II 1999	10 045 237	4 717 621[1]	5 327 616[1]	10 005[3]	9 874[3]	-0.4	207 600	48
Belgium [1] Belgique [1]	1 X 2001	10 296 350	5 035 446	5 260 904	10 251	*10 376	0.4	30 528	340
Bosnia and Herzegovina Bosnie-Herzégovine	31 III 1991	4 377 033	2 183 795[1]	2 193 238[1]	3 781[3]	*3 832[3]	0.4	51 197	75
Bulgaria [3] Bulgarie [3]	1 III 2001	7 928 901	3 862 465	4 066 436	8 170	7 824	-1.4	110 912	71
Channel Islands: Guernsey Iles Anglo-Normandes: Guernesey	29 IV 2001	59 807	29 138[1]	30 669[1]	60[3]	...	...	78	...
Channel Islands: Jersey Iles Anglo-Normandes: Jersey	11 III 2001	87 186	42 485[1]	44 701[1]	...	88[3]	...	116	755
Croatia [1] Croatie [1]	31 III 2001	4 437 460	2 135 900	2 301 560	4 381	4 442	0.5	56 538	79
Czech Republic [1] République tchèque [1]	1 III 2001	10 230 060	4 982 071	5 247 989	10 273	10 202	-0.2	78 866	129
Denmark [1,56] Danemark [1,56]	1 I 1991	5 146 469	2 536 391	2 610 078	5 337	5 387	0.3	43 094	125
Estonia Estonie	31 III 2000	1 370 052	631 851[1]	738 201[1]	1 370[3]	1 354[3]	-0.4	45 100	30
Faeroe Islands [1] Iles Féroé [1]	22 IX 1977	41 969	21 997	19 972	...	48	...	1 399	34
Finland [1] Finlande [1]	31 XII 2000	5 181 115	2 529 341	2 651 774	5 176	5 213	0.2	338 145	15
France [1,57] France [1,57]	8 III 1999	58 520 688	28 419 419	30 101 269	58 896	*59 768	0.5	551 500	108
Germany Allemagne		...	...	...	82 183[1]	82 534[1]	0.1	357 022	231

Country or area / Pays ou zone	Date	Latest census / Dernier recensement			Mid-year estimates (thousands) / Estimations au milieu de l'année (milliers)		Annual rate of increase (%) / Taux d'accroissement annuel (%)	Surface area (km²) / Superficie (km²)	Density / Densité
		Both sexes / Les deux sexes	Men / Hommes	Women / Femmes	2000	2003	2000-03	2003	2003+
Gibraltar [3,58] / Gibraltar [3,58]	12 XI 2001	27 495	13 644	13 851	27	29	1.7	6	4 760
Greece [3,59,60] / Grèce [3,59,60]	18 III 2001	10 964 020	5 431 816	5 532 204	10 008	11 024	3.2	131 957	84
Holy See * [3,14,61] / Saint-Siège * [3,14,61]	1 VII 2000	798	529	269	...	...	...	...	...
Hungary [3] / Hongrie [3]	1 II 2001	10 198 315	4 850 650	5 347 665	10 024	10 130	0.3	93 032	109
Iceland [1] / Islande [1]	1 XII 1970	204 930	103 621	101 309	281	289	0.9	103 000	3
Ireland [3] / Irlande [3]	28 IV 2002	3 917 203	1 946 164	1 971 039	3 787	3 996	1.8	70 273	57
Isle of Man [1] / Ile de Man [1]	29 IV 2001	76 315	37 372	38 943	75	77	1.1	572	135
Italy / Italie	21 X 2001	57 110 144	27 617 335 [3]	29 492 809 [3]	57 762 [1]	57 605 [1]	-0.1	301 318	191
Latvia / Lettonie	31 III 2000	2 377 383	1 094 964 [1]	1 282 419 [1]	2 373 [3]	2 325 [3]	-0.7	64 600	36
Liechtenstein [3] / Liechtenstein [3]	5 XII 2000	33 307	16 420	16 887	33	34	1.4	160	213
Lithuania [1] / Lituanie [1]	6 IV 2001	3 483 972	1 629 148	1 854 824	3 500	3 454	-0.4	65 300	53
Luxembourg [1] / Luxembourg [1]	15 II 2001	439 539	216 541	222 998	436	450	1.0	2 586	174
Malta [1,62,63] / Malte [1,62,63]	26 XI 1995	378 132	186 836	191 296	383	399	1.4	316	1 261
Monaco [1] / Monaco [1]	23 VII 1990	29 972	14 237	15 735	*32	...	...	1	...
Netherlands [1,64] / Pays-Bas [1,64]	1 I 2002	16 105 285	7 971 967	8 133 318	15 926	16 225	0.6	41 528	391
Norway [1,65] / Norvège [1,65]	3 XI 1990	4 520 947	2 240 281	2 280 666	4 491	*4 565	0.5	385 155	12
Poland [3,66,67,68] / Pologne [3,66,67,68]	20 V 2002	38 230 080	18 516 403	19 713 677	38 256	38 195	-0.1	312 685	122
Portugal [3,69] / Portugal [3,69]	12 III 2001	*10 148 259	*4 862 699	*5 285 560	10 226	10 441	0.7	91 982	114
Republic of Moldova [70] / République de Moldova [70]	12 I 1989	4 337 592	2 058 160 [3]	2 279 432 [3]	3 639 [1]	3 613 [1]	-0.2	33 851	107
Romania [1] / Roumanie [1]	18 III 2002	21 680 974	10 568 741	11 112 233	22 435	21 734	-1.1	238 391	91
Russian Federation / Fédération de Russie	9 X 2002	*145 537 200	*67 805 700 [3]	*77 731 500 [3]	146 597 [1]	144 566 [1]	-0.5	17 098 242	8
San Marino [3] / Saint-Marin [3]	30 XI 1976	19 149	9 654	9 495	27	29	2.4	61	475
Serbia and Montenegro [1,71,72,73] / Serbie-et-Monténégro [1,71,72,73]	31 III 2002	8 065 676	3 925 805	4 139 871	10 634	*8 153	...	102 173	...
Slovakia [1] / Slovaquie [1]	25 V 2001	5 379 455	2 612 515	2 766 940	5 401	5 379	-0.1	49 033	110
Slovenia [1] / Slovénie [1]	31 III 2002	*1 964 036	*958 576	*1 005 460	1 990	*1 997	0.1	20 256	99
Spain [74] / Espagne [74]	1 XI 2001	40 847 371	20 012 882 [3]	20 834 489 [3]	40 169 [1]	41 874 [1]	1.4	505 992	83

8 Population by sex, rate of population increase, surface area and density (*continued*)
8 Population selon le sexe, taux d'accroissement de la population, superficie et densité (*suite*)

| Country or area
Pays ou zone | Date | Latest census
Dernier recensement | | | Mid-year estimates
(thousands)
Estimations au milieu
de l'année (milliers) | | Annual rate of
increase (%)
Taux d'accroisse-
ment annuel (%) | Surface area
(km²)
Superficie
(km²) | Density
Densité |
		Both sexes Les deux sexes	Men Hommes	Women Femmes	2000	2003	2000-03	2003	2003+
Svalbard and Jan Mayen Is [3,75] Svalbard et îles Jan Mayen [3,75]	1 XI 1960	3 431	2 545	886	...	...	...	62 422	...
Sweden [1] Suède [1]	1 XI 1990	8 587 353	4 242 351	4 345 002	8 872	*8 958	0.3	449 964	20
Switzerland [1] Suisse [1]	5 XII 2000	7 204 055	3 519 698	3 684 357	7 184	*7 341	0.7	41 284	178
TFYR of Macedonia [76] L'ex-R.y. Macédoine [76]	1 XI 2002	2 022 547	1 015 377[1]	1 007 170[1]	2 024[3]	*2 027[3]	...	25 713	79
Ukraine [1] Ukraine [1]	5 XII 2001	48 457 102	22 441 344	26 015 758	48 889	*47 633	-0.9	603 700	79
United Kingdom [3,77,78] Royaume-Uni [3,77,78]	29 IV 2001	58 789 187	28 579 867	30 209 320	58 886	59 554	0.4	242 900	245
Oceania **Océanie**									
American Samoa [1,18] Samoa américaines [1,18]	1 IV 2000	57 291	29 264	28 027	57	58	0.3	199	291
Australia [10] Australie [10]	7 VIII 2001	18 972 350	9 362 021[3]	9 610 329[3]	19 153[1]	19 873[1]	1.2	7 741 220	3
Cook Islands [3,79] Iles Cook [3,79]	1 XII 2001	18 027	9 303	8 724	18	18	0.7	236	78
Fiji [3] Fidji [3]	25 VIII 1996	775 077	393 931	381 146	...	...	...	18 274	...
French Polynesia [3,80] Polynésie française [3,80]	7 XI 2002	245 516	...	...	231	247	2.2	4 000	62
Guam [1,18] Guam [1,18]	1 IV 2000	154 805	79 181	75 624	...	164	...	549	298
Kiribati [3,81] Kiribati [3,81]	7 XI 1995	*77 658	*38 478	*39 180	...	...	...	726	...
Marshall Islands [3] Iles Marshall [3]	1 VI 1999	50 848	26 034	24 814	53	...	...	181	...
Micronesia (Fed. States of) [1] Micronésie (Etats féd. de) [1]	1 IV 2000	107 008	54 191	52 817	119	...	...	702	...
Nauru [3] Nauru [3]	17 IV 1992	9 919	5 079	4 840	12	...	...	21	...
New Caledonia [3,82] Nouvelle-Calédonie [3,82]	16 IV 1996	196 836	100 762	96 074	211	220	1.5	18 575	12
New Zealand [1,83] Nouvelle-Zélande [1,83]	6 III 2001	3 820 749	1 863 309	1 957 440	3 858	4 009	1.3	270 534	15
Niue [3] Nioué [3]	7 IX 2001	1 788	897	891	...	...	...	260	...
Norfolk Island [3] Ile Norfolk [3]	7 VIII 2001	2 601	1 257	1 344	...	...	...	36	...
Northern Mariana Islands [3] Iles Mariannes du Nord [3]	1 IV 2000	69 221	31 984	37 237	72	76	1.8	464	164
Palau [3] Palaos [3]	15 IV 2000	19 129	...	...	19	20	1.8	459	44
Papua New Guinea [3,84] Papouasie-Nvl-Guinée [3,84]	9 VII 2000	5 190 786	2 691 744	2 499 042	5 100	...	...	462 840	...
Pitcairn [3] Pitcairn [3]	31 XII 1991	66	...	...	...	...	...	5	...
Samoa [3] Samoa [3]	5 XI 2001	176 710	92 050	84 660	171	...	...	2 831	...

Country or area	Latest census — Dernier recensement				Mid-year estimates (thousands) Estimations au milieu de l'année (milliers)		Annual rate of increase (%) Taux d'accroisse-ment annuel (%)	Surface area (km²) Superficie (km²)	Density Densité
Pays ou zone	Date	Both sexes Les deux sexes	Men Hommes	Women Femmes	2000	2003	2000-03	2003	2003+
Solomon Islands [3,85] Iles Salomon [3,85]	21 XI 1999	409 042	211 381	197 661	...	...	...	28 896	...
Tokelau [3] Tokélaou [3]	11 X 2001	1 537	761	776	...	...	...	12	...
Tonga [3,86] Tonga [3,86]	30 XI 1996	97 784	49 615	48 169	100	...	...	747	...
Tuvalu [3] Tuvalu [3]	1 XI 2002	9 561	4 729	4 832	...	...	...	26	...
Vanuatu [1] Vanuatu [1]	16 XI 1999	186 678	95 682	90 996	...	...	...	12 189	...
Wallis and Futuna Islands [3] Iles Wallis et Futuna [3]	22 VII 2003	14 944	7 494	7 450	...	...	...	200	...

Source

United Nations Statistics Division, New York, "Demographic Yearbook 2003" and the demographic statistics database.

Notes

+   Population per square kilometer of surface area in 2003. Figures are merely the quotients of population divided by surface area and are not to be considered either as reflecting density in the urban sense or as indicating the supporting power of a territory's land and resources.

[1]   De jure population.
[2]   Including the enclave of Cabinda.
[3]   De facto population.
[4]   Census results have been adjusted for under-enumeration, estimated at 1.4 per cent.
[5]   Census results, excluding Mayotte.
[6]   Comprising Bioko (which includes Pagalu) and Rio Muni (which includes Corisco and Elobeys).
[7]   For Libyan nationals only.
[8]   Data for estimates refer to national projections.
[9]   Census results have been adjusted for underenumeration, estimated at 5.1 per cent.
[10]   Mid-year estimates have been adjusted for underenumeration, at latest census.
[11]   The number of males and / or females excludes persons whose sex is not stated (18 urban, 19 rural).
[12]   Excluding the institutional population.
[13]   For 2003, updated postcensal estimates.
[14]   Population statistics are based on administrative records.
[15]   Including Carriacou and other dependencies in the Grenadines.
[16]   Including dependencies: Marie-Galante, la Désirade, les Saintes, Petite-Terre, St. Barthélemy and French part of St. Martin.
[17]   Comprising Bonaire, Curaçao, Saba, St. Eustatius and Dutch part of St. Martin.
[18]   Including armed forces stationed in the area.
[19]   Including Bequia and other islands in the Grenadines.
[20]   Excluding armed forces overseas and civilian citizens absent from country for an extended period of time.

Source

Organisation des Nations Unies, Division de statistique, New York, "Annuaire démographique 2003" et la base de données pour les statistiques démographiques.

Notes

+   Nombre d'habitants au kilomètre carré en 2003. Il s'agit simplement du quotient du chiffre de la population divisé par celui de la superficie: il ne faut pas y voir d'indication de la densité au sens urbain du terme ni de l'effectif de population que les terres et les ressources du territoire sont capables de nourrir.

[1]   Population de droit.
[2]   Y compris l'enclave de Cabinda.
[3]   Population de fait.
[4]   Les résultats du recensement ont été ajustées pour compenser les lacunes du dénombrement, estimées à 1,4 p. 100.
[5]   Les résultats du recensement, non compris Mayotte.
[6]   Comprend Bioko (qui comprend Pagalu) et Rio Muni (qui comprend Corisco et Elobeys).
[7]   Pour les nationaux libyens seulement.
[8]   Les données se referent aux projections nationales.
[9]   Les résultats du recensement ont été ajustées pour compenser les lacunes du dénombrement, estimées à 5,1 p. 100.
[10]   Les estimations au millieu de l'année tiennent compte d'une ajustement destiné à compenser les lacunes du dénombrement lors du dernierrecensement.
[11]   Il n'est pas tenu compte dans le nombre d'hommes et de femmes des personnes dont le sexe n'est pas indiqué (18 en zone urbaine et 19 en zone rurale).
[12]   Non compris la population dans les institutions.
[13]   Pour 2003, estimations post censitaires mises à jour.
[14]   La source de la statistique de la population sont des fichiers administratifs.
[15]   Y compris Carriacou et les autres dépendances du groupe des îles Grenadines.
[16]   Y compris les dépendances: Marie-Galante, la Désirade, les Saintes, Petite-Terre, Saint-Barthélemy et la partie française de Saint-Martin.
[17]   Comprend Bonaire, Curaçao, Saba, Saint-Eustache et la partie néederlandaise de Saint-Martin.
[18]   Y compris les militaires en garnison sur le territoire.
[19]   Y compris Bequia et des autres iles dans les Grenadines.
[20]   Non compris les militaires à l'étranger, et les civils hors du pays pendant une période prolongée.

[21] Data include persons in remote areas, military personnel outside the country, merchant seamen at sea, civilian seasonal workers outside the country, and other civilians outside the country, and exclude nomads, foreign military, civilian aliens temporarily in the country, transients on ships and Indian jungle population.

[22] Excluding nomadic Indian tribes.

[23] A dispute exists between the governments of Argentina and the United Kingdom of Great Britain and Northern Ireland concerning sovereignty over the Falkland Islands (Malvinas).

[24] Excluding dependencies, of which South Georgia (area 3 755 km2) had an estimated population of 499 in 1964 (494 males, 5 females). The other dependencies namely, the South Sandwich group (surface area 337 km2) and a number of smaller islands, are presumed to be uninhabited.

[25] Excluding Indian jungle population.

[26] The previous census was conducted only 16 months earlier (on 31 Mar 2003) but it was repeated because all of its data were destroyed in a fire before they could be fully processed, analyzed, and reported.

[27] Figures for male and female population do not add up to the figure for total population, because they exclude 1009 persons of unknown sex (654 urban and 355 rural).

[28] Census results, excluding nomad population.

[29] The methodology used for calculating the number of the de facto and de jure population in the 2001 census data differs as follows from the methodology used in previous censuses: the duration that defines a person as being "temporary present" or "temporary absent" is now "under one year". The previously applied definition was for 6 months.

[30] Excluding foreign diplomatic personnel and their dependants.

[31] Data for 2003 have been estimated on the basis of the annual national sample surveys on Population Changes.

[32] Estimate for 2000 have been adjusted on the basis of the Population Census of 2000.

[33] For the civilian population of 31 provinces, municipalities and autonomous regions.

[34] For statistical purposes, the data for China do not include those for the Hong Kong Special Administrative Region (Hong Kong SAR), Macao Special Administrative Region (Macao SAR) and Taiwan Province of China.

[35] Data refer to Hong Kong resident population at the census moment, which covers usual residents and mobile residents. Usual residents refer to two categories of people: (1) Hong Kong permanent residents who had stayed in Hong Kong for at least three months during the six months before or for at least three months during the six months after the census moment, regardless of whether they were in Hong Kong or not at the census moment; and (2) Hong Kong non-permanent residents who were in Hong Kong at the census moment. Mobile Residents are Hong Kong permanent residents who had stayed in Hong Kong for at least one month but less than three months during the six months before or for at least one month but less than three months during the six months after the census moment, regardless of whether they were in Hong Kong or not at the census moment.

[36] Data include all population irrespective of citizenship, who at the time of the census have resided in the country or intended to reside for a period of at least one year. It does not distinguish between those present or absent at the time of census. Data refer to government-controlled areas.

[37] Census data exclude Mao-Maram, Paomata and Purul sub-divisions of Senapati district of Manipur. The population of Manipur including the estimated population of the three sub-divisions of Senapati district is 2,291,125 (Males 1,161,173 and females 1,129,952).

[21] Y compris les personnes dans des régions éloignées, le personnel militaire en dehors du pays, les marins marchands, les ouvriers saisonniers civils de couture en dehors du pays, et autres civils en dehors du pays, et non compris les nomades, les militaires étrangers, les étrangers civils temporairement dans le pays, les transiteurs sur des bateaux et les Indiens de la jungle.

[22] Non compris les tribus d'Indiens nomades.

[23] La sourveraineté sur les îles Falkland (Malvinas) fait l'objet d'un différend entre le Gouvernement argentin et le Gouvernement du Royaume-Uni de Grande-Bretagne et d'Irlande du Nord.

[24] Non compris les dépendances, parmi lesquelles figure la Georgie du Sug (3 755 km2) avec une population estimée à 499 personnes en 1964 (494 du sexe masculin et 5 du sexe féminin). Les autres dépendances, c'est-à-dire le groupe des Sandwich de Sud (superficie: 337 km2) et certaines petites-îles, sont présumées inhabitées.

[25] Non compris les Indiens de la jungle.

[26] Le recensement précédent a eu lieu seulement 16 mois auparavant (le 31 mars 2003), mais a dû être refait parce que toutes les données ont été détruites dans un incendie avant que l'on n'ait pu les traiter et les analyser.

[27] Les chiffres relatifs à la population masculine et féminine ne correspondent pas au chiffre de la population totale, parce que l'on en a exclu 1 009 personnes de sexe inconnu (654 en zones urbaines et 355 en zones rurales).

[28] Les résultats du recensement, non compris les nomades.

[29] La méthode utilisée pour dénombrer la population présente et la population légale dans le contexte du recensement de 2001 diffère de celle qui a été appliquée lors des recensements antérieurs en ce que la durée considérée pour définir la "présence temporaire" ou "l'absence temporaire" était dorénavant fixée à "moins d'un an" alors qu'elle était de 6 mois auparavant.

[30] Non compris le personnel diplomatique étranger et les membres de leur famille les accompagnant.

[31] Les données pour 2003 ont été estimées sur la base de l'enquête annuelle ''National Sample Survey on Population Changes''.

[32] Les estimations pour 2000 ont été ajustées à partir des résultats du recensement de la population de 2000.

[33] Pour la population civile seulement de 31 provinces, municipalités et régions autonomes.

[34] Pour la présentation des statistiques, les données pour Chine ne comprennent pas la Région Administrative Spéciale de Hong Kong (Hong Kong RAS), la Région Administrative Spéciale de Macao (Macao RAS) et la province de Taiwan.

[35] Les données se rapportent à la population résidente à Hong Kong au moment du recensement. Cette population est composée des résidants habituels et des résidants mobiles. La population résidente est partagée en deux catégories: (1) les résidents permanents qui ont habité à Hong Kong au moins trois mois pendant les six mois précédents ou les six mois suivants le recensement; (2) les habitants non-permanents de Hong Kong qui étaient à Hong Kong au moment du recensement. La population mobile se rapporte aux résidants permanents de Hong Kong qui ont habité à Hong Kong pendant les six mois après le recensement pour une période comprise entre un mois et trois mois, indépendamment du fait qu'ils étaient à Hong Kong au moment du recensement au pays.

[36] Les chiffres comprennent toute la population, quelle que soit la nationalité, qui à l'époque de recensement avait résidé dans le pays, ou avait l'intention de résider, pendant une période de au moins un an. Il n'y a pas de distinction entre les personnes présentes ou absentes au moment du recensement. Les données se raportent aux zones contrôlées par le Gouvernement.

[37] Les données de recensement non compris les subdivisions Mao-Maram Paomata et Purul du district de Senapati dans l'État du Manipur. Cet État compte 2 291 125 habitants (1 161 173 hommes et 1 129 952 femmes), y compris la population estimative des trois subdivisions du district de Senapati.

38 Including data for the Indian-held part of Jammu and Kashmir, the final status of which has not yet been determined.	38 Y compris les données pour la partie du Jammu et du Cachemire occupée par l'Inde dont le statut définitif n'a pas encore été déterminé.
39 Census data include an estimated population of 459 557 persons in urban and 1 857 659 persons in rural areas that were not directly enumerated, and a population of 566 403 persons in urban and 1 717 578 persons in rural areas that decline the participation. Also included are 421 399 non permanent residents (the homeless, the crew of ships carrying national flags, boat/floating house people, remote located tribesmen and refugees).	39 Les données du recensement, y compris l'estimation de 459 557 personnes dans les zones urbaines et de 1 857 659 personnes dans les zones rurales qui n'ont pas été énumérées directement, aussi que 566 403 personnes qui n'ont pas répondu dans les zones urbaines et de 1 717 578 personnes dans les zones rurales. Y compris 421 399 résidants non permanents (les sans abri, l'équipage des bateaux portant le drapeau national, les habitants des embarcations ou des maisons flottantes, les habitants des tribus isolées et les réfugiés).
40 For the 1997 population census, data exclude population in three autonomous provinces in the north of the country.	40 Pour le recensement de 1997, la population des trois provinces autonomes dans le nord du pays est exclue.
41 Including data for East Jerusalem and Israeli residents in certain other territories under occupation by Israeli military forces since June 1967.	41 Y compris les données pour Jérusalem-Est et les résidents israéliens dans certains autres territoires occupés depuis 1967 par les forces armées israéliennes.
42 Excluding diplomatic personnel outside the country and foreign military and civilian personnel and their dependants stationed in the area.	42 Non compris le personnel diplomatique hors du pays ni les militaires et agents civils étrangers en poste sur le territoire et les membres de leur famille les accompagnant.
43 Excluding data for Jordanian territory under occupation since June 1967 by Israeli military forces. Excluding foreigners, including registered Palestinian refugees.	43 Non compris les données pour le territoire jordanien occupé depuis juin 1967 par les forces armées israéliennes. Non compris les étrangers, mais y compris les réfugiés de Palestine enregistrés.
44 Including diplomats and their families abroad, but excluding foreign diplomats, foreign military personnal, and their families in the country.	44 Y compris le personnel diplomatique et les membres de leurs familles à l'étranger, mais sans tenir compte du personnel diplomatique et militaire étranger et des membres de leurs familles.
45 Excluding Palestinian refugees in camps.	45 Non compris les réfugiés de Palestine dans les camps.
46 Sample survey, de facto.	46 Enquête par sondage, population de fait.
47 Census results have been adjusted for underenumeration.	47 Les résultats du recensement ont été ajustées pour compenser les lacunes du dénombrement.
48 Excluding Malaysian citizens and permanent residents who were away or intended to be away from the country for more than six months. Excluding Malaysian military, naval and diplomatic personnel and their families outside the country, and tourists, businessman who intended to be in Malaysia for less than six months.	48 Non compris les citoyens malaisiens et les résidents permanents qui étaient ou qui ont prévu d'être hors du pays pour six mois ou plus. Non compris le personnel militaire Malaisien, le personnel naval ou diplomatique et leurs familles hors du pays, et les touristes et les hommes d'affaires qui avaient l'intention de rester en Malaisie moins de six mois.
49 Data including estimated population from household listing from Village Development Committees and Wards which could not be enumerated at the time of census.	49 Les données incluent la population estimée par les listes des ménages des comités de développement des villages et des circonscriptions qui n'ont pas pu être énumérée au moment du recensement.
50 Total population does not include the Palestinian population living in those parts of Jerusalem governorate which were annexed by Israel in 1967, amounting to 210,209 persons. Likewise, the result does not include the estimates of not enumerated population based on the findings of the post enumeration study, i.e. 83,805 persons.	50 Les données relatives à la population totale ne comprennent pas la population palestinienne -équivalent à 210 209 personnes/habitant dans les territoires du gouvernorat de Jérusalem qui ont été annexés par Israël en 1967 Egalement, les données ne tiennent pas compte des estimations de la population calculée sur la base des résultats de l'enquête postcensitaire, équivalent à 83 805 personnes.
51 Excluding data for the Pakistan-held part of Jammu and Kashmir, the final status of which has not yet been determined.	51 Non compris les données pour le Jammu et Cachemire occupée par le Pakistan dont le statut définitif n'a pas encore été déterminé.
52 Census results, excluding transients afloat and non-locally domiciled military and civilian services personnel and their dependants and visitors.	52 Les résultats du recensment, non compris les personnes de passage à bord de navires ni les militaires et agents civils non-résidents et les membres de leur famille les accompagnant et visiteurs.
53 The Population and Housing Census 2001 did not cover the whole area of the country due to the security problems; the Census was complete in 18 districts only; in three districts it was not possible to conduct it; and in four districts it was partially conducted.	53 Le recensement de la population et de l'habitat en 2001 n' pas couvert la totalité du pays pour des problèmes de sécurité ; le recensement à été complété seulement en 18 districts ; dans 3 districts ça n'a pas été possible de conduire le recensement et dans 4 districts il a été partiellement conduit.
54 Including Palestinian refugees.	54 Y compris les réfugiés de Palestine.
55 Comprising 7 sheikdoms of Abu Dhabi, Dubai, Sharjah, Ajaman, Umm al Qaiwain, Ras al Khaimah and Fujairah, and the area lying within the modified Riyadh line as announced in October 1955.	55 Comprend les sept cheikhats de Abou Dhabi, Dabai, Ghârdja, Adjmân, Oumm-al-Quiwaïn, Ras al Khaïma et Foudjaïra, ainsi que la zone délimitée par la ligne de Riad modifiée comme il a été annoncé en octobre 1955.
56 Excluding the Faeroe Islands and Greenland.	56 Non compris les îles Féroé et Groenland.
57 Excluding Overseas Departments, namely French Guiana, Guadeloupe, Martinique and Réunion, shown separately. De jure population but excluding diplomatic personnel outside country and including members of alien armed forces not living in military camps and foreign diplomatic personnel not living in embassies or consulates.	57 Non compris les départements d'outre-mer, c'est-à-dire la Guyane française, la Guadeloupe, la Martinique et la Réunion, qui font l'objet de rubriques distinctes. Population de droit, non compris le personnel diplomatique hors du pays et y compris les militaires étrangers ne vivant pas dans des comps militaires et le personnel diplomatique étranger ne vivant pas dans les ambassades ou les consulats.
58 Excluding families of military personnel, visitors and transients.	58 Non compris les familles des militaires, ni les visiteurs et transients.

[59] Mid-year population excludes armed forces stationed outside the country, but includes alien armed forces stationed in the area.	[59] Les estimations au millieu de l'année non compris les militaires en garnison hors du pays, mais y compris les militaires étrangers en garnison sur le territoire.
[60] Census data including armed forces stationed outside the country, but excluding alien armed forces stationed in the area.	[60] Les données de recensement y compris les militaires hors du pays, mais non compris les militaires étrangers en garnison sur le territoire.
[61] Data refer to the Vatican City State.	[61] Les données se réfèrent à la Cité du Vatican.
[62] Data for estimates including work and resident permit holders and foreigners residing in Malta.	[62] Les estimations y compris les titulaires de permis de travail et de permis de séjour et les ét rangers résidant à Malte.
[63] Including foreigners residing in Malta for 12 months before the census date and excluding foreign diplomatic personnel.	[63] Y compris les les étrangers habitant à Malte pour 12 mois avant le recensement et le personnel diplomatique étrangers.
[64] Census results, based on compilation of continuous accounting and sample surveys.	[64] Les résultats du recensement, d'aprés les résultats des dénombrements et enquêtes par sondage continue.
[65] Including residents temporarily outside the country.	[65] Y compris les nationaux se trouvant temporairement hors du pays.
[66] Surface area includes inland waters as well as part of internal waters.	[66] Superficie comprends les eaux intérieures et une partie des eaux situées en deçà de la ligne de base de la mer.
[67] Average year data for 2000 contain revised data according to the final results of population census 2002.	[67] Les données annuelles moyennes pour 2000 comportent des données révisées en fonction des résultats du recensement de 2002.
[68] Excluding civilian aliens within country, but including civilian nationals temporarily outside country.	[68] Non compris les civils étrangers dans le pays, mais y compris les civils nationaux temporairement hors du pays.
[69] Including the Azores and Madeira Islands.	[69] Y compris les Açores et Madère.
[70] Data do not include information for Transnistria and the municipality of Bender.	[70] Les données ne tiennent pas compte de l'information sur la Transnistria et la municipalité de Bender.
[71] The census figure for Serbia and Montenegro consists of the final results of the population census held in the Republic of Serbia in 2002 (which was not carried out on the territory of Kosovo and Metohia) and the final results of the 2003 Census for the Republic of Montenegro.	[71] Le total pour la Serbie-et-Montenegro se consiste des résultats finales de recensement da la population de la République de Serbie du 2002 (qui n'a été pas conduit pour le territoire de Kosovo et Metohie) et les résultats finales de recensement de la population de la République de Montenegro du 2003.
[72] For 2003, without data for Kosovo and Metohia.	[72] Pour 2003, sans les donées pour le Kosovo and Metohia.
[73] For 2000, estimates of Kosovo and Metohia computed on the basis of natural increases from year 1997.	[73] Pour 2000, les estimations pour le Kosovo et la Metohia ont été calcúees sur la base des incréments naturelles depuis 1997.
[74] Including the Balearic and Canary Islands, and Alhucemas, Ceuta, Chafarinas, Melilla and Penon de Vélez de la Gomera.	[74] Y compris les Baléares et les Canaries, Al Hoceima, Ceuta, les îles Zaffarines, Melilla et Penon de Vélez de la Gomera.
[75] Inhabited only during the winter season. Census data are for total population while estimates refer to Norwegian population only. Included also in the de jure population of Norway.	[75] N'est habitée pendant la saison d'hiver. Les données de recensement se rapportent à la population totale, mais les estimations ne concernent que la population norvégienne, comprise également dans la population de droit de la Norvège.
[76] Figure for 2003 calculated on the base of census data 2002.	[76] Le chiffre pour 2003 a été calculés à partir des résultats du recensement de 2002.
[77] Population estimate for 2000 were revised in light of the local studies.	[77] Les estimations de la population pour l'année 2000 ont été révisées en fonction d'études locales.
[78] Excluding Channel Islands and Isle of Man, shown separately.	[78] Non compris les îles Anglo-Normandes et l'île de Man, qui font l'objet de rubriques distinctes.
[79] Excluding Niue, shown separately, which is part of Cook Islands, but because of remoteness is administered separately.	[79] Non compris Nioué, qui fait l'objet d'une rubricte distincte et qui fait partie des îles Cook, mais qui, en raison de son éloignement, est administrée séparément.
[80] Comprising Austral, Gambier, Marquesas, Rapa, Society and Tuamotu Islands.	[80] Comprend les îles Australes, Gambier, Marquises, Rapa, de la Societé et Tuamotou.
[81] Including Christmas, Fanning, Ocean and Washington Islands.	[81] Y compris les îles Christmas, Fanning, Océan et Washington.
[82] Including the islands of Huon, Chesterfield, Loyalty, Walpole and Belep Archipelago.	[82] Y compris les îles Huon, Chesterfield, Loyauté et Walpole, et l'archipel Belep.
[83] Including Campbell and Kermadec Islands (population 20 in 1961, surface area 148 km²) as well as Antipodes, Auckland, Bounty, Snares, Solander and Three Kings island, all of which are uninhabited.	[83] Y compris les îles Campbell et Kermadec (20 habitants en 1961, superficie: 148 km²) ainsi que les îles Antipodes, Auckland, Bounty, Snares, Solander et Three Kings, qui sont toutes inhabitées.
[84] Comprising eastern part of New Guinea, the Bismarck Archipelago, Bougainville and Buka of Solomon Islands group and about 600 smaller islands.	[84] Comprend l'est de la Nouvelle-Guinée, l'archipel Bismarck, Bougainville et Buka (ces deux dernières du groupe des Salomon) et environ 600 ilots.
[85] Comprising the Solomon Islands group (except Bougainville and Buka which are included with Papua New Guinea shown separately), Ontong, Java, Rennel and Santa Cruz Islands.	[85] Comprend les îles Salomon (à l'exception de Bougainville et de Buka dont la population est comprise dans celle de Papouasie-Nouvelle Guinée qui font l'objet d'une rubrique distincte), ainsi que les îles Ontong, Java, Rennel et Santa Cruz.
[86] Data for estimates based on the results of the 1996 population census not necessarily mid year estimated.	[86] Les estimations d'après les résultats du recensement de la population de 1996, pas nécessairement des estimations en milieu d'année.

Technical notes: table 8

Table 8 is based on detailed data on population and its growth and distribution published in the United Nations *Demographic Yearbook* [21]. Only official national population estimates reported to the United Nations Statistics Division are included in this table. For a comprehensive description of methods of evaluation and the limitations of the data, consult the *Demographic Yearbook* [21].

Unless otherwise indicated, figures refer to de facto (present-in-area) population for the present territory; surface area estimates include inland waters.

Notes techniques : tableau 8

Le *tableau 8* est fondé sur des données détaillées sur la population, sa croissance et sa distribution, publiées dans l'*Annuaire démographique* des Nations Unies [21]. Le tableau inclut seulement des estimations officielles de la population qui ont été envoyées à la Division de Statistique des Nations Unies. Pour une description complète des méthodes d'évaluation et une indication des limites des données, voir l'*Annuaire démographique* [21].

Sauf indication contraire, les chiffres se rapportent à la population effectivement présente sur le territoire tel qu'il est actuellement défini ; les estimations de superficie comprennent les étendues d'eau intérieures.

Education at the primary, secondary and tertiary levels
Number of students enrolled and percentage female

Enseignement primaire, secondaire et supérieur
Nombre d'étudiants inscrits et étudiantes féminines en pourcentage

Country or area Pays ou zone	Year [t] Année [t]	Primary education Enseignement primaire		Secondary education Enseignement secondaire		Tertiary education Enseignement supérieur	
		Total	% F	Total	% F	Total	% F
Afghanistan Afghanistan	1999	957 403	6.7	...	...	...	...
	2000	749 360	...	...	...	...	...
	2001	773 623	...	362 415	...	...	...
	2002	2 667 629	30.2	...	...	...	...
	2003	3 781 015	34.8	406 895 [1]	24.4 [1]	26 211 [1]	20.4 [1]
	2004	4 430 142	29.1	594 306	16.3	27 648	20.4
Albania Albanie	1999	292 070	48.1	363 502	48.4	38 502	59.8
	2000	283 249	48.3	363 689	48.7	40 125	59.9
	2001	274 233	48.6	377 198	48.7	40 859	61.4
	2002	263 603	47.8	382 779 [1]	47.2 [1]	42 160	62.0
	2003	252 829	48.1	396 139	48.3	43 600	62.3
Algeria Algérie	1999	4 778 870	46.6	...	...	456 358 [1]	...
	2000	4 843 313	46.8	...	...	...	...
	2001	4 720 950	46.8	...	...	549 009 [1]	...
	2002	4 691 870	47.0	3 424 208 [1]	50.1 [1]	624 788 [1]	...
	2003	4 612 574	47.0	3 548 484	50.5	682 775 [1]	...
	2004	4 507 703	47.0	3 677 107	50.7	716 452	51.0
Andorra Andorre	2002	4 108	47.4	3 132	50.3	267	49.8
	2003	4 142	47.2	3 194	50.2	306	48.7
	2004	4 264	47.1	3 250	49.9	331	48.6
Angola Angola	1999	1 057 188 [1]	46.4 [1]	300 480	45.5 [1]	7 845	39.0
	2000	...	...	354 984	45.3	...	...
	2001	...	...	413 695	44.2	...	...
	2002	...	...	...	...	12 566	39.9 [2]
	2003 [1]	...	...	...	...	12 982	39.9
Anguilla Anguilla	1999	1 569	50.2	980	52.8	...	...
	2000	1 539	50.3	1 130	50.8	...	...
	2001	1 489	48.9	1 147	51.5	...	...
	2002	1 427	49.0	1 098	50.6	...	...
	2003	1 447	49.7	1 155 [1]	51.0 [1]	...	...
	2004	1 433	50.0	1 151	51.7	...	...
Antigua and Barbuda Antigua-et-Barbuda	2000	13 025	62.0	5 276	50.2	...	...
Argentina Argentine	1999	4 820 908	49.2	3 722 449	51.0	1 600 882	61.7
	2000	4 898 224	49.1	3 832 258	50.9	1 766 933 [1]	60.3 [1]
	2001	4 900 225	49.1	3 953 677	50.8	1 918 708	59.2
	2002	4 914 441	49.2	3 976 213	50.7	2 026 735	59.3
	2003	4 674 869	49.0	3 499 181	50.9	2 101 437	59.7
Armenia Arménie	2000	166 849 [1]	48.8 [1]	389 642 [1]	49.3 [1]	62 794	53.7
	2001	155 423	48.7	384 165	50.8	68 704	54.6
	2002	143 815	48.5	377 716	50.8	75 474	53.7
	2003	134 664	48.3	364 995	49.8	73 603	53.7
	2004	144 746	48.4	392 575	49.7	79 321	55.5
Aruba Aruba	1999	9 096	48.9	6 159	50.9	1 446	53.9
	2000	9 263	48.6	6 178	50.5	1 578	60.6
	2001	9 436	48.6	6 428	51.1	1 628	60.6
	2002	9 840	48.2	6 757	51.5	1 592	60.4
	2003	9 897	48.0	6 869	51.6	1 672	59.3
	2004	10 185	47.9	6 973	50.6	1 704	60.2
Australia Australie	1999	1 885 341	48.7	2 491 404	48.8	845 636	54.1
	2000	1 905 951	48.6	2 589 474	48.9	845 132	54.3
	2001	1 914 395	48.6	2 499 676	48.4	868 689	54.2
	2002	1 933 765	48.6	2 513 670	48.0	1 012 210	54.0
	2003	1 931 817	48.6	2 568 791	48.1	1 005 977	54.1
	2004	1 934 549	48.6	2 492 235	47.8	1 002 998	54.2

Country or area Pays ou zone	Year [t] Année [t]	Primary education Enseignement primaire		Secondary education Enseignement secondaire		Tertiary education Enseignement supérieur	
		Total	%F	Total	%F	Total	%F
Austria Autriche	1999	388 777	48.5	747 681	47.6	252 893	50.0
	2000	392 407	48.4	748 659	47.7	261 229	51.0
	2001	392 339	48.5	749 135	47.7	264 669	51.8
	2002	386 484	48.5	755 581	47.5	223 735	52.7
	2003	379 920	48.6	764 426	47.5	229 802	53.0
	2004	372 963	48.7	770 391	47.4	238 522	53.3
Azerbaijan Azerbaïdjan	1999	707 239	48.7	929 065	48.9	107 783	39.0
	2000	700 136	48.9	945 393	48.9	117 077	40.0
	2001	693 760	48.2	1 020 131	48.0	120 693	41.6
	2002	668 902	48.1	1 040 175	48.1	121 475	44.2
	2003	635 652	47.7	1 094 387	47.9	121 156	44.7
	2004	607 007	47.8	1 085 632	48.0	122 770	46.0
Bahamas Bahamas	1999	33 780	48.7	38 919	48.8	...	...
	2000 [1]	33 645	48.8	39 260	48.5	...	...
	2001 [1]	33 995	49.2	39 860	48.9	...	...
	2002	34 152	49.5	31 713	51.0	...	...
	2003 [1]	34 079	49.5	29 985	50.3	...	...
	2004	34 040	49.1	28 070	51.9	...	...
Bahrain Bahreïn	1999	76 302	48.7	58 804	50.9	11 048	60.0 [1]
	2000	77 720	48.9	61 058	50.6	...	...
	2001	79 407	48.9	62 221	51.0	...	...
	2002	81 057	48.7	64 439	50.7	...	...
	2003	81 887	48.9	67 160	50.2	19 079	61.9
	2004	82 708	48.9	69 638	49.9	18 524 [1]	63.1 [1]
Bangladesh Bangladesh	1999	17 621 731	48.6	9 912 318	48.7	709 224	32.3
	2000	17 667 985	48.9	10 329 065	49.7	726 701	32.3
	2001	17 659 220	49.1	10 690 742	50.9	878 537	33.8
	2002	17 561 828	49.7	11 024 326	51.3	855 339	32.0
	2003	17 462 973	49.3	11 051 234	51.3	877 335	32.0
	2004	17 953 300	49.6	...	...	...	...
Barbados Barbade	1999	24 792	48.9	21 841	50.6	6 915	69.2
	2000	24 475	48.9	21 016	50.3	8 074	72.3
	2001	24 225	49.1	20 866	49.4	7 979	70.7
	2002	23 394	49.2	20 872	49.4	...	...
	2003	23 074	48.9	20 947	49.7	...	...
	2004	22 327	48.9	21 300	49.7	...	...
Belarus Bélarus	1999	632 083	48.3	978 496	50.2	387 347	55.8
	2000	599 732	48.4	1 001 757	49.8	411 861	56.1
	2001	560 931	48.4	992 394	49.9	437 995	56.2
	2002	511 863	48.3	982 230	49.7	463 544	56.8
	2003	437 005	48.3	997 760	49.6	488 650	57.1
	2004	403 841	47.8	969 768	49.1	507 360	57.1
Belgium Belgique	1999	762 734	48.6	1 033 484	50.6	351 788	52.7
	2000	773 742	48.6	1 057 536	51.2	355 748	52.3
	2001	771 889	48.6	1 125 256	51.4	359 265	52.8
	2002	767 787	48.7	1 149 329	51.6	366 982	53.1
	2003	761 730	48.7	1 181 327	51.3	374 532	53.3
	2004	747 111	48.8	805 778	48.0	386 110	53.8
Belize Belize	1999	44 180	48.5	21 659	51.2	...	...
	2000	44 788	48.3	23 235	50.9	...	...
	2001	45 246	48.5	24 395	50.8	...	...
	2002 [1]	46 999	48.3	25 604	50.3	...	...
	2003	47 187	48.8	27 880 [1]	50.6 [1]	527	64.9 [2]
	2004	48 996	48.7	31 224	50.3	722	70.2
Benin Bénin	1999	872 217	39.3	213 474	31.4	16 284	20.5
	2000	932 424	40.2	229 228	31.2	18 753	19.8
	2001	1 054 936	40.6	256 744 [1]	31.8 [1]	19 758 [1]	19.8 [1]
	2002	1 152 798	41.3	287 288 [1]	31.8 [1]	...	...
	2003	1 233 214	41.9	312 427 [2]	31.5 [2]	...	...
	2004	1 319 648	42.8	338 435 [1]	33.3 [1]	...	...
Bermuda Bermudes	2001	4 959	49.6	4 566	51.1	1 942	55.0
	2002	4 910	50.3	4 565	51.5	1 960 [1]	55.1 [1]

Country or area Pays ou zone	Year[t] Année[t]	Primary education Enseignement primaire		Secondary education Enseignement secondaire		Tertiary education Enseignement supérieur	
		Total	% F	Total	% F	Total	% F
Bhutan	1999	81 156	45.7	20 123	44.2	1 479[1]	36.4[1]
Bhoutan	2000	85 092	46.1	23 301	44.7	1 837[1]	33.8[1]
	2001	88 204	46.8	26 311	45.5	1 893[1]	33.8[1]
	2002[1]	91 390	47.4	29 194	45.4	...	...
Bolivia	1999	1 444 879	48.7	829 759	47.6	252 706	...
Bolivie	2000	1 492 023	48.7	876 841[1]	48.2[1]	278 763	...
	2001	1 501 040	48.8	926 190	48.3	301 984	...
	2002	1 544 430	48.8	996 577[1]	48.3[1]	311 015	...
	2003	1 531 996	48.9	1 048 881	48.4	337 914	...
	2004[1]	1 545 797	48.9	1 074 704	48.4	346 056	...
Botswana	1999	322 475	49.7	157 715	51.4	5 532	44.0
Botswana	2000	324 283	49.7	162 663[1]	51.1[1]	6 332	42.4
	2001	329 451	49.6	163 354	51.0	7 651	47.0
	2002	330 835	49.4	166 000	51.2	8 372	44.8
	2003	330 376	49.5	166 915	51.4	9 161[1]	42.8[1]
	2004	328 692	49.3	169 727[1]	51.0[1]	13 221	45.7
Brazil	1999	20 939 076	47.7	24 982 899	51.8	2 456 961	55.6
Brésil	2000	20 211 506	47.7	26 096 870	51.6	2 781 328	56.2
	2001	19 727 684	47.8	26 441 248	51.6	3 125 745	56.1
	2002	19 380 387	47.7	26 789 210	51.6	3 582 105	56.5
	2003	18 919 122	47.7	24 592 569	51.7	3 994 422	56.4
British Virgin Islands	1999	2 757	49.0	1 511	46.8	...	...
Iles Vierges britanniques	2000	2 783	49.8	1 543[1]	50.3[1]	...	...
	2001	2 775	49.7[1]	1 562	51.0	...	...
	2002	2 811	49.0	1 593	50.5	...	...
	2003	2 780	47.9	1 633	53.7	...	...
	2004	2 824	48.2	1 707	52.1	...	...
Brunei Darussalam	1999	45 822	47.0	34 426	50.8	2 917	64.6
Brunéi Darussalam	2000	44 981	47.5	36 077	49.7	3 705	65.9
	2001	44 487	47.6	36 986	49.6	3 984	64.8
	2002	44 882	47.9	38 692	49.2	4 479	63.2
	2003	45 194[1]	47.9[1]	39 646[1]	49.1[1]	4 418	63.2
	2004	46 382	47.9	42 167	49.0	4 463[1]	63.2[1]
Bulgaria	1999	411 726	48.1	699 957	48.2	270 077	59.5
Bulgarie	2000	392 876	48.1	696 073	48.1	261 321	57.3
	2001	374 361	48.1	695 474	48.2	247 006	56.3
	2002	349 616	48.2	693 289	48.1	228 394	54.0
	2003	333 016	48.2	707 251	48.1	230 513	52.8
	2004	314 221	48.3	704 678	47.7	228 468	52.5
Burkina Faso	1999	816 393	40.4	173 205	37.5	9 878	22.8
Burkina Faso	2000	852 160	40.8	189 689	39.0	...	...
	2001	901 321	41.3	199 278	39.2	12 322	25.4[1]
	2002	956 721[1]	41.7[1]	204 847[1]	39.2[1]	15 535	25.4
	2003	1 012 150	42.1	236 914	39.9	18 200	22.4
	2004	1 139 512	43.2	245 643[1]	39.9[1]	18 868[1]	22.4[1]
Burundi	1999	701 791[1]	44.5[1]	...	...	5 037	29.5
Burundi	2000	710 364[2]	44.5[2]	...	...	6 132	26.8
	2001	750 699	44.4	...	...	6 289	27.2
	2002	817 223	44.0	...	...	10 546	30.4
	2003	894 859	44.6	129 204	43.5	11 915[1]	31.9[1]
	2004	968 488	45.4	152 251	43.0	15 706	27.7
Cambodia	1999	2 127 428	45.7	318 101[1]	34.4[1]	...	...
Cambodge	2000	2 248 109	45.8	351 357	34.9	22 108	25.1
	2001	2 431 142	46.3	396 876	35.6	25 416	27.3
	2002	2 728 698	46.5	475 637	37.0	32 010	28.8
	2003	2 772 113	46.8	560 197	38.4	43 210	28.8[1]
	2004	2 762 882	47.0	631 508[1]	40.2[1]	45 370	31.3
Cameroon	1999	2 133 707	44.9	626 053[1]	45.0[1]	66 902	...
Cameroun	2000	2 237 083	45.7	699 669	...	65 697[1]	...
	2001	2 689 052	46.2	848 216	44.1	68 495	...
	2002	2 741 627[2]	45.9[2]	932 201[1]	42.5[1]	77 707	38.8[1]
	2003	2 798 523	45.7	1 019 958[2]	40.8[1]	81 318	38.8[1]
	2004	2 979 011	45.8	1 160 957	40.9[2]	83 903[2]	38.8[1]

Country or area Pays ou zone	Year[t] Année[t]	Primary education Enseignement primaire		Secondary education Enseignement secondaire		Tertiary education Enseignement supérieur	
		Total	% F	Total	% F	Total	% F
Canada	1999	2 403 709	48.8	2 564 963	48.5	1 192 570	55.7
Canada	2000	2 428 620	48.8	...	...	1 220 651	56.0
	2001	2 456 436	48.8	2 621 457	48.6	1 212 161	56.0
	2002	2 460 943[1]	48.6[1]	2 709 025[1]	48.6[1]	1 254 833	56.4
Cape Verde	1999	92 023	48.7	...	...	706	...
Cap-Vert	2000	91 636	49.0	...	...	801	51.1[1]
	2001	90 640	49.0	45 954	50.9[1]	718	51.1[2]
	2002	89 809	48.9	48 055	50.9	1 810	51.0
	2003	87 841	48.7	49 522	52.0	2 215	52.9
	2004	85 138	48.6	49 790	52.2	3 036	52.6
Cayman Islands	1999	3 231	46.8	2 151	48.4	380[1]	73.7[1]
Iles Caïmanes	2000	3 435	50.0	2 342	49.2	380[1]	73.7[1]
	2001	3 549	49.0	2 337	48.4	390	74.6
	2002	3 579	49.4	2 341	50.4	...	...
	2004	3 361	48.5	2 701	50.8	...	...
Central African Rep.	1999	...	...	...	...	6 229	16.1
Rép. centrafricaine	2000	...	...	...	...	6 323	16.2
	2001	458 585[2]	40.9[2]	70 162[1]	...	...	...
	2002	410 562[2]	40.4[2]	71 893[1]	...	...	...
	2003	414 537	41.0	...	...	...	...
	2004[1]	420 712	41.0	...	...	...	...
Chad	1999	839 932	36.7	123 408	20.7	...	...
Tchad	2000	913 547	37.8	137 269	22.1	5 901	15.0
	2001	984 224	38.7	142 031[1]	22.1[1]	6 106[1]	15.0[1]
	2002	1 085 247	39.1	184 996	24.8	...	...
	2003	1 085 342	39.3	213 249[1]	24.2[1]	...	...
	2004[1]	1 124 992	39.2	222 167	24.2	...	...
Chile	1999	1 804 612	48.4	1 304 679	50.1	450 952	47.1
Chili	2000	1 798 515	48.5	1 391 283	49.7	452 177	47.2
	2002	1 753 952	48.5	1 496 937	49.6	521 609	47.5
	2003	1 713 538	48.5	1 557 120	49.5	567 114	47.8
	2004	1 755 997	47.9	1 594 966	49.5	580 815	48.0
China[3]	1999	...	...	77 436 268	...	6 365 625	...
Chine[3]	2000	...	...	81 487 960	...	7 364 111	...
	2001	130 132 548	47.6	86 516 712	46.8[1]	9 398 581	...
	2002	125 756 891	47.3	90 722 795	...	12 143 723	...
	2003	121 662 360	47.2	95 624 760	46.8	15 186 217	43.8
	2004	120 998 605	47.2	98 762 802	47.5	19 417 044	43.8[1]
China, Hong Kong SAR	1999	476 802	48.2	...	...	...	...
Chine, Hong Kong RAS	2000	491 851	48.2	...	...	...	...
	2001	498 175	48.1	490 039	48.5	134 828	49.1
	2002	497 376	48.1	488 510	48.6	147 426	49.5
	2003	487 465	48.1	487 218	48.8	152 649	50.3
	2004	472 863	48.1	492 779	48.9	155 761	51.5
China, Macao SAR	1999	46 893	47.3	31 859	51.4	7 458	46.3
Chine, Macao RAS	2000	47 262	47.3	35 367	50.5	7 471	52.0
	2001	45 663	47.2	38 943	50.2	13 996	44.6
	2002	44 368	47.0	42 017	50.2	20 420	36.9
	2003	41 917	46.8	44 425	50.2	26 272	36.5
	2004	39 872	46.7	46 509	49.6	24 815	40.5
Colombia	1999	5 162 260	49.0	3 589 425	51.7	877 944	52.1
Colombie	2000	5 221 018	48.9	3 568 889	51.5	934 085	51.6
	2001	5 131 463	48.8	3 377 954	51.6	977 243	51.8
	2002	5 193 055	48.8	3 723 348	51.6	989 745	51.5
	2003[1]	5 207 149	48.7	3 788 991	51.6	986 680	51.5
	2004	5 259 033	48.7	4 050 525	51.6	1 112 574	51.3
Comoros	1999	82 789	45.3	28 718	44.3	649	42.7
Comores	2000	93 421	45.4[1]	28 122[1]	44.5[1]	714	41.9[1]
	2001[1]	98 564	44.8	...	...	...	...
	2002	104 274	44.3	33 874	45.3	...	...
	2003	104 274	44.3	38 272	44.9	1 707	43.2
	2004	103 809	46.2	42 919	42.5	1 779[1]	43.2[1]

Country or area Pays ou zone	Year [t] Année [t]	Primary education Enseignement primaire		Secondary education Enseignement secondaire		Tertiary education Enseignement supérieur	
		Total	% F	Total	% F	Total	% F
Congo Congo	1999	276 451	48.8	...	...	10 713	21.0
	2000	418 707	47.8	172 980	41.0	15 629	23.8
	2001	500 921	48.2	...	...	13 403	11.9
	2002	525 093	48.3	194 101[1]	42.3[1]	12 164	15.8
	2003	509 507	48.2	204 096	40.5	12 456[1]	15.8[1]
	2004	584 370	48.1	235 294[1]	45.5[1]	...	...
Cook Islands Iles Cook	1999	2 594	46.4	1 751	50.0	...	...
	2000	2 379	47.3	1 704	50.6	...	...
	2001	2 402	46.5	1 804	50.4	...	...
	2002	2 388	46.9	1 881	49.0	...	...
	2003	2 254	47.2	1 891	48.7	...	...
Costa Rica Costa Rica	1999	552 280	48.1	235 425	51.0	58 761	52.8
	2000	551 465	48.1	255 643	50.8	61 654	53.4
	2001	552 302	48.5	280 341	50.5	79 182	52.7
	2002	545 509	48.1	288 965	50.5	77 283	52.4
	2003	541 494[1]	48.1[1]	305 940	50.5[1]	79 499[1]	52.3[1]
	2004	558 084	48.3	322 722	...	108 765	54.3
Côte d'Ivoire Côte d'Ivoire	1999	1 910 820	42.6	591 549[1]	34.9[1]	96 681	26.3
	2000	1 943 501	42.7	619 969[1]	35.1[1]	...	...
	2001	2 046 861	43.2	...	...	...	...
	2002	2 116 223	42.3	736 649[1]	35.6[1]	...	...
	2003[2]	2 046 165	44.2	...	...	...	...
Croatia Croatie	1999	202 999	48.5	416 388	49.3	95 889	52.9
	2000	199 084	48.5	410 407	49.4	96 798	52.7
	2001	195 638	48.5	405 164	49.4	104 168	52.5
	2002	193 179	48.6	401 921	49.4	112 537	52.5
	2003	192 004	48.6	399 845	49.3	121 722	53.2
Cuba Cuba	1999	1 074 097	47.8	739 980	50.3	153 463	53.1
	2000	1 045 578	47.7	789 927	49.9	158 674	53.5
	2001	1 006 888	47.7	836 642	50.0	178 021	52.1
	2002	971 542	47.8	895 742	48.5	191 262	54.4
	2003	925 335	47.7	938 047	48.3	235 997	56.2
	2004	906 293	47.7	932 338	49.1	...	...
Cyprus Chypre	1999	64 248	48.4	63 050	49.5	10 842	56.0
	2000	63 952	48.5	63 054	49.8	10 414	57.1
	2001	63 637	48.5	64 065	49.1	11 934	58.0
	2002	63 717	48.6	63 871	49.0	13 927	54.8
	2003	62 868	48.6	64 711	48.9	18 272	49.5
	2004	61 731	48.8	64 534	49.2	20 849	47.9
Czech Republic République tchèque	1999	654 511	48.5	928 467	49.9	231 224	49.7
	2000	644 956	48.6	957 763	49.3	253 695	49.8
	2001	630 680	48.4	1 004 130	49.6	260 044	50.1
	2002	603 843	48.4	998 608	49.5	284 485	51.2
	2003	566 581	48.3	1 000 493	49.5	287 001	50.7
	2004	534 366	48.3	982 208	49.1	318 858	51.2
Dem. Rep. of the Congo Rép. dém. du Congo	1999	4 022 411	47.4	1 234 528	34.3	60 341[1]	...
	2000[1]	...	...	1 253 046	34.3	...	...
Denmark Danemark	1999	371 694	48.7	422 399	50.3	189 970	56.3
	2000	384 197	48.6	426 149	50.1	189 162	56.9
	2001	395 870	48.7	441 523	50.1	192 022	56.4
	2002	415 205	48.7	434 517	50.0	196 204	57.4
	2003	...	...	446 863	50.1	201 746	57.9
	2004	419 806	48.7	449 753	49.8	217 130	57.9
Djibouti Djibouti	1999	38 194	41.2	15 511	41.6	175	...
	2000	38 191	41.9	15 812	39.3	190	46.8
	2001	42 692	42.8	18 808	38.1	496	...
	2002	44 321	42.9	20 516	37.9	728	44.5
	2003	46 564[1]	43.3[1]	23 496[1]	39.3[1]	906	40.9
	2004	48 713	43.8	26 549	40.4	1 134	44.8

Country or area Pays ou zone	Year[t] Année[t]	Primary education Enseignement primaire		Secondary education Enseignement secondaire		Tertiary education Enseignement supérieur	
		Total	% F	Total	% F	Total	% F
Dominica Dominique	1999	12 044	48.3	7 126	56.6	...	...
	2000	11 774	48.3	7 429	52.8	...	...
	2001	11 430	48.3	7 456	52.2	...	...
	2002	10 984	48.0	7 500	52.1	...	...
	2003	10 460	48.3	7 724	51.7	...	...
	2004	9 872	48.3	7 477	50.4	...	...
Dominican Republic Rép. dominicaine	1999	1 315 342	48.6	610 519	55.0	...	...
	2000	1 363 609	48.4	653 558	54.8	...	...
	2001[1]	1 403 848	49.4	752 488	54.3	...	...
	2002	1 399 844	49.4	757 790	54.3	...	...
	2003	1 374 624	49.4[1]	760 293[1]	54.3[1]	286 954	61.3
	2004	1 281 885	47.8	782 690	54.3	293 565[1]	61.3[1]
Ecuador Equateur	1999	1 899 466	49.1	903 569	49.9	...	...
	2000	1 925 420	49.0	917 245	49.7	...	...
	2001	1 955 060	49.1	936 406	49.7	...	...
	2002	1 982 636	49.1	966 362	49.4	...	...
	2003	1 987 465	49.1	972 777	49.6	...	...
	2004	1 989 665	49.0	996 535	49.3	...	...
Egypt Egypte	1999[1]	8 086 230	46.7	7 671 031	46.7	2 447 088	...
	2000[1]	7 947 488	46.9	8 028 170	47.1	...	...
	2001[1]	7 856 340	47.2	8 323 597	47.3	...	...
	2002[1]	7 855 433	47.4	8 360 316	47.1	...	...
	2003	7 874 308[1]	47.6[1]	8 384 065[1]	47.3[1]	2 153 865	...
	2004[1]	7 928 380	47.9	8 329 822	47.4	2 512 399	...
El Salvador El Salvador	1999	939 877	48.2	405 998	48.8	118 491	55.1
	2000	949 077	48.0	420 959	49.2	114 675	54.3
	2001	967 748	48.1	435 571	49.5	109 946	54.2
	2002	987 676	47.8	462 501	49.6	113 366	54.2
	2003	1 016 098	48.2	488 515	49.7	116 521	53.9
	2004	1 045 485	48.2	496 209[1]	49.6[1]	120 264	54.4
Equatorial Guinea Guinée équatoriale	1999	74 940	44.0	20 056	27.0	...	...
	2000	73 307	48.8[1]	20 679[1]	37.6[1]	1 003	30.3
	2001	78 477	48.8	19 809	...	...	...
	2002	78 390	47.6	21 173[1]	36.4[1]		
Eritrea Erythrée	1999	261 963	45.2	115 393	40.9	3 994	13.5
	2000	295 941	44.9	135 209	41.1	4 135	14.3
	2001	298 691	45.0	142 124	41.6	5 505	13.4
	2002	330 278	44.3	152 723	39.3	5 507	13.4
	2003	359 299	44.4	161 273	39.2	5 755[1]	13.3[1]
	2004	374 997	44.2	194 124	36.1	4 612	13.1
Estonia Estonie	1999	126 671	47.9	115 885	50.1	48 684	57.8
	2000	123 406	47.9	116 465	49.9	53 613	58.5
	2001	117 289	47.7	118 980	49.5	57 778	60.1
	2002	108 637	47.8	123 269	49.4	60 648	61.5
	2003	100 171	47.7	123 074	49.7	63 625	61.5
	2004	92 098	47.9	124 382	49.4	65 659	61.8
Ethiopia Ethiopie	1999	4 367 929	38.0	1 859 406	38.2	52 305	18.7
	2000	4 873 683	40.0	2 167 595	37.9	67 732	21.7
	2001	5 453 405	41.6	2 692 881	37.9	87 431	21.4
	2002	5 813 817	42.5	3 133 357	37.5	101 829	26.4
	2003	6 017 305	43.1	3 463 586	37.0	147 954	25.2
	2004	6 489 947	44.5	3 920 467	37.9	172 111	25.2
Fiji Fidji	1999	115 945	48.3	98 290	51.2	...	...
	2000	114 710	48.0	97 840	50.7	...	...
	2001	115 312	48.3	96 431	50.3	...	...
	2002	114 267	48.6	97 696	50.4	...	...
	2003	113 432	48.3	99 210	50.3	12 779[1]	53.2[1]
	2004	113 449	48.0	102 023	50.1	12 783	53.1

Country or area Pays ou zone	Year[t] Année[t]	Primary education Enseignement primaire		Secondary education Enseignement secondaire		Tertiary education Enseignement supérieur	
		Total	% F	Total	% F	Total	% F
Finland	1999	382 746	48.8	479 882	51.0	262 890	54.0
Finlande	2000	388 063	48.8	490 454	51.1	270 185	53.7
	2001	392 150	48.8	493 187	51.4	279 628	53.9
	2002	393 267	48.9	492 757	51.6	283 805	54.1
	2003	392 741	48.8	496 834	51.4	291 664	53.5
	2004	387 934	48.8	425 966	50.0	299 888	53.4
France	1999	3 944 227	48.6	5 955 495	48.9	2 012 193	54.4
France	2000	3 884 560	48.6	5 928 745	48.9	2 015 344	54.2
	2001	3 837 902	48.6	5 876 047	49.0	2 031 743	54.1
	2002	3 807 739	48.6	5 851 530	49.0	2 029 179	54.8
	2003	3 791 555	48.6	5 859 127	49.1	2 119 149	55.0
	2004	3 783 197	48.6	5 826 848	49.0	2 160 300	55.0
Gabon	1999	265 244	49.7	86 543	46.3	7 473	35.7
Gabon	2000[1]	266 221	49.6	89 572	46.3	...	...
	2001	265 714	49.6	100 718[1]	...	...	...
	2002	281 871	49.5	105 191[1]	...	...	...
	2003	279 816	49.5	...	...	...	...
	2004[1]	281 371	49.4	...	...	...	...
Gambia	1999	150 403	45.9	50 351	39.3	1 169	22.7
Gambie	2000	154 664	45.9	53 351	40.5	...	...
	2001	156 839	47.6	56 755	41.4	...	...
	2002	170 922	49.6	75 339[1]	42.9[1]	...	...
	2003	174 984	49.5	74 140[1]	45.3[1]	...	...
	2004	174 836	51.1	85 489[1]	45.4[1]	1 530	19.2
Georgia	1999	302 488	48.7	440 271	48.7	130 164	52.0
Géorgie	2000	298 352	48.7	441 149	48.8	137 046	49.2
	2001	276 389	48.8	444 974	49.1	140 627	49.0
	2002	254 030	48.7	447 381	49.0	149 142	49.8
	2003	238 371	48.3	450 345	48.9	155 453	48.8
	2004	362 582	48.3	319 766	48.7	155 058	50.5
Germany	1999	3 767 460	48.5	8 185 146	48.2	...	...
Allemagne	2000	3 655 859	48.5	8 307 277	48.4	...	...
	2001	3 519 051	48.5	8 387 525	48.4	...	...
	2002	3 373 176	48.5	8 465 150	48.3	...	...
	2003	3 303 737	48.6	8 446 559	48.3	...	...
	2004	3 305 386	48.6	8 361 390	48.2	...	...
Ghana	1999	2 377 444	47.0	1 024 135	43.6	...	...
Ghana	2000	2 560 886	47.2	1 056 616	44.0	54 658	25.0
	2001	2 477 990	47.4	1 029 258	44.7	64 098	28.5
	2002	2 586 434	47.5	1 107 247[1]	44.9[1]	68 389	27.8
	2003	2 519 272	48.4	1 170 764[1]	45.0[1]	70 293	31.8
	2004	2 678 912	47.4	1 276 670	44.5	69 968	31.5
Gibraltar	1999	2 607	40.6	1 370	47.4	...	...
Gibraltar	2000	2 366	48.0	1 471	48.1	...	...
	2001	2 377	48.0	1 550	49.1		
Greece	1999	645 534	48.4	770 883	48.9	387 859	50.3
Grèce	2000	645 313	48.4	738 744	49.4	422 317	50.0
	2001	636 460	48.4	743 462	49.1	478 205	51.1
	2002	646 343	48.3	...	...	529 233	51.2
	2003	652 052	48.4	713 850	48.5	561 468	51.0
	2004	657 492	48.2	695 838	48.3	597 007	51.7
Grenada	1999[1]	...	...	9 459	55.0	...	...
Grenade	2000	16 178	48.7	10 597[1]	52.2[1]	...	...
	2001	15 974	48.4	9 517[1]	43.5[1]	...	...
	2002	17 378	48.3	14 467	52.9	...	...
	2003	16 598	49.6	14 860	48.9	...	...
	2004	15 819	48.6	13 660	51.4	...	...
Guatemala	1999	1 823 989	46.1	434 912	45.5	...	...
Guatemala	2000	1 909 389	46.8	503 884	46.9	...	...
	2001	1 971 539	47.0	547 913	47.1	...	...
	2002	2 075 694	47.2	608 420	47.0	111 739	43.0
	2003[1]	2 125 233	47.2	621 271	47.0	114 764	43.0
	2004	2 280 706	47.5	698 561	47.4	...	...

Country or area Pays ou zone	Year[t] Année[t]	Primary education Enseignement primaire		Secondary education Enseignement secondaire		Tertiary education Enseignement supérieur	
		Total	% F	Total	% F	Total	% F
Guinea	1999	726 561	38.1	171 934[1]	26.0[1]	...	...
Guinée	2000	790 497	39.8	...	...	...	...
	2001	853 623	41.1	...	...	...	...
	2002	997 645	42.1	...	...	...	...
	2003	1 073 458	42.7	310 482[1]	31.0[1]	16 858[1]	15.6[1]
	2004	1 147 388	43.3	348 780	31.3	17 218	15.6
Guinea-Bissau	1999[1]	145 288	40.3	...	...	499	15.6
Guinée-Bissau	2000	150 041	40.2	25 736	35.4	463	15.6
	2001[1]	155 033	40.2	26 543	35.5	473	15.6
Guyana	1999	107 207	49.0	66 495	49.9	...	...
Guyana	2000	108 909	48.6	69 589[1]	50.0[1]	...	...
	2001	109 292	48.9	72 028	50.3	...	...
	2002[1]	109 012	48.8	69 259	50.3	...	...
	2003	110 828	49.0	64 954	...	4 848	61.0[1]
	2004	114 161[2]	47.7[1]	...	...	6 933	65.3
Holy See Saint-Siège	1999	...	...	...	...	9 389	30.1
Honduras	1999[1]	...	...	...	...	85 000	55.7
Honduras	2000	1 094 792	49.6	...	...	90 620	56.1
	2001[1]	1 115 579	49.6	...	...	96 612	56.1
	2002[1]	...	...	...	...	110 489	58.6
	2003	...	...	...	...	119 877	58.6
	2004	1 257 358	49.0	554 810	54.6	122 874[1]	58.6[1]
Hungary	1999	503 302	48.4	1 006 546	49.3	279 397	54.2
Hongrie	2000	500 946	48.4	1 001 855	49.1	307 071	53.9
	2001	489 768	48.4	1 007 476	49.1	330 549	54.8
	2002	477 865	48.4	1 013 471	49.1	354 386	55.3
	2003	464 013	48.5	1 029 979	49.0	390 453	56.7
	2004	446 610	48.4	963 242	48.7	422 177	57.3
Iceland	1999	30 355	48.2	32 480	50.4	8 462	62.2
Islande	2000	31 282	48.3	32 133	50.7	9 667	61.9
	2001	31 786	48.5	32 186	50.4	10 184	62.7
	2002	31 465	48.6	33 486	50.3	11 584	63.2
	2003	31 470	48.4	34 587	50.4	13 347	63.7
	2004[1]	31 442	48.5	34 724	50.4	13 408	63.7
India	1999	110 985 877	43.5	67 089 892	39.3	...	...
Inde	2000	113 612 541	43.6	71 030 515	39.6	9 404 460	37.8
	2001	113 826 978	43.8	72 392 727	39.8	9 834 046	38.7
	2002	115 194 579	44.2	76 215 685	40.7	10 576 653	39.1
	2003	125 568 597	46.8	81 050 129	42.6	11 295 041	38.4
	2004	136 193 772[1]	46.8[1]	83 858 267	42.8	11 852 936	38.2
Indonesia	2000[1]	28 201 934	48.3	14 263 912	48.1	...	...
Indonésie	2001	28 690 131	48.6	14 828 085	48.8	3 017 887	42.8
	2002	28 926 377	48.6	15 140 713	49.0	3 175 833	45.9
	2003	29 050 834	48.7	15 872 535	49.0	3 441 429	43.9
	2004	29 142 093	48.7	16 353 933	49.1	3 551 092	43.8
Iran (Islamic Rep. of)	1999	8 667 147	47.4	9 726 948	47.0	1 308 150	43.4
Iran (Rép. islamique d')	2000	8 287 537	47.5	9 954 767	47.3	1 404 880	45.3
	2001	7 968 437	47.6	9 933 471	47.3	1 569 776	47.4
	2002	7 513 015	47.8	9 916 372	47.5	1 566 509	49.1
	2003	7 028 924	47.9	10 024 105	47.2	1 714 433	50.7
	2004	7 306 634	51.1	10 312 561	47.1	1 954 920	51.4
Iraq	1999	3 603 864	44.0	1 105 028	37.6	271 508	34.2
Iraq	2000	3 639 362	44.0	1 224 253	37.0	288 670	34.1
	2001	4 031 346	44.1	1 257 106	36.6	...	...
	2002	4 135 761	43.9[1]	...	...	317 993[1]	34.0[1]
	2003	4 280 602	44.5	1 477 616	40.5	...	...
	2004	4 334 609	44.3	1 706 234	38.9	412 545	36.2
Ireland	1999	456 564	48.5	346 316	50.2	151 137	53.5
Irlande	2000	449 638	48.5	338 247	50.6	160 611	54.1
	2001	443 617	48.5	328 424	50.8	166 600	54.7
	2002	445 947	48.5	323 043	51.0	176 296	55.1
	2003	447 618	48.5	320 620	50.9	181 557	55.7
	2004	450 413	48.5	320 560	50.7	188 315	55.2

9 Education at the primary, secondary and tertiary levels—Number of students enrolled and percentage female (*continued*)

Enseignement primaire, secondaire et supérieur—Nombre d'étudiants inscrits et étudiantes féminines en pourcentage (*suite*)

Country or area Pays ou zone	Year [t] Année [t]	Primary education Enseignement primaire		Secondary education Enseignement secondaire		Tertiary education Enseignement supérieur	
		Total	% F	Total	% F	Total	% F
Israel	1999	722 293	48.5	569 408	48.5	246 806	57.6
Israël	2000	738 610	48.5	587 663	48.8	255 891	57.3
	2001	748 580	48.7	594 210	48.6	270 979	56.7
	2002	760 346	48.7	606 141	48.5	299 716	56.5
	2003	769 856	48.6	603 321	48.3	301 326	55.7
	2004	775 021	48.8	607 224	48.8	301 227	55.8
Italy	1999	2 875 852	48.5	4 450 012	48.6	1 797 241	55.2
Italie	2000	2 836 333	48.6	4 404 331	...	1 770 002	55.5
	2001	2 810 337	48.5	4 473 362	48.1	1 812 325	56.0
	2002	2 789 880	48.1	4 515 802	47.8	1 854 200	56.2
	2003	2 778 877	48.4	4 528 300	48.5[1]	1 913 352	56.2
	2004	2 768 386	48.4	4 505 699	48.5	1 986 497	56.2
Jamaica	1999[1]	316 290	49.3	231 177	50.3	...	...
Jamaïque	2000	326 847	49.2	228 764	50.6	35 995	65.0
	2001	328 496	48.9	227 703	50.5[1]	42 502	66.8[1]
	2002	329 762	48.9	228 316	50.4	45 394	68.8
	2003	325 302	48.9	229 701	50.1	45 770[1]	69.9[1]
	2004	331 286	48.9	245 533	49.9	...	...
Japan	1999	7 691 872	48.8	8 958 699	49.1	3 940 756	44.7
Japon	2000	7 528 907	48.8	8 782 114	49.1	3 982 069	44.9
	2001	7 394 582	48.8	8 605 812	49.0	3 972 468	44.9
	2002	7 325 866	48.8	8 394 050	49.0	3 966 667	45.1
	2003	7 268 928	48.8	8 131 217	48.9	3 984 400	45.6
	2004	7 257 223	48.8	7 894 456	48.9	4 031 604	45.8
Jordan	1999	706 198	48.8	579 445	49.4	...	...
Jordanie	2000	723 508	48.8	583 535	49.5[1]	142 190	51.4
	2002	766 093	48.8	606 615	49.4	162 688	48.9
	2003	786 154	48.9	613 120	49.3	186 189	51.1
	2004	799 888	48.9	615 731	49.2	214 106	51.2
Kazakhstan	1999	1 248 900	49.2	1 966 471	49.2	323 949	53.4
Kazakhstan	2000	1 208 320	49.3	2 002 880	49.6	370 321	54.0
	2001	1 190 069	48.8	2 031 675	48.6	445 651	54.2
	2002	1 158 299	48.8	2 019 821	48.7	519 815	55.2
	2003	1 120 005	48.9	2 067 168	49.2	603 072	56.6
	2004	1 079 598	48.8	2 090 152	48.6	664 449	57.4
Kenya	1999	4 782 375	49.0	1 822 161	48.7	...	...
Kenya	2000	5 034 858	49.4	1 908 703	48.5	89 016	35.1
	2001	...	...	...	...	94 629	34.8
	2002	4 903 529	48.4	2 063 409	48.7	98 115[1]	34.8[1]
	2003	5 811 381	48.5	2 197 336	50.4	...	...
	2004	5 926 078	48.3	2 419 856[1]	48.1[1]	108 407	37.5
Kiribati	1999	14 328	48.7	9 270	53.3	...	...
Kiribati	2000	14 566	47.7	11 638	61.1	...	...
	2001	15 693	49.1	10 586	56.7	...	...
	2002	14 809	48.7	10 334	52.5	...	...
	2003	15 798	48.3	11 372	52.9	...	...
	2004	15 611	49.6	11 581	52.8	...	...
Korea, Republic of	1999	3 844 949	47.3	4 367 683	48.2	2 636 388	35.0
Corée, République de	2000	3 945 977	47.2	4 176 780	47.9	2 837 880	35.2
	2001	4 030 413	47.0	3 958 702	47.8	3 003 498	35.6
	2002	4 099 649	46.9	3 768 040	47.7	3 129 899	36.0
	2003	4 148 432	46.9	3 661 759	47.5	3 210 142	36.4
	2004	4 185 330	47.0	3 645 617	47.4	3 223 431	36.6
Kuwait	1999	139 691	48.8	235 106[1]	49.1[1]	32 320[1]	67.7[1]
Koweït	2000	140 182	48.9	239 997	49.5	...	...
	2001	141 419	48.9	243 757[1]	50.0[1]	...	...
	2002	148 712	48.6	243 517[1]	49.8[1]	...	...
	2003	154 056	49.0	260 695	49.7	...	...
	2004	158 271	48.9	267 251	49.9	42 076[1]	70.8[1]

Country or area Pays ou zone	Year[t] Année[t]	Primary education Enseignement primaire		Secondary education Enseignement secondaire		Tertiary education Enseignement supérieur	
		Total	% F	Total	% F	Total	% F
Kyrgyzstan	1999	469 779	49.0	633 356	50.1	131 222	50.8
Kirghizistan	2000	465 596	48.8	659 451	50.2	160 684	50.1
	2001	458 660	48.6	683 832	49.5	190 508	50.8
	2002	453 357	48.7	689 036	49.6	209 245	53.0
	2003	449 399	48.9	739 259	49.7	201 128	54.1
	2004	444 417	49.0	732 618	49.6	205 224	54.0
Lao People's Dem. Rep.	1999	827 664	45.1	240 267	40.3	12 076	32.1
Rép. dém. pop. lao	2000	831 521	45.2	264 586	40.5	14 149	33.9
	2001	828 113	45.4	288 389	41.0	16 745	36.5
	2002	852 857	45.5	320 275	41.4	23 018[2]	35.6[2]
	2003	875 300	45.6	353 362	41.9	28 117	35.8
	2004	884 629	45.9	379 579	42.2	33 760	38.0
Latvia	1999	141 408	48.3	255 381	49.9	82 042	61.6
Lettonie	2000	134 919	48.4	266 498	49.7	91 237	63.4
	2001	125 634	48.6	274 193	49.3	102 783	61.8
	2002	113 923	48.4	278 230	49.1	110 500	61.5
	2003	103 359	48.2	276 072	48.8	118 944	61.7
	2004	92 453	48.1	275 586	48.8	127 656	62.3
Lebanon	1999	394 505	48.0	372 365	51.5	113 022	50.3
Liban	2000	384 539	47.9	383 217	51.4	116 014	51.7
	2001	453 986	48.2	322 136	51.7	134 018	51.9
	2002	452 050	48.1	336 170	51.5	142 951	52.9
	2003	449 311	48.2	350 211	51.3	144 050	54.0
	2004	453 578	48.2	359 062	51.4	154 635	52.3
Lesotho	1999	365 251	51.6	73 620	57.4	4 046	63.7
Lesotho	2000	410 745	50.6	74 313	56.8	4 470[1]	61.8[1]
	2001	415 007	50.2	79 266	56.0	4 976	63.5
	2002	418 668	50.1	82 258	56.1	5 005	58.0
	2003	429 522	50.0	84 318	56.0	6 108	61.3
	2004	427 009	49.7	89 468	55.9	...	...
Liberia	1999	395 611	42.4	113 878	38.9	20 804	19.2
Libéria	2000	496 253	41.9	135 509	41.7	44 107	42.8
Libyan Arab Jamah.	1999	821 775	48.5	...	...	308 474	48.6[1]
Jamah. arabe libyenne	2000	794 293[1]	48.5[1]	...	...	290 060	48.6
	2001	766 087	49.2	...	...	324 603[1]	50.2[1]
	2002	750 204	48.8	824 538	50.5	359 146	51.4
	2003[1]	743 997	48.8	797 992	50.5	375 028	51.4
Liechtenstein	1999	1 569	48.5	...	...	...	...
Liechtenstein	2003	2 218	49.8	3 255	45.0	440	27.0
	2004	2 266	49.8	2 050	51.4	532	26.7
Lithuania	1999	219 661	48.4	406 951	49.2	107 419	60.0
Lituanie	2000	218 181	48.7	421 120	48.9	121 904	60.0
	2001	211 650	48.5	433 054	48.8	135 923	59.8
	2002	197 463	48.6	442 830	48.6	148 788	60.5
	2003	183 542	48.5	447 952	48.5	167 606	60.0
	2004	170 200	48.6	431 303	48.8	182 656	60.0
Luxembourg	1999	31 492	49.2	32 513	49.9	2 717	51.7
Luxembourg	2000	32 458	49.2	32 996	50.2	2 437	51.7[1]
	2001	33 266	48.7	33 606	50.4	2 533	53.1
	2002	33 966	48.6	34 038	50.4	2 965	52.8[1]
	2003	34 081	48.7	34 716	50.2	3 077	53.3
	2004	34 603	48.7	35 208	50.2	3 042[1]	52.9[1]
Madagascar	1999	2 012 416	49.1	346 941[1]	48.9[1]	31 013	45.7
Madagascar	2000	2 208 321	49.0	...	...	32 156	46.2
	2001	2 307 500	49.0	...	...	31 386	45.5
	2002	2 407 644	49.0	...	...	32 593	45.4
	2003	2 856 480	48.9	...	...	37 252[1]	46.3[1]
	2004	3 366 470	48.9	...	...	42 143	47.3

9 **Education at the primary, secondary and tertiary levels**— Number of students enrolled and percentage female (*continued*)
Enseignement primaire, secondaire et supérieur— Nombre d'étudiants inscrits et étudiantes féminines en pourcentage (*suite*)

Country or area Pays ou zone	Year[t] Année[t]	Primary education Enseignement primaire		Secondary education Enseignement secondaire		Tertiary education Enseignement supérieur	
		Total	% F	Total	% F	Total	% F
Malawi Malawi	1999	2 581 698	48.7	556 322	41.2	3 179	27.6
	2000	2 694 645	48.9	486 786	42.8	...	...
	2001	2 845 836	48.9	518 251	43.6	...	...
	2002	2 846 589	48.9	517 690[1]	43.6[1]	...	...
	2003	...	...	...	...	4 565	29.2
	2004	2 841 640	50.3	505 303	44.6	5 089	35.3
Malaysia Malaisie	1999	3 040 333	48.1	2 176 863	51.0	473 357	50.0
	2000	3 025 977	48.7	2 205 426	51.2	549 205	51.0
	2001	3 033 019	48.7	2 246 874	51.1	557 118	...
	2002	3 009 009	48.7	2 300 062	51.3	632 309	55.1
	2003	3 056 266	48.6	2 518 642	51.9	725 865	57.2
Maldives Maldives	1999	74 050	48.9	14 988	51.1	...	...
	2000	73 522	48.6	20 010	51.3	...	...
	2001	71 054	48.4	24 607	51.0	...	...
	2002	68 242	48.1	25 365	52.6	...	...
	2003	66 169	47.8	28 612	51.6	73	69.9
	2004	63 300	47.6	28 878[1]	51.9[1]	73[1]	69.9[1]
Mali Mali	1999	958 935	41.0	217 700	34.2	18 662	...
	2000	1 016 575	42.0	242 665[1]	35.5[1]	...	...
	2001	1 127 360	41.7	...	...	...	...
	2002	1 227 267	42.3	...	...	27 464	...
	2003	1 294 672	42.7	351 471	34.8	26 680[1]	31.5[1]
	2004	1 396 791	43.1	397 569	36.9[1]	25 803	31.5
Malta Malte	1999	34 914	48.6	...	...	5 768	51.5
	2000	34 261	48.6	36 081	48.7	6 315	53.3
	2001	33 530	48.4	36 243	47.9	7 422	54.8
	2002	32 717	48.2	36 478	48.4	7 259	56.9
	2003	31 710	48.1	37 556	48.4	8 946	57.0
	2004	31 064	48.2	41 723	46.8	7 867	55.9
Marshall Islands Iles Marshall	1999	8 209	48.2	5 957	50.5	...	...
	2000[1]	8 300	47.6	...	...	...	...
	2001[1]	8 530	47.1	...	...	888	56.4
	2002	8 757	47.0	6 353	49.5	903	56.5
	2003[1]	8 907	47.0	6 460	49.5	919	56.5
Mauritania Mauritanie	1999	346 222	48.4	63 482[1]	42.0[1]	12 912	...
	2000	355 822	48.4	65 606	41.7	...	...
	2001	360 677	48.2	76 658	42.9	9 033	16.8
	2002	375 695	48.8	78 730	43.1	8 173	21.3
	2003	394 401	49.2	84 407	44.4	9 198[1]	21.5[1]
	2004	434 181	49.4	88 926	45.3	9 292	23.7
Mauritius Maurice	1999	133 489	49.4	104 070	48.9	7 559	46.1
	2000	135 237	49.2	105 432	48.5[1]	8 256	45.0
	2001	134 085	49.3	107 846	48.8	12 469	56.9
	2002	132 432	49.4	111 766	49.4	12 602	55.8
	2003	129 616	49.4	118 234	49.2	16 764	57.9
	2004	126 226	49.3	121 743[1]	49.1[1]	17 781	57.6
Mexico Mexique	1999	14 697 915	48.6	8 721 726	49.9	1 837 884	48.3
	2000	14 765 603	48.7	9 094 103	50.2	1 962 763	48.7
	2001	14 792 528	48.8	9 357 144	50.5	2 047 895	49.0
	2002	14 843 381	48.8	9 692 976	50.9	2 147 075	49.3
	2003	14 857 191	48.8	10 188 185	51.5	2 236 791	49.6
	2004	14 781 327	48.8	10 403 853	51.2	2 322 781	50.0
Micronesia (Fed. States of) Micronésie (Etats féd. de)	1999	...	...	...	...	1 510	...
	2000[1]	...	...	...	...	1 539	...
Monaco Monaco	1999	2 022	49.9	2 883	50.9	...	...
	2000	2 008	48.5	2 929	50.9	...	...
	2001	1 985	48.9	2 971	48.4	...	...
	2004	1 831	...	3 078	...	...	...

Country or area Pays ou zone	Year[t] Année[t]	Primary education Enseignement primaire		Secondary education Enseignement secondaire		Tertiary education Enseignement supérieur	
		Total	% F	Total	% F	Total	% F
Mongolia	1999	251 476	50.2	205 229	55.5	65 272	64.9
Mongolie	2000	253 441	50.2	225 848	54.7	74 025	63.8
	2001	250 436	50.1	258 265	54.4	84 970	63.2
	2002	241 258	50.0	282 089	53.9	90 275	63.2
	2003	238 676	49.6	312 774	53.1	98 031	62.4
	2004	235 730	49.4	333 193	52.5	108 738	61.8
Montserrat	1999	392	43.9	272	47.1	...	...
Montserrat	2000	383	43.9	284	48.6	...	...
	2001	413	44.8	297	47.5	...	...
	2002	456	45.2	301	48.2	...	...
	2003[1]	465	45.2	305	48.5	...	...
	2004	468	44.7	284	48.9	...	...
Morocco	1999	3 461 940	44.0	1 469 794	43.4	273 183	41.8
Maroc	2000	3 669 605	44.8	1 541 100	43.7	276 375	42.3
	2001	3 842 000	45.6	1 608 279[1]	43.8[1]	310 258	43.7
	2002	4 029 112	46.2	1 685 063[1]	44.0[1]	315 343[1]	43.7[1]
	2003	4 101 157	46.4	1 758 057	44.5	335 755	44.9
	2004	4 070 182	46.5	1 879 483	44.8	343 599	45.7
Mozambique	1999	2 302 313	42.6	103 147	40.8	10 322	...
Mozambique	2000	2 543 820	43.0	123 810	38.4	11 619	...
	2001	2 829 787	43.5	142 553	38.8	...	...
	2002	3 023 321	44.1	180 531	39.6	...	...
	2003	...	...	...	...	17 225	32.2
	2004	3 569 473	45.3	243 428	41.1	22 256	31.6
Myanmar	1999	4 732 947	49.1	2 059 007	49.6	335 497[1]	61.2[1]
Myanmar	2000	4 857 955	49.3	2 268 402	51.2	550 705[1]	...
	2001	4 781 543	49.3	2 301 919	48.4	553 456	63.4[1]
	2002	4 778 851	49.6	2 372 593	48.1	555 060[1]	...
	2003	4 889 325	49.7	2 382 608	48.1	...	...
	2004	4 932 646	49.7	2 544 437	48.0	...	...
Namibia	1999	383 267	50.1	116 131	52.7	...	...
Namibie	2000	389 434	50.0	124 196	52.8	...	...
	2001	397 459	50.0	135 943	53.1	13 339	45.6
	2002	404 783	50.1	138 099	52.7	11 030	57.9
	2003	408 912	49.9	140 976	52.9	11 788	53.2
Nauru	2000	1 589	53.5	662	54.4	...	...
Nauru	2001	1 618	48.6	636	49.2	...	...
	2002	1 324	49.8	573	53.6	...	...
	2003	1 375	46.8	645	50.4	...	...
Nepal	1999	3 587 665	41.9	1 265 458	39.6	...	...
Népal	2000	3 780 314	42.6	1 348 212	40.1	94 401	27.5
	2001	3 623 150	44.1	1 501 503	40.2	103 290	20.7[1]
	2002	3 853 618	44.8	1 690 198	41.0	119 670	20.6
	2003	3 928 684	45.4	1 822 063	41.9	124 817	24.1
	2004	4 025 692	45.4	...	...	147 123	27.6
Netherlands	1999	1 268 093	48.3	1 364 806	47.8	469 885	49.3
Pays-Bas	2000	1 278 581	48.3	1 379 253	47.9	487 649	50.0
	2001	1 282 041	48.3	1 402 928	48.1	504 042	50.5
	2002	1 287 069	48.3	1 397 939	48.2	516 769	50.7
	2003	1 290 625	48.2	1 415 170	48.6	526 767	51.0
	2004	1 283 014	48.2	1 396 696	48.5	543 396	50.9
Netherlands Antilles	1999	25 398	48.2	15 426	53.7	2 320	53.2
Antilles néerlandaises	2000	24 911	48.4	14 418	52.4	2 561	55.5
	2001	23 650	45.9	14 652	52.6	2 433	57.7
	2002	22 924	49.2	15 093	52.2	2 285	59.7
	2003[1]	22 667	49.2	15 268	52.1	...	...
New Zealand	1999	360 621	48.6	436 901	50.1	167 308	59.0
Nouvelle-Zélande	2000	359 555	48.6	443 882	50.3	171 962	58.8
	2001	355 532	48.4	456 155	...	177 634	58.6
	2002	361 866	48.4[1]	482 959	51.6	185 099	58.8
	2003	356 442	48.5	503 692	51.3	195 511	58.6
	2004	353 062	48.5	488 994	50.6	179 452	57.3

Education at the primary, secondary and tertiary levels— Number of students enrolled and percentage female (*continued*)

Enseignement primaire, secondaire et supérieur— Nombre d'étudiants inscrits et étudiantes féminines en pourcentage (*suite*)

Country or area Pays ou zone	Year[t] Année[t]	Primary education Enseignement primaire		Secondary education Enseignement secondaire		Tertiary education Enseignement supérieur	
		Total	% F	Total	% F	Total	% F
Nicaragua	1999	830 206	49.4	321 493[1]	53.7[1]	...	...
Nicaragua	2000	838 437	49.4	333 210	53.4		
	2001	868 070	49.3	353 724	53.5	96 479[1]	52.2[1]
	2002	923 391	48.9	382 951	53.3	100 363	52.2
	2003	927 217	48.7	412 343[1]	52.7[1]	103 577[1]	52.1[1]
	2004	941 957	48.6	416 405	52.7	...	...
Niger	1999	529 806	39.2	104 933	38.0	...	...
Niger	2000	579 486	39.3	106 182[1]	38.7[1]	...	...
	2001	656 589	39.6	108 033[1]	38.9[1]	...	...
	2002	760 987	39.8	112 033	38.5	...	...
	2003	857 592	40.1	126 137	38.9	8 596[1]	27.4[1]
	2004	980 033	40.3	158 343	38.5	8 774	27.4
Nigeria	1999	17 907 008	43.8	3 844 585	46.8	699 109	43.2
Nigéria	2000[1]	18 802 361	43.8	...	...	...	...
	2001[1]	20 116 361	43.9	...	...	...	...
	2002[1]	20 742 139	44.0	...	...	...	...
	2003	24 563 004	44.0	6 313 110	43.8	1 234 218	34.6[1]
	2004	21 110 707	44.7	6 316 302	43.7	1 289 656	34.6
Niue	1999	268	46.3	268	54.1	...	...
Nioué	2000	250	46.0[1]	260[1]	51.9[1]	...	...
	2001	234	45.7	242	49.6	...	...
	2002	251	...	240	...	...	...
	2004	184	51.1	209	50.7	...	...
Norway	1999	411 878	48.7	377 640	49.4	187 482	57.4
Norvège	2000	419 805	48.7	371 659	49.4	190 943	58.4
	2001	426 475	48.7	369 943	49.3	190 054	59.2
	2002	429 445	48.7	373 015	49.3	197 064	59.6
	2003	432 618	48.6	385 009	49.3	212 395	59.7
	2004	432 345	48.7	400 159	49.5	213 845	59.6
Occupied Palestinian Terr.	1999	368 321	49.0	444 401	49.6	66 282	45.6
Terr. palestinien occupé	2000	388 163	48.9	477 378	50.1	71 207	46.5
	2001	398 978	49.0	510 214	50.6	80 543	47.4
	2002	402 370	49.0	544 935	50.3	88 930	47.9
	2003	401 372	49.0	582 736	50.2	104 567	49.5
	2004	388 948	48.9	628 495	50.1	121 928	49.5
Oman	1999	315 557	47.9	229 031	49.1	...	...
Oman	2000	315 976	48.0	242 533	49.1	18 287[1]	57.5[1]
	2001	316 889	48.2	254 496	48.9	19 297	57.9
	2002	316 633	48.3	266 923	48.6	19 864[1]	57.9[1]
	2003	314 064	48.5	279 302	48.1	...	...
	2004	306 210	48.6	286 413	47.9	33 807	56.0
Pakistan	2000	13 987 198[2]	39.1[1]	...	...	...	...
Pakistan	2001[2]	14 204 954	39.1	6 548 857	39.4	...	...
	2002	14 489 107[2]	39.1[2]	6 396 378[1]	40.4[1]	385 506[1]	43.2[1]
	2003	15 093 960	40.6	6 485 293	41.1	401 056	43.2
	2004	16 207 286	40.8	7 271 999	40.8	520 666	42.7
Palau	1999	1 901	46.6	2 177	48.7	...	...
Palaos	2000	1 942	47.7	1 901	47.9	597[1]	69.0[1]
	2001	1 897[1]	...	1 898[1]	48.2[1]	480	63.5
	2002[1]	...	...	...	...	484	63.4
	2003[1]	1 809	43.6	2 465	52.2	...	...
	2004[1]	1 796	44.7	2 451	51.4	...	...
Panama	1999	393 030	48.2	230 034	50.8	108 764	60.7
Panama	2000	400 408	48.2	234 153	50.5	118 502	62.1
	2001	408 249	48.2	244 097	50.8	117 864	62.4
	2002	419 904	48.2	251 228	50.7	117 601	62.1
	2003[1]	424 500	48.2	253 012	50.7	119 069	62.1
	2004	429 837	48.3	253 900	50.8	130 026	60.6
Papua New Guinea	1999	622 828	45.4	143 501	40.3	9 943[1]	35.2[1]
Papouasie-Nouvelle-Guinée	2000	647 804	45.1	156 144	40.9	...	...
	2001	628 358	45.2	170 271	40.3	...	...
	2002	660 425	44.8	184 651	40.8	...	...
	2003[1]	680 786	45.0	190 321	41.0	...	...

Country or area Pays ou zone	Year [t] Année [t]	Primary education Enseignement primaire		Secondary education Enseignement secondaire		Tertiary education Enseignement supérieur	
		Total	% F	Total	% F	Total	% F
Paraguay Paraguay	1999	951 481[1]	48.2[1]	425 214	50.2	66 065	57.2
	2000	966 476[1]	48.2[1]	459 260	50.1	83 088	56.9
	2001	966 548[1]	48.2[1]	497 935	49.8	96 598	57.2
	2002	962 661	48.2	519 930	49.7[1]	146 892[1]	57.6[1]
	2003	935 722	48.3	510 881	49.6	143 913[1]	57.2[1]
Peru Pérou	1999	4 349 594	49.0	2 277 813	47.7	...	...
	2000	4 338 080	49.0	2 374 178	47.5	...	...
	2001	4 317 368	49.1	2 484 775	47.5	823 995[1]	48.8[1]
	2002	4 283 046	49.1	2 539 682	47.5	831 345[1]	51.1[1]
	2003	4 200 489	49.0	2 605 247	49.4	839 584[1]	51.1[1]
	2004	4 133 386	49.0	2 661 880	49.6	896 501[1]	50.0[1]
Philippines Philippines	1999	12 502 524	48.9	5 117 459	51.3	2 208 635	54.9
	2001	12 759 918	48.9	5 386 434	51.3	2 432 002	...
	2002	12 826 218	48.7	5 816 699	51.4	2 467 267	55.6
	2003	12 970 635	48.6	6 069 063	51.5	2 427 211	55.3
	2004	13 017 973	48.5	6 308 792	51.6	2 420 997	55.2
Poland Pologne	1999	3 433 762	48.3	...	...	1 399 090	57.0
	2000	3 318 722	48.4	3 988 001	48.4	1 579 571	57.5
	2001	3 221 253	48.5	3 973 962	48.3	1 774 985	58.0
	2002	3 105 262	48.5	3 949 993	48.1	1 906 268	57.9
	2003	2 983 070	48.6	3 895 167	47.8	1 983 360	57.8
	2004	2 855 692	48.6	3 480 054	49.1	2 044 298	57.6
Portugal Portugal	1999	815 231	47.7	847 516	50.9	356 790	55.9
	2000	810 996	47.7	831 193	50.6	373 745	56.5
	2001	801 545	48.4	813 172	50.3	387 703	57.0
	2002	769 910	47.8	797 065	...	396 601	57.0
	2003	767 872	47.5	766 172	51.0	400 831	56.6
	2004	758 476	47.5	665 213	51.4	395 063	56.1
Qatar Qatar	1999	60 989	47.8	44 403	50.5	8 880[1]	71.8[1]
	2000	61 067	48.2	47 413	49.1	...	...
	2001	62 465	48.8	46 931	50.1	7 808	73.2
	2002	64 255	47.9	49 042	49.7	7 831	72.5
	2003	66 473	48.3	51 888	49.5	7 826	72.8
	2004	65 351	48.5	53 953	48.9	9 287	71.4
Republic of Moldova République de Moldova	1999	262 137	49.1	415 319	49.5	103 672	55.9
	2000	252 193	48.7	413 910	49.8	103 944	56.3
	2001	238 713	48.9	413 418	49.9	102 825	55.7
	2002	227 470	48.7	413 916	49.9	107 731	56.6
	2003	215 442	48.7	410 590	50.0	114 238	56.4
	2004	201 650	48.6	399 812	50.1	126 885	57.1
Romania Roumanie	1999	1 284 507	48.5	2 218 025	49.3	407 720	51.0
	2000	1 189 058	48.5	2 225 691	49.4	452 621	51.8
	2001	1 090 172	48.3	2 248 802	49.3	533 152	53.5
	2002	1 028 697	48.3	2 254 849	49.4	582 221	54.4
	2003	990 807	48.3	2 218 124	49.4	643 911	54.3
	2004	1 005 533	48.3	2 154 734	49.3	685 718	54.8
Russian Federation Fédération de Russie	1999	6 138 300	48.6	...	...	...	...
	2001	5 702 348	48.6	...	...	...	...
	2002	5 554 607	48.6	15 340 411[1]	49.0[1]	...	...
	2003	5 416 925	48.7	14 521 818	48.9	8 115 305[1]	56.8[1]
	2004	5 329 613	48.7	13 558 904	48.8	8 622 097[1]	57.0[1]
Rwanda Rwanda	1999	1 288 669	50.0	105 292	50.8	5 678	...
	2000	1 431 657	49.6	129 620	49.1	11 628[1]	33.7[1]
	2001	1 475 572	50.0	163 576	49.6	12 802	33.7
	2002	1 534 510	50.3	...	...	15 940	34.1
	2003	1 636 563	50.5	189 153	47.5	20 393	36.8
	2004	1 752 588	50.8	203 551	47.7	25 233	39.1

Education at the primary, secondary and tertiary levels — Number of students enrolled and percentage female (*continued*)
Enseignement primaire, secondaire et supérieur — Nombre d'étudiants inscrits et étudiantes féminines en pourcentage (*suite*)

Country or area Pays ou zone	Year [t] Année [t]	Primary education Enseignement primaire		Secondary education Enseignement secondaire		Tertiary education Enseignement supérieur	
		Total	% F	Total	% F	Total	% F
Saint Kitts and Nevis Saint-Kitts-et-Nevis	2000	6 922	48.6	4 768	50.5	...	...
	2001	6 717	49.9	4 623	53.5	...	...
	2002	6 440	49.3	4 494	50.7	...	...
	2003	6 401	49.0	4 221	54.5	...	...
	2004	6 394	50.2	4 548	50.5	...	...
Saint Lucia Sainte-Lucie	1999	25 581	49.0	11 847	56.5	...	...
	2000	25 347	49.3	12 530	57.2	...	...
	2001	25 481	48.7	12 738	56.5	...	...
	2002	24 954	48.9	12 743	56.9	221	76.9
	2003	24 573	48.4	14 110[1]	53.1[1]	...	...
	2004	23 821	48.3	14 209	52.6	2 285	77.8
St. Vincent-Grenadines St. Vincent-Grenadines	2000	19 183	48.2	9 753	53.4	...	...
	2001	19 052	48.3	9 915[1]	53.8[1]	...	...
	2002	18 130	48.4	9 606	54.1	...	...
	2003	18 629	48.7	9 624	52.0	...	...
	2004	17 536	48.4	10 398	49.1	...	...
Samoa Samoa	1999	27 297	47.6	21 748	49.5	1 871	47.5
	2000	28 026	48.1	21 681	50.4	1 182	44.3
	2001	29 203	48.1	22 185	50.4	1 179[1]	44.4[1]
	2002	30 164	47.9	22 941	50.3	...	...
	2003	31 059	47.8	23 427	50.7	...	...
	2004	31 175	48.0	23 764	50.6	...	...
San Marino Saint-Marin	2000	1 249	48.0	988	49.3	942	57.9
	2004	1 445	...	...	...	...	...
Sao Tome and Principe Sao Tomé-et-Principe	1999	23 769	48.7	...	...	...	...
	2001[1]	27 795	47.9	...	...	...	...
	2002[1]	28 780	48.3	7 367	45.4	...	...
	2003	29 347	48.5	6 753	53.5	...	...
	2004	29 784	48.7	7 423	50.5	...	...
Saudi Arabia Arabie saoudite	1999	2 259 707	48.0	1 773 725	45.9	349 599	57.0
	2000	2 285 328	48.0	1 861 755	46.3	404 094	55.9
	2001	2 308 460	48.0	1 914 465	46.3	432 348[1]	54.9[1]
	2002	2 316 166	48.1	2 020 031	45.6	444 800[1]	58.8[1]
	2003	2 342 214	47.9	1 995 443	46.3	525 344	58.2
	2004	2 385 501	47.9	2 036 608	46.0	573 732	58.7
Senegal Sénégal	1999	1 034 065	45.9[1]	237 454	38.9	29 303	...
	2000	1 107 712	46.0	249 547	39.2	...	...
	2001	1 159 721	46.5	260 738	39.5	...	...
	2002	1 197 081	47.1	289 263	39.9	...	...
	2003	1 287 093	47.5	309 959	40.6	50 375[1]	...
	2004	1 382 749	48.3	360 016	41.6	52 282	...
Serbia and Montenegro Serbie-et-Monténégro	1999	417 830	48.6	813 956	49.2	197 410	53.5
	2000	389 314	48.7	784 526	49.4	233 043	53.0
	2001	379 575	48.8	761 408	49.3	208 689	53.7
Seychelles Seychelles	1999	10 014	49.3	7 788	50.1	...	...
	2000	10 025	49.3	7 742	50.6	...	...
	2001	9 782	49.0	7 514	50.7	...	...
	2002	9 623	48.8	7 525	49.9	...	...
	2003	9 477	48.6	7 551	50.2	...	...
	2004	9 194	48.7	7 406	50.7	...	...
Sierra Leone Sierra Leone	2000	442 915	...	...	...	...	...
	2001	554 308	41.6	155 567	41.6[1]	8 795	28.8
	2002[1]	...	...	...	...	9 041	28.8
	2004	1 158 399	42.2	94 366	50.8	...	...
Slovakia Slovaquie	1999	316 601	48.5	674 405	49.5	122 886	51.7
	2000	309 399	48.5	671 670	49.4	135 914	50.4
	2001	300 189	48.7	663 555	49.3	143 909	51.3
	2002	284 312	48.7	666 238	49.2	152 182	52.1
	2003	270 004	48.5	669 578	49.1	158 089	53.1
	2004	254 906	48.5	673 712	49.3	164 667	54.1

Education at the primary, secondary and tertiary levels — Number of students enrolled and percentage female (*continued*)
Enseignement primaire, secondaire et supérieur — Nombre d'étudiants inscrits et étudiantes féminines en pourcentage (*suite*)

Country or area Pays ou zone	Year[t] Année[t]	Primary education Enseignement primaire		Secondary education Enseignement secondaire		Tertiary education Enseignement supérieur	
		Total	% F	Total	% F	Total	% F
Slovenia	1999	91 536	48.5	220 033	49.5	79 126	56.0
Slovénie	2000	86 850	49.2	218 251	49.6	83 816	56.1
	2001	86 388	48.5	224 747	49.3	91 494	56.1
	2002	86 021	48.5	220 804	48.9	99 214	57.5
	2003	87 085	48.5	217 587	48.6	101 458	56.2
	2004	93 371	48.6	187 817	48.8	104 396	56.9
Solomon Islands	1999	58 016	46.3	16 576	41.1	...	...
Iles Salomon	2000	57 364	46.1	13 527	42.1	...	...
	2001	64 986[1]	46.5[1]	16 480	43.0	...	...
	2002	66 480	46.5	21 700	42.9	...	...
	2003[1]	68 146	46.5	21 885	42.8	...	...
	2004	87 770	47.2	...	...	...	...
South Africa	1999	7 935 221	49.1	4 239 197	52.9	632 911	53.9
Afrique du Sud	2000	7 444 802	48.6	4 141 946	52.4	644 763	55.3
	2001	7 413 415	48.9	4 250 400	52.2	658 588	53.5
	2002	7 465 728	48.9	4 353 817	51.7	675 160	53.7
	2003	7 470 476	48.8	4 446 841	51.5	717 793	53.8
Spain	1999	2 579 908	48.3	3 299 469	50.3	1 786 778	53.0
Espagne	2000	2 539 995	48.4	3 245 950	50.2	1 828 987	52.9
	2001	2 505 203	48.4	3 183 282	50.0	1 833 527	52.5
	2002	2 490 744	48.3	3 106 777	50.2	1 832 760	53.1
	2003	2 488 319	48.3	3 052 662	50.0	1 840 607	53.1
	2004	2 497 513	48.4	3 048 188	50.2	1 839 903	53.8
Sri Lanka [1]	2002	1 764 300	48.9	2 344 960	50.7	...	...
Sri Lanka [1]	2003	1 702 035	49.1	2 320 093	50.6	...	...
	2004	1 612 318	...	2 332 326	49.4	...	...
Sudan	1999	2 512 824[1]	45.2[1]	964 518[1]	...	200 538	47.2
Soudan	2000	2 566 503	45.1	979 514	...	204 114[1]	47.2[1]
	2001	2 799 783	45.0	1 113 062	46.3[1]	...	...
	2002	2 889 062	45.1	1 141 199	...	...	...
	2003	3 028 127	45.5	1 291 023	44.7	...	...
	2004	3 208 186	45.5	1 292 619	47.3	...	...
Suriname	2001	64 852	48.9	41 874	53.1	...	...
Suriname	2002	64 023	48.7	42 253	57.2	5 186	62.0
	2003[1]	64 659	48.7	41 000	56.3	...	...
Swaziland	1999	213 041	48.7	61 551	50.1	4 880	47.9
Swaziland	2000	213 986	48.4	60 253	50.2	4 738	48.5
	2001	212 063	48.6	61 277	50.8	4 761[1]	...
	2002	209 037	48.1	62 676	50.4	5 193	54.6
	2003	208 444	48.5	62 401	50.2	5 369[1]	54.4[1]
	2004	...	...	...	...	6 594	52.4
Sweden	1999	763 028	49.4	963 918	54.8	335 124	57.6
Suède	2000	775 706	49.3	933 669	54.6	346 878	58.2
	2001	786 027	49.3	928 424	54.4	358 020	59.1
	2002	785 774	49.4	934 608	53.5	382 851	59.5
	2003	774 888	49.4	917 978	52.9	414 657	59.6
	2004	690 758	48.6	711 798	49.5	429 623	59.6
Switzerland	1999	529 610	48.6	544 433	46.8	156 390	41.7
Suisse	2000	538 372	48.6	549 369	47.0	156 879	42.6
	2001	537 744	48.6	553 618	47.2	163 373	42.7
	2002	536 423	48.6	550 317	47.2	170 085	43.3
	2003	535 577	48.6	555 505	47.3	185 965	44.2
	2004	532 092	48.5	563 701	47.2	195 947	44.9

Country or area Pays ou zone	Year [t] Année [t]	Primary education Enseignement primaire		Secondary education Enseignement secondaire		Tertiary education Enseignement supérieur	
		Total	% F	Total	% F	Total	% F
Syrian Arab Republic Rép. arabe syrienne	1999	2 738 083	46.8	1 029 769	46.8	...	...
	2000	2 774 922	47.0	1 069 040	46.9	...	...
	2001	2 835 023	47.2	1 124 752	46.4	...	...
	2002	2 904 569	47.2	1 182 424	46.6	...	...
	2003	2 149 474	47.5	2 119 717	47.1	...	...
	2004	2 192 764	47.6	2 249 116	47.2	...	...
Tajikistan Tadjikistan	1999	690 306	47.9	768 903	45.6	76 293	25.4
	2000	691 891	47.4	795 380	45.6	79 978	25.2
	2001	680 100	47.4	847 445	44.8	78 540	23.9
	2002	684 542	48.1	899 236	44.5	85 171	24.5
	2003	694 930	48.0	948 341	44.8	97 466	25.0
	2004	690 270	48.0	973 673	45.1	108 456	24.8
Thailand Thaïlande	1999	6 120 400	48.3	...	...	1 814 096	53.4
	2000	6 100 647	48.3	...	...	1 900 272	54.1
	2001	6 179 325	48.4	5 577 364	48.3	2 095 694	52.6
	2002	6 228 097	48.5	...	...	2 155 334	52.1
	2003 [1]	6 167 262	48.4	5 365 554	49.3	2 205 581	52.9
	2004	6 112 687	48.4	5 009 844	49.6	2 251 453	53.7
TFYR of Macedonia L'ex-R.y. Macédoine	1999	129 633	48.1	218 666	48.0	35 141	55.1
	2000	126 606	48.4	221 961	47.8	36 922	55.0
	2001	123 661	48.5	222 081	47.9	40 246	55.8
	2002	121 109	48.8	218 834	48.0	44 710	55.2
	2003	116 635	48.4	218 649	48.1	45 624	56.2
	2004	113 362	48.4	215 760	48.0	46 637	57.0
Timor-Leste Timor-Leste	2001	188 900	...	40 350 [1]	...	...	...
	2002	183 626	...	46 680	...	6 349 [2]	52.9 [2]
	2003	183 800	...	...	...	...	...
Togo Togo	1999	953 886	43.1	231 948	28.6	15 028	17.4
	2000	914 919	43.8	260 877 [1]	30.5 [1]	15 171	16.9
	2001	945 103	44.3	...	...	18 455 [1]	16.9 [1]
	2002	977 534	44.9	...	...	...	...
	2003	975 063	45.2	353 781 [1]	32.3 [1]	...	...
	2004	984 846	45.6	375 385	33.2	...	...
Tokelau Tokélaou	2000	247	48.2	180	49.4	...	...
	2001	266	46.2	202	55.9	...	...
	2002	266	45.9	202	55.9	...	...
	2003	227	50.2	191	47.6	...	...
Tonga Tonga	1999	16 783	46.4	14 710	50.0	364	54.9
	2000	16 697	46.6	14 524	49.4	526	60.5 [1]
	2001	17 033	47.2	14 127	49.2	453	60.5 [1]
	2002	17 105	47.1	14 567	49.8	600	60.5 [1]
	2003	17 891	46.9	15 743	...	668	60.5
	2004	17 113	46.9	14 032	49.2 [1]	657 [1]	59.8 [1]
Trinidad and Tobago Trinité-et-Tobago	1999	172 204	49.1	117 011	51.6	7 572	57.4
	2000	168 532	49.1	113 142 [1]	51.7 [1]	7 737	59.3
	2001	155 360	48.8	114 567 [1]	51.3 [1]	8 614	60.0
	2002	141 427 [2]	49.1 [2]	108 778 [1]	51.8 [1]	9 867	58.9
	2003	141 036	48.6	107 880 [1]	51.4 [1]	12 316	61.1
	2004	137 313 [2]	48.5 [2]	105 381 [2]	51.1 [2]	16 751	55.4
Tunisia Tunisie	1999	1 442 904	47.4	1 058 877	49.3	157 479 [1]	48.3 [1]
	2000	1 413 795	47.4	1 104 095 [1]	50.3 [1]	180 044	...
	2001	1 373 904	47.6	1 143 082	50.2	207 388	48.1 [1]
	2002	1 325 707	47.6	1 169 368	49.9	226 102	53.9
	2003	1 277 124	47.7	1 148 523	50.8	263 414	54.9
	2004	1 228 347	47.7	1 210 012	...	291 842	56.5

Country or area Pays ou zone	Year[t] Année[t]	Primary education Enseignement primaire		Secondary education Enseignement secondaire		Tertiary education Enseignement supérieur	
		Total	% F	Total	% F	Total	% F
Turkey Turquie	1999	...	...	...	...	1 464 740	39.6
	2000[1]	7 850 103	46.7			1 588 367	39.6
	2001	8 014 733[1]	47.0[1]	5 271 056[1]	42.0[1]	1 607 388	40.8
	2002	8 210 961[1]	47.2[1]	5 500 246[1]	42.5[1]	1 677 936	41.4
	2003	7 904 361[1]	47.5[1]	5 742 070[1]	42.0[1]	1 918 483	42.3
	2004	7 872 546	47.6	5 330 923	42.0	1 972 662	41.4
Turks and Caicos Islands Iles Turques et Caïques	1999	1 822	48.6	1 114	51.1	27	100.0
	2000	2 018	47.7	1 218	55.3	15[1]	100.0[1]
	2001	2 176	49.2	1 339[1]	52.7[1]	12	75.0
	2002	2 137	48.9	1 411[1]	49.8[1]	...	...
	2003	1 810	48.8	1 395[1]	49.2[1]	9	77.8[1]
	2004	2 117	50.9	1 516	48.9	6	100.0
Tuvalu Tuvalu	1999	1 360	47.6	...	...	...	...
	2000	1 517	48.1	...	...	...	...
	2001	1 427	50.2	912	46.2	...	...
	2002	1 283	51.1	...	...	...	...
	2003	1 344	50.5	...	...	...	...
	2004	1 404	49.9	...	...	...	...
Uganda Ouganda	1999	6 288 239	47.5	318 136[1]	39.7[1]	40 591	34.5[1]
	2000	6 559 013	48.2	546 977	43.4	55 767	33.8
	2001	6 900 916	48.9	570 520[1]	43.3[1]	62 586	34.5
	2002	7 354 153	49.4	687 613[1]	44.5[1]	71 544[1]	34.5[1]
	2003	7 633 314	49.3	716 736[1]	44.6[1]	74 090[1]	34.5[1]
	2004	7 377 292	49.4	732 792	44.4	88 360	38.4
Ukraine Ukraine	1999	2 200 098	48.6	5 214 106	49.8[2]	1 736 999	52.7
	2000	2 078 699	48.6	5 204 485	49.1	1 811 538	52.6
	2001	2 065 348	48.7	5 123 602	48.6[2]	1 950 755	53.1
	2002	2 047 085	48.7	4 982 947	48.9	2 134 676	53.4[2]
	2003	1 960 512	48.7	4 824 077	48.7	2 296 221	53.8[2]
	2004	1 850 734	48.6	4 445 974	48.5[2]	2 465 074	53.9[2]
United Arab Emirates Emirats arabes unis	1999	270 486	48.0	201 522	50.1	40 373[1]	67.2[1]
	2000	273 144	47.9	210 002	50.0	43 459[1]	68.5[1]
	2001	280 248	48.0	220 134	49.6	58 656[1]	66.6[1]
	2002	285 744	48.1	226 407	49.9	63 419[1]	66.4[1]
	2003	248 370	48.3	273 491	49.4	68 182[1]	66.3[1]
	2004	254 602	48.3	279 496	49.1	...	...
United Kingdom Royaume-Uni	1999	4 661 234	48.8	8 053 288	52.0	2 080 960	53.2
	2000	4 631 623	48.8	8 258 347	52.4	2 024 138	53.9
	2001	4 596 110	48.8	8 333 889	52.6	2 067 349	54.5
	2002	4 536 143	48.8	9 577 287	54.2	2 240 680	55.2
	2003	4 488 162	48.8	9 219 054	54.3	2 287 833	55.9
	2004	4 685 733	48.8	5 699 526	49.4	2 247 441	57.0
United Rep. of Tanzania Rép.-Unie de Tanzanie	1999	4 189 816	49.9	271 146[1]	44.8[1]	18 867	21.0
	2000	4 382 410	49.5	...	...	...	...
	2001	4 881 588	49.3	...	...	21 960	13.3
	2002	5 981 338	49.0	...	...	26 505[1]	23.5[1]
	2003	6 562 772	48.7	...	...	31 049	30.7
	2004	7 083 063	48.8	...	...	42 948	29.2
United States Etats-Unis	1999	24 937 931	49.5	22 444 832	...	13 769 362	55.7[1]
	2000	24 973 176	48.4	22 593 562	49.0	13 202 880	55.8
	2001	25 297 600	48.7	23 087 042	49.0	13 595 580	55.9
	2002	24 855 480	49.0	23 196 310	48.5	15 927 987	56.3
	2003	24 848 518	48.9	23 854 458	48.7	16 611 711	56.6
	2004	24 559 494	48.1	24 217 394	49.1	16 900 471	57.1
Uruguay Uruguay	1999	366 461	48.6	283 838	53.0	91 275[1]	63.0[1]
	2000	360 834	48.5	303 883	52.2	97 641[1]	64.0[1]
	2001	359 557	48.4	315 968	52.2	96 857[1]	63.7[1]
	2002	364 858	48.4	332 175	52.0	98 520[1]	65.3[1]
	2003	365 423	48.4	343 617	52.5	101 298[1]	66.3[1]

Education at the primary, secondary and tertiary levels — Number of students enrolled and percentage female (*continued*)
Enseignement primaire, secondaire et supérieur — Nombre d'étudiants inscrits et étudiantes féminines en pourcentage (*suite*)

Country or area Pays ou zone	Year [t] Année [t]	Primary education Enseignement primaire		Secondary education Enseignement secondaire		Tertiary education Enseignement supérieur	
		Total	% F	Total	% F	Total	% F
Uzbekistan	2002[1]	2 562 594	49.0	4 100 961	48.6	380 623	43.9
Ouzbékistan	2003	2 513 342	49.0	4 160 903	48.6	393 910	43.9
	2004[1]	2 440 603	49.0	4 234 948	48.5	407 582	43.9
Vanuatu	1999	34 333	47.6	8 989	45.2	643[1]	...
Vanuatu	2000	35 674	47.6	10 446	51.8	656	...
	2001	36 482	47.9	10 934	46.2	675	...
	2002	37 470	48.0	12 313	47.0	895	35.4[1]
	2003	39 388	48.1	12 800	44.0	914	36.2
	2004	38 960	47.8	13 837	44.7	955[1]	36.1[1]
Venezuela (Bolivarian Republic of)	1999	3 261 343	48.5	1 439 122	54.1	...	...
Venezuela (République bolivarienne du)	2000	3 327 797	48.5	1 543 425	53.6	668 109	58.6
	2001	3 423 480	48.5	1 677 807	53.0	...	...
	2002	3 506 780	48.5	1 811 127	52.8	927 835	51.4[1]
	2003	3 449 984	48.4	1 866 114	52.5	983 217[1]	51.0[1]
	2004	3 453 379	48.4	1 953 506	52.3		
Viet Nam	1999	10 250 214	47.2	7 400 889	46.8	810 072	42.9
Viet Nam	2000	10 063 025	47.7	7 926 126	47.0	732 187	41.6
	2001	9 751 434	47.7	8 318 192	47.1	749 253	42.1
	2002	9 336 913	47.5	8 783 340	47.4	784 675	42.8
	2003	8 841 004	47.5	9 265 801	47.4	829 459	43.0
	2004	8 350 191	47.3	9 588 698	48.0	845 313[1]	43.0[1]
Yemen	1999	2 302 787	34.9	1 041 816	26.0	164 166	20.8
Yémen	2000[1]	2 463 540	37.6	1 150 869	28.3	173 130	20.8
	2001	2 643 579	37.6	1 249 016[1]	28.3[1]	...	...
	2002	2 783 371	38.8	...	...	...	...
	2003	2 950 403	39.8	1 373 362	30.1	...	...
	2004	3 107 801	40.5	1 446 369	31.2	192 071	26.2
Zambia	1999	1 555 707	47.8	237 307	43.4[1]	23 155[1]	31.6[1]
Zambie	2000	1 589 544	48.1	276 301	44.5	24 553[1]	31.6[1]
	2001	1 625 647	48.2	304 132	43.4	...	...
	2002	1 731 579	48.1	351 442	45.2	...	...
	2004	2 251 357	48.7	363 613	44.1	...	...
Zimbabwe	1999	2 460 323	49.1	834 880	46.9	42 775[1]	...
Zimbabwe	2000	2 460 669	49.1	844 183	46.8	48 894[1]	37.4[1]
	2001	2 534 796	49.2	866 171	47.0	59 582[1]	36.7[1]
	2002	2 399 250	49.4	828 456	46.9	60 221[1]	40.8[1]
	2003	2 361 588	49.5	758 229	47.5	55 689[1]	38.8[1]

Source

United Nations Educational, Scientific and Cultural Organization, (UNESCO), Institute for Statistics, Montreal, the UNESCO Institute for Statistics database, May 2006.

Notes

t   Data relate to the calendar year in which the academic year ends.

[1] UNESCO Institute of Statistics (UIS) estimate.

[2] National estimate.

[3] For statistical purposes, the data for China do not include those for the Hong Kong Special Administrative Region (Hong Kong SAR), Macao Special Administrative Region (Macao SAR) and Taiwan Province of China.

Source

L'Institut de statistique de l'Organisation des Nations Unies pour l'éducation, la science et la culture (UNESCO), Montréal, la base de données de l'Institut de Statistiques de l'UNESCO, mai 2006.

Notes

t   Les données se réfèrent à l'année civile durant laquelle l'année scolaire se termine.

[1] Estimation de l'Institut de statistique de l'UNESCO.

[2] Estimation nationale.

[3] Pour la présentation des statistiques, les données pour Chine ne comprennent pas la Région Administrative Spéciale de Hong Kong (Hong Kong RAS), la Région Administrative Spéciale de Macao (Macao RAS) et la province de Taiwan.

10

Public expenditure on education: percentage of GNI and government expenditure

Dépenses publiques afférentes à l'éducation : pourcentage par rapport au RNB et aux dépenses du gouvernement

Country or area Pays ou zone	As % of Gross National Income (GNI) En % du Revenu National Brut (RNB)				As % of total government expenditure En % des dépenses totales du gouvernement			
	2001	2002	2003	2004	2001	2002	2003	2004
Albania [1] Albanie [1]	...	2.8	...	...	...	...	...	...
Angola [1] Angola [1]	3.2	...	...	...	...	...	...	...
Antigua and Barbuda Antigua–et–Barbuda	...	4.0	...	...	...	...	...	...
Argentina Argentine	5.0	4.1	3.6	...	13.5	13.8	14.6	...
Armenia Arménie	3.1	3.1[1]	...	...	...	...	...	...
Aruba Aruba	...	...	...	...	17.2	15.6	...	13.8
Australia Australie	5.0	5.0	4.9	...	...	...	...	...
Austria Autriche	5.9	5.8	5.6	...	11.1	...	...	...
Azerbaijan Azerbaïdjan	3.7	3.4	3.6	3.7[1]	23.1	20.7	19.2	...
Bangladesh Bangladesh	2.4	2.2	2.3	2.1	15.7	15.8	15.5	...
Barbados Barbade	7.4	7.3	7.9	7.6	18.5	16.7	17.3	...
Belarus Bélarus	...	...	5.8[1]	5.8	...	...	...	13.0
Belgium Belgique	...	6.2	6.1	...	...	...	...	...
Belize Belize	6.2	6.1[1]	5.7	5.3	20.9	20.0[1]	18.1	...
Benin [1] Bénin [1]	3.3	3.3	...	...	...	...	...	...
Bhutan Bhoutan	5.9	...	...	...	12.9	...	...	...
Bolivia Bolivie	6.1	6.4	6.6	6.7[1]	18.4	19.7	18.1	...
Botswana Botswana	2.3	...	...	...	25.6	...	...	...
Brazil Brésil	4.4	4.3	...	...	12.0	10.9	...	...
British Virgin Islands Iles Vierges britanniques	...	...	...	...	9.0	...	...	17.8
Bulgaria Bulgarie	3.6	3.6	4.4	...	...	...	...	...
Burundi Burundi	3.8	4.0	4.9[1]	5.3	21.2	13.0	...	...
Cambodia Cambodge	1.9	1.9	2.1[1]	2.2	...	...	...	...
Cameroon Cameroun	3.4	3.9[1]	4.1	4.0	12.5	14.5[1]	17.3	17.2
Canada Canada	5.3	5.4	...	...	12.5	...	...	...

Country or area Pays ou zone	As % of Gross National Income (GNI) En % du Revenu National Brut (RNB)				As % of total government expenditure En % des dépenses totales du gouvernement			
	2001	2002	2003	2004	2001	2002	2003	2004
Cape Verde Cap–Vert	...	8.1	7.7[1]	7.4	...	17.0	...	20.7
Chile Chili	...	4.4	4.3	4.1	...	18.7	19.1	18.5
China, Hong Kong SAR Chine, Hong Kong RAS	3.9	4.0	4.4	4.6	22.9	21.9	23.3	23.3
China, Macao SAR Chine, Macao RAS	3.0	...	...	...	16.0	16.1	...	...
Colombia Colombie	4.6	5.3	5.4[1]	5.1	18.0[2]	15.6	...	11.7
Comoros Comores	3.7[1]	3.9	...	...	...	24.1	...	...
Congo Congo	4.6	4.4[1]	...	...	12.6	...	...	...
Cook Islands [1] Iles Cook [1]	0.4	...	...	...	...	...	...	...
Costa Rica Costa Rica	4.9	5.2	5.3[1]	5.1	21.1	22.4	...	18.5
Côte d'Ivoire [1] Côte d'Ivoire [1]	4.8	...	...	...	...	...	...	...
Croatia Croatie	4.6[1]	4.6	...	...	...	10.0	...	...
Cuba Cuba	...	...	...	...	16.8	18.7	...	19.4
Cyprus Chypre	5.9	6.4	7.6	...	...	...	...	...
Czech Republic République tchèque	4.3	4.6	4.8	...	9.6	...	...	...
Denmark Danemark	8.6	8.6	8.5	...	15.4	...	...	...
Djibouti Djibouti	...	...	...	5.6	...	...	...	20.5
Dominican Republic Rép. dominicaine	2.4	2.4	2.5[1]	1.2	13.1	12.4	...	6.3
Ecuador [1] Equateur [1]	1.1	...	...	...	...	...	...	...
El Salvador El Salvador	2.6[1]	2.9	2.9	2.9[1]	19.9[1]	20.0	...	...
Equatorial Guinea Guinée équatoriale	2.2	...	...	...	1.6	...	...	...
Eritrea Erythrée	4.6[1]	4.1	4.1[1]	3.8	...	...	...	...
Estonia Estonie	5.8	6.0	...	...	...	...	...	...
Ethiopia Ethiopie	4.7	4.6[1]	...	...	13.8	...	...	...
Fiji Fidji	5.9	6.6	6.6[1]	6.8	19.4	20.0	...	...
Finland Finlande	6.3	6.4	6.6	...	12.7	...	...	...
France France	5.6	5.6	6.0	...	...	...	...	...
Gambia Gambie	...	3.0	2.4[1]	2.1[1]	...	8.9	...	...

Country or area	As % of Gross National Income (GNI) En % du Revenu National Brut (RNB)				As % of total government expenditure En % des dépenses totales du gouvernement			
Pays ou zone	2001	2002	2003	2004	2001	2002	2003	2004
Georgia Géorgie	2.2	2.3	2.3[1]	3.0	11.5	11.8	...	13.1
Germany Allemagne	4.6	4.8	...	...	9.7	...	...	...
Greece Grèce	3.9	4.0	4.3	...	...	...	...	...
Grenada Grenade	...	...	6.0	...	...	...	12.9	...
Guyana Guyana	9.4	9.1	7.5[1]	5.8	18.4[1]	18.4	...	...
Hungary Hongrie	5.4	5.8	6.3	...	...	...	...	...
Iceland Islande	6.7[1]	7.8[1]	8.2	...	...	...	...	...
India Inde	...	...	3.3	...	...	...	10.7	...
Indonesia Indonésie	1.1	1.0	...	...	9.6	9.0[1]	...	...
Iran (Islamic Rep. of) Iran (Rép. islamique d')	4.4	4.7	4.9	4.8	20.4	21.7	17.7	17.9
Ireland Irlande	5.1[1]	5.3	...	...	...	...	...	...
Israel Israël	7.6	7.8	7.5	...	13.8	13.7	...	...
Italy Italie	5.0	4.8	4.9	...	10.3	...	...	...
Jamaica Jamaïque	6.9	6.9	5.7	5.3	11.1	12.3	9.5	...
Japan Japon	3.5	3.5	3.6	...	10.5	...	...	...
Kazakhstan Kazakhstan	3.2[1]	3.2	3.2[1]	2.6	...	...	...	...
Kenya Kenya	6.4	7.3[1]	7.1	7.1	22.6	...	22.1	29.2
Kiribati Kiribati	8.7	9.3[1]	...	...	...	...	...	...
Korea, Republic of Corée, République de	4.3	4.2	4.6	...	14.7	15.5	16.1	...
Kuwait Koweït	...	...	...	7.6	...	...	...	17.4
Kyrgyzstan Kirghizistan	3.2	4.6	4.6[1]	...	18.6	...	...	...
Lao People's Dem. Rep. Rép. dém. pop. lao	2.1	2.8	2.4[1]	2.5	8.8	10.6	11.0[1]	...
Latvia Lettonie	5.5	5.8	5.4	...	...	...	...	...
Lebanon Liban	2.8	2.6	2.6[1]	2.5	11.1	12.3	...	12.7
Lesotho Lesotho	7.7	7.3[1]	...	...	...	...	...	...
Lithuania Lituanie	6.0	6.0	5.4	...	...	...	...	...
Madagascar Madagascar	2.9[1]	...	...	3.4	...	...	...	18.2

Country or area / Pays ou zone	As % of Gross National Income (GNI) / En % du Revenu National Brut (RNB)				As % of total government expenditure / En % des dépenses totales du gouvernement			
	2001	2002	2003	2004	2001	2002	2003	2004
Malawi / Malawi	...	...	6.2	...	...	...	...	...
Malaysia / Malaisie	8.5	8.7	8.5	...	20.0	20.3	28.0	...
Maldives / Maldives	...	8.6[1]	8.6	8.6[1]	...	...	...	...
Malta / Malte	4.7	4.6	...	...	...	...	...	...
Marshall Islands / Iles Marshall	8.6[1]	8.3	11.2	11.9[1]	...	...	15.8	...
Mauritania / Mauritanie	3.8	3.6	4.2	3.7[1]	...	...	...	...
Mauritius / Maurice	3.4	3.3	4.7	4.7	12.1	...	...	15.7
Mexico / Mexique	5.3	5.4	5.9	...	24.3	...	...	...
Mongolia / Mongolie	8.0[1]	9.0	7.4[1]	5.7	...	...	...	...
Montserrat / Montserrat	...	...	...	...	3.2	...	...	...
Morocco / Maroc	6.4	6.6	6.6[1]	6.4	25.0	26.4	...	27.8
Myanmar / Myanmar	1.3	...	...	...	18.1[2]	...	...	...
Namibia / Namibie	7.8[1]	7.5[1]	7.1	...	...	...	...	...
Nepal / Népal	3.7[1]	3.4	3.4	...	13.0[1]	13.9	14.9	...
Netherlands / Pays–Bas	5.0	5.2	5.5	...	10.7	...	...	...
Netherlands Antilles / Antilles néerlandaises	...	...	...	...	12.8	...	...	...
New Zealand / Nouvelle–Zélande	7.3	7.0	7.1	7.3	16.1	16.2	15.1	...
Nicaragua / Nicaragua	4.1[1]	3.2	3.2[1]	...	13.6[1]	15.0	...	...
Niger / Niger	2.4	2.4[1]	...	2.3	...	...	...	...
Niue / Nioué	...	...	...	...	...	10.1	...	...
Norway / Norvège	7.1	7.6	7.6	...	...	...	...	...
Oman [1] / Oman [1]	4.4	4.8	...	...	...	...	...	26.1
Pakistan / Pakistan	...	...	2.0[1]	2.0	...	...	...	...
Palau / Palaos	9.7	9.7[1]	...	...	...	...	...	...
Panama / Panama	4.6	4.5	4.7[1]	4.2[1]	7.3	7.7	...	8.9[1]
Paraguay / Paraguay	4.7	4.4	4.3	...	9.7	11.4	10.8	...
Peru / Pérou	3.0	3.1	...	...	23.5	17.1	...	...

Country or area Pays ou zone	As % of Gross National Income (GNI) En % du Revenu National Brut (RNB)				As % of total government expenditure En % des dépenses totales du gouvernement			
	2001	2002	2003	2004	2001	2002	2003	2004
Philippines Philippines	3.1	3.0	3.0	...	14.0	17.8	17.2	...
Poland Pologne	5.6	5.7	5.9	...	...	12.8	...	...
Portugal Portugal	6.1	5.9	6.0	...	12.7	...	...	...
Republic of Moldova République de Moldova	4.0	4.5	4.2[1]	...	17.0	21.4	...	...
Romania Roumanie	3.3	3.6	3.7	...	...	...	...	...
Russian Federation Fédération de Russie	3.1	3.9[1]	3.8	...	11.5	10.7[1]	12.3	...
Saint Kitts and Nevis Saint–Kitts–et–Nevis	9.1	3.7	5.0	5.0[1]	20.1	7.9[1]	12.7	...
Saint Lucia Sainte–Lucie	8.3[1]	8.4[1]	5.4[1]	5.4	...	...	...	...
St. Vincent–Grenadines St. Vincent–Grenadines	10.0[1]	10.5	11.8[1]	11.7	17.7[1]	20.3	...	...
Samoa Samoa	4.3	4.3[1]	...	...	14.6	13.7[1]	...	...
Senegal Sénégal	3.6	3.7	...	4.1	...	...	...	...
Seychelles Seychelles	...	5.7	5.7	5.7[1]	...	...	...	...
Singapore Singapour	3.7	...	...	...	...	...	...	...
Slovakia Slovaquie	4.1	4.4	4.4	...	...	...	...	...
Slovenia Slovénie	6.1	6.1	...	...	...	...	...	...
South Africa Afrique du Sud	5.4	5.4	5.2	5.5	23.4	18.5	18.5	18.1
Spain Espagne	4.5	4.5	4.6	...	11.3	...	...	...
Swaziland Swaziland	8.5	5.0	7.0	6.3	...	...	...	...
Sweden Suède	7.4	7.7	7.1	...	12.8	...	...	...
Switzerland Suisse	5.2	5.5	5.1	...	...	...	...	...
Tajikistan Tadjikistan	2.6	2.9	2.6	2.9	...	17.8	16.3	16.9
Thailand Thaïlande	5.1	...	...	4.3	28.3	...	...	27.5
TFYR of Macedonia L'ex–R.y. Macédoine	...	3.5	3.4	...	...	...	...	...
Togo Togo	...	2.7	...	...	...	13.6	...	...
Tokelau Tokélaou	...	...	...	...	...	10.7	14.5	...
Tonga Tonga	5.6[1]	4.7	5.2	4.9	13.9[1]	13.1	13.5	...
Trinidad and Tobago Trinité–et–Tobago	4.4	4.6[1]	...	...	13.4	...	...	...

Country or area Pays ou zone	As % of Gross National Income (GNI) En % du Revenu National Brut (RNB)				As % of total government expenditure En % des dépenses totales du gouvernement			
	2001	2002	2003	2004	2001	2002	2003	2004
Tunisia Tunisie	7.2	6.7	8.5	...	18.2	...	...	...
Turkey Turquie	3.7	3.6	3.8	...	...	...	...	...
Turks and Caicos Islands Iles Turques et Caïques	...	...	...	...	16.0	16.5	...	...
Tuvalu Tuvalu	...	...	...	...	...	44.0	...	...
Uganda [1] Ouganda [1]	...	...	...	5.3	...	...	...	18.3
Ukraine Ukraine	4.8	5.5	5.7	4.6	17.2	20.3	19.8	18.3
United Arab Emirates [1] Emirats arabes unis [1]	...	...	...	...	...	22.5	...	...
United Kingdom Royaume–Uni	4.7	5.2	5.4	...	11.4	11.5[1]	...	...
United States Etats–Unis	5.7	5.6	5.8	...	17.1	...	...	...
Uruguay Uruguay	3.2	2.6	2.3	...	12.8	9.6	7.9	...
Vanuatu Vanuatu	10.0	9.3	10.0	...	26.7	...	...	...
Yemen [1] Yémen [1]	10.3	...	...	...	...	...	...	...
Zambia Zambie	2.1[1]	...	...	2.9	...	...	...	14.8

Source

United Nations Educational, Scientific and Cultural Organization (UNESCO) Institute for Statistics, Montreal, the UNESCO Institute for Statistics database.

Notes

[1] UNESCO Institute of Statistics (UIS) estimate.

[2] National estimate.

Source

L'Institut de statistique de l'Organisation des Nations Unies pour l'éducation, la science et la culture (UNESCO), Montréal, la base de données de l'UNESCO.

Notes

[1] Estimation de l'Institut de statistique de l'UNESCO.

[2] Estimation nationale.

Detailed data and explanatory notes on education can be found on the UNESCO Institute for Statistics web site www.uis.unesco.org. Brief notes which pertain to the statistical information shown in tables 9 and 10 are given below.

Table 9: The definitions and classifications applied by UNESCO are those set out in the *Revised Recommendation concerning the International Standardization of Education Statistics* (1978) and the 1976 and 1997 versions of the *International Standard Classification of Education* (ISCED). Data are presented in Table 9 according to the terminology of the ISCED-97.

According to the ISCED, these educational levels are defined as follows:

- Primary education (ISCED level 1): Programmes normally designed on a unit or project basis to give pupils a sound basic education in reading, writing and mathematics along with an elementary understanding of other subjects such as history, geography, natural science, social science, art and music. Religious instruction may also be featured. It is sometimes called elementary education.
- Secondary education (ISCED levels 2 and 3): Lower secondary education (ISCED 2) is generally designed to continue the basic programmes of the primary level but the teaching is typically more subject-focused, requiring more specialized teachers for each subject area. The end of this level often coincides with the end of compulsory education. In upper secondary education (ISCED 3), the final stage of secondary education in most countries, instruction is often organized even more along subject lines and teachers typically need a higher or more subject-specific qualification than at ISCED level 2.
- Tertiary education (ISCED levels 5 and 6): Programmes with an educational content more advanced than what is offered at ISCED levels 3 and 4. The first stage of tertiary education, ISCED level 5, covers level 5A, composed of largely theoretically based programmes intended to provide sufficient qualifications for gaining entry to advanced research programmes and professions with high skill requirements; and level 5B, where programmes are generally more practical, technical and/or occupationally specific. The second stage of tertiary education, ISCED level 6, comprises programmes devoted to advanced study and original research, and leading to the award of an advanced research qualification.

The ISCED-97 also introduced a new category or level between upper secondary and tertiary education called post-secondary non-tertiary education (ISCED level 4). This level includes programmes that lie between the upper-secondary

On trouvera des données détaillées et des notes explicatives sur l'instruction sur le site Web de l'Institut de statistique de l'UNESCO www.uis.unesco.org. Ci-après figurent des notes sommaires, relatives aux principaux éléments d'information statistique figurant dans les tableaux 9 et 10.

Tableau 9 : Les définitions et classifications appliquées par l'UNESCO sont tirées de la *Recommandation révisée concernant la normalisation internationale des statistiques de l'éducation* (1978) et des versions de 1976 et de 1997 de la *Classification internationale type de l'éducation* (CITE). La terminologie utilisée dans le Tableau 9 est celle de la CITE-1997.

Dans la CITE, les niveaux d'enseignement sont définis comme suit :

- Enseignement primaire (niveau 1 de la CITE) : Programmes s'articulant normalement autour d'une unité ou d'un projet visant à donner aux élèves un solide enseignement de base en lecture, en écriture et en mathématiques et des connaissances élémentaires dans d'autres matières telles que l'histoire, la géographie, les sciences naturelles, les sciences sociales, le dessin et la musique. Dans certains cas, une instruction religieuse est aussi considérée. Appelé parfois enseignement élémentaire.
- Enseignement secondaire (niveaux 2 et 3 de la CITE) : Le premier cycle de l'enseignement secondaire (CITE 2) est généralement destiné à compléter les programmes de base de l'enseignement primaire mais dont l'enseignement est généralement plus orienté vers les matières enseignées faisant appel à des enseignants plus spécialisés. La fin de ce niveau coïncide souvent avec celle de la scolarité obligatoire. Dans le sixième cycle de l'enseignement secondaire, étape finale de l'enseignement secondaire dans plusieurs pays, l'enseignement est souvent organisé en une plus grande spécialisation et les enseignants doivent souvent être plus qualifiés ou spécialisés qu'au niveau 2 de la CITE.
- Enseignement supérieur (niveaux 5 et 6 de la CITE) : Programmes dont le contenu est plus avancé que celui offert aux niveaux 3 et 4 de la CITE. Le premier cycle de l'enseignement supérieur, niveau 5 de la CITE, couvre le niveau 5A, composé de programmes fondés dans une large mesure sur la théorie et destinés à offrir des qualifications suffisantes pour être admis à suivre des programmes de recherche de pointe ou à exercer une profession exigeant de hautes compétences; et le niveau 5B, dont les programmes sont dans une large mesure d'ordre pratique, technique et/ou spécifiquement professionnel. Le deuxième cycle de l'enseignement supérieur, niveau 6 de la CITE, comprend des programmes consacrés à des

and tertiary levels of education from an international point of view, even though they might clearly be considered as upper-secondary or tertiary programmes in a national context. They are often not significantly more advanced than programmes at ISCED 3 (upper secondary) but they serve to broaden the knowledge of participants who have already completed a programme at level 3. The students are usually older than those at level 3. ISCED 4 programmes typically last between six months and two years.

Table 10: Public expenditure on education consists of current and capital expenditures on education by local, regional and national governments, including municipalities. Household contributions are excluded. Current expenditure on education includes expenditure for goods and services consumed within the current year and which would need to be renewed if needed the following year. It includes expenditure on: staff salaries and benefits; contracted or purchased services; other resources including books and teaching materials; welfare services; and other current expenditure such as subsidies to students and households, furniture and equipment, minor repairs, fuel, telecommunications, travel, insurance and rents. Capital expenditure on education includes expenditure for assets that last longer than one year. It includes expenditure for construction, renovation and major repairs of buildings and the purchase of heavy equipment or vehicles.

études approfondies et à des travaux de recherche originaux, et conduisant à l'obtention d'un titre de chercheur hautement qualifié.

La CITE de 1997 introduit également une catégorie nouvelle, à savoir un niveau intermédiaire entre le deuxième cycle de l'enseignement secondaire et l'enseignement supérieur, appelé "enseignement post secondaire qui n'est pas du supérieur" (niveau 4 de la CITE). Programmes dont le contenu est plus avancé que celui offert aux niveaux 3 et 4 de la CITE. Le premier cycle de l'enseignement supérieur, niveau 5 de la CITE, couvre le niveau 5A, composé de programmes fondés dans une large mesure sur la théorie et destinés à offrir des qualifications suffisantes pour être admis à suivre des programmes de recherche de pointe ou à exercer une profession exigeant de hautes compétences; et le niveau 5B, dont les programmes sont dans une large mesure d'ordre pratique, technique et/ou spécifiquement professionnel. Le deuxième cycle de l'enseignement supérieur, niveau 6 de la CITE, comprend des programmes consacrés à des études approfondies et à des travaux de recherche originaux, et conduisant à l'obtention d'un titre de chercheur hautement qualifié.

Tableau 10 : Les données relatives aux dépenses publiques afférentes à l'éducation se rapportent aux dépenses courantes et en capital de l'éducation engagées par l'administration au niveau local, régional, national/central, y inclus les municipalités. Les contributions des ménages sont exclues. Les dépenses ordinaires (ou courantes) en éducation se réfèrent aux dépenses couvrant les biens et les services consommés dans l'année en cours et qui doivent être renouvelées périodiquement. Elles comprennent les dépenses en : salaires et avantages du personnel, services achetés ou assurés sous contrat, l'achat d'autres ressources y compris les manuels scolaires et du matériel pour l'enseignement, les services sociaux et d'autres dépenses de fonctionnement telles que les subventions aux étudiants et aux ménages, les fournitures et l'équipement, les réparations légères, les combustibles, les télécommunications, les voyages, les assurances et les loyers. Dépenses en capital pour l'éducation se réfèrent aux dépenses qui couvrent l'achat de biens d'une durée supérieure à une année. Elles peuvent comprendre les dépenses de construction, de rénovation et de grosses réparations de bâtiments, ainsi que l'achat d'équipements ou véhicules.

11

Food supply
Calories, protein and fat: average supply per capita per day

Disponibilités alimentaires
Calories, protéine et lipides : disponibilités moyennes par habitant, par jour

Country or area Pays ou zone	Calories (number) — Calories (nombre)			Protein (grams) — Protéine (grammes)			Fat (grams) — Lipides (grammes)		
	1990–92	1995–97	2001–03	1990–92	1995–97	2001–03	1990–92	1995–97	2001–03
World Monde	2 703.3	2 756.2	2 798.4	71.5	73.8	75.4	67.9	71.7	78.0
Africa Afrique									
Algeria Algérie	2 919.9	2 912.2	3 039.0	78.4	78.4	82.4	72.9	69.0	67.6
Angola Angola	1 782.8	1 913.4	2 072.5	39.8	41.9	44.7	44.8	39.8	43.5
Benin Bénin	2 333.0	2 438.5	2 528.1	55.4	57.1	62.0	42.8	42.5	47.9
Botswana Botswana	2 264.2	2 217.9	2 177.5	69.5	69.4	68.1	60.4	54.7	51.1
Burkina Faso Burkina Faso	2 351.0	2 406.6	2 458.8	68.6	69.6	70.7	47.1	50.5	56.0
Burundi Burundi	1 896.2	1 699.1	1 641.7	59.6	51.3	44.9	14.0	11.6	10.4
Cameroon Cameroun	2 119.8	2 117.4	2 271.0	50.8	51.5	59.1	42.9	40.6	46.0
Cape Verde Cap–Vert	3 010.8	3 063.1	3 217.4	71.8	68.1	76.2	75.2	91.3	99.3
Central African Rep. Rép. centrafricaine	1 864.7	1 850.4	1 942.2	40.2	42.8	46.1	58.1	57.1	63.9
Chad Tchad	1 782.5	1 916.7	2 163.1	52.8	56.6	66.4	46.8	58.6	67.4
Comoros Comores	1 914.7	1 827.0	1 747.3	44.4	42.7	42.3	44.9	43.6	42.2
Congo Congo	1 861.0	1 793.6	2 148.2	41.4	34.8	42.5	46.1	43.7	54.1
Côte d'Ivoire Côte d'Ivoire	2 470.9	2 553.1	2 630.8	51.4	50.6	53.7	49.9	52.4	59.0
Dem. Rep. of the Congo Rép. dém. du Congo	2 174.2	1 770.3	1 611.4	32.8	27.2	24.8	34.4	28.4	26.3
Djibouti Djibouti	1 802.2	2 017.8	2 221.7	41.0	42.8	51.3	40.4	59.3	67.3
Egypt Egypte	3 200.7	3 321.1	3 345.9	84.7	90.7	93.5	57.1	56.6	57.9
Eritrea Erythrée	...	1 579.4	1 521.0	...	51.0	46.5	...	20.4	29.0
Ethiopia Ethiopie	...	1 651.7	1 855.7	...	47.6	53.8	...	17.2	19.6
Ethiopia incl. Eritrea Ethiopie y comp. Erythrée	1 637.8	...	...	48.4	...	...	24.2	...	...
Gabon Gabon	2 452.6	2 545.8	2 667.8	70.2	74.7	72.8	47.1	49.1	55.3
Gambia Gambie	2 366.7	2 192.1	2 279.8	51.6	48.0	52.1	57.6	59.1	76.8
Ghana Ghana	2 073.3	2 446.7	2 652.9	45.5	51.0	55.1	35.3	34.7	38.0
Guinea Guinée	2 105.9	2 271.0	2 417.1	48.0	48.9	51.1	45.6	52.6	58.3
Guinea–Bissau Guinée–Bissau	2 298.0	2 166.2	2 066.6	45.6	43.0	39.5	58.5	54.1	50.6

Country or area Pays ou zone	Calories (number) — Calories (nombre)			Protein (grams) — Protéine (grammes)			Fat (grams) — Lipides (grammes)		
	1990–92	1995–97	2001–03	1990–92	1995–97	2001–03	1990–92	1995–97	2001–03
Kenya Kenya	1 980.9	2 058.4	2 147.7	54.6	57.4	59.5	45.6	47.1	49.5
Lesotho Lesotho	2 443.4	2 538.9	2 624.9	68.1	70.9	72.6	36.5	36.0	36.9
Liberia Libéria	2 211.0	2 060.2	1 943.6	39.0	37.5	31.7	53.6	66.5	51.8
Libyan Arab Jamah. Jamah. arabe libyenne	3 271.9	3 296.4	3 332.1	81.2	81.1	79.4	106.5	104.6	106.8
Madagascar Madagascar	2 084.0	2 010.2	2 036.1	49.7	47.4	46.6	31.1	30.3	28.5
Malawi Malawi	1 878.9	2 037.5	2 142.7	51.0	52.3	54.5	26.4	27.8	32.6
Mali Mali	2 215.7	2 156.0	2 224.6	62.7	61.9	62.8	48.6	44.0	45.6
Mauritania Mauritanie	2 556.6	2 688.7	2 774.8	79.1	77.6	81.0	63.6	67.6	71.2
Mauritius Maurice	2 885.9	2 914.0	2 962.6	72.0	73.1	79.7	75.3	85.9	80.3
Morocco Maroc	3 028.0	3 040.6	3 064.9	84.0	81.1	84.0	57.8	59.9	58.9
Mozambique Mozambique	1 734.9	1 853.6	2 070.4	31.4	36.1	39.3	37.8	33.8	33.2
Namibia Namibie	2 068.3	2 051.6	2 264.4	58.7	55.1	65.1	33.7	34.7	52.4
Niger Niger	2 020.8	2 002.5	2 155.6	53.3	54.5	56.8	30.6	33.7	39.1
Nigeria Nigéria	2 537.6	2 724.1	2 700.2	56.8	61.5	60.7	62.0	64.0	62.5
Rwanda Rwanda	1 947.5	1 831.0	2 066.5	47.8	43.7	48.8	17.1	17.2	15.1
Sao Tome and Principe Sao Tomé–et–Principe	2 272.2	2 231.3	2 442.7	50.7	48.5	48.4	76.7	63.4	72.8
Senegal Sénégal	2 276.0	2 251.2	2 311.7	66.3	62.7	58.4	60.1	66.3	69.0
Seychelles Seychelles	2 311.2	2 381.8	2 459.6	69.6	75.2	83.8	55.1	69.4	72.7
Sierra Leone Sierra Leone	1 990.7	2 028.6	1 931.7	42.5	43.4	44.4	56.7	59.0	45.4
South Africa Afrique du Sud	2 827.6	2 801.8	2 942.8	74.2	72.8	77.4	66.6	70.7	75.7
Sudan Soudan	2 168.8	2 327.9	2 257.2	67.4	74.6	71.2	59.7	69.3	69.4
Swaziland Swaziland	2 449.7	2 259.5	2 355.9	59.0	56.8	60.2	47.2	42.7	45.0
Togo Togo	2 150.3	2 312.6	2 321.5	50.5	55.6	53.3	44.8	49.5	47.8
Tunisia Tunisie	3 145.0	3 210.4	3 252.1	85.5	87.5	89.4	83.2	85.9	93.7
Uganda Ouganda	2 274.4	2 219.9	2 376.0	54.3	49.5	57.4	30.6	32.4	31.5
United Rep. of Tanzania Rép.–Unie de Tanzanie	2 049.6	1 876.0	1 955.8	50.0	46.4	47.4	30.5	28.5	31.5
Zambia Zambie	1 929.6	·1 922.1	1 931.3	48.5	49.2	48.1	29.5	28.1	29.4
Zimbabwe Zimbabwe	1 982.2	1 967.4	2 009.8	49.8	46.1	45.0	49.2	47.7	54.9

11

Food supply—Calories, protein and fat: average supply per capita per day (*continued*)
Disponibilités alimentaires—Calories, protéine et lipides : disponibilités moyennes par habitant, par jour (*suite*)

Country or area / Pays ou zone	Calories (number) — Calories (nombre)			Protein (grams) — Protéine (grammes)			Fat (grams) — Lipides (grammes)		
	1990–92	1995–97	2001–03	1990–92	1995–97	2001–03	1990–92	1995–97	2001–03
America, North **Amérique du Nord**									
Antigua and Barbuda Antigua–et–Barbuda	2 460.0	2 238.8	2 317.9	81.4	76.5	72.5	99.0	76.7	82.6
Bahamas Bahamas	2 618.8	2 478.8	2 707.4	78.5	77.0	91.9	87.2	77.7	95.5
Barbados Barbade	3 063.9	2 944.3	3 104.8	91.0	85.3	91.8	106.8	99.7	98.7
Belize Belize	2 650.0	2 738.2	2 839.8	65.2	63.6	75.7	68.3	70.0	69.4
Bermuda Bermudes	2 339.5	2 388.3	2 232.1	81.3	76.3	68.6	98.8	94.6	98.0
Canada Canada	3 056.3	3 283.5	3 593.7	96.3	98.8	105.6	129.9	137.9	147.3
Costa Rica Costa Rica	2 723.8	2 763.7	2 847.8	67.2	70.7	71.1	73.7	77.4	78.0
Cuba Cuba	2 716.4	2 433.5	3 185.5	62.4	54.8	78.3	70.4	42.2	53.2
Dominica Dominique	2 941.2	2 802.2	2 765.0	75.7	80.4	83.3	82.6	76.5	76.0
Dominican Republic Rép. dominicaine	2 261.5	2 290.9	2 289.2	49.6	50.4	49.3	66.1	73.8	78.4
El Salvador El Salvador	2 492.1	2 431.2	2 563.4	61.6	60.8	67.0	53.8	50.2	60.5
Grenada Grenade	2 830.0	2 935.9	2 929.2	76.9	79.0	83.6	92.6	101.0	102.2
Guatemala Guatemala	2 351.5	2 235.3	2 213.1	59.8	56.9	56.2	42.9	42.5	49.4
Haiti Haïti	1 780.4	1 881.5	2 090.6	43.6	43.5	46.9	29.5	33.8	38.0
Honduras Honduras	2 313.3	2 374.0	2 361.7	55.3	58.6	57.0	57.1	62.4	65.5
Jamaica Jamaïque	2 503.1	2 600.7	2 677.4	62.3	66.3	68.1	63.7	69.8	74.5
Mexico Mexique	3 101.0	3 118.7	3 180.2	82.0	84.2	91.2	81.6	86.3	89.1
Netherlands Antilles Antilles néerlandaises	2 511.8	2 482.6	2 591.3	80.3	75.4	79.5	82.4	87.4	73.4
Nicaragua Nicaragua	2 215.4	2 165.2	2 291.1	55.2	49.0	61.8	46.8	47.3	46.7
Panama Panama	2 316.7	2 278.2	2 255.8	61.2	61.1	63.7	67.6	68.8	65.4
Saint Kitts and Nevis Saint–Kitts–et–Nevis	2 576.7	2 450.7	2 699.1	69.8	71.0	81.1	83.3	82.6	87.1
Saint Lucia Sainte–Lucie	2 734.9	2 790.2	2 954.7	84.2	87.2	95.3	67.1	76.0	80.9
St. Vincent-Grenadines St. Vincent–Grenadines	2 299.2	2 234.3	2 580.6	59.4	60.8	71.2	70.8	61.8	67.7
Trinidad and Tobago Trinité–et–Tobago	2 632.3	2 615.3	2 764.5	62.0	59.8	65.3	71.6	69.2	76.3
United States Etats–Unis	3 501.7	3 608.2	3 768.2	108.2	111.0	114.1	139.8	139.9	156.4
America, South **Amérique du Sud**									
Argentina Argentine	2 998.2	3 162.1	2 982.6	94.7	99.8	93.8	105.5	114.5	100.0

Country or area Pays ou zone	Calories (number) — Calories (nombre)			Protein (grams) — Protéine (grammes)			Fat (grams) — Lipides (grammes)		
	1990–92	1995–97	2001–03	1990–92	1995–97	2001–03	1990–92	1995–97	2001–03
Bolivia Bolivie	2 113.6	2 183.9	2 218.0	54.1	56.9	56.6	49.9	52.2	58.1
Brazil Brésil	2 812.1	2 931.0	3 059.6	69.5	78.4	82.7	84.4	86.7	93.4
Chile Chili	2 611.6	2 776.1	2 860.5	72.8	78.6	80.3	67.4	80.4	84.6
Colombia Colombie	2 435.2	2 568.7	2 576.6	54.3	60.7	60.3	56.1	64.4	65.1
Ecuador Equateur	2 509.1	2 673.6	2 706.9	50.5	57.5	56.7	91.3	96.2	98.7
Guyana Guyana	2 347.1	2 596.3	2 727.5	60.9	70.6	76.2	34.4	49.2	55.5
Paraguay Paraguay	2 402.6	2 549.3	2 532.3	70.5	76.8	69.4	71.2	78.1	87.3
Peru Pérou	1 961.5	2 367.1	2 569.1	48.4	59.4	66.8	42.3	48.6	47.8
Suriname Suriname	2 528.4	2 636.9	2 660.8	63.9	60.4	59.5	48.9	58.6	70.9
Uruguay Uruguay	2 655.7	2 786.6	2 845.6	81.3	89.0	86.3	92.1	95.3	85.8
Venezuela (Bolivarian Rep. of) Venezuela (Rép. bolivar. du)	2 463.3	2 381.7	2 346.8	60.0	60.0	61.9	69.7	65.2	67.9
Asia Asie									
Armenia Arménie	1 847.0	2 173.6	2 260.4	58.7	60.3	67.8	30.2	45.8	47.1
Azerbaijan Azerbaïdjan	2 312.1	2 163.3	2 621.7	70.5	63.9	77.2	37.3	36.9	41.1
Bangladesh Bangladesh	2 069.9	1 997.5	2 197.9	44.4	42.9	47.5	19.0	21.7	25.1
Brunei Darussalam Brunéi Darussalam	2 797.5	2 853.9	2 849.9	78.8	89.7	82.3	70.6	76.3	73.4
Cambodia Cambodge	1 862.5	1 847.0	2 057.0	43.9	42.0	51.2	22.3	27.1	32.3
China [1] Chine [1]	2 699.4	2 903.5	2 933.8	65.3	77.0	81.8	53.2	70.2	89.2
China, Hong Kong SAR Chine, Hong Kong RAS	3 239.7	3 187.7	3 079.8	94.7	102.4	96.7	139.8	133.9	132.8
China, Macao SAR Chine, Macao RAS	2 725.0	2 614.6	2 514.5	77.1	74.1	73.8	111.6	121.0	114.2
Cyprus Chypre	3 104.0	3 187.4	3 243.7	97.0	100.1	104.7	122.0	127.5	131.8
Georgia Géorgie	2 236.8	2 361.6	2 518.0	67.4	69.4	71.0	31.2	38.4	51.9
India Inde	2 365.9	2 435.2	2 443.7	57.3	58.5	57.4	41.3	46.6	51.9
Indonesia Indonésie	2 698.5	2 885.3	2 883.4	60.8	65.9	64.1	53.1	58.3	61.4
Iran (Islamic Rep. of) Iran (Rép. islamique d')	2 978.0	3 054.0	3 091.8	79.3	80.7	83.4	63.8	66.2	60.9
Israel Israël	3 406.8	3 457.5	3 681.7	111.7	113.4	124.2	122.1	123.0	148.8
Japan Japon	2 813.2	2 838.4	2 773.4	94.0	94.6	91.6	79.6	83.9	86.0
Jordan Jordanie	2 817.7	2 658.1	2 679.9	75.9	70.3	69.0	74.0	76.0	79.9

Food supply—Calories, protein and fat: average supply per capita per day (*continued*)

Disponibilités alimentaires—Calories, protéine et lipides : disponibilités moyennes par habitant, par jour (*suite*)

Country or area / Pays ou zone	Calories (number) — Calories (nombre)			Protein (grams) — Protéine (grammes)			Fat (grams) — Lipides (grammes)		
	1990–92	1995–97	2001–03	1990–92	1995–97	2001–03	1990–92	1995–97	2001–03
Kazakhstan / Kazakhstan	3 037.9	3 118.6	2 710.6	92.9	98.3	84.9	79.4	70.4	79.6
Korea, Dem. P. R. / Corée, R. p. dém. de	2 466.7	2 165.0	2 154.8	78.5	59.7	63.1	45.6	34.7	34.6
Korea, Republic of / Corée, République de	2 997.9	3 024.0	3 040.2	81.3	84.4	89.4	59.7	67.3	78.5
Kuwait / Koweït	2 273.7	3 030.5	3 062.1	69.0	94.0	83.8	74.3	98.3	113.0
Kyrgyzstan / Kirghizistan	2 658.3	2 517.1	3 048.3	82.6	83.0	101.4	67.1	52.8	53.9
Lao People's Dem. Rep. / Rép. dém. pop. lao	2 111.1	2 148.4	2 315.4	51.1	53.0	61.5	23.0	26.3	28.5
Lebanon / Liban	3 162.5	3 166.0	3 166.5	80.2	83.0	88.5	105.6	103.3	112.7
Malaysia / Malaisie	2 830.2	2 893.2	2 871.7	68.4	76.2	75.0	97.4	85.9	84.4
Maldives / Maldives	2 377.2	2 433.2	2 560.6	77.8	89.5	106.9	46.3	51.4	66.3
Mongolia / Mongolie	2 065.5	1 955.0	2 245.5	74.0	73.4	78.6	79.1	70.5	84.0
Myanmar / Myanmar	2 633.8	2 785.2	2 901.1	64.7	69.6	78.6	41.9	45.2	49.3
Nepal / Népal	2 346.1	2 224.8	2 451.0	60.5	57.8	62.5	32.0	32.0	37.8
Occupied Palestinian Terr. / Terr. palestinien occupé	...	...	2 237.8	...	...	60.7	...	...	62.6
Pakistan / Pakistan	2 303.8	2 436.6	2 343.0	58.3	62.6	59.3	58.1	65.2	68.8
Philippines / Philippines	2 262.9	2 361.4	2 453.3	54.5	55.7	57.5	41.3	43.5	47.9
Saudi Arabia / Arabie saoudite	2 769.3	2 804.2	2 824.1	76.3	77.6	76.3	80.6	73.0	82.1
Sri Lanka / Sri Lanka	2 230.4	2 293.9	2 391.6	48.9	52.1	54.4	43.0	43.5	44.5
Syrian Arab Republic / Rép. arabe syrienne	2 831.1	2 974.3	3 055.3	71.1	71.8	77.8	84.8	99.1	100.8
Tajikistan / Tadjikistan	2 358.4	2 182.8	1 841.2	67.0	56.7	48.1	49.7	43.8	39.6
Thailand / Thaïlande	2 200.6	2 355.5	2 413.6	52.4	57.2	56.7	46.5	49.9	51.5
Timor–Leste / Timor–Leste	2 564.0	2 688.8	2 784.7	67.9	68.7	69.4	36.4	37.4	40.8
Turkey / Turquie	3 494.4	3 399.9	3 338.5	102.0	98.1	95.9	86.9	90.7	89.8
Turkmenistan / Turkménistan	2 788.1	2 536.1	2 751.8	81.9	72.5	84.8	68.7	73.3	69.9
United Arab Emirates / Emirats arabes unis	2 929.3	3 165.8	3 218.8	94.2	102.1	106.2	100.3	106.7	91.8
Uzbekistan / Ouzbékistan	2 700.2	2 673.2	2 272.8	78.6	76.9	66.7	70.9	73.9	63.9
Viet Nam / Viet Nam	2 177.1	2 376.9	2 578.4	50.3	56.6	63.2	28.4	35.8	45.5
Yemen / Yémen	2 039.2	2 026.0	2 023.9	55.2	54.7	57.1	40.0	36.5	41.0
Europe / Europe									
Albania / Albanie	2 547.1	2 804.9	2 855.5	80.6	93.8	96.4	67.8	82.2	86.2

Country or area / Pays ou zone	Calories (number) — Calories (nombre)			Protein (grams) — Protéine (grammes)			Fat (grams) — Lipides (grammes)		
	1990–92	1995–97	2001–03	1990–92	1995–97	2001–03	1990–92	1995–97	2001–03
Austria / Autriche	3 511.8	3 557.8	3 742.1	102.4	104.7	110.7	158.0	159.3	161.7
Belarus / Bélarus	3 183.9	3 250.4	2 959.9	96.8	96.1	87.2	103.8	98.4	99.2
Belgium / Belgique	...	...	3 638.7	...	...	91.7	...	...	162.2
Belgium–Luxembourg / Belgique–Luxembourg	3 580.7	3 596.4	...	104.9	101.8	...	157.0	160.0	...
Bosnia and Herzegovina / Bosnie–Herzégovine	2 505.6	2 735.4	2 711.2	71.6	81.7	72.1	37.4	52.6	58.4
Bulgaria / Bulgarie	3 287.9	2 738.7	2 851.1	100.2	83.1	88.8	111.2	86.8	95.3
Croatia / Croatie	2 420.4	2 687.1	2 767.7	60.7	67.7	73.6	77.1	76.7	87.3
Czechoslovakia–former / Tchécoslovaquie (anc.)	3 370.9	...	...	95.4	...	...	123.4	...	...
Czech Republic / République tchèque	...	3 247.1	3 243.6	...	94.0	93.2	...	109.3	114.6
Denmark / Danemark	3 229.3	3 345.8	3 450.7	100.4	103.8	109.8	133.8	133.9	139.8
Estonia / Estonie	2 549.5	2 995.4	3 157.1	108.1	95.7	89.7	79.4	91.9	95.5
Finland / Finlande	3 149.0	3 059.1	3 153.4	98.1	98.8	101.7	126.1	127.0	127.0
France / France	3 535.6	3 544.0	3 642.6	116.2	114.9	118.3	163.3	164.2	169.6
Germany / Allemagne	3 394.4	3 347.5	3 490.2	96.8	93.7	99.9	144.6	144.8	140.8
Greece / Grèce	3 571.9	3 587.6	3 682.2	112.6	115.8	117.0	142.7	148.8	145.3
Hungary / Hongrie	3 615.8	3 285.8	3 503.2	98.4	84.9	95.3	148.4	133.3	148.8
Iceland / Islande	3 095.0	3 085.1	3 243.9	113.8	114.6	123.5	121.6	117.3	129.8
Ireland / Irlande	3 624.8	3 588.5	3 694.2	114.6	108.3	116.9	133.6	131.5	135.5
Italy / Italie	3 590.9	3 517.7	3 669.6	111.1	108.4	113.3	149.4	147.2	156.5
Latvia / Lettonie	2 901.0	2 927.6	3 018.5	98.0	87.0	83.0	86.4	93.9	109.3
Lithuania / Lituanie	2 972.7	3 043.8	3 372.2	97.1	95.0	109.7	79.8	78.6	100.4
Malta / Malte	3 239.7	3 408.0	3 526.8	101.6	108.9	118.1	112.6	112.5	109.9
Netherlands / Pays–Bas	3 334.8	3 215.5	3 438.9	99.0	105.4	107.6	138.7	141.5	144.5
Norway / Norvège	3 184.2	3 273.0	3 479.1	97.4	102.7	107.3	130.7	134.0	144.5
Poland / Pologne	3 327.9	3 308.6	3 366.9	101.8	98.2	99.3	111.9	109.9	111.6
Portugal / Portugal	3 448.8	3 536.8	3 753.4	103.6	109.8	118.6	122.3	128.8	140.9
Republic of Moldova / République de Moldova	3 244.4	2 684.3	2 730.4	86.0	65.9	66.3	73.0	54.2	54.2
Romania / Roumanie	3 022.7	3 274.9	3 524.1	90.3	101.5	109.4	91.1	87.6	100.5
Russian Federation / Fédération de Russie	...	2 867.0	3 075.7	...	88.8	90.7	...	79.0	83.4

Food supply—Calories, protein and fat: average supply per capita per day (*continued*)

Disponibilités alimentaires—Calories, protéine et lipides : disponibilités moyennes par habitant, par jour (*suite*)

Country or area	Calories (number) — Calories (nombre)			Protein (grams) — Protéine (grammes)			Fat (grams) — Lipides (grammes)		
Pays ou zone	1990–92	1995–97	2001–03	1990–92	1995–97	2001–03	1990–92	1995–97	2001–03
Serbia and Montenegro Serbie–et–Monténégro	3 086.0	3 036.2	2 671.8	88.7	90.0	74.8	125.2	124.0	118.3
Slovakia Slovaquie	...	2 952.6	2 825.5	...	81.3	77.2	...	104.3	106.6
Slovenia Slovénie	2 767.4	3 005.5	2 969.4	78.9	99.9	101.9	100.1	103.8	108.0
Spain Espagne	3 304.7	3 267.1	3 405.3	105.3	105.7	113.1	143.1	144.0	154.1
Sweden Suède	2 989.8	3 088.9	3 156.9	95.9	98.0	106.5	123.1	130.5	125.4
Switzerland Suisse	3 306.9	3 290.3	3 503.4	95.1	91.0	95.6	149.7	146.8	157.0
TFYR of Macedonia L'ex–R.y. Macédoine	2 510.2	2 618.1	2 803.5	71.9	69.8	72.4	62.0	72.4	90.9
Ukraine Ukraine	3 367.9	2 844.6	3 031.8	94.0	82.2	84.2	91.7	73.2	78.6
United Kingdom Royaume–Uni	3 265.6	3 276.6	3 443.7	94.1	95.8	103.8	140.4	140.2	138.4
Oceania Océanie									
Australia Australie	3 174.8	3 126.7	3 118.2	106.8	104.4	106.8	130.5	128.9	133.8
Fiji Fidji	2 636.6	2 786.1	2 962.4	68.7	71.3	74.1	100.1	99.3	97.0
French Polynesia Polynésie française	2 863.5	2 869.8	2 895.5	89.5	93.7	99.1	102.4	108.4	124.4
Kiribati Kiribati	2 653.0	2 790.0	2 835.2	64.7	68.8	70.6	93.7	99.1	99.8
New Caledonia Nouvelle–Calédonie	2 788.3	2 790.2	2 781.8	78.1	81.3	82.4	103.7	107.7	112.7
New Zealand Nouvelle–Zélande	3 204.5	3 118.1	3 197.8	95.9	96.4	91.8	128.5	116.7	118.4
Samoa Samoa	2 568.9	2 567.7	2 913.0	70.0	67.7	83.9	116.0	115.8	132.6
Solomon Islands Iles Salomon	2 019.2	2 201.7	2 253.8	49.2	52.2	50.7	44.0	44.4	40.9
Vanuatu Vanuatu	2 528.1	2 540.7	2 590.0	59.0	59.2	60.2	98.0	92.4	86.6

Source

Food and Agriculture Organization of the United Nations (FAO), Rome, FAOSTAT Nutrition database.

Note

1 For statistical purposes, the data for China do not include those for the Hong Kong Special Administrative Region (Hong Kong SAR), Macao Special Administrative Region (Macao SAR) and Taiwan Province of China.

Source

Organisation des Nations Unies pour l'alimentation et l'agriculture (FAO), Rome, les données alimentaires de FAOSTAT.

Note

1 Pour la présentation des statistiques, les données pour Chine ne comprennent pas la Région Administrative Spéciale de Hong Kong (Hong Kong RAS), la Région Administrative Spéciale de Macao (Macao RAS) et la province de Taiwan.

12

Selected indicators of life expectancy, childbearing and mortality

Choix d'indicateurs de l'espérance de vie, de la maternité et de la mortalité

		Life expectancy at birth (years) Espérance de vie à la naissance (en années)		Total fertility rate	Mortality rates – Taux de mortalité				
					Infant Infantile (p. 1,000)	Child Juvenile (p. 1,000)			Maternal Maternale (p.100,000)
Country or area Pays ou zone	Year Année	Males Hommes	Females Femmes	Taux de fecondité	M+F	Year Année	Males Hommes	Females Femmes	2000
Africa Afrique									
Algeria Algérie	2000-2005 2005-2010	69.7 70.9	72.2 73.7	2.5 2.4	37.4 31.0	1982[1,2] 1998[1,2,3]	12.5 8.8	12.8 7.3	... 140
Angola Angola	2000-2005 2005-2010	39.2 40.5	42.2 43.4	6.8 6.4	138.8 130.0	... ...	... ...	... ...	... 1 700
Benin Bénin	2000-2005 2005-2010	53.0 55.1	54.5 56.6	5.9 5.4	105.1 97.6	... ...	... ...	... ...	... 850
Botswana Botswana	2000-2005 2005-2010	36.0 35.0	37.1 32.7	3.2 2.9	51.0 42.6	... 2001[4]	... 8.3	... 7.2	... 100
Burkina Faso Burkina Faso	2000-2005 2005-2010	46.7 48.5	48.1 50.1	6.7 6.3	121.4 115.6	... ...	... ...	... ...	... 1 000
Burundi Burundi	2000-2005 2005-2010	42.5 44.5	44.4 46.5	6.8 6.8	105.9 98.9	... ...	... ...	... ...	... 1 000
Cameroon Cameroun	2000-2005 2005-2010	45.1 45.8	46.5 46.7	4.7 4.1	94.3 90.7	... ...	... ...	... ...	... 730
Cape Verde Cap-Vert	2000-2005 2005-2010	66.8 68.3	73.0 74.5	3.8 3.4	29.8 24.6	1985[3] 1990	21.1 3.4	19.3 3.4	... 150
Central African Rep. Rép. centrafricaine	2000-2005 2005-2010	38.5 39.0	40.3 40.0	5.0 4.6	98.2 93.2	... 1988[5]	... 14.9	... 12.8	... 1 100
Chad Tchad	2000-2005 2005-2010	42.5 43.3	44.8 45.4	6.7 6.7	116.0 111.5	... ...	... ...	... ...	... 1 100
Comoros Comores	2000-2005 2005-2010	60.9 63.0	65.1 67.4	4.9 4.3	57.7 48.4	... ...	... ...	... ...	... 480
Congo Congo	2000-2005 2005-2010	50.6 52.2	53.1 54.8	6.3 6.3	72.3 68.0	... ...	... ...	... ...	... 510
Côte d'Ivoire Côte d'Ivoire	2000-2005 2005-2010	45.2 45.6	46.8 47.0	5.1 4.5	118.3 113.8	... ...	... ...	... ...	... 690
Dem. Rep. of the Congo Rép. dém. du Congo	2000-2005 2005-2010	42.1 43.6	44.1 45.8	6.7 6.7	118.5 112.5	... ...	... ...	... ...	... 990
Djibouti Djibouti	2000-2005 2005-2010	51.4 52.9	53.9 55.0	5.1 4.5	93.2 83.7	... ...	... ...	... ...	... 730
Egypt Egypte	2000-2005 2005-2010	67.5 68.9	71.8 73.5	3.3 3.0	36.7 30.1	1996 1999	2.5 2.4	2.7 2.4	... 84
Equatorial Guinea Guinée équatoriale	2000-2005 2005-2010	42.8 41.4	44.2 41.6	5.9 5.9	102.0 94.5	... ...	... ...	... ...	... 880
Eritrea Erythrée	2000-2005 2005-2010	51.5 54.1	55.4 57.8	5.5 5.1	64.6 56.9	... ...	... ...	... ...	... 630
Ethiopia Ethiopie	2000-2005 2005-2010	46.5 47.7	48.6 49.4	5.9 5.4	99.5 90.9	... ...	... ...	... ...	... 850
Gabon Gabon	2000-2005 2005-2010	53.8 53.1	55.4 53.6	4.0 3.5	57.9 51.1	... ...	... ...	... ...	... 420
Gambia Gambie	2000-2005 2005-2010	54.0 56.5	56.9 59.0	4.8 4.2	77.0 68.0	... ...	... ...	... ...	... 540
Ghana Ghana	2000-2005 2005-2010	56.2 57.6	57.2 58.5	4.4 3.8	62.3 55.6	... ...	... ...	... ...	... 540
Guinea Guinée	2000-2005 2005-2010	53.2 54.2	54.0 54.5	5.9 5.5	105.5 96.7	... ...	... ...	... ...	... 740
Guinea-Bissau Guinée-Bissau	2000-2005 2005-2010	43.1 44.3	46.2 46.7	7.1 7.1	119.7 111.0	... ...	... ...	... ...	... 1 100
Kenya Kenya	2000-2005 2005-2010	47.9 51.1	46.2 49.4	5.0 5.0	67.8 62.9	... ...	... ...	... ...	... 1 000
Lesotho Lesotho	2000-2005 2005-2010	34.9 34.2	38.1 34.3	3.7 3.3	66.5 58.7	... ...	... ...	... ...	... 550

Country or area Pays ou zone	Year Année	Life expectancy at birth (years) Espérance de vie à la naissance (en années) Males Hommes	Females Femmes	Total fertility rate Taux de fecondité	Infant Infantile (p. 1,000) M+F	Child Juvenile (p. 1,000) Year Année	Males Hommes	Females Femmes	Maternal Maternale (p.100,000) 2000
Liberia	2000-2005	41.4	43.5	6.8	141.9	...	...	...	...
Libéria	2005-2010	41.9	43.1	6.8	132.0	...	...	...	760
Libyan Arab Jamah.	2000-2005	71.4	76.1	3.0	19.2	...	...	...	...
Jamah. arabe libyenne	2005-2010	72.5	77.2	2.7	16.6	...	...	...	97
Madagascar	2000-2005	54.0	56.7	5.4	78.8	...	...	...	...
Madagascar	2005-2010	55.0	57.4	4.9	71.2	1993 [3,6]	17.0	15.1	550
Malawi	2000-2005	39.7	39.6	6.1	110.8	...	...	...	...
Malawi	2005-2010	41.6	40.6	5.7	102.6	1998 [5]	51.2	41.6	1 800
Mali	2000-2005	47.1	48.4	6.9	133.5	...	...	...	...
Mali	2005-2010	48.6	49.9	6.6	125.8	1987 [3,5]	41.5	35.7	1 200
Mauritania	2000-2005	50.9	54.1	5.8	96.7	...	...	...	...
Mauritanie	2005-2010	52.9	56.1	5.5	88.1	...	...	...	1 000
Mauritius	2000-2005	68.7[7]	75.6[7]	2.0[7]	15.0[7]	2002	0.5	0.7	...
Maurice	2005-2010	69.7[7]	76.3[7]	1.9[7]	13.8[7]	2003	0.7	0.8	24
Morocco	2000-2005	67.4	71.7	2.8	38.1	2000[3]	3.8	3.4	...
Maroc	2005-2010	68.8	73.3	2.6	31.3	2001[3]	3.7	3.3	220
Mozambique	2000-2005	41.0	42.8	5.5	100.9	...	...	...	...
Mozambique	2005-2010	41.7	41.9	5.1	90.6	1997[8,9]	61.2	51.0	1 000
Namibia	2000-2005	47.7	49.4	4.0	43.8	...	...	...	...
Namibie	2005-2010	46.6	45.1	3.5	36.6	2001[3,10,11]	18.2	19.3	300
Niger	2000-2005	44.2	44.3	7.9	152.7	...	...	...	...
Niger	2005-2010	45.4	45.4	7.5	145.4	...	...	...	1 600
Nigeria	2000-2005	43.1	43.5	5.9	114.4	...	...	...	...
Nigéria	2005-2010	44.1	44.3	5.3	108.1	...	...	...	800
Réunion	2000-2005	71.3	79.6	2.5	7.7	1987[1,12]	0.6	0.6	...
Réunion	2005-2010	72.0	80.2	2.4	7.2	1999[1,12]	0.6	0.4	41
Rwanda	2000-2005	41.9	45.3	5.7	115.5	...	...	...	...
Rwanda	2005-2010	43.1	46.1	5.2	112.3	...	...	...	1 400
Sao Tome and Principe	2000-2005	61.9	63.8	4.1	82.4	...	...	...	...
Sao Tomé-et-Principe	2005-2010	62.8	65.1	3.6	78.1	...	...	...	...
Senegal	2000-2005	54.4	56.8	5.1	83.5	...	...	...	...
Sénégal	2005-2010	55.8	58.4	4.5	77.2	...	...	...	690
Sierra Leone	2000-2005	39.3	42.0	6.5	165.1	...	...	...	...
Sierra Leone	2005-2010	40.5	43.3	6.5	159.8	...	...	...	2 000
Somalia	2000-2005	45.0	47.3	6.4	126.1	...	...	...	...
Somalie	2005-2010	47.6	50.1	6.0	113.1	...	...	...	1 100
South Africa	2000-2005	47.1	51.0	2.8	42.7	...	...	...	...
Afrique du Sud	2005-2010	44.2	43.8	2.6	38.9	1996[13,14,15]	2.4	2.1	230
Sudan	2000-2005	54.9	57.9	4.5	72.2	...	...	...	...
Soudan	2005-2010	55.6	58.2	4.0	64.9	1993[3,10,16]	34.4	28.6	590
Swaziland	2000-2005	32.5	33.4	4.0	73.1	...	...	...	...
Swaziland	2005-2010	30.8	29.2	3.5	63.8	1997[3,8]	15.8	14.2	370
Togo	2000-2005	52.3	56.2	5.4	92.5	...	...	...	...
Togo	2005-2010	54.1	57.5	4.8	87.5	...	...	...	570
Tunisia	2000-2005	71.1	75.3	2.0	22.2	1997[3]	5.1	4.2	...
Tunisie	2005-2010	72.1	76.3	1.9	19.1	1998[3]	5.9	4.7	120
Uganda	2000-2005	46.5	47.1	7.1	81.2	...	...	...	...
Ouganda	2005-2010	51.2	53.0	7.1	76.6	...	...	...	880
United Rep. of Tanzania	2000-2005	45.6	46.4	5.0	104.4	...	...	...	...
Rép.-Unie de Tanzanie	2005-2010	46.2	46.8	4.5	104.0	...	...	...	1 500
Western Sahara	2000-2005	62.2	65.7	3.9	53.3	...	...	...	...
Sahara occidental	2005-2010	64.2	68.0	3.4	44.5	...	...	...	850
Zambia	2000-2005	37.9	36.9	5.7	95.1	...	...	...	...
Zambie	2005-2010	39.6	38.6	5.2	88.4	...	...	...	750
Zimbabwe	2000-2005	37.5	36.9	3.6	62.3	...	...	...	...
Zimbabwe	2005-2010	38.2	36.3	3.2	58.8	...	...	...	1 100
America, North Amérique du Nord									
Bahamas	2000-2005	66.2	72.7	2.3	13.8	1994	1.4	0.9	...
Bahamas	2005-2010	69.0	75.3	2.2	11.4	2000	0.9	0.8	60

Country or area Pays ou zone	Year Année	Life expectancy at birth (years) Espérance de vie à la naissance (en années)		Total fertility rate Taux de fecondité	Mortality rates – Taux de mortalité					
					Infant Infantile (p. 1,000)	Child Juvenile (p. 1,000)			Maternal Maternale (p.100,000)
		Males Hommes	Females Femmes		M+F	Year Année	Males Hommes	Females Femmes	2000
Barbados	2000-2005	71.1	78.3	1.5	10.8	1987	0.8	0.2	...
Barbade	2005-2010	73.1	79.2	1.5	9.7	1988	0.5	0.5	95
Belize	2000-2005	69.5	74.5	3.2	30.5	1997[3]	6.7	6.0	...
Belize	2005-2010	69.5	74.1	2.8	28.6	1998[3]	4.8	5.3	140
Canada	2000-2005	77.3	82.4	1.5	5.1	2001[18,19,20]	0.3	0.2	...
Canada	2005-2010	78.2	83.1	1.5	4.8	2002[18,19,20]	0.2	0.2	6
Costa Rica	2000-2005	75.8	80.6	2.3	10.5	2002[3]	2.7	2.1	...
Costa Rica	2005-2010	76.5	81.2	2.1	9.9	2003	0.4	0.3	43
Cuba	2000-2005	75.3	79.1	1.6	6.1	2002	0.4	0.3	...
Cuba	2005-2010	76.8	80.3	1.6	4.9	2003[3]	1.6	1.5	33
Dominican Republic	2000-2005	63.7	70.9	2.7	34.6	...	...	...	...
Rép. dominicaine	2005-2010	65.4	72.3	2.6	29.6	...	...	...	150
El Salvador	2000-2005	67.7	73.7	2.9	26.4	2002	0.9	0.8	...
El Salvador	2005-2010	68.8	74.9	2.7	21.5	2003	0.8	0.7	150
Guadeloupe	2000-2005	74.9	81.7	2.1	7.3	1985[1,3,21]	4.8	4.2	...
Guadeloupe	2005-2010	75.9	82.4	2.0	6.7	2003[1,21]	0.3	0.3	5
Guatemala	2000-2005	63.4	70.8	4.6	38.9	1998	5.0	4.9	...
Guatemala	2005-2010	64.9	72.1	4.2	30.4	1999	3.6	3.5	240
Haiti	2000-2005	50.6	52.3	4.0	61.6	...	...	...	...
Haïti	2005-2010	52.9	54.0	3.6	56.6	...	...	...	680
Honduras	2000-2005	65.6	69.7	3.7	31.9	...	...	...	...
Honduras	2005-2010	67.2	71.4	3.3	28.4	1981	4.6	4.3	110
Jamaica	2000-2005	68.9	72.5	2.4	14.9	1989	1.4	1.1	...
Jamaïque	2005-2010	69.4	72.7	2.3	14.1	1991	1.3	1.0	87
Martinique	2000-2005	75.5	81.6	2.0	7.1	1992[1,3,21]	1.8	1.4	...
Martinique	2005-2010	76.2	82.3	1.9	6.7	2003[1,21]	0.3	0.5	4
Mexico	2000-2005	72.4	77.4	2.4	20.5	2000[10,22]	0.9	0.8	...
Mexique	2005-2010	73.7	78.6	2.2	16.7	2003[10,22]	0.9	0.8	83
Netherlands Antilles	2000-2005	72.9	79.1	2.1	13.2	1981[3,23,24]	6.5	5.9	...
Antilles néerlandaises	2005-2010	73.7	79.8	2.0	11.7	1992[23,24]	0.9	0.6	20
Nicaragua	2000-2005	67.2	71.9	3.3	30.1	2000[3]	3.5	2.7	...
Nicaragua	2005-2010	68.7	73.5	2.9	26.1	2003[3]	3.6	2.9	230
Panama	2000-2005	72.3	77.4	2.7	20.6	1998[25]	1.5	1.4	...
Panama	2005-2010	73.0	78.2	2.6	18.2	1999[3,25]	4.7	3.9	160
Puerto Rico	2000-2005	71.6	80.5	1.9	9.9	2002[22,26,27]	0.3	0.2	...
Porto Rico	2005-2010	72.6	81.1	1.9	9.1	2003[22,26,27]	0.2	0.2	25
Saint Lucia	2000-2005	70.8	73.9	2.2	14.9	2001	0.6	0.3	...
Sainte-Lucie	2005-2010	71.6	74.6	2.2	13.5	2002[3]	2.8	3.3	...
St. Vincent-Grenadines	2000-2005	68.2	73.8	2.3	25.6	1999	2.1	1.0	...
St. Vincent-Grenadines	2005-2010	69.3	74.8	2.2	22.3	2000	0.9	0.2	...
Trinidad and Tobago	2000-2005	66.9	73.0	1.6	13.7	1994	0.7	0.7	...
Trinité-et-Tobago	2005-2010	67.7	72.5	1.6	12.5	1995	0.7	0.6	160
United States	2000-2005	74.6	80.0	2.0	6.9	2002[18,28]	0.4	0.3	...
Etats-Unis	2005-2010	75.2	80.6	2.0	6.5	2003[18,28]	0.3	0.3	17
United States Virgin Is.	2000-2005	74.6	82.6	2.2	9.5	...	...	...	...
Iles Vierges américaines	2005-2010	75.4	83.2	2.1	8.6	1990[27]	1.1	...	...
America, South **Amérique du Sud**									
Argentina	2000-2005	70.6	78.1	2.4	15.0	2001[29]	0.7	0.6	...
Argentine	2005-2010	71.6	79.1	2.3	13.4	2003[29]	0.7	0.6	82
Bolivia	2000-2005	61.8	66.0	4.0	55.6	...	...	...	...
Bolivie	2005-2010	63.4	67.7	3.5	45.6	1991[3,18]	40.2	34.0	420
Brazil	2000-2005	66.4	74.4	2.4	27.4	2002[30,31]	0.7	0.6	...
Brésil	2005-2010	68.2	75.7	2.3	23.6	2003[30,31]	0.7	0.6	260
Chile	2000-2005	74.8	80.8	2.0	8.0	2002	0.4	0.4	...
Chili	2005-2010	75.5	81.5	1.9	7.2	2003	0.4	0.4	31
Colombia	2000-2005	69.2	75.3	2.6	25.6	2002[10]	0.8	0.7	...
Colombie	2005-2010	70.3	76.3	2.5	22.0	2003[3,10]	3.4	2.8	130
Ecuador	2000-2005	71.3	77.2	2.8	24.9	2002[34]	1.8	1.7	...
Equateur	2005-2010	72.1	78.0	2.6	21.1	2003[34]	1.7	1.4	130

Country or area Pays ou zone	Year Année	Life expectancy at birth (years) Espérance de vie à la naissance (en années) Males Hommes	Females Femmes	Total fertility rate Taux de fecondité	Mortality rates – Taux de mortalité Infant Infantile (p. 1,000) M+F	Child Juvenile (p. 1,000) Year Année	Males Hommes	Females Femmes	Maternal Maternale (p.100,000) 2000
French Guiana	2000-2005	72.5	78.4	3.4	14.1	...	...	...	...
Guyane française	2005-2010	73.4	79.2	3.0	12.5	2003[1]	1.0	0.8	...
Guyana	2000-2005	59.8	65.9	2.3	49.1	...	...	...	...
Guyana	2005-2010	62.3	68.4	2.1	43.2	...	...	...	170
Paraguay	2000-2005	68.6	73.1	3.9	37.0	1985[3,10]	5.4	4.8	...
Paraguay	2005-2010	69.7	74.2	3.5	34.0	1992[10]	0.7	0.6	170
Peru	2000-2005	67.3	72.4	2.9	33.4	1984[30]	4.7	4.6	...
Pérou	2005-2010	68.7	73.9	2.7	28.7	1985[3,30]	10.8	9.9	410
Suriname	2000-2005	65.8	72.5	2.6	25.6	1995[3,36]	6.2	4.7	...
Suriname	2005-2010	67.1	73.3	2.5	22.4	2000[3,36]	4.2	4.5	110
Uruguay	2000-2005	71.6	78.9	2.3	13.1	2001[10,26]	0.6	0.6	...
Uruguay	2005-2010	72.7	79.8	2.2	12.0	2002[10,26]	0.6	0.3	27
Venezuela (Bolivarian Rep. of)	2000-2005	69.9	75.8	2.7	17.5	2001[30,37]	1.2	1.1	...
Venezuela (Rép. bolivar. du)	2005-2010	70.9	76.8	2.6	15.8	2002[30,37]	0.9	0.8	96
Asia **Asie**									
Afghanistan	2000-2005	45.8	46.3	7.5	149.0	...	...	...	...
Afghanistan	2005-2010	47.4	47.9	7.1	141.9	...	...	...	1 900
Armenia	2000-2005	67.9	74.6	1.3	30.2	2001[38]	0.6	0.5	...
Arménie	2005-2010	68.4	75.1	1.4	28.9	2003[38]	0.4	0.4	55
Azerbaijan	2000-2005	63.2	70.5	1.9	75.5	2002[38]	2.5	2.4	...
Azerbaïdjan	2005-2010	63.8	71.2	1.9	72.2	2003[38]	1.8	1.8	94
Bahrain	2000-2005	72.9	75.8	2.5	13.8	2001[3,18]	3.2	2.2	...
Bahreïn	2005-2010	73.9	76.7	2.3	12.2	2002[3,18]	2.0	1.9	28
Bangladesh	2000-2005	61.8	63.4	3.3	58.8	1981[39]	14.1	15.8	...
Bangladesh	2005-2010	63.8	65.8	3.0	49.5	1986[3,39]	43.1	41.1	380
Bhutan	2000-2005	61.5	63.9	4.4	55.7	...	...	...	...
Bhoutan	2005-2010	63.6	66.1	3.8	47.8	...	...	...	420
Brunei Darussalam	2000-2005	74.2	78.9	2.5	6.1	1991[3,40]	3.0	2.6	...
Brunéi Darussalam	2005-2010	75.0	79.7	2.3	5.5	1992[3,40]	2.9	2.0	37
Cambodia	2000-2005	52.1	59.6	4.1	94.8	...	...	...	...
Cambodge	2005-2010	54.6	61.3	3.7	87.3	...	...	...	450
China	2000-2005	69.8[41]	73.3[41]	1.7[41]	34.7[41]	...	...	...	...
Chine	2005-2010	70.8[41]	74.6[41]	1.7[41]	30.7[41]	1999[3,18,43]	6.1[42]	7.3[42]	56[41]
China, Hong Kong SAR	2000-2005	78.6	84.6	0.9	3.8	2002[10,26]	0.2	0.2	...
Chine, Hong Kong RAS	2005-2010	79.3	85.1	1.0	3.7	2003[10,26]	0.2	0.2	...
China, Macao SAR	2000-2005	77.8	82.0	0.8	7.7	2002[3]	0.7	0.6	...
Chine, Macao RAS	2005-2010	78.6	82.7	0.9	7.1	2003[3]	0.2	0.3	...
Cyprus	2000-2005	76.0	81.0	1.6	6.2	2002[44,45]	0.4	0.7	...
Chypre	2005-2010	76.7	81.6	1.6	5.8	2003[44,45]	0.1	0.4	47
Georgia	2000-2005	66.5	74.3	1.5	40.5	2000[38]	0.4	0.3	...
Géorgie	2005-2010	67.1	74.8	1.4	38.7	2003[38]	0.8	0.6	32
India	2000-2005	61.7	64.7	3.1	67.6	...	...	...	...
Inde	2005-2010	63.2	66.7	2.8	59.7	...	...	...	540
Indonesia	2000-2005	64.6	68.6	2.4	42.7	...	...	...	...
Indonésie	2005-2010	67.0	70.5	2.2	33.7	...	...	...	230
Iran (Islamic Rep. of)	2000-2005	68.8	71.7	2.1	33.7	1986	3.9	1.4	...
Iran (Rép. islamique d')	2005-2010	70.1	73.4	2.0	27.5	1991	5.1	3.9	76
Iraq	2000-2005	57.3	60.4	4.8	94.3	1987	1.4	1.1	...
Iraq	2005-2010	59.5	62.5	4.2	81.5	1988[3]	5.7	4.4	250
Israel	2000-2005	77.5	81.6	2.9	5.1	2002[10,18,22,46]	0.3	0.3	...
Israël	2005-2010	78.4	82.6	2.7	4.8	2003[10,18,22,46]	0.4	0.3	17
Japan	2000-2005	78.3	85.3	1.3	3.2	2002[26,47,48]	0.3	0.2	...
Japon	2005-2010	79.1	86.4	1.4	3.1	2003[26,47,48]	0.3	0.2	10
Jordan	2000-2005	69.8	72.8	3.5	23.3	...	...	...	...
Jordanie	2005-2010	71.0	74.2	3.1	19.6	...	...	...	41
Kazakhstan	2000-2005	57.8	68.9	2.0	61.2	1999[38]	1.7	1.5	...
Kazakhstan	2005-2010	58.7	69.8	1.9	58.6	2003[38]	1.3	1.1	210
Korea, Dem. P. R.	2000-2005	60.1	66.1	2.0	45.7	...	...	...	...
Corée, R. p. dém. de	2005-2010	61.7	67.5	1.9	41.2	1993[3]	5.6	5.1	67

Selected indicators of life expectancy, childbearing and mortality (*continued*)
Choix d'indicateurs de l'espérance de vie, de la maternité et de la mortalité (*suite*)

Country or area	Year	Life expectancy at birth (years) Espérance de vie à la naissance (en années)		Total fertility rate	Mortality rates – Taux de mortalité				Maternal Maternale (p.100,000)
					Infant Infantile (p. 1,000)	Child Juvenile (p. 1,000)			
Pays ou zone	Année	Males Hommes	Females Femmes	Taux de fecondité	M+F	Year Année	Males Hommes	Females Femmes	2000
Korea, Republic of	2000-2005	73.2	80.5	1.2	3.8	2001 [49,50,51]	0.4	0.4	
Corée, République de	2005-2010	74.5	81.9	1.2	3.6	2002 [49,50,51]	0.5	0.4	20
Kuwait	2000-2005	75.1	79.4	2.4	10.3	1996 [3]	3.4	3.1	...
Koweït	2005-2010	75.8	80.2	2.3	9.6	1998	0.6	0.5	5
Kyrgyzstan	2000-2005	62.6	71.1	2.7	55.1	2002 [38,52]	2.0	1.9	...
Kirghizistan	2005-2010	63.6	71.9	2.5	51.7	2003 [38,52]	1.8	1.7	110
Lao People's Dem. Rep.	2000-2005	53.3	55.8	4.8	88.0	...	...	...	...
Rép. dém. pop. lao	2005-2010	55.3	57.8	4.3	79.6	...	...	...	650
Lebanon	2000-2005	69.7	74.0	2.3	22.5	...	...	...	...
Liban	2005-2010	70.9	75.3	2.2	18.9	...	...	...	150
Malaysia	2000-2005	70.8	75.5	2.9	10.1	1998 [53,54]	0.7	0.7	...
Malaisie	2005-2010	71.9	76.5	2.6	9.0	2000 [3,53,54]	2.0	1.7	41
Maldives	2000-2005	66.9	65.8	4.3	42.6	2002 [3,55]	3.9	4.0	...
Maldives	2005-2010	68.6	68.4	3.8	34.1	2003 [55]	1.5	0.4	110
Mongolia	2000-2005	61.9	65.9	2.5	58.2	2001	3.2	2.6	...
Mongolie	2005-2010	63.9	67.9	2.2	51.0	2003	2.1	1.6	110
Myanmar	2000-2005	57.4	62.9	2.5	74.7	...	...	...	...
Myanmar	2005-2010	58.9	64.8	2.1	66.4	...	...	...	360
Nepal	2000-2005	60.9	61.7	3.7	64.4	...	...	...	...
Népal	2005-2010	63.0	64.1	3.3	54.6	2001 [56]	4.9	3.8	740
Occupied Palestinian Terr.	2000-2005	70.8	73.9	5.6	20.9	2002 [57,58]	0.7	0.6	...
Terr. palestinien occupé	2005-2010	71.8	75.0	5.0	17.5	2003 [57,58]	0.8	0.7	100
Oman	2000-2005	72.7	75.6	3.8	15.6	...	...	...	...
Oman	2005-2010	73.7	76.8	3.2	13.4	...	...	...	87
Pakistan	2000-2005	62.7	63.1	4.3	78.6	...	...	...	...
Pakistan	2005-2010	64.6	64.9	3.7	70.5	1995 [3,59,60,61,62]	25.7	24.3	500
Philippines	2000-2005	68.1	72.4	3.2	28.1	2001 [3]	4.4	3.4	...
Philippines	2005-2010	69.5	73.8	2.8	23.3	2002 [3]	4.1	3.1	200
Qatar	2000-2005	71.1	75.9	3.0	11.6	1986	1.1	0.8	...
Qatar	2005-2010	72.2	77.1	2.8	10.2	1997	0.9	0.3	7
Saudi Arabia	2000-2005	69.9	73.8	4.1	22.5	...	...	...	...
Arabie saoudite	2005-2010	71.1	75.1	3.6	18.6	2000	0.4	1.1	23
Singapore	2000-2005	76.7	80.5	1.4	3.0	2003 [3,10,18,64]	0.8	0.6	...
Singapour	2005-2010	77.6	81.3	1.3	3.0	2004 [3,10,18,64]	0.7	0.6	30
Sri Lanka	2000-2005	71.3	76.7	2.0	17.2	1995 [3]	3.2	2.8	...
Sri Lanka	2005-2010	72.6	77.9	1.9	14.3	1996 [3]	3.4	2.8	92
Syrian Arab Republic	2000-2005	71.4	74.9	3.5	18.2	...	...	...	...
Rép. arabe syrienne	2005-2010	72.5	76.2	3.1	15.6	1984 [65]	2.8	2.9	160
Tajikistan	2000-2005	61.0	66.3	3.8	89.2	1991 [38]	5.1	4.8	...
Tadjikistan	2005-2010	61.7	67.1	3.4	85.2	1993 [38]	9.0	8.5	100
Thailand	2000-2005	66.0	73.7	1.9	19.6	1998 [3,66]	2.8	2.9	...
Thaïlande	2005-2010	68.5	75.0	1.9	17.2	1999 [3,66]	2.2	1.9	44
Timor-Leste	2000-2005	54.1	56.3	7.8	93.7	...	...	...	...
Timor-Leste	2005-2010	56.6	58.9	7.2	81.1	...	...	...	660
Turkey	2000-2005	66.3	70.9	2.5	41.6	...	...	...	...
Turquie	2005-2010	67.5	72.1	2.3	36.2	...	...	...	70
Turkmenistan	2000-2005	58.2	66.7	2.8	78.3	...	...	...	...
Turkménistan	2005-2010	59.0	67.5	2.5	74.7	...	...	...	31
United Arab Emirates	2000-2005	76.3	80.6	2.5	8.9	...	...	...	...
Emirats arabes unis	2005-2010	77.4	82.2	2.4	7.8	...	...	...	54
Uzbekistan	2000-2005	63.3	69.7	2.7	58.0	1999 [38]	3.6	3.2	...
Ouzbékistan	2005-2010	64.0	70.4	2.5	55.2	2000 [38]	2.4	2.2	24
Viet Nam	2000-2005	68.4	72.4	2.3	29.9	...	...	...	...
Viet Nam	2005-2010	69.9	73.9	2.1	25.5	...	...	...	130
Yemen	2000-2005	59.1	61.7	6.2	69.0	...	...	...	...
Yémen	2005-2010	61.3	64.1	5.7	58.7	...	...	...	570
Europe **Europe**									
Albania	2000-2005	70.9	76.7	2.3	25.0	2003 [3]	2.7	2.6	...
Albanie	2005-2010	71.7	77.4	2.2	22.4	2004	1.2	1.1	55

Country or area / Pays ou zone	Year / Année	Life expectancy at birth (years) Espérance de vie à la naissance (en années) Males Hommes	Females Femmes	Total fertility rate Taux de fecondité	Mortality rates – Taux de mortalité Infant Infantile (p. 1,000) M+F	Child Juvenile (p. 1,000) Year Année	Males Hommes	Females Femmes	Maternal Maternale (p.100,000) 2000
Austria Autriche	2000-2005	75.9	81.7	1.4	4.6	2002	0.2	0.2	...
	2005-2010	76.9	82.4	1.4	4.4	2003	0.3	0.3	4
Belarus Bélarus	2000-2005	62.4	74.0	1.2	14.9	2002[38]	0.9	0.6	...
	2005-2010	63.1	74.5	1.2	14.2	2003[38]	0.6	0.5	35
Belgium Belgique	2000-2005	75.7	81.9	1.7	4.2	2001[3,67]	1.3	1.0	...
	2005-2010	76.5	82.7	1.7	4.1	2002[3,67]	1.2	0.9	10
Bosnia and Herzegovina Bosnie-Herzégovine	2000-2005	71.3	76.7	1.3	13.5	...	...	...	...
	2005-2010	72.1	77.5	1.3	12.1	...	...	...	31
Bulgaria Bulgarie	2000-2005	68.8	75.6	1.2	13.2	2002	0.8	0.6	...
	2005-2010	69.8	76.3	1.2	12.0	2003	0.6	0.6	32
Channel Islands Iles Anglo-Normandes	2000-2005	75.9	80.8	1.4	5.5	...	...	...	...
	2005-2010	76.6	81.5	1.4	5.2	...	...	...	...
Croatia Croatie	2000-2005	71.3	78.4	1.4	6.9	2002	0.3	0.2	...
	2005-2010	72.3	79.2	1.4	6.4	2003	0.3	0.2	8
Czech Republic République tchèque	2000-2005	72.2	78.7	1.2	5.6	2002	0.3	0.2	...
	2005-2010	73.1	79.4	1.2	5.2	2003	0.1	0.1	9
Denmark Danemark	2000-2005	74.8	79.4	1.8	4.8	2002[68]	0.2	0.3	...
	2005-2010	75.5	80.1	1.8	4.7	2003[68]	0.3	0.2	5
Estonia Estonie	2000-2005	65.4	76.9	1.4	9.8	2001[3,38]	2.4	2.1	...
	2005-2010	67.0	78.0	1.4	8.8	2002[38]	0.7	0.3	63
Finland Finlande	2000-2005	75.0	81.7	1.7	3.9	2002[18,69]	0.2	0.1	...
	2005-2010	76.0	82.4	1.7	3.7	2003[18,69]	0.3	0.1	6
France France	2000-2005	75.8	83.0	1.9	4.5	2002[22,70,71]	0.3	0.2	...
	2005-2010	76.6	83.5	1.9	4.3	2003[22,70,71]	0.3	0.2	17
Germany Allemagne	2000-2005	75.6	81.4	1.3	4.5	2002[3,72]	1.0	0.9	...
	2005-2010	76.4	82.1	1.3	4.3	2003[72]	0.2	0.2	8
Greece Grèce	2000-2005	75.6	80.8	1.3	6.5	2002[3,18,73]	1.4	1.0	...
	2005-2010	76.1	81.3	1.3	6.2	2003[18,73]	0.2	0.2	9
Hungary Hongrie	2000-2005	68.4	76.7	1.3	8.3	2002	0.4	0.3	...
	2005-2010	69.8	77.7	1.3	7.6	2003	0.3	0.3	16
Iceland Islande	2000-2005	78.7	82.5	2.0	3.2	2002[3]	1.0	0.7	...
	2005-2010	79.5	83.2	1.9	3.1	2003	...	0.2	0
Ireland Irlande	2000-2005	75.1	80.3	1.9	5.5	2002[18,74]	0.3	0.3	...
	2005-2010	75.9	81.1	2.0	5.1	2003[18,74]	0.2	0.2	5
Italy Italie	2000-2005	76.8	83.0	1.3	5.2	2001	0.2	0.2	...
	2005-2010	77.5	83.6	1.4	5.0	2002	0.2	0.2	5
Latvia Lettonie	2000-2005	65.6	76.9	1.3	10.2	2001[38]	0.8	0.5	...
	2005-2010	67.2	77.8	1.3	9.4	2002[38]	0.8	0.6	42
Lithuania Lituanie	2000-2005	66.5	77.8	1.3	9.1	2002[38]	0.7	0.4	...
	2005-2010	67.9	78.6	1.3	8.4	2003[38]	0.5	0.4	13
Luxembourg Luxembourg	2000-2005	75.1	81.4	1.7	5.4	2002	0.6	0.2	...
	2005-2010	75.9	82.2	1.7	5.0	2003	0.2	0.1	28
Malta Malte	2000-2005	75.8	80.7	1.5	7.1	2002[75]	0.6	...	...
	2005-2010	76.6	81.3	1.5	6.7	2003[75]	0.1	0.1	21
Netherlands Pays-Bas	2000-2005	75.6	81.0	1.7	4.5	2002[76,77,78]	0.4	0.3	...
	2005-2010	76.3	81.6	1.7	4.4	2003[76,77,78]	0.2	0.2	16
Norway Norvège	2000-2005	76.7	81.8	1.8	3.8	2002[79]	0.3	0.3	...
	2005-2010	77.8	82.5	1.8	3.3	2003[79]	0.2	0.3	16
Poland Pologne	2000-2005	70.2	78.4	1.3	8.8	2002[3,80]	1.8	1.5	...
	2005-2010	71.2	79.0	1.2	8.1	2003[80]	0.3	0.2	13
Portugal Portugal	2000-2005	73.8	80.5	1.5	5.6	2002[22,81]	0.4	0.3	...
	2005-2010	74.6	81.2	1.5	5.2	2003[22,81]	0.3	0.3	5
Republic of Moldova République de Moldova	2000-2005	63.7	71.1	1.2	25.8	2002[38,82]	0.8	0.7	...
	2005-2010	66.0	73.1	1.2	22.6	2003[38,82]	0.9	0.8	36
Romania Roumanie	2000-2005	67.7	75.0	1.3	18.1	2002	0.9	0.7	...
	2005-2010	68.7	75.7	1.3	16.5	2003	0.8	0.6	49
Russian Federation Fédération de Russie	2000-2005	59.1	72.2	1.3	16.9	2001[3,38]	5.5	4.0	...
	2005-2010	58.7	71.8	1.4	15.9	2004[38]	0.8	0.7	67

		Life expectancy at birth (years) Espérance de vie à la naissance (en années)		Total fertility rate	Mortality rates – Taux de mortalité				
					Infant Infantile (p. 1,000)	Child Juvenile (p. 1,000)			Maternal Maternale (p.100,000)
Country or area Pays ou zone	Year Année	Males Hommes	Females Femmes	Taux de fecondité	M+F	Year Année	Males Hommes	Females Femmes	2000
Serbia and Montenegro Serbie-et-Monténégro	2000-2005	70.9	75.6	1.7	13.0	2001 [3]	3.6	2.6	...
	2005-2010	71.7	76.4	1.6	11.7	2002 [84]	0.4	0.4	11
Slovakia Slovaquie	2000-2005	70.0	77.9	1.2	7.8	2001 [85]	0.5	0.3	...
	2005-2010	71.1	78.7	1.2	7.2	2002 [85]	0.3	0.3	3
Slovenia Slovénie	2000-2005	72.6	79.9	1.2	5.5	2002	0.3	0.2	...
	2005-2010	73.5	80.7	1.2	5.1	2003	0.3	0.1	17
Spain Espagne	2000-2005	75.8	83.1	1.3	4.6	2001 [3]	1.2	1.0	...
	2005-2010	76.5	83.8	1.4	4.4	2002 [3]	1.2	1.0	4
Sweden Suède	2000-2005	77.8	82.3	1.6	3.3	2001 [3]	1.0	0.8	...
	2005-2010	78.6	83.0	1.7	3.2	2002	0.2	0.1	2
Switzerland Suisse	2000-2005	77.6	83.1	1.4	4.4	2001 [3]	1.3	1.0	...
	2005-2010	78.2	83.8	1.4	4.3	2002	0.3	0.3	7
TFYR of Macedonia L'ex-R.y. Macédoine	2000-2005	71.2	76.2	1.5	16.0	2002	0.4	0.5	...
	2005-2010	72.0	77.0	1.5	14.3	2003	0.5	0.4	23
Ukraine Ukraine	2000-2005	60.1	72.5	1.1	15.6	2001 [38]	1.0	0.7	...
	2005-2010	60.7	72.5	1.2	14.5	2003 [38]	0.9	0.7	35
United Kingdom Royaume-Uni	2000-2005	75.9	80.6	1.7	5.3	2001 [3,18,86,87]	1.3	1.1	...
	2005-2010	76.7	81.2	1.7	5.0	2003 [18,86,87]	0.3	0.2	13
Oceania Océanie									
Australia Australie	2000-2005	77.6 [88]	82.8 [88]	1.8 [88]	4.9 [88]	2002	0.3	0.2	...
	2005-2010	78.5 [88]	83.4 [88]	1.8 [88]	4.6 [88]	2003	0.2	0.2	8
Fiji Fidji	2000-2005	65.7	70.0	2.9	21.8	1985	1.8	1.2	...
	2005-2010	66.5	71.0	2.7	19.7	1986	1.2	1.3	75
French Polynesia Polynésie française	2000-2005	70.6	75.8	2.4	8.8	...	...	...	...
	2005-2010	71.7	76.8	2.3	8.0	...	...	...	20
Guam Guam	2000-2005	72.4	77.0	3.0	9.8	...	...	...	...
	2005-2010	73.3	77.9	2.7	8.8	1980 [22,27,91]	0.4	0.6	12
Micronesia (Fed. States of) Micronésie (Etats féd. de)	2000-2005	66.9	68.2	4.4	38.0	...	...	...	...
	2005-2010	67.7	69.2	4.2	34.3	...	...	...	...
New Caledonia Nouvelle-Calédonie	2000-2005	72.6	77.8	2.4	6.6	1994 [92]	1.3	1.4	...
	2005-2010	73.6	78.8	2.3	6.0	2003 [92]	1.0	0.1	10
New Zealand Nouvelle-Zélande	2000-2005	76.7	81.3	2.0	5.4	2003 [93]	0.3	0.4	...
	2005-2010	77.7	82.0	2.0	5.0	2004 [93]	0.3	0.2	7
Papua New Guinea Papouasie-Nvl-Guinée	2000-2005	54.7	55.8	4.1	70.6	...	...	...	...
	2005-2010	56.6	57.8	3.6	63.8	...	...	...	300
Samoa Samoa	2000-2005	67.1	73.5	4.4	25.7	...	...	...	...
	2005-2010	68.5	74.9	3.9	22.3	...	...	...	130
Solomon Islands Iles Salomon	2000-2005	61.6	62.9	4.3	34.3	...	...	...	...
	2005-2010	62.6	64.3	3.8	31.4	...	...	...	130
Tonga Tonga	2000-2005	70.9	73.4	3.5	21.0	1998 [3]	3.2	1.1	...
	2005-2010	71.7	74.4	3.2	19.1	1999 [3]	4.1	3.1	...
Vanuatu Vanuatu	2000-2005	66.8	70.4	4.2	34.3	...	...	...	...
	2005-2010	68.3	72.1	3.7	28.3	...	...	...	130

Source

United Nations, "World Population Prospects: The 2004 Revision" and "Demographic Yearbook, 2003"; World Health Organization, the United Nations Children's Fund and the United Nations Population Fund, "Maternal Mortality in 2000: Estimates developed by WHO, UNICEF, UNFPA".

Notes

[1] Excluding live-born infants who died before their birth was registered.

[2] For Algerian population only.

Source

Organisation des Nations Unies, "World Population Prospects: The 2004 Revision" et "Annuair démographique 2003"; Organisation mondiale de la santé, Fonds des Nations Unies pour l'enfance et Fonds des Nations Unies pour la population, "Maternal Mortality in 2000 : Estimates developed by WHO, UNICEF, UNFPA".

Notes

[1] Non compris les enfants nés vivants décédés avant l'enregistrement de leur naissance.

[2] Pour la population algérienne seulement.

[3] 0-4 years old.
[4] For 2001, data refer to last twelve months preceding census on August 2001.
[5] Based on the results of the population census.
[6] For 1993, data refer to last twelve months preceding census on August 1993.
[7] Including Agalega, Rodrigues and Saint Brandon.
[8] Data refer to last twelve months preceding census of 1997.
[9] Data exclude adjustment for underenumeration, estimated at 3.8 per cent.
[10] Data for males/females, excluding deaths of unknown sex.

[11] Deaths for 2001 refer to the period January-August 2001.

[12] Domicile population only.
[13] Excluding the former independent states (Transkei, Bophuthatswana, Venda and Ciskei).
[14] Data have been adjusted for underenumeration estimated at 6.8 per cent.

[15] Data refer to estimated population after considering HIV.

[16] For 1993, data refer to last twelve months preceding census on April 1993.
[17] Excluding the institutional population.
[18] Because of rounding, totals are not in all cases the sum of the parts.

[19] Including Canadian residents temporarily in the United States, but excluding United States residents temporarily in Canada.

[20] Excluding Newfoundland.
[21] Age classification based on year of birth rather than on completed years of age.
[22] Including unknown residence.
[23] Including residents outside the islands if one or both parents are listed in the population register of Netherlands Antilles. Except for Curaçao since 1957, excluding live-born infants dying before registration of birth. Beginning 1970, for Aruba, Bonaire and Curaçao only, and beginning 1974, excluding Aruba.

[24] Census results exclude adjustment for underenumeration.

[25] Excluding the former Canal Zone, shown separately hereunder.

[26] Including unknown sex.
[27] Including armed forces stationed in the area.
[28] De jure population, but excluding civilian citizens absent from country for extended period of time. Excluding armed forces overseas.
[29] Because of rounding, totals are not in all cases the sum of the parts. Data exclude adjustment for underenumeration, estimated at one per cent. Data for male and female categories exclude deaths of unknown sex.

[30] Excluding Indian jungle population.
[31] Data include persons in remote areas, military personel outside the country, merchant seamen at sea, civilian seasonal workers outside the country, and other civilians outside the country, and exclude nomads, foreign military, civilian aliens temporarily in the country, transients on ships and Indian jungle population.
[32] Data exclude adjustment for underenumeration, estimated at 5.6 per cent.
[33] Data exclude adjustment for underenumeration, estimated at 6.92 per cent.
[34] Excluding nomadic Indian tribes.
[35] Mid-year estimates have been adjusted for underenumeration, at latest census.

[3] De 0 à 4 ans.
[4] Pour 2001, les données se rapportent pour la dernière fois à douze mois précédant le recensement août 2001.
[5] D'après les résultats du recensement de la population.
[6] Pour 1993, les données se rapportent pour la dernière fois à douze mois précédant le recensement août 1993.
[7] Y compris Agalega, Rodrigues et Saint Brandon.
[8] Les données se réfèrent aux 12 mois précédant le recensement de 1997.
[9] Les données n'ont pas été ajustées pour compenser les lacunes du dénombrement, estimées à 3,8 p. 100.
[10] Les données pour le sexe masculin et féminin, non compris les décès dont on ignore le sexe.
[11] Le chiffer des décès de 2001 correspond à la période allant de janvier à août 2001.
[12] Pour la population dans les domiciles seulement.
[13] Non compris les anciens états indépendants (Transkei, Bophuthatswana, Venda et Ciskei).
[14] Les données ont été ajustées pour compenser les lacunes du dénombrement estimées à 6,8 p. 100.
[15] Les données portent sur la population estimée après prise en compte du VIH.
[16] Pour 1993, les données se rapportent pour la dernière fois à douze mois précédant le recensement août 1993.
[17] Non compris la population dans les institutions.
[18] Les chiffres étant arrondis, les totaux ne correspondent pas toujours rigoureusement à la somme des chiffres partiels.
[19] Y compris les résidents canadiens se trouvant temporairement aux Etats-Unis, mais ne comprennent pas les résidents des Etats-Unis se trouvant temporairement au Canada.
[20] Non compris Terre-Neuve.
[21] La classification par âge est fondée sur l'année de naissance et non sur l'âge en années révolues.
[22] Y compris la résidence inconnue.
[23] Y compris les naissances survenues parmi les résidents hors des îles si l'un des parents au moins est inscrit sur le registre de population des Antilles néerlandaises. Sauf pour Curaçao à partir de 1957, non compris les enfants nés vivants décédés avant l'enregistrement de leurs naissances. A partir de 1970, pour Aruba, Bonaire et Curaçao seulement, et à partir de 1974, non compris Aruba.
[24] Les résultats des recensements n'ont pas été ajustées pour compenser les lacunes du dénombrement.
[25] Non compris l'ancienne Zone du Canal, qui fait l'objet d'une rubrique distincte, ci-dessous.
[26] Y compris le sexe inconnu.
[27] Y compris les militaires en garnison sur le territoire.
[28] Population de droit, mais non compris les civils hors du pays pendant une période prolongée. Non compris les militaires à l'étranger.
[29] Les chiffres étant arrondis, les totaux ne correspondent pas toujours rigoureusement à la somme des chiffres partiels. Les données n'ont pas été ajustées pour compenser les lacunes du dénombrement, estimées à 1 p. 100. Les données pour le sexe masculin et féminin ne comprennent pas les décès ou on ignore le sexe.
[30] Non compris les Indiens de la jungle.
[31] Y compris les personnes dans des régions éloignées, le personel militaire en dehors du pays, les marins marchands, les ouvriers saisonniers civils de couture en dehors du pays, et autres civils en dehors du pays, et non compris les nomades, les militaires étrangers, les étrangers civils temporairement dans le pays, les transiteurs sur des bateaux et les Indiens de la jungle.
[32] Les données n'ont pas été ajustées pour compenser les lacunes du dénombrement, estimées à 5,6 p. 100.
[33] Les données n'ont pas été ajustées pour compenser les lacunes du dénombrement, estimées à 6,92 p. 100.
[34] Non compris les tribus d'Indiens nomades.
[35] Les estimations au millieu de l'année tiennent compte d'une ajustement destiné à compenser les lacunes du dénombrement lors du dernierrecensement.

12

Selected indicators of life expectancy, childbearing and mortality *(continued)*
Choix d'indicateurs de l'espérance de vie, de la maternité et de la mortalité *(suite)*

[36] Figures based on census 2003 quick count and expanded post enumeration survey (PES) to census 2003. Totals do not add up to the sum because total population include, institutional population (i.e. population in institutions such as orphanage and old people's homes and special groups (e.g. vagrants, persons on ships in the harbour and diplomats) totaling 4968 (Male 2657 Female 2294 and 17 diplomats).

[37] Based on 4 per cent sample returns.

[38] Excluding infants born alive after less than 28 weeks' gestation, of less than 1 000 grams in weight and 35 centimeters in length, who die within seven days of birth.

[39] Data exclude adjustment for underenumeration, estimated at 3.1 per cent.

[40] Data exclude adjustment for underenumeration, estimated at 1.06 per cent.

[41] For statistical purposes, the data for China do not include those for the Hong Kong Special Administrative Region (Hong Kong SAR) and Macao Special Administrative Region (Macao SAR).

[42] For statistical purposes, the data for China do not include those for the Hong Kong Special Administrative Region (Hong Kong SAR), Macao Special Administrative Region (Macao SAR) and Taiwan Province of China.

[43] Covering only the civilian population of 30 provinces, municipalities and autonomous regions. Excluding Jimmen and Mazhu Islands.

[44] Including estimates of Turkish Cypriots in the occupied area.

[45] Data refer to government controlled areas.

[46] Including data for East Jerusalem and Israeli residents in certain other territories under occupation by Israeli military forces since June 1967.

[47] For Japanese nationals in Japan only.

[48] Excluding diplomatic personnel outside the country and foreign military and civilian personnel and their dependants stationed in the area.

[49] Excluding alien armed forces, civilian aliens employed by armed forces, foreign diplomatic personnel and their dependants and Korean diplomatic personnel and their dependants outside the country.

[50] Based on the results of the Continuous Demographic Sample Survey.

[51] Excluding foreigners.

[52] Data refer to constant population as reported by national statistical authorities, meaning that it does not include migrant population.

[53] Excluding Malaysian citizens and permanent residents who were away or intended to be away from the country for more than six months. Excluding Malaysian military, naval and diplomatic personnel and their families outside the country, and tourists, businessman who intended to be in Malaysia for less than six months.

[54] Census results have been adjusted for underenumeration.

[55] Reason for discrepancy between these figures and corresponding figures shown elsewhere not ascertained.

[56] For 2001, data refer to last twelve months preceding census on June 2001.

[57] Data exclude adjustment for underenumeration, estimated at 2.4 per cent.

[58] The figures were received from the Palestinian Authority and refer to the Palestinian population.

[59] Based on the results of the Population Growth Survey.

[60] Excluding data for the Pakistan-held part of Jammu and Kashmir, the final status of which has not yet been determined.

[61] Excluding the Federal Administrative tribal areas.

[62] Data based on Population Demographic Survey. These estimates do not reflect completely accurately the actual population and vital events of the country.

[63] Excluding transients afloat and military and civilian services personnel and their dependants abroad.

[36] Les chiffres sont fondés sur le dénombrement rapide de 2003 et l'enquête postérieure au dénombrement. Les totaux ne correspondent pas à la population totale parce qu'il est tenu compte dans celle-ci de la population vivant en institutions (orphelinats, hospices) et de groupes spéciaux (vagabonds, personnes à bord de navires ancrés dans les ports et diplomates), soit 4 968 personnes (2 657 hommes et 2 294 femmes; 17 diplomates).

[37] D'après un échantillon de 4 p. 100 des bulletins de recensements.

[38] Non compris les enfants nés vivants après moins de 28 semaines de gestation, pesant moins de 1 000 grammes, mesurant moins de 35 centimètres et décédés dans les sept jours qui ont suivi leur naissance.

[39] Les données n'ont pas été ajustées pour compenser les lacunes du dénombrement, estimées à 3,1 p. 100.

[40] Les données n'ont pas été ajustées pour compenser les lacunes du dénombrement, estimées à 1,06 p. 100.

[41] Pour la présentation des statistiques, les données pour Chine ne comprennent pas la Région Administrative Spéciale de Hong Kong (Hong Kong RAS) et la Région Administrative Spéciale de Macao (Macao RAS).

[42] Pour la présentation des statistiques, les données pour Chine ne comprennent pas la Région Administrative Spéciale de Hong Kong (Hong Kong RAS), la Région Administrative Spéciale de Macao (Macao RAS) et la province de Taiwan.

[43] Pour la population civile seulement de 30 provinces, municipalités et régions autonomes. Non compris les Iles Jimmen et Mazhu.

[44] Y compris des évaluations des Chypriotes turcs dans le secteur occupé.

[45] Les données se rapportent aux zones contrôlées par le Gouvernement.

[46] Y compris les données pour Jérusalem-Est et les résidents israéliens dans certains autres territoires occupés depuis 1967 par les forces armées israéliennes.

[47] Pour les nationaux japonais au Japon seulement.

[48] Non compris le personnel diplomatique hors du pays ni les militaires et agents civils étrangers en poste sur le territoire et les membres de leur famille les accompagnant.

[49] Non compris les militaires étrangers, les civils étrangers employés par les forces armées, le personnel diplomatique étranger et les membres de leur famille les accompagnant et le personnel diplomatique coréen hors du pays et les membres de leurs familles les accompagnant.

[50] D'après les résultats d'une enquête démographique par sondage.

[51] Non compris étrangers.

[52] Les données se rapportent à la population constante déclarée par les autorités statistiques nationales; la population migrante n?est donc pas comprise.

[53] Non compris les citoyens malaisiens et les résidents permanents qui étaient ou qui ont prévu d'être hors du pays pour six mois ou plus. Non compris le personnel militaire Malaisien, le personnel naval ou diplomatique et leurs familles hors du pays, et les touristes et les hommes d'affaires qui avaient l'intention de rester en Malaisie moins de six mois.

[54] Les résultats du recensement ont été ajustées pour compenser les lacunes du dénombrement.

[55] On ne sait pas comment s'explique la divergence entre ces chiffres et les chiffres correspondants indiqués ailleurs.

[56] Pour 2001, les données se rapportent pour la dernière fois à douze mois précédant le recensement juin 2001.

[57] Les données n'ont pas été ajustées pour compenser les lacunes du dénombrement, estimées à 2,4 p. 100.

[58] Les chiffres sont fournis par l'autorité Palestinienne et comprend la population Palestinienne.

[59] D'après les résultats de la 'Population Growth Survey'.

[60] Non compris les données pour le Jammu et Cachemire occupée par le Pakistan dont le statut définitif n'a pas encore été déterminé.

[61] Non compris les zones tribales administrées par le gouvernement fédéral.

[62] D'après les résultats de l'Enquête démographique par sondage. Ces estimations ne dénotent pas d'une manière complètement ponctuelle la population actuelle et les statistiques de l'état civil du pays.

[63] Non compris les personnes de passage à bord de navires ni les militaires et agents civils et les membres de leur famille les accompagnant à l'étranger.

[64] Excluding transients afloat and non-locally domiciled military and civilian services personnel and their dependants.

[65] Including Palestinian refugees.

[66] Data exclude adjustment for underenumeration, estimated at 3.2 per cent.

[67] Including armed forces stationed outside the country, but excluding alien armed forces stationed in the area.

[68] Excluding the Faeroe Islands and Greenland.

[69] Including nationals temporarily outside the country.

[70] Including armed forces stationed outside the country.

[71] Excluding Overseas Departments, namely French Guiana, Guadeloupe, Martinique and Réunion, shown separately. De jure population but excluding diplomatic personnel outside country and including members of alien armed forces not living in military camps and foreign diplomatic personnel not living in embassies or consulates.

[72] All data shown pertaining to Germany prior to 3 October 1990 are indicated separately for the Federal Republic of Germany and the former German Democratic Republic based on their respective territories at the time indicated.

[73] Census data including armed forces stationed outside the country, but excluding alien armed forces stationed in the area.

[74] Events registered within one year of occurrence.

[75] Maltese population only.

[76] Figure differs from corresponding estimate shown elsewhere because it is a mean of end-year estimates rather than an estimate as of 1 July.

[77] Excluding persons on the Central Register of Population (containing persons belonging in the Netherlands population but having no fixed municipality of residence).

[78] Including residents outside the country if listed in a Netherlands population register.

[79] Including residents temporarily outside the country.

[80] Excluding civilian aliens within country, but including civilian nationals temporarily outside country.

[81] Including the Azores and Madeira Islands.

[82] Data do not include information for Transnistria and the municipality of Bender.

[83] Beginning with 1998, estimates of Kosovo and Metohia computed on the basis of natural increases from year 1997.

[84] From 2002, without data for Kosovo and Metohia.

[85] Includes all population with permanent residence on the territory of the Slovak Republic.

[86] For the 1991 census, excluding Northern Ireland.

[87] Data tabulated by date of occurrence for England and Wales, and by date of registration for Northern Ireland and Scotland.

[88] Including Christmas Island, Cocos (Keeling) Islands and Norfolk Island.

[89] Excluding Niue, shown separately, which is part of Cook Islands, but because of remoteness is administered separately.

[90] The resident population consisted of 14,990 (7,738 males and 7,252 females).

[91] Including United States military personnel, their dependants and contract employees.

[92] Including the islands of Huon, Chesterfield, Loyalty, Walpole and Belep Archipelago.

[93] Excluding diplomatic personnel and armed forces stationed outside country, the latter numbering 1 936 at 1966 census; also excluding alien armed forces within the country.

[64] Non compris les personnes de passage bord de navires, ni les militaires et agents civils domiciliés hors du territoire et les membres de leur famille les accompagnant.

[65] Y compris les réfugiés de Palestine.

[66] Les données n'ont pas été ajustées pour compenser les lacunes du dénombrement, estimées à 3,2 p. 100.

[67] Y compris les militaires nationaux hors du pays, mais non compris les militaires étrangers en garnison sur le territoire.

[68] Non compris les îles Féroé et Groenland.

[69] Y compris les nationaux se trouvant temporairement hors du pays.

[70] Y compris les militaires nationaux hors du pays.

[71] Non compris les départements d'outre-mer, c'est-à-dire la Guyane française, la Guadeloupe, la Martinique et la Réunion, qui font l'objet de rubriques distinctes. Population de droit, non compris le personnel diplomatique hors du pays et y compris les militaires étrangers ne vivant pas dans des camps militaires et le personnel diplomatique étranger ne vivant pas dans les ambassades ou les consulats.

[72] Toutes les données se rapportant à l'Allemagne avant le 3 octobre 1990 figurent dans deux rubriques séparées basées sur les territoires respectifs de la République fédérale de l'Allemagne et l'ancienne République démocratique allemande selon la période.

[73] Les données de recensement y compris les militaires hors du pays, mais non compris les militaires étrangers en garnison sur le territoire.

[74] Evénements enregistrés dans l'année qui suit l'événement.

[75] Population Maltaise seulement.

[76] Ce chiffre s'écarte de l'estimation correspondante indiquée ailleurs, car il s'agit d'une moyenne d'estimations de fin d'année et non d'une estimation au 1er juillet.

[77] Non compris les personnes inscrites sur le Registre central de la population (personnes appartenant à la population néerlandaise mais sans résidence fixe dans l'une des municipalités).

[78] Y compris les résidents hors du pays, s'ils sont inscrits sur un registre de population néerlandais.

[79] Y compris les nationaux se trouvant temporairement hors du pays.

[80] Non compris les civils étrangers dans le pays, mais y compris les civils nationaux temporairement hors du pays.

[81] Y compris les Açores et Madère.

[82] Les données ne tiennent pas compte de l'information sur la Transnistria et la municipalité de Bender.

[83] A partir du 1998, les estimations pour le Kosovo et la Metohia ont été calculées sur la base des incréments naturelles depuis 1997.

[84] Après 2002, sans les données pour le Kosovo and Metohie.

[85] Y compris la population de résidence permanente dans le territoire.

[86] Pour le recensement de 1991, non compris l'Irlande du Nord.

[87] Données exploitées selon l'année de l'événement pour l'Angleterre et pays de Galles et selon l'année de l'enregistrement pour Irlande du Nord et l'Ecosse.

[88] Y compris les îles Christmas, Cocos (Keeling) et Norfolk.

[89] Non compris Nioué, qui fait l'objet d'une rubrique distincte et qui fait partie des îles Cook, mais qui, en raison de son éloignement, est administrée séparément.

[90] Population résidente de 14 990 (7 738 hommes et 7 252 femmes).

[91] Y compris les militaires des Etats-Unis, les membres de leur famille les accompagnant et les agents contractuels des Etats-Unis.

[92] Y compris les îles Huon, Chesterfield, Loyauté et Walpole, et l'archipel Belep.

[93] Non compris le personnel diplomatique et les militaires hors du pays, ces derniers étant au nombre de 1 936 au recensement de 1966; non compris également les militaires étrangers en garnison dans le pays.

Table 11: Estimates on food supply are published by the Food and Agriculture Organization of the United Nations in *Food Balance Sheets* [4] and on its Web site http://faostat.fao.org, where the data give estimates of total and per capita food supplies per day available for human consumption during the reference period in terms of quantity and, by applying appropriate food composition factors for all primary and processed products, also in terms of caloric value and protein and fat content. Calorie supplies are reported in kilocalories (1 calorie = 4.19 kilojoules). Per capita supplies in terms of product weight are derived from the total supplies available for human consumption (i.e. "Food") by dividing the quantities of food by the total population actually partaking of the food supplies during the reference period, i.e. the present in-area (de facto) population within the present geographical boundaries of the country. In other words, nationals living abroad during the reference period are excluded, but foreigners living in the country are included. Adjustments are made wherever possible for part-time presence or absence, such as temporary migrants, tourists and refugees supported by special schemes (if it has not been possible to allow for the amounts provided by such schemes under imports). In almost all cases, the population figures used are the mid-year estimates published by the United Nations Population Division.

Per capita supply figures shown in the commodity balances therefore represent only the average supply available for the population as a whole and do not necessarily indicate what is actually consumed by individuals. Even if they are taken as an approximation of per capita consumption, it is important to bear in mind that there could be considerable variation in consumption between individuals.

Table 12: "Life expectancy at birth", "Infant mortality rate" and "Total fertility rate" are taken from the estimates and projections prepared by the Population Division of the United Nations Secretariat, published in *World Population Prospects: The 2004 Revision* [28].

"Life expectancy at birth" is an overall estimate of the expected average number of years to be lived by a female or male newborn. Many developing countries lack complete and reliable statistics of births and deaths based on civil registration, so various estimation techniques are used to calculate life expectancy using other sources of data, mainly population censuses and demographic surveys. Life expectancy at birth by sex gives a statistical summary of current differences in male and female mortality across all ages. However, trends and differentials in infant and child mortality rates are the predominant influence on trends and differentials in life expectancy at birth in most developing countries. Thus, life

Tableau 11 : Les estimations sur les disponibilités alimentaires sont publiées par l'Organisation des Nations Unies pour l'alimentation et l'agriculture dans les *Bilans alimentaires* [4] et sur le site Web http ://faostat.fao.org où les données donnent des estimations des disponibilités alimentaires totales et par habitant par jour pour la consommation humaine durant la période de référence, en quantité, en calories, en protéines et en lipides. Les calories sont exprimées en kilocalories (1 calorie = 4,19 kilojoules). Les disponibilités par habitant exprimées en poids du produit sont calculées à partir des disponibilités totales pour la consommation humaine (c'est-à-dire "Alimentation humaine") en divisant ce chiffre par la population totale qui a effectivement eu accès aux approvisionnements alimentaires durant la période de référence, c'est-à-dire par la population présente (de facto) dans les limites géographiques actuelles du pays. En d'autres termes, les ressortissants du pays vivant à l'étranger durant la période de référence sont exclus, mais les étrangers vivant dans le pays sont inclus. Des ajustements ont été opérés chaque fois que possible pour tenir compte des présences ou des absences de durée limitée, comme dans le cas des immigrants/émigrants temporaires, des touristes et des réfugiés bénéficiant de programmes alimentaires spéciaux (s'il n'a pas été possible de tenir compte des vivres fournis à ce titre à travers les importations). Dans la plupart des cas, les données démographiques utilisées sont les estimations au milieu de l'année publiées par la Division de la population des Nations Unies.

Les disponibilités alimentaires par habitant figurant dans les bilans ne représentent donc que les disponibilités moyennes pour l'ensemble de la population et n'indiquent pas nécessairement la consommation effective des individus. Même si elles sont considérées comme une estimation approximative de la consommation par habitant, il importe de ne pas oublier que la consommation peut varier beaucoup selon les individus.

Tableau 12 : "L'espérance de vie à la naissance", le "taux de mortalité infantile" et le "taux de fécondité" proviennent des estimations et projections de la Division de la population du Secrétariat de l'ONU, qui ont publiées dans "*World Population Prospects : The 2004 Revision*" [28].

"L'espérance de vie à la naissance" est une estimation globale du nombre d'années qu'un nouveau-né de sexe masculin ou féminin vivant, peut s'attendre à vivre. Comme dans beaucoup de pays en développement, les registres d'état civil ne permettent pas d'établir des statistiques fiables et complètes des naissances et des décès, diverses techniques d'estimation ont été utilisées pour calculer l'espérance de vie à partir d'autres sources et notamment des recensements et enquêtes démographiques. Sur la base des statistiques de

expectancy at birth is of limited usefulness in these countries in assessing levels and differentials in male and female mortality at other ages.

"Infant mortality rate" is the total number of deaths in a given year of children less than one year old divided by the total number of live births in the same year, multiplied by 1,000. It is an approximation of the number of deaths per 1,000 children born alive who die within one year of birth. In most developing countries where civil registration data are deficient, the most reliable sources are demographic surveys of households. Where these are not available, other sources and general estimates are made which are necessarily of limited reliability. Where countries lack comprehensive and accurate systems of civil registration, infant mortality statistics by sex are difficult to collect or to estimate with any degree of reliability because of reporting biases, and thus are not shown here.

"Total fertility rate" is the average number of children that would be born alive to a hypothetical cohort of women if, throughout their reproductive years, the age specific fertility rates for the specified year remained unchanged.

"Child mortality rate" is defined as the annual number of deaths among children aged 1-4 years per 1,000 population of the same age. These series have been compiled by the Statistics Division of the United Nations Secretariat for the *Demographic Yearbook* [21] and are subject to the limitations of national reporting in this field.

Data on maternal mortality are estimates developed by the World Health Organization, UNICEF and the United Nations Population Fund and published in *Maternal Mortality in 2000* [34].

l'espérance de vie par sexe, on peut calculer la différence entre la longévité des hommes et celle des femmes à tous les âges. Cependant, ce sont les tendances et les écarts des taux de mortalité infantile et juvénile qui influent de façon prépondérante sur les tendances et les écarts de l'espérance de vie à la naissance dans la plupart des pays en développement. Ainsi, l'espérance de vie à la naissance ne revêt qu'une utilité limitée dans ce pays pour évaluer les niveaux et les écarts de la mortalité des femmes et des hommes à des âges plus avancés.

Le "taux de mortalité infantile" correspond au nombre total de décès au cours d'une année donnée des enfants de moins d'un an divisé par le nombre total de naissances vivantes au cours de la même année, multiplié par 1 000. Il s'agit d'une approximation du nombre de décès pour 1 000 enfants nés vivants qui meurent la première année. Dans la plupart des pays en développement, où les données d'état civil sont déficientes, les sources les plus fiables sont les enquêtes démographiques auprès des ménages. Lorsque de telles enquêtes ne sont pas réalisées, d'autres sources sont utilisées et des estimations générales sont réalisées qui est nécessairement d'une fiabilité limitée. Lorsqu'il n'a pas dans les pays de systèmes complets et exacts d'enregistrement des faits d'état civil, les statistiques de la mortalité infantile par sexe sont difficiles à rassembler ou à estimer avec quelque fiabilité que ce soit en raison des distorsions de la notification; elles ne sont donc pas indiquées ici.

Le "taux de fécondité" est le nombre moyen d'enfants que mettrait au monde une cohorte hypothétique de femmes si, pendant toutes leurs années d'âge reproductif, les taux de fécondité par âge de l'année en question restaient inchangés.

Le "taux de mortalité juvénile" est par définition le nombre de décès d'enfants âgés de 1 à 4 ans pour 1 000 enfants de cet âge. Cette série a été compilée par la Division de statistique du Secrétariat de l'ONU pour l'*Annuaire démographique* [21] et les données qui sont incluses sont présentées sous réserve de mises en garde formulées à leur sujet.

Les données concernant la mortalité maternelle sont des estimations de l'Organisation mondiale de la santé, de l'UNICEF, et du Fonds des Nations Unies pour la Population publiées dans "*Maternal Mortality in 2000*" [34].

13

Daily newspapers
Journaux quotidiens

Country or area Pays ou zone	Number of titles — Nombre de titres				Total average daily circulation or copies printed (thousands) Diffusion moyenne ou nombre imprimé (en milliers)				Circulation or copies printed per 1000 inhabitants [t] Diffusion ou nombre imprimé pour 1000 habitants [t]			
	1997	1998	1999	2000	1997	1998	1999	2000	1997	1998	1999	2000
Africa **Afrique**												
Algeria Algérie	18	24	...	...	761	796	...	...	26.1	26.9	...	...
Angola Angola	5[1]	5[1]	...	...	129[1]	133[1]	...	...	10.0	10.1	...	...
Benin Bénin	...	...	13	...	...	...	33	...	...	...	4.7	...
Botswana Botswana	1[1]	1[1]	...	...	41[1]	41[1]	...	...	24.1	24.0	...	...
Burkina Faso Burkina Faso	4[1]	4[1]	...	...	14[1]	15[1]	...	...	1.4	1.4	...	...
Burundi Burundi	1	1	...	...	15[1]	15[1]	...	...	2.4	2.4	...	...
Cameroon Cameroun	2[1]	2[1]	...	...	92[1]	92[1]	...	...	6.6	6.4	...	...
Central African Rep. Rép. centrafricaine	3[1]	3[1]	...	...	6[1]	6[1]	...	...	1.7	1.7	...	...
Chad Tchad	2	2	...	...	2[1]	2[1]	...	...	0.2	0.2	...	...
Congo Congo	6[1]	6[1]	...	...	21[1]	21[1]	...	...	6.6	6.4	...	...
Côte d'Ivoire Côte d'Ivoire	12[1]	12[1]	...	...	235[1]	238[1]	...	...	15.1	14.9	...	...
Dem. Rep. of the Congo Rép. dém. du Congo	9[1]	9[1]	...	...	129[1]	129[1]	...	...	2.7	2.7	...	...
Egypt Egypte	14	15	16	...	2 100	2 332	2 080	...	33.0	36.0	31.5	...
Equatorial Guinea Guinée équatoriale	1[1]	1[1]	...	...	2[1]	2[1]	...	...	4.8	4.7	...	...
Ethiopia Ethiopie	2	2	...	...	23	23	...	...	0.4	0.4	...	...
Gabon Gabon	2[1]	2[1]	...	...	34[1]	35[1]	...	...	28.6	28.6	...	...
Gambia Gambie	1[1]	1	...	...	2[1]	2[1]	...	...	1.7	1.7	...	...
Ghana Ghana	4[1]	4[1]	...	...	256[1]	260[1]	...	...	13.7	13.7	...	...
Guinea–Bissau Guinée–Bissau	1[1]	1[1]	...	...	6[1]	6[1]	...	...	4.8	4.8	...	...
Kenya Kenya	4[1]	4[1]	4[2]	...	265[1]	268[1]	250[2]	...	9.2	9.1	8.3	...
Lesotho Lesotho	2[1]	2[1]	...	...	16[1]	16[1]	...	...	8.9	9.0	...	...

Country or area / Pays ou zone	Number of titles — Nombre de titres				Total average daily circulation or copies printed (thousands) / Diffusion moyenne ou nombre imprimé (en milliers)				Circulation or copies printed per 1000 inhabitants[t] / Diffusion ou nombre imprimé pour 1000 habitants[t]			
	1997	1998	1999	2000	1997	1998	1999	2000	1997	1998	1999	2000
Liberia / Libéria	6[1]	6[1]	...	...	36[1]	37[1]	...	...	14.5	13.5	...	...
Libyan Arab Jamah. / Jamah. arabe libyenne	4[1]	4[1]	...	...	71[1]	71[1]	...	...	14.2	13.9	...	...
Madagascar / Madagascar	5[1]	5[1]	...	...	68[1]	68[1]	...	...	4.6	4.5	...	...
Malawi / Malawi	5[1]	5[1]	...	...	26[1]	26[1]	...	...	2.4	2.4	...	...
Mali / Mali	3[1]	3[1]	...	...	12[1]	13[1]	...	...	1.2	1.1	...	...
Mauritius / Maurice	8	6	6	5	88	82	116	138	76.5	70.6	98.8	116.4
Morocco / Maroc	21	22	22	23	657	715	728	846	23.5	25.2	25.3	28.9
Mozambique / Mozambique	12	12	...	...	43	43	...	...	2.6	2.5	...	...
Namibia / Namibie	4[1]	4[1]	...	...	13[1]	31[1]	...	...	7.2	17.2	...	...
Niger / Niger	1[1]	1[1]	...	...	2[1]	2[1]	...	...	0.2	0.2	...	...
Nigeria / Nigéria	25[1]	25[1]	...	...	2 750[1]	2 760[1]	...	...	25.1	24.6	...	...
Rwanda / Rwanda	1[1]	1[1]	...	...	1[1]	1[1]	...	...	0.1	0.1	...	...
Senegal / Sénégal	4	5	...	...	...	...	...	...	...	...	...	...
Seychelles / Seychelles	4[1]	5[1]	...	...	46[1]	46[1]	...	...	598.0	602.2	...	...
South Africa / Afrique du Sud	17[2]	17[2]	18[2]	16[2]	1 204[2]	1 149[2]	...	1 118[2]	27.6	25.9	...	24.5
Togo / Togo	...	...	1	1	...	...	10	10	...	...	1.9	1.9
Tunisia / Tunisie	...	...	...	7	...	...	...	180	...	...	...	18.8
Uganda / Ouganda	...	4[2]	4[2]	3[2]	...	...	...	63[2]	...	...	...	2.6
Zambia / Zambie	...	...	...	...	...	...	...	228	...	...	...	21.3
America, North / Amérique du Nord												
Bermuda / Bermudes	...	...	1	1	...	...	15	15	...	...	239.7	238.6
Canada / Canada	105[2]	105[2]	106[2]	104[2]	4 979[2]	5 005[2]	5 166[2]	5 167[2]	166.8	166.1	169.9	168.4
Costa Rica / Costa Rica	6[2]	6[2]	6[2]	6[2]	...	265[2]	290[2]	275[2]	...	70.7	75.5	70.0
Cuba / Cuba	...	...	2	2	...	...	565	600	...	...	51.0	53.9
Dominican Republic / Rép. dominicaine	10	10	10	9	126	126	230	230	16.0	15.7	28.2	27.8

Country or area	Number of titles — Nombre de titres				Total average daily circulation or copies printed (thousands) / Diffusion moyenne ou nombre imprimé (en milliers)				Circulation or copies printed per 1000 inhabitants [‡] / Diffusion ou nombre imprimé pour 1000 habitants [‡]			
Pays ou zone	1997	1998	1999	2000	1997	1998	1999	2000	1997	1998	1999	2000
El Salvador / El Salvador	4	4	...	...	219	171	...	...	37.0	28.3	...	...
Mexico / Mexique	...	...	300	311	...	...	9 332	9 251	...	...	94.6	92.4
United States / Etats–Unis	1 509[2]	1 489[2]	1 483[2]	1 476[2]	56 728[2]	56 182[2]	55 979[2]	55 945[2]	206.0	201.8	199.0	196.9
America, South / Amérique du Sud												
Argentina / Argentine	101[2]	100[2]	102[2]	106[2]	2 335[2]	2 160[2]	1 944[2]	1 500[2]	65.4	59.8	53.3	40.7
Bolivia / Bolivie	27	29	...	...	863[1]	788[1]	...	...	110.4	98.8	...	...
Brazil / Brésil	400	372	465[2]	465[2]	6 892	7 163	7 245[2]	7 883[2]	41.4	42.4	42.3	45.3
Chile [2] / Chili [2]	...	...	51	53	...	...	...	...	...	...	...	...
Colombia / Colombie	25[2]	23[2]	24[2]	...	1 151[2]	1 072[2]	1 093[2]	...	28.8	26.3	26.4	...
Ecuador / Equateur	11	11	36[3]	36	569	529	1 220[3]	1 220	48.3	44.3	100.6	99.1
Guyana / Guyana	...	...	2	2	...	...	57	57	...	...	76.5	76.3
Peru / Pérou	...	57[2]	...	...	...	570[2]	...	...	...	22.7	...	...
Suriname / Suriname	2	2	...	...	29	28	...	...	67.5	65.7	...	...
Uruguay [2] / Uruguay [2]	...	...	...	4	...	...	...	...	...	...	...	...
Asia / Asie												
Armenia / Arménie	8	7	7	8	...	...	...	...	...	...	...	...
Azerbaijan / Azerbaïdjan	...	14[2]	15[2]	...	...	95[2]	80[2]	...	...	11.8	9.9	...
China [4] / Chine [4]	694[2]	740[2]	805[2]	909[2]	43 948[2]	62 989[2]	70 090[2]	75 603[2]	35.4	50.3	55.4	59.3
China, Hong Kong SAR / Chine, Hong Kong RAS	...	43[2]	48[2]	...	...	1 583[2]	1 528[2]	1 481[2]	...	244.9	233.2	223.1
China, Macao SAR / Chine, Macao RAS	...	...	10	10	...	...	158	167	...	...	359.1	377.2
Cyprus / Chypre	8	7	8	8	53	79	86	87	70.4	103.3	110.9	110.6
Georgia / Géorgie	...	...	30	35	...	...	43	26	...	...	9.1	5.4
India / Inde	5 044	5 221	...	...	46 452[5]	59 023[5]	...	...	47.9	59.8	...	...
Indonesia / Indonésie	81	172	225[2]	396[2]	4 975	4 713	4 782[2]	...	24.7	23.1	23.2	...
Iran (Islamic Rep. of) / Iran (Rép. islamique d')	...	...	105	112	...	...	...	...	...	...	...	...

Country or area Pays ou zone	Number of titles — Nombre de titres				Total average daily circulation or copies printed (thousands) Diffusion moyenne ou nombre imprimé (en milliers)				Circulation or copies printed per 1000 inhabitants [t] Diffusion ou nombre imprimé pour 1000 habitants [t]			
	1997	1998	1999	2000	1997	1998	1999	2000	1997	1998	1999	2000
Japan Japon	109[2]	108[2]	109[2]	110[2]	72 699[2]	72 410[2]	72 218[2]	71 896[2]	576.3	572.6	569.7	566.0
Jordan Jordanie	8	8	5	5	350	352	...	...	76.2	74.6	...	...
Korea, Republic of [2] Corée, République de [2]	193	108	112	116	...	...	...	...	...	...	...	...
Kyrgyzstan Kirghizistan	...	...	3	3	...	...	...	...	...	...	...	...
Lebanon Liban	...	13[2]	14[2]	13[2]	...	213[2]	225[2]	220[2]	...	64.0	66.9	64.7
Malaysia Malaisie	33	33[2]	...	31[2]	2 257	2 487[2]	...	2 191[2]	105.3	113.2	...	95.3
Mongolia Mongolie	4[2]	5[2]	5[2]	5[2]	59[2]	50[2]	40[2]	44[2]	24.2	20.4	16.2	17.6
Myanmar Myanmar	4	4	...	...	420	400	...	...	9.2	8.6	...	...
Occupied Palestinian Terr. Terr. palestinien occupé	...	...	3	3	...	...	...	...	...	...	...	...
Oman Oman	5	5	...	...	...	...	...	...	...	...	...	...
Pakistan Pakistan	359	303[2]	352	306[2]	3 915	...	5 559	5 600[2]	29.5	...	39.9	39.3
Philippines Philippines	42	...	...	...	4 712	...	...	...	66.0	...	...	...
Singapore Singapour	8[2]	8[2]	8[2]	9[2]	1 027[2]	1 062[2]	1 078[2]	1 096[2]	277.3	278.2	274.8	272.8
Sri Lanka Sri Lanka	9[2]	9[2]	...	12[2]	528[2]	524[2]	...	536[2]	27.4	26.9	...	27.0
Thailand Thaïlande	...	34[2]	...	...	4 392[2]	11 753[2]	...	...	73.6	195.1	...	...
Timor–Leste [2] Timor–Leste [2]	...	...	2	1	...	...	...	...	...	...	...	...
Turkey Turquie	980	960	560	542	...	...	...	...	...	...	...	...
Turkmenistan Turkménistan	...	...	2	2	...	...	26	32	...	...	6.0	7.0
Viet Nam Viet Nam	...	...	5	...	...	...	450[1]	...	...	...	5.8	...
Europe **Europe**												
Andorra Andorre	...	...	2	2	...	...	...	...	...	...	...	...
Austria Autriche	17[2]	17[2]	17[2]	16[2]	2 500[2]	2 669[2]	2 896[2]	2 503[2]	309.1	329.9	358.0	309.2
Belarus Bélarus	19	20	...	...	1 437	1 559	...	...	141.2	153.9	...	...
Belgium Belgique	30[2]	29[2]	28[2]	29[2]	1 605[2]	1 588[2]	1 564[2]	1 568[2]	157.2	155.1	152.2	152.2
Bulgaria Bulgarie	33[2]	33[2]	36[2]	43[2]	1 267[2]	1 112[2]	1 350[2]	1 400[2]	155.2	137.2	167.7	175.1

Country or area	Number of titles — Nombre de titres				Total average daily circulation or copies printed (thousands) Diffusion moyenne ou nombre imprimé (en milliers)				Circulation or copies printed per 1000 inhabitants [t] Diffusion ou nombre imprimé pour 1000 habitants [t]			
Pays ou zone	1997	1998	1999	2000	1997	1998	1999	2000	1997	1998	1999	2000
Croatia Croatie	11[2]	10[2]	11[2]	12[2]	503[2]	510[2]	536[2]	595[2]	108.9	111.5	118.3	132.1
Czech Republic République tchèque	99	103	104	103	...	...	...	...	...	...	...	...
Denmark Danemark	38	36	33	33	1 617	1 613	1 558	1 507	306.7	304.6	293.0	282.2
Estonia Estonie	17[2]	16[2]	17[2]	13[2]	260[2]	254[2]	273[2]	262[2]	185.0	182.7	198.1	191.7
Finland Finlande	56	56	56[6]	55[6]	2 323	2 343	2 331	2 304	452.0	454.8	451.4	445.1
France France	84[2]	86[2]	87[2]	84[2]	8 506[2]	8 268[2]	8 447[2]	8 424[2]	145.0	140.5	143.0	142.1
Germany Allemagne	402[2]	391[2]	387[2]	382[2]	25 038[2]	25 016[2]	24 565[2]	23 946[2]	305.0	304.4	298.6	290.8
Gibraltar Gibraltar	...	1	2	...	...	6	4	...	...	217.8	144.9	...
Greece Grèce	198	207	...	...	...	...	...	...	...	...	...	...
Hungary Hongrie	43[2]	40[2]	39[2]	40[2]	1 742[2]	1 700[2]	1 659[2]	1 625[2]	169.2	165.5	161.9	158.9
Iceland Islande	4	3[2]	3	3[2]	100	94[2]	93	91[2]	366.4	340.9	333.9	323.5
Ireland Irlande	6[2]	6[2]	6[2]	6[2]	552[2]	557[2]	567[2]	564[2]	150.4	150.3	151.2	148.4
Italy Italie	...	92[2]	88[2]	89[2]	5 920[2]	5 881[2]	5 914[2]	6 273[2]	103.0	102.2	102.6	108.7
Latvia Lettonie	24[2]	21[2]	27	26	284[2]	260[2]	354	327	116.8	107.9	148.1	137.8
Lithuania Lituanie	23	23	29	22	113	123	126	108	31.7	34.6	35.7	30.9
Luxembourg Luxembourg	5[2]	5[2]	5[2]	5[2]	121[2]	124[2]	124[2]	120[2]	290.1	293.0	288.9	275.7
Malta Malte	5	4	...	...	...	...	...	...	...	...	...	...
Netherlands Pays–Bas	38[2]	35[2]	35[2]	35[2]	4 753[2]	4 522[2]	4 482[2]	4 443[2]	303.9	287.5	283.4	279.5
Norway Norvège	83	81	82[7]	81[7]	2 603	2 592	2 591	2 545	589.4	583.0	579.0	565.3
Poland Pologne	66	52	46	42	...	4 168	3 870	3 928	...	107.8	100.1	101.6
Portugal Portugal	31	29[2]	28[2]	28[2]	316	673[2]	686[2]	1 026[2]	31.3	66.4	67.4	100.3
Republic of Moldova République de Moldova	5	6	6	6	480	660	...	...	111.3	153.4	...	...
Romania Roumanie	74	95	139	145[1]	...	...	...	...	...	...	...	...
Russian Federation [2] Fédération de Russie [2]	...	245	286	333	...	...	...	...	...	...	...	...
San Marino Saint–Marin	3	3	...	...	2	2	...	...	68.6	68.0	...	...

Country or area Pays ou zone	Number of titles — Nombre de titres				Total average daily circulation or copies printed (thousands) Diffusion moyenne ou nombre imprimé (en milliers)				Circulation or copies printed per 1000 inhabitants [t] Diffusion ou nombre imprimé pour 1000 habitants [t]			
	1997	1998	1999	2000	1997	1998	1999	2000	1997	1998	1999	2000
Slovakia Slovaquie	20	19	24	16	1 012	939	851	705	187.9	174.1	157.7	130.6
Slovenia Slovénie	5	5	5	5	343	340	341	335	174.3	172.8	173.3	170.3
Spain Espagne	...	...	84	87	...	...	4 191	4 003	...	...	103.7	98.3
Sweden Suède	94	94	94	90	3 881	3 820	3 750	3 627	438.1	431.1	423.0	408.6
Switzerland Suisse	78	74	81	104[2]	2 680	2 620	2 676	2 666[2]	378.9	368.7	374.8	372.0
TFYR of Macedonia L'ex–R.y. Macédoine	4	4	5	5	88	106	109	108	44.2	53.1	54.4	53.9
Ukraine Ukraine	53	41	67	61	3 495	5 059	6 107	8 683	68.9	100.7	123.0	176.8
United Kingdom Royaume–Uni	99[2]	98[2]	106[2]	108[2]	18 447[2]	18 921[2]	18 839[2]	19 159[2]	317.7	324.7	322.2	326.6
Oceania **Océanie**												
Australia Australie	49[2]	48[2]	48[2]	48[2]	3 232[2]	3 103[2]	3 083[2]	3 083[2]	175.8	166.7	163.6	161.7
New Zealand Nouvelle–Zélande	28	28	28	28	824	786	774	765	221.1	209.3	204.5	200.4

Source

United Nations Educational, Scientific and Cultural Organization (UNESCO) Institute for Statistics, Montreal, the UNESCO Institute for Statistics database.

Notes

t   Includes data from the United Nations Population Division, "World Population Prospects, The 2004 Revision".

[1]   National estimate.
[2]   Source: World Association of Newspapers.
[3]   Break in series; new source of data.
[4]   For statistical purposes, the data for China do not include those for the Hong Kong Special Administrative Region (Hong Kong SAR) and Macao Special Administrative Region (Macao SAR).
[5]   Including tri–weeklies and bi–weeklies.
[6]   Data do not include non–members of the Finnish Newspaper Association.
[7]   Data do not include Sunday issues.

Source

L'Institut de statistique de l'Organisation des Nations Unies pour l'éducation, la science et la culture (UNESCO), Montréal, la base de données de l'Institut de statistique de l'UNESCO.

Notes

t   Y compris des données du "World Population Prospects, The 2004 Revision" de la Division de la population du Secrétariat des Nations Unies.

[1]   Estimation nationale.
[2]   Source: Association Mondiale des Journaux.
[3]   Discontinuité dans la série; nouvelle source de données.
[4]   Pour la présentation des statistiques, les données pour Chine ne comprennent pas la Région Administrative Spéciale de Hong Kong (Hong Kong RAS) et la Région Administrative Spéciale de Macao (Macao RAS).
[5]   Y compris les journaux paraissant deux ou trois fois par semaine.
[6]   Les données n'incluent pas les non membres de l'Association finnoise de journaux.
[7]   Les données n'incluent pas les parutions du dimanche.

14

Cellular mobile telephone subscribers
Number

Abonnés au téléphone mobile
Nombre

Country or area Pays ou zone	1997	1998	1999	2000	2001	2002	2003	2004
Afghanistan Afghanistan	0	0	0	0	0	25 000	200 000	600 000
Albania Albanie	3 300	5 600	11 008	29 791	392 650	851 000	1 100 000	...
Algeria Algérie	17 400	18 000	72 000	86 000	100 000	400 000	1 441 400	4 682 690
American Samoa Samoa américaines	2 550	2 650	2 377	...	...	...	...	
Andorra Andorre	8 618	14 117	20 600	23 543	29 429	32 790	51 893	...
Angola Angola	7 052	9 820	24 000	25 806	86 500	130 000	332 800[1]	940 000
Anguilla Anguilla	707	787	*1 475	2 163	1 773	...	...	...
Antigua and Barbuda + Antigua–et–Barbuda +	*1 400	*1 500	8 500	22 000	25 000[2]	38 205	...	54 000
Argentina + Argentine +	2 009 073	2 670 862	3 848 869	6 487 950	6 741 791	6 566 740[1]	7 842 233	13 512 383
Armenia Arménie	5 000	7 831	8 161	17 486	25 504	71 349	114 379	203 309
Aruba Aruba	3 402	5 380	12 000	15 000	53 000	...	...	...
Australia + Australie +	4 578 000	4 918 000	6 315 000	8 562 000	11 132 000	12 575 000	14 347 000	16 449 000
Austria Autriche	1 159 700	2 292 900	4 250 393	6 117 000	6 541 000	6 736 000	7 094 502[3]	7 989 955
Azerbaijan Azerbaïdjan	40 000	65 000	370 000	420 400	730 000	794 000	1 057 000	1 782 900
Bahamas Bahamas	6 200	8 072	15 911	31 524	60 555	121 759	116 267	186 007
Bahrain Bahreïn	58 543	92 063	133 468	205 727	299 587	388 990	443 109	649 764
Bangladesh + Bangladesh +	26 000[1]	75 000	149 000	279 000	520 000[1]	1 075 000	1 365 000[1]	4 327 516
Barbados + Barbade +	8 013	12 000	20 309	28 467	53 111	97 193	140 000	200 138
Belarus Bélarus	8 167	12 155	23 457	49 353	138 329	462 630	1 118 000	...
Belgium Belgique	974 494	1 756 287	3 186 602	5 629 000	7 697 000	8 101 777[1]	8 605 834	9 131 705
Belize + Belize +	2 544	3 535	6 591	16 812	39 155	51 729	60 403	97 755
Benin Bénin	4 295	6 286	7 269	55 476	125 000[1]	218 770	236 175	...
Bermuda + Bermudes +	*10 276	12 572	12 800	13 000	13 333[2]	*30 000	40 000	49 000
Bhutan Bhoutan	0	0	0	0	0	0	7 998	17 800
Bolivia Bolivie	118 433	239 272	420 344	582 620	779 917	1 023 333	1 278 844	1 800 789

Country or area / Pays ou zone	1997	1998	1999	2000	2001	2002	2003	2004
Bosnia and Herzegovina / Bosnie–Herzégovine	9 000	25 181	52 607	93 386	444 711	748 780	1 050 000	...
Botswana [4] / Botswana [4]	0	15 190	92 000	200 000	316 000	435 000	522 840	563 782
Brazil / Brésil	4 550 000	7 368 218	15 032 698	23 188 171	28 745 769	34 880 964	46 373 266	65 605 000
British Virgin Islands [+] / Iles Vierges britanniques[+]	...	...	...	...	...	8 000	...	...
Brunei Darussalam / Brunéi Darussalam	45 000	49 129	66 000	95 000	137 000	...	...	...
Bulgaria / Bulgarie	70 000	127 000	350 000	738 000	1 550 000	2 597 548	3 500 869	4 729 731
Burkina Faso / Burkina Faso	1 503	2 730	5 036	25 245	76 000[5]	113 000[5]	227 000[5]	398 000[5]
Burundi / Burundi	619	620	800	16 320	30 687[1]	52 000	64 000	...
Cambodia / Cambodge	33 556	61 345	89 117	130 547	223 458	380 000	498 388	...
Cameroon / Cameroun	4 200	5 000	6 000	103 279	417 295	701 507	1 077 000	1 536 594
Canada / Canada	4 195 000	5 346 000	6 911 038	8 727 000	10 649 000	11 872 000	13 228 000	14 984 396
Cape Verde / Cap–Vert	20	1 020	8 068	19 729	31 507	42 949	53 342	65 780
Cayman Islands [+] / Iles Caïmanes [+]	4 109	5 170	8 410	10 700	17 000	...	...	...
Central African Rep. / Rép. centrafricaine	1 370	1 633	4 162	4 967	11 000	12 600	40 000	60 000
Chad / Tchad	0	0	0	5 500	22 000	34 200[3]	65 000	123 000
Chile / Chili	409 740	964 248	2 260 687	3 401 525	5 271 565	6 445 698[1]	7 520 280	9 566 581
China [6] / Chine [6]	13 233 000	23 863 000	43 296 000	85 260 000	144 820 000	206 005 000	269 953 000	334 824 000
China, Hong Kong SAR [+] / Chine, Hong Kong RAS [+]	2 229 862	3 174 369	4 275 048	5 447 346	5 776 360	6 395 725	7 349 202	8 148 685[7]
China, Macao SAR / Chine, Macao RAS	52 845	82 114	118 101	141 052	194 475	276 138	364 031	432 450
Colombia / Colombie	1 264 763	1 800 229	1 966 535	2 256 801	3 265 261	4 596 594	6 186 206	10 400 578
Comoros / Comores	0	0	0	0	0	0	2 000	...
Congo / Congo	...	3 390	5 000	70 000	150 000	221 800[3]	330 000	383 653
Cook Islands [+] / Iles Cook [+]	196	285	506	552	942[2]	1 499	...	...
Costa Rica / Costa Rica	64 387	108 770	138 178	211 614	326 944	502 478	778 299	923 084
Côte d'Ivoire / Côte d'Ivoire	36 000	91 212	257 134	472 952	728 545	1 027 058	1 280 696	1 531 846
Croatia / Croatie	120 420	182 500	295 000	1 033 000	*1 755 000	2 340 000	2 553 000	...
Cuba / Cuba	2 994	4 056	5 136	6 536	8 579	17 851	35 356	75 797

Cellular mobile telephone subscribers — Number (*continued*)
Abonnés au téléphone mobile — Nombre (*suite*)

Country or area Pays ou zone	1997	1998	1999	2000	2001	2002	2003	2004
Cyprus Chypre	91 968	116 429	151 649	218 324	314 355	417 933	551 752	640 515
Czech Republic République tchèque	526 339	965 476	1 944 553	4 346 009	6 947 151	8 610 177	9 708 683	10 771 270
Dem. Rep. of the Congo Rép. dém. du Congo	8 900	10 000	12 000	15 000	150 000	560 000	1 000 000	...
Denmark Danemark	1 444 016	1 931 101	2 628 585	3 363 552	3 960 165	4 477 752	4 767 277	5 165 546
Djibouti Djibouti	203	220	280	230	3 000	15 000	23 000	...
Dominica + Dominique +	*556	650	*800	*1 200	7 710	12 173	21 099	41 838
Dominican Republic Rép. dominicaine	141 592	209 384	424 434	705 431	1 270 082	1 700 609	2 122 543	2 534 063
Ecuador Equateur	126 505	242 812	383 185	482 213	859 152	1 560 861	2 398 161	4 544 174
Egypt + Egypte +	65 378	90 786	480 974	1 359 900	2 793 800	4 494 700	5 797 530	7 643 060
El Salvador El Salvador	40 163	137 114	511 365	743 628	857 782	888 818	1 149 790	1 832 579
Equatorial Guinea Guinée équatoriale	300	297	600	5 000	15 000	32 000	41 500	55 500
Eritrea Erythrée	0	0	0	0	0	0	0	20 000
Estonia Estonie	144 200	247 000	387 000	557 000	651 200	881 000	1 050 241	1 255 731
Ethiopia + Ethiopie +	0	0	6 740	17 757	27 500	50 369	97 827	178 000
Faeroe Islands Iles Féroé	4 701	6 516	10 761	16 971	24 487	30 709	38 640	...
Fiji Fidji	5 200	8 000	23 380	55 057	80 933	89 900	109 882	...
Finland Finlande	2 162 574	2 845 985	3 273 433	3 728 625	4 175 587	4 516 772	4 747 126	4 988 000
France France	5 817 300	11 210 100	21 433 500	29 052 360	36 997 400	38 585 300	41 683 100	44 551 800
French Guiana Guyane française	0	4 000	18 000	39 830	75 320	87 300	...	98 000
French Polynesia Polynésie française	5 427	11 060	21 929	39 900	67 300	90 000	...	...
Gabon Gabon	9 500	9 694	8 891	120 000	150 000	279 289	300 000	489 367
Gambia + Gambie +	4 734	5 048	5 307	*5 600	55 085	100 000	...	175 000
Georgia Géorgie	30 000	60 000	133 243	194 741	301 327	503 619	711 224	840 600
Germany Allemagne	8 276 000	13 913 000	23 446 000	48 202 000	56 126 000	59 128 000	64 800 000	71 316 000
Ghana Ghana	21 866	41 753	70 026	130 045	243 797	386 775	795 529	1 695 000
Greece Grèce	937 700	2 047 000	3 904 000	5 932 403	7 963 742	9 314 260	10 337 000	11 044 232
Greenland Groenland	6 481	8 899	13 521	15 977	16 747	19 924	...	...

Country or area Pays ou zone	1997	1998	1999	2000	2001	2002	2003	2004
Grenada Grenade	976	1 410	2 012	4 300	6 414	7 553	42 293	43 313
Guadeloupe Guadeloupe	0	14 227	88 080	169 840	292 520	323 500	...	350 000
Guam Guam	5 673	12 837[1]	20 000	27 200	32 600	...	...	...
Guatemala Guatemala	64 194	111 445	337 800	856 831	1 146 441	1 577 085	2 034 776	3 168 256
Guernsey Guernesey	7 788	11 665	15 320	21 885	31 539	36 580	41 530	43 824
Guinea Guinée	2 868	21 567	25 182	42 112	55 670	90 772	111 500	...
Guinea–Bissau Guinée–Bissau	0	0	0	0	0	0	1 275	...
Guyana Guyana	1 400	1 454	2 815	39 830	75 320	87 300	118 658	143 945
Haiti Haïti	0	10 000	25 000	55 000	91 500	140 000	320 000	400 000
Honduras Honduras	14 427	34 896	78 588	155 271	237 629	326 508	379 362	707 201
Hungary Hongrie	705 786	1 070 154	1 628 153	3 076 279	4 967 430	6 886 111	7 944 586	8 727 188[8]
Iceland Islande	65 368	104 280	172 614	214 896	248 131	260 438[1]	279 670	291 372
India + Inde +	881 839	1 195 400	1 884 311	3 577 095	6 431 520	12 687 637	26 154 405	47 300 000
Indonesia Indonésie	916 173	1 065 820	2 220 969	3 669 327	6 520 947	11 700 000	18 800 000	30 000 000
Iran (Islamic Rep. of) + Iran (Rép. islamique d') +	238 942	389 974	490 478	962 595	2 087 353	2 186 958	3 376 526	4 300 000
Iraq + Iraq +	0	0	0	0	0	20 000	80 000	574 000
Ireland + Irlande +	545 000	946 000	1 677 000	2 461 000	2 970 000	3 000 000	3 500 000	3 780 000
Israel Israël	1 672 442	2 147 000	2 880 000	4 400 000	5 900 000	6 334 000	6 500 000	7 187 500
Italy Italie	11 737 904	20 489 000	30 296 000	42 246 000	51 246 000	54 200 000[3]	56 770 000[9]	62 750 000
Jamaica + Jamaïque +	65 995	78 624	144 388	366 952	*635 000	1 187 295	1 600 000	2 200 000
Japan + 10 Japon + 10	38 253 893	47 307 592	56 845 594	66 784 374	74 819 158	81 118 324	86 654 962	91 473 940
Jersey Jersey	12 000	18 225	24 636	44 742	61 417	...	81 200	...
Jordan Jordanie	45 037[1]	82 429	118 417	388 949	865 627	1 219 597	1 325 313	1 594 513
Kazakhstan Kazakhstan	11 202	29 700	49 500	197 300	582 000	1 027 000	1 330 730	2 758 940
Kenya + Kenya +	6 767	10 756	23 757	127 404[4]	600 000	1 187 122[4]	1 590 785	2 546 157
Kiribati Kiribati	0	22	200	300	395	495	526	...
Korea, Republic of Corée, République de	6 878 786	14 018 612	23 442 724	26 816 398	29 045 596	32 342 493	33 591 758	36 586 052

Country or area Pays ou zone	1997	1998	1999	2000	2001	2002	2003	2004
Kuwait Koweït	210 000	250 000	300 000	476 000	877 920	1 227 000	1 420 000	2 000 000
Kyrgyzstan Kirghizistan	0	1 350	2 574	9 000	27 000	53 084	138 279	300 000
Lao People's Dem. Rep. Rép. dém. pop. lao	4 915	6 453	12 078	12 681	29 545	55 160	112 275	204 191
Latvia Lettonie	77 100	167 460	274 344	401 272	656 835	917 196	1 219 550	1 536 712
Lebanon [1] Liban [1]	373 900	505 300	627 000	743 000	766 754	775 104	820 000	888 000
Lesotho + Lesotho +	3 500	9 831	12 000	21 600	57 000	96 843	101 474	159 000
Liberia Libéria	0	0	0	1 500	2 000	...	47 250 [1]	...
Libyan Arab Jamah. Jamah. arabe libyenne	10 000 [1]	20 000	30 000	40 000	50 000	70 000	127 000	...
Liechtenstein [1] Liechtenstein [1]	...	7 500	9 000	10 000	11 000	11 402	...	...
Lithuania Lituanie	165 337	267 615	332 000	524 000	1 017 999	1 645 568	2 169 866	3 421 538
Luxembourg Luxembourg	67 208	130 500	209 190	303 274	409 064	473 000 [1]	539 000	...
Madagascar Madagascar	4 100	12 784	35 752	63 094	147 500	163 010	283 666	333 888
Malawi Malawi	7 000	10 500	22 500	49 000	55 730	86 047	135 114	222 135
Malaysia Malaisie	2 000 000	2 200 000	2 990 000	5 121 748	7 385 240	9 253 387	11 124 112	14 611 902
Maldives Maldives	1 290	1 606	2 926	7 638	18 894	41 899	66 466	113 246
Mali Mali	2 842	4 473	6 387	10 398	45 340	52 639	244 930	400 000
Malta Malte	17 691	22 531	37 541	114 444	239 416	276 859	289 992	...
Marshall Islands Iles Marshall	466	345	443	447	489	552	598	...
Martinique Martinique	15 000	55 000	102 000	162 080	286 120	319 900	...	349 000
Mauritania Mauritanie	0	0	0	15 300	110 463	247 238	350 954	522 400
Mauritius Maurice	42 515	60 448	102 119	180 000	272 416	348 137	326 033	510 000
Mayotte Mayotte	0	0	0	0	0	21 700	36 000	38 000
Mexico Mexique	1 740 814	3 349 475	7 731 635	14 077 880	21 757 559	25 928 266	30 097 700	38 451 135
Micronesia (Fed. States of) Micronésie (Etats féd. de)	0	0	0	0	0	100	5 869	12 782
Monaco Monaco	7 200	11 474	13 080	13 927	14 302	14 874	15 081	...
Mongolia Mongolie	2 000	9 032	34 562	154 600	195 000	216 000	319 000	...
Montserrat Montserrat	325	250	300	489	...	...	...	...

Country or area Pays ou zone	1997	1998	1999	2000	2001	2002	2003	2004
Morocco [11] Maroc [11]	74 472	116 645	369 174	2 342 000	4 771 739	6 198 670	7 359 870	9 336 878
Mozambique Mozambique	2 500	6 725	12 243	51 065	152 652	254 759	435 757	708 000
Myanmar Myanmar	8 492	8 516	11 389	13 397	22 671	47 982	66 517	92 007
Namibia + Namibie +	12 500	19 500	30 000	82 000	106 600	150 000[4]	223 671	286 095
Nauru [1] Nauru [1]	750	850	1 000	1 200	1 500	...	...	...
Nepal + Népal +	0	0	5 500	10 226	17 286[2]	21 881	50 367	179 126
Netherlands Pays–Bas	1 717 000	3 351 000	6 745 460	10 755 000	12 200 000	12 300 000	13 491 000	14 821 000
Netherlands Antilles Antilles néerlandaises	*14 500	16 000	30 000	...	...	...	200 000	200 000
New Caledonia Nouvelle–Calédonie	5 198	13 040	25 450	49 948	67 917	80 000	97 113	116 443
New Zealand + Nouvelle–Zélande +	566 200	790 000	1 395 000	1 542 000	2 288 000	2 449 000	2 599 000	3 027 000
Nicaragua Nicaragua	7 560	18 310	44 229	90 294	164 509	237 248	466 706	738 624
Niger Niger	98	1 349	2 192	2 056	2 126	16 648	76 580	148 276
Nigeria Nigéria	15 000	20 000	25 000	30 000	*400 000	1 607 931	3 149 473	9 147 209
Niue Nioué	...	...	380	410	400	...	...	...
Northern Mariana Islands Iles Mariannes du Nord	...	...	2 905[12]	3 000	...	...	...	...
Norway Norvège	1 676 763	2 106 414	2 744 793	3 367 763	3 766 431	3 911 136[1]	4 163 381	...
Occupied Palestinian Terr. [13] Terr. palestinien occupé [13]	40 000	100 000	117 000	175 941	300 000	320 000	480 000	974 345
Oman Oman	59 822	103 032	124 119	164 348	324 540	464 896	593 450	805 000
Pakistan + Pakistan +	135 027	196 096	265 614	306 493	742 606	1 698 536	2 404 400	5 022 908
Panama Panama	18 542	85 883	232 888	410 401	475 141	525 845	834 031	855 852
Papua New Guinea Papouasie–Nvl–Guinée	3 857	5 558	7 059	8 560	10 700	15 000	...	...
Paraguay Paraguay	84 240	231 520	435 611	820 810	1 150 000	1 667 018	1 770 345	1 767 824
Peru Pérou	421 814	742 642	1 013 314	1 273 857	1 793 284	2 306 944	2 930 343	4 092 558
Philippines Philippines	1 343 620	1 733 652	2 849 980	6 454 359	12 159 163	15 383 001	22 509 560	32 935 875
Poland Pologne	812 200	1 928 042	3 956 500	6 747 000	10 004 661	*13 898 471	*17 401 222	23 096 065
Portugal Portugal	1 506 958	3 074 633	4 671 458	6 664 951	7 977 537	8 528 900[3]	10 030 000	10 300 000
Puerto Rico [14] Porto Rico [14]	367 000	580 000	813 800	926 448	1 128 736	1 800 000	...	2 682 000

Country or area Pays ou zone	1997	1998	1999	2000	2001	2002	2003	2004
Qatar Qatar	43 476	65 756	84 365	120 856	177 929	266 703	376 535	490 333
Republic of Moldova République de Moldova	2 200	7 000	18 000	139 000	225 000	338 225	475 942	787 000
Réunion Réunion	26 700	50 300	111 000	276 100	421 100	489 800	565 000	...
Romania Roumanie	201 000	643 000	1 355 500	2 499 000	3 845 116	5 110 591	7 039 898	10 215 388
Russian Federation Fédération de Russie	484 883	747 160	1 370 630	3 263 200	7 750 499	17 608 756	36 500 000	74 420 000
Rwanda Rwanda	0	5 000	11 000	39 000	65 000	82 391[3]	130 720	138 728
Saint Kitts and Nevis [+] Saint–Kitts–et–Nevis [+]	205	440	700	1 200	*2 100	5 000	...	10 000
Saint Lucia [+][*] Sainte–Lucie [+][*]	1 600	1 900	2 300	2 500	2 700	14 313	...	93 000
St. Vincent–Grenadines [+] St. Vincent–Grenadines [+]	346	750	1 420	2 361	7 492	9 982	62 911	56 950
Samoa Samoa	766[15]	1 480	2 432	2 500	2 500	2 700	10 500	...
San Marino Saint–Marin	2 350	4 980	9 580	14 503	15 854	16 759	16 900	...
Sao Tome and Principe Sao Tomé–et–Principe	0	0	0	0	0	1 980	4 819	
Saudi Arabia Arabie saoudite	332 068	627 321	836 628	1 375 881	2 528 640	5 007 965	7 238 224	9 175 764
Senegal Sénégal	6 942	27 487	87 879	250 251	301 811	455 645	575 917	1 028 061
Serbia and Montenegro [*] Serbie–et–Monténégro [*]	87 000	240 000	605 697	1 303 609	1 997 809	2 750 397	3 634 613	4 729 629
Seychelles [+] Seychelles [+]	2 247	5 190	16 316	25 961	36 683	44 731	49 229	49 230
Sierra Leone Sierra Leone	0	0	0	11 940	26 895	67 000	113 214[1]	...
Singapore [+] Singapour [+]	848 600	1 094 700	1 630 800	2 747 400	2 991 600	3 344 800	3 477 100	3 860 600[4]
Slovakia Slovaquie	200 140	465 364	664 072	1 243 736	2 147 331	2 923 383	3 678 774	4 275 164
Slovenia Slovénie	93 611	161 606	631 411	1 215 601	1 470 085	1 667 234	1 739 146	...
Solomon Islands [+] Iles Salomon [+]	658	702	1 093	1 151	967	999	1 488	...
Somalia Somalie	0	0	0	80 000	85 000	100 000	200 000	500 000
South Africa [+] Afrique du Sud [+]	1 836 000	3 337 000	5 188 000	8 339 000	10 787 000	13 702 000	16 860 000	19 500 000
Spain Espagne	4 337 696	6 437 444	15 003 708	24 265 059	29 655 729	33 530 997	37 219 839	38 622 582
Sri Lanka Sri Lanka	114 888	174 202	256 655	430 202	667 662	931 580	1 393 403	2 211 158
Sudan Soudan	3 800	8 600	13 000	23 000	103 846	190 778	527 233	1 048 558
Suriname Suriname	2 258	6 007	17 500	41 048	87 000	108 363	168 522	212 819

14 Cellular mobile telephone subscribers—Number (*continued*)
Abonnés au téléphone mobile—Nombre (*suite*)

Country or area Pays ou zone	1997	1998	1999	2000	2001	2002	2003	2004
Swaziland [+] Swaziland [+]	0	4 700	14 000	33 000	55 000	68 000	85 000[4]	113 000
Sweden Suède	3 169 000	4 109 000	5 165 000	6 372 300	7 177 000	7 949 000	8 801 000	9 302 000[16]
Switzerland Suisse	1 044 379	1 698 565	3 057 509	4 638 519	5 275 791	5 736 303	6 189 000	6 275 000
Syrian Arab Republic Rép. arabe syrienne	0	0	4 000	*30 000	200 000	400 000	1 185 000	2 345 000
Tajikistan Tadjikistan	320	420	625	1 160	1 630	13 200	47 617	...
Thailand [+] Thaïlande [+]	2 203 905	1 976 957	2 339 401	3 056 000	7 550 000	16 117 000	24 864 019	27 379 000
TFYR of Macedonia L'ex–R.y. Macédoine	12 362	30 087	48 733	115 748	223 275	365 346	776 000	...
Togo Togo	2 995	7 500	17 000	50 000	95 000	170 000	220 000	
Tonga [1] Tonga [1]	120	130	140	180	236	3 354	...	
Trinidad and Tobago [+] Trinité-et-Tobago [+]	17 140	26 307	38 659	161 860	256 106	361 911	485 871	647 870
Tunisia Tunisie	7 656	38 998	55 258	119 165	389 208	574 334	1 917 530	3 562 970
Turkey Turquie	1 609 809	3 506 127	8 121 517	16 133 405	19 572 897	23 323 118	27 887 535	34 707 549
Turkmenistan Turkménistan	2 500	3 000	4 000	7 500	8 173	8 173	9 187	...
Uganda [+] Ouganda [+]	5 000	30 000	56 358	126 913	283 520	393 310	776 169	1 165 035[8]
Ukraine Ukraine	57 200	115 500	216 567	818 524	2 224 600	3 692 700	6 498 423	13 735 000
United Arab Emirates Emirats arabes unis	309 373	493 278	832 267	1 428 115	1 909 303	2 428 071	2 972 331	3 683 117
United Kingdom [+] Royaume-Uni [+]	8 841 000	14 878 000	27 185 000	43 452 000	46 283 000	49 677 000	52 984 000	61 100 000
United Rep. of Tanzania Rép.–Unie de Tanzanie	20 200	37 940	50 950	180 200	426 964	760 000	1 040 640	1 640 000
United States Etats–Unis	55 312 293	69 209 321	86 047 003	109 478 031	128 374 512	140 766 842	158 721 981	*181 105 135
United States Virgin Is. * Iles Vierges américaines *	16 000	25 000	30 000	35 000	41 000	...	...	...
Uruguay Uruguay	99 235	151 341	319 131	410 787	519 991	513 528	497 530	600 000
Uzbekistan Ouzbékistan	17 232	26 826	40 389	53 128	128 012	186 900	320 815	544 100
Vanuatu Vanuatu	207	220	300	365	350	4 900	7 800	10 504
Venezuela (Bolivarian Rep. of) Venezuela (Rép. bolivarienne)	1 071 900	2 009 757	3 784 735	5 447 172	6 472 584	6 463 561	7 015 735	8 420 980
Viet Nam Viet Nam	160 457	222 700	328 671	788 559	1 251 195	1 902 388	2 742 000	4 960 000
Yemen Yémen	12 245	16 146	27 677	32 000	152 000	411 083	700 000	1 072 000
Zambia [+] Zambie [+]	4 550[17]	8 260	28 190	98 853	121 200	139 092	241 000	300 000

Country or area Pays ou zone	1997	1998	1999	2000	2001	2002	2003	2004
Zimbabwe + Zimbabwe +	5 734	19 000	174 000	266 441	314 002	338 779	363 365	397 500

Source

International Telecommunication Union (ITU), Geneva, the ITU database.

Notes

\+   The data shown generally relate to the fiscal year used in each country, unless indicated otherwise. Countries whose reference periods coincide with the calendar year ending 31 December are not listed.

Year beginning 22 March: Iran (Islamic Republic).

Year beginning 1 April: Antigua and Barbuda, Barbados, Belize, Bermuda, British Virgin Islands, Cayman Islands, China – Hong Kong SAR, Cook Islands, Dominica, Gambia, India, Ireland, Jamaica, Japan, Lesotho, Seychelles, Singapore (beginning 1983), Solomon Islands, South Africa, St. Helena, St. Kitts and Nevis, St. Lucia, St. Vincent and the Grenadines, Swaziland, Trinidad and Tobago, United Kingdom, and Zambia.

Year ending 30 June: Australia, Bangladesh, Egypt (prior to 2000), Ethiopia, Iraq, Kenya, New Zealand (beginning 2000; prior to 2000, year ending 1 April), Pakistan, Uganda, and Zimbabwe.

Year ending 15 July: Nepal.

Year ending 30 September: Argentina, Namibia (beginning 1993), and Thailand.

[1]   ITU estimate.
[2]   As of 31 December.
[3]   September.
[4]   December.
[5]   Including Celtel subscribers.
[6]   For statistical purposes, the data for China do not include those for the Hong Kong Special Administrative Region (Hong Kong SAR) and Macao Special Administrative Region (Macao SAR).

[7]   February.
[8]   November.
[9]   30 June.
[10]   Including Personal Handyphone System.
[11]   Including Western Sahara.
[12]   As of 31 March 2000.
[13]   Users use Israel cellular network.
[14]   Data refer to the Puerto Rico Telephone Authority.
[15]   As of 10 February 1998.
[16]   June.
[17]   Zamtel (Zambian Telecommunications Company Limited) only.

Source

Union internationale des télécommunications (UIT), Genève, la base de données de l'UIT.

Notes

\+   Sauf indication contraire, les données indiquées concernent généralement l'exercice budgétaire utilisé dans chaque pays. Les pays ou territoires dont la période de référence coïncide avec l'année civile se terminant le 31 décembre ne sont pas répertoriés ci–dessous.

Exercice commençant le 22 mars : Iran (République islamique d').

Exercice commençant le 1er avril : Afrique du Sud, Antigua–et–Barbuda, Barbade, Belize, Bermudes, Chine – Hong Kong RAS, Dominique, Gambie, Îles Caïmanes, Îles Cook, Îles Salomon, Îles Vierges britanniques, Inde, Irlande, Jamaïque, Japon, Lesotho, Royaume–Uni, Saint–Kitts–et–Nevis, Saint–Vincent–et–les Grenadines, Sainte–Hélène, Sainte–Lucie, Seychelles, Singapour (à partir de 1983), Swaziland, Trinité–et–Tobago et Zambie.

Exercice se terminant le 30 juin : Australie, Bangladesh, Égypte (antérieur à 2000), Éthiopie, Iraq, Kenya, Nouvelle–Zélande (à partir de 2000; avant 2000, exercice se terminant le 1er avril), Ouganda, Pakistan et Zimbabwe.

Exercice se terminant le 15 juillet : Népal.

Exercice se terminant le 30 septembre : Argentine, Namibie (à partir de 1993), et Thaïlande.

[1]   Estimation de l'UIT.
[2]   Dès le 31 décembre.
[3]   Septembre.
[4]   Décembre.
[5]   Y compris les abonnés au Celtel.
[6]   Pour la présentation des statistiques, les données pour Chine ne comprennent pas la Région Administrative Spéciale de Hong Kong (Hong Kong RAS) et la Région Administrative Spéciale de Macao (Macao RAS).

[7]   Février.
[8]   Novembre.
[9]   30 juin.
[10]   Y compris "Personal Handyphone System".
[11]   Y compris les données de Sahara occidental.
[12]   Dès le 31 mars 2000.
[13]   Les abonnés utilisent le réseau israélien de téléphonie mobile.
[14]   Les données se réfèrent à "Puerto Rico Telephone Authority".
[15]   Dès le 10 février 1998.
[16]   Juin.
[17]   Zamtel ("Zambian Telecommunications Company Limited") seulement.

15

Telephones
Main telephone lines in operation and lines per 100 inhabitants

Téléphones
Nombre de lignes téléphoniques en service et lignes pour 100 habitants

Country or area / Pays ou zone	Number (thousands) — Nombre (en milliers)					Per 100 inhabitants — Pour 100 habitants				
	2000	2001	2002	2003	2004	2000	2001	2002	2003	2004
Afghanistan / Afghanistan	*29	29	*33	*37	*50	0.1	0.1	0.1	0.2	0.2
Albania / Albanie	153	197	220	255	...	4.9	6.4	7.1	8.3	...
Algeria / Algérie	1 761	1 880	1 908	2 200	2 288	5.8	6.1	6.1	6.9	7.1
American Samoa / Samoa américaines	*14	*15	...	...	...	25.0	25.2	...	...	...
Andorra / Andorre	34	35[1]	35[1]	35[1]	35	43.9	43.2	42.6	41.8	52.3
Angola / Angola	70[2]	80[2]	85[2]	96[2]	...	0.5	0.6	0.6	0.7	...
Anguilla / Anguilla	6	6	...	...	...	74.5	53.6	...	...	...
Antigua and Barbuda [+] / Antigua-et-Barbuda [+]	38	37[3]	38	38	38	50.0	48.1	48.8	48.4	49.4
Argentina [+] / Argentine [+]	7 894[4]	8 131[4]	7 709[4]	8 606	8 700	21.5	21.9	20.6	22.7	22.4
Armenia / Arménie	533	531	543	564	582	14.0	14.0	14.3	14.8	19.1
Aruba / Aruba	*38	37	...	...	...	37.2	35.0	...	...	...
Australia [+] / Australie [+]	10 350	10 485	10 905	10 965	10 872	54.0	54.0	55.5	55.2	54.6
Austria / Autriche	3 995[5]	3 997[5,6]	3 883[5]	3 881[5]	3 763[5]	49.9	49.6	47.9	47.7	45.9
Azerbaijan / Azerbaïdjan	801	865	924	941	984	10.2	10.8	11.4	11.4	11.6
Bahamas / Bahamas	114	123	127	132	140	37.5	40.2	40.6	41.6	44.1
Bahrain / Bahreïn	171	174	175	186	192	26.9	26.7	26.1	26.8	25.9
Bangladesh [+] / Bangladesh [+]	491	565	606	742	827	0.4	0.4	0.5	0.6	0.6
Barbados [+7] / Barbade [+7]	*124	129	133	134	136	46.3	48.1	49.4	49.7	50.1
Belarus / Bélarus	2 752	2 862	2 967	3 071	...	27.6	28.8	29.9	31.1	...
Belgium / Belgique	5 036[5]	5 132[5]	4 923[5]	4 875[5]	4 757[5]	49.1	49.8	47.5	47.0	46.0
Belize [+] / Belize [+]	36	35	31	33	34	14.9	13.7	11.4	11.3	12.9
Benin / Bénin	52	59	63	67	73	0.8	0.9	0.9	1.0	1.1
Bermuda [+] / Bermudes [+]	56	56	*56	...	...	87.0	86.9	86.2	...	...
Bhutan / Bhoutan	14	18	20	25	30	2.2	2.6	2.8	3.4	1.3
Bolivia / Bolivie	511	524	591	610	625	6.2	6.3	7.1	7.3	7.0

15

Telephones — Main telephone lines in operation and lines per 100 inhabitants (*continued*)

Téléphones — Nombre de lignes téléphoniques en service et lignes pour 100 habitants (*suite*)

Country or area / Pays ou zone	Number (thousands) — Nombre (en milliers)					Per 100 inhabitants — Pour 100 habitants				
	2000	2001	2002	2003	2004	2000	2001	2002	2003	2004
Bosnia and Herzegovina / Bosnie–Herzégovine	780[8]	847[8]	903[8]	938[8]	...	20.6	22.3	23.7	24.5	...
Botswana + / Botswana +	136	143	142	132	136	8.3	8.5	8.3	7.5	7.6
Brazil / Brésil	30 926[9]	37 431[9]	38 811[9]	39 205[9]	42 382[9]	18.2	21.8	22.3	22.2	23.5
British Virgin Islands + / Iles Vierges britanniques +	*10	*11	12[10]	...	...	52.8	50.9	53.2	...	...
Brunei Darussalam / Brunéi Darussalam	*81	*88	90	...	...	24.3	25.9	25.6	...	...
Bulgaria / Bulgarie	2 882	2 887	2 872	2 818	2 770	35.4	36.6	36.6	36.1	35.4
Burkina Faso / Burkina Faso	53	58	62	65	81	0.5	0.5	0.5	0.5	0.6
Burundi / Burundi	*20	*21	22	24	...	0.3	0.3	0.3	0.3	...
Cambodia / Cambodge	31[11]	33[11]	35[11]	36[11]	...	0.2	0.3	0.3	0.3	...
Cameroon / Cameroun	*95	*106	111	95	...	0.6	0.7	0.7	0.6	...
Canada / Canada	20 347	20 805	20 301	20 068	...	66.1	66.8	64.5	63.2	...
Cape Verde / Cap–Vert	55	64	70	72	73	12.6	14.5	15.6	15.6	15.6
Cayman Islands + / Iles Caïmanes +	35	38	...	...	...	82.1	84.9	...	...	...
Central African Rep. / Rép. centrafricaine	9	9	9	10	10	0.3	0.2	0.2	0.2	0.3
Chad / Tchad	10[12]	11[12]	12	12	13	0.1	0.1	0.2	0.2	0.2
Chile / Chili	3 303	3 478	3 467	3 252	3 318	21.7	22.6	23.0	21.4	21.5
China [13] / Chine [13]	144 829	180 368	214 222	262 747	312 443	11.2	13.7	16.7	20.3	23.8
China, Hong Kong SAR + / Chine, Hong Kong RAS +	3 926	3 898	3 832	3 806	3 780[14]	58.9	58.0	56.5	55.9	53.1
China, Macao SAR / Chine, Macao RAS	177	176	176	175	174	40.9	40.4	39.9	38.9	37.2
Colombia / Colombie	7 193	7 372[15]	7 766	7 850	8 768	17.0	17.2	17.9	17.9	19.5
Comoros / Comores	7	9	10	13	...	1.0	1.2	1.4	1.7	...
Congo / Congo	22[12]	22	22	7	14	0.8	0.7	0.7	0.2	0.4
Cook Islands + / Iles Cook +	6	6[3]	6	...	...	31.0	32.8	34.5	...	...
Costa Rica / Costa Rica	899	945	1 038	1 159	1 343	23.5	23.7	25.8	27.8	31.6
Côte d'Ivoire / Côte d'Ivoire	264	294	325	238	...	1.8	1.8	2.0	1.4	...
Croatia / Croatie	1 721	*1 781	1 825	1 871	1 888	38.5	40.7	41.7	42.8	42.7
Cuba / Cuba	489	574	666	724	768	4.4	5.1	5.9	6.4	6.8

Culture and communication — Culture et communication   115

Country or area / Pays ou zone	Number (thousands) — Nombre (en milliers)					Per 100 inhabitants — Pour 100 habitants				
	2000	2001	2002	2003	2004	2000	2001	2002	2003	2004
Cyprus / Chypre	440	435	427	424[5]	418	64.8	63.1	59.8	59.1	51.8
Czech Republic / République tchèque	3 872	3 861	3 675	3 626	3 450	37.7	37.8	36.2	36.0	33.7
Dem. Rep. of the Congo / Rép. dém. du Congo	*10	*10	*10	...	...	0.0	0.0	0.0	...	...
Denmark / Danemark	3 835[5]	3 865[5]	3 701[5]	3 613[5]	3 475[5]	72.0	72.2	68.9	66.9	64.7
Djibouti / Djibouti	10	10	10	10	11	1.5	1.5	1.5	1.5	1.6
Dominica + / Dominique +	*23	23[16]	24	22	21	29.4	29.9	30.4	28.7	29.5
Dominican Republic / Rép. dominicaine	894	955	909	909	936	11.2	11.8	10.6	10.5	10.7
Ecuador / Equateur	1 224	1 336	1 426	1 549	1 612	9.7	10.4	11.0	11.8	12.2
Egypt + / Egypte +	5 484[17]	6 695	7 736	8 736	9 464	8.6	10.4	11.5	12.7	13.5
El Salvador / El Salvador	625	650	668	753	888	10.0	10.2	10.3	11.3	13.4
Equatorial Guinea / Guinée équatoriale	*6	*7	*9	*10	...	1.4	1.5	1.7	1.8	...
Eritrea / Erythrée	31	31	36	38	39	0.8	0.8	0.9	0.9	0.9
Estonia / Estonie	523	506	475	461	444	36.3	35.4	35.1	34.1	34.0
Ethiopia + / Ethiopie +	232	284	354	435	...	0.4	0.4	0.5	0.6	...
Faeroe Islands / Iles Féroé	25	23	22	20	...	55.5	51.4	45.2	39.8	...
Falkland Is. (Malvinas) / Iles Falkland (Malvinas)	2	2	2	3	...	98.6	99.0	98.5	104.0	...
Fiji / Fidji	86[12]	92	98	102	...	10.7	11.3	11.9	12.4	...
Finland / Finlande	2 849[18]	2 806[18]	2 726[18]	2 568[18]	2 368[18]	55.0	54.0	52.4	49.2	45.4
France / France	33 987[5]	34 084[5]	34 124[5]	33 807[5]	33 870[5]	57.7	57.4	57.2	56.4	56.0
French Guiana / Guyane française	50[12]	51[12]	...	...	...	30.7	30.2	...	...	...
French Polynesia / Polynésie française	54[12]	53	53	54	...	22.7	22.2	21.7	21.4	...
Gabon / Gabon	39	37	32	38	39	3.2	3.0	2.5	2.9	2.9
Gambia + / Gambie +	*33[19]	35[19]	38[19]	...	...	2.7	2.7	2.9	...	...
Georgia / Géorgie	509[20]	569[20]	640[20]	667	683	10.1	11.4	13.0	13.6	13.5
Germany / Allemagne	50 220[5]	52 330[5]	53 670[5]	54 350[5]	54 550[5]	61.1	63.5	65.0	65.9	66.1
Ghana / Ghana	213	245	275	291	313	1.1	1.2	1.3	1.4	·1.5
Greece / Grèce	5 659	5 608[21]	5 413	5 200	5 158	53.6	52.9	49.1	45.4	47.0

Country or area / Pays ou zone	Number (thousands) — Nombre (en milliers)					Per 100 inhabitants — Pour 100 habitants				
	2000	2001	2002	2003	2004	2000	2001	2002	2003	2004
Greenland / Groenland	26	26	25	...	...	46.8	46.7	44.7	...	...
Grenada / Grenade	31	33	34	33	33	33.2	32.8	31.7	29.0	31.8
Guadeloupe / Guadeloupe	205	210[12]	...	...	...	48.0	48.7	...	...	...
Guam / Guam	74[22]	80	...	...	...	48.0	50.9	...	...	...
Guatemala / Guatemala	677	756	846	944	1 132	5.9	6.5	7.1	7.7	8.9
Guernsey / Guernesey	53[5]	55[5]	56[5]	55[5]	55[5]	84.7	97.7	99.5	99.4	...
Guinea / Guinée	24	25	26	26	...	0.3	0.3	0.3	0.3	...
Guinea–Bissau / Guinée–Bissau	11	10	11	11	...	0.9	0.8	0.9	0.8	...
Guyana / Guyana	*68	80	80	92	103	7.9	9.2	9.2	10.4	13.4
Haiti / Haïti	73[12]	80[12]	130[12]	140[12]	140[12]	0.9	1.0	1.6	1.7	1.7
Honduras / Honduras	299	310	322	334	371	4.8	4.7	4.8	4.9	5.3
Hungary / Hongrie	3 798	3 742	3 669	3 603	3 577	37.3	36.8	36.2	35.6	36.4
Iceland / Islande	196[5]	197[5]	188[5]	193[5]	190[5]	69.9	68.5	65.3	66.6	65.0
India + / Inde +	32 436	38 536	41 420[23]	42 000	43 960[24]	3.2	3.8	4.0	4.0	4.1
Indonesia / Indonésie	6 663	7 219	7 750[25]	8 477	9 990	3.2	3.5	3.7	3.9	4.5
Iran (Islamic Rep. of) + / Iran (Rép. islamique d') +	9 486	10 897	12 200	14 571	...	14.9	16.9	18.7	22.0	...
Iraq + / Iraq +	*675	675	1 128[26]	1 183[26]	*1 034	2.9	2.9	4.7	4.8	4.0
Ireland + / Irlande +	1 832[5]	1 860[5]	1 975[5]	1 955[5]	2 019[5]	48.4	48.5	50.2	49.1	50.5
Israel / Israël	2 974	3 033	3 006	3 100	3 000	47.4	46.6	45.3	45.8	43.7
Italy / Italie	27 153[5]	27 353[5,6]	27 142[5]	26 596[5,27]	25 957[5,27]	47.4	47.2	48.1	45.9	44.8
Jamaica + / Jamaïque +	507	*511	435	450	500	19.5	19.6	16.6	17.0	18.7
Japan + / Japon +	61 957	61 326	60 772	60 218	58 788	48.8	48.2	47.7	47.2	46.0
Jersey / Jersey	73	74	...	...	...	84.1	84.8	...	...	...
Jordan / Jordanie	620	660	675	623	617	12.3	12.7	12.7	11.4	11.0
Kazakhstan / Kazakhstan	1 834	1 940	2 082	2 228	2 500	11.3	12.1	13.0	14.1	16.2
Kenya + / Kenya +	292	309	321	328	299	1.0	1.0	1.0	1.0	0.9
Kiribati / Kiribati	3[12]	4	4	...	...	4.0	4.2	5.1	...	...

Country or area / Pays ou zone	Number (thousands) — Nombre (en milliers)					Per 100 inhabitants — Pour 100 habitants				
	2000	2001	2002	2003	2004	2000	2001	2002	2003	2004
Korea, Dem. P. R. / Corée, R. p. dém. de	*500	*860	*916	*980	...	2.2	3.7	3.9	4.1	...
Korea, Republic of / Corée, République de	25 863[18]	25 775[18]	25 735[18]	25 732[18]	26 058[18]	56.2	54.4	54.1	53.8	54.2
Kuwait / Koweït	467	472	482	487	497	21.3	20.8	20.4	19.6	19.2
Kyrgyzstan / Kirghizistan	376	388	395	396	...	7.7	7.9	7.9	7.9	...
Lao People's Dem. Rep. / Rép. dém. pop. lao	41	53	62	70	75	0.8	1.0	1.1	1.2	1.3
Latvia / Lettonie	735[28]	722	701	654	631	30.3	30.7	30.1	28.2	27.6
Lebanon / Liban	576	626	679	700	630	17.5	18.7	19.9	20.0	17.8
Lesotho + / Lesotho +	*22	21[16]	29[16]	35[16]	37[16]	1.0	1.0	1.3	1.6	2.1
Liberia / Libéria	*7	*7	*7	...	...	0.2	0.2	0.2	...	...
Libyan Arab Jamah. / Jamah. arabe libyenne	*605	*660	*720	*750	...	10.8	11.8	13.0	13.6	...
Liechtenstein / Liechtenstein	20	20	20	...	...	61.1	60.0	58.8	...	...
Lithuania / Lituanie	1 188[19]	1 152[19]	936[19]	824[19]	820[19]	32.2	33.0	26.9	23.9	23.8
Luxembourg / Luxembourg	331[29]	347[29]	355[29]	360[29]	...	75.5	78.9	79.7	79.8	...
Madagascar / Madagascar	55	58	59	60	...	0.4	0.4	0.4	0.4	...
Malawi / Malawi	46	55	73	85	93	0.5	0.5	0.7	0.8	0.8
Malaysia / Malaisie	4 634	4 710	4 670	4 572	4 446	19.9	19.7	19.0	18.2	17.9
Maldives / Maldives	24	27	29	30	32	9.1	9.9	10.2	10.5	9.6
Mali / Mali	39	51	57	61	75	0.4	0.5	0.5	0.6	0.7
Malta / Malte	204	208	207	208	...	52.4	53.0	52.3	52.1	...
Marshall Islands / Iles Marshall	4	4	4	4	...	7.8	8.0	8.2	8.3	...
Martinique / Martinique	172[12]	172[12]	...	...	...	44.7	44.5	...	...	...
Mauritania / Mauritanie	19	25	32	38	...	0.7	1.0	1.2	1.4	...
Mauritius / Maurice	281	307	327	348	354	23.5	25.6	27.0	28.5	28.7
Mayotte / Mayotte	10	*10	*10	...	...	6.8	6.5	6.2	...	...
Mexico / Mexique	12 332[30]	13 774[30]	14 975[30]	16 330[30]	18 073[17,30]	12.5	13.9	14.9	16.0	17.2
Micronesia (Fed. States of) / Micronésie (Etats féd. de)	10[12]	10	10	11	12	9.0	9.4	9.4	10.3	10.8
Monaco / Monaco	30	30	34	33	...	93.6	92.1	104.0	102.8	...

Country or area Pays ou zone	Number (thousands) — Nombre (en milliers)					Per 100 inhabitants — Pour 100 habitants				
	2000	2001	2002	2003	2004	2000	2001	2002	2003	2004
Mongolia Mongolie	118	124	128	138	...	5.0	5.2	5.3	5.6	...
Montserrat Montserrat	3[31]	...	...	...	...	70.3	...	...	...	...
Morocco [32] Maroc [32]	1 425	1 191	1 127	1 219	1 309	5.0	4.1	3.8	4.1	4.4
Mozambique Mozambique	86	89	84	78	...	0.5	0.5	0.5	0.4	...
Myanmar Myanmar	271	295	342	363	425	0.5	0.6	0.7	0.7	0.8
Namibia [+] Namibie [+]	110	117	121	127	128	6.2	6.4	6.5	6.6	6.4
Nauru Nauru	2[12]	2	...	...	...	15.7	16.0	...	...	...
Nepal [+] Népal [+]	267	298[3]	328	372	400	1.2	1.3	1.4	1.6	1.6
Netherlands Pays–Bas	9 889[5]	8 158[5]	8 026[5,12]	7 846[5]	7 861[5]	61.9	50.7	49.6	48.2	48.4
Netherlands Antilles Antilles néerlandaises	*80	*81	...	...	...	37.2	37.2	...	...	...
New Caledonia Nouvelle–Calédonie	51	51	52	52	53	23.8	23.1	23.2	22.7	23.0
New Zealand [+] Nouvelle–Zélande [+]	1 831	1 823	1 765	1 798	1 801	47.5	47.0	44.8	44.9	46.1
Nicaragua Nicaragua	164	158	172	205	214	3.2	3.0	3.3	3.7	3.8
Niger Niger	20	22	22	23	24	0.2	0.2	0.2	0.2	0.2
Nigeria Nigéria	553	600	702	889	1 028	0.5	0.5	0.6	0.7	0.8
Niue Nioué	1[12]	1	1	...	...	56.5	60.8	55.9	...	...
Northern Mariana Islands Iles Mariannes du Nord	21	...	...	...	...	30.9	...	...	...	...
Norway Norvège	2 401	2 338	2 317	2 228	...	53.3	51.7	50.9	48.6	...
Occupied Palestinian Terr. Terr. palestinien occupé	272	292	302	316	357	8.6	8.9	8.7	8.7	9.7
Oman Oman	222	231	228	230	240	9.2	9.3	9.0	8.8	8.2
Pakistan [+] Pakistan [+]	3 053	3 252	3 655	3 983	4 502	2.2	2.3	2.5	2.7	3.0
Panama Panama	429	382	387	380	376	15.1	13.2	12.9	12.2	11.9
Papua New Guinea Papouasie–Nvl–Guinée	65	62	62	...	...	1.3	1.2	1.1	...	...
Paraguay Paraguay	283	289[33]	273	281	...	5.2	5.1	4.7	4.7	...
Peru Pérou	1 717	1 571	1 657	1 839	2 050	6.7	6.0	6.2	6.7	7.4
Philippines Philippines	3 061	3 315	3 311	3 340	3 437	4.0	4.2	4.2	4.1	4.2
Poland Pologne	10 946[5]	11 400[5]	11 860[5]	*12 292[5]	...	28.3	29.5	30.7	31.9	...

Country or area / Pays ou zone	Number (thousands) — Nombre (en milliers)					Per 100 inhabitants — Pour 100 habitants				
	2000	2001	2002	2003	2004	2000	2001	2002	2003	2004
Portugal / Portugal	4 226[5]	4 290[5]	4 272[5]	4 197[5]	4 238[5]	42.2	41.5	41.1	40.3	42.1
Puerto Rico [34] / Porto Rico [34]	1 299[35]	1 288[35]	1 276[35]	1 213[17,35]	1 112[17,35]	34.1	33.6	33.1	31.3	28.5
Qatar / Qatar	160	167	177	185	191	26.4	26.2	26.3	26.1	30.8
Republic of Moldova / République de Moldova	584	639	719	791	863	16.0	17.6	19.9	21.9	20.3
Réunion / Réunion	280[12]	300[12]	...	...	...	40.1	41.0	...	...	...
Romania / Roumanie	3 899	4 116	4 215	4 332	4 389	17.4	18.4	19.3	20.0	19.7
Russian Federation / Fédération de Russie	32 070	33 278	35 500	36 993	...	21.8	22.7	24.2	25.3	...
Rwanda / Rwanda	18	22	25	26	23	0.2	0.3	0.3	0.3	0.3
Saint Helena + / Sainte–Hélène +	2	2[3]	2	2	...	32.9	33.7	49.4	52.4	...
Saint Kitts and Nevis + / Saint–Kitts–et–Nevis +	*22	*23	24	...	25	48.6	48.8	50.3	...	50.0
Saint Lucia + / Sainte–Lucie +	*49	50	51	...	...	31.5	31.7	32.0	...	...
St. Vincent–Grenadines + / St. Vincent–Grenadines +	25	26	27	32	19	22.0	22.7	23.4	27.3	15.7
Samoa / Samoa	9[12]	10	12	13	...	4.8	5.4	6.5	7.3	...
San Marino / Saint–Marin	20	21	21	21	...	75.2	75.9	76.3	76.6	...
Sao Tome and Principe / Sao Tomé–et–Principe	5	5	6	7	...	3.1	3.6	4.1	4.6	...
Saudi Arabia / Arabie saoudite	2 965	3 233	3 318	3 503	3 695	14.2	15.1	15.1	15.5	14.8
Senegal / Sénégal	206	237	225	229	...	2.2	2.4	2.2	2.2	...
Serbia and Montenegro / Serbie–et–Monténégro	2 406	2 444	2 493	2 612	2 685	22.6	22.9	23.3	24.3	25.5
Seychelles + / Seychelles +	21	21	21	21	21	25.4	26.2	25.4	25.6	26.2
Sierra Leone / Sierra Leone	19	23	24	...	...	0.4	0.5	0.5	...	...
Singapore + / Singapour +	1 947	1 948	1 934	1 897	1 864[16]	48.5	47.1	46.4	45.2	43.2
Slovakia / Slovaquie	1 698	1 556	1 403	1 295	1 250	31.4	28.9	23.5	20.3	23.1
Slovenia / Slovénie	785	802	808	812	...	39.5	40.2	40.5	40.7	...
Solomon Islands + / Iles Salomon +	8[36,37]	7[36,37]	7[36,37]	6[36,37]	...	1.8	1.7	1.5	1.3	...
Somalia / Somalie	*25	*35	*35	*100	*200	0.3	0.4	0.4	0.8	1.7
South Africa + / Afrique du Sud +	4 962	4 924	4 844	4 821	...	11.4	11.1	10.7	10.4	...
Spain / Espagne	17 104	17 531	17 641	17 759	17 752	42.6	43.4	42.9	41.6	43.2

Country or area / Pays ou zone	Number (thousands) — Nombre (en milliers)					Per 100 inhabitants — Pour 100 habitants				
	2000	2001	2002	2003	2004	2000	2001	2002	2003	2004
Sri Lanka / Sri Lanka	767	827	883	939	991	4.2	4.4	4.7	4.9	5.1
Sudan / Soudan	387	448	672	937	1 029	1.2	1.4	2.0	2.8	3.0
Suriname / Suriname	75	77	79	80	81	17.4	16.5	16.5	16.6	18.5
Swaziland + / Swaziland +	32	34	35	46	...	3.2	3.3	3.4	4.4	...
Sweden / Suède	6 728[5]	6 717[5]	6 579[5]	6 873[5]	...	75.8	75.4	73.6	76.6	...
Switzerland / Suisse	5 236[5]	5 383[5,38]	5 388[5]	5 323[5]	5 250[5]	72.6	74.3	74.0	72.7	70.8
Syrian Arab Republic / Rép. arabe syrienne	1 675	1 817	2 099	2 414	2 660	10.4	10.9	12.3	13.8	14.6
Tajikistan / Tadjikistan	219	227	238	245	...	3.6	3.7	3.7	3.8	...
Thailand + / Thaïlande +	5 591	6 049	6 542	6 617	6 797	9.2	9.9	10.6	10.7	11.0
TFYR of Macedonia / L'ex–R.y. Macédoine	507	539	560	525	...	25.1	26.4	27.1	25.2	...
Togo / Togo	43	48	51	61	...	0.9	1.0	1.1	1.2	...
Tonga / Tonga	10[12]	11	11	...	...	9.8	10.9	11.3	...	...
Trinidad and Tobago + / Trinité–et–Tobago +	317	312	318	320	321	24.5	24.0	24.5	24.5	24.6
Tunisia / Tunisie	955	1 056	1 149	1 164	1 204	10.0	10.9	11.7	11.8	12.1
Turkey / Turquie	18 395	18 904	18 890	18 917	19 125	28.2	27.6	27.1	26.8	26.5
Turkmenistan / Turkménistan	364	388	374	376	...	8.2	8.0	7.7	7.7	...
Turks and Caicos Islands / Iles Turques et Caïques	*6	...	...	...	...	34.3	...	...	...	...
Tuvalu / Tuvalu	*1	1	...	...	...	7.0	6.8	...	...	...
Uganda + / Ouganda +	62	56	55	61	72	0.3	0.2	0.2	0.2	0.3
Ukraine / Ukraine	10 417	10 670	10 833	11 110	12 142	21.0	21.9	22.5	23.3	25.2
United Arab Emirates / Emirats arabes unis	1 020	1 053	1 094	1 136	1 188	31.4	30.2	29.1	28.1	27.3
United Kingdom + / Royaume–Uni +	35 228[5]	35 660[5]	34 898[5]	34 591[5]	33 700[5]	58.9	59.4	59.1	59.5	56.7
United Rep. of Tanzania / Rép.–Unie de Tanzanie	174	148	162	149	...	0.5	0.4	0.5	0.4	...
United States / Etats–Unis	192 513[39]	191 697[39]	189 390[39]	183 042[39]	177 947[39]	68.4	67.2	65.8	62.9	59.9
United States Virgin Is. / Iles Vierges américaines	68	*69	69	70	71	62.9	63.5	63.1	63.0	63.9
Uruguay / Uruguay	929	951	947	938	1 000	29.0	29.6	29.4	29.0	30.9
Uzbekistan / Ouzbékistan	1 655	1 663	1 681	1 717	...	6.7	6.7	6.7	6.7	...

Country or area	Number (thousands) — Nombre (en milliers)					Per 100 inhabitants — Pour 100 habitants				
Pays ou zone	2000	2001	2002	2003	2004	2000	2001	2002	2003	2004
Vanuatu Vanuatu	7	7	7	7	7	3.5	3.4	3.3	3.2	3.1
Venezuela (Bolivarian Rep. of) Venezuela (Rép. bolivar. du)	2 536	2 705	2 842	2 956	3 346	10.5	10.9	11.3	11.5	12.8
Viet Nam Viet Nam	2 543	3 050	3 929	4 402	10 125	3.2	3.8	4.8	5.4	12.3
Yemen Yémen	347	423	542	685	798	1.9	2.2	2.8	3.4	3.9
Zambia + Zambie +	83	86	88	88	...	0.8	0.8	0.8	0.8	...
Zimbabwe + Zimbabwe +	249	254	288	306	317	2.2	2.2	2.5	2.6	2.5

Source

International Telecommunication Union (ITU), Geneva, the ITU database.

Notes

+   The data shown generally relate to the fiscal year used in each country, unless indicated otherwise. Countries whose reference periods coincide with the calendar year ending 31 December are not listed.

Year beginning 22 March: Iran (Islamic Republic).

Year beginning 1 April: Antigua and Barbuda, Barbados, Belize, Bermuda, Botswana, British Virgin Islands, Cayman Islands, China – Hong Kong, Cocos Islands, Cook Islands, Dominica, Gambia, India, Ireland, Israel (prior to 1986), Jamaica, Japan, Lesotho, Seychelles, Singapore (beginning 1983), Solomon Islands, South Africa, St. Helena, St. Kitts and Nevis, St. Lucia, St. Vincent and the Grenadines, Swaziland, Trinidad and Tobago, United Kingdom, and Zambia.

Year ending 30 June: Australia, Bangladesh, Egypt (prior to 2000), Ethiopia, Iraq, Kenya, New Zealand (beginning 2000; prior to 2000, year ending 1 April), Pakistan, Uganda, and Zimbabwe.

Year ending 15 July: Nepal.

Year ending 30 September: Argentina (beginning 1991), Namibia (beginning 1993), and Thailand.

[1]   Analogic lines + XDSI lines.
[2]   Data refer to Angola Telecom.
[3]   As of 31 December.
[4]   1994–2002 only refers to Telefónica de Argentina S.A. y Telecom Argentina S.A.. From 2002 all licensees are included (352 in 2003).

[5]   Including ISDN channels.
[6]   September.
[7]   Prior to 2002, data refer to BET and Bartel. Beginning 2002, data refer to Cable and Wireless.
[8]   Including ISDN equivalents.
[9]   Conventional telephony terminals in service.
[10]   Caribbean Telecommunications Union.
[11]   WLL lines included.
[12]   ITU estimate.
[13]   For statistical purposes, the data for China do not include those for the Hong Kong Special Administrative Region (Hong Kong SAR), Macao Special Administrative Region (Macao SAR) and Taiwan Province of China.

Source

Union internationale des télécommunications (UIT), Genève, la base de données de l'UIT.

Notes

+   Sauf indication contraire, les données indiquées concernent généralement l'exercice budgétaire utilisé dans chaque pays. Les pays ou territoires dont la période de référence coïncide avec l'année civile se terminant le 31 décembre ne sont pas répertoriés ci–dessous.

Exercice commençant le 22 mars : Iran (République islamique d').

Exercice commençant le 1er avril : Afrique du Sud, Antigua–et–Barbuda, Barbade, Belize, Bermudes, Botswana, Chine–Hong Kong, Dominique, Gambie, Îles Caïmanes, Îles des Cocos, Îles Cook, Îles Salomon, Îles Vierges britanniques, Inde, Irlande, Israël (antérieur à 1986), Jamaïque, Japon, Lesotho, Royaume–Uni, Saint–Kitts–et–Nevis, Saint–Vincent–et–les Grenadines, Sainte–Hélène, Sainte–Lucie, Seychelles, Singapour (à partir de 1983), Swaziland, Trinité–et–Tobago et Zambie.

Exercice se terminant le 30 juin : Australie, Bangladesh, Égypte (antérieur à 2000), Éthiopie, Iraq, Kenya, Nouvelle–Zélande (à partir de 2000; avant 2000, exercice se terminant le 1er avril), Ouganda, Pakistan et Zimbabwe.

Exercice se terminant le 15 juillet : Népal.

Exercice se terminant le 30 septembre : Argentine (à partir de 1991), Namibie (à partir de 1993), et Thaïlande.

[1]   Lignes analogiques et "XDSI".
[2]   Les données se réfèrent à "Angola Telecom".
[3]   Dès le 31 décembre.
[4]   Les chiffres de 1994–2002 ne concernent que Telefónica de Argentina S.A. y Telecom Argentina S.A. À partir de 2002 tous les détenteurs de licence sont compris (352 en 2003).
[5]   RNIS inclu.
[6]   Septembre.
[7]   Avant 2002, les données se réfèrent au "BET" et "Bartel". A partir de 2002 les données se réfèrent au "Cable and Wireless".
[8]   Y compris les équivalents du RNIS.
[9]   Terminaux de téléphonie conventionnelle en service.
[10]   "Caribbean Telecommunications Union".
[11]   Y compris les lignes "WLL".
[12]   Estimation de l'UIT.
[13]   Pour la présentation des statistiques, les données pour Chine ne comprennent pas la Région Administrative Spéciale de Hong Kong (Hong Kong RAS), la Région Administrative Spéciale de Macao (Macao RAS) et la province de Taiwan.

[14]	January 2005.	[14]	Janvier 2005.
[15]	Ministry of Communication estimate.	[15]	Estimation du ministère de communication.
[16]	December.	[16]	Décembre.
[17]	June.	[17]	Juin.
[18]	Telephone subscribers (Finland: from 1996 the basis for the compilation of the statistics changed).	[18]	Abonnés au téléphone. (Finland : à compter de 1996, la base de calcul des statistiques à changé).
[19]	Excluding public call offices.	[19]	Cabines publiques exclues.
[20]	Data provided by the Commission based on counts made by technical experts.	[20]	Données fournies par la Commission fondées sur un dénombrement effectué par des experts techniques.
[21]	Decrease was due to switching of users to ISDN and mobile services.	[21]	La diminution tient au fait que les usagers sont passés au RNIS et aux téléphones portables.
[22]	US Federal Communications Commission's Statistics of Communications Common Carriers.	[22]	"US Federal Communications Commission's Statistics of Communications Common Carriers".
[23]	Subscriber lines.	[23]	Lignes d'abonnés au téléphone.
[24]	October.	[24]	Octobre.
[25]	September. Telkom.	[25]	Septembre. Telkom.
[26]	Central Organisation for Statistic & IT.	[26]	Central Organisation for Statistic & IT.
[27]	Data refer to Telecom Italia Wireline.	[27]	Les données se réfèrent au "Telecom Italia Wireline".
[28]	Lattelekom.	[28]	Lattelekom.
[29]	Including digital lines.	[29]	Y compris lignes digitales.
[30]	Lines in service.	[30]	Lignes en service.
[31]	Decrease due to the reduction of population since the volcanic crisis in 1995.	[31]	Baisse due à la diminution de la population depuis l'éruption volcanique de 1995.
[32]	Including Western Sahara.	[32]	Y compris les données de Sahara occidental.
[33]	Decrease in lines available in the public sector.	[33]	Diminution des lignes disponibles dans la secteur publique.
[34]	Data refer to the Puerto Rico Telephone Authority.	[34]	Les données se réfèrent à "Puerto Rico Telephone Authority".
[35]	Switched access lines.	[35]	Lignes d'accès déviées.
[36]	Billable lines.	[36]	Lignes payables.
[37]	The number of fixed lines declined due to civil war.	[37]	Le nombre de lignes fixes a diminué en raison de la guerre civile.
[38]	SWISSCOM at September 2001.	[38]	SWISSCOM: Septembre 2001.
[39]	Data up to 1980 refer to main stations reported by FCC. From 1981, data refer to "Local Loops".	[39]	Les données pour 1980 se réfèrent aux stations principales. Dès 1981, les données se réfèrent aux "Local Loops".

Country or area Pays ou zone	1997	1998	1999	2000	2001	2002	2003	2004
Afghanistan Afghanistan	...	...	...	...	...	1 000	20 000	25 000
Albania Albanie .	1 500	2 000	2 500	3 500	10 000	12 000	30 000	75 000
Algeria Algérie	3 000	6 000	60 000	150 000	200 000	500 000	650 000	845 000
Andorra Andorre	2 000	4 500	5 000	7 000	...	...	10 049	11 000
Angola Angola	750	2 500	10 000	15 000	20 000	41 000	84 000	172 000
Antigua and Barbuda [+] Antigua–et–Barbuda [+]	2 500	3 000	4 000	5 000	7 000	10 000	14 000	20 000
Argentina [+] Argentine [+]	100 000	300 000	1 200 000	2 600 000	3 650 000	4 100 000	4 530 000	5 120 000
Armenia Arménie	3 500	4 000	30 000	40 000	50 000	60 000	140 000	150 000
Aruba Aruba	...	...	4 000	14 000	24 000	...	...	...
Australia [+] Australie [+]	1 600 000	4 200 000	5 600 000	6 600 000	7 700 000	10 500 000	11 300 000	13 000 000
Austria [1] Autriche [1]	760 000	1 230 000	1 840 000	2 700 000	3 150 000	3 340 000	3 730 000	3 900 000
Azerbaijan Azerbaïdjan	2 000	3 000	8 000	12 000	25 000	300 000	350 000	408 000
Bahamas Bahamas	3 967	6 908	11 307	13 130	16 923	60 000[2]	84 000	93 000
Bahrain Bahreïn	10 000	20 000	30 000	40 000	100 000	122 794	150 000	152 721
Bangladesh [+] Bangladesh [+]	1 000	5 000	50 000	100 000	186 000	204 000	243 000	300 000
Barbados [+3] Barbade [+3]	2 000	5 000	6 000	10 000	15 000	30 000[4]	100 000	150 000
Belarus Bélarus	5 000	7 500	50 000	187 036	430 263	808 481	1 391 903	1 600 000
Belgium Belgique	500 000	800 000	1 400 000	3 000 000	3 200 000	3 400 000	4 000 000	4 200 000
Belize [+] Belize [+]	3 000	5 000	10 000	15 000	18 000	25 000[4]	30 000	35 000
Benin Bénin	1 500	3 000	10 000	15 000	25 000	50 000	70 000	100 000
Bermuda [+] Bermudes [+]	15 000	20 000	25 000	27 000	30 000	...	36 000	39 000
Bhutan Bhoutan	...	...	750	2 250	5 000	10 000	15 000	20 000
Bolivia Bolivie	35 000	50 000	80 000	120 000	180 000	270 000	310 000	350 000
Bosnia and Herzegovina Bosnie–Herzégovine	2 000	5 000	7 000	40 000	45 000	100 000	150 000[4]	225 000
Botswana [+] Botswana [+]	5 000	10 000	19 000	25 000	50 000	60 000	60 000	60 000
Brazil [4] Brésil [4]	1 310 000	2 500 000	3 500 000	5 000 000	8 000 000	14 300 000	18 000 000	22 000 000

Country or area Pays ou zone	1997	1998	1999	2000	2001	2002	2003	2004
British Virgin Islands + Iles Vierges britanniques +	...	...	...	...	...	4 000	...	...
Brunei Darussalam Brunéi Darussalam	15 000	20 000	25 000	30 000	35 000	...	48 000	56 000
Bulgaria Bulgarie	100 000	150 000	234 600	430 000	605 000	630 000	1 545 143	2 200 000
Burkina Faso Burkina Faso	2 000	5 000	7 000	9 000	19 000	25 000	48 000	53 200
Burundi Burundi	500	1 000	2 500	5 000	7 000	8 000	14 000	25 000
Cambodia Cambodge	700	2 000	4 000	6 000	10 000	30 000	35 000	41 000
Cameroon Cameroun	1 000	2 000	20 000	40 000	45 000	60 000	100 000	167 000
Canada Canada	4 500 000	7 500 000	11 000 000	12 971 000[5]	14 000 000[6]	15 200 000[4]	17 600 000	20 000 000
Cape Verde Cap–Vert	1 000	2 000	5 000	8 000	12 000	16 000[4]	20 000	25 000
Central African Rep. Rép. centrafricaine	500	1 000	1 500	2 000	3 000	5 000	6 000	9 000
Chad Tchad	50	335	1 000	3 000	4 000	15 000	30 000	60 000
Chile Chili	156 875	250 000	625 000	2 537 308	3 102 200	3 575 000	4 000 000	4 300 000
China[7] Chine[7]	400 000	2 100 000	8 900 000	22 500 000	33 700 000	59 100 000	79 500 000	94 000 000
China, Hong Kong SAR + Chine, Hong Kong RAS +	675 000[4]	947 000[4]	1 400 000[4]	1 855 200[8]	2 601 300[8]	2 918 800[8]	3 212 800[8]	3 479 700[8]
China, Macao SAR Chine, Macao RAS	10 000	30 000	40 000	60 000	101 000	115 000	120 000	150 000
Colombia Colombie	208 000	433 000	664 000	878 000	*1 154 000	2 000 113	2 732 201[9]	3 585 688
Comoros Comores	0	200	800	1 500	2 500	3 200	5 000	8 000
Congo Congo	100	100	500	800	1 000	5 000	15 000	36 000
Cook Islands + Iles Cook +	1 200	...	2 300	2 750	3 200	3 600	...	...
Costa Rica Costa Rica	60 000	100 000	150 000	228 000	384 000	815 745	900 000	1 000 000
Côte d'Ivoire Côte d'Ivoire	3 000	10 000	20 000	40 000	70 000	90 000	240 000	300 000
Croatia Croatie	80 000	150 000	200 000	299 380	518 000	789 000	1 014 000	1 303 000
Cuba Cuba	7 500[10]	25 000[10]	34 800[10]	60 000[10]	120 000[10]	160 000[10]	98 000	150 000
Cyprus Chypre	33 000	68 000	88 000	120 000	150 000	210 000	250 000	298 000
Czech Republic République tchèque	300 000	400 000	700 000	1 000 000	1 500 000	2 600 180	*3 100 280	4 800 000
Dem. Rep. of the Congo Rép. dém. du Congo	100	200	500	3 000	6 000	50 000	...	...
Denmark Danemark	600 000[4]	1 200 000[4]	1 626 000[11]	2 090 000[11]	2 300 000[4]	2 756 000[12]	3 034 000[4]	3 762 500[4]
Djibouti Djibouti	550	650	750	1 400	3 300	4 500	6 500	9 000

Country or area Pays ou zone	1997	1998	1999	2000	2001	2002	2003	2004
Dominica + Dominique +	...	2 000	2 000	6 000	9 000	12 500	17 000	18 500
Dominican Republic Rép. dominicaine	12 000	20 000	96 000	327 118	397 333[13]	500 000	650 000	800 000
Ecuador Equateur	13 000	15 000	100 000	180 000	333 000	537 881	569 727	624 579
Egypt + Egypte +	60 000[9]	100 000[9]	200 000[9]	450 000	600 000	1 900 000	3 000 000	3 900 000
El Salvador El Salvador	15 000	25 000	50 000	70 000	150 000	300 000	550 000	587 475
Equatorial Guinea Guinée équatoriale	200	470	500	700	900	1 800	3 000	5 000
Eritrea Erythrée	300	300	900	5 000	6 000	9 000	9 500	50 000
Estonia Estonie	80 000	150 000	200 000	391 600	429 656	444 000	600 000	670 000
Ethiopia + Ethiopie +	3 000	6 000	8 000	10 000	25 000	50 000	75 000	113 000
Faeroe Islands Iles Féroé	2 000	5 000	10 000	15 000	20 000	25 000	28 000	31 000
Falkland Is. (Malvinas) Iles Falkland (Malvinas)	100[14]	...	1 600	1 700	1 900	1 900	1 900	...
Fiji Fidji	1 750	5 000	7 500	12 000	15 000	50 000	55 000	61 000
Finland [15] Finlande [15]	1 000 000	1 311 000	1 667 000	1 927 000	2 235 320	2 529 000	2 560 000	3 286 000
France France	2 485 000[16]	3 704 000[16]	5 370 000[5]	8 460 000[5]	15 653 000[17]	18 716 000[17]	21 900 000[17]	25 000 000[17]
French Guiana Guyane française	1 000	1 500	2 000	16 000	20 000	25 000	31 000	38 000
French Polynesia Polynésie française	480	3 000	8 000	15 000	15 000	20 000	35 000	61 000
Gabon Gabon	550	2 000	3 000	15 000	17 000	25 000	35 000	40 000
Gambia + Gambie +	600	2 500	9 000	12 000	18 000	25 000	35 000	49 000
Georgia Géorgie	3 000	5 000	20 000	23 000	46 500	73 500	117 020	175 600
Germany Allemagne	5 500 000	8 100 000	17 100 000	24 800 000	26 000 000	28 000 000	33 000 000	41 263 000
Ghana Ghana	5 000	6 000	20 000	30 000	*40 000	170 000	250 000	368 000
Greece Grèce	200 000	350 000	750 000	1 000 000	915 347	1 485 281	1 718 435	1 955 000
Greenland Groenland	4 434	8 187	12 102	17 841	20 000	25 000	31 000	38 000
Grenada Grenade	1 000	1 500	2 500	4 113	5 200	15 000	19 000	8 000
Guadeloupe Guadeloupe	1 000	2 000	7 000	25 000	40 000	50 000	63 000	79 000
Guam Guam	3 536	6 787	13 028	25 007	40 000	50 000	63 000	79 000
Guatemala Guatemala	10 000	50 000	65 000	80 000	200 000	400 000	550 000	756 000
Guernsey Guernesey	2 100	4 500	9 500	20 000	25 000	30 000	33 000	36 000

Country or area Pays ou zone	1997	1998	1999	2000	2001	2002	2003	2004
Guinea Guinée	300	500	5 000	8 000	15 000	35 000	40 000	46 000
Guinea–Bissau Guinée–Bissau	200	300	1 500	3 000	4 000	14 000	19 000	26 000
Guyana Guyana	1 000	2 000	30 000	50 000	100 000	125 000	140 000	145 000
Haiti Haïti	...	2 000	6 000	20 000	30 000	80 000	150 000	500 000
Honduras Honduras	10 000	18 000	35 000	55 000	90 000	168 560	185 510	222 273
Hungary Hongrie	200 000	400 000	600 000	715 000	1 480 000	1 600 000	2 400 000	2 700 000
Iceland Islande	75 000	100 000	150 000	168 000	172 000	186 600	195 000	225 610
India [+] Inde [+]	700 000	1 400 000	2 800 000	5 500 000	7 000 000	16 580 000	18 481 044 [18]	35 000 000
Indonesia Indonésie	384 000	510 000	900 000	1 900 000	4 200 000	4 500 000	8 080 000	14 508 000
Iran (Islamic Rep. of) [+] Iran (Rép. islamique d') [+]	30 000	65 000	250 000	625 000	1 005 000	3 168 000	4 800 000	550 000
Iraq [+] Iraq [+]	...	...	...	...	12 500	25 000	30 000	36 000
Ireland [+] Irlande [+]	150 000 [4]	300 000 [4]	410 000 [19]	679 000 [19]	895 000 [19]	1 102 000 [19]	1 260 000 [19]	1 079 730 [19]
Israel Israël	250 000	600 000	800 000	1 270 000	1 800 000	2 000 000	2 500 000	3 200 000
Italy Italie	1 300 000	2 600 000	8 200 000	13 200 000	15 600 000	19 800 000	22 880 000	28 870 000
Jamaica [+] Jamaïque [+]	20 000	50 000	60 000	80 000	100 000	600 000	800 000	1 067 000
Japan [+] Japon [+]	11 550 000	16 940 000 [20]	27 060 000 [20]	38 000 000 [20]	48 900 000 [20]	57 200 000 [20]	61 600 000 [20]	75 000 000 [20]
Jersey Jersey	3 000	4 000	6 000	8 000	...	...	20 000	27 000
Jordan Jordanie	27 354	60 816	120 000	127 317	234 000	307 469	444 000	600 000
Kazakhstan Kazakhstan	10 000	20 000	70 000	100 000	150 000	250 000	300 000	400 000
Kenya [+] Kenya [+]	10 000	15 000	35 000	100 000	200 000	400 000	1 000 000	1 500 000
Kiribati Kiribati	...	500	1 000	1 500	2 000	2 000	2 000	2 000
Korea, Republic of Corée, République de	1 634 000	3 103 000	10 860 000	19 040 000	24 380 000	26 270 000	29 220 000	31 580 000
Kuwait Koweït	40 000	60 000	100 000	150 000	200 000	250 000	567 000	600 000
Kyrgyzstan Kirghizistan	...	3 500	10 000	51 600	150 600	152 000	200 000	263 000
Lao People's Dem. Rep. Rép. dém. pop. lao	...	500	2 000	6 000	10 000	15 000	19 000	20 900
Latvia Lettonie	50 000	80 000	105 000	150 000	170 000	310 000	936 000	810 000
Lebanon Liban	45 000	100 000	200 000	300 000	260 000	400 000	500 000	600 000
Lesotho [+] Lesotho [+]	100	200	1 000	4 000	5 000	21 000	30 000	43 000

Country or area Pays ou zone	1997	1998	1999	2000	2001	2002	2003	2004
Liberia Libéria	100	100	300	500	1 000	...	...	...
Libyan Arab Jamah. Jamah. arabe libyenne	...	...	7 000	10 000	20 000	125 000	160 000	205 000
Liechtenstein Liechtenstein	...	...	...	12 000	15 000	20 000	...	...
Lithuania Lituanie	35 000	70 000	103 000	225 000	250 000	500 000	695 700	968 000
Luxembourg Luxembourg	30 000[4]	50 000[4]	75 000[4]	100 000[4]	160 000[21]	165 000[19]	170 000[4]	270 810[4]
Madagascar Madagascar	2 000	9 000	25 000	30 000	35 000	55 000	70 500	90 000
Malawi Malawi	500	2 000	10 000	15 000	20 000	27 000	36 000	46 140
Malaysia Malaisie	500 000	1 500 000	2 800 000	4 977 000	6 346 650	7 840 640	8 661 000	9 878 214
Maldives Maldives	800	1 500	3 000	6 000	10 000	15 000	17 000	19 000
Mali Mali	1 000	2 000	6 277	15 000	20 000	25 000	35 000	50 000
Malta Malte	15 000	25 000	30 000	51 000	99 000	120 000	190 000[4]	301 000
Marshall Islands Iles Marshall	...	...	500	800	900	1 250	1 400	2 000
Martinique Martinique	...	2 000	5 000	30 000	40 000	60 000	80 000	107 000
Mauritania Mauritanie	100	1 000	3 000	5 000	7 000	10 000	12 000	14 000
Mauritius Maurice	5 500	30 000	55 000	87 000	106 000	125 000[21]	150 000	180 000
Mayotte Mayotte	...	...	...	1 800	...	...	...	...
Mexico Mexique	595 700	1 222 379	1 822 198	#5 058 000	7 410 124	10 764 715	12 218 830	14 036 475
Micronesia (Fed. States of) Micronésie (Etats féd. de)	616	2 000	3 000	4 000	5 000	6 000	10 000	12 000
Monaco Monaco	...	...	...	13 500	15 000	15 500	16 000	...
Mongolia Mongolie	2 600	3 400	12 000	30 000	40 000	50 000	142 800	200 000
Morocco[22] Maroc[22]	6 000	40 000	50 000	200 000	400 000	700 000	1 000 000	3 500 000[23]
Mozambique Mozambique	2 000	3 500	10 000	20 000	30 000	50 000	83 000	138 000
Myanmar Myanmar	...	...	500	7 000	10 000	25 000	28 002	63 688
Namibia + Namibie +	1 000	5 000	6 000	30 000	45 000	50 000	65 000	75 000
Nauru Nauru	...	...	...	...	300	...	...	...
Nepal + Népal +	5 000	15 000	35 000	50 000	60 000[24]	80 000	100 000	175 000
Netherlands Pays–Bas	2 200 000	3 500 000	6 200 000	7 000 000	7 900 000	8 200 000	8 500 000	10 000 000
Netherlands Antilles Antilles néerlandaises	...	...	2 000	...	...	...	...	...

Country or area / Pays ou zone	1997	1998	1999	2000	2001	2002	2003	2004
New Caledonia / Nouvelle–Calédonie	2 000	4 000	12 000	30 000	40 000	50 000	60 000	70 000
New Zealand[+] / Nouvelle–Zélande[+]	550 000	750 000	1 113 000	1 515 000	1 762 000	1 908 000	2 110 000	3 200 000
Nicaragua / Nicaragua	10 000	15 000	25 000	50 000	75 000	90 000	100 000	125 000
Niger / Niger	200	300	3 000	4 000	12 000	15 000	19 000	24 000
Nigeria / Nigéria	20 000	30 000	50 000	80 000	115 000	420 000	750 000	1 769 661
Niue / Nioué	...	...	300	500	600	900	...	...
Norway / Norvège	1 300 000[4]	1 600 000[4]	1 800 000	1 950 000	1 319 400	1 398 600	1 583 300	1 792 000
Occupied Palestinian Terr. / Terr. palestinien occupé	...	...	...	35 000	60 000	105 000	145 000	160 000
Oman / Oman	10 000	20 000	50 000	90 000	120 000	180 000	210 000	245 000
Pakistan[+] / Pakistan[+]	37 800	61 900	80 000	300 000	500 000	1 000 000	1 600 000	2 000 000
Panama / Panama	15 000	30 000	45 000	90 000	168 690	220 000	260 000	300 000
Papua New Guinea / Papouasie–Nouvelle–Guinée	5 000	12 000	35 000	45 000	50 000	75 000	113 000	170 000
Paraguay / Paraguay	5 000	10 000	20 000	40 000	60 000	100 000	120 000	150 000
Peru / Pérou	100 000	300 000	500 000	800 000	*2 000 000	*2 400 000	*2 850 000	3 220 000
Philippines / Philippines	100 000	823 000	1 090 000	1 540 000	2 000 000	3 500 000	4 000 000	4 400 000
Poland / Pologne	800 000	1 581 000	2 100 000	2 800 000	3 800 000	8 880 000	*8 970 000	9 000 000
Portugal / Portugal	500 000[4]	1 000 000[4]	1 500 000[4]	1 680 200	1 860 400	2 267 200	2 674 000[4]	2 951 000[4]
Puerto Rico[25] / Porto Rico[25]	50 000	100 000	200 000	400 000	600 000	677 000	764 000	862 000
Qatar / Qatar	17 000	20 000	24 000	30 000	40 000	70 000	140 760	165 000
Republic of Moldova / République de Moldova	1 200	11 000	25 000	52 600	60 000	150 000	288 000	406 000
Réunion[26] / Réunion[26]	...	9 000	10 000	100 000	120 000	150 000	180 000	216 000
Romania / Roumanie	100 000	500 000	600 000	800 000	1 000 000	2 200 000	4 000 000	4 500 000
Russian Federation / Fédération de Russie	700 000	1 200 000	1 500 000	2 900 000	4 300 000	6 000 000	10 000 000	16 000 000
Rwanda / Rwanda	100	800	5 000	5 000	20 000	25 000	31 000	38 000
Saint Helena[+] / Sainte–Hélène[+]	...	79	300	300	400[27]	500	600	...
Saint Kitts and Nevis[+] / Saint–Kitts–et–Nevis[+]	1 000	1 500	2 000	2 700	3 600	10 000	...	...
Saint Lucia[+] / Sainte–Lucie[+]	1 500	2 000	3 000	8 000	13 000	...	34 000	55 000
St. Vincent–Grenadines[+] / St. Vincent–Grenadines[+]	1 000	2 000	3 000	3 500	5 500	6 000	7 000	8 000

Country or area Pays ou zone	1997	1998	1999	2000	2001	2002	2003	2004
Samoa Samoa	300	400	500	1 000	3 000	4 000	5 000	6 000
Sao Tome and Principe Sao Tomé-et-Principe	...	400	500	6 500	9 000	11 000	15 000	20 000
Saudi Arabia Arabie saoudite	10 000	20 000	100 000	460 000	1 016 208	1 418 880	1 500 000	1 586 000
Senegal Sénégal	2 500	7 500	30 000	40 000	100 000	105 000	225 000	482 000
Serbia and Montenegro Serbie-et-Monténégro	50 000	65 000	80 000	400 000	600 000	640 000	847 000	1 200 000
Seychelles [+] Seychelles [+]	1 000	2 000	5 000	6 000[4]	9 000[24]	11 736	12 000	20 000
Sierra Leone Sierra Leone	200	600	2 000	5 000	7 000	8 000	9 000	10 000
Singapore [+] Singapour [+]	500 000	750 000	950 000	1 300 000	1 700 000	2 100 000	2 135 034[28]	2 421 782
Slovakia Slovaquie	63 000[4]	144 539	292 359	507 029	674 039	862 833	1 375 809	2 276 000
Slovenia Slovénie	150 000	200 000	250 000	300 000	600 000	750 000	800 000	950 000
Solomon Islands [+] Iles Salomon [+]	1 500	2 000	2 000	2 000	2 000	2 200	2 500	3 000
Somalia Somalie	200	500	1 000	15 000	85 000	86 000	90 000	200 000
South Africa [+] Afrique du Sud [+]	700 000	1 266 000	1 820 000	2 400 000	2 890 000	3 100 000	3 325 000	3 566 000
Spain [29] Espagne [29]	1 110 000	1 733 000	2 830 000	5 486 000	7 388 000	7 856 000	9 789 000	14 332 800
Sri Lanka Sri Lanka	30 000	55 000	65 000	121 500	150 000	200 000	250 000	280 000
Sudan Soudan	700	2 000	5 000	30 000	150 000	300 000	937 000	1 140 000
Suriname Suriname	4 494	7 587	8 715	11 709	14 520	20 000	23 000	30 000
Swaziland [+] Swaziland [+]	900	1 000	5 000	10 000	14 000	20 000	27 000	36 000
Sweden Suède	2 100 000	2 961 000	3 666 000	4 048 000	4 600 000	5 125 000	5 655 000	6 800 000
Switzerland Suisse	548 000	939 000	1 473 000	2 096 000	2 800 000	3 000 000	3 400 000	3 500 000
Syrian Arab Republic Rép. arabe syrienne	5 000	10 000	20 000	30 000	60 000	365 000	610 000	800 000
Tajikistan Tadjikistan	...	...	2 000	3 000	3 200	3 500	4 120	5 000
Thailand [+] Thaïlande [+]	375 000	500 000	1 300 000	2 300 000	3 536 019	4 800 000	6 971 520[30]	6 972 000
TFYR of Macedonia L'ex-R.y. Macédoine	10 000	20 000	30 000	50 000	70 000	100 000	126 000	159 000
Togo Togo	10 000	15 000	30 000	100 000	150 000	200 000	210 000	221 000
Tonga Tonga	500	750	1 000	2 400	2 800	2 900	3 000	3 000
Trinidad and Tobago [+] Trinité-et-Tobago [+]	15 000	35 000	75 000	100 000	120 000[18]	138 000[18]	153 000	160 000
Tunisia Tunisie	4 000	10 000	150 000	260 000	410 000	505 500	630 000	835 000

Country or area Pays ou zone	1997	1998	1999	2000	2001	2002	2003	2004
Turkey Turquie	300 000	450 000	1 500 000	2 500 000	3 500 000	4 300 000	6 000 000	10 220 000
Turkmenistan Turkménistan	...	...	2 000	6 000	8 000	...	*20 000	36 000
Tuvalu Tuvalu	...	...	...	500	1 000	1 250	1 800	...
Uganda + Ouganda +	2 300	15 000	25 000	40 000	60 000	100 000	125 000	200 000
Ukraine Ukraine	100 000	150 000	200 000	350 000	600 000	900 000	2 500 000	3 750 000
United Arab Emirates Emirats arabes unis	90 000	200 000	458 000	765 000	976 000	1 175 516	1 373 217	1 384 837
United Kingdom + Royaume–Uni +	4 310 000[4]	8 000 000[4]	12 500 000[4]	15 800 000[31]	19 800 000[31]	25 000 000[31]	34 400 000[31]	37 600 000[31]
United Rep. of Tanzania Rép.–Unie de Tanzanie	2 500	3 000	25 000	40 000	60 000	80 000	250 000	333 000
United States Etats–Unis	60 000 000	84 587 000	102 000 000	124 000 000	142 823 000	159 000 000	161 632 400	185 000 000
United States Virgin Is. Iles Vierges américaines	7 500	10 000	12 000	15 000	20 000	30 000	...	...
Uruguay Uruguay	110 000	230 000	330 000	350 000	370 000	380 000	530 000	680 000
Uzbekistan Ouzbékistan	2 500	5 000	7 500	120 000	150 000	275 000	492 000	880 000
Vanuatu Vanuatu	250	500	1 000	4 000	5 500	7 000	7 500	7 500
Venezuela (Bolivarian Rep. of) Venezuela (Rép. bolivarienne)	90 000	322 244	680 000	820 022	1 152 502	1 274 429	1 934 791	2 312 683
Viet Nam Viet Nam	3 000	10 000	100 000	200 000	1 009 544	1 500 000	3 500 000	5 870 000
Yemen Yémen	2 500	4 000	10 000	15 000	17 000	100 000	120 000	180 000
Zambia + Zambie +	900	3 000	15 000	20 000	25 000	52 420[18]	110 000	231 000
Zimbabwe +4 Zimbabwe +4	4 000	10 000	20 000	50 000	100 000	500 000	800 000	820 000

Source

International Telecommunication Union (ITU), Geneva, the ITU database.

Notes

\+   The data shown generally relate to the fiscal year used in each country, unless indicated otherwise. Countries whose reference periods coincide with the calendar year ending 31 December are not listed.

Year beginning 22 March: Iran (Islamic Republic).

Year beginning 1 April: Antigua and Barbuda, Barbados, Belize, Bermuda, Botswana, British Virgin Islands, Cayman Islands, China – Hong Kong SAR, Cook Islands, Dominica, Gambia, India, Ireland, Jamaica, Japan, Lesotho, Seychelles, Singapore, Solomon Islands, South Africa, St. Helena, St. Kitts and Nevis, St. Lucia, St. Vincent, Swaziland, Trinidad and Tobago, United Kingdom, and Zambia.

Year ending 30 June: Australia, Bangladesh, Egypt, Ethiopia, Iraq, Kenya, New Zealand (beginning 2000; prior to 2000, year ending 1 April), Pakistan, Uganda, and Zimbabwe.

Source

Union internationale des télécommunications (UIT), Genève, la base de données de l'UIT.

Notes

\+   Sauf indication contraire, les données indiquées concernent généralement l'exercice budgétaire utilisé dans chaque pays. Les pays ou territoires dont la période de référence coïncide avec l'année civile se terminant le 31 décembre ne sont pas répertoriés ci–dessous.

Exercice commençant le 22 mars : Iran (République islamique d').

Exercice commençant le 1er avril : Afrique du Sud, Antigua–et–Barbuda, Barbade, Belize, Bermudes, Botswana, Chine – Hong Kong RAS, Dominique, Gambie, Îles Caïmanes, Îles Cook, Îles Salomon, Îles Vierges britanniques, Inde, Irlande, Jamaïque, Japon, Lesotho, Royaume–Uni, Saint–Kitts–et–Nevis, Saint–Vincent–et–les Grenadines, Sainte–Hélène, Sainte–Lucie, Seychelles, Singapour, Swaziland, Trinité–et–Tobago et Zambie.

Exercice se terminant le 30 juin : Australie, Bangladesh, Égypte, Éthiopie, Iraq, Kenya, Nouvelle–Zélande (à partir de 2000; avant 2000, exercice se terminant le 1er avril), Ouganda, Pakistan et Zimbabwe.

Year ending 15 July: Nepal.

Year ending 30 September: Argentina, Namibia (beginning 1993), and Thailand.

1 Regular users of the Internet, age 14+.
2 ITU estimate based on 3 times the number of subscribers.
3 Prior to 2002, data refer to BET and Bartel. Beginning 2002, data refer to Cable and Wireless.
4 ITU estimate.
5 Population age 15+ using in last year.
6 Population age 18+ using in last week.

7 For statistical purposes, the data for China do not include those for the Hong Kong Special Administrative Region (Hong Kong SAR) and Macao Special Administrative Region (Macao SAR).

8 Population age 10+ who accessed Internet in previous year.

9 June.
10 Including those who used only international email.

11 MR & IT, e–mail users.
12 Age 15–74 using at least once in last 3 months.

13 As of 30 September.
14 Year ending 31 March.
15 Has used at least one other Internet application besides e–mail in last 3 months. Age 15+.

16 Population age 18+, using in the last year.
17 Population age 11+ using in the last month.
18 December.
19 Age 15+.
20 PC–based only.
21 Age 12+.
22 Including Western Sahara.
23 Including users who went on the internet at least once, no matter the location.
24 As of 31 December.
25 Data refer to the Puerto Rico Telephone Authority.
26 France Télécom only.
27 Data refer to 31 December.
28 Household survey.
29 At November of year indicated. Age 15+.
30 Age 6+.
31 Population age 16+ using in the last month.

Exercice se terminant le 15 juillet : Népal.

Exercice se terminant le 30 septembre : Argentine, Namibie (à partir de 1993), et Thaïlande.

1 Utilisateurs réguliers de l'Internet âgés de plus de 14 ans.
2 Estimation de l'UIT basée sur le nombre d'abonnés multiplié par 3.
3 Avant 2002, les données se réfèrent au "BET" et "Bartel". A partir de 2002 les données se réfèrent au "Cable and Wireless".
4 Estimation de l'UIT.
5 Population âgée de plus de 15 ans utilisant au cours de l'année écoulée.
6 Population âgée de plus de 18 ans utilisant au cours de la dernière semaine.

7 Pour la présentation des statistiques, les données pour Chine ne comprennent pas la Région Administrative Spéciale de Hong Kong (Hong Kong RAS) et la Région Administrative Spéciale de Macao (Macao RAS).

8 Population âgée de plus de 10 ans s'étant branchée sur l'Internet au cours de l'année écoulée.

9 Juin.
10 Y compris ceux qui n'ont utilisé que des services internationaux de messagerie électronique.

11 "MR & IT", utilisateurs de courrier électronique.
12 Population d'âge compris entre 15 et 74 ans ayant utilisé l'Internet une fois au moins au cours des trois derniers mois.

13 Au 30 septembre.
14 Année finissant le 31 mars.
15 A utilisé au moins une application Internet autre que le courrier électronique au cours des trois derniers mois. Population âgée de plus de 15 ans.

16 Population âgée de plus de 18 ans, utilisant au cours de l'année écoulée.
17 Population âgée de plus de 11 ans utilisant au cours de dernier mois.
18 Décembre.
19 Population âgée de plus de 15 ans.
20 Pour ordinateurs personnels seulement.
21 Population âgée de plus de 12 ans.
22 Y compris les données de Sahara occidental.
23 Y compris les usagers ayant accédé à l'Internet une fois au moins quel que soit le lieu.
24 Dès le 31 décembre.
25 Les données se réfèrent à "Puerto Rico Telephone Authority".
26 France Télécom seulement.
27 Les données se réfèrent au 31 décembre.
28 L'enquête auprès des ménages.
29 En november de l'année indiquée. Population agée de plus de 15 ans.
30 Population âgée de plus de 6 ans.
31 Population âgée de plus de 16 ans utilisant au cours du dernier mois.

Table 13: The data on newspapers have been compiled from the UNESCO Institute for Statistics database (see www.uis.unesco.org). Newspapers are periodic publications intended for the general public and mainly designed to be a primary source of written information on current events connected with public affairs, international questions, politics, etc. They may also include articles on literary or other subjects as well as illustrations and advertising.

Daily newspapers are newspapers mainly reporting events that have occurred in the 24-hour period before going to press. They are issued at least 4 times a week.

Circulation figures show the average daily circulation. These figures include the number of copies sold directly, sold by subscription, or mainly distributed free of charge. Circulation figures refer to the number of copies distributed both inside the country and abroad. The figures for copies printed, unlike the circulation figures, also include the number of unsold copies (returns).

The statistics included in *Tables 14-16* were obtained from the statistics database (see www.itu.int) and the *Yearbook of Statistics, Telecommunication Services* [16] of the International Telecommunication Union.

Table 14: The number of mobile cellular telephone subscribers refers to users of portable telephones subscribing to an automatic public mobile telephone service using cellular technology which provides access to the Public Switched Telephone Network (PSTN).

Table 15: This table shows the number of main lines in operation and the main lines in operation per 100 inhabitants for the years indicated. Main telephone lines refer to the telephone lines connecting a customer's equipment to the Public Switched Telephone Network (PSTN) and which have a dedicated port on a telephone exchange. Note that in most countries, main lines also include public telephones. Main telephone lines per 100 inhabitants is calculated by dividing the number of main lines by the population and multiplying by 100.

Table 16: Internet user data is based on reported estimates, derivations based on reported Internet Access Provider subscriber counts, or calculated by multiplying the number of hosts by an estimated multiplier. However, comparisons of user data are misleading because there is no standard definition of frequency (e.g., daily, weekly, monthly) or services used (e.g., e-mail, World Wide Web).

Tableau 13 : Les données concernant les journaux proviennent de la base de données de l'Institut de statistique de l'UNESCO (voir www.uis.unesco.org). Les journaux sont les publications périodiques destinées au grand public qui ont essentiellement pour objet de constituer une source primaire d'information écrite sur les événements d'actualité concernant les affaires publiques, les questions internationales, la politique, etc. Ils peuvent aussi contenir des articles portant sur des sujets littéraires ou autres, ainsi que sur des illustrations et de la publicité.

Les quotidiens sont les journaux rapportant principalement les événements survenus dans les vingt-quatre heures précédant leur mise sous presse. Ils paraissent au moins quatre fois par semaine.

Les chiffres concernant la diffusion sont ceux de la diffusion quotidienne moyenne. Ces chiffres comprennent le nombre d'exemplaires vendus directement, vendus par abonnement ou principalement distribués gratuitement. Les chiffres concernant la diffusion se réfèrent au nombre d'exemplaires distribués aussi bien à l'étranger que dans le pays. Contrairement aux chiffres concernant la diffusion, le nombre d'exemplaires imprimés incluent les exemplaires invendus (retours).

Les données présentées dans les *Tableaux 14 à 16* proviennent de la base de données (voir www.itu.int) et l'*Annuaire statistique, Services de télécommunications* [16] de l'Union internationale des télécommunications.

Tableau 14 : Les abonnés mobiles désignent les utilisateurs de téléphones portatifs abonnés à un service automatique public de téléphones mobiles ayant accès au Réseau de téléphone public connecté (RTPC).

Tableau 15 : Ce tableau indique le nombre de lignes principales en service et les lignes principales en service pour 100 habitants pour les années indiquées. Les lignes principales sont des lignes téléphoniques qui relient l'équipement terminal de l'abonné au Réseau de téléphone public connecté (RTPC) et qui possèdent un accès individualisé aux équipements d'un central téléphonique. Pour la plupart des pays, le nombre de lignes principales en service indiqué comprend également les lignes publiques. Le nombre de lignes principales pour 100 habitants se calcule en divisant le nombre de lignes principales par la population et en multipliant par 100.

Tableau 16 : Les chiffres relatifs aux usagers d'Internet sont basés sur les estimations communiquées, calculés à partir des chiffres issus de dénombrements d'abonnés aux services de fournisseurs d'accès, ou obtenus en multipliant le nombre d'hôtes par un facteur estimatif. Mais les comparaisons de chiffres relatifs aux usagers prêtent à confusion, car il n'existe pas de définition normalisée de la fréquence (quotidienne, hebdomadaire, mensuelle) ni des services utilisés (courrier électronique, Web).

PART THREE
Economic activity

TROISIÈME PARTIE
Activité économique

Part Three of the *Yearbook* presents statistical series on production and consumption for a wide range of economic activities, and other basic series on major economic topics, for all countries or areas of the world for which data are available. Included are basic tables on national accounts, finance, labour force, wages and prices, a wide range of agricultural, mined and manufactured commodities, transport, energy, environment and research and development personnel and expenditure.

International economic topics such as external trade are covered in Part Four.

La troisième partie de l'*Annuaire* présente, pour une large gamme d'activités économiques, des séries statistiques sur la production et la consommation, et, pour tous les pays ou zones du monde pour lesquels des données sont disponibles, d'autres séries fondamentales ayant trait à des questions économiques importantes. Y figurent des tableaux de base consacrés à la comptabilité nationale, aux finances, à la main-d'oeuvre, aux salaires et aux prix, à un large éventail de produits agricoles, miniers et manufacturés, aux transports, à l'énergie, à l'environnement, au personnel employé à des travaux de recherche et développement et dépenses de recherche et développement.

Les questions économiques internationales comme le commerce extérieur sont traitées dans la quatrième partie.

Gross domestic product and gross domestic product per capita
In millions of US dollars+ at current and constant 1990 prices; per capita US dollars; real rates of growth

Produit intérieur brut et produit intérieur brut par habitant
En millions de dollars E.–U.+ aux prix courants et constants de 1990 ; par habitant en dollars E.–U. ; taux de l'accroissement réels

Country or area	1998	1999	2000	2001	2002	2003	2004	Pays ou zone
World								**Monde**
GDP at current prices	29 746 263	30 850 309	31 654 453	31 398 135	32 615 768	36 571 682	40 998 057	PIB aux prix courants
GDP per capita	5 020	5 140	5 200	5 100	5 230	5 790	6 420	PIB par habitant
GDP at constant prices	26 814 230	27 674 667	28 786 464	29 249 454	29 807 949	30 601 364	31 812 451	PIB aux prix constants
Growth rates	2.5	3.2	4.0	1.6	1.9	2.7	4.0	Taux de l'accroissement
Afghanistan								**Afghanistan**
GDP at current prices	4 394	3 851	2 713	2 618	3 573	4 399	5 252	PIB aux prix courants
GDP per capita	196	167	114	106	138	162	184	PIB par habitant
GDP at constant prices	3 973	3 482	1 961	1 777	2 285	2 644	2 842	PIB aux prix constants
Growth rates	5.2	−12.4	−43.7	−9.4	28.6	15.7	7.5	Taux de l'accroissement
Albania								**Albanie**
GDP at current prices	2 737	3 445	3 694	4 103	4 495	6 065	7 946	PIB aux prix courants
GDP per capita	892	1 125	1 207	1 338	1 461	1 960	2 554	PIB par habitant
GDP at constant prices	2 205	2 428	2 606	2 793	2 889	3 062	3 246	PIB aux prix constants
Growth rates	12.7	10.1	7.3	7.2	3.4	6.0	6.0	Taux de l'accroissement
Algeria								**Algérie**
GDP at current prices	47 841	48 641	54 462	54 935	56 220	65 172	80 783	PIB aux prix courants
GDP per capita	1 615	1 620	1 788	1 777	1 791	2 045	2 497	PIB par habitant
GDP at constant prices	69 341	71 559	73 278	74 817	77 810	83 178	86 922	PIB aux prix constants
Growth rates	5.1	3.2	2.4	2.1	4.0	6.9	4.5	Taux de l'accroissement
Andorra								**Andorre**
GDP at current prices	1 114	1 121	997	1 047	1 175	1 485	1 726	PIB aux prix courants
GDP per capita	16 886	16 996	15 109	15 832	17 705	22 276	25 786	PIB par habitant
GDP at constant prices	1 343	1 450	1 556	1 730	1 909	2 069	2 256	PIB aux prix constants
Growth rates	−3.0	8.0	7.3	11.2	10.3	8.4	9.0	Taux de l'accroissement
Angola								**Angola**
GDP at current prices	6 507	6 153	9 130	8 936	9 796	13 825	20 272	PIB aux prix courants
GDP per capita	493	456	660	629	670	919	1 309	PIB par habitant
GDP at constant prices	10 508	10 755	11 173	11 757	13 284	13 984	15 550	PIB aux prix constants
Growth rates	5.5	2.4	3.9	5.2	13.0	5.3	11.2	Taux de l'accroissement
Anguilla								**Anguilla**
GDP at current prices	100	106	108	110	113	118	130	PIB aux prix courants
GDP per capita	9 181	9 600	9 617	9 646	9 733	9 976	10 811	PIB par habitant
GDP at constant prices	81	84	85	88	86	89	90	PIB aux prix constants
Growth rates	10.3	3.7	1.3	2.6	−1.4	2.5	1.7	Taux de l'accroissement
Antigua and Barbuda								**Antigua-et-Barbuda**
GDP at current prices	545	573	585	614	632	668	692	PIB aux prix courants
GDP per capita	7 383	7 623	7 653	7 910	8 037	8 399	8 595	PIB par habitant
GDP at constant prices	431	449	456	466	480	503	508	PIB aux prix constants
Growth rates	4.4	4.1	1.5	2.3	3.0	4.7	1.0	Taux de l'accroissement
Argentina								**Argentine**
GDP at current prices	299 098	283 664	284 346	268 831	102 042	129 596	153 014	PIB aux prix courants
GDP per capita	8 285	7 771	7 707	7 212	2 711	3 410	3 988	PIB par habitant
GDP at constant prices	223 007	215 458	213 758	204 334	182 072	198 162	215 961	PIB aux prix constants
Growth rates	3.9	−3.4	−0.8	−4.4	−10.9	8.8	9.0	Taux de l'accroissement
Armenia								**Arménie**
GDP at current prices	1 892	1 845	1 912	2 118	2 376	2 805	3 615	PIB aux prix courants
GDP per capita	607	595	620	691	779	923	1 195	PIB par habitant
GDP at constant prices	1 339	1 382	1 464	1 604	1 845	2 101	2 312	PIB aux prix constants
Growth rates	7.3	3.3	5.9	9.6	15.1	13.9	10.0	Taux de l'accroissement
Aruba								**Aruba**
GDP at current prices	1 665	1 725	1 858	1 889	1 901	2 000	2 075	PIB aux prix courants
GDP per capita	18 567	18 988	20 176	20 187	19 981	20 675	21 131	PIB par habitant
GDP at constant prices	1 669	1 687	1 750	1 738	1 693	1 720	1 771	PIB aux prix constants
Growth rates	6.7	1.1	3.7	−0.7	−2.5	1.5	3.0	Taux de l'accroissement

17

Gross domestic product and gross domestic product per capita—In millions of US dollars+ at current and constant 1990 prices; per capita US dollars; real rates of growth (*continued*)

Produit intérieur brut et produit intérieur brut par habitant—En millions de dollars E.–U.+ aux prix courants et constants de 1990 ; par habitant en dollars E.–U. ; taux de l'accroissement réels (*suite*)

Country or area	1998	1999	2000	2001	2002	2003	2004	Pays ou zone
Australia								**Australie**
GDP at current prices	370 390	402 246	387 532	368 891	411 910	527 413	630 146	PIB aux prix courants
GDP per capita	19 895	21 344	20 320	19 120	21 111	26 734	31 598	PIB par habitant
GDP at constant prices	415 912	431 550	440 426	457 513	472 195	490 012	496 678	PIB aux prix constants
Growth rates	5.3	3.8	2.1	3.9	3.2	3.8	1.4	Taux de l'accroissement
Austria								**Autriche**
GDP at current prices	213 850	213 104	193 838	192 923	207 997	255 230	292 340	PIB aux prix courants
GDP per capita	26 435	26 341	23 942	23 789	25 590	31 317	35 777	PIB par habitant
GDP at constant prices	198 463	205 054	211 937	213 457	215 945	217 582	222 289	PIB aux prix constants
Growth rates	3.6	3.3	3.4	0.7	1.2	0.8	2.2	Taux de l'accroissement
Azerbaijan								**Azerbaïdjan**
GDP at current prices	4 446	4 581	5 273	5 708	6 236	7 138	8 281	PIB aux prix courants
GDP per capita	554	567	647	696	756	860	991	PIB par habitant
GDP at constant prices	3 214	3 450	3 834	4 211	4 656	5 176	5 667	PIB aux prix constants
Growth rates	10.0	7.4	11.1	9.9	10.6	11.2	9.5	Taux de l'accroissement
Bahamas								**Bahamas**
GDP at current prices	3 670	4 005	4 309	4 317	4 398	4 586	4 813	PIB aux prix courants
GDP per capita	12 538	13 482	14 296	14 119	14 182	14 585	15 099	PIB par habitant
GDP at constant prices	3 110	3 293	3 455	3 348	3 344	3 408	3 520	PIB aux prix constants
Growth rates	3.0	5.9	4.9	−3.1	−0.1	1.9	3.3	Taux de l'accroissement
Bahrain								**Bahreïn**
GDP at current prices	6 184	6 620	7 971	7 928	8 447	9 606	10 975	PIB aux prix courants
GDP per capita	9 661	10 076	11 861	11 576	12 137	13 609	15 332	PIB par habitant
GDP at constant prices	6 369	6 643	6 993	7 318	7 697	8 218	8 672	PIB aux prix constants
Growth rates	4.8	4.3	5.3	4.7	5.2	6.8	5.5	Taux de l'accroissement
Bangladesh								**Bangladesh**
GDP at current prices	46 838	48 301	48 626	48 955	51 924	57 191	61 604	PIB aux prix courants
GDP per capita	378	382	377	372	387	419	443	PIB par habitant
GDP at constant prices	46 100	48 841	51 416	53 687	56 508	60 729	63 158	PIB aux prix constants
Growth rates	4.9	5.9	5.3	4.4	5.3	7.5	4.0	Taux de l'accroissement
Barbados								**Barbade**
GDP at current prices	2 374	2 483	2 592	2 547	2 512	2 697	2 834	PIB aux prix courants
GDP per capita	8 971	9 356	9 739	9 544	9 390	10 054	10 538	PIB par habitant
GDP at constant prices	1 842	1 908	1 954	1 887	1 879	1 920	1 978	PIB aux prix constants
Growth rates	4.4	3.6	2.4	−3.4	−0.4	2.2	3.0	Taux de l'accroissement
Belarus								**Bélarus**
GDP at current prices	15 222	12 138	10 418	12 355	14 595	17 825	22 909	PIB aux prix courants
GDP per capita	1 503	1 204	1 039	1 239	1 471	1 807	2 335	PIB par habitant
GDP at constant prices	15 236	15 761	16 673	17 461	18 336	19 618	21 770	PIB aux prix constants
Growth rates	8.4	3.4	5.8	4.7	5.0	7.0	11.0	Taux de l'accroissement
Belgium								**Belgique**
GDP at current prices	250 307	251 093	228 417	227 428	245 752	304 216	352 327	PIB aux prix courants
GDP per capita	24 441	24 440	22 168	22 013	23 730	29 311	33 879	PIB par habitant
GDP at constant prices	227 906	235 180	244 298	246 054	248 278	251 404	258 729	PIB aux prix constants
Growth rates	2.0	3.2	3.9	0.7	0.9	1.3	2.9	Taux de l'accroissement
Belize								**Belize**
GDP at current prices	629	689	757	790	843	898	950	PIB aux prix courants
GDP per capita	2 723	2 910	3 125	3 188	3 327	3 469	3 594	PIB par habitant
GDP at constant prices	539	572	615	645	672	732	754	PIB aux prix constants
Growth rates	2.4	6.1	7.5	4.9	4.1	9.0	3.0	Taux de l'accroissement
Benin								**Bénin**
GDP at current prices	2 335	2 387	2 255	2 371	2 719	3 510	4 085	PIB aux prix courants
GDP per capita	344	342	313	319	355	443	500	PIB par habitant
GDP at constant prices	2 626	2 750	2 908	3 055	3 250	3 427	3 519	PIB aux prix constants
Growth rates	4.5	4.7	5.8	5.0	6.4	5.5	2.7	Taux de l'accroissement
Bermuda								**Bermudes**
GDP at current prices	3 053	3 272	3 378	3 539	3 715	3 911	4 140	PIB aux prix courants
GDP per capita	49 006	52 283	53 735	56 046	58 575	61 398	64 749	PIB par habitant
GDP at constant prices	2 409	2 495	2 546	2 588	2 639	2 691	2 745	PIB aux prix constants
Growth rates	3.4	3.6	2.1	1.7	2.0	2.0	2.0	Taux de l'accroissement

Gross domestic product and gross domestic product per capita— In millions of US dollars[+] at current and constant 1990 prices; per capita US dollars; real rates of growth (*continued*)

Produit intérieur brut et produit intérieur brut par habitant— En millions de dollars E.–U.[+] aux prix courants et constants de 1990 ; par habitant en dollars E.–U. ; taux de l'accroissement réels (*suite*)

Country or area	1998	1999	2000	2001	2002	2003	2004	Pays ou zone
Bhutan								**Bhoutan**
GDP at current prices	396	444	483	515	571	684	778	PIB aux prix courants
GDP per capita	214	235	249	260	282	331	368	PIB par habitant
GDP at constant prices	450	483	510	546	582	620	666	PIB aux prix constants
Growth rates	6.4	7.4	5.7	7.0	6.7	6.6	7.3	Taux de l'accroissement
Bolivia								**Bolivie**
GDP at current prices	8 497	8 285	8 391	8 023	7 801	7 867	8 421	PIB aux prix courants
GDP per capita	1 065	1 017	1 009	945	901	890	935	PIB par habitant
GDP at constant prices	6 845	6 874	7 031	7 137	7 333	7 513	7 797	PIB aux prix constants
Growth rates	5.0	0.4	2.3	1.5	2.8	2.5	3.8	Taux de l'accroissement
Bosnia and Herzegovina								**Bosnie-Herzégovine**
GDP at current prices	4 230	4 687	4 455	4 697	5 466	6 891	7 884	PIB aux prix courants
GDP per capita	1 169	1 250	1 158	1 204	1 394	1 759	2 017	PIB par habitant
GDP at constant prices	3 327	3 643	3 840	4 013	4 163	4 295	4 467	PIB aux prix constants
Growth rates	16.6	9.5	5.4	4.5	3.7	3.2	4.0	Taux de l'accroissement
Botswana								**Botswana**
GDP at current prices	4 771	4 654	4 889	4 903	5 045	7 341	8 441	PIB aux prix courants
GDP per capita	2 788	2 682	2 787	2 777	2 849	4 144	4 771	PIB par habitant
GDP at constant prices	5 251	5 467	5 828	6 324	6 466	6 899	7 209	PIB aux prix constants
Growth rates	8.1	4.1	6.6	8.5	2.2	6.7	4.5	Taux de l'accroissement
Brazil								**Brésil**
GDP at current prices	787 742	536 633	601 732	508 433	460 838	505 732	593 091	PIB aux prix courants
GDP per capita	4 666	3 132	3 461	2 883	2 576	2 788	3 225	PIB par habitant
GDP at constant prices	542 913	547 178	570 937	578 431	589 595	588 287	611 740	PIB aux prix constants
Growth rates	0.1	0.8	4.3	1.3	1.9	−0.2	4.0	Taux de l'accroissement
British Virgin Islands								**Iles Vierges britanniques**
GDP at current prices	593	662	691	751	798	873	943	PIB aux prix courants
GDP per capita	30 065	32 870	33 671	35 990	37 677	40 663	43 366	PIB par habitant
GDP at constant prices	387	423	429	453	480	504	539	PIB aux prix constants
Growth rates	11.4	9.1	1.6	5.6	5.8	5.2	6.8	Taux de l'accroissement
Brunei Darussalam								**Brunéi Darussalam**
GDP at current prices	3 904	4 215	4 316	4 150	4 280	4 729	5 285	PIB aux prix courants
GDP per capita	12 280	12 945	12 944	12 156	12 248	13 226	14 454	PIB par habitant
GDP at constant prices	3 915	4 016	4 129	4 253	4 390	4 527	4 579	PIB aux prix constants
Growth rates	−4.0	2.6	2.8	3.0	3.2	3.1	1.1	Taux de l'accroissement
Bulgaria								**Bulgarie**
GDP at current prices	12 737	12 955	12 600	13 599	15 568	19 859	24 406	PIB aux prix courants
GDP per capita	1 571	1 609	1 576	1 712	1 974	2 535	3 137	PIB par habitant
GDP at constant prices	15 821	16 185	17 058	17 752	18 620	19 416	20 487	PIB aux prix constants
Growth rates	4.0	2.3	5.4	4.1	4.9	4.3	5.5	Taux de l'accroissement
Burkina Faso								**Burkina Faso**
GDP at current prices	2 486	2 466	2 192	2 477	2 875	3 748	4 467	PIB aux prix courants
GDP per capita	233	225	194	213	239	302	348	PIB par habitant
GDP at constant prices	4 318	4 590	4 691	4 959	5 187	5 602	5 870	PIB aux prix constants
Growth rates	6.4	6.3	2.2	5.7	4.6	8.0	4.8	Taux de l'accroissement
Burundi								**Burundi**
GDP at current prices	896	810	711	664	630	597	677	PIB aux prix courants
GDP per capita	142	127	110	100	92	85	93	PIB par habitant
GDP at constant prices	989	980	971	993	1 037	1 032	1 087	PIB aux prix constants
Growth rates	4.6	−1.0	−0.9	2.2	4.5	−0.5	5.4	Taux de l'accroissement
Cambodia								**Cambodge**
GDP at current prices	3 035	3 306	3 606	3 721	4 012	4 140	4 357	PIB aux prix courants
GDP per capita	248	265	283	286	302	306	316	PIB par habitant
GDP at constant prices	2 586	2 764	2 975	3 141	3 313	3 490	3 640	PIB aux prix constants
Growth rates	2.1	6.9	7.7	5.6	5.5	5.3	4.3	Taux de l'accroissement
Cameroon								**Cameroun**
GDP at current prices	9 736	9 625	8 972	9 451	10 803	13 692	16 150	PIB aux prix courants
GDP per capita	683	661	604	624	699	869	1 007	PIB par habitant
GDP at constant prices	15 200	15 869	16 527	17 403	18 534	19 368	20 298	PIB aux prix constants
Growth rates	5.0	4.4	4.2	5.3	6.5	4.5	4.8	Taux de l'accroissement

Gross domestic product and gross domestic product per capita—In millions of US dollars⁺ at current and constant 1990 prices; per capita US dollars; real rates of growth (*continued*)

Produit intérieur brut et produit intérieur brut par habitant—En millions de dollars E.–U.⁺ aux prix courants et constants de 1990 ; par habitant en dollars E.–U. ; taux de l'accroissement réels (*suite*)

Country or area	1998	1999	2000	2001	2002	2003	2004	Pays ou zone
Canada								**Canada**
GDP at current prices	606 924	651 202	714 453	705 167	726 703	856 555	991 673	PIB aux prix courants
GDP per capita	20 146	21 420	23 280	22 752	23 209	27 075	31 031	PIB par habitant
GDP at constant prices	689 033	727 687	765 903	779 532	806 260	822 378	856 625	PIB aux prix constants
Growth rates	4.1	5.6	5.3	1.8	3.4	2.0	4.2	Taux de l'accroissement
Cape Verde								**Cap-Vert**
GDP at current prices	526	597	539	566	635	831	964	PIB aux prix courants
GDP per capita	1 222	1 356	1 197	1 226	1 345	1 719	1 947	PIB par habitant
GDP at constant prices	494	553	593	621	651	686	724	PIB aux prix constants
Growth rates	8.4	11.9	7.3	4.7	4.9	5.3	5.5	Taux de l'accroissement
Cayman Islands								**Iles Caïmanes**
GDP at current prices	1 237	1 280	1 357	1 438	1 524	1 615	1 702	PIB aux prix courants
GDP per capita	33 363	33 325	34 173	35 144	36 240	37 464	38 594	PIB par habitant
GDP at constant prices	735	747	755	764	773	782	792	PIB aux prix constants
Growth rates	1.5	1.5	1.2	1.2	1.2	1.2	1.2	Taux de l'accroissement
Central African Rep.								**Rép. centrafricaine**
GDP at current prices	979	988	914	922	992	1 140	1 313	PIB aux prix courants
GDP per capita	269	266	242	240	255	290	330	PIB par habitant
GDP at constant prices	1 444	1 496	1 524	1 528	1 519	1 405	1 438	PIB aux prix constants
Growth rates	4.8	3.6	1.8	0.3	−0.6	−7.5	2.3	Taux de l'accroissement
Chad								**Tchad**
GDP at current prices	1 702	1 486	1 303	1 484	1 758	2 418	4 028	PIB aux prix courants
GDP per capita	221	187	159	175	199	265	426	PIB par habitant
GDP at constant prices	2 152	2 149	2 141	2 328	2 554	2 858	3 744	PIB aux prix constants
Growth rates	5.3	−0.1	−0.4	8.7	9.7	11.9	31.0	Taux de l'accroissement
Chile								**Chili**
GDP at current prices	79 374	72 996	74 860	68 264	66 425	73 370	94 125	PIB aux prix courants
GDP per capita	5 282	4 795	4 857	4 377	4 211	4 600	5 838	PIB par habitant
GDP at constant prices	60 074	59 617	62 101	64 005	65 378	68 259	72 395	PIB aux prix constants
Growth rates	3.2	−0.8	4.2	3.1	2.1	4.4	6.1	Taux de l'accroissement
China								**Chine**
GDP at current prices	946 317	991 363	1 080 728	1 175 716	1 270 664	1 416 593	1 649 369	PIB aux prix courants
GDP per capita	768	798	863	933	1 001	1 109	1 283	PIB par habitant
GDP at constant prices	880 754	942 878	1 018 308	1 094 681	1 185 539	1 295 795	1 418 895	PIB aux prix constants
Growth rates	7.8	7.1	8.0	7.5	8.3	9.3	9.5	Taux de l'accroissement
China, Hong Kong SAR								**Chine, Hong Kong RAS**
GDP at current prices	165 241	160 636	165 359	162 833	159 943	156 679	164 612	PIB aux prix courants
GDP per capita	25 563	24 520	24 915	24 227	23 509	22 761	23 641	PIB par habitant
GDP at constant prices	102 891	106 406	117 221	117 764	119 988	123 852	133 933	PIB aux prix constants
Growth rates	−5.0	3.4	10.2	0.5	1.9	3.2	8.1	Taux de l'accroissement
China, Macao SAR								**Chine, Macao RAS**
GDP at current prices	6 505	6 134	6 198	6 207	6 759	7 900	10 276	PIB aux prix courants
GDP per capita	15 030	13 987	13 973	13 863	14 978	17 388	22 476	PIB par habitant
GDP at constant prices	4 114	3 989	4 174	4 266	4 694	5 427	6 946	PIB aux prix constants
Growth rates	−4.6	−3.0	4.6	2.2	10.0	15.6	28.0	Taux de l'accroissement
Colombia								**Colombie**
GDP at current prices	98 513	86 301	83 766	81 724	81 673	79 139	95 686	PIB aux prix courants
GDP per capita	2 421	2 084	1 989	1 908	1 876	1 789	2 130	PIB par habitant
GDP at constant prices	62 898	60 253	62 016	62 875	64 143	66 608	69 087	PIB aux prix constants
Growth rates	0.6	−4.2	2.9	1.4	2.0	3.8	3.7	Taux de l'accroissement
Comoros								**Comores**
GDP at current prices	197	204	185	200	218	285	332	PIB aux prix courants
GDP per capita	298	300	264	278	295	376	427	PIB par habitant
GDP at constant prices	242	246	244	249	255	260	265	PIB aux prix constants
Growth rates	−1.1	1.9	−1.1	2.3	2.3	2.1	1.8	Taux de l'accroissement
Congo								**Congo**
GDP at current prices	1 949	2 354	3 220	2 788	3 017	3 564	4 384	PIB aux prix courants
GDP per capita	605	707	937	786	825	946	1 129	PIB par habitant
GDP at constant prices	3 002	2 905	3 139	3 230	3 405	3 431	3 568	PIB aux prix constants
Growth rates	3.8	−3.2	8.1	2.9	5.4	0.8	4.0	Taux de l'accroissement

17 **Gross domestic product and gross domestic product per capita**—In millions of US dollars⁺ at current and constant 1990 prices; per capita US dollars; real rates of growth (*continued*)

Produit intérieur brut et produit intérieur brut par habitant—En millions de dollars E.–U.⁺ aux prix courants et constants de 1990 ; par habitant en dollars E.–U. ; taux de l'accroissement réels (*suite*)

Country or area	1998	1999	2000	2001	2002	2003	2004	Pays ou zone
Cook Islands								**Iles Cook**
GDP at current prices	75	81	81	85	102	135	162	PIB aux prix courants
GDP per capita	3 882	4 235	4 295	4 591	5 559	7 394	8 945	PIB par habitant
GDP at constant prices	66	68	78	82	85	86	89	PIB aux prix constants
Growth rates	−0.7	2.6	14.1	5.1	3.7	1.5	3.1	Taux de l'accroissement
Costa Rica								**Costa Rica**
GDP at current prices	14 100	15 796	15 947	16 403	16 839	17 485	18 395	PIB aux prix courants
GDP per capita	3 762	4 114	4 059	4 086	4 110	4 187	4 325	PIB par habitant
GDP at constant prices	10 929	11 828	12 041	12 171	12 526	13 344	13 902	PIB aux prix constants
Growth rates	8.4	8.2	1.8	1.1	2.9	6.5	4.2	Taux de l'accroissement
Côte d'Ivoire								**Côte d'Ivoire**
GDP at current prices	12 641	12 561	10 682	10 735	11 692	14 255	16 234	PIB aux prix courants
GDP per capita	790	767	638	630	674	810	908	PIB par habitant
GDP at constant prices	15 274	15 571	15 156	15 156	15 154	15 152	15 403	PIB aux prix constants
Growth rates	5.1	1.9	−2.7	0.0	0.0	0.0	1.7	Taux de l'accroissement
Croatia								**Croatie**
GDP at current prices	21 628	19 906	18 428	19 861	22 798	28 801	34 309	PIB aux prix courants
GDP per capita	4 730	4 393	4 090	4 415	5 060	6 369	7 557	PIB par habitant
GDP at constant prices	20 822	20 643	21 232	22 176	23 332	24 329	25 253	PIB aux prix constants
Growth rates	2.5	−0.9	2.9	4.4	5.2	4.3	3.8	Taux de l'accroissement
Cuba								**Cuba**
GDP at current prices	23 777	26 147	28 206	29 557	30 680	32 337	34 396	PIB aux prix courants
GDP per capita	2 155	2 359	2 535	2 648	2 741	2 882	3 059	PIB par habitant
GDP at constant prices	15 404	16 376	17 377	17 892	18 167	18 702	19 263	PIB aux prix constants
Growth rates	0.2	6.3	6.1	3.0	1.5	2.9	3.0	Taux de l'accroissement
Cyprus								**Chypre**
GDP at current prices	9 391	9 603	9 124	9 491	10 431	13 145	15 331	PIB aux prix courants
GDP per capita	12 283	12 382	11 603	11 913	12 931	16 101	18 562	PIB par habitant
GDP at constant prices	8 145	8 535	8 966	9 330	9 526	9 702	10 054	PIB aux prix constants
Growth rates	5.0	4.8	5.1	4.1	2.1	1.8	3.6	Taux de l'accroissement
Czech Republic								**République tchèque**
GDP at current prices	60 793	59 051	55 703	60 871	73 756	90 423	107 015	PIB aux prix courants
GDP per capita	5 904	5 744	5 425	5 935	7 198	8 832	10 462	PIB par habitant
GDP at constant prices	36 077	36 512	37 933	38 934	39 514	40 982	42 886	PIB aux prix constants
Growth rates	−1.1	1.2	3.9	2.6	1.5	3.7	4.6	Taux de l'accroissement
Dem. Rep. of the Congo								**Rép. dém. du Congo**
GDP at current prices	6 218	5 474¹	5 207¹	5 274¹	5 527	5 671	6 395	PIB aux prix courants
GDP per capita	130	112¹	104¹	103¹	105	105	115	PIB par habitant
GDP at constant prices	5 901	5 647¹	5 258¹	5 200¹	5 361	5 661	6 018	PIB aux prix constants
Growth rates	−1.7	−4.3	−6.9	−1.1	3.1	5.6	6.3	Taux de l'accroissement
Denmark								**Danemark**
GDP at current prices	172 428	173 123	158 225	158 955	171 100	211 082	241 438	PIB aux prix courants
GDP per capita	32 561	32 554	29 632	29 656	31 808	39 110	44 593	PIB par habitant
GDP at constant prices	159 033	163 224	167 847	170 038	170 893	172 094	176 206	PIB aux prix constants
Growth rates	2.5	2.6	2.8	1.3	0.5	0.7	2.4	Taux de l'accroissement
Djibouti								**Djibouti**
GDP at current prices	498	536	553	573	592	625	664	PIB aux prix courants
GDP per capita	743	773	774	782	790	817	852	PIB par habitant
GDP at constant prices	502	513	516	526	540	559	582	PIB aux prix constants
Growth rates	−0.2	2.2	0.7	1.9	2.6	3.5	4.1	Taux de l'accroissement
Dominica								**Dominique**
GDP at current prices	259	268	271	264	254	260	272	PIB aux prix courants
GDP per capita	3 372	3 457	3 484	3 383	3 244	3 320	3 466	PIB par habitant
GDP at constant prices	194	195	198	190	182	182	184	PIB aux prix constants
Growth rates	3.2	0.8	1.3	−4.2	−3.9	0.0	1.0	Taux de l'accroissement
Dominican Republic								**Rép. dominicaine**
GDP at current prices	20 140	22 082	25 037	27 450	27 441	21 018	23 728	PIB aux prix courants
GDP per capita	2 510	2 712	3 029	3 272	3 223	2 432	2 706	PIB par habitant
GDP at constant prices	14 655	15 849	17 079	17 760	18 522	18 442	18 806	PIB aux prix constants
Growth rates	7.4	8.1	7.8	4.0	4.3	−0.4	2.0	Taux de l'accroissement

Gross domestic product and gross domestic product per capita—In millions of US dollars[+] at current and constant 1990 prices; per capita US dollars; real rates of growth (*continued*)

Produit intérieur brut et produit intérieur brut par habitant—En millions de dollars E.–U.[+] aux prix courants et constants de 1990 ; par habitant en dollars E.–U. ; taux de l'accroissement réels (*suite*)

Country or area	1998	1999	2000	2001	2002	2003	2004	Pays ou zone
Ecuador								**Equateur**
GDP at current prices	23 255	16 674	15 934	21 024	24 311	27 201	30 015	PIB aux prix courants
GDP per capita	1 945	1 375	1 295	1 684	1 919	2 116	2 302	PIB par habitant
GDP at constant prices	13 746	12 880	13 241	13 918	14 394	14 776	15 662	PIB aux prix constants
Growth rates	2.1	−6.3	2.8	5.1	3.4	2.7	6.0	Taux de l'accroissement
Egypt								**Egypte**
GDP at current prices	90 791	100 169	103 311	95 369	92 785	81 082	88 784	PIB aux prix courants
GDP per capita	1 402	1 517	1 535	1 391	1 327	1 138	1 222	PIB par habitant
GDP at constant prices	55 847	58 853	60 927	62 868	64 826	67 497	70 723	PIB aux prix constants
Growth rates	6.1	5.4	3.5	3.2	3.1	4.1	4.8	Taux de l'accroissement
El Salvador								**El Salvador**
GDP at current prices	12 002	12 458	13 127	13 813	14 312	14 941	15 561	PIB aux prix courants
GDP per capita	1 989	2 023	2 090	2 157	2 194	2 249	2 301	PIB par habitant
GDP at constant prices	7 909	8 182	8 358	8 500	8 690	8 849	9 026	PIB aux prix constants
Growth rates	3.8	3.4	2.2	1.7	2.2	1.8	2.0	Taux de l'accroissement
Equatorial Guinea								**Guinée équatoriale**
GDP at current prices	441	724	1 216	1 791	2 186	2 594	3 862	PIB aux prix courants
GDP per capita	1 030	1 651	2 708	3 897	4 650	5 392	7 845	PIB par habitant
GDP at constant prices	684	843	963	1 594	1 926	2 122	2 411	PIB aux prix constants
Growth rates	17.7	23.2	14.2	65.6	20.9	10.2	13.6	Taux de l'accroissement
Eritrea								**Erythrée**
GDP at current prices	545	534	505	581	626	691	793	PIB aux prix courants
GDP per capita	165	156	142	157	161	171	187	PIB par habitant
GDP at constant prices	1 444	1 444	1 255	1 371	1 380	1 421	1 446	PIB aux prix constants
Growth rates	1.8	0.0	−13.1	9.2	0.7	3.0	1.8	Taux de l'accroissement
Estonia								**Estonie**
GDP at current prices	5 566	5 562	5 464	5 970	7 035	9 081	10 984	PIB aux prix courants
GDP per capita	4 003	4 036	3 997	4 400	5 218	6 771	8 227	PIB par habitant
GDP at constant prices	4 701	4 697	5 064	5 388	5 778	6 075	6 434	PIB aux prix constants
Growth rates	5.2	−0.1	7.8	6.4	7.2	5.1	5.9	Taux de l'accroissement
Ethiopia								**Ethiopie**
GDP at current prices	6 309	6 163	6 492	6 429	6 080	6 657	8 038	PIB aux prix courants
GDP per capita	97	92	95	92	84	90	106	PIB par habitant
GDP at constant prices	10 478	11 140	11 736	12 640	12 843	12 340	13 767	PIB aux prix constants
Growth rates	−0.5	6.3	5.3	7.7	1.6	−3.9	11.6	Taux de l'accroissement
Fiji								**Fidji**
GDP at current prices	1 653	1 859	1 647	1 685	1 887	2 317	2 715	PIB aux prix courants
GDP per capita	2 081	2 317	2 031	2 058	2 284	2 780	3 229	PIB par habitant
GDP at constant prices	1 535	1 676	1 629	1 673	1 745	1 797	1 865	PIB aux prix constants
Growth rates	1.2	9.2	−2.8	2.7	4.3	3.0	3.8	Taux de l'accroissement
Finland								**Finlande**
GDP at current prices	129 406	127 830	119 905	121 223	132 026	161 774	185 931	PIB aux prix courants
GDP per capita	25 118	24 755	23 163	23 355	25 364	30 988	35 515	PIB par habitant
GDP at constant prices	151 792	156 909	164 942	166 700	170 365	174 450	180 847	PIB aux prix constants
Growth rates	5.0	3.4	5.1	1.1	2.2	2.4	3.7	Taux de l'accroissement
France [2]								**France [2]**
GDP at current prices	1 472 763	1 455 813	1 327 963	1 339 750	1 457 393	1 789 064	2 046 735	PIB aux prix courants
GDP per capita	24 337	23 967	21 776	21 877	23 695	28 958	32 984	PIB par habitant
GDP at constant prices	1 401 019	1 447 942	1 506 859	1 537 771	1 556 554	1 569 031	1 605 404	PIB aux prix constants
Growth rates	3.6	3.3	4.1	2.1	1.2	0.8	2.3	Taux de l'accroissement
French Polynesia								**Polynésie française**
GDP at current prices	3 753	3 701	3 295	3 290	3 554	4 379	4 954	PIB aux prix courants
GDP per capita	16 464	15 950	13 955	13 692	14 540	17 612	19 605	PIB par habitant
GDP at constant prices	3 737	3 836	3 938	4 022	4 099	4 178	4 272	PIB aux prix constants
Growth rates	1.1	2.7	2.7	2.1	1.9	1.9	2.3	Taux de l'accroissement
Gabon								**Gabon**
GDP at current prices	4 484	4 614	5 031	4 596	4 811	5 599	6 417	PIB aux prix courants
GDP per capita	3 691	3 707	3 955	3 544	3 645	4 175	4 710	PIB par habitant
GDP at constant prices	7 147	6 340	6 217	6 337	6 333	6 394	6 490	PIB aux prix constants
Growth rates	3.5	−11.3	−1.9	1.9	−0.1	1.0	1.5	Taux de l'accroissement

Gross domestic product and gross domestic product per capita—In millions of US dollars⁺ at current and constant 1990 prices; per capita US dollars; real rates of growth (*continued*)

Produit intérieur brut et produit intérieur brut par habitant—En millions de dollars E.–U.⁺ aux prix courants et constants de 1990 ; par habitant en dollars E.–U. ; taux de l'accroissement réels (*suite*)

Country or area	1998	1999	2000	2001	2002	2003	2004	Pays ou zone
Gambia								**Gambie**
GDP at current prices	418	432	421	418	370	366	415	PIB aux prix courants
GDP per capita	338	339	320	308	265	255	281	PIB par habitant
GDP at constant prices	440	468	494	523	506	540	578	PIB aux prix constants
Growth rates	9.9	6.4	5.5	5.8	−3.2	6.7	7.1	Taux de l'accroissement
Georgia								**Géorgie**
GDP at current prices	3 613	2 800	3 044	3 207	3 397	3 990	5 113	PIB aux prix courants
GDP per capita	748	586	645	687	736	874	1 132	PIB par habitant
GDP at constant prices	3 036	3 123	3 180	3 347	3 529	3 937	4 240	PIB aux prix constants
Growth rates	3.1	2.9	1.8	5.2	5.4	11.6	7.7	Taux de l'accroissement
Germany								**Allemagne**
GDP at current prices	2 184 475	2 143 556	1 900 220	1 891 312	2 022 311	2 443 326	2 740 670	PIB aux prix courants
GDP per capita	26 578	26 056	23 076	22 945	24 511	29 586	33 162	PIB par habitant
GDP at constant prices	1 996 414	2 036 561	2 101 931	2 126 944	2 130 308	2 130 308	2 163 728	PIB aux prix constants
Growth rates	2.0	2.0	3.2	1.2	0.2	0.0	1.6	Taux de l'accroissement
Ghana								**Ghana**
GDP at current prices	7 474	7 710	4 978	5 309	6 160	7 625	8 735	PIB aux prix courants
GDP per capita	393	397	251	261	297	359	403	PIB par habitant
GDP at constant prices	8 762	9 150	9 491	9 888	10 338	10 880	11 451	PIB aux prix constants
Growth rates	4.7	4.4	3.7	4.2	4.5	5.2	5.2	Taux de l'accroissement
Greece								**Grèce**
GDP at current prices	121 958	125 628	113 491	117 508	133 329	173 212	205 224	PIB aux prix courants
GDP per capita	11 215	11 496	10 341	10 668	12 068	15 640	18 492	PIB par habitant
GDP at constant prices	98 080	101 434	105 975	110 483	114 646	119 991	124 991	PIB aux prix constants
Growth rates	3.4	3.4	4.5	4.3	3.8	4.7	4.2	Taux de l'accroissement
Grenada								**Grenade**
GDP at current prices	301	324	349	337	345	373	396	PIB aux prix courants
GDP per capita	2 982	3 197	3 440	3 314	3 390	3 661	3 872	PIB par habitant
GDP at constant prices	254	273	292	279	278	294	312	PIB aux prix constants
Growth rates	7.9	7.3	7.0	−4.4	−0.4	5.7	6.0	Taux de l'accroissement
Guatemala								**Guatemala**
GDP at current prices	19 008	17 952	18 904	20 544	22 788	24 239	26 516	PIB aux prix courants
GDP per capita	1 782	1 645	1 693	1 797	1 946	2 020	2 157	PIB par habitant
GDP at constant prices	10 612	11 020	11 418	11 685	11 947	12 200	12 517	PIB aux prix constants
Growth rates	4.8	3.8	3.6	2.3	2.2	2.1	2.6	Taux de l'accroissement
Guinea								**Guinée**
GDP at current prices	3 588	3 461	3 112	3 035	3 209	3 632	3 878	PIB aux prix courants
GDP per capita	443	419	369	352	364	403	421	PIB par habitant
GDP at constant prices	3 914	4 093	4 171	4 330	4 512	4 568	4 685	PIB aux prix constants
Growth rates	4.8	4.6	1.9	3.8	4.2	1.2	2.6	Taux de l'accroissement
Guinea-Bissau								**Guinée-Bissau**
GDP at current prices	206	225	216	200	204	240	271	PIB aux prix courants
GDP per capita	160	170	158	142	141	160	176	PIB par habitant
GDP at constant prices	228	245	263	264	245	246	249	PIB aux prix constants
Growth rates	−28.0	7.6	7.5	0.2	−7.2	0.6	1.0	Taux de l'accroissement
Guyana								**Guyana**
GDP at current prices	718	695	713	712	726	743	778	PIB aux prix courants
GDP per capita	971	937	958	955	971	992	1 037	PIB par habitant
GDP at constant prices	629	648	639	661	653	649	665	PIB aux prix constants
Growth rates	−1.7	3.0	−1.4	3.4	−1.1	−0.6	2.4	Taux de l'accroissement
Haiti								**Haïti**
GDP at current prices	3 522	3 922	3 848	3 684	3 369	2 929	3 961	PIB aux prix courants
GDP per capita	457	501	485	457	412	353	471	PIB par habitant
GDP at constant prices	2 282	2 334	2 354	2 329	2 316	2 325	2 208	PIB aux prix constants
Growth rates	3.1	2.3	0.9	−1.0	−0.6	0.4	−5.0	Taux de l'accroissement
Honduras								**Honduras**
GDP at current prices	5 262	5 424	5 898	6 266	6 441	6 799	7 371	PIB aux prix courants
GDP per capita	862	866	918	952	956	986	1 046	PIB par habitant
GDP at constant prices	4 060	3 984	4 182	4 291	4 408	4 562	4 791	PIB aux prix constants
Growth rates	2.9	−1.9	5.0	2.6	2.7	3.5	5.0	Taux de l'accroissement

17 Gross domestic product and gross domestic product per capita—In millions of US dollars⁺ at current and constant 1990 prices; per capita US dollars; real rates of growth (*continued*)

Produit intérieur brut et produit intérieur brut par habitant—En millions de dollars E.–U.⁺ aux prix courants et constants de 1990 ; par habitant en dollars E.–U. ; taux de l'accroissement réels (*suite*)

Country or area	1998	1999	2000	2001	2002	2003	2004	Pays ou zone
Hungary								**Hongrie**
GDP at current prices	47 049	48 044	46 681	51 834	64 914	82 070	100 314	PIB aux prix courants
GDP per capita	4 579	4 687	4 565	5 081	6 379	8 085	9 908	PIB par habitant
GDP at constant prices	35 593	37 071	39 000	40 502	41 917	43 150	44 974	PIB aux prix constants
Growth rates	4.9	4.2	5.2	3.8	3.5	2.9	4.2	Taux de l'accroissement
Iceland								**Islande**
GDP at current prices	7 995	8 411	8 408	7 602	8 359	10 396	12 237	PIB aux prix courants
GDP per capita	28 999	30 202	29 891	26 768	29 159	35 932	41 913	PIB par habitant
GDP at constant prices	7 355	7 680	8 116	8 327	8 152	8 498	8 938	PIB aux prix constants
Growth rates	5.7	4.4	5.7	2.6	–2.1	4.2	5.2	Taux de l'accroissement
India								**Inde**
GDP at current prices	421 961	449 846	464 936	483 644	508 033	594 802	680 682	PIB aux prix courants
GDP per capita	427	448	455	466	482	555	626	PIB par habitant
GDP at constant prices	495 636	530 969	551 900	580 333	606 995	656 768	698 509	PIB aux prix constants
Growth rates	6.0	7.1	3.9	5.2	4.6	8.2	6.4	Taux de l'accroissement
Indonesia								**Indonésie**
GDP at current prices	95 445[3]	140 001	150 196	143 034	172 971	208 309	224 997	PIB aux prix courants
GDP per capita	467[3]	678	718	675	806	958	1 022	PIB par habitant
GDP at constant prices	163 590[3]	164 884	172 996	178 967	185 569	193 180	203 086	PIB aux prix constants
Growth rates	–13.1[3]	0.8	4.9	3.5	3.7	4.1	5.1	Taux de l'accroissement
Iran (Islamic Rep. of)								**Iran (Rép. islamique d')**
GDP at current prices	104 411[4]	108 877[4]	102 930[4]	110 418[4]	135 491	137 535	165 201	PIB aux prix courants
GDP per capita	1 608[4]	1 658[4]	1 551[4]	1 648[4]	2 005	2 017	2 401	PIB par habitant
GDP at constant prices	123 838[4]	128 979[4]	132 592[4]	137 572[4]	147 597	157 987	168 362	PIB aux prix constants
Growth rates	3.2[4]	4.2[4]	2.8[4]	3.8[4]	7.3	7.0	6.6	Taux de l'accroissement
Iraq								**Iraq**
GDP at current prices	24 688[1]	31 128[1]	30 658[1]	32 658[1]	31 312[1]	17 775[1]	26 724	PIB aux prix courants
GDP per capita	1 043[1]	1 278[1]	1 223[1]	1 266[1]	1 179[1]	651[1]	952	PIB par habitant
GDP at constant prices	20 883[1]	25 956[1]	25 018[1]	26 024[1]	24 545[1]	13 682[1]	20 044	PIB aux prix constants
Growth rates	66.8	24.3	–3.6	4.0	–5.7	–44.3	46.5	Taux de l'accroissement
Ireland								**Irlande**
GDP at current prices	87 003	95 306	94 956	103 294	120 457	152 123	181 631	PIB aux prix courants
GDP per capita	23 478	25 420	24 979	26 739	30 629	37 967	44 521	PIB par habitant
GDP at constant prices	77 521	86 126	94 667	100 355	106 509	110 401	115 779	PIB aux prix constants
Growth rates	8.9	11.1	9.9	6.0	6.1	3.7	4.9	Taux de l'accroissement
Israel								**Israël**
GDP at current prices	108 405	108 664	120 988	118 691	108 913	114 898	123 109	PIB aux prix courants
GDP per capita	18 633	18 259	19 886	19 093	17 161	17 746	18 651	PIB par habitant
GDP at constant prices	88 124	90 406	98 109	97 194	96 223	97 082	101 262	PIB aux prix constants
Growth rates	3.6	2.6	8.5	–0.9	–1.0	0.9	4.3	Taux de l'accroissement
Italy								**Italie**
GDP at current prices	1 196 662	1 180 441	1 074 763	1 091 844	1 186 387	1 468 261	1 677 907	PIB aux prix courants
GDP per capita	20 789	20 481	18 622	18 891	20 497	25 332	28 913	PIB par habitant
GDP at constant prices	1 232 934	1 253 446	1 292 806	1 316 160	1 319 208	1 322 562	1 338 754	PIB aux prix constants
Growth rates	1.8	1.7	3.1	1.8	0.2	0.3	1.2	Taux de l'accroissement
Jamaica								**Jamaïque**
GDP at current prices	7 744	7 730	7 899	8 110	8 443	8 147	8 512	PIB aux prix courants
GDP per capita	3 039	3 011	3 056	3 119	3 229	3 101	3 225	PIB par habitant
GDP at constant prices	4 844	4 886	4 923	4 995	5 050	5 164	5 231	PIB aux prix constants
Growth rates	–1.1	0.9	0.8	1.5	1.1	2.3	1.3	Taux de l'accroissement
Japan								**Japon**
GDP at current prices	3 931 049	4 452 975	4 746 067	4 162 359	3 970 848	4 291 125	4 669 322	PIB aux prix courants
GDP per capita	31 086	35 130	37 361	32 700	31 138	33 594	36 501	PIB par habitant
GDP at constant prices	3 416 056	3 411 426	3 492 799	3 499 895	3 489 295	3 534 844	3 630 132	PIB aux prix constants
Growth rates	–1.0	–0.1	2.4	0.2	–0.3	1.3	2.7	Taux de l'accroissement
Jordan								**Jordanie**
GDP at current prices	7 912	8 134	8 447	8 941	9 448	9 952	10 814	PIB aux prix courants
GDP per capita	1 677	1 680	1 699	1 749	1 796	1 839	1 945	PIB par habitant
GDP at constant prices	6 013	6 197	6 451	6 767	7 093	7 327	7 730	PIB aux prix constants
Growth rates	3.0	3.1	4.1	4.9	4.8	3.3	5.5	Taux de l'accroissement

Gross domestic product and gross domestic product per capita—In millions of US dollars⁺ at current and constant 1990 prices; per capita US dollars; real rates of growth (*continued*)

Produit intérieur brut et produit intérieur brut par habitant—En millions de dollars E.–U.⁺ aux prix courants et constants de 1990 ; par habitant en dollars E.–U. ; taux de l'accroissement réels (*suite*)

Country or area	1998	1999	2000	2001	2002	2003	2004	Pays ou zone
Kazakhstan								**Kazakhstan**
GDP at current prices	22 135	16 871	18 292	22 153	24 637	30 834	40 743	PIB aux prix courants
GDP per capita	1 445	1 113	1 217	1 483	1 655	2 076	2 746	PIB par habitant
GDP at constant prices	18 258	18 748	20 594	23 384	25 664	28 058	30 696	PIB aux prix constants
Growth rates	−1.9	2.7	9.8	13.5	9.8	9.3	9.4	Taux de l'accroissement
Kenya								**Kenya**
GDP at current prices	11 465	10 553	10 454	11 185	12 225	14 376	14 841	PIB aux prix courants
GDP per capita	391	352	341	357	382	439	443	PIB par habitant
GDP at constant prices	9 975	10 104	10 087	10 202	10 310	10 481	10 718	PIB aux prix constants
Growth rates	1.6	1.3	−0.2	1.1	1.1	1.7	2.3	Taux de l'accroissement
Kiribati								**Kiribati**
GDP at current prices	46	54	48	47	53	67	79	PIB aux prix courants
GDP per capita	536	613	538	516	571	700	815	PIB par habitant
GDP at constant prices	40	45	46	47	47	48	49	PIB aux prix constants
Growth rates	5.0	13.4	1.6	1.8	0.9	3.0	1.4	Taux de l'accroissement
Korea, Dem. P. R.								**Corée, R. p. dém. de**
GDP at current prices	10 241	10 425	10 635	11 026	11 967	12 932	13 699	PIB aux prix courants
GDP per capita	476	480	486	501	540	581	612	PIB par habitant
GDP at constant prices	11 876	12 612	12 776	13 249	13 410	13 648	13 921	PIB aux prix constants
Growth rates	−1.1	6.2	1.3	3.7	1.2	1.8	2.0	Taux de l'accroissement
Korea, Republic of								**Corée, République de**
GDP at current prices	345 433	445 401	511 659	481 894	546 935	608 146	679 675	PIB aux prix courants
GDP per capita	7 485	9 582	10 938	10 244	11 572	12 813	14 266	PIB par habitant
GDP at constant prices	400 713	438 726	475 957	494 217	528 666	545 039	570 347	PIB aux prix constants
Growth rates	−6.9	9.5	8.5	3.8	7.0	3.1	4.6	Taux de l'accroissement
Kuwait								**Koweït**
GDP at current prices	25 944	30 122	37 022	34 060	35 179	41 748	51 805	PIB aux prix courants
GDP per capita	13 271	14 348	16 604	14 554	14 430	16 535	19 876	PIB par habitant
GDP at constant prices	31 357	30 796	31 388	31 610	31 447	34 502	37 001	PIB aux prix constants
Growth rates	3.7	−1.8	1.9	0.7	−0.5	9.7	7.2	Taux de l'accroissement
Kyrgyzstan								**Kirghizistan**
GDP at current prices	1 640	1 250	1 370	1 527	1 606	1 911	2 163	PIB aux prix courants
GDP per capita	342	256	277	304	316	372	416	PIB par habitant
GDP at constant prices	1 589	1 647	1 737	1 829	1 829	1 951	2 069	PIB aux prix constants
Growth rates	2.1	3.7	5.4	5.3	0.0	6.7	6.0	Taux de l'accroissement
Lao People's Dem. Rep.								**Rép. dém. pop. lao**
GDP at current prices	1 473[1]	1 603[1]	1 733	1 754	1 829	2 088	2 427	PIB aux prix courants
GDP per capita	293[1]	311[1]	328	325	331	369	419	PIB par habitant
GDP at constant prices	1 246[1]	1 337[1]	1 415	1 496	1 583	1 667	1 767	PIB aux prix constants
Growth rates	4.0	7.3	5.8	5.8	5.8	5.3	6.0	Taux de l'accroissement
Latvia								**Lettonie**
GDP at current prices	6 617	7 219	7 726	8 231	9 203	11 063	13 623	PIB aux prix courants
GDP per capita	2 746	3 019	3 256	3 492	3 929	4 748	5 876	PIB par habitant
GDP at constant prices	5 100	5 268	5 631	6 082	6 474	6 957	7 550	PIB aux prix constants
Growth rates	4.7	3.3	6.9	8.0	6.4	7.5	8.5	Taux de l'accroissement
Lebanon								**Liban**
GDP at current prices	16 165	16 458	16 462	16 791	17 462	18 443	19 946	PIB aux prix courants
GDP per capita	4 854	4 893	4 845	4 890	5 034	5 263	5 634	PIB par habitant
GDP at constant prices	5 571	5 627	5 627	5 705	5 820	5 994	6 294	PIB aux prix constants
Growth rates	3.0	1.0	0.0	1.4	2.0	3.0	5.0	Taux de l'accroissement
Lesotho								**Lesotho**
GDP at current prices	890	911	859	763	699	1 077	1 373	PIB aux prix courants
GDP per capita	507	513	481	425	389	598	764	PIB par habitant
GDP at constant prices	852	854	865	893	924	955	983	PIB aux prix constants
Growth rates	−4.6	0.2	1.3	3.2	3.5	3.3	3.0	Taux de l'accroissement
Liberia								**Libéria**
GDP at current prices	360	442	542	534	562	442	475	PIB aux prix courants
GDP per capita	133	152	177	169	175	137	146	PIB par habitant
GDP at constant prices	315	387	473	497	513	362	433	PIB aux prix constants
Growth rates	29.7	22.9	22.3	4.9	3.3	−29.5	19.7	Taux de l'accroissement

Gross domestic product and gross domestic product per capita—In millions of US dollars[+] at current and constant 1990 prices; per capita US dollars; real rates of growth (*continued*)

Produit intérieur brut et produit intérieur brut par habitant—En millions de dollars E.–U.[+] aux prix courants et constants de 1990 ; par habitant en dollars E.–U. ; taux de l'accroissement réels (*suite*)

Country or area	1998	1999	2000	2001	2002	2003	2004	Pays ou zone
Libyan Arab Jamah.								**Jamah. arabe libyenne**
GDP at current prices	27 250	30 483	33 961	28 420	19 131	19 257	19 536	PIB aux prix courants
GDP per capita	5 342	5 859	6 400	5 252	3 466	3 421	3 403	PIB par habitant
GDP at constant prices	26 134	26 162	27 002	27 896	27 840	29 399	30 222	PIB aux prix constants
Growth rates	0.4	0.1	3.2	3.3	−0.2	5.6	2.8	Taux de l'accroissement
Liechtenstein								**Liechtenstein**
GDP at current prices	2 480	2 664	2 484	2 492	2 753	3 203	3 477	PIB aux prix courants
GDP per capita	77 201	81 982	75 583	75 020	82 037	94 532	101 654	PIB par habitant
GDP at constant prices	2 186	2 414	2 491	2 472	2 480	2 471	2 489	PIB aux prix constants
Growth rates	7.8	10.4	3.2	−0.7	0.3	−0.4	0.7	Taux de l'accroissement
Lithuania								**Lituanie**
GDP at current prices	11 094	10 840	11 381	12 095	14 045	18 354	22 006	PIB aux prix courants
GDP per capita	3 127	3 078	3 252	3 474	4 051	5 313	6 391	PIB par habitant
GDP at constant prices	6 806	6 691	6 953	7 396	7 897	8 662	9 280	PIB aux prix constants
Growth rates	7.3	−1.7	3.9	6.4	6.8	9.7	7.1	Taux de l'accroissement
Luxembourg								**Luxembourg**
GDP at current prices	18 901	19 964	19 604	19 704	21 463	27 037	31 866	PIB aux prix courants
GDP per capita	44 664	46 515	45 044	44 658	47 995	59 670	69 423	PIB par habitant
GDP at constant prices	16 092	17 349	18 914	19 207	19 680	20 255	21 175	PIB aux prix constants
Growth rates	6.9	7.8	9.0	1.5	2.5	2.9	4.5	Taux de l'accroissement
Madagascar								**Madagascar**
GDP at current prices	3 741	3 721	3 878	4 530	4 397	5 469	4 029	PIB aux prix courants
GDP per capita	245	237	239	272	256	310	222	PIB par habitant
GDP at constant prices	3 336	3 492	3 660	3 880	3 387	3 712	3 935	PIB aux prix constants
Growth rates	3.9	4.7	4.8	6.0	−12.7	9.6	6.0	Taux de l'accroissement
Malawi								**Malawi**
GDP at current prices	1 715[1]	1 793	1 743	1 722	2 026	1 906	2 078	PIB aux prix courants
GDP per capita	157[1]	160	151	146	168	155	165	PIB par habitant
GDP at constant prices	2 399[1]	2 473	2 555	2 450	2 494	2 604	2 731	PIB aux prix constants
Growth rates	1.5	3.1	3.3	−4.1	1.8	4.4	4.9	Taux de l'accroissement
Malaysia								**Malaisie**
GDP at current prices	72 175	79 148	90 320	88 001	95 164	103 737	117 776	PIB aux prix courants
GDP per capita	3 287	3 520	3 927	3 746	3 970	4 245	4 731	PIB par habitant
GDP at constant prices	75 704	80 351	87 469	87 747	91 387	96 241	103 040	PIB aux prix constants
Growth rates	−7.4	6.1	8.9	0.3	4.1	5.3	7.1	Taux de l'accroissement
Maldives								**Maldives**
GDP at current prices	540	589	624	625	641	691	753	PIB aux prix courants
GDP per capita	1 966	2 086	2 151	2 098	2 096	2 204	2 345	PIB par habitant
GDP at constant prices	395	426	445	459	487	537	581	PIB aux prix constants
Growth rates	9.3	7.8	4.4	3.3	6.1	10.2	8.3	Taux de l'accroissement
Mali								**Mali**
GDP at current prices	2 914	2 830	2 584	2 923	3 238	4 233	4 945	PIB aux prix courants
GDP per capita	265	250	222	244	262	332	377	PIB par habitant
GDP at constant prices	3 709	3 819	3 698	4 146	4 322	4 581	4 787	PIB aux prix constants
Growth rates	8.4	3.0	−3.2	12.1	4.3	6.0	4.5	Taux de l'accroissement
Malta								**Malte**
GDP at current prices	3 792	3 947	3 844	3 845	4 075	4 892	5 627	PIB aux prix courants
GDP per capita	9 804	10 136	9 811	9 758	10 289	12 293	14 074	PIB par habitant
GDP at constant prices	3 736	3 929	4 128	4 039	4 112	4 120	4 173	PIB aux prix constants
Growth rates	5.0	5.2	5.1	−2.2	1.8	0.2	1.3	Taux de l'accroissement
Marshall Islands								**Iles Marshall**
GDP at current prices	96	95	99	99	103	105	107	PIB aux prix courants
GDP per capita	1 872	1 856	1 896	1 855	1 862	1 833	1 797	PIB par habitant
GDP at constant prices	60	60	59	58	61	62	62	PIB aux prix constants
Growth rates	3.0	0.8	−2.0	−1.5	4.0	2.0	0.6	Taux de l'accroissement
Mauritania								**Mauritanie**
GDP at current prices	983	964	928	967	974	1 110	1 239	PIB aux prix courants
GDP per capita	394	375	351	355	347	384	416	PIB par habitant
GDP at constant prices	1 447	1 528	1 601	1 670	1 726	1 810	1 893	PIB aux prix constants
Growth rates	3.7	5.6	4.8	4.3	3.3	4.9	4.6	Taux de l'accroissement

Gross domestic product and gross domestic product per capita—In millions of US dollars⁺ at current and constant 1990 prices; per capita US dollars; real rates of growth (*continued*)

Produit intérieur brut et produit intérieur brut par habitant—En millions de dollars E.–U.⁺ aux prix courants et constants de 1990 ; par habitant en dollars E.–U. ; taux de l'accroissement réels (*suite*)

Country or area	1998	1999	2000	2001	2002	2003	2004	Pays ou zone
Mauritius								**Maurice**
GDP at current prices	4 150	4 266	4 552	4 539	4 744	5 634	6 317	PIB aux prix courants
GDP per capita	3 571	3 634	3 839	3 790	3 922	4 613	5 123	PIB par habitant
GDP at constant prices	3 872	3 985	4 350	4 579	4 658	4 854	5 074	PIB aux prix constants
Growth rates	6.0	2.9	9.2	5.3	1.7	4.2	4.5	Taux de l'accroissement
Mexico								**Mexique**
GDP at current prices	421 008	480 600	580 792	621 866	648 629	638 745	676 148	PIB aux prix courants
GDP per capita	4 334	4 873	5 803	6 125	6 301	6 122	6 397	PIB par habitant
GDP at constant prices	334 211	346 767	369 622	369 501	372 354	377 712	394 193	PIB aux prix constants
Growth rates	5.0	3.8	6.6	0.0	0.8	1.4	4.4	Taux de l'accroissement
Micronesia (Fed. States of)								**Micronésie (Etats féd. de)**
GDP at current prices	197	194	217	221	222	222	227	PIB aux prix courants
GDP per capita	1 835	1 812	2 023	2 053	2 056	2 038	2 072	PIB par habitant
GDP at constant prices	156	151	165	166	167	168	170	PIB aux prix constants
Growth rates	−0.7	−3.5	9.3	0.5	0.9	0.1	1.5	Taux de l'accroissement
Monaco								**Monaco**
GDP at current prices	794	791	727	738	808	999	1 150	PIB aux prix courants
GDP per capita	24 337	23 967	21 776	21 877	23 695	28 958	32 984	PIB par habitant
GDP at constant prices	756	787	825	847	863	876	902	PIB aux prix constants
Growth rates	4.3	4.1	4.8	2.7	1.9	1.4	3.0	Taux de l'accroissement
Mongolia								**Mongolie**
GDP at current prices	992	906	946	1 016	1 118	1 188	1 271	PIB aux prix courants
GDP per capita	404	366	379	403	438	460	486	PIB par habitant
GDP at constant prices	1 198	1 236	1 249	1 262	1 313	1 386	1 467	PIB aux prix constants
Growth rates	3.5	3.2	1.1	1.0	4.0	5.5	5.8	Taux de l'accroissement
Montserrat								**Montserrat**
GDP at current prices	38	35	35	35	38	39	51	PIB aux prix courants
GDP per capita	6 057	7 326	8 919	9 962	10 959	10 146	12 067	PIB par habitant
GDP at constant prices	29	27	26	24	26	26	31	PIB aux prix constants
Growth rates	−10.8	−9.1	−3.6	−6.9	8.0	−1.1	20.6	Taux de l'accroissement
Morocco								**Maroc**
GDP at current prices	35 817	35 249	33 335	33 901	36 094	43 727	49 814	PIB aux prix courants
GDP per capita	1 251	1 212	1 129	1 131	1 186	1 416	1 589	PIB par habitant
GDP at constant prices	31 955	31 930	32 235	34 265	35 358	37 212	38 526	PIB aux prix constants
Growth rates	7.7	−0.1	1.0	6.3	3.2	5.2	3.5	Taux de l'accroissement
Mozambique								**Mozambique**
GDP at current prices	3 951	4 064	3 832	3 697	4 069	4 949	6 380	PIB aux prix courants
GDP per capita	230	232	214	202	218	260	328	PIB par habitant
GDP at constant prices	3 977	4 276	4 359	4 931	5 360	5 785	6 271	PIB aux prix constants
Growth rates	12.6	7.5	1.9	13.1	8.7	7.9	8.4	Taux de l'accroissement
Myanmar								**Myanmar**
GDP at current prices	5 743	6 370	7 050	7 396	9 872	9 508	10 941	PIB aux prix courants
GDP per capita	124	135	148	153	202	192	219	PIB par habitant
GDP at constant prices	8 117	9 003	10 237	11 394	12 533	12 533	12 984	PIB aux prix constants
Growth rates	5.0	10.9	13.7	11.3	10.0	0.0	3.6	Taux de l'accroissement
Namibia								**Namibie**
GDP at current prices	3 399	3 385	3 458	3 163	2 944	4 201	5 346	PIB aux prix courants
GDP per capita	1 882	1 827	1 825	1 639	1 502	2 115	2 661	PIB par habitant
GDP at constant prices	3 320	3 463	3 597	3 619	3 710	3 849	3 984	PIB aux prix constants
Growth rates	3.3	4.3	3.9	0.6	2.5	3.7	3.5	Taux de l'accroissement
Nauru								**Nauru**
GDP at current prices	32	34	33	31	36	47	58	PIB aux prix courants
GDP per capita	2 774	2 836	2 702	2 518	2 784	3 582	4 322	PIB par habitant
GDP at constant prices	31	30	30	30	30	31	32	PIB aux prix constants
Growth rates	−1.9	−1.9	−0.1	0.6	0.8	2.7	2.9	Taux de l'accroissement
Nepal								**Népal**
GDP at current prices	4 560	5 012	5 338	5 474	5 410	5 860	6 506	PIB aux prix courants
GDP per capita	195	210	218	219	212	225	245	PIB par habitant
GDP at constant prices	5 175	5 407	5 738	6 011	5 982	6 119	6 321	PIB aux prix constants
Growth rates	2.9	4.5	6.1	4.8	−0.5	2.3	3.3	Taux de l'accroissement

Gross domestic product and gross domestic product per capita—In millions of US dollars+ at current and constant 1990 prices; per capita US dollars; real rates of growth (*continued*)

Produit intérieur brut et produit intérieur brut par habitant—En millions de dollars E.–U.+ aux prix courants et constants de 1990 ; par habitant en dollars E.–U. ; taux de l'accroissement réels (*suite*)

Country or area	1998	1999	2000	2001	2002	2003	2004	Pays ou zone
Netherlands								**Pays-Bas**
GDP at current prices	393 471	398 529	370 638	384 198	418 954	512 707	579 005	PIB aux prix courants
GDP per capita	25 017	25 203	23 314	24 039	26 077	31 750	35 683	PIB par habitant
GDP at constant prices	364 857	379 436	392 589	398 191	400 455	396 937	402 649	PIB aux prix constants
Growth rates	4.3	4.0	3.5	1.4	0.6	−0.9	1.4	Taux de l'accroissement
Netherlands Antilles								**Antilles néerlandaises**
GDP at current prices	2 763	2 736	2 798	2 884	2 904	2 999	3 104	PIB aux prix courants
GDP per capita	15 443	15 476	15 931	16 406	16 412	16 768	17 164	PIB par habitant
GDP at constant prices	2 336	2 321	2 273	2 287	2 296	2 328	2 352	PIB aux prix constants
Growth rates	0.7	−0.7	−2.1	0.6	0.4	1.4	1.0	Taux de l'accroissement
New Caledonia								**Nouvelle-Calédonie**
GDP at current prices	3 158	3 055	2 681	2 770	2 971	3 618	4 080	PIB aux prix courants
GDP per capita	15 295	14 485	12 455	12 607	13 261	15 846	17 538	PIB par habitant
GDP at constant prices	2 890	2 916	2 978	2 991	3 005	3 009	3 033	PIB aux prix constants
Growth rates	−3.2	0.9	2.1	0.5	0.5	0.1	0.8	Taux de l'accroissement
New Zealand								**Nouvelle-Zélande**
GDP at current prices	54 846	57 456	52 124	51 931	60 028	80 024	97 734	PIB aux prix courants
GDP per capita	14 606	15 182	13 651	13 462	15 388	20 280	24 499	PIB par habitant
GDP at constant prices	53 617	56 391	57 684	59 689	62 454	64 700	67 948	PIB aux prix constants
Growth rates	0.5	5.2	2.3	3.5	4.6	3.6	5.0	Taux de l'accroissement
Nicaragua								**Nicaragua**
GDP at current prices	3 573	3 743	3 951	4 038	4 007	4 135	4 409	PIB aux prix courants
GDP per capita	750	770	797	798	776	785	820	PIB par habitant
GDP at constant prices	4 507	4 824	5 028	5 177	5 230	5 351	5 565	PIB aux prix constants
Growth rates	3.7	7.0	4.2	3.0	1.0	2.3	4.0	Taux de l'accroissement
Niger								**Niger**
GDP at current prices	1 978	1 913	1 666	1 772	2 016	2 380	2 685	PIB aux prix courants
GDP per capita	180	168	141	145	160	182	199	PIB par habitant
GDP at constant prices	3 160	3 109	3 101	3 321	3 420	3 603	3 636	PIB aux prix constants
Growth rates	9.9	−1.6	−0.3	7.1	3.0	5.3	0.9	Taux de l'accroissement
Nigeria								**Nigéria**
GDP at current prices	34 481[1]	35 958	48 978	50 704	49 343	61 580	76 402	PIB aux prix courants
GDP per capita	308[1]	313	416	421	401	489	594	PIB par habitant
GDP at constant prices	40 774[1]	41 916	44 168	45 530	46 235	51 180	53 214	PIB aux prix constants
Growth rates	2.3	2.8	5.4	3.1	1.5	10.7	4.0	Taux de l'accroissement
Norway								**Norvège**
GDP at current prices	150 049	158 099	166 905	169 739	190 277	220 603	250 051	PIB aux prix courants
GDP per capita	33 752	35 332	37 072	37 486	41 798	48 215	54 383	PIB par habitant
GDP at constant prices	159 336	162 736	167 353	171 915	173 817	174 468	179 553	PIB aux prix constants
Growth rates	2.6	2.1	2.8	2.7	1.1	0.4	2.9	Taux de l'accroissement
Occupied Palestinian Terr.								**Terr. palestinien occupé**
GDP at current prices	4 258	4 517	4 442	3 765	2 974	3 303	3 427	PIB aux prix courants
GDP per capita	1 453	1 486	1 410	1 155	883	950	955	PIB par habitant
GDP at constant prices	3 426	3 729	3 528	2 937	2 400	2 546	2 587	PIB aux prix constants
Growth rates	11.8	8.9	−5.4	−16.8	−18.3	6.1	1.6	Taux de l'accroissement
Oman								**Oman**
GDP at current prices	14 086	15 710	19 868	19 949	20 304	21 698	24 466	PIB aux prix courants
GDP per capita	5 983	6 539	8 136	8 072	8 146	8 642	9 656	PIB par habitant
GDP at constant prices	17 430	17 389	18 343	19 720	20 175	20 551	21 053	PIB aux prix constants
Growth rates	2.7	−0.2	5.5	7.5	2.3	1.9	2.4	Taux de l'accroissement
Pakistan								**Pakistan**
GDP at current prices	72 432	70 598	70 709	67 219	73 701	83 483	93 688	PIB aux prix courants
GDP per capita	533	507	496	461	495	550	605	PIB par habitant
GDP at constant prices	69 883	72 861	74 842	76 234	78 688	82 740	87 713	PIB aux prix constants
Growth rates	3.7	4.3	2.7	1.9	3.2	5.1	6.0	Taux de l'accroissement
Palau								**Palaos**
GDP at current prices	117	113	117	121	128	130	133	PIB aux prix courants
GDP per capita	6 288	5 970	6 076	6 194	6 520	6 602	6 717	PIB par habitant
GDP at constant prices	99	93	94	98	99	100	102	PIB aux prix constants
Growth rates	2.0	−5.4	0.3	4.5	1.1	1.5	2.0	Taux de l'accroissement

17

Gross domestic product and gross domestic product per capita—In millions of US dollars⁺ at current and constant 1990 prices; per capita US dollars; real rates of growth (*continued*)

Produit intérieur brut et produit intérieur brut par habitant—En millions de dollars E.–U.⁺ aux prix courants et constants de 1990 ; par habitant en dollars E.–U. ; taux de l'accroissement réels (*suite*)

Country or area	1998	1999	2000	2001	2002	2003	2004	Pays ou zone
Panama								**Panama**
GDP at current prices	10 933	11 456	11 621	11 808	12 272	12 862	13 557	PIB aux prix courants
GDP per capita	3 854	3 959	3 939	3 927	4 007	4 124	4 269	PIB par habitant
GDP at constant prices	9 328	9 694	9 957	10 014	10 237	10 679	11 128	PIB aux prix constants
Growth rates	7.3	3.9	2.7	0.6	2.2	4.3	4.2	Taux de l'accroissement
Papua New Guinea								**Papouasie-Nvl-Guinée**
GDP at current prices	3 764	3 706	3 864	3 470	3 434	4 167	4 756	PIB aux prix courants
GDP per capita	745	716	729	640	620	737	824	PIB par habitant
GDP at constant prices	5 185	5 708	5 708	5 862	5 981	6 143	6 296	PIB aux prix constants
Growth rates	4.7	10.1	0.0	2.7	2.0	2.7	2.5	Taux de l'accroissement
Paraguay								**Paraguay**
GDP at current prices	8 596	7 741	7 722	6 848	5 594	6 040	7 029	PIB aux prix courants
GDP per capita	1 650	1 450	1 412	1 222	975	1 028	1 168	PIB par habitant
GDP at constant prices	6 387	6 415	6 393	6 569	6 415	6 580	6 722	PIB aux prix constants
Growth rates	−0.4	0.4	−0.4	2.8	−2.3	2.6	2.2	Taux de l'accroissement
Peru								**Pérou**
GDP at current prices	56 619	51 393	53 131	53 699	56 493	60 586	67 233	PIB aux prix courants
GDP per capita	2 255	2 013	2 047	2 037	2 111	2 231	2 439	PIB par habitant
GDP at constant prices	41 825	42 196	43 430	43 510	45 621	47 338	49 515	PIB aux prix constants
Growth rates	−0.7	0.9	2.9	0.2	4.9	3.8	4.6	Taux de l'accroissement
Philippines								**Philippines**
GDP at current prices	65 171	76 157	75 912	71 216	76 732	79 330	86 429	PIB aux prix courants
GDP per capita	895	1 025	1 002	922	975	990	1 059	PIB par habitant
GDP at constant prices	54 599	56 453	59 822	60 873	63 512	66 496	70 585	PIB aux prix constants
Growth rates	−0.6	3.4	6.0	1.8	4.3	4.7	6.1	Taux de l'accroissement
Poland								**Pologne**
GDP at current prices	169 581	164 482	166 561	185 787	191 448	209 541	241 592	PIB aux prix courants
GDP per capita	4 386	4 255	4 310	4 809	4 958	5 430	6 265	PIB par habitant
GDP at constant prices	83 482	86 904	90 338	91 256	92 507	96 067	101 199	PIB aux prix constants
Growth rates	4.8	4.1	4.0	1.0	1.4	3.8	5.3	Taux de l'accroissement
Portugal								**Portugal**
GDP at current prices	112 386	115 093	106 457	109 663	120 896	147 297	167 724	PIB aux prix courants
GDP per capita	11 092	11 309	10 411	10 671	11 702	14 182	16 063	PIB par habitant
GDP at constant prices	87 547	90 874	93 945	95 557	95 955	94 858	95 765	PIB aux prix constants
Growth rates	4.6	3.8	3.4	1.7	0.4	−1.1	1.0	Taux de l'accroissement
Puerto Rico								**Porto Rico**
GDP at current prices	57 841	61 702	69 208	71 306	74 362	79 251	84 461	PIB aux prix courants
GDP per capita	15 290	16 198	18 047	18 472	19 142	20 276	21 481	PIB par habitant
GDP at constant prices	45 927	47 429	50 424	50 720	50 877	52 477	54 127	PIB aux prix constants
Growth rates	5.4	3.3	6.3	0.6	0.3	3.1	3.1	Taux de l'accroissement
Qatar								**Qatar**
GDP at current prices	10 255	12 393	17 760	17 741	19 707	23 604	28 451	PIB aux prix courants
GDP per capita	18 306	21 390	29 290	27 615	28 715	32 191	36 620	PIB par habitant
GDP at constant prices	11 827	12 204	13 097	13 923	14 945	15 438	16 874	PIB aux prix constants
Growth rates	8.4	3.2	7.3	6.3	7.3	3.3	9.3	Taux de l'accroissement
Republic of Moldova								**République de Moldova**
GDP at current prices	1 698	1 172	1 288	1 481	1 662	1 981	2 595	PIB aux prix courants
GDP per capita	395	273	301	348	392	468	615	PIB par habitant
GDP at constant prices	1 399	1 352	1 380	1 465	1 579	1 684	1 806	PIB aux prix constants
Growth rates	−6.5	−3.4	2.1	6.1	7.8	6.6	7.3	Taux de l'accroissement
Romania								**Roumanie**
GDP at current prices	42 115	35 592	37 025	40 181	45 825	57 330	73 167	PIB aux prix courants
GDP per capita	1 887	1 602	1 674	1 824	2 088	2 622	3 358	PIB par habitant
GDP at constant prices	31 925	31 558	32 236	34 088	35 834	37 684	40 809	PIB aux prix constants
Growth rates	−4.8	−1.2	2.1	5.7	5.1	5.2	8.3	Taux de l'accroissement
Russian Federation								**Fédération de Russie**
GDP at current prices	270 953	195 908	259 718	306 618	345 073	430 115	582 319	PIB aux prix courants
GDP per capita	1 838	1 332	1 772	2 100	2 374	2 974	4 047	PIB par habitant
GDP at constant prices	327 182	347 962	382 917	402 412	421 182	452 032	485 031	PIB aux prix constants
Growth rates	−5.3	6.4	10.0	5.1	4.7	7.3	7.3	Taux de l'accroissement

Gross domestic product and gross domestic product per capita— In millions of US dollars[+] at current and constant 1990 prices; per capita US dollars; real rates of growth (*continued*)

Produit intérieur brut et produit intérieur brut par habitant— En millions de dollars E.–U.[+] aux prix courants et constants de 1990 ; par habitant en dollars E.–U. ; taux de l'accroissement réels (*suite*)

Country or area	1998	1999	2000	2001	2002	2003	2004	Pays ou zone
Rwanda								**Rwanda**
GDP at current prices	2 000	1 875	1 732	1 654	1 669	1 684	1 823	PIB aux prix courants
GDP per capita	292	250	216	197	194	192	205	PIB par habitant
GDP at constant prices	2 338	2 490	2 646	2 822	3 086	3 107	3 227	PIB aux prix constants
Growth rates	9.2	6.5	6.3	6.7	9.3	0.7	3.8	Taux de l'accroissement
Saint Kitts and Nevis								**Saint-Kitts-et-Nevis**
GDP at current prices	287	305	329	344	357	371	391	PIB aux prix courants
GDP per capita	7 145	7 567	8 132	8 444	8 660	8 902	9 269	PIB par habitant
GDP at constant prices	224	232	240	245	249	255	268	PIB aux prix constants
Growth rates	1.2	3.5	3.4	2.2	1.7	2.1	5.1	Taux de l'accroissement
Saint Lucia								**Sainte-Lucie**
GDP at current prices	631	669	683	654	677	691	719	PIB aux prix courants
GDP per capita	4 148	4 365	4 424	4 202	4 312	4 369	4 506	PIB par habitant
GDP at constant prices	506	514	513	484	487	495	505	PIB aux prix constants
Growth rates	6.4	1.5	–0.1	–5.6	0.5	1.7	2.0	Taux de l'accroissement
St. Vincent-Grenadines								**St. Vincent-Grenadines**
GDP at current prices	317	330	335	346	361	376	398	PIB aux prix courants
GDP per capita	2 765	2 861	2 891	2 965	3 079	3 194	3 357	PIB par habitant
GDP at constant prices	299	312	317	321	330	343	363	PIB aux prix constants
Growth rates	5.1	4.2	1.7	1.1	2.7	4.1	5.8	Taux de l'accroissement
Samoa								**Samoa**
GDP at current prices	224	230	231	240	262	316	362	PIB aux prix courants
GDP per capita	1 290	1 307	1 301	1 339	1 450	1 731	1 968	PIB par habitant
GDP at constant prices	224	229	245	260	263	272	283	PIB aux prix constants
Growth rates	2.4	2.5	6.8	6.1	1.3	3.5	4.0	Taux de l'accroissement
San Marino								**Saint-Marin**
GDP at current prices	807	853	774	815	880	1 082	1 244	PIB aux prix courants
GDP per capita	30 481	31 952	28 708	29 975	32 087	39 107	44 607	PIB par habitant
GDP at constant prices	839	914	934	986	989	989	1 009	PIB aux prix constants
Growth rates	7.5	9.0	2.2	5.5	0.3	0.0	2.0	Taux de l'accroissement
Sao Tome and Principe								**Sao Tomé-et-Principe**
GDP at current prices	41	47	46	48	54	60	68	PIB aux prix courants
GDP per capita	304	343	332	334	367	399	447	PIB par habitant
GDP at constant prices	65	67	69	71	74	78	83	PIB aux prix constants
Growth rates	2.5	2.5	3.0	4.0	4.1	4.5	6.5	Taux de l'accroissement
Saudi Arabia								**Arabie saoudite**
GDP at current prices	145 967	161 172	188 693	183 257	188 803	212 864	244 339	PIB aux prix courants
GDP per capita	7 191	7 716	8 783	8 297	8 316	9 126	10 202	PIB par habitant
GDP at constant prices	131 488	130 504	136 850	137 602	137 778	148 108	153 466	PIB aux prix constants
Growth rates	2.8	–0.7	4.9	0.5	0.1	7.5	3.6	Taux de l'accroissement
Senegal								**Sénégal**
GDP at current prices	4 655	4 751	4 374	4 611	5 037	6 473	7 650	PIB aux prix courants
GDP per capita	473	471	423	435	464	582	672	PIB par habitant
GDP at constant prices	7 167	7 525	7 943	8 388	8 481	9 015	9 565	PIB aux prix constants
Growth rates	5.7	5.0	5.6	5.6	1.1	6.3	6.1	Taux de l'accroissement
Serbia and Montenegro								**Serbie-et-Monténégro**
GDP at current prices	15 575[1]	10 128[1]	11 011	11 727	15 572	19 397	22 895	PIB aux prix courants
GDP per capita	1 473[1]	959[1]	1 044	1 113	1 480	1 844	2 178	PIB par habitant
GDP at constant prices	15 377[1]	11 619[1]	12 363	13 043	13 538	13 674	14 494	PIB aux prix constants
Growth rates	2.5	–24.4	6.4	5.5	3.8	1.0	6.0	Taux de l'accroissement
Seychelles								**Seychelles**
GDP at current prices	608	623	599	584	699	695	709	PIB aux prix courants
GDP per capita	7 964	8 122	7 764	7 507	8 912	8 783	8 874	PIB par habitant
GDP at constant prices	554	565	564	554	555	525	515	PIB aux prix constants
Growth rates	11.2	1.9	–0.1	–1.9	0.3	–5.4	–2.0	Taux de l'accroissement
Sierra Leone								**Sierra Leone**
GDP at current prices	672	669	636	884	1 033	1 073	1 044	PIB aux prix courants
GDP per capita	157	153	141	189	211	210	196	PIB par habitant
GDP at constant prices	427	392	407	429	456	486	519	PIB aux prix constants
Growth rates	–0.8	–8.1	3.8	5.4	6.3	6.5	6.8	Taux de l'accroissement

Gross domestic product and gross domestic product per capita—In millions of US dollars⁺ at current and constant 1990 prices; per capita US dollars; real rates of growth (*continued*)

Produit intérieur brut et produit intérieur brut par habitant—En millions de dollars E.–U.⁺ aux prix courants et constants de 1990 ; par habitant en dollars E.–U. ; taux de l'accroissement réels (*suite*)

Country or area	1998	1999	2000	2001	2002	2003	2004	Pays ou zone
Singapore								**Singapour**
GDP at current prices	82 056	82 537	92 575	85 823	88 456	92 369	106 822	PIB aux prix courants
GDP per capita	21 498	21 037	23 043	20 949	21 248	21 889	25 002	PIB par habitant
GDP at constant prices	66 183	70 705	77 517	76 005	78 413	79 481	86 166	PIB aux prix constants
Growth rates	−0.8	6.8	9.6	−2.0	3.2	1.4	8.4	Taux de l'accroissement
Slovakia								**Slovaquie**
GDP at current prices	22 179	20 407	20 291	20 884	24 239	32 665	41 092	PIB aux prix courants
GDP per capita	4 113	3 781	3 757	3 866	4 487	6 047	7 607	PIB par habitant
GDP at constant prices	17 256	17 510	17 867	18 543	19 399	20 265	21 379	PIB aux prix constants
Growth rates	4.2	1.5	2.0	3.8	4.6	4.5	5.5	Taux de l'accroissement
Slovenia								**Slovénie**
GDP at current prices	20 856	21 317	19 098	19 616	22 121	27 749	32 182	PIB aux prix courants
GDP per capita	10 598	10 836	9 710	9 974	11 246	14 106	16 359	PIB par habitant
GDP at constant prices	18 983	20 037	20 817	21 374	22 085	22 643	23 679	PIB aux prix constants
Growth rates	3.6	5.6	3.9	2.7	3.3	2.5	4.6	Taux de l'accroissement
Solomon Islands								**Iles Salomon**
GDP at current prices	349	380	331	315	262	245	272	PIB aux prix courants
GDP per capita	881	933	791	733	594	540	585	PIB par habitant
GDP at constant prices	313	312	267	244	239	248	258	PIB aux prix constants
Growth rates	1.4	−0.5	−14.3	−8.7	−2.1	3.8	4.0	Taux de l'accroissement
Somalia								**Somalie**
GDP at current prices	1 926	2 017	2 052	1 303	1 219	1 537	2 088	PIB aux prix courants
GDP per capita	291	296	293	180	163	199	262	PIB par habitant
GDP at constant prices	709	724	746	768	795	823	840	PIB aux prix constants
Growth rates	2.5	2.1	3.0	3.0	3.5	3.5	2.1	Taux de l'accroissement
South Africa								**Afrique du Sud**
GDP at current prices	134 296	133 184	132 878	118 479	110 518	165 434	212 777	PIB aux prix courants
GDP per capita	3 028	2 958	2 913	2 569	2 374	3 526	4 507	PIB par habitant
GDP at constant prices	125 840	128 807	134 158	137 828	142 735	146 743	152 190	PIB aux prix constants
Growth rates	0.5	2.4	4.2	2.7	3.6	2.8	3.7	Taux de l'accroissement
Spain								**Espagne**
GDP at current prices	607 016	621 848	580 673	608 360	686 088	880 956	1 039 972	PIB aux prix courants
GDP per capita	15 086	15 381	14 261	14 796	16 488	20 903	24 386	PIB par habitant
GDP at constant prices	630 810	657 454	686 411	710 740	729 789	751 056	774 279	PIB aux prix constants
Growth rates	4.3	4.2	4.4	3.5	2.7	2.9	3.1	Taux de l'accroissement
Sri Lanka								**Sri Lanka**
GDP at current prices	15 800	15 698	16 280	15 622	16 414	18 118	19 234	PIB aux prix courants
GDP per capita	812	799	820	780	812	888	935	PIB par habitant
GDP at constant prices	12 055	12 580	13 329	13 137	13 663	14 473	15 197	PIB aux prix constants
Growth rates	4.7	4.3	6.0	−1.4	4.0	5.9	5.0	Taux de l'accroissement
Sudan								**Soudan**
GDP at current prices	9 918	9 697	11 549	13 028	14 718	17 050	19 949	PIB aux prix courants
GDP per capita	315	301	351	388	430	489	562	PIB par habitant
GDP at constant prices	19 462	20 630	22 335	23 762	25 295	26 833	28 792	PIB aux prix constants
Growth rates	6.0	6.0	8.3	6.4	6.5	6.1	7.3	Taux de l'accroissement
Suriname								**Suriname**
GDP at current prices	942	757	781	659	821	1 002	1 105	PIB aux prix courants
GDP per capita	2 210	1 759	1 800	1 507	1 863	2 260	2 475	PIB par habitant
GDP at constant prices	495	489	489	512	520	546	576	PIB aux prix constants
Growth rates	2.3	−1.4	0.0	4.9	1.4	5.2	5.3	Taux de l'accroissement
Swaziland								**Swaziland**
GDP at current prices	1 347	1 376	1 389	1 274	1 194	1 833	2 307	PIB aux prix courants
GDP per capita	1 347	1 358	1 358	1 238	1 155	1 771	2 231	PIB par habitant
GDP at constant prices	1 121	1 161	1 185	1 206	1 249	1 276	1 295	PIB aux prix constants
Growth rates	3.2	3.5	2.1	1.8	3.6	2.2	1.5	Taux de l'accroissement
Sweden								**Suède**
GDP at current prices	248 038	251 321	239 567	219 684	241 646	301 553	346 413	PIB aux prix courants
GDP per capita	27 993	28 350	26 986	24 681	27 051	33 616	38 457	PIB par habitant
GDP at constant prices	268 172	280 450	292 585	295 648	301 490	305 912	316 916	PIB aux prix constants
Growth rates	3.6	4.6	4.3	1.0	2.0	1.5	3.6	Taux de l'accroissement

Gross domestic product and gross domestic product per capita—In millions of US dollars[+] at current and constant 1990 prices; per capita US dollars; real rates of growth (*continued*)

Produit intérieur brut et produit intérieur brut par habitant—En millions de dollars E.–U.[+] aux prix courants et constants de 1990 ; par habitant en dollars E.–U. ; taux de l'accroissement réels (*suite*)

Country or area	1998	1999	2000	2001	2002	2003	2004	Pays ou zone
Switzerland								**Suisse**
GDP at current prices	269 132	264 882	246 044	250 345	276 570	321 810	357 400	PIB aux prix courants
GDP per capita	37 869	37 101	34 328	34 815	38 359	44 536	49 367	PIB par habitant
GDP at constant prices	249 254	252 527	261 646	264 371	265 231	264 296	268 725	PIB aux prix constants
Growth rates	2.8	1.3	3.6	1.0	0.3	−0.4	1.7	Taux de l'accroissement
Syrian Arab Republic								**Rép. arabe syrienne**
GDP at current prices	17 468	17 806	19 651	20 742	21 617	20 445	23 440	PIB aux prix courants
GDP per capita	1 094	1 087	1 169	1 203	1 222	1 128	1 261	PIB par habitant
GDP at constant prices	19 615	18 918	19 032	19 763	20 601	21 145	21 910	PIB aux prix constants
Growth rates	6.8	−3.6	0.6	3.8	4.2	2.6	3.6	Taux de l'accroissement
Tajikistan								**Tadjikistan**
GDP at current prices	1 320	1 087	945[1]	1 066	1 218	1 554	1 911	PIB aux prix courants
GDP per capita	220	179	153[1]	171	193	244	297	PIB par habitant
GDP at constant prices	972	1 008	1 092[1]	1 203	1 333	1 480	1 637	PIB aux prix constants
Growth rates	5.3	3.7	8.3	10.2	10.8	11.0	10.6	Taux de l'accroissement
Thailand								**Thaïlande**
GDP at current prices	111 860	122 630	122 739	115 544	126 905	143 106	160 427	PIB aux prix courants
GDP per capita	1 857	2 015	1 998	1 863	2 028	2 266	2 519	PIB par habitant
GDP at constant prices	120 676	126 044	132 042	134 863	142 153	151 921	161 644	PIB aux prix constants
Growth rates	−10.5	4.4	4.8	2.1	5.4	6.9	6.4	Taux de l'accroissement
TFYR of Macedonia								**L'ex-R.y. Macédoine**
GDP at current prices	3 580	3 673	3 587	3 437	3 791	4 666	5 264	PIB aux prix courants
GDP per capita	1 796	1 835	1 785	1 705	1 875	2 302	2 593	PIB par habitant
GDP at constant prices	3 740	3 902	4 080	3 895	3 929	4 063	4 164	PIB aux prix constants
Growth rates	3.4	4.3	4.5	−4.5	0.9	3.4	2.5	Taux de l'accroissement
Timor-Leste								**Timor-Leste**
GDP at current prices	390	270	321	387	381	341	328	PIB aux prix courants
GDP per capita	515	370	445	525	491	412	370	PIB par habitant
GDP at constant prices	203	131	151	173	178	174	175	PIB aux prix constants
Growth rates	1.0	−35.5	15.5	14.6	3.0	−2.7	0.9	Taux de l'accroissement
Togo								**Togo**
GDP at current prices	1 415	1 413	1 329	1 329	1 471	1 728	2 082	PIB aux prix courants
GDP per capita	282	272	248	240	259	296	348	PIB par habitant
GDP at constant prices	1 768	1 819	1 805	1 808	1 886	1 924	1 997	PIB aux prix constants
Growth rates	−2.2	2.9	−0.8	0.2	4.3	2.0	3.8	Taux de l'accroissement
Tonga								**Tonga**
GDP at current prices	147	149	143	129	139	162	197	PIB aux prix courants
GDP per capita	1 484	1 495	1 430	1 281	1 377	1 590	1 930	PIB par habitant
GDP at constant prices	139	143	152	154	158	163	165	PIB aux prix constants
Growth rates	2.4	2.8	6.3	1.7	2.5	3.3	1.2	Taux de l'accroissement
Trinidad and Tobago								**Trinité-et-Tobago**
GDP at current prices	6 044	6 809	8 154	8 825	8 860	10 511	11 414	PIB aux prix courants
GDP per capita	4 736	5 318	6 347	6 846	6 852	8 102	8 772	PIB par habitant
GDP at constant prices	6 708	7 311	7 841	8 176	8 731	9 882	10 492	PIB aux prix constants
Growth rates	7.5	9.0	7.3	4.3	6.8	13.2	6.2	Taux de l'accroissement
Tunisia								**Tunisie**
GDP at current prices	19 813	20 799	19 444	19 969	21 016	24 955	28 134	PIB aux prix courants
GDP per capita	2 121	2 200	2 033	2 064	2 149	2 524	2 815	PIB par habitant
GDP at constant prices	17 621	18 689	19 566	20 516	20 861	22 020	23 307	PIB aux prix constants
Growth rates	4.8	6.1	4.7	4.9	1.7	5.6	5.8	Taux de l'accroissement
Turkey								**Turquie**
GDP at current prices	200 307	184 858	199 264	145 573	184 162	239 700	301 999	PIB aux prix courants
GDP per capita	3 034	2 753	2 920	2 101	2 621	3 364	4 182	PIB par habitant
GDP at constant prices	209 331	199 474	214 154	198 103	213 835	226 226	246 431	PIB aux prix constants
Growth rates	3.1	−4.7	7.4	−7.5	7.9	5.8	8.9	Taux de l'accroissement
Turkmenistan								**Turkménistan**
GDP at current prices	2 862	3 857	4 932	6 754	8 700	10 713	12 374	PIB aux prix courants
GDP per capita	652	868	1 096	1 480	1 879	2 281	2 596	PIB par habitant
GDP at constant prices	1 963	2 287	2 413	2 517	2 524	2 606	2 737	PIB aux prix constants
Growth rates	7.1	16.5	5.5	4.3	0.3	3.3	5.0	Taux de l'accroissement

Gross domestic product and gross domestic product per capita—In millions of US dollars⁺ at current and constant 1990 prices; per capita US dollars; real rates of growth (*continued*)

Produit intérieur brut et produit intérieur brut par habitant—En millions de dollars E.–U.⁺ aux prix courants et constants de 1990 ; par habitant en dollars E.–U. ; taux de l'accroissement réels (*suite*)

Country or area	1998	1999	2000	2001	2002	2003	2004	Pays ou zone
Turks and Caicos Islands								**Iles Turques et Caïques**
GDP at current prices	166	184	200	209	216	234	250	PIB aux prix courants
GDP per capita	9 487	10 043	10 291	10 064	9 731	9 829	9 924	PIB par habitant
GDP at constant prices	117	127	133	135	138	146	152	PIB aux prix constants
Growth rates	10.9	8.7	4.9	1.6	2.0	5.6	4.3	Taux de l'accroissement
Tuvalu								**Tuvalu**
GDP at current prices	13	14	12	13	15	19	22	PIB aux prix courants
GDP per capita	1 293	1 362	1 204	1 253	1 421	1 838	2 141	PIB par habitant
GDP at constant prices	14	14	12	14	15	15	15	PIB aux prix constants
Growth rates	10.5	2.4	−12.8	13.2	5.5	2.0	1.7	Taux de l'accroissement
Uganda								**Ouganda**
GDP at current prices	6 338	6 017	5 734	5 784	6 015	6 435	7 791	PIB aux prix courants
GDP per capita	277	255	236	230	232	240	280	PIB par habitant
GDP at constant prices	6 433	6 853	7 152	7 614	7 974	8 473	8 968	PIB aux prix constants
Growth rates	9.7	6.5	4.4	6.4	4.7	6.3	5.9	Taux de l'accroissement
Ukraine								**Ukraine**
GDP at current prices	41 883	31 581	31 262	38 009	42 393	50 133	65 037	PIB aux prix courants
GDP per capita	834	636	636	783	883	1 055	1 384	PIB par habitant
GDP at constant prices	36 858	36 799	38 967	42 565	44 799	49 002	54 947	PIB aux prix constants
Growth rates	−1.9	−0.2	5.9	9.2	5.2	9.4	12.1	Taux de l'accroissement
United Arab Emirates								**Emirats arabes unis**
GDP at current prices	48 500	55 193	70 522	69 546	71 370	80 043	84 227	PIB aux prix courants
GDP per capita	16 943	18 154	21 719	19 939	19 000	19 856	19 659	PIB par habitant
GDP at constant prices	44 137	46 074	51 702	53 519	54 528	58 345	59 745	PIB aux prix constants
Growth rates	1.6	4.4	12.2	3.5	1.9	7.0	2.4	Taux de l'accroissement
United Kingdom								**Royaume-Uni**
GDP at current prices	1 421 965	1 461 301	1 438 216	1 431 371	1 564 911	1 797 867	2 124 463	PIB aux prix courants
GDP per capita	24 406	24 994	24 514	24 312	26 488	30 327	35 718	PIB par habitant
GDP at constant prices	1 176 676	1 210 301	1 257 014	1 285 948	1 308 688	1 337 406	1 379 367	PIB aux prix constants
Growth rates	3.1	2.9	3.9	2.3	1.8	2.2	3.1	Taux de l'accroissement
United Rep. of Tanzania								**Rép.-Unie de Tanzanie**
GDP at current prices	8 382	8 638	9 093	9 453	9 772	10 297	10 851	PIB aux prix courants
GDP per capita	258	261	269	274	277	287	297	PIB par habitant
GDP at constant prices	5 981	6 192	6 508	6 914	7 415	7 941	8 440	PIB aux prix constants
Growth rates	3.7	3.5	5.1	6.2	7.2	7.1	6.3	Taux de l'accroissement
United States								**Etats-Unis**
GDP at current prices	8 694 600	9 216 200	9 764 800	10 075 900	10 434 800	10 951 300	11 713 000	PIB aux prix courants
GDP per capita	31 235	32 767	34 364	35 107	36 004	37 425	39 650	PIB par habitant
GDP at constant prices	7 354 609	7 684 781	7 968 520	8 028 989	8 179 631	8 429 749	8 785 218	PIB aux prix constants
Growth rates	4.2	4.5	3.7	0.8	1.9	3.1	4.2	Taux de l'accroissement
Uruguay								**Uruguay**
GDP at current prices	22 371	20 913	20 086	18 561	12 277	11 191	13 215	PIB aux prix courants
GDP per capita	6 796	6 306	6 011	5 514	3 620	3 277	3 842	PIB par habitant
GDP at constant prices	11 792	11 507	11 341	10 961	9 735	9 972	11 199	PIB aux prix constants
Growth rates	4.2	−2.4	−1.4	−3.3	−11.2	2.4	12.3	Taux de l'accroissement
Uzbekistan								**Ouzbékistan**
GDP at current prices	14 987	17 081	13 759	9 348¹	9 902	9 975	11 788	PIB aux prix courants
GDP per capita	624	701	557	373¹	389	386	450	PIB par habitant
GDP at constant prices	13 326	13 912	14 469	15 120¹	15 755	16 448	17 188	PIB aux prix constants
Growth rates	4.4	4.4	4.0	4.5	4.2	4.4	4.5	Taux de l'accroissement
Vanuatu								**Vanuatu**
GDP at current prices	232	229	223	214	216	256	291	PIB aux prix courants
GDP per capita	1 259	1 219	1 164	1 095	1 083	1 259	1 405	PIB par habitant
GDP at constant prices	205	198	204	199	194	197	201	PIB aux prix constants
Growth rates	2.1	−3.2	2.7	−2.1	−2.8	1.6	2.1	Taux de l'accroissement
Venezuela (Bolivarian Rep. of)								**Venezuela (Rép. Bolivar. du)**
GDP at current prices	95 849	103 311	121 258	126 197	95 424	85 801	111 958	PIB aux prix courants
GDP per capita	4 081	4 313	4 966	5 072	3 764	3 324	4 260	PIB par habitant
GDP at constant prices	61 221	57 495	59 355	61 010	55 594	51 303	60 193	PIB aux prix constants
Growth rates	0.2	−6.1	3.2	2.8	−8.9	−7.7	17.3	Taux de l'accroissement

17 Gross domestic product and gross domestic product per capita — In millions of US dollars[+] at current and constant 1990 prices; per capita US dollars; real rates of growth (*continued*)

Produit intérieur brut et produit intérieur brut par habitant — En millions de dollars E.–U.[+] aux prix courants et constants de 1990 ; par habitant en dollars E.–U. ; taux de l'accroissement réels (*suite*)

Country or area	1998	1999	2000	2001	2002	2003	2004	Pays ou zone
Viet Nam								**Viet Nam**
GDP at current prices	27 210	28 684	31 173	32 685	35 064	39 046	45 819	PIB aux prix courants
GDP per capita	355	370	396	410	434	476	551	PIB par habitant
GDP at constant prices	12 006	12 579	13 433	14 359	15 376	16 492	17 729	PIB aux prix constants
Growth rates	5.8	4.8	6.8	6.9	7.1	7.3	7.5	Taux de l'accroissement
Yemen								**Yémen**
GDP at current prices	6 213	7 532	9 520	9 608	10 271	11 347	13 080	PIB aux prix courants
GDP per capita	368	433	531	519	538	576	643	PIB par habitant
GDP at constant prices	6 314	6 519	6 831	7 153	7 435	7 747	7 987	PIB aux prix constants
Growth rates	7.4	3.2	4.8	4.7	3.9	4.2	3.1	Taux de l'accroissement
Zambia								**Zambie**
GDP at current prices	3 238	3 132	3 239	3 637	3 697	4 305	5 315	PIB aux prix courants
GDP per capita	315	299	303	333	333	381	463	PIB par habitant
GDP at constant prices	3 976	4 065	4 209	4 415	4 561	4 758	4 924	PIB aux prix constants
Growth rates	−1.9	2.2	3.6	4.9	3.3	4.3	3.5	Taux de l'accroissement
Zimbabwe								**Zimbabwe**
GDP at current prices	6 275	5 964	5 628[1]	5 609[1]	5 422[1]	4 985[1]	4 546	PIB aux prix courants
GDP per capita	509	478	447[1]	442[1]	424[1]	388[1]	351	PIB par habitant
GDP at constant prices	10 409	10 035	9 267[1]	9 018[1]	8 576[1]	7 743[1]	7 343	PIB aux prix constants
Growth rates	0.5	−3.6	−7.6	−2.7	−4.9	−9.7	−5.2	Taux de l'accroissement

Source

United Nations Statistics Division, New York, the national accounts database.

Source

Organisation des Nations Unies, Division de statistique, New York, la base de données sur les comptes nationaux.

Notes

[+] In converting estimates expressed in national currency units into United States dollars, the prevailing annual average of market exchange rates as reported by the IMF has been used. For countries that are non–members of the IMF or where no annual exchange rate is available from the IMF, the conversion rate used is usually the annual average of United Nations operational rates of exchange.

It should be noted that the international comparability of data expressed in United States dollars between countries may not be entirely scientific because the exchange rates applied may, in practice, only be used for the conversion of a limited number of external transactions and may not be relevant for the much larger portion of GDP covering domestic transactions.

Alternative methods of making international comparisons have been developed in recent years. One is the Purchasing Power Parities (PPPs) which have been developed as part of the International Comparison Project; another one is the World Bank Atlas method of conversion based on the average of the exchange rates of the current year and the two immediately preceding years that have been adjusted for differences in inflation rates between individual countries and the average of G–5 countries (Germany, France, Japan, the United Kingdom, and the United States). The Statistics Division of the United Nations has developed the Price–adjusted rates of exchange method (PARE) which, like the Atlas method, is designed to adjust exchange rates that do not adequately reflect relative movements of domestic and international inflation. PARE is mainly applied to countries with fixed exchange rate regimes and countries going through a period of high inflation (e.g. transition countries from 1990–1995).

[1] Price–adjusted rates of exchange (PARE) are used for selected years for conversion to US dollars due to large distortions in the dollar levels of per capita GDP with the use of IMF market exchange rates.

[2] Including Guadeloupe, Martinique, Réunion and French Guiana.

[3] Includes Timor–Leste up to 1998.

[4] Weighted rates of exchange were used for the period 1985 – 2001.

Notes

[+] Les taux de conversion utilisés pour exprimer les chiffres nationaux en dollars des États–Unis correspondent à la moyenne annuelle des taux de change du marché donnés par le FMI. Pour les pays qui ne sont pas membres du FMI ou pour lesquels ce dernier ne publie pas de taux de change annuel, le taux utilisé pour la conversion est généralement la moyenne annuelle du taux de change utilisé pour les opérations des Nations Unies.

Il est à noter que la comparabilité internationale des données exprimées en dollars des États–Unis peut ne pas être strictement scientifique car les taux de change appliqués peuvent, dans la pratique, n'être utilisés que pour convertir un nombre restreint de transactions avec l'étranger et ne pas être pertinents pour la partie plus importante du PIB qui concerne les transactions nationales.

D'autres méthodes ont été élaborées ces dernières années pour les comparaisons internationales. L'une, celle de la parité de pouvoir d'achat (PPA), procède du Projet de comparaison internationale ; une autre méthode de conversion, celle de l'Atlas de la Banque mondiale, est basée sur la moyenne des taux de change de l'année en cours et des deux années immédiatement précédentes, ajustés en fonction des différences d'inflation entre les pays considérés et la moyenne des pays du G–5 (Allemagne, États–Unis, France, Japon, et Royaume–Uni). La Division de statistique de l'ONU a mis au point la méthode des taux de change corrigés des prix (TCCP) qui, comme celle de l'Atlas, est conçue pour corriger les taux de change qui ne rendent pas convenablement compte de l'évolution relative de l'inflation dans un pays par rapport à l'inflation à l'échelon international. Le TCCP sert surtout pour les pays à taux de change fixe et ceux qui connaissent une période de forte inflation (par ex. les pays en transition entre 1990 et 1995).

[1] Pour certaines années, on utilise les Taux de change corrigés des prix (TCCP) pour effectuer la conversion en dollars des États–Unis, en raison des aberrations importantes relevées dans les niveaux du PNB exprimés en dollars après conversion à l'aide des taux de change du marché communiqués par le FMI.

[2] Y compris Guadeloupe, Martinique, Réunion et Guyane française.

[3] Y compris Timor–Leste jusqu'en 1998.

[4] Pour la période 1985 à 2001, on a utilisé des taux de change pondérés.

18

Gross domestic product by type of expenditure at current prices
Percentage distribution

Dépenses imputées au produit intérieur brut aux prix courants
Répartition en pourcentage

Country or area Pays ou zone	Year Année	GDP in current prices (Mil. nat.cur.) PIB aux prix courant (Millions monnaie nat.)	Household final consumption expenditure Consom. finale des ménages	Govt. final consumption expenditure Consom. finale des admin. publiques	Gross fixed capital formation Formation brute de capital fixe	Changes in inventories Variation des stocks	Exports of goods and services Exportations de biens et services	Imports of goods and services Importations de biens et services
Afghanistan [+] Afghanistan [+]	2002	182 862	101.5	7.9	12.3	...	58.4	80.0
	2003	217 898[1]	96.4	8.0	12.7	...	48.5	65.6
Albania [2] Albanie [2]	2000	530 906	66.0[3]	8.9	21.3	23.7	17.6	37.5
	2001	588 663	61.1[3]	9.5	25.7	24.0	18.3	38.6
	2002	630 000	57.9[3]	10.1	23.2	33.3	19.4	43.8
Algeria Algérie	2001	4 260 811	43.4	14.7	22.7	4.8	36.4	21.8
	2002	4 537 691	43.8	15.4	24.5	6.4	35.4	25.5
	2003	5 264 187	40.4	14.8	24.0	6.3	38.2	23.8
Angola Angola	1988	239 640	45.5	32.9	14.6	0.0	32.8	25.8
	1989	278 866	48.2	28.9	11.2	0.9	33.8	23.1
	1990	308 062	44.7	28.5	11.1	0.6	38.9	23.8
Anguilla Anguilla	2001	297	80.0	17.9	32.5	...	67.2	97.7
	2002	305	80.3	17.9	28.0	...	62.4	88.6
	2003	318	82.5	17.8	29.6	...	64.0	93.9
Antigua and Barbuda Antigua–et–Barbuda	1984	468	69.8	18.5	23.6	0.0	73.7	85.6
	1985	541	71.5	18.3	28.0	0.0	75.7	93.5
	1986	642	69.7	18.9	36.1	0.0	75.2	99.9
Argentina [2] Argentine [2]	2002	312 580	61.9	12.2	12.0[4]	...	27.7	12.8
	2003	375 909	63.2	11.4	15.1[4]	...	25.0	14.2
	2004	447 307	62.9	11.1	19.1[4]	...	25.3	18.1
Armenia [2] Arménie [2]	2001	1 175 877	93.6[3]	11.3	17.7	2.1[5]	25.5	46.1
	2002	1 362 472	89.1[3]	10.0	21.1	0.6[5]	29.4	46.6
	2003	1 624 643	83.3[3]	10.2	23.0	1.3[5]	32.2	50.0
Aruba [2] Aruba [2]	2000	3 327	50.0	22.0	23.7	0.9	74.4	71.0
	2001	3 399	50.4	23.7	21.9	0.6	72.6	69.1
	2002	3 421	52.6	26.3	22.4	0.9	69.3	71.5
Australia [+ 2] Australie [+ 2]	2001	713 229	59.6	17.9	22.7	0.1	21.5	21.7
	2002	758 147	59.8	18.1	24.4	0.3	19.6	22.0
	2003	813 225	59.6	17.9	24.5	0.6	17.6	20.6
Austria [2] Autriche [2]	2002	221 008	56.2[3]	17.9	20.8	0.3[5]	48.6	43.6
	2003	226 142	56.1[3]	18.0	21.5	0.4[5]	48.2	44.3
	2004	235 441	55.8[3]	17.8	21.7	0.0[5]	51.0	46.2
Azerbaijan [2] Azerbaïdjan [2]	2002	30 312 300	62.9[3]	12.4	34.1	0.5[5]	42.8	50.0
	2003	35 732 500	60.0[3]	12.4	52.9	0.3[5]	42.0	65.5
	2004	41 872 500	56.1[3]	11.6	54.2	0.3[5]	34.7	53.8
Bahamas [2] Bahamas [2]	2002	5 400	66.5[7]	14.3	28.6	2.5	43.9	53.0
	2003	*5 502	68.4[7]	14.3	28.9	2.6	42.2	54.2
	2004	5 735[6]	69.6[7]	14.1	29.3	2.9	43.1	57.4
Bahrain Bahreïn	2001	2 981	47.5	18.5	13.4	−1.1	82.3	60.5
	2002	3 176	45.2	18.5	17.3	4.3	81.2	66.6
	2003	3 612	41.0	18.6	19.4	3.2	79.8	61.9
Bangladesh [+ 2] Bangladesh [+ 2]	2000	2 535 464	77.5	4.5	23.1	...	15.4	21.5
	2001	2 732 009	76.8	5.0	23.1	...	14.3	19.0
	2002	3 005 801	76.4	5.3	23.4	...	14.2	20.0

Country or area / Pays ou zone	Year / Année	GDP in current prices (Mil. nat.cur.) PIB aux prix courant (Millions monnaie nat.)	% of Gross domestic product – en % du Produit intérieur brut					
			Household final consumption expenditure Consom. finale des ménages	Govt. final consumption expenditure Consom. finale des admin. publiques	Gross fixed capital formation Formation brute de capital fixe	Changes in inventories Variation des stocks	Exports of goods and services Exportations de biens et services	Imports of goods and services Importations de biens et services
Barbados	1999	4 965	65.5	20.7	18.8	0.6	51.3	56.9
Barbade	2000	5 183	67.3	20.9	18.1	0.1	49.8	56.3
	2001	5 093	64.5	22.2	16.5	−0.3	50.9	53.7
Belarus [2]	2001	17 173 230	57.6[3]	21.6	22.7	1.1[5]	66.7	70.3
Bélarus [2]	2002	26 138 302	59.5[3]	21.0	22.0	0.2[5]	63.6	67.4
	2003	36 564 846	57.1[3]	21.4	25.4	1.2[5]	65.2	69.1
Belgium [2]	2002	261 124	54.1[3]	22.3	19.5	−0.3	83.7	79.2
Belgique [2]	2003	269 546	54.5[3]	22.8	18.9	0.1	81.5	77.7
	2004	283 752	54.0[3]	22.6	18.5	1.9	83.7	80.8
Belize [2]	1998	1 258	67.3	17.4	21.3	3.1	52.9	62.1
Belize [2]	1999	1 377	65.1	17.1	26.5	3.0	51.3	63.2
	2000	1 514	68.4	15.3	31.0	3.2	48.8	66.7
Benin	2002	1 956 900	78.0	12.3	18.9	−0.5	22.2	31.0
Bénin	2003	2 067 500	77.2	12.6	19.5	0.8	21.0	31.1
	2004	2 131 500	75.6	12.8	19.5	0.7	20.1	28.7
Bermuda [+][2]	2000	3 378[8]	51.5[3]	10.9	19.5	0.6[5]	47.3	34.4
Bermudes [+][2]	2001	3 539	50.2[3]	...	...	...	1.4[9]	20.4[10]
	2002	3 715	49.3[3]	...	...	...	1.5[9]	20.1[10]
Bhutan	1998	16 337	57.1	20.2	37.9	0.3	31.5	47.0
Bhoutan	1999	19 123	52.6	22.3	42.5	0.6	29.9	47.9
	2000	21 698	52.2	20.4	43.5	0.2	29.8	46.1
Bolivia	2001	53 010	76.4	15.2	14.5	−0.3	19.7	25.5
Bolivie	2002	55 933	74.8	15.4	15.9	−1.1	21.9	26.9
	2003	60 252	73.7	16.6	13.2	−2.1	23.7	25.1
Botswana [+][2]	2001	28 637	29.5[3]	30.5	24.1	−4.5	61.3	37.7
Botswana [+][2]	2002	31 922	29.2[3]	33.1	24.3	1.9	48.8	36.8
	2003	36 338	28.4[3]	33.5	24.0	5.5	44.4	34.9
Brazil [2]	2001	1 198 736	60.5	19.2	19.5	1.7	13.2	14.2
Brésil [2]	2002	1 346 028	58.0	20.1	18.3	1.4	15.5	13.4
	2003	1 556 182	56.7	19.9	17.8	2.0	16.4	12.8
British Virgin Islands [2]	1997	512	43.2	12.3	25.2	0.4	102.9	84.0
Iles Vierges britanniques [2]	1998	593	41.0	12.0	26.3	−2.0	102.7	79.8
	1999	662	40.6	11.0	24.6	−0.8	104.4	80.1
Brunei Darussalam	1982	9 126	5.5	10.0	12.4	0.0[11]	89.3	17.2
Brunéi Darussalam	1983	8 124	9.5	11.4	9.9	0.0[11]	88.3	19.0
	1984	8 069	−5.6	31.1	6.5	0.0[11]	84.5	16.5
Bulgaria [2]	2001	29 709	69.5[3]	17.4	18.2	2.4[5]	55.6	63.1
Bulgarie [2]	2002	32 335	68.8[3]	18.0	18.3	1.5[5]	53.1	59.8
	2003	34 410	69.1[3]	19.0	19.6	2.2[5]	53.2	63.0
Burkina Faso	1991	811 676	76.2	14.7	21.8	1.4	11.4	25.4
Burkina Faso	1992	812 590	76.2	14.4	21.3	−0.2	9.7	21.4
	1993	832 349	77.2	14.4	20.4	0.8	9.7	22.5
Burundi	1990	196 656	83.0	19.5	16.4	−0.6	8.0	26.2
Burundi	1991	211 898	83.9	17.0	18.1	−0.5	10.0	28.5
	1992	226 384	82.9	15.6	21.1	0.4	9.0	29.0
Cambodia [2]	2001	14 574 177	84.4[3]	5.7	19.1	1.6	55.2	64.3
Cambodge [2]	2002	15 696 011	81.4[3]	5.8	22.6	−0.4	59.1	67.3
	2003	16 451 174	80.0[3]	5.9	21.6	3.4	62.2	71.7
Cameroon [+][2]	1996	4 793 080	...	...	13.1	−0.2	24.7	17.4
Cameroun [+][2]	1997	5 370 580	...	...	12.8	0.1	24.0	19.0
	1998	5 744 000	...	...	13.5	−0.1	24.0	20.4

Country or area Pays ou zone	Year Année	GDP in current prices (Mil. nat.cur.) PIB aux prix courant (Millions monnaie nat.)	% of Gross domestic product – en % du Produit intérieur brut					
			Household final consumption expenditure Consom. finale des ménages	Govt. final consumption expenditure Consom. finale des admin. publiques	Gross fixed capital formation Formation brute de capital fixe	Changes in inventories Variation des stocks	Exports of goods and services Exportations de biens et services	Imports of goods and services Importations de biens et services
Canada [2] Canada [2]	2001	1 092 135	55.7[3]	19.3	19.9	−0.6	44.1	38.3
	2002	1 140 428	56.2[3]	19.6	19.9	−0.1	41.9	37.5
	2003	1 200 078	56.0[3]	19.7	19.8	0.6	38.3	34.4
Cape Verde Cap–Vert	1998	51 599	87.4	19.4	31.4	−0.2	19.4	57.4
	1999	61 774	81.3	19.2	34.4	3.1	19.8	57.7
	2000	64 539	86.7	18.9	30.5	0.3	20.9	57.3
Cayman Islands Iles Caïmanes	1989	474	65.0	14.1	23.2	...	60.1	68.8
	1990	590	62.5	14.2	21.4	...	64.1	58.5
	1991	616	62.5	15.1	21.8	...	58.9	52.8
Central African Rep. Rép. centrafricaine	1986	388 647	82.1	15.6	12.9	−0.1	18.2	28.6
	1987	360 942	80.6	17.5	12.9	−0.2	17.8	28.6
	1988	376 748	80.7	16.1	9.8	0.7	17.7	25.1
Chad Tchad	1999	915 000[8]	28.5	16.8	14.0	−2.6	18.1	40.7
	2000	928 000[8]	24.6	17.6	15.5	2.2	18.1	44.9
	2001	1 088 000[8]	24.5	17.3	38.7	2.1	16.9	62.0
Chile [2] Chili [2]	2001	43 537 000	63.8[3]	12.6	21.7	0.4	33.3	31.8
	2002	46 342 000	63.1[3]	12.8	21.3	0.3	34.0	31.6
	2003	50 731 000	61.6[3]	12.4	21.2	0.8	36.6	32.6
China [+ 2,12] Chine [+ 2,12]	2002	10 517 230	46.5	13.2	39.9	0.4	28.8	26.1
	2003	11 739 020	44.9	12.6	43.7	0.2	34.2	31.9
	2004	13 687 590	43.1	12.0	44.8	0.3	39.5	36.9
China Hong Kong SAR [2] Chine Hong Kong RAS [2]	2001	1 269 896	60.2[3]	10.1	26.2	−0.3	140.8	137.2
	2002	1 247 381	58.4[3]	10.5	22.9	0.5	152.1	144.4
	2003	1 220 023	57.4[3]	10.7	22.1	0.8	172.2	163.1
China Macao SAR [2] Chine Macao RAS [2]	2001	49 862	41.4[3]	12.0	10.3	0.1	97.8	61.5
	2002	54 295	39.0[3]	11.4	10.3	0.4	100.5	61.6
	2003	63 365	34.6[3]	10.4	13.3	0.4	98.6	57.3
Colombia [2] Colombie [2]	2000	174 896 258	63.0[3]	21.2	12.6	1.1[5]	21.5	19.4
	2001	188 558 786	65.6[3]	20.6	13.6	0.6[5]	20.4	20.8
	2002	204 529 738	65.8[3]	20.4	14.7	0.7[5]	19.0	20.6
Comoros Comores	1989	63 397	77.8	27.6	14.4	4.6	14.9	39.3
	1990	66 370	79.7	25.7	12.2	8.0	11.7	37.3
	1991	69 248	80.9	25.3	12.3	4.0	15.5	38.0
Costa Rica [2] Costa Rica [2]	2002	6 058 895	67.8	14.9	18.9	3.7	42.4	47.6
	2003	6 970 815	66.7	14.5	19.1	1.4	46.8	48.6
	2004	8 055 488	66.7	14.7	18.2	4.0	46.4	49.9
Côte d'Ivoire Côte d'Ivoire	1998	7 457 508	65.1[3]	13.7	14.3	0.6	41.3	34.9
	1999	7 734 000	63.2[3]	14.6	14.5	−1.3	39.7	30.8
	2000	7 605 000	67.2[3]	15.5	12.3	−1.0	39.8	33.8
Croatia [2] Croatie [2]	2002	179 390	59.9[3]	21.0	24.6	3.8	45.4	54.7
	2003	193 067	58.7[3]	20.6	27.5	2.9	47.1	56.8
	2004	207 082	58.1[3]	19.9	27.6	2.6	47.5	55.7
Cuba [2] Cuba [2]	2001	29 557	64.9	25.9	11.6	0.7	14.2	17.3
	2002	30 680	63.9	27.9	10.0	0.0	12.6	14.5
	2003	32 337	64.9	26.4	9.1	0.3	14.4	15.1
Cyprus [2] Chypre [2]	2001	6 104	64.3	17.5	17.1	−0.6	56.1	54.5
	2002	6 370	64.1	18.4	18.2	0.5	50.9	52.2
	2003	6 802	63.8	20.0	17.2	0.7	46.7	48.3
Czech Republic [2] République tchèque [2]	2002	2 414 669	51.1[3]	23.0	26.6	1.3[5]	61.5	63.6
	2003	2 550 754	50.9[3]	24.0	26.6	0.7[5]	62.4	64.6
	2004	2 750 256	50.1[3]	22.7	27.3	0.3[5]	71.7	72.1

Country or area Pays ou zone	Year Année	GDP in current prices (Mil. nat.cur.) PIB aux prix courant (Millions monnaie nat.)	% of Gross domestic product – en % du Produit intérieur brut					
			Household final consumption expenditure Consom. finale des ménages	Govt. final consumption expenditure Consom. finale des admin. publiques	Gross fixed capital formation Formation brute de capital fixe	Changes in inventories Variation des stocks	Exports of goods and services Exportations de biens et services	Imports of goods and services Importations de biens et services
Dem. Rep. of the Congo	1987	326 946	77.1	22.4	20.3	5.3	63.2	88.2
Rép. dém. du Congo	1988	622 822	...	37.2	19.0	3.7	81.0	...
	1989	2 146 811	...	14.4	13.4	3.2	46.5	...
Denmark [2]	2002	1 350 787	47.5 [3]	26.5	20.1	0.2 [5]	44.6	38.9
Danemark [2]	2003	1 390 537	47.4 [3]	26.7	19.6	0.1 [5]	42.7	36.5
	2004	1 446 471	48.1 [3]	26.7	19.7	0.4 [5]	43.5	38.4
Djibouti	1996	88 233	64.6	33.6	19.3	−0.9	40.3	56.8
Djibouti	1997	87 289	59.3	34.7	21.4	0.2	42.2	57.8
	1998	88 461	67.3	29.0	23.2	0.2	43.4	63.0
Dominica	2000	732 [8]	62.6	21.9	27.5	...	53.3	67.5
Dominique	2001	713 [8]	64.7	21.3	25.1	...	45.9	63.1
	2002	685	69.6	21.5	22.0	...	46.3	59.4
Dominican Republic [2]	1994	179 130	76.8	4.6	17.9	3.4	37.4	40.2
Rép. dominicaine [2]	1995	209 646	78.6	4.3	16.1	3.3	34.5	36.7
	1996	232 993	81.4	4.7	17.3	3.6	18.1	25.1
Ecuador [2]	2002	24 311 [13]	69.3	10.5	22.8	4.9	24.0	31.4
Equateur [2]	2003	27 201 [13]	67.9	9.5	22.8	4.9	23.8	28.8
	2004	30 015 [13]	65.8	8.9	21.8	4.9	25.8	27.2
Egypt + [2]	2001	375 203	75.2 [3]	11.8	15.9	0.7	20.4	24.0
Egypte + [2]	2002	405 256	74.2 [3]	12.2	16.4	0.7	19.5	23.0
	2003	451 154	71.3 [3]	11.6	17.2	1.0	21.8	22.8
El Salvador	2001	120 862	88.6	10.5	16.4	0.2	25.8	41.6
El Salvador	2002	125 230	88.1	10.5	16.4	−0.3	26.4	41.1
	2003	130 733	89.3	10.4	16.6	...	26.7	43.0
Equatorial Guinea	1989	42 256	54.3	22.2	19.6	0.0	40.4	36.6
Guinée équatoriale	1990	44 349	53.2	15.3	34.6	−3.1	59.7	59.7
	1991	46 429	75.9	14.4	18.4	−2.3	28.4	34.7
Estonia [2]	2001	104 338	56.2 [3]	19.0	27.0	2.2	83.9	87.4
Estonie [2]	2002	116 869	57.2 [3]	18.8	28.7	3.1	74.1	81.2
	2003	125 832	56.6 [3]	19.0	28.4	2.7	75.0	83.0
Ethiopia incl. Eritrea	1991	19 195	80.1	16.5	10.4	...	5.5	12.5
Ethiopie y comp. Erythrée	1992	20 792	86.9	10.1	9.2	...	4.5	10.7
	1993	26 671	83.8	10.6	14.2	...	8.3	16.9
Ethiopia +	1997	41 465	79.2	10.9	19.1	...	16.2	23.3
Ethiopie +	1998	44 896	78.4	14.2	19.0	...	16.2	26.4
	1999	48 949	81.4	16.0	20.8	...	14.5	30.2
Fiji	1999	3 662	54.0	16.6	13.8	1.1	60.4	64.2
Fidji	2000	3 505	59.0	18.1	11.5	1.1	59.7	67.2
	2001	3 836	57.0	17.1	13.5	1.0	55.7	60.7
Finland [2]	2002	140 284	50.7 [3]	21.6	18.9	0.4	38.6	30.2
Finlande [2]	2003	143 337	51.9 [3]	22.1	18.4	0.5	37.1	30.6
	2004	149 742	51.7 [3]	22.4	18.6	0.8	37.1	31.5
France [2]	2002	1 548 555	55.9 [3]	23.4	18.8	0.2 [5]	27.1	25.4
France [2]	2003	1 585 172	56.1 [3]	23.8	18.9	0.0 [5]	25.7	24.6
	2004	1 648 369	56.1 [3]	23.9	19.2	0.6 [5]	26.0	25.7
French Guiana	1990	6 526	64.4	35.0	47.8	−0.2	67.3	114.3
Guyane française	1991	7 404	60.1	34.4	40.5	1.5	81.1	117.6
	1992	7 976	58.9	34.2	30.8	1.5	65.4	90.8
French Polynesia	1991	305 211	63.9	39.3	18.4	−0.2	9.3	30.7
Polynésie française	1992	314 265 [8]	63.9	47.8	16.7	0.0	8.3	27.4
	1993	329 266	61.5	38.3	16.2	−0.2	10.5	26.4

Country or area Pays ou zone	Year Année	GDP in current prices (Mil. nat.cur.) PIB aux prix courant (Millions monnaie nat.)	% of Gross domestic product – en % du Produit intérieur brut					
			Household final consumption expenditure Consom. finale des ménages	Govt. final consumption expenditure Consom. finale des admin. publiques	Gross fixed capital formation Formation brute de capital fixe	Changes in inventories Variation des stocks	Exports of goods and services Exportations de biens et services	Imports of goods and services Importations de biens et services
Gabon Gabon	1987	1 020 600	48.6	23.7	26.7[4]	...	41.3	40.3
	1988	1 013 600	48.1	21.8	36.2[4]	...	37.3	43.4
	1989	1 168 066	48.4	18.4	23.3[4]	...	50.3	40.3
Gambia [+] Gambie [+]	1991	2 920	83.7	13.0	18.2[14]	...	45.3[15]	60.1[16]
	1992	3 078	81.2	13.2	22.4[14]	...	45.2[15]	61.9[16]
	1993	3 243	78.1	15.1	27.1[14]	...	36.6[15]	56.9[16]
Georgia [2] Géorgie [2]	2002	7 459	77.1[3]	9.8	21.1	1.0[5]	29.2	42.4
	2003	8 560	67.9[3]	9.2	23.4	0.7[5]	31.9	46.4
	2004	9 800	72.2[3]	14.2	25.3	0.8[5]	30.1	45.5
Germany [2] Allemagne [2]	2002	2 148 810	58.9[3]	19.2	18.3	−0.9[5]	35.7	31.2
	2003	2 164 870	59.4[3]	19.2	17.6	−0.2[5]	35.5	31.5
	2004	2 207 240	59.1[3]	18.7	17.2	0.1[5]	38.0	33.1
Ghana Ghana	1994	5 205 200	73.7	13.7	22.6	1.4[17]	22.5	33.9
	1995	7 752 600	76.2	12.1	21.1	−1.1[17]	24.5	32.8
	1996	11 339 200	76.1	12.0	20.6	0.9[17]	24.9	34.5
Greece [2] Grèce [2]	2002	141 669	67.3[3]	17.6	23.8	−0.2	20.8	29.3
	2003	153 472	66.8[3]	16.4	25.6	0.1	19.8	28.7
	2004	165 280	66.0[3]	17.1	25.5	0.0	20.9	29.5
Grenada Grenade	1990	541	64.9	20.5	38.9	3.1	44.4	71.8
	1991	567	69.2	18.8	40.0	3.7	45.4	77.1
	1992	578	66.5	19.9	32.4	2.1	38.6	59.4
Guadeloupe Guadeloupe	1990	15 201	92.8	30.8	33.9	1.1	4.9	63.5
	1991	16 415	87.3	31.0	33.0	1.0	6.1	58.4
	1992	17 972	84.1	29.3	27.8	1.3	4.5	47.0
Guatemala Guatemala	1996	95 479	87.0	5.1	13.3	−0.6	17.8	22.6
	1997	107 943	86.9	4.9	14.8	−1.0	17.9	23.6
	1998	121 548	86.6	6.2	15.7	−0.2	17.9	26.2
Guinea–Bissau Guinée–Bissau	1990	510 094	100.9	11.4	13.8	0.9	12.0	39.0
	1991	854 985	100.6	12.6	10.4	0.9	13.4	38.0
	1992	1 530 010	111.1	10.7	26.5[4]	...	8.2	56.5
Guyana Guyana	1999	123 665[8]	43.8	24.2	38.5[4]	...	−10.1[18]	...
	2000	130 013	49.9	27.5	38.5[4]	...	...	...
	2001	133 403	55.5	22.9	38.5[4]	...	...	...
Haiti [+] Haïti [+]	1997	51 578	...	...	12.5	...	11.5	27.1
	1998	59 055	...	...	12.9	...	13.2	28.6
	1999	66 425	...	...	13.1	...	13.3	28.2
Honduras Honduras	1998	70 438	67.0	10.1	28.2	2.7	46.1	54.1
	1999	77 095	68.8	11.3	29.8	4.8	41.3	56.0
	2000	87 523	70.0	12.0	27.2	4.6	42.3	56.1
Hungary [2] Hongrie [2]	2002	16 740 415	53.6[3]	23.5	23.4	1.8	64.8	67.1
	2003	18 408 815	54.9[3]	24.6	22.5	2.5	63.5	68.0
	2004	20 338 182	55.0[3]	23.7	22.6	1.6	65.1	68.0
Iceland [2] Islande [2]	2002	766 239	54.8[3]	25.7	17.7	0.0	39.9	38.1
	2003	797 487	56.6[3]	26.6	20.1	−0.2	36.2	39.3
	2004	858 921	57.8[3]	26.6	22.0	−0.4	36.8	42.7
India [+] Inde [+]	2001	22 719 840	65.4	12.5	22.1	0.1	12.8	13.7
	2002	24 633 240	64.3	11.8	22.2	0.4	14.4	15.4
	2003	27 600 250	63.8	11.3	22.7	0.3	14.8	16.1
Indonesia Indonésie	2001	1 467 655 000	66.3[3]	7.7	21.4	−3.7	42.5	34.3
	2002	1 610 565 000	69.6[3]	8.2	20.3	−4.6	35.8	29.3
	2003	1 786 691 000	69.3[3]	9.2	19.7	−3.8	31.2	25.7

Country or area Pays ou zone	Year Année	GDP in current prices (Mil. nat.cur.) PIB aux prix courant (Millions monnaie nat.)	% of Gross domestic product – en % du Produit intérieur brut					
			Household final consumption expenditure Consom. finale des ménages	Govt. final consumption expenditure Consom. finale des admin. publiques	Gross fixed capital formation Formation brute de capital fixe	Changes in inventories Variation des stocks	Exports of goods and services Exportations de biens et services	Imports of goods and services Importations de biens et services
Iran (Islamic Rep. of) [+2] Iran (Rép. islamique d') [+2]	2001	680 506 240	47.5[3]	14.2	27.6	6.0	20.2	18.5
	2002	935 828 947	44.6[3]	13.1	27.9	6.8	26.3	22.5
	2003	1 126 947 144	44.4[3]	12.9	28.3	7.2	27.5	25.1
Iraq Iraq	1998	4 570 100	79.0	7.9	3.8[4]	...	...	...
	1999	6 809 790	61.0	6.4	3.9[4]	...	...	...
	2000	7 398 604	59.7	6.2	7.3[4]	...	...	...
Ireland [2] Irlande [2]	2002	127 992	44.7[3]	15.3	22.6	0.1[5]	93.5	77.0
	2003	134 786	45.2[3]	15.8	23.6	0.4[5]	83.7	68.2
	2004	146 279	44.8[3]	14.9	25.0	...	80.2	64.7
Israel [2] Israël [2]	2001	499 173	54.5[3]	28.3	18.2	2.0	33.5	36.6
	2002	516 013	56.0[3]	29.9	17.6	0.4	35.4	39.2
	2003	523 259	56.5[3]	29.0	16.9	−0.7	36.8	38.4
Italy [2] Italie [2]	2002	1 260 598	60.1[3]	19.0	19.8	0.2[5]	27.0	26.0
	2003	1 300 929	60.5[3]	19.5	19.2	0.3[5]	25.8	25.2
	2004	1 351 328	60.1[3]	19.2	19.5	0.4[5]	26.6	25.8
Jamaica Jamaïque	2001	373 043	71.3	15.9	29.0	0.1	38.8	55.1
	2002	408 765	71.9	16.3	31.7	0.2	36.2	56.3
	2003	470 440	73.4	15.1	29.9	0.2	40.7	59.2
Japan [2] Japon [2]	2001	505 847 100	56.5[3]	17.1	25.8	0.0	10.4	9.8
	2002	497 896 800	57.1[3]	17.7	24.2	−0.2	11.2	9.9
	2003	497 485 000	56.8[3]	17.7	23.9	−0.1	11.8	10.2
Jordan Jordanie	2000	5 989	80.9[3]	23.7	21.1	1.1	41.9	68.6
	2001	6 339	81.4[3]	23.0	19.5	1.2	42.2	67.4
	2002	6 699	77.6[3]	23.0	19.3	0.8	45.3	66.0
Kazakhstan [2] Kazakhstan [2]	2001	3 250 593	57.9[3]	13.4	23.7	3.1	46.2	47.1
	2002	3 776 277	58.4[3]	11.5	24.0	3.3	47.2	46.3
	2003	4 611 975	63.7[3]	11.3	23.3	2.7	48.7	42.6
Kenya Kenya	2001	43 937	75.7	19.2	14.0	0.6	26.6	36.2
	2002	48 134	72.9	19.1	12.9	0.5	26.0	31.4
	2003	54 582	73.8	17.9	12.5	0.4	24.9	29.5
Kiribati Kiribati	1980	21	92.8	36.4	...	...	22.5	95.7
Korea Republic of [2] Corée République de [2]	2002	684 263 500	55.7[3]	12.9	29.1	0.0[5]	35.3	33.9
	2003	724 675 000	53.7[3]	13.3	29.9	0.0[5]	37.9	35.6
	2004	778 444 600	51.5[3]	13.5	29.5	0.7[5]	44.1	39.7
Kuwait Koweït	1999	8 886	50.6	27.7	14.6	0.4	47.4	40.7
	2000	10 991	42.2	22.6	7.5	...	59.4	31.7
	2001	10 057	47.7	26.3	8.6	...	54.7	37.4
Kyrgyzstan [2] Kirghizistan [2]	2001	73 883	64.8[3]	17.5	16.8	1.2[5]	36.7	37.0
	2002	75 367	67.5[3]	18.6	16.3	1.3[5]	39.6	43.3
	2003	83 872	77.9[3]	16.8	13.6	−1.8[5]	38.7	45.3
Latvia [2] Lettonie [2]	2001	5 168	62.9[3]	20.6	25.1	1.4[5]	41.6	51.7
	2002	5 689	62.7[3]	21.1	24.1	2.2[5]	41.1	51.2
	2003	6 322	63.0[3]	21.8	24.4	3.7[5]	42.3	55.1
Lebanon Liban	1994	14 992 000	110.8	10.6	36.4	...	8.4	66.3
	1995	17 779 000	107.7	9.9	36.3	...	11.0	64.9
Lesotho [2] Lesotho [2]	1999	5 565	102.8[3]	21.3	47.6	1.0	24.4	94.8[8]
	2000	5 986	101.1[3]	19.1	44.4	−2.3	29.7	92.1
	2001	6 478	101.7[3]	18.2	43.1	−2.6	39.3	99.6
Liberia Libéria	1987	1 090	65.5	13.2	11.1	0.6[19]	40.2	32.7
	1988	1 158	63.3	11.8	10.0	0.3[19]	39.0	27.8
	1989	1 194	55.0	11.9	8.1	0.3[19]	43.7	23.1

Country or area Pays ou zone	Year Année	GDP in current prices (Mil. nat.cur.) PIB aux prix courant (Millions monnaie nat.)	% of Gross domestic product – en % du Produit intérieur brut					
			Household final consumption expenditure Consom. finale des ménages	Govt. final consumption expenditure Consom. finale des admin. publiques	Gross fixed capital formation Formation brute de capital fixe	Changes in inventories Variation des stocks	Exports of goods and services Exportations de biens et services	Imports of goods and services Importations de biens et services
Libyan Arab Jamah. Jamah. arabe libyenne	1983	8 805	39.2	32.7	25.1	−1.1	42.1	38.0
	1984	8 013	38.6	33.6	25.3	0.5	41.4	39.4
	1985	8 277	37.6	31.7	19.7	0.4	37.4	26.7
Lithuania [2] Lituanie [2]	2001	48 379	65.1[3]	19.8	20.2	0.3[5]	50.0	55.4
	2002	51 643	64.5[3]	19.3	20.4	1.3[5]	53.1	58.7
	2003	56 179	64.9[3]	18.5	21.4	1.0[5]	51.8	57.6
Luxembourg [2] Luxembourg [2]	2002	22 805	42.6[3]	17.6	21.9	−0.7[5]	143.6	125.0
	2003	23 956	41.9[3]	18.2	19.8	1.3[5]	137.4	118.7
	2004	25 664	40.5[3]	18.3	19.3	0.2[5]	146.2	124.6
Madagascar Madagascar	1990	4 601 600	86.0[20]	8.0	17.0	...	15.9	26.9
	1991	4 906 400	92.2[20]	8.6	8.2	...	17.3	26.2
	1992	5 584 500	90.0[20]	8.2	11.6	...	15.6	25.3
Malawi Malawi	1994	10 319[8]	74.4[21]	28.3	12.0	...	31.8	40.7
	1995	20 923[8]	30.4[21]	21.9	11.9	...	32.2	38.2
	1996	33 918[8]	56.1[21]	17.5	11.2	...	15.5	27.1
Malaysia Malaisie	2001	334 404	45.0[3]	12.6	24.9	−1.0	116.4	98.0
	2002	361 624	44.1[3]	13.8	23.2	0.6	114.8	96.5
	2003	394 200	43.7[3]	13.9	22.1	−0.7	114.3	93.3
Maldives [2] Maldives [2]	2002	8 201	30.5	23.2	25.5	...	86.5	65.6
	2003	8 842	28.9	21.9	27.2	...	87.7	65.7
	2004	9 639	27.5	25.0	36.1	...	94.8	83.3
Mali Mali	1990	683 300	79.0	15.2	20.0	2.2	17.3	33.7
	1991	691 400	85.1	15.3	20.0	−2.4	17.5	35.5
	1992	737 400	82.2	14.2	17.6	2.7	17.8	34.6
Malta [2] Malte [2]	2001	1 731	63.0[3]	20.5	20.6	1.0[5]	80.8	86.0
	2002	1 767	62.2[3]	21.1	18.8	−1.8[5]	83.1	83.4
	2003	1 846	61.0[3]	21.0	21.3	1.9[5]	77.0	82.2
Martinique Martinique	1990	19 320	83.6	29.7	26.7	1.9	8.4	50.3
	1991	20 787	84.0	28.8	25.6	1.4	7.4	47.1
	1992	22 093	84.3	28.7	23.6	−0.9	6.8	42.5
Mauritania Mauritanie	1986	59 715	85.4	14.3	22.7	1.5	55.4	79.4
	1987	67 216	82.6	13.6	20.8	1.7	48.3	67.0
	1988	72 635	79.6	14.2	17.0	1.4	49.1	61.3
Mauritius [2] Maurice [2]	2002	142 131	62.1	12.9	22.1	−0.1	62.1	59.1
	2003	157 210	62.1	13.0	22.6	1.1	56.4	55.1
	2004	173 715	62.2	13.2	22.4	2.5	55.2	55.4
Mexico [2] Mexique [2]	2001	5 809 688	69.6[3]	11.8	20.0	0.9	27.5	29.8
	2002	6 263 137	69.1[3]	12.1	19.3	1.4	26.8	28.7
	2003	6 891 434	68.7[3]	12.4	18.9	1.6	27.9	29.5
Mongolia Mongolie	1998	833 727[1]	66.7[3]	17.3	33.5	1.6[5]	54.3	67.5
	1999	925 801[1]	68.4[3]	17.2	34.9	2.0[5]	58.5	72.5
	2000	1 018 886[1]	71.9[3]	17.7	31.6	4.6[5]	66.0	83.0
Montserrat Montserrat	1984	94	96.4	20.6	23.7	2.7	13.6	56.9
	1985	100	96.3	20.3	24.7	1.5	11.7	54.4
	1986	114	89.5	18.7	33.0	2.8	10.1	53.9
Morocco Maroc	2001	383 185	60.9	19.8	22.3	0.6	27.9	31.4
	2002	397 782	60.5	20.1	22.9	−0.2	28.9	32.2
	2003	418 655	59.3	21.0	23.5	0.3	27.9	32.0
Mozambique [2] Mozambique [2]	2001	76 544 900	69.4	13.5	20.0	5.9	21.2	29.9
	2002	96 345 300	62.5	14.0	18.0	8.8	24.1	27.3
	2003	117 690 200	59.4	15.4	15.2	11.4	24.9	26.2

Country or area Pays ou zone	Year Année	GDP in current prices (Mil. nat.cur.) PIB aux prix courant (Millions monnaie nat.)	% of Gross domestic product – en % du Produit intérieur brut					
			Household final consumption expenditure Consom. finale des ménages	Govt. final consumption expenditure Consom. finale des admin. publiques	Gross fixed capital formation Formation brute de capital fixe	Changes in inventories Variation des stocks	Exports of goods and services Exportations de biens et services	Imports of goods and services Importations de biens et services
Myanmar [+]	1996	791 980	...	...	14.9	−2.7	0.7	1.5
Myanmar [+]	1997	1 109 554	...	...	13.5	−0.9	0.6	1.3
	1998	1 559 996	...	...	11.8	−0.7	0.5	1.0
Namibia [2]	2001	27 686	58.1[3]	28.4	21.9	1.5	45.0	51.4
Namibie [2]	2002	31 550	52.6[3]	27.4	18.7	−1.5	46.5	50.1
	2003	32 309	...	28.8	22.0	0.7	39.4	46.7
Nepal [+]	2001	410 287	75.3	9.8	19.0	4.9	22.4	31.5
Népal [+]	2002	421 333	78.1	10.0	19.3	5.3	16.1	28.8
	2003	446 177	78.2	10.5	19.2	6.9	14.7	29.3
Netherlands [2]	2002	445 160	49.7[3]	24.6	20.8	−0.2[5]	62.8	57.7
Pays–Bas [2]	2003	454 276	49.4[3]	25.4	20.2	0.0[5]	61.5	56.5
	2004	466 310	48.8[3]	25.3	20.5	...	65.4	60.0
Netherlands Antilles [2]	2001	5 162	53.8[3]	21.6	25.8	0.6	82.8	84.6
Antilles néerlandaises [2]	2002	5 199	55.3[3]	20.9	25.4	0.1	80.3	81.9
	2003	5 368	55.8[3]	21.4	23.6	0.1	82.9	83.8
New Caledonia	1990	250 427	57.3	32.6[22]	24.4	−1.1	22.0	35.4
Nouvelle–Calédonie	1991	272 235	53.8	32.8[22]	23.9	1.3	20.1	32.2
	1992	281 427	56.7	33.7[22]	23.7	0.1	16.8	31.4
New Zealand [+ 2]	2001	123 532	58.5[3]	17.6	20.0	1.5[5]	35.3	33.0
Nouvelle–Zélande [+ 2]	2002	129 792	59.2[3]	17.5	20.4	0.6[5]	32.3	30.8
	2003	137 809	59.2[3]	17.6	21.7	0.8[5]	29.1	28.9
Nicaragua [2]	2002	57 099	78.7[3]	15.5	28.7	3.5	22.6	49.0
Nicaragua [2]	2003	62 458	78.9[3]	16.0	27.7	3.7	24.1	50.4
	2004	70 271	80.2[3]	15.2	30.0	3.8	25.0	54.1
Niger	2001	1 299 238	73.5	18.5	11.7	1.7	18.6	27.0
Niger	2002	1 405 430	77.0	18.1	12.1	2.4	16.4	26.0
	2003	1 383 484	77.7	17.3	12.1	4.3	16.7	28.0
Nigeria	1999	3 320 311	59.3	7.6	5.3	0.0	49.7	21.9
Nigéria	2000	4 980 943	49.1	5.2	5.4	0.0	58.9	18.6
	2001	5 639 863	60.3	4.9	7.0	0.0	55.4	27.5
Norway [2]	2002	1 519 131	44.8[3]	22.3	18.1	...	41.1	27.4
Norvège [2]	2003	1 561 915	46.0[3]	22.8	17.4	...	41.3	27.7
	2004	1 685 552	44.8[3]	22.0	18.0	...	43.7	29.5
Oman [2]	2001	7 670	43.9	22.3	12.7	0.0	57.3	36.1
Oman [2]	2002	7 807	44.1	23.1	12.7	0.1	57.1	36.8
	2003	*8 343	43.8	22.2	15.7[4]	...	55.9	37.5
Pakistan [+]	2002	4 401 699	74.5	8.8	15.5	1.3	15.4	15.5
Pakistan [+]	2003	4 821 303	73.6	9.1	14.8	1.9	16.9	16.3
	2004	5 458 063	73.1	9.1	16.4	1.7	16.0	16.2
Panama [2]	2001	11 808	61.6	13.9	15.2	2.4	72.7	65.9
Panama [2]	2002	12 272	64.3	14.8	13.6	2.2	67.5	62.3
	2003	12 862	60.5	14.3	17.2	1.9	64.0	58.0
Papua New Guinea [2]	2000	10 750	60.1	16.2	20.0	1.3	43.9	41.5
Papouasie–Nouvelle–Guinée [2]	2001	11 758	71.9	15.5	20.2	1.6	42.3	51.5
	2002	13 375	73.9	14.4	18.3	1.5	38.8	46.9
Paraguay	1993	11 991 719	81.3	6.7	22.0[23]	0.9[24]	36.9	47.9
Paraguay	1994	14 960 131	88.4	6.8	22.5[23]	0.9[24]	34.2	52.8
	1995	17 699 000	85.3	7.2	23.1[23]	0.9[24]	35.0	51.2
Peru [2]	2001	188 313	72.2	10.7	18.7	0.1	16.0	17.7
Pérou [2]	2002	198 657	71.7	10.3	17.7	1.1	16.5	17.3
	2003	210 747	71.0	10.1	17.9	0.9	17.7	17.6

Gross domestic product by type of expenditure at current prices — Percentage distribution (*continued*)
Dépenses imputées au produit intérieur brut aux prix courants — Répartition en pourcentage (*suite*)

Country or area Pays ou zone	Year Année	GDP in current prices (Mil. nat.cur.) PIB aux prix courant (Millions monnaie nat.)	% of Gross domestic product – en % du Produit intérieur brut					
			Household final consumption expenditure Consom. finale des ménages	Govt. final consumption expenditure Consom. finale des admin. publiques	Gross fixed capital formation Formation brute de capital fixe	Changes in inventories Variation des stocks	Exports of goods and services Exportations de biens et services	Imports of goods and services Importations de biens et services
Philippines Philippines	2001	3 631 474	70.6	12.2	17.9	1.0	49.2	52.3
	2002	3 959 648	69.5	11.6	17.5	0.1	49.7	50.2
	2003	4 299 932	69.5	11.0	16.6	0.0	49.1	51.7
Poland [2] Pologne [2]	2002	781 112	66.4[3]	18.1	19.0	−0.1	29.6	33.0
	2003	814 922	66.0[3]	17.6	18.4	0.5	34.4	36.9
	2004	883 656	64.9[3]	16.9	18.2	1.8	39.1	40.9
Portugal [2] Portugal [2]	2002	128 458	61.3[3]	21.2	25.0	0.6[5]	29.9	38.0
	2003	130 511	62.0[3]	21.2	22.6	0.6[5]	30.1	36.5
	2004	135 079	62.8[3]	21.3	22.6	0.9[5]	30.7	38.4
Puerto Rico [+] Porto Rico [+]	2000	69 208	54.3[3]	11.2	16.9	0.7	77.6	60.6
	2001	71 306	54.0[3]	11.7	15.9	0.4	75.9	57.9
	2002	74 362	54.0[3]	12.1	15.3	0.4	82.0	63.8
Qatar [2] Qatar [2]	2000	64 646	15.2	19.7	19.5	0.7	67.3	22.3
	2001	64 579	15.5	19.8	22.5	0.8	65.1	23.7
	2002	65 088	15.8	20.0	22.2	0.7	65.6	24.2
Republic of Moldova [2] République de Moldova [2]	2002	22 556	83.0[3]	20.2	16.3	5.3	52.5	77.4
	2003	27 619	90.6[3]	19.7	18.6	4.6	53.3	86.7
	2004	31 992	90.4[3]	15.4	21.7	3.6	48.9	80.0
Réunion Réunion	1992	33 787	76.1	28.4	28.6	2.1	3.4	38.6
	1993	33 711[8]	76.4	28.6	25.7	−0.4	3.1	36.2
	1994	35 266	78.0	28.9	28.1	0.1	2.9	38.0
Romania [2] Roumanie [2]	2002	1 514 750 900	69.0[3]	15.1	21.3	0.4[5]	35.4	41.1
	2003	1 903 353 900[25]	68.9[3]	16.0	22.2	0.7[5]	36.0	43.8
	2004	*2 387 914 300	70.4[3]	15.9	22.3	0.8[5]	37.1	46.4
Russian Federation [2] Fédération de Russie [2]	2002	10 817 536	51.2[3]	17.7	17.8	2.3[5]	35.3	24.5
	2003	13 201 074	50.7[3]	17.6	18.1	2.4[5]	35.3	23.9
	2004	16 778 775	48.6[3]	16.2	17.8	3.3[5]	34.6	22.1
Rwanda Rwanda	2000	681 455	90.2	8.9	18.0	...	6.3	23.4
	2001	732 276	90.4	9.5	17.4	...	8.7	26.1
	2002	784 000[8]	91.5	9.5	17.9	...	7.1	24.6
Saint Kitts and Nevis Saint–Kitts–et–Nevis	2001	932	51.4	20.6	53.7[4]	...	44.3	70.0
	2002	958	62.3	19.0	47.7[4]	...	43.2	72.2
	2003	997	61.2	17.7	47.1[4]	...	44.6	70.5
Saint Lucia Sainte–Lucie	2001	1 766	55.8	27.7	26.0	...	54.4	64.0
	2002	1 827	56.2	26.9	22.8	...	46.3	52.2
	2003	1 866	67.3	24.5	21.9	...	55.4	69.1
St. Vincent–Grenadines St. Vincent–Grenadines	2001	933	59.7	19.8	29.8	...	50.9	60.2
	2002	974	59.2	20.7	30.1	...	49.4	59.5
	2003	1 016	64.0	19.6	33.9	...	45.9	63.4
San Marino Saint–Marin	1997	1 279 857	...	...	38.4	3.2	234.2	238.3
	1998	1 400 841	...	...	37.0	4.9	202.0	203.8
	1999	1 551 010	...	...	41.4	5.3	197.1	200.0
Sao Tome and Principe Sao Tomé–et–Principe	1986	2 478	76.1	30.3	13.6	0.9	...	50.8
	1987	3 003	63.1	24.8	15.4	1.1	...	43.1
	1988	4 221	71.8	21.2	15.7	0.0	...	66.8
Saudi Arabia [+] Arabie saoudite [+]	2001	686 296	37.8	27.5	18.4	0.5	39.9	24.1
	2002	*707 067	36.8	26.1	18.1	1.6	41.2	23.8
	2003	*797 175	33.6	24.9	17.9	1.4	46.6	24.3
Senegal Sénégal	1998	2 746 000	75.5	11.8	17.7	2.1	29.9	37.0
	1999	2 925 000	74.3	12.7	19.6	1.1	30.4	38.0
	2000	3 114 000	72.9	14.0	17.3	5.6	29.7	39.6

Country or area Pays ou zone	Year Année	GDP in current prices (Mil. nat.cur.) PIB aux prix courant (Millions monnaie nat.)	% of Gross domestic product – en % du Produit intérieur brut					
			Household final consumption expenditure Consom. finale des ménages	Govt. final consumption expenditure Consom. finale des admin. publiques	Gross fixed capital formation Formation brute de capital fixe	Changes in inventories Variation des stocks	Exports of goods and services Exportations de biens et services	Imports of goods and services Importations de biens et services
Serbia and Montenegro Serbie–et–Monténégro	1998	148 370	70.3	28.6	11.6	−1.1[5]	23.4	32.8
	#1999[26]	191 099	68.7	28.3	12.6	−0.5[5]	11.2	20.3
	2000[26]	381 661	70.4	28.6	15.4	−6.6[5]	9.0	16.8
Seychelles Seychelles	1998	3 201	50.0	31.2	34.0	0.6	−15.8[18]	...
	1999	3 330	45.3	27.8	41.5	1.8	−16.4[18]	...
	2000	3 424	39.4	27.1	35.7	0.5	−2.6[18]	...
Sierra Leone + Sierra Leone +	1988	43 947	86.7	7.5	12.7	0.8	14.5[27]	22.3[8]
	1989	82 837	84.7	6.6	13.5	0.5	19.7[27]	25.1[8]
	1990	150 175	77.9	10.4	10.1	1.8	25.4[27]	25.7[8]
Singapore Singapour	2002	158 388	43.8	12.3	25.4	−2.6	21.4[18]	...
	2003	160 924	43.3	11.8	24.2	−9.4	32.0[18]	...
	2004	180 554	42.2	10.6	24.0	−5.7	29.7[18]	...
Slovakia [2] Slovaquie [2]	2002	1 098 658	57.7[3]	20.1	27.6	1.7[5]	71.7	78.9
	2003	1 201 196	56.5[3]	19.9	25.7	−0.2[5]	77.7	79.2
	2004	1 325 486	56.6[3]	19.4	24.7	1.6[5]	76.8	79.5
Slovenia [2] Slovénie [2]	2001	4 761 815	56.3[3]	20.5	24.5	−0.6[5]	57.6	58.3
	2002	5 314 494	54.6[3]	20.2	23.3	0.4[5]	57.6	56.1
	2003	5 747 168	54.4[3]	20.3	23.9	1.4[5]	56.5	56.5
Solomon Islands Iles Salomon	1986	253[1]	63.1	33.3	25.2	1.0	52.6	75.2[28]
	1987	293[1]	63.1	36.3	20.4	2.7	55.9	78.4[28]
	1988	367[1]	68.6	31.4	30.0	2.7	52.4	85.0[28]
Somalia Somalie	1985	87 290	90.5[20]	10.6	8.9[29]	2.9[24]	4.2[9]	17.0[30]
	1986	118 781	89.1[20]	9.7	16.8[29]	1.0[24]	5.8[9]	22.4[30]
	1987	169 608	88.8[20]	11.1	16.8[29]	4.8[24]	5.9[9]	27.2[30]
South Africa [2] Afrique du Sud [2]	2001	1 020 007	62.7	18.3	15.1	0.2	29.8	26.1
	2002	1 164 945	62.0	18.3	15.1	1.0	32.5	28.9
	2003	1 251 468	62.8	19.1	16.0	1.2	27.2	25.5
Spain [2] Espagne [2]	2002	729 004	58.2[3]	17.2	26.2	0.4	27.3	29.3
	2003	780 557	57.3[3]	17.2	27.1	0.6	26.3	28.6
	2004	837 557	57.7[3]	17.7	27.8	0.4	25.7	29.3
Sri Lanka [2] Sri Lanka [2]	2001	1 396 314	69.6	13.5	21.3	1.5	39.5[1]	45.8[1]
	2002	1 570 216	70.7	13.0	20.9	1.7	36.4	43.2
	2003	1 748 774	71.1	12.7	20.6	1.2	36.1	42.4
Sudan Soudan	1994	5 522 838	84.1	4.6	9.4	6.8	4.6	9.5
	#1996	10 330 678	81.9	7.5	12.3	9.6	8.0	19.2
	1997	16 769 372	85.6	5.4	12.2 .	5.7	10.2	19.2
Suriname Suriname	2000	1 032 979	...	24.9	68.9[31]	...	62.1	55.9
	2001	1 436 483	...	28.8	68.4[31]	...	74.8	71.9
	2002	1 926 645	...	30.5	79.1[31]	...	48.8	58.4
Swaziland +[2] Swaziland +[2]	2001	10 846	68.3	18.4	24.6	...	92.1	103.4
	2002	12 560	72.1	16.4	19.8	...	86.3	94.7
	2003	14 401	76.2	14.8	18.0	...	77.8	86.9
Sweden [2] Suède [2]	2002	2 352 938	48.6[3]	27.9	16.7	0.1[5]	44.1	37.4
	2003	2 438 447	48.7[3]	28.3	15.8	0.4[5]	43.8	37.1
	2004	2 545 750	48.1[3]	27.7	16.0	0.1[5]	46.3	38.2
Switzerland [2] Suisse [2]	2001	422 485	60.4[3]	11.6	22.2	1.4[5]	45.2	40.8
	2002	431 064	60.3[3]	11.8	21.5	−0.5[5]	44.1	37.3
	2003	433 366	60.7[3]	12.0	21.0	−0.7[5]	44.1	37.1
Syrian Arab Republic Rép. arabe syrienne	2001	954 137	59.9	12.8	20.8	...	37.7	31.1
	2002	1 014 541	59.5	12.3	20.4	...	39.8	32.0
	2003	1 052 921	60.3	13.6	23.1	...	32.9	29.9

Country or area / Pays ou zone	Year / Année	GDP in current prices (Mil. nat.cur.) PIB aux prix courant (Millions monnaie nat.)	% of Gross domestic product – en % du Produit intérieur brut					
			Household final consumption expenditure Consom. finale des ménages	Govt. final consumption expenditure Consom. finale des admin. publiques	Gross fixed capital formation Formation brute de capital fixe	Changes in inventories Variation des stocks	Exports of goods and services Exportations de biens et services	Imports of goods and services Importations de biens et services
Tajikistan [2] Tadjikistan [2]	2000	1 807	73.2[3]	8.5	9.4	2.2	85.1	74.9
	2001	2 529	74.9[3]	9.5	9.2	7.4	67.3	69.3
	2002	3 366	74.0[3]	9.1	10.8	7.2	66.2	65.4
Thailand Thaïlande	2000	4 923 263	55.9	11.3	21.9	0.9	66.8	58.1
	2001	5 133 836	57.0	11.3	23.0	1.1	66.0	59.4
	2002	5 451 854	56.5	11.2	22.9	1.1	64.7	57.5
TFYR of Macedonia [2] L'ex–R.y. Macédoine [2]	2001	233 841	70.0[3]	24.8	14.8	4.2	42.7	56.6
	2002	243 970	77.1[3]	22.4	16.6	4.1	38.0	58.2
	2003	253 454	76.5[3]	20.5	16.6	3.2	37.6	54.4
Timor–Leste Timor–Leste	2000	393	52.1	43.3	31.7	3.2	21.2	51.6
Togo Togo	1984	304 800	66.0	14.0	21.2	−1.5	51.9	51.6
	1985	332 500	66.0	14.2	22.9	5.2	48.3	56.7
	1986	363 600	69.0	14.4	23.8	5.3	35.6	48.2
Tonga + Tonga +	1999	238	97.5[3]	22.3	19.7	1.3	13.4	54.2
	2000	252	96.8[3]	21.4	20.6	0.8	16.3	56.0
	2001	274	101.8[3]	23.4	20.1	1.1	12.8	59.1
Trinidad and Tobago [2] Trinité–et–Tobago [2]	2001	55 007	56.7	13.2	18.1	1.3	55.3	44.6
	2002	55 366	57.6	17.2	19.0	0.6	51.1	45.5
	2003	66 168	50.2	16.6	16.4	1.6	56.0	40.7
Tunisia [2] Tunisie [2]	2000	26 651	60.7	15.6	26.0	1.4	44.5	48.2
	2001	28 729	61.0	15.6	26.3	1.7	47.7	52.3
	2002	29 879	62.6	16.2	25.2	0.2	45.3	49.6
Turkey Turquie	2002	277 574	66.4	14.0	16.6	4.7	29.2	30.7
	2003	359 763	66.6	13.6	15.5	7.3	27.4	30.7
	2004	430 511	66.1	13.2	17.8	7.9	28.9	34.7
Turkmenistan [2] Turkménistan [2]	2000	25 648 000	70.8[3]	...	...	...	...	...
	2001	35 118 973	70.8[3]	...	...	...	...	...
	2002	45 239 913	70.8[3]	...	...	...	...	...
Turks and Caicos Islands Iles Turques et Caïques	2000	200	59.8	28.0	33.9[4]	...	83.4	105.1
	2001	209	59.8	31.3	37.0[4]	...	86.1	114.2
	2002	216	66.4	27.8	46.3[4]	...	79.4	119.9
Tuvalu Tuvalu	1996	16[32]	...	...	67.6[4]	...	...	...
	1997	18[32]	...	...	51.2[4]	...	...	...
	1998	21[32]	...	...	54.9[4]	...	...	...
Uganda Ouganda	2001	10 154 503	80.5	14.3	19.3	0.4	11.9	25.6
	2002	10 812 390	79.9	14.9	20.2	0.4	11.6	26.5
	2003	12 637 469	79.4	13.6	21.6	0.4	13.0	27.4
Ukraine [2] Ukraine [2]	2001	204 190	56.9[3]	19.6	19.7	2.1[5]	55.5	53.8
	2002	225 810	57.0[3]	18.4	19.2	1.0[5]	55.1	50.7
	2003	264 165	56.7[3]	20.4	19.8	0.5[5]	58.4	55.8
United Arab Emirates Emirats arabes unis	1990	124 008	38.6	16.3	19.4	1.0	65.4	40.8
	1991	124 500	41.4	16.9	20.7	1.1	67.6	47.7
	1992	128 400	45.5	17.8	23.2	1.2	69.1	56.8
United Kingdom [2] Royaume–Uni [2]	2002	1 044 145	66.3[3]	20.0	16.4	0.2[5]	26.2	29.2
	2003	1 101 144	65.5[3]	20.8	16.3	0.2[5]	25.4	28.3
	2004	1 160 339	65.1[3]	21.3	16.9	0.1[5]	24.7	28.0

Country or area Pays ou zone	Year Année	GDP in current prices (Mil. nat.cur.) PIB aux prix courant (Millions monnaie nat.)	% of Gross domestic product – en % du Produit intérieur brut					
			Household final consumption expenditure Consom. finale des ménages	Govt. final consumption expenditure Consom. finale des admin. publiques	Gross fixed capital formation Formation brute de capital fixe	Changes in inventories Variation des stocks	Exports of goods and services Exportations de biens et services	Imports of goods and services Importations de biens et services
United Rep. of Tanzania [2] Rép.–Unie de Tanzanie [2]	2001	8 284 690	83.5	6.2	16.8	0.2	15.5	23.7
	2002	9 445 482	79.4	6.3	18.9	0.2	16.1	22.3
	2003	10 692 420	82.0	6.5	18.5	0.2	17.8	26.7
United States [2] Etats–Unis [2]	2001	10 075 900	70.0[3]	14.8	19.2	−0.3	10.3	13.9
	2002	10 434 800	70.7[3]	15.3	17.9	0.1	9.6	13.7
	2003	10 951 300	70.9[3]	15.6	18.0	0.0	9.6	14.1
Uruguay Uruguay	2002	260 967	73.6[3]	12.9	10.1	1.4[33]	22.0	20.0
	2003	315 681	74.6[3]	11.4	9.4	3.2[33]	26.1	24.6
	2004	379 317	74.2[3]	10.8	11.4	1.9[33]	29.6	27.9
Uzbekistan [2] Ouzbékistan [2]	1999	2 128 660	62.1[3]	20.6	27.2	−10.1	0.1[18]	...
	2000	3 255 600	61.9[3]	18.7	24.0	−4.4	−0.2[18]	...
	2001	4 868 400	61.6[3]	18.4	25.7	−5.5	−0.3[18]	...
Venezuela (Bolivarian Rep. of) [2] Venezuela (Rép. Bolivar. du) [2]	2000	79 655 700	51.7[3]	12.4	21.0	3.2[5]	29.7	18.1
	2001	88 945 600	54.9[3]	14.2	24.0	3.5[5]	22.7	19.4
	2002	107 840 200	53.5[3]	13.0	21.9	−0.8[5]	30.4	18.1
Viet Nam [2] Viet Nam [2]	2001	481 295 000	64.9	6.3	29.2	2.0	−2.3[18]	...
	2002	535 762 000	65.1	6.2	31.1	2.1	−5.2[18]	...
	2003	605 586 000	64.9	6.9	33.0	2.1	−7.6[18]	...
Yemen [2] Yémen [2]	1998	849 321	67.8	14.7	31.5	1.0	27.6	42.6
	1999	1 132 619	68.0	13.8	23.4	1.2	36.3	42.7
	2000	1 379 812	57.8	14.1	18.2	0.9	50.5	41.5
Yugoslavia SFR Yougoslavie Rfs	1988	15 833	50.1	14.2	17.2	19.9	29.5	30.4
	1989	235 395	47.4	14.4	14.5	28.0	25.3	29.2
	1990	1 147 787	66.1	17.6	14.7	7.3	23.7	29.4
Zambia Zambie	2001	13 132 693	69.9	12.8	18.7	1.4	26.9	29.7
	2002	16 260 430	69.4	13.0	21.6	1.3	23.7	29.0
	2003	20 377 051	66.6	14.6	24.8	1.3	20.6	28.0
Zimbabwe Zimbabwe	2001	709 214	89.8[3]	9.1	7.3	−1.7	14.8	19.3
	2002	1 698 180	107.4[3]	5.0	5.5	−14.3	5.5	9.2
	2003	5 518 757	112.6[3]	2.2	3.2	−16.2	1.5	3.3

Source

United Nations Statistics Division, New York, national accounts database.

Notes

+ The national accounts data relate to the fiscal year used in each country, unless indicated otherwise. Countries whose reference periods coincide with the calendar year ending 31 December are not listed below.

Year beginning 21 March: Afghanistan, Iran (Islamic Republic).

Year beginning 1 April: Bermuda, India, Myanmar, New Zealand, Nigeria (beginning 1982).

Year beginning 1 July: Australia, Bangladesh, Cameroon, Egypt, Gambia, Pakistan, Puerto Rico, Saudi Arabia, Sierra Leone, Sudan.

Year ending 30 June: Botswana, Swaziland, Tonga.

Year ending 7 July: Ethiopia.

Year ending 15 July: Nepal.

Year ending 30 September: Haiti.

Source

Organisation des Nations Unies, Division de statistique, New York, la base de données sur les comptes nationaux.

Notes

+ Sauf indication contraire, les données sur les comptes nationaux concernent l'exercice budgétaire utilisé dans chaque pays. Les pays ou territoires dont la période de référence coïncide avec l'année civile se terminant le 31 décembre ne sont pas répertoriés ci–dessous.

Exercice commençant le 21 mars: Afghanistan, Iran (République islamique d').

Exercice commençant le 1er avril: Bermudes, Inde, Myanmar, Nigéria (à partir de 1982), Nouvelle–Zélande.

Exercice commençant le 1er juillet: Arabie saoudite, Australie, Bangladesh, Cameroun, Égypte, Gambie, Pakistan, Porto Rico, Sierra Leone, Soudan.

Exercice se terminant le 30 juin: Botswana, Swaziland, Tonga.

Exercice se terminant le 7 juillet: Éthiopie.

Exercice se terminant le 15 juillet: Népal.

Exercice se terminant le 30 septembre: Haïti.

[1] Data have not been revised.	[1] Les données n'ont pas été révisées.
[2] The concepts and definitions of the System of National Accounts 1993 (1993 SNA) have been adopted.	[2] Les concepts et définitions du Système de comptabilité nationale de 1993 (SCN de 1993) ont été adoptés.
[3] Including "Non–profit institutions serving households" (NPISHs) final consumption expenditure.	[3] Y compris la consommation finale des institutions sans but lucratif au service des ménages.
[4] Gross capital formation.	[4] Formation brute de capital.
[5] Including acquisitions less disposals of valuables.	[5] Y compris les acquisitions moins cessions d'objets de valeur.
[6] Preliminary data.	[6] Données préliminaires.
[7] Derived from available data.	[7] Calculés à partir des données disponibles.
[8] Discrepancy between components and total.	[8] Ecart entre les rubriques et le total.
[9] Exports of goods only.	[9] Exportations de biens uniquement.
[10] Imports of goods only.	[10] Importations de biens uniquement.
[11] Land improvement is not included.	[11] L'amélioration des terres n'est pas comprise.
[12] For statistical purposes, the data for China do not include those for the Hong Kong Special Administrative Region (Hong Kong SAR), Macao Special Administrative Region (Macao SAR) and Taiwan Province of China.	[12] Pour la présentation des statistiques, les données pour Chine ne comprennent pas la Région Administrative Spéciale de Hong Kong (Hong Kong RAS), la Région Administrative Spéciale de Macao (Macao RAS) et la province de Taiwan.
[13] Data in US dollars.	[13] Les données sont exprimées en dollars des États–Unis.
[14] The estimates refer to central government capital formation only.	[14] Les chiffres ne concernent que la formation de capital des administrations centrales.
[15] Includes net travel and tourism income.	[15] Comprend les recettes nettes des voyages et du tourisme.
[16] Includes net freight and insurance.	[16] Comprend les montants nets du fret et de l'assurance.
[17] Cocoa is valued at cost to the Ghana Cocoa Marketing Board. Stocks of other export commodities, including minerals, are valued at export prices.	[17] Le cacao est valorisé au prix coûtant du Ghana Cocoa Marketing Board. Les stocks des autres produits d'exportation, minéraux compris, sont valorisés au prix à l'exportation.
[18] Net exports.	[18] Exportations nettes.
[19] Data in 1980 includes only increase in iron ore stocks. Beginning 1981, it includes increase in iron ore and rubber stocks.	[19] Ne comprend que l'accroissement des stocks de minerai de fer. À partir de 1981, comprend l'accroissement de minerai de fer et de caoutchouc.
[20] Obtained as a residual.	[20] Obtenu comme valeur résiduelle.
[21] Including changes in inventories.	[21] Y compris les variations des stocks.
[22] Including education and health.	[22] Y compris l'éducation et la santé.
[23] Includes communications equipment.	[23] Y compris les matériels de communication.
[24] Includes livestock only.	[24] Ne comprend que le bétail.
[25] Semi–final data.	[25] Données semi–finales.
[26] Beginning 1999, data for Kosovo and Metohia are excluded.	[26] A compter de 1999, non compris les données de Kosovo et Metohia.
[27] Includes an upward adjustment for the estimated value of diamonds smuggled out of the country.	[27] Compris un ajustement en hausse rendant compte de la valeur estimative des diamants sortis du pays en fraude.
[28] Valued f.o.b.	[28] Valeur f.o.b.
[29] Includes the value of technical assistance from abroad.	[29] Compris la valeur de l'assistance technique étrangère.
[30] Refers to imports of goods and non–factor services.	[30] Concerne les importations de biens et de services autres que les services des facteurs.
[31] Includes household and NPISH final consumption expenditure.	[31] Y compris les dépenses de consommation finale des ménages et des institutions sans but lucratif au service des ménages (ISBLSM).
[32] GDP at market prices.	[32] PIB aux prix du marché.
[33] Refers to increase in stocks of wool and livestock in the private sector, and to stocks held by the public sector.	[33] Concerne les accroissements de stocks de laine et de bétail dans le secteur privé, et les stocks dans le secteur public.
[34] Beginning 1981, estimates relate to calendar year.	[34] A partir de 1981, les estimations se réfèrent à l'année civile.

Value added by industries at current prices
Percentage distribution

Valeur ajoutée par branche d'activité aux prix courants
Répartition en pourcentage

Country or area Pays ou zone	Year Année	Value added, gross (Mil. nat. cur.) Valeur ajoutée, brut (Mil. mon. nat.)	% of value added — % de la valeur ajoutée							
			Agriculture, hunting, forestry and fishing Agriculture, chasse, sylviculture et pêche	Mining and quarrying Activités extractives	Manufac-turing Activités de fabrication	Electricity, gas and water supply Electricité, gaz et eau	Construc-tion Construc-tion	Wholesale, retail trade, restaurants and hotels Commerce, restaurants, hôtels	Transport, storage & communi-cation Transports, entépôts, communi-cations	Other activities Autres activités
Afghanistan +	2002	180 292	49.8	0.1	15.1	0.0	4.8	10.1	9.6	10.4
Afghanistan +	2003	220 393	48.5	0.2	15.1	0.4	5.5	9.2	11.3	9.7
Albania [1]	2000	490 341	28.0	0.8	11.0[2]	...	6.4	21.0	10.2	22.4
Albanie [1]	2001	546 834	26.2	0.8	10.0[2]	...	8.3	19.3	12.0	23.4
	2002	581 668	25.2	0.7	9.5[2]	...	7.6	21.1	11.0	25.0
Algeria	2001	4 075 738	10.1	36.5	6.3	1.3	7.9	12.9	8.3	16.8
Algérie	2002	4 284 371	9.7	35.5	6.2	1.3	8.6	13.2	8.5	16.9
	2003	4 991 489	10.2	38.5	5.6	1.2	8.0	12.3	8.3	15.9
Andorra	2001	1 325	0.8	...	4.7	1.6	10.8	37.7	2.8	41.6
Andorre	2002	1 401	0.7	...	5.0	1.5	10.7	38.1	2.9	41.2
	2003	1 438	0.6	...	5.6	1.4	11.7	41.1	4.0	35.6
Angola	1988	236 682	16.0	27.1	8.3	0.2	4.1	11.7[3]	3.5	29.1[3]
Angola	1989	276 075	19.3	29.7	6.2	0.2	3.3	11.4[3]	3.0	27.1[3]
	1990	305 831	18.0	32.9	5.0	0.1	2.9	10.7[3]	3.2	27.0[3]
Anguilla	2001	273[4]	2.3	0.8	1.2	3.9	11.5	33.5	13.1	33.7
Anguilla	2002	267[4]	2.7	0.8	1.3	5.5	10.8	31.3	14.2	33.4
	2003	282[4]	2.6	1.0	1.4	4.9	10.5	31.9	13.5	34.2
Antigua and Barbuda	1986	567[4]	4.3	1.7	3.8	3.5	8.9	23.6	15.6	38.5
Antigua–et–Barbuda	1987	649[4]	4.5	2.2	3.5	3.5	11.3	24.1	15.6	35.3
	1988	776[4]	4.1	2.2	3.1	4.0	12.7	23.7	14.3	35.9
Argentina [1]	2002	298 642[4,5]	10.7	6.3	21.3	1.8	2.6	13.5	7.7	36.1
Argentine [1]	2003	353 374[4,5]	11.0	5.8	23.9	1.7	3.3	14.0	8.5	31.8
	2004	414 039[4,5]	10.4	5.7	24.1	1.7	4.2	14.1	9.0	30.9
Armenia [1]	2001	1 079 085	27.9	...	22.7[2,6]	...	10.6	11.1	7.6	20.1
Arménie [1]	2002	1 245 535	25.7	...	21.4[2,6]	...	13.8	11.6	6.7	20.9
	2003	1 495 269	23.4	...	21.7[2,6]	...	17.1	11.9	6.4	19.6
Aruba [1]	2000	3 231	0.4[6]	...	3.8[7]	6.2[7]	6.0	24.4	9.0	50.3
Aruba [1]	2001	3 308	0.4[6]	...	3.3[7]	7.0[7]	5.4	23.6	9.3	51.0
	2002	3 333	0.4[6]	...	3.3[7]	6.9[7]	4.7	22.4	9.2	53.1
Australia + [1]	2001	652 346[8]	4.2	5.2	11.8	2.5[9]	6.1	13.3	8.3	48.7
Australie + [1]	2002	691 010[8]	3.1	5.0	11.9	2.5[9]	6.6	13.6	8.4	49.0
	2003	741 500[8]	3.4	4.4	11.9	2.5[9]	6.8	13.6	8.6	48.8
Austria [1]	2001	193 083	2.1	0.4	20.3	2.2	7.5	17.6	7.2	42.6
Autriche [1]	2002	197 383	2.0	0.5	20.1	2.4	7.4	17.6	7.3	42.6
	2003	202 285	2.0	0.5	19.9	2.5	7.7	17.6	7.6	42.4
Azerbaijan [1]	2002	28 057 900	15.1	31.2	8.0	1.2	9.4	8.5	10.6	15.9
Azerbaïdjan [1]	2003	33 192 400	13.4	29.6	9.3	1.2	12.1	8.1	10.8	15.5
	2004	39 014 200	12.3	30.3	9.1	1.1	14.5	8.6	10.2	13.9
Bahamas [1]	2001	5 214	2.1	0.8	4.4	3.0	7.3	22.7	8.8	50.7
Bahamas [1]	2002	5 467	2.7	1.0	4.5	3.1	7.3	22.7	9.4	49.3
	2003	5 604	2.7	1.0	4.1	3.6	7.0	22.7	9.0	49.8
Bahrain	2001	3 250[8]	0.7	22.8	11.0	1.3	3.7	9.8	6.9	43.9
Bahreïn	2002	3 459[8]	0.6	22.7	10.8	1.3	3.9	10.3	7.2	43.3
	2003	3 893[8]	0.6	23.4	10.4	1.3	3.6	9.5	6.8	44.6
Bangladesh + [1]	2001	2 635 253	22.7	1.1	15.9	1.4	8.0	14.1	9.7	27.1
Bangladesh + [1]	2002	2 898 729	21.8	1.1	15.8	1.4	7.9	14.2	10.7	27.1
	2003	3 209 680	20.5	1.1	16.0	1.4	8.1	14.4	11.2	27.3

			% of value added — % de la valeur ajoutée							
Country or area Pays ou zone	Year Année	Value added, gross (Mil. nat. cur.) Valeur ajoutée, brut (Mil. mon. nat.)	Agriculture, hunting, forestry and fishing Agriculture, chasse, sylviculture et pêche	Mining and quarrying Activités extractives	Manufac-turing Activités de fabrication	Electricity, gas and water supply Electricité, gaz et eau	Construc-tion Construc-tion	Wholesale, retail trade, restaurants and hotels Commerce, restaurants, hôtels	Transport, storage & communi-cation Transports, entépôts, communi-cations	Other activities Autres activités
Barbados Barbade	1999	4 139[4]	4.9	0.7	6.3	3.1	5.8	29.1	10.4	39.7
	2000	4 291[4]	4.4	0.7	6.3	3.3	5.8	29.0	10.3	40.1
	2001	4 223[4]	4.7	0.7	6.1	3.5	5.8	26.4	11.1	41.8
Belarus [1] Bélarus [1]	2002	22 860 668	11.6	...	29.1[2,6]	...	6.7	12.4	11.9	28.4
	2003	31 442 138	10.0	...	30.3[2,6]	...	7.1	12.5	11.2	28.8
	2004	43 037 915	10.9	...	30.8[2,6]	...	7.4	11.8	11.2	27.9
Belgium [1] Belgique [1]	2001	235 464	1.4	0.1	18.5	2.6	5.0	13.4	6.9	52.2
	2002	242 077	1.2	0.1	18.2	2.5	4.8	13.8	6.8	52.5
	2003	249 943	1.3	0.1	17.4	2.3	4.8	13.8	6.9	53.3
Belize [1] Belize [1]	1998	1 051[5,10]	19.1	0.6	13.2	3.4	5.7	18.9	10.4	37.9
	1999	1 154[5,10]	19.7	0.6	13.0	3.4	6.5	20.8	11.0	36.1
	2000	1 311[5,10]	17.2	0.7	13.1	3.3	7.1	21.6	9.9	29.8
Benin Bénin	2002	1 767 100	37.4	0.2	9.4	1.2	4.2	18.4	7.8	21.5
	2003	1 865 600	35.6	0.3	9.2	1.4	4.4	18.8	8.6	21.8
	2004	1 912 500	35.5	0.3	8.8	1.4	4.5	18.8	8.6	22.5
Bermuda +[1] Bermudes +[1]	2000	3 368[11]	0.7	0.2	2.6	2.3	6.1	16.6	7.3	64.2
	2001	3 584[11]	0.7	0.1	2.2	2.3	6.1	16.0	7.1	65.4
	2002	3 752[11]	0.7	0.2	2.2	2.2	6.2	15.7	7.2	65.6
Bhutan Bhoutan	1998	16 537[4]	36.6	1.6	9.8	11.7	10.2	7.0	8.3	14.8
	1999	18 957[4]	35.0	1.7	9.3	12.2	11.1	6.8	8.6	15.2
	2000	21 654[4]	35.9	1.6	8.0	11.6	12.5	6.8	8.6	15.0
Bolivia Bolivie	2001	48 407	14.5	6.6	14.5	3.4	3.2	11.3	12.9	33.7
	2002	50 805	14.0	6.9	14.4	3.4	3.6	11.3	13.1	33.3
	2003	54 742	14.3	8.4	14.3	3.3	2.9	11.0[5]	13.0	32.9
Bosnia and Herzegovina [1] Bosnie–Herzégovine [1]	2001	8 456	12.9	2.5	12.6	7.7	5.4	13.5	11.1	34.3
	2002	9 258	12.1	2.4	12.4	6.4	5.1	15.2	11.2	35.3
	2003	9 809	10.6	2.5	12.6	7.3	5.6	15.6	11.7	34.2
Botswana +[1] Botswana +[1]	2001	27 564	2.7	36.6	4.9	2.5	5.7	11.6	3.8	32.2
	2002	30 881	2.6	36.4	4.5	2.4	5.6	11.8	3.7	32.9
	2003	34 733	2.5	36.4	4.5	2.7	5.7	12.0	3.7	32.6
Brazil [1] Brésil [1]	2001	1 063 770[10]	8.4	2.9	22.6	3.6	8.6	7.5[3]	5.4	46.2[3]
	2002	1 199 145[10]	8.7	3.4	23.3	3.6	8.0	7.7[3]	5.3	46.2[3]
	2003	1 395 604[10]	9.9	3.9	24.2	3.4	7.2	7.7	5.6	43.4
British Virgin Islands [1] Iles Vierges britanniques [1]	1997	523	1.6[12]	0.1	4.8	2.0	6.1	30.2	11.1	44.1
	1998	606	1.5[12]	0.1	4.6	1.8	7.3	29.2	11.2	44.4
	1999	674	1.4[12]	0.1	4.0	1.7	7.3	28.0	11.7	46.0
Brunei Darussalam Brunéi Darussalam	1996	7 886	2.5	34.7[13]	...	1.0	5.8	11.9	4.8	39.3
	1997	8 268	2.6	33.6[13]	...	1.0	6.2	12.1	4.9	39.6
	1998	8 331	2.8	31.6[13]	...	1.1	6.5	12.6	5.1	40.4
Bulgaria [1] Bulgarie [1]	2001	26 356	13.4	1.5	17.5	6.0	4.6	9.4	12.8	34.8
	2002	28 526	12.1	1.4	17.4	5.7	4.5	9.4	13.8	35.6
	2003	30 089	11.4	1.5	18.3	5.7	4.5	9.2	14.1	35.4
Burkina Faso Burkina Faso	1991	780 492	33.8	0.9	14.2	0.9	5.7	1.7	4.1	1.6
	1992	782 551	32.7	0.9	15.3	1.1	5.7	1.6	4.2	1.6
	1993	808 487	33.9	0.8	14.7	1.3	5.6	1.7	4.4	1.5
Burundi Burundi	1988	149 067	48.9	1.0[2]	16.5	...	2.9	12.9	2.6	15.2
	1989	175 627	47.0	1.2[2]	18.5	...	3.3	10.8	3.3	16.0
	1990	192 050	52.4	0.8[2]	16.8	...	3.4	4.9	3.1	18.5
Cambodia [1] Cambodge [1]	1999	11 879 240	45.3	0.1	12.5	0.4	5.1	15.1	6.6	14.9
	2000	12 216 080	42.5[5]	0.3	18.2	0.4	6.0	11.7	7.2	8.8
	2001	12 573 010	41.1[5]	0.3	20.3	0.5	6.9	11.5	7.6	8.3

Country or area / Pays ou zone	Year / Année	Value added, gross (Mil. nat. cur.) / Valeur ajoutée, brut (Mil. mon. nat.)	Agriculture, hunting, forestry and fishing / Agriculture, chasse, sylviculture et pêche	Mining and quarrying / Activités extractives	Manufac-turing / Activités de fabrication	Electricity, gas and water supply / Electricité, gaz et eau	Construc-tion / Construc-tion	Wholesale, retail trade, restaurants and hotels / Commerce, restaurants, hôtels	Transport, storage & communi-cation / Transports, entrepôts, communi-cations	Other activities / Autres activités
Cameroon [+1] / Cameroun [+1]	1996	4 467 110	22.0	5.5	21.3	0.9	3.2	21.0	5.2	20.9
	1997	5 013 530	23.6	5.6	21.3	0.8	2.1	19.9	5.8	20.8
	1998	5 362 130	23.6	5.6	21.3	0.8	2.1	19.9	5.8	20.8
Canada [1] / Canada [1]	1999	909 695	2.5	3.8	19.2	3.1	5.1	13.7	7.3	45.3
	2000	999 926	2.3	6.1	19.2	2.9	5.0	13.3	7.0	44.2
	2001	1 031 199	2.2	5.7	17.8	3.0	5.3	13.6	7.1	45.2
Cape Verde / Cap–Vert	1998	49 384	11.4	1.0	7.0	2.0	8.6	21.0	20.5	28.4
	1999	58 419	14.4	1.5	6.1	1.6	8.2	21.5	20.1	26.6
	2000	60 082	13.9	1.0	5.6	1.6	8.2	22.3	21.3	26.0
Cayman Islands / Iles Caïmanes	1989	473	0.4	0.6	1.9	3.2	11.0	24.5	11.0	47.6
	1990	580	0.3	0.3	1.6	3.1	9.7	24.5	10.9	49.8
	1991	605	0.3	0.3	1.5	3.1	9.1	22.8	10.7	52.1
Central African Rep. / Rép. centrafricaine	1983	243 350	40.8	2.5	7.8 [14]	0.5	2.1	21.2 [3]	4.2	20.8 [3]
	1984	268 725	40.7	2.8	8.1 [14]	0.9	2.7	21.7 [3]	4.3	18.8 [3]
	1985	308 549	42.4	2.5	7.5 [14]	0.8	2.6	22.0 [3]	4.2	17.9 [3]
Chad / Tchad	1999	875 000 [4]	38.6	...	12.9	0.7 [15]	1.7	22.4	3.3	17.7
	2000	889 000 [4]	38.9	...	11.8	0.7 [15]	1.7	22.3	3.4	18.8
	2001	1 045 000 [4]	37.1	...	13.7	0.7 [15]	1.6	23.0	3.4	17.9
Chile [1] / Chili [1]	2002	43 628 000 [11]	5.5	7.3	19.5	3.3	7.9	10.0	7.5	39.0
	2003	48 062 000 [11]	5.7	8.9	18.9	3.2	8.3	9.8	7.5	37.6
	2004	54 363 000 [11]	5.8	14.1	18.1	3.0	8.0	8.9	7.1	35.0
China [1,16] / Chine [1,16]	2002	10 517 230	15.3	43.7 [2,13]	...	...	6.7	8.1	6.1	20.1
	2003	11 739 020	14.4	45.2 [2,13]	...	...	7.0	7.9	5.7	...
	2004	13 687 590	15.2	45.9 [2,13]	...	...	7.0	7.4	3.4	...
China, Hong Kong SAR [1] / Chine, Hong Kong RAS [1]	2001	1 310 936 [4]	0.1 [17]	0.0	4.8	3.1	4.5	24.8	9.5	53.3
	2002	1 297 806 [4]	0.1 [17]	0.0	4.2	3.2	4.1	25.0	9.9	53.5
	2003	1 262 716 [4]	0.1 [17]	0.0	3.8	3.2	3.7	25.4	9.8	54.1
China, Macao SAR [1] / Chine, Macao RAS [1]	2000	44 852	...	0.0	9.2	2.7	2.4	10.2	6.9	68.6
	2001	43 876	...	0.0	7.7	2.9	1.9	11.1	6.3	70.0
	2002	46 725	...	0.0	6.9	2.6	2.4	11.6	6.4	70.0
Colombia [1] / Colombie [1]	2000	168 124 471	13.5	6.4	15.2	3.7	3.8	11.0	7.4	38.9
	2001	180 184 781	13.0	5.2	15.1	4.5	3.7	11.1	8.1	39.3
	2002	195 547 036	12.8	5.2	15.1	4.5	4.3	11.1	8.4	38.6
Comoros / Comores	1989	64 731	40.0	...	3.9	0.8	3.4	25.1	3.9	22.8
	1990	67 992	40.4	...	4.1	0.9	3.1	25.1	4.1	22.3
	1991	71 113	40.8	...	4.2	0.9	2.7	25.1	4.2	22.1
Congo / Congo	1987	678 106	12.2	22.9	8.8	1.6	3.2	15.1	10.5	25.8
	1988	643 830	14.2	17.1	8.8	2.0	2.7	16.7	11.3	27.2
	1989	757 088	13.3	28.6	7.2	1.9	1.8	14.7	9.3	23.3
Cook Islands / Iles Cook	2000	178	13.5	...	3.4	2.2	2.8	35.4	14.0	28.7
	2001	203	11.8	...	3.4	1.5	3.4	38.4	14.8	26.6
	2002	219	11.9	...	3.2	1.4	3.7	39.7	14.6	25.6
Costa Rica [1] / Costa Rica [1]	2002	5 716 419	8.2	0.2	20.6	2.6	4.5	18.4	8.6	36.9
	2003	6 596 151	8.4	0.1	20.4	2.6	4.4	18.3	9.0	36.8
	2004	7 627 006	8.1	0.1	20.0	2.7	4.5	18.6	9.4	36.5
Côte d'Ivoire / Côte d'Ivoire	1998	6 984 000	25.6	0.6	21.9	1.6	2.3	20.4	6.0	21.3
	1999	7 449 000	23.2	0.3	22.2	2.0	3.5	21.9	5.7	21.1
	2000	7 323 000	24.8	0.3	22.4	1.6	2.9	19.0	5.5	23.2
Croatia [1] / Croatie [1]	2002	152 038	8.6	0.8	19.5	2.8	5.6	15.5	10.4	36.8
	2003	165 630	8.0	...	22.4 [2,6]	...	6.5	15.7	10.7	36.7
	2004	178 365	7.9	...	22.2 [2,6]	...	6.6	15.5	10.9	36.9

Country or area Pays ou zone	Year Année	Value added, gross (Mil. nat. cur.) Valeur ajoutée, brut (Mil. mon. nat.)	% of value added — % de la valeur ajoutée							
			Agriculture, hunting, forestry and fishing Agriculture, chasse, sylviculture et pêche	Mining and quarrying Activités extractives	Manufac-turing Activités de fabrication	Electricity, gas and water supply Electricité, gaz et eau	Construc-tion Construc-tion	Wholesale, retail trade, restaurants and hotels Commerce, restaurants, hôtels	Transport, storage & communi-cation Transports, entépôts, communi-cations	Other activities Autres activités
Cuba [1] Cuba [1]	2001	29 154	6.9	1.5	17.5	2.2	5.9	27.6	10.1	28.3
	2002	30 361	6.6	1.7	17.0	1.9	5.7	28.4	10.1	28.7
	2003	31 967	6.5	1.8	16.0	1.9	5.6	29.1	9.9	29.3
Cyprus [1] Chypre [1]	2001	5 872	3.8	0.3	9.9	2.1	7.0	22.4	9.2	45.3
	2002	6 090	3.9	0.3	9.6	2.1	7.4	21.4	8.7	46.6
	2003	6 421	4.1	0.3	9.0	2.2	7.7	20.1	8.5	48.0
Czech Republic [1] République tchèque [1]	2001	2 133 313	3.7	1.4	24.9	4.0	6.4	15.2	10.5	33.9
	2002	2 231 731	3.1	1.4	25.5	4.3	6.6	14.4	11.1	33.6
	2003	2 356 059	2.8	1.3	26.0	4.0	6.6	13.9	10.8	34.5
Denmark [1] Danemark [1]	2001	1 174 034	2.9	2.6	15.7	2.1	5.0	13.6	8.0	50.3
	2002	1 195 543	2.4	2.7	15.8	2.3	5.0	13.6	7.8	51.3
	2003	1 235 823	2.3	2.6	15.4	2.2	5.0	13.6	7.9	51.5
Djibouti Djibouti	1996	76 435	3.5 [12]	0.2	2.8	6.8 [15]	5.7	15.9	21.7	43.4
	1997	75 964	3.6 [12]	0.2	2.8	6.6 [15]	6.0	16.1	23.1	41.6
	1998	78 263	3.6 [12]	0.2	2.7	5.3 [15]	6.4	16.4	26.0	39.4
Dominica Dominique	2000	676 [4]	16.6	0.7	8.1	5.1	7.4	13.3	15.7	31.5
	2001	657 [4]	15.7	0.7	7.2	5.5	7.5	13.5	14.8	33.6
	2002	627 [4]	16.9	0.6	7.2	4.9	6.5	13.6	12.8 [5]	35.4
Dominican Republic [1] Rép. dominicaine [1]	1994	165 808	10.8	1.1	20.2	1.4	7.7	16.4	9.8	32.6
	1995	193 436	10.1	1.3	19.6	1.7	7.7	17.3	9.0	33.3
	1996	228 022	8.9	1.0	19.3	1.8	7.3	20.4	8.8	32.5
Ecuador [1] Equateur [1]	2002	22 414 [11]	9.8	12.7 [18]	7.6	1.9	8.5	17.2	16.8	25.4
	2003	25 258 [11]	8.3	14.1 [18]	6.9	1.8	8.2	16.8	18.1	25.9
	2004	27 723 [11]	7.9	15.1 [18]	6.7	1.7	8.0	16.5	18.1	25.9
Egypt + [1] Egypte + [1]	2001	401 870	0.2	8.7	16.7	1.7	1.8	11.4	4.5	20.7
	2002	428 151	0.2	9.5	16.6	1.8	1.2	12.5	4.5	19.1
	2003	475 035	0.1	10.1	16.1	2.0	1.5	12.2	5.3	18.6
El Salvador El Salvador	2001	117 569	9.7	0.4	23.7	1.8	4.8	19.8	8.9	30.8
	2002	121 847	8.7	0.5	23.8	1.8	4.9	19.7	9.2	31.3
	2003	126 581	8.7	0.5	23.7	1.8	5.0	19.5	9.3	31.4
Equatorial Guinea Guinée équatoriale	1989	40 948	56.1	...	1.3	3.1	3.7	8.8	2.0	25.0
	1990	42 765	53.6	...	1.3	3.4	3.8	7.6	2.2	28.0
	1991	43 932	53.1	...	1.4	3.1	3.0	7.6	1.9	30.0
Estonia [1] Estonie [1]	2001	94 257	5.2	0.9	17.1	2.9	5.7	14.4	15.2	38.4
	2002	105 143	4.9	0.9	17.5	2.9	6.3	14.5	14.6	38.4
	2003	112 965	4.4	1.0	17.7	2.8	6.5	14.0	15.0	38.5
Ethiopia incl. Eritrea Ethiopie y comp. Erythrée	1990	11 436 [4]	41.1	0.2	11.1	1.5	3.6	9.6 [3]	7.2	25.7 [3]
	1991	12 295 [4]	41.0	0.3	10.3	1.5	3.2	9.4 [3]	7.1	27.3 [3]
	1992	12 544 [4]	50.3	0.3	9.1	1.3	2.8	10.2 [3]	5.4	20.6 [3]
Fiji Fidji	2000	3 152	17.2	0.9	13.5	2.8	4.1	15.1	14.8	31.5
	2001	3 310	14.8	0.9	15.0	2.9	4.2	15.5	15.1	31.6
	2002	3 555	15.4	0.9	13.9	2.8	4.5	16.3	14.6	31.6
Finland [1] Finlande [1]	2001	121 184	3.5	0.3	24.4	1.8	5.6	11.5	10.6	42.3
	2002	124 782	3.5	0.3	23.2	2.1	5.3	11.8	10.7	43.1
	2003	126 750	3.4	0.3	22.6	2.3	5.3	11.9	10.8	43.6
France [1] France [1]	2002	1 392 586	2.7	0.2	14.7	1.7	5.3	13.1	6.4	55.9
	2003	1 425 634	2.6	0.2	14.0	1.8	5.6	13.0	6.3	56.6
	2004	1 478 192	2.5	0.2	13.9	1.7	5.9	12.7	6.4	56.7
French Guiana Guyane française	1990	6 454	10.1	7.6	...	0.7	12.8	13.5	7.7	47.5
	1991	7 385	7.4	7.6	...	0.5	12.1	13.1	12.3	47.0
	1992	8 052	7.2	9.0	...	0.6	10.8	11.9	11.4	49.1

			% of value added —% de la valeur ajoutée							
Country or area Pays ou zone	Year Année	Value added, gross (Mil. nat. cur.) Valeur ajoutée, brut (Mil. mon. nat.)	Agriculture, hunting, forestry and fishing Agriculture, chasse, sylviculture et pêche	Mining and quarrying Activités extractives	Manufac- turing Activités de fabrication	Electricity, gas and water supply Electricité, gaz et eau	Construc- tion Construc- tion	Wholesale, retail trade, restaurants and hotels Commerce, restaurants, hôtels	Transport, storage & communi- cation Transports, entrepôts, communi- cations	Other activities Autres activités
French Polynesia Polynésie française	1991	305 211	4.1	...	7.5[19]	1.8[19]	5.7	...	...	29.3
	1992	314 265	3.8	...	7.5[19]	2.1[19]	5.9	...	...	29.5
	1993	329 266	3.9	...	6.7[19]	2.1[19]	5.7	...	...	29.0
Gabon Gabon	1987	986 000	10.9	28.4	7.1[20]	2.7	7.2	9.2	8.1	26.5
	1988	965 700	11.2	22.6	7.3[20]	3.0	5.2	14.4	9.1	27.3
	1989	1 128 400	10.4	32.3	5.7[20]	2.5	5.5	12.4	8.2	23.1
Gambia + Gambie +	1991	2 962	22.3	0.0	5.5	0.9	4.4	39.1	10.9	17.0
	1992	3 100	18.4	0.0	5.7	1.0	4.7	41.7	11.2	17.4
	1993	3 296	20.2	0.0	5.1	1.0	4.5	38.3	12.5	18.4
Georgia [1] Géorgie [1]	2002	7 037	20.4	0.7	13.6	4.4	5.4	16.7	15.0	23.8
	2003	8 116	20.3	0.9	13.8	4.0	6.7	17.0	14.6	22.6
	2004	9 040	17.6	0.9	14.1	3.5	7.0	17.5	15.1	24.4
Germany [1] Allemagne [1]	2001	1 924 640	1.2	0.2	22.4	1.8	4.8	12.0	6.1	51.4
	2002	1 960 250	1.1	0.3	22.3	1.8	4.5	11.9	6.1	52.0
	2003	1 978 770	1.1	0.3	22.2	2.0	4.2	11.8	6.2	52.2
Ghana Ghana	1994	4 686 000	42.0	6.3	10.1	3.0	8.3	6.4	4.8	18.2
	1995	7 040 200	42.7	5.3	10.3	2.9	8.3	6.5	4.3	18.8
	1996	10 067 000	43.9	5.3	9.7	3.0	8.5	6.5	4.2	17.9
Greece [1] Grèce [1]	2001	119 231	7.0	0.6	11.9	1.8	8.4	20.6	8.4	41.2
	2002	127 089	7.1	0.7	11.6	1.8	8.2	20.3	8.6	42.2
	2003	138 822	6.7	0.6	11.5	1.8	8.7	21.0	8.5	41.5
Grenada Grenade	1989	393[5]	18.7	0.4	5.3	2.9	10.3	18.8	13.9	34.4
	1990	440	16.2	0.4	5.1	3.0	10.1	18.7	13.7	32.8
	1991	463	14.9	0.4	5.3	3.1	10.4	19.5	14.3	32.1
Guadeloupe Guadeloupe	1990	15 036	6.7	5.4[13]	...	1.0	7.4	18.3	5.9	55.2
	1991	16 278	7.3	6.1[13]	...	1.4	7.0	16.5	6.0	55.5
	1992	17 968	6.7	6.9[13]	...	1.7	6.5	16.2	7.9	54.1
Guinea–Bissau Guinée–Bissau	1989	358 875	44.6	7.9[2,13]	...	...	9.7	25.7	3.6	8.5
	1990	510 094	44.6	8.2[2,13]	...	...	10.0	25.7	3.7	7.8
	1991	854 985	44.7	8.5[2,13]	...	...	8.4	25.8	3.9	8.7
Guyana Guyana	1999	105 095[4]	41.2[12]	15.4	3.5[2]	...	4.5[21]	4.1[3]	6.8	24.5[3]
	2000	108 087[4]	36.1[12]	15.9	3.2[2]	...	4.9[21]	4.4[3]	7.8	27.7[3]
	2001	112 218[4]	35.4[12]	15.7	3.2[2]	...	5.0[21]	4.4[3]	8.6	27.8[3]
Honduras Honduras	1998	60 068[4]	19.1	1.8	18.6	5.1	5.1	12.3	5.0	33.0
	1999	65 881[4]	15.9	2.0	19.6	4.9	5.9	12.7	5.2	33.8
	2000	75 924[4]	15.0	2.0	19.8	4.8	5.7	12.8	5.2	34.7
Hungary [1] Hongrie [1]	2001	13 077 454	4.3	0.2	22.7	3.1	5.1	13.2	8.4	42.9
	2002	14 807 628	3.7	0.2	21.7	3.0	5.3	13.2	8.2	44.7
	2003	16 159 300	3.3	0.2	22.3	3.0	4.9	12.8	8.0	45.5
Iceland [1] Islande [1]	2000	583 997	8.8	0.1	13.2	3.3	8.4	14.1	7.9	44.1
	2001	674 500	9.2	0.1	14.1	3.8	8.2	12.4	7.7	44.6
	2002	697 549	9.3	0.1	12.3	3.8	7.5	12.5	8.2	46.3
India + Inde +	2001	20 814 740[4]	24.5	2.3	15.4	2.1	6.0	14.5	7.6	27.6
	2002	22 548 880[4]	22.5	2.8	15.6	2.2	6.2	14.8	7.7	28.3
	2003	25 197 850[4]	22.8	2.5	15.6	2.1	6.2	14.9	8.0	27.8
Indonesia Indonésie	2000	1 264 919 000[11]	17.2	13.9	24.9	1.3	6.1	15.7[3]	4.9	16.0[3]
	2001	1 449 398 000[11]	17.0	13.2	25.0	1.5	5.9	16.2[3]	5.2	16.1[3]
	2002	1 610 012 000[11]	17.5	11.9	25.0	1.8	5.7	16.1[3]	6.0	15.9[3]
Iran (Islamic Rep. of) +[1] Iran (Rép. islamique d') +[1]	2001	670 228 913	12.7	15.5[22]	13.5	1.6	4.2	13.4	8.4[5]	30.7
	2002	922 846 158	11.5	23.1[22]	11.5	1.6	4.5	11.9	7.1[5]	28.8
	2003	1 108 299 001	11.2	23.0[22]	11.1	1.6	4.0	11.8	7.5[5]	29.7

Value added by industries at current prices — Percentage distribution (*continued*)

Valeur ajoutée par branche d'activité aux prix courants — Répartition en pourcentage (*suite*)

Country or area / Pays ou zone	Year / Année	Value added, gross (Mil. nat. cur.) / Valeur ajoutée, brut (Mil. mon. nat.)	% of value added — % de la valeur ajoutée							
			Agriculture, hunting, forestry and fishing / Agriculture, chasse, sylviculture et pêche	Mining and quarrying / Activités extractives	Manufacturing / Activités de fabrication	Electricity, gas and water supply / Electricité, gaz et eau	Construction / Construction	Wholesale, retail trade, restaurants and hotels / Commerce, restaurants, hôtels	Transport, storage & communication / Transports, entrepôts, communications	Other activities / Autres activités
Iraq / Iraq	2001	41 494 367	6.9	74.3	1.5	0.2	1.2	6.5	6.3	3.2
	2002	41 242 664	8.5	70.4	1.5	0.2	1.6	6.4	7.9	3.5
	2003	29 894 476	8.3	68.1	1.0	0.2	0.7	6.5	7.6	7.4
Ireland [1] / Irlande [1]	2001	104 625 [8]	3.1	0.6	31.7	1.3	7.8	12.6	5.5	37.4
	2002	116 044 [8]	2.7	0.5	31.8	1.2	8.1	12.5	5.5	37.7
	2003	120 009 [8]	2.7	0.6	31.2	1.2	8.2	12.0	5.6	38.5
Israel [1] / Israël [1]	2001	450 194	1.8	...	15.5 [6]	1.8	5.0	9.4	7.4	57.2
	2002	466 601	1.8	...	15.9 [6]	2.0	4.9	9.2	7.1	58.5
	2003	467 739	1.7	...	15.6 [6]	2.2	4.9	9.3	7.6	56.8
Italy [1] / Italie [1]	2002	1 178 473	2.6	0.4	19.5	2.2	5.0	16.4	7.2	46.7
	2003	1 218 520	2.5	0.4	18.9	2.3	5.0	16.3	7.2	47.4
	2004	1 263 433	2.5	0.4	18.8	2.2	5.2	16.0	7.2	47.7
Jamaica / Jamaïque	2001	364 838	6.3	4.1	13.2	3.4	9.6	24.6 [23]	11.9	26.9
	2002	396 349	5.7	4.0	12.9	3.4	9.7	24.6 [23]	12.9	26.9
	2003	460 464	5.3	4.4	12.8	3.7	9.5	24.0 [23]	12.3	28.0
Japan [1] / Japon [1]	2001	524 599 500	1.3	0.1	20.1	2.8	6.9	13.2 [3]	6.2	49.4 [3]
	2002	518 542 200	1.3	0.1	19.6	2.7	6.6	13.0 [3]	6.1	50.4 [3]
	2003	519 381 900	1.2	0.1	20.0	2.6	6.5	12.7 [3]	6.1	50.7 [3]
Jordan / Jordanie	2000	5 255	2.3	3.3	14.6	2.6	3.9	11.8	15.6	46.0
	2001	5 568	2.2	3.2	14.2	2.5	4.1	11.9	16.3	45.5
	2002	5 954	2.3	3.2	14.9	2.6	4.2	11.3	15.7	45.8
Kazakhstan [1] / Kazakhstan [1]	2002	3 560 198	8.5	12.9	15.4	3.0	6.7	13.6	12.3	27.6
	2003	4 370 285	8.3	12.8	15.0	2.9	6.3	13.2	13.1	28.4
	2004	5 298 500	8.3	...	32.6 [2,6]	...	6.2	11.9	12.8	28.3
Kenya / Kenya	2001	39 792 [4]	18.0	0.2	12.2	1.1	4.2	24.3	7.3	32.7
	2002	43 839 [4]	16.4	0.2	12.6	1.3	4.3	25.6	8.3	31.3
	2003	50 147 [4]	15.2	0.2	13.1	1.3	4.4	25.0	8.4	32.5
Korea, Republic of [1] / Corée, République de [1]	2002	602 091 908 [11]	4.1	0.3	26.9	2.6	8.6	10.8	7.5	39.2
	2003	639 761 892 [11]	3.8	0.3	26.4	2.7	9.6	10.3	7.5	39.4
	2004	691 983 257 [11]	3.7	0.3	28.7	2.4	9.3	9.9	7.3	38.4
Kuwait / Koweït	1999	9 247 [11]	0.4	36.0	11.0	−0.5	2.6	7.5	5.3	37.8
	2000	11 399 [11]	0.4	48.6	7.0	−0.9	2.1	5.9	4.4	42.2
	2001	10 467 [11]	0.4	43.8	6.4	−1.0	2.3	6.6	4.9	36.6
Kyrgyzstan [1] / Kirghizistan [1]	2001	69 044	37.0	0.5	18.9	5.3	4.0	13.9	4.5	15.9
	2002	69 452	37.3	0.5	14.2	4.7	3.7	16.7	5.5	17.3
	2003	76 846	36.7	0.5	14.5	3.9	3.2	18.2	5.9	17.2
Lao People's Dem. Rep. / Rép. dém. pop. lao	1999	10 253 626	53.7	0.5	17.0	2.4	2.7	11.8	5.8	6.1
	2000	13 565 564	52.5	0.5	17.0	3.1	2.3	11.7	5.9	7.0
	2001	15 563 971	51.2	0.5	17.9	2.9	2.4	11.8	6.0	7.3
Latvia [1] / Lettonie [1]	2001	4 621	4.5	0.2	13.7	3.4	5.6	18.3	15.4	38.9
	2002	5 119	4.6	0.2	13.6	3.2	5.5	18.7	15.2	38.9
	2003	5 640	4.3	0.2	13.9	3.0	5.6	19.3	15.5	38.1
Lebanon / Liban	1994	14 992 000 [10,24]	12.1	...	17.7 [2,6]	...	9.5	28.8	2.8	29.5
	1995	17 779 000 [10,24]	12.6	...	17.5 [2,6]	...	9.4	30.4	2.9	28.4
Lesotho [1] / Lesotho [1]	1999	5 182 [11]	16.9	0.1	15.9	6.2	17.9	9.5	3.5	29.8
	2000	5 637 [11]	17.8	0.1	16.1	5.6	17.5	10.1	3.4	29.3
	2001	6 078 [11]	18.0	0.1	16.8	5.7	17.3	10.3	3.5	28.3
Liberia / Libéria	1987	1 009	37.8	10.4	7.2	1.9	3.2	6.0	7.5	26.0
	1988	1 080	38.2	10.7	7.4	1.7	2.7	5.9	7.3	26.1
	1989	1 119	36.7	10.9	7.3	1.7	2.4	5.7	7.1	28.3

Country or area / Pays ou zone	Year / Année	Value added, gross (Mil. nat. cur.) / Valeur ajoutée, brut (Mil. mon. nat.)	Agriculture, hunting, forestry and fishing / Agriculture, chasse, sylviculture et pêche	Mining and quarrying / Activités extractives	Manufacturing / Activités de fabrication	Electricity, gas and water supply / Electricité, gaz et eau	Construction / Construction	Wholesale, retail trade, restaurants and hotels / Commerce, restaurants, hôtels	Transport, storage & communication / Transports, entrepôts, communications	Other activities / Autres activités
Libyan Arab Jamah. Jamah. arabe libyenne	1983	8 482[4]	3.0	48.8[25]	3.2	0.9	10.4	6.1	4.6	23.0
	1984	7 681[4]	3.4	40.9[25]	3.9	1.2	11.1	7.9	5.3	26.4
	1985	8 050[4]	3.5	41.6[25]	4.5	1.3	11.4	7.0	5.0	25.8
Lithuania[1] Lituanie[1]	2001	43 609	7.0	0.7	20.1	4.1	6.0	18.7	12.3	31.0
	2002	46 530	7.0	0.6	18.9	4.1	6.3	19.1	13.4	30.5
	2003	50 876	6.2	0.6	19.6	4.6	7.1	19.2	13.3	29.5
Luxembourg[1] Luxembourg[1]	2001	22 697	0.6	0.1	10.3	1.1	5.9	12.3	9.8	59.8
	2002	24 429	0.6	0.1	9.5	1.2	6.0	11.5	9.5	61.7
	2003	26 725	0.5	0.1	9.4	1.1	5.8	11.2	8.9	63.0
Madagascar Madagascar	1983	1 187 400	44.2	15.6	...	...	...	30.4	...	9.7
	1984	1 323 100	43.9	16.2	...	...	...	30.3	...	9.7
	1985	1 500 600	43.5	16.9	...	...	...	30.1	...	9.5
Malawi Malawi	1984	1 322	37.4[26]	...	18.6	1.8	2.0	6.8	4.9	28.6
	1985	1 540	34.7[26]	...	17.5	1.5	2.2	12.8	4.8	26.4
	1986	1 694	34.5[26]	...	20.3	1.2	2.0	11.5	3.5	27.1
Malaysia Malaisie	2001	350 676	7.9	9.7	29.0	3.3	4.0	13.9	6.7	25.5
	2002	378 768	8.8	9.0	29.1	3.2	3.9	13.4	6.6	26.0
	2003	411 705	9.3	9.9	29.7	3.1	3.6	12.8	6.5	25.0
Mali Mali	1990	655 600	47.8	1.6	8.1[27]	3.8[28]	...	18.8	4.9	15.1
	1991	662 500	46.1	1.7	6.9[27]	4.3[28]	...	20.2	5.0	15.9
	1992	707 000	47.2	1.5	7.0[27]	4.4[28]	...	19.3	5.0	15.6
Malta[1] Malte[1]	2001	1 576[4]	2.6	0.3	20.8	1.8	4.3	18.0	11.5	40.7
	2002	1 588[4]	2.6	0.3	20.5	1.9	4.4	17.9	10.2	42.2
	2003	1 677[4]	2.4	0.4	20.8	1.6	4.5	17.5	10.1	42.9
Marshall Islands Iles Marshall	1999	94	8.8	0.3	3.4	2.4	11.3	18.3	5.9	49.6
	2000	97	10.0	0.3	4.6	3.2	11.1	17.6	5.4	47.9
	2001	98	10.5	0.3	4.6	3.5	11.5	17.2	5.1	47.3
Martinique Martinique	1990	18 835	5.7	7.9[13]	...	2.5	4.9	18.9	6.2	53.9
	1991	20 377	5.7	7.8[13]	...	2.4	5.3	18.9	6.3	53.6
	1992	21 869	5.1	8.1[13]	...	2.2	5.2	18.4	6.5	54.5
Mauritania Mauritanie	1987	60 302[4]	32.3	8.3	12.1	...	6.3	13.0	5.1	22.8
	1988	65 069[4]	32.4	7.7	13.0	...	6.3	13.2	5.1	22.3
	1989	75 486[4]	34.2	10.4	10.3	...	6.4	...	4.9	14.5
Mauritius[1] Maurice[1]	2002	131 972	6.0	0.1	21.4	2.3	5.5	16.9	12.8	35.0
	2003	145 054	5.9	0.1	20.3	2.4	5.8	16.4	13.0	36.1
	2004	159 505	5.7	0.1	19.7	2.2	5.7	16.8	13.1	36.7
Mexico[1] Mexique[1]	2001	5 360 426	4.0	1.4[29]	19.2[29]	1.2	5.0	20.3	11.1	37.7
	2002	5 819 424	3.8	1.3[29]	18.4[29]	1.4	5.0	19.7	10.5	39.9
	2003	6 320 022	3.8	1.3[29]	17.8[29]	1.3	5.2	20.1	10.2	40.4
Mongolia Mongolie	2000	1 043 728[30]	28.4	11.2	6.0	2.4	1.9	24.7	10.7	14.7
	2001	1 150 766[30]	24.1	8.8	7.8	2.9	1.9	27.1	12.6	14.8
	2002	1 276 277[30]	20.1	9.9	6.1	3.7	2.3	28.2	14.3	15.5
Montserrat Montserrat	1985	90[4]	4.8	1.3	5.7	3.7	7.9	18.0	11.5	47.2
	1986	103[4]	4.3	1.4	5.6	3.7	11.3	18.7	11.6	43.4
	1987	118[4]	4.1	1.3	5.7	3.2	11.5	22.1	11.1	41.0
Morocco Maroc	2001	373 322	16.0	2.0[7]	17.4	7.2[15,18]	5.2	14.2	7.0	31.0
	2002	388 315	16.5	1.9[7]	17.2	7.0[15,18]	5.0	14.2	7.4	30.9
	2003	411 150	17.1	1.6[7]	16.9	6.8[15,18]	4.8	14.0	7.3	31.5
Mozambique[1] Mozambique[1]	2001	77 025 200	22.0	0.3	13.6	3.2	8.1	24.1	10.3	18.4
	2002	96 909 300	22.4	0.3	12.0	3.8	7.3	26.2	11.3	16.8
	2003	117 640 200	21.5	0.3	11.4	3.8	7.4	27.8	12.6	15.3

		Value added, gross (Mil. nat. cur.)	Agriculture, hunting, forestry and fishing	Mining and quarrying	Manufacturing	Electricity, gas and water supply	Construction	Wholesale, retail trade, restaurants and hotels	Transport, storage & communication	Other activities
Country or area / Pays ou zone	Year / Année	Valeur ajoutée, brut (Mil. mon. nat.)	Agriculture, chasse, sylviculture et pêche	Activités extractives	Activités de fabrication	Electricité, gaz et eau	Construction	Commerce, restaurants, hôtels	Transports, entrepôts, communications	Autres activités
Myanmar [+] Myanmar [+]	1996	791 980	60.1	0.6	7.1	0.3[31]	2.4	22.6[3]	3.5	3.4[3,32]
	1997	1 109 554	59.4	0.6	7.1	0.1[31]	2.4	23.2[3]	3.9	3.1[3,32]
	1998	1 559 996	59.1	0.5	7.2	0.1[31]	2.4	23.9[3]	4.0	2.7[3,32]
Namibia [1] Namibie [1]	2001	25 245	10.2	14.5	10.3	2.5	3.1	13.8	6.1	39.5
	2002	28 565	10.5	13.8	11.2	3.0	2.1	...	7.2	38.6
	2003	29 247	10.7	7.5	12.1	2.6	3.0	...	7.9	41.4
Nepal [+] Népal [+]	2001	393 566[4]	38.4	0.5	9.0[33]	1.8	10.1	11.3	8.5	20.5
	2002	404 482[4]	39.6	0.5	8.1[33]	1.8	10.4	10.0	8.6	20.9
	2003	428 477[4]	39.6	0.5	7.9[33]	2.0	10.4	9.9	8.7	21.1
Netherlands [1] Pays–Bas [1]	2001	394 190	2.7	3.0	15.3	1.5	5.9	14.8	7.2	49.6
	2002	410 486	2.5	2.6	14.7	1.7	5.9	14.8	7.2	50.6
	2003	420 619	2.4	2.6	14.4	1.8	5.8	14.2	7.1	51.7
Netherlands Antilles [1] Antilles néerlandaises [1]	2001	4 883[34]	0.7[6]	...	5.7	4.3	3.9	16.2	9.6	59.6
	2002	4 860[34]	0.7[6]	...	5.8	3.9	4.3	18.6	9.0	57.7
	2003	5 024[34]	0.7[6]	...	5.3	4.0	4.1	18.9	8.6	58.4
New Caledonia Nouvelle–Calédonie	1994	306 748	1.9	7.4	6.6	1.5	6.0	23.0[3]	6.3	47.4[3]
	1995	329 296	1.8	8.7	6.0	1.5	5.7	22.2[3]	6.3	47.7[3]
	1996	335 482	1.7	8.5	5.7	1.6	5.0	22.8[3]	6.7	47.8[3]
New Zealand [+,1] Nouvelle–Zélande [+,1]	1999	104 217[11]	7.1	1.2	16.1	2.8	4.7	15.1	7.5	45.7
	2000	110 106[11]	8.7	1.3	16.4	2.6	4.4	14.8	7.2	44.7
	2001	118 729[11]	9.2	1.2	16.1	2.5	4.4	15.4	7.1	44.1
Nicaragua [1] Nicaragua [1]	2002	53 028	19.5	1.0	15.6	3.5	7.5	17.2	4.6	31.2
	2003	57 844	19.1	0.9	15.5	3.4	7.6	17.1	4.6	31.8
	2004	65 268	19.2	1.0	15.6	3.4	7.8	17.1	4.7	31.3
Niger Niger	2001	1 222 626	41.9	2.5	6.4	1.3	2.5	15.2	6.4	23.8
	2002	1 310 639	43.0	2.2	6.3	1.2	2.6	14.7	6.2	23.7
	2003	1 294 035	41.1	2.3	6.7	1.2	2.8	15.5	6.6	23.8
Nigeria [+] Nigéria [+]	1992	549 809	26.5	46.6	5.7	0.3	1.1	11.5[35]	1.7	6.7
	1993	701 473	33.1	35.9	6.2	0.2	1.1	14.6[35]	2.2	6.8
	1994	914 334	38.2	25.0	7.1	0.2	1.1	17.5[35]	3.5	7.3
Norway [1] Norvège [1]	2000	1 323 855	2.1	25.0	10.7	2.0	4.1	10.4	8.3	37.4
	2001	1 377 414	1.8	22.6	10.8	2.2	4.1	10.3	9.1	39.0
	2002	1 369 980	1.7	19.4	10.8	2.5	4.5	10.7	9.1	41.3
Oman [1] Oman [1]	2001	7 819[11]	2.0	42.0	8.2	1.0	2.0	12.0	6.4	26.3
	2002	7 974[11]	2.0	41.2	7.6	1.0	2.1	12.4	6.7	27.0
	2003	8 510[5,11]	1.9	38.0	8.1	1.3	2.3	12.4	6.8	26.7
Pakistan [+] Pakistan [+]	2002	4 095 212	23.6	1.6	15.7	3.3	2.3	17.6	13.3	22.6
	2003	4 479 873	23.3	1.9	16.2	3.0	2.2	17.5	13.6	22.3
	2004	5 088 321	23.1	1.7	17.1	3.3	2.6	17.6	12.9	21.8
Palau [1] Palaos [1]	1999	111	4.1	0.2	1.5	3.1	7.4	31.7	8.9	43.3
	2000	115	4.1	0.2	1.5	3.1	7.6	31.3	9.0	43.3
	2001	118	4.0	0.2	1.5	3.2	7.8	31.1	9.2	43.1
Panama [1] Panama [1]	2001	11 530	7.5	0.7	9.0	2.8	4.0	16.7	14.0	45.4
	2002	11 870	7.5	0.8	8.2	2.9	3.6	16.0	14.4	46.6
	2003	12 411	7.5	1.0	7.4	2.9	4.8	15.0	14.8	46.5
Papua New Guinea [1] Papouasie–Nvl.–Guinée [1]	2000	10 258[10]	32.2	24.0	10.0	1.4	4.4	8.8	4.3	16.5
	2001	11 226[10]	31.9	21.4	11.4	1.5	6.1	9.6	5.0	14.7
	2002	12 803[10]	34.6	16.8	11.1	1.5	7.6	11.3	4.9	13.7
Paraguay Paraguay	1993	11 991 719	24.5	0.4	16.5	3.4	5.9	30.4[3,36]	3.9	15.0[3]
	1994	14 960 131	23.7	0.4	15.7	3.9	6.0	30.5[3,36]	3.9	15.9[3]
	1995	17 699 000	24.8	0.3	15.7	4.3	6.0	29.5[3,36]	3.7	15.8[3]

			% of value added — % de la valeur ajoutée							
Country or area Pays ou zone	Year Année	Value added, gross (Mil. nat. cur.) Valeur ajoutée, brut (Mil. mon. nat.)	Agriculture, hunting, forestry and fishing Agriculture, chasse, sylviculture et pêche	Mining and quarrying Activités extractives	Manufacturing Activités de fabrication	Electricity, gas and water supply Electricité, gaz et eau	Construction Construction	Wholesale, retail trade, restaurants and hotels Commerce, restaurants, hôtels	Transport, storage & communication Transports, entêpots, communications	Other activities Autres activités
Peru [1] Pérou [1]	2001	172 436	8.3	5.4	16.1	2.5	5.7	19.5	8.7	33.7
	2002	181 803	7.9	5.9	16.2	2.4	5.9	19.3	8.5	33.9
	2003	192 100	7.6	6.6	15.7	2.4	6.0	19.2	8.8	33.8
Philippines Philippines	2001	3 631 474	15.1	0.6	22.9	3.2	4.9	16.1	6.8	30.3
	2002	3 959 648	15.1	0.8	23.1	3.1	4.7	16.0	7.0	30.2
	2003	4 299 932	14.8	1.0	23.3	3.2	4.4	15.9	7.3	30.1
Poland [1] Pologne [1]	2002	682 861 [8]	3.1	2.3	17.5	3.9	6.6	22.0	7.8	36.8
	2003	708 606 [8]	3.0	2.2	18.3	4.0	6.0	20.9	7.8	37.8
	2004	771 386 [8]	2.9	2.8	20.2	3.6	5.5	20.7	7.7	36.6
Portugal [1] Portugal [1]	2001	111 702	3.7	0.3	17.2	2.6	7.8	17.3	6.6	44.6
	2002	116 105	3.6	0.3	16.8	2.6	7.6	17.3	6.6	45.3
	2003	117 650	3.7	0.3	16.2	2.8	6.7	17.2	6.7	46.5
Puerto Rico + Porto Rico +	2000	68 491	0.5	0.1	42.4	2.3	2.5 [37]	13.2	4.6	34.4
	2001	70 975	0.3	0.1	43.0	2.3	2.5 [37]	12.8	4.7	34.3
	2002	74 297	0.3	0.1	42.1	2.4	2.3 [37]	12.6	4.5	35.7
Qatar [1] Qatar [1]	2000	65 707	0.4	59.5	5.3	1.2	3.5	5.7	3.1	21.3
	2001	65 776	0.4	56.0	5.9	1.5	4.5	6.0	3.4	22.4
	2002	66 410	0.4	56.5	5.9	1.5	4.1	5.9	3.4	22.3
Republic of Moldova [1] République de Moldova [1]	2002	20 152	23.5	0.2	16.6	2.5	3.3	13.3	11.2	29.3
	2003	24 170	20.9	0.3	17.6	2.2	3.4	13.4	12.3	29.9
	2004	28 071	20.8	0.4	16.4	1.9	4.7	13.2	13.2	29.5
Réunion Réunion	1990	27 417	4.0	9.1 [13]	...	4.7	5.9	20.5	4.0	51.7
	1991	30 371	3.7	9.1 [13]	...	4.1	7.1	19.9	4.6	51.5
	1992	32 832	3.5	9.0 [13]	...	4.1	6.8	20.0	4.5	50.1
Romania [1] Roumanie [1]	2002	1 373 001 700	12.6	2.4	25.0	3.7	6.4	11.8	10.7	27.4
	2003	1 706 964 900	13.1	30.4 [2,13]	...	...	6.7	11.9	10.6	27.3
	2004	2 152 762 800	14.4	30.0 [2,13]	...	...	6.8	48.9 [38]	...	...
Russian Federation [1] Fédération de Russie [1]	2001	7 975 813	6.8	...	28.3 [2,6]	...	7.4	22.3	9.1	26.1
	2002	9 772 333	6.0	...	27.0 [2,6]	...	7.0	22.1	9.3	28.7
	2003	11 913 786	5.4	...	27.1 [2,6]	...	7.1	22.3	9.4	28.6
Rwanda Rwanda	2000	680 822	40.7	0.3	10.0	0.6	8.9	10.4	7.3	22.0
	2001	731 919	41.4	0.5	9.9	0.5	8.5	10.2	7.5	21.5
	2002	794 978	43.1	0.5	9.5	0.4	8.1	10.0	7.5	20.9
Saint Kitts and Nevis Saint–Kitts–et–Nevis	2001	845	2.9	0.3	9.8	1.9	16.6	16.6	13.0	38.9
	2002	857	3.1	0.4	8.7	2.6	16.0	16.4	13.0	39.8
	2003	877	2.8	0.3	8.7	2.7	14.8	18.3	12.7	39.7
Saint Lucia Sainte–Lucie	2001	1 630	6.3	0.4	4.5	5.4	7.7	22.9	19.1	28.9
	2002	1 651	5.9	0.4	4.4	5.1	7.1	22.5	19.7	29.9
	2003	1 701	4.9	0.4	4.6	5.0	6.7	23.6	19.9	30.0
St. Vincent–Grenadines St. Vincent–Grenadines	2001	825	9.1	0.2	6.4	6.2	11.2	19.6	18.3	29.1
	2002	857	9.5	0.2	6.4	5.8	10.9	19.5	17.9	30.1
	2003	889	8.4	0.2	6.2	6.0	11.5	19.7	18.8	29.2
Samoa Samoa	2001	846	14.7	...	15.8	4.6	6.4	20.8	11.6	26.0
	2002	898	14.5	...	15.1	4.7	6.0	21.9	11.7	26.1
	2003	953	12.9	...	16.3	4.5	5.9	21.6	12.1	26.7
Sao Tome and Principe Sao Tomé–et–Principe	1986	2 259	29.2	...	2.3	0.3	3.4	19.4	5.3	40.1
	1987	2 797	31.5	...	1.3	1.4	3.8	17.1	5.6	39.2
	1988	3 800	32.1	...	1.7	1.0	4.2	18.8	4.1	38.1
Saudi Arabia + Arabie saoudite +	2000	710 339	4.9	36.9	9.6	1.2	5.9	6.7	4.1	30.6
	2001	693 155	5.2	33.2	10.0	1.3	6.2	7.2	4.4	32.5
	2002	711 975	5.1	33.3	10.2	1.3	6.3	7.3	4.5	32.4

Country or area Pays ou zone	Year Année	Value added, gross (Mil. nat. cur.) Valeur ajoutée, brut (Mil. mon. nat.)	Agriculture, hunting, forestry and fishing Agriculture, chasse, sylviculture et pêche	Mining and quarrying Activités extractives	Manufacturing Activités de fabrication	Electricity, gas and water supply Electricité, gaz et eau	Construction Construction	Wholesale, retail trade, restaurants and hotels Commerce, restaurants, hôtels	Transport, storage & communication Transports, entrepôts, communications	Other activities Autres activités
Senegal Sénégal	1998	2 746 000 [5]	17.9	1.0	12.3	2.3	4.0	27.5	11.1	23.1
	1999	2 925 000 [5]	18.6	1.1	12.1	2.2	4.4	27.0	11.3	22.6
	2000	3 114 000 [5]	19.4	1.1	12.0	2.2	4.3	25.7	11.9	22.4
Serbia and Montenegro Serbie–et–Monténégro	1998	134 968	18.4	5.0	22.3	4.2	5.3	10.1	10.2	24.6
	#1999 [39]	176 542	20.6	3.9	21.9	4.5	4.2	10.4	9.4	25.1
	2000 [39]	358 750	21.1	3.6	22.1	2.5	3.9	11.9	7.1	27.8
Seychelles Seychelles	1999	3 179 [5]	3.2	...	15.8 [6,27]	2.4	10.2	8.3	32.8	21.7
	2000	3 274 [5]	3.0	...	20.6 [6,27]	1.5	9.1	9.9	33.8	22.6
	2001	3 278 [5]	3.1	...	20.0 [6,27]	1.9	9.4	10.7	33.0	23.3
Sierra Leone + Sierra Leone +	1988	42 364	39.3	6.3	7.7	0.3	2.6	20.9	10.5	12.3
	1989	81 921	37.3	7.0	7.1	0.2	1.9	25.0	10.8	10.6
	1990	148 652	35.3	9.5	8.7	0.1	1.3	20.3	8.9	15.9
Singapore Singapour	2002	158 759	0.1 [40]	...	24.9	1.7	5.3	15.3	11.2	41.5
	2003	159 134	0.1 [40]	...	25.5	1.7	4.9	15.8	10.9	41.1
	2004	176 883	0.1 [40]	...	27.7	1.7	4.3	16.2	11.0	38.9
Slovakia [1] Slovaquie [1]	2002	1 002 053	4.4	0.7	21.8	3.3	5.3	15.4	11.4	37.7
	2003	1 103 653	4.0	0.6	20.8	5.1	5.3	15.0	10.8	38.4
	2004	1 226 220	3.9	0.5	21.0	5.0	5.6	15.1	10.7	38.2
Slovenia [1] Slovénie [1]	2001	4 237 439	2.9	0.6	26.9	3.0	5.9	13.8	7.0	40.1
	2002	4 728 867	3.1	0.5	26.3	3.1	5.6	13.6	6.9	40.9
	2003	5 108 742	2.6	0.5	26.7	2.9	5.7	13.9	7.1	40.6
Solomon Islands Iles Salomon	1984	199	53.5	−0.2	3.6	0.9	3.8	10.6	5.2	22.6
	1985	213	50.4	−0.7	3.8	1.0	4.2	10.4	5.1	25.8
	1986	224	48.3	−1.2	4.5	1.2	5.1	8.4	5.8	27.9
Somalia Somalie	1985	84 050 [4]	66.1	0.3	4.9	0.1	2.2	10.1	6.7	9.5
	1986	112 584 [4]	62.5	0.4	5.5	0.2	2.7	10.3	7.3	11.1
	1987	163 175 [4]	64.9	0.3	5.1	−0.5	2.9	10.7	6.8	9.8
South Africa [1] Afrique du Sud [1]	2001	928 215	3.5	8.3	19.1	2.5	2.4	14.0	9.6	40.5
	2002	1 059 789	4.2	8.7	19.8	2.4	2.3	13.5	9.4	39.8
	2003	1 134 585	3.7	7.4	19.6	2.4	2.4	13.9	9.7	41.0
Spain [1] Espagne [1]	2002	661 523	3.9	0.3	17.4	1.9	9.4	18.4	7.5	41.3
	2003	704 902	3.7	0.3	16.9	1.9	10.0	18.3	7.4	41.5
	2004	753 870	3.5	0.3	16.3	1.8	10.8	18.6	7.4	41.4
Sri Lanka [1] Sri Lanka [1]	2001	1 242 839 [4]	17.3	1.4	20.4	2.4	7.4	21.2	12.8	17.1
	2002	1 398 302 [4]	17.1	1.4	20.4	2.3	6.8	20.2	12.6	19.2
	2003	1 568 742 [4]	15.5	1.5	20.6	2.7	6.8	19.4	12.8	20.7
Sudan + Soudan +	1994	4 440 648	40.5	6.5 [13]	...	0.7	3.8	46.6 [41]	...	1.9
	#1996	9 015 824	37.1	9.6 [13]	...	0.9	5.0	44.4 [41]	...	3.0
	1997	15 865 432	40.5	9.1 [13]	...	0.8	6.9	39.8 [41]	...	2.8
Suriname Suriname	2000	1 106 507	10.8	9.5	8.6	3.1	3.1	14.5	7.8	29.7
	2001	1 507 042	11.0	8.2	6.5	3.7	3.4	12.9	7.8	30.8
	2002	2 005 762	9.3	7.7	4.9	2.9	3.1	12.1	10.3	35.8
Swaziland + [1] Swaziland + [1]	2001	7 987 [5]	13.2	0.4	33.9	1.4	5.7	8.6	4.8	22.2
	2002	8 854	...	0.5	33.7	1.4	5.7	8.9	4.9	22.0
	2003	9 564	...	0.5	34.2	1.4	5.6	9.0	4.8	22.8
Sweden [1] Suède [1]	2000	1 967 235	1.9	0.3	22.1	2.4	4.0	12.1	8.3	49.0
	2001	2 028 665	1.9	0.2	20.7	2.7	4.4	12.1	8.2	49.8
	2002	2 102 215	1.8	0.2	20.3	2.6	4.4	12.0	8.2	50.5
Switzerland [1] Suisse [1]	2000	418 520	1.5	0.2	18.8	2.5	5.3	15.3	5.9	50.5
	2001	425 688	1.4	0.2	19.2	2.6	5.4	15.6	5.9	49.8
	2002	436 539	1.3	0.2	19.0	2.4	5.5	15.4	6.1	50.2

Value added by industries at current prices — Percentage distribution (*continued*)
Valeur ajoutée par branche d'activité aux prix courants — Répartition en pourcentage (*suite*)

Country or area Pays ou zone	Year Année	Value added, gross (Mil. nat. cur.) Valeur ajoutée, brut (Mil. mon. nat.)	% of value added — % de la valeur ajoutée							
			Agriculture, hunting, forestry and fishing Agriculture, chasse, sylviculture et pêche	Mining and quarrying Activités extractives	Manufac- turing Activités de fabrication	Electricity, gas and water supply Electricité, gaz et eau	Construc- tion Construc- tion	Wholesale, retail trade, restaurants and hotels Commerce, restaurants, hôtels	Transport, storage & communi- cation Transports, entépôts, communi- cations	Other activities Autres activités
Syrian Arab Republic Rép. arabe syrienne	2001	954 137	26.0	20.3	6.5	1.0	3.1	15.9	12.7	14.7
	2002	1 014 541	25.3	19.0	6.4	1.4	3.1	17.4	12.7	15.0
	2003	1 052 921	25.3	19.5	4.2	1.4	3.6	17.0	12.8	16.2
Tajikistan [1] Tadjikistan [1]	2000	1 662	29.4	...	26.0[2,6]	...	3.7	20.1	5.3	15.6
	2001	2 302	29.1	...	24.9[2,6]	...	4.5	21.1	4.3	16.0
	2002	3 045	29.1	...	24.4[2,6]	...	4.2	22.3	4.1	15.9
Thailand Thaïlande	2000	4 440 650	10.0[5]	2.2	32.3	3.0	3.2	21.9	8.9	18.4
	2001	4 620 997	10.1[5]	2.3	31.8	3.4	3.2	21.3	9.2	18.7
	2002	4 865 776	10.5	2.4	32.1	3.4	3.2	20.4	9.0	18.9
TFYR of Macedonia [1] L'ex-R.y. Macédoine [1]	2001	199 968	11.5	0.7	19.8	5.0	5.9	14.7	10.8	31.5
	2002	202 752	12.1	0.5	18.7	4.5	5.9	15.5	10.2	32.6
	2003	220 735	13.5	0.4	18.0	5.3	6.1	15.3	9.5	31.8
Timor–Leste Timor–Leste	1996	368	30.4	1.0[42]	3.0	0.7[15]	19.9	9.7	9.9	25.4
	1997	342	33.7	1.0[42]	3.1	0.7[15]	18.1	9.1	9.7	24.6
	1998	127	41.1	0.6[42]	2.8	0.8[15]	10.6	7.2	12.0	24.9
Togo Togo	1980	223 479	28.5	9.8	7.4	1.8	6.2	20.6	6.9	5.7
	1981	242 311	28.6	9.3	6.7	1.7	4.5	21.8	7.1	6.2
Tonga + Tonga +	1999	213[4]	29.1	0.5	5.2	1.9	6.1	12.2	8.5	37.1
	2000	223[4]	26.5	0.4	5.4	1.8	6.3	14.3	8.1	37.7
	2001	244[4]	26.2	0.4	4.9	2.0	6.1	14.3	7.8	38.1
Trinidad and Tobago [1] Trinité–et–Tobago [1]	2002	57 594[11]	1.0	17.2	14.8	1.4	6.4	18.5	10.3	26.2
	2003	68 840[11]	0.9	21.4	16.5	0.8	5.9	17.1	9.7	24.8
	2004	74 236[11]	0.8	21.1	16.7	0.9	6.0	16.4	9.6	24.8
Tunisia [1] Tunisie [1]	2000	23 858[4]	13.8	2.7	21.9	2.0[15]	5.3	16.6[3]	8.9	28.8[3]
	2001	25 671[4]	13.0	2.6	22.2	2.0[15]	5.3	16.3[3]	9.3	29.2[3]
	2002	26 783[4]	11.6	2.6	22.2	2.1[15]	5.6	16.3[3]	9.5	30.0[3]
Turkmenistan [1] Turkménistan [1]	1999	20 056 000	24.8	...	31.4[2,6]	...	12.2	4.1	6.7	20.8
	2000	25 648 000	22.9	...	35.0[2,6]	...	6.8	3.5	6.6	25.1
	2001	33 863 000	24.7	...	36.6[2,6]	...	5.7	4.2	5.4	23.5
Turks and Caicos Islands Iles Turques et Caïques	2000	147	2.9	1.7	0.4	5.2	12.5	12.3	8.2	56.8
	2001	157	3.1	1.7	0.4	5.0	12.0	11.5	8.8	57.5
	2002	164	4.7	1.8	0.5	6.0	14.5	13.2	9.0	50.3
Tuvalu Tuvalu	2000	25	17.3	0.8	3.2	4.5	4.6	12.6	10.0	47.0
	2001	27	17.4	0.7	3.3	4.9	4.4	12.3	10.5	46.4
	2002	29	15.9	0.8	3.5	5.0	4.8	12.9	11.9	45.3
Uganda Ouganda	2001	9 312 930	33.6	0.8	9.9	1.4	9.2	14.2	5.7	25.2
	2002	9 892 243	31.1	0.8	9.7	1.4	9.9	14.1	6.3	26.7
	2003	11 597 319	33.6	0.7	8.7	1.3	10.0	14.2	6.9	24.6
Ukraine [1] Ukraine [1]	2001	183 296	16.1	4.6	19.4	6.1	4.0	12.9	13.4	23.4
	2002	204 342	14.5	4.9	19.8	5.6	3.7	12.7	13.5	25.4
	2003	239 869	12.0	4.8	21.2	5.2	4.1	13.4	13.3	26.0
United Arab Emirates Emirats arabes unis	1988	90 137[4]	1.8	33.2	9.1	2.3	9.8	11.3	5.6	26.8
	1989	104 730[4]	1.8	37.3	8.3	2.1	9.1	10.2	5.4	25.7
	1990	127 737[4]	1.6	45.4	7.2	1.8	7.8	8.8	4.6	22.7
United Kingdom [1] Royaume–Uni [1]	1999	823 883	1.2	2.1	18.5	1.9	5.0	15.2	7.9	48.5
	2000	872 149	1.0	2.9	17.6	1.8	5.1	15.0	7.9	49.2
	2001	914 738	0.9	2.8	16.7	1.7	5.2	14.9	7.7	50.0
United Rep. of Tanzania [1] Rép.–Unie de Tanzanie [1]	2001	7 792 480[4]	43.7	1.5	7.2[27]	1.6	5.2	11.9	4.6	24.0
	2002	8 868 717[4]	43.8	1.7	7.2[27]	1.6	5.3	11.7	4.6	24.1
	2003	9 993 889[4]	44.2	1.9	7.1[27]	1.6	5.5	11.5	4.5	23.6

Country or area Pays ou zone	Year Année	Value added, gross (Mil. nat. cur.) Valeur ajoutée, brut (Mil. mon. nat.)	% of value added — % de la valeur ajoutée							
			Agriculture, hunting, forestry and fishing Agriculture, chasse, sylviculture et pêche	Mining and quarrying Activités extractives	Manufac-turing Activités de fabrication	Electricity, gas and water supply Electricité, gaz et eau	Construc-tion Construc-tion	Wholesale, retail trade, restaurants and hotels Commerce, restaurants, hôtels	Transport, storage & communi-cation Transports, entépôts, communi-cations	Other activities Autres activités
United States [1] Etats–Unis [1]	2001	9 402 600 [4,5,24]	1.5	1.3	15.5	2.2	5.0	16.6	6.8	58.7
	2002	9 710 400 [4,5,24]	...	1.1	15.1	2.2	4.9	17.0	6.6	59.6
	2003	10 200 000 [4,5,24]	...	1.3	14.9	2.2	4.9	16.7	6.6	59.6
Uruguay Uruguay	2002	277 182 [11]	8.7	0.2	16.5	4.5	4.0	11.4	8.7	46.0
	2003	330 582 [11]	12.4	0.2	17.7	4.7	3.3	11.4	9.2	41.0
	2004	389 059 [11]	11.4	0.2	20.6	4.3	3.4	12.7	9.4	38.0
Uzbekistan [1] Ouzbékistan [1]	2000	2 788 137	34.9	...	15.8 [2,6]	...	7.0	10.9	9.3	22.2
	2002	6 565 515	34.2	...	16.7 [2,6]	...	5.6	11.3	...	22.9
	2003	8 369 111	33.3	...	17.6 [2,6]	...	5.2	10.9	...	23.3
Vanuatu Vanuatu	1999	34 016 [11]	15.5	...	4.4	1.9	2.9	38.3	11.0	26.1
	2000	35 284 [11]	14.9	...	4.2	1.7	3.0	38.0	11.6	26.7
	2001	35 712 [11]	14.3	...	3.8	1.9	3.0	37.8	12.6	26.5
Venezuela (Bolivarian Rep.of) [1] Venezuela (Rép. Bolivar. du) [1]	2000	76 304 600	4.1	18.8	19.3	2.2	8.1	9.5	6.9	31.0
	2001	84 997 600	4.4	14.7	17.8	2.4	10.0	10.1	6.8	33.7
	2002	103 987 700	4.0	19.5	17.0	2.4	9.5	9.4	6.5	31.7
Viet Nam [1] Viet Nam [1]	2001	481 295 000	23.2	9.2	19.8	3.3	5.8	17.3	4.0	17.3
	2002	535 762 000	23.0	8.6	20.6	3.4	5.9	17.3	3.9	17.2
	2003	605 586 000	21.8	9.4	20.8	3.8	5.9	16.9	3.7	17.6
Yemen [1] Yémen [1]	1998	847 533	19.4	16.4	10.2	0.9	5.3	11.2	14.4	22.2
	1999	1 132 153	16.1	29.2	8.2	0.7	4.7	9.0	11.6	20.8
	2000	1 380 603	15.3	33.8	7.5	0.7	4.2	8.6	10.3	19.4
Yugoslavia, SFR Yougoslavie, Rfs	1988	14 645	11.2	2.7	40.3	2.2	6.2	7.6	11.1	18.6
	1989	224 684	11.3	2.4	41.4	1.7	6.4	6.6	10.5	19.7
	1990	966 420	12.9	2.5	31.2	1.7	7.9	8.5	12.3	23.1
Zambia Zambie	2001	12 384 595	20.8	4.2	10.4	3.6	5.9	21.4	6.9	26.7
	2002	15 487 658	21.0	3.7	10.9	3.2	6.9	22.0	6.8	25.5
	2003	19 538 931	21.7	2.9	11.3	3.1	7.8	22.4	5.5	25.3
Zimbabwe Zimbabwe	2001	696 279 [4]	21.8	0.7	9.9	1.9 [15]	1.1	10.7	9.8	44.1
	2002	1 652 756 [4]	18.1	0.7	7.4	1.5 [15]	0.8	8.2	10.4	53.0
	2003	5 129 106 [4]	15.7	0.6	11.6	1.4 [15]	0.8	9.0	8.1	52.9

Source:

United Nations Statistics Division, New York, national accounts database.

Notes

+   The national accounts data generally relate to the fiscal year used in each country, unless indicated otherwise. Countries whose reference periods coincide with the calendar year ending 31 December are not listed below.

Year beginning 21 March: Afghanistan, Iran (Islamic Republic).
Year beginning 1 April: Bermuda, India, Myanmar, New Zealand, Nigeria (beginning 1982).
Year beginning 1 July: Australia, Bangladesh, Cameroon, Egypt, Gambia, Pakistan, Puerto Rico, Saudi Arabia, Sierra Leone, Sudan.
Year ending 30 June: Botswana, Swaziland, Tonga.
Year ending 7 July: Ethiopia.
Year ending 15 July: Nepal.
Year ending 30 September: Haiti.

Source

Organisation des Nations Unies, Division de statistique, New York, la base de données sur les comptes nationaux.

Notes

+   Sauf indication contraire, les données sur les comptes nationaux concernent généralement l'exercice budgétaire utilisé dans chaque pays. Les pays ou territoires dont la période de référence coïncide avec l'année civile se terminant le 31 décembre ne sont pas répertoriés ci–dessous.

Exercice commençant le 21 mars: Afghanistan, Iran (République islamique d').
Exercice commençant le 1er avril: Bermudes, Inde, Myanmar, Nigéria (à partir de 1982), Nouvelle–Zélande.
Exercice commençant le 1er juillet: Arabie saoudite, Australie, Bangladesh, Cameroun, Égypte, Gambie, Pakistan, Porto Rico, Sierra Leone, Soudan.
Exercice se terminant le 30 juin: Botswana, Swaziland, Tonga.
Exercice se terminant le 7 juillet: Éthiopie.
Exercice se terminant le 15 juillet: Népal.
Exercice se terminant le 30 septembre: Haïti.

[1] The concepts and definitions of the System of National Accounts 1993 (1993 SNA) have been adopted.

[2] Including electricity, gas and water.

[3] Restaurants and hotels are included in "Other activities".

[4] Value added at factor cost.

[5] Including statistical discrepancy.

[6] Including mining and quarrying.

[7] Oil refining included in "Electricity, gas and water".

[8] Financial intermediation services indirectly measured (FISIM) is distributed to uses.

[9] Including sewage services.

[10] Excluding Financial intermediation services indirectly measured (FISIM).

[11] Value added at producer's prices.

[12] Excluding hunting.

[13] Including "Manufacturing".

[14] Includes diamond cutting.

[15] Excluding gas.

[16] For statistical purposes, the data for China do not include those for the Hong Kong Special Administrative Region (Hong Kong SAR) and Macao Special Administrative Region (Macao SAR).

[17] Agriculture and fishing only.

[18] Including petroleum refining.

[19] Includes manufacturing of energy–generating products.

[20] Including repair services.

[21] Including engineering and sewage services.

[22] Including oil production.

[23] Excluding repair of motor vehicles, motorcycles and personal and household goods.

[24] Taxes less subsidies are included in the industry data.

[25] Including gas and oil production.

[26] Includes all non–monetary output.

[27] Including handicrafts.

[28] Including construction.

[29] Basic petroleum manufacturing is included in mining and quarrying.

[30] Value added at factor cost (includes taxes on production and imports, less subsidies).

[31] Electricity only. Gas and water are included in "Other activities".

[32] Including gas and water supply.

[33] Including cottage industries.

[34] Including Financial intermediation services indirectly measured (FISIM).

[35] Including import duties.

[36] Includes Financial intermediation, except insurance and pension funding.

[37] Contract construction only.

[38] Data refers to all Service industries, including Trade, Transport and telecommunications, Public Administration, and Other services.

[39] As from 1999: excluding Kosovo and Metohia.

[40] Including quarrying.

[41] Includes Transport, storage and communications; Financial intermediation, real estate, renting and business activities; and Education, health and social work; other community, social and personal services, and Private households with employed persons.

[42] Refers to non–oil and gas mining only, excludes Quarrying.

[1] Les concepts et définitions du Système de comptabilité nationale de 1993 (SCN de 1993) ont été adoptés.

[2] Y compris l'électricité, le gaz et l'eau.

[3] Restaurants et hôtels sont incluses dans "autres activités".

[4] Valeur ajoutée au coût des facteurs.

[5] Y compris une divergence statistique.

[6] Y compris les industries extractives.

[7] Le raffinage du pétrole y compris dans l'électricité, le gaz et l'eau.

[8] Services d'intermédiation financière mesurés indirectment (SIFMI) est distribué à ses utilizations.

[9] Y compris services d'égouts.

[10] Non compris les Services d'intermédiation financière mesurés indirectment (SIFMI).

[11] Valeur ajoutée aux prix à la production.

[12] Non compris le chasse.

[13] Y compris les industries manufacturières.

[14] Y compris la taille de diamant.

[15] Non compris le gaz.

[16] Pour la présentation des statistiques, les données pour Chine ne comprennent pas la Région Administrative Spéciale de Hong Kong (Hong Kong RAS) et la Région Administrative Spéciale de Macao (Macao RAS).

[17] Agriculture et la pêche seulement.

[18] Y compris le raffinage du pétrole.

[19] Y compris la fabrication de produits producteurs d'énergie.

[20] Y compris les services de réparation.

[21] Y compris génie civil et services d'égouts.

[22] Y compris la production de pétrole.

[23] Non compris les réparations de véhicules à moteur, de motorcycles et d'articles personnels et ménagers.

[24] Les impôts, moins les subventions, sont inclus dans les données sur les industries.

[25] Y compris la production de gaz et de pétrole.

[26] Y compris l'ensemble de la production non monétaire.

[27] Y compris l'artisanat.

[28] Y compris la construction.

[29] Les industries extractives y compris fabrication de produits pétroliers de base.

[30] Valeur ajoutée au coût des facteurs (y compris les taxes sur la production et les importations, moins les subventions).

[31] Seulement électricité. Le gaz et l'eau sont incluses dans les "autres activités".

[32] Y compris le gaz et l'eau.

[33] Y compris artisanat.

[34] Y compris les Services d'intermédiation financière mesurés indirectment (SIFMI).

[35] Droits d'importation compris.

[36] Y compris l'intermédiation financière sauf les assurances et la caisse des pensions.

[37] Construction sous contrat seulement.

[38] Les données concernent l'ensemble des branches de services, dont le Commerce, les Transports et télécommunications, l'Administration publique, et les Autres services.

[39] A partir de 1999: non compris Kosovo et Metohia.

[40] Y compris les carrières.

[41] Comprend Transports, entreposage et communications ; Intermédiation financière, activités immobilières, de location et commerciales ; Éducation, santé et action sociale ; Autres services communautaires, sociaux et individuels, et Ménages privés comptant des salariés.

[42] Activités extractives hormis pétrole et gaz, non compris les carrières.

Relationships among the principal national accounting aggregates
As a percentage of GDP

Relations entre les principaux agrégats de comptabilité nationale
En pourcentage du PIB

Country or area Pays ou zone	Year Année	GDP at current prices (Mil.nat. cur.) PIB aux prix courants (Millions monnaie nat.)	As a percentage of GDP – En pourcentage du PIB					
			Plus: Compensation of employees and property income from/to the rest of the world, net Plus : Rémuneration des salariés et revenus de la propriété – du et au reste du monde, net	Equals: Gross national income Égale : Revenu national brut	Plus: Net current transfers from/ to the rest of the world Plus : Transfers courants du/au reste du monde, net	Equals: Gross national disposable income Égale : Revenu national disponible brut	Less: Final consumption expenditure Moins : Dépense de consommation de finale	Equals: Gross savings Égale : Épargne brut
Algeria Algérie	2001	4 260 811	−2.9[1]	97.1	2.5	99.6	58.0	41.6
	2002	4 537 691	−3.8[1]	96.2	3.0	99.2	59.2	39.9
	2003	5 264 187	−3.6[1]	96.4	3.5	99.9	55.1	44.8
Angola Angola	1988	239 640	−11.1	88.9	−1.9	87.0	78.4	8.6
	1989	278 866	−10.5	89.5	−1.6	87.9	77.1	10.8
	1990	308 062	−12.4	87.6	−4.2	83.4	73.2	10.2
Anguilla Anguilla	2001	297	−3.2	96.8	1.1	98.0	98.0	0.0
	2002	305	−4.7	95.3	0.1	95.5	98.2	−2.7
	2003	318	−4.7	95.3	−0.1	95.3	100.3	−5.0
Argentina [2] Argentine [2]	2002	312 580	−6.2	93.8	0.4	94.2	74.1	20.1[3]
	2003	375 909	−6.0	94.0	0.4	94.4	74.6	19.7[3]
	2004	447 307	5.9	105.9	0.5	106.3	74.0	32.3[3]
Armenia [2] Arménie [2]	2001	1 175 900	−0.1	99.9	8.3	108.2	104.8	3.4
	2002	1 362 500	−0.5	99.5	7.5	107.1	99.1	8.0
	2003	1 624 600	−1.1	98.9	8.0	106.9	93.5	13.4
Aruba [2] Aruba [2]	1999	3 084	−5.0	95.0	−0.9	94.1	73.8	20.3
	2000	3 327	−4.7	95.3	−1.7	93.5	72.0	21.5
	2001	3 399	−6.6	93.4	2.7	96.1	74.1	22.1
Australia [+2] Australie [+2]	2001	713 229	−2.7	97.3	0.0	97.3	77.4	19.9
	2002	758 147	−2.8	97.2	0.0	97.1	77.8	19.3
	2003	813 225	−2.9	97.1	0.0	97.1	77.6	19.6
Austria [2] Autriche [2]	2002	221 008	−1.6	98.4	−0.9	97.5	74.2	23.4
	2003	226 142	−1.5	98.5	−1.0	97.5	74.1	23.4
	2004	235 441	−1.5	98.5	−1.1	97.4	73.6	23.8
Azerbaijan [2] Azerbaïdjan [2]	2001	26 578 000	−5.9	94.1	13.1	107.2	75.1	32.1
	2002	30 312 300	−6.2	93.8	12.7	106.5	75.3	31.2
	2003	35 732 500	−6.1	93.9	11.7	105.7	72.4	33.3
Bahamas [2] Bahamas [2]	2002	5 400[4]	−3.2[1]	96.8	0.8	97.6	80.7[6]	16.8
	2003	*5 502[4]	−2.2[1]	97.8	0.9	98.7	82.7[6]	16.0
	2004	5 735[4,5]	−1.7[1]	...	...	...	83.7[6]	...
Bahrain Bahreïn	2001	2 981	−4.1[1]	95.9	−15.9	80.0	66.0	...
	2002	3 176	−5.2	93.8	−15.6	78.2	63.7	...
	2003	3 612	−5.4[1]	94.6	−14.0	80.6	59.6	...
Bangladesh [+2] Bangladesh [+2]	2000	2 535 464	3.5	103.5	0.9	104.4	82.0	22.4
	2001	2 732 010	4.6	104.6	0.7	105.3	81.8	23.4
	2002	3 005 801	5.5	105.5	0.7	106.2	81.8	24.5
Belarus [2] Bélarus [2]	2001	17 173 200[7]	0.2	100.2	1.3	101.4	79.2	22.3
	2002	26 138 300[7]	0.1	100.1	1.2	101.3	80.5	20.7
	2003	36 564 800[7]	−0.2	99.8	1.1	100.9	78.5	22.4

Country or area Pays ou zone	Year Année	GDP at current prices (Mil.nat. cur.) PIB aux prix courants (Millions monnaie nat.)	As a percentage of GDP – En pourcentage du PIB					
			Plus: Compensation of employees and property income from/to the rest of the world, net Plus : Rémuneration des salariés et revenus de la propriété – du et au reste du monde, net	Equals: Gross national income Égale : Revenu national brut	Plus: Net current transfers from/ to the rest of the world Plus : Transfers courants du/au reste du monde, net	Equals: Gross national disposable income Égale : Revenu national disponible brut	Less: Final consumption expenditure Moins : Dépense de consommation de finale	Equals: Gross savings Égale : Épargne brut
Belgium [2] Belgique [2]	2002	261 124	2.4	102.4	–1.0	101.4	76.4	25.0
	2003	269 546	1.9	101.9	–1.2	100.7	77.2	23.4
	2004	283 752	1.4	101.4	–1.3	100.1	76.6	23.5
Belize [2] Belize [2]	1998	1 258	...	94.9	...	100.2	84.8	...
	1999	1 377	...	95.1	...	...	82.3	...
	2000	1 514	...	...	...	...	83.7	...
Benin [2] Bénin [2]	1989	479 200	...	99.2	11.1	110.2	94.4	12.6
	1990	502 300	...	...	...	...	93.6	...
	1991	535 500	...	...	...	...	94.6	...
Bermuda [+ 2] Bermudes [+ 2]	2000	3 378	4.9	104.9	...	...	72.4	...
	2001	3 539	7.0	107.0	...	...	...	...
	2002	3 715	2.8	102.8	...	...	...	...
Bhutan Bhoutan	1998	16 337 [8]	–14.2	94.1	4.2	99.0 [8]	77.3	36.6 [8]
	1999	19 123	–16.1	83.9	4.5	88.4	75.0	...
	2000	21 698	–15.9	84.1	5.8	89.8	72.6	...
Bolivia Bolivie	2000	51 884	–2.7	97.3	2.4	99.7	91.2	8.5
	2001	53 010	–2.6	97.4	4.1	101.5	91.6	9.9
	2002	55 933	–2.6	97.4	3.7	101.1	90.2	10.8
Botswana [+ 2] Botswana [+ 2]	2000	24 943	–6.0	94.0	0.0	94.0	61.6	32.4
	2001	28 671	–5.0	95.0	–0.2	94.9	59.9	34.9
	2002	32 000	–4.2 [8]	95.8	–0.1	95.7	62.1	33.6
Brazil [2] Brésil [2]	2001	1 198 736	–3.8	96.2	0.3	96.5	79.8	16.8
	2002	1 346 028	–3.9	96.1	0.5	96.7	78.2	18.5
	2003	1 556 182	–3.5	96.5	0.6	97.0	76.6	20.4
British Virgin Islands [2] Iles Vierges britanniques [2]	1997	512	–9.4 [9]	90.6	1.5	92.2	55.5	36.7
	1998	593	–8.1 [9]	92.1	2.6	94.6	53.0	41.7
	1999	662	–7.3 [9]	92.9	3.1	95.9	51.7	44.1
Bulgaria [2] Bulgarie [2]	2001	29 709	–2.2	97.8	3.7	101.5	86.9	14.6
	2002	32 335	–1.7	98.3	3.4	101.7	86.8	14.9
	2003	34 410	–2.5	97.5	3.5	101.0	88.1	12.9
Burkina Faso Burkina Faso	1991	811 676	0.3	100.3	1.5	...	90.9	...
	1992	812 590	0.2	100.2	1.9	...	90.6	...
	1993	832 349	–0.1	99.9	1.9	...	91.6	...
Burundi Burundi	1990	196 656	...	98.0	...	...	102.5	...
	1991	211 898	...	99.0	...	...	100.9	...
	1992	226 384	...	98.7	...	...	98.5	...
Cambodia Cambodge	1994	6 201 001	...	92.1	...	...	104.7	...
	1995	7 542 711	...	95.1	...	...	95.6	...
	1996	8 324 792	...	93.6	...	...	95.5	...
Cameroon [+ 2] Cameroun [+2]	1996	4 793 080	...	95.7	0.3	95.9	79.8	16.1
	1997	5 370 580	...	...	...	...	82.0	...
	1998	5 744 000	...	...	...	...	82.9	...

Country or area Pays ou zone	Year Année	GDP at current prices (Mil.nat. cur.) PIB aux prix courants (Millions monnaie nat.)	As a percentage of GDP – En pourcentage du PIB					
			Plus: Compensation of employees and property income from/to the rest of the world, net Plus : Rémuneration des salariés et revenus de la propriété – du et au reste du monde, net	Equals: Gross national income Égale : Revenu national brut	Plus: Net current transfers from/ to the rest of the world Plus : Transfers courants du/au reste du monde, net	Equals: Gross national disposable income Égale : Revenu national disponible brut	Less: Final consumption expenditure Moins : Dépense de consommation de finale	Equals: Gross savings Égale : Épargne brut
Canada [2] Canada [2]	2001	1 092 135	−2.8	97.2	0.1	97.3	75.0	22.4
	2002	1 140 428	−2.3	97.7	0.1	97.8	75.8	22.0
	2003	1 200 078	−1.9	98.1	0.0	98.1	75.7	22.4
Cape Verde Cap–Vert	1993	29 078	...	166.4	...	...	106.8	...
	1994	33 497	...	161.3	...	...	104.5	...
	1995	37 705	...	163.5	...	...	109.1	...
Cayman Islands Iles Caïmanes	1989	474	−10.8	89.2	...	92.0	79.3	12.7
	1990	590	−10.3	89.7	...	92.2	76.8	15.4
	1991	616	−9.4	90.6	...	93.0	77.6	15.4
Chile [2] Chili [2]	2002	46 342 000	−4.2	95.8	0.9	96.6	75.9	20.7
	2003	50 731 000	−6.2	93.8	0.8	94.6	74.0	20.6
	2004	57 357 000	−8.6	91.4	1.1	92.5	69.3	23.2
China [2,10] Chine [2,10]	2002	10 517 230	−1.2	98.8	...	...	...	...
	2003	11 739 020	−0.6	99.4	...	...	...	...
	2004	13 687 590	−0.2	99.8	...	...	...	...
China, Hong Kong SAR [2] Chine, Hong Kong RAS [2]	2001	1 269 896	3.2[1]	103.2	−1.1	102.1	70.4	31.8
	2002	1 247 381	1.3[1]	101.3	−1.2	100.2	68.9	31.3
	2003	1 220 023	2.8[1]	102.8	−1.2	101.6	68.1	33.5
Colombia [2] Colombie [2]	1998	140 953 206	−2.4	97.6	3.2	100.8	86.2	14.6
	1999	151 565 005	−1.8	98.2	1.9	100.1	86.6	13.6
	2000	173 729 806	−3.0	97.0	2.1	99.1	86.3	12.7
Comoros Comores	1989	63 397	...	100.7	...	...	...	...
	1990	66 370	...	99.8	12.3	112.1	105.5	6.7
	1991	69 248	...	99.6	...	...	...	...
Congo Congo	1986	640 407	−6.5	93.5	−1.3	92.2	84.4	7.8
	1987	690 523	−11.1	88.9	−1.6	87.3	77.2	10.2
	1988	658 964	−13.7	86.3	−1.8	84.5	81.2	3.3
Costa Rica [2] Costa Rica [2]	2002	6 058 895	−4.1	95.9	1.0	96.9	82.6	14.3
	2003	6 970 815	−4.5	95.5	1.2	96.7	81.3	15.4
	2004	8 055 488	−4.3	95.7	1.2	96.9	81.4	15.5
Côte d'Ivoire Côte d'Ivoire	1998	7 457 508	−5.7	94.3	−3.1	91.2	78.7	12.4
	1999	7 734 000	−6.9	92.1	−2.7	89.1	77.8	11.3[8]
	2000	7 605 000	−5.7	94.3	−3.5	90.8	82.7	8.1
Cuba [2] Cuba [2]	2001	29 557	4.6	...	...	...	...	...
	2002	30 680	1.8	...	...	...	...	...
	2003	32 337	−0.9	...	...	...	...	...
Cyprus [2] Chypre [2]	2001	6 104	...	94.4	...	...	...	...
	2002	6 370	...	95.7	...	...	...	...
	2003	6 802	...	97.1	...	...	...	...
Czech Republic [2] République tchèque [2]	2002	2 414 669	−4.8	95.2	0.6	95.8	74.1	21.7
	2003	2 550 754	−4.6	95.4	0.6	96.0	74.9	21.1
	2004	2 750 256	...	...	...	...	72.8	...

Country or area / Pays ou zone	Year / Année	GDP at current prices (Mil.nat. cur.) / PIB aux prix courants (Millions monnaie nat.)	Plus: Compensation of employees and property income from/to the rest of the world, net / Plus : Rémunération des salariés et revenus de la propriété – du et au reste du monde, net	Equals: Gross national income / Égale : Revenu national brut	Plus: Net current transfers from/ to the rest of the world / Plus : Transfers courants du/au reste du monde, net	Equals: Gross national disposable income / Égale : Revenu national disponible brut	Less: Final consumption expenditure / Moins : Dépense de consommation de finale	Equals: Gross savings / Égale : Épargne brut
Dem. Rep. of the Congo / Rép. dém. du Congo	1983	59 134	...	95.7	...	...	76.9	...
	1984	99 723	...	88.5	...	...	49.5	...
	1985	147 263	...	97.2	...	...	59.4	...
Denmark [2] / Danemark [2]	2002	1 350 787	−1.5	98.5	−2.1	96.3	74.1	22.3
	2003	1 390 537	−0.8	99.2	−2.1	97.1	74.2	23.0
	2004	1 446 471	−0.5	99.5	−2.2	97.4	74.7	22.6
Djibouti / Djibouti	1996	88 233	1.0[11]	100.0	9.4	109.4	97.3	12.1
	1997	87 289	1.2[11]	99.9	8.3	108.2	94.2	14.0
	1998	88 461	1.2[11]	99.9	8.3	108.3	96.4	11.8
Dominica / Dominique	1989	423		101.0	...	...	92.0	...
	1990	452		101.1	...	...	84.4	...
	1991	479		101.0	...	...	91.4	...
Dominican Republic [2] / Rép. dominicaine [2]	1994	179 130	−2.2	97.8	6.7	104.5	81.4	23.1
	1995	209 646	−2.3	97.7	6.2	103.9	82.9	21.0
	1996	243 973	−5.4	94.6	6.1	100.7	82.2	18.5
Ecuador [2] / Equateur [2]	2002	24 311	−5.2	94.8	6.8	101.6	79.7	21.9
	2003	27 201	−5.3	94.7	6.5	101.2	77.4	23.8
	2004	30 015	...	...	...	...	...	...
Egypt +[2] / Egypte +[2]	2001	375 203	−0.2	102.3	3.5	105.8	86.9	18.8
	2002	405 256	−0.9	101.3	4.1	105.5	86.4	19.1
	2003	451 154	−0.7	101.6	3.9	105.5	82.9	22.6
El Salvador / El Salvador	2001	120 862	−1.9	98.1	16.6	114.7	99.1	15.6
	2002	125 230	−2.3	97.7	14.1	111.9	98.6	13.3
	2003	130 733	−2.7	97.3	14.2	111.4	99.7	11.7
Estonia [2] / Estonie [2]	2001	104 338	−4.7	95.3	2.5	97.8	75.2	22.6
	2002	116 869	−4.6	95.4	1.6	96.9	76.0	20.9
	2003	125 832	−6.3	93.7	1.2	94.9	75.6	19.3
Ethiopia + / Ethiopie +	1997	41 465	−0.5[11]	99.5	7.0	106.5	...	7.0
	1998	44 896	−0.4[11]	99.6	8.3	107.9	...	8.3
	1999	48 949	−0.4[11]	99.6	7.6	107.2	...	7.6
Fiji / Fidji	1999	3 662	−4.1	95.9[6]	2.8	98.6[6]	70.6	28.1[6]
	2000	3 505	−1.3	98.7[6]	2.2	100.9[6]	77.1	23.8[6]
	2001	3 836	−4.2	95.8[6]	5.3	101.1[6]	74.1	27.0[6]
Finland [2] / Finlande [2]	2002	140 284	−0.2	99.8	−0.8	99.0	72.3	26.7
	2003	143 337	−1.3	98.7	−1.0	97.7	74.0	23.7
	2004	149 742	−0.5	99.5	−1.0	98.6	74.1	24.5
France [2] / France [2]	2002	1 548 559	0.3	100.3	−1.2	99.1	79.3	19.8
	2003	1 585 172	0.5	100.5	−1.3	99.1	80.0	19.2
	2004	1 648 368	0.5	100.5	−1.5	99.1	80.0	19.1
French Guiana / Guyane française	1990	6 526	−1.9[1]	98.1	36.3	134.4	99.4	35.0
	1991	7 404	−5.8[1]	94.2	35.9	130.1	94.5	35.6
	1992	7 976	−6.9[1]	93.1	36.4	129.6	93.1	36.4

Country or area Pays ou zone	Year Année	GDP at current prices (Mil.nat. cur.) PIB aux prix courants (Millions monnaie nat.)	Plus: Compensation of employees and property income from/to the rest of the world, net Plus : Rémuneration des salariés et revenus de la propriété – du et au reste du monde, net	Equals: Gross national income Égale : Revenu national brut	Plus: Net current transfers from/ to the rest of the world Plus : Transfers courants du/au reste du monde, net	Equals: Gross national disposable income Égale : Revenu national disponible brut	Less: Final consumption expenditure Moins : Dépense de consommation de finale	Equals: Gross savings Égale : Épargne brut
Gabon Gabon	1987	1 020 600	−6.2[1]	93.8	−4.2	89.7	72.4	17.3
	1988	1 013 600	−7.4[1]	92.6	−7.6	85.0	69.9	15.1
	1989	1 168 066	−8.6[1]	91.4	−6.1	85.3	66.8	18.5
Gambia [+] Gambie [+]	1991	2 920	...	98.3	...	115.7	96.7	19.0
	1992	3 078	...	98.7	...	114.1	94.4	19.7
	1993	3 243	...	98.5	...	114.4	93.3	21.1
Georgia [2] Géorgie [2]	#1995	3 694	−2.1	97.9	4.0	101.9	91.2	10.7
	1996	5 300	1.7	101.7	2.0	103.7	93.2	10.5
	1997	6 431	2.6	102.6	3.9	106.5	100.0	6.5
Germany [2] Allemagne [2]	2002	2 148 810	−1.2	98.8	−1.2	97.6	78.1	19.5
	2003	2 164 870	−0.7	99.3	−1.2	98.1	78.6	19.6
	2004	2 207 240	−0.5	99.5	−1.2	98.3	77.8	20.6
Ghana Ghana	1994	5 205 200	...	98.0	...	...	...	...
	1995	7 752 600	...	98.0	...	...	...	...
	1996	11 339 200	...	98.1	...	...	...	...
Greece [2] Grèce [2]	2002	141 669	0.1	100.1	0.7	100.7	84.9	15.9
	2003	153 472	0.0	100.0	0.7	100.6	83.2	17.4
	2004	165 280	0.1	100.1	0.6	100.7	83.0	17.7
Grenada Grenade	1984	275	...	98.9	...	...	99.1	...
	1985	311	...	98.9	...	...	99.0	...
	1986	350	...	99.2	...	...	97.7	...
Guadeloupe Guadeloupe	1990	15 201	−2.5[1]	97.5	37.3	134.8	123.6	11.2
	1991	16 415	−3.4[1]	96.6	35.4	132.0	118.3	13.7
	1992	17 972	−3.0[1]	97.0	36.6	133.6	113.4	20.2
Guatemala Guatemala	1996	95 479	−1.5[1]	98.5	3.4	101.9	92.1	10.2
	1997	107 943	−1.3[1]	98.7	3.4	102.1	91.8	10.8
	1998	121 548	−0.8[1]	99.2	3.8	103.0	92.8	10.6
Guinea–Bissau Guinée–Bissau	1986	46 973	−1.7[1]	98.3	2.9	101.3	102.8	−1.5
	1987	92 375	−0.5[1]	99.5	4.1	103.6	100.8	2.8
	1988	171 949	...	...	...	...	...	...
Guyana Guyana	1999	123 665	...	90.1	...	...	68.0	...
	2000	130 013	...	93.8	...	...	77.4	...
	2001	133 403	...	92.8	...	...	78.3	...
Haiti [+] Haïti [+]	1995	35 207	...	98.7	22.8	121.5	108.1	13.4
	1996	43 234	...	99.6	17.1	116.7	104.9	11.8
	1997	51 789	...	99.6	14.1	113.7	103.7	10.0
Honduras Honduras	1998	70 438	...	95.9	9.3	105.2	77.1	28.1
	1999	77 095	...	96.9	13.6	110.5	80.1	30.4
	2000	87 523	...	97.0	12.5	109.6	82.0	27.6
Hungary [2] Hongrie [2]	2002	16 740 415	−5.5	94.5	...	...	77.1	...
	2003	18 408 815	−5.0	95.0	...	...	79.5	...
	2004	20 338 182	...	...	...	...	78.8	...

Country or area Pays ou zone	Year Année	GDP at current prices (Mil.nat. cur.) PIB aux prix courants (Millions monnaie nat.)	Plus: Compensation of employees and property income from/to the rest of the world, net Plus : Rémuneration des salariés et revenus de la propriété – du et au reste du monde, net	Equals: Gross national income Égale : Revenu national brut	Plus: Net current transfers from/to the rest of the world Plus : Transfers courants du/au reste du monde, net	Equals: Gross national disposable income Égale : Revenu national disponible brut	Less: Final consumption expenditure Moins : Dépense de consommation de finale	Equals: Gross savings Égale : Épargne brut
Iceland [2] Islande [2]	2002	766 239	−0.8	99.2	0.2	99.3	80.5	18.8
	2003	797 487	−2.1	97.9	−0.1	97.8	83.1	14.6
	2004	858 921	−2.1	97.9	−0.1	97.8	84.4	13.4
India [+] Inde [+]	2001	22 719 840	−0.7	99.3	3.2	102.5	77.9	23.4
	2002	24 633 240	−0.5	99.5	3.2	102.7	76.1	26.1
	2003	27 600 250	−0.5	99.5	3.8	103.3	75.1	28.1
Indonesia Indonésie	2001	1 467 655 000	...	95.8	...	...	74.0	...
	2002	1 610 565 000	...	96.6	...	...	77.8	...
	2003	1 786 691 000	...	95.5	...	...	78.5	...
Iran (Islamic Rep. of) [+][2] Iran (Rép. islamique d') [+][2]	2001	680 506 217	0.1	100.1	0.0	100.1	61.7	38.3
	2002	935 828 854	−0.2	99.8	0.0	99.8	57.6	42.2
	2003	1 126 947 103	0.1	100.1	0.0	100.1	57.3	42.8
Iraq Iraq	1989	21 026	...	96.7	...	95.9	81.9	14.0
	1990	23 297	...	96.7	...	96.5	76.8	19.6
	1991	19 940	...	96.7	...	97.4	83.5	13.9
Ireland [2] Irlande [2]	2002	127 992	−17.3	82.7	−0.5	82.2	59.9	22.2
	2003	134 786	−16.2	83.8	−0.6	83.2	61.0	22.2
	2004	146 279	−15.2	84.8	...	...	59.8	...
Israel [2] Israël [2]	2001	499 173	−4.1	95.9	5.6	101.6	82.9	18.7
	2002	516 013	−3.7	96.3	6.2	102.5	85.8	16.7
	2003	523 259	−3.8	96.2	5.5	101.8	85.4	16.3
Italy [2] Italie [2]	2002	1 260 598	−0.8	99.2	−0.5	98.7	79.0	19.7
	2003	1 300 929	−0.8	99.2	−0.6	98.6	79.9	18.6
	2004	1 351 328	−0.6	99.4	−0.7	98.8	79.4	19.4
Jamaica Jamaïque	2001	373 043	−5.4	94.6	9.4	104.0	87.2	16.8
	2002	408 765	−7.1	92.9	11.3	104.3	88.2	16.0
	2003	470 440	−7.6	92.4	12.7	105.1	88.5	16.5
Japan [2] Japon [2]	2001	505 847 100	1.6	101.6	−0.2	101.5	73.6	26.4
	2002	497 896 800	1.6	101.6	−0.1	101.6	74.7	25.7
	2003	497 485 000	1.7	101.7	−0.1	101.6	74.5	26.4
Jordan Jordanie	2000	5 989	1.6	101.6	25.9	127.5	104.6	22.9
	2001	6 339	2.1	102.1	23.0	125.1	104.4	20.7
	2002	6 699	1.2	101.2	24.0	125.1	100.6	24.5
Kazakhstan [2] Kazakhstan [2]	2000	2 599 902	−6.2	93.8	1.4	95.1	73.6	21.5
	2001	3 250 593	−5.1	94.9	1.0	95.9	71.3	24.6
	2002	3 776 277	−4.2	95.8	0.5	96.3	69.9	26.3
Kenya Kenya	2001	43 937	...	98.9	7.2	...	94.9	...
	2002	48 134	...	98.8	5.2	...	92.1	...
	2003	54 582	...	99.4	5.7	...	91.7	...
Korea, Republic of [2] Corée, République de [2]	2002	684 263 500	0.1	100.1	−0.3	99.8	68.6	31.2
	2003	724 675 000	0.1	100.1	−0.5	99.6	67.0	32.6
	2004	778 444 600	...	100.1	−0.4	99.8	65.0	34.8

Country or area Pays ou zone	Year Année	GDP at current prices (Mil.nat. cur.) PIB aux prix courants (Millions monnaie nat.)	As a percentage of GDP – En pourcentage du PIB					
			Plus: Compensation of employees and property income from/to the rest of the world, net Plus : Rémuneration des salariés et revenus de la propriété – du et au reste du monde, net	Equals: Gross national income Égale : Revenu national brut	Plus: Net current transfers from/ to the rest of the world Plus : Transfers courants du/au reste du monde, net	Equals: Gross national disposable income Égale : Revenu national disponible brut	Less: Final consumption expenditure Moins : Dépense de consommation de finale	Equals: Gross savings Égale : Épargne brut
Kuwait Koweït	1999	8 886	17.5 [11]	117.5	−6.9	110.6	78.3	32.4
	2000	10 991	18.7 [11]	118.7	−5.5	113.2	64.8	48.5
	2001	10 057	15.1 [11]	115.1	−6.3	108.8	74.0	34.7
Kyrgyzstan [2] Kirghizistan [2]	2001	73 883	−4.2	95.8	3.4	99.1	82.3	16.8
	2002	75 367	−3.7	96.3	7.3	103.5	86.2	17.4
	2003	83 872	−3.1	96.9	5.5	102.4	94.7	7.6
Latvia [2] Lettonie [2]	2001	5 168	0.7	100.7	1.7	102.4	83.5	18.9
	2002	5 689	0.6	100.6	2.9	103.5	83.8	19.6
	2003	6 322	−0.2	99.8	4.8	104.6	84.8	19.8
Lesotho [2] Lesotho [2]	1999	5 565	25.0 [1]	126.8	17.9	144.8	122.4	22.4
	2000	5 980	25.5 [1]	125.5	17.5	142.9	120.4	22.5
	2001	6 478	23.4 [1]	123.4	20.3	143.7	119.8	23.8
Liberia Libéria	1987	1 090	...	83.2	...	...	...	...
	1988	1 158	...	84.2	...	...	...	...
	1989	1 194	...	84.9	...	...	...	...
Libyan Arab Jamah. Jamah. arabe libyenne	1983	8 805	−6.9 [11]	91.0	−0.2	90.9	72.0	18.9
	1984	8 013	−4.6 [11]	92.7	−0.3	92.4	72.2	20.2
	1985	8 277	−2.9 [11]	96.7	−0.2	96.5	69.2	27.3
Lithuania [2] Lituanie [2]	2001	48 379	−1.5	98.5	2.1	100.6	84.9	15.8
	2002	51 643	−1.2	98.8	1.6	100.4	83.8	16.6
	2003	56 179	−2.7	97.3	1.6	98.9	83.4	15.5
Luxembourg [2] Luxembourg [2]	2002	22 805	−8.5	91.5	...	...	60.2	...
	2003	23 956	−11.5	88.5	...	...	60.1	...
	2004	25 664	...	...	...	...	58.9	...
Madagascar Madagascar	1980	689 800	...	99.9	...	...	...	...
Malawi Malawi	1994	11 209	−3.6	96.4	9.2	105.6	...	...
	1995	20 246	−3.1	96.9 [8]	9.6	105.0	...	...
	1996	23 993	−1.8	98.2	3.4	101.6	...	...
Malaysia Malaisie	2001	334 404	−7.7 [1]	92.3	−2.4	89.9	57.7	32.2
	2002	361 624	−6.9 [1]	93.1	−2.9	90.1	57.9	32.2
	2003	394 200	−5.7 [1]	94.3	−2.4	91.9	57.7	34.3
Maldives [2] Maldives [2]	2002	8 200	−5.7 [1]	94.3	−5.7	88.6	53.7	35.0
	2003	8 842	−5.1 [1]	94.9	−6.4	88.5	50.8	37.7
	2004	9 640	−4.5 [1]	95.5	−6.7	88.8	52.4	36.4
Mali Mali	1990	683 300	−1.2 [1]	98.8	11.5	110.3	94.3	16.1
	1991	691 400	−1.3 [1]	98.7	13.0	111.9	100.4	11.5
	1992	737 400	−1.2 [1]	98.8	11.4	110.2	96.4	13.8
Malta Malte	1999	1 456	0.9 [1]	100.9	...	...	...	...
	2000	*1 558	−3.5 [1]	*96.5	...	...	...	...
	2001	*1 632	−0.1 [1]	*99.9	...	...	...	...
Martinique Martinique	1990	19 320	−4.2 [1]	95.8	33.7	...	113.3	...
	1991	20 787	−4.4 [1]	95.6	30.7	...	112.8	...
	1992	22 093	−3.9 [1]	96.1	33.4	...	113.1	...

Country or area Pays ou zone	Year Année	GDP at current prices (Mil.nat. cur.) PIB aux prix courants (Millions monnaie nat.)	As a percentage of GDP – En pourcentage du PIB					
			Plus: Compensation of employees and property income from/to the rest of the world, net Plus : Rémuneration des salariés et revenus de la propriété – du et au reste du monde, net	Equals: Gross national income Égale : Revenu national brut	Plus: Net current transfers from/ to the rest of the world Plus : Transfers courants du/au reste du monde, net	Equals: Gross national disposable income Égale : Revenu national disponible brut	Less: Final consumption expenditure Moins : Dépense de consommation de finale	Equals: Gross savings Égale : Épargne brut
Mauritania Mauritanie	1987	67 216	−5.1	94.9	8.1	103.0	96.2	6.7
	1988	72 635	−5.6	94.4	7.9	102.3	93.7	8.5
	1989	83 520	−3.6	96.4	9.0	105.4	...	...
Mauritius [2] Maurice [2]	2002	142 131	0.3	100.3	1.9	102.2	75.0	27.2
	2003	157 210	−0.5	99.5	1.0	100.5	75.0	25.4
	2004	173 715	−0.5	99.5	1.0	100.5	75.3	25.2
Mexico [2] Mexique [2]	2001	5 809 688	−2.2	97.8	1.5	99.3	81.4	18.0
	2002	6 263 137	−1.9	98.1	1.6	99.7	81.2	18.5
	2003	6 891 434	−1.9	98.1	2.2	100.2	81.1	19.2
Mongolia Mongolie	1996	659 698	...	98.8	...	...	...	...
	1997	846 344	...	95.0	...	...	...	...
	1998	833 727	...	99.3	...	...	...	...
Morocco Maroc	2001	383 185	−2.2[1]	0.0	10.5	108.3	80.6	27.6
	2002	397 782	−2.0[1]	0.0	9.2	107.4	80.6	26.8
	2003	418 655	−1.6[1]	0.0	9.4	107.8	80.3	27.5
Mozambique [2] Mozambique [2]	2000	58 354 600	0.8	100.8	0.1	100.9	91.5	9.4
	2001	76 544 900	−2.0	98.0	2.0	100.0	82.8	17.2[12]
	2002	96 345 300	−14.7	85.3	15.1	100.4	76.5	23.9[12]
Myanmar [+] Myanmar [+]	1996	791 980	0.0[1]	100.0	...	100.0	88.5	11.4
	1997	1 109 554	0.0[1]	100.0	...	100.0	88.1	11.9
	1998	1 559 996	0.0[1]	100.0	...	100.0	89.4	10.6
Namibia [2] Namibie [2]	2001	27 681	0.0	100.0	10.8	110.8	86.5	24.2
	2002	31 580	1.2	101.1	...	111.0	79.8	31.1
	2003	32 309	7.7	107.7	...	119.2	84.6	34.6
Nepal [+] Népal[+]	2001	410 287	3.9[1]	103.9	0.4[13]	104.3	85.1	18.8
	2002	421 333	4.4[1]	104.4	0.4[13]	104.8	88.2	16.2
	2003	446 177	5.1[1]	105.1	0.5[13]	105.6	88.7	16.4
Netherlands [2] Pays–Bas [2]	2002	445 160	−1.4	98.6	−1.0	97.6	74.3	23.4
	2003	454 276	−1.4	98.6	−1.0	97.6	74.8	22.9
	2004	466 310	−1.3	98.7	−1.2	97.4	74.1	23.3
Netherlands Antilles [2] Antilles néerlandaises [2]	2001	5 162	0.7	100.7	0.3	101.0	75.3	25.6
	2002	5 198	0.0	100.0	3.8	103.9	76.3	27.6
	2003	5 368	−0.2	99.8	3.9	103.6	77.2	26.5
New Zealand [+][2] Nouvelle–Zélande [+][2]	2001	123 532	−5.4	94.6	0.3	94.9	76.2	18.7
	2002	129 792	−5.1	94.9	0.2	95.1	76.8	18.3[8]
	2003	137 809	−4.9	95.1	0.1	95.2	76.8	18.4[8]
Nicaragua [2] Nicaragua [2]	2002	57 099	−5.0[1]	95.0	11.5	106.5	94.2	12.3
	2003	62 458	−4.6[1]	95.4	12.6	107.9	94.9	13.1
	2004	70 271	−4.4[1]	95.6	13.6	109.2	95.4	13.8
Niger Niger	2001	1 299 238	−0.8	99.2	4.1	103.2	95.0	8.2
	2002	1 405 430	−1.2	98.8	2.6	101.4	95.1	6.3
	2003	1 383 484	−1.2	98.8	2.7	101.4	95.0	6.4

Country or area / Pays ou zone	Year / Année	GDP at current prices (Mil.nat. cur.) / PIB aux prix courants (Millions monnaie nat.)	As a percentage of GDP – En pourcentage du PIB					
			Plus: Compensation of employees and property income from/to the rest of the world, net / Plus : Rémuneration des salariés et revenus de la propriété – du et au reste du monde, net	Equals: Gross national income / Égale : Revenu national brut	Plus: Net current transfers from/ to the rest of the world / Plus : Transfers courants du/au reste du monde, net	Equals: Gross national disposable income / Égale : Revenu national disponible brut	Less: Final consumption expenditure / Moins : Dépense de consommation de finale	Equals: Gross savings / Égale : Épargne brut
Nigeria [+]	1992	549 809	−11.7	88.3	2.3	90.6	77.2	13.4
Nigéria [+]	1993	701 473	−10.5	89.5	2.5	92.0	80.6	11.5
	1994	914 334	−7.2	92.8	1.2	94.0	85.5	8.5
Norway [2]	2002	1 519 131	0.3	100.3	−1.2	99.1	67.1	32.0
Norvège [2]	2003	1 561 915	0.6	100.6	−1.3	99.3	68.8	30.4
	2004	1 685 552	0.6	100.6	−1.0	99.5	66.8	32.7
Oman [2]	2001	7 670	−3.6	96.4	−7.5	88.9	66.2	22.7
Oman [2]	2002	7 807	−3.9	96.1	−7.7	88.4	67.2	21.3
	2003	8 343	−4.2	*95.8	−7.5	88.3	66.0	22.3
Pakistan [+]	2002	4 401 699	...	100.5[14]	...	...	83.3	...
Pakistan [+]	2003	4 821 303	...	103.1[14]	...	...	82.7	...
	2004	5 458 063	...	102.2[14]	...	...	82.1	...
Panama [2]	2001	11 808	−7.7	92.3	1.4	93.6	75.6	18.1[15]
Panama [2]	2002	12 272	−4.6	95.4	1.4	96.8	79.1	17.7[15]
	2003	12 862	−8.1	91.9	1.4	93.2	74.9	18.3[15]
Papua New Guinea [2]	2000	10 750	−3.6	90.5[16]	2.3	92.8	76.3	16.5
Papouasie–Nouvelle–Guinée [2]	2001	11 758	−3.5	89.7[16]	0.4	90.1	87.4	2.7
	2002	13 375	−3.0	90.2[16]	0.7	90.8	88.3	2.5
Paraguay	1993	11 991 719	...	100.4	...	100.4	88.0	12.4
Paraguay	1994	14 960 131	...	100.5	...	100.5	95.2	5.3
	1995	17 699 000	...	100.9	...	100.9	92.5	8.4
Peru	1996	148 278	...	97.3	...	...	80.6	...
Pérou	1997	172 389	...	97.5	...	...	78.7	...
	1998	183 179	...	97.7	...	...	80.9	...
Philippines	2001	3 631 474	6.8	106.8	0.6	107.4	82.9	24.5
Philippines	2002	3 959 648	6.7	106.7	0.7	107.3	81.0	26.3
	2003	4 299 932	7.4	107.4	0.8	108.2	80.5	27.7
Poland [2]	2002	781 112	−1.0	99.0	1.7	100.7	84.5	16.2
Pologne [2]	2003	814 922	−1.7	98.3	2.0	100.3	83.6	16.7
	2004	883 656	...	...	...	...	81.8	...
Portugal [2]	2002	128 458	−1.5	98.5	2.0	100.4	82.4	18.0
Portugal [2]	2003	130 511	−1.3	98.7	1.7	100.3	83.2	17.1
	2004	135 079	−2.0	98.0	1.4	99.5	84.2	15.3
Puerto Rico [+]	2000	69 208	−36.8	63.2	12.5	75.7	65.5	3.6[17]
Porto Rico [+]	2001	71 306	−37.5	62.5	13.4	75.9	65.7	4.4[17]
	2002	74 362	−36.9	63.1	13.4	76.5	66.1	3.0[17]
Republic of Moldova [2]	2000	16 020	5.0	105.0	11.2	116.2	103.0	13.1
République de Moldova [2]	2001	19 052	7.5	107.5	10.5	118.0	101.1	16.9
	2002	22 556	10.0	110.0	9.3	119.3	103.3	16.0
Réunion	1990	28 374	−2.5[1]	97.5	44.3	141.7	108.1	33.6
Réunion	1991	31 339[8]	0.1[1]	100.7	42.7	143.4	103.5	39.9
	1992	33 787	−1.5[1]	98.4	43.6	142.1	104.5	37.6

Country or area / Pays ou zone	Year / Année	GDP at current prices (Mil.nat. cur.) / PIB aux prix courants (Millions monnaie nat.)	Plus: Compensation of employees and property income from/to the rest of the world, net / Plus : Rémuneration des salariés et revenus de la propriété – du et au reste du monde, net	Equals: Gross national income / Égale : Revenu national brut	Plus: Net current transfers from/to the rest of the world / Plus : Transfers courants du/au reste du monde, net	Equals: Gross national disposable income / Égale : Revenu national disponible brut	Less: Final consumption expenditure / Moins : Dépense de consommation de finale	Equals: Gross savings / Égale : Épargne brut
Romania [2] Roumanie [2]	2002	1 514 750 900	−1.0	99.0	5.6	104.6	84.0	20.6
	2003	*1 903 353 900	...	...	...	...	84.9	...
	2004	*2 387 914 300	...	...	...	...	86.3	...
Russian Federation [2] Fédération de Russie [2]	2002	10 817 536 [18]	−1.9	98.1	−0.1	98.0	68.9	29.1
	2003	13 201 074 [18]	−3.0	97.0	−0.1	96.9	68.2	28.6
	2004	16 778 775 [18]	−2.2	97.8	−0.1	97.7	64.8	32.8 [8]
Rwanda Rwanda	1987	171 430	−1.6	98.4	2.5	100.9	93.5	7.4
	1988	177 920	−2.0	98.0	2.9	100.9	93.6	7.3
	1989	190 220	−1.2	98.8	2.4	101.3	95.4	5.9
Saint Kitts and Nevis Saint–Kitts–et–Nevis	2001	932	...	90.0	4.7 [8]	94.7	71.9	22.7
	2002	958	...	89.3	4.6	93.9	81.3	12.7
	2003	997	...	88.1	4.9	93.0	78.9	14.2
Saint Lucia Sainte–Lucie	2001	1 506	−7.5	109.7	2.5	112.2	98.0	14.1
	2002	1 524	−7.5	112.3	2.3	114.6	99.7	14.9
	2003	1 566	−8.3	110.9	2.3	113.2	109.4	3.8
St. Vincent–Grenadines St. Vincent–Grenadines	2001	933	−4.8 [8]	95.2	3.6	98.8	79.4	19.4
	2002	974	−5.3 [8]	95.1	3.4	98.5	80.0	18.5
	2003	1 016	−6.9 [8]	93.5	3.4	96.9	83.7	13.3
San Marino Saint–Marin	1997	1 279 857	...	92.2	...	76.4	...	...
	1998	1 400 841	...	90.9	...	74.2	...	...
	1999	1 551 010	...	89.3	...	73.7	...	...
Saudi Arabia [+] Arabie saoudite [+]	2000	706 657	0.5	100.5	−11.6	88.8	62.5	26.3
	2001	686 296	1.0	101.0	−11.7	89.3	65.3	24.0
	2002	*707 067	0.7	100.7	−11.8	88.9	62.9	26.0
Senegal Sénégal	1996	2 380 000	...	108.1	...	...	91.0	...
	1997	2 554 300	...	104.1	...	...	88.8	...
	1998	2 746 000	...	104.5	...	...	87.3	...
Seychelles Seychelles	1998	3 201	...	97.2	...	...	81.2	...
	1999	3 330	...	97.3	...	...	73.1	...
	2000	3 424	...	96.3	...	...	66.4	...
Sierra Leone [+] Sierra Leone [+]	1988	43 947	−0.9 [1]	100.9 [8]	0.6	101.5	94.3	7.3
	1989	82 837	−0.8 [1]	100.8 [8]	0.5	101.3	91.3	10.0
	1990	150 175	−5.0 [1]	95.0	0.7	95.7	88.4	7.3
Singapore Singapour	2002	158 388	−2.4	97.6	−1.3	96.3	56.2	40.5
	2003	160 924	−1.6	98.4	−1.2	97.2	55.1	44.0
	2004	180 554	−2.5	97.5	−1.1	96.4	52.9	44.4
Slovakia [2] Slovaquie [2]	2002	1 098 658	−0.1	99.9	0.0	99.8	77.8	22.1
	2003	1 201 196	−0.1	99.9	1.1	101.0	76.4	24.6 [12]
	2004	1 325 486	−1.0	99.0	0.3	99.3	76.0	23.3
Slovenia [2] Slovénie [2]	1992	1 017 965	−0.7 [1]	...	...	...	...	...
	1993	1 435 095	−0.4	...	...	...	...	...
Solomon Islands Iles Salomon	1984	222	−3.2 [1]	94.2	...	100.8	78.2	22.6
	1985	237	−2.3 [1]	95.0	...	101.0	91.6	9.4
	1986	253	−2.0 [1]	92.6	...	115.7	94.8	20.9

Country or area Pays ou zone	Year Année	GDP at current prices (Mil.nat. cur.) PIB aux prix courants (Millions monnaie nat.)	As a percentage of GDP – En pourcentage du PIB					
			Plus: Compensation of employees and property income from/to the rest of the world, net Plus : Rémuneration des salariés et revenus de la propriété – du et au reste du monde, net	Equals: Gross national income Égale : Revenu national brut	Plus: Net current transfers from/ to the rest of the world Plus : Transfers courants du/au reste du monde, net	Equals: Gross national disposable income Égale : Revenu national disponible brut	Less: Final consumption expenditure Moins : Dépense de consommation de finale	Equals: Gross savings Égale : Épargne brut
Somalia Somalie	1985	87 290	...	97.8	10.1	107.9	101.1	6.8
	1986	118 781	...	96.3	14.2	110.5	98.8	11.7
	1987	169 608	...	96.8	21.3	118.0	99.9	18.2
South Africa [2] Afrique du Sud [2]	2001	1 020 007	−3.2	96.8	−0.6	96.2	81.0	15.3
	2002	1 164 945	−2.5	97.5	−0.5	97.0	80.2	16.7
	2003	1 251 468	−2.0	98.0	−0.5	97.5	81.9	16.3
Spain [2] Espagne [2]	2002	729 004	−1.6	98.4	0.0	98.4	75.4	23.0
	2003	780 557	−1.6	98.4	−0.4	98.0	74.6	23.4
	2004	837 557	−1.2	98.8	−0.4	98.5	75.3	23.1
Sri Lanka [2] Sri Lanka [2]	2001	1 396 314	−1.7	98.3	6.3	104.6	83.1	21.1
	2002	1 570 216	−1.5	98.5	6.7	105.1	83.7	21.0
	2003	1 748 774	−1.1	98.9	6.7	105.6	83.7	21.1
Sudan [+] Soudan [+]	1991	421 819	...	85.5	...	104.0	86.0	18.0
	1992	948 448	...	99.7	...	102.2	88.2	14.0
	1993	1 881 289	...	99.8	...	100.6	88.3	12.3
Suriname Suriname	2000	1 032 979	−6.1	93.9	−0.3	93.6	...	...
	2001	1 436 483	−16.2	83.8	−0.1	83.7	...	...
	2002	1 926 645	−5.3	94.7	−1.0	93.7	...	...
Swaziland [2] Swaziland [2]	2001	10 846	...	104.2	2.7	106.9	86.7	20.2
	2002	12 560	...	100.5	6.1	106.5	88.6	17.9
	2003	14 401	...	103.5	6.2	109.6	91.0	18.6
Sweden [2] Suède [2]	2002	2 352 938	−0.3	99.7	−1.0	98.7	76.6	22.1
	2003	2 438 447	0.0	100.0	−0.9	99.1	77.1	22.1
	2004	2 545 750	1.2	101.2	−1.4	99.8	75.8	23.9
Switzerland [2] Suisse [2]	2001	422 485	5.6	105.6	−1.6	104.0	72.0	31.8
	2002	431 064	3.6	103.6	−2.3	101.4	72.2	29.0
	2003	433 366	7.9	107.9	...	...	72.7	...
Syrian Arab Republic Rép. arabe syrienne	2001	954 137	...	91.4	0.8	92.2	72.7	19.5
	2002	1 014 542	...	91.4	0.7	92.2	71.8	20.4
	2003	1 052 921	...	91.8	1.2	92.9	73.9	19.0
Thailand Thaïlande	2000	4 923 263	−1.6	98.4	0.5	98.9	67.3	31.6
	2001	5 133 836	−1.7	98.3	0.5	98.8	68.3	30.5
	2002	5 451 854	−1.6	98.4	0.5	98.8	67.7	31.1
TFYR of Macedonia [2] L'ex–R.y. Macédoine [2]	1991	935	...	99.4	−0.4	99.0	85.5	13.5
	1992	12 006	...	96.9	−0.4	96.6	83.8	12.8
	1993	58 145	...	97.7	0.7	98.4	88.9	9.5
Togo Togo	1984	304 800	...	...	...	...	80.0	...
	1985	332 500	...	...	...	...	80.2	...
	1986	363 600	...	...	...	...	83.4	...
Tonga [+] Tonga [+]	1981	54	6.3	106.3	23.7	130.0 [8]	136.9	15.1 [8]
	1982	64	6.9	106.9	35.8	142.7 [8]	137.9	29.0 [8]
	1983	73	4.4	104.4	27.1	130.5 [8]	140.0	10.2 [8]

Country or area Pays ou zone	Year Année	GDP at current prices (Mil.nat. cur.) PIB aux prix courants (Millions monnaie nat.)	As a percentage of GDP – En pourcentage du PIB					
			Plus: Compensation of employees and property income from/to the rest of the world, net Plus : Rémuneration des salariés et revenus de la propriété – du et au reste du monde, net	Equals: Gross national income Égale : Revenu national brut	Plus: Net current transfers from/ to the rest of the world Plus : Transfers courants du/au reste du monde, net	Equals: Gross national disposable income Égale : Revenu national disponible brut	Less: Final consumption expenditure Moins : Dépense de consommation de finale	Equals: Gross savings Égale : Épargne brut
Trinidad and Tobago [2] Trinité–et–Tobago [2]	2001	55 007	−6.1[1]	93.9	0.4	94.3	69.8	24.5
	2002	55 366	−5.4[1]	94.6	0.6	95.2	74.8	20.4
	2003	66 168	−4.2[1]	95.8	0.6	96.4	66.7	29.7
Tunisia [2] Tunisie [2]	2000	26 651	−4.7	95.3	4.1[8]	99.4	76.3	23.1
	2001	28 729	−4.6	95.4	4.8[8]	100.3	76.6	23.6
	2002	29 879	−4.5	95.5	5.3[8]	100.7	78.8	21.9
Turkey Turquie	2002	277 574	−0.9	99.1	0.0	99.1	80.4	18.7
	2003	359 763	−0.9	99.1	0.0	99.1	80.2	18.9
	2004	430 511	−0.4	99.6	...	...	79.3	...
Ukraine [2] Ukraine [2]	2000	170 070[19]	−3.0	97.0	2.9	99.9	75.3	24.6
	2001	204 190[19]	−1.8	98.2	3.9	102.2	76.6	25.6
	2002	225 810[19]	−1.4	98.6	4.6	103.2	75.4	27.7
United Arab Emirates Emirats arabes unis	1988	87 106	0.3	100.3	−1.2	99.1	65.8	33.3
	1989	100 976	0.4	100.4	−0.7	99.7	61.7	38.0
	1990	124 008	−1.0	99.0	−8.9	90.1	54.9	35.1
United Kingdom [2] Royaume–Uni [2]	2002	1 044 145	1.9	101.9	−0.6	101.3	86.3	15.0
	2003	1 101 144	1.9	101.9	−0.7	101.2	86.4	14.8
	2004	1 160 339	2.0	102.0	−0.8	101.1	86.3	14.8
United Rep. of Tanzania [2] Rép.–Unie de Tanzanie [2]	2000	7 277 800	−0.9[1]	99.0[8]	4.6	101.1	90.0	11.0
	2001	8 284 690	−0.9[1]	99.0[8]	4.2	100.9	89.7	11.2
	2002	9 374 560	−0.9[1]	98.9[8]	4.3	100.3	86.4	13.9
United States [2] Etats–Unis [2]	2001	10 075 900	0.4	101.3	−0.5	100.9	84.8	16.1
	2002	10 434 800	0.3	100.4	−0.6	99.8	86.0	13.8
	2003	10 951 300	0.5	100.3	−0.6	99.7	86.5	13.1
Uruguay Uruguay	2002	260 967	−1.0[1]	99.0	0.7	99.7	86.5	13.2
	2003	315 681	−4.5[1]	95.5	0.7	96.2	85.9	10.3
	2004	379 317	−4.2[1]	95.8	0.7	96.5	85.0	11.5
Vanuatu Vanuatu	1996	28 227	...	91.1	...	...	...	...
	1997	29 477	...	91.7	...	...	...	...
	1998	29 545	...	93.5	...	...	...	...
Venezuela (Bolivarian Rep. of) [2] Venezuela (Rép. bolivar. du) [2]	2000	79 655 700	−1.2	98.8	−0.1	98.7	64.2	34.5
	2001	88 945 600	−1.7	98.3	−0.1	98.2	69.1	29.1
	2002	107 840 200	−3.0	97.0	−0.2	96.9	66.5	30.3
Yemen [2] Yémen [2]	1998	849 321	−5.6	94.4	19.1	113.5	82.5	31.0
	1999	1 132 619	−9.3	90.7	17.2	107.9	81.8	24.7[8]
	2000	1 379 812	−13.4	86.6	17.6	104.1	71.8	37.3[8]
Zambia Zambie	1986	12 963	−18.1	81.9	−1.2	80.7	77.4	3.3
	1987	19 778	−11.4[1]	88.6	0.5	89.1	82.0	7.1
	1988	27 725	−14.2[1]	85.8	1.0	86.9	79.8	7.1
Zimbabwe Zimbabwe	2001	709 214	...	98.3	...	...	...	...
	2002	1 698 180	...	99.5	...	...	...	...
	2003	5 518 757	...	99.9	...	...	...	...

Source

United Nations Statistics Division, New York, national accounts database.

Notes

+   The national accounts data generally relate to the fiscal year used in each country, unless indicated otherwise. Countries whose reference periods coincide with the calendar year ending 31 December are not listed below.

Year beginning 21 March: Afghanistan, Iran (Islamic Republic).

Year beginning 1 April: Bermuda, India, Myanmar, New Zealand, Nigeria (beginning 1982).

Year beginning 1 July: Australia, Bangladesh, Cameroon, Egypt, Gambia, Pakistan, Puerto Rico, Saudi Arabia, Sierra Leone, Sudan.

Year ending 30 June: Botswana, Swaziland, Tonga.

Year ending 7 July: Ethiopia.

Year ending 15 July: Nepal.

Year ending 30 September: Haiti.

[1]   Property income – from and to the rest of the world, net.
[2]   The concepts and definitions of the System of National Accounts 1993 (1993 SNA) have been adopted.
[3]   Including acquisitions less disposals of valuables.
[4]   Excludes other taxes on production.
[5]   Preliminary data.
[6]   Derived from available data.
[7]   Beginning 2000, re–denomination of Belarussian roubles at 1 to 1000.
[8]   Discrepancy between components and total.
[9]   Includes social contributions.
[10] For statistical purposes, the data for China do not include those for the Hong Kong Special Administrative Region (Hong Kong SAR), Macao Special Administrative Region (Macao SAR) and Taiwan Province of China.
[11] Compensation of employees – from and to the rest of the world, net.
[12] Account does not balance.
[13] Excludes official grants.
[14] Discrepancy between net value, consumption of fixed capital and gross value.
[15] Includes capital transfers.
[16] Net national income.
[17] Discrepancy between Gross Saving, Final Consumption and Gross National Disposable Income.
[18] Re–denomination of Russian rubles at 1 to 1000.
[19] Data in karbovanets.
[20] Beginning 1981, estimates relate to calendar year.

Source

Organisation des Nations Unies, Division de statistique, New York, la base de données sur les comptes nationaux.

Notes

+   Sauf indication contraire, les données sur les comptes nationaux concernent généralement l'exercice budgétaire utilisé dans chaque pays. Les pays ou territoires dont la période de référence coïncide avec l'année civile se terminant le 31 décembre ne sont pas répertoriés ci–dessous.

Exercice commençant le 21 mars: Afghanistan, Iran (République islamique d').

Exercice commençant le 1er avril: Bermudes, Inde, Myanmar, Nigéria (à partir de 1982), Nouvelle–Zélande.

Exercice commençant le 1er juillet: Arabie saoudite, Australie, Bangladesh, Cameroun, Égypte, Gambie, Pakistan, Porto Rico, Sierra Leone, Soudan.

Exercice se terminant le 30 juin: Botswana, Swaziland, Tonga.

Exercice se terminant le 7 juillet: Éthiopie.

Exercice se terminant le 15 juillet: Népal.

Exercice se terminant le 30 septembre: Haïti.

[1]   Revenus de la propriété – du et au reste du monde, net.
[2]   Les concepts et définitions du Système de comptabilité nationale de 1993 (SCN de 1993) ont été adoptés.
[3]   Y compris les acquisitions moins cessions d'objets de valeur.
[4]   À l'exclusion des autres taxes sur la production.
[5]   Données préliminaires.
[6]   Calculés à partir des données disponibles.
[7]   A partir de 2000, instauration du nouveau rouble bélarussien par division par 1000 du rouble bélarussien ancien.
[8]   Ecart entre les rubriques et le total.
[9]   Y compris les contributions sociales.
[10] Pour la présentation des statistiques, les données pour Chine ne comprennent pas la Région Administrative Spéciale de Hong Kong (Hong Kong RAS), la Région Administrative Spéciale de Macao (Macao RAS) et la province de Taiwan.
[11] Rémunération des salariés – du et au reste du monde, net.
[12] Le compte n'est pas en équilibre.
[13] Non compris les dons officiels.
[14] Différence entre épargne brute, consommation finale et revenu national disponible.
[15] Y compris les transferts de capitaux.
[16] Revenu national net.
[17] Différence entre épargne brute, consommation finale et revenu national disponible.
[18] Instauration du nouveau rouble par division par 1000 du rouble ancien.
[19] Les données sont exprimées en karbovanets.
[20] A partir de 1981, les estimations se réfèrent à l'année civile.

21

Government final consumption expenditure by function at current prices
Percentage distribution by divisions of Classification of the Functions of Government (COFOG)

Dépenses de consommation finale des administrations publiques, par fonction, aux prix courants
Répartition en pourcentage par divisions de la Classification des fonctions des administrations publiques (COFOG)

Country or area Pays ou zone	Year Année	Total (M.nat.curr.) Totale (M.monn.nat.)	Div. 01 (%)	Div. 02 (%)	Div. 03 (%)	Div. 04 (%)	Div. 05 (%)	Div. 06 (%)	Div. 07 (%)	Div. 08 (%)	Div. 09 (%)	Div. 10 (%)
						Divisions of the Classification of the Functions of Government (COFOG) ŧ						
						Divisions de la Classification des fonctions des administrations publiques (COFOG) ŧ						
Anguilla	1999	64	42.2	...	9.4	7.8	...	3.1	15.6	...	17.2	1.6
Anguilla	2000	58	41.4	...	10.3	8.6	...	1.7	15.5	...	19.0	3.4
	2001	62	38.7	...	11.3	8.1	...	1.6	16.1	...	19.4	3.2
Antigua and Barbuda	1984	67[1]	22.8	2.2	11.4	22.5	...	6.7	9.7	0.5	15.8	8.4
Antigua-et-Barbuda	1985	81[1]	25.1	2.2	11.4	20.9	...	7.7	11.5	0.6	14.0	6.6
	1986	108[1]	26.1	2.3	11.6	21.2	...	6.4	10.0	0.5	14.7	7.2
Argentina	1996	43 617	10.8	4.5	3.2	6.0	0.2	2.1	8.4	...	5.9[2]	43.2
Argentine	1997	45 156	9.4	4.4	3.1	5.9	0.2	2.1	7.1	...	6.0[2]	42.0
	1998	46 463	9.5	4.2	3.0	5.8	0.2	2.0	6.6	...	6.0[2]	41.0
Armenia [3]	2001	84 669[4]	85.6[5]	...	...	2.9	...	3.8	...	2.0	...	0.8
Arménie [3]	2002	84 958[4]	82.8[5]	...	...	3.5	...	3.6	...	3.2	...	1.0
	2003	101 859[4]	85.3[5]	...	...	3.7	...	4.2	...	3.2	...	1.1
Australia [+3]	2000	110 021	10.3	9.4	7.9	8.1	0.0	1.3	29.6	3.4	19.8	10.1
Australie [+3]	2001	116 297	8.3	9.5	8.0	9.4	0.1	1.4	30.4	3.1	20.0	9.8
	2002	125 330	6.9	9.9	8.3	9.2	0.3	1.5	30.5	2.9	20.2	10.4
Austria [3]	2001	38 842	15.2	5.0	7.5	9.8	1.0	0.5	26.6	2.5	28.0	3.8
Autriche [3]	2002	39 622	14.8	4.8	7.5	9.8	1.0	0.5	27.2	2.6	28.0	3.8
	2003	41 085	14.6	4.9	7.6	10.0	1.1	0.5	27.4	2.5	27.8	3.5
Azerbaijan [3]	2001	3 627 000	20.6	14.7	2.2[6]	1.7[7]	...	0.0	18.4[8]	3.4	37.9	1.0
Azerbaïdjan [3]	2002	3 759 900	26.7	19.0	2.5[6]	2.0[7]	...	0.0	13.3[8]	2.5	29.1	4.8
	2003	4 426 700	26.7	19.0	2.5[6]	2.0[7]	...	0.1	13.3[8]	2.5	29.1	4.8
Bahamas [3]	1993	408	17.4	4.2	14.5	15.9	...	...	18.6	1.5[9]	24.0	4.2
Bahamas [3]	1994	511	20.2	3.7	13.3	17.2	...	...	18.0	1.6[9]	23.1	3.5
	1995	484	18.4	3.9	14.5	17.6	...	...	18.0	1.9[9]	22.1	3.9
Bangladesh [+3]	1998	88 546[10]	15.3	24.3	13.0	1.1	...	2.5	10.3	0.4	17.1	1.0
Bangladesh [+3]	1999	92 450[10]	12.9	24.0	13.4	1.1	...	3.2	12.3	0.5	16.6	1.4
	2000	105 351[10]	12.9	22.0	12.9	1.2	...	3.0	12.0	0.6	16.5	1.4
Belarus [3]	2001	1 333 900	71.3	...	0.4	24.3	...	...	...	4.0	...	...
Bélarus [3]	2002	1 948 700	72.3	...	0.6	22.3	...	...	...	4.8	...	...
	2003	2 918 400	74.1	...	0.6	20.5	...	...	...	4.8	...	...
Belgium [3]	2001	55 090	12.3	5.7	6.8	9.2	1.1	0.2	29.1	1.8	27.5	6.3
Belgique [3]	2002	58 244	12.2	5.3	7.1	9.1	1.0	0.2	28.4	2.6	27.3	6.7
	2003	61 336	12.0	5.1	7.0	8.9	1.0	0.2	29.6	2.6	26.9	6.8
Belize	1989	229	12.7	4.3	5.3	40.3	...	6.3	7.9	1.4	16.5	0.7
Belize	1990	279	12.7	3.4	7.9	37.5	...	6.7	6.8	2.6	15.3	3.3
	1991	321	16.6	3.4	7.0	32.6	...	6.1	6.6	2.4	16.8	4.0
Bermuda [+]	1985	138	36.9	2.0	...	27.1	...	6.0	3.7	2.9	21.3	3.6
Bermudes [+]	1986	141	34.4	2.1	...	28.3	...	6.4	3.9	2.9	22.2	3.8
	1987	157	34.0	2.3	...	30.1	...	6.2	3.8	2.9	21.5	3.8
Bolivia	1991	2 310	74.7	0.0	...	4.2	...	0.1	0.0	0.1	7.7	1.9
Bolivie	1992	2 833	76.2	...	...	3.0	...	0.1	0.0	0.2	8.1	1.9
	1993	3 270	75.9	...	...	2.5	...	0.2	0.0	0.2	9.0	2.4
Botswana [+3]	2000	7 525	44.0[11]	...	...	11.2	...	6.2	6.5	2.4	26.4	3.4
Botswana [+3]	2001	8 742	43.7[11]	...	...	11.0	...	5.2	6.8	2.4	27.4	3.5
	2002	10 553	45.3[11]	...	...	10.8	...	4.3	6.3	2.5	27.4	3.4
Brazil [3]	2001	230 741	73.3	...	...	...	...	...	11.2	...	15.5	...
Brésil [3]	2002	270 965	71.6	...	...	...	...	...	11.8	...	16.6	...
	2003	309 631	70.7	...	...	...	...	...	12.0	...	17.3	...
British Virgin Islands	1985	17[1]	23.3	...	10.8	20.7	...	4.1	14.9	0.8	23.6	1.8
Iles Vierges britanniques	1986	19[1]	21.8	...	11.4	22.1	...	4.4	14.5	0.7	22.7	2.4
	1987	21[1]	23.3	...	11.0	20.2	...	5.5	15.8	0.5	21.1	2.6
Brunei Darussalam	1982	914	22.9	41.4	5.5	5.0	...	0.7	5.0	4.8	14.2	0.2
Brunéi Darussalam	1983	922	24.6	35.3	6.0	5.5	...	0.7	5.7	5.7	15.2	0.2
	1984	2 512	69.3	12.8	2.7	2.5	...	0.4	2.6	2.3	6.5	0.1

Government final consumption expenditure by function at current prices — Percentage distribution by divisions of Classification of the Functions of Government (COFOG) (*continued*)

Dépenses de consommation finale des administrations publiques, par fonction, aux prix courants — Répartition en pourcentage par divisions de la Classification des fonctions des administrations publiques (COFOG) (*suite*)

Country or area Pays ou zone	Year Année	Total (M.nat.curr.) Totale (M.monn.nat.)	Div. 01 (%)	Div. 02 (%)	Div. 03 (%)	Div. 04 (%)	Div. 05 (%)	Div. 06 (%)	Div. 07 (%)	Div. 08 (%)	Div. 09 (%)	Div. 10 (%)
Burkina Faso	1982	38 198[1]	8.2	28.3	8.7	9.9	...	0.3	10.0	2.4	16.6	...
Burkina Faso	1983	38 864[1]	8.1	28.7	9.1	10.5	...	0.4	10.5	2.5	18.3	...
	1984	38 760[1]	7.3	30.4	8.7	10.8	...	0.2	10.3	2.5	19.0	...
Cameroon +	1986	476 700	30.6	12.0	...	10.6	...	6.0	5.7	2.1	19.1	0.7
Cameroun +	1987	391 000	28.3	14.7	...	7.3	...	5.0	6.1	2.3	21.6	0.8
	1988	378 400	35.5	12.4	...	6.2	...	4.9	6.0	2.2	21.5	0.9
Cayman Islands	1989	74[12]	31.1	...	14.9	20.3	...	1.4	13.5	...	13.5	4.1
Iles Caïmanes	1990	94[12]	26.6	...	14.9	19.1	...	1.1	16.0	...	14.9	4.3
	1991	103[12]	27.2	...	14.6	20.4	...	1.9	14.6	...	14.6	5.8
Chad	1996	42 080[13]	1.5[14]	24.6	4.6[15]	7.2[16]	5.3[17]	1.1[18]	5.7[19]	...	22.8	27.0[20]
Tchad	1997	40 078[13]	1.0[14]	26.6	9.5[15]	6.6[16]	5.2[17]	1.1[18]	6.9[19]	...	23.6	20.7[20]
	2001	60 157[13]	...	20.2	8.4[15]	5.9[16]	5.2[17]	1.0[18]	6.3[19]	...	25.0	28.0[20]
China, Macao SAR [3]	2000	5 901	17.9	...	28.9	10.7	0.1	0.8	17.0	5.3	10.2	9.1
Chine, Macao RAS [3]	2001	5 969	17.0	...	29.5	9.8	0.2	0.8	16.2	6.6	10.8	9.2
	2002	6 189	16.9	...	29.4	11.6	0.1	0.7	16.0	4.2	12.2	8.9
Colombia	1992	3 965 104	29.5	10.8	...	16.6	...	0.6	7.7	0.8	24.8	8.9
Colombie	1993	5 108 076	28.5	10.2	...	16.2	...	0.6	11.0	0.9	24.0	8.2
	1994	7 652 736	36.2	9.8	...	8.5	...	0.4	14.3	0.9	21.0	8.6
Cook Islands [21]	2001	75	21.3	...	5.3	22.7	...	21.3	13.3	1.3	12.0	...
Iles Cook [21]	2002	79	19.0	...	5.1	26.6	...	19.0	11.4	1.3	13.9	...
	2003	88	18.2	...	4.5	31.8	...	17.0	11.4	1.1	13.6	...
Costa Rica [3]	2000	652 654	34.3	...	...	...	...	...	32.8	...	32.8	...
Costa Rica [3]	2001	772 575	34.1	...	...	...	...	...	33.4	...	32.5	...
	2002	900 615	34.5	...	...	...	...	...	32.9	...	32.6	...
Côte d'Ivoire	1996	983 370	73.5	...	...	...	...	...	6.2	...	20.3	...
Côte d'Ivoire	1997	1 029 358	69.3	...	...	...	...	...	19.7	...	11.0	...
	1998	1 018 653	68.3	...	...	...	...	...	19.9	...	11.8	...
Croatia [3]	1996	30 973[10]	6.2	25.1	12.0	15.0	...	8.4	0.5	1.3	11.6	14.2
Croatie [3]	1997	34 395[10]	6.3	20.3	12.1	15.7	...	6.0	0.5	1.6	11.8	18.8
	1998	41 390[10]	8.2	17.8	10.3	15.6	...	6.3	2.0	1.4	11.3	19.4
Cyprus	1992	591	10.3	32.3	8.7	7.0	...	3.7	9.5	0.5	16.3	11.6
Chypre	1993	553	13.0	16.3	10.2	9.1	...	4.1	11.7	0.8	19.7	15.0
	1994	608	11.8	16.2	9.4	9.4	...	4.3	11.6	0.7	20.4	16.1
Czech Republic [3]	2002	555 198	12.0	7.0	9.4	10.4	6.5	1.1	26.8	2.8	19.5	4.5
République tchèque [3]	2003	612 645	12.7	7.7	10.1	12.2	5.3	1.0	25.4	2.7	19.1	3.7
Denmark [3]	2002	358 509	7.7	5.9	3.4	6.8	...	1.1	20.3	4.6	23.0	27.4
Danemark [3]	2003	371 839	7.5	5.9	3.4	6.9	...	1.1	20.6	4.4	23.1	27.1
	2004	385 626	7.5	5.8	3.4	6.4	...	1.1	21.0	4.4	23.3	27.0
Dominican Republic [3]	1994	8 265	66.3	...	2.7	...	...	...	12.8	...	18.1	...
Rép. dominicaine [3]	1995	9 115	61.2	...	2.7	...	...	...	12.6	...	23.4	...
	1996	10 843	61.1	...	2.3	...	...	...	12.5	...	24.1	...
Ecuador	1990	777 131[10,22]	13.0	14.5	7.0	13.9	...	4.4	4.8	0.2	27.5	6.1
Equateur	1991	1 009 000[10,22]	13.0	15.0	7.1	14.9	...	5.0	4.6	0.3	27.8	6.2
	1992	1 498 000[10,22]	12.8	15.9	7.3	16.1	...	4.3	3.9	0.2	26.8	7.8
Estonia [3]	1994	6 790	12.9	4.3	12.5	8.9	...	5.7	16.5	4.8	29.2	4.3
Estonie [3]	1995	10 350	11.2	4.5	11.2	11.4	...	5.2	17.7	5.8	27.8	3.9
	1996	12 632	11.0	4.6	11.7	11.0	...	4.2	17.3	5.6	27.8	4.1
Fiji	2000	561	18.9	12.2	9.3	16.4	...	1.0	14.7	...	27.1	0.4
Fidji	2001	566	20.4	12.0	10.0	19.4	...	1.0	12.8	...	23.9	0.5
	2002	572	16.1	9.8	10.0	18.3	...	1.3	14.3	...	29.4	0.6
Finland [3]	2001	28 393	9.9	5.7	5.5	10.2	0.9	0.3	24.6	3.3	23.1	16.4
Finlande [3]	2002	30 299	9.4	5.9	5.5	10.6	1.0	0.3	25.0	3.3	22.5	16.7
	2003	31 692	9.0	6.3	5.4	10.8	1.0	0.3	25.4	3.2	22.2	16.4
France [3]	2000	329 854	16.3	9.5	3.7	3.6	2.8	3.6	29.0	2.0	20.7	8.6
France [3]	2001	342 781	16.4	9.0	3.8	3.9	2.8	3.5	29.4	2.0	20.5	8.8
	2002	364 318	16.8	8.8	3.9	3.3	2.6	3.5	30.1	2.0	20.0	8.9

21 Government final consumption expenditure by function at current prices— Percentage distribution by divisions of Classification of the Functions of Government (COFOG) (*continued*)

Dépenses de consommation finale des administrations publiques, par fonction, aux prix courants— Répartition en pourcentage par divisions de la Classification des fonctions des administrations publiques (COFOG) (*suite*)

Country or area / Pays ou zone	Year / Année	Total (M.nat.curr.) Totale (M.monn.nat.)	Div. 01 (%)	Div. 02 (%)	Div. 03 (%)	Div. 04 (%)	Div. 05 (%)	Div. 06 (%)	Div. 07 (%)	Div. 08 (%)	Div. 09 (%)	Div. 10 (%)
Gambia [+]	1989	659[1]	23.3	...	...	25.2	...	3.6	6.3	...	10.3[23]	0.1
Gambie [+]	1990	819[1]	22.0	...	...	18.6	...	3.0	6.4	...	12.9[23]	0.1
	1991	804[1]	22.2	...	...	24.1	...	3.8	5.7	...	12.6[23]	0.1
Georgia [3]	#1993	1 213	...	1.9	8.2	30.3	...	...	0.6	0.2	5.7	0.5
Géorgie [3]	1994	119 012	...	5.4	10.1	63.6	...	...	3.2	1.2	4.8	9.0
	#1995	295	...	12.9	45.8	5.8	...	...	6.1	6.4	10.2	12.5
Germany [3]	2001	394 200	11.6	6.6	8.3	2.2	0.4	1.4	32.8	2.4	18.3	16.0
Allemagne [3]	2002	405 430	11.6	6.5	8.3	2.2	0.4	1.3	32.8	2.3	18.0	16.3
	2003	408 540	11.4	6.4	8.3	2.3	0.4	1.3	33.3	2.3	17.9	16.4
Greece [3]	2001	22 034	10.5	22.4	5.0	1.2	1.4	0.9	24.0	1.2	18.0	15.5
Grèce [3]	2002	24 243	10.9	24.5	4.9	1.1	1.4	0.9	21.1	1.2	17.9	15.9
	2003	24 497	10.5	21.1	6.2	1.3	0.1	0.7	19.9	1.3	17.8	21.1
Guinea-Bissau	1986	6 423	44.0	...	...	22.7	...	...	11.8	...	18.4	0.9
Guinée-Bissau	1987	10 776	44.0	...	...	22.7	...	...	11.8	...	18.4	1.2
Honduras	1995	3 495	27.8	9.5	...	...	...	...	20.5	...	39.1	...
Honduras	1996	4 556	26.0	8.2	...	...	...	...	27.6	...	36.7	...
	1997	5 377[10]	31.0	7.3	...	...	...	...	24.9	...	35.2	...
Hungary	1992	780 638	15.0	6.3	7.5	9.7	...	6.6	16.3	4.1	22.2	9.4
Hongrie	1993	1 013 524	15.1	12.8	7.3	8.0	...	6.0	14.4	4.0	20.4	8.7
	1994	1 145 444	17.1	6.2	8.0	9.4	...	6.3	15.7	3.6	21.4	9.3
Iceland [3]	2002	196 978	7.6	...	5.5	8.6	...	3.4	31.1	5.4	21.2	8.4
Islande [3]	2003	211 797	7.6	...	5.5	8.6	...	3.4	31.1	5.4	21.2	8.4
	2004	228 244	7.6	...	5.5	8.6	...	3.4	31.1	5.4	21.2	8.4
India [+]	2000	2 093 410	24.9[24]	29.8	...	15.9	...	1.9	6.5	0.6	16.5	3.3
Inde [+]	2001	2 229 700	23.9[24]	30.6	...	15.9	...	1.6	6.1	1.0	16.6	3.1
	2002	2 257 670	30.8[24]	31.0	...	9.1	...	2.3	6.2	0.7	16.1	3.3
Iran (Islamic Rep. of) [+][3]	2001	96 739 000	7.8	19.7	6.7	11.7	0.7	2.5	7.2	3.0	10.9	21.3
Iran (Rép. islamique d') [+][3]	2002	122 291 839	8.9	19.2	4.4	24.8	0.8	3.3	5.1	2.3	5.8	17.0
	2003	145 671 800	8.3	20.4	3.3	30.4	0.5	4.0	4.4	1.6	4.1	13.8
Ireland [3]	2000	14 392	10.5	4.1	9.0	10.6	...	4.2	36.1	1.9	16.8	6.3
Irlande [3]	2001	17 079	11.0	3.9	8.5	10.5	...	4.1	37.7	1.9	16.2	5.9
	2002	19 542	11.0	3.9	8.5	10.5	...	4.1	37.7	1.9	16.2	5.9
Israel [3]	2001	141 410	7.5	30.0	5.7	3.3	2.3	1.4	17.7	3.2	24.4	4.4
Israël [3]	2002	154 181	7.2	32.1	5.7	3.2	2.4	1.2	17.3	3.1	23.3	4.5
	2003	151 605	7.4	30.7	5.9	3.4	2.4	1.2	18.1	3.1	23.1	4.6
Italy [3]	2001	229 518	12.3	5.4	10.0	6.7	1.4	1.3	32.2	2.1	24.0	4.2
Italie [3]	2002	238 921	12.3	5.7	9.8	6.7	1.4	1.3	32.6	2.2	23.8	...
	2003	253 438	12.9	5.7	10.2	6.8	1.5	1.3	31.7	2.1	23.7	4.1
Japan [3,25]	2001	86 985 900	8.8	4.8	6.5	12.1	6.3	1.4	35.7	0.4	19.8	4.2
Japon [3,25]	2002	87 536 300	9.0	4.8	6.5	12.4	6.4	1.4	35.5	0.4	19.5	4.1
	2003	88 002 000	9.3	4.8	6.4	12.1	6.5	1.4	36.0	0.4	19.1	4.0
Jordan	1993	939	53.6[11]	...	...	...	...	...	10.2	6.4	21.9	1.0
Jordanie	1994	986	59.3[11]	...	...	...	...	...	8.2	6.0	20.4	1.0
	1995	1 111	60.0[11]	...	...	...	...	...	8.3	5.6	21.3	0.9
Kazakhstan [3]	2000	313 985	12.0	6.1	14.7	13.4	...	5.7	16.3	3.9	24.1	3.9
Kazakhstan [3]	2001	436 036	14.2	7.1	15.1	17.3	...	5.8	13.0	3.0	21.6	2.9
	2002	434 999	11.7	8.0	17.8	12.6	...	2.6	15.2	3.5	25.1	3.4
Kenya	2001	8 437	25.4	10.8	...	...	...	...	9.9	...	42.6	11.3
Kenya	2002	9 217	25.4	10.8	...	...	...	...	9.9	...	42.6	11.3
	2003	9 773	27.6	10.4	...	...	...	...	9.9	...	41.4	10.7
Korea, Republic of [3]	2000	70 097 800	14.8	20.8	9.3	12.5	1.5	0.7	14.8	1.2	20.3	4.1
Corée, République de [3]	2001	80 298 200	13.8	18.4	9.3	12.6	1.3	0.8	18.0	1.1	20.6	4.1
	2002	88 512 100	13.9	17.4	9.6	12.7	1.5	0.7	17.1	1.3	21.6	4.2
Kuwait	1997	2 452	...	55.1	...	4.3	...	3.5	10.0	4.0	19.8	3.4
Koweït	1998	2 411	...	52.2	...	4.6	...	3.5	10.4	4.3	21.3	3.7
	1999	2 463	...	51.9	...	4.5	...	3.2	10.2	4.3	22.0	3.8

Government final consumption expenditure by function at current prices — Percentage distribution by divisions of Classification of the Functions of Government (COFOG) (*continued*)

Dépenses de consommation finale des administrations publiques, par fonction, aux prix courants — Répartition en pourcentage par divisions de la Classification des fonctions des administrations publiques (COFOG) (*suite*)

Country or area Pays ou zone	Year Année	Total (M.nat.curr.) Totale (M.monn.nat.)	Divisions of the Classification of the Functions of Government (COFOG) t Divisions de la Classification des fonctions des administrations publiques (COFOG) t									
			Div. 01 (%)	Div. 02 (%)	Div. 03 (%)	Div. 04 (%)	Div. 05 (%)	Div. 06 (%)	Div. 07 (%)	Div. 08 (%)	Div. 09 (%)	Div. 10 (%)
Kyrgyzstan [3] Kirghizistan [3]	2001 2002 2003	12 912 14 033 14 116	39.9 34.4 29.4	7.3 10.5 10.8	2.2 4.1 4.4	5.5 6.2 7.0	0.4 0.5 0.4	1.9 2.1 1.7	12.6 12.6 12.5	2.3 2.0 3.0	20.9 22.1 25.1	6.2 4.8 4.9
Lesotho [3] Lesotho [3]	1999 2000 2001	1 188 1 144 1 176	25.6 27.7 27.4	... ...	19.1 20.2 20.6	4.7 5.5 6.7	... ...	10.7 11.6 11.8	13.1 13.2 14.0	... ...	6.1 8.1 7.7	... ...
Libyan Arab Jamah. Jamah. arabe libyenne	1980	2 351	68.8	...	...	7.7	...	1.2	7.4	0.9	11.5	2.3
Luxembourg [3] Luxembourg [3]	2001 2002 2003	3 729 4 018 4 361	15.3 15.4 16.4	1.4 1.4 1.5	5.3 5.4 5.5	12.2 12.2 11.7	3.9 3.6 3.6	1.7 1.5 1.4	23.4 23.4 22.7	4.4 4.4 4.6	23.8 23.9 24.1	8.7 8.7 8.8
Malaysia Malaisie	2001 2002 2003	42 265 50 015 54 913	15.4 13.9 13.4	17.1 18.5 19.5	7.8 8.7 8.8	11.8 10.5 10.0	... ...	11.4 11.7 12.0	... ...	... ...	31.2 31.1 30.3	5.4[26] 5.7[26] 5.9[26]
Maldives Maldives	1984 1985 1986	103 121 139	30.4 29.9 32.3	15.6 15.0 16.3	... ...	13.9 11.8 5.6	... ...	5.8 8.0 7.8	7.9 7.9 8.3	... ...	14.6 14.5 16.2	6.8 5.6 5.3
Malta Malte	1994 1995 1996	210 235 260	17.6 19.6 18.8	12.4 11.9 12.3	... ...	2.9 2.6 3.1	... ...	12.4 11.9 12.7	24.3 23.4 23.1	... ...	27.6 28.1 27.7	2.4 2.6 2.3
Mauritius [3] Maurice [3]	2001 2002 2003	16 749 18 290 20 390	24.9 24.7 24.1	1.7 1.6 1.4	13.9 14.7 14.6	13.3 12.6 12.4	... ...	5.8 6.5 6.4	17.8 17.2 17.1	1.9 2.0 2.5	18.6 18.4 19.0	2.2 2.4 2.5
Mexico [3] Mexique [3]	2000 2001 2002	612 621 683 377 758 495	13.2 11.7 11.6	... ...	15.4 15.4 16.0	7.6 7.4 7.5	... ...	... ...	21.2 21.6 21.2	5.1 5.2 5.1	35.9 37.1 36.9	1.6 1.6 1.6
Montserrat Montserrat	1983 1984 1985	18 19 20	15.1 19.6 18.7	0.4 0.3 0.3	10.9 10.5 11.3	27.0 27.2 24.5	... ...	0.8 -0.2 0.9	17.4 15.9 15.3	1.4 0.6 1.7	17.7 19.3 22.4	9.2 6.6 4.8
Nepal + Népal +	1986 1987 1988	5 065 5 797 6 895	14.7 16.9 15.2	11.7 13.1 7.5	9.7 8.1 11.0	23.1 34.6 37.0	... ...	2.5 3.2 3.9	8.0 8.7 3.8	6.0 0.8 1.6	23.9 27.5 24.0	0.7 0.5 1.7
Netherlands [3] Pays-Bas [3]	2001 2002 2003	100 919 109 416 115 348	7.8 7.7 7.4	6.6 6.2 6.1	6.0 6.0 6.3	13.7 13.0 12.3	1.2 1.3 1.4	4.6 4.6 4.5	17.5 18.0 18.4	2.7 2.7 2.7	18.1 17.9 18.0	21.8 22.5 22.8
Netherlands Antilles [3] Antilles néerlandaises [3]	2001 2002 2003	1 114 1 088 1 146	13.7 13.8 14.0	-0.2	12.9 13.7 14.7	2.9 2.7 2.7	4.7 4.3 4.3	10.4 8.7 9.2	14.6 15.1 14.8	1.5 1.5 1.5	15.2 15.5 15.0	24.3 24.7 23.9
New Zealand + Nouvelle-Zélande +	1992 1993 1994	12 658 12 692 12 682	22.5 22.3 22.9	8.0 8.2 7.3	9.7 10.2 10.3	5.8 5.6 5.9	... ...	... ...	20.1 19.9 20.1	... ...	26.3 26.3 26.1	7.7 7.4 7.5
Nicaragua [3] Nicaragua [3]	1998 1999 2000	5 218 7 061 8 428	21.0 18.7 20.0	4.8 4.1 4.3	9.4 8.5 8.6	28.7 30.8 33.3	1.4 1.4 1.2	... ...	12.7 14.3 12.2	0.5 0.5 0.4	17.1 15.3 15.4	3.0 4.5 3.3
Norway [3] Norvège [3]	2001 2002 2003	314 770 338 429 356 125	10.4 9.6 8.8	9.0 8.9 8.4	4.2 4.6 4.4	8.3 8.1 7.5	0.7 0.7 0.7	0.3 0.4 0.4	28.7 29.5 30.1	2.8 2.8 2.8	22.4 22.1 22.8	13.1 13.4 14.1
Oman [3] Oman [3]	2000 2001 2002	1 580 1 712 1 800	10.5 10.7 10.8	29.3[27] 33.2[27] 32.6[27]	11.6 11.3 12.0	7.7 6.8 5.9	... ... *	5.4 4.6 4.7	10.1 9.4 9.5	2.8 2.5 2.5	21.4 20.5 20.8	1.2 1.1 1.0
Pakistan + Pakistan +	2002 2003 2004	413 484 466 014 527 448	42.1 34.7 34.8	... ...	6.4 7.4 8.2	20.4 21.3 18.7	... ...	0.6 2.2 1.5	2.9 4.1 4.9	0.3 0.4 0.5	8.0 15.3 16.8	17.7 13.3 13.2
Panama [3] Panama [3]	2001 2002 2003	1 646 1 819 1 845	19.8 24.5 18.3	... ...	15.9 14.4 18.2	6.5 6.2 6.0	0.3 0.3 0.2	0.5 0.5 0.4	7.8 6.4 7.2	0.9 0.9 0.9	25.9 23.7 24.6	22.2 23.2 24.1

Government final consumption expenditure by function at current prices— Percentage distribution by divisions of Classification of the Functions of Government (COFOG) (*continued*)

Dépenses de consommation finale des administrations publiques, par fonction, aux prix courants— Répartition en pourcentage par divisions de la Classification des fonctions des administrations publiques (COFOG) (*suite*)

Country or area Pays ou zone	Year Année	Total (M.nat.curr.) Totale (M.monn.nat.)	Div. 01 (%)	Div. 02 (%)	Div. 03 (%)	Div. 04 (%)	Div. 05 (%)	Div. 06 (%)	Div. 07 (%)	Div. 08 (%)	Div. 09 (%)	Div. 10 (%)
Peru	1986	0.0	56.6	...	...	5.7	...	0.2	9.2	1.3	25.0	2.1
Pérou	1987	0.1	55.5	...	...	5.3	...	0.2	7.1	1.8	27.3	2.9
	1988	0.5	54.1	...	...	6.7	...	0.2	7.6	2.5	26.1	2.7
Portugal [3]	2001	25 596	8.7	6.8	8.4	8.4	1.9	1.7	28.2	2.6	29.3	4.0
Portugal [3]	2002	27 198	8.6	6.0	8.8	9.2	1.9	1.7	28.1	2.5	29.1	4.2
	2003	27 671	7.8	5.9	8.8	9.0	2.0	1.7	29.0	2.5	28.8	4.5
Republic of Moldova [3]	2000	2 348	26.3[5]	...	...	15.7[28]	...	1.2	18.8	...	32.2	1.2
République de Moldova [3]	2001	2 736	26.6[5]	...	...	12.1[28]	...	1.4	18.5	...	34.6	1.5
	2002	4 562	35.2[5]	...	...	7.7[28]	...	1.0	22.5	...	28.5	1.4
Romania	1993	2 473 200	36.5[11]	...	...	11.7	...	...	22.3	4.7	22.6	2.1
Roumanie	1994	6 851 800	39.0[11]	...	...	8.4	...	...	28.6	4.6	19.4	2.2
	1995	9 877 000	37.3[11]	...	...	14.5	...	...	19.0	5.5	21.4	2.3
Russian Federation [3]	2002	1 913 347	52.9[5]	...	...	0.8[29]	...	2.0[30]	21.3	2.2[31]	19.4	...
Fédération de Russie [3]	2003	2 317 770	54.0[5]	...	...	0.8[29]	...	2.9[30]	20.1	2.2[31]	18.5	...
	2004	2 718 063	53.1[5]	...	...	0.8[29]	...	3.0[30]	20.7	2.2[31]	18.7	...
St. Vincent-Grenadines	2001	186	12.4	...	11.8	23.1	...	1.1	18.3	...	25.8	7.5
St. Vincent-Grenadines	2002	202	9.9	...	11.9	22.8	...	1.5	18.8	...	25.7	7.9
	2003	199	11.1	...	12.1	22.1	...	1.5	18.6	...	25.6	8.0
San Marino	1997	354 322	18.9	0.3	4.8	9.5	...	7.2	19.5	6.2	17.4	16.2
Saint-Marin	1998	377 657	19.6	0.3	5.1	9.6	...	7.9	17.3	6.3	17.6	16.1
	1999	423 728	17.0	0.3	5.0	8.9	...	7.4	20.7	6.5	16.8	17.4
Saudi Arabia [+]	1999	154 094	19.8	27.4	...	3.4	...	4.7	11.0	2.9[32]	29.4	0.4
Arabie saoudite [+]	2000	183 804	18.0	27.9	...	4.7	...	5.3	11.7	3.0[32]	27.0	0.5
	2001	188 695	18.4	27.4	...	4.9	...	5.5	11.8	3.0[32]	26.4	0.5
Senegal	1994	258 400	8.8	14.6	8.1	4.1	...	...	5.8	1.3	31.4	...
Sénégal	1995	278 500	8.8	14.6	7.3	3.8	...	...	5.7	1.2	30.2	...
	1996	289 100	9.0	15.4	8.0	3.9	...	...	5.6	1.2	30.1	...
Seychelles	1989	475	9.4	11.5	4.9	17.1	...	2.1	11.8	3.1	29.7	2.6
Seychelles	1990	544	9.5	10.2	5.1	18.3	...	2.6	12.8	5.9	29.2	3.5
	1991	558	10.3	11.0	5.7	17.0	...	2.4	13.7	5.7	26.4	5.2
Sierra Leone [+]	1988	3 883[33]	18.5	7.2	...	28.0	...	0.8	5.9	...	13.2	1.0
Sierra Leone [+]	1989	7 620[33]	14.4	7.3	...	45.9	...	1.4	5.0	...	10.2	1.4
	1990	32 337[33]	11.9	5.6	...	27.9	...	1.0	2.1	0.0	6.2	0.6
Slovenia [3]	1991	65 845[10]	35.5	7.6	...	...	...	...	25.6	3.0	21.0	7.3
Slovénie [3]	1992	213 669[10]	34.1	7.6	...	...	...	...	28.6	2.9	19.8	7.0
	1993	297 449[10]	40.5	...	...	...	...	...	28.8	4.4	24.3	2.0
Spain	1993	10 700 500	8.4	9.6	11.8	7.5	...	3.4	24.7	3.2	22.2	5.3
Espagne	1994	10 963 200	8.0	8.7	11.9	7.4	...	3.5	25.8	3.2	22.3	4.9
	1995	11 647 100	8.3	9.0	12.5	7.4	...	3.7	24.1	3.2	22.9	4.8
Sri Lanka [3]	2001	188 353	17.4	29.7	...	9.6	...	0.5	9.6	1.6	15.7	15.9
Sri Lanka [3]	2002	204 510	23.6	22.4	...	9.4	...	0.1	10.2	3.0	13.7	17.6
	2003	221 620	24.8	22.0	...	9.2	...	0.1	12.7	0.6	13.1	17.4
Sudan [+]	1981	720	25.2[24]	18.6	...	12.4[34]	...	0.1	9.7	3.2	30.9	...
Soudan [+]	1982	854	27.7[24]	19.0	...	14.4[34]	...	0.0	8.6	2.6	27.7	...
	1983	1 113	32.4[24]	22.5	...	14.4[34]	...	-0.2	5.1	2.2	23.7	...
Sweden [3]	2001	613 332	9.1	7.2	4.8	6.4	0.2	0.6	23.8	2.7	23.4	21.6
Suède [3]	2002	657 287	9.0	6.8	4.9	6.4	0.2	0.6	24.2	2.7	23.6	21.7
	2003	690 674	9.2	6.4	4.9	6.0	0.2	0.6	24.6	2.7	23.5	22.0
Thailand	2000	557 788	25.1	24.1[35]	...	1.7	...	2.2[23]	11.4	...	34.7	0.8
Thaïlande	2001	582 518	24.4	25.8[35]	...	1.6	...	1.9[23]	12.0	...	33.6	0.7
	2002	608 164	24.8	25.1[35]	...	2.6	...	2.2[23]	11.2	...	33.3	0.8
TFYR of Macedonia [3]	1991	199	37.6	...	...	...	...	2.5	21.8	3.8	27.1	6.7
L'ex-R.y. Macédoine [3]	1992	2 302	38.3	...	...	...	...	1.2	28.9	3.0	23.4	4.7
	1993	12 472	42.6	...	...	...	...	0.4	24.3	3.4	23.5	5.5
Tonga [+]	1985	21[10]	20.7	4.2	7.0	31.9	...	...	12.2	...	13.6	1.9
Tonga [+]	1986	27[10]	22.7	3.7	7.1	29.0	...	...	11.9	...	13.8	1.9
	1987	32[10]	26.9	3.4	6.9	26.3	...	...	10.3	...	13.1	1.9

Government final consumption expenditure by function at current prices— Percentage distribution by divisions of Classification of the Functions of Government (COFOG) *(continued)*

Dépenses de consommation finale des administrations publiques, par fonction, aux prix courants— Répartition en pourcentage par divisions de la Classification des fonctions des administrations publiques (COFOG) *(suite)*

Country or area / Pays ou zone	Year / Année	Total (M.nat.curr.) / Totale (M.monn.nat.)	Div. 01 (%)	Div. 02 (%)	Div. 03 (%)	Div. 04 (%)	Div. 05 (%)	Div. 06 (%)	Div. 07 (%)	Div. 08 (%)	Div. 09 (%)	Div. 10 (%)
Trinidad and Tobago[3] Trinité-et-Tobago[3]	2001	7 548	21.7	...	20.0	16.8	...	8.5	9.6	...	22.9	0.6
	2002	8 020	21.4	...	19.5	16.4	...	8.3	10.9	...	22.8	0.6
	2003	9 574	22.0	...	20.7	17.2	...	7.0	9.1	...	23.7	0.3
Ukraine[3] Ukraine[3]	1998	22 120	32.8[5]	...	...	8.4	...	7.0	25.2[37]	2.0	23.0	...
	1999	25 866	39.2[5]	-10.9[36]	...	15.0	...	7.7	20.5[37]	1.9	25.2	...
	2000	31 667	32.5[5]	-4.7[36]	...	11.5	...	4.7	24.4[37]	2.2	27.3	...
United Kingdom[3] Royaume-Uni[3]	2001	189 724	6.7	13.5	9.4	6.3	2.1	1.9	30.5	2.1	17.6	9.9
	2002	208 866	6.8	12.6	9.6	5.8	2.2	2.2	30.6	2.2	17.6	10.5
	2003	229 892	6.5	12.6	9.4	5.9	2.1	2.3	31.1	2.2	17.2	10.8
United Rep. of Tanzania[38] Rép.-Unie de Tanzanie[38]	1992	225 639[1]	17.5	8.5	8.5	16.5	...	0.4	5.9	2.5	7.7	0.7
	1993	336 855[1]	21.5	6.8	6.8	22.6	...	0.5	5.7	2.0	7.5	0.2
	1994	408 440[1]	21.1	4.9	7.5	22.9	...	0.6	7.2	2.1	7.6	0.2
United States[3] Etats-Unis[3]	2001	1 489 050	9.8	22.2	13.0	12.0	-2.0	2.5	4.7	1.4	31.8	4.4
	2002	1 600 630	9.8	23.4	13.1	12.1	-2.0	2.5	4.4	1.4	30.8	4.6
	2003	1 712 519	9.7	25.3	12.9	11.7	-1.9	2.4	4.3	1.4	29.6	4.7
Vanuatu Vanuatu	1991	4 693[10]	20.5	8.4	...	22.6	...	18.5[39]	10.3	...	19.8	...
	1992	5 112[10]	22.6	8.7	...	21.2	...	16.1[39]	10.1	...	21.2	...
	1993	5 194[10]	27.1	9.2	...	20.1	...	13.9[39]	9.7	...	20.0	...
Venezuela (Bolivarian Rep. of)[3] Venezuela (Rép. bolivar. du)[3]	2000	9 917 000	13.4	7.4	4.6	3.9	0.5	3.8	14.6	1.3	41.9	8.6
	2001	12 663 400	13.5	7.2	6.3	4.4	0.5	3.2	14.3	1.2	41.8	7.6
	2002	14 027 200	11.9	5.2	6.1	6.4	0.5	2.9	14.9	1.1	43.2	7.8
Zimbabwe Zimbabwe	1989	5 568[40]	6.2	15.7	5.9	14.1	...	1.2	8.1	1.4	28.1	2.6
	1990	7 425[40]	28.1	13.1	4.9	20.8	...	1.6	6.5	2.0	19.9	3.1
	1991	7 788[40]	16.7	14.3	6.1	23.0	...	1.7	7.4	2.8	26.7	4.1

Source

United Nations Statistics Division, New York, national accounts database.

Notes

t   COFOG Divisions:
   Div. 01: General public services
   Div. 02: Defence
   Div. 03: Public order and safety
   Div. 04: Economic affairs
   Div. 05: Environmental protection
   Div. 06: Housing and community amenities
   Div. 07: Health
   Div. 08: Recreation, culture and religion
   Div. 09: Education
   Div. 10: Social protection

+   The national accounts data generally relate to the fiscal year used in each country, unless indicated otherwise. Countries whose reference periods coincide with the calendar year ending 31 December are not listed below.

Year beginning 21 March: Afghanistan, Iran (Islamic Republic).
Year beginning 1 April: Bermuda, India, Myanmar, New Zealand, Nigeria (beginning 1982).
Year beginning 1 July: Australia, Bangladesh, Cameroon, Egypt, Gambia, Pakistan, Puerto Rico, Saudi Arabia, Sierra Leone, Sudan.
Year ending 30 June: Botswana, Swaziland, Tonga.
Year ending 7 July: Ethiopia.
Year ending 15 July: Nepal.
Year ending 30 September: Haiti.

[1]   Central government estimates only.
[2]   Including expenditure on culture.

Source

Organisation des Nations Unies, Division de statistique, New York, la base de données sur les comptes nationaux.

Notes

t   Divisions de la COFOG:
   Div. 01: Services généraux des administrations publiques
   Div. 02: Defense
   Div. 03: Ordre et securité publics
   Div. 04: Affaires économiques
   Div. 05: Protection de l'environnement
   Div. 06: Logements et équipements collectifs
   Div. 07: Santé
   Div. 08: Loisirs, culture et culte
   Div. 09: Enseignement
   Div. 10: Protection sociale

+   Sauf indication contraire, les données sur les comptes nationaux concernent généralement l'exercice budgétaire utilisé dans chaque pays. Les pays ou territoires dont la période de référence coïncide avec l'année civile se terminant le 31 décembre ne sont pas répertoriés ci-dessous.

Exercice commençant le 21 mars: Afghanistan, Iran (République islamique d').
Exercice commençant le 1er avril: Bermudes, Inde, Myanmar, Nigéria (à partir de 1982), Nouvelle-Zélande.
Exercice commençant le 1er juillet: Arabie saoudite, Australie, Bangladesh, Cameroun, Égypte, Gambie, Pakistan, Porto Rico, Sierra Leone, Soudan.
Exercice se terminant le 30 juin: Botswana, Swaziland, Tonga.
Exercice se terminant le 7 juillet: Éthiopie.
Exercice se terminant le 15 juillet: Népal.
Exercice se terminant le 30 septembre: Haïti.

[1]   Administration centrale seulement.
[2]   Y compris dépenses de culture.

21 Government final consumption expenditure by function at current prices— Percentage distribution by divisions of Classification of the Functions of Government (COFOG) (*continued*)

Dépenses de consommation finale des administrations publiques, par fonction, aux prix courants— Répartition en pourcentage par divisions de la Classification des fonctions des administrations publiques (COFOG) (*suite*)

3 The concepts and definitions of the System of National Accounts 1993 (1993 SNA) have been adopted.
4 Data refers only to collective government consumption expenditure (excludes individual consumption).
5 Including "Defence".
6 Refers to maintenance and upkeep of public lands, lighting of streets, and fire-fighting.
7 Including maintenance and servicing of roads and units servicing agriculture.
8 Including social security.
9 Including housing and community amenities.
10 Data have not been revised.
11 Including defence and public order and safety.
12 Total government current expenditure only.
13 Excludes Office of the President, Ministries of Justice, Foreign Affairs, Information, among others.
14 Refers to inter-ministerial expenses only.
15 Refers to the Ministry of the Interior.
16 Refers to the Ministry of Finance and Planning.
17 Refers to the Ministry of Agriculture, Livestock Development and Environmental Protection.
18 Refers to the Ministry of Health, Public Services and Social Affairs.
19 Refers to the Ministry of Equipment, Transport and Telecommunication.
20 Twinning projects in the health sector.
21 General government expenditure data refer to fiscal year beginning 30 June.
22 Incuding compensation of employees and intermediate consumption of the following departmental enterprises: electricity, gas and steam, water works and supply and medical and other health services.
23 Including recreational, cultural and religion.
24 Including "Public order and safety".
25 General government expenditure data refer to fiscal year beginning 1 April.
26 Including housing and community amenities and recreation, culture and religion.
27 Data refer to defense affairs and services.
28 Includes agriculture, transport, and other branches of the economy.
29 Refers to agriculture, geology, exploration, hydrometerorology, transport, and communication.
30 Refers to housing only.
31 Refers to culture only.
32 Refers to other community and social services.
33 Central government estimates only; including development expenditure.
34 Including other functions.
35 Including justice and police.
36 Data refer to transactions in military equipment.
37 Includes includes recreational, cultural and sporting activities, and social security.
38 General government expenditure data refer to fiscal year beginning 1 July.
39 Including "Social protection".
40 Central and local government estimates only.

3 Les concepts et définitions du Système de comptabilité nationale de 1993 (SCN de 1993) ont été adoptés.
4 Les données ne concernent que les dépenses de consommation collective des administrations publiques (à l'exclusion de la consommation individuelle).
5 Y compris "Défense".
6 Entretien et aménagement des terres du domaine public, éclairage public, lutte contre les incendies.
7 Les données concernent l'entretien et le service des routes et les unités assurant des services agricoles.
8 Y compris sécurité sociale.
9 Y compris logement et équipements collectifs.
10 Les données n'ont pas été révisées.
11 Y compris défence et sureté publique.
12 Dépenses publiques courants seulement.
13 Non compris notamment le Cabinet du Président, et les Ministères de la justice, des affaires étrangères et de l'information.
14 Ne concerne que les dépenses interministères.
15 Concerne le Ministère de l'intérieur.
16 Concerne le Ministère des finances et de la planification.
17 Concerne le Ministère de l'agriculture, du développement de l'élevage et de la protection de l'environnement.
18 Concerne le Ministère de la santé, des services publics et des affaires sociales.
19 Concerne le Ministère de l'équipement, des transports et des télécommunications.
20 Projets jumelés dans le secteur de la santé.
21 Les données relatives aux dépenses générales de l'État portent sur l'année budgétaire commençant le 30 juin.
22 Y compris la rémunération des employés et la consommation intermédiaire des entreprises suivantes : électricité, gaz et vapeur, approvisionnement en eau, services médicaux et autres services sanitaires.
23 Y compris loisirs, affaires culturelles et religieuses.
24 Y compris "Ordre et securité publics".
25 Les données relatives aux dépenses générales de l'État portent sur l'année budgétaire commençant le 1e avril.
26 Y compris logement et équipements collectifs et loisirs, culture et religieuses
27 Les données se réfèrent aux affaires et services de la défense.
28 Y compris l'agriculture, les transports, et d'autres branches d'activité.
29 Les données concernent l'agriculture, la géologie, l'exploration, l'hydrométéorologie, les transports et les communications.
30 Les données ne concernent que le logement.
31 Les données ne concernent que la culture.
32 Les données concernent les autres services collectifs et sociaux.
33 Administration centrale seulement; y compris dépenses de développement.
34 Y compris les autres fonctions.
35 Y compris justice et police.
36 Ces données portent sur des transactions concernant du matériel militaire.
37 Y compris loisirs, affaires culturelles et sportives, et la sécurité sociale.
38 Les données relatives aux dépenses générales de l'État portent sur l'année budgétaire commençant le 1e juillet.
39 Y compris "protection sociale".
40 Administration centrale et locale seulement.

22

Household consumption expenditure by purpose at current prices
Percentage distribution by divisions of the Classification of Individual Consumption according to Purpose (COICOP)

Dépenses de consommation des ménages par fonction aux prix courants
Répartition en pourcentage par divisions de la Nomenclature des fonctions de la consommation individuelle (COICOP)

Country or area Pays ou zone	Year Année	Total (M.nat.curr.) Totale (M.monn. nat.)	Div. 01+02 (%)	Div. 03 (%)	Div. 04 (%)	Div. 05 (%)	Div. 06 (%)	Div. 07+08 (%)	Div. 09 (%)	Div. 10 (%)	Div. 11 (%)	Div. 12 (%)
Australia + [1] Australie + [1]	2001	424 829[2]	14.8	3.9	20.2	5.6	5.0	14.3	12.3	2.4	7.6	14.0
	2002	453 202[2]	14.7	3.9	20.0	5.6	5.3	14.5	12.0	2.4	7.6	14.0
	2003	484 935[2]	14.6	3.8	19.7	5.7	5.6	14.3	12.1	2.4	7.9	14.0
Austria [1] Autriche [1]	2001	123 554	13.8	7.0	19.3	8.4	3.3	14.7	12.1	0.5	11.4	9.4
	2002	125 274	13.8	6.9	19.2	8.2	3.3	15.1	11.9	0.6	11.9	9.3
	2003	128 070	13.5	6.7	19.2	8.2	3.3	15.5	11.8	0.6	12.1	9.1
Azerbaijan [1] Azerbaïdjan [1]	2002	18 966 300	77.5	5.7	1.3	1.7	1.8	6.1	0.3	3.3	0.4	0.6
	2003	21 413 900	77.6	5.7	1.3	1.7	1.8	6.1	0.3	3.3	0.4	0.6
	2004	23 534 100	77.6	5.7	1.3	1.7	1.8	6.1	0.3	3.3	0.4	0.6
Belarus [1] Bélarus [1]	2001	9 531 200[3]	59.6	9.4	7.2	3.9	2.2	8.4	2.2	1.0	2.5	3.7
	2002	15 113 800[3]	55.7	9.3	8.8	4.7	2.3	9.4	2.3	1.1	2.4	4.0
	2003	20 331 800[3]	52.7	8.3	11.7	4.2	2.2	11.0	2.9	1.3	2.1	3.6
Belgium [1] Belgique [1]	2001	132 573	16.6	5.5	23.6	5.7	4.0	16.6	10.0	0.6	5.4	12.0
	2002	134 617	17.3	5.6	23.6	5.8	4.4	16.6	9.4	0.6	5.5	11.3
	2003	140 223	17.5	5.4	23.5	5.7	4.5	16.5	9.1	0.6	5.3	11.9
Bolivia Bolivie	1994	21 444	34.7[4]	6.7	...	...	...	...	...	...	9.2	...
	1995	24 440	34.4[4]	6.5	...	...	...	...	...	...	9.5	...
	1996	28 200	35.7[4]	6.5	...	...	...	...	...	...	9.8	...
Botswana + [1] Botswana + [1]	1999	6 619	43.3	5.4	12.2	4.1	2.3	7.9	...	6.8	1.1	...
	2000	7 469	42.7	5.1	13.4	3.7	2.4	7.2	...	7.0	1.0	...
	2001	8 281	41.1	3.8	14.0		2.6	7.4	...	8.2	1.0	...
British Virgin Islands [1] Iles Vierges britanniques [1]	1997	221	17.2	10.9	21.3	7.2	1.8	12.7	2.3	1.4	3.2	22.2
	1998	243	16.9	9.9	22.2	7.0	2.1	12.3	2.1	1.2	3.3	23.0
	1999	269	16.4	10.4	22.3	6.7	2.6	11.5	1.9	1.1	3.0	23.8
Bulgaria [1] Bulgarie [1]	2001	21 929	31.1	3.8	23.2	3.5	3.3	19.6	3.9	0.9	8.4	2.3
	2002	23 548	28.6	3.6	22.7	3.2	3.9	21.2	4.5	1.1	8.5	2.6
	2003[5]	25 152	27.3	3.7	22.2	3.4	4.1	21.8	4.7	1.2	8.8	2.8
Canada [1] Canada [1]	2001	595 943	13.8	5.4	23.7	6.6	4.5	17.0	10.8	1.2	7.7	9.3
	2002	628 692	14.0	5.2	23.4	6.7	4.6	17.2	10.8	1.3	7.5	9.2
	2003	654 424	14.1	5.1	23.7	6.7	4.8	16.9	10.8	1.3	7.3	9.3
Cape Verde Cap-Vert	1986	13 406	61.2	2.7	14.1	7.2	0.5	...	...	...	...	...
	1987	15 134	60.4	2.9	13.6	7.2	0.6	...	...	...	...	...
	1988	17 848	62.6	2.5	13.5	6.9	0.5	...	...	...	...	...
China, Hong Kong SAR [1] Chine, Hong Kong RAS [1]	2001	670 970	14.3	15.0[6]	22.2[7]	12.7	4.6	10.9	6.5[8]	2.6	...	11.1[9]
	2002	648 315	14.6	13.6[6]	23.2[7]	12.5	4.9	10.8	7.0[8]	2.7	...	10.6[9]
	2003	630 968	14.8	13.0[6]	23.7[7]	13.0	5.0	10.3	6.8[8]	2.8	...	10.6[9]
China, Macao SAR [1] Chine, Macao RAS [1]	2001	17 492	12.6	2.9	24.8	2.4	2.1	11.8	18.5	8.6	12.6	3.7
	2002	17 657	12.1	2.9	24.6	2.3	2.2	12.0	19.3	8.7	12.1	3.7
	2003	18 602	12.5	2.5	23.5	2.3	2.2	12.4	20.4	8.4	12.1	3.6
Colombia [1] Colombie [1]	1997	78 792 148	33.4	5.5	17.6	5.7	3.6	12.8	4.6	4.7	6.2	5.8
	1998	92 065 486	33.5	5.6	17.6	5.5	3.9	12.8	4.4	5.1	6.2	5.6
	1999	95 476 502	32.9	5.3	16.6	5.6	4.2	13.6	4.7	5.5	5.8	5.6
Côte d'Ivoire Côte d'Ivoire	1996	4 015 059	51.5	5.3	7.3	3.9	0.4	9.9	1.8	0.2	2.7	16.9
	1997	4 276 928	50.4	5.3	7.3	4.1	0.5	10.1	1.9	0.2	2.6	17.6
	1998	4 768 663	50.6	5.5	7.3	4.0	0.5	9.5	1.7	0.3	1.9	18.6
Croatia [1] Croatie [1]	1999	94 101	27.0	7.3	19.7	9.3	2.6	14.6	5.2	2.7	7.5	4.3
	2000	107 866	25.2	8.7	18.8	8.3	2.6	15.2	5.1	2.5	8.4	5.1
	2001	120 709	27.5	6.9	17.7	9.8	2.2	14.8	5.0	2.5	8.2	5.5
Cyprus Chypre	1994	2 068	36.3	11.1	10.3	15.1	5.4	...	9.7	2.8	20.6	9.1
	1995	2 552	31.4	10.4	9.0	13.2	4.9	...	8.6	2.5	16.5	7.9
	1996	2 704	30.8	10.1	9.2	13.0	5.7	...	9.2	2.6	15.2	8.3
Czech Republic [1] République tchèque [1]	2001	1 242 252	26.9	5.5	21.4	5.5	1.8	13.1	11.6	0.5	7.2	6.5
	2002	1 264 794	26.1	5.3	22.6	5.4	1.7	13.1	11.8	0.5	6.6	6.8
	2003	1 322 289	25.8	5.1	22.9	5.4	1.6	13.6	11.4	0.4	6.6	7.1

Household consumption expenditure by purpose in current prices — Percentage distribution by divisions of the Classification of Individual Consumption according to Purpose (COICOP) *(continued)*

Dépenses de consommation des ménages par fonction aux prix courants — Répartition en pourcentage par divisions de la Nomenclature des fonctions de la consommation individuelle (COICOP) *(suite)*

Country or area Pays ou zone	Year Année	Total (M.nat.curr.) Totale (M.monn. nat.)	Divisions of the Classification of Individual Consumption according to Purpose (COICOP)[t] Divisions de la Nomenclature des functions de la consommation individuelle (COICOP)[t]									
			Div. 01+02 (%)	Div. 03 (%)	Div. 04 (%)	Div. 05 (%)	Div. 06 (%)	Div. 07 + 08 (%)	Div. 09 (%)	Div. 10 (%)	Div. 11 (%)	Div. 12 (%)
Denmark [1] Danemark [1]	2001	616 185	17.4	5.1	28.6	5.9	2.7	13.5	10.6	0.8	5.5	10.1
	2002	632 157	17.0	5.1	28.8	5.8	2.7	14.2	10.3	0.8	5.5	9.9
	2003	647 344	17.0	5.1	29.1	6.0	2.8	13.7	10.2	0.8	5.1	10.2
Dominican Republic [1] Rép. dominicaine [1]	1994	137 616	33.3	4.1	20.6	6.4	5.2	14.2	2.1	2.5	5.6	5.9
	1995	164 689	34.1	4.0	20.3	6.2	5.2	13.5	2.0	2.2	6.9	5.6
	1996	189 675	32.0	3.4	20.1	6.5	5.0	14.1[*]	3.1	2.2	8.8	4.8
Ecuador Equateur	1991	8 432 000	38.9	9.9	5.3[10]	7.4	4.2	...	...	...	4.2	17.5
	1992	13 147 000	38.7	9.5	5.1[10]	7.2	4.5	...	...	...	4.4	18.3
	1993	19 374 000	37.8	9.2	5.2[10]	6.6	4.6	...	...	...	4.4	18.6
Estonia [1] Estonie [1]	2001	63 232	31.8	5.8	23.9	4.7	2.2	13.1	6.9	1.3	5.3	5.0
	2002	70 857	31.2	6.2	22.8	4.9	2.2	14.2	6.9	1.3	5.4	5.1
	2003	74 596	30.6	6.2	23.0	4.7	2.5	14.1	6.8	1.5	5.4	5.2
Fiji Fidji	1989	1 197	30.9	8.6	12.4	8.6	2.0	...	...	...	...	...
	1990	1 277	31.6	8.2	13.1	7.8	2.0	...	...	...	...	...
	1991	1 405	31.2	7.9	13.2	7.9	2.0	...	...	...	...	...
Finland [1] Finlande [1]	2001	65 255	18.8	4.7	25.3	5.0	3.9	15.7	11.4	0.5	6.7	8.1
	2002	68 433	18.7	4.7	25.5	4.9	4.0	15.6	11.1	0.5	6.5	8.5
	2003	71 467	18.6	4.7	25.7	5.0	4.1	16.3	11.1	0.4	6.5	7.5
France [1] France [1]	2002	857 970	17.9	5.2	23.1	6.0	3.3	17.3	9.3	0.6	6.3	11.1
	2003	879 665	17.9	5.1	23.8	5.8	3.3	17.2	9.3	0.7	6.2	10.6
	2004	911 525	17.5	5.0	24.2	5.8	3.3	17.4	9.3	0.7	6.1	10.7
Germany [1] Allemagne [1]	2001	1 167 830	16.1	6.3	24.6	7.0	4.0	17.0	9.6	0.7	4.8	9.9
	2002	1 173 120	16.2	6.1	24.7	6.7	4.1	17.3	9.3	0.7	4.8	10.0
	2003	1 185 150	16.3	5.9	25.2	6.6	4.4	17.2	9.1	0.7	4.5	10.1
Greece [1] Grèce [1]	2002	102 602	20.5	10.4	15.7	6.4	5.6	10.9	5.8	1.7	17.3	5.8
	2003	109 773	20.1	10.2	15.7	6.3	5.8	10.8	5.8	1.7	17.7	5.8
	2004	108 570	...	...	...	...	...	...	...	...	...	...
Honduras Honduras	1984	4 742	44.6[4]	9.1	22.5	8.3	7.0	...	...	...	...	...
	1985	5 033	44.6[4]	9.1	22.5	8.3	7.0	...	...	...	...	...
	1986	5 421	44.5[4]	9.1	22.5	8.3	7.0	...	...	...	...	...
Hungary [1] Hongrie [1]	2001	8 366 833	27.7	4.6	18.4	6.7	3.6	19.8	7.8	1.1	5.0	5.4
	2002	9 184 058	27.4	4.4	18.0	6.8	3.7	20.3	7.8	1.2	4.9	5.4
	2003	10 176 737	27.0	4.3	18.2	6.9	3.8	20.5	7.9	1.3	4.8	5.3
Iceland [1] Islande [1]	2002	392 689	22.7	5.9	19.0	7.1	3.3	14.2	12.4	1.4	8.1	5.8
	2003	417 717	21.1	5.6	19.6	7.2	3.4	15.8	12.1	1.4	8.1	5.7
	2004	454 732	20.4	5.5	19.5	7.3	3.3	17.3	11.8	1.3	7.9	5.6
India + Inde +	2001	14 887 810	45.7	4.1	11.5	2.9	7.7	14.4	1.3	2.1	1.4	8.9
	2002	15 851 320	43.2	4.4	11.8	2.9	8.1	15.1	1.3	2.0	1.4	9.8
	2003	17 658 490	42.6	4.4	11.4	2.9	8.3	15.5	1.3	2.1	1.5	10.0
Iran (Islamic Rep. of) + [1] Iran (Rép. islamique d') + [1]	2001	321 298 460	30.8[4]	7.9	30.1	6.9	6.0	10.2[11]	3.4	...	...	4.8
	2002	414 570 615	30.5[4]	7.6	30.3	6.6	6.4	10.9[11]	3.4	...	...	4.3
	2003	497 482 810	31.6[4]	8.1	29.8	6.7	6.0	10.1[11]	3.3	...	...	4.4
Ireland [1] Irlande [1]	2001	50 929	14.6	6.8	19.7	7.6	2.9	13.2	7.5	1.0	17.4	9.3
	2002	54 683	14.6	6.2	20.6	7.2	3.2	13.3	6.9	1.1	17.6	9.3
	2003	57 832	13.4	5.6	21.6	7.2	3.5	13.8	6.6	1.1	17.8	9.5
Israel [1] Israël [1]	2001	266 036	21.6	3.7	26.9	9.9	4.2	13.4	6.2	3.4	3.7	7.1
	2002	281 782	21.5	3.4	29.1	9.3	4.2	13.0	5.6	3.3	3.5	7.1
	2003	288 476	22.1	3.3	28.7	9.3	4.3	12.8	5.6	3.3	3.5	7.1
Italy [1] Italie [1]	2002	760 981	17.1	9.2	19.9	9.0	3.0	15.0	7.5	0.9	9.8	8.7
	2003	789 849	17.1	9.0	20.3	9.0	3.0	15.1	7.3	1.0	9.7	8.6
	2004	817 502	16.9	8.9	20.5	8.8	2.9	15.3	7.4	1.0	9.6	8.7
Jamaica Jamaïque	1986	8 497	52.6	5.4	15.2	6.8	3.2	...	2.8	0.2	16.1	10.0
	1987	9 849	52.1	6.0	14.5	6.9	3.4	...	2.7	0.2	16.2	10.7
	1988	11 388	49.6	5.8	13.1	6.8	3.5	...	2.5	0.2	13.6	10.6
Japan [1] Japon [1]	2001	277 440 300	17.8	5.4	25.9	4.4	3.7	13.3	9.8	2.3	7.4	10.1
	2002	275 356 400	17.8	5.0	26.4	4.2	3.8	13.1	9.5	2.3	7.5	10.4
	2003	274 245 700	17.5	4.7	26.9	4.0	4.0	13.2	9.6	2.3	7.4	10.4

22 Household consumption expenditure by purpose in current prices— Percentage distribution by divisions of the Classification of Individual Consumption according to Purpose (COICOP) (continued)

Dépenses de consommation des ménages par fonction aux prix courants— Répartition en pourcentage par divisions de la Nomenclature des fonctions de la consommation individuelle (COICOP) (suite)

Country or area / Pays ou zone	Year Année	Total (M.nat.curr.) Totale (M.monn. nat.)	Divisions of the Classification of Individual Consumption according to Purpose (COICOP)[t] Divisions de la Nomenclature des functions de la consommation individuelle (COICOP)[t]									
			Div. 01+02 (%)	Div. 03 (%)	Div. 04 (%)	Div. 05 (%)	Div. 06 (%)	Div. 07 + 08 (%)	Div. 09 (%)	Div. 10 (%)	Div. 11 (%)	Div. 12 (%)
Jordan Jordanie	1984	1 375	39.6[4]	6.1	6.7	5.1	4.2[12]	...	2.9	3.4	...	...
	1985	1 415	38.5[4]	5.7	6.5	4.8	4.1[12]	...	2.9	3.4	...	...
	1986	1 238	38.8[4]	5.6	6.5	4.9	4.1[12]	...	3.0	3.4	...	...
Korea, Republic of [1] Corée, République de [1]	2002	368 882 800	17.5	4.6	16.2	4.4	4.3	17.5	8.1	5.4	7.5	14.5
	2003	376 221 300	17.5	4.4	16.9	4.2	4.5	16.8	7.8	5.9	7.7	14.4
	2004	386 113 400	18.1	4.3	17.2	4.0	4.7	16.6	7.3	6.0	7.6	14.1
Kyrgyzstan [1] Kirghizistan [1]	2001	45 932	49.9	14.4	7.7	3.1	1.6	15.7	1.6	2.0	1.5	2.4
	2002	48 681	53.8	11.8	8.4	3.4	1.4	11.9	1.5	2.6	1.3	3.8
	2003	63 352	54.0	12.9	11.2	3.1	1.7	9.6	1.7	2.1	1.0	2.6
Latvia [1] Lettonie [1]	2001	3 184	31.6	7.9	22.7	3.1	4.7	12.5	7.5	1.8	5.1	3.2
	2002	3 525	32.7	7.5	21.7	3.1	4.6	12.8	7.4	1.8	4.7	3.7
	2003	3 930	32.7	7.5	21.7	3.1	4.6	12.8	7.4	1.8	4.7	3.7
Lithuania [1] Lituanie [1]	2001	32 022	36.6	6.1	15.9	5.0	3.3	17.6	6.7	0.6	3.2	4.9
	2002	33 999	35.2	6.0	17.0	5.1	4.6	17.0	6.6	0.6	3.3	4.6
	2003	37 131	35.4	5.9	15.2	5.1	4.4	18.1	7.1	0.7	3.3	4.8
Luxembourg [1] Luxembourg [1]	2001	10 577	19.8	5.1	21.2	8.1	1.4	20.5	8.2	0.3	7.8	7.6
	2002	11 352	21.2	4.8	21.4	8.1	1.3	20.0	8.1	0.3	7.4	7.3
	2003	11 606	20.9	4.5	21.5	8.4	1.3	20.3	8.3	0.4	7.3	7.0
Malaysia Malaisie	2001	167 125	28.7	2.9	22.7	6.3	2.1	19.2[11]	5.8	...	6.4	6.0
	2002	176 886	29.4	2.4	22.2	5.8	2.2	20.0[11]	5.9	...	6.3	5.9
	2003	184 239	29.5	2.3	22.1	5.6	2.1	20.8[11]	5.7	...	6.1	5.7
Malta [1] Malte [1]	2001	1 280	22.3	6.3	8.9	8.6	2.4	19.4	9.7	1.3	14.7	6.3
	2002	1 278	22.5	6.0	9.3	9.0	2.5	19.3	9.6	1.3	14.2	6.3
	2003	1 312	22.3	6.5	9.6	9.4	2.5	18.7	9.6	1.3	14.2	6.0
Mexico [1] Mexique [1]	2001	4 074 646	26.6	3.5	12.9	8.3	4.4	19.2	2.8	3.6	7.9	10.8
	2002	4 357 960	26.7	3.4	13.1	8.4	4.6	18.5	2.8	3.8	7.7	11.1
	2003	4 767 340	26.8	3.2	13.4	8.0	4.8	18.5	2.7	3.9	7.4	11.3
Namibia [1] Namibie [1]	2001	16 550	35.9[4]	4.3	13.8	...	...	...	...	...	...	...
	2002	17 839	40.5[4]	3.8	...	...	...	...	...	...	...	...
	2003	19 015	38.9[4]	3.7	...	...	...	...	...	...	...	...
Netherlands [1] Pays-Bas [1]	2001	206 656	14.3	6.1	20.8	7.4	4.2	15.7	11.2	0.5	5.8	14.1
	2002	215 059	14.3	6.0	20.7	7.2	4.5	16.1	11.1	0.5	5.8	13.8
	2003	217 987	14.3	5.6	21.4	6.8	4.7	16.0	10.7	0.6	5.6	14.4
New Zealand + [1] Nouvelle-Zélande + [1]	2001	73 795	17.2[13]	4.6	19.5	10.4	3.2	13.9[14]	11.9[15]	...	7.4[16]	11.0[17]
	2002	78 956	17.1[13]	4.6	18.9	10.6	...	13.8[14]	...	...	7.5[16]	11.2[17]
	2003	83 746	17.1[13]	4.6	18.8	10.7	...	13.8[14]	...	...	7.5[16]	10.8[17]
Nicaragua [1] Nicaragua [1]	1998	29 759	42.8	4.9	13.2	5.4	8.2	12.4	2.8	1.2	6.9	2.2
	1999	34 144	42.0	5.0	13.3	5.5	8.1	13.1	2.8	1.2	6.8	2.2
	2000	38 906	40.8	4.8	14.6	5.4	8.2	13.5	2.8	1.4	6.4	2.2
Norway [1] Norvège [1]	2000	590 943	19.9	5.8	19.6	6.4	2.8	18.2	13.0	0.5	6.7	7.2
	2001	616 231	19.4	5.9	20.7	6.4	2.9	17.5	13.2	0.6	6.4	7.1
	2002	643 229	19.1	5.8	21.2	6.4	2.9	17.4	13.2	0.6	6.3	7.2
Panama [1] Panama [1]	1996	5 824	24.6	5.7	24.2	4.9	4.3	14.5	5.1	1.6	4.0	11.2
Peru Pérou	1986	254 987[18]	...	9.3	1.8	12.4	3.9	...	...	...	...	...
	1987	497 603[18]	...	10.1	1.4	12.5	4.4	...	...	...	...	...
	1988	3 214 245[18]	...	11.6	0.8	13.6	4.6	...	...	...	...	...
Philippines Philippines	2001	2 565 022	50.4	2.7	4.8	14.0	...	6.1[11]	...	...	...	22.0
	2002	2 750 853	49.5	2.7	4.8	13.8	...	6.6[11]	...	...	...	22.7
	2003	2 988 124	48.8	2.6	4.9	13.4	...	7.1[11]	...	...	...	23.2
Poland [1] Pologne [1]	2001	486 504[19]	27.9	4.6	23.8	4.4	4.4	13.6	7.3	1.6	3.1	9.3
	2002	510 817[19]	26.8	4.5	24.6	4.5	4.7	13.7	7.0	1.7	3.0	9.4
	2003	530 033[19]	26.0	4.4	24.8	4.5	4.7	13.8	7.2	1.7	2.9	10.0
Portugal [1] Portugal [1]	2001	77 183	22.7	7.0	10.5	7.3	4.4	20.7	6.3	1.4	9.8	9.7
	2002	80 522	22.6	7.1	10.6	7.3	4.5	20.5	6.2	1.5	9.8	10.0
	2003	82 778	22.7	7.1	10.7	7.1	4.6	19.9	6.2	1.5	10.0	10.3

22 Household consumption expenditure by purpose in current prices— Percentage distribution by divisions of the Classification of Individual Consumption according to Purpose (COICOP) (*continued*)

Dépenses de consommation des ménages par fonction aux prix courants— Répartition en pourcentage par divisions de la Nomenclature des fonctions de la consommation individuelle (COICOP) (*suite*)

Country or area Pays ou zone	Year Année	Total (M.nat.curr.) Totale (M.monn. nat.) (%)	Divisions of the Classification of Individual Consumption according to Purpose (COICOP)[t] Divisions de la Nomenclature des functions de la consommation individuelle (COICOP)[t]									
			Div. 01+02 (%)	Div. 03 (%)	Div. 04 (%)	Div. 05 (%)	Div. 06 (%)	Div. 07+08 (%)	Div. 09 (%)	Div. 10 (%)	Div. 11 (%)	Div. 12 (%)
Puerto Rico[+] Porto Rico[+]	2000	37 765	18.6	6.9	15.7	6.2	13.4	14.8	4.2	3.1	4.4	11.5
	2001	36 599	19.1	7.2	17.2	6.1	14.1	15.9	4.1	3.3	4.6	12.2
	2002	38 222	19.5	7.1	17.8	5.9	14.0	15.6	4.2	3.2	4.5	12.2
Republic of Moldova[1] République de Moldova[1]	1993	728	49.4	6.5	6.0	5.7	8.6	4.2	1.7	12.5	3.5	1.9
	1996	5 243	42.9	6.6	5.0	2.9	9.9	9.3	1.4	12.6	2.2	7.2
Saudi Arabia[+] Arabie saoudite[+]	1996	206 336	34.6[4]	7.8	14.7	9.2	0.9	17.9[11]	2.1	...	...	7.2
	1997	206 185	34.7[4]	7.7	14.7	9.1	0.9	17.8[11]	2.1	...	...	7.0
	1998	198 574	37.3[4]	8.2	15.7	9.7	1.0	18.9[11]	2.2	...	...	7.2
Sierra Leone[+] Sierra Leone[+]	1984	3 970	...	4.0	15.1	3.3	1.0	...	...	...	...	...
	1985	6 199	...	3.1	15.0	2.7	0.9	...	...	...	...	...
	1986	15 972	...	2.8	14.1	2.2	1.1	...	...	...	...	...
Singapore Singapour	1995	55 120	14.2	5.3	12.4	7.5	4.5	19.2	13.3	1.8	6.6	15.2
	1996	57 830	14.3	5.2	12.8	7.9	4.6	18.0	13.0	1.8	6.7	15.7
	1997	60 097	14.2	5.0	13.1	8.1	4.8	17.5	12.5	1.9	6.7	16.2
Slovakia[1] Slovaquie[1]	2002	633 660	27.6	4.2	22.8	5.3	2.6	13.2	9.1	0.8	8.0	6.3
	2003	671 909	26.8	3.7	26.5	4.6	2.3	13.2	8.3	0.9	7.5	6.2
	2004	736 689	25.2	3.4	27.7	4.9	2.7	13.2	8.2	1.0	7.2	6.5
South Africa[1] Afrique du Sud[1]	2001	639 800	25.8[4]	5.5	12.5	8.0	8.3	16.6[14]	4.5	3.1	3.0	12.6[17]
	2002	722 091	26.6[4]	5.4	12.4	7.9	8.6	16.4[14]	4.4	3.1	3.0	12.3[17]
	2003	786 316	26.6[4]	5.4	12.6	8.0	9.0	16.4[14]	4.2	3.1	3.0	11.6[17]
Spain[1] Espagne[1]	2002	445 472	17.9	5.9	15.7	5.5	3.4	14.3	9.2	1.6	18.1	8.5
	2003	469 643	17.7	5.6	16.0	5.5	3.5	14.3	9.3	1.5	18.3	8.3
	2004	504 513	17.3	5.4	16.0	5.3	3.5	14.7	9.4	1.5	18.6	8.3
Sri Lanka[1] Sri Lanka[1]	2000	842 546	53.5	9.7	3.6	4.7	1.7	17.8	1.7	1.5	1.0	4.7
	2001	935 020	52.6	9.8	4.2	4.7	1.7	17.6	2.1	1.5	1.3	4.5
	2002	1 043 492	52.9	9.4	4.1	4.9	1.9	17.1	1.9	1.6	1.5	4.7
Sudan[+] Soudan[+]	1981	5 386	62.8	5.6	15.8	4.6	5.2	...	...	...	...	...
	1982	7 897	60.4	7.5	15.3	5.6	5.3	...	...	...	...	...
	1983	9 385	64.7	5.3	15.2	5.5	4.1	...	...	...	...	...
Sweden[1] Suède[1]	2001	1 068 787	16.4	5.5	28.6	4.9	2.6	16.6	12.2	0.2	5.2	7.8
	2002	1 105 229	16.6	5.6	28.5	5.0	2.6	16.4	12.2	0.1	5.2	7.7
	2003	1 154 833	16.2	5.6	28.9	5.0	2.7	16.3	12.1	0.1	5.1	8.0
Switzerland[1] Suisse[1]	2001	247 441	14.6	4.4	23.5	4.7	14.2	10.4	8.6	0.5	8.1	11.1
	2002	251 497	14.6	4.2	23.6	4.7	14.3	10.3	8.5	0.5	7.7	11.6
	2003	254 102	14.7	4.0	23.6	4.6	14.6	10.1	8.5	0.5	7.9	11.5
Thailand Thaïlande	2000	2 933 383	29.9	11.2	8.7	7.0	6.6	14.3	6.6	1.0	9.4	5.4
	2001	3 106 230	30.0	10.4	8.7	6.6	6.7	15.2	6.6	1.0	9.2	5.7
	2002	3 278 730	29.4	10.1	8.5	6.6	6.4	15.9	6.8	1.0	9.2	6.2
Ukraine[1] Ukraine[1]	1997	50 617	...	...	7.4[20]	...	1.1[21]	4.9	0.2[22]	0.8	...	...
	1998	58 323	...	...	8.0[20]	...	0.9[21]	5.2	0.2[22]	1.3	...	...
	1999	71 310	...	...	7.2[20]	...	0.8[21]	5.9	0.2[22]	1.3	...	...
United Kingdom[1] Royaume-Uni[1]	2002	655 333	13.3	6.0	18.1	6.1	1.6	16.7	12.5	1.3	11.7	12.6
	2003	681 809	13.3	6.0	18.4	5.8	1.8	16.7	12.3	1.4	11.9	12.4
	2004	713 603	13.1	6.0	18.7	5.8	1.8	16.5	12.3	1.6	12.0	12.3
United States[1] Etats-Unis[1]	2001	7 062 400	9.3	4.8	17.7	5.0	17.5	13.9	9.1	2.5	6.0	14.2
	2002	7 382 400	9.2	4.7	17.8	4.8	18.3	13.3	9.0	2.6	6.0	14.2
	2003	7 763 600	9.1	4.5	17.8	4.8	18.7	13.3	9.0	2.6	6.1	14.1
Vanuatu Vanuatu	1987	8 198	47.6[4]	5.2	7.5	2.7	...	...	...	...	...	...
	1988	9 562	46.6[4]	5.5	7.4	2.7	...	...	...	...	...	...
	1989	10 545	46.0[4]	4.9	7.9	2.8	...	...	...	...	...	...
Venezuela (Bolivarian Rep. of)[1] Venezuela (Rép. Bolivar. du)[1]	2000	40 227 700	29.1[23]	6.8	13.0	8.0	6.0	15.3	4.6	4.3	8.7	4.2
	2001	47 751 600	29.2[23]	5.9	13.2	7.8	6.1	16.0	4.6	4.3	8.6	4.3
	2002	56 181 300	30.4[23]	4.8	13.5	7.5	6.1	15.5	4.4	4.5	9.0	4.4
Zimbabwe Zimbabwe	1985	3 842	25.4[4]	11.6	17.1	7.8	4.2	...	1.4	5.2	9.0	7.1[17]
	1986	4 464	23.3[4]	10.7	15.7	11.8	5.3	...	0.6	5.3	9.0	7.4[17]
	1987	4 324	20.4[4]	10.3	15.4	12.9	7.1	...	0.6	6.0	8.7	7.9[17]

22

Household consumption expenditure by purpose in current prices— Percentage distribution by divisions of the Classification of Individual Consumption according to Purpose (COICOP) *(continued)*

Dépenses de consommation des ménages par fonction aux prix courants— Répartition en pourcentage par divisions de la Nomenclature des fonctions de la consommation individuelle (COICOP) *(suite)*

Source

United Nations Statistics Division, New York, national accounts database.

Notes

t COICOP Divisions:
  Div. 01+ 02: Food, beverages, tobacco and narcotics
  Div. 03: Clothing and footwear
  Div. 04: Housing, water, electricity, gas and other fuels
  Div. 05: Furnishings, household equipment and routine household maintenance
  Div. 06: Health
  Div. 07 + 08: Transport and communication
  Div. 09: Recreation and culture
  Div. 10: Education
  Div. 11: Restaurants and hotels
  Div. 12: Miscellaneous goods and services

+ The national accounts data generally relate to the fiscal year used in each country, unless indicated otherwise. Countries whose reference periods coincide with the calendar year ending 31 December are not listed below.

Year beginning 21 March: Afghanistan, Iran (Islamic Republic).
Year beginning 1 April: Bermuda, India, Myanmar, New Zealand, Nigeria (beginning 1982).
Year beginning 1 July: Australia, Bangladesh, Cameroon, Egypt, Gambia, Pakistan, Puerto Rico, Saudi Arabia, Sierra Leone, Sudan.
Year ending 30 June: Botswana, Swaziland, Tonga.
Year ending 7 July: Ethiopia.
Year ending 15 July: Nepal.
Year ending 30 September: Haiti.

[1] The concepts and definitions of the System of National Accounts 1993 (1993 SNA) have been adopted.
[2] National concept. Data refers to final consumption expenditure of resident households in the economic territory and the rest of the world.
[3] Beginning 2000, re-denomination of Belarussian roubles at 1 to 1000.
[4] Food and non-alcoholic beverages only.
[5] Preliminary data.
[6] Including personal effects.
[7] Including housing maintenance charges.
[8] Including hotel expenditures.
[9] Including restaurant expenditure.
[10] Including transport and communication.
[11] Transport only.
[12] Including personal care.
[13] Alcoholic beverages, tobacco and narcotics only.
[14] Excluding communication, which is included in "Miscellaneous goods and services".
[15] Including education.
[16] Including expenditure on alcohol consumed in chartered clubs, taverns and hotels and restaurants.
[17] Including communication.
[18] Thousands.
[19] Final consumption expenditure of resident households in the economic territory and the rest of the world.
[20] Data refers to housing and communal services only.
[21] Including recreational, cultural and sporting activities.
[22] Refers to culture, art, and mass media.
[23] Excluding narcotics.

Source

Organisation des Nations Unies, Division de statistique, New York, base de données sur les comptes nationaux.

Notes

t Divisions de la COICOP:
  Div. 01 + 02: Alimentation, boissons, tabac et stupéfiants
  Div. 03: Articles d'habillement et chaussures
  Div. 04: Logement, eau, gaz, électricité et autres combustibles
  Div. 05: Meubles, articles de ménage et entretien courant de l'habitation
  Div. 06: Santé
  Div. 07 + 08: Transports et communication
  Div. 09: Loisirs et culture
  Div. 10: Enseignement
  Div. 11: Restaurants et hôtels
  Div. 12: Biens et services divers

+ Sauf indication contraire, les données sur les comptes nationaux concernent généralement l'exercice budgétaire utilisé dans chaque pays. Les pays ou territoires dont la période de référence coïncide avec l'année civile se terminant le 31 décembre ne sont pas répertoriés ci-dessous.

Exercice commençant le 21 mars: Afghanistan, Iran (République islamique d').
Exercice commençant le 1er avril: Bermude, Inde, Myanmar, Nigéria (à partir de 1982), Nouvelle-Zélande.
Exercice commençant le 1er juillet: Arabie saoudite, Australie, Bangladesh, Cameroun, Égypte, Gambie, Pakistan, Porto Rico, Sierra Leone, Soudan.
Exercice se terminant le 30 juin: Botswana, Swaziland, Tonga.
Exercice se terminant le 7 juillet: Éthiopie.
Exercice se terminant le 15 juillet: Népal.
Exercice se terminant le 30 septembre: Haïti.

[1] Les concepts et définitions du Système de comptabilité nationale de 1993 (SCN de 1993) ont été adoptés.
[2] Concept national. Les données concernent les dépenses de consommation finale des ménages résidant dans le territoire économique et le reste du monde.
[3] A partir de 2000, instauration du nouveau rouble bélarussien par division par 1000 du rouble bélarussien ancien.
[4] Alimentation et boissons non alcoolisées seulement.
[5] Données préliminaires.
[6] Y compris effects personnels.
[7] Y compris coût d'entretien du logement.
[8] Y compris les dépenses d'hôtel.
[9] Y compris les dépenses de restauration.
[10] Y compris transports et communications.
[11] Transports seulement.
[12] Y compris les soins personnels.
[13] Boissons alcoolisées, tabac et stupéfiants seulement.
[14] À l'exclusion des communications, déjà incluses dans la rubrique "autres".
[15] Y compris l'enseignement.
[16] Y compris les dépenses consacrées à l'alcool consommé dans les clubs, les bars, les hôtels et restaurants.
[17] Y compris communications.
[18] En milliers.
[19] Dépenses de consommation finale des ménages résidant dans le territoire économique et le reste du monde.
[20] Les données concernent le logement et les services collectifs.
[21] Y compris loisirs, affaires culturelles et sportives.
[22] Concerne la culture, les arts et les médias.
[23] À l'exclusion des stupéfiants.

# Index numbers of industrial production
1995 = 100

# Indices de la production industrielle
1995 = 100

Country or area and industry [ISIC Rev. 3] Pays ou zone et industrie [CITI Rév. 3]	1997	1998	1999	2000	2001	2002	2003	2004
Africa — Afrique								
Algeria — Algérie								
Total industry [CDE] Total, industrie [CDE]	89.6	95.7	96.0	97.3	97.0	98.1	99.3	99.7
Total mining [C] Total, industries extractives [C]	84.1	87.3	93.0	98.2	95.3	102.3	103.0	91.0
Total manufacturing [D] Total, industries manufacturières [D]	82.3	89.7	88.3	86.8	86.0	84.5	81.7	79.7
Food, beverages and tobacco — Aliments, boissons et tabac	93.4	107.1	105.5	96.1	84.0	68.0	53.9	45.5
Textiles, wearing apparel, leather, footwear Textiles, habillement, cuir et chaussures	63.7	69.5	51.0	45.7	41.3	43.6	43.0	39.0
Chemicals, petroleum, rubber and plastic products Prod. chimiques, pétroliers, caoutch. et plast.	100.9	99.7	103.8	104.8	108.8	106.0	104.3	93.6
Basic metals — Métaux de base	53.9	62.9	75.1	72.2	77.9	85.9	105.1	105.0
Metal products — Produits métalliques	60.7	64.7	72.0	74.5	85.5	82.6	79.0	87.2
Electricity [E] Electricité [E]	108.5	118.0	126.4	129.4	135.9	141.8	151.1	159.8
Burkina Faso — Burkina Faso								
Total industry [CDE] Total, industrie [CDE]	117.8	136.7	116.8	127.0	128.4	135.0	139.0	...
Cameroon [1] — Cameroun [1]								
Total industry [DE] Total, industrie [DE]	117.1	121.1	128.5	130.1	129.6	133.4	142.5	...
Total manufacturing [D] Total, industries manufacturières [D]	117.5	121.1	120.4	113.2	131.7	133.2	139.7	...
Electricity, gas and water [E] Electricité, gaz et eau [E]	113.7	121.0	127.0	128.3	118.1	133.2	139.9	...
Côte d'Ivoire — Côte d'Ivoire								
Total industry [CDE] Total, industrie [CDE]	125.0	138.8	143.2	132.0	126.5	121.0	...	...
Total mining [C] Total, industries extractives [C]	220.0	165.5	169.5	146.5	99.1	177.8	...	...
Total manufacturing [D] Total, industries manufacturières [D]	119.2	139.5	139.6	126.9	121.5	107.0	...	...
Food, beverages and tobacco — Aliments, boissons et tabac	116.8	127.1	139.5	133.0	130.2	108.9	...	...
Textiles and wearing apparel Textiles et habillement	117.6	164.0	157.6	106.4	92.8	70.2	...	...
Chemicals, petroleum, rubber and plastic products Prod. chimiques, pétroliers, caoutch. et plast.	124.6	137.8	129.0	121.9	120.9	126.5	...	...
Metal products — Produits métalliques	108.2	112.8	106.5	89.5	76.2	83.4	...	...
Electricity and water [E] Electricité et eau [E]	132.8	134.7	157.0	156.5	159.7	172.5	...	...
Egypt [2] — Egypte [2]								
Total industry [CDE] Total, industrie [CDE]	124.5	127.2	134.6	132.8	138.2	146.6	180.6	198.2
Total mining [C] Total, industries extractives [C]	113.8	99.3	143.8	148.7	168.1	185.6	299.7	363.1
Total manufacturing [D] Total, industries manufacturières [D]	134.0	144.7	133.8	127.3	125.2	132.8	163.6	179.5

Country or area and industry [ISIC Rev. 3] Pays ou zone et industrie [CITI Rév. 3]	1997	1998	1999	2000	2001	2002	2003	2004
Food, beverages and tobacco — Aliments, boissons et tabac	118.0	147.1	153.1	170.5	127.1	126.3	109.7	110.1
Textiles and wearing apparel Textiles et habillement	117.5	113.8	111.8	100.1	92.8	93.3	97.2	83.8
Chemicals, petroleum, rubber and plastic products Prod. chimiques, pétroliers, caoutch. et plast.	129.5	97.8	121.2	106.6	125.6	130.2	152.4	144.8
Basic metals — Métaux de base	110.0	139.0	156.3	164.2	146.5	167.0	232.8	183.0
Metal products — Produits métalliques	182.7	236.8	173.3	163.0	143.7	154.2	136.4	139.0
Electricity, gas and water [E] Electricité, gaz et eau [E]	110.6	117.3	127.1	137.4	151.6	181.9	197.1	212.2
Ethiopia [2] — Ethiopie [2]								
Total industry [CDE] Total, industrie [CDE]	105.9	106.2	118.0	122.5	127.5	133.9	139.4	147.8
Total mining [C] Total, industries extractives [C]	127.8	140.6	153.9	168.6	183.7	200.2	220.2	221.8
Total manufacturing [D] Total, industries manufacturières [D]	106.6	105.3	119.8	123.9	128.7	134.0	138.9	147.5
Electricity and water [E] Electricité et eau [E]	98.1	101.7	103.1	107.1	110.8	118.7	123.3	132.6
Gabon — Gabon								
Total industry [DE] Total, industrie [DE]	110.0	118.4	121.8	114.1	127.5	132.9	...	...
Total manufacturing [D] Total, industries manufacturières [D]	112.4	115.8	121.7	110.5	125.3	128.8	...	...
Food, beverages and tobacco — Aliments, boissons et tabac	105.0	111.0	105.1	114.1	128.3	119.7	...	...
Chemicals and petroleum products Produits chimiques et pétroliers	126.3	131.8	141.0	110.7	119.6	150.5	...	...
Electricity and water [E] Electricité et eau [E]	107.0	121.8	121.8	118.5	130.3	138.2	...	...
Ghana — Ghana								
Total industry [CDE] [3] Total, industrie [CDE] [3]	96.6	103.3	109.3	110.9	138.3	138.4	138.0	...
Total mining [C] Total, industries extractives [C]	109.3	140.8	158.8	153.8	154.9	147.7	154.9	...
Total manufacturing [D] Total, industries manufacturières [D]	91.9	94.3	98.4	101.7	136.7	139.6	141.0	...
Food, beverages and tobacco — Aliments, boissons et tabac	106.9	107.6	101.4	102.0	156.4	190.9	...	...
Textiles, wearing apparel, leather, footwear Textiles, habillement, cuir et chaussures	101.3	102.0	102.2	102.6	105.5	109.5	...	...
Chemicals, petroleum, rubber and plastic products Prod. chimiques, pétroliers, caoutch. et plast.	110.7	90.3	97.5	106.0	100.8	106.9	...	...
Basic metals — Métaux de base	124.5	114.1	133.1	133.2	92.1	76.7	...	...
Metal products — Produits métalliques	125.3	121.8	119.7	119.8	117.7	96.1	...	...
Electricity [E] Electricité [E]	112.2	115.9	119.6	117.8	128.1	118.9	96.2	98.5
Kenya — Kenya								
Total industry [CD] [3] Total, industrie [CD] [3]	111.2	120.9	108.5	106.7	108.0	108.7	110.4	113.4
Total mining [C] Total, industries extractives [C]	111.6	110.6	122.3	110.6	138.2	114.3	123.1	126.6
Total manufacturing [D] Total, industries manufacturières [D]	111.2	121.2	108.2	106.6	107.3	108.6	110.1	113.1
Food, beverages and tobacco — Aliments, boissons et tabac	97.7	99.6	97.2	95.5	95.3	99.0	100.5	100.5
Textiles, wearing apparel, leather, footwear Textiles, habillement, cuir et chaussures	90.0	89.4	87.7	89.9	91.8	93.3	81.3	81.3

Country or area and industry [ISIC Rev. 3] Pays ou zone et industrie [CITI Rév. 3]	1997	1998	1999	2000	2001	2002	2003	2004
Chemicals, petroleum, rubber and plastic products Prod. chimiques, pétroliers, caoutch. et plast.	115.3	121.5	125.8	133.2	144.2	148.1	157.1	157.1
Metal products — Produits métalliques	114.0	100.1	95.1	84.5	84.9	83.2	86.0	86.0
Madagascar — Madagascar								
Total industry [CDE] Total, industrie [CDE]	119.9	123.9	129.0	147.8	158.9	129.4	165.4	171.6
Total mining [C] Total, industries extractives [C]	106.8	124.8	75.2	109.2	108.6	74.0	87.6	91.3
Total manufacturing [D] Total, industries manufacturières [D]	122.1	124.5	131.0	148.3	160.9	124.9	166.7	173.1
Food, beverages and tobacco — Aliments, boissons et tabac	97.6	107.6	131.8	139.1	150.6	132.2	160.1	163.8
Textiles, wearing apparel, leather, footwear Textiles, habillement, cuir et chaussures	100.6	97.8	112.6	109.0	130.5	78.6	100.1	102.0
Chemicals, petroleum, rubber and plastic products Prod. chimiques, pétroliers, caoutch. et plast.	157.8	146.7	145.9	163.8	184.2	114.3	195.4	203.4
Metal products — Produits métalliques	121.9	129.7	133.5	113.1	126.8	105.2	124.1	121.2
Electricity, gas and water [E] Electricité, gaz et eau [E]	112.3	121.1	129.7	152.4	159.0	158.0	177.0	182.5
Malawi — Malawi								
Total industry [DE] Total, industrie [DE]	102.7	99.4	90.4	91.2	81.8	81.9	79.7	...
Total manufacturing [D] Total, industries manufacturières [D]	100.2	94.4	81.2	80.2	68.1	68.2	66.1	...
Food, beverages and tobacco — Aliments, boissons et tabac	103.1	65.1	50.0	48.5	43.4	41.4	34.4	...
Textiles, wearing apparel, leather, footwear Textiles, habillement, cuir et chaussures	146.2	181.8	222.5	137.3	111.9	60.7	60.9	...
Electricity and water [E] Electricité et eau [E]	112.8	120.3	118.7	128.1	131.6	137.7	134.7	...
Mali — Mali								
Total industry [DE] Total, industrie [DE]	121.5	140.2	133.4	...	...	...	...	...
Food, beverages and tobacco — Aliments, boissons et tabac	110.1	104.3	98.7	...	...	...	...	...
Wearing apparel Habillement	138.4	141.4	121.8	...	...	...	...	...
Chemicals and chemical products Produits chimiques	106.5	101.2	91.3	...	...	...	...	...
Mauritius — Maurice								
Total industry [CDE] Total, industrie [CDE]	111.6	118.6	121.8	132.9	139.8	136.9	135.8	134.8
Total mining [C] Total, industries extractives [C]	110.2	113.5	116.9	120.4	113.4	57.8	58.3	58.6
Total manufacturing [D] Total, industries manufacturières [D]	112.9	119.7	122.4	132.9	139.1	136.1	134.1	132.6
Food, beverages and tobacco — Aliments, boissons et tabac	110.4	113.7	108.5	121.3	127.8	129.1	134.8	144.4
Textiles, wearing apparel, leather, footwear Textiles, habillement, cuir et chaussures	114.9	121.9	129.3	137.1	142.8	133.1	124.3	111.7
Chemicals, petroleum, rubber and plastic products Prod. chimiques, pétroliers, caoutch. et plast.	105.0	114.0	120.9	130.3	130.9	133.1	162.5	142.1
Basic metals — Métaux de base	107.4	118.2	124.1	130.3	137.6	161.8	145.9	146.6
Metal products — Produits métalliques	108.4	119.1	124.8	130.2	131.8	130.4	162.5	221.5
Electricity, gas and water [E] Electricité, gaz et eau [E]	116.4	128.5	139.6	171.9	190.1	194.6	205.8	211.3

Country or area and industry [ISIC Rev. 3] Pays ou zone et industrie [CITI Rév. 3]	1997	1998	1999	2000	2001	2002	2003	2004
Morocco — Maroc								
Total industry [CDE] [3] Total, industrie [CDE] [3]	108.3	110.6	111.8	114.6	119.7	123.8	128.1	133.3
Total mining [C] [4] Total, industries extractives [C] [4]	111.6	109.8	107.5	103.8	106.3	109.0	104.3	112.7
Total manufacturing [D] [5] Total, industries manufacturières [D] [5]	107.5	110.2	112.7	116.6	120.4	124.0	128.3	132.2
Food, beverages and tobacco — Aliments, boissons et tabac	101.8	112.4	114.6	120.6	130.0	131.6	136.5	146.3
Textiles, wearing apparel, leather, footwear Textiles, habillement, cuir et chaussures	108.9	110.7	109.2	110.5	109.1	108.9	105.8	105.1
Chemicals, petroleum, rubber and plastic products Prod. chimiques, pétroliers, caoutch. et plast.	108.6	109.5	116.5	118.1	123.3	127.8	126.0	133.2
Basic metals — Métaux de base	110.5	109.3	122.0	122.2	130.8	152.1	170.5	168.4
Metal products — Produits métalliques	102.5	103.0	109.6	114.9	120.1	123.3	130.4	133.4
Electricity [E] Electricité [E]	111.2	112.6	109.7	111.1	126.6	135.8	147.6	158.0
Nigeria — Nigéria								
Total industry [CDE] Total, industrie [CDE]	109.2	104.0	...	...	...	...	...	...
Total mining [C] Total, industries extractives [C]	113.7	107.8	...	...	...	...	...	...
Total manufacturing [D] Total, industries manufacturières [D]	101.6	97.7	...	...	...	...	...	...
Electricity [E] Electricité [E]	95.7	92.2	...	...	...	...	...	...
Senegal — Sénégal								
Total industry [CDE] Total, industrie [CDE]	98.0	102.9	104.4	99.7	100.5	125.6	130.7	145.8
Total mining [C] Total, industries extractives [C]	105.6	104.5	122.4	123.7	107.8	120.0	154.6	140.3
Total manufacturing [D] [3] Total, industries manufacturières [D] [3]	94.5	100.1	99.6	91.7	90.0	123.9	121.3	142.7
Food, beverages and tobacco — Aliments, boissons et tabac	84.9	95.2	96.5	93.7	77.4	94.6	102.4	129.7
Textiles Textiles	106.1	101.0	82.2	79.2	98.9	50.2	70.9	56.9
Chemicals, petroleum, rubber and plastic products Prod. chimiques, pétroliers, caoutch. et plast.	111.7	108.5	79.5	101.3	84.6	124.0	115.8	117.1
Metal products — Produits métalliques	89.9	92.2	89.7	91.4	43.8	75.1	76.6	76.5
Electricity and water [E] Electricité et eau [E]	108.7	113.0	116.1	121.3	137.2	133.4	157.6	159.3
South Africa — Afrique du Sud								
Total industry [CDE] [3] Total, industrie [CDE] [3]	105.7	102.8	101.8	104.5	106.7	110.8	111.1	116.2
Total mining [C] Total, industries extractives [C]	100.3	99.2	97.2	95.8	97.1	98.3	101.9	107.8
Total manufacturing [D] Total, industries manufacturières [D]	106.4	102.8	102.2	106.0	109.0	113.9	111.8	116.5
Food and beverages Aliments et boissons	102.0	103.0	101.8	99.0	104.0	101.0	102.9	110.8
Textiles, wearing apparel, leather, footwear Textiles, habillement, cuir et chaussures	104.2	97.2	96.3	93.5	91.1	97.4	90.1	93.9
Chemicals, petroleum, rubber and plastic products Prod. chimiques, pétroliers, caoutch. et plast.	99.6	101.1	103.3	104.5	107.8	115.8	111.3	115.7

Country or area and industry [ISIC Rev. 3] Pays ou zone et industrie [CITI Rév. 3]	1997	1998	1999	2000	2001	2002	2003	2004
Basic metals — Métaux de base	101.7	110.9	106.3	116.3	121.3	131.3	129.4	132.4
Metal products — Produits métalliques	100.5	105.0	105.4	116.0	121.2	127.7	126.1	130.6
Electricity [E] Electricité [E]	112.6	110.0	108.8	112.9	112.5	118.2	125.5	131.0
Swaziland — Swaziland								
Total industry [CDE] [3] Total, industrie [CDE] [3]	112.0	114.1	109.7	109.6	110.7	126.3	...	...
Total mining [C] Total, industries extractives [C]	78.4	99.6	85.6	65.9	52.8	59.0	...	...
Total manufacturing [D] Total, industries manufacturières [D]	112.6	114.0	109.0	110.1	111.1	128.0	...	...
Electricity, gas and water [E] Electricité, gaz et eau [E]	115.1	120.4	126.4	117.9	124.4	126.0	...	...
Tunisia — Tunisie								
Total industry [CDE] Total, industrie [CDE]	107.2	114.6	120.7	128.3	136.0	135.8	135.6	142.1
Total mining [C] Total, industries extractives [C]	102.6	109.8	112.9	109.6	106.1	106.9	101.8	106.1
Total manufacturing [D] Total, industries manufacturières [D]	108.2	115.9	122.5	133.2	144.1	143.0	143.5	150.5
Food, beverages and tobacco — Aliments, boissons et tabac	113.4	117.9	132.7	143.4	144.1	152.2	156.1	166.0
Textiles, wearing apparel, leather, footwear Textiles, habillement, cuir et chaussures	106.0	114.6	117.8	133.0	147.7	144.1	136.6	135.8
Chemicals, petroleum, rubber and plastic products Prod. chimiques, pétroliers, caoutch. et plast.	105.7	108.1	108.3	112.1	113.0	116.1	114.4	113.2
Basic metals — Métaux de base	105.0	100.3	119.6	124.5	118.5	96.2	78.6	64.8
Metal products — Produits métalliques	111.7	129.9	141.3	153.7	169.9	172.1	181.6	201.1
Electricity and water [E] Electricité et eau [E]	108.4	114.5	124.7	131.7	140.3	146.7	154.1	161.7
Uganda — Ouganda								
Total manufacturing [D] Total, industries manufacturières [D]	137.9	153.5	165.1	164.4	168.1	196.8	...	...
Food, beverages and tobacco — Aliments, boissons et tabac	125.9	138.8	148.5	82.2	147.1	159.6	...	...
Textiles, wearing apparel, leather, footwear Textiles, habillement, cuir et chaussures	168.3	148.2	155.9	121.1	87.6	110.5	...	...
Chemicals, rubber and plastic prod. Prod. chimiques, caoutchouc et plastiques	146.9	174.8	192.1	199.1	227.0	203.4	...	...
Basic metals — Métaux de base	255.6	280.7	319.3	286.8	307.3	523.8	...	...
Metal products — Produits métalliques	106.4	81.9	73.1	65.6	58.3	103.9	...	...
United Rep. of Tanzania — Rép.-Unie de Tanzanie								
Total manufacturing [D] Total, industries manufacturières [D]	106.7	115.4	119.2	137.0	142.6	162.0	199.2	214.4
Food, beverages and tobacco — Aliments, boissons et tabac	133.7	139.8	130.5	156.4	167.2	175.7	204.6	245.3
Textiles, leather and footwear Textiles, cuir et chaussures	91.2	104.6	106.0	185.4	241.9	341.4	852.8	1 793.0
Chemicals, rubber and plastic prod. Prod. chimiques, caoutchouc et plastiques	82.8	80.0	86.6	138.1	127.6	113.4	128.6	122.9
Basic metals — Métaux de base	29.2	81.3	16.7	127.0	134.9	182.5	447.6	457.8
Metal products — Produits métalliques	119.9	122.3	132.1	120.3	113.5	104.0	119.7	121.0
Zambia — Zambie								
Total industry [CDE] Total, industrie [CDE]	103.3	103.8	91.0	93.3	98.1	96.7	105.5	114.0

Country or area and industry [ISIC Rev. 3] Pays ou zone et industrie [CITI Rév. 3]	1997	1998	1999	2000	2001	2002	2003	2004
Total mining [C] Total, industries extractives [C]	114.5	129.5	92.8	96.1	109.5	107.1	121.8	139.7
Total manufacturing [D] Total, industries manufacturières [D]	94.8	82.0	87.5	95.4	91.9	92.9	100.6	106.2
Food, beverages and tobacco — Aliments, boissons et tabac	54.7	52.2	57.2	57.6	64.8	70.3	74.5	78.9
Textiles and wearing apparel Textiles et habillement	220.2	166.5	185.0	189.1	128.6	136.6	140.9	138.3
Chemicals, petroleum, rubber and plastic products Prod. chimiques, pétroliers, caoutch. et plast.	148.7	115.6	123.1	173.7	118.0	128.2	138.3	147.7
Basic metals — Métaux de base	62.8	74.3	77.5	80.8	45.7	47.7	54.9	56.6
Metal products — Produits métalliques	64.9	69.5	57.9	64.4	61.4	45.7	54.2	56.8
Electricity and water [E] Electricité et eau [E]	101.8	93.5	94.6	96.1	110.9	102.7	102.6	99.5
Zimbabwe — Zimbabwe								
Total industry [CDE] [3] Total, industrie [CDE] [3]	106.8	109.9	103.2	96.6	87.8	79.7	72.6	...
Total mining [C] Total, industries extractives [C]	90.9	108.6	103.4	95.0	81.7	83.5	83.0	...
Total manufacturing [D] Total, industries manufacturières [D]	112.9	112.0	103.7	97.4	88.6	76.1	69.3	61.0
Food, beverages and tobacco — Aliments, boissons et tabac	105.7	111.8	101.6	108.8	90.2	71.5	63.2	56.8
Textiles, wearing apparel, leather, footwear Textiles, habillement, cuir et chaussures	125.4	137.7	148.3	132.2	130.0	103.3	73.4	85.1
Chemicals, petroleum, rubber and plastic products Prod. chimiques, pétroliers, caoutch. et plast.	126.8	120.0	107.0	75.5	75.4	78.6	67.5	66.4
Basic metals and metal products Métaux de base et produits métalliques	96.2	81.1	78.7	76.7	68.4	59.5	62.4	48.3
Electricity [E] Electricité [E]	94.1	87.3	94.6	93.2	104.5	112.7	115.5	127.1
America, North — Amérique du Nord								
Barbados — Barbade								
Total industry [CDE] Total, industrie [CDE]	104.3	112.1	112.9	111.1	104.3	104.8	104.0	106.1
Total mining [C] Total, industries extractives [C]	72.4	126.8	155.4	122.6	102.8	86.8	81.8	81.6
Total manufacturing [D] Total, industries manufacturières [D]	104.3	109.1	107.2	106.5	98.3	98.8	97.8	99.4
Food, beverages and tobacco — Aliments, boissons et tabac	106.2	114.5	112.7	109.8	106.7	109.0	108.8	109.2
Wearing apparel Habillement	94.4	69.2	65.0	69.9	44.1	32.9	30.8	32.2
Chemicals and petroleum products Produits chimiques et pétroliers	118.6	105.3	104.7	83.8	78.7	75.5	72.8	91.9
Metal products — Produits métalliques	103.3	87.5	80.8	78.9	54.9	53.7	47.0	53.2
Electricity and gas [E] Electricité et gaz [E]	107.8	117.3	123.6	123.5	128.0	130.2	133.7	136.8
Belize — Belize								
Total industry [DE] Total, industrie [DE]	106.0	105.0	105.0	120.0	120.2	115.7	...	...
Total manufacturing [D] Total, industries manufacturières [D]	105.2	101.8	107.2	125.4	125.2	119.6	...	...
Food, beverages and tobacco — Aliments, boissons et tabac	105.2	102.4	107.0	124.8	125.3	119.6	...	...
Wearing apparel Habillement	100.9	108.6	108.4	89.1	76.3	59.9	...	...

Country or area and industry [ISIC Rev. 3] Pays ou zone et industrie [CITI Rév. 3]	1997	1998	1999	2000	2001	2002	2003	2004
Chemicals and chemical products Produits chimiques	80.9	80.1	94.8	87.5	89.2	102.2	...	...
Metal products — Produits métalliques	66.1	54.6	46.3	40.2	31.0	29.4	...	...
Electricity and water [E] Electricité et eau [E]	111.0	122.3	93.1	91.4	93.3	94.6	...	...
Canada — Canada								
Total industry [CDE] Total, industrie [CDE]	106.2	109.9	116.1	125.9	121.3	123.3	124.3	128.5
Total mining [C] Total, industries extractives [C]	104.1	105.7	105.5	108.8	109.3	108.0	115.0	119.0
Total manufacturing [D] Total, industries manufacturières [D]	107.7	113.0	121.8	135.0	128.6	131.2	131.4	136.3
Food, beverages and tobacco — Aliments, boissons et tabac	100.0	105.2	104.8	109.0	114.9	115.9	114.7	118.7
Textiles, wearing apparel, leather, footwear Textiles, habillement, cuir et chaussures	102.8	106.2	104.0	120.0	116.8	111.2	102.7	95.2
Chemicals, petroleum, rubber and plastic products Prod. chimiques, pétroliers, caoutch. et plast.	99.8	101.8	106.4	117.8	119.0	125.8	127.6	133.8
Basic metals — Métaux de base	107.2	116.3	120.5	130.5	128.6	132.6	132.1	134.6
Metal products — Produits métalliques	109.3	116.5	134.4	155.3	135.0	133.4	132.0	140.2
Electricity, gas and water [E] Electricité, gaz et eau [E]	101.4	99.6	100.9	101.4	99.4	102.1	100.3	101.0
Costa Rica — Costa Rica								
Total industry [DE] [3] Total, industrie [DE] [3]	108.2	120.1	146.3	143.9	133.6	138.5	149.9	153.8
Total manufacturing [D] Total, industries manufacturières [D]	108.2	120.5	150.3	145.9	132.7	137.1	149.1	152.4
Food, beverages and tobacco — Aliments, boissons et tabac	109.3	115.9	118.7	117.3	112.7	110.1	112.8	112.0
Textiles, wearing apparel, leather, footwear Textiles, habillement, cuir et chaussures	87.5	91.5	83.1	74.1	67.0	65.8	63.5	60.7
Chemicals, petroleum, rubber and plastic products Prod. chimiques, pétroliers, caoutch. et plast.	101.7	100.1	100.6	103.4	106.1	115.8	119.9	129.2
Metal products — Produits métalliques	109.7	113.8	112.1	108.4	98.9	106.4	107.9	108.1
Electricity and water [E] Electricité et eau [E]	108.2	117.7	125.0	133.0	138.5	145.8	154.4	161.4
Cuba — Cuba								
Total industry [CDE] Total, industrie [CDE]	117.0	111.4	118.7	128.2	...	...	...	...
Total mining [C] Total, industries extractives [C]	108.1	121.8	163.7	201.9	...	...	...	...
Total manufacturing [D] Total, industries manufacturières [D]	114.2	113.4	116.7	126.8	...	...	...	...
Food, beverages and tobacco — Aliments, boissons et tabac	110.9	116.5	127.1	127.0	...	...	...	...
Textiles, wearing apparel, leather, footwear Textiles, habillement, cuir et chaussures	118.2	122.5	132.8	126.0	...	...	...	...
Chemicals, petroleum, rubber and plastic products Prod. chimiques, pétroliers, caoutch. et plast.	114.0	94.6	94.4	122.7	...	...	...	...
Basic metals — Métaux de base	141.4	149.9	147.8	158.0	...	...	...	...
Metal products — Produits métalliques	165.4	110.1	136.8	121.9	...	...	...	...
Electricity and water [E] Electricité et eau [E]	113.4	113.4	116.3	120.5	...	...	...	...
Dominican Republic — Rép. dominicaine								
Total industry [CDE] Total, industrie [CDE]	111.1	115.5	121.9	131.6	130.8	136.0	132.5	...

Country or area and industry [ISIC Rev. 3] Pays ou zone et industrie [CITI Rév. 3]	1997	1998	1999	2000	2001	2002	2003	2004
Total mining [C] Total, industries extractives [C]	105.6	88.8	87.4	99.0	83.6	81.3	88.4	...
Total manufacturing [D] Total, industries manufacturières [D]	110.8	117.1	124.2	133.6	131.8	137.1	133.4	...
Electricity [E] Electricité [E]	121.4	138.3	149.5	159.8	189.1	203.9	186.7	...
El Salvador — El Salvador								
Total industry [CDE] Total, industrie [CDE]	110.2	117.5	121.7	126.4	131.7	135.6	138.8	...
Total mining [C] Total, industries extractives [C]	107.5	113.2	113.7	108.4	121.1	127.7	132.9	...
Total manufacturing [D] Total, industries manufacturières [D]	109.9	117.2	121.5	126.5	131.6	135.4	138.5	...
Food, beverages and tobacco — Aliments, boissons et tabac	106.2	111.4	114.3	118.0	123.0	123.9	125.0	...
Textiles, wearing apparel, leather, footwear Textiles, habillement, cuir et chaussures	102.2	108.4	111.7	113.7	106.4	107.6	112.7	...
Chemicals, petroleum, rubber and plastic products Prod. chimiques, pétroliers, caoutch. et plast.	106.9	114.4	124.2	121.7	127.3	130.3	131.8	...
Basic metals and metal products Métaux de base et produits métalliques	117.4	129.9	132.3	135.3	139.4	142.9	145.2	...
Electricity [E] Electricité [E]	142.0	156.8	160.2	146.0	155.9	167.3	174.9	...
Haiti [6] — Haïti [6]								
Total industry [DE] [3] Total, industrie [DE] [3]	108.1	112.2	115.2	120.8	114.8	116.6	122.6	124.8
Total manufacturing [D] Total, industries manufacturières [D]	102.0	107.4	110.9	118.2	120.9	122.9	128.1	130.4
Food, beverages and tobacco — Aliments, boissons et tabac	112.6	112.0	149.8	173.4	179.8	182.5	183.4	188.8
Chemicals and chemical products Produits chimiques	94.2	101.7	101.9	104.7	108.3	110.9	126.9	125.3
Electricity [E] Electricité [E]	131.6	130.7	132.0	130.8	91.0	92.2	101.3	102.9
Honduras — Honduras								
Total industry [CDE] Total, industrie [CDE]	113.0	117.1	120.3	127.5	132.0	137.4	143.3	...
Total mining [C] Total, industries extractives [C]	112.5	116.7	122.9	125.0	124.0	129.2	133.3	...
Total manufacturing [D] Total, industries manufacturières [D]	111.0	114.8	117.8	124.3	130.8	135.7	140.7	...
Food, beverages and tobacco — Aliments, boissons et tabac	149.0	162.9	180.0	195.9	213.5	228.9	244.1	...
Textiles, wearing apparel, leather, footwear Textiles, habillement, cuir et chaussures	166.0	193.6	221.4	246.3	271.7	289.4	306.9	...
Chemicals, petroleum, rubber and plastic products Prod. chimiques, pétroliers, caoutch. et plast.	128.1	144.8	162.4	178.4	191.0	204.0	218.7	...
Basic metals — Métaux de base	136.6	143.7	155.9	174.8	194.0	208.3	224.6	...
Metal products — Produits métalliques	134.0	153.4	174.4	193.1	211.8	227.4	244.9	...
Electricity, gas and water [E] Electricité, gaz et eau [E]	124.2	130.2	132.9	147.0	144.3	152.3	164.4	...
Mexico — Mexique								
Total industry [CDE] [7] Total, industrie [CDE] [7]	120.3	128.0	134.0	142.0	137.2	137.0	136.7	142.0
Total mining [C] Total, industries extractives [C]	112.9	116.0	113.6	117.9	119.6	120.1	124.5	127.7

Country or area and industry [ISIC Rev. 3] Pays ou zone et industrie [CITI Rév. 3]	1997	1998	1999	2000	2001	2002	2003	2004
Total manufacturing [D] Total, industries manufacturières [D]	121.8	130.8	136.4	145.8	140.2	139.3	137.5	142.7
Food, beverages and tobacco — Aliments, boissons et tabac	106.7	113.7	118.3	122.9	125.8	128.2	130.4	134.0
Textiles and wearing apparel Textiles et habillement	127.8	132.6	136.9	144.2	131.9	124.2	115.7	117.6
Chemicals, petroleum, rubber and plastic products Prod. chimiques, pétroliers, caoutch. et plast.	113.8	120.7	123.5	127.6	122.7	122.3	124.2	129.0
Basic metals — Métaux de base	131.9	137.3	137.8	141.9	131.8	133.5	139.0	147.3
Metal products — Produits métalliques	145.7	162.4	173.6	197.2	183.6	179.8	171.1	179.8
Electricity [E] Electricité [E]	110.1	112.1	129.8	133.7	136.7	138.1	140.3	143.6
Panama — Panama								
Total industry [CDE] [3] Total, industrie [CDE] [3]	110.2	115.6	112.2	110.3	107.2	109.5	112.5	116.9
Total mining [C] Total, industries extractives [C]	151.7	187.2	225.9	218.9	187.6	247.6	192.7	198.9
Total manufacturing [D] Total, industries manufacturières [D]	105.6	109.9	105.3	100.0	93.4	94.7	96.0	98.4
Food, beverages and tobacco — Aliments, boissons et tabac	110.7	119.7	111.8	108.3	106.9	106.9	108.4	111.7
Textiles, wearing apparel, leather, footwear Textiles, habillement, cuir et chaussures	85.2	80.4	68.9	62.1	56.1	47.0	35.0	29.9
Chemicals, petroleum, rubber and plastic products Prod. chimiques, pétroliers, caoutch. et plast.	121.5	126.5	125.8	116.9	117.3	120.6	121.7	120.8
Basic metals — Métaux de base	148.9	124.3	177.1	135.6	55.1	69.9	70.6	77.0
Metal products — Produits métalliques	111.0	116.3	112.3	120.3	111.0	71.8	69.0	69.5
Electricity and water [E] Electricité et eau [E]	120.3	127.6	126.3	132.7	138.1	142.0	150.1	159.0
Trinidad and Tobago — Trinité-et-Tobago								
Total industry [DE] Total, industrie [DE]	112.5	125.3	139.0	146.4	157.6	187.7	205.5	...
Total manufacturing [D] [3] Total, industries manufacturières [D] [3]	113.1	125.8	140.1	148.7	162.2	193.3	213.7	...
Food, beverages and tobacco — Aliments, boissons et tabac	122.3	174.0	183.3	234.2	267.4	222.4	227.5	...
Textiles, leather and footwear Textiles, cuir et chaussures	135.6	180.8	364.1	458.0	434.1	447.1	724.8	...
Chemicals and petroleum products Produits chimiques et pétroliers	134.5	175.6	236.6	270.6	264.1	361.5	477.1	...
Metal products — Produits métalliques	110.6	154.3	154.4	155.5	172.2	208.8	264.4	...
Electricity [E] Electricité [E]	106.3	120.1	127.1	121.5	106.4	125.9	114.4	...
United States — Etats-Unis								
Total industry [CDE] Total, industrie [CDE]	111.9	118.5	123.7	129.2	124.5	124.2	124.0	129.2
Total mining [C] Total, industries extractives [C]	103.4	101.9	96.8	99.1	100.0	95.8	95.3	94.5
Total manufacturing [D] Total, industries manufacturières [D]	113.5	121.1	127.4	133.1	127.5	127.0	127.0	133.0
Food, beverages and tobacco — Aliments, boissons et tabac	101.4	104.8	104.1	105.6	105.5	106.0	106.1	108.6
Textiles, wearing apparel, leather, footwear Textiles, habillement, cuir et chaussures	100.0	96.4	94.0	90.9	79.3	72.0	64.2	61.3
Chemicals, petroleum, rubber and plastic products Prod. chimiques, pétroliers, caoutch. et plast.	109.2	112.1	113.8	114.9	111.4	116.1	115.1	119.2

Country or area and industry [ISIC Rev. 3] Pays ou zone et industrie [CITI Rév. 3]	1997	1998	1999	2000	2001	2002	2003	2004
Basic metals — Métaux de base	106.6	108.3	108.1	104.6	94.6	96.3	93.2	98.4
Metal products — Produits métalliques	130.7	152.8	182.9	209.4	219.3	217.4	238.7	273.4
Electricity and gas [E] Electricité et gaz [E]	102.9	105.6	108.5	111.7	111.2	114.6	115.1	117.9
America, South — Amérique du Sud								
Argentina — Argentine								
Total manufacturing [D] Total, industries manufacturières [D]	116.3	115.9	103.8	101.8	90.4	81.6	95.8	109.0
Food, beverages and tobacco — Aliments, boissons et tabac	105.1	107.3	107.2	103.5	94.5	90.0	101.5	111.8
Textiles, wearing apparel, leather, footwear Textiles, habillement, cuir et chaussures	111.0	98.7	78.2	78.2	67.1	56.1	76.6	85.4
Chemicals, petroleum, rubber and plastic products Prod. chimiques, pétroliers, caoutch. et plast.	116.4	117.1	111.4	112.2	102.8	98.4	109.9	117.8
Basic metals — Métaux de base	124.2	129.5	99.7	103.4	97.5	103.2	114.8	126.3
Metal products — Produits métalliques	124.5	120.0	91.6	88.4	73.2	58.7	75.7	95.9
Bolivia — Bolivie								
Total industry [CDE] [3] Total, industrie [CDE] [3]	104.8	109.8	104.6	104.1	102.2	102.6	104.7	103.6
Total mining [C] Total, industries extractives [C]	100.6	106.7	95.1	93.6	90.5	90.7	91.4	85.5
Total manufacturing [D] Total, industries manufacturières [D]	108.4	112.0	113.4	113.8	113.0	113.3	117.0	121.1
Food, beverages and tobacco — Aliments, boissons et tabac	106.3	111.8	114.9	119.7	122.5	126.2	128.7	129.7
Textiles, wearing apparel, leather, footwear Textiles, habillement, cuir et chaussures	105.1	103.5	92.9	95.7	81.9	77.5	86.5	87.8
Chemicals, petroleum, rubber and plastic products Prod. chimiques, pétroliers, caoutch. et plast.	121.5	123.5	122.0	113.3	110.8	111.5	118.2	138.9
Basic metals — Métaux de base	108.4	84.7	87.1	90.5	79.1	82.4	89.2	90.0
Metal products — Produits métalliques	92.9	95.0	88.2	75.6	69.7	60.4	48.9	51.3
Electricity, gas and water [E] Electricité, gaz et eau [E]	118.5	126.2	131.6	135.6	136.5	141.7	143.8	148.0
Brazil — Brésil								
Total industry [CD] Total, industrie [CD]	105.6	103.4	102.9	109.6	111.3	114.4	114.4	124.0
Total mining [C] Total, industries extractives [C]	117.3	131.4	142.5	159.4	164.9	196.1	205.3	214.1
Total manufacturing [D] Total, industries manufacturières [D]	104.7	101.3	99.7	105.8	107.2	107.8	107.5	116.7
Food, beverages and tobacco — Aliments, boissons et tabac	107.2	106.3	108.7	106.6	110.8	108.9	106.5	111.8
Textiles, wearing apparel, leather, footwear Textiles, habillement, cuir et chaussures	89.7	85.1	84.4	89.5	83.6	85.0	78.1	82.8
Chemicals, petroleum, rubber and plastic products Prod. chimiques, pétroliers, caoutch. et plast.	109.3	111.8	112.7	114.2	112.6	111.0	109.6	114.9
Basic metals and metal products Métaux de base et produits métalliques	108.9	104.9	103.5	113.2	113.4	117.5	124.6	128.7
Metal products — Produits métalliques	99.9	96.7	94.0	108.1	117.2	124.4	128.9	147.1
Chile — Chili								
Total industry [CDE] [3] Total, industrie [CDE] [3]	115.6	118.8	124.8	130.1	132.2	132.9	140.6	152.6
Total mining [C] Total, industries extractives [C]	134.8	142.5	164.6	173.7	176.4	170.2	181.3	199.1
Total manufacturing [D] Total, industries manufacturières [D]	108.0	109.0	108.7	112.3	113.6	116.5	122.6	132.3

Country or area and industry [ISIC Rev. 3] Pays ou zone et industrie [CITI Rév. 3]	1997	1998	1999	2000	2001	2002	2003	2004
Food, beverages and tobacco — Aliments, boissons et tabac	102.6	100.2	101.6	104.5	108.3	111.4	115.0	123.5
Textiles, wearing apparel, leather, footwear Textiles, habillement, cuir et chaussures	90.2	77.6	68.7	67.2	59.3	56.2	61.8	69.2
Chemicals, petroleum, rubber and plastic products Prod. chimiques, pétroliers, caoutch. et plast.	116.5	123.2	128.3	140.6	148.1	153.1	163.9	178.9
Basic metals — Métaux de base	111.3	119.9	123.5	92.3	96.5	95.6	111.1	140.9
Metal products — Produits métalliques	113.4	107.6	99.3	104.7	106.6	100.4	100.7	107.0
Electricity [E] Electricité [E]	121.2	129.9	139.6	147.4	153.7	157.7	168.4	181.9
Colombia — Colombie								
Total manufacturing [D] Total, industries manufacturières [D]	99.6	98.2	85.0	93.2	94.3	95.3	98.8	103.8
Food, beverages and tobacco — Aliments, boissons et tabac	101.5	102.2	93.2	92.7	94.3	100.5	102.6	105.6
Textiles, wearing apparel, leather, footwear Textiles, habillement, cuir et chaussures	101.3	119.0	102.7	120.6	117.0	109.3	117.5	120.2
Chemicals, petroleum, rubber and plastic products Prod. chimiques, pétroliers, caoutch. et plast.	98.3	94.6	86.0	93.1	89.7	92.3	97.5	104.0
Basic metals — Métaux de base	107.0	97.9	93.3	123.7	118.0	125.1	158.1	171.8
Metal products — Produits métalliques	100.0	91.4	66.6	75.1	83.7	85.0	83.6	95.9
Ecuador — Equateur								
Total manufacturing [D] Total, industries manufacturières [D]	104.4	105.2	100.0	114.9	127.6	130.9	...	...
Food, beverages and tobacco — Aliments, boissons et tabac	103.3	105.9	104.5	107.7	119.6	123.4	...	...
Textiles, leather and footwear Textiles, cuir et chaussures	104.0	101.3	95.8	114.7	118.0	119.5	...	...
Chemicals, petroleum, rubber and plastic products Prod. chimiques, pétroliers, caoutch. et plast.	104.7	106.8	97.0	107.4	112.5	116.4	...	...
Basic metals — Métaux de base	102.4	102.7	95.5	127.1	129.6	132.8	...	...
Metal products — Produits métalliques	100.8	101.6	67.1	97.0	151.8	153.6	...	...
Paraguay — Paraguay								
Total manufacturing [D] Total, industries manufacturières [D]	97.6	98.6	98.6	99.6	101.0	97.8	97.2	...
Food, beverages and tobacco — Aliments, boissons et tabac	105.0	106.6	110.0	112.5	114.2	117.9	117.2	...
Textiles, wearing apparel, leather, footwear Textiles, habillement, cuir et chaussures	81.2	88.3	84.9	92.3	99.1	82.4	87.1	...
Chemicals, petroleum, rubber and plastic products Prod. chimiques, pétroliers, caoutch. et plast.	76.9	72.0	68.6	64.2	67.3	63.3	60.7	...
Basic metals — Métaux de base	90.7	86.3	82.5	83.2	79.9	84.2	88.7	...
Metal products — Produits métalliques	99.1	99.1	99.1	99.1	99.1	99.1	95.5	...
Peru — Pérou								
Total industry [CDE] Total, industrie [CDE]	109.5	108.7	109.7	112.9	113.2	118.7	123.4	129.4
Total mining [C] Total, industries extractives [C]	114.6	118.9	134.5	137.7	151.3	170.2	181.9	191.7
Total manufacturing [D] Total, industries manufacturières [D]	106.9	103.1	102.4	108.3	109.1	113.5	115.8	124.0
Food, beverages and tobacco — Aliments, boissons et tabac	103.8	99.0	112.4	122.0	118.1	122.3	123.0	129.7
Textiles, wearing apparel, leather, footwear Textiles, habillement, cuir et chaussures	107.2	99.9	97.2	110.1	105.6	109.5	114.5	130.5
Chemicals, petroleum, rubber and plastic products Prod. chimiques, pétroliers, caoutch. et plast.	118.3	114.1	114.3	118.6	122.9	128.1	129.7	135.2
Basic metals — Métaux de base	115.6	121.4	121.9	128.1	132.7	129.1	132.9	135.2

Country or area and industry [ISIC Rev. 3] Pays ou zone et industrie [CITI Rév. 3]	1997	1998	1999	2000	2001	2002	2003	2004
Metal products — Produits métalliques	98.3	91.7	75.6	83.4	82.1	78.8	81.3	83.7
Electricity [E] Electricité [E]	119.5	126.9	130.7	134.8	137.0	143.8	151.5	158.5
Suriname — Suriname								
Total industry [CDE] Total, industrie [CDE]	107.6	106.7	99.0	...	...	...	...	...
Total mining [C] Total, industries extractives [C]	168.9	194.2	...	...	...	...	...	...
Total manufacturing [D] Total, industries manufacturières [D]	104.5	86.5	79.3	...	...	...	...	...
Food, beverages and tobacco — Aliments, boissons et tabac	118.4	125.8	142.2	...	...	...	...	...
Electricity, gas and water [E] Electricité, gaz et eau [E]	140.4	159.6	86.2	62.8	...	...	...	...
Uruguay — Uruguay								
Total manufacturing [D] Total, industries manufacturières [D]	118.3	125.0	122.6	127.5	129.6	136.7	147.2	178.4
Food, beverages and tobacco — Aliments, boissons et tabac	119.0	123.3	122.4	115.8	108.1	108.1	110.4	132.0
Textiles, wearing apparel, leather, footwear Textiles, habillement, cuir et chaussures	108.6	89.4	64.3	65.0	53.4	41.5	48.7	56.9
Chemicals, petroleum, rubber and plastic products Prod. chimiques, pétroliers, caoutch. et plast.	98.6	113.6	102.9	111.3	102.1	97.2	112.2	137.3
Basic metals — Métaux de base	107.0	111.5	105.2	101.0	99.7	99.7	120.3	152.8
Metal products — Produits métalliques	83.8	115.8	92.5	111.9	85.5	41.1	29.9	43.9
Venezuela (Bolivarian Republic of) — Venezuela (République bolivarienne du)								
Total industry [CDE] Total, industrie [CDE]	100.1	98.6	89.4	94.2	97.8	87.2	81.7	99.9
Total mining [C] Total, industries extractives [C]	109.5	101.3	89.0	102.6	105.4	110.0	100.6	112.4
Total manufacturing [D] Total, industries manufacturières [D]	99.1	99.8	86.8	92.4	95.9	79.8	72.7	93.7
Electricity and water [E] Electricité et eau [E]	106.0	110.3	109.8	114.8	120.7	123.7	124.7	134.0
Asia — Asie								
Armenia — Arménie								
Total industry [CDE] Total, industrie [CDE]	102.4	100.2	105.5	112.3	118.3	135.6	156.1	155.8
Total mining [C] Total, industries extractives [C]	110.2	143.1	166.3	207.4	248.3	297.0	332.3	304.1
Total manufacturing [D] Total, industries manufacturières [D]	101.9	97.1	107.3	114.7	125.7	157.5	187.7	189.5
Food, beverages and tobacco — Aliments, boissons et tabac	113.5	101.4	112.1	117.0	123.7	138.0	203.0	149.8
Textiles, wearing apparel, leather, footwear Textiles, habillement, cuir et chaussures	133.0	117.5	75.1	73.0	84.4	84.6	108.9	108.9
Chemicals, petroleum, rubber and plastic products Prod. chimiques, pétroliers, caoutch. et plast.	78.1	93.0	101.5	115.3	97.9	83.1	81.3	81.3
Basic metals — Métaux de base	44.5	184.7	151.3	318.0	460.1	566.8	670.5	670.5
Metal products — Produits métalliques	81.0	68.2	74.4	88.1	120.2	102.4	131.1	131.1
Electricity and gas [E] Electricité et gaz [E]	105.2	105.7	100.0	102.6	95.1	81.4	83.4	83.4
Azerbaijan — Azerbaïdjan								
Total industry [CDE] Total, industrie [CDE]	93.6	95.6	99.1	105.9	111.3	115.2	119.8	126.6

Country or area and industry [ISIC Rev. 3] Pays ou zone et industrie [CITI Rév. 3]	1997	1998	1999	2000	2001	2002	2003	2004
Total mining [C] Total, industries extractives [C]	97.3	121.2	145.3	146.9	155.5	159.4	161.6	165.3
Total manufacturing [D] Total, industries manufacturières [D]	90.7	80.1	72.8	83.9	86.2	90.9	108.2	119.2
Electricity, gas and water [E] Électricité, gaz et eau [E]	98.6	103.6	104.6	107.8	108.4	113.5	132.1	135.5
Bangladesh [2] — Bangladesh [2]								
Total industry [CDE] Total, industrie [CDE]	110.3	112.5	121.4	131.5	140.9	147.6	157.2	164.8
Total mining [C] Total, industries extractives [C]	106.4	113.5	114.6	134.5	150.8	158.4	170.1	180.9
Total manufacturing [D] Total, industries manufacturières [D]	109.8	120.0	123.8	132.8	139.9	146.2	155.8	162.8
Food, beverages and tobacco — Aliments, boissons et tabac	94.4	99.4	98.0	105.2	108.3	125.2	129.6	133.4
Textiles, wearing apparel, leather, footwear Textiles, habillement, cuir et chaussures	111.8	122.8	127.7	132.3	141.9	149.0	156.0	166.5
Chemicals, petroleum, rubber and plastic products Prod. chimiques, pétroliers, caoutch. et plast.	99.1	104.4	98.2	103.5	112.7	113.5	133.9	134.9
Basic metals — Métaux de base	94.3	105.1	89.3	93.0	103.0	107.9	111.7	114.2
Metal products — Produits métalliques	108.5	151.9	116.6	117.5	117.3	123.9	120.4	126.1
Electricity [E] Électricité [E]	109.3	118.8	127.3	135.8	149.8	160.5	170.2	184.1
China, Hong Kong SAR — Chine, Hong Kong RAS								
Total industry [DE] [3] Total, industrie [DE] [3]	96.6	90.2	84.7	85.1	82.4	76.3	71.1	73.4
Total manufacturing [D] Total, industries manufacturières [D]	95.6	87.2	81.7	81.2	77.7	70.0	63.6	65.5
Food, beverages and tobacco — Aliments, boissons et tabac	98.6	89.7	88.2	85.5	84.0	90.9	80.4	85.0
Textiles and wearing apparel Textiles et habillement	93.9	86.2	84.1	86.9	86.7	80.8	77.9	76.3
Chemicals and other non-metallic mineral products Prod. chimiques et minéraux non-métalliques	101.4	88.1	74.9	64.1	59.1	48.9	49.6	48.7
Basic metals and metal products Métaux de base et produits métalliques	91.3	84.0	80.0	79.2	72.5	56.0	44.5	49.5
Electricity and gas [E] Électricité et gaz [E]	104.6	111.9	106.8	113.4	117.0	122.7	126.4	131.3
China, Macao SAR [8] — Chine, Macao RAS [8]								
Total industry [CDE] Total, industrie [CDE]	100.0	100.9	101.2	112.6	106.2	106.0	108.2	...
Total mining [C] Total, industries extractives [C]	100.0	99.3	75.0	36.0	71.9	80.9	101.1	...
Total manufacturing [D] Total, industries manufacturières [D]	100.0	97.9	98.8	113.2	103.6	100.9	101.4	...
Electricity and gas [E] Électricité et gaz [E]	100.0	110.1	109.1	112.6	115.1	122.8	129.8	...
Cyprus — Chypre								
Total industry [CDE] Total, industrie [CDE]	96.7	99.4	100.9	105.4	105.1	105.2	113.7	115.5
Total mining [C] Total, industries extractives [C]	101.4	121.1	130.2	135.3	129.0	143.6	149.0	150.3
Total manufacturing [D] Total, industries manufacturières [D]	94.3	95.4	96.3	100.1	98.2	95.8	104.0	105.2
Food, beverages and tobacco — Aliments, boissons et tabac	93.9	94.5	98.1	102.0	100.8	96.9	98.7	97.3

Country or area and industry [ISIC Rev. 3] Pays ou zone et industrie [CITI Rév. 3]	1997	1998	1999	2000	2001	2002	2003	2004
Textiles, wearing apparel, leather, footwear Textiles, habillement, cuir et chaussures	80.2	81.7	76.0	70.1	67.2	55.3	39.8	34.6
Chemicals, petroleum, rubber and plastic products Prod. chimiques, pétroliers, caoutch. et plast.	102.9	101.7	101.8	102.6	105.7	107.0	101.5	94.9
Metal products — Produits métalliques	100.0	103.2	109.2	117.4	120.6	132.2	121.7	124.5
Electricity, gas and water [E] Electricité, gaz et eau [E]	107.8	116.0	123.5	131.7	141.6	153.6	165.1	170.4
India [9] — Inde [9]								
Total industry [CDE] Total, industrie [CDE]	113.1	117.8	125.6	131.9	135.4	143.2	153.3	165.6
Total mining [C] Total, industries extractives [C]	104.9	104.1	105.1	108.1	109.5	115.9	122.0	127.1
Total manufacturing [D] Total, industries manufacturières [D]	114.5	119.5	128.0	134.9	138.7	147.1	158.0	171.8
Food, beverages and tobacco — Aliments, boissons et tabac	110.9	113.3	118.9	125.8	124.6	140.8	142.6	147.6
Textiles, wearing apparel, leather, footwear Textiles, habillement, cuir et chaussures	112.9	109.7	117.0	123.9	123.9	126.0	127.1	137.6
Chemicals, petroleum, rubber and plastic products Prod. chimiques, pétroliers, caoutch. et plast.	116.4	125.2	134.8	146.4	154.3	160.4	172.7	192.7
Basic metals — Métaux de base	109.5	106.8	112.1	114.2	119.1	130.1	142.0	150.0
Metal products — Produits métalliques	113.2	125.2	137.7	145.2	145.1	156.2	178.3	199.8
Electricity [E] Electricité [E]	110.8	118.0	126.6	131.7	135.7	140.1	147.1	154.7
Indonesia — Indonésie								
Total industry [CDE] [3] Total, industrie [CDE] [3]	105.2	97.6	95.1	108.2	111.5	115.8	122.8	136.2
Total mining [C] Total, industries extractives [C]	103.3	103.8	96.9	117.7	124.6	137.9	148.4	170.1
Total manufacturing [D] Total, industries manufacturières [D]	106.0	86.7	88.3	91.5	90.5	84.2	87.2	90.9
Food, beverages and tobacco — Aliments, boissons et tabac	100.8	93.5	87.3	85.4	83.7	80.1	91.0	97.9
Textiles, wearing apparel, leather, footwear Textiles, habillement, cuir et chaussures	95.8	84.0	89.2	90.0	83.0	79.7	79.0	71.8
Chemicals, petroleum, rubber and plastic products Prod. chimiques, pétroliers, caoutch. et plast.	113.8	104.3	109.6	106.7	102.3	91.8	99.8	104.3
Basic metals — Métaux de base	104.1	81.1	89.3	109.3	111.6	98.1	77.2	73.8
Metal products — Produits métalliques	106.5	50.5	59.4	95.3	110.1	99.5	102.0	140.9
Electricity [E] Electricité [E]	130.1	147.6	167.5	185.2	187.2	183.8	184.2	186.2
Iran (Islamic Rep. of) — Iran (Rép. islamique d')								
Total manufacturing [D] Total, industries manufacturières [D]	108.6	130.3	135.8	141.2	146.6	152.0	157.5	162.9
Food and beverages Aliments et boissons	119.2	123.5	131.7	139.3	133.8	159.4	175.8	179.7
Textiles, wearing apparel, leather, footwear Textiles, habillement, cuir et chaussures	109.5	104.9	102.0	97.7	98.9	105.6	99.8	98.9
Chemicals, rubber and plastic prod. Prod. chimiques, caoutchouc et plastiques	117.7	115.2	124.4	129.6	137.6	147.5	160.7	181.9
Metal products — Produits métalliques	146.4	154.2	173.3	187.1	212.2	339.0	458.4	604.3
Israel — Israël								
Total industry [CD] Total, industrie [CD]	107.2	110.2	111.8	123.1	117.0	114.8	114.4	...

Country or area and industry [ISIC Rev. 3] Pays ou zone et industrie [CITI Rév. 3]	1997	1998	1999	2000	2001	2002	2003	2004
Total mining [C] Total, industries extractives [C]	104.9	109.2	108.2	105.6	107.8	116.3	112.9	...
Total manufacturing [D] Total, industries manufacturières [D]	107.3	110.3	112.0	123.6	116.8	114.8	114.5	...
Food, beverages and tobacco — Aliments, boissons et tabac	103.1	103.9	105.3	105.5	104.3	102.8	...	...
Textiles Textiles	94.6	97.7	102.3	96.6	88.4	84.6	...	...
Chemicals, petroleum, rubber and plastic products Prod. chimiques, pétroliers, caoutch. et plast.	108.8	119.1	118.1	122.1	124.4	136.4	...	...
Basic metals — Métaux de base	107.4	101.1	100.6	102.5	95.2	86.6	...	...
Metal products — Produits métalliques	107.5	106.6	104.4	114.4	108.7	106.1	...	...
Japan — Japon								
Total industry [CDE] Total, industrie [CDE]	106.0	99.0	99.9	105.5	98.7	97.6	100.6	106.0
Total mining [C] Total, industries extractives [C]	92.8	86.4	86.1	85.8	85.5	80.3	81.9	81.9
Total manufacturing [D] Total, industries manufacturières [D]	106.0	98.5	99.3	105.2	98.0	96.8	99.9	105.4
Food, beverages and tobacco — Aliments, boissons et tabac	100.4	97.8	98.6	99.0	98.2	97.1	97.3	95.4
Textiles, wearing apparel, leather, footwear Textiles, habillement, cuir et chaussures	92.6	82.4	77.1	70.9	63.9	56.7	52.1	48.4
Chemicals, petroleum, rubber and plastic products Prod. chimiques, pétroliers, caoutch. et plast.	104.0	100.5	103.1	104.2	103.4	102.9	104.5	105.2
Basic metals — Métaux de base	103.7	92.0	91.5	100.1	97.0	98.5	102.0	104.8
Metal products — Produits métalliques	110.3	102.7	105.7	117.5	104.7	105.8	112.7	124.2
Electricity and gas [E] Electricité et gaz [E]	105.6	106.8	108.2	111.5	111.7	112.6	114.2	118.1
Jordan — Jordanie								
Total industry [CDE] Total, industrie [CDE]	99.6	102.1	102.5	109.6	122.5	129.9	118.8	133.0
Total mining [C] Total, industries extractives [C]	104.0	99.4	106.6	108.4	110.9	119.0	116.5	112.1
Total manufacturing [D] Total, industries manufacturières [D]	100.9	104.1	102.0	110.0	125.0	132.3	119.5	136.0
Food, beverages and tobacco — Aliments, boissons et tabac	83.4	107.7	119.0	140.5	166.4	199.4	201.9	227.1
Textiles, wearing apparel, leather, footwear Textiles, habillement, cuir et chaussures	100.6	100.5	82.9	74.9	55.8	60.2	60.6	65.9
Chemicals, petroleum, rubber and plastic products Prod. chimiques, pétroliers, caoutch. et plast.	109.2	103.0	94.7	97.1	107.8	106.8	102.1	112.6
Basic metals — Métaux de base	78.1	64.4	75.3	70.7	88.1	84.2	92.0	101.2
Electricity [E] Electricité [E]	112.1	123.9	130.1	136.0	139.9	147.8	146.4	165.6
Korea, Republic of — Corée, République de								
Total industry [CDE] Total, industrie [CDE]	113.6	106.2	131.9	154.1	155.0	167.6	175.8	194.3
Total mining [C] Total, industries extractives [C]	94.0	72.7	78.6	77.5	77.4	80.4	79.8	77.4
Total manufacturing [D] Total, industries manufacturières [D]	113.1	105.6	132.0	154.6	154.9	167.5	175.9	194.7
Food, beverages and tobacco — Aliments, boissons et tabac	104.0	95.2	103.1	106.0	111.6	114.6	114.9	117.8
Textiles, wearing apparel, leather, footwear Textiles, habillement, cuir et chaussures	82.9	69.7	74.0	75.1	68.3	65.6	58.2	54.3

Country or area and industry [ISIC Rev. 3] Pays ou zone et industrie [CITI Rév. 3]	1997	1998	1999	2000	2001	2002	2003	2004
Chemicals, petroleum, rubber and plastic products Prod. chimiques, pétroliers, caoutch. et plast.	125.4	115.1	128.0	134.6	136.5	141.2	146.2	152.6
Basic metals — Métaux de base	112.2	98.7	112.7	122.2	124.0	130.1	136.8	143.8
Metal products — Produits métalliques	120.5	119.0	163.2	204.1	207.5	243.8	274.2	338.1
Electricity and gas [E] Electricité et gaz [E]	123.2	119.0	133.7	149.9	160.3	172.4	181.9	192.5
Malaysia — Malaisie								
Total industry [CDE] Total, industrie [CDE]	122.8	114.0	124.3	148.1	142.0	148.4	162.3	180.6
Total mining [C] Total, industries extractives [C]	108.4	109.6	106.1	105.9	108.8	110.7	116.7	123.4
Total manufacturing [D] Total, industries manufacturières [D]	126.2	113.3	127.7	159.8	149.2	156.0	171.5	194.1
Food, beverages and tobacco — Aliments, boissons et tabac	117.8	113.1	127.1	150.9	158.8	166.0	183.9	190.8
Textiles, wearing apparel, leather, footwear Textiles, habillement, cuir et chaussures	103.9	97.8	101.4	112.0	103.9	97.7	94.6	86.0
Chemicals, petroleum, rubber and plastic products Prod. chimiques, pétroliers, caoutch. et plast.	136.6	134.8	152.7	174.4	169.0	171.7	202.5	225.6
Basic metals — Métaux de base	132.5	- 93.7	134.6	141.6	140.8	144.1	159.7	166.7
Metal products — Produits métalliques	125.4	111.1	128.2	179.4	155.9	167.9	182.4	216.4
Electricity [E] Electricité [E]	128.8	133.2	138.3	146.8	159.4	174.2	186.1	201.5
Mongolia — Mongolie								
Total industry [CDE] Total, industrie [CDE]	101.9	186.2	106.7	108.9	121.9	122.7	...	...
Total mining [C] Total, industries extractives [C]	125.5	116.5	121.0	128.1	141.1	128.0	...	...
Total manufacturing [D] Total, industries manufacturières [D]	82.1	73.3	71.1	65.9	81.1	97.8	...	...
Food and beverages Aliments et boissons	70.8	69.6	60.7	59.5	70.4	66.1	...	...
Textiles, wearing apparel, leather, footwear Textiles, habillement, cuir et chaussures	80.8	80.6	88.4	83.0	121.6	149.5	...	...
Chemicals and chemical products Produits chimiques	96.1	103.0	108.0	108.4	117.3	135.4	...	...
Basic metals — Métaux de base	167.3	143.1	145.1	133.3	158.9	254.3	...	...
Electricity and gas [E] Electricité et gaz [E]	93.7	98.1	101.1	103.6	108.4	103.0	...	...
Pakistan [1] — Pakistan [1]								
Total industry [CDE] Total, industrie [CDE]	104.8	107.8	108.3	114.2	122.2	133.6	155.1	176.4
Total mining [C] Total, industries extractives [C]	96.1	101.0	104.1	113.1	112.2	124.1	129.0	133.5
Total manufacturing [D] Total, industries manufacturières [D]	105.3	109.1	109.1	116.3	123.4	134.3	159.0	183.5
Electricity [E] Electricité [E]	105.1	100.5	103.9	98.2	117.5	133.0	137.1	141.7
Singapore — Singapour								
Total manufacturing [D] Total, industries manufacturières [D]	108.2	107.7	122.6	141.3	124.8	135.4	139.5	158.9
Food, beverages and tobacco — Aliments, boissons et tabac	98.9	87.8	92.0	93.4	97.3	94.6	94.3	95.9
Textiles, wearing apparel, leather, footwear Textiles, habillement, cuir et chaussures	79.1	84.4	88.1	101.1	86.3	72.6	70.9	69.1

Country or area and industry [ISIC Rev. 3] Pays ou zone et industrie [CITI Rév. 3]	1997	1998	1999	2000	2001	2002	2003	2004
Chemicals, petroleum, rubber and plastic products Prod. chimiques, pétroliers, caoutch. et plast.	119.7	136.0	159.9	167.9	174.0	227.1	247.2	292.3
Basic metals — Métaux de base	105.2	87.3	92.7	98.4	99.0	101.6	87.3	103.7
Metal products — Produits métalliques	102.3	100.0	114.5	138.0	115.5	120.4	123.2	140.7
Sri Lanka — Sri Lanka								
Total manufacturing [D] Total, industries manufacturières [D]	91.0	97.2	99.4	101.0	104.7	109.2	110.0	113.3
Food, beverages and tobacco — Aliments, boissons et tabac	89.4	94.4	99.5	104.4	107.3	111.8	117.9	122.5
Textiles, wearing apparel, leather, footwear Textiles, habillement, cuir et chaussures	116.4	123.8	131.1	152.0	149.0	145.5	141.7	153.5
Chemicals, petroleum, rubber and plastic products Prod. chimiques, pétroliers, caoutch. et plast.	95.1	101.6	107.9	118.0	121.7	123.6	128.7	135.1
Basic metals — Métaux de base	90.7	97.4	104.2	107.2	108.8	113.3	117.6	127.8
Metal products — Produits métalliques	120.1	128.7	137.5	146.4	150.1	154.9	158.5	162.8
Syrian Arab Republic — Rép. arabe syrienne								
Total industry [CDE] Total, industrie [CDE]	107.0	109.0	109.0	109.0	112.3	118.8	111.2	...
Total mining [C] Total, industries extractives [C]	101.0	102.0	101.0	97.0	93.1	95.1	97.0	...
Total manufacturing [D] Total, industries manufacturières [D]	109.0	110.0	110.0	109.0	105.7	110.1	95.9	...
Food, beverages and tobacco — Aliments, boissons et tabac	108.0	102.1	108.3	107.6	112.4	123.9	119.3	...
Textiles, wearing apparel, leather, footwear Textiles, habillement, cuir et chaussures	106.9	108.3	113.7	126.3	134.9	140.5	132.3	...
Chemicals, petroleum, rubber and plastic products Prod. chimiques, pétroliers, caoutch. et plast.	109.6	109.3	95.1	95.1	112.9	109.0	96.3	...
Basic metals — Métaux de base	163.0	159.0	147.0	138.0	150.4	131.1	127.0	...
Metal products — Produits métalliques	88.9	85.4	93.2	60.6	107.4	90.4	75.8	...
Electricity and water [E] Électricité et eau [E]	115.0	129.0	142.0	155.0	164.3	172.1	181.4	
Tajikistan — Tadjikistan								
Total industry [CDE] Total, industrie [CDE]	74.4	81.4	86.0	95.3	109.3	116.3	120.9	...
Total mining [C] Total, industries extractives [C]	118.8	131.3	131.3	125.0	129.7	132.8	135.9	...
Total manufacturing [D] Total, industries manufacturières [D]	65.9	68.3	78.0	85.4	100.0	107.3	112.2	...
Electricity, gas and water [E] Électricité, gaz et eau [E]	109.5	112.6	126.3	112.6	116.8	121.1	124.2	...
Thailand — Thaïlande								
Total manufacturing [D] Total, industries manufacturières [D]	107.8	96.5	108.6	111.9	113.5	123.3	138.4	149.8
Turkey — Turquie								
Total industry [CDE] Total, industrie [CDE]	117.2	118.6	114.3	121.2	110.7	121.1	131.8	144.5
Total mining [C] Total, industries extractives [C]	109.4	121.7	109.6	106.6	97.9	89.9	86.9	90.4
Total manufacturing [D] Total, industries manufacturières [D]	118.8	118.9	113.9	121.3	109.7	121.7	133.0	146.8
Food, beverages and tobacco — Aliments, boissons et tabac	118.1	120.4	119.2	124.3	122.3	126.3	133.5	129.4
Textiles, wearing apparel, leather, footwear Textiles, habillement, cuir et chaussures	115.1	111.6	105.0	114.2	108.4	118.9	121.1	121.8

Country or area and industry [ISIC Rev. 3] Pays ou zone et industrie [CITI Rév. 3]	1997	1998	1999	2000	2001	2002	2003	2004
Chemicals, petroleum, rubber and plastic products Prod. chimiques, pétroliers, caoutch. et plast.	118.5	120.4	118.3	123.1	116.2	130.5	142.0	155.8
Basic metals — Métaux de base	118.1	118.7	116.5	120.9	114.9	126.4	141.4	157.9
Metal products — Produits métalliques	140.4	138.5	127.6	148.2	115.0	144.3	173.3	227.7
Electricity, gas and water [E] Electricité, gaz et eau [E]	119.6	128.7	135.0	144.9	142.3	150.0	162.7	173.8
Europe — Europe								
Albania — Albanie								
Total industry [CDE] Total, industrie [CDE]	53.6	82.5	59.7	121.3	91.3	...	...	...
Total mining [C] Total, industries extractives [C]	54.5	56.2	41.4	36.4	32.1	...	...	...
Total manufacturing [D] Total, industries manufacturières [D]	74.8	68.5	77.7	116.0	77.6	...	...	...
Electricity, gas and water [E] Electricité, gaz et eau [E]	116.0	114.6	121.5	104.5	81.5	...	...	...
Austria — Autriche								
Total industry [CDE] Total, industrie [CDE]	107.4	116.2	123.2	134.1	138.5	139.6	142.5	150.9
Total mining [C] Total, industries extractives [C]	96.7	103.9	107.4	112.3	109.8	113.4	112.9	105.4
Total manufacturing [D] Total, industries manufacturières [D]	108.0	117.8	124.9	137.3	140.5	139.6	143.6	153.6
Food, beverages and tobacco — Aliments, boissons et tabac	108.4	113.2	117.1	121.2	123.2	127.0	127.2	129.1
Textiles, wearing apparel, leather, footwear Textiles, habillement, cuir et chaussures	95.3	97.5	90.8	88.9	87.3	86.5	84.9	79.6
Chemicals, petroleum, rubber and plastic products Prod. chimiques, pétroliers, caoutch. et plast.	103.7	112.1	116.8	126.6	132.1	127.7	131.8	138.4
Basic metals — Métaux de base	111.2	114.6	113.9	126.5	134.8	136.1	136.7	145.0
Metal products — Produits métalliques	111.5	128.4	142.3	162.2	165.1	166.9	170.9	189.8
Electricity, gas and water [E] Electricité, gaz et eau [E]	104.8	106.6	112.9	114.6	129.0	137.3	138.2	138.2
Belarus — Bélarus								
Total industry [CDE] Total, industrie [CDE]	122.4	137.5	152.0	163.8	173.7	181.6	194.6	225.0
Total mining [C] Total, industries extractives [C]	111.7	118.6	123.9	117.5	130.7	134.8	147.5	160.5
Total manufacturing [D] Total, industries manufacturières [D]	123.6	139.3	154.2	167.0	176.4	184.3	197.2	228.6
Electricity [E] Electricité [E]	103.9	96.2	101.4	98.7	97.6	100.6	101.5	114.7
Belgium — Belgique								
Total industry [CDE] Total, industrie [CDE]	105.4	108.9	110.1	115.5	115.0	116.7	117.5	121.5
Total mining [C] Total, industries extractives [C]	113.4	116.6	125.2	138.1	139.5	182.2	173.9	177.0
Total manufacturing [D] Total, industries manufacturières [D]	105.4	108.4	109.7	116.2	116.1	117.1	117.7	122.7
Food, beverages and tobacco — Aliments, boissons et tabac	105.0	107.3	103.0	107.3	111.3	117.3	121.2	127.2
Textiles, wearing apparel, leather, footwear Textiles, habillement, cuir et chaussures	93.9	91.0	85.2	87.0	83.2	80.4	77.5	79.4
Chemicals, petroleum, rubber and plastic products Prod. chimiques, pétroliers, caoutch. et plast.	113.7	115.1	122.5	134.9	131.8	140.3	148.3	156.7

Country or area and industry [ISIC Rev. 3] Pays ou zone et industrie [CITI Rév. 3]	1997	1998	1999	2000	2001	2002	2003	2004
Basic metals — Métaux de base	98.2	101.2	101.5	106.9	94.7	95.5	97.9	89.6
Metal products — Produits métalliques	105.3	111.8	112.3	119.2	122.1	116.8	112.8	120.8
Electricity, gas and water [E] Electricité, gaz et eau [E]	105.6	112.7	112.8	109.8	106.9	109.6	112.4	110.1
Bulgaria — Bulgarie								
Total industry [CDE] Total, industrie [CDE]	85.8	78.5	72.2	78.2	79.9	83.6	96.4	113.5
Total mining [C] Total, industries extractives [C]	93.3	90.9	78.6	80.7	73.7	73.3	78.4	90.3
Total manufacturing [D] Total, industries manufacturières [D]	84.2	74.8	69.7	74.7	75.7	81.3	98.1	120.4
Food, beverages and tobacco — Aliments, boissons et tabac	75.5	78.2	73.8	73.3	71.1	71.9	85.9	99.5
Textiles, wearing apparel, leather, footwear Textiles, habillement, cuir et chaussures	91.8	87.9	75.2	85.5	94.1	115.7	153.0	167.6
Chemicals, petroleum, rubber and plastic products Prod. chimiques, pétroliers, caoutch. et plast.	84.4	61.9	61.7	69.7	70.7	67.7	80.4	86.1
Basic metals — Métaux de base	100.7	82.7	69.6	80.9	67.7	72.9	92.7	168.4
Metal products — Produits métalliques	87.2	84.0	71.4	72.3	76.5	87.9	101.3	125.3
Electricity, gas and water [E] Electricité, gaz et eau [E]	98.6	109.2	95.0	112.3	121.7	120.0	123.3	125.3
Croatia — Croatie								
Total industry [CDE] Total, industrie [CDE]	110.0	114.2	112.5	114.4	121.3	127.9	133.1	138.0
Total mining [C] Total, industries extractives [C]	96.6	94.2	96.0	97.8	99.7	116.7	119.4	115.4
Total manufacturing [D] Total, industries manufacturières [D]	105.2	108.6	105.4	108.5	115.4	120.5	126.7	131.8
Food, beverages and tobacco — Aliments, boissons et tabac	95.8	99.1	94.1	94.3	100.5	106.1	111.5	114.7
Textiles, wearing apparel, leather, footwear Textiles, habillement, cuir et chaussures	89.1	88.3	79.4	78.4	82.1	74.4	70.7	60.3
Chemicals, petroleum, rubber and plastic products Prod. chimiques, pétroliers, caoutch. et plast.	91.6	88.8	91.5	96.7	92.4	96.8	95.2	99.1
Basic metals — Métaux de base	114.1	133.3	115.6	120.6	125.7	113.3	119.1	149.5
Metal products — Produits métalliques	111.4	118.4	120.4	121.1	137.0	143.6	153.8	165.4
Electricity, gas and water [E] Electricité, gaz et eau [E]	155.7	169.3	181.0	172.4	180.7	183.8	189.8	197.8
Czech Republic — République tchèque								
Total industry [CDE] Total, industrie [CDE]	106.5	108.2	104.7	105.7	117.6	123.2	130.4	143.3
Total mining [C] Total, industries extractives [C]	98.5	92.8	81.6	88.2	89.4	89.7	90.1	89.3
Total manufacturing [D] Total, industries manufacturières [D]	108.1	110.9	107.9	108.2	121.8	128.4	135.8	150.4
Food, beverages and tobacco — Aliments, boissons et tabac	108.0	107.8	107.2	103.4	104.9	108.4	111.4	111.7
Textiles, wearing apparel, leather, footwear Textiles, habillement, cuir et chaussures	95.4	92.0	81.1	90.4	92.7	89.9	86.6	85.8
Chemicals, petroleum, rubber and plastic products Prod. chimiques, pétroliers, caoutch. et plast.	108.0	107.1	105.1	101.5	117.8	125.1	135.6	145.7
Basic metals — Métaux de base	92.6	86.2	69.0	58.7	60.5	59.5	60.5	76.9
Metal products — Produits métalliques	125.2	139.9	145.9	157.1	191.1	201.3	215.9	239.5
Electricity, gas and water [E] Electricité, gaz et eau [E]	100.9	99.4	95.9	102.1	103.8	103.9	113.1	114.2

Country or area and industry [ISIC Rev. 3] Pays ou zone et industrie [CITI Rév. 3]	1997	1998	1999	2000	2001	2002	2003	2004
Denmark — Danemark								
Total industry [CD] Total, industrie [CD]	106.2	109.4	109.6	115.5	117.2	119.1	118.2	118.6
Total mining [C] Total, industries extractives [C]	87.8	93.0	93.5	93.8	92.3	97.6	95.8	100.7
Total manufacturing [D] Total, industries manufacturières [D]	106.4	109.5	109.7	115.6	117.9	119.1	118.5	117.9
Food, beverages and tobacco — Aliments, boissons et tabac	103.1	98.3	101.6	103.3	103.3	111.0	117.9	114.4
Textiles, wearing apparel, leather, footwear Textiles, habillement, cuir et chaussures	102.8	105.1	101.1	103.2	93.4	88.2	83.9	70.2
Chemicals, petroleum, rubber and plastic products Prod. chimiques, pétroliers, caoutch. et plast.	111.6	116.1	130.7	141.7	152.3	155.4	150.9	139.4
Basic metals — Métaux de base	103.4	107.0	98.0	120.3	109.1	82.6	88.3	81.6
Metal products — Produits métalliques	106.7	112.8	109.3	116.1	121.4	123.3	121.2	123.0
Estonia — Estonie								
Total industry [CDE] Total, industrie [CDE]	117.9	122.7	118.6	135.9	148.0	160.1	177.6	191.6
Total mining [C] Total, industries extractives [C]	105.3	100.7	87.0	91.7	95.0	109.7	115.4	105.4
Total manufacturing [D] Total, industries manufacturières [D]	121.1	127.9	124.7	145.3	160.2	174.1	192.9	211.8
Food, beverages and tobacco — Aliments, boissons et tabac	108.6	103.3	83.1	89.0	97.7	99.6	102.1	106.3
Textiles, wearing apparel, leather, footwear Textiles, habillement, cuir et chaussures	127.5	134.0	135.6	160.6	179.4	193.2	205.3	198.2
Chemicals, rubber and plastic prod. Prod. chimiques, caoutchouc et plastiques	126.0	123.7	115.7	133.7	161.6	179.5	224.4	236.9
Basic metals — Métaux de base	111.2	167.2	162.5	181.2	277.7	360.7	621.6	435.0
Metal products — Produits métalliques	121.8	142.0	149.4	188.3	203.8	236.2	275.8	323.6
Electricity and gas [E] Electricité et gaz [E]	103.0	99.3	93.9	94.3	95.5	96.0	109.7	111.3
Finland — Finlande								
Total industry [CDE] Total, industrie [CDE]	112.0	122.3	129.3	144.5	144.7	147.7	149.4	156.5
Total mining [C] Total, industries extractives [C]	127.0	92.7	128.1	99.4	120.0	131.1	131.7	110.1
Total manufacturing [D] Total, industries manufacturières [D]	111.8	123.5	130.9	147.9	147.2	150.1	150.7	158.7
Food, beverages and tobacco — Aliments, boissons et tabac	106.3	106.8	110.7	109.3	113.4	116.4	118.7	119.1
Textiles, wearing apparel, leather, footwear Textiles, habillement, cuir et chaussures	101.4	100.5	100.4	98.3	100.2	98.1	90.0	85.3
Chemicals, petroleum, rubber and plastic products Prod. chimiques, pétroliers, caoutch. et plast.	108.2	114.5	117.2	127.7	127.1	125.9	125.8	127.5
Basic metals — Métaux de base	112.0	118.2	122.5	129.4	129.0	130.0	133.4	138.3
Metal products — Produits métalliques	118.1	140.1	154.2	191.3	194.0	198.1	197.0	214.6
Electricity, gas and water [E] Electricité, gaz et eau [E]	108.9	110.2	109.9	110.9	117.1	118.6	131.7	133.4
France — France								
Total industry [CDE] Total, industrie [CDE]	103.9	107.7	110.2	114.4	115.9	114.2	113.6	116.4
Total mining [C] Total, industries extractives [C]	88.0	86.9	86.8	88.4	87.4	83.0	82.0	80.6
Total manufacturing [D] Total, industries manufacturières [D]	104.4	108.6	111.2	115.6	116.9	114.9	114.0	116.8

Country or area and industry [ISIC Rev. 3] Pays ou zone et industrie [CITI Rév. 3]	1997	1998	1999	2000	2001	2002	2003	2004
Food, beverages and tobacco — Aliments, boissons et tabac	104.3	105.0	106.7	104.6	105.4	108.3	107.5	107.8
Textiles, wearing apparel, leather, footwear Textiles, habillement, cuir et chaussures	85.6	82.7	74.1	66.9	62.6	55.2	49.1	45.2
Chemicals, petroleum, rubber and plastic products Prod. chimiques, pétroliers, caoutch. et plast.	108.3	113.3	115.1	121.4	123.8	123.6	126.8	130.7
Basic metals — Métaux de base	104.0	106.5	104.0	111.4	108.9	106.6	103.2	105.3
Metal products — Produits métalliques	107.8	115.0	121.6	130.4	133.1	130.5	128.9	133.6
Electricity, gas and water [E] Electricité, gaz et eau [E]	102.1	103.6	105.6	108.6	112.1	112.1	115.2	117.3
Germany — Allemagne								
Total industry [CDE] Total, industrie [CDE]	103.4	107.2	108.4	114.5	114.8	113.5	114.0	117.4
Total mining [C] Total, industries extractives [C]	92.2	85.8	85.5	79.6	74.2	73.1	72.6	70.3
Total manufacturing [D] Total, industries manufacturières [D]	103.6	108.0	109.3	116.3	116.9	115.5	115.7	119.3
Food, beverages and tobacco — Aliments, boissons et tabac	103.9	103.3	106.3	108.8	108.2	108.8	108.6	109.4
Textiles, wearing apparel, leather, footwear Textiles, habillement, cuir et chaussures	90.8	88.8	81.7	79.9	76.5	70.6	65.7	63.5
Chemicals, petroleum, rubber and plastic products Prod. chimiques, pétroliers, caoutch. et plast.	107.2	108.9	111.9	115.7	113.7	117.1	117.8	120.9
Basic metals — Métaux de base	104.1	105.2	101.3	109.6	110.9	111.6	109.5	113.7
Metal products — Produits métalliques	105.8	114.1	115.9	127.8	131.0	129.0	130.3	136.1
Electricity and gas [E] Electricité et gaz [E]	104.6	104.7	105.1	106.5	104.6	104.9	108.7	111.4
Greece — Grèce								
Total industry [CDE] Total, industrie [CDE]	102.8	112.0	114.2	122.5	120.3	121.3	121.6	123.0
Total mining [C] Total, industries extractives [C]	103.9	102.6	96.4	109.3	111.9	122.7	116.3	116.7
Total manufacturing [D] Total, industries manufacturières [D]	101.9	110.2	109.2	114.8	111.9	111.8	111.4	112.6
Food, beverages and tobacco — Aliments, boissons et tabac	102.4	111.8	111.6	113.5	115.4	116.8	114.2	121.0
Textiles, wearing apparel, leather, footwear Textiles, habillement, cuir et chaussures	92.7	91.4	85.9	86.6	80.7	77.0	75.1	69.4
Chemicals, petroleum, rubber and plastic products Prod. chimiques, pétroliers, caoutch. et plast.	110.7	124.8	121.6	130.9	132.2	136.4	137.8	129.9
Basic metals — Métaux de base	106.2	98.3	109.7	125.5	129.7	138.3	136.7	143.8
Metal products — Produits métalliques	97.5	108.0	110.4	119.1	106.9	101.8	104.0	106.2
Electricity and gas [E] Electricité et gaz [E]	104.5	120.0	135.1	151.0	149.6	152.2	163.2	165.5
Hungary — Hongrie								
Total industry [CDE] Total, industrie [CDE]	114.8	129.0	142.4	168.4	175.0	180.7	192.6	208.8
Total mining [C] Total, industries extractives [C]	93.9	74.7	75.1	68.2	79.4	71.9	69.4	75.9
Total manufacturing [D] Total, industries manufacturières [D]	118.5	137.7	154.6	186.8	194.6	201.6	215.8	235.9
Food, beverages and tobacco — Aliments, boissons et tabac	92.4	93.1	95.3	101.6	100.8	102.7	101.8	99.3
Textiles, wearing apparel, leather, footwear Textiles, habillement, cuir et chaussures	98.9	112.4	121.6	133.8	136.7	130.0	117.9	112.2
Chemicals, petroleum, rubber and plastic products Prod. chimiques, pétroliers, caoutch. et plast.	101.7	105.9	100.2	107.6	109.8	114.4	116.3	125.2

Country or area and industry [ISIC Rev. 3] Pays ou zone et industrie [CITI Rév. 3]	1997	1998	1999	2000	2001	2002	2003	2004
Basic metals — Métaux de base	122.4	118.8	113.5	132.2	127.8	133.2	144.0	153.9
Metal products — Produits métalliques	158.7	216.4	297.8	402.2	407.5	421.9	499.8	588.1
Electricity and gas [E] Electricité et gaz [E]	106.0	106.0	102.9	101.4	101.4	105.8	110.1	110.6
Ireland — Irlande								
Total industry [CDE] Total, industrie [CDE]	127.0	152.2	174.6	201.6	222.0	237.9	249.0	249.8
Total mining [C] Total, industries extractives [C]	84.7	78.0	92.9	114.7	114.6	108.9	132.7	129.8
Total manufacturing [D] Total, industries manufacturières [D]	129.2	156.8	180.4	208.8	230.5	247.8	259.1	259.5
Food, beverages and tobacco — Aliments, boissons et tabac	103.5	109.0	114.4	120.4	128.3	133.3	138.4	145.7
Textiles, wearing apparel, leather, footwear Textiles, habillement, cuir et chaussures	100.3	102.1	90.1	73.6	77.4	55.2	48.1	46.4
Chemicals, rubber and plastic prod. Prod. chimiques, caoutchouc et plastiques	157.1	218.7	273.0	310.4	378.5	469.0	488.5	443.8
Basic metals — Métaux de base	95.1	90.4	91.5	94.2	84.3	83.0	79.4	75.3
Metal products — Produits métalliques	126.0	143.8	161.6	213.3	224.4	208.5	235.8	255.7
Electricity, gas and water [E] Electricité, gaz et eau [E]	110.1	113.0	122.6	129.0	137.4	141.9	146.1	152.0
Italy — Italie								
Total industry [CDE] Total, industrie [CDE]	102.4	104.3	104.4	107.7	107.1	105.3	104.3	104.8
Total mining [C] Total, industries extractives [C]	108.5	107.9	107.8	98.4	90.8	106.2	108.2	106.0
Total manufacturing [D] Total, industries manufacturières [D]	102.2	103.9	103.6	106.7	106.1	103.7	101.9	102.3
Food, beverages and tobacco — Aliments, boissons et tabac	102.2	104.4	107.6	109.9	113.9	114.9	117.3	116.0
Textiles, wearing apparel, leather, footwear Textiles, habillement, cuir et chaussures	102.1	99.9	95.2	95.6	95.3	88.5	85.3	82.0
Chemicals, petroleum, rubber and plastic products Prod. chimiques, pétroliers, caoutch. et plast.	105.2	106.8	106.3	108.4	106.5	107.4	106.4	108.2
Basic metals — Métaux de base	102.0	101.8	94.1	100.8	96.8	95.7	97.0	101.4
Metal products — Produits métalliques	102.2	104.0	102.5	106.5	105.0	101.3	98.2	98.3
Electricity and gas [E] Electricité et gaz [E]	103.4	107.3	111.4	118.3	119.0	120.7	126.8	130.4
Latvia — Lettonie								
Total industry [CDE] Total, industrie [CDE]	120.1	123.8	101.7	104.9	112.1	118.6	126.4	134.0
Total mining [C] Total, industries extractives [C]	110.4	117.2	123.9	134.9	141.4	154.2	162.4	180.2
Total manufacturing [D] Total, industries manufacturières [D]	125.6	130.2	103.6	108.4	116.5	123.8	133.5	141.8
Food, beverages and tobacco — Aliments, boissons et tabac	127.7	124.0	102.0	100.6	107.0	112.7	119.4	126.9
Textiles, wearing apparel, leather, footwear Textiles, habillement, cuir et chaussures	138.9	140.8	121.3	133.1	137.9	136.8	132.3	132.2
Chemicals, rubber and plastic prod. Prod. chimiques, caoutchouc et plastiques	115.6	105.5	56.5	48.7	54.7	63.2	60.3	71.8
Basic metals — Métaux de base	139.7	237.6	325.9	325.8	379.9	373.4	456.4	493.6
Metal products — Produits métalliques	103.2	91.7	72.9	91.3	94.5	102.7	117.3	126.0
Electricity, gas and water [E] Electricité, gaz et eau [E]	97.4	98.5	92.5	89.8	94.6	98.8	101.6	106.7

Country or area and industry [ISIC Rev. 3] Pays ou zone et industrie [CITI Rév. 3]	1997	1998	1999	2000	2001	2002	2003	2004
Lithuania — Lituanie								
Total industry [CDE] Total, industrie [CDE]	108.9	117.8	104.6	110.1	127.7	131.6	152.8	169.4
Total mining [C] Total, industries extractives [C]	136.3	185.7	177.1	198.1	263.1	250.8	271.8	251.2
Total manufacturing [D] Total, industries manufacturières [D]	106.6	115.4	102.8	111.9	129.6	133.3	152.1	170.1
Food, beverages and tobacco — Aliments, boissons et tabac	102.9	107.1	97.6	103.6	106.1	103.9	113.0	117.6
Textiles, wearing apparel, leather, footwear Textiles, habillement, cuir et chaussures	111.6	109.9	111.9	121.3	132.1	131.0	130.1	126.2
Chemicals, petroleum, rubber and plastic products Prod. chimiques, pétroliers, caoutch. et plast.	120.7	137.5	134.2	143.0	143.6	169.2	185.3	195.4
Basic metals — Métaux de base	69.2	79.3	172.2	255.8	265.3	211.0	155.5	121.0
Metal products — Produits métalliques	103.2	114.4	117.3	134.5	153.2	180.9	231.6	272.7
Electricity, gas and water [E] Electricité, gaz et eau [E]	96.8	99.9	80.7	68.7	79.1	83.3	108.1	116.0
Luxembourg — Luxembourg								
Total industry [CDE] Total, industrie [CDE]	105.3	114.5	116.3	122.1	126.1	128.4	134.7	143.8
Total mining [C] Total, industries extractives [C]	89.4	100.2	107.8	108.8	111.5	100.6	89.0	87.8
Total manufacturing [D] Total, industries manufacturières [D]	106.1	115.7	117.7	123.6	126.9	128.7	134.2	142.0
Food and beverages Aliments et boissons	99.6	101.2	105.6	106.6	122.1	124.1	121.2	126.7
Textiles, wearing apparel, leather, footwear Textiles, habillement, cuir et chaussures	93.2	98.8	91.6	98.4	100.0	102.3	107.3	107.6
Chemicals, rubber and plastic prod. Prod. chimiques, caoutchouc et plastiques	109.9	129.6	119.5	128.3	137.8	149.0	159.4	165.7
Basic metals — Métaux de base	102.9	90.1	114.2	120.6	118.7	115.1	118.2	123.7
Metal products — Produits métalliques	106.9	121.6	122.0	122.5	117.2	116.0	119.0	127.0
Electricity and gas [E] Electricité et gaz [E]	98.2	102.0	99.8	106.9	116.0	124.6	140.0	159.2
Malta — Malte								
Total industry [CDE] Total, industrie [CDE]	95.9	97.8	98.5	111.8	102.7	...	...	...
Total mining [C] Total, industries extractives [C]	112.1	112.9	113.8	152.5	155.5	...	...	...
Total manufacturing [D] Total, industries manufacturières [D]	94.1	95.2	96.2	110.1	100.0	...	...	...
Food, beverages and tobacco — Aliments, boissons et tabac	106.5	109.6	112.6	115.9	114.2	...	...	...
Textiles, wearing apparel, leather, footwear Textiles, habillement, cuir et chaussures	109.7	111.8	113.4	113.3	117.1	...	...	...
Chemicals, petroleum, rubber and plastic products Prod. chimiques, pétroliers, caoutch. et plast.	102.5	104.4	105.4	91.5	81.9	...	...	...
Metal products — Produits métalliques	92.0	92.8	93.7	104.4	96.9	...	...	...
Electricity and water [E] Electricité et eau [E]	104.1	105.9	106.8	110.8	114.1	...	...	...
Netherlands — Pays-Bas								
Total industry [CDE] Total, industrie [CDE]	102.6	104.8	106.3	110.0	110.5	110.1	107.5	110.2
Total mining [C] Total, industries extractives [C]	104.2	103.3	100.0	97.8	103.6	104.7	101.5	117.5

Country or area and industry [ISIC Rev. 3] Pays ou zone et industrie [CITI Rév. 3]	1997	1998	1999	2000	2001	2002	2003	2004
Total manufacturing [D] Total, industries manufacturières [D]	103.2	106.3	108.9	113.6	112.8	111.9	108.9	109.3
Food, beverages and tobacco — Aliments, boissons et tabac	102.1	102.1	103.8	105.3	105.4	107.8	104.8	104.3
Textiles, wearing apparel, leather, footwear Textiles, habillement, cuir et chaussures	99.9	103.9	105.0	112.2	105.8	102.8	97.2	93.3
Chemicals, petroleum, rubber and plastic products Prod. chimiques, pétroliers, caoutch. et plast.	99.4	100.3	105.2	111.3	114.1	118.2	121.9	121.9
Basic metals — Métaux de base	105.5	107.6	107.9	109.9	109.0	106.9	109.5	121.8
Metal products — Produits métalliques	105.6	109.8	111.5	120.4	118.3	112.8	107.3	108.6
Electricity, gas and water [E] Electricité, gaz et eau [E]	97.6	97.9	96.1	97.8	100.5	102.1	103.5	104.2
Norway — Norvège								
Total industry [CDE] Total, industrie [CDE]	109.0	107.7	107.5	110.7	109.2	110.3	105.8	107.8
Total mining [C] [10] Total, industries extractives [C] [10]	116.1	109.1	109.8	115.7	119.3	117.7	115.7	113.8
Total manufacturing [D] Total, industries manufacturières [D]	105.8	108.8	106.3	103.0	102.0	101.1	96.7	98.2
Food, beverages and tobacco — Aliments, boissons et tabac	102.9	102.1	98.8	97.1	96.3	93.7	89.8	90.0
Textiles, wearing apparel, leather, footwear Textiles, habillement, cuir et chaussures	99.9	95.1	83.1	76.4	72.4	65.5	56.3	54.1
Chemicals, petroleum, rubber and plastic products Prod. chimiques, pétroliers, caoutch. et plast.	103.3	105.7	105.9	104.3	104.2	102.4	102.4	104.7
Basic metals — Métaux de base	106.6	111.7	115.2	116.3	111.3	109.1	109.5	120.6
Metal products — Produits métalliques	108.1	117.3	115.2	109.6	109.9	110.9	103.7	103.9
Electricity and gas [E] Electricité et gaz [E]	90.8	94.9	99.4	115.7	98.5	105.2	86.9	88.0
Poland — Pologne								
Total industry [CDE] Total, industrie [CDE]	121.7	127.4	133.5	143.5	144.1	146.1	158.9	179.1
Total mining [C] Total, industries extractives [C]	99.7	86.6	83.2	82.1	77.9	75.5	74.1	76.4
Total manufacturing [D] Total, industries manufacturières [D]	126.6	134.9	142.4	153.7	153.5	156.3	172.8	198.0
Food, beverages and tobacco — Aliments, boissons et tabac	118.3	127.0	129.0	130.1	134.0	138.6	146.0	154.7
Textiles, wearing apparel, leather, footwear Textiles, habillement, cuir et chaussures	118.1	120.0	115.9	114.5	110.3	109.4	108.4	108.1
Chemicals, petroleum, rubber and plastic products Prod. chimiques, pétroliers, caoutch. et plast.	121.3	124.9	132.8	147.1	153.2	163.0	186.8	208.0
Basic metals — Métaux de base	112.9	107.2	97.2	106.5	89.6	85.8	89.3	107.3
Metal products — Produits métalliques	136.6	152.3	163.8	180.1	181.2	187.2	215.9	268.8
Electricity, gas and water [E] Electricité, gaz et eau [E]	102.8	104.7	107.1	116.9	126.4	126.1	126.7	128.1
Portugal — Portugal								
Total industry [CDE] Total, industrie [CDE]	109.6	114.0	117.6	118.1	121.6	121.2	121.3	118.1
Total mining [C] Total, industries extractives [C]	103.3	105.2	102.2	103.8	105.8	100.2	90.7	94.6
Total manufacturing [D] Total, industries manufacturières [D]	110.0	112.8	114.4	114.8	117.3	117.8	117.2	116.4
Food, beverages and tobacco — Aliments, boissons et tabac	105.4	109.3	113.5	116.8	119.3	122.7	122.1	125.2
Textiles, wearing apparel, leather, footwear Textiles, habillement, cuir et chaussures	95.1	91.4	86.2	80.4	81.1	77.1	71.2	66.2

Country or area and industry [ISIC Rev. 3] Pays ou zone et industrie [CITI Rév. 3]	1997	1998	1999	2000	2001	2002	2003	2004
Chemicals, petroleum, rubber and plastic products Prod. chimiques, pétroliers, caoutch. et plast.	107.7	110.3	115.0	114.2	113.5	120.1	122.9	123.5
Basic metals — Métaux de base	109.9	112.5	126.3	124.1	114.6	115.5	114.2	117.3
Metal products — Produits métalliques	121.9	130.7	134.8	136.2	141.8	141.4	146.4	146.5
Electricity and gas [E] Electricité et gaz [E]	113.1	124.3	144.3	145.6	158.7	150.4	158.6	132.8
Romania — Roumanie								
Total industry [CDE] Total, industrie [CDE]	98.7	81.9	77.7	83.2	90.4	94.3	97.5	101.5
Total mining [C] Total, industries extractives [C]	95.0	81.6	76.1	79.8	84.3	79.8	79.6	80.8
Total manufacturing [D] Total, industries manufacturières [D]	100.8	82.5	78.5	85.1	93.9	99.8	103.7	109.2
Food, beverages and tobacco — Aliments, boissons et tabac	86.2	85.0	85.9	97.2	117.4	130.7	137.3	130.2
Textiles, wearing apparel, leather, footwear Textiles, habillement, cuir et chaussures	111.1	71.8	73.8	82.5	91.3	95.1	105.0	102.1
Chemicals, petroleum, rubber and plastic products Prod. chimiques, pétroliers, caoutch. et plast.	75.3	64.7	59.1	66.9	67.6	72.8	77.0	92.0
Basic metals — Métaux de base	93.0	92.4	63.9	79.9	90.7	110.4	89.4	100.9
Metal products — Produits métalliques	119.5	97.0	92.2	84.2	88.4	90.4	97.4	106.0
Electricity, gas and water [E] Electricité, gaz et eau [E]	88.8	77.8	72.9	72.7	70.9	68.4	69.9	67.2
Russian Federation — Fédération de Russie								
Total industry [CDE] Total, industrie [CDE]	93.3	88.8	96.7	105.2	108.3	111.7	121.6	130.5
Total mining [C] Total, industries extractives [C]	97.2	94.9	98.7	105.0	111.3	118.8	129.1	137.5
Total manufacturing [D] Total, industries manufacturières [D]	91.6	85.9	96.9	107.5	109.6	110.8	122.2	133.4
Food, beverages and tobacco — Aliments, boissons et tabac	91.3	90.2	100.8	104.9	113.6	121.9	131.1	135.4
Textiles, wearing apparel, leather, footwear Textiles, habillement, cuir et chaussures	78.0	71.2	82.6	101.1	109.7	109.2	112.3	106.0
Chemicals, petroleum, rubber and plastic products Prod. chimiques, pétroliers, caoutch. et plast.	94.4	87.9	104.7	117.6	119.0	120.8	126.1	130.3
Basic metals — Métaux de base	100.3	94.6	103.2	119.0	121.2	127.1	136.3	140.5
Metal products — Produits métalliques	89.7	79.8	91.7	106.7	108.0	101.0	124.3	145.2
Electricity and gas [E] Electricité et gaz [E]	95.5	93.3	92.2	95.9	97.2	101.9	105.3	105.4
Serbia and Montenegro — Serbie-et-Monténégro								
Total industry [CDE] Total, industrie [CDE]	117.2	121.2	91.7	102.1	102.3	104.2	101.4	109.1
Total mining [C] Total, industries extractives [C]	106.0	105.4	86.0	93.8	81.9	83.6	84.6	83.6
Total manufacturing [D] Total, industries manufacturières [D]	127.8	133.4	94.7	108.4	109.3	112.6	107.5	118.3
Food, beverages and tobacco — Aliments, boissons et tabac	98.2	113.5	109.5	110.5	107.5	116.3	113.8	117.8
Textiles, wearing apparel, leather, footwear Textiles, habillement, cuir et chaussures	112.3	127.2	90.3	106.4	108.0	86.6	61.3	58.6
Chemicals, petroleum, rubber and plastic products Prod. chimiques, pétroliers, caoutch. et plast.	194.1	226.0	124.6	141.3	164.2	170.4	184.8	213.4

Country or area and industry [ISIC Rev. 3] / Pays ou zone et industrie [CITI Rév. 3]	1997	1998	1999	2000	2001	2002	2003	2004
Basic metals — Métaux de base	177.4	192.6	105.2	142.2	138.3	146.9	149.7	195.9
Metal products — Produits métalliques	120.3	134.4	94.7	114.8	101.5	106.7	96.3	108.9
Electricity, gas and water [E] / Electricité, gaz et eau [E]	108.4	109.3	103.1	104.6	105.3	103.1	106.5	108.2
Slovakia — Slovaquie								
Total industry [CDE] / Total, industrie [CDE]	103.8	108.6	106.3	115.2	123.1	130.9	137.6	143.3
Total mining [C] / Total, industries extractives [C]	117.7	104.7	103.8	101.6	88.2	113.5	107.1	95.0
Total manufacturing [D] / Total, industries manufacturières [D]	104.0	110.4	106.6	116.6	128.2	138.8	149.3	156.3
Electricity, gas and water [E] / Electricité, gaz et eau [E]	101.5	95.6	98.4	105.1	103.2	97.1	92.2	95.7
Slovenia — Slovénie								
Total industry [CDE] / Total, industrie [CDE]	102.0	105.8	105.3	111.9	115.1	117.9	119.5	127.0
Total mining [C] / Total, industries extractives [C]	102.3	102.0	97.8	95.5	87.7	94.6	100.2	104.7
Total manufacturing [D] / Total, industries manufacturières [D]	101.4	105.4	105.4	112.9	116.0	118.3	120.2	128.2
Food, beverages and tobacco — Aliments, boissons et tabac	101.5	101.8	101.6	110.2	113.9	109.4	111.4	106.6
Textiles, wearing apparel, leather, footwear / Textiles, habillement, cuir et chaussures	96.8	94.8	85.9	89.2	83.2	71.2	63.1	57.3
Chemicals, petroleum, rubber and plastic products / Prod. chimiques, pétroliers, caoutch. et plast.	107.2	109.4	110.1	122.8	130.1	135.4	149.3	161.7
Basic metals — Métaux de base	80.6	81.6	88.9	100.4	105.4	107.7	119.1	130.9
Metal products — Produits métalliques	90.9	102.2	104.7	111.8	119.5	126.1	132.0	144.3
Electricity [E] / Electricité [E]	109.0	112.7	107.5	109.1	118.1	126.2	121.0	123.2
Spain — Espagne								
Total industry [CDE] / Total, industrie [CDE]	106.1	111.9	114.8	119.3	117.9	118.0	119.9	122.0
Total mining [C] / Total, industries extractives [C]	91.9	92.0	90.1	91.1	88.2	87.7	87.7	83.5
Total manufacturing [D] / Total, industries manufacturières [D]	106.6	113.2	115.8	119.7	117.3	117.8	119.6	121.0
Food, beverages and tobacco — Aliments, boissons et tabac	104.6	109.1	109.3	108.3	109.5	113.7	116.3	118.1
Textiles, wearing apparel, leather, footwear / Textiles, habillement, cuir et chaussures	99.5	101.5	99.4	97.6	94.4	85.6	79.4	73.8
Chemicals, petroleum, rubber and plastic products / Prod. chimiques, pétroliers, caoutch. et plast.	107.0	112.6	118.7	119.7	119.7	125.1	130.0	129.8
Basic metals — Métaux de base	103.8	108.5	109.5	124.7	120.2	127.9	129.4	137.4
Metal products — Produits métalliques	111.5	121.0	122.7	128.8	123.8	119.5	121.3	123.9
Electricity and gas [E] / Electricité et gaz [E]	107.0	108.4	115.1	124.9	130.3	130.3	134.0	143.4
Sweden — Suède								
Total industry [CDE] / Total, industrie [CDE]	105.4	110.3	113.4	119.9	118.6	118.5	120.1	126.4
Total mining [C] / Total, industries extractives [C]	92.8	94.6	96.6	97.9	96.3	99.4	96.3	105.2

Country or area and industry [ISIC Rev. 3] Pays ou zone et industrie [CITI Rév. 3]	1997	1998	1999	2000	2001	2002	2003	2004
Total manufacturing [D] Total, industries manufacturières [D]	106.1	111.2	114.8	122.0	120.6	121.8	124.8	130.2
Food, beverages and tobacco — Aliments, boissons et tabac	102.8	103.8	103.7	102.5	105.7	103.1	98.8	100.0
Textiles, wearing apparel, leather, footwear Textiles, habillement, cuir et chaussures	97.7	94.5	86.9	87.8	87.0	83.3	82.2	84.8
Chemicals, petroleum, rubber and plastic products Prod. chimiques, pétroliers, caoutch. et plast.	110.2	113.0	117.2	125.7	133.7	140.4	151.2	160.2
Basic metals — Métaux de base	105.8	105.6	105.1	110.6	120.9	126.2	124.4	131.7
Metal products — Produits métalliques	108.8	116.8	123.6	135.5	130.4	125.2	129.0	141.0
Electricity, gas and water [E] Electricité, gaz et eau [E]	101.9	106.2	105.2	106.0	104.5	94.8	87.7	97.8
Switzerland — Suisse								
Total industry [CDE] Total, industrie [CDE]	104.6	108.4	112.2	121.7	120.8	114.6	114.6	119.7
Total mining [C] Total, industries extractives [C]	100.5	87.9	93.4	94.2	94.7	93.3	92.6	96.5
Total manufacturing [D] Total, industries manufacturières [D]	104.9	109.1	112.7	123.2	121.8	115.4	115.3	120.8
Food, beverages and tobacco — Aliments, boissons et tabac	92.2	88.2	86.8	88.5	85.8	90.6	90.1	91.2
Textiles and wearing apparel Textiles et habillement	99.0	93.1	87.5	87.7	79.7	74.4	70.2	77.0
Chemicals and chemical products Produits chimiques	125.7	135.8	152.0	163.0	172.0	181.7	197.3	206.4
Basic metals and metal products Métaux de base et produits métalliques	106.3	108.6	108.8	123.9	123.5	108.6	104.5	105.8
Electricity, gas and water [E] Electricité, gaz et eau [E]	101.5	102.4	108.1	107.6	112.2	107.6	109.8	109.3
TFYR of Macedonia — L'ex-R.y. Macédoine								
Total industry [CDE] Total, industrie [CDE]	104.7	109.5	106.7	110.4	99.2	93.9	98.3	96.1
Ukraine — Ukraine								
Total industry [CDE] Total, industrie [CDE]	93.1	91.6	95.9	109.0	123.1	131.2	152.2	170.1
Total mining [C] Total, industries extractives [C]	97.9	95.3	98.3	104.6	108.1	110.6	116.7	121.5
Total manufacturing [D] Total, industries manufacturières [D]	94.5	93.7	97.1	113.2	132.7	144.5	170.8	195.7
Electricity, gas and water [E] Electricité, gaz et eau [E]	90.8	90.6	88.3	89.2	91.2	92.5	94.9	93.9
United Kingdom — Royaume-Uni								
Total industry [CDE] Total, industrie [CDE]	102.8	103.9	105.1	107.1	105.4	102.8	102.3	103.1
Total mining [C] Total, industries extractives [C]	102.2	104.3	108.6	105.3	99.4	99.1	94.1	86.5
Total manufacturing [D] Total, industries manufacturières [D]	102.5	103.3	104.1	106.6	105.2	101.9	102.0	103.9
Food, beverages and tobacco — Aliments, boissons et tabac	103.6	102.3	101.9	101.2	102.1	103.1	103.0	104.4
Textiles, wearing apparel, leather, footwear Textiles, habillement, cuir et chaussures	96.9	89.4	83.2	80.3	71.6	66.2	64.6	53.5
Chemicals, petroleum, rubber and plastic products Prod. chimiques, pétroliers, caoutch. et plast.	101.5	102.2	103.4	107.5	110.2	109.3	109.5	111.9

Country or area and industry [ISIC Rev. 3] Pays ou zone et industrie [CITI Rév. 3]	1997	1998	1999	2000	2001	2002	2003	2004
Basic metals — Métaux de base	102.9	101.1	97.3	94.0	91.7	81.8	79.4	82.7
Metal products — Produits métalliques	105.5	108.9	112.6	119.3	115.1	105.4	104.5	107.3
Electricity, gas and water [E] Electricité, gaz et eau [E]	105.3	108.7	111.6	114.1	116.7	116.1	117.5	120.1
Oceania — Océanie								
Australia [2] — Australie [2]								
Total industry [CDE] Total, industrie [CDE]	105.2	108.6	110.0	112.5	116.7	118.2	120.3	120.0
Total mining [C] Total, industries extractives [C]	109.1	112.5	113.3	121.5	129.4	128.9	126.9	122.9
Total manufacturing [D] Total, industries manufacturières [D]	104.4	107.8	110.0	110.9	113.7	116.7	120.3	121.4
Food, beverages and tobacco — Aliments, boissons et tabac	105.1	113.6	117.6	119.3	124.6	123.5	124.1	123.6
Textiles, wearing apparel, leather, footwear Textiles, habillement, cuir et chaussures	94.1	95.9	96.0	92.5	85.4	74.5	66.9	63.0
Chemicals, petroleum, rubber and plastic products Prod. chimiques, pétroliers, caoutch. et plast.	108.0	110.9	112.4	116.2	118.9	122.7	133.2	129.5
Basic metals and metal products Métaux de base et produits métalliques	106.2	108.9	109.9	107.4	110.1	114.3	118.1	121.1
Electricity, gas and water [E] Electricité, gaz et eau [E]	101.1	104.7	106.3	108.6	110.2	109.6	110.6	111.4
Fiji — Fidji								
Total industry [CDE] Total, industrie [CDE]	115.1	119.2	129.7	122.8	136.3	137.2	134.0	149.5
Total mining [C] Total, industries extractives [C]	141.3	113.3	134.5	116.3	117.1	113.6	106.9	122.7
Total manufacturing [D] Total, industries manufacturières [D]	113.8	121.6	130.6	123.1	140.0	139.7	136.2	152.9
Food, beverages and tobacco — Aliments, boissons et tabac	86.1	89.1	96.7	88.6	97.5	104.8	111.3	119.5
Textiles and wearing apparel Textiles et habillement	169.3	220.9	240.6	227.3	297.6	261.3	232.8	290.5
Chemicals and chemical products Produits chimiques	113.5	124.7	109.2	95.0	92.3	110.4	92.2	106.7
Electricity and water [E] Electricité et eau [E]	110.7	114.5	125.9	123.9	114.6	123.2	136.0	147.5
New Zealand [11] — Nouvelle-Zélande [11]								
Total industry [CDE] Total, industrie [CDE]	104.6	103.6	101.0	104.7	107.2	108.4	115.3	114.6
Total mining [C] [12] Total, industries extractives [C] [12]	112.5	113.9	112.0	116.7	118.6	120.0	123.4	113.8
Total manufacturing [D] Total, industries manufacturières [D]	103.5	102.8	99.2	104.1	106.8	108.5	115.8	117.5
Food, beverages and tobacco — Aliments, boissons et tabac	104.3	108.6	104.9	106.7	109.2	111.1	123.7	125.0
Textiles, wearing apparel, leather, footwear Textiles, habillement, cuir et chaussures	103.2	95.3	93.2	96.8	85.6	88.4	91.5	87.7
Chemicals, petroleum, rubber and plastic products Prod. chimiques, pétroliers, caoutch. et plast.	102.0	95.8	93.2	96.1	102.1	98.9	102.2	92.9
Basic metals and metal products Métaux de base et produits métalliques	105.3	104.5	101.7	108.3	115.0	120.2	125.4	133.6
Electricity, gas and water [E] Electricité, gaz et eau [E]	97.3	97.3	100.8	95.9	97.7	94.7	102.5	103.4

Source

United Nations Statistics Division, New York, the index numbers of industrial production database.

Notes

[1] Twelve months beginning 1 July of the year stated.
[2] Twelve months ending 30 June of the year stated.
[3] Calculated by the Statistics Division of the United Nations from component national indices.
[4] Excluding coal mining and crude petroleum.
[5] Excluding petroleum refineries.
[6] Twelve months ending 30 September of the year stated.
[7] Including construction.
[8] Base: 1997=100.
[9] Twelve months beginning 1 April of the year stated.
[10] Excluding gas and oil extraction.
[11] Twelve months ending 31 March of the year stated.
[12] Including forestry and fishing.

Source

Organisation des Nations Unies, Division de statistique, New York, la base de données pour les indices de la production industrielle.

Notes

[1] Période de 12 mois commençant le 1er juillet de l'année indiquée.
[2] Période de 12 mois finissant le 30 juin de l'année indiquée.
[3] Calculé par la Division de Statistiques de l'Organisation des Nations Unies à partir d'indices nationaux plus détaillés.
[4] Non compris l'extraction du charbon et de pétrole brut.
[5] Non compris les raffineries de pétrole.
[6] Période de 12 mois finissant le 30 septembre de l'année indiquée.
[7] Y compris la construction.
[8] Base: 1997=100.
[9] Période de 12 mois commençant le 1er avril de l'année indiquée.
[10] Non compris l'extraction de gaz et de pétrole brut.
[11] Période de 12 mois finissant le 31 mars de l'année indiquée.
[12] Y compris l'exploitation forestière et la pêche.

Detailed internationally comparable data on national accounts are compiled and published annually by the Statistics Division, Department of Economic and Social Affairs of the United Nations Secretariat. Data for national accounts aggregates for countries or areas are based on the concepts and definitions contained in *A System of National Accounts* (1968 SNA) [55] and in *System of National Accounts 1993* (1993 SNA) [56]. A summary of the conceptual framework, classifications and definitions of transactions is found in the annual United Nations publication, *National Accounts Statistics: Main Aggregates and Detailed Tables* [26], which presents, in the form of analytical tables, a summary of selected principal national accounts aggregates based on official detailed national accounts data of over 200 countries and areas. Every effort has been made to present the estimates of the various countries or areas in a form designed to facilitate international comparability. The data for the majority of countries or areas has been compiled according to the 1968 SNA. Data for those countries or areas which have started to follow the concepts and definitions of the 1993 SNA is indicated with a footnote. To the extent possible, any other differences in concept, scope, coverage and classification are footnoted as well. Detailed footnotes identifying these differences are also available in the annual national accounts publication mentioned above. Such differences should be taken into account in order to avoid misleading comparisons among countries or areas.

Table 17 shows gross domestic product (GDP) and GDP per capita in US dollars at current prices, and GDP at constant 1990 prices and the corresponding real rates of growth. The table is designed to facilitate international comparisons of levels of income generated in production. In order to present comparable coverage for as many countries as possible, the official GDP national currency data are supplemented by estimates prepared by the Statistics Division, based on a variety of data derived from national and international sources. The conversion rates used to translate national currency data into US dollars are the period averages of market exchange rates (MERs) for members of the International Monetary Fund (IMF). These rates, which are published in the *International Financial Statistics* [13], are communicated to the IMF by national central banks and consist of three types: (a) market rates, determined largely by market forces; (b) official rates, determined by government authorities; and (c) principal rates for countries maintaining multiple exchange rate arrangements. Market rates always take priority and official rates are used only when a free market rate is not available.

For non-members of the IMF, averages of the United Nations operational rates, used for accounting purposes in

La Division de statistique du Département des affaires économiques et sociales du Secrétariat de l'Organisation des Nations Unies établit et publie chaque année des données détaillées, comparables au plan international, sur les comptes nationaux. Les données relatives aux agrégats des différents pays et territoires sont établies en fonction des concepts et des définitions du *Système de comptabilité nationale* (SCN de 1968) [55] et du *Système de comptabilité nationale* (SCN de 1993) [56]. On trouvera un résumé de l'appareil conceptuel, des classifications et des définitions des opérations dans *National Accounts Statistics : Main Aggregates and Detailed Tables* [26], publication annuelle des Nations Unies, qui présente, sous forme de tableaux analytiques, un choix d'agrégats essentiels de comptabilité nationale, issus des comptes nationaux détaillés de plus que 200 pays et territoires. On n'a rien négligé pour présenter les chiffres des différents pays et territoires sous une forme facilitant les comparaisons internationales. Pour la plupart des pays, les chiffres ont été établis selon le SCN de 1968. Les données des pays et territoires qui ont commencé à appliquer les concepts et les définitions du SCN de 1993 sont signalées par une note. Dans la mesure du possible, on signale également au moyen de notes les cas où les concepts, la portée, la couverture et la classification ne seraient pas les mêmes. Il y a en outre des notes détaillées explicitant ces différences dans la publication annuelle mentionnée plus haut. Il y a lieu de tenir compte de ces différences pour éviter de tenter des comparaisons qui donneraient matière à confusion.

Le *tableau 17* fait apparaître le produit intérieur brut (PIB) total et par habitant, exprimé en dollars des États-Unis aux prix courants et à prix constants (base 1990), ainsi que les taux de croissance correspondants. Le tableau est conçu pour faciliter les comparaisons internationales du revenu issu de la production. Afin que la couverture soit comparable pour le plus grand nombre possible de pays, la Division de statistique s'appuie non seulement sur les chiffres officiels du PIB exprimé dans la monnaie nationale, mais aussi sur diverses données provenant de sources nationales et internationales. Les taux de conversion utilisés pour exprimer les données nationales en dollars des États-Unis sont, pour les membres du Fonds monétaire international (FMI), les moyennes pour la période considérée des taux de change du marché. Ces derniers, publiés dans *Statistiques financières internationales* [13], sont communiqués au FMI par les banques centrales des pays et reposent sur trois types de taux : a) taux du marché, déterminés dans une large mesure par les facteurs du marché; b) taux officiels, déterminés par les pouvoirs publics; c) taux principaux, pour les pays pratiquant différents arrangements en matière de taux de change. On donne toujours la priorité aux taux du marché, n'utilisant les taux officiels que lorsqu'on n'a pas de taux du marché libre.

United Nations transactions with member countries, are applied. These are based on official, commercial and/or tourist rates of exchange.

It should be noted that there are practical constraints in the use of MERs for conversion purposes. Their use may result in excessive fluctuations or distortions in the dollar income levels of a number of countries particularly in those with multiple exchange rates, those coping with inordinate levels of inflation or countries experiencing misalignments caused by market fluctuations. Caution is therefore urged when making inter-country comparisons of incomes as expressed in US dollars.

The GDP at constant price series, based primarily on data officially provided by countries or areas and partly on estimates made by the Statistics Division, are transformed into index numbers and rebased to 1990=100. The resulting data are then converted into US dollars at the rate prevailing in the base year 1990. The growth rates are based on the estimates of GDP at constant 1990 prices. The growth rate of the year in question is obtained by dividing the GDP of that year by the GDP of the preceding year.

Table 18 features the percentage distribution of GDP at current prices by expenditure breakdown. It shows the portions of GDP spent on consumption by the household sector (including the non-profit institutions serving households) and the government, the portions spent on gross fixed capital formation, on changes in inventories, and on exports of goods and services, deducting imports of goods and services. The percentages are derived from official data reported to the United Nations by the countries and published in the annual national accounts publication.

Table 19 shows the percentage distribution of value added originating from the various industry components of the *International Standard Industrial Classification of All Economic Activities, Revision 3* (ISIC Rev. 3) [47]. This table reflects the economic structure of production in the different countries or areas. The percentages are based on official gross value added at basic current prices broken down by the kind of economic activity: agriculture, hunting, forestry and fishing (categories A+B); mining and quarrying (C); manufacturing (D); electricity, gas and water supply (E); construction (F); wholesale and retail trade, repair of motor vehicles, motorcycles and personal and household goods, restaurants and hotels (G+H); transport, storage and communication (I) and other activities comprised of financial intermediation (J), real estate, renting and business activities (K), public administration and defence, compulsory social security (L), education (M), health and social work (N), other community, social and personal service activities (O) and private households with employed persons (P).

Pour les pays qui ne sont pas membres du FMI, on utilise les moyennes des taux de change opérationnels de l'ONU (qui servent à des fins comptables pour les opérations de l'ONU avec les pays qui en sont membres). Ces taux reposent sur les taux de change officiels, les taux du commerce et/ou les taux touristiques.

Il faut noter que l'utilisation des taux de change du marché pour la conversion des données se heurte à des obstacles pratiques. On risque, ce faisant, d'aboutir à des fluctuations excessives ou à des distorsions du revenu en dollars de certains pays, surtout dans le cas des pays qui pratiquent plusieurs taux de change et de ceux qui connaissent des taux d'inflation exceptionnels ou des décalages provenant des fluctuations du marché. Les comparaisons de revenu entre pays sont donc sujettes à caution lorsqu'on se fonde sur le revenu exprimé en dollars des États-Unis.

La série de statistiques du PIB à prix constants est fondée principalement sur des données officiellement communiquées par les pays, et en partie sur des estimations de la Division de statistique; les données permettent de calculer des indices, la base 100 correspondant à 1990. Les chiffres ainsi obtenus sont alors convertis en dollars des États-Unis au taux de change de l'année de base (1990). Les taux de croissance sont calculés à partir des estimations du PIB aux prix constants de 1990. Le taux de croissance de l'année considérée est obtenu en divisant le PIB de l'année par celui de l'année précédente.

Le *tableau 18* montre la répartition (en pourcentage) du PIB aux prix courants par catégorie de dépense. Il indique la part du PIB consacrée aux dépenses de consommation du secteur des ménages (y compris les institutions sans but lucratif au service des ménages) et des administrations publiques et celle qui est consacrée à l'investissement fixe brut, celle qui correspond aux variations de stocks et celle qui correspond aux exportations de biens et services, déduction faite des importations de biens et services. Ces pourcentages sont calculés à partir des chiffres officiels communiqués à l'ONU par les pays, publiés dans l'ouvrage annuel.

Le *tableau 19* montre la répartition (en pourcentage) de la valeur ajoutée par branche d'activité, selon le classement retenu dans la *Classification internationale type, par industrie, de toutes les branches d'activité économique, Révision 3* (CITI Rev. 3) [47]. Il rend donc compte de la structure économique de la production dans chaque pays. Les pourcentages sont établis à partir des chiffres officiels de valeur ajoutée brute aux prix de base courants, répartis selon les différentes catégories d'activité économique : agriculture, chasse, sylviculture et pêche (catégories A + B); activités extractives (C); activités de fabrication (D); production et distribution d'électricité, de gaz et d'eau (E); construction (F); commerce de gros et de détail, réparation de

Table 20 presents the relationships among the principal national accounting aggregates, namely: gross domestic product (GDP), gross national income (GNI), gross national disposable income (GNDI) and gross savings. GNI is the term used in the 1993 SNA instead of the term Gross National Product (GNP) which was used in the 1968 SNA. The ratio of each aggregate to GDP is derived cumulatively by adding net primary income (or net factor income) from the rest of the world, (GNI); adding net current transfers from the rest of the world, (GNDI) and deducting final consumption to arrive at gross saving.

Table 21 presents the distribution of government final consumption expenditure by function at current prices. The breakdown by function includes: general public services; defence; public order and safety; economic affairs, environmental protection; housing and community amenities; health; recreation, culture and religion; education; and social protection. The government expenditure is equal to the service produced by general government for its own use. These services are not sold; they are valued in the GDP at their cost to the government.

Table 22 shows the distribution of household final consumption expenditure in the domestic market by purpose at current prices. The percentage shares include: food, beverages, tobacco and narcotics; clothing and footwear; housing, water, electricity, gas and other fuels; furnishings, household equipment and routine maintenance of the house; health; transport and communication; recreation and culture; education; restaurants and hotels; and miscellaneous goods and services.

Table 23: The national indices in this table are shown for the categories "Mining and Quarrying", "Manufacturing" and "Electricity, gas and water". These categories are classified according to Tabulation Categories C, D and E of the ISIC Revision 3 [47] at the 2-digit level. Major deviations from ISIC in the scope of the indices for the above categories are indicated by footnotes to the table.

The category "Total industry" covers Mining, Manufacturing and Electricity, gas and water. The indices for "Total industry", however, are the combination of the components shown and share all deviations from ISIC as footnoted for the component series.

The weights used in the calculation of the indices for a particular country are the value added contribution to the gross domestic product (GDP) of the given industry during the base year (value added = output – intermediate consumption). These value added contributions are measured at factor cost. Ideally, every five years the base year is changed, the corresponding base weights are updated and the indices of subsequent years are rebased.

Currently, the national indices have been rebased to 1995=100.

véhicules automobiles, de motocycles et de biens personnels et domestiques, hôtels et restaurants (G + H); transports, entreposage et communications (I) et intermédiation financière (J); immobilier, locations et activités de services aux entreprises (K); administration publique et défense, sécurité sociale obligatoire (L); éducation (M); santé et action sociale (N); autres activités de services collectifs, sociaux et personnels (O); et ménages privés employant du personnel domestique (P).

Le *tableau 20* montre les rapports entre les principaux agrégats de la comptabilité nationale, à savoir le produit intérieur brut (PIB), le revenu national brut (RNB), le revenu national brut disponible et l'épargne brute. Le revenu national brut est l'agrégat qui remplace dans le SCN de 1993 le produit national brut, utilisé dans le SCN de 1968. Chacun d'entre eux est obtenu par rapport au PIB, en ajoutant les revenus primaires nets (ou revenus nets de facteurs) engendrés dans le reste du monde, pour obtenir le revenu national brut; en ajoutant les transferts courants nets reçus de non-résidents, pour obtenir le revenu national disponible; en soustrayant la consommation finale pour obtenir l'épargne brute.

Le *tableau 21* donne la répartition des dépenses de consommation finale des administrations publiques, par fonction, aux prix courants. La répartition par fonction est la suivante : services généraux des administrations publiques; défense; ordre et sécurité publiques; affaires économiques; protection de l'environnement; logements et équipements collectifs; santé; loisirs, culture et culte; enseignement; protection sociale. Les dépenses des administrations sont considérées comme égales aux services produits par l'administration pour son propre usage. Ces services ne sont pas vendus et ils sont évalués, dans le PIB, à leur coût pour l'administration.

Le *tableau 22* donne la répartition des dépenses de consommation finale des ménages sur le marché intérieur par fonction aux prix courants. La répartition en pourcentage distingue les rubriques suivantes : alimentation, boissons, tabac et stupéfiants; articles d'habillement et chaussures; logement, eau, gaz, électricité et autres combustibles; meubles, articles de ménage et entretien courant de l'habitation; santé; transports et communication; loisirs et culture; enseignement; restaurants et hôtels; et autres fonctions, y compris les biens et services divers.

Tableau 23 : Les indices nationaux de ce tableau sont donnés pour les catégories "Industries extractives et carrières", "Industries manufacturières" et "Électricité, gaz et eau". Les catégories correspondent à celles des catégories C, D et E de la *Classification internationale type, par industrie, de toutes les branches d'activité économique* (CITI Rev. 3) [47] au niveau des classes à deux chiffres. Tous les indices pour lesquels les catégories s'écartent sensiblement de celles de la CITI sont signalés en note au tableau.

La catégorie "Ensemble de l'industrie" comprend les Industries extractives et carrières, les Industries manufacturières et l'Électricité, gaz et eau. Les indices pour "Ensemble de l'industrie", toutefois, combinent les composantes indiquées et présentent tous les écarts par rapport à la CITI que signalent les notes concernant les séries des composantes.

Les coefficients de pondération utilisés pour le calcul des indices d'un pays donné correspondent à la part de la valeur ajoutée de la branche considérée dans le produit intérieur brut (PIB) pendant l'année de référence (valeur ajoutée = production – consommation intermédiaire). Cette part de la valeur ajoutée est mesurée au coût des facteurs. En principe, l'année de référence change tous les cinq ans, les coefficients de pondération correspondants sont actualisés et les indices des années suivantes sont calculés sur une nouvelle base. À l'heure actuelle, la nouvelle base des indices est 1995 = 100.

24

Rates of discount of central banks
Per cent per annum, end of period

Taux d'escompte des banques centrales
Pour cent par année, fin de la période

Country or area Pays ou zone	1996	1997	1998	1999	2000	2001	2002	2003	2004	2005
Albania [1] Albanie [1]	24.00	32.00	23.44	18.00	10.82	7.00	8.50	6.50	5.25	...
Algeria [2] Algérie [2]	13.00	11.00	9.50	8.50	6.00	6.00	5.50	4.50	4.00	4.00
Angola Angola	2.00	48.00	58.00	120.00	150.00	150.00	150.00	150.00	95.00	...
Anguilla Anguilla	9.00	8.00	8.00	8.00	8.00	7.00	7.00	6.50	6.50	6.50
Antigua and Barbuda Antigua-et-Barbuda	9.00	8.00	8.00	8.00	8.00	7.00	7.00	6.50	6.50	6.50
Armenia [3] Arménie [3]	60.00	54.00	39.00	43.00	25.00	15.00	13.50	7.00	3.75	3.50
Aruba [1,2] Aruba [1,2]	9.50	9.50	9.50	6.50	6.50	6.50	6.50	5.00	5.00	5.00
Austria [4] Autriche [4]	2.50	2.50	2.50	...	...	...	...	...	...	...
Azerbaijan [2,3] Azerbaïdjan [2,3]	20.00	12.00	14.00	10.00	10.00	10.00	7.00	7.00	7.00	9.00
Bahamas [1,2] Bahamas [1,2]	6.50	6.50	6.50	5.75	5.75	5.75	5.75	5.75	5.75	5.25
Bangladesh Bangladesh	7.00	8.00	8.00	7.00	7.00	6.00	6.00	5.00	5.00	5.00
Barbados [1] Barbade [1]	12.50	9.00	9.00	10.00	10.00	7.50	7.50	7.50	7.50	...
Belarus [2,3] Bélarus [2,3]	8.30	8.90	9.60	23.40	80.00	48.00	38.00	28.00	17.00	11.00
Belgium [4] Belgique [4]	2.50	2.75	2.75	...	...	...	...	...	...	...
Belize [5] Belize [5]	12.00	12.00	12.00	12.00	12.00	12.00	12.00	12.00	12.00	12.00
Benin [2] Bénin [2]	6.00	6.00	6.00	6.00	6.00	6.00	6.00	4.50	4.00	4.00
Bolivia Bolivie	16.50	13.25	14.10	12.50	10.00	8.50	12.50	7.50	6.00	5.25
Botswana [1,2] Botswana [1,2]	13.00	12.00	12.75	13.75	14.25	14.25	15.25	14.25	14.25	14.50
Brazil Brésil	25.34	45.09	39.41	21.37	18.52	21.43	30.42	23.92	24.55	25.34
Bulgaria [1] Bulgarie [1]	180.00	6.65	5.08	4.46	4.63	4.65	3.31	2.83	2.37	2.05
Burkina Faso [1] Burkina Faso [1]	6.00	6.00	6.00	6.00	6.00	6.00	6.00	4.50	4.00	4.00
Burundi [6] Burundi [6]	10.00	12.00	12.00	12.00	14.00	14.00	15.50	14.50	14.50	14.50
Cameroon [2] Cameroun [2]	7.75	7.50	7.00	7.30	7.00	6.50	6.30	6.00	6.00	5.50
Canada [1] Canada [1]	3.25	4.50	5.25	5.00	6.00	2.50	3.00	3.00	2.75	3.50
Central African Rep. [2] Rép. centrafricaine [2]	7.75	7.50	7.00	7.60	7.00	6.50	6.30	6.00	6.00	5.50

Country or area Pays ou zone	1996	1997	1998	1999	2000	2001	2002	2003	2004	2005
Chad [2] Tchad [2]	7.75	7.50	7.00	7.60	7.00	6.50	6.30	6.00	6.00	5.50
Chile Chili	11.75	7.96	9.12	7.44	8.73	6.50	3.00	2.45	2.25	4.50
China [1] Chine [1]	9.00	8.55	4.59	3.24	3.24	3.24	2.70	2.70	3.33	3.33
China, Hong Kong SAR Chine, Hong Kong RAS	6.00	7.00	6.25	7.00	8.00	3.25	2.75	2.50	3.75	5.75
Colombia [2] Colombie [2]	35.05	31.32	42.28	23.05	18.28	16.40	12.73	12.95	12.76	11.30
Comoros [2] Comores [2]	...	...	...	6.36	5.63	5.89	4.79	3.82	3.55	3.59
Congo [2] Congo [2]	7.75	7.50	7.00	7.60	7.00	6.50	6.30	6.00	6.00	5.50
Costa Rica [2] Costa Rica [2]	35.00	31.00	37.00	34.00	31.50	28.75	31.25	26.00	26.00	27.00
Côte d'Ivoire Côte d'Ivoire	6.00	6.00	6.00	6.00	6.00	6.00	6.00	4.50	4.00	4.00
Croatia [2] Croatie [2]	6.50	5.90	5.90	7.90	5.90	5.90	4.50	4.50	4.50	4.50
Cyprus [2] Chypre [2]	7.50	7.00	7.00	7.00	7.00	5.50	5.00	4.50	5.50	4.25
Czech Republic [1] République tchèque [1]	12.40	14.75	9.50	5.25	5.25	4.50	2.75	2.00	2.50	2.00
Dem. Rep. of the Congo [2] Rép. dém. du Congo [2]	238.00	13.00	22.00	120.00	120.00	140.00	24.00	8.00	...	...
Denmark Danemark	3.25	3.50	3.50	3.00	4.75	3.25	2.86	2.00	2.00	2.25
Dominica Dominique	9.00	8.00	8.00	8.00	8.00	7.00	7.00	6.50	6.50	6.50
Ecuador Equateur	46.38	37.46	61.84	64.40	13.16	16.44	14.55	11.19	9.86	9.61
Egypt Egypte	13.00	12.25	12.00	12.00	12.00	11.00	10.00	10.00	10.00	...
Equatorial Guinea [2] Guinée équatoriale [2]	7.75	7.50	7.00	7.60	7.00	6.50	6.30	6.00	6.00	5.50
Euro Area [2,7,8] Zone euro [2,7,8]	...	...	...	4.00	5.75	4.25	3.75	3.00	3.00	3.25
Fiji [1] Fidji [1]	6.00	1.88	2.50	2.50	8.00	1.75	1.75	1.75	2.25	2.75
Finland [1,2,4] Finlande [1,2,4]	4.00	4.00	3.50	...	...	...	...	...	...	...
Gabon [2] Gabon [2]	7.75	7.50	7.00	7.60	7.00	6.50	6.30	6.00	6.00	5.50
Gambia [2] Gambie [2]	14.00	14.00	12.00	10.50	10.00	13.00	18.00	29.00	28.00	...
Germany [4] Allemagne [4]	2.50	2.50	2.50	...	...	...	...	...	...	...
Ghana Ghana	45.00	45.00	37.00	27.00	27.00	27.00	24.50	21.50	18.50	...
Greece [1,2,4] Grèce [1,2,4]	16.50	14.50	...	11.81	8.10	...	...	...	...	...
Grenada Grenade	9.00	8.00	8.00	8.00	8.00	7.00	7.00	6.50	6.50	6.50

Rates of discount of central banks— Per cent per annum, end of period (*continued*)
Taux d'escompte des banques centrales— Pour cent par année, fin de la période (*suite*)

Country or area Pays ou zone	1996	1997	1998	1999	2000	2001	2002	2003	2004	2005
Guinea [3] Guinée [3]	18.00	15.00	...	...	11.50	16.25	16.25	16.25	16.25	...
Guinea-Bissau Guinée-Bissau	6.00	6.00	6.00	6.00	6.00	6.00	6.00	4.50	4.00	4.00
Guyana Guyana	12.00	11.00	11.25	13.25	11.75	8.75	6.25	5.50	6.00	6.00
Hungary Hongrie	23.00	20.50	17.00	14.50	11.00	9.75	8.50	12.50	9.50	6.00
Iceland Islande	5.70	6.55	8.50	10.00	12.40	12.00	8.20	7.70	10.25	...
India [1] Inde [1]	12.00	9.00	9.00	8.00	8.00	6.50	6.25	6.00	6.00	...
Indonesia [2] Indonésie [2]	12.80	20.00	38.44	12.51	14.53	17.62	12.93	8.31	7.43	12.75
Iran (Islamic Rep. of) Iran (Rép. islamique d')	...	...	...	...	...	...	...	11.68	11.70	...
Ireland [4,9] Irlande [4,9]	6.25	6.75	4.06	...	...	...	...	...	...	...
Israel [2] Israël [2]	15.30	13.72	13.47	11.20	8.21	5.67	9.18	5.20	3.90	...
Italy [4] Italie [4]	7.50	5.50	3.00	...	...	...	...	...	...	...
Japan Japon	0.50	0.50	0.50	0.50	0.50	0.10	0.10	0.10	0.10	0.10
Jordan Jordanie	8.50	7.75	9.00	8.00	6.50	5.00	4.50	2.50	3.75	...
Kazakhstan [2,3] Kazakhstan [2,3]	35.00	18.50	25.00	18.00	14.00	9.00	7.50	7.00	7.00	8.00
Kenya Kenya	26.88	32.27	17.07	26.46	...	...	...	...	...	...
Korea, Dem. P. R. Corée, R. p. dém. de	5.00	5.00	3.00	3.00	3.00	2.50	2.50	2.50	2.00	...
Kuwait [2] Koweït [2]	7.25	7.50	7.00	6.75	7.25	4.25	3.25	3.25	4.75	6.00
Lao People's Dem. Rep. [1,2] Rép. dém. pop. lao [1,2]	35.00	...	35.00	34.89	35.17	35.00	20.00	20.00	20.00	...
Latvia Lettonie	9.50	4.00	4.00	4.00	3.50	3.50	3.00	3.00	4.00	4.00
Lebanon Liban	25.00	30.00	30.00	25.00	20.00	20.00	20.00	20.00	20.00	12.00
Lesotho Lesotho	17.00	15.60	19.50	19.00	15.00	13.00	16.19	15.00	13.00	13.00
Libyan Arab Jamah. Jamah. arabe libyenne	...	...	3.00	5.00	5.00	5.00	5.00	5.00	4.00	3.00
Malawi Malawi	27.00	23.00	43.00	47.00	50.23	46.80	40.00	35.00	25.00	25.00
Maldives Maldives	...	...	...	...	...	18.00	18.54	19.00	18.25	18.00
Mali [2] Mali [2]	6.00	6.00	6.00	6.00	6.00	6.00	6.00	4.50	4.00	4.00
Malta Malte	5.50	5.50	5.50	4.75	4.75	4.25	3.75	3.00	3.00	3.25
Mauritius Maurice	11.82	10.46	17.19	...	...	...	...	...	...	...

Country or area Pays ou zone	1996	1997	1998	1999	2000	2001	2002	2003	2004	2005
Mongolia [1] Mongolie [1]	109.00	45.50	23.30	11.40	8.65	8.60	9.90	11.50	15.75	4.40
Montserrat Montserrat	9.00	8.00	8.00	8.00	8.00	7.00	7.00	6.50	6.50	6.50
Morocco [2] Maroc [2]	...	...	6.04	5.42	5.00	4.71	3.79	3.25	3.25	3.25
Mozambique [2] Mozambique [2]	32.00	12.95	9.95	9.95	9.95	9.95	9.95	9.95	9.95	9.95
Myanmar [1] Myanmar [1]	15.00	15.00	15.00	12.00	10.00	10.00	10.00	10.00	10.00	10.00
Namibia [2,10] Namibie [2,10]	17.75	16.00	18.75	11.50	11.25	9.25	12.75	7.75	7.50	7.00
Nepal Népal	11.00	9.00	9.00	9.00	7.50	6.50	5.50	5.50	5.50	...
Netherlands Antilles Antilles néerlandaises	6.00	6.00	6.00	6.00	6.00	6.00	6.00	...	...	...
New Zealand Nouvelle-Zélande	8.80	9.70	5.60	5.00	6.50	4.75	5.75	5.00	6.50	7.25
Niger Niger	6.00	6.00	6.00	6.00	6.00	6.00	6.00	4.50	4.00	4.00
Nigeria Nigéria	13.50	13.50	13.50	18.00	14.00	20.50	16.50	15.00	15.00	...
Norway Norvège	6.00	5.50	10.00	7.50	9.00	8.50	8.50	4.25	3.75	4.25
Pakistan Pakistan	20.00	18.00	16.50	13.00	13.00	10.00	7.50	7.50	7.50	9.00
Papua New Guinea Papouasie-Nvl-Guinée	14.86	9.49	17.07	16.66	9.79	11.73	11.71	15.50	12.67	9.67
Paraguay Paraguay	15.00	20.00	20.00	20.00	20.00	20.00	20.00	20.00	20.00	20.00
Peru Pérou	18.16	15.94	18.72	17.80	14.00	5.00	4.50	3.25	3.75	4.00
Philippines Philippines	11.70	14.64	12.40	7.89	13.81	8.30	4.19	5.53	8.36	5.70
Poland Pologne	22.00	24.50	18.25	19.00	21.50	14.00	7.75	5.75	7.00	4.75
Portugal [4] Portugal [4]	6.70	5.31	3.00	...	...	...	...	...	...	...
Russian Federation [3] Fédération de Russie [3]	48.00	28.00	60.00	55.00	25.00	25.00	21.00	16.00	13.00	12.00
Rwanda Rwanda	16.00	10.75	11.38	11.19	11.69	13.00	13.00	14.50	14.50	...
Saint Kitts and Nevis Saint-Kitts-et-Nevis	9.00	8.00	8.00	8.00	8.00	7.00	7.00	6.50	6.50	6.50
Saint Lucia Sainte-Lucie	9.00	8.00	8.00	8.00	8.00	7.00	7.00	6.50	6.50	6.50
St. Vincent-Grenadines St. Vincent-Grenadines	9.00	8.00	8.00	8.00	8.00	7.00	7.00	6.50	6.50	6.50
Sao Tome and Principe Sao Tomé-et-Principe	35.00	55.00	29.50	17.00	17.00	15.50	15.50	14.50	14.50	...
Senegal Sénégal	6.00	6.00	6.00	6.00	6.00	6.00	6.00	4.50	4.00	4.00
Seychelles Seychelles	11.00	11.00	5.50	5.50	5.50	5.50	5.50	4.67	3.51	3.87

Country or area Pays ou zone	1996	1997	1998	1999	2000	2001	2002	2003	2004	2005
Slovakia Slovaquie	8.80	8.80	8.80	8.80	8.80	7.75	6.50	6.00	4.00	3.00
Slovenia [1,2] Slovénie [1,2]	11.00	11.00	11.00	9.00	11.00	12.00	10.50	7.25	5.00	5.00
South Africa Afrique du Sud	17.00	16.00	19.32	12.00	12.00	9.50	13.50	8.00	7.50	7.00
Spain [1,2,4] Espagne [1,2,4]	6.25	4.75	3.00	...	...	...	...	...	...	...
Sri Lanka [1] Sri Lanka [1]	17.00	17.00	17.00	16.00	25.00	...	18.00	15.00	15.00	...
Swaziland [2] Swaziland [2]	16.75	15.75	18.00	12.00	11.00	9.50	13.50	8.00	7.50	7.00
Sweden [1] Suède [1]	3.50	2.50	2.00	1.50	2.00	2.00	4.50	3.00	2.00	...
Switzerland Suisse	1.00	1.00	1.00	0.50	3.20	1.59	0.50	0.11	0.54	0.73
Syrian Arab Republic Rép. arabe syrienne	5.00	5.00	5.00	5.00	5.00	5.00	5.00	...	...	...
Tajikistan [2,3] Tadjikistan [2,3]	...	76.00	36.40	20.10	20.60	20.00	24.75	15.00	10.00	9.00
Thailand Thaïlande	10.50	12.50	12.50	4.00	4.00	3.75	3.25	2.75	3.50	5.50
TFYR of Macedonia [1] L'ex-R.y. Macédoine [1]	9.20	8.90	8.90	8.90	7.90	10.70	10.70	6.50	6.50	6.50
Togo Togo	6.00	6.00	6.00	6.00	6.00	6.00	6.00	4.50	4.00	4.00
Trinidad and Tobago [1] Trinité-et-Tobago [1]	13.00	13.00	13.00	13.00	13.00	13.00	7.25	7.00	7.00	8.00
Tunisia Tunisie	7.88	...	...	...	...	...	...	...	...	...
Turkey Turquie	50.00	67.00	67.00	60.00	60.00	60.00	55.00	43.00	38.00	...
Uganda [1,2] Ouganda [1,2]	15.85	14.08	9.10	15.75	18.86	8.88	13.08	25.62	16.15	...
Ukraine [2,3] Ukraine [2,3]	40.00	35.00	60.00	45.00	27.00	12.50	7.00	7.00	9.00	9.50
United Rep. of Tanzania Rép.-Unie de Tanzanie	19.00	16.20	17.60	20.20	10.70	8.70	9.18	12.34	14.42	19.33
United States Etats-Unis	5.00	5.00	4.50	5.00	6.00	1.25	0.75	2.00	3.15	5.15
Uruguay [2,11] Uruguay [2,11]	160.30	95.50	73.70	66.39	57.26	71.66	316.01	...	...	...
Vanuatu Vanuatu	...	...	7.00	7.00	7.00	6.50	6.50	6.50	6.50	6.25
Venezuela (Bolivarian Rep. of) Venezuela (Rép. bolivarienne)	45.00	45.00	60.00	38.00	38.00	37.00	40.00	28.50	28.50	28.50
Viet Nam [2,3] Viet Nam [2,3]	18.90	10.80	12.00	6.00	6.00	4.80	4.80	5.00	5.00	...
Yemen [2] Yémen [2]	28.51	15.00	19.95	18.53	15.89	15.16	13.13	...	...	...
Zambia [2] Zambie [2]	47.00	17.70	...	32.93	25.67	40.10	27.87	14.35	16.68	14.81
Zimbabwe [1] Zimbabwe [1]	27.00	31.50	39.50	74.41	57.84	57.20	29.65	300.00	110.00	540.00

Source	Source
International Monetary Fund (IMF), Washington, D.C., "International Financial Statistics," February 2006 and the IMF database.	Fonds monétaire international (FMI), Washington, D.C.,"Statistiques Financières Internationales," février 2006 et la base de données du FMI.

Notes	Notes
[1] Central Bank rate.	[1] Taux de la Banque centrale.
[2] Period average.	[2] Moyenne pour la période.
[3] Refinance rate.	[3] Taux de refinancement.
[4] Beginning 1999, see Euro Area. For Greece, beginning 2001.	[4] A partir de 1999, voir la Zone euro. Grèce, à partir de 2001.
[5] Monetary Authority of Belize lending rate.	[5] Taux prêteur de l'Autorité monétaire du Belize.
[6] Avances ordinaires à l'état.	[6] Avances ordinaires à l'état.
[7] Marginal lending facility rate.	[7] Taux de facilité de prêt marginal.
[8] "Euro Area" is an official descriptor for the European Economic and Monetary Union (EMU). The participating member states of the EMU are Austria, Belgium, Finland, France, Germany, Greece (beginning 2001), Ireland, Italy, Luxembourg, Netherlands, Portugal, and Spain.	[8] L'expression "zone euro" est un intitulé officiel pour l'Union économique et monétaire (UEM) européene. L'UEM est composée des pays membres suivants : Allemagne, Autriche, Belgique, Espagne, Finlande, France, Grèce (à partir de 2001), Irlande, Italie, Luxembourg, Pays-Bas et Portugal.
[9] Short-term facility rate.	[9] Taux de facilité à court terme.
[10] Bank of Namibia overdraft rate.	[10] Taux de découvert à la Bank of Namibia.
[11] Domestic currency.	[11] Monnaie locale.

Short-term interest rates
Treasury bill and money market rates: per cent per annum

Taux d'intérêt à court terme
Taux des bons du Trésor et du marché monétaire : pour cent par année

Country or area — Pays ou zone	1996	1997	1998	1999	2000	2001	2002	2003	2004	2005
Albania — Albanie										
Treasury bill Bons du trésor	17.81	32.59	27.49	17.54	10.80	7.72	9.49	8.81	6.79	...
Algeria — Algérie										
Money market Marché monétaire	18.09	13.00	10.00	9.99	6.45	2.84	3.13	1.91	1.09	2.01
Treasury bill Bons du trésor	...	...	9.96	10.05	7.95	5.69	1.80	1.25	0.15	1.30
Anguilla — Anguilla										
Money market Marché monétaire	5.25	5.25	5.25	5.25	5.25	5.64	6.32	6.07	4.67	4.01
Antigua and Barbuda — Antigua-et-Barbuda										
Money market Marché monétaire	5.25	5.25	5.25	5.25	5.25	5.64	6.32	6.07	4.67	4.01
Treasury bill Bons du trésor	7.00	7.00	7.00	7.00	7.00	7.00	7.00	7.00	7.00	7.00
Argentina — Argentine										
Money market Marché monétaire	6.23	6.63	6.81	6.99	8.15	24.90	41.35	3.74	1.96	4.11
Money market B [1] Marché monétaire B [1]	5.91	6.39	6.55	6.07	7.53	12.76	13.01	1.64	2.03	2.86
Armenia — Arménie										
Money market Marché monétaire	48.56	36.41	27.84	23.65	18.63	19.40	12.29	7.51	4.18	3.17
Treasury bill Bons du trésor	43.95	57.54	46.99	55.10	24.40	20.59	14.75	11.91	5.27	4.05
Australia — Australie										
Money market Marché monétaire	7.20	5.50	4.99	4.78	5.90	5.06	4.55	4.81	5.25	5.46
Treasury bill A [2] Bons du trésor A [2]	7.02	5.29	4.84	4.76	5.98	4.80	...	...	...	...
Austria [3] — Autriche [3]										
Money market Marché monétaire	3.19	3.27	3.36	...	...	...	...	...	...	...
Azerbaijan — Azerbaïdjan										
Treasury bill Bons du trésor	...	12.23	14.10	18.31	16.73	16.51	14.12	8.00	4.62	7.52
Bahamas — Bahamas										
Treasury bill Bons du trésor	4.45	4.35	3.84	1.97	1.03	1.94	2.50	1.78	0.56	0.14
Bahrain — Bahreïn										
Money market B [4] Marché monétaire B [4]	5.69	...	5.69	5.58	6.89	3.85	2.02	1.24	1.74	...
Treasury bill Bons du trésor	5.49	5.68	5.53	5.46	6.56	3.78	1.75	1.13	1.56	...
Barbados — Barbade										
Treasury bill Bons du trésor	6.85	3.61	5.61	5.83	5.29	3.14	2.10	1.41	1.20	...
Belgium — Belgique										
Money market B [3,5] Marché monétaire B [3,5]	3.24	3.46	3.58	...	...	...	...	...	...	...
Treasury bill Bons du trésor	3.19	3.38	3.51	2.72	4.02	4.16	3.17	2.23	1.97	2.02
Belize [6] — Belize [6]										
Treasury bill B Bons du trésor B	3.78	3.51	3.83	5.91	5.91	5.91	4.59	3.22	3.22	3.22

Country or area — Pays ou zone	1996	1997	1998	1999	2000	2001	2002	2003	2004	2005
Benin [7] — Bénin [7]										
Money market A Marché monétaire A	4.95	4.95	4.95	4.95	4.95	4.95	4.95	4.95	4.95	4.95
Bolivia — Bolivie										
Money market Marché monétaire	20.27	13.97	12.57	13.49	7.40	6.99	8.41	4.07	4.05	3.53
Money market B [1] Marché monétaire B [1]	9.54	7.85	9.26	8.29	5.68	3.57	2.96	2.12	3.02	3.37
Treasury bill Bons du trésor	19.93	13.65	12.33	14.07	10.99	11.48	12.41	9.92	7.41	4.96
Treasury bill B [1] Bons du trésor B [1]	9.89	7.15	7.48	7.84	7.02	4.19	3.56	2.53	3.34	2.85
Brazil — Brésil										
Money market Marché monétaire	27.45	25.00	29.50	26.26	17.59	17.47	19.11	23.37	16.24	19.12
Treasury bill Bons du trésor	25.73	24.79	28.57	26.39	18.51	20.06	19.43	22.11	17.14	18.93
Treasury bill B [1] Bons du trésor B [1]	15.13	11.60	15.04	...	...	11.46	...	...	...	...
Bulgaria — Bulgarie										
Money market B [4] Marché monétaire B [4]	119.88	66.43	2.48	2.93	3.02	3.74	2.47	1.95	1.95	2.03
Treasury bill Bons du trésor	114.31	78.35	6.02	5.43	4.21	4.57	4.29	2.81	2.64	...
Burkina Faso [7] — Burkina Faso [7]										
Money market A Marché monétaire A	4.95	4.95	4.95	4.95	4.95	4.95	4.95	4.95	4.95	4.95
Canada — Canada										
Money market A [8] Marché monétaire A [8]	4.32	3.26	4.87	4.74	5.52	4.11	2.45	2.93	2.25	2.66
Treasury bill Bons du trésor	4.21	3.26	4.73	4.72	5.49	3.77	2.59	2.87	2.22	2.73
Chile — Chili										
Money market Marché monétaire	...	...	...	...	10.09	6.81	4.08	2.72	1.88	3.48
China, Hong Kong SAR — Chine, Hong Kong RAS										
Money market Marché monétaire	5.13	4.50	5.50	5.75	7.13	2.69	1.50	0.07	0.13	4.25
Treasury bill Bons du trésor	4.45	7.50	5.04	4.94	5.69	1.69	1.35	-0.08	0.07	3.65
China, Macao SAR [4] — Chine, Macao RAS [4]										
Money market B Marché monétaire B	5.60	7.54	5.41	5.70	6.29	2.11	1.48	0.11	0.27	4.09
Colombia [4] — Colombie [4]										
Money market B Marché monétaire B	28.37	23.83	35.00	18.81	10.87	10.43	6.06	6.95	7.01	6.18
Côte d'Ivoire [7] — Côte d'Ivoire [7]										
Money market A Marché monétaire A	4.95	4.95	4.95	4.95	4.95	4.95	4.95	4.95	4.95	4.95
Croatia — Croatie										
Money market Marché monétaire	17.60	9.71	11.16	10.21	6.78	3.42	1.75	3.31	5.11	3.10
Cyprus — Chypre										
Money market Marché monétaire	6.85	4.82	4.80	5.15	5.96	4.93	3.42	3.35	4.01	3.27
Treasury bill Bons du trésor	6.05	5.38	5.59	5.59	6.01	...	...	3.56	...	...
Czech Republic — République tchèque										
Money market Marché monétaire	12.67	17.50	10.08	5.58	5.42	4.69	2.63	2.08	2.56	2.17
Treasury bill Bons du trésor	11.91	11.21	10.51	5.71	5.37	5.06	2.72	2.04	2.57	1.96

Country or area — Pays ou zone	1996	1997	1998	1999	2000	2001	2002	2003	2004	2005
Denmark [5] — Danemark [5]										
Money market B Marché monétaire B	3.98	3.71	4.27	3.37	4.98	...	3.56	2.38	2.16	2.20
Dominica — Dominique										
Money market Marché monétaire	5.25	5.25	5.25	5.25	5.25	5.64	6.32	6.07	4.67	4.01
Treasury bill Bons du trésor	6.40	6.40	6.40	6.40	6.40	6.40	6.40	6.40	6.40	6.40
Dominican Republic — Rép. dominicaine										
Money market Marché monétaire	14.70	13.01	16.68	15.30	18.28	13.47	14.50	24.24	36.76	12.57
Egypt — Egypte										
Treasury bill Bons du trésor	...	8.80	8.80	9.00	9.10	7.20	5.50	6.90	9.90	...
El Salvador — El Salvador										
Money market Marché monétaire	...	10.43	9.43	10.68	6.93	5.28	4.40	3.86	4.36	5.18
Estonia — Estonie										
Money market Marché monétaire	3.53	6.45	11.66	5.39	5.68	5.31	3.88	2.92	2.50	2.38
Ethiopia — Ethiopie										
Treasury bill Bons du trésor	7.22	3.97	3.48	3.65	2.74	3.06	1.30	1.31	0.56	...
Euro Area [9] — Zone euro [9]										
Money market A Marché monétaire A	5.09	4.38	3.96	2.97	4.39	4.26	3.32	2.34	2.11	2.19
Fiji — Fidji										
Money market A [10] Marché monétaire A [10]	2.43	1.91	1.27	1.27	2.58	0.79	0.92	0.86	0.90	1.28
Treasury bill Bons du trésor	2.98	2.60	2.00	2.00	3.63	1.51	1.66	1.06	1.56	1.94
Finland [11] — Finlande [11]										
Money market B Marché monétaire B	3.63	3.23	3.57	2.96	4.39	4.26	3.32	2.33	2.11	2.18
France — France										
Money market B [3,5] Marché monétaire B [3,5]	3.73	3.24	3.39	...	...	...	...	...	...	...
Treasury bill Bons du trésor	3.84	3.35	3.45	2.72	4.23	4.26	3.28	2.27	...	...
Treasury bill A [12] Bons du trésor A [12]	3.84	3.35	3.45	2.72	4.23	4.26	3.28	2.27	...	...
Georgia — Géorgie										
Money market Marché monétaire	43.39	26.58	43.26	34.61	18.17	17.52	27.69	16.88	11.87	7.71
Treasury bill Bons du trésor	...	...	...	...	...	29.93	43.42	44.26	19.16	...
Germany — Allemagne										
Money market B [5] Marché monétaire B [5]	3.27	3.18	3.41	2.73	4.11	4.37	3.28	2.32	2.05	...
Treasury bill Bons du trésor	3.30	3.32	3.42	2.88	4.32	3.66	2.97	1.98	2.00	...
Ghana — Ghana										
Money market Marché monétaire	...	...	...	...	...	...	...	24.71	15.73	...
Treasury bill B [13] Bons du trésor B [13]	41.64	42.77	34.33	26.37	36.28	40.96	25.11	27.25	16.57	...
Greece [3,14] — Grèce [3,14]										
Money market A Marché monétaire A	13.80	12.80	13.99	...	...	...	...	...	...	...

Country or area — Pays ou zone	1996	1997	1998	1999	2000	2001	2002	2003	2004	2005
Grenada — Grenade										
Money market Marché monétaire	5.25	5.25	5.25	5.25	5.25	5.64	6.32	6.07	4.67	4.01
Treasury bill Bons du trésor	6.50	6.50	6.50	6.50	6.50	7.00	7.00	6.50	5.50	5.50
Guatemala — Guatemala										
Money market Marché monétaire	...	7.77	6.62	9.23	9.33	10.58	9.11	6.65	6.16	6.54
Guinea-Bissau — Guinée-Bissau										
Money market Marché monétaire	4.95	4.95	4.95	4.95	4.95	4.95	4.95	4.95	4.95	4.95
Guyana — Guyana										
Treasury bill Bons du trésor	11.35	8.91	8.33	11.31	9.88	7.78	4.94	3.04	3.62	3.79
Haiti — Haïti										
Treasury bill Bons du trésor	...	14.13	16.21	7.71	12.33	13.53	7.56	20.50	12.24	...
Hungary — Hongrie										
Treasury bill Bons du trésor	23.96	20.13	17.83	14.68	11.03	10.79	8.91	8.22	11.32	6.95
Iceland — Islande										
Money market Marché monétaire	6.96	7.38	8.12	9.24	11.61	14.51	11.21	5.14	6.22	...
Treasury bill B [15] Bons du trésor B [15]	6.97	7.04	7.40	8.61	11.12	11.03	8.01	4.93	6.04	...
India [5] — Inde [5]										
Money market B Marché monétaire B	11.04	5.29	...	...	...	...	...	...	...	...
Indonesia [5] — Indonésie [5]										
Money market B Marché monétaire B	13.96	27.82	62.79	23.58	10.32	15.03	13.54	7.76	5.38	6.78
Ireland — Irlande										
Money market A [16] Marché monétaire A [16]	5.74	6.43	3.23	3.14	4.84	3.31	2.88	2.08	2.13	...
Treasury bill Bons du trésor	5.36	6.03	5.37	...	...	...	...	...	...	...
Israel — Israël										
Treasury bill Bons du trésor	15.34	13.39	11.33	11.41	8.81	6.50	7.38	7.00	4.78	4.34
Italy — Italie										
Money market Marché monétaire	8.82	6.88	4.99	2.95	4.39	4.26	3.32	2.33	2.10	2.18
Treasury bill Bons du trésor	8.46	6.33	4.59	3.01	4.53	4.05	3.26	2.19	2.08	2.17
Jamaica — Jamaïque										
Treasury bill Bons du trésor	37.95	21.14	25.65	20.75	18.24	16.71	15.54	25.94	15.47	13.39
Japan [5] — Japon [5]										
Money market B Marché monétaire B	0.47	0.48	0.37	0.06	0.11	0.06	0.01	0.00	0.00	0.00
Jordan — Jordanie										
Money market Marché monétaire	...	...	...	5.19	5.28	4.63	3.49	2.58	2.18	...
Kazakhstan — Kazakhstan										
Treasury bill Bons du trésor	28.91	15.15	23.59	15.63	6.59	5.28	5.20	5.86	3.28	3.28
Kenya — Kenya										
Treasury bill Bons du trésor	22.25	22.87	22.83	13.87	12.05	12.60	8.95	3.51	3.17	8.43

Country or area — Pays ou zone	1996	1997	1998	1999	2000	2001	2002	2003	2004	2005
Korea, Republic of — Corée, République de										
Money market Marché monétaire	12.44	13.24	14.98	5.01	5.16	4.69	4.21	4.00	3.65	...
Money market B [17] Marché monétaire B [17]	11.75	13.39	15.10	8.86	9.35	7.05	6.56	5.43	4.73	...
Kuwait — Koweït										
Money market B [18] Marché monétaire B [18]	6.93	6.98	...	...	...	...	...	...	...	...
Money market A [19] Marché monétaire A [19]	6.98	7.05	7.24	6.32	6.82	4.62	2.99	2.47	2.14	2.83
Kyrgyzstan — Kirghizistan										
Money market Marché monétaire	...	...	43.98	43.71	24.26	11.92	...	...	...	3.24
Treasury bill Bons du trésor	40.10	35.83	43.67	47.19	32.26	19.08	10.15	7.21	4.94	4.40
Lao People's Dem. Rep. — Rép. dém. pop. lao										
Treasury bill Bons du trésor	...	...	23.66	30.00	29.94	22.70	21.41	24.87	20.37	...
Latvia — Lettonie										
Money market Marché monétaire	13.08	3.76	4.42	4.72	2.97	5.23	3.01	2.86	3.25	2.49
Treasury bill Bons du trésor	16.27	4.73	5.27	6.23	4.85	5.63	3.52	3.24	...	...
Lebanon — Liban										
Treasury bill Bons du trésor	15.19	13.42	12.70	11.57	11.18	11.18	10.90	...	5.25	5.22
Lesotho — Lesotho										
Treasury bill Bons du trésor	13.89	14.83	15.47	12.45	9.06	9.49	11.34	11.96	8.55	7.21
Libyan Arab Jamah. [20] — Jamah. arabe libyenne [20]										
Money market B Marché monétaire B	...	...	4.00	4.00	4.00	4.00	4.00	4.00	4.00	...
Lithuania — Lituanie										
Money market Marché monétaire	20.26	9.55	6.12	6.26	3.60	3.37	2.21	1.79	1.53	1.97
Money market B [1] Marché monétaire B [1]	...	...	5.52	5.05	6.10	4.03	1.92	1.72	1.73	2.59
Treasury bill Bons du trésor	20.95	8.64	10.69	11.14	9.27	5.68	3.72	2.61	...	...
Luxembourg [3,4] — Luxembourg [3,4]										
Money market B Marché monétaire B	3.29	3.36	3.48	...	...	...	...	...	...	...
Madagascar — Madagascar										
Money market Marché monétaire	10.00	...	11.24	...	16.00	...	...	10.50	16.50	16.50
Treasury bill Bons du trésor	...	...	...	...	...	10.28	...	11.94	12.95	18.84
Malawi — Malawi										
Treasury bill Bons du trésor	30.83	18.31	32.98	42.85	39.52	42.41	41.75	39.32	28.58	24.36
Malaysia — Malaisie										
Money market A [21] Marché monétaire A [21]	6.92	7.61	8.46	3.38	2.66	2.79	2.73	2.74	2.70	2.72
Treasury bill A [12] Bons du trésor A [12]	6.41	6.41	6.86	3.53	2.86	2.79	2.73	2.79	2.40	2.48
Maldives [5] — Maldives [5]										
Money market B Marché monétaire B	6.80	6.80	6.80	6.80	6.80	...	...	...	...	...
Mali [7] — Mali [7]										
Money market A Marché monétaire A	4.95	4.95	4.95	4.95	4.95	4.95	4.95	4.95	4.95	4.95

Country or area — Pays ou zone	1996	1997	1998	1999	2000	2001	2002	2003	2004	2005
Malta [12] — Malte [12]										
Treasury bill A Bons du trésor A	4.99	5.08	5.41	5.15	4.89	4.93	4.03	3.29	2.94	3.18
Mauritius — Maurice										
Money market Marché monétaire	9.96	9.43	8.99	10.01	7.66	7.25	6.20	3.22	1.33	2.45
Mexico — Mexique										
Money market B [22] Marché monétaire B [22]	33.61	21.91	26.89	24.10	16.96	12.89	8.17	6.83	7.15	9.59
Treasury bill Bons du trésor	31.39	19.80	24.76	21.41	15.24	11.31	7.09	6.23	6.82	9.20
Montserrat — Montserrat										
Money market Marché monétaire	5.25	5.25	5.25	5.25	5.25	5.64	6.32	6.07	4.67	4.01
Morocco — Maroc										
Money market Marché monétaire	8.42	7.89	6.30	5.64	5.41	4.44	2.99	3.22	2.39	2.78
Mozambique — Mozambique										
Money market Marché monétaire	...	...	...	9.92	16.12	25.00	20.40	13.34	9.87	6.35
Treasury bill Bons du trésor	...	...	...	...	16.97	24.77	29.55	15.31	12.37	9.10
Namibia — Namibie										
Money market Marché monétaire	15.00	15.41	17.14	13.17	9.19	9.53	10.46	10.03	6.93	6.87
Treasury bill Bons du trésor	15.25	15.69	17.24	13.28	10.26	9.29	11.00	10.51	7.78	7.09
Nepal — Népal										
Treasury bill Bons du trésor	11.51	2.52	3.70	4.30	5.30	5.00	3.80	3.85	2.40	...
Netherlands [3,5] — Pays-Bas [3,5]										
Money market B Marché monétaire B	2.89	3.07	3.21	...	...	...	...	...	...	...
Netherlands Antilles [12] — Antilles néerlandaises [12]										
Treasury bill A Bons du trésor A	5.66	5.77	5.82	6.15	6.15	6.15	4.96	2.80	3.86	3.52
New Zealand — Nouvelle-Zélande										
Money market Marché monétaire	9.38	7.38	6.86	4.33	6.12	5.76	5.40	5.33	5.77	6.76
Treasury bill A [23] Bons du trésor A [23]	9.09	7.53	7.10	4.58	6.39	5.56	5.52	5.21	5.85	6.53
Niger [7] — Niger [7]										
Money market A Marché monétaire A	4.95	4.95	4.95	4.95	4.95	4.95	4.95	4.95	4.95	4.95
Nigeria — Nigéria										
Treasury bill Bons du trésor	12.25	12.00	12.26	17.82	15.50	17.50	19.03	14.79	14.34	...
Norway [5] — Norvège [5]										
Money market B Marché monétaire B	4.97	3.77	6.03	6.87	6.72	7.38	7.05	4.45	2.17	2.26
Pakistan — Pakistan										
Money market B [5] Marché monétaire B [5]	11.40	12.10	10.76	9.04	8.57	8.49	5.53	2.14	2.70	6.83
Treasury bill A [24] Bons du trésor A [24]	13.61	15.74	...	...	8.38	10.71	6.08	1.93	2.48	7.18
Panama — Panama										
Money market Marché monétaire	...	...	...	...	...	...	2.22	1.50	1.90	3.13
Papua New Guinea [25] — Papouasie-Nvl-Guinée [25]										
Treasury bill A Bons du trésor A	14.44	9.94	21.18	22.70	17.00	12.36	10.93	18.69	8.85	...

Country or area — Pays ou zone	1996	1997	1998	1999	2000	2001	2002	2003	2004	2005
Paraguay — Paraguay										
Money market Marché monétaire	16.35	12.48	20.74	17.26	10.70	13.45	13.19	13.02	1.33	2.29
Philippines — Philippines										
Money market Marché monétaire	12.77	16.16	13.90	10.16	10.84	9.75	7.15	6.97	7.05	7.31
Treasury bill A [26] Bons du trésor A [26]	12.34	12.89	15.00	10.00	9.91	9.73	5.49	5.87	7.32	6.13
Poland — Pologne										
Money market Marché monétaire	20.63	22.43	20.59	13.58	18.16	16.23	9.39	5.76	6.03	5.34
Treasury bill Bons du trésor	20.32	21.58	19.09	13.14	16.62	...	...	...	...	...
Portugal — Portugal										
Money market A [3,27] Marché monétaire A [3,27]	7.38	5.78	4.34	2.71	...	...	...	...	...	...
Treasury bill Bons du trésor	5.75	4.43	...	...	...	...	...	...	...	...
Republic of Moldova — République de Moldova										
Money market Marché monétaire	...	28.10	30.91	32.60	20.77	11.04	5.13	11.51	13.19	...
Money market B [1] Marché monétaire B [1]	...	...	...	11.88	6.86	9.06	4.80	2.51	0.78	...
Treasury bill Bons du trésor	39.01	23.63	30.54	28.49	22.20	14.24	5.89	15.08	11.89	
Romania [26] — Roumanie [26]										
Treasury bill A Bons du trésor A	51.09	85.72	63.99	74.21	51.86	42.18	27.03	...	...	...
Russian Federation — Fédération de Russie										
Money market Marché monétaire	47.65	20.97	50.56	14.79	7.14	10.10	8.19	3.77	3.33	2.68
Treasury bill Bons du trésor	86.07	23.43	...	...	12.12	12.45	12.72	5.35	...	...
Saint Kitts and Nevis — Saint-Kitts-et-Nevis										
Money market Marché monétaire	5.25	5.25	5.25	5.25	5.25	5.64	6.32	6.07	4.67	4.01
Treasury bill Bons du trésor	6.50	6.50	6.50	6.50	6.50	7.50	7.50	7.17	7.00	7.00
Saint Lucia — Sainte-Lucie										
Money market Marché monétaire	5.25	5.25	5.25	5.25	5.25	5.64	6.32	6.07	4.67	4.01
Treasury bill Bons du trésor	7.00	7.00	7.00	7.00	7.00	6.80	6.80	6.33	6.40	...
St. Vincent-Grenadines — St. Vincent-Grenadines										
Money market Marché monétaire	5.25	5.25	5.25	5.25	5.25	5.64	6.32	6.07	4.67	4.01
Treasury bill Bons du trésor	6.50	6.50	6.50	6.50	6.50	7.00	7.00	5.73	4.60	4.85
Senegal — Sénégal										
Money market Marché monétaire	4.95	4.95	4.95	4.95	4.95	4.95	4.95	4.95	4.95	4.95
Seychelles — Seychelles										
Treasury bill Bons du trésor	11.55	10.50	8.13	5.00	5.00	5.00	5.00	4.61	3.17	3.34
Sierra Leone — Sierra Leone										
Treasury bill Bons du trésor	29.25	12.71	22.10	32.42	26.22	13.74	15.15	15.68	26.14	22.98

Country or area — Pays ou zone	1996	1997	1998	1999	2000	2001	2002	2003	2004	2005
Singapore — Singapour										
Money market A [14] Marché monétaire A [14]	2.93	4.35	5.00	2.04	2.57	1.99	0.96	0.74	1.04	2.28
Treasury bill Bons du trésor	1.38	2.32	2.12	1.12	2.18	1.69	0.81	0.64	0.96	2.04
Slovakia — Slovaquie										
Money market Marché monétaire	...	...	...	...	8.08	7.76	6.33	6.08	3.82	3.02
Slovenia — Slovénie										
Money market Marché monétaire	13.98	9.71	7.45	6.87	6.95	6.90	4.93	5.59	4.40	3.73
Treasury bill Bons du trésor	...	...	...	8.63	10.94	10.88	8.73	6.53	4.17	3.66
Solomon Islands [12] — Iles Salomon [12]										
Treasury bill A Bons du trésor A	12.75	12.88	6.00	6.00	7.05	8.23	6.87	5.85	6.00	...
South Africa — Afrique du Sud										
Money market Marché monétaire	15.54	15.59	17.11	13.06	9.54	8.49	11.11	10.93	7.15	6.62
Treasury bill Bons du trésor	15.04	15.26	16.53	12.85	10.11	9.68	11.16	10.67	7.53	6.91
Spain — Espagne										
Money market B [5] Marché monétaire B [5]	7.65	5.49	4.34	2.72	4.11	4.36	3.28	2.31	2.04	2.09
Treasury bill Bons du trésor	7.23	5.02	3.79	3.01	4.61	3.92	3.34	2.21	2.17	2.19
Sri Lanka — Sri Lanka										
Money market B [28] Marché monétaire B [28]	24.33	18.42	15.74	16.69	17.30	21.24	12.33	9.68	8.87	...
Treasury bill Bons du trésor	17.40	...	12.59	12.51	14.02	17.57	12.47	8.09	7.71	...
Swaziland — Swaziland										
Money market Marché monétaire	9.77	10.35	10.63	8.86	5.54	5.06	7.31	6.98	4.12	3.47
Treasury bill Bons du trésor	13.68	14.37	13.09	11.19	8.30	7.16	8.59	10.61	7.94	7.07
Sweden — Suède										
Money market B [5] Marché monétaire B [5]	6.28	4.21	4.24	3.14	3.81	4.09	4.19	3.29	...	...
Treasury bill A [29] Bons du trésor A [29]	5.79	4.11	4.19	3.12	3.95	...	4.07	3.04	...	...
Switzerland — Suisse										
Money market Marché monétaire	1.78	1.35	1.22	0.93	3.50	1.65	0.44	0.09	0.55	0.63
Treasury bill Bons du trésor	1.72	1.45	1.32	1.17	2.93	2.68	0.94	0.16	0.37	0.71
Thailand — Thaïlande										
Money market Marché monétaire	9.23	14.59	13.02	1.77	1.95	2.00	1.76	1.31	1.23	2.62
Togo [7] — Togo [7]										
Money market A Marché monétaire A	4.95	4.95	4.95	4.95	4.95	4.95	4.95	4.95	4.95	4.95
Trinidad and Tobago — Trinité-et-Tobago										
Treasury bill Bons du trésor	10.44	9.83	11.93	10.40	10.56	8.55	4.83	4.71	4.77	4.86
Tunisia — Tunisie										
Money market Marché monétaire	8.64	6.88	6.89	5.99	5.88	6.04	5.93	5.14	5.00	5.00

Country or area — Pays ou zone	1996	1997	1998	1999	2000	2001	2002	2003	2004	2005
Turkey — Turquie										
Money market B [4] Marché monétaire B [4]	76.24	70.32	74.60	73.53	56.72	91.95	49.51	36.16	21.57	...
Treasury bill Bons du trésor	...	...	...	...	25.18	85.33	59.50	34.90	21.95	...
Uganda [26] — Ouganda [26]										
Treasury bill A Bons du trésor A	11.71	10.59	7.77	7.43	13.19	11.00	5.85	16.87	9.02	...
Ukraine — Ukraine										
Money market Marché monétaire	...	22.05	40.41	44.98	18.34	16.57	5.50	7.90	6.34	4.16
Money market B [1] Marché monétaire B [1]	...	...	10.61	5.44	6.27	5.87	3.14	3.61	2.15	2.85
United Kingdom — Royaume-Uni										
Money market A [30] Marché monétaire A [30]	5.96	6.61	7.21	5.20	5.77	5.08	3.89	3.59	4.29	4.70
Treasury bill Bons du trésor	5.78	6.48	6.82	5.04	5.80	4.77	3.86	3.55	4.43	4.55
Treasury bill B [31] Bons du trésor B [31]	5.89	6.62	7.23	5.14	5.83	4.79	3.96	3.55	4.44	4.59
United Rep. of Tanzania — Rép.-Unie de Tanzanie										
Treasury bill Bons du trésor	15.30	9.59	11.83	10.05	9.78	4.14	3.55	6.26	8.35	10.67
United States — Etats-Unis										
Money market B [32] Marché monétaire B [32]	5.30	5.46	5.35	4.97	6.24	3.89	1.67	1.13	1.35	3.21
Money market A [33] Marché monétaire A [33]	5.41	5.57	5.34	5.18	6.31	3.61	1.69	1.11	1.49	3.38
Treasury bill Bons du trésor	5.02	5.07	4.82	4.66	5.84	3.45	1.61	1.01	1.38	3.17
Uruguay — Uruguay										
Money market Marché monétaire	28.47	23.43	20.48	13.96	14.82	22.10	86.10	20.76	3.57	...
Treasury bill Bons du trésor	29.20	23.18	...	...	...	...	...	32.53	14.75	...
Treasury bill B [1] Bons du trésor B [1]	5.36	5.18	...	...	...	...	...	...	...	...
Vanuatu [34] — Vanuatu [34]										
Money market B Marché monétaire B	6.00	6.00	8.65	6.99	5.58	5.50	5.50	5.50	5.50	5.50
Venezuela (Bolivarian Republic of) — Venezuela (République bolivarienne du)										
Money market Marché monétaire	16.70	12.47	18.58	7.48	8.14	13.33	28.87	13.23	4.38	2.62
Viet Nam — Viet Nam										
Treasury bill Bons du trésor	...	...	...	...	5.42	5.49	5.92	5.83	...	...
Yemen — Yémen										
Treasury bill Bons du trésor	25.20	15.97	12.53	20.57	14.16	13.25	11.55	12.92	13.84	...
Zambia — Zambie										
Treasury bill Bons du trésor	52.78	29.48	24.94	36.19	31.37	44.28	34.54	29.97	12.60	16.32
Zimbabwe — Zimbabwe										
Money market A [9] Marché monétaire A [9]	26.18	25.15	37.22	53.13	64.98	21.52	32.35	110.05	129.58	...
Treasury bill Bons du trésor	24.53	22.07	32.78	50.48	64.78	17.60	28.51	52.73	125.68	185.11

Source

International Monetary Fund (IMF), Washington, D.C., "International Financial Statistics,"February 2005 and the IMF database.

Notes

+ The naming conventions for money market rates and treasury bill yields sometimes vary among countries. In this table, three money market and treasury bill descriptions are used: (i) "Money market"/"Treasury bill", (ii) "Money market A"/"Treasury bill A" and (iii) "Money market B"/"Treasury bill B". These distinctions are shown for those countries for which more than one type of money market rate or treasury bill yield is differentiated by the International Monetary Fund in "International Financial Statistics". In general, "Money market A" and "Treasury bill A" refer to those interest rates or yields whose durations have been specified (e.g. overnight, one month, 91 days, etc.) and "Money market B" and "Treasury bill B" refer to all others containing specific descriptors such as "call money rate", "foreign currency", "interbank", "discounted rate", etc.

[1] Foreign currency.
[2] 13 weeks.
[3] Beginning 1999, see Euro Area. For Greece, beginning 2001, see Euro Area.
[4] Interbank.
[5] Call money rate.
[6] Discount rate.
[7] Overnight advances.
[8] Overnight rate.
[9] Interbank rate (3-month maturity).
[10] Overnight interbank.
[11] Average cost of Central Bank debt.
[12] 3 months.
[13] Discounted.
[14] 3-month interbank rate.
[15] Yield.
[16] 1-month fixed rate.
[17] Corporate bond rate.
[18] Central Bank bill rate.
[19] Interbank deposit rate (3 months).
[20] Interbank call loans (maximum rate).
[21] Interbank overnight.
[22] Bankers' acceptances.
[23] New issue rate: 3-month treasury bills.
[24] 6 months.
[25] 182 days.
[26] 91 days.
[27] Up-to-5-days interbank deposit.
[28] Interbank call loans.
[29] 3-month discount notes.
[30] Overnight interbank minimum.
[31] Bond equivalent.
[32] Federal funds rate.
[33] Commercial paper (3 months).
[34] Interbank borrowing rate.

Source

Fonds monétaire international (FMI), Washington, D.C., "Statistiques Financières Internationales", février 2005 et la base de données du FMI.

Notes

+ La manière dont par convention on dénomme les taux du marché monétaire et le rendement des bons du Trésor peut varier selon les pays. Dans le tableau, on utilise trois termes pour le marché monétaire et les bons du Trésor : i) "Marché monétaire"/"Bons du Trésor", ii) "Marché monétaire A"/"Bons du Trésor A", iii) "Marché monétaire B"/"Bons du Trésor B". Ces distinctions apparaissent pour les pays où le Fonds monétaire international (FMI) distingue dans Statistiques financières internationales plus d'un type de taux du marché monétaire ou de rendement de bons du Trésor. En général, "Marché monétaire A" et "Bons du Trésor A" désignent les taux d'intérêt ou les rendements dont la durée a été précisée (au jour le jour, à un mois, à 91 jours, etc.), "Marché monétaire B" et "Bons du Trésor B" désignant tous les autres assortis de descripteurs précis tels que taux de l'argent au jour le jour, en devises, interbancaire, taux escompté, etc.

[1] Devises.
[2] Treize semaines.
[3] À compter de 1999, voir zone euro. Pour la Grèce, à compter de 2001, voir zone euro.
[4] Interbancaire.
[5] Taux de l'argent au jour le jour.
[6] Taux de l'escompte.
[7] Taux des avances à un jour.
[8] Taux à un jour.
[9] Taux interbancaire (maturité à 3 mois).
[10] Taux interbancaire à un jour.
[11] Coût moyen de la dette à la Banque centrale.
[12] Trois mois.
[13] Taux actualisé.
[14] Taux interbancaire à trois mois.
[15] Rendement.
[16] Taux forfaitaire à un mois.
[17] Taux des obligations de société.
[18] Taux d'escompte de la Banque Centrale (a trois mois).
[19] Taux des dépôts interbancaires (à trois mois).
[20] Prêts interbancaires remboursables sur demande (taux maximum).
[21] Taux interbancaire au jour le jour.
[22] Traite bancaire.
[23] Taux des émissions nouvelles : bons du Trésor à trois mois.
[24] Six mois.
[25] Cent quatre-vingt-deux jours.
[26] Quatre-vingt-onze jours.
[27] Dépôts interbancaires jusqu'à cinq jours.
[28] Prêts interbancaires remboursables sur demande.
[29] Billets à escompte à trois mois.
[30] Taux minimum des prêts interbancaires à un jour.
[31] Équivalant à obligation.
[32] Taux des fonds du système fédérale.
[33] Effet de commerce (à trois mois).
[34] Taux des prêts interbancaires.

Detailed information and current figures relating to tables 24 and 25 are contained in *International Financial Statistics*, published by the International Monetary Fund [13] (see also www.imf.org) and in the United Nations *Monthly Bulletin of Statistics* [25].

Table 24: The discount rates shown represent the rates at which the central bank lends or discounts eligible paper for deposit money banks, typically shown on an end-of-period basis.

Table 25: The rates shown represent short-term treasury bill rates and money market rates. The treasury bill rate is the rate at which short-term securities are issued or traded in the market. The money market rate is the rate on short-term lending between financial institutions.

The naming conventions for money market rates and treasury bill yields sometimes vary among countries. In table 25, three money market and treasury bill descriptions are used: (i) "Money market"/"Treasury bill", (ii) "Money market A"/ "Treasury bill A" and (iii) "Money market B"/"Treasury bill B". These distinctions are shown for those countries for which more than one type of money market rate or treasury bill yield is differentiated by the International Monetary Fund in *International Financial Statistics*. In this table, "Money market A" and "Treasury bill A" generally refer to those interest rates or yields whose durations have been specified (e.g. overnight, one month, 91 days, etc.) and "Money market B" and "Treasury bill B" refer to all others containing specific descriptors such as "call money rate", "foreign currency", "interbank", "discounted rate", etc.

Les informations détaillées et les chiffres courants concernant les tableaux 24 et 25 figurent dans les *Statistiques financières internationales* publiées par le Fonds monétaire international 13] (voir aussi www.imf.org) et dans le *Bulletin mensuel de statistique* des Nations Unies [25].

Tableau 24 : Les taux d'escomptes indiqués représentent les taux que la banque centrale applique à ses prêts ou auquel elle réescompte les effets escomptables des banques créatrices de monnaie (généralement, taux de fin de période).

Tableau 25 : Les taux indiqués représentent le taux des bons du Trésor et le taux du marché monétaire à court terme. Le taux des bons du Trésor est le taux auquel les effets à court terme sont émis ou négociés sur le marché. Le taux du marché monétaire est le taux prêteur à court terme entre institutions financières.

La manière dont par convention on dénomme les taux du marché monétaire et le rendement des bons du Trésor peut varier selon les pays. Dans le tableau 25, on utilise trois termes pour le marché monétaire et les bons du Trésor : i) "Marché monétaire"/"Bons du Trésor", ii) "Marché monétaire A"/"Bons du Trésor A", iii) "Marché monétaire B"/"Bons du Trésor B". Ces distinctions apparaissent pour les pays où le Fonds monétaire international distingue dans *Statistiques financières internationales* plus d'un type de taux du marché monétaire ou de rendement de bons du Trésor. En général, dans ce tableau, "Marché monétaire A" et "Bons du Trésor A" désignent les taux d'intérêt ou les rendements dont la durée a été précisée (au jour le jour, à un mois, à 91 jours, etc.), "Marché monétaire B" et "Bons du Trésor B" désignant tous les autres assortis de descripteurs précis tels que taux de l'argent au jour le jour, en devises, interbancaire, taux escompté, etc.

26

Unemployment
Number (thousands) and percentage unemployed, by sex

Chômage
Nombre (milliers) et pourcentage des chômeurs, par sexe

Country or area, source§ — Pays ou zone, source§	1997	1998	1999	2000	2001	2002	2003	2004
Albania — Albanie								
MF [BA] [1]	...	...	...	...	...	...	166.0	...
M [BA] [1]	...	...	...	...	...	...	88.0	...
F [BA] [1]	...	...	...	...	...	...	78.0	...
%MF [BA] [1]	...	...	...	...	...	...	15.2	...
%M [BA] [1]	...	...	...	...	...	...	13.2	...
%F [BA] [1]	...	...	...	...	...	...	18.3	...
MF [A]	...	...	...	...	305.5	...	...	...
M [A]	...	...	...	...	150.1	...	...	...
F [A]	...	...	...	...	155.4	...	...	...
MF [FB]	193.5	235.0	239.8	215.1	180.5	172.4	163.0	157.0
M [FB]	110.0	127.0	130.0	113.0	96.0	91.0	86.0	82.0
F [FB]	83.5	108.0	109.8	102.1	84.5	81.4	77.0	75.0
%MF [FB]	14.9	17.7	18.4	16.8	16.4	15.8	15.0	14.4
%M [FB]	13.8	15.8	16.4	14.9	14.2	13.6	12.9	12.4
%F [FB]	16.6	20.9	21.4	19.3	19.9	19.1	18.2	17.5
Algeria [1,2] — Algérie [1,2]								
MF [BA]	...	...	...	...	2 339.4	...	2 078.3	1 671.5
M [BA]	...	...	...	...	1 934.9	...	1 759.9	1 370.4
F [BA]	...	...	...	...	404.5	...	318.3	301.1
%MF [BA]	...	...	...	...	27.3	...	23.7	17.7
%M [BA]	...	...	...	...	26.6	...	23.4	17.5
%F [BA]	...	...	...	...	31.4	...	25.4	18.1
Anguilla [1] — Anguilla [1]								
MF [BA]	...	...	0.6[3]	...	0.4[4]	0.5[5]	...	...
M [BA]	...	...	0.2[3]	...	0.2[4]	0.2[5]	...	...
F [BA]	...	...	0.4[3]	...	0.2[4]	0.3[5]	...	...
%MF [BA]	...	...	8.3[3]	...	6.7[4]	7.8[5]	...	...
%M [BA]	...	...	4.6[3]	...	6.5[4]	6.3[5]	...	...
%F [BA]	...	...	12.1[3]	...	7.0[4]	9.5[5]	...	...
Argentina [6] — Argentine [6]								
MF [BA]	1 375.1[7,8]	1 203.1[7,8]	1 359.6[7,8]	1 460.9[7,8]	1 709.8[7,8]	1 955.8[7,8]	1 583.6[9]	...
M [BA]	731.4[7,8]	673.0[7,8]	764.9[7,8]	809.9[7,8]	1 021.9[7,8]	1 175.2[7,8]	949.0[9]	...
F [BA]	643.7[7,8]	530.1[7,8]	594.7[7,8]	651.0[7,8]	688.4[7,8]	780.6[7,8]	634.6[9]	...
%MF [BA]	14.9[7,8]	12.8[7,8]	14.1[7,8]	15.0[7,8]	17.4[7,8]	19.6[7,8]	15.6[9]	...
%M [BA]	13.0[7,8]	11.9[7,8]	13.3[7,8]	14.1[7,8]	17.4[7,8]	20.2[7,8]	16.3[9]	...
%F [BA]	17.9[7,8]	14.2[7,8]	15.2[7,8]	16.4[7,8]	17.2[7,8]	18.8[7,8]	14.7[9]	...
Armenia — Arménie								
MF [BA] [1,10]	423.7	...	...	...	...	...	...	...
M [BA] [1,10]	247.0	...	...	...	...	...	...	...
F [BA] [1,10]	176.7	...	...	...	...	...	...	...
%MF [BA] [1,10]	36.4	...	...	...	...	...	...	...
%M [BA] [1,10]	38.0	...	...	...	...	...	...	...
%F [BA] [1,10]	34.4	...	...	...	...	...	...	...
MF [FB] [11,12]	174.4	133.8	175.0	153.9	138.4	127.3	118.6	108.6
M [FB] [11,12]	49.7	40.9	62.3	54.4	47.1	85.7	37.0	32.3
F [FB] [11,12]	124.7	92.8	112.7	99.5	91.3	41.6	81.6	76.3
%MF [FB] [11,12]	10.8	9.4	11.2	11.7	10.4	10.8	10.1	9.4
%M [FB] [11,12]	6.3	5.6	7.6	8.0	6.9	7.2	5.9	5.2
%F [FB] [11,12]	15.1	13.3	15.0	15.7	14.1	14.5	14.4	13.6
Aruba [1] — Aruba [1]								
MF [BA]	3.3	...	...	...	...	...	...	...
M [BA]	1.7	...	...	...	...	...	...	...
F [BA]	1.6	...	...	...	...	...	...	...

Country or area, source[§] — Pays ou zone, source[§]	1997	1998	1999	2000	2001	2002	2003	2004
Australia [1,13] — Australie [1,13]								
MF [BA]	769.1	728.1	654.9	607.5	667.1	636.9	607.4	570.6
M [BA]	449.4	428.1	379.5	347.7	383.8	363.5	330.0	308.8
F [BA]	319.7	300.0	275.4	259.8	283.3	273.4	277.3	261.7
%MF [BA]	8.4	7.8	7.0	6.4	6.9	6.4	6.0	5.6
%M [BA]	8.6	8.1	7.2	6.5	7.1	6.6	5.9	5.5
%F [BA]	8.1	7.5	6.8	6.2	6.6	6.2	6.2	5.7
Austria [1] — Autriche [1]								
MF [BA]	164.8[14]	165.0[14]	146.7[14]	138.8[14]	142.5[14]	161.0[14]	168.8[14]	194.6[15]
M [BA]	87.3[14]	88.4[14]	81.7[14]	73.8[14]	77.0[14]	91.7[14]	94.7[14]	98.0[15]
F [BA]	77.5[14]	76.6[14]	65.0[14]	65.0[14]	65.5[14]	69.3[14]	74.3[14]	96.6[15]
%MF [BA]	4.2[14]	4.2[14]	3.8[14]	3.6[14]	3.6[14]	4.0[14]	4.3[14]	4.9[15]
%M [BA]	3.9[14]	4.0[14]	3.7[14]	3.3[14]	3.5[14]	4.1[14]	4.3[14]	4.5[15]
%F [BA]	4.6[14]	4.6[14]	3.9[14]	3.8[14]	3.8[14]	3.9[14]	4.2[14]	5.4[15]
MF [FB]	233.3	237.8	221.7	194.3	203.9	232.4	240.1	243.9
M [FB]	128.5	129.4	121.5	107.5	115.3	134.4	139.7	140.3
F [FB]	104.8	108.4	100.2	86.8	88.6	98.0	100.4	103.6
%MF [FB]	7.1	7.2	6.7	5.8	6.1	6.9	7.0	7.1
%M [FB]	6.9	6.9	6.5	5.8	6.2	7.2	7.5	7.5
%F [FB]	7.4	7.5	6.9	5.9	5.9	6.4	6.5	6.6
Azerbaijan [16] — Azerbaïdjan [16]								
MF [FB]	38.3	42.3	45.2	43.7	48.4	51.0	54.4	55.9
M [FB]	16.2	18.2	19.6	19.3	21.8	23.1	25.3	26.7
F [FB]	22.1	24.1	25.6	24.5	26.6	27.9	29.1	29.3
%MF [FB]	1.0	1.1	1.2	1.2	1.3	1.3	1.4	1.4
%M [FB]	0.8	0.9	1.0	1.0	1.1	1.2	1.3	1.3
%F [FB]	1.2	1.4	1.4	1.4	1.5	1.5	1.6	1.6
Bahamas [1,17] — Bahamas [1,17]								
MF [BA]	14.7	12.1	12.3	...	11.3	15.3	18.8	...
M [BA]	6.5	4.5	5.0	...	5.7	7.6	8.8	...
F [BA]	8.2	7.6	7.3	...	5.6	7.7	10.1	...
%MF [BA]	9.8	7.8	7.8	...	6.9	9.1	10.8	...
%M [BA]	8.3	5.7	6.0	...	7.1	9.1	10.8	...
%F [BA]	11.3	9.8	9.7	...	6.8	8.8	10.0	...
Bahrain — Bahreïn								
MF [A]	...	...	...	...	16.1	...	...	...
M [A]	...	...	...	...	9.4	...	...	...
F [A]	...	...	...	...	6.7	...	...	...
MF [FB] [18,19]	6.1	4.1	3.8	6.2	...	8.7	11.8	6.3
M [FB] [18,19]	4.1	2.7	2.6	4.2	...	4.4	6.0	3.1
F [FB] [18,19]	2.0	1.4	1.1	2.0	...	4.4	5.7	3.2
Bangladesh [1,20] — Bangladesh [1,20]								
MF [BA]	...	...	...	1 750.0	...	...	2 002.0	...
M [BA]	...	...	...	1 083.0	...	...	1 500.0	...
F [BA]	...	...	...	666.0	...	...	502.0	...
%MF [BA]	...	...	...	3.3	...	...	4.3	...
%M [BA]	...	...	...	3.2	...	...	4.2	...
%F [BA]	...	...	...	3.3	...	...	4.9	...
Barbados [1] — Barbade [1]								
MF [BA]	20.1	16.8	14.4	13.3	14.3	14.8	16.0	14.3
M [BA]	8.1	6.0	5.6	5.5	6.0	6.4	7.1	6.7
F [BA]	11.9	10.9	8.8	7.9	8.3	8.4	8.9	7.5
%MF [BA]	14.5	12.3	10.5	9.4	9.9	10.3	11.0	9.8
%M [BA]	11.3	8.4	7.7	7.5	8.0	8.2	9.6	9.0
%F [BA]	17.8	16.4	13.3	11.5	11.9	12.4	12.6	10.6
Belarus [11,21] — Bélarus [11,21]								
MF [FB]	126.2	105.9	95.4	95.8	102.9	130.5	136.1	83.0
M [FB]	42.1	35.3	34.2	37.6	40.9	47.8	46.1	25.5
F [FB]	84.1	70.6	61.2	58.2	62.0	82.7	90.0	57.5

Country or area, source[§] — Pays ou zone, source[§]	1997	1998	1999	2000	2001	2002	2003	2004
%MF [FB]	2.8	2.3	2.1	2.1	2.3	3.0	3.1	1.9
%M [FB]	1.9	1.6	1.6	1.7	1.9	2.3	1.2	...
%F [FB]	3.6	3.0	2.6	2.4	2.6	3.5	3.9	...
Belgium — Belgique								
MF [BA] [1]	375.1[17]	384.0[17]	375.2	308.5	286.4	332.1	364.3	...
M [BA] [1]	173.2[17]	179.3[17]	179.4	144.6	147.9	168.1	193.0	...
F [BA] [1]	201.9[17]	204.7[17]	195.8	163.9	138.4	164.0	171.3	...
%MF [BA] [1]	8.9[17]	9.1[17]	8.6	7.0	6.6	7.5	8.2	...
%M [BA] [1]	7.1[17]	7.3[17]	7.2	5.8	6.0	6.7	7.7	...
%F [BA] [1]	11.5[17]	11.4[17]	10.4	8.7	7.5	8.7	8.9	...
MF [FB] [22]	570.0	541.0	507.5	474.4	469.7	491.5	538.1	...
M [FB] [22]	249.6	237.4	224.7	208.7	210.9	228.0	253.1	...
F [FB] [22]	320.5	303.6	282.9	265.8	258.9	263.4	285.1	...
%MF [FB] [22]	13.1	12.4	11.6	10.9	10.8	11.2	12.3	...
%M [FB] [22]	10.2	9.7	9.2	8.6	8.7	9.4	10.4	...
%F [FB] [22]	16.8	15.9	14.7	13.8	13.4	13.6	14.7	...
Belize [17,23] — Belize [17,23]								
MF [BA]	10.3	12.3	11.5	...	8.6	9.5	...	...
M [BA]	4.8	5.9	5.3	...	3.6	4.7	...	...
F [BA]	5.5	6.3	6.1	...	5.0	4.7	...	...
%MF [BA]	12.7	14.3	12.8	...	9.1	10.0	...	...
%M [BA]	8.9	10.6	9.0	...	5.8	7.5	...	...
%F [BA]	20.3	21.3	20.3	...	15.4	15.3	...	...
Bolivia [6] — Bolivie [6]								
MF [BA]	...	...	164.5	183.2	214.9	221.6	...	...
M [BA]	...	...	76.9	83.3	99.4	97.4	...	...
F [BA]	...	...	87.6	99.9	115.5	124.2	...	...
%MF [BA]	...	...	4.3	4.8	5.2	5.5	...	...
%M [BA]	...	...	3.7	3.9	4.5	4.3	...	...
%F [BA]	...	...	5.1	5.9	6.2	6.9	...	...
Botswana [24] — Botswana [24]								
MF [BA]	...	115.7	...	90.7	109.5[25]	...	...	...
M [BA]	...	56.7	...	46.3	51.9[25]	...	...	...
F [BA]	...	59.0	...	44.5	57.6[25]	...	...	...
%MF [BA]	...	20.8	...	15.8	19.6[25]	...	...	...
%M [BA]	...	18.6	...	14.7	16.4[25]	...	...	...
%F [BA]	...	23.6	...	17.2	23.9[25]	...	...	...
Brazil [2,6,26] — Brésil [2,6,26]								
MF [BA]	5 881.8	6 922.6	7 639.1	...	7 853.4	7 958.5	8 640.0	...
M [BA]	2 854.9	3 301.1	3 667.9	...	3 674.9	3 685.1	3 972.8	...
F [BA]	3 026.9	3 621.5	3 971.2	...	4 178.5	4 273.3	4 667.1	...
%MF [BA]	7.8	9.0	9.6	...	9.4	9.2	9.7	...
%M [BA]	6.4	7.2	7.9	...	7.5	7.4	7.8	...
%F [BA]	10.0	11.6	12.1	...	11.9	11.6	12.3	...
Brunei Darussalam [19] — Brunéi Darussalam [19]								
MF [FB]	5.5	6.5	5.2	7.0	8.6	5.6	7.1	...
M [FB]	2.1	2.6	2.1	2.7	3.3	2.1	3.1	...
F [FB]	3.4	3.8	3.1	4.3	5.3	3.4	4.0	...
Bulgaria — Bulgarie								
MF [BA] [27]	491.4[28]	438.8[28]	486.7[28]	559.0[28]	661.1[28]	599.2[28]	449.1	399.8
M [BA] [27]	265.0[28]	240.8[28]	258.6[28]	306.3[28]	363.2[28]	328.7[28]	246.1	221.6
F [BA] [27]	226.4[28]	198.0[28]	228.1[28]	252.6[28]	297.8[28]	270.4[28]	203.0	178.2
%MF [BA] [27]	13.7[28]	12.2[28]	14.1[28]	16.3[28]	19.4[28]	17.6[28]	13.7	12.0
%M [BA] [27]	13.9[28]	12.6[28]	14.0[28]	16.7[28]	20.2[28]	18.3[28]	14.1	12.5
%F [BA] [27]	13.5[28]	11.8[28]	14.1[28]	15.9[28]	18.4[28]	16.9[28]	13.2	11.5
MF [FB] [11]	523.5[29]	465.2[29]	610.6[29]	682.8	662.3	602.5	500.7	450.6[30]
M [FB] [11]	236.5[29]	211.1[29]	284.5[29]	323.4	321.1	281.1	227.1	201.6[30]
F [FB] [11]	287.1[29]	254.1[29]	326.1[29]	359.4	341.2	321.5	273.6	249.0[30]
%MF [FB] [11]	13.7[29]	12.2[29]	16.0[29]	17.9	17.3	16.3	13.5	12.2[30]

26

Unemployment—Number (thousands) and percentage unemployed, by sex (*continued*)
Chômage—Nombre (milliers) et pourcentage des chômeurs, par sexe (*suite*)

Country or area, source[§] — Pays ou zone, source[§]	1997	1998	1999	2000	2001	2002	2003	2004
Burkina Faso [19,31] — Burkina Faso [19,31]								
MF [FB]	9.2	9.4	7.5	6.6	...	...	...	...
M [FB]	7.6	7.8	6.2	5.4	...	...	...	...
F [FB]	1.6	1.6	1.4	1.2	...	...	...	...
Burundi [19,32] — Burundi [19,32]								
MF [FB]	1.6	2.8	0.7	...	...	...	...	...
%MF [FB]	...	...	14.0	...	...	...	...	...
%M [FB]	...	...	15.0	...	...	...	...	...
%F [FB]	...	...	13.2	...	...	...	...	...
Cambodia [6,33] — Cambodge [6,33]								
MF [BA]	...	...	...	133.6	115.8	...	...	...
M [BA]	...	...	...	55.0	44.9	...	...	...
F [BA]	...	...	...	78.6	71.0	...	...	...
%MF [BA]	...	...	...	2.5	1.8	...	...	...
%M [BA]	...	...	...	2.1	1.5	...	...	...
%F [BA]	...	...	...	2.8	2.2	...	...	...
Cameroon [1] — Cameroun [1]								
MF [A]	...	...	...	...	468.0	...	...	...
M [A]	...	...	...	...	263.0	...	...	...
F [A]	...	...	...	...	205.0	...	...	...
%MF [A]	...	...	...	...	7.5	...	...	...
%M [A]	...	...	...	...	8.2	...	...	...
%F [A]	...	...	...	...	6.7	...	...	...
Canada [1,34,35] — Canada [1,34,35]								
MF [BA]	1 382.0	1 277.6	1 185.2	1 083.5	1 164.1	1 272.2	1 288.9	1 233.7
M [BA]	768.2	715.4	662.7	596.0	655.3	725.6	722.4	684.8
F [BA]	613.8	562.2	522.5	487.6	508.7	546.6	566.5	548.9
%MF [BA]	9.2	8.4	7.6	6.8	7.2	7.7	7.6	7.2
%M [BA]	9.3	8.6	7.8	7.0	7.5	8.1	8.0	7.5
%F [BA]	9.0	8.1	7.3	6.7	6.9	7.1	7.2	6.8
Cayman Islands [36] — Iles Caïmanes [36]								
MF [BA]	0.9	...	...	...	...	...	...	...
M [BA]	0.3	...	...	...	...	...	...	...
F [BA]	0.6	...	...	...	...	...	...	...
%MF [BA]	4.1	...	...	...	...	...	...	...
%M [BA]	3.2	...	...	...	...	...	...	...
%F [BA]	5.1	...	...	...	...	...	...	...
Chile [1,37] — Chili [1,37]								
MF [BA]	303.6	419.2	529.1	489.4	469.4	468.7	453.1	494.7
M [BA]	180.8	271.1	322.9	312.5	302.6	298.5	279.2	280.8
F [BA]	122.8	148.1	206.2	176.9	166.9	170.2	173.9	213.9
%MF [BA]	5.3	7.2	8.9	8.3	7.9	7.8	7.4	7.8
%M [BA]	4.7	7.0	8.2	8.0	7.6	7.5	6.9	6.9
%F [BA]	6.6	7.6	10.3	9.0	8.4	8.5	8.3	9.5
China [1,11,38,39] — Chine [1,11,38,39]								
MF [E]	5 768.0	5 710.0	5 750.0	5 950.0	6 810.0	7 700.0	8 000.0	8 270.0
M [E]	2 737.0	2 705.0	...	...	...	...	...	...
F [E]	3 031.0	3 005.0	...	...	...	...	...	...
%MF [E]	3.0	3.1	3.1	3.1	3.6	4.0	4.3	4.2
China, Hong Kong SAR [1,40] — Chine, Hong Kong RAS [1,40]								
MF [BA]	71.2	154.1	207.5	166.9	174.8	255.5	277.2[41]	241.4
M [BA]	45.2	101.2	140.6	109.6	118.3	164.8	181.4[41]	153.3
F [BA]	26.0	52.9	66.9	57.3	56.5	90.7	95.8[41]	88.1
%MF [BA]	2.2	4.7	6.2	4.9	5.1	7.3	7.9[41]	6.8
%M [BA]	2.3	5.2	7.2	5.6	6.0	8.4	9.3[41]	7.8
%F [BA]	2.0	4.0	4.9	4.1	3.9	6.0	6.2[41]	5.6
China, Macao SAR [23,42] — Chine, Macao RAS [23,42]								
MF [BA]	6.5	9.5	13.2	14.2	13.9	13.4	12.9	11.0
M [BA]	4.1	6.4	9.1	9.8	9.4	8.9	8.2	6.7

Country or area, source[9] — Pays ou zone, source[9]	1997	1998	1999	2000	2001	2002	2003	2004
F [BA]	2.4	3.1	4.2	4.4	4.4	4.4	4.7	4.3
%MF [BA]	3.2	4.6	6.3	6.8	6.4	6.3	6.0	4.8
%M [BA]	3.7	5.7	8.0	8.6	8.1	7.9	7.1	5.5
%F [BA]	2.6	3.3	4.4	4.6	4.4	4.5	4.7	4.0
Colombia [43] — Colombie [43]								
MF [BA]	782.1[44]	998.3[44]	1 415.4[44]	1 526.0[44]	2 846.0[6]	3 084.4[6]	2 878.1[6]	2 766.7[6]
M [BA]	353.5[44]	457.2[44]	649.8[44]	660.2[44]	1 303.5[6]	1 440.7[6]	1 274.0[6]	1 243.1[6]
F [BA]	428.6[44]	541.1[44]	765.6[44]	865.8[44]	1 542.5[6]	1 643.8[6]	1 604.1[6]	1 523.6[6]
%MF [BA]	12.1[44]	15.0[44]	20.1[44]	20.5[44]	14.7[6]	15.7[6]	14.2[6]	13.6[6]
%M [BA]	9.8[44]	12.5[44]	17.2[44]	16.9[44]	11.6[6]	12.7[6]	11.0[6]	10.6[6]
%F [BA]	15.1[44]	18.0[44]	23.3[44]	24.5[44]	19.1[6]	19.7[6]	18.5[6]	17.7[6]
Costa Rica [24,45] — Costa Rica [24,45]								
MF [BA]	74.3	76.5	83.3	71.9	100.4	108.5	117.2	114.9
M [BA]	43.5	40.6	45.6	41.2	55.8	61.6	66.0	62.5
F [BA]	30.8	36.0	37.7	30.8	44.6	46.9	51.2	52.4
%MF [BA]	5.7	5.6	6.0	5.2	6.1	6.4	6.7	6.5
%M [BA]	4.9	4.4	4.9	4.4	5.2	5.6	5.8	5.4
%F [BA]	7.5	8.0	8.2	6.9	7.6	7.9	8.2	8.5
Croatia — Croatie								
MF [BA][1]	175.2[46]	198.5	234.0	297.2	276.2	265.8	255.7	249.7
M [BA][1]	90.7[46]	100.9	117.4	149.8	134.8	129.7	127.7	120.0
F [BA][1]	84.5[46]	97.5	116.6	147.4	141.4	136.0	128.1	129.7
%MF [BA][1]	9.9[46]	11.9	13.5	16.1	15.8	14.8	14.3	13.8
%M [BA][1]	9.5[46]	11.4	12.8	15.0	14.2	13.4	13.1	1.2
%F [BA][1]	10.4[46]	12.1	14.5	17.3	17.9	16.6	15.7	15.7
MF [FB]	278.0	288.0	322.0	358.0	380.0	390.0	330.0	310.0
M [FB]	141.0	139.0	153.0	169.0	177.0	177.0	140.0	129.0
F [FB]	137.0	149.0	169.0	189.0	203.0	213.0	190.0	181.0
%MF [FB]	17.5	17.2	19.1	21.1	22.0	22.3	19.2	...
%M [FB]	16.5	15.6	17.2	19.0	19.5	19.3	15.5	...
%F [FB]	18.6	19.0	21.2	23.4	24.7	25.6	23.2	...
Cyprus [1,47] — Chypre [1,47]								
MF [BA][48]	...	...	16.9	14.5	12.8	10.8	14.1	16.7
M [BA][48]	...	...	7.7	5.5	4.8	4.7	7.1	7.0
F [BA][48]	...	...	9.1	8.9	8.1	6.0	7.0	9.7
%MF [BA][48]	...	...	5.7	4.9	4.0	3.3	4.1	4.7
%M [BA][48]	...	...	4.3	3.2	2.6	2.6	3.8	3.5
%F [BA][48]	...	...	7.9	7.4	5.7	4.2	4.6	6.2
MF [FB]	10.4	10.4	11.4	10.9	9.5	10.6	12.0	12.7
M [FB]	5.0	5.4	5.6	5.3	4.5	4.7	5.1	5.4
F [FB]	5.4	5.0	5.8	5.7	5.0	5.9	6.8	7.2
%MF [FB]	3.4	3.3	3.6	3.4	2.9	3.2	3.5	3.6
%M [FB]	2.7	2.8	2.9	2.7	2.3	2.3	2.5	2.6
%F [FB]	4.5	4.2	4.8	4.4	3.8	4.3	5.0	5.1
Czech Republic — République tchèque								
MF [BA][1]	248.0[49]	336.0	454.0	455.0	418.0	374.0	399.0	426.0
M [BA][1]	113.0[49]	146.0	211.0	212.0	193.0	169.0	175.0	201.0
F [BA][1]	136.0[49]	190.0	243.0	243.0	225.0	205.0	224.0	225.0
%MF [BA][1]	4.8[49]	6.5	8.7	8.8	8.1	7.3	7.8	8.3
%M [BA][1]	3.9[49]	5.0	7.3	7.3	6.8	5.9	6.1	7.0
%F [BA][1]	6.0[49]	8.3	10.5	10.6	9.9	9.0	9.9	9.9
MF [FB][11]	269.0	387.0	488.0	457.0	462.0	514.0	542.0	542.0
M [FB][11]	117.0	182.0	240.0	227.0	230.0	257.0	270.0	266.0
F [FB][11]	152.0	205.0	248.0	230.0	232.0	257.0	272.0	276.0
%MF [FB][11]	5.2	7.5	9.4	8.8	8.9	9.8	10.3	9.5
%M [FB][11]	4.1	6.3	8.2	7.8	7.9	8.7	9.2	8.3
%F [FB][11]	6.7	9.0	10.8	10.0	10.1	11.2	11.8	10.9
Denmark — Danemark								
MF [BA][50]	174.2	155.3	158.0	131.1	137.0	134.0	157.6	162.6

Country or area, source[6] — Pays ou zone, source[6]	1997	1998	1999	2000	2001	2002	2003	2004
M [BA] [50]	74.8	68.5	71.0	61.2	66.0	66.0	75.7	79.9
F [BA] [50]	99.5	86.9	87.0	69.8	71.0	68.0	81.8	82.7
%MF [BA] [50]	6.1	5.5	5.5	4.6	4.8	4.7	5.5	5.6
%M [BA] [50]	4.9	4.5	4.8	4.0	4.4	4.4	5.0	5.2
%F [BA] [50]	7.6	6.6	6.5	5.2	5.3	5.1	6.2	6.1
MF [FB] [51]	220.2	182.7	158.2	150.5	145.1	144.7	170.6	176.4
M [FB] [51]	99.4	81.0	72.8	68.5	66.5	68.8	83.3	84.6
F [FB] [51]	120.8	101.8	85.4	82.0	78.6	75.9	87.3	91.8
%MF [FB] [51]	7.9	6.6	5.7	5.4	5.2	5.2	6.2	6.4
%M [FB] [51]	6.7	5.5	4.9	4.6	4.5	4.7	5.7	5.8
%F [FB] [51]	9.3	7.8	6.5	6.0	5.9	5.8	6.6	7.0
Dominica [1] — Dominique [1]								
MF [BA]	7.7	...	...	...	...	...	...	...
M [BA]	3.6	...	...	...	...	...	...	...
F [BA]	4.2	...	...	...	...	...	...	...
%MF [BA]	23.1	...	...	...	...	...	...	...
%M [BA]	19.6	...	...	...	...	...	...	...
%F [BA]	27.2	...	...	...	...	...	...	...
Dominican Republic [6] — Rép. dominicaine [6]								
MF [BA]	503.7	486.1	477.9	491.4	556.3	596.3	619.7	723.7
M [BA]	199.0	201.7	175.8	174.7	208.0	215.5	243.0	252.5
F [BA]	304.7	284.3	302.1	316.8	348.2	380.8	376.8	471.2
%MF [BA]	16.0	14.4	13.8	13.9	15.6	16.1	16.7	18.4
%M [BA]	9.5	9.3	7.8	7.9	9.3	9.4	10.6	10.5
%F [BA]	28.6	23.8	24.9	23.8	26.0	26.6	26.6	30.7
Ecuador [6] — Equateur [6]								
MF [BA]	311.6[33]	409.3[33]	543.5[33]	333.1[33]	450.9[5]	352.9[33]	461.1[33]	362.1[33]
M [BA]	143.4[33]	175.5[33]	239.5[33]	138.3[33]	169.0[5]	136.2[33]	215.0[33]	160.7[33]
F [BA]	168.3[33]	233.8[33]	304.0[33]	194.8[33]	282.0[5]	216.7[33]	246.1[33]	201.4[33]
%MF [BA]	9.2[33]	11.5[33]	14.0[33]	9.0[33]	11.0[5]	9.3[33]	11.5[33]	8.6[33]
%M [BA]	7.0[33]	8.4[33]	10.8[33]	6.2[33]	7.1[5]	6.0[33]	9.1[33]	6.6[33]
%F [BA]	12.7[33]	16.0[33]	19.6[33]	13.1[33]	16.2[5]	14.0[33]	15.0[33]	11.4[33]
Egypt [52,53] — Egypte [52,53]								
MF [BA]	1 446.4	1 447.5	1 480.5	1 698.0	1 783.0	2 020.6	2 240.7	...
M [BA]	701.5	703.0	726.2	743.5	851.8	983.2	1 186.7	...
F [BA]	744.9	744.5	754.3	954.5	931.2	1 037.4	1 054.0	...
%MF [BA]	8.4	8.2	8.1	9.0	9.2	10.2	11.0	...
%M [BA]	5.2	5.1	5.1	5.1	5.6	6.3	7.5	...
%F [BA]	19.8	19.9	19.4	22.7	22.6	23.9	23.3	...
El Salvador [6] — El Salvador [6]								
MF [BA]	180.0	175.7	170.2	173.7	183.5	160.2	187.2	183.9
M [BA]	136.0	119.9	125.2	136.8	128.8	123.6	148.6	142.7
F [BA]	44.0	55.8	45.0	36.9	54.7	36.6	38.6	41.1
%MF [BA]	8.0	7.3	7.0	7.0	7.0	6.2	6.9	6.8
%M [BA]	9.5	8.2	8.5	9.1	8.1	8.1	9.2	8.7
%F [BA]	5.3	6.0	4.6	3.6	5.2	3.5	3.7	3.8
Estonia — Estonie								
MF [BA] [27]	65.8[55]	66.1[55]	80.5[55]	89.9	83.1	67.2	66.2	63.6
M [BA] [27]	35.6[55]	37.4[55]	45.7[55]	49.5	43.7	36.1	34.2	34.7
F [BA] [27]	30.2[55]	28.7[55]	34.8[55]	40.5	39.3	31.0	32.0	28.9
%MF [BA] [27]	9.6[55]	9.8[55]	12.2[55]	13.6	12.6	10.3	10.0	9.7
%M [BA] [27]	10.1[55]	10.8[55]	13.4[55]	14.5	12.9	10.8	10.2	10.4
%F [BA] [27]	9.2[55]	8.8[55]	10.9[55]	12.6	12.2	9.7	9.9	8.9
MF [FB] [54]	...	18.8	44.0	46.3	54.1	48.2	43.3	...
%MF [FB] [54]	...	2.2	5.1	5.3	6.5	5.9	5.3	...
Ethiopia — Ethiopie								
MF [BA] [6,10,56]	...	...	...	...	...	...	...	845.9
M [BA] [6,10,56]	...	...	...	...	...	...	...	304.5
F [BA] [6,10,56]	...	...	...	...	...	...	...	541.4

Country or area, source§ — Pays ou zone, source§	1997	1998	1999	2000	2001	2002	2003	2004
%MF [BA] [6,10,56]	...	...	...	...	...	...	...	22.9
%M [BA] [6,10,56]	...	...	...	...	...	...	...	15.8
%F [BA] [6,10,56]	...	...	...	...	...	...	...	30.6
MF [FB] [20]	34.6	29.5	25.7	...	...	...	...	...
M [FB] [20]	19.1	16.6	14.3	...	...	...	...	...
F [FB] [20]	15.4	12.9	11.4	...	...	...	...	...
Finland — Finlande								
MF [BA] [27]	314.0	285.0	261.0	253.0	238.0	237.0	235.0	229.0
M [BA] [27]	160.0	143.0	130.0	122.0	117.0	123.0	124.0	118.0
F [BA] [27]	154.0	142.0	131.0	131.0	121.0	114.0	111.0	111.0
%MF [BA] [27]	12.5	11.3	10.1	9.7	9.1	9.1	9.0	8.8
%M [BA] [27]	12.1	10.7	9.6	8.9	8.6	9.1	9.2	8.7
%F [BA] [27]	13.0	11.9	10.7	10.6	9.7	9.1	8.9	8.9
MF [FB] [1,57,58]	398.0	362.0	337.0	321.0	302.0	294.0	288.0	288.0
M [FB] [1,57,58]	207.0	183.0	169.0	162.0	153.0	154.0	153.0	152.0
F [FB] [1,57,58]	191.0	179.0	168.0	159.0	149.0	140.0	135.0	136.0
France — France								
MF [BA] [1]	3 104.9[60]	3 006.6[60]	3 014.3[61]	2 590.2[60]	2 285.0[60]	2 341.0[60]	2 655.9	2 727.2
M [BA] [1]	1 495.7[60]	1 411.0[60]	1 424.6[61]	1 185.0[60]	1 004.0[60]	1 122.5[60]	1 283.4	1 326.5
F [BA] [1]	1 609.2[60]	1 595.6[60]	1 589.7[61]	1 405.1[60]	1 281.0[60]	1 218.5[60]	1 372.5	1 400.8
%MF [BA] [1]	12.3[60]	11.8[60]	11.7[61]	10.0[60]	8.8[60]	8.9[60]	9.7	9.9
%M [BA] [1]	10.8[60]	10.2[60]	10.2[61]	8.5[60]	7.1[60]	7.9[60]	8.7	9.0
%F [BA] [1]	14.1[60]	13.8[60]	13.6[61]	11.9[60]	10.7[60]	10.1[60]	10.9	11.1
MF [FB] [54,59]	3 108.6	2 981.5	2 792.0	2 354.5	2 117.0	2 254.9	2 390.4	2 439.9
M [FB] [54,59]	1 549.6	1 466.4	1 368.0	1 137.3	1 035.6	1 154.8	1 247.5	1 266.0
F [FB] [54,59]	1 559.0	1 515.1	1 423.9	1 217.2	1 081.4	1 100.1	1 142.9	1 173.9
MF [E] [1]	3 109.3	2 993.4	2 844.3	2 516.6	2 324.8	2 441.3	2 655.8	2 727.2
M [E] [1]	1 488.7	1 403.9	1 329.2	1 140.7	1 050.0	1 169.4	1 283.3	1 326.5
F [E] [1]	1 620.6	1 589.5	1 515.8	1 375.9	1 274.8	1 271.8	1 372.5	1 400.8
%MF [E] [1]	12.1	11.5	10.8	9.5	8.7	9.0	9.7	10.0
%M [E] [1]	10.6	9.9	9.3	7.9	7.3	8.0	8.8	9.1
%F [E] [1]	13.9	13.5	12.7	11.4	10.4	10.2	10.8	11.0
French Guiana [1,28] — Guyane française [1,28]								
MF [BA]	15.0	16.2	15.5	15.2	15.0	13.5	14.1	15.2
M [BA]	8.0	9.1	7.8	7.3	7.4	6.4	6.6	7.3
F [BA]	7.0	7.1	7.7	7.9	7.6	7.1	7.5	8.0
%MF [BA]	25.6	26.5	26.6	25.8	26.3	23.4	24.5	26.3
%M [BA]	22.2	23.9	22.8	21.2	23.0	19.8	20.5	22.6
%F [BA]	30.7	30.7	32.1	32.2	30.5	27.8	29.6	30.8
Georgia — Géorgie								
MF [BA] [1]	...	294.7	277.5	212.2	235.6	265.0	235.9	257.6
M [BA] [1]	...	161.8	160.1	116.7	126.9	155.5	124.2	143.2
F [BA] [1]	...	132.9	117.4	95.5	108.7	109.5	111.7	114.4
%MF [BA] [1]	...	14.5	13.8	10.8	11.0	12.3	11.5	12.6
%M [BA] [1]	...	15.4	15.3	11.1	11.6	13.7	11.5	13.4
%F [BA] [1]	...	13.9	12.2	10.5	10.7	10.7	11.5	11.8
MF [FB] [11]	118.2	85.5	92.2	101.0	97.8	21.9[62]	42.9	46.6
M [FB] [11]	51.7	45.5	38.9	46.5	40.1	12.1[62]	23.2	24.1
F [FB] [11]	66.5	40.0	53.3	54.1	57.7	9.8[62]	19.7	22.5
%MF [FB] [11]	5.0	4.2	5.0	3.5	5.5	1.2[62]	...	...
Germany — Allemagne								
MF [BA] [1]	3 890.0[17]	3 849.0[17]	3 503.0[17]	3 127.0[17]	3 150.0[17]	3 486.0[17]	4 023.0[64]	4 388.0[65]
M [BA] [1]	2 083.0[17]	2 074.0[17]	1 905.0[17]	1 691.0[64]	1 754.0[17]	1 982.0[17]	2 316.0[64]	2 551.0[65]
F [BA] [1]	1 806.0[17]	1 775.0[17]	1 598.0[17]	1 436.0[64]	1 396.0[17]	1 504.0[17]	1 707.0[64]	1 836.0[65]
%MF [BA] [1]	9.8[17]	9.7[17]	8.8[17]	7.9[64]	7.9[17]	8.7[17]	10.0[64]	11.0[65]
%M [BA] [1]	9.2[17]	9.2[17]	8.4[17]	7.6[64]	7.8[17]	8.9[17]	10.4[64]	11.5[65]
%F [BA] [1]	10.6[17]	10.4[17]	9.2[17]	8.3[64]	7.9[17]	8.5[17]	9.5[64]	10.3[65]
MF [FB] [2,63]	4 308.0	3 965.0	3 943.0	3 685.0	3 743.0	3 942.0	4 207.0	4 381.0[62]
M [FB] [2,63]	2 220.5	2 046.8	2 013.0	1 899.0	1 961.0	2 133.0	2 296.0	2 449.0[62]

Country or area, source§ — Pays ou zone, source§	1997	1998	1999	2000	2001	2002	2003	2004
F [FB] [2,63]	2 087.6	1 918.6	1 930.0	1 786.0	1 782.0	1 809.0	1 911.0	1 932.0[62]
%MF [FB] [2,63]	12.5	11.4	11.2	10.0	10.0	10.9	11.2	11.7
%M [FB] [2,63]	11.6	10.7	10.5	9.6	9.9	11.4	11.6	12.5
%F [FB] [2,63]	13.5	12.2	12.0	10.4	10.1	10.3	11.7	10.8
Gibraltar [66] — Gibraltar [66]								
MF [FB]	1.7	0.5	0.4	0.4	0.4	0.5	0.5	0.4
M [FB]	1.1	0.3	0.3	0.3	0.2	0.3	0.3	0.3
F [FB]	0.6	0.2	0.1	0.1	0.2	0.2	0.2	0.2
Greece [48] — Grèce [48]								
MF [BA]	440.4[67]	475.1[1]	522.5[1]	490.8[1]	448.2[1]	428.0[1]	403.0[1]	...
M [BA]	173.0[67]	187.3[1]	200.0[1]	192.3[1]	175.9[1]	165.7[1]	155.2[1]	...
F [BA]	267.3[67]	287.8[1]	322.5[1]	298.6[1]	272.2[1]	262.3[1]	247.8[1]	...
%MF [BA]	10.3[67]	10.6[1]	11.6[1]	11.0[1]	10.2[1]	9.6[1]	8.9[1]	...
%M [BA]	6.6[67]	6.9[1]	7.4[1]	7.2[1]	6.7[1]	6.2[1]	5.8[1]	...
%F [BA]	15.9[67]	16.4[1]	17.9[1]	16.6[1]	15.4[1]	14.7[1]	13.6[1]	...
Guadeloupe [1,28] — Guadeloupe [1,28]								
MF [BA]	52.7	55.9	55.0	49.4	43.7	41.5	44.0	40.3
M [BA]	23.4	24.5	22.3	21.7	19.1	19.0	20.9	17.5
F [BA]	29.3	31.4	32.7	27.7	24.6	22.5	23.1	22.8
%MF [BA]	29.5	30.7	29.8	25.7	27.6	25.7	26.9	24.7
%M [BA]	25.0	25.3	23.2	21.2	23.4	22.6	24.6	21.0
%F [BA]	34.4	36.8	37.1	30.8	32.0	29.1	29.4	28.5
Guatemala [6] — Guatemala [6]								
MF [BA]	...	...	79.8	64.9	62.2	154.3	172.2	...
M [BA]	...	...	59.2	40.3	34.4	77.1	79.4	...
F [BA]	...	...	20.6	24.6	27.8	77.2	92.8	...
%MF [BA]	...	...	1.9	1.4	1.3	3.1	3.4	...
%M [BA]	...	...	2.2	1.4	1.3	2.5	2.5	...
%F [BA]	...	...	1.4	1.5	1.4	4.3	4.9	...
Honduras [6] — Honduras [6]								
MF [BA]	69.4[3]	87.7[60]	89.3[60]	...	103.4[3]	93.7[3]	130.3[60]	153.2[64]
M [BA]	45.4[3]	55.5[60]	56.7[60]	...	62.0[3]	...	...	81.0[64]
F [BA]	23.9[3]	32.2[60]	32.6[60]	...	41.4[3]	...	...	72.2[64]
%MF [BA]	3.2[3]	3.9[60]	3.7[60]	...	4.2[3]	3.8[3]	5.1[3]	5.9[64]
%M [BA]	3.2[3]	3.8[60]	3.7[60]	...	4.0[3]	...	...	4.7[64]
%F [BA]	3.2[3]	4.2[60]	3.8[60]	...	4.8[3]	...	...	8.3[64]
Hungary — Hongrie								
MF [BA] [27]	348.8	313.0	284.7	262.5	232.9	238.8[68]	244.5	252.9
M [BA] [27]	214.1	189.2	170.7	159.5	142.7	138.0[68]	138.5	136.8
F [BA] [27]	134.7	123.8	114.0	103.0	90.2	100.8[68]	106.0	116.1
%MF [BA] [27]	8.7	7.8	7.0	6.4	5.7	5.8[68]	5.6	6.1
%M [BA] [27]	9.5	8.5	7.5	7.0	6.3	6.1[68]	6.1	6.1
%F [BA] [27]	7.8	7.0	6.3	5.6	5.0	5.4[68]	5.3	6.1
MF [FB] [11]	464.0	404.1	404.5	372.4	342.8	344.9	359.9	400.6
M [FB] [11]	261.4	222.7	220.1	202.2	188.7	186.8	189.4	209.6
F [FB] [11]	202.6	181.3	184.4	170.2	154.1	158.1	170.5	191.0
%MF [FB] [11]	10.4	9.6	9.6	...	...	...	8.4	...
%M [FB] [11]	...	...	...	...	...	...	7.9	...
%F [FB] [11]	...	...	...	...	...	...	8.9	...
Iceland — Islande								
MF [BA] [69,70]	5.7	4.2	3.1	3.7	3.7	5.3	...	...
M [BA] [69,70]	2.6	1.8	1.2	1.5	1.8	3.1	...	...
F [BA] [69,70]	3.1	2.4	1.9	2.2	1.9	2.2	...	...
%MF [BA] [69,70]	3.9	2.7	2.0	2.3	2.3	3.3	...	...
%M [BA] [69,70]	3.3	2.3	1.5	1.8	2.0	3.6	...	...
%F [BA] [69,70]	4.5	3.3	2.6	2.9	2.5	2.9	...	...
MF [FB] [54]	5.2	3.8	2.6	1.9	2.0	3.6	4.9	...
M [FB] [54]	2.0	1.4	1.0	0.7	0.8	1.8	2.5	...
F [FB] [54]	3.2	2.4	1.6	1.1	1.2	1.8	2.4	...

26

Unemployment—Number (thousands) and percentage unemployed, by sex (*continued*)
Chômage—Nombre (milliers) et pourcentage des chômeurs, par sexe (*suite*)

Country or area, source[§] — Pays ou zone, source[§]	1997	1998	1999	2000	2001	2002	2003	2004
%MF [FB] [54]	3.9	2.8	1.9	1.3	1.4	2.5	3.4	...
%M [FB] [54]	2.6	1.8	1.2	0.9	1.0	2.1	3.0	...
%F [FB] [54]	5.5	4.0	2.7	1.9	1.9	3.0	3.9	...
India — Inde								
MF [BA]	9 323.4[5]	12 541.7[56]	...	16 634.0[61]	...	...	...	...
M [BA]	7 106.8[5]	9 489.4[56]	...	11 837.5[61]	...	...	...	...
F [BA]	2 216.6[5]	3 052.3[56]	...	4 796.5[61]	...	...	...	...
%MF [BA]	2.6[5]	3.6[56]	...	4.3[61]	...	...	...	...
%M [BA]	2.6[5]	3.5[56]	...	4.3[61]	...	...	...	...
%F [BA]	2.4[5]	3.8[56]	...	4.3[61]	...	...	...	...
MF [FB] [11,19,23]	39 140.0	40 090.0	40 371.0	41 344.0	41 996.0	41 171.0	41 389.0	40 458.0
M [FB] [11,19,23]	30 107.0	30 563.0	30 438.0	30 887.0	31 111.0	30 521.0	30 636.0	29 746.0
F [FB] [11,19,23]	9 033.0	9 526.0	9 933.0	10 457.0	10 885.0	10 650.0	10 752.0	10 712.0
Indonesia [1] — Indonésie [1]								
MF [BA] [71]	4 197.3	5 062.5	6 030.3	5 813.2	8 005.0	9 132.1	...	...
M [BA] [71]	...	2 862.2	...	...	...	...	...	...
F [BA] [71]	...	2 200.3	...	...	...	...	...	...
%MF [BA] [71]	4.7	5.5	6.4	6.1	8.1	9.1	...	...
MF [FB]	1 542.2	...	1 191.8	...	...	...	...	...
Iraq [1] — Iraq [1]								
%MF [BA]	...	...	...	...	...	...	28.1	
%M [BA]	...	...	...	...	...	...	30.2	
%F [BA]	...	...	...	...	...	...	16.0	
Ireland — Irlande								
MF [BA] [1,72]	159.0	126.6	96.9	74.9	65.4	77.2	82.1	84.2
M [BA] [1,72]	97.1	78.8	59.4	44.9	39.8	48.8	51.7	54.4
F [BA] [1,72]	62.0	47.8	37.5	30.0	25.6	28.3	30.4	29.8
%MF [BA] [1,72]	10.3	7.8	5.7	4.3	3.7	4.2	4.4	4.4
%M [BA] [1,72]	10.4	8.1	5.9	4.3	3.8	4.6	4.7	4.9
%F [BA] [1,72]	10.3	7.4	5.5	4.2	3.5	3.7	3.9	3.7
MF [FB] [54]	254.4	227.1	193.2	155.4	142.3	162.5	172.4	166.0
M [FB] [54]	155.8	135.7	111.6	88.7	83.0	96.3	100.2	96.1
F [FB] [54]	98.5	91.4	81.6	66.7	59.3	66.2	72.2	70.0
%MF [FB] [54]	10.1	7.4	5.5	4.1	3.9	4.4	4.6	4.4
Isle of Man — Ile de Man								
MF [A] [1,56]	...	...	...	...	0.6	...	...	...
M [A] [1,56]	...	...	...	...	0.4	...	...	...
F [A] [1,56]	...	...	...	...	0.3	...	...	...
%MF [A] [1,56]	...	...	...	...	1.6	...	...	...
%M [A] [1,56]	...	...	...	...	1.7	...	...	...
%F [A] [1,56]	...	...	...	...	1.5	...	...	...
MF [FB]	0.7	0.4	0.3	0.2	0.2	0.2	0.3	0.4
M [FB]	0.5	0.3	0.2	0.2	0.1	0.1	0.2	0.3
F [FB]	0.2	0.1	0.1	0.1	0.1	0.1	0.1	0.1
%MF [FB]	...	...	0.8	0.6	0.5	0.5	0.8	1.0
%M [FB]	...	...	1.0	0.8	0.6	0.7	1.0	1.3
%F [FB]	...	...	0.5	0.4	0.3	0.4	0.5	0.6
Israel [1] — Israël [1]								
MF [BA]	169.8	193.4[73]	208.5	213.8	233.9	262.4	279.9	...
M [BA]	84.6	100.4[73]	108.8	111.7	120.9	138.4	142.8	...
F [BA]	85.2	93.0[73]	99.7	102.1	113.0	124.0	137.1	...
%MF [BA]	7.7	8.5[73]	8.9	8.8	9.4	10.3	10.7	...
%M [BA]	6.8	8.0[73]	8.5	8.4	8.9	10.1	10.2	...
%F [BA]	8.8	9.2[73]	9.4	9.2	9.9	10.6	11.3	...
Italy [1] — Italie [1]								
MF [BA]	2 688.0	2 745.0	2 669.0	2 495.0	2 267.0	2 163.0	2 096.0	...
M [BA]	1 294.0	1 313.0	1 266.0	1 179.0	1 066.0	1 016.0	996.0	...
F [BA]	1 394.0	1 431.0	1 404.0	1 316.0	1 201.0	1 147.0	1 100.0	...
%MF [BA]	11.5	11.7	11.4	10.5	9.5	9.0	8.7	...

Country or area, source[§] — Pays ou zone, source[§]	1997	1998	1999	2000	2001	2002	2003	2004
%M [BA]	9.0	9.1	8.8	8.1	7.3	6.9	6.7	...
%F [BA]	15.6	16.0	15.7	14.5	13.0	12.2	11.6	...
Jamaica [23] — Jamaïque [23]								
MF [BA]	186.9	175.0	175.2	171.8	165.4[74]	171.8	128.9	136.8
M [BA]	64.8	61.4	61.4	62.5	63.4[74]	65.7	47.6	54.0
F [BA]	122.1	113.5	113.8	109.2	102.1[74]	106.1	81.3	82.8
%MF [BA]	16.5	15.5	15.7	15.5	15.0[74]	14.3	10.9	11.4
%M [BA]	10.6	10.0	10.0	10.2	10.3[74]	9.9	7.2	8.1
%F [BA]	23.5	22.1	22.4	22.3	21.0[74]	19.8	15.6	15.7
Japan [1] — Japon [1]								
MF [BA]	2 300.0	2 790.0	3 170.0	3 190.0	3 400.0	3 590.0	3 500.0	3 130.0
M [BA]	1 350.0	1 680.0	1 940.0	1 960.0	2 090.0	2 190.0	2 150.0	1 920.0
F [BA]	950.0	1 110.0	1 230.0	1 230.0	1 310.0	1 400.0	1 350.0	1 210.0
%MF [BA]	3.4	4.1	4.7	4.7	5.0	5.4	5.3	4.7
%M [BA]	3.4	4.2	4.8	4.9	5.2	5.5	5.5	4.9
%F [BA]	3.4	4.0	4.5	4.5	4.7	5.1	4.9	4.4
Kazakhstan — Kazakhstan								
MF [BA] [1]	...	...	...	...	780.3	690.7	672.1	658.8
M [BA] [1]	...	...	...	...	338.0	283.8	281.4	281.1
F [BA] [1]	...	...	...	...	442.3	406.9	390.7	377.7
%MF [BA] [1]	...	...	...	...	10.4	9.3	8.8	8.4
%M [BA] [1]	...	...	...	...	8.9	7.5	7.2	7.0
%F [BA] [1]	...	...	...	...	12.0	11.2	10.4	9.8
MF [FB] [16]	257.5	251.9	251.4	231.4	216.1	193.7	142.8	117.7
M [FB] [16]	86.0	95.5	102.0	...	...	...	...	...
F [FB] [16]	171.5	156.4	149.4	...	...	...	...	...
%MF [FB] [16]	3.8	3.7	3.9	3.7	2.9	2.6	1.8	1.5
%M [FB] [16]	2.4	2.6	...	...	...	...	...	...
%F [FB] [16]	5.5	5.0	...	...	...	...	...	...
MF [E]	967.8	925.8	950.0	906.4	...	...	...	...
%MF [E]	13.0	13.1	13.5	12.8	...	...	...	...
Korea, Republic of [1] — Corée, République de [1]								
MF [BA]	556.0	1 461.0	1 353.0	979.0[75]	899.0	752.0	818.0	860.0
M [BA]	352.0	983.0	911.0	647.0[75]	591.0	491.0	508.0	534.0
F [BA]	204.0	478.0	442.0	332.0[75]	308.0	261.0	310.0	326.0
%MF [BA]	2.6	6.8	6.3	4.4[75]	4.0	3.3	3.6	3.7
%M [BA]	2.8	7.6	7.1	5.0[75]	4.5	3.7	3.8	3.9
%F [BA]	2.3	5.6	5.1	3.6[75]	3.3	2.8	3.3	3.4
Kuwait [16] — Koweït [16]								
MF [FD]	8.4	8.7	8.9	9.3	9.5	15.1	...	...
M [FD]	7.0	7.1	7.3	7.5	7.6	9.4	...	...
F [FD]	1.3	1.5	1.7	1.8	1.9	5.6	...	...
%MF [FD]	0.7	0.7	0.7	0.8	0.8	1.1	...	...
%M [FD]	0.8	0.8	0.8	0.8	0.8	1.0	...	...
%F [FD]	0.5	0.5	0.6	0.7	0.6	1.7	...	...
Kyrgyzstan — Kirghizistan								
MF [BA] [1,76]	...	...	...	...	...	265.5	...	...
M [BA] [1,76]	...	...	...	...	...	132.6	...	...
F [BA] [1,76]	...	...	...	...	...	132.9	...	...
%MF [BA] [1,76]	...	...	...	...	...	12.5	...	...
%M [BA] [1,76]	...	...	...	...	...	11.2	...	...
%F [BA] [1,76]	...	...	...	...	...	14.3	...	...
MF [FB]	54.6	55.9	54.7	58.3	60.5	60.2	57.4	...
M [FB]	22.7	22.6	24.2	27.1	28.0	27.6	26.5	...
F [FB]	31.9	33.3	30.6	31.2	32.5	32.6	30.9	...
Latvia — Lettonie								
MF [BA] [77]	176.7	162.4	161.4	158.7	144.7	134.5	119.2	118.6
M [BA] [77]	92.3	86.4	88.7	87.0	81.9	74.9	61.7	61.7
F [BA] [77]	84.4	76.0	72.7	71.7	62.7	59.6	57.5	56.9

Country or area, source[§] — Pays ou zone, source[§]	1997	1998	1999	2000	2001	2002	2003	2004
%MF [BA] [77]	15.1	14.1	14.3	14.4	13.1	12.0	10.6	10.4
%M [BA] [77]	15.4	14.4	15.0	15.4	14.4	12.9	10.7	10.6
%F [BA] [77]	14.9	13.8	13.5	13.5	11.7	11.0	10.5	10.3
MF [FB] [16,78]	84.9	111.4	109.5	93.3	91.6	89.7	90.6	90.8
M [FB] [16,78]	34.5	46.2	46.7	39.5	39.1	37.0	37.6	37.3
F [FB] [16,78]	50.4	65.2	62.8	53.8	52.6	52.7	53.0	53.5
%MF [FB] [16,78]	7.0	9.2	9.1	7.8	7.7	8.5	8.6	8.5
%M [FB] [16,78]	5.6	7.5	7.6	6.5	6.4	6.7	6.8	...
%F [FB] [16,78]	8.5	11.0	10.7	9.2	9.0	10.5	10.6	...
Lesotho [1] — Lesotho [1]								
MF [A]	215.9	...	...	...	...	...	...	...
M [A]	80.2	...	...	...	...	...	...	...
F [A]	135.7	...	...	...	...	...	...	...
%MF [A]	39.3	...	...	...	...	...	...	...
%M [A]	30.7	...	...	...	...	...	...	...
%F [A]	47.1	...	...	...	...	...	...	...
Lithuania — Lituanie								
MF [BA]	257.2 [23]	226.7 [1]	249.0 [1]	273.7 [1]	284.0 [1]	224.4 [1]	203.9 [1]	184.4 [1]
M [BA]	137.1 [23]	130.9 [1]	140.5 [1]	158.5 [1]	165.6 [1]	121.1 [1]	105.4 [1]	90.6 [1]
F [BA]	120.1 [23]	95.8 [1]	108.5 [1]	115.2 [1]	118.4 [1]	103.3 [1]	98.4 [1]	93.8 [1]
%MF [BA]	14.1 [23]	13.2 [1]	14.6 [1]	16.4 [1]	17.4 [1]	13.8 [1]	12.4 [1]	12.8 [1]
%M [BA]	14.2 [23]	14.7 [1]	16.2 [1]	18.8 [1]	19.9 [1]	14.6 [1]	12.7 [1]	11.4 [1]
%F [BA]	13.9 [23]	12.2 [1]	11.6 [1]	13.0 [1]	14.7 [1]	12.9 [1]	12.2 [1]	13.2 [1]
MF [FB] [16]	120.2 [79]	122.8 [79]	177.4 [79]	225.9 [79]	224.0 [79]	191.2 [79]	158.8 [79]	126.4 [80]
M [FB] [16]	58.3 [79]	61.7 [79]	94.6 [79]	123.1 [79]	117.7 [79]	95.1 [79]	73.7 [79]	53.8 [80]
F [FB] [16]	61.9 [79]	61.1 [79]	82.8 [79]	102.8 [79]	106.3 [79]	96.1 [79]	85.1 [79]	72.6 [80]
%MF [FB] [16]	6.7 [79]	6.5 [79]	10.0 [79]	12.6 [79]	12.9 [79]	10.9 [79]	9.8 [79]	6.0 [80]
%M [FB] [16]	6.6 [79]	6.5 [79]	10.6 [79]	13.5 [79]	13.5 [79]	10.8 [79]	9.0 [79]	5.1 [80]
%F [FB] [16]	6.9 [79]	7.0 [79]	9.3 [79]	11.6 [79]	12.2 [79]	11.0 [79]	10.5 [79]	7.0 [80]
Luxembourg [81] — Luxembourg [81]								
MF [FB]	6.4 [82]	5.5	5.4	5.0	4.9	5.8	7.6	8.7
M [FB]	3.6 [82]	2.9	2.8	2.6	2.6	3.2	4.1	4.7
F [FB]	2.8 [82]	2.6	2.5	2.3	2.3	2.7	3.5	4.0
%MF [FB]	3.3 [82]	3.1	2.9	2.7	2.7	3.0	3.8	4.2
Madagascar [83] — Madagascar [83]								
MF [BA]	...	...	...	...	...	383.0	...	...
M [BA]	...	...	...	...	...	149.8	...	...
F [BA]	...	...	...	...	...	233.2	...	...
%MF [BA]	...	...	...	...	...	4.5	...	...
%M [BA]	...	...	...	...	...	3.5	...	...
%F [BA]	...	...	...	...	...	5.6	...	...
Malaysia — Malaisie								
MF [BA] [63]	214.9	284.0	313.7	286.9	342.4	343.6	369.8	...
M [BA] [63]	129.6	185.3	212.3	182.7	212.3	210.5	235.8	...
F [BA] [63]	85.3	98.7	101.4	104.2	130.1	133.1	134.0	...
%MF [BA] [63]	2.5	3.2	3.4	3.0	3.5	3.5	3.6	...
%M [BA] [63]	2.2	3.1	3.5	3.0	3.4	3.3	3.6	...
%F [BA] [63]	2.8	3.3	3.3	3.1	3.8	3.8	3.6	...
MF [FB] [1,19]	23.1	33.4	31.8	34.3	33.5	37.2	34.8	...
Maldives [24] — Maldives [24]								
MF [A]	...	...	...	1.7	...	...	...	...
M [A]	...	...	...	0.9	...	...	...	...
F [A]	...	...	...	0.8	...	...	...	...
Malta — Malte								
MF [BA] [1]	...	...	...	10.3	10.1	11.0	12.1	11.5 [11]
M [BA] [1]	...	...	...	7.3	6.8	7.2	7.8	7.1 [11]
F [BA] [1]	...	...	...	3.0	3.2	3.8	4.3	4.4 [11]
%MF [BA] [1]	...	...	...	6.7	6.4	7.0	7.6	7.2 [11]
%M [BA] [1]	...	...	...	6.8	6.2	6.6	7.1	6.4 [11]

Country or area, source§ — Pays ou zone, source§	1997	1998	1999	2000	2001	2002	2003	2004
%F [BA] [1]	...	...	...	6.4	7.0	7.7	8.7	9.0[11]
MF [FB] [11,84]	7.1	7.4	7.7	6.6	6.8	6.8	8.2[62]	8.1
M [FB] [11,84]	6.0	6.4	6.6	5.7	5.6	5.6	6.6[62]	6.5
F [FB] [11,84]	1.1	1.0	1.1	0.9	1.1	1.2	1.6[62]	1.6
%MF [FB] [11,84]	5.0	5.1	5.3	4.5	4.7	4.7	5.7[62]	5.4
%M [FB] [11,84]	5.8	6.1	6.3	5.4	5.4	5.4	6.4[62]	6.1
%F [FB] [11,84]	2.8	2.5	2.6	2.2	2.7	2.9	3.8[62]	3.8
Marshall Islands [1] — Iles Marshall [1]								
MF [A]	...	...	4.5	...	...	...	...	...
M [A]	...	...	2.7	...	...	...	...	...
F [A]	...	...	1.9	...	...	...	...	...
%MF [A]	...	...	30.9	...	...	...	...	...
%M [A]	...	...	27.6	...	...	...	...	...
%F [A]	...	...	37.3	...	...	...	...	...
Martinique [1,28] — Martinique [1,28]								
MF [BA]	49.1	48.5	46.9	44.1	39.8	35.8[85]	36.1	35.9
M [BA]	22.7	22.6	20.9	18.9	16.3	15.4[85]	16.1	15.9
F [BA]	26.4	25.9	26.0	25.2	23.6	20.4[85]	20.1	20.0
%MF [BA]	28.8	29.3	28.1	26.3	24.7	22.3	22.3	22.4
%M [BA]	25.4	26.3	24.5	22.1	20.1	19.2	19.9	19.9
%F [BA]	32.6	32.4	32.0	30.8	29.3	25.4	24.6	24.7
Mauritius — Maurice								
MF [BA] [1]	...	...	...	...	...	...	...	45.1
M [BA] [1]	...	...	...	...	...	...	...	20.3
F [BA] [1]	...	...	...	...	...	...	...	24.8
%MF [BA] [1]	...	...	...	...	...	...	...	8.5
%M [BA] [1]	...	...	...	...	...	...	...	5.8
%F [BA] [1]	...	...	...	...	...	...	...	13.5
MF [FB] [1,86]	10.7	10.7	12.1	18.0	21.6	22.0	23.4	22.0
M [FB] [1,86]	4.6	4.6	5.3	8.6	10.5	10.1	10.1	10.5
F [FB] [1,86]	6.0	6.1	6.8	9.5	11.1	11.9	13.3	11.4
MF [E]	32.2	34.4	39.0	45.0	47.7	50.8	54.4	...
M [E]	18.5	20.4	23.8	28.5	30.5	29.6	31.7	...
F [E]	13.7	14.0	15.2	16.5	17.2	21.2	22.7	...
%MF [E]	6.6	6.9	7.7	8.8	9.1	9.7	10.2	...
%M [E]	5.6	6.1	7.0	8.3	8.8	8.5	9.0	...
%F [E]	8.5	8.5	9.0	9.6	9.8	12.0	12.6	...
Mexico [24,48] — Mexique [24,48]								
MF [BA]	984.9	903.6	695.0	659.4	687.4	783.7	882.5	1 092.7
M [BA]	544.7	526.2	395.4	407.1	422.8	505.0	560.4	656.6
F [BA]	440.2	377.5	299.6	252.3	264.6	278.8	322.1	436.2
%MF [BA]	2.6	2.3	1.8	1.6	1.7	1.9	2.1	2.5
%M [BA]	2.1	2.0	1.5	1.5	1.6	1.9	2.1	2.3
%F [BA]	3.4	2.8	2.2	1.8	1.9	2.0	2.3	2.8
Mongolia [16] — Mongolie [16]								
MF [FB]	63.7	49.8	39.8	38.6	40.3	30.9	33.3	35.6
M [FB]	31.1	23.8	18.1	17.8	18.5	14.1	15.3	15.9
F [FB]	32.6	26.0	21.6	20.7	21.9	16.8	18.1	19.6
%MF [FB]	7.7	5.9	4.7	4.6	4.6	3.5	3.5	3.6
%M [FB]	7.3	5.4	4.1	4.1	4.2	3.4	3.2	3.3
%F [FB]	8.1	6.4	5.3	5.0	5.1	3.8	3.8	3.9
Morocco [1] — Maroc [1]								
MF [BA]	...	...	1 432.2	1 394.3	1 275.0	1 202.7	1 299.0	...
M [BA]	...	...	1 044.8	1 035.5	952.0	878.4	922.4	...
F [BA]	...	...	387.9	358.7	323.0	324.3	376.6	...
%MF [BA]	...	...	13.9	13.6	12.5	11.6	11.9	...
%M [BA]	...	...	14.2	13.8	12.5	11.6	11.5	...
%F [BA]	...	...	13.3	13.0	12.5	12.5	13.0	...

Country or area, source[§] — Pays ou zone, source[§]	1997	1998	1999	2000	2001	2002	2003	2004
Myanmar [87] — Myanmar [87]								
MF [FB]	535.3	451.5	425.3	382.1	398.4	435.7	326.5	291.3
Namibia [88] — Namibie [88]								
MF [BA]	211.4	...	...	220.6	...	...	...	...
M [BA]	88.0	...	...	89.4	...	...	...	...
F [BA]	123.4	...	...	131.3	...	...	...	...
%MF [BA]	35.0	...	...	33.8	...	...	...	...
%M [BA]	29.0	...	...	28.3	...	...	...	...
%F [BA]	40.0	...	...	39.0	...	...	...	...
Netherlands — Pays-Bas								
MF [BA] [63]	422.0	337.0	277.0	262.0	220.0	261.0	355.0	...
M [BA] [63]	196.0	155.0	124.0	118.0	101.0	131.0	194.0	...
F [BA] [63]	227.0	181.0	153.0	144.0	119.0	129.0	162.0	...
%MF [BA] [63]	5.5	4.4	3.5	3.3	2.7	3.1	4.3	...
%M [BA] [63]	4.5	3.5	2.8	2.6	2.2	2.8	4.2	...
%F [BA] [63]	7.0	5.5	4.5	4.2	3.4	3.6	4.4	...
MF [FB] [81,89]	375.0	286.0	221.5	187.0	146.0	170.0	255.0	...
M [FB] [81,89]	199.0	156.0	115.0	98.0	77.0	91.0	144.0	...
F [FB] [81,89]	176.0	132.0	106.0	90.0	69.0	79.0	111.0	...
%MF [FB] [81]	5.5	4.1	3.2	2.6	2.0	2.3	3.4	...
%M [FB] [81]	4.8	3.7	2.7	2.3	1.8	2.1	3.3	...
%F [FB] [81]	6.5	4.8	3.7	3.1	2.4	2.6	3.5	...
Netherlands Antilles [1,90] — Antilles néerlandaises [1,90]								
MF [BA] [91]	10.1	10.5[85]	...	8.5	...	9.1	9.3	...
M [BA] [91]	4.3	4.7[85]	...	3.7	...	4.1	4.0	...
F [BA] [91]	5.8	5.8[85]	...	4.8	...	4.9	5.3	...
%MF [BA]	15.3	16.6	...	14.2	15.8	15.6	15.1	...
%M [BA]	12.4	13.7	...	12.0	...	...	...	...
%F [BA]	18.4	19.2	...	16.2	...	...	...	...
New Caledonia [54] — Nouvelle-Calédonie [54]								
MF [FB]	7.9	8.3	8.8	9.4	9.9	10.5	10.2	...
M [FB]	...	...	3.9	4.2	4.4	4.8	4.6	...
F [FB]	...	...	4.9	5.2	5.4	5.7	5.6	...
New Zealand — Nouvelle-Zélande								
MF [BA] [1]	123.3	139.1	127.8	113.4	102.3	102.5	93.9	82.0
M [BA] [1]	67.9	77.4	72.4	63.4	56.2	54.6	48.0	39.5
F [BA] [1]	55.5	61.8	55.4	50.0	46.1	47.9	45.9	42.4
%MF [BA] [1]	6.6	7.5	6.8	6.0	5.3	5.2	4.7	3.9
%M [BA] [1]	6.6	7.6	7.0	6.1	5.4	5.1	4.4	3.5
%F [BA] [1]	6.7	7.4	6.5	5.8	5.3	5.3	5.0	4.4
MF [FB] [92,93]	168.9	193.9	221.4	226.9	192.2	168.3	...	...
M [FB] [92,93]	107.3	...	127.2	120.3	103.5	89.1	...	...
F [FB] [92,93]	61.6	...	94.1	106.6	88.7	79.2	...	...
Nicaragua [6] — Nicaragua [6]								
MF [E]	208.4	215.5	185.1	178.0	122.5	135.3	...	...
M [E]	138.2	142.9	122.8	118.0	77.3	84.0	...	...
F [E]	70.2	72.6	62.3	60.0	45.2	51.3	...	...
%MF [E]	13.3	13.3	10.9	9.8	11.3	12.2	...	...
%M [E]	12.6	8.8	...	...	...	...	...	...
%F [E]	14.8	14.5	...	...	...	...	...	...
Norway — Norvège								
MF [BA] [70]	92.0	74.0	75.0	81.0	84.0	92.0	107.0	106.0
M [BA] [70]	48.0	40.0	42.0	46.0	46.0	52.0	62.0	62.0
F [BA] [70]	44.0	34.0	33.0	35.0	38.0	40.0	45.0	45.0
%MF [BA] [70]	4.0	3.2	3.2	3.4	3.6	3.9	4.5	4.5
%M [BA] [70]	3.9	3.2	3.4	3.6	3.7	4.1	4.9	4.9
%F [BA] [70]	4.2	3.3	3.0	3.2	3.4	3.6	4.0	4.0
MF [FB] [54]	73.5	56.0	59.6[41]	62.6	62.7	75.2	92.6	91.6
M [FB] [54]	39.9	29.8	33.5[41]	36.3	35.7	42.6	54.0	52.2

Country or area, source§ — Pays ou zone, source§	1997	1998	1999	2000	2001	2002	2003	2004
F [FB] [54]	33.6	26.2	26.0[41]	26.4	27.0	32.6	38.6	39.4
%MF [FB] [54]	3.3	2.4	2.6[41]	2.7	2.7	3.2	3.9	3.9
%M [FB] [54]	...	...	...	...	...	...	4.3	4.1
%F [FB] [54]	...	...	...	...	...	...	3.5	3.5
Occupied Palestinian Terr. — Terr. palestinien occupé								
MF [BA]	121.0[1]	92.0[1]	79.0[1]	98.8[1]	170.5[6]	217.5[6]	194.3[6]	212.2[6]
M [BA]	104.1[1]	79.2[1]	66.1[1]	85.4[1]	158.0[6]	201.5[6]	172.2[6]	185.8[6]
F [BA]	16.9[1]	12.8[1]	12.9[1]	13.4[1]	12.5[6]	16.0[6]	22.1[6]	26.4[6]
%MF [BA]	20.3[1]	14.4[1]	11.8[1]	14.1[1]	25.2[6]	31.2[6]	25.4[6]	26.7[6]
%M [BA]	20.3[1]	14.4[1]	11.6[1]	14.4[1]	26.9[6]	33.5[6]	26.7[6]	28.0[6]
%F [BA]	20.1[1]	15.2[1]	13.0[1]	12.3[1]	14.0[6]	17.0[6]	18.4[6]	20.0[6]
Pakistan — Pakistan								
MF [BA] [6,94]	2 254.0	2 279.0	2 334.0	3 127.0	3 181.0	3 506.0	...	...
M [BA] [6,94]	1 317.0	1 386.0	1 419.0	2 046.0	2 082.0	2 381.0	...	...
F [BA] [6,94]	937.0	893.0	915.0	1 081.0	1 099.0	1 125.0	...	...
%MF [BA] [6,94]	6.1	5.9	5.9	7.8	7.8	8.3	...	...
%M [BA] [6,94]	4.2	4.2	4.2	6.1	6.1	6.7	...	...
%F [BA] [6,94]	16.8	15.0	15.0	17.3	17.3	16.5	...	...
MF [FB] [19,95]	262.0	212.0	217.0	469.0	477.0	493.0	...	...
M [FB] [19,95]	184.0	186.0	190.0	421.0	428.0	442.0	...	...
F [FB] [19,95]	78.0	26.0	27.0	48.0	49.0	51.0	...	...
Panama [1,96] — Panama [1,96]								
MF [BA]	140.3	147.1	128.0	147.0	169.7	172.4	170.4	158.3
M [BA]	72.5	69.5	62.1	77.7	92.0	86.5	82.9	75.6
F [BA]	67.8	77.6	65.9	69.3	77.8	85.9	87.3	82.7
%MF [BA]	13.4	13.6	11.8	13.5	14.7	14.1	13.6	12.3
%M [BA]	10.7	10.0	8.9	11.1	12.2	11.2	10.5	9.4
%F [BA]	18.1	19.9	16.9	18.0	19.3	19.2	18.8	17.2
Papua New Guinea — Papouasie-Nouvelle-Guinée								
MF [A]	...	...	...	68.6	...	...	...	...
M [A]	...	...	...	53.7	...	...	...	...
F [A]	...	...	...	15.0	...	...	...	...
%MF [A]	...	...	...	2.8	...	...	...	...
%M [A]	...	...	...	4.3	...	...	...	...
%F [A]	...	...	...	1.3	...	...	...	...
Paraguay [6] — Paraguay [6]								
MF [BA]	121.7[97]	...	...	198.7[98]	...	272.6	206.0	...
M [BA]	66.1[97]	...	...	108.5[98]	...	141.9	105.6	...
F [BA]	55.6[97]	...	...	89.9[98]	...	130.9	100.4	...
%MF [BA]	5.4[97]	...	6.8	7.6[98]	...	10.8	8.1	...
%M [BA]	4.5[97]	...	...	6.8[98]	...	9.0	6.7	...
%F [BA]	6.8[97]	...	...	8.9[98]	...	13.6	10.1	...
Peru [23] — Pérou [23]								
MF [BA]	565.0[10,99]	582.5[10,99]	624.9[10,99]	566.5[10,99]	651.5[10,99]	359.0[100]	386.0[101]	394.4[102]
M [BA]	279.9[10,99]	274.4[10,99]	322.8[10,99]	318.8[10,99]	327.5[10,99]	173.4[100]	187.9[101]	207.0[102]
F [BA]	285.1[10,99]	308.1[10,99]	302.2[10,99]	247.7[10,99]	324.0[10,99]	185.7[100]	198.1[101]	187.4[102]
%MF [BA]	7.7[10,99]	7.8[10,99]	8.0[10,99]	7.4[10,99]	7.9[10,99]	9.7[100]	10.3[101]	10.5[102]
%M [BA]	6.8[10,99]	6.5[10,99]	7.5[10,99]	7.3[10,99]	7.2[10,99]	8.3[100]	9.0[101]	9.4[102]
%F [BA]	8.9[10,99]	9.3[10,99]	8.6[10,99]	7.5[10,99]	8.7[10,99]	11.6[100]	11.9[101]	12.0[102]
Philippines [1,91] — Philippines [1,91]								
MF [BA]	2 377.0	3 016.0	2 931.0	3 133.0	3 269.0	3 423.0	3 567.0	3 888.0
M [BA]	1 411.0	1 857.0	1 835.0	1 978.0	1 912.0	2 076.0	2 183.0	2 312.0
F [BA]	966.0	1 159.0	1 096.0	1 156.0	1 356.0	1 346.0	1 384.0	1 576.0
%MF [BA]	7.9	9.6	9.6	10.1	9.8	10.2	10.2	10.9
%M [BA]	7.5	9.5	9.7	10.3	9.4	10.1	10.1	10.4
%F [BA]	8.5	9.8	9.3	9.9	10.3	10.2	10.3	11.7
Poland — Pologne								
MF [BA]	1 923.0[1]	1 808.0[1]	2 391.0[1,104]	2 785.0[1]	3 170.0[27]	3 431.0[27]	3 329.0[27]	3 230.0[27]
M [BA]	889.0[1]	843.0[1]	1 147.0[1,104]	1 344.0[1]	1 583.0[27]	1 779.0[27]	1 741.0[27]	1 681.0[27]

Unemployment—Number (thousands) and percentage unemployed, by sex (*continued*)
Chômage—Nombre (milliers) et pourcentage des chômeurs, par sexe (*suite*)

Country or area, source⁵ — Pays ou zone, source⁵	1997	1998	1999	2000	2001	2002	2003	2004
F [BA]	1 035.0[1]	965.0[1]	1 244.0[1,104]	1 440.0[1]	1 587.0[27]	1 652.0[27]	1 588.0[27]	1 550.0[27]
%MF [BA]	11.2[1]	10.5[1]	13.9[1,104]	16.1[1]	18.2[27]	19.9[27]	19.6[27]	19.0[27]
%M [BA]	9.6[1]	9.1[1]	12.4[1,104]	14.4[1]	16.9[27]	19.1[27]	19.0[27]	18.2[27]
%F [BA]	13.2[1]	12.3[1]	15.8[1,104]	18.1[1]	19.8[27]	20.9[27]	20.4[27]	19.9[27]
MF [FB] [16,103]	1 826.4	1 831.4	2 349.8	2 702.6	3 115.1	3 217.0[62]	3 175.7	2 999.6
M [FB] [16,103]	723.2	760.1	1 042.5	1 211.0	1 473.0	1 571.2[62]	1 541.0	1 431.1
F [FB] [16,103]	1 103.2	1 071.3	1 307.3	1 491.6	1 642.1	1 645.8[62]	1 634.7	1 568.5
%MF [FB] [16,103]	10.3	10.4	13.1	15.1	17.5	20.0[62]	20.0	19.1
Portugal — Portugal								
MF [BA]	324.1[105]	251.9[1]	225.8[1]	205.5[1]	213.5[1]	270.5[1]	342.3[1]	...
M [BA]	158.5[105]	110.6[1]	108.9[1]	89.3[1]	91.6[1]	121.4[1]	160.9[1]	...
F [BA]	165.6[105]	141.3[1]	116.9[1]	116.2[1]	122.0[1]	149.1[1]	181.4[1]	...
%MF [BA]	6.7[105]	4.9[1]	4.4[1]	3.9[1]	4.0[1]	5.0[1]	6.3[1]	...
%M [BA]	6.0[105]	3.9[1]	3.9[1]	3.1[1]	3.2[1]	4.1[1]	5.5[1]	...
%F [BA]	7.5[105]	6.2[1]	5.0[1]	4.9[1]	5.0[1]	6.0[1]	7.2[1]	...
MF [FB]	442.9	400.6	356.8	327.4	324.7	344.6	427.3	...
M [FB]	187.0	165.3	144.9	128.7	127.0	139.6	182.3	...
F [FB]	255.8	235.4	211.9	198.8	197.7	205.3	245.0	...
Puerto Rico [54,58] — Porto Rico [54,58]								
MF [BA]	176.0	175.0	153.0	132.0	147.0	166.0	167.0	149.0
M [BA]	112.0	112.0	102.0	91.0	98.0	103.0	101.0	94.0
F [BA]	64.0	63.0	51.0	42.0	49.0	63.0	66.0	55.0
%MF [BA]	13.5	13.3	11.8	10.1	11.4	12.3	12.0	10.6
%M [BA]	14.4	14.4	13.2	11.8	13.0	13.2	12.8	11.8
%F [BA]	12.1	11.8	9.6	7.7	9.1	10.9	10.9	9.0
Qatar [1] — Qatar [1]								
MF [BA]	6.6[106]	...	...	...	12.6[56]	...	...	...
M [BA]	4.5[106]	...	...	...	6.1[56]	...	...	...
F [BA]	2.1[106]	...	...	...	6.5[56]	...	...	...
%MF [BA]	2.3[106]	...	...	...	3.9[56]	...	...	...
%M [BA]	1.8[106]	...	...	...	2.3[56]	...	...	...
%F [BA]	5.2[106]	...	...	...	12.6[56]	...	...	...
Republic of Moldova — République de Moldova								
MF [BA] [1]	...	...	187.2	140.1	117.7	110.0	117.1	116.5
M [BA] [1]	...	...	113.6	80.6	70.1	64.4	69.9	70.1
F [BA] [1]	...	...	73.6	59.5	47.6	45.4	47.2	46.4
%MF [BA] [1]	...	...	11.1	8.5	7.3	6.8	7.9	8.1
%M [BA] [1]	...	...	13.3	9.7	8.7	8.1	9.6	10.0
%F [BA] [1]	...	...	8.9	7.2	5.9	5.5	6.4	6.3
MF [FB] [11]	28.0	32.0	34.9	28.9	27.6	24.0	19.7	21.0
M [FB] [11]	10.3	13.0	13.3	11.9	13.6	11.7	10.3	11.7
F [FB] [11]	17.7	19.0	21.6	17.0	14.0	12.3	9.4	9.3
%MF [FB] [11]	1.5	1.9	2.1	2.3	2.2	2.1	2.0	2.0
Romania — Roumanie								
MF [BA] [1]	706.5	732.4	789.9	821.2	750.0	845.3[107]	691.8	799.5
M [BA] [1]	364.2	410.3	462.5	481.6	436.1	494.1[107]	408.0	490.8
F [BA] [1]	342.2	322.1	327.4	339.6	313.9	351.2[107]	283.7	308.7
%MF [BA] [1]	6.0	6.3	6.8	7.1	6.6	8.4[107]	7.0	8.0
%M [BA] [1]	5.7	6.5	7.4	7.7	7.1	8.9[107]	7.5	9.0
%F [BA] [1]	6.4	6.1	6.2	6.4	5.9	7.7[107]	6.4	6.9
MF [FB] [11]	881.4	1 025.1	1 130.3	1 007.1	826.9	760.6	658.9	557.9
M [FB] [11]	452.8	539.9	600.2	535.5	445.8	421.1	372.6	323.3
F [FB] [11]	428.6	485.2	530.1	471.6	381.1	339.5	286.3	234.6
%MF [FB] [11]	8.9	10.4	11.8	10.5	8.8	8.4	7.4	6.2
%M [FB] [11]	8.5	10.4	12.1	10.8	9.2	8.9	7.8	6.8
%F [FB] [11]	9.3	10.4	11.6	10.1	8.4	7.8	6.6	5.6
Russian Federation — Fédération de Russie								
MF [BA] [91,108]	8 058.0	8 876.0	9 323.0	7 138.0	6 303.0	6 153.0	5 716.0	5 775.0
M [BA] [91,108]	4 371.0	4 787.0	4 966.0	3 781.0	3 411.0	3 322.0	3 064.0	2 902.0

Country or area, source[§] — Pays ou zone, source[§]	1997	1998	1999	2000	2001	2002	2003	2004
F [BA] [91,108]	3 687.0	4 090.0	4 293.0	3 357.0	2 892.0	2 831.0	2 652.0	2 872.0
%MF [BA] [91,108]	11.8	13.3	12.6	9.8	8.9	7.9	8.0	7.8
%M [BA] [91,108]	12.2	13.6	12.8	10.2	9.3	7.9	8.3	7.6
%F [BA] [91,108]	11.5	13.0	12.3	9.4	8.5	7.9	7.8	8.0
MF [FB] [11]	1 998.7	1 929.0	1 263.4	1 037.0	1 122.7	1 309.4	1 600.0	...
M [FB] [11]	721.0	682.0	383.0	322.2	359.5	412.8	...	...
F [FB] [11]	1 278.0	1 247.0	880.0	714.8	763.2	896.6	...	...
%MF [FB] [11]	11.3	13.3	...	...	...	...	...	...
Saint Helena — Sainte-Hélène								
MF [A] [88]	...	0.4	...	...	...	...	...	...
M [A] [88]	...	0.3	...	...	...	...	...	...
F [A] [88]	...	0.2	...	...	...	...	...	...
MF [FB]	0.4	0.5	0.4	0.3	...	...	...	...
M [FB]	0.3	0.3	0.3	0.2	...	...	...	...
F [FB]	0.1	0.1	0.1	0.1	...	...	...	...
Saint Lucia [1] — Sainte-Lucie [1]								
MF [BA]	14.4	15.5	13.2	12.5	...	...	...	...
M [BA]	6.8	7.1	6.1	5.1	...	...	...	...
F [BA]	7.6	8.5	7.2	7.5	...	...	...	...
%MF [BA]	20.5	21.6	18.1	16.4	...	...	...	...
%M [BA]	17.7	18.0	16.0	12.6	...	...	...	...
%F [BA]	23.8	26.0	20.3	20.7	...	...	...	...
San Marino [16,109] — Saint-Marin [16,109]								
MF [E]	0.5	0.6	0.4	0.4	0.5	0.7	0.6	0.6
M [E]	0.1	0.1	0.1	0.1	0.2	0.2	0.2	0.1
F [E]	0.4	0.4	0.3	0.3	0.4	0.5	0.5	0.4
%MF [E]	4.4	4.1	3.0	2.8	2.6	3.6	3.1	2.8
%M [E]	1.9	1.8	1.6	1.7	1.4	1.6	1.5	1.1
%F [E]	7.3	6.9	4.6	4.1	4.3	6.3	5.5	5.2
Saudi Arabia [1] — Arabie saoudite [1]								
MF [BA]	...	...	254.1	273.6	281.2	326.6	...	...
M [BA]	...	...	183.8	194.3	202.6	225.0	...	...
F [BA]	...	...	70.3	79.3	78.6	103.7	...	...
%MF [BA]	...	...	4.3	4.6	4.6	5.2	...	...
%M [BA]	...	...	3.7	3.8	3.9	4.2	...	...
%F [BA]	...	...	8.1	9.3	9.1	11.5	...	...
Serbia and Montenegro — Serbie-et-Monténégro								
MF [BA] [1,91]	613.1	617.0	528.0 [111]	480.5 [111]	490.2 [111]	517.3 [111]	562.4 [111]	...
M [BA] [1,91]	310.8	303.4	248.9 [111]	223.6 [111]	242.5 [111]	261.5 [111]	306.4 [111]	...
F [BA] [1,91]	302.3	313.6	279.0 [111]	257.0 [111]	247.7 [111]	255.8 [111]	256.0 [111]	...
%MF [BA] [1,91]	13.8	13.7	13.7 [111]	12.6 [111]	12.8 [111]	13.8 [111]	15.2 [111]	...
%M [BA] [1,91]	12.2	11.8	11.7 [111]	10.6 [111]	11.1 [111]	12.4 [111]	14.4 [111]	...
%F [BA] [1,91]	16.1	16.1	16.2 [111]	15.2 [111]	15.0 [111]	15.8 [111]	16.4 [111]	...
MF [FB] [19]	814.1 [110]	837.6 [110]	811.1 [112]	805.8 [112]	850.0 [112]	923.2 [112]	1 019.0 [112]	...
M [FB] [19]	...	364.5 [110]	349.3 [112]	346.0 [112]	369.6 [112]	408.7 [112]	461.2 [112]	...
F [FB] [19]	...	473.1 [110]	461.8 [112]	459.8 [112]	480.4 [112]	514.5 [112]	557.8 [112]	...
%MF [FB] [19]	...	18.6 [110]	21.1 [112]	21.2 [112]	22.3 [112]	24.7 [112]	27.6 [112]	...
%M [FB] [19]	...	14.2 [110]	16.4 [112]	20.5 [112]	22.6 [112]	...	...	...
%F [FB] [19]	...	24.3 [110]	26.8 [112]	21.8 [112]	22.1 [112]	...	...	...
Singapore — Singapour								
MF [BA] [1,28]	45.5	62.1	90.1	97.5 [4]	72.9	111.2	116.4	...
M [BA] [1,28]	26.8	35.5	51.4	53.5 [4]	41.7	65.0	65.6	...
F [BA] [1,28]	18.7	26.6	38.7	44.0 [4]	31.2	46.2	50.8	...
%MF [BA] [1,28]	2.4	3.2	4.6	4.4 [4]	3.4	5.2	5.4	...
%M [BA] [1,28]	2.4	3.2	4.5	4.0 [4]	3.5	5.4	5.5	...
%F [BA] [1,28]	2.4	3.3	4.6	5.1 [4]	3.4	5.0	5.3	...
MF [FB] [23]	2.6	4.4	5.9	4.2	6.4	11.6	13.9	...
M [FB] [23]	1.2	2.3	3.2	2.3	3.2	5.6	6.8	...
F [FB] [23]	1.4	2.1	2.7	1.8	3.2	6.0	7.1	...

26

Unemployment—Number (thousands) and percentage unemployed, by sex (*continued*)

Chômage—Nombre (milliers) et pourcentage des chômeurs, par sexe (*suite*)

Country or area, source[6] — Pays ou zone, source[6]	1997	1998	1999	2000	2001	2002	2003	2004
Slovakia — Slovaquie								
MF [BA] [1,113]	297.5	317.1	416.8	485.2	508.0	486.9	459.2	481.0
M [BA] [1,113]	151.8	167.5	226.6	265.5	282.5	263.9	246.5	250.0
F [BA] [1,113]	145.7	149.6	190.2	219.7	225.5	223.0	212.7	231.0
%MF [BA] [1,113]	11.8	12.5	16.2	18.6	19.2	18.5	17.4	18.1
%M [BA] [1,113]	10.9	11.9	16.0	18.6	19.5	18.4	17.2	17.3
%F [BA] [1,113]	12.8	13.2	16.4	18.6	18.8	18.7	17.7	19.1
MF [FB]	336.7	379.5	485.2	517.9	520.6	513.2	443.4	409.0
M [FB]	162.9	193.0	265.8	283.7	284.7	280.8	240.0	211.0
F [FB]	173.8	186.5	219.4	234.2	235.9	232.4	203.4	198.0
%MF [FB]	12.9	13.7	17.3	18.2	18.3	17.8	15.2	14.3
%M [FB]	11.7	13.3	17.9	18.8	18.9	19.0	15.3	13.7
%F [FB]	14.3	14.1	16.6	17.6	17.5	16.5	15.0	14.9
Slovenia [1] — Slovénie [1]								
MF [BA] [48]	69.0	75.0	71.0	69.0	57.0	58.0	63.0	61.0
M [BA] [48]	36.0	40.0	37.0	36.0	29.0	30.0	32.0	31.0
F [BA] [48]	33.0	35.0	34.0	33.0	28.0	28.0	31.0	30.0
%MF [BA] [48]	7.1	7.7	7.4	7.2	5.9	5.9	6.6	6.1
%M [BA] [48]	7.0	7.6	7.2	7.0	5.6	5.7	6.1	5.7
%F [BA] [48]	7.3	7.7	7.6	7.4	6.3	6.3	7.1	6.4
MF [FB]	125.2	126.1	119.0	106.6	101.9	102.6	97.7	92.8
M [FB]	64.1	63.2	58.8	52.5	50.2	50.1	46.1	43.6
F [FB]	61.1	62.9	60.2	54.1	51.7	52.1	51.6	49.3
%MF [FB]	14.4	14.5	13.6	12.2	11.6	11.6	11.2	10.6
%M [FB]	13.6	13.4	12.4	11.1	10.4	10.4	9.7	9.1
%F [FB]	15.3	15.7	15.0	13.5	12.9	13.1	13.0	12.4
South Africa — Afrique du Sud								
MF [BA] [66]	...	...	3 158.0[36]	4 208.0[116]	4 383.0[116]	4 788.0[116]	4 910.0[117]	4 271.5[117]
M [BA] [66]	...	...	1 480.0[36]	2 015.0[116]	2 114.0[116]	2 252.0[116]	2 328.0[117]	2 055.0[117]
F [BA] [66]	...	...	1 677.0[36]	2 194.0[116]	2 268.0[116]	2 535.0[116]	2 581.0[117]	2 216.5[117]
%MF [BA] [66]	...	...	23.3[36]	26.3[116]	28.0[116]	30.0[116]	29.7[117]	27.1[117]
%M [BA] [66]	...	...	19.8[36]	24.1[116]	25.5[116]	26.7[116]	26.6[117]	23.5[117]
%F [BA] [66]	...	...	27.8[36]	28.7[116]	30.7[116]	33.6[116]	33.4[117]	31.6[117]
MF [FB] [1,114,115]	309.6	...	...	...	...	...	...	...
M [FB] [1,114,115]	207.8	...	...	...	...	...	...	...
F [FB] [1,114,115]	101.8	...	...	...	...	...	...	...
%MF [FB]	5.4	...	...	...	...	...	...	...
Spain — Espagne								
MF [BA] [54]	3 464.1	3 176.8	2 722.2	2 496.4	1 904.4	2 155.3	2 242.2	2 213.6
M [BA] [54]	1 629.7	1 417.7	1 158.3	1 037.4	828.1	929.3	976.4	970.8
F [BA] [54]	1 834.4	1 759.1	1 563.9	1 458.9	1 076.3	1 226.0	1 265.8	1 242.8
%MF [BA] [54]	20.6	18.6	15.6	13.9	10.6	11.5	11.5	11.0
%M [BA] [54]	15.8	13.6	10.9	9.6	7.5	8.2	8.4	8.2
%F [BA] [54]	28.2	26.5	22.9	20.4	15.2	16.4	16.0	15.0
MF [FB] [81]	2 118.7	1 889.5	1 651.6	1 557.5	1 529.9	1 621.5	1 657.6	1 670.6
M [FB] [81]	968.4	818.2	682.2	615.9	601.5	656.4	672.3	674.8
F [FB] [81]	1 150.3	1 071.3	969.4	941.6	928.4	965.1	985.3	995.8
Sri Lanka [6] — Sri Lanka [6]								
MF [BA]	...	611.3[118,119]	612.7[99,118]	546.1[118,119]	565.9[118,119]	632.8[118,119]	700.4[119,120]	679.1[99,120]
M [BA]	...	277.5[118,119]	330.7[99,118]	290.2[118,119]	309.5[118,119]	305.8[118,119]	323.8[119,120]	318.5[99,120]
F [BA]	...	333.8[118,119]	282.0[99,118]	255.9[118,119]	256.4[118,119]	327.0[118,119]	376.6[119,120]	360.6[99,120]
%MF [BA]	10.7[118,119]	10.6[118,119]	9.1[99,118]	8.0[118,119]	7.7[118,119]	8.7[118,119]	9.2[119,120]	8.5[99,120]
%M [BA]	8.0[118,119]	7.1[118,119]	7.4[99,118]	6.4[118,119]	5.8[118,119]	6.5[118,119]	6.4[119,120]	6.0[99,120]
%F [BA]	16.2[118,119]	16.2[118,119]	12.6[99,118]	11.1[118,119]	11.7[118,119]	12.8[118,119]	14.6[119,120]	13.5[99,120]
Suriname [1] — Suriname [1]								
MF [BA]	9.7	10.5	11.8[121]	...	...	...	...	...
M [BA]	4.4	4.6	5.4[121]	...	...	...	...	...
F [BA]	5.3	5.8	6.5[121]	...	...	...	...	...
%MF [BA]	10.5	10.6	14.0[121]	...	...	...	...	...

Country or area, source[§] — Pays ou zone, source[§]	1997	1998	1999	2000	2001	2002	2003	2004
%M [BA]	7.4	7.2	10.0[121]	...	...	...	...	...
%F [BA]	16.0	17.0	20.0[121]	...	...	...	...	...
Sweden — Suède								
MF [BA] [81]	342.0	276.0	241.0	203.0	175.0	176.0	217.0	246.0
M [BA] [81]	188.0	154.0	133.0	114.0	99.0	101.0	123.0	137.0
F [BA] [81]	154.0	122.0	107.0	89.0	76.0	76.0	94.0	109.0
%MF [BA] [81]	8.0	6.5	5.6	4.7	4.0	4.0	4.9	5.5
%M [BA] [81]	8.4	6.9	5.9	5.0	4.3	4.4	5.3	5.9
%F [BA] [81]	7.5	6.0	5.2	4.3	3.6	3.6	4.4	5.1
MF [FB] [1]	367.0	285.6	276.7	231.2	193.0	185.8	223.0	239.2
M [FB] [1]	199.5	156.3	151.7	126.9	107.2	105.4	127.4	135.1
F [FB] [1]	167.4	129.3	125.0	104.3	85.8	80.4	95.6	104.1
%MF [FB] [1]	8.6	6.7	6.4	5.3	4.4	4.2	4.9	5.5
%M [FB] [1]	8.9	7.0	6.7	5.6	4.7	4.6	5.3	5.9
%F [FB] [1]	8.2	6.4	6.1	5.0	4.1	3.8	4.4	5.1
Switzerland [1] — Suisse [1]								
MF [BA] [48]	162.1	141.8	121.6	105.9	100.6	119.0	170.0	178.0
M [BA] [48]	94.7	70.0	59.2	51.0	37.9	62.0	86.0	89.0
F [BA] [48]	67.4	71.8	62.4	54.9	62.6	57.0	84.0	89.0
%MF [BA] [48]	4.1	3.6	3.1	2.7	2.5	2.9	4.1	4.3
%M [BA] [48]	4.3	3.2	2.7	2.3	1.7	2.8	3.8	3.9
%F [BA] [48]	3.9	4.1	3.5	3.1	3.5	3.1	4.5	4.7
MF [FB]	188.3	139.7	98.6	72.0	67.2	100.5	145.7	153.1
M [FB]	108.7	77.1	52.6	37.8	35.4	55.9	81.7	83.6
F [FB]	79.6	62.6	46.0	34.2	31.8	44.6	64.0	69.5
%MF [FB]	5.2	3.9	2.7	1.8	1.7	2.5	3.7[122]	3.9[122]
%M [FB]	4.9	3.5	2.4	1.7	1.6	2.5	3.7[122]	3.8[122]
%F [FB]	5.7	4.4	3.3	2.0	1.8	2.6	3.7[122]	4.0[122]
Syrian Arab Republic [1] — Rép. arabe syrienne [1]								
MF [BA]	...	...	...	...	613.4	637.8	...	...
M [BA]	...	...	...	...	348.4	355.8	...	...
F [BA]	...	...	...	...	265.0	282.0	...	...
%MF [BA]	...	...	...	...	11.2	11.7	...	...
%M [BA]	...	...	...	...	8.0	8.3	...	...
%F [BA]	...	...	...	...	23.9	24.1	...	...
Tajikistan — Tadjikistan								
MF [FB]	51.1	...	...	...	...	...	...	...
M [FB]	24.1	...	...	...	...	...	...	...
F [FB]	27.0	...	...	...	...	...	...	...
%MF [FB]	2.7	...	...	...	...	...	...	...
%M [FB]	2.4	...	...	...	...	...	...	...
%F [FB]	2.9	...	...	...	...	...	...	...
Thailand [123,124] — Thaïlande [123,124]								
MF [BA]	292.5	1 137.9	985.7	812.6	896.3	616.3	543.7	548.9
M [BA]	154.4	625.2	546.4	454.5	511.2	372.1	314.7	324.2
F [BA]	138.1	512.7	439.3	358.0	385.1	244.2	229.0	224.7
%MF [BA]	0.9	3.4	3.0	2.4	2.6	1.8	1.5	1.5
%M [BA]	0.8	3.4	3.0	2.4	2.7	2.0	1.6	1.6
%F [BA]	0.9	3.4	3.0	2.3	2.5	1.6	1.4	1.4
TFYR of Macedonia — L'ex-R.y. Macédoine								
MF [BA] [1,17]	...	...	...	...	263.2	263.5	315.9	309.3
M [BA] [1,17]	...	...	...	...	149.4	159.1	191.9	186.2
F [BA] [1,17]	...	...	...	...	113.8	104.3	124.0	123.1
%MF [BA] [1,17]	...	...	...	...	30.5	31.9	36.7	37.2
%M [BA] [1,17]	...	...	...	...	29.5	31.7	37.0	36.7
%F [BA] [1,17]	...	...	...	...	32.0	32.3	36.3	37.8
MF [FB] [19]	253.0	...	...	...	354.0	371.0	384.0	...
M [FB] [19]	138.0	...	...	...	...	208.0	216.0	...
F [FB] [19]	115.0	...	...	...	...	163.0	168.0	...
%MF [FB] [19]	40.6	46.6	51.5	53.7	...	...	...	...

Country or area, source⁶ — Pays ou zone, source⁶	1997	1998	1999	2000	2001	2002	2003	2004
Trinidad and Tobago [1,125] — **Trinité-et-Tobago** [1,125]								
MF [BA]	81.2	79.4	74.0	69.6	62.4	61.1	...	...
M [BA]	41.3	39.0	37.9	36.1	30.7	27.9	...	...
F [BA]	39.9	40.4	36.1	33.5	31.7	33.2	...	...
%MF [BA]	15.0	14.2	13.1	12.2	10.8	10.4	...	...
%M [BA]	12.3	11.3	10.9	10.2	8.6	7.8	...	...
%F [BA]	19.4	18.9	16.8	15.2	14.4	14.5	...	...
Tunisia — **Tunisie**								
MF [BA] [1]	474.7	...	509.9	510.8	503.9	523.7	509.3	...
%MF [BA] [1]	15.7	...	15.8	15.6	15.0	14.9	14.3	...
MF [FB] [19,87]	...	...	...	77.0	71.9	73.5	77.9	...
M [FB] [19,87]	...	...	...	42.7	40.5	40.5	41.6	...
F [FB] [19,87]	...	...	...	34.3	31.5	33.1	36.2	...
Turkey — **Turquie**								
MF [BA]	1 463.0[24]	1 528.0[24]	1 774.0[24]	1 497.0[1,75]	1 967.0[1]	2 464.0[1]	2 493.0[1]	2 498.0[1]
M [BA]	1 007.0[24]	1 107.0[24]	1 275.0[24]	1 111.0[1,75]	1 485.0[1]	1 826.0[1]	1 830.0[1]	1 878.0[1]
F [BA]	456.0[24]	421.0[24]	499.0[24]	387.0[1,75]	482.0[1]	638.0[1]	663.0[1]	620.0[1]
%MF [BA]	6.7[24]	6.8[24]	7.7[24]	6.5[1,75]	8.4[1]	10.3[1]	10.5[1]	10.3[1]
%M [BA]	6.3[24]	6.8[24]	7.7[24]	6.6[1,75]	8.7[1]	10.7[1]	10.7[1]	10.5[1]
%F [BA]	7.8[24]	6.9[24]	7.5[24]	6.3[1,75]	7.5[1]	9.4[1]	10.1[1]	9.7[1]
MF [FB] [11,23]	463.0	465.2	487.5	730.5	718.7	464.3	587.4	...
M [FB] [11,23]	382.1	386.0	413.8	591.9	582.9	379.8	469.4	...
F [FB] [11,23]	81.2	79.2	73.7	138.6	135.8	84.5	118.0	...
Uganda [6,126] — **Ouganda** [6,126]								
MF [BA]	...	...	...	...	...	...	346.0	...
M [BA]	...	...	...	...	...	...	128.0	...
F [BA]	...	...	...	...	...	...	218.0	...
%MF [BA]	...	...	...	...	...	...	3.2	...
%M [BA]	...	...	...	...	...	...	2.5	...
%F [BA]	...	...	...	...	...	...	3.9	...
Ukraine — **Ukraine**								
MF [BA] [127]	2 330.1[36]	2 937.1[76]	2 614.3[68]	2 655.8	2 455.0	2 140.7	2 008.0	1 906.7
M [BA] [127]	1 216.9[36]	1 515.1[76]	1 346.5[68]	1 357.4	1 263.0	1 106.5	1 055.7	1 001.6
F [BA] [127]	1 113.2[36]	1 422.0[76]	1 267.8[68]	1 298.4	1 192.0	1 034.2	952.3	905.1
%MF [BA] [127]	8.9[36]	11.3[76]	11.6[68]	11.6	10.9	9.6	9.1	8.6
%M [BA] [127]	9.5[36]	11.9[76]	11.8[68]	11.6	11.0	9.8	9.4	8.9
%F [BA] [127]	8.4[36]	10.8[76]	11.3[68]	11.6	10.8	9.5	8.7	8.3
MF [FB] [16,21]	637.1	1 003.2	1 174.5	1 155.2	1 008.1	1 034.2	988.9	981.8
M [FB] [16,21]	220.6	382.8	444.9	424.8	362.5	369.2	361.3	361.9
F [FB] [16,21]	416.5	620.4	729.6	730.4	645.6	665.0	627.6	619.9
%MF [FB] [16,21]	2.7	4.3	5.5	5.5	4.8	5.0	4.8	4.8
%M [FB] [16,21]	1.8	3.2	4.0	3.8	3.3	3.4	3.4	3.4
%F [FB] [16,21]	3.7	5.5	7.3	7.2	6.4	6.7	6.3	6.3
United Arab Emirates — **Emirats arabes unis**								
MF [E]	...	...	...	41.0	...	...	...	...
M [E]	...	...	...	34.7	...	...	...	...
F [E]	...	...	...	6.3	...	...	...	...
%MF [E]	...	...	...	2.3	...	...	...	...
%M [E]	...	...	...	2.2	...	...	...	...
%F [E]	...	...	...	2.6	...	...	...	...
United Kingdom — **Royaume-Uni**								
MF [BA] [128,129]	2 037.3	1 776.4	1 751.7	1 619.1	1 412.9	1 519.4	1 414.0	1 361.0
M [BA] [128,129]	1 305.8	1 097.8	1 095.2	991.5	864.1	933.5	866.2	788.1
F [BA] [128,129]	731.5	678.6	656.5	627.6	548.8	585.9	547.8	572.9
%MF [BA] [128,129]	7.1	6.1	6.0	5.5	4.8	5.1	4.8	4.6
%M [BA] [128,129]	8.1	6.8	6.7	6.1	5.3	5.6	5.5	5.0
%F [BA] [128,129]	5.7	5.3	5.1	4.8	4.2	4.4	4.1	4.2
MF [FA] [58,130,131,132,133,134]	1 602.4	1 362.4	1 263.1	1 102.3	983.0	958.8	945.9	...

Country or area, source[§] — Pays ou zone, source[§]	1997	1998	1999	2000	2001	2002	2003	2004
M [FA] [58,130,131,132,133,134]	1 225.5	1 037.7	963.5	839.6	746.8	723.8	707.6	...
F [FA] [58,130,132,134]	377.3	324.7	299.5	262.6	236.2	235.0	238.5	...
%MF [FA] [58,130,131,132,133,134]	5.7	4.7	4.3	3.8	3.3	3.2	3.1	...
%M [FA] [58,130,131,132,133,134]	7.7	6.5	6.0	5.2	4.6	4.4	4.3	...
%F [FA] [58,130,132,134]	2.9	2.5	2.3	2.0	1.7	1.7	1.7	...
United Rep. of Tanzania [6,135,136] — Rép.-Unie de Tanzanie [6,135,136]								
MF [BA]	...	...	...	...	912.8	...	...	...
M [BA]	...	...	...	...	388.4	...	...	...
F [BA]	...	...	...	...	524.4	...	...	...
%MF [BA]	...	...	...	...	5.1	...	...	...
%M [BA]	...	...	...	...	4.4	...	...	...
%F [BA]	...	...	...	...	5.8	...	...	...
United States [54] — Etats-Unis [54]								
MF [BA]	6 739.0	6 210.0	5 880.0	5 655.0	6 742.0	8 378.0	8 774.0	8 149.0
M [BA]	3 577.0	3 266.0	3 066.0	2 954.0	3 663.0	4 597.0	4 906.0	4 456.0
F [BA]	3 162.0	2 944.0	2 814.0	2 701.0	3 079.0	3 781.0	3 868.0	3 694.0
%MF [BA]	4.9	4.5	4.2	4.0	4.8	5.8	6.0	5.5
%M [BA]	4.9	4.4	4.1	3.9	4.8	5.9	6.3	5.6
%F [BA]	5.0	4.6	4.3	4.1	4.7	5.6	5.7	5.4
United States Virgin Is. [137] — Iles Vierges américaines [137]								
MF [FB]	2.7	...	...	...	...	...	...	...
%MF [FB]	5.9	...	...	...	...	...	...	...
Uruguay [10,23] — Uruguay [10,23]								
MF [BA]	151.5	123.8	137.7	167.7	193.2	211.3	208.5	...
M [BA]	...	53.7	59.4	74.7	80.4	93.3	92.2	...
F [BA]	...	70.1	78.3	93.0	112.8	118.0	116.2	...
%MF [BA]	11.4	10.1	11.3	13.6	15.3	17.0	16.9	...
%M [BA]	9.0	7.8	8.7	10.9	11.5	13.5	13.5	...
%F [BA]	14.7	13.0	14.6	17.0	19.7	21.2	20.8	...
Venezuela (Bolivarian Republic of) [1] — Venezuela (République bolivarienne du) [1]								
MF [BA]	1 060.7	1 092.6	1 525.5	1 423.5	1 435.8	1 822.6	...	...
M [BA]	592.4	616.4	877.8	867.7	827.1	998.6	...	...
F [BA]	468.3	476.2	647.8	555.8	608.7	824.0	...	...
%MF [BA]	11.4	11.2	14.9	13.9	13.2	15.8	...	...
%M [BA]	9.8	9.9	13.6	13.4	12.4	14.3	...	...
%F [BA]	14.2	13.4	17.1	14.8	14.6	18.1	...	...
Viet Nam [1,45] — Viet Nam [1,45]								
MF [BA]	1 051.1	866.2	908.9	885.7	1 109.6	871.0	949.0	...
M [BA]	581.2	456.1	438.6	468.0	460.9	398.0	402.4	...
F [BA]	469.9	410.1	470.3	417.7	648.7	473.0	546.6	...
%MF [BA]	2.9	2.3	2.3	2.3	2.8	2.1	2.3	...
%M [BA]	3.2	2.4	2.3	2.4	2.3	1.9	1.9	...
%F [BA]	2.6	2.2	2.4	2.1	3.2	2.3	2.6	...
Yemen [1] — Yémen [1]								
MF [BA]	...	...	469.0	...	...	...	...	...
M [BA]	...	...	389.6	...	...	...	...	...
F [BA]	...	...	79.4	...	...	...	...	...
%MF [BA]	...	...	11.5	...	...	...	...	...
%M [BA]	...	...	12.5	...	...	...	...	...
%F [BA]	...	...	8.2	...	...	...	...	...
Zambia [24] — Zambie [24]								
MF [A]	...	508.0	...	...	...	...	...	...
M [A]	...	281.0	...	...	...	...	...	...
F [A]	...	227.0	...	...	...	...	...	...
%MF [A]	...	12.0	...	...	...	...	...	...
%M [A]	...	13.0	...	...	...	...	...	...
%F [A]	...	12.0	...	...	...	...	...	...

Country or area, source§ — Pays ou zone, source§	1997	1998	1999	2000	2001	2002	2003	2004
Zimbabwe [1] — Zimbabwe [1]								
MF [BA]	341.1	...	297.8	...	...	...	...	...
M [BA]	219.4	...	187.1	...	...	...	...	...
F [BA]	121.8	...	110.7	...	...	...	...	...
%MF [BA]	6.9	...	6.0	...	...	...	...	...
%M [BA]	8.7	...	7.3	...	...	...	...	...
%F [BA]	5.1	...	4.6	...	...	...	...	...

Source

International Labour Office (ILO), Geneva, the ILO labour statistics database and the "Yearbook of Labour Statistics 2005".

Notes

§ Data sources:
   A: Population census.
   B: Household surveys.
   BA: Labour force sample surveys.
   E: Official estimates.
   FA: Insurance records.
   FB: Employment office records.
   FD: Administration reports.

[1] Persons aged 15 years and over.
[2] September of each year.
[3] September.
[4] Population census.
[5] July.
[6] Persons aged 10 years and over.
[7] Prior to 2003, 28 urban agglomerations.
[8] May and October of each year.
[9] May. 31 Urban agglomerations.
[10] Urban areas.
[11] December of each year.
[12] Persons aged 16 to 63 years.
[13] Estimates based on 1996 census of population benchmarks.

[14] Prior to 2004: including conscripts.
[15] Excluding conscripts.
[16] 31 December of each year.
[17] April of each year.
[18] Private sector.
[19] Work applicants.
[20] Year ending in June of the year indicated.
[21] Men aged 16 to 59 years; women aged 16 to 54 years.
[22] Beginning April 1985, excluding some elderly unemployed no longer applicants for work.
[23] Persons aged 14 years and over.
[24] Persons aged 12 years and over.
[25] Population census; August.
[26] Excluding rural population of Rondônia, Acre, Amazonas, Roraima, Pará and Amapá.
[27] Persons aged 15 to 74 years.
[28] June of each year.
[29] Men aged 16 to 60 years; women aged 16 to 55 years. After 1999, age limits vary according to the year.
[30] Men aged 16 to 62.5 years; women aged 16 to 57 years.
[31] Four employment offices.
[32] Bujumbura.
[33] November of each year.
[34] Excluding full-time members of the armed forces.
[35] Excluding residents of the Territories and indigenous persons living on reserves.
[36] October.

Source

Bureau international du Travail (BIT), Genève, la base de données du BIT et "l'Annuaire des statistiques du travail 2005".

Notes

§ Sources de données :
   A: Recensement de la population.
   B: Enquêtes auprès des ménages.
   BA: Enquêtes par sondage sur la main-d'œuvre.
   E: Evaluations officielles.
   FA: Fichiers des assurances.
   FB: Fichiers des bureaux de placement.
   FD: Rapports administratifs.

[1] Personnes âgées de 15 ans et plus.
[2] Septembre de chaque année.
[3] Septembre.
[4] Recensement de population.
[5] Juillet.
[6] Personnes âgées de 10 ans et plus.
[7] Avant 2003, 28 agglomérations urbaines.
[8] Mai et octobre de chaque année.
[9] Mai. 31 agglomérations urbaines.
[10] Régions urbaines.
[11] Décembre de chaque année.
[12] Personnes âgées de 16 à 63 ans.
[13] Estimations basées sur les données de calage du recensement de population de 1996.

[14] Avant 2004: y compris les conscrits.
[15] Non compris les conscrits.
[16] 31 décembre de chaque année.
[17] Avril de chaque année.
[18] Secteur privé.
[19] Demandeurs d'emploi.
[20] Année se terminant en juin de l'année indiquée.
[21] Hommes âgés de 16 à 59 ans; femmes âgées de 16 à 54 ans.
[22] A partir d'avril 1985 : non compris certains chômeurs âgés devenus non demandeurs d'emploi.
[23] Personnes âgées de 14 ans et plus.
[24] Personnes âgées de 12 ans et plus.
[25] Recensement de population; août.
[26] Non compris la population rurale de Rondônia, Acre, Amazonas, Roraima, Pará et Amapá.
[27] Personnes âgées de 15 à 74 ans.
[28] Juin de chaque année.
[29] Hommes âgés de 16 à 60 ans; femmes âgées de 16 à 55 ans. Après 1999, les limites d'âge varient selon l'année.
[30] Hommes âgés de 16 à 62,5 ans; femmes âgées de 16 à 57 ans.
[31] Quatre bureaux de placement.
[32] Bujumbura.
[33] Novembre de chaque année.
[34] Non compris les membres à temps complet des forces armées.
[35] Non compris les habitants des Territoires et les populations indigènes vivant dans les réserves.
[36] Octobre.

37 Fourth quarter of each year.
38 For statistical purposes, the data for China do not include those for the Hong Kong Special Administrative Region (Hong Kong SAR), Macao Special Administrative Region (Macao SAR) and Taiwan Province of China.
39 Unemployed in urban areas.
40 Excluding unpaid family workers who worked for one hour or more.

41 Methodology revised.
42 February, May, August and November.
43 Beginning 1991: estimates based on the 1993 Census results.

44 Prior to 2001: 7 main cities; Sep. of each year. Persons aged 12 years and over.
45 July of each year.
46 June.
47 The data relate to the government-controlled areas.
48 Second quarter of each year.
49 Excluding persons on child care leave actively seeking a job.

50 Persons aged 15 to 66 years.
51 Persons aged 16 to 66 years.
52 Prior to 1997: persons aged 12 to 64 years. Beginning 1997, persons aged 15 to 64 years.
53 Prior to 2003: May and November of each year. Beginning 2003, January, April, July and October.
54 Persons aged 16 years and over.
55 Prior to 2000: second quarter of each year.
56 April.
57 Excluding elderly unemployment pensioners no longer seeking work.
58 Excluding persons temporarily laid off.
59 Beginning October 1982, series revised on the basis of new administrative procedures adopted in 1986.
60 March of each year.
61 January.
62 Beginning this year, methodology revised; data not strictly comparable.

63 Persons aged 15 to 64 years.
64 May.
65 March.
66 Persons aged 15 to 65 years.
67 Prior to 1998: persons aged 14 years and over.
68 Estimates based on the 2001 Population Census results.

69 April and November of each year.
70 Persons aged 16 to 74 years.
71 May of each year.
72 Prior to 1998: April of each year. Beginning 1998, March - May of each year.
73 Beginning 1998: methodology revised.
74 First and second quarters.
75 Estimates based on the 2000 Population Census results.

76 November.
77 Persons aged 15 years and over. Beginning 2002, persons aged 15 to 74 years.
78 Age limits vary according to the year.
79 Men aged 16 to 61 years; women aged 16-57 years.
80 Men aged 16 to 62 years; women aged 16-59.5 years.
81 Persons aged 16 to 64 years.
82 Revised series.
83 Totals include persons still attending school (incl. full-time tertiary students).
84 Persons aged 16 to 61 years.
85 Methodology revised; data not strictly comparable.
86 Excluding Rodrigues.
87 Persons aged 18 years and over.

37 Quatrième trimestre de chaque année.
38 Pour la présentation des statistiques, les données pour Chine ne comprennent pas la Région Administrative Spéciale de Hong Kong (Hong Kong RAS), la Région Administrative Spéciale de Macao (Macao RAS) et la province de Taiwan.
39 Chômeurs dans les régions urbaines.
40 Non compris les travailleurs familiaux non rémunérés ayant travaillé une heure ou plus.
41 Méthodologie révisée.
42 Février, mai, août et novembre.
43 A partir de 1991: estimations basées sur les résultats du Recensement de 1993.
44 Avant 2001: 7 villes principales; sept. de chaque année. Personnes âgées de 10 ans et plus.
45 Juillet de chaque année.
46 Juin.
47 Les données se réfèrent aux régions sous contrôle gouvernemental.
48 Deuxième trimestre de chaque année.
49 Non compris les personnes en congé parental cherchant activement un travail.
50 Personnes âgées de 15 à 66 ans.
51 Personnes âgées de 16 à 66 ans.
52 Avant 1997: personnes âgées de 12 à 64 ans. A partir de 1997, personnes âgées de 15 à 64 ans.
53 Avant 2003: mai et novembre de chaque année. A partir de 2003, Janvier, avril, juillet et octobre.
54 Personnes âgées de 16 ans et plus.
55 Avant 2000: deuxième trimestre de chaque année.
56 Avril.
57 Non compris chômeurs âgés devenus non demandeurs d'emploi.
58 Non compris les personnes temporairement mises à pied.
59 A partir d'octobre, série révisée sur la base de nouvelles procédures administratives adoptées en 1986.
60 Mars de chaque année.
61 Janvier.
62 A partir de cette année, méthodologie révisée; les données ne sont pas strictement comparables.
63 Personnes âgées de 15 à 64 ans.
64 Mai.
65 Mars.
66 Personnes âgées de 15 à 65 ans.
67 Avant 1998 : personnes âgées de 14 ans et plus.
68 Estimations basées sur les résultats du Recensement de la population de 2001.
69 Avril et novembre de chaque année.
70 Personnes âgées de 16 à 74 ans.
71 Mai de chaque année.
72 Avant 1998: avril de chaque année. A partir de 1998: Mars - mai de chaque année.
73 A partir de 1998: méthodologie révisée.
74 Premier et deuxième trimestres.
75 Estimations basées sur les résultats du recensement de la population de 2000.
76 Novembre.
77 Personnes âgées de 15 ans et plus. A partir de 2002, Personnes âgées de 15 à 74 ans.
78 Les limites d'âge varient selon l'année.
79 Hommes âgés de 16 à 61 ans; femmes âgées de 16 à 57 ans.
80 Hommes âgés de 16 à 62 ans; femmes âgées de 16 à 59,5 ans.
81 Personnes âgées de 16 à 64 ans.
82 Série révisée.
83 Les totaux incluent les personnes encore en cours d'études (y compris les étudiants à plein temps de l'enseignement supérieur).
84 Personnes âgées de 16 à 61 ans.
85 Méthodologie révisée; les données ne sont pas strictement comparables.
86 Non compris Rodrigues.
87 Personnes âgées de 18 ans et plus.

[88] Persons aged 15 to 69 years.
[89] Beginning 1983, persons seeking work for 20 hours or more a week.

[90] Curaçao.
[91] October of each year.
[92] Including students seeking vacation work.
[93] Persons aged 15 to 60 years.
[94] July of preceding year to June of current year.
[95] Persons aged 18 to 60 years.
[96] August of each year.
[97] Year beginning in August of year indicated.
[98] Year beginning in September of year indicated.
[99] Third quarter.
[100] Metropolitan Lima; Oct.
[101] Metropolitan Lima; July.
[102] Metropolitan Lima; August.
[103] Men aged 18 to 64 years; women aged 18 to 59 years (with the exception of juvenile graduates).
[104] First and fourth quarters.
[105] Prior to 1998: persons aged 14 years and over. Estimates based the 2001 Census results.
[106] March 1997 Population and Housing Census.
[107] Estimates based on the 2002 Population Census results.

[108] Persons aged 15 to 72 years.
[109] Persons aged 15 years and over; prior to 1996: 14 years and over.
[110] Including Kosovo and Metohia.
[111] Beginning 1999, data for Kosovo and Metohia are excluded.
[112] Excluding Kosovo and Metohia.
[113] Excluding persons on child-care leave.
[114] Excluding Transkei, Bophuthatswana, Venda, Ciskei, Kwazulu, KaNgwane, Qwa Qwa, Gazankulu, Lebowa and KwaNdebele.
[115] Whites, Coloureds and Asians; eligibility rules for registration not specified.
[116] February and September.
[117] March and Sep. of each year
[118] Excluding Northern and Eastern provinces.
[119] First quarter of each year.
[120] Excluding Northern province.
[121] First semester.
[122] Beginning 2003, rates calculated on basis of 2000 Census.
[123] Third round (August) of each year.
[124] Persons aged 13 years and over.
[125] Beginning 1987, excluding unemployed not previously employed.
[126] Year ending in April of the year indicated.
[127] Persons aged 15-70 years.
[128] March - May of each year.
[129] Men aged 16 to 64 years; women aged 16-59 years.
[130] Beginning September 1988: excluding most under 18-years-old.

[131] Beginning September 1989: excluding some men formerly employed in the coal mining industry.
[132] Beginning February 1986: data not strictly comparable as a result of changes in compilation date.
[133] Beginning April 1983, excluding some categories of men aged 60 and over.
[134] Claimants at unemployment benefits offices.
[135] Tanganyika.
[136] Year ending in March of the year indicated.
[137] Persons aged 16 to 65 years.

[88] Personnes âgées de 15 à 69 ans.
[89] A partir de 1983, personnes en quête de travail pour 20 heures ou plus par semaine.
[90] Curaçao.
[91] Octobre de chaque année.
[92] Y compris les étudiants qui cherchent un emploi pendant les vacances.
[93] Personnes âgées de 15 à 60 ans.
[94] Juillet de l'année précédente à juin de l'année en cours.
[95] Personnes âgées de 18 à 60 ans.
[96] Août de chaque année.
[97] Année commençant en août de l'année indiquée.
[98] Année commençant en septembre del'année indiquée.
[99] Troisième trimestre.
[100] Lima métropolitaine; oct.
[101] Lima métropolitaine; juillet.
[102] Lima métropolitaine; aôut.
[103] Hommes âgés de 18 à 64 ans; femmes âgées de 18 à 59 ans (à l'exception des jeunes diplômés).
[104] Première et quatrième trimestres.
[105] Avant 1998: personnes âgées de 14 ans et plus. Estimations basées sur les résultats du Recensement de 2001.
[106] Recensement de la population et de l'habitat de mars 1997.
[107] Estimations basées sur les résultats du Recensement de la population de 2002
[108] Personnes âgées de 15 à 72 ans.
[109] Personnes âgées de 15 ans et plus; avant 1996 : 14 ans et plus.
[110] Y compris Kosovo et Metohia.
[111] A compter de 1999, non compris les données de Kosovo et Metohia.
[112] Non compris Kosovo et Metohia.
[113] Non compris les personnes en congé parental.
[114] Non compris Transkei, Bophuthatswana, Venda, Ciskei, Kwazulu, KaNgwane, Qwa Qwa, Gazankulu, Lebowa et KwaNdebele.
[115] Blancs, personnes de couleur et asiatiques; conditions d'éligibilité pour l'enregistrement non spécifiées.
[116] Février et septembre.
[117] Mars et sept. de chaque année.
[118] Non compris les provinces du Nord et de l'Est.
[119] Le primer trimestre de chaque année.
[120] Non compris la province du Nord.
[121] Premier trimestre.
[122] A partir de 2003, taux calculés sur la base du Recensement de 2000.
[123] Troisième enquête (août) de chaque année.
[124] Personnes âgées de 13 ans et plus.
[125] A partir de 1987, non compris les chômeurs n'ayant jamais travaillé.
[126] Année se terminant en avril de l'année indiquée.
[127] Personnes âgées de 15 à 70 ans.
[128] Mars - mai de chaque année.
[129] Hommes âgés de 16 à 64 ans; femmes âgées de 16 à 59 ans.
[130] A compter de septembre 1988 non compris la plupart des moins de 18 ans.
[131] A compter de september 1989 : non compris hommes ayant précédement travaillé dans l'industrie charbonnière.
[132] A partir de février 1986: données non strictement comparables en raison d'un changement de date de traitement.
[133] A compter d'avril 1983, non compris certaines catégories d'hommes âgés de 60 ans et plus.
[134] Demandeurs auprès des bureaux de prestations de chômage.
[135] Tanganyika.
[136] Année se terminant en mars de l'année indiquée.
[137] Personnes âgées de 16 à 65 ans.

Technical notes: table 26

Detailed data on labour force and related topics are published in the ILO *Yearbook of Labour Statistics* [11] and on the ILO web site http://laborsta.ilo.org. The series shown in the *Statistical Yearbook* give an overall picture of the availability and disposition of labour resources and, in conjunction with other macroeconomic indicators, can be useful for an overall assessment of economic performance. The ILO *Yearbook of Labour Statistics* provides a comprehensive description of the methodology underlying the labour series. Brief definitions of the major categories of labour statistics are given below.

"Unemployment" is defined to include persons above a certain age and who, during a specified period of time were:

(a) "Without work", i.e. were not in paid employment or self-employment;

(b) "Currently available for work", i.e. were available for paid employment or self employment during the reference period; and

(c) "Seeking work", i.e. had taken specific steps in a specified period to find paid employment or self-employment.

Persons not considered to be unemployed include:

(a) Persons intending to establish their own business or farm, but who had not yet arranged to do so and who were not seeking work for pay or profit;

(b) Former unpaid family workers not at work and not seeking work for pay or profit.

For various reasons, national definitions of employment and unemployment often differ from the recommended international standard definitions and thereby limit international comparability. Inter-country comparisons are also complicated by a variety of types of data collection systems used to obtain information on employed and unemployed persons.

Table 26: Figures are presented in absolute numbers and in percentages. Data are normally annual averages of monthly, quarterly or semi annual data.

The series generally represent the total number of persons wholly unemployed or temporarily laid off. Percentage figures, where given, are calculated by comparing the number of unemployed to the total members of that group of the labour force on which the unemployment data are based.

Notes techniques : tableau 26

Des données détaillées sur la main-d'oeuvre et des sujets connexes sont publiées dans l'*Annuaire des Statistiques du Travail* du BIT [11] et sur le site Web du BIT http://laborsta.ilo.org. Les séries indiquées dans l'*Annuaire des Statistiques* donnent un tableau d'ensemble des disponibilités de main-d'œuvre et de l'emploi de ces ressources et, combinées à d'autres indicateurs économiques, elles peuvent être utiles pour une évaluation générale de la performance économique. L'*Annuaire des statistiques du Travail* du BIT donne une description complète de la méthodologie employée pour établir les séries sur la main-d'œuvre. On trouvera ci-dessous quelques brèves définitions des grandes catégories de statistiques du travail.

Par "chômeurs", on entend les personnes dépassant un âge déterminé et qui, pendant une période donnée, étaient:

a) "sans emploi", c'est-à-dire sans emploi rémunéré ou indépendant;

b) "disponibles", c'est-à-dire qui pouvaient être engagées pour un emploi rémunéré ou pouvaient s'adonner à un emploi indépendant au cours de la période de référence; et

c) "à la recherche d'un emploi", c'est-à-dire qui avaient pris des mesures précises à un certain moment pour trouver un emploi rémunéré ou un emploi indépendant.

Ne sont pas considérés comme chômeurs:

a) Les personnes qui, pendant la période de référence, avaient l'intention de créer leur propre entreprise ou exploitation agricole, mais n'avaient pas encore pris les dispositions nécessaires à cet effet et qui n'étaient pas à la recherche d'un emploi en vue d'une rémunération ou d'un profit;

b) Les anciens travailleurs familiaux non rémunérés qui n'avaient pas d'emploi et n'étaient pas à la recherche d'un emploi en vue d'une rémunération ou d'un profit.

Pour diverses raisons, les définitions nationales de l'emploi et du chômage diffèrent souvent des définitions internationales types recommandées, limitant ainsi les possibilités de comparaison entre pays. Ces comparaisons se trouvent en outre compliquées par la diversité des systèmes de collecte de données utilisés pour recueillir des informations sur les personnes employées et les chômeurs.

Tableau 26 : Les chiffres sont présentés en valeur absolue et en pourcentage. Les données sont normalement des moyennes annuelles des données mensuelles, trimestrielles ou semestrielles.

Les séries représentent généralement le nombre total des chômeurs complets ou des personnes temporairement mises à pied. Les données en pourcentage, lorsqu'elles figurent dans le tableau, sont calculées en comparant le nombre de chômeurs au nombre total des personnes du groupe de main-d'œuvre sur lequel sont basées les données relatives au chômage.

Wages in manufacturing
By hour, day, week or month

Salaires dans les industries manufacturières
Par heure, jour, semaine ou mois

Country or area § Pays ou zone §	1997	1998	1999	2000	2001	2002	2003	2004
Albania (lek) — Albanie (lek)								
MF(I) - month mois	9 121.0	9 674.0	10 734.0	11 708.0	14 056.0	14 334.0	16 572.0	...
Anguilla (EC dollar) — Anguilla (dollar des Caraïbes orientales)								
MF(I) - month mois	...	...	...	1 494.7	...	...	...	...
Argentina [1,2] (Argentine peso) — Argentine [1,2] (peso argentin)								
MF(II) - hour heure	4.1	4.1	4.2	4.2	4.3	...	...	...
Armenia (dram) — Arménie (dram)								
MF(I) - month mois	17 656.0	21 278.0	24 515.0	29 307.0	35 848.0	40 362.0	53 048.0	...
Australia [3,4] (Australian dollar) — Australie [3,4] (dollar australien)								
MF(I) - hour heure	...	17.4	...	18.2	...	20.5	...	22.8
M(I) - hour heure	...	18.0	...	19.1	...	20.8	...	23.4
F(I) - hour heure	...	15.2	...	16.8	...	18.5	...	19.9
Austria (Austrian schilling, euro) — Autriche (schilling autrichien, euro)								
MF(I) - month mois	27 776.0[5]	28 455.0[5]	29 136.0[5]	2 417.0	2 501.0	2 289.0	2 358.0	...
M(I) - month mois	30 667.0[5]	31 471.0[5]	32 195.0[5]	2 738.0	2 837.0	2 524.0	2 594.0	...
F(I) - month mois	21 051.0[5]	21 480.0[5]	22 009.0[5]	1 662.0	1 716.0	1 738.0	1 795.0	...
MF(II) - month mois	24 878.0[5]	25 471.0[5]	26 104.0[5]	1 973.0	2 046.0	2 052.0	2 112.0	...
M(II) - month mois	27 275.0[5]	27 972.0[5]	28 646.0[5]	2 186.0	2 271.0	2 249.0	2 309.0	...
F(II) - month mois	17 929.0[5]	18 248.0[5]	18 702.0[5]	1 353.0	1 394.0	1 470.0	1 512.0	...
MF(V) - month mois	33 095.0[5]	33 829.0[5]	34 547.0[5]	3 191.0	3 273.0	...	...	...
M(V) - month mois	38 147.0[5]	39 050.0[5]	39 793.0[5]	3 879.0	3 979.0	...	...	...
F(V) - month mois	24 904.0[5]	25 396.0[5]	25 981.0[5]	2 032.0	2 090.0	...	...	...
Azerbaijan (manat) — Azerbaïdjan (manat)								
MF(I) - month mois	200 030.1	202 082.6	244 087.1	284 272.3	303 163.6	348 815.6	445 436.5	491 330.2
Bahrain [6,7] (Bahrain dinar) — Bahreïn [6,7] (dinar de Bahreïn)								
MF(I) - month mois	...	257.0	227.0	231.0	215.0	228.0	230.0	234.0
M(I) - month mois	...	276.0	250.0	255.0	241.0	252.0	250.0	249.0
F(I) - month mois	...	125.0	109.0	107.0	100.0	111.0	125.0	138.0
Belarus [8,9] (Belarussian rouble) — Bélarus [8,9] (rouble bélarussien)								
MF(I) - month mois	3 260.3	7 924.6	34 587.5	87.4[10]	165.0	220.3	297.0	...
M(I) - month mois	3 620.3	8 606.2	38 540.7	97.2[10]	181.9	245.8	334.2	...
F(I) - month mois	2 926.4	7 304.7	31 051.0	78.7[10]	150.4	198.8	265.5	...
Belgium [11] (euro) — Belgique [11] (euro)								
MF(I) - month mois	...	...	2 205.0	...	...	2 535.0	...	...
M(I) - month mois	...	...	2 284.0	...	...	...	...	...
F(I) - month mois	...	...	1 843.0	...	...	...	...	...
Bolivia [12] (boliviano) — Bolivie [12] (boliviano)								
MF(II) - month mois	873.0	972.0	1 055.0	1 120.0[13]	...	...	...	...
Botswana [14] (pula) — Botswana [14] (pula)								
MF(I) - month mois	598.0[16]	695.0[15]	785.0[16]	783.0[16]	891.0[16]	889.0[16]	944.0[15]	...
M(I) - month mois	...	821.0[15]	1 004.0[16]	1 067.0[16]	...	1 200.0[16]	1 296.0[15]	...
F(I) - month mois	...	447.0[15]	588.0[16]	555.0[16]	681.0[16]	651.0[16]	671.0[15]	...
Brazil [8] (real) — Brésil [8] (real)								
MF(I) - month mois	737.7	717.4	752.2	763.1	844.6	901.9	...	...
M(I) - month mois	826.5	800.6	844.5	854.2	946.9	1 009.8	...	...
F(I) - month mois	486.7	487.8	505.5	524.0	576.5	618.6	...	...
Bulgaria [17] (lev) — Bulgarie [17] (lev)								
MF(I) - month mois	148 460.0	194 612.0	203.0[18]	219.0	227.0	236.0	246.0	269.0
M(I) - month mois	172 043.0	224 492.0	232.0[18]	257.0	271.0	284.0	293.0	...
F(I) - month mois	123 423.0	163 045.0	172.0[18]	181.0	185.0	192.0	203.0	...
Cambodia [6] (riel) — Cambodge [6] (riel)								
MF(II) - month mois	...	243 000.0	...	...	243 000.0	...	...	...

Country or area § Pays ou zone §	1997	1998	1999	2000	2001	2002	2003	2004
Canada [19] (Canadian dollar) — Canada [19] (dollar canadien)								
MF(I) - week semaine	752.4	770.9	782.4	796.9	808.1	830.1	842.4	859.0
MF(II) - hour heure [20]	17.2	17.6	17.8	18.3	18.6	19.1	19.7	20.2
Chile [21,22] (Chilean peso) — Chili [21,22] (peso chilien)								
MF(I) - month mois	189 753.0	200 773.0	203 540.0	208 257.0	213 394.0	218 740.0	221 860.0	229 575.0
China [23,24] (yuan) — Chine [23,24] (yuan)								
MF(I) - month mois	494.4	588.7	649.5	729.2	814.5	916.8	1 041.3	...
China, Hong Kong SAR (Hong Kong dollar) — Chine, Hong Kong RAS (dollar de Hong Kong)								
MF(I) - month mois [25,26]	...	...	...	...	...	...	10 000.0	
MF(II) - day jour	322.6	335.3	334.7	335.4	342.6	326.1	322.2	324.3
M(II) - day jour	423.8	430.6	422.6	428.8	428.5	419.2	406.1	380.4
F(II) - day jour	258.8	262.9	268.9	278.1	280.6	268.2	262.7	280.0
MF(V) - month mois	11 331.2	11 711.6	11 853.0	11 869.7	12 133.1	11 950.7	11 508.8	11 498.1
M(V) - month mois	12 165.2	12 555.7	12 893.2	12 697.1	12 929.7	12 810.2	12 082.7	11 880.7
F(V) - month mois	10 467.0	10 915.9	10 846.7	11 101.4	11 395.0	11 123.2	11 021.1	11 139.3
China, Macao SAR [26] (Macao pataca) — Chine, Macao RAS [26] (pataca de Macao)								
MF(VI) - month mois	3 260.0	3 080.0	2 921.0	2 960.0	2 760.0	2 766.0	2 840.0	2 992.0
M(VI) - month mois	4 981.0	4 762.0	4 738.0	4 690.0	4 525.0	4 479.0	4 380.0	4 846.0
F(VI) - month mois	2 808.0	2 656.0	2 510.0	2 613.0	2 431.0	2 435.0	2 544.0	2 656.0
Colombia (Colombian peso) — Colombie (peso colombien)								
MF(I) - month mois	322 695.0 [16,28]	441 965.0 [16,28]	455 252.0 [16,28]	...	...	353 590.0 [27,29]	442 510.0 [27]	468 406.0 [27]
M(I) - month mois [27]	...	...	...	...	...	457 189.0 [29]	531 791.0	557 571.0
F(I) - month mois [27]	...	...	...	...	...	258 415.0 [29]	347 588.0	365 782.0
MF(VI) - month mois [16,28]	329 437.0	446 445.0	427 313.0	420 734.0	...	...	...	...
Costa Rica [30] (Costa Rican colón) — Costa Rica [30] (colón costa-ricien)								
MF(I) - month mois	75 672.0	85 899.0	97 774.5	108 777.0	128 207.0	...	...	...
M(I) - month mois	78 917.0	91 493.0	106 594.0	115 642.0	135 707.0	...	...	173 054.0
F(I) - month mois	67 531.0	73 122.0	77 969.3	93 773.0	112 596.0	...	...	135 471.0
Croatia [31] (kuna) — Croatie [31] (kuna)								
MF(I) - month mois	3 358.0	3 681.0	3 869.0	4 100.0	4 465.0	4 794.0	4 952.0	...
M(I) - month mois	...	...	...	...	...	...	5 412.0	...
F(I) - month mois	...	...	...	...	...	...	4 196.0	...
Cuba [32] (Cuban peso) — Cuba [32] (peso cubain)								
MF(I) - month mois	212.0	214.0	225.0	234.0	245.0	263.0 [33]	...	...
Cyprus [11,21,34] (Cyprus pound) — Chypre [11,21,34] (livre chypriote)								
MF(I) - hour heure	3.6	3.7	3.9	4.0	4.3	4.5	4.6	4.8
M(I) - hour heure	4.4	4.5	4.7	4.8	4.9	5.2	5.4	5.7
F(I) - hour heure	2.7	2.7	2.8	2.9	3.2	3.2	3.4	3.5
MF(II) - hour heure	3.2	3.3	3.4	3.5	3.7	3.9	4.1	4.2
M(II) - hour heure	3.8	4.0	4.1	4.2	4.3	4.6	4.8	5.0
F(II) - hour heure	2.4	2.5	2.6	2.7	2.8	2.7	2.9	2.9
MF(II) - week semaine	117.5	...	...	...	152.4	157.3	165.7	169.4
M(II) - week semaine	145.0	166.5	185.9	...	176.6	186.3	194.9	203.3
F(II) - week semaine	92.4	96.4	100.2	...	109.0	105.5	113.5	108.8
Czech Republic [35] (Czech koruna) — République tchèque [35] (couronne tchèque)								
MF(I) - month mois	10 411.0	11 513.0	12 271.0	13 188.0	14 130.0	14 897.0	15 842.0	17 035.0
Denmark [6,36] (Danish krone) — Danemark [6,36] (couronne danoise)								
MF(I) - hour heure	167.3	174.6	182.3	188.6	199.1	207.0	215.3	...
M(I) - hour heure	176.5	183.3	192.2	197.6	207.7	215.3	223.8	...
F(I) - hour heure	147.4	154.8	160.3	166.7	178.8	186.8	194.5	...
Dominican Republic (Dominican peso) — Rép. dominicaine (peso dominicain)								
MF(I) - hour heure	19.2	19.9	27.1	24.1	28.2	29.4	32.7	50.8
Ecuador (sucre, US dollar) — Equateur (sucre, dollar des Etats-Unis)								
MF(I) - month mois	2 179.7 [9,37]	3 252.0 [9,37]	4 158.3 [9,37]	346.7 [37]	203.7	...	...	...
MF(II) - hour heure	4 380.4 [37]	6 119.0 [37]	8 556.2 [37]	0.8 [37]	1.3	...	...	...

Country or area § Pays ou zone §	1997	1998	1999	2000	2001	2002	2003	2004
Egypt [7,11] (Egyptian pound) — Egypte [7,11] (livre égyptienne)								
MF(II) - week semaine	103.0	107.0	121.0	125.0	136.0	147.0	150.0	...
M(II) - week semaine	107.0	112.0	125.0	131.0	142.0	154.0	157.0	...
F(II) - week semaine	80.0	77.0	94.0	87.0	97.0	104.0	104.0	...
El Salvador (El Salvadoran colón, US dollar) — El Salvador (cólon salvadorien, dollar des Etats-Unis)								
MF(I) - month mois	...	1 993.4[39]	1 746.6[39]	1 790.0[39]	1 750.4[39]	208.7[39]	209.6	...
M(I) - month mois	...	2 348.5[39]	2 157.8[39]	2 241.1[39]	2 117.4[39]	253.8[39]	249.6	...
F(I) - month mois	...	1 646.0[39]	1 337.1[39]	1 370.4[39]	1 370.5[39]	167.7[39]	171.2	...
MF(II) - hour heure [38]	...	10.3[39]	10.7[39]	10.1[39]	...	1.2[39]	1.3	...
M(II) - hour heure [38]	...	12.0[39]	12.1[39]	11.4[39]	10.3[39]	1.3[39]	1.5	...
F(II) - hour heure [38]	...	9.0[39]	9.2[39]	9.0[39]	9.5[39]	1.1[39]	1.2	...
Estonia (Estonian kroon) — Estonie (couronne estonienne)								
MF(I) - month mois	3 578.0	4 081.0	4 117.0	4 772.0	5 149.0	5 665.0	6 177.0	6 696.0
Fiji [40] (Fiji dollar) — Fidji [40] (dollar des Fidji)								
MF(II) - day jour	15.1	14.5	15.2	...	...	...	...	...
MF(II) - hour heure	2.2	2.2	...	...	...	...	...	...
Finland [41] (Finnish markka, euro) — Finlande [41] (markka finlandais, euro)								
MF(I) - month mois	11 677.0[42]	12 054.0[42]	12 510.0[42]	13 124.0[42]	2 275.0	2 357.0	...	...
M(I) - month mois	12 523.0[42]	12 880.0[42]	13 305.0[42]	13 939.0[42]	2 402.0	2 475.0	...	...
F(I) - month mois	9 842.0[42]	10 237.0[42]	10 683.0[42]	11 239.0[42]	1 969.0	2 063.0	...	...
France [43] (euro) — France [43] (euro)								
MF(I) - month mois	...	...	1 459.4	1 477.0	1 506.9	1 562.7	...	...
M(I) - month mois	...	...	1 573.8	1 591.0	1 618.5	1 668.8	...	...
F(I) - month mois	...	...	1 191.8	1 205.9	1 241.7	1 307.9	...	...
French Guiana (French franc, euro) — Guyane française (franc français, euro)								
MF(I) - hour heure	...	70.0[44]	70.7[44]	11.2	11.8	...	...	...
M(I) - hour heure	...	74.0[44]	74.5[44]	11.9	12.5	...	...	...
French Polynesia (CFP franc) — Polynésie française (franc CFP)								
M(I) - month mois	181 707.0	186 911.0	187 996.0	196 279.0	202 046.0	205 866.0	213 876.0	...
F(I) - month mois	149 640.0	153 351.0	160 946.0	165 206.0	176 580.0	177 719.0	186 653.0	...
Gambia [45,46] (dalasi) — Gambie [45,46] (dalasi)								
MF(I) - month mois	...	969.7	...	...	...	...	...	...
Georgia (lari) — Géorgie (lari)								
MF(I) - month mois	51.2	68.9	87.4	99.3	120.8	143.4	152.5	...
M(I) - month mois	...	...	101.1	111.2	141.5	165.1	174.9	...
F(I) - month mois	...	...	63.3	69.3	82.7	101.6	108.4	...
Germany (deutsche mark, euro) — Allemagne (deutsche mark, euro)								
MF(II) - hour heure	26.2[47]	26.8[47]	27.5[47]	27.8[47]	14.4	14.7	15.1	15.4
M(II) - hour heure	27.4[47]	28.0[47]	28.8[47]	29.1[47]	15.1	15.4	15.7	16.0
F(II) - hour heure	20.3[47]	20.8[47]	21.4[47]	21.4[47]	11.1	11.4	11.6	11.9
Gibraltar [11,49] (Gibraltar pound) — Gibraltar [11,49] (livre de Gibraltar)								
MF(II) - hour heure	...	6.6	6.8	6.4	6.6	7.0	7.2	8.0
M(II) - hour heure	...	6.8	7.0	6.6	6.7	7.2	7.2	8.1
F(II) - hour heure	...	4.9	5.3	5.3	5.7	5.7	5.9	6.0
MF(II) - week semaine	226.3	339.3	320.0	291.6	299.5	311.3	323.8	...
M(II) - week semaine	243.3	358.9	332.6	299.8	306.4	339.5	333.2	...
F(II) - week semaine	172.5	192.9	210.4	213.8	233.9	237.1	235.5	...
Greece [7,50] (drachma) — Grèce [7,50] (drachma)								
MF(II) - hour heure	1 470.5	1 539.8	...	...	...	...	...	...
M(II) - hour heure	1 585.9	1 653.0	...	...	...	...	...	...
F(II) - hour heure	1 287.8	1 355.8	...	...	...	...	...	...
MF(V) - month mois	399 599.0	423 142.0	...	...	...	...	...	...
M(V) - month mois	430 889.0	456 488.0	...	...	...	...	...	...
F(V) - month mois	303 900.0	323 153.0	...	...	...	...	...	...
Guadeloupe (French franc, euro) — Guadeloupe (franc français, euro)								
MF(I) - hour heure	...	62.1[44]	62.7[44]	9.8	10.3	...	...	...
M(I) - hour heure	...	65.2[44]	66.0[44]	10.4	10.8	...	...	...
F(I) - hour heure	...	58.2[44]	58.7[44]	9.2	9.7	...	...	...

Country or area § Pays ou zone §	1997	1998	1999	2000	2001	2002	2003	2004
Guatemala (quetzal) — Guatemala (quetzal)								
MF(I) - month mois	1 430.1	1 541.0	1 602.3	1 655.3	1 732.3	1 837.3	...	...
Hungary [41] (forint) — Hongrie [41] (forint)								
MF(I) - month mois	58 915.0[51]	68 872.0[51]	76 099.0[52]	88 551.0[52]	101 700.0[52]	114 297.0[52]	124 770.0[52]	136 520.0[52]
M(I) - month mois	68 396.0[51]	79 892.0[51]	86 866.0[52]	100 351.0[52]	115 830.0[52]	127 916.0[52]	140 244.0[52]	...
F(I) - month mois	46 897.0[51]	54 985.0[51]	61 898.0[52]	72 962.0[52]	82 761.0[52]	94 882.0[52]	102 585.0[52]	...
Iceland [29] (Icelandic króna) — Islande [29] (couronne islandaise)								
MF(I) - hour heure [53]	...	828.0	864.0	945.0	1 049.0	1 108.0	1 173.0	1 234.0
M(I) - hour heure [53]	...	902.0	957.0	1 044.0	1 153.0	1 216.0	1 295.0	1 353.0
F(I) - hour heure [53]	...	730.0	760.0	814.0	905.0	968.0	1 003.0	1 079.0
MF(I) - month mois [54]	...	128 300.0[27]	136 200.0	149 200.0	166 400.0	176 800.0	186 100.0	194 900.0
M(I) - month mois [54]	...	139 900.0[27]	150 800.0	164 600.0	182 600.0	194 000.0	206 000.0	214 000.0
F(I) - month mois [54]	...	114 600.0[27]	121 300.0	129 900.0	145 700.0	156 600.0	161 200.0	173 200.0
India (Indian rupee) — Inde (roupie indienne)								
MF(II) - month mois	1 137.3	1 211.1	1 548.5	1 280.8	1 893.2	1 158.6	...	...
Indonesia [8,9,55] (Indonesian rupiah) — Indonésie [8,9,55] (roupie indonésien)								
MF(II) - week semaine	52.4	64.2	75.3	98.0	129.2			
Iran (Islamic Rep. of) (Iranian rial) — Iran (Rép. islamique d') (rial iranien)								
MF(I) - month mois	471 489.0	567 630.0	698 899.0	867 526.0	1 014 285.0	...	...	...
M(I) - month mois	477 540.0	575 371.0	709 212.0	880 779.0	1 029 232.0	...	...	...
F(I) - month mois	385 983.0	455 132.0	554 231.0	685 514.0	828 265.0	...	...	...
Ireland [7] (euro) — Irlande [7] (euro)								
MF(II) - hour heure	8.8	9.3	9.8	10.4	11.5	12.3	12.9	13.5
M(II) - hour heure	9.7	10.2	10.7	11.4	12.4	13.3	13.8	14.4
F(II) - hour heure	7.2	7.6	8.0	8.6	9.4	10.1	10.7	11.2
MF(II) - week semaine	360.0	374.8	396.6	423.2	457.0	483.0	514.8	535.0
M(II) - week semaine	413.1	428.8	453.0	477.7	512.4	538.9	568.9	589.7
F(II) - week semaine	273.6	285.4	298.2	324.7	347.3	365.2	393.8	407.3
Isle of Man [40] (pound sterling) — Ile de Man [40] (livre sterling)								
MF(I) - hour heure	7.1	7.8	9.1	8.5	9.0	10.3	9.7	10.4
M(I) - hour heure	7.6	9.0	9.5	9.2	9.2	10.9	11.0	10.3
F(I) - hour heure	5.7	5.7	7.5	6.8	8.5	7.7	7.5	10.7
MF(I) - week semaine	292.7	313.3	377.1	366.9	361.4	392.0	409.6	412.4
M(I) - week semaine	320.5	366.0	408.9	407.3	381.5	417.3	504.5	455.4
F(I) - week semaine	215.8	209.6	241.1	258.2	278.3	292.8	253.9	265.2
Israel (new sheqel) — Israël (nouveau sheqel)								
MF(I) - hour heure	35.0	39.0	42.0	44.0	...	...	...	...
MF(I) - month mois [56,57]	...	...	...	...	9 088.0	9 179.0	9 218.0	...
Italy [58,59] (euro) — Italie [58,59] (euro)								
MF(II) - hour heure	105.7	108.6	110.9	113.1	101.4	104.2	106.9	110.0
MF(V) - hour heure	106.4	109.6	112.1	114.4	101.6	104.5	107.2	110.7
Jamaica (Jamaican dollar) — Jamaïque (dollar jamaïcain)								
MF(I) - week semaine	4 203.8	4 302.2	5 549.4	5 208.8	5 725.2	6 092.9	...	...
Japan [60,61] (yen) — Japon [60,61] (yen)								
MF(I) - month mois	287 200.0	289 600.0	291 100.0	293 100.0	297 500.0	296 400.0	296 500.0	...
M(I) - month mois	325 600.0	327 900.0	327 700.0	328 100.0	331 400.0	328 300.0	327 800.0	...
F(I) - month mois	184 500.0	187 300.0	189 000.0	190 700.0	195 000.0	195 600.0	195 800.0	...
Jordan [11] (Jordan dinar) — Jordanie [11] (dinar jordanien)								
MF(I) - day jour	5.7	5.9	5.5[62]	...	...	...	...	...
M(I) - day jour	6.0	6.2	5.8[62]	...	...	...	...	...
F(I) - day jour	3.6	3.7	4.0[62]	...	...	...	...	...
MF(I) - month mois	192.9	198.5	172.0	189.0	185.0	186.7	...	...
M(I) - month mois	203.5	210.6	180.0	198.0	195.0	196.0	...	...
F(I) - month mois	119.1	122.2	123.0	131.0	126.0	129.3	...	...
Kazakhstan (tenge) — Kazakhstan (tenge)								
MF(I) - month mois	11 092.0	11 357.0	13 821.0	17 717.0	19 982.0	22 130.0	24 823.0	30 234.0
M(I) - month mois	...	12 246.0	14 991.0	19 510.0	22 184.0	24 479.0	27 515.0	33 542.0
F(I) - month mois	...	9 641.0	11 433.0	13 981.0	15 597.0	17 433.0	19 382.0	23 433.0

Country or area § Pays ou zone §	1997	1998	1999	2000	2001	2002	2003	2004
Kenya [40,63] (Kenya shilling) — Kenya [40,63] (shilling du Kenya)								
MF(I) - month mois	5 510.8	...	...	...	...	...	...	...
M(I) - month mois	5 294.3	...	...	...	...	...	...	...
F(I) - month mois	6 509.5	...	...	...	...	...	...	...
Korea, Republic of [9,21,64] (Korean won) — Corée, République de [9,21,64] (won coréen)								
MF(I) - month mois	1 326.2	1 284.5	1 475.5	1 601.5	1 702.4	1 907.0	2 075.0	...
M(I) - month mois	1 527.2	1 467.3	1 686.3	1 826.4	1 936.4	2 177.0	...	...
F(I) - month mois	852.0	820.1	933.1	1 055.8	1 121.3	1 211.0	...	...
Kuwait (Kuwaiti dinar) — Koweït (dinar koweïtien)								
MF(I) - hour heure	1.2	1.2	1.2	1.4	...	...	...	...
Kyrgyzstan (Kyrgyz som) — Kirghizistan (som kirghize)								
MF(I) - month mois	844.7	1 405.8	1 962.3	2 020.1	2 390.6	2 833.5	3 182.6	...
Latvia [65] (lats) — Lettonie [65] (lats)								
MF(I) - month mois	114.7	128.3	129.0	135.1	140.3	145.5	159.3	176.4
M(I) - month mois	121.5	136.1	137.5	146.0	150.9	157.3	172.8	192.1
F(I) - month mois	107.9	119.2	118.5	122.9	127.1	131.1	142.0	155.9
Lithuania (litas) — Lituanie (litas)								
MF(I) - hour heure [66,67]	4.9[68]	5.9[68]	6.2[68]	6.2	6.3	6.5	6.6	6.9
M(I) - hour heure [66,67]	5.4[68]	6.6[68]	6.9[68]	6.9	7.1	7.2	7.5	7.7
F(I) - hour heure [66,67]	4.4[68]	5.1[68]	5.4[68]	5.5	5.5	5.7	5.8	5.9
MF(I) - month mois [41,68]	824.0	973.0	1 010.0	...	...	...	...	...
M(I) - month mois [41,68]	909.0	1 089.0	1 135.0	...	...	...	...	...
F(I) - month mois [41,68]	733.0	847.0	875.0	...	...	...	...	...
Luxembourg [11] (Luxembourg franc, euro) — Luxembourg [11] (franc luxembourgeois, euro)								
MF(II) - hour heure	465.0[69]	470.0[69]	12.2	12.5	12.6	13.1	13.5	14.2
M(II) - hour heure	485.0[69]	490.0[69]	12.7	13.1	13.1	13.6	14.0	14.7
F(II) - hour heure	335.0[69]	337.0[69]	8.7	9.4	9.5	9.8	10.2	10.6
MF(V) - month mois	145 433.0[69]	144 697.0[69]	3 680.0	3 995.0	3 816.0	3 941.0	4 090.0	4 189.0
M(V) - month mois	156 574.0[69]	155 036.0[69]	3 944.0	3 995.0	4 104.0	4 251.0	4 412.0	4 510.0
F(V) - month mois	97 209.0[69]	98 614.0[69]	2 535.0	2 621.0	2 710.0	2 782.0	2 911.0	3 030.0
Malaysia (ringgit) — Malaisie (ringgit)								
MF(I) - month mois	1 210.0	...	...	1 387.8	1 530.7	...	...	...
M(I) - month mois	1 449.0	...	...	...	...	...	...	...
F(I) - month mois	912.0	...	...	...	...	...	...	...
Malta (Maltese lira) — Malte (lire maltaise)								
MF(VI) - hour heure	...	...	...	2.1	2.2	2.3	2.3	2.3
M(VI)- hour heure	...	...	...	2.2	2.4	2.4	2.5	2.6
F(VI) - hour heure	...	...	...	1.8	1.9	2.1	2.2	2.2
Mauritius [70] (Mauritian rupee) — Maurice [70] (roupie mauricienne)								
MF(I) - month mois [7]	...	...	5 142.0	5 544.0	5 856.0	6 155.0	6 668.0	7 299.0
MF(II) - day jour [71]	148.7	161.4	166.0	174.3	...	...	...	...
MF(V) - month mois [7]	6 282.0	6 912.0	7 034.0	7 638.0	...	...	...	...
Mexico (Mexican peso) — Mexique (peso mexicain)								
MF(I) - day jour	78.0	92.0	108.7	125.6	143.6	...	...	...
MF(I) - hour heure	...	10.8	12.3	15.3	17.8	18.0	19.4	...
M(I) - hour heure	...	11.8	13.5	16.7	19.3	19.8	21.2	...
F(I) - hour heure	...	8.7	9.9	12.3	14.7	14.4	15.7	...
MF(I) - month mois	1 635.3	2 090.2	2 392.0	2 910.5	3 367.6	3 537.5	3 737.7	3 858.8
M(I) - month mois	1 798.0	2 307.0	2 646.6	3 254.0	3 740.8	3 963.0	4 136.9	4 230.4
F(I) - month mois	1 274.2	1 624.4	1 854.4	2 242.6	2 634.9	2 712.3	2 918.0	3 112.3
MF(II) - hour heure	12.4	14.8	17.8	20.8	23.5	25.2	26.9	...
Mongolia [9] (togrog) — Mongolie [9] (togrog)								
MF(I) - month mois	...	...	...	66.0[27]	...	68.7	82.7	92.8
M(I) - month mois	...	...	...	60.0[27]	65.9	69.3	86.9	98.1
F(I) - month mois	...	...	...	70.0[27]	64.8	68.2	75.6	89.1
Myanmar [72,73] (kyat) — Myanmar [72,73] (kyat)								
M(II) - hour heure	...	...	...	13.5	19.0	20.8	22.8	29.9
F(II) - hour heure	...	...	...	20.8	17.5	19.6	20.3	27.2

Country or area § Pays ou zone §	1997	1998	1999	2000	2001	2002	2003	2004
Netherlands [8,74,75] (Netherlands guilder, euro) — **Pays-Bas** [8,74,75] (florin néerlandais, euro)								
MF(I) - hour heure	31.1	32.0	33.3	34.4	...	...	...	...
M(I) - hour heure	32.3	33.4	34.7	35.8	...	...	...	...
F(I) - hour heure	24.8	25.7	26.9	28.0	...	...	...	...
MF(I) - month mois [76]	4 472.0	4 614.0	4 797.0	4 958.0	...	...	...	...
M(I) - month mois [76]	4 601.0	4 750.0	4 932.0	5 099.0	...	...	...	...
F(I) - month mois [76]	3 567.0	3 684.0	3 870.0	4 001.0	...	...	...	...
Netherlands Antilles [77] (Netherlands Antillean guilder) — **Antilles néerlandaises** [77] (florin des Antilles néerlandaises)								
MF(I) - month mois	2 591.0	2 462.0	...	2 565.0	...	...	...	...
New Caledonia (CFP franc) — **Nouvelle-Calédonie** (franc CFP)								
MF(I) - month mois	...	...	255 118.0	...	...	...	...	...
M(I) - month mois	...	...	275 779.0	...	...	...	...	...
F(I) - month mois	...	...	224 335.0	...	...	...	...	...
New Zealand [78,79,80] (New Zealand dollar) — **Nouvelle-Zélande** [78,79,80] (dollar néo-zélandais)								
MF(I) - hour heure	15.6	16.0	16.5	17.0	17.4	18.0	18.8	19.3
M(I) - hour heure	16.5	16.9	17.4	17.9	18.3	18.9	19.8	20.2
F(I) - hour heure	12.9	13.4	13.9	14.5	14.8	15.3	15.9	16.6
Nicaragua (córdoba) — **Nicaragua** (córdoba)								
MF(I) - month mois	2 724.0	2 846.0	3 097.7	3 221.9	3 272.9	3 276.0	3 279.0	3 283.0
Norway (Norwegian krone) — **Norvège** (couronne norvégienne)								
MF(I) - month mois [11,41,74]	20 005.0	21 417.0	22 441.0	23 388.0	24 426.0	25 991.0	26 944.0	27 920.0
M(I) - month mois [11,41,74]	20 571.0	22 017.0	23 039.0	23 964.0	25 006.0	26 623.0	27 625.0	28 588.0
F(I) - month mois [11,41,74]	17 839.0	19 109.0	20 017.0	21 091.0	22 051.0	23 483.0	24 260.0	25 290.0
MF(II) - hour heure [34,63]	118.9	125.5[81]	...	...	...	...	...	...
M(II) - hour heure [34,63]	121.6	128.3[81]	...	...	...	...	...	...
F(II) - hour heure [34,63]	106.1	112.4[81]	...	...	...	...	...	...
Occupied Palestinian Terr. [82,83] (new shekel) — **Terr. palestinien occupé** [82,83] (nouveau shekel)								
MF(I) - day jour	49.9	57.3	65.4	68.8	68.0	70.1	68.5	66.8
M(I) - day jour	53.2	61.1	69.3	73.2	73.5	74.7	71.7	70.9
F(I) - day jour	27.5	32.6	32.4	36.0	35.2	36.8	41.6	30.8
Pakistan (Pakistan rupee) — **Pakistan** (roupie pakistanaise)								
MF(I) - month mois	3 211.5	3 706.0	2 865.8	2 981.0	3 002.2	4 113.7	...	...
Panama [26,84] (balboa) — **Panama** [26,84] (balboa)								
MF(VI) - hour heure	...	...	...	...	...	1.8	1.7	1.9
M(VI)- hour heure	...	...	...	...	...	1.8	1.7	1.9
F(VI) - hour heure	...	...	...	...	...	1.9	1.8	2.1
Paraguay (guaraní) — **Paraguay** (guaraní)								
MF(I) - month mois	...	...	...	813 765.0	639 988.0	739 738.0	816 428.0	...
M(I) - month mois	...	...	...	995 539.0	746 213.0	880 891.0	966 821.0	...
F(I) - month mois	...	...	...	402 798.0	408 608.0	453 064.0	514 766.0	...
Peru (new sol) — **Pérou** (nouveau sol)								
MF(II) - day jour	24.5[38]	24.9[38]	25.6[38]	27.2[38]	27.1[38,85]	28.1[86]	27.2[38,87]	28.0[38,87]
MF(V) - month mois	1 875.2[38]	2 067.0[38]	2 155.6[38]	2 315.7[38]	2 286.8[38,85]	2 430.2[86]	2 356.1[38,87]	2 460.0[38,87]
Philippines [7,88] (Philippine peso) — **Philippines** [7,88] (peso philippin)								
MF(I) - month mois	7 283.0	7 734.0	8 347.0	...	9 644.0	...	...	...
M(I) - month mois	8 065.0	8 522.0	9 453.0	...	...	...	...	...
F(I) - month mois	6 310.0	6 810.0	7 168.0	...	...	...	...	...
Poland [63] (zloty) — **Pologne** [63] (zloty)								
MF(I) - month mois	1 014.9	1 164.4	1 598.9	1 756.4	1 866.5	1 911.5	1 980.7	2 134.4
Portugal (Portuguese escudo) — **Portugal** (escudo portugais)								
MF(I) - month mois	116 100.0	120 803.0	122 327.0	...	...	...	...	...
M(I) - month mois	136 900.0	140 720.0	146 138.0	...	...	...	...	...
F(I) - month mois	88 900.0	94 837.0	94 057.0	...	...	...	...	...
MF(II) - hour heure	539.0	...	...	...	...	...	...	...
M(II) - hour heure	626.0	...	...	...	...	...	...	...
F(II) - hour heure	434.0	...	...	...	...	...	...	...
Puerto Rico (US dollar) — **Porto Rico** (dollar des Etats-Unis)								
MF(II) - hour heure	8.0	8.4	8.9	9.4	9.8	10.3	10.5	10.8

Country or area § Pays ou zone §	1997	1998	1999	2000	2001	2002	2003	2004
Qatar [22,82] (Qatar riyal) — Qatar [22,82] (riyal qatarien)								
MF(VI) - month mois	…	…	…	…	1 546.0	…	…	…
M(VI) - month mois	…	…	…	…	1 543.0	…	…	…
F(VI) - month mois	…	…	…	…	2 987.0	…	…	…
Republic of Moldova [35] (Moldovan leu) — République de Moldova [35] (leu moldove)								
MF(I) - month mois	352.0	399.0	492.6	677.7	813.1	971.8	1 216.1	1 417.8
Romania (Romanian leu) — Roumanie (leu roumain)								
MF(I) - month mois	826 902.0	1 198 560.0	1 712 748.0	2 535 223.0	3 734 701.0	4 632 583.0	5 804 147.0	…
M(I) - month mois	…	…	…	…	…	…	6 662 800.0	…
F(I) - month mois	…	…	…	…	…	…	4 915 058.0	…
Russian Federation (ruble) — Fédération de Russie (ruble)								
MF(I) - month mois	919.0[10]	1 026.0	1 580.0	2 371.0	…	4 439.1	5 603.3	
Rwanda [89] (Rwanda franc) — Rwanda [89] (franc rwandais)								
MF(I) - month mois	27 659.0	…	…	…	…	…	…	…
Saint Helena [90] (pound sterling) — Sainte-Hélène [90] (livre sterling)								
MF(I) - month mois	236.3	246.8	237.5	263.1	263.4	296.8	…	…
M(I) - month mois	242.2	276.1	251.8	272.5	272.9	317.1	…	…
F(I) - month mois	215.7	129.9	195.3	222.4	229.0	229.5	…	…
Saint Lucia [91] (EC dollar) — Sainte-Lucie [91] (dollar des Caraïbes orientales)								
M(II) - hour heure [92]	…	…	…	5.3	6.3	5.3	…	…
F(II) - hour heure [93]	…	…	…	4.4	4.1	4.5	…	…
M(V) - hour heure	…	…	…	10.8	10.0	21.5	…	…
F(V) - hour heure	…	…	…	8.2	10.2	14.9	…	…
M(V) - month mois	…	…	…	1 919.8	1 656.3	2 901.7	…	…
F(V) - month mois	…	…	…	1 477.3	1 588.0	2 435.1	…	…
St. Vincent-Grenadines (EC dollar) — St. Vincent-Grenadines (dollar des Caraïbes orientales)								
MF(II) - day jour	25.0	25.0	25.8	25.8	26.5	26.5	…	…
San Marino (Italian lira, euro) — Saint-Marin (lire italienne, euro)								
MF(I) - day jour [94]	142 712.0	149 357.0	157 158.0	…	…	…	…	…
MF(I) - month mois	…	…	…	…	3 289 004.2[95]	1 868.2	1 922.1	1 900.0
Saudi Arabia (Saudi Arabian riyal) — Arabie saoudite (riyal saoudien)								
MF(I) - week semaine	657.0	…	…	…	…	…	…	…
Serbia and Montenegro (Yugoslav dinar) — Serbie-et-Monténégro (dinar yougoslave)								
MF(I) - month mois	647.0[13,96]	823.0[96]	1 053.0[13,96,97]	2 230.0[96,97]	4 786.0[96,97]	11 065.0[96,97]	12 996.0[97]	
Seychelles (Seychelles rupee) — Seychelles (roupie seychelloises)								
MF(I) - month mois	2 727.0	2 853.0	2 962.0	3 067.0	3 235.0	3 300.0	2 986.0	3 042.0
Singapore (Singapore dollar) — Singapour (dollar singapourien)								
MF(I) - month mois	2 486.7	2 716.0[98]	2 803.0	3 036.0	3 117.0	3 154.0	3 265.0	3 350.0
M(I) - month mois	2 999.7	3 311.0[98]	3 384.0	3 653.0	3 752.0	3 762.0	3 881.0	…
F(I) - month mois	1 811.0	1 916.0[98]	2 007.0	2 181.0	2 226.0	2 283.0	2 374.0	…
Slovakia [99] (Slovak koruna) — Slovaquie [99] (couronne slovaque)								
MF(I) - month mois	9 197.0	9 980.0	10 758.0	11 722.0	12 908.0	13 837.0	14 873.0	16 378.0
Slovenia (tolar) — Slovénie (tolar)								
MF(I) - month mois	118 960.0	132 080.0	144 110.0	161 296.0	178 596.0	196 220.0	211 060.0	226 029.0
South Africa (rand) — Afrique du Sud (rand)								
MF(I) - month mois	3 408.0	3 803.0	4 018.0	4 323.0	4 701.0	5 197.0[81]	…	…
Spain [100] (peseta) — Espagne [100] (peseta)								
MF(I) - hour heure	1 372.0	1 429.0	1 463.0	1 499.0[81]	…	…	…	…
Sri Lanka [73] (Sri Lanka rupee) — Sri Lanka [73] (roupie sri-lankaise)								
MF(II) - day jour	166.3	174.2	199.2	222.5	230.7	273.1	306.3	309.0
M(II) - day jour	167.8	175.6	203.9	222.6	233.1	278.1	311.2	312.1
F(II) - day jour	142.5	145.7	165.8	185.6	201.3	235.1	253.0	270.0
MF(II) - hour heure	18.2	20.3	22.0	24.9	27.1	31.9	33.2	35.5
M(II) - hour heure	18.4	20.8	22.3	25.3	27.5	32.1	33.6	35.8
F(II) - hour heure	16.3	16.4	18.1	20.4	22.6	28.0	28.9	31.2

Country or area § Pays ou zone §	1997	1998	1999	2000	2001	2002	2003	2004
Swaziland [6,40] (lilangeni) — Swaziland [6,40] (lilangeni)								
M(III) - month mois [101]	2 948.0	...	...	...	...	...	...	...
F(III) - month mois [101]	1 850.0	...	...	...	...	...	...	...
M(IV) - month mois [102]	863.0	...	...	...	...	...	...	...
F(IV) - month mois [102]	542.0	...	...	...	...	...	...	...
Sweden [103,104] (Swedish krona) — Suède [103,104] (couronne suédoise)								
MF(II) - hour heure	101.2[87]	105.1[105]	106.9[105]	111.3[105]	114.9[16]	118.2[16]	122.0[16]	126.1[16]
M(II) - hour heure	103.3[87]	107.0[105]	108.7[105]	113.3[105]	116.9[16]	120.2[16]	124.1[16]	128.4[16]
F(II) - hour heure	93.4[87]	97.6[105]	99.6[105]	103.4[105]	106.6[16]	109.4[16]	112.9[16]	116.8[16]
Switzerland [106] (Swiss franc) — Suisse [106] (franc suisse)								
MF(I) - month mois	...	5 717.0	...	5 862.0	...	6 155.0	...	...
M(I) - month mois	...	6 128.0	...	6 296.0	...	6 552.0	...	...
F(I) - month mois	...	4 413.0	...	4 550.0	...	4 926.0	...	...
Tajikistan [107] (somoni) — Tadjikistan [107] (somoni)								
MF(I) - month mois	14 977.0	...	...	...	...	...	...	...
Thailand (baht) — Thaïlande (baht)								
MF(II) - month mois	...	...	...	5 839.0	6 064.6	...	...	...
M(II) - month mois	...	...	...	6 612.0	7 112.7	...	...	...
F(II) - month mois	...	...	...	5 052.0	5 122.4	...	...	...
TFYR of Macedonia [83] (TFYR Macedonian denar) — L'ex-R.y. Macédoine [83] (denar de l'ex-R.Y. Macédoine)								
MF(I) - month mois	...	...	...	...	9 577.0	9 944.0	10 028.0	10 486.0
Trinidad and Tobago (Trinidad and Tobago dollar) — Trinité-et-Tobago (dollar de la Trinité-et-Tobago)								
MF(I) - week semaine	865.4	908.7	938.8	1 170.1	1 161.2	1 161.6	...	...
Turkey [7] (new Turkish Lira) — Turquie [7] (nouveau livre turque)								
MF(I) - day jour [9]	3 215.5	5 859.0	10 477.2	16 225.0	21 882.0	...	...	...
MF(I) - hour heure [108,109]	428.7	781.6	1 397.0	2 163.3	2 917.6	...	...	...
MF(I) - month mois [108,110]	77 171.2	140 683.6	251 453.0	389 395.8	525 175.7	...	...	...
Ukraine (hryvnia) — Ukraine (hryvnia)								
MF(I) - month mois	148.8	159.7	191.3	270.7	368.3	441.3	552.9	700.6
M(I) - month mois	...	...	...	...	...	509.0	640.8	809.0
F(I) - month mois	...	...	...	...	...	358.9	443.5	562.9
United Kingdom (pound sterling) — Royaume-Uni (livre sterling)								
MF(I) - hour heure	7.5[111,112]	9.4[113,114]	9.8[113,115]	10.1[113,115]	10.7[113,115]	11.1[113,115]	11.7[113,115]	10.5[111,112]
M(I) - hour heure	8.2[111,112]	10.0[113,114]	10.3[113,115]	10.6[113,115]	11.2[113,115]	11.6[113,115]	12.1[113,115]	11.0[111,112]
F(I) - hour heure	5.7[111,112]	7.3[113,114]	7.7[113,115]	8.0[113,115]	8.5[113,115]	9.0[113,115]	9.6[113,115]	9.1[111,112]
MF(I) - week semaine	330.0[111,112]	392.4[113,114]	402.7[113,115]	417.2[113,115]	439.9[113,115]	455.6[113,115]	476.5[113,115]	438.0[111,112]
M(I) - week semaine	358.0[111,112]	423.1[113,114]	431.7[113,115]	445.6[113,115]	464.9[113,115]	482.9[113,115]	503.0[113,115]	462.0[111,112]
F(I) - week semaine	236.0[111,112]	273.7[113,114]	299.3[113,115]	312.1[113,115]	332.2[113,115]	350.8[113,115]	372.8[113,115]	346.0[111,112]
United States [116,117] (US dollar) — Etats-Unis [116,117] (dollar des Etats-Unis)								
MF(II) - hour heure	13.1	13.5	13.9	14.3	14.8	15.3	15.7	16.1
United States Virgin Is. (US dollar) — Iles Vierges américaines (dollar des Etats-Unis)								
MF(II) - hour heure	18.1	...	...	...	...	...	...	...
Uruguay [38,45] (Uruguayan peso) — Uruguay [38,45] (peso uruguayen)								
MF(I) - month mois	...	...	...	6 855.0	6 856.0	...	...	...
Uzbekistan (Uzbek sum) — Ouzbékistan (sum ouzbek)								
MF(I) - month mois	3 681.0	5 424.0	8 823.0	...	...	...	...	...
Venezuela (Bolivarian Republic of) [13] (bolívar) — Venezuela (République bolivarienne du) [13] (bolívar)								
MF(I) - month mois	141 122.0	...	...	...	...	...	...	...
Zimbabwe (Zimbabwe dollar) — Zimbabwe (dollar zimbabwéen)								
MF(I) - hour heure	16.4	20.5	29.4	45.9	80.2	144.0	...	...
MF(I) - month mois	2 619.8	3 276.8	4 700.4	7 351.1	12 823.7	...	...	...

Source

International Labour Office (ILO), Geneva, the ILO labour statistics database and the "Yearbook of Labour Statistics 2005".
Data are classified according to ISIC Rev. 3 except for the following countries whose data are classified according to Rev.2:

Source

Bureau international du Travail (BIT), Genève, la base de données du BIT et "Annuaire des statistiques du travail 2005".
Les données sont classifiées selon la CITI-Rév. 3 à l'exception des données des pays suivants qui sont classifiées selon la CITI-Rév. 2:

Albania: prior to 1992; Anguilla: prior to 1996; Argentina: prior to 1995; Australia: prior to 1996; Austria: prior to 1995; Azerbaijan: prior to 1997; Belgium: prior to 1995; Bolivia: prior to 1996; Botswana: prior to 1998; Brazil: prior to 1994; British Virgin Islands: prior to 1998; Bulgaria: prior to 1996; Canada: prior to 1993; China: prior to 1995; China, Macao SAR: prior to 1998; Colombia: prior to 2001; Costa Rica: prior to 1999; Croatia: prior to 1996; Cyprus: prior to 1998; Denmark: prior to 1993; Ecuador: prior to 1995; Egypt: prior to 1996; El Salvador: prior to 1997; Finland: prior to 1995; France: prior to 1997; Gambia: prior to 1988; Germany: prior to 1996; Gibraltar: prior to 1998; Hungary: prior to 1992; Ireland: prior to 1999; Isle of Man: prior to 1995; Israel: prior to 1994; Italy: prior to 1996; Jordan: prior to 1994; Kazakhstan: prior to 1993; Korea, Republic of: prior to 1993; Luxembourg: prior to 1995; Mauritius: prior to 1999; Mexico: prior to 1995; Netherlands Antilles: prior to 1989; Netherlands: prior to 1994; New Zealand: prior to 1998; Norway: prior to 1997; Panama: prior to 1996; Paraguay: prior to 2000; Peru: prior to 1995; Philippines: prior to 1996; Poland: prior to 1993; Portugal: prior to 1998; Republic of Moldova: prior to 1996; Romania: prior to 1994; Russian Federation: prior to 1997; San Marino: prior to 2000; Seychelles: prior to 1986; Singapore: prior to 1998; Slovakia: prior to 1990; Slovenia: prior to 1994; Spain: prior to 1996; Sweden: prior to 1993; Switzerland: prior to 1994; Thailand: prior to 2001; Turkey: prior to 1997; Ukraine: prior to 2002; United States: prior to 1993; Uruguay: prior to 2000; Yugoslavia: prior to 1990.

Albanie: avant 1992; Allemagne: avant 1996; Anguilla: avant 1996; Antilles néerlandaises: avant 1989; Argentine: avant 1995; Australie: avant 1996; Autriche: avant 1995; Azerbaïdjan: avant 1997; Belgium: avant 1995; Bolivie: avant 1996; Botswana: avant 1998; Brésil: avant 1994; Bulgarie: avant 1996; Canada: avant 1993; Chine: avant 1995; Chine, Macao RAS: avant 1998; Chypre: avant 1998; Colombie: avant 2001; Corée, République de: avant 1993; Costa Rica: avant 1999; Croatie: avant 1996; Danemark: avant 1993; Egypte: avant 1996; El Salvador: avant 1997; Equateur: avant 1995; Espagne: avant 1996; Etats-Unis: avant 1993; Fédération de Russie: avant 1997; Finlande: avant 1995; France: avant 1997; Gambie: avant 1988; Gibraltar: avant 1998; Hongrie: avant 1992; Ile de Man: avant 1995; Iles Vierges britanniques: avant 1998; Irlande: avant 1999; Israël: avant 1994; Italie: avant 1996; Jordanie: avant 1994; Kazakhstan: avant 1993; Luxembourg: avant 1995; Maurice: avant 1999; Mexique: avant 1995; Norvège: avant 1997; Nouvelle-Zélande: avant 1998; Panama: avant 1996; Paraguay: avant 2000; Pays-Bas: avant 1994; Pérou: avant 1995; Philippines: avant 1996; Pologne: avant 1993; Portugal: avant 1998; République de Moldova: avant 1996; Roumanie: avant 1994; Saint-Marin: avant 2000; Seychelles: avant 1986; Singapour: avant 1998; Slovaquie: avant 1990; Slovénie: avant 1994; Suède: avant 1993; Suisse: avant 1994; Thaïlande: avant 2001; Turquie: avant 1997; Ukraine: avant 2002; Uruguay: avant 2000; Yougoslavie: avant 1990.

Notes

§ I.   Employees.
  II.   Wage earners.
  III.   Skilled wage earners.
  IV.   Unskilled wage earners.
  V.   Salaried employees.
  VI.   Total employment.

[1] Production and related workers.
[2] Local units with 10 or more workers.
[3] May of each year.
[4] Full-time adult non-managerial employees.
[5] Prior to 2000: ATS;1 Euro = 13.7603 ATS.
[6] Private sector.
[7] Establishments with 10 or more persons employed.
[8] December of each year.
[9] Figures in thousands.
[10] New denomination: 1 new rouble = 1,000 old roubles.
[11] October of each year.
[12] Main cities, except Pando.
[13] September.
[14] Citizens only.
[15] March.
[16] September of each year.
[17] Employees under labour contract.
[18] New denomination: 1 new lev = 1,000 old leva.
[19] Including overtime.
[20] Employees paid by the hour.
[21] Including family allowances and the value of payments in kind.
[22] April of each year.
[23] State-owned units, urban collective-owned units and other ownership units.
[24] For statistical purposes, the data for China do not include those for the Hong Kong Special Administrative Region (Hong Kong SAR), Macao Special Administrative Region (Macao SAR) and Taiwan Province of China.
[25] Including outworkers.
[26] Median.
[27] Fourth quarter.

Notes

§ I.   Salariés.
  II.   Ouvriers.
  III.   Ouvriers qualifiés.
  IV.   Ouvriers non qualifiés.
  V.   Employés.
  VI.   Emploi total.

[1] Ouvriers à la production et assimilés.
[2] Unités locales occupant 10 ouvriers et plus.
[3] Mai de chaque année.
[4] Salariés adultes à plein temps, non compris les cadres dirigeants.
[5] Avant 2000: ATS; 1 Euro = 13,7603 ATS.
[6] Secteur privé.
[7] Etablissements occupant 10 personnes et plus.
[8] Décembre de chaque année.
[9] Données en milliers.
[10] Nouvelle dénomination: 1 nouveau rouble = 1,000 anciens roubles.
[11] Octobre de chaque année.
[12] Villes prinipales, sauf Pando.
[13] Septembre.
[14] Nationaux seulement.
[15] Mars.
[16] Septembre de chaque année.
[17] Salariés sous contrat de travail.
[18] Nouvelle dénomination: 1 nouveau lev = 1,000 anciens leva.
[19] Y compris les heures supplémentaires.
[20] Salariés rémunérés à l'heure.
[21] Y compris les allocations familiales et la valeur des paiements en nature.
[22] Avril de chaque année.
[23] Unités d'Etat, unités collectives urbaines et autres.
[24] Pour la présentation des statistiques, les données pour Chine ne comprennent pas la Région Administrative Spéciale de Hong Kong (Hong Kong RAS), la Région Administrative Spéciale de Macao (Macao RAS) et la province de Taiwan.
[25] Y compris les travailleurs externes.
[26] Médiane.
[27] Quatrième trimestre.

28 Seven main cities.	28 Sept villes principales.
29 Methodology revised.	29 Méthodologie révisée.
30 Usual hours; main occupation; July of each year.	30 Heures habituelles; occupation principale; juillet de chaque année.
31 Excluding employees in craft and trade.	31 Non compris les salariés dans l'artisanat et dans le commerce.
32 State sector (civilian).	32 Secteur d'Etat (civils).
33 Incl. employment-related allowances received from the State.	33 Y compris les allocations en espèces liées à l'emploi et reçues de l'Etat.
34 Adults.	34 Adultes.
35 Enterprises with 20 or more employees.	35 Entreprises occupant 20 salariés et plus.
36 Excluding young people aged less than 18 years and trainees.	36 Non compris les jeunes gens âgés de moins de 18 ans et les apprentis.
37 Prior to March 2000: sucres; 25,000 sucres =1 US dollar.	37 Avant mars 2000: sucres; 25 000 sucres = 1 dollar EU.
38 Urban areas.	38 Régions urbaines.
39 Prior to 2002: colones; 8.75 colones=1 US dollar.	39 Avant 2002: colones; 8.75 colones=1 dollar EU.
40 June of each year.	40 Juin de chaque année.
41 Full-time employees.	41 Salariés à plein temps.
42 Prior to 2001: FIM; 1 Euro = 5.94573 FIM.	42 Avant 2001: FIM; 1 Euro = 5.94573 FIM.
43 Net earnings.	43 Gains nets.
44 Prior to 2000: FRF; 1 Euro=6.55957 FRF.	44 Avant 2000: FRF; 1 Euro=6,55957 FRF.
45 Establishments with 5 or more persons employed.	45 Entreprises occupant 5 salariés et plus.
46 Survey results influenced by a low response rate.	46 Résultats de l'enquête influencés par un taux de réponse faible.
47 Prior to 2001: DEM; 1 Euro = 1.95583 DEM.	47 Avant 2001: DEM; 1 Euro = 1.95583 DEM.
48 Prior to 1999: DEM; 1 Euro=1.95583 DEM.	48 Avant 1999: DEM; 1 Euro=1.95583 DEM.
49 Excluding part-time workers and juveniles.	49 Non compris les travailleurs à temps partiel et les jeunes.
50 Prior to 1999: GRD; 1 Euro = 340.750 GRD.	50 Avant 1999: GRD; 1 Euro=340.750 GRD.
51 Prior to 1999: enterprises with more than 20 employees.	51 Avant 1999: entreprises occupant moins de 20 salariés.
52 Enterprises with 5 or more employees.	52 Entreprises occupant 5 salariés et plus.
53 Adult employees; excluding irregular bonuses and the value of payments in kind.	53 Salariés adultes; non compris les prestations versées irrégulièrement et la valeur des paiements en nature.
54 Adult employees; excluding overtime payments and payments in kind.	54 Salariés adultes; non compris la rémunération des heures supplémentaires et la valeur des paiements en nature.
55 Production workers.	55 Travailleurs à la production.
56 Israeli workers only.	56 Travailleurs israéliens seulement.
57 Including payments subject to income tax.	57 Y compris les versements soumis à l'impôt sur le revenu.
58 Index of hourly wage rates.	58 Indice des taux de salaires horaires
59 December 2000=100.	59 Décembre 2000=100.
60 Private sector; establishments with 10 or more regular employees; June of each year .	60 Secteur privé; établissements occupant 10 salariés stables ou plus; juin de chaque années.
61 Regular scheduled cash earnings.	61 Gains en espèce tarifés réguliers.
62 Prior to 1999: establishments with 5 or more persons employed.	62 Avant 1999: établissements occupant 5 personnes et plus.
63 Including the value of payments in kind.	63 Y compris la valeur des paiements en nature.
64 Establishments with 10 or more regular employees.	64 Etablissements occupant 10 salariés stables ou plus.
65 Beginning 1997: first quarter of each year.	65 A partir de 1997 : le primer trimestre de chaque année.
66 Excluding individual unincorporated enterprises.	66 Non compris les entreprises individuelles non constituées en société.
67 All employees converted into full-time units.	67 Ensemble des salariés convertis en unités à plein temps.
68 April.	68 Avril.
69 Prior to 1999: LUF; 1 Euro = 40.3399 LUF.	69 Avant 1999: LUF; 1 Euro=40.3399 LUF.
70 March of each year.	70 Mars de chaque année.
71 Wage-earners on daily rates of pay.	71 Ouvriers rémunérés sur la base de taux de salaire journaliers.
72 Regular employees.	72 Salariés stables.
73 March and Sep. of each year	73 Mars et sept. de chaque année.
74 Excluding overtime payments.	74 Non compris la rémunération des heures supplémentaires.
75 Prior to 2001: NLG; 1 Euro = 2.20371 NLG.	75 Avant 2001: NGL; 1 Euro = 2.20371 NLG.
76 Full-time employees only.	76 Salariés à plein temps seulement.
77 Curaçao.	77 Curaçao.
78 February of each year.	78 Février de chaque année.
79 Establishments with the equivalent of more than 0.5 full-time paid employees.	79 Etablissements occupant plus de l'équivalent de 0.5 salarié à plein temps.
80 Full-time equivalent employees.	80 Salariés en équivalents à plein temps.
81 Series discontinued.	81 Série arrêtée.
82 Persons aged 15 years and over.	82 Personnes âgées de 15 ans et plus.
83 Net earnings.	83 Gains nets.

[84] August.	[84] Août.
[85] Average of the first three quarters.	[85] Moyenne des trois premiers trimestres.
[86] Metropolitan Lima.	[86] Lima métropolitaine.
[87] Second quarter.	[87] Deuxième trimestre.
[88] Computed on the basis of annual wages.	[88] Calculés sur la base de salaires annuels.
[89] June.	[89] Juin.
[90] Year ending in March of the year indicated.	[90] Année se terminant en mars de l'année indiquée.
[91] Unweighted survey results.	[91] Résultats d'enquête non pondérés.
[92] Per month.	[92] Par mois.
[93] Minimum rates actually paid.	[93] Taux minima effectivement payés.
[94] Prior to 2000: ITL; 1 Euro=1936.27 ITL.	[94] Avant 2000: ITL; 1 Euro=1936,27 ITL.
[95] Prior to 2002: ITL; 1 Euro=1936.27 ITL.	[95] Avant 2002: ITL; 1 Euro=1936,27 ITL.
[96] Prior to 2002: excl. private sector; net earnings.	[96] Avant 2002: non compris le secteur privé; gains nets.
[97] As from 1999: excluding Kosovo and Metohia.	[97] A partir de 1999: non compris Kosovo et Metohia.
[98] Methodology revised; data not strictly comparable.	[98] Méthodologie révisée; les données ne sont pas strictement comparables.
[99] Excluding enterprises with less than 20 employees.	[99] Non compris les entreprises occupant moins de 20 salariés.
[100] Prior to 2001: ESP; 1 Euro = 166.386 ESP.	[100] Avant 2001: ESP; 1 Euro = 166,386 ESP.
[101] Skilled wage earners.	[101] Ouvriers qualifiés.
[102] Unskilled wage earners.	[102] Ouvriers non qualifiés.
[103] Excl. holidays, sick-leave and overtime payments.	[103] Non compris les versements pour les vacances, congés maladie ainsi que la rémunération des heures supplémentaires.
[104] Private sector; adults.	[104] Secteur privé; adultes.
[105] September-October of each year.	[105] Septembre-Octobre de chaque année.
[106] Standardised monthly earnings (40 hours x 4 1/3 weeks).	[106] Gains mensuels standardisés (40 heures x 4 1/3 semaines).
[107] Including major divisions 2 and 4.	[107] Y compris les branches 2 et 4.
[108] Figures in thousands; Jan - June.	[108] Chiffres en milliers; jan - juin.
[109] Excluding overtime payments and irregular bonuses and allowances.	[109] Non compris la rémunération des heures supplémentaires et les prestations versées irrégulièrement.
[110] Including overtime payments and irregular bonuses and allowances.	[110] Y compris la rémunération des heures supplémentaires et les prestations versées irrégulièrement.
[111] Average: spring of each year.	[111] Moyenne: printemps de chaque année.
[112] Full-time employees; labour force sample survey.	[112] Salariés à plein temps, enquête par sondage sur la main d'oeuvre.
[113] Including overtime payments.	[113] Y compris la rémunération des heures supplémentaires.
[114] Results with imputation and weighting. New series: revised methodology. April; full-time employees on adult rates.	[114] Résultats après imputation et pondération. Nouvelle série: méthodologie révisée. Avril; salariés à plein temps rémunérés sur la base de taux de salaires pour adultes.
[115] Results with imputation and weighting. April; full-time employees on adult rates.	[115] Résultats après imputation et pondération. Avril; salariés à plein temps rémunérés sur la base de taux de salaires pour adultes.
[116] National classification not strictly compatible with ISIC.	[116] Classification nationale non strictement compatible avec la CITI.
[117] Private sector; production workers.	[117] Secteur privé. Travailleurs à la production.

28

Producer price indices
Index base: 2000 = 100

Indices des prix à la production
Indices base: 2000 = 100

Country or area	1998	1999	2000	2001	2002	2003	2004	Pays ou zone
Argentina								**Argentine**
Domestic supply [1,2]	100	96	100	98	173	204	219	Offre intérieure [1,2]
Domestic production	100	96	100	98	168	200	216	Production intérieure
Agricultural products [2]	129	103	100	98	233	264	271	Produits agricoles [2]
Industrial products [2,3]	102	99	100	96	158	190	205	Produits industriels [2,3]
Imported goods [3]	106	100	100	97	253	258	265	Produits importés [3]
Australia [4,5]								**Australie** [4,5]
Domestic supply	94	96	100	102	103	105	107	Offre intérieure
Domestic production	93	97	100	102	104	106	113	Production intérieure
Agricultural products	87	96	100	118	123	123	...	Produits agricoles
Industrial products [2,3,6]	92	96	100	103	...	104	108	Produits industriels [2,3,6]
Imported goods	94	92	100	...	101	93	88	Produits importés
Raw materials	89	93	100	102	101	101	104	Matières premières
Intermediate goods	91	94	100	101	102	102	104	Produits intermédiaires
Consumer goods	94	96	100	102	105	104	103	Biens de consommation
Capital goods	93	96	100	102	105	106	109	Biens d'équipement
Austria								**Autriche**
Domestic supply [2,7]	97	96	100	102	101	103	108	Offre intérieure [2,7]
Agricultural products	100	98	100	104	102	108	109	Produits agricoles
Intermediate goods	...	...	100	...	...	102	113	Produits intermédiaires
Consumer goods [2]	97	97	100	102	103	105	106	Biens de consommation [2]
Capital goods [2]	103	102	100	100	100	100	100	Biens d'équipement [2]
Bangladesh [5]								**Bangladesh** [5]
Domestic supply [2,7]	95	102	100	100	102	108	112	Offre intérieure [2,7]
Agricultural products [2,8]	94	103	100	99	102	108	112	Produits agricoles [2,8]
Industrial products [2,3,8]	100	93	100	101	105	107	110	Produits industriels [2,3,8]
Raw materials	...	102	100	101	103	113	107	Matières premières
Belarus [9]								**Bélarus** [9]
Industrial products	...	...	...	...	1 729 746	2 376 575	2 949 064	Produits industriels
Consumer goods	...	311 826	...	...	2 066 288	2 525 710	3 066 546	Biens de consommation
Capital goods	...	231 992	...	...	1 633 020	2 351 105	2 950 505	Biens d'équipement
Belgium								**Belgique**
Domestic production	...	...	100	...	102	103	107	Production intérieure
Agricultural products [2]	98	97	100	104	...	...	...	Produits agricoles [2]
Industrial products	92	92	100	100	101	100	...	Produits industriels
Intermediate goods	87	87	100	101	101	102	108	Produits intermédiaires
Consumer goods	98	97	100	98	99	97	99	Biens de consommation
Capital goods	101	100	100	100	100	100	...	Biens d'équipement
Bolivia								**Bolivie**
Industrial products	93	95	100	102	104	107	...	Produits industriels
Raw materials	113	106	100	107	108	117	...	Matières premières
Consumer goods	90	93	100	101	103	106	...	Biens de consommation
Capital goods	97	98	100	103	109	110	...	Biens d'équipement
Botswana								**Botswana**
Domestic supply	91	95	100	105	112	123	...	Offre intérieure
Brazil								**Brésil**
Domestic supply [10]	73	85	100	113	130	164	185	Offre intérieure [10]
Agricultural products [10]	70	82	100	117	142	186	197	Produits agricoles [10]
Industrial products [10]	74	86	100	111	127	161	180	Produits industriels [10]
Raw materials [10]	71	85	100	113	133	169	191	Matières premières [10]
Consumer goods [10]	73	84	100	109	130	165	176	Biens de consommation [10]
Capital goods	81	90	100	109	121	147	...	Biens d'équipement
Bulgaria								**Bulgarie**
Domestic supply	83	85	100	104	105	110	117	Offre intérieure
Canada [11]								**Canada** [11]
Raw materials	75	82	100	99	98	100	...	Matières premières
Chile								**Chili**
Domestic supply	85	90	100	108	115	123	126	Offre intérieure
Domestic production	86	90	100	106	112	120	126	Production intérieure
Agricultural products	95	92	100	99	113	113	120	Produits agricoles
Industrial products [7]	85	90	100	107	112	121	125	Produits industriels [7]
Imported goods	83	91	100	114	124	131	125	Produits importés

Country or area	1998	1999	2000	2001	2002	2003	2004	Pays ou zone
China, Hong Kong SAR								**Chine, Hong Kong RAS**
Industrial products	101	100	100	98	93	95	98	Produits industriels
Colombia [12]								**Colombie** [12]
Domestic supply [2]	80	84	100	107	117	124	...	Offre intérieure [2]
Domestic production	81	85	100	108	115	123	...	Production intérieure
Agricultural products	84	87	100	108	117	120	...	Produits agricoles
Industrial products	79	83	100	107	116	124	...	Produits industriels
Imported goods	77	80	100	105	121	127	...	Produits importés
Raw materials	77	83	100	107	116	127	...	Matières premières
Intermediate goods	80	83	100	106	116	124	...	Produits intermédiaires
Capital goods	...	82	100	106	122	...	...	Biens d'équipement
Croatia								**Croatie**
Agricultural products	99	97	100	108	92	91	95	Produits agricoles
Industrial products	89	91	100	104	95	95	98	Produits industriels
Consumer goods	99	99	100	100	101	104	102	Biens de consommation
Capital goods	92	95	100	98	96	93	92	Biens d'équipement
Cyprus [13]								**Chypre** [13]
Industrial products	92	94	100	...	...	108	...	Produits industriels
Czech Republic								**République tchèque**
Agricultural products	104	92	100	108	98	96	...	Produits agricoles
Industrial products	94	95	100	103	...	102	...	Produits industriels
Denmark								**Danemark**
Domestic supply [2,10]	94	94	100	102	102	102	105	Offre intérieure [2,10]
Domestic production [2,10]	94	95	100	103	103	105	109	Production intérieure [2,10]
Imported goods [10]	93	93	100	101	100	99	100	Produits importés [10]
Raw materials	80	78	100	99	94	94	106	Matières premières
Consumer goods	97	98	100	103	104	105	107	Biens de consommation
Ecuador								**Equateur**
Domestic supply	19	38	100	100	...	...	125	Offre intérieure
Domestic production	27	46	100	117	...	...	...	Production intérieure
Agricultural products	...	...	100	117	...	...	...	Produits agricoles
Egypt [5]								**Egypte** [5]
Domestic supply [7]	101	102	100	98	...	...	139	Offre intérieure [7]
Raw materials	103	102	100	98	...	...	162	Matières premières
Intermediate goods	105	101	100	98	...	...	143	Produits intermédiaires
Capital goods	104	101	100	99	...	...	146	Biens d'équipement
El Salvador								**El Salvador**
Domestic supply [14]	99	97	100	...	...	...	...	Offre intérieure [14]
Domestic production	96	99	100	...	...	...	...	Production intérieure
Imported goods	97	97	100	...	...	...	...	Produits importés
Finland								**Finlande**
Domestic supply	93	92	100	100	99	98	100	Offre intérieure
Domestic production	94	94	100	102	101	101	101	Production intérieure
Industrial products	...	...	100	...	96	95	96	Produits industriels
Imported goods	88	89	100	97	94	94	97	Produits importés
Raw materials	92	90	100	98	99	96	99	Matières premières
Consumer goods [15]	98	99	100	102	93	98	96	Biens de consommation [15]
Capital goods	97	97	100	101	94	90	89	Biens d'équipement
France								**France**
Agricultural products	102	98	100	103	...	...	...	Produits agricoles
Intermediate goods	97	96	100	102	101	101	104	Produits intermédiaires
Consumer goods	...	...	100	...	...	101	101	Biens de consommation
Capital goods	...	...	100	...	...	101	101	Biens d'équipement
Germany								**Allemagne**
Domestic supply	98	97	100	104	104	103	104	Offre intérieure
Agricultural products	99	94	100	104	98	98	99	Produits agricoles
Industrial products	100	99	100	106	106	104	106	Produits industriels
Imported goods	89	90	100	101	...	96	97	Produits importés
Intermediate goods	100	...	100	111	111	100	102	Produits intermédiaires
Consumer goods	102	...	100	106	106	104	104	Biens de consommation
Capital goods	102	...	100	92	93	102	102	Biens d'équipement

Country or area	1998	1999	2000	2001	2002	2003	2004	Pays ou zone
Greece								**Grèce**
Domestic supply [16,17]	92	94	100	103	105	107	111	Offre intérieure [16,17]
Domestic production [16,17]	93	95	100	102	105	108	110	Production intérieure [16,17]
Agricultural products [16,18]	96	98	100	110	122	133	...	Produits agricoles [16,18]
Industrial products [16,17]	92	95	100	103	105	108	...	Produits industriels [16,17]
Imported goods [16,17]	93	94	100	102	102	103	104	Produits importés [16,17]
Intermediate goods	...	...	100	105	105	106	109	Produits intermédiaires
Consumer goods	...	...	100	105	108	111	116	Biens de consommation
Capital goods	...	...	100	101	102	103	107	Biens d'équipement
Guatemala								**Guatemala**
Domestic supply	87	91	100	105	109	114	120	Offre intérieure
Domestic production	88	91	100	107	112	115	121	Production intérieure
Agricultural products	87	91	100	108	109	112	112	Produits agricoles
Industrial products	89	90	100	106	...	117	127	Produits industriels
Imported goods	87	91	100	103	106	112	118	Produits importés
India [19]								**Inde** [19]
Domestic supply	94	97	100	105	107	113	120	Offre intérieure
Agricultural products	91	95	100	97	102	108	99	Produits agricoles
Industrial products [3]	98	100	100	102	111	109	117	Produits industriels [3]
Raw materials [20]	94	98	100	100	97	110	119	Matières premières [20]
Indonesia								**Indonésie**
Domestic supply [17]	79	88	100	114	117	120	130	Offre intérieure [17]
Domestic production	73	80	100	116	126	130	135	Production intérieure
Agricultural products	65	88	100	124	134	134	138	Produits agricoles
Industrial products [3]	75	95	100	111	122	127	133	Produits industriels [3]
Imported goods [17]	90	93	100	112	111	109	120	Produits importés [17]
Raw materials	79	78	100	110	110	116	137	Matières premières
Intermediate goods	84	91	100	114	119	119	130	Produits intermédiaires
Consumer goods	68	90	100	119	...	126	129	Biens de consommation
Capital goods	84	99	100	108	107	107	112	Biens d'équipement
Iran (Islamic Rep. of) [2,8]								**Iran (Rép. islamique d')** [2,8]
Domestic supply	73	85	100	110	119	...	...	Offre intérieure
Domestic production	74	86	100	...	...	...	...	Production intérieure
Agricultural products	73	87	100	108	122	...	...	Produits agricoles
Industrial products	61	75	100	93	97	...	...	Produits industriels
Imported goods	75	85	100	149	...	...	...	Produits importés
Raw materials	73	83	100	112	118	...	...	Matières premières
Ireland								**Irlande**
Domestic supply [2,21]	94	94	100	100	103	98	...	Offre intérieure [2,21]
Agricultural products [2,21]	98	93	100	105	100	91	102	Produits agricoles [2,21]
Industrial products [2,3,21]	94	95	100	102	101	92	...	Produits industriels [2,3,21]
Capital goods [8]	94	96	100	98	92	80	...	Biens d'équipement [8]
Israel [17]								**Israël** [17]
Industrial products	92	98	100	101	105	108	113	Produits industriels
Italy								**Italie**
Domestic supply [2,17]	95	94	100	102	102	105	107	Offre intérieure [2,17]
Intermediate goods	92	91	100	102	100	103	108	Produits intermédiaires
Consumer goods	98	98	100	102	104	107	108	Biens de consommation
Capital goods	98	99	100	101	102	103	105	Biens d'équipement
Japan								**Japon**
Domestic supply [2]	102	99	100	100	99	96	97	Offre intérieure [2]
Domestic production	101	100	100	99	98	98	96	Production intérieure
Agricultural products [8]	99	103	100	101	100	98	102	Produits agricoles [8]
Industrial products [8]	101	100	100	99	98	95	96	Produits industriels [8]
Imported goods	91	91	100	96	94	93	104	Produits importés
Raw materials	93	88	100	104	104	108	117	Matières premières
Intermediate goods	101	99	100	100	99	97	99	Produits intermédiaires
Consumer goods	103	101	100	100	99	95	95	Biens de consommation
Capital goods	105	102	100	99	97	89	87	Biens d'équipement
Jordan [2]								**Jordanie** [2]
Domestic supply	106	104	100	99	97	98	106	Offre intérieure

Country or area	1998	1999	2000	2001	2002	2003	2004	Pays ou zone
Korea, Republic of								**Corée, République de**
Domestic supply	100	98	100	100	99	101	108	Offre intérieure
Agricultural products [8,22]	94	104	100	104	106	113	127	Produits agricoles [8,22]
Industrial products	101	98	100	98	96	98	105	Produits industriels
Raw materials	88	81	100	102	104	110	132	Matières premières
Intermediate goods	106	96	100	100	96	98	107	Produits intermédiaires
Consumer goods	98	100	100	101	100	102	105	Biens de consommation
Capital goods	108	103	100	99	95	94	96	Biens d'équipement
Kuwait								**Koweït**
Domestic supply	101	100	100	102	105	107	...	Offre intérieure
Domestic production	100	100	100	100	102	102	...	Production intérieure
Agricultural products	100	97	100	96	103	106	...	Produits agricoles
Industrial products	101	100	100	102	105	...	...	Produits industriels
Imported goods	101	99	100	102	106	109	...	Produits importés
Raw materials	97	99	100	105	108	...	...	Matières premières
Intermediate goods	106	102	100	100	104	...	...	Produits intermédiaires
Consumer goods	100	99	100	100	103	...	...	Biens de consommation
Capital goods	103	100	100	106	115	...	...	Biens d'équipement
Latvia								**Lettonie**
Domestic supply	104	99	100	102	...	106	115	Offre intérieure
Lithuania								**Lituanie**
Domestic supply	81	84	100	98	93	92	100	Offre intérieure
Luxembourg								**Luxembourg**
Industrial products	100	96	100	101	100	100	109	Produits industriels
Imported goods	96	94	100	103	104	107	116	Produits importés
Intermediate goods	100	94	100	99	97	98	111	Produits intermédiaires
Consumer goods [15]	98	99	100	109	111	105	105	Biens de consommation [15]
Capital goods	97	97	100	102	104	105	109	Biens d'équipement
Malaysia								**Malaisie**
Domestic supply	100	97	100	95	99	105	114	Offre intérieure
Domestic production	100	97	100	94	99	106	117	Production intérieure
Imported goods	99	99	100	100	99	100	102	Produits importés
Mexico								**Mexique**
Domestic supply [7,23]	299	346	100	106	110	119	126	Offre intérieure [7,23]
Agricultural products	266	332	100	110	115	128	136	Produits agricoles
Industrial products	...	343	100	104	107	116	120	Produits industriels
Raw materials	80	89	100	...	103	116	...	Matières premières
Consumer goods [8,23]	307	346	100	106	118	120	124	Biens de consommation [8,23]
Capital goods [7,8,23]	284	326	100	105	108	117	130	Biens d'équipement [7,8,23]
Morocco								**Maroc**
Domestic supply [24]	132	134	...	...	...	...	...	Offre intérieure [24]
Agricultural products	98	96	100	99	102	97	97	Produits agricoles
Industrial products	96	96	100	98	97	98	103	Produits industriels
Netherlands								**Pays-Bas**
Agricultural products [25,26]	96	93	100	105	103	...	...	Produits agricoles [25,26]
Industrial products	92	93	100	92	92	93	96	Produits industriels
Imported goods	77	80	100	74	72	72	78	Produits importés
Raw materials	82	84	100	82	80	80	86	Matières premières
Intermediate goods	91	90	100	91	10	92	96	Produits intermédiaires
Consumer goods	90	91	100	90	90	92	94	Biens de consommation
Capital goods	98	99	100	95	97	99	100	Biens d'équipement
New Zealand								**Nouvelle-Zélande**
Agricultural products [2]	89	89	100	124	123	112	113	Produits agricoles [2]
Industrial products [2,27]	92	93	100	105	105	103	106	Produits industriels [2,27]
Intermediate goods [28]	93	94	100	107	107	106	108	Produits intermédiaires [28]
Norway								**Norvège**
Domestic supply	94	96	100	105	105	106	107	Offre intérieure
Domestic production	...	...	100	105	106	106	107	Production intérieure
Industrial products	94	96	100	102	101	102	105	Produits industriels
Imported goods	97	95	100	106	...	...	...	Produits importés
Raw materials	92	93	100	99	88	89	98	Matières premières
Intermediate goods	97	97	100	101	99	99	104	Produits intermédiaires
Consumer goods	96	98	100	104	104	104	106	Biens de consommation
Capital goods	98	99	100	102	104	97	108	Biens d'équipement

Country or area	1998	1999	2000	2001	2002	2003	2004	Pays ou zone
Oman [29]								**Oman** [29]
Domestic supply	...	...	100	104	102	104	107	Offre intérieure
Pakistan [5]								**Pakistan** [5]
Domestic supply [2,7]	95	96	100	102	108	113	120	Offre intérieure [2,7]
Agricultural products	98	98	100	102	106	108	119	Produits agricoles
Industrial products	95	98	100	102	104	109	113	Produits industriels
Raw materials	109	104	100	101	116	125	122	Matières premières
Panama								**Panama**
Domestic supply	90	92	100	97	94	95	100	Offre intérieure
Peru								**Pérou**
Domestic supply	91	96	100	101	100	102	109	Offre intérieure
Domestic production	92	96	100	101	100	102	107	Production intérieure
Agricultural products [30]	115	105	100	104	97	97	107	Produits agricoles [30]
Industrial products [3,8]	89	94	100	102	101	103	108	Produits industriels [3,8]
Imported goods	86	94	100	101	100	103	108	Produits importés
Philippines [31]								**Philippines** [31]
Domestic supply	93	98	100	102	106	...	...	Offre intérieure
Portugal								**Portugal**
Domestic supply	85	86	100	101	92	104	106	Offre intérieure
Intermediate goods	96	95	100	101	98	101	103	Produits intermédiaires
Consumer goods	97	97	100	104	102	106	106	Biens de consommation
Capital goods	...	...	100	102	102	103	105	Biens d'équipement
Romania								**Roumanie**
Industrial products	45	65	100	140	175	209	248	Produits industriels
Serbia and Montenegro								**Serbie-et-Monténégro**
Domestic supply [32]	100	135	...	...	...	...	...	Offre intérieure [32]
Agricultural products	27	39	100	170	...	...	...	Produits agricoles
Industrial products	34	48	100	185	...	...	...	Produits industriels
Consumer goods	38	54	100	201	...	...	...	Biens de consommation
Capital goods	28	44	100	143	...	...	...	Biens d'équipement
Singapore								**Singapour**
Domestic supply [7]	89	91	100	98	97	99	102	Offre intérieure [7]
Domestic production [2,3]	94	94	100	98	101	97	96	Production intérieure [2,3]
Imported goods	90	92	100	100	100	100	99	Produits importés
Slovakia [24]								**Slovaquie** [24]
Agricultural products	...	...	...	...	...	139	151	Produits agricoles
Slovenia								**Slovénie**
Agricultural products [33]	123	124	...	...	...	...	...	Produits agricoles [33]
Industrial products	91	93	100	109	115	118	123	Produits industriels
Intermediate goods	...	...	100	109	114	116	123	Produits intermédiaires
Consumer goods	90	94	100	110	118	123	126	Biens de consommation
Capital goods	92	96	100	104	107	106	108	Biens d'équipement
South Africa								**Afrique du Sud**
Domestic supply [34]	87	91	100	108	124	126	127	Offre intérieure [34]
Domestic production [34]	89	93	100	108	122	127	130	Production intérieure [34]
Agricultural products	94	96	100	113	140	132	131	Produits agricoles
Industrial products [3]	90	93	100	108	122	125	128	Produits industriels [3]
Imported goods	81	87	100	110	127	122	117	Produits importés
Spain								**Espagne**
Domestic supply [17]	94	95	100	102	102	104	107	Offre intérieure [17]
Consumer goods	97	99	100	104	106	108	111	Biens de consommation
Capital goods	98	99	100	101	103	104	106	Biens d'équipement
Sri Lanka								**Sri Lanka**
Domestic supply	94	93	100	...	...	...	...	Offre intérieure
Domestic production	89	91	100	...	...	...	...	Production intérieure
Imported goods	86	85	100	...	...	...	...	Produits importés
Consumer goods	101	101	100	...	...	...	...	Biens de consommation
Capital goods	96	104	100	...	...	...	...	Biens d'équipement
Sweden [17,35]								**Suède** [17,35]
Domestic supply [2]	94	95	100	103	104	103	105	Offre intérieure [2]
Domestic production [2]	97	96	100	103	103	103	106	Production intérieure [2]
Imported goods	90	93	100	105	105	102	105	Produits importés

Producer price indices — Index base: 2000 = 100 (*continued*)
Indices des prix à la production — Indices base: 2000 = 100 (*suite*)

Country or area	1998	1999	2000	2001	2002	2003	2004	Pays ou zone
Switzerland								**Suisse**
Domestic supply [2,7]	99	97	100	100	...	...	...	Offre intérieure [2,7]
Domestic production [2,7]	100	99	100	101	...	...	...	Production intérieure [2,7]
Agricultural products [2]	98	95	100	110	...	...	...	Produits agricoles [2]
Industrial products	102	101	100	99	...	...	...	Produits industriels
Imported goods [7]	96	94	100	98	...	...	...	Produits importés [7]
Raw materials	96	93	100	89	...	...	...	Matières premières
Intermediate goods	101	...	100	101	...	...	...	Produits intermédiaires
Consumer goods	99	99	100	102	...	...	...	Biens de consommation
Capital goods	100	...	100	101	...	...	...	Biens d'équipement
Syrian Arab Republic								**Rép. arabe syrienne**
Domestic supply	105	105	100	96	101	...	...	Offre intérieure
Agricultural products [24]	...	141	...	...	...	...	...	Produits agricoles [24]
Raw materials	99	104	100	99	100	...	...	Matières premières
Intermediate goods	103	94	100	...	...	...	...	Produits intermédiaires
Consumer goods [24]	149	149	...	...	...	...	...	Biens de consommation [24]
Thailand								**Thaïlande**
Domestic supply [2,10]	94	88	100	93	94	108	...	Offre intérieure [2,10]
Agricultural products	118	102	100	105	116	128	...	Produits agricoles
Industrial products [3]	99	96	100	102	103	106	...	Produits industriels [3]
Raw materials	125	99	100	108	111	120	...	Matières premières
Intermediate goods	105	101	100	101	101	108	...	Produits intermédiaires
Consumer goods	106	98	100	105	110	116	...	Biens de consommation
Capital goods	...	97	100	103	106	106	...	Biens d'équipement
TFYR of Macedonia								**L'ex-R.y. Macédoine**
Domestic supply	92	92	100	...	...	...	...	Offre intérieure
Agricultural products	109	103	100	...	...	...	...	Produits agricoles
Industrial products	92	92	100	...	...	...	...	Produits industriels
Consumer goods	97	98	100	...	...	...	...	Biens de consommation
Capital goods	97	99	100	...	...	...	...	Biens d'équipement
Trinidad and Tobago								**Trinité-et-Tobago**
Domestic supply [24]	124	126	126	128	129	130	...	Offre intérieure [24]
Industrial products	97	99	100	101	101	103	...	Produits industriels
Tunisia								**Tunisie**
Agricultural products	96	97	100	102	107	111	116	Produits agricoles
Industrial products	97	99	100	102	105	108	111	Produits industriels
Turkey								**Turquie**
Domestic supply [2,17,36]	43	66	100	162	243	305	368	Offre intérieure [2,17,36]
Agricultural products	51	72	100	142	223	298	...	Produits agricoles
Industrial products	41	64	100	167	247	306	...	Produits industriels
United Kingdom								**Royaume-Uni**
Domestic supply	98	99	100	100	100	101	104	Offre intérieure
Domestic production	97	98	100	100	100	102	104	Production intérieure
Agricultural products	120	102	100	107	100	110	178	Produits agricoles
Industrial products [3]	100	99	100	100	101	101	102	Produits industriels [3]
Imported goods	90	89	100	98	94	96	95	Produits importés
Raw materials	94	93	100	100	96	96	99	Matières premières
Intermediate goods	95	96	100	100	97	100	107	Produits intermédiaires
Consumer goods	97	99	100	102	103	104	106	Biens de consommation
Capital goods	101	101	100	99	99	96	94	Biens d'équipement
United States								**Etats-Unis**
Domestic supply [2]	94	95	100	101	99	104	110	Offre intérieure [2]
Agricultural products [2]	105	99	100	104	99	112	125	Produits agricoles [2]
Industrial products [2,37]	93	94	100	101	98	103	109	Produits industriels [2,37]
Raw materials	81	82	100	99	90	113	132	Matières premières
Intermediate goods	95	95	100	100	99	104	110	Produits intermédiaires
Consumer goods	93	95	100	102	101	105	110	Biens de consommation
Capital goods	99	99	100	101	100	101	102	Biens d'équipement
Uruguay [38]								**Uruguay** [38]
Domestic supply [2,7]	94	94	100	...	...	...	...	Offre intérieure [2,7]
Domestic production	94	94	100	107	141	195	...	Production intérieure
Agricultural products	102	93	100	110	166	250	...	Produits agricoles
Industrial products [7]	92	94	100	106	132	177	...	Produits industriels [7]
Imported goods	83	88	100	...	...	...	...	Produits importés

Country or area	1998	1999	2000	2001	2002	2003	2004	Pays ou zone
Venezuela (Bolivarian Rep.)								**Venezuela (Rép. bolivarienne)**
Domestic supply [7]	76	88	100	115	...	253	...	Offre intérieure [7]
Domestic production [7]	73	86	100	115	...	237	...	Production intérieure [7]
Agricultural products [7]	44	61	100	141	...	159	...	Produits agricoles [7]
Industrial products [7]	76	88	100	112	...	191	...	Produits industriels [7]
Imported goods [7]	82	91	100	108	...	294	...	Produits importés [7]
Raw materials	80	85	100	123	...	...	...	Matières premières
Zimbabwe [24]								**Zimbabwe [24]**
Domestic supply	662	1 048	...	...	...	...	...	Offre intérieure
Domestic production	661	1 048	...	...	...	...	...	Production intérieure

Source

United Nations Statistics Division, New York, price statistics database.

Source

Organisation des Nations Unies, Division de statistique, New York, la base de données pour les statistiques des prix.

Notes

[1] Domestic agricultural products only.
[2] Including exported products.
[3] Manufacturing industry only.
[4] Including service industries.
[5] Annual average refers to average of 12 months ending June.
[6] Prices relate only to products for sale or transfer to other sectors or for use as capital equipment.
[7] Excluding mining and quarrying.
[8] Including imported products.
[9] Index base: 1993 = 100.
[10] Agricultural products and products of manufacturing industry.
[11] Valued at purchasers' values.
[12] Beginning 1999, annual average refers to average of 12 months ending May.
[13] For government-controlled areas.
[14] San Salvador.
[15] Durable goods only.
[16] Finished products only.
[17] Excluding electricity, gas and water.
[18] Including mining and quarrying.
[19] Annual average refers to average of 12 months ending March.
[20] Primary articles include food, non-food articles and minerals.
[21] Excluding Value Added Tax.
[22] Including marine foods.
[23] Mexico City.
[24] Index base: 1990 = 100.
[25] Excluding forestry, fishing and hunting.
[26] Crop growing production only, excluding livestock production.
[27] Including all outputs of manufacturing.
[28] Including all industrial inputs.
[29] Muscat.
[30] Excluding fishing.
[31] Metro Manila.
[32] Index base: 1998 = 100.
[33] Index base: 1995 = 100.
[34] Excluding gold mining.
[35] Excluding agriculture.
[36] Excluding industrial finished goods.
[37] Excluding foods and feeds production.
[38] Montevideo.

Notes

[1] Produits agricoles interiérs seulement.
[2] Y compris les produits exportés.
[3] Industries manufacturières seulement.
[4] Y compris industries de service.
[5] Le moyen annuel est le moyen de douze mois finissant juin.
[6] Uniquement les prix des produits destinés à être vendus ou transférés à d'autres secteurs ou à être utilisés comme biens d'équipment.
[7] Non compris les industries extractives.
[8] Y compris les produits importés.
[9] Indice base: 1993 = 100.
[10] Produits agricoles et produits des industries manufacturières.
[11] A la valeur d'acquisition.
[12] A partir de 1999, la moyenne annuelle est la moyenne de 12 mois finissant mai.
[13] Pour les zones contrôlées par le Gouvernement.
[14] San Salvador.
[15] Biens durables seulement.
[16] Produits finis uniquement.
[17] Non compris l'électricité, le gaz et l'eau.
[18] Y compris les industries extractives.
[19] Le moyen annuel est le moyen de douze mois finissant mars.
[20] Les articles primaires comprennent des articles des produits alimentaires, non- alimentaires et des minéraux.
[21] Non compris taxe sur la valeur ajoutée.
[22] Y compris l'alimentation marine.
[23] Mexico.
[24] Indice base: 1990 = 100.
[25] Non compris sylviculture, pêche et chasse.
[26] Cultures uniquement, non compris les produits de l'élevage.
[27] Y compris toute la production du secteur manufacturière.
[28] Tous les intrants industriels.
[29] Muscat.
[30] Non compris la pêche.
[31] L'agglomération de Manille.
[32] Indice base : 1998 = 100.
[33] Indice base : 1995 = 100.
[34] Non compris l'extraction de l'or.
[35] Non compris l'agriculture.
[36] Non compris les produits finis industriels.
[37] Non compris les produits alimentaires et d'affourage.
[38] Montevideo.

Consumer price indices
General and food (Index base: 2000 = 100)

Indices des prix à la consommation
Généraux et alimentation (Indices base : 2000 = 100)

Country or area	1997	1998	1999	2000	2001	2002	2003	2004	Pays ou zone
Albania									**Albanie**
General	82.5	99.6	100.0	100.0	103.1[2]	108.4	110.8	114.0	Généraux
Food (1992 = 100) [1]	357.8	433.2	431.9	...	...	...	...	...	Alimentation (1992 = 100) [1]
Food	...	...	...	100.0	103.7	110.2	115.0	114.9	Alimentation
Algeria									**Algérie**
General	92.8	98.6	100.6	100.0	103.5	105.8	109.5	114.5	Généraux
Food	94.7	101.2	102.2	100.0	104.4	106.2	111.0	116.4	Alimentation
American Samoa									**Samoa américaines**
General [3]	95.7[4]	...	98.2[5]	100.0	101.4	103.6	108.6	116.3	Généraux [3]
Food	100.9[4]	...	99.9[5]	100.0	101.6	103.1	109.7	123.5	Alimentation
Angola [6]									**Angola** [6]
General	3.3	6.8	23.5	100.0	252.6	527.6[2]	1 045.8	1 501.2	Généraux
Food	3.0	6.7	25.7	100.0	251.1	508.6[2]	...	...	Alimentation
Anguilla									**Anguilla**
General	89.6	91.9	92.5	100.0	102.3[2]	102.9	106.1	111.0	Généraux
Food	97.7	96.9	98.9	100.0	101.9[2]	102.4	99.8	104.0	Alimentation
Antigua and Barbuda									**Antigua-et-Barbuda**
General	95.0	98.2	99.3	100.0	101.5	...	...	...	Généraux
Food	93.9	95.3	98.2	100.0	103.6	...	...	...	Alimentation
Argentina [6,7]									**Argentine** [6,7]
General	101.2	102.1	100.9	100.0[2]	98.9	124.5	141.3	147.5	Généraux
Food	104.9	106.6	102.7	100.0[2]	98.1	132.0	157.3	165.1	Alimentation
Armenia									**Arménie**
General	92.1	100.1	100.8	100.0	103.1	104.2[2]	109.2	116.3	Généraux
Food	106.1	112.6	106.3	100.0	104.7	107.0[2]	114.4	125.8	Alimentation
Aruba									**Aruba**
General	92.3	94.0	96.1	100.0	102.9[2]	106.3	110.2	113.0	Généraux
Food	94.3	96.2	98.2	100.0	103.3[2]	106.7	110.1	114.4	Alimentation
Australia									**Australie**
General	93.5	94.3	95.7	100.0	104.4	107.6	110.5	113.1	Généraux
Food	91.9	94.4	97.6	100.0	106.5	110.4	114.4	117.1	Alimentation
Austria									**Autriche**
General	96.3	97.1	97.7	100.0[2]	102.7	104.5	105.9	108.1	Généraux
Food	97.3	99.0	98.9	100.0[2]	103.3	105.2	107.3	109.5	Alimentation
Azerbaijan									**Azerbaïdjan**
General	108.2	107.4	98.2	100.0	101.5	104.4	106.7	113.9	Généraux
Food [8]	111.3	109.8	97.7	100.0	102.7	106.5	109.9	120.9	Alimentation [8]
Bahamas									**Bahamas**
General	95.9	97.2	98.4	100.0	102.1	104.2	107.4	108.6	Généraux
Food	96.1	98.2	98.4	100.0	102.1	104.1	104.7	107.8	Alimentation
Bahrain									**Bahreïn**
General	102.4	102.1	100.7	100.0	98.8	98.3	100.0	...	Généraux
Food	101.2	102.3	101.3	100.0	98.6	97.6	96.2	...	Alimentation
Bangladesh [9]									**Bangladesh** [9]
General	84.9	92.2	97.9	100.0	101.5	105.4	111.5[2]	118.4	Généraux
Food	82.1	90.7	98.0	100.0	100.8	103.4	110.1[2]	118.3	Alimentation
Barbados									**Barbade**
General	97.3	96.1	97.6	100.0	102.6[2]	103.0	104.6	106.1	Généraux
Food	99.4	95.2	97.5	100.0	105.2[2]	107.1	110.1	115.0	Alimentation
Belarus									**Bélarus**
General	5.5	9.5	37.2	100.0	161.1	229.8	295.0	348.3	Généraux
Food	5.2	9.1	37.7	100.0	156.8	217.9	267.6	320.1	Alimentation

Country or area	1997	1998	1999	2000	2001	2002	2003	2004	Pays ou zone
Belgium									**Belgique**
General	95.5	96.4	97.5	100.0	102.5	104.2	105.8	108.0	Généraux
Food	97.2	98.9	99.1	100.0	104.2	106.5	108.7	110.4	Alimentation
Belize									**Belize**
General	101.5	100.6	99.4	100.0	101.2	103.4	106.1	...	Généraux
Food [8]	102.1	101.1	99.4	100.0	100.5	101.6	104.2	...	Alimentation [8]
Benin [6]									**Bénin [6]**
General	90.4	95.6	95.9	100.0	103.9	106.5	108.1	109.0	Généraux
Food [1]	92.4	99.2	98.8	100.0	102.3	108.0	105.5	104.7	Alimentation [1]
Bermuda									**Bermudes**
General	93.2	95.1	97.4	100.0	102.9	105.3	108.6	112.5	Généraux
Food	93.6	95.8	97.8	100.0	102.0	103.5	105.6	108.2	Alimentation
Bhutan									**Bhoutan**
General	81.4	90.0	96.1	100.0	103.4	106.0	107.6	...	Généraux
Food [8]	84.0	93.6	99.1	100.0	101.5	103.6	104.5	...	Alimentation [8]
Bolivia [10]									**Bolivie [10]**
General	86.9	93.6	95.6	100.0	101.6	102.5	105.9	110.6	Généraux
Food	94.3	99.5	97.9	100.0	100.6	99.7	103.2	109.3	Alimentation
Botswana									**Botswana**
General	80.2	85.5	92.2	100.0	106.6	115.1	125.8	134.4	Généraux
Food	84.2	89.4	95.5	100.0	102.6	112.2	125.0	130.9	Alimentation
Brazil									**Brésil**
General	86.3	89.1	93.4	100.0	106.8	115.9	132.9	141.7	Généraux
Food	89.5	92.0	95.1	100.0	106.7	117.0	140.8	146.5	Alimentation
British Virgin Islands									**Iles Vierges britanniques**
General	91.1	95.1	97.3	100.0	103.1	103.5	107.2	108.3	Généraux
Food	96.0	98.9	99.7	100.0	104.3	105.3	107.1	108.4	Alimentation
Brunei Darussalam									**Brunéi Darussalam**
General	99.3	98.8	98.8	100.0	100.6	98.3 [2]	98.6	99.5	Généraux
Food	99.8	100.2	100.0	100.0	100.5	100.8 [2]	100.0	101.7	Alimentation
Bulgaria									**Bulgarie**
General	74.5	88.4	90.6	100.0	107.4	113.6	116.3	123.4	Généraux
Food (1995 = 100)	2 665.6	2 962.4	...	...	...	...	...	...	Alimentation (1995 = 100)
Food	...	...	90.7	100.0	106.5	106.5	105.4	112.5	Alimentation
Burkina Faso [6]									**Burkina Faso [6]**
General	96.1	101.4 [2]	100.3	100.0	104.9	107.3	109.5	109.0	Généraux
Food	101.4	113.1 [2]	106.1	100.0	108.8	112.2	110.3	104.9	Alimentation
Burundi [6]									**Burundi [6]**
General	68.4	77.0	79.6	100.0	108.1	106.7	118.1	...	Généraux
Food	67.9	76.4	77.2	100.0	100.6	95.5	107.5	...	Alimentation
Cambodia [6]									**Cambodge [6]**
General	84.4	96.9	100.8	100.0	99.4 [2]	102.7	103.9	107.9	Généraux
Food [11]	84.4	96.2	103.5	100.0	98.0 [2]	99.7	101.2	107.6	Alimentation [11]
Cameroon									**Cameroun**
General	94.0	97.0	98.8	100.0	104.4	107.4	108.1	...	Généraux
Food	93.7	96.8	97.8	100.0	107.0	112.1	111.4	...	Alimentation
Canada									**Canada**
General	94.8	95.7	97.4	100.0	102.6	104.8	107.8	109.8	Généraux
Food	95.9	97.4	98.7	100.0	104.5	107.2	109.1	111.3	Alimentation
Cape Verde									**Cap-Vert**
General	94.2	98.2	102.5	100.0	99.6	105.4	106.5	104.5	Généraux
Food	94.0	98.3	101.8	100.0	105.3	...	...	...	Alimentation
Cayman Islands									**Iles Caïmanes**
General	88.5	91.1	97.4	100.0	101.1	103.6	104.3	108.9	Généraux
Food	95.0	96.4	98.4	100.0	103.5	105.7	109.1	113.9	Alimentation
Central African Rep. [6]									**Rép. centrafricaine [6]**
General [3]	99.9	99.4	97.1	100.0	103.7	105.2	110.9	108.6	Généraux [3]
Food	102.1	99.4	96.3	100.0	104.7	106.8	112.4	107.2	Alimentation

Country or area	1997	1998	1999	2000	2001	2002	2003	2004	Pays ou zone
Chad [6]									Tchad [6]
General	101.1	105.6	96.7	100.0	112.4	117.5	116.4[12]	116.6[2]	Généraux
Food	102.7	106.0	92.9	100.0	119.3	125.8	124.2[12]	...	Alimentation
Chile [6]									Chili [6]
General	88.7	93.2[2]	96.3	100.0	103.6	106.1	109.1	110.3	Généraux
Food	94.8	98.3[2]	98.6	100.0	100.8	102.9	105.8	104.4	Alimentation
China									Chine
General	102.1	101.3	99.9	100.0	100.7	99.9	101.1	...	Généraux
Food	110.7	107.2	102.7	100.0	100.0	99.4	102.8	...	Alimentation
China, Hong Kong SAR									Chine, Hong Kong RAS
General (1990 = 100)	105.1	108.1	103.8	...	...	...	...	...	Généraux (1990 = 100)
General	...	...	...	100.0	98.4	95.4	93.0	92.6	Généraux
Food (1990 = 100)	102.1	104.1	102.2	...	...	...	...	...	Alimentation (1990 = 100)
Food	...	...	...	100.0	99.2	97.1	95.7	96.7	Alimentation
China, Macao SAR									Chine, Macao RAS
General (1990 = 100) [3]	157.6[2]	157.9	...	...	...	...	...	...	Généraux (1990 = 100) [3]
General	...	...	101.6	100.0[2]	98.0	95.4	93.9	94.9	Généraux
Food	105.5[2]	106.2	101.5	100.0[2]	98.6	96.5	95.2	97.4	Alimentation
Colombia [13]									Colombie [13]
General	68.2	82.1[2]	91.3	100.0	108.6	116.5	125.0	132.5	Généraux
Food	70.8	86.9[2]	91.7	100.0	108.7	118.4	127.2	134.6	Alimentation
Congo [6]									Congo [6]
General	98.8	96.9	100.9	100.0	100.1	104.4	103.8	106.4	Généraux
Food	101.1	100.7	105.5	100.0	98.3	102.9	96.9	90.8	Alimentation
Cook Islands [6]									Iles Cook [6]
General	94.9	95.7[2]	96.9	100.0	108.7	112.3	114.6	115.6	Généraux
Food [14]	94.9	96.3[2]	96.8	100.0	109.3	116.9	119.9	120.9	Alimentation [14]
Costa Rica [15]									Costa Rica [15]
General	73.3	81.9	90.1	100.0	111.3	121.5	132.9	149.3	Généraux
Food [1]	72.6	83.0	91.1	100.0	110.8	121.8	133.3	151.6	Alimentation [1]
Côte d'Ivoire [6]									Côte d'Ivoire [6]
General	92.5	96.8	97.5	100.0	104.4	107.6	111.1	112.7	Généraux
Food (1996 = 100) [1]	...	...	...	...	...	125.6	130.6	125.6	Alimentation (1996 = 100) [1]
Croatia									Croatie
General	86.2	91.7	95.0	100.0	104.5[2]	106.3	108.2	110.4	Généraux
Food	93.2	99.1	99.6	100.0	102.1[2]	102.3	104.0	105.5	Alimentation
Cyprus									Chypre
General	92.4	94.5[2]	96.0	100.0	102.0	104.8	109.2	111.7	Généraux
Food (1990 = 100) [1]	138.8	144.5	...	...	...	...	...	...	Alimentation (1990 = 100) [1]
Food	...	...	94.8	100.0	104.1	108.9	114.4	119.0	Alimentation
Czech Republic									République tchèque
General	85.1	94.2	96.2	100.0[2]	104.7	106.6	106.6	109.7	Généraux
Food [16]	94.8	100.7	98.2	100.0[2]	104.3	104.3	104.0	109.0	Alimentation [16]
Denmark									Danemark
General	93.1	94.8	97.1	100.0[2]	102.4	104.8	107.0	108.3	Généraux
Food	95.0	97.0	97.7	100.0[2]	103.9	106.1	107.7	106.6	Alimentation
Dominica									Dominique
General	97.0	98.0	99.1	100.0	...	...	...	...	Généraux
General (2001 = 100)	...	...	...	...	100.0	100.2	...	...	Généraux (2001 = 100)
Food	100.1	100.0	100.3	100.0	...	...	...	...	Alimentation
Food (2001 = 100)	...	...	...	...	100.0	101.5	...	...	Alimentation (2001 = 100)
Dominican Republic [17]									Rép. dominicaine [17]
General	83.2	87.2[2]	92.8	100.0	108.9	114.6	146.0	221.2	Généraux
Food [1]	88.8[2]	94.5	99.6	100.0	106.1	110.7	140.1	237.0	Alimentation [1]
Ecuador									Equateur
General	24.6	33.5	51.0	100.0	137.7	154.9	167.1	171.7	Généraux
Food [18]	23.3	32.9	45.3	100.0	131.2	141.7	145.8	146.9	Alimentation [18]

Country or area	1997	1998	1999	2000	2001	2002	2003	2004	Pays ou zone
Egypt									**Egypte**
General	89.3	92.5	97.4[2]	100.0	102.2	105.0	109.5	127.5[2]	Généraux
Food [8]	88.1	91.5	97.6[2]	100.0	101.1	105.3	112.3	...	Alimentation [8]
Food (2004 = 100)	...	...	...	...	...	...	...	100.0	Alimentation (2004 = 100)
El Salvador [10]									**El Salvador [10]**
General	94.9	97.4	97.8	100.0	103.7	105.7	107.9	112.7	Généraux
Food	99.6	101.2	99.7	100.0	104.6	106.6	108.6	115.5	Alimentation
Equatorial Guinea [6]									**Guinée équatoriale [6]**
General	...	...	...	100.0	108.8	117.0	125.5	130.9	Généraux
Food (1990 = 100)	162.4	177.2	178.2	...	...	...	...	...	Alimentation (1990 = 100)
Food	...	...	...	100.0	111.5	122.2	130.0	135.7	Alimentation
Estonia									**Estonie**
General	86.0[2]	93.1	96.2	100.0	105.8	109.5	111.0	114.4	Généraux
Food [19]	96.8	101.5	97.6	100.0	108.3	111.6	109.6	114.2	Alimentation [19]
Ethiopia [6]									**Ethiopie [6]**
General [3]	93.7	94.5	98.1	100.0	94.5[2]	93.7	100.7	105.8	Généraux [3]
Food (1990 = 100) [14]	90.9	92.5	101.1	...	...	...	...	...	Alimentation (1990 = 100) [14]
Food [14]	...	...	...	100.0	87.6[2]	85.7	98.8	102.4	Alimentation [14]
Faeroe Islands									**Iles Féroé**
General	87.4	91.3	96.1	100.0	104.9	105.2[2]	106.5	107.2	Généraux
Food	82.4	89.3	97.5	100.0	106.2	108.9[2]	109.4	109.9	Alimentation
Falkland Is. (Malvinas) [6]									**Iles Falkland (Malvinas) [6]**
General	89.8	92.1	96.0[2]	100.0	101.3	102.0	103.2	...	Généraux
Food (1990 = 100)	123.9	...	...	...	...	...	...	...	Alimentation (1990 = 100)
Fiji									**Fidji**
General	91.7	97.0	98.9	100.0	104.3	105.0	109.4	112.5	Généraux
Food [20]	94.3	101.5	103.3	100.0	104.1	104.6	111.0	115.2	Alimentation [20]
Finland									**Finlande**
General	94.3	95.6	96.7	100.0[2]	102.6	104.2	105.1	105.3	Généraux
Food	97.6	99.3	99.0	100.0[2]	104.4	107.4	108.1	108.9	Alimentation
France									**France**
General	97.2	97.8[2]	98.3	100.0	101.7	103.6	105.8	108.0	Généraux
Food	95.9	97.4[2]	98.0	100.0	105.1	107.8	110.2	110.9	Alimentation
French Guiana									**Guyane française**
General	97.9	98.4[2]	98.6	100.0	101.6	103.1	105.2	106.4	Généraux
Food	98.4	99.4[2]	98.5	100.0	102.7	105.3	109.3	109.8	Alimentation
French Polynesia									**Polynésie française**
General	96.9	98.2	99.0	100.0	101.0	103.9	104.3[2]	104.8	Généraux
Food	98.4	99.2	99.2	100.0	102.2	107.4	108.2[2]	110.6	Alimentation
Gabon [6]									**Gabon [6]**
General	97.9	100.2	99.5	100.0	102.1	102.3	104.4	104.9	Généraux
Food	97.2	100.1	99.5	100.0	105.0	...	...	...	Alimentation
Gambia [6]									**Gambie [6]**
General	94.5	95.5	99.2	100.0	104.5	113.5	132.8	151.7	Généraux
Food	92.6	95.9	99.8	100.0	99.3	117.2	141.2	164.0	Alimentation
Georgia [21]									**Géorgie [21]**
General	77.9	80.7	96.1	100.0	104.7	110.5	115.8	...	Généraux
Food [8]	80.2	83.3	98.7	100.0	106.6	114.6	122.7	...	Alimentation [8]
Germany									**Allemagne**
General	96.6	97.6	98.1	100.0[2]	102.0	103.4	104.5	106.2	Généraux
Food	100.8	101.8	100.5	100.0[2]	104.5	105.3	105.2	104.8	Alimentation
Ghana									**Ghana**
General	59.8	71.1[2]	79.9	100.0	132.9	151.8	193.3	217.7	Généraux
Food	68.0	82.3[2]	89.4	100.0	123.2	145.6	181.6	211.8	Alimentation
Gibraltar									**Gibraltar**
General	97.0	98.1	98.9[2]	100.0	101.8	102.5	105.2	107.6	Généraux
Food	95.7	97.7	99.2[2]	100.0	103.5	107.1	111.3	115.1	Alimentation

Country or area	1997	1998	1999	2000	2001	2002	2003	2004	Pays ou zone
Greece									**Grèce**
General	90.1	94.4	96.9[2]	100.0	103.4	107.1	110.9	114.1	Généraux
Food	91.8	95.9	98.1[2]	100.0	105.1	110.7	116.2	116.8	Alimentation
Greenland									**Groenland**
General	96.7	97.6	98.3	100.0	103.0	107.2	109.0	112.0	Généraux
Food (1990 = 100)	94.5	96.4	...	...	...	...	...	...	Alimentation (1990 = 100)
Food	...	...	97.3	100.0	103.4	107.6	109.8	111.4	Alimentation
Grenada									**Grenade**
General	96.0	97.4	97.9	100.0	103.2[2]	104.3	106.6	...	Généraux
Food	97.8[1]	99.1[1]	99.2[1]	100.0[1]	101.8	101.4	102.1	...	Alimentation
Guadeloupe									**Guadeloupe**
General	98.1	99.6[2]	100.0	100.0	102.6	105.0	107.1	108.6	Généraux
Food	98.9	101.7[2]	101.2	100.0	105.3	108.0	111.7	113.1	Alimentation
Guam									**Guam**
General	96.5	96.1	95.8	100.0	98.8	99.2	100.8	...	Généraux
Food	93.8	95.1	94.6	100.0	106.1	112.8	119.1	...	Alimentation
Guatemala [6]									**Guatemala** [6]
General	84.1	89.7	94.4	100.0	107.3[2]	116.0	122.5	131.8	Généraux
Food	89.7	93.8	95.8	100.0	110.0[2]	121.5	128.5	141.7	Alimentation
Guinea [6]									**Guinée** [6]
General	85.2	89.5	93.5	100.0	105.4	108.4	122.4	141.1[2]	Généraux
Food	82.8	91.2	96.2	100.0			...	...	Alimentation
Guinea-Bissau									**Guinée-Bissau**
General (2003 = 100)	...	...	...	...	...	...	100.0	100.9	Généraux (2003 = 100)
Food [1]	88.2	95.2	93.2	100.0	...	...	...	...	Alimentation [1]
Food (2003 = 100) [1]	...	...	...	...	...	...	100.0	101.1	Alimentation (2003 = 100) [1]
Guyana [6]									**Guyana** [6]
General	83.8	87.6	94.3	100.0	102.7	108.2	114.6	120.0	Généraux
Food [8]	85.2	88.3	96.0	100.0	100.6	104.4	108.5	113.3	Alimentation [8]
Haiti [7]									**Haïti** [7]
General	73.1	80.8	87.8	100.0	114.0	125.3	174.5	214.3	Généraux
Food [1]	81.5	89.4	91.1	100.0	115.5	127.4	174.2	223.2	Alimentation [1]
Honduras									**Honduras**
General	74.3	84.5	94.3	100.0[2]	109.6	118.0	127.1	137.5	Généraux
Food	79.0	88.3	95.2	100.0[2]	108.7	112.8	117.0	124.9	Alimentation
Hungary									**Hongrie**
General	72.4	82.8	91.1	100.0	109.2	115.0	120.3	128.5	Généraux
Food	77.8	89.0	91.6	100.0	113.8	119.9	123.2	131.2	Alimentation
Iceland [22]									**Islande** [22]
General	90.6	92.1	95.2	100.0	106.7	111.8	114.2	117.8	Généraux
Food	90.7	93.0	96.2	100.0	107.4	111.1	108.4	109.7	Alimentation
India [23]									**Inde** [23]
General	81.2	91.8	96.1	100.0	103.9	108.2	112.5	116.6	Généraux
Food	84.1	96.7	98.2	100.0	102.2	104.9	108.4	111.5	Alimentation
Indonesia									**Indonésie**
General	50.7	80.0[2]	96.4[24]	100.0[24]	111.5[24]	124.7[24]	133.0	141.3[2,24]	Généraux
Food	43.7	84.0[2]	105.0[24]	100.0[24]	108.5[24]	120.2[24]	121.2	128.3[2,24]	Alimentation
Iran (Islamic Rep. of)									**Iran (Rép. islamique d')**
General	61.5	73.4	88.8[2]	100.0	111.4	129.0	149.2	165.6	Généraux
Food [8]	59.8	73.9	91.8[2]	100.0	107.3	128.2	143.7	162.3	Alimentation [8]
Ireland									**Irlande**
General	91.0[2]	93.1	94.7	100.0	104.8[2]	109.7	113.5	116.0	Généraux
Food	89.5[2]	93.3	96.4	100.0	107.0[2]	110.7	112.3	112.0	Alimentation
Isle of Man									**Ile de Man**
General	92.8	95.4	97.3	100.0[2]	101.7	104.1	107.3	112.8	Généraux
Food	88.2	93.6	97.0	100.0[2]	104.9	113.0	119.6	126.3	Alimentation

Country or area	1997	1998	1999	2000	2001	2002	2003	2004	Pays ou zone
Israel									**Israël**
General	89.2	94.0[2]	98.9	100.0	101.1	106.8[2]	107.5[2]	107.1	Généraux
Food	86.5	91.3[2]	97.7	100.0	102.6	105.4[2]	108.4[2]	108.0	Alimentation
Italy [25]									**Italie** [25]
General	94.1	95.9	97.5	100.0	102.8	105.4	108.2	110.5	Généraux
Food	96.9	98.0	98.4[26]	100.0	104.1	107.9	111.3	113.7	Alimentation
Jamaica									**Jamaïque**
General	80.3	87.3	92.4	100.0	107.0	114.6	126.4	143.6	Généraux
Food	85.4	91.4	93.4	100.0	103.4	109.7	120.2	136.5	Alimentation
Japan									**Japon**
General	100.4	101.0	100.7	100.0[2]	99.3	98.4	98.1	98.1	Généraux
Food	101.1	102.5	102.0	100.0[2]	99.4	98.6	98.4	99.3	Alimentation
Jordan									**Jordanie**
General	95.8[2]	98.8	99.3	100.0	101.8	103.6[2]	105.3	108.9	Généraux
Food	97.7[2]	101.6	100.7	100.0	100.3	100.5[2]	103.1	107.8	Alimentation
Kazakhstan									**Kazakhstan**
General	76.2	81.6	88.4	100.0	108.4	114.7	122.1	130.5	Généraux
Food [1]	76.8	80.3	86.2	100.0	111.5	119.0	127.3	137.1	Alimentation [1]
Kenya [6,13]									**Kenya** [6,13]
General	87.0	92.0	94.5	100.0[2]	103.6	105.3	116.7	133.5	Généraux
Food	91.9	95.2	96.8	100.0[2]	102.4	103.9	120.9	143.8	Alimentation
Kiribati [6]									**Kiribati** [6]
General	94.5[2]	97.9	99.6	100.0	106.0	109.4	111.4	...	Généraux
Food	87.5[4]	...	...	100.0[2]	106.1	109.7	112.8	...	Alimentation
Korea, Republic of									**Corée, République de**
General	90.2	97.0	97.8	100.0[2]	104.1	106.9	110.7	114.7	Généraux
Food	88.7	96.5	99.2	100.0[2]	103.5	107.7	112.4	119.5	Alimentation
Kuwait									**Koweït**
General	95.2	95.4	98.2	100.0	101.7	102.3[2]	104.3	...	Généraux
Food	94.5	94.7	99.0	99.8	99.8	101.1[2]	103.5	...	Alimentation
Kyrgyzstan									**Kirghizistan**
General	56.1	62.0	84.2	100.0	106.9	109.1	112.5	...	Généraux
Food	54.2	59.9	83.6	100.0	105.7	105.9	108.9	...	Alimentation
Lao People's Dem. Rep.									**Rép. dém. pop. lao**
General (1996 = 100)	119.6	227.3	519.1	...	...	...	...	...	Généraux (1996 = 100)
Food (1996 = 100)	125.3	241.7	529.0	...	...	...	...	...	Alimentation (1996 = 100)
Latvia									**Lettonie**
General	90.9	95.2	97.4	100.0[2]	102.5	104.5	107.5	114.2	Généraux
Food	99.1	100.4	99.4	100.0[2]	104.8	108.4	111.2	119.5	Alimentation
Lebanon [6]									**Liban** [6]
General (1990 = 100)	447.1	...	...	...	...	...	...	...	Généraux (1990 = 100)
General	...	...	...	100.0	97.0	95.3	...	...	Généraux
Food (1990 = 100)	377.1	...	...	...	...	...	...	...	Alimentation (1990 = 100)
Lesotho									**Lesotho**
General [3]	80.4[2]	86.7	94.2	100.0	106.9	119.3	129.0	135.5	Généraux [3]
Food	81.5	88.9	95.6	100.0	106.5	134.8	142.4	148.1	Alimentation
Lithuania									**Lituanie**
General	93.6	98.3	99.1	100.0[2]	101.3	101.6	100.4	101.6	Généraux
Food	106.8	106.7	102.5	100.0[2]	103.5	102.8	99.0	101.2	Alimentation
Luxembourg									**Luxembourg**
General [29]	95.0	96.0	96.9	100.0	102.7	104.8	106.9	109.3	Généraux [29]
Food [19]	94.3	96.8	98.0	100.0	104.8	108.9	111.0	113.0	Alimentation [19]
Madagascar [6]									**Madagascar** [6]
General [3]	76.6	81.3	89.4	100.0	107.4	125.1	123.0	140.0	Généraux [3]
Food	73.6	78.0	87.5	100.0	101.9	117.2	112.9	...	Alimentation
Malawi									**Malawi**
General	41.1	53.3	77.2	100.0[2]	122.7	140.8	154.3	172.0	Généraux
Food	45.7	58.4	83.5	100.0[2]	117.6	136.4	143.6	154.4	Alimentation

Country or area	1997	1998	1999	2000	2001	2002	2003	2004	Pays ou zone
Malaysia									**Malaisie**
General	91.1	95.9	98.5	100.0[2]	101.4	103.2	104.4	105.9	Généraux
Food	86.1	93.8	98.1	100.0[2]	100.7	101.4	102.7	105.0	Alimentation
Maldives [6]									**Maldives** [6]
General	99.7	98.3	101.2	100.0	100.7	101.6	98.7	105.0	Généraux
Food [1]	105.8	100.8	105.0	100.0	102.1	105.7	99.3	115.2	Alimentation [1]
Mali [6]									**Mali** [6]
General	98.0	101.9[2]	100.7	100.0	105.1	110.4	109.1	105.6	Généraux
Food (1990 = 100)	144.4	...	...	...	...	...	...	...	Alimentation (1990 = 100)
Food [30]	...	108.8	104.7	100.0	108.0	115.8	111.1	103.3	Alimentation [30]
Malta									**Malte**
General	93.3	95.6	97.6	100.0	102.9	105.1	105.7[2]	108.7	Généraux
Food	95.7	97.6	98.5	100.0	106.0	107.4	109.2[2]	109.5	Alimentation
Marshall Islands [6]									**Iles Marshall** [6]
General	94.7	96.8	98.4	100.0	101.8	103.0	100.1	...	Généraux
Food	97.1	99.3	100.2	100.0	100.3	102.7	102.5	...	Alimentation
Martinique									**Martinique**
General	97.4	98.6[2]	99.0	100.0	102.1	104.2	106.4	108.6	Généraux
Food [8]	97.6	100.3[2]	100.1	100.0	104.1	109.4	113.0	115.4	Alimentation [8]
Mauritania									**Mauritanie**
General	86.2	93.1	96.8	100.0	104.7	108.9	114.4	124.2[2]	Généraux
Food	85.4	92.9	96.3	100.0	106.5	111.3	117.9[31]	131.2[2]	Alimentation
Mauritius									**Maurice**
General	84.0[2]	89.8	96.0	100.0	105.4	112.2[2]	116.5	122.1	Généraux
Food	85.9[2]	92.8	98.7	100.0	104.0	112.2[2]	115.4	122.3	Alimentation
Mexico									**Mexique**
General	67.6	78.3	91.3	100.0	106.4	111.7[2]	116.8	123.3	Généraux
Food [1]	69.9	81.2	94.1	100.0	105.4	109.6[2]	115.1	122.9	Alimentation [1]
Mongolia									**Mongolie**
General	76.2	83.3	89.6	100.0	106.3[2]	107.3	112.8	121.1	Généraux
Food [1]	82.2	84.0	87.0[2]	100.0	101.5	98.5	105.5	118.5	Alimentation [1]
Morocco									**Maroc**
General	94.9	97.5	98.2	100.0	100.6	103.4	104.6	106.2	Généraux
Food [8]	96.4	99.4	98.5	100.0	99.0	103.2	104.6	106.2	Alimentation [8]
Mozambique [6]									**Mozambique** [6]
General	85.0	86.2	88.7	100.0	109.1	127.4	144.5	162.7	Généraux
Food	95.9	94.6	89.4	100.0	107.9	126.4	147.9	...	Alimentation
Myanmar									**Myanmar**
General	65.9	82.6	100.1	100.0	121.1	190.2	259.8	...	Généraux
Food	67.4	84.1	102.6	100.0	119.5	201.2	274.3	...	Alimentation
Namibia [6]									**Namibie** [6]
General	79.4	84.3	91.5	100.0	109.3	121.7	130.4	135.5	Généraux
Food	86.3	88.6	93.5	100.0	111.5	133.2	144.1	147.1	Alimentation
Nepal									**Népal**
General	81.9	91.3	97.7	100.0	102.7	105.9	112.0	115.2	Généraux
Food	82.7	95.4	102.8	100.0	101.3	104.4	110.1	112.9	Alimentation
Netherlands									**Pays-Bas**
General	93.5	95.4	97.5	100.0[2]	104.2	107.6	109.9	111.2	Généraux
Food	95.8	97.9	99.2	100.0[2]	107.0	110.9	111.7	107.8	Alimentation
Netherlands Antilles [6]									**Antilles néerlandaises** [6]
General	93.1	94.1	94.5	100.0	101.8	102.1	104.3	105.7	Généraux
Food	91.1	92.2	94.1	100.0	103.4	107.3	109.5	114.7	Alimentation
New Caledonia [6]									**Nouvelle-Calédonie** [6]
General	97.1	98.3	98.5	100.0	102.3	104.1	105.4	106.2	Généraux
Food	97.4	98.5	99.4	100.0	102.6	105.0	107.0	108.2	Alimentation
New Zealand									**Nouvelle-Zélande**
General	96.4	97.6[2]	97.5	100.0	102.6	105.4	107.2	109.7	Généraux
Food	94.7	97.7[2]	98.7	100.0	106.0	109.4	109.4	110.3	Alimentation

Country or area	1997	1998	1999	2000	2001	2002	2003	2004	Pays ou zone
Nicaragua [6]									**Nicaragua [6]**
General	71.3	80.6	89.6	100.0	107.4[2]	111.6	117.4	127.3	Généraux
Food	79.0	90.3	95.2	100.0	108.6[2]	111.8	115.9	127.6	Alimentation
Niger [6]									**Niger [6]**
General [3]	94.6	99.4[2]	97.2	100.0	104.0	106.7	105.1	105.2	Généraux [3]
Food	95.5[25]	102.4[2,8]	97.0[8]	100.0[8]	107.1[8]	111.9[8]	106.7[8]	105.1[8]	Alimentation
Nigeria									**Nigéria**
General	79.5	87.7	93.5	100.0	118.9	134.2	153.1[2]	...	Généraux
Food	90.7	96.7	97.6	100.0	128.0	144.8	153.8[2]	...	Alimentation
Niue									**Nioué**
General	94.3	95.7	96.6	100.0	106.8	109.7	112.3[2]	116.6[32]	Généraux
Food	94.4	94.5	94.9	100.0	111.2	115.1	118.3[2]	121.2[32]	Alimentation
Norfolk Island									**Ile Norfolk**
General	90.1	93.5	96.4	100.0	103.1	...	...	...	Généraux
Food	93.9	95.6	97.2	100.0	104.5	...	...	...	Alimentation
Northern Mariana Islands [6]									**Iles Mariannes du Nord [6]**
General	97.0	96.7	98.0	100.0	99.2	99.4	98.4[2]	99.3	Généraux
Food	102.3	101.9	100.6	100.0	96.6	93.0	90.7[2]	94.9	Alimentation
Norway									**Norvège**
General	92.7	94.8[2]	97.0	100.0	103.0	104.4	106.9	107.4	Généraux
Food (1990 = 100)	110.4	...	...	...	...	...	...	...	Alimentation (1990 = 100)
Food	...	95.4	98.2	100.0	98.1	96.5	99.7	101.5	Alimentation
Occupied Palestinian Terr.									**Terr. palestinien occupé**
General	87.3	92.2	97.3	100.0	101.2	107.0	111.7	115.1	Généraux
Food	87.6	94.0	98.4	100.0	99.5	102.1	106.8	109.1	Alimentation
Oman [6]									**Oman [6]**
General	101.2	100.7	101.2	100.0	99.0	98.3	97.9	98.3	Généraux
Food [8]	101.8	101.5	101.3	100.0	99.4	98.3	98.2	98.5	Alimentation [8]
Pakistan									**Pakistan**
General	86.6	92.0	95.8	100.0	103.2	107.4[2]	110.5	118.7	Généraux
Food	88.2	93.3	96.9	100.0	101.8	105.9[2]	108.6	120.2	Alimentation
Panama [10]									**Panama [10]**
General	96.8	97.3	98.5	100.0	100.3	101.3	102.7	...	Généraux
General (2003 = 100)	...	...	...	...	...	...	100.0	100.4	Généraux (2003 = 100)
Food	99.0	99.4	99.3	100.0	99.6	98.9	100.2	...	Alimentation
Food (2003 = 100)	...	...	...	...	...	...	100.0	101.3	Alimentation (2003 = 100)
Papua New Guinea									**Papouasie-Nvl-Guinée**
General	66.3	75.3	86.5	100.0	109.3	122.2	140.2	...	Généraux
Food	66.4	75.3	88.0	100.0	109.6	128.3	145.3	...	Alimentation
Paraguay [6]									**Paraguay [6]**
General	77.1	86.0	91.8	100.0	107.3	118.5	135.4	141.3	Généraux
Food	80.5	89.5	92.3	100.0	103.8	114.4	139.3	149.7	Alimentation
Peru [6,7]									**Pérou [6,7]**
General	86.9	93.2	96.4	100.0	102.0	102.2[2]	104.5	108.3	Généraux
Food	91.9	99.5	99.3	100.0	100.5	100.2[2]	101.0	106.6	Alimentation
Philippines									**Philippines**
General	81.9	89.8	95.9	100.0[2]	106.8	110.1	113.9	120.6	Généraux
Food [1]	85.6	93.1	98.0	100.0[2]	104.7	107.1	109.4	116.3	Alimentation [1]
Poland									**Pologne**
General (1990 = 100)	767.0	...	...	...	...	...	...	...	Généraux (1990 = 100)
General	...	84.7	90.9	100.0	105.5	107.5	108.4	112.2	Généraux
Food (1990 = 100) [18]	620.1	...	...	...	...	...	...	...	Alimentation (1990 = 100) [18]
Food [18]	...	89.4	91.2	100.0	105.1	104.6	103.0	108.6	Alimentation [18]
Portugal									**Portugal**
General [3]	92.5[2]	95.0	97.2	100.0	104.3	108.0[2]	111.6	114.2	Généraux [3]
Food [33]	92.7[2]	95.9	97.9	100.0	106.5	108.1[2]	110.9	112.1	Alimentation [33]
Puerto Rico									**Porto Rico**
General	84.4	88.9	94.0	100.0	107.0	113.6	122.5	137.1	Généraux
Food	74.0	83.1	91.7	100.0	114.1	127.8	145.8	176.3	Alimentation

Country or area	1997	1998	1999	2000	2001	2002	2003	2004	Pays ou zone
Qatar									**Qatar**
General	93.6	96.3	98.4	100.0	...	...	...	...	Généraux
Food [8]	95.7	99.6	99.6	100.0	...	...	...	...	Alimentation [8]
Republic of Moldova									**République de Moldova**
General	50.8	54.7	76.2	100.0	109.8	115.6	129.2	145.3	Généraux
Food	53.1	55.2	73.3	100.0	110.7	115.5	131.2	147.9	Alimentation
Réunion									**Réunion**
General	96.1	97.3[2]	98.2	100.0	102.3	105.1	106.3	108.1	Généraux
Food	97.5	100.2[2]	99.3	100.0	101.5	108.3	107.5	107.5	Alimentation
Romania									**Roumanie**
General	29.6	47.1	68.6	100.0	134.5	164.8	189.9	212.5	Généraux
Food	36.7	54.4	69.6	100.0	135.7	160.5	184.1	201.5	Alimentation
Russian Federation									**Fédération de Russie**
General	34.9	44.6[2]	82.8	100.0	121.5[2]	140.6	159.9	177.3	Généraux
Food	34.0	43.3[2]	85.1	100.0	120.6[2]	135.3	150.4	165.9	Alimentation
Rwanda [6]									**Rwanda [6]**
General	92.9[34]	98.6	96.2	100.0	103.4	105.4	113.2[2]	126.7	Généraux
Food	106.7	116.2	99.1	100.0	106.0	104.7	119.2[2]	141.7	Alimentation
Saba									**Saba**
General	93.1	97.1	99.4	100.0	100.6	101.4	102.2	103.3	Généraux
Food	86.4	94.4	99.3	100.0	99.6	99.4	100.8	103.2	Alimentation
Saint Helena									**Sainte-Hélène**
General	95.4	96.6	98.6	100.0	103.5	...	...	...	Généraux
General (2002 = 100)	...	...	...	...	...	100.0	100.0	...	Généraux (2002 = 100)
Food	99.5	98.2	99.4	100.0	102.6	...	...	...	Alimentation
Food (2002 = 100)	...	...	...	...	...	100.0	103.8	...	Alimentation (2002 = 100)
Saint Kitts and Nevis [6]									**Saint-Kitts-et-Nevis [6]**
General	91.6	94.7	97.9	100.0	...	...	...	...	Généraux
Food	93.1	97.3	97.7	100.0	...	...	...	...	Alimentation
Saint Lucia									**Sainte-Lucie**
General	90.6	93.2	96.4	100.0	105.2	105.0	106.0	107.6	Généraux
Food	92.1	96.0	98.8	100.0	103.2	101.9	104.1	104.9	Alimentation
Saint Pierre and Miquelon									**Saint-Pierre-et-Miquelon**
General	90.3	91.3	92.2	100.0	102.3	...	...	...	Généraux
Food	91.3	93.5	94.5	100.0	103.5	...	...	...	Alimentation
St. Vincent-Grenadines [6]									**St. Vincent-Grenadines [6]**
General	96.8	98.8	99.8	100.0	100.8[2]	101.5	101.8	104.8	Généraux
Food	103.2	100.6	101.1	100.0	101.0[2]	101.6	100.9	105.6	Alimentation
Samoa									**Samoa**
General [3]	111.9	98.6	98.9[2]	100.0	103.7	112.2	112.3	130.5[2]	Généraux [3]
Food	131.4	101.1	100.1[2]	100.0	105.1	117.3	115.1	146.2[2]	Alimentation
San Marino									**Saint-Marin**
General	91.7	93.8	96.8	100.0	...	...	...	...	Généraux
General (2003 = 100)	...	...	...	...	...	...	100.0	101.4	Généraux (2003 = 100)
Food	94.3	96.8	98.9	100.0	...	...	...	...	Alimentation
Food (2003 = 100)	...	...	...	...	...	...	100.0	103.3	Alimentation (2003 = 100)
Saudi Arabia [35]									**Arabie saoudite [35]**
General	102.1[36]	102.0[36]	100.6[36]	100.0[36]	99.2[36]	98.6[36]	97.2	99.5[2]	Généraux
Food [8]	102.4[36]	103.6[36]	100.9[36]	100.0[36]	100.6[36]	100.0[36]	96.9	104.4[2]	Alimentation [8]
Senegal [6]									**Sénégal [6]**
General	97.5	98.5[2]	99.2	100.0	103.0	105.4	105.3	105.8	Généraux
Food	97.3[25]	100.9[2,8]	101.2[8]	100.0[8]	104.9[8]	110.2[8]	109.5[8]	110.3[8]	Alimentation
Serbia and Montenegro									**Serbie-et-Monténégro**
General	28.6	37.2	53.9	100.0	189.2	220.4	241.2	267.2	Généraux
Food	25.2	33.6	48.7	100.0	188.2	200.4	202.0	224.5	Alimentation
Seychelles									**Seychelles**
General	86.3	88.6	94.2	100.0	106.0[2]	106.2	109.6	...	Généraux
Food	97.1	99.5	98.6	100.0	104.9[2]	105.6	108.1	...	Alimentation

Country or area	1997	1998	1999	2000	2001	2002	2003	2004	Pays ou zone
Sierra Leone [6]									Sierra Leone [6]
General	55.5	75.3	100.9	100.0	102.2	98.8	106.3	...	Généraux
Food	56.8	74.8	100.4	100.0	105.2	104.4	112.2	...	Alimentation
Singapore									Singapour
General	98.8	98.6[2]	98.7	100.0	101.0	100.6	101.1	102.8[2]	Généraux
Food	98.3	98.5[2]	99.4	100.0	100.5	100.5	101.1	103.2[2]	Alimentation
Slovakia									Slovaquie
General	75.7	80.8	89.3	100.0	107.1[2]	110.7	120.2	129.2	Généraux
Food	87.4	92.5	94.9	100.0	105.8[2]	107.3	111.0	116.4	Alimentation
Slovenia [10]									Slovénie [10]
General	80.2	86.5	91.8	100.0	108.4	116.5	123.0	127.4	Généraux
Food	84.0	91.2	94.8	100.0	109.0	117.5	123.1	124.2	Alimentation
Solomon Islands [6]									Iles Salomon [6]
General	77.0	86.5	93.6	100.0	107.8	119.5	129.4	138.7	Généraux
Food	74.2	83.7	93.1	100.0	108.9	122.1	125.0	136.8	Alimentation
South Africa									Afrique du Sud
General	84.5	90.3	95.0	100.0[2]	105.7	115.4	122.1	123.8	Généraux
Food	83.3	88.5	92.8	100.0[2]	105.4	122.0	131.9	134.9	Alimentation
Spain									Espagne
General	92.8	94.5	96.7	100.0	...	...	...	...	Généraux
General (2001 = 100)	...	...	...	...	100.0	103.5	106.7	109.9	Généraux (2001 = 100)
Food	95.7	96.8	98.0	100.0	...	...	...	...	Alimentation
Food (2001 = 100)	...	...	...	...	100.0	104.7	109.0	113.2	Alimentation (2001 = 100)
Sri Lanka [6]									Sri Lanka [6]
General	82.3	90.0	94.2	100.0	114.2	125.1	133.0	143.0	Généraux
Food	83.0	92.1	95.7	100.0	115.2	127.5	134.9	145.5	Alimentation
Suriname [6]									Suriname [6]
General (2001 = 100)	19.1	22.8	45.3	77.4[37]	100.0[2]	115.9	...	156.9	Généraux (2001 = 100)
Food (2001 = 100)	22.3	25.5	48.6	80.5[37]	100.0[2]	118.1	...	157.8	Alimentation (2001 = 100)
Swaziland									Swaziland
General	79.9	85.9	91.0	100.0	107.7	120.2	129.0	133.5	Généraux
Food	85.8	89.3	93.7	100.0	106.5	129.8	145.7	155.7	Alimentation
Sweden									Suède
General	98.9	98.7	99.1	100.0	102.4	104.6	106.6	107.0	Généraux
Food	97.4	98.5	100.0	100.0	102.9	106.2	106.5	106.1	Alimentation
Switzerland									Suisse
General	97.7	97.7	98.5	100.0[2]	101.0	101.7	102.3	103.1	Généraux
Food	97.7	98.6	98.5	100.0[2]	102.1	104.5	105.9	106.5	Alimentation
Syrian Arab Republic									Rép. arabe syrienne
General	103.3	102.8	100.8	100.0	100.4	101.4	109.3[2]	114.1	Généraux
Food	108.8	106.3	102.1	100.0	100.2	99.6	107.3[2]	112.8	Alimentation
Tajikistan									Tadjikistan
General	4.5	64.0	80.6	100.0	...	...	...	...	Généraux
Food (1990 = 100) [38]	7 172.0	...	...	...	...	...	...	...	Alimentation (1990 = 100) [38]
Thailand									Thaïlande
General	90.8	98.2	98.5	100.0[2]	101.6	102.3	104.1	107.0[2]	Généraux
Food	93.0	102.0	101.1	100.0[2]	100.7	101.0	104.7	109.4[2]	Alimentation
TFYR of Macedonia									L'ex-R.y. Macédoine
General	95.3	95.2	94.5	100.0	105.5	107.4	108.7	108.2	Généraux
Food	102.2	102.0	100.4	100.0	106.9	108.8	107.3	104.0	Alimentation
Togo [6]									Togo [6]
General	99.9	98.2[2]	98.2	100.0	109.7	107.1	106.0	106.5	Généraux
Food	199.9[1]	109.0[30]	103.5[30]	100.0[30]	...	109.3[30]	104.4[30]	103.0[30]	Alimentation
Tonga									Tonga
General [3]	87.2	90.1	93.7	100.0	108.3	119.5[2]	133.5	148.1	Généraux [3]
Food	89.0	94.5	99.7	100.0	111.8	130.6[2]	143.1	156.0	Alimentation
Trinidad and Tobago									Trinité-et-Tobago
General	88.4	93.4	96.6	100.0	105.6	109.9	114.2[2]	118.3	Généraux
Food	73.9	85.0	92.3	100.0	114.0	125.6	142.9[2]	161.1	Alimentation

Consumer price indices—General and food (Index base: 2000 = 100) (*continued*)

Indices des prix à la consommation—Généraux et alimentation (Indices base : 2000 = 100) (*suite*)

Country or area	1997	1998	1999	2000	2001	2002	2003	2004	Pays ou zone
Tunisia									Tunisie
General	91.7	94.6	97.1	100.0[2]	102.0	104.8	107.6	111.5	Généraux
Food	91.1	93.5	95.6	100.0[2]	102.0	106.1	109.7	115.1	Alimentation
Turkey									Turquie
General	21.2	39.2	64.5	100.0	154.4	223.8	280.4	310.1	Généraux
Food [8]	24.6	44.9	66.8	100.0	150.3	225.3	290.0	316.1	Alimentation [8]
Tuvalu [6]									Tuvalu [6]
General	92.4	93.1	96.2	100.0	101.5	106.7[2]	110.2	113.3	Généraux
Food	95.1	95.2	99.0	100.0	105.3	109.4[2]	117.4	120.8	Alimentation
Uganda									Ouganda
General	90.8	91.5	96.8	100.0	101.9	101.6	110.5	114.5	Généraux
Food	94.6	92.6	99.0	100.0	96.6	92.5	106.7	111.4	Alimentation
Ukraine									Ukraine
General	57.5	63.6	78.0	100.0	112.0	112.8	118.7	129.4	Généraux
Food [1]	52.0	58.2	74.3	100.0	114.4	114.4	121.5	135.1	Alimentation [1]
United Arab Emirates									Emirats arabes unis
General	94.7	96.6	98.6	100.0[2]	102.8	105.8	109.1	114.6	Généraux
Food [30]	95.2	97.0	99.5	100.0[2]	101.0	102.4	104.7	112.0	Alimentation [30]
United Kingdom									Royaume-Uni
General	92.5	95.7	97.1	100.0	101.8	103.5	106.5	109.6	Généraux
Food	98.7	100.0	100.3	100.0	103.3	104.0	105.4	106.0	Alimentation
United Rep. of Tanzania [39]									Rép.-Unie de Tanzanie [39]
General	77.5	87.5	94.4	100.0	105.1[2]	106.2	109.8	114.5	Généraux
Food	75.1	86.1	93.6	100.0	106.1[2]	107.1	112.0	118.6	Alimentation
United States [40]									Etats-Unis [40]
General	93.2	94.7	96.7	100.0	102.8	104.5	106.9	109.7	Généraux
Food	93.7	95.8	97.8	100.0	103.2	105.0	107.3	111.0	Alimentation
Uruguay [6]									Uruguay [6]
General	81.6[2]	90.3	95.5	100.0	104.4	118.9	142.0	155.0	Généraux
Food	82.6[2]	91.3	94.6	100.0	103.1	117.2	142.5	159.2	Alimentation
Vanuatu									Vanuatu
General	92.6	95.6	97.5[2]	100.0	103.6	105.7	108.8	110.4	Généraux
Food	93.6	96.6	98.0[2]	100.0	102.2	102.7	105.0	108.5	Alimentation
Venezuela (Bolivarian Republic of) [6]									Venezuela (Rép. bolivarienne) [6]
General	51.3	69.6	86.0	100.0[2]	112.5	137.8	180.6	219.9	Généraux
Food	57.5	79.8	93.3	100.0[2]	116.1	149.0	205.2	274.6	Alimentation
Viet Nam									Viet Nam
General	90.4	97.4	101.6	100.0	99.7	103.7	107.0	115.0	Généraux
Food [1]	90.8	99.8	104.0	100.0	98.6	106.1	108.7	119.8	Alimentation [1]
Yemen									Yémen
General	83.0	88.0	95.6	100.0	111.9	125.6	139.2	...	Généraux
Food	81.5	86.1	95.0	100.0	115.7	121.2	141.4	...	Alimentation
Zambia									Zambie
General	50.2	62.6	79.3	100.0	121.4	148.4	180.1	212.5	Généraux
Food [1]	53.4	66.6	81.6	100.0	118.9	151.1	184.5	...	Alimentation [1]
Zimbabwe									Zimbabwe
General	30.7	40.5	64.2	100.0	176.7	424.3	2 255.8	8 625.7	Généraux
Food	28.7	40.0	67.1	100.0	164.1	407.7	2 238.4	8 792.0	Alimentation

Source

International Labour Office (ILO), Geneva, the ILO labour statistics database and the "Yearbook of Labour Statistics 2005".

Notes

[1] Including alcoholic beverages and tobacco.
[2] Series linked to former series.
[3] Excluding rent.

Source

Bureau international du Travail (BIT), Genève, la base de données du BIT et "l'Annuaire des statistiques du travail 2005".

Notes

[1] Y compris les boissons alcoolisées et le tabac.
[2] Série enchaînée à la précédente.
[3] Non compris le groupe "Loyer".

[4] Average of the first three quarters.	[4] Moyenne des trois premiers trimestres.
[5] Series linked to former series; average of the last three quarters.	[5] Série enchaînée à la précédente; moyenne des trois derniers trimestres.
[6] Data refer to the index of the capital city.	[6] Les données se réfèrent a l'indice de la ville principale.
[7] Metropolitan area.	[7] Région métropolitaine.
[8] Including tobacco.	[8] Y compris le tabac.
[9] Government officials.	[9] Fonctionnaires.
[10] Urban areas.	[10] Régions urbaines.
[11] Beginning 1997, including tobacco.	[11] A partir 1997, y compris le tabac.
[12] January-October.	[12] Janvier-octobre.
[13] Low-income group.	[13] Familles à revenu modique.
[14] Excluding beverages.	[14] Non compris les boissons.
[15] Central area.	[15] Région centrale.
[16] Including tobacco, beverages and public catering.	[16] Y compris le tabac, les boissons et la restauration.
[17] Including direct taxes.	[17] Y compris les impôts directs.
[18] Including alcoholic beverages.	[18] Y compris les boissons alcoolisées.
[19] Excluding alcoholic beverages and tobacco.	[19] Non compris les boissons alcoolisées et le tabac.
[20] Excluding beverages and tobacco.	[20] Non compris les boissons et le tabac.
[21] Five cities.	[21] Cinq villes.
[22] Annual averages are based on the months Feb.-Dec. and the mean of January both years.	[22] Les moyennes annuelles sont basées sur les mois de fév.-déc. et la moyenne de janvier des deux années.
[23] Industrial workers.	[23] Travailleurs de l'industrie.
[24] Since November 1999: excluding Dili.	[24] A partir de novembre 1999: non compris Dili.
[25] Excluding tobacco.	[25] Non compris le tabac.
[26] Prior to 1999: including alcoholic beverages.	[26] Avant 1999 : y compris les boissons alcooliques.
[27] June of each year.	[27] Juin de chaque année.
[28] Index base: June 2000=100.	[28] Indice base : juin 2000=100.
[29] Beginning July 1987, including Rent.	[29] A partir de juillet 1987, y compris le groupe "loyer".
[30] Including beverages and tobacco.	[30] Y compris les boissons et le tabac.
[31] January-November.	[31] Janvier-novembre.
[32] Average of the last three quarters.	[32] Moyenne des trois derniers trimestres.
[33] Excluding alcoholic beverages.	[33] Non compris les boissons alcooliques.
[34] 10 months' average.	[34] Moyenne de 10 mois.
[35] All cities.	[35] Ensemble des villes.
[36] Middle-income group.	[36] Familles à revenu moyen.
[37] April-December.	[37] Avril-décembre.
[38] Due to lack of space, multiply each figure by 100.	[38] En raison du manque de place, multiplier chaque chiffre par 100.
[39] Tanganyika.	[39] Tanganyika.
[40] All urban consumers.	[40] Tous les consommateurs urbains.

Table 27: The series generally relate to the average earnings per worker in manufacturing industries, according to the *International Standard Industrial Classification of All Economic Activities* (ISIC) Revision 2 or Revision 3 [47]. The data are published in the ILO *Yearbook of Labour Statistics* [11] and on the ILO web site http://laborsta.ilo.org and generally cover all employees (i.e. wage earners and salaried employees) of both sexes, irrespective of age. Data which refer exclusively to wage earners (i.e. manual or production workers), salaried employees (i.e. non-manual workers), or to total employment are also shown when available. Earnings generally include bonuses, cost of living allowances, taxes, social insurance contributions payable by the employed person and, in some cases, payments in kind, and normally exclude social insurance contributions payable by the employers, family allowances and other social security benefits. The time of year to which the figures refer is not the same for all countries. In some cases, the series may show wage rates instead of earnings; this is indicated in footnotes.

Table 28: The producer price index (PPI) can be generally described as an index for measuring the average change in the prices of goods and services either as they leave the place of production or as they enter the production process. As such, producer price indices can represent input prices (at purchasers' prices) and output prices (at basic or producer prices) with different levels of aggregation.

The industrial coverage of the PPI can vary across countries. Normally, the PPIs refer to indices related to the agricultural, mining, manufacturing, transport and telecommunications, and public utilities sectors. Many countries are progressively developing service industry PPIs for incorporation within their larger PPI frameworks. PPI prices should be actual transaction prices recorded at the time the transaction occurs (i.e. when ownership changes).

PPIs can be calculated in a number of different combinations. In this publication, the PPIs are classified according to the following scheme:

(a)   Components of supply
       Domestic supply
       Domestic production for domestic
       market
       Agricultural products
       Industrial products
       Imported goods

(b)   Stage of processing
       Raw materials
       Intermediate goods

Tableau 27 : Les séries se rapportent généralement aux gains moyens des salariés des industries manufacturières (activités de fabrication), suivant la *Classification internationale type, par industrie, de toutes les branches d'activité économique* (CITI, Rev. 2 ou Rev.3) [47]. Les données sont publiées dans l'*Annuaire des statistiques du travail* du BIT [11] et sur le site Web du BIT http://laborsta.ilo.org et généralement portent sur l'ensemble des salariés (qu'ils perçoivent un salaire ou un traitement au mois) des deux sexes, indépendamment de leur âge. Les données qui portent exclusivement sur les salariés horaires (ouvriers, travailleurs manuels), sur les employés percevant un traitement (travailleurs autres que manuels, cadres), ou sur l'emploi total sont aussi présentées si elles sont disponibles. Les gains comprennent en général les primes, les indemnités pour coût de la vie, les impôts, les cotisations de sécurité sociale à la charge de l'employé, et dans certains cas des paiements en nature, mais ne comprennent pas en règle générale la part patronale des cotisations d'assurance sociale, les allocations familiales et les autres prestations de sécurité sociale. La période de l'année visée par les données n'est pas la même pour tous les pays. Dans certains cas, les séries présentent les taux horaires et non pas les gains, ce présente qui est alors signalé en note.

Tableau 28 : L'indice des prix à la production peut être caractérisé de manière générale comme un indice permettant de mesurer le changement moyen des prix des biens et des services soit au moment où ils quittent le lieu de production soit au moment où ils arrivent au processus de production. Les indices des prix à la production peuvent donc représenter les prix des intrants (aux prix d'acquisition) et les prix à la sortie de fabrique (aux prix de base, ou prix à la production), les agrégats étant de différents niveaux.

Les branches d'activité couvertes par l'indice des prix à la production peuvent n'être pas les mêmes d'un pays à l'autre. Normalement, l'indice concerne l'agriculture, les industries extractives, les industries manufacturières, les transports et télécommunications et les services publics de distribution. Nombre de pays mettent peu à peu au point des indices des prix à la production pour les services, de manière à pouvoir les intégrer à leurs indices des prix à la production plus généraux. Les prix servant pour ces indices doivent être des prix effectifs de transaction enregistrés au moment où s'effectue la transaction (au moment où le propriétaire change).

Les indices des prix à la production peuvent se calculer selon plusieurs combinaisons différentes. Dans la présente publication, on les classe de la manière ci-après :

a)   Eléments de l'offre
      Offre intérieure
      Production nationale pour le marché

(c)   End-use
        Consumer goods
        Capital goods

Though a few countries are still compiling the wholesale price index (WPI), which is the precedent of the PPI, the WPI has been replaced in most countries by the PPI because of the broader coverage provided by the PPI in terms of products and industries and the conceptual concordance between the PPI and the System of National Accounts. The WPI would normally cover the price of products as they flow from the wholesaler to the retailer and is an index for measuring the price level changes in markets other than retail.

For a more detailed explanation about the PPI, please refer to the *Producer Price Index Manual: Theory and Practice* published by the International Monetary Fund in 2004.

Table 29: Unless otherwise stated, the consumer price index covers all the main classes of expenditure on all items and on food. Monthly data for many of these series may be found in the United Nations *Monthly Bulletin of Statistics* [25].

intérieur
        Produits agricoles
        Produits industriels
        Produits importés

b)   Stade de la transformation
        Matières premières
        Produits intermédiaires

c)   Utilisation finale
        Biens de consommation
        Biens d'équipement

Même s'il y a encore quelques pays qui compilent l'indice des prix de gros, qui est l'ancêtre de l'indice des prix à la production, la plupart l'ont remplacé par ce dernier, qui offre une couverture plus large de produits et de branches d'activité, et coïncide dans ses concepts avec le Système de comptabilité nationale. L'indice des prix de gros suivait normalement le prix des produits à mesure qu'ils passaient du grossiste au détaillant il permet de mesurer les changements du niveau des prix sur les marchés autres que le marché de détail.

Pour un complément de détails sur l'indice des prix à la production, on se reportera au *Producer Price Index Manual, Theory and Practice* publié par le Fonds monétaire international en 2004.

Tableau 29 : Sauf indication contraire, les indices des prix à la consommation donnés englobent tous les groupes principaux de dépenses pour l'ensemble des prix et alimentation. Les données mensuelles pour plusieurs de ces séries figurent dans le *Bulletin mensuel de statistique* [25].

30

Agricultural production
Index base: 1999-01 = 100

Production agricole
Indices base : 1999-01 = 100

Country or area Pays ou zone	Agriculture — Agriculture					Food — Produits alimentaires				
	2000	2001	2002	2003	2004	2000	2001	2002	2003	2004
World Monde	100.2	101.6	103.3	106.0	110.1	100.2	101.5	103.4	106.2	109.8
Africa Afrique	99.6	101.5	102.9	106.6	108.2	99.8	101.4	103.2	107.3	108.5
Algeria Algérie	95.5	103.6	104.9	117.6	116.7	95.4	103.6	104.9	117.8	116.8
Angola Angola	100.3	111.3	111.6	113.8	112.5	100.2	111.6	112.0	114.2	112.9
Benin Bénin	103.1	102.0	111.5	128.4	132.1	101.6	102.1	108.3	133.2	137.4
Botswana Botswana	98.9	107.5	108.2	101.8	104.2	98.8	107.5	108.4	101.8	104.3
Burkina Faso Burkina Faso	86.4	112.3	116.3	123.7	124.6	85.0	114.3	112.6	120.7	115.2
Burundi Burundi	95.2	103.8	108.7	106.8	103.9	95.5	104.6	107.2	107.4	104.4
Cameroon Cameroun	100.1	102.1	101.7	102.6	104.5	100.2	102.3	103.4	104.4	104.7
Cape Verde Cap-Vert	96.9	96.9	91.3	94.0	91.8	96.9	96.9	91.3	94.0	91.8
Central African Rep. Rép. centrafricaine	102.2	105.0	105.0	102.8	104.6	102.1	105.0	106.4	106.2	108.2
Chad Tchad	92.7	108.5	107.3	107.0	113.1	93.4	109.0	107.5	111.0	112.2
Comoros Comores	100.2	102.0	101.5	104.4	104.6	100.2	102.0	101.5	104.4	104.6
Congo Congo	100.3	101.1	105.0	107.5	108.8	100.3	101.1	104.9	107.3	108.8
Côte d'Ivoire Côte d'Ivoire	103.6	96.5	96.4	96.3	98.0	102.0	99.6	98.9	99.8	101.2
Dem. Rep. of the Congo Rép. dém. du Congo	100.1	98.2	97.3	97.9	97.2	100.0	98.5	97.0	98.0	97.5
Djibouti Djibouti	99.6	99.7	103.0	109.6	109.6	99.6	99.7	103.0	109.6	109.6
Egypt Egypte	102.2	100.2	103.8	107.6	110.9	102.7	99.3	103.7	108.6	110.9
Equatorial Guinea Guinée équatoriale	100.3	98.2	93.0	94.1	94.1	100.4	98.1	92.2	93.4	93.4
Eritrea Erythrée	92.2	98.3	76.6	87.1	86.4	92.1	98.2	76.4	87.0	86.3
Ethiopia Ethiopie	98.4	107.9	110.7	107.6	112.2	98.3	108.2	111.4	108.2	112.1
Gabon Gabon	101.0	100.4	101.2	101.8	101.7	101.0	100.4	101.2	101.8	101.7
Gambia Gambie	100.6	109.2	65.4	71.8	69.1	100.6	109.2	65.3	71.7	69.0
Ghana Ghana	99.2	102.4	112.9	115.9	120.6	99.2	102.6	113.3	116.3	121.0

Country or area Pays ou zone	Agriculture — Agriculture					Food — Produits alimentaires				
	2000	2001	2002	2003	2004	2000	2001	2002	2003	2004
Guinea Guinée	98.7	103.5	104.9	108.4	111.0	98.1	103.2	107.2	111.0	113.8
Guinea-Bissau Guinée-Bissau	100.3	103.7	101.8	104.3	109.7	100.4	103.6	101.6	104.1	109.7
Kenya Kenya	96.4	105.1	104.9	109.5	104.8	96.1	104.9	105.0	109.9	104.3
Lesotho Lesotho	100.0	104.4	98.4	97.2	105.9	99.9	104.5	98.2	97.0	106.0
Liberia Libéria	102.4	100.6	98.1	98.2	100.7	102.9	99.8	95.8	95.6	97.3
Libyan Arab Jamah. Jamah. arabe libyenne	96.9	94.4	98.8	101.6	104.4	96.9	94.2	98.8	101.6	104.3
Madagascar Madagascar	99.6	99.5	97.5	99.4	107.3	99.8	99.5	98.1	99.6	107.6
Malawi Malawi	103.6	105.9	78.8	86.6	94.0	102.6	108.6	78.1	87.5	95.6
Mali Mali	87.8	106.6	99.6	115.1	113.8	94.5	100.7	99.3	108.6	109.6
Mauritania Mauritanie	101.7	100.2	105.8	108.3	108.8	101.7	100.2	105.8	108.3	108.8
Mauritius Maurice	101.3	116.8	101.9	106.2	105.6	101.4	117.1	102.1	106.6	105.9
Morocco Maroc	93.8	104.3	112.2	122.9	131.5	93.6	104.3	112.3	123.4	132.1
Mozambique Mozambique	94.5	100.3	102.1	105.3	105.3	95.1	99.4	101.1	104.0	104.0
Namibia Namibie	105.5	94.6	101.2	114.6	114.1	105.7	94.3	100.9	114.5	114.0
Niger Niger	92.2	107.2	109.9	118.5	116.9	91.9	107.8	110.4	120.0	118.4
Nigeria Nigéria	100.5	99.4	101.7	103.2	106.2	100.5	99.4	101.7	103.2	106.2
Réunion Réunion	99.6	100.1	99.2	102.6	102.6	99.6	100.1	99.2	102.6	102.6
Rwanda Rwanda	103.7	99.5	124.1	112.8	112.8	104.0	99.2	124.9	113.5	113.2
Sao Tome and Principe Sao Tomé-et-Principe	100.8	102.2	103.4	108.1	109.1	100.8	102.2	103.5	108.2	109.2
Senegal Sénégal	101.2	96.2	61.9	84.3	83.6	101.3	95.4	60.8	82.3	81.6
Seychelles Seychelles	100.6	98.4	98.8	80.2	91.8	100.4	98.5	99.0	78.8	91.6
Sierra Leone Sierra Leone	94.2	103.6	108.6	114.5	113.5	94.1	103.5	108.7	114.6	113.5
South Africa Afrique du Sud	104.8	99.9	105.2	104.7	105.3	105.2	99.9	106.0	105.3	105.9
Sudan Soudan	97.2	106.1	102.7	112.6	108.5	97.3	105.8	102.7	112.4	107.8
Swaziland Swaziland	97.7	95.4	101.8	103.2	103.3	98.3	96.8	104.3	105.8	105.9
Togo Togo	97.1	98.7	109.3	108.9	110.4	97.5	97.1	104.2	104.3	104.2

Country or area Pays ou zone	Agriculture — Agriculture					Food — Produits alimentaires				
	2000	2001	2002	2003	2004	2000	2001	2002	2003	2004
Tunisia Tunisie	97.9	87.4	83.6	123.5	101.5	97.8	87.2	83.4	123.9	101.6
Uganda Ouganda	98.6	104.2	108.5	105.3	109.3	99.4	104.5	108.3	105.7	109.2
United Rep. of Tanzania Rép.-Unie de Tanzanie	99.8	102.9	104.5	103.7	107.6	100.5	101.9	104.9	104.4	105.6
Zambia Zambie	97.8	93.9	94.2	104.6	104.6	100.5	96.0	96.2	108.0	108.0
Zimbabwe Zimbabwe	106.7	99.9	81.1	78.3	75.5	105.4	100.3	81.9	88.8	86.4
America, North Amérique du Nord	**101.1**	**99.5**	**98.4**	**101.4**	**107.2**	**101.4**	**99.2**	**98.7**	**101.7**	**106.9**
Antigua and Barbuda Antigua-et-Barbuda	99.7	102.0	103.5	105.9	107.9	99.7	102.0	103.5	105.8	107.8
Bahamas Bahamas	88.5	92.2	91.7	100.7	104.8	88.5	92.2	91.7	100.7	104.8
Barbados Barbade	104.9	97.1	93.5	93.9	100.8	104.9	97.1	93.5	93.9	100.8
Belize Belize	103.0	105.7	101.5	102.7	116.7	103.0	105.6	101.4	102.6	116.6
Canada Canada	102.3	92.3	87.0	95.5	101.1	102.6	92.3	87.0	95.7	101.6
Costa Rica Costa Rica	100.3	100.4	98.0	103.3	97.9	99.8	100.7	98.6	104.9	99.4
Cuba Cuba	105.2	104.6	106.6	107.9	109.3	105.3	104.8	106.7	108.1	109.6
Dominica Dominique	102.3	94.9	93.2	90.8	98.3	102.3	94.8	93.1	90.6	98.2
Dominican Republic Rép. dominicaine	98.8	105.2	109.1	107.7	103.1	98.2	105.6	108.7	107.0	102.6
El Salvador El Salvador	100.3	97.5	98.2	96.5	98.6	102.3	99.4	103.0	101.0	104.8
Grenada Grenade	103.0	91.3	102.4	98.7	98.7	103.0	91.3	102.4	98.7	98.7
Guadeloupe Guadeloupe	97.7	102.3	104.6	102.9	102.9	97.7	102.3	104.6	102.9	102.9
Guatemala Guatemala	100.3	102.0	102.7	103.1	100.8	99.4	103.0	106.4	105.8	104.4
Haiti Haïti	103.1	99.2	101.6	103.3	100.5	103.1	99.3	101.7	103.3	100.6
Honduras Honduras	102.1	104.0	109.2	108.5	108.6	101.7	102.7	111.3	113.4	111.0
Jamaica Jamaïque	95.3	101.8	97.0	97.2	99.4	95.3	101.8	97.0	97.2	99.4
Martinique Martinique	103.9	94.3	101.9	97.2	99.2	103.9	94.3	101.9	97.2	99.2
Mexico Mexique	98.7	103.3	101.9	105.3	107.4	98.8	103.6	102.7	106.1	107.8
Nicaragua Nicaragua	103.9	103.6	109.8	117.6	120.1	104.1	105.7	113.2	121.9	123.1
Panama Panama	100.2	99.5	100.8	100.8	103.3	100.5	99.2	100.8	100.8	103.7

Country or area Pays ou zone	Agriculture — Agriculture					Food — Produits alimentaires				
	2000	2001	2002	2003	2004	2000	2001	2002	2003	2004
Puerto Rico Porto Rico	105.6	100.1	98.8	97.2	98.9	105.7	99.9	98.8	96.4	98.2
Saint Kitts and Nevis Saint-Kitts-et-Nevis	99.8	98.9	99.3	99.5	100.0	99.8	98.9	99.3	99.5	100.0
Saint Lucia Sainte-Lucie	99.5	91.0	101.6	93.6	91.8	99.5	91.0	101.6	93.6	91.8
St. Vincent-Grenadines St. Vincent-Grenadines	100.1	102.9	107.0	107.8	103.9	100.1	103.0	107.1	107.9	104.0
Trinidad and Tobago Trinité-et-Tobago	105.2	104.6	129.6	119.1	117.7	105.2	104.6	129.8	118.9	117.5
United States Etats-Unis	101.2	99.6	98.8	101.3	108.1	101.6	99.2	99.1	101.5	107.5
America, South **Amérique du Sud**	**99.7**	**102.6**	**106.7**	**112.2**	**116.4**	**99.7**	**102.4**	**106.4**	**112.6**	**115.5**
Argentina Argentine	99.8	99.6	97.9	103.3	101.7	100.0	99.6	98.3	103.9	102.0
Bolivia Bolivie	103.7	101.9	109.1	115.7	110.5	104.2	101.3	108.8	115.8	110.3
Brazil Brésil	99.4	103.9	111.8	118.5	126.1	99.2	103.6	110.9	118.9	124.3
Chile Chili	98.9	106.0	104.8	107.8	112.5	98.9	106.2	105.0	108.0	112.8
Colombia Colombie	100.7	102.6	104.1	107.3	109.7	100.5	102.5	103.7	107.1	109.7
Ecuador Equateur	98.8	103.7	102.9	105.8	105.5	98.9	103.3	104.8	107.6	107.2
Falkland Is. (Malvinas) Iles Falkland (Malvinas)	100.8	99.4	122.9	99.4	99.4	102.9	96.4	96.7	96.7	96.7
French Guiana Guyane française	95.3	109.0	97.6	99.2	99.1	95.3	109.0	97.6	99.2	99.1
Guyana Guyana	102.4	99.1	95.4	106.1	105.3	102.4	99.1	95.3	106.1	105.2
Paraguay Paraguay	95.8	104.3	98.3	111.9	116.5	96.0	103.1	101.4	114.4	115.0
Peru Pérou	101.6	103.0	109.0	111.4	109.5	101.3	103.3	109.6	112.2	110.2
Suriname Suriname	95.2	103.4	88.9	95.9	100.6	95.2	103.4	88.9	95.9	100.6
Uruguay Uruguay	102.6	88.1	93.2	101.1	113.0	102.8	87.6	94.4	103.1	115.5
Venezuela (Bolivarian Republic of) Venezuela (Rép. bolivarienne)	100.6	104.7	102.6	95.3	98.0	100.7	104.8	102.9	95.6	98.3
Asia **Asie**	**100.2**	**102.6**	**105.4**	**109.5**	**113.0**	**100.2**	**102.6**	**105.6**	**109.7**	**112.4**
Armenia Arménie	96.0	103.3	108.5	114.8	139.9	95.2	103.6	108.8	115.9	140.6
Azerbaijan Azerbaïdjan	101.4	108.0	112.9	116.7	119.5	100.3	109.4	116.2	118.5	121.1
Bahrain Bahreïn	104.4	89.0	86.6	101.2	99.0	104.4	89.0	86.6	101.2	99.0
Bangladesh Bangladesh	102.8	100.7	102.9	106.0	104.6	102.9	100.5	103.0	106.1	104.6

Country or area	Agriculture — Agriculture					Food — Produits alimentaires				
Pays ou zone	2000	2001	2002	2003	2004	2000	2001	2002	2003	2004
Bhutan Bhoutan	90.1	97.9	91.3	96.1	94.5	90.0	97.9	91.3	96.1	94.5
Brunei Darussalam Brunéi Darussalam	98.7	114.3	105.9	105.6	121.2	98.7	114.3	105.9	105.6	121.3
Cambodia Cambodge	99.4	103.2	98.8	114.2	105.6	99.1	103.6	99.3	114.2	105.4
China [1] Chine [1]	100.2	103.8	109.0	112.2	118.1	100.2	103.5	109.1	112.6	117.8
Cyprus Chypre	101.8	99.5	102.9	103.6	105.1	101.8	99.5	102.8	103.5	105.0
Georgia Géorgie	92.0	98.2	92.5	106.1	99.1	93.3	100.0	93.7	108.2	100.8
India Inde	99.0	102.0	97.8	105.3	106.0	99.1	102.4	98.0	104.9	104.7
Indonesia Indonésie	100.7	102.0	109.1	114.6	119.0	100.6	102.1	108.1	113.8	117.4
Iran (Islamic Rep. of) Iran (Rép. islamique d')	100.3	98.8	110.8	112.6	114.5	100.2	99.0	111.4	113.2	115.4
Israel Israël	105.1	101.6	104.2	106.4	107.9	105.7	101.5	104.5	106.8	108.2
Japan Japon	100.5	98.6	99.2	95.2	97.7	100.6	98.6	99.2	95.3	97.7
Jordan Jordanie	111.4	100.0	137.4	117.3	118.1	111.2	100.2	136.9	117.2	118.2
Kazakhstan Kazakhstan	90.9	108.3	109.7	106.9	104.9	90.2	107.8	110.0	106.0	103.1
Korea, Dem. P. R. Corée, R. p. dém. de	96.1	105.9	107.6	109.5	109.3	95.8	106.2	107.8	109.9	109.7
Korea, Republic of Corée, République de	100.4	100.7	94.0	91.4	91.5	100.3	100.9	94.3	91.9	92.1
Kuwait Koweït	91.7	116.0	117.1	123.1	125.9	91.6	116.0	117.1	123.1	125.9
Kyrgyzstan Kirghizistan	100.3	104.9	98.8	102.6	97.8	99.5	105.7	100.6	104.4	97.9
Lao People's Dem. Rep. Rép. dém. pop. lao	104.8	106.4	115.3	110.8	115.3	102.9	107.1	117.0	113.8	116.8
Lebanon Liban	105.4	93.7	100.6	98.9	100.4	105.9	93.3	101.1	99.3	100.8
Malaysia Malaisie	99.0	104.7	106.2	114.9	121.3	98.3	104.9	106.3	114.9	120.0
Maldives Maldives	103.3	103.9	113.7	113.9	115.0	103.3	103.9	113.7	113.9	115.0
Mongolia Mongolie	109.4	84.2	101.4	93.8	93.5	109.7	83.6	101.9	93.8	93.6
Myanmar Myanmar	99.7	108.1	111.2	118.5	115.3	99.6	108.2	111.4	118.8	115.4
Nepal Népal	100.3	103.4	106.3	111.5	110.7	100.3	103.3	106.3	111.5	110.5
Occupied Palestinian Terr. Terr. palestinien occupé	93.8	105.6	107.8	102.4	106.3	93.8	105.6	107.8	102.4	106.3
Oman Oman	97.5	101.6	93.3	84.5	92.1	97.4	101.7	93.2	84.3	92.1

Country or area Pays ou zone	Agriculture — Agriculture					Food — Produits alimentaires				
	2000	2001	2002	2003	2004	2000	2001	2002	2003	2004
Pakistan Pakistan	101.7	99.1	100.6	104.4	112.8	102.0	99.4	101.5	106.0	110.6
Philippines Philippines	99.7	104.2	109.2	111.6	115.2	99.8	104.2	109.4	111.8	115.5
Qatar Qatar	111.6	80.9	108.2	146.6	143.9	111.6	80.9	108.2	146.6	143.9
Saudi Arabia Arabie saoudite	92.8	115.4	112.9	116.4	118.5	92.7	115.5	113.0	116.5	118.6
Singapore Singapour	66.4	72.3	66.9	70.9	70.2	66.4	72.3	66.9	70.9	70.2
Sri Lanka Sri Lanka	101.8	98.8	101.0	103.5	96.8	101.6	98.8	100.4	104.0	95.6
Syrian Arab Republic Rép. arabe syrienne	103.0	106.9	118.3	115.2	118.8	102.7	107.8	125.3	119.7	121.7
Tajikistan Tadjikistan	98.9	112.2	115.5	135.7	147.7	104.4	106.8	122.2	129.9	145.8
Thailand Thaïlande	100.5	103.9	104.2	108.6	106.7	100.4	103.9	104.4	109.0	104.7
Timor-Leste Timor-Leste	99.4	101.2	108.7	108.1	112.0	99.3	99.7	109.0	108.3	112.9
Turkey Turquie	104.2	96.3	102.0	103.5	103.6	104.6	96.2	101.8	103.8	103.9
Turkmenistan Turkménistan	102.3	101.0	103.8	118.4	122.1	100.8	106.8	116.6	127.9	131.0
United Arab Emirates Emirats arabes unis	141.0	63.9	62.9	60.2	64.0	141.1	63.8	62.7	60.1	63.7
Uzbekistan Ouzbékistan	100.9	101.4	105.3	106.1	107.3	101.8	101.8	107.4	111.1	105.2
Viet Nam Viet Nam	100.7	104.4	112.4	117.4	124.1	100.4	103.8	112.8	117.6	124.4
Yemen Yémen	99.1	107.1	106.3	105.6	110.5	99.1	107.1	106.3	105.4	110.5
Europe **Europe**	**100.1**	**99.8**	**101.6**	**97.8**	**104.2**	**100.1**	**99.8**	**101.7**	**97.9**	**104.4**
Albania Albanie	100.2	102.6	103.6	106.6	104.2	100.1	103.3	104.6	108.0	105.1
Austria Autriche	97.5	100.1	99.0	95.9	102.2	97.5	100.1	99.0	95.9	102.2
Belarus Bélarus	98.5	102.8	103.4	102.3	116.4	98.3	102.8	103.5	102.1	116.0
Bosnia and Herzegovina Bosnie-Herzégovine	87.7	97.6	98.8	91.6	98.1	87.7	97.6	98.3	91.6	98.0
Bulgaria Bulgarie	97.6	101.7	106.6	93.8	108.7	98.3	100.6	105.3	92.2	107.7
Croatia Croatie	95.3	98.9	113.4	86.8	96.9	95.3	98.8	113.5	86.6	96.7
Czech Republic République tchèque	97.1	101.5	96.7	88.5	104.6	97.1	101.5	96.7	88.5	104.6
Denmark Danemark	99.9	100.5	99.7	100.6	101.4	99.9	100.6	99.7	100.6	101.4
Estonia Estonie	98.1	96.8	98.7	100.4	102.1	98.1	96.8	98.7	100.4	102.1

30

Agricultural production—Index base: 1999-01 = 100 (*continued*)
Production agricole—Indices base : 1999-01 = 100 (*suite*)

Country or area Pays ou zone	Agriculture—Agriculture					Food—Produits alimentaires				
	2000	2001	2002	2003	2004	2000	2001	2002	2003	2004
Finland Finlande	102.9	101.7	104.8	101.4	103.6	102.9	101.7	104.8	101.4	103.6
France France	101.3	95.3	102.1	94.7	101.6	101.3	95.3	102.1	94.7	101.6
Germany Allemagne	100.1	99.5	96.7	92.9	102.9	100.1	99.6	96.8	92.9	102.9
Greece Grèce	102.4	98.5	95.0	85.0	93.9	102.4	97.6	95.9	85.4	95.3
Hungary Hongrie	93.5	111.8	96.9	94.1	111.7	93.5	111.9	96.9	94.0	111.9
Iceland Islande	101.1	100.9	103.3	104.1	103.1	100.8	100.6	104.6	105.3	104.3
Ireland Irlande	99.2	98.3	95.0	95.9	98.4	99.2	98.3	95.0	95.8	98.4
Italy Italie	99.7	97.7	94.2	90.6	97.9	99.7	97.6	94.2	90.5	98.1
Latvia Lettonie	98.8	99.0	108.1	107.3	117.3	98.8	99.0	108.1	107.4	117.4
Lithuania Lituanie	109.2	90.9	105.5	115.4	112.2	109.2	91.0	105.5	115.2	112.2
Malta Malte	99.2	97.6	97.1	102.4	106.8	99.2	97.6	97.1	102.3	106.8
Netherlands Pays-Bas	100.5	94.5	97.2	92.3	95.1	100.5	94.5	97.1	92.3	95.1
Norway Norvège	99.2	96.8	97.1	99.3	99.5	99.3	96.8	97.1	99.3	99.5
Poland Pologne	98.0	102.3	101.4	102.3	106.5	98.1	102.4	101.6	102.5	106.7
Portugal Portugal	100.8	95.2	101.7	96.6	98.8	100.8	95.2	101.7	96.6	98.9
Republic of Moldova République de Moldova	102.7	103.7	111.5	105.6	113.2	102.1	104.8	113.7	108.4	115.7
Romania Roumanie	88.1	107.6	101.8	106.9	122.8	88.1	107.8	101.7	107.2	123.2
Russian Federation Fédération de Russie	100.1	104.2	113.2	105.9	111.4	100.0	104.2	113.3	105.9	111.4
Serbia and Montenegro Serbie-et-Monténégro	99.8	98.7	103.5	100.4	113.8	99.9	98.6	103.3	100.5	114.2
Slovakia Slovaquie	91.5	100.8	104.6	92.8	106.9	91.5	100.8	104.6	92.7	107.0
Slovenia Slovénie	101.5	99.2	106.4	102.4	108.5	101.5	99.2	106.4	102.4	108.5
Spain Espagne	102.8	102.2	101.7	108.0	105.6	103.0	102.4	101.8	108.2	105.9
Sweden Suède	101.4	99.7	100.8	99.7	99.3	101.5	99.8	100.8	99.8	99.4
Switzerland Suisse	102.6	98.9	101.1	99.7	99.6	102.6	98.9	101.1	99.7	99.6
TFYR of Macedonia L'ex-R.y. Macédoine	102.9	93.1	84.8	94.9	106.8	104.3	93.0	84.3	95.7	108.5
Ukraine Ukraine	100.6	108.0	110.7	98.2	115.4	100.6	108.1	110.7	98.2	115.4

30

Agricultural production—Index base: 1999-01 = 100 (*continued*)
Production agricole—Indices base : 1999-01 = 100 (*suite*)

Country or area / Pays ou zone	Agriculture — Agriculture					Food — Produits alimentaires				
	2000	2001	2002	2003	2004	2000	2001	2002	2003	2004
United Kingdom / Royaume-Uni	102.3	92.5	100.1	98.4	97.9	102.4	92.7	100.3	98.5	98.0
Oceania / Océanie	**98.9**	**102.6**	**89.5**	**99.4**	**96.6**	**98.5**	**103.1**	**91.1**	**102.6**	**98.8**
Australia / Australie	98.0	102.1	82.9	95.0	89.6	97.4	102.7	84.4	98.9	91.9
Fiji / Fidji	101.8	95.8	99.1	93.9	95.6	101.8	95.7	99.2	93.8	95.5
French Polynesia / Polynésie française	102.6	102.8	111.2	110.1	111.7	102.6	102.9	111.2	110.1	111.7
Guam / Guam	99.9	100.1	103.9	103.7	107.0	99.9	100.1	103.9	103.7	107.0
Kiribati / Kiribati	97.4	98.9	100.5	101.0	107.3	97.4	98.9	100.5	101.0	107.3
Micronesia (Fed. States of) / Micronésie (Etats féd. de)	100.0	100.0	100.1	100.1	100.1	100.0	100.0	100.1	100.1	100.1
New Caledonia / Nouvelle-Calédonie	98.8	100.2	100.6	100.9	103.0	98.9	100.1	100.7	101.0	103.0
New Zealand / Nouvelle-Zélande	101.1	104.7	106.2	111.6	115.0	100.9	105.3	107.1	112.8	116.4
Papua New Guinea / Papouasie-Nouvelle-Guinée	101.7	99.7	103.3	104.9	106.3	101.4	100.6	104.2	105.9	107.7
Samoa / Samoa	100.7	102.0	101.6	103.3	103.3	100.7	102.0	101.7	103.3	103.3
Solomon Islands / Iles Salomon	98.4	94.1	96.1	100.5	143.0	98.4	94.1	96.1	100.5	143.2
Tonga / Tonga	99.3	99.9	103.5	102.2	102.2	99.3	99.9	103.5	102.2	102.2
Vanuatu / Vanuatu	97.9	99.0	89.8	94.0	97.3	97.9	99.0	89.8	94.0	97.3

Source

Food and Agriculture Organization of the United Nations (FAO), Rome, FAOSTAT data, 2005, last accessed August 2005, and the "FAO Production Yearbook".

Note

[1] For statistical purposes, the data for China do not include those for the Hong Kong Special Administrative Region (Hong Kong SAR) and Macao Special Administrative Region (Macao SAR).

Source

Organisation des Nations Unies pour l'alimentation et l'agriculture (FAO), Rome, données FAOSTAT, année 2005, dernier accès août 2005, et "l'Annuaire FAO de la production".

Note

[1] Pour la présentation des statistiques, les données pour Chine ne comprennent pas la Région Administrative Spéciale de Hong Kong (Hong Kong RAS) et la Région Administrative Spéciale de Macao (Macao RAS).

31

Cereals
Production: thousand metric tons

Céréales
Production : milliers de tonnes

Region, country or area Région, pays ou zone	1995	1996	1997	1998	1999	2000	2001	2002	2003	2004
World Monde	1 897 364	2 072 342	2 095 363	2 084 214	2 085 780	2 060 540	2 107 829	2 036 818	2 081 039	2 264 030
Africa Afrique	97 542	125 194	110 186	115 715	113 983	112 091	115 548	116 920	129 634	127 737
Algeria Algérie	2 140	4 902	870	3 026	2 021	935	2 659	1 953	4 266	3 994
Angola Angola	296	525	457	621	550	520	597	566	663	626[1]
Benin Bénin	734	714	877	867	974	993	943	926	1 232	1 102[1]
Botswana Botswana	45	114	45	16	21	25	24	36	38	45[1]
Burkina Faso Burkina Faso	2 308	2 482	2 014	2 657	2 700	2 286	3 109	3 119	3 564	3 063
Burundi Burundi	*269	*273	*305	261	265	245	273	282	287[1]	280
Cameroon Cameroun	1 180	1 296	1 267	1 412	1 185	1 275	1 356	1 388[1]	1 412[1]	1 412[1]
Cape Verde Cap-Vert	8	10	5	5	36	24	20	5	*12	*4
Central African Rep. Rép. centrafricaine	113	126	138	148	161	166	183	193	202	202[1]
Chad Tchad	907	878	986	1 312	1 231	930	1 321	1 212	*1 423	1 394
Comoros Comores	21	21	21	21	21	21	21	21	21[1]	21[1]
Congo Congo	9	*10	10	11	7	8	8	8	9[1]	9[1]
Côte d'Ivoire Côte d'Ivoire	1 409	1 793	1 961	1 873	2 121	2 039	1 898	2 059	1 808	2 205
Dem. Rep. of the Congo Rép. dém. du Congo	1 475	1 557	1 584	1 675	1 648	1 623	1 600	1 574	1 569	1 570
Egypt Egypte	16 097	16 542	18 071	17 964	19 401	20 106	18 561	19 425	19 796	20 261
Eritrea Erythrée	*123	*83	95	458	319	121	208	63	105	102
Ethiopia Ethiopie	6 740	9 379	9 473	7 197	8 379	8 005	9 578	9 042	8 720	9 280
Gabon Gabon	29	29	25	27	28	27	26	25	32	32[1]
Gambia Gambie	98	103	100	106	151	176	200	139	171	162
Ghana Ghana	1 797	1 770	1 669	1 788	1 686	1 711	1 627	2 155	2 041	1 943
Guinea Guinée	825	876	927	982	1 042	973	1 031	1 094	1 161	1 142
Guinea-Bissau Guinée-Bissau	201	175	140	139	145	178	160	150	154	193
Kenya Kenya	3 230	2 669	2 700	2 927	2 802	2 591	3 369	3 045	3 351	2 709

Region, country or area / Région, pays ou zone	1995	1996	1997	1998	1999	2000	2001	2002	2003	2004
Lesotho / Lesotho	81	257	206	169	174	179	242	195	180	248[1]
Liberia / Libéria	*56	*94	168	209	196	183	*145	*110	*100	*110
Libyan Arab Jamah. / Jamah. arabe libyenne	146	160	206	213[1]	213	217	218	212	213[1]	213
Madagascar / Madagascar	2 642	2 685	2 742	2 610	2 756	2 660	2 853	2 787	3 129	3 391
Malawi / Malawi	1 778	1 943	1 349	1 904	2 636	2 631	1 742	1 711	2 142	1 847
Mali / Mali	2 189	2 219	2 138	2 548	2 894	2 310	2 584	2 532	2 788	2 728
Mauritania / Mauritanie	222	234	154	189	194	180	124	113	153[1]	153[1]
Mauritius / Maurice	0	0	0	0	0	1	0	0	0	0[1]
Morocco / Maroc	1 783	10 104	4 098	6 632	3 846	2 002	4 607	5 293	7 972	8 591
Mozambique / Mozambique	1 127	1 379	1 531	1 688	1 822	1 473	1 478	1 769	1 812	1 813[1]
Namibia / Namibie	66	89	185	70	74	121	107	100	107	98[1]
Niger / Niger	2 096	2 232	1 719	2 973	2 853	2 127	3 161	3 289	3 309	3 169
Nigeria / Nigéria	22 513	21 665	21 853	22 040	22 405	21 370	20 090	21 844	22 616	22 783
Réunion / Réunion	17	16	17[1]	17[1]	17[1]	17[1]	17[1]	17[1]	17[1]	17[1]
Rwanda / Rwanda	143	183	223	194	179	240	285	308	298	319
Sao Tome and Principe / Sao Tomé-et-Principe	4	5	4	*1	1	2	3[1]	3[1]	3[1]	3[1]
Senegal / Sénégal	1 059	976	781	717	1 131	1 026	962	785	1 452	*1 200
Sierra Leone / Sierra Leone	408	444	467	373	280	222	259	304	309	309
South Africa / Afrique du Sud	7 511	13 668	13 250	10 221	10 065	14 528	10 732	13 053	11 825	12 225
Sudan / Soudan	3 305	5 202	4 209	5 583	3 066	3 259	5 339	3 721	6 380	3 792
Swaziland / Swaziland	152	121	139	119	125	92	75	77	70	71[1]
Togo / Togo	591	687	748	624	759	737	715	804	816	787
Tunisia / Tunisie	647	2 894	1 081	1 697	1 837	1 118	1 391	550	2 312	2 155
Uganda / Ouganda	2 030	1 588	1 625	2 085	2 178	2 112	2 309	2 368	2 413	2 625
United Rep. of Tanzania / Rép.-Unie de Tanzanie	4 774	5 016	3 324	4 465	4 088	4 327	4 262	4 575	4 261	4 458
Zambia / Zambie	870	1 573	1 137	798	1 003	1 050	750	745	1 365	1 364[1]
Zimbabwe / Zimbabwe	988	3 147	2 785	1 879	1 997	2 538	1 897	756	1 259	1 227

Region, country or area Région, pays ou zone	1995	1996	1997	1998	1999	2000	2001	2002	2003	2004
America, North **Amérique du Nord**	**359 327**	**429 347**	**419 748**	**434 836**	**422 699**	**427 692**	**405 926**	**369 924**	**435 687**	**478 105**
Barbados Barbade	1[1]	1[1]	1[1]	1[1]	0[1]	0[1]	0[1]	0	0	0
Belize Belize	43	56	60	52	62	48	57	57	56	49
Canada Canada	49 344	58 494	49 557	50 993	54 078	51 038	43 391	36 303	50 174	52 680
Costa Rica Costa Rica	210	266	282	263	322	315	239	202	229	234
Cuba Cuba	501	718	818	619	797	826	900	1 001	1 076	910[1]
Dominican Republic Rép. dominicaine	548	535	564	530	605	610	771	766	656	687
El Salvador El Salvador	899	867	773	783	857	779	760	814	791	822
Guatemala Guatemala	1 164	1 140	954	1 164	1 134	1 161	1 199	1 155	*1 147	1 172
Haiti Haïti	410[1]	412	490[1]	403	475[1]	431	363	374[1]	398[1]	367[1]
Honduras Honduras	770	784	757	590	562	607	603	447	592	597
Jamaica Jamaïque	4	4	3	2	2	2	2	2	1	1[1]
Mexico Mexique	26 883	29 311	28 062	29 123	27 419	27 991	31 057	28 772	30 315	30 251
Nicaragua Nicaragua	622	674	608	618	559	765	755	911	972	878
Panama Panama	310	316	269	233	265	303	342	324	374	381
Puerto Rico Porto Rico	1[1]	1[1]	1	1	1[1]	0[1]	0[1]	0[1]	0[1]	0[1]
St. Vincent-Grenadines St. Vincent-Grenadines	2	1	1	2	1	1	1	1	1	1
Trinidad and Tobago Trinité-et-Tobago	15	23	12	12	7	7	5	7	6	6[1]
United States Etats-Unis	277 600	335 744	336 536	349 445	335 553	342 809	325 480	298 788	348 897	389 068
America, South **Amérique du Sud**	**91 833**	**93 330**	**99 127**	**96 004**	**100 786**	**104 188**	**113 714**	**103 339**	**123 710**	**122 119**
Argentina Argentine	24 307	30 700	35 907	37 808	35 036	38 749	35 922	32 071	33 961	34 212
Bolivia Bolivie	1 092	1 139	920	1 146	1 128	1 256	1 279	1 257	1 486	1 341[1]
Brazil Brésil	49 642	44 962	44 876	40 743	47 431	45 897	57 117	50 879	66 895	64 049
Chile Chili	2 766	2 578	3 077	3 098	2 168	2 590	3 116	3 380	3 693	3 956
Colombia Colombie	3 435	3 177	3 207	2 893	3 400	3 765	3 827	3 794	4 062	4 450
Ecuador Equateur	1 900	1 947	1 815	1 485	1 847	1 909	1 644	1 940	1 967	1 802
French Guiana Guyane française	25	31	31	25	20	20	32	22	23	24[1]

Region, country or area / Région, pays ou zone	1995	1996	1997	1998	1999	2000	2001	2002	2003	2004
Guyana / Guyana	532	547	576	526	565	453	498	446	*506	506[1]
Paraguay / Paraguay	1 522	1 210	1 450	1 156	1 156	1 003	1 455	1 371	1 710	2 002
Peru / Pérou	2 132	2 338	2 584	2 840	3 402	3 556	3 741	3 847	3 927	3 389
Suriname / Suriname	242	229	213	189	180	164	191	157	194	195[1]
Uruguay / Uruguay	1 811	2 222	2 057	1 961	2 219	1 880	1 749	1 606	2 171	2 523
Venezuela (Bolivarian Rep. of) / Venezuela (Rép. bolivarienne)	2 428	2 250	2 413	2 134	2 234	2 948	3 143	2 569	3 116	3 671
Asia / Asie	**944 371**	**996 942**	**992 861**	**1 016 746**	**1 036 022**	**996 192**	**1 001 291**	**990 134**	**996 906**	**1 037 612**
Armenia / Arménie	257	323	259	328	302	225	367	416	310	456
Azerbaijan / Azerbaïdjan	909	1 000	1 119	918	1 069	1 496	1 956	2 133	1 993	*2 091
Bangladesh / Bangladesh	27 703	29 620	29 674	31 577	36 403	39 539	38 014	39 270	40 667	39 232
Bhutan / Bhoutan	151[1]	164[1]	173	173	157	107	115[1]	93	108	97[1]
Brunei Darussalam / Brunéi Darussalam	*1	*0	*0	*0	0	0	0	0	1	1
Cambodia / Cambodge	3 503	3 469	3 457	3 558	4 136	4 183	4 285	3 971	4 901	4 426
China [2,3] / Chine [2,3]	418 664	453 665	445 931	458 396	455 193	407 336	398 395	399 998	376 123	413 568
Cyprus / Chypre	145	141	48	66	127	48	127	142	142	107
Georgia / Géorgie	501	630	892	589	771	418	704	662	742	663
India / Inde	210 013	218 750	223 232	226 877	236 206	234 866	242 964	214 570	233 406	233 360
Indonesia / Indonésie	57 990	60 409	58 148	59 406	60 070	61 575	59 808	61 144	63 024	65 416
Iran (Islamic Rep. of) / Iran (Rép. islamique d')	17 032	16 083	15 823	18 979	14 186	12 874	14 945	19 861	20 930	21 610
Israel / Israël	309	264	187	249	122	183	242	271	324	294
Japan / Japon	14 122	13 668	13 320	11 934	12 283	12 796	12 255	12 184	10 826	12 041
Jordan / Jordanie	125	97	96	76	27	57	48	115	80	91
Kazakhstan / Kazakhstan	9 476	11 210	12 359	6 380	14 248	11 539	15 866	15 929	14 743	12 347
Korea, Dem. P. R. / Corée, R. p. dém. de	3 787	2 596	2 867	4 420	3 837	2 945	3 880	4 211	4 319	4 456
Korea, Republic of / Corée, République de	6 877	7 617	7 676	7 132	7 458	7 501	7 860	7 083	6 355	7 153
Kuwait / Koweït	2	3	2	3	7	6	6	11	8	8[1]
Kyrgyzstan / Kirghizistan	912	1 325	1 610	1 608	1 618	1 550	1 795	1 712	1 633	1 709

Region, country or area Région, pays ou zone	1995	1996	1997	1998	1999	2000	2001	2002	2003	2004
Lao People's Dem. Rep. Rép. dém. pop. lao	1 466	1 490	1 738	1 784	2 199	2 319	2 447	2 541	2 518	2 733
Lebanon Liban	100	94	90	103	93	123	153	140	146	145[1]
Malaysia Malaisie	2 170	2 273	2 168	1 994	2 094	2 206	2 162	2 267	2 331	2 259
Mongolia Mongolie	261	220	240	195	170	142	142	153	184	154
Myanmar Myanmar	18 483	18 204	17 217	17 636	20 774	21 964	22 717	22 695	24 152	22 892
Nepal Népal	6 078	6 378	6 350	6 390	6 930	7 116	7 120	7 215	7 684	7 591
Occupied Palestinian Terr. Terr. palestinien occupé	66	51	43	52	14	67	38	77	68	68[1]
Oman Oman	6[1]	6[1]	6[1]	5	5	6	6	6	6	6[1]
Pakistan Pakistan	25 036	25 395	25 260	27 985	27 756	30 461	27 048	27 172	28 964	30 509
Philippines Philippines	14 702	15 629	15 600	12 377	16 371	16 901	17 480	17 590	18 116	19 910
Qatar Qatar	4	5	6	6	6	6	5	6	6[1]	6[1]
Saudi Arabia Arabie saoudite	2 669	1 932	2 339	2 202	2 454	2 167	2 590	2 853	2 949	2 792
Sri Lanka Sri Lanka	2 850	2 099	2 269	2 731	2 894	2 896	2 728	2 890	3 107	2 541
Syrian Arab Republic Rép. arabe syrienne	6 094	5 990	4 322	5 270	3 301	3 511	6 919	5 930	6 223	5 249
Tajikistan Tadjikistan	249	548	559	491	465	545	478	688	868	*883
Thailand Thaïlande	26 413	27 144	27 635	28 265	28 661	30 519	31 212	30 512	31 646	31 350
Timor-Leste Timor-Leste	150	159	137	96	149	*139	*123	147	*136	136[1]
Turkey Turquie	28 134	29 344	29 761	33 187	28 886	32 249	29 571	30 831	30 807	33 967
Turkmenistan Turkménistan	1 102	545	759	1 278	1 567	1 751	1 832	2 461	2 667	2 783
United Arab Emirates Emirats arabes unis	1	1	0	0	0	0	0	0	0	0[1]
Uzbekistan Ouzbékistan	3 223	3 558	3 768	4 132	4 311	3 914	4 056	5 535	6 030	5 071
Viet Nam Viet Nam	26 141	27 933	29 175	30 758	33 147	34 535	34 270	36 958	37 705	39 571
Yemen Yémen	810	660	646	833	694	672	700	560	418	488
Europe **Europe**	**376 120**	**390 949**	**441 193**	**386 683**	**376 011**	**385 039**	**431 495**	**436 553**	**355 249**	**466 198**
Albania Albanie	645	504	602	606	498	566	503	519	489	522
Austria Autriche	4 455	4 493	5 009	4 776	4 809	4 494	4 830	4 461	3 996	5 009
Belarus Bélarus	5 315	5 482	5 928	4 497	3 413	4 565	4 871	5 710	5 116	*6 585

Region, country or area / Région, pays ou zone	1995	1996	1997	1998	1999	2000	2001	2002	2003	2004
Belgium / Belgique	...	...	...	...	...	2 513	2 359	2 639	2 561	2 951
Belgium-Luxembourg / Belgique-Luxembourg	2 144	2 571	2 393	2 601	2 449	...	...	...	...	...
Bosnia and Herzegovina / Bosnie-Herzégovine	671	841	1 242	1 327	1 369	930	1 138	1 308	802	1 159
Bulgaria / Bulgarie	6 548	3 404	6 187	5 378	5 260	4 387	6 076	6 776	3 819	7 463
Croatia / Croatie	2 760	2 762	3 179	3 210	2 883	2 770	3 396	3 722	2 355	3 268[1]
Czech Republic / République tchèque	6 611	6 654	6 995	6 676	6 935	6 460	7 347	6 780	5 759	8 796
Denmark / Danemark	9 150	9 218	9 529	9 334	8 774	9 413	9 423	8 807	9 051	8 963
Estonia / Estonie	513	629	651	576	402	697	558	525	506	600
Finland / Finlande	3 333	3 708	3 807	2 773	2 879	4 095	3 670	3 936	3 788	3 616
France / France	53 545	62 599	63 432	68 664	64 342	65 698	60 237	69 657	54 940	70 534
Germany / Allemagne	39 863	42 136	45 486	44 575	44 461	45 271	49 686	43 391	39 426	51 097
Greece / Grèce	4 903	4 894	4 970	4 611	4 576	4 968	4 930	4 799	4 534	4 584
Hungary / Hongrie	11 299	11 344	14 139	13 038	11 392	10 036	15 046	11 703	8 770	16 749
Ireland / Irlande	1 796	2 142	1 944	1 866	2 011	2 174	2 165	1 964	2 147	2 142[1]
Italy / Italie	19 693	20 900	19 917	20 731	21 068	20 661	20 034	21 256	17 864	22 864
Latvia / Lettonie	692	964	1 040	964	786	929	930	1 033	932	*1 060
Lithuania / Lituanie	1 907	2 615	2 945	2 717	2 048	2 657	2 344	2 531	2 623	*2 859
Luxembourg / Luxembourg	...	...	...	...	...	153	144	169	164	180
Malta / Malte	7	7	11	11	11	12	12	12	12	12
Netherlands / Pays-Bas	1 505	1 659	1 449	1 497	1 368	1 732	1 672	1 652	1 861	1 754
Norway / Norvège	1 227	1 345	1 288	1 358	1 218	1 300	1 219	1 142	1 291	1 427
Poland / Pologne	25 905	25 298	25 399	27 159	25 750	22 341	26 960	26 877	23 391	28 174
Portugal / Portugal	1 446	1 673	1 559	1 622	1 678	1 608	1 298	1 497	1 182	1 287
Republic of Moldova / République de Moldova	2 611	1 976	3 487	2 428	2 142	1 905	2 550	2 539	1 583	*2 830
Romania / Roumanie	19 883	14 200	22 107	15 453	17 038	10 500	18 900	14 364	12 973	24 232
Russian Federation / Fédération de Russie	61 902	67 589	86 801	46 937	53 845	64 326	83 398	84 859	65 562	76 231
Serbia and Montenegro / Serbie-et-Monténégro	9 246	7 294	10 355	8 667	8 615	5 391	9 040	8 327	5 541	9 585

Region, country or area Région, pays ou zone	1995	1996	1997	1998	1999	2000	2001	2002	2003	2004
Slovakia Slovaquie	3 489	3 322	3 740	3 485	2 829	2 201	3 412	3 193	2 490	3 793
Slovenia Slovénie	453	487	544	557	477	494	499	614	402	586
Spain Espagne	11 574	22 366	19 324	22 557	17 988	24 556	18 050	21 710	21 449	24 743
Sweden Suède	4 791	5 954	5 986	5 618	4 931	5 670	5 391	5 462	5 352	5 508
Switzerland Suisse	1 281	1 348	1 223	1 263	1 055	1 206	1 094	1 101	878	1 035[1]
TFYR of Macedonia L'ex-R.y. Macédoine	725	546	610	660	638	563	475	556	472	684
Ukraine Ukraine	32 360	23 448	34 393	25 724	23 950	23 807	38 879	37 994	19 663	40 979
United Kingdom Royaume-Uni	21 870	24 576	23 523	22 768	22 125	23 989	18 959	22 966	21 511	22 338
Oceania **Océanie**	**28 172**	**36 582**	**32 249**	**34 230**	**36 279**	**35 338**	**39 855**	**19 947**	**39 854**	**32 259**
Australia Australie	27 390	35 647	31 237	33 340	35 370	34 448	38 878	18 975	38 916	31 341
Fiji Fidji	20	19	19	6	18	14	16	14	17	16[1]
New Caledonia Nouvelle-Calédonie	1	2	2	2	2	5	5	4	6	4[1]
New Zealand Nouvelle-Zélande	752	904	980	869	873	854	938	936	899	882
Papua New Guinea Papouasie-Nvl-Guinée	8	9	10	10	11	11	13	13	10	11
Solomon Islands Iles Salomon	0[1]	0[1]	0[1]	*1	*5	5[1]	5[1]	5[1]	5[1]	6[1]
Vanuatu Vanuatu	1[1]	1[1]	1	1	1[1]	1[1]	1[1]	1[1]	1[1]	1[1]

Source

Food and Agriculture Organization of the United Nations (FAO), Rome, FAOSTAT data, 2005, last accessed August 2005.

Notes

[1] FAO estimate.
[2] Data generally include those for Taiwan Province of China.
[3] For statistical purposes, the data for China do not include those for the Hong Kong Special Administrative Region (Hong Kong SAR) and Macao Special Administrative Region (Macao SAR).

Source

Organisation des Nations Unies pour l'alimentation et l'agriculture (FAO), Rome, données FAOSTAT, année 2005, dernier accès août 2005.

Notes

[1] Estimation de la FAO.
[2] Les données comprennent en général les chiffres pour la province de Taiwan.
[3] Pour la présentation des statistiques, les données pour Chine ne comprennent pas la Région Administrative Spéciale de Hong Kong (Hong Kong RAS) et la Région Administrative Spéciale de Macao (Macao RAS).

Oil crops
Production in oil equivalent: thousand metric tons

Cultures oléagineuses
Production en équivalent d'huile : milliers de tonnes

Region, country or area / Région, pays ou zone	1995	1996	1997	1998	1999	2000	2001	2002	2003	2004
World / Monde	91 857	93 446	98 036	102 645	109 104	110 043	112 135	114 148	123 169	132 727
Africa / Afrique	6 089	7 073	6 593	6 781	7 608	7 066	7 169	7 204	7 524	7 530
Algeria / Algérie	41	81	82	40	93	60	57	54	49	49[1]
Angola / Angola	72	74	73	75	72	75	79	82	82[1]	82[1]
Benin / Bénin	93	100	93	97	100	102	110	125	118	115
Botswana / Botswana	1	2	2	3	3	3	3[1]	3[1]	3	3[1]
Burkina Faso / Burkina Faso	90	106	98	118	130	88	156	160	167	177
Burundi / Burundi	7	6	6	6	6	5	5	5	5[1]	5[1]
Cameroon / Cameroun	217	273	220	238	249	262	265	270	287	291[1]
Cape Verde / Cap-Vert	1	1	1	1	1	1	1	1	1	1
Central African Rep. / Rép. centrafricaine	58	56	61	61	66	64	71	72	73	73[1]
Chad / Tchad	113	122	146	174	143	143	177	174	168	177
Comoros / Comores	9	10	10	10	10	10	10	10	10[1]	10[1]
Congo / Congo	27	27	25	25	27	27	27	27	27[1]	27[1]
Côte d'Ivoire / Côte d'Ivoire	390	416	374	401	399	422	335	409	446	431
Dem. Rep. of the Congo / Rép. dém. du Congo	372	356	337	340	335	331	329	333	340	341
Egypt / Egypte	206	224	211	189	223	218	252	243	215	239
Equatorial Guinea / Guinée équatoriale	7[1]	7[1]	6[1]	6[1]	6	6[1]	6[1]	6[1]	6[1]	6[1]
Eritrea / Erythrée	11	7	6	8	7	7	7	6	9	8
Ethiopia / Ethiopie	85	121	86	83	80	86	105	99	98	137
Gabon / Gabon	13	12	13	12	12	13	13[1]	12	13[1]	13[1]
Gambia / Gambie	26	18	27	26	41	46	50	25	27	26
Ghana / Ghana	216	202	210	249	240	246	260	338	315	312
Guinea / Guinée	118	126	131	131	137	143	148	154	161	170
Guinea-Bissau / Guinée-Bissau	19	19	20	20	20	21	20	20	21	21

Oil crops — Production in oil equivalent: thousand metric tons (*continued*)
Cultures oléagineuses — Production en équivalent d'huile : milliers de tonnes (*suite*)

Region, country or area Région, pays ou zone	1995	1996	1997	1998	1999	2000	2001	2002	2003	2004
Kenya Kenya	32	34	34	35	42	40	40[1]	39	39[1]	39[1]
Liberia Libéria	41	53	50	50	50	50	50	50	50	50
Libyan Arab Jamah. Jamah. arabe libyenne	41	45	47	49	66	42	39	40	40	47
Madagascar Madagascar	28	30	31	30	31	30	30	28	28	29
Malawi Malawi	21	29	28	34	44	40	50	54	63	54
Mali Mali	103	101	104	105	138	98	103	89	102	100
Mauritania Mauritanie	2	2	2	2	2[1]	2[1]	2[1]	2[1]	2[1]	2[1]
Mauritius Maurice	1	0	1	0	0	0	0	0	1	1[1]
Morocco Maroc	104	229	158	196	133	109	118	120	136	142
Mozambique Mozambique	112	118	124	132	132	87	86	86	87	88[1]
Namibia Namibie	0	0	0	0	1	1	1[1]	1	1[1]	1[1]
Niger Niger	33	61	28	36	35	41	49	40	73	73[1]
Nigeria Nigéria	1 887	2 033	2 158	2 202	2 378	2 399	2 342	2 366	2 414	2 471
Rwanda Rwanda	4	3	3	3	3	5	6	6	7	7
Sao Tome and Principe Sao Tomé-et-Principe	4	5	5	5	5	7	7[1]	7[1]	8[1]	8[1]
Senegal Sénégal	250	207	177	184	316	330	297	93	154	161
Sierra Leone Sierra Leone	71	74	78	64	55	51	52	52[1]	57[1]	56[1]
South Africa Afrique du Sud	278	417	273	324	598	314	406	487	335	369
Sudan Soudan	444	491	503	409	493	447	477	487	562	564
Swaziland Swaziland	2	4	5	6	5	2	2	2	2[1]	2[1]
Togo Togo	40	47	44	43	41	39	44	46	47	47
Tunisia Tunisie	72	347	116	215	255	128	40	84	271[1]	84[1]
Uganda Ouganda	101	99	100	106	116	122	131	137	137	139
United Rep. of Tanzania Rép.-Unie de Tanzanie	139	141	134	120	127	133	144	139	137	155
Zambia Zambie	22	32	29	28	36	35	23	26	26	26[1]
Zimbabwe Zimbabwe	52	92	108	79	95	125	131	77	87	85

Region, country or area Région, pays ou zone	1995	1996	1997	1998	1999	2000	2001	2002	2003	2004
America, North **Amérique du Nord**	**17 155**	**17 553**	**19 779**	**20 913**	**20 864**	**20 490**	**20 452**	**19 073**	**18 864**	**22 795**
Belize Belize	1	1	0	0	0	0	0	0	0	0
Canada Canada	3 361	2 718	3 350	3 908	4 333	3 591	2 532	2 454	3 389	3 799
Costa Rica Costa Rica	106	110	115	122	122	151	165	143	171	210
Cuba Cuba	6	7	8	9	9	13	15	17	17	17
Dominica [1] Dominique [1]	2	2	2	1	1	1	1	1	1	1
Dominican Republic Rép. dominicaine	49	50	48	50	52	48	51	51	54	54
El Salvador El Salvador	15	15	15	15	16	14	16	6	10	17
Grenada [1] Grenade [1]	1	1	1	1	1	1	1	1	1	1
Guatemala Guatemala	59	73	82	84	95	104	117	138	138	141
Haiti Haïti	13[1]	13	14[1]	12	13[1]	12	12	12[1]	12[1]	12[1]
Honduras Honduras	91	94	92	108	106	111	149	146	180	193
Jamaica Jamaïque	23	25	24	23	23	23	23	23	23	23[1]
Mexico Mexique	331	347	365	392	378	316	332	272	325	333
Nicaragua Nicaragua	28	32	31	27	35	33	37	37	42	44
Panama Panama	2	2	2	2	14	15	15	15	15	16
Puerto Rico Porto Rico	1	1	1	0	1	1	1	1	1	1[1]
Saint Lucia [1] Sainte-Lucie [1]	2	2	3	1	3	2	2	2	2	2
St. Vincent-Grenadines St. Vincent-Grenadines	1	1	1	1	1	0	1	1	0	0
Trinidad and Tobago [1] Trinité-et-Tobago [1]	3	3	3	3	3	3	3	3	2	2
United States Etats-Unis	13 062	14 057	15 622	16 153	15 658	16 050	16 979	15 749	14 480	17 928
America, South **Amérique du Sud**	**11 499**	**11 157**	**11 568**	**14 135**	**14 918**	**15 090**	**16 139**	**17 912**	**20 581**	**19 689**
Argentina Argentine	4 854	4 921	4 483	6 083	6 780	6 399	6 345	7 220	7 939	7 149
Bolivia Bolivie	183	180	231	249	223	275	223	317	364	381
Brazil Brésil	5 057	4 573	5 270	6 198	6 229	6 696	7 720	8 570	10 233	10 040
Chile Chili	15	16	16	23	32	25	31	6	13	13
Colombia Colombie	469	492	523	498	583	608	639	616	622	742

Oil crops— Production in oil equivalent: thousand metric tons (*continued*)
Cultures oléagineuses— Production en équivalent d'huile : milliers de tonnes (*suite*)

Region, country or area Région, pays ou zone	1995	1996	1997	1998	1999	2000	2001	2002	2003	2004
Ecuador Equateur	221	226	275	299	200	259	274	287	291	308
Guyana Guyana	10	15	16	8	10	11	6	6	7	6
Paraguay Paraguay	490	520	542	599	625	623	714	660	824	736
Peru Pérou	65	70	61	53	60	67	66	63	65	72
Suriname Suriname	3	1	1	1	1	1	1	2	2	1[1]
Uruguay Uruguay	54	51	51	37	71	17	31	76	131	143
Venezuela (Bolivarian Rep. of) Venezuela (Rép. bolivarienne)	78	91	99	86	102	109	87	89	90	97
Asia Asie	**44 187**	**45 650**	**46 815**	**46 952**	**49 473**	**52 827**	**54 469**	**55 981**	**60 246**	**65 717**
Azerbaijan Azerbaïdjan	24	24	13	12	11	10	11	13	17	20
Bangladesh Bangladesh	161	159	162	163	162	158	154	153	148	146
Bhutan Bhoutan	1[1]	1[1]	1[1]	1[1]	1[1]	1	1[1]	1	1	1[1]
Cambodia Cambodge	15	20	25	18	22	21	20	25	26[1]	26[1]
China [2,3] Chine [2,3]	12 513	12 162	12 463	12 890	13 585	15 140	15 143	15 347	14 819	16 618
Cyprus Chypre	3	3	2	3	4	5	4	6	3	7[1]
Georgia Géorgie	3	2	13	10	17	2	18	9	11	9
India Inde	8 708	9 313	8 975	8 772	7 819	7 934	7 639	6 628	8 478	9 021
Indonesia Indonésie	7 472	7 928	8 384	8 986	9 272	10 248	11 296	12 973	14 381	16 134
Iran (Islamic Rep. of) Iran (Rép. islamique d')	91	105	101	105	93	109	101	95	96	94
Israel Israël	36	39	34	33	23	32	25	30	23	30
Japan Japon	38	45	36	36	42	51	59	56	49	57
Jordan Jordanie	14	20	13	30	8	30	14	40	26	26[1]
Kazakhstan Kazakhstan	82	57	56	67	91	93	122	143	185	176
Korea, Dem. P. R. Corée, R. p. dém. de	73	76	68	65	65	67	67	69	69	69
Korea, Republic of Corée, République de	57	53	54	50	43	45	45	41	33	38
Kyrgyzstan Kirghizistan	14	20	20	24	31	30	34	39	41	49
Lao People's Dem. Rep. Rép. dém. pop. lao	9	9	9	10	8	8	8	8	8	9
Lebanon Liban	15[1]	24	23	25	17	44	21	43	21	42[1]

Region, country or area Région, pays ou zone	1995	1996	1997	1998	1999	2000	2001	2002	2003	2004
Malaysia Malaisie	9 080	9 691	10 438	9 572	12 079	12 429	13 480	13 539	15 135	15 790
Maldives Maldives	*2	*2	*2	*2	*1	*2	*3	*5	5[1]	5[1]
Myanmar Myanmar	376	433	416	392	406	456	597	610	718	697
Nepal Népal	48	47	49	45	49	49	53	54	51	54
Occupied Palestinian Terr. Terr. palestinien occupé	29	11	22	8	35	9	32	19	20	20
Pakistan Pakistan	763	717	734	715	867	818	798	790	865	1 170
Philippines Philippines	1 660	1 626	1 851	1 731	1 646	1 763	1 783	1 905	1 936	1 945
Saudi Arabia Arabie saoudite	2	2	2	2	2	3	2	2	2	2
Sri Lanka Sri Lanka	277	255	264	254	284	310	277	240	258	258
Syrian Arab Republic Rép. arabe syrienne	171	237	207	290	202	317	232	319	220	327
Tajikistan Tadjikistan	39	29	33	34	28	31	42	49	53	54
Thailand Thaïlande	779	806	834	863	968	921	1 004	977	1 039	1 073
Timor-Leste Timor-Leste	2	2	2	3	3	3	3	3	3	3
Turkey Turquie	745	959	721	994	767	978	666	1 037	801	950
Turkmenistan Turkménistan	125	42	61	68	125	74	60	48	67	*71
Uzbekistan Ouzbékistan	398	343	373	327	344	299	309	301	272	338
Viet Nam Viet Nam	291	315	280	276	276	260	270	288	293	314
Yemen Yémen	7	8	9	10	10	11	11	11	11	11[1]
Europe **Europe**	**12 010**	**10 948**	**12 104**	**12 343**	**14 382**	**12 935**	**12 415**	**12 907**	**14 632**	**15 581**
Albania Albanie	9	7	8	12	11	9	10	7	7	7
Austria Autriche	134	71	76	97	120	88	93	92	79	98
Belarus Bélarus	22	20	20	30	34	42	49	35	31	78
Belgium Belgique	...	...	...	...	...	11	11	12	11	14
Belgium-Luxembourg Belgique-Luxembourg	14	14	14	15	19	...	...	...	...	...
Bosnia and Herzegovina Bosnie-Herzégovine	2	2	*2	*2	*2	2	2	2	2	3
Bulgaria Bulgarie	326	225	189	224	259	187	178	275	334	458
Croatia Croatie	38	26	28	52	71	49	47	66	56	60

Oil crops— Production in oil equivalent: thousand metric tons (*continued*)

Cultures oléagineuses— Production en équivalent d'huile : milliers de tonnes (*suite*)

Region, country or area / Région, pays ou zone	1995	1996	1997	1998	1999	2000	2001	2002	2003	2004
Czech Republic / République tchèque	280	221	237	297	412	362	413	314	229	422
Denmark / Danemark	119	96	112	137	158	113	81	83	135	178
Estonia / Estonie	3	4	4	7	11	15	16	24	26	28
Finland / Finlande	49	34	35	24	34	27	38	39	36	28
France / France	1 946	1 986	2 221	2 195	2 530	2 134	1 819	1 941	1 952	2 167
Germany / Allemagne	1 245	821	1 169	1 394	1 721	1 423	1 617	1 490	1 421	2 041
Greece / Grèce	616	571	571	581	672	682	627	679	548	613
Hungary / Hongrie	368	420	289	342	474	277	351	416	465	621
Ireland / Irlande	5	4	5	6	2	3	3	3	3	3[1]
Italy / Italie	1 139	888	1 241	1 018	1 222	1 020	1 071	998	946	959
Latvia / Lettonie	1	1	1	1	4	4	5	13	15	40
Lithuania / Lituanie	10	10	15	29	45	32	25	41	47	79
Luxembourg / Luxembourg	...	...	...	...	...	3	3	5	5	6
Netherlands / Pays-Bas	5	3	3	3	4	3	3	3	3	3[1]
Norway / Norvège	*5	*5	*5	5	4	3	7	7	5	*4
Poland / Pologne	531	177	231	425	438	368	410	366	306	496
Portugal / Portugal	87	84	78	81	86	75	81	67	73	74
Republic of Moldova / République de Moldova	96	130	83	83	120	112	106	132	163	138
Romania / Roumanie	407	473	382	493	613	338	392	455	668	736
Russian Federation / Fédération de Russie	1 865	1 274	1 283	1 370	1 839	1 759	1 238	1 658	2 193	2 217
Serbia and Montenegro / Serbie-et-Monténégro	146	196	138	146	166	166	170	162	188	237
Slovakia / Slovaquie	94	100	105	91	146	102	143	151	129	185
Slovenia / Slovénie	1	1	0	0	0	0	0	1	0	1
Spain / Espagne	645	1 544	1 890	1 494	1 086	1 511	1 888	1 311	1 945	1 449
Sweden / Suède	76	54	50	49	73	49	41	62	52	91
Switzerland / Suisse	18	18	21	21	18	20	21	26	25	*29
TFYR of Macedonia / L'ex-R.y. Macédoine	10	10	7	6	11	8	6	7	7	6

Region, country or area Région, pays ou zone	1995	1996	1997	1998	1999	2000	2001	2002	2003	2004
Ukraine Ukraine	1 203	888	972	968	1 216	1 486	994	1 401	1 835	1 391
United Kingdom Royaume-Uni	497	568	617	646	764	455	453	564	694	623
Oceania **Océanie**	**916**	**1 067**	**1 176**	**1 521**	**1 859**	**1 634**	**1 491**	**1 070**	**1 320**	**1 415**
American Samoa [1] Samoa américaines [1]	1	1	1	1	1	1	1	1	1	1
Australia Australie	382	435	565	880	1 223	971	901	482	732	742
Cocos (Keeling) Islands Iles des Cocos (Keeling)	1[1]	*1	*1	*1	*1	*1	1[1]	1[1]	1[1]	1[1]
Cook Islands Iles Cook	1[1]	1[1]	1	1	1[1]	1[1]	1[1]	1[1]	0	0
Fiji Fidji	25[1]	28[1]	28	27	22	22	22	22	20[1]	18[1]
French Polynesia [1] Polynésie française [1]	12	12	11	8	9	10	10	11	11	11
Guam Guam	5[1]	*7	*7	*7	*7	*7	7[1]	7[1]	7[1]	7[1]
Kiribati Kiribati	*11	*13	*13	*14	*14	*12	*12	*12	*12	13[1]
Marshall Islands [1] Iles Marshall [1]	5	5	4	3	2	2	2	2	2	2
New Caledonia [1] Nouvelle-Calédonie [1]	2	2	2	2	2	2	2	2	2	2
New Zealand Nouvelle-Zélande	2	2	2	2	2	2	2	2	2	2
Papua New Guinea Papouasie-Nvl-Guinée	337	426	394	424	464	510	439	442	445	476
Samoa Samoa	20[1]	21[1]	21[1]	20[1]	17[1]	18	18[1]	18[1]	18[1]	18[1]
Solomon Islands Iles Salomon	69	69	71	72	49	33	28	27	27	81
Tonga Tonga	5	5[1]	6[1]	7[1]	8	8	8[1]	8[1]	8[1]	8[1]
Vanuatu Vanuatu	36	38	48	51	37	33	36	31	31	32[1]

Source

Food and Agriculture Organization of the United Nations (FAO), Rome, FAOSTAT data, 2005, last accessed August 2005.

Notes

[1] FAO estimate.
[2] Data generally include those for Taiwan Province of China.

[3] For statistical purposes, the data for China do not include those for the Hong Kong Special Administrative Region (Hong Kong SAR) and Macao Special Administrative Region (Macao SAR).

Source

Organisation de Nations Unies pour l'alimentation et l'agriculture (FAO), Rome, données FAOSTAT, année 2005, dernier accès août 2005.

Notes

[1] Estimation de la FAO.
[2] Les données comprennent en général les chiffres pour la province de Taiwan.

[3] Pour la présentation des statistiques, les données pour Chine ne comprennent pas la Région Administrative Spéciale de Hong Kong (Hong Kong RAS) et la Région Administrative Spéciale de Macao (Macao RAS).

33

Roundwood
Production (solid volume of roundwood without bark): million cubic metres

Bois rond
Production (volume solide de bois rond sans écorce) : millions de mètres cubes

Region, country or area Région, pays ou zone	1995	1996	1997	1998	1999	2000	2001	2002	2003	2004
World Monde	3 251.1	3 234.1	3 304.3	3 224.2	3 292.4	3 356.7	3 284.3	3 301.0	3 347.5	3 401.9
Africa Afrique	568.3	576.2	582.5	584.9	588.3	592.8	589.8	597.5	608.6	621.7
Algeria Algérie	6.8	7.0	7.2	7.3	7.4	7.2	7.4	7.5	7.5	7.6
Angola Angola	3.8	3.8	3.9	4.0	4.2	4.3	4.3	4.4	4.5	4.6
Benin Bénin	6.1	6.2	6.2	6.2	6.2	6.2[1]	0.5	0.5	0.5	0.5[1]
Botswana [1] Botswana [1]	0.7	0.7	0.7	0.7	0.7	0.7	0.7	0.7	0.8	0.8
Burkina Faso Burkina Faso	10.8	11.0	11.1	11.3	7.8	8.0	8.0[1]	7.2	7.3	12.9[1]
Burundi Burundi	6.8	7.1	7.4[1]	7.7	5.6	5.8	8.3[1]	8.4[1]	8.6[1]	8.7[1]
Cameroon Cameroun	12.3	12.6	12.2	11.1	10.9	11.0	10.5	10.6	10.9	11.0[1]
Central African Rep. Rép. centrafricaine	3.6	3.2	3.4	3.5	2.9	3.0	3.0	2.9	2.8	2.8
Chad [1] Tchad [1]	5.9	6.0	6.2	6.3	6.5	6.6	6.8	6.9	7.0	7.1
Congo Congo	2.5	2.2	2.7	2.7	2.4	2.4	2.4	2.4	2.5	2.5
Côte d'Ivoire Côte d'Ivoire	11.9	11.7	11.6	11.8	11.7	11.9	12.1	11.6	11.6[1]	11.7[1]
Dem. Rep. of the Congo Rép. dém. du Congo	62.1	63.7	64.9	66.0	67.3[1]	68.6[1]	69.7[1]	70.9[1]	72.2[1]	73.4[1]
Egypt Egypte	15.5[1]	15.8	16.0[1]	16.1	16.3	16.4	16.6[1]	16.8[1]	16.9[1]	17.1[1]
Equatorial Guinea Guinée équatoriale	0.8	0.8[1]	0.8[1]	0.8[1]	0.8[1]	0.8[1]	0.8[1]	0.8[1]	0.8[1]	0.8[1]
Eritrea Erythrée	1.9	1.9	2.0	2.1	2.2	2.2[1]	2.3[1]	1.3	1.3[1]	2.4[1]
Ethiopia Ethiopie	82.5	83.7	85.5	86.5	88.2	89.9	91.3	92.7	94.1	95.5
Gabon Gabon	2.8	2.9	3.3	3.3[1]	2.8	3.1	3.1[1]	2.2	4.1	4.1[1]
Gambia Gambie	0.6	0.6	0.6	0.6	0.6	0.7[1]	0.7[1]	0.7[1]	0.7[1]	0.8[1]
Ghana Ghana	22.0	21.9	22.0	21.9	21.8	21.7	21.9	21.8	22.1	22.1[1]
Guinea Guinée	12.6[1]	12.7[1]	8.7	8.7	12.2[1]	12.1[1]	12.1[1]	12.2[1]	12.2[1]	12.3[1]
Guinea-Bissau [1] Guinée-Bissau [1]	0.6	0.6	0.6	0.6	0.6	0.6	0.6	0.6	0.6	0.6
Kenya Kenya	20.8	21.0	21.3	21.3	21.5	21.6	21.7	21.8	22.0	22.2
Lesotho Lesotho	1.5	1.5	1.6	1.6	2.0[1]	2.0[1]	2.0[1]	2.0[1]	2.0[1]	2.0[1]
Liberia Libéria	3.0[1]	3.1	3.5	4.1	4.5[1]	5.1[1]	5.3[1]	5.5[1]	5.7[1]	5.9[1]

Region, country or area Région, pays ou zone	1995	1996	1997	1998	1999	2000	2001	2002	2003	2004
Libyan Arab Jamah. [1] Jamah. arabe libyenne [1]	0.6	0.6	0.7	0.7	0.7	0.7	0.7	0.7	0.7	0.7
Madagascar Madagascar	9.8	10.1	9.2	9.2	9.5	9.7	10.0	10.3	10.6	10.9
Malawi [1] Malawi [1]	5.4	5.3	5.3	5.4	5.4	5.5	5.5	5.5	5.6	5.6
Mali Mali	4.8	4.9	5.0[1]	5.0[1]	5.1[1]	5.1[1]	5.2[1]	5.3[1]	5.3[1]	5.4[1]
Mauritania [1] Mauritanie [1]	1.3	1.3	1.3	1.4	1.4	1.4	1.5	1.5	1.5	1.6
Morocco Maroc	1.5	1.5	0.8	1.7	1.1	1.1	1.0	0.9	0.9	0.9
Mozambique Mozambique	17.9	17.9[1]	18.0[1]	18.0[1]	18.0[1]	18.0[1]	18.0[1]	18.0[1]	18.0[1]	18.0[1]
Niger Niger	7.2[1]	7.4[1]	7.6[1]	7.8[1]	8.0[1]	8.2[1]	3.3	8.6[1]	8.8[1]	9.0[1]
Nigeria Nigéria	65.0	66.2	67.7	67.8	68.3[1]	68.8[1]	69.1[1]	69.5[1]	69.9[1]	70.3[1]
Rwanda Rwanda	5.4	5.8	7.4	7.5	7.8	5.4	5.5	5.5	5.5[1]	5.5[1]
Senegal [1] Sénégal [1]	5.6	5.7	5.8	5.8	5.9	5.9	5.9	6.0	6.0	6.0
Sierra Leone [1] Sierra Leone [1]	4.7	4.7	5.1	5.2	5.3	5.5	5.5	5.5	5.5	5.5
Somalia [1] Somalie [1]	7.6	8.0	8.3	8.6	9.0	9.3	9.6	9.9	10.3	10.6
South Africa [2] Afrique du Sud [2]	32.0	32.4	33.2	30.6	30.6	30.6	30.6	30.6	33.2	33.2
Sudan [1] Soudan [1]	18.3	18.4	18.4	18.6	18.7	18.9	19.0	19.2	19.4	19.7
Swaziland Swaziland	1.5	1.5	1.5	0.9	0.9	0.9	0.9	0.9	0.9	0.9
Togo Togo	5.5	5.5	5.6	5.7	5.7	5.8	5.8	5.8	5.9	5.9[1]
Tunisia Tunisie	2.2	2.2	2.3	2.3	2.3	2.3	2.3	2.3	2.3	2.4
Uganda Ouganda	34.9	35.4	36.0	36.4	36.9	37.3[1]	37.8[1]	38.3[1]	38.9[1]	39.4[1]
United Rep. of Tanzania Rép.-Unie de Tanzanie	22.6	22.8	22.9	23.0	23.1	23.1	23.3	23.4	23.6	23.8
Zambia [1] Zambie [1]	8.2	8.1	8.0	8.0	8.1	8.1	8.1	8.1	8.1	8.1
Zimbabwe Zimbabwe	8.4	8.6	8.9	9.0	9.3	9.1	9.1	9.1	9.1	9.1
America, North **Amérique du Nord**	**777.4**	**770.8**	**769.6**	**764.4**	**756.0**	**762.0**	**730.0**	**735.3**	**733.7**	**754.4**
Bahamas Bahamas	0.1	0.1	0.1	0.0	0.0	0.0	0.0	0.0	0.0	0.0
Belize [1] Belize [1]	0.2	0.2	0.2	0.2	0.2	0.2	0.2	0.2	0.2	0.2
Canada Canada	188.4	189.8	191.2	176.9	193.9	201.8	187.6	192.1	190.2	199.6
Costa Rica Costa Rica	5.2	5.2	5.2	5.2	5.2	5.2	5.2	5.2	5.1	5.1
Cuba Cuba	3.6[1]	3.5[1]	3.5[1]	3.5[1]	1.6	1.8	1.7	2.8	2.6	3.6[1]

Roundwood — Production (solid volume of roundwood without bark): million cubic metres (*continued*)
Bois rond — Production (volume solide de bois rond sans écorce) : millions de mètres cubes (*suite*)

Region, country or area Région, pays ou zone	1995	1996	1997	1998	1999	2000	2001	2002	2003	2004
Dominican Republic [1] Rép. dominicaine [1]	0.6	0.6	0.6	0.6	0.6	0.6	0.6	0.6	0.6	0.6
El Salvador El Salvador	4.7	4.3	5.2	5.1	5.2	5.2	5.2	5.2	4.8[1]	4.9[1]
Guatemala Guatemala	13.6	13.5	13.8	14.1[1]	14.7	15.0	15.3	15.7	16.1	16.4[1]
Haiti [1] Haïti [1]	2.1	2.2	2.2	2.2	2.2	2.2	2.2	2.2	2.2	2.2
Honduras Honduras	9.1	9.3	9.4	9.5	9.6	9.5	9.6	9.7	9.5	9.5[1]
Jamaica Jamaïque	0.6	0.8	0.8	0.8	0.9	0.9[1]	0.9[1]	0.9[1]	0.9[1]	0.9[1]
Mexico Mexique	42.5	43.3	44.3	45.0	45.4	45.7	45.2	45.3	45.5	45.7
Nicaragua Nicaragua	5.8	5.9	5.8	5.9[1]	5.9[1]	6.0[1]	5.9	6.0	6.0	6.0[1]
Panama Panama	1.5	1.4	1.4	1.3	1.3	1.3	1.3	1.4	1.4	1.4[1]
Trinidad and Tobago Trinité-et-Tobago	0.2	0.1	0.1	0.1	0.1	0.1	0.1	0.1	0.1	0.1[1]
United States Etats-Unis	499.3	490.6	485.9	494.0	469.3	466.5	449.1	448.0	448.5	458.3
America, South **Amérique du Sud**	**307.2**	**305.6**	**304.4**	**305.8**	**325.6**	**331.3**	**332.2**	**333.7**	**337.6**	**342.3**
Argentina Argentine	10.6	11.4	6.9	5.7	10.6	10.0	9.3	9.3	9.3	9.3
Bolivia Bolivie	2.9	2.9	3.0	2.9	2.6	2.6	2.7	2.7	2.9	2.9
Brazil Brésil	211.1	212.3	213.5	213.7	231.6	235.4	236.4	237.5	238.5	239.6
Chile Chili	34.6	29.8	30.0	31.7	34.0	36.6	37.8	37.8	40.2	40.6
Colombia Colombie	9.5	9.5	9.6	10.1	10.6	13.1	12.5	11.6	10.0	10.0
Ecuador Equateur	10.7	11.3	12.1	11.5	5.5	5.7	6.1	6.2	6.3	6.3
French Guiana [1] Guyane française [1]	0.1	0.1	0.1	0.1	0.1	0.1	0.1	0.1	0.1	0.2
Guyana Guyana	1.4	1.4	1.5	1.3	1.3	1.2	1.2	1.2	1.2	1.2
Paraguay Paraguay	9.3	9.3	9.4	9.5	9.6	9.6[1]	9.7[1]	9.8[1]	9.9[1]	10.0[1]
Peru Pérou	8.0	7.9	8.4	9.2	9.2	9.3	8.6	8.8	10.3	10.5
Suriname Suriname	0.1	0.3	0.2	0.2	0.1	0.2	0.2	0.2	0.2	0.2
Uruguay Uruguay	4.6	4.7	5.0	5.2	5.1	2.9	3.0	3.4	3.7	6.4
Venezuela (Bolivarian Rep. of) Venezuela (Rép. bolivar. du)	4.3	4.6	4.7	4.6	5.3	4.7	4.6	5.1	5.0	5.1
Asia **Asie**	**1 052.1**	**1 066.5**	**1 071.7**	**1 044.4**	**1 036.4**	**1 019.7**	**1 007.6**	**999.4**	**1 000.2**	**998.9**
Afghanistan [1] Afghanistan [1]	2.6	2.7	2.8	2.9	3.0	3.0	3.1	3.1	3.1	3.2
Armenia Arménie	0.0	0.0	0.1	0.0	0.0	0.1	0.0	0.1	0.1	0.1

Region, country or area / Région, pays ou zone	1995	1996	1997	1998	1999	2000	2001	2002	2003	2004
Bangladesh / Bangladesh	28.5	28.5	28.5	28.5	28.5	28.5	28.4	28.0	28.0	28.0
Bhutan / Bhoutan	3.9[1]	4.0[1]	4.0[1]	4.1[1]	4.3	4.4	4.4[1]	4.5	4.5	4.6[1]
Brunei Darussalam [1] / Brunéi Darussalam [1]	0.2	0.2	0.2	0.2	0.2	0.2	0.2	0.2	0.2	0.2
Cambodia / Cambodge	12.0	11.9[1]	11.8[1]	11.6[1]	11.2	10.3	10.0	9.9	9.7[1]	9.5[1]
China [3,4] / Chine [3,4]	305.7	312.8	311.2	298.5	291.4	287.5	284.9	284.2	286.1	286.1
India / Inde	313.4	296.8	296.5	296.3	296.6	296.1	296.7	319.4	321.0	322.7
Indonesia / Indonésie	143.6	143.1	139.1	135.6	130.2	122.5	112.2	115.6	112.0	109.1
Iran (Islamic Rep. of) / Iran (Rép. islamique d')	1.5	1.4	1.5	1.3	1.1	1.1	1.3	0.7	0.7	0.8
Iraq / Iraq	0.1[1]	0.1[1]	0.2	0.2	0.1[1]	0.1[1]	0.1[1]	0.1[1]	0.1[1]	0.1[1]
Israel / Israël	0.1	0.1	0.1	0.1	0.1	0.1	0.0	0.0	0.0	0.0
Japan / Japon	23.1	23.2	22.3	19.6	19.0	18.1	15.9	15.2	15.3	15.3
Jordan [1] / Jordanie [1]	0.2	0.2	0.1	0.2	0.2	0.2	0.2	0.2	0.2	0.3
Kazakhstan / Kazakhstan	0.3	0.3	0.3	0.0[1]	*0.5	0.6	*0.7	*0.5	*0.3	0.3[1]
Korea, Dem. P. R. / Corée, R. p. dém. de	5.6	6.1[1]	6.5[1]	6.9[1]	6.9[1]	7.0[1]	7.1[1]	7.1[1]	7.2[1]	7.2[1]
Korea, Republic of / Corée, République de	3.8	3.6	3.5	3.9	4.1	4.0	4.0	4.1	4.1	4.1
Lao People's Dem. Rep. / Rép. dém. pop. lao	6.7	6.5	6.5	6.4[1]	6.7[1]	6.4	6.5	6.3	6.3[1]	6.3[1]
Lebanon / Liban	0.1[1]	0.1[1]	0.1[1]	0.1[1]	0.0	0.0	0.1[1]	0.1[1]	0.1[1]	0.1[1]
Malaysia / Malaisie	39.3	35.1	36.0	26.4	26.6	18.4	19.4	21.1	21.3	21.3
Mongolia [1] / Mongolie [1]	0.6	0.6	0.6	0.6	0.6	0.6	0.6	0.6	0.6	0.6
Myanmar / Myanmar	21.1	21.5	34.8	34.3	37.6	38.1	39.4	38.9	39.8	39.8[1]
Nepal / Népal	13.1[1]	13.1[1]	13.2[1]	13.9	13.9	14.0	14.0	14.0[1]	14.0[1]	14.0[1]
Pakistan / Pakistan	24.2	29.0	30.9	31.8	33.1	33.6	33.2	27.7	28.0	28.3
Philippines / Philippines	17.2	40.3	41.0	42.0	43.0	44.0	44.4	16.0	16.0	15.9
Sri Lanka / Sri Lanka	10.4	10.4	6.8	6.6	6.6	6.6	6.5	6.5	6.4	6.3
Syrian Arab Republic [1] / Rép. arabe syrienne [1]	0.1	0.1	0.1	0.1	0.1	0.1	0.1	0.1	0.1	0.1
Thailand / Thaïlande	23.5	23.4	23.4	23.4	23.4	26.8	27.5	28.1	27.9[1]	27.8[1]
Turkey / Turquie	19.3	19.4	18.1	17.7	16.6	15.9	15.3	16.1	15.8	15.8
Viet Nam / Viet Nam	31.6	31.6	31.3	31.0	30.2	30.9	30.8[1]	30.7[1]	30.7[1]	30.6[1]

Roundwood—Production (solid volume of roundwood without bark): million cubic metres (*continued*)

Bois rond—Production (volume solide de bois rond sans écorce) : millions de mètres cubes (*suite*)

Region, country or area Région, pays ou zone	1995	1996	1997	1998	1999	2000	2001	2002	2003	2004
Yemen [1] Yémen [1]	0.2	0.3	0.3	0.3	0.3	0.3	0.3	0.3	0.3	0.4
Europe **Europe**	**494.4**	**463.8**	**523.6**	**472.4**	**531.7**	**591.8**	**564.2**	**578.2**	**607.7**	**624.9**
Albania Albanie	0.4	0.4	0.4	*0.0	0.2	0.4	0.3	0.3	0.3	0.3[1]
Austria Autriche	14.4	15.6	15.3	14.0	14.1	13.3	13.5	14.8	17.1	16.5
Belarus Bélarus	10.0	15.7	17.6	5.9	6.6	6.1	6.5	6.9	7.5	7.5
Belgium Belgique	...	...	...	...	4.8	4.5[1]	4.2	4.5	4.8	4.8[1]
Belgium-Luxembourg Belgique-Luxembourg	4.1	4.0	4.0	4.8	...	...	...	...	...	...
Bosnia and Herzegovina Bosnie-Herzégovine	0.0	0.0	4.0	*4.1	*4.1	4.3	3.8	4.2	4.1	4.0
Bulgaria Bulgarie	2.8	3.2	3.0	3.2	4.4	4.8	4.0	4.8	4.8	4.8
Croatia Croatie	2.6	2.5	3.1	3.4	3.5	3.7	3.5	3.6	3.8	3.8
Czech Republic République tchèque	12.4	12.6	13.5	14.0	14.2	14.4	14.4	14.5	15.1	15.6
Denmark Danemark	2.3	2.3	2.1	1.6	1.6	3.0	1.6	1.4	1.6	1.6
Estonia Estonie	3.7	3.9	5.4	6.1	6.7	8.9	10.2	10.5	10.5	10.3
Finland Finlande	50.2	46.6	51.3	53.7	53.6	54.3	52.2	53.0	53.8	53.8
France France	43.4	40.4	41.1	35.5	36.0	45.8	39.8	35.4	32.8	34.6
Germany Allemagne	39.3	37.0	38.2	39.1	37.6	53.7	39.5	42.4	51.2	54.5
Greece Grèce	2.0	2.0	1.7	1.7	2.2	2.2	1.9	1.6	1.7	1.7
Hungary Hongrie	4.3	3.7	4.2	4.2	5.2	5.9	5.8	5.8	5.8	5.7
Ireland Irlande	2.2	2.3	2.2	2.3	2.6	2.7	2.5	2.6	2.7	2.5
Italy Italie	9.7	9.1	9.1	9.6	11.1	9.3	8.1	7.5	8.2	8.7
Latvia Lettonie	6.9	8.1	8.7	10.0	14.0	14.3	12.8	13.5	12.9	12.4
Lithuania Lituanie	6.0	5.5	5.1	4.9	4.9	5.5	5.7	6.1	6.3	6.1
Luxembourg Luxembourg	...	...	...	...	0.3	0.3[1]	0.3	0.3	0.3	0.3
Netherlands Pays-Bas	1.1	1.0	1.1	1.0	1.0	1.0	0.9	0.8	1.0	1.0
Norway Norvège	9.0	8.4	8.3	8.2	8.4	8.2	9.0	8.7	8.3	8.8
Poland Pologne	20.4	20.3	21.7	23.1	24.3	26.0	25.0	27.1	30.8	32.6
Portugal Portugal	9.4	9.0	9.0	8.5	9.0	10.8	8.9	8.7	9.7	9.7
Republic of Moldova République de Moldova	0.0	0.4	0.4	0.4	0.0	0.1	0.1	0.1[1]	0.1[1]	0.1[1]

Region, country or area Région, pays ou zone	1995	1996	1997	1998	1999	2000	2001	2002	2003	2004
Romania Roumanie	12.2	12.3	13.5	11.6	12.7	13.1	12.4	15.2	15.4	15.8
Russian Federation Fédération de Russie	116.2	96.8	134.7	95.0	143.6	158.1	164.7	165.0	174.0	182.0
Serbia and Montenegro Serbie-et-Monténégro	3.1	3.1	2.8	2.7	2.5	3.4	2.5	2.9	3.2	3.5
Slovakia Slovaquie	5.3	5.5	4.9	5.5	5.8	6.2	5.8	5.8	6.4	7.2
Slovenia Slovénie	1.9	2.0	2.2	2.1	2.1	2.3	2.3	2.3	2.6	2.6
Spain Espagne	16.1	15.6	15.6	14.9	14.8	14.3	15.1	15.8	16.1	16.3
Sweden Suède	63.6	56.3	60.2	60.6	58.7	63.3	63.2	66.6	67.1	67.3
Switzerland Suisse	4.7	4.1	4.5	4.3	4.7	9.2	5.7	4.6	5.1	4.7
TFYR of Macedonia L'ex-R.y. Macédoine	0.8	0.8	0.8	0.7	0.8	1.1	0.7	0.7	0.8	0.8[1]
Ukraine Ukraine	6.3	6.3	6.1	8.5	7.9	9.9	*9.9	12.3	13.8	14.9
United Kingdom Royaume-Uni	7.6	7.1	7.5	7.3	7.5	7.5	7.6	7.6	8.0	8.1
Oceania **Océanie**	**51.7**	**51.2**	**52.7**	**52.3**	**54.5**	**59.0**	**60.4**	**56.8**	**59.8**	**59.8**
Australia Australie	24.3	24.4	25.2	26.8	26.6	30.4	31.1	26.2	29.8	29.8
Fiji Fidji	0.6	0.6	0.5	0.5	0.5	0.5	0.5	0.4	0.4	0.4
New Zealand Nouvelle-Zélande	16.9	16.4	17.1	15.3	17.7	19.3	20.7	22.1	21.4	21.4
Papua New Guinea Papouasie-Nvl-Guinée	8.8	8.8	8.8	8.6	8.6	7.7	7.2	7.2	7.2	7.2
Samoa [1] Samoa [1]	0.1	0.1	0.1	0.1	0.1	0.1	0.1	0.1	0.1	0.1
Solomon Islands Iles Salomon	0.9	0.9[1]	0.9[1]	0.9[1]	0.9[1]	0.9[1]	0.7	0.7[1]	0.7[1]	0.7[1]
Vanuatu Vanuatu	0.1[1]	0.1[1]	0.1[1]	0.1	0.1	0.1	0.1	0.1[1]	0.1[1]	0.1[1]

Source

Food and Agriculture Organization of the United Nations (FAO), Rome, FAOSTAT data , 2005, last accessed October 2005, and the "FAO Yearbook of Forest Products".

Notes

[1] FAO estimate.

[2] Data include those for Namibia.

[3] For statistical purposes, the data for China do not include those for the Hong Kong Special Administrative Region (Hong Kong SAR) and Macao Special Administrative Region (Macao SAR).

[4] Data include those for Taiwan Province of China.

Source

Organisation des Nations Unies pour l'alimentation et l'agriculture (FAO), Rome, données FAOSTAT, année 2005, dernier accés octobre 2005, et "l'Annuaire FAO des produits forestiers".

Notes

[1] Estimation de la FAO.

[2] Les données comprennent les chiffres pour la Namibie.

[3] Pour la présentation des statistiques, les données pour Chine ne comprennent pas la Région Administrative Spéciale de Hong Kong (Hong Kong RAS) et la Région Administrative Spéciale de Macao (Macao RAS).

[4] Les données comprennent les chiffres pour la province de Taiwan.

Fish production
Capture and aquaculture: metric tons

Production halieutique
Capture et aquaculture : tonnes

Country or area Pays ou zone	Capture production — Captures					Aquaculture production — Production de l'aquaculture				
	2000	2001	2002	2003	2004	2000	2001	2002	2003	2004
Afghanistan [1] Afghanistan [1]	1 000	800	900	900	1 000	...	...	...	...	...
Albania Albanie	3 320	3 310	3 655	2 800 [1]	3 563	307	286	860	1 473	1 569
Algeria Algérie	113 157	133 623	134 320	141 528	140 000 [1]	351	454	476	417 [1]	586 [1]
American Samoa Samoa américaines	832	3 649	6 971	4 984	4 043	...	...	...	...	...
Angola Angola	239 351	254 519	254 807	211 539	240 005	...	...	...	...	...
Anguilla Anguilla	250 [1]	250 [1]	250 [1]	250 [1]	250	...	...	...	...	...
Antigua and Barbuda Antigua-et-Barbuda	1 754	1 824	2 374	2 587	2 527	...	...	...	...	...
Argentina Argentine	921 795	948 974	958 482	915 994	951 412	1 784	1 340	1 457	1 647	1 848
Armenia Arménie	1 133	866	465	569	218	893	1 331	1 020	1 064	813
Aruba Aruba	163	163	163 [1]	160 [1]	162	...	...	...	...	...
Australia Australie	190 358	191 371	197 184	212 817	228 038	31 746	35 403	38 569	40 308	39 331
Austria Autriche	439	362	350	372	400	2 847	2 393	2 333	2 233	2 267
Azerbaijan Azerbaïdjan	18 797	10 893	11 334	6 694	9 281	120	170	168	243	15
Bahamas Bahamas	11 070	9 290	12 192	12 611	11 347	2 [1]	13	25	42	10
Bahrain Bahreïn	11 718	11 230	11 204	13 638	14 259	12	0	3	4	8
Bangladesh Bangladesh	1 004 264	1 068 417	1 103 855	1 141 241	1 187 274	657 120	712 640	786 604	856 956	914 752
Barbados Barbade	3 100	2 676	2 500	2 500 [1]	2 500 [1]	...	...	...	...	...
Belarus Bélarus	553	943	5 877	6 925	890	6 716	4 666	6 523	5 393	4 150
Belgium Belgique	29 800	30 209	29 028	26 831	26 575	1 871	1 630	1 600	1 010 [1]	1 200 [1]
Belize Belize	51 540	16 396	24 753	5 245	2 907	3 630	4 460	4 400	10 160	11 428
Benin Bénin	32 324	38 415	40 663	41 893	39 988	...	...	7	7 [1]	7
Bermuda Bermudes	286	315	393	358	379	...	...	...	...	...
Bhutan Bhoutan	300 [1]	300 [1]	300 [1]	300 [1]	300 [1]	30 [1]	30 [1]	...	...	...
Bolivia Bolivie	6 106	5 940	6 300 [1]	6 599	6 746	405	320	418	375	450

Country or area Pays ou zone	Capture production — Captures					Aquaculture production — Production de l'aquaculture				
	2000	2001	2002	2003	2004	2000	2001	2002	2003	2004
Bosnia and Herzegovina Bosnie-Herzégovine	2 000[1]	2 000[1]	2 000[1]	2 000[1]	2 000[1]	...	...	4 685	6 635	6 394
Botswana Botswana	166	118	139	122	161	...	...	...	...	...
Brazil Brésil	666 846	730 378	755 582	712 144	746 217	172 450	203 710	242 590	277 640	269 699
British Virgin Islands Iles Vierges britanniques	43	837	1 062	2 771	1 262	...	...	...	...	...
Brunei Darussalam Brunéi Darussalam	2 487	1 597	2 058	2 226	2 428	113	99	157	160	708
Bulgaria Bulgarie	6 998	6 520	15 008	12 033	8 250	3 654	2 935	2 308	4 465	2 489
Burkina Faso Burkina Faso	8 500	8 500	8 500	9 000	9 000[1]	5	5	5	5	5[1]
Burundi Burundi	17 315	8 964	11 000[1]	14 697	13 431	100	100[1]	150[1]	200	200[1]
Cambodia Cambodge	284 368	428 200	406 182	364 357	305 817	14 430	14 000	14 600	18 500	20 835
Cameroon Cameroun	112 109	111 031	120 135	107 801	108 000[1]	50	150[1]	330	320	330[1]
Canada Canada	997 553	1 041 063	1 062 867	1 110 547	1 173 827	127 665	153 046	170 746	150 624	145 018
Cape Verde Cap-Vert	10 821	8 890	7 762	8 721	8 446	...	...	...	...	...
Cayman Islands Iles Caïmanes	125	125	125	125	125	...	...	...	...	...
Central African Rep. Rép. centrafricaine	15 000[1]	15 000[1]	15 000[1]	15 000[1]	15 000[1]	120[1]	125[1]	...	...	...
Chad Tchad	83 200	80 000[1]	75 000[1]	70 000[1]	70 000[1]	...	...	...	...	...
Channel Islands Iles Anglo-Normandes	3 589	3 927	3 449	3 526	3 201	390	487	580	684	775
Chile Chili	4 300 474	3 797 352	4 272 317	3 612 912	4 935 376	391 587	566 096	545 655	563 435	674 979
China [2] Chine [2]	16 987 325	16 529 389	16 553 144	16 755 653	16 892 793	24 580 671	26 050 101	27 767 251	28 886 199	30 614 968
China, Hong Kong SAR Chine, Hong Kong RAS	157 012	173 972	169 790	157 444	167 544	4 988	5 627	4 302	4 857	4 615
China, Macao SAR [1] Chine, Macao RAS [1]	1 500	1 500	1 500	1 500	1 500	...	...	...	...	...
Colombia Colombie	129 644	137 376[1]	148 000[1]	157 794	151 313	61 786	57 660[1]	57 160[1]	60 895	60 072
Comoros Comores	13 200	12 180	13 102	14 115	14 935	...	...	...	...	...
Congo Congo	45 958	48 830	51 003	46 972	43 502	26	25	26	27	25[1]
Cook Islands Iles Cook	650[1]	600[1]	1 678[1]	2 611[1]	3 279	0	0	0	0	0
Costa Rica Costa Rica	35 398	34 733	32 938	29 327	20 817	9 708	10 520	17 892	20 546	24 708
Côte d'Ivoire Côte d'Ivoire	75 772	73 556	79 689[1]	68 903	54 398	1 197	1 025	806	866	866

Country or area Pays ou zone	Capture production — Captures					Aquaculture production — Production de l'aquaculture				
	2000	2001	2002	2003	2004	2000	2001	2002	2003	2004
Croatia Croatie	21 062	18 489	21 230	19 946	30 164	6 674	10 166	8 416	7 605	10 147
Cuba Cuba	70 036	56 152	33 861	41 466	37 274	32 780	25 569	27 044	26 897	27 562
Cyprus Chypre	67 482	81 058	1 968	1 791	1 567	1 878	1 883	1 862	1 821	2 425
Czech Republic République tchèque	4 654	4 646	4 983	5 127	4 528	19 475	20 098	19 210	19 670	19 384
Dem. Rep. of the Congo Rép. dém. du Congo	209 300[1]	214 600[1]	220 000[1]	220 000[1]	220 000[1]	2 076	2 744	2 965	2 965[1]	2 965[1]
Denmark Danemark	1 534 089	1 510 694	1 442 348	1 036 154	1 089 986	43 609	41 573	32 026	37 771	42 252
Djibouti Djibouti	270	260	260	260[1]	260[1]	...	...	...	...	...
Dominica Dominique	1 200[1]	1 200[1]	1 270	1 100[1]	1 020[1]	7	7[1]	3	3[1]	3[1]
Dominican Republic Rép. dominicaine	11 029	13 217	17 261	18 097	14 223	2 125	2 647	3 554	1 944[1]	2 000[1]
Ecuador Equateur	592 547	586 563	318 642	397 864	335 811	61 311	52 428[1]	55 638[1]	65 227[1]	63 579[1]
Egypt Egypte	384 314	428 651	425 170	430 809	393 494	340 093	342 864	376 296	445 181	471 535
El Salvador El Salvador	9 590	19 010	34 455	35 410	42 415	261	395	781	1 131	2 219
Equatorial Guinea Guinée équatoriale	3 634	3 500[1]	3 500[1]	3 500[1]	3 500[1]	...	...	...	...	...
Eritrea Erythrée	12 612	8 820	7 832	6 689	7 404	...	...	...	...	...
Estonia Estonie	113 146	105 167	101 453	79 082	87 906	225	467	257	372	252
Ethiopia Ethiopie	15 681	15 390	12 300	9 213	10 005	0	0	0	0	0
Faeroe Islands Iles Féroé	454 399	515 909	525 946	620 991	599 386	32 610	51 749	50 952	65 517	41 879
Falkland Is. (Malvinas) Iles Falkland (Malvinas)	75 478	68 332	53 261	74 898	55 369	0	0	0	0	21
Fiji Fidji	40 000[1]	42 972	38 800	34 685	46 635	1 779	1 717	401	144	99
Finland Finlande	156 431	150 056	142 301	121 954	135 879	15 400	15 739	15 132	12 558	12 821
France France	634 992	615 784	631 599	638 795	597 018	266 770	251 620	251 970	239 814	243 870
French Guiana Guyane française	4 837[1]	4 694[1]	4 968[1]	5 565[1]	5 514[1]	31	37	38	37	37
French Polynesia Polynésie française	13 899	15 404	15 543	14 100[1]	12 200[1]	53	66	65	65[1]	60
Gabon Gabon	47 826	42 871	41 571	45 958	45 960	558	102	83	80	80
Gambia Gambie	29 016	34 527	45 769	36 864	31 423	...	...	...	...	...
Georgia Géorgie	1 791	1 636	1 811	3 306	2 951	86	80	52	56	72

Country or area Pays ou zone	Capture production — Captures					Aquaculture production — Production de l'aquaculture				
	2000	2001	2002	2003	2004	2000	2001	2002	2003	2004
Germany Allemagne	205 689	211 282	224 452	260 867	262 103	65 891	53 409	49 852	74 280	57 233
Ghana Ghana	452 070	447 181	371 178	390 756	399 370	5 000	6 000	6 000[1]	938	950
Greece Grèce	99 332	94 190	96 343	93 383	93 220	95 418	97 512	87 928	101 434	97 068
Greenland Groenland	159 711	158 485	195 624	175 321	216 302	...	...	...	...	...
Grenada Grenade	1 701	2 250	2 171	2 544	2 039	4	0	0	0	0
Guadeloupe Guadeloupe	10 100	10 100	10 100	10 100	10 100	14	14	23	31	31
Guam Guam	275	278	231	162	180	232[1]	232[1]	233[1]	...	...
Guatemala Guatemala	39 203	30 514[1]	24 164	24 134	13 831[1]	3 963	5 100[1]	7 978[1]	6 346[1]	4 508[1]
Guinea Guinée	91 513	105 402	92 755	118 845	92 550	0	0	0	0	0
Guinea-Bissau [1] Guinée-Bissau [1]	6 315	6 848	7 324	6 153	6 200	...	...	...	...	...
Guyana Guyana	48 887	53 405	48 017	59 696	56 717	606	608	608	608[1]	608[1]
Haiti Haïti	6 200[1]	6 800[1]	7 300[1]	7 800[1]	8 300	...	...	...	...	...
Honduras Honduras	14 507[1]	18 159[1]	10 086[1]	10 516[1]	14 939[1]	9 080	12 130	14 557	20 035	22 520
Hungary Hongrie	7 101	6 638	6 750	6 536	7 242	12 886	13 056	11 574	11 870	12 744
Iceland Islande	1 982 524	1 980 715	2 129 705	1 978 135	1 728 085	3 623	4 371	3 585	6 214	8 868
India Inde	3 666 427	3 777 092	3 736 603	3 712 149	3 615 724	1 942 204	2 119 839	2 187 189	2 312 971	2 472 335
Indonesia Indonésie	4 082 810	4 242 270	4 322 764	4 627 149	4 811 320	788 500	864 276	914 071	996 659	1 045 051
Iran (Islamic Rep. of) Iran (Rép. islamique d')	383 990	351 140	324 853	350 122	369 990	40 550	62 550	76 817	91 714	104 330
Iraq Iraq	20 767	33 300	35 900	17 200	14 687	1 745	2 000[1]	2 000[1]	2 000[1]	12 196
Ireland Irlande	276 292	356 430	282 338	266 218	280 229	51 247	60 940	62 568	62 516	58 359
Isle of Man Ile de Man	3 552	3 112	3 127	2 984	2 627	...	...	...	...	...
Israel Israël	5 818	5 024	5 043	4 055	3 340	20 098	21 318	22 256	20 776	22 303
Italy Italie	302 149	310 397	269 846	295 694	287 084	213 525	218 269	183 962	191 662	117 786
Jamaica Jamaïque	5 540	12 294	7 797	8 702	13 471	4 512	4 512[1]	6 150	2 969	4 142
Japan Japon	4 985 894	4 703 147	4 360 664[1]	4 670 452	4 401 341	762 824	799 946	826 715	823 873	776 421
Jordan Jordanie	550	520	526	481	494	569	540	515	650	487

Country or area / Pays ou zone	Capture production — Captures					Aquaculture production — Production de l'aquaculture				
	2000	2001	2002	2003	2004	2000	2001	2002	2003	2004
Kazakhstan / Kazakhstan	36 620	21 654	24 910	25 371	33 896	813[1]	417	778	820	589
Kenya / Kenya	215 106	164 151	144 512	120 051	126 867	512	1 009	798	1 012	1 035
Kiribati / Kiribati	25 566	32 377	31 638	31 357	31 600[1]	14	18	14	9	9[1]
Korea, Dem. P. R. / Corée, R. p. dém. de	212 850[1]	206 500	205 000[1]	205 000[1]	205 000[1]	66 700[1]	63 700[1]	63 700[1]	63 700[1]	63 700[1]
Korea, Republic of / Corée, République de	1 824 995	1 990 722	1 671 420	1 642 905	1 575 337	293 420	294 484	296 783	387 791	405 748
Kuwait / Koweït	6 977	5 846	5 360	4 059	4 833	376	195	195[1]	366	375[1]
Kyrgyzstan / Kirghizistan	52	57	48	14	7	58	144	94	12	20
Lao People's Dem. Rep. / Rép. dém. pop. lao	29 250	31 000[1]	33 440	29 800	29 800[1]	42 066	50 000[1]	59 716	64 900	64 900
Latvia / Lettonie	136 403	128 176	113 677	114 543	125 391	325	463	430	637	545
Lebanon / Liban	3 666	3 670	3 970	3 898	3 866	400	300	790	790	790
Lesotho / Lesotho	32	24	40	42	45	8	8	8[1]	4	2
Liberia / Libéria	11 726	11 286	11 000[1]	10 700[1]	10 359	22	14	14[1]	14[1]	...
Libyan Arab Jamah. / Jamah. arabe libyenne	44 887	46 239	46 666	46 666[1]	46 073[1]	100[1]	100[1]	...	58[1]	266[1]
Lithuania / Lituanie	78 988	150 831	150 146	157 205	158 140	1 996	2 001	1 750	2 356	2 697
Madagascar / Madagascar	132 093	135 583	141 284	140 838	128 958	7 280[1]	7 749	9 713	9 507	8 743
Malawi / Malawi	50 000[1]	40 619	41 329	53 543	56 463	530[1]	568	642	666	733
Malaysia / Malaisie	1 289 245	1 234 733	1 275 555	1 287 084	1 335 764	151 773	158 158	165 119	167 160	171 270
Maldives / Maldives	118 963	127 184	163 388	155 415	158 576	...	...	...	...	...
Mali / Mali	109 870	100 000[1]	100 000[1]	100 000[1]	100 000[1]	30	500[1]	1 008	1 008[1]	1 008[1]
Malta / Malte	1 074	895	1 074	1 132	1 134	1 746	1 235	1 116	887	868
Marshall Islands / Iles Marshall	8 060	36 274	39 452	38 375	47 172	...	...	...	...	...
Martinique / Martinique	6 310	6 200	6 200[1]	6 200	6 200	51	51	80	100	92
Mauritania / Mauritanie	109 456[1]	135 142[1]	149 131[1]	141 898[1]	199 380	...	...	...	...	...
Mauritius / Maurice	9 615	10 986	10 706	11 136	10 227	87	59	56	33	350
Mayotte / Mayotte	6 088	10 052	4 754	3 464	2 306	3[1]	3[1]	...	...	170
Mexico / Mexique	1 315 581	1 398 592	1 450 673	1 451 278	1 450 063	53 918	76 075	73 675	89 037[1]	89 037[1]

Country or area / Pays ou zone	Capture production — Captures					Aquaculture production — Production de l'aquaculture				
	2000	2001	2002	2003	2004	2000	2001	2002	2003	2004
Micronesia (Fed. States of) Micronésie (Etats féd. de)	23 138[1]	19 199[1]	23 257[1]	32 381[1]	29 234	0	0	0	0	0
Monaco [1] Monaco [1]	3	3	3	3	3	...	...	...	...	...
Mongolia Mongolie	425	117	129	200[1]	305	...	...	...	...	...
Montserrat Montserrat	50[1]	50[1]	46	50[1]	50[1]	...	...	...	...	...
Morocco Maroc	875 215	1 083 953	894 977	885 131	894 608	1 889	1 403	1 670	1 538	1 718
Mozambique Mozambique	37 729	30 074	36 462	43 933[1]	44 683[1]	0	0	677	409	446
Myanmar Myanmar	1 093 200	1 187 880	1 284 340	1 343 860	1 586 660	98 912	121 266	190 120	252 010	400 360
Namibia Namibie	589 904	547 498	624 891	636 296	570 708	50[1]	50[1]	50	50[1]	50[1]
Nauru Nauru	109[1]	61[1]	22	44	18	...	...	...	...	...
Nepal Népal	16 700	16 700	17 900	18 888	19 947	15 023	16 570	17 100	17 680	20 000
Netherlands Pays-Bas	495 774	518 163	464 036	526 280	521 636	75 339	57 064	54 442	67 025	78 925
Netherlands Antilles Antilles néerlandaises	19 882[1]	22 805[1]	12 901[1]	23 070[1]	600[1]	5[1]	5[1]	...	...	...
New Caledonia Nouvelle-Calédonie	3 386	3 309	3 417[1]	3 513	3 500[1]	1 761	1 887	1 911	1 775	2 284
New Zealand Nouvelle-Zélande	553 254	567 504	576 076	550 313	539 587	85 640	76 024	86 583	84 642	92 219
Nicaragua Nicaragua	22 525	19 528	16 421	15 326	19 297	5 435	5 750	6 089	7 005	7 880
Niger Niger	16 250	20 800	23 560	55 860	51 466	15	21	40	40	40
Nigeria Nigéria	441 377	452 146	481 056	475 162	465 251	25 718	24 398	30 663	30 677	43 950
Niue [1] Nioué [1]	200	200	200	200	200	...	...	...	...	...
Northern Mariana Islands Iles Mariannes du Nord	189	197	198	173	167	...	...	...	...	...
Norway Norvège	2 699 365	2 686 944	2 740 344	2 548 975	2 522 225	491 329	510 748	550 209	582 767	637 993
Occupied Palestinian Terr. Terr. palestinien occupé	2 623	1 950	2 379	1 508	2 951	...	...	...	...	...
Oman Oman	120 421	129 907	142 670	138 481	165 029	0	0	0	352	503
Pakistan Pakistan	614 069	600 798	599 104	564 743	556 438	12 485	16 405	12 440	12 061	13 557[1]
Palau Palaos	1 096	1 084	1 027	1 047	1 079	2	2	4	4	5
Panama Panama	215 532	265 500[1]	229 736	215 398	192 485	1 779[1]	3 127	3 638[1]	6 228	7 048
Papua New Guinea Papouasie-Nvl-Guinée	96 578[1]	122 483[1]	150 653[1]	187 900[1]	233 800[1]	12	15	15[1]	15[1]	...

Country or area Pays ou zone	Capture production — Captures					Aquaculture production — Production de l'aquaculture				
	2000	2001	2002	2003	2004	2000	2001	2002	2003	2004
Paraguay [1] Paraguay [1]	28 000	25 000	24 000	23 000	22 000	103	570	1 000	1 300	2 100
Peru Pérou	10 657 308	7 983 108	8 765 186	6 085 912	9 613 180	6 512	7 628	11 614	13 768	22 199
Philippines Philippines	1 896 661	1 949 076	2 030 622	2 165 904	2 211 570	393 863	434 661	443 537	459 615	512 220
Pitcairn [1] Pitcairn [1]	8	8	5	5	5	...	...	...	...	...
Poland Pologne	217 682	225 064	223 440	180 254	192 109	35 795	35 460	32 709	34 526	35 258
Portugal Portugal	190 893	193 265	202 845	212 949	221 429	7 537	8 209	8 288	8 033	6 700
Puerto Rico Porto Rico	4 154	3 794	2 529	2 919	2 428	154	414	442	269	417
Qatar Qatar	7 140	8 864	7 155	11 295	11 134	0	1	0	0	0
Republic of Moldova République de Moldova	344	387	565	343	487	990	1 189	1 765	2 638	4 470
Réunion Réunion	4 082	3 889	2 872	2 904	3 373	142	130	110	121	107
Romania Roumanie	7 372	7 637	6 989	10 050	5 086	9 727	10 818	9 248	9 042	8 137
Russian Federation Fédération de Russie	3 973 473	3 628 422	3 232 282	3 281 448	2 941 533	74 124	89 945	101 330	108 684	109 802
Rwanda Rwanda	6 726	6 828	7 000[1]	7 400	7 400[1]	270	435	612[1]	1 027	1 027[1]
Saint Helena Sainte-Hélène	719	866	598	985	1 061	...	...	...	...	...
Saint Kitts and Nevis Saint-Kitts-et-Nevis	469	555	355	400[1]	477	...	...	...	...	...
Saint Lucia Sainte-Lucie	1 855	1 983	1 637	1 462	1 508	1	1	2	2[1]	1
Saint Pierre and Miquelon Saint-Pierre-et-Miquelon	6 485	3 802	3 692	3 831	4 311	...	...	...	...	...
St. Vincent-Grenadines St. Vincent-Grenadines	27 694	52 485	44 529	4 782	8 625	...	...	...	...	...
Samoa Samoa	13 004	11 800[1]	9 900[1]	6 600[1]	4 719	0	0	0	0	0
Sao Tome and Principe Sao Tomé-et-Principe	3 500[1]	3 400[1]	3 300[1]	3 283	4 141	...	...	...	...	...
Saudi Arabia Arabie saoudite	49 080	55 331	57 211	55 440	55 418	6 004	8 218	6 744	11 824	11 172
Senegal Sénégal	431 716	433 202	405 824	478 484	445 263	104	105	109	98	204
Serbia and Montenegro Serbie-et-Monténégro	1 103	1 015	1 403	1 066	1 371	2 844	2 688	2 450	2 607	4 019
Seychelles Seychelles	32 776	53 534	63 209	85 784	93 740	425	282	234	1 084	1 175
Sierra Leone Sierra Leone	74 730	75 210	82 990	96 926	134 440	30[1]	30[1]	...	...	...
Singapore Singapour	5 371	3 342	2 769	2 085	2 173	5 112	4 443	5 027	5 024	5 406

Country or area Pays ou zone	Capture production — Captures					Aquaculture production — Production de l'aquaculture				
	2000	2001	2002	2003	2004	2000	2001	2002	2003	2004
Slovakia Slovaquie	1 368	1 531	1 746	1 646	1 603	887	999	829	881	1 180
Slovenia Slovénie	1 856	1 827	1 686	1 281	1 022	1 181	1 262	1 289	1 353	1 569
Solomon Islands Iles Salomon	25 352[1]	29 642[1]	31 105[1]	39 849[1]	36 563[1]	15[1]	15[1]	...	...	
Somalia [1] Somalie [1]	20 800	27 500	27 500	27 500	27 500	...	...	...	...	...
South Africa Afrique du Sud	643 525	750 346	766 480	822 882	881 939	3 951	4 177	4 505[1]	4 896	3 167
Spain Espagne	1 045 675	1 092 829	892 549	896 442	803 336	312 171	312 647	322 714	313 288	363 181
Sri Lanka Sri Lanka	284 806	281 150	300 240	281 500	283 860	4 420	3 610	2 651	3 462	2 513
Sudan Soudan	53 000	58 000	57 000	59 000	59 000[1]	1 000	1 000	1 600	1 600[1]	1 600[1]
Suriname Suriname	20 826[1]	24 865	25 242[1]	28 180	32 777	345	422	422[1]	260	288
Swaziland Swaziland	70[1]	70[1]	70[1]	70[1]	70[1]	69[1]	72[1]	...	...	...
Sweden Suède	338 534	311 817	294 964	286 875	269 922	4 834	6 773	5 618	6 334	5 989
Switzerland Suisse	1 659	1 715	1 544	1 815	1 602	1 100	1 135	1 135	1 100	1 205
Syrian Arab Republic Rép. arabe syrienne	6 572	8 291	9 178	8 911	8 528	6 797	5 880	5 988	7 217	8 682
Tajikistan Tadjikistan	78[1]	137	181	158	184	86	99	143	167	26
Thailand Thaïlande	2 997 394	2 833 911	2 842 508	2 849 697	2 845 088	738 155	814 121	954 567	1 064 378	1 172 866
TFYR of Macedonia L'ex-R.y. Macédoine	208	128	148	162	213	1 626	1 053	883	910	959
Timor-Leste Timor-Leste	362	356	350[1]	350[1]	350[1]	...	...	...	...	...
Togo Togo	22 277	23 163	20 946	27 485	28 013	102	120	1 025	1 221	1 525[1]
Tokelau [1] Tokélaou [1]	200	200	200	200	200	...	...	...	...	...
Tonga Tonga	3 760	4 673	4 791	4 435	1 673	14	19	14	20	0
Trinidad and Tobago Trinité-et-Tobago	8 613	10 763	12 596	9 740	9 709	22	7	7[1]	7[1]	...
Tunisia Tunisie	95 550	98 482	96 685	90 341	110 272	1 553	1 868	1 975	2 130	2 524
Turkey Turquie	503 348	527 733	566 682	507 772	550 482	79 031	67 244	61 165	79 943	94 010
Turkmenistan Turkménistan	12 228	12 749	12 812	14 543	14 992	68	43	38	24	16
Turks and Caicos Islands Iles Turques et Caïques	5 713	6 419	5 767	5 100	5 679	15[1]	20[1]	30	25	4
Tuvalu Tuvalu	500[1]	500[1]	600[1]	1 500	2 080	...	...	...	5	1

Country or area / Pays ou zone	Capture production — Captures					Aquaculture production — Production de l'aquaculture				
	2000	2001	2002	2003	2004	2000	2001	2002	2003	2004
Uganda / Ouganda	219 356	220 726	221 898	241 810	371 789	820	2 360	4 915	5 500	5 539
Ukraine / Ukraine	391 831	360 914	265 599	222 349	202 676	30 969	31 037	30 819	25 616	26 223[1]
United Arab Emirates / Emirats arabes unis	105 456	112 561	97 574	95 150	90 000[1]	0	0	0	2 300	570[1]
United Kingdom / Royaume-Uni	747 571	741 045	689 891	635 486	652 405	152 485	170 516	179 036[1]	181 838[1]	207 203
United Rep. of Tanzania / Rép.-Unie de Tanzanie	332 779	335 900	323 530	351 125	347 795	210	300	630	2	11
United States / Etats-Unis	4 717 638	4 944 336	4 937 305	4 938 956	4 959 826	456 045	479 254	497 346	544 329	606 549
United States Virgin Is. / Iles Vierges américaines	1 100[1]	1 200[1]	1 300[1]	1 492	1 519	0	0	0	0	0
Uruguay / Uruguay	113 335	105 137	108 765	117 269	122 989	85	17	17	24	21
Uzbekistan / Ouzbékistan	3 306	2 341	1 564	1 349	1 230	5 652	3 988	3 824	3 118	3 093
Vanuatu / Vanuatu	70 461[1]	35 176[1]	41 017[1]	55 913	94 787	...	...	...	...	1
Venezuela (Bolivarian Rep. of) / Venezuela (Rép. bolivar. du)	356 835	411 648	513 848	524 449	490 000[1]	13 410	16 622	17 860	19 821	22 210
Viet Nam / Viet Nam	1 623 312	1 724 758	1 802 598	1 856 105	1 879 488	498 517	588 098[1]	703 041[1]	937 502	1 198 617
Wallis and Futuna Islands / Iles Wallis et Futuna	300[1]	300[1]	300[1]	300	300[1]	...	...	...	...	...
Yemen / Yémen	114 750	142 198	179 584	228 116	256 300	...	...	...	...	...
Zambia / Zambie	66 671	65 000[1]	65 000[1]	65 000[1]	65 000[1]	4 240[1]	4 520[1]	4 630[1]	4 501	5 125
Zimbabwe / Zimbabwe	13 114	13 000[1]	13 000[1]	13 000[1]	13 000[1]	2 151	2 285	2 213	2 600	2 955

Source

Food and Agriculture Organization of the United Nations (FAO), Rome, FISHSTAT database.

Notes

[1] FAO estimate.
[2] For statistical purposes, the data for China do not include those for the Hong Kong Special Administrative Region (Hong Kong SAR), Macao Special Administrative Region (Macao SAR) and Taiwan Province of China.

Source

Organisation des Nations Unies pour l'alimentation et l'agriculture (FAO), Rome, les données des pêches de FISHSTAT.

Notes

[1] Estimation de la FAO.
[2] Pour la présentation des statistiques, les données pour Chine ne comprennent pas la Région Administrative Spéciale de Hong Kong (Hong Kong RAS), la Région Administrative Spéciale de Macao (Macao RAS) et la province de Taiwan.

The series shown on agriculture and fishing have been furnished by the Food and Agriculture Organization of the United Nations (FAO). They refer mainly to the long-term trends in the growth of agricultural output and the food supply, the output of principal agricultural commodities and fish production.

Agricultural production is defined to include all crops and livestock products except those used for seed and fodder and other intermediate uses in agriculture; for example deductions are made for eggs used for hatching. Intermediate input of seeds and fodder and similar items refer to both domestically produced and imported commodities. For further details, reference may be made to FAO Yearbooks [3, 5, 6, 7, 8, 9]. FAO data are also available through the Internet at http://faostat.fao.org.

Table 30: "Agriculture" relates to the production of all crops and livestock products. The "Food Index" includes those commodities which are considered edible and contain nutrients.

The index numbers of agricultural output and food production are calculated by the Laspeyres formula with the base year period 1999–2001. The latter is provided in order to diminish the impact of annual fluctuations in agricultural output during base years on the indices for the period. Production quantities of each commodity are weighted by 1999–2001 average national producer prices and summed for each year. The index numbers are based on production data for a calendar year. These may differ in some instances from those actually produced and published by the individual countries themselves due to variations in concepts, coverage, weights and methods of calculation. Efforts have been made to estimate these methodological differences to achieve a better international comparability of data. The series include a large amount of estimates made by FAO in cases where no official or semi official figures are available from the countries.

Detailed data on agricultural production are published by FAO in its *Production Yearbook* [5].

Table 31: The data on the production of cereals relate to crops harvested for dry grain only. Cereals harvested for hay, green feed or used for grazing are excluded.

Table 32: Oil crops, or oil bearing crops, are those crops yielding seeds, nuts or fruits which are used mainly for the extraction of culinary or industrial oils, excluding essential oils. In this table, data for oil crops represent the total production of oil seeds, oil nuts and oil fruits harvested in the year indicated and expressed in terms of oil equivalent. That is to say, these figures do not relate to the actual production of vegetable oils, but to the potential production if the to-

Les séries présentées sur l'agriculture et la pêche ont été fournies par l'Organisation des Nations Unies pour l'alimentation et l'agriculture (FAO) et portent principalement sur les tendances à long terme de la croissance de la production agricole et des approvisionnements alimentaires, et sur la production des principales denrées agricoles et la production halieutique.

La production agricole se définit comme comprenant l'ensemble des produits agricoles et des produits de l'élevage à l'exception de ceux utilisés comme semences et comme aliments pour les animaux, et pour les autres utilisations intermédiaires en agriculture; par exemple, on déduit les œufs utilisés pour la reproduction. L'apport intermédiaire de semences et d'aliments pour les animaux et d'autres éléments similaires se rapportent à la fois à des produits locaux et importés. Pour tous détails complémentaires, on se reportera aux annuaires de la FAO [3, 5, 6, 7, 8, 9]. Des statistiques peuvent également être consultées sur le site Web de la FAO http://faostat.fao.org.

Tableau 30 : "L'agriculture" se rapporte à la production de tous les produits de l'agriculture et de l'élevage. "L'indice des produits alimentaires" comprend les produits considérés comme comestibles et qui contiennent des éléments nutritifs.

Les indices de la production agricole et de la production alimentaire sont calculés selon la formule de Laspeyres avec les années 1999–2001 pour période de base. Le choix d'une période de plusieurs années permet de diminuer l'incidence des fluctuations annuelles de la production agricole pendant les années de base sur les indices pour cette période. Les quantités produites de chaque denrée sont pondérées par les prix nationaux moyens à la production de 1999–2001, et additionnées pour chaque année. Les indices sont fondés sur les données de production d'une année civile. Ils peuvent différer dans certains cas des indices effectivement établis et publiés par les pays eux-mêmes par suite de différences dans les concepts, la couverture, les pondérations et les méthodes de calcul. On s'est efforcé d'estimer ces différences méthodologiques afin de rendre les données plus facilement comparables à l'échelle internationale. Les séries comprennent une grande quantité d'estimations faites par la FAO dans les cas où les pays n'auraient pas fourni de chiffres officiels ou semi-officiels.

Des chiffres détaillés de production sont publiés dans l'*Annuaire de la production* de la FAO [5].

Tableau 31 : Les données sur la production de céréales se rapportent uniquement aux céréales récoltées pour le grain sec; celles cultivées pour le foin, le fourrage vert ou le pâturage en sont exclues.

tal amounts produced from all oil crops were processed into oil in producing countries in the same year in which they were harvested. Naturally, the total production of oil crops is never processed into oil in its entirety, since depending on the crop, important quantities are also used for seed, feed and food. However, although oil extraction rates vary from country to country, in this table the same extraction rate for each crop has been applied for all countries. Moreover, it should be borne in mind that the crops harvested during the latter months of the year are generally processed into oil during the following year.

In spite of these deficiencies in coverage, extraction rates and time reference, the data reported here are useful as they provide a valid indication of year to year changes in the size of total oil crop production. The actual production of vegetable oils in the world is about 80 percent of the production reported here. In addition, about two million tonnes of vegetable oils are produced every year from crops which are not included among those defined above. The most important of these oils are maize germ oil and rice bran oil. The actual world production of cake/meal derived from oil crops is also about 80 percent of the production reported.

Table 33: The data on roundwood refer to wood in the rough, wood in its natural state as felled or otherwise harvested, with or without bark, round, split, roughly squared or in other form (i.e. roots, stumps, burls, etc.). It may also be impregnated (e.g. telegraph poles) or roughly shaped or pointed. It comprises all wood obtained from removals, i.e. the quantities removed from forests and from trees outside the forest, including wood recovered from natural, felling and logging losses during the period—calendar year or forest year.

Table 34: The data cover (i) capture production from marine and inland fisheries and (ii) aquaculture, and are expressed in terms of live weight. They include fish, crustaceans and molluscs but exclude sponges, corals, pearls, seaweed, crocodiles, and aquatic mammals (such as whales and dolphins).

The flag of the vessel is considered as the paramount indication of the nationality of the catch. Marine fisheries data include landings by domestic craft in foreign ports and exclude landings by foreign craft in domestic ports.

To separate aquaculture from capture fisheries production, at least two criteria must apply i.e., the human intervention in one or more of the phases of the growth cycle, and individual, corporate or state ownership of the organism reared and harvested.

Data on aquaculture production are published in the FAO *Yearbook of Fishery Statistics, Aquaculture Production* [6]; capture production statistics are published in the FAO *Yearbook of Fishery Statistics, Capture Production* [7].

Tableau 32 : On désigne sous le nom de cultures oléagineuses l'ensemble des cultures produisant des graines, des noix ou des fruits, essentiellement destinées à l'extraction d'huiles alimentaires ou industrielles, à l'exclusion des huiles essentielles. Dans ce tableau, les chiffres se rapportent à la production totale de graines, noix et fruits oléagineux récoltés au cours de l'année de référence et sont exprimés en équivalent d'huile. En d'autres termes, ces chiffres ne se rapportent pas à la production effective mais à la production potentielle d'huiles végétales dans l'hypothèse où les volumes totaux de produits provenant de toutes les cultures d'oléagineux seraient transformés en huile dans les pays producteurs l'année même où ils ont été récoltés. Bien entendu, la production totale d'oléagineux n'est jamais transformée intégralement en huile, car des quantités importantes qui varient suivant les cultures sont également utilisées pour les semailles, l'alimentation animale et l'alimentation humaine. Toutefois, bien que les taux d'extraction d'huile varient selon les pays, on a appliqué dans ce tableau le même taux à tous les pays pour chaque oléagineux. En outre, il ne faut pas oublier que les produits récoltés au cours des derniers mois de l'année sont généralement transformés en huile dans le courant de l'année suivante.

En dépit de ces imperfections qui concernent le champ d'application, les taux d'extraction et les périodes de référence, les chiffres présentés ici sont utiles, car ils donnent une indication valable des variations de volume que la production totale d'oléagineux enregistre d'une année à l'autre. La production mondiale effective d'huiles végétales atteint 80 pour cent environ de la production indiquée ici. En outre, environ 2 millions de tonnes d'huiles végétales sont produites chaque année à partir de cultures non comprises dans les catégories définies ci dessus. Les principales sont l'huile de germes de maïs et l'huile de son de riz. La production mondiale effective tourteau/farine d'oléagineux représente environ 80 pour cent de la production indiquée.

Tableau 33 : Les données sur le bois rond se réfèrent au bois brut, bois à l'état naturel, tel qu'il a été abattu ou récolté autrement, avec ou sans écorce, fendu, grossièrement équarri ou sous une autre forme (par exemple, racines, souches, loupes, etc.). Il peut être également imprégné (par exemple, dans le cas des poteaux télégraphiques) et dégrossi ou taillé en pointe. Cette catégorie comprend tous les bois provenant des quantités enlevées en forêt ou provenant des arbres poussant hors forêt, y compris le volume récupéré sur les déchets naturels et les déchets d'abattage et de transport pendant la période envisagée (année civile ou forestière).

Tableau 34 : Les données ont trait i) à la pêche maritime et intérieure et ii) à l'aquaculture, et sont exprimées en poids vif. Elles comprennent poissons, crustacés et mollusques,

mais excluent éponges, coraux, perles, algues, crocodiles et les mammifères aquatiques (baleines, dauphins, etc.).

Le pavillon du navire est considéré comme la principale indication de la nationalité de la prise. Les données de pêche maritime comprennent les quantités débarquées par des bateaux nationaux dans des ports étrangers et excluent les quantités débarquées par des bateaux étrangers dans des ports nationaux.

Pour séparer la production d'aquaculture de la pêche de capture, au moins deux critères doivent se vérifier, c'est-à-dire l'intervention humaine dans une ou plusieurs des phases du cycle de croissance, et l'appartenance de l'organisme élevé et récolté à une personne physique, à une personne morale ou à l'état.

Les données sur la production de l'aquaculture sont publiées dans l'*Annuaire statistique des pêches, production de l'aquaculture* [6]; celles sur les captures sont publiées dans l'*Annuaire statistique des pêches, captures* [7].

Sugar
Production and consumption: thousand metric tons; consumption per capita: kilograms

Sucre
Production et consommation : milliers de tonnes ; consommation per habitant : kilogrammes

Country or area	1998	1999	2000	2001	2002	2003	2004	Pays ou zone
World								Monde
Production	125 890	135 002	130 004	130 659	142 076	148 361	148 267	Production
Consumption	123 209	126 631	127 357	131 709	137 667	141 403	146 606	Consommation
Consumption per cap. (kg.)	20	21	21	21	22	22	23	Consom. par hab. (kg.)
Afghanistan								Afghanistan
Consumption *	55	60	60	60	70	90	120	Consommation *
Consumption per cap. (kg.)	3	3	3	3	3	4	4	Consom. par hab. (kg.)
Albania								Albanie
Production *	3	3	3	3	3	3	3	Production *
Consumption *	65	65	68	68	75	85	88	Consommation *
Consumption per cap. (kg.)	20	20	22	22	24	27	28	Consom. par hab. (kg.)
Algeria								Algérie
Consumption *	800	900	935	965	1 040	1 100	1 135	Consommation *
Consumption per cap. (kg.)	27	29	31	31	29	34	41	Consom. par hab. (kg.)
Angola								Angola
Production *	32	32	...	...	...	...	...	Production *
Consumption *	85	120	130	155	185	195	205	Consommation *
Consumption per cap. (kg.)	7	10	10	11	13	13	13	Consom. par hab. (kg.)
Argentina								Argentine
Production	1 749	*1 882	*1 580	*1 630	*1 680	1 952	1 857	Production
Consumption	*1 350	*1 450	*1 485	*1 520	*1 515	1 515	1 574	Consommation
Consumption per cap. (kg.)	38	40	41	41	40	40	41	Consom. par hab. (kg.)
Armenia								Arménie
Consumption *	65	70	72	73	74	87	87	Consommation *
Consumption per cap. (kg.)	17	18	19	19	23	27	27	Consom. par hab. (kg.)
Australia								Australie
Production	5 085	5 514	4 417	4 768	5 614	5 315	5 530	Production
Consumption	1 003	*1 005	1 049	1 068	1 100	1 089	1 043	Consommation
Consumption per cap. (kg.)	54	53	55	55	56	55	52	Consom. par hab. (kg.)
Azerbaijan								Azerbaïdjan
Consumption	157	*160	*160	*160	*165	*175	*180	Consommation
Consumption per cap. (kg.)	20	20	20	20	20	21	22	Consom. par hab. (kg.)
Bahamas								Bahamas
Consumption	10	10	11	8	9	11	12	Consommation
Consumption per cap. (kg.)	36	35	35	28	32	37	36	Consom. par hab. (kg.)
Bangladesh								Bangladesh
Production	*159	*162	*110	109	229	*166	*125	Production
Consumption *	400	440	500	550	635	695	790	Consommation *
Consumption per cap. (kg.)	3	3	4	4	5	5	6	Consom. par hab. (kg.)
Barbados								Barbade
Production	46	53	58	*50	*45	*36	*35	Production
Consumption	15	*15	*15	*15	*15	*15	*15	Consommation
Consumption per cap. (kg.)	55	56	56	56	50	56	62	Consom. par hab. (kg.)
Belarus								Bélarus
Production	180	151	186	196	162	*255	*340	Production
Consumption	405[1]	*357	380	422	410	*410	*415	Consommation
Consumption per cap. (kg.)	39	35	38	42	41	42	42	Consom. par hab. (kg.)
Belize								Belize
Production	123	124	128	114	119	111	125	Production
Consumption	15	15	15	12[2]	12	12	12	Consommation
Consumption per cap. (kg.)	64	61	58	46	44	44	42	Consom. par hab. (kg.)
Benin								Bénin
Production *	4	4	5	5	5	4	4	Production *
Consumption	*40	*45	*46	22	*28	*35	*36	Consommation
Consumption per cap. (kg.)	7	8	8	3	4	5	6	Consom. par hab. (kg.)
Bermuda								Bermudes
Consumption	2	1	2	2	2	2	2	Consommation
Consumption per cap. (kg.)	25	17	25	25	14	25	46	Consom. par hab. (kg.)

Country or area	1998	1999	2000	2001	2002	2003	2004	Pays ou zone
Bolivia								Bolivie
Production	282	293	311	390	426	387	464	Production
Consumption	287	290	*293	*295	*300	*305	*310	Consommation
Consumption per cap. (kg.)	36	36	35	35	34	34	34	Consom. par hab. (kg.)
Bosnia and Herzegovina								Bosnie-Herzégovine
Consumption *	75	80	90	110	120	130	130	Consommation *
Consumption per cap. (kg.)	21	21	23	27	31	30	26	Consom. par hab. (kg.)
Botswana								Botswana
Consumption	45	45	46	46	47	48	48	Consommation
Consumption per cap. (kg.)	29	28	28	27	27	27	27	Consom. par hab. (kg.)
Brazil								Brésil
Production	19 168	20 646	16 464	20 336	23 567	25 956	28 248	Production
Consumption	*9 150	*9 500	*9 725	*9 800	10 520	10 217	10 857	Consommation
Consumption per cap. (kg.)	57	57	58	57	60	58	59	Consom. par hab. (kg.)
Brunei Darussalam								Brunéi Darussalam
Consumption	7	5	6	10	10	11	11	Consommation
Consumption per cap. (kg.)	20	15	18	29	29	32	32	Consom. par hab. (kg.)
Bulgaria								Bulgarie
Production *	5	2	2	3	3	3	3	Production *
Consumption *	260	225	230	240	255	265	270	Consommation *
Consumption per cap. (kg.)	32	28	28	30	33	34	35	Consom. par hab. (kg.)
Burkina Faso								Burkina Faso
Production	*30	30	*30	*35	*40	*40	*40	Production
Consumption *	50	45	50	55	60	65	65	Consommation *
Consumption per cap. (kg.)	5	4	4	5	6	6	5	Consom. par hab. (kg.)
Burundi								Burundi
Production	24	23	24	20	20	22	22	Production
Consumption	22	23	24	23	25	26	27	Consommation
Consumption per cap. (kg.)	4	4	4	4	3	4	5	Consom. par hab. (kg.)
Cambodia								Cambodge
Consumption *	65	75	85	90	115	120	130	Consommation *
Consumption per cap. (kg.)	5	6	7	7	9	9	10	Consom. par hab. (kg.)
Cameroon								Cameroun
Production	*46	*52	41	94	104	120	*125	Production
Consumption	*90	*95	*95	112	145	145	*150	Consommation
Consumption per cap. (kg.)	6	7	6	8	10	10	10	Consom. par hab. (kg.)
Canada								Canada
Production *	104	118	123	95	64	85	115	Production *
Consumption *	1 200	1 200	1 235	1 240	1 255	1 400	1 425	Consommation *
Consumption per cap. (kg.)	40	39	40	40	40	44	45	Consom. par hab. (kg.)
Cape Verde								Cap-Vert
Consumption *	14	13	13	15	16	17	17	Consommation *
Consumption per cap. (kg.)	33	31	31	34	36	37	36	Consom. par hab. (kg.)
Central African Rep.								Rép. centrafricaine
Consumption *	5	4	4	4	5	6	9	Consommation *
Consumption per cap. (kg.)	1	1	1	1	1	2	2	Consom. par hab. (kg.)
Chad								Tchad
Production *	31	32	32	32	32	33	30	Production *
Consumption *	55	55	57	57	65	75	75	Consommation *
Consumption per cap. (kg.)	7	7	7	7	15	8	4	Consom. par hab. (kg.)
Chile								Chili
Production	511	487	457	*430	576	374	401	Production
Consumption	728	729	683	*685	*690	700	673	Consommation
Consumption per cap. (kg.)	49	49	45	44	46	46	44	Consom. par hab. (kg.)
China [3]								Chine 3
Production	8 904	8 527	7 616	7 161	9 805	11 433	10 912	Production
Consumption *	8 300	8 300	8 500	8 900	9 975	11 065	11 613	Consommation *
Consumption per cap. (kg.)	7	7	7	7	8	9	9	Consom. par hab. (kg.)
China, Hong Kong SAR								Chine, Hong Kong RAS
Consumption *	180	180	181	185	180	195	195	Consommation *
Consumption per cap. (kg.)	28	27	27	28	27	29	29	Consom. par hab. (kg.)
China, Macao SAR								Chine, Macao RAS
Consumption	7	7	7	7	8	8	8	Consommation
Consumption per cap. (kg.)	17	16	17	17	17	20	21	Consom. par hab. (kg.)

Sugar—Production and consumption: thousand metric tons; consumption per capita: kilograms (*continued*)
Sucre—Production et consommation : milliers de tonnes ; consommation par habitant : kilogrammes (*suite*)

Country or area	1998	1999	2000	2001	2002	2003	2004	Pays ou zone
Colombia								Colombie
Production	2 126	2 241	2 391	2 260	2 523	2 646	2 740	Production
Consumption [4]	1 240	1 281	1 343	1 309	1 356	1 348	1 521	Consommation [4]
Consumption per cap. (kg.)	30	31	32	30	31	30	34	Consom. par hab. (kg.)
Comoros								Comores
Consumption	5	5	6	8	9	9	9	Consommation
Consumption per cap. (kg.)	8	7	8	11	11	11	11	Consom. par hab. (kg.)
Congo								Congo
Production	*45	*35	*40	*45	33	*45	*55	Production
Consumption	*30	*30	*35	*45	32	*50	*55	Consommation
Consumption per cap. (kg.)	11	10	12	15	10	15	16	Consom. par hab. (kg.)
Costa Rica								Costa Rica
Production	*381	*378	338	358	*360	*358	*405	Production
Consumption	*210	*210	208	*210	*225	*230	*230	Consommation
Consumption per cap. (kg.)	62	61	57	54	55	49	43	Consom. par hab. (kg.)
Côte d'Ivoire								Côte d'Ivoire
Production	126	152	189	*155	*170	*145	*120	Production
Consumption	137	*170	*180	*190	*200	*205	*210	Consommation
Consumption per cap. (kg.)	9	11	11	11	11	11	12	Consom. par hab. (kg.)
Croatia								Croatie
Production	151	114	57	131	160	116	173	Production
Consumption *	180	175	175	175	180	185	190	Consommation *
Consumption per cap. (kg.)	40	39	40	40	41	42	43	Consom. par hab. (kg.)
Cuba								Cuba
Production	3 291	3 875	4 057	3 748	3 522	2 278	*2 600	Production
Consumption	713	711	705	698	698	682	*700	Consommation
Consumption per cap. (kg.)	64	64	63	62	62	60	62	Consom. par hab. (kg.)
Cyprus								Chypre
Consumption	*30	*30	*31	32	*33	*36	...	Consommation
Consumption per cap. (kg.)	40	40	41	42	47	47	...	Consom. par hab. (kg.)
Czech Republic								République tchèque
Production	535	420	434	484	523	522	...	Production
Consumption	438	*450	440	*450	*475	399	...	Consommation
Consumption per cap. (kg.)	43	44	43	44	47	39	...	Consom. par hab. (kg.)
Dem. Rep. of the Congo								Rép. dém. du Congo
Production	51	65	75	60	65	65	60	Production
Consumption *	80	75	75	75	85	85	90	Consommation *
Consumption per cap. (kg.)	2	2	2	1	2	2	2	Consom. par hab. (kg.)
Djibouti								Djibouti
Consumption	10	12	13	13	13	14	15	Consommation
Consumption per cap. (kg.)	16	19	20	20	20	21	23	Consom. par hab. (kg.)
Dominican Republic								Rép. dominicaine
Production	409	421	438	491	516	525	*530	Production
Consumption	337	*350	298	352	366	322	*360	Consommation
Consumption per cap. (kg.)	42	42	35	41	45	37	39	Consom. par hab. (kg.)
Ecuador								Equateur
Production	354	601	*500	*495	*475	*505	*490	Production
Consumption *	410	425	440	465	480	485	485	Consommation *
Consumption per cap. (kg.)	34	34	35	36	36	36	36	Consom. par hab. (kg.)
Egypt								Egypte
Production	*1 152	*1 269	*1 450	*1 585	*1 490	*1 425	1 489	Production
Consumption *	2 075	2 150	2 250	2 325	2 400	2 500	2 600	Consommation *
Consumption per cap. (kg.)	34	34	35	34	35	36	37	Consom. par hab. (kg.)
El Salvador								El Salvador
Production	487	585	562	527	476	530	555	Production
Consumption	237	234	236	244	217	209	212	Consommation
Consumption per cap. (kg.)	39	38	38	38	33	33	33	Consom. par hab. (kg.)
Eritrea								Erythrée
Consumption	10	8	8	8	9	15	16	Consommation
Consumption per cap. (kg.)	3	2	2	2	2	4	4	Consom. par hab. (kg.)
Estonia								Estonie
Consumption *	55	65	70	73	73	80	...	Consommation *
Consumption per cap. (kg.)	38	46	49	53	49	60	...	Consom. par hab. (kg.)

Country or area	1998	1999	2000	2001	2002	2003	2004	Pays ou zone
Ethiopia								**Ethiopie**
Production	173	235	251	*305	287	*295	*325	Production
Consumption	185	199	246	*240	211	*260	*295	Consommation
Consumption per cap. (kg.)	3	3	4	4	3	4	4	Consom. par hab. (kg.)
EU 25 [5]								**UE 25** [5]
Production	17 398	18 731	17 854	15 500	18 268	16 578	21 843	Production
Consumption	13 819	15 007	14 112	13 588	14 370	14 137	17 691	Consommation
Consumption per cap. (kg.)	37	40	37	36	38	37	39	Consom. par hab. (kg.)
Fiji								**Fidji**
Production	278	377	353	327	334	330	330	Production
Consumption [6]	44	38	41	45	53	55	58	Consommation [6]
Consumption per cap. (kg.)	55	47	51	56	64	66	69	Consom. par hab. (kg.)
Gabon								**Gabon**
Production	*17	*16	*17	*18	*18	25	*19	Production
Consumption *	17	18	19	19	20	21	21	Consommation *
Consumption per cap. (kg.)	15	15	15	15	16	16	16	Consom. par hab. (kg.)
Gambia								**Gambie**
Consumption *	45	50	58	60	65	70	75	Consommation *
Consumption per cap. (kg.)	37	36	41	42	41	47	54	Consom. par hab. (kg.)
Georgia								**Géorgie**
Consumption *	100	105	108	110	120	125	135	Consommation *
Consumption per cap. (kg.)	19	21	21	22	27	27	27	Consom. par hab. (kg.)
Ghana								**Ghana**
Consumption *	140	145	150	155	170	185	200	Consommation *
Consumption per cap. (kg.)	8	8	8	8	8	9	10	Consom. par hab. (kg.)
Gibraltar								**Gibraltar**
Consumption	3	3	3	2	2	2	2	Consommation
Consumption per cap. (kg.)	100	83	83	73	55	60	89	Consom. par hab. (kg.)
Guatemala								**Guatemala**
Production	1 682	1 687	1 675	1 661	1 910	1 801	2 092	Production
Consumption	408	460	468	496	534	585	585	Consommation
Consumption per cap. (kg.)	38	42	41	43	45	48	47	Consom. par hab. (kg.)
Guinea								**Guinée**
Production *	22	25	25	25	25	26	26	Production *
Consumption *	80	85	90	95	100	110	110	Consommation *
Consumption per cap. (kg.)	10	11	11	12	12	13	12	Consom. par hab. (kg.)
Guinea-Bissau								**Guinée-Bissau**
Consumption	4	5	7	7	7	8	9	Consommation
Consumption per cap. (kg.)	4	4	6	6	6	6	7	Consom. par hab. (kg.)
Guyana								**Guyana**
Production	263	336	273	284	331	*302	*320	Production
Consumption	25	25	24	24	24	*25	*26	Consommation
Consumption per cap. (kg.)	32	32	31	35	31	32	33	Consom. par hab. (kg.)
Haiti								**Haïti**
Production *	5	5	5	5	5	...	...	Production *
Consumption *	130	160	165	165	170	175	175	Consommation *
Consumption per cap. (kg.)	17	21	21	20	21	21	20	Consom. par hab. (kg.)
Honduras								**Honduras**
Production	*277	190	*320	316	*320	300	357	Production
Consumption	*230	235	236	237	*240	249	250	Consommation
Consumption per cap. (kg.)	37	37	37	39	33	36	36	Consom. par hab. (kg.)
Hungary								**Hongrie**
Production [7]	461	446	309	434	347	257	...	Production [7]
Consumption [7]	386	399	367	317	313	282	...	Consommation [7]
Consumption per cap. (kg.)	38	40	37	31	31	28	...	Consom. par hab. (kg.)
Iceland								**Islande**
Consumption *	13	12	13	12	12	12	12	Consommation *
Consumption per cap. (kg.)	46	43	46	43	41	42	41	Consom. par hab. (kg.)
India								**Inde**
Production	14 281	17 406	20 247	19 906	19 525	21 702	14 432	Production
Consumption	15 272	16 278	16 546	17 274	17 857	18 625	19 858	Consommation
Consumption per cap. (kg.)	16	17	17	17	17	18	19	Consom. par hab. (kg.)

35

Sugar— Production and consumption: thousand metric tons; consumption per capita: kilograms (*continued*)
Sucre— Production et consommation : milliers de tonnes ; consommation par habitant : kilogrammes (*suite*)

Country or area	1998	1999	2000	2001	2002	2003	2004	Pays ou zone
Indonesia								Indonésie
Production	1 493	*1 490	*1 685	*1 850	*2 150	*1 780	*2 225	Production
Consumption	2 736	*3 000	*3 375	*3 500	*3 675	*3 800	*3 915	Consommation
Consumption per cap. (kg.)	14	15	16	17	17	18	18	Consom. par hab. (kg.)
Iran (Islamic Rep. of)								Iran (Rép. islamique d')
Production	863	*940	*920	*900	*995	*1 270	*1 310	Production
Consumption *	1 800	1 900	1 960	1 965	1 975	2 025	2 060	Consommation *
Consumption per cap. (kg.)	29	30	31	31	30	31	31	Consom. par hab. (kg.)
Iraq								Iraq
Consumption *	350	400	405	425	500	650	675	Consommation *
Consumption per cap. (kg.)	16	18	18	17	21	22	19	Consom. par hab. (kg.)
Israel								Israël
Consumption *	360	370	380	400	410	425	440	Consommation *
Consumption per cap. (kg.)	60	61	62	62	62	59	56	Consom. par hab. (kg.)
Jamaica								Jamaïque
Production	183	212	210	205	175	154	181	Production
Consumption	120	98	129	136	126	129	111	Consommation
Consumption per cap. (kg.)	47	38	49	52	49	50	43	Consom. par hab. (kg.)
Japan								Japon
Production	870	913	842	823	901	934	976	Production
Consumption	2 427	2 541	2 413	2 339	2 433	2 415	2 403	Consommation
Consumption per cap. (kg.)	19	20	19	18	19	19	19	Consom. par hab. (kg.)
Jordan								Jordanie
Consumption	*150	*180	*185	*190	*200	216	*225	Consommation
Consumption per cap. (kg.)	32	38	38	38	40	43	45	Consom. par hab. (kg.)
Kazakhstan								Kazakhstan
Production	*40	*25	*30	*25	46	62	40	Production
Consumption	307	303	312	365	438	442	450	Consommation
Consumption per cap. (kg.)	20	20	21	25	30	30	30	Consom. par hab. (kg.)
Kenya								Kenya
Production	488	512	437	377	537	448	562	Production
Consumption	*600	662	663	*625	652	692	728	Consommation
Consumption per cap. (kg.)	20	22	22	21	21	22	22	Consom. par hab. (kg.)
Korea, Dem. P. R.								Corée, R. p. dém. de
Consumption *	30	60	65	70	70	75	85	Consommation *
Consumption per cap. (kg.)	1	3	3	3	3	3	4	Consom. par hab. (kg.)
Korea, Republic of								Corée, République de
Consumption [8]	986	966	1 012	1 086	1 114	1 134	1 171	Consommation [8]
Consumption per cap. (kg.)	21	21	21	23	23	24	24	Consom. par hab. (kg.)
Kuwait								Koweït
Consumption *	70	70	73	75	80	80	85	Consommation *
Consumption per cap. (kg.)	35	33	33	33	35	33	32	Consom. par hab. (kg.)
Kyrgyzstan								Kirghizistan
Production	36	45	57	29	41	75	88	Production
Consumption *	110	100	110	110	115	120	120	Consommation *
Consumption per cap. (kg.)	23	21	22	22	23	24	24	Consom. par hab. (kg.)
Lao People's Dem. Rep.								Rép. dém. pop. lao
Consumption *	16	20	21	25	30	30	35	Consommation *
Consumption per cap. (kg.)	3	4	4	5	6	6	6	Consom. par hab. (kg.)
Latvia								Lettonie
Production [7]	71	72	68	56	77	75	...	Production [7]
Consumption [7]	*85	82	78	*78	*78	73	...	Consommation [7]
Consumption per cap. (kg.)	35	34	32	33	33	31	...	Consom. par hab. (kg.)
Lebanon								Liban
Production	37	40	34	...	...	...	...	Production
Consumption	*125	*130	122	*135	*140	*145	*150	Consommation
Consumption per cap. (kg.)	37	38	35	38	36	39	43	Consom. par hab. (kg.)
Liberia								Libéria
Consumption	10	8	10	9	10	10	10	Consommation
Consumption per cap. (kg.)	4	3	3	3	3	3	3	Consom. par hab. (kg.)
Libyan Arab Jamah.								Jamah. arabe libyenne
Consumption *	220	220	225	230	240	250	260	Consommation *
Consumption per cap. (kg.)	44	43	43	43	45	47	49	Consom. par hab. (kg.)

Country or area	1998	1999	2000	2001	2002	2003	2004	Pays ou zone
Lithuania								**Lituanie**
Production [7]	137	121	137	118	150	143	...	Production [7]
Consumption [7]	119	*110	95	111	89	89	...	Consommation [7]
Consumption per cap. (kg.)	32	30	26	32	26	26	...	Consom. par hab. (kg.)
Madagascar								**Madagascar**
Production	*95	*85	*70	*50	32	27	26	Production
Consumption	*93	*95	*98	*98	104	117	129	Consommation
Consumption per cap. (kg.)	6	6	6	6	7	7	8	Consom. par hab. (kg.)
Malawi								**Malawi**
Production	210	187	209	*205	261	*257	*255	Production
Consumption	158	137	127	*140	*145	*150	*155	Consommation
Consumption per cap. (kg.)	15	12	11	13	13	14	15	Consom. par hab. (kg.)
Malaysia								**Malaisie**
Production *	100	107	108	105	110	80	80	Production *
Consumption *	1 035	1 040	1 045	1 050	1 090	1 175	1 215	Consommation *
Consumption per cap. (kg.)	47	46	45	44	44	46	47	Consom. par hab. (kg.)
Maldives								**Maldives**
Consumption	8	5	6	5	5	5	5	Consommation
Consumption per cap. (kg.)	30	18	22	16	18	17	15	Consom. par hab. (kg.)
Mali								**Mali**
Production *	33	31	32	32	32	34	35	Production *
Consumption *	80	75	80	80	90	95	95	Consommation *
Consumption per cap. (kg.)	7	7	7	8	7	11	17	Consom. par hab. (kg.)
Malta								**Malte**
Consumption * [7]	20	22	23	23	23	25	...	Consommation * [7]
Consumption per cap. (kg.)	53	56	58	59	59	63	...	Consom. par hab. (kg.)
Mauritania								**Mauritanie**
Consumption *	120	125	130	135	135	140	140	Consommation *
Consumption per cap. (kg.)	48	48	49	50	51	50	47	Consom. par hab. (kg.)
Mauritius								**Maurice**
Production	667	396	604	685	553	538	606	Production
Consumption	43	42	42	44	43	41	42	Consommation
Consumption per cap. (kg.)	37	36	35	36	35	34	34	Consom. par hab. (kg.)
Mexico								**Mexique**
Production	5 287	5 030	4 816	5 614	5 073	5 442	5 672	Production
Consumption	4 293	4 400	4 619	4 857	5 069	5 328	5 300	Consommation
Consumption per cap. (kg.)	44	45	46	48	49	52	50	Consom. par hab. (kg.)
Mongolia								**Mongolie**
Consumption	19	10	20	20	21	22	23	Consommation
Consumption per cap. (kg.)	8	4	8	8	8	9	10	Consom. par hab. (kg.)
Morocco								**Maroc**
Production	499	522	556	*530	*505	*505	*540	Production
Consumption	1 002	1 018	1 034	*1 050	*1 100	1 057	*1 150	Consommation
Consumption per cap. (kg.)	36	36	36	36	37	35	39	Consom. par hab. (kg.)
Mozambique								**Mozambique**
Production	39	46	*45	*60	*170	*225	205	Production
Consumption	*60	*70	*90	*95	*110	*120	134	Consommation
Consumption per cap. (kg.)	4	4	5	5	5	7	7	Consom. par hab. (kg.)
Myanmar								**Myanmar**
Production	51	43	75	*125	*125	*135	*150	Production
Consumption	31	69	*85	*90	*120	*135	*150	Consommation
Consumption per cap. (kg.)	1	2	2	2	2	3	3	Consom. par hab. (kg.)
Namibia								**Namibie**
Consumption *	40	45	46	47	48	50	55	Consommation *
Consumption per cap. (kg.)	22	25	26	26	27	28	31	Consom. par hab. (kg.)
Nepal								**Népal**
Production *	120	150	110	65	110	125	140	Production *
Consumption *	105	110	115	120	125	125	130	Consommation *
Consumption per cap. (kg.)	5	5	5	5	5	5	5	Consom. par hab. (kg.)
Netherlands Antilles								**Antilles néerlandaises**
Consumption *	15	20	21	22	25	25	25	Consommation *
Consumption per cap. (kg.)	71	95	96	96	114	99	87	Consom. par hab. (kg.)

Country or area	1998	1999	2000	2001	2002	2003	2004	Pays ou zone
New Zealand								**Nouvelle-Zélande**
Consumption	158	198	212	*215	*220	*225	*230	Consommation
Consumption per cap. (kg.)	42	52	56	56	56	56	57	Consom. par hab. (kg.)
Nicaragua								**Nicaragua**
Production	330	351	398	*390	*370	333	*440	Production
Consumption	217	179	157	*160	*175	*190	*200	Consommation
Consumption per cap. (kg.)	45	36	31	31	31	35	37	Consom. par hab. (kg.)
Niger								**Niger**
Production *	5	10	10	10	10	15	10	Production *
Consumption *	45	50	55	55	65	70	70	Consommation *
Consumption per cap. (kg.)	5	5	5	5	5	6	7	Consom. par hab. (kg.)
Nigeria								**Nigéria**
Production	*15	*17	36	7	7	...	...	Production
Consumption	*700	*700	*760	975	1 317	1 046	1 222	Consommation
Consumption per cap. (kg.)	7	6	7	8	11	8	10	Consom. par hab. (kg.)
Norway								**Norvège**
Consumption *	185	185	186	186	186	186	186	Consommation *
Consumption per cap. (kg.)	42	42	41	41	41	41	41	Consom. par hab. (kg.)
Pakistan								**Pakistan**
Production	3 503	3 709	2 053	2 720	3 334	4 063	4 481	Production
Consumption	*3 085	*3 196	*3 295	*3 390	*3 490	3 875	4 004	Consommation
Consumption per cap. (kg.)	24	24	24	24	25	26	27	Consom. par hab. (kg.)
Panama								**Panama**
Production	181	183	161	146	150	147	*160	Production
Consumption *	75	85	95	105	110	113	115	Consommation *
Consumption per cap. (kg.)	27	30	33	36	36	38	40	Consom. par hab. (kg.)
Papua New Guinea								**Papouasie-Nouvelle-Guinée**
Production	36	38	35	35	37	35	35	Production
Consumption	41	47	41	45	53	50	46	Consommation
Consumption per cap. (kg.)	8	8	7	7	8	7	6	Consom. par hab. (kg.)
Paraguay								**Paraguay**
Production *	114	112	90	95	115	116	115	Production *
Consumption *	105	108	108	110	110	115	115	Consommation *
Consumption per cap. (kg.)	20	20	20	20	19	19	19	Consom. par hab. (kg.)
Peru								**Pérou**
Production	570	*655	*725	*755	*850	*970	813	Production
Consumption	*850	*900	*925	*950	*975	*995	967	Consommation
Consumption per cap. (kg.)	34	36	36	36	36	36	35	Consom. par hab. (kg.)
Philippines								**Philippines**
Production	1 549	1 913	1 826	1 895	1 988	2 245	2 423	Production
Consumption	1 958	1 854	2 052	1 974	2 059	2 117	2 102	Consommation
Consumption per cap. (kg.)	27	25	28	26	26	26	25	Consom. par hab. (kg.)
Poland								**Pologne**
Production [7]	2 242	1 968	2 104	1 626	2 038	1 912	...	Production [7]
Consumption [7]	1 708	*1 720	*1 730	*1 740	*1 745	*1 760	...	Consommation [7]
Consumption per cap. (kg.)	44	45	45	45	45	46	...	Consom. par hab. (kg.)
Republic of Moldova								**République de Moldova**
Production	186	108	102	130	*125	107	111	Production
Consumption	*150	*125	*105	*105	*110	*115	106	Consommation
Consumption per cap. (kg.)	41	34	29	29	26	32	29	Consom. par hab. (kg.)
Romania								**Roumanie**
Production	189	86	54	71	75	57	*55	Production
Consumption *	520	530	550	565	570	590	584	Consommation *
Consumption per cap. (kg.)	23	24	25	25	26	27	27	Consom. par hab. (kg.)
Russian Federation								**Fédération de Russie**
Production	1 370	1 651	1 705	1 757	1 757	1 892	2 496	Production
Consumption	*5 450	5 565	5 707	5 848	6 673	*6 850	*6 700	Consommation
Consumption per cap. (kg.)	37	38	39	41	47	47	46	Consom. par hab. (kg.)
Rwanda								**Rwanda**
Consumption *	3	3	3	10	11	11	11	Consommation *
Consumption per cap. (kg.)	0	0	0	1	1	1	1	Consom. par hab. (kg.)

Country or area	1998	1999	2000	2001	2002	2003	2004	Pays ou zone
Saint Kitts and Nevis								**Saint-Kitts-et-Nevis**
Production	24	*20	*20	*20	*20	*22	*20	Production
Consumption *	2	2	3	3	3	4	5	Consommation *
Consumption per cap. (kg.)	50	50	63	50	50	51	49	Consom. par hab. (kg.)
Samoa								**Samoa**
Production	2	2	2	2	2	2	2	Production
Consumption	3	2	2	2	3	4	4	Consommation
Consumption per cap. (kg.)	10	8	8	8	12	15	15	Consom. par hab. (kg.)
Saudi Arabia								**Arabie saoudite**
Consumption *	550	570	595	620	650	690	720	Consommation *
Consumption per cap. (kg.)	29	29	29	28	30	29	28	Consom. par hab. (kg.)
Senegal								**Sénégal**
Production	90	*95	*90	*95	*95	*90	*90	Production
Consumption *	170	170	165	170	175	180	180	Consommation *
Consumption per cap. (kg.)	18	18	17	17	17	17	17	Consom. par hab. (kg.)
Serbia and Montenegro								**Serbie-et-Monténégro**
Production	213	248	*170	209	*230	*270	*335	Production
Consumption *	300	300	275	300	300	310	315	Consommation *
Consumption per cap. (kg.)	28	28	26	28	28	29	30	Consom. par hab. (kg.)
Sierra Leone								**Sierra Leone**
Production *	6	7	7	7	7	5	6	Production *
Consumption *	15	15	20	20	21	22	25	Consommation *
Consumption per cap. (kg.)	4	4	5	4	4	4	5	Consom. par hab. (kg.)
Singapore								**Singapour**
Consumption *	270	280	285	300	305	310	310	Consommation *
Consumption per cap. (kg.)	69	71	69	73	73	75	76	Consom. par hab. (kg.)
Slovakia								**Slovaquie**
Production [7]	170	213	140	173	197	171	...	Production [7]
Consumption [7]	*220	*225	*230	*235	*240	206	...	Consommation [7]
Consumption per cap. (kg.)	41	42	43	44	45	38	...	Consom. par hab. (kg.)
Slovenia								**Slovénie**
Production [7]	51	*60	44	*50	44	55	...	Production [7]
Consumption * [7]	90	95	105	90	90	100	...	Consommation * [7]
Consumption per cap. (kg.)	45	48	53	45	45	50	...	Consom. par hab. (kg.)
Somalia								**Somalie**
Production *	19	20	15	20	20	20	20	Production *
Consumption *	150	170	180	185	190	200	200	Consommation *
Consumption per cap. (kg.)	19	20	21	20	19	20	21	Consom. par hab. (kg.)
South Africa								**Afrique du Sud**
Production	2 985	2 547	2 691	2 311	2 767	2 418	2 234	Production
Consumption	1 508	1 386	1 453	1 341	1 478	1 436	1 484	Consommation
Consumption per cap. (kg.)	36	32	33	30	33	32	32	Consom. par hab. (kg.)
Sri Lanka								**Sri Lanka**
Production	20	*19	*15	*20	*20	*21	*60	Production
Consumption *	550	550	560	575	600	620	640	Consommation *
Consumption per cap. (kg.)	30	29	29	31	32	36	33	Consom. par hab. (kg.)
Sudan								**Soudan**
Production	610	635	680	719	744	686	789	Production
Consumption	*450	*450	430	523	568	568	624	Consommation
Consumption per cap. (kg.)	15	15	14	17	18	17	19	Consom. par hab. (kg.)
Suriname								**Suriname**
Production *	5	7	10	10	10	5	5	Production *
Consumption *	18	18	19	19	20	20	20	Consommation *
Consumption per cap. (kg.)	44	42	45	46	39	42	44	Consom. par hab. (kg.)
Swaziland								**Swaziland**
Production	537	571	553	567	675	616	594	Production
Consumption	101	103	105	107	107	109	112	Consommation
Consumption per cap. (kg.)	113	113	113	107	112	99	98	Consom. par hab. (kg.)
Switzerland								**Suisse**
Production	191	177	*231	*187	222	185	*225	Production
Consumption	*305	328	*375	*385	393	463	*410	Consommation
Consumption per cap. (kg.)	43	46	52	53	54	63	55	Consom. par hab. (kg.)

Sugar—Production and consumption: thousand metric tons; consumption per capita: kilograms (*continued*)

Sucre—Production et consommation : milliers de tonnes ; consommation par habitant : kilogrammes (*suite*)

Country or area	1998	1999	2000	2001	2002	2003	2004	Pays ou zone
Syrian Arab Republic								Rép. arabe syrienne
Production	107	*102	*100	121	*120	*120	*105	Production
Consumption *	715	720	730	745	760	775	790	Consommation *
Consumption per cap. (kg.)	46	45	45	45	44	44	44	Consom. par hab. (kg.)
Tajikistan								Tadjikistan
Consumption *	65	60	60	60	70	80	85	Consommation *
Consumption per cap. (kg.)	11	10	9	10	11	13	15	Consom. par hab. (kg.)
Thailand								Thaïlande
Production	4 143	5 456	6 157	5 370	6 438	7 737	7 462	Production
Consumption	1 834	1 776	1 816	1 955	1 978	2 073	2 303	Consommation
Consumption per cap. (kg.)	30	29	29	31	31	33	36	Consom. par hab. (kg.)
TFYR of Macedonia								L'ex-R.y. Macédoine
Production	40	43	32	20	*20	33	28	Production
Consumption *	60	80	80	80	80	85	85	Consommation *
Consumption per cap. (kg.)	30	40	39	39	39	42	42	Consom. par hab. (kg.)
Togo								Togo
Consumption *	42	45	45	45	45	48	50	Consommation *
Consumption per cap. (kg.)	10	10	10	10	10	10	10	Consom. par hab. (kg.)
Trinidad and Tobago								Trinité-et-Tobago
Production	79	92	115	89	104	67	43	Production
Consumption	72	70	78	79	70	70	*75	Consommation
Consumption per cap. (kg.)	56	55	60	61	54	59	68	Consom. par hab. (kg.)
Tunisia								Tunisie
Production	15	9	2	...	...	...	...	Production
Consumption	287	292	294	309	319	*330	335	Consommation
Consumption per cap. (kg.)	31	31	31	32	33	33	34	Consom. par hab. (kg.)
Turkey								Turquie
Production	2 784	2 491	2 273	2 360	2 128	2 136	2 053	Production
Consumption	2 074	1 836	*1 925	1 973	1 782	1 725	1 894	Consommation
Consumption per cap. (kg.)	33	29	29	29	26	24	26	Consom. par hab. (kg.)
Turkmenistan								Turkménistan
Production	...	...	...	...	...	1	2	Production
Consumption *	70	70	70	70	70	75	75	Consommation *
Consumption per cap. (kg.)	16	15	15	15	15	15	14	Consom. par hab. (kg.)
Uganda								Ouganda
Production *	111	137	130	140	160	180	190	Production *
Consumption *	150	150	155	160	180	195	210	Consommation *
Consumption per cap. (kg.)	7	7	7	7	7	8	10	Consom. par hab. (kg.)
Ukraine								Ukraine
Production	2 041	1 640	1 686	1 802	*1 545	1 690	*1 945	Production
Consumption	1 739	*1 800	*1 875	*2 005	*2 100	*2 300	*2 300	Consommation
Consumption per cap. (kg.)	34	36	38	41	43	48	49	Consom. par hab. (kg.)
United Rep. of Tanzania								Rép.-Unie de Tanzanie
Production	*110	114	*130	*115	187	218	211	Production
Consumption	*200	*200	*208	*200	165	218	221	Consommation
Consumption per cap. (kg.)	6	6	6	6	5	6	6	Consom. par hab. (kg.)
United States								Etats-Unis
Production	7 159	*8 243	8 080	7 774	6 805	7 964	7 647	Production
Consumption	9 049	9 067	9 051	9 139[9]	9 079	8 844	8 994	Consommation
Consumption per cap. (kg.)	34	33	32	32	32	30	31	Consom. par hab. (kg.)
Uruguay								Uruguay
Production *	14	9	8	7	7	6	7	Production *
Consumption	*115	101	*102	*105	*110	*115	*120	Consommation
Consumption per cap. (kg.)	35	31	30	31	33	34	35	Consom. par hab. (kg.)
Uzbekistan								Ouzbékistan
Production	11	*20	11	*7	*7	...	...	Production
Consumption *	410	435	450	475	490	495	495	Consommation *
Consumption per cap. (kg.)	17	18	18	19	19	20	20	Consom. par hab. (kg.)
Venezuela (Bolivarian Rep. of)								Venezuela (Rép. bolivar. du)
Production *	590	535	645	585	550	510	694	Production *
Consumption *	855	870	893	910	925	930	1 020	Consommation *
Consumption per cap. (kg.)	37	37	37	37	37	36	39	Consom. par hab. (kg.)

Country or area	1998	1999	2000	2001	2002	2003	2004	Pays ou zone
Viet Nam								**Viet Nam**
Production	657	*878	1 155	*850	*890	*975	*1 070	Production
Consumption *	700	750	810	875	950	1 005	1 035	Consommation *
Consumption per cap. (kg.)	9	10	10	11	12	13	13	Consom. par hab. (kg.)
Yemen								**Yémen**
Consumption *	375	390	410	425	445	470	480	Consommation *
Consumption per cap. (kg.)	22	22	22	23	23	24	23	Consom. par hab. (kg.)
Zambia								**Zambie**
Production	173	*210	*190	199	233	230	245	Production
Consumption	*85	*115	*145	102	116	104	115	Consommation
Consumption per cap. (kg.)	8	11	14	11	11	9	10	Consom. par hab. (kg.)
Zimbabwe								**Zimbabwe**
Production	572	583	571	548	565	482	456	Production
Consumption	305	376	374	305	335	315	311	Consommation
Consumption per cap. (kg.)	24	29	30	24	27	25	27	Consom. par hab. (kg.)

Source

International Sugar Organization (ISO), London, the ISO database and the "Sugar Yearbook 2004".

Notes

[1] Including non-human consumption: 1998-15,652 tons.
[2] Including store losses of 1,159 tons and accidental losses of 129 tons.

[3] For statistical purposes, the data for China do not include those for the Hong Kong Special Administrative Region (Hong Kong SAR), Macao Special Administrative Region (Macao SAR) and Taiwan Province of China.

[4] Including non-human consumption: 1983-6,710 tons; 1984-19,797 tons; 1985-79,908 tons; 1986-98,608 tons; 1987-147,262 tons; 1988-122,058 tons; 1989-52,230 tons; 1991-13,541 tons; 1994-12,178 tons; 1995-10,211 tons; 1996-14,648 tons; 1997-13,893 tons; 1998-17,082 tons; 1999-42,635 tons; 2000-31,836 tons; 2001-13,534 tons; 2002-16,750 tons.

[5] For member states of this grouping, see Annex I – Other groupings.

[6] Including 11,572 tons sold to other Pacific Island nations in 1994; 12,520 tons in 1995; 14,154 tons in 1996; 13,109 tons in 1997; 6,444 tons in 2001 and 10,686 tons in 2004.

[7] Beginning 2004, data for Cyprus, Czech Republic, Estonia, Hungary, Latvia, Lithuania, Malta, Poland, Slovakia, Slovenia are incorporated in the European Union data.

[8] Including consumption of mono-sodium glutamate, lysine and other products: 1987-44,600 tons; 1988-92,200 tons; 1989-94,500 tons; 1990-89,400 tons; 1991-77,300 tons; 1992-75,800 tons; 1993-89,800 tons; 1994-170,384 tons; 1995-200,863 tons; 1996-257,700 tons; 1997-257,310 tons; 1998-258,247 tons; 1999-152,739 tons; 2000-159,027 tons; 2001-210,498 tons; 2002-197,939 tons; 2003-226,191 tons; 2004-235,773 tons.

[9] Including 19,780 tons used for livestock feed.

Source

Organisation internationale du sucre (OIS), Londres, la base de données de l'OIS et "l'Annuaire du sucre 2004".

Notes

[1] Dont la consommation non humaine: 1998-15 652 tonnes.
[2] Y compris des pertes de 1.159 tonnes au cours du stockage et des pertes accidentelles de 129 tonnes.

[3] Pour la présentation des statistiques, les données pour Chine ne comprennent pas la Région Administrative Spéciale de Hong Kong (Hong Kong RAS), la Région Administrative Spéciale de Macao (Macao RAS) et la province de Taiwan.

[4] Dont consommation non humaine : 1983-6.701 tonnes; 1984-19.797 tonnes; 1985-79.908 tonnes; 1986-98.608 tonnes; 1987-147.262 tonnes; 1988-122.058 tonnes; 1989-52.230 tonnes; 1991-13.541 tonnes; 1994-12.178 tonnes; 1995-10.211 tonnes; 1996-14.648 tonnes; 1997-13.893 tonnes; 1998-17.082 tonnes; 1999-42.635 tonnes; 2000-31.836 tonnes; 2001-13.534 tonnes; 2002-16.750 tonnes.

[5] Pour les Etats membres de ce groupements, voir annexe I – Autres groupements.

[6] Y compris 11.572 tonnes vendues à autres îles pacifiques en 1994; 12.520 tonnes en 1995; 14.154 tonnes en 1996; 13.109 tonnes en 1997; et 6.444 tonnes en 2001 et 10.686 tonnes en 2004.

[7] A partir de 2004, les données pour Chypre, République tchèque, Estonie, Hongrie, Lettonie, Lituanie, Malta, Pologne, Slovaquie, Slovénie sont inclus dans la Union européen.

[8] Y compris la consommation des produits du glutamate monosodium, lysine et autres: 1987-44.600 tonnes ; 1988-92.200 tonnes; 1989-94.500 tonnes; 1990-89.400 tonnes; 1991-77.300 tonnes ; 1992-75.800 tonnes; 1993-89.800 tonnes; 1994-170.384 tonnes; 1995-200.863 tonnes; 1996-257.700 tonnes; 1997-257.310 tonnes; 1998-258.247 tonnes; 1999-152.739 tonnes; 2000-159.027 tonnes; 2001-210.498 tonnes; 2002-197.939 tonnes; 2003-226.191 tonnes; 2004-235.773 tonnes.

[9] Y compris 19.780 tonnes utilisées pour les aliments du bétail.

36

Meat
Production: thousand metric tons

Viande
Production : milliers de tonnes

Country or area	1997	1998	1999	2000	2001	2002	2003	2004	Pays ou zone
World									**Monde**
Total	**151 810**	**157 384**	**159 519**	**161 306**	**162 553**	**167 895**	**172 047**	**175 762**	**Totale**
Beef and veal	55 412	55 269	56 312	56 904	56 086	57 801	58 434	59 153	Bœuf et veau
Buffalo	2 842	2 880	2 966	2 994	2 953	3 018	2 998	3 124	Buffle
Goat	3 294	3 499	3 590	3 738	3 853	4 042	4 266	4 370	Chèvre
Mutton and lamb	7 167	7 311	7 380	7 587	7 603	7 715	7 928	8 225	Mouton et agneau
Pork	83 095	88 425	89 270	90 083	92 057	95 319	98 421	100 889	Porc
Africa									**Afrique**
Total	6 293	6 436	6 571	6 828	6 789	6 937	7 130	7 212	Totale
Beef and veal	3 598	3 685	3 775	3 993	3 952	4 074	4 191	4 228	Bœuf et veau
Buffalo	256	266	277	288	189	203	229	230	Buffle
Goat	763	773	782	790	808	823	845	855	Chèvre
Mutton and lamb	1 002	1 035	1 051	1 066	1 094	1 080	1 104	1 121	Mouton et agneau
Pork	675	676	687	691	746	756	761	779	Porc
Algeria									**Algérie**
Total	281	282	293	309	282	293	298	302	Totale
Beef and veal	102	103	117	133	105	116[1]	121	*125	Bœuf et veau
Goat [1]	12	12	12	12	12	12	12	12	Chèvre [1]
Mutton and lamb	167	167	163	164	165[1]	165[1]	165[1]	165[1]	Mouton et agneau
Angola									**Angola**
Total	115	123	124	125	125	123	123	123	Totale
Beef and veal [1]	77	85	85	85	85	85	85	85	Bœuf et veau [1]
Goat [1]	8	8	9	10	10	9	9	9	Chèvre [1]
Mutton and lamb [1]	1	1	1	1	1	1	1	1	Mouton et agneau [1]
Pork [1]	29	29	29	29	29	28	28	28	Porc [1]
Benin									**Bénin**
Total	29	29	28	28	29	30	31	32	Totale
Beef and veal [1]	16	20	19	18	19	20	20	21	Bœuf et veau [1]
Goat [1]	4	4	4	4	4	4	4	5	Chèvre [1]
Mutton and lamb [1]	2	2	2	3	3	3	3	3	Mouton et agneau [1]
Pork [1]	6	3	2	4	3	4	4	4	Porc [1]
Botswana									**Botswana**
Total	48	46	35	38	40	39	35	37	Totale
Beef and veal	38[1]	37[1]	27[1]	29[1]	32[1]	31[1]	27	28[1]	Bœuf et veau
Goat [1]	7	6	6	6	6	6	6	6	Chèvre [1]
Mutton and lamb [1]	2	2	2	2	2	2	2	2	Mouton et agneau [1]
Pork [1]	0	1	0	1	0	0	0	0	Porc [1]
Burkina Faso									**Burkina Faso**
Total	91	94	96	100	95	103	106	109	Totale
Beef and veal [1]	50	51	52	55	49	55	57	58	Bœuf et veau [1]
Goat [1]	22	22	22	23	23	25	26	27	Chèvre [1]
Mutton and lamb [1]	13	13	13	14	14	14	14	14	Mouton et agneau [1]
Pork [1]	8	8	8	9	9	9	10	10	Porc [1]
Burundi									**Burundi**
Total	17	18	17	17	17	17	17	17	Totale
Beef and veal	9[1]	10[1]	9	9	9[1]	9[1]	9[1]	9[1]	Bœuf et veau
Goat	3[1]	3[1]	3	3	3[1]	3[1]	3[1]	3[1]	Chèvre
Mutton and lamb [1]	1	1	1	1	1	1	1	1	Mouton et agneau [1]
Pork [1]	4	4	4	4	4	4	4	4	Porc [1]
Cameroon									**Cameroun**
Total	116	120	133	141	143	143	143	143	Totale
Beef and veal	76[1]	77[1]	*91	*93	*95	95[1]	95[1]	95[1]	Bœuf et veau
Goat [1]	13	14	14	16	16	16	16	16	Chèvre [1]
Mutton and lamb [1]	15	15	16	16	16	16	16	16	Mouton et agneau [1]
Pork [1]	12	14	12	16	16	16	16	16	Porc [1]
Cape Verde									**Cap-Vert**
Total	6	8	8	7	8	8	8	8	Totale
Beef and veal	1[1]	1	0	0	1[1]	0[1]	0[1]	0[1]	Bœuf et veau
Pork	5[1]	6	7[1]	7	7[1]	7[1]	7[1]	7[1]	Porc

Country or area	1997	1998	1999	2000	2001	2002	2003	2004	Pays ou zone
									Rép. centrafricaine
Central African Rep.									
Total	70	72	72	90	91	94	97	101	Totale
Beef and veal	*50	*51	*51	67	67	69	71[1]	*74	Bœuf et veau
Goat	8	8[1]	8[1]	*10	10[1]	11	12[1]	12[1]	Chèvre
Mutton and lamb	1	1[1]	1[1]	1[1]	1[1]	1[1]	2[1]	2[1]	Mouton et agneau
Pork	12	12[1]	12[1]	*12	13[1]	13	13	*14	Porc
Chad									**Tchad**
Total	102	110	108	105	109	110	113	115	Totale
Beef and veal [1]	73	80	78	74	77	76	78	80	Bœuf et veau [1]
Goat [1]	18	18	18	19	20	20	21	21	Chèvre [1]
Mutton and lamb [1]	11	11	11	12	12	13	13	13	Mouton et agneau [1]
Comoros									**Comores**
Total	1	1	2	1	1	2	2	2	Totale
Beef and veal [1]	1	1	1	1	1	1	1	1	Bœuf et veau [1]
Goat [1]	0	0	1	0	0	0	0	0	Chèvre [1]
Congo									**Congo**
Total	5	4	5	5	5	5	5	5	Totale
Beef and veal [1]	1	1	2	2	2	2	2	2	Bœuf et veau [1]
Goat [1]	1	1	1	1	1	1	1	1	Chèvre [1]
Pork [1]	2	2	2	2	2	2	2	2	Porc [1]
Côte d'Ivoire									**Côte d'Ivoire**
Total	72	75	70	71	69	76	72	73	Totale
Beef and veal	50	52	47	48	46	53	51	52	Bœuf et veau
Goat	*5	*5	*5	*5	5[1]	4[1]	4[1]	4[1]	Chèvre
Mutton and lamb	*6	*7	*6	5	5	5	5[1]	5[1]	Mouton et agneau
Pork	11[1]	11[1]	13[1]	*13	14[1]	14[1]	12[1]	12[1]	Porc
Dem. Rep. of the Congo									**Rép. dém. du Congo**
Total	68	68	64	61	59	57	57	57	Totale
Beef and veal	16	14	14	14	13	12	12	12	Bœuf et veau
Goat	21	22	19	19	19	18	18	18	Chèvre
Mutton and lamb	3	3	3	3	3	3	3	3	Mouton et agneau
Pork	29	29	27	26	25	24	24	24	Porc
Djibouti									**Djibouti**
Total	8	8	9	11	11	11	11	11	Totale
Beef and veal [1]	4	4	4	6	6	6	6	6	Bœuf et veau [1]
Goat [1]	2	2	2	2	2	2	2	2	Chèvre [1]
Mutton and lamb [1]	2	2	2	2	2	2	2	2	Mouton et agneau [1]
Egypt									**Egypte**
Total	600	616	593	622	516	537	595	607	Totale
Beef and veal	248[1]	252	233	*256	*247	252	287	298[1]	Bœuf et veau
Buffalo	256	266	277	288	189	203	229	230[1]	Buffle
Goat	30	30	30	25[1]	25[1]	26	26	26[1]	Chèvre
Mutton and lamb	64	65	50[1]	50	53	52	50	50[1]	Mouton et agneau
Pork	3[1]	3[1]	3	*3	*3	3[1]	3[1]	3[1]	Porc
Eritrea									**Erythrée**
Total	25	27	28	29	27	26	29	29	Totale
Beef and veal [1]	14	16	16	16	15	14	17	17	Bœuf et veau [1]
Goat [1]	5	5	6	6	6	6	6	6	Chèvre [1]
Mutton and lamb [1]	5	6	6	6	6	6	7	7	Mouton et agneau [1]
Ethiopia									**Ethiopie**
Total	332	340	355	357	371	430	418	416	Totale
Beef and veal	270	274	290	294[1]	304[1]	353[1]	338[1]	331[1]	Bœuf et veau
Goat [1]	25	28	27	26	29	29	29	29	Chèvre [1]
Mutton and lamb [1]	36	36	36	36	38	48	50	55	Mouton et agneau [1]
Pork [1]	1	1	1	1	1	1	2	2	Porc [1]
Gabon									**Gabon**
Total	5	5	5	5	5	5	5	5	Totale
Beef and veal [1]	1	1	1	1	1	1	1	1	Bœuf et veau [1]
Mutton and lamb [1]	1	1	1	1	1	1	1	1	Mouton et agneau [1]
Pork [1]	3	3	3	3	3	3	3	3	Porc [1]
Gambia									**Gambie**
Total	5	5	5	5	4	5	5	5	Totale
Beef and veal [1]	3	3	3	3	3	3	3	3	Bœuf et veau [1]
Goat [1]	0	0	0	0	1	1	1	1	Chèvre [1]

Country or area	1997	1998	1999	2000	2001	2002	2003	2004	Pays ou zone
Ghana									**Ghana**
Total	44	45	45	54	55	55	57	59	Totale
Beef and veal [1]	21	21	21	24	24	24	24	25	Bœuf et veau [1]
Goat [1]	6	7	7	10	11	11	12	12	Chèvre [1]
Mutton and lamb [1]	6	7	7	9	10	10	10	11	Mouton et agneau [1]
Pork	11[1]	11[1]	10[1]	11[1]	11[1]	10[1]	10[1]	11	Porc
Guinea									**Guinée**
Total	35	37	39	41	43	44	45	47	Totale
Beef and veal [1]	27	29	30	32	33	34	34	35	Bœuf et veau [1]
Goat [1]	4	4	4	4	5	5	5	6	Chèvre [1]
Mutton and lamb [1]	3	3	3	3	4	4	4	4	Mouton et agneau [1]
Pork	1	2	2	2	2	2	2	2	Porc
Guinea-Bissau									**Guinée-Bissau**
Total	16	16	17	17	17	17	18	18	Totale
Beef and veal [1]	4	4	4	5	5	5	5	5	Bœuf et veau [1]
Goat [1]	1	1	1	1	1	1	1	1	Chèvre [1]
Mutton and lamb [1]	1	1	1	1	1	1	1	1	Mouton et agneau [1]
Pork [1]	10	10	11	11	11	11	11	11	Porc [1]
Kenya									**Kenya**
Total	330	333	352	355	370	365	393	408	Totale
Beef and veal	261	270	279	287	295	295	305[1]	319	Bœuf et veau
Goat [1]	34	30	34	31	34	34	36	36	Chèvre [1]
Mutton and lamb [1]	24	22	28	26	26	25	34	34	Mouton et agneau [1]
Pork	12	11	11	11	15[1]	11	19[1]	19[1]	Porc
Lesotho									**Lesotho**
Total	18	17	17	16	17	17	17	17	Totale
Beef and veal [1]	10	10	9	8	9	9	9	9	Bœuf et veau [1]
Goat [1]	2	1	2	2	2	2	2	2	Chèvre [1]
Mutton and lamb [1]	4	3	3	3	3	3	3	3	Mouton et agneau [1]
Pork [1]	2	3	3	3	3	3	3	3	Porc [1]
Liberia									**Libéria**
Total	6	6	6	7	7	7	7	7	Totale
Beef and veal [1]	1	1	1	1	1	1	1	1	Bœuf et veau [1]
Goat [1]	1	1	1	1	1	1	1	1	Chèvre [1]
Mutton and lamb [1]	1	1	1	1	1	1	1	1	Mouton et agneau [1]
Pork [1]	4	4	4	4	4	4	4	4	Porc [1]
Libyan Arab Jamah.									**Jamah. arabe libyenne**
Total	79	89	56	42	45	40	40	40	Totale
Beef and veal [1]	40	44	16	8	6	6	6	6	Bœuf et veau [1]
Goat [1]	6	6	6	6	6	6	6	6	Chèvre [1]
Mutton and lamb [1]	33	39	34	27	32	27	27	27	Mouton et agneau [1]
Madagascar									**Madagascar**
Total	229	229	221	218	197	190	194	225	Totale
Beef and veal [1]	147	148	148	148	119	112	115	147	Bœuf et veau [1]
Goat [1]	7	6	6	5	6	6	6	6	Chèvre [1]
Mutton and lamb [1]	3	2	2	2	2	2	3	2	Mouton et agneau [1]
Pork [1]	72	72	65	63	70	70	70	70	Porc [1]
Malawi									**Malawi**
Total	37	40	40	44	42	43	43	43	Totale
Beef and veal [1]	12	14	15	16	16	16	16	16	Bœuf et veau [1]
Goat [1]	6	6	5	6	6	6	6	6	Chèvre [1]
Pork [1]	19	19	20	22	20	21	21	21	Porc [1]
Mali									**Mali**
Total	146	152	151	140	155	178	195	184	Totale
Beef and veal [1]	88	91	89	76	85	103	113	98	Bœuf et veau [1]
Goat [1]	32	32	35	36	39	42	46	48	Chèvre [1]
Mutton and lamb [1]	23	26	25	26	29	31	34	36	Mouton et agneau [1]
Pork [1]	2	2	2	2	2	2	2	2	Porc [1]
Mauritania									**Mauritanie**
Total	39	43	47	55	58	60	61	62	Totale
Beef and veal [1]	13	14	14	21	22	22	23	23	Bœuf et veau [1]
Goat [1]	10	11	12	12	13	14	14	14	Chèvre [1]
Mutton and lamb [1]	17	19	21	22	23	24	24	25	Mouton et agneau [1]

Country or area	1997	1998	1999	2000	2001	2002	2003	2004	Pays ou zone
Mauritius									**Maurice**
Total	3	4	4	4	3	3	4	2	Totale
Beef and veal	2	3	3	3	2	2	3	1[1]	Bœuf et veau
Pork	1	1	1	1	1	1	1	1[1]	Porc
Morocco									**Maroc**
Total	268	258	282	288	305	30J	272	273	Totale
Beef and veal	125	120	135	140	159	170	150	148	Bœuf et veau
Goat	22	22	20	22	21	20[1]	21[1]	21[1]	Chèvre
Mutton and lamb	120	115	126	125	125	110	100	103	Mouton et agneau
Pork	1	1	1	*1	1[1]	1[1]	1[1]	1[1]	Porc
Mozambique									**Mozambique**
Total	53	53	54	54	54	54	54	54	Totale
Beef and veal [1]	38	38	38	38	38	38	38	38	Bœuf et veau [1]
Goat [1]	2	2	2	2	2	2	2	2	Chèvre [1]
Mutton and lamb [1]	1	1	1	1	1	1	1	1	Mouton et agneau [1]
Pork [1]	13	13	13	13	13	13	13	13	Porc [1]
Namibia									**Namibie**
Total	41	45	54	74	71	79	98	97	Totale
Beef and veal [1]	30	38	45	64	58	61	78	77	Bœuf et veau [1]
Goat [1]	5	4	5	5	4	5	5	5	Chèvre [1]
Mutton and lamb [1]	5	2	4	5	8	13	14	14	Mouton et agneau [1]
Pork [1]	1	1	1	1	1	1	1	1	Porc [1]
Niger									**Niger**
Total	76	78	81	82	84	71	79	79	Totale
Beef and veal	38[1]	39[1]	40[1]	*41	*42	35[1]	37[1]	37[1]	Bœuf et veau
Goat [1]	23	23	25	25	25	22	25	25	Chèvre [1]
Mutton and lamb [1]	14	14	15	15	16	13	15	15	Mouton et agneau [1]
Pork [1]	1	1	1	1	1	1	1	1	Porc [1]
Nigeria									**Nigéria**
Total	654	664	680	671	698	711	721	736	Totale
Beef and veal	294	297	298	279[1]	279[1]	280[1]	280[1]	280[1]	Bœuf et veau
Goat [1]	133	133	137	139	140	142	142	147	Chèvre [1]
Mutton and lamb [1]	87	89	91	95	94	97	99	101	Mouton et agneau [1]
Pork [1]	140	144	153	158	185	193	200	208	Porc [1]
Réunion									**Réunion**
Total	14	13	14	14	14	14	14	14	Totale
Beef and veal	2	2	2	2	2	2[1]	2[1]	2[1]	Bœuf et veau
Pork	13	11	12	12	12	12[1]	12[1]	12[1]	Porc
Rwanda									**Rwanda**
Total	19	21	24	24	26	27	28	30	Totale
Beef and veal [1]	14	16	18	17	19	20	21	23	Bœuf et veau [1]
Goat [1]	2	2	2	3	3	3	3	3	Chèvre [1]
Mutton and lamb [1]	1	1	1	1	1	1	1	1	Mouton et agneau [1]
Pork [1]	3	2	3	3	3	3	3	3	Porc [1]
Senegal									**Sénégal**
Total	81	83	85	89	90	87	85	90	Totale
Beef and veal	47[1]	47[1]	48[1]	50[1]	48	45	43	48[1]	Bœuf et veau
Goat [1]	15	16	16	16	17	16	17	17	Chèvre [1]
Mutton and lamb	14[1]	15[1]	15[1]	15[1]	16	15	15	16[1]	Mouton et agneau
Pork	5[1]	5[1]	6[1]	8[1]	9	11	10	10[1]	Porc
Seychelles									**Seychelles**
Total	1	1	1	1	1	1	1	1	Totale
Pork [1]	1	1	1	1	1	1	1	1	Porc [1]
Sierra Leone									**Sierra Leone**
Total	10	10	10	9	10	9	9	9	Totale
Beef and veal [1]	6	6	7	5	5	5	5	5	Bœuf et veau [1]
Mutton and lamb [1]	1	1	1	1	1	1	1	1	Mouton et agneau [1]
Pork [1]	2	2	2	2	2	2	2	2	Porc [1]
South Africa									**Afrique du Sud**
Total	756	743	784	880	828	833	905	904	Totale
Beef and veal	503	496	513	622	577	580	635	625	Bœuf et veau
Goat [1]	37	37	36	36	36	36	36	36	Chèvre [1]
Mutton and lamb	91	91	112	118	104	105	107	108	Mouton et agneau
Pork	125	119	123	104	111	112	127	134	Porc

Country or area	1997	1998	1999	2000	2001	2002	2003	2004	Pays ou zone
Sudan									**Soudan**
Total	505	529	532	557	592	595	595	595	Totale
Beef and veal [1]	250	265	276	296	320	325	325	325	Bœuf et veau [1]
Goat	122	123	114	118	122 [1]	126 [1]	126 [1]	126 [1]	Chèvre
Mutton and lamb [1]	133	141	142	143	150	144	144	144	Mouton et agneau [1]
Swaziland									**Swaziland**
Total	18	18	18	22	12	16	16	16	Totale
Beef and veal	*14	14 [1]	14 [1]	18	8	13	13 [1]	13 [1]	Bœuf et veau
Goat [1]	2	2	2	3	3	2	2	2	Chèvre [1]
Mutton and lamb [1]	0	0	1	0	0	0	0	0	Mouton et agneau [1]
Pork [1]	1	1	1	1	1	1	1	1	Porc [1]
Togo									**Togo**
Total	16	15	16	17	17	18	18	18	Totale
Beef and veal [1]	5	5	5	5	6	6	6	6	Bœuf et veau [1]
Goat [1]	3	3	3	4	4	4	4	4	Chèvre [1]
Mutton and lamb [1]	3	3	3	3	4	4	4	4	Mouton et agneau [1]
Pork [1]	5	4	4	4	5	5	5	5	Porc [1]
Tunisia									**Tunisie**
Total	106	112	120	124	129	128	132	133	Totale
Beef and veal	50	53	58	60	62	60	63	63 [1]	Bœuf et veau
Goat	8	9	9	10	10	10	10	10 [1]	Chèvre
Mutton and lamb	47	50	53	54	57	58	60	60 [1]	Mouton et agneau
Uganda									**Ouganda**
Total	186	194	200	204	214	221	207	203	Totale
Beef and veal	89	93 [1]	96 [1]	97 [1]	101 [1]	106	110 [1]	106 [1]	Bœuf et veau
Goat	22	23 [1]	24 [1]	25 [1]	25 [1]	25 [1]	29 [1]	29 [1]	Chèvre
Mutton and lamb [1]	5	5	5	5	6	6	8	8	Mouton et agneau [1]
Pork [1]	71	73	75	77	81	84	60	60	Porc [1]
United Rep. of Tanzania									**Rép.-Unie de Tanzanie**
Total	241	247	267	277	284	300	301	300	Totale
Beef and veal [1]	193	198	215	225	230	246	246	246	Bœuf et veau [1]
Goat [1]	27	27	29	29	30	31	31	31	Chèvre [1]
Mutton and lamb [1]	11	11	11	10	10	10	10	10	Mouton et agneau [1]
Pork [1]	11	11	12	13	13	13	13	13	Porc [1]
Zambia									**Zambie**
Total	55	55	61	56	57	57	57	57	Totale
Beef and veal [1]	42	41	47	41	41	41	41	41	Bœuf et veau [1]
Goat [1]	3	3	4	5	5	5	5	5	Chèvre [1]
Mutton and lamb [1]	0	0	0	1	1	1	1	1	Mouton et agneau [1]
Pork [1]	10	10	11	10	11	11	11	11	Porc [1]
Zimbabwe									**Zimbabwe**
Total	98	99	122	135	142	139	138	138	Totale
Beef and veal	74 [1]	74 [1]	95	101	101 [1]	99 [1]	97 [1]	97 [1]	Bœuf et veau
Goat [1]	12	12	13	13	13	13	13	13	Chèvre [1]
Mutton and lamb [1]	0	0	1	1	1	1	1	1	Mouton et agneau [1]
Pork	12 [1]	13 [1]	13	20 [1]	27 [1]	27 [1]	28 [1]	28 [1]	Porc
America, North									**Amérique du Nord**
Total	25 236	26 411	27 188	27 334	27 238	28 147	27 798	27 651	Totale
Beef and veal	14 715	14 924	15 345	15 541	15 244	15 752	15 280	14 805	Bœuf et veau
Goat	47	49	48	51	52	55	55	54	Chèvre
Mutton and lamb	167	162	162	162	162	165	161	160	Mouton et agneau
Pork	10 309	11 275	11 633	11 580	11 780	12 175	12 301	12 631	Porc
Antigua and Barbuda									**Antigua-et-Barbuda**
Total	1	1	1	1	1	1	1	1	Totale
Beef and veal [1]	0	0	0	0	1	1	1	1	Bœuf et veau [1]
Barbados									**Barbade**
Total	4	3	3	3	2	2	2	2	Totale
Beef and veal	1	1	1	1	0	0	0	0	Bœuf et veau
Pork	3 [1]	3 [1]	2	2	2	1	2	2	Porc
Belize									**Belize**
Total	2	2	2	2	3	3	3	3	Totale
Beef and veal	2	1	1	1	1	2	2	3	Bœuf et veau
Pork	1	1	1	1	1	1	1	1	Porc

Country or area	1997	1998	1999	2000	2001	2002	2003	2004	Pays ou zone
Canada									**Canada**
Total	2 356	2 584	2 841	2 916	3 007	3 167	3 089	3 406	Totale
Beef and veal	1 089	1 182	1 264	1 263	1 262	1 294	1 190	*1 460	Bœuf et veau
Mutton and lamb	10	10	11	13	14	15	16	16[1]	Mouton et agneau
Pork	1 257	1 392	1 566	1 640	1 731	1 858	1 882	*1 930	Porc
Costa Rica									**Costa Rica**
Total	107	107	113	113	110	104	110	107	Totale
Beef and veal	86	82	84	82	74	68	74	69	Bœuf et veau
Pork	21	25	29	31	36	36	36	38	Porc
Cuba									**Cuba**
Total	139	159	181	178	159	165	160	176	Totale
Beef and veal	71	74	76	76	75	66	56	70[1]	Bœuf et veau
Goat	1[1]	1[1]	1	2	2	2	2	3[1]	Chèvre
Mutton and lamb	4[1]	4[1]	5	6[1]	6	7	7	8[1]	Mouton et agneau
Pork	65	81	99	94	76	90	94	96[1]	Porc
Dominica									**Dominique**
Total	1	1	1	1	1	1	1	1	Totale
Beef and veal [1]	1	1	1	1	1	1	1	1	Bœuf et veau [1]
Dominican Republic									**Rép. dominicaine**
Total	146	146	124	131	135	137	138	122	Totale
Beef and veal	79	80	66	69	71	72	72[1]	56[1]	Bœuf et veau
Goat [1]	2	1	1	1	1	1	1	1	Chèvre [1]
Pork	64	64	58	61	63	64	65[1]	65[1]	Porc
El Salvador									**El Salvador**
Total	46	44	48	46	43	49	38	34	Totale
Beef and veal	35	34	34	35	35	40	29	27	Bœuf et veau
Pork	10[1]	10[1]	14[1]	11[1]	9[1]	9[1]	9[1]	8	Porc
Guadeloupe									**Guadeloupe**
Total	5	5	5	5	5	5	5	5	Totale
Beef and veal	3	3	3	3[1]	3[1]	3[1]	3[1]	3[1]	Bœuf et veau
Pork	1[1]	1[1]	1[1]	1[1]	1[1]	1	1[1]	1[1]	Porc
Guatemala									**Guatemala**
Total	85	85	88	88	89	90	91	91	Totale
Beef and veal	54	54	62	62[1]	62[1]	63[1]	63[1]	63[1]	Bœuf et veau
Mutton and lamb [1]	2	2	2	1	1	1	1	1	Mouton et agneau [1]
Pork	28	28	24	25[1]	25[1]	26[1]	26[1]	26[1]	Porc
Haiti									**Haïti**
Total	59	64	64	76	79	82	83	82	Totale
Beef and veal	28	31	31[1]	40	41[1]	42[1]	43[1]	43[1]	Bœuf et veau
Goat	*5	*5	5[1]	6	7[1]	7[1]	7[1]	6[1]	Chèvre
Mutton and lamb	*1	*1	1[1]	1	1[1]	1[1]	1[1]	1[1]	Mouton et agneau
Pork	25	27	27[1]	28	31[1]	33[1]	33[1]	33[1]	Porc
Honduras									**Honduras**
Total	73	66	64	65	65	73	67	64	Totale
Beef and veal	63	57	55	55	55	62	57	54	Bœuf et veau
Pork	9	9	9	10	10	11[1]	10[1]	10	Porc
Jamaica									**Jamaïque**
Total	23	19	23	22	22	21	22	22	Totale
Beef and veal	15	12	15	14	13	14	15[1]	15[1]	Bœuf et veau
Goat [1]	2	2	2	2	2	2	2	2	Chèvre [1]
Pork	7	6	7	7	6	5	5[1]	5[1]	Porc
Martinique									**Martinique**
Total	4	4	4	4	4	4	4	4	Totale
Beef and veal	2	2	2	2	2	2	2[1]	2[1]	Bœuf et veau
Pork	1	2	2	2	2	2	2[1]	2[1]	Porc
Mexico									**Mexique**
Total	2 345	2 409	2 462	2 511	2 578	2 618	2 623	2 685	Totale
Beef and veal	1 340	1 380	1 400	1 409	1 445	1 468	1 504	1 543	Bœuf et veau
Goat	35	38	37	39	39	42	42	42	Chèvre
Mutton and lamb	30	30	31	33	36	38	42	42	Mouton et agneau
Pork	939	961	994	1 030	1 058	1 070	1 035	1 058	Porc

Country or area	1997	1998	1999	2000	2001	2002	2003	2004	Pays ou zone
Montserrat									Montserrat
Total	1	1	1	1	1	1	1	1	Totale
Beef and veal [1]	1	1	1	1	1	1	1	1	Bœuf et veau [1]
Nicaragua									Nicaragua
Total	57	52	52	58	60	66	72	77	Totale
Beef and veal	52	46	46[1]	53[1]	54	60	66	70	Bœuf et veau
Pork	5	6	6	6	6	6	6	7	Porc
Panama									Panama
Total	79	83	81	81	70	72	72	74	Totale
Beef and veal	60	64	60	59	52	54	52	54[1]	Bœuf et veau
Pork	19	19	21	22	18	18	20	21[1]	Porc
Puerto Rico									Porto Rico
Total	29	28	27	25	23	20	21	22	Totale
Beef and veal	16	14[1]	18	15	13	11	9	10[1]	Bœuf et veau
Pork	13	14[1]	9	9	10	9	12	12[1]	Porc
Saint Kitts and Nevis [2]									Saint-Kitts-et-Nevis [2]
Total	0	0	0	1	1	1	1	1	Totale
Saint Lucia									Sainte-Lucie
Total	1	1	1	1	1	1	1	1	Totale
Beef and veal [1]	1	1	1	1	1	1	1	1	Bœuf et veau [1]
Pork [1]	1	1	1	1	1	1	1	1	Porc [1]
St. Vincent-Grenadines									St. Vincent-Grenadines
Total	1	1	1	1	1	1	1	1	Totale
Pork [1]	1	1	1	1	1	1	1	1	Porc [1]
Trinidad and Tobago									Trinité-et-Tobago
Total	4	3	3	3	3	4	4	4	Totale
Beef and veal	1	1	1	1	1	1	1	1[1]	Bœuf et veau
Pork	2	2	2	2	2	3	3	3[1]	Porc
United States									Etats-Unis
Total	19 667	20 540	20 994	21 001	20 774	21 457	21 187	20 663	Totale
Beef and veal	11 714	11 803	12 123	12 298	11 982	12 427	12 039	11 261	Bœuf et veau
Mutton and lamb	118	114	113	106	101	*101	*92	*90	Mouton et agneau
Pork	7 835	8 623	8 758	8 597	8 691	8 929	9 056	9 312	Porc
United States Virgin Is.									Iles Vierges américaines
Total	1	1	1	1	1	1	1	1	Totale
Beef and veal [1]	1	1	1	1	1	1	1	1	Bœuf et veau [1]
America, South									Amérique du Sud
Total	14 871	14 533	15 444	15 897	15 752	16 334	16 880	17 758	Totale
Beef and veal	11 188	10 816	11 628	11 860	11 630	12 054	12 310	13 057	Bœuf et veau
Goat	71	76	79	82	78	81	83	83	Chèvre
Mutton and lamb	254	238	244	250	251	227	226	236	Mouton et agneau
Pork	3 359	3 403	3 493	3 706	3 794	3 973	4 260	4 381	Porc
Argentina									Argentine
Total	2 938	2 710	2 988	2 991	2 718	2 718	2 832	2 911	Totale
Beef and veal	2 712	2 469	2 720	2 718	2 461	2 493	2 621	2 700[1]	Bœuf et veau
Goat [1]	7	9	9	9	9	9	10	10	Chèvre [1]
Mutton and lamb	*58	*48	*45	50[1]	50[1]	50[1]	52[1]	52[1]	Mouton et agneau
Pork	161	184	215	214	198	165	150	150[1]	Porc
Bolivia									Bolivie
Total	236	248	250	258	280	288	296	304	Totale
Beef and veal	147	155	155	160[1]	161	165	168	172	Bœuf et veau
Goat [1]	6	6	6	6	6	6	6	6	Chèvre [1]
Mutton and lamb	15	15	15	16	16	17	18	18	Mouton et agneau
Pork [1]	69	72	74	76	97	101	104	108	Porc [1]
Brazil									Brésil
Total	8 373	8 296	8 923	9 289	9 571	10 046	10 398	11 001	Totale
Beef and veal	5 922	5 794	6 413	6 579	6 824	7 139	7 231	7 774	Bœuf et veau
Goat [1]	31	34	38	39	39	40	41	41	Chèvre [1]
Mutton and lamb [1]	70	68	71	72	72	69	68	76	Mouton et agneau [1]
Pork	2 350[1]	2 400[1]	2 400[1]	2 600[1]	2 637	2 798	3 059	3 110	Porc

Country or area	1997	1998	1999	2000	2001	2002	2003	2004	Pays ou zone
Chile									**Chili**
Total	486	508	488	504	537	566	572	587	Totale
Beef and veal	262	256	226	226	218	200	192	208	Bœuf et veau
Goat [1]	5	5	5	5	5	5	5	5	Chèvre [1]
Mutton and lamb	10	11	13	11	11	10	10	10	Mouton et agneau
Pork	209	235	244	261	303	351	365	364	Porc
Colombia									**Colombie**
Total	879	854	835	864	812	797	801	822	Totale
Beef and veal	763	766	716	745	700[1]	675[1]	670[1]	690[1]	Bœuf et veau
Goat	6	6	6	7[1]	6[1]	6[1]	7[1]	7[1]	Chèvre
Mutton and lamb	7[1]	6[1]	6	*7	7[1]	6[1]	7[1]	7[1]	Mouton et agneau
Pork	103	75	107	105	98	109	118	119[1]	Porc
Ecuador									**Equateur**
Total	270	265	282	286	325	344	370	373	Totale
Beef and veal	156	158	164	*171	189	191	206	212[1]	Bœuf et veau
Goat	1[1]	1[1]	1[1]	2	1	2	2	2[1]	Chèvre
Mutton and lamb	6[1]	6[1]	6[1]	6	6[1]	7[1]	8[1]	8[1]	Mouton et agneau
Pork	107[1]	100	110	108	128	145	154	*150	Porc
Falkland Is. (Malvinas)									**Iles Falkland (Malvinas)**
Total	1	1	1	1	1	1	1	1	Totale
Mutton and lamb [1]	1	1	1	1	1	1	1	1	Mouton et agneau [1]
French Guiana									**Guyane française**
Total	2	2	2	2	1	1	1	1	Totale
Pork	1	1	1	1	1	1	1[1]	1[1]	Porc
Guyana									**Guyana**
Total	3	3	3	3	3	3	3	3	Totale
Beef and veal	2	2	2	2	*2	2[1]	2[1]	2[1]	Bœuf et veau
Mutton and lamb [1]	1	1	1	1	1	1	1	1	Mouton et agneau [1]
Pork [1]	1	1	1	1	1	1	1	1	Porc [1]
Paraguay									**Paraguay**
Total	347	353	369	356	306	286	302	374	Totale
Beef and veal	226	*231	*246	239	200	205	215	215	Bœuf et veau
Goat [1]	1	1	1	1	1	1	1	1	Chèvre [1]
Mutton and lamb [1]	3	3	3	2	2	3	3	2	Mouton et agneau [1]
Pork [1]	117	119	120	114	103	78	84	156	Porc [1]
Peru									**Pérou**
Total	233	223	236	246	261	264	270	280	Totale
Beef and veal	118	124	134	136	138	142	145	152	Bœuf et veau
Goat	6	6	7	7	6	6	7	*7	Chèvre
Mutton and lamb	22	23	30	31	32	32	32	34	Mouton et agneau
Pork	87	71	66	72	85	85	86	88	Porc
Suriname									**Suriname**
Total	3	3	3	3	3	3	3	4	Totale
Beef and veal	2	2	2	2	2	2	2[1]	2[1]	Bœuf et veau
Pork	1	1	1	1	1	1	1[1]	1[1]	Porc
Uruguay									**Uruguay**
Total	536	531	536	530	391	462	468	539	Totale
Beef and veal	454	450	458	453	*317	412	424	496	Bœuf et veau
Mutton and lamb	*60	*55	*51	*51	51[1]	31	27	27	Mouton et agneau
Pork	22	26	27	26	23	20	17	16[1]	Porc
Venezuela (Bolivarian Rep. of)									**Venezuela (Rép. bolivar. du)**
Total	565	535	527	564	544	554	563	558	Totale
Beef and veal	423	408	391	429	418	429	435	433	Bœuf et veau
Goat	7	7	5	7	4	5	5	5	Chèvre
Mutton and lamb	2	2	3	2	2	2	2	2	Mouton et agneau
Pork	133	118	128	126	119	119	120	118	Porc
Asia									**Asie**
Total	62 235	65 764	66 198	68 259	70 434	73 419	76 605	79 916	Totale
Beef and veal	10 266	10 657	10 847	11 157	11 071	11 631	12 217	12 688	Bœuf et veau
Buffalo	2 584	2 612	2 687	2 704	2 763	2 813	2 767	2 892	Buffle
Goat	2 272	2 459	2 539	2 679	2 782	2 944	3 145	3 238	Chèvre
Mutton and lamb	3 169	3 247	3 337	3 481	3 545	3 782	3 988	4 335	Mouton et agneau
Pork	43 944	46 791	46 787	48 238	50 273	52 250	54 487	56 762	Porc

Meat—Production: thousand metric tons (*continued*)
Viande—Production : milliers de tonnes (*suite*)

Country or area	1997	1998	1999	2000	2001	2002	2003	2004	Pays ou zone
Armenia									Arménie
Total	45	47	45	48	45	46	48	49	Totale
Beef and veal	35	35	32	31	29	30	30	33	Bœuf et veau
Mutton and lamb	5	5	5	8	7	6	6	7	Mouton et agneau
Pork	5	7	8	9	9	10	12	9	Porc
Azerbaijan									Azerbaïdjan
Total	76	83	88	92	95	101	107	118	Totale
Beef and veal	48	50	52	56	57	63	67	*73	Bœuf et veau
Mutton and lamb	26	32	35	35	37	38	39	*44	Mouton et agneau
Pork	2	1	2	1	1	1	2	*1	Porc
Bahrain									Bahreïn
Total	7	7	9	8	8	9	8	8	Totale
Beef and veal	1[1]	1[1]	1[1]	1[1]	1[1]	1[1]	1[1]	1	Bœuf et veau
Goat [1]	0	1	1	0	5	6	5	6	Chèvre [1]
Mutton and lamb [1]	6	5	8	7	3	1	2	2	Mouton et agneau [1]
Bangladesh									Bangladesh
Total	295	293	304	308	310	322	317	317	Totale
Beef and veal	*166	161	*171	*173	*174	*178	180[1]	180[1]	Bœuf et veau
Buffalo	*3	4	*4	*4	*4	*4	4[1]	4[1]	Buffle
Goat	*124	126	*127	*129	*129	*137	130[1]	130[1]	Chèvre
Mutton and lamb	*3	3	*3	*3	*3	*3	3[1]	3[1]	Mouton et agneau
Bhutan									Bhoutan
Total	7	7	8	7	6	6	7	7	Totale
Beef and veal [1]	6	5	6	5	5	5	5	5	Bœuf et veau [1]
Pork [1]	1	1	1	1	1	1	1	1	Porc [1]
Brunei Darussalam									Brunéi Darussalam
Total	1	1	5	3	3	4	4	4	Totale
Beef and veal [1]	1	1	5	3	3	3	3	3	Bœuf et veau [1]
Buffalo [1]	0	0	0	0	0	1	1	1	Buffle [1]
Cambodia									Cambodge
Total	148	152	154	171	175	172	183	169	Totale
Beef and veal [1]	41	42	42	57	58	53	54	54	Bœuf et veau [1]
Buffalo [1]	10	10	9	10	9	9	10	13	Buffle [1]
Pork [1]	97	100	103	105	108	110	120	103	Porc [1]
China [3,4]									Chine [3,4]
Total	43 720	47 075	47 496	49 501	51 422	53 410	56 132	59 042	Totale
Beef and veal *	4 106	4 486	4 711	4 991	5 131	5 480	6 019	6 494	Bœuf et veau *
Buffalo *	325	339	367	361	379	387	305	328	Buffle *
Goat *	942	1 111	1 182	1 304	1 390	1 490	1 683	1 753	Chèvre *
Mutton and lamb *	1 190	1 239	1 335	1 440	1 540	1 680	1 892	2 201	Mouton et agneau *
Pork	37 156	39 900	39 900	41 406	42 982	44 374	46 233	*48 267	Porc
Cyprus [5]									Chypre [5]
Total	60	61	64	67	66	68	70	70	Totale
Beef and veal	5	4	4	4	4	4	4[1]	5[1]	Bœuf et veau
Goat	4	5	6	6	7	8	8[1]	8[1]	Chèvre
Mutton and lamb	4	5	4	4	4	5	5[1]	5[1]	Mouton et agneau
Pork	46	47	49	52	51	52	53[1]	53[1]	Porc
Georgia									Géorgie
Total	109	93	89	94	89	93	95	92	Totale
Beef and veal	56	43	41	48	47	49	50	47	Bœuf et veau
Mutton and lamb	7	8	7	9	8	8	8	8	Mouton et agneau
Pork	47	42	41	37	35	36	37	37	Porc
India									Inde
Total	3 886	3 936	3 987	4 030	4 067	4 102	4 138	4 177	Totale
Beef and veal [1]	1 378	1 401	1 421	1 442	1 452	1 463	1 473	1 483	Bœuf et veau [1]
Buffalo [1]	1 365	1 382	1 399	1 416	1 433	1 450	1 467	1 483	Buffle [1]
Goat [1]	458	462	466	467	469	470	473	475	Chèvre [1]
Mutton and lamb [1]	222	226	228	229	230	233	236	239	Mouton et agneau [1]
Pork [1]	462	466	473	476	483	487	490	497	Porc [1]

Country or area	1997	1998	1999	2000	2001	2002	2003	2004	Pays ou zone
Indonesia									**Indonésie**
Total	1 141	1 092	984	877	939	1 011	1 083	1 146	Totale
Beef and veal	354	343	309	340	339	330	370	380	Bœuf et veau
Buffalo	47	46	48	46	44	42	41	46	Buffle
Goat	65	48	45	45	49	58	64	70	Chèvre
Mutton and lamb	42	34	32	33	45	69	81	85	Mouton et agneau
Pork [1]	633	622	550	413	463	512	528	567	Porc [1]
Iran (Islamic Rep. of)									**Iran (Rép. islamique d')**
Total	734	753	694	716	730	747	776	786	Totale
Beef and veal	317	324	286	269	274	284	312[1]	320[1]	Bœuf et veau
Buffalo [1]	11	11	11	12	12	13	13	13	Buffle [1]
Goat	105	109	104	110	111	105	105[1]	105[1]	Chèvre
Mutton and lamb	301	309	293	326	333	345	346[1]	348[1]	Mouton et agneau
Israel [6]									**Israël [6]**
Total	65	63	63	86	86	89	106	108	Totale
Beef and veal	46	44	46	64	62	64	81	82	Bœuf et veau
Goat	*1	2[1]	2	2	2	2	2	3	Chèvre
Mutton and lamb	*6	*5	*5	*5	*5	5[1]	5[1]	5[1]	Mouton et agneau
Pork	12	12	9	15	16	16	17	18	Porc
Japan									**Japon**
Total	1 819	1 820	1 818	1 787	1 690	1 783	1 770	1 784	Totale
Beef and veal	530	529	540	530	459	537	496	513	Bœuf et veau
Pork	1 288	1 291	1 277	1 256	1 232	1 246	1 274	1 270	Porc
Jordan									**Jordanie**
Total	15	14	11	10	10	8	10	10	Totale
Beef and veal	4	3	4	3	4	3	5[1]	5[1]	Bœuf et veau
Goat	3	4	3	2	2	1	2[1]	2[1]	Chèvre
Mutton and lamb	9	*7	4	5	5	4	4[1]	4[1]	Mouton et agneau
Kazakhstan									**Kazakhstan**
Total	627	546	540	535	566	585	606	642	Totale
Beef and veal	398	348	344	306	288	297	*320	*340	Bœuf et veau
Goat	*5	5	*4	*4	*5	7	*7	*8	Chèvre
Mutton and lamb	143	114	*95	91	92	94	*94	*99	Mouton et agneau
Pork	82	79	98	133	181	187	*185	*195	Porc
Korea, Dem. P. R.									**Corée, R. p. dém. de**
Total	108	139	163	171	178	179	181	180	Totale
Beef and veal [1]	19	20	20	20	21	22	22	21	Bœuf et veau [1]
Goat [1]	5	7	9	10	11	11	11	11	Chèvre [1]
Mutton and lamb [1]	1	1	1	1	1	1	1	1	Mouton et agneau [1]
Pork [1]	84	112	134	140	145	146	147	147	Porc [1]
Korea, Republic of									**Corée, République de**
Total	1 237	1 318	1 342	1 225	1 163	1 219	1 334	1 289	Totale
Beef and veal	338	376	342	306	233	211	*182	*187	Bœuf et veau
Goat [1]	4	3	3	3	3	3	3	2	Chèvre [1]
Pork	896	939	996	916	928	1 005	*1 149	*1 100	Porc
Kuwait									**Koweït**
Total	41	41	36	36	33	40	39	39	Totale
Beef and veal [1]	2	2	2	2	2	2	2	2	Bœuf et veau [1]
Goat [1]	1	0	1	1	0	1	1	1	Chèvre [1]
Mutton and lamb [1]	39	38	34	34	31	37	37	37	Mouton et agneau [1]
Kyrgyzstan									**Kirghizistan**
Total	164	169	170	168	170	171	160	166	Totale
Beef and veal	95	95	95	101	100	105	94	96	Bœuf et veau
Goat	1	3	3	4	7	7	7	*7	Chèvre
Mutton and lamb	*43	*41	43	39	37	37	37	*37	Mouton et agneau
Pork	26	30	29	24	26	23	22	25	Porc
Lao People's Dem. Rep.									**Rép. dém. pop. lao**
Total	61	63	70	61	66	70	76	67	Totale
Beef and veal	14	15	19	16	17	20	22	21[1]	Bœuf et veau
Buffalo	16	16	19	17	17	17	18	18[1]	Buffle
Goat [1]	0	0	0	0	0	0	1	0	Chèvre [1]
Pork	31	31	32	28	32	32	36	27[1]	Porc

Country or area	1997	1998	1999	2000	2001	2002	2003	2004	Pays ou zone
Lebanon									Liban
Total	57	43	63	68	65	73	71	71	Totale
Beef and veal [1]	44	31	51	58	43	55	53	53	Bœuf et veau [1]
Goat [1]	4	3	3	3	3	3	3	3	Chèvre [1]
Mutton and lamb [1]	7	5	6	6	17	14	14	14	Mouton et agneau [1]
Pork [1]	3	3	2	2	2	2	2	2	Porc [1]
Malaysia									Malaisie
Total	306	282	181	178	205	216	223	231	Totale
Beef and veal [1]	18	18	18	15	16	18	20	21	Bœuf et veau [1]
Buffalo [1]	4	4	3	3	3	4	4	5	Buffle [1]
Goat [1]	1	1	1	1	1	1	1	1	Chèvre [1]
Pork	282	260	159	160	185	193	198	203	Porc
Mongolia									Mongolie
Total	191	220	234	234	172	252	217	215	Totale
Beef and veal	87	99	105	113	67	84	80[1]	80[1]	Bœuf et veau
Goat	26	30	32	30	28	38	34[1]	35[1]	Chèvre
Mutton and lamb	79	90	97	90	77	130	103[1]	100[1]	Mouton et agneau
Pork	0	0	0	1	1	1[1]	1[1]	1[1]	Porc
Myanmar									Myanmar
Total	216	220	237	244	256	263	277	280	Totale
Beef and veal [1]	99	101	101	102	104	108	112	114	Bœuf et veau [1]
Buffalo [1]	20	20	20	20	21	22	22	23	Buffle [1]
Goat	6	7	7	7	7	8	9[1]	9[1]	Chèvre
Mutton and lamb	2	2	2	2	2	2	2[1]	2[1]	Mouton et agneau
Pork [1]	89	91	107	113	121	123	132	132	Porc [1]
Nepal									Népal
Total	211	217	220	224	228	232	236	241	Totale
Beef and veal [1]	48	48	48	48	47	47	48	48	Bœuf et veau [1]
Buffalo	113	117	120	122	125	128	131	134	Buffle
Goat	35	36	36	37	38	39	40	41	Chèvre
Mutton and lamb	3	3	3	3	3	3	3	3	Mouton et agneau
Pork	12	13	14	15	15	16	16	15	Porc
Occupied Palestinian Terr.									Terr. palestinien occupé
Total	22	22	23	25	19	21	26	26	Totale
Beef and veal [1]	11	12	12	14	11	8	8	10	Bœuf et veau [1]
Goat [1]	3	3	3	4	3	4	5	4	Chèvre [1]
Mutton and lamb [1]	8	7	7	7	5	10	13	12	Mouton et agneau [1]
Oman									Oman
Total	23	21	21	22	23	25	27	31	Totale
Beef and veal [1]	4	4	5	4	4	4	4	4	Bœuf et veau [1]
Goat [1]	6	4	4	5	6	8	10	14	Chèvre [1]
Mutton and lamb [1]	13	13	13	13	13	13	13	13	Mouton et agneau [1]
Pakistan									Pakistan
Total	1 261	1 291	1 323	1 353	1 388	1 423	1 459	1 530	Totale
Beef and veal	398	405	413	420	428	437	445	*395	Bœuf et veau
Buffalo	429	441	454	466	480	494	508	598	Buffle
Goat	279	289	300	310	321	333	345	*355	Chèvre
Mutton and lamb	155	156	156	157	159	159	161	182[1]	Mouton et agneau
Philippines									Philippines
Total	1 121	1 175	1 265	1 304	1 353	1 625	1 636	1 669	Totale
Beef and veal	137	156	190	190	183	183	181	179	Bœuf et veau
Buffalo	52	56	69	72	72	76	76	80	Buffle
Goat	*31	*31	33	34	33	34	33	*34	Chèvre
Pork	901	933	973	1 008	1 064	1 332	1 346	1 376	Porc
Qatar									Qatar
Total	8	8	6	7	9	9	9	9	Totale
Beef and veal [1]	0	0	0	1	0	0	0	0	Bœuf et veau [1]
Goat [1]	1	1	1	1	1	1	1	1	Chèvre [1]
Mutton and lamb [1]	7	7	5	6	8	8	8	8	Mouton et agneau [1]
Saudi Arabia									Arabie saoudite
Total	107	110	119	120	120	120	121	121	Totale
Beef and veal	*16	*21	*21	*22	*22	*22	*22	23[1]	Bœuf et veau
Goat	21[1]	20	21	*22	*22	*22	23[1]	23[1]	Chèvre
Mutton and lamb	*70	*69	*77	*76	*76	*76	76[1]	76[1]	Mouton et agneau

Country or area	1997	1998	1999	2000	2001	2002	2003	2004	Pays ou zone
Singapore									**Singapour**
Total	84	84	31	21	23	21	19	20	Totale
Pork	84	84	31[1]	21[1]	23	21	19	20[1]	Porc
Sri Lanka									**Sri Lanka**
Total	38	33	31	36	34	35	36	37	Totale
Beef and veal	25	25	24	29	27	28	29	30[1]	Bœuf et veau
Buffalo [1]	8	4	4	4	3	3	3	3	Buffle [1]
Goat	2	2	2	2	2	2	1	1[1]	Chèvre
Pork	2	2	2	2	2	2	2	2[1]	Porc
Syrian Arab Republic									**Rép. arabe syrienne**
Total	196	204	229	236	216	236	260	260	Totale
Beef and veal	42	43	47	47	42	47	47	47[1]	Bœuf et veau
Goat	5	6	5	5	5	5	5[1]	5[1]	Chèvre
Mutton and lamb	148	154	177	184	169	184[1]	207[1]	207[1]	Mouton et agneau
Tajikistan									**Tadjikistan**
Total	29	28	28	28	28	34	42	41	Totale
Beef and veal	26	15	*15	*12	*15	*19	*23	*23	Bœuf et veau
Mutton and lamb	3	13	*13	*16	*13	*14	*19	*18	Mouton et agneau
Thailand									**Thaïlande**
Total	819	723	685	695	862	884	883	810	Totale
Beef and veal	206[1]	183[1]	170[1]	167[1]	172[1]	178[1]	180[1]	115	Bœuf et veau
Buffalo	79[1]	69[1]	60[1]	52[1]	58[1]	58[1]	59[1]	38	Buffle
Goat [1]	1	1	1	1	1	1	1	1	Chèvre [1]
Pork [1]	533	469	454	475	632	646	642	657	Porc [1]
Timor-Leste									**Timor-Leste**
Total	12	12	8	8	10	10	10	12	Totale
Beef and veal [1]	1	2	1	1	1	1	1	1	Bœuf et veau [1]
Buffalo [1]	0	0	1	1	1	1	1	1	Buffle [1]
Goat [1]	1	1	1	0	0	0	0	0	Chèvre [1]
Pork [1]	10	9	6	6	8	8	8	10	Porc [1]
Turkey									**Turquie**
Total	763	738	723	733	685	662	604	602	Totale
Beef and veal	380	359	350	355	332	328	290	290[1]	Bœuf et veau
Buffalo	6	5	5	4	2	2	2	2[1]	Buffle
Goat	*54	*57	*55	53[1]	48[1]	47[1]	45[1]	44[1]	Chèvre
Mutton and lamb	*324	*317	*313	321[1]	303[1]	286[1]	267[1]	267[1]	Mouton et agneau
Turkmenistan									**Turkménistan**
Total	107	123	127	143	164	181	197	208	Totale
Beef and veal	55	61	63	*72	84[1]	*92	*101	106[1]	Bœuf et veau
Goat	*3	*3	*3	*5	5[1]	*6	*6	7[1]	Chèvre
Mutton and lamb	*48	*58	*60	*66	75[1]	*83	*90	95[1]	Mouton et agneau
Pork	1	1	1	*1	*0	*0	*0	0[1]	Porc
United Arab Emirates									**Emirats arabes unis**
Total	46	40	47	40	31	38	27	29	Totale
Beef and veal [1]	7	8	21	15	8	9	10	10	Bœuf et veau [1]
Goat [1]	7	7	8	8	9	11	10	10	Chèvre [1]
Mutton and lamb [1]	32	24	18	16	14	17	7	9	Mouton et agneau [1]
Uzbekistan									**Ouzbékistan**
Total	457	497	463	484	490	495	514	516	Totale
Beef and veal	387	400	*371	*390	*394	*397	*413	420[1]	Bœuf et veau
Mutton and lamb	*66	82	*73	*79	*81	*83	*86	81[1]	Mouton et agneau
Pork	4	15	*20	*15	*15	*15	*16	15[1]	Porc
Viet Nam									**Viet Nam**
Total	1 323	1 396	1 502	1 599	1 715	1 860	2 014	2 240	Totale
Beef and veal	72	79	89	92	98	102	108	120	Bœuf et veau
Buffalo [1]	92	84	90	92	97	99	100	101	Buffle [1]
Goat [1]	5	5	5	5	5	5	6	7	Chèvre [1]
Pork	1 154	1 228	1 318	1 409	1 515	1 654	1 800	2 012	Porc
Yemen									**Yémen**
Total	86	90	93	99	105	111	115	116	Totale
Beef and veal	43	45	47	52	56	59	60	60[1]	Bœuf et veau
Goat [1]	21	22	22	23	24	25	26	26	Chèvre [1]
Mutton and lamb [1]	22	23	24	24	25	27	29	30	Mouton et agneau [1]

Country or area	1997	1998	1999	2000	2001	2002	2003	2004	Pays ou zone
Europe									**Europe**
Total	39 108	39 963	39 881	38 694	37 824	38 723	39 165	38 822	Totale
Beef and veal	13 168	12 575	12 124	11 772	11 458	11 666	11 681	11 601	Bœuf et veau
Buffalo	3	2	2	3	2	2	2	2	Buffle
Goat	130	131	131	124	120	123	121	123	Chèvre
Mutton and lamb	1 466	1 468	1 439	1 415	1 275	1 296	1 304	1 304	Mouton et agneau
Pork	24 341	25 786	26 184	25 381	24 969	25 636	26 056	25 792	Porc
Albania									**Albanie**
Total	55	55	58	63	63	66	68	67	Totale
Beef and veal	*33	*32	*34	*36	*35	*38	40	39[1]	Bœuf et veau
Goat	*4	*6	*6	7	7	7	7	7[1]	Chèvre
Mutton and lamb	*11	*11	*12	*12	12[1]	12	12	12[1]	Mouton et agneau
Pork	*7	*7	*6	*8	*8	*9	*9	9[1]	Porc
Austria									**Autriche**
Total	823	865	894	832	837	873	878	877	Totale
Beef and veal	206	197	203	203	215	212	208	215[1]	Bœuf et veau
Goat	1	1	1	1	1	1	1[1]	1[1]	Chèvre
Mutton and lamb	7	7	6	7	7	7	*7	7[1]	Mouton et agneau
Pork *	610	661	684	620	614	653	663	654	Porc *
Belarus									**Bélarus**
Total	557	593	576	517	537	529	514	543	Totale
Beef and veal	256	271	262	213	231	227	211	*223	Bœuf et veau
Mutton and lamb	3	3	3	3	3	2	2	*2	Mouton et agneau
Pork	298	320	311	302	303	301	301	*318	Porc
Belgium									**Belgique**
Total	...	...	...	1 322	1 353	1 349	1 305	1 334	Totale
Beef and veal	...	...	...	275	285	305	275	280[1]	Bœuf et veau
Mutton and lamb	...	...	...	4	5	3	4[1]	4[1]	Mouton et agneau
Pork	...	...	...	1 042	1 062	1 041	1 026	1 050[1]	Porc
Belgium-Luxembourg									**Belgique-Luxembourg**
Total	1 377	1 393	1 290	...	...	...	...	...	Totale
Beef and veal	340	303	281	...	...	...	...	...	Bœuf et veau
Mutton and lamb	4	4	5	...	...	...	...	...	Mouton et agneau
Pork	1 033	1 085	1 005	...	...	...	...	...	Porc
Bosnia and Herzegovina									**Bosnie-Herzégovine**
Total	24	27	27	26	27	26	24	24	Totale
Beef and veal	10	12	12[1]	*13	*13	13[1]	13[1]	13[1]	Bœuf et veau
Mutton and lamb	3[1]	3[1]	3[1]	3	3[1]	3[1]	3[1]	3[1]	Mouton et agneau
Pork [1]	11	12	12	11	11	10	8	8	Porc [1]
Bulgaria									**Bulgarie**
Total	333	356	387	363	358	347	349	364	Totale
Beef and veal	*56	*55	*61	*60	*69	*48	*53	70[1]	Bœuf et veau
Buffalo	1[1]	1[1]	1[1]	1[1]	1[1]	0	0	0[1]	Buffle
Goat *	6	7	8	8	7	7	7	7	Chèvre *
Mutton and lamb *	44	46	50	51	44	47	39	37	Mouton et agneau *
Pork	227	248	267	243	237	245[1]	250[1]	250[1]	Porc
Croatia									**Croatie**
Total	83	88	96	94	92	94	93	95	Totale
Beef and veal	26	26	28	28	26	27	28	23[1]	Bœuf et veau
Mutton and lamb	*2	*2	4	2	2	2	3	2[1]	Mouton et agneau
Pork	*55	*60	64	*64	*64	*65	*62	70[1]	Porc
Czech Republic									**République tchèque**
Total	623	613	576	526	525	523	517	486	Totale
Beef and veal	156	134	121	108	109	106	104	97	Bœuf et veau
Mutton and lamb	*3	3	3	1	1	1	1	1	Mouton et agneau
Pork	464	476	452	417	415	416	411	388	Porc
Denmark									**Danemark**
Total	1 697	1 793	1 800	1 780	1 871	1 914	1 911	1 912	Totale
Beef and veal	175	162	157	154	153	154	148	148[1]	Bœuf et veau
Mutton and lamb	2	2	1	1	2	1	2	2[1]	Mouton et agneau
Pork	1 521	1 629	1 642	1 625	1 716	1 759	1 762	1 762[1]	Porc

Country or area	1997	1998	1999	2000	2001	2002	2003	2004	Pays ou zone
Estonia									Estonie
Total	49	52	53	46	48	57	53	53	Totale
Beef and veal	19	19	22	15	14	17	13	14	Bœuf et veau
Pork	30	32	31	30	34	40	40	39	Porc
Faeroe Islands									Iles Féroé
Total	1	1	1	1	1	1	1	1	Totale
Mutton and lamb [1]	1	1	1	1	1	1	1	1	Mouton et agneau [1]
Finland									Finlande
Total	281	279	273	265	264	276	290	292	Totale
Beef and veal	100	94	90	91	90	91	96	93	Bœuf et veau
Mutton and lamb	1	1	1	1	1	1	1	1	Mouton et agneau
Pork	180	185	182	173	174	184	193	198	Porc
France									France
Total	4 089	4 104	4 100	3 980	4 022	4 121	4 107	4 041	Totale
Beef and veal	1 720	1 632	1 609	1 528	1 566	1 640	1 632	*1 590	Bœuf et veau
Goat	9	9	6	7	7	7	7	7[1]	Chèvre
Mutton and lamb	141	135	132	133	134	128	129	*124	Mouton et agneau
Pork	2 219	2 328	2 353	2 312	2 315	2 346	2 339	*2 320	Porc
Germany									Allemagne
Total	5 056	5 246	5 521	5 334	5 482	5 471	5 512	5 634	Totale
Beef and veal	1 448	1 367	1 374	1 304	1 362	1 316	1 226	1 258	Bœuf et veau
Mutton and lamb	44	44	44	48	46	44	46	*52	Mouton et agneau
Pork	3 564	3 834	4 103	3 982	4 074	4 110	4 239	4 323	Porc
Greece									Grèce
Total	349	352	350	330	319	328	320	335	Totale
Beef and veal	72	73	67	63	60	62	62	75[1]	Bœuf et veau
Goat	54	55	56	44	43	45	44[1]	44[1]	Chèvre
Mutton and lamb	89	90	90	81	79	82	80[1]	81[1]	Mouton et agneau
Pork	133	134	138	141	137	139	*134	135[1]	Porc
Hungary									Hongrie
Total	638	619	680	684	610	690	692	654	Totale
Beef and veal	55	47	51	67	52	48	61	51[1]	Bœuf et veau
Mutton and lamb	2	3	4	4	3	3[1]	1	3[1]	Mouton et agneau
Pork	581	570	626	613	556	640	631	600[1]	Porc
Iceland									Islande
Total	15	16	17	18	18	18	19	18	Totale
Beef and veal	3	3	4	4	4	4	4	4[1]	Bœuf et veau
Mutton and lamb	8	8	9	10	9	9	9	9[1]	Mouton et agneau
Pork	4	4	5	5	5	6	6	6[1]	Porc
Ireland									Irlande
Total	866	921	984	890	898	838	849	856	Totale
Beef and veal	568	594	644	577	579	540	568	570[1]	Bœuf et veau
Mutton and lamb	79	86	90	83	78	67	*64	*63	Mouton et agneau
Pork	220	242	250	230	241	231	217	223[1]	Porc
Italy									Italie
Total	2 633	2 598	2 711	2 701	2 710	2 735	2 778	2 821	Totale
Beef and veal	1 159	1 111	1 164	1 152	1 133	1 134	1 127	*1 142	Bœuf et veau
Buffalo	2	1	1	1	1	2	1	1[1]	Buffle
Goat	4	3	4	4	4	4	3	*4	Chèvre
Mutton and lamb	72	70	70	65	62	58	58	*56	Mouton et agneau
Pork	1 396	1 412	1 472	1 479	1 510	1 536	1 589	*1 618	Porc
Latvia									Lettonie
Total	63	63	57	54	51	52	58	59	Totale
Beef and veal	26	26	23	22	19	16	21	*22	Bœuf et veau
Pork	37	36	35	32	32	36	37	*37	Porc
Lithuania									Lituanie
Total	178	178	170	161	120	140	157	175	Totale
Beef and veal	90	81	77	75	47	45	52	*60	Bœuf et veau
Mutton and lamb	1	1	1	1	1	1	1	*1	Mouton et agneau
Pork	87	96	91	85	72	95	105	114	Porc

Country or area	1997	1998	1999	2000	2001	2002	2003	2004	Pays ou zone
Luxembourg									**Luxembourg**
Total	...	...	...	30	23	30	30	29	Totale
Beef and veal	...	...	...	17	11	19	18	18[1]	Bœuf et veau
Pork	...	...	...	13	11	11	13	12[1]	Porc
Malta									**Malte**
Total	12	12	12	11	12	12	11	11	Totale
Beef and veal	2	2	2	2	2	2	1	1[1]	Bœuf et veau
Pork	10	10	10	9	10	10	10	10[1]	Porc
Netherlands									**Pays-Bas**
Total	1 956	2 277	2 237	2 112	1 822	1 778	1 629	1 684	Totale
Beef and veal	565	535	508	471	372	384	364	381	Bœuf et veau
Goat	0	0	*1	*0	0[1]	0[1]	0[1]	0[1]	Chèvre
Mutton and lamb	15	17	18	18	18	17	15	16	Mouton et agneau
Pork	1 376	1 725	1 711	1 623	1 432	1 377	1 250	1 287	Porc
Norway									**Norvège**
Total	220	221	228	218	219	223	214	212	Totale
Beef and veal	88	91	96	91	86	86	83	83[1]	Bœuf et veau
Mutton and lamb	26	23	23	23	24	25	25	24[1]	Mouton et agneau
Pork	105	106	109	103	109	112	106	105[1]	Porc
Poland									**Pologne**
Total	2 323	2 457	2 429	2 273	2 167	2 306	2 528	2 418	Totale
Beef and veal	429	430	385	349	316	281	317	317[1]	Bœuf et veau
Mutton and lamb	3	1	2	1	1	1	1	1[1]	Mouton et agneau
Pork	1 891	2 026	2 043	1 923	1 849	2 023	2 209	*2 100	Porc
Portugal									**Portugal**
Total	442	454	468	455	437	461	458	460	Totale
Beef and veal	109	96	97	100	95	106	105	105[1]	Bœuf et veau
Goat	3	3	3	2	2	2	2	2[1]	Chèvre
Mutton and lamb	24	23	22	24	22	24	22	23[1]	Mouton et agneau
Pork	306	332	346	329	317	330	329	330[1]	Porc
Republic of Moldova									**République de Moldova**
Total	104	86	85	71	62	64	62	64	Totale
Beef and veal	35	24	21	18	16	16	16	*23	Bœuf et veau
Mutton and lamb	3	4	4	3	3	3	3	*3	Mouton et agneau
Pork	66	58	61	50	44	45	43	*38	Porc
Romania									**Roumanie**
Total	916	824	806	717	657	687	785	613	Totale
Beef and veal	185	150	153	162	145	156	185	163	Bœuf et veau
Goat	5	3	4	4	4	3	5	6	Chèvre
Mutton and lamb	59	53	54	49	48	51	62	68	Mouton et agneau
Pork	667	617	595	502	460	476	533	376	Porc
Russian Federation									**Fédération de Russie**
Total	4 140	3 931	3 497	3 603	3 505	3 676	3 829	3 703	Totale
Beef and veal	2 394	2 247	1 868	1 894	1 873	1 957	1 990	1 907	Bœuf et veau
Goat	21	22	20	20	20	20	19	21[1]	Chèvre
Mutton and lamb	178	156	124	119	114	115	114	120[1]	Mouton et agneau
Pork	1 546	1 505	1 485	1 569	1 498	1 583	1 706	1 656	Porc
Serbia and Montenegro									**Serbie-et-Monténégro**
Total	871	870	861	852	752	803	760	773	Totale
Beef and veal	*209	*216	*185	*194	*165	*166	*164	170[1]	Bœuf et veau
Goat [1]	1	1	1	1	1	1	1	1	Chèvre [1]
Mutton and lamb	30	29	22	23	22	19	21	20	Mouton et agneau
Pork *	632	625	653	635	565	617	574	582	Porc *
Slovakia									**Slovaquie**
Total	322	288	272	213	193	198	200	180	Totale
Beef and veal	66	59	50	48	38	42	40	41	Bœuf et veau
Mutton and lamb	2	2	1	2	2	2	2	2	Mouton et agneau
Pork	255	227	220	164	153	154	158	136	Porc
Slovenia									**Slovénie**
Total	114	113	120	104	117	106	117	119	Totale
Beef and veal	54	48	48	43	49	43	52	47	Bœuf et veau
Mutton and lamb	1	1	1	1	1	1	1	1[1]	Mouton et agneau
Pork	59	65	71	60	66	62	64	71	Porc

Country or area	1997	1998	1999	2000	2001	2002	2003	2004	Pays ou zone
Spain									**Espagne**
Total	3 238	3 645	3 792	3 805	3 891	4 001	4 146	4 152	Totale
Beef and veal	592	651	661	651	651	679	706	714	Bœuf et veau
Goat	16	16	17	16	15	15	14	14	Chèvre
Mutton and lamb	229	233	221	232	236	237	236	233	Mouton et agneau
Pork	2 401	2 744	2 893	2 905	2 989	3 070	3 190	3 191	Porc
Sweden									**Suède**
Total	482	477	474	431	423	434	432	430	Totale
Beef and veal	149	143	145	150	143	147	141	138[1]	Bœuf et veau
Mutton and lamb	4	3	4	4	4	4	4	4[1]	Mouton et agneau
Pork	329	330	325	277	276	284	288	288[1]	Porc
Switzerland									**Suisse**
Total	373	385	380	359	378	382	379	381	Totale
Beef and veal	152	147	146	128	138	140	139	140[1]	Bœuf et veau
Goat	0	1	1	1	0	0	0	0	Chèvre
Mutton and lamb	6	6	6	6	6	6	6	7[1]	Mouton et agneau
Pork	214	232	226	225	234	236	234	234[1]	Porc
TFYR of Macedonia									**L'ex-R.y. Macédoine**
Total	23	20	20	20	21	22	24	25	Totale
Beef and veal	7	6	7	6	*7	7	9	9	Bœuf et veau
Mutton and lamb	7	6	4	5[1]	6[1]	5	6	7	Mouton et agneau
Pork	9	9	9	9	8	11	10	9	Porc
Ukraine									**Ukraine**
Total	1 664	1 482	1 467	1 447	1 253	1 320	1 371	1 244	Totale
Beef and veal	930	793	791	754	646	704	723	*658	Bœuf et veau
Goat	4	4	4	8	7	9	9	*8	Chèvre
Mutton and lamb	20	17	15	9	8	8	8	*8	Mouton et agneau
Pork	710	668	656	676	591	599	631	*570	Porc
United Kingdom									**Royaume-Uni**
Total	2 121	2 209	2 113	1 987	1 689	1 775	1 693	1 685	Totale
Beef and veal	688	699	679	705	645	694	687	700[1]	Bœuf et veau
Mutton and lamb	342	375	392	383	267	307	316	310[1]	Mouton et agneau
Pork	1 091	1 135	1 042	899	777	774	690	675[1]	Porc
Oceania									**Océanie**
Total	4 066	4 278	4 237	4 295	4 516	4 336	4 470	4 403	Totale
Beef and veal	2 478	2 611	2 593	2 581	2 731	2 625	2 754	2 774	Bœuf et veau
Buffalo	0	0	0	0	0	0	0	0	Buffle
Goat	11	11	11	13	13	16	17	16	Chèvre
Mutton and lamb	1 109	1 161	1 145	1 213	1 277	1 165	1 143	1 070	Mouton et agneau
Pork	468	495	487	488	495	529	555	543	Porc
Australia [7]									**Australie** [7]
Total	2 729	2 948	3 009	3 043	3 210	3 081	3 104	3 014	Totale
Beef and veal	1 810	1 955	2 011	1 988	2 119	2 028	2 073	2 033	Bœuf et veau
Goat [1]	9	8	8	11	11	14	14	14	Chèvre [1]
Mutton and lamb	566	616	628	680	715	644	597	561	Mouton et agneau
Pork	344	369	362	364	365	396	420	406	Porc
Cook Islands									**Iles Cook**
Total	1	1	1	1	1	1	1	1	Totale
Pork [1]	1	1	1	1	1	1	1	1	Porc [1]
Fiji									**Fidji**
Total	14	14	14	14	14	14	13	13	Totale
Beef and veal [1]	9	9	9	9	9	9	8	8	Bœuf et veau [1]
Goat	1	1[1]	1[1]	1[1]	1	1	1	1[1]	Chèvre
Pork [1]	4	3	4	4	4	4	4	4	Porc [1]
French Polynesia									**Polynésie française**
Total	1	1	1	2	1	1	1	1	Totale
Pork	1	1	1	1	1	1	1	1[1]	Porc
Kiribati									**Kiribati**
Total	1	1	1	1	1	1	1	1	Totale
Pork [1]	1	1	1	1	1	1	1	1	Porc [1]

Country or area	1997	1998	1999	2000	2001	2002	2003	2004	Pays ou zone
Micronesia (Fed. States of)									Micronésie (Etats féd. de)
Total	1	1	1	1	1	1	1	1	Totale
Pork [1]	1	1	1	1	1	1	1	1	Porc [1]
New Caledonia									Nouvelle-Calédonie
Total	5	6	6	5	5	5	5	5	Totale
Beef and veal	4	4	4	4	4	4	4	4[1]	Bœuf et veau
Pork	1	1	1	1	1[1]	1[1]	1[1]	1[1]	Porc
New Zealand [6]									Nouvelle-Zélande [6]
Total	1 240	1 231	1 129	1 153	1 201	1 146	1 256	1 284	Totale
Beef and veal	646	634	561	572	590	576	660	*720	Bœuf et veau
Goat	2	2	2	1	2	1	1	1[1]	Chèvre
Mutton and lamb	543	545	517	533	562	521	546	509	Mouton et agneau
Pork	49	50	49	47	47	47	48	53[1]	Porc
Papua New Guinea									Papouasie-Nouvelle-Guinée
Total	59	61	61	61	67	71	71	67	Totale
Beef and veal [1]	2	3	3	3	3	3	3	3	Bœuf et veau [1]
Pork [1]	56	58	58	58	64	68	68	64	Porc [1]
Samoa									Samoa
Total	4	4	4	5	5	5	5	5	Totale
Beef and veal [1]	1	1	1	1	1	1	1	1	Bœuf et veau [1]
Pork	3[1]	3[1]	3[1]	4[1]	4	4[1]	4[1]	4[1]	Porc
Solomon Islands									Iles Salomon
Total	3	3	3	3	3	3	3	3	Totale
Beef and veal [1]	1	1	1	1	1	1	1	1	Bœuf et veau [1]
Pork [1]	2	2	2	2	2	2	2	2	Porc [1]
Tonga									Tonga
Total	2	2	2	2	2	2	2	2	Totale
Pork [1]	1	1	1	1	1	1	1	1	Porc [1]
Vanuatu									Vanuatu
Total	7	6	7	7	6	5	6	6	Totale
Beef and veal	4	4	4	4	3	3	3	3[1]	Bœuf et veau
Pork [1]	3	3	3	3	3	3	3	3	Porc [1]

Source

Food and Agriculture Organization of the United Nations (FAO), Rome, FAOSTAT data, 2005, last accessed September 2005, and *FAO Production Yearbook*.

Notes

[1] FAO estimate.

[2] Including Anguilla.

[3] Data include those for Taiwan Province of China.

[4] For statistical purposes, the data for China do not include those for the Hong Kong Special Administrative Region (Hong Kong SAR) and Macao Special Administrative Region (Macao SAR).

[5] The data relate to the government-controlled areas.

[6] Data refer to fiscal years ending 30 September.

[7] Data refer to fiscal years ending 30 June.

Source

Organisation des Nations Unies pour l'alimentation et l'agriculture (FAO), Rome, données FAOSTAT, année 2005, dernier accès septembre 2005 et *Annuaire FAO de la production*.

Notes

[1] Estimation de la FAO.

[2] Y compris Anguilla.

[3] Les données comprennent les chiffres pour la province de Taiwan.

[4] Pour la présentation des statistiques, les données pour Chine ne comprennent pas la Région Administrative Spéciale de Hong Kong (Hong Kong RAS) et la Région Administrative Spéciale de Macao (Macao RAS).

[5] Les données se réfèrent aux régions sous contrôle gouvernemental.

[6] Les données se réfèrent aux exercices budgétaires finissant le 30 septembre.

[7] Les données se réfèrent aux exercices budgétaires finissant le 30 juin.

37

Beer
Production: thousand hectoliters

Bière
Production : milliers d'hectolitres

Country or area Pays ou zone	1994	1995	1996	1997	1998	1999	2000	2001	2002	2003
Albania Albanie	72	89	9	151	93	87	86	117	150	144
Algeria Algérie	398	402	377	370	382	383	453	435	283	186
Angola [1] Angola [1]	...	280	797	1 150	1 288	1 609	...	...	...	...
Argentina Argentine	11 272	10 913	11 615	12 687	12 395	12 448	12 685	12 390	11 990	...
Armenia Arménie	70	53	29	50	133	84	79	100	71	73
Australia [2] Australie [2]	17 840	17 700	17 424	17 349	17 570	17 378	17 679	17 449	17 445	17 270
Austria Autriche	10 070	9 767	9 445	9 303	8 837	8 884	8 725	8 528	8 745	8 980
Azerbaijan Azerbaïdjan	114	22	13	16	12	69	71	116	125	133
Barbados Barbade	73	74	76	75	87	76	69	67	68	69
Belarus Bélarus	1 489	1 518	2 013	2 413	2 604	2 728	2 371	2 174	2 026	2 056
Belgium Belgique	15 055	15 110	14 648	14 758	14 763	15 094 [3]	15 509 [3]	15 068 [3]	15 063 [3]	15 924 [3]
Belize Belize	56	49	41	37	42	66	92	...	...	...
Benin [4] Bénin [4]	277	330	349	364	329	347	...	...	...	...
Bolivia Bolivie	1 262	*1 429	...	1 870	1 862	1 657	...	...	...	...
Bosnia and Herzegovina Bosnie-Herzégovine	...	...	537	745	844	975	676 [5]	480 [5]	652 [5]	1 316
Botswana Botswana	1 305	1 366	1 351	1 005	1 019	1 591	1 976	1 692	1 396	1 198
Brazil Brésil	52 556	67 284	63 559	66 582	66 453	62 491	66 954	67 905	64 576	59 961
Bulgaria Bulgarie	4 792	4 331	4 402	3 031	3 796	4 045	4 048	4 093	3 952	4 396
Burkina Faso [4] Burkina Faso [4]	...	372	435	460	501	516	...	...	...	...
Burundi Burundi	1 383	1 404	1 228	1 161	1 036	1 084	892	702	752	876
Cameroon Cameroun	2 073	2 933	...	3 124	3 370	3 373	3 340	3 740	4 196	4 597
Canada Canada	...	...	...	...	24 352	24 605	24 515	25 551	25 368	...
Central African Rep. Rép. centrafricaine	450	269	175 [4]	209 [4]	219 [4]	243 [4]	...	...	...	...
Chad Tchad	110	95	134 [4]	123 [4]	...	...	...	...	...	...
Chile Chili	3 303	3 551	3 459	3 640	3 666	3 343	3 221	3 374	3 401	3 490

Country or area Pays ou zone	1994	1995	1996	1997	1998	1999	2000	2001	2002	2003
China [6,7] Chine [6,7]	115 752	128 406	137 664	154 610	162 693	...	...	...	...	...
China, Hong Kong SAR Chine, Hong Kong RAS	...	983	897	894	...	...	...	...	...	...
Colombia Colombie	15 739	20 525	...	18 290	16 461	14 213	...	...	...	...
Croatia Croatie	3 122	3 166	3 292	3 607	3 759	3 663	3 847	3 799	3 624	3 679
Cuba Cuba	...	...	...	...	...	2 009	2 136	2 197	2 331	2 313
Cyprus Chypre	359	352	331	333	365	405	409	404	383	367
Czech Republic République tchèque	17 876	17 687	18 057	18 558	18 290	17 945	17 796	17 734	17 987	18 216
Denmark [8] Danemark [8]	9 410	9 903	9 591	9 181	8 044	8 205	7 455	7 233	8 202	8 352
Dominica Dominique	...	3	14	11	11	8	11	9	10	...
Dominican Republic Rép. dominicaine	2 190	2 082	...	2 593	2 993	3 484	3 666	3 176	3 554	...
Ecuador Equateur	1 131	3 201	2 163	238	633	555	353	...	...	...
Egypt Egypte	360	360	380	...	...	...	...	...	...	...
Estonia Estonie	477	492	459	543	744	957	950	1 015	1 044	1 040
Ethiopia Ethiopie	634[9]	724[9]	876[9]	843[9]	831[9]	921[9]	1 111[9]	1 605[9]	1 812	2 123
Fiji Fidji	160	150	170	170	170	185	179	184	199	150
Finland Finlande	4 524	4 702	4 980	4 840	4 341	4 733	4 559	4 650	4 777	4 606
France France	17 688	18 311	17 140	17 010	16 551	16 623	15 993	15 716	15 344	15 437
Gabon Gabon	801	816	...	801	847	778	812	867	792	754
Georgia Géorgie	63	65	48	79	97	126	234	257	273	284
Germany Allemagne	113 428	111 875	108 938	108 729	106 993	107 479	106 877	106 372	...	98 933
Greece Grèce	4 376	4 024	3 766	3 950	3 886	4 129	4 223	4 502	...	2 804[3]
Grenada Grenade	24	...	...	...	...	...	...	...	...	...
Guatemala Guatemala	805	1 471	1 655	1 303	1 363	1 443	1 406	...	...	...
Guyana Guyana	97	97	112	129	131	129	118	81	...	...
Hungary Hongrie	8 082	7 697	7 270	6 973	7 163	6 996	7 194	7 142	7 275	7 245
Iceland Islande	54	52	63	64	71	77	88	123	103	108
India [10] Inde [10]	2 778	3 700	4 255	4 331	4 332	3 632	3 025	2 352	2 696	3 609

Country or area / Pays ou zone	1994	1995	1996	1997	1998	1999	2000	2001	2002	2003
Indonesia / Indonésie	779	1 136	...	531	502	401	...	437	237	...
Iran (Islamic Rep. of) [11] / Iran (Rép. islamique d') [11]	...	...	...	130	155	127	145	...	...	...
Ireland / Irlande	...	8 132	10 765	12 095	12 580 [12]	...	...	...	...	...
Israel / Israël	508	...	...	...	...	...	...	...	...	...
Italy / Italie	10 258	10 616	9 559	10 379	11 073	11 123	11 173	11 375	11 208	12 032
Jamaica / Jamaïque	760	662	690	674	670	656	697	784	774	585
Japan [13] / Japon [13]	71 007	67 971	69 082	66 370	61 759	58 901	54 638	48 131	43 000	39 589
Kazakhstan / Kazakhstan	...	812	636	693	850	824	1 357	1 732	2 020	2 348
Kenya / Kenya	3 250	3 474	2 759	2 703	2 630	1 885	2 029	1 843	1 919	2 223
Korea, Republic of / Corée, République de	17 176	17 554	17 210	16 907	14 080	14 866	16 544	17 765	18 224	17 863
Kyrgyzstan / Kirghizistan	12	12	14	14	13	12	12	9	7	8
Lao People's Dem. Rep. / Rép. dém. pop. lao	102	151	...	...	...	...	...	...	...	...
Latvia / Lettonie	638	653	645	715	721	953	945	997	1 199	1 337
Lithuania / Lituanie	1 353	1 093	1 139	1 413	1 559	1 848	2 105	2 193	2 688	2 642
Luxembourg / Luxembourg	531	518	483	481	469	450	438	397	386	391
Madagascar / Madagascar	219	246	347	234	297	446	467	502	439	...
Malawi / Malawi	811	289	277	780	678	684	739	1 033	...	...
Mali / Mali	43	52	60	...	...	...	...	...	...	...
Mauritius / Maurice	283	309	312	340	376	358	375	386	376	401
Mexico / Mexique	45 060	44 205	48 111	51 315	54 569	57 905	59 851	61 632	63 530	65 462
Mozambique / Mozambique	118	244	374	631	75	95	989	982	779	1 048
Myanmar [14] / Myanmar [14]	13	...	...	...	...	...	...	...	...	...
Nepal [15] / Népal [15]	149	168	183	215	139	188	217	233	...	...
Netherlands / Pays-Bas	21 200	22 380	22 670	23 780	23 040	23 799	24 956	24 605 [8]	24 774 [8]	25 699
New Zealand / Nouvelle-Zélande	3 568 [8]	3 488 [8]	3 435 [8]	3 214	3 206	3 148	2 980	3 070	3 093	3 127
Nigeria / Nigéria	1 561	1 461	...	...	...	...	...	...	...	...
Norway / Norvège	...	2 255	...	2 396	1 833	2 651	...	2 462	2 377	...

Country or area Pays ou zone	1994	1995	1996	1997	1998	1999	2000	2001	2002	2003
Panama Panama	1 291	1 274	1 229	1 335	1 448	1 461	1 399	...	...	...
Peru Pérou	6 957	7 817	7 435	7 431	6 557	6 168	5 706	*5 296	6 180	*6 483
Poland Pologne	14 099	15 205	16 667	19 281	21 017	23 360	25 231	25 163	26 875	28 622
Portugal Portugal	6 902	7 220	6 958	6 766	7 072	6 945	7 090	6 830	7 125	7 545
Puerto Rico Porto Rico	438	397	360	317	263	259	...	...	...	...
Republic of Moldova [17] République de Moldova [17]	233	276	226	238	278	202	249	318	438	566
Romania Roumanie	9 047	8 768	8 118	7 651	9 989	11 133	12 664	12 087	11 602	13 292
Russian Federation Fédération de Russie	21 800	21 400	20 800	26 100	33 631	44 484	51 563	63 780	70 266	75 540
Saint Kitts and Nevis Saint-Kitts-et-Nevis	18	17	20	19	20	20	20	20	20	...
Serbia and Montenegro Serbie-et-Monténégro	5 043	5 611	5 987	6 106	6 630	6 786 [18]	6 734	6 063	5 764	6 049
Seychelles Seychelles	58	58	63	71	72	68	70	72	76	...
Slovakia Slovaquie	4 974	4 369	4 666	5 577	4 478	4 473	4 491	4 520	4 800	4 630
Slovenia Slovénie	2 075	2 087	2 223	2 138	2 000	2 022	2 571	2 546 [19]	...	...
Spain Espagne	25 587	25 396	24 520	24 786	22 428	26 007	26 388	26 802	28 631	31 028
Suriname Suriname	69	65	72	...	...	...	...	...	...	...
Sweden Suède	5 379	5 471	5 318	5 078	4 763	4 718	4 686	4 522	4 527	4 248
Switzerland [8] Suisse [8]	3 828	3 672	...	...	...	...	...	...	...	...
Syrian Arab Republic Rép. arabe syrienne	102	102	102	97	97	121	91	100	104	100
Tajikistan Tadjikistan	67	47	6	6	9	7	4	8	9	...
Thailand Thaïlande	5 230	6 473	7 591	8 742	9 770	10 422	11 650	12 380	12 750	16 020
TFYR of Macedonia L'ex-R.y. Macédoine	725	620	622	600	578	652	661	618	657	680
Trinidad and Tobago Trinité-et-Tobago	482	428	419	407	517	522	625	...	...	...
Tunisia Tunisie	689	659	662	780	813	912	1 066	1 087	1 100	997
Turkey Turquie	6 019	6 946	7 381	7 656	7 130	7 188	7 649	7 441	7 845	8 363
Turkmenistan Turkménistan	218	113	17	44	29	37	52	79	84	...
Uganda Ouganda	308	512	642	896	1 105	1 178	1 261	1 079	989	...
Ukraine Ukraine	9 087	7 102	6 025	6 125	6 842	8 407	10 765	13 059	15 000	16 994

Country or area Pays ou zone	1994	1995	1996	1997	1998	1999	2000	2001	2002	2003
United Kingdom Royaume-Uni	66 161	59 337	61 262	64 816	60 915	62 510	54 206	57 032	60 646	64 008
United Rep. of Tanzania Rép.-Unie de Tanzanie	...	...	...	...	...	1 674	1 830	1 756	1 759	1 941
United States [20] Etats-Unis [20]	237 987	...	233 485	...	...	...	...	...	...	...
Uruguay Uruguay	...	998	913	939	860	741	706	629	507	415
Uzbekistan Ouzbékistan	1 291	724	677	619	569[21]	422[21]	609[21]	...	...	...
Viet Nam Viet Nam	...	4 650	5 330	5 810	6 700	*6 480	7 791	8 712	9 398	11 189

Source

United Nations Statistics Division, New York, the industrial statistics database and the *Industrial Commodity Statistics Yearbook 2003*.

Notes

[1] Source: Economist Intelligence Unit (London).
[2] Twelve months ending 30 June of the year stated.
[3] Incomplete coverage.
[4] Source: Afristat: Sub-Saharan African Observatory of Economics and Statistics (Bamako, Mali).
[5] Excluding the Federation of Bosnia and Herzegovina.
[6] Original data in metric tons.
[7] For statistical purposes, the data for China do not include those for the Hong Kong Special Administrative Region (Hong Kong SAR), Macao Special Administrative Region (Macao SAR) and Taiwan Province of China.
[8] Sales.
[9] Twelve months ending 7 July of the year stated.
[10] Production by large- and medium-scale establishments only.
[11] Production by establishments employing 10 or more persons.
[12] Beginning 1999, data are confidential.
[13] Twelve months beginning 1 April of the year stated.
[14] Government production only.
[15] Twelve months beginning 16 July of the year stated.
[16] Production by establishments employing 20 or more persons.
[17] Excluding the Transnistria region.
[18] Beginning 1999, data for Kosovo are not included.
[19] Beginning 2002, data are confidential
[20] Twelve months ending 30 September of the year stated.
[21] Source: *Statistical Yearbook for Asia and the Pacific*, United Nations Economic and Social Commission for Asia and the Pacific (Bangkok).

Source

Organisation des Nations Unies, Division de statistique, New York, la base de données pour les statistiques industrielles et l'*Annuaire de statistiques industrielles par produit 2003*.

Notes

[1] Source : Economist Intelligence Unit (London).
[2] Période de 12 mois finissant le 30 juin de l'année indiquée.
[3] Couverture incomplète.
[4] Source : Afristat: Sub-Saharan African Observatory of Economics and Statistics (Bamako, Mali).
[5] Non compris la Fédération de Bosnie et Herzegovine.
[6] Données d'origine exprimées en tonnes.
[7] Pour la présentation des statistiques, les données pour Chine ne comprennent pas la Région Administrative Spéciale de Hong Kong (Hong Kong RAS), la Région Administrative Spéciale de Macao (Macao RAS) et la province de Taiwan.
[8] Ventes.
[9] Période de 12 mois finissant le 7 juillet de l'année indiquée.
[10] Production des grandes et moyennes entreprises seulement.
[11] Production des établissements occupant 10 personnes ou plus.
[12] A partir de 1999, les données sont confidentielles.
[13] Période de 12 mois commençant le 1er avril de l'année indiquée.
[14] Production de l'Etat seulement.
[15] Période de 12 mois commençant le 16 juillet de l'année indiquée.
[16] Production des établissements occupant 20 personnes ou plus.
[17] Non compris la région de Transnistrie.
[18] A partir de 1999, non compris les données de Kosovo.
[19] A partir de l'année 2002, les données sont confidentielles.
[20] Période de 12 mois finissant le 30 septembre de l'année indiquée.
[21] Source : *Annuaire des Statistiques de l'Asie et Pacifique*, Conseil Economique et Social des Nations Unis pour l'Asie et le Pacifique (Bangkok).

Cigarettes
Production: millions

Cigarettes
Production : millions

Country or area Pays ou zone	1994	1995	1996	1997	1998	1999	2000	2001	2002	2003
Albania Albanie	929[1]	685[1]	483[1]	414[1]	764[1]	647[1]	372[1]	126[1]	50	15
Algeria [1] Algérie [1]	16 345	...	...	...	...	...	...	...	...	...
Argentina Argentine	1 975	1 963	1 971	1 940	1 967	1 996	1 843	1 739	1 812	...
Armenia Arménie	2 014	1 043	...	815	2 489	3 132	2 109	1 623	2 815	3 222
Austria Autriche	16 429	16 297	...	...	...	...	...	...	...	...
Azerbaijan Azerbaïdjan	3 179	1 926	766	827	241	416	2 362	6 808	6 296	6 611
Bangladesh [2] Bangladesh [2]	12 655	17 379	16 222	18 601	19 889	19 558	19 732	20 120	20 384	22 499
Barbados Barbade	150[1]	65	...	...	...	...	...	...	...	...
Belarus Bélarus	7 378	6 228	6 267	6 787	7 296	9 259	10 356	11 182	10 524	10 464
Belgium Belgique	21 366	18 826	17 471	18 061	17 519	14 713[3]	...	...	...	...
Belize Belize	101	95	79	88	94	91	84	...	...	...
Bolivia Bolivie	1 490	...	...	1 484	1 537	1 404	...	...	...	...
Bosnia and Herzegovina Bosnie-Herzégovine	...	...	3 198	3 886	4 830	5 974	491[4]	690[4]	662[4]	5 062
Bulgaria Bulgarie	53 664	74 603	57 238	43 315	33 181	25 715	26 681	26 659	23 785	25 407
Burundi Burundi	585	523	450	377	317	353	286	293	312	354
Cameroon Cameroun	...	...	...	2 704	3 084	3 249	2 984	2 814	2 785	1 903
Canada Canada	...	50 775	49 362	47 263	48 730	47 224	46 068	44 403	41 267	...
Central African Rep. Rép. centrafricaine	21	30	...	...	...	...	...	...	...	...
Chad Tchad	508	569	...	...	...	...	...	...	...	...
Chile Chili	10 801	10 891	11 569	12 522	12 904	13 271	13 796	13 305	13 839	13 776
China, Hong Kong SAR [5] Chine, Hong Kong RAS [5]	24 747	22 767	21 386	20 929	13 470[6]	...	...	...	...	...
China, Macao SAR [1,7] Chine, Macao RAS [1,7]	450	450	450[8]	...	...	...	...	...	...	...
Colombia Colombie	11 566	10 491	...	11 662	12 472	15 182	...	...	...	...
Costa Rica [1,7] Costa Rica [1,7]	16	16	16	...	...	...	...	...	...	...

Country or area Pays ou zone	1994	1995	1996	1997	1998	1999	2000	2001	2002	2003
Croatia Croatie	12 672	12 110	11 548	11 416	11 987	12 785	13 692	14 738	15 047	15 613
Cyprus Chypre	2 493	2 528	2 728	3 662	4 362	4 783	4 980	3 803	3 418	3 538
Denmark [9] Danemark [9]	11 448	11 902	11 804	12 262	12 392	11 749	11 413	11 089	12 039	12 898
Dominican Republic Rép. dominicaine	4 696	4 092	4 192	3 972	4 098	4 005	3 898	3 338	3 509	...
Ecuador Equateur	2 515	1 734	1 745	1 678	1 997	2 178	2 773	...		2 975
Egypt Egypte	39 145	42 469	46 000	50 000	52 000	51 000	53 000	...	...	...
El Salvador El Salvador	...	1 701	1 756	...	...	...	...	...	...	...
Estonia Estonie	2 287	1 864	954	...	...	...	...	...	...	...
Ethiopia Ethiopie	1 468 [10]	1 583 [10]	1 862 [10]	2 024 [10]	2 029 [10]	1 829 [10]	1 931 [10]	1 904 [10]	1 511	1 511
Fiji Fidji	483	437	439	450	410	446	396	442	479	418
Finland Finlande	7 232	6 542	5 910	...	...	4 877	3 981	3 999	4 130	3 946
France France	48 188	46 361	46 931	44 646	43 304	42 405	42 398	39 000	39 600	36 900
Gabon Gabon	288	297	...	331	463	670	859	880	860	...
Georgia Géorgie	3 256	1 840	1 183	917	601	1 327	296	1 615	1 894	2 972
Germany Allemagne	222 791	...	...	...	...	...	...	...	...	...
Ghana Ghana	...	...	...	1 747	1 399	1 158	1 166	1 481	1 800	...
Greece Grèce	32 843	39 291	38 268	36 909	21 427	34 322	34 381	33 256	...	34 872 [3]
Grenada Grenade	15	...	...	...	...	...	...	...	...	...
Guatemala Guatemala	1 390	2 616	1 725	2 198	4 184	4 376	4 262	...	...	...
Guyana Guyana	314	318	400	221	...	...	...	...	...	...
Haiti Haïti	722	...	...	...	...	...	...	...	...	...
Honduras Honduras	...	...	...	...	3 814	4 586	5 655	5 984	6 010	...
Hungary Hongrie	29 518	25 709	27 594	26 057	26 849	22 985	21 608	20 787	19 492	20 189
India Inde	71 038 [11]	69 589 [11]	73 841 [11]	83 162 [11]	79 313 [11]	82 504 [11]	75 085 [11]	60 577 [12]	54 991 [12]	49 769 [12]
Iran (Islamic Rep. of) Iran (Rép. islamique d')	7 939 [12]	9 787 [13]	11 860 [13]	10 304 [13]	14 335 [13]	20 143 [13]	13 811 [13]	13 359 [13]	13 580 [13]	...
Ireland Irlande	7 000 [1,7]	7 500 [1,7]	7 500 [1,7]	4 605	6 452	6 176	6 461	6 807	6 599 [14]	...
Israel [1] Israël [1]	5 638	4 933	4 793	...	...	...	...	...	...	...

Country or area Pays ou zone	1994	1995	1996	1997	1998	1999	2000	2001	2002	2003
Italy Italie	55 175[1]	50 247[1]	51 489[1]	51 894[1]	50 785	45 159	43 694[1]	45 368[1]	37 342	40 350
Jamaica Jamaïque	1 273	1 216	1 219	1 175	1 160	1 073	995	1 027	1 049	889
Jordan Jordanie	4 191	3 675	4 738	1 853[15]	1 144[15]	*1 602[15]	*1 300[15]	...	...	...
Kazakhstan Kazakhstan	9 393	12 080	19 121	24 109	21 747	18 773	19 293	21 395	23 453	25 715
Kenya Kenya	7 319	7 932	8 436	...	...	8 896	6 009	5 850	4 631	4 753
Korea, Republic of Corée, République de	90 774	87 959	94 709	96 725	101 011	95 995	94 531	94 116	94 433	123 166
Kyrgyzstan Kirghizistan	1 943	1 332	975	716	862	2 103	3 169	3 013	2 927	3 102
Lao People's Dem. Rep. Rép. dém. pop. lao	936	1 062	...	856[16]	1 104[16]	...	...	...	...	...
Latvia Lettonie	2 093	2 101	1 876	1 775	2 018	1 916[14]	...	...	...	...
Lebanon [1] Liban [1]	...	535[17]	539	793	672	945	1 009	...	...	...
Lithuania Lituanie	3 860	4 876	4 538	5 755	7 427	8 217	7 207[18]	...	...	...
Madagascar [1] Madagascar [1]	2 003	2 354	2 957	2 826	3 303	...	...	...	...	...
Malawi Malawi	1 127	1 160	975	731	501	...	...	...	...	...
Malaysia Malaisie	15 762[1]	15 918[1]	16 896[1]	20 236[1]	18 410[1]	15 504[1]	27 271[1]	25 618	23 079	23 971
Mali Mali	20	22	21	...	...	...	...	...	...	...
Mauritius Maurice	1 300	1 215	1 193	1 144	1 034	979	1 049	861	928	938
Mexico Mexique	53 402	56 821	59 907	57 618	60 407	59 492	56 383	56 057	54 704	52 128
Mozambique Mozambique	343	106	250	250	950	1 084	1 417	1 359	1 255	1 390
Myanmar [19] Myanmar [19]	440	752	1 727	1 991	2 040	2 270	2 559	2 650	2 657	2 806
Nepal [20] Népal [20]	6 894	7 430	8 067	7 944	8 127	7 315	6 584	6 979	...	...
Netherlands [9,21] Pays-Bas [9,21]	88 069	97 727	...	...	...	...	...	...	...	...
New Zealand Nouvelle-Zélande	3 396[9]	3 338[9]	3 660[9]	3 449	3 263	3 010	2 916	2 396	2 509	2 176
Nicaragua Nicaragua	...	...	...	1 580	1 789	780[22]	...	...	...	...
Nigeria Nigéria	338	256	...	...	...	...	...	...	...	...
Pakistan [2] Pakistan [2]	35 895	32 747	45 506	46 101	48 215	51 579	46 976	58 259	55 318	49 365
Panama Panama	1 204	1 136	663	752	...	...	...	...	...	...
Peru Pérou	2 752	3 041	3 358	3 028	3 115	3 580	3 605	*3 310	3 766	*2 707

Country or area Pays ou zone	1994	1995	1996	1997	1998	1999	2000	2001	2002	2003
Philippines [1,7] Philippines [1,7]	7 300	7 440	7 440	...	...	...	...	...	...	...
Poland Pologne	98 394	100 627	95 293	95 798	96 741	95 056	83 800	81 697	80 865	82 253
Portugal Portugal	13 610	13 215	12 780	13 234	15 781	17 742	21 377	23 479	25 261	25 294
Republic of Moldova [23] République de Moldova [23]	8 001	7 108	9 657	9 539	7 512	8 731	9 262	9 421	6 310	7 126
Romania Roumanie	14 532[24]	14 747[24]	16 536[24]	25 943[24]	...	...	...	...	...	37 149
Russian Federation Fédération de Russie	91 601	99 545	112 319	140 077	195 806	266 031	333 953	355 632	382 503	376 132
Serbia and Montenegro Serbie-et-Monténégro	12 972	12 686	13 176	10 988	14 597	13 126[25]	14 451	13 968	15 388	...
Seychelles Seychelles	49	56	62	70	61	60	40	36	24	...
Slovenia Slovénie	4 722	4 543	4 909	5 767	7 555	8 032	7 855[18]	...	...	...
Spain Espagne	81 886	78 676	77 675	77 315	81 940	74 873	74 799[18]	...	...	...
Sri Lanka Sri Lanka	5 656	5 822	6 160	5 712	5 797	5 333	4 889	*4 973	...	...
Suriname Suriname	443	472	483	...	...	...	...	...	...	...
Sweden Suède	8 032	7 193	7 251	6 237	5 692	6 060	5 958	5 979	...	...
Switzerland Suisse	39 906	41 976	42 955	37 638	34 453	32 139	34 299	33 565	37 160	38 140
Syrian Arab Republic [1] Rép. arabe syrienne [1]	7 773	9 699	8 528	10 137	10 398	10 991	11 097	12 007	12 863	13 412
Tajikistan Tadjikistan	1 644	964	604	153	191	209	667	1 155	585	...
Thailand Thaïlande	45 359	43 020	48 173	43 387	34 585	31 146	30 732	29 807	30 772	31 908
Trinidad and Tobago Trinité-et-Tobago	593	920	1 102	1 386	1 680	1 945	2 050	...	...	...
Tunisia Tunisie	7 128	7 421	7 159	7 735	9 813	11 066	12 231	12 354	13 230	13 227
Turkey Turquie	85 093[1]	80 700[1]	73 787[1]	74 984[1]	81 616[1]	75 135[1]	76 613[1]	77 160	131 938	111 881
Uganda Ouganda	1 459	1 576	1 702	1 846	1 866	1 602	1 344	1 220	1 092	...
Ukraine Ukraine	47 083	48 033	44 900	54 488	59 275	54 052	58 774	69 731	81 088	96 980
United Kingdom Royaume-Uni	165 479	155 103	166 496	167 670	152 998	143 794	139 125	109 025	124 896	95 578
United Rep. of Tanzania Rép.-Unie de Tanzanie	3 383	3 699	3 733	4 710	...	3 371	3 745	3 491	3 778	3 920
United States Etats-Unis	725 500	746 500	754 500	719 600	679 700	611 929	...	...	...	...
Uruguay Uruguay	...	3 561	6 018	6 872	10 187	11 161	10 894	9 616	8 449	5 718
Uzbekistan Ouzbékistan	3 379	2 742	5 172	8 521	7 582[16]	10 668[16]	7 766[16]	...	...	...

Country or area Pays ou zone	1994	1995	1996	1997	1998	1999	2000	2001	2002	2003
Viet Nam Viet Nam	...	42 940[26]	...	...	43 900[26]	42 940[26]	56 716	61 504	67 504	77 412
Yemen Yémen	5 423[1,7]	6 540	6 740	6 800	5 980	5 760	4 780	6 020	5 780	5 960

Source

United Nations Statistics Division, New York, the industrial statistics database and *Industrial Commodity Statistics Yearbook 2003*.

Notes

[1] Original data in units of weight. Computed on the basis of one million cigarettes per ton.
[2] Twelve months ending 30 June of the year stated.
[3] Incomplete coverage.
[4] Excluding the Federation of Bosnia and Herzegovina.
[5] Including cigarillos.
[6] Beginning 1999, data are confidential.
[7] Source: Food and Agriculture Organization of the United Nations (FAO), (Rome).
[8] Beginning 1997, data are confidential.
[9] Sales.
[10] Twelve months ending 7 July of the year stated.
[11] Production by large- and medium-scale establishments only.
[12] Production by establishments employing 50 or more persons.
[13] Production by establishments employing 10 or more persons.
[14] 2003 data are confidential.
[15] Source: *Bulletin of Industrial Statistics for the Arab Countries*, United Nations Economic and Social Commission for Western Asia (Beirut).
[16] Source: *Statistical Yearbook for Asia and the Pacific*, United Nations Economic and Social Commission for Asia and the Pacific (Bangkok).
[17] Break in series; data prior to the sign not comparable to following years.
[18] Beginning 2001, data are confidential.
[19] Government production only.
[20] Twelve months beginning 16 July of the year stated.
[21] Production by establishments employing 20 or more persons.
[22] Beginning August 1999, national production discontinued.
[23] Excluding the Transnistria region.
[24] Including cigars.
[25] Beginning 1999, data for Kosovo are not included.
[26] Source: *Country Economic Review*, Asian Development Bank (Manila).

Source

Organisation des Nations Unies, Division de statistique, New York, la base de données pour les statistiques industrielles et *Annuaire de statistiques industrielles par produit 2003*.

Notes

[1] Données d'origine exprimées en poids. Calcul sur la base d'un million cigarettes par tonne.
[2] Période de 12 mois finissant le 30 juin de l'année indiquée.
[3] Couverture incomplète.
[4] Non compris la Fédération de Bosnie et Herzegovine.
[5] Y compris les cigarillos.
[6] A partir de 1999, les données sont confidentielles.
[7] Source : Organisation des Nations Unies pour l'alimentation et l'agriculture (FAO), (Rome).
[8] A partir 1997, les données sont confidentielles.
[9] Ventes.
[10] Période de 12 mois finissant le 7 juillet de l'année indiquée.
[11] Production des grandes et moyennes entreprises seulement.
[12] Production des établissements occupant 50 personnes ou plus.
[13] Production des établissements occupant 10 personnes ou plus.
[14] Pour 2003, les données sont confidentielles.
[15] Source : *Bulletin of Industrial Statistics for the Arab Countries*, Commission économique et sociale pour l'Asie occidentale (Beyrouth).
[16] Source : *Annuaire des Statistiques de l'Asie et Pacifique*, Conseil Economique et Social des Nations Unies pour l'Asie et le Pacifique (Bangkok).
[17] Marque une interruption dans la série et la non-comparabilité des données précédant le symbole.
[18] A partir de 2001, les données sont confidentielles.
[19] Production de l'Etat seulement.
[20] Période de 12 mois commençant le 16 juillet de l'année indiquée.
[21] Production des établissements occupant 20 personnes ou plus.
[22] A partir d'août 1999, la production nationale a été discontinuée.
[23] Non compris la région de Transnistria.
[24] Y compris les cigares.
[25] A partir de 1999, non compris les données de Kosovo.
[26] Source : *La Revue Economique du Pays*, La Banque de Développement Asiatique (Manila).

39 Fabrics
Woven cotton, wool, cellulosic and non-cellulosic fibres: million square metres

Tissus
Tissus de coton, laines, fibres cellulosiques et non cellulosiques : miillions de mètres carrés

Country or area — Pays ou zone	1995	1996	1997	1998	1999	2000	2001	2002	2003
Armenia — Arménie									
Cotton — Coton	0	1	0	0	0	0	0	0	0
Australia [1] — Australie [1]									
Cotton — Coton	52	64	61	62	56	47	39	34	26
Wool — Laines	8	7	6	7	6	5	4	0	0
Austria — Autriche									
Cotton — Coton	101	96	95	101	74	58	62	56	95
Wool — Laines	2	12	13	17	13	15[2]	...	...	...
Azerbaijan — Azerbaïdjan									
Cotton — Coton	58	24	17	7	1	1	3	3	3
Wool — Laines	1	0	0	0	0	0	...	...	...
Non-cellulosic — Non cellulosiques	...	...	...	...	...	0	0	0	1
Bangladesh [1] — Bangladesh [1]									
Cotton — Coton	63	63	63	63	63	63	63	63	63
Belarus — Bélarus									
Cotton — Coton	34	45	48	72	50	65	56	57	57
Wool — Laines	8	8	9	10	10	9	7	5	5
Cellulosic — Cellulosiques	35	39	67	77	71	62	...	...	...
Belgium [3] — Belgique [3]									
Cotton — Coton	256	294	298	311	301	...	...	...	...
Cellulosic — Cellulosiques	590	602	656	712	712	...	...	...	...
Non-cellulosic — Non cellulosiques	288	297	316	305	302	...	...	...	...
Bolivia — Bolivie									
Cotton — Coton	*0[4]	...	985	637	397				
Cellulosic * [4] — Cellulosiques * [4]	2	...	...	...	...				
Bosnia and Herzegovina — Bosnie-Herzégovine									
Cotton — Coton	...	...	...	...	...	...	...	...	7
Cellulosic — Cellulosiques	...	1	1[5]	1[5]	2[5]	1[5]	0[5]	1[5]	1[5]
Brazil [4] — Brésil [4]									
Cotton — Coton	1 354	1 318	1 278	1 209	1 270	1 339	...	...	...
Bulgaria — Bulgarie									
Cotton — Coton	93[6]	85[6]	98[6]	96[4]	62[4]	59[4]	...	...	...
Wool — Laines	20[6]	18[6]	17[6]	10[4,6]	8[4,6]	8[4,6]	8	9	7
Cameroon [4] — Cameroun [4]									
Cotton — Coton	24	...	...	...	...	...	...	...	...
Chile [4] — Chili [4]									
Cotton — Coton	29	34	31	27	21	25	...	...	...
China [4,7] — Chine [4,7]									
Cotton — Coton	31 091	24 987	29 730	28 800	29 875	33 102	...	...	...
Wool — Laines	1 079	758	640	442	451	459	...	...	...
China, Hong Kong SAR — Chine, Hong Kong RAS									
Cotton — Coton	658	540	506	341[10]	366[10]	306[10]	378[10]	333[10]	221[10]
China, Macao SAR — Chine, Macao RAS									
Cotton — Coton	8	9	9	10	11	7	0	...	...
Colombia — Colombie									
Cotton [4] — Coton [4]	90	...	88	76	54	...	...	...	...
Wool [4] — Laines [4]	1	...	1	1	1	...	...	...	...
Cellulosic [4] — Cellulosiques [4]	...	...	78	69	...	...	...	...	...
Non-cellulosic — Non cellulosiques	22[3]	...	20[4]	21[4]	16[4]	...	...	...	...

Country or area—Pays ou zone	1995	1996	1997	1998	1999	2000	2001	2002	2003
Croatia—Croatie									
Cotton—Coton	22	19	34	39	34	34	37	35	35
Wool—Laines	7	5	3	2	2	2	2	1	3
Cellulosic—Cellulosiques	8	5	6	7	7	6	1	0	0
Non-cellulosic—Non cellulosiques	1	3	5	5	2	2	2	2	3
Czech Republic—République tchèque									
Cotton—Coton	358	330	346	331	265	313	341	373	376
Wool—Laines	32	30	28	28	17	14	14	13	16
Cellulosic—Cellulosiques	...	...	...	...	...	14	14	13	16
Non-cellulosic—Non cellulosiques	...	...	...	...	...	32	34	34	35
Denmark [11]—Danemark [11]						265	290	284	306
Cotton—Coton	...	5	19	6	2	1	0	...	...
Wool—Laines	1	1	1	0	0	1	2	2	1
Ecuador [4]—Equateur [4]									
Wool—Laines	3	2	0	2	2	...	...	...	...
Cellulosic—Cellulosiques	36	21	...	21	20	...	...	...	...
Egypt—Egypte									
Cotton—Coton	414	1 561	1 474	1 559	1 524	1 559	...	...	...
Wool—Laines	14	8	8	8	7	6	...	...	...
Estonia—Estonie									
Cotton—Coton	90	120	130	127	95	124	117	119	116
Ethiopia—Ethiopie									
Cotton—Coton	50[12]	48[12]	35[12]	38[12]	43[12]	38[12]	45[12]	45	41
Non-cellulosic—Non cellulosiques	5[12]	5[12]	4[12]	5[12]	4[12]	3[12]	1[12]	1	1
Finland—Finlande									
Cotton [6]—Coton [6]	8	9	...	...	...	...	...	...	...
Non-cellulosic—Non cellulosiques	8	8	...	...	...	...	...	...	...
France—France									
Cotton—Coton	682[3]	672[3]	689[3]	658[3]	702[3]	579	548	486	448
Georgia—Géorgie									
Cotton—Coton	1	1	0	0	0	...	...	...	...
Germany—Allemagne									
Cotton—Coton	444	466	489	506	432	452	544	390	376
Wool—Laines	87	87	87	79	63	57	56	45	35
Cellulosic—Cellulosiques	387	325	311	335	294	290	163	211	210
Non-cellulosic—Non cellulosiques	942	851	914	934	938	945	866	902	827
Greece—Grèce									
Cotton—Coton	72[14]	...	...	29	...	...	27	...	36[10]
Wool—Laines	2	2	3	3	...	...	2	...	3[10]
Non-cellulosic—Non cellulosiques	15[15,16]	...	...	...	...	...	...	...	5[10]
Hungary [6]—Hongrie [6]									
Cotton—Coton	66	...	79	44	48	47	40	33	25
Wool—Laines	1	...	0	...	...	...	...	...	...
Cellulosic—Cellulosiques	12	...	...	2	0	0	0	0	...
Non-cellulosic—Non cellulosiques	6	...	...	#95	231	255	291	291	260
Italy [3]—Italie [3]									
Cotton—Coton	1 585	1 555	1 609	1 657	1 570	...	...	...	...
Wool—Laines	433	431	445	396	...	...	...	...	...
Japan—Japon									
Cotton—Coton	1 029	916	917	842	774	664	603	541	507
Wool—Laines	249[17]	247[17]	247[17]	213[17]	199[17]	98[17]	95	88	78
Cellulosic—Cellulosiques	409	441	456	390	352	273	241	211	201
Non-cellulosic—Non cellulosiques	2 050[17]	1 997[17]	2 041[17]	1 743[17]	1 581[17]	1 573[17]	1 484	1 293	1 218

Country or area — Pays ou zone	1995	1996	1997	1998	1999	2000	2001	2002	2003
Kazakhstan — Kazakhstan									
Cotton — Coton	21	21	14	10	9	5	8	14	20
Wool — Laines	3	2	2	1	0	0	0	1	...
Kenya — Kenya									
Cotton — Coton	22	28	29	22	20	16	15	15	10
Wool — Laines	1	1	...	...	...	...	...	...	...
Korea, Republic of — Corée, République de									
Cotton [6] — Coton [6]	379	...	...	...	...	...	...	...	...
Wool — Laines	18	17	14	7	6	9	9	9	7
Non-cellulosic — Non cellulosiques	2 594	...	...	...	...	...	...	...	...
Kyrgyzstan — Kirghizistan									
Cotton — Coton	21	25	20	13	12	6	6	2	1
Wool — Laines	2	3	3	2	1	1	0	0	0
Latvia — Lettonie									
Cotton — Coton	2	6	9	12	12	13	15	22	29
Lithuania — Lituanie									
Cotton — Coton	35	35	62	64	57	55	44	42	34
Wool — Laines	10	13	12	14	11	15	22	21	22
Cellulosic — Cellulosiques	...	...	38	40	35	14	5	11	11
Non-cellulosic — Non cellulosiques	8	6	5	7	5	5	5	5	4
Madagascar — Madagascar									
Cotton — Coton	34[4]	27[4]	32[4]	23[4]	20	23	30	20	
Mexico [3] — Mexique [3]									
Cotton — Coton	304	282	271	300	285	311	...	...	...
Wool — Laines	12	16	20	19	19	18	...	...	...
Non-cellulosic — Non cellulosiques	489	624	638	623	626	622	...	...	...
Myanmar [4,19] — Myanmar [4,19]									
Cotton — Coton	16	12	11	13	21	26	...	...	...
Nepal [4] — Népal [4]									
Non-cellulosic — Non cellulosiques	20	25	25	26	24	33	...	...	...
Nigeria — Nigéria									
Cotton — Coton	113	...	...	...	...	...	...	...	...
Norway [3] — Norvège [3]									
Cotton — Coton	6	7	...	...	*8	6[10]	...	...	...
Wool — Laines	2	2	2	2	...	...	...	...	...
Pakistan [20] — Pakistan [20]									
Cotton — Coton	322	327	333	340	385	437	490	568	582
Poland — Pologne									
Cotton [6,21] — Coton [6,21]	263	295	303	275	234	298	285	261	237
Wool — Laines	50[6,22]	50[6,22]	49[6,22]	45[6,22]	35[6,22]	9[23]	10	6	8
Cellulosic [6] — Cellulosiques [6]	25	26	28	27	18	...	...	...	...
Non-cellulosic [6] — Non cellulosiques [6]	79	69	67	60	40	...	...	...	...
Portugal — Portugal									
Cotton — Coton	418	401	412	444	399	394	398	352	305
Wool — Laines	8	6	6	8	9	11	12	9	5
Cellulosic — Cellulosiques	24	10	11	9	8	10	8	7	8
Non-cellulosic — Non cellulosiques	103	121	127	142	165	169	152	136	133
Romania — Roumanie									
Cotton [6] — Coton [6]	275	212	173	170	143	145	154	160	161
Wool [6] — Laines [6]	68	50	34	22	18	13	17	14	11
Non-cellulosic — Non cellulosiques	...	...	...	...	...	...	...	...	27
Russian Federation — Fédération de Russie									
Cotton — Coton	1 401	1 120	1 374	1 241	1 455	2 026	2 209	2 173	2 169
Wool — Laines	107	67	63	52	61	67	67	55	52
Cellulosic [4] — Cellulosiques [4]	29	14	11	8	...	...	...	...	...
Non-cellulosic [4] — Non cellulosiques [4]	85	51	45	42	...	...	...	...	...

39

Fabrics — Woven cotton, wool, cellulosic and non-cellulosic fibres: million square metres (*continued*)
Tissus — Tissus de coton, laines, fibres cellulosiques et non cellulosiques : millions de mètres carrés (*suite*)

Country or area — Pays ou zone	1995	1996	1997	1998	1999	2000	2001	2002	2003
Serbia and Montenegro — Serbie-et-Monténégro									
Cotton — Coton	19[25,26]	22[25,26]	18[25,26]	23[25,26]	21[25,26,28]	20[25,26]	19[25,26]	11[25,26]	4[10]
Wool — Laines	11[25,27]	11[25,27]	10[25,27]	9[25,27]	7[28]	6	7	5	3
Cellulosic — Cellulosiques	2	1	1	1	0[28]	0	0	0	
Slovakia — Slovaquie									
Cotton — Coton	90	57	61[4]	125[3]	32[3]	49[3]	5	...	31
Wool — Laines	10[4]	11[4]	11[4]	10[3]	7[3]	9[3]	...	...	7
Cellulosic — Cellulosiques	...	...	...	...	...	...	...	...	13
Non-cellulosic — Non cellulosiques	...	...	...	#79[3]	68[3]	73[3]	...	...	5
Slovenia — Slovénie									
Cotton — Coton	71	53	...	42	40	38	44	32	29
Wool — Laines	7	3	...	...	1	2	2[29]	...	1
Cellulosic — Cellulosiques	24	10	...	...	4	3[2]	...	...	...
Non-cellulosic — Non cellulosiques	...	32	...	...	30	47	33[30]	...	...
South Africa — Afrique du Sud									
Cotton — Coton	228	246	269	223	224	219	216	215	198
Wool[31] — Laines[31]	10	9	9	8	7	7	8	9	8
Spain — Espagne									
Cotton — Coton	689	...	...	...	...	...	...	...	...
Wool[3] — Laines[3]	15	...	...	...	...	...	...	...	...
Non-cellulosic[3,32] — Non cellulosiques[3,32]	1 003	...	...	...	...	...	...	...	...
Sweden[3] — Suède[3]									
Cellulosic[33] — Cellulosiques[33]	2	...	...	...	...	...	...	...	...
Non-cellulosic — Non cellulosiques	23	38	28	28	21	18	...	...	...
Switzerland — Suisse									
Cotton[4] — Coton[4]	70	...	...	...	...	...	...	...	...
Wool[31] — Laines[31]	5	...	...	...	...	...	...	...	...
Syrian Arab Republic[3] — Rép. arabe syrienne[3]									
Cotton — Coton	184	186	198	199	186	175	...	...	...
Wool — Laines	4	5	8	14	19	18	...	...	...
Tajikistan — Tadjikistan									
Cotton — Coton	28	27	8	13	12	12	14	20	17
TFYR of Macedonia — L'ex-R.y. Macédoine									
Cotton — Coton	15	16	8	12	6	6	3	4	3
Wool — Laines	6	4	4	4	3	2	3	0	0
Cellulosic — Cellulosiques	1	1	1	1	0	0	0	...	...
Turkey[4] — Turquie[4]									
Cotton — Coton	414	395	580	479	471	567	...	...	...
Wool — Laines	50	59	78	77	78	91	...	...	...
Cellulosic — Cellulosiques	225	246	224	240	215	228	...	...	...
Turkmenistan — Turkménistan									
Cotton — Coton	17	18	14	22	21	34	61	78	...
Wool — Laines	3	3	3	3	...	...	...	...	...
Uganda — Ouganda									
Cotton — Coton	...	...	...	5	7	5	6	8	...
Ukraine — Ukraine									
Cotton — Coton	87	54	28	57	27	37	46	57	27
Wool — Laines	19	12	14	8	6	8	7	7	7
Cellulosic[4] — Cellulosiques[4]	9	3	3	3	2	1	...	...	...
Non-cellulosic[4] — Non cellulosiques[4]	6	3	2	3	2	4	...	...	...
United Kingdom[4] — Royaume-Uni[4]									
Cotton — Coton	96	99	93	88	...	...	...	...	...

Country or area — Pays ou zone	1995	1996	1997	1998	1999	2000	2001	2002	2003
United Rep. of Tanzania — Rép.-Unie de Tanzanie									
Cotton — Coton	10	13	27	...	42	65	75	99	117
United States — Etats-Unis									
Cotton — Coton	3 753	4 010	4 246	3 974[34]	3 721[34]	3 718[34]	3 101[34]	2 947[34]	2 423[34]
Wool — Laines	136	127	138	111[34]	65[34]	57[34]	44[34]	23[34]	19[34]
Uzbekistan — Ouzbékistan									
Cotton — Coton	456	445	425	314[35]	333[35]	360[35]	...	...	...
Wool — Laines	1	1	0	...	...	...	...	...	...

Source

United Nations Statistics Division, New York, the industrial statistics database and *Industrial Commodity Statistics Yearbook 2003*.

Notes

1. Twelve months ending 30 June of the year stated.
2. Beginning 2001, data are confidential.
3. Original data in metric tons.
4. Original data in metres.
5. Excluding the Federation of Bosnia and Herzegovina.
6. After undergoing finishing processes.
7. For statistical purposes, the data for China do not include those for the Hong Kong Special Administrative Region (Hong Kong SAR), Macao Special Administrative Region (Macao SAR) and Taiwan Province of China.
8. 1996 data are confidential.
9. Beginning 1998, data are confidential.
10. Incomplete coverage.
11. Sales.
12. Twelve months ending 7 July of the year stated.
13. Beginning 2000, data are confidential.
14. Including cotton fabrics after undergoing finishing processes.
15. Including fabrics after undergoing finishing processes.
16. Including mixed fabrics.
17. Including finished fabrics and blanketing made of synthetic fibers.
18. 2003 data are confidential.
19. Production by government-owned enterprises only.
20. Factory production only.
21. Including fabrics of cotton substitutes.
22. Including fabrics of wool substitutes.
23. Since 2000, the former "Polish Systematic Nomenclature of Products", has been replaced by the "Polish Classification of Products and Services", impacting range change of some data.
24. Excluding the Transnistria region.
25. Including cellulosic fabrics.
26. Including mixed cotton fabrics.
27. Including mixed wool fabrics.
28. Beginning 1999, data for Kosovo are not included.
29. 2002 data are confidential.
30. Beginning 2002, data are confidential
31. Pure woollen fabrics only.
32. Including woven cellulosic fabrics.
33. Including woven non-cellulosic fabrics.
34. Shipments.
35. Source: *Statistical Yearbook for Asia and the Pacific*, United Nations Economic and Social Council for Asia and the Pacific (Bangkok).

Source

Organisation des Nations Unies, Division de statistique, New York, la base de données pour les statistiques industrielles et *Annuaire de statistiques industrielles par produit 2003*.

Notes

1. Période de 12 mois finissant le 30 juin de l'année indiquée.
2. A partir de 2001, les données sont confidentielles.
3. Données d'origine exprimées en tonnes.
4. Données d'origine exprimées en mètres.
5. Non compris la Fédération de Bosnie et Herzegovina.
6. Après opérations de finition.
7. Pour la présentation des statistiques, les données pour Chine ne comprennent pas la Région Administrative Spéciale de Hong Kong (Hong Kong RAS), la Région Administrative Spéciale de Macao (Macao RAS) et la province de Taiwan.
8. Pour 1996, les données sont confidentielles.
9. A partir de 1998, les données sont confidentielles.
10. Couverture incomplète.
11. Ventes.
12. Période de 12 mois finissant le 7 juillet de l'année indiquée.
13. A partir de 2000, les données sont confidentielles.
14. Y compris les tissus de cotton, après opérations de finition.
15. Y compris les tissus, après opérations de finition.
16. Y compris les tissus mélangés.
17. Y compris les tissus finis et les couvertures en fibres synthétiques.
18. Pour 2003, les données sont confidentielles.
19. Production des établissements d'Etat seulement.
20. Production des fabriques seulement.
21. Y compris les tissus de succédanés de coton.
22. Y compris les tissus de succédanés de laine.
23. A partir de l'année 2000, la "Nomenclature Systematique Polonaise des Produits", a été remplacé par la "Classification Polonaise des Produits et Sérvices", ayant un effet à l'ordre des quelques données.
24. Non compris la région de Transnistria.
25. Y compris les tissus en fibres cellulosiques.
26. Y compris les tissus de cotton mélangé.
27. Y compris les tissus de laine mélangée.
28. A partir de 1999, non compris les données de Kosovo.
29. Pour 2002, les données sont confidentielles.
30. A partir de l'année 2002, les données sont confidentiels.
31. Tissus de laine pure seulement.
32. Y compris les tissus en fibres cellulosiques.
33. Y compris les tissus en fibres non cellulosiques.
34. Expéditions.
35. Source : *Statistical Yearbook for Asia and the Pacific*, United Nations Economic and Social Council for Asia and the Pacific (Bangkok).

40

Leather footwear
Production: thousand pairs

Chaussures de cuir
Production : milliers de paires

Country or area Pays ou zone	1994	1995	1996	1997	1998	1999	2000	2001	2002	2003
Afghanistan Afghanistan	...	...	...	...	...	...	...	...	8	...
Albania Albanie	266	267	...	...	...	...	...	...	...	...
Algeria Algérie	6 467	3 986	2 320	2 542	2 149	1 529	1 222	1 214	929	718
Armenia Arménie	1 749	726	305	122	65	31	63	51	36	23
Australia [1] Australie [1]	315[2]	278[2]	...	...	...	...	9 697	8 129	6 340	5 596
Austria [3] Autriche [3]	12 767	...	...	...	...	...	...	...	...	...
Azerbaijan Azerbaïdjan	3 505	815	546	318	315	54	122	220	339	457
Bangladesh Bangladesh	...	...	...	2 856	2 877	2 792	3 244	3 300	3 442	...
Belarus Bélarus	30 896	14 893	12 480	17 697	18 502	16 538	15 388	13 796	11 664	10 855
Belgium Belgique	383	361	325	276	253	317[4]	172[4]	165[4]	70[4]	46[4]
Bolivia Bolivie	1 903	1 675	...	615	175	251	...	...	...	...
Bosnia and Herzegovina Bosnie-Herzégovine	...	...	2 171	2 354	1 341	2 082	...	...	...	1 078
Brazil Brésil	272 276	261 901	293 309	279 956	276 635	145 393	146 938	151 042	164 882	164 545
Bulgaria Bulgarie	10 244	11 980	8 915	6 838	6 401	4 591	4 790	4 054	7 036	6 675
Canada Canada	...	...	...	...	*1 397	11 505	10 508	11 342	9 432	...
Cape Verde Cap-Vert	...	192	...	...	...	...	...	...	...	...
Chile Chili	8 317	7 410	7 134	7 008	6 777	6 237	5 735	5 251	5 280	6 257
China, Hong Kong SAR Chine, Hong Kong RAS	1 541	2 147	1 499	752[5]	178[5]	200[5]	437[5]	602[5]	523[5]	572[5]
China, Macao SAR Chine, Macao RAS	2 008	2 568	2 103	3 755	3 505	8 799	12 602	10 168	10 465	*12 131
Colombia Colombie	20 933	18 277	...	18 736[6]	16 635[6]	12 541[6]	...	...	...	...
Croatia Croatie	12 459	9 521	9 271	9 598	9 350	8 367	8 402	9 722	8 458	8 338
Cyprus [7] Chypre [7]	3 820	3 444	2 507	2 192	2 100	1 208	1 416	1 081	1 014	744
Czech Republic République tchèque	23 323	22 115	21 572	13 455	10 099	7 146	6 109	5 202	3 157	2 391
Denmark [8] Danemark [8]	...	...	8 387	10 118	10 444	10 114	10 025	1 954	2 136	2 050
Ecuador Equateur	1 672	1 744	1 507	12	8	19	9	...	...	37

Country or area Pays ou zone	1994	1995	1996	1997	1998	1999	2000	2001	2002	2003
Egypt Egypte	48 394	48 444	48 300	48 131	48 171	...	49 077	...	...	...
Estonia Estonie	827	682	711	793	803	840	909	912	1 269	1 451
Ethiopia Ethiopie	2 871[9]	3 751[9]	3 773[9]	6 925[9]	6 252[9]	7 477[7,9]	5 022[9]	6 358	6 677[7,9]	7 138[7,9]
Finland Finlande	3 421	3 186	3 220	2 928	3 499	2 650	2 612	2 133	2 840	2 695
France France	154 898[7]	151 704[7]	139 442[7]	135 447[7]	125 524[7]	114 540[7]	98 496	85 620	66 276	52 906
Georgia Géorgie	224	50	48	101	95	101	90	45	25	19
Germany Allemagne	58 790	45 491	40 675	36 948	38 441	36 581	32 898	27 019	...	...
Greece Grèce	6 922	7 032	6 769	6 202	5 716	4 941	4 994	4 938	...	4 342[4]
Hungary Hongrie	14 224	12 595	...	...	...	14 386	15 045	15 536	15 175	12 581
Iceland Islande	...	...	9	8	...	...	...	...	...	...
India Inde	158 263[10]	181 462[10]	157 095[10]	137 837[10]	180 490[10]	134 524[10]	141 941[10]	157 923	162 908	168 677
Indonesia Indonésie	324 357[11]	278 863[11]	...	287 409[11]	305 729[11]	377 786[11]	325 169	325 169	306 761	...
Iran (Islamic Rep. of) Iran (Rép. islamique d')	17 598[12]	29 807[13]	28 310[13]	8 721[13]	7 156[13]	5 257[13]	4 833[13]	4 585[13]	...	...
Ireland Irlande	...	460	440	328	235	203	126	116	*80	...
Japan Japon	51 503[14]	49 525[14]	48 819[14]	47 573[14]	42 573[14]	37 546[14]	35 961[14]	34 776	29 657	27 478
Jordan Jordanie	...	...	...	...	565	277	354	268	235	...
Kazakhstan Kazakhstan	100	*2	*0	3	27	423	686	1 034	667	809
Kenya Kenya	1 774	1 009	1 041	899	828	1 174	1 348	1 451	1 510	1 556
Korea, Republic of Corée, République de	16 806	15 309	...	...	...	...	...	...	...	...
Kyrgyzstan Kirghizistan	1 512	755	605	332	135	85	129	189	171	238
Lao People's Dem. Rep. Rép. dém. pop. lao	480	450	...	...	...	...	...	...	...	...
Latvia Lettonie	1 633	1 032	939	753	753	451	371	294	284	376
Lithuania Lituanie	1 565	1 961	2 004	1 663	1 654	1 783	747	776	870	618
Madagascar Madagascar	180	136	158	126	115	460	570	568	...	...
Malawi Malawi	...	...	...	1 591	2 023	1 727	1 467	1 340	...	...
Mali Mali	106	99	98	...	...	...	...	...	...	...
Mexico Mexique	56 948	44 006	50 340	52 586	47 072	43 916	42 434	38 526	36 153	32 872

Leather footwear—Production: thousand pairs (*continued*)
Chaussures de cuir—Production : milliers de paires (*suite*)

Country or area Pays ou zone	1994	1995	1996	1997	1998	1999	2000	2001	2002	2003
Mongolia Mongolie	407	325	146	41	33	7	6	17	10	5
Mozambique Mozambique	87	29	...	12	10	7	7	2	*12	*17
Nepal [15] Népal [15]	700	685	649	550	550	*605	650	709	...	...
Netherlands Pays-Bas	5 455 [16]	5 492 [16]	1 146	952	1 030	991	...	...	...	...
New Zealand [1,6] Nouvelle-Zélande [1,6]	3 590	3 119	2 676	2 222	1 484	1 650	...	...	...	...
Nigeria Nigéria	1 182	1 255	...	...	...	...	...	...	...	...
Panama Panama	1 418	1 287	1 058	1 104	753	799	...	...	...	...
Peru Pérou	...	...	...	...	3 523	2 921	2 499	1 016	498	*312
Poland Pologne	53 236	59 783	66 620	68 513	54 491	48 538	*885 [17]	*1 141	*1 194	*888
Portugal Portugal	71 802	68 239	69 439	71 949	68 176	76 632	75 716	76 894	73 191	67 272
Republic of Moldova [18] République de Moldova [18]	2 267	1 506	1 429	1 032	739	705	998	1 078	1 689	2 181
Romania Roumanie	45 666	48 239	44 838	34 365	30 341	30 491	36 863	38 289	39 777	77 114
Russian Federation Fédération de Russie	92 429	62 538	43 548	40 658	27 958	29 864	32 939	37 034	42 237	47 382
Serbia and Montenegro Serbie-et-Monténégro	8 824	5 982	6 461	6 848	6 976	3 892 [19]	4 248	4 351	2 983	...
Slovakia Slovaquie	13 577	46 438	13 188	10 300	9 772	7 643	8 503	8 994	9 555	13 496
Slovenia Slovénie	8 913	7 145	6 139	5 976	5 882	4 779	4 691	4 690	4 256	3 906
South Africa [7] Afrique du Sud [7]	44 373	42 871	38 858	35 486	29 581	24 257	20 195	17 552	19 699	17 137
Spain Espagne	104 788	140 141	155 218	165 417	177 464 [20]	...	...	165 399	163 467 [21]	...
Sweden Suède	676	372	1 104	1 202	430	956	944	912	1 246	1 080
Switzerland Suisse	3 272	2 497	...	...	...	...	...	...	...	...
Syrian Arab Republic Rép. arabe syrienne	286	1 737	1 769	2 459	2 640	3 094	3 341	4 461	3 988	...
Tajikistan Tadjikistan	929	612	394	107	123	72	110	100	84	40
TFYR of Macedonia L'ex-R.y. Macédoine	1 760	1 121	*1 230	*1 509	*1 722	*2 172	*2 059	1 246	1 654	1 586
Tunisia Tunisie	14 100	16 580	18 380	20 300	...	...	...	...	...	...
Turkey Turquie	4 686	5 668	6 059	5 643	5 222	6 590	33 589	37 299	42 280	*35 245
Turkmenistan Turkménistan	1 938	1 910	1 546	1 108	561	416	478	444	253	300
Uganda Ouganda	...	...	...	...	1 471	1 725	1 696	1 979	1 978	...

Country or area Pays ou zone	1994	1995	1996	1997	1998	1999	2000	2001	2002	2003
Ukraine Ukraine	50 223	26 745	17 385	13 246	14 875	11 863[22]	13 468[22]	15 155[22]	15 016[22]	15 939[22]
United Kingdom Royaume-Uni	69 637	61 141	62 157	55 418	44 862	37 148	28 313	...	...	...
United Rep. of Tanzania Rép.-Unie de Tanzanie	89	339	121	152	...	71	1 756	...	...	...
United States Etats-Unis	160 651	146 979	127 315	127 876	115 808	85 332[23]	58 870[23]	55 612[23]	41 166[23]	22 375[23]
Uzbekistan Ouzbékistan	28 202	5 654	5 591	5 547	...	...	...	...	...	...
Viet Nam Viet Nam	...	46 440	61 785	79 289	77 037	*81 780	140 335	143 080	147 921	168 867
Yemen Yémen	192	218	280	283	301	313	229	231	225	*157

Source

United Nations Statistics Division, New York, the industrial statistics database and *Industrial Commodity Statistics Yearbook 2003*.

Notes

[1] Twelve months ending 30 June of the year stated.
[2] Excluding sporting footwear.
[3] Beginning 1995, data are confidential.
[4] Incomplete coverage.
[5] Excluding other footwear for confidentiality purposes.
[6] Including rubber and plastic footwear.
[7] Including rubber footwear.
[8] Sales.
[9] Twelve months ending 7 July of the year stated.
[10] Production by large- and medium-scale establishments only.
[11] Including plastic footwear.
[12] Production by establishments employing 50 or more persons.
[13] Production by establishments employing 10 or more persons.
[14] Shipments. Production by establishments employing 10 or more persons.
[15] Twelve months beginning 16 July of the year stated.
[16] Sales. Including rubber footwear. Production by establishments employing 20 or more persons.
[17] Since 2000, the former "Polish Systematic Nomenclature of Products", has been replaced by the "Polish Classification of Products and Services", impacting range change of some data.
[18] Excluding the Transnistria region.
[19] Beginning 1999, data for Kosovo are not included.
[20] 1999-2000 data are confidential.
[21] 2003 data are confidential.
[22] Including footwear for men, women and children.
[23] Including non-leather footwear.

Source

Organisation des Nations Unies, Division de statistique, New York, la base de données pour les statistiques industrielles et *Annuaire de statistiques industrielles par produit 2003*.

Notes

[1] Période de 12 mois finissant le 30 juin de l'année indiquée.
[2] Non compris les chaussures sportif.
[3] A partir de 1995, les données sont confidentielles.
[4] Couverture incomplète.
[5] A l'exclusion d'autres chaussures, pour raisons de confidentialité.
[6] Y compris les chaussures en caoutchouc et en matière plastique.
[7] Y compris les chaussures en caoutchouc.
[8] Ventes.
[9] Période de 12 mois finissant le 7 juillet de l'année indiquée.
[10] Production des grandes et moyennes entreprises seulement.
[11] Y compris les chaussures en matière plastique.
[12] Production des établissements occupant 50 personnes ou plus.
[13] Production des établissements occupant 10 personnes ou plus.
[14] Expéditions. Production des établissements occupant 10 personnes ou plus.
[15] Période de 12 mois commençant le 16 juillet de l'année indiquée.
[16] Ventes. Y compris les chaussures en caoutchouc. Production des établissements occupant 20 personnes ou plus.
[17] A partir de l'année 2000, la "Nomenclature Systematique Polonaise des Produits", a été remplacé par la " Classification Polonaise des Produits et Sérvices", ayant un effet à l'ordre des quelques données.
[18] Non compris la région de Transnistria.
[19] A partir de 1999, non compris les données de Kosovo.
[20] Pour 1999-2000, les données sont confidentielles.
[21] Pour 2003, les données sont confidentielles.
[22] Y compris les chaussures pour hommes, dames et enfants.
[23] Y compris les chaussures en matières autres que le cuir.

Sawnwood
Production (sawn): thousand cubic metres

Sciages
Production (sciés) : milliers de mètres cubes

Region, country or area Région, pays ou zone	1995	1996	1997	1998	1999	2000	2001	2002	2003	2004
World Monde	391 977	387 236	393 626	377 570	385 702	387 405	379 806	393 829	399 271	409 385
Africa Afrique	8 243	7 867	7 505	7 423	7 415	8 350	7 973	7 496	8 370	8 370
Algeria [1] Algérie [1]	13	13	13	13	13	13	13	13	13	13
Angola [1] Angola [1]	5	5	5	5	5	5	5	5	5	5
Benin Bénin	15	11	12	13	13	13 [1]	32	46	31	31 [1]
Burkina Faso Burkina Faso	1	1	2	1	1	1 [1]	1 [1]	2	2	2 [1]
Burundi Burundi	43	33	33 [1]	33 [1]	80 [1]	83 [1]	83 [1]	83 [1]	83 [1]	83 [1]
Cameroon Cameroun	676 [1]	685 [1]	560	588	600	1 154	800	652	658	658 [1]
Central African Rep. Rép. centrafricaine	70	61	72	91	79	102	150	97	69	69 [1]
Chad Tchad	2	2	2 [1]	2 [1]	2 [1]	2 [1]	2 [1]	2 [1]	2 [1]	2 [1]
Congo Congo	62	59	64	73	74	93	126	170	315	315 [1]
Côte d'Ivoire Côte d'Ivoire	706	596	613	623	611	603	630	620	620 [1]	620 [1]
Dem. Rep. of the Congo Rép. dém. du Congo	65	85	90	80	70	70	60	40	40 [1]	40 [1]
Egypt Egypte	0	0	0	3	4	4	4 [1]	4 [1]	4 [1]	4 [1]
Equatorial Guinea Guinée équatoriale	4	4 [1]	4 [1]	4 [1]	4 [1]	4 [1]	4 [1]	4 [1]	4 [1]	4 [1]
Ethiopia Ethiopie	40	33	60	60 [1]	60 [1]	60 [1]	60 [1]	14	18	18 [1]
Gabon Gabon	100 [1]	50 [1]	30 [1]	60	98	88	112	176	231	231 [1]
Gambia [1] Gambie [1]	1	1	1	1	1	1	1	1	1	1
Ghana Ghana	612	604	575	590	454	475	480	461	496	496 [1]
Guinea Guinée	85	85 [1]	25	26	26 [1]	26 [1]	26 [1]	26 [1]	26 [1]	26 [1]
Guinea-Bissau [1] Guinée-Bissau [1]	16	16	16	16	16	16	16	16	16	16
Kenya Kenya	185 [1]	185 [1]	185 [1]	185 [1]	185 [1]	185 [1]	84	78	78	78 [1]
Liberia Libéria	90 [1]	90 [1]	90 [1]	6	4	10	20	30	30 [1]	30 [1]
Libyan Arab Jamah. [1] Jamah. arabe libyenne [1]	31	31	31	31	31	31	31	31	31	31
Madagascar Madagascar	84 [1]	84 [1]	84 [1]	84 [1]	102	485	400	95	95 [1]	95 [1]
Malawi [1] Malawi [1]	45	45	45	45	45	45	45	45	45	45

Region, country or area Région, pays ou zone	1995	1996	1997	1998	1999	2000	2001	2002	2003	2004
Mali [1] Mali [1]	13	13	13	13	13	13	13	13	13	13
Mauritius Maurice	2	3	3 [1]	5	5	3	3	3 [1]	3 [1]	3 [1]
Morocco [1] Maroc [1]	83	83	83	83	83	83	83	83	83	83
Mozambique Mozambique	42	42 [1]	33	28	28 [1]	28 [1]	28 [1]	28 [1]	28 [1]	28 [1]
Niger [1] Niger [1]	4	4	4	4	4	4	4	4	4	4
Nigeria Nigéria	2 356	2 178	2 000	2 000 [1]	2 000 [1]	2 000 [1]	2 000 [1]	2 000 [1]	2 000 [1]	2 000 [1]
Réunion [1] Réunion [1]	2	2	2	2	2	2	2	2	2	2
Rwanda Rwanda	54	59	74	76	79	79 [1]	79 [1]	79 [1]	79 [1]	79 [1]
Sao Tome and Principe [1] Sao Tomé-et-Principe [1]	5	5	5	5	5	5	5	5	5	5
Senegal [1] Sénégal [1]	23	23	23	23	23	23	23	23	23	23
Sierra Leone [1] Sierra Leone [1]	5	5	5	5	5	5	5	5	5	5
Somalia [1] Somalie [1]	14	14	14	14	14	14	14	14	14	14
South Africa [2] Afrique du Sud [2]	1 574	1 574 [1]	1 574 [1]	1 498	1 498 [1]	1 498 [1]	1 498 [1]	1 498 [1]	*2 171	2 171 [1]
Sudan Soudan	45	45 [1]	45 [1]	51 [1]	51 [1]	51 [1]	51 [1]	51 [1]	51 [1]	51 [1]
Swaziland Swaziland	90 [1]	100 [1]	102	102 [1]	102 [1]	102 [1]	102 [1]	102 [1]	102 [1]	102 [1]
Togo Togo	14	15	17	18	21	19	15	13	13	13 [1]
Tunisia [1] Tunisie [1]	20	20	20	20	20	20	20	20	20	20
Uganda Ouganda	200	215	229	245	264	264 [1]	264 [1]	264 [1]	264 [1]	264 [1]
United Rep. of Tanzania [1] Rép.-Unie de Tanzanie [1]	24	24	24	24	24	24	24	24	24	24
Zambia [1] Zambie [1]	320	245	157	157	157	157	157	157	157	157
Zimbabwe Zimbabwe	401	418	465	416	438	386	397	397 [1]	397 [1]	397 [1]
America, North **Amérique du Nord**	**133 770**	**137 752**	**141 554**	**141 383**	**148 105**	**146 828**	**145 196**	**152 581**	**148 518**	**153 559**
Bahamas [1] Bahamas [1]	1	1	1	1	1	1	1	1	1	1
Belize [1] Belize [1]	35	35	35	35	35	35	35	35	35	35
Canada Canada	45 444	47 025	47 665	47 185	50 412	50 465	53 708	58 481	56 892	60 655
Costa Rica Costa Rica	780 [1]	780 [1]	780 [1]	780 [1]	780 [1]	812	812 [1]	812 [1]	812 [1]	812 [1]
Cuba Cuba	130 [1]	130 [1]	130 [1]	130 [1]	146 [1]	179	190	147 [1]	181 [1]	181 [1]
El Salvador El Salvador	70 [1]	70 [1]	58	58 [1]	58 [1]	58 [1]	58 [1]	68	68	68 [1]

Sawnwood — Production (sawn): thousand cubic metres (*continued*)
Sciages — Production (sciés) : milliers de mètres cubes (*suite*)

Region, country or area / Région, pays ou zone	1995	1996	1997	1998	1999	2000	2001	2002	2003	2004
Guadeloupe [1] / Guadeloupe [1]	1	1	1	1	1	1	1	1	1	1
Guatemala / Guatemala	355	355[1]	355[1]	308	235	340	340	340	366	366[1]
Haiti [1] / Haïti [1]	14	14	14	14	14	14	14	14	14	14
Honduras / Honduras	231	322	379	369	419	442	419	470	421	421[1]
Jamaica / Jamaïque	63	64	65	66	66[1]	66[1]	66[1]	66[1]	66[1]	66[1]
Martinique [1] / Martinique [1]	1	1	1	1	1	1	1	1	1	1
Mexico / Mexique	2 329	2 543	2 961	3 260	3 110[1]	3 110[1]	3 387	3 387[1]	3 387[1]	3 387[1]
Nicaragua / Nicaragua	74	160	148	148[1]	148[1]	148[1]	65	45	45[1]	45[1]
Panama / Panama	37	19	17	8	46	48	42	26	26[1]	26[1]
Trinidad and Tobago / Trinité-et-Tobago	64	29	38	27	18	32	41	43	43	43[1]
United States / Etats-Unis	84 140	86 202	88 906	88 991	92 615	91 076	86 015	88 643	86 159	87 436
America, South / Amérique du Sud	**28 390**	**29 990**	**29 926**	**29 799**	**28 292**	**32 865**	**32 154**	**33 202**	**33 977**	**34 056**
Argentina / Argentine	1 329	1 711	1 170	1 377	1 408	821	2 130	2 130[1]	2 130[1]	2 130[1]
Bolivia / Bolivie	162	181	180	515	244	239	308	299	347	347[1]
Brazil / Brésil	19 091	19 091[1]	19 091[1]	18 591	17 280	23 100	20 850	21 200	21 200[1]	21 200[1]
Chile / Chili	3 802	4 140	4 661	4 551	5 254	5 698	5 872	6 439	7 004	7 004[1]
Colombia / Colombie	644	1 134	1 085	910	730	587	539	527	599	599[1]
Ecuador / Equateur	1 696	1 886	2 075	2 079	1 455	715	794	750	750[1]	750[1]
French Guiana [1] / Guyane française [1]	15	15	15	15	15	15	15	15	15	15
Guyana / Guyana	101	97	57	50	50	29	30	31	38	38[1]
Paraguay [1] / Paraguay [1]	400	500	550	550	550	550	550	550	550	550
Peru / Pérou	630	693	482	590	835	646	506	626	557	*646
Suriname / Suriname	29	40	41	41	28	60	56	47	56	46
Uruguay / Uruguay	269[1]	269[1]	269[1]	269[1]	269[1]	203	203	224	230	230[1]
Venezuela (Bolivarian Rep. of) / Venezuela (Rép. bolivar. du)	222	233	250	261	174	202	301	364	501	501[1]
Asia / Asie	**96 652**	**92 094**	**90 251**	**71 957**	**71 581**	**61 947**	**60 587**	**64 012**	**67 636**	**67 634**
Afghanistan [1] / Afghanistan [1]	400	400	400	400	400	400	400	400	400	400
Armenia / Arménie	0	0	0	0	0	4	4	4	3	2
Azerbaijan / Azerbaïdjan	0	0	0	0	0	1	0	0[1]	0	0[1]

Region, country or area / Région, pays ou zone	1995	1996	1997	1998	1999	2000	2001	2002	2003	2004
Bangladesh / Bangladesh	70[1]	70[1]	70[1]	70[1]	70[1]	70[1]	70[1]	255	388	388[1]
Bhutan [1] / Bhoutan [1]	18	18	18	18	22	31	31	31	31	31
Brunei Darussalam [1] / Brunéi Darussalam [1]	90	90	90	90	90	90	90	90	90	90
Cambodia / Cambodge	140	100	71	40	26	20	5	10	4	4[1]
China [3,4] / Chine [3,4]	25 603[1]	27 410[1]	20 982	18 716[1]	16 700[1]	7 345[1]	8 549	9 431	12 211[1]	12 211[1]
Cyprus / Chypre	15	16	14	11	12	9	9	7	6	5
Georgia / Géorgie	0	*5	*5	*5	*10	*10	*20	*20	*50	50[1]
India / Inde	17 460[1]	10 624[1]	18 520[1]	8 400	8 400	7 900	7 900	10 990	11 880	11 880[1]
Indonesia / Indonésie	6 638	7 338	7 238	7 125	6 625	6 500	6 750	6 230	6 250	6 250[1]
Iran (Islamic Rep. of) / Iran (Rép. islamique d')	159	144	141	129	96	106	106[1]	170	180	180[1]
Iraq / Iraq	8[1]	8[1]	8[1]	12	12[1]	12[1]	12[1]	12[1]	12[1]	12[1]
Japan / Japon	24 493[1]	23 844[1]	21 709	18 625	17 952	17 094	15 485	14 402	13 929	13 929[1]
Kazakhstan / Kazakhstan	0	0	0	*182	183	244	224	232	*265	265[1]
Korea, Dem. P. R. [1] / Corée, R. p. dém. de [1]	280	280	280	280	280	280	280	280	280	280
Korea, Republic of / Corée, République de	3 440	4 291	4 759	2 240	4 300	4 544	4 420	4 410	4 380	4 380[1]
Kyrgyzstan / Kirghizistan	0	0	2	*23	*23	*6	*6	6[1]	6[1]	6[1]
Lao People's Dem. Rep. / Rép. dém. pop. lao	465	320	560	250[1]	350[1]	208	227	182	182[1]	182[1]
Lebanon [1] / Liban [1]	9	9	9	9	9	9	9	9	9	9
Malaysia / Malaisie	8 382[1]	8 382[1]	7 326	5 091	5 237	5 590	4 696	4 643	4 769	4 769[1]
Mongolia / Mongolie	61	170[1]	200[1]	300[1]	300[1]	300[1]	300[1]	300[1]	300[1]	300[1]
Myanmar / Myanmar	347[1]	351	372	299	298	545	671	1 012	1 007	1 007[1]
Nepal / Népal	620[1]	620[1]	620[1]	630	630	630	630	630[1]	630[1]	630[1]
Pakistan / Pakistan	1 266	1 280	1 024	1 051	1 075	1 087	1 180	1 180[1]	1 180[1]	1 180[1]
Philippines / Philippines	286	313	351	222	288	151	199	163	246	246[1]
Singapore [1] / Singapour [1]	25	25	25	25	25	25	25	25	25	25
Sri Lanka / Sri Lanka	6	5	5	5	5	29	61	61[1]	61[1]	61[1]
Syrian Arab Republic [1] / Rép. arabe syrienne [1]	9	9	9	9	9	9	9	9	9	9
Thailand / Thaïlande	426	307	426	103	178	220	233	288	288[1]	288[1]
Turkey / Turquie	4 331	4 268	3 833	4 891	5 039	5 528	5 036	5 579	5 615	5 615[1]

Sawnwood— Production (sawn): thousand cubic metres (*continued*)

Sciages— Production (sciés) : milliers de mètres cubes (*suite*)

Region, country or area Région, pays ou zone	1995	1996	1997	1998	1999	2000	2001	2002	2003	2004
Viet Nam Viet Nam	1 606	1 398	1 184	2 705	2 937	2 950	2 950	2 950[1]	2 950[1]	2 950[1]
Europe **Europe**	**117 917**	**112 606**	**117 378**	**119 718**	**122 822**	**129 354**	**126 372**	**127 899**	**132 209**	**137 205**
Albania Albanie	5[1]	5[1]	5	28	35	90	197	97	97[1]	97[1]
Austria Autriche	7 804	8 200	8 450	8 737	9 628	10 390	10 227	10 415	10 473	11 133
Belarus Bélarus	1 545[1]	1 545[1]	1 545[1]	*2 131	2 175	1 808	2 058	2 182	2 304	2 304[1]
Belgium Belgique	...	...	...	...	1 056	*1 150	1 275	1 175	1 215	1 215[1]
Belgium-Luxembourg Belgique-Luxembourg	1 150	1 100	1 150	1 267	...	...	...	...	...	...
Bosnia and Herzegovina Bosnie-Herzégovine	20	20	320	*330	*330	*320	*310	738	888	888[1]
Bulgaria Bulgarie	253[1]	253[1]	253[1]	253[1]	325	312	332	332[1]	332[1]	332[1]
Croatia Croatie	578	598	644	676	685	642	574	640	585	582
Czech Republic République tchèque	3 490	3 405	3 393	3 427	3 584	4 106	3 889	3 800	3 805	3 940
Denmark Danemark	583[1]	583[1]	583[1]	238	344	364	283	244	248	196
Estonia Estonie	350	400	729[1]	850	1 200	1 436	1 623	1 825	1 954	2 000
Finland Finlande	9 940	9 780	11 430	12 300	12 768	13 420	12 770	13 390	13 745	13 544
France France	9 848	9 600	9 607	10 220	10 236	10 536	10 518	9 815	9 539	9 860
Germany Allemagne	14 105	14 267	14 730	14 972	16 096	16 340	16 131	17 119	17 596	19 051
Greece Grèce	337[1]	337[1]	130	137	140	123	123[1]	196	196	196[1]
Hungary Hongrie	230	285	317	298	308	291	264	293	299	205
Ireland Irlande	678	687	642	675	811	888	925	818	1 005	939
Italy Italie	1 850	1 650	1 751	1 600	1 630	1 630	1 600	1 605	1 590	1 580
Latvia Lettonie	1 300	1 614	2 700	3 200	3 640	3 900	3 840	3 947	3 951	3 920
Lithuania Lituanie	940	1 450	1 250	1 150	1 150	1 300	1 200	1 300	1 400	1 450
Luxembourg Luxembourg	...	...	...	...	133	133[1]	133[1]	133[1]	133[1]	133[1]
Netherlands Pays-Bas	426	359	401	349	362	390	268	258	269	273
Norway Norvège	2 210	2 420	2 520	2 525	2 336	2 280	2 253	2 225	2 186	2 230
Poland Pologne	3 842	3 747	4 214	4 320	4 137	4 262	3 083	3 180	3 360	3 850
Portugal Portugal	1 731	1 731[1]	1 731[1]	1 490	1 430	1 427	1 492	1 298	1 383	1 383[1]
Republic of Moldova République de Moldova	25	29	30	30	6	5	5[1]	5[1]	5[1]	5[1]
Romania Roumanie	1 777	1 693	1 861	2 200	2 818	3 396	3 059	3 696	4 246	4 588

Region, country or area Région, pays ou zone	1995	1996	1997	1998	1999	2000	2001	2002	2003	2004
Russian Federation Fédération de Russie	26 500	21 913	20 600	19 580	19 100	20 000	19 600	*19 240	20 155	21 500
Serbia and Montenegro Serbie-et-Monténégro	304	378	391	438	364	504	391	432	514	575
Slovakia Slovaquie	646	629	767	1 265	1 265[1]	1 265[1]	1 265[1]	1 265[1]	1 651	1 837
Slovenia Slovénie	511	496	510	664	455	439	460	506	511	461
Spain Espagne	3 262	3 080	3 080	3 178	3 178[1]	3 760	4 275	3 524	3 630	3 730
Sweden Suède	14 944	14 370	15 669	15 124	14 858	16 176	15 988	16 172	16 800	16 900
Switzerland Suisse	1 479	1 355	1 280	1 400[1]	1 525	1 625	1 400	1 392	1 345	1 505
TFYR of Macedonia L'ex-R.y. Macédoine	42	40	34	27	37	36	23	20	21	21[1]
Ukraine Ukraine	2 917	2 296	2 306	2 258	2 141	2 127	1 995	*1 950	*2 019	2 019[1]
United Kingdom Royaume-Uni	2 295	2 291	2 356	2 382	2 537	2 482	2 543	2 671	2 759	2 763
Oceania **Océanie**	**7 006**	**6 927**	**7 013**	**7 291**	**7 486**	**8 061**	**7 524**	**8 640**	**8 561**	**8 561**
Australia Australie	3 691	3 530	3 481	3 711	3 673	3 983	3 525	4 119	4 049	4 049[1]
Fiji Fidji	102	102[1]	133	131	64	72	72	84	84[1]	84[1]
New Caledonia [1] Nouvelle-Calédonie [1]	3	3	3	3	3	3	3	3	3	3
New Zealand Nouvelle-Zélande	2 950	3 032	3 136	3 178	3 653	3 910	3 821	4 301	4 292	4 292[1]
Papua New Guinea Papouasie-Nvl-Guinée	218	218[1]	218[1]	218[1]	40	40	40	70	70[1]	70[1]
Samoa [1] Samoa [1]	21	21	21	21	21	21	21	21	21	21
Solomon Islands [1] Iles Salomon [1]	12	12	12	12	12	12	12	12	12	12
Tonga Tonga	1[1]	1[1]	1[1]	2	2[1]	2[1]	2[1]	2[1]	2[1]	2[1]
Vanuatu Vanuatu	7[1]	7[1]	7[1]	15	18	18	28	28[1]	28[1]	28[1]

Source

Food and Agriculture Organization of the United Nations (FAO), Rome, FAOSTAT data , 2005, last accessed October 2005, and *FAO Yearbook of Forest Products.*

Notes

[1] FAO estimate.
[2] Data include those for Namibia.
[3] For statistical purposes, the data for China do not include those for the Hong Kong Special Administrative Region (Hong Kong SAR) and Macao Special Administrative Region (Macao SAR).
[4] Data include those for Taiwan Province of China.

Source

Organisation des Nations Unies pour l'alimentation et l'agriculture (FAO), Rome, données FAOSTAT, année 2005, dernier accés octobre 2005, et *Annuaire FAO des produits forestiers.*

Notes

[1] Estimation de la FAO.
[2] Les données comprennent les chiffres pour la Namibie.
[3] Pour la présentation des statistiques, les données pour Chine ne comprennent pas la Région Administrative Spéciale de Hong Kong (Hong Kong RAS) et la Région Administrative Spéciale de Macao (Macao RAS).
[4] Les données comprennent les chiffres pour la province de Taiwan.

42

Paper and paperboard
Production: thousand metric tons

Papiers et cartons
Production : milliers de tonnes

Region, country or area Région, pays ou zone	1995	1996	1997	1998	1999	2000	2001	2002	2003	2004
World Monde	282 591	284 302	301 316	301 671	315 544	323 706	320 208	324 670	328 226	336 765
Africa Afrique	2 624	2 634	2 885	3 027	2 902	3 020	3 223	3 234	3 303	3 600
Algeria Algérie	*78	*56	*65	94[1]	26[1]	41[1]	41[1]	41[1]	41[1]	41[1]
Cameroon Cameroun	5[1]	5[1]	0	0	0[1]	0[1]	0[1]	0[1]	0[1]	0[1]
Central African Rep. Rép. centrafricaine	8	8	3	3	3	3	3	3	3	3
Dem. Rep. of the Congo [1] Rép. dém. du Congo [1]	3	3	3	3	3	3	3	3	3	3
Egypt Egypte	*221	221[1]	*282	343[1]	343[1]	440[1]	460[1]	460[1]	460[1]	460[1]
Ethiopia Ethiopie	6	8	10	6	10	12	12[1]	11[1]	11[1]	11[1]
Kenya Kenya	*113	129	129[1]	129[1]	129[1]	129[1]	67	80	80	147
Libyan Arab Jamah. [1] Jamah. arabe libyenne [1]	6	6	6	6	6	6	6	6	6	6
Madagascar Madagascar	4	3	4	13	7	11[1]	10[1]	9[1]	9[1]	9[1]
Morocco Maroc	106	106	107	110	109	109	129	129[1]	129[1]	129[1]
Mozambique Mozambique	1[1]	1[1]	0	0	0[1]	0[1]	0[1]	0[1]	0[1]	0[1]
Nigeria Nigéria	6	21	19	19	19	19	19	19	19	19
South Africa [2] Afrique du Sud [2]	1 871	1 871[1]	2 047	2 105	2 041	2 041[1]	2 267	2 267[1]	2 336	2 566
Sudan [1] Soudan [1]	3	3	3	3	3	3	3	3	3	3
Tunisia Tunisie	*90	90[1]	97	88	*94	94[1]	94[1]	94[1]	94[1]	94[1]
Uganda [1] Ouganda [1]	3	3	3	3	3	3	3	3	3	3
United Rep. of Tanzania [1] Rép.-Unie de Tanzanie [1]	25	25	25	25	25	25	25	25	25	25
Zambia [1] Zambie [1]	2	2	4	4	4	4	4	4	4	4
Zimbabwe Zimbabwe	81	81	81	76	80	80[1]	80[1]	80[1]	80[1]	80[1]
America, North Amérique du Nord	107 536	105 823	111 272	109 388	113 123	111 427	105 528	106 518	105 248	108 600
Canada Canada	18 713	18 414	18 969	18 875	20 280	20 921	19 834	20 226	20 120	20 578
Costa Rica [1] Costa Rica [1]	20	20	20	20	20	20	20	20	20	20
Cuba [1] Cuba [1]	57	57	57	57	57	57	57	25	24	18

Region, country or area / Région, pays ou zone	1995	1996	1997	1998	1999	2000	2001	2002	2003	2004
Dominican Republic / Rép. dominicaine	7	21	21[1]	130	130[1]	130[1]	130[1]	130[1]	130[1]	130[1]
El Salvador / El Salvador	17	56	56[1]	56[1]	56[1]	56[1]	56[1]	56[1]	56[1]	56[1]
Guatemala / Guatemala	31	31[1]	31[1]	31[1]	31[1]	31[1]	31[1]	31[1]	31[1]	31[1]
Honduras / Honduras	90	103	88	95	95[1]	95[1]	95[1]	95[1]	95[1]	95[1]
Jamaica / Jamaïque	0	0[1]	0[1]	0[1]	0[1]	0[1]	0[1]	0[1]	0[1]	0[1]
Mexico / Mexique	*3 047	3 047[1]	3 491	3 673	3 784	3 865	4 056	4 056[1]	4 060	4 060[1]
Panama / Panama	28[1]	28[1]	28[1]	0	0	0[1]	0[1]	0[1]	0[1]	0[1]
United States / Etats-Unis	85 526	84 046	88 511	86 451	88 670	86 252	81 249	81 879	80 712	83 612
America, South / Amérique du Sud	**9 204**	**9 247**	**9 970**	**9 562**	**9 664**	**10 243**	**11 258**	**11 428**	**12 039**	**12 602**
Argentina / Argentine	1 025	991	1 133	978	1 012	1 270	1 338	1 417[1]	1 394	1 507
Bolivia / Bolivie	2	2	2[1]	2[1]	0[1]	0[1]	0[1]	0[1]	0[1]	0[1]
Brazil / Brésil	5 856	5 885	6 475	6 524	6 255	6 473	7 354	7 354[1]	7 811	8 221
Chile / Chili	573	680	614	598	824	861	876	1 016	1 098	1 098[1]
Colombia / Colombie	690	693	704	712	733	771[1]	771[1]	847[1]	866[1]	899[1]
Ecuador / Equateur	83	86	91	91[1]	91[1]	91[1]	91[1]	94[1]	101	101[1]
Paraguay[1] / Paraguay[1]	13	13	13	13	13	13	13	13	13	13
Peru / Pérou	140	140[1]	140[1]	63	63[1]	83[1]	86[1]	88[1]	91[1]	91[1]
Uruguay / Uruguay	86	86[1]	*90	88[1]	92[1]	87[1]	88[1]	89[1]	89[1]	96[1]
Venezuela (Bolivarian Republic of) / Venezuela (Rép. Bolivarienne)	736	671	708	493[1]	581	594[1]	641[1]	510[1]	576[1]	576[1]
Asia / Asie	**77 457**	**81 636**	**85 108**	**85 484**	**91 734**	**94 865**	**97 385**	**98 004**	**99 238**	**99 001**
Armenia / Arménie	0	0	0	0	0	20	1	2	2	2[1]
Azerbaijan / Azerbaïdjan	0	0	0	0	0	28	146	144	148[1]	148[1]
Bangladesh / Bangladesh	120[1]	90[1]	70	46	46[1]	46[1]	46[1]	46[1]	46[1]	46[1]
China[3,4] / Chine[3,4]	28 517	30 913	31 663	32 203	34 137	35 439	37 929	37 929[1]	37 929[1]	37 929[1]
India / Inde	*3 025	3 025[1]	2 922	3 320	3 845	3 794	4 094	4 105[1]	4 145[1]	4 145[1]
Indonesia / Indonésie	*3 425	*4 121	*4 822	5 487	6 978	6 977	6 995	6 995[1]	6 995[1]	7 223
Iran (Islamic Rep. of) / Iran (Rép. islamique d')	205	205	205	20	25	46	46[1]	46[1]	46[1]	46[1]

Region, country or area Région, pays ou zone	1995	1996	1997	1998	1999	2000	2001	2002	2003	2004
Iraq Iraq	18[1]	18[1]	18[1]	20	20[1]	20[1]	20[1]	20[1]	20[1]	20[1]
Israel Israël	275	275[1]	275[1]	242	275[1]	275[1]	275	275[1]	275[1]	275[1]
Japan Japon	29 664	30 014	31 014	29 886	30 631	31 828	30 717	30 686	30 457	30 457[1]
Jordan Jordanie	31	31	32	32	32	19[1]	27[1]	25[1]	25[1]	25[1]
Kazakhstan Kazakhstan	0	0	0	0	3	24	47	64	58	58[1]
Korea, Dem. P. R.[1] Corée, R. p. dém. de [1]	80	80	80	80	80	80	80	80	80	80
Korea, Republic of Corée, République de	*6 878	7 681	8 334	7 750	8 875	9 308	9 332	9 812	10 148	10 148[1]
Kyrgyzstan Kirghizistan	0	0	0	0	0	2[1]	7[1]	16[1]	16[1]	16[1]
Lebanon[1] Liban [1]	42	42	42	42	42	42	42	42	42	42
Malaysia Malaisie	665	674	711	761	859	791	851	851[1]	968[1]	968[1]
Myanmar Myanmar	15	15	39	41	37	39	42	49	45	45[1]
Nepal[1] Népal [1]	13	13	13	13	13	13	13	13	13	13
Pakistan Pakistan	420	447	500	527	574	592	1 165	1 165[1]	1 165[1]	700[1]
Philippines Philippines	*613	613[1]	613[1]	987	1 010	1 107	1 056	1 056[1]	1 056[1]	1 056[1]
Singapore Singapour	*87	87[1]	87[1]	87[1]	87[1]	87[1]	87[1]	87[1]	87[1]	87[1]
Sri Lanka Sri Lanka	28	25	25[1]	25[1]	25[1]	24[1]	25[1]	25[1]	25[1]	25[1]
Syrian Arab Republic[1] Rép. arabe syrienne [1]	1	1	1	1	1	1	1	1	1	1
Thailand Thaïlande	1 970	2 036	2 271	2 367[1]	2 434	2 312	2 445	2 444[1]	3 420	3 420[1]
Turkey Turquie	1 240	1 105	1 246	1 357	1 349	1 567	1 513	1 643	1 643[1]	1 643[1]
Viet Nam Viet Nam	*125	125[1]	125[1]	190	356	384	384[1]	384[1]	384[1]	384[1]
Europe **Europe**	**82 615**	**81 777**	**88 774**	**90 825**	**94 740**	**100 438**	**99 299**	**101 966**	**104 494**	**109 059**
Albania Albanie	44[1]	44[1]	44[1]	44[1]	1	3	3[1]	3[1]	3[1]	3[1]
Austria Autriche	3 599	3 653	3 816	4 009	4 142	4 386	4 250	4 419	4 565	4 852
Belarus Bélarus	131	131	131	195	208	236	224	216	279	279[1]
Belgium Belgique	...	...	...	...	1 727	1 727	1 662	1 704	1 746	1 746[1]
Belgium-Luxembourg Belgique-Luxembourg	1 088[1]	1 432	1 432[1]	1 831	...	...	...	...	...	...
Bulgaria Bulgarie	150	150	150	153	126	136	171[1]	171[1]	171[1]	171[1]

Region, country or area Région, pays ou zone	1995	1996	1997	1998	1999	2000	2001	2002	2003	2004
Croatia Croatie	325	304	393	403	417	406[1]	451	467	463	464
Czech Republic République tchèque	738	714	772	768	770	804	864	870	920	933
Denmark Danemark	345[1]	345[1]	391	393	397	263[1]	389[1]	384[1]	388[1]	402[1]
Estonia Estonie	42	53	35	43	48	54[1]	70[1]	75[1]	64	66[1]
Finland Finlande	10 942	10 442	12 149	12 703	12 947	13 509	12 502	12 789	13 058	14 036
France France	8 619	8 556	9 143	9 161	9 603	10 006	9 625	9 809	9 939	10 249
Germany Allemagne	14 827	14 733	15 930	16 311	16 742	18 182	17 879	18 526	19 310	20 392
Greece Grèce	750[1]	750[1]	478	622	545	496	495	264[1]	264	264[1]
Hungary Hongrie	321	363	820	434	473	506	495[1]	517	546	579[1]
Ireland Irlande	0	0[1]	0[1]	42	42	43	43[1]	44[1]	45[1]	45[1]
Italy Italie	6 810	6 954	8 032	8 254	8 568	9 129	8 926	9 317	9 491	9 667
Latvia Lettonie	6	8	16	18	19	16[1]	24[1]	33[1]	38	38[1]
Lithuania Lituanie	29	31	25	37	37	53	68[1]	78	92[1]	99[1]
Netherlands Pays-Bas	2 967	2 987	3 159	3 180	3 256	3 332	3 174	3 346	3 339	3 459
Norway Norvège	2 261	2 096	2 129	2 260	2 241	2 300	2 220	2 114	2 186	2 294
Poland Pologne	1 477	1 528	1 660	1 718	1 839	1 934	2 086[1]	2 342	2 456	2 640
Portugal Portugal	977	1 026	1 080	1 136	1 163	1 290[1]	1 419[1]	1 537	1 536[1]	1 536[1]
Romania Roumanie	364	332	324	301	289	340	395	370	443	462
Russian Federation Fédération de Russie	4 073	3 224	3 339	3 595	4 535	5 310	5 625	5 978	6 377	6 789
Serbia and Montenegro Serbie-et-Monténégro	245	249	300	326	230	180	241	254	148	159
Slovakia Slovaquie	327	467	526	597	803	925	988	710	674	798[1]
Slovenia Slovénie	449	456	430	491	417	411	633	704	511	558
Spain Espagne	3 684	3 768	3 968	3 545	4 435	4 765	5 131	5 365	5 437	5 490
Sweden Suède	9 159	9 018	9 756	9 879	10 071	10 786	10 534	10 724	11 062	11 589
Switzerland Suisse	1 435	1 461	1 583	1 592	1 748	1 616	1 750	1 805	1 818	1 777
TFYR of Macedonia L'ex-R.y. Macédoine	34	21	21	15	14	17	15	19	18[1]	18[1]
Ukraine Ukraine	305	293	264	293	311	411	480	532	618	702

Region, country or area Région, pays ou zone	1995	1996	1997	1998	1999	2000	2001	2002	2003	2004
United Kingdom Royaume-Uni	6 093	6 189	6 479	6 477	6 576	6 868	6 467	6 481	6 489	6 503
Oceania **Océanie**	**3 155**	**3 185**	**3 308**	**3 385**	**3 381**	**3 713**	**3 515**	**3 519**	**3 903**	**3 903**
Australia Australie	2 252	2 320	2 418	2 541	2 564	2 836	2 672	2 645	3 090	3 090[1]
New Zealand Nouvelle-Zélande	903	865	890	844	817	877	843	874	813	813[1]

Source

Food and Agriculture Organization of the United Nations (FAO), Rome, FAOSTAT data, 2006, last accessed February 2006, and *FAO Yearbook of Forest Products*.

Notes

[1] FAO estimate.

[2] Data include those for Namibia.

[3] For statistical purposes, the data for China do not include those for the Hong Kong Special Administrative Region (Hong Kong SAR) and Macao Special Administrative Region (Macao SAR).

[4] Data include those for Taiwan Province of China.

Source

Organisation des Nations Unies pour l'alimentation et l'agriculture (FAO), Rome, données FAOSTAT, année 2006, dernier accès février 2006, et *Annuaire FAO des produits forestiers*.

Notes

[1] Estimation de la FAO.

[2] Les données comprennent les chiffres pour la Namibie.

[3] Pour la présentation des statistiques, les données pour Chine ne comprennent pas la Région Administrative Spéciale de Hong Kong (Hong Kong RAS) et la Région Administrative Spéciale de Macao (Macao RAS).

[4] Les données comprennent les chiffres pour la province de Taiwan.

Cement
Production: thousand metric tons

Ciment
Production : milliers de tonnes

Country or area Pays ou zone	1994	1995	1996	1997	1998	1999	2000	2001	2002	2003
Afghanistan Afghanistan	*115[1]	*115[1]	*116[1]	*116[1]	*116[1]	*120[1]	50[1]	16	27	24
Albania Albanie	240	240	204	100	84	108	180	301	348	578
Algeria Algérie	6 093	6 783	7 470	7 146	7 836	7 685	8 700	8 710	8 941	8 192
Angola [1] Angola [1]	*240	*200	*270	301	*350	207	201	*200	*250	250
Argentina Argentine	6 306	5 477	5 117	6 769	7 092	7 187	6 121	5 545	3 910	3 900[1]
Armenia Arménie	122	228	281	293	314	287	219	275	355	384
Australia Australie	7 017	6 606	6 397[2]	6 701	7 235[2]	7 705[2]	7 937[2]	6 786[2]	7 236[2]	7 517[2]
Austria Autriche	4 828	3 843[1]	3 900[3]	...	...	...	...	...	...	...
Azerbaijan Azerbaïdjan	467	196	223	303	201	171	251	523	848	1 012
Bahrain Bahreïn	...	...	192[1]	172	230	156[1]	89[1]	89[1]	67[1]	70[1]
Bangladesh [2] Bangladesh [2]	324	316	426	610	543	1 514	1 868	2 340	2 514	2 565
Barbados Barbade	76	76	108	176	257	257	268	250	298	325
Belarus Bélarus	1 488	1 235	1 467	1 876	2 035	1 998	1 847	1 803	2 171	2 472
Belgium Belgique	7 542	7 501	6 996	6 996	6 852	7 463	7 150[1]	*7 500[1]	*8 000[1]	8 000[1]
Benin [1] Bénin [1]	465	579	*360	*450	*200	*200	*250	*250	*250	*250
Bhutan *[1] Bhoutan *[1]	120	140	160	160	150	150	150	160	160	160
Bolivia Bolivie	776	877	897	1 048	1 167	1 201	1 072	983	1 010[1]	1 000[1]
Bosnia and Herzegovina Bosnie-Herzégovine	...	...	200	414	563	683	164[4]	145[4]	213[4]	891
Brazil Brésil	25 229	28 256	34 559	37 995	39 942	40 248	39 559	38 735	38 104	34 010
Brunei Darussalam Brunéi Darussalam	...	...	...	...	...	222	241	234	220	235[1]
Bulgaria Bulgarie	1 910	2 070	2 137	1 654	1 742	2 060	2 209	2 088	2 173	2 406
Burkina Faso [1] Burkina Faso [1]	...	...	...	50	50	*50	*50	*50	*50	*30
Cambodia [1] Cambodge [1]	...	...	...	...	150	...	...	...	...	...
Cameroon Cameroun	*479[1]	522	305[1]	633	740	825	956	980	937	949
Canada Canada	10 584	10 440	11 587	11 736[5]	12 168	12 643	12 753	12 793	13 081	14 063[1]

Country or area Pays ou zone	1994	1995	1996	1997	1998	1999	2000	2001	2002	2003
Chile Chili	3 001	3 304	3 627	3 718	3 890	2 508	2 686	3 145	3 522 [1]	3 550 [1]
China [6] Chine [6]	421 180	475 606	491 189	511 738	536 000	573 000	597 000	661 040	725 000	862 081
China, Hong Kong SAR Chine, Hong Kong RAS	1 927	1 913	2 027	1 925	1 539	1 387	1 284	1 279	1 206	1 189
Colombia Colombie	9 273	9 908	...	10 878	8 673	6 677	7 131	6 776	6 633	*6 800 [1]
Congo Congo	87	98	43	20	0	0	0	...	...	...
Costa Rica [1] Costa Rica [1]	940	865	830	940	1 085	1 100	1 150	1 100	1 100	1 130
Côte d'Ivoire [1] Côte d'Ivoire [1]	*1 100	*1 000	*1 000	1 100	650	650	650	650	650	650
Croatia Croatie	2 055	1 708	1 842	2 134	3 873	2 712	2 852	3 246	3 378	3 571
Cuba Cuba	1 085 [7]	1 456 [7]	1 438	1 701	1 713	1 797	1 643	1 335	1 336	1 357
Cyprus Chypre	1 053	1 024	1 021	910	1 207	1 157	1 398	1 367	1 445	1 638
Czech Republic République tchèque	5 252	4 831	5 016	4 874	4 599	4 241	4 093	3 591	3 249	3 502
Dem. Rep. of the Congo [1] Rép. dém. du Congo [1]	166	235	241	125	134	159	161	192	*190	190
Denmark [8] Danemark [8]	2 427	2 584	2 629	2 683	2 667	2 534	2 639	2 678	2 698	2 642
Dominican Republic Rép. dominicaine	1 276	1 450	1 642	1 822	1 872	2 295	2 505	2 746	3 050	2 907 [1]
Ecuador Equateur	2 452	2 549	2 601	2 900 [1]	2 539	2 262	2 800 [1]	2 947	3 113	3
Egypt Egypte	13 544	14 237	15 569	15 569	15 480	11 933	25 101	26 811	*28 000 [1]	29 100 [1]
El Salvador El Salvador	915 [7]	914 [7]	948 [1]	1 020 [1]	1 065 [1]	1 031 [1]	1 064 [1]	1 174 [1]	1 318 [1]	1 391 [1]
Eritrea [1] Erythrée [1]	...	...	...	60	50	*45	*45	*45	*45	*45
Estonia Estonie	403	418	388	422	321	358	329	405	466	506
Ethiopia Ethiopie	464 [9]	609 [9]	672 [9]	775 [9]	783 [9]	767 [9]	816 [9]	819	919	890
Fiji Fidji	94	91	84	96	89	99	87	99	102	100
Finland Finlande	864	907	975	*960 [1]	*1 104	*1 164	1 422	1 325	1 198	1 493
France France	20 020	19 724	18 337	18 309	19 434	20 302	20 000 [1]	20 652	20 244	20 544
French Guiana [1] Guyane française [1]	...	...	...	51	88	*88	*88	*58	*62	*62
Gabon Gabon	126 [1]	154 [1]	185	200	198	162	166	240	257	261
Georgia Géorgie	89	59	85	94	199	341	348	335	347	345
Germany Allemagne	40 217	38 858	37 006	37 210	38 464	39 970	38 088	33 689	32 012 [10]	...

Country or area Pays ou zone	1994	1995	1996	1997	1998	1999	2000	2001	2002	2003
Ghana Ghana	1 350[1]	*1 300[1]	*1 500[1]	1 446	1 573	1 851	1 673	1 490	1 414	1 900[1]
Greece Grèce	12 633	10 914	13 391	13 660	14 207	13 624	14 147	15 563	15 500[1]	18 742[11]
Guadeloupe Guadeloupe	283	*230	*230[1]	*230[1]	*230[1]	*230[1]	*230[1]	*230[1]	*230[1]	*230[1]
Guatemala Guatemala	1 163[7]	1 257	1 173	1 480	1 496	2 120	2 039	1 976	2 068	1 650[1]
Guinea [1] Guinée [1]	...	...	...	260	277	297	300	315	360	360
Haiti Haïti	228[7]	...	...	...	...	...	...	204[1]	290[1]	200[1]
Honduras Honduras	1 000[7]	995[7]	952[1]	*1 041[1]	896[1]	980[1]	1 100[1]	*1 100[1]	*1 100[1]	1 000[1]
Hungary Hongrie	2 793	2 875	2 747	2 811	2 999	2 980	3 326	3 452	3 510	3 573
Iceland Islande	81	82	90	110	118	131	144	125	83	85
India Inde	63 461	67 722	73 261	82 873	87 646	100 230	99 227	106 491	111 778	117 035
Indonesia Indonésie	24 564	23 136	*24 648	20 702	*22 344	22 806	27 789[1]	18 629	34 640[1]	35 000[1]
Iran (Islamic Rep. of) Iran (Rép. islamique d')	16 250[12]	16 904[12]	17 703[12]	16 994[13]	20 049[12]	22 219[13]	23 277[13]	24 755[13]	23 670[13]	30 000[1]
Iraq [1] Iraq [1]	*2 000	2 108	*1 600	*1 700	*2 000	*5 000	*6 000	*6 000	*6 834	*1 000
Ireland Irlande	1 623[1]	1 730[1]	1 933[1]	2 100[1]	*2 000[14]	*2 000[14]	...	...	...	...
Israel Israël	4 800	6 204	6 723	5 916	6 476[1]	6 354[1]	*5 703[1]	*4 700[1]	*5 150[1]	*5 150[1]
Italy Italie	32 698	33 716	33 327	33 718	35 512	36 827	39 588	40 494	42 050	43 903
Jamaica Jamaïque	445	518	559	588	558	504[7]	521[7]	596[1]	614	605
Japan Japon	91 624	90 474	94 492	91 938	81 328	80 120	81 097	76 550	71 828	68 766
Jordan Jordanie	3 392	3 415	3 512	3 250	2 650	2 688	2 640	3 149	3 557	3 515[1]
Kazakhstan Kazakhstan	2 033	1 772	1 115	657	622	838	1 175	2 029	2 129	2 581
Kenya Kenya	1 470	1 670	1 575	1 580	1 453	1 389	1 367	1 319	1 537	1 649
Korea, Dem. P. R. [1] Corée, R. p. dém. de [1]	*17 000	*17 000	*17 000	7 000	7 000	*4 000	*4 600	*5 160	*5 320	*5 500
Korea, Republic of Corée, République de	52 088	56 101	58 434	60 317	46 791	48 579	51 417	53 062	56 823	60 725
Kuwait Koweït	1 232	*1 363	1 113[15]	1 370	2 310	947	1 187	921	1 584	1 863
Kyrgyzstan Kirghizistan	426	310	546	658	709	386	453	469	533	757
Lao People's Dem. Rep. Rép. dém. pop. lao	...	59	78[1]	84[1]	80[1]	*80[1]	*92[1]	*92[1]	*240[1]	*250[1]
Latvia Lettonie	244	204	325	246	366	301[16]	...	...	...	...

Country or area Pays ou zone	1994	1995	1996	1997	1998	1999	2000	2001	2002	2003
Lebanon Liban	2 948	3 470	3 430	3 126	3 316	2 714	2 808	2 890	2 852[1]	2 950[1]
Liberia *[1] Libéria *[1]	3	5	15	7	10	15	71	63	54	30
Libyan Arab Jamah.[1] Jamah. arabe libyenne[1]	4 000	3 000	3 000	3 000	3 000	*3 000	*3 000	*3 000	*3 300	*3 300
Lithuania Lituanie	736	649	656	714	788	666	573	529	606	597
Luxembourg Luxembourg	711	714	667	683	699	742	749	725	729	709
Madagascar Madagascar	...	38	44	36	44	46[1]	48[1]	51	34	33[1]
Malawi Malawi	122	124	88	70	83	104	156[1]	111	174[1]	190[1]
Malaysia Malaisie	9 928	10 713	12 349	12 668	10 397	10 104	11 445	13 820	14 336	17 243
Mali Mali	14	13	21	10[1]	10[1]	10[1]	10[1]	...	...	...
Martinique Martinique	231	*225	*220[1]	*220[1]	*220[1]	*220[1]	*220[1]	*220[1]	*220[1]	*220[1]
Mauritania Mauritanie	374	120[1]	120[1]	*125[1]	134[1]	*100[1]	*110[1]	*110[1]	*110[1]	*110[1]
Mexico Mexique	31 594	25 295	28 174	29 685	30 915	31 958	33 429	32 239	33 478	33 729
Mongolia Mongolie	86	109	106	*112[1]	109	104	92	68	148	162
Morocco Maroc	6 284	6 399	6 585	7 236	7 155	7 194	7 497	8 058	8 057	10 400[1]
Mozambique Mozambique	62	146	179	217	264	266	348	421	435	668
Myanmar[17] Myanmar[17]	477	525	513	524	371	343	400	384	462	581
Nepal Népal	315[18]	327[18]	309[18]	227[18]	139[18]	191[18]	206[18]	215[18]	*290[1]	*395[1]
Netherlands Pays-Bas	3 180[1]	3 180[1]	3 140[1]	3 230	3 200	3 200	3 200	*3 450[1]	*3 400[1]	*3 400[1]
New Caledonia Nouvelle-Calédonie	97	99	89	84	89	93	91	100	100	100[1]
New Zealand[1] Nouvelle-Zélande[1]	*900	*950	974	976	950	*1 030	*1 070	*1 080	*1 090	*1 100
Nicaragua Nicaragua	309[1]	324[1]	360[1]	361	412	536	568	588	*543	*570
Niger Niger	26	31	29[1]	*30[1]	*30[1]	*30[1]	*40[1]	*40[1]	*55[1]	*55[1]
Nigeria Nigéria	1 275	1 573	2 545[1]	2 520[1]	2 700[1]	*2 500[1]	*2 500[1]	*2 400[1]	*2 100[1]	*2 100[1]
Norway Norvège	1 464	1 613	1 690	1 724[1]	1 676[1]	1 827[1]	1 851[1]	*1 870[1]	1 850[1]	1 860[1]
Oman Oman	1 191[19]	1 280[19]	1 206[19]	1 233[19]	1 217[19]	1 990[19]	1 815[19]	1 370[1]	*1 400[1]	1 400[1]
Pakistan[2] Pakistan[2]	8 100	7 913	9 567	9 536	9 364	9 635	9 314	9 674	9 935	10 845
Panama Panama	678[7]	658[7]	651	752	814	976	849[7]	*760[1]	*760[1]	*770[1]

Country or area Pays ou zone	1994	1995	1996	1997	1998	1999	2000	2001	2002	2003
Paraguay Paraguay	529	624	627	603	586	556	516	505	447	505
Peru Pérou	3 177	3 645	3 678	4 092	4 069	3 799	3 684	3 589	4 120	*4 202
Philippines Philippines	9 576	10 566	12 429[1]	14 681	12 888	12 557	11 959	11 378	11 396	10 000[1]
Poland Pologne	13 834	13 914	13 959	15 003	14 970	15 555	15 046	12 074	11 206	11 653
Portugal Portugal	7 756	8 030	8 444	9 395	9 784	10 079	10 343	10 162	9 761	8 567
Puerto Rico Porto Rico	1 356	1 398	1 508	1 586	1 646	1 757	...	...	...	...
Qatar Qatar	470	475	486	584	857	959	1 029	1 209	*1 350[1]	*1 400[1]
Republic of Moldova [20] République de Moldova [20]	39	49	40	122	74	50	222	158	279	255
Réunion Réunion	321	313	229	200	342	263	258	*380[1]	*380[1]	*380[1]
Romania Roumanie	5 998	6 842	6 956	6 553	7 300	6 252	8 411	5 668	5 680	5 992
Russian Federation Fédération de Russie	37 220	36 466	27 791	26 688	26 018	28 529	32 389	35 271	37 706	40 998
Rwanda Rwanda	10	36	42	61	60	66	71[1]	91[1]	101[1]	115[1]
Saudi Arabia Arabie saoudite	17 013	15 772	16 391	15 448	15 776	16 381	18 296	20 963	23 452	23 000[1]
Senegal Sénégal	697	694	810	854	847	1 030	*1 000[1]	*1 000[1]	*2 150[1]	*2 150[1]
Serbia and Montenegro Serbie-et-Monténégro	1 612	1 696	2 212	2 011	2 253	1 575[21]	2 117	2 418	2 396	2 075
Sierra Leone [1] Sierra Leone [1]	...	...	...	...	100	45	73	113	144	170
Singapore [1] Singapour [1]	*3 100	*3 200	*3 300	*3 300	2 340	1 660	1 150	*600	*200	150
Slovakia Slovaquie	2 879	2 981	4 234	5 856	3 066	3 084	3 045	3 123	3 141	3 147
Slovenia Slovénie	1 667	1 807	1 064	1 113	1 149	1 222	1 252[22]	...	...	...
South Africa Afrique du Sud	7 068	7 437	7 664	7 891	7 676	8 211	8 715	8 036[1]	8 525[1]	8 883[1]
Spain Espagne	25 884	27 220	26 339	27 860	27 943 [1,23]	...	...	...	...	...
Sri Lanka Sri Lanka	*925[1]	956	670	966	2 151	2 354	2 432	2 123	973	1 163
Sudan [1] Soudan [1]	*160	391	*380	276	*198	231	146	190	*220	320
Suriname Suriname	18	*60[1]	*60[1]	*65[1]	*65[1]	*60[1]	*60[1]	*65[1]	*65[1]	*65[1]
Sweden Suède	2 138	2 550	2 503	2 272	2 372	2 293	2 613	2 644	2 765	2 545
Switzerland [1] Suisse [1]	*4 370	4 024	3 638	3 568	*3 600	3 548	3 771	3 950	*4 000	3 800
Syrian Arab Republic Rép. arabe syrienne	4 344	4 804	4 817	4 838	5 016	5 134	4 631	5 428	5 399	5 224

Cement — Production: thousand metric tons (*continued*)
Ciment — Production : milliers de tonnes (*suite*)

Country or area Pays ou zone	1994	1995	1996	1997	1998	1999	2000	2001	2002	2003
Tajikistan Tadjikistan	178	78	49	36	18	33	55	69	89	166
Thailand Thaïlande	29 929	34 051	38 749	37 136	22 722	25 354	25 499	27 913	31 679	32 530
TFYR of Macedonia L'ex-R.y. Macédoine	486	523	490	610	461	563	801	630	777	832
Togo [1] Togo [1]	286	350	413	421	500	*600	*700	*800	*800	*800
Trinidad and Tobago Trinité-et-Tobago	583	559	617	677	700	740	743	697	744	750 [1]
Tunisia Tunisie	4 605	4 998	4 566	4 378	4 588	4 864	5 647	5 721	6 020	6 039
Turkey Turquie	29 356	33 153	35 214	36 035	38 175	34 215	36 238	30 111	32 546	35 215
Turkmenistan Turkménistan	690	437	438	601	750	780	420	448	486	200
Uganda Ouganda	45	84	195	290	321	347	367	431	506	505 [1]
Ukraine Ukraine	11 435	7 627	5 021	5 101	5 591	5 828	5 311	5 786	7 157	8 923
United Arab Emirates Emirats arabes unis	4 968 [15]	5 071 [15]	6 000 [1]	6 330 [1]	7 066 [1]	*7 069 [1]	*6 100 [1]	*6 100 [1]	*6 500 [1]	*6 600 [1]
United Kingdom Royaume-Uni	12 307	11 805	12 214	12 638 [1]	12 409 [1]	12 697 [1]	12 452 [1]	11 854 [1]	*12 000 [1]	12 000 [1]
United Rep. of Tanzania Rép.-Unie de Tanzanie	686	739	726	621	778 [1]	833	833	880	1 026	1 186
United States Etats-Unis	77 948	76 906	79 266	82 582	83 931	85 952	87 846	88 900	89 732	92 843
Uruguay Uruguay	701	593	631	818	940	839	688	1 015 [1]	437	446
Uzbekistan Ouzbékistan	4 780	3 419	3 277	3 286	3 358 [24]	3 331 [24]	3 284 [24]	3 722 [24]	*4 000 [1]	*4 000 [1]
Venezuela (Bolivarian Rep. of) Venezuela (Rép. bolivarienne du)	4 562	*6 900	7 556 [1]	8 145 [1]	8 202 [1]	*8 500 [1]	*8 600 [1]	*8 700 [1]	*7 000 [1]	*7 000 [1]
Viet Nam Viet Nam	*4 700 [1]	5 828	6 585	8 019	9 738	*10 489	13 298	16 073	21 121	24 127
Yemen Yémen	898	1 100	1 028	1 038	1 195	1 454	1 406	1 449	1 561	1 541
Zambia Zambie	280 [1]	312 [1]	348 [1]	384 [1]	351 [1]	300 [1]	335	309	343	424
Zimbabwe Zimbabwe	624	948	996	954	1 115	1 105	1 000	549	*600 [1]	*400 [1]

Source

United Nations Statistics Division, New York, the industrial statistics database and *Industrial Commodity Statistics Yearbook 2003*.

Notes

[1] Source: *U. S. Geological Survey* (Washington, D. C.).
[2] Twelve months ending 30 June of the year stated.
[3] Beginning 1997, data are confidential.
[4] Excluding the Federation of Bosnia and Herzegovina.

Source

Organisation des Nations Unies, Division de statistique, New York, la base de données pour les statistiques industrielles et *Annuaire de statistiques industrielles par produit 2003*.

Notes

[1] Source : *U. S. Geological Survey* (Washington, D. C.).
[2] Période de 12 mois finissant le 30 juin de l'année indiquée.
[3] A partir 1997, les données sont confidentielles.
[4] Non compris la Fédération de Bosnie et Herzegovine.

[5] Shipments.

[6] For statistical purposes, the data for China do not include those for the Hong Kong Special Administrative Region (Hong Kong SAR), Macao Special Administrative Region (Macao SAR) and Taiwan Province of China.

[7] Source: United Nations Economic Commission for Latin America and the Caribbean (Santiago).

[8] Sales.

[9] Twelve months ending 7 July of the year stated.

[10] 2003 data are confidential.

[11] Incomplete coverage.

[12] Production by establishments employing 50 or more persons.

[13] Production by establishments employing 10 or more persons.

[14] Official figures communicated directly to the Statistics Division of the United Nations.

[15] Source: Arab Gulf Cooperation Council (Riyadh).

[16] Beginning 2002, data are confidential

[17] Government production only.

[18] Twelve months beginning 16 July of the year stated.

[19] Source: *Bulletin of Industrial Statistics for the Arab Countries*, United Nations Economic and Social Commission for Western Asia (Beirut).

[20] Excluding the Transnistria region.

[21] Beginning 1999, data for Kosovo are not included.

[22] Beginning 2001, data are confidential.

[23] Beginning 1999, data are confidential.

[24] Source: *Country Economic Review*, Asian Development Bank (Manila).

[5] Expéditions.

[6] Pour la présentation des statistiques, les données pour Chine ne comprennent pas la Région Administrative Spéciale de Hong Kong (Hong Kong RAS), la Région Administrative Spéciale de Macao (Macao RAS) et la province de Taiwan.

[7] Source : Commission économique des Nations Unies pour l'Amérique Latine et des Caraïbes (Santiago).

[8] Ventes.

[9] Période de 12 mois finissant le 7 juillet de l'année indiquée.

[10] Pour 2003, les données sont confidentielles.

[11] Couverture incomplète.

[12] Production des établissements occupant 50 personnes ou plus.

[13] Production des établissements occupant 10 personnes ou plus.

[14] Données officielles fournies directement à la Division de statistique des Nations Unies.

[15] Source : Arab Gulf Cooperation Council (Riyadh).

[16] A partir de l'année 2002, les données sont confidentiels.

[17] Production de l'Etat seulement.

[18] Période de 12 mois commençant le 16 juillet de l'année indiquée.

[19] Source : *Bulletin of Industrial Statistics for the Arab Countries*, Commission économique et sociale pour l'Asie occidentale (Beyrouth).

[20] Non compris la région de Transnistria.

[21] A partir de 1999, non compris les données de Kosovo.

[22] A partir de 2001, les données sont confidentielles.

[23] A partir de 1999, les données sont confidentielles.

[24] Source : *La Revue Economique du Pays*, La Banque de Développement Asiatique (Manila).

44

Sulphuric acid
Production: thousand metric tons

Acide sulfurique
Production : milliers de tonnes

Country or area Pays ou zone	1994	1995	1996	1997	1998	1999	2000	2001	2002	2003
Albania Albanie	4	...	0	0	0	0	0	...	...	...
Algeria Algérie	40	45	42	55	45	48	36	22	59	57
Argentina Argentine	204	226	220	...	...	...	...	...	...	...
Australia [1] Australie [1]	833	...	...	...	...	...	...	...	...	...
Azerbaijan Azerbaïdjan	56	24	31	53	24	26	52	10	19	24
Bangladesh [1] Bangladesh [1]	6	5	9	4	4	4	5	4	3	0
Belarus Bélarus	291	437	549	698	640	614	584	534	524	574
Belgium [2] Belgique [2]	717	673	678	668	596	666	721	723	705	623
Bolivia Bolivie	3	*1	...	831	754	620	...	...	...	...
Brazil Brésil	4 112	4 043	4 308	4 638	4 624	4 882	5 221	5 211	5 586	6 047
Bulgaria Bulgarie	428	454	525	556	506	456	644	620	751[3]	...
Canada Canada	4 059	3 844	4 278	*4 100	4 333	4 194	3 804	3 846	3 887	...
Chile Chili	1 174	1 427	1 518	1 864	1 983	2 436	2 363	2 736	2 720	2 866
China [4] Chine [4]	15 365	18 110	18 836	20 369	21 710	23 560	24 270	26 963	30 504	33 712
Colombia Colombie	103	86	...	95	93	92	...	...	...	...
Croatia Croatie	206	233	223	202	164	193	200	126	135	123
Czech Republic République tchèque	337	340	345	333	327	318	274	241	220	293
Denmark Danemark	5[5]	25[5]	19[5]	2[5]	...	0[6]	...	...	...	...
Egypt Egypte	112	133	299	84	82	83	75	...	...	...
Finland Finlande	1 084	1 159	1 288	2 182	2 496	2 857	1 211	914	854	1 035
France France	2 227	2 382[6]	2 263[6]	2 250[6]	2 214[6]	2 177[6]	2 181	2 051	1 930	1 624
Germany Allemagne	2 781[6]	1 387	1 225	1 370	1 601	1 618	1 474	1 504	1 640	1 536
Greece Grèce	623	753	1 544	1 655	814	911	966	515	...	484[2]
Hungary Hongrie	80[7]	114[7]	94[7]	89[7]	62[7]	53[7]	80[7]	...	59	73
India Inde	3 745	4 402	4 988	4 830	5 366	5 686	5 540	5 178	5 988	6 076

Country or area / Pays ou zone	1994	1995	1996	1997	1998	1999	2000	2001	2002	2003
Indonesia / Indonésie	35	35	...	224	314	981	...	...	...	...
Iran (Islamic Rep. of) [8] / Iran (Rép. islamique d') [8]	...	...	...	141	170	144	182	...	...	...
Italy / Italie	1 975	2 161	2 214	2 214	2 013	1 017	1 048	988	1 043	1 058
Japan / Japon	6 594	6 888	6 851	6 828	6 739	6 943	7 059	6 727	6 763	6 534
Jordan [9] / Jordanie [9]	...	...	...	1	2	2	2	1		...
Kazakhstan / Kazakhstan	681	695	653	635	605	685	635	695	710	735
Kenya [9] / Kenya [9]	...	...	...	20	20	20	20	20	20	...
Kuwait [9] / Koweït [9]	5	10	10	10	10	10	100	150	150	150
Lebanon [9] / Liban [9]	...	...	...	174	262	249	400	400	480	...
Lithuania / Lituanie	212	344	425	504	619	800	809	465	874	1 002
Mexico / Mexique	375	...	...	...	...	...	...	...	...	...
Netherlands / Pays-Bas	...	500[6]	418[6]	356[6]	429[6]	485[10]	...	...	...	...
Pakistan [1] / Pakistan [1]	102	80	69	31	28	27	58	57	59	56
Peru / Pérou	215	216	429	411	541	592	594	*623	574	*633
Poland / Pologne	1 452	1 861	1 761	1 741	1 707	1 505	1 948	1 845	1 861	1 980
Portugal [6] / Portugal [6]	2	3	10	11	15	16[10]	...	...	...	...
Romania / Roumanie	491	477	422	329	229	234	181	58	58	21
Russian Federation / Fédération de Russie	6 334	6 946	5 764	6 247	5 840	7 148	8 258	8 209	8 458	8 759
Serbia and Montenegro / Serbie-et-Monténégro	24	87	231	177	211	30[11]	98	68	74	25
Slovakia / Slovaquie	...	...	62[6]	73	68	16	15	36	37[3]	...
Slovenia / Slovénie	123	116	103	109	128	126	133[12]	...	...	...
Spain / Espagne	1 375	2 847	2 265	2 817	3 896[6,13]	...	...	...	...	...
Sweden / Suède	487	507	572[6]	566	383	415	359	363	255	391
Syrian Arab Republic [9] / Rép. arabe syrienne [9]	...	...	...	214	256	193	318	320	344	...
TFYR of Macedonia / L'ex-R.y. Macédoine	72	82	99	105	101	88	109	101	95	45
Tunisia / Tunisie	4 161	4 239	4 423	4 256	4 657	4 858	...	...	...	...
Turkey / Turquie	730	765	798[6]	947	913	828	678	576	630	...

Country or area Pays ou zone	1994	1995	1996	1997	1998	1999	2000	2001	2002	2003
Turkmenistan Turkménistan	70	76	120	31	47	104	93	64	122	...
Ukraine Ukraine	1 646	1 593	1 577	1 438	1 354	1 393	1 036	1 040	935	1 131
United Kingdom Royaume-Uni	1 266	1 293	643[6]	698	716	908	581	485	844	...
United States Etats-Unis	11 300[14]	11 500[14]	10 900[14]	10 700[14]	10 600[14]	1 320[15]	1 030[15]	982[15]	772[15]	683[15]
Uzbekistan Ouzbékistan	805	1 016	984	870	856[16]	897[16]	823[16]	...	...	...
Viet Nam Viet Nam	...	10	18	15	23	*24	36	36	40	45

Source

United Nations Statistics Division, New York, the industrial statistics database and *Industrial Commodity Statistics Yearbook 2003.*

Notes

[1] Twelve months ending 30 June of the year stated.

[2] Incomplete coverage.

[3] 2003 data are confidential.

[4] For statistical purposes, the data for China do not include those for the Hong Kong Special Administrative Region (Hong Kong SAR), Macao Special Administrative Region (Macao SAR) and Taiwan Province of China.

[5] Sales.

[6] Source : United Nations Economic Commission for Europe (Geneva).

[7] Including regenerated sulphuric acid.

[8] Production by establishments employing 10 or more persons.

[9] Source: *U. S. Geological Survey* (Washington, D. C.).

[10] Beginning 2000, data are confidential.

[11] Beginning 1999, data for Kosovo are not included.

[12] Beginning 2001, data are confidential.

[13] Beginning 1999, data are confidential.

[14] Sold or used by producers.

[15] Recovered as by-product from smelters.

[16] Source: *Statistical Yearbook for Asia and the Pacific*, United Nations Economic and Social Council for Asia and the Pacific (Bangkok).

Source

Organisation des Nations Unies, Division de statistique, New York, la base de données pour les statistiques industrielles et *Annuaire de statistiques industrielles par produit 2003.*

Notes

[1] Période de 12 mois finissant le 30 juin de l'année indiquée.

[2] Couverture incomplète.

[3] Pour 2003, les données sont confidentielles.

[4] Pour la présentation des statistiques, les données pour Chine ne comprennent pas la Région Administrative Spéciale de Hong Kong (Hong Kong RAS), la Région Administrative Spéciale de Macao (Macao RAS) et la province de Taiwan.

[5] Ventes.

[6] Source : Commission économique des Nations Unies pour l'Europe (Genève).

[7] Y compris l'acide sulfurique régénéré.

[8] Production des établissements occupant 10 personnes ou plus.

[9] Source : *U. S. Geological Survey* (Washington, D. C.).

[10] A partir de 2000, les données sont confidentielles.

[11] A partir de 1999, non compris les données de Kosovo.

[12] A partir de 2001, les données sont confidentielles.

[13] A partir de 1999, les données sont confidentielles.

[14] Vendu ou utilisé par les producteurs.

[15] Obtenus à partir des sous-produits des fonderies.

[16] Source : *Statistical Yearbook for Asia and the Pacific*, Commission économique et sociale pour l'Asie et le Pacifique (Bangkok).

45

Pig iron and crude steel
Production : thousand metric tons

Fonte et acier brut
Production : milliers de tonnes

Country or area	1996	1997	1998	1999	2000	2001	2002	2003	Pays ou zone
Albania									**Albanie**
Crude steel, ingots [1]	22	22	22	16	65	72	81	86	Acier brut (lingots) [1]
Pig iron, steel-making * [2]	10	10	10	10	10	10	...	...	Fonte d'affinage * [2]
Algeria									**Algérie**
Crude steel, ingots	590[1]	361[1]	581[1]	675[1]	689[1]	861[1]	991	964	Acier brut (lingots)
Pig iron, steel-making	850[3]	526[3]	757[3]	807[3]	762[3]	895[3]	959	1 026	Fonte d'affinage
Angola * [2]									**Angola * [2]**
Crude steel, ingots	9	9	9	9	9	9	...	...	Acier brut (lingots)
Argentina									**Argentine**
Crude steel, castings [4]	11	...	...	...	7	5	5	5	Acier brut pour moulages [4]
Crude steel, ingots	4 069[1]	4 157[1]	4 210[1]	3 797[1]	4 472[1]	4 100[1,4]	4 363	5 030[1,4]	Acier brut (lingots)
Pig iron, steel-making [3,4]	1 966	2 080	2 122	1 984	2 188	1 917	2 180	2 404	Fonte d'affinage [3,4]
Australia									**Australie**
Crude steel, ingots [1]	7 944[5]	8 088[5]	8 356[5]	7 678[5]	6 742[5]	7 033[4]	7 527[4]	7 544[4]	Acier brut (lingots) [1]
Pig iron, steel-making	7 554[3,5]	7 545[3,5]	7 928[3,5]	7 047	7 049	6 017	6 106	6 116	Fonte d'affinage
Austria									**Autriche**
Crude steel, castings *	3 359	3 831	3 858[7]	...	...	...	...	...	Acier brut pour moulages *
Crude steel, ingots	1 083	1 350	1 425	1 406	1 417	1 539	1 447	1 191	Acier brut (lingots)
Pig iron, steel-making [2]	3 416	3 965	4 022[7]	...	...	...	...	...	Fonte d'affinage [2]
Azerbaijan									**Azerbaïdjan**
Crude steel, castings	3	25	8	0	0	0	0	1	Acier brut pour moulages
Crude steel, ingots	0	0	0	0	...	2	0	0	Acier brut (lingots)
Bahrain [8]									**Bahreïn [8]**
Pig iron, foundry	...	4 000	4 000	...	...	...	...	...	Fonte de moulage
Bangladesh									**Bangladesh**
Crude steel, ingots	27[5]	23[5]	35[2]	36[2]	*35[2]	35[2]	35	...	Acier brut (lingots)
Belarus									**Bélarus**
Crude steel, castings	91	110	111	114	121	125	123	121	Acier brut pour moulages
Crude steel, ingots	795	1 110	1 300	1 335	1 502	1 487	1 484	1 573	Acier brut (lingots)
Belgium									**Belgique**
Crude steel, castings [4]	66	21	21	21	21	20	21	21	Acier brut pour moulages [4]
Crude steel, ingots	10 752[1]	10 728[1]	11 400[1]	10 908[1]	11 592[1]	10 740[1]	11 316[1]	11 113[1]	Acier brut (lingots)
Pig iron, steel-making	8 628	8 076	8 616	8 436	8 472	7 728	7 992	7 813[3,4]	Fonte d'affinage
Bosnia and Herzegovina									**Bosnie-Herzégovine**
Crude steel, ingots	52	77	88	61	77[4]	84[4]	70[4]	103	Acier brut (lingots)
Pig iron, steel-making	*100[2]	*100[2]	*100[2]	*100[2]	*100[2]	*100[2]	...	28	Fonte d'affinage
Brazil									**Brésil**
Crude steel, castings	11	15	16	21	22	26	32	31	Acier brut pour moulages
Crude steel, ingots	25 226	26 138	25 744	24 975	27 843	26 691	29 572	31 116	Acier brut (lingots)
Pig iron, steel-making [3]	23 978	25 013	25 111	24 549	27 723	27 391	29 694	32 039	Fonte d'affinage [3]
Bulgaria									**Bulgarie**
Crude steel, castings [4]	21	22	...	...	...	...	...	...	Acier brut pour moulages [4]
Crude steel, ingots	2 457[1]	2 628[1]	2 242[4]	1 889[4]	2 022[4]	1 972[4]	1 860[4]	2 317[4]	Acier brut (lingots)
Pig iron, foundry	23	30	...	...	...	...	...	...	Fonte de moulage
Pig iron, steel-making	1 481	1 613	1 390[3,4]	1 152[3,4]	1 220[3,4]	1 211[3,4]	1 072[3,4]	1 386[3,4]	Fonte d'affinage
Canada									**Canada**
Crude steel, castings [4]	98	95	97	99	98	97	95	98	Acier brut pour moulages [4]
Crude steel, ingots [4]	14 637	15 458	15 833	16 136	16 496	15 179	15 907	15 829	Acier brut (lingots) [4]
Pig iron, steel-making [3]	8 638[4]	9 567[4]	8 937[4]	8 857[4]	8 904	8 302	8 670[4]	8 554[4]	Fonte d'affinage [3]
Chile [4]									**Chili [4]**
Crude steel, castings	0	0	0	18	0	...	...	...	Acier brut pour moulages
Crude steel, ingots	1 178	1 168	1 171	1 272	1 352	1 250	1 280	1 380	Acier brut (lingots)
Pig iron, steel-making	996	941	993	1 030	1 024	927	964	988	Fonte d'affinage
China [9]									**Chine [9]**
Crude steel, castings [4]	2 110	1 840	1 349	1 222	1 199	1 310	1 420	1 654	Acier brut pour moulages [4]
Crude steel, ingots	100 056[1]	108 942[1]	115 590[1]	124 260	128 500	151 634	182 366	222 336	Acier brut (lingots)
Pig iron, steel-making	107 225	115 114	118 629	125 392	131 015	155 543	170 846	213 667	Fonte d'affinage

Country or area	1996	1997	1998	1999	2000	2001	2002	2003	Pays ou zone
China, Hong Kong SAR * [4]									Chine, Hong Kong RAS * [4]
Crude steel, ingots	100	...	...	...	...	...	...	...	Acier brut (lingots)
Colombia [4]									Colombie [4]
Crude steel, castings	5	4	3	2	1	...	...	...	Acier brut pour moulages
Crude steel, ingots	689	731	633	533	658	640	670	670	Acier brut (lingots)
Pig iron, steel-making [3]	286	324	256	264	285	319	311	283	Fonte d'affinage [3]
Croatia									Croatie
Crude steel, castings	1 [4]	1	1	1	1	2	1	0	Acier brut pour moulages
Crude steel, ingots	46	69	100	75	68	54	0	0	Acier brut (lingots)
Cuba									Cuba
Crude steel, ingots	229	335	283	303	327	270 [4]	268 [4]	210 [4]	Acier brut (lingots)
Czech Republic									République tchèque
Crude steel, castings [4]	276	217	219	236	168	146	163	149	Acier brut pour moulages [4]
Crude steel, ingots	6 519 [1]	6 593 [1]	6 059 [1]	5 453 [1]	2 613	2 430	2 333	6 634 [4]	Acier brut (lingots)
Pig iron, steel-making	4 898 [3]	5 276 [3]	5 165 [3]	4 137 [3]	4 603 [3]	4 651	4 819	5 181	Fonte d'affinage
Dem. Rep. of the Congo * [4]									Rép. dém. du Congo * [4]
Crude steel, ingots	30	30	30	30	30	30	30	30	Acier brut (lingots)
Denmark [10]									Danemark [10]
Crude steel, ingots	4	3	4	4	5	5	5	4	Acier brut (lingots)
Dominican Republic [4]									Rép. dominicaine [4]
Crude steel, ingots	36	43	39	...	...	...	...	...	Acier brut (lingots)
Ecuador [4]									Equateur [4]
Crude steel, ingots	20	44	46	53	65	61	67	80	Acier brut (lingots)
Egypt [4]									Egypte [4]
Crude steel, castings	30	25	50	50	...	...	...	...	Acier brut pour moulages
Crude steel, ingots	2 580	2 700	2 820	2 580	2 840	3 800	4 315	4 400	Acier brut (lingots)
Pig iron, foundry [11]	1 235	1 514	1 357	1 020	990	1 160	1 100	*1 080	Fonte de moulage [11]
El Salvador [1,4]									El Salvador [1,4]
Crude steel, ingots	41	45	43	34	41	39	49	57	Acier brut (lingots)
Estonia [4]									Estonie [4]
Crude steel, castings	3	3	2	1	1	...	...	1	Acier brut pour moulages
Crude steel, ingots	...	...	...	...	...	1 [1]	1 [1]	...	Acier brut (lingots)
Finland									Finlande
Crude steel, castings	20	23	23 [4]	19 [4]	22 [4]	23 [4]	22 [4]	22 [4]	Acier brut pour moulages
Crude steel, ingots	3 281	3 711	3 929 [4]	3 937 [4]	4 075 [4]	3 916 [4]	3 981 [4]	4 744 [4]	Acier brut (lingots)
Pig iron, steel-making	2 457	2 784	2 916	2 954 [3,4]	2 983 [3,4]	2 852 [3,4]	8 178	3 092 [3,4]	Fonte d'affinage
France									France
Crude steel, castings	220	224	225	223	216 [4]	210 [4]	3 [4]	2 [4]	Acier brut pour moulages
Crude steel, ingots	17 413	19 543	19 901	19 977	20 738 [4]	19 133 [4]	20 255 [4]	19 756 [4]	Acier brut (lingots)
Pig iron, foundry	561	646	710	896 [6]	672	600	624	708	Fonte de moulage
Pig iron, steel-making	11 547	12 778	12 892	12 956	13 916 [3,4]	12 270	12 600	12 036	Fonte d'affinage
Georgia									Géorgie
Crude steel, castings	82	1	0	0 [12]	...	...	...	...	Acier brut pour moulages
Crude steel, ingots	83	103	56	7	...	...	...	...	Acier brut (lingots)
Pig iron, foundry	2	3	1	1	0	3	3	1	Fonte de moulage
Pig iron, steel-making	2	1	0	...	0	...	...	...	Fonte d'affinage
Germany									Allemagne
Crude steel, castings [4]	296	295	324	296	300	323	309	310	Acier brut pour moulages [4]
Crude steel, ingots	39 496 [6]	10 296	9 895	9 585	9 880	10 289	#44 706 [4]	44 499 [4]	Acier brut (lingots)
Pig iron, foundry [6]	168	183	190	580	...	...	...	...	Fonte de moulage [6]
Pig iron, steel-making	27 172 [6]	30 279 [6]	29 515 [6]	27 354 [3,6]	30 845 [3,4]	29 184 [3,4]	29 427 [3,4]	29 481 [3,4]	Fonte d'affinage
Ghana [4]									Ghana [4]
Crude steel, ingots	26	25	25	25	25	25	25	*25	Acier brut (lingots)
Greece									Grèce
Crude steel, ingots	852 [1]	1 020 [1]	1 104 [1]	960 [1]	1 088 [4]	1 281 [4]	1 835 [4]	1 701 [4]	Acier brut (lingots)
Guatemala [4]									Guatemala [4]
Crude steel, ingots	...	...	...	...	167	202	216	226	Acier brut (lingots)
Hungary									Hongrie
Crude steel, castings	7	...	...	...	...	...	...	...	Acier brut pour moulages
Crude steel, ingots	2 060 [13]	1 819 [13]	1 940	1 920	1 970	2 065	2 138	2 045	Acier brut (lingots)
Pig iron, steel-making	1 496 [3,4]	1 140 [3,4]	1 259 [3,4]	1 310 [3,4]	1 340 [3,4]	1 226	1 335	1 333 [3,4]	Fonte d'affinage

Country or area	1996	1997	1998	1999	2000	2001	2002	2003	Pays ou zone
India									**Inde**
Crude steel, castings	467	438	419	435	398	454	528	459	Acier brut pour moulages
Crude steel, ingots	12 972	12 978	23 463[4]	24 275[4]	26 900[4]	27 270[4]	28 800[4]	31 760[4]	Acier brut (lingots)
Pig iron, foundry	3 304	3 427	2 976	3 201	3 105	3 886	5 059	5 197	Fonte de moulage
Pig iron, steel-making [3,4]	20 453	21 096	20 194	20 139	21 321	21 875	24 315	26 550	Fonte d'affinage [3,4]
Indonesia [4]									**Indonésie** [4]
Crude steel, ingots	4 109	3 816	2 699	2 891	2 848	2 781	2 462	2 042	Acier brut (lingots)
Iran (Islamic Rep. of) [4]									**Iran (Rép. islamique d')** [4]
Crude steel, ingots	5 415	6 322	5 602	6 070	6 600	6 916	7 321	7 869	Acier brut (lingots)
Pig iron, steel-making [3]	1 852	2 150	2 117	2 112	2 202	2 183	2 182	2 231	Fonte d'affinage [3]
Iraq [2]									**Iraq** [2]
Crude steel, ingots	*300	*200	*200	*200	50	50	...	...	Acier brut (lingots)
Ireland									**Irlande**
Crude steel, ingots	336[1]	337[4]	358[4]	335[4,12]	...	...	...	...	Acier brut (lingots)
Israel [4]									**Israël** [4]
Crude steel, ingots	265	270	280	280	280	280	280	*280	Acier brut (lingots)
Italy									**Italie**
Crude steel, castings	106	101	137	139	137	137	137	136	Acier brut pour moulages
Crude steel, ingots	24 285	25 769	25 645	24 641	26 623	26 526	26 302	26 696	Acier brut (lingots)
Pig iron, foundry	214	245	275	165	168	298	102	144	Fonte de moulage
Pig iron, steel-making	10 107	11 232	10 516	10 664	11 007	10 263	9 775	10 149	Fonte d'affinage
Japan									**Japon**
Crude steel, castings	594	580	461	415	426	419	369	374	Acier brut pour moulages
Crude steel, ingots	98 207	103 965	93 087	93 777	106 018	102 447	107 376	110 136	Acier brut (lingots)
Pig iron, foundry	900	849	702	603	514	523	466	605	Fonte de moulage
Pig iron, steel-making	73 697	77 671	74 279	73 917	80 557	78 313	80 513	81 486	Fonte d'affinage
Jordan									**Jordanie**
Crude steel, castings [2]	...	30	30	30	30	30	...	...	Acier brut pour moulages [2]
Crude steel, ingots [4]	30	30	30	30	30	30	134	*135	Acier brut (lingots) [4]
Kazakhstan									**Kazakhstan**
Crude steel, castings	81	3 880	3 116	4 105	4 799	4 691	4 866	5 069	Acier brut pour moulages
Crude steel, ingots	3 135	3 816	3 116	4 105	4 150	4 135	4 240	4 316	Acier brut (lingots)
Pig iron, foundry	2 536	3 089	2 594	3 438	4 010	3 907	4 009	4 138	Fonte de moulage
Kenya [4]									**Kenya** [4]
Crude steel, ingots	20	20	20	20	20	20	20	*20	Acier brut (lingots)
Korea, Dem. P. R.									**Corée, R. p. dém. de**
Crude steel, ingots [2]	*1 500[1]	*1 000[1]	*1 000[1]	*1 000[1]	*1 000[1]	1 000	...	...	Acier brut (lingots) [2]
Pig iron, steel-making [3,4]	500	500	250	250	250	250	250	*250	Fonte d'affinage [3,4]
Korea, Republic of									**Corée, République de**
Crude steel, castings [4]	139	124	119	117	119	122	122	147	Acier brut pour moulages [4]
Crude steel, ingots	39 643[1]	43 405[1]	40 299[1]	41 502[1]	43 423[1]	44 199[1]	45 482[1]	46 561	Acier brut (lingots)
Pig iron, steel-making	23 010[3]	22 712[3]	23 093[3]	23 328[3]	24 943[3]	26 182[3]	26 879[3]	27 468	Fonte d'affinage
Latvia									**Lettonie**
Crude steel, castings	3	3	2	2[4]	...	2[4]	2[4]	2[4]	Acier brut pour moulages
Crude steel, ingots	290	462	469	480[4]	496[4]	513[4]	518[4]	518[4]	Acier brut (lingots)
Libyan Arab Jamah. [4]									**Jamah. arabe libyenne** [4]
Crude steel, ingots	863	897	874	966	1 055	846	886	1 007	Acier brut (lingots)
Lithuania									**Lituanie**
Crude steel, castings	0	1	1	1	0	0	0	0	Acier brut pour moulages
Crude steel, ingots [1]	1[13]	1[13]	1[13]	0[14]	0[14]	...	...	...	Acier brut (lingots) [1]
Luxembourg									**Luxembourg**
Crude steel, ingots	2 501	2 580	2 477	2 600	2 571	2 725	2 719[4]	2 670	Acier brut (lingots)
Pig iron, steel-making	829	438	0	0	0	0	...	...	Fonte d'affinage
Malaysia [4]									**Malaisie** [4]
Crude steel, ingots	3 216	2 962	1 903	2 770	3 650	4 100	4 722	3 960	Acier brut (lingots)
Mauritania [4]									**Mauritanie** [4]
Crude steel, castings	5	5	5	5	5	5	5	*5	Acier brut pour moulages
Mexico									**Mexique**
Crude steel, castings [4]	20	16	13	6	5	3	2	1	Acier brut pour moulages [4]
Crude steel, ingots	9 852[1]	10 560[1]	10 812	...	...	13 297[1,4]	14 009[4]	15 178[4]	Acier brut (lingots)
Pig iron, foundry	...	6 174	6 272	6 803	6 713	5 262	5 943	6 747	Fonte de moulage
Pig iron, steel-making [3]	4 230	4 450	4 532	4 822[4]	4 856[4]	4 373[4]	3 996[4]	4 183[4]	Fonte d'affinage [3]

Pig iron and crude steel—Production : thousand metric tons (*continued*)

Fonte et acier brut—Production : milliers de tonnes (*suite*)

Country or area	1996	1997	1998	1999	2000	2001	2002	2003	Pays ou zone
Mongolia [2]									**Mongolie** [2]
Crude steel, castings	...	...	16	13	13	10	16	...	Acier brut pour moulages
Morocco [4]									**Maroc** [4]
Crude steel, castings	5	5	5	5	5	5	5	*5	Acier brut pour moulages
Pig iron, steel-making [3]	15	15	15	15	15	15	15	*15	Fonte d'affinage [3]
Myanmar									**Myanmar**
Crude steel, ingots * [4]	25	25	25	25	25	25	25	25	Acier brut (lingots) * [4]
Pig iron, steel-making [2]	1	0	2	2	2	2	2	...	Fonte d'affinage [2]
Netherlands									**Pays-Bas**
Crude steel, ingots	6 326	6 641	6 377	6 075	5 666 [4]	6 037 [4]	6 118 [4]	6 572 [4]	Acier brut (lingots)
Pig iron, steel-making	5 544 [15]	5 805 [15]	5 562 [15]	5 320	4 969	5 305 [3,4]	5 367 [3,4]	5 846 [3,4]	Fonte d'affinage
New Zealand [4]									**Nouvelle-Zélande** [4]
Crude steel, ingots	808	758	756	775	702	826	765	853	Acier brut (lingots)
Pig iron, steel-making [3]	619	534	609	620	603	646	617	700	Fonte d'affinage [3]
Nigeria [4]									**Nigéria** [4]
Crude steel, ingots	12	...	...	...				...	Acier brut (lingots)
Norway [4]									**Norvège** [4]
Crude steel, castings	6	7	4	4	4	5	4	4	Acier brut pour moulages
Crude steel, ingots	505	578	633	606	675	635	694	699	Acier brut (lingots)
Pig iron, steel-making [3]	70	70	70	70	70	70	108	*110	Fonte d'affinage [3]
Pakistan									**Pakistan**
Crude steel, castings [16]	416 [2]	479 [2]	494 [2]	*500 [2]	*500 [2]	*1 094 [4]	*970 [4]	...	Acier brut pour moulages [16]
Pig iron, steel-making	1 002 [17]	1 069 [17]	1 016	989	1 107	1 071	1 043	1 140	Fonte d'affinage
Paraguay									**Paraguay**
Crude steel, ingots [4]	96	66	56	56	77	71	80	91	Acier brut (lingots) [4]
Pig iron, steel-making	104 [2]	79 [2]	66 [2]	61 [2]	43	39	44	50	Fonte d'affinage
Peru [4]									**Pérou** [4]
Crude steel, castings	5	27	5	47	7	5	5	*5	Acier brut pour moulages
Crude steel, ingots	573	580	625	512	744	685	605	665	Acier brut (lingots)
Pig iron, steel-making [3]	273	264	283	197	327	316	240	226	Fonte d'affinage [3]
Philippines [4]									**Philippines** [4]
Crude steel, castings	290	200	100	80	...	75	83	75	Acier brut pour moulages
Crude steel, ingots	630	780	780	450	426	425	467	425	Acier brut (lingots)
Poland									**Pologne**
Crude steel, castings [4]	234	382	310	300	300	100	100	100	Acier brut pour moulages [4]
Crude steel, ingots	12 274 [4]	11 210	9 605 [4]	8 548 [4]	10 200 [4]	8 710 [4]	8 270 [4]	9 010 [4]	Acier brut (lingots)
Pig iron, foundry	219	263	288	197	246	97	52	47	Fonte de moulage
Pig iron, steel-making	6 321	7 032	5 841	5 036	6 245	5 343	5 245	5 585	Fonte d'affinage
Portugal									**Portugal**
Crude steel, castings [4]	30	25	29	26	33	23	24	20	Acier brut pour moulages [4]
Crude steel, ingots [4]	840	879	907	1 012	1 055	705 [18]	...	...	Acier brut (lingots) [4]
Pig iron, steel-making	420	431 [3,4]	387 [3,4]	389 [3,4]	379 [3,4]	82 [3,4]	...	...	Fonte d'affinage
Qatar									**Qatar**
Crude steel, castings	...	...	...	...	...	714	...	...	Acier brut pour moulages
Crude steel, ingots [4]	616	608	637	629	729	891	1 027	1 055	Acier brut (lingots) [4]
Pig iron, steel-making [8]	...	593	597	...	...	...	...	...	Fonte d'affinage [8]
Republic of Moldova [19]									**République de Moldova** [19]
Crude steel, ingots [4]	646	811	735	790	902	960	510	845	Acier brut (lingots) [4]
Romania									**Roumanie**
Crude steel, castings	133	115	69	39	70	...	...	5 692	Acier brut pour moulages
Crude steel, ingots	6 083	6 675	6 336	4 392	4 672	4 936	5 490	. 496	Acier brut (lingots)
Pig iron, foundry	187	167	145	69	47	31	15	24	Fonte de moulage
Pig iron, steel-making	3 838	4 390	4 396	2 900	3 019	3 212	3 964	4 075	Fonte d'affinage
Russian Federation									**Fédération de Russie**
Crude steel, castings	2 625	2 758	2 459	3 125	3 633	3 718	3 755	5 089	Acier brut pour moulages
Crude steel, ingots	46 628	45 744	41 214	48 392	55 517	55 312	56 128	57 750	Acier brut (lingots)
Pig iron, foundry	793	890	1 061	1 032	1 140	1 306	1 415	1 458	Fonte de moulage
Pig iron, steel-making	36 286	36 387	33 521	39 663	43 352	43 634	45 199	47 249	Fonte d'affinage
Saudi Arabia [4]									**Arabie saoudite** [4]
Crude steel, ingots	2 683	2 539	2 356	2 610	2 981	3 413	3 570	3 944	Acier brut (lingots)

Country or area	1996	1997	1998	1999	2000	2001	2002	2003	Pays ou zone
Serbia and Montenegro									Serbie-et-Monténégro
Crude steel, castings	8	7	7	4[20]	5	4	4	...	Acier brut pour moulages
Crude steel, ingots	37	39	38	25[20]	21	22	17	...	Acier brut (lingots)
Pig iron, steel-making	565	907[6]	792	135[20]	563	461	485	635	Fonte d'affinage
Singapore [4]									Singapour [4]
Crude steel, ingots	531	383	499	590	603	456	460	561	Acier brut (lingots)
Slovakia									Slovaquie
Crude steel, castings	...	...	3 179	3 419	3 520	3 753	4 103[21]	...	Acier brut pour moulages
Crude steel, ingots	253	255	36	16	17	17	11[21]	...	Acier brut (lingots)
Pig iron, steel-making	2 928	3 072[6]	2 756[6]	2 897[6]	3 166	3 255[3,4]	3 533	3 892[3,4]	Fonte d'affinage
Slovenia									Slovénie
Crude steel, castings	4	2	3	3	3[22]	...	...	...	Acier brut pour moulages
Crude steel, ingots	90	97	95	76	92	462[4]	89[4,21]	...	Acier brut (lingots)
South Africa [4]									Afrique du Sud [4]
Crude steel, castings	90	81	79	90	81	97	87	96	Acier brut pour moulages
Crude steel, ingots	7 909	8 230	7 427	7 766	8 399	8 724	9 008	9 384	Acier brut (lingots)
Pig iron, steel-making [3]	6 014	6 192	6 893	6 005	6 292	5 820	5 823	6 234	Fonte d'affinage [3]
Spain									Espagne
Crude steel, castings [4]	125	125	129	129	133	142	150	150	Acier brut pour moulages [4]
Crude steel, ingots [4]	12 029	13 558	14 698	14 753	15 741	16 362	16 260	16 320	Acier brut (lingots) [4]
Pig iron, steel-making [4]	4 127	3 927	4 236	4 058	4 059	4 219	4 021	3 645	Fonte d'affinage [4]
Sri Lanka * [1,4]									Sri Lanka * [1,4]
Crude steel, ingots	30	30	30	30	30	30	30	30	Acier brut (lingots)
Sweden									Suède
Crude steel, castings [4]	28	31	29	28	28	30	33	29	Acier brut pour moulages [4]
Crude steel, ingots	4 880	5 117	5 143	5 038[4]	3 566	5 518[4]	4 180	3 985	Acier brut (lingots)
Pig iron, steel-making [3]	1 223	1 317	1 272	1 281	1 411	1 433	1 452	3 710[4]	Fonte d'affinage [3]
Switzerland [4]									Suisse [4]
Crude steel, ingots	700	789	800	800	1 000	1 000	1 000	*1 000	Acier brut (lingots)
Pig iron, foundry * [11]	100	100	80	80	80	80	80	82	Fonte de moulage * [11]
Syrian Arab Republic [1,4]									Rép. arabe syrienne [1,4]
Crude steel, ingots	70	70	70	70	70	70	70	*70	Acier brut (lingots)
Thailand									Thaïlande
Crude steel, castings [4]	...	...	...	...	0	...	...	...	Acier brut pour moulages [4]
Crude steel, ingots	2 143[4]	2 101	1 619	1 474	1 650	1 710	2 538[4]	3 572[4]	Acier brut (lingots)
TFYR of Macedonia									L'ex-R.y. Macédoine
Crude steel, castings	...	...	...	...	...	228	232	296	Acier brut pour moulages
Crude steel, ingots	21	27	45	47	*161	218	225	291	Acier brut (lingots)
Pig iron, steel-making * [2]	20	...	...	...	...	...	...	...	Fonte d'affinage * [2]
Trinidad and Tobago [1,4]									Trinité-et-Tobago [1,4]
Crude steel, ingots	695	736	777	726	741	668	817	903	Acier brut (lingots)
Tunisia									Tunisie
Crude steel, castings	186	195	171	231	237	239	201	86	Acier brut pour moulages
Pig iron, foundry	145	152	123	180	195	192	152	36	Fonte de moulage
Turkey									Turquie
Crude steel, castings	4 505	4 717	4 431	4 449	4 374	4 561	4 461	4 884	Acier brut pour moulages
Crude steel, ingots	12 684	13 078	12 571	12 372	12 677	12 260	11 475	12 455	Acier brut (lingots)
Pig iron, foundry	363	337	171	192	250	237	157	149	Fonte de moulage
Pig iron, steel-making [3,4]	5 253	5 565	5 286	5 181	5 333	5 289	5 003	5 706	Fonte d'affinage [3,4]
Uganda									Ouganda
Crude steel, castings * [4]	30	30	30	30	30	30	30	30	Acier brut pour moulages * [4]
Crude steel, ingots [2]	*12[1]	*7[1]	*7[1]	*8[1]	*7[1]	7	...	...	Acier brut (lingots) [2]
Ukraine									Ukraine
Crude steel, castings	385	343	342	320	482	500	872	1 514	Acier brut pour moulages
Crude steel, ingots	22 333	25 629	24 447	27 393	31 782	33 523	34 546	37 524	Acier brut (lingots)
Pig iron, foundry	278	444	302	305	353	157	131	184	Fonte de moulage
Pig iron, steel-making	17 832	20 616	20 937	23 010	25 699	26 379	27 633	29 529	Fonte d'affinage
United Arab Emirates [4]									Emirats arabes unis [4]
Crude steel, ingots	90	90	90	90	90	90	90	90	Acier brut (lingots)

Pig iron and crude steel — Production : thousand metric tons (*continued*)

Fonte et acier brut — Production : milliers de tonnes (*suite*)

Country or area	1996	1997	1998	1999	2000	2001	2002	2003	Pays ou zone
United Kingdom									Royaume-Uni
Crude steel, castings	188	186	185	128	146 [4]	150 [4]	147 [4]	148 [4]	Acier brut pour moulages
Crude steel, ingots	17 804	18 313	17 130	16 156	15 009 [4]	13 393 [4]	11 520 [4]	13 120 [4]	Acier brut (lingots)
Pig iron, steel-making	12 830	13 056	12 746	12 139	10 890 [3,4]	9 870 [3,4]	8 561 [3,4]	10 228 [3,4]	Fonte d'affinage
United States									Etats-Unis
Crude steel, castings [4]	34	34	26	21	21	18	...	2	Acier brut pour moulages [4]
Crude steel, ingots [1]	95 500	98 500	98 600	97 400	102 000	90 100	91 600	93 700	Acier brut (lingots) [1]
Pig iron, steel-making [3]	49 400	49 600	48 200	46 300	47 900	42 100	40 200	40 600	Fonte d'affinage [3]
Uruguay [4]									Uruguay [4]
Crude steel, ingots	34	39	52	45	38	31	34	41	Acier brut (lingots)
Uzbekistan [4]									Ouzbékistan [4]
Crude steel, ingots	444	365	344	340	403	429	446	495	Acier brut (lingots)
Venezuela (Bolivarian Rep. of) [4]									Venezuela (Rép. bolivar. du) [4]
Crude steel, ingots	3 956	3 987	3 553	3 261	3 835	3 813	4 164	3 930	Acier brut (lingots)
Viet Nam									Viet Nam
Crude steel, castings [4]	0	3	1	0	0	0	0	1	Acier brut pour moulages [4]
Crude steel, ingots	311 [4]	*330	306 [4]	308 [4]	109	318 [4]	409 [4]	543 [4]	Acier brut (lingots)
Pig iron, steel-making [3,4]	52	41	48	66	47	48	146	200	Fonte d'affinage [3,4]
Zimbabwe [4]									Zimbabwe [4]
Crude steel, ingots	210	215	210	255	260	149	105	152	Acier brut (lingots)
Pig iron, steel-making [3]	219	216	217	270	277	156	122	185	Fonte d'affinage [3]

Source

United Nations Statistics Division, New York, the industrial statistics database and *Industrial Commodity Statistics Yearbook 2003*.

Notes

[1] Including crude steel for casting.

[2] Source: *U. S. Geological Survey* (Washington, D. C.).

[3] Including foundry pig iron.

[4] Source: International Iron and Steel Institute (Brussels).

[5] Twelve months ending 30 June of the year stated.

[6] Source: *Annual Bulletin of Steel Statistics for Europe, America and Asia*, United Nations Economic Commission for Europe (Geneva).

[7] Beginning 1999, data are confidential.

[8] Source: Organisation of the Islamic Conference (Jeddah, Saudi Arabia).

[9] For statistical purposes, the data for China do not include those for the Hong Kong Special Administrative Region (Hong Kong SAR), Macao Special Administrative Region (Macao SAR) and Taiwan Province of China.

[10] Sales.

[11] Including pig iron for steel making.

[12] Beginning 2000, data are confidential.

[13] Source: Eurostat (Luxembourg).

[14] Source: *Statistical Yearbook for Asia and the Pacific*, United Nations Economic and Social Commission for Asia and the Pacific (Bangkok).

[15] Sales. Production by establishments employing 20 or more persons.

[16] Including ingots.

[17] Source: *Country Economic Review*, Asian Development Bank (Manila).

[18] Beginning 2002, data are confidential

[19] Excluding the Transnistria region.

[20] Beginning 1999, data for Kosovo are not included.

[21] 2003 data are confidential.

[22] Beginning 2001, data are confidential.

Source

Organisation des Nations Unies, Division de statistique, New York, la base de données pour les statistiques industrielles et *Annuaire de statistiques industrielles par produit 2003*.

Notes

[1] Y compris l'acier pour les moulage.

[2] Source : *U. S. Geological Survey* (Washington, D. C.).

[3] Y compris la fonte de moulage.

[4] Source : Institut international de sidérurgique (Bruxelles).

[5] Période de 12 mois finissant le 30 juin de l'année indiquée.

[6] Source : *Bulletin annuel de statistiques de l'acier pour l'Europe, l'Amérique et l'Asie*, Commission économique des Nations Unies pour l'Europe (Genève).

[7] A partir de 1999, les données sont confidentielles.

[8] Source : Organisation de la Conférence islamique (Jeddah, Arabie saoudite).

[9] Pour la présentation des statistiques, les données pour Chine ne comprennent pas la Région Administrative Spéciale de Hong Kong (Hong Kong RAS), la Région Administrative Spéciale de Macao (Macao RAS) et la province de Taiwan.

[10] Ventes.

[11] Y compris la fonte d'affinage.

[12] A partir de 2000, les données sont confidentielles.

[13] Source : Eurostat (Luxembourg).

[14] Source : *Annuaire des Statistiques de l'Asie et Pacifique*, Conseil Economique et Social des Nations Unis pour l'Asie et le Pacifique (Bangkok).

[15] Ventes. Production des établissements occupant 20 personnes ou plus.

[16] Y compris l'acier brut (lingots).

[17] Source : *La Revue Economique du Pays*, La Banque de Développement Asiatique (Manila).

[18] A partir de l'année 2002, les données sont confidentielles.

[19] Non compris la région de Transnistria.

[20] A partir de 1999, non compris les données de Kosovo.

[21] Pour 2003, les données sont confidentielles.

[22] A partir de 2001, les données sont confidentielles.

Aluminium
Production : thousand metric tons

Aluminium
Production : milliers de tonnes

Country or area Pays ou zone	1994	1995	1996	1997	1998	1999	2000	2001	2002	2003
Argentina — Argentine										
Primary — Neuf	173	183	185	187	187	206	261	248	269	...
Secondary [1] — Récupéré [1]	14	10	16	13	17	14	23	23	...	...
Australia [2] — Australie [2]										
Primary — Neuf	1 384	1 285	1 331	1 395	1 589	1 686	1 742	1 788	1 809	1 855
Secondary [1] — Récupéré [1]	55	...	...	...	...	...	...	...	...	...
Austria — Autriche										
Secondary — Récupéré	53[1]	94[1]	98[1]	119[1]	126	143[1]	158[1]	158[1]	150[3]	...
Azerbaijan [3] — Azerbaïdjan [3]										
Primary — Neuf	*5	4	1	5	...	...	...	...	...	...
Bahrain — Bahreïn										
Primary — Neuf	451	449	456	490[3]	501[3]	502	512	510[3]	517[3]	...
Bosnia and Herzegovina [3] — Bosnie-Herzégovine [3]										
Primary — Neuf	*10	*10	*10	*15	...	...	*95	*96	104	...
Brazil — Brésil										
Primary — Neuf	1 185[1]	1 188[1]	1 197[1]	1 189[1]	1 208[1]	1 250[3]	1 277[3]	1 140[3]	1 318[3]	1 381[3]
Secondary — Récupéré	91[1]	117[1]	146[1]	163[1]	180[1]	190[3]	210[3]	200[3]	215[3]	254[3]
Bulgaria [3] — Bulgarie [3]										
Secondary — Récupéré	...	...	4	3	4	4	4	...	...	...
Cameroon — Cameroun										
Primary — Neuf	81[1]	71	82[1]	98	89	93	100	181	72	79
Canada — Canada										
Primary — Neuf	2 255[1]	2 172[1]	2 283[1]	2 327	2 374	2 390	2 373	2 583	2 709	...
Secondary [1] — Récupéré [1]	97	97	101	106	111	112	148	...	180	...
China [4] — Chine [4]										
Primary — Neuf	1 498	1 870	1 896	2 180	2 362	2 809	2 989	3 576	4 511	5 866
Croatia — Croatie										
Primary — Neuf	26	31	33	...	16	14	14	15	15[3]	0
Czech Republic [3] — République tchèque [3]										
Secondary — Récupéré	...	...	45	45	45	40	40	...	...	...
Denmark [5] — Danemark [5]										
Secondary — Récupéré	22	28	27	35	34	34	32	33	...	...
Egypt [6] — Egypte [6]										
Primary — Neuf	149	136	150	119	187[1]	193[3]	193[3]	193[3]	...	...
Finland — Finlande										
Secondary — Récupéré	*4	*5	*5	38[3,7]	41[3]	43[3]	45[3]	34[3]	30[3]	...
France — France										
Primary — Neuf	481	364	380	399	424	455	441	460	463	445
Secondary — Récupéré	227[8]	...	...	236	239	239	260	253	250	240
Germany — Allemagne										
Primary — Neuf	503	576	577	572[3]	612[3]	634[3]	644[3]	652[3]	653[3]	661[3]
Secondary — Récupéré	56	531[3]	417[3]	432[3]	453[3]	483[3]	572[3]	620[3]	666[3]	680[3]
Ghana [1] — Ghana [1]										
Primary — Neuf	141	135	137	152	56	114	156	162	...	...
Greece — Grèce										
Primary — Neuf	142	132	141	132	146	161	168[3]	163[3]	164[3]	...
Hungary — Hongrie										
Primary — Neuf	31	35	94	98	92	89	34[3]	34[3]	35[3]	...
Secondary [3] — Récupéré [3]	...	...	64	63	64	54	55	76	75	...

Aluminium — Production : thousand metric tons (*continued*)
Aluminium — Production : milliers de tonnes (*suite*)

Country or area / Pays ou zone	1994	1995	1996	1997	1998	1999	2000	2001	2002	2003
Iceland — Islande										
Primary — Neuf	99	100	102	123	160	161	167	169	194	286
India — Inde										
Primary — Neuf	479	518	516	539	542[3]	614[3]	644[3]	624[3]	671[3]	...
Indonesia [1] — Indonésie [1]										
Primary — Neuf	222	228	223	219	133	112	191	209	...	...
Iran (Islamic Rep. of) [1] — Iran (Rép. islamique d') [1]										
Primary — Neuf	116	115	78	91	111	138	140	145	...	...
Secondary — Récupéré	26	26	26	26	26	26	10	10	...	...
Italy — Italie										
Primary — Neuf	175	178	184	188	187	187	190	188	190	191
Secondary — Récupéré	376	412	377	443	503	502	568	578	591	594
Japan — Japon										
Primary — Neuf	41	46	46	53	35	35	41	27	40	44
Secondary — Récupéré	1 175[8]	1 181[8]	1 191[8]	1 277[8]	1 155[8]	1 158[8]	1 214[8]	1 171	...	...
Kenya [3] — Kenya [3]										
Secondary — Récupéré	...	...	...	2	1	1	1	1	...	...
Mexico — Mexique										
Primary — Neuf	29	33	69	71	68	70	63	56	38	34
Secondary [3] — Récupéré [3]	46	59	98	123	218	363	350	350	...	...
Mozambique — Mozambique										
Primary — Neuf	...	...	...	...	...	...	54[3]	266[3]	273[3]	408
Netherlands — Pays-Bas										
Primary — Neuf	230	216	227[3]	232[3]	264[3]	286[3]	300[3]	294[3]	300[3]	...
Secondary — Récupéré	175	192	150[3]	150	102	105	105	120[3]	120[3]	...
New Zealand — Nouvelle-Zélande										
Primary — Neuf	269[1]	273[1]	285[1]	310[1]	318[3]	327[3]	328[3]	322[3]	335[3]	...
Secondary — Récupéré	8[1]	8[1]	8[1]	8[1]	21[3]	21[3]	22[3]	22[3]	22[3]	...
Norway — Norvège										
Primary — Neuf	857	847	863	919[1]	996[1]	1 020[3]	1 026[3]	1 067[3]	1 096[3]	1 192[3]
Secondary — Récupéré	49[1]	72[1]	60[1]	59[1]	62[1]	178[3]	255[3]	224[3]	271[3]	257[3]
Poland — Pologne										
Primary — Neuf	50	56	52	54	54	51	47	45	49	45
Portugal — Portugal										
Secondary — Récupéré	12	14[1]	16[1]	16[1]	18[1]	18[1]	18[1]	18[1]	0	0
Romania — Roumanie										
Primary — Neuf	120[8,9]	141[8,9]	141[8,9]	162[8,9]	174[8,9]	174[8,9]	179	182	187	197
Secondary [8] — Récupéré [8]	3	3	4	2	1[9]	0[9]	2[9]	1[9]	3[9]	8[9]
Russian Federation [3] — Fédération de Russie [3]										
Primary — Neuf	2 670	2 724	2 874	2 906	3 005	3 146	3 245	3 300	3 347	...
Serbia and Montenegro — Serbie-et-Monténégro										
Primary — Neuf	4	17	37	66	61	73[11]	88	100	112	117
Secondary — Récupéré	0	0	0	1	...	...	...	...	...	...
Slovakia — Slovaquie										
Primary — Neuf	4	25	311	110[1]	115	109[1]	110[1]	110	112	166
Secondary — Récupéré	...	...	...	...	6	...	...	...	...	12
Slovenia — Slovénie										
Primary — Neuf	77	58	27	9	10	9	9[12]	...	...	...
South Africa [3] — Afrique du Sud [3]										
Primary — Neuf	172	229	570	673	677	679	674	663	676	...
Spain — Espagne										
Primary — Neuf	338[1]	362[1]	362[1]	360[1]	360[1]	364[1]	366[1]	376[1]	380[3]	...
Secondary [1] — Récupéré [1]	104	107	154	173	210	224	240	240	...	...
Suriname — Suriname										
Primary — Neuf	27	28	29	32[3]	29[3]	10[3]	...	...	...	...

Country or area Pays ou zone	1994	1995	1996	1997	1998	1999	2000	2001	2002	2003
Sweden [3] — Suède [3]										
Primary — Neuf	84	95	98	98	96	99	101	102	101	101
Secondary — Récupéré	33	23	24	24	25	25	26	25	28	30
Switzerland — Suisse										
Primary — Neuf	24	21	27[1]	27[1]	32[1]	34[1]	36[1]	36[1]	36[3]	...
Secondary — Récupéré	6[1]	5[1]	6[1]	8[1]	15[1]	6[1]	6[1]	6[1]	6[3]	...
Tajikistan — Tadjikistan										
Primary — Neuf	237	237	198	189	196	229	269[13]	289[13]	308[3]	...
TFYR of Macedonia — L'ex-R.y. Macédoine										
Total — Totale	7	5	5	5	7	6	4	...	...	...
Turkey — Turquie										
Primary — Neuf	60	62	62	62	62	62	62	62	63	63
Ukraine [3] — Ukraine [3]										
Primary — Neuf	*100	*98	*90	101	107	115	104	106	112	...
Secondary — Récupéré	40	40	40	...	71	111	129	130	130	...
United Arab Emirates [3] — Emirats arabes unis [3]										
Primary — Neuf	...	...	...	...	352	440	470	500	536	...
United Kingdom — Royaume-Uni										
Primary — Neuf	231[8]	238[8]	240[8]	248[3]	258[3]	272[3]	305[3]	341[3]	344[3]	343[3]
Secondary — Récupéré	224	230	261	258[3]	236[3]	275[3]	285[3]	249[3]	205[3]	205[3]
United States — Etats-Unis										
Primary — Neuf	3 299	3 375	3 577	3 603	3 713	3 779	3 668	2 637	2 707	2 703
Secondary [8] — Récupéré [8]	3 090	3 190	3 310	3 550	3 440	3 700	3 450	2 970	2 930	2 820
Uzbekistan [3] — Ouzbékistan [3]										
Secondary — Récupéré	...	...	3	3	3	3	3	...	...	...
Venezuela Bolivarian Republic of) — Venezuela (République bolivarienne du)										
Primary — Neuf	585[1]	627[1]	635[1]	641[1]	584[1]	567[1]	569[1]	572[1]	570[3]	...
Secondary [1] — Récupéré [1]	32	28	21	27	33	27	24	24	...	...

Source

United Nations Statistics Division, New York, the industrial statistics database and *Industrial Commodity Statistics Yearbook 2003*.

Notes

[1] Source: World Metal Statistics, (London).

[2] Twelve months ending 30 June of the year stated.

[3] Source: *U. S. Geological Survey* (Washington, D. C.).

[4] For statistical purposes, the data for China do not include those for the Hong Kong Special Administrative Region (Hong Kong SAR), Macao Special Administrative Region (Macao SAR) and Taiwan province of China.

[5] Sales.

[6] Including aluminium plates, shapes and bars.

[7] Break in series; data prior to the sign not comparable to following years.

[8] Including alloys.

[9] Including pure content of virgin alloys.

[10] Gold refined, including gold recovered as a by-product.

[11] Beginning 1999, data for Kosovo are not included.

[12] 2003 data are confidential.

[13] Source: *Country Economic Review*, Asian Development Bank (Manila).

Source

Organisation des Nations Unies, Division de statistique, New York, la base de données pour les statistiques industrielles et *Annuaire de statistiques industrielles par produit 2003*.

Notes

[1] Source : "World Metal Statistics," (Londres).

[2] Période de 12 mois finissant le 30 juin de l'année indiquée.

[3] Source : *U. S. Geological Survey* (Washington, D. C.).

[4] Pour la présentation des statistiques, les données pour Chine ne comprennent pas la Région Administrative Spéciale de Hong Kong (Hong Kong RAS), la Région Administrative Spéciale de Macao (Macao RAS) et la province de Taiwan.

[5] Ventes.

[6] Aluminium de deuxième fusion produit de débris de metal.

[7] Marque une interruption dans la série et la non-comparabilité des données précédant le symbole.

[8] Y compris les alliages.

[9] Y compris la teneur pure des alliages de première fusion.

[10] Or raffiné, y compris récupéré comme sous-produit.

[11] A partir de 1999, non compris les données de Kosovo.

[12] Pour 2003, les données sont confidentielles.

[13] Source : *La Revue Economique du Pays*, Banque de Développement Asiatique (Manila).

Radio and television receivers
Production: thousands

Récepteurs de radio et de télévision
Production : milliers

Country or area Pays ou zone	Radio receivers — Récepteurs de radio					Television receivers — Récepteurs de télévision				
	1999	2000	2001	2002	2003	1999	2000	2001	2002	2003
Algeria Algérie	...	...	...	...	...	173	194	245	289	292
Argentina Argentine	...	...	...	...	...	1 335	1 556	1 201	219	...
Bangladesh Bangladesh	13	13	14	10	13	107	127	133	143	140
Belarus Bélarus	195	101	56	47	33	516	532	727	738	690
Bosnia and Herzegovina Bosnie-Herzégovine	...	...	...	...	...	2	...	...	...	...
Brazil Brésil	2 039	1 629	1 184	965	783	4 328	6 078	5 463	5 750	5 603
Bulgaria [1] Bulgarie [1]	0	...	...	...	...	4	...	...	...	...
China [2] Chine [2]	...	...	...	...	...	49 113	45 012	46 110	58 057	75 302
Colombia Colombie	...	...	...	...	...	19	...	...	...	...
Czech Republic République tchèque	...	...	...	...	...	707	1 141	...	...	...
Denmark [3] Danemark [3]	...	...	...	...	...	88	99	92	83	68
Egypt Egypte	...	...	...	...	...	30	27	...	...	...
Finland Finlande	...	...	...	...	...	...	92	130	115	88
France France	2 961	3 195	3 508	3 357	3 498	3 811	4 203	4 977	5 375	5 657
Georgia Géorgie	...	...	...	...	...	1	2 [4]	...	...	...
Germany Allemagne	4 021	4 025	4 746	5 823 [5]	...	1 335	1 533	...	...	621
Hungary Hongrie	2 412	2 320	3 459	3 789	2 989	...	...	...	...	...
India Inde	0	0	0	0	0	2 561	2 399	1 979	2 191	3 572
Indonesia Indonésie	4 937 [6]	...	...	...	...	15 924	...	21 519	23 680	...
Iran (Islamic Rep. of) [7] Iran (Rép. islamique d') [7]	114	139	129	275		904	859	816	...	...
Italy Italie	...	...	...	...		1 627	1 350	1 208	1 212	1 055
Japan Japon	2 678	2 384	1 972	2 138	1 856	4 386	3 382	2 862	3 130	3 051
Jordan Jordanie	...	...	...	...		15	14	18	...	...

Country or area Pays ou zone	Radio receivers — Récepteurs de radio					Television receivers — Récepteurs de télévision				
	1999	2000	2001	2002	2003	1999	2000	2001	2002	2003
Kazakhstan Kazakhstan	0	0	0	...	...	112	338	347	358	503
Korea, Republic of Corée, République de	...	...	...	...	...	15 556	10 054	9 321	9 157	7 336
Kyrgyzstan Kirghizistan	...	...	...	...	...	1	3	6	6	8
Latvia Lettonie	2[5]	...	...	...	...	...	...	...	...	...
Lithuania Lituanie	...	...	...	...	...	187	207	143	348	687
Malaysia Malaisie	32 957	36 348	28 839	21 735	27 634	7 611	10 551	9 501	10 410	9 915
Pakistan Pakistan	...	...	...	...	...	128	122	97	450	765
Poland Pologne	132	109	13	10	28	5 121	6 287	7 502	7 795	6 818
Portugal Portugal	5 939	8 042	8 627	8 559	7 301	...	...	...	...	...
Republic of Moldova [8] République de Moldova [8]	10	18	3	5	3	3	2	2	8	10
Romania Roumanie	0[6]	0	0	0	0	56	32	29	60	90
Russian Federation Fédération de Russie	332	390	281	253	278	281	1 116	1 024	1 980	2 383
Serbia and Montenegro Serbie-et-Monténégro	0[9]	0	0	...	...	13[9]	6	5	5	2
Slovakia Slovaquie	...	...	...	...	...	311	431	594	712[5]	...
Slovenia Slovénie	0	0	...	...	...	244	349[10]	...	...	...
South Africa Afrique du Sud	...	...	...	...	...	273	290	260	271	359
Spain Espagne	357	57	85	52	47	...	...	...	...	...
Syrian Arab Republic Rép. arabe syrienne	...	...	...	...	...	150	169	139	164	148
Tunisia Tunisie	...	...	...	...	...	104	99	117	78	62
Turkey Turquie	...	...	...	...	...	6 941	8 789	8 025	12 463	15 036
Ukraine Ukraine	27	36	26	33	29	81	62	148	159	415
United Kingdom Royaume-Uni	...	505				...	...	...	...	...
United States [11] Etats-Unis [11]	...	...	...	...	...	10 914	9 272	8 264	8 811	8 221
Uzbekistan [12] Ouzbékistan [12]	...	...	...	...	...	50	26	...	...	...

Source

United Nations Statistics Division, New York, the industrial statistics database and *Industrial Commodity Statistics Yearbook 2003*.

Notes

1 Beginning 2000, data are confidential.

2 For statistical purposes, the data for China do not include those for the Hong Kong Special Administrative Region (Hong Kong SAR), Macao Special Administrative Region (Macao SAR) and Taiwan Province of China.

3 Sales.

4 2001-2002 data are confidential.

5 2003 data are confidential.

6 Including radios with tape recording units.

7 Production by establishments employing 10 or more persons.

8 Excluding the Transnistria region.

9 Beginning 1999, data for Kosovo are not included.

10 Beginning 2001, data are confidential.

11 Shipments.

12 Source: *Statistical Yearbook for Asia and the Pacific*, United Nations Economic and Social Commission for Asia and the Pacific (Bangkok).

Source

Organisation des Nations Unies, Division de statistique, New York, la base de données pour les statistiques industrielles et *Annuaire de statistiques industrielles par produit 2003*.

Notes

1 A partir de 2000, les données sont confidentielles.

2 Pour la présentation des statistiques, les données pour Chine ne comprennent pas la Région Administrative Spéciale de Hong Kong (Hong Kong RAS), la Région Administrative Spéciale de Macao (Macao RAS) et la province de Taiwan.

3 Ventes.

4 Pour 2001 et 2002, les données sont confidentielles.

5 Pour 2003, les données sont confidentielles.

6 Y compris les récepteurs de radio avec appareil enregistreur à bande magnétique incorporés.

7 Production des établissements occupant 10 personnes ou plus.

8 Non compris la région de Transnistria.

9 A partir de 1999, non compris les données de Kosovo.

10 A partir de 2001, les données sont confidentielles.

11 Expéditions.

12 Source : *Statistical Yearbook for Asia and the Pacific*, Commission économique et sociale pour l'Asie et le Pacifique (Bangkok).

48

Passenger cars
Production: thousands

Voitures de tourisme
Production : milliers

Country or area Pays ou zone	1994	1995	1996	1997	1998	1999	2000	2001	2002	2003
Argentina [1] Argentine [1]	338	227	269	366	353	225	239	...	...	...
Australia Australie	310	294	305	301	336	323	330	328	327	358 [2]
Brazil [3] Brésil [3]	367	271	245	253	242	221	260	296	326	344
Canada Canada	...	...	...	...	1 302	1 482	1 496	1 297	1 350	...
Colombia [4] Colombie [4]	65	66	63	69	50	25	38	...	...	...
Ecuador Equateur	...	...	...	...	27	...	...	...	...	...
Egypt Egypte	7	8	14	13	13	12	11	...	...	...
Finland Finlande	...	...	0 [1]	...	...	34	38	41	41	20
France France	3 176	3 052	...	3 352	3 932	4 265	4 652	3 182 [5]	3 498	3 704
Germany Allemagne	4 222	...	4 713 [1]	...	...	...	...	...	...	...
Hungary Hongrie	...	...	...	...	90	125	...	...	...	122
India Inde	262 [6]	331 [6]	400 [6]	384 [6]	393 [6]	577 [6]	506	573	575	801
Indonesia Indonésie	85	19	...	11	56	39	...	74	...	...
Italy Italie	1 340 [6]	1 422 [6]	1 244 [6]	1 563 [6]	1 379 [6]	1 384 [6]	1 423 [6]	1 272 [6]	1 126 [6]	1 023
Japan Japon	7 801	7 611	7 864	8 491	8 056	8 100	8 363	8 118	8 618	8 478
Korea, Republic of Corée, République de	1 755 [1]	1 999 [1]	2 256 [1]	2 313 [1]	1 577 [1]	2 158 [1]	2 626 [1]	2 477 [1]	2 653 [1]	2 767
Mexico Mexique	887	705	802	858	947	988	1 294	1 273	1 247	1 028
Poland Pologne	338	366	441	520	592	647	532	364	288	334
Romania Roumanie	56	70	97	109	104	89	64	57	66	76
Russian Federation Fédération de Russie	798	835	868	986	840	954	969	1 022	981	1 012
Serbia and Montenegro Serbie-et-Monténégro	8	8	9	10	12	8 [7]	12	7	11	11
Slovakia Slovaquie	8	22	32	42	125	127	181	277	226	...
Slovenia Slovénie	74	88	89	96	127	119	123	119	127	118
Spain [1,8] Espagne [1,8]	2 146	2 254	2 334	2 278	2 468	2 473	2 619	2 406	2 470	2 518
Sweden Suède	193	...	207	219	214	235	278	272	260	292

Passenger cars—Production: thousands (*continued*)
Voitures de tourisme—Production : milliers (*suite*)

Country or area Pays ou zone	1994	1995	1996	1997	1998	1999	2000	2001	2002	2003
Ukraine Ukraine	94	59	7	2	26	10	17	26	44	102
United Kingdom Royaume-Uni	1 654	1 735	1 707	1 818	1 709	...	...	...	...	...
United States * [9] Etats-Unis * [9]	6 614	...	...	...	...	...	...	...	...	...
Uzbekistan Ouzbékistan	...	...	25[10]	65[10]	54[10]	58[10]	32[5]	32[5]	...	...

Source

United Nations Statistics Division, New York, the industrial statistics database and *Industrial Commodity Statistics Yearbook 2003*.

Notes

[1] Including assembly.

[2] Twelve months ending 30 June of the year stated.

[3] Excluding station wagons.

[4] Source: United Nations Economic Commission for Latin America and the Caribbean (Santiago).

[5] Source: International Organization of Motor Vehicle Manufacturers (Paris).

[6] Excluding production for armed forces.

[7] Beginning 1999, data for Kosovo are not included.

[8] Sales.

[9] Factory sales.

[10] Source: *Statistical Yearbook*, Commonwealth of Independent States (Moscow).

Source

Organisation des Nations Unies, Division de statistique, New York, la base de données pour les statistiques industrielles et *Annuaire de statistiques industrielles par produit 2003*.

Notes

[1] Y compris le montage.

[2] Période de 12 mois finissant le 30 juin de l'année indiquée.

[3] Non compris les stations-wagons.

[4] Source : Commission économique des Nations Unies pour l'Amérique Latine et des Caraïbes (Santiago).

[5] Source : Organisation internationale des constructeurs d'automobiles (Paris).

[6] Non compris la production destinée aux forces armées.

[7] A partir de 1999, non compris les données de Kosovo.

[8] Ventes.

[9] Ventes des fabriques.

[10] Source : *Annuaire des Statistiques*, Communauté d'Etats indépendants (Moscou).

Refrigerators for household use
Production: thousands

Réfrigérateurs à usage domestique
Production : milliers

Country or area Pays ou zone	1994	19954	1996	1997	1998	1999	2000	2001	2002	2003
Algeria Algérie	119	131	137	175	215	181	117	64	153	150
Antigua and Barbuda [1] Antigua-et-Barbuda [1]	3	...	...	...	...	...	...	...	...	...
Argentina Argentine	494	49	45	401	424	354	325	246	162	...
Australia Australie	444	423	403	398	441	427	...	...	...	...
Azerbaijan Azerbaïdjan	97	25	7	0	3	1	1	2	4	5
Belarus Bélarus	742	746	754	795	802	802	812	830	856	886
Brazil Brésil	2 721	3 242	3 776	3 592	3 034	2 796	2 921	3 371	3 037	3 544
Bulgaria Bulgarie	69	49	36	21	56	45	18	145	202	244
Chile Chili	221	272	213	268	229	242	271	280	230	232
China [2] Chine [2]	7 681	9 185	9 797	10 444	10 600	12 100	12 790	13 513	15 989	19 645
Colombia Colombie	465	465	...	...	...	...	...	...	...	...
Denmark [3] Danemark [3]	808	1 502	1 276	1 523	1 589	1 560	1 475	1 225	1 173	1 128
Ecuador Equateur	111	156	17	133	88	38	55	...	...	142
Egypt Egypte	236	236	250	2	5	3	...	...	...	...
Finland Finlande	134	104	68	102	107	...	...	...	0	...
France France	554	...	...	490	640	509	555	542	528	544
Germany Allemagne	3 794	...	2 747	...	...	...	...	...	...	...
Greece [4,5] Grèce [4,5]	...	...	...	...	...	...	...	...	...	381
Guyana Guyana	5	...	...	...	...	...	...	...	...	...
Hungary Hongrie	603	714	736	835	708	849	995	1 058	1 119	1 312
India Inde	1 668	1 913	1 705	1 600	1 902	2 012	2 009	2 469	2 735	3 715
Indonesia Indonésie	469	291	...	573	417	240	774	...	...	...
Iran (Islamic Rep. of) Iran (Rép. islamique d')	629[6]	575[7]	756[7]	786[7]	860[7]	798[7]	791[7]	...	...	...
Italy Italie	5 033	5 908	5 402	5 562	6 280	6 582	6 987	6 936	7 088	6 715

Refrigerators for household use — Production: thousands (*continued*)

Réfrigérateurs à usage domestique — Production : milliers (*suite*)

Country or area Pays ou zone	1994	19954	1996	1997	1998	1999	2000	2001	2002	2003
Japan Japon	4 952	5 013	5 163	5 369	4 851	4 543	4 224	3 875	3 317	2 859
Korea, Republic of Corée, République de	3 943	3 975	4 292	4 257	3 790	4 735	5 224	5 128	6 124	5 637
Kyrgyzstan Kirghizistan	3	1	0	0	...	...	...	...	...	...
Lithuania Lituanie	183	187	138	172	154	153	154	260	346	355
Malaysia Malaisie	266	295	257	249	206	194	215	186	172	187
Mexico Mexique	1 356	1 256	1 447	1 942	1 986	2 083	2 049	2 071	2 222	2 162
Nigeria Nigéria	20	19	...	...	...	...	...	...	...	...
Peru Pérou	86	161	81	101	118	42	51	*68	64	*46
Poland Pologne	605	585	584	705	714	726	693	589	645	1 001
Portugal Portugal	244	...	173	211	257	304	308	257	281	262
Republic of Moldova [8] République de Moldova [8]	53	24	1	2	0	...	...	...	...	...
Romania [5] Roumanie [5]	383	435	446	429	366	323	341	313	390	489
Russian Federation Fédération de Russie	2 283	1 531	966	1 108	956	1 041	1 151	1 542	1 733	2 004
Serbia and Montenegro Serbie-et-Monténégro	41	50	51	81	48	5 [9]	20	0	10	...
Slovakia Slovaquie	371	330	393	258	228	206	177	27	2 [10]	...
Slovenia Slovénie	797	863	592	692	756	780	841 [11]	...	...	...
South Africa [12] Afrique du Sud [12]	321	365	411	388	399	440	508	662	702	711
Spain Espagne	1 461	1 269	1 260	1 960	2 415	2 107	2 153 [11]	...	...	...
Sweden Suède	582	610	478	523	545	604	620	609	635	581
Syrian Arab Republic Rép. arabe syrienne	148	156	155	138	137	120	96	110	113	
Tajikistan Tadjikistan	3	0	1	2	1	2	2	2	1	1
Thailand Thaïlande	...	...	2 246	2 384	1 631 [13]	...	...	...	...	...
TFYR of Macedonia L'ex-R.y. Macédoine	95	51	20	12	*4	0	0	0		
Trinidad and Tobago Trinité-et-Tobago	3	1	0	...	...	...	...	...	...	...
Tunisia Tunisie	129	...	...	...	...	...	...	...	...	...
Turkey Turquie	1 258	1 680	1 612	1 945	1 993	2 083	2 405	2 245	3 017	4 011

Country or area Pays ou zone	1994	19954	1996	1997	1998	1999	2000	2001	2002	2003
Ukraine Ukraine	653	562	431	382	390	409	451	509	583	788
United Kingdom Royaume-Uni	1 094	1 256	1 225	1 251	1 095	931	892	821	751	745
United States [14,15] Etats-Unis [14,15]	11 276	11 005	11 132	12 092	11 279	11 716	12 355	11 776	11 145	11 639
Uzbekistan Ouzbékistan	20	19	13	13	16[16]	2[16]	1[16]	...	...	...

Source

United Nations Statistics Division, New York, the industrial statistics database and *Industrial Commodity Statistics Yearbook 2003*.

Notes

[1] Twelve months beginning 21 March of the year stated.

[2] For statistical purposes, the data for China do not include those for the Hong Kong Special Administrative Region (Hong Kong SAR), Macao Special Administrative Region (Macao SAR) and Taiwan Province of China.

[3] Sales.

[4] Incomplete coverage.

[5] Including freezers.

[6] Production by establishments employing 50 or more persons.

[7] Production by establishments employing 10 or more persons.

[8] Excluding the Transnistria region.

[9] Beginning 1999, data for Kosovo are not included.

[10] 2003 data are confidential.

[11] Beginning 2001, data are confidential.

[12] Including deep freezers and deep freeze-refrigerator combinations.

[13] Beginning 1999, series discontinued.

[14] Electric domestic refrigerators only.

[15] Shipments.

[16] Source: *Statistical Yearbook for Asia and the Pacific*, United Nations Economic and Social Commission for Asia and the Pacific (Bangkok).

Source

Organisation des Nations Unies, Division de statistique, New York, la base de données pour les statistiques industrielles et *Annuaire de statistiques industrielles par produit 2003*.

Notes

[1] Période de 12 mois commençant le 21 mars de l'année indiquée.

[2] Pour la présentation des statistiques, les données pour Chine ne comprennent pas la Région Administrative Spéciale de Hong Kong (Hong Kong RAS), la Région Administrative Spéciale de Macao (Macao RAS) et la province de Taiwan.

[3] Ventes.

[4] Couverture incomplète.

[5] Y compris les congélateurs.

[6] Production des établissements occupant 50 personnes ou plus.

[7] Production des établissements occupant 10 personnes ou plus.

[8] Non compris la région de Transnistria.

[9] A partir de 1999, non compris les données de Kosovo.

[10] Pour 2003, les données sont confidentielles.

[11] A partir de 2001, les données sont confidentielles.

[12] Y compris congélateurs-conservateurs et congélateurs combinés avec un réfrigérateur.

[13] A partir de 1999, les séries ont été discontinuées.

[14] Réfrigérateurs électriques de ménage seulement.

[15] Expéditions.

[16] Source : *Statistical Yearbook for Asia and the Pacific*, Commission économique et sociale pour l'Asie et le Pacifique (Bangkok).

Washing machines for household use
Production: thousands

Machines à laver à usage domestique
Production : milliers

Country or area Pays ou zone	1994	1995	1996	1997	1998	1999	2000	2001	2002	2003
Argentina Argentine	702	458	524	603	...	279	317	295	162	...
Armenia Arménie	0	1	0	...	...	...	...	...	...	...
Australia Australie	314	310	266	268	321	354	...	...	...	...
Belarus Bélarus	77	37	61	88	91	92	88	81	66	63
Brazil Brésil	1 461	1 681	2 160	2 095	1 851	1 940	2 302	2 257	2 260	2 266
Bulgaria Bulgarie	41	26	24	5	...	2	1	0[1]	...	...
Chile Chili	447	434	310	...	...	...	...	...	...	...
China [2] Chine [2]	10 941	9 484	10 747	12 545	12 073	13 422	14 430	13 416	15 989	...
Colombia Colombie	50	45	...	...	...	...	...	...	...	...
Ecuador Equateur	...	11	12	...	...	...	...	...	...	...
Egypt Egypte	209	198	200	201	201	252	...	...	...	...
France France	2 244[4]	2 200[4]	1 868[4]	1 933[4]	1 941[4]	2 229[4]	2 751	3 259	3 404	3 618
Germany Allemagne	...	2 703	2 816	3 035	3 370	4 768	4 611	4 542	4 751	4 856
Greece Grèce	20	15	10	...	...	...	...	...	...	5[5]
Indonesia Indonésie	44	13	...	86	33	48	110	92	96	...
Iran (Islamic Rep. of) Iran (Rép. islamique d')	79[6]	98[7]	159[7]	194[7]	190[7]	183[7]	189[7]	213[7]	260[7]	...
Italy Italie	6 251	6 996	7 135	7 967	8 119	7 367	8 186	8 507	8 884	9 687
Japan Japon	5 042	4 876	5 006	4 818	4 468	4 287	4 179	4 059	3 524	3 133
Kazakhstan Kazakhstan	88	46	23	11	3	2	5	11	17	20
Korea, Republic of Corée, République de	2 443	2 827	2 878	2 967	2 643	2 822	3 271	3 529	4 183	4 977
Kyrgyzstan Kirghizistan	17	4	3	2	0	...	...	...	...	...
Latvia Lettonie	10	8	3	3	2	...	...	...	...	...
Mexico Mexique	1 185	882	1 091	1 448	1 512	1 593	1 720	1 636	1 657	1 547
Peru Pérou	5	6	3	1	0	0	0	*0	0	0
Poland Pologne	449	419	445	412	416	448	564	759	915	977

Country or area Pays ou zone	1994	1995	1996	1997	1998	1999	2000	2001	2002	2003
Republic of Moldova [8] République de Moldova [8]	81	49	54	46	43	18	25	25	40	48
Romania Roumanie	109	125	138	82	36	28	25	24	29	35
Russian Federation Fédération de Russie	2 122	1 294	762	800	862	999	954	1 039	1 369	1 330
Serbia and Montenegro Serbie-et-Monténégro	63	36	33	33	30	12 [9]	10	5	4	...
Slovenia Slovénie	200	220	291	405	474	447	488 [10]	...	...	...
South Africa Afrique du Sud	55	57	55	44	44	45	35	34	...	...
Spain Espagne	1 632	1 655	1 945	2 270	2 281 [11]	...	...	...	2 702 [12]	...
Sweden Suède	113	106	103	120	119	122	117	137	128	124
Syrian Arab Republic Rép. arabe syrienne	50	78	80	72	68	65	66	62	85	...
Thailand Thaïlande	...	...	541	794	800 [13]	...	...	...	...	...
Turkey Turquie	780	873	1 015	1 485	1 408	1 249	1 346	1 034	1 687	2 471
Ukraine Ukraine	422	213	149	147	138	127	125	166	232	251
United Kingdom Royaume-Uni	...	...	...	1 148	1 111	...	...	...	...	...
United States Etats-Unis	7 081 [4]	6 605 [4]	6 873 [4]	6 942 [4]	7 504 [4]	7 991 [4]	8 043	7 992 [4]	8 959 [4]	9 531 [4]
Uzbekistan Ouzbékistan	9	14	4	4	5 [14]	0 [14]	0 [14]	...	...	...

Source

United Nations Statistics Division, New York, the industrial statistics database and *Industrial Commodity Statistics Yearbook 2003.*

Notes

[1] Beginning 2002, data are confidential
[2] For statistical purposes, the data for China do not include those for the Hong Kong Special Administrative Region (Hong Kong SAR), Macao Special Administrative Region (Macao SAR) and Taiwan Province of China.
[3] Sales.
[4] Shipments.
[5] Incomplete coverage.
[6] Production by establishments employing 50 or more persons.
[7] Production by establishments employing 10 or more persons.
[8] Excluding the Transnistria region.
[9] Beginning 1999, data for Kosovo are not included.
[10] Beginning 2001, data are confidential.
[11] 1999-2001, data are confidential.
[12] 2003 data are confidential.
[13] Beginning 1999, series discontinued.
[14] Source: *Statistical Yearbook*, Commonwealth of Independent States (Moscow).

Source

Organisation des Nations Unies, Division de statistique, New York, la base de données pour les statistiques industrielles et *Annuaire de statistiques industrielles par produit 2003.*

Notes

[1] A compter de l'année 2002, les données sont confidentiels.
[2] Pour la présentation des statistiques, les données pour Chine ne comprennent pas la Région Administrative Spéciale de Hong Kong (Hong Kong RAS), la Région Administrative Spéciale de Macao (Macao RAS) et la province de Taiwan.
[3] Ventes.
[4] Expéditions.
[5] Couverture incomplète.
[6] Production des établissements occupant 50 personnes ou plus.
[7] Production des établissements occupant 10 personnes ou plus.
[8] Non compris la région de Transnistria.
[9] A partir de 1999, non compris les données de Kosovo.
[10] Pour 2001, les données sont confidentielles.
[11] Pour 1999-2001, les données sont confidentielles.
[12] Pour 2003, les données sont confidentielles.
[13] A partir de 1999, les séries ont été discontinuées.
[14] Source : *Statistical Yearbook*, Commonwealth of Independent States (Moscow).

51

Machine tools
Production: number

Machines-outils
Production : nombre

Country or area — Pays ou zone	1994	1995	1996	1997	1998	1999	2000	2001	2002	2003
Algeria — Algérie										
Lathes Tours	118	196	189	110	14	...	38	27	30	47
Milling machines Fraiseuses	124	119	124	75	80	72	69	44	65	43
Armenia — Arménie										
Lathes Tours	395	190	141	81	71	33	40	47	115	95
Milling machines Fraiseuses	63	73	47	188	82	27	19	40	34	4
Metal-working presses Presses pour de travail de métaux	29	43	34	31	18	11	11	3	0	0
Austria — Autriche										
Lathes Tours	709	1 482	1 452	801	1 914[1]	...	...	1 091	1 031[3]	...
Milling machines Fraiseuses	209	625	362	284	279[2]	...	...	...	...	...
Azerbaijan — Azerbaïdjan										
Drilling and boring machines Perceuses	102	112	49	24	29	1	...	...	...	...
Bangladesh[4] — Bangladesh[4]										
Lathes Tours	1	...	...	...	...	...	...	...	...	...
Belarus — Bélarus										
Drilling and boring machines Perceuses	1 846	1 309	1 158	1 438	1 712	1 661	1 923	1 652	1 930	1 866
Lathes Tours	57	70	93	117	131	96	122	146	150	141
Milling machines Fraiseuses	0	1	3	5	3	2	16	34	40	14
Metal-working presses Presses pour de travail de métaux	63	61	35	22	14	30	30	27	22	15
Belgium[5] — Belgique[5]										
Metal-working presses Presses pour de travail de métaux	...	...	...	...	...	343	312	279	...	...
Brazil — Brésil										
Metal-working presses Presses pour de travail de métaux	1 836	1 858	1 657	1 678	1 531	1 102	1 386	1 285	1 047	762
Bulgaria — Bulgarie										
Drilling and boring machines Perceuses	850	864	953	906	*1 025	*940	1 436	1 212	936	749
Lathes Tours	1 979	2 496	2 513	2 315	1 761	1 611	1 563	1 916	1 814	2 104
Milling machines Fraiseuses	200	227	295	412	104	139	218	306	243	216
China, Hong Kong SAR — Chine, Hong Kong RAS										
Drilling and boring machines Perceuses	12 177	3 607	1 571	1 234	1 464	1 386	1 019[6]	...	...	6 265
Colombia — Colombie										
Lathes Tours	155	112	...	...	...	...	...	...	...	...
Metal-working presses Presses pour de travail de métaux	22 661	26 344	...	...	...	...	...	...	...	...

Country or area — Pays ou zone	1994	1995	1996	1997	1998	1999	2000	2001	2002	2003
Croatia — Croatie										
Drilling and boring machines Perceuses	...	4 369	3 212	66	31	28	16	4	0	0
Lathes Tours	...	52	68	98	144	186	122	74	152	0
Milling machines Fraiseuses	...	77	90	165	224	196	162	206	96	0
Czech Republic — République tchèque										
Drilling and boring machines Perceuses	...	...	1 235	1 263	1 352	986	982	840	620	486
Lathes Tours	685	735	943	932	994	989	1 046	1 254	1 044	861
Milling machines Fraiseuses	...	...	1 109	1 039	1 117	821	860	906	658	558
Metal-working presses Presses pour de travail de métaux	60	114	231	239	...	...	...	...	...	...
Finland — Finlande										
Drilling and boring machines Perceuses	88	106	109	...	67	13	89	56	56	60
Lathes Tours	2	3	2	...	...	...	...	...	...	...
Metal-working presses Presses pour de travail de métaux	180	1 764	2 159	2 101	2 285	2 315	2 735	2 400	2 339	2 760
France [8] — France [8]										
Lathes Tours	546	...	...	...	...	...	...	...	...	...
Milling machines Fraiseuses	394	...	...	...	...	...	...	...	...	...
Metal-working presses Presses pour de travail de métaux	605	...	...	...	...	...	...	...	...	...
Georgia — Géorgie										
Lathes Tours	109	57	18	28	21	2 [6]	...	...	9	23
Germany — Allemagne										
Drilling and boring machines Perceuses	15 955	13 049	11 730	...	11 396	14 440	...	...	7 904	6 520
Lathes Tours	5 322	8 232	6 375	5 542	6 070	5 754	6 027	20 845	...	3 127
Milling machines Fraiseuses	6 327	...	5 213	5 335	5 348	5 755	6 806	21 355 [3]	...	...
Metal-working presses Presses pour de travail de métaux	23 284	16 399	...	21 531	...	...	21 170	...	16 636 [3]	...
Greece [5] — Grèce [5]										
Metal-working presses Presses pour de travail de métaux	...	...	...	...	...	...	...	...	...	15
Hungary — Hongrie										
Drilling and boring machines Perceuses	15	4	...	...	212	...	167	154	49	...
Lathes Tours	33	7	...	...	...	51	100	...	223	...
Milling machines Fraiseuses	3	...	...	...	...	...	...	...	...	...
India [9] — Inde [9]										
Lathes Tours	6 747	6 279	4 685	4 881	6 902	12 436	21 579	20 469	14 623	7 677
Indonesia — Indonésie										
Drilling and boring machines Perceuses	...	12 155	...	...	5 153	14	...	...	43	...
Lathes Tours	96	166	...	23	4	4	...	...	...	...

Country or area — Pays ou zone	1994	1995	1996	1997	1998	1999	2000	2001	2002	2003
Iran (Islamic Rep. of) — Iran (Rép. islamique d')										
Drilling and boring machines Perceuses	...	...	...	500[10]	2[10]	20[10]	29	35	...	...
Lathes [10] Tours [10]	...	...	...	1 720	2 836	1 529	1 474	1 691	...	...
Metal-working presses [10] Presses pour de travail de métaux [10]	...	...	...	230	751	1 518	1 516	1 444	...	...
Japan — Japon										
Drilling and boring machines Perceuses	11 936	14 678	16 414	17 097	12 531	9 377	12 784	10 225	...	...
Lathes Tours	14 961	20 339	21 443	23 357	22 652	16 924	22 027	19 813	14 758	17 105
Milling machines Fraiseuses	1 791	1 832	2 198	2 368	2 019	1 022	1 260	1 042	...	...
Metal-working presses Presses pour de travail de métaux	9 531	10 512	10 068	11 575	8 546	7 285	8 884	6 992	4 132	4 960
Korea, Republic of — Corée, République de										
Drilling and boring machines [11] Perceuses [11]	11 107	10 861	8 025	8 741	1 491	2 805		...	...	...
Lathes Tours	10 265	12 526	11 094	8 357	4 809	6 542	8 482	7 577	7 182	7 532
Milling machines Fraiseuses	4 667	5 293	3 952	2 900	825	2 242	3 731	2 496	2 634	2 341
Latvia — Lettonie										
Lathes Tours	87	36	26	20	29	...	...	...	...	...
Milling machines Fraiseuses	44	44	9	26	78	...	...	...	...	...
Lithuania — Lituanie										
Drilling and boring machines Perceuses	...	749	437	333	192	171	109	84	99	89
Lathes Tours	27	64	4	1	6	6	6	5	0	0
Milling machines Fraiseuses	341	255	213	161	130	58	55	48	23	42
Poland — Pologne										
Drilling and boring machines Perceuses	998	771	840	1 253	917	624	...	...	...	...
Lathes Tours	900	1 012	1 037	900	963	732	748	1 055	665	658
Milling machines Fraiseuses	260	274	281	354	257	222	180	141	138	113
Metal-working presses Presses pour de travail de métaux	8	2	2	15	...	...	...	1[12]	0	0
Portugal — Portugal										
Metal-working presses Presses pour de travail de métaux	649	...	...	...	...	...	...	...	...	...
Romania — Roumanie										
Drilling and boring machines Perceuses	...	...	...	...	...	...	...	...	...	560
Lathes Tours	312	471	587	681	573	330	307	388	281	49
Milling machines Fraiseuses	162	341	458	403	321	333	242	236	155	244
Metal-working presses Presses pour de travail de métaux	...	...	...	...	...	...	...	...	...	87

Country or area — Pays ou zone	1994	1995	1996	1997	1998	1999	2000	2001	2002	2003
Russian Federation — Fédération de Russie										
Drilling and boring machines Perceuses	5 291	5 021	3 088	2 522	1 877	1 898	1 669	1 333	1 211	1 303
Lathes Tours	3 807	3 269	2 095	2 135	1 798	1 681	2 067	2 444	1 959	1 597
Milling machines Fraiseuses	1 560	897	622	591	641	724	1 163	1 128	796	710
Serbia and Montenegro — Serbie-et-Monténégro										
Drilling and boring machines Perceuses	206	328	100	106	133	111[13]	97	...	...	...
Lathes Tours	135	206	110	256	213	231[13]	181	...	...	...
Metal-working presses Presses pour de travail de métaux	54	114	53	47	66	29[13]	28	...	...	...
Slovakia — Slovaquie										
Drilling and boring machines Perceuses	...	...	...	...	...	...	866	921	947	...
Lathes Tours	1 566	1 549	3 121	3 084	1 660	1 786	1 769	1 699	1 321	1 165
Milling machines Fraiseuses	...	...	...	...	6	1	9	39	59	...
Metal-working presses Presses pour de travail de métaux	301	282	199	73	276	195	147	151	110	88
Slovenia — Slovénie										
Drilling and boring machines Perceuses	...	...	...	4	0[14]	...	...	...	...	...
Milling machines Fraiseuses	26	27	...	...	...	...	...	...	...	...
Metal-working presses Presses pour de travail de métaux	153	215	719	...	...	...	91	121	59	42
Spain — Espagne										
Drilling and boring machines Perceuses	1 738	2 313	2 185	2 689	3 317	4 732	4 976	4 548[15]	...	3 416
Lathes Tours	1 713	2 475	2 887	3 080	3 509	3 559	3 492	4 240	3 143	2 785
Milling machines Fraiseuses	1 458	1 600	1 852	1 605	2 986	3 075	3 964	3 066	2 678	1 769
Metal-working presses Presses pour de travail de métaux	723	5 452	...	...	...	...	...	...	...	...
Sweden — Suède										
Drilling and boring machines Perceuses	...	...	...	3 158	3 661	3 003	2 232	1 933	1 956	1 422
Lathes Tours	...	...	259	40	22	25	17	18	23	0
Milling machines Fraiseuses	27	25	...	...	...	...	...	...	...	...
Turkey — Turquie										
Drilling and boring machines Perceuses	185	12	57	22	21	7	85	67	47	...
Lathes Tours	59	12	16	0	0	0	0	0	0	0
Milling machines Fraiseuses	107	84	169	75	1	0	50	11	5	...

Country or area— Pays ou zone	1994	1995	1996	1997	1998	1999	2000	2001	2002	2003
Ukraine — Ukraine										
Drilling and boring machines Perceuses	3 745	1 337	563	750	418	306	225	306	86	155
Lathes Tours	867	808	338	352	234	213	260	293	195	87
Milling machines Fraiseuses	195	90	48	161	168	45	77	36	28	16
Metal-working presses Presses pour de travail de métaux	117	146	35	42	38	29	34	25	20	8
United Kingdom — Royaume-Uni										
Drilling and boring machines Perceuses	1 061	...	...	...	...	...	...	...	...	...
Lathes Tours	2 941	3 568	3 845	3 102	3 478	2 047	...	...	...	...
Milling machines Fraiseuses	856	493	268	529	...	...	132	...	...	...
Metal-working presses Presses pour de travail de métaux	615	...	...	827	...	...	...	...	...	...
United States [8] — Etats-Unis [8]										
Drilling and boring machines Perceuses	...	10 465	7 927	6 234	5 812	5 096	4 277	2 803	1 958	2 812
Lathes Tours	3 662	4 643	4 190	5 058	5 089	3 807	3 278	2 949	1 793	1 816
Milling machines Fraiseuses	4 087	4 747	4 102	4 240	3 416	2 749	3 545	1 990	369	531
Metal-working presses Presses pour de travail de métaux	10 947	5 045	11 023	12 084	12 559	12 301	11 079	10 059	7 682	7 053

Source

United Nations Statistics Division, New York, the industrial statistics database and *Industrial Commodity Statistics Yearbook 2003*.

Notes

[1] 1999-2000 data are confidential.

[2] Beginning 1999, data are confidential.

[3] 2003 data are confidential.

[4] Twelve months ending 30 June of the year stated.

[5] Incomplete coverage.

[6] 2001-2002 data are confidential.

[7] Sales.

[8] Shipments.

[9] All metal-cutting machines.

[10] Production by establishments employing 10 or more persons.

[11] Drilling machines only.

[12] Since 2000, the former "Polish Systematic Nomenclature of Products", has been replaced by the "Polish Classification of Products and Services", impacting range change of some data.

[13] Beginning 1999, data for Kosovo are not included.

[14] Beginning 2001, data are confidential.

[15] 2002 data are confidential.

Source

Organisation des Nations Unies, Division de statistique, New York, la base de données pour les statistiques industrielles et *Annuaire de statistiques industrielles par produit 2003*.

Notes

[1] Pour 1999-2000, les données sont confidentielles.

[2] A partir de 1999, les données sont confidentielles.

[3] Pour 2003, les données sont confidentielles.

[4] Période de 12 mois finissant le 30 juin de l'année indiquée.

[5] Couverture incomplète.

[6] Pour 2001 et 2002, les données sont confidentielles.

[7] Ventes.

[8] Expéditions.

[9] Machines-outils tous types pour le travail des métaux.

[10] Production des établissements occupant 10 personnes ou plus.

[11] Perceuses seulement.

[12] A partir de l'année 2000, la "Nomenclature Systematique Polonaise des Produits", a été remplacé par la " Classification Polonaise des Produits et Sérvices", ayant un effet à l'ordre des quelques données.

[13] A partir de 1999, non compris les données de Kosovo.

[14] A partir de 2001, les données sont confidentielles.

[15] Pour 2002, les données sont confidentielles.

Country or area Pays ou zone	1994	1995	1996	1997	1998	1999	2000	2001	2002	2003
Algeria — Algérie										
Assembled Assemblés	1 230	2 570	2 136	1 293	1 798	1 583	1 719	2 811	2 561	2 059
Argentina [1] — Argentine [1]										
Produced Fabriqués	64 022	...	...	...	...	...	...	...	...	...
Armenia — Arménie										
Produced Fabriqués	446	232	114	27	51	2	...	...	...	...
Austria [2] — Autriche [2]										
Produced Fabriqués	3 098	...	...	...	...	...	...	...	...	...
Azerbaijan — Azerbaïdjan										
Produced Fabriqués	8	2	1	0	0	0	0	...	...	...
Bangladesh — Bangladesh										
Assembled Assemblés	430	830	797	887	788	793	629	714	718	720
Belarus — Bélarus										
Produced Fabriqués	21 264	12 902	10 671	13 002	12 799	13 370	14 656	16 524	16 544	18 126
Brazil [3] — Brésil [3]										
Produced Fabriqués	64 137	70 495	48 712	63 744	63 773	55 277	71 686	77 431	68 558	78 938
Bulgaria — Bulgarie										
Produced Fabriqués	321	259	66	43[4]	...	...	...	...	...	...
Chile [5] — Chili [5]										
Assembled Assemblés	15 960	...	...	...	...	...	...	...	...	...
China [6] — Chine [6]										
Produced Fabriqués	662 600	595 997	625 100	573 600	...	...	...	...	...	...
Colombia — Colombie										
Assembled Assemblés	15 660[5]	...	...	736	903	219	...	...	...	...
Croatia — Croatie										
Produced Fabriqués	...	5	8	10	96	10	0	0	0	...
Czech Republic — République tchèque										
Produced Fabriqués	30 103	22 052	27 036	39 537	39 098	23 113	23 641	4 701	...	...
Egypt — Egypte										
Produced Fabriqués	1 379	1 241	738	328	467	444	180	...	...	...
Finland — Finlande										
Produced Fabriqués	546[1]	540[1]	492[1]	493[1]	687[1]	721[1]	655[1]	646[1]	596[1]	702

Lorries (trucks) — Production or assembly from imported parts: number (*continued*)
Camions — Production ou montage avec des pièces importées : nombre (*suite*)

Country or area Pays ou zone	1994	1995	1996	1997	1998	1999	2000	2001	2002	2003
France — France										
Produced Fabriqués	453 344	381 360	...	440 244	608 369	627 588	741 780	760 791	791 948	780 600
Georgia — Géorgie										
Produced Fabriqués	137	209	95	82	39	38	45	4	5	...
Germany — Allemagne										
Produced Fabriqués	259 575	...	240 604[1]	272 916[1]	292 581[1]	291 817	299 151	282 758	256 131	275 934
Greece — Grèce										
Assembled Assemblés	...	57	128	...	219	...	...	...	...	284[7,8]
India [5,9] — Inde [5,9]										
Produced Fabriqués	163 200	...	...	...	...	...	...	...	...	...
Indonesia — Indonésie										
Produced Fabriqués	2 890	4 755	...	575	...	...	...	...	...	...
Iran (Islamic Rep. of) — Iran (Rép. islamique d')										
Assembled Assemblés	15 785[10]	8 836[11]	19 777[11]	16 689[11]	42 446[11]	38 130[11]	50 942[11]	52 720[11]	...	...
Israel — Israël										
Assembled Assemblés	1 260	1 217	1 199	...	...	...	...	...	...	...
Italy — Italie										
Produced Fabriqués	191 288	234 354	188 852	256 062	278 322	288 038	283 094	280 731	266 406	267 430
Japan — Japon										
Produced Fabriqués	2 689 340	2 519 319	2 417 370	2 410 124	1 930 965	1 742 111	1 719 584	1 596 080	1 566 411	1 735 469
Kazakhstan — Kazakhstan										
Produced Fabriqués	...	200[3]	20[3]	30[3]	100[3]	271	225	105	343	103
Kenya — Kenya										
Assembled Assemblés	428	1 103	1 430	...	...	...	...	...	...	...
Korea, Republic of — Corée, République de										
Produced Fabriqués	332 263[1]	331 328[1]	340 179[1]	297 565[1]	182 218[1]	264 212[1]	265 448[1]	254 233[1]	288 992[1]	246 742
Kyrgyzstan — Kirghizistan										
Produced Fabriqués	206	8	1	12	...	...	...	...	...	...
Latvia — Lettonie										
Assembled Assemblés	...	...	...	...	...	5	...	...	...	...
Lithuania — Lituanie										
Assembled Assemblés	...	...	...	...	...	...	...	...	126	182
Malaysia — Malaisie										
Assembled Assemblés	42 618[12]	55 961[12]	78 571[12]	94 977[12]	19 693[12]	44 951[12]	55 721[12]	62 722	72 327	81 308

Country or area Pays ou zone	1994	1995	1996	1997	1998	1999	2000	2001	2002	2003
Mexico — Mexique										
Produced Fabriqués	217 359	210 072	396 377	468 931	445 125	451 880	542 809	521 357	492 904	505 811
Myanmar[13] — Myanmar[13]										
Assembled Assemblés	846	500	550	255	31	102	135	204	208	223
Netherlands[14,15] — Pays-Bas[14,15]										
Produced Fabriqués	13 938	15 818	...	...	...	...	...	...	...	...
Nigeria — Nigéria										
Assembled Assemblés	696	715	...	...	...	...	...	...	...	...
Pakistan — Pakistan										
Assembled Assemblés	6 522[16]	5 857[16]	9 864[16]	12 733[16]	11 736[16]	9 210[16]	7 633[16]	7 917[16]	9 632	14 124
Poland[17] — Pologne[17]										
Produced Fabriqués	21 356	30 662	44 159	57 254	56 080	62 719	58 104	24 670	20 986	18 497
Romania — Roumanie										
Produced Fabriqués	3 044	3 098	3 142	1 956	1 263	900	762	352	476	4
Russian Federation — Fédération de Russie										
Produced Fabriqués	185 018	142 483	134 130	145 850[3]	141 484[3]	176 207[3]	184 489[3]	172 597[3]	172 552[3]	192 937[3]
Serbia and Montenegro — Serbie-et-Monténégro										
Produced Fabriqués	685	708	824	1 278	1 139	425[18]	711	590	595	487
Slovakia — Slovaquie										
Produced Fabriqués	369	663	1 421	709	312	72	37	70[19]	...	...
Slovenia — Slovénie										
Produced Fabriqués	397	277	195	...	...	16	16[19]	...	...	...
South Africa — Afrique du Sud										
Assembled Assemblés	118 221	147 792	132 383	132 338	117 092	113 310	130 589	125 873	128 615	124 885
Spain[1,14] — Espagne[1,14]										
Produced Fabriqués	32 217	50 255	73 319	280 708	343 699	366 702	404 249	402 518	368 360	433 653
Sweden — Suède										
Produced Fabriqués	...	...	...	51 378	30 582	30 399	32 546	29 455	29 390	32 588
Thailand[5] — Thaïlande[5]										
Assembled Assemblés	324 780	...	...	...	...	...	...	...	...	...
Trinidad and Tobago[5] — Trinité-et-Tobago[5]										
Assembled Assemblés	621	...	...	...	...	...	...	...	...	...
Tunisia — Tunisie										
Assembled Assemblés	1 084	616	954	1 003	1 016	770	1 130	1 391	1 437	765

Lorries (trucks) — Production or assembly from imported parts: number (*continued*)

Camions — Production ou montage avec des pièces importées : nombre (*suite*)

Country or area / Pays ou zone	1994	1995	1996	1997	1998	1999	2000	2001	2002	2003
Turkey — Turquie										
Assembled / Assemblés	21 591	35 930	50 471	73 946	67 985	44 457	77 514	30 112	67 986	95 297
Ukraine — Ukraine										
Produced / Fabriqués	11 741	6 492	4 164	3 386	4 768	7 769	11 185	6 747	2 343	1 265
United Kingdom — Royaume-Uni										
Produced / Fabriqués	372 633	247 022	188 215	189 464	185 152	...	...	...	...	...
United Rep. of Tanzania [20] — Rép.-Unie de Tanzanie [20]										
Assembled / Assemblés	115	0	0	0	...	...	...	...	...	...
Uzbekistan [3] — Ouzbékistan [3]										
Produced / Fabriqués	...	300	30	20	60	300	...	...	...	...

Source

United Nations Statistics Division, New York, the industrial statistics database and *Industrial Commodity Statistics Yearbook 2003*.

Notes

[1] Including assembly.
[2] Beginning 1995, data are confidential.
[3] Trucks only.
[4] 2001-2002 data are confidential.
[5] Including motor coaches and buses.
[6] For statistical purposes, the data for China do not include those for the Hong Kong Special Administrative Region (Hong Kong SAR), Macao Special Administrative Region (Macao SAR) and Taiwan Province of China.
[7] Incomplete coverage.
[8] Including lorries (trucks), including articulated vehicles, produced.
[9] Excluding production for armed forces.
[10] Production by establishments employing 50 or more persons.
[11] Production by establishments employing 10 or more persons.
[12] Including vans and buses.
[13] Government production only.
[14] Sales.
[15] Beginning 1986, production by establishments employing 20 or more persons.
[16] Twelve months ending 30 June of the year stated.
[17] Including special-purpose vehicles.
[18] Beginning 1999, data for Kosovo are not included.
[19] Beginning 2002, data are confidential
[20] Including buses.

Source

Organisation des Nations Unies, Division de statistique, New York, la base de données pour les statistiques industrielles et *Annuaire de statistiques industrielles par produit 2003*.

Notes

[1] Y compris le montage.
[2] A partir de 1995, les données sont confidentielles.
[3] Camions seulement.
[4] Pour 2001 et 2002, les données sont confidentielles.
[5] Y compris les autocars et autobus.
[6] Pour la présentation des statistiques, les données pour Chine ne comprennent pas la Région Administrative Spéciale de Hong Kong (Hong Kong RAS), la Région Administrative Spéciale de Macao (Macao RAS) et la province de Taiwan.
[7] Couverture incomplète.
[8] Comprend les camions produits, y compris les ensembles articulés.
[9] Non compris la production destinée aux forces armées.
[10] Production des établissements occupant 50 personnes ou plus.
[11] Production des établissements occupant 10 personnes ou plus.
[12] Y compris les autobus et les camionnettes.
[13] Production de l'Etat seulement.
[14] Ventes.
[15] A partir de 1986, production des établissements occupant 20 personnes ou plus.
[16] Période de 12 mois finissant le 30 juin de l'année indiquée.
[17] Y compris véhicules à usages spéciaux.
[18] A partir de 1999, non compris les données de Kosovo.
[19] A compter de l'année 2002, les données sont confidentiels.
[20] Y compris les autobus.

Industrial activity includes mining and quarrying, manufacturing and the production of electricity, gas and water. These activities correspond to the major divisions 2, 3 and 4 respectively of the *International Standard Industrial Classification of All Economic Activities* [47].

Many of the tables are based primarily on data compiled for the United Nations *Industrial Commodity Statistics Yearbook* [23]. Data taken from alternate sources are footnoted.

The methods used by countries for the computation of industrial output are, as a rule, consistent with those described in the United Nations *International Recommendations for Industrial Statistics* [46] and provide a satisfactory basis for comparative analysis. In some cases, however, the definitions and procedures underlying computations of output differ from approved guidelines. The differences, where known, are indicated in the footnotes to each table.

Table 35: The statistics on sugar were obtained from the database and the *Sugar Yearbook* [14] of the International Sugar Organization. The data shown cover the production and consumption of centrifugal sugar from both beet and cane, and refer to calendar years.

The consumption data relate to the apparent consumption of centrifugal sugar in the country concerned, including sugar used for the manufacture of sugar-containing products whether exported or not and sugar used for purposes other than human consumption as food. Unless otherwise specified, the statistics are expressed in terms of raw value (i.e. sugar polarizing at 96 degrees). The world and regional totals also include data for countries not shown separately whose sugar consumption was less than 10,000 metric tons.

Table 36: The data refer to meat from animals slaughtered within the national boundaries irrespective of the origin of the animals. Production figures of beef, veal, buffalo meat, pork (including bacon and ham), mutton, lamb and goat meat are in terms of carcass weight, excluding edible offals, tallow and lard. All data refer to total meat production, i.e. from both commercial and farm slaughter.

Table 37: The data refer to beer made from malt, including ale, stout, porter.

Table 38 presents data on cigarettes only, unless otherwise indicated.

Table 39: The data on cotton fabrics refer to woven fabrics of cotton at the loom stage before undergoing finishing processes such as bleaching, dyeing, printing, mercerizing, lazing, etc.; those on wool refer to woollen and worsted fabrics before undergoing finishing processes. Fabrics of fine hair are excluded.

The data on woven fabrics of cellulosic and non-cellulosic fibres include fabrics of continuous and discontinuous rayon

L'activité industrielle comprend les industries extractives (mines et carrières), les industries manufacturières et la production d'électricité, de gaz et d'eau. Ces activités correspondent aux grandes divisions 2, 3 et 4, respectivement, de la *Classification internationale type par industrie de toutes les branches d'activité économique* [47].

Un grand nombre de ces tableaux sont établis principalement sur la base de données compilées pour l'*Annuaire de statistiques industrielles par produit* des Nations Unies [23]. Les données tirées d'autres sources sont signalées par une note.

En règle générale, les méthodes employées par les pays pour le calcul de leur production industrielle sont conformes à celles dans *Recommandations internationales concernant les statistiques industrielles* des Nations Unies [46] et offrent une base satisfaisante pour une analyse comparative. Toutefois, dans certains cas, les définitions des méthodes sur lesquelles reposent les calculs de la production diffèrent des directives approuvées. Lorsqu'elles sont connues, les différences sont indiquées par une note.

Tableau 35 : Les données sur le sucre proviennent de la base de données et de l'*Annuaire du sucre* [14] de l'Organisation internationale du sucre. Les données présentées portent sur la production et la consommation de sucre centrifugé à partir de la betterave et de la canne à sucre, et se rapportent à des années civiles.

Les données de la consommation se rapportent à la consommation apparente de sucre centrifugé dans le pays en question, y compris le sucre utilisé pour la fabrication de produits à base de sucre, exportés ou non, et le sucre utilisé à d'autres fins que pour la consommation alimentaire humaine. Sauf indication contraire, les statistiques sont exprimés en valeur brute (sucre polarisant à 96 degrés). Les totaux mondiaux et régionaux comprennent également les données relatives aux pays où la consommation de sucre est inférieure à 10.000 tonnes.

Le *tableau 36* indique la production de viande provenant des animaux abattus à l'intérieur des frontières nationales, quelle que soient leurs origines. Les chiffres de production de viande de bœuf, de veau, de buffle, de porc (y compris le bacon et le jambon), de mouton et d'agneau (y compris la viande de chèvre) se rapportent à la production en poids de carcasses et ne comprennent pas le saindoux, le suif et les abats comestibles. Toutes les données se rapportent à la production totale de viande, c'est-à-dire à la fois aux animaux abattus à des fins commerciales et des animaux sacrifiés à la ferme.

Tableau 37 : Les données se rapportent à la bière produite à partir du malte, y compris ale, stout et porter (bière anglaise, blonde et brune).

Le *tableau 38* se rapporte seulement aux cigarettes, sauf indication contraire.

and acetate fibres, and non-cellulosic fibres other than textile glass fibres. Pile and chenille fabrics at the loom stage are also included.

Table 40: The data refer to the total production of leather footwear for children, men and women and all other footwear such as footwear with outer soles of wood or cork, sports footwear and orthopedic leather footwear. House slippers and sandals of various types are included, but rubber footwear is excluded.

Table 41: The data refer to the aggregate of sawnwood and sleepers, coniferous or non coniferous. The data cover wood planed, unplaned, grooved, tongued and the like, sawn lengthwise or produced by a profile chipping process, and planed wood which may also be finger jointed, tongued or grooved, chamfered, rabbeted, V jointed, beaded and so on. Wood flooring is excluded. Sleepers may be sawn or hewn.

Table 42 presents statistics on the production of all paper and paper board. The data cover newsprint, printing and writing paper, construction paper and paperboard, household and sanitary paper, special thin paper, wrapping and packaging paper and paperboard.

Table 43: Statistics on all hydraulic cements used for construction (portland, metallurgic, aluminous, natural, and so on) are shown.

Table 44: The data refer to H_2SO_4 in terms of pure monohydrate sulphuric acid, including the sulphuric acid equivalent of oleum or fuming sulphuric acid.

Table 45: The data on pig iron include foundry and steel making pig iron. Figures on crude steel include both ingots and steel for castings. The series are based on data compiled for the United Nations *Industrial Commodity Statistics Yearbook* [23]. In selected cases, data are obtained from the United States Bureau of Mines (Washington, D.C.), the Latin American Iron and Steel Institute (Santiago) and the United Nations Economic Commission for Europe (Geneva).

Pig iron is iron in liquid or solid form, containing at least 3 per cent of carbon and possibly one or more of the following elements within the weight limits specified: less than 6 per cent of silicon, less than 6 per cent of manganese, and less than 3 per cent of phosphorus. It may also contain small proportions of other elements, for example, chromium and nickel. Foundry pig iron is pig iron for use in making cast iron, including forge pig iron and pig iron for direct casting. Steel-making pig iron is distinguished from foundry pig iron on the basis of the uses to which it is put. Steel-making pig iron is pig iron for use in making crude steel.

Crude steel is steel (including alloy steel) in the form in which it emerges from the Bassemer, Thomas, open-hearth or electric process or from one of the various oxygen-blowing processes. Puddled iron is excluded. Steel ingots are primary

Tableau 39 : Les données sur les tissus de coton et de laine se rapportent aux tissus de coton, avant les opérations de finition, c'est-à-dire avant d'être blanchis teints, imprimés, mercerisés, glacés, etc., et aux tissus de laine cardée ou peignée, avant les opérations de finition. A l'exclusion des tissus de poils fins.

Les données sur les tissus de fibres cellulosiques et non-cellulosiques comprennent les tissus sortant du métier à tisser de fibres de rayonne et d'acétate et tissus composés de fibres non cellulosiques, autres que les fibres de verre, continues ou discontinues. Cette rubrique comprend les velours, peluches, tissus boucles et tissus chenille.

Tableau 40 : Les données se rapportent à la production totale de chaussures de cuir pour enfants, hommes et dames et toutes les autres chaussures telles que chaussures à semelles en bois ou en liège, les chaussures pour sports et orthopédiques en cuir. Les chaussures en caoutchouc ne sont pas compris.

Tableau 41 : Les données font référence à un agrégat des sciages de bois de conifères et de non-conifères et des traverses de chemins de fer. Elles comprennent les bois rabotés, non rabotés, rainés, languetés, etc. sciés en long ou obtenus à l'aide d'un procédé de profilage par enlèvement de copeaux et les bois rabotés qui peuvent être également à joints digitiformes languetés ou rainés, chanfreinés, à feuillures, à joints en V, à rebords, etc. Cette rubrique ne comprend pas les éléments de parquet en bois. Les traverses de chemin de fer comprennent les traverses sciées ou équaries à la hache.

Le *tableau 42* présente les statistiques sur la production de tout papier et carton. Les données comprennent le papier journal, les papiers d'impression et d'écriture, les papiers et cartons de construction, les papiers de ménage et les papiers hygiéniques, les papiers minces spéciaux, les papiers d'empaquetage et d'emballage et carton.

Tableau 43 : Les données sur tous les ciments hydrauliques utilisés dans la construction (portland métallurgique, alumineux, naturel, etc.) sont présentées.

Tableau 44 : Les données se rapportent au H_2SO_4 sur la base de l'acide sulfurique monohydraté, y compris l'équivalent en acide sulfurique de l'oléum ou acide sulfurique fumant.

Tableau 45 : Les données se rapportent à la production de fonte et d'acier. Les données sur l'acier brut comprennent les lingots et l'acier pour moulage. Les séries sont basées sur l'*Annuaire des statistiques industrielles par produit* des Nations Unies [23]. Dans certains cas, les données proviennent du United States Bureau of Mines (Washington, D.C.), de l'Institut latino-américain du fer et de l'acier (Santiago) et de la Commission économique pour l'Europe (Genève).

La fonte est du fer à l'état liquide ou solide contenant au moins 3 p. 100 de carbone et pouvant contenir un ou plusieurs des éléments suivants dans les limites de poids indiquées : moins de 6 p. 100 de silicium, moins de 6 p. 100 de

products for rolling or forging obtained by casting the molten steel into moulds which are usually square, rectangular or octagonal in cross-section with one end thicker than the other, to facilitate removal from the mould. Continuously-cast blooms, billets and slabs are included as ingots.

Table 46: The data refer to aluminium obtained by electrolytic reduction of alumina (primary) and re-melting metal waste or scrap (secondary).

Table 47: The data on radio receivers include complete receiving sets, irrespective of frequencies covered, made for home, automobile and general use, including battery sets. Radio-gramophone combinations are also included.

The data on television receivers include household television receivers, colour, of all kinds (table models, consoles, television sets incorporating a radio receiver or a gramophone).

Table 48: Passenger cars include three-and four-wheeled road motor vehicles other than motorcycle combinations, intended for the transport of passengers and seating not more than nine persons (including the driver), which are manufactured wholly or mainly from domestically-produced parts and passenger cars shipped in "knocked-down" form for assembly abroad.

Table 49: The data refer to refrigerators of the compression type or of the absorption type, of the sizes commonly used in private households. Insulated cabinets to contain an active refrigerating element (block ice) but no machine are excluded.

Table 50: These washing machines usually include electrically-driven paddles or rotating cylinders (for keeping the cleaning solution circulating through the fabrics) or alternative devices. Washing machines with attached wringers or centrifugal spin driers, and centrifugal spin driers designed as independent units, are included.

Table 51: The data on machine tools presented in this table include drilling and boring machines, lathes, milling machines, and metal-working presses. Drilling and boring machines refer to metal-working machines fitted with a baseplate, stand or other device for mounting on the floor, or on a bench, wall or another machine. Lathes refer to metal-working lathes of all kinds, whether or not automatic, including slide lathes, vertical lathes, capstan and turret lathes, production (or copying) lathes. Milling machines refer to metal-working machines designed to work a plane or profile surface by means of rotating tools, known as milling cutters. Metal-working presses are mechanical, hydraulic and pneumatic presses used for forging, stamping, cutting out, etc. Forge hammers are excluded. Detailed product definitions are given in the United Nations *Industrial Commodity Statistics Yearbook* [23].

Table 52 presents data on lorries, distinguishing between lorries assembled from imported parts and those manufactured wholly or mainly from domestically-produced parts.

manganèse et moins de 3 p. 100 de phosphore. Elle peut aussi contenir de faibles proportions d'autres éléments, tels que le chrome et le nickel. La fonte de moulage est de la fonte servant à la fabrication de pièces mouleés en fonte et comprend notamment la fonte pour forge et la fonte pour moulages de première coulé. La fonte d'affinage ne se distingue de la fonte de moulage que par sa destination. La fonte d'affinage est de la fonte servant à la fabrication d'acier brut.

On entend par acier brut l'acier (y compris l'acier allié) produit par les procédés Bessemer, Thomas, Martin ou électrique ou par les procédés à l'oxygène. Cette rubrique ne comprend pas le fer puddlé. Les lingots d'acier sont des produits de base destinés à être transformés par laminage ou forgeage et obtenus en coulant l'acier liquide dans des lingotières qui sont ordinairement de section carrée, rectangulaire ou octogonale et dont l'une des extrémités est plus épaisse que l'autre pour faciliter le démoulage. Les blooms, les billettes et les brames obtenus par coulée continue sont classés parmi les lingots.

Tableau 46 : Les données se rapportent à la production d'aluminium obtenue par réduction électrolytique de l'alumine (production primaire) et par refusion de déchets métalliques (production secondaire).

Tableau 47 : Les données sur les récepteurs de radio comprennent les récepteurs complets, d'appartement, d'automobiles et d'usage général, y compris les postes à piles quelles que soient les longueurs d'ondes captées. Cette rubrique comprend les récepteurs avec phonographes ou tourne-disques incorporés.

Les données sur les récepteurs de télévision comprennent de tous genres pour usage privé en noir et couleurs (récepteurs de table, récepteurs-meubles, etc., même avec appareils récepteur de radio diffusion, phonographe ou tourne-disques incorporés).

Tableau 48 : Les voitures de tourisme comprennent les véhicules automobiles routiers à trois ou quatre roues, autres que les motocycles, destinés au transport de passagers, dont le nombre de places assises (y compris celle du conducteur) est inférieur ou égal à neuf et qui sont construits entièrement ou principalement avec des pièces fabriqués dans le pays, et les voitures destinées au transport de passagers exportées en pièces détachées pour être montées à l'étranger.

Tableau 49 : Les données se rapportent aux appareils frigorifiques du type à compression ou à absorption de la taille des appareils communément utilisés dans les ménages. Cette rubrique ne comprend pas les glacières conçues pour contenir un élément frigorifique actif (glace en bloc) mais non pour contenir équipement frigorifique.

Tableau 50 : Ces machines à laver comprennent généralement des pales ou des cylindres rotatifs (destinés à assurer le brassage continu du liquide et du linge) ou des dispositifs à

Both include road motor vehicles designed for the conveyance of goods, including vehicles specially equipped for the transport of certain goods, and articulated vehicles (that is, units made up of a road motor vehicle and a semi-trailer). Ambulances, prison vans and special purpose lorries and vans, such as fire-engines are excluded.

mouvements alternés, mus électriquement. Cette rubrique comprend les machines à laver avec essoreuses à rouleau ou essoreuses centrifuges et les essoreuses centrifuges conçues comme des appareils indépendants.

Tableau 51 : Les données sur les machines-outils présentés dans ce tableau comprennent les perceuses, tours, fraiseuses, et presses pour le travail des métaux. Perceuses se rapportent aux machines-outils pour le travail des métaux, munies d'un socle, d'un pied ou d'un autre dispositif permettant de les fixer au sol, à un établi, à une paroi ou à une autre machine. Tours se rapportent aux tours à métaux, de tous types, automatiques ou non, y compris les tours parallèles, les tours verticaux, les tours à revolver, les tours à reproduire. Fraiseuses se rapportent aux machines-outils pour le travail des métaux conçues pour usiner une surface plane ou un profil au moyen d'outils tournants appelés fraises. Presses pour le travail des métaux se rapportent aux presses à commande mécanique, hydraulique et pneumatique servant à forger, à estamper, à matricer etc. Cette rubrique ne comprend pas les outils agissant par chocs. Pour plus de détails sur les description des produits se reporter à l'*Annuaire des statistiques industrielles par produit* [23] des Nations Unies.

Le *tableau 52* présente les données sur les camions et fait la distinction entre les camions assemblés à partir de pièces importées et les camions qui sont montés entièrement ou principalement avec des pièces importées. Les deux comprennent les véhicules automobiles routiers conçus pour le transport des marchandises, y compris les véhicules spécialement équipés pour le transport de certaines marchandises, et les véhicules articulés (c'est-à-dire les ensembles composés d'un véhicule automobile routier et d'une semi-remorque). Cette rubrique ne comprend pas les ambulances, les voitures cellulaires et les camions à usages spéciaux, tels que les voitures-pompes à incendie.

53

Railways: traffic
Passenger and net ton-kilometres: millions

Chemins de fer : trafic
Voyageurs et tonnes-kilomètres nettes : millions

Country or area Pays ou zone	1995	1996	1997	1998	1999	2000	2001	2002	2003	2004
Albania — Albanie										
Passenger-kilometres Voyageurs-kilomètres	197	168	95	116	121	183	138	123	105	...
Net ton-kilometres Tonnes-kilomètres nettes	53	42	23	25	26	28	19	20	31	...
Algeria — Algérie										
Passenger-kilomètres Voyageurs-kilomètres	1 574	1 826	1 360	1 163	1 069	1 142	981		...	...
Net ton-kilometres Tonnes-kilomètres nettes	1 946	2 194	2 892	2 174	2 033	1 980	1 990	...		...
Argentina — Argentine										
Passenger-kilomètres [1] Voyageurs-kilomètres [1]	7 017	8 524	9 324	9 652	9 102	8 939	7 975	6 586	...	...
Net ton-kilometres Tonnes-kilomètres nettes	7 613	8 505	9 835	9 852	9 101	8 696	8 989	9 444	...	...
Armenia — Arménie										
Passenger-kilometres Voyageurs-kilomètres	166	84	84	52	46	47	48	48	41	30
Net ton-kilometres Tonnes-kilomètres nettes	403	351	381	419	323	354	344	452	529	678
Australia [2] — Australie [2]										
Passenger-kilometres Voyageurs-kilomètres	...	...	...	...	...	...	99	106	113	...
Net ton-kilometres Tonnes-kilomètres nettes	99 727	104 311	114 500	125 200	127 400	134 200	134 109	139 700	158 070	...
Austria — Autriche										
Passenger-kilometres Voyageurs-kilomètres	9 625	9 689	8 140	7 971	7 997	8 206	8 240	8 300	8 249	8 295
Net ton-kilometres Tonnes-kilomètres nettes	13 715	13 909	14 791	15 348	15 556	17 110	17 387	17 627	17 836	19 027
Azerbaijan — Azerbaïdjan										
Passenger-kilometres Voyageurs-kilomètres	791	558	489	533	422	493	537	584	654	789
Net ton-kilometres Tonnes-kilomètres nettes	2 409	2 778	3 515	4 702	5 052	5 770	6 141	6 980	7 719	7 536
Bangladesh [3] — Bangladesh [3]										
Passenger-kilometres Voyageurs-kilomètres	4 037	3 333	3 754	3 855	...	...	...	...	...	...
Net ton-kilometres Tonnes-kilomètres nettes	760	689	782	804	...	...	...	...		
Belarus — Bélarus										
Passenger-kilometres [4] Voyageurs-kilomètres [4]	12 505	11 657	12 909	13 268	16 874	17 722	15 264	14 349	13 308	13 893
Net ton-kilometres Tonnes-kilomètres nettes	25 510	26 018	30 636	30 370	30 529	31 425	29 727	34 169	38 402	40 331
Belgium — Belgique										
Passenger-kilometres Voyageurs-kilomètres	6 757	6 788	6 984	7 097	7 354	7 755	8 036	8 249	8 264	8 675
Net ton-kilometres Tonnes-kilomètres nettes	7 287	7 244	7 465	7 600	7 392	7 674	7 080	7 297	7 293	7 691
Benin — Bénin										
Passenger-kilometres Voyageurs-kilomètres	116	117	121	119	121	121	101	...	...	...
Net ton-kilometres Tonnes-kilomètres nettes	207	178	218	221	215	314	316	482	...	...

Country or area Pays ou zone	1995	1996	1997	1998	1999	2000	2001	2002	2003	2004
Bolivia — Bolivie										
Passenger-kilometres Voyageurs-kilomètres	240	197	225	270	271	259	267	280	283	286
Net ton-kilometres Tonnes-kilomètres nettes	758	780	839	908	832	856	750	873	901	1 058
Botswana — Botswana										
Passenger-kilometres Voyageurs-kilomètres	110	81	82	71	75	...	...	...	...	...
Net ton-kilometres Tonnes-kilomètres nettes	687	668	1 049	1 278	1 037	874	704	920	637	...
Brazil — Brésil										
Passenger-kilometres [5] Voyageurs-kilomètres [5]	9 936	9 048	7 876	7 224	6 528	5 852	...	...	...	...
Net ton-kilometres [6] Tonnes-kilomètres nettes [6]	136 460	128 976	138 724	142 446	140 957	154 870	162 235	170 177	182 644	205 711
Bulgaria — Bulgarie										
Passenger-kilometres Voyageurs-kilomètres	4 693	5 065	5 886	4 740	3 819	3 472	2 990	2 598	2 517	2 404
Net ton-kilometres Tonnes-kilomètres nettes	8 595[7]	7 549[7]	7 444[7]	6 152[7]	5 297[7]	5 538[7]	4 904[7]	4 627[7]	5 274	5 211
Cambodia — Cambodge										
Passenger-kilometres Voyageurs-kilomètres	38	22	51	44	50	15	...	...	...	...
Net ton-kilometres Tonnes-kilomètres nettes	6	4	37	76	76	91	...	...	...	...
Cameroon — Cameroun										
Passenger-kilometres Voyageurs-kilomètres	301	306[8]	283[8]	292[8]	311[8]	711[8]	303[8]	308	322	...
Net ton-kilometres Tonnes-kilomètres nettes	607	869[8]	850[8]	888[8]	916[8]	1 063[8]	1 159[8]	1 179	1 090	...
Canada — Canada										
Passenger-kilometres Voyageurs-kilomètres	1 473	1 519	1 515	1 458	1 593	1 533	1 553	1 597	1 434	...
Net ton-kilometres Tonnes-kilomètres nettes	280 474	282 489	306 943	299 508	298 836	321 894	321 291	318 315	318 345	...
Chile — Chili										
Passenger-kilometres Voyageurs-kilomètres	691	644	552	519	638	737	871	770	829	820
Net ton-kilometres Tonnes-kilomètres nettes	2 262	2 366	2 330	2 650	2 896	3 135	3 318	3 338	3 575	3 898
China [9,10] — Chine [9,10]										
Passenger-kilometres Voyageurs-kilomètres	354 570	334 759	358 486	377 342	413 593	453 260	476 682	496 938	478 861	571 217
Net ton-kilometres Tonnes-kilomètres nettes	1 304 953	1 310 616	1 326 988	1 256 008	1 291 033	1 377 049	1 469 414	1 565 842	1 724 665	1 928 880
China, Hong Kong SAR [11] — Chine, Hong Kong RAS [11]										
Passenger-kilometres Voyageurs-kilomètres	3 662	3 914	4 172	4 252	4 321	4 533	4 559	4 618	4 256	4 485
Net ton-kilometres Tonnes-kilomètres nettes	41	30	24	15	15	15	12	13	11	9
Colombia — Colombie										
Passenger-kilometres Voyageurs-kilomètres	58	257	232	204	160	50	55	37	17	25
Congo — Congo										
Passenger-kilometres Voyageurs-kilomètres	302	360	235	242	8	84	171	76	...	...
Net ton-kilometres Tonnes-kilomètres nettes	267	289	139	135	16	85	228	307	...	...

Country or area Pays ou zone	1995	1996	1997	1998	1999	2000	2001	2002	2003	2004
Croatia — Croatie										
Passenger-kilometres [12] Voyageurs-kilomètres [12]	1 139	1 205	1 158	1 092	1 137	1 252	1 241	1 195	1 163	1 213
Net ton-kilometres Tonnes-kilomètres nettes	1 974[12]	1 717[12]	1 876[12]	2 001[12]	1 849[12]	1 928[12]	2 249[12]	2 206[13]	2 487[13]	2 493[13]
Cuba — Cuba										
Passenger-kilometres Voyageurs-kilomètres	2 188	2 156	1 962	1 750	1 499	1 737	1 758	1 681	2 046	1 781
Net ton-kilometres Tonnes-kilomètres nettes	745	871	859	822	806	808	842	811	792	694
Czech Republic — République tchèque										
Passenger-kilometres Voyageurs-kilomètres	8 005	8 111	7 721	7 018	6 954	7 300	7 299	6 597	6 518	6 589[15]
Net ton-kilometres [14] Tonnes-kilomètres nettes [14]	22 623	22 338	21 010	18 709	16 713	17 496	16 882	15 810	15 862	15 091[15]
Denmark — Danemark										
Passenger-kilometres Voyageurs-kilomètres	4 684	4 621	4 978	5 163	5 113	5 327	5 521	5 541	5 620	5 730
Net ton-kilometres [16] Tonnes-kilomètres nettes [16]	1 985	1 757	1 983	2 058	1 938	2 025	1 961	1 906	1 985	2 147
Ecuador — Equateur										
Passenger-kilometres Voyageurs-kilomètres	47	51	47	44	5	5	32	33	4	2
Net ton-kilometres Tonnes-kilomètres nettes	3	1	...	14	...	...	...	...	...	...
Egypt [2] — Egypte [2]										
Passenger-kilometres Voyageurs-kilomètres	52 839	55 888	60 617	64 077	68 423	57 859	38 106	39 083	46 185	52 682
Net ton-kilometres Tonnes-kilomètres nettes	4 073	4 117	3 969	4 012	3 464	4 184	4 138	4 188	4 104	4 663
El Salvador — El Salvador										
Passenger-kilometres Voyageurs-kilomètres	5	7	7	6	8	10	11	...	...	...
Net ton-kilometres Tonnes-kilomètres nettes	13	17	17	24	19	13	8	...	...	...
Estonia — Estonie										
Passenger-kilometres Voyageurs-kilomètres	421	309	261	236	238	263	183	177	182	193
Net ton-kilometres Tonnes-kilomètres nettes	3 846	4 198	5 141	6 079	7 295	8 102	8 557	9 697	9 670	10 487
Ethiopia [17,18] — Ethiopie [17,18]										
Passenger-kilometres Voyageurs-kilomètres	293	218	206	151	150	152	173	123	82	...
Net ton-kilometres Tonnes-kilomètres nettes	93	104	106	90	116	116	80	85	97	...
Finland — Finlande										
Passenger-kilometres Voyageurs-kilomètres	3 184	3 254	3 376	3 377	3 415	3 405	3 282	3 318	3 338	3 352
Net ton-kilometres [19] Tonnes-kilomètres nettes [19]	9 293	8 806	9 856	9 885	9 753	10 107	9 857	9 664	10 047	10 105
France — France										
Passenger-kilometres Voyageurs-kilomètres	55 560	59 770	61 830	64 460	66 590	69 870	71 550	73 530	72 200	74 300
Net ton-kilometres [20] Tonnes-kilomètres nettes [20]	49 170	50 500	54 820	55 090	54 350	55 450	50 400	50 040	47 000	45 000
Georgia — Géorgie										
Passenger-kilometres Voyageurs-kilomètres	371	380	294	397	355	453	401	401	387	614
Net ton-kilometres Tonnes-kilomètres nettes	1 246	1 141	2 006	2 574	3 160	3 912	4 481	5 075	5 539	4 856

Country or area Pays ou zone	1995	1996	1997	1998	1999	2000	2001	2002	2003	2004
Germany — Allemagne										
Passenger-kilometres Voyageurs-kilomètres	74 970	75 975	73 917	72 389	73 587	75 111	75 314	70 819	70 784	72 563
Net ton-kilometres [21] Tonnes-kilomètres nettes [21]	68 046	67 227	72 703	73 560	71 356	76 032	74 260	75 414	78 463	86 409
Ghana — Ghana										
Passenger-kilometres Voyageurs-kilomètres	233	211	177	192	129	83	53	61	86	80
Net ton-kilometres Tonnes-kilomètres nettes	157	151	148	138	151	165	220	244	242	216
Greece — Grèce										
Passenger-kilometres Voyageurs-kilomètres	1 569	1 752	1 783	1 552	1 453	1 629	1 783	1 836	1 574	1 669
Net ton-kilometres Tonnes-kilomètres nettes	306[22]	350[22]	330[22]	322[22]	347[22]	427[22]	380[22]	327[22]	457	592
Guatemala — Guatemala										
Net ton-kilometres Tonnes-kilomètres nettes	14 242	836	...	...	...	...	...	...	...	...
Hungary — Hongrie										
Passenger-kilometres Voyageurs-kilomètres	8 441	8 582	8 669	8 884	9 514	9 693	10 005	10 531	10 286	10 544
Net ton-kilometres Tonnes-kilomètres nettes	8 422	7 634	8 149	8 150	7 734	8 095	7 731	7 752	8 109	8 749
India [23] — Inde [23]										
Passenger-kilometres Voyageurs-kilomètres	341 999	357 013	379 897	403 884	430 666	457 022	490 912	515 044	541 208	...
Net ton-kilometres Tonnes-kilomètres nettes	270 489	277 567	284 249	281 513	305 201	312 371	333 228	353 194	381 241	...
Indonesia — Indonésie										
Passenger-kilometres Voyageurs-kilomètres	15 500	15 223	15 518	16 970	17 820	19 228	18 270	16 329	15 031	15 078
Net ton-kilometres Tonnes-kilomètres nettes	4 172	4 700	5 030	4 963	5 035	4 997	4 859	4 450	4 355	4 691
Iran (Islamic Rep. of) — Iran (Rép. islamique d')										
Passenger-kilometres Voyageurs-kilomètres	7 294	7 044	6 103	5 637	6 451	7 128	8 043	8 582	9 314[24]	10 012[24]
Net ton-kilometres Tonnes-kilomètres nettes	11 865	13 638	14 400	12 638	14 082	14 179	14 613	15 842	18 048[24]	18 182[24]
Iraq — Iraq										
Passenger-kilometres Voyageurs-kilomètres	2 198	1 169	1 200	825	503	381	460	573	154	...
Net ton-kilometres [25] Tonnes-kilomètres nettes [25]	1 120	908	942	750	821	746	933	1 684	435	...
Ireland — Irlande										
Passenger-kilometres Voyageurs-kilomètres	1 291	1 295	1 388	1 421	1 458	1 389	1 515	1 628	1 601	1 582
Net ton-kilometres Tonnes-kilomètres nettes	602	570	522	466	526	491	516	426	398	399
Israel — Israël										
Passenger-kilometres Voyageurs-kilomètres	269	294	346	383	529	781	961	1 116	1 278	1 423
Net ton-kilometres Tonnes-kilomètres nettes	1 176	1 152	992	1 049	1 128	1 173	1 098	1 102	1 112	1 173
Italy — Italie										
Passenger-kilometres Voyageurs-kilomètres	49 700	50 300	49 500	47 285	49 424	47 133	46 675	...	...	...
Net ton-kilometres [25] Tonnes-kilomètres nettes [25]	24 050	23 314	25 285	24 704	23 781	24 995	24 352	...	...	...

Country or area / Pays ou zone	1995	1996	1997	1998	1999	2000	2001	2002	2003	2004
Japan — Japon										
Passenger-kilometres / Voyageurs-kilomètres	393 907	400 712	301 510	391 073	384 943	384 906	385 403	382 892	382 035	385 282
Net ton-kilometres / Tonnes-kilomètres nettes	23 695	24 991	18 661	23 136	22 676	22 131	22 363	21 984	22 549	22 643
Jordan — Jordanie										
Passenger-kilometres / Voyageurs-kilomètres	1	1	2	2	2	2	4	3	1	1
Net ton-kilometres / Tonnes-kilomètres nettes	698	735	625	596	585	671	371	531	497	563
Kazakhstan — Kazakhstan										
Passenger-kilometres / Voyageurs-kilomètres	13 159	14 188	12 802	10 668	8 859	10 215	10 384	10 449	10 686	11 849
Net ton-kilometres / Tonnes-kilomètres nettes	124 502	112 688	106 425	103 045	91 700	124 983	135 653	133 088	147 672	163 455
Kenya — Kenya										
Passenger-kilometres / Voyageurs-kilomètres	363	385	393	432	306	302	216	306	295	279
Net ton-kilometres / Tonnes-kilomètres nettes	1 371	1 338	1 068	1 111	1 492	1 557	1 603	1 638	1 789	1 399
Korea, Republic of — Corée, République de										
Passenger-kilometres / Voyageurs-kilomètres	29 292	29 580	30 073	32 977	28 606	28 528	28 882	27 492	27 228	28 459
Net ton-kilometres / Tonnes-kilomètres nettes	13 838	12 947	12 710	10 372	10 072	10 803	10 492	10 784	11 057	10 641
Kyrgyzstan — Kirghizistan										
Passenger-kilometres / Voyageurs-kilomètres	87	92	93	59	31	44	50	43	50	45
Net ton-kilometres / Tonnes-kilomètres nettes	403	481	472	466	354	338	332	395	562	715
Latvia — Lettonie										
Passenger-kilometres / Voyageurs-kilomètres	1 256	1 149	1 154	1 059	984	715	706	744	764	811
Net ton-kilometres [16] / Tonnes-kilomètres nettes [16]	9 757	12 412	13 970	12 995	12 210	13 310	14 179	15 020	17 955	18 618
Lithuania — Lituanie										
Passenger-kilometres / Voyageurs-kilomètres	1 130	953	842	800	745	611	533	498	432	443
Net ton-kilometres [26] / Tonnes-kilomètres nettes [26]	7 220	8 103	8 622	8 265	7 849	8 918	7 741	9 767	11 457	11 637
Luxembourg — Luxembourg										
Passenger-kilometres / Voyageurs-kilomètres	286	284	295	300	310	332	346	268	262	...
Net ton-kilometres / Tonnes-kilomètres nettes	566	574	613	624	660	683	634	613	562	...
Madagascar — Madagascar										
Passenger-kilometres / Voyageurs-kilomètres	...	...	81	35	28	19	...	...	...	...
Net ton-kilometres [7,27] / Tonnes-kilomètres nettes [7,27]	...	...	81	71	44	26	...	...	...	...
Malawi [23] — Malawi [23]										
Passenger-kilometres / Voyageurs-kilomètres	22	26	17	21	19	25	22	42	30	30
Net ton-kilometres / Tonnes-kilomètres nettes	74	57	46	55	62	80	66	64	18	26
Malaysia — Malaisie										
Passenger-kilometres / Voyageurs-kilomètres	1 270 [28]	1 385	1 508	1 411	1 333	1 241	1 199	1 138	1 031	1 152
Net ton-kilometres / Tonnes-kilomètres nettes	1 421	1 398	1 338	993	909	918	1 095	1 073	887	1 017

Country or area Pays ou zone	1995	1996	1997	1998	1999	2000	2001	2002	2003	2004
Mali — Mali										
Net ton-kilometres Tonnes-kilomètres nettes	254	405	...	...	...	...	...	...	...	...
Mexico — Mexique										
Passenger-kilometres Voyageurs-kilomètres	1 899	1 799	1 508	460	254	82	67	66	78	...
Net ton-kilometres Tonnes-kilomètres nettes	37 613	41 723	42 442	46 873	47 273	48 333	47 353	47 809	54 171	...
Mongolia — Mongolie										
Passenger-kilometres Voyageurs-kilomètres	680	733	951	981	1 010	1 067	1 062	1 067	1 039	1 219
Net ton-kilometres Tonnes-kilomètres nettes	2 280	2 529	2 554	2 815	3 492	4 283	5 288	6 461	7 253	8 878
Morocco — Maroc										
Passenger-kilometres Voyageurs-kilomètres	1 564	1 776	1 856	1 875	1 880	1 956	2 019	2 145	2 374	...
Net ton-kilometres Tonnes-kilomètres nettes	4 621	4 757	4 835	4 827	4 795	4 650	4 699	4 974	5 246	...
Mozambique — Mozambique										
Passenger-kilometres Voyageurs-kilomètres	251	358	387	155	145	130	142	138	82	106
Net ton-kilometres Tonnes-kilomètres nettes	886	983	896	765	737	605	778	808	778	794
Myanmar — Myanmar										
Passenger-kilometres Voyageurs-kilomètres	4 178	4 294	3 784	3 948	4 112	4 451	4 447	4 804	4 284	4 164
Net ton-kilometres [7] Tonnes-kilomètres nettes [7]	659	748	674	988	1 049	1 222	1 218	1 196	1 016	886
Netherlands — Pays-Bas										
Passenger-kilometres Voyageurs-kilomètres	13 499	13 695	13 875	14 107	14 281	14 666	14 392	14 288	13 848	13 439
Net ton-kilometres Tonnes-kilomètres nettes	3 097	3 163	3 435	3 793	3 988	4 522	4 293	4 323	4 962	5 225
New Zealand [2] — Nouvelle-Zélande [2]										
Net ton-kilometres Tonnes-kilomètres nettes	3 202	3 260	3 505	3 547	3 636	4 040	...	...	...	...
Nigeria — Nigéria										
Passenger-kilometres Voyageurs-kilomètres	161	170	179	...	...	...	...	...	...	...
Net ton-kilometres Tonnes-kilomètres nettes	108	114	120	...	...	...	...	...	...	...
Norway — Norvège										
Passenger-kilometres Voyageurs-kilomètres	2 381	2 449	2 561	2 652	2 733	2 707	2 594	2 543	2 474	2 657
Net ton-kilometres Tonnes-kilomètres nettes	2 684	2 804	2 975	2 948	2 894	2 955	2 887	3 019	2 627	2 804
Pakistan [3] — Pakistan [3]										
Passenger-kilometres Voyageurs-kilomètres	18 905	19 114	18 771	18 979	18 761	19 292	20 004	19 793	20 346	22 987
Net ton-kilometres Tonnes-kilomètres nettes	5 078	4 538	4 444	3 939	3 612	3 799	4 681	4 594	4 568	4 789
Panama — Panama										
Passenger-kilometres Voyageurs-kilomètres	1 069[29]	122[29]	9[31]	...	...	...	24 576[31]	35 693[30]	52 324	53 377
Net ton-kilometres Tonnes-kilomètres nettes	1 728[30]	710[30]	306[30,31]	...	...	...	4 896[30,31]	20 665[30]	41 863	52 946
Paraguay — Paraguay										
Net ton-kilometres Tonnes-kilomètres nettes	4	3	2	1	1	1	0	1	...	...

Railways: traffic — Passenger and net ton-kilometres: millions (*continued*)
Chemins de fer : trafic — Voyageurs et tonnes-kilomètres nettes : millions (*suite*)

Country or area Pays ou zone	1995	1996	1997	1998	1999	2000	2001	2002	2003	2004
Peru [7] — Pérou [7]										
Passenger-kilometres Voyageurs-kilomètres	231	222	206	180	69	107	124	99	103	...
Net ton-kilometres Tonnes-kilomètres nettes	843	878	839	890	677	874	1 154	1 112	1 117	...
Philippines — Philippines										
Passenger-kilometres Voyageurs-kilomètres	163	69	175	181	171	123	110	93	83	84
Net ton-kilometres Tonnes-kilomètres nettes	4	0[32]	...	...	...	49	67	63	69	76
Poland — Pologne										
Passenger-kilometres Voyageurs-kilomètres	26 635	26 569	25 806	25 664	26 198	24 093	22 469	20 809	19 638	18 690
Net ton-kilometres Tonnes-kilomètres nettes	69 116	68 332	68 651	61 760	55 471	54 448	47 913	47 756	49 595	52 332
Portugal — Portugal										
Passenger-kilometres Voyageurs-kilomètres	4 840	4 503[33]	4 563[33]	4 602[33]	4 380	3 834	3 898	3 926	3 585	3 693
Net ton-kilometres Tonnes-kilomètres nettes	2 342	2 178[33]	2 632[33]	2 340[33]	2 562	2 569	2 498	2 583	2 443	2 589
Republic of Moldova — République de Moldova										
Passenger-kilometres [4] Voyageurs-kilomètres [4]	1 019	882	789	656	343	315	325	355	352	346
Net ton-kilometres Tonnes-kilomètres nettes	3 134	2 897	2 937	2 575	1 191	1 513	1 980	2 748	3 019	3 006
Romania — Roumanie										
Passenger-kilometres [34] Voyageurs-kilomètres [34]	18 879	18 356	15 795	13 422	12 304	11 632	10 966	8 502	8 529	8 638
Net ton-kilometres Tonnes-kilomètres nettes	17 907	24 254	22 111	16 619	14 679	16 354	16 102	15 218	15 039	17 022
Russian Federation — Fédération de Russie										
Passenger-kilometres Voyageurs-kilomètres	192 200	181 200	170 300	152 900	141 000	167 100	157 900	152 900	157 600	164 300
Net ton-kilometres Tonnes-kilomètres nettes	1 214 000	1 131 000	1 100 000	1 020 000	1 205 000	1 373 000	1 434 000	1 510 000	1 669 000	1 802 000
Saudi Arabia — Arabie saoudite										
Passenger-kilometres Voyageurs-kilomètres	159	170	192	222	224	270	285	236	232	301
Net ton-kilometres Tonnes-kilomètres nettes	728	691	726	856	938	849	802	688	778	892
Senegal — Sénégal										
Passenger-kilometres Voyageurs-kilomètres	194	103	78	63	71	74	88	105	129	122[35]
Net ton-kilometres Tonnes-kilomètres nettes	475	474	446	435	401	361	321	345	375	358[35]
Serbia and Montenegro — Serbie-et-Monténégro										
Passenger-kilometres Voyageurs-kilomètres	2 611	1 830	1 744	1 622	860	1 436	1 262	1 141	970	962
Net ton-kilometres [7] Tonnes-kilomètres nettes [7]	1 855	2 062	2 432	2 793	1 267	1 969	2 042	2 328	2 646	3 258
Slovakia — Slovaquie										
Passenger-kilometres Voyageurs-kilomètres	4 202	3 769	3 057	3 092	2 968	2 870	2 805	2 682	2 316	2 228
Net ton-kilometres Tonnes-kilomètres nettes	13 674	12 017	12 373	11 753	9 859	11 234	10 929	10 383	10 113	9 702
Slovenia — Slovénie										
Passenger-kilometres Voyageurs-kilomètres	595	613	616	645	623	705	715	749	777	764
Net ton-kilometres Tonnes-kilomètres nettes	3 076	2 550	2 852	2 859	2 784	2 857	2 837	3 018	3 274	3 466[36]

Country or area Pays ou zone	1995	1996	1997	1998	1999	2000	2001	2002	2003	2004
South Africa [37,38] — Afrique du Sud [37,38]										
Passenger-kilometres Voyageurs-kilomètres	1 007	1 198	1 393	1 775	1 794	3 930	...	...	...	...
Net ton-kilometres Tonnes-kilomètres nettes	98 798	99 818	99 773	103 866	102 777	106 786	...	...	...	...
Spain — Espagne										
Passenger-kilometres Voyageurs-kilomètres	16 582	16 637	17 883	18 875	18 143 [39]	19 958 [40]	20 649 [40]	21 019 [40]	20 874 [40]	20 578 [40]
Net ton-kilometres [7] Tonnes-kilomètres nettes [7]	10 419	10 219	11 488	11 801	11 489 [39]	12 071 [40]	12 217 [40]	12 146 [40]	12 299 [40]	11 963 [40]
Sri Lanka [41] — Sri Lanka [41]										
Passenger-kilometres Voyageurs-kilomètres	3 321	3 103	3 146	3 073	3 104	3 208	3 979	4 079	4 627	4 684
Net ton-kilometres Tonnes-kilomètres nettes	136	107	98	105	103	88	109	131	129	134
Swaziland — Swaziland										
Net ton-kilometres Tonnes-kilomètres nettes	743	684	670	653	677	753	746	728	726	710
Sweden — Suède										
Passenger-kilometres Voyageurs-kilomètres	6 833	6 953 [42]	7 022 [42]	7 210 [42]	7 701 [42]	8 243	8 732	8 984	9 051	...
Net ton-kilometres Tonnes-kilomètres nettes	19 391	18 846 [42]	19 181 [42]	19 163 [42]	19 090 [42]	20 088 [42]	19 547 [42]	19 197	20 141	
Switzerland — Suisse										
Passenger-kilometres Voyageurs-kilomètres	13 408	13 326	14 104	...	...	...	...	...		
Net ton-kilometres Tonnes-kilomètres nettes	8 626	7 847	8 629	...	...	...	...	...		
Syrian Arab Republic — Rép. arabe syrienne										
Passenger-kilometres Voyageurs-kilomètres	498	454	294	182	187	197	307	384	525	692
Net ton-kilometres Tonnes-kilomètres nettes	1 285	1 864	1 472	1 430	1 577	1 568	1 492	1 814	1 885	1 923
Tajikistan [43] — Tadjikistan [43]										
Passenger-kilometres Voyageurs-kilomètres	134	95	129	121	61	73	32	42	50	50
Net ton-kilometres Tonnes-kilomètres nettes	2 115	1 719	1 384	1 458	1 282	1 326	1 248	1 086	1 086	1 118
Thailand [41] — Thaïlande [41]										
Passenger-kilometres Voyageurs-kilomètres	12 975	12 205	11 804	10 947	9 894	9 935	10 321	10 378	10 251	9 332
Net ton-kilometres Tonnes-kilomètres nettes	3 242	3 286	3 410	2 874	2 929	3 384	3 724	3 898	3 976	4 085
TFYR of Macedonia — L'ex-R.y. Macédoine										
Passenger-kilometres Voyageurs-kilomètres	65	120	141	150	150	176	133	98	92	94
Net ton-kilometres Tonnes-kilomètres nettes	169	271	279	408	380	527	462	334	373	426
Tunisia — Tunisie										
Passenger-kilometres [22] Voyageurs-kilomètres [22]	996	988	1 094	1 133	1 196	1 258	1 285	1 265	...	...
Net ton-kilometres [7,44] Tonnes-kilomètres nettes [7,44]	2 317	2 329	2 338	2 349	2 365	2 274	2 279	2 250	...	...
Turkey — Turquie										
Passenger-kilometres Voyageurs-kilomètres	5 797	5 229	5 840	6 161	6 146	5 833	5 568	5 204	5 878	5 237
Net ton-kilometres Tonnes-kilomètres nettes	8 632	9 018	9 717	8 466	8 446	9 895	7 562	7 224	8 669	9 417
Uganda — Ouganda										
Passenger-kilometres Voyageurs-kilomètres	30	25	5 [45]	...	...	...	...	...	...	...
Net ton-kilometres Tonnes-kilomètres nettes	245	184	144	148	200	219	217	217	212	229

Country or area Pays ou zone	1995	1996	1997	1998	1999	2000	2001	2002	2003	2004
Ukraine — Ukraine										
Passenger-kilometres Voyageurs-kilomètres	63 759	59 080	54 540	49 938	47 600	51 767	49 661	50 544	52 558	51 726
Net ton-kilometres Tonnes-kilomètres nettes	195 762	160 384	160 433	158 693	156 336	172 840	177 465	193 141	225 287	233 987
United Kingdom [23,46] — Royaume-Uni [23,46]										
Passenger-kilometres Voyageurs-kilomètres	30 039	32 135	34 950	36 270	38 500	38 200	39 100	39 700	40 900	42 400
Net ton-kilometres Tonnes-kilomètres nettes	13 136	15 144	16 949	17 369	18 200	18 100	19 400	18 700	18 900	20 700
United States — États-Unis										
Passenger-kilometres [47] Voyageurs-kilomètres [47]	8 924	8 127	8 317	8 539	8 581	8 852	8 950	8 594	9 141	8 869
Net ton-kilometres Tonnes-kilomètres nettes	1 906 300 [48]	1 984 654 [48]	1 974 337 [48]	2 015 138 [48]	2 098 066 [48]	2 145 632 [48]	2 188 827 [48]	2 205 716 [48]	2 270 741	...
Uruguay — Uruguay										
Passenger-kilometres Voyageurs-kilomètres	...	...	17	14	10	9	9	8	11	11
Net ton-kilometres Tonnes-kilomètres nettes	184	182	204	244	272	239	209	178	188	297
Uzbekistan — Ouzbékistan										
Passenger-kilometres Voyageurs-kilomètres	3	2	2	2	2	2	2	2	2	2
Net ton-kilometres Tonnes-kilomètres nettes	17	20	17	16	14	15	16	18	19	18
Venezuela (Bolivarian Republic of) — Venezuela (Rép. bolivarienne)										
Passenger-kilometres Voyageurs-kilomètres	12	15	...	...	...	...	...	...	...	...
Net ton-kilometres Tonnes-kilomètres nettes	53	45	54	79	54	59	81	32	12	22
Viet Nam — Viet Nam										
Passenger-kilometres Voyageurs-kilomètres	2 133	2 261	2 476	2 542	2 722	3 200	3 426	3 697	4 069	4 376
Net ton-kilometres Tonnes-kilomètres nettes	1 751	1 684	1 533	1 369	1 446	1 955	2 054	2 392	2 725	2 745
Yemen — Yémen										
Passenger-kilometres Voyageurs-kilomètres	2 051	2 260	2 492	...	...	...	...	...	...	...
Zambia — Zambie										
Passenger-kilometres Voyageurs-kilomètres	778	749	755	586						
Net ton-kilometres Tonnes-kilomètres nettes	90	666	758	702						
Zimbabwe [2,49] — Zimbabwe [2,49]										
Net ton-kilometres Tonnes-kilomètres nettes	7 180	4 990	5 115	9 122	4 375	3 326	3 100	4 088	...	...

Source

United Nations Statistics Division, New York, transport statistics database.

Notes

[1] Including urban transport only.
[2] Data refer to fiscal years ending 30 June.
[3] Data refer to fiscal years beginning 1 July.

[4] Including passengers carried without revenues.
[5] Including urban railways traffic.
[6] Including service traffic, animals, baggage and parcels.

Source

Organisation des Nations Unies, Division de statistique, New York, la base de données pour les statistiques des transports.

Notes

[1] Les chemins de fer urbains seulement.
[2] Les données se réfèrent aux exercices budgétaires finissant le 30 juin.
[3] Les données se réfèrent aux exercices budgétaires commençant le 1er juillet.
[4] Y compris passagers transportés gratuitement.
[5] Y compris le trafic de chemins-de-fer urbains.
[6] Y compris le trafic de service, les animaux, les baggages et les colis.

53

Railways: traffic— Passenger and net ton-kilometres: millions (*continued*)
Chemins de fer : trafic— Voyageurs et tonnes-kilomètres nettes : millions (*suite*)

7 Including service traffic.

8 From 1996 to 2001, annual data cover 12 months ending June.

9 For statistical purposes, the data for China do not include those for the Hong Kong Special Administrative Region (Hong Kong SAR), Macao Special Administrative Region (Macao SAR) and Taiwan Province of China.

10 May include service traffic.

11 Kowloon - Canton Railway only.

12 Beginning 1993, railway transport of passengers includes urban transport of passengers.

13 Excluding privately-owned wagons.

14 Including only state-owned railways.

15 Preliminary data.

16 Including passengers' baggage and parcel post (Latvia: also mail).

17 Including traffic of the Djibouti portion of the Djibouti-Addis Ababa line.

18 Data refer to fiscal years beginning 7 July.

19 Beginning 1995, wagon loads traffic only.

20 Including passengers' baggage.

21 Including service traffic and baggage.

22 Including military traffic (Greece: also government traffic).

23 Data refer to fiscal years beginning 1 April.

24 Data refer to fiscal years ending 20 March.

25 Excluding livestock.

26 Prior to 1994, data refer to operated ton-kilometres which is the weight in tons of freight carried multiplied by the distance in kilometres actually run; beginning 1994, data refer to net ton-kilometres which is the weight in tons of freight carried multiplied by distance in kilometres for which payments were made.

27 Including baggage and service traffic.

28 Data refer to Peninsular Malaysia only.

29 Panama Railway and National Railway of Chiriqui.

30 Panama Railway only.

31 Beginning August 1997, railway operations closed. Beginning July 2001, Panama Railway resumed operations.

32 Freight train operations suspended from November 1995 to August 1996 due to typhoon damages.

33 Excluding river traffic of the railway company.

34 Including military and government personnel.

35 National estimation.

36 Prior to 2004, data are based on goods movements (origin/destination of goods irrespective of modes of transport). Since 2004 data are based on journeys (place of loading/unloading from rail vehicle).

37 Beginning 1988, excluding Namibia.

38 Data refer to fiscal years ending 31 March.

39 RENFE only.

40 RENFE and narrow-gauge trains.

41 Data refer to fiscal years ending 30 September.

42 Including Swedish State Railways and MTAB.

43 Beginning 1992, decline due to border changes affecting the Dushanbe branch of the Sredne-Asiatskaya (Central Asia) Railway Co.

44 Ordinary goods only.

45 Beginning late 1997, passenger services suspended.

46 Excluding Northern Ireland.

47 Includes National Passenger Railroad Corporation (Amtrak) only.

48 Class I railways only.

49 Including traffic in Botswana.

7 Y compris le trafic de service.

8 Pour la période de 1996 à 2001, les données années se réfèrent aux douze mois finissant 30 juin.

9 Pour la présentation des statistiques, les données pour Chine ne comprennent pas la Région Administrative Spéciale de Hong Kong (Hong Kong RAS), la Région Administrative Spéciale de Macao (Macao RAS) et la province de Taiwan.

10 Le trafic de service peut être compris.

11 Chemin de fer de Kowloon-Canton seulement.

12 A compter de l'annee 1993 y compris le transport urbain de passagers.

13 Non compris wagons privés.

14 Y compris chemins-de-fer de l'état seulement.

15 Données préliminaires.

16 Y compris les bagages des voyageurs et les colis postaux (Lettonie : courrier aussi).

17 Y compris le trafic de la ligne Djibouti-Addis Abeba en Djibouti.

18 Les données se réfèrent aux exercices budgétaires commençant le 7 juillet.

19 A compter de 1995, y compris trafic de charge de waggon seulement.

20 Y compris les bagages des voyageurs.

21 Y compris les transports pour les besoins du service et les bagages.

22 Y compris le trafic militaire (Grèce : et de l'Etat aussi).

23 Les données se réfèrent aux exercices budgétaires commençant le 1er avril.

24 Les données se réfèrent aux exercices budgétaires finissant le 20 mars.

25 Non compris le bétail.

26 Avant 1994, les données se réfèrent aux tonnes-kilomètres transportées, c'est-à-dire le produit du poids et de la distance effectivement parcourue. A partir de l'année 1994, l'unité utilisée est la tonne-kilomètre nette, c'est-à-dire le produit du poids et de la distance pour lequel un paiement a été effectué.

27 Y compris bagages et les transports pour les besoins du service.

28 Les données se rapportent à Malaisie péninsulaire seulement.

29 Chemin de fer de Panama et chemin de fer national de Chiriqui.

30 Chemin de fer de Panama seulement.

31 A cessé de fonctionner en août 1997. A compter de juillet 2001, le Chemin de fer de Panama a recommencé des opérations.

32 Les opérations de train de marchandises interrompues pendant la période de novembre 1995 à août 1996 à cause des dommages de typhon.

33 Non compris le trafic fluvial de la compagnie des chemins de fer.

34 Y compris les militaires et les fonctionnaires.

35 Estimation nationale.

36 Avant 2004, les données sont basées sur le mouvement des marchandises (origine/destination quel que soit le mode de transport). À partir de 2004, les données sont basées sur les trajets (lieu de chargement/de déchargement des wagons).

37 A partir de 1988, non compris la Namibie.

38 Les données se réfèrent aux exercices budgétaires finissant le 31 mars.

39 RENFE seulement.

40 Réseau national des chemins de fer espagnols et chemins de fer à voie étroite.

41 Les données se réfèrent aux exercices budgétaires finissant le 30 septembre.

42 Y compris chemins-de-fer de l'état y MTAB.

43 A compter de 1992, réduction imputable à des changements de frontière affectant la ligne de Douchanbé de la la Société des chemins de fer d'Asie centrale.

44 Petite vitesse seulement.

45 A compter de l'année de 1997, transport passager interrompu.

46 Non compris l'Irlande du Nord.

47 Y compris National Passenger Railroad Corporation (Amtrak) seulement.

48 Réseaux de catégorie 1 seulement.

49 Y compris le trafic en Botswana.

Motor vehicles in use
Passenger cars and commercial vehicles: thousands

Véhicules automobiles en circulation
Voitures de tourisme et véhicules utilitaires : milliers de véhicules

Country or area Pays ou zone	1995	1996	1997	1998	1999	2000	2001	2002	2003	2004
Afghanistan — Afghanistan										
Passenger cars Voitures de tourisme	1.6	4.1	4.6	4.9	5.4	6.2	8.6[1]	8.6[1]	...	...
Commercial vehicles Véhicules utilitaires	0.6	4.5	5.3	5.4	6.2	7.0	4.5[1]	4.5[1]	...	...
Albania — Albanie										
Passenger cars Voitures de tourisme	58.6	67.2	76.8	90.7	99.0	114.5	133.5	148.5	174.7	...
Commercial vehicles Véhicules utilitaires	29.1	30.6	33.2	37.1	40.9	43.0	73.0	73.0	88.8	...
Algeria — Algérie										
Passenger cars Voitures de tourisme	1 562.0	1 588.0	1 615.0	1 634.0	1 677.0	1 692.0	1 708.0	1 739.0	...	...
Commercial vehicles Véhicules utilitaires	933.0	958.0	953.0	964.0	987.0	996.0	1 002.0	1 010.0	...	...
American Samoa — Samoa américaines										
Passenger cars Voitures de tourisme	4.7	5.4	5.3	5.7	6.2	...	...	...	...	...
Commercial vehicles Véhicules utilitaires	0.4	0.5	0.5	0.7	0.7	...	...	...	...	...
Angola [1] — Angola [1]										
Passenger cars Voitures de tourisme	...	...	103.4	107.1	117.2	117.2	117.2	117.2	...	...
Commercial vehicles Véhicules utilitaires	...	...	107.6	110.5	118.3	118.3	118.3	118.3	...	...
Antigua and Barbuda — Antigua-et-Barbuda										
Passenger cars Voitures de tourisme	15.1	21.6[2]	23.7[2]	24.0[2]	...	...	...	...	...	...
Commercial vehicles Véhicules utilitaires	4.8	...	...	...	...	...	...	...	...	...
Argentina — Argentine										
Passenger cars Voitures de tourisme	4 665.0	4 783.9	4 904.3	5 047.8	5 056.7	5 386.7	...	...	...	...
Commercial vehicles Véhicules utilitaires	1 233.0	4 254.0	1 172.0	1 094.0	1 029.0	1 004.0	...	...	...	...
Australia — Australie										
Passenger cars Voitures de tourisme	8 661.0[3]	9 022.0	9 240.0[4]	9 527.0[4]	9 686.0[4]	...	9 836.0[5]	10 101.0[5]	10 366.0[5]	10 629.0[4]
Commercial vehicles Véhicules utilitaires	1 990.0[3]	2 076.0	2 112.0[4]	2 178.0[4]	2 112.0[4]	...	2 256.0[5]	2 314.0[5]	2 381.0[5]	2 467.0[4]
Austria [6] — Autriche [6]										
Passenger cars Voitures de tourisme	3 593.6	3 690.7	3 782.5	3 887.2	4 009.6	4 097.1	4 182.0	3 987.1	4 054.3	4 109.0
Commercial vehicles [7] Véhicules utilitaires [7]	710.1	721.1	736.2	752.1	767.8	779.7	787.9	765.6	765.7	775.0
Azerbaijan — Azerbaïdjan										
Passenger cars Voitures de tourisme	278.3	273.7	271.3	281.3	307.0	332.1	343.0	350.6	370.4	404.0
Commercial vehicles Véhicules utilitaires	125.5	122.9	115.6	117.6	122.8	133.4	127.6	120.4	129.3	108.0[8]
Bahamas — Bahamas										
Passenger cars Voitures de tourisme	67.1	86.6[9]	89.7[9]	86.6[1]	97.5[1]	80.0[1]	80.0[1]	90.0[1]	...	112.8
Commercial vehicles Véhicules utilitaires	13.7	16.9[9]	17.6[9]	...	...	...	...	...	...	3.5

Country or area Pays ou zone	1995	1996	1997	1998	1999	2000	2001	2002	2003	2004
Bahrain — Bahreïn										
Passenger cars Voitures de tourisme	135.4	140.0	147.9	160.2	169.6	175.7	187.0	...	...	...
Commercial vehicles Véhicules utilitaires	30.5	31.5	32.8	34.5	35.7	36.8	38.4	...	...	...
Bangladesh — Bangladesh										
Passenger cars Voitures de tourisme	51.1	55.8	61.2	65.0	...	...	...	...	...	...
Commercial vehicles Véhicules utilitaires	111.7	126.8	138.1	145.9	...	...	...	...	...	...
Barbados — Barbade										
Passenger cars [10] Voitures de tourisme [10]	47.2	49.8	53.6	57.5	62.1	...	...	...	...	...
Commercial vehicles [11] Véhicules utilitaires [11]	7.1	6.9	7.9	8.6	9.4	...	...	...	...	...
Belarus — Bélarus										
Passenger cars Voitures de tourisme	939.6	1 035.8	1 132.8	1 279.2	1 351.1	1 421.9	1 467.6	1 552.4	1 656.2	1 708.0
Belgium — Belgique										
Passenger cars Voitures de tourisme	4 270.0	4 336.0	4 412.0	4 489.0	4 580.0	4 675.0	4 737.0	4 784.0	4 818.0	4 871.0
Commercial vehicles Véhicules utilitaires	457.0	472.0	491.0	510.0	539.0	563.0	587.0	602.0	619.0	641.0
Belize [9,12] — Belize [9,12]										
Passenger cars Voitures de tourisme	16.1	17.0	19.1	19.3	24.2	26.1	28.8	32.6	...	...
Commercial vehicles Véhicules utilitaires	3.0	3.1	3.6	3.7	6.5	6.4	7.6	7.8	...	...
Benin [1] — Bénin [1]										
Passenger cars Voitures de tourisme	7.3	7.3	7.3	7.3	...	103.4	103.4	135.7	135.7	...
Commercial vehicles Véhicules utilitaires	5.7	5.8	6.0	6.2	...	96.6	96.6	18.8	19.2	...
Bermuda — Bermudes										
Passenger cars Voitures de tourisme	21.1	21.2	21.6	22.0	22.6	20.0	20.3	20.8	21.0	21.5
Commercial vehicles Véhicules utilitaires	4.5	4.2	4.2	4.5	4.4	4.6	4.8	4.8	4.7	4.8
Bolivia — Bolivie										
Passenger cars Voitures de tourisme	201.9	220.3	234.1	178.3	166.0	234.0	244.0	249.0	264.0	294.0
Commercial vehicles Véhicules utilitaires	112.2	119.8	124.8	110.4	99.0	139.0	146.0	150.0	158.0	174.0
Botswana — Botswana										
Passenger cars Voitures de tourisme	31.0	27.0	28.0	37.0	45.0	48.0	54.0	60.0	65.0	74.0
Commercial vehicles Véhicules utilitaires	64.0	48.0	52.0	59.0	68.0	78.0	83.0	89.0	93.0	99.0
Brazil [1] — Brésil [1]										
Passenger cars Voitures de tourisme	10 320.5	12 666.0	9 385.8	10 828.8	11 630.7	14 820.0	15 210.0	16 606.1	...	...
Commercial vehicles Véhicules utilitaires	2 520.4	2 896.0	2 087.5	2 429.5	2 630.1	3 300.0	4 256.7	4 509.6	...	...
British Virgin Islands — Iles Vierges britanniques										
Passenger cars Voitures de tourisme	5.0 [2]	5.6	5.8	5.9	6.0	6.1	7.1	7.4	8.1	9.1
Commercial vehicles Véhicules utilitaires	1.3	1.3	1.4	1.4	1.5	1.4	1.6	1.8	1.6	2.2

Country or area Pays ou zone	1995	1996	1997	1998	1999	2000	2001	2002	2003	2004
Brunei Darussalam — Brunéi Darussalam										
Passenger cars Voitures de tourisme	142.0	150.0	163.0	171.0	176.0	183.0	189.0	200.0	212.0	226.0
Commercial vehicles Véhicules utilitaires	16.0	17.0	18.0	19.0	19.0	19.0	20.0	20.0	21.0	22.0
Bulgaria — Bulgarie										
Passenger cars Voitures de tourisme	1 647.6	1 707.0	1 730.5	1 809.4	1 908.4	1 992.8	2 085.7	2 174.1	2 309.3	2 438.0
Commercial vehicles Véhicules utilitaires	264.0	271.0	273.0	284.0	294.0	302.0	313.0	323.0	337.0	354.0
Burkina Faso — Burkina Faso										
Passenger cars Voitures de tourisme	35.5[1]	35.5[1]	35.5[1]	25.3[1]	26.3	26.5[1]	26.5[1]	26.5[1]	26.5[1]	...
Commercial vehicles Véhicules utilitaires	19.5[1]	19.5[1]	19.5[1]	14.9[1]	19.6	22.6[1]	22.6[1]	22.6[1]	22.6[1]	...
Burundi[1] — Burundi[1]										
Passenger cars Voitures de tourisme	8.2	8.2	8.2	6.6	6.9	7.0	7.0	7.0	7.0	...
Commercial vehicles Véhicules utilitaires	11.8	11.8	11.8	9.3	9.3	9.3	9.3	9.3	9.3	...
Cambodia — Cambodge										
Passenger cars Voitures de tourisme	8.0	6.3	8.4	8.0	8.5	8.3	...	...	...	...
Commercial vehicles Véhicules utilitaires	2.1	1.4	1.8	1.6	1.5	3.1	...	...	...	...
Cameroon — Cameroun										
Passenger cars Voitures de tourisme	94.7	100.9	102.2	105.8	110.7	115.9	134.5	151.9	173.1	...
Commercial vehicles Véhicules utilitaires	39.6	40.6	41.6	43.2	45.3	47.4	51.1	37.4	57.4	...
Canada[6] — Canada[6]										
Passenger cars Voitures de tourisme	13 182.9	13 251.1	13 486.9	13 887.3	16 538.0	16 861.0	17 054.8	17 543.6	17 756.0	17 920.0
Commercial vehicles Véhicules utilitaires	3 420.3	3 476.2	3 526.9	3 625.8	649.1[13]	668.0[13]	654.5[14]	644.3[14]	660.4[14]	675.0[14]
Cape Verde — Cap-Vert										
Passenger cars Voitures de tourisme	8.0	9.3	10.3	11.4	13.5	...	...	...	...	...
Commercial vehicles Véhicules utilitaires	2.0	2.2	2.5	2.8	3.1	...	...	...	...	...
Cayman Islands — Iles Caïmanes										
Passenger cars Voitures de tourisme	13.5	14.9	16.0	15.8	17.9	19.8	20.3	22.6	...	...
Commercial vehicles Véhicules utilitaires	3.1	3.4	3.7	3.6	4.1	4.4	4.5	4.8	...	...
Central African Rep. — Rép. centrafricaine										
Passenger cars Voitures de tourisme	8.9	...	...	4.5[1]	4.9[1]	5.3[1]	5.3[1]	5.3[1]	...	...
Commercial vehicles Véhicules utilitaires	3.5	...	...	5.4[1]	5.8[1]	6.3[1]	6.3[1]	6.3[1]	...	...
Chad[15] — Tchad[15]										
Passenger cars Voitures de tourisme	8.7	...	...	...	...	...	...	...	...	...
Commercial vehicles Véhicules utilitaires	12.4	...	...	...	...	...	...	...	...	...
Chile — Chili										
Passenger cars Voitures de tourisme	1 026.0	1 121.2	1 175.8	1 236.9	1 323.8	1 334.0[17]	1 368.0[17]	1 389.0[17]	1 419.0[17]	1 505.0[17]
Commercial vehicles Véhicules utilitaires	540.0[16]	585.7[16]	635.2[16]	672.2[16]	708.5[16]	701.3	712.9	734.0	737.6	756.0

Country or area Pays ou zone	1995	1996	1997	1998	1999	2000	2001	2002	2003	2004
China [18] — Chine [18]										
Passenger cars Voitures de tourisme	4 179.0	4 880.2	5 805.6	6 548.3	7 402.3	8 537.3	9 939.6	12 023.7	14 788.0	17 359.0
Commercial vehicles Véhicules utilitaires	5 854.3	5 750.3	6 012.3	6 278.9	6 769.5	7 163.7	7 652.8	8 122.2	8 535.0	8 930.0
China, Hong Kong SAR — Chine, Hong Kong RAS										
Passenger cars Voitures de tourisme	303.3	311.2	332.8	336.2	339.6	350.4	358.6	358.9	357.0	363.0
Commercial vehicles Véhicules utilitaires	134.2	133.7	135.9	133.4	132.3	133.2	132.0	130.8	129.5	131.0
China, Macao SAR [19] — Chine, Macao RAS [19]										
Passenger cars Voitures de tourisme	34.5	38.9	42.9	46.3	47.8	48.9	49.9	53.3	57.0	61.3
Commercial vehicles Véhicules utilitaires	6.2	6.3	6.6	6.6	7.4	7.1	6.6	6.9	7.1	7.5
Colombia — Colombie										
Passenger cars Voitures de tourisme	1 542.0	1 642.5	1 746.1	1 860.4	1 907.3	1 947.0	1 987.8	2 042.2	2 099.3	2 119.6
Commercial vehicles Véhicules utilitaires	285.1	299.2	312.6	327.4	334.7	342.5	348.8	355.7	360.5	343.5
Congo [1] — Congo [1]										
Passenger cars Voitures de tourisme	29.0	29.0	29.0	24.9	26.2	29.7	29.7	...	...	...
Commercial vehicles Véhicules utilitaires	16.6	16.6	16.6	19.2	20.4	23.1	23.1	...	...	...
Costa Rica — Costa Rica										
Passenger cars Voitures de tourisme	254.8[6]	272.9[6]	294.1	316.8	326.5	342.0	354.4	367.8	582.0	621.0
Commercial vehicles Véhicules utilitaires	141.4[6]	151.1[6]	153.1	164.8	169.8	177.9	184.3	191.3	195.0	199.0
Côte d'Ivoire [1] — Côte d'Ivoire [1]										
Passenger cars Voitures de tourisme	111.9	74.2	76.2	98.4	109.6	113.9	113.9	113.9	...	...
Commercial vehicles Véhicules utilitaires	50.3	35.3	35.3	45.4	54.1	54.9	54.9	54.9	...	...
Croatia — Croatie										
Passenger cars Voitures de tourisme	710.9	835.7	932.3	1 000.0	1 063.5	1 124.8	1 195.5	1 244.3	1 293.4	1 338.0
Commercial vehicles Véhicules utilitaires	77.4	99.5	114.5	120.6	123.4	127.2	134.3	143.5	153.1	160.0
Cuba [20] — Cuba [20]										
Commercial vehicles Véhicules utilitaires	18.0	16.0	17.0	18.0	20.0	23.0	23.0	23.0	24.0	24.0
Cyprus — Chypre										
Passenger cars Voitures de tourisme	219.7	226.8	235.0	249.2	257.0	267.6	280.1	287.6	302.5	336.0
Commercial vehicles Véhicules utilitaires	104.9	108.0	109.7	113.6	115.8	119.6	123.2	123.3	125.7	126.0
Czech Republic — République tchèque										
Passenger cars [21] Voitures de tourisme [21]	3 113.5	3 192.5[24]	3 391.5[24]	3 493.0[24]	3 439.7[24]	3 438.9[24]	3 529.8[24]	3 647.1[24]	3 706.0[24]	3 816.0[24]
Commercial vehicles [22,23] Véhicules utilitaires [22,23]	490.0	281.1[24]	305.1[24]	320.6[24]	329.9[24]	339.3[24]	364.1[24]	397.6[24]	414.0[24]	445.0[24]
Dem. Rep. of the Congo [1] — Rép. dém. du Congo [1]										
Passenger cars Voitures de tourisme	...	...	...	172.6	172.6	...	...	...	...	...
Commercial vehicles Véhicules utilitaires	...	...	...	28.2	34.6	...	...	...	...	...

Country or area Pays ou zone	1995	1996	1997	1998	1999	2000	2001	2002	2003	2004
Denmark [6,25] — Danemark [6,25]										
Passenger cars Voitures de tourisme	1 679.0	1 738.9	1 783.1	1 817.1	1 843.8	1 854.1	1 872.6	1 888.3	1 894.6	1 916.0
Commercial vehicles Véhicules utilitaires	347.4	353.7	359.8	371.5	387.2	398.8	406.2	415.7	426.9	450.0
Dominica — Dominique										
Passenger cars Voitures de tourisme	7.4	7.9	8.3	8.7	...	...	...	...	...	...
Commercial vehicles [26] Véhicules utilitaires [26]	2.9	3.3	3.3	3.4	...	...	...	...	...	...
Dominican Republic — Rép. dominicaine										
Passenger cars Voitures de tourisme	183.8	271.0	331.0	384.7	445.9	455.6	561.3	616.0	652.0	630.0
Commercial vehicles Véhicules utilitaires	117.5	164.8	202.3	236.7	247.2	283.0	284.7	336.0	355.0	341.0
Ecuador — Equateur										
Passenger cars Voitures de tourisme	254.0	268.0	277.0	301.0	322.0	336.0	326.0	358.0	394.0	411.0
Commercial vehicles Véhicules utilitaires	244.0	248.0	256.0	258.0	272.0	281.0	268.0	278.0	297.0	306.0
Egypt — Egypte										
Passenger cars Voitures de tourisme	1 313.0	1 372.0	1 439.0	1 525.0	1 616.0	1 700.0	1 767.0	1 847.0	1 881.0	1 960.0
Commercial vehicles Véhicules utilitaires	466.0	484.0	508.0	539.0	577.0	600.0	624.0	650.0	686.0	715.0
El Salvador — El Salvador										
Passenger cars Voitures de tourisme	113.8	121.8	129.8	136.6	142.2	148.0	...	...	...	...
Commercial vehicles Véhicules utilitaires	209.9	218.6	227.3	235.4	243.0	250.8	...	...	...	...
Estonia — Estonie										
Passenger cars Voitures de tourisme	383.4	406.6	427.7	451.0	458.7	463.9	407.3	400.7	434.0	471.2
Commercial vehicles Véhicules utilitaires	72.6	78.1	83.1	86.9	87.2	88.8	86.1	85.5	88.8	91.0
Ethiopia [27] — Ethiopie [27]										
Passenger cars Voitures de tourisme	60.0	62.4	66.2	68.9	71.0	73.1	76.0	81.2	...	...
Commercial vehicles Véhicules utilitaires	23.3	29.0	30.3	34.0	34.6	39.4	43.7	44.5	...	...
Fiji — Fidji										
Passenger cars [28] Voitures de tourisme [28]	49.7	51.7	53.0	55.0	58.0	61.0	66.0	70.0	75.0	81.0
Commercial vehicles [29] Véhicules utilitaires [29]	47.5	48.5	49.0	50.0	51.0	52.0	53.0	54.0	56.0	57.0
Finland — Finlande										
Passenger cars Voitures de tourisme	1 900.9	1 942.8	1 948.1	2 021.1	2 082.6	2 134.7	2 160.6	2 194.7	2 274.6	2 346.7
Commercial vehicles [8] Véhicules utilitaires [8]	260.1	266.9	275.4	289.7	303.2	314.2	322.3	329.7	337.5	365.9
France — France										
Passenger cars Voitures de tourisme	25 100.0	25 500.0	26 090.0	26 810.0	27 480.0	28 060.0	28 700.0	29 160.0	29 560.0	29 700.0
Commercial vehicles [30] Véhicules utilitaires [30]	5 374.0	5 437.0	5 561.0	5 680.0	5 790.0	5 933.0	6 083.0	6 178.0	6 424.0	...
French Guiana [1] — Guyane française [1]										
Passenger cars Voitures de tourisme	26.5	28.2	28.2	32.9	32.9	32.9	32.9	32.9	...	...
Commercial vehicles Véhicules utilitaires	8.1	8.9	9.4	11.9	11.9	11.9	11.9	11.9	...	...

Country or area Pays ou zone	1995	1996	1997	1998	1999	2000	2001	2002	2003	2004
Gabon [15] — Gabon [15]										
Passenger cars Voitures de tourisme	23.0	...	...	...	...	...	...	...	...	...
Commercial vehicles Véhicules utilitaires	10.0	...	...	...	...	...	...	...	...	...
Gambia — Gambie										
Passenger cars Voitures de tourisme	6.4	...	...	...	...	...	...	...	...	...
Commercial vehicles Véhicules utilitaires	3.5	...	...	...	...	...	...	...	...	...
Georgia — Géorgie										
Passenger cars Voitures de tourisme	361.0	324.0	266.0	260.0	248.0	245.0	248.0	252.0	255.0	377.0[31]
Commercial vehicles Véhicules utilitaires	104.0	91.0	80.0	71.0	69.0	67.0	70.0 .	70.0	69.0	84.0[31]
Germany [32] — Allemagne [32]										
Passenger cars Voitures de tourisme	40 404.3	40 987.5	41 372.0	41 673.8	42 323.7	42 839.9	43 772.2	44 383.3	44 657.3	45 022.9
Commercial vehicles Véhicules utilitaires	3 232.0	3 271.7	3 294.0	3 332.7	3 422.1	...	3 566.6	3 596.3	3 550.8	3 505.4
Ghana — Ghana										
Passenger cars Voitures de tourisme	31.0[1]	31.0[1]	32.0[1]	64.0[1]	90.0[1]	92.0	91.0	91.0	92.0	...
Commercial vehicles Véhicules utilitaires	36.0[1]	38.0[1]	38.0[1]	109.0[1]	120.0[1]	120.0	121.0	124.0	124.0	...
Gibraltar — Gibraltar										
Passenger cars Voitures de tourisme	18.4	...	...	...	...	...	...	13.0	13.0	14.0
Commercial vehicles Véhicules utilitaires	1.0	...	...	...	...	...	...	...	...	...
Greece — Grèce										
Passenger cars Voitures de tourisme	2 205.0	2 339.0	2 500.0	2 676.0	2 929.0	3 195.0	3 424.0	3 646.0	3 840.0	4 074.0
Commercial vehicles Véhicules utilitaires	908.0	940.0	978.0	1 014.0	1 051.0	1 085.0	1 113.0	1 136.0	1 158.0	1 186.0
Greenland [6] — Groenland [6]										
Passenger cars Voitures de tourisme	1.9	2.6	1.8	2.0	2.4	1.9	2.5	2.5	...	...
Commercial vehicles Véhicules utilitaires	1.4	1.2	1.5	1.4	1.5	0.9	1.7	1.8	...	...
Grenada — Grenade										
Passenger cars [33] Voitures de tourisme [33]	9.0	9.7	10.7	12.0	13.3	14.6	15.8	...	...	...
Commercial vehicles Véhicules utilitaires	2.2	2.4	2.7	3.1	3.6	3.9	4.2	...	...	...
Guadeloupe [1] — Guadeloupe [1]										
Passenger cars Voitures de tourisme	97.0	106.5	107.6	117.7	117.7	117.7	117.7	117.7	...	...
Commercial vehicles Véhicules utilitaires	28.9	32.5	34.1	31.4	31.4	31.4	31.4	31.4	...	...
Guam — Guam										
Passenger cars Voitures de tourisme	79.8	79.1	67.8	69.0	66.4	64.5	45.5	52.7	...	...
Commercial vehicles Véhicules utilitaires	34.7	33.8	28.9	28.9	27.4	26.6	19.3	21.9	...	...
Guatemala — Guatemala										
Passenger cars [2] Voitures de tourisme [2]	...	...	...	373.2	553.3	1 026.7	1 101.6	1 143.2	1 217.3	1 328.1
Commercial vehicles Véhicules utilitaires	...	...	...	21.2	...	...	...	...	...	...

Country or area Pays ou zone	1995	1996	1997	1998	1999	2000	2001	2002	2003	2004
Guinea [15] — Guinée [15]										
Passenger cars Voitures de tourisme	23.2	...	...	...	...	...	...	...	...	...
Commercial vehicles Véhicules utilitaires	13.0	...	...	...	...	...	...	...	...	...
Guyana [1] — Guyana [1]										
Passenger cars Voitures de tourisme	...	...	...	61.3	61.3	61.3	61.3	61.3	...	...
Commercial vehicles Véhicules utilitaires	...	...	...	15.5	15.5	15.5	15.5	15.5	...	...
Haiti — Haïti										
Passenger cars Voitures de tourisme	49.0	59.0	...	...	93.0	...	...	...	...	...
Commercial vehicles Véhicules utilitaires	29.0	35.0	...	...	61.6	...	...	...	...	...
Honduras — Honduras										
Passenger cars Voitures de tourisme	44.2	46.3	50.3	73.1	46.0	...	...	...	...	...
Commercial vehicles Véhicules utilitaires	48.0	48.6	49.1	53.9	39.3	...	...	...	...	...
Hungary — Hongrie										
Passenger cars Voitures de tourisme	2 245.4	2 264.2	2 297.1	2 218.0	2 255.5	2 364.7	2 482.8	2 629.5	2 777.2	2 828.0
Commercial vehicles Véhicules utilitaires	345.0[19]	351.3[19]	360.9[19]	355.4[19]	363.0[19]	370.0	384.0	399.3	409.9	414.0
Iceland — Islande										
Passenger cars Voitures de tourisme	119.2	124.9	132.5	140.4	151.4	158.9	159.9	161.7	166.9	175.4
Commercial vehicles [34] Véhicules utilitaires [34]	16.0	16.6	17.5	18.1	19.4	21.1	21.7	22.0	22.9	24.8
India — Inde										
Passenger cars Voitures de tourisme	3 841.0	4 204.0	4 672.0	5 138.0	5 556.0	6 143.0	7 058.0	7 613.0	8 619.0	...
Commercial vehicles [35] Véhicules utilitaires [35]	5 623.0	6 330.0	6 931.0	7 588.0	7 991.0	8 596.0	9 377.0	9 730.0	10 889.0	...
Indonesia — Indonésie										
Passenger cars Voitures de tourisme	2 107.0	2 409.0	2 640.0	2 769.0	2 898.0	3 039.0	3 261.8	3 403.0	3 885.0	...
Commercial vehicles Véhicules utilitaires	2 025.0	2 030.0	2 160.0	2 221.0	2 273.0	2 373.0	2 447.0	2 580.0	2 846.0	...
Iran (Islamic Rep. of) [1,36] — Iran (Rép. islamique d') [1,36]										
Passenger cars Voitures de tourisme	819.6	454.2	572.9	684.5	847.9	1 139.5	1 246.9	1 545.2	...	...
Commercial vehicles Véhicules utilitaires	589.2	346.4	346.4	355.1	378.8	384.9	384.9	431.2	...	...
Iraq — Iraq										
Passenger cars Voitures de tourisme	719.0	722.0	724.0	729.0	735.0	740.0	744.0	753.0	...	...
Commercial vehicles Véhicules utilitaires	320.0	323.0	324.0	328.0	332.0	336.0	340.0	345.0	...	...
Ireland [37] — Irlande [37]										
Passenger cars [38,39] Voitures de tourisme [38,39]	999.7	1 067.8	1 145.9	1 209.2	1 283.4	1 333.9	1 402.3	1 467.0	1 528.0	...
Commercial vehicles [26] Véhicules utilitaires [26]	150.5	155.9	168.2	181.0	199.0	217.3	231.7	245.0	264.0	...
Israel — Israël										
Passenger cars Voitures de tourisme	1 131.0	1 195.1	1 252.0	1 298.0	1 341.3	1 422.0	1 474.0	1 522.1	1 545.4	1 593.0
Commercial vehicles Véhicules utilitaires	263.0	279.0	292.0	297.9	308.8	328.0	345.2	354.9	356.6	364.0

Country or area Pays ou zone	1995	1996	1997	1998	1999	2000	2001	2002	2003	2004
Italy — Italie										
Passenger cars Voitures de tourisme	30 149.6	30 467.1	30 741.9	31 370.8	31 953.2	32 583.8	33 239.0[1]	33 706.0	34 310.0	33 973.0
Commercial vehicles Véhicules utilitaires	2 863.5	3 177.7	3 253.7	3 336.4	3 409.5	3 377.6	3 541.2[1]	3 752.0	3 934.0	4 016.0
Jamaica — Jamaïque										
Passenger cars Voitures de tourisme	104.0	121.0	157.0	140.0[1]	140.0[1]	129.0[1]	129.0[1]	...	...	...
Commercial vehicles Véhicules utilitaires	49.0	53.0	56.0	55.0[1]	57.0[1]	58.0[1]	65.2[1]	...	...	...
Japan [40] — Japon [40]										
Passenger cars [41] Voitures de tourisme [41]	44 680.0	46 869.0	48 611.0	49 896.0	51 165.0	52 738.0	53 541.2	54 540.5	55 213.0	55 995.0
Commercial vehicles Véhicules utilitaires	20 676.0	20 334.0	19 859.0	19 821.0	18 869.0	18 463.6	18 103.6	17 716.3	17 314.6	17 014.0
Jordan [6] — Jordanie [6]										
Passenger cars Voitures de tourisme	188.0	193.0	191.0	202.0	213.0	255.8	290.0	357.0	365.0	396.0
Commercial vehicles Véhicules utilitaires	76.7	87.0	95.0	101.0	94.0	103.0	112.0	146.0	163.0	176.0
Kazakhstan — Kazakhstan										
Passenger cars Voitures de tourisme	1 034.1	997.5	973.3	971.2	987.7	1 000.3	1 057.8	1 062.6	1 149.0	1 204.0
Commercial vehicles Véhicules utilitaires	390.9	360.4	315.3	277.1	257.4	256.6	268.5	280.3	299.0	307.0
Kenya — Kenya										
Passenger cars Voitures de tourisme	172.8	202.7	211.9	225.1	238.9	244.8	255.4	270.0	286.0	308.0
Commercial vehicles Véhicules utilitaires	163.3	187.7	196.1	239.4	249.8	256.2	263.7	273.0	285.0	299.0
Korea, Republic of [42] — Corée, République de [42]										
Passenger cars Voitures de tourisme	6 006.3	6 893.6	7 586.5	7 580.9	7 837.2	8 083.9	8 889.3	9 737.4	10 278.9	10 621.0
Commercial vehicles Véhicules utilitaires	2 429.2	2 625.6	2 791.2	2 854.0	3 291.3	3 938.2	3 985.4	4 169.7	4 263.0	4 267.0
Kuwait — Koweït										
Passenger cars Voitures de tourisme	662.9	701.2	540.0	585.0	624.0	690.0	715.0	756.0	781.0	849.0
Commercial vehicles Véhicules utilitaires	153.5	160.0	115.0	124.0	130.0	134.0	116.0	142.0	154.0	172.0
Kyrgyzstan — Kirghizistan										
Passenger cars Voitures de tourisme	197.5	172.4	176.1	187.7	187.3	189.8	189.8	188.7	189.0	196.0
Latvia — Lettonie										
Passenger cars Voitures de tourisme	331.8	379.9	431.8	482.7	525.6	556.8	586.2	619.1	648.9	686.0
Commercial vehicles Véhicules utilitaires	85.1	90.2	95.4	96.5	101.8	108.6	111.0	113.9	115.6	118.0
Lebanon — Liban										
Passenger cars Voitures de tourisme	1 197.5	1 250.5	1 299.4[43]	1 335.7[43]	1 370.6[43]	1 370.8[43]	1 370.9[43]	...	...	...
Commercial vehicles Véhicules utilitaires	84.7	87.4	92.1[43]	95.4[43]	98.2[43]	100.2[43]	102.4[43]	...	...	...
Liberia [1] — Libéria [1]										
Passenger cars Voitures de tourisme	17.4	17.4	17.4	17.4	15.3	17.1	17.1	17.1	...	...
Commercial vehicles Véhicules utilitaires	10.7	10.7	10.7	10.7	11.9	12.8	12.8	12.8	...	...

Country or area Pays ou zone	1995	1996	1997	1998	1999	2000	2001	2002	2003	2004
Libyan Arab Jamah. — Jamah. arabe libyenne										
Passenger cars Voitures de tourisme	763.2[15]	796.3	859.0	...	...	549.6[44]	552.7[44]	...	...	...
Commercial vehicles Véhicules utilitaires	353.0[15]	357.5	362.4	...	...	177.4[44]	195.5[44]	...	...	...
Lithuania — Lituanie										
Passenger cars Voitures de tourisme	718.5	785.1	882.1	980.9	1 089.3	1 172.4	1 133.5	1 180.9	1 256.9	1 315.9
Commercial vehicles Véhicules utilitaires	125.9	104.8	108.6	114.6	112.2	113.7	115.6	120.9	126.1	130.0
Luxembourg — Luxembourg										
Passenger cars Voitures de tourisme	229.0	231.7	236.8	244.1	253.4	272.1	280.7	287.2	293.4	300.0
Commercial vehicles Véhicules utilitaires	26.1	25.5	26.2	27.3	28.8	48.6	48.7	50.0	51.7	53.0
Madagascar — Madagascar										
Passenger cars Voitures de tourisme	11.1[1]	11.1[1]	11.3[1]	64.0	...	...	...	...	...	...
Commercial vehicles Véhicules utilitaires	13.3[1]	13.9[1]	15.5[1]	9.1	...	...	...	...	...	...
Malawi [6] — Malawi [6]										
Passenger cars Voitures de tourisme	1.5	1.6	2.0	...	...	...	...	...	2.0	2.0
Commercial vehicles Véhicules utilitaires	2.2	1.9	3.0	...	...	...	...	...	2.0	3.0
Malaysia [45] — Malaisie [45]										
Passenger cars Voitures de tourisme	256.4	325.7	379.5	163.8	300.4	350.4	400.4	423.3	431.5	482.0
Commercial vehicles [8] Véhicules utilitaires [8]	74.9	102.7	96.5	19.0	28.6	36.8	40.1	42.8	48.0	53.0
Maldives — Maldives										
Passenger cars Voitures de tourisme	1.0	1.0	1.0	1.0	2.0	2.0	2.0	2.0	2.0	2.0
Commercial vehicles Véhicules utilitaires	1.0	1.0	1.0	1.0	1.0	1.0	1.0	1.0	1.0	1.0
Mali — Mali										
Passenger cars Voitures de tourisme	6.3	6.3[1]	6.3[1]	15.8[1]	17.6[1]	18.9[1]	18.9[1]	...	...	...
Commercial vehicles Véhicules utilitaires	7.2	7.6[1]	7.6[1]	21.5[1]	28.1[1]	31.7[1]	31.7[1]	...	...	...
Malta — Malte										
Passenger cars Voitures de tourisme	199.3	166.2	183.8	191.8	201.8	210.9	219.0	227.2	235.9	241.0
Commercial vehicles Véhicules utilitaires	40.8	39.4	47.4	49.5	51.2	51.4	52.6	53.3	54.6	56.0
Martinique [1] — Martinique [1]										
Passenger cars Voitures de tourisme	95.0	...	...	...	...	...	...	...	...	...
Commercial vehicles Véhicules utilitaires	21.5	...	...	...	...	...	...	...	...	...
Mauritania [1] — Mauritanie [1]										
Passenger cars Voitures de tourisme	5.1	5.2	5.3	8.6	9.9	12.2	12.2	12.2	...	...
Commercial vehicles Véhicules utilitaires	5.6	6.0	6.3	16.7	17.3	18.2	18.2	18.2	...	...
Mauritius — Maurice										
Passenger cars Voitures de tourisme	63.6	68.1	73.4	78.5	83.0	87.5	92.7	98.9	105.3	115.0
Commercial vehicles Véhicules utilitaires	24.4	25.3	26.6	29.1	31.7	34.2	36.5	38.0	39.3	40.0

Country or area / Pays ou zone	1995	1996	1997	1998	1999	2000	2001	2002	2003	2004
Mexico [6] — Mexique [6]										
Passenger cars / Voitures de tourisme	8 074.0	8 437.0	9 023.0	9 761.0	10 281.0	10 985.0	12 270.0	13 370.0	...	...
Commercial vehicles / Véhicules utilitaires	3 751.0	3 773.0	4 034.0	4 282.0	4 569.0	5 214.0	5 772.0	6 289.0	...	...
Morocco [19] — Maroc [19]										
Passenger cars / Voitures de tourisme	992.0	1 018.1	1 060.3	1 108.7	1 161.9	1 211.1	1 253.0	1 295.5	...	...
Commercial vehicles / Véhicules utilitaires	343.2	351.6	365.7	382.0	400.3	415.7	431.0	444.0	...	...
Mozambique — Mozambique										
Passenger cars [46] / Voitures de tourisme [46]	30.0	36.0	45.0	35.0	...	...	...	...	99.0	112.0
Commercial vehicles [47] / Véhicules utilitaires [47]	10.0	10.0	9.0	13.0	...	...	...	...	35.0	40.0
Myanmar [6] — Myanmar [6]										
Passenger cars / Voitures de tourisme	145.4	171.3	177.9	177.6	171.1	173.9	175.4	178.0	183.0	188.0
Commercial vehicles / Véhicules utilitaires	63.1	68.3	74.8	75.9	83.4	90.4	98.9	113.0	121.0	131.0
Nepal — Népal										
Passenger cars / Voitures de tourisme	34.5	39.8	42.8	46.9	49.4	47.5	59.1	63.5	...	...
Commercial vehicles / Véhicules utilitaires	113.8	131.8	147.9	164.2	185.8	51.6	66.0	72.7	...	...
Netherlands [6,48] — Pays-Bas [6,48]										
Passenger cars / Voitures de tourisme	5 581.0	5 664.0	5 810.0	5 931.0	6 120.0	6 343.0	6 539.0	6 711.0	6 855.0	6 908.0
Commercial vehicles / Véhicules utilitaires	654.0	666.0	695.0	738.0	806.0	884.0	950.0	997.0	1 039.0	1 070.0
New Caledonia — Nouvelle-Calédonie										
Passenger cars / Voitures de tourisme	53.0	55.0	58.0	76.0[2]	80.0[2]	87.0[2]	89.0[2]	93.0[2]	96.0[2]	...
Commercial vehicles [1] / Véhicules utilitaires [1]	18.0	21.0	23.0	...	...	...	...	...	...	...
New Zealand [5] — Nouvelle-Zélande [5]										
Passenger cars / Voitures de tourisme	1 665.0	1 655.8	1 697.2	1 768.2	1 855.8	1 905.6	1 936.8	1 988.9	2 041.7	2 148.0
Commercial vehicles / Véhicules utilitaires	411.9	403.1	407.8	422.6	433.6	438.1	436.3	443.0	451.8	472.0
Nicaragua — Nicaragua										
Passenger cars / Voitures de tourisme	44.9	50.7	57.6	62.9	67.9	73.0	82.2	...	...	...
Commercial vehicles / Véhicules utilitaires	56.7	63.8	72.8	81.7	91.1	98.1	107.7	...	...	...
Niger — Niger										
Passenger cars / Voitures de tourisme	2.4	2.7	2.1	2.7	3.9	3.7	4.7	5.3	5.3	9.3
Commercial vehicles / Véhicules utilitaires	1.3	0.6	0.7	0.7	1.0	1.2	1.3	1.5	1.9	3.8
Nigeria [49] — Nigéria [49]										
Passenger cars / Voitures de tourisme	46.1	40.7	52.3	...	...	...	...	...	...	...
Commercial vehicles / Véhicules utilitaires	8.6	10.5	13.5	...	...	...	...	...	...	...
Norway [6] — Norvège [6]										
Passenger cars / Voitures de tourisme	1 684.7	1 661.2	1 758.0	1 786.0	1 813.6	1 851.9	1 872.9	1 899.7	1 933.6	1 978.0
Commercial vehicles [50] / Véhicules utilitaires [50]	382.0	392.1	412.2	427.0	440.0	451.0	462.2	464.8	470.3	480.0

Country or area / Pays ou zone	1995	1996	1997	1998	1999	2000	2001	2002	2003	2004
Oman — Oman										
Passenger cars [51] / Voitures de tourisme [51]	202.3	216.2	245.1	279.1	310.4	344.0	359.2	390.0	324.0	...
Commercial vehicles [14] / Véhicules utilitaires [14]	89.3	92.0	101.2	110.7	117.6	124.6	132.9	140.2	109.1	...
Pakistan [6,52] — Pakistan [6,52]										
Passenger cars / Voitures de tourisme	773.0	816.0	863.0	930.0	1 004.0	1 066.0	1 131.0	1 171.0	1 280.0	1 373.0
Commercial vehicles / Véhicules utilitaires	306.0	334.0	352.0	379.0	406.0	435.0	463.0	489.0	517.0	657.0
Panama — Panama										
Passenger cars / Voitures de tourisme	178.3	188.3	198.7	212.6	222.4	223.1	219.4	225.0	234.0	245.0
Commercial vehicles / Véhicules utilitaires	60.4	60.5	64.2	68.4	71.9	74.4	70.3	74.0	75.0	80.0
Papua New Guinea — Papouasie-Nvl-Guinée										
Passenger cars / Voitures de tourisme	20.0[15]	21.7[1]	21.7[1]	21.7[1]	18.8[1]	24.9[1]	24.9[1]	24.9[1]	...	...
Commercial vehicles / Véhicules utilitaires	35.0[15]	81.1[1]	85.5[1]	89.7[1]	87.0[1]	87.8[1]	87.8[1]	87.8[1]	...	...
Paraguay — Paraguay										
Passenger cars / Voitures de tourisme	294.1	305.5	272.1	357.7	401.7	415.8	...	...	325.0	...
Commercial vehicles / Véhicules utilitaires	41.1	42.0	36.9	48.0	53.6	56.4	...	...	50.0	...
Peru — Pérou										
Passenger cars / Voitures de tourisme	505.8	557.0	595.8	645.9	684.5	716.9	750.6	834.2	906.6	...
Commercial vehicles / Véhicules utilitaires	357.0	379.5	389.9	409.8	429.7	446.0	458.4	508.0	555.3	...
Philippines — Philippines										
Passenger cars / Voitures de tourisme	1 624.9	1 803.7	1 934.7	1 993.2	2 084.7	2 156.1	2 218.6	2 401.9	1 096.0	1 229.0
Commercial vehicles / Véhicules utilitaires	221.0	249.7	274.8	263.1	276.6	282.3	285.3	291.7	287.0	302.0
Poland — Pologne										
Passenger cars / Voitures de tourisme	7 517.3	8 054.4	8 533.5	8 890.8	9 282.8	9 991.3	10 503.1	11 028.9	11 243.8	11 975.0
Commercial vehicles / Véhicules utilitaires	1 440.1	1 517.6	1 569.9	1 644.4	1 762.9	1 962.7	2 062.9	2 247.3	2 396.0	2 476.0
Portugal [53] — Portugal [53]										
Passenger cars [54] / Voitures de tourisme [54]	3 751.0	4 002.6[55]	4 272.5[55]	4 587.3[55]	4 931.7[55]	5 260.3	5 537.1	5 787.7	5 995.0	...
Commercial vehicles / Véhicules utilitaires	1 218.8	1 292.2[55]	1 383.9[55]	1 492.4[55]	1 600.1[55]	1 727.9	1 828.1	1 908.9	1 973.4	...
Puerto Rico [52] — Porto Rico [52]										
Passenger cars / Voitures de tourisme	1 609.0	1 738.0	1 853.0	1 975.0	2 058.0	2 047.0	2 076.0	2 059.0	2 079.0	2 211.0
Commercial vehicles / Véhicules utilitaires	65.0	70.0	74.0	80.0	86.0	86.0	118.0	89.0	90.0	70.0
Qatar — Qatar										
Passenger cars / Voitures de tourisme	143.4	151.9	164.7	178.0	188.0	199.6	213.3	230.1	...	...
Commercial vehicles / Véhicules utilitaires	69.5	73.8	79.1	85.0	88.9	92.9	98.0	109.7	...	...
Republic of Moldova [56] — République de Moldova [56]										
Passenger cars / Voitures de tourisme	165.9	173.6	206.0	222.8	232.3	238.4	256.5	268.9	266.0	280.0
Commercial vehicles [57] / Véhicules utilitaires [57]	12.9	11.5	10.4	9.2	8.1	6.9	6.3	5.7	5.2	5.0

Country or area Pays ou zone	1995	1996	1997	1998	1999	2000	2001	2002	2003	2004
Réunion — Réunion										
Passenger cars Voitures de tourisme	142.1	150.6	159.3	167.9	180.6	247.8[2]	258.4[2]	271.1[2]	280.8[2]	309.0[2]
Commercial vehicles Véhicules utilitaires	43.6	46.2	49.0	51.6	54.0	...	...	...	...	...
Romania — Roumanie										
Passenger cars Voitures de tourisme	2 197.0	2 392.0	2 447.0	2 594.0	2 702.0	2 778.0	2 881.0	2 973.0	3 088.0	3 225.0
Commercial vehicles Véhicules utilitaires	385.0	409.0	430.0	446.0	458.0	468.0	479.0	488.0	505.0	526.0
Russian Federation [58] — Fédération de Russie [58]										
Passenger cars Voitures de tourisme	14 195.3	15 464.3	17 631.6	18 819.6	19 624.4	20 246.9	21 152.1	22 342.3	23 271.4	24 091.3
Commercial vehicles Véhicules utilitaires	3 078.1	3 041.2	4 277.6	4 260.0	4 082.7	4 122.0	4 217.7	4 331.1	4 363.3	4 470.1
Rwanda — Rwanda										
Passenger cars Voitures de tourisme	1.2	3.2	5.8	7.7	9.2	10.7	...	...	...	...
Commercial vehicles Véhicules utilitaires	1.7	4.6	9.0	11.3	13.6	16.3	...	...	...	...
Saint Kitts and Nevis — Saint-Kitts-et-Nevis										
Passenger cars Voitures de tourisme	5.2	5.5	6.3	6.3	7.7	8.0	8.0	9.0	9.0	9.0
Commercial vehicles Véhicules utilitaires	2.3	2.5	2.4	2.9	3.9	4.0	3.0	3.0	3.0	3.0
Saint Lucia — Sainte-Lucie										
Passenger cars Voitures de tourisme	12.5	13.5	17.0	19.4	21.4	23.0	24.8	23.8	...	...
Commercial vehicles Véhicules utilitaires	...	10.8	8.1	8.4	8.8	9.0	9.2	9.8	...	...
St. Vincent-Grenadines — St. Vincent-Grenadines										
Passenger cars Voitures de tourisme	5.3	6.1	7.4	8.0	8.7	9.1	9.9	10.0	11.0	...
Commercial vehicles Véhicules utilitaires	3.7	3.2	3.8	4.1	3.9	4.0	4.0	4.0	4.0	...
Saudi Arabia [2,59] — Arabie saoudite [2,59]										
Passenger cars Voitures de tourisme	6 111.1	6 333.9	6 580.0	7 046.2	7 553.9	8 049.1	8 467.0	9 009.1	9 484.9	9 946.6
Senegal — Sénégal										
Passenger cars Voitures de tourisme	106.0	112.0	118.0	132.0	150.0	169.0	193.0	126.0[60]	166.0[60]	147.0[60]
Commercial vehicles Véhicules utilitaires	48.0	51.0	54.0	59.0	65.0	71.0	79.0	39.0[60]	53.0[60]	46.0[60]
Serbia and Montenegro — Serbie-et-Monténégro										
Passenger cars Voitures de tourisme	...	...	...	...	1 667.9	1 392.6	1 481.4	1 446.6	1 494.5	1 554.1
Commercial vehicles [61] Véhicules utilitaires [61]	...	...	...	...	150.5	132.9	140.2	139.2	146.0	158.4
Seychelles — Seychelles										
Passenger cars Voitures de tourisme	5.5	6.2	6.7	6.5	6.4	5.9	5.4	5.9	6.2	...
Commercial vehicles Véhicules utilitaires	1.9	2.0	2.1	2.2	2.2	2.3	2.2	2.4	2.4	...
Sierra Leone [1] — Sierra Leone [1]										
Passenger cars Voitures de tourisme	32.4	32.4	32.4	18.5	19.2	20.1	11.4	11.4	...	...
Commercial vehicles Véhicules utilitaires	11.9	11.9	11.9	14.8	14.8	15.8	15.8	7.8	...	...

Country or area / Pays ou zone	1995	1996	1997	1998	1999	2000	2001	2002	2003	2004
Singapore — Singapour										
Passenger cars / Voitures de tourisme	363.9	384.5	396.4	395.2	403.2	413.5	426.4	425.7	427.1	437.5
Commercial vehicles / Véhicules utilitaires	140.0	142.7	144.8	142.6	141.3	137.2	139.9	138.6	137.7	139.6
Slovakia — Slovaquie										
Passenger cars / Voitures de tourisme	1 015.8	1 058.4	1 135.9	1 196.1	1 236.4	1 274.2	1 292.8	1 326.9	1 356.2	1 197.0
Commercial vehicles / Véhicules utilitaires	131.5	127.2	135.0	144.4	149.4	153.2	161.5	171.3	183.0	175.0
Slovenia — Slovénie										
Passenger cars / Voitures de tourisme	709.6	740.9	778.3	813.4	848.3	868.3	884.2	896.7	913.7	936.0
Commercial vehicles / Véhicules utilitaires	40.2	42.6	44.9	46.4	48.5	50.8	52.6	54.3	56.1	59.0
Somalia [15] — Somalie [15]										
Passenger cars / Voitures de tourisme	12.0	...	...	...	...	...	...	...	...	...
Commercial vehicles / Véhicules utilitaires	12.0	...	...	...	...	...	...	...	...	...
South Africa — Afrique du Sud										
Passenger cars / Voitures de tourisme	3 830.8[1]	3 846.8[1]	3 664.0[1]	3 540.6[1]	3 966.3[62]	...	...	...	...	
Commercial vehicles / Véhicules utilitaires	1 625.5[1]	1 653.5[1]	1 868.0[1]	1 736.0[1]	2 248.1[63]	...	...	...	...	
Spain — Espagne										
Passenger cars / Voitures de tourisme	14 212.3	14 753.8	15 297.4	16 050.1	16 847.4	17 449.2	18 150.8	18 732.6	18 688.0[64]	19 542.0[64]
Commercial vehicles / Véhicules utilitaires	3 071.6	3 200.3	3 360.1	3 561.5	3 788.7	3 977.9	4 161.1	4 315.8	4 419.0[64]	4 666.0[64]
Sri Lanka [6] — Sri Lanka [6]										
Passenger cars / Voitures de tourisme	228.9	246.5	261.6	284.3	309.5	335.0[65]	353.7[65]	386.6	443.9	507.0
Commercial vehicles / Véhicules utilitaires	184.3	191.5	199.2	211.2	227.1	238.3	245.7	255.3	268.4	280.0
Sudan — Soudan										
Passenger cars / Voitures de tourisme	30.8[15]	...	...	38.0[1]	40.6[1]	46.0[1]	46.4[1]	47.3[1]	...	...
Commercial vehicles / Véhicules utilitaires	35.9[15]	...	...	50.4[1]	53.9[1]	60.5[1]	61.8[1]	62.5[1]	...	...
Suriname — Suriname										
Passenger cars / Voitures de tourisme	49.0	46.0	50.0	55.0	60.0	61.0	55.0	64.0	71.0	76.0
Commercial vehicles / Véhicules utilitaires	17.3	19.5	20.5	21.1	22.5	23.5	21.7	26.4	29.3	29.9
Swaziland [9] — Swaziland [9]										
Passenger cars / Voitures de tourisme	28.1	29.0	39.9	33.9	35.8	37.9	39.9	41.5	46.4	49.0
Commercial vehicles / Véhicules utilitaires	35.9	37.3	40.2	42.5	45.1	47.6	49.9	51.8	56.2	63.0
Sweden — Suède										
Passenger cars / Voitures de tourisme	3 630.8	3 654.9	3 702.8	3 792.1	3 889.9	3 999.3	4 018.5	4 044.9	4 078.0	4 116.3
Commercial vehicles / Véhicules utilitaires	322.3	326.5	336.6	353.2	369.1	388.8	409.9	423.0	435.3	453.4
Switzerland [37] — Suisse [37]										
Passenger cars / Voitures de tourisme	3 229.0	3 268.0	3 323.0	3 383.0	3 467.0	3 545.0	3 630.0	3 701.0	...	...
Commercial vehicles / Véhicules utilitaires	299.0	301.0	303.0	306.0	314.0	319.0	327.0	333.0	...	...

Country or area / Pays ou zone	1995	1996	1997	1998	1999	2000	2001	2002	2003	2004
Syrian Arab Republic — Rép. arabe syrienne										
Passenger cars / Voitures de tourisme	167.0	174.0	176.0	179.0	181.0	182.0	194.0	228.0	253.0	281.0
Commercial vehicles / Véhicules utilitaires	224.0	251.0	269.0	283.0	314.0	346.0	349.0	367.0	382.0	394.0
Tajikistan — Tadjikistan										
Passenger cars / Voitures de tourisme	166.4	151.5	154.1	146.6	141.7	117.1	...	...	...	...
Commercial vehicles / Véhicules utilitaires	9.8	9.6	10.2	13.3	16.4	16.8	...	...	...	...
Thailand — Thaïlande										
Passenger cars [66] / Voitures de tourisme [66]	1 913.2	2 098.6	2 350.4	2 529.2	2 650.5	2 665.4	2 864.0	3 259.5	3 398.8	2 993.0
Commercial vehicles [67] / Véhicules utilitaires [67]	2 735.6	3 149.3	3 534.9	3 746.7	4 065.3	4 220.1	4 373.4	4 579.7	4 678.7	4 366.0
TFYR of Macedonia — L'ex-R.y. Macédoine										
Passenger cars / Voitures de tourisme	286.0	284.0	289.0	289.0	290.0	300.0	309.6	307.6	*300.0	...
Commercial vehicles / Véhicules utilitaires	29.2	29.0	29.6	29.9	30.1	31.8	33.9	33.0	*32.0	...
Togo [1] — Togo [1]										
Passenger cars / Voitures de tourisme	74.7	74.7	74.7	27.2	36.0	51.4	51.4	51.4	...	...
Commercial vehicles / Véhicules utilitaires	34.6	34.6	34.6	11.0	17.6	24.5	24.5	24.5	...	...
Tonga — Tonga										
Passenger cars / Voitures de tourisme	8.0	9.0	9.0	10.0	11.0	5.0	5.0	6.0	7.0	...
Commercial vehicles / Véhicules utilitaires	8.0	10.0	9.0	9.0	10.0	4.0	4.0	6.0	7.0	...
Trinidad and Tobago — Trinité-et-Tobago										
Passenger cars / Voitures de tourisme	167.0	180.0	194.0	213.0	229.0	...	...	...	...	...
Commercial vehicles / Véhicules utilitaires	42.0	45.0	48.0	51.0	54.0	...	...	...	...	...
Tunisia — Tunisie										
Passenger cars / Voitures de tourisme	356.0	379.0	415.0	446.0	482.0	517.0	553.0	...	...	...
Commercial vehicles [68] / Véhicules utilitaires [68]	189.0	202.0	217.0	233.0	250.0	266.0	282.0	...	...	...
Turkey — Turquie										
Passenger cars [69] / Voitures de tourisme [69]	3 058.5	3 274.1	3 570.1	3 838.3	4 072.3	4 422.2	4 534.8	4 600.1	4 700.3	5 400.0
Commercial vehicles [34] / Véhicules utilitaires [34]	1 010.2	1 083.9	1 215.7	1 353.6	1 443.2	1 583.7	1 629.9	1 679.1	1 794.1	2 379.0
Uganda — Ouganda										
Passenger cars / Voitures de tourisme	28.9	35.4	42.0	46.9	48.4	49.0	53.1	54.2	56.8	60.0
Commercial vehicles / Véhicules utilitaires	44.1	52.5	59.1	66.8	72.6	74.3	79.9	82.3	87.6	96.0
Ukraine — Ukraine										
Passenger cars / Voitures de tourisme	4 603.1	4 872.3	5 024.0	5 127.3	5 210.8	5 250.1	5 312.6	5 400.0[70]	5 524.0	5 446.0[70]
Commercial vehicles / Véhicules utilitaires	951.0	925.0	918.0	900.0	880.0	838.0	809.0	938.0[70]	940.0	917.0[70]
United Arab Emirates — Emirats arabes unis										
Passenger cars / Voitures de tourisme	321.6	346.3	695.7[1]	693.5[1]	717.3[1]	745.3[1]	794.1[1]	...	...	...
Commercial vehicles / Véhicules utilitaires	84.2	89.3	385.7[1]	420.2[1]	440.6[1]	453.1[1]	477.9[1]	...	...	...

54

Motor vehicles in use—Passenger cars and commercial vehicles: thousands (*continued*)

Véhicules automobiles en circulation—Voitures de tourisme et véhicules utilitaires : milliers de véhicules (*suite*)

Country or area Pays ou zone	1995	1996	1997	1998	1999*	2000	2001	2002	2003	2004
United Kingdom [71] — Royaume-Uni [71]										
Passenger cars Voitures de tourisme	21 949.9	22 819.0	23 450.0	23 922.0	24 628.0	25 067.0	25 816.0	26 493.0	26 992.0	27 807.0
Commercial vehicles Véhicules utilitaires	2 987.3	3 035.0	3 104.0	3 167.0	3 333.0	3 333.0	3 425.0	3 527.0	3 552.0	3 849.0
United Rep. of Tanzania [1] — Rép.-Unie de Tanzanie [1]										
Passenger cars Voitures de tourisme	13.8	13.8	13.8	31.2	33.9	35.6	35.6	35.6	...	...
Commercial vehicles Véhicules utilitaires	37.5	42.5	42.5	87.3	98.8	98.8	98.8	98.8	...	...
United States — Etats-Unis										
Passenger cars [72] Voitures de tourisme [72]	193 963.4	198 662.0	199 973.0	203 168.7	207 788.4	212 706.4	221 821.1	220 932.0	222 701.4	...
Commercial vehicles Véhicules utilitaires	7 404.9	7 707.4	7 780.8	8 447.8	8 520.2	8 768.8	8 607.2	8 687.9	8 688.6	...
Uruguay — Uruguay										
Passenger cars Voitures de tourisme	464.5	485.1	516.9	578.3	662.3	669.7	652.0	622.0	372.0	372.0
Commercial vehicles Véhicules utilitaires	45.8	48.4	50.3	53.9	57.8	58.0	30.0	50.0	54.0	54.0
Vanuatu [1] — Vanuatu [1]										
Passenger cars Voitures de tourisme	7.4	2.7	2.7	2.5	2.6	2.6	2.5	6.0	...	...
Commercial vehicles Véhicules utilitaires	1.8	3.2	3.5	3.8	4.1	4.4	4.5	4.6	...	...
Venezuela (Bolivarian Republic of) — Venezuela (République bolivarienne du)										
Passenger cars Voitures de tourisme	1 823.0	1 393.5	1 313.9	1 402.9	1 420.0	1 326.2	1 372.0	2 092.0	2 173.0	2 466.0
Commercial vehicles Véhicules utilitaires	581.0	664.6	352.1	786.2	846.0	1 078.6	1 107.9	615.0	630.0	677.0
Viet Nam — Viet Nam										
Commercial vehicles Véhicules utilitaires	39.1 [73]	41.5 [73]	41.5 [73]	49.4 [73]	57.8 [73]	69.9 [73]	88.0 [73]	89.0 [73]	213.0	206.0
Yemen — Yémen										
Passenger cars Voitures de tourisme	224.1	259.4	327.1	380.6	301.2 [43]	323.1 [43]	346.6 [43]	...	...	...
Commercial vehicles Véhicules utilitaires	291.7	345.3	413.1	422.1	534.0 [43]	560.3 [43]	587.9 [43]	...	...	...
Zambia — Zambie										
Passenger cars Voitures de tourisme	5.7	3.7	...	...	...	...	...	...	...	...
Commercial vehicles Véhicules utilitaires	7.3	3.9	...	...	...	...	...	...	...	...
Zimbabwe — Zimbabwe										
Passenger cars Voitures de tourisme	384.0	422.4	464.7	521.0	534.6	544.5	556.0	571.0	585.0	598.0
Commercial vehicles Véhicules utilitaires	37.9	42.2	46.4	54.3	58.5	67.7	81.0	84.0	100.0	103.0

Source

United Nations Statistics Division, New York, transport statistics database.

Notes

[1] Source: *World Automotive Market Report*, Motor and Equipment Manufacturers Association (Research Triangle Park, North Carolina).
[2] Including commercial vehicles.
[3] Prior to 1996, all data have different collection months.
[4] As of 31 October.

Source

Organisation des Nations Unies, Division de statistique, New York, la base de données pour les statistiques des transports.

Notes

[1] Source : *World Automotive Market Report*, Motor and Equipment Manufacturers Association (Research Triangle Park, North Carolina).
[2] Y compris véhicules utilitaires.
[3] Avant 1996, les mois de collecte des données sont tous différents.
[4] Dès le 31 octobre.

5 Data refer to fiscal years ending 31 March.	5 Les données se réfèrent aux exercices budgétaires finissant le 31 mars.
6 Including vehicles operated by police or other governmental security organizations.	6 Y compris véhicules de la police ou d'autres services gouvernementales d'ordre public.
7 Including farm tractors.	7 Y compris tracteurs agricoles.
8 Excluding tractors.	8 Non compris tracteurs.
9 Excluding government vehicles.	9 Non compris les véhicules des administrations publiques.
10 Including buses and coaches.	10 Y compris autobus et autocars.
11 Including pick-ups.	11 Y compris fourgonnettes.
12 Number of licensed vehicles.	12 Nombre de véhicules automobiles licensés.
13 Including only vehicles (trucks) weighing 4,500 kilograms to 14,999 kilograms and vehicles (tractor-trailers and Class A trucks) weighing 15,000 kilograms or more.	13 Y compris seulement véhicules (camions) pesant de 4.500 kilogrammes à 14.999 kilogrammes et véhicules (semi-remorques et camions de Classe A) pesant 15.000 kilogrammes ou plus.
14 Trucks only.	14 Camions seulement.
15 Source: *AAMA Motor Vehicle Facts and Figures*, American Automobile Manufacturers Association (Michigan).	15 Source : *AAMA Motor Vehicle Facts and Figures*, American Automobile Manufacturers Association (Michigan).
16 Including special-purpose vehicles and mini-buses.	16 Y compris véhicules à usages spéciaux et mini-buses.
17 Including mini-buses.	17 Y compris minibuses.
18 For statistical purposes, the data for China do not include those for the Hong Kong Special Administrative Region (Hong Kong SAR), Macao Special Administrative Region (Macao SAR) and Taiwan Province of China.	18 Pour la présentation des statistiques, les données pour Chine ne comprennent pas la Région Administrative Spéciale de Hong Kong (Hong Kong RAS), la Région Administrative Spéciale de Macao (Macao RAS) et la province de Taiwan.
19 Including special-purpose vehicles.	19 Y compris véhicules à usages spéciaux.
20 Including specialized enterprises only.	20 Ne comprend que les entrerises spécialisées.
21 Including vans.	21 Y compris fourgons.
22 Excluding vans.	22 Non compris fourgons.
23 Including special-purpose commercial vehicles and farm tractors.	23 Y compris véhicules utilitaires à usages spéciaux et tracteurs agricoles.
24 Beginning 1996, methodological change in calculation.	24 Changement de méthode de calcul introduit en 1996.
25 Excluding Faeroe Islands.	25 Non compris les Iles Féroés.
26 Including large public service excavators and trench diggers.	26 Y compris les grosses excavatrices et machines d'excavation de tranchées de travaux publics.
27 Data refer to fiscal years ending 7 July.	27 Les données se réfèrent aux exercices budgétaires finissant le 7 juillet.
28 Including private and government cars, rental and hired cars.	28 Y compris les voitures particulières et celles des administrations publiques, les voitures de location et de louage.
29 Including pick-ups, ambulances, light and heavy fire engines and all other vehicles such as trailers, cranes, loaders, forklifts, etc.	29 Y compris les fourgonnettes, les ambulances, les voitures de pompiers légères pompiers légères et lourdes, et tous autres véhicles tels que remoques, grues, chargeuses, chariots élévateurs à fourches, etc.
30 Including only trailers and semi-trailer combinations less than 10 years old.	30 Y compris les légères remoques et semi-remorques de moins de 10 ans seulement.
31 As at 20 October 2005.	31 Données au 20 octobre 2005.
32 Beginning 2001, data refer to fiscal years ending 1 January. For all previous years data refer to fiscal years ending 1 July.	32 A compter de l'année 2001, les données se réfèrent aux exercices budgétaires finissant le 1er janvier. Pour toutes les années antérieures, les données se réfèrent aux exercices budgétaires finissant le 1er juillet.
33 Including "other, not specified", registered motor vehicles.	33 Y compris "autres, non-spécifiés", véhicules automobiles enregistrés.
34 Excluding tractors and semi-trailer combinations.	34 Non compris ensembles tracteur-remorque et semi-remorque.
35 Including goods vehicles, tractors, trailers, three-wheeled passengers and goods vehicles and other miscellaneous vehicles which are not separately classified.	35 Y compris véhicules de transport de marchandises, camions-remorques, remorques, véhicules à trois roues (passagers et marchandises) et autres véhicules divers qui ne font pas l'objet d'une catégories separée.
36 Data refer to fiscal years ending 20 March.	36 Les données se réfèrent aux exercices budgétaires finissant le 20 mars.
37 Data refer to fiscal years ending 30 September.	37 Les données se réfèrent aux exercices budgétaires finissant le 30 septembre.
38 Including mini-buses equipped for transport of nine to fifteen passengers.	38 Y compris mini-buses ayant une capacité de neuf à quinze passagers.
39 Including school buses.	39 Y compris l'autobus de l'école.
40 Excluding small vehicles.	40 Non compris véhicules petites.
41 Including cars with a seating capacity of up to 10 persons.	41 Y compris véhicules comptant jusqu'à 10 places.
42 Number of registered motor vehicles.	42 Nombre de véhicules automobiles enregistrès.
43 Source: United Nations Economic and Social Commission for Western Asia (ESCWA).	43 Source : Commission économique et sociale pour l'Asie occidentale (CESAO).
44 Excluding government passenger-cars.	44 Non compris les voitures de tourisme du gouvernement.
45 Registration of new motor vehicles only.	45 Immatriculation de véhicules automobiles neufs seulement.
46 Light vehicles carrying passengers and goods.	46 Véhicules légers (passagers et marchandises).
47 Heavy vehicles carrying passengers and goods.	47 Véhicules lourds (passagers et marchandises).
48 Excluding diplomatic corps vehicles.	48 Non compris véhicules des diplomates.

54

Motor vehicles in use — Passenger cars and commercial vehicles: thousands (*continued*)

Véhicules automobiles en circulation — Voitures de tourisme et véhicules utilitaires : milliers de véhicules (*suite*)

[49] Newly registered.

[50] Including hearses (Norway: registered before 1981).

[51] Excluding taxis.

[52] Data refer to fiscal years beginning 1 July.

[53] Excluding Madeira and Azores.

[54] Including light miscellaneous vehicles.

[55] Including vehicles no longer in circulation.

[56] Excluding the Transnistria region.

[57] For the period 1980-1994, including motor vehicles for general use owned by Ministry of Transport. Beginning 1995, including motor vehicles owned by enterprises with main activity as road transport enterprises.

[58] Beginning 1997, data provided by State Inspection for security of road traffic of the Russian Federation Ministry of Internal Affairs.

[59] Including motorcycles.

[60] Including registration of new motor vehicles.

[61] Excluding semi-trailers.

[62] Including all mini-buses and passenger vehicles which transport fewer than 12 persons.

[63] Including vehicles which transport 12 persons or more and all light and heavy load vehicles, whether self-propelled or semi-trailer.

[64] Not including temporarily dropped-out vehicles.

[65] Including three-wheelers.

[66] Including micro-buses and passenger pick-ups.

[67] Including pick-ups, taxis, cars for hire, small rural buses.

[68] Including trailers.

[69] Including vehicles seating not more than eight persons, including the driver.

[70] As of 1 August.

[71] Figures prior to 1992 were derived from vehicle taxation class; beginning 1992, figures derived from vehicle body type.

[72] Including motorcycles (prior to 1993 only), mini-vans, sport-utility vehicles and pick-up trucks.

[73] Data prior to 2003 refer only to data under the management of Ministry of Transport of Viet Nam.

[49] Enregistrés récemment.

[50] Y compris corbillards (Norvège : enregistrés avant 1981).

[51] Non compris taxis.

[52] Les données se réfèrent aux exercices budgétaires commençant le 1er juillet.

[53] Non compris Madère et Azores.

[54] Y compris les véhicules légers divers.

[55] Y compris véhicules retirés de la circulation.

[56] Non compris la région de Transnistria.

[57] Pour la période 1980 - 1994, y compris les véhicules à moteur d'usage général appartenant au Ministère des transports. A partir de 1995, y compris les véhicules pour les entreprises de transport.

[58] A partir de 1997, données fournies par l'Inspecteurat d'Etat pour la sécurité routière du Ministère de l'Intérieur de la Fédération de Russie.

[59] Y compris motocyclettes.

[60] Y compris immatriculation de automobiles véhicules neufs.

[61] Non compris semi-remorques.

[62] Y compris tous les minibus et véhicules qui transportant moins de 12 passagers.

[63] Y compris véhicules transportant 12 personnes ou plus et tous véhicules poids légèrs ou poids lourds, auto-propulsés ou semi-remorque.

[64] Non compris les véhicules temporairement inutilisés.

[65] Y compris véhicules à trois roues.

[66] Y compris les microbus et les camionnettes de transport de passagers.

[67] Y compris les camionnettes, les taxis, les voitures de louage, les petits autobus ruraux.

[68] Y compris remorques.

[69] Y compris véhicules dont le nombre de places assises (y compris celle du conducteur) n'est pas supérieur à huit.

[70] Dès le 1er août.

[71] Les chiffres antérieurs à 1992 ont été calculés selon les catégories fiscales de véhicules; à partir de 1992, ils ont été calculés selan les types de carrosserie.

[72] Y compris motocyclettes (antérieur à 1993 seulement), fourgonnettes, véhicules de la classe quatre-x-quatre et camionettes légères.

[73] Les données avant l'année 2003 se réfèrent seulement aux données de Ministère des transports.

Merchant shipping: fleets
All ships, oil tankers, and ore and bulk carrier fleets: thousand gross registered tons

Transports maritimes : flotte marchande
Tous les navires, pétroliers, et minéraliers et transporteurs de vracs : milliers de tonneaux de jauge brute

Country or area	1997	1998	1999	2000	2001	2002	2003	2004	Pays ou zone
World									**Monde**
All ships	522 197	531 893	543 610	558 054	574 551	585 583	605 218	633 321	Tous les navires
Oil tankers	147 108	151 036	154 092	155 429	156 068	154 559	159 273	165 345	Pétroliers
Ore and bulk carriers	162 169	158 565	158 957	161 186	168 000	169 954	171 689	181 444	Minéral. et transp. de vracs
Albania									**Albanie**
All ships	30	29	21	24	25	49	70	73	Tous les navires
Algeria									**Algérie**
All ships	983	1 005	1 005	961	964	936	872	862	Tous les navires
Oil tankers	34	33	33	19	19	19	17	15	Pétroliers
Ore and bulk carriers	172	172	172	173	173	173	173	173	Minéral. et transp. de vracs
Angola									**Angola**
All ships	68	74	66	66	63	55	45	48	Tous les navires
Oil tankers	3	3	3	3	3	3	1	3	Pétroliers
Anguilla									**Anguilla**
All ships	2	1	1	1	1	1	1	1	Tous les navires
Antigua and Barbuda									**Antigua-et-Barbuda**
All ships	2 214	2 788	3 622	4 224	4 688	5 066	6 005	6 915	Tous les navires
Oil tankers	4	7	5	5	5	3	3	3	Pétroliers
Ore and bulk carriers	174	294	196	194	251	206	376	604	Minéral. et transp. de vracs
Argentina									**Argentine**
All ships	579	499	477	464	422	423	434	437	Tous les navires
Oil tankers	105	102	100	83	49	51	51	51	Pétroliers
Ore and bulk carriers	34	34	34	34	34	34	34	34	Minéral. et transp. de vracs
Australia									**Australie**
All ships	2 607	2 188	2 084	1 912	1 888	1 861	1 906	1 972	Tous les navires
Oil tankers	380	226	226	226	226	264	264	317	Pétroliers
Ore and bulk carriers	1 036	893	801	624	624	573	578	539	Minéral. et transp. de vracs
Austria									**Autriche**
All ships	83	68	71	90	35	30	32	34	Tous les navires
Azerbaijan									**Azerbaïdjan**
All ships	633	651	654	647	641	633	638	664	Tous les navires
Oil tankers	180	176	176	176	175	175	176	200	Pétroliers
Bahamas									**Bahamas**
All ships	25 523	27 716	29 483	31 445	33 386	35 798	34 752	35 388	Tous les navires
Oil tankers	10 810	11 982	13 158	13 504	14 469	14 574	13 431	12 359	Pétroliers
Ore and bulk carriers	4 728	4 990	4 943	4 833	5 339	5 249	5 513	6 336	Minéral. et transp. de vracs
Bahrain									**Bahreïn**
All ships	194	284	292	256	338	288	276	294	Tous les navires
Oil tankers	55	54	54	1	81	81	81	81	Pétroliers
Ore and bulk carriers	33	33	33	43	43	43	43	58	Minéral. et transp. de vracs
Bangladesh									**Bangladesh**
All ships	419	414	378	370	388	432	447	456	Tous les navires
Oil tankers	59	59	61	62	63	63	63	63	Pétroliers
Ore and bulk carriers	7	6	6	6	6	6	6	26	Minéral. et transp. de vracs
Barbados									**Barbade**
All ships	888	688	725	733	687	328	468	580	Tous les navires
Oil tankers	350	350	350	350	350	8	8	30	Pétroliers
Ore and bulk carriers	268	174	174	174	174	174	228	251	Minéral. et transp. de vracs
Belgium									**Belgique**
All ships	169	127	132	144	151	187	1 393	3 973	Tous les navires
Oil tankers	2	4	4	4	4	4	330	1 904	Pétroliers
Ore and bulk carriers	...	...	...	...	...	...	176	1 147	Minéral. et transp. de vracs
Belize									**Belize**
All ships	1 761	2 382	2 368	2 251	1 828	1 473	1 534	1 687	Tous les navires
Oil tankers	338	360	321	348	311	236	110	75	Pétroliers
Ore and bulk carriers	195	190	210	178	145	159	172	210	Minéral. et transp. de vracs

55 Merchant shipping: fleets—All ships, oil tankers, and ore and bulk carrier fleets: thousand gross registered tons (*continued*)

Transports maritimes : flotte marchande—Tous les navires, pétroliers, et minéraliers et transporteurs de vracs : milliers de tonneaux de jauge brute (*suite*)

Country or area	1997	1998	1999	2000	2001	2002	2003	2004	Pays ou zone
Benin									**Bénin**
All ships	1	1	1	1	1	1	1	1	Tous les navires
Bermuda									**Bermudes**
All ships	4 610	4 811	6 187	5 752	5 313	4 798	4 844	6 166	Tous les navires
Oil tankers	2 069	2 144	2 652	2 152	1 661	898	572	730	Pétroliers
Ore and bulk carriers	1 018	1 089	1 910	1 911	1 885	1 863	1 851	1 851	Minéral. et transp. de vracs
Bolivia									**Bolivie**
All ships	2	16	179	178	174	358	420	303	Tous les navires
Oil tankers	...	...	18	25	65	242	253	214	Pétroliers
Ore and bulk carriers	...	7	49	28	25	14	9	4	Minéral. et transp. de vracs
Brazil									**Brésil**
All ships	4 372	4 171	3 933	3 809	3 687	3 449	3 258	2 628	Tous les navires
Oil tankers	1 854	1 825	1 770	1 642	1 564	1 397	1 311	1 115	Pétroliers
Ore and bulk carriers	1 706	1 501	1 453	1 437	1 418	1 334	1 217	761	Minéral. et transp. de vracs
British Virgin Islands									**Iles Vierges britanniques**
All ships	5	4	4	74	3	23	87	3	Tous les navires
Oil tankers	...	...	...	...	...	...	63	...	Pétroliers
Brunei Darussalam									**Brunéi Darussalam**
All ships	369	362	362	362	363	483	480	479	Tous les navires
Oil tankers	0	0	0	0	0	1	1	1	Pétroliers
Bulgaria									**Bulgarie**
All ships	1 128	1 091	1 036	990	955	889	748	790	Tous les navires
Oil tankers	163	145	145	143	114	114	...	...	Pétroliers
Ore and bulk carriers	542	532	518	518	517	517	527	567	Minéral. et transp. de vracs
Cambodia									**Cambodge**
All ships	439	616	999	1 447	1 997	2 426	2 048	1 821	Tous les navires
Oil tankers	...	...	7	31	111	141	140	83	Pétroliers
Ore and bulk carriers	146	169	305	405	511	626	455	444	Minéral. et transp. de vracs
Cameroon									**Cameroun**
All ships	11	13	14	14	14	17	187	185	Tous les navires
Oil tankers	...	...	...	...	...	...	170	170	Pétroliers
Canada									**Canada**
All ships	2 527	2 501	2 496	2 658	2 727	2 798	2 723	2 664	Tous les navires
Oil tankers	254	255	250	329	338	400	400	387	Pétroliers
Ore and bulk carriers	1 352	1 352	1 338	1 307	1 321	1 295	1 210	1 098	Minéral. et transp. de vracs
Cape Verde									**Cap-Vert**
All ships	21	20	21	21	17	16	21	21	Tous les navires
Oil tankers	1	1	1	1	1	1	1	1	Pétroliers
Cayman Islands									**Iles Caïmanes**
All ships	844	1 282	1 165	1 796	2 054	2 377	2 802	2 609	Tous les navires
Oil tankers	114	318	123	304	519	704	957	587	Pétroliers
Ore and bulk carriers	282	455	526	634	602	632	672	856	Minéral. et transp. de vracs
Channel Islands									**Iles Anglo-Normandes**
All ships	3	2	2	2	1	1	1	1	Tous les navires
Chile									**Chili**
All ships	722	753	820	842	880	880	964	947	Tous les navires
Oil tankers	93	100	100	100	100	139	144	184	Pétroliers
Ore and bulk carriers	213	188	203	217	224	170	196	189	Minéral. et transp. de vracs
China [1]									**Chine** [1]
All ships	16 339	16 503	16 315	16 499	16 646	17 316	18 428	20 369	Tous les navires
Oil tankers	2 014	2 029	2 084	2 250	2 352	2 480	2 847	3 471	Pétroliers
Ore and bulk carriers	6 464	6 832	6 648	6 618	6 634	6 876	7 171	7 863	Minéral. et transp. de vracs
China, Hong Kong SAR									**Chine, Hong Kong RAS**
All ships	5 771	6 171	7 973	10 242	13 710	16 164	20 507	26 085	Tous les navires
Oil tankers	22	340	515	734	1 537	2 450	4 146	5 799	Pétroliers
Ore and bulk carriers	4 211	4 208	5 233	6 947	8 740	9 862	11 879	...	Minéral. et transp. de vracs
China, Macao SAR									**Chine, Macao RAS**
All ships	2	2	4	4	4	4	2	2	Tous les navires
Colombia									**Colombie**
All ships	118	112	97	81	66	68	71	75	Tous les navires
Oil tankers	6	6	6	6	6	6	6	6	Pétroliers
Ore and bulk carriers	...	...	...	...	...	...	...	3	Minéral. et transp. de vracs

55 Merchant shipping: fleets—All ships, oil tankers, and ore and bulk carrier fleets: thousand gross registered tons (*continued*)

Transports maritimes : flotte marchande—Tous les navires, pétroliers, et minéraliers et transporteurs de vracs : milliers de tonneaux de jauge brute (*suite*)

Country or area	1997	1998	1999	2000	2001	2002	2003	2004	Pays ou zone
Comoros									**Comores**
All ships	2	1	1	20	54	407	417	389	Tous les navires
Oil tankers	...	...	...	...	37	273	71	71	Pétroliers
Ore and bulk carriers	...	...	...	...	...	59	145	102	Minéral. et transp. de vracs
Congo									**Congo**
All ships	7	4	4	3	3	3	3	3	Tous les navires
Cook Islands									**Iles Cook**
All ships	6	7	7	6	5	8	18	26	Tous les navires
Oil tankers	...	...	...	...	...	...	3	3	Pétroliers
Costa Rica									**Costa Rica**
All ships	6	6	6	6	3	4	5	5	Tous les navires
Côte d'Ivoire									**Côte d'Ivoire**
All ships	11	10	10	9	9	9	9	9	Tous les navires
Oil tankers	1	1	1	1	1	1	1	1	Pétroliers
Croatia									**Croatie**
All ships	871	896	869	734	775	835	848	1 016	Tous les navires
Oil tankers	13	11	11	9	9	8	6	90	Pétroliers
Ore and bulk carriers	469	517	504	438	527	499	517	602	Minéral. et transp. de vracs
Cuba									**Cuba**
All ships	203	158	130	120	101	103	90	126	Tous les navires
Oil tankers	8	8	3	3	3	20	20	49	Pétroliers
Ore and bulk carriers	2	2	2	2	5	5	5	6	Minéral. et transp. de vracs
Cyprus									**Chypre**
All ships	23 653	23 302	23 641	23 206	22 762	22 997	22 054	21 283	Tous les navires
Oil tankers	3 779	3 848	3 987	4 165	3 803	3 602	3 449	3 674	Pétroliers
Ore and bulk carriers	11 819	11 090	11 511	11 437	11 776	12 374	12 145	11 289	Minéral. et transp. de vracs
Czech Republic									**République tchèque**
All ships	16	...	...	...	...	...	...	...	Tous les navires
Ore and bulk carriers	16	...	...	...	...	...	...	...	Minéral. et transp. de vracs
Dem. Rep. of the Congo									**Rép. dém. du Congo**
All ships	15	13	13	13	13	13	13	13	Tous les navires
Denmark									**Danemark**
All ships	5 754	5 687	5 809	6 823	6 913	7 403	7 567	7 582	Tous les navires
Oil tankers	741	379	494	1 171	1 230	1 522	1 383	1 237	Pétroliers
Ore and bulk carriers	522	522	464	356	204	124	50	48	Minéral. et transp. de vracs
Djibouti									**Djibouti**
All ships	4	4	4	4	2	3	4	5	Tous les navires
Dominica									**Dominique**
All ships	3	3	2	2	2	4	40	304	Tous les navires
Oil tankers	...	...	...	...	...	2	11	143	Pétroliers
Ore and bulk carriers	...	...	...	...	...	...	0	21	Minéral. et transp. de vracs
Dominican Republic									**Rép. dominicaine**
All ships	11	9	10	10	9	9	13	13	Tous les navires
Oil tankers	1	...	...	...	...	...	...	...	Pétroliers
Ecuador									**Equateur**
All ships	145	171	309	301	306	313	324	265	Tous les navires
Oil tankers	80	93	223	219	219	219	218	162	Pétroliers
Egypt									**Egypte**
All ships	1 288	1 368	1 368	1 346	1 350	1 275	1 151	1 143	Tous les navires
Oil tankers	223	210	209	208	207	223	223	225	Pétroliers
Ore and bulk carriers	575	613	601	546	586	512	432	432	Minéral. et transp. de vracs
El Salvador									**El Salvador**
All ships	1	1	2	2	1	6	6	6	Tous les navires
Equatorial Guinea									**Guinée équatoriale**
All ships	35	59	44	46	37	29	31	28	Tous les navires
Oil tankers	...	5	...	...	...	...	...	...	Pétroliers
Eritrea									**Erythrée**
All ships	7	7	16	16	21	21	21	21	Tous les navires
Oil tankers	...	2	2	2	2	2	2	2	Pétroliers
Estonia									**Estonie**
All ships	602	522	453	379	347	357	358	335	Tous les navires
Oil tankers	6	7	8	6	9	9	9	7	Pétroliers
Ore and bulk carriers	160	96	65	33	33	33	33	...	Minéral. et transp. de vracs

Merchant shipping: fleets—All ships, oil tankers, and ore and bulk carrier fleets: thousand gross registered tons (*continued*)

Transports maritimes : flotte marchande—Tous les navires, pétroliers, et minéraliers et transporteurs de vracs : milliers de tonneaux de jauge brute (*suite*)

Country or area	1997	1998	1999	2000	2001	2002	2003	2004	Pays ou zone
Ethiopia									**Ethiopie**
All ships	86	83	96	92	82	82	82	79	Tous les navires
Oil tankers	...	2	2	2	2	2	2	...	Pétroliers
Faeroe Islands									**Iles Féroé**
All ships	105	103	104	103	195	200	160	181	Tous les navires
Oil tankers	2	2	2	2	80	80	6	6	Pétroliers
Falkland Is. (Malvinas)									**Iles Falkland (Malvinas)**
All ships	38	39	45	53	55	54	52	50	Tous les navires
Fiji									**Fidji**
All ships	36	29	29	29	29	27	23	30	Tous les navires
Oil tankers	3	3	3	3	3	1	...	...	Pétroliers
Finland									**Finlande**
All ships	1 559	1 629	1 658	1 620	1 595	1 545	1 452	1 429	Tous les navires
Oil tankers	303	303	303	304	304	275	265	257	Pétroliers
Ore and bulk carriers	80	90	90	90	105	60	60	54	Minéral. et transp. de vracs
France [2]									**France** [2]
All ships	4 570	4 738	4 766	4 681	4 495	4 574	4 745	4 900	Tous les navires
Oil tankers	2 049	2 248	2 198	2 108	1 900	1 709	1 898	2 012	Pétroliers
Ore and bulk carriers	355	354	539	538	355	354	354	1	Minéral. et transp. de vracs
Gabon									**Gabon**
All ships	35	27	16	13	13	13	13	13	Tous les navires
Oil tankers	1	1	1	1	1	1	1	1	Pétroliers
Ore and bulk carriers	24	12	...	...	...	...	...	...	Minéral. et transp. de vracs
Gambia									**Gambie**
All ships	2	2	2	2	2	2	2	33	Tous les navires
Oil tankers	...	...	...	...	...	...	...	4	Pétroliers
Georgia									**Géorgie**
All ships	128	118	132	119	277	569	815	974	Tous les navires
Oil tankers	73	73	76	8	21	41	38	17	Pétroliers
Ore and bulk carriers	0	0	0	0	5	126	223	342	Minéral. et transp. de vracs
Germany									**Allemagne**
All ships	6 950	8 084	6 514	6 552	6 300	6 546	6 112	8 246	Tous les navires
Oil tankers	17	9	8	29	51	49	48	1	Pétroliers
Ore and bulk carriers	2	2	2	2	2	1	1	49	Minéral. et transp. de vracs
Ghana									**Ghana**
All ships	130	115	118	119	123	126	121	117	Tous les navires
Oil tankers	2	6	6	6	7	8	8	3	Pétroliers
Ore and bulk carriers	...	...	...	...	...	...	0	0	Minéral. et transp. de vracs
Gibraltar									**Gibraltar**
All ships	297	314	451	604	816	961	993	1 142	Tous les navires
Oil tankers	263	233	288	342	342	341	128	126	Pétroliers
Ore and bulk carriers	...	...	16	16	85	19	19	19	Minéral. et transp. de vracs
Greece									**Grèce**
All ships	25 288	25 225	24 833	26 402	28 678	28 783	32 203	32 041	Tous les navires
Oil tankers	11 894	12 587	13 158	13 681	14 889	14 562	16 717	15 998	Pétroliers
Ore and bulk carriers	9 472	8 771	7 709	8 077	9 026	9 255	10 401	11 068	Minéral. et transp. de vracs
Grenada									**Grenade**
All ships	1	1	1	1	1	1	3	3	Tous les navires
Guatemala									**Guatemala**
All ships	1	1	5	5	5	9	5	6	Tous les navires
Oil tankers	...	...	...	...	...	...	...	0	Pétroliers
Guinea									**Guinée**
All ships	9	11	11	11	11	12	14	13	Tous les navires
Oil tankers	...	...	...	...	...	...	2	...	Pétroliers
Guinea-Bissau									**Guinée-Bissau**
All ships	6	6	6	7	6	6	6	6	Tous les navires
Guyana									**Guyana**
All ships	17	16	14	16	15	15	32	33	Tous les navires
Oil tankers	0	0	0	0	0	0	1	1	Pétroliers
Haiti									**Haïti**
All ships	2	1	1	1	1	1	1	1	Tous les navires

55 Merchant shipping: fleets—All ships, oil tankers, and ore and bulk carrier fleets: thousand gross registered tons (*continued*)

Transports maritimes : flotte marchande—Tous les navires, pétroliers, et minéraliers et transporteurs de vracs : milliers de tonneaux de jauge brute (*suite*)

Country or area	1997	1998	1999	2000	2001	2002	2003	2004	Pays ou zone
Honduras									Honduras
All ships	1 053	1 083	1 220	1 111	967	933	813	784	Tous les navires
Oil tankers	107	108	131	143	184	214	136	129	Pétroliers
Ore and bulk carriers	114	77	133	101	74	73	68	103	Minéral. et transp. de vracs
Hungary									Hongrie
All ships	27	15	12	...	...	4	8	...	Tous les navires
Iceland									Islande
All ships	215	198	192	187	193	187	187	194	Tous les navires
Oil tankers	2	2	2	2	1	1	0	0	Pétroliers
India									Inde
All ships	6 934	6 777	6 915	6 662	6 688	6 142	6 961	7 518	Tous les navires
Oil tankers	2 515	2 530	2 698	2 526	2 522	2 564	3 676	4 228	Pétroliers
Ore and bulk carriers	3 013	2 832	2 748	2 663	2 706	2 249	2 000	1 973	Minéral. et transp. de vracs
Indonesia									Indonésie
All ships	3 195	3 252	3 241	3 384	3 613	3 723	3 840	4 072	Tous les navires
Oil tankers	844	841	830	805	831	827	895	964	Pétroliers
Ore and bulk carriers	335	358	380	335	344	324	389	379	Minéral. et transp. de vracs
Iran (Islamic Rep. of)									Iran (Rép. islamique d')
All ships	3 553	3 347	3 546	4 234	3 944	4 128	4 852	3 203	Tous les navires
Oil tankers	1 844	1 592	1 754	2 101	1 846	2 145	2 927	992	Pétroliers
Ore and bulk carriers	1 015	990	957	1 148	1 142	1 073	1 032	5 324	Minéral. et transp. de vracs
Iraq									Iraq
All ships	572	511	511	511	241	188	161	163	Tous les navires
Oil tankers	422	361	361	361	102	59	51	52	Pétroliers
Ireland									Irlande
All ships	235	184	219	248	300	280	471	...	Tous les navires
Oil tankers	3	0	0	0	...	...	...	...	Pétroliers
Ore and bulk carriers	...	...	8	26	26	26	88	...	Minéral. et transp. de vracs
Isle of Man									Ile de Man
All ships	4 759	4 203	4 729	5 431	6 057	5 672	6 416	7 169	Tous les navires
Oil tankers	2 401	1 893	2 409	2 877	3 154	2 761	3 377	3 058	Pétroliers
Ore and bulk carriers	831	783	732	795	911	923	861	1 551	Minéral. et transp. de vracs
Israel									Israël
All ships	794	752	728	612	611	765	766	740	Tous les navires
Oil tankers	1	1	1	1	1	1	1	1	Pétroliers
Ore and bulk carriers	12	...	...	...	...	...	...	...	Minéral. et transp. de vracs
Italy									Italie
All ships	6 194	6 819	8 048	9 049	9 655	9 596	10 246	10 956	Tous les navires
Oil tankers	1 608	1 547	1 660	1 639	1 426	1 104	1 244	1 466	Pétroliers
Ore and bulk carriers	1 303	1 525	1 851	2 049	1 829	1 518	1 396	1 469	Minéral. et transp. de vracs
Jamaica									Jamaïque
All ships	10	4	4	4	23	75	57	131	Tous les navires
Oil tankers	2	2	2	2	2	2	2	2	Pétroliers
Ore and bulk carriers	...	...	...	...	...	44	45	102	Minéral. et transp. de vracs
Japan									Japon
All ships	18 516	17 780	17 063	15 257	14 565	13 918	13 562	13 180	Tous les navires
Oil tankers	5 510	5 434	5 006	3 742	3 341	3 160	2 872	2 756	Pétroliers
Ore and bulk carriers	4 558	3 869	3 556	3 243	3 093	2 776	2 732	2 639	Minéral. et transp. de vracs
Jordan									Jordanie
All ships	43	42	42	42	42	69	224	195	Tous les navires
Oil tankers	...	...	...	...	...	...	137	32	Pétroliers
Ore and bulk carriers	40	21	21	11	...	...	...	...	Minéral. et transp. de vracs
Kazakhstan									Kazakhstan
All ships	10	9	9	11	13	12	15	26	Tous les navires
Oil tankers	...	...	...	...	...	...	...	1	Pétroliers
Kenya									Kenya
All ships	21	21	21	21	19	19	18	19	Tous les navires
Oil tankers	5	5	5	5	5	5	5	5	Pétroliers
Kiribati									Kiribati
All ships	6	4	4	4	4	4	4	4	Tous les navires
Oil tankers	2	...	...	...	...	...	...	...	Pétroliers

55 Merchant shipping: fleets—All ships, oil tankers, and ore and bulk carrier fleets: thousand gross registered tons (*continued*)

Transports maritimes : flotte marchande—Tous les navires, pétroliers, et minéraliers et transporteurs de vracs : milliers de tonneaux de jauge brute (*suite*)

Country or area	1997	1998	1999	2000	2001	2002	2003	2004	Pays ou zone
Korea, Dem. P. R.									**Corée, R. p. dém. de**
All ships	667	631	658	653	698	870	959	1 123	Tous les navires
Oil tankers	5	6	6	6	12	16	19	36	Pétroliers
Ore and bulk carriers	96	50	53	63	63	153	120	152	Minéral. et transp. de vracs
Korea, Republic of									**Corée, République de**
All ships	7 430	5 694	5 735	6 200	6 395	7 050	6 757	7 826	Tous les navires
Oil tankers	385	328	404	607	843	841	771	486	Pétroliers
Ore and bulk carriers	3 542	2 809	2 708	2 915	2 874	3 431	3 225	4 079	Minéral. et transp. de vracs
Kuwait									**Koweït**
All ships	1 984	2 459	2 456	2 415	2 292	2 256	2 324	2 378	Tous les navires
Oil tankers	1 313	1 662	1 644	1 628	1 628	1 628	1 685	1 685	Pétroliers
Ore and bulk carriers	...	17	17	17	17	17	17	71	Minéral. et transp. de vracs
Lao People's Dem. Rep.									**Rép. dém. pop. lao**
All ships	3	2	2	2	2	2	2	2	Tous les navires
Latvia									**Lettonie**
All ships	319	118	118	98	68	89	91	294	Tous les navires
Oil tankers	137	9	9	7	4	4	3	139	Pétroliers
Lebanon									**Liban**
All ships	297	263	322	363	302	229	193	184	Tous les navires
Oil tankers	2	1	1	1	1	1	1	1	Pétroliers
Ore and bulk carriers	124	108	152	191	126	83	50	50	Minéral. et transp. de vracs
Liberia									**Libéria**
All ships	60 058	60 492	54 107	51 451	51 784	50 400	52 435	53 899	Tous les navires
Oil tankers	26 699	26 361	21 298	19 759	18 733	18 638	20 357	21 093	Pétroliers
Ore and bulk carriers	17 711	16 739	14 426	10 533	11 747	10 947	10 399	10 616	Minéral. et transp. de vracs
Libyan Arab Jamah.									**Jamah. arabe libyenne**
All ships	686	567	439	434	251	165	157	130	Tous les navires
Oil tankers	511	395	267	267	81	7	7	7	Pétroliers
Lithuania									**Lituanie**
All ships	510	481	424	434	393	435	442	453	Tous les navires
Oil tankers	5	4	4	4	5	5	3	3	Pétroliers
Ore and bulk carriers	110	110	110	100	80	80	80	80	Minéral. et transp. de vracs
Luxembourg									**Luxembourg**
All ships	820	932	1 343	1 079	1 469	1 494	1 006	690	Tous les navires
Oil tankers	165	244	543	311	630	495	333	178	Pétroliers
Ore and bulk carriers	86	86	93	6	14	14	...	...	Minéral. et transp. de vracs
Madagascar									**Madagascar**
All ships	40	42	43	44	43	35	35	33	Tous les navires
Oil tankers	11	11	11	11	11	5	5	5	Pétroliers
Malaysia									**Malaisie**
All ships	4 842	5 209	5 245	5 328	5 207	5 394	5 746	6 057	Tous les navires
Oil tankers	689	854	918	868	871	767	1 061	1 552	Pétroliers
Ore and bulk carriers	1 305	1 448	1 513	1 568	1 447	1 509	1 444	1 204	Minéral. et transp. de vracs
Maldives									**Maldives**
All ships	98	101	90	78	67	58	64	78	Tous les navires
Oil tankers	6	6	4	3	4	5	5	7	Pétroliers
Malta									**Malte**
All ships	22 984	24 075	28 205	28 170	27 053	26 331	25 134	22 353	Tous les navires
Oil tankers	9 043	9 848	12 151	11 595	10 546	9 398	8 423	6 067	Pétroliers
Ore and bulk carriers	8 623	8 616	9 984	10 533	10 661	11 574	11 361	10 687	Minéral. et transp. de vracs
Marshall Islands									**Iles Marshall**
All ships	6 314	6 442	6 762	9 745	11 719	14 673	17 628	22 495	Tous les navires
Oil tankers	3 388	3 561	4 313	5 462	5 955	7 177	9 779	12 875	Pétroliers
Ore and bulk carriers	1 666	1 602	1 255	2 067	2 747	3 310	2 958	3 292	Minéral. et transp. de vracs
Mauritania									**Mauritanie**
All ships	43	48	49	49	47	48	48	49	Tous les navires
Mauritius									**Maurice**
All ships	275	206	150	91	97	63	68	79	Tous les navires
Oil tankers	53	...	...	...	...	...	...	...	Pétroliers
Ore and bulk carriers	4	4	4	4	4	10	10	10	Minéral. et transp. de vracs

55 Merchant shipping: fleets—All ships, oil tankers, and ore and bulk carrier fleets: thousand gross registered tons (*continued*)

Transports maritimes : flotte marchande—Tous les navires, pétroliers, et minéraliers et transporteurs de vracs : milliers de tonneaux de jauge brute (*suite*)

Country or area	1997	1998	1999	2000	2001	2002	2003	2004	Pays ou zone
Mexico									Mexique
All ships	1 145	1 085	918	883	908	937	973	1 008	Tous les navires
Oil tankers	435	409	464	460	454	455	459	482	Pétroliers
Ore and bulk carriers	...	...	...	...	...	...	9	19	Minéral. et transp. de vracs
Micronesia (Fed. States of)									Micronésie (Etats féd. de)
All ships	9	10	10	10	9	13	18	18	Tous les navires
Mongolia									Mongolie
All ships	...	...	...	...	...	...	337	360	Tous les navires
Oil tankers	...	...	...	...	...	...	4	2	Pétroliers
Ore and bulk carriers	...	...	...	...	...	...	64	138	Minéral. et transp. de vracs
Morocco									Maroc
All ships	417	444	448	467	461	502	504	523	Tous les navires
Oil tankers	12	12	12	12	9	4	4	4	Pétroliers
Mozambique									Mozambique
All ships	39	35	36	37	38	37	36	36	Tous les navires
Myanmar									Myanmar
All ships	568	492	540	446	380	402	433	444	Tous les navires
Oil tankers	3	3	3	3	3	3	3	3	Pétroliers
Ore and bulk carriers	298	283	301	231	162	185	246	246	Minéral. et transp. de vracs
Namibia									Namibie
All ships	55	55	55	63	66	69	75	92	Tous les navires
Netherlands									Pays-Bas
All ships	3 880	4 263	4 814	5 168	5 605	5 664	5 703	5 623	Tous les navires
Oil tankers	18	16	25	29	37	46	48	53	Pétroliers
Ore and bulk carriers	68	77	77	10	9	10	4	4	Minéral. et transp. de vracs
Netherlands Antilles									Antilles néerlandaises
All ships	1 067	971	1 110	1 235	1 250	1 391	1 511	1 662	Tous les navires
Oil tankers	158	135	135	135	0	0	4	12	Pétroliers
Ore and bulk carriers	108	...	...	2	72	42	161	200	Minéral. et transp. de vracs
New Zealand									Nouvelle-Zélande
All ships	367	336	265	180	175	180	205	206	Tous les navires
Oil tankers	61	73	73	20	50	50	50	50	Pétroliers
Ore and bulk carriers	12	12	12	12	12	12	12	12	Minéral. et transp. de vracs
Nicaragua									Nicaragua
All ships	4	4	4	4	4	4	4	5	Tous les navires
Nigeria									Nigéria
All ships	452	452	432	438	404	411	419	429	Tous les navires
Oil tankers	250	252	265	265	287	285	287	301	Pétroliers
Ore and bulk carriers	...	...	...	...	...	...	10	10	Minéral. et transp. de vracs
Norway									Norvège
All ships	22 839	23 136	23 446	22 604	22 591	22 195	20 509	18 936	Tous les navires
Oil tankers	9 244	8 993	9 195	7 949	7 575	6 936	4 948	3 978	Pétroliers
Ore and bulk carriers	3 908	4 041	3 913	3 863	4 048	4 216	4 079	3 736	Minéral. et transp. de vracs
Oman									Oman
All ships	15	15	17	19	20	19	16	17	Tous les navires
Pakistan									Pakistan
All ships	435	401	308	260	247	247	322	301	Tous les navires
Oil tankers	50	50	50	50	50	50	155	155	Pétroliers
Ore and bulk carriers	158	125	30	...	...	...	...	...	Minéral. et transp. de vracs
Panama									Panama
All ships	91 128	98 222	105 248	114 382	122 352	124 729	125 722	131 452	Tous les navires
Oil tankers	21 272	22 680	23 856	27 588	28 528	28 758	26 095	26 911	Pétroliers
Ore and bulk carriers	38 617	40 319	42 726	45 734	49 947	50 189	51 283	54 189	Minéral. et transp. de vracs
Papua New Guinea									Papouasie-Nvl-Guinée
All ships	60	61	65	73	77	72	73	75	Tous les navires
Oil tankers	4	3	3	2	2	2	5	4	Pétroliers
Ore and bulk carriers	...	...	...	...	...	...	4	4	Minéral. et transp. de vracs
Paraguay									Paraguay
All ships	44	45	43	45	47	47	45	44	Tous les navires
Oil tankers	4	4	4	4	4	4	3	3	Pétroliers

55 Merchant shipping: fleets—All ships, oil tankers, and ore and bulk carrier fleets: thousand gross registered tons (*continued*)

Transports maritimes : flotte marchande—Tous les navires, pétroliers, et minéraliers et transporteurs de vracs : milliers de tonneaux de jauge brute (*suite*)

Country or area	1997	1998	1999	2000	2001	2002	2003	2004	Pays ou zone
Peru									**Pérou**
All ships	337	270	285	257	240	240	224	227	Tous les navires
Oil tankers	76	31	31	19	14	15	15	15	Pétroliers
Ore and bulk carriers	...	...	15	...	...	...	...	...	Minéral. et transp. de vracs
Philippines									**Philippines**
All ships	8 849	8 508	7 650	7 002	6 030	5 320	5 116	5 137	Tous les navires
Oil tankers	163	162	159	154	142	146	200	312	Pétroliers
Ore and bulk carriers	5 951	5 597	4 822	4 366	3 751	3 065	2 814	2 693	Minéral. et transp. de vracs
Poland									**Pologne**
All ships	1 878	1 424	1 319	1 119	618	586	282	163	Tous les navires
Oil tankers	5	5	5	6	5	5	5	5	Pétroliers
Ore and bulk carriers	1 360	1 082	993	851	391	391	126	...	Minéral. et transp. de vracs
Portugal									**Portugal**
All ships	952	1 130	1 165	1 191	1 199	1 100	1 156	1 336	Tous les navires
Oil tankers	349	416	416	354	424	424	412	557	Pétroliers
Ore and bulk carriers	128	188	160	261	214	156	173	134	Minéral. et transp. de vracs
Qatar									**Qatar**
All ships	648	744	749	715	691	623	562	575	Tous les navires
Oil tankers	263	263	263	214	214	210	210	184	Pétroliers
Ore and bulk carriers	142	142	142	142	142	142	...	...	Minéral. et transp. de vracs
Republic of Moldova									**République de Moldova**
All ships	...	...	...	...	...	...	...	4	Tous les navires
Romania									**Roumanie**
All ships	2 345	2 088	1 221	767	638	622	563	427	Tous les navires
Oil tankers	249	204	68	67	64	64	63	53	Pétroliers
Ore and bulk carriers	865	788	320	138	143	139	145	49	Minéral. et transp. de vracs
Russian Federation									**Fédération de Russie**
All ships	12 282	11 090	10 649	10 486	10 248	10 380	10 431	8 639	Tous les navires
Oil tankers	1 646	1 608	1 429	1 402	1 430	1 504	1 684	1 347	Pétroliers
Ore and bulk carriers	1 568	1 031	889	864	783	782	805	800	Minéral. et transp. de vracs
Saint Helena									**Sainte-Hélène**
All ships	1	1	1	1	1	1	2	1	Tous les navires
St. Vincent-Grenadines									**St. Vincent-Grenadines**
All ships	8 374	7 875	7 105	7 026	7 073	6 584	6 318	6 324	Tous les navires
Oil tankers	1 061	913	569	450	459	313	284	274	Pétroliers
Ore and bulk carriers	3 202	2 858	2 656	2 672	3 019	2 716	2 654	2 670	Minéral. et transp. de vracs
Samoa									**Samoa**
All ships	1	3	3	2	10	10	10	10	Tous les navires
Sao Tome and Principe									**Sao Tomé-et-Principe**
All ships	3	10	42	173	190	86	84	58	Tous les navires
Oil tankers	...	...	1	7	11	7	1	1	Pétroliers
Ore and bulk carriers	...	...	...	10	62	17	17	17	Minéral. et transp. de vracs
Saudi Arabia									**Arabie saoudite**
All ships	1 164	1 278	1 208	1 260	1 133	1 472	1 364	1 678	Tous les navires
Oil tankers	203	220	218	219	224	664	586	907	Pétroliers
Ore and bulk carriers	12	12	...	...	...	...	...	...	Minéral. et transp. de vracs
Senegal									**Sénégal**
All ships	51	51	48	50	48	47	46	41	Tous les navires
Serbia and Montenegro									**Serbie-et-Monténégro**
All ships	2	5	4	4	3	1	1	6	Tous les navires
Seychelles									**Seychelles**
All ships	5	18	24	22	34	65	64	67	Tous les navires
Sierra Leone									**Sierra Leone**
All ships	19	19	17	17	13	23	23	27	Tous les navires
Oil tankers	1	1	3	...	...	9	9	14	Pétroliers
Singapore									**Singapour**
All ships	18 875	20 370	21 780	21 491	21 023	21 148	23 241	26 283	Tous les navires
Oil tankers	7 787	8 781	9 619	9 118	8 647	8 528	9 343	11 488	Pétroliers
Ore and bulk carriers	4 358	4 585	4 695	4 753	4 800	4 958	5 530	5 756	Minéral. et transp. de vracs
Slovakia									**Slovaquie**
All ships	15	15	15	15	15	7	29	126	Tous les navires
Ore and bulk carriers	...	...	...	...	...	7	23	42	Minéral. et transp. de vracs

55
Merchant shipping: fleets—All ships, oil tankers, and ore and bulk carrier fleets: thousand gross registered tons (*continued*)

Transports maritimes : flotte marchande—Tous les navires, pétroliers, et minéraliers et transporteurs de vracs : milliers de tonneaux de jauge brute (*suite*)

Country or area	1997	1998	1999	2000	2001	2002	2003	2004	Pays ou zone
Slovenia									Slovénie
All ships	2	2	2	2	2	2	2	1	Tous les navires
Solomon Islands									Iles Salomon
All ships	10	10	10	9	8	8	7	8	Tous les navires
Somalia									Somalie
All ships	11	11	6	7	6	6	6	7	Tous les navires
Oil tankers	...	...	1	1	1	1	1	1	Pétroliers
South Africa									Afrique du Sud
All ships	383	384	379	380	382	144	171	167	Tous les navires
Oil tankers	3	3	3	3	3	3	3	2	Pétroliers
Spain									Espagne
All ships	1 688	1 838	1 903	2 030	2 148	2 371	2 651	2 869	Tous les navires
Oil tankers	510	585	583	600	598	603	603	413	Pétroliers
Ore and bulk carriers	39	42	42	42	42	42	27	115	Minéral. et transp. de vracs
Sri Lanka									Sri Lanka
All ships	217	189	195	150	154	81	141	157	Tous les navires
Oil tankers	5	5	5	2	6	6	43	8	Pétroliers
Ore and bulk carriers	95	77	77	77	77	...	...	...	Minéral. et transp. de vracs
Sudan									Soudan
All ships	42	43	43	43	43	33	24	16	Tous les navires
Oil tankers	1	1	1	1	1	1	1	1	Pétroliers
Suriname									Suriname
All ships	8	6	6	5	5	5	5	5	Tous les navires
Oil tankers	2	2	2	2	2	2	2	2	Pétroliers
Sweden									Suède
All ships	2 754	2 552	2 947	2 887	2 958	3 178	3 579	3 667	Tous les navires
Oil tankers	307	105	102	103	101	81	68	108	Pétroliers
Ore and bulk carriers	38	32	32	29	29	29	43	41	Minéral. et transp. de vracs
Switzerland									Suisse
All ships	434	383	439	429	502	559	589	487	Tous les navires
Ore and bulk carriers	389	349	393	393	463	503	477	371	Minéral. et transp. de vracs
Syrian Arab Republic									Rép. arabe syrienne
All ships	415	428	440	465	498	472	477	447	Tous les navires
Oil tankers	...	...	...	1	1	1	1	1	Pétroliers
Ore and bulk carriers	14	22	30	26	54	61	49	42	Minéral. et transp. de vracs
Thailand									Thaïlande
All ships	2 158	1 999	1 956	1 945	1 771	1 880	2 269	2 890	Tous les navires
Oil tankers	411	364	361	364	231	209	277	292	Pétroliers
Ore and bulk carriers	567	491	476	443	392	457	577	943	Minéral. et transp. de vracs
Togo									Togo
All ships	2	2	43	5	8	13	15	20	Tous les navires
Tonga									Tonga
All ships	12	22	25	25	338	291	170	109	Tous les navires
Oil tankers	...	...	...	...	31	41	12	2	Pétroliers
Ore and bulk carriers	...	...	...	...	49	39	39	6	Minéral. et transp. de vracs
Trinidad and Tobago									Trinité-et-Tobago
All ships	19	19	22	22	27	27	28	34	Tous les navires
Oil tankers	...	...	1	1	1	1	...	1	Pétroliers
Tunisia									Tunisie
All ships	180	193	200	208	203	186	174	175	Tous les navires
Oil tankers	7	22	20	20	20	20	...	2	Pétroliers
Ore and bulk carriers	38	27	17	17	17	17	17	17	Minéral. et transp. de vracs
Turkey									Turquie
All ships	6 567	6 251	6 325	5 833	5 897	5 659	4 951	4 679	Tous les navires
Oil tankers	514	503	584	625	772	625	430	408	Pétroliers
Ore and bulk carriers	4 444	4 023	3 939	3 303	3 178	2 904	2 532	2 369	Minéral. et transp. de vracs
Turkmenistan									Turkménistan
All ships	39	38	44	42	46	46	47	43	Tous les navires
Oil tankers	3	2	2	2	6	6	6	6	Pétroliers
Ore and bulk carriers	...	...	5	3	3	3	3	3	Minéral. et transp. de vracs
Turks and Caicos Islands									Iles Turques et Caïques
All ships	2	1	1	1	1	1	1	1	Tous les navires

55 Merchant shipping: fleets—All ships, oil tankers, and ore and bulk carrier fleets: thousand gross registered tons (*continued*)

Transports maritimes : flotte marchande—Tous les navires, pétroliers, et minéraliers et transporteurs de vracs : milliers de tonneaux de jauge brute (*suite*)

Country or area	1997	1998	1999	2000	2001	2002	2003	2004	Pays ou zone
Tuvalu									**Tuvalu**
All ships	55	49	43	59	36	38	61	138	Tous les navires
Oil tankers	...	...	...	...	...	...	4	35	Pétroliers
Ukraine									**Ukraine**
All ships	2 690	2 033	1 775	1 546	1 408	1 350	1 379	1 145	Tous les navires
Oil tankers	89	62	56	56	45	39	34	30	Pétroliers
Ore and bulk carriers	254	207	161	100	100	100	100	100	Minéral. et transp. de vracs
United Arab Emirates									**Emirats arabes unis**
All ships	924	933	786	979	746	703	799	799	Tous les navires
Oil tankers	426	369	248	240	233	221	274	271	Pétroliers
Ore and bulk carriers	20	20	20	0	0	0	36	13	Minéral. et transp. de vracs
United Kingdom									**Royaume-Uni**
All ships	3 486	4 085	4 331	5 532	6 029	8 045	10 844	11 123	Tous les navires
Oil tankers	476	625	544	538	562	515	549	535	Pétroliers
Ore and bulk carriers	64	48	33	52	78	665	869	894	Minéral. et transp. de vracs
United Rep. of Tanzania									**Rép.-Unie de Tanzanie**
All ships	46	36	36	38	38	47	39	39	Tous les navires
Oil tankers	5	4	4	4	4	8	8	8	Pétroliers
United States									**Etats-Unis**
All ships	11 789	11 852	12 026	11 111	10 907	10 371	10 409	10 744	Tous les navires
Oil tankers	3 372	3 436	3 491	3 176	2 965	2 296	2 159	2 031	Pétroliers
Ore and bulk carriers	1 275	1 268	1 268	1 271	1 339	1 291	1 280	1 236	Minéral. et transp. de vracs
Uruguay									**Uruguay**
All ships	121	107	62	67	73	75	76	76	Tous les navires
Oil tankers	48	48	6	6	6	6	6	6	Pétroliers
Vanuatu									**Vanuatu**
All ships	1 578	1 602	1 444	1 379	1 496	1 381	1 618	1 756	Tous les navires
Oil tankers	14	11	11	11	4	55	...	...	Pétroliers
Ore and bulk carriers	620	708	518	506	529	518	756	771	Minéral. et transp. de vracs
Venezuela (Bolivarian Rep. of)									**Venezuela (Rép. Bolivarienne)**
All ships	705	665	657	667	872	865	847	1 011	Tous les navires
Oil tankers	275	222	222	212	374	376	377	515	Pétroliers
Ore and bulk carriers	111	126	116	126	121	121	121	142	Minéral. et transp. de vracs
Viet Nam									**Viet Nam**
All ships	766	784	865	1 002	1 074	1 131	1 251	1 428	Tous les navires
Oil tankers	22	63	105	136	158	162	241	239	Pétroliers
Ore and bulk carriers	94	94	94	122	122	150	172	198	Minéral. et transp. de vracs
Wallis and Futuna Islands									**Iles Wallis et Futuna**
All ships	111	111	159	135	183	158	114	75	Tous les navires
Oil tankers	75	75	75	50	50	25	...	...	Pétroliers
Yemen									**Yémen**
All ships	26	25	25	28	74	78	79	33	Tous les navires
Oil tankers	2	2	2	5	51	51	51	5	Pétroliers

Source

Lloyd's Register of Shipping, London, *World Fleet Statistics 2004* and previous issues.

Notes

1 For statistical purposes, the data for China do not include those for the Hong Kong Special Administrative Region (Hong Kong SAR), Macao Special Administrative Region (Macao SAR) and Taiwan Province of China.
2 Including the French Antarctic Territory.

Source

Lloyd's Register of Shipping, Londres, *World Fleet Statistics 2004* et éditions précédentes.

Notes

1 Pour la présentation des statistiques, les données pour Chine ne comprennent pas la Région Administrative Spéciale de Hong Kong (Hong Kong RAS), la Région Administrative Spéciale de Macao (Macao RAS) et la province de Taiwan.
2 Y compris le territoire antarctique français.

56

International maritime transport
Vessels entered and cleared: thousand net registered tons

Transports maritimes internationaux
Navires entrés et sortis : milliers de tonneaux de jauge nette

Country or area — Pays ou zone	1995	1996	1997	1998	1999	2000	2001	2002	2003	2004
Albania — Albanie										
Vessels entered Navires entrés	1 002	1 218	1 053	1 419	1 115	2 212	2 558	2 673	2 876	...
Vessels cleared Navires sortis	309	213	123	61	29	72	69	64	208	...
Algeria [1] — Algérie [1]										
Vessels entered Navires entrés	88 502	93 913	103 201	106 256	113 681	117 918	118 994	130 950		...
Vessels cleared Navires sortis	88 865	93 676	103 187	106 036	113 627	117 937	119 074	130 706		
American Samoa [2] — Samoa américaines [2]										
Vessels entered Navires entrés	526	452	725	589	884	184	167	186	191	...
Vessels cleared Navires sortis	526	452	725	589	884	184	167	186	191	...
Antigua and Barbuda — Antigua-et-Barbuda										
Vessels entered Navires entrés	...	57 386	94 907	...	...	...	...	...	...	...
Vessels cleared Navires sortis	...	544 328	667 126	...	...	...	...	...	...	...
Australia [1,2,3] — Australie [1,2,3]										
Vessels entered Navires entrés	...	...	125 809	158 849	177 127	186 434	180 107	163 358[4]	175 655[4]	203 673
Vessels cleared Navires sortis	...	...	125 667	158 828	177 199	185 920	179 319	163 334[4]	175 129[4]	204 215
Azerbaijan — Azerbaïdjan										
Vessels entered Navires entrés	925	1 022	2 007	3 967	4 015	5 118	...	...	...	...
Vessels cleared Navires sortis	1 751	1 702	1 737	1 483	624	703	...	...	...	...
Bahrain — Bahreïn										
Vessels entered Navires entrés	1	2	2	...	...	...	...	...	...	...
Bangladesh [5] — Bangladesh [5]										
Vessels entered Navires entrés	6 013	5 928	5 488	5 794	6 509	...	...	...	...	...
Vessels cleared Navires sortis	3 094	3 136	2 866	2 556	2 949	...	...	...	...	...
Barbados — Barbade										
Vessels entered Navires entrés	12 780	14 002	15 146	16 893	14 470	15 875	...	...	...	...
Belgium — Belgique										
Vessels entered Navires entrés	253 427	297 664	337 862	367 684	386 211	415 640	436 927	447 105	427 039	451 691
Vessels cleared Navires sortis	210 144	297 610	333 694	360 987	375 519	404 159	422 703	439 863	419 680	444 956
Benin — Bénin										
Vessels entered Navires entrés	1 192	1 321	1 296	1 289	1 095	1 184	1 260	1 307	1 539	...
Vessels cleared Navires sortis	...	...	5 377	5 961	...	...	7 992	8 569	8 450	...
Brazil — Brésil										
Vessels entered Navires entrés	79 732	82 593	86 720	92 822	78 774	84 423	88 562	...	...	...
Vessels cleared Navires sortis	197 955	192 889	209 331	216 273	217 810	237 170	258 962	...	...	...

Country or area — Pays ou zone	1995	1996	1997	1998	1999	2000	2001	2002	2003	2004
Brunei Darussalam — Brunéi Darussalam										
Vessels entered Navires entrés	...	...	...	...	...	...	...	1 735	...	...
Vessels cleared Navires sortis	...	...	...	...	...	...	...	1 732	...	...
Cambodia [6] — Cambodge [6]										
Vessels entered Navires entrés	647	726	715	781	1 056	1 313	...	...	...	...
Vessels cleared Navires sortis	214	145	293	319	191	179	...	...	...	...
Cameroon [3,7] — Cameroun [3,7]										
Vessels entered Navires entrés	1 543	1 157	1 159	1 154	1 234	1 215	1 243	1 278	...	...
Canada [8] — Canada [8]										
Vessels entered Navires entrés	62 415	66 166	74 422	81 539	82 976	90 925	92 790	91 899	93 612	...
Vessels cleared Navires sortis	114 040	117 452	124 999	120 349	122 282	128 549	121 712	120 212	126 234	...
Cape Verde — Cap-Vert										
Vessels entered Navires entrés	3 628	3 601	3 590	4 296	...	...	...	...	...	...
China, Hong Kong SAR — Chine, Hong Kong RAS										
Vessels entered Navires entrés	216 437	229 444	250 303	261 694	267 255	300 606	340 027	372 415	386 224	399 031
Vessels cleared Navires sortis	217 539	229 474	250 399	261 552	267 419	300 522	340 163	372 574	386 292	399 025
China, Macao SAR [3] — Chine, Macao RAS [3]										
Vessels cleared Navires sortis	...	...	...	...	...	10 736[1,9]	1 975	2 820	2 451	2 364
Colombia — Colombie										
Vessels entered Navires entrés	10 295	11 268	12 814	15 003	12 902	13 400	14 148	14 555	15 431	16 269
Vessels cleared Navires sortis	37 444	45 576	43 530	61 327	67 280	66 878	66 669	63 132	70 787	79 539
Congo — Congo										
Vessels entered Navires entrés	6 449	7 645	...	8 045	8 507	8 529	8 522	9 432	...	...
Vessels cleared Navires sortis	1 342	1 878	...	1 732	1 706	1 781	1 921	2 015	...	...
Costa Rica — Costa Rica										
Vessels entered Navires entrés	4 202	4 135	3 555	4 024	2 168	2 019	1 923	2 101	2 780	2 724
Vessels cleared Navires sortis	3 070	2 992	2 941	3 405	2 168	2 019	1 923	2 101	2 780	2 724
Croatia — Croatie										
Vessels entered Navires entrés	6 023	13 587[1]	16 131[1]	16 410[1]	14 685[1]	13 925[1]	22 425[1]	24 436[1]	31 024[1]	42 929[1]
Vessels cleared Navires sortis	4 297	10 393[1]	11 502[1]	11 912[1]	11 374[1]	12 686[1]	20 560[1]	20 577[1]	26 457[1]	39 508[1]
Cuba [10] — Cuba [10]										
Vessels entered Navires entrés	...	...	...	1 348	2 696	3 840	4 716	2 505	1 399	1 100
Vessels cleared Navires sortis	...	...	...	1 371	766	657	512	268	317	174
Cyprus — Chypre										
Vessels entered Navires entrés	15 700	19 033	16 478	15 955	18 001	20 571	20 310	19 969	19 169	18 359
Dominica — Dominique										
Vessels entered Navires entrés	2 252	2 289	2 145	2 218	...	...	...	...	...	...

Country or area — Pays ou zone	1995	1996	1997	1998	1999	2000	2001	2002	2003	2004
Dominican Republic — Rép. dominicaine										
Vessels entered Navires entrés	8 751	9 238	10 113	10 719	13 603	14 245	13 892	14 560	14 256	12 730
Vessels cleared Navires sortis	1 162	1 341	1 822	1 673	1 609	2 170	2 507	1 749	1 957	2 144
Ecuador — Equateur										
Vessels entered Navires entrés	3 665	3 283	3 263	3 158	2 019	4 711	3 064	5 408	8 948	12 721
Vessels cleared Navires sortis	18 010	17 450	18 277	16 937	18 051	16 779	18 761	18 755	37 147	46 981
Egypt — Egypte										
Vessels entered Navires entrés	48 008	47 824	48 866	40 834	36 333	69 801	73 888	78 484	41 028	50 931
Vessels cleared Navires sortis	41 257	43 386	40 924	33 711	32 186	54 142	63 741	61 339	19 923	32 077
El Salvador — El Salvador										
Vessels entered Navires entrés	3 185	3 345	5 633	7 969	3 374	12 986	9 312	13 820	6 983	...
Vessels cleared Navires sortis	625	822	550	490	566	1 431	1 560	3 833	694	...
Estonia [1] — Estonie [1]										
Vessels entered Navires entrés	...	...	...	...	...	112 455	115 405	134 467	146 239	155 726
Vessels cleared Navires sortis	...					112 541	115 294	134 728	146 059	156 066
Fiji — Fidji										
Vessels entered Navires entrés	4 065	4 070[11]	...	...	...	...	...	...	...	...
Finland [3] — Finlande [3]										
Vessels entered Navires entrés	127 711	131 338	144 923	148 690	153 149	155 556	157 730	166 143	175 237	195 107
Vessels cleared Navires sortis	132 880	135 651	148 366	150 969	154 700	152 070	157 639	166 291	174 836	195 180
France [12,13] — France [12,13]										
Vessels entered Navires entrés	1 921 826	2 202 359	2 235 239	2 164 285	2 080 509	2 120 282	2 252 518	2 438 562	...	...
Germany — Allemagne										
Vessels entered Navires entrés	221 226	251 500	260 553	263 470	271 978	959 448[1]	953 366[1]	958 945[1]	1 000 824[1]	1 079 643[1]
Vessels cleared Navires sortis	197 339	229 959	235 110	237 071	249 225	938 028[1]	953 287[1]	958 503[1]	999 749[1]	1 093 136[1]
Gibraltar — Gibraltar										
Vessels entered Navires entrés	256	222	190	156	161	208	180	155	133	...
Greece — Grèce										
Vessels entered Navires entrés	38 573	38 549	38 704	43 786	44 662	45 072	45 973	...	...	...
Vessels cleared Navires sortis	21 940	21 356	19 359	21 865	22 302	22 526	23 970	...	...	...
Guatemala — Guatemala										
Vessels entered Navires entrés	3 976	3 680	4 505	5 950	5 986	6 246	6 095	5 855	6 627	9 534
Vessels cleared Navires sortis	2 854	3 275	3 815	4 565	4 362	4 714	4 633	4 135	5 020	5 211
Haïti [14] — Haïti [14]										
Vessels entered Navires entrés	1 285	1 680	1 304	...	...	...	...	...	...	...
India [15,16] — Inde [15,16]										
Vessels entered Navires entrés	47 857	48 358	47 055	48 512	60 850	55 466	55 982	47 582	59 011	...
Vessels cleared Navires sortis	48 497	44 494	45 819	39 031	41 187	38 043	41 716	44 244	50 744	...

Country or area — Pays ou zone	1995	1996	1997	1998	1999	2000	2001	2002	2003	2004
Indonesia — Indonésie										
Vessels entered Navires entrés	163 597	259 096	286 314	246 838	252 893	303 587	331 164	342 166	333 236	...
Vessels cleared Navires sortis	48 753	75 055	97 885	82 711	73 938	79 813	83 115	85 554	...	...
Iran (Islamic Rep. of) — Iran (Rép. islamique d')										
Vessels entered Navires entrés	14 686	17 155	27 756	46 937	62 828	65 008	67 199	70 956	78 253[17]	86 842[17]
Ireland [3] — Irlande [3]										
Vessels entered Navires entrés	45 968	54 602	165 925[1]	176 228[1]	190 818[1]	196 713	210 882	216 460	218 429	218 355
Vessels cleared Navires sortis	15 890	16 787	16 463[1]	16 669[1]	17 645[1]	17 954	17 234	16 863	17 183	16 323
Italy — Italie										
Vessels entered Navires entrés	181 733	190 910	226 977	250 830	277 384	211 242	222 594	264 678	288 050	278 306
Vessels cleared Navires sortis	96 505	160 757	132 532	152 655	167 550	137 864	149 902	187 194	200 772	191 187
Jamaica — Jamaïque										
Vessels entered Navires entrés	10 531	12 339	12 815	...	...	...	...	...	...	...
Vessels cleared Navires sortis	5 730	6 043	6 457	6 553	...	...	...	...	...	...
Japan — Japon										
Vessels entered Navires entrés	412 163[3]	422 256[3]	438 111[3]	425 193[3]	446 482[3]	461 903[3]	459 840[3]	461 420[3]	491 619[3]	494 187
Jordan — Jordanie										
Vessels entered Navires entrés	1 848	2 265	2 572	2 190	2 351	2 505	2 673	2 789	2 694	2 888
Vessels cleared Navires sortis	534	470	423	418	...	...	...	...	...	...
Kenya — Kenya										
Vessels entered Navires entrés	7 973[3,7]	8 694[3,7]	8 442[3,7]	8 561[3,7]	8 188[3,7]	9 126[3,7]	10 600[3,7]	10 564	11 931	12 920
Korea, Republic of — Corée, République de										
Vessels entered Navires entrés	487 834	537 163	578 373	586 629	691 166	755 225	770 284	819 677	858 660	922 142
Vessels cleared Navires sortis	485 374	542 600	584 164	595 072	693 598	737 999	776 250	828 211	864 522	932 277
Kuwait — Koweït										
Vessels entered Navires entrés	10 723	9 676	9 171	9 357	10 711	10 842	2 189	2 052	3 199	3 531
Vessels cleared Navires sortis	1 222	1 223	1 285	1 178	1 201	1 071	1 071	1 178	1 262	1 279
Latvia [1] — Lettonie [1]										
Vessels entered Navires entrés	...	...	...	...	...	...	...	...	...	19 001
Vessels cleared Navires sortis	...	...	...	...	...	...	...	...	...	54 737
Libyan Arab Jamah. — Jamah. arabe libyenne										
Vessels entered Navires entrés	5 142	5 638	5 980	6 245	5 304	2 721	2 538	...	...	...
Vessels cleared Navires sortis	751	624	647	739	815	1 009	949	...	...	...
Lithuania [1,3] — Lituanie [1,3]										
Vessels entered Navires entrés	25 642	32 187	34 259	35 680	32 438	37 138	34 310	38 532	42 844	44 402
Vessels cleared Navires sortis	25 477	31 383	34 161	35 658	32 419	37 044	33 932	38 269	42 712	44 115
Madagascar [3] — Madagascar [3]										
Vessels entered Navires entrés	...	...	4 169	3 920	2 629	4 842	...	...	...	...

Country or area — Pays ou zone	1995	1996	1997	1998	1999	2000	2001	2002	2003	2004
Malaysia — Malaisie										
Vessels entered Navires entrés	115 494	154 191	164 525	160 663	183 262	198 380	221 752	242 116	257 997	270 874
Vessels cleared Navires sortis	134 172	146 827	154 832	155 237	172 876	191 771	214 133	230 724	249 729	265 917
Malta — Malte										
Vessels entered Navires entrés	9 404	9 830	11 597	13 738	16 725	17 299	23 829	25 136	24 415	23 896
Vessels cleared Navires sortis	2 887	3 779	4 976	2 493	5 084	7 528	23 752	25 161	24 393	23 931
Mauritius — Maurice										
Vessels entered Navires entrés	5 356[3]	4 999[3]	5 485[3]	5 925[3]	6 725[3]	6 387[3]	7 026[3]	8 595[3]	8 399[3]	7 800
Vessels cleared Navires sortis	5 313[3]	5 140[3]	5 263[3]	5 924[3]	6 129[3]	6 087[3]	6 482[3]	7 871[3]	8 843[3]	8 662
Mexico — Mexique										
Vessels entered Navires entrés	19 697	27 533	33 317	43 185	44 814	51 814	50 380	51 718	52 811	...
Vessels cleared Navires sortis	103 355	117 598	125 571	125 682	119 284	124 880	129 020	130 536	139 645	...
Morocco [1,18] — Maroc [1,18]										
Vessels entered Navires entrés	160 233	164 961	196 619	219 617	266 956	263 637	271 696	304 024	300 535	...
Myanmar — Myanmar										
Vessels entered Navires entrés	2 388	2 806	1 868	3 458	4 014	5 458	5 863	3 367	3 157	2 652
Vessels cleared Navires sortis	1 624	1 962	1 689	1 783	3 651	3 206	999	797	1 059	762
Netherlands [1] — Pays-Bas [1]										
Vessels entered Navires entrés	431 997	441 281	456 522	472 977	497 058	535 322	548 082	562 910	587 662	621 695
Vessels cleared Navires sortis	280 667	291 089	290 813	301 559	342 220	365 975	379 887	396 830	413 449	431 834
New Zealand [1] — Nouvelle-Zélande [1]										
Vessels entered Navires entrés	48 827	...	...	...	...	...	...	...	...	...
Vessels cleared Navires sortis	42 985	...	...	...	...	...	...	...	...	...
Nigeria — Nigéria										
Vessels entered Navires entrés	1 846[19]	2 043	2 464	...	...	...	...	...	...	...
Vessels cleared Navires sortis	1 852[19]	2 104	2 510	...	...	...	...	...	...	...
Norway — Norvège										
Vessels entered Navires entrés	139 252[21]	147 192[21]	148 060[21]	148 764[21]	155 805[21]	...	...	...	...	136 277[20]
Vessels cleared [20] Navires sortis [20]	...	...	...	...	...	...	...	...	...	136 277
Oman — Oman										
Vessels entered Navires entrés	2 099	2 155	2 226	2 102	2 087	2 142	2 457	2 688	2 667	...
Vessels cleared Navires sortis	1 309	5 529	6 781	7 147	7 008	...	...	...	...	...
Pakistan [5] — Pakistan [5]										
Vessels entered Navires entrés	21 268	22 632	26 915	26 502	26 702	27 005	26 453	27 262	30 485	32 468
Vessels cleared Navires sortis	7 411	7 728	5 748	6 983	7 296	7 500	9 173	11 861	18 483	16 798

Country or area — Pays ou zone	1995	1996	1997	1998	1999	2000	2001	2002	2003	2004
Panama — Panama										
Vessels entered Navires entrés	2 766	3 263	4 431	9 879	12 008	13 301	13 765	11 459	13 833	18 627
Vessels cleared Navires sortis	1 972	2 367	2 927	6 453	7 298	7 369	9 694	9 735	11 973	17 441
Peru — Pérou										
Vessels entered Navires entrés	7 454	7 515	6 701	7 675	6 948	6 901	7 150	8 260	9 403	...
Vessels cleared Navires sortis	4 640	4 731	6 082	4 668	5 696	6 499	6 637	6 112	6 535	...
Philippines — Philippines										
Vessels entered Navires entrés	40 876	...	...	...	...	...	...	...	...	...
Vessels cleared Navires sortis	27 829	...	...	...	...	...	...	...	...	...
Poland — Pologne										
Vessels entered Navires entrés	18 316	20 997	24 280	25 549	24 161	26 176	26 568	25 976	29 063	30 237
Vessels cleared Navires sortis	25 269	25 566	28 877	30 065	30 062	32 225	31 730	32 802	39 658	37 963
Portugal — Portugal										
Vessels entered Navires entrés	36 095	...	...	...	84 077	85 423 [1,22]	82 659 [1,22]	85 423 [1,22]	89 025 [1,22]	91 436 [1,22]
Vessels cleared Navires sortis	...	...	...	...	84 666	85 348 [1,22]	82 537 [1,22]	85 560 [1,22]	89 627 [1,22]	91 899 [1,22]
Réunion [18] — Réunion [18]										
Vessels entered Navires entrés	2 715	2 595	2 755	3 065	3 059	3 266	3 364	3 195	3 435	3 891
Russian Federation [3] — Fédération de Russie [3]										
Vessels entered Navires entrés	...	...	...	67 110	82 544	76 376	83 581	117 306	107 786	...
Vessels cleared Navires sortis	...	...	...	68 830	82 939	76 369	81 830	100 620	106 937	...
Saint Helena — Sainte-Hélène										
Vessels entered Navires entrés	55	...	...	...	...	...	...	...	...	...
Saint Lucia — Sainte-Lucie										
Vessels entered Navires entrés	4 755	5 317	6 803	...	...	...	...	...	...	...
St. Vincent-Grenadines — St. Vincent-Grenadines										
Vessels entered Navires entrés	932	1 204	1 253	1 274	1 478	1 674	1 790	1 506	1 560	1 641
Vessels cleared Navires sortis	932	1 204	1 253	1 274	1 478	1 674	1 790	1 506	1 560	1 641
Samoa — Samoa										
Vessels entered Navires entrés	579	544	662	685	827	...	...	...	...	...
Senegal — Sénégal										
Vessels entered Navires entrés	2 395	2 542	2 460	2 467	2 511	2 205	2 235	2 360	2 097	2 085
Vessels cleared Navires sortis	2 395	2 542	2 460	2 467	2 511	2 213	2 235	2 360	2 019	2 067
Serbia and Montenegro — Serbie-et-Monténégro										
Vessels entered Navires entrés	805	1 960	1 828	1 589	1 859	2 057	2 165	1 780	3 282	...
Vessels cleared Navires sortis	769	1 155	1 360	1 091	1 091	1 368	1 148	1 373	2 922	...
Seychelles — Seychelles										
Vessels entered Navires entrés	879	872	1 059	1 099	1 139	1 105	1 023	1 276	1 332	...

Country or area — Pays ou zone	1995	1996	1997	1998	1999	2000	2001	2002	2003	2004
Singapore [23] — Singapour [23]										
Vessels entered Navires entrés	104 014	117 723	130 333	140 922	141 523	145 383	146 265	142 745	...	...
Vessels cleared Navires sortis	104 123	117 662	130 237	140 838	141 745	145 415	146 322	142 765	...	...
Slovakia [24] — Slovaquie [24]										
Vessels entered Navires entrés	374	401	367	381	336	347	335	327	289	335
Slovenia — Slovénie										
Vessels entered Navires entrés	4 280	5 067	5 960	6 686	7 762	6 605	6 444	6 825	7 943	8 947
Vessels cleared Navires sortis	2 388	2 251	3 254	3 652	4 394	3 969	3 986	4 430	4 865	5 149
South Africa [1] — Afrique du Sud [1]										
Vessels entered Navires entrés	13 285	14 075	14 383	13 559	12 695	12 041	12 763	13 593	14 311	...
Vessels cleared Navires sortis	515 278	586 492	629 033	631 059	606 231	577 520	634 997	688 975	706 199	...
Spain — Espagne										
Vessels entered Navires entrés	154 134	149 874	152 951	170 817	184 362	194 911	198 696	212 985	218 507	...
Vessels cleared Navires sortis	48 176	51 657	54 243	56 449	56 817	59 247	59 297	61 510	67 404	...
Sri Lanka — Sri Lanka										
Vessels entered Navires entrés	25 368	29 882	33 188	36 011	37 399	37 418	34 690	39 336	41 831	40 894
Suriname — Suriname										
Vessels entered Navires entrés	1 167	1 270	1 307	1 411	1 344	1 120	1 212	1 185	1 317	1 518
Vessels cleared Navires sortis	1 926	2 018	2 135	2 206	2 391	2 186	2 306	2 138	2 174	2 142
Sweden [1] — Suède [1]										
Vessels entered Navires entrés	82 386	88 828	95 655	101 977	158 718[25]	935 481[26]	925 202[26]	953 350[26]	960 929[26]	1 000 644[26,27]
Vessels cleared Navires sortis	73 139	79 888	82 877	84 722	143 200[25]	917 926[26]	910 735[26]	937 947[26]	947 954[26]	990 452[26,27]
Syrian Arab Republic [3] — Rép. arabe syrienne [3]										
Vessels entered [7] Navires entrés [7]	2 884	2 901	2 640	2 622	2 928	2 798	2 827	2 979	3 012	3 711
Vessels cleared Navires sortis	2 701	2 792	2 573	2 562	2 845	2 696	2 791	2 900	2 928	3 524
Thailand — Thaïlande										
Vessels entered Navires entrés	98 759	93 033	84 052	62 339	71 094	68 079	...	...	...	...
Vessels cleared Navires sortis	28 689	22 231	23 757	24 920	31 125	33 154	...	...	...	...
Tunisia [1] — Tunisie [1]										
Vessels entered Navires entrés	36 205	38 513	42 749	43 546	52 441	56 632	58 610	...	...	...
Vessels cleared Navires sortis	36 232	38 541	42 561	43 513	52 464	56 551	58 595	...	...	...
Turkey — Turquie										
Vessels entered Navires entrés	57 170	59 861	78 474	142 303[1]	136 456[1]	152 191[1]	125 997[1]	...	...	...
Vessels cleared Navires sortis	56 221	58 766	77 952	89 712[1]	88 761[1]	92 406[1]	96 867[1]	...	...	...
Ukraine — Ukraine										
Vessels entered Navires entrés	4 270	3 287	3 108	4 843	5 085	6 840	7 404	7 605	10 955	11 675
Vessels cleared Navires sortis	21 916	21 550	28 765	36 027	44 030	42 704	49 310	62 197	56 171	65 436

Country or area — Pays ou zone	1995	1996	1997	1998	1999	2000	2001	2002	2003	2004
United States [8,28] — Etats-Unis [8,28]										
Vessels entered Navires entrés	352 411	371 107	410 157	431 565	440 341	464 358	451 929	488 385	524 327	538 513
Vessels cleared Navires sortis	303 707	305 250	318 435	327 092	302 344	332 445	310 973	341 558	342 707	347 086
Uruguay — Uruguay										
Vessels entered Navires entrés	5 414	5 505	5 844	5 262	4 386	5 257	5 196	4 689	4 806	5 067
Vessels cleared Navires sortis	24 608	24 975	26 844	24 499	21 596	19 985	20 197	21 515	22 264	22 262
Venezuela (Bolivarian Rep. of) — Venezuela (Rép.bolivarienne)										
Vessels entered Navires entrés	21 009	...	...	...	...	...	...	...	...	...
Vessels cleared Navires sortis	8 461	...	...	...	...	...	...	...	...	...
Yemen — Yémen										
Vessels entered Navires entrés	10 353	10 477	10 268	11 210	12 085	12 898	13 846	14 575	16 182	15 395
Vessels cleared Navires sortis	10 524	4 562	5 958	9 851	10 724	11 658	11 668	10 758	10 794	...

Source

United Nations Statistics Division, New York, transport statistics database.

Notes

[1] Gross registered tons.
[2] Data refer to fiscal years ending 30 June.
[3] Including vessels in ballast.
[4] Incomplete coverage.
[5] Data refer to fiscal years beginning 1 July.

[6] Sihanoukville Port and Phnom Penh Port.
[7] All entrances counted.
[8] Including Great Lakes international traffic (Canada: also St. Lawrence).

[9] Including passenger vessels entered from and departed for Mainland China and Hong Kong SAR.
[10] Cuban vessels only.
[11] Beginning 1997, series discontinued.
[12] Including national maritime transport.
[13] Taxable volume in thousands of cubic metres.
[14] Port-au-Prince.
[15] Data refer to fiscal years beginning 1 April.
[16] Excluding minor and intermediate ports.
[17] Data refer to fiscal years ending 20 March.
[18] Including vessels cleared.
[19] Data cover only the first three quarters of the year.
[20] Excluding fishing vessels, ferries and cruise vessels.
[21] Gross tonnage for a sample of Norwegian ports.
[22] Excluding the Azores.
[23] Vessels exceeding 75 gross registered tons.
[24] Inland waterway system.
[25] Break in series. Beginning this year, data are based on a survey of all ports in Sweden.
[26] Including all passenger vessels and ferries.
[27] Beginning 2004, including cruise passenger vessels.
[28] Excluding traffic with United States Virgin Islands.

Source

Organisation des Nations Unies, Division de statistique, New York, la base de données pour les statistiques des transports.

Notes

[1] Tonneaux de jauge brute.
[2] Les données se réfèrent aux exercices budgétaires finissant le 30 juin.
[3] Y compris navires sur lest.
[4] Couverture incomplète.
[5] Les données se réfèrent aux exercices budgétaires commençant le 1er juillet.
[6] Port de Sihanoukville et Port de Phnom Penh.
[7] Toutes entrées comprises.
[8] Y compris trafic international des Grands Lacs (Canada: et du St. Laurent).
[9] Y compris les navires à passagers en provenance de Chine continentale et de la RAS de Hong Kong, ou en partance pour ces deux destinations.
[10] Navires de Cuba seulement.
[11] A compter de 1997, série arrêtée.
[12] Y compris transports martimes nationaux.
[13] Volume taxable en milliers de mètres cubes.
[14] Port-au-Prince.
[15] Les données se réfèrent aux exercices budgétaires commençant le 1er avril.
[16] Non compris les ports petits et moyens.
[17] Les données se réfèrent aux exercices budgétaires finissant le 20 mars.
[18] Y compris navires sortis.
[19] Les données se réfèrent aux premières trois trimestres de l'année.
[20] Non compris les bateaux de pêche, les bacs et les navires de croisière.
[21] Tonnage brute pour un échantillon de ports norvègiens.
[22] Non compris les Açores.
[23] Navires dépassant 75 tonneaux de jauge brute.
[24] Transport fluvial.
[25] Discontinuité dans la série. A compter de cette année, les données sont basées sur une enquête menée auprès de tous les ports de Suède.
[26] Y compris tous les navires à passagers et les transbordeurs.
[27] A compter de 2004, y compris navires de croisière.
[28] Non compris le trafic avec les Iles Vierges américaines.

Civil aviation: scheduled airline traffic
Passengers carried (thousands); kilometres (millions)

Aviation civile : trafic régulier des lignes aériennes
Passagers transportés (milliers) ; kilomètres (millions)

Region, country or area, and traffic	Total traffic (domestic and international) Trafic total (intérieur et international)				International traffic Trafic international				Région, pays ou zone et trafic
	2000	2001	2002	2003	2000	2001	2002	2003	
World									**Monde**
Kilometres flown	25 155	25 277	25 403	26 264	12 043	12 097	11 873	12 314	Kilomètres parcourus
Passengers carried	1 655 164	1 623 491	1 639 009	1 691 233	538 200	531 749	547 618	561 229	Passagers transportés
Passenger-kilomètres	3 014 211	2 929 426	2 964 891	3 019 104	1 778 860	1 715 562	1 736 523	1 738 507	Passagers-kilomètres
Total tonne-kilometres	400 740	385 385	397 109	407 670	271 482	259 477	267 151	268 424	Tonnes-kilomètres totales
Africa [1]									**Afrique** [1]
Kilometres flown	595	595	582	621	456	451	438	463	Kilomètres parcourus
Passengers carried	32 057	30 933	30 225	30 534	18 420	18 108	17 991	17 264	Passagers transportés
Passenger-kilomètres	66 637	66 548	65 742	66 504	57 204	57 741	57 125	56 650	Passagers-kilomètres
Total tonne-kilometres	8 278	8 236	7 864	8 136	7 331	7 337	6 988	7 137	Tonnes-kilomètres totales
Algeria									**Algérie**
Kilometres flown	34	42	42	41	19	25	27	27	Kilomètres parcourus
Passengers carried	2 997	3 419	3 002	3 293	1 863	2 076	1 876	2 019	Passagers transportés
Passenger-kilomètres	3 051	3 501	3 257	3 415	2 389	2 722	2 605	2 672	Passagers-kilomètres
Total tonne-kilometres	287	338	313	328	225	264	251	258	Tonnes-kilomètres totales
Angola									**Angola**
Kilometres flown	6	5	5	5	5	3	3	4	Kilomètres parcourus
Passengers carried	235	193	190	198	142	101	101	99	Passagers transportés
Passenger-kilomètres	619	465	470	479	565	413	417	417	Passagers-kilomètres
Total tonne-kilometres	116	92	92	98	111	87	87	92	Tonnes-kilomètres totales
Benin [2]									**Bénin** [2]
Kilometres flown	3	1	...	...	3	1	...	...	Kilomètres parcourus
Passengers carried	77	46	...	...	77	46	...	...	Passagers transportés
Passenger-kilomètres	216	130	...	...	216	130	...	...	Passagers-kilomètres
Total tonne-kilometres	32	19	...	...	32	19	...	...	Tonnes-kilomètres totales
Botswana									**Botswana**
Kilometres flown	3	3	3	3	2	2	2	2	Kilomètres parcourus
Passengers carried	164	170	179	189	121	123	124	131	Passagers transportés
Passenger-kilomètres	74	77	80	83	53	55	54	55	Passagers-kilomètres
Total tonne-kilometres	7	7	8	8	5	5	5	5	Tonnes-kilomètres totales
Burkina Faso [2]									**Burkina Faso** [2]
Kilometres flown	4	2	1	1	4	2	1	1	Kilomètres parcourus
Passengers carried	144	100	53	54	128	83	37	36	Passagers transportés
Passenger-kilomètres	253	158	29	29	247	154	24	24	Passagers-kilomètres
Total tonne-kilometres	35	22	3	3	35	21	2	2	Tonnes-kilomètres totales
Cameroon									**Cameroun**
Kilometres flown	6	5	11	9	5	4	9	8	Kilomètres parcourus
Passengers carried	312	247	322	315	221	157	235	225	Passagers transportés
Passenger-kilomètres	646	489	646	629	580	423	585	562	Passagers-kilomètres
Total tonne-kilometres	115	91	79	77	108	84	73	70	Tonnes-kilomètres totales
Cape Verde									**Cap-Vert**
Kilometres flown	6	4	4	5	4	3	3	3	Kilomètres parcourus
Passengers carried	264	243	237	253	120	87	87	86	Passagers transportés
Passenger-kilomètres	356	276	279	285	307	240	242	242	Passagers-kilomètres
Total tonne-kilometres	34	27	26	27	29	23	23	23	Tonnes-kilomètres totales
Central African Rep. [2]									**Rép. centrafricaine** [2]
Kilometres flown	3	1	...	...	3	1	...	...	Kilomètres parcourus
Passengers carried	77	46	...	...	77	46	...	...	Passagers transportés
Passenger-kilomètres	216	130	...	...	216	130	...	...	Passagers-kilomètres
Total tonne-kilometres	32	19	...	...	32	19	...	...	Tonnes-kilomètres totales

57 Civil aviation: scheduled airline traffic — Passengers carried (thousands); kilometres (millions) (*continued*)

Aviation civile : trafic régulier des lignes aériennes — Passagers transportés (milliers) ; kilomètres (millions) (*suite*)

Region, country or area, and traffic	Total traffic (domestic and international) Trafic total (intérieur et international)				International traffic Trafic international				Région, pays ou zone et trafic
	2000	2001	2002	2003	2000	2001	2002	2003	
Chad [2]									**Tchad [2]**
Kilometres flown	3	1	...	...	3	1	...	...	Kilomètres parcourus
Passengers carried	77	46	...	...	77	46	...	...	Passagers transportés
Passenger-kilomètres	216	130	...	...	216	130	...	...	Passagers-kilomètres
Total tonne-kilomètres	32	19	...	...	32	19	...	...	Tonnes-kilomètres totales
Congo [2]									**Congo [2]**
Kilometres flown	4	3	1	1	3	2	0	0	Kilomètres parcourus
Passengers carried	128	95	47	52	81	49	2	2	Passagers transportés
Passenger-kilomètres	245	157	27	31	222	134	4	4	Passagers-kilomètres
Total tonne-kilomètres	34	22	3	3	32	19	0	0	Tonnes-kilomètres totales
Côte d'Ivoire [2]									**Côte d'Ivoire [2]**
Kilometres flown	3	1	...	...	3	1	...	...	Kilomètres parcourus
Passengers carried	108	46	...	...	103	46	...	...	Passagers transportés
Passenger-kilomètres	242	130	...	...	240	130	...	...	Passagers-kilomètres
Total tonne-kilomètres	34	19	...	...	34	19	...	...	Tonnes-kilomètres totales
Egypt									**Egypte**
Kilometres flown	64	64	64	63	58	59	59	58	Kilomètres parcourus
Passengers carried	4 522	4 389	4 527	4 181	2 860	2 981	3 141	2 916	Passagers transportés
Passenger-kilomètres	8 828	8 893	9 000	8 103	8 065	8 241	8 357	7 517	Passagers-kilomètres
Total tonne-kilomètres	1 085	1 051	1 068	975	1 015	991	1 009	921	Tonnes-kilomètres totales
Ethiopia									**Ethiopie**
Kilometres flown	29	32	34	35	26	28	31	32	Kilomètres parcourus
Passengers carried	945	1 028	1 103	1 147	683	754	831	881	Passagers transportés
Passenger-kilomètres	2 753	2 953	3 287	3 573	2 641	2 835	3 170	3 460	Passagers-kilomètres
Total tonne-kilomètres	383	402	442	484	373	392	432	474	Tonnes-kilomètres totales
Gabon									**Gabon**
Kilometres flown	8	7	7	8	7	5	5	5	Kilomètres parcourus
Passengers carried	447	374	366	386	244	173	173	170	Passagers transportés
Passenger-kilomètres	847	637	643	655	774	565	571	571	Passagers-kilomètres
Total tonne-kilomètres	135	107	106	112	128	100	100	104	Tonnes-kilomètres totales
Ghana									**Ghana**
Kilometres flown	9	18	12	12	9	18	12	12	Kilomètres parcourus
Passengers carried	314	301	256	241	314	301	256	241	Passagers transportés
Passenger-kilomètres	1 204	1 233	912	906	1 204	1 233	912	906	Passagers-kilomètres
Total tonne-kilomètres	162	157	107	101	162	157	107	101	Tonnes-kilomètres totales
Kenya									**Kenya**
Kilometres flown	34	32	36	41	27	27	31	35	Kilomètres parcourus
Passengers carried	1 555	1 418	1 600	1 732	973	990	1 148	1 250	Passagers transportés
Passenger-kilomètres	3 271	3 706	3 939	4 245	3 040	3 522	3 754	4 050	Passagers-kilomètres
Total tonne-kilomètres	377	427	465	527	355	410	448	509	Tonnes-kilomètres totales
Libyan Arab Jamah.									**Jamah. arabe libyenne**
Kilometres flown	4	4	4	8	...	...	...	4	Kilomètres parcourus
Passengers carried	601	583	559	742	...	...	...	115	Passagers transportés
Passenger-kilomètres	409	409	409	825	...	...	...	346	Passagers-kilomètres
Total tonne-kilomètres	33	33	33	69	...	...	...	31	Tonnes-kilomètres totales
Madagascar									**Madagascar**
Kilometres flown	14	12	5	9	9	7	2	4	Kilomètres parcourus
Passengers carried	667	566	391	452	183	146	241	140	Passagers transportés
Passenger-kilomètres	1 146	835	319	715	907	654	266	562	Passagers-kilomètres
Total tonne-kilomètres	137	103	48	74	114	86	42	60	Tonnes-kilomètres totales
Malawi									**Malawi**
Kilometres flown	3	3	3	4	2	2	2	2	Kilomètres parcourus
Passengers carried	116	113	105	109	64	66	67	68	Passagers transportés
Passenger-kilomètres	210	221	140	147	136	148	80	86	Passagers-kilomètres
Total tonne-kilomètres	22	23	14	16	15	16	8	11	Tonnes-kilomètres totales

57

Civil aviation: scheduled airline traffic—Passengers carried (thousands); kilometres (millions) (*continued*)

Aviation civile : trafic régulier des lignes aériennes—Passagers transportés (milliers) ; kilomètres (millions) (*suite*)

Region, country or area, and traffic	Total traffic (domestic and international) Trafic total (intérieur et international)				International traffic Trafic international				Région, pays ou zone et trafic
	2000	2001	2002	2003	2000	2001	2002	2003	
Mali [2]									**Mali [2]**
Kilometres flown	3	1	...	...	3	1	...	...	Kilomètres parcourus
Passengers carried	77	46	...	...	77	46	...	...	Passagers transportés
Passenger-kilomètres	216	130	...	...	216	130	...	...	Passagers-kilomètres
Total tonne-kilomètres	32	19	...	...	32	19	...	...	Tonnes-kilomètres totales
Mauritania [2]									**Mauritanie [2]**
Kilometres flown	4	2	1	1	3	2	0	0	Kilomètres parcourus
Passengers carried	185	156	106	116	98	61	15	14	Passagers transportés
Passenger-kilomètres	275	174	45	49	238	147	17	17	Passagers-kilomètres
Total tonne-kilomètres	37	23	4	5	34	21	2	2	Tonnes-kilomètres totales
Mauritius									**Maurice**
Kilometres flown	29	30	30	33	27	29	29	32	Kilomètres parcourus
Passengers carried	949	1 002	1 006	1 043	865	913	909	929	Passagers transportés
Passenger-kilomètres	4 888	5 194	5 084	5 243	4 837	5 140	5 026	5 175	Passagers-kilomètres
Total tonne-kilomètres	647	669	667	687	643	664	661	680	Tonnes-kilomètres totales
Morocco									**Maroc**
Kilometres flown	64	63	58	59	60	59	55	56	Kilomètres parcourus
Passengers carried	3 671	3 681	3 146	2 638	2 800	2 766	2 501	2 049	Passagers transportés
Passenger-kilomètres	7 185	7 112	6 045	4 905	6 904	6 820	5 834	4 710	Passagers-kilomètres
Total tonne-kilomètres	722	715	626	528	693	687	605	507	Tonnes-kilomètres totales
Mozambique									**Mozambique**
Kilometres flown	6	7	7	6	3	3	3	3	Kilomètres parcourus
Passengers carried	260	264	282	281	93	85	98	103	Passagers transportés
Passenger-kilomètres	376	353	397	405	207	169	201	214	Passagers-kilomètres
Total tonne-kilomètres	41	39	43	43	24	20	23	23	Tonnes-kilomètres totales
Namibia									**Namibie**
Kilometres flown	8	9	9	11	6	6	6	8	Kilomètres parcourus
Passengers carried	247	215	222	266	212	179	179	222	Passagers transportés
Passenger-kilomètres	740	754	760	930	720	734	734	904	Passagers-kilomètres
Total tonne-kilomètres	151	151	98	139	149	149	95	136	Tonnes-kilomètres totales
Niger [2]									**Niger [2]**
Kilometres flown	3	1	...	...	3	1	...	...	Kilomètres parcourus
Passengers carried	77	46	...	...	77	46	...	...	Passagers transportés
Passenger-kilomètres	216	130	...	...	216	130	...	...	Passagers-kilomètres
Total tonne-kilomètres	32	19	...	...	32	19	...	...	Tonnes-kilomètres totales
Nigeria									**Nigéria**
Kilometres flown	7	4	6	12	2	1	1	4	Kilomètres parcourus
Passengers carried	507	529	512	520	48	33	41	51	Passagers transportés
Passenger-kilomètres	565	402	522	638	63	25	27	15	Passagers-kilomètres
Total tonne-kilomètres	57	37	57	61	8	3	3	2	Tonnes-kilomètres totales
Sao Tome and Principe									**Sao Tomé-et-Principe**
Kilometres flown	0	0	0	0	0	0	0	0	Kilomètres parcourus
Passengers carried	35	35	34	36	21	21	21	21	Passagers transportés
Passenger-kilomètres	14	14	14	15	7	7	7	7	Passagers-kilomètres
Total tonne-kilomètres	1	1	1	1	1	1	1	1	Tonnes-kilomètres totales
Senegal [2]									**Sénégal [2]**
Kilometres flown	3	4	7	6	3	4	7	6	Kilomètres parcourus
Passengers carried	98	176	231	130	77	145	199	96	Passagers transportés
Passenger-kilomètres	222	319	572	388	216	304	554	378	Passagers-kilomètres
Total tonne-kilomètres	32	116	20	35	32	109	18	34	Tonnes-kilomètres totales
Seychelles									**Seychelles**
Kilometres flown	9	9	12	12	8	9	11	11	Kilomètres parcourus
Passengers carried	394	420	518	413	127	153	250	187	Passagers transportés
Passenger-kilomètres	807	925	1 397	986	795	917	1 387	976	Passagers-kilomètres
Total tonne-kilomètres	94	101	153	114	93	100	152	113	Tonnes-kilomètres totales

Region, country or area, and traffic	Total traffic (domestic and international) Trafic total (intérieur et international)				International traffic Trafic international				Région, pays ou zone et trafic
	2000	2001	2002	2003	2000	2001	2002	2003	
Sierra Leone									**Sierra Leone**
Kilometres flown	1	1	1	1	1	1	1	1	Kilomètres parcourus
Passengers carried	19	14	14	14	19	14	14	14	Passagers transportés
Passenger-kilomètres	93	73	74	74	93	73	74	74	Passagers-kilomètres
Total tonne-kilometres	18	13	13	13	18	13	13	13	Tonnes-kilomètres totales
South Africa									**Afrique du Sud**
Kilometres flown	151	167	170	188	87	92	94	104	Kilomètres parcourus
Passengers carried	8 001	7 948	8 167	9 160	2 483	2 693	2 834	2 996	Passagers transportés
Passenger-kilomètres	21 015	22 061	22 914	24 666	15 857	17 192	17 953	18 852	Passagers-kilomètres
Total tonne-kilometres	2 579	2 746	2 853	3 125	2 041	2 225	2 330	2 505	Tonnes-kilomètres totales
Sudan									**Soudan**
Kilometres flown	6	6	6	7	5	5	5	5	Kilomètres parcourus
Passengers carried	414	415	409	420	265	270	270	264	Passagers transportés
Passenger-kilomètres	748	761	767	786	639	652	659	659	Passagers-kilomètres
Total tonne-kilometres	101	98	98	103	87	85	85	88	Tonnes-kilomètres totales
Swaziland									**Swaziland**
Kilometres flown	2	...	...	...	2	...	...	...	Kilomètres parcourus
Passengers carried	90	...	...	...	90	...	...	...	Passagers transportés
Passenger-kilomètres	68	...	...	...	68	...	...	...	Passagers-kilomètres
Total tonne-kilometres	6	...	...	...	6	...	...	...	Tonnes-kilomètres totales
Togo [2]									**Togo** [2]
Kilometres flown	3	1	...	...	3	1	...	...	Kilomètres parcourus
Passengers carried	77	46	...	...	77	46	...	...	Passagers transportés
Passenger-kilomètres	216	130	...	...	216	130	...	...	Passagers-kilomètres
Total tonne-kilometres	32	19	...	...	32	19	...	...	Tonnes-kilomètres totales
Tunisia									**Tunisie**
Kilometres flown	27	26	24	25	27	26	24	25	Kilomètres parcourus
Passengers carried	1 908	1 926	1 789	1 720	1 908	1 926	1 789	1 720	Passagers transportés
Passenger-kilomètres	2 690	2 696	2 511	2 459	2 690	2 696	2 511	2 459	Passagers-kilomètres
Total tonne-kilometres	284	283	266	261	284	283	266	261	Tonnes-kilomètres totales
Uganda									**Ouganda**
Kilometres flown	2	2	2	2	2	2	2	2	Kilomètres parcourus
Passengers carried	39	41	41	40	39	41	41	40	Passagers transportés
Passenger-kilomètres	215	235	237	237	215	235	237	237	Passagers-kilomètres
Total tonne-kilometres	40	42	42	44	40	42	42	44	Tonnes-kilomètres totales
United Rep. of Tanzania									**Rép.-Unie de Tanzanie**
Kilometres flown	4	4	3	4	3	3	2	3	Kilomètres parcourus
Passengers carried	193	175	134	150	90	77	67	61	Passagers transportés
Passenger-kilomètres	198	181	136	151	146	134	93	102	Passagers-kilomètres
Total tonne-kilometres	21	21	14	16	15	15	9	10	Tonnes-kilomètres totales
Zambia									**Zambie**
Kilometres flown	2	2	2	2	1	0	0	1	Kilomètres parcourus
Passengers carried	90	49	47	45	45	12	12	17	Passagers transportés
Passenger-kilomètres	51	16	16	14	38	5	5	6	Passagers-kilomètres
Total tonne-kilometres	5	1	1	1	4	0	0	1	Tonnes-kilomètres totales
Zimbabwe									**Zimbabwe**
Kilometres flown	17	15	8	6	14	14	7	5	Kilomètres parcourus
Passengers carried	605	308	251	201	288	188	155	102	Passagers transportés
Passenger-kilomètres	771	723	674	437	653	674	635	391	Passagers-kilomètres
Total tonne-kilometres	228	224	87	58	217	219	83	54	Tonnes-kilomètres totales
America, North [1]									**Amérique du Nord** [1]
Kilometres flown	11 553	11 414	11 368	11 962	2 754	2 779	2 621	2 635	Kilomètres parcourus
Passengers carried	721 303	674 391	662 629	683 665	98 240	91 893	91 547	89 609	Passagers transportés
Passenger-kilomètres	1 226 291	1 158 788	1 141 876	1 160 350	387 991	364 771	351 728	339 970	Passagers-kilomètres
Total tonne-kilometres	147 429	138 072	140 694	145 046	57 021	54 267	54 552	52 048	Tonnes-kilomètres totales

Region, country or area, and traffic	Total traffic (domestic and international) Trafic total (intérieur et international)				International traffic Trafic international				Région, pays ou zone et trafic
	2000	2001	2002	2003	2000	2001	2002	2003	
Antigua and Barbuda									**Antigua-et-Barbuda**
Kilometres flown	10	12	11	12	10	12	11	12	Kilomètres parcourus
Passengers carried	1 426	1 369	1 287	1 428	1 426	1 369	1 287	1 428	Passagers transportés
Passenger-kilomètres	298	304	301	325	298	304	301	325	Passagers-kilomètres
Total tonne-kilometres	28	30	30	32	28	30	30	32	Tonnes-kilomètres totales
Bahamas									**Bahamas**
Kilometres flown	7	7	6	6	3	4	4	4	Kilomètres parcourus
Passengers carried	1 861	1 626	1 543	1 601	1 016	975	886	984	Passagers transportés
Passenger-kilomètres	415	391	369	388	280	286	266	287	Passagers-kilomètres
Total tonne-kilometres	47	48	47	48	32	35	33	35	Tonnes-kilomètres totales
Canada									**Canada**
Kilometres flown	598	567	885	870	370	357	387	338	Kilomètres parcourus
Passengers carried	25 281	24 204	36 202	36 264	12 775	12 135	13 370	12 191	Passagers transportés
Passenger-kilomètres	69 985	68 804	80 426	76 328	47 408	46 436	49 540	45 875	Passagers-kilomètres
Total tonne-kilometres	8 293	7 979	9 942	8 816	5 882	5 624	6 422	5 406	Tonnes-kilomètres totales
Costa Rica									**Costa Rica**
Kilometres flown	20	24	22	20	18	22	18	16	Kilomètres parcourus
Passengers carried	878	738	680	750	742	631	512	584	Passagers transportés
Passenger-kilomètres	2 358	2 152	1 784	1 671	2 334	2 143	1 766	1 654	Passagers-kilomètres
Total tonne-kilometres	252	179	107	122	250	178	105	120	Tonnes-kilomètres totales
Cuba									**Cuba**
Kilometres flown	20	19	15	19	16	17	12	16	Kilomètres parcourus
Passengers carried	1 007	882	589	664	598	567	339	429	Passagers transportés
Passenger-kilomètres	2 964	3 171	1 887	2 036	2 769	3 019	1 795	1 945	Passagers-kilomètres
Total tonne-kilometres	335	361	223	224	312	340	210	211	Tonnes-kilomètres totales
El Salvador									**El Salvador**
Kilometres flown	34	26	26	34	30	26	26	34	Kilomètres parcourus
Passengers carried	2 476	1 692	1 804	2 271	1 960	1 692	1 804	2 182	Passagers transportés
Passenger-kilomètres	3 020	2 907	3 300	3 644	2 829	2 907	3 300	3 616	Passagers-kilomètres
Total tonne-kilometres	302	308	309	339	284	308	309	336	Tonnes-kilomètres totales
Jamaica									**Jamaïque**
Kilometres flown	32	46	41	48	32	46	41	48	Kilomètres parcourus
Passengers carried	1 922	1 946	2 016	1 838	1 922	1 946	2 016	1 838	Passagers transportés
Passenger-kilomètres	4 087	4 412	4 912	5 005	4 087	4 412	4 912	5 005	Passagers-kilomètres
Total tonne-kilometres	400	471	589	484	400	471	589	484	Tonnes-kilomètres totales
Mexico									**Mexique**
Kilometres flown	359	363	337	344	160	157	144	149	Kilomètres parcourus
Passengers carried	20 894	20 173	19 619	19 642	6 137	5 743	5 312	5 383	Passagers transportés
Passenger-kilomètres	30 299	29 621	28 264	28 927	15 059	14 511	13 347	13 517	Passagers-kilomètres
Total tonne-kilometres	3 061	3 029	3 216	3 300	1 635	1 606	1 689	1 739	Tonnes-kilomètres totales
Nicaragua									**Nicaragua**
Kilometres flown	1	...	...	...	1	...	...	...	Kilomètres parcourus
Passengers carried	61	...	...	...	61	...	...	...	Passagers transportés
Passenger-kilomètres	72	...	...	...	72	...	...	...	Passagers-kilomètres
Total tonne-kilometres	7	...	...	...	7	...	...	...	Tonnes-kilomètres totales
Panama									**Panama**
Kilometres flown	34	40	38	43	34	40	38	43	Kilomètres parcourus
Passengers carried	1 117	1 115	1 048	1 313	1 117	1 115	1 048	1 313	Passagers transportés
Passenger-kilomètres	2 604	3 004	2 974	3 529	2 604	3 004	2 974	3 529	Passagers-kilomètres
Total tonne-kilometres	312	317	317	375	312	317	317	375	Tonnes-kilomètres totales
Trinidad and Tobago									**Trinité-et-Tobago**
Kilometres flown	28	29	28	31	28	29	28	31	Kilomètres parcourus
Passengers carried	1 254	1 388	1 269	1 084	1 126	1 079	1 164	972	Passagers transportés
Passenger-kilomètres	2 765	2 723	2 875	2 671	2 754	2 697	2 866	2 662	Passagers-kilomètres
Total tonne-kilometres	300	288	295	276	299	285	294	275	Tonnes-kilomètres totales

57 Civil aviation: scheduled airline traffic—Passengers carried (thousands); kilometres (millions) (*continued*)

Aviation civile : trafic régulier des lignes aériennes—Passagers transportés (milliers) ; kilomètres (millions) (*suite*)

Region, country or area, and traffic	Total traffic (domestic and international) Trafic total (intérieur et international)				International traffic Trafic international				Région, pays ou zone et trafic
	2000	2001	2002	2003	2000	2001	2002	2003	
United States									**Etats-Unis**
Kilometres flown	10 386	10 268	9 946	10 526	2 030	2 057	1 901	1 937	Kilomètres parcourus
Passengers carried	661 461	618 149	595 561	615 944	68 037	63 793	63 008	61 639	Passagers transportés
Passenger-kilomètres	1 105 728	1 040 472	1 014 132	1 035 277	305 895	284 299	270 076	261 070	Passagers-kilomètres
Total tonne-kilometres	133 937	124 982	125 555	130 979	47 431	44 999	44 496	42 991	Tonnes-kilomètres totales
America, South									**Amérique du Sud**
Kilometres flown	1 049	1 050	1 013	910	412	401	385	375	Kilomètres parcourus
Passengers carried	64 647	67 124	67 697	62 578	12 992	12 821	11 929	12 120	Passagers transportés
Passenger-kilomètres	91 229	85 648	85 545	87 140	51 849	45 190	44 985	48 069	Passagers-kilomètres
Total tonne-kilomètres	12 245	11 486	11 234	11 440	8 174	7 307	6 904	7 346	Tonnes-kilomètres totales
Argentina									**Argentine**
Kilometres flown	160	107	102	104	58	28	38	48	Kilomètres parcourus
Passengers carried	8 904	5 809	5 257	5 946	2 305	1 032	1 248	1 709	Passagers transportés
Passenger-kilomètres	15 535	8 330	9 844	12 381	9 287	3 580	5 568	7 764	Passagers-kilomètres
Total tonne-kilometres	1 751	883	956	1 218	1 171	445	556	787	Tonnes-kilomètres totales
Bolivia									**Bolivie**
Kilometres flown	20	18	18	22	15	13	12	14	Kilomètres parcourus
Passengers carried	1 757	1 557	1 509	1 771	657	550	446	568	Passagers transportés
Passenger-kilomètres	1 809	1 567	1 432	1 744	1 403	1 201	982	1 311	Passagers-kilomètres
Total tonne-kilometres	181	159	148	187	143	124	106	145	Tonnes-kilomètres totales
Brazil									**Brésil**
Kilometres flown	519	547	529	443	151	155	137	123	Kilomètres parcourus
Passengers carried	31 819	34 286	35 890	32 293	3 903	3 819	3 387	3 448	Passagers transportés
Passenger-kilomètres	45 812	46 603	46 092	44 192	22 812	21 502	20 761	20 252	Passagers-kilomètres
Total tonne-kilometres	5 712	5 726	5 763	5 447	3 246	3 050	2 950	2 875	Tonnes-kilomètres totales
Chile									**Chili**
Kilometres flown	108	110	108	107	67	73	70	71	Kilomètres parcourus
Passengers carried	5 175	5 316	4 987	5 247	2 059	2 200	2 120	2 387	Passagers transportés
Passenger-kilomètres	10 859	11 520	11 094	12 187	7 678	8 308	8 110	9 140	Passagers-kilomètres
Total tonne-kilometres	2 296	2 329	2 110	2 237	1 955	1 981	1 785	1 913	Tonnes-kilomètres totales
Colombia									**Colombie**
Kilometres flown	120	122	114	110	65	65	57	54	Kilomètres parcourus
Passengers carried	8 570	9 604	9 425	8 665	1 773	2 090	1 842	1 714	Passagers transportés
Passenger-kilomètres	8 662	8 657	8 271	8 299	5 366	5 082	4 272	4 210	Passagers-kilomètres
Total tonne-kilometres	1 384	1 386	1 281	1 390	1 046	1 031	871	953	Tonnes-kilomètres totales
Ecuador									**Equateur**
Kilometres flown	12	8	7	9	6	3	2	0	Kilomètres parcourus
Passengers carried	1 319	1 285	1 184	1 521	163	87	61	16	Passagers transportés
Passenger-kilomètres	1 042	715	626	674	544	188	112	9	Passagers-kilomètres
Total tonne-kilometres	108	70	64	64	62	21	13	1	Tonnes-kilomètres totales
Guyana									**Guyana**
Kilometres flown	2	1	...	...	2	1	...	...	Kilomètres parcourus
Passengers carried	73	48	...	...	73	48	...	...	Passagers transportés
Passenger-kilomètres	299	175	...	...	299	175	...	...	Passagers-kilomètres
Total tonne-kilometres	30	17	...	...	30	17	...	...	Tonnes-kilomètres totales
Paraguay									**Paraguay**
Kilometres flown	5	6	6	6	4	5	5	5	Kilomètres parcourus
Passengers carried	266	281	269	299	249	266	254	288	Passagers transportés
Passenger-kilomètres	270	294	279	320	266	290	274	318	Passagers-kilomètres
Total tonne-kilometres	24	26	25	29	24	26	25	29	Tonnes-kilomètres totales
Peru									**Pérou**
Kilometres flown	24	38	38	44	8	21	22	29	Kilomètres parcourus
Passengers carried	1 595	1 844	2 092	2 226	145	442	500	547	Passagers transportés
Passenger-kilomètres	1 555	2 627	2 340	2 796	548	1 605	1 279	1 727	Passagers-kilomètres
Total tonne-kilometres	196	357	317	382	95	254	208	265	Tonnes-kilomètres totales

57 Civil aviation: scheduled airline traffic— Passengers carried (thousands); kilometres (millions) *(continued)*

Aviation civile : trafic régulier des lignes aériennes— Passagers transportés (milliers) ; kilomètres (millions) *(suite)*

Region, country or area, and traffic	Total traffic (domestic and international) Trafic total (intérieur et international)				International traffic Trafic international				Région, pays ou zone et trafic
	2000	2001	2002	2003	2000	2001	2002	2003	
Suriname									**Suriname**
Kilometres flown	6	5	5	5	5	5	5	4	Kilometres parcourus
Passengers carried	233	203	191	258	227	198	186	253	Passagers transportés
Passenger-kilometres	1 151	898	889	1 470	1 149	896	887	1 469	Passagers-kilomètres
Total tonne-kilometres	130	103	101	183	129	103	101	183	Tonnes-kilomètres totales
Uruguay									**Uruguay**
Kilometres flown	8	7	7	8	8	7	7	8	Kilometres parcourus
Passengers carried	642	559	525	464	642	559	525	464	Passagers transportés
Passenger-kilometres	747	582	577	1 029	747	582	577	1 029	Passagers-kilomètres
Total tonne-kilometres	82	65	64	118	82	65	64	118	Tonnes-kilomètres totales
Venezuela (Bolivarian Rep. of)									**Venezuela (Rép. bolivar. du)**
Kilometres flown	66	80	79	50	23	24	28	17	Kilometres parcourus
Passengers carried	4 295	6 334	6 369	3 887	795	1 534	1 361	726	Passagers transportés
Passenger-kilometres	3 487	3 681	4 103	2 048	1 750	1 781	2 162	841	Passagers-kilomètres
Total tonne-kilometres	350	364	405	187	190	190	227	78	Tonnes-kilomètres totales
Asia [1]									**Asie** [1]
Kilometres flown	4 627	4 862	5 142	5 370	2 959	2 998	3 142	3 205	Kilometres parcourus
Passengers carried	379 120	392 265	415 500	421 400	143 253	143 124	155 426	145 094	Passagers transportés
Passenger-kilometres	737 948	744 611	801 800	779 549	544 206	533 154	572 818	534 442	Passagers-kilomètres
Total tonne-kilometres	109 528	108 917	119 357	119 004	90 964	87 626	96 207	94 180	Tonnes-kilomètres totales
Afghanistan									**Afghanistan**
Kilometres flown	3	...	...	...	2	...	...	...	Kilometres parcourus
Passengers carried	150	...	...	...	40	...	...	...	Passagers transportés
Passenger-kilometres	143	...	...	...	101	...	...	...	Passagers-kilomètres
Total tonne-kilometres	21	...	...	...	17	...	...	...	Tonnes-kilomètres totales
Armenia									**Arménie**
Kilometres flown	7	9	8	8	7	9	8	8	Kilometres parcourus
Passengers carried	298	369	408	370	298	369	408	370	Passagers transportés
Passenger-kilometres	572	706	747	716	572	706	747	716	Passagers-kilomètres
Total tonne-kilometres	61	81	73	70	61	81	73	70	Tonnes-kilomètres totales
Azerbaijan									**Azerbaïdjan**
Kilometres flown	10	10	11	12	7	8	8	9	Kilometres parcourus
Passengers carried	546	544	575	684	146	147	171	245	Passagers transportés
Passenger-kilometres	503	511	579	751	272	282	347	497	Passagers-kilomètres
Total tonne-kilometres	93	112	128	135	70	89	105	111	Tonnes-kilomètres totales
Bahrain [3]									**Bahreïn** [3]
Kilometres flown	28	28	27	40	28	28	27	40	Kilometres parcourus
Passengers carried	1 382	1 250	1 256	1 850	1 382	1 250	1 256	1 850	Passagers transportés
Passenger-kilometres	3 185	3 076	2 944	4 494	3 185	3 076	2 944	4 494	Passagers-kilomètres
Total tonne-kilometres	510	525	523	769	510	525	523	769	Tonnes-kilomètres totales
Bangladesh									**Bangladesh**
Kilometres flown	25	27	27	29	23	26	26	27	Kilometres parcourus
Passengers carried	1 331	1 450	1 536	1 579	969	1 110	1 172	1 205	Passagers transportés
Passenger-kilometres	3 988	4 395	4 580	4 662	3 910	4 323	4 503	4 583	Passagers-kilomètres
Total tonne-kilometres	632	599	684	704	626	593	677	697	Tonnes-kilomètres totales
Bhutan									**Bhoutan**
Kilometres flown	1	1	2	2	1	1	2	2	Kilometres parcourus
Passengers carried	34	35	41	36	34	35	41	36	Passagers transportés
Passenger-kilometres	47	47	61	56	47	47	61	56	Passagers-kilomètres
Total tonne-kilometres	4	4	6	5	4	4	6	5	Tonnes-kilomètres totales
Brunei Darussalam									**Brunéi Darussalam**
Kilometres flown	25	26	27	28	25	26	27	28	Kilometres parcourus
Passengers carried	864	1 008	1 036	956	864	1 008	1 036	956	Passagers transportés
Passenger-kilometres	3 001	3 624	3 715	3 591	3 001	3 624	3 715	3 591	Passagers-kilomètres
Total tonne-kilometres	410	458	496	473	410	458	496	473	Tonnes-kilomètres totales

57 Civil aviation: scheduled airline traffic—Passengers carried (thousands); kilometres (millions) (*continued*)

Aviation civile : trafic régulier des lignes aériennes—Passagers transportés (milliers) ; kilomètres (millions) (*suite*)

Region, country or area, and traffic	Total traffic (domestic and international) Trafic total (intérieur et international)				International traffic Trafic international				Région, pays ou zone et trafic
	2000	2001	2002	2003	2000	2001	2002	2003	
Cambodia									**Cambodge**
Kilometres flown	...	...	2	2	...	...	1	1	Kilomètres parcourus
Passengers carried	...	...	125	165	...	...	13	70	Passagers transportés
Passenger-kilomètres	...	...	61	106	...	...	14	82	Passagers-kilomètres
Total tonne-kilomètres	...	...	9	12	...	...	5	11	Tonnes-kilomètres totales
China [4]									**Chine** [4]
Kilometres flown	854	1 017	1 149	1 195	153	165	199	209	Kilomètres parcourus
Passengers carried	61 892	72 661	83 672	86 041	6 417	6 604	8 050	6 641	Passagers transportés
Passenger-kilomètres	90 960	105 870	123 908	124 591	22 232	23 699	28 821	24 346	Passagers-kilomètres
Total tonne-kilomètres	11 603	13 802	16 200	17 641	4 465	4 529	5 400	6 246	Tonnes-kilomètres totales
China, Hong Kong SAR									**Chine, Hong Kong RAS**
Kilometres flown	251	251	231	272	251	251	231	272	Kilomètres parcourus
Passengers carried	14 378	14 064	15 636	13 025	14 378	14 064	15 636	13 025	Passagers transportés
Passenger-kilomètres	50 248	48 268	53 148	46 402	50 248	48 268	53 148	46 402	Passagers-kilomètres
Total tonne-kilomètres	9 933	9 693	10 821	10 278	9 933	9 693	10 821	10 278	Tonnes-kilomètres totales
China, Macao SAR									**Chine, Macao RAS**
Kilometres flown	14	16	18	15	14	16	18	15	Kilomètres parcourus
Passengers carried	1 532	1 706	1 728	1 212	1 532	1 706	1 728	1 212	Passagers transportés
Passenger-kilomètres	1 730	1 908	2 056	1 566	1 730	1 908	2 056	1 566	Passagers-kilomètres
Total tonne-kilomètres	195	213	236	198	195	213	236	198	Tonnes-kilomètres totales
Cyprus									**Chypre**
Kilometres flown	21	22	25	30	21	22	25	30	Kilomètres parcourus
Passengers carried	1 396	1 503	1 705	1 883	1 396	1 503	1 705	1 883	Passagers transportés
Passenger-kilomètres	2 785	3 012	3 436	3 935	2 785	3 012	3 436	3 935	Passagers-kilomètres
Total tonne-kilomètres	297	314	355	408	297	314	355	408	Tonnes-kilomètres totales
Georgia									**Géorgie**
Kilometres flown	4	4	4	6	4	4	4	6	Kilomètres parcourus
Passengers carried	118	111	112	180	118	111	112	180	Passagers transportés
Passenger-kilomètres	230	235	230	384	230	235	230	384	Passagers-kilomètres
Total tonne-kilomètres	23	23	23	37	23	23	23	37	Tonnes-kilomètres totales
India									**Inde**
Kilometres flown	202	221	244	277	65	78	81	94	Kilomètres parcourus
Passengers carried	17 303	17 419	17 633	19 455	3 748	4 291	4 049	4 348	Passagers transportés
Passenger-kilomètres	25 905	25 708	27 478	31 196	13 798	13 888	15 052	17 221	Passagers-kilomètres
Total tonne-kilomètres	2 903	2 854	3 035	3 410	1 693	1 682	1 797	2 011	Tonnes-kilomètres totales
Indonesia									**Indonésie**
Kilometres flown	138	150	159	211	48	50	62	40	Kilomètres parcourus
Passengers carried	9 916	10 397	12 113	20 358	2 192	2 217	2 513	1 984	Passagers transportés
Passenger-kilomètres	16 764	16 169	18 419	21 274	10 706	9 793	10 298	6 487	Passagers-kilomètres
Total tonne-kilomètres	1 865	1 978	1 879	2 164	1 252	1 269	1 093	776	Tonnes-kilomètres totales
Iran (Islamic Rep. of)									**Iran (Rép. islamique d')**
Kilometres flown	66	73	75	89	25	30	28	34	Kilomètres parcourus
Passengers carried	8 722	9 533	9 892	11 664	1 775	1 916	1 942	2 282	Passagers transportés
Passenger-kilomètres	8 202	8 793	8 616	10 231	3 220	3 439	3 022	3 761	Passagers-kilomètres
Total tonne-kilomètres	801	854	835	1 002	350	370	329	401	Tonnes-kilomètres totales
Israel									**Israël**
Kilometres flown	92	83	90	89	82	74	81	83	Kilomètres parcourus
Passengers carried	4 443	3 989	3 708	3 678	3 102	2 695	2 482	2 581	Passagers transportés
Passenger-kilomètres	14 507	13 514	12 234	12 465	14 127	13 146	11 862	12 157	Passagers-kilomètres
Total tonne-kilomètres	2 200	2 083	2 437	2 535	2 166	2 050	2 404	2 507	Tonnes-kilomètres totales
Japan									**Japon**
Kilometres flown	878	853	853	834	471	447	443	420	Kilomètres parcourus
Passengers carried	109 123	107 823	109 038	103 650	20 571	18 487	18 839	14 411	Passagers transportés
Passenger-kilomètres	174 149	162 290	164 134	146 856	102 683	90 194	90 595	73 610	Passagers-kilomètres
Total tonne-kilomètres	23 868	21 717	22 470	21 071	17 572	15 426	16 075	14 643	Tonnes-kilomètres totales

57 Civil aviation: scheduled airline traffic — Passengers carried (thousands); kilometres (millions) (*continued*)

Aviation civile : trafic régulier des lignes aériennes — Passagers transportés (milliers) ; kilomètres (millions) (*suite*)

Region, country or area, and traffic	Total traffic (domestic and international) Trafic total (intérieur et international)				International traffic Trafic international				Région, pays ou zone et trafic
	2000	2001	2002	2003	2000	2001	2002	2003	
Jordan									**Jordanie**
Kilometres flown	37	36	37	36	37	36	37	36	Kilomètres parcourus
Passengers carried	1 282	1 178	1 300	1 353	1 282	1 178	1 300	1 353	Passagers transportés
Passenger-kilomètres	4 207	3 848	4 146	4 498	4 207	3 848	4 146	4 498	Passagers-kilomètres
Total tonne-kilometres	591	530	577	602	591	530	577	602	Tonnes-kilomètres totales
Kazakhstan									**Kazakhstan**
Kilometres flown	15	16	25	31	10	10	13	17	Kilomètres parcourus
Passengers carried	461	501	757	1 010	234	247	305	405	Passagers transportés
Passenger-kilomètres	1 208	1 268	1 730	2 149	916	945	1 141	1 404	Passagers-kilomètres
Total tonne-kilometres	133	137	184	222	104	105	127	151	Tonnes-kilomètres totales
Korea, Dem. P. R.									**Corée, R. p. dém. de**
Kilometres flown	1	1	1	1	1	1	1	1	Kilomètres parcourus
Passengers carried	83	79	84	75	83	79	84	75	Passagers transportés
Passenger-kilomètres	37	33	35	32	37	33	35	32	Passagers-kilomètres
Total tonne-kilometres	5	5	5	5	5	5	5	5	Tonnes-kilomètres totales
Korea, Republic of									**Corée, République de**
Kilometres flown	367	361	400	370	309	304	343	311	Kilomètres parcourus
Passengers carried	34 331	33 710	34 832	33 373	12 137	12 215	14 077	13 051	Passagers transportés
Passenger-kilomètres	62 837	60 143	65 852	57 624	54 926	52 403	58 249	50 104	Passagers-kilomètres
Total tonne-kilometres	13 302	12 265	13 875	12 134	12 526	11 503	13 123	11 402	Tonnes-kilomètres totales
Kuwait									**Koweït**
Kilometres flown	37	37	41	39	37	37	41	39	Kilomètres parcourus
Passengers carried	2 113	2 085	2 299	2 186	2 113	2 085	2 299	2 186	Passagers transportés
Passenger-kilomètres	6 134	6 010	6 706	6 311	6 134	6 010	6 706	6 311	Passagers-kilomètres
Total tonne-kilometres	805	777	867	795	805	777	867	795	Tonnes-kilomètres totales
Kyrgyzstan									**Kirghizistan**
Kilometres flown	6	6	5	6	5	5	4	5	Kilomètres parcourus
Passengers carried	241	192	174	206	114	102	85	103	Passagers transportés
Passenger-kilomètres	423	363	315	372	373	326	280	332	Passagers-kilomètres
Total tonne-kilometres	44	39	35	39	39	35	32	35	Tonnes-kilomètres totales
Lao People's Dem. Rep.									**Rép. dém. pop. lao**
Kilometres flown	2	2	2	3	1	1	1	1	Kilomètres parcourus
Passengers carried	211	211	220	219	61	61	65	58	Passagers transportés
Passenger-kilomètres	85	86	91	90	38	38	40	37	Passagers-kilomètres
Total tonne-kilometres	9	9	9	9	4	4	5	4	Tonnes-kilomètres totales
Lebanon									**Liban**
Kilometres flown	20	20	20	20	20	20	20	20	Kilomètres parcourus
Passengers carried	806	816	874	935	806	816	874	935	Passagers transportés
Passenger-kilomètres	1 484	1 658	1 749	1 905	1 484	1 658	1 749	1 905	Passagers-kilomètres
Total tonne-kilometres	223	229	244	253	223	229	244	253	Tonnes-kilomètres totales
Malaysia									**Malaisie**
Kilometres flown	220	217	232	247	171	169	176	179	Kilomètres parcourus
Passengers carried	16 561	16 107	16 275	16 710	7 390	7 197	7 527	6 949	Passagers transportés
Passenger-kilomètres	37 939	35 658	36 923	38 415	32 905	31 011	32 191	32 309	Passagers-kilomètres
Total tonne-kilometres	5 346	5 233	5 345	5 689	4 875	4 807	4 920	5 126	Tonnes-kilomètres totales
Maldives									**Maldives**
Kilometres flown	6	7	1	2	4	4	...	...	Kilomètres parcourus
Passengers carried	315	367	58	60	222	226	...	...	Passagers transportés
Passenger-kilomètres	425	447	26	28	385	385	...	...	Passagers-kilomètres
Total tonne-kilometres	54	56	2	3	50	49	...	...	Tonnes-kilomètres totales
Mongolia									**Mongolie**
Kilometres flown	6	6	7	9	3	4	5	5	Kilomètres parcourus
Passengers carried	254	255	270	289	118	136	153	139	Passagers transportés
Passenger-kilomètres	520	574	661	691	401	470	560	552	Passagers-kilomètres
Total tonne-kilometres	51	52	69	71	41	43	59	58	Tonnes-kilomètres totales

Region, country or area, and traffic	Total traffic (domestic and international) Trafic total (intérieur et international)				International traffic Trafic international				Région, pays ou zone et trafic
	2000	2001	2002	2003	2000	2001	2002	2003	
Myanmar									**Myanmar**
Kilometres flown	...	...	15	16	...	...	11	11	Kilomètres parcourus
Passengers carried	...	...	1 186	1 117	...	...	776	691	Passagers transportés
Passenger-kilomètres	...	...	1 154	1 083	...	...	932	848	Passagers-kilomètres
Total tonne-kilometres	...	...	106	100	...	...	85	78	Tonnes-kilomètres totales
Nepal									**Népal**
Kilometres flown	10	9	10	8	9	8	9	6	Kilomètres parcourus
Passengers carried	643	641	681	356	506	517	553	279	Passagers transportés
Passenger-kilomètres	1 155	1 153	1 211	663	1 135	1 135	1 191	652	Passagers-kilomètres
Total tonne-kilometres	121	119	127	64	119	117	125	63	Tonnes-kilomètres totales
Oman [3]									**Oman** [3]
Kilometres flown	32	33	32	45	31	31	31	43	Kilomètres parcourus
Passengers carried	2 118	1 980	2 104	2 777	1 942	1 817	1 931	2 617	Passagers transportés
Passenger-kilomètres	4 148	4 026	4 133	5 899	4 002	3 889	3 989	5 765	Passagers-kilomètres
Total tonne-kilometres	549	518	485	746	533	502	468	731	Tonnes-kilomètres totales
Pakistan									**Pakistan**
Kilometres flown	76	71	61	68	57	54	47	52	Kilomètres parcourus
Passengers carried	5 294	6 012	4 141	4 522	2 785	2 690	2 205	2 433	Passagers transportés
Passenger-kilomètres	12 054	11 649	10 680	11 880	10 103	9 854	9 089	10 154	Passagers-kilomètres
Total tonne-kilometres	1 452	1 438	1 322	1 432	1 243	1 241	1 141	1 239	Tonnes-kilomètres totales
Philippines									**Philippines**
Kilometres flown	67	69	79	75	50	52	53	53	Kilomètres parcourus
Passengers carried	5 756	5 652	6 449	6 435	2 343	2 501	2 547	2 416	Passagers transportés
Passenger-kilomètres	13 063	13 454	14 216	13 904	10 958	11 483	11 753	11 387	Passagers-kilomètres
Total tonne-kilometres	1 661	1 666	1 755	1 729	1 438	1 457	1 497	1 468	Tonnes-kilomètres totales
Qatar [3]									**Qatar** [3]
Kilometres flown	48	50	65	59	48	50	65	59	Kilomètres parcourus
Passengers carried	2 673	2 778	3 571	3 184	2 673	2 778	3 571	3 184	Passagers transportés
Passenger-kilomètres	6 042	6 510	8 608	8 003	6 042	6 510	8 608	8 003	Passagers-kilomètres
Total tonne-kilometres	823	876	1 095	1 003	823	876	1 095	1 003	Tonnes-kilomètres totales
Saudi Arabia									**Arabie saoudite**
Kilometres flown	133	126	124	125	79	73	71	72	Kilomètres parcourus
Passengers carried	12 566	12 836	13 564	13 822	4 246	4 218	4 622	4 801	Passagers transportés
Passenger-kilomètres	20 229	20 217	20 804	20 801	13 807	13 495	13 818	13 693	Passagers-kilomètres
Total tonne-kilometres	2 836	2 633	2 748	2 739	2 173	1 945	2 031	2 014	Tonnes-kilomètres totales
Singapore									**Singapour**
Kilometres flown	346	350	361	341	346	350	361	341	Kilomètres parcourus
Passengers carried	16 704	16 374	17 257	14 737	16 704	16 374	17 257	14 737	Passagers transportés
Passenger-kilomètres	71 786	70 232	75 620	65 387	71 786	70 232	75 620	65 387	Passagers-kilomètres
Total tonne-kilometres	12 986	12 595	14 140	13 062	12 986	12 595	14 140	13 062	Tonnes-kilomètres totales
Sri Lanka									**Sri Lanka**
Kilometres flown	47	34	29	34	47	34	29	34	Kilomètres parcourus
Passengers carried	1 756	1 719	1 741	1 958	1 756	1 719	1 741	1 958	Passagers transportés
Passenger-kilomètres	6 840	6 641	6 327	6 910	6 840	6 641	6 327	6 910	Passagers-kilomètres
Total tonne-kilometres	1 125	822	778	864	1 125	822	778	864	Tonnes-kilomètres totales
Syrian Arab Republic									**Rép. arabe syrienne**
Kilometres flown	15	15	16	9	14	14	15	9	Kilomètres parcourus
Passengers carried	750	761	824	940	640	647	705	908	Passagers transportés
Passenger-kilomètres	1 422	1 465	1 609	1 744	1 381	1 422	1 565	1 727	Passagers-kilomètres
Total tonne-kilometres	149	153	169	173	145	149	165	171	Tonnes-kilomètres totales
Tajikistan									**Tadjikistan**
Kilometres flown	4	6	9	10	4	5	8	8	Kilomètres parcourus
Passengers carried	168	274	397	413	99	202	316	291	Passagers transportés
Passenger-kilomètres	286	573	864	854	257	542	829	803	Passagers-kilomètres
Total tonne-kilometres	29	54	82	84	26	51	79	79	Tonnes-kilomètres totales

57 Civil aviation: scheduled airline traffic — Passengers carried (thousands); kilometres (millions) (*continued*)

Aviation civile : trafic régulier des lignes aériennes — Passagers transportés (milliers) ; kilomètres (millions) (*suite*)

Region, country or area, and traffic	Total traffic (domestic and international) Trafic total (intérieur et international)				International traffic Trafic international				Région, pays ou zone et trafic
	2000	2001	2002	2003	2000	2001	2002	2003	
Thailand									**Thaïlande**
Kilometres flown	172	182	194	204	147	158	173	175	Kilomètres parcourus
Passengers carried	17 392	17 662	18 112	17 892	11 054	11 343	12 537	11 774	Passagers transportés
Passenger-kilomètres	42 236	44 142	48 337	45 449	38 676	40 584	45 084	41 910	Passagers-kilomètres
Total tonne-kilometres	5 571	5 702	6 241	5 920	5 215	5 345	5 913	5 579	Tonnes-kilomètres totales
Turkey									**Turquie**
Kilometres flown	142	143	140	142	106	108	108	111	Kilomètres parcourus
Passengers carried	11 513	10 604	10 640	10 745	5 075	4 990	5 276	5 239	Passagers transportés
Passenger-kilomètres	16 492	16 058	16 818	16 451	12 938	12 907	13 822	13 343	Passagers-kilomètres
Total tonne-kilometres	1 865	1 996	2 117	2 071	1 555	1 679	1 813	1 756	Tonnes-kilomètres totales
Turkmenistan									**Turkménistan**
Kilometres flown	20	22	22	22	10	11	11	12	Kilomètres parcourus
Passengers carried	1 284	1 407	1 407	1 412	315	345	345	307	Passagers transportés
Passenger-kilomètres	1 466	1 608	1 608	1 538	1 007	1 104	1 104	1 005	Passagers-kilomètres
Total tonne-kilometres	144	156	156	150	102	110	110	102	Tonnes-kilomètres totales
United Arab Emirates [3]									**Emirats arabes unis [3]**
Kilometres flown	123	136	159	207	123	136	159	207	Kilomètres parcourus
Passengers carried	6 893	7 676	9 667	11 610	6 893	7 676	9 667	11 610	Passagers transportés
Passenger-kilomètres	22 691	26 202	33 125	41 504	22 691	26 202	33 125	41 504	Passagers-kilomètres
Total tonne-kilometres	3 649	4 148	5 261	6 760	3 649	4 148	5 261	6 760	Tonnes-kilomètres totales
Uzbekistan									**Ouzbékistan**
Kilometres flown	39	57	39	40	30	45	32	33	Kilomètres parcourus
Passengers carried	1 745	2 256	1 451	1 466	950	1 379	1 036	1 048	Passagers transportés
Passenger-kilomètres	3 732	5 268	3 835	3 889	3 332	4 806	3 600	3 646	Passagers-kilomètres
Total tonne-kilometres	417	580	417	424	380	538	396	401	Tonnes-kilomètres totales
Viet Nam									**Viet Nam**
Kilometres flown	34	40	50	48	21	27	34	32	Kilomètres parcourus
Passengers carried	2 878	3 427	4 082	3 969	1 165	1 472	1 790	1 644	Passagers transportés
Passenger-kilomètres	4 499	5 621	6 676	6 246	3 099	4 083	4 895	4 459	Passagers-kilomètres
Total tonne-kilometres	524	645	756	726	375	479	562	523	Tonnes-kilomètres totales
Yemen									**Yémen**
Kilometres flown	16	18	16	18	15	17	15	17	Kilomètres parcourus
Passengers carried	842	841	869	844	585	601	632	622	Passagers transportés
Passenger-kilomètres	1 588	1 580	1 598	1 956	1 498	1 497	1 518	1 876	Passagers-kilomètres
Total tonne-kilometres	179	174	180	225	170	166	172	217	Tonnes-kilomètres totales
Europe [1]									**Europe [1]**
Kilometres flown	6 482	6 512	6 375	6 658	5 033	5 069	4 907	5 247	Kilomètres parcourus
Passengers carried	409 735	408 675	407 556	442 326	251 520	251 317	256 067	283 043	Passagers transportés
Passenger-kilomètres	777 230	756 247	749 172	807 101	656 321	633 100	627 052	679 838	Passagers-kilomètres
Total tonne-kilometres	109 339	104 713	104 172	110 017	97 401	92 635	92 152	97 479	Tonnes-kilomètres totales
Albania									**Albanie**
Kilometres flown	3	2	2	2	3	2	2	2	Kilomètres parcourus
Passengers carried	137	146	138	159	137	146	138	159	Passagers transportés
Passenger-kilomètres	101	93	96	121	101	93	96	121	Passagers-kilomètres
Total tonne-kilometres	9	8	9	11	9	8	9	11	Tonnes-kilomètres totales
Austria									**Autriche**
Kilometres flown	139	134	130	130	135	130	126	126	Kilomètres parcourus
Passengers carried	6 642	6 550	7 070	6 903	6 261	6 188	6 646	6 461	Passagers transportés
Passenger-kilomètres	14 232	13 875	13 794	14 558	14 121	13 770	13 682	14 440	Passagers-kilomètres
Total tonne-kilometres	1 885	1 786	1 859	1 983	1 874	1 776	1 847	1 971	Tonnes-kilomètres totales
Belarus									**Bélarus**
Kilometres flown	7	7	7	7	7	7	7	7	Kilomètres parcourus
Passengers carried	211	222	205	234	211	222	203	232	Passagers transportés
Passenger-kilomètres	317	339	308	338	317	339	308	337	Passagers-kilomètres
Total tonne-kilometres	31	33	30	32	31	33	29	32	Tonnes-kilomètres totales

Region, country or area, and traffic	Total traffic (domestic and international) Trafic total (intérieur et international)				International traffic Trafic international				Région, pays ou zone et trafic
	2000	2001	2002	2003	2000	2001	2002	2003	
Belgium									**Belgique**
Kilometres flown	216	186	115	103	216	186	115	103	Kilomètres parcourus
Passengers carried	10 738	8 489	2 342	2 904	10 738	8 489	2 342	2 904	Passagers transportés
Passenger-kilometres	19 379	15 320	2 606	3 958	19 379	15 320	2 606	3 958	Passagers-kilomètres
Total tonne-kilometres	2 921	2 356	890	961	2 921	2 356	890	961	Tonnes-kilomètres totales
Bosnia and Herzegovina									**Bosnie-Herzégovine**
Kilometres flown	2	1	1	1	2	1	1	1	Kilomètres parcourus
Passengers carried	69	65	66	73	69	65	66	73	Passagers transportés
Passenger-kilometres	48	44	43	47	48	44	43	47	Passagers-kilomètres
Total tonne-kilometres	6	6	5	6	6	6	5	6	Tonnes-kilomètres totales
Bulgaria									**Bulgarie**
Kilometres flown	14	6	1	7	12	5	1	7	Kilomètres parcourus
Passengers carried	535	234	63	311	466	185	38	270	Passagers transportés
Passenger-kilometres	834	362	57	457	804	342	47	442	Passagers-kilomètres
Total tonne-kilometres	70	31	5	42	68	29	4	41	Tonnes-kilomètres totales
Croatia									**Croatie**
Kilometres flown	10	11	11	12	9	9	10	10	Kilomètres parcourus
Passengers carried	929	1 063	1 127	1 267	583	688	736	795	Passagers transportés
Passenger-kilometres	644	736	783	869	538	622	665	726	Passagers-kilomètres
Total tonne-kilometres	61	70	74	81	51	59	63	68	Tonnes-kilomètres totales
Czech Republic									**République tchèque**
Kilometres flown	39	42	44	53	39	41	44	52	Kilomètres parcourus
Passengers carried	2 229	2 566	2 809	3 391	2 204	2 523	2 760	3 339	Passagers transportés
Passenger-kilometres	3 313	3 576	3 855	4 938	3 306	3 564	3 842	4 923	Passagers-kilomètres
Total tonne-kilometres	333	351	378	485	332	350	377	483	Tonnes-kilomètres totales
Denmark [5]									**Danemark** [5]
Kilometres flown	85	92	81	78	76	83	72	73	Kilomètres parcourus
Passengers carried	5 923	6 382	6 322	5 886	4 305	4 845	5 013	4 855	Passagers transportés
Passenger-kilometres	6 128	6 952	7 453	7 202	5 543	6 380	6 956	6 968	Passagers-kilomètres
Total tonne-kilometres	810	876	925	885	747	814	870	863	Tonnes-kilomètres totales
Estonia									**Estonie**
Kilometres flown	6	6	6	7	6	6	6	7	Kilomètres parcourus
Passengers carried	278	277	304	395	275	275	298	389	Passagers transportés
Passenger-kilometres	235	246	283	415	235	246	280	413	Passagers-kilomètres
Total tonne-kilometres	23	24	27	39	23	24	27	39	Tonnes-kilomètres totales
Finland									**Finlande**
Kilometres flown	92	95	91	97	70	74	73	80	Kilomètres parcourus
Passengers carried	6 427	6 698	6 416	6 184	3 622	3 960	4 012	3 971	Passagers transportés
Passenger-kilometres	7 556	8 195	8 807	9 056	6 270	6 923	7 649	7 981	Passagers-kilomètres
Total tonne-kilometres	984	920	1 025	1 086	871	808	924	991	Tonnes-kilomètres totales
France [6]									**France** [6]
Kilometres flown	961	888	856	860	643	630	602	620	Kilomètres parcourus
Passengers carried	52 581	49 008	47 834	47 641	24 103	23 549	23 894	23 904	Passagers transportés
Passenger-kilometres	113 438	112 308	114 698	112 260	75 250	75 804	79 164	79 027	Passagers-kilomètres
Total tonne-kilometres	15 639	15 126	15 507	15 293	11 871	11 593	12 049	12 029	Tonnes-kilomètres totales
Germany									**Allemagne**
Kilometres flown	850	861	927	1 070	736	738	801	952	Kilomètres parcourus
Passengers carried	58 679	56 389	61 890	72 693	38 568	37 251	42 818	53 645	Passagers transportés
Passenger-kilometres	114 124	111 303	124 246	149 672	105 552	103 102	116 020	141 313	Passagers-kilomètres
Total tonne-kilometres	18 495	18 004	19 425	21 937	17 619	17 161	18 594	21 097	Tonnes-kilomètres totales
Greece									**Grèce**
Kilometres flown	90	95	82	80	70	68	58	55	Kilomètres parcourus
Passengers carried	7 937	8 430	7 579	7 657	3 384	3 320	3 015	2 855	Passagers transportés
Passenger-kilometres	9 841	9 801	8 587	7 650	8 504	8 212	7 194	6 177	Passagers-kilomètres
Total tonne-kilometres	1 067	1 029	891	785	939	879	760	640	Tonnes-kilomètres totales

Region, country or area, and traffic	Total traffic (domestic and international) Trafic total (intérieur et international)				International traffic Trafic international				Région, pays ou zone et trafic
	2000	2001	2002	2003	2000	2001	2002	2003	
Hungary									**Hongrie**
Kilometres flown	42	39	39	46	42	39	39	46	Kilomètres parcourus
Passengers carried	2 198	2 075	2 134	2 362	2 198	2 075	2 134	2 362	Passagers transportés
Passenger-kilomètres	3 573	3 146	3 116	3 130	3 573	3 146	3 116	3 130	Passagers-kilomètres
Total tonne-kilometres	377	324	312	314	377	324	312	314	Tonnes-kilomètres totales
Iceland									**Islande**
Kilometres flown	34	32	26	25	34	32	26	25	Kilomètres parcourus
Passengers carried	1 432	1 358	1 199	1 134	1 432	1 358	1 199	1 134	Passagers transportés
Passenger-kilomètres	3 937	3 714	3 188	2 998	3 937	3 714	3 188	2 998	Passagers-kilomètres
Total tonne-kilometres	491	475	413	378	491	475	413	378	Tonnes-kilomètres totales
Ireland									**Irlande**
Kilometres flown	106	119	138	197	104	118	138	197	Kilomètres parcourus
Passengers carried	13 983	15 451	19 729	28 923	13 431	15 093	19 630	28 890	Passagers transportés
Passenger-kilomètres	13 664	13 917	18 575	27 441	13 584	13 871	18 552	27 433	Passagers-kilomètres
Total tonne-kilometres	1 396	1 458	1 756	2 573	1 389	1 454	1 754	2 572	Tonnes-kilomètres totales
Italy									**Italie**
Kilometres flown	392	393	351	398	274	270	235	265	Kilomètres parcourus
Passengers carried	30 418	31 031	28 245	36 077	12 246	12 153	10 989	13 613	Passagers transportés
Passenger-kilomètres	44 389	40 950	34 328	40 823	34 271	30 706	24 735	28 559	Passagers-kilomètres
Total tonne-kilometres	6 136	5 568	4 798	5 343	5 147	4 574	3 859	4 171	Tonnes-kilomètres totales
Latvia									**Lettonie**
Kilometres flown	7	6	6	7	7	6	6	7	Kilomètres parcourus
Passengers carried	278	255	265	340	278	255	265	340	Passagers transportés
Passenger-kilomètres	236	180	184	245	236	180	184	245	Passagers-kilomètres
Total tonne-kilometres	22	17	18	23	22	17	18	23	Tonnes-kilomètres totales
Lithuania									**Lituanie**
Kilometres flown	10	10	10	10	10	10	10	10	Kilomètres parcourus
Passengers carried	284	304	304	329	284	304	303	329	Passagers transportés
Passenger-kilomètres	322	347	355	395	322	347	355	395	Passagers-kilomètres
Total tonne-kilometres	31	33	34	37	31	33	34	37	Tonnes-kilomètres totales
Luxembourg									**Luxembourg**
Kilometres flown	61	66	70	74	61	66	70	74	Kilomètres parcourus
Passengers carried	871	886	823	854	871	886	823	854	Passagers transportés
Passenger-kilomètres	557	586	437	548	557	586	437	548	Passagers-kilomètres
Total tonne-kilometres	3 573	3 821	4 197	4 397	3 573	3 821	4 197	4 397	Tonnes-kilomètres totales
Malta									**Malte**
Kilometres flown	26	25	22	22	26	25	22	22	Kilomètres parcourus
Passengers carried	1 365	1 340	1 399	1 309	1 365	1 340	1 399	1 309	Passagers transportés
Passenger-kilomètres	2 384	2 359	2 305	2 174	2 384	2 359	2 305	2 174	Passagers-kilomètres
Total tonne-kilometres	229	227	221	209	229	227	221	209	Tonnes-kilomètres totales
Monaco									**Monaco**
Kilometres flown	1	1	1	1	1	1	1	1	Kilomètres parcourus
Passengers carried	83	78	104	95	83	78	104	95	Passagers transportés
Passenger-kilomètres	2	2	7	6	2	2	7	6	Passagers-kilomètres
Total tonne-kilometres	0	0	1	1	0	0	1	1	Tonnes-kilomètres totales
Netherlands [7]									**Pays-Bas** [7]
Kilometres flown	445	425	424	429	444	424	423	428	Kilomètres parcourus
Passengers carried	19 556	19 261	22 119	22 590	19 393	19 128	22 000	22 482	Passagers transportés
Passenger-kilomètres	73 030	68 793	68 979	68 688	73 008	68 775	68 962	68 673	Passagers-kilomètres
Total tonne-kilometres	11 811	11 154	11 244	11 331	11 809	11 152	11 243	11 329	Tonnes-kilomètres totales
Norway [5]									**Norvège** [5]
Kilometres flown	149	149	129	127	71	74	64	66	Kilomètres parcourus
Passengers carried	15 182	14 556	13 699	12 806	4 646	4 659	4 474	4 407	Passagers transportés
Passenger-kilomètres	10 367	10 461	10 546	10 506	5 870	6 140	6 444	6 726	Passagers-kilomètres
Total tonne-kilometres	1 218	1 224	1 231	1 211	777	793	822	834	Tonnes-kilomètres totales

Region, country or area, and traffic	Total traffic (domestic and international) Trafic total (intérieur et international)				International traffic Trafic international				Région, pays ou zone et trafic
	2000	2001	2002	2003	2000	2001	2002	2003	
Poland									**Pologne**
Kilometres flown	55	70	66	68	51	64	59	61	Kilomètres parcourus
Passengers carried	2 341	2 670	2 846	3 252	1 928	2 078	2 196	2 495	Passagers transportés
Passenger-kilomètres	4 757	4 915	5 111	5 434	4 635	4 739	4 921	5 213	Passagers-kilomètres
Total tonne-kilomètres	547	562	581	608	537	547	565	589	Tonnes-kilomètres totales
Portugal									**Portugal**
Kilometres flown	105	112	117	128	87	94	100	110	Kilomètres parcourus
Passengers carried	6 721	6 650	6 796	7 590	4 019	4 003	4 403	4 994	Passagers transportés
Passenger-kilomètres	11 217	11 182	12 109	13 562	9 594	9 540	10 674	11 904	Passagers-kilomètres
Total tonne-kilomètres	1 252	1 236	1 314	1 455	1 088	1 071	1 169	1 289	Tonnes-kilomètres totales
Republic of Moldova									**République de Moldova**
Kilometres flown	4	5	5	5	4	5	5	5	Kilomètres parcourus
Passengers carried	118	120	129	179	118	120	129	179	Passagers transportés
Passenger-kilomètres	125	146	161	223	125	146	161	223	Passagers-kilomètres
Total tonne-kilomètres	13	14	15	22	13	14	15	22	Tonnes-kilomètres totales
Romania									**Roumanie**
Kilometres flown	30	26	21	26	29	24	19	24	Kilomètres parcourus
Passengers carried	1 218	1 139	959	1 255	1 105	1 036	858	1 034	Passagers transportés
Passenger-kilomètres	2 098	1 856	1 593	1 696	2 053	1 816	1 555	1 634	Passagers-kilomètres
Total tonne-kilomètres	202	178	153	160	198	175	150	155	Tonnes-kilomètres totales
Russian Federation									**Fédération de Russie**
Kilometres flown	534	568	653	602	189	198	196	199	Kilomètres parcourus
Passengers carried	17 688	20 301	20 892	22 723	5 480	6 688	6 667	6 972	Passagers transportés
Passenger-kilomètres	42 950	48 321	49 890	53 894	17 584	19 638	19 552	20 478	Passagers-kilomètres
Total tonne-kilomètres	4 948	5 292	5 580	6 018	2 285	2 305	2 395	2 513	Tonnes-kilomètres totales
Serbia and Montenegro									**Serbie-et-Monténégro**
Kilometres flown	...	13	17	18	...	11	14	16	Kilomètres parcourus
Passengers carried	...	1 117	1 185	1 298	...	615	767	871	Passagers transportés
Passenger-kilomètres	...	897	1 081	1 199	...	750	949	1 061	Passagers-kilomètres
Total tonne-kilomètres	...	85	98	156	...	72	87	137	Tonnes-kilomètres totales
Slovakia									**Slovaquie**
Kilometres flown	2	2	3	5	2	1	2	4	Kilomètres parcourus
Passengers carried	57	43	83	190	44	34	53	159	Passagers transportés
Passenger-kilomètres	108	85	94	220	103	82	85	211	Passagers-kilomètres
Total tonne-kilomètres	10	11	9	20	10	11	8	19	Tonnes-kilomètres totales
Slovenia									**Slovénie**
Kilometres flown	10	11	12	13	10	11	12	13	Kilomètres parcourus
Passengers carried	628	690	721	758	628	690	721	758	Passagers transportés
Passenger-kilomètres	563	657	678	700	563	657	678	700	Passagers-kilomètres
Total tonne-kilomètres	55	63	66	67	55	63	66	67	Tonnes-kilomètres totales
Spain									**Espagne**
Kilometres flown	418	460	442	473	235	268	261	279	Kilomètres parcourus
Passengers carried	39 712	41 470	40 381	42 507	11 911	12 807	12 858	13 515	Passagers transportés
Passenger-kilomètres	52 427	55 324	54 044	57 594	35 003	37 295	36 511	38 723	Passagers-kilomètres
Total tonne-kilomètres	5 635	5 897	5 715	6 096	3 966	4 173	4 040	4 268	Tonnes-kilomètres totales
Sweden [5]									**Suède [5]**
Kilometres flown	167	167	130	129	92	96	81	86	Kilomètres parcourus
Passengers carried	13 354	13 123	12 421	11 873	5 901	5 811	5 958	5 900	Passagers transportés
Passenger-kilomètres	11 192	11 277	11 663	11 638	7 765	7 879	8 643	8 846	Passagers-kilomètres
Total tonne-kilomètres	1 387	1 384	1 427	1 410	1 064	1 059	1 137	1 142	Tonnes-kilomètres totales
Switzerland									**Suisse**
Kilometres flown	317	304	256	218	311	299	252	216	Kilomètres parcourus
Passengers carried	17 268	16 915	13 292	10 118	15 800	15 567	12 311	9 642	Passagers transportés
Passenger-kilomètres	36 625	33 470	26 704	23 295	36 339	33 211	26 501	23 186	Passagers-kilomètres
Total tonne-kilomètres	5 616	4 970	3 720	3 617	5 588	4 945	3 699	3 605	Tonnes-kilomètres totales

Region, country or area, and traffic	Total traffic (domestic and international) Trafic total (intérieur et international)				International traffic Trafic international				Région, pays ou zone et trafic
	2000	2001	2002	2003	2000	2001	2002	2003	
TFYR of Macedonia									**L'ex-R.y. Macédoine**
Kilometres flown	10	5	3	3	10	5	3	3	Kilomètres parcourus
Passengers carried	599	315	166	201	599	315	166	201	Passagers transportés
Passenger-kilomètres	740	377	236	280	740	377	236	280	Passagers-kilomètres
Total tonne-kilometres	70	36	21	25	70	36	21	25	Tonnes-kilomètres totales
Ukraine									**Ukraine**
Kilometres flown	32	30	32	38	25	26	27	30	Kilomètres parcourus
Passengers carried	951	986	1 120	1 476	704	816	882	1 054	Passagers transportés
Passenger-kilomètres	1 387	1 418	1 578	2 351	1 240	1 322	1 443	2 115	Passagers-kilomètres
Total tonne-kilometres	145	149	156	231	132	140	144	211	Tonnes-kilomètres totales
United Kingdom [8]									**Royaume-Uni** [8]
Kilometres flown	1 013	1 049	1 048	1 087	893	921	925	965	Kilomètres parcourus
Passengers carried	70 115	70 021	72 381	76 389	52 131	51 703	52 802	55 604	Passagers transportés
Passenger-kilomètres	170 388	158 717	156 594	166 518	162 865	151 059	148 305	157 503	Passagers-kilomètres
Total tonne-kilometres	21 839	19 914	20 041	20 689	21 191	19 257	19 335	19 942	Tonnes-kilomètres totales
Oceania [1]									**Océanie** [1]
Kilometres flown	850	843	923	743	429	399	381	389	Kilomètres parcourus
Passengers carried	48 303	50 103	55 401	50 731	13 776	14 485	14 656	14 099	Passagers transportés
Passenger-kilomètres	114 876	117 585	120 757	118 460	81 288	81 605	82 815	79 537	Passagers-kilomètres
Total tonne-kilometres	13 921	13 961	13 789	14 027	10 590	10 304	10 348	10 234	Tonnes-kilomètres totales
Australia									**Australie**
Kilometres flown	558	556	640	482	248	238	212	204	Kilomètres parcourus
Passengers carried	32 578	33 477	39 022	36 400	7 508	8 530	7 961	7 452	Passagers transportés
Passenger-kilomètres	81 689	84 931	86 138	83 886	53 007	54 549	52 583	49 244	Passagers-kilomètres
Total tonne-kilometres	9 806	10 050	9 726	9 524	6 936	7 008	6 694	6 212	Tonnes-kilomètres totales
Fiji									**Fidji**
Kilometres flown	23	23	20	21	16	14	16	17	Kilomètres parcourus
Passengers carried	586	613	715	766	399	407	450	516	Passagers transportés
Passenger-kilomètres	2 385	2 391	2 906	2 233	2 355	2 355	2 872	2 190	Passagers-kilomètres
Total tonne-kilometres	309	306	368	298	307	302	365	294	Tonnes-kilomètres totales
Marshall Islands									**Iles Marshall**
Kilometres flown	1	1	1	1	0	0	0	0	Kilomètres parcourus
Passengers carried	16	19	25	27	1	1	1	1	Passagers transportés
Passenger-kilomètres	22	25	32	36	2	2	2	1	Passagers-kilomètres
Total tonne-kilometres	2	2	3	4	0	0	0	0	Tonnes-kilomètres totales
Nauru									**Nauru**
Kilometres flown	3	3	3	3	3	3	3	3	Kilomètres parcourus
Passengers carried	161	164	175	156	161	164	175	156	Passagers transportés
Passenger-kilomètres	287	287	302	275	287	287	302	275	Passagers-kilomètres
Total tonne-kilometres	28	29	30	28	28	29	30	28	Tonnes-kilomètres totales
New Zealand									**Nouvelle-Zélande**
Kilometres flown	198	190	180	164	121	101	96	109	Kilomètres parcourus
Passengers carried	10 781	11 467	11 285	10 334	3 673	3 443	3 746	4 042	Passagers transportés
Passenger-kilomètres	23 374	23 069	23 323	23 280	20 338	19 414	19 802	20 440	Passagers-kilomètres
Total tonne-kilometres	3 006	2 846	2 787	3 203	2 762	2 453	2 463	2 902	Tonnes-kilomètres totales
Papua New Guinea									**Papouasie-Nvl-Guinée**
Kilometres flown	17	17	18	11	7	6	6	5	Kilomètres parcourus
Passengers carried	1 100	1 188	1 235	691	271	276	296	127	Passagers transportés
Passenger-kilomètres	1 036	1 110	1 175	576	628	628	660	334	Passagers-kilomètres
Total tonne-kilometres	118	124	133	76	77	77	82	50	Tonnes-kilomètres totales
Samoa									**Samoa**
Kilometres flown	2	2	2	4	1	1	1	3	Kilomètres parcourus
Passengers carried	164	173	182	198	88	90	97	121	Passagers transportés
Passenger-kilomètres	290	291	306	279	281	281	295	270	Passagers-kilomètres
Total tonne-kilometres	28	29	31	27	28	28	29	26	Tonnes-kilomètres totales

57

Civil aviation: scheduled airline traffic — Passengers carried (thousands); kilometres (millions) (*continued*)

Aviation civile : trafic régulier des lignes aériennes — Passagers transportés (milliers) ; kilomètres (millions) (*suite*)

Region, country or area, and traffic	Total traffic (domestic and international) Trafic total (intérieur et international)				International traffic Trafic international				Région, pays ou zone et trafic
	2000	2001	2002	2003	2000	2001	2002	2003	
Solomon Islands									**Iles Salomon**
Kilometres flown	3	4	4	2	1	1	1	1	Kilomètres parcourus
Passengers carried	75	81	85	68	18	18	19	23	Passagers transportés
Passenger-kilomètres	50	52	55	59	37	37	39	47	Passagers-kilomètres
Total tonne-kilometres	6	6	6	6	4	4	5	5	Tonnes-kilomètres totales
Tonga									**Tonga**
Kilometres flown	1	1	1	1	...	...	...	...	Kilomètres parcourus
Passengers carried	52	57	58	61	...	...	...	...	Passagers transportés
Passenger-kilomètres	11	13	14	15	...	...	...	...	Passagers-kilomètres
Total tonne-kilometres	1	1	1	1	...	...	...	...	Tonnes-kilomètres totales
Vanuatu									**Vanuatu**
Kilometres flown	3	3	3	3	3	3	3	3	Kilomètres parcourus
Passengers carried	102	97	104	83	102	97	104	83	Passagers transportés
Passenger-kilomètres	221	212	223	176	221	212	223	176	Passagers-kilomètres
Total tonne-kilometres	22	21	23	18	22	21	23	18	Tonnes-kilomètres totales

Source

International Civil Aviation Organization (ICAO), Montreal, the ICAO Integrated Statistical Database (ISDB).

Notes

1   The statistics of France, the Netherlands, Portugal, United Kingdom and United States have been distributed between two or more regions - France (Europe, Africa, North America and Oceania), Netherlands (Europe and North America), Portugal (1997-1999 only; Europe and Asia), United Kingdom (Europe, Asia and North America) and United States (North America and Oceania).

2   Includes apportionment (1/10) of the traffic of Air Afrique, a multinational airline with headquarters in Côte d'Ivoire and operated by 10 African states unitl 1991. From 1992 includes apportionment (1/11) of the traffic of Air Afrique and operated by 11 African states.

3   Includes apportionment (1/4) of the traffic of Gulf Air, a multinational airline with headquarters in Bahrain and operated by four Gulf States.

4   For statistical purposes, the data for China do not include those for the Hong Kong Special Administrative Region (Hong Kong SAR), Macao Special Administrative Region (Macao SAR) and Taiwan Province of China.

5   Includes the apportionment of international operations performed by Scandinavian Airlines System (SAS): Denmark (2/7), Norway (2/7), Sweden (3/7).

6   Includes data for airlines based in the territories and dependancies of France.

7   Includes data for airlines based in the territories and dependancies of Netherlands.

8   Includes data for airlines based in the territories and dependancies of United Kingdom.

Source

Organisation de l'aviation civile internationale (OACI), Montréal, la base de données statistiques intégrée (ISDB).

Notes

1   Les statistiques de la France, des Pays-Bas, du Portugal, du Royaume-Uni et des Etats-Unis concernent deux régions ou plus; France (Europe, Afrique, Amérique du Nord et Océanie), Pays-Bas (Europe et Amérique du Nord), Portugal (1997 à 1999 seulement; Europe et Asie), Royaume-Uni (Europe, Asie et Amérqiue du Nord) et Etats-Unis (Amérique du Nord et Océanie).

2   Ces chiffres comprennent une partie du trafic (1/10) assurée par Air Afrique, compagnie aérienne multinationale dont le siège est situé en Côte d'Ivoire et est exploitée conjointement par 10 Etats Africains jusqu'à 1991. A partir de 1992 ces chiffres comprennent une partie du trafic (1/11) assurée par Air Afrique et exploitée conjointement par11 Etats Africains.

3   Ces chiffres comprennent une partie du trafic (1/4) assurée par Gulf Air, compagnie aérienne multinationale dont le siège est situé en Bahreïn et est exploitée conjointement par 4 Etats Gulf.

4   Pour la présentation des statistiques, les données pour Chine ne comprennent pas la Région Administrative Spéciale de Hong Kong (Hong Kong RAS), la Région Administrative Spéciale de Macao (Macao RAS) et la province de Taiwan.

5   Y compris une partie des vols internationaux effectués par le SAS; Danemark (2/7), Norvège (2/7) et Suède (3/7).

6   Y compris les données relatives aux compagnies aériennes ayant des bases d'opérations dans les territoires et dépendances de France.

7   Y compris les données relatives aux compagnies aériennes ayant des bases d'opérations dans les territoires et dépendances des Pays-Bas.

8   Y compris les données relatives aux compagnies aériennes ayant des bases d'opération dans les territoires et dépendances du Royaume-Uni.

Table 53: Data refer to domestic and international traffic on all railway lines within each country shown, except railways entirely within an urban unit, and plantation, industrial mining, funicular and cable railways. The figures relating to passenger-kilometres include all passengers except military, government and railway personnel when carried without revenue. Those relating to ton-kilometres are freight net ton-kilometres and include both fast and ordinary goods services but exclude service traffic, mail, baggage and non-revenue governmental stores.

Table 54: For years in which a census or registration took place, the census or registration figure is shown; for other years, unless otherwise indicated, the officially estimated number of vehicles in use is shown. The time of year to which the figures refer is variable. Special purpose vehicles such as two- or three-wheeled cycles and motorcycles, trams, trolley-buses, ambulances, hearses and military vehicles operated by police or other governmental security organizations are excluded. Passenger cars include vehicles seating not more than nine persons (including the driver), such as taxis, jeeps and station wagons. Commercial vehicles include: vans, lorries (trucks), buses, tractor and semi-trailer combinations but exclude trailers and farm tractors.

Table 55: Data refer to merchant fleets registered in each country as at 31 December, except for data prior to 1992 which refer to 30 June of the year stated. They are given in gross registered tons (100 cubic feet or 2.83 cubic metres) and represent the total volume of all the permanently enclosed spaces of the vessels to which the figures refer. Vessels without mechanical means of propulsion are excluded, but sailing vessels with auxiliary power are included.

Data are shown for all ships (cargo carrying ships and ships of miscellaneous activities), oil tanker fleets, and for ore and bulk carrier fleets. The data are published by Lloyd's Register of Shipping in *World Fleet Statistics* [17]. (See also www.lrfairplay.com).

Table 56: The figures for vessels entered and cleared, unless otherwise stated, represent the sum of the net registered tonnage of sea-going foreign and domestic merchant vessels (power and sailing) entered with cargo from or cleared with cargo to a foreign port and refer to only one entrance or clearance for each foreign voyage. Net registered tonnage refers to the internal capacity of a vessel measured in units of 100 cubic feet less the space occupied by boilers, engines, shaft alleys, chain lockers, officer's and crew quarters and other spaces not available for carrying passengers or freight. Where possible, the data exclude vessels "in ballast", i.e. entering without unloading or clearing without loading goods.

Tableau 53 : Les données se rapportent au trafic intérieur et international de toutes les lignes de chemins de fer du pays indiqué, à l'exception des lignes situées entièrement à l'intérieur d'une agglomération urbaine ou desservant une plantation ou un complexe industriel minier, des funiculaires et des téléfériques. Les chiffres relatifs aux voyageurs-kilomètres se rapportent à tous les voyageurs sauf les militaires, les fonctionnaires et le personnel des chemins de fer, qui sont transportés gratuitement. Les chiffres relatifs aux tonnes-kilomètres se rapportent aux tonnes-kilomètres nettes de fret et comprennent les services rapides et ordinaires de transport de marchandises, à l'exception des transports pour les besoins du service, du courrier, des bagages et des marchandises transportées gratuitement pour les besoins de l'Etat.

Tableau 54 : Pour les années où a eu lieu un recensement ou un enregistrement des véhicules, le chiffre indiqué est le résultat de cette opération; pour les autres années, sauf indication contraire, le chiffre indiqué correspond à l'estimation officielle du nombre de véhicules en circulation. L'époque de l'année à laquelle se rapportent les chiffres varie. Les véhicules à usage spécial, tels que les cycles à deux ou trois roues et motocyclettes, les tramways, les trolley-bus, les ambulances, les corbillards, les véhicules militaires utilisés par la police ou par d'autres services publics de sécurité ne sont pas compris dans ces chiffres. Les voitures de tourisme comprennent les véhicules automobiles dont le nombre de places assises (y compris celle du conducteur) est inférieur ou égal à neuf, tels que les taxis, jeeps et breaks. Les véhicules utilitaires comprennent les fourgons, camions, autobus et autocars, les ensembles tracteurs-remorques et semi-remorques, mais ne comprennent pas les remorques et les tracteurs agricoles.

Tableau 55 : Les données se rapportent à la flotte marchande enregistrée dans chaque pays au 31 décembre de l'année indiquée à l'exception des données qui se rapportent aux années avant 1992, qui se réfèrent à la flotte marchande au 30 juin. Elles sont exprimées en tonneaux de jauge brute (100 pieds cubes ou 2,83 mètres cubes) et représentent le volume total de tous les espaces clos en permanence dans les navires auxquels elle s'appliquent. Elles excluent les navires sans moteur, mais pas les voiliers avec moteurs auxiliaires.

Les données sont présentées pour tous les navires, pour la flotte des pétroliers, et pour la flotte des minéraliers et des transporteurs de vrac et d'huile. Les données sont publiées par Lloyd's Register of Shipping dans *World Fleet Statistics* [17]. (Voir aussi www.lrfairplay.com).

Tableau 56 : Sauf indication contraire, les données relatives aux navires entrés et sortis représentent la jauge nette totale des navires marchands de haute mer (à moteur ou à voile) nationaux ou étrangers, qui entrent ou sortent chargés, en pro-

Table 57: Data for total traffic cover both domestic and international scheduled services operated by airlines registered in each country. Scheduled services include supplementary services occasioned by overflow traffic on regularly scheduled trips and preparatory flights for newly scheduled services. The data are prepared by the International Civil Aviation Organization (see also www.icao.int).

venance ou à destination d'un port étranger. On ne compte qu'une seule entrée et une seule sortie pour chaque voyage international. Le tonnage enregistré net concerne la capacité intérieure d'un navire, mesurée en unités de 100 pieds cubes, moins l'espace occupé par les chaudières, les moteurs, les tunnels d'arbre, les soutes aux chaînes, les emménagements des officiers et des marins, et les autres espaces qui ne sont pas disponibles pour le transport de passagers ou de fret. Dans la mesure du possible, le tableau exclut les navires sur lest (c'est-à-dire les navires entrant sans décharger ou sortant sans avoir chargé).

Tableau 57 : Les données relatives au trafic total se rapportent aux services réguliers, intérieurs ou internationaux des compagnies de transport aérien enregistrées dans chaque pays. Les services réguliers comprennent aussi les vols supplémentaires nécessités par un surcroît d'activité des services réguliers et les vols préparatoires en vue de nouveaux services réguliers. Les données sont préparées par l'Organisation de l'aviation civile internationale (voir aussi www.icao.int).

Production, trade and consumption of commercial energy
Thousand metric tons of oil equivalent and kilograms per capita

Production, commerce et consommation d'énergie commerciale
Milliers de tonnes d'équivalent pétrole et kilogrammes par habitant

Region, country or area	Year / Année	Primary energy production — Production d'énergie primaire					Changes in stocks / Variations des stocks	Imports / Importations	Exports / Exportations
		Total / Totale	Solids / Solides	Liquids / Liquides	Gas / Gaz	Electricity / Electricité			
World	2000	9 202 839	2 139 262	3 768 449	2 340 310	954 817	−50 294	3 652 215	3 628 613
	2001	9 386 609	2 289 458	3 755 240	2 381 696	960 215	54 727	3 713 279	3 662 696
	2002	9 528 831	2 397 209	3 721 932	2 434 779	974 911	9 683	3 760 255	3 619 959
	2003	9 890 057	2 568 362	3 855 277	2 495 245	971 174	9 286	3 918 771	3 855 051
Africa	2000	712 635	161 388	421 358	119 475	10 414	829	76 745	435 669
	2001	718 547	162 261	424 677	121 555	10 054	4 322	76 771	433 551
	2002	720 329	162 863	420 116	126 168	11 181	−1 697	81 306	429 124
	2003	761 999	171 748	445 309	133 592	11 350	263	83 517	466 588
Algeria	2000	175 176	...	96 895	78 276	5	−728	651	114 124
	2001	168 306	...	94 964	73 336	6	−523	681	107 119
	2002	176 338	...	99 524	76 808	5	*−26	968	113 119
	2003	183 979	...	106 319	77 637	23	*−182	817	121 462
Angola	2000	37 347	...	36 742	*527	78	490	356	34 829
	2001	37 074	...	36 505	*481	87	124	448	34 828
	2002	44 750	...	44 089	563	98	−80	423	42 564
	2003	43 887	...	43 126	*654	107	−166	588	41 717
Benin	2000	35	...	35	...	0	−9	574	61
	2001	35	...	35	...	0	17	823	238
	2002	40	...	40	...	0	21	946	274
	2003	20	...	20	...	0	18	1 043	329
Burkina Faso	2000	8	...	...	...	8	...	*341	...
	2001	10	...	...	...	10	...	*347	...
	2002	10	...	...	...	10	...	*359	...
	*2003	10	...	...	...	10	...	345	...
Burundi	2000	13	*4	...	...	9	...	*93	...
	2001	14	*4	...	...	10	2	*87	...
	2002	15	*4	...	...	11	...	*93	...
	*2003	15	4	...	...	11	...	86	...
Cameroon	2000	7 649	...	7 353	...	296	5	186	6 456
	2001	7 331	...	7 032	...	299	−13	15	5 995
	2002	6 719	...	6 445	...	274	−64	98	5 521
	2003	6 729	...	6 425	...	303	−124	89	5 521
Cape Verde *	2000	...	...	...	...	...	...	46	...
	2001	...	...	...	...	...	...	50	...
	2002	...	...	...	...	...	...	50	...
	2003	...	...	...	...	...	...	49	...
Central African Rep. *	2000	7	...	...	...	7	1	107	...
	2001	7	...	...	...	7	2	111	...
	2002	7	...	...	...	7	...	111	...
	2003	7	...	...	...	7	...	105	...
Chad *	2000	...	...	...	...	...	...	63	...
	2001	...	...	...	...	...	...	60	...
	2002	...	...	...	...	...	...	59	...
	2003	...	...	...	...	...	...	58	...
Comoros *	2000	0	...	...	...	0	...	28	...
	2001	0	...	...	...	0	...	27	...
	2002	0	...	...	...	0	...	27	...
	2003	0	...	...	...	0	...	30	...
Congo	2000	13 852	...	13 710	117	26	...	23	13 041
	2001	12 907	...	12 761	117	29	...	26	11 874
	2002	12 415	...	12 263	118	34	...	31	11 485
	2003	11 333	...	11 187	*116	29	...	31	10 414
Côte d'Ivoire	2000	1 925	...	364	1 409	152	*1	3 175	2 397
	2001	1 876	...	302	1 419	155	...	3 048	2 246
	2002	2 337	...	750	1 438	149	...	3 211	2 349
	2003	2 481	...	1 056	1 267	158	...	2 992	2 817

Production, trade and consumption of commercial energy—Thousand metric tons of oil equivalent and kilograms per capita (*continued*)

Production, commerce et consommation d'énergie commerciale—Milliers de tonnes d'équivalent pétrole et kilogrammes par habitant (*suite*)

Bunkers — Soutes			Consumption — Consommation							
Air / Avion	Sea / Maritime	Unallocated / Non distribué	Per capita / Par habitant	Total / Totale	Solids / Solides	Liquids / Liquides	Gas / Gaz	Electricity / Electricité	Year / Année	Région, pays ou zone
105 358	148 448	529 107	1 356	8 493 823	2 227 119	2 959 357	2 352 676	954 671	2000	Monde
103 407	140 792	529 447	1 357	8 608 818	2 291 228	2 993 416	2 363 382	960 792	2001	
104 009	145 705	538 871	1 381	8 870 857	2 425 844	3 020 338	2 448 748	975 927	2002	
106 106	142 248	577 765	1 398	9 118 372	2 608 885	3 044 205	2 494 279	971 003	2003	
4 106	7 468	55 758	363	285 549	117 430	102 192	55 472	10 456	2000	Afrique
3 769	7 581	53 177	364	292 919	118 210	104 341	60 091	10 277	2001	
3 647	6 733	54 676	376	309 152	122 668	111 081	64 112	11 291	2002	
3 630	7 803	50 699	376	316 532	127 011	111 627	66 682	11 212	2003	
*248	246	33 195	939	28 743	538	8 916	19 293	-4	2000	Algérie
*312	138	32 579	946	29 363	572	8 849	19 934	7	2001	
*319	243	31 313	1 031	32 337	714	9 926	21 694	3	2002	
*273	270	30 664	1 015	32 309	761	10 133	21 390	24	2003	
463	...	201	165	1 720	...	1 115	*527	78	2000	Angola
502	...	221	174	1 847	...	1 279	*481	87	2001	
431	...	212	188	2 046	...	1 384	563	98	2002	
301	...	215	215	2 408	...	1 647	*654	107	2003	
22	...	...	81	535	...	503	...	32	2000	Bénin
21	...	...	85	583	...	543	...	39	2001	
24	...	0	95	669	...	623	...	46	2002	
26	...	0	95	690	...	646	...	44	2003	
...	...	...	*30	*350	...	*341	...	8	2000	Burkina Faso
...	...	...	*29	*356	...	*347	...	10	2001	
...	...	...	*29	*369	...	*359	...	10	2002	
...	...	...	28	356	...	345	...	10	*2003	
*7	...	...	15	98	*4	*82	...	12	2000	Burundi
*9	...	...	*13	*90	*4	*73	...	13	2001	
*9	...	...	14	98	*4	*80	...	14	2002	
9	...	...	13	92	4	74	...	14	*2003	
59	19	73	82	1 224	...	928	...	296	2000	Cameroun
62	20	83	78	1 198	...	899	...	299	2001	
71	18	66	77	1 205	...	931	...	274	2002	
71	14	86	77	1 249	...	945	...	303	2003	
...	...	...	107	46	...	46	...	...	2000	Cap-Vert *
...	...	...	111	50	...	50	...	...	2001	
...	...	...	109	50	...	50	...	...	2002	
...	...	...	105	49	...	49	...	...	2003	
17	...	...	26	97	...	89	...	7	2000	Rép. centrafricaine *
20	...	...	26	97	...	89	...	7	2001	
20	...	...	26	99	...	91	...	7	2002	
21	...	...	29	92	...	84	...	7	2003	
21	...	...	5	42	...	42	...	...	2000	Tchad *
19	...	...	5	41	...	41	...	...	2001	
19	...	...	5	40	...	40	...	...	2002	
19	...	...	4	39	...	39	...	...	2003	
...	...	...	48	28	...	28	...	0	2000	Comores *
...	...	...	45	27	...	27	...	0	2001	
...	...	...	44	27	...	27	...	0	2002	
...	...	...	47	30	...	30	...	0	2003	
...	...	486	112	348	...	183	117	48	2000	Congo
...	...	649	127	410	...	238	117	55	2001	
...	...	590	111	371	...	187	118	65	2002	
...	...	518	127	432	...	256	*116	60	2003	
*99	93	-214	166	2 724	...	1 270	1 409	45	2000	Côte d'Ivoire
107	93	-236	160	2 715	...	1 240	1 419	55	2001	
*96	91	210	161	2 803	...	1 351	1 438	14	2002	
*108	91	284	121	2 173	...	862	1 267	43	2003	

58 **Production, trade and consumption of commercial energy**—Thousand metric tons of oil equivalent and kilograms per capita (*continued*)

Production, commerce et consommation d'énergie commerciale—Milliers de tonnes d'équivalent pétrole et kilogrammes par habitant (*suite*)

Region, country or area	Year / Année	Primary energy production — Production d'énergie primaire					Changes in stocks / Variations des stocks	Imports / Importations	Exports / Exportations
		Total / Totale	Solids / Solides	Liquids / Liquides	Gas / Gaz	Electricity / Electricité			
Dem. Rep. of the Congo	2000	1 740	67	1 157	...	516	−59	500	1 331
	2001	1 801	69	1 226	...	506	...	500	1 339
	2002	1 744	71	1 152	...	521	...	505	1 268
	2003	1 694	74	1 084	...	536	...	513	1 203
Djibouti *	2000	...	...	...	...	...	...	562	...
	2001	...	...	...	...	...	...	563	...
	2002	...	...	...	...	...	...	573	...
	2003	...	...	...	...	...	...	582	...
Egypt	2000	61 869	37	42 030	18 567	1 234	878	4 824	9 446
	2001	63 414	36	39 820	22 367	1 191	1 251	4 383	11 048
	2002	65 647	27	40 021	24 280	1 319	247	2 869	9 899
	2003	67 879	28	40 733	*26 036	1 083	*436	2 423	10 332
Equatorial Guinea	2000	5 911	...	5 911	...	*0	...	*54	5 909
	2001	10 451	...	10 450	...	*0	...	*54	*10 450
	2002	11 609	...	11 609	...	*0	...	*56	11 609
	2003	10 310	...	10 309	...	*0	...	*55	10 309
Eritrea	2000	...	...	...	...	...	...	203	...
	2001	...	...	...	...	...	13	234	...
	2002	...	...	...	...	...	−22	191	...
	2003	...	...	...	...	...	21	258	...
Ethiopia	2000	165	...	...	...	165	−53	1 803	...
	2001	164	...	...	...	164	−234	1 911	...
	2002	181	...	...	...	181	−241	1 960	...
	2003	203	...	...	...	203	−272	2 047	...
Gabon	2000	15 668	...	15 485	113	69	−169	144	15 044
	2001	15 176	...	15 010	91	76	−104	174	14 402
	2002	14 170	...	13 989	102	79	−162	71	13 434
	2003	11 250	...	11 067	106	77	−163	116	10 713
Gambia	2000	...	...	...	...	...	...	93	*2
	2001	...	...	...	...	...	...	*96	*2
	*2002	...	...	...	...	...	...	97	2
	*2003	...	...	...	...	...	...	97	2
Ghana	2000	568	...	...	...	568	...	2 234	332
	2001	568	...	...	...	568	...	2 452	375
	2002	433	...	...	...	433	−6	2 602	345
	2003	334	...	...	...	334	−6	2 609	224
Guinea *	2000	35	...	...	...	35	...	395	...
	2001	37	...	...	...	37	...	398	...
	2002	38	...	...	...	38	...	400	...
	2003	38	...	...	...	38	...	405	...
Guinea-Bissau *	2000	...	...	...	...	...	...	94	...
	2001	...	...	...	...	...	...	97	...
	2002	...	...	...	...	...	...	100	...
	2003	...	...	...	...	...	...	100	...
Kenya	2000	450	...	...	...	450	...	3 808	451
	2001	548	...	...	...	548	...	3 539	569
	2002	601	...	...	...	601	...	2 880	404
	2003	958	...	...	...	958	...	2 973	322
Liberia *	2000	17	...	...	...	17	...	148	1
	2001	17	...	...	...	17	...	159	1
	2002	17	...	...	...	17	...	163	1
	2003	18	...	...	...	18	...	166	1
Libyan Arab Jamah.	2000	73 852	...	68 512	5 340	...	...	...	54 828
	2001	72 513	...	66 900	5 613	...	...	...	53 103
	2002	68 491	...	62 851	5 640	...	...	...	48 642
	2003	76 269	...	70 457	5 812	...	...	...	56 107
Madagascar	2000	45	...	...	...	45	...	785	*20
	2001	46	...	...	...	46	...	800	*20
	2002	47	...	...	...	47	...	803	*20
	*2003	47	...	...	...	47	...	806	20

Production, trade and consumption of commercial energy—Thousand metric tons of oil equivalent and kilograms per capita (*continued*)

Production, commerce et consommation d'énergie commerciale—Milliers de tonnes d'équivalent pétrole et kilogrammes par habitant (*suite*)

Bunkers — Soutes			Consumption — Consommation							
Air Avion	Sea Maritime	Unallocated Non distribué	Per capita Par habitant	Total Totale	Solids Solides	Liquids Liquides	Gas Gaz	Electricity Electricité	Year Année	Région, pays ou zone
*95	2	0	17	871	220	245	...	406	2000	Rép. dém. du Congo
*96	2	...	16	864	218	247	...	398	2001	
*96	2	...	16	883	225	247	...	410	2002	
*97	2	...	16	904	232	249	...	423	2003	
70	363	...	298	128	...	128	...	...	2000	Djibouti *
70	363	...	296	129	...	129	...	...	2001	
75	378	...	267	119	...	119	...	...	2002	
81	380	...	266	122	...	122	...	...	2003	
560	2 674	9 673	679	43 461	831	22 836	18 567	1 228	2000	Egypte
491	2 642	5 111	724	47 254	824	22 888	22 367	1 176	2001	
480	1 963	4 606	770	51 322	647	25 120	24 280	1 276	2002	
490	2 736	4 928	*756	*51 380	476	23 861	*26 036	1 008	2003	
...	...	2	*115	*54	...	*54	...	*0	2000	Guinée équatoriale
...	...	...	*112	*54	...	*54	...	*0	2001	
...	...	...	*114	*57	...	*56	...	*0	2002	
...	...	...	*109	*56	...	*55	...	*0	2003	
9	...	...	44	194	...	194	...	...	2000	Erythrée
11	8	...	46	202	...	202	...	...	2001	
8	...	...	46	205	...	205	...	...	2002	
11	1	...	50	224	...	224	...	...	2003	
79	...	747	19	1 193	...	1 029	...	165	2000	Ethiopie
97	...	752	22	1 460	...	1 296	...	164	2001	
92	...	756	23	1 533	...	1 353	...	181	2002	
89	...	*760	24	1 673	...	1 470	...	203	2003	
*59	194	165	421	520	...	338	113	69	2000	Gabon
*72	144	257	456	578	...	412	91	76	2001	
*79	144	147	462	600	...	418	102	79	2002	
*72	145	*-16	461	614	...	431	106	77	2003	
...	...	...	66	91	...	91	...	...	2000	Gambie
...	...	...	66	94	...	94	...	...	2001	
...	...	...	65	95	...	95	...	...	*2002	
...	...	...	63	95	...	95	...	...	*2003	
102	...	227	109	2 140	...	1 531	...	609	2000	Ghana
91	...	452	105	2 103	...	1 521	...	582	2001	
94	...	498	102	2 104	...	1 625	...	479	2002	
140	...	613	94	1 972	...	1 631	...	342	2003	
22	...	...	47	408	...	373	...	35	2000	Guinée *
22	...	...	47	413	...	376	...	37	2001	
22	...	...	47	415	...	378	...	38	2002	
22	...	...	47	421	...	383	...	38	2003	
10	...	...	65	83	...	83	...	...	2000	Guinée-Bissau *
10	...	...	66	86	...	86	...	...	2001	
10	...	...	67	90	...	90	...	...	2002	
10	...	...	66	90	...	90	...	...	2003	
...	84	463	106	3 259	47	2 744	...	469	2000	Kenya
...	84	287	101	3 147	47	2 542	...	557	2001	
...	84	-79	97	3 072	70	2 382	...	620	2002	
...	13	29	109	3 567	65	2 529	...	972	2003	
3	13	...	55	148	...	131	...	17	2000	Libéria *
3	12	...	58	160	...	143	...	17	2001	
3	13	...	58	163	...	146	...	17	2002	
3	13	...	59	167	...	149	...	18	2003	
433	89	4 556	2 636	13 946	...	9 332	4 614	...	2000	Jamah. arabe libyenne
221	89	4 647	2 672	14 453	...	9 558	4 895	...	2001	
218	89	4 720	2 680	14 822	...	9 755	5 068	...	2002	
213	89	4 675	2 683	15 186	...	10 054	5 131	...	2003	
2	*17	142	42	648	*7	*597	...	45	2000	Madagascar
2	*17	146	41	661	*7	*608	...	46	2001	
2	*17	143	*41	*668	*7	*614	...	47	2002	
2	17	143	40	671	7	617	...	47	*2003	

Production, trade and consumption of commercial energy— Thousand metric tons of oil equivalent and kilograms per capita (*continued*)

Production, commerce et consommation d'énergie commerciale— Milliers de tonnes d'équivalent pétrole et kilogrammes par habitant (*suite*)

Region, country or area	Year Année	Primary energy production — Production d'énergie primaire					Changes in stocks Variations des stocks	Imports Importations	Exports Exportations
		Total Totale	Solids Solides	Liquids Liquides	Gas Gaz	Electricity Electricité			
Malawi	2000	*74	...	...	...	*74	...	*263	0
	2001	*75	...	...	...	*75	...	*267	0
	2002	*75	...	...	...	*75	...	*268	0
	2003	*75	...	...	...	*75	...	283	*0
Mali *	2000	20	...	...	...	20	...	200	...
	2001	20	...	...	...	20	...	201	...
	2002	20	...	...	...	20	...	203	...
	2003	20	...	...	...	20	...	203	...
Mauritania	*2000	3	...	...	...	3	...	853	...
	*2001	3	...	...	...	3	...	859	...
	2002	*3	...	...	...	*3	...	844	...
	*2003	3	...	...	...	3	...	849	...
Mauritius	2000	8	...	...	...	8	−71	1 113	...
	2001	6	...	...	...	6	6	1 219	...
	2002	*7	...	...	...	*7	*−44	1 154	...
	2003	10	...	...	...	10	−30	1 185	...
Morocco	2000	144	22	13	42	67	−42	11 349	911
	2001	146	1	10	42	93	336	12 736	1 220
	2002	143	...	13	40	90	−84	11 904	723
	2003	192	...	10	39	143	93	11 409	296
Mozambique	2000	778	17	...	1	760	−2	459	686
	2001	778	20	...	1	757	27	793	660
	2002	1 123	31	...	2	1 090	10	930	945
	2003	937	26	...	2	909	30	1 006	752
Niger *	2000	123	123	...	...	...	...	273	...
	2001	123	123	...	...	...	...	275	...
	2002	125	125	...	...	...	...	281	...
	2003	125	125	...	...	...	...	281	...
Nigeria	2000	124 570	2	112 333	11 740	494	95	7 008	108 732
	2001	131 650	2	117 090	14 039	518	699	3 559	110 312
	2002	116 606	30	102 621	13 236	718	−159	4 756	95 210
	2003	136 663	16	118 076	17 896	674	−397	7 755	119 229
Réunion	2000	*48	...	...	...	*48	...	777	...
	2001	48	...	...	...	48	...	769	...
	2002	*49	...	...	...	*49	...	768	...
	*2003	50	...	...	...	50	...	774	...
Rwanda	2000	*14	...	...	*0	*14	...	*196	0
	2001	*15	...	...	*0	*14	...	*200	0
	2002	*15	...	...	*0	*14	...	*207	1
	*2003	15	...	...	0	14	...	207	1
Saint Helena	2000	...	...	...	...	...	...	4	...
	2001	...	...	...	...	...	...	4	...
	2002	...	...	...	...	...	...	4	...
	*2003	...	...	...	...	...	...	4	...
Sao Tome and Principe	2000	*1	...	...	...	*1	...	30	...
	*2001	1	...	...	...	1	...	31	...
	*2002	1	...	...	...	1	...	31	...
	*2003	1	...	...	...	1	...	31	...
Senegal	2000	2	...	1	1	...	−1	1 532	94
	2001	1	...	...	1	...	49	1 566	47
	2002	3	...	...	3	...	...	1 528	70
	2003	10	...	...	10	...	70	1 712	190
Seychelles	2000	...	...	...	...	...	...	301	...
	2001	...	...	...	...	...	...	323	...
	2002	...	...	...	...	...	...	282	...
	*2003	...	...	...	...	...	...	287	...
Sierra Leone *	2000	...	...	...	...	...	...	315	4
	2001	...	...	...	...	...	...	327	4
	2002	...	...	...	...	...	...	337	4
	2003	...	...	...	...	...	...	340	4

58   **Production, trade and consumption of commercial energy**—Thousand metric tons of oil equivalent and kilograms per capita (*continued*)

Production, commerce et consommation d'énergie commerciale—Milliers de tonnes d'équivalent pétrole et kilogrammes par habitant (*suite*)

Bunkers — Soutes			Consumption — Consommation						Year	
Air Avion	Sea Maritime	Unallocated Non distribué	Per capita Par habitant	Total Totale	Solids Solides	Liquids Liquides	Gas Gaz	Electricity Electricité	Année	Région, pays ou zone
*19	...	...	*30	*319	*12	*233	...	*74	2000	Malawi
*20	...	...	*30	*322	*13	*235	...	*75	2001	
*20	...	...	*29	*323	*13	*236	...	*75	2002	
*21	...	...	*29	*337	14	249	...	*75	2003	
18	...	...	20	202	...	182	...	20	2000	Mali *
18	...	...	20	203	...	183	...	20	2001	
18	...	...	19	206	...	185	...	20	2002	
18	...	...	19	206	...	185	...	20	2003	
17	30	...	303	808	4	801	...	3	*2000	Mauritanie
18	32	...	295	812	4	805	...	3	*2001	
*18	*32	...	282	797	*4	790	...	*3	2002	
18	32	...	275	802	5	794	...	3	*2003	
91	220	...	744	882	177	697	...	8	2000	Maurice
78	203	...	781	937	209	722	...	6	2001	
96	*169	...	777	940	*219	714	...	*7	2002	
92	135	...	816	998	221	766	...	10	2003	
294	13	989	325	9 328	2 813	6 206	42	267	2000	Maroc
287	13	1 045	342	9 980	3 571	6 142	42	225	2001	
291	13	1 017	340	10 087	3 682	6 156	40	208	2002	
301	13	674	340	10 223	3 423	6 496	39	265	2003	
40	1	...	29	511	0	399	1	112	2000	Mozambique
35	3	...	47	847	0	404	1	442	2001	
32	5	...	57	1 061	6	416	2	637	2002	
22	38	...	59	1 101	15	441	2	642	2003	
23	...	...	36	374	123	232	...	18	2000	Niger *
23	...	...	35	376	123	234	...	18	2001	
24	...	...	34	381	125	238	...	18	2002	
24	...	...	33	381	125	238	...	18	2003	
572	473	4 188	153	17 517	*5	10 375	6 643	494	2000	Nigéria
432	729	5 301	151	17 735	*5	11 360	5 851	518	2001	
388	721	5 582	162	19 621	33	12 941	5 928	718	2002	
400	975	4 755	156	19 456	18	11 857	6 907	674	2003	
...	15	...	1 123	809	...	761	...	*48	2000	Réunion
...	10	...	1 103	807	...	759	...	48	2001	
...	9	...	1 087	809	...	759	...	*49	2002	
...	9	...	1 079	815	...	765	...	50	*2003	
*10	...	...	*27	*200	...	*178	*0	*22	2000	Rwanda
*10	...	...	*27	*204	...	*179	*0	*25	2001	
*12	...	...	*27	*208	...	*180	*0	*28	2002	
12	...	...	26	209	...	182	0	27	*2003	
...	...	...	587	4	...	4	...	...	2000	Sainte-Hélène
...	...	...	587	4	...	4	...	...	2001	
...	...	...	587	4	...	4	...	...	2002	
...	...	...	587	4	...	4	...	...	*2003	
...	...	...	191	31	...	30	...	*1	2000	Sao Tomé-et-Principe
...	...	...	191	32	...	31	...	1	*2001	
...	...	...	186	32	...	31	...	1	*2002	
...	...	...	179	32	...	31	...	1	*2003	
265	77	2	106	1 095	...	1 095	1	...	2000	Sénégal
226	75	56	105	1 114	...	1 114	1	...	2001	
186	75	4	110	1 197	...	1 194	3	...	2002	
*209	9	6	111	1 238	...	1 228	10	...	2003	
32	*81	...	2 316	188	...	188	...	...	2000	Seychelles
31	*81	...	2 609	211	...	211	...	...	2001	
*24	*78	...	2 222	180	...	180	...	...	2002	
26	80	...	2 230	181	...	181	...	...	*2003	
19	86	59	33	147	...	147	...	...	2000	Sierra Leone *
19	87	63	34	154	...	154	...	...	2001	
24	88	67	32	154	...	154	...	...	2002	
24	88	69	29	155	...	155	...	...	2003	

Production, trade and consumption of commercial energy—Thousand metric tons of oil equivalent and kilograms per capita (*continued*)

Production, commerce et consommation d'énergie commerciale—Milliers de tonnes d'équivalent pétrole et kilogrammes par habitant (*suite*)

Region, country or area	Year Année	Primary energy production — Production d'énergie primaire					Changes in stocks Variations des stocks	Imports Importations	Exports Exportations
		Total Totale	Solids Solides	Liquids Liquides	Gas Gaz	Electricity Electricité			
South Africa [1]	2000	171 541	157 865	8 252	1 554	3 869	184	21 219	55 184
	2001	173 053	159 011	8 777	2 019	3 246	2 302	23 107	55 089
	2002	174 597	159 733	9 178	2 002	3 684	−1 285	28 485	57 374
	2003	183 657	168 893	8 970	2 045	3 749	731	27 899	60 171
Sudan	2000	8 968	...	8 866	...	102	184	512	7 288
	2001	10 511	...	10 404	...	106	277	353	8 320
	2002	12 158	...	12 047	...	111	131	309	9 492
	2003	13 363	...	13 263	...	100	135	350	10 470
Togo	2000	0	...	...	...	0	1	497	...
	2001	0	...	...	...	0	−66	352	...
	2002	0	...	...	...	0	...	428	...
	2003	*0	...	...	...	*0	...	702	...
Tunisia	2000	5 493	...	3 698	1 788	7	185	5 269	4 174
	2001	5 425	...	3 389	2 030	7	212	5 379	3 844
	2002	5 466	...	3 523	1 935	8	116	5 455	3 973
	2003	5 193	...	3 206	1 970	17	113	5 411	3 573
Uganda	2000	135	...	...	...	135	...	452	*17
	2001	143	...	...	...	143	...	471	*14
	2002	144	...	...	...	144	...	483	*14
	*2003	144	...	...	...	144	...	488	14
United Rep. of Tanzania	2000	240	55	...	...	184	...	758	...
	2001	276	55	...	...	221	...	911	...
	2002	289	55	...	...	234	...	1 046	...
	2003	258	39	...	...	219	...	1 118	...
Western Sahara *	2000	...	...	...	...	...	...	85	...
	2001	...	...	...	...	...	...	85	...
	2002	...	...	...	...	...	...	85	...
	2003	...	...	...	...	...	...	85	...
Zambia	2000	781	114	...	...	667	38	494	163
	2001	900	120	...	...	780	45	572	288
	2002	903	124	...	...	779	52	597	239
	2003	949	130	...	...	819	56	627	251
Zimbabwe	2000	3 360	3 080	...	...	280	−98	1 500	144
	2001	3 078	2 820	...	...	258	−102	1 331	144
	2002	2 992	2 663	...	...	329	−99	1 278	144
	2003	2 876	2 415	...	...	461	−102	1 130	144
America, North	2000	2 348 852	586 670	721 290	732 503	308 389	−54 113	821 190	378 555
	2001	2 387 758	616 079	723 694	748 360	299 625	62 158	852 778	382 392
	2002	2 373 765	595 410	730 281	736 649	311 425	−21 724	836 166	385 459
	2003	2 353 218	579 708	740 136	725 741	307 633	−10 476	881 229	406 834
Antigua and Barbuda *	2000	...	...	...	...	...	...	171	7
	2001	...	...	...	...	...	...	171	7
	2002	...	...	...	...	...	...	180	6
	2003	...	...	...	...	...	...	190	8
Aruba	2000	120	...	120	...	...	...	*633	...
	2001	120	...	120	...	...	...	*637	...
	2002	120	...	120	...	...	...	*652	...
	2003	120	...	120	...	...	...	*661	...
Bahamas *	2000	...	...	...	...	...	2	2 915	2 096
	2001	...	...	...	...	...	2	2 915	2 096
	2002	...	...	...	...	...	3	3 064	2 103
	2003	...	...	...	...	...	50	3 162	2 206
Barbados	2000	112	...	77	35	...	−12	519	77
	2001	93	...	63	30	...	−16	531	63
	2002	107	...	80	27	...	27	545	53
	2003	98	...	74	24	...	...	531	74
Belize	2000	8	...	...	...	8	...	277	...
	2001	8	...	...	...	8	...	272	...
	*2002	8	...	...	...	8	...	286	...
	*2003	9	...	...	...	9	...	300	...

Production, trade and consumption of commercial energy — Thousand metric tons of oil equivalent and kilograms per capita *(continued)*

Production, commerce et consommation d'énergie commerciale — Milliers de tonnes d'équivalent pétrole et kilogrammes par habitant *(suite)*

Bunkers — Soutes			Consumption — Consommation							
Air Avion	Sea Maritime	Unallocated Non distribué	Per capita Par habitant	Total Totale	Solids Solides	Liquids Liquides	Gas Gaz	Electricity Electricité	Year Année	Région, pays ou zone
...	2 645	660	2 643	134 086	109 538	18 861	1 554	4 133	2000	Afrique du Sud [1]
...	2 704	1 598	2 635	134 467	109 747	19 052	2 019	3 648	2001	
...	2 469	4 590	2 732	139 933	114 216	19 610	2 002	4 105	2002	
...	2 622	2 124	2 845	145 908	119 226	20 757	2 045	3 880	2003	
110	8	89	58	1 799	...	1 697	...	102	2000	Soudan
124	8	84	65	2 051	...	1 945	...	106	2001	
130	8	156	79	2 551	...	2 440	...	111	2002	
136	8	96	86	2 868	...	2 768	...	100	2003	
25	...	...	100	472	...	428	...	44	2000	Togo
18	...	...	83	400	...	355	...	45	2001	
24	...	...	81	404	...	365	...	39	2002	
74	...	...	123	628	...	599	...	30	2003	
...	...	51	664	6 352	74	3 679	2 592	8	2000	Tunisie
...	...	45	693	6 703	67	3 755	2 874	8	2001	
...	...	40	694	6 793	57	3 859	2 873	3	2002	
...	...	35	699	6 882	16	3 872	2 978	15	2003	
...	...	...	24	570	...	449	...	121	2000	Ouganda
...	...	...	25	600	...	471	...	129	2001	
...	...	...	25	612	...	483	...	129	2002	
...	...	...	24	617	...	488	...	129	*2003	
58	23	...	28	917	55	673	...	189	2000	Rép.-Unie de Tanzanie
65	23	...	32	1 099	55	823	...	221	2001	
69	23	...	36	1 243	55	954	...	234	2002	
74	23	...	36	1 279	39	1 021	...	219	2003	
6	...	...	322	79	...	79	...	...	2000	Sahara occidental *
6	...	...	314	79	...	79	...	...	2001	
6	...	...	308	79	...	79	...	...	2002	
6	...	...	301	79	...	79	...	...	2003	
40	...	3	96	1 031	76	448	...	507	2000	Zambie
42	...	38	100	1 060	79	479	...	502	2001	
43	...	38	105	1 127	80	496	...	551	2002	
45	...	42	110	1 182	85	519	...	579	2003	
87	...	...	402	4 727	2 907	1 102	...	719	2000	Zimbabwe
79	...	...	362	4 287	2 664	1 016	...	608	2001	
75	...	...	348	4 149	2 511	964	...	674	2002	
68	...	...	324	3 895	2 280	881	...	735	2003	
23 612	33 499	136 261	5 541	2 652 228	582 467	999 948	761 492	308 320	2000	Amérique du Nord
21 840	24 462	141 265	5 302	2 608 419	577 500	1 009 831	721 544	299 543	2001	
21 223	28 308	137 801	5 333	2 658 863	582 315	1 011 268	753 598	311 683	2002	
20 659	24 137	148 742	5 245	2 644 551	587 154	1 026 015	723 845	307 537	2003	
45	...	...	1 787	118	...	118	...	...	2000	Antigua-et-Barbuda *
45	...	...	1 760	118	...	118	...	...	2001	
50	...	...	1 852	124	...	124	...	...	2002	
49	...	...	1 959	133	...	133	...	...	2003	
*68	...	*445	*2 628	*239	...	*239	...	...	2000	Aruba
*70	...	*445	*2 621	*241	...	*241	...	...	2001	
*73	...	*450	*2 643	*248	...	*248	...	...	2002	
*75	...	*455	*2 610	*251	...	*251	...	...	2003	
37	184	...	2 052	595	1	594	...	...	2000	Bahamas *
37	184	...	2 031	595	1	594	...	...	2001	
40	229	...	2 332	688	1	686	...	...	2002	
43	244	...	2 084	619	2	617	...	...	2003	
207	...	...	1 345	359	...	324	35	...	2000	Barbade
207	...	...	1 379	370	...	340	30	...	2001	
207	...	0	1 355	364	...	337	27	...	2002	
*207	...	-1	1 293	349	...	325	24	...	2003	
29	*12	...	977	244	...	234	...	10	2000	Belize
17	*12	...	980	252	...	241	...	11	2001	
19	12	...	994	263	...	253	...	11	*2002	
22	12	...	1 005	275	...	264	...	11	*2003	

58 Production, trade and consumption of commercial energy — Thousand metric tons of oil equivalent and kilograms per capita (*continued*)

Production, commerce et consommation d'énergie commerciale — Milliers de tonnes d'équivalent pétrole et kilogrammes par habitant (*suite*)

| Region, country or area | Year Année | Primary energy production — Production d'énergie primaire | | | | | Changes in stocks Variations des stocks | Imports Importations | Exports Exportations |
		Total Totale	Solids Solides	Liquids Liquides	Gas Gaz	Electricity Electricité			
Bermuda *	2000	...	...	...	...	...	...	171	...
	2001	...	...	...	...	...	...	171	...
	2002	...	...	...	...	...	...	185	...
	2003	...	...	...	...	...	...	185	...
British Virgin Islands *	2000	...	...	...	...	...	...	20	...
	2001	...	...	...	...	...	...	20	...
	2002	...	...	...	...	...	...	23	...
	2003	...	...	...	...	...	...	26	...
Canada	2000	384 342	35 276	134 245	164 952	49 869	−9 377	67 181	189 230
	2001	390 053	35 759	136 240	169 328	48 726	−2 764	71 168	195 560
	2002	396 578	32 919	142 990	170 760	49 909	−3 469	68 525	194 490
	2003	397 123	30 374	150 612	167 476	48 662	−6 835	75 267	194 050
Cayman Islands *	2000	...	...	...	...	...	...	113	...
	2001	...	...	...	...	...	...	113	...
	2002	...	...	...	...	...	...	117	...
	2003	...	...	...	...	...	...	123	...
Costa Rica	2000	1 343	...	...	...	1 343	−30	1 812	203
	2001	1 350	...	...	...	1 350	0	1 884	183
	2002	1 496	...	...	...	1 496	87	2 049	229
	2003	1 327	...	...	...	1 327	−4	2 105	104
Cuba	2000	3 227	...	2 698	521	8	398	5 856	...
	2001	3 435	...	2 889	540	6	236	5 295	...
	2002	4 172	...	3 632	531	9	*104	5 167	...
	2003	4 290	...	3 684	598	8	128	4 528	...
Dominica	2000	3	...	...	...	3	...	34	...
	2001	2	...	...	...	2	...	37	...
	*2002	2	...	...	...	2	...	40	...
	*2003	3	...	...	...	3	...	47	...
Dominican Republic	2000	66	...	...	...	66	...	6 323	...
	2001	48	...	...	...	48	...	6 291	...
	2002	76	...	...	...	76	...	6 643	...
	2003	103	...	...	...	103	...	6 481	...
El Salvador	2000	777	...	...	...	777	−12	2 172	299
	2001	931	...	...	...	931	−21	2 205	320
	2002	952	...	...	...	952	17	2 236	318
	2003	1 008	...	...	...	1 008	8	2 262	191
Greenland *	2000	...	...	...	...	...	...	192	7
	2001	...	...	...	...	...	...	194	7
	2002	...	...	...	...	...	...	195	7
	2003	...	...	...	...	...	...	196	7
Grenada	2000	...	...	...	...	...	...	78	...
	2001	...	...	...	...	...	1	83	...
	2002	...	...	...	...	...	...	81	...
	2003	...	...	...	...	...	...	83	...
Guadeloupe *	2000	...	...	...	...	...	...	590	...
	2001	...	...	...	...	...	...	601	...
	2002	...	...	...	...	...	...	624	...
	2003	...	...	...	...	...	...	635	...
Guatemala	2000	1 328	...	1 131	...	197	−92	3 038	1 103
	2001	1 316	...	1 150	...	166	−82	3 196	1 091
	2002	1 492	...	1 345	...	146	...	3 402	1 298
	2003	1 561	...	1 348	...	213	...	3 349	1 385
Haiti	2000	24	...	...	...	24	...	476	...
	2001	24	...	...	...	24	...	525	...
	2002	22	...	...	...	22	...	575	...
	2003	22	...	...	...	22	...	550	...
Honduras	2000	194	...	...	...	194	108	1 602	1
	2001	204	...	...	...	204	162	1 866	1
	2002	211	...	...	...	211	242	2 052	...
	2003	187	...	...	...	187	259	2 204	...

Production, trade and consumption of commercial energy—Thousand metric tons of oil equivalent and kilograms per capita (*continued*)

Production, commerce et consommation d'énergie commerciale—Milliers de tonnes d'équivalent pétrole et kilogrammes par habitant (*suite*)

Bunkers — Soutes			Consumption — Consommation							
Air Avion	Sea Maritime	Unallocated Non distribué	Per capita Par habitant	Total Totale	Solids Solides	Liquids Liquides	Gas Gaz	Electricity Electricité	Year Année	Région, pays ou zone
17	...	...	2 456	155	...	155	...	...	2000	Bermudes *
17	...	...	2 495	155	...	155	...	...	2001	
19	...	...	2 679	166	...	166	...	...	2002	
19	...	...	2 679	166	...	166	...	...	2003	
...	...	...	816	20	...	20	...	...	2000	Iles Vierges britanniques *
...	...	...	979	20	...	20	...	...	2001	
...	...	...	1 079	23	...	23	...	...	2002	
...	...	...	1 171	26	...	26	...	...	2003	
1 008	1 076	11 756	8 401	257 830	28 813	99 652	82 563	46 804	2000	Canada
1 054	1 076	12 367	8 186	253 930	27 725	99 551	79 917	46 737	2001	
907	1 159	15 597	8 176	256 420	26 699	99 712	81 821	48 187	2002	
699	880	16 246	8 444	267 350	26 456	104 757	88 051	48 086	2003	
19	...	...	2 361	94	...	94	...	...	2000	Iles Caïmanes *
19	...	...	2 303	94	...	94	...	...	2001	
21	...	...	2 413	97	...	97	...	...	2002	
22	...	...	2 422	102	...	102	...	...	2003	
...	...	-7	762	2 989	...	1 687	...	1 302	2000	Costa Rica
...	...	46	731	3 005	...	1 676	...	1 329	2001	
...	...	74	751	3 155	18	1 677	...	1 460	2002	
...	...	149	750	3 184	49	1 815	...	1 320	2003	
217	15	69	747	8 384	11	7 844	521	8	2000	Cuba
187	15	228	718	8 064	9	7 509	540	6	2001	
*166	15	280	778	8 774	9	8 225	531	9	2002	
131	...	353	726	8 205	10	7 589	598	8	2003	
...	...	...	514	37	...	34	...	3	2000	Dominique
...	...	...	559	40	...	37	...	2	2001	
...	...	...	614	43	...	40	...	2	*2002	
...	...	...	704	49	...	47	...	3	*2003	
71	...	502	693	5 815	65	5 684	...	66	2000	Rép. dominicaine
76	...	606	663	5 656	142	5 466	...	48	2001	
80	...	489	709	6 149	163	5 910	...	76	2002	
92	...	632	664	5 860	740	5 012	4	103	2003	
71	...	82	400	2 510	1	1 672	...	837	2000	El Salvador
72	...	81	419	2 683	1	1 725	...	957	2001	
66	...	45	421	2 742	1	1 756	...	985	2002	
70	...	66	442	2 935	1	1 898	...	1 037	2003	
...	...	...	3 292	184	...	184	...	...	2000	Groenland *
...	...	...	3 329	186	...	186	...	...	2001	
...	...	...	3 347	187	...	187	...	...	2002	
...	...	...	3 306	188	...	188	...	...	2003	
*8	...	...	738	69	...	69	...	...	2000	Grenade
*7	...	...	793	75	...	75	...	...	2001	
*7	...	...	782	73	...	73	...	...	2002	
*8	...	...	795	75	...	75	...	...	2003	
92	...	...	1 165	498	...	498	...	...	2000	Guadeloupe *
95	...	...	1 170	506	...	506	...	...	2001	
102	...	...	1 195	522	...	522	...	...	2002	
103	...	...	1 210	531	...	531	...	...	2003	
50	122	177	264	3 006	151	2 720	...	136	2000	Guatemala
46	122	180	270	3 155	140	2 870	...	145	2001	
37	122	110	277	3 327	273	2 941	...	113	2002	
41	122	...	273	3 363	258	2 925	...	179	2003	
28	...	...	61	473	...	449	...	24	2000	Haïti
34	...	...	60	515	...	490	...	24	2001	
35	...	...	65	563	...	540	...	22	2002	
19	...	...	63	553	...	531	...	22	2003	
36	...	...	255	1 651	95	1 338	...	218	2000	Honduras
23	...	...	283	1 884	86	1 567	...	231	2001	
24	...	...	293	1 998	99	1 652	...	247	2002	
26	...	...	301	2 106	118	1 772	...	215	2003	

Production, trade and consumption of commercial energy — Thousand metric tons of oil equivalent and kilograms per capita (*continued*)

Production, commerce et consommation d'énergie commerciale — Milliers de tonnes d'équivalent pétrole et kilogrammes par habitant (*suite*)

Region, country or area	Year Année	Primary energy production — Production d'énergie primaire					Changes in stocks Variations des stocks	Imports Importations	Exports Exportations
		Total Totale	Solids Solides	Liquids Liquides	Gas Gaz	Electricity Electricité			
Jamaica	2000	10	...	...	...	10	164	3 867	219
	2001	5	...	...	...	5	...	3 657	85
	2002	8	...	...	...	8	−116	3 487	107
	2003	10	...	...	...	10	35	3 802	129
Martinique *	2000	...	...	...	...	...	...	885	208
	2001	...	...	...	...	...	...	899	213
	2002	...	...	...	...	...	...	962	225
	2003	...	...	...	...	...	...	667	225
Mexico	2000	225 689	3 548	177 211	34 856	10 074	1 346	24 440	95 265
	2001	231 570	3 529	183 398	35 123	9 520	48	21 842	96 857
	2002	234 832	3 348	186 131	36 017	9 336	380	22 681	102 040
	2003	247 899	2 948	197 344	37 751	9 857	−1 021	22 553	109 494
Montserrat *	2000	...	...	...	...	...	...	18	...
	2001	...	...	...	...	...	...	18	...
	2002	...	...	...	...	...	...	20	...
	2003	...	...	...	...	...	...	22	...
Netherlands Antilles	2000	...	...	...	...	...	...	14 125	8 760
	2001	...	...	...	...	...	...	15 284	9 815
	2002	...	...	...	...	...	...	13 691	8 367
	2003	...	...	...	...	...	...	13 271	8 028
Nicaragua	2000	133	...	...	...	133	−41	1 216	30
	2001	194	...	...	...	194	26	1 331	19
	2002	86	...	...	...	86	−35	1 227	12
	2003	259	...	...	...	259	5	1 263	17
Panama	2000	294	...	...	...	294	−22	2 969	1 218
	2001	215	...	...	...	215	79	2 918	659
	2002	292	...	...	...	292	−156	2 144	482
	2003	243	...	...	...	243	−20	2 054	208
Saint Kitts and Nevis *	2000	...	...	...	...	...	...	34	...
	2001	...	...	...	...	...	...	34	...
	2002	...	...	...	...	...	...	38	...
	2003	...	...	...	...	...	...	42	...
Saint Lucia	2000	...	...	...	...	...	...	108	...
	2001	...	...	...	...	...	...	105	...
	*2002	...	...	...	...	...	...	102	...
	*2003	...	...	...	...	...	...	110	...
Saint Pierre and Miquelon	2000	...	...	...	...	...	...	*22	...
	2001	...	...	...	...	...	...	*22	...
	*2002	...	...	...	...	...	...	24	...
	*2003	...	...	...	...	...	...	28	...
St. Vincent-Grenadines	2000	2	...	...	...	2	...	52	...
	2001	2	...	...	...	2	...	59	...
	2002	2	...	...	...	2	...	62	...
	*2003	3	...	...	...	3	...	65	...
Trinidad and Tobago	2000	19 596	...	7 344	12 252	...	168	5 056	12 752
	2001	20 205	...	7 105	13 100	...	228	5 022	12 677
	2002	23 456	...	8 193	15 263	...	275	4 732	14 515
	2003	31 852	...	8 627	23 225	...	298	4 706	22 146
United States [2]	2000	1 711 584	547 846	398 463	519 887	245 388	−46 715	674 226	67 079
	2001	1 737 980	576 792	392 728	530 239	238 222	64 259	703 412	62 738
	2002	1 709 851	559 143	387 790	514 051	248 866	−19 082	690 356	61 206
	2003	1 667 101	546 386	378 327	496 667	245 720	−3 381	729 762	68 561
America, South	2000	528 096	33 755	350 811	94 216	49 313	495	80 828	253 179
	2001	525 128	36 594	346 114	93 663	48 756	2 290	81 948	254 844
	2002	515 090	36 322	331 201	97 259	50 308	13 830	80 805	239 919
	2003	505 690	39 812	317 831	95 443	52 604	4 144	78 393	234 659
Argentina	2000	83 169	153	41 256	37 664	4 096	−733	3 784	23 399
	2001	84 474	120	42 082	37 239	5 033	−17	2 855	27 244
	2002	81 256	57	40 477	36 110	4 612	167	2 445	25 352
	2003	84 432	53	39 716	39 772	4 892	25	1 962	24 233

Production, trade and consumption of commercial energy—Thousand metric tons of oil equivalent and kilograms per capita (*continued*)

Production, commerce et consommation d'énergie commerciale—Milliers de tonnes d'équivalent pétrole et kilogrammes par habitant (*suite*)

Bunkers — Soutes			Consumption — Consommation							
Air Avion	Sea Maritime	Unallocated Non distribué	Per capita Par habitant	Total Totale	Solids Solides	Liquids Liquides	Gas Gaz	Electricity Electricité	Year Année	Région, pays ou zone
162	30	112	1 238	3 189	50	3 129	...	10	2000	Jamaïque
161	30	217	1 220	3 169	37	3 127	...	5	2001	
195	30	37	1 237	3 242	62	3 173	...	8	2002	
195	30	25	1 282	3 397	60	3 328	...	10	2003	
...	40	51	1 522	586	...	586	...	...	2000	Martinique *
...	40	52	1 536	594	...	594	...	...	2001	
...	44	75	1 588	618	...	618	...	...	2002	
...	44	-223	1 588	621	...	621	...	...	2003	
2 620	1 348	18 115	1 330	131 435	5 331	78 685	37 270	10 149	2000	Mexique
2 602	1 107	22 068	1 302	130 730	5 052	77 790	38 363	9 525	2001	
2 507	796	20 524	1 289	131 265	5 179	74 109	42 624	9 354	2002	
2 552	815	21 790	1 324	136 822	5 631	74 735	46 673	9 783	2003	
...	1	...	2 756	17	...	17	...	...	2000	Montserrat *
...	1	...	2 067	17	...	17	...	...	2001	
...	1	...	2 325	19	...	19	...	...	2002	
...	1	...	2 296	21	...	21	...	...	2003	
70	1 708	2 356	6 871	1 230	...	1 230	...	...	2000	Antilles néerlandaises
71	1 709	2 077	9 261	1 611	...	1 611	...	...	2001	
75	1 704	1 702	10 585	1 842	...	1 842	...	...	2002	
80	1 712	1 888	8 738	1 564	...	1 564	...	...	2003	
27	...	67	250	1 266	...	1 123	...	143	2000	Nicaragua
25	...	67	267	1 389	...	1 193	...	196	2001	
15	...	69	234	1 252	...	1 165	...	87	2002	
12	...	118	249	1 369	...	1 111	...	258	2003	
...	4	199	652	1 863	42	1 517	...	304	2000	Panama
...	5	245	740	2 145	44	1 892	...	208	2001	
...	2	115	678	1 993	32	1 671	...	291	2002	
...	2	...	676	2 106	...	1 878	...	228	2003	
...	...	...	869	34	...	34	...	...	2000	Saint-Kitts-et-Nevis *
...	...	...	869	34	...	34	...	...	2001	
...	...	...	975	38	...	38	...	...	2002	
...	...	...	1 080	42	...	42	...	...	2003	
...	...	...	731	108	...	108	...	...	2000	Sainte-Lucie
...	...	...	667	105	...	105	...	...	2001	
...	...	...	644	102	...	102	...	*2002		
...	...	...	682	110	...	110	...	*2003		
...	4	...	*2 625	*18	...	*18	...	...	2000	Saint-Pierre-et-Miquelon
...	4	...	*2 625	*18	...	*18	...	...	2001	
...	5	...	2 770	19	...	19	...	*2002		
...	6	...	3 065	21	...	21	...	*2003		
...	...	...	467	54	...	52	...	2	2000	St. Vincent-Grenadines
...	...	...	528	61	...	59	...	2	2001	
...	...	...	555	64	...	62	...	2	2002	
...	...	...	578	68	...	65	...	3	*2003	
59	278	1 510	7 639	9 885	...	725	9 160	...	2000	Trinité-et-Tobago
61	339	1 141	8 293	10 781	...	751	10 030	...	2001	
8	668	1 518	8 580	11 205	...	700	10 505	...	2002	
8	744	1 554	9 034	11 808	...	705	11 103	...	2003	
18 670	28 677	100 826	8 055	2 217 272	547 909	789 116	631 942	248 305	2000	Etats-Unis [2]
16 913	19 818	101 444	7 641	2 176 220	544 263	799 178	592 663	240 116	2001	
16 569	23 521	96 716	7 703	2 221 277	549 780	802 580	618 090	250 828	2002	
16 186	19 525	105 688	7 532	2 190 283	553 830	812 790	577 392	246 272	2003	
1 992	5 127	36 725	908	311 405	21 057	147 075	94 074	49 199	2000	Amérique du Sud
1 959	5 632	32 633	882	309 718	19 694	148 207	93 140	48 677	2001	
1 936	5 755	23 521	873	310 934	19 148	144 163	97 449	50 175	2002	
2 145	5 490	30 118	846	307 528	19 730	139 311	96 199	52 287	2003	
...	507	4 583	1 599	59 196	437	20 823	33 735	4 201	2000	Argentine
...	570	5 543	1 440	53 988	340	16 857	31 607	5 183	2001	
1	502	5 859	1 366	51 821	290	15 072	31 337	5 121	2002	
...	588	6 223	1 441	55 325	524	15 074	34 402	5 325	2003	

Production, trade and consumption of commercial energy—Thousand metric tons of oil equivalent and kilograms per capita (*continued*)

Production, commerce et consommation d'énergie commerciale—Milliers de tonnes d'équivalent pétrole et kilogrammes par habitant (*suite*)

Region, country or area	Year Année	Primary energy production — Production d'énergie primaire					Changes in stocks Variations des stocks	Imports Importations	Exports Exportations
		Total Totale	Solids Solides	Liquids Liquides	Gas Gaz	Electricity Electricité			
Bolivia	2000	*5 496	...	1 877	*3 454	165	*–323	350	2 170
	2001	*7 185	...	2 082	*4 919	183	*–192	354	3 853
	2002	8 125	...	2 117	5 818	189	*–268	300	4 934
	2003	7 253	...	1 856	5 205	193	11	284	4 156
Brazil	2000	103 225	3 024	65 700	6 744	27 757	991	45 872	6 280
	2001	104 797	2 512	68 669	6 852	26 764	–3 026	48 394	12 580
	2002	115 877	2 285	76 584	8 793	28 215	–1 455	46 754	19 228
	2003	120 536	2 064	79 173	9 501	29 798	–184	41 812	20 121
Chile	2000	4 326	256	480	1 949	1 641	530	19 287	556
	2001	4 730	403	508	1 954	1 864	304	18 394	681
	2002	4 776	303	476	2 002	1 994	384	19 034	784
	2003	4 541	403	433	1 761	1 944	342	20 501	1 219
Colombia	2000	69 630	24 792	36 012	6 067	2 758	–940	456	46 892
	2001	68 943	28 237	31 529	6 442	2 735	232	479	45 123
	2002	67 232	28 503	29 450	6 436	*2 844	3 065	480	41 433
	2003	69 316	32 517	27 652	6 161	2 987	616	334	45 292
Ecuador	2000	22 041	...	21 081	229	730	479	1 022	15 147
	2001	22 057	...	21 216	233	608	457	1 403	14 830
	2002	21 519	...	20 564	236	719	718	1 695	14 078
	2003	22 526	...	21 520	388	618	1 134	1 530	14 923
Falkland Is. (Malvinas) *	2000	3	3	...	...	...	...	9	...
	2001	3	3	...	...	...	...	10	...
	2002	3	3	...	...	...	...	10	...
	2003	3	3	...	...	...	...	11	...
French Guiana	*2000	...	...	...	...	...	...	313	...
	*2001	...	...	...	...	...	...	320	...
	2002	...	...	...	...	...	...	325	...
	*2003	...	...	...	...	...	...	326	...
Guyana	2000	*0	...	...	...	*0	–4	537	...
	2001	*0	...	...	...	*0	...	558	...
	2002	1	...	...	...	1	–1	545	...
	*2003	1	...	...	...	1	...	553	...
Paraguay	2000	4 599	...	...	...	4 599	44	1 179	4 070
	2001	3 896	...	...	...	3 896	19	1 192	3 365
	2002	4 145	...	...	...	4 145	11	1 261	3 597
	2003	4 451	...	...	...	4 451	–71	1 226	3 885
Peru	2000	7 670	11	5 536	679	1 444	139	5 556	2 295
	2001	7 697	12	5 406	710	1 569	48	5 666	3 074
	2002	7 791	15	5 420	750	1 606	662	6 095	3 270
	2003	7 797	10	5 332	805	1 650	1 030	7 009	3 808
Suriname	2000	716	...	603	...	113	...	280	192
	2001	758	...	644	...	115	...	230	138
	2002	732	...	616	...	116	...	248	132
	2003	706	...	589	...	117	...	268	129
Uruguay	2000	606	...	...	...	606	–57	2 182	153
	2001	791	...	...	...	791	–28	2 095	213
	2002	820	...	...	...	820	–241	1 612	237
	2003	733	...	...	...	733	129	2 017	258
Venezuela (Bolivarian Rep. of)	2000	226 615	5 516	178 266	37 430	5 403	368	...	152 025
	2001	219 797	5 306	173 978	35 314	5 199	4 491	...	143 743
	2002	202 814	5 155	155 498	37 114	5 046	10 788	...	126 874
	2003	183 394	4 762	141 561	31 851	5 220	1 111	561	116 635
Asia	2000	3 134 114	830 966	1 571 941	533 016	198 191	–5 460	1 248 043	1 397 390
	2001	3 227 120	930 843	1 540 899	553 508	201 870	–9 830	1 243 982	1 395 801
	2002	3 341 047	1 058 032	1 491 775	589 711	201 528	5 036	1 285 331	1 304 244
	2003	3 628 487	1 221 610	1 580 234	629 730	196 913	5 832	1 350 186	1 430 277
Afghanistan	2000	*137	1	...	*109	*27	*10	*236	...
	2001	*146	18	...	*102	*27	*10	*130	...
	2002	*143	15	...	*102	*27	...	*133	...
	2003	*154	25	...	*102	*28	...	*133	...

58 Production, trade and consumption of commercial energy—Thousand metric tons of oil equivalent and kilograms per capita (continued)

Production, commerce et consommation d'énergie commerciale—Milliers de tonnes d'équivalent pétrole et kilogrammes par habitant (suite)

| Bunkers — Soutes | | | Consumption — Consommation | | | | | | | |
Air Avion	Sea Maritime	Unallocated Non distribué	Per capita Par habitant	Total Totale	Solids Solides	Liquids Liquides	Gas Gaz	Electricity Electricité	Year Année	Région, pays ou zone
...	...	*362	*457	*3 637	...	1 968	*1 502	166	2000	Bolivie
...	...	403	*408	*3 474	...	1 951	*1 339	184	2001	
...	...	*377	389	3 382	...	1 891	1 300	190	2002	
...	...	93	368	3 277	...	1 889	1 195	194	2003	
667	2 961	14 051	740	124 147	13 513	70 316	8 749	31 570	2000	Brésil
585	3 335	13 332	733	126 385	13 353	71 896	11 117	30 019	2001	
722	3 660	12 575	732	127 901	12 874	69 904	13 762	31 360	2002	
1 100	3 218	12 183	703	125 910	13 057	65 682	14 180	32 992	2003	
...	219	751	1 417	21 557	3 759	10 504	5 652	1 641	2000	Chili
57	243	641	1 376	21 199	2 860	10 126	6 349	1 864	2001	
2	194	962	1 378	21 483	2 907	10 088	6 494	1 994	2002	
6	372	812	1 413	22 291	2 864	10 319	7 164	1 944	2003	
625	231	2 812	484	20 466	2 698	8 939	6 067	2 762	2000	Colombie
625	231	2 152	489	21 058	2 723	9 173	6 442	2 720	2001	
630	235	1 086	485	21 264	2 445	9 592	6 436	*2 792	2002	
589	221	1 970	470	20 960	2 746	9 163	6 161	2 891	2003	
...	306	1 065	480	6 066	...	5 107	229	730	2000	Equateur
...	257	700	560	7 217	...	6 373	233	610	2001	
...	266	759	564	7 393	...	6 434	236	724	2002	
...	258	658	531	7 084	...	5 981	388	715	2003	
...	...	...	3 972	12	3	9	...	...	2000	Iles Falkland (Malvinas) *
...	...	...	4 387	13	3	10	...	...	2001	
...	...	...	4 387	13	3	10	...	...	2002	
...	...	...	4 725	14	3	11	...	...	2003	
4	...	...	1 888	310	...	310	...	...	*2000	Guyane française
4	...	...	1 857	316	...	316	...	...	*2001	
*4	...	...	1 837	321	...	321	...	...	2002	
4	...	...	1 778	322	...	322	...	...	*2003	
12	...	...	696	529	...	529	...	*0	2000	Guyana
13	...	...	714	545	...	544	...	*0	2001	
*13	...	...	697	533	...	533	...	1	2002	
13	...	...	705	540	...	540	...	1	*2003	
14	...	-1	300	1 651	...	1 122	...	529	2000	Paraguay
7	...	0	301	1 696	...	1 165	...	531	2001	
20	...	1	308	1 777	...	1 223	...	554	2002	
26	...	1	310	1 836	...	1 269	...	567	2003	
346	...	-345	421	10 791	521	8 148	679	1 444	2000	Pérou
358	...	-97	379	9 980	366	7 336	710	1 569	2001	
201	...	-456	382	10 209	610	7 243	750	1 606	2002	
139	...	-668	387	10 496	525	7 516	805	1 650	2003	
...	...	196	1 458	608	...	495	...	113	2000	Suriname
...	...	198	1 557	652	...	538	...	115	2001	
...	...	162	1 630	686	...	570	...	116	2002	
...	...	138	1 671	707	...	590	...	117	2003	
45	288	36	700	2 324	1	1 653	31	640	2000	Uruguay
49	343	163	638	2 145	1	1 432	29	683	2001	
40	329	66	591	2 001	1	1 309	19	671	2002	
32	316	35	581	1 979	1	1 251	54	673	2003	
279	617	13 215	2 476	60 111	126	17 152	37 430	5 403	2000	Venezuela (Rép. bolivar. du)
260	653	9 600	2 467	61 050	47	20 491	35 314	5 199	2001	
302	569	2 130	2 463	62 150	17	19 972	37 114	5 046	2002	
235	517	8 672	2 209	56 786	10	19 705	31 851	5 220	2003	
24 069	55 504	230 005	722	2 680 650	984 182	972 880	524 684	198 904	2000	Asie
24 721	54 900	233 598	738	2 771 912	1 047 457	972 458	549 417	202 581	2001	
27 204	55 740	259 474	781	2 974 680	1 183 674	998 771	590 034	202 201	2002	
28 173	55 329	277 148	822	3 181 915	1 342 623	1 016 133	626 219	196 940	2003	
*5	...	...	*16	*357	1	*212	*109	*35	2000	Afghanistan
*5	...	...	*12	*261	18	*106	*102	*35	2001	
*5	...	...	*13	*271	15	*119	*102	*36	2002	
*8	...	...	*12	*279	25	*116	*102	*37	2003	

58

Production, trade and consumption of commercial energy — Thousand metric tons of oil equivalent and kilograms per capita *(continued)*

Production, commerce et consommation d'énergie commerciale — Milliers de tonnes d'équivalent pétrole et kilogrammes par habitant *(suite)*

Region, country or area	Year / Année	Primary energy production — Production d'énergie primaire					Changes in stocks / Variations des stocks	Imports / Importations	Exports / Exportations
		Total / Totale	Solids / Solides	Liquids / Liquides	Gas / Gaz	Electricity / Electricité			
Armenia	2000	632	...	...	...	632	...	1 606	70
	2001	602	...	...	...	602	...	1 620	60
	2002	738	...	...	...	738	...	1 323	57
	2003	692	...	...	...	692	...	1 471	50
Azerbaijan	2000	19 436	...	14 043	5 262	132	−82	415	7 614
	2001	20 033	...	14 934	4 987	112	113	3 166	10 677
	2002	20 168	...	15 359	4 635	174	−101	3 778	11 491
	2003	20 239	...	15 407	4 620	212	−3	3 888	10 971
Bahrain	2000	*17 576	...	9 733	*7 843	...	−85	3 523	10 362
	2001	17 929	...	9 513	8 416	...	−365	2 886	10 160
	2002	*18 457	...	9 620	*8 836	...	−549	3 177	9 987
	2003	18 760	...	9 807	*8 953	...	−603	3 286	10 344
Bangladesh	2000	8 385	...	103	8 201	81	−134	3 395	...
	2001	9 369	...	100	9 184	85	30	4 217	...
	2002	9 846	...	93	9 662	92	21	4 210	...
	2003	10 579	...	90	10 393	97	146	4 228	...
Bhutan *	2000	191	35	...	...	156	...	84	144
	2001	198	35	...	...	163	...	87	145
	2002	200	36	...	...	163	...	85	147
	2003	198	35	...	...	163	...	85	149
Brunei Darussalam	2000	21 027	...	10 501	10 526	...	−102	...	18 126
	2001	21 257	...	10 615	10 642	...	15	1	18 299
	2002	21 801	...	11 114	10 687	...	9	9	18 832
	2003	22 626	...	11 105	11 522	...	−30	6	19 941
Cambodia *	2000	4	...	...	...	4	...	177	...
	2001	3	...	...	...	3	...	178	...
	2002	3	...	...	...	3	...	182	...
	2003	3	...	...	...	3	...	178	...
China [3]	2000	716 442	498 501	163 163	31 282	23 496	−4 541	101 115	57 922
	2001	807 232	579 810	164 123	34 880	28 419	79	91 062	72 889
	2002	925 365	689 310	167 167	37 564	31 324	5 105	102 388	72 821
	2003	1 078 416	832 667	169 770	40 272	35 708	4 787	126 046	80 872
China, Hong Kong SAR	2000	...	...	...	...	...	−128	19 758	1 631
	2001	...	...	...	...	...	578	20 432	1 461
	2002	...	...	...	...	...	43	21 064	1 305
	2003	...	...	...	...	...	−64	21 616	1 436
China, Macao SAR	2000	...	...	...	...	...	−13	542	...
	2001	...	...	...	...	...	23	597	...
	2002	...	...	...	...	...	−8	613	...
	2003	...	...	...	...	...	−4	626	0
Cyprus	2000	...	...	...	...	...	18	2 384	...
	2001	...	...	...	...	...	−30	2 413	...
	2002	...	...	...	...	...	22	2 408	...
	2003	...	...	...	...	...	−46	2 557	...
Georgia	2000	680	4	110	62	504	−2	1 756	98
	2001	613	1	99	37	477	−25	1 514	154
	2002	675	4	74	16	582	−43	1 347	112
	2003	723	5	140	17	561	−23	1 500	124
India	2000	259 212	188 433	36 473	23 345	10 960	−2 549	93 539	3 634
	2001	263 934	192 641	36 381	23 354	11 558	−1 798	91 928	6 451
	2002	276 168	202 906	37 361	25 096	10 805	−826	99 130	7 323
	2003	290 272	215 929	37 225	25 689	11 429	976	105 898	11 233
Indonesia	2000	215 048	53 774	88 087	70 048	3 140	−3 313	22 130	114 759
	2001	221 550	64 754	85 851	67 631	3 314	−7 027	26 109	125 654
	2002	232 619	72 142	84 041	73 267	*3 168	*−1 076	27 879	120 612
	2003	235 096	76 525	78 631	76 615	3 326	−571	28 068	129 943
Iran (Islamic Rep. of)	2000	253 089	976	196 708	54 981	424	...	5 403	146 765
	2001	242 132	966	183 367	57 364	435	232	7 185	130 475
	2002	245 661	860	179 069	65 036	695	−138	8 679	111 820
	2003	275 247	843	200 527	72 923	954	−132	10 571	136 408

Production, trade and consumption of commercial energy—Thousand metric tons of oil equivalent and kilograms per capita (*continued*)

Production, commerce et consommation d'énergie commerciale—Milliers de tonnes d'équivalent pétrole et kilogrammes par habitant (*suite*)

Bunkers — Soutes			Consumption — Consommation							
Air Avion	Sea Maritime	Unallocated Non distribué	Per capita Par habitant	Total Totale	Solids Solides	Liquids Liquides	Gas Gaz	Electricity Electricité	Year Année	Région, pays ou zone
63	...	...	629	2 105	...	267	1 246	592	2000	Arménie
60	...	...	631	2 102	...	263	1 269	570	2001	
60	...	...	585	1 944	13	271	953	708	2002	
27	...	...	549	2 086	19	316	1 082	668	2003	
121	...	1 020	1 389	11 179	...	5 457	5 548	174	2000	Azerbaïdjan
222	...	730	1 415	11 457	...	3 234	8 053	170	2001	
271	...	839	1 407	11 445	...	3 072	8 075	298	2002	
338	...	506	1 517	12 315	...	3 683	8 285	347	2003	
365	...	1 763	*13 626	*8 694	...	850	*7 843	...	2000	Bahreïn
353	...	1 271	14 344	9 395	...	980	8 416	...	2001	
426	...	2 025	*14 501	*9 745	...	908	*8 836	...	2002	
477	...	1 903	*14 405	*9 925	...	972	*8 953	...	2003	
123	36	617	81	11 139	330	2 526	8 201	81	2000	Bangladesh
202	36	598	90	12 721	350	3 102	9 184	85	2001	
209	36	497	92	13 292	350	3 189	9 662	92	2002	
236	36	480	103	13 910	350	3 070	10 393	97	2003	
...	...	...	65	131	46	48	...	36	2000	Bhoutan *
...	...	...	68	140	46	50	...	44	2001	
...	...	...	66	138	43	53	...	42	2002	
...	...	...	59	134	42	49	...	42	2003	
...	...	530	7 607	2 472	...	1 005	1 468	...	2000	Brunéi Darussalam
...	...	*527	7 213	2 416	...	1 014	1 402	...	2001	
...	...	*554	7 081	2 414	...	1 038	1 376	...	2002	
...	...	481	6 458	2 241	...	841	1 400	...	2003	
...	...	...	14	180	...	177	...	4	2000	Cambodge *
...	...	...	14	180	...	178	...	3	2001	
...	...	...	14	185	...	182	...	3	2002	
...	...	...	13	181	...	178	...	3	2003	
...	4 161	51 387	556	708 628	481 624	172 942	31 282	22 779	2000	Chine [3]
...	4 285	51 186	599	769 855	530 534	176 743	34 880	27 697	2001	
...	4 324	58 086	685	887 417	637 715	183 589	35 425	30 687	2002	
...	2 842	64 950	796	1 051 011	776 193	200 847	38 896	35 075	2003	
2 100	3 407	...	1 913	12 748	3 816	5 924	2 232	776	2000	Chine, Hong Kong RAS
2 461	3 777	...	1 807	12 155	3 994	5 153	2 253	755	2001	
3 179	4 997	...	1 700	11 540	4 479	4 232	2 140	689	2002	
2 874	5 410	...	1 702	11 960	5 743	4 205	1 376	635	2003	
...	...	...	1 288	555	...	538	...	17	2000	Chine, Macao RAS
...	...	...	1 323	574	...	558	...	17	2001	
...	...	...	1 418	621	...	604	...	17	2002	
...	...	...	1 430	631	...	615	...	15	2003	
277	192	16	2 721	1 880	37	1 844	...	...	2000	Chypre
337	191	35	2 692	1 879	40	1 839	...	...	2001	
304	138	45	2 689	1 899	41	1 858	...	...	2002	
330	124	37	2 953	2 111	40	2 072	...	...	2003	
26	...	4	439	2 312	16	711	1 060	525	2000	Géorgie
10	...	13	378	1 975	14	559	903	499	2001	
13	...	14	372	1 925	14	535	755	621	2002	
13	...	54	401	2 055	30	527	858	640	2003	
702	...	31 813	314	319 150	203 840	80 893	23 345	11 072	2000	Inde
*707	...	30 010	310	320 492	206 686	78 777	23 354	11 675	2001	
*273	...	35 715	317	332 812	216 857	79 938	25 096	10 920	2002	
*1 135	...	36 496	324	346 330	227 655	81 413	25 689	11 574	2003	
420	77	25 232	475	100 003	13 852	49 554	33 458	3 140	2000	Indonésie
480	77	29 419	475	99 055	18 123	45 699	31 919	3 314	2001	
539	77	33 352	507	106 994	21 013	44 690	38 123	*3 168	2002	
*527	*17	29 496	472	103 751	14 272	46 282	39 871	3 326	2003	
887	638	-10 858	1 902	121 061	1 764	60 862	58 073	361	2000	Iran (Rép. islamique d')
905	639	*247	1 810	116 818	1 226	53 909	61 274	409	2001	
*803	606	*6 820	2 051	134 430	1 301	63 615	68 803	711	2002	
*774	585	*7 148	2 122	141 034	1 260	63 667	75 103	1 003	2003	

Production, trade and consumption of commercial energy—Thousand metric tons of oil equivalent and kilograms per capita (*continued*)

Production, commerce et consommation d'énergie commerciale—Milliers de tonnes d'équivalent pétrole et kilogrammes par habitant (*suite*)

Region, country or area	Year Année	Primary energy production — Production d'énergie primaire					Changes in stocks Variations des stocks	Imports Importations	Exports Exportations
		Total Totale	Solids Solides	Liquids Liquides	Gas Gaz	Electricity Electricité			
Iraq	2000	130 029	...	127 116	2 861	53	...	52	105 036
	2001	119 499	...	116 940	2 507	53	...	16	91 481
	2002	102 072	...	99 928	2 089	56	...	...	72 440
	2003	67 148	...	65 693	1 417	37	...	...	41 777
Israel	2000	100	86	4	9	1	−774	21 982	3 298
	2001	105	91	4	9	1	143	22 340	2 834
	2002	117	101	5	8	3	−429	22 670	2 788
	2003	110	96	3	8	3	*−527	22 772	3 092
Japan	2000	100 051	1 719	620	2 443	95 270	3 541	416 840	5 062
	2001	99 395	1 860	595	2 410	94 529	−2 765	405 109	5 434
	2002	91 151	...	608	2 690	87 852	−1 406	412 262	4 953
	2003	78 087	...	670	2 751	74 667	−448	423 596	4 697
Jordan	2000	221	...	2	216	3	−106	4 778	0
	2001	235	...	2	229	4	97	4 878	0
	2002	222	...	2	215	5	1	5 059	0
	2003	249	...	2	244	4	−23	5 244	0
Kazakhstan	2000	79 399	31 840	35 716	11 195	648	−305	6 721	42 030
	2001	84 941	32 971	40 446	10 829	695	43	7 879	47 844
	2002	97 271	35 625	47 722	13 159	765	41	12 250	52 251
	2003	107 302	39 104	51 976	15 480	742	39	12 570	62 970
Korea, Dem. P. R.	2000	19 669	18 792	...	...	877	38	1 253	252
	2001	20 205	19 293	...	...	912	106	1 498	210
	2002	19 204	18 291	...	...	913	106	1 487	210
	2003	19 633	18 625	...	...	1 008	103	1 490	210
Korea, Republic of	2000	30 789	1 867	...	...	28 922	3 543	192 500	34 613
	2001	31 341	1 717	...	...	29 624	2 222	191 280	32 813
	2002	33 035	1 493	...	...	31 543	3 112	188 527	25 067
	2003	35 920	1 484	...	...	34 437	5 401	190 833	22 762
Kuwait [4]	2000	116 875	...	108 379	8 495	...	...	398	84 549
	2001	114 679	...	106 367	8 313	...	...	261	82 724
	2002	108 296	...	100 842	7 455	...	...	483	76 732
	2003	123 677	...	114 991	8 686	...	...	589	86 434
Kyrgyzstan	2000	1 416	133	77	30	1 177	−42	1 289	278
	2001	1 323	147	76	31	1 069	−56	1 075	217
	2002	1 174	143	76	28	928	−28	1 591	236
	2003	1 336	123	69	25	1 119	−23	1 630	303
Lao People's Dem. Rep. *	2000	260	158	...	...	102	...	140	61
	2001	300	196	...	...	104	...	143	63
	2002	307	200	...	...	107	...	144	64
	2003	307	200	...	...	108	...	144	65
Lebanon	2000	76	...	...	...	76	−13	4 851	...
	2001	*72	...	...	...	*72	−36	5 184	...
	2002	106	...	...	...	106	−15	5 100	...
	2003	69	...	...	...	69	...	5 909	...
Malaysia	2000	*76 854	242	33 415	*42 559	638	289	16 396	42 011
	2001	*77 643	344	35 329	*41 417	553	−488	18 741	42 979
	2002	*80 979	223	37 581	*42 719	456	734	17 779	43 599
	2003	*84 451	107	39 140	*44 710	495	−587	19 993	45 862
Maldives	2000	...	...	...	...	...	...	227	61
	2001	...	...	...	...	...	...	374	*67
	2002	...	...	...	...	...	...	423	*80
	2003	...	...	...	...	...	...	225	*78
Mongolia	2000	1 548	1 548	...	...	...	...	489	0
	2001	1 626	1 626	...	...	...	...	525	2
	2002	1 742	1 742	...	...	...	...	496	1
	2003	1 742	1 742	...	...	...	...	524	101
Myanmar	2000	6 853	358	577	5 755	163	−70	1 425	4 740
	2001	7 074	412	674	5 832	157	17	1 148	5 113
	2002	7 465	344	883	6 046	192	−272	963	5 220
	2003	*9 121	609	984	*7 335	194	−92	922	6 361

Production, trade and consumption of commercial energy—Thousand metric tons of oil equivalent and kilograms per capita (*continued*)

Production, commerce et consommation d'énergie commerciale—Milliers de tonnes d'équivalent pétrole et kilogrammes par habitant (*suite*)

Bunkers — Soutes			Consumption — Consommation							
Air Avion	Sea Maritime	Unallocated Non distribué	Per capita Par habitant	Total Totale	Solids Solides	Liquids Liquides	Gas Gaz	Electricity Electricité	Year Année	Région, pays ou zone
485	...	-556	1 082	25 116	...	22 203	2 861	53	2000	Iraq
527	...	1 256	1 100	26 251	...	23 691	2 507	53	2001	
516	...	3 911	1 028	25 206	...	23 061	2 089	56	2002	
418	...	2 726	884	22 226	...	20 772	1 417	37	2003	
4	187	271	3 036	19 096	7 500	11 711	9	-124	2000	Israël
4	177	-558	3 082	19 844	8 132	11 823	9	-119	2001	
4	269	-294	3 112	20 447	8 828	11 728	8	-117	2002	
*4	272	68	2 985	19 973	8 963	11 126	8	-124	2003	
6 417	5 229	20 685	3 752	475 959	106 413	201 425	72 850	95 270	2000	Japon
6 166	4 570	17 074	3 729	474 025	109 222	196 569	73 705	94 529	2001	
6 989	5 091	13 490	3 723	474 297	112 948	199 702	73 794	87 852	2002	
6 721	5 129	19 793	3 653	465 790	116 752	195 462	78 910	74 667	2003	
251	11	77	946	4 766	...	4 543	216	7	2000	Jordanie
221	2	115	903	4 677	...	4 422	229	26	2001	
223	...	95	931	4 962	...	4 715	215	32	2002	
184	...	95	956	5 238	...	4 963	244	31	2003	
208	...	5 512	2 596	38 675	21 161	6 349	10 260	905	2000	Kazakhstan
163	...	5 840	2 625	38 930	20 936	7 489	9 655	850	2001	
171	...	6 794	3 383	50 264	26 194	8 057	15 116	898	2002	
184	...	7 065	3 274	49 615	28 866	6 809	13 324	615	2003	
...	...	12	926	20 621	18 730	1 014	...	877	2000	Corée, R. p. dém. de
...	...	17	954	21 369	19 339	1 119	...	912	2001	
...	...	17	903	20 359	18 323	1 122	...	913	2002	
...	...	15	918	20 795	18 662	1 125	...	1 008	2003	
568	6 264	22 994	3 285	155 307	42 979	64 909	18 497	28 922	2000	Corée, République de
654	6 146	21 379	3 367	159 407	45 592	64 214	19 977	29 624	2001	
923	5 862	19 648	3 504	166 951	48 640	64 450	22 318	31 543	2002	
1 201	6 542	19 855	3 561	170 992	49 904	63 247	23 405	34 437	2003	
378	481	12 806	8 703	19 059	...	10 563	8 495	...	2000	Koweït [4]
404	414	12 518	8 318	18 881	...	10 569	8 313	...	2001	
465	538	12 774	7 775	18 270	...	10 816	7 455	...	2002	
717	556	15 077	8 840	21 481	...	12 795	8 686	...	2003	
...	...	4	502	2 466	460	435	638	933	2000	Kirghizistan
...	...	-2	452	2 239	290	386	652	910	2001	
...	...	2	512	2 555	491	368	826	869	2002	
...	...	4	522	2 683	579	443	682	980	2003	
...	...	...	65	339	158	123	...	57	2000	Rép. dém. pop. lao *
...	...	...	70	380	196	127	...	56	2001	
...	...	...	70	386	200	126	...	60	2002	
...	...	...	68	387	200	125	...	62	2003	
129	15	...	1 372	4 796	141	4 459	...	196	2000	Liban
132	15	...	1 455	5 145	141	4 824	...	180	2001	
129	15	...	1 412	5 077	141	4 784	...	152	2002	
*129	...	...	1 569	5 848	141	5 639	...	69	2003	
1 573	212	2 961	*1 986	*46 203	2 307	19 126	*24 132	638	2000	Malaisie
1 764	153	5 079	*1 996	*46 898	2 909	19 832	*23 603	553	2001	
1 786	90	4 322	*2 012	*48 227	3 676	20 277	*23 818	456	2002	
1 854	71	7 479	*2 028	*49 766	5 336	19 592	*24 343	495	2003	
...	...	...	613	166	...	166	...	...	2000	Maldives
...	...	...	1 111	307	...	307	...	...	2001	
...	...	...	1 218	342	...	342	...	...	2002	
...	...	...	510	147	...	147	...	...	2003	
...	...	...	846	2 037	1 578	444	...	16	2000	Mongolie
...	...	...	880	2 150	1 633	501	...	15	2001	
...	...	...	904	2 236	1 742	482	...	13	2002	
...	...	...	835	2 165	1 642	509	...	14	2003	
64	2	243	69	3 300	43	1 763	1 331	163	2000	Myanmar
69	3	346	55	2 673	49	1 386	1 081	157	2001	
72	2	492	60	2 914	52	1 552	1 118	192	2002	
82	3	155	*71	*3 534	97	1 759	*1 485	194	2003	

Production, trade and consumption of commercial energy — Thousand metric tons of oil equivalent and kilograms per capita (*continued*)

Production, commerce et consommation d'énergie commerciale — Milliers de tonnes d'équivalent pétrole et kilogrammes par habitant (*suite*)

| Region, country or area | Year Année | Primary energy production — Production d'énergie primaire |||||| Changes in stocks Variations des stocks | Imports Importations | Exports Exportations |
		Total Totale	Solids Solides	Liquids Liquides	Gas Gaz	Electricity Electricité			
Nepal	2000	152	12	...	...	140	...	1 011	11
	2001	166	7	...	...	159	...	1 069	12
	2002	191	8	...	...	182	...	866	16
	2003	202	8	...	...	195	...	932	18
Oman	2000	56 686	...	47 750	8 936	...	−935	179	49 378
	2001	61 574	...	47 880	13 694	...	−1 233	301	53 620
	2002	60 042	...	44 993	15 049	...	−1 263	385	50 027
	2003	57 647	...	41 119	16 528	...	−1 564	381	47 198
Pakistan	2000	24 302	1 498	2 893	18 148	1 763	...	16 973	356
	2001	25 562	1 464	2 969	19 130	2 000	...	17 756	433
	2002	27 072	1 574	3 276	19 995	2 227	...	16 898	239
	2003	28 701	1 566	3 312	21 446	2 376	...	16 741	240
Philippines	2000	11 375	640	55	10	10 671	116	22 674	975
	2001	10 363	581	63	126	9 593	−518	21 697	571
	2002	12 060	786	273	1 586	9 414	*−411	20 496	963
	2003	13 062	869	651	2 417	9 125	116	20 179	881
Qatar	2000	60 870	...	35 379	25 491	...	−1 322	...	46 418
	2001	65 390	...	39 109	26 281	...	−574	...	48 180
	2002	69 106	...	40 246	28 860	...	1 868	...	48 238
	2003	71 182	...	41 018	30 164	...	2 601	...	49 522
Saudi Arabia [4]	2000	486 693	...	443 850	42 843	...	...	...	366 308
	2001	477 945	...	429 110	48 835	...	−54	604	349 137
	2002	439 974	...	391 412	48 562	...	1 516	1 036	306 018
	2003	518 200	...	463 654	54 546	...	264	122	372 882
Singapore	2000	...	...	...	...	...	609	80 566	35 295
	2001	...	...	...	...	...	1 728	84 145	35 556
	2002	...	...	...	...	...	85	86 064	38 474
	2003	...	...	...	...	...	−3 077	84 547	41 819
Sri Lanka	2000	275	...	...	...	275	103	3 837	...
	2001	268	...	...	...	268	−45	3 567	...
	2002	232	...	...	...	232	76	3 898	...
	2003	285	...	...	...	285	−104	3 510	...
Syrian Arab Republic	2000	34 187	...	28 413	*5 496	278	...	1 898	17 720
	2001	34 453	...	29 123	*5 037	293	...	4 345	20 897
	2002	37 745	...	31 317	*6 127	301	...	1 528	20 083
	2003	34 655	...	28 152	*6 262	241	*11	1 185	16 999
Tajikistan	2000	1 262	12	18	36	1 197	...	1 952	341
	2001	1 274	12	18	36	1 208	...	2 034	353
	2002	1 355	27	16	27	1 285	...	2 144	337
	2003	1 460	26	18	30	1 386	...	2 039	398
Thailand	2000	30 897	7 790	7 287	15 301	520	−1 514	40 502	6 805
	2001	33 317	8 630	7 731	16 413	543	−335	45 898	7 435
	2002	34 960	8 623	8 576	17 117	644	−1 364	48 100	8 092
	2003	35 938	8 289	10 116	16 904	629	−938	52 235	7 873
Timor-Leste *	2002	7 315	...	7 315	...	...	...	53	7 245
	2003	7 315	...	7 315	...	...	...	53	7 245
Turkey	2000	19 738	13 665	2 765	585	2 724	−399	53 606	636
	2001	18 418	13 462	2 523	286	2 148	−222	50 177	1 448
	2002	17 545	11 785	2 422	346	2 991	−223	55 629	2 251
	2003	16 520	10 534	2 353	513	3 120	437	62 833	3 729
Turkmenistan	2000	50 266	...	7 779	42 486	0	...	87	34 889
	2001	55 143	...	8 688	46 455	0	...	87	38 255
	2002	58 540	...	10 183	48 356	0	...	87	40 624
	2003	63 972	...	10 399	53 572	0	...	87	45 373
United Arab Emirates	2000	160 497	...	125 018	35 479	...	...	8 261	110 029
	2001	157 096	...	122 045	35 051	...	...	6 260	103 688
	2002	152 618	...	113 978	38 640	...	...	5 215	93 977
	2003	169 405	...	129 518	39 887	...	...	4 353	107 800

Production, trade and consumption of commercial energy — Thousand metric tons of oil equivalent and kilograms per capita (*continued*)

Production, commerce et consommation d'énergie commerciale — Milliers de tonnes d'équivalent pétrole et kilogrammes par habitant (*suite*)

Bunkers — Soutes			Consumption — Consommation							
Air Avion	Sea Maritime	Unallocated Non distribué	Per capita Par habitant	Total Totale	Solids Solides	Liquids Liquides	Gas Gaz	Electricity Electricité	Year Année	Région, pays ou zone
53	...	...	48	1 100	301	650	...	149	2000	Népal
38	...	...	50	1 184	344	673	...	167	2001	
43	...	...	41	997	160	659	...	179	2002	
40	...	...	44	1 077	204	683	...	190	2003	
212	62	-32	3 229	8 180	...	2 822	5 358	...	2000	Oman
261	50	177	3 433	9 000	...	3 105	5 895	...	2001	
369	34	246	4 059	11 013	...	3 587	7 426	...	2002	
369	1	418	4 134	11 605	...	3 555	8 050	...	2003	
126	16	747	283	40 030	2 161	17 958	18 148	1 763	2000	Pakistan
120	24	1 302	291	41 439	2 122	18 188	19 130	2 000	2001	
164	13	1 257	284	42 297	2 323	17 752	19 995	2 227	2002	
285	42	1 513	282	43 361	2 659	16 879	21 446	2 376	2003	
536	210	2 053	395	30 160	4 182	15 298	10	10 671	2000	Philippines
596	217	1 816	377	29 378	4 196	15 463	126	9 593	2001	
610	226	*473	386	30 696	4 125	15 570	1 586	9 414	2002	
588	185	1 627	370	29 843	3 949	14 352	2 417	9 125	2003	
...	...	9	26 722	15 766	...	3 967	11 800	...	2000	Qatar
...	...	31	29 588	17 753	...	5 797	11 956	...	2001	
...	...	-31	31 198	19 031	...	6 889	12 142	...	2002	
...	...	-52	30 825	19 111	...	6 636	12 475	...	2003	
2 484	2 118	16 893	4 743	98 890	...	56 048	42 843	...	2000	Arabie saoudite [4]
2 498	2 150	6 636	5 512	118 182	...	69 346	48 835	...	2001	
2 546	2 200	9 160	5 425	119 571	...	71 009	48 562	...	2002	
2 593	2 216	10 976	5 708	129 389	...	74 843	54 546	...	2003	
1 282	18 520	11 765	3 158	13 094	...	11 778	1 316	...	2000	Singapour
*1 282	20 215	11 716	3 290	13 649	...	11 663	1 986	...	2001	
*1 238	19 962	12 621	3 292	13 684	...	10 460	3 223	...	2002	
*1 259	20 658	9 667	3 255	14 220	...	9 234	4 986	...	2003	
105	159	195	183	3 551	1	3 274	...	275	2000	Sri Lanka
68	154	137	188	3 521	1	3 253	...	268	2001	
100	158	126	193	3 670	1	3 436	...	232	2002	
114	114	160	184	3 512	68	3 159	...	285	2003	
135	...	1 448	1 028	16 782	3	11 005	*5 496	278	2000	Rép. arabe syrienne
95	...	1 417	980	16 389	3	11 056	*5 037	293	2001	
*109	...	1 757	1 011	17 324	2	10 894	*6 127	301	2002	
*100	...	1 959	956	16 772	...	10 268	*6 262	241	2003	
5	...	13	461	2 855	58	788	698	1 311	2000	Tadjikistan
5	...	13	479	2 937	58	1 005	549	1 324	2001	
4	...	12	498	3 145	73	1 022	698	1 353	2002	
4	...	15	493	3 081	72	1 111	511	1 387	2003	
...	...	4 831	992	61 277	11 090	32 209	17 220	758	2000	Thaïlande
...	...	4 393	1 079	67 723	12 744	32 150	22 060	768	2001	
...	...	5 261	1 120	71 071	12 768	33 853	23 586	863	2002	
...	...	7 423	1 175	73 814	13 281	35 802	23 914	817	2003	
...	...	70	56	53	...	53	...	...	2002	Timor-Leste *
...	...	70	54	53	...	53	...	...	2003	
523	406	4 113	1 010	68 066	24 230	26 773	14 051	3 012	2000	Turquie
521	237	4 052	913	62 558	20 311	24 875	14 867	2 504	2001	
867	537	3 328	954	66 414	20 525	26 244	16 383	3 262	2002	
904	626	3 091	989	70 567	22 067	25 628	19 702	3 169	2003	
...	...	682	3 121	14 782	...	2 729	12 122	-68	2000	Turkménistan
...	...	1 021	3 380	15 954	...	3 276	12 768	-90	2001	
...	...	1 292	3 486	16 710	...	3 351	13 449	-91	2002	
...	...	964	3 641	17 722	...	3 543	14 271	-92	2003	
1 006	9 466	12 298	12 357	35 958	...	6 775	29 183	...	2000	Emirats arabes unis
988	8 722	14 113	12 029	35 845	...	7 099	28 746	...	2001	
1 271	7 980	14 599	13 116	40 005	...	7 733	32 273	...	2002	
1 302	6 738	15 904	13 466	42 013	...	8 494	33 519	...	2003	

Production, trade and consumption of commercial energy— Thousand metric tons of oil equivalent and kilograms per capita (*continued*)

Production, commerce et consommation d'énergie commerciale— Milliers de tonnes d'équivalent pétrole et kilogrammes par habitant (*suite*)

Region, country or area	Year Année	Primary energy production — Production d'énergie primaire					Changes in stocks Variations des stocks	Imports Importations	Exports Exportations
		Total Totale	Solids Solides	Liquids Liquides	Gas Gaz	Electricity Electricité			
Uzbekistan	2000	60 099	706	7 814	51 074	505	16	1 213	6 521
	2001	60 718	732	7 482	51 991	512	17	1 164	6 616
	2002	60 938	666	7 354	52 373	545	16	991	5 467
	2003	60 880	512	7 871	51 951	546	12	991	4 694
Viet Nam	2000	27 819	8 126	16 625	1 245	1 823	1 234	8 782	18 842
	2001	29 650	9 073	17 201	1 247	2 129	−210	9 125	20 548
	2002	33 027	11 130	17 183	2 573	2 141	...	10 111	21 504
	2003	34 061	11 690	17 148	3 011	2 212	...	10 437	21 588
Yemen	2000	21 434	...	21 434	...	...	...	1 984	18 147
	2001	21 505	...	21 505	...	...	63	1 551	17 208
	2002	21 639	...	21 639	...	...	420	2 007	17 457
	2003	21 320	...	21 320	...	...	568	2 425	17 082
Europe	2000	2 226 586	358 502	662 129	823 712	382 243	6 966	1 392 058	1 015 667
	2001	2 258 834	360 561	678 043	826 242	393 988	−3 739	1 423 329	1 034 065
	2002	2 304 806	354 660	710 338	845 556	394 251	10 399	1 442 339	1 095 098
	2003	2 368 782	364 400	736 195	871 557	396 630	7 622	1 489 624	1 149 236
Albania	2000	732	9	317	10	395	...	634	19
	2001	632	7	311	8	306	...	778	6
	2002	729	20	393	13	302	...	914	79
	2003	854	21	375	13	445	...	861	34
Austria	2000	6 860	325	1 083	1 704	3 747	−124	21 859	2 557
	2001	6 582	314	1 019	1 635	3 613	−1 004	23 212	2 987
	2002	6 827	368	1 050	1 776	3 633	0	24 407	2 975
	2003	6 630	300	1 021	1 974	3 335	−114	26 596	3 262
Belarus	2000	2 554	462	1 853	237	2	94	29 930	7 311
	2001	2 546	454	1 854	235	3	−17	29 305	6 654
	2002	2 579	502	1 848	227	2	155	31 986	8 887
	2003	2 470	411	1 822	234	2	−190	33 883	9 878
Belgium	2000	12 945	226	...	2	12 716	−547	73 367	23 302
	2001	12 373	131	...	...	12 242	788	73 902	22 044
	2002	12 598	104	...	...	12 494	−724	72 879	23 353
	2003	12 564	78	...	...	12 487	1	76 959	23 222
Bosnia and Herzegovina	2000	4 587	4 148	...	...	438	...	1 248	221
	2001	4 110	3 672	...	...	438	−536	1 256	202
	2002	4 638	4 185	...	...	453	283	1 304	183
	2003	4 299	3 835	...	...	465	−96	1 437	272
Bulgaria	2000	9 436	4 382	42	14	4 998	−135	11 256	2 565
	2001	9 752	4 407	34	20	5 290	−206	11 787	2 761
	2002	9 892	4 326	37	18	5 510	493	11 233	2 349
	2003	9 346	4 513	30	14	4 788	−326	11 278	2 089
Croatia	2000	3 559	...	1 546	1 506	507	−89	6 000	1 510
	2001	3 813	...	1 421	1 826	566	−114	6 147	1 645
	2002	3 776	...	1 383	1 926	467	364	7 018	1 637
	2003	3 731	...	1 318	1 989	424	−128	7 170	1 795
Czech Republic	2000	27 899	23 741	175	188	3 794	−1 089	18 258	7 414
	2001	28 485	24 105	183	136	4 062	−365	19 374	7 603
	2002	28 618	23 090	265	128	5 135	16	19 523	7 637
	2003	30 389	23 019	317	146	6 907	−16	19 791	7 744
Denmark	2000	26 405	...	17 798	8 240	367	−386	13 065	21 971
	2001	25 715	...	16 904	8 438	373	−89	12 526	20 135
	2002	27 037	...	18 161	8 453	422	−648	11 965	21 934
	2003	26 649	...	18 161	8 008	480	−152	14 109	21 721
Estonia	2000	2 724	2 724	...	...	0	−13	2 026	170
	2001	2 748	2 748	...	...	1	−125	2 023	150
	2002	2 951	2 950	...	...	1	27	1 827	177
	2003	3 440	3 439	...	...	1	86	1 975	253
Faeroe Islands	2000	7	...	...	...	7	...	*215	...
	2001	7	...	...	...	7	...	*215	...
	2002	8	...	...	...	8	...	*217	...
	2003	8	...	...	...	8	...	*219	...

58 **Production, trade and consumption of commercial energy**—Thousand metric tons of oil equivalent and kilograms per capita (*continued*)

Production, commerce et consommation d'énergie commerciale—Milliers de tonnes d'équivalent pétrole et kilogrammes par habitant (*suite*)

Bunkers — Soutes			Consumption — Consommation							
Air Avion	Sea Maritime	Unallocated Non distribué	Per capita Par habitant	Total Totale	Solids Solides	Liquids Liquides	Gas Gaz	Electricity Electricité	Year Année	Région, pays ou zone
...	...	1 708	2 144	53 067	689	5 805	45 958	615	2000	Ouzbékistan
...	...	1 490	2 153	53 758	714	5 701	46 788	555	2001	
...	...	1 590	2 162	54 856	650	5 488	48 180	538	2002	
...	...	1 273	2 142	55 892	499	6 281	48 573	539	2003	
101	...	58	211	16 365	5 466	7 832	1 245	1 823	2000	Viet Nam
148	...	165	229	18 126	6 280	8 469	1 247	2 129	2001	
172	...	187	267	21 275	6 896	9 665	2 573	2 141	2002	
159	...	199	277	22 553	7 280	10 049	3 011	2 212	2003	
124	97	1 391	209	3 660	...	3 660	...	...	2000	Yémen
113	85	1 661	217	3 927	...	3 927	...	...	2001	
105	117	1 424	220	4 122	...	4 122	...	...	2002	
94	126	1 342	234	4 533	...	4 533	...	...	2003	
48 722	45 622	67 452	2 837	2 434 215	467 757	695 137	889 796	381 524	2000	Europe
47 717	47 091	67 569	2 906	2 489 460	466 621	718 435	910 611	393 793	2001	
47 145	48 019	63 438	2 900	2 483 045	461 638	713 047	914 001	394 359	2002	
48 424	48 433	70 519	2 960	2 534 173	476 338	708 525	952 327	396 983	2003	
41	...	150	333	1 156	19	645	10	481	2000	Albanie
44	...	142	349	1 218	22	731	8	456	2001	
44	...	188	380	1 332	23	813	13	483	2002	
49	...	214	402	1 418	23	858	13	523	2003	
554	...	685	3 130	25 047	3 624	10 546	7 248	3 629	2000	Autriche
540	...	882	3 290	26 390	3 754	11 323	7 681	3 632	2001	
499	...	1 049	3 323	26 710	3 806	11 443	7 768	3 693	2002	
428	...	1 153	3 532	28 496	3 994	12 285	8 399	3 817	2003	
...	...	2 071	2 300	23 007	901	5 630	15 854	622	2000	Bélarus
...	...	2 341	2 293	22 873	755	5 334	16 070	714	2001	
...	...	2 850	2 285	22 674	674	5 073	16 360	566	2002	
...	...	3 460	2 350	23 205	648	4 938	17 029	590	2003	
1 483	5 508	3 921	5 142	52 645	8 391	16 302	14 864	13 089	2000	Belgique
1 122	5 384	2 933	5 262	54 005	7 929	18 397	14 654	13 025	2001	
*1 187	7 034	3 687	4 941	50 941	6 711	16 210	14 874	13 147	2002	
1 478	7 097	4 716	5 119	53 010	6 256	17 704	16 013	13 038	2003	
...	...	...	1 506	5 613	4 148	860	258	347	2000	Bosnie-Herzégovine
...	...	...	1 505	5 699	4 208	877	270	344	2001	
...	...	...	1 431	5 475	3 901	936	280	357	2002	
...	...	...	1 451	5 561	3 931	971	292	366	2003	
80	65	794	2 120	17 322	6 332	3 129	3 260	4 601	2000	Bulgarie
104	97	532	2 306	18 251	7 078	3 434	3 045	4 695	2001	
125	107	766	2 197	17 287	6 413	3 231	2 673	4 969	2002	
160	139	1 053	2 238	17 509	7 209	3 203	2 780	4 316	2003	
33	18	571	1 716	7 516	475	3 733	2 456	851	2000	Croatie
21	29	517	1 772	7 863	529	3 922	2 574	838	2001	
20	24	437	1 871	8 312	654	4 252	2 635	770	2002	
24	22	165	2 032	9 024	764	4 881	2 620	759	2003	
160	...	1 284	3 735	38 388	21 113	6 004	8 339	2 932	2000	République tchèque
135	...	1 368	3 810	39 118	20 570	6 377	8 930	3 241	2001	
168	...	1 656	3 788	38 664	19 658	6 220	8 630	4 156	2002	
203	...	1 653	3 978	40 596	20 019	6 345	8 719	5 513	2003	
785	1 353	-357	3 021	16 104	3 927	6 806	4 946	424	2000	Danemark
800	1 141	-211	3 078	16 465	4 131	6 862	5 149	323	2001	
692	941	-307	3 053	16 389	4 080	6 921	5 145	244	2002	
719	991	-105	3 328	17 584	5 618	7 039	5 182	-255	2003	
20	107	...	3 256	4 467	3 055	756	736	-79	2000	Estonie
17	102	...	3 385	4 627	3 073	817	790	-53	2001	
20	120	...	3 258	4 434	3 010	821	662	-59	2002	
19	*107	...	3 652	4 952	3 537	820	756	-162	2003	
...	...	...	*4 923	*222	...	*215	...	7	2000	Iles Féroé
...	...	...	*4 816	*222	...	*215	...	7	2001	
...	...	...	*4 880	*224	...	*217	...	8	2002	
...	...	...	*4 924	*226	...	*219	...	8	2003	

Production, trade and consumption of commercial energy—Thousand metric tons of oil equivalent and kilograms per capita (*continued*)

Production, commerce et consommation d'énergie commerciale—Milliers de tonnes d'équivalent pétrole et kilogrammes par habitant (*suite*)

Region, country or area	Year Année	Primary energy production — Production d'énergie primaire					Changes in stocks Variations des stocks	Imports Importations	Exports Exportations
		Total Totale	Solids Solides	Liquids Liquides	Gas Gaz	Electricity Electricité			
Finland	2000	8 365	1 231	...	...	7 134	285	22 312	4 776
	2001	8 531	1 446	...	...	7 085	−114	22 372	4 773
	2002	8 962	2 211	...	...	6 751	−1 114	23 145	5 218
	2003	8 615	1 850	...	...	6 766	572	27 107	5 682
France [5]	2000	120 126	2 176	1 687	1 673	114 591	3 631	162 473	26 100
	2001	121 470	1 412	1 653	1 678	116 727	−1 667	160 882	22 951
	2002	124 185	1 306	1 536	*1 612	119 730	2 208	161 571	22 593
	2003	125 028	1 454	1 421	1 425	120 729	−452	166 160	24 631
Germany	2000	126 802	59 236	3 169	17 087	47 309	−4 392	230 285	27 920
	2001	124 938	56 497	3 281	17 196	47 964	−4 026	240 951	26 695
	2002	124 460	56 891	3 513	17 256	46 800	−3 191	235 148	27 243
	2003	123 744	56 034	3 694	17 184	46 833	−1 619	240 115	27 680
Gibraltar	2000	...	...	...	...	...	...	1 155	...
	2001	...	...	...	...	...	...	1 187	...
	2002	...	...	...	...	...	...	1 208	...
	2003	...	...	...	...	...	...	1 239	...
Greece	2000	9 096	8 369	281	47	399	182	25 992	3 173
	2001	9 234	8 691	193	45	305	−78	26 199	3 205
	2002	9 830	9 231	191	47	360	1 019	27 290	3 711
	2003	9 673	8 947	138	34	553	−913	28 502	5 300
Hungary	2000	11 486	2 894	2 122	2 754	3 716	145	16 414	2 114
	2001	11 228	2 869	1 902	2 754	3 703	−790	17 099	2 571
	2002	11 130	2 686	2 167	2 619	3 659	127	18 441	2 821
	2003	10 349	2 743	2 175	2 541	2 889	466	20 090	2 660
Iceland	2000	1 684	...	...	...	1 684	38	910	...
	2001	1 814	...	...	...	1 814	−3	812	...
	2002	1 832	...	...	...	1 832	−24	827	...
	2003	1 819	...	...	...	1 819	−52	801	...
Ireland	2000	2 289	1 065	...	1 065	158	−63	13 678	1 261
	2001	1 848	966	...	732	150	131	15 036	1 338
	2002	1 541	636	...	753	152	−35	15 181	1 481
	2003	1 956	1 220	...	605	132	271	14 876	1 585
Italy [6]	2000	28 791	3	4 592	15 146	9 050	4 561	175 809	19 588
	2001	27 289	88	4 102	13 879	9 220	−2 133	170 738	19 921
	2002	27 759	103	5 541	13 316	8 801	3 652	176 454	19 229
	2003	26 905	157	5 576	12 644	8 529	−2 244	181 198	21 200
Latvia	2000	258	16	...	...	243	−100	2 473	59
	2001	260	16	...	...	244	−226	2 800	40
	2002	245	32	...	...	213	−179	2 789	44
	2003	201	2	...	...	199	80	3 186	9
Lithuania	2000	2 579	10	316	...	2 253	160	7 679	3 275
	2001	3 505	8	471	...	3 026	−149	9 659	5 652
	2002	4 204	11	434	...	3 758	−147	9 387	5 458
	2003	4 519	10	382	...	4 126	129	10 548	6 248
Luxembourg	2000	76	...	...	...	76	49	3 772	81
	2001	78	...	...	...	78	−29	3 856	95
	2002	88	...	...	...	88	16	4 324	270
	2003	81	...	...	...	81	6	4 510	253
Malta	2000	...	...	...	...	...	6	825	...
	2001	...	...	...	...	...	...	755	...
	2002	...	...	...	...	...	...	801	...
	2003	...	...	...	...	...	...	909	...
Netherlands	2000	61 241	...	2 423	57 709	1 109	2 384	117 690	89 799
	2001	65 398	...	2 335	61 944	1 120	166	127 447	103 805
	2002	64 599	...	3 143	60 344	1 112	−933	123 422	102 302
	2003	62 362	...	3 139	58 051	1 172	−356	119 667	98 306
Norway [7]	2000	225 355	424	162 026	50 916	11 990	304	4 819	200 822
	2001	230 046	1 200	164 190	54 432	10 225	−1 989	5 519	205 129
	2002	240 806	1 431	162 420	*65 783	11 172	−43	4 685	210 893
	2003	242 251	1 976	157 451	*73 680	9 143	1 081	5 540	216 354

58

Production, trade and consumption of commercial energy—Thousand metric tons of oil equivalent and kilograms per capita (*continued*)

Production, commerce et consommation d'énergie commerciale—Milliers de tonnes d'équivalent pétrole et kilogrammes par habitant (*suite*)

Bunkers—Soutes			Consumption—Consommation							
Air / Avion	Sea / Maritime	Unallocated / Non distribué	Per capita / Par habitant	Total / Totale	Solids / Solides	Liquids / Liquides	Gas / Gaz	Electricity / Electricité	Year / Année	Région, pays ou zone
346	680	-1 692	5 083	26 282	5 094	9 228	3 805	8 156	2000	Finlande
355	582	-1 909	5 253	27 217	6 226	8 927	4 121	7 942	2001	
351	655	-1 442	5 474	28 439	6 706	9 861	4 096	7 777	2002	
362	650	-1 236	5 703	29 691	8 302	9 665	4 541	7 183	2003	
5 160	3 028	11 156	3 931	233 524	15 098	70 546	39 264	108 615	2000	France [5]
4 644	2 720	11 323	4 061	242 381	12 625	78 121	40 789	110 845	2001	
4 806	2 645	9 076	4 077	244 427	13 654	75 979	41 676	113 117	2002	
5 080	2 852	10 480	4 129	248 598	14 691	75 068	43 786	115 053	2003	
7 105	2 198	6 854	3 863	317 401	83 707	106 714	79 408	47 572	2000	Allemagne
6 927	2 239	7 219	3 973	326 835	85 200	109 803	83 527	48 278	2001	
6 870	2 396	7 925	3 862	318 364	83 131	104 071	83 503	47 660	2002	
6 976	2 640	7 998	3 879	320 185	83 430	102 409	87 549	46 796	2003	
4	1 041	...	3 950	111	...	111	...	...	2000	Gibraltar
4	1 069	...	4 060	114	...	114	...	...	2001	
4	1 088	...	4 131	116	...	116	...	...	2002	
4	1 115	...	4 277	120	...	120	...	...	2003	
818	3 633	-1 136	2 606	28 417	9 181	16 944	1 895	398	2000	Grèce
761	3 528	-864	2 642	28 881	9 604	16 885	1 871	520	2001	
761	3 158	-1 377	2 716	29 849	9 612	17 625	2 003	609	2002	
785	3 237	-1 145	2 806	30 911	9 700	18 226	2 253	733	2003	
220	...	1 496	2 341	23 925	3 464	5 747	10 702	4 012	2000	Hongrie
219	...	1 421	2 442	24 906	3 516	5 506	11 908	3 976	2001	
206	...	975	2 501	25 443	3 429	5 970	12 019	4 025	2002	
202	...	1 326	2 542	25 784	3 520	5 563	13 215	3 486	2003	
133	69	...	8 438	2 354	98	572	...	1 684	2000	Islande
115	47	...	8 719	2 468	92	562	...	1 814	2001	
101	67	...	8 765	2 516	96	587	...	1 832	2002	
103	68	...	8 653	2 501	91	591	...	1 819	2003	
585	152	124	3 682	13 908	2 906	7 016	3 820	167	2000	Irlande
703	163	-42	3 814	14 593	3 019	7 460	3 985	129	2001	
746	150	6	3 686	14 374	2 937	7 152	4 090	195	2002	
731	172	65	3 534	14 008	2 799	6 916	4 061	232	2003	
3 508	2 721	969	3 000	173 253	12 690	83 279	64 420	12 864	2000	Italie [6]
3 410	2 834	-1 052	3 025	175 048	13 529	83 543	64 596	13 380	2001	
3 199	3 001	-1 843	3 054	176 974	14 008	85 656	64 158	13 152	2002	
3 599	3 233	537	3 133	181 778	15 272	83 156	70 438	12 912	2003	
27	...	...	1 152	2 745	113	1 021	1 215	396	2000	Lettonie
27	198	...	1 278	3 021	102	1 101	1 412	406	2001	
28	194	...	1 257	2 948	75	1 022	1 436	415	2002	
36	190	...	1 317	3 072	63	1 085	1 498	426	2003	
27	94	-65	1 927	6 767	109	2 196	2 324	2 138	2000	Lituanie
10	102	-33	2 174	7 581	98	2 384	2 414	2 685	2001	
12	112	169	2 298	7 988	165	2 182	2 441	3 200	2002	
22	111	222	2 407	8 334	211	1 994	2 651	3 478	2003	
322	...	...	7 825	3 396	125	1 957	745	569	2000	Luxembourg
348	...	...	8 018	3 520	110	2 074	772	563	2001	
377	...	...	8 445	3 749	93	2 103	1 171	383	2002	
392	...	...	8 795	3 940	78	2 279	1 183	400	2003	
87	43	...	1 772	689	...	689	...	...	2000	Malte
59	23	...	1 722	673	...	673	...	...	2001	
90	23	...	1 742	688	...	688	...	...	2002	
79	23	...	2 031	806	...	806	...	...	2003	
3 273	13 514	-7 725	4 897	77 687	7 809	28 550	38 592	2 736	2000	Pays-Bas
3 205	14 765	-8 050	4 939	78 953	7 756	29 068	39 522	2 606	2001	
3 340	14 707	-15 842	5 244	84 448	8 245	33 832	39 850	2 521	2002	
3 289	13 771	-15 503	5 096	82 521	8 474	31 389	40 024	2 633	2003	
357	832	3 694	5 395	24 166	1 075	8 727	4 013	10 351	2000	Norvège [7]
362	816	5 160	5 793	26 088	944	8 508	6 104	10 532	2001	
399	670	8 098	*5 631	*25 474	813	7 496	*6 828	10 337	2002	
211	567	2 536	*5 941	*27 042	789	9 348	*7 085	9 820	2003	

Production, trade and consumption of commercial energy—Thousand metric tons of oil equivalent and kilograms per capita *(continued)*

Production, commerce et consommation d'énergie commerciale—Milliers de tonnes d'équivalent pétrole et kilogrammes par habitant *(suite)*

Region, country or area	Year / Année	Primary energy production — Production d'énergie primaire					Changes in stocks / Variations des stocks	Imports / Importations	Exports / Exportations
		Total / Totale	Solids / Solides	Liquids / Liquides	Gas / Gaz	Electricity / Electricité			
Poland	2000	75 804	71 109	654	3 684	357	−606	29 931	18 547
	2001	76 502	71 488	768	3 883	364	−588	31 070	19 370
	2002	76 087	71 049	729	3 968	341	1 158	31 804	19 343
	2003	76 207	71 132	766	4 015	294	325	32 190	18 157
Portugal	2000	1 091	...	...	...	1 091	−275	22 443	1 555
	2001	1 349	...	...	...	1 349	193	22 250	1 289
	2002	824	...	...	...	824	−485	22 744	1 216
	2003	1 501	...	...	...	1 501	492	22 943	1 575
Republic of Moldova	2000	5	...	...	...	5	−7	3 035	...
	2001	6	...	...	...	6	16	3 336	...
	2002	10	...	...	...	10	−14	3 126	1
	2003	6	...	...	...	6	51	3 479	12
Romania	2000	26 332	5 129	6 313	12 195	2 695	−155	11 025	2 767
	2001	26 741	5 788	6 262	11 986	2 705	312	12 688	2 904
	2002	25 969	5 268	6 099	11 784	2 819	262	13 945	4 525
	2003	25 654	5 724	5 915	11 595	2 421	−184	13 909	3 795
Russian Federation	2000	993 407	99 623	322 014	523 381	48 389	5 436	30 098	392 562
	2001	1 021 947	103 615	346 187	521 203	50 942	6 684	22 400	403 831
	2002	1 061 658	99 718	377 550	533 169	51 220	8 016	22 438	446 143
	2003	1 135 400	107 591	419 001	555 725	53 083	12 172	25 555	494 260
Serbia and Montenegro	2000	10 597	7 893	979	693	1 032	...	2 202	161
	2001	10 221	7 745	900	506	1 071	...	4 157	436
	2002	10 417	8 189	813	405	1 011	...	5 131	553
	2003	10 593	8 601	774	371	847	...	5 419	400
Slovakia	2000	6 020	1 068	59	148	4 745	109	15 968	3 614
	2001	6 185	1 003	111	168	4 904	−430	15 887	4 047
	2002	6 423	997	108	161	5 157	113	16 397	4 121
	2003	6 153	907	83	185	4 978	−133	16 413	4 183
Slovenia	2000	2 554	974	1	6	1 572	54	4 222	685
	2001	2 603	899	...	6	1 699	−204	4 053	579
	2002	2 761	1 019	1	5	1 736	−52	4 119	538
	2003	2 685	1 050	...	5	1 630	20	4 406	594
Spain	2000	27 970	7 967	459	165	19 379	1 236	103 893	5 921
	2001	29 629	7 539	583	524	20 983	−454	102 712	5 107
	2002	27 780	7 189	559	519	19 512	2 059	111 781	4 855
	2003	28 575	6 811	510	219	21 035	−90	113 661	5 492
Sweden	2000	21 983	223	...	...	21 760	*39	30 753	11 626
	2001	25 926	263	...	...	25 663	528	30 094	11 051
	2002	23 871	332	...	...	23 539	−1 671	29 701	9 989
	2003	22 576	345	...	...	22 231	1 242	32 850	10 487
Switzerland [8]	2000	10 309	...	...	...	10 309	−406	17 215	3 331
	2001	10 669	...	...	...	10 669	−178	18 568	3 500
	2002	10 285	...	...	...	10 285	39	18 243	3 370
	2003	10 346	...	...	...	10 346	−160	18 094	3 464
TFYR of Macedonia	2000	2 130	2 029	...	...	101	−97	1 271	185
	2001	2 242	2 189	...	...	54	−56	1 147	232
	2002	2 112	2 047	...	...	65	197	1 299	194
	2003	2 111	1 993	...	...	118	−54	1 279	331
Ukraine	2000	73 876	32 246	3 780	16 678	21 172	...	69 042	7 565
	2001	73 588	31 765	3 791	17 101	20 931	...	71 433	8 753
	2002	73 141	30 700	3 822	17 420	21 199	...	76 600	12 762
	2003	77 224	33 210	4 061	17 896	22 057	...	80 753	19 584
United Kingdom	2000	278 652	18 797	128 439	108 464	22 952	−3 262	86 816	121 139
	2001	268 824	19 238	119 586	105 909	24 091	3 014	97 696	112 603
	2002	264 174	18 068	118 576	103 854	23 676	−542	97 067	117 014
	2003	251 866	17 026	108 065	103 005	23 771	−2 096	99 950	106 727
Oceania	2000	252 556	167 982	40 920	37 388	6 267	989	33 352	148 152
	2001	269 221	183 118	41 813	38 368	5 922	−475	34 472	162 043
	2002	273 795	189 921	38 220	39 436	6 218	3 839	34 308	166 115
	2003	271 880	191 084	35 571	39 182	6 043	1 901	35 822	167 457

Production, trade and consumption of commercial energy—Thousand metric tons of oil equivalent and kilograms per capita (*continued*)

Production, commerce et consommation d'énergie commerciale—Milliers de tonnes d'équivalent pétrole et kilogrammes par habitant (*suite*)

Bunkers — Soutes			Consumption — Consommation							
Air Avion	Sea Maritime	Unallocated Non distribué	Per capita Par habitant	Total Totale	Solids Solides	Liquids Liquides	Gas Gaz	Electricity Electricité	Year Année	Région, pays ou zone
370	290	1 354	2 219	85 780	57 769	17 128	11 073	-191	2000	Pologne
349	265	1 441	2 244	86 736	57 750	17 664	11 537	-215	2001	
425	275	2 503	2 179	84 187	56 479	16 731	11 244	-267	2002	
288	289	1 650	2 294	87 688	57 998	17 750	12 520	-580	2003	
572	675	1 269	1 936	19 739	3 892	12 415	2 261	1 171	2000	Portugal
591	482	1 378	1 916	19 665	3 176	12 613	2 507	1 369	2001	
599	491	1 047	2 004	20 700	3 585	13 093	3 035	987	2002	
635	589	1 260	1 911	19 893	3 381	11 840	2 931	1 741	2003	
21	...	...	832	3 026	97	421	2 350	158	2000	République de Moldova
18	...	...	911	3 309	69	464	2 587	189	2001	
19	...	...	864	3 131	73	529	2 295	234	2002	
12	...	...	943	3 408	89	583	2 433	302	2003	
127	...	1 586	1 472	33 033	6 875	8 314	15 210	2 635	2000	Roumanie
114	...	1 399	1 568	34 701	7 487	9 969	14 654	2 592	2001	
97	...	943	1 564	34 087	7 800	8 562	15 153	2 573	2002	
118	...	710	1 616	35 124	8 111	8 394	16 376	2 242	2003	
8 997	...	20 230	4 058	596 279	94 529	99 889	354 681	47 180	2000	Fédération de Russie
9 253	...	22 140	4 164	602 439	90 620	100 530	361 711	49 578	2001	
9 601	...	20 190	4 169	600 146	90 498	97 467	362 074	50 107	2002	
9 755	...	23 631	4 336	621 137	91 188	97 103	380 913	51 932	2003	
30	...	160	1 147	12 448	8 191	1 261	1 704	1 291	2000	Serbie-et-Monténégro
49	...	499	1 234	13 396	7 914	2 139	1 924	1 418	2001	
59	...	467	1 336	14 469	8 521	2 617	1 935	1 396	2002	
64	...	597	1 381	14 951	8 930	2 867	2 066	1 087	2003	
...	...	1 569	3 092	16 696	3 940	1 821	6 422	4 513	2000	Slovaquie
...	...	250	3 384	18 205	4 036	2 723	6 858	4 588	2001	
...	...	477	3 367	18 109	3 885	2 901	6 523	4 800	2002	
...	...	409	3 366	18 107	4 205	2 814	6 303	4 784	2003	
24	...	-37	3 043	6 050	1 345	2 280	966	1 459	2000	Slovénie
27	...	...	3 142	6 254	1 417	2 345	945	1 546	2001	
28	...	...	3 193	6 366	1 542	2 274	911	1 638	2002	
26	...	...	3 234	6 452	1 508	2 291	1 008	1 645	2003	
2 723	6 118	6 209	2 744	109 656	21 319	51 655	16 921	19 761	2000	Espagne
2 774	6 846	7 138	2 747	110 929	19 351	52 064	18 234	21 280	2001	
2 668	7 008	6 868	2 842	116 102	22 161	53 122	20 848	19 971	2002	
2 799	7 144	7 840	2 865	119 051	20 379	53 787	23 741	21 144	2003	
699	1 384	1 284	4 255	37 704	2 408	12 271	863	22 162	2000	Suède
712	1 417	1 367	4 609	40 946	2 712	12 225	973	25 036	2001	
527	1 224	2 313	4 623	41 189	2 799	13 400	990	24 000	2002	
513	1 645	2 744	4 339	38 796	2 648	11 826	988	23 334	2003	
1 528	11	36	3 191	23 024	137	10 481	2 705	9 701	2000	Suisse [8]
1 489	12	-108	3 375	24 521	148	11 786	2 816	9 771	2001	
1 330	8	-50	3 253	23 831	137	11 033	2 764	9 897	2002	
1 211	10	-24	3 261	23 940	143	10 797	2 921	10 079	2003	
29	...	21	1 612	3 263	2 243	849	60	110	2000	L'ex-R.y. Macédoine
23	...	7	1 564	3 183	2 340	672	80	91	2001	
39	...	8	1 463	2 972	2 003	753	83	133	2002	
7	...	7	1 529	3 099	2 077	748	74	200	2003	
681	...	275	2 704	134 395	34 413	9 909	69 232	20 841	2000	Ukraine
317	...	1 313	2 746	134 638	33 322	11 397	69 251	20 668	2001	
302	...	2 916	2 764	133 760	32 626	11 826	68 376	20 931	2002	
373	...	4 736	2 798	133 284	35 856	11 327	64 469	21 632	2003	
7 793	2 088	10 701	3 807	227 009	37 144	68 520	97 173	24 171	2000	Royaume-Uni
8 072	2 231	9 068	3 868	231 531	41 406	68 800	96 340	24 985	2001	
7 406	1 923	9 685	3 817	225 755	37 634	68 265	95 456	24 400	2002	
7 673	1 770	9 367	3 849	228 375	40 407	68 514	95 498	23 956	2003	
2 858	1 228	2 906	4 281	129 777	54 227	42 125	27 158	6 267	2000	Océanie
3 403	1 127	1 206	4 441	136 389	61 746	40 144	28 578	5 922	2001	
2 854	1 151	-40	4 302	134 183	56 402	42 008	29 555	6 218	2002	
3 075	1 057	540	4 168	133 672	56 028	42 593	29 007	6 043	2003	

Production, trade and consumption of commercial energy—Thousand metric tons of oil equivalent and kilograms per capita (*continued*)

Production, commerce et consommation d'énergie commerciale—Milliers de tonnes d'équivalent pétrole et kilogrammes par habitant (*suite*)

Region, country or area	Year Année	Primary energy production — Production d'énergie primaire					Changes in stocks Variations des stocks	Imports Importations	Exports Exportations
		Total Totale	Solids Solides	Liquids Liquides	Gas Gaz	Electricity Electricité			
Australia	2000	233 878	165 805	34 906	31 688	1 479	931	25 147	141 907
	2001	250 542	180 906	35 800	32 374	1 462	−81	26 119	155 611
	2002	254 915	187 396	32 376	33 733	1 410	3 890	25 555	159 651
	2003	254 566	188 150	30 145	34 812	1 458	2 230	26 663	161 148
Cook Islands *	2000	...	...	...	...	...	...	19	...
	2001	...	...	...	...	...	...	19	...
	2002	...	...	...	...	...	...	19	...
	2003	...	...	...	...	...	...	21	...
Fiji	2000	*37	...	...	...	*37	...	528	*86
	2001	*36	...	...	...	*36	...	603	*110
	*2002	36	...	...	...	36	...	603	110
	*2003	37	...	...	...	37	...	597	109
French Polynesia	2000	10	...	...	...	10	...	251	...
	2001	9	...	...	...	9	...	226	...
	2002	8	...	...	...	8	...	276	...
	*2003	8	...	...	...	8	...	272	...
Kiribati	2000	...	...	...	...	...	...	11	...
	2001	...	...	...	...	...	...	10	...
	*2002	...	...	...	...	...	...	10	...
	*2003	...	...	...	...	...	...	10	...
Nauru *	2000	...	...	...	...	...	...	50	...
	2001	...	...	...	...	...	...	52	...
	2002	...	...	...	...	...	...	52	...
	2003	...	...	...	...	...	...	53	...
New Caledonia	2000	39	...	...	...	39	...	*596	*12
	2001	32	...	...	...	32	...	*602	*12
	*2002	32	...	...	...	32	...	602	12
	*2003	32	...	...	...	32	...	617	12
New Zealand	2000	14 498	2 177	2 080	*5 622	4 620	58	5 766	2 267
	2001	14 444	2 212	2 019	*5 916	4 298	−394	5 862	2 391
	2002	14 645	2 525	1 850	*5 624	4 647	−51	6 213	2 423
	2003	13 079	2 933	1 432	*4 289	4 424	−328	6 587	2 268
Niue *	2000	...	...	...	...	...	...	1	...
	2001	...	...	...	...	...	...	1	...
	2002	...	...	...	...	...	...	1	...
	2003	...	...	...	...	...	...	1	...
Palau *	2000	2	...	...	...	2	...	96	...
	2001	2	...	...	...	2	...	91	...
	2002	2	...	...	...	2	...	91	...
	2003	2	...	...	...	2	...	96	...
Papua New Guinea	2000	*4 090	...	*3 934	*78	78	...	*716	*3 880
	2001	*4 152	...	*3 994	*79	79	...	*713	*3 919
	*2002	4 152	...	3 994	79	79	...	713	3 919
	*2003	4 153	...	3 994	80	79	...	725	3 920
Samoa *	2000	3	...	...	...	3	...	46	...
	2001	3	...	...	...	3	...	48	...
	2002	3	...	...	...	3	...	48	...
	2003	3	...	...	...	3	...	51	...
Solomon Islands *	2000	...	...	...	...	...	...	57	...
	2001	...	...	...	...	...	...	59	...
	2002	...	...	...	...	...	...	59	...
	2003	...	...	...	...	...	...	61	...
Tonga	2000	...	...	...	...	...	...	41	...
	2001	...	...	...	...	...	...	37	...
	*2002	...	...	...	...	...	...	37	...
	*2003	...	...	...	...	...	...	39	...
Vanuatu *	2000	...	...	...	...	...	...	27	...
	2001	...	...	...	...	...	...	29	...
	2002	...	...	...	...	...	...	29	...
	2003	...	...	...	...	...	...	30	...

58
Production, trade and consumption of commercial energy — Thousand metric tons of oil equivalent and kilograms per capita (*continued*)

Production, commerce et consommation d'énergie commerciale — Milliers de tonnes d'équivalent pétrole et kilogrammes par habitant (*suite*)

Bunkers — Soutes			Consumption — Consommation							
Air Avion	Sea Maritime	Unallocated Non distribué	Per capita Par habitant	Total Totale	Solids Solides	Liquids Liquides	Gas Gaz	Electricity Electricité	Year Année	Région, pays ou zone
2 067	909	2 652	5 771	110 559	53 023	34 600	21 457	1 479	2000	Australie
2 605	788	1 163	6 013	116 575	60 290	32 240	22 583	1 462	2001	
2 061	733	20	5 804	114 114	54 962	33 889	23 852	1 410	2002	
2 247	733	542	5 738	114 329	53 959	34 275	24 637	1 458	2003	
9	...	...	486	9	...	9	...	...	2000	Iles Cook *
9	...	...	486	9	...	9	...	...	2001	
9	...	...	462	9	...	9	...	...	2002	
10	...	...	513	10	...	10	...	...	2003	
*135	*41	...	372	303	*13	254	...	*37	2000	Fidji
*98	*41	...	475	390	*11	343	...	*36	2001	
98	41	...	469	390	11	343	...	36	*2002	
98	36	...	466	391	10	344	...	37	*2003	
*4	*32	...	964	225	...	214	...	10	2000	Polynésie française
*5	*38	...	809	192	...	183	...	9	2001	
*5	*38	...	996	240	...	232	...	8	2002	
5	36	...	976	238	...	230	...	8	*2003	
...	...	...	136	11	...	11	...	...	2000	Kiribati
...	...	...	121	10	...	10	...	...	2001	
...	...	...	118	10	...	10	...	...	*2002	
...	...	...	111	10	...	10	...	...	*2003	
6	...	...	3 666	44	...	44	...	...	2000	Nauru *
7	...	...	3 749	45	...	45	...	...	2001	
7	...	...	3 460	45	...	45	...	...	2002	
7	...	...	3 537	46	...	46	...	...	2003	
*18	*10	...	*2 817	*594	*81	*475	...	39	2000	Nouvelle-Calédonie
*19	*10	...	*2 771	*593	*81	*480	...	32	2001	
19	10	...	2 732	593	81	480	...	32	*2002	
19	10	...	2 667	608	83	493	...	32	*2003	
580	232	233	4 422	16 893	1 110	5 541	*5 623	4 620	2000	Nouvelle-Zélande
620	247	3	4 511	17 440	1 365	5 862	*5 916	4 298	2001	
615	326	-100	4 511	17 646	1 348	6 027	*5 624	4 647	2002	
648	238	-42	4 292	16 882	1 976	6 192	*4 289	4 424	2003	
...	...	...	508	1	...	1	...	...	2000	Nioué *
...	...	...	508	1	...	1	...	...	2001	
...	...	...	508	1	...	1	...	...	2002	
...	...	...	508	1	...	1	...	...	2003	
14	...	...	4 381	83	...	81	...	2	2000	Palaos *
13	...	...	4 008	80	...	78	...	2	2001	
13	...	...	4 008	80	...	78	...	2	2002	
14	...	...	3 964	83	...	81	...	2	2003	
*21	*3	*20	*184	*883	*1	*726	*78	78	2000	Papouasie-Nouvelle-Guinée
*23	*3	*40	*179	*881	*1	*722	*79	79	2001	
23	3	40	175	881	1	722	79	79	*2002	
23	3	40	160	892	1	732	80	79	*2003	
...	...	...	292	49	...	46	...	3	2000	Samoa *
...	...	...	324	51	...	48	...	3	2001	
...	...	...	322	51	...	48	...	3	2002	
...	...	...	309	54	...	51	...	3	2003	
2	...	...	124	55	...	55	...	...	2000	Iles Salomon *
2	...	...	127	57	...	57	...	...	2001	
2	...	...	124	57	...	57	...	...	2002	
2	...	...	125	59	...	59	...	...	2003	
1	...	...	403	40	...	40	...	...	2000	Tonga
1	...	...	357	36	...	36	...	...	2001	
1	...	...	357	36	...	36	...	...	*2002	
1	...	...	377	38	...	38	...	...	*2003	
...	...	...	135	27	...	27	...	...	2000	Vanuatu *
...	...	...	142	29	...	29	...	...	2001	
...	...	...	138	29	...	29	...	...	2002	
...	...	...	140	30	...	30	...	...	2003	

Production, trade and consumption of commercial energy — Thousand metric tons of oil equivalent and kilograms per capita (*continued*)

Production, commerce et consommation d'énergie commerciale — Milliers de tonnes d'équivalent pétrole et kilogrammes par habitant (*suite*)

Source

United Nations Statistics Division, New York, *Energy Statistics Yearbook 2003* and the energy statistics database.

Notes

[1] Refers to the Southern African Customs Union.

[2] Includes the 50 states and the District of Columbia. Oil statistics as well as coal trade statistics also include Puerto Rico, Guam, the U.S. Virgin Islands, American Samoa, Johnston Atoll, Midway Islands, Wake Island and the Northern Mariana Islands.

[3] For statistical purposes, the data for China do not include those for the Hong Kong Special Administrative Region (Hong Kong SAR), Macao Special Administrative Region (Macao SAR) and Taiwan Province of China.

[4] Including part of the Neutral Zone.

[5] Including Monaco.

[6] Including San Marino.

[7] Including Svalbard and Jan Mayen Islands.

[8] Including Liechtenstein.

Source

Organisation des Nations Unies, Division de statistique, New York, *Annuaire des statistiques de l'énergie 2003* et la base de données pour les statistiques énergétiques.

Notes

[1] Se réfèrent à l'Union douanière d'afrique australe.

[2] Englobent les 50 Etats fédérés et le District de Columbia. Les statistiques sur le pétrole et sur les échanges de charbon concernent également Porto Rico, l'Ile de Guam, les Iles Vierges des Etats-Unis, le Territoire non incorporé des Samoa américaines, l'Ile Johnston, les Iles Midway, l'Ile de Wake et les Iles Mariannes-du-Nord.

[3] Pour la présentation des statistiques, les données pour Chine ne comprennent pas la Région Administrative Spéciale de Hong Kong (Hong Kong RAS), la Région Administrative Spéciale de Macao (Macao RAS) et la province de Taiwan.

[4] Y compris une partie de la Zone Neutrale.

[5] Y compris Monaco.

[6] Y compris Saint-Marin.

[7] Y compris îles Svalbard et Jan Mayen.

[8] Y compris Liechtenstein.

Production of selected energy commodities
Thousand metric tons of oil equivalent

Production des principaux biens de l'énergie
Milliers de tonnes d'équivalent pétrole

Region, country or area Région, pays ou zone	Year Année	Hard coal, lignite and peat Houille, lignite et tourbe	Briquettes and cokes Agglomérés et cokes	Crude petroleum and NGL Pétrole brut et GNL	Light petroleum products Produits pétroliers légers	Heavy petroleum products Produits pétroliers lourds	Other petroleum products Autres produits pétroliers	LPG and refinery gas GLP et gas de raffinerie	Natural gas Gaz naturel	Electricity Electricité
World Monde	2000	2 139 262	232 331	3 768 449	1 400 167	1 643 084	278 241	217 224	2 340 310	1 820 646
	2001	2 289 458	235 988	3 755 240	1 399 830	1 647 133	283 702	222 526	2 381 696	1 836 661
	2002	2 397 209	240 489	3 721 932	1 419 644	1 638 842	291 497	228 660	2 434 779	1 892 494
	2003	2 568 362	267 836	3 855 277	1 439 599	1 682 838	294 177	236 220	2 495 245	1 940 496
Africa Afrique	2000	161 388	2 635	421 358	44 428	66 864	3 716	5 344	119 475	40 527
	2001	162 261	2 897	424 677	48 260	71 383	4 287	5 731	121 555	41 852
	2002	162 863	2 881	420 116	48 394	73 473	4 426	6 166	126 168	44 933
	2003	171 748	2 516	445 309	47 935	72 578	3 888	5 823	133 592	46 356
Algeria Algérie	2000	...	297	96 895	7 979	11 574	360	593	78 276	2 185
	2001	...	321	94 964	8 094	12 241	405	619	73 336	2 290
	2002	...	418	99 524	7 848	11 915	432	653	76 808	2 378
	2003	...	417	106 319	7 797	12 386	445	662	77 637	2 543
Angola Angola	2000	...	...	36 742	591	1 156	9	73	*527	124
	2001	...	...	36 505	579	1 199	8	76	*481	141
	2002	...	...	44 089	582	1 265	7	86	563	152
	2003	...	...	43 126	591	1 297	6	89	*654	172
Benin Bénin	2000	...	...	35	...	...	...	...	...	7
	2001	...	...	35	...	...	...	...	...	6
	2002	...	...	40	...	...	...	...	...	5
	2003	...	...	20	...	...	...	...	...	7
Burkina Faso * Burkina Faso *	2000	...	...	...	...	...	...	...	...	34
	2001	...	...	...	...	...	...	...	...	34
	2002	...	...	...	...	...	...	...	...	34
	2003	...	...	...	...	...	...	...	...	35
Burundi Burundi	2000	*4	...	...	...	...	...	...	...	9
	2001	*4	...	...	...	...	...	...	...	10
	2002	*4	...	...	...	...	...	...	...	11
	*2003	4	...	...	...	...	...	...	...	11
Cameroon Cameroun	2000	...	...	7 353	665	859	22	28	...	299
	2001	...	...	7 032	687	783	22	30	...	305
	2002	...	...	6 445	469	690	22	20	...	284
	2003	...	...	6 425	609	777	22	23	...	317
Cape Verde * Cap-Vert *	2000	...	...	...	...	...	...	...	...	4
	2001	...	...	...	...	...	...	...	...	4
	2002	...	...	...	...	...	...	...	...	4
	2003	...	...	...	...	...	...	...	...	4
Central African Rep. * Rép. centrafricaine *	2000	...	...	...	...	...	...	...	...	9
	2001	...	...	...	...	...	...	...	...	9
	2002	...	...	...	...	...	...	...	...	9
	2003	...	...	...	...	...	...	...	...	9
Chad * Tchad *	2000	...	...	...	...	...	...	...	...	8
	2001	...	...	...	...	...	...	...	...	8
	2002	...	...	...	...	...	...	...	...	8
	2003	...	...	...	...	...	...	...	...	9
Comoros * Comores *	2000	...	...	...	...	...	...	...	...	2
	2001	...	...	...	...	...	...	...	...	2
	2002	...	...	...	...	...	...	...	...	2
	2003	...	...	...	...	...	...	...	...	2
Congo Congo	2000	...	...	13 710	104	284	10	2	117	26
	2001	...	...	12 761	137	373	11	3	117	29
	2002	...	...	12 263	107	302	10	2	118	34
	2003	...	...	11 187	117	405	10	4	*116	29

Region, country or area / Région, pays ou zone	Year / Année	Hard coal, lignite and peat / Houille, lignite et tourbe	Briquettes and cokes / Agglomérés et cokes	Crude petroleum and NGL / Pétrole brut et GNL	Light petroleum products / Produits pétroliers légers	Heavy petroleum products / Produits pétroliers lourds	Other petroleum products / Autres produits pétroliers	LPG and refinery gas / GLP et gas de raffinerie	Natural gas / Gaz naturel	Electricity / Electricité
Côte d'Ivoire	2000	...	...	364	1 230	1 559	226	110	1 409	414
Côte d'Ivoire	2001	...	...	302	1 189	1 555	287	101	1 419	422
	2002	...	...	750	1 171	1 434	321	96	1 438	456
	2003	...	...	1 056	1 116	1 071	268	73	1 267	438
Dem. Rep. of the Congo	2000	67	...	1 157	...	...	...	...	...	518
Rép. dém. du Congo	2001	69	...	1 226	...	...	...	...	...	507
	2002	71	...	1 152	...	...	...	...	...	522
	2003	74	...	1 084	...	...	...	...	...	538
Djibouti *	2000	...	...	...	...	...	...	...	...	17
Djibouti *	2001	...	...	...	...	...	...	...	...	17
	2002	...	...	...	...	...	...	...	...	18
	2003	...	...	...	...	...	...	...	...	18
Egypt	2000	37	730	42 030	10 308	16 911	1 554	941	18 567	6 049
Egypte	2001	36	968	39 820	11 216	17 228	1 608	993	22 367	6 605
	2002	27	920	40 021	12 302	17 731	1 673	1 093	24 280	7 391
	2003	28	657	40 733	*12 855	18 796	1 729	1 139	*26 036	*7 906
Equatorial Guinea	2000	...	...	5 911	...	...	...	...	...	*2
Guinée équatoriale	2001	...	...	10 450	...	...	...	...	...	*2
	2002	...	...	11 609	...	...	...	...	...	*2
	2003	...	...	10 309	...	...	...	...	...	*2
Eritrea	2000	...	...	...	...	...	...	...	...	18
Erythrée	2001	...	...	...	...	...	...	...	...	20
	2002	...	...	...	...	...	...	...	...	22
	2003	...	...	...	...	...	...	...	...	24
Ethiopia	2000	...	...	...	...	...	*2	3	...	167
Ethiopie	2001	...	...	...	...	...	*2	3	...	166
	2002	...	...	...	...	...	*2	3	...	182
	2003	...	...	...	...	...	*2	*3	...	205
Gabon	2000	...	...	15 485	236	452	41	41	113	125
Gabon	2001	...	...	15 010	218	394	43	40	91	132
	2002	...	...	13 989	250	474	47	45	102	136
	2003	...	...	11 067	251	512	*48	*45	106	141
Gambia	2000	...	...	...	...	...	...	...	...	11
Gambie	2001	...	...	...	...	...	...	...	...	12
	2002	...	...	...	...	...	...	...	...	13
	*2003	...	...	...	...	...	...	...	...	13
Ghana	2000	...	...	...	415	624	*33	44	...	621
Ghana	2001	...	...	...	467	617	*35	42	...	676
	2002	...	...	...	511	648	*15	64	...	628
	2003	...	...	...	564	714	*15	70	...	508
Guinea *	2000	...	...	...	...	...	...	...	...	66
Guinée *	2001	...	...	...	...	...	...	...	...	68
	2002	...	...	...	...	...	...	...	...	69
	2003	...	...	...	...	...	...	...	...	69
Guinea-Bissau *	2000	...	...	...	...	...	...	...	...	5
Guinée-Bissau *	2001	...	...	...	...	...	...	...	...	5
	2002	...	...	...	...	...	...	...	...	5
	2003	...	...	...	...	...	...	...	...	5
Kenya	2000	...	...	...	765	1 129	31	98	...	623
Kenya	2001	...	...	...	617	973	31	91	...	717
	2002	...	...	...	547	939	25	87	...	701
	2003	...	...	...	577	936	22	108	...	1 027
Liberia *	2000	...	...	...	...	...	...	...	...	45
Libéria *	2001	...	...	...	...	...	...	...	...	46
	2002	...	...	...	...	...	...	...	...	46
	2003	...	...	...	...	...	...	...	...	47
Libyan Arab Jamah.	2000	...	...	68 512	5 497	9 552	149	914	5 340	1 333
Jamah. arabe libyenne	2001	...	...	66 900	5 575	9 678	149	915	5 613	1 386
	2002	...	...	62 851	5 484	9 533	156	901	5 640	1 492
	2003	...	...	70 457	5 359	9 323	163	884	5 812	1 629

Region, country or area Région, pays ou zone	Year Année	Hard coal, lignite and peat Houille, lignite et tourbe	Briquettes and cokes Agglomérés et cokes	Crude petroleum and NGL Pétrole brut et GNL	Light petroleum products Produits pétroliers légers	Heavy petroleum products Produits pétroliers lourds	Other petroleum products Autres produits pétroliers	LPG and refinery gas GLP et gas de raffinerie	Natural gas Gaz naturel	Electricity Electricité
Madagascar	2000	...	...	...	*181	*132	*10	*7	...	69
Madagascar	2001	...	...	...	*186	*132	*10	*7	...	72
	2002	...	...	...	*187	*134	*10	*7	...	72
	*2003	...	...	...	189	134	10	7	...	72
Malawi *	2000	...	...	...	...	...	...	...	...	76
Malawi *	2001	...	...	...	...	...	...	...	...	77
	2002	...	...	...	...	...	...	...	...	77
	2003	...	...	...	...	...	...	...	...	77
Mali *	2000	...	...	...	...	...	...	...	...	35
Mali *	2001	...	...	...	...	...	...	...	...	36
	2002	...	...	...	...	...	...	...	...	36
	2003	...	...	...	...	...	...	...	...	36
Mauritania *	2000	...	...	...	...	...	...	...	...	14
Mauritanie *	2001	...	...	...	...	...	...	...	...	14
	2002	...	...	...	...	...	...	...	...	14
	2003	...	...	...	...	...	...	...	...	15
Mauritius	2000	...	...	...	...	...	...	...	...	153
Maurice	2001	...	...	...	...	...	...	...	...	164
	*2002	...	...	...	...	...	...	...	...	168
	2003	...	...	...	...	...	...	...	...	177
Morocco	2000	22	...	13	1 313	4 701	270	389	42	1 179
Maroc	2001	1	...	10	1 318	4 831	241	386	42	1 343
	2002	...	...	13	1 175	4 339	237	370	40	1 434
	2003	...	...	10	887	3 289	58	158	39	1 557
Mozambique	2000	17	...	...	...	...	...	...	1	761
Mozambique	2001	20	...	...	...	...	...	...	1	761
	2002	31	...	...	...	...	...	...	2	1 093
	2003	26	...	...	...	...	...	...	2	912
Niger *	2000	123	...	...	...	...	...	...	...	20
Niger *	2001	123	...	...	...	...	...	...	...	21
	2002	125	...	...	...	...	...	...	...	21
	2003	125	...	...	...	...	...	...	...	21
Nigeria	2000	2	...	112 333	1 784	2 489	330	132	11 740	1 267
Nigéria	2001	2	...	117 090	4 405	5 251	729	311	14 039	1 329
	2002	30	...	102 621	4 323	5 091	696	327	13 236	1 853
	2003	16	...	118 076	1 982	3 261	288	153	17 896	1 736
Réunion *	2000	...	...	...	...	...	...	...	...	135
Réunion *	2001	...	...	...	...	...	...	...	...	136
	2002	...	...	...	...	...	...	...	...	139
	2003	...	...	...	...	...	...	...	...	139
Rwanda *	2000	...	...	...	...	...	...	...	0	15
Rwanda *	2001	...	...	...	...	...	...	...	0	15
	2002	...	...	...	...	...	...	...	0	15
	2003	...	...	...	...	...	...	...	0	15
Saint Helena	2000	...	...	...	...	...	...	...	...	1
Sainte-Hélène	2001	...	...	...	...	...	...	...	...	1
	2002	...	...	...	...	...	...	...	...	1
	*2003	...	...	...	...	...	...	...	...	1
Sao Tome and Principe *	2000	...	...	...	...	...	...	...	...	2
Sao Tomé-et-Principe *	2001	...	...	...	...	...	...	...	...	2
	2002	...	...	...	...	...	...	...	...	2
	2003	...	...	...	...	...	...	...	...	2
Senegal	2000	...	...	1	267	631	10	18	1	127
Sénégal	2001	...	...	...	222	627	10	16	1	142
	2002	...	...	...	271	633	9	18	3	*148
	2003	...	...	...	331	783	9	21	10	*184
Seychelles	2000	...	...	...	...	...	...	...	...	16
Seychelles	2001	...	...	...	...	...	...	...	...	18
	2002	...	...	...	...	...	...	...	...	19
	*2003	...	...	...	...	...	...	...	...	19

Region, country or area Région, pays ou zone	Year Année	Hard coal, lignite and peat Houille, lignite et tourbe	Briquettes and cokes Agglomérés et cokes	Crude petroleum and NGL Pétrole brut et GNL	Light petroleum products Produits pétroliers légers	Heavy petroleum products Produits pétroliers lourds	Other petroleum products Autres produits pétroliers	LPG and refinery gas GLP et gas de raffinerie	Natural gas Gaz naturel	Electricity Electricité
Sierra Leone * Sierra Leone *	2000	...	...	...	67	128	31	...	...	21
	2001	...	...	...	68	130	32	...	...	22
	2002	...	...	...	72	130	32	...	...	22
	2003	...	...	...	72	130	32	...	...	22
Somalia * Somalie *	2000	...	...	...	...	...	...	...	...	24
	2001	...	...	...	...	...	...	...	...	24
	2002	...	...	...	...	...	...	...	...	24
	2003	...	...	...	...	...	...	...	...	24
South Africa [1] Afrique du Sud [1]	2000	157 865	1 188	8 252	11 772	12 329	625	1 653	1 554	21 178
	2001	159 011	1 225	8 777	11 510	12 833	640	1 730	2 019	21 043
	2002	159 733	1 181	9 178	11 062	15 448	706	1 993	2 002	22 036
	2003	168 893	1 113	8 970	12 493	15 744	734	1 943	2 045	22 355
Sudan Soudan	2000	...	...	8 866	720	1 150	...	179	...	211
	2001	...	...	10 404	1 057	1 226	...	237	...	220
	2002	...	...	12 047	1 271	1 427	...	265	...	249
	2003	...	...	13 263	1 407	1 617	...	312	...	288
Togo Togo	2000	...	...	...	...	...	...	...	...	7
	2001	...	...	...	...	...	...	...	...	7
	2002	...	...	...	...	...	...	...	...	10
	*2003	...	...	...	...	...	...	...	...	11
Tunisia Tunisie	2000	...	...	3 698	526	1 192	...	120	1 788	868
	2001	...	...	3 389	567	1 065	...	120	2 030	933
	2002	...	...	3 523	606	1 075	...	122	1 935	970
	2003	...	...	3 206	573	1 117	...	112	1 970	1 017
Uganda Ouganda	2000	...	...	...	...	...	...	...	...	135
	2001	...	...	...	...	...	...	...	...	143
	2002	...	...	...	...	...	...	...	...	144
	*2003	...	...	...	...	...	...	...	...	144
United Rep. of Tanzania Rép.-Unie de Tanzanie	2000	55	...	...	...	...	...	...	...	213
	2001	55	...	...	...	...	...	...	...	241
	2002	55	...	...	...	...	...	...	...	249
	2003	39	...	...	...	...	...	...	...	236
Western Sahara * Sahara occidental *	2000	...	...	...	...	...	...	...	...	8
	2001	...	...	...	...	...	...	...	...	8
	2002	...	...	...	...	...	...	...	...	8
	2003	...	...	...	...	...	...	...	...	8
Zambia Zambie	2000	114	*9	...	8	13	1	1	...	671
	2001	120	*8	...	147	247	22	12	...	784
	2002	124	*7	...	157	266	24	14	...	783
	2003	130	*6	...	166	284	25	16	...	823
Zimbabwe Zimbabwe	2000	3 080	410	...	...	...	...	...	...	602
	2001	2 820	375	...	...	...	...	...	...	680
	2002	2 663	355	...	...	...	...	...	...	738
	2003	2 415	322	...	...	...	...	...	...	757
America, North **Amérique du Nord**	2000	586 670	15 906	721 290	533 081	317 126	116 542	65 524	732 503	595 511
	2001	616 079	14 736	723 694	528 916	326 456	113 690	64 676	748 360	578 271
	2002	595 410	13 003	730 281	538 976	311 433	114 087	65 762	736 649	598 514
	2003	579 708	13 306	740 136	541 569	323 031	116 990	68 870	725 741	598 377
Antigua and Barbuda * Antigua-et-Barbuda *	2000	...	...	...	...	...	...	...	...	9
	2001	...	...	...	...	...	...	...	...	9
	2002	...	...	...	...	...	...	...	...	9
	2003	...	...	...	...	...	...	...	...	9
Aruba Aruba	2000	...	...	120	...	...	...	...	...	67
	2001	...	...	120	...	...	...	...	...	69
	2002	...	...	120	...	...	...	...	...	70
	2003	...	...	120	...	...	...	...	...	70
Bahamas Bahamas	2000	...	...	...	...	...	...	...	...	147
	2001	...	...	...	...	...	...	...	...	152
	2002	...	...	...	...	...	...	...	...	162
	2003	...	...	...	...	...	...	...	...	171

Region, country or area / Région, pays ou zone	Year / Année	Hard coal, lignite and peat / Houille, lignite et tourbe	Briquettes and cokes / Agglomérés et cokes	Crude petroleum and NGL / Pétrole brut et GNL	Light petroleum products / Produits pétroliers légers	Heavy petroleum products / Produits pétroliers lourds	Other petroleum products / Autres produits pétroliers	LPG and refinery gas / GLP et gas de raffinerie	Natural gas / Gaz naturel	Electricity / Electricité
Barbados	2000	...	...	77	...	...	...	...	35	68
Barbade	2001	...	...	63	...	...	...	...	30	71
	2002	...	...	80	...	...	...	...	27	74
	2003	...	...	74	...	...	...	1	24	75
Belize	2000	...	...	...	...	...	...	...	...	15
Belize	2001	...	...	...	...	...	...	...	...	13
	*2002	...	...	...	...	...	...	...	...	14
	*2003	...	...	...	...	...	...	...	...	15
Bermuda	2000	...	...	...	...	...	...	...	...	52
Bermudes	2001	...	...	...	...	...	...	...	...	53
	2002	...	...	...	...	...	...	...	...	55
	2003	...	...	...	...	...	...	...	...	57
British Virgin Islands	*2000	...	...	...	...	...	...	...	...	4
Iles Vierges britanniques	*2001	...	...	...	...	...	...	...	...	4
	2002	...	...	...	...	...	...	...	...	3
	*2003	...	...	...	...	...	...	...	...	4
Canada	2000	35 276	2 121	134 245	42 784	35 126	12 127	5 695	164 952	64 815
Canada	2001	35 759	2 080	136 240	43 666	36 406	12 315	6 020	169 328	64 136
	2002	32 919	2 049	142 990	45 311	36 509	12 345	7 260	170 760	64 910
	2003	30 374	2 077	150 612	45 481	39 520	12 747	7 575	167 476	63 584
Cayman Islands	*2000	...	...	...	...	...	...	...	...	28
Iles Caïmanes	*2001	...	...	...	...	...	...	...	...	28
	2002	...	...	...	...	...	...	...	...	35
	2003	...	...	...	...	...	...	...	...	36
Costa Rica	2000	...	...	...	...	9	...	...	...	1 350
Costa Rica	2001	...	...	...	39	240	8	...	...	1 360
	2002	...	...	...	69	383	4	2	...	1 511
	2003	...	...	...	97	398	32	2	...	1 363
Cuba	2000	...	...	2 698	843	1 184	163	141	521	1 293
Cuba	2001	...	...	2 889	825	1 366	192	135	540	1 316
	2002	...	...	3 632	602	1 123	189	100	531	1 350
	2003	...	...	3 684	811	1 123	236	168	598	1 368
Dominica	2000	...	...	...	...	...	...	...	...	7
Dominique	2001	...	...	...	...	...	...	...	...	7
	*2002	...	...	...	...	...	...	...	...	7
	*2003	...	...	...	...	...	...	...	...	7
Dominican Republic	2000	...	...	...	535	940	...	42	...	734
Rép. dominicaine	2001	...	...	...	501	778	...	41	...	886
	2002	...	...	...	564	883	...	41	...	990
	2003	...	...	...	550	862	...	46	...	1 162
El Salvador	2000	...	...	...	198	698	28	32	...	940
El Salvador	2001	...	...	...	183	745	29	33	...	1 084
	2002	...	...	...	189	675	26	30	...	1 121
	2003	...	...	...	208	678	24	26	...	1 145
Greenland *	2000	...	...	...	...	...	...	...	...	23
Groenland *	2001	...	...	...	...	...	...	...	...	23
	2002	...	...	...	...	...	...	...	...	23
	2003	...	...	...	...	...	...	...	...	23
Grenada	2000	...	...	...	...	...	...	...	...	12
Grenade	2001	...	...	...	...	...	...	...	...	13
	2002	...	...	...	...	...	...	...	...	13
	2003	...	...	...	...	...	...	...	...	13
Guadeloupe	*2000	...	...	...	...	...	...	...	...	105
Guadeloupe	*2001	...	...	...	...	...	...	...	...	105
	2002	...	...	...	...	...	...	...	...	100
	2003	...	...	...	...	...	...	...	...	100
Guatemala	2000	...	...	1 131	200	604	26	21	...	520
Guatemala	2001	...	...	1 150	189	559	54	21	...	504
	2002	...	...	1 345	144	415	39	16	...	532
	2003	...	...	1 348	...	...	...	...	...	564

Region, country or area Région, pays ou zone	Year Année	Hard coal, lignite and peat Houille, lignite et tourbe	Briquettes and cokes Agglomérés et cokes	Crude petroleum and NGL Pétrole brut et GNL	Light petroleum products Produits pétroliers légers	Heavy petroleum products Produits pétroliers lourds	Other petroleum products Autres produits pétroliers	LPG and refinery gas GLP et gas de raffinerie	Natural gas Gaz naturel	Electricity Electricité
Haiti	2000	...	...	...	...	...	...	...	...	47
Haïti	2001	...	...	...	...	...	...	...	...	51
	2002	...	...	...	...	...	...	...	...	47
	2003	...	...	...	...	...	...	...	...	46
Honduras	2000	...	...	...	...	...	...	...	...	315
Honduras	2001	...	...	...	...	...	...	...	...	337
	2002	...	...	...	...	...	...	...	...	358
	2003	...	...	...	...	...	...	...	...	390
Jamaica	2000	...	...	...	223	714	17	11	...	570
Jamaïque	2001	...	...	...	225	607	17	11	...	572
	2002	...	...	...	269	831	18	15	...	596
	2003	...	...	...	200	651	14	8	...	615
Martinique	*2000	...	...	...	301	440	...	24	...	96
Martinique	*2001	...	...	...	305	443	...	26	...	96
	2002	...	...	...	*311	*476	...	*28	...	101
	*2003	...	...	...	314	477	...	28	...	102
Mexico	2000	3 548	1 400	177 211	20 065	37 347	4 608	3 004	34 856	23 580
Mexique	2001	3 529	1 377	183 398	20 737	38 690	3 507	2 948	35 123	23 860
	2002	3 348	968	186 131	21 053	38 731	3 720	2 968	36 017	24 385
	2003	2 948	1 008	197 344	23 325	37 788	3 383	3 789	37 751	25 502
Montserrat	2000	...	...	...	...	...	...	...	...	1
Montserrat	2001	...	...	...	...	...	...	...	...	1
	2002	...	...	...	...	...	...	. ...	...	2
	2003	...	...	...	...	...	...	...	...	2
Netherlands Antilles	2000	...	...	...	2 809	6 918	2 615	131	...	96
Antilles néerlandaises	2001	...	...	...	2 839	7 936	2 679	128	...	94
	2002	...	...	...	2 521	6 676	2 498	129	...	94
	2003	...	...	...	2 645	6 353	2 215	136	...	93
Nicaragua	2000	...	...	...	177	623	11	31	...	300
Nicaragua	2001	...	...	...	178	715	9	35	...	372
	2002	...	...	...	187	607	6	26	...	283
	2003	...	...	...	184	593	13	24	...	443
Panama	2000	...	...	...	361	1 684	27	75	...	420
Panama	2001	...	...	...	395	1 606	33	78	...	441
	2002	...	...	...	194	634	24	87	...	455
	2003	...	...	...	...	...	...	...	...	480
Saint Kitts and Nevis	*2000	...	...	...	...	...	...	...	...	9
Saint-Kitts-et-Nevis	*2001	...	...	...	...	...	...	...	...	9
	2002	...	...	...	...	...	...	...	...	9
	2003	...	...	...	...	...	...	...	...	11
Saint Lucia	2000	...	...	...	...	...	...	...	...	24
Sainte-Lucie	2001	...	...	...	...	...	...	...	...	25
	2002	...	...	...	...	...	...	...	...	25
	*2003	...	...	...	...	...	...	...	...	26
Saint Pierre and Miquelon *	2000	...	...	...	...	...	...	...	...	4
Saint-Pierre-et-Miquelon *	2001	...	...	...	...	...	...	...	...	4
	2002	...	...	...	...	...	...	...	...	4
	2003	...	...	...	...	...	...	...	...	4
St. Vincent-Grenadines	2000	...	...	...	...	...	...	...	...	8
St. Vincent-Grenadines	2001	...	...	...	...	...	...	...	...	9
	2002	...	...	...	...	...	...	...	...	9
	*2003	...	...	...	...	...	...	...	...	9
Trinidad and Tobago	2000	...	...	7 344	2 183	5 056	76	337	12 252	469
Trinité-et-Tobago	2001	...	...	7 105	2 122	5 170	94	311	13 100	485
	2002	...	...	8 193	2 111	4 716	58	340	15 263	485
	2003	...	...	8 627	2 130	4 763	49	321	23 225	554
Turks and Caicos Islands *	2000	...	...	...	...	...	...	...	...	0
Iles Turques et Caïques *	2001	...	...	...	...	...	...	...	...	0
	2002	...	...	...	...	...	...	...	...	1
	2003	...	...	...	...	...	...	...	...	1

Region, country or area / Région, pays ou zone	Year / Année	Hard coal, lignite and peat / Houille, lignite et tourbe	Briquettes and cokes / Agglomérés et cokes	Crude petroleum and NGL / Pétrole brut et GNL	Light petroleum products / Produits pétroliers légers	Heavy petroleum products / Produits pétroliers lourds	Other petroleum products / Autres produits pétroliers	LPG and refinery gas / GLP et gas de raffinerie	Natural gas / Gaz naturel	Electricity / Électricité
United States [2]	2000	547 846	12 385	398 463	462 401	225 783	96 842	55 981	519 887	499 386
États-Unis [2]	2001	576 792	11 278	392 728	456 710	231 195	94 751	54 890	530 239	482 081
	2002	559 143	9 986	387 790	465 451	218 775	95 160	54 719	514 051	500 679
	2003	546 386	10 221	378 327	465 624	229 825	98 277	56 746	496 667	500 337
America, South	**2000**	**33 755**	**7 065**	**350 811**	**70 193**	**108 335**	**16 491**	**14 121**	**94 216**	**63 002**
Amérique du Sud	**2001**	**36 594**	**6 948**	**346 114**	**70 082**	**112 576**	**15 907**	**15 164**	**93 663**	**63 055**
	2002	**36 322**	**6 858**	**331 201**	**67 241**	**108 945**	**15 971**	**15 164**	**97 259**	**64 295**
	2003	**39 812**	**6 885**	**317 831**	**61 940**	**109 743**	**14 405**	**15 218**	**95 443**	**67 836**
Argentina	2000	153	740	41 256	9 845	12 837	2 216	2 018	37 664	8 752
Argentine	2001	120	721	42 082	8 110	12 812	2 058	2 077	37 239	9 003
	2002	57	666	40 477	8 335	11 330	2 092	2 031	36 110	8 333
	2003	53	748	39 716	8 158	12 035	2 312	2 188	39 772	9 288
Bolivia	2000	...	...	1 877	731	386	439	190	*3 454	334
Bolivie	2001	...	...	2 082	647	411	501	189	*4 919	342
	2002	...	...	2 117	656	449	499	204	5 818	360
	2003	...	...	1 856	632	500	506	194	5 205	367
Brazil	2000	3 024	5 604	65 700	26 037	43 787	5 948	7 697	6 744	31 064
Brésil	2001	2 512	5 559	68 669	26 552	45 842	5 740	8 308	6 852	30 751
	2002	2 285	5 421	76 584	25 023	45 187	5 888	8 627	8 793	32 149
	2003	2 064	5 256	79 173	24 601	46 039	5 137	8 793	9 501	33 723
Chile	2000	256	442	480	3 253	5 349	662	621	1 949	3 549
Chili	2001	403	454	508	3 550	5 414	754	698	1 954	3 777
	2002	303	541	476	3 282	5 206	694	558	2 002	3 912
	2003	403	638	433	3 311	5 721	748	523	1 761	4 195
Colombia	2000	24 792	261	36 012	6 587	5 535	1 804	1 101	6 067	3 779
Colombie	2001	28 237	197	31 529	6 897	6 321	1 804	1 195	6 442	3 757
	2002	28 503	211	29 450	6 446	6 432	1 804	1 198	6 436	*3 891
	2003	32 517	215	27 652	6 763	6 140	1 795	1 216	6 161	4 101
Ecuador	2000	...	...	21 081	1 622	5 656	242	148	229	988
Équateur	2001	...	...	21 216	1 875	5 582	295	131	233	950
	2002	...	...	20 564	1 853	5 361	291	107	236	1 022
	2003	...	...	21 520	1 838	5 237	285	174	388	994
Falkland Is. (Malvinas) *	2000	3	...	...	...	...	...	...	...	1
Îles Falkland (Malvinas) *	2001	3	...	...	...	...	...	...	...	1
	2002	3	...	...	...	...	...	...	...	1
	2003	3	...	...	...	...	...	...	...	1
French Guiana *	2000	...	...	...	...	...	...	...	...	39
Guyane française *	2001	...	...	...	...	...	...	...	...	39
	2002	...	...	...	...	...	...	...	...	41
	2003	...	...	...	...	...	...	...	...	40
Guyana	2000	...	...	...	...	...	...	...	...	77
Guyana	2001	...	...	...	...	...	...	...	...	78
	*2002	...	...	...	...	...	...	...	...	80
	*2003	...	...	...	...	...	...	...	...	77
Paraguay	2000	...	...	...	18	88	...	...	...	4 599
Paraguay	2001	...	...	...	17	85	...	...	...	3 897
	2002	...	...	...	14	83	...	...	...	4 145
	2003	...	...	...	12	72	...	...	...	4 451
Peru	2000	11	18	5 536	3 458	4 773	259	383	679	1 713
Pérou	2001	12	18	5 406	3 091	5 103	143	367	710	1 787
	2002	15	19	5 420	2 881	5 092	193	353	750	1 890
	2003	10	28	5 332	2 964	5 234	104	398	805	1 972
Suriname	2000	...	...	603	...	282	...	...	...	125
Suriname	2001	...	...	644	...	351	...	...	...	126
	2002	...	...	616	...	372	...	...	...	127
	2003	...	...	589	...	369	...	...	...	129
Uruguay	2000	...	...	...	493	1 249	177	131	...	653
Uruguay	2001	...	...	...	455	1 081	229	131	...	796
	2002	...	...	...	318	834	91	90	...	826
	2003	...	...	...	387	1 071	54	95	...	738

Region, country or area Région, pays ou zone	Year Année	Hard coal, lignite and peat Houille, lignite et tourbe	Briquettes and cokes Agglomérés et cokes	Crude petroleum and NGL Pétrole brut et GNL	Light petroleum products Produits pétroliers légers	Heavy petroleum products Produits pétroliers lourds	Other petroleum products Autres produits pétroliers	LPG and refinery gas GLP et gas de raffinerie	Natural gas Gaz naturel	Electricity Electricité
Venezuela (Bolivarian Rep. of)	2000	5 516	...	178 266	18 150	28 393	4 742	1 833	37 430	7 328
Venezuela (Rép. bolivar. du)	2001	5 306	...	173 978	18 887	29 575	4 383	2 069	35 314	7 750
	2002	5 155	...	155 498	18 432	28 601	4 419	1 997	37 114	7 517
	2003	4 762	...	141 561	13 273	27 324	3 465	1 636	31 851	7 760
Asia	**2000**	**830 966**	**132 783**	**1 571 941**	**426 863**	**628 083**	**63 596**	**62 071**	**533 016**	**509 352**
Asie	**2001**	**930 843**	**137 643**	**1 540 899**	**430 247**	**606 882**	**67 527**	**66 647**	**553 508**	**526 364**
	2002	**1 058 032**	**145 589**	**1 491 775**	**441 186**	**610 599**	**71 236**	**69 890**	**589 711**	**552 282**
	2003	**1 221 610**	**169 959**	**1 580 234**	**458 488**	**636 144**	**75 700**	**71 789**	**629 730**	**582 043**
Afghanistan	2000	1	...	...	...	...	...	...	*109	*41
Afghanistan	2001	18	...	...	...	...	...	...	*102	*40
	2002	15	...	...	...	...	...	...	*102	*41
	2003	25	...	...	...	...	...	...	*102	*42
Armenia	2000	...	...	...	...	...	...	...	...	863
Arménie	2001	...	...	...	...	...	...	...	...	842
	2002	...	...	...	...	...	...	...	...	874
	2003	...	...	...	...	...	...	...	...	823
Azerbaijan	2000	...	...	14 043	1 837	6 022	87	259	5 262	1 608
Azerbaïdjan	2001	...	...	14 934	1 621	4 210	85	245	4 987	1 631
	2002	...	...	15 359	1 578	4 163	135	197	4 635	1 681
	2003	...	...	15 407	1 904	4 113	124	256	4 620	1 831
Bahrain	2000	...	...	9 733	4 884	7 732	209	295	*7 843	542
Bahreïn	2001	...	...	9 513	4 964	7 358	321	295	8 416	583
	2002	...	...	9 620	4 892	7 106	243	283	*8 836	626
	2003	...	...	9 807	4 890	7 340	236	291	*8 953	668
Bangladesh	2000	...	...	103	466	345	534	55	8 201	1 356
Bangladesh	2001	...	...	100	459	339	525	62	9 184	1 496
	2002	...	...	93	492	312	422	55	9 662	1 605
	2003	...	...	90	474	300	406	50	10 393	1 695
Bhutan *	2000	35	...	...	...	...	...	...	...	156
Bhoutan *	2001	35	...	...	...	...	...	...	...	163
	2002	36	...	...	...	...	...	...	...	163
	2003	35	...	...	...	...	...	...	...	163
Brunei Darussalam	2000	...	...	10 501	396	221	...	60	10 526	244
Brunéi Darussalam	2001	...	...	10 615	409	231	...	54	10 642	250
	2002	...	...	11 114	418	225	...	66	10 687	261
	2003	...	...	11 105	431	245	...	64	11 522	273
Cambodia *	2000	...	...	...	...	...	...	...	...	13
Cambodge *	2001	...	...	...	...	...	...	...	...	9
	2002	...	...	...	...	...	...	...	...	11
	2003	...	...	...	...	...	...	...	...	11
China [3]	2000	498 501	82 729	163 163	75 105	92 210	12 197	16 908	31 282	119 511
Chine [3]	2001	579 810	89 158	164 123	74 649	94 455	12 291	17 091	34 880	129 620
	2002	689 310	96 780	167 167	79 103	96 506	13 528	18 239	37 564	145 479
	2003	832 667	120 697	169 770	87 348	106 475	15 078	20 304	40 272	171 619
China, Hong Kong SAR	2000	...	...	...	...	...	...	...	...	2 694
Chine, Hong Kong RAS	2001	...	...	...	...	...	...	...	...	2 789
	2002	...	...	...	...	...	...	...	...	2 951
	2003	...	...	...	...	...	...	...	...	3 054
China, Macao SAR	2000	...	...	...	...	...	...	...	...	135
Chine, Macao RAS	2001	...	...	...	...	...	...	...	...	138
	2002	...	...	...	...	...	...	...	...	146
	2003	...	...	...	...	...	...	...	...	154
Cyprus	2000	...	...	...	197	900	36	62	...	290
Chypre	2001	...	...	...	196	874	42	53	...	305
	2002	...	...	...	199	787	54	57	...	326
	2003	...	...	...	193	691	46	51	...	348
Georgia	2000	4	...	110	2	15	2	...	...	638
Géorgie	2001	1	...	99	...	12	7	...	37	597
	2002	4	...	74	...	14	8	...	16	624
	2003	5	...	140	...	15	8	...	17	612

Region, country or area / Région, pays ou zone	Year / Année	Hard coal, lignite and peat / Houille, lignite et tourbe	Briquettes and cokes / Agglomérés et cokes	Crude petroleum and NGL / Pétrole brut et GNL	Light petroleum products / Produits pétroliers légers	Heavy petroleum products / Produits pétroliers lourds	Other petroleum products / Autres produits pétroliers	LPG and refinery gas / GLP et gas de raffinerie	Natural gas / Gaz naturel	Electricity / Électricité
India Inde	2000	188 433	7 924	36 473	29 922	51 205	11 663	4 344	23 345	51 190
	2001	192 641	7 560	36 381	31 973	52 459	11 568	4 929	23 354	*53 128
	2002	202 906	7 872	37 361	33 681	52 218	12 778	5 256	25 096	54 696
	2003	215 929	8 452	37 225	37 352	55 249	14 163	5 641	25 689	57 573
Indonesia Indonésie	2000	53 774	...	88 087	18 692	25 935	1 788	2 589	70 048	9 826
	2001	64 754	...	85 851	18 485	19 385	1 871	2 526	67 631	10 535
	2002	72 142	...	84 041	19 204	18 160	1 919	2 741	73 267	11 083
	2003	76 525	...	78 631	19 746	20 416	2 086	2 801	76 615	11 713
Iran (Islamic Rep. of) Iran (Rép. islamique d')	2000	976	809	196 708	22 035	50 065	4 161	1 767	54 981	10 433
	2001	966	798	183 367	21 821	39 546	4 522	1 786	57 364	11 182
	2002	860	812	179 069	21 868	49 834	4 199	3 759	65 036	12 105
	2003	843	772	200 527	21 248	48 082	4 508	4 080	72 923	13 121
Iraq Iraq	2000	...	...	127 116	5 794	15 794	855	1 705	2 861	2 839
	2001	...	...	116 940	6 248	15 211	922	1 839	2 507	2 869
	2002	...	...	99 928	6 122	14 629	898	1 791	2 089	3 008
	2003	...	...	65 693	5 480	14 047	804	1 603	1 417	2 533
Israel Israël	2000	86	...	4	4 079	6 820	330	508	9	3 694
	2001	91	...	4	4 085	6 727	344	567	9	3 770
	2002	101	...	5	3 861	6 218	374	524	8	3 904
	2003	96	...	3	4 057	6 431	221	516	8	4 062
Japan Japon	2000	1 719	24 436	620	89 772	96 385	11 196	13 982	2 443	149 932
	2001	1 860	24 566	595	90 166	91 028	11 032	13 800	2 410	148 047
	2002	...	25 819	608	91 174	91 638	10 735	13 485	2 690	145 270
	2003	...	25 884	670	90 394	92 239	11 013	13 007	2 751	134 758
Jordan Jordanie	2000	...	...	2	1 167	2 391	130	222	216	634
	2001	...	...	2	1 115	2 387	150	202	229	649
	2002	...	...	2	1 164	2 407	191	200	215	699
	2003	...	...	2	1 119	2 417	214	199	244	690
Kazakhstan Kazakhstan	2000	31 840	2 657	35 716	1 468	4 353	757	736	11 195	4 441
	2001	32 971	2 655	40 446	1 730	4 991	1 083	1 669	10 829	4 760
	2002	35 625	2 654	47 722	1 861	5 104	1 078	2 007	13 159	5 016
	2003	39 104	2 885	51 976	1 901	4 816	995	1 854	15 480	5 488
Korea, Dem. P. R. Corée, R. p. dém. de	2000	18 792	...	...	159	220	...	...	...	1 668
	2001	19 293	...	...	237	328	...	...	...	1 737
	2002	18 291	...	...	238	328	...	...	...	1 701
	2003	18 625	...	...	232	319	...	...	...	1 809
Korea, Republic of Corée, République de	2000	1 867	9 118	...	49 210	66 508	3 155	3 261	...	44 452
	2001	1 717	8 065	...	47 779	64 507	3 249	3 676	...	46 624
	2002	1 493	6 704	...	46 627	57 475	3 899	3 783	...	49 759
	2003	1 484	6 154	...	43 053	58 992	3 828	3 561	...	52 995
Kuwait [4] Koweït [4]	2000	...	...	108 379	14 049	19 951	268	1 358	8 495	2 825
	2001	...	...	106 367	13 867	16 713	300	1 388	8 313	2 995
	2002	...	...	100 842	15 006	18 833	458	1 319	7 455	3 173
	2003	...	...	114 991	17 070	21 877	504	1 503	8 686	3 423
Kyrgyzstan Kirghizistan	2000	133	...	77	65	71	...	...	30	1 283
	2001	147	...	76	50	83	...	...	31	1 175
	2002	143	...	76	42	70	...	...	28	1 025
	2003	123	...	69	28	62	...	...	25	1 206
Lao People's Dem. Rep. * Rép. dém. pop. lao *	2000	158	...	...	...	...	...	...	...	105
	2001	196	...	...	...	...	...	...	...	108
	2002	200	...	...	...	...	...	...	...	111
	2003	200	...	...	...	...	...	...	...	111
Lebanon Liban	2000	...	...	...	...	...	...	...	...	831
	*2001	...	...	...	...	...	...	...	...	839
	2002	...	...	...	...	...	...	...	...	831
	2003	...	...	...	...	...	...	...	...	907
Malaysia Malaisie	2000	242	...	33 415	7 847	10 584	2 585	1 048	*42 559	5 952
	2001	344	...	35 329	8 888	10 723	3 116	1 163	*41 417	6 139
	2002	223	...	37 581	8 432	10 725	2 219	1 153	*42 719	6 381
	2003	107	...	39 140	8 921	10 817	2 715	1 159	*44 710	6 745

Region, country or area / Région, pays ou zone	Year / Année	Hard coal, lignite and peat / Houille, lignite et tourbe	Briquettes and cokes / Agglomérés et cokes	Crude petroleum and NGL / Pétrole brut et GNL	Light petroleum products / Produits pétroliers légers	Heavy petroleum products / Produits pétroliers lourds	Other petroleum products / Autres produits pétroliers	LPG and refinery gas / GLP et gas de raffinerie	Natural gas / Gaz naturel	Electricity / Electricité
Maldives	2000	...	...	...	...	...	...	...	...	9
Maldives	2001	...	...	...	...	...	...	...	...	10
	2002	...	...	...	...	...	...	...	...	11
	2003	...	...	...	...	...	...	...	...	12
Mongolia	2000	1 548	...	...	...	...	...	...	...	252
Mongolie	2001	1 626	...	...	...	...	...	...	...	259
	2002	1 742	...	...	...	...	...	...	...	268
	2003	1 742	...	...	...	...	...	...	...	270
Myanmar	2000	358	...	577	342	565	41	48	5 755	440
Myanmar	2001	412	...	674	312	484	41	50	5 832	403
	2002	344	...	883	362	550	44	57	6 046	504
	2003	609	...	984	457	373	33	45	*7 335	534
Nepal	2000	12	...	...	...	...	...	...	...	143
Népal	2001	7	...	...	...	...	...	...	...	161
	2002	8	...	...	...	...	...	...	...	183
	2003	8	...	...	...	...	...	...	...	195
Oman	2000	...	...	47 750	824	3 080	25	35	8 936	784
Oman	2001	...	...	47 880	717	2 516	25	*35	13 694	837
	2002	...	...	44 993	1 004	3 139	25	*44	15 049	888
	2003	...	...	41 119	902	3 130	25	54	16 528	921
Pakistan	2000	1 498	...	2 893	2 415	3 743	415	69	18 148	5 724
Pakistan	2001	1 464	...	2 969	2 786	5 491	418	202	19 130	6 208
	2002	1 574	...	3 276	3 039	5 931	384	217	19 995	6 628
	2003	1 566	...	3 312	2 798	6 016	459	223	21 446	6 813
Philippines	2000	640	...	55	4 213	9 926	220	791	10	12 897
Philippines	2001	581	...	63	4 236	9 246	232	888	126	12 129
	2002	786	...	273	3 832	9 191	101	790	1 586	12 097
	2003	869	...	651	3 551	7 773	133	710	2 417	12 151
Qatar	2000	...	...	35 379	956	1 543	...	111	25 491	786
Qatar	2001	...	...	39 109	1 119	1 189	...	88	26 281	856
	2002	...	...	40 246	2 247	1 651	...	119	28 860	941
	2003	...	...	41 018	2 860	1 405	...	207	30 164	1 033
Saudi Arabia [4]	2000	...	...	443 850	28 226	48 693	1 591	3 322	42 843	10 315
Arabie saoudite [4]	2001	...	...	429 110	26 632	51 596	3 219	4 331	48 835	11 496
	2002	...	...	391 412	26 685	49 682	3 970	3 554	48 562	12 189
	2003	...	...	463 654	29 745	54 536	4 599	3 359	54 546	13 158
Singapore	2000	...	...	...	15 521	17 644	2 922	961	...	2 723
Singapour	2001	...	...	...	14 545	17 557	3 187	932	...	2 846
	2002	...	...	...	13 691	17 367	3 970	890	...	2 981
	2003	...	...	...	14 571	16 018	3 678	947	...	3 038
Sri Lanka	2000	...	...	...	633	1 507	167	69	...	589
Sri Lanka	2001	...	...	...	584	1 344	112	59	...	570
	2002	...	...	...	630	1 521	84	70	...	598
	2003	...	...	...	539	1 370	98	66	...	667
Syrian Arab Republic	2000	...	6	28 413	2 265	9 233	1 055	326	*5 496	2 169
Rép. arabe syrienne	2001	...	6	29 123	2 393	9 609	1 034	326	*5 037	2 297
	2002	...	3	31 317	2 373	9 175	1 083	319	*6 127	2 409
	2003	...	6	28 152	2 324	8 714	1 049	311	*6 262	2 540
Tajikistan	2000	12	...	18	13	...	...	...	36	1 225
Tadjikistan	2001	12	...	18	13	...	...	...	36	1 237
	2002	27	...	16	12	...	...	...	27	1 316
	2003	26	...	18	12	...	...	...	30	1 420
Thailand	2000	7 790	...	7 287	9 695	20 399	1 005	2 431	15 301	8 255
Thaïlande	2001	8 630	...	7 731	9 835	20 297	1 145	3 154	16 413	8 809
	2002	8 623	...	8 576	10 174	20 504	951	3 582	17 117	9 376
	2003	8 289	...	10 116	10 237	21 736	914	3 340	16 904	10 062
Timor-Leste *	2002	...	...	7 315	...	...	...	...	...	26
Timor-Leste *	2003	...	...	7 315	...	...	...	...	...	26

Region, country or area / Région, pays ou zone	Year / Année	Hard coal, lignite and peat / Houille, lignite et tourbe	Briquettes and cokes / Agglomérés et cokes	Crude petroleum and NGL / Pétrole brut et GNL	Light petroleum products / Produits pétroliers légers	Heavy petroleum products / Produits pétroliers lourds	Other petroleum products / Autres produits pétroliers	LPG and refinery gas / GLP et gas de raffinerie	Natural gas / Gaz naturel	Electricity / Électricité
Turkey Turquie	2000	13 665	2 048	2 765	5 920	14 695	2 176	1 323	585	10 802
	2001	13 462	1 812	2 523	6 523	15 830	2 030	1 395	286	10 624
	2002	11 785	1 820	2 422	7 141	15 734	2 160	1 437	346	11 210
	2003	10 534	2 037	2 353	7 277	16 174	2 051	1 401	513	12 159
Turkmenistan Turkménistan	2000	...	...	7 779	1 424	3 803	...	369	42 486	847
	2001	...	...	8 688	1 591	4 157	...	418	46 455	912
	2002	...	...	10 183	1 635	4 021	...	422	48 356	920
	2003	...	...	10 399	1 708	4 330	...	425	53 572	929
United Arab Emirates Emirats arabes unis	2000	...	...	125 018	6 814	7 756	474	554	35 479	3 435
	2001	...	...	122 045	9 265	9 513	465	735	35 051	3 713
	2002	...	...	113 978	10 237	10 182	469	795	38 640	4 006
	2003	...	...	129 518	10 299	10 196	539	803	39 887	4 260
Uzbekistan Ouzbékistan	2000	706	11	7 814	2 226	3 613	855	247	51 074	4 028
	2001	732	...	7 482	2 197	3 538	819	237	51 991	4 085
	2002	666	...	7 354	2 089	3 421	805	233	52 373	4 241
	2003	512	...	7 871	2 398	3 931	862	250	51 951	4 248
Viet Nam Viet Nam	2000	8 126	...	16 625	...	...	...	...	1 245	*2 802
	2001	9 073	...	17 201	...	...	...	...	1 247	3 155
	2002	11 130	...	17 183	...	...	...	...	2 573	*3 597
	2003	11 690	...	17 148	...	...	...	...	3 011	*4 041
Yemen Yémen	2000	...	...	21 434	1 912	1 650	62	63	...	294
	2001	...	...	21 505	1 868	1 607	69	70	...	313
	2002	...	...	21 639	1 875	1 384	74	103	...	324
	2003	...	...	21 320	2 025	1 412	107	95	...	352
Europe Europe	2000	358 502	71 467	662 129	303 412	507 011	75 230	67 717	823 712	588 372
	2001	360 561	71 453	678 043	301 280	514 384	79 735	67 843	826 242	602 456
	2002	354 660	69 900	710 338	302 239	518 920	83 623	69 266	845 556	606 856
	2003	364 400	72 988	736 195	308 436	525 918	80 907	72 136	871 557	620 197
Albania Albanie	2000	9	...	317	42	116	139	10	10	407
	2001	7	...	311	53	107	138	9	8	318
	2002	20	...	393	31	166	182	9	13	317
	2003	21	...	375	12	141	188	8	13	450
Austria Autriche	2000	325	943	1 083	2 468	4 750	1 368	349	1 704	5 316
	2001	314	949	1 019	2 549	5 053	1 578	328	1 635	5 361
	2002	368	950	1 050	2 524	5 047	1 714	331	1 776	5 375
	2003	300	950	1 021	2 363	4 959	1 636	364	1 974	5 434
Belarus Bélarus	2000	462	588	1 853	2 223	8 492	541	684	237	2 244
	2001	454	517	1 854	2 052	8 306	657	629	235	2 154
	2002	502	485	1 848	1 988	9 728	645	686	227	2 275
	2003	411	516	1 822	2 124	9 734	714	602	234	2 290
Belgium Belgique	2000	226	2 176	...	10 305	20 607	6 389	1 473	2	15 653
	2001	131	2 262	...	10 224	19 921	9 089	1 356	0	14 976
	2002	104	2 084	...	10 568	20 186	14 662	1 398	...	15 346
	2003	78	2 010	...	11 048	21 819	12 012	1 400	...	15 570
Bosnia and Herzegovina Bosnie-Herzégovine	2000	4 148	...	...	...	...	...	...	...	897
	2001	3 672	...	...	...	...	...	...	...	888
	2002	4 185	...	...	...	...	...	...	...	928
	2003	3 835	...	...	...	...	...	...	...	968
Bulgaria Bulgarie	2000	4 382	1 093	42	1 683	3 080	253	274	14	6 701
	2001	4 407	992	34	1 872	3 093	328	314	20	7 203
	2002	4 326	942	37	1 672	3 036	201	228	18	7 209
	2003	4 513	1 144	30	1 871	2 618	595	216	14	6 682
Croatia Croatie	2000	...	...	1 546	1 597	2 792	355	571	1 506	920
	2001	...	...	1 421	1 523	2 687	303	506	1 826	1 047
	2002	...	...	1 383	1 519	2 717	385	557	1 926	1 057
	2003	...	...	1 318	1 576	2 928	371	590	1 989	1 091
Czech Republic République tchèque	2000	23 741	2 279	175	1 637	3 060	1 285	272	188	8 696
	2001	24 105	2 362	183	1 946	3 050	1 125	326	136	9 001
	2002	23 090	2 382	265	1 911	2 821	1 505	283	128	9 845
	2003	23 019	2 400	317	2 042	3 070	1 442	308	146	11 685

Region, country or area / Région, pays ou zone	Year / Année	Hard coal, lignite and peat / Houille, lignite et tourbe	Briquettes and cokes / Agglomérés et cokes	Crude petroleum and NGL / Pétrole brut et GNL	Light petroleum products / Produits pétroliers légers	Heavy petroleum products / Produits pétroliers lourds	Other petroleum products / Autres produits pétroliers	LPG and refinery gas / GLP et gas de raffinerie	Natural gas / Gaz naturel	Electricity / Électricité
Denmark Danemark	2000	...	...	17 798	2 910	5 010	...	489	8 240	3 109
	2001	...	...	16 904	2 917	4 821	...	485	8 438	3 248
	2002	...	...	18 161	2 724	4 867	...	469	8 453	3 381
	2003	...	...	18 161	2 817	5 008	5	501	8 008	3 979
Estonia Estonie	2000	2 724	54	...	...	...	...	...	...	732
	2001	2 748	69	...	...	...	...	...	...	730
	2002	2 950	66	...	...	...	...	...	...	733
	2003	3 439	74	...	...	...	...	...	...	874
Faeroe Islands Iles Féroé	2000	...	...	...	...	...	...	...	...	15
	2001	...	...	...	...	...	...	...	...	17
	2002	...	...	...	...	...	...	...	...	21
	2003	...	...	...	...	...	...	...	...	23
Finland Finlande	2000	1 231	573	...	5 222	6 721	351	804	...	9 953
	2001	1 446	573	...	4 708	6 428	341	630	...	10 388
	2002	2 211	575	...	5 687	6 595	546	696	...	10 343
	2003	1 850	564	...	5 469	6 369	840	752	...	11 222
France [5] France [5]	2000	2 176	3 677	1 687	30 465	46 017	8 607	5 472	1 673	119 101
	2001	1 412	3 551	1 653	29 706	46 848	8 537	5 675	1 678	120 982
	2002	1 306	3 172	1 536	29 217	44 331	7 645	4 981	*1 612	124 565
	2003	1 454	3 184	1 421	29 632	46 633	8 178	5 420	1 425	125 894
Germany Allemagne	2000	59 236	8 872	3 169	42 351	60 092	8 733	7 428	17 087	78 812
	2001	56 497	7 554	3 281	40 659	60 720	8 296	7 174	17 196	80 394
	2002	56 891	7 420	3 513	40 742	60 240	8 271	7 412	17 256	77 993
	2003	56 034	7 776	3 694	41 310	61 489	8 200	7 777	17 184	80 411
Gibraltar Gibraltar	2000	...	...	...	...	...	...	...	...	11
	2001	...	...	...	...	...	...	...	...	11
	2002	...	...	...	...	...	...	...	...	11
	2003	...	...	...	...	...	...	...	...	12
Greece Grèce	2000	8 369	51	281	7 222	13 174	891	1 321	47	4 630
	2001	8 691	50	193	6 748	12 829	919	1 345	45	4 618
	2002	9 231	66	191	6 616	12 832	945	1 277	47	4 696
	2003	8 947	76	138	6 630	13 533	1 046	1 261	34	5 028
Hungary Hongrie	2000	2 894	705	2 122	2 508	3 932	738	466	2 754	5 508
	2001	2 869	519	1 902	2 663	3 865	617	474	2 754	5 604
	2002	2 686	306	2 167	2 751	3 497	830	296	2 619	5 551
	2003	2 743	432	2 175	2 910	3 535	725	267	2 541	4 864
Iceland Islande	2000	...	...	...	...	...	...	...	...	1 685
	2001	...	...	...	...	...	...	...	...	1 814
	2002	...	...	...	...	...	...	...	...	1 833
	2003	...	...	...	...	...	...	...	...	1 819
Ireland Irlande	2000	1 065	154	...	925	2 298	27	114	1 065	2 075
	2001	966	152	...	964	2 312	5	143	732	2 156
	2002	636	159	...	1 049	2 007	...	153	753	2 170
	2003	1 220	159	...	1 029	1 999	...	157	605	2 176
Italy [6] Italie [6]	2000	3	3 153	4 592	27 942	56 314	6 596	5 563	15 146	28 008
	2001	88	3 380	4 102	28 553	56 753	6 822	5 672	13 879	28 084
	2002	103	2 846	5 541	28 866	56 613	7 059	5 497	13 316	*28 140
	2003	157	2 679	5 576	30 230	56 821	6 989	5 704	12 644	29 404
Latvia Lettonie	2000	16	1	...	...	...	...	...	...	356
	2001	16	0	...	...	...	...	...	...	368
	2002	32	...	...	...	...	...	...	...	342
	2003	2	...	...	...	...	...	...	...	342
Lithuania Lituanie	2000	10	5	316	2 118	2 263	209	433	...	2 456
	2001	8	4	471	2 770	3 202	216	710	...	3 256
	2002	11	5	434	2 626	3 096	246	731	...	3 999
	2003	10	7	382	2 819	3 464	257	731	...	4 386
Luxembourg Luxembourg	2000	...	...	...	...	...	...	...	...	101
	2001	...	...	...	...	...	...	...	...	102
	2002	...	...	...	...	...	...	...	...	316
	2003	...	...	...	...	...	...	...	...	311

Region, country or area Région, pays ou zone	Year Année	Hard coal, lignite and peat Houille, lignite et tourbe	Briquettes and cokes Agglomérés et cokes	Crude petroleum and NGL Pétrole brut et GNL	Light petroleum products Produits pétroliers légers	Heavy petroleum products Produits pétroliers lourds	Other petroleum products Autres produits pétroliers	LPG and refinery gas GLP et gas de raffinerie	Natural gas Gaz naturel	Electricity Electricité
Malta Malte	2000 2001 2002 2003	... ...	... ...	... ...	... ...	... ...	... ...	... ...	... ...	165 167 176 192
Netherlands Pays-Bas	2000 2001 2002 2003	... ...	1 448 1 507 1 448 1 466	2 423 2 335 3 143 3 139	35 026 35 663 32 890 35 050	33 388 33 133 32 417 33 321	6 287 6 562 6 292 6 604	7 692 8 184 9 215 9 592	57 709 61 944 60 344 58 051	8 395 8 757 8 938 9 023
Norway [7] Norvège [7]	2000 2001 2002 2003	424 1 200 1 431 1 976	... ...	162 026 164 190 162 420 157 451	5 616 5 107 5 012 5 550	8 707 8 207 7 590 8 421	169 183 173 195	1 053 801 721 823	50 916 54 432 *65 783 *73 680	12 047 10 297 11 241 9 225
Poland Pologne	2000 2001 2002 2003	71 109 71 488 71 049 71 132	6 071 6 045 5 894 6 833	654 768 729 766	5 835 5 954 5 722 5 698	10 853 10 641 9 704 10 047	1 255 1 254 1 576 1 680	981 942 953 988	3 684 3 883 3 968 4 015	12 486 12 523 12 395 13 040
Portugal Portugal	2000 2001 2002 2003	... ...	248 45	... ...	4 331 4 451 4 347 4 821	6 824 7 280 7 236 7 396	1 113 1 218 725 907	301 404 371 412	... ...	3 826 4 081 4 039 4 099
Republic of Moldova * République de Moldova *	2000 2001 2002 2003	... ...	... ...	... ...	... ...	... ...	... ...	... ...	... ...	285 308 278 294
Romania Roumanie	2000 2001 2002 2003	5 129 5 788 5 268 5 724	1 016 890 1 176 1 032	6 313 6 262 6 099 5 915	3 658 3 896 4 633 4 157	5 317 6 043 6 444 5 596	1 088 1 122 1 251 1 226	1 095 1 196 1 129 1 265	12 195 11 986 11 784 11 595	5 421 5 586 5 672 5 601
Russian Federation Fédération de Russie	2000 2001 2002 2003	99 623 103 615 99 718 107 591	18 454 18 880 19 895 19 945	322 014 346 187 377 550 419 001	37 627 38 345 40 147 40 643	102 855 105 988 111 881 110 609	14 476 15 752 14 012 10 691	21 344 20 613 20 987 22 070	523 381 521 203 533 169 555 725	98 408 100 684 101 556 105 361
Serbia and Montenegro Serbie-et-Monténégro	2000 2001 2002 2003	7 893 7 745 8 189 8 601	299 305 320 361	979 900 813 774	461 743 987 953	649 1 544 1 971 2 184	95 208 255 277	36 87 95 86	693 506 405 371	*2 936 *3 021 *3 015 *3 041
Slovakia Slovaquie	2000 2001 2002 2003	1 068 1 003 997 907	1 101 1 095 1 165 1 217	59 111 108 83	2 286 2 199 2 277 2 322	2 695 3 154 2 991 3 016	883 487 538 470	89 541 485 500	148 168 161 185	5 585 5 749 5 930 5 808
Slovenia Slovénie	2000 2001 2002 2003	974 899 1 019 1 050	... ...	1 ... 1 ...	83	98	7 5 4 8	... ...	6 6 5 5	2 005 2 164 2 231 2 117
Spain Espagne	2000 2001 2002 2003	7 967 7 539 7 189 6 811	1 787 1 915 1 900 1 804	459 583 559 510	18 054 17 254 16 624 16 636	33 329 32 158 33 145 31 994	6 195 6 140 5 884 7 020	3 279 3 255 3 252 2 994	165 524 519 219	30 189 31 447 32 092 33 316
Sweden Suède	2000 2001 2002 2003	223 263 332 345	768 769 720 863	... ...	6 121 5 661 5 328 5 337	14 227 13 658 12 092 12 170	1 064 1 148 1 167 1 046	338 304 296 392	... ...	22 523 26 518 24 538 23 461
Switzerland [8] Suisse [8]	2000 2001 2002 2003	... ...	... ...	... ...	1 607 1 632 1 653 1 496	2 622 2 823 2 777 2 674	149 179 166 172	376 384 432 375	... ...	10 537 10 876 10 497 10 570
TFYR of Macedonia L'ex-R.y. Macédoine	2000 2001 2002 2003	2 029 2 189 2 047 1 993	... ...	... ...	307 250 195 301	636 507 426 667	... ...	9 12 10 23	... ...	586 547 524 579

Region, country or area Région, pays ou zone	Year Année	Hard coal, lignite and peat Houille, lignite et tourbe	Briquettes and cokes Agglomérés et cokes	Crude petroleum and NGL Pétrole brut et GNL	Light petroleum products Produits pétroliers légers	Heavy petroleum products Produits pétroliers lourds	Other petroleum products Autres produits pétroliers	LPG and refinery gas GLP et gas de raffinerie	Natural gas Gaz naturel	Electricity Electricité
Ukraine	2000	32 246	11 657	3 780	2 878	5 854	853	370	16 678	28 279
Ukraine	2001	31 765	13 244	3 791	4 525	10 251	1 808	785	17 101	28 205
	2002	30 700	12 749	3 822	5 187	13 193	2 137	995	17 420	28 589
	2003	33 210	14 316	4 061	4 912	14 302	2 440	1 155	17 896	29 756
United Kingdom	2000	18 797	4 294	128 439	37 905	40 239	5 112	5 031	108 464	47 314
Royaume-Uni	2001	19 238	3 823	119 586	35 695	39 003	4 699	4 560	105 909	48 810
	2002	18 068	3 177	118 576	36 746	39 275	4 607	5 321	103 854	48 699
	2003	17 026	3 180	108 065	36 678	39 406	4 971	5 404	103 005	49 801
Oceania	2000	167 982	2 477	40 920	22 190	15 664	2 666	2 446	37 388	23 882
Océanie	2001	183 118	2 311	41 813	21 046	15 453	2 557	2 465	38 368	24 662
	2002	189 921	2 258	38 220	21 607	15 471	2 154	2 412	39 436	25 614
	2003	191 084	2 182	35 571	21 231	15 423	2 287	2 384	39 182	25 687
Australia	2000	165 805	2 477	34 906	19 804	13 260	2 449	2 217	31 688	17 867
Australie	2001	180 906	2 311	35 800	18 607	13 156	2 359	2 239	32 374	18 680
	2002	187 396	2 258	32 376	19 081	12 938	1 966	2 168	33 733	19 465
	2003	188 150	2 182	30 145	18 754	12 989	2 052	2 169	34 812	19 614
Cook Islands	2000	...	...	...	...	...	...	...	...	2
Iles Cook	2001	...	...	...	...	...	...	...	...	2
	2002	...	...	...	...	...	...	...	...	2
	2003	...	...	...	...	...	...	...	...	2
Fiji *	2000	...	...	...	...	...	...	...	...	45
Fidji *	2001	...	...	...	...	...	...	...	...	45
	2002	...	...	...	...	...	...	...	...	45
	2003	...	...	...	...	...	...	...	...	45
French Polynesia	2000	...	...	...	...	...	...	...	...	35
Polynésie française	2001	...	...	...	...	...	...	...	...	43
	2002	...	...	...	...	...	...	...	...	44
	*2003	...	...	...	...	...	...	...	...	43
Kiribati	2000	...	...	...	...	...	...	...	...	1
Kiribati	2001	...	...	...	...	...	...	...	...	1
	*2002	...	...	...	...	...	...	...	...	1
	*2003	...	...	...	...	...	...	...	...	1
Nauru *	2000	...	...	...	...	...	...	...	...	3
Nauru *	2001	...	...	...	...	...	...	...	...	3
	2002	...	...	...	...	...	...	...	...	3
	2003	...	...	...	...	...	...	...	...	3
New Caledonia	2000	...	...	...	...	...	...	...	...	141
Nouvelle-Calédonie	2001	...	...	...	...	...	...	...	...	149
	*2002	...	...	...	...	...	...	...	...	149
	*2003	...	...	...	...	...	...	...	...	149
New Zealand	2000	2 177	...	2 080	2 367	2 372	217	229	*5 622	5 634
Nouvelle-Zélande	2001	2 212	...	2 019	2 419	2 267	198	226	*5 916	5 588
	2002	2 525	...	1 850	2 506	2 503	188	244	*5 624	5 753
	2003	2 933	...	1 432	2 458	2 404	235	215	*4 289	5 675
Palau *	2000	...	...	...	...	...	...	...	...	15
Palaos *	2001	...	...	...	...	...	...	...	...	14
	2002	...	...	...	...	...	...	...	...	14
	2003	...	...	...	...	...	...	...	...	15
Papua New Guinea	2000	...	...	*3 934	*19	*31	...	...	*78	121
Papouasie-Nouvelle-Guinée	2001	...	...	*3 994	*20	*30	...	...	*79	120
	*2002	...	...	3 994	20	30	...	...	79	120
	*2003	...	...	3 994	20	30	...	...	80	120
Samoa *	2000	...	...	...	...	...	...	...	...	8
Samoa *	2001	...	...	...	...	...	...	...	...	9
	2002	...	...	...	...	...	...	...	...	9
	2003	...	...	...	...	...	...	...	...	9
Solomon Islands *	2000	...	...	...	...	...	...	...	...	3
Iles Salomon *	2001	...	...	...	...	...	...	...	...	3
	2002	...	...	...	...	...	...	...	...	3
	2003	...	...	...	...	...	...	...	...	3

Region, country or area Région, pays ou zone	Year Année	Hard coal, lignite and peat Houille, lignite et tourbe	Briquettes and cokes Agglomérés et cokes	Crude petroleum and NGL Pétrole brut et GNL	Light petroleum products Produits pétroliers légers	Heavy petroleum products Produits pétroliers lourds	Other petroleum products Autres produits pétroliers	LPG and refinery gas GLP et gas de raffinerie	Natural gas Gaz naturel	Electricity Electricité
Tonga *	2000	...	...	...	...	...	...	...	...	3
Tonga *	2001	...	...	...	...	...	...	...	...	3
	2002	...	...	...	...	...	...	...	...	3
	2003	...	...	...	...	...	...	...	...	3
Vanuatu *	2000	...	...	...	...	...	...	...	...	4
Vanuatu *	2001	...	...	...	...	...	...	...	...	4
	2002	...	...	...	...	...	...	...	...	4
	2003	...	...	...	...	...	...	...	...	4

Source

United Nations Statistics Division, New York, *Energy Statistics Yearbook 2003* and the energy statistics database.

Notes

[1] Refers to the Southern African Customs Union.

[2] Includes the 50 states and the District of Columbia. Oil statistics as well as coal trade statistics also include Puerto Rico, Guam, the U.S. Virgin Islands, American Samoa, Johnston Atoll, Midway Islands, Wake Island and the Northern Mariana Islands.

[3] For statistical purposes, the data for China do not include those for the Hong Kong Special Administrative Region (Hong Kong SAR), Macao Special Administrative Region (Macao SAR) and Taiwan Province of China.

[4] Including part of the Neutral Zone.

[5] Including Monaco.

[6] Including San Marino.

[7] Including Svalbard and Jan Mayen Islands.

[8] Including Liechtenstein.

Source

Organisation des Nations Unies, Division de statistique, New York, *Annuaire des statistiques de l'énergie 2003* et la base de données pour les statistiques énergétiques.

Notes

[1] Se réfèrent à l'Union douanière d'afrique australe.

[2] Englobent les 50 Etats fédérés et le District de Columbia. Les statistiques sur le pétrole et sur les échanges de charbon concernent également Porto Rico, l'Ile de Guam, les Iles Vierges des Etats-Unis, le Territoire non incorporé des Samoa américaines, l'Ile Johnston, les Iles Midway, l'Ile de Wake et les Iles Mariannes-du-Nord.

[3] Pour la présentation des statistiques, les données pour Chine ne comprennent pas la Région Administrative Spéciale de Hong Kong (Hong Kong RAS), la Région Administrative Spéciale de Macao (Macao RAS) et la province de Taiwan.

[4] Y compris une partie de la Zone Neutrale.

[5] Y compris Monaco.

[6] Y compris Saint-Marin.

[7] Y compris îles Svalbard et Jan Mayen.

[8] Y compris Liechtenstein.

Tables 58 and 59: Data are presented in metric tons of oil equivalent (TOE), to which the individual energy commodities are converted in the interests of international uniformity and comparability.

To convert from original units to TOE, the data in original units (metric tons, terajoules, kilowatt hours, cubic metres) are multiplied by conversion factors. For a list of the relevant conversion factors and a detailed description of methods, see the United Nations *Energy Statistics Yearbook* and related methodological publications [22, 42, 43].

Table 58: Included in the production of commercial primary energy for solids are hard coal, lignite, peat and oil shale; liquids are comprised of crude petroleum and natural gas liquids; gas comprises natural gas; and electricity is comprised of primary electricity generation from hydro, nuclear, geothermal, wind, tide, wave and solar sources.

In general, data on stocks refer to changes in stocks of producers, importers and/or industrial consumers at the beginning and end of each year.

International trade of energy commodities is based on the "general trade" system, that is, all goods entering and leaving the national boundary of a country are recorded as imports and exports.

Sea/air bunkers refer to the amounts of fuels delivered to ocean-going ships or aircraft of all flags engaged in international traffic. Consumption by ships engaged in transport in inland and coastal waters, or by aircraft engaged in domestic flights, is not included.

Data on consumption refer to "apparent consumption" and are derived from the formula "production + imports – exports – bunkers +/– stock changes". Accordingly, the series on apparent consumption may in some cases represent only an indication of the magnitude of actual gross inland availability.

Included in the consumption of commercial energy for solids are consumption of primary forms of solid fuels, net imports and changes in stocks of secondary fuels; liquids are comprised of consumption of energy petroleum products including feedstocks, natural gasolene, condensate, refinery gas and input of crude petroleum to thermal power plants; gases include the consumption of natural gas, net imports and changes in stocks of gasworks and coke oven gas; and electricity is comprised of production of primary electricity and net imports of electricity.

Table 59: The definitions of the energy commodities are as follows:

* Hard coal: Coal that has a high degree of coalification with a gross calorific value above 23,865 kJ/kg (5,700 kcal/kg) on an ash free but moist basis, and a mean random reflectance of vitrinite of at least 0.6. Slurries, middlings and other low-grade coal products, which cannot

Tableaux 58 et 59 : Les données relatives aux divers produits énergétiques ont été converties en tonnes d'équivalent pétrole (TEP), dans un souci d'uniformité et pour permettre les comparaisons entre la production de différents pays.

Pour passer des unités de mesure d'origine à l'unité commune, les données en unités d'origine (tonnes, terajoules, kilowatt-heures, mètres cubes) sont multipliées par des facteurs de conversion. Pour une liste des facteurs de conversion appropriée et pour des descriptions détaillées des méthodes appliquées, se reporter à l'*Annuaire des statistiques de l'énergie des Nations Unies* et aux publications méthodologiques apparentées [22, 42, 43].

Tableau 58 : Sont compris dans la production d'énergie primaire commerciale : pour les solides, la houille, le lignite, la tourbe et le schiste bitumineux; pour les liquides, le pétrole brut et les liquides de gaz naturel; pour les gaz, le gaz naturel; pour l'électricité, l'électricité primaire de source hydraulique, nucléaire, géothermique, éolienne, marémotrice, des vagues et solaire.

En général, les variations des stocks se rapportent aux différences entre les stocks des producteurs, des importateurs ou des consommateurs industriels au début et à la fin de chaque année.

Le commerce international des produits énergétiques est fondé sur le système du "commerce général", c'est-à-dire que tous les biens entrant sur le territoire national d'un pays ou en sortant sont respectivement enregistrés comme importations et exportations.

Les soutes maritimes/aériens se rapportent aux quantités de combustibles livrées aux navires de mer et aéronefs assurant des liaisons commerciales internationales, quel que soit leur pavillon. La consommation des navires effectuant des opérations de transport sur les voies navigables intérieures ou dans les eaux côtières n'est pas incluse, tout comme celle des aéronefs effectuant des vols intérieurs.

Les données sur la consommation se rapportent à la "consommation apparente" et sont obtenues par la formule "production + importations – exportations – soutes +/– variations des stocks". En conséquence, les séries relatives à la consommation apparente peuvent occasionnellement ne donner qu'une indication de l'ordre de grandeur des disponibilités intérieures brutes réelles.

Sont compris dans la consommation d'énergie commerciale : pour les solides, la consommation de combustibles solides primaires, les importations nettes et les variations de stocks de combustibles solides secondaires; pour les liquides, la consommation de produits pétroliers énergétiques y compris les charges d'alimentation des usines de traitement, l'essence naturelle, le condensat et le gaz de raffinerie ainsi que le pétrole brut consommé dans les centrales thermiques pour la production d'électricité; pour les gaz, la consommation de gaz naturel, les importations nettes et les variations de stocks de gaz d'usines à

be classified according to the type of coal from which they are obtained, are included under hard coal.

- Lignite: Non-agglomerating coal with a low degree of coalification which retained the anatomical structure of the vegetable matter from which it was formed. Its gross calorific value is less than 17,435 kJ/kg (4,165 kcal/kg), and it contains greater than 31 per cent volatile matter on a dry mineral matter free basis.
- Peat: A solid fuel formed from the partial decomposition of dead vegetation under conditions of high humidity and limited air access (initial stage of coalification). Only peat used as fuel is included.
- Patent fuel (hard coal briquettes): A composition fuel manufactured from coal fines by shaping with the addition of a binding agent (pitch).
- Lignite briquettes: A composition fuel manufactured from lignite. The lignite is crushed, dried and molded under high pressure into an even-shaped briquette without the addition of binders.
- Peat briquettes: A composition fuel manufactured from peat. Raw peat, after crushing and drying, is molded under high pressure into an even-shaped briquette without the addition of binders.
- Coke: The solid residue obtained from coal or lignite by heating it to a high temperature in the absence or near absence of air. It is high in carbon and low in moisture and volatile matter. Several categories are distinguished: coke oven coke; gas coke; and brown coal coke.
- Crude oil: A mineral oil consisting of a mixture of hydrocarbons of natural origin, yellow to black in color, of variable density and viscosity. Data in this category also includes lease or field condensate (separator liquids) which is recovered from gaseous hydrocarbons in lease separation facilities, as well as synthetic crude oil, mineral oils extracted from bituminous minerals such as shales and bituminous sand, and oils from coal liquefaction.
- Natural gas liquids (NGL): Liquid or liquefied hydrocarbons produced in the manufacture, purification and stabilization of natural gas. NGLs include, but are not limited to, ethane, propane, butane, pentane, natural gasolene, and plant condensate.
- Light petroleum products: Light products are defined in the table as liquid products obtained by distillation of crude petroleum at temperatures between 30°C and 350°C, and/or which have a specific gravity between 0.625 and 0.830. They comprise: aviation gasolene; motor gasolene; natural gasolene; jet fuel; kerosene; naphtha; and white spirit/industrial spirit.
- Heavy petroleum products: are defined in the table as products obtained by the distillation of crude petroleum at temperatures above 350°C, and which have a specific gravity higher than 0.83. Products which are not used

gaz et de gaz de cokerie; pour l'électricité, la production d'électricité primaire et les importations nettes d'électricité.

Tableau 59 : Les définitions des produits énergétiques sont données ci-après :

- Houille : Charbon à haut degré de houillification et à pouvoir calorifique brut supérieur à 23.865 kJ/kg (5.700 kcal/kg), valeur mesurée pour un combustible exempt de cendres, mais humide et ayant un indice moyen de réflectance de la vitrinite au moins égal à 0,6. Les schlamms, les mixtes et autres produits du charbon de faible qualité qui ne peuvent être classés en fonction du type de charbon dont ils sont dérivés, sont inclus dans cette rubrique.
- Lignite : Le charbon non agglutinant d'un faible degré de houillification qui a gardé la structure anatomique des végétaux dont il est issu. Son pouvoir calorifique supérieur est inférieur à 17.435 kJ/kg (4.165 kcal/kg) et il contient plus de 31% de matières volatiles sur produit sec exempt de matières minérales.
- Tourbe : Combustible solide issu de la décomposition partielle de végétaux morts dans des conditions de forte humidité et de faible circulation d'air (phase initiale de la houillification). N'est prise en considération ici que la tourbe utilisée comme combustible.
- Agglomérés (briquettes de houille) : Combustibles composites fabriqués par moulage au moyen de fines de charbon avec l'addition d'un liant (brai).
- Briquettes de lignite : Combustibles composites fabriqués au moyen de lignite. Le lignite est broyé, séché et moulé sous pression élevée pour donner une briquette de forme régulière sans l'addition d'un élément liant.
- Briquettes de tourbe : Combustibles composites fabriqués au moyen de tourbe. La tourbe brute, après broyage et séchage, est moulée sous pression élevée pour donner une briquette de forme régulière sans l'addition d'un élément liant.
- Coke : Résidu solide obtenu lors de la distillation de houille ou de lignite en l'absence totale ou presque total d'air. Il a un haut contenu de carbone, et a peu d'humidité et matières volatiles. On distingue plusieurs catégories de coke : coke de four; coke de gaz; et coke de lignite.
- Pétrole brut : Huile minérale constituée d'un mélange d'hydrocarbures d'origine naturelle, de couleur variant du jaune au noir, d'une densité et d'une viscosité variable. Figurent également dans cette rubrique les condensats directement récupérés sur les sites d'exploitation des hydrocarbures gazeux (dans les installations prévues pour la séparation des phases liquide et gazeuse), le pétrole brut synthétique, les huiles minérales brutes extraites des roches bitumineuses telles que schistes, sables asphaltiques et les huiles issues de la liquéfaction du charbon.
- Liquides de gaz naturel (LGN) : Hydrocarbures liquides ou liquéfiés produits lors de la fabrication, de la purification et de la stabilisation du gaz naturel. Les liquides de

for energy purposes, such as insulating oils, lubricants, paraffin wax, bitumen and petroleum coke, are excluded. Heavy products comprise residual fuel oil and gas diesel oil (distillate fuel oil).

- Liquefied petroleum gas (LPG): Hydrocarbons which are gaseous under conditions of normal temperature and pressure but are liquefied by compression or cooling to facilitate storage, handling and transportation. It comprises propane, butane, or a combination of the two. Also included is ethane from petroleum refineries or natural gas producers' separation and stabilization plants.

- Refinery gas: Non condensable gas obtained during distillation of crude oil or treatment of oil products (e.g. cracking) in refineries. It consists mainly of hydrogen, methane, ethane and olefins.

- Natural gas: Gases consisting mainly of methane occurring naturally in underground deposits. It includes both non associated gas (originating from fields producing only hydrocarbons in gaseous form) and associated gas (originating from fields producing both liquid and gaseous hydrocarbons), as well as methane recovered from coal mines and sewage gas. Production of natural gas refers to dry marketable production, measured after purification and extraction of natural gas liquids and sulphur. Extraction losses and the amounts that have been reinjected, flared, and vented are excluded from the data on production.

- Electricity production refers to gross production, which includes the consumption by station auxiliaries and any losses in the transformers that are considered integral parts of the station. Included also is total electric energy produced by pumping installations without deduction of electric energy absorbed by pumping.

gaz naturel comprennent l'éthane, le propane, le butane, le pentane, l'essence naturelle et les condensats d'usine, sans que la liste soit limitative.

- Produits pétroliers légers sont définis ici comme des produits liquides obtenus par distillation du pétrole brut à des températures comprises entre 30°C et 350°C et/ou ayant une densité comprise entre 0,625 et 0,830. Ces produits sont les suivants : l'essence aviation; l'essence auto; l'essence naturelle; les carburéacteurs du type essence et du type kérosène; le pétrole lampant; les naphtas; et le white spirit/essences spéciales.

- Produits pétroliers lourds sont définis ici comme des produits obtenus par distillation du pétrole brut à des températures supérieures à 350°C et ayant une densité supérieure à 0,83. En sont exclus les produits qui ne sont pas utilisés à des fins énergétiques, tels que les huiles isolantes, les lubrifiants, les paraffines, le bitume et le coke de pétrole. Les produits lourds comprennent le mazout résiduel et le gazole/carburant diesel (mazout distillé).

- Gaz de pétrole liquéfiés (GPL) : Hydrocarbures qui sont à l'état gazeux dans des conditions de température et de pression normales mais sont liquéfiés par compression ou refroidissement pour en faciliter l'entreposage, la manipulation et le transport. Dans cette rubrique figurent le propane et le butane ou un mélange de ces deux hydrocarbures. Est également inclus l'éthane produit dans les raffineries ou dans les installations de séparation et de stabilisation des producteurs de gaz naturel.

- Gaz de raffinerie : Comprend les gaz non condensables obtenus dans les raffineries lors de la distillation du pétrole brut ou du traitement des produits pétroliers (par craquage par exemple). Il s'agit principalement d'hydrogène, de méthane, d'éthane et d'oléfines.

- Gaz naturel : Est constitué de gaz, méthane essentiellement, extraits de gisements naturels souterrains. Il peut s'agir aussi bien de gaz non associé (provenant de gisements qui produisent uniquement des hydrocarbures gazeux) que de gaz associé (provenant de gisements qui produisent à la fois des hydrocarbures liquides et gazeux) ou de méthane récupéré dans les mines de charbon et le gaz de gadoues. La production de gaz naturel se rapporte à la production de gaz commercialisable sec, mesurée après purification et extraction des condensats de gaz naturel et du soufre. Les quantités réinjectées, brûlées à la torchère ou éventées et les pertes d'extraction sont exclues des données sur la production.

- La production d'électricité se rapporte à la production brute, qui comprend la consommation des équipements auxiliaires des centrales et les pertes au niveau des transformateurs considérés comme faisant partie intégrante de ces centrales, ainsi que la quantité totale d'énergie électrique produite par les installations de pompage sans déductions de l'énergie électrique absorbée par ces dernières.

60

Land
Terres

Country or area Pays ou zone	2003			Net change — Variation nette		2005	
	Land area Superficie des terres	Arable land Terre arables	Permanent crops Cultures permanentes	1990 – 2003		Protected areas Aires protégées	Protected areas Aires protégées
				Arable land Terres arables	Permanent crops Cultures permanentes		
	Area in thousand hectares — Superficie en milliers de hectares						% [1]
Africa **Afrique**							
Algeria Algérie	238 174	7 545 [2]	670 [2]	464	116	11 969.9	5.0
Angola Angola	124 670	3 300 [2]	290 [2]	400	−210	15 458.0	12.1
Benin Bénin	11 062	2 650 [2]	267 [2]	1 035	162	2 642.8	23.0
Botswana Botswana	56 673	377 [2]	3 [2]	−41	0	17 565.0	30.2
Burkina Faso Burkina Faso	27 360	4 840 [2]	60 [2]	1 320	5	4 208.2	15.4
Burundi Burundi	2 568	990 [2]	365 [2]	60	5	154.8	5.6
Cameroon Cameroun	46 540	5 960 [2]	1 200 [2]	20	−30	4 319.7	8.9
Cape Verde Cap-Vert	403	46 [2]	3 [2]	5	1	1.4	0.0
Central African Rep. Rép. centrafricaine	62 298	1 930 [2]	94 [2]	10	8	9 776.9	15.7
Chad Tchad	125 920	3 600 [2]	30 [2]	327	3	11 977.3	9.3
Comoros Comores	223	80 [2]	52 [2]	2	17	40.4	2.7
Congo Congo	34 150	495 [2]	52 [2]	16	10	4 874.0	14.1
Côte d'Ivoire Côte d'Ivoire	31 800	3 300 [2]	3 600 [2]	870	100	5 485.4	16.4
Dem. Rep. of the Congo Rép. dém. du Congo	226 705	6 700 [2]	1 100 [2]	30	−90	19 740.6	8.4
Djibouti Djibouti	2 318	1 [2]	...	0	...	0.0	0.0
Egypt Egypte	99 545	2 922 [2]	502 [2]	638	138	14 074.4	13.3
Equatorial Guinea Guinée équatoriale	2 805	130 [2]	100 [2]	0	0	586.0	14.3
Eritrea Erythrée	10 100	562 [2]	3 [2]	...	...	500.6	3.2
Ethiopia Ethiopie	100 000	11 056 [2]	713 [2]	...	...	18 619.8	16.9
Gabon Gabon	25 767	325 [2]	170 [2]	30	8	4 648.4	16.2
Gambia Gambie	1 000	315 [2]	5 [2]	133	0	56.5	4.1
Ghana Ghana	22 754	4 185 [2]	2 200 [2]	1 485	700	3 687.2	14.7

Country or area Pays ou zone	2003			Net change — Variation nette		2005	
				1990 – 2003			
	Land area Superficie des terres	Arable land Terre arables	Permanent crops Cultures permanentes	Arable land Terres arables	Permanent crops Cultures permanentes	Protected areas Aires protégées	Protected areas Aires protégées
	Area in thousand hectares — Superficie en milliers de hectares						% [1]
Guinea Guinée	24 572	1 100 [2]	650 [2]	372	150	1 591.3	6.1
Guinea-Bissau Guinée-Bissau	2 812	300 [2]	250 [2]	0	133	404.0	7.3
Kenya Kenya	56 914	4 650 [2]	562 [2]	450	62	7 522.1	12.7
Lesotho Lesotho	3 035	330 [2]	4 [2]	13	0	6.8	0.2
Liberia Libéria	9 632	382 [2]	220 [2]	−18	5	1 578.5	12.7
Libyan Arab Jamah. Jamah. arabe libyenne	175 954	1 815 [2]	335 [2]	10	−15	220.9	0.1
Madagascar Madagascar	58 154	2 950 [2]	600 [2]	230	−5	1 845.8	2.6
Malawi Malawi	9 408	2 450 [2]	140 [2]	635	25	1 940.5	16.4
Mali Mali	122 019	4 660 [2]	40 [2]	2 607	0	2 633.3	2.1
Mauritania Mauritanie	102 522	488 [2]	12 [2]	88	6	1 749.0	1.7
Mauritius Maurice	203	100 [2]	6 [2]	0	0	16.2	0.9
Mayotte Mayotte	...	...	...	...	...	6.4	17.2
Morocco Maroc	44 630	8 484	892	−223	156	567.3	1.2
Mozambique Mozambique	78 409	4 350 [2]	230 [2]	900	0	7 526.0	8.6
Namibia Namibie	82 329	815 [2]	5 [2]	155	3	12 488.4	14.6
Niger Niger	126 670	14 483 [2]	17 [2]	3 447	6	8 414.1	6.6
Nigeria Nigéria	91 077	30 500 [2]	2 900 [2]	961	365	5 710.2	6.1
Réunion Réunion	250	35	4	−12	−1	24.6	3.0
Rwanda Rwanda	2 467	1 200 [2]	270 [2]	320	−35	200.8	7.6
Saint Helena Sainte-Hélène	31	4 [2]	...	2	...	11.9	38.3
Sao Tome and Principe Sao Tomé-et-Principe	96	8 [2]	47 [2]	6	8	...	...
Senegal Sénégal	19 253	2 460 [2]	47 [2]	135	22	2 242.2	10.8
Seychelles Seychelles	46	1 [2]	6 [2]	0	1	45.2	1.0
Sierra Leone Sierra Leone	7 162	570 [2]	75 [2]	84	21	324.4	3.9
Somalia Somalie	62 734	1 045 [2]	26 [2]	23	6	524.6	0.7

		Net change — Variation nette				
	2003			1990 – 2003		2005
Country or area Pays ou zone	Land area Superficie des terres	Arable land Terre arables	Permanent crops Cultures permanentes	Arable land Terres arables	Permanent crops Cultures permanentes	Protected areas Aires protégées	Protected areas Aires protégées
	Area in thousand hectares — Superficie en milliers de hectares						% [1]
South Africa Afrique du Sud	121 447	14 753	959	1 313	99	7 905.2	6.1
Sudan Soudan	237 600	17 000 [2]	420 [2]	4 000	185	12 009.0	4.7
Swaziland Swaziland	1 720	178 [2]	14 [2]	−2	2	60.1	3.5
Togo Togo	5 439	2 510 [2]	120 [2]	410	30	650.1	11.2
Tunisia Tunisie	15 536	2 790	2 140	−119	198	257.9	1.3
Uganda Ouganda	19 710	5 200 [2]	2 150 [2]	200	300	6 336.8	26.3
United Rep. of Tanzania Rép.-Unie de Tanzanie	88 359	4 000 [2]	1 100 [2]	500	200	37 660.4	38.4
Western Sahara Sahara occidental	...	...	...	...	...	1 888.9	7.1
Zambia Zambie	74 339	5 260 [2]	29 [2]	11	10	31 234.1	41.5
Zimbabwe Zimbabwe	38 685	3 220 [2]	130 [2]	330	10	5 752.5	14.7
America, North **Amérique du Nord**							
Anguilla Anguilla	...	...	...	...	...	0.0	0.1
Antigua and Barbuda Antigua-et-Barbuda	44	8 [2]	2 [2]	0	0	6.6	0.9
Aruba Aruba	19	2 [2]	...	0	...	0.3	0.1
Bahamas Bahamas	1 001	8 [2]	4 [2]	0	2	281.4	0.9
Barbados Barbade	43	16 [2]	1 [2]	0	0	0.3	0.1
Belize Belize	2 281	70 [2]	32 [2]	18	7	1 260.4	30.4
Bermuda Bermudes	5	1 [2]	...	0	...	15.4	5.2
British Virgin Islands Iles Vierges britanniques	15	3 [2]	1 [2]	0	0	5.2	34.6
Canada Canada	909 351	45 660 [2]	6 455 [2]	156	94	86 602.1	6.8
Cayman Islands Iles Caïmanes	26	1 [2]	...	0	...	24.1	92.7
Costa Rica Costa Rica	5 106	225 [2]	300 [2]	−35	50	1 750.9	23.3
Cuba Cuba	10 982	3 063 [2]	725 [2]	32	−85	3 519.3	15.1
Dominica Dominique	75	5 [2]	16 [2]	0	5	20.4	4.5
Dominican Republic Rép. dominicaine	4 838	1 096 [2]	500 [2]	46	50	2 045.1	32.6

		2003		Net change — Variation nette		2005	
				1990 – 2003			
Country or area Pays ou zone	Land area Superficie des terres	Arable land Terre arables	Permanent crops Cultures permanentes	Arable land Terres arables	Permanent crops Cultures permanentes	Protected areas Aires protégées	Protected areas Aires protégées
	Area in thousand hectares — Superficie en milliers de hectares						% [1]
El Salvador El Salvador	2 072	660 [2]	250 [2]	110	−10	25.8	0.9
Grenada Grenade	34	2 [2]	10 [2]	0	0	0.7	0.2
Guadeloupe Guadeloupe	169	20	5	−1	−3	40.5	3.0
Guatemala Guatemala	10 843	1 440 [2]	610 [2]	140	125	3 585.9	30.8
Haiti Haïti	2 756	780 [2]	320 [2]	0	0	7.4	0.1
Honduras Honduras	11 189	1 068 [2]	360 [2]	−394	2	2 976.2	20.0
Jamaica Jamaïque	1 083	174 [2]	110 [2]	55	10	364.7	13.5
Martinique Martinique	106	10	11	0	1	65.5	10.5
Mexico Mexique	190 869	24 800 [2]	2 500 [2]	800	600	19 618.6	8.7
Montserrat Montserrat	10	2 [2]	...	0	...	1.1	10.7
Netherlands Antilles Antilles néerlandaises	80	8 [2]	...	0	...	14.5	1.1
Nicaragua Nicaragua	12 140	1 925 [2]	236 [2]	625	41	2 940.6	18.2
Panama Panama	7 443	548 [2]	147 [2]	49	−8	3 279.5	24.6
Puerto Rico Porto Rico	887	33 [2]	50 [2]	−32	0	64.9	2.5
Saint Kitts and Nevis Saint-Kitts-et-Nevis	36	7 [2]	1 [2]	−1	−1	2.6	9.7
Saint Lucia Sainte-Lucie	61	4 [2]	14 [2]	−1	1	10.4	2.4
Saint Pierre and Miquelon Saint-Pierre-et-Miquelon	23	3 [2]	...	0	...	12.7	52.8
St. Vincent-Grenadines St. Vincent-Grenadines	39	7 [2]	7 [2]	2	0	8.3	1.3
Trinidad and Tobago Trinité-et-Tobago	513	75 [2]	47 [2]	1	1	32.2	1.8
Turks and Caicos Islands Iles Turques et Caïques	43	1 [2]	...	0	...	71.7	166.8
United States Etats-Unis	915 896	173 450 [2]	2 050 [2]	−12 292	16	242 134.3	23.2
United States Virgin Is. Iles Vierges américaines	35	2 [2]	1 [2]	−2	0	18.3	3.0
America, South Amérique du Sud							
Argentina Argentine	273 669	27 900 [2]	1 000 [2]	1 500	−20	18 142.2	6.2
Bolivia Bolivie	108 438	3 050 [2]	206 [2]	950	51	21 701.2	19.8

	Net change — Variation nette					
	2003			1990 – 2003		2005
Country or area Pays ou zone	Land area Superficie des terres	Arable land Terre arables	Permanent crops Cultures permanentes	Arable land Terres arables	Permanent crops Cultures permanentes	Protected areas Aires protégées	Protected areas Aires protégées
	Area in thousand hectares — Superficie en milliers de hectares						% [1]
Brazil Brésil	845 942[2]	59 000[2]	7 600[2]	8 319	873	163 886.7	18.7
Chile Chili	74 880	1 982[2]	325[2]	−820	78	21 357.0	20.8
Colombia Colombie	103 870	2 293	1 557	−1 012	−138	37 412.3	31.6
Ecuador Equateur	27 684	1 620[2]	1 365[2]	16	44	20 893.1	53.5
Falkland Is. (Malvinas) Iles Falkland (Malvinas)	1 217	...	...	...	...	11.3	0.9
French Guiana Guyane française	8 815	12	4	2	2	530.6	5.4
Guyana Guyana	19 685	480[2]	30[2]	0	8	486.0	2.2
Paraguay Paraguay	39 730	3 040[2]	96[2]	930	7	2 366.4	5.8
Peru Pérou	128 000	3 700[2]	610[2]	200	190	17 925.7	13.3
Suriname Suriname	15 600	58[2]	10[2]	1	−1	1 981.2	11.5
Uruguay Uruguay	17 502	1 370[2]	42[2]	110	−3	72.5	0.4
Venezuela (Bolivarian Rep. of) Venezuela (Rép. bolivarienne du)	88 205	2 600[2]	800[2]	−232	22	65 973.8	62.9
Asia **Asie**							
Afghanistan Afghanistan	65 209	7 910[2]	138	0	8	218.6	0.3
Armenia Arménie	2 820	500[2]	60[2]	...	...	299.1	10.0
Azerbaijan Azerbaïdjan	8 260	1 786	226	...	...	632.8	7.3
Bahrain Bahreïn	71	2[2]	4[2]	0	2	6.0	1.3
Bangladesh Bangladesh	13 017	7 976[2]	443[2]	−1 161	143	240.9	1.3
Bhutan Bhoutan	4 700	108[2]	20[2]	−5	1	1 240.8	26.4
Brunei Darussalam Brunéi Darussalam	527	12[2]	5[2]	9	1	342.1	38.3
Cambodia Cambodge	17 652	3 700[2]	107[2]	5	7	4 346.5	21.6
China [3] Chine [3]	932 743[4]	142 615	12 235	18 937[4]	4 516[4]	147 225.0	14.9
China, Hong Kong SAR Chine, Hong Kong RAS	...	...	...	...	...	54.7	51.5
Cyprus Chypre	924	100	40	−6	−11	92.0	4.0
Georgia Géorgie	6 949	802	264	...	...	304.0	4.0

		2003		Net change — Variation nette		2005	
				1990 – 2003			
Country or area Pays ou zone	Land area Superficie des terres	Arable land Terre arables	Permanent crops Cultures permanentes	Arable land Terres arables	Permanent crops Cultures permanentes	Protected areas Aires protégées	Protected areas Aires protégées
	Area in thousand hectares — Superficie en milliers de hectares						% [1]
India Inde	297 319	160 519 [2]	9 220 [2]	−2 269	2 570	18 862.9	5.4
Indonesia Indonésie	181 157	21 000 [2]	13 400 [2]	747	1 680	46 536.3	9.1
Iran (Islamic Rep. of) Iran (Rép. islamique d')	163 620	16 117 [2]	2 131	927	821	11 273.9	6.6
Iraq Iraq	43 737	5 750 [2]	269 [2]	450	−21	0.5	0.0
Israel Israël	2 171	342 [2]	86 [2]	−1	−2	407.5	16.2
Japan Japon	36 450 [2]	4 397	339	−371	−136	6 428.9	8.6
Jordan Jordanie	8 824	295 [2]	105 [2]	5	15	973.4	10.9
Kazakhstan Kazakhstan	269 970	22 550 [2]	136 [2]	...	...	7 791.9	2.9
Korea, Dem. P. R. Corée, R. p. dém. de	12 041	2 700 [2]	200 [2]	412	20	315.9	2.4
Korea, Republic of Corée, République de	9 873	1 646 [2]	200 [2]	−307	44	703.7	3.9
Kuwait Koweït	1 782	15 [2]	3 [2]	11	2	59.7	2.6
Kyrgyzstan Kirghizistan	19 180	1 310 [2]	55 [2]	...	...	715.2	3.6
Lao People's Dem. Rep. Rép. dém. pop. lao	23 080	950 [2]	81 [2]	151	20	3 790.4	16.0
Lebanon Liban	1 023	170 [2]	143 [2]	−13	21	7.8	0.5
Malaysia Malaisie	32 855	1 800 [2]	5 785 [2]	100	537	8 328.6	17.3
Maldives Maldives	30	4 [2]	9 [2]	0	5	0.0	0.0
Mongolia Mongolie	156 650	1 198 [2]	2 [2]	−172	1	21 791.2	13.9
Myanmar Myanmar	65 755	10 093	888	526	386	3 853.2	4.6
Nepal Népal	14 300	2 365 [2]	125 [2]	78	59	2 395.8	16.3
Occupied Palestinian Terr. Terr. palestinien occupé	602	79 [2]	116	−32	1	...	...
Oman Oman	30 950	37 [2]	43 [2]	2	−2	2 982.8	11.3
Pakistan Pakistan	77 088	19 458 [2]	672 [2]	−1 026	216	7 531.1	9.1
Philippines Philippines	29 817	5 700 [2]	5 000 [2]	220	600	6 372.7	6.5
Qatar Qatar	1 100	18 [2]	3 [2]	8	2	13.7	0.6
Saudi Arabia Arabie saoudite	214 969	3 600 [2]	198	210	107	82 859.4	37.1

Country or area / Pays ou zone	Land area 2003 Superficie des terres	Arable land 2003 Terre arables	Permanent crops 2003 Cultures permanentes	Net change — Variation nette 1990 – 2003 Arable land Terres arables	Net change — Variation nette 1990 – 2003 Permanent crops Cultures permanentes	Protected areas 2005 Aires protégées	Protected areas 2005 Aires protégées
	Area in thousand hectares — Superficie en milliers de hectares						% [1]
Singapore / Singapour	67	1[2]	1[2]	0	0	3.0	2.2
Sri Lanka / Sri Lanka	6 463	916[2]	1 000[2]	41	−25	1 654.6	17.2
Syrian Arab Republic / Rép. arabe syrienne	18 378[2]	4 593[2]	828[2]	−292	87	357.3	1.9
Tajikistan / Tadjikistan	13 996	930[2]	127[2]	...	...	2 602.9	18.2
Thailand / Thaïlande	51 089	14 133[2]	3 554	−3 361	445	11 185.5	19.0
Timor-Leste / Timor-Leste	1 487	122[2]	68[2]	12	10	187.6	1.2
Turkey / Turquie	76 963	23 358	2 655	−1 289	−375	3 353.2	3.9
Turkmenistan / Turkménistan	46 993	2 200[2]	66[2]	...	...	1 978.2	4.1
United Arab Emirates / Emirats arabes unis	8 360	64	190	29	170	455.9	4.0
Uzbekistan / Ouzbékistan	42 540	4 700[2]	340[2]	...	...	2 050.3	4.6
Viet Nam / Viet Nam	32 549	6 680[2]	2 300[2]	1 341	1 255	1 772.6	3.6
Yemen / Yémen	52 797	1 537[2]	132	14	29	0.0	0.0
Europe / Europe							
Albania / Albanie	2 740	578	121	−1	−4	102.9	2.9
Andorra / Andorre	47	1[2]	...	0		3.3	7.2
Austria / Autriche	8 245	1 391[2]	71[2]	−35	−8	2 347.5	28.0
Belarus / Bélarus	20 748	5 557[2]	124[2]	...	...	1 315.3	6.3
Belgium / Belgique	...	...	...	...	...	105.2	3.3
Bosnia and Herzegovina / Bosnie-Herzégovine	5 120	1 004	97	...	...	27.1	0.5
Bulgaria / Bulgarie	11 063	3 323	211	−533	−89	1 118.4	9.5
Croatia / Croatie	5 592	1 460	124	...	...	572.4	6.5
Czech Republic / République tchèque	7 727	3 062	237	...	...	1 245.1	15.8
Denmark / Danemark	4 243	2 266	8	−295	−2	98 744.6[5]	44.0[5]
Estonia / Estonie	4 239	545	16	...	...	2 147.3	30.9
Faeroe Islands / Iles Féroé	140	3[2]	...	0	...	...	...

Country or area Pays ou zone	2003			Net change — Variation nette		2005	
				1990 – 2003			
	Land area Superficie des terres	Arable land Terre arables	Permanent crops Cultures permanentes	Arable land Terres arables	Permanent crops Cultures permanentes	Protected areas Aires protégées	Protected areas Aires protégées
	Area in thousand hectares — Superficie en milliers de hectares						% [1]
Finland Finlande	30 459	2 210	8	−59	2	3 069.8	7.8
France France	55 010	18 451	1 122	452	−69	8 281.8	13.3
Germany Allemagne	34 895	11 827	213	−144	−230	11 244.6	30.0
Gibraltar Gibraltar	1	...	...	...	...	0.0	3.5
Greece Grèce	12 890	2 698	1 133	−201	65	688.4	2.8
Hungary Hongrie	9 209	4 612	192	−442	−42	830.0	8.9
Iceland Islande	10 025	7		0	...	980.7	5.6
Ireland Irlande	6 889	*1 182	2	141	−1	80.7	0.7
Italy Italie	29 411	*7 959	2 738[2]	−1 053	−222	5 724.4	12.5
Latvia Lettonie	6 205	1 821	29	...	...	1 069.8	13.9
Liechtenstein Liechtenstein	16	4[2]	...	0	...	6.4	40.1
Lithuania Lituanie	6 268	2 926	59	...	...	714.3	10.6
Luxembourg Luxembourg	...	...	...	...	...	44.1	17.0
Malta Malte	32	10[2]	*1	−2	0	5.9	1.4
Monaco Monaco	...	...	...	...	...	0.1	25.5
Netherlands Pays-Bas	3 388	912	32	33	2	799.3	14.6
Norway Norvège	30 625	873	...	9	...	8 727.3[6]	20.1[6]
Poland Pologne	30 624	12 587	314	−1 801	−31	9 052.7	27.1
Portugal Portugal	9 150	1 590[2]	721[2]	−754	−60	779.0	5.0
Republic of Moldova République de Moldova	3 287	1 845	298	...	...	47.3	1.4
Romania Roumanie	22 995	9 414	458	−36	−133	1 231.5	5.1
Russian Federation Fédération de Russie	1 638 098	122 559	1 814	...	...	161 714.8	8.8
San Marino Saint-Marin	6	1[2]	...	0	...	...	...
Serbia and Montenegro Serbie-et-Monténégro	10 200	3 390	327	...	...	387.1	3.8
Slovakia Slovaquie	4 808	1 433	131	...	...	1 234.7	25.2

Country or area Pays ou zone	2003 Land area Superficie des terres	2003 Arable land Terre arables	2003 Permanent crops Cultures permanentes	Net change — Variation nette 1990 – 2003 Arable land Terres arables	Net change — Variation nette 1990 – 2003 Permanent crops Cultures permanentes	2005 Protected areas Aires protégées	2005 Protected areas Aires protégées
	Area in thousand hectares — Superficie en milliers de hectares						% [1]
Slovenia Slovénie	2 014	173	29	...	...	149.8	7.3
Spain Espagne	49 921	13 738	4 977	−1 597	140	4 807.1	7.7
Sweden Suède	41 033	2 669	*3	−176	−1	4 912.0	9.2
Switzerland Suisse	4 000	409	24	18	3	1 185.2	28.7
TFYR of Macedonia L'ex-R.y. Macédoine	2 543	566[2]	46[2]	...	...	183.3	7.1
Ukraine Ukraine	57 935	32 480	907	...	...	2 246.8	3.4
United Kingdom Royaume-Uni	24 193	5 660	48	−960	−18	5 438.3	13.2
Oceania **Océanie**							
American Samoa Samoa américaines	20	2[2]	3[2]	0	1	20.4	101.8
Australia Australie	768 230[7]	47 600[2]	335[2]	−300	154	148 953.0	17.5
Christmas Is. Ile Christmas	13	...	...	...	...	8.7	62.3
Cocos (Keeling) Islands Iles des Cocos (Keeling)	1	...	...	...	...	0.1	5.6
Cook Islands Iles Cook	24	4[2]	2[2]	2	−2	2.3	9.9
Fiji Fidji	1 827	200[2]	85[2]	40	5	49.3	0.3
French Polynesia Polynésie française	366	3[2]	22[2]	1	1	24.9	0.1
Guam Guam	55	2[2]	10[2]	0	0	14.8	27.0
Kiribati Kiribati	73	2[2]	35[2]	0	−2	112.5	1.5
Marshall Islands Iles Marshall	18	2[2]	8[2]	...	...	75.7	0.7
Micronesia (Fed. States of) Micronésie (Etats féd. de)	70	4[2]	32[2]	...	...	7.2	0.1
Nauru Nauru	2	...	...	...	...	...	...
New Caledonia Nouvelle-Calédonie	1 828	6[2]	4[2]	−3	−2	220.9	2.2
New Zealand Nouvelle-Zélande	26 799	1 500[2]	1 872[2]	−1 011	518	8 753.6	19.6
Niue Nioué	26	3[2]	4[2]	0	1	5.5	21.0
Norfolk Island Ile Norfolk	4	...	...	...	...	0.7	23.2
Northern Mariana Islands Iles Mariannes du Nord	46	6[2]	2[2]	...	...	2.8	5.8

		Net change — Variation nette					
			2003		1990 – 2003		2005
Country or area Pays ou zone	Land area Superficie des terres	Arable land Terre arables	Permanent crops Cultures permanentes	Arable land Terres arables	Permanent crops Cultures permanentes	Protected areas Aires protégées	Protected areas Aires protégées
	Area in thousand hectares — Superficie en milliers de hectares						% [1]
Palau Palaos	46	4	2	–18	–38	134.8	0.4
Papua New Guinea Papouasie-Nouvelle-Guinée	45 286	225[2]	650[2]	33	70	4 399.6	3.6
Samoa Samoa	283	60[2]	69[2]	5	2	23.9	1.8
Solomon Islands Iles Salomon	2 799	18[2]	59[2]	1	7	41.2	0.2
Tokelau Tokélaou	1	...	...	...	...	1.0	100.0
Tonga Tonga	72	15[2]	11[2]	–1	–1	1 010.5	27.8
Tuvalu Tuvalu	3	...	2[2]	...	0	3.3	0.0
Vanuatu Vanuatu	1 219	20[2]	85[2]	0	0	19.4	0.2
Wallis and Futuna Islands Iles Wallis et Futuna	14	1[2]	5[2]	0	0	0.1	0.4

Source

Food and Agriculture Organization of the United Nations (FAO), Rome, FAOSTAT data, 2005, last accessed January 2006, and the United Nations Environment Programme (UNEP), World Conservation Monitoring Centre, Protected Areas database.

Notes

[1] Calculated by the United Nations Statistics Division from data provided by the World Conservation Monitoring Centre. Calculations are based on total area, which includes land area and inland waters. Percentages may be inflated due to the inclusion of marine protected areas.

[2] FAO estimate.

[3] For statistical purposes, the data for China do not include those for the Hong Kong Special Administrative Region (Hong Kong SAR) and Macao Special Administrative Region (Macao SAR).

[4] Data include those for Taiwan Province of China.

[5] Beginning 1998, including Greenland.

[6] Including Svalbard, Jan Mayen and Bouvet Islands.

[7] Includes about 27 million hectares of cultivated grassland.

Source

Organisation des Nations Unies pour l'alimentation et l'agriculture (FAO), Rome, données FAOSTAT, 2005, dernier accès janvier 2006, et le Programme des Nations Unies pour l'environnement (PNUE), Centre mondial de surveillance pour la conservation, la base de données sur les aires protégées.

Notes

[1] Calculés par la Division de statistique sur les données fournies par le Centre mondial de surveillance pour la conservation. Les calculations sont basées sur la superficie totale des pays, qui comprend la superficie des terres et celle des eaux intérieures. Les pourcentages sont majorés, du fait qu'on tient compte des zones marines protégées.

[2] Estimation de la FAO.

[3] Pour la présentation des statistiques, les données pour Chine ne comprennent pas la Région Administrative Spéciale de Hong Kong (Hong Kong RAS) et la Région Administrative Spéciale de Macao (Macao RAS).

[4] Les données comprennent les chiffres pour la province de Taiwan.

[5] A partir de 1998, y compris le Groenland

[6] Y compris les îles Svalbard, Jan Mayen et Bouvet.

[7] Y compris 27 million d'hectares d'herbages cultivés.

CO₂ emission estimates

From fossil fuel combustion, cement production and gas flared (thousand metric tons of carbon dioxide)

Estimation des émissions de CO₂

Dues à la combustion de combustibles fossiles, à la production de ciment et au gaz brûlés à la torchère (milliers de tonnes de dioxyde de carbone)

Country or area / Pays ou zone	1994	1995	1996	1997	1998	1999	2000	2001	2002	2003
Afghanistan / Afghanistan	1 293	1 242	1 177	1 097	1 040	966	907	642	671	704
Albania / Albanie	1 928	1 877	1 829	1 439	1 578	2 142	2 150	2 332	2 563	3 045
Algeria / Algérie	86 422	94 768	96 646	88 038	178 301	164 481	165 863	161 727	166 017	163 946
Angola / Angola	4 202	11 313	9 996	6 314	5 770	6 595	6 609	7 128	7 662	8 634
Antigua and Barbuda / Antigua-et-Barbuda	310	323	323	338	335	350	353	353	372	399
Argentina / Argentine	120 760	119 474	127 017	131 635	133 317	141 973	137 562	125 972	119 933	127 728
Armenia / Arménie	2 856	3 413	2 566	3 239	3 364	3 016	3 467	3 543	2 989	3 432
Aruba / Aruba	1 782	1 804	1 834	1 874	1 696	1 711	2 093	2 099	2 136	2 157
Australia [1] / Australie [1]	295 560	305 610	315 790	322 490	339 720	348 950	354 370	360 630	363 810	371 700
Austria [1] / Autriche [1]	60 200	63 120	66 560	66 530	66 220	64 610	65 450	69 280	70 990	76 210
Azerbaijan / Azerbaïdjan	41 717	32 705	30 416	28 883	30 455	32 770	29 811	27 805	27 924	29 223
Bahamas / Bahamas	1 723	1 732	1 732	1 744	1 794	1 797	1 800	1 800	2 086	1 873
Bahrain / Bahreïn	15 027	15 866	15 611	17 334	18 456	18 028	18 682	18 104	21 327	21 912
Bangladesh / Bangladesh	18 432	22 622	23 836	24 859	23 800	24 967	27 786	32 310	33 542	34 690
Barbados / Barbade	748	828	850	899	1 144	1 212	1 187	1 216	1 225	1 192
Belarus [1] / Bélarus [1]	66 780	61 450	60 890	61 450	58 740	56 590	52 020	52 100	51 690	52 590
Belgium [1] / Belgique [1]	122 520	123 620	127 710	122 170	127 380	121 990	123 820	123 360	122 980	126 200
Belize / Belize	375	378	307	390	372	602	691	713	747	780
Benin / Bénin	1 268	1 328	1 267	1 218	1 215	1 566	1 618	1 738	1 975	2 045
Bermuda / Bermudes	458	455	464	464	464	464	464	464	498	498
Bhutan / Bhoutan	216	251	302	391	388	385	395	403	401	387
Bolivia / Bolivie	7 941	8 129	8 741	9 850	10 335	10 649	9 867	9 207	9 093	7 908
Bosnia and Herzegovina / Bosnie-Herzégovine	4 047	4 049	5 276	12 664	16 547	15 663	19 448	19 792	18 925	19 161
Botswana / Botswana	3 483	3 516	3 115	3 203	3 820	3 531	4 097	3 919	4 100	4 123
Brazil / Brésil	235 064	250 024	276 911	289 113	301 599	303 396	308 024	316 478	312 897	298 902
British Virgin Islands / Iles Vierges britanniques	52	52	58	58	58	58	58	58	68	77

CO₂ emission estimates—From fossil fuel combustion, cement production and gas flared
(thousand metric tons of carbon dioxide) (*continued*)

Estimation des émissions de CO₂—Dues à la combustion de combustibles fossiles, à la production de ciment
et au gaz brûlés à la torchère (milliers de tonnes de dioxyde de carbone) (*suite*)

Country or area Pays ou zone	1994	1995	1996	1997	1998	1999	2000	2001	2002	2003
Brunei Darussalam Brunéi Darussalam	5 106	5 214	5 154	5 502	3 408	4 334	5 742	5 495	5 275	4 558
Bulgaria [1] Bulgarie [1]	61 280	64 730	63 160	61 580	54 300	50 530	49 900	51 470	48 760	53 320
Burkina Faso Burkina Faso	949	974	983	994	1 012	1 088	1 064	1 054	1 081	1 041
Burundi Burundi	213	216	222	229	229	244	262	235	256	236
Cambodia Cambodge	538	551	601	588	588	525	532	560	547	535
Cameroon Cameroun	3 652	4 174	4 595	3 213	3 212	3 082	3 434	3 402	3 430	3 543
Canada [1] Canada [1]	479 550	492 430	505 470	517 070	527 820	542 720	565 680	558 970	567 790	586 070
Cape Verde Cap-Vert	117	117	123	123	123	138	138	147	147	144
Cayman Islands Iles Caïmanes	286	286	283	283	283	280	283	283	289	304
Central African Rep. Rép. centrafricaine	237	237	237	246	249	264	267	267	273	252
Chad Tchad	95	95	101	114	114	123	126	123	120	117
Chile Chili	41 244	44 277	50 505	58 171	57 502	62 618	59 539	55 228	57 251	58 591
China [2] Chine [2]	2 962 916	3 202 835	3 345 058	3 293 751	3 116 650	2 819 844	2 776 528	3 012 075	3 489 489	4 151 412
China, Hong Kong SAR Chine, Hong Kong RAS	29 883	29 919	27 532	28 891	37 344	40 063	37 552	35 931	34 705	37 865
China, Macao SAR Chine, Macao RAS	1 275	1 232	1 410	1 490	1 561	1 518	1 638	1 696	1 837	1 868
Colombia Colombie	66 428	59 105	59 867	64 875	65 564	56 481	58 249	56 198	53 399	55 631
Comoros Comores	65	68	68	68	71	80	83	80	80	89
Congo Congo	2 110	1 549	1 704	2 338	776	824	1 050	1 249	1 068	1 380
Cook Islands Iles Cook	22	22	22	22	22	28	28	28	28	31
Costa Rica Costa Rica	5 241	4 866	4 738	4 974	5 329	5 524	5 539	5 629	5 674	6 340
Côte d'Ivoire Côte d'Ivoire	4 998	6 878	8 126	7 914	2 955	7 134	5 889	5 555	7 171	5 723
Croatia [1] Croatie [1]	15 670	16 250	16 970	18 060	18 950	19 680	19 380	19 770	20 910	23 000
Cuba Cuba	31 900	25 402	26 678	24 637	24 321	25 357	25 436	24 332	26 874	25 295
Cyprus Chypre	5 265	5 138	5 282	5 428	5 941	6 020	6 432	6 450	6 541	7 291
Czech Republic [1] République tchèque [1]	130 630	131 400	132 780	137 360	128 270	121 090	127 900	128 000	123 050	127 120
Dem. Rep. of the Congo Rép. dém. du Congo	2 598	2 554	2 574	2 500	2 537	2 249	1 649	1 667	1 724	1 789
Denmark [1] Danemark [1]	64 700	61 670	75 180	65 660	61 580	58 750	54 430	56 020	55 660	60 750

61

CO₂ emission estimates — From fossil fuel combustion, cement production and gas flared
(thousand metric tons of carbon dioxide) (*continued*)

Estimation des émissions de CO₂ — Dues à la combustion de combustibles fossiles, à la production de ciment
et au gaz brûlés à la torchère (milliers de tonnes de dioxyde de carbone) (*suite*)

Country or area Pays ou zone	1994	1995	1996	1997	1998	1999	2000	2001	2002	2003
Djibouti Djibouti	369	372	366	366	366	384	387	390	360	366
Dominica Dominique	71	80	74	80	77	80	101	111	120	138
Dominican Republic Rép. dominicaine	12 685	16 101	17 562	18 253	18 700	18 889	20 133	20 251	21 518	21 347
Ecuador Equateur	13 544	22 703	24 226	18 560	22 663	21 641	21 366	24 004	24 619	23 245
Egypt Egypte	84 876	95 181	102 139	107 930	121 684	124 798	139 034	132 740	141 631	139 893
El Salvador El Salvador	4 428	5 293	4 898	5 763	5 798	5 704	5 748	5 953	6 034	6 553
Equatorial Guinea Guinée équatoriale	126	126	132	144	147	166	169	163	169	166
Eritrea Erythrée	182	295	349	525	591	622	609	634	643	702
Estonia [1] Estonie [1]	21 380	19 310	20 260	20 220	18 320	16 770	16 850	17 100	17 310	19 110
Ethiopia Ethiopie	2 920	2 136	3 731	4 278	5 029	5 075	5 826	6 653	6 837	7 347
Faeroe Islands Iles Féroé	513	621	633	636	642	648	648	648	654	661
Falkland Is. (Malvinas) Iles Falkland (Malvinas)	38	41	44	47	38	38	38	42	42	46
Fiji Fidji	828	891	924	761	731	833	857	1 117	1 117	1 120
Finland [1] Finlande [1]	61 090	58 070	63 410	62 280	59 510	59 240	57 610	63 190	64 950	73 190
France [1,3] France [1,3]	389 010	395 330	408 720	403 050	422 340	411 210	405 050	410 760	403 150	408 160
Gabon Gabon	3 431	3 729	3 622	3 700	1 615	1 432	1 472	1 967	1 685	1 225
Gambia Gambie	209	215	215	215	234	255	270	280	283	283
Georgia Géorgie	6 025	2 285	4 012	4 286	4 962	4 352	4 541	3 753	3 382	3 732
Germany [1] Allemagne [1]	905 630	902 210	924 910	893 530	885 200	857 420	860 090	873 860	863 880	865 370
Ghana Ghana	4 988	5 333	5 651	6 286	6 314	6 464	6 203	6 833	7 361	7 745
Gibraltar Gibraltar	356	301	181	86	310	323	335	344	350	363
Greece [1] Grèce [1]	87 200	87 340	89 550	94 290	98 860	98 240	104 110	106 330	106 160	109 980
Greenland Groenland	504	504	516	522	529	541	556	562	565	568
Grenada Grenade	166	172	175	206	191	206	206	221	218	221
Guatemala Guatemala	6 843	7 172	6 658	7 604	8 759	8 935	10 205	10 563	11 009	10 711
Guinea Guinée	1 188	1 206	1 230	1 236	1 241	1 276	1 280	1 297	1 326	1 341
Guinea-Bissau Guinée-Bissau	227	230	230	234	230	249	252	261	270	270

61

CO₂ emission estimates — From fossil fuel combustion, cement production and gas flared
(thousand metric tons of carbon dioxide) (*continued*)

Estimation des émissions de CO₂ — Dues à la combustion de combustibles fossiles, à la production de ciment
et au gaz brûlés à la torchère (milliers de tonnes de dioxyde de carbone) (*suite*)

Country or area Pays ou zone	1994	1995	1996	1997	1998	1999	2000	2001	2002	2003
Guyana Guyana	1 327	1 475	1 521	1 595	1 656	1 687	1 601	1 647	1 610	1 632
Haiti Haïti	301	943	1 094	1 426	1 232	1 315	1 343	1 571	1 764	1 741
Honduras Honduras	3 340	3 884	3 966	4 161	4 653	4 746	5 034	5 718	6 044	6 507
Hungary [1] Hongrie [1]	61 600	60 870	62 220	60 480	60 140	60 020	57 800	59 360	57 700	60 460
Iceland [1] Islande [1]	2 200	2 220	2 310	2 410	2 290	2 460	2 310	2 190	2 240	2 180
India Inde	861 637	909 017	1 004 413	1 027 134	1 065 813	1 105 747	1 160 949	1 167 169	1 231 881	1 275 608
Indonesia Indonésie	223 577	225 853	271 988	279 883	208 060	248 487	276 024	288 641	326 520	295 596
Iran (Islamic Rep. of) Iran (Rép. islamique d')	291 885	277 201	302 699	313 601	306 476	275 187	293 622	299 894	370 414	382 092
Iraq Iraq	71 195	74 075	68 054	66 841	70 839	70 806	72 942	81 996	87 883	73 007
Ireland [1] Irlande [1]	34 110	34 760	35 950	38 310	40 250	42 130	44 160	46 460	45 810	44 450
Israel Israël	46 008	51 934	52 038	60 421	59 365	58 482	64 228	64 262	68 406	68 427
Italy [1] Italie [1]	417 250	446 660	438 860	443 120	452 980	460 270	467 550	472 010	471 400	487 280
Jamaica Jamaïque	8 638	9 711	10 204	10 639	9 738	9 778	10 327	10 637	10 315	10 737
Japan [1] Japon [1]	1 198 160	1 213 080	1 234 760	1 242 030	1 195 180	1 228 370	1 238 960	1 213 610	1 247 760	1 259 430
Jordan Jordanie	13 644	13 604	14 198	14 431	14 557	14 583	15 540	15 518	16 385	17 117
Kazakhstan Kazakhstan	197 138	165 747	138 818	128 073	122 459	112 232	121 314	125 029	157 395	159 494
Kenya Kenya	6 532	7 499	9 270	8 275	10 046	10 180	10 426	9 228	7 909	8 790
Kiribati Kiribati	22	22	37	28	34	31	34	31	31	31
Korea, Dem. P. R. Corée, R. p. dém. de	259 855	259 559	256 893	234 881	64 982	71 456	77 028	79 985	76 194	77 601
Korea, Republic of Corée, République de	343 393	374 213	408 595	424 573	364 070	394 318	428 005	435 492	446 190	456 751
Kuwait [4] Koweït [4]	35 883	54 767	48 981	51 081	66 005	68 493	70 692	67 481	66 061	78 602
Kyrgyzstan Kirghizistan	6 092	4 632	5 803	5 626	5 993	4 686	4 649	3 853	4 957	5 328
Lao People's Dem. Rep. Rép. dém. pop. lao	300	315	530	718	820	889	1 012	1 168	1 252	1 254
Latvia [1] Lettonie [1]	11 450	8 960	9 160	8 740	8 130	7 410	6 850	7 410	7 340	7 430
Lebanon Liban	12 753	13 632	13 811	15 658	16 014	16 613	15 366	16 541	16 390	18 998
Liberia Libéria	312	322	336	348	386	401	429	462	466	464
Libyan Arab Jamah. Jamah. arabe libyenne	39 284	43 780	40 279	48 610	45 176	44 284	46 739	48 096	49 183	50 274

61

CO₂ emission estimates—From fossil fuel combustion, cement production and gas flared (thousand metric tons of carbon dioxide) (*continued*)

Estimation des émissions de CO₂—Dues à la combustion de combustibles fossiles, à la production de ciment et au gaz brûlés à la torchère (milliers de tonnes de dioxyde de carbone) (*suite*)

Country or area Pays ou zone	1994	1995	1996	1997	1998	1999	2000	2001	2002	2003
Liechtenstein [1] Liechtenstein [1]	...	...	...	...	...	...	...	...	...	240
Lithuania [1] Lituanie [1]	...	...	...	...	15 660	...	...	13 330	12 700	12 290
Luxembourg [1] Luxembourg [1]	12 000	9 550	...	...	7 700	5 430	8 920	5 480	10 220	10 690
Madagascar Madagascar	1 269	1 263	1 361	1 648	1 738	1 922	2 271	2 317	2 317	2 345
Malawi Malawi	702	714	699	744	779	829	814	836	835	885
Malaysia Malaisie	92 800	119 186	122 445	124 472	114 057	108 097	126 599	136 017	141 529	156 680
Maldives Maldives	221	277	320	369	335	467	501	925	1 032	442
Mali Mali	462	467	488	525	519	541	544	547	553	553
Malta Malte	2 708	2 951	3 133	3 339	2 105	2 305	2 108	2 062	2 111	2 467
Mauritania Mauritanie	3 069	2 946	2 945	2 935	2 441	2 478	2 485	2 534	2 488	2 503
Mauritius Maurice	1 626	1 833	1 953	2 000	2 198	2 469	2 771	2 970	2 983	3 150
Mexico Mexique	387 448	368 048	371 355	388 751	390 883	392 362	396 663	408 280	399 932	416 698
Monaco [1] Monaco [1]	120	120	120	120	120	120	130	130	130	130
Mongolia Mongolie	7 951	7 927	8 049	7 717	7 712	7 561	7 509	7 890	8 293	7 987
Montserrat Montserrat	37	43	40	46	52	49	49	49	55	61
Morocco Maroc	29 677	30 380	31 216	31 885	31 995	32 893	34 295	38 031	38 514	37 968
Mozambique Mozambique	1 065	1 114	1 043	1 128	1 118	1 175	1 335	1 348	1 419	1 571
Myanmar Myanmar	6 227	6 931	7 201	7 419	8 015	8 765	9 096	7 776	8 845	9 467
Namibia Namibie	28	1 693	1 832	1 855	1 951	1 743	1 750	2 069	2 128	2 331
Nauru Nauru	135	138	138	138	138	135	135	138	138	141
Nepal Népal	1 701	2 039	2 490	2 785	2 252	3 225	3 234	3 456	2 714	2 955
Netherlands [1] Pays-Bas [1]	165 550	169 660	177 320	170 180	172 160	166 930	168 870	174 350	173 930	176 860
Netherlands Antilles Antilles néerlandaises	5 408	5 319	4 956	7 368	3 395	3 232	3 291	3 334	3 395	4 059
New Zealand [1] Nouvelle-Zélande [1]	27 210	27 160	28 180	30 430	29 060	30 500	31 010	32 980	33 010	34 700
Nicaragua Nicaragua	2 551	2 841	2 930	3 138	3 424	3 628	3 774	3 981	3 934	3 917
Niger Niger	1 089	1 132	1 138	1 141	1 138	1 168	1 185	1 191	1 209	1 209
Nigeria Nigéria	46 699	33 389	38 594	40 223	40 217	44 824	46 627	48 682	53 520	52 276

CO₂ emission estimates — From fossil fuel combustion, cement production and gas flared (thousand metric tons of carbon dioxide) (*continued*)

Estimation des émissions de CO₂ — Dues à la combustion de combustibles fossiles, à la production de ciment et au gaz brûlés à la torchère (milliers de tonnes de dioxyde de carbone) (*suite*)

Country or area Pays ou zone	1994	1995	1996	1997	1998	1999	2000	2001	2002	2003
Niue Nioué	3	3	3	3	3	3	3	3	3	3
Norway [1] Norvège [1]	37 270	37 230	40 390	40 570	40 770	41 630	41 140	42 660	41 240	43 220
Oman Oman	15 158	15 896	15 237	15 607	16 682	20 830	21 967	24 465	30 350	32 309
Pakistan Pakistan	84 631	84 619	94 260	94 516	97 576	100 505	106 195	105 529	111 215	114 356
Palau Palaos	230	240	246	240	243	243	243	234	234	243
Panama Panama	4 785	3 474	4 884	5 965	5 964	5 643	5 762	7 008	5 841	6 035
Papua New Guinea Papouasie-Nvl-Guinée	2 506	2 410	2 412	2 455	2 351	2 431	2 431	2 482	2 482	2 515
Paraguay Paraguay	3 500	3 967	3 757	4 196	4 506	4 509	3 692	3 827	4 002	4 143
Peru Pérou	23 064	23 533	23 872	26 448	26 617	28 271	27 356	26 419	25 966	26 198
Philippines Philippines	56 086	62 896	65 878	77 280	75 889	73 027	78 071	76 730	78 128	77 095
Poland [1] Pologne [1]	371 590	348 170	372 530	361 630	337 450	329 700	314 810	317 840	308 280	...
Portugal [1] Portugal [1]	49 260	53 180	50 280	53 450	58 050	64 770	63 610	64 690	68 840	64 290
Qatar Qatar	31 029	31 779	32 928	37 545	33 801	32 956	36 426	42 611	46 252	46 262
Republic of Moldova République de Moldova	12 080	11 198	11 531	10 801	9 636	6 494	6 579	7 077	6 734	7 240
Romania [1] Roumanie [1]	126 590	132 660	138 480	123 750	108 410	91 690	94 370	98 510	105 400	111 390
Russian Federation [1] Fédération de Russie [1]	1 660 000	1 589 000	1 495 000	1 529 000	1 505 000	1 509 000	...	...	...	...
Rwanda Rwanda	483	493	509	531	536	567	573	586	594	602
Saint Helena Sainte-Hélène	6	12	15	15	18	22	12	12	12	12
Saint Kitts and Nevis Saint-Kitts-et-Nevis	89	95	101	101	101	101	101	101	114	126
Saint Lucia Sainte-Lucie	261	307	323	301	215	316	323	313	304	326
St. Vincent-Grenadines St. Vincent-Grenadines	120	129	132	132	163	166	154	175	184	194
Samoa Samoa	123	132	132	132	132	138	138	144	144	151
Sao Tome and Principe Sao Tomé-et-Principe	74	77	77	77	80	89	89	92	92	92
Saudi Arabia [4] Arabie saoudite [4]	322 219	244 568	273 205	248 230	221 253	232 390	272 308	282 812	288 651	302 884
Senegal Sénégal	3 855	3 470	3 717	3 244	3 405	3 673	4 001	4 318	4 711	4 846
Serbia and Montenegro Serbie-et-Monténégro	38 003	40 088	46 127	49 241	51 872	36 710	40 879	43 688	47 244	50 023
Seychelles Seychelles	187	191	197	415	439	513	565	642	544	547

CO₂ emission estimates — From fossil fuel combustion, cement production and gas flared
(thousand metric tons of carbon dioxide) (*continued*)

Estimation des émissions de CO₂ — Dues à la combustion de combustibles fossiles, à la production de ciment
et au gaz brûlés à la torchère (milliers de tonnes de dioxyde de carbone) (*suite*)

Country or area Pays ou zone	1994	1995	1996	1997	1998	1999	2000	2001	2002	2003
Sierra Leone Sierra Leone	502	505	544	553	529	514	553	603	631	653
Singapore Singapour	64 323	46 890	53 772	62 209	56 332	55 986	56 574	56 608	55 589	47 885
Slovakia [1] Slovaquie [1]	42 440	43 840	44 390	44 660	43 650	42 630	40 150	42 600	42 250	43 050
Slovenia [1] Slovénie [1]	13 940	14 790	15 600	16 050	15 800	15 160	15 240	16 220	16 290	16 100
Solomon Islands Iles Salomon	154	160	160	160	160	166	166	172	172	178
Somalia Somalie	12	12	0	0	...	...	...	...	...	...
South Africa Afrique du Sud	313 018	325 744	324 022	332 868	335 164	331 760	326 687	332 672	356 253	364 853
Spain [1] Espagne [1]	244 850	255 450	242 720	262 550	270 830	295 900	308 250	310 460	331 080	331 760
Sri Lanka Sri Lanka	5 407	5 801	6 979	7 569	7 748	8 528	10 199	10 195	10 754	10 321
Sudan Soudan	4 096	4 245	3 895	5 346	4 631	5 099	5 539	6 375	8 125	9 007
Suriname Suriname	2 141	2 159	2 107	2 119	2 141	2 153	2 129	2 266	2 254	2 242
Swaziland Swaziland	484	454	343	399	531	797	1 005	983	970	957
Sweden [1] Suède [1]	58 690	57 590	61 170	56 780	57 460	54 710	52 430	53 450	54 830	56 000
Switzerland [1] Suisse [1]	42 640	43 370	43 920	43 150	44 440	44 560	43 660	44 460	43 650	44 720
Syrian Arab Republic Rép. arabe syrienne	43 606	43 320	43 759	40 253	47 410	48 975	48 381	47 466	50 413	49 036
Tajikistan Tadjikistan	5 087	5 174	5 786	5 093	5 128	5 119	4 000	4 345	4 771	4 662
Thailand Thaïlande	158 401	181 603	202 870	210 227	186 517	197 110	201 714	217 266	230 827	246 372
TFYR of Macedonia L'ex-R.y. Macédoine	10 353	10 701	11 751	10 643	12 058	11 196	11 417	11 394	10 394	10 545
Timor-Leste Timor-Leste	...	...	...	...	...	...	...	...	163	163
Togo Togo	791	894	1 002	935	1 095	1 479	1 634	1 466	1 493	2 200
Tonga Tonga	108	111	111	114	111	129	120	108	108	114
Trinidad and Tobago Trinité-et-Tobago	19 316	20 268	20 944	18 538	20 119	23 954	25 344	25 854	27 800	28 699
Tunisia Tunisie	15 952	15 735	16 868	16 950	18 017	18 115	19 742	20 539	20 864	20 909
Turkey Turquie	155 903	171 182	188 475	198 336	202 368	200 114	221 967	200 135	208 478	220 409
Turkmenistan Turkménistan	33 503	34 649	31 390	29 954	26 071	35 143	35 678	39 715	42 136	43 413
Uganda Ouganda	746	955	1 053	1 137	1 337	1 390	1 526	1 622	1 697	1 713
Ukraine [1] Ukraine [1]	428 040	408 350	379 670	350 300	300 540	295 800	293 880	293 160	292 770	313 140

61

CO₂ emission estimates — From fossil fuel combustion, cement production and gas flared (thousand metric tons of carbon dioxide) (*continued*)

Estimation des émissions de CO₂ — Dues à la combustion de combustibles fossiles, à la production de ciment et au gaz brûlés à la torchère (milliers de tonnes de dioxyde de carbone) (*suite*)

Country or area / Pays ou zone	1994	1995	1996	1997	1998	1999	2000	2001	2002	2003
United Arab Emirates / Emirats arabes unis	76 181	73 640	43 531	47 973	104 236	109 449	115 750	116 941	126 590	135 285
United Kingdom [1] / Royaume-Uni [1]	559 110	550 320	572 220	548 440	551 180	540 990	545 300	562 270	545 290	557 460
United Rep. of Tanzania / Rép.-Unie de Tanzanie	2 408	3 549	3 464	2 886	2 557	2 542	2 654	3 133	3 592	3 811
United States [1,3] / Etats-Unis [1,3]	5 268 050	5 319 380	5 500 170	5 579 980	5 607 160	5 677 970	5 858 200	5 744 780	5 796 760	5 841 500
Uruguay / Uruguay	4 022	4 528	5 252	5 271	5 219	6 155	4 895	4 528	4 351	4 380
Uzbekistan / Ouzbékistan	112 096	99 240	101 773	101 743	117 732	117 295	118 821	120 034	122 330	123 840
Vanuatu / Vanuatu	61	65	83	86	80	80	80	86	86	89
Venezuela (Bolivarian Republic of) / Venezuela (Rép. bolivarienne)	166 286	148 721	155 261	153 235	164 107	162 424	162 917	158 123	135 761	144 227
Viet Nam / Viet Nam	26 327	29 871	35 320	45 698	47 847	48 347	53 739	60 437	71 661	76 242
Western Sahara / Sahara occidental	203	209	212	221	224	237	240	240	240	240
Yemen / Yémen	11 200	11 261	14 946	15 488	12 211	13 911	14 643	16 225	16 219	17 082
Zambia / Zambie	2 421	2 174	1 873	2 392	2 314	1 819	1 828	1 919	1 980	2 200
Zimbabwe / Zimbabwe	18 803	16 082	15 907	15 233	15 100	16 734	14 828	13 549	12 714	11 487

Source

Carbon Dioxide Information Analysis Center (CDIAC) of the Oak Ridge National Laboratory, Oak Ridge, Tennessee, U.S.A., database on national CO₂ emission estimates from fossil fuel burning, cement production and gas flaring, and the Secretariat of the United Nations Framework Convention on Climate Change (UNFCCC), Bonn, Secretariat of the UNFCCC database.

The majority of the data have been taken from the CDIAC database; all other data have been taken from the UNFCCC database and are footnoted accordingly.

Notes

[1] Source: Secretariat of the UNFCCC.
[2] For statistical purposes, the data for China do not include those for the Hong Kong Special Administrative Region (Hong Kong SAR), Macao Special Administrative Region (Macao SAR) and Taiwan Province of China.
[3] Including territories.
[4] Including part of the Neutral Zone.

Source

Carbon Dioxide Information Analysis Center (CDIAC) of the Oak Ridge National Laboratory, Oak Ridge, Tennessee, U.S.A., database on national CO₂ emission estimates from fossil fuel burning, cement production and gas flaring, et Secrétariat de la convention-cadre concernant les changements climatiques (CCCC) des Nations Unies, Bonn, la base de données du Secrétariat de la CCCC.

La majorité des données proviennent de la base de données du CDIAC ; les autres, qui proviennent de la base de données du Secrétariat de la CCCC, sont signalées par une note.

Notes

[1] Source : Secrétariat de la CCC des Nations Unies.
[2] Pour la présentation des statistiques, les données pour Chine ne comprennent pas la Région Administrative Spéciale de Hong Kong (Hong Kong RAS), la Région Administrative Spéciale de Macao (Macao RAS) et la province de Taiwan.
[3] Y compris les territoires.
[4] Y compris une partie de la Zone Neutre.

Ozone-depleting chlorofluorocarbons (CFCs)
Consumption: ozone-depleting potential (ODP) metric tons

Chlorofluorocarbones (CFC) qui appauvrissent la couche d'ozone
Consommation : tonnes de potentiel de destruction de l'ozone (PDO)

Country or area Pays ou zone	1995	1996	1997	1998	1999	2000	2001	2002	2003	2004
Afghanistan Afghanistan	380	380	380	...	...	...	...	...	...	178
Albania Albanie	40	40	42	47	53	62	69	50	35	37
Algeria Algérie	2 292	2 292	1 774	1 549	1 502	1 475	1 022	1 762	1 762	1 045
Angola Angola	115	115	115	116	...	107	115	105	104	76
Antigua and Barbuda Antigua-et-Barbuda	12	10	10	26	−2	5	3	4	1	2
Argentina Argentine	6 366	4 202	3 524	3 546	4 316	2 397	3 293	2 139	2 255	2 212
Armenia Arménie	202	197	191	186	9	25	163	173	173	111
Australia Australie	2 585	234	184	195	274	6	6	10	1	−62
Azerbaijan Azerbaïdjan	...	456	201	152	100	88	52	12	10	15
Bahamas Bahamas	70	72	53	55	54	66	63	55	25	19
Bahrain Bahreïn	122	137	147	150	129	113	106	95	86	65
Bangladesh Bangladesh	281	628	832	830	801	805	808	328	333	295
Barbados Barbade	25	22	17	22	17	8	12	9	9	14
Belarus Bélarus	579	524	372	256	194	0	0	0	0	0
Belize Belize	22	25	26	25	25	16	28	22	15	12
Benin Bénin	62	58	60	54	57	55	54	36	17	11
Bolivia Bolivie	82	87	58	74	72	79	77	65	32	42
Bosnia and Herzegovina Bosnie-Herzégovine	3	21	49	45	151	176	200	244	230	188
Botswana Botswana	8	5	7	3	3	2	4	4	5	3
Brazil Brésil	10 896	10 872	9 810	9 543	11 612	9 275	6 231	3 001	3 224	1 871
Brunei Darussalam Brunéi Darussalam	65	80	90	63	37	47	31	43	32	60
Bulgaria Bulgarie	322	4	0	0	0	0	0	0	0	0
Burkina Faso Burkina Faso	34	38	38	37	31	25	20	16	13	11
Burundi Burundi	56	59	62	64	60	54	46	19	9	4
Cambodia Cambodge	94	94	94	94	94	94	94	94	87	70

62

Ozone-depleting chlorofluorocarbons (CFCs) — Consumption: ozone-depleting potential (ODP) metric tons (*continued*)
Chlorofluorocarbones (CFC) qui appauvrissent la couche d'ozone — Consommation : tonnes de potentiel de destruction de l'ozone (PDO) (*suite*)

Country or area Pays ou zone	1995	1996	1997	1998	1999	2000	2001	2002	2003	2004
Cameroon Cameroun	231	280	260	312	362	369	364	226	221	149
Canada Canada	4 816	129	136	42	−5	10	0	−13	0	0
Cape Verde Cap-Vert	2	2	2	2	2	2	2	2	2	2
Central African Rep. Rép. centrafricaine	27	6	0	7	1	4	4	4	4	4
Chad Tchad	33	35	36	38	37	37	32	27	23	14
Chile Chili	933	878	674	738	658	576	470	370	424	231
China [1] Chine [1]	75 291	47 089	51 076	55 414	42 983	39 124	33 923	30 621	22 809	17 902
Colombia Colombie	2 156	2 302	2 166	1 224	986	1 149	1 165	907	1 058	899
Comoros Comores	2	2	3	4	2	3	2	2	1	1
Congo Congo	14	13	9	7	9	11	2	5	7	5
Cook Islands Iles Cook	2	2	1	1	0	0	...	...	0	0
Costa Rica Costa Rica	159	497	95	204	152	106	145	137	143	112
Côte d'Ivoire Côte d'Ivoire	354	384	144	268	166	206	148	107	93	79
Croatia Croatie	194	184	280	86	142	171	114	140	89	78
Cuba Cuba	546	664	665	531	571	534	504	489	481	445
Cyprus Chypre	165	141	143	81	115	165	138	132	63	...
Czech Republic République tchèque	369	50	12	8	11	5	3	4	−4	...
Dem. Rep. of the Congo Rép. dém. du Congo	793	735	469	689	368	387	639	569	567	329
Djibouti Djibouti	23	22	19	21	21	21	18	16	12	9
Dominica Dominique	1	2	2	2	1	2	2	3	1	1
Dominican Republic Rép. dominicaine	634	559	427	311	752	402	486	330	266	310
Ecuador Equateur	315	269	320	272	153	230	207	230	256	147
Egypt Egypte	1 640	1 732	1 632	1 540	1 374	1 267	1 335	1 294	1 102	1 048
El Salvador El Salvador	330	312	278	195	110	99	117	102	97	76
Estonia Estonie	765	−442	45	70	56	16	0	0	0	...
Ethiopia Ethiopie	33	34	35	38	39	39	35	30	28	16

62

Ozone-depleting chlorofluorocarbons (CFCs) — Consumption: ozone-depleting potential (ODP) metric tons (*continued*)

Chlorofluorocarbones (CFC) qui appauvrissent la couche d'ozone — Consommation : tonnes de potentiel de destruction de l'ozone (PDO) (*suite*)

Country or area Pays ou zone	1995	1996	1997	1998	1999	2000	2001	2002	2003	2004
Fiji Fidji	60	27	14	13	9	0	0	0	0	0
Gabon Gabon	7	11	12	12	8	14	6	5	5	5
Gambia Gambie	23	21	28	11	7	6	6	5	5	0
Georgia Géorgie	13	23	31	26	22	22	19	16	13	9
Ghana Ghana	44	14	49	50	47	47	36	21	32	36
Grenada Grenade	7	5	7	4	3	3	1	2	2	2
Guatemala Guatemala	231	236	207	189	191	188	265	240	147	65
Guinea Guinée	37	44	46	42	40	38	35	31	26	17
Guinea-Bissau Guinée-Bissau	26	26	27	27	26	26	27	27	29	25
Guyana Guyana	91	41	28	29	40	24	20	14	10	12
Haiti Haïti	169	169	169	...	...	169	169	181	116	133
Honduras Honduras	118	523	354	157	335	172	122	131	219	168
Hungary Hongrie	566	0	4	1	1	0	0	0	−1	...
India Inde	6 402	6 937	6 703	5 265	4 143	5 614	4 514	3 918	2 632	2 242
Indonesia Indonésie	8 351	9 012	7 635	6 183	5 866	5 411	5 003	5 506	4 829	3 925
Iran (Islamic Rep. of) Iran (Rép. islamique d')	4 140	3 692	5 883	5 571	4 399	4 157	4 205	4 438	4 089	3 472
Israel Israël	1 095	7	0	0	0	0	0	0	0	0
Jamaica Jamaïque	82	91	107	199	210	60	49	32	16	16
Japan Japon	23 064	−614	−113	−208	23	24	6	20	4	0
Jordan Jordanie	535	627	857	647	398	354	321	90	74	58
Kazakhstan Kazakhstan	...	826	669	1 025	730	524	290	112	30	11
Kenya Kenya	301	167	251	245	241	203	169	152	169	132
Kiribati Kiribati	1	1	1	0	0	0	0	0	0	0
Korea, Dem. P. R. Corée, R. p. dém. de	825	267	233	112	106	77	321	299	587	7
Korea, Republic of Corée, République de	10 039	8 220	9 220	5 299	7 403	7 395	6 802	6 647	5 172	5 012
Kuwait Koweït	485	472	485	399	450	420	354	349	247	233

Country or area Pays ou zone	1995	1996	1997	1998	1999	2000	2001	2002	2003	2004
Kyrgyzstan Kirghizistan	82	67	70	57	52	53	53	38	33	23
Lao People's Dem. Rep. Rép. dém. pop. lao	43	43	43	43	44	45	41	42	35	23
Latvia Lettonie	665	307	23	25	22	35	0	0	0	...
Lebanon Liban	820	735	621	475	463	528	533	492	480	347
Lesotho Lesotho	6	6	4	3	3	2	2	2	1	1
Liberia Libéria	45	67	56	31	18	41	25	33	26	14
Libyan Arab Jamah. Jamah. arabe libyenne	773	730	647	660	894	985	985	985	704	459
Liechtenstein Liechtenstein	1	0	0	0	0	0	0	0	0	0
Lithuania Lituanie	361	289	100	104	85	37	0	0	0	...
Madagascar Madagascar	19	21	104	24	26	12	10	8	7	7
Malawi Malawi	62	56	56	57	50	22	19	19	19	11
Malaysia Malaisie	3 427	3 038	3 348	2 334	2 010	1 980	1 947	1 606	1 174	1 129
Maldives Maldives	6	0	8	1	1	5	14	3	0	0
Mali Mali	104	109	111	113	37	29	27	26	26	25
Malta Malte	63	70	60	107	97	68	63	10	14	...
Marshall Islands Iles Marshall	1	1	1	1	1	1	0	0	0	0
Mauritania Mauritanie	23	8	16	15	13	14	15	15	14	7
Mauritius Maurice	24	36	27	39	19	19	14	7	4	3
Mexico Mexique	4 859	4 859	4 157	3 483	2 838	3 060	2 224	1 947	1 983	3 208
Micronesia (Fed. States of) Micronésie (Etats féd. de)	1	1	1	1	1	1	1	2	2	1
Mongolia Mongolie	7	12	13	13	12	11	9	7	6	4
Morocco Maroc	707	814	886	924	871	564	435	669	475	329
Mozambique Mozambique	20	22	13	3	14	10	8	10	2	...
Myanmar Myanmar	49	59	55	52	31	26	39	44	52	30
Namibia Namibie	27	19	19	16	17	22	24	20	17	8
Nauru Nauru	1	1	1	0	0	0	0	0	0	0

Country or area Pays ou zone	1995	1996	1997	1998	1999	2000	2001	2002	2003	2004
Nepal Népal	25	27	29	33	25	94	0	0	0	0
New Zealand Nouvelle-Zélande	189	2	0	0	0	−3	0	−5	0	−1
Nicaragua Nicaragua	110	83	56	37	53	44	35	55	30	48
Niger Niger	19	18	59	61	58	40	29	27	25	23
Nigeria Nigéria	1 536	4 548	4 866	4 762	4 286	4 095	3 666	3 287	2 662	2 116
Norway Norvège	3	3	3	−16	−60	−40	−48	−73	−66	−55
Oman Oman	230	265	250	261	260	282	207	179	134	99
Pakistan Pakistan	2 104	1 671	1 264	1 196	1 422	1 945	1 666	1 647	1 124	805
Palau Palaos	2	1	2	2	0	1	1	0	1	1
Panama Panama	440	355	358	346	301	250	180	195	168	135
Papua New Guinea Papouasie-Nouvelle-Guinée	10	63	36	45	35	48	15	35	23	17
Paraguay Paraguay	211	180	240	113	345	153	116	97	92	141
Peru Pérou	367	243	259	327	296	347	189	197	178	146
Philippines Philippines	3 382	3 039	2 747	2 130	2 088	2 905	2 049	1 644	1 422	1 390
Poland Pologne	1 756	549	308	314	187	175	179	202	126	...
Qatar Qatar	91	102	111	121	89	86	85	87	95	64
Republic of Moldova République de Moldova	85	51	83	40	11	32	23	30	19	20
Romania Roumanie	544	763	720	582	338	361	186	359	362	117
Russian Federation Fédération de Russie	20 990	12 345	10 986	11 821	14 824	23 821	0	0	258	374
Rwanda Rwanda	26	30	34	38	30	30	30	30	30	27
Saint Kitts and Nevis Saint-Kitts-et-Nevis	4	3	4	2	3	7	7	5	3	3
Saint Lucia Sainte-Lucie	8	8	8	6	3	4	4	8	3	1
St. Vincent-Grenadines St. Vincent-Grenadines	2	1	2	2	10	6	7	6	3	2
Samoa Samoa	4	5	5	3	6	1	2	2	0	0
Sao Tome and Principe Sao Tomé-et-Principe	5	4	5	4	3	4	4	4	5	4
Saudi Arabia Arabie saoudite	1 828	1 668	1 899	1 922	1 710	1 594	1 593	1 531	1 300	1 150

62

Ozone-depleting chlorofluorocarbons (CFCs) — Consumption: ozone-depleting potential (ODP) metric tons (*continued*)

Chlorofluorocarbones (CFC) qui appauvrissent la couche d'ozone — Consommation : tonnes de potentiel de destruction de l'ozone (PDO) (*suite*)

Country or area Pays ou zone	1995	1996	1997	1998	1999	2000	2001	2002	2003	2004
Senegal Sénégal	151	178	138	128	121	117	98	72	51	40
Serbia and Montenegro Serbie-et-Monténégro	820	896	832	519	549	310	263	372	412	283
Seychelles Seychelles	4	2	2	2	1	1	1	2	1	0
Sierra Leone Sierra Leone	67	87	82	81	76	76	93	81	66	65
Singapore Singapour	774	37	−179	17	24	22	22	1	11	7
Slovakia Slovaquie	381	0	1	1	1	2	3	1	1	...
Slovenia Slovénie	354	1	0	0	0	0	3	0	1	...
Solomon Islands Iles Salomon	2	2	2	1	6	0	1	0	1	1
Somalia Somalie	241	241	242	247	49	66	87	98	108	97
South Africa Afrique du Sud	1 680	0	98	155	117	81	16	87	61	62
Sri Lanka Sri Lanka	520	498	318	250	216	220	190	185	180	156
Sudan Soudan	635	430	306	295	295	292	266	253	216	203
Suriname Suriname	41	41	42	42	43	44	46	46	12	9
Swaziland Swaziland	35	22	16	2	2	0	1	1	2	3
Switzerland Suisse	275	−43	−41	−28	−5	−6	−2	−3	−9	−19
Syrian Arab Republic Rép. arabe syrienne	2 370	2 260	2 044	1 246	1 281	1 175	1 392	1 202	1 125	928
Tajikistan Tadjikistan	32	35	48	56	51	28	28	12	5	0
Thailand Thaïlande	8 248	5 550	4 448	3 783	3 611	3 568	3 375	2 177	1 857	1 358
TFYR of Macedonia L'ex-R.y. Macédoine	558	514	487	63	192	49	47	34	49	9
Togo Togo	50	34	35	37	42	37	35	35	34	26
Tonga Tonga	2	1	1	0	83	0	1	1	0	0
Trinidad and Tobago Trinité-et-Tobago	111	114	135	156	82	101	79	64	63	35
Tunisia Tunisie	758	882	970	791	566	555	570	466	363	271
Turkey Turquie	3 789	3 759	3 870	3 985	1 791	820	731	699	441	258
Turkmenistan Turkménistan	56	30	26	25	19	21	58	10	43	58
Uganda Ouganda	12	13	14	11	12	13	13	13	4	0

Ozone-depleting chlorofluorocarbons (CFCs) — Consumption: ozone-depleting potential (ODP) metric tons (*continued*)
Chlorofluorocarbones (CFC) qui appauvrissent la couche d'ozone — Consommation : tonnes de potentiel de destruction de l'ozone (PDO) (*suite*)

Country or area Pays ou zone	1995	1996	1997	1998	1999	2000	2001	2002	2003	2004
Ukraine Ukraine	746	1 401	1 405	1 101	951	839	1 077	120	78	80
United Arab Emirates Emirats arabes unis	514	511	563	737	529	476	423	370	317	291
United Rep. of Tanzania Rép.-Unie de Tanzanie	280	294	188	132	89	215	131	71	148	99
United States Etats-Unis	35 530	1 331	743	2 706	2 904	2 613	2 805	1 357	1 605	1 154
Uruguay Uruguay	232	172	193	194	111	107	102	75	111	91
Uzbekistan Ouzbékistan	294	260	53	120	53	42	15	0	0	0
Venezuela (Bolivarian Rep. of) Venezuela (Rép. bolivarienne du)	3 220	3 041	3 704	3 214	1 922	2 706	2 546	1 553	1 313	2 945
Viet Nam Viet Nam	480	520	500	392	294	220	243	236	244	241
Yemen Yémen	2 350	1 674	1 364	1 061	1 041	1 045	1 023	960	759	746
Zambia Zambie	23	30	29	27	24	23	12	11	10	10
Zimbabwe Zimbabwe	462	457	435	390	229	145	259	129	117	113

Source

United Nations Environment Programme (UNEP) Ozone Secretariat (Nairobi).

Note

[1] Data include those for China, Hong Kong SAR and the Taiwan Province of China.

Source

Sécretariat de l'ozone du programme des Nations Unies pour l'environnement (PNUE) (Nairobi).

Note

[1] Les données comprennent les chiffres pour Chine, Hong Kong RAS et la province de Taiwan.

Table 60: The data on land are compiled by the Food and Agriculture Organization of the United Nations (FAO). The protected areas data are taken from the United Nations Environment Programme (UNEP) World Conservation Monitoring Centre.

FAO's definitions of the land categories are as follows:

- *Land area*: Total area excluding area under inland water bodies. The definition of inland water bodies generally includes major rivers and lakes.
- *Arable land*: Land under temporary crops (double-cropped areas are counted only once); temporary meadows for mowing or pasture; land under market and kitchen gardens; and land temporarily fallow (less than five years). Abandoned land resulting from shifting cultivation is not included in this category. Data for "arable land" are not meant to indicate the amount of land that is potentially cultivable.
- *Permanent crops*: Land cultivated with crops that occupy the land for long periods and need not be replanted after each harvest, such as cocoa, coffee and rubber. This category includes land under flowering shrubs, fruit trees, nut trees and vines, but excludes land under trees grown for wood or timber.

The *United Nations List of Protected Areas* [31] is the definitive list of the world's national parks and reserves. It is compiled by the UNEP World Conservation Monitoring Centre working in close collaboration with the World Conservation Union (IUCN) World Commission on Protected Areas. Information is provided by national protected areas authorities and the secretariats of international conventions and programmes.

Countries vary considerably in their mechanisms for creating and maintaining systems of protected areas. In order to facilitate international comparisons for protected areas, IUCN has adopted a definition of a protected area which is, an area of land and/or sea especially dedicated to the protection and maintenance of biological diversity, and of natural and associated cultural resources, and managed through legal or other effective means.

IUCN has defined a series of six protected area management categories, based on primary management objectives. These categories are as follows: Ia: Strict Nature Reserve; Ib: Wilderness Area; II: National Park; III: Natural Monument; IV: Habitat/Species Management Area; V: Protected Landscape/Seascape; and VI: Managed Resource Protected Area.

Table 61: The sources of the data presented on the emissions of carbon dioxide (CO_2) are the Carbon Dioxide Information Analysis Center (CDIAC) of the Oak Ridge National Laboratory in the USA and the Secretariat of the

Tableau 60 : Les données relatives aux terres sont compilées par l'Organisation des Nations Unies pour l'alimentation et l'agriculture (FAO). Les données relatives aux aires protégées viennent du Centre mondial de surveillance pour la conservation du Programme des Nations Unies pour l'environnement (PNUE).

Les définitions de la FAO en ce qui concerne les terres sont les suivantes :

- *Superficie totale des terres* : Superficie totale, à l'exception des eaux intérieures. Les eaux intérieures désignent généralement les principaux fleuves et lacs.
- *Terres arables* : Terres affectées aux cultures temporaires (les terres sur lesquelles est pratiquée la double culture ne sont comptabilisées qu'une fois), prairies temporaires à faucher ou à pâturer, jardins maraîchers ou potagers et terres en jachère temporaire (moins de cinq ans). Cette définition ne comprend pas les terres abandonnées du fait de la culture itinérante. Les données relatives aux terres arables ne peuvent être utilisées pour calculer la superficie des terres aptes à l'agriculture.
- *Cultures permanentes* : Superficie des terres avec des cultures qui occupent la terre pour de longues périodes et qui ne nécessitent pas d'être replantées après chaque récolte, comme le cacao, le café et le caoutchouc. Cette catégorie comprend les terres plantées d'arbustes à fleurs, d'arbres fruitiers, d'arbres à noix et de vignes, mais ne comprend pas les terres plantées d'arbres destinés à la coupe.

La *Liste des Nations Unies des zones protégées* [31] est la liste la plus fiable des parcs et réserves naturels du monde. Elle est établie par le Centre mondial de surveillance pour la conservation du PNUE, en collaboration étroite avec la Commission mondiale des aires protégées de l'Union mondiale pour la nature (UICN). Les renseignements sont communiqués par les services nationaux responsables des aires protégées et les secrétariats des conventions et programmes internationaux.

Les mécanismes nationaux de création et d'entretien des systèmes de zones protégées sont très différents d'un pays à l'autre. Pour faciliter les comparaisons internationales, l'UICN a adopté une définition des aires protégées, zone terrestre ou marine (ou les deux) spécialement consacrée à la protection et à la sauvegarde de la diversité biologique et des ressources naturelles, ainsi que des ressources culturelles qui y sont associées, dont la gestion est assurée par des moyens juridiques ou autres moyens efficaces.

L'UICN a défini une série de six catégories de gestion des aires protégées, en fonction des objectifs principaux : Ia : Réserve naturelle intégrale; Ib : Zone vierge; II : Parc national; III : Monument naturel; IV : Aire de gestion des habitats/des

United Nations Framework Convention on Climate Change (UNFCCC). The majority of the data have been taken from the CDIAC database. The data taken from the UNFCCC database are footnoted accordingly.

The CDIAC estimates of CO_2 emissions are derived primarily from United Nations energy statistics on the consumption of liquid and solid fuels and gas consumption and flaring, and from cement production estimates from the Bureau of Mines of the U.S. Department of Interior. The emissions presented in the table are in units of 1,000 metric tons of carbon dioxide (CO_2); to convert CO_2 into carbon, multiply the data by 0.272756. Full details of the procedures for calculating emissions are given in *Global, Regional, and National Annual C02 Emissions Estimates from Fossil Fuel Burning, Hydraulic Cement Production, and Gas Flaring* [2] and in the CDIAC web site (see http://cdiac.esd.ornl.gov). Relative to other industrial sources for which CO_2 emissions are estimated, statistics on gas flaring activities are sparse and sporadic. In countries where gas flaring activities account for a considerable proportion of the total CO_2 emissions, the sporadic nature of gas flaring statistics may produce spurious or misleading trends in national CO_2 emissions over the period covered by the table.

The UNFCCC data in the table are indicated by a footnote, and cover countries parties to Annex I of the United Nations Framework Convention on Climate Change.

Table 62: Chlorofluorocarbons (CFCs) are synthetic compounds formerly used as refrigerants and aerosol propellants and known to be harmful to the ozone layer of the atmosphere. In the Montreal Protocol on Substances that Deplete the Ozone Layer, CFCs to be measured are found in vehicle air conditioning units, domestic and commercial refrigeration and air conditioning/heat pump equipment, aerosol products, portable fire extinguishers, insulation boards, panels and pipe covers, and pre-polymers.

The Parties to the Montreal Protocol on Substances that Deplete the Ozone Layer report data on CFCs to the Ozone Secretariat of the United Nations Environment Programme. The data on CFCs are shown in ozone depleting potential (ODP) tons that are calculated by multiplying the quantities in metric tons reported by the Parties, by the ODP of that substance, and added together.

Consumption is defined as production plus imports, minus exports of controlled substances. Feedstocks are exempt and are therefore subtracted from the imports and/or production. Similarly, the destroyed amounts are also subtracted. Negative numbers can occur when destruction and/or exports exceed production plus imports, implying that the destruction and/or exports are from stockpiles.

espèces; V : Paysage terrestre/marin protégé; VI : Aire protégée de ressources naturelles.

Tableau 61 : Les données sur les émissions de dioxyde de carbone (CO_2) proviennent du Carbon Dioxide Information Analysis Center (CDIAC) du Oak Ridge National Laboratory (États-Unis) et du Secrétariat de la convention-cadre concernant les changements climatiques (CCCC) des Nations Unies. La majorité des données proviennent de la base de données du CDIAC. Les données qui proviennent du Secrétariat de la CCCC sont signalées par une note.

Les estimations du Carbon Dioxide Information Analysis Center sont obtenues essentiellement à partir des statistiques de l'énergie des Nations Unies relatives à la consommation de combustibles liquides et solides, à la production et à la consommation de gaz de torche, et des chiffres de production de ciment du Bureau of Mines du Department of Interior des États-Unis. Les émissions sont indiquées en milliers de tonnes de dioxyde de carbone (à multiplier par 0,272756 pour avoir les chiffres de carbone). On peut voir dans le détail les méthodes utilisées pour calculer les émissions dans *Global, Regional, and National Annual CO_2 Emissions Estimates from Fossil Fuel Burning, Hydraulic Cement Production, and Gas Flaring* [2] et sur le site Web du Carbon Dioxide Information Analysis Center (voir http ://cdiac.esd.ornl.gov). Par rapport à d'autres sources industrielles pour lesquelles on calcule les émissions de CO_2, les statistiques sur la production de gaz de torche sont rares et sporadiques. Dans les pays où cette production représente une proportion considérable de l'ensemble des émissions de dioxyde de carbone, on peut voir apparaître de ce fait des chiffres parasites ou trompeurs pour ce qui est des tendances des émissions nationales de dioxyde de carbone durant la période visée par le tableau.

Les données provenant du secrétariat de la Convention-cadre sont signalées par une note, et couvrent les pays qui sont parties à l'Annexe 1 de la Convention-cadre des Nations Unies sur les changements climatiques.

Tableau 62 : Les chlorofluorocarbones (CFC) sont des substances de synthèse utilisées comme réfrigérants et propulseurs d'aérosols, dont on sait qu'elles appauvrissent la couche d'ozone. Aux termes du Protocole de Montréal relatif à des substances qui appauvrissent la couche d'ozone, la production de certains CFC doit être mesurée : ils sont utilisés dans les climatiseurs de véhicules, le matériel domestique et commercial de réfrigération et de climatisation (pompes à chaleur), les produits sous forme d'aérosols, les extincteurs d'incendie portables, les planches, panneaux et gaines isolants, et les prépolymères.

Les Parties au Protocole de Montréal communiquent leurs données concernant les CFC au secrétariat de l'ozone du Programme des Nations Unies pour l'environnement. Les

données sur les CFC, indiquées en tonnes de potentiel de destruction de l'ozone (PDO), sont calculées en multipliant le nombre de tonnes signalé par les Parties par le potentiel de destruction coefficient de la substance considérée, et en faisant la somme de ces PDO.

La consommation est définie comme production de substances contrôlées, plus les importations, moins les exportations. Les produits intermédiaires de l'industrie sont exemptés, et on les soustrait donc des importations et/ou de la production. De même, on soustrait aussi les quantités détruites. On peut obtenir des quantités négatives, lorsque les quantités détruites et/ou exportées sont supérieures à la somme production + importations, ce qui signifie que les quantités détruites ou exportées ont été prélevées sur les stocks accumulés.

63

Human resources in research and development (R & D)
Full-time equivalent (FTE)

Personnel employé dans la recherche et le développement (R–D)
Equivalent temps plein (ETP)

Country or area Pays ou zone	Year Année	Total R & D personnel Total du personnel de R–D	Researchers Chercheurs		Technicians and equivalent staff Techniciens et personnel assimilé		Other supporting staff Autre personnel de soutien
			Total M & W Total H & F	Women Femmes	Total M & W Total H & F	Women Femmes	Total M & W Total H & F
American Samoa [1,2] — Samoa américaines [1,2]	2002	5	5	...	...	...	...
Argentina — Argentine	1999	36 939	26 004	12 297	10 935[3]	...	...
	2000	37 515	26 420	12 819	11 095[3]	...	...
	2001	37 444	25 656	12 675	11 788[3]	...	...
	2002	37 413	26 083	13 210	11 330[3]	...	...
	2003	39 393	27 367	13 905	12 026[3]	...	...
Armenia [1,2] — Arménie [1,2]	1999	5 764	4 443	...	413	...	908
	2000	5 817	4 598	2 565	373	...	846
	2001	6 260	5 087	2 175	415	...	758
	2002	6 268	4 927	2 314	451	...	890
	2003	5 763	4 667	...	313	...	783
Australia — Australie	2000	95 621	66 001	...	...	...	...
	2002	106 838	73 344	...	...	...	...
Austria — Autriche	2002	38 893[4]	24 124[4]	3 811[4,5]	10 194[5]	2 683[5]	4 575[5]
Azerbaijan [2] — Azerbaïdjan [2]	1999	15 678	10 161	4 883	1 349	...	4 168
	2000	15 809	10 168	4 971	1 478	...	4 163
	2001	15 929	10 139	5 069	1 552	...	4 238
	2002	16 019	10 195	5 236	1 609	...	4 215
Belarus [2] — Bélarus [2]	1999	27 982	18 817	8 851	2 452	...	6 713
	2000	29 032	19 707	9 099	2 574	...	6 751
	2001	28 186	19 133	8 648	2 332	...	6 721
	2002	26 871	18 557	8 361	2 050	...	6 264
Belgium — Belgique	1999	49 466	29 732	...	10 890[5]	...	8 844[5]
	2000	53 391	30 540	7 786[5]	14 428[5]	4 263[5]	8 424[5]
	2001	55 949	32 237	8 254[5]	15 038[5]	4 497[5]	8 675[5]
	2002[5]	52 038	30 652	8 306	15 358	4 498	6 028
	2003[5]	52 240	30 901	8 575	15 293	4 572	6 046
	2004[5,6]	53 938	31 880	...	...	...	...
Bermuda [2] — Bermudes [2]	1999	569	...	...	...	...	...
	2000	558	...	...	...	...	...
	2001	545	...	...	...	...	...
	2002	556	...	...	...	...	...
Bolivia — Bolivie	1999	830	600	237	200	130	30
	2000	820	600	231	170	111	50
	#2001	1 200	1 050	415	50	30	100
	2002	1 190	1 040	...	50	...	100
Brazil — Brésil	2000	117 541	59 838	...	57 703[3]	...	...
Brunei Darussalam — Brunéi Darussalam	2002	140	99	79[2]	...	...	...
	2003	140	98	78[2]	...	...	...
Bulgaria — Bulgarie	1999	16 087	10 580	4 656	3 829	2 578	1 678
	2000	15 259	9 479	4 354	3 833	2 441	1 947
	2001	14 949	9 217	4 247	3 786	2 355	1 946
	2002	15 029	9 223	4 353	3 713	2 374	2 093
	2003	15 453	9 589	4 535	3 735	2 294	2 129
	2004	15 647	9 827	...	...	...	...
Canada — Canada	1999	153 197	98 813	...	...	...	...
	2000	167 861	108 492	...	...	...	...
	*2001[7]	178 980	114 957	...	...	...	...
	*2002[7]	177 120	112 624	...	...	...	...

Country or area / Pays ou zone	Year / Année	Total R & D personnel / Total du personnel de R–D	Researchers / Chercheurs — Total M & W / Total H & F	Women / Femmes	Technicians and equivalent staff / Techniciens et personnel assimilé — Total M & W / Total H & F	Women / Femmes	Other supporting staff / Autre personnel de soutien — Total M & W / Total H & F
Cape Verde [1] — Cap-Vert [1]	2000	28	21	...	...	...	7
	2001	130	45	...	14	...	71
	2002	151	60	56[2]	15	...	76
Chile — Chili	1999	10 774	6 157	...	4 617[3]	...	...
	2000	11 073	6 328	...	4 745[3]	...	...
	2001	11 173	6 446	...	4 727[3]	...	...
	2002	...	6 942	2 273	...	...	...
	2003	...	7 085	2 308	...	...	...
China [8] — Chine [8]	1999[4]	821 700	531 100	...	...	...	...
	#2000	922 131	695 062	...	...	...	...
	2001	956 500	742 700	...	...	...	...
	2002	1 035 197	810 525	...	...	...	...
	2003	1 094 831	862 108	...	...	...	...
	2004	1 152 617	926 252	...	...	...	...
China, Hong Kong SAR — Chine, Hong Kong RAS	1999	10 118	7 922	...	1 302	...	896
	2000	9 802	7 728	...	1 374	...	699
	2001	11 041	9 149	...	1 162	...	730
	2002	12 890	10 639	...	1 532	...	719
China, Macao SAR [1] — Chine, Macao RAS [1]	1999	18	12	2	6	...	...
	2000	28	18	2	10	2	...
Colombia — Colombie	1999	5 925	4 065	1 507	1 860[3]	883[3]	...
	2000	6 262	4 240	1 599	2 022[3]	960[3]	...
	#2001	4 383	3 136	1 185	1 247[3]	610[3]	...
	2002	5 534	3 539	1 359	1 995[3]	992[3]	...
	2003	8 216	4 829	1 797	3 387[3]	1 664[3]	...
Congo [1] — Congo [1]	1999	227	110	15	114	22	3
	2000	217	102	13	111	22	4
Costa Rica [2] — Costa Rica [2]	1999	...	1 412	...	...	...	...
Croatia — Croatie	1999	8 827	5 523	2 426	1 615	954	1 689
	2000	10 399	6 772	2 929	1 750	...	1 877
	2001	10 043	6 656	2 964	1 676	...	1 711
	2002	12 960	8 572	3 651	1 981	1 086[5]	2 407
	2003[5]	9 148	5 861	2 799	2 056	1 046	1 231
Cuba [2] — Cuba [2]	1999	29 063	5 468	...	23 595[3]	...	...
	2000	29 568	5 378	...	24 190[3]	...	...
	2001	32 721	5 849	...	26 872[3]	...	...
	2002	34 326	6 057	...	28 269[3]	...	...
	2003	33 478	6 027	...	27 451[3]	...	...
Cyprus — Chypre	1999	681	278	81	197	71	205
	2000	680	303	91	195	68	181
	2001	689	333	105	186	65	169
	2002	822	435	137	206	80	181
	2003	922	490	157	239	87	194
	*2004	940	520	...	...	...	...
Czech Republic — République tchèque	1999	24 106	13 535	7 528[2]	7 403[5]	...	3 168[5]
	2000	24 198	13 852	3 551[5]	7 319[5]	3 038[5]	3 027[5]
	2001	26 107	14 987	3 853[5]	8 109[5]	3 447[5]	3 011[5]
	2002	26 032	14 974	3 917[5]	8 090[5]	3 216[5]	2 968[5]
	2003	27 957	15 809	4 121[5]	9 001[5]	3 347[5]	3 147[5]
	2004	28 765	16 300	9 730[2]	...	...	...
Denmark — Danemark	1999	36 452	18 945[9]	4 986[5]	17 508[5]	7 150[5]	...
	2000[5]	37 693	...	...	...	...	...
	2001	39 893	19 453[9,10]	5 559[5]	20 439[5,10]	8 752[5]	3 380[5,10]
	2002	42 406	#25 546	6 801[5]	#13 070[5]	6 913[5]	3 790[5]
	2003	43 298	25 546	7 349[5]	14 640[5]	7 180[5]	3 111[5]
	*2004[5]	44 321	27 159	...	...	...	...

Country or area Pays ou zone	Year Année	Total R & D personnel Total du personnel de R–D	Researchers Chercheurs Total M & W Total H & F	Women Femmes	Technicians and equivalent staff Techniciens et personnel assimilé Total M & W Total H & F	Women Femmes	Other supporting staff Autre personnel de soutien Total M & W Total H & F
Ecuador — Equateur	#2001	...	514	125	516[2,3]	...	...
	2002	#1 271[2]	550	126	575[2,3]	...	...
	2003	1 555[2]	645	184	710[2,3]	...	...
El Salvador — El Salvador	1999	...	199	36	...	...	...
	#2000	...	293	109	...	...	...
Estonia — Estonie	1999	4 545	3 002	1 252	750	529	793
	2000	3 710	2 666	1 109	530	368	514
	2001	3 694	2 631	1 079	471	296	592
	2002	4 129	3 059	1 262	524	317	546
	2003	4 144	3 017	1 273	573	362	554
	*2004	4 735	3 369	...	...	...	...
Finland — Finlande	1999	50 604	32 676[9]	12 355[2,9]	17 928[5]	9 498[2,5]	...
	2000	52 604	34 847[9]	12 904[2,9]	...	...	...
	2001	53 424	36 889[9]	13 814[2,9]	...	...	...
	2002	55 044	38 632[9]	15 025[2,9]	...	...	...
	2003	57 196	41 724[9]	15 931[2,9]	...	...	...
	2004[5]	58 281	41 004	...	...	...	...
France — France	1999	314 452	160 424	...	...	...	...
	2000	#327 466	#172 070	58 124[2,4]	...	...	...
	2001	333 518	177 372	59 630[2,4]	...	...	...
	2002	343 718	186 420	64 253[2,4]	...	...	...
	2003	346 078	192 790	66 713[2,5]	...	...	...
Gabon [1,2] — Gabon [1,2]	2004	188	80	25	68	...	40
Georgia [2] — Géorgie [2]	1999	15 138	12 786	...	2 353	...	...
	2000	12 726	11 071	...	1 655	...	...
	2001	12 391	10 871	...	1 520	...	...
	2002	14 893	11 997	6 165	1 246	...	1 650
Germany — Allemagne	1999	479 599	254 691	36 616[5]	126 420[5]	78 836[5]	98 488[11]
	2000	484 734	257 874[7]	...	...	...	...
	2001	480 606	264 385	42 588[5]	119 414[5]	...	96 807[11]
	2002	480 004	265 812[7]	...	118 376[5]	...	95 815[5]
	2003	472 533	268 943	43 422[5]	89 956[5]	...	113 634[5]
	2004[5,7]	469 100	269 500	...	...	...	...
Greece — Grèce	1999	26 382	14 748	12 105[2]	5 839[5]	5 673[2,5]	5 796[5]
	2001	30 226	14 371	9 295[2]	9 636[5]	5 796[2,5]	6 219[5]
	2003[5]	*31 822	*15 390	10 416[2]	9 908	2 653	6 524
	2004[5]	*31 843	*15 680	5 155	...	...	...
Guinea [1,2] — Guinée [1,2]	2000	3 711	2 117	122	768	...	826
Honduras [2] — Honduras [2]	2000	2 167	479	160	1 688[3]	712[3]	...
	2001	2 262	525	164	1 737[3]	677[3]	...
	2002	2 321	516	149	1 805[3]	830[3]	...
	2003	2 280	539	143	1 741[3]	731[3]	...
Hungary [12] — Hongrie [12]	1999	21 329	12 579	7 554[2]	5 037[5]	...	3 713[5]
	2000	23 534	14 406	9 537[2]	5 166[5]	4 844[2,5]	3 962[5]
	2001	22 942	14 666	9 363[2]	4 752[5]	4 896[2,5]	3 524[5]
	2002	23 703	14 965	10 039[2]	4 936[5]	5 590[2,5]	3 802[5]
	2003	23 311	15 180	10 647[2]	4 641[5]	5 552[2,5]	3 490[5]
	2004	*22 826	*14 904	10 484[2]	...	...	...
Iceland — Islande	1999	2 390	1 578	501[5]	461[5]	169[5]	352[5]
	2000[5,7]	2 646	...	...	...	...	...
	2001	2 901	1 859[10]	641[5]	587[5,10]	269[5]	463[5,10]
	2002[7]	2 797	...	...	...	...	...
	2003	2 940	1 917	690[5]	594[5]	248[5]	429[5]
	2004[5]	3 050	1 987	...	...	...	...

Country or area Pays ou zone	Year Année	Total R & D personnel Total du personnel de R–D	Researchers Chercheurs Total M & W Total H & F	Women Femmes	Technicians and equivalent staff Techniciens et personnel assimilé Total M & W Total H & F	Women Femmes	Other supporting staff Autre personnel de soutien Total M & W Total H & F
Iran (Islamic Rep. of) [2] — Iran (Rép. islamique d') [2]	2001	56 454	31 256	6 670	25 198	...	
Ireland — Irlande	1999	11 929[7]	7 877[7,10]	...	2 581[5,10]	...	1 491[5,10]
	2000[7]	12 761	8 516	...	...	...	...
	2001	13 317	8 949	...	...	...	...
	2002	13 581[7]	9 376[7]	2 602[5]	2 410[5]	586[5]	1 797[5]
	2003	14 450	10 039[10]	2 883[5]	*2 489[5,10]	633[5]	*1 846[5,10]
	2004	15 713[7]	10 910[7]	4 895[2]			
Italy — Italie	1999	142 506	65 098[10]	26 450[2]	77 620[5,10]	...	...
	2000	150 066	66 110	27 908[2]	...	...	...
	2001	153 905	66 702	28 176[2]	...	...	...
	2002	164 023	71 242	31 220[2]	...	...	...
	2003[5]	161 828	70 332	20 105	...	...	...
Japan — Japon	1999	919 132	658 910	...	84 527[5]	...	175 695[5]
	2000	896 847	647 572	...	78 951[5]	...	170 324[5]
	2001	892 057	675 898	85 207[2]	68 754[5]	22 433[2,5]	147 405[5]
	2002	#857 300	#646 547	88 674[2]	67 040[5]	22 964[2,5]	143 713[5]
	2003	882 414	675 330	96 133[2]	67 389[5]	24 650[2,5]	139 695[5]
Kazakhstan — Kazakhstan	1999	13 850	9 624	4 678	1 179	...	3 047
	2000	12 829	9 009	4 544	1 183	...	2 637
	2001	13 156	9 223	4 624	1 140	...	2 793
	2002	13 720	9 366	4 558	1 364	...	2 990
Korea, Republic of [1] — Corée, République de [1]	1999	137 874	100 210	13 009[2]	...	...	...
	2000	138 077	108 370	16 385[2]	...	...	...
	2001	165 715	136 337	19 930[2]	...	...	...
	2002	172 270	141 917	22 057[2]	...	...	...
	2003	186 214	151 254	22 613[2]	...	...	...
Kuwait [1,2] — Koweït [1,2]	1999	742	186	37	375	...	181
	2000	744	181	35	383	...	180
	2001	757	174	36	403	...	180
	2002	766	169	33	420	...	177
Kyrgyzstan [2] — Kirghizistan [2]	1999	3 088	2 284	1 114	205	...	599
	2000	2 886	2 121	1 028	194	...	571
	2001	2 958	2 099	1 001	248	...	611
	2002	...	2 065	1 019	257	...	600
Latvia — Lettonie	1999	4 301	2 626	1 277	726	419[5]	949
	#2000	5 449	3 814	1 881	635	371[5]	1 000
	2001	5 476	3 497	1 927	809	536[5]	1 170
	2002	5 294	3 451	1 835	660	367[5]	1 183
	2003[5]	4 858	3 203	1 707	742	416	913
	2004[5]	5 103	3 324	...	...	...	...
Lesotho [1,2] — Lesotho [1,2]	2002	...	81	31[4]	47	...	68
Lithuania — Lituanie	1999	12 794	8 539	...	1 983	...	2 272
	2000	11 791	7 777	3 388	1 774	1 156	2 240
	2001	11 949	8 075	3 766	1 725	1 215	2 149
	2002	9 531	6 326	2 989	1 490	1 058	1 715
	2003	9 648	6 606	3 196	1 476	1 029	1 566
	2004	10 557	7 356	...	...	...	...
Luxembourg — Luxembourg	2000	3 663	1 646	...	#1 673[5]	...	344[11]
	2003	4 010	1 949	322[5]	1 685[5]	...	376[5]
Madagascar [1] — Madagascar [1]	1999	1 114	227	...	862	...	25
	2000	985	240	...	730	...	15
Malaysia — Malaisie	2000	10 060	6 423	2 045	921	...	2 716
	2002	10 731	7 157	2 451	1 379	...	2 195

Country or area Pays ou zone	Year Année	Total R & D personnel Total du personnel de R–D	Researchers Chercheurs Total M & W Total H & F	Women Femmes	Technicians and equivalent staff Techniciens et personnel assimilé Total M & W Total H & F	Women Femmes	Other supporting staff Autre personnel de soutien Total M & W Total H & F
Malta — Malte	1999	45	...	...	...	...	...
	2000	79	...	...	...	...	...
	2002	475	272	...	45	...	158
	2003	413	276	...	...	...	...
	*2004	395	272	...	...	...	...
Mexico — Mexique	1999	39 736[7]	21 879[10]	...	9 161[7,10,13]	...	8 656[7,10,13]
	*2001	43 455	25 751[7,10]	...	9 803[7,10]	...	8 531[7,10]
	2002[7,13]	46 092	27 626	...	9 881	...	8 586
Mongolia [2] — Mongolie [2]	1999	1 955	1 794	...	...	...	161
	2000	2 113	1 631	...	294	150	188
	2001	2 302	1 898	...	215	...	189
	2002	2 313	1 738	...	177	...	398
Morocco [2] — Maroc [2]	1999	...	24 035[1]	4 957[4]	...	...	...
	2000	...	23 991[1]	5 061[4]	...	...	...
	2001	...	24 890[1]	5 133[4]	...	...	...
	2002	...	23 559[1]	6 049[4]	...	...	...
Mozambique [1,2,4] — Mozambique [1,2,4]	2002	2 467	468	...	1 999[3]	...	...
Myanmar [1] — Myanmar [1]	1999	2 797	510	2 527[2]	2 238	...	49
	2001	4 373	574	2 793[2]	3 754	...	46
	2002	7 418	837	4 038[2]	6 499	...	82
Nepal — Népal	2002	6 500	1 500	450[2]	3 500	...	1 500
Netherlands — Pays-Bas	1999	86 774	40 390	...	22 397[5]	...	23 985[5]
	2000	87 999	42 088	...	24 347[5]	...	21 563[5]
	2001	89 207	45 517	...	22 264[5]	...	21 428[5]
	2002	87 415	43 539	...	22 647[5]	...	21 231[5]
	2003[5]	85 987	37 928	...	27 861	...	20 198
	2004[5]	*89 522	40 269[7]	...	...	...	...
New Zealand — Nouvelle-Zélande	1999	13 085	8 768	...	...	...	...
	#2001	17 768	13 133	8 657[2]	...	...	...
	2003[14]	21 410	15 568	...	...	...	...
Nicaragua [2,15] — Nicaragua [2,15]	2002	456	226	96	200[3]	...	...
Norway — Norvège	1999	25 400	18 295[9]	8 615[2,9]	7 107[5]	...	...
	2001	27 068	20 048[10]	9 883[2,9]	6 876[5,10]	...	...
	2002	27 335	...	...	...	...	...
	2003	29 014	20 989	10 505[2]	8 025[5]	6 521[2,5]	...
Pakistan [1,2] — Pakistan [1,2]	2002	...	12 820[11]	1 332[4]	...	...	...
Panama — Panama	#1999	962	288	101	674[3]	241[3]	...
	2000	964	286	112	678[3]	245[3]	...
	2001	894	276	98	618[3]	207[3]	...
	2002	1 469	297	110	1 172[3]	407[3]	...
	2003	1 512	304	111	1 208[3]	423[3]	...
Paraguay — Paraguay	2001	1 149	481	241	669[3]	408[3]	...
	2002	1 106	455	228	651[3]	362[3]	...
Poland — Pologne	1999	82 368	56 433	...	15 362[5]	...	10 573[5]
	2000	78 925	55 174	33 572[2]	13 648[5]	10 578[2,5]	10 103[5]
	2001	78 027	56 918	...	12 385[5]	...	8 724[5]
	2002	76 214	56 725	...	11 435[5]	...	8 054[5]
	2003	77 040	58 595	22 068[5]	10 881[5]	8 430[2,5]	7 564[5]
	2004[5]	78 362	60 944	...	...	...	...
Portugal — Portugal	1999	20 806	15 752	12 255[2]	2 479[5]	...	2 576[5]
	2000[7]	21 888	16 738	12 914[2]	2 676[5]	...	2 473[5]
	2001	22 970	17 725	7 940[5,7]	2 874[5]	1 056[5,7]	2 371[5]
	2002[7]	24 250	18 984	8 538[5]	3 031[5]	1 164[5]	2 235[5]
	2003	25 529	20 242	9 136[5]	3 189[5]	1 272[5]	2 098[5]

Human resources in research and development (R & D) — Full-time equivalent (FTE) *(continued)*
Personnel employé dans la recherche et le développement (R–D) — Equivalent temps plein (ETP) *(suite)*

Country or area Pays ou zone	Year Année	Total R & D personnel Total du personnel de R–D	Researchers Chercheurs Total M & W Total H & F	Women Femmes	Technicians and equivalent staff Techniciens et personnel assimilé Total M & W Total H & F	Women Femmes	Other supporting staff Autre personnel de soutien Total M & W Total H & F
Republic of Moldova [2]	1999	2 479	722	208	1 005	...	752
République de Moldova [2]	2000	2 395	737	212	967	...	691
	2001	2 262	738	222	888	...	636
	2002	2 201	729	221	855	...	617
Romania — Roumanie	1999	44 091	23 473	10 335[5]	8 843[5]	5 155[5]	11 775[5]
	2000	33 892	20 476	8 785[5]	6 482[5]	3 853[5]	6 934[5]
	2001	32 639	19 726	8 551[5]	5 952[5]	3 447[5]	6 961[5]
	2002	32 799	20 286	9 181[5]	6 436[5]	3 540[5]	6 077[5]
	2003	33 077	20 965	9 340[5]	5 434[5]	3 174[5]	6 678[5]
	2004	33 361	21 257	...	...	...	...
Russian Federation — Fédération de Russie	1999	989 291	497 030	186 264[2,4]	80 498[5]	...	411 763[5]
	2000	1 007 257	506 420	187 792[2,4]	83 490[5]	...	417 348[5]
	2001	1 008 091	505 778	185 609[2,4]	83 914[5]	...	418 399[5]
	2002	986 854	491 944	179 120[2,4]	83 413[5]	...	411 497[5]
	2003	973 382	487 477	177 538[2,4]	80 514[5]	...	405 391[5]
	2004	951 569	477 647	172 177[2,4]	...	...	...
Saint Helena [1] — Sainte-Hélène [1]	1999	40	4	1	38	13	...
	2000	33	2	...	8	4	23
Saint Lucia [2] — Sainte-Lucie [2]	1999	311	74	10[4]	237	...	...
St. Vincent-Grenadines [2]	2001	129	20	...	109	...	...
St. Vincent-Grenadines [2]	2002	131	21	...	110	...	...
Saudi Arabia [1,2] — Arabie saoudite [1,2]	1999	3 515	1 218	216	1 353	...	944
	2000	3 601	1 218	220	1 427	...	956
	2001	3 708	1 239	225[4]	1 498	...	971
	2002	4 182	1 513	263	1 674	...	995
Serbia and Montenegro [1,2]	1999	24 198	12 163	4 755	5 651	...	6 384
Serbie-et-Monténégro [1,2]	2000	23 117	11 969	4 815	5 448	...	5 700
	2001	19 415	10 071	4 246	4 518	...	4 826
	2002	21 291	10 855	4 663	4 631	...	5 805
Seychelles [1] — Seychelles [1]	2002	7	2	...	3	...	3
Singapore — Singapour	1999	15 097	12 598	...	1 450	...	1 049
	2000	19 365	16 633	...	1 360	...	1 372
	2001	19 453	16 741	...	1 435	...	1 277
	2002	21 871	18 120	5 517[2]	1 586	...	2 165
	2003	23 514	20 024	...	...	...	...
	2004	25 492	21 359	...	...	...	...
Slovakia — Slovaquie	1999	14 849	9 204	3 516[5]	3 858[5]	2 198[5]	1 787[5]
	2000	15 221	9 955	3 867[5]	3 597[5]	1 979[5]	1 669[5]
	2001	14 422	9 585	3 817[5]	3 323[5]	1 798[5]	1 514[5]
	2002	13 631	9 181	3 749[5]	3 032[5]	1 586[5]	1 418[5]
	2003	13 353	9 626	3 946[5]	2 483[5]	1 433[5]	1 244[5]
	2004	14 329	10 718	7 152[2]	2 402[5]	...	1 209[5]
Slovenia — Slovénie	1999	8 495	4 427	1 487[5]	1 783[5]	758[5]	2 285[5]
	2000	8 568	4 336	1 525[5]	1 776[5]	773[5]	2 456[5]
	2001	8 608	4 498	1 547[5]	1 796[5]	778[5]	2 314[5]
	2002	8 615	4 642	1 606[5]	3 140[5]	1 199[5]	833[5]
	2003[7]	8 731	4 815	1 653[5]	3 148[5]	1 180[5]	768[5]
	2004[5,7]	8 830	5 003	...	...	...	...
South Africa — Afrique du Sud	2001	21 195	14 182	4 922	3 374	...	3 639
Spain — Espagne	1999	102 237	61 568	19 989[5]	23 593[5]	6 483[5]	17 076[5]
	2000	120 618	76 670	...	25 622[7]	...	18 326[5,7]
	2001	125 750	80 081	28 208[5]	28 460[5]	7 437[5]	17 209[5]
	2002	134 258	83 318	29 767[5]	30 376[5]	9 561[5]	20 564[5]
	2003	151 487	92 523	33 985[5]	36 278[5]	11 381[5]	22 687[5]

Country or area Pays ou zone	Year Année	Total R & D personnel Total du personnel de R–D	Researchers Chercheurs Total M & W Total H & F	Women Femmes	Technicians and equivalent staff Techniciens et personnel assimilé Total M & W Total H & F	Women Femmes	Other supporting staff Autre personnel de soutien Total M & W Total H & F
Sri Lanka [1] — Sri Lanka [1]	2000	16 851[2]	2 537	1 294[2,4]	1 551[2]	...	7 493[2]
Sudan [2] — Soudan [2]	1999	14 923	7 300	1 554	2 947	...	4 676
	2000	15 333	7 500	1 644	3 028	...	4 805
	2001	16 050	7 850	1 664	3 170	...	5 030
	2002	18 604	9 100	2 754	3 674	...	5 830
	2003	18 808	9 200	2 784[7]	3 714	...	5 894
	2004	19 772	9 340	2 830[7]	4 641	...	5 791
Sweden — Suède	1999	66 674	39 921	...	...	...	...
	2001	72 190	45 995	...	...	...	...
	2003	72 978	47 836	25 391[2,5]	...	...	...
	2004[5]	72 459	48 784	...	...	...	...
Switzerland — Suisse	2000	52 284	25 808	7 064[2]	16 620[5]	3 612[2,5]	9 857[5]
Thailand — Thaïlande	1999	20 048	10 418	...	5 281	...	4 349
	2001	32 011	17 710	...	7 110	...	7 191
	2003	42 379	18 114	13 607[2]	13 139	...	11 126
TFYR of Macedonia — L'ex-R.y. Macédoine	1999	1 838	1 136	511	239	...	463
	2000	1 786	1 106	521	234	...	446
	2001	1 630	1 057	504	199	...	374
	2002	1 519	1 018	489	140	...	361
Trinidad and Tobago [2] — Trinité-et-Tobago [2]	2000	1 589	447	153	1 142	445	...
	2001	...	509	192	...	...	...
	2003	...	518	208	...	...	...
Tunisia — Tunisie	1999	8 589	6 911	...	326	...	1 352
	2000	9 229	7 516	...	341	...	1 372
	2001	10 090	8 515	...	294	...	1 281
	2002	11 510	9 910	...	329	...	1 271
Turkey — Turquie	1999	24 267[4]	20 065	19 317[2]	2 371[5]	776[2,5]	1 831[5]
	2000	27 003[4]	23 083	23 173[2]	2 361[5]	901[2,5]	1 559[5]
	2001	27 698[4]	22 702	8 527[5]	2 560[5]	434[5]	2 436[5]
	2002	28 964[4]	23 995	8 211[5]	2 567[5]	415[5]	2 402[5]
Uganda [2] — Ouganda [2]	1999	1 102	503	189	309	...	290
	2000	1 187	549	206	330	...	308
	2001	1 278	568	210[11]	366	...	344
Ukraine [2] — Ukraine [2]	1999	166 551	94 726	...	31 273	...	40 552
	2000	156 372	89 192	...	31 536	...	35 644
	2001	147 116	86 366	36 164	26 975	...	33 775
	2002	142 763	85 211	36 557	22 236	...	35 316
	2003	139 470	83 890	...	20 951	...	34 629
United States — Etats-Unis	1999	...	1 260 920	...	...	...	...
	2000[16]	...	1 289 262	...	...	...	...
	2001[16]	...	1 320 096	...	...	...	...
	2002[16]	...	1 334 628	...	...	...	...
United States Virgin Is. [1] Iles Vierges américaines [1]	1999	31	9	...	6	...	16
	2000	33	11	2	6	...	16
	2001	34	13	2	7	...	14
	2002	37	12	2	6	...	19
Uruguay — Uruguay	1999	792	724	327	68[3]	31[3]	...
	2000	1 097	922	401	175[3]	64[3]	...
	2002	1 412	1 242	596	170[3]	40[3]	...
Venezuela (Bolivarian Rep. of) [2] Venezuela (Rép. bolivarienne du) [2]	1999	...	4 435	...	...	...	...
	2000	...	4 688	1 969	...	...	...
	2001	...	4 756	1 998	...	...	...
	2002	...	5 580	2 541	...	...	...
	2003	...	6 100	2 818	...	...	...
Zambia [1] — Zambie [1]	1999	2 098	536	76	163	7	1 399

Source

United Nations Educational, Scientific and Cultural Organization (UNESCO) Institute for Statistics, Montreal, the UNESCO Institute of Statistics database.

Countries covered by OECD: Australia, Austria, Belgium, Canada, Czech Republic, Denmark, Finland, France, Germany, Greece, Hungary, Iceland, Ireland, Italy, Japan, Korea, Luxembourg, Mexico, Netherlands, New Zealand, Norway, Poland, Portugal, Slovakia, Spain, Sweden, Switzerland, Turkey, United Kingdom, United States. Non members: China, Israel, Romania, Russian Federation, Singapore, Slovenia.

Countries covered by the Science and Technology Indicators Network (RICYT): Argentina, Bolivia, Brazil, Chile, Colombia, Costa Rica, Cuba, Ecuador, El Salvador, Honduras, Nicaragua, Panama, Paraguay, Peru, Trinidad & Tobago, Uruguay, Venezuela.

Countries covered by EUROSTAT: Bulgaria, Cyprus, Estonia, Lithuania, Malta.

Notes

[1] Partial data.

[2] Head count instead of Full-time equivalent.

[3] Includes other supporting staff.

[4] Underestimated or based on underestimated data.

[5] Source: EUROSTAT.

[6] EUROSTAT estimation.

[7] National estimation.

[8] For statistical purposes, the data for China do not include those for the Hong Kong Special Administrative Region (Hong Kong SAR), Macao Special Administrative Region (Macao SAR) and Taiwan Province of China.

[9] University graduates instead of researchers.

[10] The sum of the breakdown does not add to the total.

[11] UIS estimation.

[12] Defence excluded (all or mostly).

[13] Source: National statistical publication(s).

[14] Source: OECD.

[15] Source: RICYT.

[16] OECD estimation.

Source

L'Institut de statistique de l'Organisation des Nations Unies pour l'éducation, la science et la culture (UNESCO), Montréal, la base de données de l'Institut de statistique de l'UNESCO.

Pays dont la source est OCDE : Allemagne, Australie, Autriche, Belgique, Canada, Corée, Danemark, Espagne, Etats-Unis, Fédération de Russie, Finlande, France, Grèce, Hongrie, Islande, Irlande, Italie, Japon, Luxembourg, Mexique, Norvège, Nouvelle-Zélande, Pays-Bas, Pologne, Portugal, République tchèque, Royaume-Uni, Slovaquie, Suède, Suisse, Turquie. Non-membres : Chine, Israël, Roumanie, Singapour, Slovénie.

Pays dont la source est Red IberoAmericana de Indicadores de Ciencia y Tecnologia (RICYT) : Argentine, Bolivie, Brésil, Chili, Colombie, Costa Rica, Cuba, Ecuador, El Salvador, Honduras, Nicaragua, Panama, Paraguay, Pérou, Trinité-et-Tobago, Uruguay, Venezuela.

Pays dont la source est EUROSTAT : Bulgarie, Chypre, Estonie, Lithuanie, Malte.

Notes

[1] Données partielles.

[2] Personnes physiques au lieu d'Equivalents temps plein.

[3] Y compris autre personnel de soutien.

[4] Sous-estimé ou basé sur des données sous-estimées.

[5] Source : EUROSTAT.

[6] Estimation de EUROSTAT.

[7] Estimation nationale.

[8] Pour la présentation des statistiques, les données pour Chine ne comprennent pas la Région Administrative Spéciale de Hong Kong (Hong Kong RAS), la Région Administrative Spéciale de Macao (Macao RAS) et la province de Taiwan.

[9] Diplômes universitaires au lieu de chercheurs.

[10] La somme de toutes les valeurs diffère du total.

[11] Estimation de l'ISU.

[12] A l'exclusion de la défense (en totalité ou en grande partie).

[13] Source : Publications des statistiques nationales.

[14] Source : OCDE.

[15] Source : RICYT.

[16] Estimation de l'OCDE.

64

Gross domestic expenditure on R & D by source of funds
National currency

Dépenses intérieures brutes de recherche et développement par source de financement
Monnaie nationale

Country or area (monetary unit) Pays ou zone (unité monétaire)	Year Année	Gross domestic expenditure on R&D (000) Dépenses int. brutes de R–D (000)	Source of funds (%) — Source de financement (%)					
			Business enterprises Enterprises	Gov't Etat	Higher education Enseignement supérieur	Private non-profit institut. Institutions privées sans but lucratif	Funds from abroad Fonds de l'étranger	Not distributed Non répartis
American Samoa (US dollar) [1] Samoa américaines (dollar des Etats-Unis) [1]	2001	1 117	...	...	...	...	...	...
Argentina (Argentine peso) Argentine (peso argentin)	2001	1 140 900	...	...	...	...	...	...
	2002	1 215 500	22.5	41.8	32.2	2.2	1.2	...
	2003	1 541 700	26.1	44.2	25.9	2.3	1.4	...
Armenia (dram) [1] Arménie (dram) [1]	2000	1 904 200	...	73.3	...	...	...	26.7
	2001	3 290 900	...	54.6	...	...	1.4	43.9
	2002	3 440 900	...	55.2[2,3]	...	...	11.2	33.6
Australia (Australian dollar) Australie (dollar australien)	1998	8 918 200	45.9	46.9	4.7	...	2.5	...
	2000	10 417 100	46.3	45.5	4.7	...	3.5	...
	2002	12 842 700	48.8	42.4	4.7	...	4.1	...
Austria (euro) [4] Autriche (euro) [4]	2002	4 684 310	44.6	33.6	0.4	...	21.4	...
	2003	*4 974 680	43.9	34.7	0.4	...	21.0	...
	*2004	5 346 080	43.4	35.8	0.4	...	20.4	...
Azerbaijan (manat) Azerbaïdjan (manat)	2000	79 263 000	...	...	...	...	...	...
	2001	90 368 000	24.0	44.8	31.2	...	...	...
	2002	91 407 000	21.1	54.4	24.5	...	...	...
Belarus (Belarussian rouble) Bélarus (rouble bélarussien)	2000	65 955 300[5]	23.8	62.6	1.1	...	12.5	...
	2001	121 717 400	24.3	65.6	1.1	...	9.0	...
	2002	162 291 500	24.4	63.4	2.2	...	10.1	...
Belgium (euro) Belgique (euro)	2001	5 373 380	63.4	22.0	2.1[6]	0.4[6]	12.1	...
	2002	*5 122 320	59.4[6]	21.3[6]	2.6[6]	2.4[6]	14.3[6]	...
	2003	*5 089 200	60.3[6]	21.7[6]	2.7[6]	2.4[6]	12.9[6]	...
Bermuda (Bermuda dollar) Bermudes (dollar des Bermudes)	1997	1 726	...	...	...	...	...	...
Bolivia (boliviano) Bolivie (boliviano)	2000	149 300	22.0	22.0	32.0	15.0	9.0	...
	2001	157 900	18.0	21.0	33.0	17.0	11.0	...
	2002	156 800	16.0	20.0	31.0	19.0	14.0	...
Brazil (real) Brésil (real)	2001	12 221 140	37.3	35.3	27.4	...	...	...
	2002	13 125 940	39.5	31.5	29.1	...	...	...
	2003	14 851 310	41.0	30.4	28.6	...	...	...
Bulgaria (lev) Bulgarie (lev)	2002	158 330	24.8	69.8	0.2	0.2	5.0	...
	2003	173 009	26.8	66.9	0.4	0.2	5.8	...
	2004	193 946	...	...	...	...	...	...
Burkina Faso (CFA franc) [1] Burkina Faso (franc CFA) [1]	1996	2 095 056	...	...	...	...	...	...
	1997	2 586 462	...	...	...	...	...	...
Canada (Canadian dollar) Canada (dollar canadien)	2002	23 382 000[7]	51.3[7]	23.1[7]	14.8[7]	2.7[7]	8.2	...
	2003	23 992 000[7]	*49.3[7]	24.5[7]	14.9[7]	2.6[7]	8.6	...
	*2004	25 259 000[7]	47.9[7]	25.4[7]	15.6[7]	2.7[7]	8.3	...
Chile (Chilean peso) Chili (peso chilien)	2001	228 761 525	24.9	68.9	...	2.1	4.1	...
	2002	326 632 138	#34.4	#53.9	...	#0.3	#11.0	...
	2003	303 001 483	35.2	50.5	...	0.5	13.3	...
China (yuan) [8] Chine (yuan) [8]	2002	128 760 000	...	...	...	...	...	...
	2003	153 963 000	60.1[9]	29.9[9]	...	...	2.0[9]	8.0
	2004	196 661 000	...	...	...	...	...	...
China, Hong Kong SAR (Hong Kong dollar) Chine, Hong Kong RAS (dollar de Hong Kong)	2000	6 218 400	22.8	76.7	...	...	0.5	...
	2001	7 087 300	31.4	67.4	0.1	...	1.2	...
	2002	7 543 600	35.3	62.8	0.2	...	1.7	...

Gross domestic expenditure on R & D by source of funds—National currency (*continued*)

Dépenses intérieures brutes de recherche et développement par source de financement—Monnaie nationale (*suite*)

Country or area (monetary unit) Pays ou zone (unité monétaire)	Year Année	Gross domestic expenditure on R&D (000) Dépenses int. brutes de R–D (000)	Source of funds (%) — Source de financement (%)					
			Business enterprises Enterprises	Gov't Etat	Higher education Enseignement supérieur	Private non-profit institut. Institutions privées sans but lucratif	Funds from abroad Fonds de l'étranger	Not distributed Non répartis
Colombia (Colombian peso) Colombie (peso colombien)	1999	302 038 500	45.0	24.0	29.0	2.0	...	...
	2000	306 385 210	48.4	16.6	33.6	1.4	...	...
	2001	313 720 990	46.9	13.2	38.3	1.7	...	...
Costa Rica (Costa Rican colón) Costa Rica (colón costa-ricien)	1998	9 335 632	...	...	...	...	...	...
	1999	14 969 633	...	...	...	...	...	...
	2000	19 033 194	...	...	...	...	...	...
Croatia (kuna) Croatie (kuna)	2001	1 780 379	43.1	55.8[2,3]	...	...	1.1	...
	2002	2 006 307	44.2	54.2[2,3]	...	...	1.6	...
	2003[6]	2 209 000	42.1	55.9	...	...	2.2	...
Cuba (Cuban peso) Cuba (peso cubain)	2001	179 100	36.2	57.6	...	...	6.2	...
	2002	189 600	35.0	60.0	...	...	5.0	...
	2003	209 100	35.0	60.0	...	...	5.0	...
Cyprus (Cyprus pound) Chypre (livre chypriote)	2002	19 440	17.4	61.7	3.8	2.0	15.1	...
	2003	23 933	19.8	59.9	3.8	2.3	13.9	...
	*2004	26 500	...	...	...	...	...	...
Czech Republic (Czech koruna) République tchèque (couronne tchèque)	2002	29 552 200	53.7	42.1	0.5[6]	1.0[6]	2.7	...
	2003	32 246 600	51.5	41.8	1.2[6]	1.0[6]	4.6	...
	2004	35 083 039	52.8	41.9	1.6[3]	...	3.7	...
Denmark (Danish krone) Danemark (couronne danoise)	2002	34 432 000	...	...	...	...	...	...
	2003	36 739 700	61.3	26.5	2.7[3]	...	9.5	...
	*2004[6]	38 034 000	...	...	...	...	...	...
Ecuador (sucre) Equateur (sucre)	2001	12 600	...	...	...	...	...	...
	2002	15 800	...	...	...	...	...	...
	2003	18 600	...	...	...	...	...	...
Egypt (Egyptian pound) [1] Egypte (livre égyptienne) [1]	1998	572 200	...	...	...	...	...	...
	1999	573 700	...	...	...	...	...	...
	2000	654 600	...	...	...	...	...	...
El Salvador (El Salvadoran colón) El Salvador (cólon salvadorien)	1998	84 437	1.2	51.9	13.2	10.4	23.4	...
Estonia (Estonian kroon) Estonie (couronne estonienne)	2002	872 000	29.2	53.8	2.4	0.2	14.4	...
	2003	1 046 200	...	...	...	...	...	...
	*2004	1 294 000	...	...	...	...	...	...
Finland (euro) Finlande (euro)	2002	4 830 330	69.5	26.1	0.2[6]	1.0[6]	3.1	...
	2003	5 005 020	70.0	25.7	0.2[6]	0.9[6]	3.2	...
	2004[6]	5 253 400	...	...	...	...	...	...
France (euro) France (euro)	2002	34 527 250	52.1	38.3	1.6	...	8.0	...
	2003	34 569 100	50.8	39.0	1.9	...	8.4	...
	*2004	35 648 100	...	...	...	...	...	...
Georgia (lari) Géorgie (lari)	2000	11 963	...	...	...	...	...	...
	2001	16 113	...	...	...	...	...	...
	2002	21 478	...	...	...	...	...	...
Germany (euro) Allemagne (euro)	2002	53 363 750	65.5[4]	31.6[4]	0.5[3,4]	...	2.4[4]	...
	2003	54 538 430	66.3	31.2[4]	0.3[3]	...	2.3	...
	2004[4]	55 100 000	67.1	30.4	0.3[3]	...	2.3	...
Greece (euro) Grèce (euro)	2001	851 500	33.1	46.6	1.6[6]	0.4[6]	18.4	...
	2003	950 560	30.7	47.4	2.6[6]	1.2[6]	18.1	...
	*2004[6]	966 700	...	...	...	...	...	...
Guam (US dollar) [1] Guam (dollar des Etats-Unis) [1]	2001	3 813	...	...	...	...	...	...
Honduras (lempira) Honduras (lempira)	2001	45 400	...	...	...	...	...	...
	2002	54 000	...	...	...	...	...	...
	2003	60 200	...	...	...	...	...	...

Gross domestic expenditure on R & D by source of funds — National currency (*continued*)

Dépenses intérieures brutes de recherche et développement par source de financement — Monnaie nationale (*suite*)

Country or area (monetary unit) / Pays ou zone (unité monétaire)	Year / Année	Gross domestic expenditure on R&D (000) Dépenses int. brutes de R–D (000)	Source of funds (%) — Source de financement (%)					
			Business enterprises Enterprises	Gov't Etat	Higher education Enseignement supérieur	Private non-profit institut. Institutions privées sans but lucratif	Funds from abroad Fonds de l'étranger	Not distributed Non répartis
Hungary (forint) [10]	2002	171 470 200	29.7	58.6	0.3	...	10.4	1.2
Hongrie (forint) [10]	2003	175 772 900	30.7	58.0	0.4	...	10.7	...
	*2004	179 749 900	37.5	51.3	0.6	...	10.5	...
Iceland (Icelandic króna)	2002[4]	24 097 030	...	...	...	...	...	...
Islande (couronne islandaise)	2003	23 720 000	43.9	40.1	1.5	...	14.5	...
	2004[6]	25 862 000	...	...	...	...	...	...
India (Indian rupee)	1998	129 015 400	21.6	75.4	2.9	...	...	...
Inde (roupie indienne)	1999	150 902 200	22.3[3,4]	75.1[4]	2.6[4]	...	...	...
	2000	176 602 100	23.0[3,4]	74.7[4]	2.4[4]	...	...	...
Ireland (euro)	2002[4]	1 435 800	63.4	28.0	1.5	...	7.2	...
Irlande (euro)	2003	1 607 500	59.5	30.4	1.6	...	8.5	...
	*2004	1 775 000	57.3	32.0	1.7	...	8.9	...
Israel (new sheqel) * [10]	2002	24 730 000	...	...	...	...	...	...
Israël (nouveau sheqel) * [10]	2003	23 682 000	...	...	...	...	...	...
	2004	24 452 000	...	...	...	...	...	...
Italy (euro)	2001	13 572 200	...	...	...	...	...	...
Italie (euro)	2002	14 599 500	...	...	...	...	...	...
	2003[6]	14 769 000	...	...	...	...	...	...
Jamaica (Jamaican dollar)	2001	207 700	...	...	...	...	...	...
Jamaïque (dollar jamaïcain)	2002	286 800	...	...	...	...	...	...
Japan (yen)	2001	15 542 822 000	73.0	18.6[11]	6.8[4,6]	#1.2[6]	0.4	...
Japon (yen)	2002	15 551 513 000	73.9	18.2[11]	6.5[4,6]	1.1[6]	0.4	...
	2003	15 683 403 000	74.5	17.7[11]	6.3[4,6]	1.2[6]	0.3	...
Kazakhstan (tenge)	1999	3 706 880	56.2	40.2		1.2	2.3	...
Kazakhstan (tenge)	2000	4 706 882	55.6	41.3	0.1	0.8	2.3	...
	2001	7 154 075	58.1	38.3	...	0.9	2.8	...
Korea, Republic of (Korean won) [1]	2001	16 110 522 000	72.5	25.0	2.1	...	0.5	...
Corée, République de (won coréen) [1]	2002	17 325 082 000	72.2	25.4	2.0	...	0.4	...
	2003	19 068 682 000	74.0	23.9	1.7	...	0.4	...
Kuwait (Kuwaiti dinar) [1]	2000	14 512	20.9	79.1	...	...	...	...
Koweït (dinar koweïtien) [1]	2001	19 136	20.1	79.9	...	...	...	...
	2002	20 864	20.0	80.0	...	...	...	...
Kyrgyzstan (Kyrgyz som)	2000	102 200	23.7	41.7	2.0	...	32.7	...
Kirghizistan (som kirghize)	2001	127 000	40.6	41.6	0.7	...	17.2	...
	2002	149 300	52.7	45.9	0.1	...	1.2	...
Latvia (lats)	2002	24 132	21.7	42.7[2]	...	...	35.6	...
Lettonie (lats)	2003[6]	24 167	33.2	46.4	...	...	20.4	...
	2004[6]	31 068	...	...	...	...	...	...
Lesotho (loti) [1]								
Lesotho (loti) [1]	2002	500	...	...	...	...	...	...
Lithuania (litas)	2002	344 700	27.9	65.0	...	...	7.1	...
Lituanie (litas)	2003	381 800	16.7	64.6	4.8	0.1	13.8	...
	2004	472 700	...	...	...	...	...	...
Luxembourg (euro)	2000	363 900	90.7	7.7		...	1.7	...
Luxembourg (euro)	2003	425 800	80.4	11.2	0.2	...	8.3	...
Madagascar (Malagasy ariary) [1]	1998	22 467 000	...	...	...	...	...	...
Madagascar (ariary malgache) [1]	1999	22 425 000	...	...	...	...	...	...
	2000	31 428 000	...	...	...	...	...	...
Malaysia (ringgit)	1998	1 127 010	61.4	31.8	3.2	...	3.7	...
Malaisie (ringgit)	2000	1 671 500	...	...	...	...	...	...
	2002	2 500 600	51.5	32.1	4.9	...	11.5	...

		Gross domestic expenditure on R&D (000)	Source of funds (%) — Source de financement (%)					
Country or area (monetary unit) Pays ou zone (unité monétaire)	Year Année	Dépenses int. brutes de R–D (000)	Business enterprises Enterprises	Gov't Etat	Higher education Enseignement supérieur	Private non-profit institut. Institutions privées sans but lucratif	Funds from abroad Fonds de l'étranger	Not distributed Non répartis
Malta (Maltese lira) [6] Malte (lire maltaise) [6]	2002 2003 2004	4 850 4 881 5 339	18.6	59.8	... ...	... ...	21.6	... ...
Mauritius (Mauritian rupee) [1] Maurice (roupie mauricienne) [1]	2001 2002 2003	487 265 533 883 529 139	... ...	... ...	... ...	... ...	... ...	... ...
Mexico (Mexican peso) Mexique (peso mexicain)	2000 2001 2002[12]	20 491 700 22 917 500 24 861 000	29.5 29.8 30.6	63.0 59.1 61.0	6.0[12] 9.1[12] 7.1	0.6[12] 0.8[12] 0.3	0.9 1.3 1.0	... ...
Mongolia (togrog) [1] Mongolie (togrog) [1]	2000 2001 2002	2 296 000 2 821 500 3 522 700	... ...	... ...	... ...	... ...	... ...	... ...
Morocco (Moroccan dirham) Maroc (dirham marocain)	1998 2001 2002	1 097 800 2 706 510 2 447 850						
Mozambique (metical) [1,13] Mozambique (metical) [1,13]	2002	501 580 800	...	34.7	...	...	65.3	...
Myanmar (kyat) [1,14] Myanmar (kyat) [1,14]	2000 2001	2 886 055 2 535 022	... ...	... ...	... ...	... ...	... ...	... ...
Nepal (Nepalese rupee) [13] Népal (roupie népalaise) [13]	2002 2002	9 122 008 2 807 000	... ...	... ...	... ...	... ...	... ...	... ...
Netherlands (euro) Pays-Bas (euro)	2002 2003[6] *2004[6]	8 018 200 8 376 000 8 657 000	50.0 50.9 ...	37.1 36.8 ...	0.1[6] 0.1 ...	1.1[6] 0.9 ...	11.7 11.3 ...	... ...
New Zealand (New Zealand dollar) Nouvelle-Zélande (dollar néo-zélandais)	1999 #2001 2003	1 091 380 1 416 200 1 593 100	34.1 37.8[13] 38.5	50.6 47.1[13] 45.1	11.0 10.0[13] 9.6	... ...	4.3 6.7[13] 6.8	... ...
Nicaragua (córdoba) Nicaragua (córdoba)	1997 2002	27 000 26 000	... ...	... ...	... ...	... ...	... ...	... ...
Norway (Norwegian krone) Norvège (couronne norvégienne)	2001 2002 2003	24 443 700 25 440 000 27 301 700	51.7 ... 49.2	39.8 ... 41.9	0.5[6] ... 0.6[6]	0.9[6] ... 0.8[6]	7.1 ... 7.4	... ...
Pakistan (Pakistan rupee) Pakistan (roupie pakistanaise)	2000[1] #2001[4] #2002[4]	4 908 030 7 017 890 9 785 470	... ...	... ...	... ...	... ...	... ...	... ...
Panama (balboa) Panama (balboa)	2001 2002 2003	45 100 44 460 43 970	10.2 0.6 0.6	32.8 26.2 25.5	0.6 2.1 1.8	1.2 0.2 1.0	55.2 70.9 71.1	... ...
Paraguay (guaraní) Paraguay (guaraní)	2001 2002	23 367 270 30 821 390	3.9 ...	51.1 63.1	4.0 12.7	0.8 2.3	40.1 21.8	... ...
Peru (new sol) Pérou (nouveau sol)	2001 2002 2003	202 540 204 530 220 950	... ...	... ...	... ...	... ...	... ...	... ...
Poland (zloty) Pologne (zloty)	2002 2003 2004[6]	4 522 100 4 558 300 5 155 400	30.1 30.3 ...	61.9 62.7 ...	2.9[6] 2.1[6] ...	0.3[6] 0.3[6] ...	4.8 4.6 ...	... ...
Portugal (euro) Portugal (euro)	2001 2002[4] 2003	1 038 430 1 029 010 1 019 580	31.5 31.6 31.7	61.0 60.5 60.1	0.8[6] 1.1[6] 1.3[6]	1.6[6] 1.8[6] 1.9[6]	5.1 5.0 5.0	... ...
Republic of Moldova (Moldovan leu) République de Moldova (leu moldove)	1996 1997	68 069 71 941	... 51.4	... 47.8	... 0.2	... ...	... 0.6	... ...

Gross domestic expenditure on R & D by source of funds—National currency (*continued*)

Dépenses intérieures brutes de recherche et développement par source de financement—Monnaie nationale (*suite*)

Country or area (monetary unit) / Pays ou zone (unité monétaire)	Year / Année	Gross domestic expenditure on R&D (000) / Dépenses int. brutes de R–D (000)	Source of funds (%) — Source de financement (%)					
			Business enterprises / Enterprises	Gov't / Etat	Higher education / Enseignement supérieur	Private non-profit institut. / Institutions privées sans but lucratif	Funds from abroad / Fonds de l'étranger	Not distributed / Non répartis
Romania (Romanian leu)	2002	5 743 861 000	41.6	48.4	3.0	...	7.1	...
Roumanie (leu roumain)	2003	7 620 646 000	45.4	47.6	1.5	...	5.5	...
	2004[6]	9 528 718 000	...	...	...	...	...	...
Russian Federation (ruble)	2002	135 004 490	33.1	58.4	0.3[6]	0.1[6]	8.0	...
Fédération de Russie (ruble)	2003	169 862 370	30.8	59.6	0.5[6]	0.2[6]	9.0	...
	2004	196 039 900	31.4	60.6	0.4[3]	...	7.6	...
Saint Helena (pound sterling) [1]	1998	30 082	...	...	...	...	...	...
Sainte-Hélène (livre sterling) [1]	1999	40 390	...	...	...	...	...	...
	2000	51 156	...	...	...	...	...	...
Saint Lucia (EC dollar) [13]	1998	13 597	...	...	...	...	...	...
Sainte-Lucie (dollar des Caraïbes orientales) [13]	1999	6 814	...	...	...	...	...	...
St. Vincent-Grenadines (EC dollar)								
St. Vincent-Grenadines (dollar des Caraïbes orientales)	2001	500	...	...	...	...	...	...
	2002	1 500	...	...	...	...	...	...
Serbia and Montenegro (Yugoslav dinar) [1]	2000	8 137	...	...	...	...	...	...
Serbie-et-Monténégro (dinar yougoslave) [1]	2001	9 023	...	...	...	...	...	...
	2002	11 788	...	...	...	...	...	...
Seychelles (Seychelles rupee) [1]								
Seychelles (roupie seychelloises) [1]	2002	4 080	...	89.7	...	3.4	6.9	...
Singapore (Singapore dollar)	2002	3 404 660	49.9	41.8	0.7	0.5	7.2	...
Singapour (dollar singapourien)	2003[15]	3 424 470	51.6	41.6	0.6	...	6.2	...
	2004[15]	4 061 900	54.3	36.6	2.3	...	6.8	...
Slovakia (Slovak koruna)	2002	6 333 000[16]	53.6[13]	44.1	0.1[6]	0.2[6]	2.1[13]	...
Slovaquie (couronne slovaque)	2003	7 016 000[16]	45.1[13]	50.8	0.3[6]	0.4[6]	3.3[13]	...
	2004	6 965 000[16]	38.3[13]	57.1	...	...	4.3[13]	...
Slovenia (tolar)	2002	81 445 300	60.0	35.6	0.6[6]	...	3.7	...
Slovénie (tolar)	2003[4]	88 263 000	59.3	35.3	1.4[6]	...	4.0	...
	2004[4,6]	99 933 000	...	...	...	...	...	...
South Africa (rand)								
Afrique du Sud (rand)	2001	7 488 076	53.3	35.2	...	5.4	6.1	...
Spain (euro)	2001	6 227 160	47.2	39.9	5.3[3]	...	7.7	...
Espagne (euro)	2002	7 193 540	48.9	39.1	4.5[6]	0.7[6]	6.8	...
	2003	8 213 040	48.4	40.1	5.4[6]	0.4[6]	5.7	...
Sri Lanka (Sri Lanka rupee)	1996	1 410 000	1.7	52.8	21.2	...	24.4	...
Sri Lanka (roupie sri-lankaise)	2000[1]	1 810 000	7.7	51.7	18.5	...	4.5	17.5
Sudan (Sudanese dinar)	2002	15 400 000	...	...	...	...	...	...
Soudan (dinar soudanaise)	2003	15 650 000	...	...	...	...	...	...
	2004	16 373 000	...	...	...	...	...	...
Sweden (Swedish krona)	2001	96 794 600[16]	71.6	21.3	3.8[3]	...	3.4	...
Suède (couronne suédoise)	2003	97 100 000[16]	65.0	23.5	0.4[6]	3.9[6]	7.3	...
	2004[6]	95 131 000	...	...	...	...	...	...
Switzerland (Swiss franc)	1996	9 990 000	67.5	26.9	1.3[6]	1.2[6]	3.1	...
Suisse (franc suisse)	2000	10 675 000	69.1	23.2	2.1[6]	1.4[6]	4.3	...
Thailand (baht)	2001	13 485 888	...	...	...	...	...	...
Thaïlande (baht)	2002[4]	13 302 039	...	...	...	...	...	...
	2003	15 499 201	41.8	38.6	15.1	0.6	2.6	1.3
TFYR of Macedonia (TFYR Macedonian denar)	2000	1 041 518	...	...	...	...	...	...
L'ex-R.y. Macédoine (denar de l'ex-R.Y. Macédoine)	2001	739 758	...	...	...	...	...	...
	2002	632 520	...	...	...	...	...	...
Trinidad and Tobago (Trinidad and Tobago dollar)	2001	57 300	...	...	...	...	...	...
Trinité-et-Tobago (dollar de la Trinité-et-Tobago)	2002	76 000	...	...	...	...	...	...
	2003	81 900	...	...	...	...	...	...

Country or area (monetary unit) Pays ou zone (unité monétaire)	Year Année	Gross domestic expenditure on R&D (000) Dépenses int. brutes de R–D (000)	Source of funds (%) — Source de financement (%)					
			Business enterprises Enterprises	Gov't Etat	Higher education Enseignement supérieur	Private non-profit institut. Institutions privées sans but lucratif	Funds from abroad Fonds de l'étranger	Not distributed Non répartis
Tunisia (Tunisian dinar)	2000	122 000	5.7	55.3	35.7	...	3.3	...
Tunisie (dinar tunisien)	2001	153 000	6.9	53.9	34.3	...	4.9	...
	2002	188 000	8.0	51.1	35.1	...	5.9	...
Turkey (new Turkish Lira)	2000	798 440	42.9	50.6	...	5.3[6]	1.2	...
Turquie (nouveau livre turque)	2001	1 291 890	44.9	48.0	...	6.3[6]	0.8	...
	2002	1 843 290	41.3	50.6	...	6.9[6]	1.3	...
Uganda (Uganda shilling)	1999	53 213 400	2.2[4]	6.6[4]	0.6[4]	0.3[4]	90.2[4]	...
Ouganda (shilling ougandais)	2000	65 685 450	2.2[4]	6.6[4]	0.6[4]	0.3[4]	90.3[4]	...
	2001	81 215 540	...	...	...	...	...	...
Ukraine (hryvnia)	2000	2 046 339	...	...	...	...	...	...
Ukraine (hryvnia)	2001	2 432 520	32.0	41.4	0.3	0.4	22.8	3.0
	2002	2 611 702	33.4	37.4	0.4	0.4	26.2	2.3
United Kingdom (pound sterling)	2001	18 623 200	46.9	29.1	5.7	...	18.2	...
Royaume-Uni (livre sterling)	2002	19 816 700	46.1	27.8	1.0[6]	4.9[6]	20.2	...
	2003	20 821 400	43.9	31.3	1.0[6]	4.5[6]	19.4	...
United States (US dollar)	2002	*276 260 200[17]	65.4[17,18]	29.2[17]	*2.6[6]	2.7[4,6]	...	...
Etats-Unis (dollar des Etats-Unis)	*2003	292 437 410[17]	63.8[17,18]	30.8[17]	2.8[6]	2.9[6]	...	...
	*2004	312 535 430[17]	63.7[17,18]	31.0[17]	...	...	...	5.4
United States Virgin Is. (US dollar) [1]	2000	1 433	...	...	...	...	...	...
Iles Vierges américaines (dollar des Etats-Unis) [1]	2001	1 649	...	...	...	...	...	...
	2002	1 564	...	...	...	...	...	...
Uruguay (Uruguayan peso)	1999	609 655	35.6	9.4	47.1	...	7.9	...
Uruguay (peso uruguayen)	2000	577 855	39.3	20.3	35.7	...	4.8	...
	2002	688 880	46.7	17.1	31.4	0.1	4.7	...
Venezuela (Bolivarian Rep. of) (bolívar)	2001	438 321 680[13]	27.3	55.5	17.2	...	...	...
Venezuela (Rép. bolivarienne du) (bolívar)	2002	431 199 400[13]	22.9	59.1	18.0	...	...	...
	2003	390 550 100[13]	#1.0	#71.6	#27.4	...	...	...
Zambia (Zambia kwacha) [1]	1996	479 570	...	...	...	...	...	...
Zambie (kwacha zambie) [1]	1997	417 000	...	...	...	...	...	...

Source

United Nations Educational, Scientific and Cultural Organization (UNESCO) Institute for Statistics, Montreal, the UNESCO Institute of Statistics database.

Countries covered by OECD: Australia, Austria, Belgium, Canada, Czech Republic, Denmark, Finland, France, Germany, Greece, Hungary, Iceland, Ireland, Italy, Japan, Korea, Luxembourg, Mexico, Netherlands, New Zealand, Norway, Poland, Portugal, Slovakia, Spain, Sweden, Switzerland, Turkey, United Kingdom, United States. Non members: China, Israel, Romania, Russian Federation, Slovenia.

Countries covered by Red Ibero Americana de Indicadores de Ciencia y Tecnologia (RICYT): Argentina, Bolivia, Brazil, Chile, Colombia, Costa Rica, Cuba, Ecuador, El Salvador, Honduras, Jamaica, Nicaragua, Panama, Paraguay, Peru, Trinidad & Tobago, Uruguay, Venezuela.

Countries covered by EUROSTAT: Bulgaria, Cyprus, Estonia, Lithuania.

Source

L'Institut de statistique de l'Organisation des Nations Unies pour l'éducation, la science et la culture (UNESCO), Montréal, la base de données de l'Institut de statistique de l'UNESCO.

Pays dont la source est OCDE : Allemagne, Australie, Autriche, Belgique, Canada, Corée, Danemark, Espagne, Etats-Unis, Fédération de Russie, Finlande, France, Grèce, Hongrie, Islande, Irlande, Italie, Japon, Luxembourg, Mexique, Norvège, Nouvelle-Zélande, Pays-Bas, Pologne, Portugal, République tchèque, Royaume-Uni, Slovaquie, Suède, Suisse, Turquie. Non-membres : Chine, Israël, Roumanie, Slovénie.

Pays dont la source est Red IberoAmericana de Indicadores de Ciencia y Tecnologia (RICYT) : Argentine, Bolivie, Brésil, Chili, Colombie, Costa Rica, Cuba, Ecuador, El Salvador, Honduras, Jamaïque, Nicaragua, Panama, Paraguay, Pérou, Trinité-et-Tobago, Uruguay, Venezuela.

Pays dont la source est EUROSTAT : Bulgarie, Chypre, Estonie, Lituanie.

Notes

[1] Partial data.
[2] Includes higher education.
[3] Includes private non-profit institutions.
[4] National estimation.
[5] Denomination change.

Notes

[1] Données partielles.
[2] Y compris l'enseignement supérieur.
[3] Y compris institutions privées sans but lucratif.
[4] Estimation nationale.
[5] Changement de dénomination.

6 Source: EUROSTAT.

7 Source: National statistical publication(s).

8 For statistical purposes, the data for China do not include those for the Hong Kong Special Administrative Region (Hong Kong SAR), Macao Special Administrative Region (Macao SAR) and Taiwan Province of China.

9 The sum of the breakdown does not add to the total.

10 Defence excluded (all or mostly).

11 OECD estimation.

12 Source: RICYT.

13 Overestimated or based on overestimated data.

14 UIS estimation.

15 Source: OECD.

16 Underestimated or based on underestimated data.

17 Excludes most or all capital expenditure.

18 Including funds from abroad.

6 Source : EUROSTAT.

7 Source : Publications des statistiques nationales.

8 Pour la présentation des statistiques, les données pour Chine ne comprennent pas la Région Administrative Spéciale de Hong Kong (Hong Kong RAS), la Région Administrative Spéciale de Macao (Macao RAS) et la province de Taiwan.

9 La somme de toutes les valeurs diffère du total.

10 A l'exclusion de la défense (en totalité ou en grande partie).

11 Estimation de l'OCDE.

12 Source : RICYT.

13 Surestimé ou fondé sur des données surestimées.

14 Estimation de l'ISU.

15 Source : OCDE.

16 Sous-estimé ou basé sur des données sous-estimées.

17 A l'exclusion des dépenses d'équipement (en totalité ou en grande partie).

18 Y compris les fonds étrangers.

Table 63: The data presented on human resources in research and development (R&D) are compiled by the UNESCO Institute for Statistics. Data for certain countries are provided to UNESCO by OECD, EUROSTAT and the Network on Science and Technology Indicators (RICYT).

The definitions and classifications applied by UNESCO in the table are based on those set out in the *Recommendation concerning the International Standardization of Statistics on Science and Technology* (UNESCO, 1978) and in the *Frascati Manual* (OECD, 2002).

The three categories of personnel shown are defined as follows:

* *Researchers* are professionals engaged in the conception or creation of new knowledge, products, processes, methods and systems, and in the planning and management of R&D projects. Postgraduate students at the PhD level (ISCED level 6) engaged in R&D are also considered as researchers.
* *Technicians and equivalent staff* comprise persons whose main tasks require technical knowledge and experience in one or more fields of engineering, physical and life sciences, or social sciences and humanities. They participate in R&D by performing scientific and technical tasks involving the application of concepts and operational methods, normally under the supervision of researchers. As distinguished from technicians participating in the R&D under the supervision of researchers in engineering, physical and life sciences, equivalent staff perform corresponding R&D tasks in the social sciences and humanities.
* *Other supporting staff* includes skilled and unskilled craftsmen, secretarial and clerical staff participating in or directly associated with R&D projects. Included in this category are all managers and administrators dealing mainly with financial and personnel matters and general administration, insofar as their activities are a direct service to R&D.

Headcount data reflect the total number of persons employed in R&D, independently from their dedication. Full-time equivalent may be thought of as one person-year. Thus, a person who normally spends 30% of his/her time on R&D and the rest on other activities (such as teaching, university administration and student counselling) should be considered as 0.3 FTE. Similarly, if a full-time R&D worker is employed at an R&D unit for only six months, this results in an FTE of 0.5.

More information can be found on the UNESCO Institute for Statistics web site www.uis.unesco.org.

Table 64: The data presented on gross domestic expenditure on research and development are compiled by the UNESCO

Tableau 63 : Les données présentées sur le personnel employé dans la recherche et le développement (R-D) sont compilées par l'Institut de statistique de l'UNESCO. Les données de certains pays ont été fournies à l'UNESCO par l'OCDE, EUROSTAT et la Red de Indicadores de Ciencia y Tecnología (RICYT).

Les définitions et classifications appliquées par l'UNESCO sont basées sur la *Recommandation concernant la normalisation internationale des statistiques relatives à la science et à la technologie* (UNESCO, 1978) et sur le *Manuel de Frascati* (OCDE, 2002).

Les trois catégories du personnel présentées sont définies comme suivant :

* Les *chercheurs* sont des spécialistes travaillant à la conception ou à la création de connaissances, de produits, de procédés, de méthodes et de systèmes, et dans la planification et la gestion de projets de R-D. Les étudiants diplômés ayant des activités de R-D sont également considérés comme des chercheurs.
* *Techniciens et personnel assimilé* comprend des personnes dont les tâches principales requièrent des connaissances et une expérience technique dans un ou plusieurs domaines de l'ingénierie, des sciences physiques et de la vie ou des sciences sociales et humaines. Ils participent à la R-D en exécutant des tâches scientifiques et techniques faisant intervenir l'application de principes et de méthodes opérationnelles, généralement sous le contrôle de chercheurs. Pour se distinguer des techniciens qui participent à la R-D sous le contrôle de chercheurs dans les domaines de l'ingénierie, des sciences physiques et de la vie, le personnel assimilé effectue des travaux correspondants dans les sciences sociales et humaines.
* *Autre personnel de soutien* comprend les travailleurs, qualifiés ou non, et le personnel de secrétariat et de bureau qui participent à l'exécution des projets de R-D ou qui sont directement associés à l'exécution de tels projets. Sont inclus dans cette catégorie les gérants et administrateurs qui s'occupent principalement de problèmes financiers, le personnel et l'administration en général, dans la mesure où leurs activités ont une relation directe avec la R-D.

Personnes physiques est le nombre total de personnes qui sont principalement ou partiellement affectées à la R-D. Ce dénombrement inclut les employés à 'temps plein' et les employés à 'temps partiel'. Équivalent temps plein (ETP) peut être considéré comme une année-personne. Ainsi, une personne qui consacre 30% de son temps en R&D et le reste à d'autres activités (enseignement, administration universitaire ou direction d'étudiants) compte pour 0,3 ETP en R&D. De façon analo-

Institute for Statistics. Data for certain countries are provided to UNESCO by OECD, EUROSTAT and the Network on Science and Technology Indicators (RICYT).

Gross domestic expenditure on R&D (GERD) is total intramural expenditure on R&D performed on the national territory during a given period. It includes R&D performed within a country and funded from abroad but excludes payments made abroad for R&D.

The sources of funds for GERD are classified according to the following five categories:

- *Business enterprise funds* include funds allocated to R&D by all firms, organizations and institutions whose primary activity is the market production of goods and services (other than the higher education sector) for sale to the general public at an economically significant price, and those private non-profit institutes mainly serving these firms, organizations and institutions.
- *Government funds* refer to funds allocated to R&D by the central (federal), state or local government authorities. These include all departments, offices and other bodies which furnish, but normally do not sell to the community, those common services, other than higher education, which cannot be conveniently and economically provided, as well as those that administer the state and the economic and social policy of the community. Public enterprises funds are included in the business enterprise funds sector. These authorities also include private non-profit institutes controlled and mainly financed by government.
- *Higher education funds* include funds allocated to R&D by institutions of higher education comprising all universities, colleges of technology, other institutes of post-secondary education, and all research institutes, experimental stations and clinics operating under the direct control of or administered by or associated with higher educational establishments.
- *Private non-profit funds* are funds allocated to R&D by non-market, private non-profit institutions serving the general public, as well as by private individuals and households.
- *Funds from abroad* refer to funds allocated to R&D by institutions and individuals located outside the political frontiers of a country except for vehicles, ships, aircraft and space satellites operated by domestic organizations and testing grounds acquired by such organizations, and by all international organizations (except business enterprises) including their facilities and operations within the country's borders.

The absolute figures for R&D expenditure should not be compared country by country. Such comparisons would re-

gue, si un employé travaille à temps plein dans un centre de R&D pendant six mois seulement, il compte pour 0,5 ETP.

Pour tout renseignement complémentaire, voir le site Web de l'Institut de statistique de l'UNESCO www.uis.unesco.org.

Tableau 64 : Les données présentées sur les dépenses intérieures brutes de recherche et développement sont compilées par l'Institut de statistique de l'UNESCO. Les données de certains pays ont été fournies à l'UNESCO par l'OCDE, EUROSTAT et la Red de Indicadores de Ciencia y Tecnología (RICYT).

La dépense intérieure brute de R-D (DIRD) est la dépense totale intra-muros afférente aux travaux de R-D exécutés sur le territoire national pendant une période donnée. Elle comprend la R-D exécutée sur le territoire national et financée par l'étranger mais ne tient pas compte des paiements effectués à l'étranger pour des travaux de R-D.

Les sources de financement pour la DIRD sont classées selon les cinq catégories suivantes :

- *Les fonds des entreprises* incluent les fonds alloués à la R-D par toutes les firmes, organismes et institutions dont l'activité première est la production marchande de biens ou de services (autres que dans le secteur d'enseignement supérieur) en vue de leur vente au public, à un prix qui correspond à la réalité économique, et les institutions privées sans but lucratif principalement au service de ces entreprises, organismes et institutions.
- *Les fonds de l'Etat* sont les fonds fournis à la R-D par le gouvernement central (fédéral), d'état ou par les autorités locales. Ceci inclut tous les ministères, bureaux et autres organismes qui fournissent, sans normalement les vendre, des services collectifs autres que d'enseignement supérieur, qu'il n'est pas possible d'assurer de façon pratique et économique par d'autres moyens et qui, de surcroît, administrent les affaires publiques et appliquent la politique économique et sociale de la collectivité. Les fonds des entreprises publiques sont compris dans ceux du secteur des entreprises. Les fonds de l'Etat incluent également les institutions privées sans but lucratif contrôlées et principalement financées par l'Etat.
- *Les fonds de l'enseignement supérieur* inclut les fonds fournis à la R-D par les établissements d'enseignement supérieur tels que toutes les universités, grandes écoles, instituts de technologie et autres établissements post-secondaires, ainsi que tous les instituts de recherche, les stations d'essais et les cliniques qui travaillent sous le contrôle direct des établissements d'enseignement supérieur ou qui sont administrés par ces derniers ou leur sont associés.
- *Les fonds d'institutions privées à but non lucratif* sont les fonds destinés à la R-D par les institutions privées sans

quire the conversion of national currencies into a common currency by means of special R&D exchange rates. Official exchange rates do not always reflect the real costs of R&D activities and comparisons are based on such rates can result in misleading conclusions, although they can be used to indicate a gross order of magnitude.

More information can be found on the UNESCO Institute for Statistics web site www.uis.unesco.org.

but lucratif non marchandes au service du public, ainsi que par les simples particuliers ou les ménages.

- *Les fonds étrangers* concernent les fonds destinés à la R-D par les institutions et les individus se trouvant en dehors des frontières politiques d'un pays, à l'exception des véhicules, navires, avions et satellites utilisés par des institutions nationales, ainsi que des terrains d'essai acquis par ces institutions, et par toutes les organisations internationales (à l'exception des entreprises), y compris leurs installations et leurs activités à l'intérieur des frontières d'un pays.

Il faut éviter de comparer les chiffres absolus concernant les dépenses de R-D d'un pays à l'autre. On ne pourrait procéder à des comparaisons détaillées qu'en convertissant en une même monnaie les sommes libellées en monnaie nationale au moyen de taux de change spécialement applicables aux activités de R-D. Les taux de change officiels ne reflètent pas toujours le coût réel des activités de R-D, et les comparaisons établies sur la base de ces taux peuvent conduire à des conclusions trompeuses; toutefois, elles peuvent être utilisées pour donner une idée de l'ordre de grandeur.

Pour tout renseignement complémentaire, voir le site Web de l'Institut de statistique de l'UNESCO www.uis.unesco.org.

Part Four of the *Yearbook* presents statistics on international economic relations in areas of international merchandise trade, international tourism, balance of payments and assistance to developing countries. The series cover all countries or areas of the world for which data have been made available.

La quatrième partie de l'*Annuaire* présente des statistiques sur les relations économiques internationales dans les domaines du commerce international des marchandises, du tourisme international, de la balance des paiements et de l'assistance aux pays en développement. Les séries couvrent tous les pays ou les zones du monde pour lesquels des données sont disponibles.

Total imports and exports

Imports c.i.f., exports f.o.b. and balance, value in million US dollars

Importations et exportations totales

Importations c.a.f., exportations f.o.b. et balance, valeur en millions de dollars E.-U.

Country or area	Sys. [t]	1998	1999	2000	2001	2002	2003	2004	Pays ou zone
World									Monde
Imports		5 295 267	5 513 766	6 227 647	5 996 900	6 212 922	7 235 995	8 787 237	Importations
Exports		5 217 133	5 409 483	6 066 873	5 828 631	6 100 946	7 074 122	8 566 994	Exportations
Developed economies [1,2]									Economies développées [1,2]
Imports		3 799 158	3 980 288	4 386 109	4 220 649	4 339 109	5 034 439	5 991 344	Importations
Exports		3 699 412	3 756 622	4 018 950	3 902 776	4 035 762	4 641 211	5 467 252	Exportations
Balance		−99 746	−223 666	−367 159	−317 873	−303 346	−393 228	−524 092	Balance
Asia and the Pacific									Asie et le Pacifique
Imports		342 692	376 016	447 181	406 268	399 696	456 637	538 070	Importations
Exports		440 990	468 737	538 649	460 616	470 892	525 948	623 439	Exportations
Balance		98 299	92 720	91 469	54 348	71 196	69 312	85 370	Balance
Australia									Australie
Imports	G	64 630	69 158	71 537	63 890	72 693	89 090	109 378	Importations
Exports	G	55 893	56 080	63 878	63 389	65 036	71 548	86 426	Exportations
Balance		−8 737	−13 078	−7 659	−501	−7 657	−17 542	−22 952	Balance
Japan									Japon
Imports	G	280 632	310 039	379 491	349 189	337 209	383 085	454 592	Importations
Exports	G	388 135	417 659	479 227	403 616	416 730	471 999	565 743	Exportations
Balance		107 503	107 620	99 736	54 427	79 520	88 914	111 150	Balance
New Zealand									Nouvelle–Zélande
Imports	G	12 496	14 299	13 906	13 308	15 047	18 565	23 201	Importations
Exports	G	12 028	12 477	13 297	13 730	14 380	16 505	20 373	Exportations
Balance		−468	−1 822	−608	422	−667	−2 060	−2 828	Balance
Europe – Develop. economies [3]									Europe – Economies dévelop. [3]
Imports		2 370 610	2 395 006	2 523 929	2 492 315	2 595 308	3 122 821	3 761 422	Importations
Exports		2 422 162	2 419 352	2 505 579	2 532 808	2 698 222	3 205 839	3 828 634	Exportations
Balance		51 552	24 346	−18 349	40 492	102 913	83 017	67 212	Balance
Andorra									Andorre
Imports	S	1 077	...	...	...	...	...	...	Importations
Exports	S	58	...	...	...	...	...	...	Exportations
Balance		−1 019	...	...	...	...	...	...	Balance
Austria									Autriche
Imports	S	68 187	69 557	68 986	70 461	72 881	88 265	108 866	Importations
Exports	S	62 747	64 126	64 167	66 671	70 891	87 567	109 004	Exportations
Balance		−5 441	−5 431	−4 819	−3 789	−1 990	−698	138	Balance
Belgium [4]									Belgique [4]
Imports	S	162 212	164 610	176 992	178 715	198 125	234 795	285 516	Importations
Exports	S	177 666	178 976	187 876	190 361	215 877	255 516	306 536	Exportations
Balance		15 454	14 366	10 884	11 646	17 752	20 721	21 020	Balance
Croatia									Croatie
Imports	G	8 383	7 799	7 887	9 147	10 714	14 209	16 589	Importations
Exports	G	4 541	4 303	4 432	4 666	4 899	6 187	8 024	Exportations
Balance		−3 842	−3 496	−3 455	−4 481	−5 815	−8 022	−8 565	Balance
Czech Republic [5]									République tchèque [5]
Imports	S	28 814	28 087	32 180	36 473	40 736	51 245	67 923	Importations
Exports	S	26 417	26 245	29 057	33 399	38 488	48 715	66 844	Exportations
Balance		−2 396	−1 842	−3 123	−3 075	−2 249	−2 530	−1 079	Balance
Denmark									Danemark
Imports	S	46 334	44 518	44 364	44 132	48 890	56 227	66 580	Importations
Exports	S	48 843	50 398	50 390	51 077	56 308	65 280	75 834	Exportations
Balance		2 509	5 880	6 025	6 945	7 418	9 052	9 255	Balance
Estonia [3,6]									Estonie [3,6]
Imports	G	4 611	4 094	4 242	4 285	4 810	6 500	8 487	Importations
Exports	G	3 130	2 937	3 132	3 279	3 444	4 531	5 870	Exportations
Balance		−1 482	−1 157	−1 109	−1 006	−1 367	−1 968	−2 617	Balance

Total imports and exports—Imports c.i.f., exports f.o.b., and balance, value in million US dollars (*continued*)
Importations et exportations totales—Importations c.a.f., exportations f.o.b. et balance, valeur en millions de dollars E.-U. (*suite*)

Country or area	Sys. [t]	1998	1999	2000	2001	2002	2003	2004	Pays ou zone
Faeroe Islands									Iles Féroé
Imports	G	387	470	532	498	...	...	...	Importations
Exports	G	435	468	472	514	...	...	...	Exportations
Balance		48	−2	−60	16	...	...	...	Balance
Finland									Finlande
Imports	G	32 301	31 617	33 900	32 114	33 642	41 600	50 069	Importations
Exports	G	42 963	41 841	45 482	42 802	44 671	52 513	60 739	Exportations
Balance		10 662	10 224	11 582	10 688	11 029	10 913	10 670	Balance
France [7]									France [7]
Imports	S	290 273	294 927	311 029	302 015	312 061	370 617	442 711	Importations
Exports	S	305 991	302 482	300 083	297 188	311 791	365 605	424 331	Exportations
Balance		15 718	7 556	−10 947	−4 826	−271	−5 013	−18 380	Balance
Germany [8]									Allemagne [8]
Imports	S	471 448	473 551	495 450	486 053	490 157	604 729	718 269	Importations
Exports	S	543 431	542 884	550 222	571 460	615 705	751 824	911 859	Exportations
Balance		71 983	69 334	54 772	85 407	125 548	147 095	193 591	Balance
Gibraltar									Gibraltar
Imports		424	485	480	440	385	468	...	Importations
Exports		124	120	126	125	148	147	...	Exportations
Balance		−299	−365	−354	−315	−236	−320	...	Balance
Greece									Grèce
Imports	S	29 388	28 720	29 221	29 928	31 164	44 375	51 559	Importations
Exports	S	10 732	10 475	10 747	9 483	10 315	13 195	14 996	Exportations
Balance		−18 656	−18 244	−18 474	−20 444	−20 849	−31 180	−36 564	Balance
Greenland									Groenland
Imports	G	410	409	364	366	398	492	559	Importations
Exports	G	255	276	271	283	323	412	482	Exportations
Balance		−155	−134	−93	−83	−76	−81	−77	Balance
Hungary [9,10]									Hongrie [9,10]
Imports	S	25 678	27 923	31 955	33 724	37 787	47 602	59 636	Importations
Exports	S	22 991	24 950	28 016	30 530	34 512	42 532	54 893	Exportations
Balance		−2 687	−2 973	−3 939	−3 194	−3 276	−5 070	−4 744	Balance
Iceland									Islande
Imports	G	2 489	2 503	2 591	2 253	2 274	2 788	3 551	Importations
Exports	G	2 050	2 005	1 891	2 021	2 227	2 386	2 896	Exportations
Balance		−438	−498	−700	−232	−47	−403	−654	Balance
Ireland									Irlande
Imports	G	44 635	47 195	51 444	51 305	51 508	53 315	61 404	Importations
Exports	G	64 479	71 221	77 097	83 020	87 497	92 431	104 202	Exportations
Balance		19 844	24 026	25 653	31 715	35 990	39 117	42 798	Balance
Italy									Italie
Imports	S	218 459	220 327	238 071	236 128	246 613	297 405	354 765	Importations
Exports	S	245 716	235 180	239 934	244 253	254 219	299 468	353 785	Exportations
Balance		27 257	14 852	1 863	8 125	7 606	2 063	−980	Balance
Latvia [3]									Lettonie [3]
Imports	S	3 191	2 945	3 187	3 504	4 053	5 242	6 934	Importations
Exports	S	1 811	1 723	1 867	2 001	2 284	2 893	3 917	Exportations
Balance		−1 380	−1 222	−1 320	−1 504	−1 769	−2 350	−3 018	Balance
Lithuania [3]									Lituanie [3]
Imports	G	5 364	4 627	5 219	6 060	7 524	9 668	12 282	Importations
Exports	G	3 235	2 754	3 548	4 279	5 231	6 970	9 274	Exportations
Balance		−2 129	−1 873	−1 671	−1 781	−2 294	−2 698	−3 008	Balance
Luxembourg									Luxembourg
Imports	S	10 238	11 045	10 718	11 153	11 602	13 679	16 717	Importations
Exports	S	7 923	7 895	7 950	8 239	8 499	9 950	12 187	Exportations
Balance		−2 315	−3 150	−2 768	−2 914	−3 103	−3 728	−4 529	Balance
Malta									Malte
Imports	G	2 666	2 841	3 400	2 726	2 840	3 399	3 832	Importations
Exports	G	1 833	1 980	2 443	1 958	2 223	2 468	2 641	Exportations
Balance		−834	−861	−957	−768	−616	−931	−1 191	Balance

Total imports and exports—Imports c.i.f., exports f.o.b., and balance, value in million US dollars (*continued*)

Importations et exportations totales—Importations c.a.f., exportations f.o.b. et balance, valeur en millions de dollars E.-U. (*suite*)

Country or area	Sys. [t]	1998	1999	2000	2001	2002	2003	2004	Pays ou zone
Netherlands									Pays–Bas
Imports	S	187 754	187 530	198 882	195 552	193 657	233 091	283 734	Importations
Exports	S	201 382	200 290	213 447	216 155	221 367	258 915	317 936	Exportations
Balance		13 628	12 760	14 565	20 603	27 711	25 824	34 202	Balance
Norway									Norvège
Imports	G	37 478	34 172	34 351	32 954	34 889	39 284	48 062	Importations
Exports	G	40 405	45 474	60 063	59 193	59 576	67 103	81 716	Exportations
Balance		2 926	11 302	25 712	26 239	24 687	27 818	33 654	Balance
Poland									Pologne
Imports	S	46 803	45 778	48 970	50 378	55 141	68 153	89 094	Importations
Exports	S	27 370	27 323	31 684	36 159	41 032	53 699	74 831	Exportations
Balance		–19 433	–18 455	–17 285	–14 219	–14 108	–14 453	–14 264	Balance
Portugal									Portugal
Imports	S	38 539	39 826	38 192	39 422	38 326	40 843	49 225	Importations
Exports	S	24 816	25 228	23 279	24 449	25 536	30 714	33 023	Exportations
Balance		–13 723	–14 599	–14 913	–14 973	–12 791	–10 129	–16 201	Balance
Slovakia									Slovaquie
Imports	S	13 725	11 688	13 413	15 501	17 460	23 760	30 469	Importations
Exports	S	10 721	10 062	11 889	12 641	14 478	21 966	27 605	Exportations
Balance		–3 004	–1 625	–1 524	–2 860	–2 983	–1 794	–2 864	Balance
Slovenia									Slovénie
Imports	S	10 111	10 083	10 116	10 148	10 933	13 854	17 571	Importations
Exports	S	9 051	8 546	8 732	9 252	10 357	12 767	15 879	Exportations
Balance		–1 060	–1 537	–1 384	–895	–576	–1 087	–1 692	Balance
Spain									Espagne
Imports	S	133 164	144 438	152 901	153 634	163 575	208 553	257 672	Importations
Exports	S	109 240	109 966	113 348	115 175	123 563	156 024	182 156	Exportations
Balance		–23 923	–34 473	–39 553	–38 459	–40 012	–52 529	–75 516	Balance
Sweden									Suède
Imports	G	68 633	68 721	72 982	63 471	66 410	84 222	100 436	Importations
Exports	G	85 003	84 772	86 962	75 789	81 370	102 405	123 223	Exportations
Balance		16 370	16 050	13 980	12 318	14 960	18 183	22 787	Balance
Switzerland									Suisse
Imports	S	73 885	75 440	76 104	77 086	79 129	92 014	106 645	Importations
Exports	S	75 439	76 124	74 867	78 126	83 922	97 165	114 138	Exportations
Balance		1 554	684	–1 237	1 041	4 793	5 152	7 493	Balance
United Kingdom									Royaume–Uni
Imports	G	314 036	317 963	334 371	320 956	335 458	380 821	451 715	Importations
Exports	G	271 851	268 203	281 525	267 357	276 315	304 268	341 621	Exportations
Balance		–42 185	–49 760	–52 846	–53 599	–59 143	–76 553	–110 094	Balance
North America – Develop. economies [1]									**Amer. du Nord – Economies dével.** [1]
Imports		1 085 856	1 209 266	1 415 000	1 322 065	1 344 105	1 454 981	1 691 852	Importations
Exports		836 259	868 533	974 721	909 352	866 649	909 424	1 015 179	Exportations
Balance		–249 596	–340 732	–440 278	–412 713	–477 456	–545 557	–676 674	Balance
Bermuda									Bermudes
Imports	G	629	712	720	721	...	838	...	Importations
Exports	G	45	...	...	...	...	52	...	Exportations
Balance		–584	...	...	...	...	–786	...	Balance
Canada [5]									Canada [5]
Imports	G	201 061	214 791	238 812	221 757	221 961	239 083	273 084	Importations
Exports	G	214 335	238 422	276 645	259 857	252 408	272 696	304 456	Exportations
Balance		13 274	23 631	37 833	38 100	30 447	33 613	31 371	Balance
United States [11]									Etats–Unis [11]
Imports	G	944 353	1 059 440	1 259 300	1 179 180	1 200 230	1 303 050	1 525 680	Importations
Exports	G	682 138	695 797	781 918	729 100	693 103	724 771	818 520	Exportations
Balance		–262 215	–363 643	–477 382	–450 080	–507 127	–578 279	–707 160	Balance
South–eastern Europe									**Europe du Sud–Est**
Imports		27 288	25 334	29 538	34 028	39 580	51 255	66 764	Importations
Exports		17 464	16 170	19 549	20 902	24 360	30 922	40 484	Exportations
Balance		–9 825	–9 164	–9 989	–13 125	–15 219	–20 333	–26 280	Balance

65 Total imports and exports—Imports c.i.f., exports f.o.b., and balance, value in million US dollars (*continued*)

Importations et exportations totales—Importations c.a.f., exportations f.o.b. et balance, valeur en millions de dollars E.-U. (*suite*)

Country or area	Sys. [t]	1998	1999	2000	2001	2002	2003	2004	Pays ou zone
Albania									Albanie
Imports	G	829	1 140	1 091	1 331	1 504	1 864	2 269	Importations
Exports	G	205	264	261	305	330	453	596	Exportations
Balance		−624	−876	−829	−1 026	−1 173	−1 411	−1 673	Balance
Bosnia and Herzegovina									Bosnie−Herzégovine
Imports	S	2 921	3 276	3 083	3 342	3 912	4 777	...	Importations
Exports	S	594	749	1 067	1 031	1 015	1 372	...	Exportations
Balance		−2 327	−2 528	−2 017	−2 311	−2 897	−3 405	...	Balance
Bulgaria									Bulgarie
Imports	S	4 954	5 454	6 505	7 263	7 987	10 887	14 467	Importations
Exports	S	4 197	3 964	4 809	5 115	5 749	7 540	9 931	Exportations
Balance		−757	−1 490	−1 696	−2 148	−2 238	−3 346	−4 536	Balance
Romania									Roumanie
Imports	S	11 821	10 392	13 055	15 561	17 862	24 003	32 664	Importations
Exports	S	8 300	8 505	10 367	11 391	13 876	17 619	23 485	Exportations
Balance		−3 521	−1 887	−2 688	−4 170	−3 986	−6 384	−9 179	Balance
Serbia and Montenegro									Serbie−et−Monténégro
Imports	S	4 849	3 296	3 711	4 837	...	...	...	Importations
Exports	S	2 858	1 498	1 723	1 903	...	...	...	Exportations
Balance		−1 991	−1 798	−1 988	−2 934	...	...	...	Balance
TFYR of Macedonia									L'ex−R.y. Macédoine
Imports	S	1 915	1 776	2 094	1 694	1 995	2 300	2 875	Importations
Exports	S	1 311	1 191	1 323	1 158	1 116	1 363	1 661	Exportations
Balance		−604	−585	−771	−536	−880	−937	−1 214	Balance
CIS+ [3]									CEI+ [3]
Imports		80 739	61 169	70 973	82 977	89 349	108 324	149 323	Importations
Exports		103 139	102 572	143 613	142 864	152 996	183 758	261 686	Exportations
Balance		22 401	41 403	72 640	59 887	63 647	75 434	112 363	Balance
Asia – Former USSR									Asia – ex-URSS
Imports		12 959	11 878	13 710	16 144	16 081	19 894	26 655	Importations
Exports		11 524	12 790	18 172	18 625	19 669	23 895	32 634	Exportations
Balance		−1 435	912	4 462	2 481	3 589	4 002	5 979	Balance
Armenia									Arménie
Imports	S	902	800	882	874	991	1 269	1 318	Importations
Exports	S	221	232	294	343	507	678	705	Exportations
Balance		−682	−568	−588	−532	−484	−591	−613	Balance
Azerbaijan									Azerbaïdjan
Imports	G	1 077	1 036	1 172	1 431	1 666	2 626	3 516	Importations
Exports	G	606	930	1 745	2 314	2 167	2 590	3 615	Exportations
Balance		−470	−106	573	883	502	−36	99	Balance
Georgia									Géorgie
Imports	G	878	585	720	752	794	1 141	...	Importations
Exports	G	191	241	326	316	351	478	...	Exportations
Balance		−687	−343	−393	−436	−443	−663	...	Balance
Kazakhstan									Kazakhstan
Imports	G	4 314	3 655	5 040	6 446	6 584	8 409	12 781	Importations
Exports	G	5 334	5 872	8 812	8 639	9 670	12 927	20 093	Exportations
Balance		1 020	2 217	3 772	2 193	3 086	4 518	7 312	Balance
Kyrgyzstan									Kirghizistan
Imports	S	842	600	554	467	587	717	941	Importations
Exports	S	514	454	505	476	486	582	719	Exportations
Balance		−328	−146	−50	9	−101	−135	−222	Balance
Tajikistan									Tadjikistan
Imports	G	711	664	675	688	721	864	...	Importations
Exports	G	597	689	784	652	737	772	...	Exportations
Balance		−114	25	109	−36	16	−92	...	Balance
Uzbekistan									Ouzbékistan
Imports	G	3 289	3 111	2 947	3 137	2 712	...	...	Importations
Exports	G	3 528	3 236	3 265	3 265	2 988	...	...	Exportations
Balance		240	125	317	128	276	...	...	Balance

65

Total imports and exports—Imports c.i.f., exports f.o.b., and balance, value in million US dollars (*continued*)

Importations et exportations totales—Importations c.a.f., exportations f.o.b. et balance, valeur en millions de dollars E.-U. (*suite*)

Country or area	Sys. [t]	1998	1999	2000	2001	2002	2003	2004	Pays ou zone
Europe – Former USSR									**Europe – ex-URSS**
Imports		67 779	49 291	57 263	66 833	73 269	88 431	122 668	Importations
Exports		91 615	89 782	125 441	124 239	133 327	159 863	229 052	Exportations
Balance		23 836	40 491	68 178	57 406	60 058	71 432	106 384	Balance
Belarus									Bélarus
Imports	G	8 549	6 674	8 646	8 286	9 092	11 558	16 346	Importations
Exports	G	7 070	5 909	7 326	7 451	8 021	9 946	13 752	Exportations
Balance		−1 480	−765	−1 320	−836	−1 071	−1 612	−2 594	Balance
Republic of Moldova									République de Moldova
Imports	G	1 024	586	776	893	1 039	1 403	1 773	Importations
Exports	G	644	474	472	568	644	789	980	Exportations
Balance		−380	−112	−305	−325	−395	−614	−793	Balance
Russian Federation									Fédération de Russie
Imports	G	43 530	30 185	33 884	41 879	46 161	52 449	75 554	Importations
Exports	G	71 265	71 817	103 070	99 955	106 705	126 048	181 648	Exportations
Balance		27 735	41 632	69 186	58 076	60 544	73 599	106 094	Balance
Ukraine									Ukraine
Imports	G	14 676	11 846	13 956	15 775	16 977	23 021	28 996	Importations
Exports	G	12 637	11 582	14 573	16 265	17 957	23 080	32 672	Exportations
Balance		−2 039	−264	617	490	980	59	3 676	Balance
Northern Africa									**Afrique du Nord**
Imports		48 664	47 501	46 672	47 267	49 966	53 593	61 975	Importations
Exports		30 888	37 259	48 248	44 924	45 760	52 880	59 673	Exportations
Balance		−17 776	−10 242	1 577	−2 342	−4 206	−713	−2 302	Balance
Algeria									Algérie
Imports	S	9 372	9 139	9 025	9 750	11 809	...	...	Importations
Exports	S	10 026	12 754	20 539	18 325	18 530	...	...	Exportations
Balance		654	3 615	11 515	8 575	6 721	...	...	Balance
Egypt [12]									Egypte [12]
Imports	S	16 166	16 022	14 010	12 756	12 552	11 170	12 859	Importations
Exports	S	3 130	3 559	4 691	4 128	4 708	6 327	7 530	Exportations
Balance		−13 036	−12 463	−9 319	−8 628	−7 844	−4 842	−5 329	Balance
Libyan Arab Jamah.									Jamah. arabe libyenne
Imports	G	4 708	4 158	3 731	4 391	4 400	4 322	...	Importations
Exports	G	5 072	7 933	10 415	8 903	8 017	11 433	...	Exportations
Balance		364	3 775	6 684	4 512	3 617	7 110	...	Balance
Morocco									Maroc
Imports	S	10 290	9 925	11 534	11 037	11 868	...	...	Importations
Exports	S	7 153	7 367	6 956	7 144	7 848	...	...	Exportations
Balance		−3 137	−2 558	−4 577	−3 893	−4 020	...	...	Balance
Tunisia									Tunisie
Imports	G	8 350	8 475	8 567	9 529	9 526	10 910	12 738	Importations
Exports	G	5 738	5 872	5 850	6 631	6 874	8 027	9 685	Exportations
Balance		−2 613	−2 603	−2 717	−2 898	−2 652	−2 883	−3 053	Balance
Sub–Saharan Africa									**Afrique sud-saharienne**
Imports		81 745	77 518	79 411	82 459	83 661	105 622	126 976	Importations
Exports		71 336	78 551	92 780	87 581	90 226	111 306	142 013	Exportations
Balance		−10 408	1 034	13 369	5 122	6 565	5 684	15 037	Balance
Angola									Angola
Imports	S	2 079	3 109	3 040	3 179	...	3 407	3 573	Importations
Exports	S	3 543	5 397	7 702	6 380	7 510	9 237	12 974	Exportations
Balance		1 463	2 288	4 663	3 201	...	5 831	9 401	Balance
Benin									Bénin
Imports	S	736	749	613	623	725	892	854	Importations
Exports	S	407	422	392	204	242	272	300	Exportations
Balance		−328	−327	−221	−419	−483	−620	−553	Balance
Botswana									Botswana
Imports	G	2 320	2 197	2 469	1 816	1 934	...	...	Importations
Exports	G	2 075	2 645	2 681	2 480	2 318	...	...	Exportations
Balance		−245	447	213	664	384	...	...	Balance

Total imports and exports—Imports c.i.f., exports f.o.b., and balance, value in million US dollars (*continued*)

Importations et exportations totales—Importations c.a.f., exportations f.o.b. et balance, valeur en millions de dollars E.-U. (*suite*)

Country or area	Sys. [t]	1998	1999	2000	2001	2002	2003	2004	Pays ou zone
Burkina Faso									Burkina Faso
Imports	G	732	568	654	649	704	926	1 108	Importations
Exports	G	319	216	241	263	292	369	511	Exportations
Balance		−412	−353	−413	−386	−412	−557	−597	Balance
Burundi									Burundi
Imports	S	158	118	148	139	129	157	176	Importations
Exports	S	65	54	50	39	30	38	47	Exportations
Balance		−93	−64	−98	−101	−99	−119	−129	Balance
Cameroon									Cameroun
Imports	S	1 491	1 323	1 278	1 580	2 848	...	...	Importations
Exports	S	1 843	1 520	1 534	2 102	2 278	...	...	Exportations
Balance		352	198	256	522	−570	...	...	Balance
Cape Verde									Cap–Vert
Imports	G	231	262	237	248	293	...	...	Importations
Exports	G	10	11	11	10	11	...	...	Exportations
Balance		−220	−251	−227	−238	−282	...	...	Balance
Central African Rep.									Rép. centrafricaine
Imports	S	146	131	118	107	120	117	159	Importations
Exports	S	151	147	161	142	146	128	101	Exportations
Balance		5	15	44	35	26	11	−58	Balance
Chad									Tchad
Imports	S	356	317	316	680	1 640	...	...	Importations
Exports	S	262	244	184	189	184	...	...	Exportations
Balance		−94	−73	−133	−491	−1 456	...	...	Balance
Congo									Congo
Imports	S	682	820	464	...	...	...	...	Importations
Exports	S	1 374	1 555	2 477	...	...	...	...	Exportations
Balance		692	735	2 013	...	...	...	...	Balance
Côte d'Ivoire									Côte d'Ivoire
Imports	S	3 358	2 763	2 395	2 420	2 466	3 335	...	Importations
Exports	S	4 610	4 673	3 897	3 955	5 265	5 850	...	Exportations
Balance		1 252	1 910	1 502	1 536	2 799	2 515	...	Balance
Djibouti									Djibouti
Imports	G	158	153	...	...	...	...	...	Importations
Exports	G	12	12	...	...	...	...	...	Exportations
Balance		−146	−140	...	...	...	...	...	Balance
Eritrea									Erythrée
Imports	G	356	382	...	...	...	...	...	Importations
Exports	G	26	20	...	...	...	...	...	Exportations
Balance		−330	−362	...	...	...	...	...	Balance
Equatorial Guinea									Guinée équatoriale
Imports	G	317	425	451	...	...	...	...	Importations
Exports	G	438	708	1 097	...	...	...	...	Exportations
Balance		122	284	646	...	...	...	...	Balance
Ethiopia									Ethiopie
Imports	G	1 512	1 538	1 261	1 813	1 666	...	...	Importations
Exports	G	560	469	486	456	480	...	...	Exportations
Balance		−951	−1 069	−775	−1 357	−1 185	...	...	Balance
Gabon									Gabon
Imports	S	1 103	844	996	858	...	...	...	Importations
Exports	S	1 916	2 401	2 465	2 646	...	...	...	Exportations
Balance		813	1 557	1 470	1 788	...	...	...	Balance
Gambia									Gambie
Imports	G	228	192	188	134	148	...	229	Importations
Exports	G	21	5	15	3	2	...	10	Exportations
Balance		−207	−187	−172	−131	−146	...	−219	Balance
Ghana									Ghana
Imports	G	2 561	3 505	2 973	...	...	...	...	Importations
Exports	G	1 792	...	...	...	...	...	...	Exportations
Balance		−769	...	...	...	...	...	...	Balance

Total imports and exports—Imports c.i.f., exports f.o.b., and balance, value in million US dollars (*continued*)

Importations et exportations totales—Importations c.a.f., exportations f.o.b. et balance, valeur en millions de dollars E.-U. (*suite*)

Country or area	Sys. ^{t}	1998	1999	2000	2001	2002	2003	2004	Pays ou zone
Guinea–Bissau									Guinée–Bissau
Imports	G	63	51	49	62	59	69	...	Importations
Exports	G	27	51	62	63	54	69	...	Exportations
Balance		−36	0	13	1	−4	0	...	Balance
Kenya									Kenya
Imports	G	3 195	2 833	3 105	3 189	3 245	3 725	4 553	Importations
Exports	G	2 007	1 747	1 734	1 943	2 116	2 411	2 684	Exportations
Balance		−1 188	−1 086	−1 372	−1 246	−1 129	−1 314	−1 869	Balance
Lesotho									Lesotho
Imports	G	863	781	728	681	785	1 021	...	Importations
Exports	G	194	172	221	280	373	480	657	Exportations
Balance		−670	−609	−507	−401	−412	−541	...	Balance
Madagascar									Madagascar
Imports	S	544	582	733	744	508	1 218	...	Importations
Exports	S	557	589	828	696	505	855	...	Exportations
Balance		13	7	95	−48	−3	−363	...	Balance
Malawi									Malawi
Imports	G	515	673	533	563	695	786	933	Importations
Exports	G	430	453	379	449	407	525	483	Exportations
Balance		−85	−221	−153	−113	−288	−261	−449	Balance
Mali									Mali
Imports	S	761	605	593	731	706	977	...	Importations
Exports	S	561	571	546	724	874	991	...	Exportations
Balance		−199	−34	−47	−7	168	15	...	Balance
Mauritius									Maurice
Imports	G	2 073	2 248	2 091	1 987	2 159	2 364	2 778	Importations
Exports	G	1 645	1 588	1 551	1 628	1 801	1 899	2 005	Exportations
Balance		−428	−659	−540	−359	−358	−465	−774	Balance
Mozambique									Mozambique
Imports	S	805	1 161	1 158	...	...	...	...	Importations
Exports	S	234	268	364	...	...	...	...	Exportations
Balance		−571	−893	−794	...	...	...	...	Balance
Namibia									Namibie
Imports	G	1 636	1 609	1 539	1 546	...	...	...	Importations
Exports	G	1 224	1 233	1 317	1 182	...	...	...	Exportations
Balance		−412	−376	−222	−364	...	...	...	Balance
Niger									Niger
Imports	S	470	336	326	332	371	410	521	Importations
Exports	S	334	288	285	272	282	206	207	Exportations
Balance		−136	−49	−41	−59	−90	−204	−315	Balance
Nigeria									Nigéria
Imports	G	9 211	8 588	8 721	11 586	7 547	10 853	14 164	Importations
Exports	G	9 855	13 856	20 975	17 261	15 107	19 887	31 148	Exportations
Balance		644	5 268	12 254	5 675	7 560	9 033	16 984	Balance
Rwanda									Rwanda
Imports	G	284	250	211	250	203	245	284	Importations
Exports	G	60	60	52	85	56	58	98	Exportations
Balance		−224	−190	−159	−165	−147	−187	−186	Balance
Senegal									Sénégal
Imports	G	1 455	1 377	1 342	1 431	1 598	2 353	2 837	Importations
Exports	G	968	1 030	924	1 005	1 062	1 128	1 271	Exportations
Balance		−487	−347	−418	−426	−536	−1 226	−1 567	Balance
Seychelles									Seychelles
Imports	G	384	434	342	476	420	413	498	Importations
Exports	G	122	145	194	216	228	211	183	Exportations
Balance		−261	−289	−149	−260	−192	−202	−315	Balance
Sierra Leone									Sierra Leone
Imports	S	95	80	149	182	264	303	286	Importations
Exports	S	7	6	13	29	49	92	139	Exportations
Balance		−88	−74	−136	−153	−216	−211	−148	Balance

Country or area	Sys.[t]	1998	1999	2000	2001	2002	2003	2004	Pays ou zone
South Africa [13,14]									Afrique du Sud [13,14]
Imports	G	29 252	26 697	29 700	28 264	29 281	41 120	48 585	Importations
Exports	G	26 371	26 708	29 987	29 283	29 733	36 503	46 026	Exportations
Balance		−2 881	11	287	1 019	452	−4 617	−2 559	Balance
Sudan [15]									Soudan [15]
Imports	G	1 915	1 415	1 553	1 586	2 446	2 736	...	Importations
Exports	G	596	780	1 807	1 699	1 949	2 542	3 778	Exportations
Balance		−1 319	−635	254	113	−497	−194	...	Balance
Swaziland									Swaziland
Imports	G	1 071	1 068	1 031	1 129	983	...	...	Importations
Exports	G	963	937	896	1 054	937	...	...	Exportations
Balance		−108	−131	−135	−75	−45	...	...	Balance
Togo									Togo
Imports	S	589	486	485	516	579	844	558	Importations
Exports	S	421	389	361	357	427	616	367	Exportations
Balance		−168	−97	−124	−159	−152	−228	−191	Balance
Uganda									Ouganda
Imports	G	1 414	1 342	1 512	1 594	1 112	1 251	2 021	Importations
Exports	G	501	517	469	457	442	563	885	Exportations
Balance		−913	−825	−1 043	−1 137	−670	−689	−1 136	Balance
United Rep. of Tanzania									Rép.–Unie de Tanzanie
Imports	G	1 453	1 550	1 523	1 715	1 661	2 125	2 513	Importations
Exports	G	589	543	663	777	902	1 129	1 336	Exportations
Balance		−864	−1 007	−860	−937	−758	−995	−1 177	Balance
Latin America and the Carib.									**Amérique latine et Caraïbes**
Imports		334 309	322 717	373 093	364 889	341 143	352 599	427 432	Importations
Exports		276 587	293 987	352 271	338 120	342 110	372 073	457 437	Exportations
Balance		−57 723	−28 730	−20 821	−26 769	967	19 474	30 005	Balance
Caribbean									**Caraïbes**
Imports		21 633	22 488	24 968	24 779	25 064	25 168	26 170	Importations
Exports		9 007	8 808	10 610	10 399	9 869	11 535	12 959	Exportations
Balance		−12 626	−13 680	−14 358	−14 379	−15 195	−13 632	−13 211	Balance
Anguilla									Anguilla
Imports	S	71	92	95	78	70	...	...	Importations
Exports	S	3	3	4	3	4	...	...	Exportations
Balance		−68	−89	−90	−75	−66	...	...	Balance
Antigua and Barbuda									Antigua–et–Barbuda
Imports	G	385	414	...	...	...	...	...	Importations
Exports	G	36	38	...	...	...	...	...	Exportations
Balance		−349	−376	...	...	...	...	...	Balance
Aruba									Aruba
Imports	S	815	782	835	841	841	848	875	Importations
Exports	S	29	29	173	149	128	83	80	Exportations
Balance		−786	−753	−662	−693	−713	−764	−796	Balance
Bahamas [16]									Bahamas [16]
Imports	G	1 873	1 757	2 074	1 912	1 728	1 762	1 586	Importations
Exports	G	300	462	576	423	446	425	357	Exportations
Balance		−1 573	−1 295	−1 498	−1 489	−1 282	−1 337	−1 228	Balance
Barbados									Barbade
Imports	G	1 010	1 108	1 156	1 087	1 039	1 133	1 308	Importations
Exports	G	252	264	272	259	206	210	219	Exportations
Balance		−758	−844	−884	−827	−833	−923	−1 089	Balance
Dominica									Dominique
Imports	S	132	138	148	131	116	126	144	Importations
Exports	S	62	56	54	44	43	39	40	Exportations
Balance		−70	−83	−95	−88	−74	−87	−104	Balance
Dominican Republic [5,17]									Rép. dominicaine [5,17]
Imports	G	4 897	5 207	6 416	5 937	6 037	5 266	...	Importations
Exports	G	880	805	966	805	834	1 041	...	Exportations
Balance		−4 016	−4 402	−5 450	−5 132	−5 204	−4 225	...	Balance

Country or area	Sys. [t]	1998	1999	2000	2001	2002	2003	2004	Pays ou zone
Grenada									Grenade
Imports	S	200	...	...	...	...	...	...	Importations
Exports	S	27	...	...	...	...	...	...	Exportations
Balance		−173	...	...	...	...	...	...	Balance
Haiti									Haïti
Imports	G	800	1 035	1 040	1 017	1 122	1 187	1 317	Importations
Exports	G	320	338	313	275	279	346	394	Exportations
Balance		−480	−697	−727	−742	−842	−841	−923	Balance
Jamaica									Jamaïque
Imports	G	3 033	2 899	3 302	3 361	3 533	3 637	3 772	Importations
Exports	G	1 312	1 241	1 295	1 220	1 114	1 175	1 390	Exportations
Balance		−1 721	−1 658	−2 007	−2 140	−2 419	−2 462	−2 382	Balance
Saint Kitts and Nevis									Saint–Kitts–et–Nevis
Imports	S	131	135	172	166	178	...	...	Importations
Exports	S	42	44	49	52	55	...	...	Exportations
Balance		−89	−91	−123	−114	−122	...	...	Balance
Saint Lucia									Sainte–Lucie
Imports	S	335	355	355	355	309	403	...	Importations
Exports	S	62	56	43	44	44	62	...	Exportations
Balance		−273	−299	−312	−311	−265	−341	...	Balance
St. Vincent–Grenadines									St. Vincent–Grenadines
Imports	S	193	201	163	186	174	200	228	Importations
Exports	S	50	49	47	41	38	38	37	Exportations
Balance		−143	−152	−116	−144	−136	−162	−190	Balance
Trinidad and Tobago									Trinité–et–Tobago
Imports	S	2 999	2 740	3 308	3 569	3 643	3 892	...	Importations
Exports	S	2 258	2 803	4 274	4 280	3 881	5 178	...	Exportations
Balance		−741	63	965	711	237	1 286	...	Balance
Latin America									**Amérique latine**
Imports		312 676	300 229	348 125	340 111	316 079	327 431	401 262	Importations
Exports		267 579	285 180	341 661	327 721	332 241	360 538	444 478	Exportations
Balance		−45 097	−15 050	−6 463	−12 390	16 162	33 106	43 216	Balance
Argentina									Argentine
Imports	S	31 377	25 508	25 280	20 320	8 990	13 834	22 320	Importations
Exports	S	26 434	23 309	26 341	26 543	25 650	29 566	34 453	Exportations
Balance		−4 944	−2 200	1 061	6 223	16 660	15 732	12 132	Balance
Belize									Belize
Imports	G	295	370	524	517	525	552	514	Importations
Exports	G	172	186	218	169	169	205	213	Exportations
Balance		−123	−184	−306	−348	−356	−347	−301	Balance
Bolivia									Bolivie
Imports	G	1 983	1 755	1 830	1 708	1 770	1 616	1 844	Importations
Exports	G	1 104	1 051	1 230	1 285	1 299	1 598	2 146	Exportations
Balance		−879	−704	−600	−423	−471	−18	302	Balance
Brazil									Brésil
Imports	G	60 652	51 759	58 631	58 351	49 599	50 706	65 950	Importations
Exports	G	51 140	48 011	55 086	58 223	60 362	73 084	96 475	Exportations
Balance		−9 512	−3 748	−3 545	−128	10 763	22 378	30 525	Balance
Chile									Chili
Imports	S	19 882	15 987	18 507	17 429	17 091	19 381	24 871	Importations
Exports	S	16 323	17 162	19 210	18 272	18 180	21 524	32 025	Exportations
Balance		−3 559	1 175	703	843	1 089	2 143	7 154	Balance
Colombia									Colombie
Imports	G	14 635	10 659	11 539	12 834	12 738	13 892	16 746	Importations
Exports	G	10 890	11 575	13 043	12 290	11 911	12 671	16 224	Exportations
Balance		−3 744	917	1 505	−544	−827	−1 221	−522	Balance
Costa Rica									Costa Rica
Imports	S	6 239	6 355	6 389	6 569	7 188	7 663	8 268	Importations
Exports	S	5 526	6 662	5 850	5 021	5 264	6 102	6 297	Exportations
Balance		−713	308	−539	−1 547	−1 924	−1 560	−1 971	Balance

Country or area	Sys.[t]	1998	1999	2000	2001	2002	2003	2004	Pays ou zone
Ecuador									Equateur
Imports	G	5 576	3 017	3 721	5 363	6 431	6 534	7 861	Importations
Exports	G	4 203	4 451	4 927	4 678	5 042	6 038	7 655	Exportations
Balance		−1 373	1 434	1 206	−685	−1 390	−496	−206	Balance
El Salvador									El Salvador
Imports	S	3 121	3 140	3 795	3 866	3 902	4 375	4 891	Importations
Exports	S	1 256	1 177	1 332	1 213	1 238	1 255	1 475	Exportations
Balance		−1 865	−1 963	−2 463	−2 653	−2 664	−3 120	−3 416	Balance
Guatemala									Guatemala
Imports	S	4 651	4 560	5 171	5 606	6 304	6 722	7 812	Importations
Exports	S	2 563	2 494	2 711	2 464	2 473	2 632	2 939	Exportations
Balance		−2 088	−2 066	−2 460	−3 143	−3 831	−4 090	−4 873	Balance
Guyana									Guyana
Imports	S	...	...	...	584	563	1 021	680	Importations
Exports	S	485	523	498	478	493	634	593	Exportations
Balance		...	...	...	−106	−70	−387	−87	Balance
Honduras									Honduras
Imports	S	2 535	2 676	2 855	2 942	2 981	3 276	3 916	Importations
Exports	S	1 533	1 164	1 380	1 324	1 321	1 332	1 537	Exportations
Balance		−1 002	−1 512	−1 475	−1 617	−1 660	−1 943	−2 379	Balance
Mexico [5,18]									Mexique [5,18]
Imports	G	125 373	141 975	174 500	168 276	168 679	170 490	197 347	Importations
Exports	G	117 460	136 391	166 367	158 547	160 682	165 396	189 083	Exportations
Balance		−7 913	−5 584	−8 133	−9 729	−7 997	−5 094	−8 264	Balance
Nicaragua									Nicaragua
Imports	G	1 492	1 861	1 805	1 775	1 754	1 879	2 212	Importations
Exports	G	573	546	643	589	561	605	756	Exportations
Balance		−919	−1 315	−1 163	−1 186	−1 193	−1 275	−1 457	Balance
Panama [19]									Panama [19]
Imports	S	3 398	3 516	3 379	2 964	2 982	3 086	3 594	Importations
Exports	S	784	822	859	911	846	864	944	Exportations
Balance		−2 614	−2 694	−2 519	−2 053	−2 136	−2 222	−2 651	Balance
Paraguay									Paraguay
Imports	S	2 471	1 725	2 050	1 989	...	...	...	Importations
Exports	S	1 014	741	869	990	951	1 242	1 626	Exportations
Balance		−1 457	−984	−1 181	−999	...	...	...	Balance
Peru [5]									Pérou [5]
Imports	S	8 262	6 793	7 407	7 273	7 440	8 244	9 812	Importations
Exports	S	5 757	6 088	6 955	7 026	7 714	9 091	12 617	Exportations
Balance		−2 505	−706	−452	−248	274	846	2 805	Balance
Suriname									Suriname
Imports	G	551	616	574	461	500	704	...	Importations
Exports	G	508	506	560	403	466	636	...	Exportations
Balance		−43	−110	−14	−58	−33	−68	...	Balance
Uruguay									Uruguay
Imports	G	3 811	3 357	3 466	3 061	1 964	2 206	2 918	Importations
Exports	G	2 771	2 237	2 295	2 060	1 861	2 198	2 950	Exportations
Balance		−1 040	−1 120	−1 171	−1 000	−103	−8	31	Balance
Venezuela (Bolivarian Rep. of)									Venezuela (Rép. Bolivar. du)
Imports	G	15 818	14 064	16 213	18 323	12 963	9 256	16 679	Importations
Exports	G	17 193	20 190	31 413	25 353	25 890	23 990	33 929	Exportations
Balance		1 376	6 126	15 200	7 030	12 927	14 734	17 250	Balance
Eastern Asia									**Asie orientale**
Imports		376 074	426 862	562 865	526 268	588 133	747 663	986 584	Importations
Exports		453 319	484 756	595 471	561 550	638 202	794 972	1 041 255	Exportations
Balance		77 244	57 893	32 606	35 282	50 069	47 310	54 671	Balance
China [20]									Chine [20]
Imports	S	140 237	165 699	225 094	243 553	295 171	413 062	560 683	Importations
Exports	S	183 712	194 931	249 203	266 098	325 591	437 899	593 439	Exportations
Balance		43 475	29 232	24 109	22 545	30 420	24 837	32 756	Balance

65 Total imports and exports—Imports c.i.f., exports f.o.b., and balance, value in million US dollars (*continued*)

Importations et exportations totales—Importations c.a.f., exportations f.o.b. et balance, valeur en millions de dollars E.-U. (*suite*)

Country or area	Sys.[t]	1998	1999	2000	2001	2002	2003	2004	Pays ou zone
China, Hong Kong SAR									Chine, Hong Kong RAS
Imports	G	184 518	179 520	212 805	201 076	207 644	231 896	271 158	Importations
Exports	G	174 002	173 885	201 860	189 894	200 092	223 762	259 314	Exportations
Balance		−10 516	−5 635	−10 945	−11 182	−7 552	−8 134	−11 844	Balance
China, Macao SAR									Chine, Macao RAS
Imports	G	1 955	2 040	2 255	2 386	2 530	2 755	3 478	Importations
Exports	G	2 141	2 200	2 539	2 300	2 356	2 581	2 812	Exportations
Balance		186	160	284	−87	−174	−174	−666	Balance
Korea, Republic of									Corée, République de
Imports	G	93 282	119 725	160 481	141 098	152 126	178 827	224 463	Importations
Exports	G	132 313	143 685	172 267	150 439	162 470	193 817	253 845	Exportations
Balance		39 031	23 960	11 786	9 341	10 344	14 990	29 382	Balance
Mongolia									Mongolie
Imports	G	503	513	615	638	691	801	1 011	Importations
Exports	G	345	454	536	521	524	616	853	Exportations
Balance		−158	−59	−79	−116	−167	−185	−158	Balance
Southern Asia									**Asie australe**
Imports		81 208	85 380	93 502	94 546	104 886	130 562	164 020	Importations
Exports		64 270	74 325	90 966	86 951	97 251	113 973	140 398	Exportations
Balance		−16 938	−11 055	−2 536	−7 595	−7 635	−16 589	−23 622	Balance
Bangladesh									Bangladesh
Imports	G	6 978	7 685	8 358	8 349	7 913	9 516	11 266	Importations
Exports	G	3 831	3 919	4 787	4 826	4 566	5 263	6 597	Exportations
Balance		−3 147	−3 766	−3 572	−3 523	−3 348	−4 253	−4 669	Balance
Bhutan									Bhoutan
Imports	G	134	182	175	191	196	249	...	Importations
Exports	G	108	116	103	106	113	133	...	Exportations
Balance		−26	−66	−73	−85	−84	−116	...	Balance
India [21]									Inde [21]
Imports	G	42 999	46 971	51 563	50 391	56 495	71 239	94 070	Importations
Exports	G	33 463	35 666	42 378	43 352	49 232	57 086	71 798	Exportations
Balance		−9 536	−11 305	−9 185	−7 038	−7 264	−14 153	−22 271	Balance
Maldives									Maldives
Imports	G	354	402	389	393	392	471	645	Importations
Exports	G	74	64	76	76	90	113	122	Exportations
Balance		−280	−338	−313	−317	−301	−358	−522	Balance
Nepal									Népal
Imports	G	1 245	1 422	1 573	1 475	1 419	1 754	1 870	Importations
Exports	G	474	602	804	738	567	662	756	Exportations
Balance		−772	−820	−768	−737	−851	−1 092	−1 114	Balance
Iran (Islamic Rep. of) [22,23]									Iran (Rép. islamique d') [22,23]
Imports	S	14 323	12 683	14 347	17 626	21 180	27 676	...	Importations
Exports	S	13 118	21 030	28 461	23 904	28 186	33 788	...	Exportations
Balance		−1 205	8 347	14 114	6 278	7 006	6 112	...	Balance
Pakistan									Pakistan
Imports	G	9 331	10 216	10 864	10 192	11 227	13 038	17 949	Importations
Exports	G	8 515	8 431	9 028	9 238	9 908	11 930	13 379	Exportations
Balance		−816	−1 786	−1 836	−953	−1 319	−1 107	−4 570	Balance
Sri Lanka									Sri Lanka
Imports	G	5 905	5 870	6 281	5 973	6 105	6 672	7 973	Importations
Exports	G	4 787	4 594	5 433	4 815	4 699	5 125	5 757	Exportations
Balance		−1 118	−1 276	−848	−1 158	−1 406	−1 547	−2 216	Balance
South–eastern Asia									**Asie du Sud–Est**
Imports		288 028	307 442	377 216	343 545	358 279	395 388	492 667	Importations
Exports		329 043	359 752	428 917	384 491	405 684	451 281	545 104	Exportations
Balance		41 016	52 310	51 701	40 946	47 404	55 893	52 437	Balance
Brunei Darussalam									Brunéi Darussalam
Imports	S	1 401	1 342	1 098	1 148	1 003	1 244	1 298	Importations
Exports	S	1 913	2 579	3 877	3 401	3 742	4 144	4 606	Exportations
Balance		513	1 237	2 778	2 253	2 739	2 901	3 308	Balance

Country or area	Sys. [t]	1998	1999	2000	2001	2002	2003	2004	Pays ou zone
Cambodia									Cambodge
Imports	S	1 129	1 243	1 424	1 456	1 675	1 732	...	Importations
Exports	S	933	1 040	1 123	1 296	1 489	1 771	...	Exportations
Balance		−195	−203	−302	−160	−186	38	...	Balance
Indonesia									Indonésie
Imports	S	35 280	33 321	43 595	37 534	38 310	42 243	52 076	Importations
Exports	S	50 370	51 243	65 403	57 361	60 164	64 107	71 261	Exportations
Balance		15 090	17 922	21 808	19 827	21 854	21 864	19 185	Balance
Lao People's Dem. Rep.									Rép. dém. pop. lao
Imports	S	553	525	535	528	431	524	506	Importations
Exports	S	370	311	330	331	298	378	361	Exportations
Balance		−183	−214	−205	−197	−133	−146	−145	Balance
Malaysia									Malaisie
Imports	G	58 278	65 385	81 963	73 867	79 868	81 949	105 299	Importations
Exports	G	73 255	84 617	98 230	88 006	93 264	99 370	125 745	Exportations
Balance		14 977	19 231	16 266	14 139	13 396	17 421	20 446	Balance
Philippines									Philippines
Imports	G	31 542	32 569	36 887	34 944	37 202	39 502	42 345	Importations
Exports	G	29 449	36 577	39 794	32 664	36 510	37 028	39 689	Exportations
Balance		−2 093	4 008	2 907	−2 280	−692	−2 474	−2 656	Balance
Myanmar									Myanmar
Imports	G	2 695	2 323	2 401	2 877	2 348	2 092	...	Importations
Exports	G	1 077	1 136	1 647	2 382	3 046	2 485	...	Exportations
Balance		−1 617	−1 187	−755	−496	698	392	...	Balance
Singapore									Singapour
Imports	G	104 728	111 062	134 546	116 004	116 441	127 935	163 851	Importations
Exports	G	109 905	114 682	137 806	121 755	125 177	144 183	179 611	Exportations
Balance		5 177	3 620	3 259	5 752	8 736	16 248	15 760	Balance
Thailand									Thaïlande
Imports	S	42 971	50 343	61 924	61 962	64 645	75 805	95 353	Importations
Exports	S	54 458	58 440	69 057	64 968	68 108	80 333	97 413	Exportations
Balance		11 487	8 098	7 133	3 006	3 463	4 528	2 061	Balance
Viet Nam									Viet Nam
Imports	G	11 500	11 742	15 638	15 999	19 000	24 863	31 091	Importations
Exports	G	9 361	11 540	14 449	15 100	16 530	20 176	25 625	Exportations
Balance		−2 139	−202	−1 189	−899	−2 470	−4 687	−5 466	Balance
Western Asia									**Asie occidentale**
Imports		170 909	172 135	200 874	192 885	210 673	247 387	310 177	Importations
Exports		167 171	200 541	270 946	253 866	264 017	316 254	405 377	Exportations
Balance		−3 738	28 406	70 071	60 982	53 344	68 867	95 200	Balance
Bahrain									Bahreïn
Imports	G	3 566	3 698	4 634	4 306	5 012	5 116	6 345	Importations
Exports	G	3 270	4 363	6 195	5 577	5 794	6 364	7 562	Exportations
Balance		−296	665	1 561	1 271	782	1 248	1 217	Balance
Cyprus [24]									Chypre [24]
Imports	G	3 687	3 618	3 846	3 922	4 086	4 462	5 730	Importations
Exports	G	1 062	995	951	976	843	836	1 155	Exportations
Balance		−2 625	−2 623	−2 895	−2 946	−3 243	−3 626	−4 575	Balance
Israel [25]									Israël [25]
Imports	S	29 342	33 166	37 686	35 449	35 517	36 303	42 864	Importations
Exports	S	22 993	25 794	31 404	29 081	29 347	31 784	38 618	Exportations
Balance		−6 349	−7 371	−6 282	−6 368	−6 170	−4 519	−4 245	Balance
Jordan									Jordanie
Imports	G	3 828	3 717	4 597	4 871	5 076	5 743	8 128	Importations
Exports	G	1 802	1 832	1 899	2 294	2 770	3 082	3 950	Exportations
Balance		−2 026	−1 885	−2 698	−2 577	−2 306	−2 662	−4 179	Balance
Kuwait									Koweït
Imports	S	8 617	7 617	7 157	7 869	9 007	10 993	12 005	Importations
Exports	S	9 553	12 164	19 436	16 203	15 369	20 678	28 729	Exportations
Balance		936	4 547	12 279	8 334	6 362	9 685	16 724	Balance

Country or area	Sys.[t]	1998	1999	2000	2001	2002	2003	2004	Pays ou zone
Lebanon									Liban
Imports	G	7 070	6 207	6 230	7 293	6 447	7 171	9 354	Importations
Exports	G	662	677	715	870	1 046	1 524	1 748	Exportations
Balance		−6 408	−5 530	−5 515	−6 423	−5 401	−5 647	−7 606	Balance
Occupied Palestinian Terr.									Terr. palestinien occupé
Imports	S	...	...	2 383	...	...	...	...	Importations
Exports	S	...	...	401	...	...	...	...	Exportations
Balance		...	...	−1 982	...	...	...	...	Balance
Oman									Oman
Imports	G	5 682	4 674	5 040	5 798	6 005	6 572	8 865	Importations
Exports	G	5 508	7 238	11 319	11 074	11 172	11 669	13 341	Exportations
Balance		−173	2 564	6 279	5 276	5 166	5 096	4 476	Balance
Qatar									Qatar
Imports	S	3 409	2 499	3 252	3 758	4 052	4 897	6 004	Importations
Exports	S	4 880	7 212	11 594	10 706	10 771	13 193	...	Exportations
Balance		1 471	4 713	8 342	6 948	6 719	8 295	...	Balance
Saudi Arabia									Arabie saoudite
Imports	S	30 013	27 973	30 197	31 181	32 269	36 915	44 517	Importations
Exports	S	38 822	50 693	77 480	67 973	72 453	93 245	125 728	Exportations
Balance		8 809	22 720	47 283	36 792	40 184	56 331	81 211	Balance
Syrian Arab Republic									Rép. arabe syrienne
Imports	S	3 895	3 832	4 055	4 757	5 097	5 120	7 070	Importations
Exports	S	2 890	3 464	4 674	5 254	6 831	5 731	5 384	Exportations
Balance		−1 005	−368	620	497	1 734	611	−1 686	Balance
Turkey									Turquie
Imports	S	45 921	40 671	54 503	41 399	49 663	65 637	96 368	Importations
Exports	S	26 974	26 587	27 775	31 334	34 561	46 576	61 683	Exportations
Balance		−18 947	−14 084	−26 728	−10 065	−15 101	−19 061	−34 685	Balance
United Arab Emirates									Emirats arabes unis
Imports	G	24 728	33 231	35 009	37 293	42 652	51 955	...	Importations
Exports	G	42 666	43 307	49 878	48 773	52 163	65 826	...	Exportations
Balance		17 938	10 076	14 869	11 480	9 511	13 872	...	Balance
Yemen									Yémen
Imports	S	2 172	2 006	2 326	2 309	2 345	2 367	...	Importations
Exports	S	1 501	2 438	4 078	3 214	3 315	3 325	...	Exportations
Balance		−671	432	1 751	905	970	958	...	Balance
Non Petrol. Exports [26]									Pétrole non Compris [26]
Exports		60 768	73 025	102 397	100 182	92 853	86 061	79 766	Exportations
Oceania – Developing economies									Océanie – Economies en dévelop.
Imports		7 146	7 419	7 394	7 388	8 145	9 162	9 975	Importations
Exports		4 505	4 948	5 161	4 605	4 577	5 489	6 315	Exportations
Balance		−2 641	−2 472	−2 232	−2 783	−3 568	−3 673	−3 660	Balance
Cook Islands									Iles Cook
Imports	G	38	41	50	47	47	...	...	Importations
Exports	G	3	4	9	7	5	...	...	Exportations
Balance		−35	−38	−41	−40	−42	...	...	Balance
Fiji									Fidji
Imports	G	721	903	826	794	898	1 171	1 274	Importations
Exports	G	510	609	581	537	549	680	...	Exportations
Balance		−211	−293	−245	−257	−349	−491	...	Balance
French Polynesia									Polynésie française
Imports	S	968	886	930	1 016	1 268	1 558	...	Importations
Exports	S	189	229	197	175	170	151	...	Exportations
Balance		−779	−658	−733	−841	−1 098	−1 407	...	Balance
Kiribati [5]									Kiribati [5]
Imports	G	33	41	39	...	...	...	...	Importations
Exports	G	6	9	6	...	...	...	...	Exportations
Balance		−27	−32	−33	...	...	...	...	Balance
Marshall Islands									Iles Marshall
Imports	G	67	...	68	...	...	...	...	Importations
Exports	G	6	8	7	...	...	...	...	Exportations
Balance		−62	...	−61	...	...	...	...	Balance

Country or area	Sys. [t]	1998	1999	2000	2001	2002	2003	2004	Pays ou zone
Micronesia (Fed. States of) [5]	S								Micronésie (Etats féd. de) [5]
Imports		49	12	...	...	...	...	...	Importations
New Caledonia									Nouvelle–Calédonie
Imports	S	938	1 006	923	931	...	...	...	Importations
Exports	S	382	467	604	443	...	...	...	Exportations
Balance		−555	−539	−318	−489	...	...	...	Balance
Palau									Palaos
Imports	S	66	78	123	...	...	...	...	Importations
Exports	S	11	11	...	...	...	...	...	Exportations
Balance		−55	−67	...	...	...	...	...	Balance
Papua New Guinea									Papouasie–Nvl–Guinée
Imports	G	1 232	1 194	1 151	1 071	1 235	1 358	1 680	Importations
Exports	G	1 772	1 880	2 095	1 805	1 641	2 206	2 558	Exportations
Balance		540	686	944	734	406	849	879	Balance
Samoa									Samoa
Imports	S	97	115	106	120	127	128	155	Importations
Exports	S	15	20	14	16	14	15	11	Exportations
Balance		−82	−95	−92	−104	−114	−113	−145	Balance
Solomon Islands									Iles Salomon
Imports	S	150	109	98	87	67	82	100	Importations
Exports	S	118	123	65	23	30	77	74	Exportations
Balance		−32	14	−33	−64	−37	−5	−26	Balance
Tonga									Tonga
Imports	G	69	73	69	73	89	93	...	Importations
Exports	G	8	12	9	7	15	18	...	Exportations
Balance		−61	−60	−61	−66	−74	−76	...	Balance
Vanuatu									Vanuatu
Imports	G	93	98	87	86	90	105	128	Importations
Exports	G	34	26	26	19	19	27	37	Exportations
Balance		−60	−72	−60	−67	−71	−78	−91	Balance
Additional country groupings — Groupement supplémentaires de pays									
ANCOM+									ANCOM+
Imports		46 233	36 241	40 636	45 442	41 282	39 488	52 866	Importations
Exports		39 107	43 309	57 495	50 573	51 795	53 333	72 494	Exportations
Balance		−7 126	7 067	16 858	5 131	10 514	13 845	19 628	Balance
APEC+									CEAP+
Imports		2 283 488	2 508 425	3 030 007	2 825 630	2 922 386	3 297 296	4 008 766	Importations
Exports		2 267 717	2 410 347	2 829 939	2 595 407	2 669 153	2 998 312	3 635 766	Exportations
Balance		−15 771	−98 078	−200 069	−230 223	−253 233	−298 984	−373 000	Balance
ASEAN+									ANASE+
Imports		288 028	307 442	377 216	343 545	358 279	395 167	492 400	Importations
Exports		329 043	359 752	428 917	384 491	405 684	451 252	545 073	Exportations
Balance		41 016	52 310	51 701	40 946	47 404	56 085	52 673	Balance
CACM +									MCAC +
Imports		18 037	18 592	20 015	20 758	22 129	23 914	27 099	Importations
Exports		11 451	12 043	11 916	10 612	10 856	11 926	13 003	Exportations
Balance		−6 587	−6 549	−8 099	−10 146	−11 272	−11 988	−14 096	Balance
CARICOM+									CARICOM+
Imports		12 249	12 172	13 433	13 396	13 478	14 919	15 721	Importations
Exports		5 501	6 160	7 640	7 146	6 675	8 502	9 723	Exportations
Balance		−6 748	−6 012	−5 793	−6 250	−6 802	−6 417	−5 998	Balance
COMESA+									COMESA+
Imports		37 990	37 129	34 795	34 657	35 183	36 031	43 551	Importations
Exports		19 350	20 781	25 301	23 013	25 624	33 352	40 212	Exportations
Balance		−18 640	−16 347	−9 495	−11 643	−9 559	−2 679	−3 340	Balance
ECOWAS +									CEDEAO +
Imports		21 103	20 261	19 419	22 736	19 365	25 469	31 655	Importations
Exports		19 959	24 712	30 538	27 085	26 646	32 389	45 069	Exportations
Balance		−1 144	4 451	11 119	4 349	7 282	6 920	13 414	Balance

Total imports and exports—Imports c.i.f., exports f.o.b., and balance, value in million US dollars (*continued*)

Importations et exportations totales—Importations c.a.f., exportations f.o.b. et balance, valeur en millions de dollars E.-U. (*suite*)

Country or area	Sys. [t]	1998	1999	2000	2001	2002	2003	2004	Pays ou zone
EFTA+									AELE+
Imports		113 852	112 114	113 046	112 293	116 292	134 086	158 257	Importations
Exports		117 894	123 602	136 822	139 340	145 725	166 654	198 750	Exportations
Balance		4 042	11 488	23 776	27 047	29 433	32 567	40 492	Balance
EMCCA +									CEMAC +
Imports		4 095	3 859	3 622	4 160	6 724	7 646	9 202	Importations
Exports		5 983	6 575	7 919	8 730	9 379	11 258	14 274	Exportations
Balance		1 888	2 716	4 297	4 571	2 655	3 612	5 071	Balance
LAIA +									ALAI +
Imports		292 212	279 753	326 285	318 096	292 674	301 456	371 946	Importations
Exports		256 401	272 560	329 142	316 693	320 971	347 838	430 608	Exportations
Balance		−35 810	−7 193	2 857	−1 403	28 298	46 383	58 662	Balance
LDC+									PMA+
Imports		38 120	38 580	39 760	42 071	43 918	51 617	57 719	Importations
Exports		23 540	26 187	33 166	31 953	34 794	40 004	47 828	Exportations
Balance		−14 580	−12 394	−6 594	−10 118	−9 125	−11 612	−9 891	Balance
MERCOSUR+									MERCOSUR+
Imports		98 310	82 349	89 427	83 720	62 379	68 840	93 591	Importations
Exports		81 358	74 298	84 591	87 816	88 823	106 089	135 503	Exportations
Balance		−16 952	−8 051	−4 836	4 096	26 444	37 250	41 912	Balance
NAFTA+									ALENA+
Imports		1 210 558	1 350 497	1 588 750	1 489 591	1 511 990	1 624 557	1 888 306	Importations
Exports		953 704	1 004 901	1 141 068	1 067 883	1 027 313	1 074 797	1 204 253	Exportations
Balance		−256 854	−345 596	−447 682	−421 709	−484 677	−549 760	−684 053	Balance
OECD+									OCDE+
Imports		4 026 560	4 247 300	4 738 702	4 532 782	4 665 663	5 392 652	6 439 055	Importations
Exports		3 951 793	4 040 283	4 360 457	4 216 838	4 364 095	5 009 992	5 924 807	Exportations
Balance		−74 767	−207 017	−378 245	−315 943	−301 568	−382 660	−514 247	Balance
OPEC+									OPEP+
Imports		157 235	155 265	173 894	182 066	187 441	216 596	256 338	Importations
Exports		208 919	256 923	361 429	317 907	326 735	379 873	482 149	Exportations
Balance		51 684	101 659	187 535	135 840	139 294	163 277	225 811	Balance
EU [25]									UE [25]
Imports		...	2 275 686	2 403 970	2 371 980	2 469 483	2 975 396	3 587 670	Importations
Exports		...	2 290 909	2 363 768	2 388 174	2 546 857	3 032 028	3 620 816	Exportations
Balance		...	15 223	−40 202	16 194	77 374	56 632	33 146	Balance
Extra–EU–[25,27]									Extra–UE–[25,27]
Imports		...	794 370	916 360	880 949	889 941	1 064 066	1 279 221	Importations
Exports		...	732 804	788 642	801 722	854 122	999 810	1 203 136	Exportations
Balance		...	−61 566	−127 718	−79 227	−35 819	−64 255	−76 085	Balance

Source

United Nations Statistics Division, New York, trade statistics database.

Notes

t   Systems of trade : Two systems of recording trade, the General trade system (G) and the Special trade system (S), are in common use. They differ mainly in the way warehoused and re-exported goods are recorded. See the Technical notes for an explanation of the trade systems.

+   For member states of this grouping, see Annex I – Other groupings. The totals have been re-calculated for all periods shown according to the current composition.

Notes

[1]   This classification is intended for statistical convenience and does not, necessarily, express a judgement about the stage reached by a particular country in the development process.

Source

Organisation des Nations Unies, Division de statistique, New York, la base de données pour les statistiques du commerce extérieur.

Notes

t   Systèmes de commerce : Deux systèmes d'enregistrement du commerce sont couramment utilisés, le Commerce général (G) et le Commerce spécial (S). Ils ne diffèrent que par la façon dont sont enregistées les merchandises entreposées et les merchandises réexportées. Voir les Notes techniques pour une explication des Systèmes de commerce.

+   Pour les Etats membres de ce groupements, voir annexe I – Autres groupements. Les totaux ont été récalculés pour toutes les périodes données suivant la composition présente.

Notes

[1]   Cette classification est utilisée pour plus de commodité dans la presentation des statistique et n'implique pas nécessairement un jugement quant au stade de développement auquel est parvenu un pays donné.

65 **Total imports and exports** — Imports c.i.f., exports f.o.b., and balance, value in million US dollars (*continued*)

Importations et exportations totales — Importations c.a.f., exportations f.o.b. et balance, valeur en millions de dollars E.-U. (*suite*)

[2] Developed Economies of the Asia-Pacific region, Europe, and North America.

[3] Prior to 1992 Estonia, Latvia, and Lithuania were included in the region CIS as members of the former USSR, and hence not included in the region Development countries - Europe.

[4] Economic Union of Belgium and Luxembourg. Intertrade between the two countries is excluded. Beginning January 1997, data refer to Belgium only and include trade between Belgium and Luxembourg.

[5] Imports FOB.

[6] Beginning January 1994, foreign trade statistics exclude re-exports.

[7] Beginning 1997, trade data for France include the import and export values of French Guiana, Guadeloupe, Martinique, and Réunion.

[8] Prior to January 1991, excludes trade conducted in accordance with the supplementary protocol to the treaty on the basis of relations between the Federal Republic of Germany and the former German Democratic Republic.

[9] Prior to 1996 data exclude customs free zones, repairs on goods, and operational leasing.

[10] Data exclude re-exports; Hungary beginning 1989; Estonia beginning January 1994.

[11] Including the trade of the U.S. Virgin Islands and Puerto Rico but excluding shipments of merchandise between the United States and its other possessions (Guam, American Samoa, etc.). Data include imports and exports of non-monetary gold.

[12] Imports exclude petroleum imported without stated value. Exports cover domestic exports.

[13] Exports include gold.

[14] Beginning in January 1998, foreign trade data refer to South Africa only, excluding intra-trade of the Southern African Common Customs Area. Prior to January 1998, trade data refer to the Southern African Common Customs Area, which includes Botswana, Lesotho, Namibia, South Africa and Swaziland.

[15] Year ending June 30 through 1994. Year ending December 31 thereafter.

[16] Beginning 1990, trade statistics exclude certain oil and chemical products.

[17] Export and import values exclude trade in the processing zone.

[18] Trade data include maquiladoras and exclude goods from customs-bonded warehouses. Total exports include revaluation and exports of silver.

[19] Exports include re-exports and petroleum products.

[20] For statistical purposes, the data for China do not include those for the Hong Kong Special Administrative Region (Hong Kong SAR), Macao Special Administrative Region (Macao SAR) and Taiwan Province of China.

[21] Excluding military goods, fissionable materials, bunkers, ships, and aircraft.

[22] Year ending 20 March of the years stated.

[23] Data include oil and gas. Data on the value and volume of oil exports and on the value of total exports are rough estimates based on information published in various petroleum industry journals.

[24] For government-controlled areas.

[25] Imports and exports net of returned goods. The figures also exclude Judea and Samaria and the Gaza area.

[26] Data refer to total exports less petroleum exports of Asia Middle East countries where petroleum, in this case, is the sum of SITC groups 333, 334 and 335.

[27] Excluding intra-EU trade.

[2] Économies développées de la région Asie-Pacifique, de l'Europe, et de l'Amérique de Nord.

[3] Avant 1992, l'Estonie, Lettonie et Lituanie étaient inclus dans la région CEI comme membres de l'ancienne URSS, et puis n'étaient pas inclus dans la région Pays développés - Europe.

[4] L'Union économique belgo-luxembourgeoise. Non compris le commerce entre ces pays. A partir de janvier 1997, les données se rapportent à Belgique seulement et recouvrent les échanges entre la Belgique et le Luxembourg

[5] Importations FOB.

[6] A partir de janvier 1994, les statistiques du commerce extérieur non compris les réexportations.

[7] A compter de 1997, les valeurs de commerce pour la France comprennent les valeurs des importations et des exportations de la Guyane française, la Guadeloupe, la Martinique, et la Réunion.

[8] Avant janvier 1991, non compris le commerce effectué en accord avec le protocole additionnel au traité définissant la base des relations entre la République Fédérale d'Allemagne et l'ancienne République Démocratique Allemande.

[9] Avant 1996 les données excluent des zones franches, des réparations sur des marchandises, et le crédit-bail opérationnel.

[10] Les données non compris les réexportations. Hongrie à compter de 1989; Estonie à compter de 1994.

[11] Y compris le commerce des Iles Vierges américaines et de Porto Rico mais non compris les échanges de marchandise, entre les Etats-Unis et leurs autres possessions (Guam, Samoa americaines, etc.). Les données comprennent les importations et exportations d'or non-monétaire.

[12] Non compris le petrole brute dont la valeur des importations ne sont pas stipulée. Les exportations sont les exportations d'intérieur.

[13] Les exportations comprennent l'or.

[14] A compter de janvier 1998, les données sur le commerce extérieur ne se rapportent qu'à l'Afrique du Sud. et ne tiennent pas compte des échanges commerciaux entre les pays de l'Union douanière de l'Afrique du Sud. qui incluait l'Afrique du Sud, Botswana, Lesotho, Namibie, et Swaziland.

[15] Année finissant juin 30 à 1994. Année finissant décembre 31 ensuite.

[16] A compter de 1990, les statistiques commerciales font exclusion de certains produits pétroliers et chimiques.

[17] Les valeurs à l'exportation et à l'importation excluent le commerce de la zone de transformation.

[18] Les statistiques du commerce extérieur comprennent maquiladoras et ne comprennent pas les marchandises provenant des entrepôts en douane. Les exportations comprennent la réévaluation et les données sur les exportations d'argent.

[19] Exportations comprennent re-exportations et produits pétroliers.

[20] Pour la présentation des statistiques, les données pour Chine ne comprennent pas la Région Administrative Spéciale de Hong Kong (Hong Kong RAS), la Région Administrative Spéciale de Macao (Macao RAS) et la province de Taiwan.

[21] A l'exclusion des marchandises militaires, des matières fissibles, des soutes, des bateaux, et de l'avion.

[22] Année finissant le 20 mars de l'année indiquée.

[23] Les données comprennent le pétrole et le gaz. La valeur des exportations de pétrole et des exportations totales sont des évaluations grossières basées sur l'information pubilée à divers journaux d'industrie de pétrole.

[24] Pour les zones contrôlées par le gouvernement.

[25] Importations et exportations nets, ne comprenant pas les marchandises retournées. Sont également exclues les données de la Judée et de Samaria et ainsi que la zone de Gaza.

[26] Les données se rapportent aux exportations totales moins les exportations pétrolières de moyen-orient d'Asie. Dans ce cas, le pétrole est la somme des groupes CTCI 333, 334 et 335.

[27] Non compris le commerce de l'intra-UE.

# 66 Total imports and exports: index numbers
2000 = 100

# Importations et exportations : indices
2000 = 100

Country or area	1995	1996	1997	1998	1999	2001	2002	2003	2004	Pays ou zone
Argentina										**Argentine**
Imports: volume	61	82	108	117	101	83	38	58	87	Imp. : volume
Imports: unit value	124	115	112	106	100	97	94	94	102	Imp. : valeur unitaire
Exports: volume	94	77	88	98	97	104	105	110	118	Exp. : volume
Exports: unit value	120	118	114	102	91	97	93	102	111	Exp. : valeur unitaire
Terms of trade	97	103	102	97	91	99	99	108	110	Termes de l'echange
Purchasing power of exports	92	79	90	94	89	104	104	119	129	Pouvoir d'achat des export.
Australia										**Australie**
Imports: volume	63	69	77	84	92	96	108	120	...	Imp. : volume
Imports: unit value [1]	117	117	111	102	102	94	95	104	111	Imp. : valeur unitaire [1]
Exports: volume	69	77	87	87	91	103	104	102	...	Exp. : volume
Exports: unit value [1]	117	118	114	101	96	98	100	111	129	Exp. : valeur unitaire [1]
Terms of trade	100	101	103	100	94	104	106	106	116	Termes de l'echange
Purchasing power of exports	68	77	90	86	86	107	110	108	...	Pouvoir d'achat des export.
Austria										**Autriche**
Imports: volume	56	58	73	84	92	106	103	111	132	Imp. : volume
Imports: unit value	181	163	134	124	115	97	100	114	125	Imp. : valeur unitaire
Exports: volume	52	55	72	82	100	109	113	119	139	Exp. : volume
Exports: unit value	182	166	135	126	105	95	101	114	126	Exp. : valeur unitaire
Terms of trade	101	102	101	102	91	98	101	100	101	Termes de l'echange
Purchasing power of exports	53	56	72	83	91	107	114	119	140	Pouvoir d'achat des export.
Belgium [2]										**Belgique [2]**
Imports: volume	78	82	85	91	91	101	109	111	118	Imp. : volume
Imports: unit value	121	119	110	106	102	100	103	120	137	Imp. : valeur unitaire
Exports: volume	77	78	84	88	91	102	111	113	121	Exp. : volume
Exports: unit value	126	123	112	111	105	99	104	121	135	Exp. : valeur unitaire
Terms of trade	104	103	102	104	102	100	101	100	99	Termes de l'echange
Purchasing power of exports	79	81	86	92	93	102	112	113	120	Pouvoir d'achat des export.
Bolivia										**Bolivie**
Exports: volume	94	96	101	96	88	107	129	145	173	Exp. : volume
Exports: unit value	128	126	90	79	78	92	81	90	122	Exp. : valeur unitaire
Brazil										**Brésil**
Imports: volume	95	97	94	98	92	100	97	100	111	Imp. : volume
Imports: unit value	95	99	125	105	96	100	87	86	101	Imp. : valeur unitaire
Exports: volume	82	81	85	94	93	111	121	131	157	Exp. : volume
Exports: unit value	103	106	113	100	94	95	91	101	112	Exp. : valeur unitaire
Terms of trade	108	108	90	95	98	95	105	117	110	Termes de l'echange
Purchasing power of exports	89	88	77	89	91	106	126	154	173	Pouvoir d'achat des export.
Bulgaria										**Bulgarie**
Imports: unit value	...	...	...	...	...	94	96	112	123	Imp. : valeur unitaire
Exports: unit value	...	...	...	...	...	95	96	118	126	Exp. : valeur unitaire
Terms of trade	...	...	...	...	...	101	100	105	102	Termes de l'echange
Canada										**Canada**
Imports: volume [3]	63	67	79	86	96	94	96	99	109	Imp. : volume [3]
Imports: unit value [3]	102	102	101	94	96	99	98	102	108	Imp. : valeur unitaire [3]
Exports: volume	66	70	76	82	91	96	96	94	101	Exp. : volume
Exports: unit value	99	100	98	97	106	98	95	106	115	Exp. : valeur unitaire
Terms of trade	97	98	97	103	110	99	97	104	107	Termes de l'echange
Purchasing power of exports	64	69	73	85	101	95	93	98	108	Pouvoir d'achat des export.
China, Hong Kong SAR										**Chine, Hong Kong RAS**
Imports: volume	81	85	91	85	85	98	106	119	136	Imp. : volume
Imports: unit value	111	110	107	102	100	97	93	93	95	Imp. : valeur unitaire
Exports: volume	77	81	86	82	85	97	105	120	138	Exp. : volume
Exports: unit value	110	110	108	104	101	98	95	94	95	Exp. : valeur unitaire
Terms of trade	99	100	100	102	101	101	102	101	99	Termes de l'echange
Purchasing power of exports	76	81	86	84	86	98	107	121	137	Pouvoir d'achat des export.

Country or area	1995	1996	1997	1998	1999	2001	2002	2003	2004	Pays ou zone
Colombia										**Colombie**
Imports: unit value	121	122	120	110	103	98	95	95	103	Imp. : valeur unitaire
Exports: unit value	111	104	115	103	96	89	84	87	96	Exp. : valeur unitaire
Terms of trade	92	85	96	93	93	91	89	92	93	Termes de l'échange
Czech Republic										**République tchèque**
Imports: unit value [3]	123	122	110	105	100	101	107	123	138	Imp. : valeur unitaire [3]
Exports: unit value	125	123	111	114	105	102	111	130	148	Exp. : valeur unitaire
Terms of trade	101	101	101	108	105	101	104	105	107	Termes de l'échange
Denmark										**Danemark**
Imports: volume	81	82	88	93	93	102	108	107	114	Imp. : volume
Imports: unit value	128	126	114	113	108	98	102	119	133	Imp. : valeur unitaire
Exports: volume	78	80	84	86	92	103	109	108	112	Exp. : volume
Exports: unit value	131	129	115	112	108	99	103	123	136	Exp. : valeur unitaire
Terms of trade	102	102	101	99	100	101	101	103	102	Termes de l'échange
Purchasing power of exports	80	81	85	85	92	104	110	111	114	Pouvoir d'achat des export.
Dominica										**Dominique**
Imports: volume	...	95	90	94	97	98	82	...	...	Imp. : volume
Imports: unit value	...	96	97	116	95	95	91	...	...	Imp. : valeur unitaire
Exports: volume	79	105	101	94	92	78	72	...	...	Exp. : volume
Exports: unit value	113	104	134	113	113	101	101	...	...	Exp. : valeur unitaire
Terms of trade	...	108	137	98	119	106	111	...	...	Termes de l'échange
Purchasing power of exports	...	113	139	91	110	82	80	...	...	Pouvoir d'achat des export.
Ecuador										**Equateur**
Imports: volume	100	96	133	166	96	119	148	161	168	Imp. : volume
Exports: volume	100	102	102	96	93	101	99	106	133	Exp. : volume
Exports: unit value	76	88	85	64	77	88	94	106	118	Exp. : valeur unitaire
Finland										**Finlande**
Imports: volume	75	81	88	95	96	97	104	103	108	Imp. : volume
Imports: unit value	119	115	105	102	101	98	97	116	131	Imp. : valeur unitaire
Exports: volume	71	75	85	89	92	99	104	106	112	Exp. : volume
Exports: unit value	124	118	106	105	102	96	94	108	117	Exp. : valeur unitaire
Terms of trade	104	102	101	103	101	97	97	94	89	Termes de l'échange
Purchasing power of exports	74	77	85	92	93	97	101	99	100	Pouvoir d'achat des export.
France [4]										**France** [4]
Imports: unit value	149	146	130	129	108	100	99	119	128	Imp. : valeur unitaire
Exports: unit value	159	154	137	137	114	108	109	131	102	Exp. : valeur unitaire
Terms of trade	106	106	106	106	105	108	110	110	80	Termes de l'échange
Germany [5,6]										**Allemagne** [5,6]
Imports: volume	67	71	77	85	89	101	100	110	121	Imp. : volume
Imports: unit value	139	129	115	111	104	97	98	111	121	Imp. : valeur unitaire
Exports: volume	64	69	77	83	87	103	104	115	129	Exp. : volume
Exports: unit value	149	138	121	118	111	99	102	119	129	Exp. : valeur unitaire
Terms of trade	107	107	105	107	107	102	104	107	107	Termes de l'échange
Purchasing power of exports	69	74	81	89	93	105	109	123	139	Pouvoir d'achat des export.
Greece										**Grèce**
Imports: volume	63	69	70	85	90	...	...	...	...	Imp. : volume
Imports: unit value [1]	134	133	120	117	113	99	105	127	140	Imp. : valeur unitaire [1]
Exports: volume	67	72	80	90	96	...	...	...	...	Exp. : volume
Exports: unit value [1]	124	129	117	111	107	98	105	126	143	Exp. : valeur unitaire [1]
Terms of trade	93	97	98	95	95	99	100	99	102	Termes de l'échange
Purchasing power of exports	62	69	78	86	91	...	...	...	...	Pouvoir d'achat des export.
Honduras										**Honduras**
Exports: volume	70	80	60	77	70	133	118	94	109	Exp. : volume
Exports: unit value	126	117	133	134	101	101	95	83	102	Exp. : valeur unitaire
Hungary [7,8]										**Hongrie** [7,8]
Imports: volume	43	46	58	72	83	104	109	120	137	Imp. : volume
Imports: unit value	124	123	114	111	106	101	107	123	135	Imp. : valeur unitaire
Exports: volume	43	45	58	71	82	108	114	124	146	Exp. : volume
Exports: unit value	128	125	117	116	108	101	107	122	134	Exp. : valeur unitaire
Terms of trade	104	102	103	104	103	100	100	100	99	Termes de l'échange
Purchasing power of exports	44	45	60	74	84	107	114	124	144	Pouvoir d'achat des export.

Country or area	1995	1996	1997	1998	1999	2001	2002	2003	2004	Pays ou zone
Iceland										**Islande**
Imports: volume	60	70	74	92	96	90	...	...	...	Imp. : volume
Imports: unit value	113	113	105	104	101	97	...	...	...	Imp. : valeur unitaire
Exports: volume	86	94	96	93	100	107	...	...	...	Exp. : volume
Exports: unit value	110	106	102	110	106	99	...	...	...	Exp. : valeur unitaire
Terms of trade	98	94	97	105	104	102	...	...	...	Termes de l'echange
Purchasing power of exports	84	88	92	97	104	109	...	...	...	Pouvoir d'achat des export.
India [9]										**Inde** [9]
Imports: volume	74	73	81	92	101	105	115	139	...	Imp. : volume
Imports: unit value	100	104	103	91	96	96	104	108	...	Imp. : valeur unitaire
Exports: volume	67	72	68	70	81	104	126	134	...	Exp. : volume
Exports: unit value	107	103	117	107	101	94	92	104	...	Exp. : valeur unitaire
Terms of trade	108	99	114	117	105	98	89	96	...	Termes de l'echange
Purchasing power of exports	72	71	77	82	85	102	112	129	...	Pouvoir d'achat des export.
Indonesia										**Indonésie**
Exports: volume	81	86	110	102	84	121	100	97	101	Exp. : volume
Exports: unit value	103	109	104	81	65	90	96	103	120	Exp. : valeur unitaire
Ireland										**Irlande**
Imports: volume	53	58	67	79	86	99	97	90	98	Imp. : volume
Imports: unit value	121	119	114	109	107	100	101	112	121	Imp. : valeur unitaire
Exports: volume	46	50	58	72	84	105	104	99	110	Exp. : volume
Exports: unit value	120	119	114	110	110	99	104	115	116	Exp. : valeur unitaire
Terms of trade	99	100	100	101	103	98	102	103	96	Termes de l'echange
Purchasing power of exports	45	50	58	73	86	103	107	103	106	Pouvoir d'achat des export.
Israel										**Israël**
Imports: volume	71	76	77	77	88	93	93	92	103	Imp. : volume
Imports: unit value	111	111	106	100	97	99	99	104	112	Imp. : valeur unitaire
Exports: volume	59	63	69	74	80	96	97	101	116	Exp. : volume
Exports: unit value	103	103	102	99	100	96	96	100	106	Exp. : valeur unitaire
Terms of trade	92	93	96	99	103	98	98	96	95	Termes de l'echange
Purchasing power of exports	54	58	67	73	82	94	95	97	109	Pouvoir d'achat des export.
Italy										**Italie**
Imports: volume	80	76	83	90	93	99	99	100	102	Imp. : volume
Imports: unit value	109	115	106	103	99	100	105	125	144	Imp. : valeur unitaire
Exports: volume	94	92	94	94	92	101	99	96	98	Exp. : volume
Exports: unit value	105	115	108	109	107	101	108	130	149	Exp. : valeur unitaire
Terms of trade	96	100	101	107	108	101	103	104	103	Termes de l'echange
Purchasing power of exports	90	92	95	100	99	102	101	100	101	Pouvoir d'achat des export.
Japan										**Japon**
Imports: volume	81	85	87	82	90	99	100	107	115	Imp. : volume
Imports: unit value	109	108	103	90	91	87	86	91	101	Imp. : valeur unitaire
Exports: volume	80	81	91	90	91	90	97	102	113	Exp. : volume
Exports: unit value	115	106	97	91	95	94	89	96	104	Exp. : valeur unitaire
Terms of trade	106	98	94	101	105	107	104	105	103	Termes de l'echange
Purchasing power of exports	85	80	85	90	96	97	101	108	116	Pouvoir d'achat des export.
Jordan										**Jordanie**
Imports: volume	85	92	90	85	84	103	104	109	136	Imp. : volume
Imports: unit value	96	103	101	100	97	102	105	115	130	Imp. : valeur unitaire
Exports: volume	84	82	88	90	93	123	142	152	190	Exp. : volume
Exports: unit value	111	117	114	107	105	101	102	102	114	Exp. : valeur unitaire
Terms of trade	116	113	113	107	107	99	97	88	87	Termes de l'echange
Purchasing power of exports	98	93	99	97	100	122	137	135	166	Pouvoir d'achat des export.
Kenya										**Kenya**
Imports: volume	90	89	95	96	87	...	...	...	...	Imp. : volume
Imports: unit value	102	101	107	105	98	...	...	...	...	Imp. : valeur unitaire
Exports: unit value	117	112	128	125	101	...	...	...	...	Exp. : valeur unitaire
Terms of trade	114	110	120	119	103	...	...	...	...	Termes de l'echange

Country or area	1995	1996	1997	1998	1999	2001	2002	2003	2004	Pays ou zone
Korea, Republic of										**Corée, République de**
Imports: volume	74	85	87	65	84	98	110	118	132	Imp. : volume
Imports: unit value	117	112	107	88	87	91	88	96	107	Imp. : valeur unitaire
Exports: volume	46	54	62	74	83	101	114	133	163	Exp. : volume
Exports: unit value	162	141	131	103	100	87	83	85	92	Exp. : valeur unitaire
Terms of trade	139	125	122	117	114	95	95	89	85	Termes de l'echange
Purchasing power of exports	64	68	76	86	95	96	108	119	139	Pouvoir d'achat des export.
Libyan Arab Jamah.										**Jamah. arabe libyenne**
Imports: volume	171	185	208	156	147	173	214	...	...	Imp. : volume
Imports: unit value	119	96	93	96	114	83	47	...	...	Imp. : valeur unitaire
Exports: volume	132	123	129	94	108	110	95	...	...	Exp. : volume
Exports: unit value	76	73	62	52	70	85	86	...	...	Exp. : valeur unitaire
Terms of trade	64	76	67	54	62	102	182	...	...	Termes de l'echange
Purchasing power of exports	84	93	87	51	67	113	172	...	...	Pouvoir d'achat des export.
Malaysia										**Malaisie**
Imports: volume	...	...	...	...	...	92	97	...	...	Imp. : volume
Imports: unit value	...	...	...	...	...	98	99	...	...	Imp. : valeur unitaire
Exports: volume	75	...	...	...	...	96	102	...	...	Exp. : volume
Exports: unit value	...	...	...	...	...	94	93	...	...	Exp. : valeur unitaire
Terms of trade	...	...	...	...	...	96	94	...	...	Termes de l'echange
Purchasing power of exports	...	...	...	...	...	92	96	...	...	Pouvoir d'achat des export.
Mauritius										**Maurice**
Imports: unit value	118	122	106	99	100	97	99	113	138	Imp. : valeur unitaire
Exports: unit value	118	127	111	111	106	92	98	110	123	Exp. : valeur unitaire
Terms of trade	100	104	105	112	106	95	98	97	89	Termes de l'echange
Mexico										**Mexique**
Imports: unit value	...	98	99	98	97	...	...	...	...	Imp. : valeur unitaire
Exports: unit value	...	96	95	90	93	...	...	...	...	Exp. : valeur unitaire
Terms of trade	...	98	96	91	96	...	...	...	...	Termes de l'echange
Morocco										**Maroc**
Imports: volume	66	63	66	82	89	99	104	...	...	Imp. : volume
Exports: volume	79	77	82	84	91	102	106	...	...	Exp. : volume
Netherlands										**Pays-Bas**
Imports: volume	73	76	81	89	96	97	95	98	107	Imp. : volume
Imports: unit value	128	123	113	108	103	101	102	117	130	Imp. : valeur unitaire
Exports: volume	72	75	82	88	92	102	103	106	117	Exp. : volume
Exports: unit value	130	124	114	109	101	100	100	116	127	Exp. : valeur unitaire
Terms of trade	102	101	101	101	98	98	98	99	97	Termes de l'echange
Purchasing power of exports	73	76	83	88	90	100	101	104	114	Pouvoir d'achat des export.
New Zealand										**Nouvelle-Zélande**
Imports: volume	83	85	88	91	103	102	111	124	142	Imp. : volume
Imports: unit value	122	125	118	99	100	94	98	109	118	Imp. : valeur unitaire
Exports: volume	84	88	93	92	95	103	109	112	119	Exp. : volume
Exports: unit value	123	125	117	99	99	101	99	111	129	Exp. : valeur unitaire
Terms of trade	101	100	99	99	99	107	102	102	109	Termes de l'echange
Purchasing power of exports	84	88	92	92	93	110	111	115	130	Pouvoir d'achat des export.
Norway [10]										**Norvège** [10]
Imports: volume [11]	69	76	83	94	94	101	103	106	118	Imp. : volume [11]
Imports: unit value [11]	145	141	127	118	109	98	104	116	127	Imp. : valeur unitaire [11]
Exports: volume [11]	78	88	93	93	95	105	107	107	108	Exp. : volume [11]
Exports: unit value [11]	88	93	86	71	78	93	94	104	127	Exp. : valeur unitaire [11]
Terms of trade	60	66	68	61	71	95	91	90	100	Termes de l'echange
Purchasing power of exports	47	58	63	56	68	99	97	97	109	Pouvoir d'achat des export.
Pakistan										**Pakistan**
Imports: volume	94	92	94	90	101	112	123	123	142	Imp. : volume
Imports: unit value	99	96	97	86	93	94	95	109	122	Imp. : valeur unitaire
Exports: volume	73	87	82	79	89	102	109	110	103	Exp. : volume
Exports: unit value	118	115	115	118	109	94	90	96	103	Exp. : valeur unitaire
Terms of trade	120	120	118	137	118	100	95	89	85	Termes de l'echange
Purchasing power of exports	88	105	97	109	105	102	104	98	87	Pouvoir d'achat des export.

Country or area	1995	1996	1997	1998	1999	2001	2002	2003	2004	Pays ou zone
Panama [12]										**Panama** [12]
Exports: volume	...	...	143	105	...	81	84	...		Exp. : volume
Papua New Guinea										**Papouasie-Nvl-Guinée**
Exports: unit value	99	95	98	80	79	90	85	101	126	Exp. : valeur unitaire
Peru										**Pérou**
Exports: volume	79	86	91	78	88	114	126	122	135	Exp. : volume
Exports: unit value	88	87	90	70	75	84	87	97	100	Exp. : valeur unitaire
Philippines										**Philippines**
Imports: volume	83	98	106	85	95	114	116	...	...	Imp. : volume
Imports: unit value [1]	174	180	162	121	118	80	84	...	...	Imp. : valeur unitaire [1]
Exports: volume	56	62	74	80	87	89	105	...	...	Exp. : volume
Exports: unit value [1]	141	146	134	105	121	84	77	...	...	Exp. : valeur unitaire [1]
Terms of trade	81	82	83	87	103	104	91	...	...	Termes de l'echange
Purchasing power of exports	45	51	61	70	89	92	96	...	...	Pouvoir d'achat des export.
Poland										**Pologne**
Imports: volume	48	62	75	90	94	103	111	120	141	Imp. : volume
Imports: unit value [1]	117	122	114	114	106	100	102	116	130	Imp. : valeur unitaire [1]
Exports: volume	57	63	72	76	81	112	121	144	170	Exp. : volume
Exports: unit value [1]	126	122	113	115	108	102	107	118	139	Exp. : valeur unitaire [1]
Terms of trade	108	100	99	101	102	102	105	102	107	Termes de l'echange
Purchasing power of exports	62	63	71	77	82	114	127	146	182	Pouvoir d'achat des export.
Portugal										**Portugal**
Imports: volume	...	...	...	...	...	97	94	94	...	Imp. : volume
Imports: unit value [1]	138	130	115	110	106	89	91	110	...	Imp. : valeur unitaire [1]
Exports: volume	...	...	...	...	...	95	95	97	...	Exp. : volume
Exports: unit value [1]	144	131	119	116	109	93	96	112	...	Exp. : valeur unitaire [1]
Terms of trade	105	101	104	106	103	105	106	102	...	Termes de l'echange
Purchasing power of exports	...	...	...	...	...	99	101	99	...	Pouvoir d'achat des export.
Republic of Moldova										**République de Moldova**
Imports: volume	...	...	...	...	...	118	139	180	...	Imp. : volume
Imports: unit value	...	...	...	...	...	97	92	95	...	Imp. : valeur unitaire
Exports: volume	...	...	...	...	...	122	142	170	...	Exp. : volume
Exports: unit value	...	...	...	...	...	93	87	88	...	Exp. : valeur unitaire
Terms of trade	...	...	...	...	...	96	95	93	...	Termes de l'echange
Purchasing power of exports	...	...	...	...	...	117	134	158	...	Pouvoir d'achat des export.
Romania										**Roumanie**
Imports: volume	...	...	...	...	...	124	143	...	...	Imp. : volume
Imports: unit value	...	144	133	117	105	96	96	...	...	Imp. : valeur unitaire
Exports: volume	...	...	...	...	...	112	132	...	...	Exp. : volume
Exports: unit value	...	126	118	109	102	98	102	...	...	Exp. : valeur unitaire
Terms of trade	...	88	89	93	97	102	106	...	...	Termes de l'echange
Purchasing power of exports	...	...	...	...	...	114	139	...	...	Pouvoir d'achat des export.
Russian Federation										**Fédération de Russie**
Imports: volume	...	...	...	...	...	130	153	...	...	Imp. : volume
Exports: volume	...	...	...	...	...	103	114	...	...	Exp. : volume
Seychelles										**Seychelles**
Imports: volume	46	77	68	83	105	...	...	...	...	Imp. : volume
Imports: unit value	148	144	146	136	120	...	...	...	...	Imp. : valeur unitaire
Exports: volume	21	38	51	51	78	...	...	...	...	Exp. : volume
Exports: unit value	94	88	110	143	114	...	...	...	...	Exp. : valeur unitaire
Terms of trade	63	61	75	105	94	...	...	...	...	Termes de l'echange
Purchasing power of exports	13	23	38	54	73	...	...	...	...	Pouvoir d'achat des export.
Singapore										**Singapour**
Imports: volume	80	85	92	83	88	89	96	...	...	Imp. : volume
Imports: unit value [1]	115	114	107	93	93	97	96	99	104	Imp. : valeur unitaire [1]
Exports: volume	71	76	81	82	86	95	100	116	140	Exp. : volume
Exports: unit value [1]	120	120	112	97	96	93	91	90	93	Exp. : valeur unitaire [1]
Terms of trade	104	105	105	104	103	96	94	91	89	Termes de l'echange
Purchasing power of exports	75	79	85	86	89	91	95	106	126	Pouvoir d'achat des export.

Country or area	1995	1996	1997	1998	1999	2001	2002	2003	2004	Pays ou zone
South Africa [10,13]										**Afrique du Sud** [10,13]
Imports: volume	87	94	99	101	93	100	103	...	...	Imp. : volume
Imports: unit value	117	107	107	99	98	94	94	115	...	Imp. : valeur unitaire
Exports: volume	76	83	88	90	91	101	100	...	...	Exp. : volume
Exports: unit value	123	114	113	104	100	95	96	123	...	Exp. : valeur unitaire
Terms of trade	106	106	106	105	102	100	103	107	...	Termes de l'echange
Purchasing power of exports	80	89	93	94	92	102	103	...	...	Pouvoir d'achat des export.
Spain										**Espagne**
Imports: volume	...	...	...	...	92	104	109	117	129	Imp. : volume
Imports: unit value [1]	127	125	112	108	102	96	99	116	131	Imp. : valeur unitaire [1]
Exports: volume	...	...	...	...	89	104	107	114	120	Exp. : volume
Exports: unit value [1]	132	131	117	115	109	98	102	121	134	Exp. : valeur unitaire [1]
Terms of trade	104	105	105	107	106	101	103	104	102	Termes de l'echange
Purchasing power of exports	...	...	...	...	94	106	111	118	123	Pouvoir d'achat des export.
Sri Lanka										**Sri Lanka**
Imports: volume	73	73	82	89	90	91	101	111	...	Imp. : volume
Imports: unit value	...	...	...	...	...	98	90	...	...	Imp. : valeur unitaire
Exports: volume	71	74	82	81	84	92	93	98	106	Exp. : volume
Exports: unit value	99	102	105	110	101	97	91	97	102	Exp. : valeur unitaire
Terms of trade	...	...	...	...	...	98	101	...	...	Termes de l'echange
Purchasing power of exports	...	...	...	...	...	90	94	...	...	Pouvoir d'achat des export.
Sweden										**Suède**
Imports: volume	69	71	78	86	89	95	94	100	108	Imp. : volume
Imports: unit value [1]	120	122	110	104	103	93	99	117	132	Imp. : valeur unitaire [1]
Exports: volume	67	70	78	85	90	98	101	106	117	Exp. : volume
Exports: unit value [1]	131	132	117	112	106	90	94	111	121	Exp. : valeur unitaire [1]
Terms of trade	109	108	107	107	104	97	95	95	92	Termes de l'echange
Purchasing power of exports	73	76	83	91	93	96	96	101	108	Pouvoir d'achat des export.
Switzerland										**Suisse**
Imports: volume	75	76	80	87	93	101	99	100	104	Imp. : volume
Imports: unit value	136	129	116	112	107	100	105	121	135	Imp. : valeur unitaire
Exports: volume	80	81	87	91	93	103	105	105	111	Exp. : volume
Exports: unit value	131	126	111	110	109	101	107	124	137	Exp. : valeur unitaire
Terms of trade	96	97	96	99	103	101	102	102	102	Termes de l'echange
Purchasing power of exports	77	79	83	90	95	104	106	107	113	Pouvoir d'achat des export.
Thailand										**Thaïlande**
Imports: volume	113	102	91	67	82	89	99	108	121	Imp. : volume
Imports: unit value	100	111	109	98	95	109	103	110	125	Imp. : valeur unitaire
Exports: volume	70	63	68	73	82	94	107	117	124	Exp. : volume
Exports: unit value	117	127	122	107	102	99	92	99	114	Exp. : valeur unitaire
Terms of trade	116	114	112	109	107	91	89	90	92	Termes de l'echange
Purchasing power of exports	82	72	76	80	88	86	96	105	113	Pouvoir d'achat des export.
Turkey										**Turquie**
Imports: volume	49	63	78	76	75	75	91	121	153	Imp. : volume
Imports: unit value	123	116	106	101	96	100	98	106	120	Imp. : valeur unitaire
Exports: volume	64	70	79	87	90	122	142	173	199	Exp. : volume
Exports: unit value	128	123	117	112	104	97	96	105	122	Exp. : valeur unitaire
Terms of trade	104	106	111	111	109	98	97	99	102	Termes de l'echange
Purchasing power of exports	67	74	88	96	98	119	137	171	203	Pouvoir d'achat des export.
United Kingdom										**Royaume-Uni**
Imports: volume	66	72	79	86	91	105	110	112	119	Imp. : volume
Imports: unit value [1]	116	114	112	106	104	94	96	104	115	Imp. : valeur unitaire [1]
Exports: volume	73	79	85	86	89	103	101	101	102	Exp. : volume
Exports: unit value [1]	116	116	115	111	106	94	98	108	121	Exp. : valeur unitaire [1]
Terms of trade	100	101	103	104	102	99	102	104	105	Termes de l'echange
Purchasing power of exports	73	80	88	90	91	102	103	105	107	Pouvoir d'achat des export.

Country or area	1995	1996	1997	1998	1999	2001	2002	2003	2004	Pays ou zone
United States [14]										**Etats-Unis** [14]
Imports: volume	61	64	72	81	90	97	101	107	118	Imp. : volume
Imports: unit value [1]	101	102	99	93	94	96	94	97	102	Imp. : valeur unitaire [1]
Exports: volume [15]	72	77	86	88	90	94	90	93	101	Exp. : volume [15]
Exports: unit value [1,15]	104	104	103	100	98	99	98	100	104	Exp. : valeur unitaire [1,15]
Terms of trade	103	103	104	107	105	103	104	103	101	Termes de l'echange
Purchasing power of exports	74	79	89	94	95	97	94	96	102	Pouvoir d'achat des export.
Uruguay										**Uruguay**
Imports: unit value	112	112	108	101	96	94	87	...	...	Imp. : valeur unitaire
Exports: unit value	125	122	119	118	101	98	93	...	...	Exp. : valeur unitaire
Terms of trade	112	109	110	117	106	104	106	...	...	Termes de l'echange
Venezuela (Bolivarian Rep. of) [1]										**Venezuela (Rép. bolivarienne du)** [1]
Imports: unit value	105	99	98	102	102	105	105	112	123	Imp. : valeur unitaire

Source

United Nations Statistics Division, New York, trade statistics database.

Notes

[1] Price index numbers.
[2] Prior to 1997, the data refer to the Economic Union of Belgium and Luxembourg and intertrade between the two countries is excluded. Beginning January 1997, data refer to Belgium only and include trade between Belgium and Luxembourg.
[3] Imports FOB.
[4] Beginning 1997, trade data for France include the import and export values of French Guiana, Guadeloupe, Martinique, and Réunion.
[5] Prior to 1991, data refer to the Federal Republic of Germany.
[6] Prior to January 1991, excludes trade conducted in accordance with the supplementary protocol to the treaty on the basis of relations between the Federal Republic of Germany and the former German Democratic Republic.
[7] Beginning 1989, data exclude re-exports.
[8] Prior to 1996 data exclude customs free zones, repairs on goods, and operational leasing.
[9] Excluding military goods, fissionable materials, bunkers, ships, and aircraft.
[10] Exports include gold.
[11] Index numbers exclude ships.
[12] Exports include re-exports and petroleum products.
[13] Beginning in January 1998, foreign trade data refer to South Africa only, excluding intra-trade of the Southern African Common Customs Area. Prior to January 1998, trade data refer to the Southern African Common Customs Area, which includes Botswana, Lesotho, Namibia, South Africa and Swaziland.
[14] Including the trade of the U.S. Virgin Islands and Puerto Rico but excluding shipments of merchandise between the United States and its other possessions (Guam, American Samoa, etc.). Data include imports and exports of non-monetary gold.
[15] Excluding military goods.

Source

Organisation des Nations Unies, Division de statistique, New York, la base de données pour les statistiques du commerce extérieur.

Notes

[1] Indices de prix.
[2] Avant 1997, les données se rapportent à l'Union économique belgo-luxembourgeoise et ne comprennent pas le commerce entre ces pays. A partir de janvier 1997, les données se rapportent à Belgique seulement et recouvrent les échanges entre la Belgique et le Luxembourg.
[3] Importations FOB.
[4] A compter de 1997, les valeurs de commerce pour la France comprennent les valeurs des importations et des exportations de la Guyane française, la Guadeloupe, la Martinique, et la Réunion.
[5] Avant 1991, les données se rapportent à la République Fédérale d'Allemagne.
[6] Avant janvier 1991, non compris le commerce effectué en accord avec le protocole additionnel au traité définissant la base des relations entre la République Fédérale d'Allemagne et l'ancienne République Démocratique Allemande.
[7] A compter 1989, les données non compris les réexportations.
[8] Avant 1996 les données excluent des zones franches, des réparations sur des marchandises, et le crédit-bail opérationnel.
[9] A l'exclusion des marchandises militaires, des matières fissibles, des soutes, des bateaux, et de l'avion.
[10] Les exportations comprennent l'or.
[11] Non compris les navires.
[12] Exportations comprennent re-exportations et produits pétroliers.
[13] A compter de janvier 1998, les données sur le commerce extérieur ne se rapportent qu'à l'Afrique du Sud. et ne tiennent pas compte des échanges commerciaux entre les pays de l'Union douanière de l'Afrique du Sud. qui incluait l'Afrique du Sud, Botswana, Lesotho, Namibie, et Swaziland.
[14] Y compris le commerce des Iles Vierges américaines et de Porto Rico mais non compris les échanges de marchandise, entre les Etats-Unis et leurs autres possessions (Guam, Samoa americaines, etc.). Les données comprennent les importations et exportations d'or non-monétaire.
[15] Non compris les importations des economistes militaires.

Manufactured goods exports
Unit value and volume indices: 2000 = 100; value: thousand million US dollars

Exportations des produits manufacturés
Indices de valeur unitaire et de volume : 2000 = 100; valeur : milliards de dollars des E.-U.

Country or area — Pays ou zone	1994	1995	1996	1997	1998	1999	2001	2002	2003	2004
Total — Total										
Unit value indices, US $ [1] Ind. de valeur unitaire, $ des E.-U. [1]	111	122	117	110	108	103	98	98	104	...
Unit value indices, SDR Ind. de valeur unitaire, DTS	102	106	106	104	105	99	102	99	98	...
Volume indices [1] Indices de volume [1]	61	66	71	80	82	89	101	105	113	...
Value, thousand million US $ [1] Valeur, milliards de $ des E.-U. [1]	3 141.8	3 744.2	3 872.7	4 068.5	4 104.4	4 205.0	4 572.9	4 730.7	5 401.8	...
Developed economies — Economies développées										
Unit value indices, US $ Ind. de valeur unitaire, $ des E.-U.	110	122	118	110	109	105	98	99	107	116
Unit value indices, SDR Ind. de valeur unitaire, DTS	101	106	107	105	107	101	102	100	102	102
Volume indices Indices de volume	66	71	75	84	85	90	103	104	107	116
Value, thousand million US $ Valeur, milliards de $ des E.-U.	2 346.2	2 774.6	2 847.2	2 959.8	2 993.4	3 031.7	3 240.2	3 278.5	3 699.0	4 320.2
Americas — Amériques										
Unit value indices, US $ Ind. de valeur unitaire, $ des E.-U.	97	100	99	101	100	99	99	100	103	106
Volume indices Indices de volume	66	73	78	87	89	93	103	90	90	100
Value, thousand million US $ Valeur, milliards de $ des E.-U.	490.1	557.0	593.7	667.7	675.6	703.7	781.4	685.2	704.0	803.0
Canada — Canada										
Unit value indices, US $ Ind. de valeur unitaire, $ des E.-U.	101	104	105	106	101	99	97	96	103	112
Unit value indices, national currency Ind. de val. unitaire, monnaie nat.	93	96	97	99	101	99	102	102	98	98
Volume indices Indices de volume	65	74	76	80	88	99	104	103	101	107
Value, thousand million US $ Valeur, milliards de $ des E.-U.	109.2	128.2	134.0	142.9	148.7	165.6	168.8	166.5	173.6	200.0
United States — Etats-Unis										
Unit value indices, US $ [2] Ind. de valeur unitaire, $ des E.-U. [2]	95	98	98	99	100	99	100	102	103	104
Unit value indices, national currency [2] Ind. de val. unitaire, monnaie nat. [2]	95	98	98	99	100	99	100	102	103	104
Volume indices Indices de volume	67	73	79	89	89	91	103	86	87	97
Value, thousand million US $ Valeur, milliards de $ des E.-U.	380.9	428.8	459.7	524.8	527.0	538.1	612.6	518.8	530.4	603.0
Europe — Europe										
Unit value indices, US $ Ind. de valeur unitaire, $ des E.-U.	116	134	129	116	116	109	99	100	111	121
Volume indices Indices de volume	64	68	73	82	85	89	106	111	116	124
Value, thousand million US $ Valeur, milliards de $ des E.-U.	1 432.4	1 741.3	1 803.1	1 830.8	1 894.1	1 866.9	2 011.5	2 133.5	2 472.7	2 891.8

Manufactured goods exports — Unit value and volume indices: 2000 = 100; value: thousand million US dollars (*continued*)

Exportations des produits manufacturés — Indices de valeur unitaire et de volume : 2000 = 100; valeur : milliards de dollars des E.-U. (*suite*)

Country or area — Pays ou zone	1994	1995	1996	1997	1998	1999	2001	2002	2003	2004
Austria — Autriche										
Unit value indices, US $ [3] Ind. de valeur unitaire, $ des E.-U. [3]	178	205	185	152	141	118	94	100	...	...
Unit value indices, national currency [3] Ind. de val. unitaire, monnaie nat. [3]	136	139	132	125	117	102	98	98	...	...
Volume indices Indices de volume	46	50	57	70	73	86	124	115	...	...
Value, thousand million US $ Valeur, milliards de $ des E.-U.	40.9	51.4	52.3	53.1	51.7	50.4	58.3	57.1	77.7	96.7
Belgium — Belgique										
Unit value indices, US $ [4] Ind. de valeur unitaire, $ des E.-U. [4]	109	127	123	113	112	106	98	104	125	141
Unit value indices, national currency Ind. de val. unitaire, monnaie nat.	...	...	...	...	...	...	...	...	103	105
Volume indices Indices de volume	67	69	71	77	85	89	105	141	112	119
Value, thousand million US $ Valeur, milliards de $ des E.-U.	110.7	133.1	133.3	131.2	143.3	142.5	156.7	222.8	211.9	253.1
Denmark — Danemark										
Unit value indices, US $ Ind. de valeur unitaire, $ des E.-U.	116	134	130	118	116	112	100	103	122	136
Unit value indices, national currency Ind. de val. unitaire, monnaie nat.	91	93	93	96	96	97	102	100	101	101
Volume indices Indices de volume	66	69	71	81	84	95	105	114	119	119
Value, thousand million US $ Valeur, milliards de $ des E.-U.	24.3	29.4	29.2	30.2	31.2	33.8	33.5	37.2	46.4	51.4
Finland — Finlande										
Unit value indices, US $ Ind. de valeur unitaire, $ des E.-U.	101	128	121	109	107	104	95	100	117	120
Unit value indices, national currency Ind. de val. unitaire, monnaie nat.	81	87	86	88	89	90	98	98	96	89
Volume indices Indices de volume	63	68	72	81	89	89	103	98	98	109
Value, thousand million US $ Valeur, milliards de $ des E.-U.	25.1	34.7	34.8	35.1	38.0	36.7	38.9	38.9	45.4	51.8
France — France										
Unit value indices, US $ Ind. de valeur unitaire, $ des E.-U.	123	139	135	120	120	113	98	84	101	111
Unit value indices, national currency Ind. de val. unitaire, monnaie nat.	96	97	97	98	100	98	101	83	83	82
Volume indices Indices de volume	61	64	68	76	82	86	119	120	118	127
Value, thousand million US $ Valeur, milliards de $ des E.-U.	187.2	222.9	229.4	225.8	244.3	242.5	290.2	251.9	298.5	351.8
Germany — Allemagne										
Unit value indices, US $ Ind. de valeur unitaire, $ des E.-U.	130	150	140	121	124	111	99	104	118	128
Unit value indices, national currency Ind. de val. unitaire, monnaie nat.	99	101	99	99	103	97	102	102	96	95
Volume indices Indices de volume	61	63	68	79	80	86	105	107	114	128
Value, thousand million US $ Valeur, milliards de $ des E.-U.	380.4	455.8	459.7	455.3	477.9	461.1	499.2	534.8	644.3	790.3

Manufactured goods exports—Unit value and volume indices: 2000 = 100; value: thousand million US dollars (*continued*)

Exportations des produits manufacturés—Indices de valeur unitaire et de volume : 2000 = 100; valeur : milliards de dollars des E.-U. (*suite*)

Country or area — Pays ou zone	1994	1995	1996	1997	1998	1999	2001	2002	2003	2004
Greece — Grèce										
Unit value indices, US $ Ind. de valeur unitaire, $ des E.-U.	141	149	143	122	113	107	...	...	...	...
Unit value indices, national currency Ind. de val. unitaire, monnaie nat.	93	95	94	91	91	90	...	...	...	...
Volume indices Indices de volume	57	66	73	84	93	86	...	...	...	...
Value, thousand million US $ Valeur, millards de $ des E.-U.	4.9	6.0	6.3	6.2	6.3	5.6	6.0	5.7	8.7	10.0
Ireland — Irlande										
Unit value indices, US $ [4] Ind. de valeur unitaire, $ des E.-U. [4]	113	125	124	104	96	...	...	...	...	...
Volume indices Indices de volume	33	38	46	63	86	...	...	...	...	...
Value, thousand million US $ Valeur, millards de $ des E.-U.	24.3	31.2	37.0	42.8	53.6	59.6	75.1	77.7	79.4	88.7
Italy — Italie										
Unit value indices, US $ [4] Ind. de valeur unitaire, $ des E.-U. [4]	107	120	123	112	119	113	100	...	104	...
Volume indices Indices de volume	75	82	87	90	87	86	105	...	119	
Value, thousand million US $ Valeur, millards de $ des E.-U.	170.6	209.0	226.9	215.0	219.7	206.7	223.2	226.1	262.5	309.7
Netherlands — Pays-Bas										
Unit value indices, US $ [5] Ind. de valeur unitaire, $ des E.-U. [5]	119	141	132	117	115	109	104	104	117	128
Unit value indices, national currency [5] Ind. de val. unitaire, monnaie nat. [5]	90	94	93	96	95	95	107	102	96	95
Volume indices Indices de volume	59	64	68	89	83	88	115	117	124	138
Value, thousand million US $ Valeur, millards de $ des E.-U.	89.9	113.9	114.0	133.5	121.7	122.2	152.8	154.6	186.1	224.7
Portugal — Portugal										
Unit value indices, US $ [4] Ind. de valeur unitaire, $ des E.-U. [4]	116	137	129	116	113	108	99	...	...	...
Volume indices Indices de volume	61	68	73	80	89	94	103	...	...	...
Value, thousand million US $ Valeur, millards de $ des E.-U.	14.9	19.5	19.9	19.5	21.1	21.3	21.4	23.1	27.5	...
Spain — Espagne										
Unit value indices, US $ [4] Ind. de valeur unitaire, $ des E.-U. [4]	98	113	113	100	98	...	...	...	...	...
Volume indices Indices de volume	66	71	80	92	96	...	...	...	...	...
Value, thousand million US $ Valeur, millards de $ des E.-U.	57.7	71.4	80.5	82.3	84.8	88.7	91.4	99.0	124.0	...
Sweden — Suède										
Unit value indices, US $ Ind. de valeur unitaire, $ des E.-U.	106	131	132	117	112	106	...	...	...	...
Unit value indices, national currency Ind. de val. unitaire, monnaie nat.	89	102	97	97	97	96	...	...	...	...
Volume indices Indices de volume	75	77	76	91	91	100	...	...	...	...
Value, thousand million US $ Valeur, millards de $ des E.-U.	53.4	67.4	67.7	71.4	68.7	71.1	58.7	66.9	82.4	101.0

Manufactured goods exports— Unit value and volume indices: 2000 = 100; value: thousand million US dollars (*continued*)

Exportations des produits manufacturés— Indices de valeur unitaire et de volume : 2000 = 100; valeur : milliards de dollars des E.-U. (*suite*)

Country or area — Pays ou zone	1994	1995	1996	1997	1998	1999	2001	2002	2003	2004
United Kingdom — Royaume-Uni										
Unit value indices, US $ Ind. de valeur unitaire, $ des E.-U.	105	116	115	115	114	108	94	97	109	120
Unit value indices, national currency Ind. de val. unitaire, monnaie nat.	103	111	111	106	104	101	98	98	101	99
Volume indices Indices de volume	69	75	82	89	89	90	96	103	102	104
Value, thousand million US $ Valeur, millards de $ des E.-U.	168.7	201.3	218.4	237.7	236.4	225.6	210.2	232.6	258.1	290.2
Iceland — Islande										
Unit value indices, US $ [4] Ind. de valeur unitaire, $ des E.-U. [4]	90	128	118	113	100	...	...	...	...	...
Volume indices Indices de volume	56	52	56	64	72	...	...	...	...	...
Value, thousand million US $ Valeur, millards de $ des E.-U.	0.3	0.4	0.4	0.4	0.4	0.6	0.7	0.7	...	...
Norway — Norvège										
Unit value indices, US $ Ind. de valeur unitaire, $ des E.-U.	109	135	127	116	112	106	97	100	110	126
Unit value indices, national currency Ind. de val. unitaire, monnaie nat.	87	97	93	93	96	94	99	91	89	96
Volume indices Indices de volume	62	65	68	88	95	96	92	110	110	112
Value, thousand million US $ Valeur, millards de $ des E.-U.	11.2	14.5	14.4	17.0	17.7	16.8	14.8	18.3	20.3	23.5
Switzerland — Suisse										
Unit value indices, US $ [4] Ind. de valeur unitaire, $ des E.-U. [4]	106	128	126	112	111	109	104	109	...	...
Volume indices Indices de volume	80	78	78	83	87	94	97	99	...	...
Value, thousand million US $ Valeur, millards de $ des E.-U.	66.7	77.8	77.5	72.9	75.7	80.0	78.8	84.5	96.8	113.7
Other developed economies — Autres economies développées										
Unit value indices, US $ Ind. de valeur unitaire, $ des E.-U.	109	118	110	104	99	98	94	91	97	108
Volume indices Indices de volume	74	77	78	85	82	90	91	96	102	110
Value, thousand million US $ Valeur, millards de $ des E.-U.	423.7	476.2	450.4	461.3	423.7	461.0	447.4	459.8	522.3	625.4
Australia — Australie										
Unit value indices, US $ Ind. de valeur unitaire, $ des E.-U.	110	121	117	112	98	97	90	92	101	133
Unit value indices, national currency Ind. de val. unitaire, monnaie nat.	87	94	87	87	90	87	104	97	89	104
Volume indices Indices de volume	56	61	79	86	83	91	101	104	101	88
Value, thousand million US $ Valeur, millards de $ des E.-U.	13.1	15.6	19.8	20.4	17.3	18.7	19.3	20.2	21.7	25.0
Israel — Israël										
Unit value indices, US $ Ind. de valeur unitaire, $ des E.-U.	74	77	77	75	77	83	98	97	100	104
Volume indices Indices de volume	71	75	82	94	95	98	95	95	99	118
Value, thousand million US $ Valeur, millards de $ des E.-U.	15.5	17.1	18.8	20.8	21.7	24.2	27.6	27.5	29.5	36.5

Manufactured goods exports—Unit value and volume indices: 2000 = 100; value: thousand million US dollars (*continued*)

Exportations des produits manufacturés—Indices de valeur unitaire et de volume : 2000 = 100; valeur : milliards de dollars des E.-U. (*suite*)

Country or area — Pays ou zone	1994	1995	1996	1997	1998	1999	2001	2002	2003	2004
Japan — Japon										
Unit value indices, US $ Ind. de valeur unitaire, $ des E.-U.	111	119	110	104	100	98	94	92	97	107
Unit value indices, national currency Ind. de val. unitaire, monnaie nat.	105	103	111	117	121	104	110	106	105	107
Volume indices Indices de volume	76	79	79	85	81	89	89	94	100	110
Value, thousand million US $ Valeur, millards de $ des E.-U.	381.1	425.8	393.6	402.1	369.6	397.5	378.0	391.8	443.3	534.1
New Zealand — Nouvelle-Zélande										
Unit value indices, US $ Ind. de valeur unitaire, $ des E.-U.	118	134	131	122	101	96	98	99	112	125
Unit value indices, national currency Ind. de val. unitaire, monnaie nat.	90	93	86	84	85	83	105	97	88	86
Volume indices Indices de volume	68	70	73	80	92	99	108	105	109	116
Value, thousand million US $ Valeur, millards de $ des E.-U.	3.8	4.4	4.5	4.6	4.3	4.5	5.0	4.9	5.7	6.8
South Africa — Afrique du Sud										
Unit value indices, US $ Ind. de valeur unitaire, $ des E.-U.	155	190	165	...	...	...	...	...	...	...
Unit value indices, national currency Ind. de val. unitaire, monnaie nat.	79	99	102	...	...	...	...	...	...	...
Volume indices Indices de volume	43	46	55	...	...	...	...	...	...	...
Value, thousand million US $ Valeur, millards de $ des E.-U.	10.3	13.4	13.8	13.3	10.8	16.1	17.5	15.3	22.0	...
Developing economies — Economies en dévelop.										
Unit value indices, US $ Ind. de valeur unitaire, $ des E.-U.	113	120	114	108	104	97	98	96	97	...
Unit value indices, SDR Ind. de valeur unitaire, DTS	104	104	104	103	101	93	102	98	92	...
Volume indices Indices de volume	50	57	64	73	76	86	96	107	124	...
Value, thousand million US $ Valeur, millards de $ des E.-U.	795.6	969.6	1 025.5	1 108.7	1 111.0	1 173.3	1 332.7	1 452.2	1 702.8	...
China, Hong Kong SAR — Chine, Hong Kong RAS										
Unit value indices, US $ Ind. de valeur unitaire, $ des E.-U.	109	111	111	107	104	102	95	93	93	94
Unit value indices, national currency Ind. de val. unitaire, monnaie nat.	108	110	110	106	103	101	96	93	93	94
Volume indices Indices de volume	111	113	104	107	100	93	88	93	70	71
Value, thousand million US $ Valeur, millards de $ des E.-U.	27.1	28.2	25.8	25.7	23.3	21.2	18.9	19.4	14.7	15.1
India — Inde										
Unit value indices, US $ Ind. de valeur unitaire, $ des E.-U.	119	117	94	113	107	121	92	99	...	...
Unit value indices, national currency Ind. de val. unitaire, monnaie nat.	83	84	74	92	98	116	95	107	...	...
Volume indices Indices de volume	48	57	74	65	67	69	105	115	...	...
Value, thousand million US $ Valeur, millards de $ des E.-U.	20.2	23.3	24.3	26.0	25.3	29.3	33.6	39.9	48.8	...

67 Manufactured goods exports—Unit value and volume indices: 2000 = 100; value: thousand million US dollars (*continued*)

Exportations des produits manufacturés—Indices de valeur unitaire et de volume : 2000 = 100; valeur : milliards de dollars des E.-U. (*suite*)

Country or area—Pays ou zone	1994	1995	1996	1997	1998	1999	2001	2002	2003	2004
Korea, Republic of—Corée, République de										
Unit value indices, US $ Ind. de valeur unitaire, $ des E.-U.	127	134	123	112	100	94	91	81	81	90
Unit value indices, national currency Ind. de val. unitaire, monnaie nat.	92	93	89	95	125	101	105	91	87	93
Volume indices Indices de volume	45	55	60	68	74	88	96	99	120	147
Value, thousand million US $ Valeur, millards de $ des E.-U.	89.9	115.5	116.0	120.0	116.3	130.6	137.3	125.4	153.0	207.9
Pakistan—Pakistan										
Unit value indices, US $ Ind. de valeur unitaire, $ des E.-U.	97	113	111	117	115	106	100	96	101	108
Unit value indices, national currency Ind. de val. unitaire, monnaie nat.	56	68	76	91	99	100	117	109	111	119
Volume indices Indices de volume	85	77	90	82	79	90	101	113	140	137
Value, thousand million US $ Valeur, millards de $ des E.-U.	6.4	6.7	7.8	7.4	7.1	7.4	7.8	8.4	10.9	11.4
Singapore—Singapour										
Unit value indices, US $ Ind. de valeur unitaire, $ des E.-U.	123	127	123	116	105	101	98	100	99	98
Volume indices Indices de volume	55	67	72	77	75	82	89	90	104	129
Value, thousand million US $ Valeur, millards de $ des E.-U.	80.5	101.0	106.0	106.6	94.2	99.7	103.7	106.7	122.8	151.7
Turkey—Turquie										
Unit value indices, US $ [6] Ind. de valeur unitaire, $ des E.-U. [6]	118	139	127	116	109	105	99	96	108	124
Volume indices Indices de volume	50	52	60	76	85	89	115	139	165	192
Value, thousand million US $ Valeur, millards de $ des E.-U.	13.3	16.3	17.3	20.0	21.0	21.2	26.0	30.3	40.4	54.2

Source

United Nations Statistics Division, New York, trade statistics database.

Notes

[1] Excludes trade of the countries of Eastern Europe and the former USSR.
[2] Beginning 1989, derived from price indices; national unit value index is discontinued.
[3] Series linked at 1988 and 1995 by a factor calculated by the United Nations Statistics Division.
[4] Beginning 1981, indices are calculated by the United Nations Statistics Division; for Netherlands beginning 1988, for Belgium 1988 to 1992 and for Switzerland 1988 to 1995.
[5] Derived from sub-indices using current weights; for Netherlands 1989 to 1996.
[6] Industrial product.

Source

Organisation des Nations Unies, Division de statistique, New York, la base de données pour les statistiques du commerce extérieur.

Notes

[1] Non compris le commerce des pays de l'Europe de l'Est et l'ex-URSS.
[2] A partir de 1989, calculés à partir des indices des prix; l'indice de la valeur unitaire nationale est discontinué.
[3] Les series sont enchaînées à 1988 et 1995 par un facteur calculé par la Division de Statistique des Nations Unies.
[4] A partir de 1981, les indices sont calculés par la Division de statistique des Nations Unies; pour la Pays-Bas 1988, pour la Belgique 1988-1992 et pour la Suisse 1988 to 1995.
[5] Calculés à partir de sous-indices à coéfficients de pondération correspondant à la période en cours; pour les Pays-Bas de 1989 à 1996.
[6] Produit industriel.

Tables 65-67: Current data (annual, monthly and/or quarterly) for most of the series are published regularly by the Statistics Division in the United Nations *Monthly Bulletin of Statistics* [25]. More detailed descriptions of the tables and notes on methodology appear in the United Nations publications *International Trade Statistics: Concepts and Definitions* [48] and the *International Trade Statistics Yearbook* [24]. More detailed data including series for individual countries showing the value in national currencies for imports and exports and notes on these series can be found in the *International Trade Statistics Yearbook* [24] and in the *Monthly Bulletin of Statistics* [25].

Data are obtained from national published sources, from data supplied by the governments for publication in United Nations publications and from publications of other United Nations agencies.

Territory

The statistics reported by each country refer to its customs area, which in most cases coincides with its geographical area.

Systems of trade

Two systems of recording trade are in common use, differing mainly in the way warehoused and re-exported goods are recorded:

(a) Special trade (S): special imports are the combined total of imports for direct domestic consumption (including transformation and repair) and withdrawals from bonded warehouses or free zones for domestic consumption. Special exports comprise exports of national merchandise, namely, goods wholly or partly produced or manufactured in the country, together with exports of nationalized goods. (Nationalized goods are goods which, having been included in special imports, are then exported without transformation);

(b) General trade (G): general imports are the combined total of imports for direct domestic consumption and imports into bonded warehouses or free zones. General exports are the combined total of national exports and re-exports. Re-exports, in the general trade system, consist of the outward movement of nationalized goods plus goods which, after importation, move outward from bonded warehouses or free zones without having been transformed.

Tableaux 65-67 : La Division de statistique des Nations Unies publie régulièrement dans le *Bulletin mensuel de statistique* [25] des données courantes (annuelles, mensuelles et/ou trimestrielles) pour la plupart des séries de ces tableaux. Des descriptions plus détaillées des tableaux et des notes méthodologiques figurent dans les publications des Nations Unies *Statistiques du commerce international, Concepts et définitions* [48] et l'*Annuaire statistique du Commerce international* [24]. Des données plus détaillées, comprenant des séries indiquant la valeur en monnaie nationale des importations et des exportations des divers pays et les notes accompagnant ces séries figurent dans l'*Annuaire statistique du Commerce international* [24] et dans le *Bulletin mensuel de statistique* [25].

Les données proviennent de publications nationales et des informations fournies par les gouvernements pour les publications des Nations Unies ainsi que de publications d'autres institutions des Nations Unies.

Territoire

Les statistiques fournies par chaque pays se rapportent au territoire douanier de ce pays. Le plus souvent, ce territoire coïncide avec l'étendue géographique du pays.

Systèmes de commerce

Deux systèmes d'enregistrement du commerce sont couramment utilisés, et ne diffèrent que par la façon dont sont enregistrées les marchandises entreposées et les marchandises réexportées :

a) Commerce spécial (S) : les importations spéciales représentent le total combiné des importations destinées directement à la consommation intérieure (transformations et réparations comprises) et les marchandises retirées des entrepôts douaniers ou des zones franches pour la consommation intérieure. Les exportations spéciales comprennent les exportations de marchandises nationales, c'est-à-dire des biens produits ou fabriqués en totalité ou en partie dans le pays, ainsi que les exportations de biens nationalisés. (Les biens nationalisés sont des biens qui, ayant été inclus dans les importations spéciales, sont ensuite réexportés tels quels).

b) Commerce général (G) : les importations générales sont le total combiné des importations destinées directement à la consommation intérieure et des importations placées en entrepôt douanier ou destinées aux zones franches. Les exportations générales sont le total combiné des exportations de biens nationaux et

Valuation

Goods are, in general, valued according to the transaction value. In the case of imports, the transaction value is the value at which the goods were purchased by the importer plus the cost of transportation and insurance to the frontier of the importing country (c.i.f. valuation). In the case of exports, the transaction value is the value at which the goods were sold by the exporter, including the cost of transportation and insurance to bring the goods onto the transporting vehicle at the frontier of the exporting country (f.o.b. valuation).

Currency conversion

Conversion of values from national currencies into United States dollars is done by means of external trade conversion factors which are generally weighted averages of exchange rates, the weight being the corresponding monthly or quarterly value of imports or exports.

Coverage

The statistics relate to merchandise trade. Merchandise trade is defined to include, as far as possible, all goods which add to or subtract from the material resources of a country as a result of their movement into or out of the country. Thus, ordinary commercial transactions, government trade (including foreign aid, war reparations and trade in military goods), postal trade and all kinds of silver (except silver coins after their issue), are included in the statistics. Since their movement affects monetary rather than material resources, monetary gold, together with currency and titles of ownership after their issue into circulation, are excluded.

Commodity classification

The commodity classification of trade is in accordance with the United Nations Standard International Trade Classification (SITC) [53].

World and regional totals

The regional, economic and world totals have been adjusted: (a) to include estimates for countries or areas for which full data are not available; (b) to include insurance and freight for imports valued f.o.b.; (c) to include countries or areas not listed separately; (d) to approximate special trade; (e) to approximate calendar years; and (f) where possible, to eliminate incomparabilities owing to geographical changes, by adjusting the figures for periods before the change to be comparable to those for periods after the change.

des réexportations. Ces dernières, dans le système du commerce général, comprennent les exportations de biens nationalisés et de biens qui, après avoir été importés, sortent des entrepôts de douane ou des zones franches sans avoir été transformés.

Evaluation

En général, les marchandises sont évaluées à la valeur de la transaction. Dans le cas des importations, cette valeur est celle à laquelle les marchandises ont été achetées par l'importateur plus le coût de leur transport et de leur assurance jusqu'à la frontière du pays importateur (valeur c.a.f.). Dans le cas des exportations, la valeur de la transaction est celle à laquelle les marchandises ont été vendues par l'exportateur, y compris le coût de transport et d'assurance des marchandises jusqu'à leur chargement sur le véhicule de transport à la frontière du pays exportateur (valeur f.à.b.).

Conversion des monnaies

La conversion en dollars des Etats-Unis de valeurs exprimées en monnaie nationale se fait par application de coefficients de conversion du commerce extérieur, qui sont généralement les moyennes pondérées des taux de change, le poids étant la valeur mensuelle ou trimestrielle correspondante des importations ou des exportations.

Couverture

Les statistiques se rapportent au commerce des marchandises. Le commerce des marchandises se définit comme comprenant, dans toute la mesure du possible, toutes les marchandises que l'ajoute ou retranche aux ressources matérielles d'un pays suite à leur importation ou à leur exportation par ce pays. Ainsi, les transactions commerciales ordinaires, le commerce pour le compte de l'Etat (y compris l'aide extérieure, les réparations pour dommages de guerre et le commerce des fournitures militaires), le commerce par voie postale et les transactions de toutes sortes sur l'argent (à l'exception des transactions sur les pièces d'argent après leur émission) sont inclus dans ces statistiques. La monnaie or ainsi que la monnaie et les titres de propriété après leur mise en circulation sont exclus, car leurs mouvements influent sur les ressources monétaires plutôt que sur les ressources matérielles.

Classification par marchandise

La classification par marchandise du commerce extérieur est celle adoptée dans la Classification type pour le commerce international des Nations Unies (CTCI) [53].

Volume and unit value index numbers

These index numbers show the changes in the volume of imports or exports (volume index) and the average price of imports or exports (unit value index).

Description of tables

Table 65: World imports and exports are the sum of imports and exports of Developed economies, Developing economies and other. The regional totals for imports and exports and have been adjusted to exclude the re-exports of countries or areas comprising each region. Estimates for certain countries or areas not shown separately as well as for those shown separately but for which no data are yet available are included in the regional and world totals. Export and import values in terms of U.S. dollars are derived by the United Nations Statistics Division from data published in national publications, from data in the replies to the *Monthly Bulletin of Statistics* questionnaires and from data published by the International Monetary Fund (IMF) in the publication International Financial Statistics [13].

Table 66: These index numbers show the changes in the volume (quantum index) and the average price (unit value index) of total imports and exports. The terms of trade figures are calculated by dividing export unit value indices by the corresponding import unit value indices. The product of the net terms of trade and the volume index of exports is called the index of the purchasing power of exports. The footnotes to countries appearing in table 65 also apply to the index numbers in this table.

Table 67: Manufactured goods are defined here to comprise sections 5 through 8 of the Standard International Trade Classification (SITC). These sections are: chemicals and related products, manufactured goods classified chiefly by material, machinery and transport equipment and miscellaneous manufactured articles. The economic and geographic groupings in this table are in accordance with those of table 65, although table 65 includes more detailed geographical sub-groups which make up the groupings "other developed market economies" and "developing market economies" of this table.

The unit value indices are obtained from national sources, except those of a few countries which the United Nations Statistics Division compiles using their quantity and value figures. For countries that do not compile indices for manufactured goods exports conforming to the above definition, sub-indices are aggregated to approximate an index of SITC sections 5-8. Unit value indices obtained from national indices are rebased, where necessary, so that 2000 = 100. Indices in national currency are converted into US dollars using conversion factors obtained by dividing the weighted average exchange

Totaux mondiaux et régionaux

Les totaux économiques, régionaux et mondiaux ont été ajustés de manière : a) à inclure les estimations pour les pays ou régions pour lesquels on ne disposait pas de données complètes; b) à inclure l'assurance et le fret dans la valeur f.o.b. des importations; c) à inclure les pays ou régions non indiqués séparément; d) à donner une approximation du commerce spécial; e) à les ramener à des années civiles; et f) à éliminer, dans la mesure du possible, les données non comparables par suite de changements géographiques, en ajustant les chiffres correspondant aux périodes avant le changement de manière à les rendre comparables à ceux des périodes après le changement.

Indices de volume et de valeur unitaire

Ces indices indiquent les variations du volume des importations ou des exportations (indice de volume) et du prix moyen des importations ou des exportations (indice de valeur unitaire).

Description des tableaux

Tableau 65 : Les importations et les exportations totales pour le monde se composent des importations et exportations des Economies développées, des Economies en développement et des autres. Les totaux régionaux pour importations et exportations ont été ajustés pour exclure les re-exportations des pays ou zones que comprennent une région donnée. Les totaux régionaux et mondiaux comprennent des estimations pour certains pays ou zones ne figurant pas séparément mais pour lesquels les données ne sont pas encore disponibles. Les valeurs en dollars des E.U. des exportations et des importations ont été obtenues par la Division de statistique des Nations Unies à partir des réponses aux questionnaires du *Bulletin Mensuel de Statistique*, des données publiées par le Fonds Monétaire International dans la publication Statistiques financières internationales [13].

Tableau 66 : Ces indices indiquent les variations du volume (indice de quantum) et du prix moyen (indice de valeur unitaire) des importations et des exportations totales. Les chiffres relatifs aux termes de l'échange se calculent en divisant les indices de valeur unitaire des exportations par les indices correspondants de valeur unitaire des importations. Le produit de la valeur nette des termes de l'échange et de l'indice du volume des exportations est appelé indice du pouvoir d'achat des exportations. Les notes figurant au bas du tableau 65 concernant certains pays s'appliquent également aux indices du présent tableau.

Tableau 67 : Les produits manufacturés se définissent comme correspondant aux sections 5 à 8 de la Classification type pour le commerce international (CTCI). Ces sections sont :

rate of a given currency in the current period by the weighted average exchange rate in the base period. All aggregate unit value indices are current period weighted.

The indices in Special Drawing Rights (SDRs) are calculated by multiplying the equivalent aggregate indices in United States dollars by conversion factors obtained by dividing the SDR/US$ exchange rate in the current period by the rate in the base period.

The volume indices are derived from the value data and the unit value indices. All aggregate volume indices are base period weighted.

produits chimiques et produits liés connexes, biens manufacturés classés principalement par matière première, machines et équipements de transport et articles divers manufacturés. Les groupements économiques et géographiques de ce tableau sont conformes à ceux du tableau 65; toutefois, le tableau 65 comprend des subdivisions géographiques plus détaillées qui composent les groupements "autres pays développés à économie de marché" et "pays en développement à économie de marché" du présent tableau.

Les indices de valeur unitaire sont obtenus de sources nationales, à l'exception de ceux de certains pays que la Division de statistique des Nations Unies compile en utilisant les chiffres de ces pays relatifs aux quantités et aux valeurs. Pour les pays qui n'établissent pas d'indices conformes à la définition ci-dessus pour leurs exportations de produits manufacturés, on fait la synthèse de sous-indices de manière à établir un indice proche de celui des sections 5 à 8 de la CTCI. Le cas échéant, les indices de valeur unitaire obtenus à partir des indices nationaux sont ajustés sur la base 2000 = 100. On convertit les indices en monnaie nationale en indices en dollars des Etats-Unis en utilisant des facteurs de conversion obtenus en divisant la moyenne pondérée des taux de change d'une monnaie donnée pendant la période courante par la moyenne pondérée des taux de change de la période de base. Tous les indices globaux de valeur unitaire sont pondérés pour la période courante.

On calcule les indices en droits de tirages spéciaux (DTS) en multipliant les indices globaux équivalents en dollars des Etats-Unis par les facteurs de conversion obtenus en divisant le taux de change DTS/dollars E.U. de la période courante par le taux correspondant de la période de base.

On détermine les indices de volume à partir des données de valeur et des indices de valeur unitaire. Tous les indices globaux de volume sont pondérés par rapport à la période de base.

Tourist/visitor arrivals by region of origin
Arrivées de touristes/visiteurs par région de provenance

Country or area of destination and region of origin [+]	Series / Série	2000	2001	2002	2003	2004	Pays ou zone de destination et région de provenance [+]
Albania	VFN						Albanie
Total		317 149	342 908	469 691	557 210	645 409	Totale
Africa		244	66	75	233	174	Afrique
Americas		13 977	13 596	15 790	18 895	25 519	Amériques
Europe		295 149	320 477	439 151	531 927	609 821	Europe
Asia, East/S.East/Oceania		1 932	2 035	2 901	3 805	4 288	Asie, Est/S.-Est/Océanie
Southern Asia		355	309	351	424	410	Asie du Sud
Western Asia		1 439	1 074	752	896	775	Asie occidentale
Region not specified		4 053	5 351	10 671	1 030	4 422	Région non spécifiée
Algeria	VFN						Algérie
Total [1]		865 984	901 446	988 060	1 166 287	1 233 719	Totale [1]
Africa		55 508	62 661	72 041	111 941	131 066	Afrique
Americas		3 207	3 220	4 626	4 949	6 830	Amériques
Europe		98 563	107 162	140 844	157 093	198 230	Europe
Asia, East/S.East/Oceania		5 080	5 373	9 491	8 260	9 401	Asie, Est/S.-Est/Océanie
Western Asia		13 180	17 843	24 143	22 671	23 035	Asie occidentale
Region not specified		690 446	705 187	736 915	861 373	865 157	Région non spécifiée
American Samoa	TFN						Samoa américaines
Total		44 158	36 009	...	...	...	Totale
Africa		14	10	...	...	...	Afrique
Americas		7 763	7 339	...	...	...	Amériques
Europe		887	493	...	...	...	Europe
Asia, East/S.East/Oceania		35 326	28 084	...	...	...	Asie, Est/S.-Est/Océanie
Southern Asia		53	23	...	...	...	Asie du Sud
Western Asia		24	10	...	...	...	Asie occidentale
Region not specified		91	50	...	...	...	Région non spécifiée
Andorra	TFR						Andorre
Total		2 949 087	3 516 261	3 387 586	3 137 738	2 791 116	Totale
Europe		2 949 087	3 516 261	3 387 586	3 137 738	2 791 116	Europe
Angola	TFR						Angola
Total		50 765	67 379	90 532	106 625	194 329	Totale
Africa		8 343	14 580	16 618	30 915	41 873	Afrique
Americas		7 666	9 192	15 044	14 770	34 045	Amériques
Europe		30 868	38 176	52 169	55 190	101 180	Europe
Asia, East/S.East/Oceania		3 028	4 391	4 746	5 396	16 061	Asie, Est/S.-Est/Océanie
Southern Asia		661	661	828	...	...	Asie du Sud
Western Asia		199	379	1 127	354	1 170	Asie occidentale
Anguilla	TFR						Anguilla
Total [2]		43 789	47 965	43 969	46 915	53 987	Totale [2]
Americas		33 127	38 726	37 511	39 295	44 429	Amériques
Europe		9 422	8 027	5 383	6 308	8 037	Europe
Region not specified		1 240	1 212	1 075	1 312	1 521	Région non spécifiée
Antigua and Barbuda	TFR						Antigua-et-Barbuda
Total [2,3]		206 871	193 176	198 185	224 032	245 456	Totale [2,3]
Americas		107 438	107 275	108 235	112 809	129 316	Amériques
Western Asia		90 049	78 115	81 907	98 665	113 033	Asie occidentale
Region not specified		9 384	7 786	8 043	12 558	3 107	Région non spécifiée
Argentina	TFN						Argentine
Total [2]		2 909 468	2 620 464	2 820 039	2 995 271	*3 352 573	Totale [2]
Americas		2 480 150	2 157 191	2 419 591	2 424 735	2 653 088	Amériques
Europe		354 050	370 933	323 729	455 998	555 148	Europe
Region not specified		75 268	92 340	76 719	114 538	144 337	Région non spécifiée
Armenia	TCER						Arménie
Total		45 222	123 262	162 089	206 094	262 959	Totale
Africa		48	62	89	133	184	Afrique

Country or area of destination and region of origin [+]	Series / Série	2000	2001	2002	2003	2004	Pays ou zone de destination et région de provenance [·]
Americas		8 117	41 408	46 088	58 258	75 496	Amériques
Europe		25 487	47 896	79 761	98 884	127 242	Europe
Asia, East/S.East/Oceania		787	2 762	3 369	5 669	9 355	Asie, Est/S.-Est/Océanie
Southern Asia		8 704	18 350	19 090	23 995	27 551	Asie du Sud
Western Asia		2 079	12 784	13 692	19 155	23 131	Asie occidentale
Aruba	TFR						**Aruba**
Total		721 224	691 419	642 627	641 906	728 157	Totale
Americas		670 271	642 995	595 350	584 651	665 489	Amériques
Europe		47 063	44 961	43 970	54 711	60 428	Europe
Asia, East/S.East/Oceania		215	169	209	162	211	Asie, Est/S.-Est/Océanie
Region not specified		3 675	3 294	3 098	2 382	2 029	Région non spécifiée
Australia	VFR						**Australie**
Total [4]		4 931 336	4 855 669	4 841 152	4 745 855	5 214 981	Totale [4]
Africa		78 629	73 453	68 244	69 535	67 711	Afrique
Americas		620 927	577 450	556 186	537 494	561 454	Amériques
Europe		1 212 422	1 196 661	1 198 361	1 228 033	1 261 477	Europe
Asia, East/S.East/Oceania		2 911 569	2 893 463	2 924 158	2 811 834	3 205 477	Asie, Est/S.-Est/Océanie
Southern Asia		60 011	65 967	60 687	63 264	75 233	Asie du Sud
Western Asia		35 166	34 724	30 962	34 432	43 484	Asie occidentale
Region not specified		12 612	13 951	2 554	1 263	145	Région non spécifiée
Austria	TCER						**Autriche**
Total [5]		17 982 204	18 180 079	18 610 925	19 077 630	19 372 816	Totale [5]
Africa		35 511	35 737	25 779	27 206	32 114	Afrique
Americas		933 841	787 930	646 863	599 474	673 695	Amériques
Europe		16 084 063	16 474 203	16 983 956	17 386 722	17 445 939	Europe
Asia, East/S.East/Oceania		623 939	576 226	593 583	618 852	755 406	Asie, Est/S.-Est/Océanie
Southern Asia		35 357	32 159	39 011	29 619	39 882	Asie du Sud
Western Asia		28 858	33 320	28 524	37 667	43 202	Asie occidentale
Region not specified		240 635	240 504	293 209	378 090	382 578	Région non spécifiée
Azerbaijan	TFR						**Azerbaïdjan**
Total		680 909	766 992	834 351	1 013 811	1 348 655	Totale
Africa		...	...	108	320	661	Afrique
Americas		...	...	6 532	7 951	12 358	Amériques
Europe		359 176	272 273	581 633	746 916	1 050 943	Europe
Asia, East/S.East/Oceania		...	...	2 748	4 271	6 051	Asie, Est/S.-Est/Océanie
Southern Asia		242 360	321 882	241 352	252 669	275 147	Asie du Sud
Western Asia		1	...	1 978	1 684	2 143	Asie occidentale
Region not specified		79 372	172 837	...	...	1 352	Région non spécifiée
Bahamas	TFR						**Bahamas**
Total		1 543 959	1 537 780	1 513 151	1 510 169	1 561 312	Totale
Africa		1 627	469	1 166	1 409	1 427	Afrique
Americas		1 406 513	1 417 578	1 406 458	1 392 578	1 455 375	Amériques
Europe		105 432	94 897	80 140	93 714	84 121	Europe
Asia, East/S.East/Oceania		15 524	11 350	8 080	6 285	6 890	Asie, Est/S.-Est/Océanie
Southern Asia		360	291	377	381	347	Asie du Sud
Western Asia		648	548	347	346	616	Asie occidentale
Region not specified		13 855	12 647	16 583	15 456	12 536	Région non spécifiée
Bahrain	VFN						**Bahreïn**
Total [2]		3 868 738	4 387 930	4 830 943	4 844 497	5 667 331	Totale [2]
Africa		32 442	38 907	46 663	59 989	76 325	Afrique
Americas		120 801	139 550	177 089	192 206	200 481	Amériques
Europe		215 951	235 484	256 437	260 698	333 920	Europe
Asia, East/S.East/Oceania		107 445	135 121	187 058	211 749	267 978	Asie, Est/S.-Est/Océanie
Southern Asia		331 893	391 812	521 796	561 050	648 003	Asie du Sud
Western Asia		3 060 206	3 447 056	3 641 900	3 558 805	4 140 624	Asie occidentale
Bangladesh	TFN						**Bangladesh**
Total		199 211	207 199	207 246	244 509	271 270	Totale
Africa		1 787	1 561	1 297	2 012	2 147	Afrique
Americas		15 110	19 230	17 538	30 795	37 404	Amériques
Europe		46 036	50 184	46 641	63 749	77 307	Europe

Country or area of destination and region of origin †	Series Série	2000	2001	2002	2003	2004	Pays ou zone de destination et région de provenance
Asia, East/S.East/Oceania		38 429	37 937	41 019	42 824	51 230	Asie, Est/S.-Est/Océanie
Southern Asia		93 709	94 382	97 623	102 503	99 939	Asie du Sud
Western Asia		3 893	3 811	3 128	2 626	3 243	Asie occidentale
Region not specified		247	94	...	...	...	Région non spécifiée
Barbados	TFR						**Barbade**
Total		544 696	507 078	497 899	531 211	551 502	Totale
Africa		646	852	626	668	753	Afrique
Americas		278 391	256 125	275 144	291 623	301 268	Amériques
Europe		262 331	247 165	219 006	233 791	245 919	Europe
Asia, East/S.East/Oceania		2 334	2 021	2 103	4 027	2 679	Asie, Est/S.-Est/Océanie
Southern Asia		460	454	503	466	627	Asie du Sud
Western Asia		170	160	101	160	145	Asie occidentale
Region not specified		364	301	416	476	111	Région non spécifiée
Belarus	TFN						**Bélarus**
Total [6]		59 855	61 358	63 336	64 190	67 297	Totale [6]
Africa		123	67	58	65	47	Afrique
Americas		2 972	4 883	2 999	3 522	5 892	Amériques
Europe		55 655	55 007	56 833	57 916	58 524	Europe
Asia, East/S.East/Oceania		633	791	2 766	1 833	2 150	Asie, Est/S.-Est/Océanie
Southern Asia		177	278	279	472	269	Asie du Sud
Western Asia		295	332	401	382	415	Asie occidentale
Belgium	TCER						**Belgique**
Total [7]		6 457 325	6 451 513	6 719 653	6 689 998	6 709 740	Totale [7]
Africa		64 094	64 293	60 026	62 755	60 872	Afrique
Americas		448 770	427 918	399 576	368 814	382 249	Amériques
Europe		5 549 692	5 592 062	5 798 298	5 846 966	5 800 440	Europe
Asia, East/S.East/Oceania		297 402	267 755	347 725	294 364	318 231	Asie, Est/S.-Est/Océanie
Southern Asia		23 448	26 644	38 542	32 362	33 152	Asie du Sud
Western Asia		20 363	19 140	17 724	17 502	17 664	Asie occidentale
Region not specified		53 556	53 701	57 762	67 235	97 132	Région non spécifiée
Belize	TFN						**Belize**
Total [1]		195 765	195 956	199 521	220 574	230 835	Totale [1]
Africa		296	271	374	337	349	Afrique
Americas		150 102	148 981	154 321	174 784	185 254	Amériques
Europe		27 674	29 736	29 115	33 530	32 768	Europe
Asia, East/S.East/Oceania		3 226	3 524	3 411	3 754	4 285	Asie, Est/S.-Est/Océanie
Western Asia		361	445	405	370	481	Asie occidentale
Region not specified		14 106	12 999	11 895	7 799	7 698	Région non spécifiée
Benin	TFR						**Bénin**
Total		96 146	87 555	72 288	175 000 [8]	173 500 [8]	Totale
Africa		50 140	49 619	49 387	148 646	147 536	Afrique
Americas		4 651	602	1 281	471	360	Amériques
Europe		39 881	36 226	21 090	25 403	25 157	Europe
Asia, East/S.East/Oceania		518	498	220	225	261	Asie, Est/S.-Est/Océanie
Southern Asia		322	262	115	137	125	Asie du Sud
Western Asia		634	151	185	112	61	Asie occidentale
Region not specified		...	197	10	6	...	Région non spécifiée
Bermuda	TFR						**Bermudes**
Total [3]		332 191	278 153	284 024	256 579	271 613	Totale [3]
Americas		287 341	241 268	243 793	222 396	235 545	Amériques
Europe		35 918	28 508	30 669	25 938	25 867	Europe
Asia, East/S.East/Oceania		1 126	868	861	503	834	Asie, Est/S.-Est/Océanie
Region not specified		7 806	7 509	8 701	7 742	9 367	Région non spécifiée
Bhutan	TFN						**Bhoutan**
Total		7 559	6 393	5 599	6 261	9 249	Totale
Africa		7	27	17	14	14	Afrique
Americas		3 024	2 367	2 142	2 025	3 601	Amériques
Europe		3 029	2 530	2 020	2 764	3 899	Europe
Asia, East/S.East/Oceania		1 425	1 368	1 306	1 413	1 676	Asie, Est/S.-Est/Océanie

Country or area of destination and region of origin	Series Série	2000	2001	2002	2003	2004	Pays ou zone de destination et région de provenance
Southern Asia		50	14	16	13	15	Asie du Sud
Region not specified		24	87	98	32	44	Région non spécifiée
Bolivia	THSN						**Bolivie**
Total [9]		381 077	378 551	382 185	367 036	390 888	Totale [9]
Africa		1 117	862	977	1 117	1 278	Afrique
Americas		219 636	215 131	217 678	209 715	227 280	Amériques
Europe		142 170	145 969	147 236	140 913	143 413	Europe
Asia, East/S.East/Oceania		18 154	16 589	16 294	15 291	18 917	Asie, Est/S.-Est/Océanie
Bonaire	TFR						**Bonaire**
Total		51 269	50 395	52 085	62 179	63 156	Totale
Americas		33 067	33 816	33 548	32 771	34 330	Amériques
Europe		17 950	16 326	18 152	29 079	28 203	Europe
Asia, East/S.East/Oceania		16	31	...	...	...	Asie, Est/S.-Est/Océanie
Region not specified		236	222	385	329	623	Région non spécifiée
Bosnia and Herzegovina	TCER						**Bosnie-Herzégovine**
Total		170 937	138 528	159 763	165 465	190 300	Totale
Americas		10 155	8 365	8 286	7 339	8 442	Amériques
Europe		151 870	125 189	145 883	152 246	176 588	Europe
Asia, East/S.East/Oceania		1 464	1 131	1 496	1 870	2 177	Asie, Est/S.-Est/Océanie
Southern Asia		1 839	367	122	189	116	Asie du Sud
Western Asia		174	193	93	94	132	Asie occidentale
Region not specified		5 435	3 283	3 883	3 727	2 845	Région non spécifiée
Botswana	TFR						**Botswana**
Total [1]		1 103 795	1 048 845	1 036 558	975 465	...	Totale [1]
Africa		913 641	884 772	901 730	865 957	...	Afrique
Americas		27 360	25 279	17 631	12 827	...	Amériques
Europe		65 813	56 041	48 669	39 433	...	Europe
Asia, East/S.East/Oceania		14 834	12 461	11 441	9 123	...	Asie, Est/S.-Est/Océanie
Southern Asia		2 305	2 407	2 017	1 216	...	Asie du Sud
Region not specified		79 842	67 885	55 070	46 909	...	Région non spécifiée
Brazil	TFR						**Brésil**
Total		5 313 463	4 772 575	3 784 898	4 132 847	4 793 703	Totale
Africa		34 503	36 352	40 259	52 489	64 678	Afrique
Americas		3 803 069	3 131 693	2 205 618	2 396 832	2 703 442	Amériques
Europe		1 320 325	1 445 576	1 414 962	1 543 559	1 860 259	Europe
Asia, East/S.East/Oceania		121 791	127 394	108 201	128 640	155 605	Asie, Est/S.-Est/Océanie
Western Asia		11 174	11 326	7 118	5 595	6 064	Asie occidentale
Region not specified		22 601	20 234	8 740	5 732	3 655	Région non spécifiée
British Virgin Islands	TFR						**Iles Vierges britanniques**
Total		272 356	295 625	281 696	317 758	...	Totale
Americas		235 463	258 994	250 013	261 201	...	Amériques
Europe		34 122	33 270	28 511	49 952	...	Europe
Region not specified		2 771	3 361	3 172	6 605	...	Région non spécifiée
Brunei Darussalam	VFN						**Brunéi Darussalam**
Total		984 093	840 272	...	...	...	Totale
Americas		9 469	6 408	...	...	...	Amériques
Europe		41 728	30 387	...	...	...	Europe
Asia, East/S.East/Oceania		912 667	779 627	...	...	...	Asie, Est/S.-Est/Océanie
Southern Asia		16 168	13 283	...	...	...	Asie du Sud
Western Asia		781	...	...	...	...	Asie occidentale
Region not specified		3 280	10 567	...	...	...	Région non spécifiée
Bulgaria	VFR						**Bulgarie**
Total [10,11]		4 922 118	5 103 797	5 562 917	6 240 932	6 981 597	Totale [10,11]
Africa		3 523	2 984	3 778	3 848	...	Afrique
Americas		42 435	52 124	46 934	54 701	65 393	Amériques
Europe		4 780 489	4 950 963	5 426 164	6 088 039	6 677 212	Europe
Asia, East/S.East/Oceania		23 674	23 873	21 957	26 521	...	Asie, Est/S.-Est/Océanie
Southern Asia		15 917	12 916	9 498	11 613	...	Asie du Sud
Western Asia		17 403	14 811	14 144	15 132	...	Asie occidentale
Region not specified		38 677	46 126	40 442	41 078	238 992	Région non spécifiée

Country or area of destination and region of origin †	Series Série	2000	2001	2002	2003	2004	Pays ou zone de destination et région de provenance †
Burkina Faso	THSN						Burkina Faso
Total [1]		125 699	128 449	150 204	163 123	222 201	Totale [1]
Africa		47 208	50 241	55 144	65 459	96 385	Afrique
Americas		7 539	8 041	9 840	10 025	12 991	Amériques
Europe		62 978	62 870	73 076	76 743	99 742	Europe
Asia, East/S.East/Oceania		3 540	2 695	3 760	3 271	4 550	Asie, Est/S.-Est/Océanie
Western Asia		652	593	876	1 447	1 982	Asie occidentale
Region not specified		3 782	4 009	7 508	6 178	6 551	Région non spécifiée
Burundi	TFN						Burundi
Total [12]		29 000	36 000	...	...	...	Totale [12]
Africa		14 000	17 000	...	...	...	Afrique
Americas		2 000	2 000	...	...	...	Amériques
Europe		12 000	14 000	...	...	...	Europe
Asia, East/S.East/Oceania		1 000	3 000	...	...	...	Asie, Est/S.-Est/Océanie
Cambodia	TFR						Cambodge
Total		351 661 [13]	408 377 [13]	786 526	701 014	1 055 202 [14]	Totale
Americas		42 156	43 905	113 144	88 662	122 169	Amériques
Europe		65 657	66 088	218 950	183 353	242 811	Europe
Asia, East/S.East/Oceania		152 383	158 407	409 489	412 245	589 230	Asie, Est/S.-Est/Océanie
Southern Asia		2 967	4 691	4 459	5 286	7 132	Asie du Sud
Region not specified		88 498	135 286	40 484	11 468	93 860	Région non spécifiée
Cameroon	THSN						Cameroun
Total		277 070	220 578	226 019	...	189 856	Totale
Africa		88 618	100 282	104 695	...	80 013	Afrique
Americas		23 124	12 611	13 506	...	11 593	Amériques
Europe		150 096	99 624	98 570	...	83 272	Europe
Asia, East/S.East/Oceania		8 308	4 168	4 882	...	4 248	Asie, Est/S.-Est/Océanie
Western Asia		5 539	1 087	1 153	...	4 583	Asie occidentale
Region not specified		1 385	2 806	3 213	...	6 147	Région non spécifiée
Canada	TFR						Canada
Total		19 627 415 [15]	19 679 392 [15]	20 056 988	17 534 298	*19 095 342	Totale
Africa		64 588	61 264	54 111	52 437	58 210	Afrique
Americas		15 604 782	15 973 802	16 576 444	14 588 791	15 468 775	Amériques
Europe		2 498 863	2 323 626	2 095 148	1 872 693	2 202 397	Europe
Asia, East/S.East/Oceania		1 340 222	1 195 365	1 209 706	900 328	1 221 981	Asie, Est/S.-Est/Océanie
Southern Asia		73 998	78 435	79 073	79 792	96 342	Asie du Sud
Western Asia		44 962	46 900	42 506	40 257	47 637	Asie occidentale
Cape Verde	THSR						Cap-Vert
Total		115 015	134 169	125 852	150 048	157 052	Totale
Africa		4 469	3 392	10 003	5 225	10 034	Afrique
Americas		2 035	2 382	1 665	1 740	1 472	Amériques
Europe		100 555	121 508	105 790	134 749	136 304	Europe
Region not specified		7 956	6 887	8 394	8 334	9 242	Région non spécifiée
Cayman Islands	TFR						Iles Caïmanes
Total [3]		354 087	334 071	302 797	293 513	...	Totale [3]
Africa		404	400	353	373	...	Afrique
Americas		327 479	310 175	281 796	272 381	...	Amériques
Europe		23 595	21 428	18 705	19 001	...	Europe
Asia, East/S.East/Oceania		1 975	1 514	1 382	1 201	...	Asie, Est/S.-Est/Océanie
Southern Asia		326	233	238	274	...	Asie du Sud
Western Asia		93	84	100	65	...	Asie occidentale
Region not specified		215	237	223	218	...	Région non spécifiée
Central African Rep.	TFN						Rép. centrafricaine
Total [3]		11 217	9 873	2 910	5 687	8 156	Totale [3]
Africa		5 379	4 970	1 455	3 111	3 501	Afrique
Americas		904	697	176	374	449	Amériques
Europe		3 604	3 454	1 025	1 881	3 674	Europe
Asia, East/S.East/Oceania		1 163	449	170	288	317	Asie, Est/S.-Est/Océanie
Western Asia		117	51	15	18	192	Asie occidentale
Region not specified		50	252	69	15	23	Région non spécifiée

Country or area of destination and region of origin [*]	Series Série	2000	2001	2002	2003	2004	Pays ou zone de destination et région de provenance [·]
Chad	THSN						Tchad
Total		43 034	56 850	32 334	20 960	...	Totale
Africa		12 542	16 911	7 514	5 131	...	Afrique
Americas		8 216	5 122	6 485	4 368	...	Amériques
Europe		21 306	31 889	15 225	10 029	...	Europe
Asia, East/S.East/Oceania		436	1 623	1 000	293	...	Asie, Est/S.-Est/Océanie
Western Asia		534	924	2 110	1 139	...	Asie occidentale
Region not specified		...	381	...	...	...	Région non spécifiée
Chile	TFN						Chili
Total		1 742 407	1 723 107	1 412 315	1 613 523	1 785 024	Totale
Africa		2 392	2 495	2 476	2 872	3 653	Afrique
Americas		1 456 648	1 429 293	1 119 232	1 242 956	1 360 342	Amériques
Europe		240 144	249 985	245 494	309 008	344 774	Europe
Asia, East/S.East/Oceania		36 996	37 155	40 786	54 476	69 883	Asie, Est/S.-Est/Océanie
Southern Asia		2 746	1 807	1 697	2 039	3 605	Asie du Sud
Western Asia		912	721	728	637	812	Asie occidentale
Region not specified		2 569	1 651	1 902	1 535	1 955	Région non spécifiée
China [16,17]	VFN						Chine [16,17]
Total		83 443 881	89 012 924	97 908 252	91 662 082	109 038 218	Totale
Africa		54 015	62 827	84 541	91 949	154 223	Afrique
Americas		1 217 091	1 278 383	1 509 574	1 132 937	1 789 500	Amériques
Europe		2 537 222	2 732 112	3 007 483	2 789 888	4 096 999	Europe
Asia, East/S.East/Oceania		79 311 825	84 610 214	92 865 905	87 214 341	102 393 763	Asie, Est/S.-Est/Océanie
Southern Asia		210 347	277 288	380 512	383 121	514 163	Asie du Sud
Western Asia		34 658	37 202	52 122	46 856	84 376	Asie occidentale
Region not specified		78 723	14 898	8 115	2 990	5 194	Région non spécifiée
China, Hong Kong SAR	TFR						Chine, Hong Kong RAS
Total		8 813 500	8 878 200	10 688 700	9 676 300	13 655 100	Totale
Africa		22 700	23 100	20 700	68 100	91 100	Afrique
Americas		1 104 400	1 050 500	1 094 900	713 400	1 091 600	Amériques
Europe		639 300	602 600	617 400	588 000	888 700	Europe
Asia, East/S.East/Oceania		6 517 200	6 656 700	8 366 700	8 154 000	11 368 600	Asie, Est/S.-Est/Océanie
Southern Asia		108 500	125 800	131 400	113 700	159 500	Asie du Sud
Western Asia		59 400	52 800	57 200	39 100	55 600	Asie occidentale
Region not specified		362 000	366 700	400 400	...	...	Région non spécifiée
China, Macao SAR	VFN						Chine, Macao RAS
Total [18]		9 162 212	10 278 973	11 530 841	11 887 876	16 672 556	Totale [18]
Africa		4 334	4 092	4 407	4 657	5 897	Afrique
Americas		117 989	118 817	128 219	95 502	147 953	Amériques
Europe		148 361	130 265	127 614	94 078	128 887	Europe
Asia, East/S.East/Oceania		8 871 880	10 005 009	11 249 556	11 673 256	16 361 807	Asie, Est/S.-Est/Océanie
Southern Asia		17 008	17 731	17 719	17 324	23 771	Asie du Sud
Western Asia		773	938	899	1 147	1 843	Asie occidentale
Region not specified		1 867	2 121	2 427	1 912	2 398	Région non spécifiée
Colombia	VFN						Colombie
Total [19]		557 281	615 623	566 761	624 909	790 940	Totale [19]
Africa		1 155	991	970	886	929	Afrique
Americas		413 405	468 908	428 403	485 259	618 262	Amériques
Europe		127 205	129 475	117 500	125 073	155 651	Europe
Asia, East/S.East/Oceania		12 674	12 015	11 854	11 271	13 294	Asie, Est/S.-Est/Océanie
Southern Asia		1 344	1 320	1 226	1 119	1 404	Asie du Sud
Western Asia		1 313	1 769	1 062	1 004	1 399	Asie occidentale
Region not specified		185	1 145	5 746	297	1	Région non spécifiée
Comoros	TFN						Comores
Total [3]		23 893	19 356	18 936	14 229	17 603	Totale [3]
Africa		15 812	11 820	8 715	5 590	6 344	Afrique
Americas		230	167	60	26	162	Amériques
Europe		7 240	6 932	9 490	8 003	10 562	Europe

Country or area of destination and region of origin	Series Série	2000	2001	2002	2003	2004	Pays ou zone de destination et région de provenance
Asia, East/S.East/Oceania		153	102	64	610	165	Asie, Est/S.-Est/Océanie
Region not specified		458	335	607	...	370	Région non spécifiée
Congo	THSR						**Congo**
Total		18 797	27 363	21 611	...	...	Totale
Africa		9 300	11 750	11 006	...	...	Afrique
Americas		785	874	694	...	...	Amériques
Europe		8 294	12 029	8 752	...	...	Europe
Region not specified		418	2 710	1 159	...	...	Région non spécifiée
Cook Islands	TFR						**Iles Cook**
Total [20]		72 994	74 575	72 781	78 328	83 333	Totale [20]
Americas		12 726	13 413	11 505	11 390	8 445	Amériques
Europe		23 683	22 816	19 630	21 559	20 410	Europe
Asia, East/S.East/Oceania		36 359	38 061	41 277	45 008	53 962	Asie, Est/S.-Est/Océanie
Region not specified		226	285	369	371	516	Région non spécifiée
Costa Rica	TFN						**Costa Rica**
Total		1 088 075	1 131 406	1 113 359	1 238 692	1 452 926	Totale
Africa		789	837	900	1 048	1 194	Afrique
Americas		907 381	952 087	927 509	1 017 831	1 213 784	Amériques
Europe		156 562	156 571	164 263	198 242	215 072	Europe
Asia, East/S.East/Oceania		15 993	14 648	16 140	16 403	16 043	Asie, Est/S.-Est/Océanie
Region not specified		7 350	7 263	4 547	5 168	6 833	Région non spécifiée
Croatia	TCER						**Croatie**
Total [21]		5 831 180	6 544 217	6 944 345	7 408 590	7 911 874	Totale [21]
Americas		66 869	67 316	74 938	84 470	119 485	Amériques
Europe		5 719 995	6 428 582	6 806 518	7 244 346	7 692 506	Europe
Asia, East/S.East/Oceania		23 305	26 675	36 068	43 173	58 370	Asie, Est/S.-Est/Océanie
Region not specified		21 011	21 644	26 821	36 601	41 513	Région non spécifiée
Cuba	VFR						**Cuba**
Total		1 773 986	1 774 541	1 686 162	1 905 682	2 048 572	Totale
Africa		7 262	6 565	5 641	6 679	5 868	Afrique
Americas		783 425	834 660	787 729	916 818	1 025 756	Amériques
Europe		949 328	898 110	859 129	942 052	976 727	Europe
Asia, East/S.East/Oceania		27 103	28 586	27 354	32 463	33 861	Asie, Est/S.-Est/Océanie
Southern Asia		4 442	4 273	4 096	5 559	4 176	Asie du Sud
Western Asia		2 168	1 866	1 737	1 514	1 517	Asie occidentale
Region not specified		258	481	476	597	667	Région non spécifiée
Curaçao	TFR						**Curaçao**
Total [3]		191 246	204 603	217 963	221 395	223 439	Totale [3]
Americas		121 421	124 616	141 006	125 794	128 873	Amériques
Europe		65 476	73 190	70 390	91 384	89 752	Europe
Region not specified		4 349	6 797	6 567	4 217	4 814	Région non spécifiée
Cyprus	TFR						**Chypre**
Total		2 686 205	2 696 732	2 418 238	2 303 247	2 349 012	Totale
Africa		10 247	7 424	6 890	6 750	4 945	Afrique
Americas		38 737	30 185	26 734	23 245	22 923	Amériques
Europe		2 553 853	2 591 565	2 323 568	2 207 434	2 263 128	Europe
Asia, East/S.East/Oceania		18 680	13 695	11 697	12 266	14 812	Asie, Est/S.-Est/Océanie
Southern Asia		8 825	7 652	3 383	3 130	536	Asie du Sud
Western Asia		52 158	45 261	45 170	49 413	41 076	Asie occidentale
Region not specified		3 705	950	796	1 009	1 592	Région non spécifiée
Czech Republic	TCEN						**République tchèque**
Total		4 666 305	5 193 973	4 579 015	5 075 756	6 061 225	Totale
Africa		14 122	15 482	12 017	14 097	15 394	Afrique
Americas		284 537	279 410	235 328	282 239	380 056	Amériques
Europe		4 167 620	4 649 830	4 097 526	4 528 009	5 314 123	Europe
Asia, East/S.East/Oceania		200 026	249 251	234 144	251 411	351 652	Asie, Est/S.-Est/Océanie
Dem. Rep. of the Congo	TFN						**Rép. dém. du Congo**
Total		102 770	54 813	28 179	35 141	...	Totale
Africa		96 594	37 793	9 088	20 380	...	Afrique

Country or area of destination and region of origin	Series Série	2000	2001	2002	2003	2004	Pays ou zone de destination et région de provenance
Americas		495	2 746	3 678	2 568	...	Amériques
Europe		5 681	10 682	11 273	9 037	...	Europe
Asia, East/S.East/Oceania		...	3 592	4 140	3 156	...	Asie, Est/S.-Est/Océanie
Denmark	TCER						**Danemark**
Total [22]		3 534 513	3 683 977	3 435 563	3 473 808	3 357 989	Totale [22]
Americas		84 071	89 383	79 513	78 382	84 890	Amériques
Europe		3 313 057	3 455 308	3 220 983	3 253 489	3 117 228	Europe
Asia, East/S.East/Oceania		47 534	46 455	49 299	46 850	51 145	Asie, Est/S.-Est/Océanie
Region not specified		89 851	92 831	85 768	95 087	104 726	Région non spécifiée
Dominica	TFR						**Dominique**
Total		69 598	66 393	69 193	73 140	79 388	Totale
Americas		57 383	54 214	58 153	61 079	67 384	Amériques
Europe		11 147	10 825	10 131	10 749	5 969	Europe
Asia, East/S.East/Oceania		427	...	455	...	...	Asie, Est/S.-Est/Océanie
Region not specified		641	1 354	454	1 312	6 035	Région non spécifiée
Dominican Republic	TFR						**Rép. dominicaine**
Total [1,3,23]		2 972 552	2 868 915	2 793 209	3 268 182	*3 443 205	Totale [1,3,23]
Americas		1 152 622	1 238 611	1 260 558	1 493 912	1 591 605	Amériques
Europe		1 282 801	1 141 968	1 030 981	1 249 200	1 269 571	Europe
Asia, East/S.East/Oceania		2 628	1 809	1 294	1 588	1 665	Asie, Est/S.-Est/Océanie
Region not specified		534 501	486 527	500 376	523 482	580 364	Région non spécifiée
Ecuador	VFN						**Equateur**
Total [2]		627 090	640 561	682 962	760 776	818 927	Totale [2]
Africa		1 507	1 588	2 107	1 720	2 191	Afrique
Americas		503 056	510 714	549 927	617 088	662 019	Amériques
Europe		103 893	112 390	113 435	124 137	133 495	Europe
Asia, East/S.East/Oceania		18 633	15 863	17 493	17 831	21 195	Asie, Est/S.-Est/Océanie
Region not specified		1	6	...	...	27	Région non spécifiée
Egypt	VFN						**Egypte**
Total [2]		5 506 179	4 648 485	5 191 678	6 044 160	8 103 609	Totale [2]
Africa		147 425	145 554	161 497	183 035	244 662	Afrique
Americas		340 770	251 462	171 458	187 828	257 418	Amériques
Europe		3 805 389	3 132 459	3 583 791	4 203 687	5 919 575	Europe
Asia, East/S.East/Oceania		280 831	209 888	213 771	226 756	296 189	Asie, Est/S.-Est/Océanie
Southern Asia		39 304	39 536	46 110	51 042	63 310	Asie du Sud
Western Asia		889 886	867 911	1 012 613	1 188 994	1 317 883	Asie occidentale
Region not specified		2 574	1 675	2 438	2 818	4 572	Région non spécifiée
El Salvador	TFN						**El Salvador**
Total		794 678	734 627	950 597	857 378	966 416	Totale
Africa		...	...	...	424	582	Afrique
Americas		719 615	659 611	872 588	812 192	923 127	Amériques
Europe		27 012	21 731	26 523	34 782	33 053	Europe
Asia, East/S.East/Oceania		3 075	3 239	3 726	8 898	9 654	Asie, Est/S.-Est/Océanie
Region not specified		44 976	50 046	47 760	1 082	...	Région non spécifiée
Eritrea	VFN						**Erythrée**
Total [1]		70 355	113 024	100 828	80 029	87 298	Totale [1]
Africa		4 023	7 092	8 185	3 147	4 503	Afrique
Americas		2 093	2 829	2 094	2 321	2 559	Amériques
Europe		6 276	9 734	8 378	8 367	10 142	Europe
Asia, East/S.East/Oceania		2 960	2 568	1 700	1 953	2 484	Asie, Est/S.-Est/Océanie
Southern Asia		562	2 231	2 549	2 580	2 420	Asie du Sud
Western Asia		1 512	4 021	3 565	2 857	4 196	Asie occidentale
Region not specified		52 929	84 549	74 357	58 804	60 994	Région non spécifiée
Estonia	TCER						**Estonie**
Total		...	984 550	1 003 383	1 112 746	1 374 414	Totale
Africa		...	...	...	542	641	Afrique
Americas		...	16 878	15 601	14 823	23 448	Amériques
Europe		...	948 540	967 167	1 080 977	1 333 979	Europe
Asia, East/S.East/Oceania		...	6 907	6 587	10 663	13 456	Asie, Est/S.-Est/Océanie
Region not specified		...	12 225	14 028	5 741	2 890	Région non spécifiée

Country or area of destination and region of origin [*]	Series Série	2000	2001	2002	2003	2004	Pays ou zone de destination et région de provenance [*]
Ethiopia	TFN						Ethiopie
Total [12,24]		135 954	148 438	156 327	179 910	...	Totale [12,24]
Africa		48 796	61 234	59 640 .	82 152	...	Afrique
Americas		14 279	14 514	19 433	27 456	...	Amériques
Europe		34 941	32 540	34 280	43 647	...	Europe
Asia, East/S.East/Oceania		6 951	7 478	7 916	7 645	...	Asie, Est/S.-Est/Océanie
Southern Asia		3 480	3 244	3 778	3 602	...	Asie du Sud
Western Asia		8 605	9 908	9 189	14 366	...	Asie occidentale
Region not specified		18 902	19 520	22 091	1 042	...	Région non spécifiée
Fiji	TFR						Fidji
Total [2]		294 070	348 014	397 859	430 800	...	Totale [2]
Americas		63 066	68 263	68 617	69 313	...	Amériques
Europe		51 721	51 425	65 047	71 641	...	Europe
Asia, East/S.East/Oceania		177 697	226 190	261 690	288 321	...	Asie, Est/S.-Est/Océanie
Region not specified		1 586	2 136	2 505	1 525	...	Région non spécifiée
Finland	TCER						Finlande
Total		1 970 816	1 999 300	2 042 540	2 047 444	2 083 487 [25]	Totale
Africa		4 051	4 603	3 646	3 370	3 185	Afrique
Americas		123 479	119 946	108 446	102 034	111 245	Amériques
Europe		1 589 433	1 615 004	1 659 534	1 683 624	1 698 936	Europe
Asia, East/S.East/Oceania		133 491	142 083	157 635	146 652	167 808	Asie, Est/S.-Est/Océanie
Southern Asia		5 610	5 849	5 285	5 361	5 965	Asie du Sud
Western Asia		2 023	3 408	3 857	3 463	3 168	Asie occidentale
Region not specified		112 729	108 407	104 137	102 940	93 180	Région non spécifiée
France	TFR						France
Total		77 190 000	75 202 000	77 012 000	75 048 000	*75 121 000	Totale
Africa		1 074 000	921 000	924 000	889 000	895 000	Afrique
Americas		5 699 000	5 291 000	4 639 000	3 954 000	4 206 000	Amériques
Europe		67 580 000	66 491 000	69 078 000	68 072 000	67 711 000	Europe
Asia, East/S.East/Oceania		2 353 000	2 114 000	2 080 000	1 890 000	2 058 000	Asie, Est/S.-Est/Océanie
Western Asia		399 000	325 000	249 000	210 000	237 000	Asie occidentale
Region not specified		85 000	60 000	42 000	33 000	14 000	Région non spécifiée
French Guiana	TFR						Guyane française
Total		...	...	65 000	...	...	Totale
Americas		...	...	17 550	...	...	Amériques
Europe		...	...	44 850	...	...	Europe
Region not specified		...	...	2 600	...	...	Région non spécifiée
French Polynesia	TFR						Polynésie française
Total [2,3]		252 200 [26]	227 547	188 998	212 692	211 828	Totale [2,3]
Africa		...	280	253	294	257	Afrique
Americas		...	106 875	72 468	89 454	86 032	Amériques
Europe		...	83 556	76 100	80 182	79 944	Europe
Asia, East/S.East/Oceania		...	36 386	39 697	42 235	45 083	Asie, Est/S.-Est/Océanie
Southern Asia		...	43	46	62	75	Asie du Sud
Western Asia		...	191	182	163	172	Asie occidentale
Region not specified		252 200	216	252	302	265	Région non spécifiée
Gabon	TFN						Gabon
Total [27]		155 432	169 191	208 348	222 257	...	Totale [27]
Africa		37 712	42 433	52 408	55 487	...	Afrique
Americas		2 000	2 700	...	...	...	Amériques
Europe		112 000	118 631	...	...	...	Europe
Asia, East/S.East/Oceania		1 000	1 330	...	...	...	Asie, Est/S.-Est/Océanie
Western Asia		2 000	2 987	...	...	...	Asie occidentale
Region not specified		720	1 110	155 940	166 770	...	Région non spécifiée
Gambia	TFN						Gambie
Total [28]		78 710	57 231	81 005	73 485	90 095	Totale [28]
Africa		804	409	726	4 542	1 330	Afrique
Americas		910	821	1 075	643	3 248	Amériques

Country or area of destination and region of origin [+]	Series Série	2000	2001	2002	2003	2004	Pays ou zone de destination et région de provenance [+]
Europe		74 643	54 468	77 155	63 625	81 955	Europe
Region not specified		2 353	1 533	2 049	4 675	3 562	Région non spécifiée
Georgia	TFR						**Géorgie**
Total		387 258	302 215	298 469	313 442	368 312	Totale
Africa		326	730	681	586	1 029	Afrique
Americas		10 958	7 719	8 213	8 722	11 231	Amériques
Europe		357 798	281 691	275 332	288 648	342 596	Europe
Asia, East/S.East/Oceania		7 327	5 265	6 872	6 563	4 942	Asie, Est/S.-Est/Océanie
Southern Asia		6 058	5 289	5 838	6 683	6 636	Asie du Sud
Western Asia		2 167	1 261	1 253	1 835	1 564	Asie occidentale
Region not specified		2 624	260	280	405	314	Région non spécifiée
Germany	TCER						**Allemagne**
Total		18 983 264	17 861 293	17 969 396	18 399 093	20 136 979	Totale
Africa		159 991	147 387	143 714	143 156	146 454	Afrique
Americas		2 865 485	2 334 247	2 150 961	2 048 770	2 337 209	Amériques
Europe		13 515 662	13 093 176	13 288 813	13 877 895	14 918 028	Europe
Asia, East/S.East/Oceania		1 799 132	1 651 279	1 715 992	1 605 064	1 931 265	Asie, Est/S.-Est/Océanie
Western Asia		106 459	116 740	128 054	142 732	160 110	Asie occidentale
Region not specified		536 535	518 464	541 862	581 476	643 913	Région non spécifiée
Ghana	TFN						**Ghana**
Total [1]		398 998	438 828	482 637	530 827	583 821	Totale [1]
Africa		135 754	149 305	164 210	180 609	...	Afrique
Americas		33 509	36 855	40 534	44 581	...	Amériques
Europe		98 909	108 782	119 642	131 587	...	Europe
Asia, East/S.East/Oceania		19 191	21 106	23 214	25 532	...	Asie, Est/S.-Est/Océanie
Western Asia		3 026	3 329	3 661	4 026	...	Asie occidentale
Region not specified		108 609	119 451	131 376	144 492	583 821	Région non spécifiée
Greece	TFN						**Grèce**
Total [29]		13 095 545	14 057 035	14 179 999	13 969 393	...	Totale [29]
Africa		24 244	24 421	22 265	19 184	...	Afrique
Americas		300 213	231 675	217 369	219 391	...	Amériques
Europe		12 464 615	13 482 560	13 630 328	13 459 272	...	Europe
Asia, East/S.East/Oceania		231 255	243 122	242 040	212 791	...	Asie, Est/S.-Est/Océanie
Southern Asia		3 330	4 424	4 252	3 919	...	Asie du Sud
Western Asia		71 888	70 833	63 745	54 836	...	Asie occidentale
Grenada	TFN						**Grenade**
Total [1]		128 864	123 351	132 416	142 355	133 865	Totale [1]
Africa		612	632	494	522	562	Afrique
Americas		62 214	66 036	76 572	80 126	77 126	Amériques
Europe		46 325	40 170	38 976	43 167	36 222	Europe
Asia, East/S.East/Oceania		1 394	1 279	980	1 062	722	Asie, Est/S.-Est/Océanie
Western Asia		122	166	115	109	132	Asie occidentale
Region not specified		18 197	15 068	15 279	17 369	19 101	Région non spécifiée
Guadeloupe	THSR						**Guadeloupe**
Total		623 134 [30]	379 000 [31]	...	438 819 [31]	455 981 [31]	Totale
Americas		125 871	13 000		...		Amériques
Europe		495 385	361 000		386 737	406 204	Europe
Region not specified		1 878	5 000	...	52 082	49 777	Région non spécifiée
Guam	TFR						**Guam**
Total [20]		1 286 807	1 159 071	1 058 704	909 506	1 156 891	Totale [20]
Americas		42 284	42 545	42 975	41 160	46 754	Amériques
Europe		1 618	1 312	1 436	...	1 511	Europe
Asia, East/S.East/Oceania		1 231 413	1 077 140	984 373	808 623	1 068 997	Asie, Est/S.-Est/Océanie
Region not specified		11 492	38 074	29 920	59 723	39 629	Région non spécifiée
Guatemala	TFN						**Guatemala**
Total		826 240	835 492	884 190	880 223	1 181 526	Totale
Americas		688 121	676 176	712 261	703 841	1 006 614	Amériques
Europe		119 202	134 869	144 846	150 920	149 871	Europe
Asia, East/S.East/Oceania		16 852	22 490	24 370	21 999	23 167	Asie, Est/S.-Est/Océanie

Country or area of destination and region of origin [+]	Series Série	2000	2001	2002	2003	2004	Pays ou zone de destination et région de provenance [+]
Western Asia		382	418	590	603	365	Asie occidentale
Region not specified		1 683	1 539	2 123	2 860	1 509	Région non spécifiée
Guinea	TFN						**Guinée**
Total		32 598[32]	37 677	42 507	43 966[32]	44 622	Totale
Africa		12 679	17 851	21 868	15 771	13 330	Afrique
Americas		3 689	3 557	3 430	3 546	4 378	Amériques
Europe		14 352	12 928	11 646	15 162	15 500	Europe
Asia, East/S.East/Oceania		1 185	1 703	2 447	1 940	2 454	Asie, Est/S.-Est/Océanie
Southern Asia		384	552	794	732	985	Asie du Sud
Western Asia		309	726	1 705	1 042	566	Asie occidentale
Region not specified		...	360	617	5 773	7 409	Région non spécifiée
Guinea-Bissau	TFN						**Guinée-Bissau**
Total [3]		...	7 754	...	...	...	Totale [3]
Africa		...	2 052	...	...	...	Afrique
Americas		...	433	...	...	...	Amériques
Europe		...	3 824	...	...	...	Europe
Asia, East/S.East/Oceania		...	159	...	...	...	Asie, Est/S.-Est/Océanie
Southern Asia		...	103	...	...	...	Asie du Sud
Western Asia		...	169	...	...	...	Asie occidentale
Region not specified		...	1 014	...	...	...	Région non spécifiée
Guyana	TFR						**Guyana**
Total		105 042	99 317	104 341[33]	100 911[33]	121 989[33]	Totale
Americas		96 125	88 861	94 620	91 022	111 078	Amériques
Europe		7 229	8 689	8 190	8 136	9 056	Europe
Region not specified		1 688	1 767	1 531	1 753	1 855	Région non spécifiée
Haiti	TFR						**Haïti**
Total		140 492	141 632	140 112	136 031	96 439	Totale
Americas		128 048	129 041	126 683	125 214	90 615	Amériques
Europe		10 960	11 132	11 312	7 659	4 246	Europe
Region not specified		1 484	1 459	2 117	3 158	1 578	Région non spécifiée
Honduras	TFN						**Honduras**
Total		470 727	517 914	549 500	610 535	672 103	Totale
Africa		204	242	297	206	220	Afrique
Americas		420 112	460 223	493 330	557 262	613 474	Amériques
Europe		43 022	50 242	48 681	45 152	49 710	Europe
Asia, East/S.East/Oceania		6 914	6 662	6 727	7 115	7 826	Asie, Est/S.-Est/Océanie
Southern Asia		168	173	209	260	283	Asie du Sud
Western Asia		132	136	96	102	108	Asie occidentale
Region not specified		175	236	160	438	482	Région non spécifiée
Hungary	TCEN						**Hongrie**
Total [34]		2 992 401	3 070 261	3 013 116	2 948 224	3 269 868	Totale [34]
Africa		...	7 122	5 739	5 756	12 379	Afrique
Americas		203 241	181 147	169 967	173 862	202 180	Amériques
Europe		2 619 881	2 730 416	2 688 940	2 626 677	2 860 588	Europe
Asia, East/S.East/Oceania		107 366	92 817	82 781	77 189	104 805	Asie, Est/S.-Est/Océanie
Region not specified		61 913	58 759	65 689	64 740	89 916	Région non spécifiée
Iceland	TCEN						**Islande**
Total		633 901	672 156	704 633	771 323	836 230	Totale
Americas		64 686	74 398	69 342	72 174	74 857	Amériques
Europe		535 271	553 309	593 315	642 762	706 580	Europe
Asia, East/S.East/Oceania		5 459	6 734	7 048	9 013	10 520	Asie, Est/S.-Est/Océanie
Region not specified		28 485	37 715	34 928	47 374	44 273	Région non spécifiée
India	TFN						**Inde**
Total [2]		2 649 378	2 537 282	2 384 364	2 726 214	3 457 477	Totale [2]
Africa		90 914	86 718	80 317	89 201	111 712	Afrique
Americas		455 436	439 672	459 462	540 128	690 169	Amériques
Europe		954 911	890 359	796 613	942 061	1 256 814	Europe
Asia, East/S.East/Oceania		363 754	336 543	327 976	393 281	511 681	Asie, Est/S.-Est/Océanie
Southern Asia		673 917	672 133	630 653	666 889	790 698	Asie du Sud

68 Tourist/visitor arrivals by region of origin (*continued*)
Arrivées de touristes/visiteurs par région de provenance (*suite*)

Country or area of destination and region of origin	Series / Série	2000	2001	2002	2003	2004	Pays ou zone de destination et région de provenance
Western Asia		68 506	67 380	66 051	68 917	80 498	Asie occidentale
Region not specified		41 940	44 477	23 292	25 737	15 905	Région non spécifiée
Indonesia	TFR						**Indonésie**
Total		5 064 217	5 153 620	5 033 400	4 467 021	5 321 165	Totale
Africa		37 573	40 282	36 503	30 244	24 095	Afrique
Americas		232 117	243 097	222 052	175 546	199 397	Amériques
Europe		799 769	861 970	808 067	605 904	750 589	Europe
Asia, East/S.East/Oceania		3 909 094	3 920 183	3 877 195	3 575 842	4 254 430	Asie, Est/S.-Est/Océanie
Southern Asia		50 260	51 223	51 596	48 114	54 317	Asie du Sud
Western Asia		35 404	36 865	37 987	31 371	38 337	Asie occidentale
Iraq	VFN						**Iraq**
Total		78 457	126 654	...	...	...	Totale
Africa		256	127	...	...	...	Afrique
Americas		183	32	...	...	...	Amériques
Europe		1 461	501	...	...	...	Europe
Asia, East/S.East/Oceania		134	110	...	...	...	Asie, Est/S.-Est/Océanie
Southern Asia		76 367	124 434	...	...	...	Asie du Sud
Western Asia		56	20	...	...	...	Asie occidentale
Region not specified		...	1 430	...	...	...	Région non spécifiée
Ireland	TFR						**Irlande**
Total		6 646 000	6 353 000	6 476 000	6 764 000	6 982 000	Totale
Africa		27 000	32 000	29 000	...		Afrique
Americas		1 068 000	915 000	860 000	893 000	956 000	Amériques
Europe		5 329 000	5 189 000	5 387 000	5 623 000	5 706 000	Europe
Asia, East/S.East/Oceania		222 000	217 000	200 000	131 000	177 000	Asie, Est/S.-Est/Océanie
Region not specified		...	...		117 000	143 000	Région non spécifiée
Israel	TFR						**Israël**
Total [2]		2 416 756	1 195 689	861 859	1 063 381	1 505 606	Totale [2]
Africa		45 381	35 597	29 323	29 547	40 122	Afrique
Americas		683 917	350 484	260 912	347 622	486 508	Amériques
Europe		1 442 158	703 607	484 353	598 231	857 133	Europe
Asia, East/S.East/Oceania		111 238	53 231	35 885	42 384	65 953	Asie, Est/S.-Est/Océanie
Southern Asia		19 052	14 262	10 745	10 172	15 155	Asie du Sud
Western Asia		107 882	30 842	28 356	23 159	28 561	Asie occidentale
Region not specified		7 128	7 666	12 285	12 266	12 174	Région non spécifiée
Italy	TFN						**Italie**
Total [37]		41 180 719	39 562 697	39 798 969	39 604 118	37 070 775	Totale [37]
Africa		200 711	192 538	179 251	122 472	205 617	Afrique
Americas		2 251 610	2 158 479	2 064 520	1 680 228	2 988 244	Amériques
Europe		37 197 924	35 839 204	36 001 041	36 583 819	32 521 819	Europe
Asia, East/S.East/Oceania		1 346 817	1 199 891	1 382 734	1 074 563	1 088 281	Asie, Est/S.-Est/Océanie
Southern Asia		90 641	75 108	89 329	67 001	135 290	Asie du Sud
Western Asia		93 016	97 477	82 093	76 035	129 760	Asie occidentale
Region not specified		...	...	1	...	1 764	Région non spécifiée
Jamaica	TFR						**Jamaïque**
Total [3,12]		1 322 690	1 276 516	1 266 366	1 350 285	1 414 786	Totale [3,12]
Africa		1 388	1 271	1 131	1 084	1 139	Afrique
Americas		1 108 727	1 083 499	1 076 044	1 119 679	1 161 840	Amériques
Europe		200 269	181 891	179 902	219 406	242 904	Europe
Asia, East/S.East/Oceania		11 194	8 725	8 292	9 051	7 971	Asie, Est/S.-Est/Océanie
Southern Asia		670	731	530	643	554	Asie du Sud
Western Asia		361	334	392	363	350	Asie occidentale
Region not specified		81	65	75	59	28	Région non spécifiée
Japan	TFN						**Japon**
Total [2]		4 757 146	4 771 555	5 238 963	5 211 725	6 137 905	Totale [2]
Africa		14 512	14 640	16 698	16 434	16 946	Afrique
Americas		899 277	866 137	927 598	824 345	951 074	Amériques
Europe		624 850	630 128	688 250	665 187	744 142	Europe
Asia, East/S.East/Oceania		3 148 918	3 189 259	3 528 489	3 625 013	4 337 788	Asie, Est/S.-Est/Océanie

Country or area of destination and region of origin	Series Série	2000	2001	2002	2003	2004	Pays ou zone de destination et région de provenance
Southern Asia		63 725	66 120	72 580	76 217	83 856	Asie du Sud
Western Asia		3 154	3 062	3 394	3 166	3 285	Asie occidentale
Region not specified		2 710	2 209	1 954	1 363	814	Région non spécifiée
Jordan	TFN						**Jordanie**
Total [1]		1 580 430	1 671 510	2 384 472	2 353 087	2 852 803	Totale [1]
Africa		17 285	17 497	19 582	17 537	19 938	Afrique
Americas		91 309	51 768	51 908	64 545	93 477	Amériques
Europe		332 524	285 113	313 467	314 858	374 428	Europe
Asia, East/S.East/Oceania		42 226	29 309	43 251	43 883	60 121	Asie, Est/S.-Est/Océanie
Southern Asia		21 346	16 782	36 421	27 034	37 885	Asie du Sud
Western Asia		730 365	897 296	1 497 960	1 464 910	1 780 755	Asie occidentale
Region not specified		345 375	373 745	421 883	420 320	486 199	Région non spécifiée
Kazakhstan	VFR						**Kazakhstan**
Total		1 682 604	2 692 590	3 677 921	3 249 344	4 291 040	Totale
Africa		441	1 687	1 159	1 050	1 506	Afrique
Americas		18 017	19 134	24 699	23 207	32 345	Amériques
Europe		1 583 711	2 585 032	3 569 412	3 125 313	4 125 909	Europe
Asia, East/S.East/Oceania		68 835	68 649	65 929	73 917	96 660	Asie, Est/S.-Est/Océanie
Southern Asia		9 177	10 049	12 437	17 811	20 849	Asie du Sud
Western Asia		2 423	2 234	3 330	2 917	1 984	Asie occidentale
Region not specified		...	5 805	955	5 129	11 787	Région non spécifiée
Kenya	VFR						**Kenya**
Total [38]		1 036 628	995 066	1 001 297	1 146 099	...	Totale [38]
Africa		282 458	270 734	272 429	311 819	...	Afrique
Americas		88 216	84 555	85 083	97 389	...	Amériques
Europe		595 162	571 615	575 197	658 384	...	Europe
Asia, East/S.East/Oceania		45 903	44 003	44 278	50 681	...	Asie, Est/S.-Est/Océanie
Southern Asia		24 889	23 858	24 007	27 479	...	Asie du Sud
Region not specified		...	301	303	347	...	Région non spécifiée
Kiribati	TFN						**Kiribati**
Total [3]		4 842	4 555	...	...	...	Totale [3]
Americas		1 202	1 303	...	...	...	Amériques
Europe		152	213	...	...	...	Europe
Asia, East/S.East/Oceania		2 229	2 474	...	...	...	Asie, Est/S.-Est/Océanie
Region not specified		1 259	565	...	...	...	Région non spécifiée
Korea, Republic of	VFN						**Corée, République de**
Total [39]		5 321 792	5 147 204	5 347 468	4 753 604	5 818 138	Totale [39]
Africa		14 085	15 511	16 322	14 834	14 649	Afrique
Americas		534 519	506 787	556 440	505 067	610 562	Amériques
Europe		479 238	454 777	536 261	514 403	531 257	Europe
Asia, East/S.East/Oceania		3 916 518	3 787 356	3 829 548	3 334 633	4 252 976	Asie, Est/S.-Est/Océanie
Southern Asia		95 677	88 338	81 648	86 000	95 398	Asie du Sud
Western Asia		4 232	7 850	10 715	8 045	11 155	Asie occidentale
Region not specified		277 523	286 585	316 534	290 622	302 141	Région non spécifiée
Kuwait	VFN						**Koweït**
Total		1 944 233	2 071 616	2 315 568	2 602 300	3 056 093	Totale
Africa		17 093	18 495	24 407	26 167	29 144	Afrique
Americas		39 389	39 261	50 267	103 447	115 260	Amériques
Europe		71 409	69 166	80 650	94 168	125 509	Europe
Asia, East/S.East/Oceania		95 263	99 139	117 923	124 868	158 006	Asie, Est/S.-Est/Océanie
Southern Asia		518 160	577 813	648 075	745 679	855 730	Asie du Sud
Western Asia		1 191 168	1 264 107	1 391 296	1 505 733	1 769 220	Asie occidentale
Region not specified		11 751	3 635	2 950	2 238	3 224	Région non spécifiée
Kyrgyzstan	TFR						**Kirghizistan**
Total		58 756	98 558	139 589	341 990 [40]	398 078 [40]	Totale
Americas		4 615	4 388	11 936	12 744	12 266	Amériques
Europe		50 649	44 733	88 148	269 575	356 982	Europe
Asia, East/S.East/Oceania		2 394	8 384	11 333	14 005	16 766	Asie, Est/S.-Est/Océanie
Southern Asia		598	1 588	3 400	5 395	5 864	Asie du Sud

Country or area of destination and region of origin [†]	Series Série	2000	2001	2002	2003	2004	Pays ou zone de destination et région de provenance [†]
Western Asia		75	73	45	...	...	Asie occidentale
Region not specified		425	39 392	24 727	40 271	6 200	Région non spécifiée
Lao People's Dem. Rep.	VFN						**Rép. dém. pop. lao**
Total		737 208	673 823	735 662	636 361	894 806	Totale
Americas		42 111	34 370	46 704	39 453	47 153	Amériques
Europe		89 703	84 153	107 439	97 314	116 180	Europe
Asia, East/S.East/Oceania		599 908	549 112	575 268	495 253	728 262	Asie, Est/S.-Est/Océanie
Southern Asia		4 346	4 137	3 763	2 932	1 845	Asie du Sud
Region not specified		1 140	2 051	2 488	1 409	1 366	Région non spécifiée
Latvia	TCER						**Lettonie**
Total		268 083	322 916	360 927	414 924	545 366	Totale
Africa		136	86	87	151	83	Afrique
Americas		11 574	13 427	15 014	14 128	21 091	Amériques
Europe		240 686	297 865	332 107	386 070	500 979	Europe
Asia, East/S.East/Oceania		6 816	7 782	7 611	7 603	9 511	Asie, Est/S.-Est/Océanie
Southern Asia		285	278	403	294	308	Asie du Sud
Western Asia		257	94	158	131	196	Asie occidentale
Region not specified		8 329	3 384	5 547	6 547	13 198	Région non spécifiée
Lebanon	TFN						**Liban**
Total [41]		741 648	837 072	956 464	1 015 793	1 278 469	Totale [41]
Africa		24 183	29 995	37 240	39 453	45 095	Afrique
Americas		89 962	101 199	108 329	120 239	152 175	Amériques
Europe		228 960	237 411	250 817	267 077	337 337	Europe
Asia, East/S.East/Oceania		55 638	54 266	60 543	65 581	92 285	Asie, Est/S.-Est/Océanie
Southern Asia		51 313	82 183	95 647	102 035	128 120	Asie du Sud
Western Asia		288 083	329 945	403 000	421 148	520 230	Asie occidentale
Region not specified		3 509	2 073	888	260	3 227	Région non spécifiée
Lesotho	VFR						**Lesotho**
Total		301 759	294 644	287 280	329 301	303 530	Totale
Africa		292 704	285 804	278 662	302 924	290 295	Afrique
Americas		906	885	861	2 842	1 375	Amériques
Europe		6 036	5 893	5 746	12 569	7 568	Europe
Asia, East/S.East/Oceania		2 113	2 062	2 011	4 009	2 551	Asie, Est/S.-Est/Océanie
Region not specified		...	...	...	6 957	1 741	Région non spécifiée
Libyan Arab Jamah.	VFN						**Jamah. arabe libyenne**
Total [42]		962 559	952 934 [43]	857 952 [43]	957 896 [43]	999 343 [43]	Totale [42]
Africa		533 223	514 887	438 881	457 721	482 704	Afrique
Americas		647	677	1 943	1 926	2 201	Amériques
Europe		34 296	39 857	36 418	42 056	45 657	Europe
Asia, East/S.East/Oceania		1 669	5 646	6 611	6 601	6 942	Asie, Est/S.-Est/Océanie
Southern Asia		977	4 065	4 325	4 031	3 704	Asie du Sud
Western Asia		391 747	387 802	369 774	445 561	458 124	Asie occidentale
Region not specified		...	...	...	...	11	Région non spécifiée
Liechtenstein	THSR						**Liechtenstein**
Total		61 550	56 475	48 727	49 002	48 501	Totale
Africa		224	193	223	214	198	Afrique
Americas		4 728	3 667	2 852	2 414	2 739	Amériques
Europe		54 759	51 018	43 990	44 740	43 836	Europe
Asia, East/S.East/Oceania		1 839	1 597	1 662	1 634	1 728	Asie, Est/S.-Est/Océanie
Lithuania	TCER						**Lituanie**
Total		299 976	353 889	393 126	438 299	590 043	Totale
Africa		220	290	271	400	525	Afrique
Americas		15 120	15 256	15 673	16 324	22 385	Amériques
Europe		272 202	321 788	357 990	400 338	538 078	Europe
Asia, East/S.East/Oceania		9 133	10 649	9 808	11 003	15 472	Asie, Est/S.-Est/Océanie
Region not specified		3 301	5 906	9 384	10 234	13 583	Région non spécifiée
Luxembourg	TCER						**Luxembourg**
Total		851 589	842 733	884 672	867 047	874 117	Totale
Americas		42 372	36 048	33 136	28 562	29 759	Amériques

Country or area of destination and region of origin	Series Série	2000	2001	2002	2003	2004	Pays ou zone de destination et région de provenance
Europe		780 110	776 027	809 401	801 137	803 014	Europe
Region not specified		29 107	30 658	42 135	37 348	41 344	Région non spécifiée
Madagascar	TFN						**Madagascar**
Total		160 071	170 208	61 674	139 000	228 785	Totale
Africa		24 534	31 488	6 218	17 000	39 302	Afrique
Americas		6 402	6 808	1 880	4 000	9 180	Amériques
Europe		110 449	119 144	43 172	100 000	175 727	Europe
Asia, East/S.East/Oceania		2 055	3 404	617	2 000	3 432	Asie, Est/S.-Est/Océanie
Region not specified		16 631	9 364	9 787	16 000	1 144	Région non spécifiée
Malawi	TFR						**Malawi**
Total		228 106	266 300	382 647	424 000	*470 640	Totale
Africa		179 000	184 900	299 485	324 870	360 605	Afrique
Americas		10 000	23 000	15 251	18 070	20 058	Amériques
Europe		26 106	51 100	55 710	67 500	74 925	Europe
Asia, East/S.East/Oceania		10 000	7 300	5 542	9 940	11 033	Asie, Est/S.-Est/Océanie
Southern Asia		3 000	...	1 659	3 620	4 019	Asie du Sud
Western Asia		...	...	5 000		...	Asie occidentale
Malaysia	TFR						**Malaisie**
Total [44]		10 221 582	12 775 073	13 292 010	10 576 915	15 703 406	Totale [44]
Africa		74 314	161 926	148 102	133 762	136 587	Afrique
Americas		307 692	321 841	283 216	270 157	271 901	Amériques
Europe		590 304	703 724	636 972	456 351	540 306	Europe
Asia, East/S.East/Oceania		8 716 429	10 832 535	11 456 003	9 073 882	13 983 381	Asie, Est/S.-Est/Océanie
Southern Asia		180 016	212 083	244 351	209 120	248 673	Asie du Sud
Western Asia		44 346	107 775	126 239	78 324	124 331	Asie occidentale
Region not specified		308 481	435 189	397 127	355 319	398 227	Région non spécifiée
Maldives	TFN						**Maldives**
Total [3]		467 154	460 984	484 680	563 593	616 716	Totale [3]
Africa		2 311	2 060	3 002	3 984	5 325	Afrique
Americas		7 108	6 814	7 487	7 660	9 385	Amériques
Europe		362 196	364 105	373 428	443 093	475 707	Europe
Asia, East/S.East/Oceania		73 411	68 967	77 289	83 640	99 735	Asie, Est/S.-Est/Océanie
Southern Asia		20 648	17 007	20 533	21 580	22 047	Asie du Sud
Western Asia		1 480	2 031	2 941	3 636	4 517	Asie occidentale
Mali	THSN						**Mali**
Total		86 469	88 639	95 851	110 365	112 654	Totale
Africa		18 962	19 241	21 165	27 816	29 256	Afrique
Americas		9 306	8 393	9 232	9 393	12 494	Amériques
Europe		48 304	50 694	55 763	62 744	64 252	Europe
Asia, East/S.East/Oceania		1 020	1 081	1 189	1 200	3 117	Asie, Est/S.-Est/Océanie
Western Asia		2 206	2 445	2 567	2 712	1 524	Asie occidentale
Region not specified		6 671	6 785	5 935	6 500	2 011	Région non spécifiée
Malta	TFN						**Malte**
Total		1 215 712	1 180 145	1 133 814	1 126 601	1 156 028 [45]	Totale
Africa		9 691	8 694	9 086	...	...	Afrique
Americas		26 934	27 945	27 005	20 657	18 720	Amériques
Europe		1 103 945	1 079 862	1 039 904	939 793	975 864	Europe
Asia, East/S.East/Oceania		21 162	22 246	25 020	...	...	Asie, Est/S.-Est/Océanie
Southern Asia		1 944	1 613	1 549	...	...	Asie du Sud
Western Asia		46 287	33 771	25 484	20 218	12 831	Asie occidentale
Region not specified		5 749	6 014	5 766	145 933	148 613	Région non spécifiée
Marshall Islands	TFR						**Iles Marshall**
Total		5 246 [3]	5 444 [3]	6 002 [3]	7 195 [3]	9 007 [20]	Totale
Americas		2 022	1 994	2 156	2 189	2 099	Amériques
Europe		129	115	147	196	160	Europe
Asia, East/S.East/Oceania		2 884	3 073	3 397	4 422	4 466	Asie, Est/S.-Est/Océanie
Region not specified		211	262	302	388	2 282	Région non spécifiée
Martinique	TFR						**Martinique**
Total		526 291	460 382	446 689	453 159	470 890	Totale

68

Tourist/visitor arrivals by region of origin (*continued*)
Arrivées de touristes/visiteurs par région de provenance (*suite*)

Country or area of destination and region of origin [+]	Series Série	2000	2001	2002	2003	2004	Pays ou zone de destination et région de provenance [+]
Americas		80 168	54 744	70 378	71 559	73 011	Amériques
Europe		443 046	403 316	371 978	379 922	396 138	Europe
Region not specified		3 077	2 322	4 333	1 678	1 741	Région non spécifiée
Mauritius	TFR						**Maurice**
Total		656 453	660 318	681 648	702 018	718 861	Totale
Africa		163 763	168 319	172 351	173 996	175 295	Afrique
Americas		7 643	8 055	7 451	8 106	8 380	Amériques
Europe		440 279	437 615	451 791	465 620	477 347	Europe
Asia, East/S.East/Oceania		24 083	24 534	24 694	21 934	27 026	Asie, Est/S.-Est/Océanie
Southern Asia		19 598	20 946	22 869	27 277	26 558	Asie du Sud
Western Asia		591	729	2 287	4 800	3 883	Asie occidentale
Region not specified		496	120	205	285	372	Région non spécifiée
Mexico	TFR						**Mexique**
Total [12]		20 641 358	19 810 459	19 666 677	18 665 384	*20 617 741	Totale [12]
Americas		19 949 917	19 172 090	19 133 397	18 155 315	19 705 631	Amériques
Europe		400 566	362 480	479 174	443 366	...	Europe
Region not specified		290 875	275 889	54 106	66 703	912 110	Région non spécifiée
Micronesia (Fed. States of)	TFR						**Micronésie (Etats féd. de)**
Total [46]		20 501	15 253	19 059	18 169	18 967	Totale [46]
Americas		8 991	7 074	8 441	7 674	7 668	Amériques
Europe		1 465	1 205	1 483	1 522	1 403	Europe
Asia, East/S.East/Oceania		9 891	6 890	9 045	8 885	9 775	Asie, Est/S.-Est/Océanie
Region not specified		154	84	90	88	121	Région non spécifiée
Monaco	THSN						**Monaco**
Total		300 185	269 925	262 520	234 638	250 159	Totale
Africa		2 459	2 372	2 440	2 228	2 230	Afrique
Americas		43 622	35 991	31 096	22 660	24 370	Amériques
Europe		210 506	195 531	194 244	177 922	179 542	Europe
Asia, East/S.East/Oceania		19 311	13 473	12 143	9 781	12 653	Asie, Est/S.-Est/Océanie
Western Asia		4 173	3 325	4 024	3 320	3 367	Asie occidentale
Region not specified		20 114	19 233	18 573	18 727	27 997	Région non spécifiée
Mongolia	TFN						**Mongolie**
Total		137 374	165 899	228 719	201 153	300 537	Totale
Africa		154	180	143	209	263	Afrique
Americas		5 831	6 296	7 973	6 863	12 198	Amériques
Europe		61 639	79 368	97 674	72 345	98 592	Europe
Asia, East/S.East/Oceania		69 257	79 492	122 106	120 691	188 250	Asie, Est/S.-Est/Océanie
Southern Asia		412	462	655	803	966	Asie du Sud
Western Asia		78	93	155	229	249	Asie occidentale
Region not specified		3	8	13	13	19	Région non spécifiée
Montserrat	TFR						**Montserrat**
Total [3,12]		10 337	9 800	9 623	8 414	9 569	Totale [3,12]
Americas		7 231	7 143	6 778	5 938	6 594	Amériques
Europe		2 592	2 419	2 581	2 271	2 663	Europe
Region not specified		514	238	264	205	312	Région non spécifiée
Morocco	TFN						**Maroc**
Total [1]		4 239 962	4 342 150	4 303 446	4 761 271	5 476 713	Totale [1]
Africa		88 689	96 694	91 698	103 194	123 070	Afrique
Americas		178 625	149 103	119 229	107 877	127 974	Amériques
Europe		1 918 545	1 864 450	1 868 540	1 880 177	2 309 433	Europe
Asia, East/S.East/Oceania		49 486	43 459	44 242	41 651	48 874	Asie, Est/S.-Est/Océanie
Southern Asia		5 107	5 548	6 053	5 383	6 486	Asie du Sud
Western Asia		78 514	85 391	85 996	78 639	84 298	Asie occidentale
Region not specified		1 920 996	2 097 505	2 087 688	2 544 350	2 776 578	Région non spécifiée
Mozambique	VFR						**Mozambique**
Total		...	404 093	942 885	726 099	711 060	Totale
Africa		...	367 593	848 259	591 647	623 240	Afrique
Americas		...	...	10 401	5 035	5 647	Amériques
Europe		...	36 500	53 691	42 698	56 508	Europe

Country or area of destination and region of origin [+]	Series Série	2000	2001	2002	2003	2004	Pays ou zone de destination et région de provenance [+]
Asia, East/S.East/Oceania		...	...	5 721	...	...	Asie, Est/S.-Est/Océanie
Region not specified		...	...	24 813	86 719	25 665	Région non spécifiée
Myanmar	TFN						**Myanmar**
Total [47]		207 665	204 862	217 212	205 610	241 938	Totale [47]
Africa		304	312	430	390	395	Afrique
Americas		15 312	16 671	17 824	16 426	20 451	Amériques
Europe		54 905	57 490	65 477	60 364	65 411	Europe
Asia, East/S.East/Oceania		129 347	122 327	124 280	115 614	141 683	Asie, Est/S.-Est/Océanie
Southern Asia		6 534	6 646	7 179	11 668	12 167	Asie du Sud
Western Asia		1 263	1 416	2 022	1 148	1 831	Asie occidentale
Namibia	TFR						**Namibie**
Total		...	670 497	757 201	695 221	...	Totale
Africa		...	536 203	591 612	525 885	...	Afrique
Americas		...	9 056	9 625	11 775	...	Amériques
Europe		...	112 182	140 781	141 834	...	Europe
Asia, East/S.East/Oceania		...	...	3 430	4 280	...	Asie, Est/S.-Est/Océanie
Region not specified		...	13 056	11 753	11 447	...	Région non spécifiée
Nepal	TFR						**Népal**
Total		463 646	361 237	275 468	338 132	385 297	Totale
Africa		2 038	2 038	1 117	1 501	1 346	Afrique
Americas		52 964	42 751	25 110	25 156	29 791	Amériques
Europe		169 367	142 483	97 026	111 822	131 999	Europe
Asia, East/S.East/Oceania		111 667	88 005	67 985	91 582	97 357	Asie, Est/S.-Est/Océanie
Southern Asia		127 602	85 960	84 230	108 071	124 804	Asie du Sud
Region not specified		8	...	...	...	...	Région non spécifiée
Netherlands	TCER						**Pays-Bas**
Total		10 003 100	9 499 800	9 595 300	9 180 600	9 646 500	Totale
Africa		107 800	140 500	172 800	130 600	117 300	Afrique
Americas		1 215 800	1 202 900	1 099 700	996 100	1 131 500	Amériques
Europe		7 957 000	7 478 800	7 591 600	7 431 800	7 644 000	Europe
Asia, East/S.East/Oceania		722 500	677 600	731 200	622 100	753 700	Asie, Est/S.-Est/Océanie
New Caledonia	TFR						**Nouvelle-Calédonie**
Total [12]		109 587	100 515	103 933	101 983	99 515	Totale [12]
Africa		583	592	520	489	615	Afrique
Americas		2 523	1 870	2 141	1 753	1 676	Amériques
Europe		33 651	27 652	32 683	32 492	29 992	Europe
Asia, East/S.East/Oceania		72 129	69 980	67 998	65 382	65 892	Asie, Est/S.-Est/Océanie
Region not specified		701	421	591	1 867	1 340	Région non spécifiée
New Zealand	VFR						**Nouvelle-Zélande**
Total [12,48]		1 786 765	1 909 381	2 045 064	2 104 420	2 334 153	Totale [12,48]
Africa		19 268	21 331	20 679	19 395	18 673	Afrique
Americas		245 000	240 296	261 273	266 245	275 699	Amériques
Europe		371 684	387 222	423 200	460 938	488 674	Europe
Asia, East/S.East/Oceania		1 068 991	1 158 944	1 240 381	1 271 657	1 468 307	Asie, Est/S.-Est/Océanie
Southern Asia		10 494	14 988	19 410	17 028	17 830	Asie du Sud
Western Asia		4 741	5 474	5 922	7 048	8 122	Asie occidentale
Region not specified		66 587	81 126	74 199	62 109	56 848	Région non spécifiée
Nicaragua	TFN						**Nicaragua**
Total		485 909	482 869	471 622	525 775	614 782	Totale
Africa		563	560	287	378	515	Afrique
Americas		437 062	432 474	417 226	464 176	552 846	Amériques
Europe		38 357	40 153	44 730	49 147	52 564	Europe
Asia, East/S.East/Oceania		9 189	8 940	8 732	10 674	8 326	Asie, Est/S.-Est/Océanie
Southern Asia		531	590	549	1 254	437	Asie du Sud
Western Asia		128	131	64	89	76	Asie occidentale
Region not specified		79	21	34	57	18	Région non spécifiée
Niger	TFN						**Niger**
Total [3]		45 700	52 000	39 000	...	...	Totale [3]
Africa		28 000	37 000	26 000	...	...	Afrique

Country or area of destination and region of origin [+]	Series Série	2000	2001	2002	2003	2004	Pays ou zone de destination et région de provenance [+]
Americas		2 700	2 000	2 000	...	...	Amériques
Europe		14 000	11 000	9 000	...	...	Europe
Asia, East/S.East/Oceania		1 000	1 000	2 000	...	...	Asie, Est/S.-Est/Océanie
Western Asia		...	1 000	...	...	...	Asie occidentale
Nigeria	VFN						**Nigéria**
Total		1 491 767	1 752 948	2 045 543	2 253 115	2 646 411	Totale
Africa		1 050 993	1 234 733	1 450 814	1 554 308	1 825 312	Afrique
Americas		58 242	68 435	80 412	94 486	111 020	Amériques
Europe		230 316	270 056	317 317	372 846	438 093	Europe
Asia, East/S.East/Oceania		91 997	108 097	110 832	130 228	153 020	Asie, Est/S.-Est/Océanie
Southern Asia		33 978	36 335	44 701	52 523	61 714	Asie du Sud
Western Asia		25 034	29 414	34 560	40 608	47 714	Asie occidentale
Region not specified		1 207	5 878	6 907	8 116	9 538	Région non spécifiée
Niue	TFR						**Nioué**
Total [3,49]		1 647	1 407	2 084	2 706	2 550	Totale [3,49]
Americas		155	193	252	178	138	Amériques
Europe		104	174	275	235	168	Europe
Asia, East/S.East/Oceania		1 370	1 023	1 387	2 247	2 217	Asie, Est/S.-Est/Océanie
Region not specified		18	17	170	46	27	Région non spécifiée
Northern Mariana Islands	VFN						**Iles Mariannes du Nord**
Total		528 608	444 284	475 547	459 458	535 873	Totale
Africa		36	...	...	...	...	Afrique
Americas		52 331	35 460	36 451	34 670	37 334	Amériques
Europe		2 166	566	598	439	666	Europe
Asia, East/S.East/Oceania		473 883	407 104	437 322	422 811	494 826	Asie, Est/S.-Est/Océanie
Southern Asia		93	...	...	...	...	Asie du Sud
Western Asia		49	...	...	...	...	Asie occidentale
Region not specified		50	1 154	1 176	1 538	3 047	Région non spécifiée
Norway	TFN						**Norvège**
Total [50]		3 104 000	3 073 000	3 111 000	3 269 000	3 600 000	Totale [50]
Americas		141 000	141 000	126 000	144 000	174 000	Amériques
Europe		2 855 000	2 817 000	2 868 000	3 009 000	3 281 000	Europe
Region not specified		108 000	115 000	117 000	116 000	145 000	Région non spécifiée
Occupied Palestinian Terr.	VFR						**Terr. palestinien occupé**
Total		1 055 000	81 472 [51]	9 453 [51]	46 356 [51]	...	Totale
Africa		21 000	1 682	88	337	...	Afrique
Americas		211 000	23 377	1 402	5 836	...	Amériques
Europe		717 000	24 571	4 656	18 569	...	Europe
Asia, East/S.East/Oceania		43 000	7 286	1 073	8 111	...	Asie, Est/S.-Est/Océanie
Southern Asia		21 000	1 742	113	561	...	Asie du Sud
Western Asia		42 000	58	...	...	...	Asie occidentale
Region not specified		...	22 756	2 121	12 942	...	Région non spécifiée
Oman	THSN						**Oman**
Total		571 110	562 119	602 109	629 986	...	Totale
Africa		18 352	20 191	15 527	19 035	...	Afrique
Americas		34 089	48 574	36 717	36 356	...	Amériques
Europe		227 143	197 279	186 320	163 855	...	Europe
Asia, East/S.East/Oceania		98 295	36 913	47 012	51 026	...	Asie, Est/S.-Est/Océanie
Southern Asia		65 555	77 033	69 818	101 971	...	Asie du Sud
Western Asia		127 676	154 554	165 879	204 586	...	Asie occidentale
Region not specified		...	27 575	80 836	53 157	...	Région non spécifiée
Pakistan	TFN						**Pakistan**
Total		556 707	499 719	498 059	500 918	647 993	Totale
Africa		16 499	14 877	11 620	11 721	12 521	Afrique
Americas		89 783	82 159	87 884	85 910	103 104	Amériques
Europe		257 504	205 140	215 280	192 854	280 877	Europe
Asia, East/S.East/Oceania		50 011	42 711	43 920	43 521	59 503	Asie, Est/S.-Est/Océanie
Southern Asia		108 603	123 957	116 449	146 655	160 345	Asie du Sud

Country or area of destination and region of origin [+]	Series Série	2000	2001	2002	2003	2004	Pays ou zone de destination et région de provenance [+]
Western Asia		33 107	30 466	22 329	19 593	28 365	Asie occidentale
Region not specified		1 200	409	577	664	3 278	Région non spécifiée
Palau	TFR						Palaos
Total [52]		57 732	54 111	58 560	68 296	94 894	Totale [52]
Americas		6 704	5 375	4 774	4 511	6 507	Amériques
Europe		974	930	834	818	1 837	Europe
Asia, East/S.East/Oceania		48 630	46 191	51 504	61 400	84 449	Asie, Est/S.-Est/Océanie
Region not specified		1 424	1 615	1 448	1 567	2 101	Région non spécifiée
Panama	VFR						Panama
Total [53]		395 551	410 605	426 154	468 686[43]	498 415[43]	Totale [53]
Africa		318	412	334	354	335	Afrique
Americas		353 102	367 028	375 518	410 957	438 872	Amériques
Europe		30 904	31 876	38 417	43 355	45 254	Europe
Asia, East/S.East/Oceania		11 173	11 194	11 864	13 968	13 919	Asie, Est/S.-Est/Océanie
Western Asia		54	95	21	52	35	Asie occidentale
Papua New Guinea	TFR						Papouasie-Nouvelle-Guinée
Total		58 448	54 235	53 761	56 282	59 013	Totale
Africa		210	244	271	193	241	Afrique
Americas		7 191	6 142	6 990	5 215	5 440	Amériques
Europe		5 198	5 161	4 733	4 218	4 739	Europe
Asia, East/S.East/Oceania		43 191	40 148	39 316	45 999	47 963	Asie, Est/S.-Est/Océanie
Southern Asia		2 656	2 540	2 451	657	630	Asie du Sud
Region not specified		2	...	...	...	...	Région non spécifiée
Paraguay	TFN						Paraguay
Total [4]		288 515[54]	278 672[55]	250 423[55]	268 175[55]	309 287[55]	Totale [4]
Africa		...	139	161	185	211	Afrique
Americas		285 977	260 112	231 727	248 364	284 325	Amériques
Europe		...	15 411	13 915	15 375	19 788	Europe
Asia, East/S.East/Oceania		...	3 010	4 620	4 251	4 718	Asie, Est/S.-Est/Océanie
Southern Asia		...	...	...	...	148	Asie du Sud
Western Asia		...	...	...	...	96	Asie occidentale
Region not specified		2 538	...	...	...	1	Région non spécifiée
Peru	TFN						Pérou
Total		800 491	900 514	967 958	1 027 901	1 208 228[56]	Totale
Africa		1 594	1 796	1 873	1 993	2 343	Afrique
Americas		534 944	533 730	575 920	725 928	853 279	Amériques
Europe		209 289	221 151	240 652	248 071	291 591	Europe
Asia, East/S.East/Oceania		48 239	38 420	45 696	49 193	57 823	Asie, Est/S.-Est/Océanie
Southern Asia		1 366	1 107	1 204	1 265	1 487	Asie du Sud
Western Asia		195	146	123	115	135	Asie occidentale
Region not specified		4 864	104 164	102 490	1 336	1 570	Région non spécifiée
Philippines	TFR						Philippines
Total [1]		1 992 169	1 796 893	1 932 677	1 907 226	2 291 352	Totale [1]
Africa		1 192	1 685	1 465	1 442	1 700	Afrique
Americas		510 862	451 008	453 667	444 264	545 867	Amériques
Europe		252 195	201 815	183 910	177 338	212 305	Europe
Asia, East/S.East/Oceania		1 021 967	985 941	1 154 439	1 128 540	1 359 256	Asie, Est/S.-Est/Océanie
Southern Asia		24 092	22 193	20 822	21 543	24 997	Asie du Sud
Western Asia		14 711	16 073	18 500	16 736	20 683	Asie occidentale
Region not specified		167 150	118 178	99 874	117 363	126 544	Région non spécifiée
Poland	TCER						Pologne
Total		3 117 146	3 151 513	3 145 439	3 331 870	3 934 064	Totale
Africa		4 758	3 788	5 051	6 009	5 483	Afrique
Americas		216 404	201 289	189 177	182 309	232 723	Amériques
Europe		2 742 901	2 791 284	2 818 036	3 022 645	3 521 865	Europe
Asia, East/S.East/Oceania		67 584	64 127	64 206	66 951	98 239	Asie, Est/S.-Est/Océanie
Southern Asia		5 555	6 550	6 238	4 843	8 659	Asie du Sud
Western Asia		3 143	3 189	2 621	3 780	4 403	Asie occidentale
Region not specified		76 801	81 286	60 110	45 333	62 692	Région non spécifiée

Country or area of destination and region of origin [†]	Series Série	2000	2001	2002	2003	2004	Pays ou zone de destination et région de provenance [†]
Portugal	TFR						**Portugal**
Total [2,57]		12 096 680	12 167 200	11 644 231	11 707 228	11 616 899	Totale [2,57]
Americas		563 992	536 248	463 847	480 544	494 343	Amériques
Europe		11 125 806	11 281 780	10 849 103	10 887 861	10 754 110	Europe
Asia, East/S.East/Oceania		42 595	40 053	43 964	40 055	44 019	Asie, Est/S.-Est/Océanie
Region not specified		364 287	309 119	287 317	298 768	324 427	Région non spécifiée
Puerto Rico	TFR						**Porto Rico**
Total [58]		3 341 400	3 551 200	3 087 100	3 238 300	*3 541 000	Totale [58]
Americas		2 500 800	2 635 000	2 230 400	2 470 500	2 754 400	Amériques
Region not specified		840 600	916 200	856 700	767 800	786 600	Région non spécifiée
Qatar	THSR						**Qatar**
Total [59]		377 979	375 954	586 645	556 965	732 454	Totale [59]
Europe		105 758	56 426	102 983	88 620	195 732	Europe
Asia, East/S.East/Oceania		62 031	59 755	107 832	127 348	145 974	Asie, Est/S.-Est/Océanie
Western Asia		166 375	231 456	312 063	282 538	295 335	Asie occidentale
Region not specified		43 815	28 317	63 767	58 459	95 413	Région non spécifiée
Republic of Moldova	VFN						**République de Moldova**
Total [60]		18 964	15 690	20 161	23 598	26 045	Totale [60]
Africa		20	27	40	45	71	Afrique
Americas		1 109	1 148	1 788	2 556	2 564	Amériques
Europe		17 230	14 028	17 631	20 152	22 686	Europe
Asia, East/S.East/Oceania		398	377	411	295	307	Asie, Est/S.-Est/Océanie
Southern Asia		48	30	10	25	25	Asie du Sud
Western Asia		159	80	281	525	392	Asie occidentale
Réunion	TFR						**Réunion**
Total		430 000	424 000	426 000	432 000	430 000	Totale
Africa		44 240	45 805	30 625	27 367	26 222	Afrique
Europe		364 548	347 215	356 828	366 725	370 474	Europe
Region not specified		21 212	30 980	38 547	37 908	33 304	Région non spécifiée
Romania	VFR						**Roumanie**
Total		5 263 715	4 938 375	4 793 722	5 594 828	6 600 115	Totale
Africa		5 131	4 735	4 984	5 461	6 585	Afrique
Americas		94 642	96 012	102 481	115 373	139 463	Amériques
Europe		5 074 204	4 757 141	4 603 867	5 391 609	6 360 587	Europe
Asia, East/S.East/Oceania		37 260	36 393	41 703	41 610	49 309	Asie, Est/S.-Est/Océanie
Southern Asia		16 909	13 971	12 423	12 856	15 344	Asie du Sud
Western Asia		33 647	28 181	27 105	26 867	27 760	Asie occidentale
Region not specified		1 922	1 942	1 159	1 052	1 067	Région non spécifiée
Russian Federation	VFN						**Fédération de Russie**
Total		21 169 100	21 594 788	23 308 711	22 521 059	22 064 213	Totale
Africa		38 438	34 463	31 473	28 985	29 217	Afrique
Americas		292 865	305 601	342 594	420 857	477 338	Amériques
Europe		19 269 425	19 704 037	21 097 290	20 236 821	19 607 077	Europe
Asia, East/S.East/Oceania		838 803	868 636	1 150 430	1 106 605	1 313 669	Asie, Est/S.-Est/Océanie
Southern Asia		44 970	48 236	57 708	58 804	62 927	Asie du Sud
Western Asia		32 983	24 341	28 312	31 792	31 765	Asie occidentale
Region not specified		651 616	609 474	600 904	637 195	542 220	Région non spécifiée
Rwanda	TFR						**Rwanda**
Total		104 216	113 185 [61]	...	...	...	Totale
Africa		93 058	99 928	...	...	...	Afrique
Americas		2 250	2 785	...	...	...	Amériques
Europe		6 412	8 395	...	...	...	Europe
Asia, East/S.East/Oceania		751	699	...	...	...	Asie, Est/S.-Est/Océanie
Southern Asia		1 241	1 045	...	...	...	Asie du Sud
Western Asia		504	333	...	...	...	Asie occidentale
Saba	TFR						**Saba**
Total		9 120	9 005	10 778	10 260	11 012	Totale
Americas		6 695	7 036	4 380	...	4 764	Amériques

Country or area of destination and region of origin †	Series Série	2000	2001	2002	2003	2004	Pays ou zone de destination et région de provenance †
Europe		848	1 354	4 565	4 732	5 043	Europe
Region not specified		1 577	615	1 833	5 528	1 205	Région non spécifiée
Saint Eustatius	TFR						**Saint-Eustache**
Total [62]		9 072	9 597	9 781	10 451	11 056	Totale [62]
Americas		3 393	3 447	3 403	3 483	3 732	Amériques
Europe		3 988	4 499	4 600	5 272	5 505	Europe
Region not specified		1 691	1 651	1 778	1 696	1 819	Région non spécifiée
Saint Kitts and Nevis	TFR						**Saint-Kitts-et-Nevis**
Total [3]		73 149	70 565	67 531	...	...	Totale [3]
Americas		45 407	59 285	60 023	...	...	Amériques
Europe		15 155	8 726	5 464	...	...	Europe
Region not specified		12 587	2 554	2 044	...	...	Région non spécifiée
Saint Lucia	TFR						**Sainte-Lucie**
Total [2]		269 850	250 132	253 463	276 948	*298 431	Totale [2]
Americas		168 150	165 239	175 390	183 349	197 433	Amériques
Europe		98 869	82 672	76 199	90 193	96 793	Europe
Asia, East/S.East/Oceania		503	205	278	373	282	Asie, Est/S.-Est/Océanie
Region not specified		2 328	2 016	1 596	3 033	3 923	Région non spécifiée
Saint Maarten	TFN						**Saint-Martin**
Total [63]		432 292	402 649	380 801	427 587	475 032	Totale [63]
Americas		271 753	269 613	259 506	301 018	338 241	Amériques
Europe		121 819	97 449	87 147	88 259	96 404	Europe
Region not specified		38 720	35 587	34 148	38 310	40 387	Région non spécifiée
St. Vincent-Grenadines	TFR						**St. Vincent-Grenadines**
Total [3]		72 895	70 686	77 631	78 535	86 722	Totale [3]
Americas		...	50 572	58 465	60 315	66 871	Amériques
Europe		...	18 850	17 997	17 201	18 652	Europe
Region not specified		72 895	1 264	1 169	1 019	1 199	Région non spécifiée
Samoa	TFR						**Samoa**
Total		87 688	88 263	88 971	92 486	98 155	Totale
Americas		9 422	8 837	9 095	8 959	8 311	Amériques
Europe		6 396	5 797	4 762	5 136	4 756	Europe
Asia, East/S.East/Oceania		71 314	73 403	74 833	78 155	84 882	Asie, Est/S.-Est/Océanie
Region not specified		556	226	281	236	206	Région non spécifiée
San Marino	VFN						**Saint-Marin**
Total [64]		3 071 005	3 035 650	3 102 453	2 882 207	2 812 488	Totale [64]
Region not specified		3 071 005	3 035 650	3 102 453	2 882 207	2 812 488	Région non spécifiée
Sao Tome and Principe	TFR						**Sao Tomé-et-Principe**
Total		7 137	7 569	...	...	...	Totale
Africa		1 141	2 615	...	...	...	Afrique
Americas		...	456	...	...	...	Amériques
Europe		3 818	4 380	...	...	...	Europe
Asia, East/S.East/Oceania		...	62	...	...	...	Asie, Est/S.-Est/Océanie
Southern Asia		...	23	...	...	...	Asie du Sud
Western Asia		...	33	...	...	...	Asie occidentale
Region not specified		2 178	...	...	...	...	Région non spécifiée
Saudi Arabia	TFN						**Arabie saoudite**
Total		6 585 326	6 726 620	7 511 299	7 332 233	8 599 430	Totale
Africa		566 204	535 099	606 791	525 045	675 441	Afrique
Americas		53 725	47 109	51 964	46 496	53 190	Amériques
Europe		338 449	304 894	338 580	334 159	424 297	Europe
Asia, East/S.East/Oceania		630 023	595 847	660 329	612 340	752 905	Asie, Est/S.-Est/Océanie
Southern Asia		1 380 304	1 371 162	1 618 928	1 868 897	1 932 990	Asie du Sud
Western Asia		3 598 746	3 853 143	4 212 598	3 923 873	4 752 257	Asie occidentale
Region not specified		17 875	19 366	22 092	21 423	8 350	Région non spécifiée
Senegal	THSN						**Sénégal**
Total		389 433	396 254	426 825	353 539	363 490	Totale
Africa		96 834	77 623	86 037	85 664	89 660	Afrique
Americas		13 192	10 683	9 536	10 025	12 431	Amériques
Europe		274 035	301 087	322 631	252 568	242 944	Europe

Country or area of destination and region of origin [+]	Series / Série	2000	2001	2002	2003	2004	Pays ou zone de destination et région de provenance [+]
Asia, East/S.East/Oceania		2 669	2 208	1 864	2 273	3 705	Asie, Est/S.-Est/Océanie
Western Asia		988	915	994	1 253	1 672	Asie occidentale
Region not specified		1 715	3 738	5 763	1 756	13 078	Région non spécifiée
Serbia and Montenegro	TCEN						**Serbie-et-Monténégro**
Total		238 957	351 333	448 223	481 070	579 886	Totale
Americas		3 631	10 555	14 593	16 812	16 837	Amériques
Europe		222 074	327 263	418 676	449 932	545 288	Europe
Asia, East/S.East/Oceania		2 360	3 089	3 442	4 156	5 631	Asie, Est/S.-Est/Océanie
Region not specified		10 892	10 426	11 512	10 170	12 130	Région non spécifiée
Seychelles	TFR						**Seychelles**
Total		130 046	129 762	132 246	122 038	120 765	Totale
Africa		13 746	13 821	13 819	13 578	12 598	Afrique
Americas		6 239	6 854	3 670	3 477	4 030	Amériques
Europe		104 545	103 270	108 246	99 961	98 654	Europe
Asia, East/S.East/Oceania		2 716	2 624	2 678	1 977	2 135	Asie, Est/S.-Est/Océanie
Southern Asia		1 288	1 690	1 810	1 275	1 437	Asie du Sud
Western Asia		1 512	1 503	2 023	1 770	1 911	Asie occidentale
Sierra Leone	TFR						**Sierra Leone**
Total [3]		15 713	24 067	28 463	38 107	43 560	Totale [3]
Africa		4 810	11 427	13 519	23 341	24 446	Afrique
Americas		2 454	3 211	3 785	4 699	4 790	Amériques
Europe		5 658	6 250	7 403	6 460	9 476	Europe
Asia, East/S.East/Oceania		1 923	1 812	2 134	1 995	2 257	Asie, Est/S.-Est/Océanie
Western Asia		868	1 367	1 622	1 612	2 591	Asie occidentale
Singapore	VFR						**Singapour**
Total [65]		7 691 399	7 522 163	7 567 110	6 127 288	8 328 658	Totale [65]
Africa		92 003	81 150	70 117	55 997	70 626	Afrique
Americas		482 984	433 552	416 375	314 728	422 167	Amériques
Europe		1 138 518	1 124 435	1 112 156	885 146	1 081 336	Europe
Asia, East/S.East/Oceania		5 347 318	5 297 821	5 426 216	4 426 234	6 072 654	Asie, Est/S.-Est/Océanie
Southern Asia		516 293	508 302	490 262	415 151	626 153	Asie du Sud
Western Asia		70 628	71 516	46 770	29 844	55 449	Asie occidentale
Region not specified		43 655	5 387	5 214	188	273	Région non spécifiée
Slovakia	TCEN						**Slovaquie**
Total		1 045 614 [66]	1 219 099	1 398 740	1 386 791	1 401 189	Totale
Africa		2 670	3 131	2 960	2 581	2 482	Afrique
Americas		35 821	35 922	33 352	33 981	38 712	Amériques
Europe		980 250	1 147 970	1 326 492	1 316 120	1 316 705	Europe
Asia, East/S.East/Oceania		25 417	30 089	34 130	32 258	42 249	Asie, Est/S.-Est/Océanie
Southern Asia		1 117	1 515	1 437	1 305	384	Asie du Sud
Western Asia		238	334	224	241	314	Asie occidentale
Region not specified		101	138	145	305	343	Région non spécifiée
Slovenia	TCEN						**Slovénie**
Total		1 089 549	1 218 721	1 302 019	1 373 137	1 498 843	Totale
Americas		30 221	33 344	36 232	35 945	45 880	Amériques
Europe		1 037 797	1 159 864	1 235 856	1 307 775	1 410 662	Europe
Asia, East/S.East/Oceania		11 725	15 065	17 430	17 141	24 237	Asie, Est/S.-Est/Océanie
Region not specified		9 806	10 448	12 501	12 276	18 064	Région non spécifiée
South Africa	TFR						**Afrique du Sud**
Total [67]		5 872 243	5 787 368	6 429 583	6 504 890	6 677 839	Totale [67]
Africa		4 233 528	4 130 975	4 452 762	4 450 212	4 638 355	Afrique
Americas		248 353	241 991	254 586	262 496	290 625	Amériques
Europe		1 042 110	1 028 236	1 274 365	1 338 976	1 303 468	Europe
Asia, East/S.East/Oceania		192 324	193 955	229 128	224 610	241 750	Asie, Est/S.-Est/Océanie
Southern Asia		25 951	28 012	34 062	41 018	36 172	Asie du Sud
Western Asia		11 227	13 062	14 955	15 048	16 037	Asie occidentale
Region not specified		118 750	151 137	169 725	172 530	151 432	Région non spécifiée
Spain	TFR						**Espagne**
Total		47 897 915	50 093 557	52 326 766	50 853 822	52 429 836	Totale
Americas		2 518 590	2 174 344	2 079 643	1 893 950	2 079 065	Amériques

Country or area of destination and region of origin	Series Série	2000	2001	2002	2003	2004	Pays ou zone de destination et région de provenance
Europe		44 499 469	46 827 387	49 303 582	47 835 345	49 238 605	Europe
Asia, East/S.East/Oceania		300 828	265 047	240 637	237 392	150 583	Asie, Est/S.-Est/Océanie
Region not specified		579 028	826 779	702 904	887 135	961 583	Région non spécifiée
Sri Lanka	TFR						**Sri Lanka**
Total [2]		400 414	336 794	393 171	500 642	566 202	Totale [2]
Africa		894	952	1 611	1 991	1 855	Afrique
Americas		17 766	16 412	20 421	25 744	30 500	Amériques
Europe		267 664	211 049	208 374	265 802	298 776	Europe
Asia, East/S.East/Oceania		58 197	49 079	66 084	84 145	91 076	Asie, Est/S.-Est/Océanie
Southern Asia		51 552	53 758	90 189	116 171	133 532	Asie du Sud
Western Asia		4 341	5 544	6 492	6 789	10 463	Asie occidentale
Sudan	TFN						**Soudan**
Total		38 000	50 000	51 580	52 291	60 577	Totale
Africa		5 000	7 000	7 000	7 000	9 000	Afrique
Americas		4 000	4 000	...	...	...	Amériques
Europe		9 000	11 000	12 000	14 000	17 000	Europe
Asia, East/S.East/Oceania		7 000	10 000	13 000	14 000	17 000	Asie, Est/S.-Est/Océanie
Southern Asia		4 000	5 000	...	...	...	Asie du Sud
Western Asia		9 000	13 000		...	...	Asie occidentale
Region not specified		...	...	19 580	17 291	17 577	Région non spécifiée
Suriname	TFN						**Suriname**
Total [69]		56 843	54 341	60 223	82 298	74 887	Totale [69]
Africa		65	31	32	187	177	Afrique
Americas		7 909	3 362	4 307	6 903	7 986	Amériques
Europe		46 285	49 475	54 477	74 153	64 011	Europe
Asia, East/S.East/Oceania		2 187	1 375	1 306	998	2 522	Asie, Est/S.-Est/Océanie
Southern Asia		85	98	68	55	165	Asie du Sud
Region not specified		312	...	33	2	26	Région non spécifiée
Swaziland	THSR						**Swaziland**
Total [59]		280 870	283 177	255 927	218 813	352 040	Totale [59]
Africa		177 216	145 169	173 420	110 054	151 879	Afrique
Americas		10 823	20 217	10 380	11 092	4 968	Amériques
Europe		84 514	84 988	40 483	87 999	110 709	Europe
Asia, East/S.East/Oceania		7 053	5 676	5 244	2 343	3 485	Asie, Est/S.-Est/Océanie
Region not specified		1 264	27 127	26 400	7 325	80 999	Région non spécifiée
Sweden	TFR						**Suède**
Total [70]		...	7 431 000	7 459 000	7 627 000	...	Totale [70]
Africa		...	37 000	42 000	46 000	...	Afrique
Americas		...	546 000	413 000	467 000	...	Amériques
Europe		...	6 437 000	6 656 000	6 696 000	...	Europe
Asia, East/S.East/Oceania		...	411 000	348 000	380 000	...	Asie, Est/S.-Est/Océanie
Region not specified		...	...	...	38 000	...	Région non spécifiée
Switzerland	THSR						**Suisse**
Total		7 821 158	7 454 855	6 867 696	6 530 108	...	Totale
Africa		77 345	79 164	74 195	72 786	...	Afrique
Americas		1 198 553	1 026 667	871 279	757 015	...	Amériques
Europe		5 343 044	5 277 161	4 906 368	4 821 157	...	Europe
Asia, East/S.East/Oceania		1 079 068	937 554	865 244	727 005	...	Asie, Est/S.-Est/Océanie
Southern Asia		71 912	72 291	80 430	84 685	...	Asie du Sud
Western Asia		51 236	62 018	70 180	67 460	...	Asie occidentale
Syrian Arab Republic	TCEN						**Rép. arabe syrienne**
Total [71,72]		...	...	1 657 779	2 084 956	3 029 964	Totale [71,72]
Africa		...	...	63 008	73 487	89 664	Afrique
Americas		...	...	16 577	43 901	57 032	Amériques
Europe		...	...	113 436	204 445	313 956	Europe
Asia, East/S.East/Oceania		...	...	6 228	25 897	36 852	Asie, Est/S.-Est/Océanie
Southern Asia		...	...	293 628	228 357	217 947	Asie du Sud
Western Asia		...	...	1 055 832	1 470 289	2 259 703	Asie occidentale
Region not specified		...	...	109 070	38 580	54 810	Région non spécifiée

Country or area of destination and region of origin	Series Série	2000	2001	2002	2003	2004	Pays ou zone de destination et région de provenance
Tajikistan	VFR						**Tadjikistan**
Total		7 673	5 200	...	...	...	Totale
Africa		72	...	...	...	...	Afrique
Americas		796	887	...	...	...	Amériques
Europe		4 921	3 300	...	...	...	Europe
Asia, East/S.East/Oceania		1 093	467	...	...	...	Asie, Est/S.-Est/Océanie
Southern Asia		668	512	...	...	...	Asie du Sud
Western Asia		123	34	...	...	...	Asie occidentale
Thailand	TFR						**Thaïlande**
Total [1]		9 578 826	10 132 509	10 872 976	10 082 109	11 737 413	Totale [1]
Africa		80 389	90 963	89 449	67 117	82 711	Afrique
Americas		584 967	604 041	640 143	576 589	692 827	Amériques
Europe		2 242 466	2 395 806	2 549 507	2 320 810	2 706 062	Europe
Asia, East/S.East/Oceania		6 134 335	6 491 790	6 955 047	6 510 374	7 500 931	Asie, Est/S.-Est/Océanie
Southern Asia		339 413	333 248	390 745	390 335	468 316	Asie du Sud
Western Asia		127 053	146 102	174 176	139 228	199 856	Asie occidentale
Region not specified		70 203	70 559	73 909	77 656	86 710	Région non spécifiée
TFYR of Macedonia	TCEN						**L'ex-R.y. Macédoine**
Total		224 016	98 946	122 861	157 692	165 306	Totale
Americas		17 023	7 846	7 773	8 373	8 362	Amériques
Europe		198 298	87 396	110 878	143 387	151 215	Europe
Asia, East/S.East/Oceania		2 803	1 082	1 566	2 362	2 143	Asie, Est/S.-Est/Océanie
Region not specified		5 892	2 622	2 644	3 570	3 586	Région non spécifiée
Togo	THSR						**Togo**
Total		59 541	56 629	57 539	60 592	82 686	Totale
Africa		29 546	33 554	28 636	31 334	43 842	Afrique
Americas		2 050	2 343	1 975	1 785	2 738	Amériques
Europe		25 376	17 680	24 097	24 484	30 018	Europe
Asia, East/S.East/Oceania		1 271	1 311	1 125	1 452	3 492	Asie, Est/S.-Est/Océanie
Western Asia		1 203	1 619	1 680	1 495	2 500	Asie occidentale
Region not specified		95	122	26	42	96	Région non spécifiée
Tonga	TFR						**Tonga**
Total [3]		34 694	32 386	36 588	40 110	...	Totale [3]
Africa		53	55	92	...	...	Afrique
Americas		8 005	6 706	7 860	7 930	...	Amériques
Europe		5 977	4 601	4 082	4 131	...	Europe
Asia, East/S.East/Oceania		20 557	20 920	24 477	27 932	...	Asie, Est/S.-Est/Océanie
Southern Asia		102	104	77	...	...	Asie du Sud
Region not specified		...	...	...	117	...	Région non spécifiée
Trinidad and Tobago	TFR						**Trinité-et-Tobago**
Total [3]		398 559	383 101	384 212	409 069	442 596	Totale [3]
Africa		996	935	997	935	1 017	Afrique
Americas		309 122	285 882	308 018	324 175	347 181	Amériques
Europe		82 661	89 002	71 133	79 236	89 512	Europe
Asia, East/S.East/Oceania		3 507	3 874	2 670	3 313	2 925	Asie, Est/S.-Est/Océanie
Southern Asia		1 196	1 492	1 164	1 136	1 411	Asie du Sud
Western Asia		279	262	219	239	221	Asie occidentale
Region not specified		798	1 654	11	35	329	Région non spécifiée
Tunisia	TFN						**Tunisie**
Total [2]		5 057 513	5 387 300	5 063 538	5 114 303	5 997 929	Totale [2]
Africa		666 199	676 236	786 053	872 251	984 538	Afrique
Americas		31 275	28 486	21 920	22 192	29 008	Amériques
Europe		3 615 793	3 609 526	2 918 526	2 840 307	3 482 052	Europe
Asia, East/S.East/Oceania		8 343	7 804	7 167	6 833	7 109	Asie, Est/S.-Est/Océanie
Western Asia		712 545	1 046 184	1 310 607	1 355 878	1 471 752	Asie occidentale
Region not specified		23 358	19 064	19 265	16 842	23 470	Région non spécifiée
Turkey	TFN						**Turquie**
Total		9 585 695	10 782 673	12 789 827	13 340 956	16 826 062	Totale
Africa		106 289	118 870	130 758	119 122	131 148	Afrique

Country or area of destination and region of origin [+]	Series Série	2000	2001	2002	2003	2004	Pays ou zone de destination et région de provenance [+]
Americas		360 920	326 732	253 804	213 136	282 586	Amériques
Europe		8 234 233	9 473 313	11 359 447	11 871 694	14 946 162	Europe
Asia, East/S.East/Oceania		233 669	247 202	280 607	241 996	288 326	Asie, Est/S.-Est/Océanie
Southern Asia		397 348	342 218	450 787	522 054	660 787	Asie du Sud
Western Asia		242 352	262 894	303 860	359 281	498 095	Asie occidentale
Region not specified		10 884	11 444	10 564	13 673	18 958	Région non spécifiée
Turks and Caicos Islands	TFR						**Iles Turques et Caïques**
Total		152 291	165 920	154 961	...	...	Totale
Americas		136 211	148 025	140 349	...	...	Amériques
Europe		11 829	11 086	10 634	...	...	Europe
Asia, East/S.East/Oceania		113	57	35	...	...	Asie, Est/S.-Est/Océanie
Region not specified		4 138	6 752	3 943	...	...	Région non spécifiée
Tuvalu	TFN						**Tuvalu**
Total		1 079	1 140	1 313	1 377	1 290	Totale
Americas		59	65	92	130	79	Amériques
Europe		62	102	108	97	108	Europe
Asia, East/S.East/Oceania		922	957	1 075	1 101	1 043	Asie, Est/S.-Est/Océanie
Region not specified		36	16	38	49	60	Région non spécifiée
Uganda	TFR						**Ouganda**
Total		192 755	205 287	254 212	304 656	512 379	Totale
Africa		131 687	149 907	192 278	233 043	405 706	Afrique
Americas		11 947	12 922	14 785	16 409	23 438	Amériques
Europe		36 050	30 395	33 850	39 207	48 847	Europe
Asia, East/S.East/Oceania		4 899	4 757	4 188	4 845	8 150	Asie, Est/S.-Est/Océanie
Southern Asia		5 538	5 514	6 439	7 647	12 139	Asie du Sud
Western Asia		2 032	1 792	1 836	1 976	3 133	Asie occidentale
Region not specified		602	...	836	1 529	10 966	Région non spécifiée
Ukraine	TFR						**Ukraine**
Total		6 430 940	9 174 165	10 516 665	12 513 883	...	Totale
Africa		15 296	5 227	4 748	12 367	...	Afrique
Americas		70 542	64 096	52 632	83 451	...	Amériques
Europe		6 283 415	9 061 051	10 408 714	12 345 396	...	Europe
Asia, East/S.East/Oceania		26 625	17 107	21 900	26 362	...	Asie, Est/S.-Est/Océanie
Southern Asia		11 363	7 453	9 866	13 978	...	Asie du Sud
Western Asia		18 436	13 399	14 777	18 720	...	Asie occidentale
Region not specified		5 263	5 832	4 028	13 609	...	Région non spécifiée
United Arab Emirates	THSN						**Emirats arabes unis**
Total [73]		3 906 545	4 133 531	5 445 367	5 871 023	...	Totale [73]
Africa		173 601	218 162	310 722	306 872	...	Afrique
Americas		139 474	149 802	238 749	254 362	...	Amériques
Europe		1 076 813	1 115 373	1 468 015	1 584 792	...	Europe
Asia, East/S.East/Oceania		263 609	284 878	395 061	427 506	...	Asie, Est/S.-Est/Océanie
Southern Asia		568 453	590 378	807 094	921 698	...	Asie du Sud
Western Asia		1 088 753	1 220 738	1 556 533	1 583 258	...	Asie occidentale
Region not specified		595 842	554 200	669 193	792 535	...	Région non spécifiée
United Kingdom	VFR						**Royaume-Uni**
Total		25 211 000	22 835 000	24 181 000	24 715 000	27 754 000	Totale
Africa		618 000	630 000	631 000	569 000	639 000	Afrique
Americas		5 287 000	4 582 000	4 619 000	4 326 000	4 692 000	Amériques
Europe		16 307 000	15 060 000	16 409 000	17 371 000	19 582 000	Europe
Asia, East/S.East/Oceania		2 256 000	1 834 000	1 854 000	1 809 000	2 086 000	Asie, Est/S.-Est/Océanie
Southern Asia		314 000	326 000	308 000	294 000	371 000	Asie du Sud
Western Asia		429 000	403 000	360 000	346 000	384 000	Asie occidentale
United Rep. of Tanzania	VFR						**Rép.-Unie de Tanzanie**
Total		501 669	525 122	575 296	576 198	582 807	Totale
Africa		201 934	213 013	249 601	267 940	256 455	Afrique
Americas		49 001	45 544	59 077	49 781	53 437	Amériques
Europe		157 470	162 225	191 982	191 025	221 865	Europe
Asia, East/S.East/Oceania		38 299	46 605	30 087	27 208	22 928	Asie, Est/S.-Est/Océanie

68 Tourist/visitor arrivals by region of origin (*continued*)
Arrivées de touristes/visiteurs par région de provenance (*suite*)

Country or area of destination and region of origin	Series Série	2000	2001	2002	2003	2004	Pays ou zone de destination et région de provenance
Southern Asia		24 626	28 060	27 867	26 502	16 528	Asie du Sud
Western Asia		30 339	29 675	16 682	13 742	11 594	Asie occidentale
United States	TFR						**Etats-Unis**
Total		51 236 701	46 926 868	43 581 707	41 218 213	46 085 257	Totale
Africa		295 090	286 783	241 011	236 067	240 488	Afrique
Americas		30 356 382	29 597 703	28 036 856	26 368 298	29 194 830	Amériques
Europe		12 052 331	9 906 957	8 964 202	8 981 711	10 055 657	Europe
Asia, East/S.East/Oceania		7 921 004	6 535 276	5 888 710	5 192 366	6 086 708	Asie, Est/S.-Est/Océanie
Southern Asia		362 634	362 792	324 315	329 660	370 315	Asie du Sud
Western Asia		249 260	237 357	126 613	110 111	137 259	Asie occidentale
United States Virgin Is.	THSN						**Iles Vierges américaines**
Total		607 342	597 437	585 684	623 394	608 125	Totale
Africa		179	170	828	134	287	Afrique
Americas		533 421	540 598	494 324	531 270	565 827	Amériques
Europe		12 450	8 708	6 144	7 747	15 814	Europe
Asia, East/S.East/Oceania		798	389	333	363	377	Asie, Est/S.-Est/Océanie
Region not specified		60 494	47 572	84 055	83 880	25 820	Région non spécifiée
Uruguay	VFN						**Uruguay**
Total [1]		2 235 887	2 136 446	1 353 872	1 508 055	1 870 858	Totale [1]
Americas		1 758 399	1 708 380	1 030 738	1 159 580	1 457 944	Amériques
Europe		85 039	70 009	56 159	73 230	97 223	Europe
Asia, East/S.East/Oceania		6 515	5 531	5 618	6 230	7 221	Asie, Est/S.-Est/Océanie
Western Asia		201	2 627	170	131	489	Asie occidentale
Region not specified		385 733	349 899	261 187	268 884	307 981	Région non spécifiée
Uzbekistan	TFR						**Ouzbékistan**
Total		301 900	344 900	331 500	231 000	261 600	Totale
Africa		...	1 000	1 000	1 000	1 000	Afrique
Americas		6 000	10 000	4 100	2 000	12 000	Amériques
Europe		72 000	109 000	99 800	51 000	68 600	Europe
Asia, East/S.East/Oceania		195 900	192 900	195 100	145 000	140 000	Asie, Est/S.-Est/Océanie
Southern Asia		7 000	8 000	8 000	8 000	10 000	Asie du Sud
Western Asia		21 000	24 000	23 500	24 000	30 000	Asie occidentale
Vanuatu	TFR						**Vanuatu**
Total		57 591	53 300	49 461	50 400	61 454	Totale
Americas		1 547	1 413	1 438	1 625	1 954	Amériques
Europe		3 401	2 683	2 948	3 003	3 388	Europe
Asia, East/S.East/Oceania		51 803	48 234	44 256	44 876	55 027	Asie, Est/S.-Est/Océanie
Region not specified		840	970	819	896	1 085	Région non spécifiée
Venezuela (Bolivarian Rep. of)	TFN						**Venezuela (Rép. bolivar. du)**
Total		469 047	584 399	431 677	336 974	*491 754	Totale
Africa		380	819	518	438	640	Afrique
Americas		172 071	280 101	185 276	154 334	217 699	Amériques
Europe		288 037	290 914	237 250	175 159	263 531	Europe
Asia, East/S.East/Oceania		3 286	6 835	3 756	3 201	4 475	Asie, Est/S.-Est/Océanie
Southern Asia		256	468	302	270	344	Asie du Sud
Western Asia		462	643	432	371	492	Asie occidentale
Region not specified		4 555	4 619	4 143	3 201	4 573	Région non spécifiée
Viet Nam	VFR						**Viet Nam**
Total [12]		2 140 000	2 330 050	2 627 988	2 428 735	2 927 873	Totale [12]
Africa		1 707	...	...	...	...	Afrique
Americas		241 708	266 433	303 519	258 991	326 286	Amériques
Europe		271 183	307 722	343 360	293 636	354 735	Europe
Asia, East/S.East/Oceania		1 398 885	1 484 799	1 694 624	1 669 541	2 008 366	Asie, Est/S.-Est/Océanie
Southern Asia		6 639	8 086	...	...		Asie du Sud
Region not specified		219 878	263 010	286 485	206 567	238 486	Région non spécifiée
Yemen	THSN						**Yémen**
Total		72 836	75 579	98 020	154 667	273 732	Totale
Africa		5 658	4 867	3 045	8 627	7 798	Afrique
Americas		8 161	2 879	4 429	12 932	17 099	Amériques

Country or area of destination and region of origin +	Série	2000	2001	2002	2003	2004	Pays ou zone de destination et région de provenance
Europe		24 825	26 920	15 828	13 033	28 608	Europe
Asia, East/S.East/Oceania		8 788	6 209	11 303	16 666	41 493	Asie, Est/S.-Est/Océanie
Western Asia		25 404	34 704	63 415	103 409	178 734	Asie occidentale
Zambia	TFR						**Zambie**
Total		457 419	*491 991	*565 073	412 675	515 000	Totale
Africa		294 479	316 736	363 783	298 485	366 918	Afrique
Americas		27 469	29 546	33 935	22 667	29 053	Amériques
Europe		105 409	113 375	130 218	71 363	91 863	Europe
Asia, East/S.East/Oceania		27 709	29 803	34 230	17 297	23 107	Asie, Est/S.-Est/Océanie
Southern Asia		2 353	2 531	2 907	2 863	4 059	Asie du Sud
Zimbabwe	VFR						**Zimbabwe**
Total		1 966 582	2 217 429	2 041 202	2 256 205	1 854 488	Totale
Africa		1 496 802	1 737 186	1 760 097	1 942 052	1 523 090	Afrique
Americas		117 532	111 727	65 194	61 181	75 161	Amériques
Europe		271 570	265 236	149 995	169 938	155 767	Europe
Asia, East/S.East/Oceania		80 678	103 280	65 916	68 414	90 405	Asie, Est/S.-Est/Océanie
Southern Asia		...	...	...	12 411	6 316	Asie du Sud
Western Asia		...	...	...	2 209	3 749	Asie occidentale

Source

World Tourism Organization (UNWTO), Madrid, UNWTO statistics database and *Yearbook of Tourism Statistics*, 2005 edition.

Notes

+   For a listing of the Member States of the regions of origin, see Annex I, with the following exceptions:

Africa includes the countries and territories listed under Africa in Annex I but excludes Egypt, Guinea-Bissau, Liberia, Libyan Arab Jamahiriya, Mozambique and Western Sahara.

Americas is as shown in Annex I, but excludes Falkland Islands (Malvinas), French Guyana, Greenland and Saint Pierre and Miquelon.

Europe is as shown in Annex I, but excludes Andorra, Channel Islands, Faeroe Islands, Holy See, Isle of Man and Svalbard and Jan Mayen Islands. The Europe group also includes Armenia, Azerbaijan, Cyprus, Israel, Kyrgyzstan, Turkey and Turkmenistan.

Asia, East and South East/Oceania includes the countries and territories listed under Eastern Asia and South-eastern Asia in Annex I (except for Timor-Leste), and under Oceania except for Christmas Island, Cocos Island, Norfolk Island, Nauru, Wake Island, Johnston Island, Midway Islands, Pitcairn, Tokelau and Wallis and Futuna Islands. The Asia, East and South East/Oceania group also includes Taiwan Province of China.

Southern Asia is as shown in Annex I under South-central Asia, but excludes Kazakhstan, Kyrgyzstan, Tajikistan, Turkmenistan and Uzbekistan.

Western Asia is as shown in Annex I but excludes Armenia, Azerbaijan, Cyprus, Georgia, Israel, Occupied Palestinian Territory, and Turkey. The Western Asia group also includes Egypt and the Libyan Arab Jamahiriya.

TFN: Arrivals of non-resident tourists at national borders (excluding same-day visitors), by nationality

TFR: Arrivals of non-resident tourists at national borders (excluding same- day visitors), by country of residence.

TCEN: Arrivals of non-resident tourists in all types of accommodation establishments, by nationality.

Source

Organisation mondiale du tourisme (OMT), Madrid, la base de données de l'OMT, et *Annuaire des statistiques du tourisme*, 2005 édition.

Notes

+   On se reportera à l'Annexe I pour les États Membres classés dans les différentes régions de provenance, avec les exceptions ci-après ;

Afrique – Comprend les États et territoires énumérés à l'Annexe I, sauf l'Égypte, la Guinée-Bissau, le Libéria, la Jamahiriya arabe libyenne, le Mozambique et le Sahara occidental.

Amériques – Comprend les États et territoires énumérés à l'Annexe I, sauf les îles Falkland (Malvinas), le Groënland, la Guyane française et Saint-Pierre-et-Miquelon.

Europe – Comprend les États et territoires énumérés à l'Annexe I, sauf l'Andorre, les îles Anglo-normandes, les îles Féroé, l'île de Man, le Saint-Siège et les îles Svalbard et Jan Mayen. Le Groupe comprend en revanche l'Arménie, l'Azerbaïdjan, Chypre, Israël, l'Kirghizistan, la Turquie et le Turkménistan.

L'Asie de l'Est et du Sud-Est/Océanie – Comprend les États et territoires énumérés à l'Annexe I dans les Groupes Asie de l'Est et Asie de Sud-Est sauf le Timor-Leste, et les États et territoires énumérés dans le Groupe Océanie sauf les îles Christmas, les îles Cocos, l'île Johnston, les îles Midway, Nauru, l'îles Norfolk, Pitcairn, Tokélou, l'île Wake et Wallis-et-Futuna. Le Groupe Asie de l'Est et du Sud-Est/Océanie comprend en revanche la Province chinoise de Taiwan.

Asie du Sud – Comprend les États et territoires énumérés à l'Annexe I, sauf le Kazakhstan, le Kirghizistan, l'Ouzbékistan, le Tadjikistan et le Turkménistan.

Asie occidentale – Comprend les États et territoires énumérés à l'Annexe I, sauf l'Arménie, l'Azerbaïdjan, Chypre, la Géorgie, Israël, le territoire Palestinien Occupé et la Turquie. Le Groupe comprend en revanche l'Égypte et la Jamahiriya arabe libyenne.

TFN : Arrivées de touristes non résidents aux frontières nationales (a l'exclusion de visiteurs de la journée), par nationalité.

TFR : Arrivées de touristes non résidents aux frontières nationales (a l'exclusion de visiteurs de la journée), par pays de résidence.

TCEN : Arrivées de touristes non résidents dans tous les types d'établissements d'hébergement, par nationalité.

TCER: Arrivals of non-resident tourists in all types of accommodation establishments, by country of residence.

THSN: Arrivals of non-resident tourists in hotels and similar establishments, by nationality.

THSR: Arrivals of non-resident tourists in hotels and similar establishments, by country of residence.

VFN: Arrivals of non-resident visitors at national borders (including tourists and same-day visitors), by nationality.

VFR: Arrivals of non-resident visitors at national borders (including tourists and same-day visitors), by country of residence.

Note: Footnotes on the totals also apply to the other regions.

[1] Arrivals of nationals residing abroad are included in the total and are all accounted for in "Region not specified" only.

[2] Excluding nationals of the country residing abroad.

[3] Air arrivals.

[4] Excluding nationals residing abroad and crew members.

[5] Including private accommodation.

[6] Organized tourism.

[7] Hotels establishments, campings, holiday centres, holiday villages and specific categories of accommodation.

[8] Estimates.

[9] International tourist arrivals in hotels of regional capitals.

[10] Including transit visitors.

[11] Excluding children without own passports.

[12] Arrivals of nationals residing abroad are included in the total and are also accounted for in the individual regions.

[13] Air arrivals at Pochentong and Siem Reap Airports. "Region not specified" 1998 to 2001: including arrivals at Siem Reap Airport by direct-flights; 2000: 87,012; 2001: 133,688.

[14] Arrivals in the Phreah Vihear Province are included in the total and are all accounted for in "Region not specified": 2004 - 67,843.

[15] Different types of methodological changes that affect the estimates for 2000 and 2001 for expenditures and characteristics of International Tourists to Canada, have been introduced in 2002. Therefore, Statistics Canada advises not to compare the estimates for 2000 and 2001 with the years prior because of these methodological changes for the non-count estimates.

[16] For statistical purposes, the data for China do not include those for the Hong Kong Special Administrative Region (Hong Kong SAR), Macao Special Administrative Region (Macao SAR) and Taiwan Province of China.

[17] Including ethnic Chinese arriving from Hong Kong Special Administrative Region of China, Macao Special Administrative Region of China and Taiwan Province of China and overseas Chinese, of which most same-day visitors are from Hong Kong Special Administrative Region of China and Macao Special Administrative Region of China.

[18] Including arrivals by sea, land and by air (helicopter). Including stateless and Chinese people who do not have permanent residency in Hong Kong SAR, China.

[19] Source: "Departamento Administrativo de Seguridad (DAS)".

[20] Air and sea arrivals.

[21] Including arrivals in ports of nautical tourism.

TCER : Arrivées de touristes non résidents dans tous les types d'établissements d'hébergement, par pays de résidence.

THSN : Arrivées de touristes non résidents dans les hôtels et établissements assimilés, par nationalité.

THSR : Arrivées de touristes non résidents dans les hôtels et établissements assimilés, par pays de résidence.

VFN : Arrivées de visiteurs non résidents aux frontières nationales (y compris touristes et visiteurs de la journée), par nationalité.

VFR : Arrivées de visiteurs non résidents aux frontières nationales (y compris touristes et visiteurs de la journée), par pays de résidence.

Note : Les notes de pied en les totales se réfèrent aussi aux autres régions.

[1] Les arrivées de nationaux résidant à l'étranger sont comprises dans le total, et sont toutes comptabilisées uniquement dans la catégorie "Région non spécifiée" seulement.

[2] A l'exclusion des nationaux du pays résidant à l'étranger.

[3] Arrivées par voie aérienne.

[4] A l'exclusion des nationaux du pays résidant à l'étranger et des membres des équipages.

[5] Y compris hébergement privé.

[6] Tourisme organisé.

[7] Établissements hôteliers, terrains de camping, centres de vacances, villages de vacances et catégories spécifiques d'hébergement.

[8] Estimations.

[9] Arrivées de touristes internationaux dans les hôtels des capitales de département.

[10] Y compris les visiteurs en transit.

[11] A l'exclusion d'enfants sans passeports personnels.

[12] Les arrivées de nationaux résidant à l'étranger sont comprises dans le total, et comptabilisées aussi dans chacune des régions.

[13] Arrivées par voie aérienne aux aéroports de Pochentong et de Siem Reap. "Région non spécifiée" 1998 à 2001 : y compris les arrivées à l'aéroport de Siem Reap en vols directs; 2000 : 87.012; 2001 : 133.688.

[14] Les arrivées dans la province de Phreah Vihear sont comprises dans le total, et sont toutes prises en compte dans "Région non spécifiée" : 2004 – 67.843.

[15] En 2002, il a été adopté différents types de changements méthodologiques qui ont eu des effets sur les estimations des dépenses et des caractéristiques des touristes internationaux ayant visité le Canada en 2000 et 2001. Pour 2000 et 2001, Statistique Canada conseille par conséquent de ne pas comparer les estimations ne reposant pas sur des comptages aux données des années précédentes.

[16] Pour la présentation des statistiques, les données pour Chine ne comprennent pas la Région Administrative Spéciale de Hong Kong (Hong Kong RAS), la Région Administrative Spéciale de Macao (Macao RAS) et la province de Taïwan.

[17] Y compris les arrivées de personnes d'origine ethnique chinoise en provenance de la région administrative spéciale de Hong Kong, de la région administrative spéciale de Macao et de la province chinoise de Taïwan, et chinois de l'étranger, la plupart visiteurs de la journée (excursionnistes) en provenance de la région administrative spéciale de Hong Kong et de la région administrative spéciale de Macao.

[18] Y compris les arrivées par mer, terre et air (hélicoptère). Y compris les aptrides et les chinois qui ne résident pas de manière permanente à Hong Kong SAR, Chine.

[19] Source : Departamento Administrativo de Seguridad (DAS).

[20] Arrivées par voie aérienne et maritime.

[21] Y compris les arrivées dans des ports à tourisme nautique.

[22] New coverage from 2000.

[23] Excluding the passengers at Herrera airport.

[24] Arrivals through all ports of entry.

[25] Due to a change in the methodology, data are not comparable to previous years.

[26] Figure estimated by the Institut de la Statistique (ISPF). Due to problems of E/D card distributions, the breakdown by country of origin could not be elaborated.

[27] Arrivals of non-resident tourists at Libreville airport.

[28] Charter tourists only.

[29] Data based on surveys.

[30] Arrivals at 175 traditional hotel establishments.

[31] Estimates for continental Guadeloupe (without Saint-Martin and Saint-Barthelemy).

[32] Air arrivals at Conakry airport.

[33] Arrivals to Timehri airport only.

[34] Collective accommodation establishments.

[35] Departures.

[36] Due to the introduction of Schengen in March 2001, the data collection on arrivals and departures at the Icelandic borders was changed. From 2002 this data collection is done by the Icelandic Tourist Board.

[37] Excluding seasonal and border workers.

[38] Excluding nationals of the country residing abroad. All data are estimates, projected using 1989 market shares. Source: Economic survey various years.

[39] Including nationals residing abroad and crew members.

[40] New data source: Department of Customs Control.

[41] Excluding Syrian nationals, Palestinians and students.

[42] Travellers.

[43] Preliminary data.

[44] Including Singapore residents crossing the frontier by road through Johore Causeway.

[45] Data based on departures by air and by sea.

[46] Arrivals in the States of Kosrae, Chuuk, Pohnpei and Yap.

[47] Including tourist arrivals through border entry points to Yangon.

[48] Data regarding to short term movements are compiled from a random sample of passenger declarations. Including nationals of the country residing abroad. Source: Statistics New Zealand, External Migration.

[49] Including Niuans residing usually in New Zealand.

[50] Figures are based on "The Guest survey" carried out by Institute of Transport Economics.

[51] Arrivals to the West Bank only; excluding Jerusalem and the Gaza Strip due to the lack of control on the borders of these regions.

[52] Air arrivals (Palau International Airport).

[53] Total number of visitors broken down by permanent residence who arrived in Panama at Tocumen International Airport.

[54] Inbound and outbound tourism survey - Central Bank of Paraguay.

[22] Nouvelle couverture depuis 2000.

[23] A l'exclusion des passagers à l'aéroport de Herrera.

[24] Arrivées à travers tous les ports d'entrée.

[25] Dû à un changement dans la méthodologie, l'information n'est pas comparable à celle des années précédentes.

[26] Estimation réalisée par l'Institut de la Statistique (ISPF). En raison de problèmes de distribution de formulaires, la ventilation par pays d'origine n'a pas pu être réalisée.

[27] Arrivées de touristes non résidents à l'aéroport de Libreville.

[28] Arrivées en vols à la demande seulement.

[29] Données obtenues au moyen d'enquêtes.

[30] Arrivées dans 175 établissements hôteliers.

[31] Estimations pour la Guadeloupe continentale (sans Saint-Martin et Saint-Barthélemy).

[32] Arrivées par voie aérienne à l'aéroport de Conakry.

[33] Arrivées à l'aéroport de Timehri seulement.

[34] Etablissements d'hébergement collectif.

[35] Départs.

[36] Suite à l'application des accords de Schengen à partir de mars 2001, la collecte des données sur les arrivées et les départs aux postes-frontières islandais a subi des changements. Depuis 2002, le Icelandic Tourist Board est chargé de la collecte de ces données.

[37] A l'exclusion des travailleurs saisoniers et frontaliers.

[38] A l'exclusion des nationaux du pays résidant à l'étranger. Toutes les données représentent des estimations, dont la projection a été faite sur la base des taux de marché de l'année 1989. Source : Enquête économique de diverses années.

[39] Y compris les nationaux résidant à l'étranger et membres des équipages.

[40] Nouvelle source d'information : Département du Contrôle douanier.

[41] A l'exclusion des ressortissants syriens, palestiniens et sous-études.

[42] Voyaeurs.

[43] Données préliminaires.

[44] Y compris les résidents de Singapour traversant la frontière par voie terrestre à travers le Johore Causeway.

[45] Données tirées des départs par voies aérienne et maritime.

[46] Arrivées dans les États de Kosrae, Chuuk, Pohnpei et Yap.

[47] Comprenant les arrivées de touristes aux postes-frontières de Yangon.

[48] Les données relatives aux mouvements de courte durée sont obtenues à partir d'un échantillon aléatoire de déclarations des passagers. Y compris les nationaux du pays résidant à l'étranger. Source : Statistiques de la Nouvelle Zélande, Immigration.

[49] Y compris les nationaux de Niue résidant habituellement en Nouvelle-Zélande.

[50] Les chiffres se fondent sur "l'enquête auprès de la clientèle" de l'Institut d'économie des transports.

[51] Uniquement arrivées en Cisjordanie; Jérusalem et la bande de Gaza sont exclus en raison du manque de contrôle aux frontières dans ces zones.

[52] Arrivées par voie aérienne (Aéroport international de Palau).

[53] Nombre total de visiteurs arrivées au Panama par l'aéroport international de Tocúmen.

[54] Enquête sur le tourisme récepteur et sur le tourisme émetteur – Banque Centrale du Paraguay.

⁵⁵ E/D cards in the Silvio Petirossi airport and passenger counts at the national border crossings - National Police and SENATUR.

⁵⁶ Preliminary estimates.

⁵⁷ Including arrivals from abroad to insular possessions of Madeira and the Azores.

⁵⁸ Arrivals by air. Fiscal year July to June. Source: Junta de Planificación de Puerto Rico.

⁵⁹ Arrivals in hotels only.

⁶⁰ Visitors who enjoyed the services of the economic agents officially registered under tourism activity and accommodation (excluding the regions of the left bank of the Dniestr and the municipality of Bender).

⁶¹ January-November.

⁶² Excluding Netherlands Antillean residents.

⁶³ Arrivals at Princess Juliana International airport. Including visitors to St. Maarten (the French side of the island).

⁶⁴ Including Italian visitors.

⁶⁵ Excluding Malaysian citizens arriving by land.

⁶⁶ Excluding arrivals in private accommodation = 7,086.

⁶⁷ Excluding arrivals by work and contract workers.

⁶⁸ Including arrivals by purpose of holiday, business, study, work, transit, border traffic and contract workers.

⁶⁹ Arrivals at Zanderij Airport.

⁷⁰ Data according to IBIS-Survey (Incoming Visitors to Sweden) during the years 2001 to 2003, (no data collected before 2001 or after 2003). Source: Swedish Tourist Authority and Statistics Sweden.

⁷¹ Data source: The survey of Incoming Tourism in 2002 and 2004.

⁷² Excluding private accommodation.

⁷³ Domestic tourism and arrivals of nationals residing abroad are included in the total and are all accounted for in "region not specified" only.

⁵⁵ Cartes d'embarquement et de débarquement à l'aéroport Silvio Petirossi et comptages des passagers lors du franchissement des frontières nationales – Police Nationale et SENATUR.

⁵⁶ Estimations préliminaires.

⁵⁷ Y compris les arrivées en provenance de l'étranger aux possessions insulaires de Madère et des Açores.

⁵⁸ Arrivées par voie aérienne. Année fiscale de juillet à juin. Source : Junta de Planificación de Puerto Rico.

⁵⁹ Arrivées dans les hôtels uniquement.

⁶⁰ Visiteurs qui ont bénéficié des services des agents économiques officiellement enregistrés avec le type d'activité tourisme et des unités d'hébergement qui leur appartiennent (à l'exception des régions de la partie gauche du Dniestr et de la municipalité de Bender).

⁶¹ Janvier-novembre.

⁶² A l'exclusion des résidents des Antilles Néerlandaises.

⁶³ Arrivées à l'aéroport international Princess Juliana. Y compris les visiteurs à Saint-Martin (partie française de l'île).

⁶⁴ Y compris les visiteurs italiens.

⁶⁵ Non compris les arrivées de malaysiens par voie terrestre.

⁶⁶ A l'exclusion des arrivées dans l'hébergement privé = 7.086.

⁶⁷ À l'exclusion des arrivées par travail et les travailleurs contractuels.

⁶⁸ Y compris les arrivées par motif de vacances, affaires, études, travail, transit, trafic frontalier et travailleurs contractuels.

⁶⁹ Arrivées à l'aéroport de Zanderij.

⁷⁰ Données reposant sur l'enquête IBIS (auprès des visiteurs du tourisme récepteur) portant sur les années 2001 à 2003 (aucune donnée n'a été collectée avant 2001 ni après 2003). Source : Swedish Tourist Authority et Statistics Sweden.

⁷¹ Source des données : enquête du tourisme récepteur en 2002 et 2004.

⁷² À l'exclusion de l'hébergement chez des particuliers.

⁷³ Les touristes nationaux et les arrivées de nationaux résidant à l'étranger sont compris dans le total, et sont tous pris en compte uniquement dans "région non spécifiée".

Tourist/visitor arrivals and tourism expenditure

Arrivées de touristes/visiteurs et dépenses touristiques

Country or area Pays ou zone	Number of tourist/visitor arrivals (thousands) Nombre d'arrivées de touristes/visiteurs (milliers)					Tourism expenditure (million US dollars) t Dépenses touristiques (millions de dollars E. -U.) t				
	2000	2001	2002	2003	2004	2000	2001	2002	2003	2004
Albania Albanie	32[1]	34[1]	36[1]	41[1]	42[1]	398	451	492	537	756[2]
Algeria Algérie	866[3,4]	901[3,4]	988[3,4]	1 166[3,4]	1 234[3,4]	102[2]	100[2]	110[2]	112[2]	178[2]
American Samoa [5] Samoa américaines [5]	44	36	...	...	...	...	...	...	...	...
Andorra [5] Andorre [5]	2 949	3 516	3 387	3 138	2 791	...	...	...	...	...
Angola Angola	51[5]	67[5]	91[5]	107[5]	194[5]	34	36	51	63	82
Anguilla Anguilla	44[5,6]	48[5,6]	44[5,6]	47[5,6]	54[5,6]	56[7]	62[7]	57[7]	60[2,7]	69[2,7]
Antigua and Barbuda Antigua-et-Barbuda	207[3,5]	193[3,5]	198[3,5]	224[3,5]	245[3,5]	291[7]	272[7]	274[7]	300[7,8]	337[7,8]
Argentina Argentine	2 909[5,6]	2 620[5,6]	2 820[5,6]	2 995[5,6]	3 353[5,6]	3 195	2 756	1 716	2 306	2 990
Armenia Arménie	45[9]	123[9]	162[9]	206[9]	263[9]	52	81	82	90	103
Aruba Aruba	721[5]	691[5]	643[5]	642[5]	728[5]	850	828	833	861	1 052
Australia Australie	4 530[5]	4 435[5]	4 420[5]	4 354[5]	4 774[5]	12 196	11 629	12 230	14 521	17 946
Austria Autriche	17 982[9]	18 180[9]	18 611[9]	19 078[9]	19 373[9]	11 483	12 033	13 047	16 342	18 401
Azerbaijan Azerbaïdjan	681[5]	767[5]	834[5]	1 014[5]	1 349[5]	68	57	63	70	79
Bahamas Bahamas	1 544[5]	1 538[5]	1 513[5]	1 510[5]	1 561[5]	1 753	1 665	1 773	1 770	1 897
Bahrain Bahreïn	2 420[5]	2 789[5]	3 167[5]	2 955[5]	3 514[5]	854	886	986	1 206	1 504
Bangladesh Bangladesh	199[5]	207[5]	207[5]	245[5]	271[5]	50[7]	48[7]	57[7]	57[7]	67[7]
Barbados Barbade	545[5]	507[5]	498[5]	531[5]	552[5]	734	706	666	767	*810[7,10]
Belarus Bélarus	60[5,11]	61[5,11]	63[5,11]	64[5,11]	67[5,11]	188	272	295	339	379
Belgium Belgique	6 457[9]	6 452[9]	6 720[9]	6 690[9]	6 710[9]	6 592[2,7]	6 903[2,7]	7 590	8 802	10 044
Belize Belize	196[5]	196[5]	200[5]	221[5]	231[5]	116[7]	103[7]	103[7]	117[7]	133[7]
Benin Bénin	96[5]	88[5]	72[5]	175[5,12]	174[5,12]	77	86	95	108	...
Bermuda Bermudes	332[5]	278[5]	284[5]	257[5]	272[5]	431[2]	351[2]	379[2]	370[2]	394[2]
Bhutan Bhoutan	8[5]	6[5]	6[5]	6[5]	9[5]	10[2]	9[2]	8[2]	8[2]	13[2]
Bolivia Bolivie	319[5]	316[5]	334[5]	370[5]	405[5]	101	119	144	244	265

Country or area / Pays ou zone	Number of tourist/visitor arrivals (thousands) Nombre d'arrivées de touristes/visiteurs (milliers)					Tourism expenditure (million US dollars) † Dépenses touristiques (millions de dollars E.-U.) †				
	2000	2001	2002	2003	2004	2000	2001	2002	2003	2004
Bonaire / Bonaire	51[5]	50[5]	52[5]	62[5]	63[5]	59[13]	64[13]	65[13]	84[13]	84[13]
Bosnia and Herzegovina / Bosnie-Herzégovine	171[9]	139[9]	160[9]	165[9]	190[9]	246	279	307	399	514
Botswana / Botswana	1 104[5]	1 049[5]	1 037[5]	975[5]	...	227	235	324	459	549[7,14]
Brazil / Brésil	5 313[5]	4 773[5]	3 785[5]	4 133[5]	4 794[5]	1 969	1 845	2 142	2 673	3 389
British Virgin Islands / Iles Vierges britanniques	272[5]	296[5]	282[5]	318[5]	305[5]	345[2]	374[2]	357[2]	425[2]	391[2]
Brunei Darussalam [4] / Brunéi Darussalam [4]	984	840	...	...	...	...	...	...	...	...
Bulgaria / Bulgarie	2 785[5,15]	3 186[5,15]	3 433[5,15]	4 048[5,15]	4 630[5,15]	1 364	1 223	1 466	2 106	2 718
Burkina Faso / Burkina Faso	126[1]	128[1]	150[1]	163[1]	222[1]	23	25	...	...	...
Burundi / Burundi	29[3,5]	36[3,5]	...	...	...	1	1	2	1	...
Cambodia / Cambodge	466[5]	605[5]	787[5]	701[5]	1 055[5]	345	429	509	441	674
Cameroon / Cameroun	277[1]	221[1]	226[1]	...	190[1]	39[2]	...	...	...	...
Canada / Canada	19 627[5,16]	19 679[5,16]	20 057[5,16]	17 534[5,16]	19 095[5,16]	13 035	12 680	12 748	12 236	14 925
Cape Verde / Cap-Vert	115[1]	134[1]	126[1]	150[1]	157[1]	64	77	101	137	125[7,17]
Cayman Islands / Iles Caïmanes	354[5]	334[5]	303[5]	294[5]	260[5]	559[2]	585[2]	607[2]	518[2]	...
Central African Rep. / Rép. centrafricaine	11[5]	10[5]	3[5]	5[5]	6[5]	5[18]	5[18]	3[18]	4[2,18]	4[2,18]
Chad / Tchad	43[1]	57[1]	32[1]	21[1]	...	14[18]	23[18]	25[18]	...	...
Chile / Chili	1 742[5]	1 723[5]	1 412[5]	1 614[5]	1 785[5]	1 179	1 184	1 221	1 241	1 554
China / Chine	31 229[5]	33 167[5]	36 803[5]	32 970[5]	41 761[5]	17 318	19 006	21 742	18 708	27 755
China, Hong Kong SAR / Chine, Hong Kong RAS	8 814[5]	8 878[5]	10 689[5]	9 676[5]	13 655[5]	8 198[19]	7 926[19]	9 851[19]	9 048[19]	11 815[19]
China, Macao SAR / Chine, Macao RAS	5 197[5,20]	5 842[5,20]	6 565[5,20]	6 309[5,20]	8 324[5,20]	3 205[19]	3 745[19]	4 440[19]	5 303[19]	7 344[19]
Colombia / Colombie	557[4]	616[4]	567[4]	625[4]	791[4]	1 313	1 483	1 237	1 167	1 340
Comoros / Comores	24[5]	19[5]	19[5]	14[5]	18[5]	15[2]	9[2]	11[2]	8[2]	10[2]
Congo / Congo	19[1]	27[1]	22[1]	...	...	12	23	26	20[7]	...
Cook Islands / Iles Cook	73[5]	75[5]	73[5]	78[5]	83[5]	36[2]	38[2]	46[2]	69[2]	72[2]
Costa Rica / Costa Rica	1 088[5]	1 131[5]	1 113[5]	1 239[5]	1 453[5]	1 477	1 339	1 292	1 424	1 585
Côte d'Ivoire / Côte d'Ivoire	...	...	...	...	...	53	58	56	76	76[7]

Country or area Pays ou zone	Number of tourist/visitor arrivals (thousands) Nombre d'arrivées de touristes/visiteurs (milliers)					Tourism expenditure (million US dollars) t Dépenses touristiques (millions de dollars E. -U.) t				
	2000	2001	2002	2003	2004	2000	2001	2002	2003	2004
Croatia Croatie	5 831[9]	6 544[9]	6 944[9]	7 409[9]	7 912[9]	2 871	3 463	3 953	6 581	7 191
Cuba Cuba	1 741[5]	1 736[5]	1 656[5]	1 847[5]	2 017[5]	1 737[2]	1 692[2]	1 633[2]	1 846[2]	1 915[2]
Curaçao Curaçao	191[5]	205[5]	218[5]	221[5]	223[5]	227[2]	253[2]	273[2]	284[2]	295[2]
Cyprus Chypre	2 686[5]	2 697[5]	2 418[5]	2 303[5]	2 349[5]	2 137	2 203	2 146	2 244	2 550
Czech Republic République tchèque	4 666[9]	5 194[9]	4 579[9]	5 076[9]	6 061[9]	2 973[7]	3 104[7]	3 376	4 069	4 956
Dem. Rep. of the Congo[5] Rép. dém. du Congo[5]	103	55	28	35	...	...	...	...	...	...
Denmark Danemark	3 535[21]	3 684[21]	3 436[21]	3 474[21]	3 358[21]	3 671[7]	4 003[7]	4 791[7]	5 271[7]	5 652[7]
Djibouti Djibouti	20[1]	22[1]	23[1]	23[1]	26[1]	...	...	...	7[22]	7[22]
Dominica Dominique	70[5]	66[5]	69[5]	73[5]	79[5]	48[7]	46[7]	46[7]	52[7,8]	60[7,8]
Dominican Republic Rép. dominicaine	2 978[3,5]	2 882[3,5]	2 811[3,5]	3 282[3,5]	3 450[3,5]	2 860[7]	2 798[7]	2 730[7]	3 128[7]	3 180[7]
Ecuador Equateur	627[4,6]	641[4,6]	683[4,6]	761[4,6]	819[4,6]	451	438	449	408	369
Egypt Egypte	5 116[5]	4 357[5]	4 906[5]	5 746[5]	7 795[5]	4 657	4 119	4 133	4 704	6 328
El Salvador El Salvador	795[5,6]	735[5,6]	951[5,6]	857[5,6]	966[5,6]	437	452	521	569	632
Equatorial Guinea[18] Guinée équatoriale[18]	...	...	...	...	...	5	14	...	...	...
Eritrea Erythrée	70[3,4]	113[3,4]	101[3,4]	80[3,4]	87[3,4]	36[2]	74[2]	73[2]	...	73[2]
Estonia Estonie	1 220[5]	1 320[5]	1 362[5]	1 462[5]	1 750[5,23]	654	661	737	881	1 102
Ethiopia Ethiopie	136[5,24]	148[5,24]	156[5,24]	180[5,24]	210[5,24]	205	218	261	336	457
Fiji Fidji	294[5,6]	348[5,6]	398[5,6]	431[5,6]	499[5,6]	182[2,7]	197[2,7]	254[2,7]	521[2]	573[2]
Finland Finlande	2 714[5]	2 826[5]	2 875[5]	2 601[5]	2 840[5]	2 035	2 066	2 242	2 677	2 867
France France	77 190[5,25]	75 202[5,25]	77 012[5,25]	75 048[5,25]	75 121[5,25]	30 981[7]	30 363[7]	32 437[7]	36 617[7]	40 686[7]
French Guiana Guyane française	...	65[5]	65[5]	...	...	...	42[2]	45[2]	...	...
French Polynesia Polynésie française	252[26]	228[5,6]	189[5,6]	213[5,6]	212[5,6]	...	...	471	651	767
Gabon Gabon	155[5,27]	169[5,27]	208[5,27]	222[5,27]	...	99	46	77	84	...
Gambia Gambie	79[5,28]	57[5,28]	81[5,28]	73[5,28]	90[5,28]	...	48[29]	48[29]	51[29]	59[29]
Georgia Géorgie	387[5]	302[5]	298[5]	313[5]	368[5]	107	136	144	172	209
Germany Allemagne	18 983[9]	17 861[9]	17 969[9]	18 399[9]	20 137[9]	24 943	24 175	26 680	30 149	35 589

69 Tourist/visitor arrivals and tourism expenditure (*continued*)
Arrivées de touristes/visiteurs et dépenses touristiques (*suite*)

Country or area Pays ou zone	Number of tourist/visitor arrivals (thousands) Nombre d'arrivées de touristes/visiteurs (milliers)					Tourism expenditure (million US dollars) t Dépenses touristiques (millions de dollars E. -U.) t				
	2000	2001	2002	2003	2004	2000	2001	2002	2003	2004
Ghana Ghana	399[3,5]	439[3,5]	483[3,5]	531[3,5]	584[3,5]	357	374	383	441	495
Greece Grèce	13 096[5,30]	14 057[5,30]	14 180[5,30]	13 969[5,30]	...	9 262	9 216	10 005	10 842	12 809
Grenada Grenade	129[5]	123[5]	132[5]	142[5]	134[5]	93[7]	84[7]	92[7]	104[7,8]	92[7,8]
Guadeloupe Guadeloupe	603[31]	521[31]	...	439[32]	456[32]	418[2]	...	...	...	...
Guam [5] Guam [5]	1 287	1 159	1 059	910	1 157	...	...	...	...	...
Guatemala Guatemala	826[5]	835[5]	884[5]	880[5]	1 182[5]	498	588	647	646	806
Guinea Guinée	33[5,33]	38[5]	43[5]	44[5,33]	45[5]	18	22	...	32	...
Guinea-Bissau Guinée-Bissau	...	8[5]	...	...	...	...	3[7]	2[7]	3	...
Guyana Guyana	105[5]	99[5]	104[5,34]	101[5,34]	122[5,34]	80	65	53	28	30
Haiti Haïti	140[5]	142[5]	140[5]	136[5]	96[5]	128[7]	105[7]	112[7]	93[7]	...
Honduras Honduras	471[5]	518[5]	550[5]	611[5]	672[5]	263	260	305	358	403
Hungary Hongrie	2 992[9]	3 070[9]	3 013[9]	2 948[9]	3 270[9]	3 809	4 191	3 774	4 119	4 084
Iceland Islande	634[9]	672[9]	705[9]	771[9]	836[9]	386	383	415	486	558
India Inde	2 649[5,6]	2 537[5,6]	2 384[5,6]	2 726[5,6]	3 457[5,6]	3 718	3 497	3 476	4 128	...
Indonesia Indonésie	5 064[5]	5 153[5]	5 033[5]	4 467[5]	5 321[5]	4 975[7]	5 277[7]	5 797	4 461	5 226
Iran (Islamic Rep. of) Iran (Rép. islamique d')	1 342[5]	1 402[5]	1 585[5]	1 546[5]	1 659[5]	677[35]	1 122[35]	1 607[35]	1 266[35]	1 324[35]
Iraq Iraq	78[4]	127[4]	...	...	...	2[7,36]	15[7,36]	45[7,36]	...	...
Ireland Irlande	6 646[5,37]	6 353[5,37]	6 476[5,37]	6 764[5,37]	6 982[5,37]	3 517	3 789	4 229	5 206	5 962
Israel Israël	2 417[5,6]	1 196[5,6]	862[5,6]	1 063[5,6]	1 506[5,6]	4 585[38]	2 769[38]	2 325[38]	2 408[38]	2 819[38]
Italy Italie	41 181[5,39]	39 563[5,39]	39 799[5,39]	39 604[5,39]	37 071[5,39]	28 706	26 916	28 192	32 592	37 872
Jamaica Jamaïque	1 323[5,40]	1 277[5,40]	1 266[5,40]	1 350[5,40]	1 415[5,40]	1 577	1 494	1 482	1 621	1 733
Japan Japon	4 757[5,6]	4 772[5,6]	5 239[5,6]	5 212[5,6]	6 138[5,6]	5 970	5 750	6 069	11 476	14 343
Jordan Jordanie	1 580[41]	1 672[41]	2 384[41]	2 353[41]	2 853[41]	935	884	1 254	1 266	1 621
Kazakhstan Kazakhstan	1 471[5]	1 845[5]	2 832[5]	2 410[5]	3 073[5]	403	502	680	638	793
Kenya Kenya	899[5]	841[5]	838[5]	927[5]	1 199[5]	500	536	513	611	808
Kiribati Kiribati	5[5,42]	5[5,42]	5[5,42]	5[5,42]	3[5,42]	3[2]	3[2]	...	...	...

Country or area Pays ou zone	Number of tourist/visitor arrivals (thousands) Nombre d'arrivées de touristes/visiteurs (milliers)					Tourism expenditure (million US dollars) t Dépenses touristiques (millions de dollars E. -U.) t				
	2000	2001	2002	2003	2004	2000	2001	2002	2003	2004
Korea, Republic of Corée, République de	5 322[5,43]	5 147[5,43]	5 347[5,43]	4 753[5,43]	5 818[5,43]	8 527	7 919	7 621	7 005	7 870
Kuwait Koweït	78[1]	73[1]	96[1]	94[1]	91[1]	395	283	323	328	414
Kyrgyzstan Kirghizistan	59[5]	99[5]	140[5]	342[5,44]	398[5,44]	20	32	53	65	97
Lao People's Dem. Rep. Rép. dém. pop. lao	191[5]	173[5]	215[5]	196[5]	236[5]	114[7]	104[7]	113[2,7]	87[2,7]	119[2,7]
Latvia Lettonie	509[45]	591[45]	848[45]	971[45]	1 079[45]	172	154	200	271	343
Lebanon Liban	742[5,46]	837[5,46]	956[5,46]	1 016[5,46]	1 278[5,46]	742[47]	837[47]	4 284[7]	6 782	5 931
Lesotho Lesotho	302[4]	295[4]	287[4]	329[4]	304[4]	24[7]	23[7]	20[7]	28[7]	34[7]
Libyan Arab Jamah. Jamah. arabe libyenne	174[5]	169[5]	135[5]	142[5]	149[5]	84	90	202	243	261
Liechtenstein [1] Liechtenstein [1]	62	56	49	49	49	...	...	...	...	...
Lithuania Lituanie	1 083[5]	1 271[5]	1 428[5]	1 491[5]	1 800[5]	430	425	556	700	874
Luxembourg Luxembourg	852[9]	843[9]	885[9]	867[9]	874[9]	1 686[7]	1 780[7]	2 577	3 134	3 889
Madagascar Madagascar	160[5]	170[5]	62[5]	139[5]	229[5]	152	149	62	118	265[2]
Malawi Malawi	228[48]	266[48]	383[48]	424[48]	471[48]	30	40	45	43	24[7,49]
Malaysia Malaisie	10 222[5,50]	12 775[5,50]	13 292[5,50]	10 577[5,50]	15 703[5,50]	5 873	7 627	8 084	6 799	8 198[7,51]
Maldives Maldives	467[5]	461[5]	485[5]	564[5]	617[5]	321[7]	327[7]	337[7]	402[7]	471[7]
Mali Mali	86[1,52]	89[1,52]	96[1,52]	110[1,52]	113[1,52]	47	91	105	136	148[2]
Malta Malte	1 216[5]	1 180[5]	1 134[5]	1 127[5]	1 158[5]	754	721	714	856	963
Marshall Islands Iles Marshall	5[5]	5[5]	6[5]	7[5]	9[5,53]	4[2]	4[2]	4[2]	...	...
Martinique Martinique	526[5]	460[5]	447[5]	453[5]	471[5]	302[2]	245[2]	237[2]	247[2]	291[2]
Mauritania [5] Mauritanie [5]	30	...	...	...	...	...	...	...	...	...
Mauritius Maurice	656[5]	660[5]	682[5]	702[5]	719[5]	732	820	829	960	1 156
Mexico Mexique	20 641[3,5]	19 810[3,5]	19 667[3,5]	18 665[3,5]	20 618[3,5]	9 133	9 190	9 547	10 058	11 566
Micronesia (Fed. States of) Micronésie (Etats féd. de)	21[5,54]	15[5,54]	19[5,54]	18[5,54]	19[5,54]	15[2]	15[2]	17[2]	17[2]	...
Monaco [1] Monaco [1]	300	270	263	235	250	...	...	...	...	...
Mongolia Mongolie	137[55]	166[55]	229[55]	201[55]	301[55]	43	49	143	154	205
Montserrat Montserrat	10[5]	10[5]	10[5]	8[5]	10[5]	9[7]	8[7]	9[7]	7[7,8]	9[7,8]

69 Tourist/visitor arrivals and tourism expenditure (*continued*)
Arrivées de touristes/visiteurs et dépenses touristiques (*suite*)

Country or area Pays ou zone	Number of tourist/visitor arrivals (thousands) Nombre d'arrivées de touristes/visiteurs (milliers)					Tourism expenditure (million US dollars) † Dépenses touristiques (millions de dollars E.-U.) †				
	2000	2001	2002	2003	2004	2000	2001	2002	2003	2004
Morocco Maroc	4 278[3,5]	4 380[3,5]	4 453[3,5]	4 761[3,5]	5 477[3,5]	2 280	2 966	3 157	3 802	4 541
Mozambique Mozambique	...	323[5]	541[5]	441[5]	470[5]	74[7]	64[7]	65	106	96
Myanmar Myanmar	208[5,56]	205[5,56]	217[5,56]	206[5,56]	242[5,56]	195	132	136	70	98
Namibia Namibie	656[5]	670[5]	757[5]	695[5]	...	160[7]	264	251	383	426
Nepal Népal	464[5,57]	361[5,57]	275[5,57]	338[5,57]	385[5,57]	219	191	135	233	260
Netherlands Pays-Bas	10 003[9]	9 500[9]	9 595[9]	9 181[9]	9 646[9]	11 285	11 147	11 745	9 249[7]	10 417[7]
New Caledonia Nouvelle-Calédonie	110[3,5]	101[3,5]	104[3,5]	102[3,5]	100[3,5]	111[2,7]	94[2,7]	156[7]	196[7]	241[7]
New Zealand Nouvelle-Zélande	1 787[4]	1 909[4]	2 045[4]	2 104[4]	2 334[4]	2 267[7]	2 360[7]	3 006[7]	3 976[7]	5 069[7]
Nicaragua Nicaragua	486[5]	483[5]	472[5]	526[5]	615[5]	133	138	138	164	191
Niger Niger	50[1]	53[1]	58[1]	55[1]	...	23[7]	30[7]	20[7]	29	...
Nigeria Nigéria	813[5]	850[5]	887[5]	924[5]	962[5]	186	168	256	58	49
Niue [5,58] Nioué [5,58]	2	1	2	3	3	...	...	...	...	...
Northern Mariana Islands [5] Iles Marianes du Nord [5]	517	438	466	452	525	...	...	...	...	...
Norway Norvège	3 104[5,59]	3 073[5,59]	3 111[5,59]	3 269[5,59]	3 600[5,59]	2 521	2 380	2 581	2 955	3 400
Occupied Palestinian Terr. Terr. palestinien occupé	330[5]	49[5]	40[5]	40[5]	...	226[19]	7[19]	1[19]	4[19]	...
Oman Oman	571[1]	829[5,60]	817[5,60]	630[1]	...	377	419	447	547	708
Pakistan Pakistan	557[5]	500[5]	498[5]	501[5]	648[5]	551	533	562	620	763
Palau Palaos	58[5,61]	54[5,61]	59[5,61]	68[5,61]	95[5,61]	53[2]	59[2]	47[2]	76[2]	97[2]
Panama Panama	484[5]	519[5]	534[5]	566[5]	621[5]	628	665	710	809	903
Papua New Guinea Papouasie-Nouvelle-Guinée	58[5]	54[5]	54[5]	56[5]	59[5]	7[7]	5[7]	...	...	...
Paraguay Paraguay	289[62]	279[63]	250[63]	268[63]	309[63]	88	91	76	81	84
Peru Pérou	800[5]	901[5]	968[5]	1 028[5]	1 208[5]	861	763	863	1 001	1 169
Philippines Philippines	1 992[3,5]	1 797[3,5]	1 933[3,5]	1 907[3,5]	2 291[3,5]	2 377	1 822	1 827	1 820	2 412
Poland Pologne	17 400[5]	15 000[5]	13 980[5]	13 720[5]	14 290[5]	6 128	5 121	4 971	4 733	6 499
Portugal Portugal	12 097[5,64]	12 167[5,64]	11 644[5,64]	11 707[5,64]	11 617[5,64]	6 027	6 238	6 559	7 565	8 922
Puerto Rico Porto Rico	3 341[5,65]	3 551[5,65]	3 087[5,65]	3 238[5,65]	3 541[5,65]	2 388[66]	2 728[66]	2 486[66]	2 677[66]	3 024[66]

Country or area Pays ou zone	Number of tourist/visitor arrivals (thousands) Nombre d'arrivées de touristes/visiteurs (milliers)					Tourism expenditure (million US dollars) ŧ Dépenses touristiques (millions de dollars E. -U.) ŧ				
	2000	2001	2002	2003	2004	2000	2001	2002	2003	2004
Qatar Qatar	378[1]	376[1]	587[1]	557[1]	732[1]	128[67]	272[67]	285[67]	369[67]	498[67]
Republic of Moldova République de Moldova	18[5,68]	16[5,68]	18[5,68]	21[5,68]	24[5,68]	57	58	72	83	119
Réunion Réunion	430[5]	424[5]	426[5]	432[5]	430[5]	296[2]	281[2]	329[2]	413[2]	448[2]
Romania Roumanie	5 264[4]	4 938[4]	4 794[4]	5 595[4]	6 600[4]	394	419	400	523	607
Russian Federation Fédération de Russie	...	19 457[5]	21 279[5]	20 443[5]	19 892[5]	3 430[7]	4 726	5 429	5 879	6 958
Rwanda Rwanda	104[5]	113[5,69]	...	...	...	27	29	31[7]	30[7]	44[7]
Saba[5] Saba[5]	9	9	11	10	11	...	...	...	...	...
Saint Eustatius[5,70] Saint-Eustache[5,70]	9	10	10	10	11	...	...	...	...	...
Saint Kitts and Nevis Saint-Kitts-et-Nevis	73[5]	71[5]	69[5]	91[5]	118[5]	58[7]	62[7]	57[7]	75[7,8]	107[7,8]
Saint Lucia Sainte-Lucie	270[5,6]	250[5,6]	253[5,6]	277[5,6]	298[5,6]	279[7]	237[7]	215[7]	282[7,8]	326[7,8]
Saint Maarten Saint-Martin	432[5,71]	403[5,71]	381[5,71]	428[5,71]	475[5,71]	511[72]	484[72]	489[72]	538[72]	613[72]
St. Vincent-Grenadines St. Vincent-Grenadines	73[5]	71[5]	78[5]	79[5]	87[5]	75[7]	80[7]	83[7]	85[2,7]	96[2,7]
Samoa Samoa	88[5]	88[5]	89[5]	92[5]	98[5]	41[2,7]	40[2,7]	45[2,7]	52[2,7]	71[2,7]
San Marino[5,73] Saint-Marin[5,73]	43	49	45	41	42	...	...	...	...	...
Sao Tome and Principe Sao Tomé-et-Principe	7[5]	8[5]	...	...	...	10[7]	10[7]	10[7]	...	...
Saudi Arabia Arabie saoudite	6 585[5]	6 727[5]	7 511[5]	7 332[5]	8 599[5]	...	...	3 418[2]	...	6 540[2]
Senegal Sénégal	389[1]	396[1]	427[1]	354[1]	363[1]	152	175	210	269	...
Serbia and Montenegro Serbie-et-Monténégro	239[9]	351[9]	448[9]	481[9]	580[9]	30[2,7]	54[2,7]	97[2,7]	201[2,7]	...
Seychelles Seychelles	130[5]	130[5]	132[5]	122[5]	121[5]	221	210	242	258[74]	256[74]
Sierra Leone Sierra Leone	16[5]	24[5]	28[5]	38[5]	44[5]	11[7]	14[7]	38[7]	60[7]	58[7]
Singapore Singapour	6 917[5]	6 725[5]	6 997[5]	5 705[5]	...	5 142[7]	4 627[7]	4 437[7]	3 790[7]	5 093[7]
Slovakia Slovaquie	1 053[9]	1 219[9]	1 399[9]	1 387[9]	1 401[9]	441	649[2]	742	876	932[2]
Slovenia Slovénie	1 090[9]	1 219[9]	1 302[9]	1 373[9]	1 499[9]	1 016	1 059	1 152	1 427	1 726
Solomon Islands[7,75] Iles Salomon[7,75]	...	...	...	...	...	4	5	1	2	4
South Africa Afrique du Sud	5 872[5,76]	5 787[5,76]	6 430[5,76]	6 505[5,76]	6 678[5,76]	3 338	3 256	3 695	6 147	6 729
Spain Espagne	47 898[5]	50 094[5]	52 327[5]	50 854[5]	52 430[5]	33 833	35 970	37 371	45 967	51 125

Country or area Pays ou zone	Number of tourist/visitor arrivals (thousands) Nombre d'arrivées de touristes/visiteurs (milliers)					Tourism expenditure (million US dollars) t Dépenses touristiques (millions de dollars E. -U.) t				
	2000	2001	2002	2003	2004	2000	2001	2002	2003	2004
Sri Lanka Sri Lanka	400[5,6]	337[5,6]	393[5,6]	501[5,6]	566[5,6]	388	347	594	709	808
Sudan Soudan	38[5]	50[5]	52[5]	52[5]	61[5]	5[7]	3[7]	23[7]	18[7]	21[7]
Suriname Suriname	58[5,77]	54[5,77]	60[5,77]	82[5,77]	138[5]	42	26	17	18	52
Swaziland Swaziland	281[1]	283[1]	256[1]	461[1]	459[1]	40	32	68	113	109
Sweden Suède	2 746[9,78]	7 431[5,79]	7 458[5,79]	7 627[5,79]	...	4 825	5 200	5 671	6 548	7 245[2]
Switzerland Suisse	7 821[1]	7 455[1]	6 868[1]	6 530[1]	...	10 124	10 013	9 742	11 048	12 208
Syrian Arab Republic Rép. arabe syrienne	1 416[80]	1 318[80]	2 870[3,5]	2 788[3,5]	3 032[3,5]	1 082[7]	1 150[7]	970[7]	877	1 888
Tajikistan Tadjikistan	4[5]	4[5]	...	...	...	...	...	5	7	9
Thailand Thaïlande	9 579[3,5]	10 133[3,5]	10 873[3,5]	10 082[3,5]	11 737[3,5]	9 936	9 380	10 388	10 456	13 054
TFYR of Macedonia L'ex-R.y. Macédoine	224[9]	99[9]	123[9]	158[9]	165[9]	88	49	55	65	77
Togo Togo	60[1]	57[1]	58[1]	61[1]	83[1]	11	14	16	26	...
Tonga Tonga	35[5]	32[5]	37[5]	40[5]	41[5]	7[81]	6[81]	8[81]	15[81]	15[81]
Trinidad and Tobago Trinité-et-Tobago	399[5]	383[5]	384[5]	409[5]	443[5]	371	361	402	437	568[2]
Tunisia Tunisie	5 058[5,6]	5 387[5,6]	5 064[5,6]	5 114[5,6]	5 998[5,6]	1 978	2 061	1 832	1 935	2 432
Turkey Turquie	9 586[5]	10 783[5]	12 790[5]	13 341[5]	16 826[5]	7 636[7]	10 067[82]	11 901[82]	13 203[7,83]	15 888[7,83]
Turks and Caicos Islands Iles Turques et Caïques	152[5]	166[5]	155[5]	164[5]	...	285[2]	311[2]	292[2]	...	...
Tuvalu [5] Tuvalu [5]	1	1	1	1	1	...	...	...	...	...
Uganda Ouganda	193[5]	205[5]	254[5]	305[5]	512[5]	165[7]	193	202	219	306
Ukraine Ukraine	6 431[5]	9 174[5]	10 517[5]	12 514[5]	15 629[5]	563	759	1 001	1 204	1 512
United Arab Emirates Emirats arabes unis	3 907[1,84]	4 134[1,84]	5 445[1,84]	5 871[1,84]	...	1 063[2]	1 200[2]	1 332[2]	1 439[2]	1 594[2]
United Kingdom Royaume-Uni	25 209[4]	22 835[4]	24 180[4]	24 715[4]	27 755[4]	29 978	26 137	27 819	30 738	37 193
United Rep. of Tanzania Rép.-Unie de Tanzanie	459[5]	501[5]	550[5]	552[5]	566[5]	381	444	448	468	610
United States Etats-Unis	51 237[5,85]	46 927[5,85]	43 582[5,85]	41 218[5,85]	46 085[5,85]	118 630	106 705	101 798	98 947	112 780
United States Virgin Is. Iles Vierges américaines	546[5]	527[5]	520[5]	538[5]	544[5]	1 206[2]	1 234[2]	1 195[2]	1 257[2]	1 357[2]
Uruguay Uruguay	1 968[5]	1 892[5]	1 258[5]	1 420[5]	1 756[5]	827	700	409	419	579
Uzbekistan Ouzbékistan	302[5]	345[5]	332[5]	231[5]	262[5]	63[2]	72[2]	68[2]	48[2]	57[2]

Country or area	Number of tourist/visitor arrivals (thousands) Nombre d'arrivées de touristes/visiteurs (milliers)					Tourism expenditure (million US dollars) ŧ Dépenses touristiques (millions de dollars E. -U.) ŧ				
Pays ou zone	2000	2001	2002	2003	2004	2000	2001	2002	2003	2004
Vanuatu Vanuatu	58[5]	53[5]	49[5]	50[5]	61[5]	69	58	62	71	...
Venezuela (Bolivarian Rep. of) Venezuela (Rép. bolivar. du)	469[5]	584[5]	432[5]	337[5]	492[5]	469	677	484	378	531
Viet Nam Viet Nam	1 383[5]	1 599[5]	2 628[4]	2 429[4]	2 928[4]	...	...	...	...	...
Yemen Yémen	73[1]	76[1]	98[1]	155[1]	274[1]	73[7]	38[7]	38[7]	139[7]	139[7]
Zambia Zambie	457[5]	492[5]	565[5]	413[5]	515[5]	111[19]	117[19]	134[19]	149[19]	161[19]
Zimbabwe Zimbabwe	1 868[5]	2 068[5]	2 041[4]	2 256[4]	1 854[4]	125[2]	81[2]	76[2]	61[2]	194[2]

Source

World Tourism Organization (UNWTO), Madrid, the UNWTO Statistics Database.

Notes

ŧ   The majority of the data have been provided to the UNWTO by the International Monetary Fund (IMF). Exceptions are footnoted.

[1]   Arrivals of non-resident tourists in hotels and similar establishments; Albania, Qatar, Niger and Swaziland: arrivals in hotels only.

[2]   Figures provided by the country to the World Tourism Organisation (UNWTO).

[3]   Including nationals of the country residing abroad.

[4]   Arrivals of non-resident visitors at national borders (including tourists and same-day visitors).

[5]   Arrivals of non-resident tourists at national borders (excluding same-day visitors); Antigua and Barbuda, Australia, Bermuda, Cayman Islands, Comoros, Cuba, Curaçao, Dominican Republic, Madagascar, Maldives, Marshall Islands, Montserrat, Niue, Northern Mariana Islands, Saint Kitts and Nevis, St. Vincent-Grenadines, Sierra Leone, Tonga, Trinidad and Tobago: arrivals by air only.

[6]   Excluding nationals of the country residing abroad.

[7]   Excluding passenger transport.

[8]   Source: Eastern Caribbean Central Bank.

[9]   Arrivals of non-resident tourists in all types of tourism accommodation establishments.

[10]   Source: Central Bank of Barbados.

[11]   Organized tourism.

[12]   Country estimates.

[13]   Source: Central Bank of the Netherlands Antilles. Excluding passenger transport.

[14]   Source: Bank of Bostwana.

[15]   Excluding children without own passports.

[16]   Different types of methodological changes that affect the estimates for 2000 and 2001 for expenditures and characteristics of International Tourists to Canada, have been introduced in 2002. Therefore, Statistics Canada advises not to compare the estimates for 2000 and 2001 with the years prior because of these methodological changes for the non-count estimates.

[17]   Source: Banco de Cabo Verde.

[18]   Source: Banque des Etats de l'Afrique Centrale (B.E.A.C.).

Source

Organisation mondiale du tourisme (OMT), Madrid, la base de données de l'OMT.

Notes

ŧ   La majorité des données proviennent que l'Organisation mondiale du tourisme (OMT) a fournis à l'Organisation mondiale du tourisme (OMT). Les exceptions sont signalées par une note.

[1]   Arrivées de touristes non résidents dans les hôtels et établissements assimilés; Albanie, Qatar, Niger et Swaziland : arrivées dans les hôtels uniquement.

[2]   Les chiffres de dépense sont ceux que le pays a fournis à l'Organisation mondiale du tourisme (OMT).

[3]   Y compris les nationaux du pays résidant à l'étranger.

[4]   Arrivées de visiteurs non résidents aux frontières nationales (y compris touristes et visiteurs de la journée).

[5]   Arrivées de touristes non résidents aux frontières nationales(à l'exclusion de visiteurs de la journée); Antigua-et-Barbuda, Australie, Bermudes, Iles Caïmanes, Comores, Cuba, Curaçao, République dominicaine, Madagascar, Maldives, Iles Marshall, Montserrat, Nioué, Iles Mariannes du Nord, Saint-Kitts-et-Nevis, St. Vincent-et-les-Grenadines, Sierra Leone, Tonga, Trinité-et-Tobago : arrivées par voie aérienne seulement.

[6]   A l'exclusion des nationaux du pays résidant à l'étranger.

[7]   Non compris le transport de passagers.

[8]   Source : Eastern Caribbean Central Bank.

[9]   Arrivées de touristes non résidents dans tous les types d'établissements d'hébergement touristique.

[10]   Source : Central Bank of Barbados.

[11]   Tourisme organisé.

[12]   Estimations du pays.

[13]   Source : Central Bank of the Netherlands Antilles. Non compris le transport de passagers.

[14]   Source : Bank of Bostwana.

[15]   A l'exclusion d'enfants sans passeports personnels.

[16]   En 2002, il a été adopté différents types de changements méthodologiques qui ont eu des effets sur les estimations des dépenses et des caractéristiques des touristes internationaux ayant visité le Canada en 2000 et 2001. Pour 2000 et 2001, Statistique Canada conseille par conséquent de ne pas comparer les estimations ne reposant pas sur des comptages aux données des années précédentes.

[17]   Source : Banco de Cabo Verde.

[18]   Source : Banque des Etats de l'Afrique Centrale (B.E.A.C.).

69

Tourist/visitor arrivals and tourism expenditure (*continued*)
Arrivées de touristes/visiteurs et dépenses touristiques (*suite*)

19 The expenditure figures used were the ones provided by the country to UNWTO, as this data series is more complete than that provided by the International Monetary Fund (IMF).

20 Regional estimates.

21 Arrivals of non-resident tourists in all types of accommodation establishments. New coverage from 2000.

22 Excluding passenger transport. Source: Banque centrale de Djibouti.

23 Calculated on the basis of accommodation statistics and *Foreign Visitor Survey* carried out by the Statistical Office of Estonia. Starting from 2004, border statistics are not collected any more.

24 Arrivals through all ports of entry. Including nationals residing abroad.

25 Estimates based on the 1996 survey at national borders. Data revised from 1996.

26 Arrivals of non-resident tourists at national borders. Excluding nationals residing abroad. The figure of 252,200 has been estimated by the Institut de la Statistique (ISPF). Due to problems of E/D card distributions, the brekdown by country of origin could not be elaborated.

27 Arrivals of non-resident tourists at Libreville airport.

28 Charter tourists only.

29 Source: Central Bank of the Gambia.

30 Data based on surveys.

31 Arrivals of non-resident tourists in all types of accommodation establishments. Air arrivals. Excluding the north islands (Saint Martin and Saint Barthelemy).

32 Arrivals of non-resident tourists in all types of accommodation establishments. Air arrivals. Air arrivals in hotels only. Excluding the north islands (Saint Martin and Saint Barthelemy).

33 Air arrivals at Conakry airport.

34 Arrivals to Timehri airport only.

35 Source: Central Bank of Islamic Republic of Iran.

36 Source: Central Bank of Iraq.

37 Including tourists from Northern Ireland.

38 Including the expenditures of foreign workers in Israel.

39 Excluding seasonal and border workers.

40 Including nationals residing abroad; E/D cards.

41 Arrivals of non-resident tourists at national borders. Including nationals residing abroad. New series. Data revised from 1998.

42 Arrivals at Tarawa and Christmas Islands.

43 Including nationals residing abroad and crew members.

44 New data source: Department of Customs Control.

45 Departures. Survey of persons crossing the state border.

46 Excluding Syrian nationals.

47 Figures provided by the country to World Tourism Organisation. Due to lack of data on international tourism receipts concerning statistics on inbound tourism, the Department of Internet and Statistics Service of the Ministry of Tourism considers that a tourist spends an average of US$ 1,000.

48 Departures.

49 Source: Reserve Bank of Malawi.

50 Including Singapore residents crossing the frontier by road through Johore Causeway.

51 Source: Department of Statistics Malaysia.

52 Air arrivals.

53 Air and sea arrivals.

54 Arrivals in the States of Kosrae, Chuuk, Pohnpei and Yap.

19 Les données de dépense sont celles que le pays a fournies à l'OMT car il s'agit d'une série plus complète que celle obtenue du Fonds monétaire international (FMI).

20 Les estimation régionale.

21 Arrivées de touristes non résidents dans tous les types d'établissements d'hébergement. Nouvelle couverture depuis 2000.

22 Non compris le transport de passagers. Source : Banque centrale de Djibouti.

23 Calculé sur la base des statistiques d'hébergement et de la "Foreign Visitor Survey" menée par la "Statistical Office of Estonia". À partir de 2004, les statistiques de frontière ne sont plus collectées.

24 Arrivées à travers tous les ports d'entrée. Y compris les nationaux résidant à l'étranger.

25 Estimation à partir de l'enquête aux frontières 1996. Données révisées depuis 1996.

26 Arrivées de touristes non résidents aux frontières nationales. A l'exclusion des nationaux résidant à l'étranger. Estimation de la fréquentation touristique (252.200) réalisée par l'Institut de la Statistique (ISPF). En raison de problèmes de distribution de formulaires, la ventilation par pays d'origine n'a pu être réalisée.

27 Arrivées de touristes non résidents à l'aéroport de Libreville.

28 Arrivées en vols à la demande seulement.

29 Source : Central Bank of the Gambia.

30 Données obtenues au moyen d'enquêtes.

31 Arrivées de touristes non résidents dans tous les types d'établissements d'hébergement. Arrivées par voie aérienne. À l'exclusion des îles du nord (Saint Martin et Saint Barthélemy).

32 Arrivées de touristes non résidents dans tous les types d'établissements d'hébergement. Arrivées par voie aérienne. Arrivées par voie aérienne dans les hôtels seulement. À l'exclusion des îles du nord (Saint Martin et Saint Barthélemy).

33 Arrivées par voie aérienne à l'aéroport de Conakry.

34 Arrivées à l'aéroport de Timehri seulement.

35 Source : Central Bank of Islamic Republic of Iran.

36 Source : Central Bank of Iraq.

37 Y compris touristes à Irlande du Nord.

38 Y compris les dépenses des travailleurs étrangers en Israël.

39 A l'exclusion des travailleurs saisoniers et frontaliers.

40 Y compris les nationaux résidant à l'étranger ; cartes d'embarquement.

41 Arrivées de touristes non résidents aux frontières nationales. Y compris les nationaux résidant à l'étranger. Nouvelle série. Données révisées depuis 1998.

42 Arrivées aux Iles Tarawa et Christmas.

43 Y compris les nationaux résidant à l'étranger et membres des équipages.

44 Nouvelle source d'information : Département du Contrôle douanier.

45 Départs. Enquête auprès des personnes qui traversent les frontières du pays.

46 A l'exclusion des ressortissants syriens.

47 Les chiffres sont ceux que le pays a fournis à l'Organnisation mondiale du tourisme. Du fait d'un manque de données sur les recettes du tourisme international concernant les statistiques sur le tourisme récepteur, le Département Internet et Service Statistique du Ministère du Tourisme considère qu'un touriste dépense en moyenne 1.000$EU.

48 Départs.

49 Source : Reserve Bank of Malawi.

50 Y compris les résidents de Singapour traversant la frontière par voie terrestre à travers le Johore Causeway.

51 Source : Department of Statistics Malaysia.

52 Arrivées par voie aérienne.

53 Arrivées par voie aérienne et maritime.

54 Arrivées dans les États de Kosrae, Chuuk, Pohnpei et Yap.

#	English	French

55 Arrivals of non-resident tourists at national borders (excluding same-day visitors). Excluding diplomats and foreign residents in Mongolia.

55 Arrivées de touristes non résidents aux frontières nationales(à l'exclusion de visiteurs de la journée). A l'exclusion des diplomates et des étrangers résidant en Mongolie.

56 Including tourist arrivals through border entry points to Yangon.

56 Comprenant les arrivées de touristes aux postes-frontières de Yangon.

57 Including arrivals from India.

57 Y compris les arrivées à Inde.

58 Arrivals by air, including Niueans residing usually in New Zealand.

58 Arrivées par voie aérienne et y compris les nationaux de Niue résidant habituellement en Nouvelle-Zélande.

59 Figures are based on "The Guest survey" carried out by Institute of Transport Economics.

59 Les chiffres se fondent sur "l'enquête auprès de la clientèle" de l'Institut d'économie des transports.

60 Inbound Tourism Survey.

60 Enquête sur le tourisme récepteur.

61 Air arrivals (Palau International Airport).

61 Arrivées par voie aérienne (Aéroport international de Palau).

62 Arrivals of non-resident tourists at national borders. Excluding nationals residing abroad and crew members. Inbound and outbound tourism survey - Central Bank of Paraguay.

62 Arrivées de touristes non résidents aux frontières nationales. À l'exclusion des nationaux résidant à l'étranger et membres des équipages. Enquête sur le tourisme récepteur et sur le tourisme émetteur – Banque centrale du Paraguay.

63 Arrivals of non-resident tourists at national borders. Excluding nationals residing abroad and crew members. E/D cards in the "Silvio Petirossi" airport and passenger counts at the national border crossings - National Police and SENATUR.

63 Arrivées de touristes non résidents aux frontières nationales. À l'exclusion des nationaux résidant à l'étranger et membres des équipages. Cartes d'embarquement et de débarquement à l'aéroport Silvio Petirossi et comptages des passagers lors du franchissement des frontières nationales – Police nationale et SENATUR.

64 Including arrivals from abroad to insular possessions of Madeira and the Azores. Excluding nationals residing abroad.

64 Y compris les arrivées en provenance de l'étranger aux possessions insulaires de Madère et des Açores. A l'exclusion des nationaux résidant à l'étranger.

65 Arrivals by air. Fiscal year July to June. Source: Junta de Planificación de Puerto Rico.

65 Arrivées par voie aérienne. Année fiscale de juillet à juin. Source : Junta de Planificación de Puerto Rico.

66 Fiscal years (July-June). Figures are those provided by the country to the World Tourism Organisation.

66 Années fiscales (juillet-juin). Les chiffres sont ceux que le pays a fournis à l'Organisation mondiale du tourisme mais ils ne figurent pas dans les données du Fonds monétaire international.

67 Source: Qatar Central Bank. Excluding passenger transport.

67 Source : Qatar Central Bank. Non compris le transport de passagers.

68 Visitors who enjoyed the services of the economic agents officially registered under tourism activity and accommodation (excluding the regions of the left bank of the Dniestr and the municipality of Bender).

68 Visiteurs qui ont bénéficié des services des agents économiques officiellement enregistrés avec le type d'activité tourisme et des unités d'hébergement qui leur appartiennent (à l'exception des régions de la partie gauche du Dniestr et de la municipalité de Bender).

69 January-November.

69 Janvier-novembre.

70 Excluding Netherlands Antillean residents.

70 A l'exclusion des résidents des Antilles Néerlandaises.

71 Including air arrivals to Saint Maarten (the French side of the island).

71 Y compris les arrivées par voie aérienne à Saint-Martin (côté français de l'île).

72 Including the estimates for Saba and Saint Eustatius. Excluding passenger transport. Source: Central Bank of the Netherlands Antilles.

72 Y compris estimations pour Saba et Saint-Eustache. Non compris le transport de passagers. Source : "Central Bank of the Netherlands Antilles".

73 Including Italian visitors.

73 Y compris les visiteurs italiens.

74 Source: Central Bank of Seychelles.

74 Source : Central Bank of Seychelles.

75 Source: Central Bank of Solomon Islands.

75 Source : Central Bank of Solomon Islands.

76 Excluding arrivals by work and contract workers.

76 À l'exclusion des arrivées par travail et les travailleurs contractuels.

77 Arrivals at Zanderij Airport.

77 Arrivées à l'aéroport de Zanderij.

78 Excluding camping.

78 Camping exclu.

79 Data according to IBIS-Survey (Incoming Visitors to Sweden) during the years 2001 to 2003, (no data collected before 2001 or after 2003). Source: Swedish Tourist Authority and Statistics Sweden.

79 Données reposant sur l'enquête IBIS (auprès des visiteurs du tourisme récepteur) portant sur les années 2001 à 2003 (aucune donnée n'a été collectée avant 2001 ni après 2003). Source : Swedish Tourist Authority et Statistics Sweden.

80 Arrivals of non-resident tourists in all types of accommodation establishments. Excluding private accommodation.

80 Arrivals of non-resident tourists in all types of accommodation establishments. À l'exclusion de l'hébergement privé.

81 Source: National Reserve Bank of Tonga. Excluding passenger transport.

81 Source : National Reserve Bank of Tonga. Non compris le transport de passagers.

82 Country data. Including expenditure of the nationals residing abroad. Excluding passenger transport.

82 Données du pays. Y compris les dépenses des nationaux résidant à l'étranger. Non compris le transport de passagers.

83 Including expenditure of the nationals residing abroad.

83 Y compris dépenses des nationaux résidant à l'étranger.

84 Including nationals residing abroad. Arrivals in hotels only. Including domestic tourism.

84 Y compris les nationaux résidant à l'étranger. Arrivées dans les hôtels seulement. Y compris le tourisme interne.

85 Including Mexicans staying one or more nights in the United States.

85 Incluyant Mexicains passant 1 nuit ou plus aux EU.

70

Tourism expenditure in other countries
Total, travel and passenger transport: million US dollars

Dépenses touristiques dans d'autres pays
Totale, voyage et transport de passager : millions de dollars E.-U.

Country or area	2000	2001	2002	2003	2004	Pays ou zone
Albania						Albanie
Total	290	269	387	507	668[1]	Totale
Travel	272	257	366	489	641[1]	Voyage
Passenger transport	18	12	21	18	27[1]	Transport de passagers
Algeria [1]						Algérie [1]
Total	193	194	248	255	394	Totale
Angola						Angola
Total	146	80	53	49	86	Totale
Travel	136	66	19	12	39	Voyage
Passenger transport	10	14	34	37	47	Transport de passagers
Anguilla						Anguilla
Travel	9	9	8	9[1]	10[1]	Voyage
Antigua and Barbuda						Antigua-et-Barbuda
Travel	31	32	33	35[2]	38[2]	Voyage
Argentina						Argentine
Total	5 460	4 888	2 744	2 997	3 561	Totale
Travel	4 425	3 893	2 328	2 511	2 964	Voyage
Passenger transport	1 035	995	416	486	597	Transport de passagers
Armenia						Arménie
Total	56	59	85	97	102	Totale
Travel	40	40	54	67	65	Voyage
Passenger transport	16	19	31	30	37	Transport de passagers
Aruba						Aruba
Total	159	155	174	209	258	Totale
Travel	143	135	162	190	228	Voyage
Passenger transport	16	20	12	19	30	Transport de passagers
Australia						Australie
Total	8 496	7 894	8 526	10 137	13 004	Totale
Travel	6 103	5 701	6 104	7 347	9 410	Voyage
Passenger transport	2 393	2 193	2 422	2 790	3 594	Transport de passagers
Austria						Autriche
Total	9 231	9 787	10 301	12 894	12 811	Totale
Travel	8 463	8 956	9 460	11 757	11 252	Voyage
Passenger transport	768	831	841	1 137	1 559	Transport de passagers
Azerbaijan						Azerbaïdjan
Total	138	119	111	120	140	Totale
Travel	132	109	106	111	126	Voyage
Passenger transport	6	10	5	9	14	Transport de passagers
Bahamas						Bahamas
Total	348	342	338	404	469	Totale
Travel	261	256	244	305	316	Voyage
Passenger transport	87	86	94	99	153	Transport de passagers
Bahrain						Bahreïn
Total	425	423	550	492	528	Totale
Travel	224	250	380	372	387	Voyage
Passenger transport	201	173	170	120	141	Transport de passagers
Bangladesh						Bangladesh
Total	471	341	309	389	442	Totale
Travel	290	165	113	165	161	Voyage
Passenger transport	181	176	196	224	281	Transport de passagers
Barbados						Barbade
Total	141	149	146	154	...	Totale
Travel	94	101	99	105	...	Voyage
Passenger transport	47	48	47	49	...	Transport de passagers

Tourism expenditure in other countries—Total, travel and passenger transport: million US dollars (*continued*)

Dépenses touristiques dans d'autres pays—Totale, voyage et transport de passager : millions de dollars E.-U. (*suite*)

Country or area	2000	2001	2002	2003	2004	Pays ou zone
Belarus						Bélarus
Total	274	533	593	510	574	Totale
Travel	243	501	559	473	524	Voyage
Passenger transport	31	32	34	37	50	Transport de passagers
Belgium						Belgique
Total	...	...	11 198	13 267	15 295	Totale
Travel	9 429[1]	9 782[1]	10 176	12 159	13 884	Voyage
Passenger transport	...	...	1 022	1 108	1 411	Transport de passagers
Belize						Belize
Total	44	44	46	48	44	Totale
Travel	40	41	43	44	41	Voyage
Passenger transport	4	3	3	4	3	Transport de passagers
Benin						Bénin
Total	50	48	49	53	...	Totale
Travel	12	17	20	21	...	Voyage
Passenger transport	38	31	29	32	...	Transport de passagers
Bolivia						Bolivie
Total	116	114	114	198	219	Totale
Travel	77	83	80	139	148	Voyage
Passenger transport	39	31	34	59	71	Transport de passagers
Bonaire [3]						Bonaire [3]
Travel	3	2	2	3	4	Voyage
Bosnia and Herzegovina						Bosnie-Herzégovine
Total	107	105	124	163	169	Totale
Travel	88	83	97	124	124	Voyage
Passenger transport	19	22	27	39	45	Transport de passagers
Botswana						Botswana
Total	209	215	197	235	...	Totale
Travel	198	204	184	230	276[4]	Voyage
Passenger transport	11	11	13	5	...	Transport de passagers
Brazil						Brésil
Total	4 548	3 765	2 929	2 874	3 752	Totale
Travel	3 894	3 199	2 396	2 261	2 871	Voyage
Passenger transport	654	566	533	613	881	Transport de passagers
Bulgaria						Bulgarie
Total	764	647	757	1 065	1 356	Totale
Travel	538	456	533	750	955	Voyage
Passenger transport	226	191	224	315	401	Transport de passagers
Burkina Faso						Burkina Faso
Total	30	35	...	...	...	Totale
Travel	20	22	...	...	...	Voyage
Passenger transport	10	13	...	...	...	Transport de passagers
Burundi						Burundi
Travel	14	12	14	15	...	Voyage
Cambodia						Cambodge
Total	52	59	64	60	80	Totale
Travel	33	37	38	36	48	Voyage
Passenger transport	19	22	26	24	32	Transport de passagers
Canada						Canada
Total	15 125	14 635	14 214	16 365	19 730	Totale
Travel	12 438	11 961	11 679	13 393	15 985	Voyage
Passenger transport	2 687	2 674	2 535	2 972	3 745	Transport de passagers
Cape Verde						Cap-Vert
Total	41	55	63	89	...	Totale
Travel	36	47	56	71	94[5]	Voyage
Passenger transport	5	8	7	18	...	Transport de passagers
Central African Rep. [6]						Rép. centrafricaine [6]
Total	33	29	29	31[1]	32[1]	Totale
Chad [6]						Tchad [6]
Total	56	56	80	...	...	Totale

Country or area	2000	2001	2002	2003	2004	Pays ou zone
Chile						Chili
Total	904	939	932	1 034	1 196	Totale
Travel	620	708	673	775	892	Voyage
Passenger transport	284	231	259	259	304	Transport de passagers
China [7]						Chine [7]
Total	14 169	14 992	16 759	16 716	21 360	Totale
Travel	13 114	13 909	15 398	15 187	19 149	Voyage
Passenger transport	1 055	1 083	1 361	1 529	2 211	Transport de passagers
Colombia						Colombie
Total	1 453	1 556	1 355	1 323	1 644	Totale
Travel	1 060	1 164	1 075	1 036	1 290	Voyage
Passenger transport	393	392	280	287	354	Transport de passagers
Congo						Congo
Total	59	82	85	...	...	Totale
Travel	50	65	70	53	...	Voyage
Passenger transport	9	17	15	...	...	Transport de passagers
Costa Rica						Costa Rica
Total	551	434	430	434	481	Totale
Travel	485	364	345	353	406	Voyage
Passenger transport	66	70	85	81	75	Transport de passagers
Côte d'Ivoire						Côte d'Ivoire
Total	291	289	490	551	...	Totale
Travel	189	187	358	387	360	Voyage
Passenger transport	102	102	132	164	...	Transport de passagers
Croatia						Croatie
Total	635	677	852	709	872	Totale
Travel	568	606	781	672	839	Voyage
Passenger transport	67	71	71	37	33	Transport de passagers
Cyprus						Chypre
Total	543	568	588	722	902	Totale
Travel	413	428	516	632	806	Voyage
Passenger transport	130	140	72	90	96	Transport de passagers
Czech Republic						République tchèque
Total	...	...	1 797	2 177	2 659	Totale
Travel	1 276	1 386	1 597	1 934	2 279	Voyage
Passenger transport	...	...	200	243	380	Transport de passagers
Denmark						Danemark
Travel	4 669	4 861	5 838	6 659	7 279	Voyage
Djibouti [8]						Djibouti [8]
Travel	...	...	...	3	3	Voyage
Dominica						Dominique
Travel	9	9	9	9 [2]	9 [2]	Voyage
Dominican Republic						Rép. dominicaine
Total	440	425	429	408	448	Totale
Travel	309	291	295	272	310	Voyage
Passenger transport	131	134	134	136	138	Transport de passagers
Ecuador						Equateur
Total	416	465	507	500	577	Totale
Travel	299	340	364	354	391	Voyage
Passenger transport	117	125	143	146	186	Transport de passagers
Egypt						Egypte
Total	1 206	1 248	1 309	1 465	1 543	Totale
Travel	1 072	1 132	1 266	1 321	1 257	Voyage
Passenger transport	134	116	43	144	286	Transport de passagers
El Salvador						El Salvador
Total	219	247	266	277	321	Totale
Travel	165	195	191	196	240	Voyage
Passenger transport	54	52	75	81	81	Transport de passagers
Equatorial Guinea [6]						Guinée équatoriale [6]
Total	19	30	...	...	...	Totale

Country or area	2000	2001	2002	2003	2004	Pays ou zone
Estonia						Estonie
Total	253	253	305	404	481	Totale
Travel	204	192	231	319	400	Voyage
Passenger transport	49	61	74	85	81	Transport de passagers
Ethiopia						Ethiopie
Total	80	50	56	63	61	Totale
Travel	74	44	45	50	60	Voyage
Passenger transport	6	6	11	13	1	Transport de passagers
Fiji [1]						Fidji [1]
Total	...	...	...	87	118	Totale
Travel	83	65	55	69	94	Voyage
Passenger transport	...	...	...	18	24	Transport de passagers
Finland						Finlande
Total	2 293	2 442	2 437	2 956	3 597	Totale
Travel	1 852	1 852	2 006	2 435	2 822	Voyage
Passenger transport	441	590	431	521	775	Transport de passagers
France						France
Travel	17 906	18 109	19 518	23 396	28 520	Voyage
French Polynesia						Polynésie française
Total	...	...	264	335	425	Totale
Travel	...	...	180	236	311	Voyage
Passenger transport	...	...	84	99	114	Transport de passagers
Gabon						Gabon
Total	183	256	237	239	...	Totale
Travel	84	225	197	194	...	Voyage
Passenger transport	99	31	40	45	...	Transport de passagers
Georgia						Géorgie
Total	129	136	189	170	196	Totale
Travel	110	107	149	130	147	Voyage
Passenger transport	19	29	40	40	49	Transport de passagers
Germany						Allemagne
Total	57 888	56 709	59 486	72 597	78 553	Totale
Travel	52 824	51 810	52 660	64 629	70 614	Voyage
Passenger transport	5 064	4 899	6 826	7 968	7 939	Transport de passagers
Ghana						Ghana
Total	162	165	184	216	270	Totale
Travel	100	105	119	138	186	Voyage
Passenger transport	62	60	65	78	84	Transport de passagers
Greece						Grèce
Total	4 564	4 189	2 453	2 439	2 880	Totale
Travel	4 558	4 177	2 436	2 431	2 872	Voyage
Passenger transport	6	12	17	8	8	Transport de passagers
Grenada						Grenade
Travel	8	8	8	8 [2]	8 [2]	Voyage
Guatemala						Guatemala
Total	216	267	329	373	456	Totale
Travel	182	226	276	312	391	Voyage
Passenger transport	34	41	53	61	65	Transport de passagers
Guinea						Guinée
Total	13	26	38	36	29	Totale
Travel	9	18	31	26	25	Voyage
Passenger transport	4	8	7	10	4	Transport de passagers
Guinea-Bissau						Guinée-Bissau
Total	...	6	10	21	...	Totale
Travel	...	3	5	13	...	Voyage
Passenger transport	...	3	5	8	...	Transport de passagers
Guyana						Guyana
Total	77	62	44	30	37	Totale
Travel	69	55	38	26	32	Voyage
Passenger transport	8	7	6	4	5	Transport de passagers

Country or area	2000	2001	2002	2003	2004	Pays ou zone
Haiti						Haïti
Passenger transport	155	150	156	154	...	Transport de passagers
Honduras						Honduras
Total	194	205	221	256	269	Totale
Travel	120	128	149	200	210	Voyage
Passenger transport	74	77	72	56	59	Transport de passagers
Hungary						Hongrie
Total	1 722	1 887	2 211	2 700	2 908	Totale
Travel	1 651	1 808	2 133	2 594	2 848	Voyage
Passenger transport	71	79	78	106	60	Transport de passagers
Iceland						Islande
Total	...	...	372	522	695	Totale
Travel	471	372	370	521	693	Voyage
Passenger transport	...	...	2	1	2	Transport de passagers
India						Inde
Total	3 278	5 099	4 990	4 758	...	Totale
Travel	2 690	3 006	2 988	3 510	...	Voyage
Passenger transport	588	2 093	2 002	1 248	...	Transport de passagers
Indonesia						Indonésie
Total	...	...	5 042	4 427	4 570	Totale
Travel	3 197	3 406	3 289	3 082	3 507	Voyage
Passenger transport	...	...	1 753	1 345	1 063	Transport de passagers
Iran (Islamic Rep. of) [9]						Iran (Rép. islamique d') [9]
Total	671	714	3 990	4 120	4 353	Totale
Travel	668	708	3 750	3 842	4 053	Voyage
Passenger transport	3	6	240	278	300	Transport de passagers
Iraq [10]						Iraq [10]
Travel	9	31	26	...	...	Voyage
Ireland						Irlande
Total	2 626	2 956	3 835	4 832	5 287	Totale
Travel	2 525	2 858	3 755	4 736	5 173	Voyage
Passenger transport	101	98	80	96	114	Transport de passagers
Israel						Israël
Total	3 733	3 887	3 323	3 342	3 663	Totale
Travel	2 804	2 945	2 543	2 550	2 796	Voyage
Passenger transport	929	942	780	792	867	Transport de passagers
Italy						Italie
Total	18 169	16 997	19 636	23 731	24 062	Totale
Travel	15 685	14 795	16 924	20 589	20 460	Voyage
Passenger transport	2 484	2 202	2 712	3 142	3 602	Transport de passagers
Jamaica						Jamaïque
Total	238	227	274	269	318	Totale
Travel	209	206	258	252	286	Voyage
Passenger transport	29	21	16	17	32	Transport de passagers
Japan						Japon
Total	42 643	35 526	34 977	36 506	48 175	Totale
Travel	31 884	26 531	26 656	28 959	38 252	Voyage
Passenger transport	10 759	8 995	8 321	7 547	9 923	Transport de passagers
Jordan						Jordanie
Total	387	421	505	503	585	Totale
Travel	350	378	453	452	524	Voyage
Passenger transport	37	43	52	51	61	Transport de passagers
Kazakhstan						Kazakhstan
Total	483	761	863	783	917	Totale
Travel	408	673	757	669	764	Voyage
Passenger transport	75	88	106	114	153	Transport de passagers
Kenya						Kenya
Total	156	183	...	...	...	Totale
Travel	132	143	126	127	108	Voyage
Passenger transport	24	40	...	...	...	Transport de passagers

Country or area	2000	2001	2002	2003	2004	Pays ou zone
Korea, Republic of						Corée, République de
Total	7 945	8 349	11 440	11 063	13 103	Totale
Travel	7 132	7 617	10 465	10 103	11 986	Voyage
Passenger transport	813	732	975	960	1 117	Transport de passagers
Kuwait						Koweït
Total	2 851	3 208	3 413	3 752	4 140	Totale
Travel	2 494	2 843	3 021	3 349	3 692	Voyage
Passenger transport	357	365	392	403	448	Transport de passagers
Kyrgyzstan						Kirghizistan
Total	23	19	18	24	63	Totale
Travel	16	12	10	17	50	Voyage
Passenger transport	7	7	8	7	13	Transport de passagers
Lao People's Dem. Rep.						Rép. dém. pop. lao
Travel	8	0	...	...	...	Voyage
Latvia						Lettonie
Total	281	255	267	365	429	Totale
Travel	247	223	230	328	378	Voyage
Passenger transport	34	32	37	37	51	Transport de passagers
Lebanon						Liban
Total	...	...	...	3 319	3 719	Totale
Travel	...	...	2 683	2 943	3 170	Voyage
Passenger transport	...	...	...	376	549	Transport de passagers
Lesotho						Lesotho
Total	12	12	16	30	37	Totale
Travel	9	9	14	26	30	Voyage
Passenger transport	3	3	2	4	7	Transport de passagers
Libyan Arab Jamah.						Jamah. arabe libyenne
Total	495	572	654	689	789	Totale
Travel	397	445	586	557	603	Voyage
Passenger transport	98	127	68	132	186	Transport de passagers
Lithuania						Lituanie
Total	261	227	334	476	646	Totale
Travel	253	219	326	471	639	Voyage
Passenger transport	8	8	8	5	7	Transport de passagers
Luxembourg						Luxembourg
Total	...	...	2 159	2 697	3 372	Totale
Travel	1 309	1 464	2 138	2 675	3 333	Voyage
Passenger transport	...	...	21	22	39	Transport de passagers
Madagascar						Madagascar
Total	140	179	109	67	184 [1]	Totale
Travel	116	130	91	64	134 [1]	Voyage
Passenger transport	24	49	18	3	50 [1]	Transport de passagers
Malawi						Malawi
Total	53	53	86	48	...	Totale
Travel	50	41	78	38	50 [11]	Voyage
Passenger transport	3	12	8	10	...	Transport de passagers
Malaysia						Malaisie
Total	2 543	3 391	3 330	3 401	...	Totale
Travel	2 075	2 614	2 618	2 846	3 093 [12]	Voyage
Passenger transport	468	777	712	555	...	Transport de passagers
Maldives						Maldives
Total	60	59	60	60	75	Totale
Travel	46	45	46	46	56	Voyage
Passenger transport	14	14	14	14	19	Transport de passagers
Mali						Mali
Total	66	65	62	94	98 [1]	Totale
Travel	40	36	36	48	50 [1]	Voyage
Passenger transport	26	29	26	46	48 [1]	Transport de passagers
Malta						Malte
Total	224	204	180	238	295	Totale
Travel	200	180	154	215	256	Voyage
Passenger transport	24	24	26	23	39	Transport de passagers

Country or area	2000	2001	2002	2003	2004	Pays ou zone
Mauritius						Maurice
Total	203	216	224	236	277	Totale
Travel	182	198	204	216	255	Voyage
Passenger transport	21	18	20	20	22	Transport de passagers
Mexico						Mexique
Total	6 365	6 685	7 087	7 252	8 034	Totale
Travel	5 499	5 702	6 060	6 253	6 959	Voyage
Passenger transport	866	983	1 027	999	1 075	Transport de passagers
Micronesia (Fed. States of) [1]						Micronésie (Etats féd. de) [1]
Total	5	6	6	6	...	Totale
Mongolia						Mongolie
Total	54	59	125	144	207	Totale
Travel	51	55	119	138	193	Voyage
Passenger transport	3	4	6	6	14	Transport de passagers
Montserrat						Montserrat
Travel	2	2	2	2[2]	2[2]	Voyage
Morocco						Maroc
Total	507	589	670	845	913	Totale
Travel	426	389	444	548	575	Voyage
Passenger transport	81	200	226	297	338	Transport de passagers
Mozambique						Mozambique
Total	122	132	115	141	140	Totale
Travel	108	114	113	140	134	Voyage
Passenger transport	14	18	2	1	6	Transport de passagers
Myanmar						Myanmar
Total	30	32	34	36	32	Totale
Travel	25	27	29	32	29	Voyage
Passenger transport	5	5	5	4	3	Transport de passagers
Namibia						Namibie
Travel	86	71	55	74	88	Voyage
Nepal						Népal
Total	109	128	108	119	205	Totale
Travel	73	80	69	81	154	Voyage
Passenger transport	36	48	39	38	51	Transport de passagers
Netherlands						Pays-Bas
Total	13 649	13 061	14 201	...	...	Totale
Travel	12 191	11 994	12 976	14 583	17 216	Voyage
Passenger transport	1 458	1 067	1 225	...	...	Transport de passagers
New Caledonia						Nouvelle-Calédonie
Travel	...	...	104	128	167	Voyage
New Zealand						Nouvelle-Zélande
Travel	1 533	1 332	1 489	1 782	2 358	Voyage
Nicaragua						Nicaragua
Total	126	128	125	139	158	Totale
Travel	78	76	69	75	86	Voyage
Passenger transport	48	52	56	64	72	Transport de passagers
Niger						Niger
Total	32	33	29	39	...	Totale
Travel	26	26	17	22	...	Voyage
Passenger transport	6	7	12	17	...	Transport de passagers
Nigeria						Nigéria
Total	610	858	910	2 076	1 469	Totale
Travel	591	831	881	1 795	1 161	Voyage
Passenger transport	19	27	29	281	308	Transport de passagers
Norway						Norvège
Total	4 850	4 671	5 542	6 943	8 788	Totale
Travel	4 558	4 363	5 121	6 605	8 383	Voyage
Passenger transport	292	308	421	338	405	Transport de passagers
Occupied Palestinian Terr. [13]						Terr. palestinien occupé [13]
Travel	309	488	...	...	...	Voyage

Tourism expenditure in other countries—Total, travel and passenger transport: million US dollars (*continued*)

Dépenses touristiques dans d'autres pays—Totale, voyage et transport de passager : millions de dollars E.-U. (*suite*)

Country or area	2000	2001	2002	2003	2004	Pays ou zone
Oman						Oman
Total	629	701	701	752	795	Totale
Travel	471	518	531	579	616	Voyage
Passenger transport	158	183	170	173	179	Transport de passagers
Pakistan						Pakistan
Total	574	555	491	1 163	1 590	Totale
Travel	250	252	255	925	1 267	Voyage
Passenger transport	324	303	236	238	323	Transport de passagers
Palau [1]						Palaos [1]
Total	2	2	2	2	2	Totale
Panama						Panama
Total	241	227	252	290	344	Totale
Travel	188	174	179	208	239	Voyage
Passenger transport	53	53	73	82	105	Transport de passagers
Papua New Guinea						Papouasie-Nvl-Guinée
Travel	50	38	...	...	...	Voyage
Paraguay						Paraguay
Total	154	130	118	115	121	Totale
Travel	81	72	65	67	71	Voyage
Passenger transport	73	58	53	48	50	Transport de passagers
Peru						Pérou
Total	641	774	780	794	821	Totale
Travel	423	546	580	598	620	Voyage
Passenger transport	218	228	200	196	201	Transport de passagers
Philippines						Philippines
Total	1 321	1 565	1 260	1 442	1 558	Totale
Travel	1 005	1 229	871	1 206	1 315	Voyage
Passenger transport	316	336	389	236	243	Transport de passagers
Poland						Pologne
Total	3 415	3 594	3 364	3 002	4 157	Totale
Travel	3 313	3 495	3 202	2 801	3 841	Voyage
Passenger transport	102	99	162	201	316	Transport de passagers
Portugal						Portugal
Total	2 754	2 606	2 632	2 982	3 359	Totale
Travel	2 228	2 114	2 125	2 409	2 762	Voyage
Passenger transport	526	492	507	573	597	Transport de passagers
Puerto Rico [14]						Porto Rico [14]
Total	1 333	1 456	1 319	1 420	1 584	Totale
Travel	931	1 004	928	985	1 085	Voyage
Passenger transport	402	452	391	435	499	Transport de passagers
Qatar [15]						Qatar [15]
Travel	307	366	423	471	691	Voyage
Republic of Moldova						République de Moldova
Total	86	90	109	124	157	Totale
Travel	73	75	95	105	135	Voyage
Passenger transport	13	15	14	19	22	Transport de passagers
Romania						Roumanie
Total	447	475	448	572	672	Totale
Travel	425	449	396	479	539	Voyage
Passenger transport	22	26	52	93	133	Transport de passagers
Russian Federation						Fédération de Russie
Total	...	9 760	11 713	13 427	16 527	Totale
Travel	8 848	9 285	11 284	12 880	15 730	Voyage
Passenger transport	...	475	429	547	797	Transport de passagers
Rwanda						Rwanda
Total	35	33	...	...	...	Totale
Travel	22	20	24	26	31	Voyage
Passenger transport	13	13	...	...	...	Transport de passagers
Saint Kitts and Nevis						Saint-Kitts-et-Nevis
Travel	9	8	8	8 [2]	9 [2]	Voyage

Country or area	2000	2001	2002	2003	2004	Pays ou zone
Saint Lucia						Sainte-Lucie
Travel	33	32	34	36[2]	38[2]	Voyage
Saint Maarten [3,16]						Saint-Martin [3,16]
Travel	127	137	140	143	110	Voyage
St. Vincent-Grenadines						St. Vincent-Grenadines
Travel	9	10	10	11[1]	12[1]	Voyage
Sao Tome and Principe						Sao Tomé-et-Principe
Total	2	2	2	...	...	Totale
Travel	1	1	1	...	...	Voyage
Passenger transport	2	1	1	...	...	Transport de passagers
Saudi Arabia [1]						Arabie saoudite [1]
Total	...	...	7 370	4 165	4 262	Totale
Senegal						Sénégal
Total	125	112	112	129	...	Totale
Travel	47	43	43	55	...	Voyage
Passenger transport	78	69	69	74	...	Transport de passagers
Seychelles						Seychelles
Total	30	29	44	52[17]	53[17]	Totale
Travel	22	21	34	34[17]	32[17]	Voyage
Passenger transport	8	8	10	18[17]	21[17]	Transport de passagers
Sierra Leone						Sierra Leone
Total	35	42	39	38	30	Totale
Travel	32	42	39	37	30	Voyage
Passenger transport	3	0	0	1	0	Transport de passagers
Singapore						Singapour
Travel	4 535	5 874	6 343	5 470	7 750	Voyage
Slovakia						Slovaquie
Total	341	340[1]	506	662	903[1]	Totale
Travel	296	289[1]	442	573	745[1]	Voyage
Passenger transport	45	51[1]	64	89	158[1]	Transport de passagers
Slovenia						Slovénie
Total	544	560	647	805	940	Totale
Travel	511	528	608	752	871	Voyage
Passenger transport	33	32	39	53	69	Transport de passagers
Solomon Islands [18]						Iles Salomon [18]
Travel	10	7	6	4	9	Voyage
South Africa						Afrique du Sud
Total	2 684	2 366	2 251	3 670	3 661	Totale
Travel	2 085	1 878	1 811	2 889	2 680	Voyage
Passenger transport	599	488	440	781	981	Transport de passagers
Spain						Espagne
Total	7 264	7 897	8 733	10 544	13 337	Totale
Travel	5 476	5 960	6 662	8 285	11 078	Voyage
Passenger transport	1 788	1 937	2 071	2 259	2 259	Transport de passagers
Sri Lanka						Sri Lanka
Total	383	404	438	462	499	Totale
Travel	240	251	263	279	296	Voyage
Passenger transport	143	153	175	183	203	Transport de passagers
Sudan						Soudan
Travel	55	74	91	119	176	Voyage
Suriname						Suriname
Total	67	62	54	68	85	Totale
Travel	23	23	10	6	14	Voyage
Passenger transport	44	39	44	62	71	Transport de passagers
Swaziland						Swaziland
Total	65	48	40	44	54	Totale
Travel	64	47	39	43	52	Voyage
Passenger transport	1	1	1	1	2	Transport de passagers

Country or area	2000	2001	2002	2003	2004	Pays ou zone
Sweden						Suède
Total	8 959	7 916	8 221	9 375	11 309[1]	Totale
Travel	8 048	6 921	7 301	8 296	9 946[1]	Voyage
Passenger transport	911	995	920	1 079	1 363[1]	Transport de passagers
Switzerland						Suisse
Total	8 276	8 179	8 347	9 194	10 599	Totale
Travel	6 335	6 235	6 674	7 463	8 779	Voyage
Passenger transport	1 941	1 944	1 673	1 731	1 820	Transport de passagers
Syrian Arab Republic						Rép. arabe syrienne
Total	...	...	...	734	698	Totale
Travel	669	670	760	700	650	Voyage
Passenger transport	...	...	...	34	48	Transport de passagers
Tajikistan						Tadjikistan
Travel	...	...	2	2	3	Voyage
Thailand						Thaïlande
Total	3 218	3 334	3 888	3 539	5 343	Totale
Travel	2 772	2 924	3 303	2 921	4 514	Voyage
Passenger transport	446	410	585	618	829	Transport de passagers
TFYR of Macedonia						L'ex-R.y. Macédoine
Total	58	60	61	71	84	Totale
Travel	34	39	45	48	55	Voyage
Passenger transport	24	21	16	23	29	Transport de passagers
Togo						Togo
Total	15	20	26	37	...	Totale
Travel	2	5	5	7	...	Voyage
Passenger transport	13	15	21	30	...	Transport de passagers
Tonga						Tonga
Travel	...	3	3	...	...	Voyage
Trinidad and Tobago						Trinité-et-Tobago
Total	190	172	208	143	141[1]	Totale
Travel	147	151	186	107	96[1]	Voyage
Passenger transport	43	21	22	36	45[1]	Transport de passagers
Tunisia						Tunisie
Total	310	322	303	355	427	Totale
Travel	263	273	260	300	340	Voyage
Passenger transport	47	49	43	55	87	Transport de passagers
Turkey						Turquie
Travel	1 713	1 738	1 881	2 113	2 524	Voyage
Uganda						Ouganda
Travel	...	...	...	...	121	Voyage
Ukraine						Ukraine
Total	561	676	794	953	1 193	Totale
Travel	470	566	657	789	996	Voyage
Passenger transport	91	110	137	164	197	Transport de passagers
United Arab Emirates [1]						Emirats arabes unis [1]
Total	3 019	3 321	3 654	3 959	4 475	Totale
United Kingdom						Royaume-Uni
Total	47 009	46 123	50 651	57 921	68 778	Totale
Travel	38 262	37 931	41 744	47 853	56 428	Voyage
Passenger transport	8 747	8 192	8 907	10 068	12 350	Transport de passagers
United Rep. of Tanzania						Rép.-Unie de Tanzanie
Total	369	380	365	384	446	Totale
Travel	337	342	341	362	422	Voyage
Passenger transport	32	38	24	22	24	Transport de passagers
United States						Etats-Unis
Total	91 317	85 453	81 707	81 927	93 217	Totale
Travel	67 043	62 820	61 738	60 970	69 516	Voyage
Passenger transport	24 274	22 633	19 969	20 957	23 701	Transport de passagers

Country or area	2000	2001	2002	2003	2004	Pays ou zone
Uruguay						Uruguay
Total	381	333	243	236	281	Totale
Travel	281	252	178	169	194	Voyage
Passenger transport	100	81	65	67	87	Transport de passagers
Vanuatu						Vanuatu
Total	...	...	11	14	...	Totale
Travel	9	8	9	12	...	Voyage
Passenger transport	...	...	2	2	...	Transport de passagers
Venezuela (Bolivarian Rep. of)						Venezuela (Rép. bolivar. du)
Total	1 647	1 718	1 546	1 311	1 603	Totale
Travel	1 058	1 108	981	859	1 076	Voyage
Passenger transport	589	610	565	452	527	Transport de passagers
Yemen						Yémen
Total	127	136	135	134	183	Totale
Travel	70	79	78	77	126	Voyage
Passenger transport	57	57	57	57	57	Transport de passagers
Zambia						Zambie
Total	102	...	...	...	...	Totale
Travel	44	57[1]	67[1]	77[1]	89[1]	Voyage
Passenger transport	58	...	...	...	...	Transport de passagers

Source

World Tourism Organization (UNWTO), Madrid, UNWTO statistics database and *Yearbook of Tourism Statistics*, 2005 edition. The majority of the data have been provided to the UNWTO by the International Monetary Fund (IMF). Exceptions are footnoted.

Notes

[1] Figures provided by the country to the World Tourism Organisation (UNWTO).

[2] Source: Eastern Caribbean Central Bank.

[3] Source: Central Bank of the Netherlands Antilles.

[4] Source: Bank of Bostwana.

[5] Source: Banco de Cabo Verde.

[6] Source: Banque des Etats de l'Afrique Centrale (B.E.A.C.).

[7] For statistical purposes, the data for China do not include those for the Hong Kong Special Administrative Region (Hong Kong SAR), Macao Special Administrative Region (Macao SAR) and Taiwan Province of China.

[8] Source: Banque centrale de Djibouti.

[9] Source: Central Bank of Islamic Republic of Iran.

[10] Central Bank.

[11] Source: Reserve Bank of Malawi.

[12] Source: Department of Statistics Malaysia.

[13] West Bank and Gaza.

[14] Fiscal years (July-June). The expenditure figures are those provided by the country to UNWTO, which do not appear in the International Monetary Fund data.

[15] Source: Qatar Central Bank.

[16] Including the estimates for Saba and Saint Eustatius. Excluding passenger transport. Source: Central Bank of the Netherlands Antilles.

[17] Source: Central Bank of Seychelles.

[18] Source: Central Bank of Solomon Islands.

Source

Organisation mondiale du tourisme (OMT), Madrid, la base de données de l'OMT, et *Annuaire des statistiques du tourisme*, 2005 édition. La majorité des données sont celles que le Fonds monétaire international (FMI) a fournis à l'Organisation mondiale du tourisme (OMT). Les exceptions sont signalées par une note.

Notes

[1] Les chiffres de dépense sont ceux que le pays a fournis à l'Organisation mondiale du tourisme (OMT).

[2] Source : Eastern Caribbean Central Bank.

[3] Source : Central Bank of the Netherlands Antilles.

[4] Source : Bank of Bostwana.

[5] Source : Banco de Cabo Verde.

[6] Source : Banque des Etats de l'Afrique Centrale (B.E.A.C.).

[7] Pour la présentation des statistiques, les données pour Chine ne comprennent pas la Région Administrative Spéciale de Hong Kong (Hong Kong RAS), la Région Administrative Spéciale de Macao (Macao RAS) et la province de Taiwan.

[8] Source : Banque centrale de Djibouti.

[9] Source : Central Bank of Islamic Republic of Iran.

[10] Banque centrale.

[11] Source : Reserve Bank of Malawi.

[12] Source : Department of Statistics Malaysia.

[13] Cisjordanie et Gaza.

[14] Années fiscales (juillet-juin). Les chiffres de dépense sont ceux que le pays a fournis à l'OMT mais ils ne figurent pas dans les données du Fonds monétaire international.

[15] Source : Qatar Central Bank.

[16] Y compris estimations pour Saba et Saint-Eustache. Non compris le transport de passagers. Source : Central Bank of the Netherlands Antilles.

[17] Source : Central Bank of Seychelles.

[18] Source : Central Bank of Solomon Islands.

The data on international tourism have been supplied by the United Nations World Tourism Organization (UNWTO) from detailed tourism information published in the *Compendium of Tourism Statistics* [36] and in the *Tourism Factbook* online available from http://www.unwto.org/statistics/index.htm.

For statistical purposes, the term "international visitor" describes "any person who travels to a country other than that in which he/she has his/her usual residence but outside his/her usual environment for a period not exceeding 12 months and whose main purpose of visit is other than the exercise of an activity remunerated from within the country visited".

International visitors include: (a) *tourists* (overnight visitors): "visitors who stay at least one night in a collective or private accommodation in the country visited"; and (b) *same-day visitors*: "visitors who do not spend the night in a collective or private accommodation in the country visited". The figures do not include immigrants, residents in a frontier zone, persons domiciled in one country or area and working in an adjoining country or area, members of the armed forces and diplomats and consular representatives when they travel from their country of origin to the country in which they are stationed and vice-versa. The figures also exclude persons in transit who do not formally enter the country through passport control, such as air transit passengers who remain for a short period in a designated area of the air terminal or ship passengers who are not permitted to disembark. This category includes passengers transferred directly between airports or other terminals. Other passengers in transit through a country are classified as visitors.

Tables 68 and 69: Data on arrivals of non-resident (or international) visitors may be obtained from different sources. In some cases data are obtained from border statistics derived from administrative records (police, immigration, traffic counts and other types of controls) border surveys and registrations at accommodation establishments.

Unless otherwise stated, table 68 shows the number of non-resident tourist/visitor arrivals at national borders classified by their region of origin. Totals correspond to the total number of arrivals from the regions indicated in the table. However, these totals may not correspond to the number of tourist arrivals shown in table 69. The latter excludes same-day visitors except when indicated whereas they may be included in table 68.

When a person visits the same country several times a year, an equal number of arrivals is recorded. Likewise, if a person visits several countries during the course of a single trip, his/her arrival in each country is recorded separately. Consequently, arrivals cannot be assumed to be equal to the number of persons traveling.

Les données sur le tourisme international ont été fournies par l'Organisation mondiale du tourisme (l'OMT) qui publie des renseignements détaillés sur le tourisme dans *le Compendium de statistiques du tourisme* [36] et dans le *Tourism Factbook* en ligne au http://www.unwto.org/statistics/index.htm.

A des fins statistiques, l'expression "visiteur international" désigne "toute personne qui se rend dans un pays autre que celui où elle a son lieu de résidence habituelle, mais différent de son environnement habituel, pour une période de 12 mois au maximum, dans un but principal autre que celui d'y exercer une profession rémunérée".

Entrent dans cette catégorie: (a) *les touristes* (visiteurs passant la nuit), c'est à dire "les visiteurs qui passent une nuit au moins en logement collectif ou privé dans le pays visité"; et (b) *les visiteurs ne restant que la journée*, c'est à dire "les visiteurs qui ne passent pas la nuit en logement collectif ou privé dans le pays visité". Ces chiffres ne comprennent pas les immigrants, les résidents frontaliers, les personnes domiciliées dans une zone ou un pays donné et travaillant dans une zone ou pays limitrophe, les membres des forces armées et les membres des corps diplomatique et consulaire lorsqu'ils se rendent de leur pays d'origine au pays où ils sont en poste, et vice versa. Ne sont pas non plus inclus les voyageurs en transit, qui ne pénètrent pas officiellement dans le pays en faisant contrôler leurs passeports, tels que les passagers d'un vol en escale, qui demeurent pendant un court laps de temps dans une aire distincte de l'aérogare, ou les passagers d'un navire qui ne sont pas autorisés à débarquer. Cette catégorie comprend également les passagers transportés directement d'une aérogare à l'autre ou à un autre terminal. Les autres passagers en transit dans un pays sont classés parmi les visiteurs.

Tableaux 68 et 69: Les données relatives aux arrivées des visiteurs non résidents (ou internationaux) peuvent être obtenues de différentes sources. Dans certains cas, elles proviennent des statistiques des frontières tirées des registres administratifs (contrôles de police, de l'immigration, de la circulation et autres effectués aux frontières nationales) et des enquêtes statistiques aux frontières et des enregistrements d'établissements d'hébergement touristique.

Sauf indication contraire, le tableau 68 indique le nombre d'arrivées de touristes/visiteurs non résidents aux frontières nationales par région de provenance. Les totaux correspondent au nombre total d'arrivées de touristes des régions indiquées sur le tableau. Les chiffres totaux peuvent néanmoins, ne pas coïncider avec le nombre des arrivées de touristes indiqué dans le tableau 69, qui sauf indication contraire ne comprend pas les visiteurs ne restant que la journée, lesquels peuvent au contraire être inclus dans les chiffres du tableau 68.

Expenditure associated with tourism activity of visitors has been traditionally identified with the travel item of the Balance of Payments (BOP): in the case of inbound tourism, those expenditures in the country of reference associated with non-resident visitors are registered as "credits" in the BOP and refer to "travel receipts".

The new conceptual framework approved by the United Nations Statistical Commission in relation to the measurement of tourism macroeconomic activity (the so-called Tourism Satellite Account) considers that "tourism industries and products" includes transport of passengers. Consequently, a better estimate of tourism-related expenditures by resident and non-resident visitors in an international scenario would be, in terms of the BOP, the value of the travel item plus that of the passenger transport item.

Nevertheless, users should be aware that BOP estimates include, in addition to expenditures associated with visitors, those related to other types of individuals.

The data published should allow international comparability and therefore correspond to those published by the International Monetary Fund (and provided by the Central Banks). Exceptions are footnoted.

Table 70: Indicators on expenditure (in other countries) are equivalent to those for inbound tourism but are registered as "debits" in the BOP's *travel and passenger transport* items. The data published are also provided by the International Monetary Fund and the same previous warning is applicable.

More detailed tourism information from the United Nations World Tourism Organization is available in the *Compendium of Tourism Statistics* [36] and from http://www.unwto.org/statistics/index.htm; information on the balance of payments are published by the International Monetary Fund in the *Balance of Payments Statistics Yearbook* [12].

Lorsqu'une personne visite le même pays plusieurs fois dans l'année, il est enregistré un nombre égal d'arrivées. En outre, si une personne visite plusieurs pays au cours d'un seul et même voyage, son arrivée dans chaque pays est enregistrée séparément. Par conséquent, on ne peut pas partir du postulat que les arrivées sont égales au nombre de personnes qui voyagent.

Les dépenses associées à l'activité touristique des visiteurs sont traditionnellement identifiées au poste «Voyages» de la balance des paiements. Dans le cas du tourisme récepteur, ces dépenses associées aux visiteurs non résidents sont enregistrées dans la balance des paiements comme des «crédits» et il s'agit de «recettes au titre des voyages».

Le cadre conceptuel approuvé par la Commission de statistique de l'Organisation des Nations Unies concernant l'évaluation de l'activité touristique à l'échelle macroéconomique (cadre qu'il est convenu d'appeler compte satellite du tourisme) considère que la notion «industries et produits touristiques» englobe le transport de passagers. Par conséquent, une meilleure estimation des dépenses liées au tourisme international que font les visiteurs résidents et non résidents serait, sous l'angle de la balance des paiements, la somme des valeurs des postes «Voyages» et «Transport de passagers».

Néanmoins, les utilisateurs doivent être conscients que les estimations de la balance des paiements comprennent, outre les dépenses associées aux visiteurs, celles liées à d'autres types d'individus.

Les données publiées doivent permettre la comparabilité internationale et donc correspondre à celles publiées par le Fonds monétaire international (FMI) qui viennent des banques centrales. Les exceptions sont signalées par une note de pied.

Tableau 70: Les indicateurs relatifs aux dépenses touristiques dans d'autres pays sont équivalents à ceux du tourisme récepteur mais ils sont enregistrés comme «débits» aux postes «Voyages» et «Transport de passagers» de la balance des paiements. Les données publiées sont également fournies par le FMI. Il y a lieu de faire la même mise en garde que plus haut.

On trouvera plus de renseignements publiés par l'Organisation mondiale du tourisme dans le *Compendium des statistiques du tourisme* [36] et au http://www.unwto.org/statistics/index.htm; des renseignements sur la balance des paiements sont publiés par le Fonds monétaire international dans *Balance of Payments Statistics Yearbook* [12].

Summary of balance of payments
Millions of US dollars

Résumé des balances des paiements
Millions de dollars des E.-U.

Country or area	1998	1999	2000	2001	2002	2003	2004	Pays ou zone
Albania								**Albanie**
Goods: Exports fob	208.0	275.0	255.7	304.5	330.2	447.2	...	Biens : exportations, fab
Goods: Imports fob	−811.7	−938.0	−1 070.0	−1 331.6	−1 485.4	−1 783.5	...	Biens : importations, fab
Serv. & Income: Credit	172.6	354.9	563.7	696.8	733.3	914.5	...	Serv. & revenu : crédit
Serv. & Income: Debit	−138.0	−173.3	−438.6	−457.6	−610.8	−827.0	...	Serv. & revenu : débit
Current Trans.,nie: Credit	560.8	508.9	629.0	647.5	683.7	924.2	...	Transf. cour.,nia : crédit
Current Transfers: Debit	−56.9	−182.9	−96.1	−76.9	−58.6	−82.3	...	Transf. courants : débit
Capital Acct.,nie: Credit	31.0	22.6	78.0	117.7	121.2	157.0	...	Compte de cap.,nia : crédit
Capital Account: Debit	0.0	0.0	0.0	0.0	0.0	0.0	...	Compte de capital : débit
Financial Account, nie	15.4	33.7	188.4	110.0	213.4	200.6	...	Compte d'op. fin., nia
Net Errors and Omissions	71.1	206.2	9.8	136.3	108.5	147.4	...	Erreurs et omissions nettes
Reserves & Related Items	−52.4	−107.1	−119.9	−146.7	−35.6	−98.1	...	Rés. et postes appareutés
Angola								**Angola**
Goods: Exports fob	3 542.9	5 156.5	7 920.7	6 534.3	8 327.9	9 508.2	13 475.0	Biens : exportations, fab
Goods: Imports fob	−2 079.4	−3 109.1	−3 039.5	−3 179.2	−3 760.1	−5 480.1	−5 831.8	Biens : importations, fab
Serv. & Income: Credit	156.3	177.1	301.7	225.5	224.5	213.3	355.8	Serv. & revenu : crédit
Serv. & Income: Debit	−3 638.4	−3 990.7	−4 414.7	−5 102.1	−4 974.4	−5 059.9	−7 319.4	Serv. & revenu : débit
Current Trans.,nie: Credit	238.2	154.5	123.5	208.3	142.3	186.2	124.4	Transf. cour.,nia : crédit
Current Transfers: Debit	−86.7	−98.7	−96.0	−117.8	−110.3	−87.3	−117.9	Transf. courants : débit
Capital Acct.,nie: Credit	8.4	6.8	18.3	3.9	0.0	0.0	0.0	Compte de cap.,nia : crédit
Capital Account: Debit	0.0	0.0	0.0	0.0	0.0	0.0	0.0	Compte de capital : débit
Financial Account, nie	368.3	1 739.6	−445.6	950.0	−356.7	1 370.5	−628.2	Compte d'op. fin., nia
Net Errors and Omissions	378.5	−78.9	−50.6	−308.6	150.5	−388.2	282.3	Erreurs et omissions nettes
Reserves & Related Items	1 112.0	42.9	−317.8	785.6	356.3	−262.8	−340.3	Rés. et postes appareutés
Anguilla								**Anguilla**
Goods: Exports fob	3.5	2.9	4.4	3.6	4.4	...	...	Biens : exportations, fab
Goods: Imports fob	−63.0	−80.9	−83.3	−68.5	−61.6	...	...	Biens : importations, fab
Serv. & Income: Credit	81.0	72.5	68.9	72.3	67.1	...	...	Serv. & revenu : crédit
Serv. & Income: Debit	−43.6	−45.2	−47.5	−44.5	−45.4	...	...	Serv. & revenu : débit
Current Trans.,nie: Credit	9.3	8.2	11.1	9.8	8.5	...	...	Transf. cour.,nia : crédit
Current Transfers: Debit	−6.2	−8.6	−8.1	−8.6	−8.4	...	...	Transf. courants : débit
Capital Acct.,nie: Credit	7.0	9.3	11.1	10.1	8.1	...	...	Compte de cap.,nia : crédit
Capital Account: Debit	−1.3	−1.3	−1.3	−1.3	−1.3	...	...	Compte de capital : débit
Financial Account, nie	11.6	58.8	41.0	20.2	17.3	...	...	Compte d'op. fin., nia
Net Errors and Omissions	3.7	−13.9	4.1	10.7	13.1	...	...	Erreurs et omissions nettes
Reserves & Related Items	−1.8	−1.8	−0.4	−3.9	−1.8	...	...	Rés. et postes appareutés
Antigua and Barbuda								**Antigua-et-Barbuda**
Goods: Exports fob	37.4	37.4	49.7	38.6	44.8	...	...	Biens : exportations, fab
Goods: Imports fob	−320.8	−352.7	−342.4	−321.2	−335.6	...	...	Biens : importations, fab
Serv. & Income: Credit	441.4	450.9	431.9	421.4	404.4	...	...	Serv. & revenu : crédit
Serv. & Income: Debit	−203.0	−212.4	−214.4	−212.4	−221.7	...	...	Serv. & revenu : débit
Current Trans.,nie: Credit	12.4	23.6	18.4	22.5	23.0	...	...	Transf. cour.,nia : crédit
Current Transfers: Debit	−14.1	−4.1	−9.1	−13.4	−17.4	...	...	Transf. courants : débit
Capital Acct.,nie: Credit	156.3	17.6	39.3	11.9	13.9	...	...	Compte de cap.,nia : crédit
Capital Account: Debit	0.0	0.0	0.0	0.0	0.0	...	...	Compte de capital : débit
Financial Account, nie	−56.7	52.1	42.1	60.0	84.6	...	...	Compte d'op. fin., nia
Net Errors and Omissions	−44.0	−2.1	−21.8	8.4	11.7	...	...	Erreurs et omissions nettes
Reserves & Related Items	−8.9	−10.4	6.2	−16.0	−7.7	...	...	Rés. et postes appareutés
Argentina								**Argentine**
Goods: Exports fob	26 433.7	23 308.6	26 341.0	26 542.7	25 650.6	29 938.8	34 550.2	Biens : exportations, fab
Goods: Imports fob	−29 530.9	−24 103.2	−23 889.1	−19 157.8	−8 473.1	−13 134.2	−21 311.1	Biens : importations, fab
Serv. & Income: Credit	10 987.7	10 793.8	12 355.7	10 474.5	6 316.7	7 308.4	8 660.1	Serv. & revenu : crédit
Serv. & Income: Debit	−22 836.6	−22 395.4	−24 187.2	−21 574.8	−15 390.7	−16 676.1	−19 259.3	Serv. & revenu : débit
Current Trans.,nie: Credit	801.8	790.2	792.0	855.7	798.5	921.6	1 103.6	Transf. cour.,nia : crédit

Country or area	1998	1999	2000	2001	2002	2003	2004	Pays ou zone
Current Transfers: Debit	−337.8	−336.9	−392.9	−431.2	−234.4	−376.7	−462.9	Transf. courants : débit
Capital Acct.,nie: Credit	91.5	160.6	120.8	164.7	410.2	76.7	47.2	Compte de cap.,nia : crédit
Capital Account: Debit	−18.6	−11.5	−14.9	−8.2	−4.1	−6.6	−4.3	Compte de capital : débit
Financial Account, nie	18 935.9	14 448.1	7 852.7	−14 971.0	−20 686.2	−15 864.4	−10 447.9	Compte d'op. fin., nia
Net Errors and Omissions	−436.5	−641.8	−154.4	−3 299.5	−1 789.9	−1 264.8	131.1	Erreurs et omissions nettes
Reserves & Related Items	−4 090.3	−2 012.7	1 176.4	21 405.0	13 402.4	9 077.4	6 993.4	Rés. et postes apparentés
Armenia								**Arménie**
Goods: Exports fob	228.9	247.3	309.9	353.1	513.8	696.1	738.3	Biens : exportations, fab
Goods: Imports fob	−806.3	−721.4	−773.4	−773.3	−882.5	−1 130.2	−1 196.3	Biens : importations, fab
Serv. & Income: Credit	234.3	229.4	240.7	290.3	320.4	373.3	557.4	Serv. & revenu : crédit
Serv. & Income: Debit	−252.2	−236.5	−243.6	−243.6	−272.9	−347.2	−591.5	Serv. & revenu : débit
Current Trans.,nie: Credit	203.0	200.6	208.5	200.8	199.7	245.0	389.1	Transf. cour.,nia : crédit
Current Transfers: Debit	−25.6	−26.5	−20.5	−26.8	−26.3	−26.5	−58.7	Transf. courants : débit
Capital Acct.,nie: Credit	9.7	16.9	29.5	32.6	70.2	92.1	40.2	Compte de cap.,nia : crédit
Capital Account: Debit	0.0	−4.3	−1.2	−2.5	−2.1	−2.2	−5.9	Compte de capital : débit
Financial Account, nie	390.4	286.2	249.9	175.1	147.8	174.5	161.0	Compte d'op. fin., nia
Net Errors and Omissions	18.4	13.1	17.0	11.1	−4.8	−1.6	−0.8	Erreurs et omissions nettes
Reserves & Related Items	−0.6	−4.8	−16.9	−16.7	−63.2	−73.4	−32.8	Rés. et postes apparentés
Aruba								**Aruba**
Goods: Exports fob	1 164.8	1 390.5	2 525.9	2 423.9	1 487.9	2 049.5	2 715.2	Biens : exportations, fab
Goods: Imports fob	−1 518.2	−1 995.6	−2 582.7	−2 369.2	−2 018.2	−2 378.4	−2 986.2	Biens : importations, fab
Serv. & Income: Credit	932.6	966.5	1 064.4	1 044.1	1 030.9	1 079.3	1 275.9	Serv. & revenu : crédit
Serv. & Income: Debit	−593.2	−737.9	−710.6	−715.3	−765.0	−802.9	−889.9	Serv. & revenu : débit
Current Trans.,nie: Credit	29.3	34.5	36.9	40.2	34.9	40.1	40.1	Transf. cour.,nia : crédit
Current Transfers: Debit	−34.1	−79.3	−108.7	−98.2	−109.8	−123.3	−144.6	Transf. courants : débit
Capital Acct.,nie: Credit	10.2	6.5	16.3	8.5	28.5	122.5	28.7	Compte de cap.,nia : crédit
Capital Account: Debit	−5.0	−5.0	−5.0	−10.0	−7.2	−21.7	−10.3	Compte de capital : débit
Financial Account, nie	64.2	443.7	−262.8	−230.4	334.9	−10.6	−28.2	Compte d'op. fin., nia
Net Errors and Omissions	0.6	−20.9	11.5	−10.8	23.4	9.2	1.0	Erreurs et omissions nettes
Reserves & Related Items	−51.3	−2.8	15.0	−82.8	−40.2	36.4	−1.6	Rés. et postes apparentés
Australia								**Australie**
Goods: Exports fob	55 883.6	56 096.0	64 024.9	63 625.2	65 013.1	70 526.5	87 096.1	Biens : exportations, fab
Goods: Imports fob	−61 215.2	−65 856.9	−68 865.5	−61 889.6	−70 529.7	−85 861.5	−105 238.0	Biens : importations, fab
Serv. & Income: Credit	22 938.0	25 094.1	28 039.0	25 644.1	27 160.0	32 385.0	40 353.7	Serv. & revenu : crédit
Serv. & Income: Debit	−35 661.9	−37 516.4	−38 456.6	−35 255.0	−38 047.6	−46 585.7	−61 964.3	Serv. & revenu : débit
Current Trans.,nie: Credit	2 650.6	3 002.7	2 621.8	2 242.4	2 309.9	2 767.4	3 145.1	Transf. cour.,nia : crédit
Current Transfers: Debit	−2 932.7	−3 031.7	−2 669.1	−2 221.4	−2 373.4	−2 927.3	−3 414.0	Transf. courants : débit
Capital Acct.,nie: Credit	1 315.3	1 534.7	1 405.9	1 319.8	1 298.0	1 663.9	0.0	Compte de cap.,nia : crédit
Capital Account: Debit	−645.6	−715.5	−790.9	−728.9	−854.8	−928.3	0.0	Compte de capital : débit
Financial Account, nie	15 204.0	27 613.2	12 953.5	8 155.2	16 798.1	36 233.8	39 960.2	Compte d'op. fin., nia
Net Errors and Omissions	423.8	485.3	372.4	204.0	−651.4	−396.8	443.3	Erreurs et omissions nettes
Reserves & Related Items	2 040.0	−6 705.5	1 364.7	−1 095.7	−122.1	−6 877.1	−1 165.9	Rés. et postes apparentés
Austria								**Autriche**
Goods: Exports fob	63 299.1	64 421.7	64 684.0	66 900.2	73 667.5	89 621.7	112 068.0	Biens : exportations, fab
Goods: Imports fob	−66 983.3	−68 050.8	−67 420.7	−68 169.3	−70 079.7	−88 480.4	−109 020.0	Biens : importations, fab
Serv. & Income: Credit	39 715.8	43 978.5	43 333.2	45 382.1	49 202.0	59 132.8	67 721.9	Serv. & revenu : crédit
Serv. & Income: Debit	−39 356.2	−44 973.7	−44 108.5	−46 547.6	−50 401.2	−58 617.5	−67 249.0	Serv. & revenu : débit
Current Trans.,nie: Credit	2 940.4	2 924.8	2 914.2	3 266.8	3 815.3	4 388.1	5 314.0	Transf. cour.,nia : crédit
Current Transfers: Debit	−4 874.0	−4 956.1	−4 266.6	−4 468.4	−5 638.9	−6 682.8	−8 070.3	Transf. courants : débit
Capital Acct.,nie: Credit	483.3	554.6	530.2	483.3	1 011.9	896.6	760.2	Compte de cap.,nia : crédit
Capital Account: Debit	−830.6	−820.0	−962.1	−1 012.5	−1 389.7	−888.1	−1 105.4	Compte de capital : débit
Financial Account, nie	9 534.8	4 788.7	3 407.2	1 794.9	−4 713.2	−2 463.9	−1 812.2	Compte d'op. fin., nia
Net Errors and Omissions	−447.2	−39.7	1 143.2	482.3	2 803.4	1 070.3	−456.8	Erreurs et omissions nettes
Reserves & Related Items	−3 481.9	2 171.9	745.8	1 888.4	1 722.6	2 023.5	1 849.3	Rés. et postes apparentés
Azerbaijan								**Azerbaïdjan**
Goods: Exports fob	677.8	1 025.2	1 858.3	2 078.9	2 304.9	2 624.6	3 743.0	Biens : exportations, fab
Goods: Imports fob	−1 723.9	−1 433.4	−1 539.0	−1 465.1	−1 823.3	−2 723.1	−3 581.7	Biens : importations, fab
Serv. & Income: Credit	370.0	267.8	315.7	331.3	399.3	484.6	557.3	Serv. & revenu : crédit
Serv. & Income: Debit	−752.3	−541.1	−875.9	−1 073.5	−1 719.6	−2 541.2	−3 496.4	Serv. & revenu : débit

Country or area	1998	1999	2000	2001	2002	2003	2004	Pays ou zone
Current Trans.,nie: Credit	145.0	134.5	135.0	176.5	228.2	225.1	262.6	Transf. cour.,nia : crédit
Current Transfers: Debit	−80.9	−52.8	−62.0	−99.9	−157.9	−90.9	−74.1	Transf. courants : débit
Capital Acct.,nie: Credit	0.0	0.0	0.0	0.0	18.4	15.0	24.0	Compte de cap.,nia : crédit
Capital Account: Debit	−0.7	0.0	0.0	0.0	−47.1	−38.1	−28.1	Compte de capital : débit
Financial Account, nie	1 326.0	690.2	493.4	126.0	918.0	2 279.7	2 960.2	Compte d'op. fin., nia
Net Errors and Omissions	−20.1	42.4	0.0	−0.9	−86.7	−111.8	−49.9	Erreurs et omissions nettes
Reserves & Related Items	59.2	−132.9	−325.6	−73.4	−34.2	−123.8	−317.0	Rés. et postes appareutés
Bahamas								**Bahamas**
Goods: Exports fob	362.9	406.8	464.8	416.9	422.1	426.5	471.2	Biens : exportations, fab
Goods: Imports fob	−1 737.1	−1 677.2	−1 983.1	−1 804.2	−1 749.0	−1 758.5	−1 811.5	Biens : importations, fab
Serv. & Income: Credit	1 680.9	2 193.4	2 290.1	1 988.9	2 169.5	2 133.8	2 322.1	Serv. & revenu : crédit
Serv. & Income: Debit	−1 336.3	−1 453.2	−1 482.8	−1 356.6	−1 308.2	−1 324.0	−1 436.0	Serv. & revenu : débit
Current Trans.,nie: Credit	45.0	218.3	88.5	120.9	55.4	59.8	264.7	Transf. cour.,nia : crédit
Current Transfers: Debit	−10.8	−12.5	−10.5	−10.9	−13.0	−11.1	−13.9	Transf. courants : débit
Capital Acct.,nie: Credit	0.0	0.0	0.0	0.0	0.0	0.0	0.0	Compte de cap.,nia : crédit
Capital Account: Debit	−11.7	−14.5	−16.4	−21.3	−24.5	−37.4	−47.9	Compte de capital : débit
Financial Account, nie	817.7	616.1	429.9	264.6	405.0	535.5	359.4	Compte d'op. fin., nia
Net Errors and Omissions	308.6	−212.0	158.4	370.8	102.9	85.5	75.2	Erreurs et omissions nettes
Reserves & Related Items	−119.2	−65.2	61.0	30.9	−60.1	−110.1	−183.3	Rés. et postes appareutés
Bahrain								**Bahreïn**
Goods: Exports fob	3 270.2	4 362.8	6 242.7	5 657.1	5 887.3	6 720.9	7 620.7	Biens : exportations, fab
Goods: Imports fob	−3 298.7	−3 468.4	−4 393.6	−4 047.1	−4 697.3	−5 319.2	−6 135.4	Biens : importations, fab
Serv. & Income: Credit	5 488.8	5 977.4	7 261.4	4 744.7	2 746.8	2 526.6	4 102.5	Serv. & revenu : crédit
Serv. & Income: Debit	−5 577.9	−6 089.3	−7 290.0	−4 863.6	−3 130.4	−2 645.3	−4 052.6	Serv. & revenu : débit
Current Trans.,nie: Credit	65.2	36.7	22.4	22.9	14.7	0.0	0.0	Transf. cour.,nia : crédit
Current Transfers: Debit	−725.0	−856.2	−1 012.7	−1 286.9	−871.5	−1 082.2	−1 120.0	Transf. courants : débit
Capital Acct.,nie: Credit	100.0	100.0	50.0	100.0	101.6	50.0	50.0	Compte de cap.,nia : crédit
Capital Account: Debit	0.0	0.0	0.0	0.0	0.0	0.0	0.0	Compte de capital : débit
Financial Account, nie	22.5	229.9	−29.8	−417.1	−1 234.1	493.1	−390.8	Compte d'op. fin., nia
Net Errors and Omissions	638.3	−267.7	−650.3	213.5	1 217.8	−700.3	83.5	Erreurs et omissions nettes
Reserves & Related Items	16.6	−25.3	−200.1	−123.5	−34.8	−43.7	−157.9	Rés. et postes appareutés
Bangladesh								**Bangladesh**
Goods: Exports fob	5 141.5	5 458.3	6 399.2	6 084.7	6 102.4	7 050.1	8 150.7	Biens : exportations, fab
Goods: Imports fob	−6 715.7	−7 535.5	−8 052.9	−8 133.4	−7 780.1	−9 492.0	−11 157.1	Biens : importations, fab
Serv. & Income: Credit	815.4	872.0	893.4	828.8	905.4	1 068.2	1 185.6	Serv. & revenu : crédit
Serv. & Income: Debit	−1 443.2	−1 655.2	−1 965.0	−1 883.4	−1 727.7	−2 072.8	−2 405.3	Serv. & revenu : débit
Current Trans.,nie: Credit	2 172.9	2 501.4	2 426.5	2 572.8	3 245.4	3 586.2	3 960.5	Transf. cour.,nia : crédit
Current Transfers: Debit	−5.9	−5.3	−7.0	−4.9	−6.0	−8.2	−12.9	Transf. courants : débit
Capital Acct.,nie: Credit	238.7	364.1	248.7	235.4	363.7	386.7	142.1	Compte de cap.,nia : crédit
Capital Account: Debit	0.0	0.0	0.0	0.0	0.0	0.0	0.0	Compte de capital : débit
Financial Account, nie	−116.0	−446.9	−256.0	262.1	−256.2	289.0	665.0	Compte d'op. fin., nia
Net Errors and Omissions	201.0	258.0	282.4	−106.0	−349.3	81.1	−25.0	Erreurs et omissions nettes
Reserves & Related Items	−288.5	189.2	30.7	143.9	−497.4	−888.5	−503.4	Rés. et postes appareutés
Barbados								**Barbade**
Goods: Exports fob	270.1	275.3	286.4	271.2	253.0	264.2	293.1	Biens : exportations, fab
Goods: Imports fob	−920.7	−989.4	−1 030.3	−952.3	−955.0	−1 065.6	−1 264.1	Biens : importations, fab
Serv. & Income: Credit	1 087.1	1 096.1	1 160.4	1 141.5	1 113.5	1 240.5	1 299.2	Serv. & revenu : crédit
Serv. & Income: Debit	−551.7	−596.4	−639.8	−664.9	−665.4	−700.9	−752.9	Serv. & revenu : débit
Current Trans.,nie: Credit	78.4	94.0	108.9	125.6	120.1	126.5	125.8	Transf. cour.,nia : crédit
Current Transfers: Debit	−26.2	−27.7	−31.0	−32.3	−34.3	−34.5	−38.2	Transf. courants : débit
Capital Acct.,nie: Credit	0.7	0.7	1.8	1.3	0.0	0.0	0.0	Compte de cap.,nia : crédit
Capital Account: Debit	0.0	0.0	0.0	0.0	0.0	0.0	0.0	Compte de capital : débit
Financial Account, nie	55.1	120.3	289.2	284.8	118.6	202.6	134.5	Compte d'op. fin., nia
Net Errors and Omissions	1.2	63.4	32.1	47.4	25.1	34.4	45.4	Erreurs et omissions nettes
Reserves & Related Items	6.1	−36.3	−177.6	−222.4	24.4	−67.3	157.3	Rés. et postes appareutés
Belarus								**Bélarus**
Goods: Exports fob	6 172.3	5 646.4	6 640.5	7 334.1	7 964.7	10 072.9	13 916.8	Biens : exportations, fab
Goods: Imports fob	−7 673.4	−6 216.4	−7 524.6	−8 140.8	−8 879.0	−11 328.5	−15 982.5	Biens : importations, fab
Serv. & Income: Credit	951.9	774.1	1 026.0	1 169.3	1 385.3	1 626.2	1 896.1	Serv. & revenu : crédit

Country or area	1998	1999	2000	2001	2002	2003	2004	Pays ou zone
Serv. & Income: Debit	−562.9	−501.6	−635.0	−911.1	−981.1	−1 016.2	−1 158.0	Serv. & revenu : débit
Current Trans.,nie: Credit	120.9	137.0	177.1	202.6	260.4	291.7	378.7	Transf. cour.,nia : crédit
Current Transfers: Debit	−25.3	−33.2	−22.4	−48.5	−61.5	−69.6	−94.0	Transf. courants : débit
Capital Acct.,nie: Credit	261.3	131.1	125.6	132.3	119.8	133.2	128.3	Compte de cap.,nia : crédit
Capital Account: Debit	−91.2	−70.7	−56.2	−76.0	−67.1	−64.3	−79.5	Compte de capital : débit
Financial Account, nie	354.8	399.5	140.1	265.0	482.5	231.9	872.5	Compte d'op. fin., nia
Net Errors and Omissions	172.3	−246.3	254.2	−5.4	−126.9	41.4	306.7	Erreurs et omissions nettes
Reserves & Related Items	319.3	−19.9	−125.3	78.5	−97.1	81.4	−185.1	Rés. et postes appareutés
Belgium								**Belgique**
Goods: Exports fob	...	...	...	...	169 166.0	204 964.0	245 457.0	Biens : exportations, fab
Goods: Imports fob	...	...	...	...	−159 648.0	−194 007.0	−235 718.0	Biens : importations, fab
Serv. & Income: Credit	...	...	...	...	74 193.8	86 169.1	100 588.4	Serv. & revenu : crédit
Serv. & Income: Debit	...	...	...	...	−67 759.4	−78 000.0	−91 750.6	Serv. & revenu : débit
Current Trans.,nie: Credit	...	...	...	...	5 275.2	6 512.5	7 930.0	Transf. cour.,nia : crédit
Current Transfers: Debit	...	...	...	...	−9 615.9	−12 902.6	−14 555.6	Transf. courants : débit
Capital Acct.,nie: Credit	...	...	...	...	218.9	267.2	399.3	Compte de cap.,nia : crédit
Capital Account: Debit	...	...	...	...	−803.5	−1 219.0	−828.2	Compte de capital : débit
Financial Account, nie	...	...	...	...	−6 482.9	1 381.2	639.4	Compte d'op. fin., nia
Net Errors and Omissions	...	...	...	...	−4 578.8	−14 890.2	−13 135.1	Erreurs et omissions nettes
Reserves & Related Items	...	...	...	...	35.0	1 725.1	973.6	Rés. et postes appareutés
Belgium-Luxembourg [1]								**Belgique-Luxembourg** [1]
Goods: Exports fob	153 558.0	161 263.0	164 677.0	163 498.0	...	...	...	Biens : exportations, fab
Goods: Imports fob	−146 577.0	−154 237.0	−162 086.0	−159 790.0	...	...	...	Biens : importations, fab
Serv. & Income: Credit	103 332.2	117 183.2	125 461.8	129 219.4	...	...	...	Serv. & revenu : crédit
Serv. & Income: Debit	−93 725.8	−105 292.2	−112 493.2	−119 314.9	...	...	...	Serv. & revenu : débit
Current Trans.,nie: Credit	7 005.7	7 040.6	7 013.9	7 315.7	...	...	...	Transf. cour.,nia : crédit
Current Transfers: Debit	−11 425.5	−11 871.8	−11 192.8	−11 535.3	...	...	...	Transf. courants : débit
Capital Acct.,nie: Credit	323.1	449.2	222.5	479.7	...	...	...	Compte de cap.,nia : crédit
Capital Account: Debit	−436.3	−502.7	−435.8	−454.1	...	...	...	Compte de capital : débit
Financial Account, nie	−16 042.8	−13 470.1	−9 232.8	−7 978.4	...	...	...	Compte d'op. fin., nia
Net Errors and Omissions	1 893.0	−2 430.2	−2 893.9	2.5	...	...	...	Erreurs et omissions nettes
Reserves & Related Items	2 095.0	1 867.4	959.0	−1 442.1	...	...	...	Rés. et postes appareutés
Belize								**Belize**
Goods: Exports fob	186.2	261.5	281.8	269.1	309.7	315.5	306.9	Biens : exportations, fab
Goods: Imports fob	−290.9	−375.8	−478.4	−477.7	−496.9	−522.3	−480.8	Biens : importations, fab
Serv. & Income: Credit	147.7	158.7	165.1	165.6	160.9	182.8	203.1	Serv. & revenu : crédit
Serv. & Income: Debit	−138.3	−151.7	−184.3	−196.1	−203.3	−228.7	−263.7	Serv. & revenu : débit
Current Trans.,nie: Credit	38.4	41.9	61.1	51.0	49.1	47.7	54.3	Transf. cour.,nia : crédit
Current Transfers: Debit	−2.8	−2.3	−1.3	−1.8	−2.1	−2.5	−2.2	Transf. courants : débit
Capital Acct.,nie: Credit	0.0	1.8	1.6	2.1	10.3	2.4	5.0	Compte de cap.,nia : crédit
Capital Account: Debit	−1.9	−1.3	−4.1	−1.3	−1.1	−0.9	−0.8	Compte de capital : débit
Financial Account, nie	23.5	96.0	205.1	172.3	140.3	206.8	129.6	Compte d'op. fin., nia
Net Errors and Omissions	24.5	−4.0	5.1	14.0	24.9	−9.3	16.9	Erreurs et omissions nettes
Reserves & Related Items	13.7	−24.8	−51.6	2.8	8.2	8.4	31.6	Rés. et postes appareutés
Benin								**Bénin**
Goods: Exports fob	414.3	421.5	392.4	373.5	447.8	540.8	...	Biens : exportations, fab
Goods: Imports fob	−572.6	−635.2	−516.1	−553.0	−678.9	−818.7	...	Biens : importations, fab
Serv. & Income: Credit	173.4	206.0	167.3	176.6	177.3	198.6	...	Serv. & revenu : crédit
Serv. & Income: Debit	−235.9	−255.8	−235.2	−234.8	−259.8	−318.3	...	Serv. & revenu : débit
Current Trans.,nie: Credit	102.0	87.1	91.3	87.3	93.2	56.6	...	Transf. cour.,nia : crédit
Current Transfers: Debit	−32.7	−14.9	−10.7	−10.0	−18.6	−7.5	...	Transf. courants : débit
Capital Acct.,nie: Credit	66.6	69.9	73.4	48.6	37.6	34.9	...	Compte de cap.,nia : crédit
Capital Account: Debit	0.0	0.0	−0.1	0.0	0.0	−0.5	...	Compte de capital : débit
Financial Account, nie	−8.9	25.4	10.8	39.6	−61.4	32.1	...	Compte d'op. fin., nia
Net Errors and Omissions	7.1	7.3	6.7	3.6	2.1	182.0	...	Erreurs et omissions nettes
Reserves & Related Items	86.7	88.7	20.3	68.7	260.5	100.0	...	Rés. et postes appareutés
Bolivia								**Bolivie**
Goods: Exports fob	1 104.0	1 051.2	1 246.1	1 284.8	1 298.7	1 597.9	2 146.0	Biens : exportations, fab
Goods: Imports fob	−1 759.5	−1 539.0	−1 610.2	−1 580.0	−1 638.7	−1 497.5	−1 724.7	Biens : importations, fab

Country or area	1998	1999	2000	2001	2002	2003	2004	Pays ou zone
Serv. & Income: Credit	378.6	416.7	363.7	357.1	359.8	434.7	489.3	Serv. & revenu : crédit
Serv. & Income: Debit	−729.8	−803.0	−832.7	−732.0	−741.2	−924.9	−1 069.1	Serv. & revenu : débit
Current Trans.,nie: Credit	352.3	414.7	420.0	431.6	407.8	494.2	488.4	Transf. cour.,nia : crédit
Current Transfers: Debit	−11.7	−28.6	−33.2	−35.5	−38.4	−42.8	−44.7	Transf. courants : débit
Capital Acct.,nie: Credit	9.9	0.0	0.0	0.0	0.0	0.0	0.0	Compte de cap.,nia : crédit
Capital Account: Debit	0.0	0.0	0.0	0.0	0.0	0.0	0.0	Compte de capital : débit
Financial Account, nie	1 181.6	868.2	461.8	440.7	649.0	36.5	152.8	Compte d'op. fin., nia
Net Errors and Omissions	−400.7	−353.2	−54.8	−202.7	−639.8	−159.5	−365.4	Erreurs et omissions nettes
Reserves & Related Items	−124.7	−27.0	39.4	36.0	342.7	61.5	−72.6	Rés. et postes appareutés
Bosnia and Herzegovina								**Bosnie-Herzégovine**
Goods: Exports fob	663.8	831.8	1 129.8	1 134.2	1 109.7	1 477.5	2 086.7	Biens : exportations, fab
Goods: Imports fob	−3 779.5	−4 128.7	−3 894.2	−4 092.0	−4 449.4	−5 636.8	−6 656.2	Biens : importations, fab
Serv. & Income: Credit	1 314.5	1 230.8	1 088.2	1 121.9	1 127.0	1 329.9	1 398.4	Serv. & revenu : crédit
Serv. & Income: Debit	−329.6	−355.4	−358.9	−364.7	−410.4	−532.0	−580.3	Serv. & revenu : débit
Current Trans.,nie: Credit	1 846.2	1 960.8	1 647.6	1 523.2	1 523.9	1 738.8	1 999.6	Transf. cour.,nia : crédit
Current Transfers: Debit	−86.3	−86.4	−75.4	−72.9	−101.9	−122.8	−166.5	Transf. courants : débit
Capital Acct.,nie: Credit	495.2	625.3	546.4	395.5	412.4	462.1	405.7	Compte de cap.,nia : crédit
Capital Account: Debit	0.0	0.0	0.0	0.0	0.0	0.0	0.0	Compte de capital : débit
Financial Account, nie	−589.9	−699.9	−460.2	750.7	159.7	855.8	890.1	Compte d'op. fin., nia
Net Errors and Omissions	105.7	25.3	112.8	85.5	97.2	340.8	648.6	Erreurs et omissions nettes
Reserves & Related Items	359.9	596.4	263.9	−481.5	531.9	86.7	−26.0	Rés. et postes appareutés
Botswana								**Botswana**
Goods: Exports fob	2 060.6	2 658.2	2 675.4	2 314.5	2 318.6	3 024.4	...	Biens : exportations, fab
Goods: Imports fob	−1 983.1	−1 873.5	−1 773.2	−1 604.1	−1 642.3	−2 127.2	...	Biens : importations, fab
Serv. & Income: Credit	877.6	761.0	702.9	718.8	757.9	1 046.8	...	Serv. & revenu : crédit
Serv. & Income: Debit	−1 025.5	−1 214.0	−1 277.0	−1 008.8	−1 503.3	−1 750.8	...	Serv. & revenu : débit
Current Trans.,nie: Credit	460.9	474.4	426.1	383.0	400.4	538.3	...	Transf. cour.,nia : crédit
Current Transfers: Debit	−220.8	−222.6	−209.0	−185.5	−188.1	−248.2	...	Transf. courants : débit
Capital Acct.,nie: Credit	44.2	33.5	51.5	18.7	29.7	42.5	...	Compte de cap.,nia : crédit
Capital Account: Debit	−12.4	−12.9	−13.3	−12.9	−14.0	−20.0	...	Compte de capital : débit
Financial Account, nie	−202.4	−231.0	−214.0	−509.4	−217.3	−378.8	...	Compte d'op. fin., nia
Net Errors and Omissions	45.1	21.1	−1.9	55.7	119.0	44.5	...	Erreurs et omissions nettes
Reserves & Related Items	−44.2	−394.1	−367.4	−170.0	−60.6	−171.5	...	Rés. et postes appareutés
Brazil								**Brésil**
Goods: Exports fob	51 136.0	48 011.0	55 085.6	58 222.6	60 361.8	73 084.1	96 475.2	Biens : exportations, fab
Goods: Imports fob	−57 739.0	−49 272.0	−55 783.3	−55 572.2	−47 240.5	−48 290.2	−62 834.7	Biens : importations, fab
Serv. & Income: Credit	12 545.0	11 125.0	13 119.1	12 601.5	12 846.6	13 785.7	15 782.5	Serv. & revenu : crédit
Serv. & Income: Debit	−41 207.0	−36 952.0	−38 167.0	−40 104.0	−35 994.4	−37 268.9	−40 980.2	Serv. & revenu : débit
Current Trans.,nie: Credit	1 795.0	1 969.0	1 827.7	1 933.8	2 626.9	3 132.0	3 582.5	Transf. cour.,nia : crédit
Current Transfers: Debit	−359.0	−281.0	−306.6	−296.2	−237.0	−265.5	−314.3	Transf. courants : débit
Capital Acct.,nie: Credit	488.0	361.0	300.2	328.2	464.4	535.4	764.4	Compte de cap.,nia : crédit
Capital Account: Debit	−113.0	−22.0	−27.7	−364.2	−31.5	−37.2	−424.9	Compte de capital : débit
Financial Account, nie	20 063.0	8 056.0	29 376.2	20 331.3	−3 908.9	−156.6	−3 307.4	Compte d'op. fin., nia
Net Errors and Omissions	−2 910.7	239.6	2 557.1	−498.3	−153.9	−932.7	−2 144.1	Erreurs et omissions nettes
Reserves & Related Items	16 301.7	16 765.4	−7 981.3	3 417.5	11 266.4	−3 586.3	−6 599.1	Rés. et postes appareutés
Bulgaria								**Bulgarie**
Goods: Exports fob	4 193.5	4 006.4	4 824.6	5 112.9	5 692.1	7 540.6	9 847.7	Biens : exportations, fab
Goods: Imports fob	−4 574.2	−5 087.4	−6 000.2	−6 693.4	−7 286.6	−10 059.1	−13 214.0	Biens : importations, fab
Serv. & Income: Credit	2 094.1	2 053.8	2 496.0	2 475.5	2 684.7	3 494.1	4 480.3	Serv. & revenu : crédit
Serv. & Income: Debit	−2 005.3	−1 924.6	−2 313.9	−2 377.3	−2 464.3	−3 526.6	−4 262.8	Serv. & revenu : débit
Current Trans.,nie: Credit	261.5	328.7	354.1	598.5	653.6	865.5	1 291.3	Transf. cour.,nia : crédit
Current Transfers: Debit	−31.5	−29.0	−64.3	−100.2	−106.2	−169.9	−197.3	Transf. courants : débit
Capital Acct.,nie: Credit	0.0	0.0	25.0	0.0	0.0	0.0	0.0	Compte de cap.,nia : crédit
Capital Account: Debit	0.0	−2.4	−0.1	−0.1	−0.1	−0.3	−0.1	Compte de capital : débit
Financial Account, nie	266.8	720.9	781.3	662.8	1 750.2	2 640.9	3 263.7	Compte d'op. fin., nia
Net Errors and Omissions	−299.2	29.9	34.5	694.7	−208.3	−55.7	521.3	Erreurs et omissions nettes
Reserves & Related Items	94.3	−96.2	−137.0	−373.4	−715.1	−729.5	−1 730.2	Rés. et postes appareutés

Country or area	1998	1999	2000	2001	2002	2003	2004	Pays ou zone
Burkina Faso								**Burkina Faso**
Goods: Exports fob	...	...	205.6	223.5	...	...	...	Biens : exportations, fab
Goods: Imports fob	...	...	−517.7	−509.3	...	...	...	Biens : importations, fab
Serv. & Income: Credit	...	...	44.9	51.7	...	...	...	Serv. & revenu : crédit
Serv. & Income: Debit	...	...	−173.5	−180.9	...	...	...	Serv. & revenu : débit
Current Trans.,nie: Credit	...	...	87.6	72.0	...	...	...	Transf. cour.,nia : crédit
Current Transfers: Debit	...	...	−38.9	−37.9	...	...	...	Transf. courants : débit
Capital Acct.,nie: Credit	...	...	175.9	165.2	...	...	...	Compte de cap.,nia : crédit
Capital Account: Debit	...	...	0.0	0.0	...	...	...	Compte de capital : débit
Financial Account, nie	...	...	19.2	25.2	...	...	...	Compte d'op. fin., nia
Net Errors and Omissions	...	...	5.1	3.4	...	...	...	Erreurs et omissions nettes
Reserves & Related Items	...	...	191.8	187.0	...	...	...	Rés. et postes appareutés
Burundi								**Burundi**
Goods: Exports fob	64.0	55.0	49.1	39.2	31.0	37.5	...	Biens : exportations, fab
Goods: Imports fob	−123.5	−97.3	−107.9	−108.3	−104.8	−130.0	...	Biens : importations, fab
Serv. & Income: Credit	8.1	6.3	6.4	7.1	7.1	6.9	...	Serv. & revenu : crédit
Serv. & Income: Debit	−53.5	−36.6	−57.2	−53.7	−55.8	−63.6	...	Serv. & revenu : débit
Current Trans.,nie: Credit	56.8	51.4	58.3	79.6	115.5	115.5	...	Transf. cour.,nia : crédit
Current Transfers: Debit	−3.3	−1.8	−1.8	−2.9	−3.3	−3.5	...	Transf. courants : débit
Capital Acct.,nie: Credit	0.0	0.0	0.0	0.0	0.0	0.0	...	Compte de cap.,nia : crédit
Capital Account: Debit	0.0	0.0	0.0	0.0	−0.5	−0.9	...	Compte de capital : débit
Financial Account, nie	−7.8	−6.5	−7.5	−4.0	−40.5	−50.0	...	Compte d'op. fin., nia
Net Errors and Omissions	−18.8	−19.0	−34.2	−31.2	3.9	−12.6	...	Erreurs et omissions nettes
Reserves & Related Items	78.1	48.6	94.8	74.3	47.2	100.9	...	Rés. et postes appareutés
Cambodia								**Cambodge**
Goods: Exports fob	2 775.9	1 424.2	1 961.2	2 490.1	1 753.8	2 027.2	2 475.5	Biens : exportations, fab
Goods: Imports fob	−4 046.2	−2 075.5	−2 792.0	−3 430.8	−2 318.0	−2 559.9	−3 193.3	Biens : importations, fab
Serv. & Income: Credit	225.2	345.3	495.5	582.1	654.8	569.8	815.6	Serv. & revenu : crédit
Serv. & Income: Debit	−328.4	−441.6	−517.7	−542.7	−601.9	−640.7	−757.1	Serv. & revenu : débit
Current Trans.,nie: Credit	269.0	322.7	361.0	351.8	391.7	455.4	431.1	Transf. cour.,nia : crédit
Current Transfers: Debit	−5.6	−7.6	−7.3	−8.3	−9.3	−10.3	−12.3	Transf. courants : débit
Capital Acct.,nie: Credit	89.5	78.7	79.8	102.8	76.7	53.2	68.9	Compte de cap.,nia : crédit
Capital Account: Debit	−94.3	−67.7	−44.2	−58.0	−63.4	−53.3	−64.9	Compte de capital : débit
Financial Account, nie	227.3	191.4	178.1	138.0	236.4	166.8	332.2	Compte d'op. fin., nia
Net Errors and Omissions	876.4	219.7	306.5	391.1	−20.0	−8.2	6.3	Erreurs et omissions nettes
Reserves & Related Items	11.3	10.5	−20.9	−16.1	−100.9	0.0	−102.0	Rés. et postes appareutés
Canada								**Canada**
Goods: Exports fob	220 539.0	248 494.0	289 022.0	271 849.0	263 919.0	285 912.0	330 112.0	Biens : exportations, fab
Goods: Imports fob	−204 617.0	−220 203.0	−243 975.0	−226 132.0	−227 431.0	−244 836.0	−279 430.0	Biens : importations, fab
Serv. & Income: Credit	55 665.9	58 275.0	64 975.3	55 626.6	59 731.4	64 204.9	77 107.6	Serv. & revenu : crédit
Serv. & Income: Debit	−79 971.6	−85 350.3	−91 154.6	−86 081.1	−83 360.3	−92 095.9	−106 043.6	Serv. & revenu : débit
Current Trans.,nie: Credit	3 406.8	3 796.0	4 122.1	4 499.5	4 387.0	4 721.6	5 608.5	Transf. cour.,nia : crédit
Current Transfers: Debit	−2 862.9	−3 247.1	−3 367.8	−3 480.2	−3 790.7	−4 546.4	−5 354.7	Transf. courants : débit
Capital Acct.,nie: Credit	3 793.7	3 861.6	4 045.3	4 191.4	3 599.0	3 454.2	3 948.5	Compte de cap.,nia : crédit
Capital Account: Debit	−457.5	−461.5	−464.1	−470.7	−453.9	−611.6	−555.0	Compte de capital : débit
Financial Account, nie	4 944.4	−5 968.2	−14 500.0	−11 609.4	−11 663.0	−18 287.9	−23 577.7	Compte d'op. fin., nia
Net Errors and Omissions	4 555.1	6 736.1	−4 983.6	−6 220.3	−5 122.9	−1 170.1	−4 651.0	Erreurs et omissions nettes
Reserves & Related Items	−4 996.3	−5 933.1	−3 720.0	−2 172.2	185.2	3 255.1	2 835.6	Rés. et postes appareutés
Cape Verde								**Cap-Vert**
Goods: Exports fob	32.7	26.0	38.3	37.2	41.8	52.8	...	Biens : exportations, fab
Goods: Imports fob	−218.8	−239.0	−225.7	−231.5	−278.0	−343.9	...	Biens : importations, fab
Serv. & Income: Credit	89.0	107.0	112.6	137.2	159.2	237.2	...	Serv. & revenu : crédit
Serv. & Income: Debit	−98.7	−126.2	−117.9	−131.7	−160.3	−233.0	...	Serv. & revenu : débit
Current Trans.,nie: Credit	142.5	167.1	146.3	155.5	181.6	229.0	...	Transf. cour.,nia : crédit
Current Transfers: Debit	−5.1	−9.0	−11.7	−22.5	−15.7	−19.3	...	Transf. courants : débit
Capital Acct.,nie: Credit	19.0	4.5	10.8	24.4	8.6	21.1	...	Compte de cap.,nia : crédit
Capital Account: Debit	0.0	0.0	0.0	0.0	0.0	0.0	...	Compte de capital : débit
Financial Account, nie	37.0	127.8	31.5	38.5	80.7	5.5	...	Compte d'op. fin., nia
Net Errors and Omissions	13.3	−8.7	−12.0	−23.9	−7.7	−5.4	...	Erreurs et omissions nettes
Reserves & Related Items	−10.8	−49.3	27.8	16.7	−10.1	56.0	...	Rés. et postes appareutés

Country or area	1998	1999	2000	2001	2002	2003	2004	Pays ou zone
Chile								**Chili**
Goods: Exports fob	16 322.8	17 162.3	19 210.2	18 271.8	18 179.8	21 523.6	32 024.9	Biens : exportations, fab
Goods: Imports fob	−18 363.1	−14 735.1	−17 091.4	−16 428.2	−15 794.2	−18 001.7	−23 005.7	Biens : importations, fab
Serv. & Income: Credit	5 148.1	4 781.3	5 680.6	5 596.7	5 499.2	6 385.0	7 466.1	Serv. & revenu : crédit
Serv. & Income: Debit	−7 488.6	−7 751.6	−9 254.9	−8 967.2	−9 047.4	−11 608.4	−16 147.0	Serv. & revenu : débit
Current Trans.,nie: Credit	809.9	840.9	765.3	713.0	954.3	928.5	1 395.2	Transf. cour.,nia : crédit
Current Transfers: Debit	−347.5	−198.4	−207.3	−286.2	−371.7	−329.1	−343.8	Transf. courants : débit
Capital Acct.,nie: Credit	0.0	0.0	0.0	0.0	83.0	0.0	5.1	Compte de cap.,nia : crédit
Capital Account: Debit	0.0	0.0	0.0	0.0	0.0	0.0	0.0	Compte de capital : débit
Financial Account, nie	1 966.2	237.1	787.4	1 361.8	1 634.3	1 661.2	−524.3	Compte d'op. fin., nia
Net Errors and Omissions	−239.0	−1 083.0	426.6	−860.7	−952.2	−916.3	−1 062.0	Erreurs et omissions nettes
Reserves & Related Items	2 191.3	746.5	−316.5	599.0	−185.0	357.2	191.5	Rés. et postes appareutés
China [2]								**Chine** [2]
Goods: Exports fob	183 529.0	194 716.0	249 131.0	266 075.0	325 651.0	438 270.0	593 393.0	Biens : exportations, fab
Goods: Imports fob	−136 915.0	−158 734.0	−214 657.0	−232 058.0	−281 484.0	−393 618.0	−534 410.0	Biens : importations, fab
Serv. & Income: Credit	29 479.0	34 578.0	42 980.4	42 722.0	48 088.5	62 828.3	82 978.2	Serv. & revenu : crédit
Serv. & Income: Debit	−48 900.0	−54 389.0	−63 246.9	−67 830.0	−69 817.5	−79 239.4	−96 199.5	Serv. & revenu : débit
Current Trans.,nie: Credit	4 661.0	5 368.0	6 860.8	9 125.0	13 795.4	18 482.5	24 326.3	Transf. cour.,nia : crédit
Current Transfers: Debit	−382.0	−424.0	−549.5	−633.0	−810.9	−848.3	−1 428.2	Transf. courants : débit
Capital Acct.,nie: Credit	0.0	0.0	0.0	0.0	0.0	0.0	0.0	Compte de cap.,nia : crédit
Capital Account: Debit	−47.0	−26.0	−35.3	−54.0	−49.6	−48.1	−69.3	Compte de capital : débit
Financial Account, nie	−6 275.0	5 204.0	1 957.9	34 832.0	32 341.0	52 774.0	110 729.0	Compte d'op. fin., nia
Net Errors and Omissions	−18 901.8	−17 640.5	−11 747.9	−4 732.5	7 503.5	17 985.4	26 834.2	Erreurs et omissions nettes
Reserves & Related Items	−6 248.2	−8 652.5	−10 693.1	−47 446.5	−75 216.9	−116 586.0	−206 153.0	Rés. et postes appareutés
China, Hong Kong SAR								**Chine, Hong Kong RAS**
Goods: Exports fob	175 833.0	174 719.0	202 698.0	190 926.0	200 300.0	224 656.0	260 263.0	Biens : exportations, fab
Goods: Imports fob	−183 666.0	−177 878.0	−210 891.0	−199 257.0	−205 353.0	−230 435.0	−269 575.0	Biens : importations, fab
Serv. & Income: Credit	79 762.0	82 433.3	94 913.0	89 192.6	86 111.9	89 736.2	106 177.7	Serv. & revenu : crédit
Serv. & Income: Debit	−67 825.4	−67 486.9	−78 056.6	−69 296.6	−66 751.4	−65 650.6	−79 013.3	Serv. & revenu : débit
Current Trans.,nie: Credit	668.7	569.5	538.2	605.1	777.4	528.7	625.5	Transf. cour.,nia : crédit
Current Transfers: Debit	−2 265.0	−2 109.3	−2 208.3	−2 384.6	−2 673.3	−2 365.5	−2 610.7	Transf. courants : débit
Capital Acct.,nie: Credit	377.4	103.3	56.5	41.3	30.6	132.2	1 151.5	Compte de cap.,nia : crédit
Capital Account: Debit	−2 759.0	−1 883.3	−1 602.2	−1 215.3	−2 042.1	−1 197.0	−1 480.1	Compte de capital : débit
Financial Account, nie	−8 475.8	1 060.9	4 165.4	−6 626.3	−19 750.5	−20 952.6	−20 093.5	Compte d'op. fin., nia
Net Errors and Omissions	1 560.9	499.2	431.2	2 698.8	6 972.8	6 541.5	7 840.8	Erreurs et omissions nettes
Reserves & Related Items	6 789.1	−10 027.7	−10 043.7	−4 684.0	2 377.4	−993.8	−3 286.2	Rés. et postes appareutés
China, Macao SAR								**Chine, Macao RAS**
Goods: Exports fob	...	...	...	...	2 357.8	2 584.8	2 815.6	Biens : exportations, fab
Goods: Imports fob	...	...	...	...	−3 277.5	−3 677.8	−4 657.0	Biens : importations, fab
Serv. & Income: Credit	...	...	...	...	5 207.2	5 999.2	8 444.2	Serv. & revenu : crédit
Serv. & Income: Debit	...	...	...	...	−1 539.5	−1 722.2	−2 413.0	Serv. & revenu : débit
Current Trans.,nie: Credit	...	...	...	...	89.9	102.6	97.8	Transf. cour.,nia : crédit
Current Transfers: Debit	...	...	...	...	−98.9	−107.5	−124.5	Transf. courants : débit
Capital Acct.,nie: Credit	...	...	...	...	161.5	113.4	301.8	Compte de cap.,nia : crédit
Capital Account: Debit	...	...	...	...	−22.7	−25.4	−27.8	Compte de capital : débit
Financial Account, nie	...	...	...	...	−1 085.9	−1 676.6	−1 667.4	Compte d'op. fin., nia
Net Errors and Omissions	...	...	...	...	−1 499.3	−1 066.1	−1 671.9	Erreurs et omissions nettes
Reserves & Related Items	...	...	...	...	−292.5	−524.4	−1 097.8	Rés. et postes appareutés
Colombia								**Colombie**
Goods: Exports fob	11 480.1	12 037.3	13 722.2	12 848.0	12 316.0	13 825.0	17 245.9	Biens : exportations, fab
Goods: Imports fob	−13 930.0	−10 262.1	−11 089.6	−12 268.9	−12 077.5	−13 257.8	−15 877.9	Biens : importations, fab
Serv. & Income: Credit	2 904.3	2 863.4	3 099.5	3 104.0	2 578.2	2 471.4	2 940.4	Serv. & revenu : crédit
Serv. & Income: Debit	−6 062.4	−5 422.2	−6 644.7	−7 130.7	−6 861.9	−7 362.3	−8 914.1	Serv. & revenu : débit
Current Trans.,nie: Credit	912.3	1 703.0	1 911.4	2 655.5	3 008.3	3 567.6	3 925.2	Transf. cour.,nia : crédit
Current Transfers: Debit	−161.9	−248.4	−238.2	−301.5	−304.2	−235.0	−269.5	Transf. courants : débit
Capital Acct.,nie: Credit	0.0	0.0	0.0	0.0	0.0	0.0	0.0	Compte de cap.,nia : crédit
Capital Account: Debit	0.0	0.0	0.0	0.0	0.0	0.0	0.0	Compte de capital : débit
Financial Account, nie	3 306.9	−551.0	50.1	2 465.0	1 279.8	742.1	3 136.4	Compte d'op. fin., nia
Net Errors and Omissions	153.1	−431.9	51.1	−146.0	200.1	61.0	283.2	Erreurs et omissions nettes
Reserves & Related Items	1 397.6	311.9	−861.7	−1 225.4	−138.9	188.0	−2 469.5	Rés. et postes appareutés

Country or area	1998	1999	2000	2001	2002	2003	2004	Pays ou zone
Congo								**Congo**
Goods: Exports fob	1 367.8	1 560.1	2 491.8	2 055.3	2 288.8	1 461.1	...	Biens : exportations, fab
Goods: Imports fob	−558.4	−522.7	−455.3	−681.3	−691.1	−449.9	...	Biens : importations, fab
Serv. & Income: Credit	121.6	175.6	150.5	159.1	171.0	89.0	...	Serv. & revenu : crédit
Serv. & Income: Debit	−1 168.5	−1 438.4	−1 557.7	−1 546.2	−1 793.3	−1 095.3	...	Serv. & revenu : débit
Current Trans.,nie: Credit	10.0	14.9	38.9	18.3	12.9	9.6	...	Transf. cour.,nia : crédit
Current Transfers: Debit	−13.0	−20.2	−20.1	−33.5	−22.7	−17.1	...	Transf. courants : débit
Capital Acct.,nie: Credit	0.0	10.3	8.9	13.3	5.3	9.9	...	Compte de cap.,nia : crédit
Capital Account: Debit	−0.2	−0.1	−0.6	−0.7	0.0	0.0	...	Compte de capital : débit
Financial Account, nie	−715.9	−336.2	−821.8	−653.1	−464.3	−58.5	...	Compte d'op. fin., nia
Net Errors and Omissions	−72.0	−99.0	−77.6	−11.8	−219.7	−110.3	...	Erreurs et omissions nettes
Reserves & Related Items	1 028.6	655.6	242.8	680.6	713.1	161.5	...	Rés. et postes appareutés
Costa Rica								**Costa Rica**
Goods: Exports fob	5 538.3	6 576.4	5 813.4	4 923.2	5 269.9	6 163.0	6 369.7	Biens : exportations, fab
Goods: Imports fob	−5 937.4	−5 996.2	−6 023.8	−5 743.3	−6 537.1	−7 294.4	−7 832.7	Biens : importations, fab
Serv. & Income: Credit	1 526.1	1 864.3	2 179.0	2 096.7	2 187.8	2 240.3	2 727.7	Serv. & revenu : crédit
Serv. & Income: Debit	−1 761.0	−3 215.0	−2 768.7	−2 144.5	−2 017.4	−2 250.3	−2 311.9	Serv. & revenu : débit
Current Trans.,nie: Credit	190.5	201.4	203.8	266.4	296.9	368.6	371.2	Transf. cour.,nia : crédit
Current Transfers: Debit	−77.3	−97.5	−110.5	−111.1	−116.2	−156.0	−155.5	Transf. courants : débit
Capital Acct.,nie: Credit	0.0	0.0	8.9	12.4	5.7	26.1	9.4	Compte de cap.,nia : crédit
Capital Account: Debit	0.0	0.0	0.0	0.0	0.0	0.0	0.0	Compte de capital : débit
Financial Account, nie	199.0	683.1	−34.6	320.4	844.8	594.3	707.7	Compte d'op. fin., nia
Net Errors and Omissions	−182.5	213.1	391.0	243.9	28.2	82.3	80.9	Erreurs et omissions nettes
Reserves & Related Items	504.3	−229.7	341.4	136.0	37.4	226.1	33.5	Rés. et postes appareutés
Côte d'Ivoire								**Côte d'Ivoire**
Goods: Exports fob	4 606.4	4 661.5	3 888.0	3 945.9	5 274.8	5 787.7	6 902.1	Biens : exportations, fab
Goods: Imports fob	−2 886.4	−2 766.1	−2 401.8	−2 417.8	−2 455.6	−3 230.9	−4 167.7	Biens : importations, fab
Serv. & Income: Credit	783.5	749.0	623.9	715.2	726.6	834.9	927.5	Serv. & revenu : crédit
Serv. & Income: Debit	−2 400.1	−2 378.2	−2 021.4	−1 994.4	−2 315.6	−2 610.2	−2 897.5	Serv. & revenu : débit
Current Trans.,nie: Credit	148.2	136.8	79.4	88.5	131.9	196.4	202.9	Transf. cour.,nia : crédit
Current Transfers: Debit	−541.7	−522.6	−409.4	−398.7	−593.8	−683.3	−664.8	Transf. courants : débit
Capital Acct.,nie: Credit	35.9	17.4	9.9	11.5	9.1	14.1	11.5	Compte de cap.,nia : crédit
Capital Account: Debit	−10.3	−3.6	−1.4	−1.4	−0.8	−0.4	−2.7	Compte de capital : débit
Financial Account, nie	−417.1	−580.6	−365.2	−69.8	−1 034.6	−1 041.7	−1 124.4	Compte d'op. fin., nia
Net Errors and Omissions	32.1	−21.5	−10.3	35.0	−20.3	−53.8	32.2	Erreurs et omissions nettes
Reserves & Related Items	649.6	707.9	608.3	86.1	278.4	787.2	780.8	Rés. et postes appareutés
Croatia								**Croatie**
Goods: Exports fob	4 580.6	4 394.7	4 567.2	4 759.3	5 003.9	6 308.0	8 209.9	Biens : exportations, fab
Goods: Imports fob	−8 652.1	−7 693.3	−7 770.2	−8 860.0	−10 652.2	−14 216.0	−16 560.3	Biens : importations, fab
Serv. & Income: Credit	4 343.9	3 978.9	4 414.4	5 306.8	6 015.7	9 077.3	10 179.6	Serv. & revenu : crédit
Serv. & Income: Debit	−2 446.2	−2 721.1	−2 562.3	−2 916.9	−3 374.4	−4 708.6	−5 211.2	Serv. & revenu : débit
Current Trans.,nie: Credit	919.1	967.6	1 098.2	1 192.7	1 375.0	1 741.4	1 974.0	Transf. cour.,nia : crédit
Current Transfers: Debit	−213.3	−335.0	−217.8	−209.3	−284.6	−334.4	−488.2	Transf. courants : débit
Capital Acct.,nie: Credit	24.1	28.2	24.2	138.2	450.2	95.6	37.3	Compte de cap.,nia : crédit
Capital Account: Debit	−5.0	−3.4	−3.6	−4.6	−6.8	−11.7	−8.9	Compte de capital : débit
Financial Account, nie	1 610.3	2 868.6	1 790.2	2 200.7	2 993.1	4 783.1	2 917.6	Compte d'op. fin., nia
Net Errors and Omissions	−0.9	−1 027.5	−684.6	−209.3	−705.4	−1 333.9	−981.5	Erreurs et omissions nettes
Reserves & Related Items	−160.5	−457.9	−655.6	−1 397.6	−814.6	−1 400.8	−68.2	Rés. et postes appareutés
Cyprus								**Chypre**
Goods: Exports fob	1 064.6	1 000.3	950.9	975.2	855.1	924.6	1 156.9	Biens : exportations, fab
Goods: Imports fob	−3 490.4	−3 309.5	−3 556.6	−3 552.5	−3 702.6	−4 055.0	−5 216.2	Biens : importations, fab
Serv. & Income: Credit	4 065.0	4 440.2	4 640.5	4 899.0	4 902.6	5 800.0	6 877.5	Serv. & revenu : crédit
Serv. & Income: Debit	−1 393.0	−2 404.4	−2 700.1	−2 697.9	−2 624.2	−3 161.0	−3 919.0	Serv. & revenu : débit
Current Trans.,nie: Credit	94.0	145.5	236.8	147.3	271.9	402.4	594.2	Transf. cour.,nia : crédit
Current Transfers: Debit	−48.9	−42.4	−59.6	−93.3	−160.6	−241.6	−416.7	Transf. courants : débit
Capital Acct.,nie: Credit	0.0	0.0	19.3	27.1	22.2	41.3	183.1	Compte de cap.,nia : crédit
Capital Account: Debit	0.0	0.0	−14.5	−21.5	−27.6	−21.0	−57.8	Compte de capital : débit
Financial Account, nie	−420.2	844.9	530.3	965.1	939.6	9.1	1 198.9	Compte d'op. fin., nia
Net Errors and Omissions	46.2	−35.6	−55.2	−37.9	−87.4	113.5	−29.4	Erreurs et omissions nettes
Reserves & Related Items	82.5	−639.0	8.2	−610.6	−389.0	187.6	−371.4	Rés. et postes appareutés

Summary of balance of payments—Millions of US dollars (*continued*)
Résumé des balances des paiements—Millions de dollars des E.-U. (*suite*)

Country or area	1998	1999	2000	2001	2002	2003	2004	Pays ou zone
Czech Republic								**République tchèque**
Goods: Exports fob	25 885.5	26 258.9	29 019.3	33 403.6	38 479.7	48 705.2	66 874.0	Biens : exportations, fab
Goods: Imports fob	−28 532.5	−28 161.3	−32 114.5	−36 481.6	−40 719.7	−51 224.4	−67 749.8	Biens : importations, fab
Serv. & Income: Credit	9 377.8	8 907.7	8 791.3	9 324.8	9 134.3	10 470.7	12 434.8	Serv. & revenu : crédit
Serv. & Income: Debit	−8 556.0	−9 058.8	−8 758.8	−9 989.3	−12 071.2	−14 285.4	−17 389.1	Serv. & revenu : débit
Current Trans.,nie: Credit	1 066.5	1 309.7	948.0	958.9	1 464.7	1 662.6	1 802.3	Transf. cour.,nia : crédit
Current Transfers: Debit	−549.7	−722.0	−575.1	−488.9	−552.6	−1 114.2	−1 567.2	Transf. courants : débit
Capital Acct.,nie: Credit	13.8	18.4	5.8	2.4	6.7	7.1	218.1	Compte de cap.,nia : crédit
Capital Account: Debit	−11.6	−20.5	−10.9	−11.3	−10.7	−10.0	−813.1	Compte de capital : débit
Financial Account, nie	2 908.2	3 079.8	3 834.9	4 569.3	10 621.3	5 620.1	7 164.8	Compte d'op. fin., nia
Net Errors and Omissions	288.3	27.4	−296.4	499.3	265.7	610.8	−712.3	Erreurs et omissions nettes
Reserves & Related Items	−1 890.4	−1 639.3	−843.6	−1 787.1	−6 618.2	−442.5	−262.6	Rés. et postes appareutés
Denmark								**Danemark**
Goods: Exports fob	47 907.8	49 786.6	50 083.9	50 466.3	55 472.6	64 537.1	75 050.2	Biens : exportations, fab
Goods: Imports fob	−44 021.5	−43 128.4	−43 442.8	−43 048.4	−47 810.3	−54 839.8	−65 523.6	Biens : importations, fab
Serv. & Income: Credit	25 612.8	29 071.6	35 604.6	35 871.5	35 931.7	42 852.0	49 088.4	Serv. & revenu : crédit
Serv. & Income: Debit	−30 026.4	−29 947.5	−36 969.5	−35 869.2	−37 110.4	−42 050.1	−48 514.8	Serv. & revenu : débit
Current Trans.,nie: Credit	3 442.8	4 238.8	3 395.2	3 718.9	3 466.2	4 614.6	5 119.5	Transf. cour.,nia : crédit
Current Transfers: Debit	−4 923.7	−6 974.0	−6 409.6	−6 290.9	−6 489.3	−8 150.7	−9 279.0	Transf. courants : débit
Capital Acct.,nie: Credit	81.3	372.2	320.1	300.1	411.0	344.2	511.4	Compte de cap.,nia : crédit
Capital Account: Debit	−31.3	−244.6	−331.5	−285.6	−258.5	−350.8	−498.2	Compte de capital : débit
Financial Account, nie	−1 489.1	7 413.5	−3 311.3	−5 712.2	3 819.2	−5 128.6	−19 023.2	Compte d'op. fin., nia
Net Errors and Omissions	−792.3	−1 024.3	−4 460.4	4 166.8	−1 886.5	2 846.3	11 643.7	Erreurs et omissions nettes
Reserves & Related Items	4 239.4	−9 564.0	5 521.3	−3 317.2	−5 545.5	−4 674.2	1 425.5	Rés. et postes appareutés
Dominica								**Dominique**
Goods: Exports fob	63.2	56.0	54.7	44.4	42.9	...	...	Biens : exportations, fab
Goods: Imports fob	−116.4	−121.6	−130.4	−115.7	−102.4	...	...	Biens : importations, fab
Serv. & Income: Credit	93.1	105.4	94.4	79.0	82.4	...	...	Serv. & revenu : crédit
Serv. & Income: Debit	−75.7	−89.2	−89.8	−74.3	−74.9	...	...	Serv. & revenu : débit
Current Trans.,nie: Credit	19.9	20.5	25.1	24.8	20.6	...	...	Transf. cour.,nia : crédit
Current Transfers: Debit	−7.2	−6.9	−7.0	−7.3	−6.7	...	...	Transf. courants : débit
Capital Acct.,nie: Credit	14.9	12.1	12.4	18.1	20.6	...	...	Compte de cap.,nia : crédit
Capital Account: Debit	−0.1	−0.3	−1.5	−0.1	−0.1	...	...	Compte de capital : débit
Financial Account, nie	−2.2	38.4	43.4	25.0	8.9	...	...	Compte d'op. fin., nia
Net Errors and Omissions	14.1	−3.3	−0.9	9.6	17.0	...	...	Erreurs et omissions nettes
Reserves & Related Items	−3.5	−11.0	−0.5	−3.5	−8.3	...	...	Rés. et postes appareutés
Dominican Republic								**Rép. dominicaine**
Goods: Exports fob	4 980.5	5 136.7	5 736.7	5 276.3	5 165.0	5 470.8	5 750.0	Biens : exportations, fab
Goods: Imports fob	−7 597.3	−8 041.1	−9 478.5	−8 779.3	−8 837.7	−7 626.8	−7 844.6	Biens : importations, fab
Serv. & Income: Credit	2 669.7	3 068.6	3 527.3	3 381.5	3 371.2	3 809.5	3 848.8	Serv. & revenu : crédit
Serv. & Income: Debit	−2 377.8	−2 441.2	−2 714.3	−2 646.8	−2 765.7	−2 953.2	−2 852.9	Serv. & revenu : débit
Current Trans.,nie: Credit	2 016.9	1 997.1	2 095.6	2 232.0	2 451.9	2 512.2	2 671.5	Transf. cour.,nia : crédit
Current Transfers: Debit	−30.4	−149.3	−193.3	−204.5	−182.6	−176.3	−173.9	Transf. courants : débit
Capital Acct.,nie: Credit	0.0	0.0	0.0	0.0	0.0	0.0	0.0	Compte de cap.,nia : crédit
Capital Account: Debit	0.0	0.0	0.0	0.0	0.0	0.0	0.0	Compte de capital : débit
Financial Account, nie	688.1	1 061.0	1 596.6	1 707.4	383.0	−15.9	−710.3	Compte d'op. fin., nia
Net Errors and Omissions	−338.6	−480.4	−618.5	−451.9	−139.3	−1 568.2	−143.7	Erreurs et omissions nettes
Reserves & Related Items	−11.1	−151.4	48.4	−514.7	554.2	548.0	−544.8	Rés. et postes appareutés
Ecuador								**Equateur**
Goods: Exports fob	4 326.2	4 615.5	5 137.2	4 781.5	5 198.3	6 196.6	7 813.0	Biens : exportations, fab
Goods: Imports fob	−5 457.9	−3 027.9	−3 742.6	−5 178.7	−6 196.0	−6 268.0	−7 492.4	Biens : importations, fab
Serv. & Income: Credit	797.7	804.7	919.8	909.7	913.9	909.3	954.0	Serv. & revenu : crédit
Serv. & Income: Debit	−2 531.4	−2 563.7	−2 745.2	−2 846.0	−2 967.1	−3 081.3	−3 325.5	Serv. & revenu : débit
Current Trans.,nie: Credit	933.0	1 188.2	1 436.8	1 685.9	1 709.5	1 794.1	1 912.8	Transf. cour.,nia : crédit
Current Transfers: Debit	−166.1	−98.7	−85.0	−47.1	−57.8	−22.4	−19.2	Transf. courants : débit
Capital Acct.,nie: Credit	22.7	11.3	8.1	21.4	23.6	26.1	28.1	Compte de cap.,nia : crédit
Capital Account: Debit	−8.6	−9.2	−9.5	−84.1	−8.0	−9.0	−10.0	Compte de capital : débit
Financial Account, nie	1 447.6	−1 343.5	−6 602.3	1 031.5	1 069.1	231.9	320.3	Compte d'op. fin., nia
Net Errors and Omissions	−147.3	−521.0	−14.5	−532.1	93.9	292.6	153.7	Erreurs et omissions nettes
Reserves & Related Items	784.1	944.3	5 697.3	258.0	220.6	−70.1	−334.8	Rés. et postes appareutés

Country or area	1998	1999	2000	2001	2002	2003	2004	Pays ou zone
Egypt								**Egypte**
Goods: Exports fob	4 403.0	5 236.5	7 061.0	7 024.9	7 117.7	8 987.3	12 319.6	Biens : exportations, fab
Goods: Imports fob	−14 617.0	−15 164.8	−15 382.0	−13 959.6	−12 879.4	−13 188.6	−18 895.3	Biens : importations, fab
Serv. & Income: Credit	10 171.0	11 281.5	11 674.0	10 510.7	10 018.4	11 651.4	14 768.8	Serv. & revenu : crédit
Serv. & Income: Debit	−7 567.0	−7 496.4	−8 496.0	−7 921.6	−7 594.2	−7 305.5	−8 838.1	Serv. & revenu : débit
Current Trans.,nie: Credit	5 166.0	4 563.8	4 224.0	4 055.6	4 001.6	3 707.8	4 614.6	Transf. cour.,nia : crédit
Current Transfers: Debit	−122.0	−55.4	−52.0	−98.4	−41.7	−109.1	−47.9	Transf. courants : débit
Capital Acct.,nie: Credit	0.0	0.0	0.0	0.0	0.0	0.0	0.0	Compte de cap.,nia : crédit
Capital Account: Debit	0.0	0.0	0.0	0.0	0.0	0.0	0.0	Compte de capital : débit
Financial Account, nie	1 901.0	−1 421.4	−1 646.0	189.8	−3 332.7	−5 725.0	−4 460.8	Compte d'op. fin., nia
Net Errors and Omissions	−721.9	−1 557.6	586.8	−1 146.1	1 906.5	1 574.9	−45.3	Erreurs et omissions nettes
Reserves & Related Items	1 386.9	4 613.8	2 030.2	1 344.7	803.8	406.8	584.4	Rés. et postes apparentés
El Salvador								**El Salvador**
Goods: Exports fob	2 459.5	2 534.3	2 963.2	2 891.6	3 019.7	3 152.6	3 329.6	Biens : exportations, fab
Goods: Imports fob	−3 765.2	−3 890.4	−4 702.8	−4 824.1	−4 884.7	−5 428.0	−5 948.8	Biens : importations, fab
Serv. & Income: Credit	699.8	753.3	839.7	872.5	942.4	993.8	1 115.7	Serv. & revenu : crédit
Serv. & Income: Debit	−1 011.7	−1 218.0	−1 327.7	−1 388.6	−1 505.5	−1 596.7	−1 683.9	Serv. & revenu : débit
Current Trans.,nie: Credit	1 534.1	1 590.5	1 830.3	2 373.5	2 111.1	2 200.2	2 634.4	Transf. cour.,nia : crédit
Current Transfers: Debit	−7.3	−9.0	−33.2	−75.2	−88.2	−85.9	−58.6	Transf. courants : débit
Capital Acct.,nie: Credit	28.9	78.8	109.4	199.3	209.4	113.4	100.5	Compte de cap.,nia : crédit
Capital Account: Debit	−0.3	−0.2	−0.4	−0.4	−0.5	−0.5	−0.8	Compte de capital : débit
Financial Account, nie	1 034.3	574.5	287.5	230.3	688.0	1 239.8	426.4	Compte d'op. fin., nia
Net Errors and Omissions	−668.9	−206.0	−11.5	−456.6	−615.3	−272.4	45.4	Erreurs et omissions nettes
Reserves & Related Items	−303.3	−207.8	45.5	177.7	123.5	−316.2	40.0	Rés. et postes apparentés
Eritrea								**Erythrée**
Goods: Exports fob	28.1	20.7	36.8	...	...	...	...	Biens : exportations, fab
Goods: Imports fob	−508.3	−510.2	−471.4	...	...	...	...	Biens : importations, fab
Serv. & Income: Credit	93.3	56.0	70.1	...	...	...	...	Serv. & revenu : crédit
Serv. & Income: Debit	−194.3	−106.7	−38.9	...	...	...	...	Serv. & revenu : débit
Current Trans.,nie: Credit	293.3	346.5	306.1	...	...	...	...	Transf. cour.,nia : crédit
Current Transfers: Debit	−4.9	−15.1	−7.3	...	...	...	...	Transf. courants : débit
Capital Acct.,nie: Credit	2.7	0.6	0.0	...	...	...	...	Compte de cap.,nia : crédit
Capital Account: Debit	0.0	0.0	0.0	...	...	...	...	Compte de capital : débit
Financial Account, nie	197.0	196.3	63.2	...	...	...	...	Compte d'op. fin., nia
Net Errors and Omissions	−66.5	12.8	−22.9	...	...	...	...	Erreurs et omissions nettes
Reserves & Related Items	159.5	−0.9	64.3	...	...	...	...	Rés. et postes apparentés
Estonia								**Estonie**
Goods: Exports fob	2 690.1	2 453.1	3 311.4	3 359.7	3 532.2	4 608.3	5 970.3	Biens : exportations, fab
Goods: Imports fob	−3 805.4	−3 330.6	−4 079.5	−4 148.4	−4 621.3	−6 162.1	−7 936.3	Biens : importations, fab
Serv. & Income: Credit	1 613.2	1 623.5	1 616.5	1 820.6	1 915.8	2 481.4	3 257.7	Serv. & revenu : crédit
Serv. & Income: Debit	−1 124.7	−1 153.1	−1 258.1	−1 522.7	−1 656.3	−2 166.9	−2 888.8	Serv. & revenu : débit
Current Trans.,nie: Credit	172.9	153.7	144.7	181.4	174.3	232.6	457.3	Transf. cour.,nia : crédit
Current Transfers: Debit	−24.6	−41.3	−29.1	−29.4	−61.3	−109.5	−291.8	Transf. courants : débit
Capital Acct.,nie: Credit	2.1	1.4	16.8	5.5	20.1	55.7	90.5	Compte de cap.,nia : crédit
Capital Account: Debit	−0.3	−0.2	−0.2	−0.4	−1.0	−8.2	−6.8	Compte de capital : débit
Financial Account, nie	508.1	418.2	392.9	269.4	751.5	1 274.8	1 700.7	Compte d'op. fin., nia
Net Errors and Omissions	5.9	−5.5	12.2	22.3	15.3	−36.7	−81.5	Erreurs et omissions nettes
Reserves & Related Items	−37.3	−119.3	−127.6	41.9	−69.3	−169.4	−271.2	Rés. et postes apparentés
Ethiopia								**Ethiopie**
Goods: Exports fob	560.3	467.4	486.1	455.6	480.2	496.4	680.2	Biens : exportations, fab
Goods: Imports fob	−1 359.8	−1 387.2	−1 131.4	−1 625.8	−1 455.0	−1 895.0	−2 813.8	Biens : importations, fab
Serv. & Income: Credit	412.5	490.3	522.4	539.4	599.7	780.6	1 035.7	Serv. & revenu : crédit
Serv. & Income: Debit	−519.8	−516.8	−541.6	−572.8	−617.3	−751.7	−1 024.4	Serv. & revenu : débit
Current Trans.,nie: Credit	589.8	500.7	697.9	854.3	876.4	1 266.5	1 407.8	Transf. cour.,nia : crédit
Current Transfers: Debit	−15.7	−19.7	−23.1	−52.1	−53.8	−68.5	−35.9	Transf. courants : débit
Capital Acct.,nie: Credit	1.4	1.8	0.0	0.0	0.0	0.0	0.0	Compte de cap.,nia : crédit
Capital Account: Debit	0.0	0.0	0.0	0.0	0.0	0.0	0.0	Compte de capital : débit
Financial Account, nie	−21.3	−180.1	28.4	−178.4	−69.6	265.5	−105.5	Compte d'op. fin., nia
Net Errors and Omissions	−7.9	407.2	−228.1	−200.9	−881.3	−267.2	239.5	Erreurs et omissions nettes
Reserves & Related Items	360.4	236.3	189.5	780.8	1 120.7	173.4	616.6	Rés. et postes apparentés

Country or area	1998	1999	2000	2001	2002	2003	2004	Pays ou zone
Euro Area								**Zone euro**
Goods: Exports fob	878 060.0	870 374.0	910 536.0	925 621.0	1 003 300.0	1 176 010.0	1 404 350.0	Biens : exportations, fab
Goods: Imports fob	−756 110.0	−790 048.0	−881 918.0	−860 339.0	−881 172.0	−1 059 220.0	−1 277 170.0	Biens : importations, fab
Serv. & Income: Credit	481 592.0	485 081.0	511 798.0	533 089.0	547 773.0	628 157.0	757 477.0	Serv. & revenu : crédit
Serv. & Income: Debit	−519 148.0	−540 155.0	−556 709.0	−555 771.0	−561 655.0	−657 498.0	−757 027.0	Serv. & revenu : débit
Current Trans.,nie: Credit	70 062.7	69 683.3	62 260.2	70 974.6	79 858.6	90 629.9	99 666.6	Transf. cour.,nia : crédit
Current Transfers: Debit	−123 105.0	−118 356.0	−111 955.0	−116 662.0	−126 252.0	−154 573.0	−168 618.0	Transf. courants : débit
Capital Acct.,nie: Credit	19 851.5	20 309.7	16 811.8	15 574.8	18 110.9	26 519.5	29 294.0	Compte de cap.,nia : crédit
Capital Account: Debit	−5 934.8	−6 725.8	−7 763.8	−9 798.1	−8 555.7	−11 334.2	−7 547.9	Compte de capital : débit
Financial Account, nie	−86 053.5	4 662.0	47 606.5	−54 532.3	−45 010.8	−41 507.6	−24 122.1	Compte d'op. fin., nia
Net Errors and Omissions	31 150.0	−6 400.3	−6 820.4	35 330.6	−23 763.3	−32 404.8	−71 701.2	Erreurs et omissions nettes
Reserves & Related Items	9 637.0	11 576.6	16 152.4	16 512.0	−2 635.1	35 227.5	15 403.0	Rés. et postes appareutés
Fiji								**Fidji**
Goods: Exports fob	428.9	537.7	...	...	...	...	...	Biens : exportations, fab
Goods: Imports fob	−614.6	−653.3	...	...	...	...	...	Biens : importations, fab
Serv. & Income: Credit	557.8	572.4	...	...	...	...	...	Serv. & revenu : crédit
Serv. & Income: Debit	−462.6	−472.6	...	...	...	...	...	Serv. & revenu : débit
Current Trans.,nie: Credit	45.3	42.7	...	...	...	...	...	Transf. cour.,nia : crédit
Current Transfers: Debit	−14.7	−14.2	...	...	...	...	...	Transf. courants : débit
Capital Acct.,nie: Credit	100.6	59.3	...	...	...	...	...	Compte de cap.,nia : crédit
Capital Account: Debit	−40.0	−45.3	...	...	...	...	...	Compte de capital : débit
Financial Account, nie	28.7	−104.0	...	...	...	...	...	Compte d'op. fin., nia
Net Errors and Omissions	−24.6	32.5	...	...	...	...	...	Erreurs et omissions nettes
Reserves & Related Items	−4.9	44.9	...	...	...	...	...	Rés. et postes appareutés
Finland								**Finlande**
Goods: Exports fob	43 393.4	41 983.0	45 703.2	42 979.6	44 856.0	52 736.5	61 202.6	Biens : exportations, fab
Goods: Imports fob	−30 902.9	−29 815.1	−32 018.9	−30 320.8	−31 974.0	−39 789.6	−48 362.7	Biens : importations, fab
Serv. & Income: Credit	10 934.6	12 185.7	13 442.2	14 399.7	15 147.3	16 972.3	22 693.2	Serv. & revenu : crédit
Serv. & Income: Debit	−15 087.1	−15 327.2	−17 428.7	−17 677.5	−17 268.5	−21 810.2	−24 832.4	Serv. & revenu : débit
Current Trans.,nie: Credit	1 522.7	1 658.0	1 611.4	1 562.0	1 731.8	2 020.3	2 112.7	Transf. cour.,nia : crédit
Current Transfers: Debit	−2 521.1	−2 639.7	−2 334.0	−2 238.7	−2 344.2	−3 010.3	−3 115.8	Transf. courants : débit
Capital Acct.,nie: Credit	90.7	85.3	110.8	93.1	92.6	108.5	124.3	Compte de cap.,nia : crédit
Capital Account: Debit	0.0	−36.3	−7.4	−9.8	−3.8	−4.5	0.0	Compte de capital : débit
Financial Account, nie	−1 722.3	−6 414.4	−8 841.0	−10 942.2	−8 603.5	−12 193.5	−11 086.4	Compte d'op. fin., nia
Net Errors and Omissions	−5 412.2	−1 666.6	113.7	2 564.8	−1 746.8	4 462.2	2 170.3	Erreurs et omissions nettes
Reserves & Related Items	−295.8	−12.8	−351.3	−410.1	113.1	508.4	−905.8	Rés. et postes appareutés
France								**France**
Goods: Exports fob	303 025.0	299 949.0	298 198.0	294 621.0	307 196.0	361 913.0	421 113.0	Biens : exportations, fab
Goods: Imports fob	−278 084.0	−283 010.0	−301 817.0	−291 785.0	−299 557.0	−358 487.0	−429 050.0	Biens : importations, fab
Serv. & Income: Credit	151 623.2	153 329.4	153 308.6	156 403.9	144 166.9	187 486.8	218 518.0	Serv. & revenu : crédit
Serv. & Income: Debit	−125 732.6	−115 739.1	−117 853.3	−115 903.2	−126 341.9	−159 664.8	−197 187.3	Serv. & revenu : débit
Current Trans.,nie: Credit	19 653.9	18 766.1	17 871.6	17 278.8	19 765.5	24 049.9	26 041.9	Transf. cour.,nia : crédit
Current Transfers: Debit	−32 786.3	−31 786.8	−31 127.1	−31 857.4	−34 231.6	−43 494.8	−47 816.7	Transf. courants : débit
Capital Acct.,nie: Credit	2 098.5	1 991.2	1 923.2	1 102.3	906.6	1 929.0	3 202.7	Compte de cap.,nia : crédit
Capital Account: Debit	−632.4	−566.9	−531.1	−1 410.4	−1 098.2	−10 160.3	−1 058.2	Compte de capital : débit
Financial Account, nie	−29 288.9	−50 473.2	−32 549.0	−33 247.2	−20 338.3	13 537.5	4 127.2	Compte d'op. fin., nia
Net Errors and Omissions	9 939.3	6 091.5	10 142.9	−770.1	5 567.5	−15 835.1	6 218.2	Erreurs et omissions nettes
Reserves & Related Items	−19 815.1	1 448.4	2 432.6	5 566.6	3 965.1	−1 274.3	−4 108.1	Rés. et postes appareutés
Gabon								**Gabon**
Goods: Exports fob	1 907.6	2 498.8	3 320.6	2 613.8	2 555.9	3 178.5	...	Biens : exportations, fab
Goods: Imports fob	−1 163.2	−910.5	−798.1	−847.5	−942.0	−1 042.8	...	Biens : importations, fab
Serv. & Income: Credit	277.0	365.1	226.2	198.2	161.6	257.7	...	Serv. & revenu : crédit
Serv. & Income: Debit	−1 563.5	−1 520.0	−1 684.7	−1 368.8	−1 308.0	−1 637.9	...	Serv. & revenu : débit
Current Trans.,nie: Credit	36.6	42.6	16.0	34.3	4.7	7.2	...	Transf. cour.,nia : crédit
Current Transfers: Debit	−90.0	−85.6	−79.1	−112.6	−135.9	−188.2	...	Transf. courants : débit
Capital Acct.,nie: Credit	3.6	5.7	0.0	2.9	2.6	43.1	...	Compte de cap.,nia : crédit
Capital Account: Debit	−1.8	−0.3	−0.3	−0.1	0.0	0.0	...	Compte de capital : débit
Financial Account, nie	−224.1	−756.9	−567.8	−674.0	−451.4	−564.1	...	Compte d'op. fin., nia
Net Errors and Omissions	94.7	−74.8	−152.4	−104.0	−109.6	−154.4	...	Erreurs et omissions nettes
Reserves & Related Items	723.1	435.9	−280.5	257.8	222.1	100.9	...	Rés. et postes appareutés

Country or area	1998	1999	2000	2001	2002	2003	2004	Pays ou zone
Georgia								**Géorgie**
Goods: Exports fob	299.9	329.5	459.0	496.1	601.7	830.6	1 092.5	Biens : exportations, fab
Goods: Imports fob	−994.5	−863.4	−970.5	−1 045.6	−1 084.7	−1 466.6	−2 008.6	Biens : importations, fab
Serv. & Income: Credit	608.7	428.3	385.0	411.8	552.8	620.1	790.3	Serv. & revenu : crédit
Serv. & Income: Debit	−397.9	−288.5	−277.4	−302.3	−484.0	−533.8	−637.4	Serv. & revenu : débit
Current Trans.,nie: Credit	219.9	228.7	163.2	246.4	222.0	211.1	389.1	Transf. cour.,nia : crédit
Current Transfers: Debit	−11.8	−33.0	−28.3	−18.1	−29.0	−36.2	−51.5	Transf. courants : débit
Capital Acct.,nie: Credit	0.0	0.0	0.0	0.0	27.1	27.9	44.2	Compte de cap.,nia : crédit
Capital Account: Debit	−6.1	−7.1	−4.8	−5.2	−8.6	−8.0	−3.4	Compte de capital : débit
Financial Account, nie	348.8	135.5	92.8	209.7	19.2	322.7	479.0	Compte d'op. fin., nia
Net Errors and Omissions	−170.5	55.7	187.4	34.9	−6.0	−17.0	1.6	Erreurs et omissions nettes
Reserves & Related Items	103.5	14.3	−6.4	−27.7	189.7	49.1	−95.7	Rés. et postes appareutés
Germany								**Allemagne**
Goods: Exports fob	541 379.0	541 924.0	549 113.0	569 676.0	616 620.0	752 441.0	909 451.0	Biens : exportations, fab
Goods: Imports fob	−465 263.0	−472 278.0	−491 895.0	−480 479.0	−488 786.0	−604 513.0	−719 477.0	Biens : importations, fab
Serv. & Income: Credit	169 222.4	176 316.8	189 784.3	179 923.0	200 589.4	232 912.0	274 696.0	Serv. & revenu : crédit
Serv. & Income: Debit	−230 123.0	−244 953.0	−250 578.0	−241 570.2	−256 252.0	−297 058.0	−325 671.0	Serv. & revenu : débit
Current Trans.,nie: Credit	15 964.1	17 071.6	14 976.3	14 835.9	15 375.4	18 425.6	19 363.3	Transf. cour.,nia : crédit
Current Transfers: Debit	−46 302.6	−43 630.2	−41 001.5	−39 318.8	−41 906.5	−50 868.6	−54 592.7	Transf. courants : débit
Capital Acct.,nie: Credit	3 310.8	3 010.0	9 407.2	1 869.0	2 091.3	3 226.2	3 299.5	Compte de cap.,nia : crédit
Capital Account: Debit	−2 591.8	−3 161.2	−3 218.8	−2 195.9	−2 317.8	−2 873.4	−2 786.2	Compte de capital : débit
Financial Account, nie	20 008.0	−26 881.9	28 993.7	−16 130.8	−43 269.5	−53 208.1	−138 536.0	Compte d'op. fin., nia
Net Errors and Omissions	−1 588.9	38 467.1	−10 804.2	7 924.4	−4 124.4	831.9	32 445.8	Erreurs et omissions nettes
Reserves & Related Items	−4 015.9	14 114.8	5 222.2	5 466.1	1 978.8	683.9	1 806.9	Rés. et postes appareutés
Ghana								**Ghana**
Goods: Exports fob	2 090.8	2 005.5	1 936.3	1 867.1	2 015.2	2 562.4	2 784.6	Biens : exportations, fab
Goods: Imports fob	−2 991.6	−3 279.9	−2 766.6	−2 968.5	−2 707.0	−3 276.1	−4 297.3	Biens : importations, fab
Serv. & Income: Credit	467.6	482.8	519.8	548.0	569.6	651.4	746.8	Serv. & revenu : crédit
Serv. & Income: Debit	−822.4	−792.8	−706.9	−730.2	−809.8	−1 081.7	−1 300.8	Serv. & revenu : débit
Current Trans.,nie: Credit	751.0	637.9	649.3	978.4	912.2	1 408.4	1 831.0	Transf. cour.,nia : crédit
Current Transfers: Debit	−17.1	−17.8	−18.4	−19.4	−12.2	−9.2	0.0	Transf. courants : débit
Capital Acct.,nie: Credit	0.0	0.0	0.0	0.0	0.0	0.0	0.0	Compte de cap.,nia : crédit
Capital Account: Debit	0.0	0.0	0.0	0.0	0.0	0.0	0.0	Compte de capital : débit
Financial Account, nie	560.9	746.0	369.3	392.2	−38.7	347.3	201.6	Compte d'op. fin., nia
Net Errors and Omissions	−11.5	81.9	−352.1	−189.1	57.1	−98.8	20.9	Erreurs et omissions nettes
Reserves & Related Items	−27.6	136.4	369.3	121.5	13.6	−503.6	13.2	Rés. et postes appareutés
Greece								**Grèce**
Goods: Exports fob	...	8 544.7	10 201.5	10 615.0	9 865.4	12 577.8	15 739.0	Biens : exportations, fab
Goods: Imports fob	...	−26 495.6	−30 440.4	−29 702.0	−31 320.6	−38 183.6	−47 360.0	Biens : importations, fab
Serv. & Income: Credit	...	19 082.3	22 046.1	21 340.7	21 673.8	26 827.5	36 158.3	Serv. & revenu : crédit
Serv. & Income: Debit	...	−12 498.8	−14 978.5	−15 240.6	−13 307.1	−18 048.3	−22 189.6	Serv. & revenu : débit
Current Trans.,nie: Credit	...	4 956.5	4 115.8	4 592.0	5 535.6	7 202.2	7 900.6	Transf. cour.,nia : crédit
Current Transfers: Debit	...	−884.0	−764.2	−1 005.0	−2 028.8	−2 930.4	−3 396.3	Transf. courants : débit
Capital Acct.,nie: Credit	...	2 318.2	2 243.5	2 320.0	1 706.9	1 584.5	3 278.0	Compte de cap.,nia : crédit
Capital Account: Debit	...	−107.0	−131.2	−167.0	−177.2	−173.5	−288.1	Compte de capital : débit
Financial Account, nie	...	7 477.5	10 830.0	536.7	11 578.3	6 169.3	6 508.3	Compte d'op. fin., nia
Net Errors and Omissions	...	41.6	−549.8	1 010.9	−1 663.2	252.0	372.9	Erreurs et omissions nettes
Reserves & Related Items	...	−2 435.5	−2 572.8	5 699.4	−1 863.4	4 722.5	3 277.0	Rés. et postes appareutés
Grenada								**Grenade**
Goods: Exports fob	45.9	74.3	83.0	63.6	42.0	...	...	Biens : exportations, fab
Goods: Imports fob	−183.0	−184.6	−220.9	−196.8	−181.4	...	...	Biens : importations, fab
Serv. & Income: Credit	123.9	148.1	157.8	137.1	137.2	...	...	Serv. & revenu : crédit
Serv. & Income: Debit	−97.5	−110.0	−124.3	−124.0	−137.1	...	...	Serv. & revenu : débit
Current Trans.,nie: Credit	34.2	26.8	30.4	31.0	31.8	...	...	Transf. cour.,nia : crédit
Current Transfers: Debit	−5.0	−7.6	−10.2	−9.4	−8.7	...	...	Transf. courants : débit
Capital Acct.,nie: Credit	30.4	33.1	34.2	44.4	33.9	...	...	Compte de cap.,nia : crédit
Capital Account: Debit	−1.8	−1.9	−2.1	−2.0	−2.0	...	...	Compte de capital : débit
Financial Account, nie	55.8	27.6	63.7	47.3	108.2	...	...	Compte d'op. fin., nia
Net Errors and Omissions	1.3	−1.0	−4.9	14.8	7.4	...	...	Erreurs et omissions nettes
Reserves & Related Items	−4.1	−4.7	−6.6	−5.8	−31.2	...	...	Rés. et postes appareutés

Country or area	1998	1999	2000	2001	2002	2003	2004	Pays ou zone
Guatemala								**Guatemala**
Goods: Exports fob	2 846.9	2 780.6	3 085.1	2 859.8	2 818.9	3 059.9	3 429.5	Biens : exportations, fab
Goods: Imports fob	−4 255.7	−4 225.7	−4 742.0	−5 142.0	−5 791.0	−6 175.7	−7 189.1	Biens : importations, fab
Serv. & Income: Credit	731.3	775.7	991.4	1 362.3	1 306.5	1 237.9	1 351.5	Serv. & revenu : crédit
Serv. & Income: Debit	−1 066.9	−1 071.4	−1 249.4	−1 329.8	−1 545.5	−1 623.1	−1 785.9	Serv. & revenu : débit
Current Trans.,nie: Credit	742.9	754.4	908.2	1 024.3	2 077.7	2 558.9	3 048.6	Transf. cour.,nia : crédit
Current Transfers: Debit	−37.6	−39.5	−42.9	−27.5	−101.5	−97.0	−42.9	Transf. courants : débit
Capital Acct.,nie: Credit	71.0	68.4	85.5	93.4	124.2	133.8	135.3	Compte de cap.,nia : crédit
Capital Account: Debit	0.0	0.0	0.0	0.0	0.0	0.0	0.0	Compte de capital : débit
Financial Account, nie	1 136.7	637.5	1 520.7	1 546.7	1 196.5	1 516.3	1 597.8	Compte d'op. fin., nia
Net Errors and Omissions	66.8	195.0	86.1	87.2	−64.7	−60.8	63.5	Erreurs et omissions nettes
Reserves & Related Items	−235.4	125.0	−642.7	−474.4	−21.1	−550.1	−608.3	Rés. et postes appareutés
Guinea								**Guinée**
Goods: Exports fob	693.0	635.7	666.3	731.1	708.6	609.3	725.6	Biens : exportations, fab
Goods: Imports fob	−572.0	−581.7	−587.1	−561.9	−668.5	−644.3	−688.4	Biens : importations, fab
Serv. & Income: Credit	119.7	137.9	91.4	114.1	96.6	146.3	95.1	Serv. & revenu : crédit
Serv. & Income: Debit	−516.3	−471.3	−386.0	−432.6	−382.2	−431.6	−312.3	Serv. & revenu : débit
Current Trans.,nie: Credit	116.2	80.0	88.6	91.6	70.5	194.6	55.1	Transf. cour.,nia : crédit
Current Transfers: Debit	−24.3	−15.1	−28.5	−44.5	−24.8	−61.7	−49.9	Transf. courants : débit
Capital Acct.,nie: Credit	0.0	0.0	0.0	0.0	91.9	57.6	0.0	Compte de cap.,nia : crédit
Capital Account: Debit	0.0	0.0	0.0	0.0	0.0	0.0	−30.2	Compte de capital : débit
Financial Account, nie	8.0	117.1	8.4	−12.1	−115.1	58.6	77.7	Compte d'op. fin., nia
Net Errors and Omissions	17.8	21.4	83.9	−2.2	143.1	−157.2	68.6	Erreurs et omissions nettes
Reserves & Related Items	157.8	75.9	62.9	116.5	79.8	228.5	58.6	Rés. et postes appareutés
Guinea-Bissau								**Guinée-Bissau**
Goods: Exports fob	...	...	...	62.9	54.4	65.0	...	Biens : exportations, fab
Goods: Imports fob	...	...	...	−61.7	−58.5	−65.3	...	Biens : importations, fab
Serv. & Income: Credit	...	...	...	5.0	7.8	8.1	...	Serv. & revenu : crédit
Serv. & Income: Debit	...	...	...	−42.8	−37.5	−47.1	...	Serv. & revenu : débit
Current Trans.,nie: Credit	...	...	...	9.8	30.2	39.7	...	Transf. cour.,nia : crédit
Current Transfers: Debit	...	...	...	0.0	−5.1	−6.8	...	Transf. courants : débit
Capital Acct.,nie: Credit	...	...	...	25.0	40.4	42.8	...	Compte de cap.,nia : crédit
Capital Account: Debit	...	...	...	0.3	−1.5	0.0	...	Compte de capital : débit
Financial Account, nie	...	...	...	−17.3	−21.4	−13.1	...	Compte d'op. fin., nia
Net Errors and Omissions	...	...	...	5.9	−3.0	6.2	...	Erreurs et omissions nettes
Reserves & Related Items	...	...	...	13.0	−5.9	−29.4	...	Rés. et postes appareutés
Guyana								**Guyana**
Goods: Exports fob	545.1	522.3	502.9	485.4	490.1	508.0	584.0	Biens : exportations, fab
Goods: Imports fob	−552.9	−518.7	−550.1	−541.0	−513.9	−525.3	−598.1	Biens : importations, fab
Serv. & Income: Credit	153.7	158.2	181.0	182.1	180.1	161.5	168.0	Serv. & revenu : crédit
Serv. & Income: Debit	−245.5	−250.3	−263.0	−266.1	−262.5	−234.3	−230.4	Serv. & revenu : débit
Current Trans.,nie: Credit	74.3	76.1	100.8	98.1	128.7	127.4	139.7	Transf. cour.,nia : crédit
Current Transfers: Debit	−30.3	−37.1	−53.8	−54.1	−88.7	−84.2	−93.4	Transf. courants : débit
Capital Acct.,nie: Credit	13.1	15.5	16.3	31.9	31.1	43.8	45.9	Compte de cap.,nia : crédit
Capital Account: Debit	0.0	0.0	0.0	0.0	0.0	0.0	0.0	Compte de capital : débit
Financial Account, nie	65.9	52.9	110.5	84.4	54.3	35.0	−7.0	Compte d'op. fin., nia
Net Errors and Omissions	−36.4	2.7	−4.4	5.5	−4.5	−22.1	35.9	Erreurs et omissions nettes
Reserves & Related Items	13.0	−21.6	−40.2	−26.2	−14.7	−9.8	−44.6	Rés. et postes appareutés
Haiti								**Haïti**
Goods: Exports fob	294.8	343.3	331.7	305.2	274.4	333.2	...	Biens : exportations, fab
Goods: Imports fob	−822.1	−1 017.5	−1 086.7	−1 055.4	−980.4	−1 115.8	...	Biens : importations, fab
Serv. & Income: Credit [3]	179.0	188.0	172.0	139.0	148.0	136.0	...	Serv. & revenu : crédit [3]
Serv. & Income: Debit	−229.5	−247.2	−273.2	−251.9	−265.3	−273.3	...	Serv. & revenu : débit
Current Trans.,nie: Credit	606.5	673.7	771.0	768.6	775.7	906.8	...	Transf. cour.,nia : crédit
Current Transfers: Debit	0.0	0.0	0.0	0.0	0.0	0.0	...	Transf. courants : débit
Capital Acct.,nie: Credit	0.0	0.0	0.0	0.0	0.0	0.0	...	Compte de cap.,nia : crédit
Capital Account: Debit	0.0	0.0	0.0	0.0	0.0	0.0	...	Compte de capital : débit
Financial Account, nie	186.8	85.3	−16.0	82.5	−17.3	−76.5	...	Compte d'op. fin., nia
Net Errors and Omissions	−181.3	1.0	44.3	6.9	−3.1	85.0	...	Erreurs et omissions nettes
Reserves & Related Items	−34.2	−26.5	56.9	5.2	67.9	4.6	...	Rés. et postes appareutés

Country or area	1998	1999	2000	2001	2002	2003	2004	Pays ou zone
Honduras								**Honduras**
Goods: Exports fob	2 047.9	1 756.3	2 011.6	1 935.5	1 977.1	2 094.4	2 411.2	Biens : exportations, fab
Goods: Imports fob	−2 370.5	−2 509.6	−2 669.6	−2 769.4	−2 806.1	−3 059.0	−3 678.5	Biens : importations, fab
Serv. & Income: Credit	436.6	554.6	597.4	579.3	588.5	647.1	703.6	Serv. & revenu : crédit
Serv. & Income: Debit	−710.4	−738.1	−849.1	−888.6	−871.4	−977.9	−1 079.7	Serv. & revenu : débit
Current Trans.,nie: Credit	241.7	354.6	717.9	894.0	946.7	1 085.0	1 358.8	Transf. cour.,nia : crédit
Current Transfers: Debit	−40.1	−42.4	−70.4	−89.9	−99.0	−104.0	−128.4	Transf. courants : débit
Capital Acct.,nie: Credit	29.4	110.9	30.1	36.7	23.6	22.4	21.8	Compte de cap.,nia : crédit
Capital Account: Debit	0.0	0.0	0.0	0.0	0.0	0.0	0.0	Compte de capital : débit
Financial Account, nie	113.9	203.4	−28.8	123.6	158.2	72.2	724.1	Compte d'op. fin., nia
Net Errors and Omissions	96.1	122.0	104.3	104.8	63.7	21.9	35.3	Erreurs et omissions nettes
Reserves & Related Items	155.4	188.3	156.6	74.1	18.7	197.9	−368.3	Rés. et postes appareutés
Hungary								**Hongrie**
Goods: Exports fob	23 698.2	25 607.7	28 761.7	31 080.5	34 792.1	43 474.8	56 053.6	Biens : exportations, fab
Goods: Imports fob	−25 583.2	−27 777.8	−31 674.5	−33 317.7	−36 911.0	−46 753.3	−59 051.2	Biens : importations, fab
Serv. & Income: Credit	6 653.3	6 115.9	7 065.8	8 330.9	8 653.2	10 071.6	12 132.5	Serv. & revenu : crédit
Serv. & Income: Debit	−8 403.0	−8 154.1	−8 514.4	−9 702.3	−11 718.7	−14 691.1	−18 294.2	Serv. & revenu : débit
Current Trans.,nie: Credit	509.7	711.2	673.7	780.6	1 069.8	1 283.3	1 632.6	Transf. cour.,nia : crédit
Current Transfers: Debit	−266.4	−277.5	−316.3	−376.6	−578.8	−616.2	−1 315.5	Transf. courants : débit
Capital Acct.,nie: Credit	408.0	509.0	458.3	417.5	238.5	240.0	517.6	Compte de cap.,nia : crédit
Capital Account: Debit	−219.3	−479.5	−188.0	−100.6	−47.9	−267.4	−189.9	Compte de capital : débit
Financial Account, nie	4 438.8	6 469.0	4 960.0	2 774.7	2 564.9	7 368.3	11 957.0	Compte d'op. fin., nia
Net Errors and Omissions	−285.2	−388.8	−174.1	29.0	145.4	225.8	−1 461.3	Erreurs et omissions nettes
Reserves & Related Items	−950.8	−2 335.0	−1 052.2	83.9	1 792.4	−335.6	−1 981.2	Rés. et postes appareutés
Iceland								**Islande**
Goods: Exports fob	1 927.4	2 009.0	1 901.9	2 015.8	2 239.8	2 385.7	2 896.5	Biens : exportations, fab
Goods: Imports fob	−2 278.6	−2 316.2	−2 376.0	−2 090.6	−2 090.2	−2 595.9	−3 415.3	Biens : importations, fab
Serv. & Income: Credit	1 073.6	1 059.0	1 190.9	1 257.6	1 427.3	1 748.8	2 217.2	Serv. & revenu : crédit
Serv. & Income: Debit	−1 263.3	−1 330.4	−1 554.3	−1 509.1	−1 463.3	−2 056.8	−2 736.6	Serv. & revenu : débit
Current Trans.,nie: Credit	4.3	4.8	6.1	8.0	36.4	12.5	10.3	Transf. cour.,nia : crédit
Current Transfers: Debit	−18.3	−14.9	−15.6	−17.3	−22.0	−27.9	−27.1	Transf. courants : débit
Capital Acct.,nie: Credit	8.9	17.4	17.5	15.3	13.7	14.9	31.6	Compte de cap.,nia : crédit
Capital Account: Debit	−13.5	−18.2	−20.6	−11.5	−15.1	−20.2	−34.9	Compte de capital : débit
Financial Account, nie	682.7	863.8	846.4	172.3	38.4	530.9	2 158.5	Compte d'op. fin., nia
Net Errors and Omissions	−91.1	−188.8	−70.4	111.3	−103.6	314.7	−898.0	Erreurs et omissions nettes
Reserves & Related Items	−32.0	−85.6	74.1	48.3	−61.4	−306.5	−202.1	Rés. et postes appareutés
India								**Inde**
Goods: Exports fob	34 075.7	36 877.3	43 246.6	44 793.2	51 141.1	59 338.2	...	Biens : exportations, fab
Goods: Imports fob	−44 828.0	−45 556.2	−53 886.5	−51 211.0	−54 700.4	−68 208.4	...	Biens : importations, fab
Serv. & Income: Credit	13 497.2	16 428.5	19 204.8	20 860.4	22 666.3	27 175.1	...	Serv. & revenu : crédit
Serv. & Income: Debit	−19 982.5	−22 900.6	−26 600.7	−27 765.3	−28 138.3	−33 939.5	...	Serv. & revenu : débit
Current Trans.,nie: Credit	10 401.8	11 957.9	13 548.4	15 140.1	16 788.5	22 832.7	...	Transf. cour.,nia : crédit
Current Transfers: Debit	−67.4	−34.9	−113.9	−407.1	−697.7	−344.9	...	Transf. courants : débit
Capital Acct.,nie: Credit	0.0	0.0	2 757.8	2 226.8	1 408.7	5 594.9	...	Compte de cap.,nia : crédit
Capital Account: Debit	0.0	0.0	−2 042.0	−1 483.9	−1 306.6	−1 756.0	...	Compte de capital : débit
Financial Account, nie	8 583.9	9 578.6	9 623.4	7 252.2	11 882.4	14 791.5	...	Compte d'op. fin., nia
Net Errors and Omissions	1 389.9	313.2	330.8	−715.0	−191.0	182.9	...	Erreurs et omissions nettes
Reserves & Related Items	−3 070.7	−6 663.7	−6 068.8	−8 690.4	−18 853.0	−25 666.5	...	Rés. et postes appareutés
Indonesia								**Indonésie**
Goods: Exports fob	50 371.0	51 241.9	65 407.4	57 364.6	59 165.1	64 391.3	72 166.8	Biens : exportations, fab
Goods: Imports fob	−31 942.1	−30 598.5	−40 365.4	−34 668.5	−35 651.9	−39 547.8	−50 614.6	Biens : importations, fab
Serv. & Income: Credit	6 388.8	6 489.1	7 671.6	7 504.9	7 980.6	6 347.4	18 920.8	Serv. & revenu : crédit
Serv. & Income: Debit	−22 187.0	−23 263.3	−26 538.0	−24 820.0	−25 410.4	−24 672.4	−38 504.2	Serv. & revenu : débit
Current Trans.,nie: Credit	1 466.4	1 913.6	1 816.4	1 520.0	2 210.5	2 052.7	2 432.7	Transf. cour.,nia : crédit
Current Transfers: Debit	0.0	0.0	0.0	0.0	−470.4	−184.0	−1 293.3	Transf. courants : débit
Capital Acct.,nie: Credit	0.0	0.0	0.0	0.0	0.0	0.0	0.0	Compte de cap.,nia : crédit
Capital Account: Debit	0.0	0.0	0.0	0.0	0.0	0.0	0.0	Compte de capital : débit
Financial Account, nie	−9 633.1	−5 944.3	−7 895.8	−7 616.9	−1 103.1	−949.5	2 996.7	Compte d'op. fin., nia
Net Errors and Omissions	2 099.3	2 077.0	3 829.3	701.0	−1 762.6	−3 790.6	−5 783.7	Erreurs et omissions nettes
Reserves & Related Items	3 436.8	−1 915.6	−3 925.6	15.0	−4 957.9	−3 647.3	−321.1	Rés. et postes appareutés

Country or area	1998	1999	2000	2001	2002	2003	2004	Pays ou zone
Iran (Islamic Rep. of)								**Iran (Rép. islamique d')**
Goods: Exports fob	13 118.0	21 030.0	28 345.0	...	...	...	...	Biens : exportations, fab
Goods: Imports fob	−14 286.0	−13 433.0	−15 207.0	...	...	...	...	Biens : importations, fab
Serv. & Income: Credit	2 023.0	1 397.0	1 786.0	...	...	...	...	Serv. & revenu : crédit
Serv. & Income: Debit	−3 491.0	−2 930.0	−2 900.0	...	...	...	...	Serv. & revenu : débit
Current Trans.,nie: Credit	500.0	508.0	539.0	...	...	...	...	Transf. cour.,nia : crédit
Current Transfers: Debit	−3.0	17.0	82.0	...	...	...	...	Transf. courants : débit
Capital Acct.,nie: Credit	0.0	0.0	0.0	...	...	...	...	Compte de cap.,nia : crédit
Capital Account: Debit	0.0	0.0	0.0	...	...	...	...	Compte de capital : débit
Financial Account, nie	2 270.0	−5 894.0	−10 189.0	...	...	...	...	Compte d'op. fin., nia
Net Errors and Omissions	−1 121.7	−243.5	−1 372.5	...	...	...	...	Erreurs et omissions nettes
Reserves & Related Items	990.7	−451.5	−1 083.5	...	...	...	...	Rés. et postes appareutés
Ireland								**Irlande**
Goods: Exports fob	78 562.0	67 830.6	73 530.0	77 622.9	84 215.6	88 590.3	99 712.7	Biens : exportations, fab
Goods: Imports fob	−53 172.1	−44 243.7	−48 520.0	−50 360.0	−50 768.6	−51 708.5	−60 206.5	Biens : importations, fab
Serv. & Income: Credit	42 165.6	40 130.3	46 151.0	52 315.6	57 100.1	76 156.1	94 449.7	Serv. & revenu : crédit
Serv. & Income: Debit	−68 425.3	−64 725.4	−72 432.0	−80 540.4	−92 343.5	−113 475.8	−135 776.3	Serv. & revenu : débit
Current Trans.,nie: Credit	7 428.5	5 308.1	4 142.9	7 399.6	7 538.2	7 026.8	6 685.3	Transf. cour.,nia : crédit
Current Transfers: Debit	−5 542.6	−4 054.9	−3 387.8	−7 127.8	−6 842.3	−6 499.9	−6 288.3	Transf. courants : débit
Capital Acct.,nie: Credit	1 326.7	674.4	1 167.1	719.2	656.1	617.3	682.5	Compte de cap.,nia : crédit
Capital Account: Debit	−108.3	−81.0	−92.8	−84.1	−144.4	−491.1	−162.8	Compte de capital : débit
Financial Account, nie	4 686.1	−4 184.9	7 912.1	16.4	468.2	−3 480.8	3 851.1	Compte d'op. fin., nia
Net Errors and Omissions	−3 708.0	1 373.2	−8 509.2	433.8	−170.9	1 375.3	−4 381.9	Erreurs et omissions nettes
Reserves & Related Items	−3 212.4	1 973.5	38.6	−395.2	291.6	1 890.2	1 434.6	Rés. et postes appareutés
Israel								**Israël**
Goods: Exports fob	23 113.7	25 816.0	31 188.1	27 966.9	27 535.1	30 098.4	36 584.6	Biens : exportations, fab
Goods: Imports fob	−26 618.5	−30 567.0	−34 728.1	−31 713.5	−31 970.8	−33 161.0	−39 486.8	Biens : importations, fab
Serv. & Income: Credit	12 034.9	14 399.9	18 255.8	14 632.4	13 645.8	15 371.3	17 158.7	Serv. & revenu : crédit
Serv. & Income: Debit	−15 863.0	−17 607.0	−22 428.1	−19 157.2	−17 260.0	−17 885.4	−19 012.9	Serv. & revenu : débit
Current Trans.,nie: Credit	6 682.7	7 122.0	7 466.9	7 798.6	8 124.3	7 497.1	7 306.5	Transf. cour.,nia : crédit
Current Transfers: Debit	−606.4	−809.4	−984.5	−1 106.8	−1 362.4	−1 125.4	−1 076.3	Transf. courants : débit
Capital Acct.,nie: Credit	577.0	568.7	455.2	678.9	150.6	465.3	524.0	Compte de cap.,nia : crédit
Capital Account: Debit	0.0	0.0	0.0	0.0	0.0	0.0	0.0	Compte de capital : débit
Financial Account, nie	1 454.6	2 004.0	1 877.4	945.6	−1 575.9	−2 636.8	−4 255.7	Compte d'op. fin., nia
Net Errors and Omissions	−936.3	−1 064.2	−829.9	307.9	1 800.4	1 209.9	572.6	Erreurs et omissions nettes
Reserves & Related Items	161.3	137.0	−272.8	−352.8	912.9	166.6	1 685.3	Rés. et postes appareutés
Italy								**Italie**
Goods: Exports fob	242 572.0	235 856.0	240 473.0	244 931.0	252 618.0	298 118.0	352 166.0	Biens : exportations, fab
Goods: Imports fob	−206 941.0	−212 420.0	−230 925.0	−229 392.0	−239 206.0	−286 641.0	−341 255.0	Biens : importations, fab
Serv. & Income: Credit	118 867.5	105 148.5	95 226.8	96 250.6	103 742.6	120 546.5	136 924.9	Serv. & revenu : crédit
Serv. & Income: Debit	−127 015.2	−115 118.3	−106 281.1	−106 663.3	−121 020.0	−143 335.1	−153 410.1	Serv. & revenu : débit
Current Trans.,nie: Credit	14 402.3	16 776.2	15 797.4	16 136.5	20 871.1	20 649.5	21 854.1	Transf. cour.,nia : crédit
Current Transfers: Debit	−21 887.4	−22 132.3	−20 073.0	−21 915.3	−26 374.9	−28 743.7	−31 417.2	Transf. courants : débit
Capital Acct.,nie: Credit	3 359.4	4 571.9	4 172.1	2 098.0	2 060.1	4 950.3	4 112.6	Compte de cap.,nia : crédit
Capital Account: Debit	−1 001.5	−1 608.0	−1 293.0	−1 251.8	−2 140.4	−2 009.2	−1 467.7	Compte de capital : débit
Financial Account, nie	−18 074.0	−17 414.7	7 504.3	−3 569.7	11 223.5	20 437.4	8 165.2	Compte d'op. fin., nia
Net Errors and Omissions	−25 753.7	−1 710.8	−1 355.2	2 787.5	1 395.0	−2 857.8	1 483.9	Erreurs et omissions nettes
Reserves & Related Items	21 471.9	8 051.1	−3 247.0	587.9	−3 169.1	−1 114.9	2 843.6	Rés. et postes appareutés
Jamaica								**Jamaïque**
Goods: Exports fob	1 613.4	1 499.1	1 562.8	1 454.4	1 309.1	1 385.6	1 601.6	Biens : exportations, fab
Goods: Imports fob	−2 743.9	−2 685.6	−3 004.3	−3 072.6	−3 179.6	−3 328.2	−3 546.1	Biens : importations, fab
Serv. & Income: Credit	1 926.7	2 144.2	2 218.8	2 115.2	2 133.3	2 355.3	2 566.7	Serv. & revenu : crédit
Serv. & Income: Debit	−1 758.0	−1 821.3	−1 965.5	−2 169.9	−2 423.7	−2 375.1	−2 577.5	Serv. & revenu : débit
Current Trans.,nie: Credit	727.6	757.9	969.4	1 090.7	1 337.9	1 523.5	1 892.0	Transf. cour.,nia : crédit
Current Transfers: Debit	−99.6	−110.6	−148.6	−176.6	−251.0	−334.4	−445.9	Transf. courants : débit
Capital Acct.,nie: Credit	20.3	19.1	29.6	15.2	18.9	19.3	35.8	Compte de cap.,nia : crédit
Capital Account: Debit	−29.0	−30.0	−27.4	−37.5	−35.8	−19.2	−33.6	Compte de capital : débit
Financial Account, nie	337.3	94.8	853.9	1 660.5	909.9	313.3	1 214.7	Compte d'op. fin., nia
Net Errors and Omissions	49.1	−4.0	29.7	−14.4	−60.9	28.4	−14.1	Erreurs et omissions nettes
Reserves & Related Items	−43.9	136.4	−518.4	−865.0	242.0	431.6	−693.6	Rés. et postes appareutés

Summary of balance of payments—Millions of US dollars (*continued*)
Résumé des balances des paiements—Millions de dollars des E.-U. (*suite*)

Country or area	1998	1999	2000	2001	2002	2003	2004	Pays ou zone
Japan								**Japon**
Goods: Exports fob	374 044.0	403 694.0	459 513.0	383 592.0	395 581.0	449 119.0	538 999.0	Biens : exportations, fab
Goods: Imports fob	−251 655.0	−280 369.0	−342 797.0	−313 378.0	−301 751.0	−342 723.0	−406 866.0	Biens : importations, fab
Serv. & Income: Credit	162 747.0	153 046.8	166 437.3	167 611.2	157 189.9	172 831.7	210 943.0	Serv. & revenu : crédit
Serv. & Income: Debit	−157 544.9	−149 628.7	−153 662.7	−142 122.7	−133 649.2	−135 499.7	−163 142.1	Serv. & revenu : débit
Current Trans.,nie: Credit	5 531.1	6 211.5	7 380.4	6 151.7	10 037.9	6 507.5	6 907.2	Transf. cour.,nia : crédit
Current Transfers: Debit	−14 373.3	−18 350.3	−17 211.1	−14 056.0	−14 960.4	−14 019.8	−14 782.4	Transf. courants : débit
Capital Acct.,nie: Credit	1 568.7	745.9	780.9	994.7	914.6	392.4	437.3	Compte de cap.,nia : crédit
Capital Account: Debit	−16 022.9	−17 213.4	−10 039.5	−3 863.5	−4 236.0	−4 390.5	−5 231.1	Compte de capital : débit
Financial Account, nie	−114 816.0	−38 845.4	−78 312.7	−48 160.3	−63 380.5	71 924.4	22 493.7	Compte d'op. fin., nia
Net Errors and Omissions	4 357.0	16 965.2	16 865.9	3 718.4	388.2	−16 988.5	−28 904.6	Erreurs et omissions nettes
Reserves & Related Items	6 164.4	−76 256.3	−48 955.0	−40 487.0	−46 133.7	−187 153.0	−160 854.0	Rés. et postes appareutés
Jordan								**Jordanie**
Goods: Exports fob	1 802.4	1 831.9	1 899.3	2 294.4	2 770.0	3 081.6	3 882.9	Biens : exportations, fab
Goods: Imports fob	−3 404.0	−3 292.0	−4 073.7	−4 301.5	−4 500.9	−5 077.9	−7 261.1	Biens : importations, fab
Serv. & Income: Credit	2 132.0	2 169.3	2 307.3	2 131.2	2 259.1	2 232.6	2 615.4	Serv. & revenu : crédit
Serv. & Income: Debit	−2 228.8	−2 177.7	−2 257.4	−2 187.1	−2 255.2	−2 263.6	−2 471.4	Serv. & revenu : débit
Current Trans.,nie: Credit	1 984.3	2 154.9	2 611.3	2 365.8	2 524.3	3 501.0	3 562.5	Transf. cour.,nia : crédit
Current Transfers: Debit	−271.9	−281.4	−427.4	−306.9	−260.1	−295.1	−346.3	Transf. courants : débit
Capital Acct.,nie: Credit	81.1	87.6	64.9	21.6	68.8	93.5	2.0	Compte de cap.,nia : crédit
Capital Account: Debit	0.0	0.0	0.0	0.0	0.0	0.0	0.0	Compte de capital : débit
Financial Account, nie	−177.3	230.9	270.9	−319.0	474.8	−199.4	−307.2	Compte d'op. fin., nia
Net Errors and Omissions	−454.0	28.7	297.7	57.7	−150.5	275.5	501.7	Erreurs et omissions nettes
Reserves & Related Items	536.1	−752.1	−692.9	243.9	−930.3	−1 348.2	−178.6	Rés. et postes appareutés
Kazakhstan								**Kazakhstan**
Goods: Exports fob	5 870.5	5 988.7	9 288.1	8 927.8	10 026.9	13 232.6	20 603.1	Biens : exportations, fab
Goods: Imports fob	−6 671.7	−5 645.0	−7 119.7	−7 944.4	−8 039.8	−9 553.6	−13 817.6	Biens : importations, fab
Serv. & Income: Credit	999.8	1 041.1	1 191.6	1 485.0	1 774.2	1 967.6	2 421.8	Serv. & revenu : crédit
Serv. & Income: Debit	−1 545.9	−1 712.5	−3 242.7	−4 096.3	−4 899.4	−5 754.6	−8 189.6	Serv. & revenu : débit
Current Trans.,nie: Credit	141.4	174.7	352.2	394.4	425.9	278.6	352.9	Transf. cour.,nia : crédit
Current Transfers: Debit	−19.0	−18.0	−103.2	−156.0	−312.1	−443.3	−841.1	Transf. courants : débit
Capital Acct.,nie: Credit	65.9	61.1	66.4	99.2	109.8	123.1	114.4	Compte de cap.,nia : crédit
Capital Account: Debit	−435.0	−295.1	−356.9	−284.2	−229.7	−150.9	−134.6	Compte de capital : débit
Financial Account, nie	2 229.1	1 299.2	1 307.0	2 613.7	1 359.1	2 765.8	4 605.6	Compte d'op. fin., nia
Net Errors and Omissions	−1 078.4	−641.6	−812.7	−654.5	320.2	−931.9	−1 116.0	Erreurs et omissions nettes
Reserves & Related Items	443.3	−252.6	−570.1	−384.7	−535.1	−1 533.5	−3 999.0	Rés. et postes appareutés
Kenya								**Kenya**
Goods: Exports fob	2 017.0	1 756.7	1 782.2	1 891.4	2 162.5	2 412.2	2 722.7	Biens : exportations, fab
Goods: Imports fob	−3 028.7	−2 731.8	−3 044.0	−3 238.2	−3 159.0	−3 554.8	−4 320.2	Biens : importations, fab
Serv. & Income: Credit	871.7	966.2	1 038.4	1 135.4	1 053.5	1 212.8	1 524.1	Serv. & revenu : crédit
Serv. & Income: Debit	−909.4	−761.3	−896.8	−933.1	−824.1	−818.7	−953.8	Serv. & revenu : débit
Current Trans.,nie: Credit	578.6	685.3	926.6	804.8	632.1	818.6	649.7	Transf. cour.,nia : crédit
Current Transfers: Debit	−4.5	−4.7	−5.8	−1.6	−1.9	−2.3	−0.9	Transf. courants : débit
Capital Acct.,nie: Credit	84.3	55.4	49.6	51.5	82.1	163.1	145.2	Compte de cap.,nia : crédit
Capital Account: Debit	0.0	0.0	0.0	0.0	−0.9	0.0	0.0	Compte de capital : débit
Financial Account, nie	562.1	165.7	269.8	148.1	−173.9	406.3	39.6	Compte d'op. fin., nia
Net Errors and Omissions	−88.6	−165.5	−127.1	151.7	213.2	−211.9	202.7	Erreurs et omissions nettes
Reserves & Related Items	−82.6	34.0	7.2	−10.0	16.4	−425.2	−9.0	Rés. et postes appareutés
Korea, Republic of								**Corée, République de**
Goods: Exports fob	132 251.0	145 375.0	176 221.0	151 478.0	163 414.0	197 289.0	257 745.0	Biens : exportations, fab
Goods: Imports fob	−90 586.2	−116 912.0	−159 267.0	−137 990.0	−148 637.0	−175 337.0	−219 584.0	Biens : importations, fab
Serv. & Income: Credit	28 239.5	29 773.4	36 909.0	35 704.5	35 287.4	40 132.3	50 151.3	Serv. & revenu : crédit
Serv. & Income: Debit	−32 853.7	−35 583.4	−42 178.1	−40 774.7	−43 052.6	−47 230.2	−58 195.2	Serv. & revenu : débit
Current Trans.,nie: Credit	6 736.6	6 421.3	6 500.1	6 686.7	7 313.9	7 859.3	9 179.4	Transf. cour.,nia : crédit
Current Transfers: Debit	−3 416.2	−4 552.4	−5 933.8	−7 071.9	−8 932.2	−10 763.9	−11 683.4	Transf. courants : débit
Capital Acct.,nie: Credit	463.6	95.1	97.8	42.4	46.5	58.5	72.2	Compte de cap.,nia : crédit
Capital Account: Debit	−292.5	−484.4	−713.0	−773.4	−1 133.3	−1 456.9	−1 844.8	Compte de capital : débit
Financial Account, nie	−8 381.0	12 708.8	12 725.2	3 024.6	7 338.3	15 307.8	10 091.7	Compte d'op. fin., nia
Net Errors and Omissions	−6 231.2	−3 581.2	−570.8	2 951.4	123.6	−67.8	2 743.1	Erreurs et omissions nettes
Reserves & Related Items	−25 930.1	−33 260.2	−23 790.0	−13 277.6	−11 769.0	−25 791.1	−38 675.0	Rés. et postes appareutés

Country or area	1998	1999	2000	2001	2002	2003	2004	Pays ou zone
Kuwait								**Koweït**
Goods: Exports fob	9 617.5	12 223.5	19 478.3	16 238.3	15 366.2	21 794.5	30 220.6	Biens : exportations, fab
Goods: Imports fob	−7 714.4	−6 708.0	−6 451.5	−7 046.4	−8 124.0	−9 882.2	−10 919.6	Biens : importations, fab
Serv. & Income: Credit	8 925.2	7 654.0	9 137.7	7 088.8	5 356.8	6 868.9	10 166.3	Serv. & revenu : crédit
Serv. & Income: Debit	−6 838.3	−6 156.1	−5 536.4	−5 879.4	−6 202.4	−6 986.3	−8 035.3	Serv. & revenu : débit
Current Trans.,nie: Credit	98.4	98.5	84.8	52.2	49.4	67.1	88.2	Transf. cour.,nia : crédit
Current Transfers: Debit	−1 873.6	−2 102.4	−2 040.7	−2 129.2	−2 194.7	−2 446.2	−2 636.6	Transf. courants : débit
Capital Acct.,nie: Credit	288.8	716.1	2 236.3	2 950.9	1 707.7	1 463.0	475.1	Compte de cap.,nia : crédit
Capital Account: Debit	−210.0	−13.1	−19.6	−19.6	−36.2	−33.6	−40.7	Compte de capital : débit
Financial Account, nie	−2 920.4	−5 706.0	−13 773.4	−6 312.7	−5 162.6	−11 942.5	−19 820.2	Compte d'op. fin., nia
Net Errors and Omissions	884.6	911.5	−847.4	−2 038.1	−1 733.2	−726.8	1 127.7	Erreurs et omissions nettes
Reserves & Related Items	−257.9	−918.1	−2 268.2	−2 904.8	973.1	1 824.1	−625.5	Rés. et postes appareutés
Kyrgyzstan								**Kirghizistan**
Goods: Exports fob	535.1	462.6	510.9	480.3	498.1	590.3	733.2	Biens : exportations, fab
Goods: Imports fob	−755.7	−551.1	−506.9	−449.5	−572.1	−723.8	−904.5	Biens : importations, fab
Serv. & Income: Credit	75.4	75.9	78.8	92.1	148.3	160.0	220.1	Serv. & revenu : crédit
Serv. & Income: Debit	−267.4	−239.5	−247.7	−197.8	−212.1	−218.8	−332.4	Serv. & revenu : débit
Current Trans.,nie: Credit	2.2	1.1	42.9	22.8	60.7	100.4	200.6	Transf. cour.,nia : crédit
Current Transfers: Debit	−2.0	−1.2	−2.4	−4.5	−2.9	−7.0	−17.6	Transf. courants : débit
Capital Acct.,nie: Credit	26.4	24.0	22.8	9.2	35.1	36.1	33.7	Compte de cap.,nia : crédit
Capital Account: Debit	−34.5	−39.2	−34.2	−41.2	−43.0	−36.9	−53.6	Compte de capital : débit
Financial Account, nie	299.8	244.2	99.8	54.5	108.7	24.9	185.7	Compte d'op. fin., nia
Net Errors and Omissions	63.5	−2.9	3.1	21.3	−0.3	121.7	79.5	Erreurs et omissions nettes
Reserves & Related Items	57.2	26.1	32.9	12.9	−20.4	−46.8	−144.5	Rés. et postes appareutés
Lao People's Dem. Rep.								**Rép. dém. pop. lao**
Goods: Exports fob	342.1	338.2	330.3	311.1	...	...	...	Biens : exportations, fab
Goods: Imports fob	−506.8	−527.7	−535.3	−527.9	...	...	...	Biens : importations, fab
Serv. & Income: Credit	151.9	140.5	183.0	171.9	...	...	...	Serv. & revenu : crédit
Serv. & Income: Debit	−137.3	−101.7	−102.7	−71.3	...	...	...	Serv. & revenu : débit
Current Trans.,nie: Credit	0.0	80.2	116.3	33.7	...	...	...	Transf. cour.,nia : crédit
Current Transfers: Debit	0.0	−50.6	0.0	0.0	...	...	...	Transf. courants : débit
Capital Acct.,nie: Credit	49.4	0.0	0.0	0.0	...	...	...	Compte de cap.,nia : crédit
Capital Account: Debit	−6.3	0.0	0.0	0.0	...	...	...	Compte de capital : débit
Financial Account, nie	−43.4	−46.9	126.1	135.7	...	...	...	Compte d'op. fin., nia
Net Errors and Omissions	−103.8	−165.1	−74.2	−57.2	...	...	...	Erreurs et omissions nettes
Reserves & Related Items	254.2	333.1	−43.4	3.9	...	...	...	Rés. et postes appareutés
Latvia								**Lettonie**
Goods: Exports fob	2 011.2	1 889.1	2 079.5	2 242.8	2 545.0	3 170.8	4 221.2	Biens : exportations, fab
Goods: Imports fob	−3 141.4	−2 916.1	−3 123.3	−3 578.2	−4 024.0	−5 174.2	−7 001.8	Biens : importations, fab
Serv. & Income: Credit	1 315.8	1 182.0	1 365.2	1 457.2	1 527.6	1 874.5	2 279.8	Serv. & revenu : crédit
Serv. & Income: Debit	−959.6	−902.1	−887.7	−892.2	−936.3	−1 311.4	−1 950.1	Serv. & revenu : débit
Current Trans.,nie: Credit	137.3	113.8	405.8	373.4	537.9	924.2	1 289.0	Transf. cour.,nia : crédit
Current Transfers: Debit	−12.8	−21.0	−210.6	−229.2	−274.6	−394.4	−604.1	Transf. courants : débit
Capital Acct.,nie: Credit	14.1	12.6	40.0	49.9	26.5	79.9	150.3	Compte de cap.,nia : crédit
Capital Account: Debit	0.0	0.0	−4.8	−8.9	−5.6	−3.6	−6.8	Compte de capital : débit
Financial Account, nie	601.1	768.4	413.2	899.7	686.8	889.2	1 956.6	Compte d'op. fin., nia
Net Errors and Omissions	96.9	38.3	−74.4	−0.1	−71.3	24.3	68.8	Erreurs et omissions nettes
Reserves & Related Items	−62.6	−165.0	−2.9	−314.5	−12.1	−79.4	−402.8	Rés. et postes appareutés
Lebanon								**Liban**
Goods: Exports fob	...	...	...	...	1 017.7	1 444.3	1 598.2	Biens : exportations, fab
Goods: Imports fob	...	...	...	...	−5 979.4	−6 666.9	−8 703.5	Biens : importations, fab
Serv. & Income: Credit	...	...	...	...	4 996.2	10 972.5	11 015.6	Serv. & revenu : crédit
Serv. & Income: Debit	...	...	...	...	−4 497.2	−11 540.9	−10 431.4	Serv. & revenu : débit
Current Trans.,nie: Credit	...	...	...	...	2 591.1	4 079.1	5 325.2	Transf. cour.,nia : crédit
Current Transfers: Debit	...	...	...	...	−2 513.4	−3 750.7	−3 609.4	Transf. courants : débit
Capital Acct.,nie: Credit	...	...	...	...	12.8	30.0	53.7	Compte de cap.,nia : crédit
Capital Account: Debit	...	...	...	...	0.0	−0.7	−3.3	Compte de capital : débit
Financial Account, nie	...	...	...	...	3 349.9	4 003.0	4 817.3	Compte d'op. fin., nia
Net Errors and Omissions	...	...	...	...	−1 196.2	−2 572.1	−402.6	Erreurs et omissions nettes
Reserves & Related Items	...	...	...	...	2 218.5	4 002.5	340.1	Rés. et postes appareutés

Country or area	1998	1999	2000	2001	2002	2003	2004	Pays ou zone
Lesotho								**Lesotho**
Goods: Exports fob	193.4	172.5	211.1	278.6	357.3	475.0	707.3	Biens : exportations, fab
Goods: Imports fob	−866.0	−779.2	−727.6	−678.6	−762.7	−994.4	−1 302.0	Biens : importations, fab
Serv. & Income: Credit	411.2	368.7	331.4	275.8	241.7	354.1	443.0	Serv. & revenu : crédit
Serv. & Income: Debit	−175.8	−130.7	−105.2	−105.7	−84.5	−139.3	−172.4	Serv. & revenu : débit
Current Trans.,nie: Credit	158.0	149.4	139.8	137.2	123.3	171.8	250.7	Transf. cour.,nia : crédit
Current Transfers: Debit	−1.2	−1.6	−1.0	−2.5	−1.7	−1.9	−2.5	Transf. courants : débit
Capital Acct.,nie: Credit	22.9	15.2	22.0	16.8	23.5	27.5	33.4	Compte de cap.,nia : crédit
Capital Account: Debit	0.0	0.0	0.0	0.0	0.0	0.0	0.0	Compte de capital : débit
Financial Account, nie	316.1	135.8	85.2	88.6	92.0	98.2	63.3	Compte d'op. fin., nia
Net Errors and Omissions	56.8	29.0	62.1	155.4	−166.4	−56.6	−15.8	Erreurs et omissions nettes
Reserves & Related Items	−115.6	40.8	−17.8	−165.7	177.6	65.7	−4.9	Rés. et postes appareutés
Libyan Arab Jamah.								**Jamah. arabe libyenne**
Goods: Exports fob	5 326.2	7 275.8	13 508.0	10 985.0	9 851.0	14 664.0	17 425.0	Biens : exportations, fab
Goods: Imports fob	−4 929.9	−4 302.0	−4 129.0	−4 825.0	−7 408.0	−7 200.0	−8 768.0	Biens : importations, fab
Serv. & Income: Credit	572.3	605.0	895.0	868.0	1 650.0	2 029.0	1 776.0	Serv. & revenu : crédit
Serv. & Income: Debit	−1 095.3	−1 223.8	−2 047.0	−2 883.0	−3 197.0	−4 178.0	−4 404.0	Serv. & revenu : débit
Current Trans.,nie: Credit	4.3	6.9	16.0	20.0	13.0	255.0	254.0	Transf. cour.,nia : crédit
Current Transfers: Debit	−228.8	−226.0	−503.0	−748.0	−792.0	−1 928.0	−2 578.0	Transf. courants : débit
Capital Acct.,nie: Credit	0.0	0.0	0.0	0.0	0.0	0.0	0.0	Compte de cap.,nia : crédit
Capital Account: Debit	0.0	0.0	0.0	0.0	0.0	0.0	0.0	Compte de capital : débit
Financial Account, nie	−466.9	−1 045.3	−149.0	−711.0	89.0	−167.0	1 047.0	Compte d'op. fin., nia
Net Errors and Omissions	392.0	−402.8	−1 133.0	−1 412.7	71.7	−458.7	979.9	Erreurs et omissions nettes
Reserves & Related Items	426.1	−688.0	−6 458.0	−1 293.3	−277.7	−3 016.3	−5 732.0	Rés. et postes appareutés
Lithuania								**Lituanie**
Goods: Exports fob	3 961.6	3 146.7	4 050.4	4 889.0	6 028.4	7 657.8	9 306.3	Biens : exportations, fab
Goods: Imports fob	−5 479.9	−4 551.3	−5 154.1	−5 997.0	−7 343.3	−9 362.0	−11 688.9	Biens : importations, fab
Serv. & Income: Credit	1 233.6	1 206.4	1 244.3	1 362.7	1 655.3	2 113.2	2 799.3	Serv. & revenu : crédit
Serv. & Income: Debit	−1 248.4	−1 158.6	−1 058.0	−1 085.8	−1 289.9	−1 981.0	−2 599.3	Serv. & revenu : débit
Current Trans.,nie: Credit	240.4	167.4	246.8	262.0	231.7	301.5	612.1	Transf. cour.,nia : crédit
Current Transfers: Debit	−5.4	−4.6	−4.3	−4.5	−2.9	−7.8	−154.2	Transf. courants : débit
Capital Acct.,nie: Credit	0.9	2.7	2.6	1.5	56.8	68.3	288.1	Compte de cap.,nia : crédit
Capital Account: Debit	−2.6	−6.0	−0.4	−0.1	−0.4	−0.8	−1.0	Compte de capital : débit
Financial Account, nie	1 443.9	1 060.7	702.4	777.6	1 048.4	1 642.3	1 141.2	Compte d'op. fin., nia
Net Errors and Omissions	282.9	−42.2	128.3	153.6	78.5	181.2	191.8	Erreurs et omissions nettes
Reserves & Related Items	−426.8	178.7	−158.0	−359.0	−462.7	−612.7	104.4	Rés. et postes appareutés
Luxembourg								**Luxembourg**
Goods: Exports fob	8 557.1	8 565.1	8 635.4	8 995.7	9 535.2	11 040.5	13 670.0	Biens : exportations, fab
Goods: Imports fob	−10 881.4	−11 151.3	−11 055.6	−11 394.8	−11 598.9	−13 976.7	−17 110.7	Biens : importations, fab
Serv. & Income: Credit	60 897.8	65 065.6	70 701.0	72 246.9	69 501.4	76 554.9	94 682.6	Serv. & revenu : crédit
Serv. & Income: Debit	−56 524.5	−60 252.7	−65 258.4	−67 649.0	−64 724.6	−71 142.0	−86 379.9	Serv. & revenu : débit
Current Trans.,nie: Credit	2 185.2	2 281.7	2 750.0	2 268.5	3 582.1	3 724.6	4 435.1	Transf. cour.,nia : crédit
Current Transfers: Debit	−2 608.3	−2 858.7	−3 210.8	−2 793.5	−3 884.8	−4 334.3	−5 735.5	Transf. courants : débit
Capital Acct.,nie: Credit	0.0	0.0	0.0	0.0	63.7	53.9	32.6	Compte de cap.,nia : crédit
Capital Account: Debit	0.0	0.0	0.0	0.0	−180.6	−204.4	−274.3	Compte de capital : débit
Financial Account, nie	0.0	0.0	0.0	0.0	−2 742.9	−1 649.7	−3 579.0	Compte d'op. fin., nia
Net Errors and Omissions	0.0	0.0	0.0	0.0	484.7	40.9	267.1	Erreurs et omissions nettes
Reserves & Related Items	0.0	0.0	0.0	0.0	−35.3	−107.6	−8.2	Rés. et postes appareutés
Madagascar								**Madagascar**
Goods: Exports fob	538.2	584.0	823.7	928.2	485.6	855.5	...	Biens : exportations, fab
Goods: Imports fob	−692.7	−742.5	−997.5	−955.0	−602.7	−1 109.3	...	Biens : importations, fab
Serv. & Income: Credit	315.6	346.7	386.5	374.5	250.2	286.5	...	Serv. & revenu : crédit
Serv. & Income: Debit	−538.6	−519.3	−586.2	−617.2	−498.7	−640.0	...	Serv. & revenu : débit
Current Trans.,nie: Credit	109.5	110.9	121.9	114.2	88.0	348.9	...	Transf. cour.,nia : crédit
Current Transfers: Debit	−32.7	−31.8	−31.3	−14.9	−20.6	−180.4	...	Transf. courants : débit
Capital Acct.,nie: Credit	102.7	128.8	115.0	112.8	57.7	140.4	...	Compte de cap.,nia : crédit
Capital Account: Debit	0.0	0.0	0.0	0.0	0.0	0.0	...	Compte de capital : débit
Financial Account, nie	−76.3	−13.6	−30.7	−138.6	−54.0	−118.4	...	Compte d'op. fin., nia
Net Errors and Omissions	−25.0	32.4	38.6	−56.9	11.1	51.9	...	Erreurs et omissions nettes
Reserves & Related Items	299.2	104.3	160.0	252.9	283.5	364.8	...	Rés. et postes appareutés

Country or area	1998	1999	2000	2001	2002	2003	2004	Pays ou zone
Malawi								**Malawi**
Goods: Exports fob	539.6	448.4	403.1	427.9	422.4	...	...	Biens : exportations, fab
Goods: Imports fob	−500.6	−575.0	−462.0	−472.2	−573.2	...	...	Biens : importations, fab
Serv. & Income: Credit	43.0	74.8	67.5	55.8	55.4	...	...	Serv. & revenu : crédit
Serv. & Income: Debit	−209.7	−235.3	−217.7	−214.0	−266.4	...	...	Serv. & revenu : débit
Current Trans.,nie: Credit	134.1	137.7	143.1	148.8	170.0	...	...	Transf. cour.,nia : crédit
Current Transfers: Debit	−10.8	−8.2	−7.6	−6.2	−8.9	...	...	Transf. courants : débit
Capital Acct.,nie: Credit	0.0	0.0	0.0	0.0	0.0	...	...	Compte de cap.,nia : crédit
Capital Account: Debit	0.0	0.0	0.0	0.0	0.0	...	...	Compte de capital : débit
Financial Account, nie	237.8	219.6	188.8	213.4	134.0	...	...	Compte d'op. fin., nia
Net Errors and Omissions	−407.6	−28.8	−23.9	−221.5	156.7	...	...	Erreurs et omissions nettes
Reserves & Related Items	174.1	−33.3	−91.4	68.0	−90.0	...	...	Rés. et postes apparentés
Malaysia								**Malaisie**
Goods: Exports fob	71 882.8	84 096.8	98 429.1	87 980.5	93 382.8	104 999.0	...	Biens : exportations, fab
Goods: Imports fob	−54 377.8	−61 452.6	−77 602.4	−69 597.4	−75 247.7	−79 288.7	...	Biens : importations, fab
Serv. & Income: Credit	13 058.9	13 922.5	15 926.6	16 301.8	17 017.2	17 025.7	...	Serv. & revenu : crédit
Serv. & Income: Debit	−18 572.7	−22 234.8	−26 341.1	−25 246.3	−25 182.0	−26 907.9	...	Serv. & revenu : débit
Current Trans.,nie: Credit	727.8	800.8	756.2	536.8	661.3	507.7	...	Transf. cour.,nia : crédit
Current Transfers: Debit	−3 190.3	−2 529.1	−2 680.5	−2 688.7	−3 441.8	−2 955.1	...	Transf. courants : débit
Capital Acct.,nie: Credit	0.0	0.0	0.0	0.0	0.0	0.0	...	Compte de cap.,nia : crédit
Capital Account: Debit	0.0	0.0	0.0	0.0	0.0	0.0	...	Compte de capital : débit
Financial Account, nie	−2 549.7	−6 619.0	−6 275.5	−3 892.4	−3 142.4	−3 196.3	...	Compte d'op. fin., nia
Net Errors and Omissions	3 038.8	−1 272.8	−3 220.9	−2 394.2	−390.5	−4.2	...	Erreurs et omissions nettes
Reserves & Related Items	−10 017.7	−4 711.9	1 008.8	−1 000.3	−3 656.8	−10 180.6	...	Rés. et postes apparentés
Maldives								**Maldives**
Goods: Exports fob	95.6	91.5	108.7	110.2	132.3	152.0	181.0	Biens : exportations, fab
Goods: Imports fob	−311.5	−353.9	−342.0	−346.3	−344.7	−414.3	−567.3	Biens : importations, fab
Serv. & Income: Credit	339.9	351.8	358.8	362.2	368.5	438.3	515.6	Serv. & revenu : crédit
Serv. & Income: Debit	−135.6	−148.2	−150.0	−155.2	−152.2	−165.6	−208.9	Serv. & revenu : débit
Current Trans.,nie: Credit	20.3	20.4	19.3	19.9	10.6	12.7	6.9	Transf. cour.,nia : crédit
Current Transfers: Debit	−30.6	−40.5	−46.2	−49.6	−50.2	−54.9	−61.1	Transf. courants : débit
Capital Acct.,nie: Credit	0.0	0.0	0.0	0.0	0.0	0.0	0.0	Compte de cap.,nia : crédit
Capital Account: Debit	0.0	0.0	0.0	0.0	0.0	0.0	0.0	Compte de capital : débit
Financial Account, nie	60.2	76.2	40.2	35.5	73.5	56.3	152.5	Compte d'op. fin., nia
Net Errors and Omissions	−18.2	11.4	6.9	−6.5	2.3	1.7	25.4	Erreurs et omissions nettes
Reserves & Related Items	−20.2	−8.6	4.3	29.7	−40.1	−26.2	−44.1	Rés. et postes apparentés
Mali								**Mali**
Goods: Exports fob	556.2	571.0	545.1	725.2	875.1	927.8	...	Biens : exportations, fab
Goods: Imports fob	−558.2	−605.5	−592.1	−734.7	−712.5	−988.3	...	Biens : importations, fab
Serv. & Income: Credit	112.7	141.3	119.6	173.3	205.5	245.6	...	Serv. & revenu : crédit
Serv. & Income: Debit	−433.4	−473.4	−453.6	−609.5	−663.3	−663.5	...	Serv. & revenu : débit
Current Trans.,nie: Credit	151.6	145.8	157.2	160.7	182.1	265.5	...	Transf. cour.,nia : crédit
Current Transfers: Debit	−37.1	−32.2	−30.8	−25.0	−35.7	−58.1	...	Transf. courants : débit
Capital Acct.,nie: Credit	124.0	113.4	101.6	107.5	104.4	113.7	...	Compte de cap.,nia : crédit
Capital Account: Debit	0.0	−0.1	0.0	−0.1	−0.2	0.0	...	Compte de capital : débit
Financial Account, nie	48.0	116.9	220.4	146.2	188.6	290.1	...	Compte d'op. fin., nia
Net Errors and Omissions	−9.7	9.5	−4.8	9.4	−6.1	4.6	...	Erreurs et omissions nettes
Reserves & Related Items	45.9	13.4	−62.6	47.0	−137.8	−137.4	...	Rés. et postes apparentés
Malta								**Malte**
Goods: Exports fob	1 824.5	2 017.3	2 479.0	2 002.3	2 311.4	2 503.2	2 654.3	Biens : exportations, fab
Goods: Imports fob	−2 497.5	−2 680.2	−3 232.6	−2 568.4	−2 668.0	−3 189.3	−3 496.2	Biens : importations, fab
Serv. & Income: Credit	1 692.2	2 454.7	2 000.7	1 930.0	1 978.7	2 222.5	2 316.1	Serv. & revenu : crédit
Serv. & Income: Debit	−1 298.4	−1 956.2	−1 742.1	−1 537.3	−1 572.6	−1 765.7	−1 947.1	Serv. & revenu : débit
Current Trans.,nie: Credit	115.0	120.4	101.8	190.5	249.3	204.5	221.3	Transf. cour.,nia : crédit
Current Transfers: Debit	−57.2	−77.9	−76.4	−182.3	−287.2	−255.5	−296.9	Transf. courants : débit
Capital Acct.,nie: Credit	33.3	31.1	24.1	4.4	8.5	18.6	87.4	Compte de cap.,nia : crédit
Capital Account: Debit	−4.7	−5.4	−5.5	−2.9	−1.9	−1.4	−3.3	Compte de capital : débit
Financial Account, nie	294.4	428.2	215.8	132.5	209.7	238.0	48.4	Compte d'op. fin., nia
Net Errors and Omissions	89.3	−93.8	13.4	286.1	60.0	169.1	209.4	Erreurs et omissions nettes
Reserves & Related Items	−190.9	−238.3	221.9	−255.0	−287.9	−144.0	206.6	Rés. et postes apparentés

Country or area	1998	1999	2000	2001	2002	2003	2004	Pays ou zone
Mauritania								**Mauritanie**
Goods: Exports fob	358.6	...	...	...	...	...	...	Biens : exportations, fab
Goods: Imports fob	−318.7	...	...	...	...	...	...	Biens : importations, fab
Serv. & Income: Credit	36.4	...	...	...	...	...	...	Serv. & revenu : crédit
Serv. & Income: Debit	−186.6	...	...	...	...	...	...	Serv. & revenu : débit
Current Trans.,nie: Credit	198.3	...	...	...	...	...	...	Transf. cour.,nia : crédit
Current Transfers: Debit	−10.8	...	...	...	...	...	...	Transf. courants : débit
Capital Acct.,nie: Credit	0.0	...	...	...	...	...	...	Compte de cap.,nia : crédit
Capital Account: Debit	0.0	...	...	...	...	...	...	Compte de capital : débit
Financial Account, nie	−25.9	...	...	...	...	...	...	Compte d'op. fin., nia
Net Errors and Omissions	−8.1	...	...	...	...	...	...	Erreurs et omissions nettes
Reserves & Related Items	−43.2	...	...	...	...	...	...	Rés. et postes appareutés
Mauritius								**Maurice**
Goods: Exports fob	1 669.3	1 589.2	1 552.2	1 628.2	1 801.3	1 898.1	2 004.3	Biens : exportations, fab
Goods: Imports fob	−1 933.3	−2 107.9	−1 944.4	−1 846.0	−2 012.6	−2 201.1	−2 579.4	Biens : importations, fab
Serv. & Income: Credit	964.8	1 078.6	1 118.8	1 297.2	1 228.6	1 327.1	1 507.4	Serv. & revenu : crédit
Serv. & Income: Debit	−792.4	−787.7	−827.4	−871.0	−859.4	−983.4	−1 089.1	Serv. & revenu : débit
Current Trans.,nie: Credit	186.8	196.4	167.6	193.1	195.3	163.0	168.1	Transf. cour.,nia : crédit
Current Transfers: Debit	−91.8	−92.8	−103.8	−125.5	−103.8	−110.6	−118.7	Transf. courants : débit
Capital Acct.,nie: Credit	0.0	0.0	0.0	0.4	0.0	0.0	0.0	Compte de cap.,nia : crédit
Capital Account: Debit	−0.8	−0.5	−0.6	−1.8	−1.9	−0.9	−1.6	Compte de capital : débit
Financial Account, nie	−26.0	180.5	258.0	−240.2	84.2	89.7	8.9	Compte d'op. fin., nia
Net Errors and Omissions	−41.9	133.9	10.1	−86.3	9.4	40.4	72.7	Erreurs et omissions nettes
Reserves & Related Items	65.4	−189.7	−230.6	51.8	−341.1	−222.4	27.5	Rés. et postes appareutés
Mexico								**Mexique**
Goods: Exports fob	117 539.0	136 362.0	166 121.0	158 780.0	161 046.0	164 766.0	187 999.0	Biens : exportations, fab
Goods: Imports fob	−125 373.0	−141 975.0	−174 458.0	−168 397.0	−168 679.0	−170 546.0	−196 810.0	Biens : importations, fab
Serv. & Income: Credit	16 570.1	16 208.9	19 732.1	18 026.8	16 790.5	16 474.8	19 053.5	Serv. & revenu : crédit
Serv. & Income: Debit	−30 741.3	−30 813.8	−37 010.9	−35 391.7	−32 929.9	−33 168.9	−34 556.4	Serv. & revenu : débit
Current Trans.,nie: Credit	6 015.2	6 313.3	6 999.4	9 336.4	10 287.3	13 879.5	17 108.4	Transf. cour.,nia : crédit
Current Transfers: Debit	−27.2	−26.9	−29.5	−21.9	−35.2	−37.2	−80.1	Transf. courants : débit
Capital Acct.,nie: Credit	0.0	0.0	0.0	0.0	0.0	0.0	0.0	Compte de cap.,nia : crédit
Capital Account: Debit	0.0	0.0	0.0	0.0	0.0	0.0	0.0	Compte de capital : débit
Financial Account, nie	19 899.7	17 869.1	23 245.9	26 248.5	24 759.1	19 128.7	13 617.2	Compte d'op. fin., nia
Net Errors and Omissions	−712.5	312.0	2 526.5	−1 266.8	−3 879.7	−680.0	−2 227.5	Erreurs et omissions nettes
Reserves & Related Items	−3 170.0	−4 249.5	−7 126.2	−7 314.5	−7 359.1	−9 817.4	−4 104.1	Rés. et postes appareutés
Mongolia								**Mongolie**
Goods: Exports fob	462.4	454.3	535.8	523.2	524.0	627.3	872.1	Biens : exportations, fab
Goods: Imports fob	−524.2	−510.7	−608.4	−623.8	−680.2	−826.9	−901.0	Biens : importations, fab
Serv. & Income: Credit	87.9	82.5	90.7	128.3	198.0	221.8	355.0	Serv. & revenu : crédit
Serv. & Income: Debit	−156.5	−152.3	−182.3	−222.2	−284.5	−282.5	−531.3	Serv. & revenu : débit
Current Trans.,nie: Credit	5.5	17.6	25.0	40.3	126.9	167.1	230.9	Transf. cour.,nia : crédit
Current Transfers: Debit	−3.6	−3.6	−16.9	0.0	−42.3	−54.9	−50.2	Transf. courants : débit
Capital Acct.,nie: Credit	0.0	0.0	0.0	0.0	0.0	0.0	0.0	Compte de cap.,nia : crédit
Capital Account: Debit	0.0	0.0	0.0	0.0	0.0	0.0	0.0	Compte de capital : débit
Financial Account, nie	126.2	69.6	89.9	107.0	157.4	5.0	−23.2	Compte d'op. fin., nia
Net Errors and Omissions	−50.2	23.6	−19.3	−32.2	14.1	−5.9	1.4	Erreurs et omissions nettes
Reserves & Related Items	52.5	19.0	85.5	79.4	−13.4	149.0	46.3	Rés. et postes appareutés
Montserrat								**Montserrat**
Goods: Exports fob	1.2	1.3	1.1	0.7	1.5	...	...	Biens : exportations, fab
Goods: Imports fob	−19.4	−19.3	−19.0	−17.1	−22.4	...	...	Biens : importations, fab
Serv. & Income: Credit	13.8	21.4	17.3	15.5	15.6	...	...	Serv. & revenu : crédit
Serv. & Income: Debit	−23.3	−28.7	−22.9	−26.0	−27.8	...	...	Serv. & revenu : débit
Current Trans.,nie: Credit	33.2	26.5	18.9	23.7	28.1	...	...	Transf. cour.,nia : crédit
Current Transfers: Debit	−2.2	−2.7	−1.9	−2.5	−3.2	...	...	Transf. courants : débit
Capital Acct.,nie: Credit	7.2	5.0	7.3	9.7	14.6	...	...	Compte de cap.,nia : crédit
Capital Account: Debit	−3.6	−3.6	−2.9	−2.0	−2.1	...	...	Compte de capital : débit
Financial Account, nie	3.9	−5.9	3.6	−3.2	−0.1	...	...	Compte d'op. fin., nia
Net Errors and Omissions	2.6	−4.7	−5.1	3.2	−2.6	...	...	Erreurs et omissions nettes
Reserves & Related Items	−13.5	10.7	3.5	−2.1	−1.7	...	...	Rés. et postes appareutés

Country or area	1998	1999	2000	2001	2002	2003	2004	Pays ou zone
Morocco								Maroc
Goods: Exports fob	7 143.7	7 509.0	7 418.6	7 141.8	7 838.9	8 771.4	9 921.9	Biens : exportations, fab
Goods: Imports fob	−9 462.6	−9 956.6	−10 653.6	−10 163.7	−10 900.3	−13 116.6	−16 408.4	Biens : importations, fab
Serv. & Income: Credit	3 020.3	3 301.7	3 310.2	4 355.0	4 736.6	5 848.4	7 215.3	Serv. & revenu : crédit
Serv. & Income: Debit	−3 189.9	−3 174.9	−3 032.7	−3 277.2	−3 528.4	−4 023.7	−4 627.0	Serv. & revenu : débit
Current Trans.,nie: Credit	2 437.7	2 246.1	2 574.2	3 670.3	3 441.0	4 213.7	4 974.4	Transf. cour.,nia : crédit
Current Transfers: Debit	−95.0	−96.0	−117.7	−120.1	−115.4	−141.1	−154.5	Transf. courants : débit
Capital Acct.,nie: Credit	0.1	0.2	0.1	0.0	0.0	0.0	0.0	Compte de cap.,nia : crédit
Capital Account: Debit	−10.2	−8.8	−6.0	−8.9	−6.1	−10.1	−8.0	Compte de capital : débit
Financial Account, nie	−644.1	−13.0	−773.5	−966.2	−1 336.3	−1 090.8	69.2	Compte d'op. fin., nia
Net Errors and Omissions	160.4	123.5	114.0	229.6	−181.9	−297.1	−247.1	Erreurs et omissions nettes
Reserves & Related Items	639.5	68.8	1 166.4	−860.5	52.0	−154.3	−735.7	Rés. et postes apparentés
Mozambique								Mozambique
Goods: Exports fob	244.6	283.8	364.0	726.0	809.8	1 043.9	1 503.9	Biens : exportations, fab
Goods: Imports fob	−735.6	−1 090.0	−1 046.0	−997.3	−1 476.5	−1 648.1	−1 849.7	Biens : importations, fab
Serv. & Income: Credit	332.5	353.0	404.7	305.7	391.5	359.8	330.1	Serv. & revenu : crédit
Serv. & Income: Debit	−584.0	−620.5	−717.2	−909.0	−1 232.3	−795.3	−905.4	Serv. & revenu : débit
Current Trans.,nie: Credit	313.2	256.3	337.3	254.6	827.0	293.2	370.5	Transf. cour.,nia : crédit
Current Transfers: Debit	0.0	−94.6	−106.4	−37.1	−188.7	−70.0	−56.7	Transf. courants : débit
Capital Acct.,nie: Credit	0.0	180.3	226.8	256.7	222.5	271.2	581.2	Compte de cap.,nia : crédit
Capital Account: Debit	0.0	0.0	0.0	0.0	−0.4	−0.5	−3.1	Compte de capital : débit
Financial Account, nie	300.4	403.9	83.2	−24.8	−731.7	372.8	−46.5	Compte d'op. fin., nia
Net Errors and Omissions	−263.8	1.5	37.5	−59.6	−60.0	208.2	216.4	Erreurs et omissions nettes
Reserves & Related Items	392.7	326.3	416.1	484.9	1 438.8	−35.3	−140.7	Rés. et postes apparentés
Myanmar								Myanmar
Goods: Exports fob	1 077.3	1 293.9	1 661.6	2 521.8	2 421.1	2 709.7	2 926.7	Biens : exportations, fab
Goods: Imports fob	−2 478.2	−2 181.3	−2 165.4	−2 443.7	−2 022.1	−1 911.6	−1 998.7	Biens : importations, fab
Serv. & Income: Credit	644.1	563.8	513.3	444.4	462.6	278.5	295.1	Serv. & revenu : crédit
Serv. & Income: Debit	−380.2	−345.7	−496.9	−910.6	−929.2	−1 190.9	−1 245.4	Serv. & revenu : débit
Current Trans.,nie: Credit	638.1	384.8	289.8	248.9	187.6	118.0	160.6	Transf. cour.,nia : crédit
Current Transfers: Debit	−0.3	−0.3	−14.1	−14.3	−23.4	−23.0	−26.7	Transf. courants : débit
Capital Acct.,nie: Credit	0.0	0.0	0.0	0.0	0.0	0.0	0.0	Compte de cap.,nia : crédit
Capital Account: Debit	0.0	0.0	0.0	0.0	0.0	0.0	0.0	Compte de capital : débit
Financial Account, nie	540.9	251.2	212.8	347.7	−32.0	137.1	125.2	Compte d'op. fin., nia
Net Errors and Omissions	18.7	−12.4	−24.5	−14.3	−19.1	−78.9	−142.7	Erreurs et omissions nettes
Reserves & Related Items	−60.4	45.9	23.4	−179.8	−45.4	−38.9	−94.0	Rés. et postes apparentés
Namibia								Namibie
Goods: Exports fob	1 278.3	1 196.8	1 309.5	1 147.0	1 071.6	1 262.0	1 827.5	Biens : exportations, fab
Goods: Imports fob	−1 450.9	−1 401.3	−1 310.0	−1 349.0	−1 282.5	−1 726.0	−2 110.3	Biens : importations, fab
Serv. & Income: Credit	553.8	594.4	469.8	493.7	455.8	704.0	850.9	Serv. & revenu : crédit
Serv. & Income: Debit	−622.8	−554.1	−558.8	−544.8	−357.7	−303.4	−602.7	Serv. & revenu : débit
Current Trans.,nie: Credit	418.2	380.4	419.2	346.7	270.4	426.2	642.1	Transf. cour.,nia : crédit
Current Transfers: Debit	−14.7	−58.4	−37.0	−35.6	−29.9	−27.2	−34.9	Transf. courants : débit
Capital Acct.,nie: Credit	24.2	23.2	112.9	96.0	40.9	68.6	77.6	Compte de cap.,nia : crédit
Capital Account: Debit	−0.4	−0.3	−0.3	−0.2	−0.2	−0.4	−0.5	Compte de capital : débit
Financial Account, nie	−145.6	−288.9	−488.6	−500.0	−346.8	−663.7	−717.0	Compte d'op. fin., nia
Net Errors and Omissions	15.7	−41.2	−100.7	−12.6	−31.8	−69.3	−69.7	Erreurs et omissions nettes
Reserves & Related Items	−55.8	149.3	184.1	358.8	210.3	329.1	136.9	Rés. et postes apparentés
Nepal								Népal
Goods: Exports fob	482.0	612.3	776.1	720.5	632.0	703.2	763.6	Biens : exportations, fab
Goods: Imports fob	−1 239.1	−1 494.2	−1 590.1	−1 485.7	−1 425.4	−1 665.9	−1 812.5	Biens : importations, fab
Serv. & Income: Credit	610.6	710.9	578.1	483.6	362.1	420.8	523.9	Serv. & revenu : crédit
Serv. & Income: Debit	−222.7	−240.9	−235.1	−273.5	−308.0	−335.2	−451.2	Serv. & revenu : débit
Current Trans.,nie: Credit	326.0	182.3	189.0	240.2	828.1	1 022.5	1 090.6	Transf. cour.,nia : crédit
Current Transfers: Debit	−24.1	−26.9	−16.7	−24.3	−33.2	−25.4	−62.8	Transf. courants : débit
Capital Acct.,nie: Credit	0.0	0.0	0.0	0.0	102.4	24.8	15.7	Compte de cap.,nia : crédit
Capital Account: Debit	0.0	0.0	0.0	0.0	0.0	0.0	0.0	Compte de capital : débit
Financial Account, nie	212.9	−24.5	76.1	−216.9	−404.8	−354.1	−508.9	Compte d'op. fin., nia
Net Errors and Omissions	134.0	58.3	145.7	256.5	−66.6	309.9	339.9	Erreurs et omissions nettes
Reserves & Related Items	−279.7	222.7	77.0	299.6	313.4	−100.6	101.7	Rés. et postes apparentés

Country or area	1998	1999	2000	2001	2002	2003	2004	Pays ou zone
Netherlands								**Pays-Bas**
Goods: Exports fob	196 041.0	195 694.0	205 271.0	203 201.0	209 516.0	262 340.0	315 124.0	Biens : exportations, fab
Goods: Imports fob	−175 611.0	−179 747.0	−187 471.0	−184 015.0	−190 950.0	−226 591.0	−272 179.0	Biens : importations, fab
Serv. & Income: Credit	85 047.4	95 589.7	94 824.5	94 706.5	96 441.7	121 844.7	153 877.7	Serv. & revenu : crédit
Serv. & Income: Debit	−85 264.8	−89 498.7	−99 141.9	−97 343.7	−97 449.2	−120 838.4	−134 457.8	Serv. & revenu : débit
Current Trans.,nie: Credit	3 798.7	4 563.6	4 399.1	4 475.2	4 960.6	7 506.4	8 816.9	Transf. cour.,nia : crédit
Current Transfers: Debit	−10 980.6	−10 917.6	−10 617.6	−11 214.3	−11 500.9	−14 571.9	−16 768.7	Transf. courants : débit
Capital Acct.,nie: Credit	1 037.4	1 684.9	2 216.3	1 117.8	856.9	1 426.5	1 668.4	Compte de cap.,nia : crédit
Capital Account: Debit	−1 457.2	−1 898.8	−2 313.8	−4 317.3	−1 402.3	−4 080.5	−2 811.5	Compte de capital : débit
Financial Account, nie	−14 397.6	−9 857.1	−7 604.1	−3 851.6	−4 527.0	−24 212.3	−53 457.0	Compte d'op. fin., nia
Net Errors and Omissions	−553.0	−10 223.6	657.3	−3 109.8	−6 077.0	−3 640.5	−826.7	Erreurs et omissions nettes
Reserves & Related Items	2 339.4	4 611.0	−219.4	350.7	132.0	817.0	1 013.3	Rés. et postes appareutés
Netherlands Antilles								**Antilles néerlandaises**
Goods: Exports fob	465.6	467.0	676.1	638.2	575.5	681.5	799.8	Biens : exportations, fab
Goods: Imports fob	−1 513.2	−1 584.2	−1 661.7	−1 752.4	−1 602.4	−1 684.4	−1 967.7	Biens : importations, fab
Serv. & Income: Credit	1 655.1	1 619.7	1 739.4	1 753.3	1 719.0	1 795.6	1 950.4	Serv. & revenu : crédit
Serv. & Income: Debit	−720.6	−783.3	−836.7	−850.7	−859.7	−908.7	−940.1	Serv. & revenu : débit
Current Trans.,nie: Credit	137.2	179.6	246.6	217.0	365.5	399.1	319.6	Transf. cour.,nia : crédit
Current Transfers: Debit	−161.0	−175.8	−214.3	−216.2	−256.6	−276.3	−254.0	Transf. courants : débit
Capital Acct.,nie: Credit	91.3	109.8	31.3	37.9	29.3	32.8	80.2	Compte de cap.,nia : crédit
Capital Account: Debit	−4.4	−1.5	−1.4	−0.6	−1.6	−6.6	−0.8	Compte de capital : débit
Financial Account, nie	58.0	69.5	−122.2	351.6	32.3	−52.1	−52.7	Compte d'op. fin., nia
Net Errors and Omissions	17.4	24.5	13.4	39.8	51.0	46.3	71.3	Erreurs et omissions nettes
Reserves & Related Items	−25.5	74.7	129.6	−217.7	−52.3	−27.1	−5.8	Rés. et postes appareutés
New Zealand								**Nouvelle-Zélande**
Goods: Exports fob	12 245.6	12 656.8	13 529.7	13 919.7	14 517.3	16 834.5	20 458.1	Biens : exportations, fab
Goods: Imports fob	−11 333.5	−13 028.0	−12 849.9	−12 448.5	−14 351.3	−17 290.8	−21 888.8	Biens : importations, fab
Serv. & Income: Credit	4 642.9	5 304.5	5 125.1	4 968.7	6 238.2	7 822.5	9 374.4	Serv. & revenu : crédit
Serv. & Income: Debit	−7 991.7	−8 617.8	−8 503.2	−7 880.8	−8 759.5	−10 868.3	−14 222.2	Serv. & revenu : débit
Current Trans.,nie: Credit	680.9	609.5	634.1	578.1	616.0	792.6	827.7	Transf. cour.,nia : crédit
Current Transfers: Debit	−400.9	−440.5	−397.6	−390.5	−495.8	−647.1	−748.3	Transf. courants : débit
Capital Acct.,nie: Credit	263.1	260.2	238.3	821.5	1 122.3	965.7	888.5	Compte de cap.,nia : crédit
Capital Account: Debit	−443.7	−476.8	−418.0	−378.3	−357.2	−457.9	−586.2	Compte de capital : débit
Financial Account, nie	1 580.3	1 973.6	1 243.5	1 758.0	1 040.4	3 354.8	8 859.3	Compte d'op. fin., nia
Net Errors and Omissions	271.1	1 946.9	1 255.2	−1 135.1	1 516.1	276.8	−2 333.8	Erreurs et omissions nettes
Reserves & Related Items	486.0	−188.4	142.8	187.2	−1 086.5	−782.7	−628.6	Rés. et postes appareutés
Nicaragua								**Nicaragua**
Goods: Exports fob	761.0	748.6	880.6	894.7	916.8	1 049.6	1 362.9	Biens : exportations, fab
Goods: Imports fob	−1 509.6	−1 819.8	−1 801.5	−1 804.3	−1 834.4	−2 021.3	−2 452.0	Biens : importations, fab
Serv. & Income: Credit	209.7	244.9	252.0	237.8	234.7	264.3	299.0	Serv. & revenu : crédit
Serv. & Income: Debit	−479.0	−562.2	−575.9	−607.1	−546.8	−560.8	−600.9	Serv. & revenu : débit
Current Trans.,nie: Credit	331.3	460.1	452.9	482.5	462.4	518.9	618.8	Transf. cour.,nia : crédit
Current Transfers: Debit	0.0	0.0	0.0	0.0	0.0	0.0	0.0	Transf. courants : débit
Capital Acct.,nie: Credit	194.4	307.2	308.9	294.7	248.2	286.0	283.5	Compte de cap.,nia : crédit
Capital Account: Debit	0.0	0.0	0.0	0.0	0.0	0.0	0.0	Compte de capital : débit
Financial Account, nie	231.6	525.5	49.1	12.9	188.8	83.1	61.0	Compte d'op. fin., nia
Net Errors and Omissions	−141.3	−299.5	−21.9	−3.7	−70.7	−89.3	30.1	Erreurs et omissions nettes
Reserves & Related Items	401.9	395.2	455.8	492.5	401.0	469.5	397.6	Rés. et postes appareutés
Niger								**Niger**
Goods: Exports fob	334.0	286.8	283.1	272.5	279.4	351.8	...	Biens : exportations, fab
Goods: Imports fob	−403.9	−335.4	−323.7	−331.3	−371.2	−488.5	...	Biens : importations, fab
Serv. & Income: Credit	48.3	48.1	50.6	69.0	63.8	80.6	...	Serv. & revenu : crédit
Serv. & Income: Debit	−188.8	−172.5	−161.4	−174.4	−189.7	−235.9	...	Serv. & revenu : débit
Current Trans.,nie: Credit	76.1	57.4	63.8	87.9	65.1	82.9	...	Transf. cour.,nia : crédit
Current Transfers: Debit	−18.1	−21.5	−16.5	−16.0	−12.3	−9.5	...	Transf. courants : débit
Capital Acct.,nie: Credit	69.6	62.0	55.4	40.2	91.9	92.4	...	Compte de cap.,nia : crédit
Capital Account: Debit	0.0	0.0	0.0	0.0	−0.1	−0.1	...	Compte de capital : débit
Financial Account, nie	48.9	47.6	97.5	60.5	69.1	97.1	...	Compte d'op. fin., nia
Net Errors and Omissions	17.5	25.6	−13.6	13.8	−8.6	−14.6	...	Erreurs et omissions nettes
Reserves & Related Items	16.3	2.0	−35.1	−22.2	12.5	43.8	...	Rés. et postes appareutés

Country or area	1998	1999	2000	2001	2002	2003	2004	Pays ou zone
Nigeria								**Nigéria**
Goods: Exports fob	8 971.2	12 876.3	19 132.0	17 991.8	15 613.4	22 629.1	23 657.2	Biens : exportations, fab
Goods: Imports fob	−9 211.3	−8 588.0	−8 717.0	−11 096.5	−10 875.6	−10 499.0	−11 095.8	Biens : importations, fab
Serv. & Income: Credit	1 216.6	1 219.3	2 050.5	1 852.3	2 707.3	3 554.8	3 493.4	Serv. & revenu : crédit
Serv. & Income: Debit	−6 789.5	−6 293.5	−6 665.6	−7 636.4	−7 775.3	−7 232.4	−6 042.3	Serv. & revenu : débit
Current Trans.,nie: Credit	1 574.2	1 301.1	1 637.4	1 372.5	1 422.3	1 062.8	2 272.7	Transf. cour.,nia : crédit
Current Transfers: Debit	−4.7	−9.4	−8.4	−5.9	−9.0	−11.6	−20.9	Transf. courants : débit
Capital Acct.,nie: Credit	0.0	0.0	0.0	0.0	0.0	0.0	0.0	Compte de cap.,nia : crédit
Capital Account: Debit	0.0	0.0	0.0	0.0	0.0	0.0	0.0	Compte de capital : débit
Financial Account, nie	1 502.5	−4 002.3	−6 219.3	−3 034.6	−8 554.4	−11 799.0	−4 486.8	Compte d'op. fin., nia
Net Errors and Omissions	−131.8	−41.1	1 879.6	779.5	2 782.1	1 035.1	713.7	Erreurs et omissions nettes
Reserves & Related Items	2 872.8	3 537.7	−3 089.2	−222.7	4 689.2	1 260.1	−8 491.3	Rés. et postes appareutés
Norway								**Norvège**
Goods: Exports fob	40 887.8	46 224.3	60 463.3	59 526.5	59 616.1	69 072.6	82 993.2	Biens : exportations, fab
Goods: Imports fob	−38 826.6	−35 501.5	−34 488.0	−33 055.0	−35 276.5	−40 803.4	−49 417.6	Biens : importations, fab
Serv. & Income: Credit	22 350.9	21 978.4	23 904.2	25 159.0	28 011.4	32 214.3	38 462.9	Serv. & revenu : crédit
Serv. & Income: Debit	−22 872.7	−22 879.9	−22 743.8	−23 840.4	−25 599.5	−29 197.3	−34 948.1	Serv. & revenu : débit
Current Trans.,nie: Credit	1 500.5	1 680.7	1 604.8	1 759.7	1 810.3	2 008.0	2 408.4	Transf. cour.,nia : crédit
Current Transfers: Debit	−3 033.7	−3 124.3	−2 889.5	−3 378.7	−4 089.0	−4 968.1	−5 053.8	Transf. courants : débit
Capital Acct.,nie: Credit	43.7	40.5	134.7	113.3	43.9	964.2	105.4	Compte de cap.,nia : crédit
Capital Account: Debit	−159.9	−156.4	−225.4	−117.6	−235.0	−286.1	−259.7	Compte de capital : débit
Financial Account, nie	60.7	431.4	−13 394.7	−27 392.6	−9 237.8	−19 372.7	−20 745.2	Compte d'op. fin., nia
Net Errors and Omissions	−6 334.6	−2 709.5	−8 679.7	−1 120.0	−9 320.5	−9 286.0	−8 318.3	Erreurs et omissions nettes
Reserves & Related Items	6 384.0	−5 983.7	−3 685.8	2 345.9	−5 723.5	−345.6	−5 227.0	Rés. et postes appareutés
Oman								**Oman**
Goods: Exports fob	5 520.0	7 237.0	11 318.0	11 073.0	11 172.0	11 670.0	13 345.0	Biens : exportations, fab
Goods: Imports fob	−5 213.0	−4 299.0	−4 593.0	−5 310.0	−5 636.0	−6 086.0	−7 873.0	Biens : importations, fab
Serv. & Income: Credit	727.2	600.3	743.1	809.8	765.3	893.1	1 091.0	Serv. & revenu : crédit
Serv. & Income: Debit	−2 730.9	−2 559.6	−2 887.5	−3 155.6	−3 332.2	−3 925.0	−4 294.0	Serv. & revenu : débit
Current Trans.,nie: Credit	0.0	0.0	0.0	0.0	0.0	0.0	0.0	Transf. cour.,nia : crédit
Current Transfers: Debit	−1 466.9	−1 438.2	−1 451.2	−1 531.9	−1 602.1	−1 672.3	−1 826.0	Transf. courants : débit
Capital Acct.,nie: Credit	20.3	15.6	33.8	7.8	36.9	26.0	26.0	Compte de cap.,nia : crédit
Capital Account: Debit	−26.5	−18.2	−26.0	−18.2	−30.7	−15.6	−5.0	Compte de capital : débit
Financial Account, nie	1 488.8	127.9	−370.0	−219.7	−1 080.6	−279.4	990.0	Compte d'op. fin., nia
Net Errors and Omissions	910.5	539.0	−503.9	−640.5	16.2	45.1	−971.5	Erreurs et omissions nettes
Reserves & Related Items	770.6	−204.8	−2 263.4	−1 014.7	−308.8	−655.9	−482.5	Rés. et postes appareutés
Pakistan								**Pakistan**
Goods: Exports fob	7 850.0	7 673.0	8 739.0	9 131.0	9 832.0	11 869.0	13 297.0	Biens : exportations, fab
Goods: Imports fob	−9 834.0	−9 520.0	−9 896.0	−9 741.0	−10 428.0	−11 978.0	−16 693.0	Biens : importations, fab
Serv. & Income: Credit	1 487.0	1 492.0	1 498.0	1 572.0	2 557.0	3 148.0	2 970.1	Serv. & revenu : crédit
Serv. & Income: Debit	−4 524.0	−4 105.0	−4 588.0	−4 519.0	−4 655.0	−5 698.0	−7 917.1	Serv. & revenu : débit
Current Trans.,nie: Credit	2 801.0	3 582.0	4 200.0	5 496.0	6 593.0	6 300.0	7 666.0	Transf. cour.,nia : crédit
Current Transfers: Debit	−28.0	−42.0	−38.0	−61.0	−45.0	−68.0	−140.0	Transf. courants : débit
Capital Acct.,nie: Credit	0.0	0.0	0.0	0.0	40.0	1 140.0	596.0	Compte de cap.,nia : crédit
Capital Account: Debit	0.0	0.0	0.0	0.0	0.0	−2.0	−5.0	Compte de capital : débit
Financial Account, nie	−1 873.0	−2 364.0	−3 099.0	−389.0	−784.0	−1 751.0	−1 810.0	Compte d'op. fin., nia
Net Errors and Omissions	1 011.2	768.1	556.9	707.6	974.0	−52.4	685.2	Erreurs et omissions nettes
Reserves & Related Items	3 109.8	2 515.9	2 627.1	−2 196.6	−4 084.0	−2 907.6	1 350.8	Rés. et postes appareutés
Panama								**Panama**
Goods: Exports fob	6 331.8	5 288.1	5 838.5	5 992.4	5 314.7	5 071.9	6 133.4	Biens : exportations, fab
Goods: Imports fob	−7 627.3	−6 628.1	−6 981.4	−6 688.6	−6 349.8	−6 274.2	−7 721.7	Biens : importations, fab
Serv. & Income: Credit	3 570.8	3 348.0	3 569.7	3 376.8	3 231.1	3 283.9	3 511.8	Serv. & revenu : crédit
Serv. & Income: Debit	−3 449.9	−3 337.9	−3 276.3	−3 077.0	−2 535.3	−2 830.7	−3 278.8	Serv. & revenu : débit
Current Trans.,nie: Credit	195.2	202.7	208.7	277.9	298.8	310.6	323.3	Transf. cour.,nia : crédit
Current Transfers: Debit	−36.6	−31.6	−31.7	−51.8	−55.0	−64.2	−95.3	Transf. courants : débit
Capital Acct.,nie: Credit	50.9	3.0	1.7	1.6	0.0	0.0	0.0	Compte de cap.,nia : crédit
Capital Account: Debit	0.0	0.0	0.0	0.0	0.0	0.0	0.0	Compte de capital : débit
Financial Account, nie	1 249.2	1 836.9	331.8	1 301.0	194.3	−13.5	407.5	Compte d'op. fin., nia
Net Errors and Omissions	−389.1	−490.1	262.5	−498.6	45.2	247.6	323.6	Erreurs et omissions nettes
Reserves & Related Items	105.0	−191.0	76.5	−633.7	−144.0	268.6	396.1	Rés. et postes appareutés

Country or area	1998	1999	2000	2001	2002	2003	2004	Pays ou zone
Papua New Guinea								**Papouasie-Nvl-Guinée**
Goods: Exports fob	1 773.3	1 927.4	2 094.1	1 812.9	...	...	...	Biens : exportations, fab
Goods: Imports fob	−1 078.3	−1 071.4	−998.8	−932.4	...	...	...	Biens : importations, fab
Serv. & Income: Credit	339.0	266.1	274.7	305.1	...	...	...	Serv. & revenu : crédit
Serv. & Income: Debit	−1 073.6	−1 019.0	−1 014.4	−912.2	...	...	...	Serv. & revenu : débit
Current Trans.,nie: Credit	82.4	60.3	62.4	75.9	...	...	...	Transf. cour.,nia : crédit
Current Transfers: Debit	−71.6	−68.7	−72.7	−67.3	...	...	...	Transf. courants : débit
Capital Acct.,nie: Credit	9.7	7.8	7.2	5.9	...	...	...	Compte de cap.,nia : crédit
Capital Account: Debit	−9.7	−7.8	−7.2	−5.9	...	...	...	Compte de capital : débit
Financial Account, nie	−179.7	16.0	−254.1	−151.9	...	...	...	Compte d'op. fin., nia
Net Errors and Omissions	−12.5	14.3	13.1	−1.6	...	...	...	Erreurs et omissions nettes
Reserves & Related Items	221.0	−125.0	−104.5	−128.6	...	...	...	Rés. et postes appareutés
Paraguay								**Paraguay**
Goods: Exports fob	3 548.6	2 312.4	2 329.0	1 889.7	1 858.0	2 175.3	2 811.7	Biens : exportations, fab
Goods: Imports fob	−3 941.5	−2 752.9	−2 866.1	−2 503.6	−2 137.9	−2 450.5	−3 203.0	Biens : importations, fab
Serv. & Income: Credit	891.8	787.9	855.8	811.1	764.1	749.0	771.6	Serv. & revenu : crédit
Serv. & Income: Debit	−836.2	−688.0	−658.3	−630.1	−507.5	−505.9	−554.1	Serv. & revenu : débit
Current Trans.,nie: Credit	178.3	176.7	178.3	168.0	117.5	166.0	195.7	Transf. cour.,nia : crédit
Current Transfers: Debit	−1.0	−1.5	−1.5	−1.5	−1.6	−1.5	−1.5	Transf. courants : débit
Capital Acct.,nie: Credit	5.4	19.6	3.0	15.0	4.0	15.0	16.0	Compte de cap.,nia : crédit
Capital Account: Debit	0.0	0.0	0.0	0.0	0.0	0.0	0.0	Compte de capital : débit
Financial Account, nie	312.9	89.2	63.9	148.2	40.5	173.2	113.0	Compte d'op. fin., nia
Net Errors and Omissions	−141.6	−244.3	−243.4	52.9	−262.8	−87.8	120.5	Erreurs et omissions nettes
Reserves & Related Items	−16.7	300.9	339.3	50.2	125.7	−232.8	−270.0	Rés. et postes appareutés
Peru								**Pérou**
Goods: Exports fob	5 756.8	6 088.2	6 955.3	7 025.7	7 713.9	9 090.7	12 616.0	Biens : exportations, fab
Goods: Imports fob	−8 194.1	−6 743.0	−7 365.9	−7 220.6	−7 421.8	−8 255.0	−9 824.2	Biens : importations, fab
Serv. & Income: Credit	2 560.6	2 248.4	2 265.7	2 125.4	1 900.1	2 017.3	2 245.5	Serv. & revenu : crédit
Serv. & Income: Debit	−4 421.6	−4 023.2	−4 380.0	−4 116.5	−4 298.4	−5 015.2	−6 509.1	Serv. & revenu : débit
Current Trans.,nie: Credit	988.9	992.4	1 007.9	1 050.1	1 051.6	1 233.6	1 467.0	Transf. cour.,nia : crédit
Current Transfers: Debit	−11.7	−26.8	−8.6	−8.5	−8.3	−6.1	−6.2	Transf. courants : débit
Capital Acct.,nie: Credit	20.8	25.0	24.2	32.0	14.4	13.8	37.2	Compte de cap.,nia : crédit
Capital Account: Debit	−78.1	−79.4	−275.4	−174.9	−121.2	−121.2	−123.3	Compte de capital : débit
Financial Account, nie	1 772.7	544.5	1 015.3	1 533.9	1 982.8	820.1	2 375.1	Compte d'op. fin., nia
Net Errors and Omissions	364.7	111.6	631.4	185.0	196.5	783.5	177.7	Erreurs et omissions nettes
Reserves & Related Items	1 241.1	862.2	130.2	−431.5	−1 009.8	−561.5	−2 455.7	Rés. et postes appareutés
Philippines								**Philippines**
Goods: Exports fob	29 496.0	34 211.0	37 295.0	31 243.0	34 377.0	35 342.0	38 728.0	Biens : exportations, fab
Goods: Imports fob	−29 524.0	−29 252.0	−33 481.0	−31 986.0	−33 970.0	−40 797.0	−45 109.0	Biens : importations, fab
Serv. & Income: Credit	13 917.0	12 885.0	11 776.0	10 300.0	11 001.0	6 639.0	7 650.0	Serv. & revenu : crédit
Serv. & Income: Debit	−12 778.0	−11 137.0	−9 769.0	−8 681.0	−7 528.0	−8 590.0	−8 785.0	Serv. & revenu : débit
Current Trans.,nie: Credit	758.0	607.0	552.0	517.0	594.0	9 009.0	9 858.0	Transf. cour.,nia : crédit
Current Transfers: Debit	−323.0	−95.0	−115.0	−70.0	−91.0	−207.0	−262.0	Transf. courants : débit
Capital Acct.,nie: Credit	0.0	44.0	74.0	12.0	2.0	41.0	5.0	Compte de cap.,nia : crédit
Capital Account: Debit	0.0	−52.0	−36.0	−24.0	−21.0	−18.0	−28.0	Compte de capital : débit
Financial Account, nie	483.0	−2 250.0	−4 042.0	−745.0	−2 399.0	−1 716.0	−2 977.0	Compte d'op. fin., nia
Net Errors and Omissions	−749.9	−1 310.9	−2 629.6	−270.5	−2 075.7	218.1	−666.9	Erreurs et omissions nettes
Reserves & Related Items	−1 279.1	−3 650.1	375.5	−295.5	110.7	78.9	1 586.9	Rés. et postes appareutés
Poland								**Pologne**
Goods: Exports fob	32 467.0	30 060.0	35 902.0	41 663.0	46 742.0	61 007.0	81 862.0	Biens : exportations, fab
Goods: Imports fob	−45 303.0	−45 132.0	−48 209.0	−49 324.0	−53 991.0	−66 732.0	−87 484.0	Biens : importations, fab
Serv. & Income: Credit	13 066.0	10 200.0	12 648.0	12 378.0	11 985.0	13 282.0	15 577.0	Serv. & revenu : crédit
Serv. & Income: Debit	−10 028.0	−9 829.0	−12 702.0	−12 981.0	−13 023.0	−16 392.0	−25 956.0	Serv. & revenu : débit
Current Trans.,nie: Credit	3 520.0	2 898.0	3 008.0	3 737.0	4 181.0	5 316.0	8 282.0	Transf. cour.,nia : crédit
Current Transfers: Debit	−623.0	−684.0	−628.0	−848.0	−903.0	−1 080.0	−2 638.0	Transf. courants : débit
Capital Acct.,nie: Credit	117.0	95.0	110.0	113.0	46.0	60.0	1 144.0	Compte de cap.,nia : crédit
Capital Account: Debit	−54.0	−40.0	−76.0	−37.0	−53.0	−106.0	−146.0	Compte de capital : débit
Financial Account, nie	13 282.0	10 462.0	10 221.0	3 173.0	7 180.0	8 686.0	8 204.0	Compte d'op. fin., nia
Net Errors and Omissions	−519.6	2 125.6	350.2	1 698.7	−1 515.8	−2 834.7	1 955.6	Erreurs et omissions nettes
Reserves & Related Items	−5 924.4	−155.6	−624.2	427.3	−648.2	−1 206.3	−800.6	Rés. et postes appareutés

Country or area	1998	1999	2000	2001	2002	2003	2004	Pays ou zone
Portugal								**Portugal**
Goods: Exports fob	20 881.4	24 899.4	24 663.4	24 335.3	26 086.7	32 054.9	37 107.9	Biens : exportations, fab
Goods: Imports fob	−31 568.0	−39 326.4	−39 194.9	−38 572.0	−39 275.9	−46 232.5	−55 773.9	Biens : importations, fab
Serv. & Income: Credit	11 058.7	13 520.1	13 586.7	14 814.7	15 257.4	18 560.5	21 399.0	Serv. & revenu : crédit
Serv. & Income: Debit	−10 826.5	−13 352.1	−14 154.8	−15 619.9	−14 468.4	−16 288.7	−19 339.9	Serv. & revenu : débit
Current Trans.,nie: Credit	5 120.5	6 079.3	5 415.3	5 582.3	5 445.5	6 443.2	7 160.5	Transf. cour.,nia : crédit
Current Transfers: Debit	−1 726.5	−2 234.3	−2 063.1	−2 233.8	−2 641.1	−3 191.0	−3 711.4	Transf. courants : débit
Capital Acct.,nie: Credit	2 261.2	2 641.9	1 680.6	1 277.6	2 110.9	3 245.6	3 126.8	Compte de cap.,nia : crédit
Capital Account: Debit	−149.9	−183.4	−168.9	−208.9	−205.4	−235.9	−322.3	Compte de capital : débit
Financial Account, nie	4 799.6	9 172.3	10 871.6	10 828.2	7 726.2	−430.5	9 911.0	Compte d'op. fin., nia
Net Errors and Omissions	604.7	−1 000.8	−265.1	649.0	981.8	−380.5	−1 420.8	Erreurs et omissions nettes
Reserves & Related Items	−455.2	−215.9	−370.7	−852.5	−1 017.5	6 455.1	1 863.1	Rés. et postes appareutés
Republic of Moldova								**République de Moldova**
Goods: Exports fob	643.6	474.3	476.8	564.6	659.7	805.9	994.1	Biens : exportations, fab
Goods: Imports fob	−1 031.7	−611.5	−770.3	−879.7	−1 037.5	−1 428.1	−1 748.2	Biens : importations, fab
Serv. & Income: Credit	288.8	256.2	303.9	345.3	446.9	595.1	827.2	Serv. & revenu : crédit
Serv. & Income: Debit	−300.9	−273.7	−319.1	−286.9	−377.0	−411.4	−507.1	Serv. & revenu : débit
Current Trans.,nie: Credit	110.9	111.5	213.6	236.0	255.6	331.7	399.0	Transf. cour.,nia : crédit
Current Transfers: Debit	−45.5	−35.4	−13.1	−15.9	−19.3	−27.5	−35.2	Transf. courants : débit
Capital Acct.,nie: Credit	2.1	1.5	2.8	1.1	0.8	3.5	5.3	Compte de cap.,nia : crédit
Capital Account: Debit	−2.5	−0.4	−17.1	−21.8	−16.1	−16.3	−16.1	Compte de capital : débit
Financial Account, nie	5.2	−34.6	126.4	17.0	63.1	62.0	103.9	Compte d'op. fin., nia
Net Errors and Omissions	−22.8	−3.8	−9.1	15.5	−23.3	69.3	121.3	Erreurs et omissions nettes
Reserves & Related Items	352.8	115.9	5.2	24.7	47.1	15.7	−144.1	Rés. et postes appareutés
Romania								**Roumanie**
Goods: Exports fob	8 302.0	8 503.0	10 366.0	11 385.0	13 876.0	17 618.0	23 485.0	Biens : exportations, fab
Goods: Imports fob	−10 927.0	−9 595.0	−12 050.0	−14 354.0	−16 487.0	−22 155.0	−30 150.0	Biens : importations, fab
Serv. & Income: Credit	1 489.0	1 517.0	2 072.0	2 487.0	2 760.0	3 400.0	4 047.0	Serv. & revenu : crédit
Serv. & Income: Debit	−2 534.0	−2 348.0	−2 603.0	−2 890.0	−3 210.0	−4 035.0	−7 461.0	Serv. & revenu : débit
Current Trans.,nie: Credit	886.0	804.0	1 079.0	1 417.0	1 808.0	2 200.0	4 188.0	Transf. cour.,nia : crédit
Current Transfers: Debit	−133.0	−178.0	−219.0	−274.0	−272.0	−339.0	−491.0	Transf. courants : débit
Capital Acct.,nie: Credit	39.0	46.0	37.0	108.0	100.0	223.0	669.0	Compte de cap.,nia : crédit
Capital Account: Debit	0.0	−1.0	−1.0	−13.0	−7.0	−10.0	−26.0	Compte de capital : débit
Financial Account, nie	2 042.0	697.0	2 102.0	2 938.0	4 079.0	4 400.0	10 761.0	Compte d'op. fin., nia
Net Errors and Omissions	193.4	794.5	125.0	730.6	−856.0	−288.8	1 167.1	Erreurs et omissions nettes
Reserves & Related Items	642.6	−239.5	−908.0	−1 534.6	−1 791.0	−1 013.2	−6 189.1	Rés. et postes appareutés
Russian Federation								**Fédération de Russie**
Goods: Exports fob	74 444.1	75 550.7	105 033.0	101 884.0	107 301.0	135 929.0	183 207.0	Biens : exportations, fab
Goods: Imports fob	−58 015.1	−39 536.5	−44 861.6	−53 763.7	−60 965.8	−76 069.7	−97 382.1	Biens : importations, fab
Serv. & Income: Credit	16 673.6	12 948.3	14 317.3	18 241.3	19 288.0	27 285.6	30 670.8	Serv. & revenu : crédit
Serv. & Income: Debit	−32 546.7	−24 947.8	−27 718.9	−31 610.0	−35 757.1	−51 349.8	−57 256.3	Serv. & revenu : débit
Current Trans.,nie: Credit	307.6	1 182.9	807.5	744.1	1 352.5	2 537.0	3 640.5	Transf. cour.,nia : crédit
Current Transfers: Debit	−644.4	−581.6	−738.1	−1 561.3	−2 102.8	−2 922.4	−4 317.1	Transf. courants : débit
Capital Acct.,nie: Credit	1 704.3	884.9	11 543.0	2 124.9	7 528.2	613.8	860.4	Compte de cap.,nia : crédit
Capital Account: Debit	−2 086.5	−1 212.9	−867.2	−11 502.8	−19 924.2	−1 608.8	−2 486.1	Compte de capital : débit
Financial Account, nie	−11 408.9	−17 007.6	−33 855.4	−3 308.3	1 345.3	3 059.9	−3 242.4	Compte d'op. fin., nia
Net Errors and Omissions	−9 806.3	−8 983.7	−9 736.6	−9 982.4	−6 501.8	−9 712.7	−7 054.5	Erreurs et omissions nettes
Reserves & Related Items	21 378.4	1 703.5	−13 923.1	−11 266.0	−11 563.4	−27 762.2	−46 640.4	Rés. et postes appareutés
Rwanda								**Rwanda**
Goods: Exports fob	64.2	61.5	68.4	93.3	67.2	59.2	97.9	Biens : exportations, fab
Goods: Imports fob	−233.0	−246.9	−223.2	−245.2	−233.3	−217.8	−257.9	Biens : importations, fab
Serv. & Income: Credit	57.0	58.5	73.1	80.0	73.7	82.7	108.2	Serv. & revenu : crédit
Serv. & Income: Debit	−205.6	−211.7	−228.5	−223.2	−228.7	−235.3	−268.4	Serv. & revenu : débit
Current Trans.,nie: Credit	251.4	209.9	232.9	210.5	215.3	246.4	332.2	Transf. cour.,nia : crédit
Current Transfers: Debit	−16.8	−12.7	−17.0	−17.9	−20.4	−19.9	−18.3	Transf. courants : débit
Capital Acct.,nie: Credit	0.0	70.2	62.1	50.2	66.2	41.1	60.6	Compte de cap.,nia : crédit
Capital Account: Debit	0.0	0.0	0.0	0.0	−0.3	0.0	0.0	Compte de capital : débit
Financial Account, nie	−16.7	−33.2	10.7	−44.1	81.1	38.7	89.1	Compte d'op. fin., nia
Net Errors and Omissions	92.3	32.3	−109.6	26.0	−41.5	17.4	−42.9	Erreurs et omissions nettes
Reserves & Related Items	7.1	72.1	131.1	70.3	20.8	−12.5	−100.5	Rés. et postes appareutés

71

Summary of balance of payments — Millions of US dollars (*continued*)
Résumé des balances des paiements — Millions de dollars des E.-U. (*suite*)

Country or area	1998	1999	2000	2001	2002	2003	2004	Pays ou zone
Saint Kitts and Nevis								**Saint-Kitts-et-Nevis**
Goods: Exports fob	44.4	45.0	51.5	55.0	64.4	...	...	Biens : exportations, fab
Goods: Imports fob	−131.0	−135.2	−172.7	−166.6	−177.6	...	...	Biens : importations, fab
Serv. & Income: Credit	105.4	107.5	104.1	103.7	96.1	...	...	Serv. & revenu : crédit
Serv. & Income: Debit	−92.2	−120.2	−111.7	−114.1	−123.3	...	...	Serv. & revenu : débit
Current Trans.,nie: Credit	33.7	24.1	69.9	26.6	28.3	...	...	Transf. cour.,nia : crédit
Current Transfers: Debit	−6.6	−3.6	−7.3	−10.6	−11.9	...	...	Transf. courants : débit
Capital Acct.,nie: Credit	8.4	6.0	6.2	10.5	14.8	...	...	Compte de cap.,nia : crédit
Capital Account: Debit	−0.2	−0.2	−0.2	−0.2	−0.2	...	...	Compte de capital : débit
Financial Account, nie	45.7	95.5	70.2	103.9	106.9	...	...	Compte d'op. fin., nia
Net Errors and Omissions	3.4	−16.0	−14.4	3.3	12.2	...	...	Erreurs et omissions nettes
Reserves & Related Items	−11.0	−2.8	4.4	−11.6	−9.7	...	...	Rés. et postes appareutés
Saint Lucia								**Sainte-Lucie**
Goods: Exports fob	70.4	60.9	63.1	54.4	70.0	...	...	Biens : exportations, fab
Goods: Imports fob	−295.1	−312.0	−312.5	−272.1	−277.0	...	...	Biens : importations, fab
Serv. & Income: Credit	322.9	308.6	325.0	286.0	260.7	...	...	Serv. & revenu : crédit
Serv. & Income: Debit	−177.9	−176.8	−172.0	−157.4	−170.6	...	...	Serv. & revenu : débit
Current Trans.,nie: Credit	29.6	32.1	28.9	27.5	28.6	...	...	Transf. cour.,nia : crédit
Current Transfers: Debit	−10.1	−9.6	−11.4	−13.4	−15.6	...	...	Transf. courants : débit
Capital Acct.,nie: Credit	25.4	25.8	16.5	27.5	22.5	...	...	Compte de cap.,nia : crédit
Capital Account: Debit	−0.8	−0.7	−2.3	−1.1	−1.1	...	...	Compte de capital : débit
Financial Account, nie	58.5	66.2	70.9	43.7	68.4	...	...	Compte d'op. fin., nia
Net Errors and Omissions	−13.2	9.5	−1.4	16.9	19.2	...	...	Erreurs et omissions nettes
Reserves & Related Items	−9.8	−4.0	−4.8	−12.1	−5.2	...	...	Rés. et postes appareutés
St. Vincent-Grenadines								**St. Vincent-Grenadines**
Goods: Exports fob	50.1	49.6	51.8	42.8	40.5	...	...	Biens : exportations, fab
Goods: Imports fob	−170.0	−177.1	−144.4	−152.0	−157.2	...	...	Biens : importations, fab
Serv. & Income: Credit	110.4	129.1	129.4	133.7	139.9	...	...	Serv. & revenu : crédit
Serv. & Income: Debit	−95.8	−88.6	−82.5	−78.4	−77.5	...	...	Serv. & revenu : débit
Current Trans.,nie: Credit	21.6	23.4	24.7	23.2	23.7	...	...	Transf. cour.,nia : crédit
Current Transfers: Debit	−8.6	−9.0	−8.4	−10.6	−11.6	...	...	Transf. courants : débit
Capital Acct.,nie: Credit	14.8	9.1	6.9	10.0	11.9	...	...	Compte de cap.,nia : crédit
Capital Account: Debit	−1.3	−1.3	−1.3	−1.3	−1.3	...	...	Compte de capital : débit
Financial Account, nie	92.1	54.4	24.6	49.7	12.7	...	...	Compte d'op. fin., nia
Net Errors and Omissions	−5.3	14.7	13.2	−8.1	13.0	...	...	Erreurs et omissions nettes
Reserves & Related Items	−8.0	−4.4	−14.0	−9.1	6.0	...	...	Rés. et postes appareutés
Samoa								**Samoa**
Goods: Exports fob	20.4	18.2	...	...	...	...	...	Biens : exportations, fab
Goods: Imports fob	−96.9	−115.7	...	...	...	...	...	Biens : importations, fab
Serv. & Income: Credit	68.5	64.1	...	...	...	...	...	Serv. & revenu : crédit
Serv. & Income: Debit	−31.5	−26.9	...	...	...	...	...	Serv. & revenu : débit
Current Trans.,nie: Credit	64.1	44.7	...	...	...	...	...	Transf. cour.,nia : crédit
Current Transfers: Debit	−4.6	−3.1	...	...	...	...	...	Transf. courants : débit
Capital Acct.,nie: Credit	0.0	27.1	...	...	...	...	...	Compte de cap.,nia : crédit
Capital Account: Debit	0.0	−2.7	...	...	...	...	...	Compte de capital : débit
Financial Account, nie	−5.0	−0.7	...	...	...	...	...	Compte d'op. fin., nia
Net Errors and Omissions	−9.6	2.1	...	...	...	...	...	Erreurs et omissions nettes
Reserves & Related Items	−5.5	−7.0	...	...	...	...	...	Rés. et postes appareutés
Sao Tome and Principe								**Sao Tomé-et-Principe**
Goods: Exports fob	4.7	3.9	2.7	3.3	5.1	...	...	Biens : exportations, fab
Goods: Imports fob	−16.9	−21.9	−25.1	−24.4	−28.0	...	...	Biens : importations, fab
Serv. & Income: Credit [3]	6.6	12.5	13.6	12.8	13.4	...	...	Serv. & revenu : crédit [3]
Serv. & Income: Debit	−15.6	−17.1	−14.6	−16.7	−18.2	...	...	Serv. & revenu : débit
Current Trans.,nie: Credit	10.7	6.4	4.4	4.0	4.9	...	...	Transf. cour.,nia : crédit
Current Transfers: Debit	0.0	0.0	0.0	0.0	0.0	...	...	Transf. courants : débit
Capital Acct.,nie: Credit	3.9	9.3	12.0	15.2	12.1	...	...	Compte de cap.,nia : crédit
Capital Account: Debit	0.0	0.0	0.0	0.0	0.0	...	...	Compte de capital : débit
Financial Account, nie	0.3	4.4	3.3	1.7	3.7	...	...	Compte d'op. fin., nia
Net Errors and Omissions	0.3	0.1	−1.7	2.7	0.0	...	...	Erreurs et omissions nettes
Reserves & Related Items	6.0	2.6	5.5	1.5	7.0	...	...	Rés. et postes appareutés

Summary of balance of payments—Millions of US dollars (*continued*)
Résumé des balances des paiements—Millions de dollars des E.-U. (*suite*)

Country or area	1998	1999	2000	2001	2002	2003	2004	Pays ou zone
Saudi Arabia								**Arabie saoudite**
Goods: Exports fob	38 770.1	50 688.9	77 480.5	67 972.8	72 464.3	93 244.1	125 998.0	Biens : exportations, fab
Goods: Imports fob	−27 497.9	−25 683.2	−27 704.0	−28 607.0	−29 624.3	−33 867.7	−41 050.4	Biens : importations, fab
Serv. & Income: Credit	10 525.1	11 176.1	8 123.7	9 132.3	8 891.3	8 689.6	10 129.6	Serv. & revenu : crédit
Serv. & Income: Debit	−19 895.4	−21 712.7	−28 093.3	−23 924.9	−23 904.6	−25 134.7	−29 495.8	Serv. & revenu : débit
Current Trans.,nie: Credit	0.0	0.0	0.0	0.0	0.0	0.0	0.0	Transf. cour.,nia : crédit
Current Transfers: Debit	−15 034.0	−14 058.1	−15 490.1	−15 219.7	−15 953.6	−14 883.3	−13 655.1	Transf. courants : débit
Capital Acct.,nie: Credit	0.0	0.0	0.0	0.0	0.0	0.0	0.0	Compte de cap.,nia : crédit
Capital Account: Debit	0.0	0.0	0.0	0.0	0.0	0.0	0.0	Compte de capital : débit
Financial Account, nie	12 414.1	2 403.6	−11 652.0	−11 262.2	−9 137.1	−26 439.9	−47 428.2	Compte d'op. fin., nia
Net Errors and Omissions	0.0	0.0	0.0	0.0	0.0	0.0	0.0	Erreurs et omissions nettes
Reserves & Related Items	717.9	−2 814.6	−2 664.8	1 908.8	−2 736.0	−1 608.1	−4 497.8	Rés. et postes appareutés
Senegal								**Sénégal**
Goods: Exports fob	967.7	1 027.1	919.8	1 003.1	1 066.5	1 257.0	...	Biens : exportations, fab
Goods: Imports fob	−1 280.6	−1 372.8	−1 336.6	−1 428.4	−1 603.9	−2 065.5	...	Biens : importations, fab
Serv. & Income: Credit	501.6	496.0	463.2	459.6	521.4	655.5	...	Serv. & revenu : crédit
Serv. & Income: Debit	−607.3	−629.5	−592.7	−580.0	−669.4	−813.9	...	Serv. & revenu : débit
Current Trans.,nie: Credit	254.7	225.4	274.9	353.6	414.4	595.6	...	Transf. cour.,nia : crédit
Current Transfers: Debit	−83.6	−66.3	−61.0	−53.4	−45.8	−65.2	...	Transf. courants : débit
Capital Acct.,nie: Credit	98.8	99.0	83.6	146.1	127.1	150.9	...	Compte de cap.,nia : crédit
Capital Account: Debit	−0.4	−0.5	−0.3	−0.1	−0.2	−0.6	...	Compte de capital : débit
Financial Account, nie	−109.7	−54.8	27.1	−102.6	−88.2	2.5	...	Compte d'op. fin., nia
Net Errors and Omissions	10.7	8.2	−9.0	7.9	30.8	10.8	...	Erreurs et omissions nettes
Reserves & Related Items	248.1	268.2	231.0	194.1	247.3	272.8	...	Rés. et postes appareutés
Seychelles								**Seychelles**
Goods: Exports fob	122.8	145.7	194.8	216.4	236.7	286.4	300.5	Biens : exportations, fab
Goods: Imports fob	−334.6	−369.7	−311.6	−421.9	−376.3	−377.6	−416.9	Biens : importations, fab
Serv. & Income: Credit	252.9	285.8	303.5	304.6	314.0	342.4	335.0	Serv. & revenu : crédit
Serv. & Income: Debit	−157.5	−188.3	−232.3	−221.4	−301.3	−273.6	−255.9	Serv. & revenu : débit
Current Trans.,nie: Credit	9.8	10.1	4.3	7.9	7.8	9.0	11.2	Transf. cour.,nia : crédit
Current Transfers: Debit	−11.4	−10.8	−10.0	−8.9	−11.6	−2.8	−1.9	Transf. courants : débit
Capital Acct.,nie: Credit	21.7	16.5	0.9	9.4	5.0	7.4	1.0	Compte de cap.,nia : crédit
Capital Account: Debit	0.0	0.0	0.0	0.0	0.0	0.0	0.0	Compte de capital : débit
Financial Account, nie	27.1	13.9	−32.1	52.3	−64.0	−152.6	−190.6	Compte d'op. fin., nia
Net Errors and Omissions	−4.3	−2.1	−20.8	14.4	0.5	39.8	32.5	Erreurs et omissions nettes
Reserves & Related Items	73.6	99.1	103.3	47.1	189.1	121.6	185.3	Rés. et postes appareutés
Sierra Leone								**Sierra Leone**
Goods: Exports fob	31.6	6.3	12.8	29.2	59.8	110.8	154.1	Biens : exportations, fab
Goods: Imports fob	−88.8	−86.8	−136.9	−165.1	−254.9	−310.7	−252.5	Biens : importations, fab
Serv. & Income: Credit	25.9	28.5	49.7	56.3	56.6	67.7	65.5	Serv. & revenu : crédit
Serv. & Income: Debit	−66.6	−115.0	−125.5	−125.7	−101.9	−110.5	−160.6	Serv. & revenu : débit
Current Trans.,nie: Credit	65.2	68.6	92.3	120.7	170.8	167.6	122.0	Transf. cour.,nia : crédit
Current Transfers: Debit	−0.6	−1.0	−4.7	−13.2	−3.6	−5.0	−2.8	Transf. courants : débit
Capital Acct.,nie: Credit	0.0	0.0	0.0	0.4	50.6	71.0	81.3	Compte de cap.,nia : crédit
Capital Account: Debit	0.0	0.0	0.0	−0.1	0.0	0.0	0.0	Compte de capital : débit
Financial Account, nie	10.6	−27.3	124.6	30.1	10.0	28.1	57.4	Compte d'op. fin., nia
Net Errors and Omissions	24.7	110.5	−2.5	97.2	−7.4	−47.6	−59.5	Erreurs et omissions nettes
Reserves & Related Items	−2.1	16.1	−9.8	−29.6	20.1	28.6	−4.9	Rés. et postes appareutés
Singapore								**Singapour**
Goods: Exports fob	117 717.0	124 468.0	149 228.0	133 744.0	137 747.0	158 440.0	197 343.0	Biens : exportations, fab
Goods: Imports fob	−104 306.0	−112 026.0	−136 505.0	−118 036.0	−120 166.0	−130 310.0	−166 104.0	Biens : importations, fab
Serv. & Income: Credit	35 812.7	42 599.2	45 193.1	42 889.6	44 118.0	49 139.6	56 587.4	Serv. & revenu : crédit
Serv. & Income: Debit	−29 832.9	−39 241.6	−44 820.3	−43 042.3	−44 831.7	−49 181.0	−58 785.1	Serv. & revenu : débit
Current Trans.,nie: Credit	130.6	134.8	127.5	122.4	125.7	129.7	134.0	Transf. cour.,nia : crédit
Current Transfers: Debit	−1 250.9	−1 160.6	−1 287.6	−1 295.6	−1 266.1	−1 267.2	−1 278.2	Transf. courants : débit
Capital Acct.,nie: Credit	0.0	0.0	0.0	0.0	0.0	0.0	0.0	Compte de cap.,nia : crédit
Capital Account: Debit	−225.8	−191.0	−162.8	−161.2	−160.4	−167.6	−182.5	Compte de capital : débit
Financial Account, nie	−17 985.4	−13 696.2	−5 526.5	−18 525.3	−10 296.1	−19 633.4	−12 873.5	Compte d'op. fin., nia
Net Errors and Omissions	2 930.6	3 302.3	504.1	3 436.8	−3 943.3	−475.4	−2 753.2	Erreurs et omissions nettes
Reserves & Related Items	−2 989.5	−4 188.2	−6 750.5	866.8	−1 327.0	−6 674.6	−12 087.3	Rés. et postes appareutés

Country or area	1998	1999	2000	2001	2002	2003	2004	Pays ou zone
Slovakia								**Slovaquie**
Goods: Exports fob	10 720.2	10 201.3	11 896.1	...	14 460.1	21 944.0	...	Biens : exportations, fab
Goods: Imports fob	−13 070.9	−11 310.3	−12 790.6	...	−16 625.7	−22 592.7	...	Biens : importations, fab
Serv. & Income: Credit	2 729.4	2 167.7	2 508.9	...	3 153.6	4 204.4	...	Serv. & revenu : crédit
Serv. & Income: Debit	−2 870.8	−2 411.8	−2 428.5	...	−3 141.5	−4 082.3	...	Serv. & revenu : débit
Current Trans.,nie: Credit	645.0	466.0	343.8	...	480.5	536.5	...	Transf. cour.,nia : crédit
Current Transfers: Debit	−279.3	−268.1	−224.0	...	−281.9	−291.8	...	Transf. courants : débit
Capital Acct.,nie: Credit	82.8	171.0	105.7	...	130.1	195.0	...	Compte de cap.,nia : crédit
Capital Account: Debit	−12.4	−13.4	−14.8	...	−20.0	−92.9	...	Compte de capital : débit
Financial Account, nie	1 911.5	1 788.8	1 472.4	...	5 230.1	1 661.1	...	Compte d'op. fin., nia
Net Errors and Omissions	−333.1	−14.3	50.7	...	298.3	26.8	...	Erreurs et omissions nettes
Reserves & Related Items	477.6	−777.0	−919.7	...	−3 683.6	−1 508.0	...	Rés. et postes appareutés
Slovenia								**Slovénie**
Goods: Exports fob	9 090.9	8 623.2	8 807.9	9 342.8	10 471.1	12 916.3	16 064.6	Biens : exportations, fab
Goods: Imports fob	−9 882.9	−9 858.3	−9 946.9	−9 962.3	−10 718.9	−13 538.5	−17 322.1	Biens : importations, fab
Serv. & Income: Credit	2 437.5	2 302.3	2 321.7	2 422.2	2 785.4	3 417.0	4 188.6	Serv. & revenu : crédit
Serv. & Income: Debit	−1 880.9	−1 885.0	−1 845.8	−1 901.0	−2 337.0	−2 987.3	−3 638.5	Serv. & revenu : débit
Current Trans.,nie: Credit	299.8	334.9	340.8	390.0	452.1	508.0	677.7	Transf. cour.,nia : crédit
Current Transfers: Debit	−182.4	−215.3	−225.4	−260.8	−317.9	−400.8	−640.0	Transf. courants : débit
Capital Acct.,nie: Credit	3.5	3.3	6.8	3.3	72.0	92.8	179.4	Compte de cap.,nia : crédit
Capital Account: Debit	−5.0	−4.0	−3.3	−6.9	−230.3	−283.7	−313.6	Compte de capital : débit
Financial Account, nie	215.8	576.1	680.4	1 204.3	1 847.5	499.9	643.3	Compte d'op. fin., nia
Net Errors and Omissions	61.4	41.5	42.1	53.0	−207.4	86.5	−135.9	Erreurs et omissions nettes
Reserves & Related Items	−157.8	81.4	−178.3	−1 284.6	−1 816.7	−310.2	296.5	Rés. et postes appareutés
Solomon Islands								**Iles Salomon**
Goods: Exports fob	141.8	164.6	...	...	...	...	...	Biens : exportations, fab
Goods: Imports fob	−159.9	−110.0	...	...	...	...	...	Biens : importations, fab
Serv. & Income: Credit	57.2	61.8	...	...	...	...	...	Serv. & revenu : crédit
Serv. & Income: Debit	−64.5	−109.9	...	...	...	...	...	Serv. & revenu : débit
Current Trans.,nie: Credit	56.4	41.5	...	...	...	...	...	Transf. cour.,nia : crédit
Current Transfers: Debit	−22.9	−26.5	...	...	...	...	...	Transf. courants : débit
Capital Acct.,nie: Credit	6.9	9.2	...	...	...	...	...	Compte de cap.,nia : crédit
Capital Account: Debit	−0.3	0.0	...	...	...	...	...	Compte de capital : débit
Financial Account, nie	16.9	−33.8	...	...	...	...	...	Compte d'op. fin., nia
Net Errors and Omissions	−14.4	−1.6	...	...	...	...	...	Erreurs et omissions nettes
Reserves & Related Items	−17.2	4.7	...	...	...	...	...	Rés. et postes appareutés
South Africa								**Afrique du Sud**
Goods: Exports fob	29 198.8	28 534.0	31 949.7	31 063.6	31 772.1	38 700.1	48 236.9	Biens : exportations, fab
Goods: Imports fob	−27 207.6	−24 525.6	−27 252.2	−25 808.8	−27 016.0	−35 269.5	−48 518.4	Biens : importations, fab
Serv. & Income: Credit	6 870.3	7 001.0	7 556.8	7 130.2	6 851.7	10 766.2	12 268.6	Serv. & revenu : crédit
Serv. & Income: Debit	−10 316.9	−10 758.2	−11 518.4	−11 494.0	−10 368.0	−15 677.6	−17 956.9	Serv. & revenu : débit
Current Trans.,nie: Credit	60.1	66.2	106.4	126.1	139.1	251.7	257.2	Transf. cour.,nia : crédit
Current Transfers: Debit	−803.8	−992.7	−1 032.9	−864.6	−695.5	−1 094.3	−1 729.9	Transf. courants : débit
Capital Acct.,nie: Credit	24.4	20.5	19.0	15.8	20.2	43.6	54.7	Compte de cap.,nia : crédit
Capital Account: Debit	−80.4	−82.3	−71.0	−47.0	−35.1	0.0	−2.3	Compte de capital : débit
Financial Account, nie	4 041.2	3 153.6	73.3	−1 188.3	−1 451.8	−1 961.4	7 394.3	Compte d'op. fin., nia
Net Errors and Omissions	−1 741.5	−500.2	648.8	1 044.8	460.8	3 886.8	6 319.8	Erreurs et omissions nettes
Reserves & Related Items	−44.6	−1 916.2	−479.6	22.1	322.4	354.4	−6 324.1	Rés. et postes appareutés
Spain								**Espagne**
Goods: Exports fob	112 310.0	112 919.0	115 769.0	117 522.0	127 162.0	158 049.0	184 153.0	Biens : exportations, fab
Goods: Imports fob	−133 949.0	−144 732.0	−152 856.0	−152 039.0	−161 794.0	−203 205.0	−249 983.0	Biens : importations, fab
Serv. & Income: Credit	64 379.5	67 265.7	71 014.7	75 520.2	81 379.2	99 832.6	115 626.9	Serv. & revenu : crédit
Serv. & Income: Debit	−53 137.3	−56 416.4	−58 496.0	−66 266.9	−71 480.3	−86 539.5	−105 116.9	Serv. & revenu : débit
Current Trans.,nie: Credit	12 556.2	13 129.7	11 122.0	12 087.8	13 419.8	16 495.2	19 217.9	Transf. cour.,nia : crédit
Current Transfers: Debit	−9 411.4	−10 026.0	−9 629.8	−10 402.8	−11 278.2	−16 370.2	−19 278.0	Transf. courants : débit
Capital Acct.,nie: Credit	7 080.6	7 986.8	5 786.6	5 781.8	8 117.8	10 984.0	11 595.0	Compte de cap.,nia : crédit
Capital Account: Debit	−662.3	−1 063.1	−989.3	−970.6	−881.7	−1 709.7	−994.2	Compte de capital : débit
Financial Account, nie	−13 074.8	−10 894.7	15 250.0	17 888.2	18 655.5	5 903.6	39 626.8	Compte d'op. fin., nia
Net Errors and Omissions	−445.9	−964.2	149.1	−461.3	390.3	1 069.9	−1 259.2	Erreurs et omissions nettes
Reserves & Related Items	14 353.9	22 795.1	2 880.1	1 341.2	−3 690.1	15 489.5	6 412.0	Rés. et postes appareutés

Summary of balance of payments — Millions of US dollars (*continued*)
Résumé des balances des paiements — Millions de dollars des E.-U. (*suite*)

Country or area	1998	1999	2000	2001	2002	2003	2004	Pays ou zone
Sri Lanka								**Sri Lanka**
Goods: Exports fob	4 808.0	4 596.2	5 439.6	4 816.9	4 699.2	5 133.2	5 757.2	Biens : exportations, fab
Goods: Imports fob	−5 313.4	−5 365.5	−6 483.6	−5 376.9	−5 495.1	−6 004.8	−7 199.8	Biens : importations, fab
Serv. & Income: Credit	1 130.8	1 131.1	1 087.7	1 463.3	1 343.6	1 580.4	1 683.3	Serv. & revenu : crédit
Serv. & Income: Debit	−1 756.2	−1 833.0	−2 070.3	−2 124.0	−1 912.1	−2 020.5	−2 268.1	Serv. & revenu : débit
Current Trans.,nie: Credit	1 054.5	1 078.1	1 165.7	1 155.4	1 287.1	1 413.9	1 563.9	Transf. cour.,nia : crédit
Current Transfers: Debit	−151.3	−168.2	−182.7	−171.7	−190.2	−208.6	−213.7	Transf. courants : débit
Capital Acct.,nie: Credit	84.6	85.2	55.0	55.2	70.9	80.5	70.8	Compte de cap.,nia : crédit
Capital Account: Debit	−4.7	−5.2	−5.7	−5.3	−5.9	−6.5	−6.6	Compte de capital : débit
Financial Account, nie	345.1	413.4	447.2	−136.0	−195.9	−218.8	−132.5	Compte d'op. fin., nia
Net Errors and Omissions	26.3	−27.3	186.2	15.0	136.2	−113.9	−189.3	Erreurs et omissions nettes
Reserves & Related Items	−223.6	95.2	360.8	308.1	262.2	365.0	934.8	Rés. et postes appareutés
Sudan								**Soudan**
Goods: Exports fob	595.7	780.1	1 806.7	1 698.7	1 949.1	2 542.2	3 777.8	Biens : exportations, fab
Goods: Imports fob	−1 732.2	−1 256.0	−1 366.3	−1 395.1	−2 293.8	−2 536.1	−3 586.2	Biens : importations, fab
Serv. & Income: Credit	29.5	100.7	32.0	32.4	161.4	46.5	66.0	Serv. & revenu : crédit
Serv. & Income: Debit	−214.6	−398.1	−1 227.2	−1 232.2	−1 456.2	−1 709.5	−2 199.1	Serv. & revenu : débit
Current Trans.,nie: Credit	731.8	702.2	651.3	730.4	1 085.9	1 218.4	1 580.2	Transf. cour.,nia : crédit
Current Transfers: Debit	−366.7	−393.7	−453.3	−452.5	−454.5	−516.8	−509.6	Transf. courants : débit
Capital Acct.,nie: Credit	13.0	45.8	16.5	11.9	0.0	0.0	0.0	Compte de cap.,nia : crédit
Capital Account: Debit	−67.2	−68.7	−135.8	−105.2	0.0	0.0	0.0	Compte de capital : débit
Financial Account, nie	333.4	435.3	431.6	561.2	761.2	1 284.4	1 427.8	Compte d'op. fin., nia
Net Errors and Omissions	750.5	167.2	368.4	−0.5	492.2	−2.4	225.5	Erreurs et omissions nettes
Reserves & Related Items	−73.2	−114.8	−123.9	150.9	−245.3	−326.6	−782.4	Rés. et postes appareutés
Suriname								**Suriname**
Goods: Exports fob	349.7	342.0	399.1	437.0	369.3	487.8	782.2	Biens : exportations, fab
Goods: Imports fob	−376.9	−297.9	−246.1	−297.2	−321.9	−458.0	−740.1	Biens : importations, fab
Serv. & Income: Credit	78.5	87.0	104.1	64.8	46.9	70.7	156.9	Serv. & revenu : crédit
Serv. & Income: Debit	−203.9	−158.7	−222.7	−287.3	−216.8	−254.8	−349.5	Serv. & revenu : débit
Current Trans.,nie: Credit	1.3	1.8	1.2	2.1	12.9	24.8	75.8	Transf. cour.,nia : crédit
Current Transfers: Debit	−3.6	−3.3	−3.3	−3.0	−21.4	−29.5	−63.0	Transf. courants : débit
Capital Acct.,nie: Credit	6.6	3.5	2.3	1.5	5.9	9.2	18.9	Compte de cap.,nia : crédit
Capital Account: Debit	0.0	0.0	0.0	0.0	0.0	−0.2	0.0	Compte de capital : débit
Financial Account, nie	30.5	−21.6	−139.1	104.1	−38.1	−36.5	−23.5	Compte d'op. fin., nia
Net Errors and Omissions	125.9	42.8	114.3	56.1	144.1	193.7	218.4	Erreurs et omissions nettes
Reserves & Related Items	−8.1	4.4	−9.8	−78.1	19.1	−7.2	−76.1	Rés. et postes appareutés
Swaziland								**Swaziland**
Goods: Exports fob	967.8	936.7	905.0	1 042.5	1 029.2	1 625.6	1 938.3	Biens : exportations, fab
Goods: Imports fob	−1 073.8	−1 068.1	−1 041.1	−1 124.2	−938.7	−1 508.1	−1 913.9	Biens : importations, fab
Serv. & Income: Credit	259.3	233.5	381.6	270.3	245.9	398.9	660.1	Serv. & revenu : crédit
Serv. & Income: Debit	−379.1	−268.3	−427.5	−279.8	−341.4	−446.6	−662.5	Serv. & revenu : débit
Current Trans.,nie: Credit	242.7	241.4	234.1	229.7	198.5	333.3	424.4	Transf. cour.,nia : crédit
Current Transfers: Debit	−110.3	−110.2	−127.0	−195.3	−136.0	−287.0	−332.2	Transf. courants : débit
Capital Acct.,nie: Credit	0.0	0.0	0.1	0.2	0.5	0.0	0.0	Compte de cap.,nia : crédit
Capital Account: Debit	0.0	0.0	0.0	−0.4	−0.1	0.0	−0.6	Compte de capital : débit
Financial Account, nie	139.7	48.0	16.7	−67.3	−54.4	−27.3	−110.2	Compte d'op. fin., nia
Net Errors and Omissions	4.1	13.4	51.7	67.7	−29.3	−133.0	−21.9	Erreurs et omissions nettes
Reserves & Related Items	−50.5	−26.3	6.5	56.5	25.8	44.1	18.5	Rés. et postes appareutés
Sweden								**Suède**
Goods: Exports fob	85 179.0	87 568.0	87 431.0	76 200.0	84 172.4	102 080.0	125 214.0	Biens : exportations, fab
Goods: Imports fob	−67 547.3	−71 854.2	−72 215.7	−62 368.4	−67 541.3	−83 147.0	−101 799.0	Biens : importations, fab
Serv. & Income: Credit	34 515.3	39 774.8	40 325.8	39 931.0	42 027.1	53 587.8	67 535.6	Serv. & revenu : crédit
Serv. & Income: Debit	−44 069.9	−45 907.3	−45 577.0	−43 805.3	−43 001.6	−51 408.1	−58 648.0	Serv. & revenu : débit
Current Trans.,nie: Credit	2 266.0	2 340.6	2 602.5	2 577.6	3 345.4	3 576.9	3 680.3	Transf. cour.,nia : crédit
Current Transfers: Debit	−5 703.7	−5 939.6	−5 950.1	−5 838.8	−6 217.7	−1 845.4	−8 497.9	Transf. courants : débit
Capital Acct.,nie: Credit	1 502.2	1 288.6	1 225.7	1 110.7	529.4	552.2	590.7	Compte de cap.,nia : crédit
Capital Account: Debit	−634.0	−3 431.9	−841.2	−601.2	−608.6	−598.7	−497.0	Compte de capital : débit
Financial Account, nie	5 960.7	−1 412.9	−3 296.6	1 824.2	−10 703.8	−20 163.3	−34 769.1	Compte d'op. fin., nia
Net Errors and Omissions	−8 214.5	−544.6	−3 533.9	−10 077.8	−1 336.3	−558.0	6 090.7	Erreurs et omissions nettes
Reserves & Related Items	−3 253.8	−1 881.4	−170.5	1 048.2	−665.0	−2 076.4	1 099.7	Rés. et postes appareutés

Country or area	1998	1999	2000	2001	2002	2003	2004	Pays ou zone
Switzerland								**Suisse**
Goods: Exports fob	93 781.7	91 787.0	94 810.0	95 897.3	100 786.0	115 443.0	138 225.0	Biens : exportations, fab
Goods: Imports fob	−92 848.7	−90 937.2	−92 738.8	−94 257.7	−94 139.2	−108 484.0	−122 487.0	Biens : importations, fab
Serv. & Income: Credit	72 775.8	79 358.0	91 379.7	81 387.6	72 109.9	98 757.7	114 943.9	Serv. & revenu : crédit
Serv. & Income: Debit	−43 939.5	−46 480.5	−55 869.0	−55 245.8	−48 385.2	−55 620.4	−64 430.2	Serv. & revenu : débit
Current Trans.,nie: Credit	2 647.0	7 539.0	6 539.6	9 699.3	10 598.6	13 161.7	14 169.5	Transf. cour.,nia : crédit
Current Transfers: Debit	−7 221.9	−12 688.3	−10 749.1	−14 937.5	−16 385.2	−18 552.1	−20 174.5	Transf. courants : débit
Capital Acct.,nie: Credit	754.9	52.5	489.6	2 313.9	273.9	492.1	336.4	Compte de cap.,nia : crédit
Capital Account: Debit	−616.1	−567.7	−4 030.7	−791.1	−1 433.1	−1 158.9	−1 745.4	Compte de capital : débit
Financial Account, nie	−31 161.5	−33 040.0	−30 136.6	−36 868.7	−22 832.0	−25 147.8	−66 342.2	Compte d'op. fin., nia
Net Errors and Omissions	7 007.8	2 292.2	−3 909.0	13 425.0	1 955.1	−15 486.1	9 123.2	Erreurs et omissions nettes
Reserves & Related Items	−1 179.2	2 685.1	4 214.1	−622.1	−2 548.9	−3 404.6	−1 618.2	Rés. et postes appareutés
Syrian Arab Republic								**Rép. arabe syrienne**
Goods: Exports fob	3 142.0	3 806.0	5 146.0	5 706.0	6 668.0	5 762.0	5 561.2	Biens : exportations, fab
Goods: Imports fob	−3 320.0	−3 590.0	−3 723.0	−4 282.0	−4 458.0	−4 430.0	−5 935.0	Biens : importations, fab
Serv. & Income: Credit	2 035.0	2 007.0	2 044.0	2 160.0	1 809.0	1 613.0	2 999.1	Serv. & revenu : crédit
Serv. & Income: Debit	−2 330.0	−2 511.0	−2 891.0	−2 856.0	−3 058.0	−2 945.0	−3 094.0	Serv. & revenu : débit
Current Trans.,nie: Credit	533.0	491.0	495.0	512.0	499.0	743.0	690.0	Transf. cour.,nia : crédit
Current Transfers: Debit	−2.0	−2.0	−10.0	−19.0	−20.0	−15.0	−16.0	Transf. courants : débit
Capital Acct.,nie: Credit	27.0	80.0	63.0	17.0	20.0	20.0	20.0	Compte de cap.,nia : crédit
Capital Account: Debit	0.0	0.0	0.0	0.0	0.0	0.0	−2.0	Compte de capital : débit
Financial Account, nie	196.0	173.0	−139.0	−244.0	−250.0	−138.0	−60.0	Compte d'op. fin., nia
Net Errors and Omissions	153.1	−195.0	−171.0	26.4	−160.4	85.0	253.8	Erreurs et omissions nettes
Reserves & Related Items	−434.1	−259.0	−814.0	−1 020.4	−1 049.6	−695.0	−417.1	Rés. et postes appareutés
Tajikistan								**Tadjikistan**
Goods: Exports fob	...	...	...	...	699.1	906.2	1 096.9	Biens : exportations, fab
Goods: Imports fob	...	...	...	...	−822.9	−1 025.7	−1 232.4	Biens : importations, fab
Serv. & Income: Credit	...	...	...	...	70.2	89.5	124.6	Serv. & revenu : crédit
Serv. & Income: Debit	...	...	...	...	−147.2	−192.8	−271.8	Serv. & revenu : débit
Current Trans.,nie: Credit	...	...	...	...	201.7	285.1	348.4	Transf. cour.,nia : crédit
Current Transfers: Debit	...	...	...	...	−16.1	−67.0	−122.8	Transf. courants : débit
Capital Acct.,nie: Credit	...	...	...	...	0.0	0.0	0.0	Compte de cap.,nia : crédit
Capital Account: Debit	...	...	...	...	0.0	0.0	0.0	Compte de capital : débit
Financial Account, nie	...	...	...	...	72.4	62.7	93.4	Compte d'op. fin., nia
Net Errors and Omissions	...	...	...	...	−55.6	−30.0	−32.5	Erreurs et omissions nettes
Reserves & Related Items	...	...	...	...	−1.7	−27.9	−3.9	Rés. et postes appareutés
Thailand								**Thaïlande**
Goods: Exports fob	52 752.9	56 775.1	67 893.6	63 082.3	66 089.0	78 083.3	94 978.5	Biens : exportations, fab
Goods: Imports fob	−36 514.9	−42 761.8	−56 193.0	−54 538.8	−57 008.2	−66 908.7	−84 395.8	Biens : importations, fab
Serv. & Income: Credit	16 479.3	17 726.9	18 103.1	16 857.7	18 746.7	18 813.5	22 159.5	Serv. & revenu : crédit
Serv. & Income: Debit	−18 889.1	−19 665.6	−21 076.5	−19 810.1	−21 416.6	−22 976.2	−28 258.0	Serv. & revenu : débit
Current Trans.,nie: Credit	819.8	805.6	951.6	990.0	978.4	1 325.7	2 479.3	Transf. cour.,nia : crédit
Current Transfers: Debit	−405.4	−452.5	−365.7	−389.2	−375.0	−384.8	−331.0	Transf. courants : débit
Capital Acct.,nie: Credit	0.0	0.0	0.0	0.0	0.0	0.0	0.0	Compte de cap.,nia : crédit
Capital Account: Debit	0.0	0.0	0.0	0.0	0.0	0.0	0.0	Compte de capital : débit
Financial Account, nie	−14 110.3	−11 073.0	−10 434.3	−3 657.7	−2 887.3	−7 626.3	−701.1	Compte d'op. fin., nia
Net Errors and Omissions	−2 828.2	33.4	−685.3	−258.4	1 409.7	191.4	−221.4	Erreurs et omissions nettes
Reserves & Related Items	2 696.0	−1 388.3	1 806.4	−2 275.7	−5 536.7	−517.9	−5 709.9	Rés. et postes appareutés
TFYR of Macedonia								**L'ex-R.y. Macédoine**
Goods: Exports fob	1 291.5	1 190.0	1 320.7	1 155.4	1 112.2	1 362.7	1 672.4	Biens : exportations, fab
Goods: Imports fob	−1 806.6	−1 685.8	−2 011.1	−1 681.8	−1 916.5	−2 210.6	−2 784.5	Biens : importations, fab
Serv. & Income: Credit	172.8	297.0	358.3	297.2	304.0	387.2	492.5	Serv. & revenu : crédit
Serv. & Income: Debit	−277.6	−297.4	−355.2	−357.1	−356.0	−428.9	−586.1	Serv. & revenu : débit
Current Trans.,nie: Credit	542.7	618.5	788.2	725.7	535.7	778.9	836.9	Transf. cour.,nia : crédit
Current Transfers: Debit	−192.5	−154.8	−173.3	−383.0	−37.2	−38.2	−46.0	Transf. courants : débit
Capital Acct.,nie: Credit	0.0	0.0	0.3	3.6	9.9	0.0	0.0	Compte de cap.,nia : crédit
Capital Account: Debit	−1.8	0.0	0.0	−2.3	−1.7	−6.7	−4.6	Compte de capital : débit
Financial Account, nie	329.9	14.2	290.3	325.7	257.2	237.0	439.6	Compte d'op. fin., nia
Net Errors and Omissions	−15.1	159.9	61.0	2.3	−29.7	−26.0	7.8	Erreurs et omissions nettes
Reserves & Related Items	−43.3	−141.7	−279.2	−85.6	122.1	−55.4	−28.0	Rés. et postes appareutés

Country or area	1998	1999	2000	2001	2002	2003	2004	Pays ou zone
Togo								**Togo**
Goods: Exports fob	420.3	391.5	361.8	357.2	424.2	597.7	...	Biens : exportations, fab
Goods: Imports fob	−553.5	−489.4	−484.6	−516.1	−575.6	−754.5	...	Biens : importations, fab
Serv. & Income: Credit	120.4	108.6	94.7	97.7	116.2	121.6	...	Serv. & revenu : crédit
Serv. & Income: Debit	−217.0	−209.1	−179.5	−185.1	−195.9	−254.4	...	Serv. & revenu : débit
Current Trans.,nie: Credit	101.8	73.6	73.3	88.3	113.0	161.4	...	Transf. cour.,nia : crédit
Current Transfers: Debit	−12.2	−2.2	−5.4	−11.1	−21.8	−33.8	...	Transf. courants : débit
Capital Acct.,nie: Credit	6.1	6.9	8.7	21.4	13.6	20.6	...	Compte de cap.,nia : crédit
Capital Account: Debit	0.0	0.0	0.0	0.0	0.0	0.0	...	Compte de capital : débit
Financial Account, nie	114.1	155.5	162.8	151.2	150.8	142.9	...	Compte d'op. fin., nia
Net Errors and Omissions	2.7	−3.7	5.0	−5.4	5.0	−10.2	...	Erreurs et omissions nettes
Reserves & Related Items	17.2	−31.6	−36.8	2.0	−29.6	8.6	...	Rés. et postes appareutés
Tonga								**Tonga**
Goods: Exports fob	...	...	...	6.7	18.1	...	...	Biens : exportations, fab
Goods: Imports fob	...	...	...	−63.7	−73.4	...	...	Biens : importations, fab
Serv. & Income: Credit	...	...	...	25.3	29.2	...	...	Serv. & revenu : crédit
Serv. & Income: Debit	...	...	...	−29.8	−35.7	...	...	Serv. & revenu : débit
Current Trans.,nie: Credit	...	...	...	62.5	74.5	...	...	Transf. cour.,nia : crédit
Current Transfers: Debit	...	...	...	−11.7	−16.1	...	...	Transf. courants : débit
Capital Acct.,nie: Credit	...	...	...	11.7	14.1	...	...	Compte de cap.,nia : crédit
Capital Account: Debit	...	...	...	−2.1	−0.7	...	...	Compte de capital : débit
Financial Account, nie	...	...	...	0.8	−3.2	...	...	Compte d'op. fin., nia
Net Errors and Omissions	...	...	...	2.1	0.0	...	...	Erreurs et omissions nettes
Reserves & Related Items	...	...	...	−1.7	−6.9	...	...	Rés. et postes appareutés
Trinidad and Tobago								**Trinité-et-Tobago**
Goods: Exports fob	2 258.0	2 815.8	4 290.3	4 304.2	3 920.0	5 204.9	...	Biens : exportations, fab
Goods: Imports fob	−2 998.9	−2 752.2	−3 321.5	−3 586.1	−3 682.3	−3 911.7	...	Biens : importations, fab
Serv. & Income: Credit	735.8	671.5	634.7	682.5	700.7	763.4	...	Serv. & revenu : crédit
Serv. & Income: Debit	−660.7	−742.2	−1 097.1	−1 018.0	−916.5	−1 130.5	...	Serv. & revenu : débit
Current Trans.,nie: Credit	58.4	68.9	63.9	64.0	96.2	100.8	...	Transf. cour.,nia : crédit
Current Transfers: Debit	−36.2	−31.2	−26.0	−30.6	−41.7	−42.2	...	Transf. courants : débit
Capital Acct.,nie: Credit	0.0	0.0	0.0	0.0	0.0	0.0	...	Compte de cap.,nia : crédit
Capital Account: Debit	0.0	0.0	0.0	0.0	0.0	0.0	...	Compte de capital : débit
Financial Account, nie	471.5	38.3	173.7	321.5	397.3	34.4	...	Compte d'op. fin., nia
Net Errors and Omissions	252.2	93.2	−276.9	−235.3	−358.0	−610.3	...	Erreurs et omissions nettes
Reserves & Related Items	−80.2	−162.1	−441.1	−502.2	−115.7	−408.8	...	Rés. et postes appareutés
Tunisia								**Tunisie**
Goods: Exports fob	5 724.0	5 873.3	5 840.2	6 628.2	6 857.1	8 027.4	9 679.1	Biens : exportations, fab
Goods: Imports fob	−7 875.5	−8 014.5	−8 093.0	−8 996.9	−8 980.6	−10 296.8	−12 113.5	Biens : importations, fab
Serv. & Income: Credit	2 847.9	3 009.5	2 860.6	3 006.9	2 753.0	3 017.6	3 743.2	Serv. & revenu : crédit
Serv. & Income: Debit	−2 203.3	−2 212.1	−2 254.4	−2 460.5	−2 506.1	−2 785.5	−3 397.1	Serv. & revenu : débit
Current Trans.,nie: Credit	851.8	919.7	854.3	1 016.2	1 155.6	1 342.7	1 564.1	Transf. cour.,nia : crédit
Current Transfers: Debit	−20.2	−17.7	−29.2	−34.1	−24.6	−35.7	−30.5	Transf. courants : débit
Capital Acct.,nie: Credit	82.5	72.5	8.8	55.6	83.0	66.0	113.2	Compte de cap.,nia : crédit
Capital Account: Debit	−22.0	−13.5	−5.8	−2.8	−7.7	−7.0	−5.6	Compte de capital : débit
Financial Account, nie	489.1	1 083.3	646.4	1 062.8	856.7	1 109.9	1 456.5	Compte d'op. fin., nia
Net Errors and Omissions	−12.0	37.6	−32.8	13.1	−46.4	−56.0	−32.0	Erreurs et omissions nettes
Reserves & Related Items	137.6	−738.1	205.0	−288.4	−140.0	−382.6	−977.3	Rés. et postes appareutés
Turkey								**Turquie**
Goods: Exports fob	30 662.0	28 842.0	30 721.0	34 373.0	40 124.0	51 206.0	67 001.0	Biens : exportations, fab
Goods: Imports fob	−44 714.0	−39 027.0	−52 680.0	−38 106.0	−47 407.0	−65 216.0	−90 925.0	Biens : importations, fab
Serv. & Income: Credit	26 360.0	19 231.0	23 265.0	18 812.0	17 288.0	21 332.0	26 698.0	Serv. & revenu : crédit
Serv. & Income: Debit	−15 839.0	−15 281.0	−15 899.0	−14 682.0	−13 962.0	−16 386.0	−19 444.0	Serv. & revenu : débit
Current Trans.,nie: Credit	5 649.0	5 011.0	4 866.0	3 051.0	2 482.0	1 088.0	1 165.0	Transf. cour.,nia : crédit
Current Transfers: Debit	−134.0	−120.0	−92.0	−58.0	−46.0	−61.0	−38.0	Transf. courants : débit
Capital Acct.,nie: Credit	0.0	0.0	0.0	0.0	0.0	0.0	0.0	Compte de cap.,nia : crédit
Capital Account: Debit	0.0	0.0	0.0	0.0	0.0	0.0	0.0	Compte de capital : débit
Financial Account, nie	−840.0	4 979.0	8 584.0	−14 644.0	1 159.0	7 098.0	17 039.0	Compte d'op. fin., nia
Net Errors and Omissions	−703.1	1 719.5	−2 698.5	−1 633.5	148.4	5 026.1	2 811.7	Erreurs et omissions nettes
Reserves & Related Items	−440.9	−5 354.5	3 933.5	12 887.5	213.6	−4 087.1	−4 307.7	Rés. et postes appareutés

Country or area	1998	1999	2000	2001	2002	2003	2004	Pays ou zone
Uganda								**Ouganda**
Goods: Exports fob	510.2	483.5	449.9	475.6	480.7	563.0	705.3	Biens : exportations, fab
Goods: Imports fob	−1 166.3	−989.1	−949.7	−975.4	−1 054.5	−1 240.9	−1 458.9	Biens : importations, fab
Serv. & Income: Credit	227.0	231.1	266.3	260.1	257.0	322.0	483.0	Serv. & revenu : crédit
Serv. & Income: Debit	−788.0	−581.7	−624.3	−706.4	−691.3	−694.3	−903.4	Serv. & revenu : débit
Current Trans.,nie: Credit	714.6	329.7	340.0	882.8	1 015.3	893.9	1 150.7	Transf. cour.,nia : crédit
Current Transfers: Debit	0.0	−184.2	−307.6	−304.2	−367.1	−195.9	−176.5	Transf. courants : débit
Capital Acct.,nie: Credit	49.5	0.0	0.0	0.0	0.0	0.0	0.0	Compte de cap.,nia : crédit
Capital Account: Debit	0.0	0.0	0.0	0.0	0.0	0.0	0.0	Compte de capital : débit
Financial Account, nie	372.8	253.3	320.5	441.7	177.8	359.3	326.8	Compte d'op. fin., nia
Net Errors and Omissions	39.7	2.0	40.6	17.0	7.1	−9.9	−4.4	Erreurs et omissions nettes
Reserves & Related Items	40.6	455.4	464.3	−91.0	175.1	2.8	−122.5	Rés. et postes appareutés
Ukraine								**Ukraine**
Goods: Exports fob	13 699.0	13 189.0	15 722.0	17 091.0	18 669.0	23 739.0	33 432.0	Biens : exportations, fab
Goods: Imports fob	−16 283.0	−12 945.0	−14 943.0	−16 893.0	−17 959.0	−23 221.0	−29 691.0	Biens : importations, fab
Serv. & Income: Credit	4 044.0	3 967.0	3 943.0	4 162.0	4 847.0	5 468.0	6 676.0	Serv. & revenu : crédit
Serv. & Income: Debit	−3 538.0	−3 259.0	−4 089.0	−4 414.0	−4 304.0	−5 279.0	−6 189.0	Serv. & revenu : débit
Current Trans.,nie: Credit	868.0	754.0	967.0	1 516.0	1 967.0	2 270.0	2 671.0	Transf. cour.,nia : crédit
Current Transfers: Debit	−86.0	−48.0	−119.0	−60.0	−46.0	−86.0	−95.0	Transf. courants : débit
Capital Acct.,nie: Credit	0.0	0.0	0.0	8.0	28.0	11.0	21.0	Compte de cap.,nia : crédit
Capital Account: Debit	−3.0	−10.0	−8.0	−5.0	−11.0	−28.0	−14.0	Compte de capital : débit
Financial Account, nie	−1 340.0	−879.0	−752.0	−191.0	−1 065.0	264.0	−4 234.0	Compte d'op. fin., nia
Net Errors and Omissions	−817.9	−953.1	−148.2	−220.8	−895.5	−965.4	−53.7	Erreurs et omissions nettes
Reserves & Related Items	3 456.9	184.1	−572.8	−993.2	−1 230.5	−2 172.6	−2 523.3	Rés. et postes appareutés
United Kingdom								**Royaume-Uni**
Goods: Exports fob	271 723.0	268 884.0	284 378.0	273 661.0	279 846.0	308 272.0	349 759.0	Biens : exportations, fab
Goods: Imports fob	−307 851.0	−315 896.0	−334 228.0	−332 138.0	−350 689.0	−386 514.0	−460 361.0	Biens : importations, fab
Serv. & Income: Credit	282 990.0	280 777.0	323 810.0	321 972.0	320 493.0	359 164.0	448 947.0	Serv. & revenu : crédit
Serv. & Income: Debit	−239 614.2	−261 100.9	−295 930.2	−285 827.0	−261 351.0	−290 895.0	−360 604.0	Serv. & revenu : débit
Current Trans.,nie: Credit	20 470.8	21 656.0	16 422.9	21 008.3	19 122.4	20 218.1	23 008.7	Transf. cour.,nia : crédit
Current Transfers: Debit	−34 348.9	−33 609.2	−31 136.9	−30 522.8	−31 990.5	−36 437.3	−43 045.3	Transf. courants : débit
Capital Acct.,nie: Credit	2 506.6	2 632.3	3 942.6	4 792.8	3 507.2	4 591.5	6 596.0	Compte de cap.,nia : crédit
Capital Account: Debit	−1 647.2	−1 385.0	−1 633.5	−3 064.6	−2 183.2	−2 445.7	−3 143.2	Compte de capital : débit
Financial Account, nie	16 934.9	34 857.3	26 050.9	23 229.6	13 291.2	46 081.8	28 124.0	Compte d'op. fin., nia
Net Errors and Omissions	−11 421.2	2 148.2	13 624.7	2 432.6	9 320.0	−24 627.4	11 125.6	Erreurs et omissions nettes
Reserves & Related Items	257.0	1 035.9	−5 300.4	4 456.5	634.7	2 591.9	−406.8	Rés. et postes appareutés
United Rep. of Tanzania								**Rép.-Unie de Tanzanie**
Goods: Exports fob	589.5	543.3	663.3	811.7	911.6	1 156.6	1 278.1	Biens : exportations, fab
Goods: Imports fob	−1 365.3	−1 415.4	−1 367.6	−1 631.4	−1 526.5	−1 980.4	−2 184.1	Biens : importations, fab
Serv. & Income: Credit	590.0	643.4	677.7	768.0	743.9	796.8	979.6	Serv. & revenu : crédit
Serv. & Income: Debit	−1 124.9	−943.2	−862.8	−818.2	−766.8	−926.6	−1 129.2	Serv. & revenu : débit
Current Trans.,nie: Credit	426.6	445.6	463.3	496.4	482.8	624.7	680.8	Transf. cour.,nia : crédit
Current Transfers: Debit	−35.5	−109.0	−72.9	−83.1	−61.9	−64.5	−62.3	Transf. courants : débit
Capital Acct.,nie: Credit	422.9	347.8	420.4	1 049.3	793.6	709.5	385.4	Compte de cap.,nia : crédit
Capital Account: Debit	0.0	0.0	0.0	0.0	0.0	0.0	0.0	Compte de capital : débit
Financial Account, nie	77.6	565.2	492.6	−1 365.2	−917.7	−25.1	218.5	Compte d'op. fin., nia
Net Errors and Omissions	−90.3	−156.7	−415.7	721.5	668.1	103.7	33.4	Erreurs et omissions nettes
Reserves & Related Items	509.4	79.0	1.3	50.9	−327.0	−394.7	−200.2	Rés. et postes appareutés
United States								**Etats-Unis**
Goods: Exports fob	672 377.0	686 271.0	774 632.0	721 842.0	685 933.0	716 710.0	811 030.0	Biens : exportations, fab
Goods: Imports fob	−917 113.0	−1 029 990.0	−1 224 420.0	−1 145 930.0	−1 164 740.0	−1 260 750.0	−1 472 960.0	Biens : importations, fab
Serv. & Income: Credit	522 953.0	574 095.0	647 771.0	573 600.0	562 136.0	615 686.0	719 945.0	Serv. & revenu : crédit
Serv. & Income: Debit	−438 936.0	−479 907.0	−555 202.0	−487 061.0	−494 490.0	−520 152.0	−645 159.0	Serv. & revenu : débit
Current Trans.,nie: Credit	9 635.8	8 881.2	10 827.9	8 526.2	11 987.3	14 693.8	17 919.7	Transf. cour.,nia : crédit
Current Transfers: Debit	−62 953.9	−59 435.7	−69 608.2	−60 435.3	−76 033.2	−85 863.4	−98 850.5	Transf. courants : débit
Capital Acct.,nie: Credit	933.0	1 085.0	1 077.0	1 041.0	1 074.0	1 102.0	1 126.0	Compte de cap.,nia : crédit
Capital Account: Debit	−1 635.0	−5 973.0	−2 006.0	−2 265.0	−2 437.0	−4 316.0	−2 775.0	Compte de capital : débit
Financial Account, nie	76 511.7	227 399.0	486 663.0	405 152.0	503 999.0	559 122.0	581 789.0	Compte d'op. fin., nia
Net Errors and Omissions	144 959.0	68 843.7	−69 442.7	−9 546.7	−23 734.8	−37 757.2	85 130.1	Erreurs et omissions nettes
Reserves & Related Items	−6 731.3	8 727.0	−294.9	−4 926.7	−3 692.5	1 529.4	2 804.0	Rés. et postes appareutés

Country or area	1998	1999	2000	2001	2002	2003	2004	Pays ou zone
Uruguay								**Uruguay**
Goods: Exports fob	2 829.3	2 290.6	2 383.8	2 139.4	1 922.1	2 281.1	3 021.3	Biens : exportations, fab
Goods: Imports fob	−3 601.4	−3 187.2	−3 311.1	−2 914.7	−1 873.8	−2 097.8	−2 990.2	Biens : importations, fab
Serv. & Income: Credit	1 927.1	1 997.1	2 057.2	1 954.5	1 207.1	1 044.5	1 343.8	Serv. & revenu : crédit
Serv. & Income: Debit	−1 689.5	−1 681.6	−1 723.6	−1 696.6	−1 005.4	−1 365.9	−1 567.0	Serv. & revenu : débit
Current Trans.,nie: Credit	75.0	78.4	48.0	48.0	83.7	94.9	97.8	Transf. cour.,nia : crédit
Current Transfers: Debit	−16.0	−4.9	−20.5	−18.3	−11.5	−12.3	−8.6	Transf. courants : débit
Capital Acct.,nie: Credit	0.0	0.0	0.0	0.0	0.0	0.0	0.0	Compte de cap.,nia : crédit
Capital Account: Debit	0.0	0.0	0.0	0.0	0.0	0.0	0.0	Compte de capital : débit
Financial Account, nie	545.1	147.1	779.3	457.3	−1 927.5	4.2	−39.4	Compte d'op. fin., nia
Net Errors and Omissions	285.5	250.9	−46.6	334.4	−2 291.8	1 009.3	446.7	Erreurs et omissions nettes
Reserves & Related Items	−355.1	109.6	−166.5	−304.0	3 897.1	−957.9	−304.4	Rés. et postes appareutés
Vanuatu								**Vanuatu**
Goods: Exports fob	33.8	25.7	27.2	19.9	20.2	26.8	...	Biens : exportations, fab
Goods: Imports fob	−76.2	−84.5	−76.9	−78.0	−78.4	−91.8	...	Biens : importations, fab
Serv. & Income: Credit	134.9	135.8	148.5	136.5	103.8	119.0	...	Serv. & revenu : crédit
Serv. & Income: Debit	−86.2	−98.2	−101.9	−94.2	−73.9	−90.2	...	Serv. & revenu : débit
Current Trans.,nie: Credit	15.6	18.7	27.4	39.5	5.9	4.8	...	Transf. cour.,nia : crédit
Current Transfers: Debit	−31.2	−30.8	−38.0	−38.3	−8.8	−9.9	...	Transf. courants : débit
Capital Acct.,nie: Credit	25.4	23.9	31.9	46.1	10.6	10.4	...	Compte de cap.,nia : crédit
Capital Account: Debit	−46.3	−73.7	−55.5	−62.1	−12.9	−15.1	...	Compte de capital : débit
Financial Account, nie	17.4	56.2	19.3	12.8	20.7	39.6	...	Compte d'op. fin., nia
Net Errors and Omissions	6.0	3.6	−0.9	7.5	−5.6	−5.0	...	Erreurs et omissions nettes
Reserves & Related Items	6.9	23.2	18.8	10.3	18.4	11.3	...	Rés. et postes appareutés
Venezuela (Bolivarian Rep. of)								**Venezuela (Rép. Bolivar. du)**
Goods: Exports fob	17 707.0	20 963.0	33 529.0	26 667.0	26 781.0	27 170.0	38 748.0	Biens : exportations, fab
Goods: Imports fob	−16 755.0	−14 492.0	−16 865.0	−19 211.0	−13 360.0	−10 687.0	−17 318.0	Biens : importations, fab
Serv. & Income: Credit	3 902.0	3 624.0	4 231.0	3 979.0	2 487.0	2 607.0	2 662.0	Serv. & revenu : crédit
Serv. & Income: Debit	−9 085.0	−7 916.0	−8 872.0	−9 304.0	−8 152.0	−7 662.0	−10 173.0	Serv. & revenu : débit
Current Trans.,nie: Credit	169.0	203.0	261.0	356.0	288.0	257.0	180.0	Transf. cour.,nia : crédit
Current Transfers: Debit	−370.0	−270.0	−431.0	−504.0	−445.0	−237.0	−269.0	Transf. courants : débit
Capital Acct.,nie: Credit	0.0	0.0	0.0	0.0	0.0	0.0	0.0	Compte de cap.,nia : crédit
Capital Account: Debit	0.0	0.0	0.0	0.0	0.0	0.0	0.0	Compte de capital : débit
Financial Account, nie	2 689.0	−516.0	−2 969.0	−211.0	−9 246.0	−4 942.0	−8 716.0	Compte d'op. fin., nia
Net Errors and Omissions	−1 662.3	−538.0	−2 926.2	−3 601.4	−2 781.3	−1 052.0	−2 959.2	Erreurs et omissions nettes
Reserves & Related Items	3 405.3	−1 058.0	−5 957.8	1 829.4	4 428.3	−5 454.0	−2 154.8	Rés. et postes appareutés
Viet Nam								**Viet Nam**
Goods: Exports fob	9 361.0	11 540.0	14 448.0	15 027.0	16 706.0	...	...	Biens : exportations, fab
Goods: Imports fob	−10 350.0	−10 568.0	−14 073.0	−14 546.0	−17 760.0	...	...	Biens : importations, fab
Serv. & Income: Credit	2 743.0	2 635.0	3 033.0	3 128.0	3 115.0	...	...	Serv. & revenu : crédit
Serv. & Income: Debit	−3 950.0	−3 611.0	−4 034.0	−4 177.0	−4 586.0	...	...	Serv. & revenu : débit
Current Trans.,nie: Credit	1 122.0	1 181.0	1 732.0	1 250.0	1 921.0	...	...	Transf. cour.,nia : crédit
Current Transfers: Debit	0.0	0.0	0.0	0.0	0.0	...	...	Transf. courants : débit
Capital Acct.,nie: Credit	0.0	0.0	0.0	0.0	0.0	...	...	Compte de cap.,nia : crédit
Capital Account: Debit	0.0	0.0	0.0	0.0	0.0	...	...	Compte de capital : débit
Financial Account, nie	1 646.0	1 058.0	−316.0	371.0	2 090.0	...	...	Compte d'op. fin., nia
Net Errors and Omissions	−534.9	−925.0	−680.1	−846.7	−1 037.7	...	...	Erreurs et omissions nettes
Reserves & Related Items	−37.1	−1 310.0	−109.9	−206.3	−448.3	...	...	Rés. et postes appareutés
Yemen								**Yémen**
Goods: Exports fob	1 503.7	2 478.3	3 797.2	3 366.9	3 620.7	3 934.3	4 675.7	Biens : exportations, fab
Goods: Imports fob	−2 288.8	−2 120.5	−2 484.4	−2 600.4	−2 932.0	−3 557.4	−3 858.6	Biens : importations, fab
Serv. & Income: Credit	243.4	239.9	360.5	344.9	301.1	416.6	473.3	Serv. & revenu : crédit
Serv. & Income: Debit	−1 106.3	−1 471.0	−1 736.2	−1 717.2	−1 835.4	−2 011.9	−2 509.5	Serv. & revenu : débit
Current Trans.,nie: Credit	1 223.5	1 262.1	1 471.9	1 344.4	1 456.9	1 442.1	1 493.1	Transf. cour.,nia : crédit
Current Transfers: Debit	−47.7	−30.7	−72.4	−71.4	−73.1	−75.0	−49.4	Transf. courants : débit
Capital Acct.,nie: Credit	2.2	1.5	338.9	49.5	0.0	5.5	163.3	Compte de cap.,nia : crédit
Capital Account: Debit	0.0	0.0	0.0	0.0	0.0	0.0	0.0	Compte de capital : débit
Financial Account, nie	−418.0	−415.1	−376.2	−53.5	−156.8	19.7	−68.6	Compte d'op. fin., nia
Net Errors and Omissions	307.0	129.4	295.1	−110.0	43.3	156.4	53.3	Erreurs et omissions nettes
Reserves & Related Items	580.9	−74.0	−1 594.4	−553.2	−424.7	−330.3	−372.5	Rés. et postes appareutés

71

Summary of balance of payments—Millions of US dollars (*continued*)
Résumé des balances des paiements—Millions de dollars des E.-U. (*suite*)

Country or area	1998	1999	2000	2001	2002	2003	2004	Pays ou zone
Zambia								**Zambie**
Goods: Exports fob	818.0	772.0	757.0	...	...	...	...	Biens : exportations, fab
Goods: Imports fob	−971.0	−870.0	−978.0	...	...	...	...	Biens : importations, fab
Serv. & Income: Credit	146.3	150.5	160.6	...	...	...	...	Serv. & revenu : crédit
Serv. & Income: Debit	−539.7	−483.4	−505.9	...	...	...	...	Serv. & revenu : débit
Current Trans.,nie: Credit	0.0	0.0	0.0	...	...	...	...	Transf. cour.,nia : crédit
Current Transfers: Debit	−27.0	−16.0	−18.0	...	...	...	...	Transf. courants : débit
Capital Acct.,nie: Credit	203.0	196.0	153.0	...	...	...	...	Compte de cap.,nia : crédit
Capital Account: Debit	0.0	0.0	0.0	...	...	...	...	Compte de capital : débit
Financial Account, nie	−263.7	−173.9	−273.6	...	...	...	...	Compte d'op. fin., nia
Net Errors and Omissions	−37.4	−229.4	184.8	...	...	...	...	Erreurs et omissions nettes
Reserves & Related Items	671.4	654.2	520.2	...	...	...	...	Rés. et postes appareutés

Source

International Monetary Fund (IMF), Washington, D.C., *International Financial Statistics*, March 2006 and the IMF database.

Notes

1   BLEU trade data refer to the Belgium-Luxembourg Economic Union and exclude transactions between the two countries. Beginning in 1997, trade data are for Belgium only, which includes trade between Belgium and Luxembourg.

2   For statistical purposes, the data for China do not include those for the Hong Kong Special Administrative Region (Hong Kong SAR), Macao Special Administrative Region (Macao SAR) and Taiwan Province of China.

3   Services only.

Source

Fonds monétaire international (FMI), Washington, D.C., *Statistiques Financières Internationales*, mars 2006 et la base de données du FMI.

Notes

1   Les données sur le commerce extérieur se rapportent à l'Union économique belgo-luxembourgeoise (UEBL) et ne couvrent pas les transactions entre les deux pays. A compter de 1997, les données sur le commerce extérieur ne se rapportent qu'à la Belgique, et recouvrent les échanges entre la Belgique et le Luxembourg.

2   Pour la présentation des statistiques, les données pour Chine ne comprennent pas la Région Administrative Spéciale de Hong Kong (Hong Kong RAS), la Région Administrative Spéciale de Macao (Macao RAS) et la province de Taiwan.

3   Service seulement.

A balance of payments can be broadly described as the record of an economy's international economic transactions. It shows (a) transactions in goods, services and income between an economy and the rest of the world, (b) changes of ownership and other changes in that economy's monetary gold, special drawing rights (SDRs) and claims on and liabilities to the rest of the world, and (c) unrequited transfers and counterpart entries needed to balance in the accounting sense any entries for the foregoing transactions and changes which are not mutually offsetting.

The balance of payments are presented on the basis of the methodology and presentation of the fifth edition of the *Balance of Payments Manual* (BPM5) [39], published by the International Monetary Fund in September 1993. The BPM5 incorporates several major changes to take account of developments in international trade and finance over the past decade, and to better harmonize the Fund's balance of payments methodology with the methodology of the 1993 *System of National Accounts* (SNA) [56]. The Fund's balance of payments has been converted for all periods from the BPM4 basis to the BPM5 basis; thus the time series conform to the BPM5 methodology with no methodological breaks.

The detailed definitions concerning the content of the basic categories of the balance of payments are given in the *Balance of Payments Manual* (fifth edition) [39]. Brief explanatory notes are given below to clarify the scope of the major items.

Goods: Exports f.o.b. and Goods: Imports f.o.b. are both measured on the "free-on-board" (f.o.b.) basis—that is, by the value of the goods at the border of the exporting country; in the case of imports, this excludes the cost of freight and insurance incurred beyond the border of the exporting country.

Services and income covers transactions in real resources between residents and non residents other than those classified as merchandise, including (a) shipment and other transportation services, including freight, insurance and other distributive services in connection with the movement of commodities, (b) travel, i.e. goods and services acquired by non resident travellers in a given country and similar acquisitions by resident travellers abroad, and (c) investment income which covers income of non residents from their financial assets invested in the compiling economy (debit) and similar income of residents from their financial assets invested abroad (credit).

Current Transfers, n.i.e.: Credit comprises all current transfers received by the reporting country, except those made to the country to finance its "overall balance", hence, the label "n.i.e." (not included elsewhere). (Note: some of the capital and financial accounts labelled "n.i.e." denote that *Exceptional Financing items and Liabilities Constituting Foreign Authorities' Reserves* (LCFARs) have been excluded.)

La balance des paiements peut se définir d'une façon générale comme le relevé des transactions économiques internationales d'une économie. Elle indique a) les transactions sur biens, services et revenus entre une économie et le reste du monde, b) les transferts de propriété et autres variations intervenues au niveau des avoirs en or monétaire de cette économie, de ses avoirs en droits de tirages spéciaux (DTS) ainsi que de ses créances financières sur le reste du monde ou de ses engagements financiers envers lui et c) les "inscriptions de transferts sans contrepartie" et de "contrepartie" destinées à équilibrer, d'un point de vue comptable, les transactions et changements précités qui ne se compensent pas réciproquement.

Les données de balance des paiements sont présentées conformément à la méthodologie et à la classification recommandées dans la cinquième édition du *Manuel de la balance des paiements* [39], publiée en septembre 1993 par le Fonds monétaire international. La cinquième édition fait état de plusieurs changements importants qui ont été opérés de manière à rendre compte de l'évolution des finances et des changes internationaux pendant la décennie écoulée et à harmoniser davantage la méthodologie de la balance des paiements du FMI avec celle du *Système de comptabilité nationale* (SCN) [56] de 1993. Les statistiques incluses dans la balance des paiements du FMI ont été converties et sont désormais établies, pour toutes les périodes, sur la base de la cinquième et non plus de la quatrième édition; en conséquence, les séries chronologiques sont conformes aux principes de la cinquième édition, sans rupture due à des différences d'ordre méthodologique.

Les définitions détaillées relatives au contenu des postes fondamentaux de la balance des paiements figurent dans le *Manuel de la balance des paiements* (cinquième édition) [39]. De brèves notes explicatives sont présentées ci-après pour clarifier la portée de ces principales rubriques.

Les Biens : exportations, f.à.b. et Biens : importations, f.à.b. sont évalués sur la base f.à.b. (franco à bord) —c'est-à-dire à la frontière du pays exportateur; dans le cas des importations, cette valeur exclut le coût du fret et de l'assurance au-delà de la frontière du pays exportateur.

Services et revenus : transactions en ressources effectuées entre résidents et non résidents, autres que celles qui sont considérées comme des marchandises, notamment : a) expéditions et autres services de transport, y compris le fret, l'assurance et les autres services de distribution liés aux mouvements de marchandises; b) voyages, à savoir les biens et services acquis par des voyageurs non résidents dans un pays donné et achats similaires faits par des résidents voyageant à l'étranger; et c) revenus des investissements, qui correspondent aux revenus que les non résidents tirent de leurs avoirs financiers placés dans l'économie déclarante

Capital Account, n.i.e.: Credit refers mainly to capital transfers linked to the acquisition of a fixed asset other than transactions relating to debt forgiveness plus the disposal of nonproduced, nonfinancial assets. *Capital Account: Debit* refers mainly to capital transfers linked to the disposal of fixed assets by the donor or to the financing of capital formation by the recipient, plus the acquisition of nonproduced, nonfinancial assets.

Financial Account, n.i.e. is the net sum of the balance of direct investment, portfolio investment, and other investment transactions.

Net Errors and Omissions is a residual category needed to ensure that all debit and credit entries in the balance of payments statement sum to zero and reflects statistical inconsistencies in the recording of the credit and debit entries.

Reserves and Related Items is the sum of transactions in reserve assets, LCFARs, exceptional financing, and use of Fund credit and loans.

For further information see *International Financial Statistics* [13] and www.imf.org.

(débit) et les revenus similaires que les résidents tirent de leurs avoirs financiers placés à l'étranger (crédit).

Les transferts courants, n.i.a : Crédit englobent tous les transferts courants reçus par l'économie qui établit sa balance des paiements, à l'exception de ceux qui sont destinés à financer sa "balance globale"—c'est ce qui explique la mention "n.i.a." (non inclus ailleurs). (Note : comptes de capital et d'opérations financières portent la mention "n.i.a.", ce qui signifie que les postes de *Financement exceptionnel et les Engagements constituant des réserves pour les autorités étrangères* ont été exclus de ces composantes du compte de capital et d'opérations financières.

Le Compte de capital, n.i.a. : crédit retrace principalement les transferts de capital liés à l'acquisition d'un actif fixe autres que les transactions ayant trait à des remises de dettes plus les cessions d'actifs non financiers non produits. Le *Compte de capital débit* retrace principalement les transferts de capital liés à la cession d'actifs fixes par le donateur ou au financement de la formation de capital par le bénéficiaire, plus les acquisitions d'actifs non financiers non produits.

Le solde du Compte d'op. Fin., n.i.a. (compte d'opérations financières, n.i.a.) est la somme des soldes des investissements directs, des investissements de portefeuille et des autres investissements.

Le poste des Erreurs et omissions nettes est une catégorie résiduelle qui est nécessaire pour assurer que la somme de toutes les inscriptions effectuées au débit et au crédit est égal à zéro et qui laisse apparaître les écarts entre les montants portés au débit et ceux qui sont inscrits au crédit.

Le montant de Réserves et postes apparentés est égal à la somme de transactions afférentes aux avoirs de réserve, aux engagements constituant des réserves pour les autorités étrangères, au financement exceptionnel et à l'utilisation des crédits et des prêts du FMI.

Pour plus de renseignements, voir *Statistiques financières internationales* [13] et www.imf.org.

Exchange rates
National currency per US dollar

Cours des changes
Valeur du dollar des États-Unis en monnaie nationale

Country or area — Pays ou zone	1996	1997	1998	1999	2000	2001	2002	2003	2004	2005
Afghanistan [1,2] (afghani) — Afghanistan [1,2] (afghani)										
End of period Fin de période	3.000	3.000	3.000	46.791	...	47.259	44.875	48.865	48.220	...
Period average Moyenne sur période	2.500	3.000	3.000	45.106	61.629	65.690	41.459	48.773	47.845	...
Albania (lek) — Albanie (lek)										
End of period Fin de période	103.070	149.140	140.580	135.120	142.640	136.550	133.740	106.580	92.640	...
Period average Moyenne sur période	104.499	148.933	150.633	137.691	143.709	143.485	140.155	121.863	102.780	...
Algeria (Algerian dinar) — Algérie (dinar algérien)										
End of period Fin de période	56.186	58.414	60.353	69.314	75.343	77.820	79.723	72.613	72.614	73.380
Period average Moyenne sur période	54.749	57.707	58.739	66.574	75.260	77.215	79.682	77.395	72.061	73.276
Angola (readjusted kwanza) — Angola (réajusté kwanza)										
End of period Fin de période	0.202	0.262	0.697	5.580	16.818	31.949	58.666	79.082	85.988	...
Period average Moyenne sur période	0.128	0.229	0.393	2.791	10.041	22.058	43.530	74.606	83.541	...
Anguilla (EC dollar) — Anguilla (dollar des Caraïbes orientales)										
End of period Fin de période	2.700	2.700	2.700	2.700	2.700	2.700	2.700	2.700	2.700	2.700
Antigua and Barbuda (EC dollar) — Antigua-et-Barbuda (dollar des Caraïbes orientales)										
End of period Fin de période	2.700	2.700	2.700	2.700	2.700	2.700	2.700	2.700	2.700	2.700
Argentina [3] (Argentine peso) — Argentine [3] (peso argentin)										
End of period Fin de période	1.000	1.000	1.000	1.000	1.000	1.000	3.320	2.905	2.959	3.012
Period average Moyenne sur période	1.000	1.000	1.000	1.000	1.000	1.000	3.063	2.901	2.923	2.904
Armenia (dram) — Arménie (dram)										
End of period Fin de période	435.070	494.980	522.030	523.770	552.180	561.810	584.890	566.000	485.840	450.190
Period average Moyenne sur période	414.042	490.847	504.915	535.062	539.526	555.078	573.353	578.763	533.451	457.687
Aruba (Aruban florin) — Aruba (florin de Aruba)										
End of period Fin de période	1.790	1.790	1.790	1.790	1.790	1.790	1.790	1.790	1.790	1.790
Australia (Australian dollar) — Australie (dollar australien)										
End of period Fin de période	1.256	1.532	1.629	1.530	1.805	1.959	1.766	1.333	1.284	1.363
Period average Moyenne sur période	1.278	1.347	1.592	1.550	1.725	1.933	1.841	1.542	1.360	1.310
Austria [4] (Austrian schilling, euro) — Autriche [4] (schilling autrichien, euro)										
End of period Fin de période	10.954	12.633	11.747	...	...	...	...	...	...	...
Period average Moyenne sur période	10.587	12.204	12.379	...	...	...	...	...	...	...
Azerbaijan [5] (manat) — Azerbaïdjan [5] (manat)										
End of period Fin de période	0.820	0.778	0.778	0.876	0.913	0.955	0.979	0.985	0.981	0.919
Period average Moyenne sur période	0.860	0.797	0.774	0.824	0.895	0.931	0.972	0.982	0.983	0.945
Bahamas [1] (Bahamian dollar) — Bahamas [1] (dollar des Bahamas)										
End of period Fin de période	1.000	1.000	1.000	1.000	1.000	1.000	1.000	1.000	1.000	1.000

Country or area — Pays ou zone	1996	1997	1998	1999	2000	2001	2002	2003	2004	2005
Bahrain (Bahrain dinar) — Bahreïn (dinar de Bahreïn)										
End of period Fin de période	0.376	0.376	0.376	0.376	0.376	0.376	0.376	0.376	0.376	0.376
Bangladesh [1] (taka) — Bangladesh [1] (taka)										
End of period Fin de période	42.450	45.450	48.500	51.000	54.000	57.000	57.900	58.782	60.742	66.210
Period average Moyenne sur période	41.794	43.892	46.906	49.085	52.142	55.807	57.888	58.150	59.513	64.328
Barbados (Barbados dollar) — Barbade (dollar de la Barbade)										
End of period Fin de période	2.000	2.000	2.000	2.000	2.000	2.000	2.000	2.000	2.000	2.000
Belarus (Belarussian rouble) — Bélarus (rouble bélarussien)										
End of period Fin de période	15.500	30.740	106.000	320.000	1 180.000	1 580.000	1 920.000	2 156.000	2 170.000	2 152.000
Period average Moyenne sur période	13.230	26.021	46.128	249.295	876.750	1 390.000	1 790.920	2 051.270	2 160.260	2 153.820
Belgium [4] (Belgian franc, euro) — Belgique [4] (franc belge, euro)										
End of period Fin de période	32.005	36.920	34.575	...	...	...	...	...	...	...
Period average Moyenne sur période	30.962	35.774	36.299	...	...	...	...	...	...	...
Belize (Belize dollar) — Belize (dollar du Belize)										
End of period Fin de période	2.000	2.000	2.000	2.000	2.000	2.000	2.000	2.000	2.000	2.000
Benin [6] (CFA franc) — Bénin [6] (franc CFA)										
End of period Fin de période	523.700	598.810	562.210	652.953	704.951	744.306	625.495	519.364	481.578	556.037
Period average Moyenne sur période	511.552	583.669	589.952	615.699	711.976	733.039	696.988	581.200	528.285	527.468
Bhutan (ngultrum) — Bhoutan (ngultrum)										
End of period Fin de période	35.930	39.280	42.480	43.490	46.750	48.180	48.030	45.605	43.585	45.065
Period average Moyenne sur période	35.433	36.313	41.259	43.055	44.942	47.186	48.610	46.583	45.317	44.100
Bolivia [7] (boliviano) — Bolivie [7] (boliviano)										
End of period Fin de période	5.185	5.365	5.645	5.990	6.390	6.820	7.490	7.830	8.050	8.040
Period average Moyenne sur période	5.075	5.254	5.510	5.812	6.184	6.607	7.170	7.659	7.936	8.066
Bosnia and Herzegovina (convertible mark) — Bosnie-Herzégovine (mark convertible)										
End of period Fin de période	...	1.792	1.673	1.947	2.102	2.219	1.865	1.549	1.436	1.658
Period average Moyenne sur période	...	1.734	1.760	1.836	2.123	2.186	2.078	1.733	1.575	1.573
Botswana (pula) — Botswana (pula)										
End of period Fin de période	3.644	3.810	4.458	4.632	5.362	6.983	5.468	4.443	4.281	5.513
Period average Moyenne sur période	3.324	3.651	4.226	4.624	5.102	5.841	6.328	4.950	4.693	5.110
Brazil [8] (real) — Brésil [8] (real)										
End of period Fin de période	1.039	1.116	1.209	1.789	1.955	2.320	3.533	2.888	2.654	2.340
Period average Moyenne sur période	1.005	1.078	1.161	1.815	1.830	2.358	2.921	3.077	2.925	2.434
Brunei Darussalam (Brunei dollar) — Brunéi Darussalam (dollar du Brunéi)										
End of period Fin de période	1.400	1.676	1.661	1.666	1.732	1.851	1.737	1.701	1.634	1.664
Period average Moyenne sur période	1.410	1.485	1.674	1.695	1.724	1.792	1.791	1.742	1.690	1.664

Country or area — Pays ou zone	1996	1997	1998	1999	2000	2001	2002	2003	2004	2005
Bulgaria (lev) — Bulgarie (lev)										
End of period Fin de période	0.487	1.777	1.675	1.947	2.102	2.219	1.885	1.549	1.436	1.658
Period average Moyenne sur période	0.178	1.682	1.760	1.836	2.123	2.185	2.077	1.733	1.575	1.574
Burkina Faso [6] (CFA franc) — Burkina Faso [6] (franc CFA)										
End of period Fin de période	523.700	598.810	562.210	652.953	704.951	744.306	625.495	519.364	481.578	556.037
Period average Moyenne sur période	511.552	583.669	589.952	615.699	711.976	733.039	696.988	581.200	528.285	527.468
Burundi (Burundi franc) — Burundi (franc burundais)										
End of period Fin de période	322.350	408.380	505.160	628.580	778.200	864.200	1 071.230	1 093.000	1 109.510	...
Period average Moyenne sur période	302.747	352.351	447.766	563.563	720.673	830.353	930.749	1 082.620	1 100.910	...
Cambodia (riel) — Cambodge (riel)										
End of period Fin de période	2 713.000	3 452.000	3 770.000	3 770.000	3 905.000	3 895.000	3 930.000	3 984.000	4 027.000	4 112.000
Period average Moyenne sur période	2 624.080	2 946.250	3 744.420	3 807.830	3 840.750	3 916.330	3 912.080	3 973.330	4 016.250	4 092.500
Cameroon [6] (CFA franc) — Cameroun [6] (franc CFA)										
End of period Fin de période	523.700	598.810	562.210	652.953	704.951	744.306	625.495	519.364	481.578	556.037
Period average Moyenne sur période	511.552	583.669	589.952	615.699	711.976	733.039	696.988	581.200	528.285	527.468
Canada (Canadian dollar) — Canada (dollar canadien)										
End of period Fin de période	1.370	1.429	1.531	1.443	1.500	1.593	1.580	1.292	1.204	1.165
Period average Moyenne sur période	1.364	1.385	1.484	1.486	1.485	1.549	1.569	1.401	1.301	1.212
Cape Verde (Cape Verde escudo) — Cap-Vert (escudo du Cap-Vert)										
End of period Fin de période	85.165	96.235	94.255	109.765	118.506	125.122	105.149	87.308	80.956	93.473
Period average Moyenne sur période	82.592	93.177	98.158	103.502	119.687	123.228	117.168	97.703	88.808	88.670
Central African Rep. [6] (CFA franc) — Rép. centrafricaine [6] (franc CFA)										
End of period Fin de période	523.700	598.810	562.210	652.953	704.951	744.306	625.495	519.364	481.578	556.037
Period average Moyenne sur période	511.552	583.669	589.952	615.699	711.976	733.039	696.988	581.200	528.285	527.468
Chad [6] (CFA franc) — Tchad [6] (franc CFA)										
End of period Fin de période	523.700	598.810	562.210	652.953	704.951	744.306	625.495	519.364	481.578	556.037
Period average Moyenne sur période	511.552	583.669	589.952	615.699	711.976	733.039	696.988	581.200	528.285	527.468
Chile [1] (Chilean peso) — Chili [1] (peso chilien)										
End of period Fin de période	424.970	439.810	473.770	530.070	572.680	656.200	712.380	599.420	559.830	514.210
Period average Moyenne sur période	412.267	419.295	460.288	508.777	539.588	634.938	688.936	691.433	609.369	560.090
China [1] (yuan) — Chine [1] (yuan)										
End of period Fin de période	8.298	8.280	8.279	8.280	8.277	8.277	8.277	8.277	8.277	8.070
Period average Moyenne sur période	8.314	8.290	8.279	8.278	8.279	8.277	8.277	8.277	8.277	8.194
China, Hong Kong SAR (Hong Kong dollar) — Chine, Hong Kong RAS (dollar de Hong Kong)										
End of period Fin de période	7.736	7.746	7.746	7.771	7.796	7.797	7.798	7.763	7.774	7.753
Period average Moyenne sur période	7.734	7.742	7.745	7.758	7.791	7.799	7.799	7.787	7.788	7.777

Country or area — Pays ou zone	1996	1997	1998	1999	2000	2001	2002	2003	2004	2005
China, Macao SAR (Macao pataca) — Chine, Macao RAS (pataca de Macao)										
End of period Fin de période	7.968	7.982	7.980	8.005	8.034	8.031	8.033	7.997	8.010	7.987
Period average Moyenne sur période	7.966	7.975	7.979	7.992	8.026	8.034	8.033	8.021	8.022	8.011
Colombia (Colombian peso) — Colombie (peso colombien)										
End of period Fin de période	1 005.330	1 293.580	1 507.520	1 873.770	2 187.020	2 301.330	2 864.790	2 780.820	2 412.100	2 282.350
Period average Moyenne sur période	1 036.690	1 140.960	1 426.040	1 756.230	2 087.900	2 299.630	2 504.240	2 877.650	2 628.610	2 320.750
Comoros [9] (Comorian franc) — Comores [9] (franc comorien)										
End of period Fin de période	392.773	449.105	421.655	489.715	528.714	558.230	469.122	389.523	361.183	417.028
Period average Moyenne sur période	383.660	437.747	442.459	461.775	533.982	549.779	522.741	435.900	396.214	395.601
Congo [6] (CFA franc) — Congo [6] (franc CFA)										
End of period Fin de période	523.700	598.810	562.210	652.953	704.951	744.306	625.495	519.364	481.578	556.037
Period average Moyenne sur période	511.552	583.669	589.952	615.699	711.976	733.039	696.988	581.200	528.285	527.468
Costa Rica (Costa Rican colón) — Costa Rica (colón costa-ricien)										
End of period Fin de période	220.110	244.290	271.420	298.190	318.020	341.670	378.720	418.530	458.610	496.680
Period average Moyenne sur période	207.689	232.598	257.229	285.685	308.187	328.871	359.818	398.662	437.935	477.787
Côte d'Ivoire [6] (CFA franc) — Côte d'Ivoire [6] (franc CFA)										
End of period Fin de période	523.700	598.810	562.210	652.953	704.951	744.306	625.495	519.364	481.578	556.037
Period average Moyenne sur période	511.552	583.669	589.952	615.699	711.976	733.039	696.988	581.200	528.285	527.468
Croatia (kuna) — Croatie (kuna)										
End of period Fin de période	5.540	6.303	6.248	7.648	8.155	8.356	7.146	6.119	5.637	6.234
Period average Moyenne sur période	5.434	6.101	6.362	7.112	8.277	8.340	7.869	6.704	6.036	5.947
Cyprus (Cyprus pound) — Chypre (livre chypriote)										
End of period Fin de période	0.470	0.526	0.498	0.575	0.617	0.650	0.547	0.465	0.425	0.484
Period average Moyenne sur période	0.466	0.514	0.518	0.543	0.622	0.643	0.611	0.517	0.469	0.464
Czech Republic (Czech koruna) — République tchèque (couronne tchèque)										
End of period Fin de période	27.332	34.636	29.855	35.979	37.813	36.259	30.141	25.654	22.365	24.588
Period average [1] Moyenne sur période [1]	27.145	31.698	32.281	34.569	38.598	38.035	32.739	28.209	25.700	23.957
Dem. Rep. of the Congo [10] (Congo franc) — Rép. dém. du Congo [10] (franc congolais)										
End of period Fin de période	1 156.000	1 060.000	2.450	4.500	50.000	313.600	382.140	369.590	453.080	431.279
Period average Moyenne sur période	501.849	1 313.450	1.607	4.018	21.818	206.617	346.485	405.340	401.041	472.618
Denmark (Danish krone) — Danemark (couronne danoise)										
End of period Fin de période	5.945	6.826	6.387	7.399	8.021	8.410	7.082	5.958	5.468	6.324
Period average Moyenne sur période	5.799	6.605	6.701	6.976	8.083	8.323	7.895	6.588	5.991	5.997
Djibouti (Djibouti franc) — Djibouti (franc djiboutien)										
End of period Fin de période	177.721	177.721	177.721	177.721	177.721	177.721	177.721	177.721	177.721	177.721
Dominica (EC dollar) — Dominique (dollar des Caraïbes orientales)										
End of period Fin de période	2.700	2.700	2.700	2.700	2.700	2.700	2.700	2.700	2.700	2.700

Exchange rates—National currency per US dollar (*continued*)
Cours des changes—Valeur du dollar des Etats-Unis en monnaie nationale (*suite*)

Country or area — Pays ou zone	1996	1997	1998	1999	2000	2001	2002	2003	2004	2005
Dominican Republic [1] (Dominican peso) — Rép. dominicaine [1] (peso dominicain)										
End of period / Fin de période	14.062	14.366	15.788	16.039	16.674	17.149	21.194	37.250	31.109	34.879
Period average / Moyenne sur période	13.775	14.266	15.267	16.033	16.415	16.952	18.610	30.831	42.120	30.409
Ecuador [1] (sucre) — Equateur [1] (sucre)										
End of period / Fin de période	3 635.000	4 428.000	6 825.000	20 243.000	25 000.000	25 000.000	25 000.000	25 000.000	25 000.000	25 000.000
Period average / Moyenne sur période	3 189.470	3 998.270	5 446.570	11 786.800	24 988.400	25 000.000	25 000.000	25 000.000	25 000.000	25 000.000
Egypt [1] (Egyptian pound) — Egypte [1] (livre égyptienne)										
End of period / Fin de période	3.388	3.388	3.388	3.405	3.690	4.490	4.500	6.153	6.131	5.732
Period average / Moyenne sur période	3.392	3.389	3.388	3.395	3.472	3.973	4.500	5.851	6.196	5.779
El Salvador [1] (El Salvadoran colón) — El Salvador [1] (colón salvadorien)										
End of period / Fin de période	8.755	8.755	8.755	8.755	8.755	8.750	8.750	8.750	8.750	8.750
Period average / Moyenne sur période	8.755	8.756	8.755	8.755	8.755	8.750	8.750	8.750	8.750	8.750
Equatorial Guinea [6] (CFA franc) — Guinée équatoriale [6] (franc CFA)										
End of period / Fin de période	523.700	598.810	562.210	652.953	704.951	744.306	625.495	519.364	481.578	556.037
Period average / Moyenne sur période	511.552	583.669	589.952	615.699	711.976	733.039	696.988	581.200	528.285	527.468
Eritrea (Nakfa) — Erythrée (Nakfa)										
End of period / Fin de période	6.426	7.125	7.597	9.600	10.200	13.798	14.131	13.788	13.788	...
Period average / Moyenne sur période	6.358	6.837	7.362	8.153	9.625	11.310	13.958	13.878	13.788	...
Estonia (Estonian kroon) — Estonie (couronne estonienne)										
End of period / Fin de période	12.440	14.336	13.410	15.562	16.820	17.692	14.936	12.410	11.471	13.221
Period average / Moyenne sur période	12.038	13.882	14.075	14.678	16.969	17.478	16.612	13.856	12.596	12.584
Ethiopia (Ethiopian birr) — Ethiopie (birr éthiopien)										
End of period / Fin de période	6.426	6.864	7.503	8.134	8.314	8.558	8.581	8.621	8.652	...
Period average / Moyenne sur période	6.352	6.709	7.116	7.942	8.217	8.458	8.568	8.600	8.636	...
Euro Area [11] (euro) — Zone euro [11] (euro)										
End of period / Fin de période	...	...	...	0.995	1.075	1.135	0.954	0.792	0.734	0.848
Period average / Moyenne sur période	...	...	...	0.939	1.085	1.118	1.063	0.886	0.805	0.804
Fiji (Fiji dollar) — Fidji (dollar des Fidji)										
End of period / Fin de période	1.384	1.549	1.986	1.966	2.186	2.309	2.065	1.722	1.645	1.745
Period average / Moyenne sur période	1.403	1.444	1.987	1.970	2.129	2.277	2.187	1.896	1.733	1.691
Finland [4] (Finnish markka, euro) — Finlande [4] (markka finlandais, euro)										
End of period / Fin de période	4.644	5.421	5.096	...	...	...	...	...	...	...
Period average / Moyenne sur période	4.594	5.191	5.344	...	...	...	...	...	...	...
France [4] (French franc, euro) — France [4] (franc français, euro)										
End of period / Fin de période	5.237	5.988	5.622	...	...	...	...	...	...	...
Period average / Moyenne sur période	5.116	5.837	5.900	...	...	...	...	...	...	...

Country or area — Pays ou zone	1996	1997	1998	1999	2000	2001	2002	2003	2004	2005
Gabon [6] (CFA franc) — Gabon [6] (franc CFA)										
End of period Fin de période	523.700	598.810	562.210	652.953	704.951	744.306	625.495	519.364	481.578	556.037
Period average Moyenne sur période	511.552	583.669	589.952	615.699	711.976	733.039	696.988	581.200	528.285	527.468
Gambia (dalasi) — Gambie (dalasi)										
End of period Fin de période	9.892	10.530	10.991	11.547	14.888	16.932	23.392	30.960	29.674	...
Period average Moyenne sur période	9.789	10.200	10.643	11.395	12.788	15.687	19.918	27.306	30.030	...
Georgia (lari) — Géorgie (lari)										
End of period Fin de période	1.276	1.304	1.800	1.930	1.975	2.060	2.090	2.075	1.825	1.793
Period average Moyenne sur période	1.263	1.298	1.390	2.025	1.976	2.073	2.196	2.146	1.917	1.813
Germany [4] (deutsche mark, euro) — Allemagne [4] (deutsche mark, euro)										
End of period Fin de période	1.555	1.792	1.673	...	...	...	...	...	...	...
Period average Moyenne sur période	1.505	1.734	1.760	...	...	...	...	...	...	...
Ghana [1] (cedi) — Ghana [1] (cedi)										
End of period Fin de période	1 754.390	2 272.730	2 325.580	3 535.140	7 047.650	7 321.940	8 438.820	8 852.320	9 054.260	9 130.820
Period average Moyenne sur période	1 637.230	2 050.170	2 314.150	2 669.300	5 455.060	7 170.760	7 932.700	8 677.370	9 004.630	9 072.540
Greece [4] (drachma, euro) — Grèce [4] (drachma, euro)										
End of period Fin de période	247.020	282.610	282.570	328.440	365.620	...	...	...	...	...
Period average Moyenne sur période	240.712	273.058	295.529	305.647	365.399	...	...	...	...	...
Grenada (EC dollar) — Grenade (dollar des Caraïbes orientales)										
End of period Fin de période	2.700	2.700	2.700	2.700	2.700	2.700	2.700	2.700	2.700	2.700
Guatemala (quetzal) — Guatemala (quetzal)										
End of period Fin de période	5.966	6.177	6.848	7.821	7.731	8.001	7.807	8.041	7.748	7.610
Period average Moyenne sur période	6.050	6.065	6.395	7.386	7.763	7.859	7.822	7.941	7.947	7.634
Guinea (Guinean franc) — Guinée (franc guinéen)										
End of period Fin de période	1 039.130	1 144.950	1 298.030	1 736.000	1 882.270	1 988.330	1 976.000	2 000.000	2 550.000	...
Period average Moyenne sur période	1 004.020	1 095.330	1 236.830	1 387.400	1 746.870	1 950.560	1 975.840	1 984.930	2 225.030	...
Guinea-Bissau [12] (CFA franc) — Guinée-Bissau [12] (franc CFA)										
End of period Fin de période	537.482	598.810	562.210	652.953	704.951	744.306	625.495	519.364	481.578	556.037
Period average Moyenne sur période	405.745	583.669	589.952	615.699	711.976	733.039	696.988	581.200	528.285	527.468
Guyana [1] (Guyana dollar) — Guyana [1] (dollar guyanais)										
End of period Fin de période	141.250	144.000	162.250	180.500	184.750	189.500	191.750	194.250	199.750	200.250
Period average Moyenne sur période	140.375	142.401	150.519	177.995	182.430	187.321	190.665	193.878	198.307	199.875
Haiti [1] (gourde) — Haïti [1] (gourde)										
End of period Fin de période	15.093	17.311	16.505	17.965	22.524	26.339	37.609	42.085	37.232	43.000
Period average Moyenne sur période	15.701	16.655	16.766	16.938	21.171	24.429	29.251	42.367	38.352	40.449
Honduras [1] (lempira) — Honduras [1] (lempira)										
End of period Fin de période	12.869	13.094	13.808	14.504	15.141	15.920	16.923	17.748	18.633	18.895
Period average Moyenne sur période	11.705	13.004	13.385	14.213	14.839	15.474	16.433	17.345	18.206	18.832

Exchange rates—National currency per US dollar (*continued*)
Cours des changes—Valeur du dollar des Etats-Unis en monnaie nationale (*suite*)

Country or area—Pays ou zone	1996	1997	1998	1999	2000	2001	2002	2003	2004	2005
Hungary (forint) — Hongrie (forint)										
End of period Fin de période	164.930	203.500	219.030	252.520	284.730	279.030	225.160	207.920	180.290	213.580
Period average Moyenne sur période	152.647	186.789	214.402	237.146	282.179	286.490	257.887	224.307	202.746	199.582
Iceland (Icelandic króna) — Islande (couronne islandaise)										
End of period Fin de période	66.890	72.180	69.320	72.550	84.700	102.950	80.580	70.990	61.040	62.980
Period average Moyenne sur période	66.500	70.904	70.958	72.335	78.616	97.425	91.662	76.709	70.192	62.982
India (Indian rupee) — Inde (roupie indienne)										
End of period Fin de période	35.930	39.280	42.480	43.490	46.750	48.180	48.030	45.605	43.585	45.065
Period average Moyenne sur période	35.433	36.313	41.259	43.055	44.942	47.186	48.610	46.583	45.317	44.100
Indonesia (Indonesian rupiah) — Indonésie (roupie indonésien)										
End of period Fin de période	2 383.000	4 650.000	8 025.000	7 085.000	9 595.000	10 400.000	8 940.000	8 465.000	9 290.000	9 830.000
Period average Moyenne sur période	2 342.300	2 909.380	10 013.600	7 855.150	8 421.780	10 260.900	9 311.190	8 577.130	8 938.850	9 704.740
Iran (Islamic Rep. of) (Iranian rial) — Iran (Rép. islamique d') (rial iranien)										
End of period Fin de période	1 749.140	1 754.260	1 750.930	1 752.290	2 262.930	1 750.950	7 951.980	8 272.110	8 793.000	9 091.000
Period average Moyenne sur période	1 750.760	1 752.920	1 751.860	1 752.930	1 764.430	1 753.560	6 906.960	8 193.890	8 613.990	8 963.960
Iraq [1] (Iraqi dinar) — Iraq [1] (dinar iraquien)										
End of period Fin de période	0.311	0.311	0.311	0.311	0.311	0.311	0.311	...	...	...
Ireland [4] (Irish pound, euro) — Irlande [4] (livre irlandaise, euro)										
End of period Fin de période	0.595	0.699	0.672	...	...	...	...	...	...	...
Period average Moyenne sur période	0.625	0.660	0.702	...	...	...	...	...	...	...
Israel (new sheqel) — Israël (nouveau sheqel)										
End of period Fin de période	3.251	3.536	4.161	4.153	4.041	4.416	4.737	4.379	4.308	4.603
Period average Moyenne sur période	3.192	3.449	3.800	4.140	4.077	4.206	4.738	4.554	4.482	4.488
Italy [4] (Italian lira, euro) — Italie [4] (lire italienne, euro)										
End of period Fin de période	1 530.570	1 759.190	1 653.100	...	...	...	...	...	...	...
Period average Moyenne sur période	1 542.950	1 703.100	1 736.210	...	...	...	...	...	...	...
Jamaica (Jamaican dollar) — Jamaïque (dollar jamaïcain)										
End of period Fin de période	34.865	36.341	37.055	41.291	45.415	47.286	50.762	60.517	61.450	64.381
Period average Moyenne sur période	37.120	35.405	36.550	39.044	42.986	45.996	48.416	57.741	61.197	62.281
Japan (yen) — Japon (yen)										
End of period Fin de période	116.000	129.950	115.600	102.200	114.900	131.800	119.900	107.100	104.120	117.970
Period average Moyenne sur période	108.779	120.991	130.905	113.907	107.765	121.529	125.388	115.933	108.193	110.218
Jordan (Jordan dinar) — Jordanie (dinar jordanien)										
End of period Fin de période	0.709	0.709	0.709	0.709	0.709	0.709	0.709	0.709	0.709	0.709
Period average Moyenne sur période	0.709	0.709	0.709	0.709	0.709	0.709	0.709	0.709	0.709	0.709
Kazakhstan (tenge) — Kazakhstan (tenge)										
End of period Fin de période	73.300	75.550	83.800	138.200	144.500	150.200	154.600	144.220	130.000	133.980
Period average Moyenne sur période	67.303	75.438	78.303	119.523	142.133	146.736	153.279	149.576	136.035	132.880

Country or area — Pays ou zone	1996	1997	1998	1999	2000	2001	2002	2003	2004	2005
Kenya (Kenya shilling) — Kenya (shilling du Kenya)										
End of period / Fin de période	55.021	62.678	61.906	72.931	78.036	78.600	77.072	76.139	77.344	72.367
Period average / Moyenne sur période	57.115	58.732	60.367	70.326	76.176	78.563	78.749	75.936	79.174	75.554
Kiribati (Australian dollar) — Kiribati (dollar australien)										
End of period / Fin de période	1.256	1.532	1.629	1.530	1.805	1.959	1.766	1.333	1.284	1.363
Period average / Moyenne sur période	1.278	1.347	1.592	1.550	1.725	1.933	1.841	1.542	1.360	1.310
Korea, Republic of (Korean won) — Corée, République de (won coréen)										
End of period / Fin de période	844.200	1 695.000	1 204.000	1 138.000	1 264.500	1 313.500	1 186.200	1 192.600	1 035.100	1 011.600
Period average / Moyenne sur période	804.453	951.289	1 401.440	1 188.820	1 130.960	1 290.990	1 251.090	1 191.610	1 145.320	1 024.120
Kuwait (Kuwaiti dinar) — Koweït (dinar koweïtien)										
End of period / Fin de période	0.300	0.305	0.302	0.304	0.305	0.308	0.300	0.295	0.295	0.292
Period average / Moyenne sur période	0.299	0.303	0.305	0.304	0.307	0.307	0.304	0.298	0.295	0.292
Kyrgyzstan (Kyrgyz som) — Kirghizistan (som kirghize)										
End of period / Fin de période	16.700	17.375	29.376	45.429	48.304	47.719	46.095	44.190	41.625	41.301
Period average / Moyenne sur période	12.810	17.363	20.838	39.008	47.704	48.378	46.937	43.648	42.650	41.012
Lao People's Dem. Rep. (kip) — Rép. dém. pop. lao (kip)										
End of period / Fin de période	935.000	2 634.500	4 274.000	7 600.000	8 218.000	9 490.000	10 680.000	10 467.000	10 376.500	10 743.000
Period average / Moyenne sur période	921.022	1 259.980	3 298.330	7 102.020	7 887.640	8 954.580	10 056.300	10 569.000	10 585.500	10 655.200
Latvia (lats) — Lettonie (lats)										
End of period / Fin de période	0.556	0.590	0.569	0.583	0.613	0.638	0.594	0.541	0.516	0.593
Period average / Moyenne sur période	0.551	0.581	0.590	0.585	0.607	0.628	0.618	0.572	0.540	0.565
Lebanon (Lebanese pound) — Liban (livre libanaise)										
End of period / Fin de période	1 552.000	1 527.000	1 508.000	1 507.500	1 507.500	1 507.500	1 507.500	1 507.500	1 507.500	1 507.500
Period average / Moyenne sur période	1 571.440	1 539.450	1 516.130	1 507.840	1 507.500	1 507.500	1 507.500	1 507.500	1 507.500	1 507.500
Lesotho [1] (loti) — Lesotho [1] (loti)										
End of period / Fin de période	4.683	4.868	5.860	6.155	7.569	12.127	8.640	6.640	5.630	6.325
Period average / Moyenne sur période	4.299	4.608	5.528	6.110	6.940	8.609	10.541	7.565	6.460	6.359
Liberia [1] (Liberian dollar) — Libéria [1] (dollar libérien)										
End of period / Fin de période	1.000	1.000	43.250	39.500	42.750	49.500	65.000	50.500	54.500	56.500
Period average / Moyenne sur période	1.000	1.000	41.508	41.903	40.953	48.583	61.754	59.379	54.906	57.096
Libyan Arab Jamah. (Libyan dinar) — Jamah. arabe libyenne (dinar libyen)										
End of period / Fin de période	0.441	0.470	0.450	0.462	0.540	0.650	1.210	1.300	1.244	1.352
Period average / Moyenne sur période	0.437	0.461	0.468	0.464	0.512	0.605	1.271	1.293	1.305	1.308
Lithuania (litas) — Lituanie (litas)										
End of period / Fin de période	4.000	4.000	4.000	4.000	4.000	4.000	3.311	2.762	2.535	2.910
Period average / Moyenne sur période	4.000	4.000	4.000	4.000	4.000	4.000	3.677	3.061	2.781	2.774

Country or area—Pays ou zone	1996	1997	1998	1999	2000	2001	2002	2003	2004	2005
Luxembourg [4] (Luxembourg franc, euro) — Luxembourg [4] (franc luxembourgeois, euro)										
End of period Fin de période	32.005	36.920	34.575	...	...	...	...	...	...	...
Period average Moyenne sur période	30.962	35.774	36.299	...	...	...	...	...	...	...
Madagascar [13] (Malagasy ariary) — Madagascar [13] (ariary malgache)										
End of period Fin de période	865.694	1 056.930	1 080.440	1 308.640	1 310.090	1 326.240	1 286.950	1 219.620	1 869.400	2 159.820
Period average Moyenne sur période	812.250	1 018.180	1 088.280	1 256.760	1 353.500	1 317.700	1 366.390	1 238.330	1 868.860	2 003.030
Malawi (Malawi kwacha) — Malawi (kwacha malawien)										
End of period Fin de période	15.323	21.228	43.884	46.438	80.076	67.294	87.139	108.566	108.943	...
Period average Moyenne sur période	15.309	16.444	31.073	44.088	59.544	72.197	76.687	97.433	108.898	...
Malaysia (ringgit) — Malaisie (ringgit)										
End of period Fin de période	2.529	3.892	3.800	3.800	3.800	3.800	3.800	3.800	3.800	3.780
Period average Moyenne sur période	2.516	2.813	3.924	3.800	3.800	3.800	3.800	3.800	3.800	3.787
Maldives [14] (rufiyaa) — Maldives [14] (rufiyaa)										
End of period Fin de période	11.770	11.770	11.770	11.770	11.770	12.800	12.800	12.800	12.800	12.800
Period average Moyenne sur période	11.770	11.770	11.770	11.770	11.770	12.242	12.800	12.800	12.800	12.800
Mali [6] (CFA franc) — Mali [6] (franc CFA)										
End of period Fin de période	523.700	598.810	562.210	652.953	704.951	744.306	625.495	519.364	481.578	556.037
Period average Moyenne sur période	511.552	583.669	589.952	615.699	711.976	733.039	696.988	581.200	528.285	527.468
Malta (Maltese lira) — Malte (lire maltaise)										
End of period Fin de période	0.360	0.391	0.377	0.412	0.438	0.452	0.399	0.343	0.319	0.363
Period average Moyenne sur période	0.361	0.386	0.389	0.399	0.438	0.450	0.434	0.377	0.345	0.346
Mauritania (ouguiya) — Mauritanie (ouguiya)										
End of period Fin de période	142.450	168.350	205.780	225.000	252.300	264.120	268.710	265.600	...	...
Period average Moyenne sur période	137.222	151.853	188.476	209.514	238.923	255.629	271.739	263.030	...	...
Mauritius (Mauritian rupee) — Maurice (roupie mauricienne)										
End of period Fin de période	17.972	22.265	24.784	25.468	27.882	30.394	29.197	26.088	28.204	30.667
Period average Moyenne sur période	17.948	21.057	23.993	25.186	26.250	29.129	29.962	27.902	27.499	29.496
Mexico [1] (Mexican peso) — Mexique [1] (peso mexicain)										
End of period Fin de période	7.851	8.083	9.865	9.514	9.572	9.142	10.313	11.236	11.265	10.778
Period average Moyenne sur période	7.600	7.919	9.136	9.560	9.456	9.342	9.656	10.789	11.286	10.898
Micronesia (Fed. States of) (US dollar) — Micronésie (Etats féd. de) (dollar des Etats-Unis)										
End of period Fin de période	1.000	1.000	1.000	1.000	1.000	1.000	1.000	1.000	1.000	1.000
Mongolia (togrog) — Mongolie (togrog)										
End of period Fin de période	693.510	813.160	902.000	1 072.370	1 097.000	1 102.000	1 125.000	1 168.000	1 209.000	...
Period average Moyenne sur période	548.403	789.993	840.828	1 021.870	1 076.670	1 097.700	1 110.310	1 146.540	1 185.280	...
Montserrat (EC dollar) — Montserrat (dollar des Caraïbes orientales)										
End of period Fin de période	2.700	2.700	2.700	2.700	2.700	2.700	2.700	2.700	2.700	2.700

Country or area — Pays ou zone	1996	1997	1998	1999	2000	2001	2002	2003	2004	2005
Morocco (Moroccan dirham) — Maroc (dirham marocain)										
End of period Fin de période	8.800	9.714	9.255	10.087	10.619	11.560	10.167	8.750	8.218	9.249
Period average Moyenne sur période	8.716	9.527	9.604	9.804	10.626	11.303	11.021	9.574	8.868	8.865
Mozambique [1] (metical) — Mozambique [1] (metical)										
End of period Fin de période	11 377.000	11 543.000	12 366.000	13 300.000	17 140.500	23 320.400	23 854.300	23 856.700	18 899.300	24 183.000
Period average Moyenne sur période	11 293.700	11 543.600	11 874.600	12 775.100	15 227.200	20 703.600	23 678.000	23 782.300	22 581.300	23 061.000
Myanmar (kyat) — Myanmar (kyat)										
End of period Fin de période	5.917	6.306	6.043	6.199	6.530	6.770	6.258	5.726	5.479	5.953
Period average Moyenne sur période	5.861	6.184	6.274	6.223	6.426	6.684	6.573	6.076	5.746	5.761
Namibia (Namibia dollar) — Namibie (Dollar namibia)										
End of period Fin de période	4.683	4.868	5.860	6.155	7.569	12.127	8.640	6.640	5.630	6.325
Period average Moyenne sur période	4.299	4.608	5.528	6.110	6.940	8.609	10.541	7.565	6.460	6.359
Nepal (Nepalese rupee) — Népal (roupie népalaise)										
End of period Fin de période	57.030	63.300	67.675	68.725	74.300	76.475	78.300	74.040	71.800	74.050
Period average Moyenne sur période	56.692	58.010	65.976	68.239	71.094	74.949	77.877	76.141	73.674	71.368
Netherlands [4] (Netherlands guilder, euro) — Pays-Bas [4] (florin néerlandais, euro)										
End of period Fin de période	1.744	2.017	1.889	...	...	...	...	...	...	...
Period average Moyenne sur période	1.686	1.951	1.984	...	...	...	...	...	...	...
Netherlands Antilles (Netherlands Antillean guilder) — Antilles néerlandaises (florin des Antilles néerlandaises)										
End of period Fin de période	1.790	1.790	1.790	1.790	1.790	1.790	1.790	1.790	1.790	1.790
New Zealand (New Zealand dollar) — Nouvelle-Zélande (dollar néo-zélandais)										
End of period Fin de période	1.416	1.719	1.898	1.921	2.272	2.407	1.899	1.539	1.392	1.468
Period average Moyenne sur période	1.455	1.512	1.868	1.890	2.201	2.379	2.162	1.722	1.509	1.420
Nicaragua [1,15] (córdoba) — Nicaragua [1,15] (córdoba)										
End of period Fin de période	8.924	9.995	11.194	12.318	13.057	13.841	14.671	15.552	16.329	17.146
Period average Moyenne sur période	8.436	9.448	10.582	11.809	12.684	13.372	14.251	15.105	15.937	16.733
Niger [6] (CFA franc) — Niger [6] (franc CFA)										
End of period Fin de période	523.700	598.810	562.210	652.953	704.951	744.306	625.495	519.364	481.578	556.037
Period average Moyenne sur période	511.552	583.669	589.952	615.699	711.976	733.039	696.988	581.200	528.285	527.468
Nigeria [1] (naira) — Nigéria [1] (naira)										
End of period Fin de période	21.886	21.886	21.886	97.950	109.550	112.950	126.400	136.500	132.350	129.000
Period average Moyenne sur période	21.884	21.886	21.886	92.338	101.697	111.231	120.578	129.222	132.888	131.274
Norway (Norwegian krone) — Norvège (couronne norvégienne)										
End of period Fin de période	6.443	7.316	7.600	8.040	8.849	9.012	6.966	6.680	6.040	6.770
Period average Moyenne sur période	6.450	7.073	7.545	7.799	8.802	8.992	7.984	7.080	6.741	6.443
Oman (rial Omani) — Oman (rial omani)										
End of period Fin de période	0.385	0.385	0.385	0.385	0.385	0.385	0.385	0.385	0.385	0.385

Exchange rates — National currency per US dollar (*continued*)
Cours des changes — Valeur du dollar des Etats-Unis en monnaie nationale (*suite*)

Country or area — Pays ou zone	1996	1997	1998	1999	2000	2001	2002	2003	2004	2005
Pakistan (Pakistan rupee) — Pakistan (roupie pakistanaise)										
End of period Fin de période	40.120	44.050	45.885	51.785	58.029	60.864	58.534	57.215	59.124	59.830
Period average Moyenne sur période	36.079	41.112	45.047	49.501	53.648	61.927	59.724	57.752	58.258	59.515
Panama (balboa) — Panama (balboa)										
End of period Fin de période	1.000	1.000	1.000	1.000	1.000	1.000	1.000	1.000	1.000	1.000
Papua New Guinea (kina) — Papouasie-Nouvelle-Guinée (kina)										
End of period Fin de période	1.347	1.751	2.096	2.695	3.072	3.762	4.019	3.333	3.125	...
Period average Moyenne sur période	1.319	1.438	2.074	2.571	2.782	3.389	3.895	3.564	3.223	...
Paraguay (guaraní) — Paraguay (guaraní)										
End of period Fin de période	2 109.670	2 360.000	2 840.190	3 328.860	3 526.900	4 682.000	7 103.590	6 114.960	6 250.000	6 120.000
Period average Moyenne sur période	2 056.810	2 177.860	2 726.490	3 119.070	3 486.350	4 105.930	5 716.260	6 424.340	5 974.580	6 177.960
Peru [16] (new sol) — Pérou [16] (nouveau sol)										
End of period Fin de période	2.600	2.730	3.160	3.510	3.527	3.444	3.514	3.463	3.282	3.430
Period average Moyenne sur période	2.453	2.664	2.930	3.383	3.490	3.507	3.517	3.479	3.413	3.296
Philippines (Philippine peso) — Philippines (peso philippin)										
End of period Fin de période	26.288	39.975	39.059	40.313	49.998	51.404	53.096	55.569	56.267	53.067
Period average Moyenne sur période	26.216	29.471	40.893	39.089	44.192	50.993	51.604	54.203	56.040	55.086
Poland (zloty) — Pologne (zloty)										
End of period Fin de période	2.876	3.518	3.504	4.148	4.143	3.986	3.839	3.741	2.990	3.261
Period average Moyenne sur période	2.696	3.279	3.475	3.967	4.346	4.094	4.080	3.889	3.658	3.236
Portugal [4] (Portuguese escudo, euro) — Portugal [4] (escudo portugais, euro)										
End of period Fin de période	156.385	183.326	171.829	...	...	...	...	...	...	...
Period average Moyenne sur période	154.244	175.312	180.104	...	...	...	...	...	...	...
Qatar (Qatar riyal) — Qatar (riyal qatarien)										
End of period Fin de période	3.640	3.640	3.640	3.640	3.640	3.640	3.640	3.640	3.640	3.640
Republic of Moldova (Moldovan leu) — République de Moldova (leu moldove)										
End of period Fin de période	4.674	4.661	8.323	11.590	12.383	13.091	13.822	13.220	12.461	12.832
Period average Moyenne sur période	4.605	4.624	5.371	10.516	12.434	12.865	13.571	13.945	12.330	12.600
Romania [1,17] (Romanian leu) — Roumanie [1,17] (leu roumain)										
End of period Fin de période	0.404	0.802	1.095	1.826	2.593	3.160	3.350	3.260	2.907	3.108
Period average Moyenne sur période	0.308	0.717	0.888	1.533	2.171	2.906	3.306	3.320	3.264	2.914
Russian Federation [18] (ruble) — Fédération de Russie [18] (ruble)										
End of period Fin de période	5.560	5.960	20.650	27.000	28.160	30.140	31.784	29.455	27.749	28.783
Period average Moyenne sur période	5.121	5.785	9.705	24.620	28.129	29.169	31.349	30.692	28.814	28.284
Rwanda (Rwanda franc) — Rwanda (franc rwandais)										
End of period Fin de période	304.161	304.843	320.128	349.170	430.316	455.820	511.854	571.390	565.578	553.720
Period average Moyenne sur période	306.098	301.321	313.717	337.831	393.435	442.801	476.327	537.658	574.622	555.936

Country or area — Pays ou zone	1996	1997	1998	1999	2000	2001	2002	2003	2004	2005
Saint Kitts and Nevis (EC dollar) — Saint-Kitts-et-Nevis (dollar des Caraïbes orientales)										
End of period Fin de période	2.700	2.700	2.700	2.700	2.700	2.700	2.700	2.700	2.700	2.700
Saint Lucia (EC dollar) — Sainte-Lucie (dollar des Caraïbes orientales)										
End of period Fin de période	2.700	2.700	2.700	2.700	2.700	2.700	2.700	2.700	2.700	2.700
St. Vincent-Grenadines (EC dollar) — St. Vincent-Grenadines (dollar des Caraïbes orientales)										
End of period Fin de période	2.700	2.700	2.700	2.700	2.700	2.700	2.700	2.700	2.700	2.700
Samoa (tala) — Samoa (tala)										
End of period Fin de période	2.434	2.766	3.010	3.018	3.341	3.551	3.217	2.778	2.673	2.764
Period average Moyenne sur période	2.462	2.559	2.948	3.013	3.286	3.478	3.376	2.973	2.781	2.710
San Marino [4] (Italian lira, euro) — Saint-Marin [4] (lire italienne, euro)										
End of period Fin de période	1 530.570	1 759.190	1 653.100	...	...	...	...	...	...	...
Period average Moyenne sur période	1 542.950	1 703.100	1 736.210	...	...	...	...	...	...	...
Sao Tome and Principe (dobra) — Sao Tomé-et-Principe (dobra)										
End of period Fin de période	2 833.210	6 969.730	6 885.000	7 300.000	8 610.650	9 019.710	9 191.840	9 455.900	9 971.000	...
Period average Moyenne sur période	2 203.160	4 552.510	6 883.240	7 118.960	7 978.170	8 842.110	9 088.330	9 347.580	...	...
Saudi Arabia (Saudi Arabian riyal) — Arabie saoudite (riyal saoudien)										
End of period Fin de période	3.750	3.750	3.750	3.750	3.750	3.750	3.750	3.750	3.750	3.745
Period average Moyenne sur période	3.750	3.750	3.750	3.750	3.750	3.750	3.750	3.750	3.750	3.747
Senegal [6] (CFA franc) — Sénégal [6] (franc CFA)										
End of period Fin de période	523.700	598.810	562.210	652.953	704.951	744.306	625.495	519.364	481.578	556.037
Period average Moyenne sur période	511.552	583.669	589.952	615.699	711.976	733.039	696.988	581.200	528.285	527.468
Seychelles (Seychelles rupee) — Seychelles (roupie seychelloises)										
End of period Fin de période	4.995	5.125	5.452	5.368	6.269	5.752	5.055	5.500	5.500	5.500
Period average Moyenne sur période	4.970	5.026	5.262	5.343	5.714	5.858	5.480	5.401	5.500	5.500
Sierra Leone (leone) — Sierra Leone (leone)										
End of period Fin de période	909.091	1 333.330	1 590.760	2 276.050	1 666.670	2 161.270	2 191.730	2 562.180	2 860.490	2 932.520
Period average Moyenne sur période	920.732	981.482	1 563.620	1 804.200	2 092.120	1 986.150	2 099.030	2 347.940	2 701.300	2 889.590
Singapore (Singapore dollar) — Singapour (dollar singapourien)										
End of period Fin de période	1.400	1.676	1.661	1.666	1.732	1.851	1.737	1.701	1.634	1.664
Period average Moyenne sur période	1.410	1.485	1.674	1.695	1.724	1.792	1.791	1.742	1.690	1.664
Slovakia (Slovak koruna) — Slovaquie (couronne slovaque)										
End of period Fin de période	31.895	34.782	36.913	42.266	47.389	48.467	40.036	32.975	28.496	31.948
Period average [1] Moyenne sur période [1]	30.654	33.616	35.233	41.363	46.035	48.355	45.327	36.773	32.257	31.018
Slovenia (tolar) — Slovénie (tolar)										
End of period Fin de période	141.480	169.180	161.200	196.771	227.377	250.946	221.071	189.367	176.243	202.430
Period average Moyenne sur période	135.364	159.688	166.134	181.769	222.656	242.749	240.248	207.114	192.381	192.705

Exchange rates — National currency per US dollar (*continued*)
Cours des changes — Valeur du dollar des Etats-Unis en monnaie nationale (*suite*)

Country or area — Pays ou zone	1996	1997	1998	1999	2000	2001	2002	2003	2004	2005
Solomon Islands (Solomon Islands dollar) — Iles Salomon (dollar des Iles Salomon)										
End of period Fin de période	3.622	4.748	4.859	5.076	5.099	5.565	7.457	7.491	7.508	7.576
Period average Moyenne sur période	3.566	3.717	4.816	4.838	5.089	5.278	6.749	7.506	7.485	7.530
South Africa [1] (rand) — Afrique du Sud [1] (rand)										
End of period Fin de période	4.683	4.868	5.860	6.155	7.569	12.127	8.640	6.640	5.630	6.325
Period average Moyenne sur période	4.299	4.608	5.528	6.110	6.940	8.609	10.541	7.565	6.460	6.359
Spain [4] (peseta, euro) — Espagne [4] (peseta, euro)										
End of period Fin de période	131.275	151.702	142.607	...	...	...	...	...	...	...
Period average Moyenne sur période	126.662	146.414	149.395	...	...	...	...	...	...	...
Sri Lanka (Sri Lanka rupee) — Sri Lanka (roupie sri-lankaise)										
End of period Fin de période	56.705	61.285	68.297	72.170	82.580	93.159	96.725	96.738	104.605	102.117
Period average Moyenne sur période	55.271	58.995	64.450	70.635	77.005	89.383	95.662	96.521	101.194	100.498
Sudan [1] (Sudanese dinar) — Soudan [1] (dinar soudanaise)										
End of period Fin de période	144.928	172.206	237.801	257.700	257.350	261.430	261.680	260.160	250.630	230.540
Period average Moyenne sur période	125.079	157.574	200.802	252.550	257.123	258.702	263.306	260.983	257.905	243.606
Suriname [19] (Surinamese dollar) — Suriname [19] (dolar surinamais)										
End of period Fin de période	401.000	401.000	401.000	987.500	2 178.500	2 178.500	2 515.000	2 625.000	2 715.000	2 740.000
Period average Moyenne sur période	401.258	401.000	401.000	859.437	1 322.470	2 178.500	2 346.750	2 601.330	2 733.580	2 731.670
Swaziland (lilangeni) — Swaziland (lilangeni)										
End of period Fin de période	4.683	4.868	5.860	6.155	7.569	12.127	8.640	6.640	5.630	6.325
Period average Moyenne sur période	4.299	4.608	5.528	6.110	6.940	8.609	10.541	7.565	6.460	6.359
Sweden (Swedish krona) — Suède (couronne suédoise)										
End of period Fin de période	6.871	7.877	8.061	8.525	9.535	10.668	8.825	7.189	6.615	7.958
Period average Moyenne sur période	6.706	7.635	7.950	8.262	9.162	10.329	9.737	8.086	7.349	7.473
Switzerland (Swiss franc) — Suisse (franc suisse)										
End of period Fin de période	1.346	1.455	1.377	1.600	1.637	1.677	1.387	1.237	1.132	1.314
Period average Moyenne sur période	1.236	1.451	1.450	1.502	1.689	1.688	1.559	1.347	1.244	1.245
Syrian Arab Republic [1] (Syrian pound) — Rép. arabe syrienne [1] (livre syrienne)										
End of period Fin de période	11.225	11.225	11.225	11.225	11.225	11.225	11.225	11.225	11.225	11.225
Tajikistan (somoni) — Tadjikistan (somoni)										
End of period Fin de période	0.328	0.747	0.978	1.436	2.200	2.550	3.000	2.957	3.037	3.199
Period average Moyenne sur période	0.296	0.562	0.777	1.238	2.076	2.372	2.764	3.061	2.971	3.117
Thailand (baht) — Thaïlande (baht)										
End of period Fin de période	25.610	47.247	36.691	37.470	43.268	44.222	43.152	39.591	39.061	41.030
Period average Moyenne sur période	25.343	31.364	41.359	37.814	40.112	44.432	42.960	41.485	40.222	40.220
TFYR of Macedonia (TFYR Macedonian denar) — L'ex-R.y. Macédoine (denar de l'ex-R.Y. Macédoine)										
End of period Fin de période	41.411	55.421	51.836	60.339	66.328	69.172	58.598	49.050	45.068	51.859
Period average Moyenne sur période	39.981	50.004	54.462	56.902	65.904	68.037	64.350	54.322	49.410	49.284

Country or area — Pays ou zone	1996	1997	1998	1999	2000	2001	2002	2003	2004	2005
Togo [6] (CFA franc) — Togo [6] (franc CFA)										
End of period / Fin de période	523.700	598.810	562.210	652.953	704.951	744.306	625.495	519.364	481.578	556.037
Period average / Moyenne sur période	511.552	583.669	589.952	615.699	711.976	733.039	696.988	581.200	528.285	527.468
Tonga (pa'anga) — Tonga (pa'anga)										
End of period / Fin de période	1.213	1.362	1.616	1.608	1.977	2.207	2.229	2.020	1.912	2.060
Period average / Moyenne sur période	1.232	1.264	1.492	1.599	1.759	2.124	2.195	2.142	1.972	1.949
Trinidad and Tobago (Trinidad and Tobago dollar) — Trinité-et-Tobago (dollar de la Trinité-et-Tobago)										
End of period / Fin de période	6.195	6.300	6.597	6.300	6.300	6.290	6.300	6.300	6.300	6.310
Period average / Moyenne sur période	6.005	6.252	6.298	6.299	6.300	6.233	6.249	6.295	6.299	6.300
Tunisia (Tunisian dinar) — Tunisie (dinar tunisien)										
End of period / Fin de période	0.999	1.148	1.101	1.253	1.385	1.468	1.334	1.208	1.199	1.363
Period average / Moyenne sur période	0.973	1.106	1.139	1.186	1.371	1.439	1.422	1.289	1.246	1.297
Turkey [20] (new Turkish Lira) — Turquie [20] (nouveau livre turque)										
End of period / Fin de période	0.108	0.206	0.315	0.541	0.673	1.450	1.644	1.397	1.340	1.345
Period average / Moyenne sur période	0.081	0.152	0.261	0.419	0.625	1.226	1.507	1.501	1.426	1.344
Turkmenistan (Turkmen manat) — Turkménistan (manat turkmene)										
End of period / Fin de période	4 070.000	4 165.000	5 200.000	5 200.000	5 200.000	5 200.000	...	...	...	...
Period average / Moyenne sur période	3 257.670	4 143.420	4 890.170	5 200.000	5 200.000	5 200.000	...	...	...	...
Uganda [1] (Uganda shilling) — Ouganda [1] (shilling ougandais)										
End of period / Fin de période	1 029.590	1 140.110	1 362.690	1 506.040	1 766.680	1 727.400	1 852.570	1 935.320	1 738.590	1 816.860
Period average / Moyenne sur période	1 046.080	1 083.010	1 240.310	1 454.830	1 644.480	1 755.660	1 797.550	1 963.720	1 810.300	1 780.670
Ukraine (hryvnia) — Ukraine (hryvnia)										
End of period / Fin de période	1.889	1.899	3.427	5.216	5.435	5.299	5.332	5.332	5.305	5.050
Period average / Moyenne sur période	1.830	1.862	2.450	4.130	5.440	5.372	5.327	5.333	5.319	5.125
United Arab Emirates (UAE dirham) — Emirats arabes unis (dirham des EAU)										
End of period / Fin de période	3.671	3.673	3.673	3.673	3.673	3.673	3.673	3.673	3.673	3.673
United Kingdom (pound sterling) — Royaume-Uni (livre sterling)										
End of period / Fin de période	0.589	0.605	0.601	0.619	0.670	0.690	0.620	0.560	0.518	0.581
Period average / Moyenne sur période	0.641	0.611	0.604	0.618	0.661	0.695	0.667	0.613	0.546	0.550
United Rep. of Tanzania (Tanzania shilling) — Rép.-Unie de Tanzanie (shilling tanzanien)										
End of period / Fin de période	595.640	624.570	681.000	797.330	803.260	916.300	976.300	1 063.620	1 042.960	1 165.510
Period average / Moyenne sur période	579.977	612.123	664.671	744.759	800.409	876.412	966.583	1 038.420	1 089.330	1 128.930
United States (US dollar) — Etats-Unis (dollar des Etats-Unis)										
End of period / Fin de période	1.000	1.000	1.000	1.000	1.000	1.000	1.000	1.000	1.000	1.000
Period average / Moyenne sur période	1.000	1.000	1.000	1.000	1.000	1.000	1.000	1.000	1.000	1.000

Country or area — Pays ou zone	1996	1997	1998	1999	2000	2001	2002	2003	2004	2005
Uruguay (Uruguayan peso) — Uruguay (peso uruguayen)										
End of period Fin de période	8.713	10.040	10.817	11.615	12.515	14.768	27.200	29.300	26.350	24.100
Period average Moyenne sur période	7.972	9.442	10.472	11.339	12.100	13.319	21.257	28.209	28.704	24.479
Uzbekistan (Uzbek sum) — Ouzbékistan (sum ouzbek)										
End of period Fin de période	...	...	...	140.000	...	...	...	...	...	...
Period average Moyenne sur période	40.067	62.917	94.492	124.625	236.608	...	...	...	...	...
Vanuatu (vatu) — Vanuatu (vatu)										
End of period Fin de période	110.770	124.310	129.780	128.890	142.810	146.740	133.170	111.810	106.530	112.330
Period average Moyenne sur période	111.719	115.873	127.517	129.075	137.643	145.313	139.198	122.189	111.790	109.246
Venezuela (Bolivarian Republic of) (bolívar) — Venezuela (République bolivarienne du) (bolívar)										
End of period Fin de période	476.500	504.250	564.500	648.250	699.750	763.000	1 401.250	1 598.000	1 918.000	2 147.000
Period average Moyenne sur période	417.333	488.635	547.556	605.717	679.960	723.666	1 160.950	1 606.960	1 891.330	2 089.750
Viet Nam (dong) — Viet Nam (dong)										
End of period Fin de période	11 149.000	12 292.000	13 890.000	14 028.000	14 514.000	15 084.000	15 403.000	15 646.000	15 777.000	...
Period average Moyenne sur période	11 032.600	11 683.300	13 268.000	13 943.200	14 167.700	14 725.200	15 279.500	15 509.600	...	...
Yemen (Yemeni rial) — Yémen (rial yéménite)										
End of period Fin de période	126.910	130.460	141.650	159.100	165.590	173.270	179.010	184.310	185.870	...
Period average Moyenne sur période	94.157	129.281	135.882	155.718	161.718	168.672	175.625	183.448	184.776	...
Zambia (Zambia kwacha) — Zambie (kwacha zambie)										
End of period Fin de période	1 282.690	1 414.840	2 298.920	2 632.190	4 157.830	3 830.400	4 334.400	4 645.480	4 771.310	3 508.980
Period average Moyenne sur période	1 207.900	1 314.500	1 862.070	2 388.020	3 110.840	3 610.940	4 398.590	4 733.270	4 778.880	4 463.500
Zimbabwe (Zimbabwe dollar) — Zimbabwe (dollar zimbabwéen)										
End of period Fin de période	10.839	18.608	37.369	38.139	55.066	55.036	55.036	823.723	5 729.270	77 964.600
Period average Moyenne sur période	10.002	12.111	23.679	38.301	44.418	55.052	55.036	697.424	5 068.660	22 363.600

Source

International Monetary Fund (IMF), Washington, D.C., *International Financial Statistics*, March 2006 and the IMF database.

Notes

[1] Principal rate.

[2] In October 2002, Afghanistan redenominated its currency. One afghani is equal to 1,000 old afghanis.

[3] Pesos per million US dollars through 1983, per thousand US dollars through 1988 and per US dollar up to 2001. A unified floating exchange rate regime was introduced on 11 Feb. 2002, with the exchange rate determined by market conditions.

[4] Beginning 1999, see Euro Area. For Greece, beginning 2001.

[5] The manat, which was first introduced on 15 August 1992 and circulated alongside the Russian ruble at a fixed rate of 10 rubles per manat, became the sole legal tender in Azerbaijan on 1 January 1994. On 1 January 2006, the new manat, equivalent to 5,000 old manats, was introduced.

Source

Fonds monétaire international (FMI), Washington, D.C., *Statistiques Financières Internationales*, mars 2006 et la base de données du FMI.

Notes

[1] Taux principal.

[2] L'Afghanistan a changé en octobre 2002 la valeur de sa monnaie : un afghani vaut 1 000 afghanis anciens.

[3] Pesos par million de dollars des États-Unis jusqu'en 1983, par millier de dollars des États-Unis jusqu'en 1988 et par dollar des États-Unis apres 2001. Un régime de taux de change flottant unifié a été introduit le 11 février 2002, le taux de change étant déterminé par le marché.

[4] A partir de 1999, voir la Zone euro. Grèce, à partir de 2001.

[5] Le manat, introduit d'abord le 15 août 1992 et circulant parallèlement au rouble russe, au taux fixe de 10 roubles pour un manat, est la seule monnaie ayant cours légal en Azerbaïdjan depuis le 1er janvier 1994. Le nouveau manat, valant 5 000 manats anciens, a été introduit le 1er janvier 2006.

6 Prior to January 1999, the official rate was pegged to the French franc. On 12 January 1994, the CFA franc was devalued to CFAF 100 per French franc from CFAF 50 at which it had been fixed since 1948. From 1 January 1999, the CFAF is pegged to the euro at a rate of CFA francs 655.957 per euro.

7 Bolivianos per million US dollars through 1983, per thousand US dollars for 1984, and per US dollar thereafter.

8 Reals per trillion US dollars through 1983, per billion US dollars 1984-1988, per million US dollars 1989-1992, and per US dollar thereafter.

9 The official rate is pegged to the French franc. Beginning January 12, 1994, the CFA franc was devalued to CFAF 75 per French franc from CFAF 50 at which it had been fixed since 1948.

10 New Zaires per million US dollars through 1990, per thousand US dollars for 1991-1995, and per US dollar thereafter.

11 "Euro Area" is an official descriptor for the European Economic and Monetary Union (EMU). The participating member states of the EMU are Austria, Belgium, Finland, France, Germany, Greece (beginning 2001), Ireland, Italy, Luxembourg, Netherlands, Portugal, and Spain.

12 Prior to January 1999, the official rate was pegged to the French franc at CFAF 100 per French franc. The CFA franc was adopted as national currency as of May 2, 1997. The Guinean peso and the CFA franc were set at PG65 per CFA franc. From January 1, 1999, the CFAF is pegged to the euro at a rate of CFA franc 655.957 per euro.

13 Effective 1 January 2005, Madagascar announced a new currency, the ariary. One ariary is equal to 5 Malagasy francs.

14 Effective 19 October 1994, the official rate of the rufiyaa was pegged to the US dollar at a rate of Rf 11.77 per US dollar. Effective 25 July 2001, the rufiyaa was devalued and fixed at Rf 12.80 per US dollar.

15 Gold córdobas per billion US dollars through 1987, per million US dollars for 1988, per thousand US dollars for 1989-1990 and per US dollar thereafter.

16 New soles per billion US dollars through 1987, per million US dollars for 1988-1989, and per US dollar thereafter.

17 Effective 1 July 2005, Romania redenominated its currency. One new leu is equal to 10,000 old lei.

18 The post-1 January 1998 ruble is equal to 1,000 pre-January 1998 rubles.

19 On 1 January 2004, the Surinamese dollar, equal to 1,000 Surinamese guilders, replaced the guilder as the currency unit.

20 Effective 1 January 2005, Turkey adopted a new currency, the new Turkish lira. One new Turkish lira (yeni Türk lirasi) is equal to 1,000,000 Turkish lira (Türk lirasi).

6 Avant janvier 1999, le taux officiel était établi par référence au franc français. Le 12 janvier 1994, le franc CFA a été dévalué; son taux par rapport au franc français, auquel il est rattaché depuis 1948, est passé de 50 à 100 francs CFA pour 1 franc français. A compter du 1er janvier 1999, le taux officiel est établi par référence à l'euro à un taux de 655,957 francs CFA pour un euro.

7 Bolivianos par million de dollars des États-Unis jusqu'en 1983, par millier de dollars des États-Unis en 1984, et par dollar des États-Unis après cette date.

8 Reals par trillion de dollars des États-Unis jusqu'en 1983, par millard de dollars des États-Unis 1984-1988, par million de dollars des États-Unis 1989-1992, et par dollar de l'État-Unis après cette date.

9 Le taux de change officiel est raccroché au taux de change du franc français. Le 12 janvier 1994, le CFA a été dévalué de 50 par franc français, valeur qu'il avait conservée depuis 1948, à 75 par franc français.

10 Nouveaux zaïres par million de dollars des États-Unis jusqu'en 1990, par millier de dollars des États-Unis en 1991 et 1995, et par dollar des États-Unis après cette date.

11 L'expression "zone euro" est un intitulé officiel pour l'Union économique et monétaire (UEM) européene. L'UEM est composée des pays membres suivants : Allemagne, Autriche, Belgique, Espagne, Finlande, France, Grèce (à partir de 2001), Irlande, Italie, Luxembourg, Pays-Bas et Portugal.

12 Avant janvier 1999, le taux de change officiel était fixé à 100 francs CFA pour un franc français. Le franc CFA avait été adopté comme monnaie nationale à compter du 2 mai 1997. Le taux de change du peso guinéen par rapport au franc CFA a été établi à 65 pesos guinéens pour 1 franc CFA. A compter du 1er janvier 1999, le taux officiel est établi par référence à l'euro : 655,957 francs CFA pour un euro.

13 À compter du 1er janvier 2005, Madagascar a adopté une nouvelle monnaie, l'ariary, qui vaut 5 francs malgaches.

14 À compter du 19 octobre 1994, le taux de change officiel du rufiyaa est indexé sur le dollar des États-Unis, et établi à 11,77 Rf pour 1 dollar. À compter du 25 juillet 2001, le rufiyaa a été dévalué et le taux de change fixe est de 12,80 Rf pour 1 dollar.

15 Córdobas d'or par milliard de dollars des États-Unis jusqu'en 1987, par million de dollars en 1988, par millier de dollars des États-Unis en 1989-1990 et par dollar des États Unis après cette date.

16 Nouveaux soles par milliard de dollars des États-Unis jusqu'en 1987, par million de dollars des États-Unis en 1988-1989 et par dollar des États-Unis après cette date.

17 À compter du 1er juillet 2005, la Roumanie a changé la valeur de sa monnaie : un nouveau leu vaut 10.000 lei anciens.

18 Le rouble ayant cours après le 1er janvier 1998 vaut 1.000 roubles de la période antérieure à cette date.

19 Le 1er janvier 2004, le dollar de Suriname, égal à 1.000 florins de Suriname, a remplacé le florin comme unité monétaire.

20 À compter du 1er janvier 2005, la Turquie a adopté une nouvelle monnaie, la nouvelle livre turque (yeni Türk lirasi), qui vaut 1.000.000 de livres turques (Türk lirasi).

73

Total external and public/publicly guaranteed long-term debt of developing countries
Millions of US dollars
A. Total external debt [+]

Total de la dette extérieure et dette publique extérieure à long terme garantie par l'Etat des pays en développement
Millions de dollars des E.-U.
A. Total de la dette extérieure [+]

Developing economies	1998	1999	2000	2001	2002	2003	2004	Economies en développement
Total long-term debt	1 893 959	1 939 851	1 906 754	1 863 304	1 919 840	2 045 215	2 040 791	Total de la dette à long terme
Public and publicly guaranteed	1 394 997	1 405 168	1 363 432	1 325 664	1 375 430	1 450 089	1 459 114	Dette publique ou garantie par l'Etat
Official creditors	789 845	809 013	781 048	751 638	778 908	826 485	800 704	Créanciers publics
Multilateral	317 326	333 652	333 265	338 540	358 648	381 447	382 783	Multilatéraux
IBRD	108 455	111 329	112 145	112 530	111 303	109 036	104 526	BIRD
IDA	84 088	86 604	86 843	89 220	100 613	113 842	117 488	IDA
Bilateral	472 520	475 361	447 783	413 098	420 261	445 039	417 920	Bilatéraux
Private creditors	605 152	596 155	582 384	574 027	596 522	623 604	658 411	Créanciers privés
Bonds	323 040	341 974	372 050	372 346	396 396	426 772	465 268	Obligations
Commercial banks	197 660	170 447	139 718	135 923	139 667	141 729	144 173	Banques commerciales
Other private	84 452	83 735	70 615	65 758	60 459	55 103	48 969	Autres institutions privées
Private non-guaranteed	498 962	534 683	543 322	537 640	544 410	595 126	581 677	Dette privée non garantie
Undisbursed debt	280 323	303 574	235 691	212 501	211 511	213 033	...	Dette (montants non versés)
Official creditors	215 688	243 434	182 310	168 825	170 649	163 535	...	Créanciers publics
Private creditors	64 634	60 140	53 381	43 676	40 862	49 498	...	Créanciers privés
Commitments	188 869	147 798	147 823	144 355	111 117	129 257	...	Engagements
Official creditors	85 390	66 228	51 023	64 288	50 684	42 849	...	Créanciers publics
Private creditors	103 480	81 570	96 801	80 067	60 432	86 408	...	Créanciers privés
Disbursements	281 342	259 599	247 595	244 272	248 695	299 949	294 094	Versements
Public and publicly guaranteed	158 667	142 758	137 838	119 535	112 786	124 250	158 205	Dette publique ou garantie par l'Etat
Official creditors	63 630	60 595	53 976	51 340	46 277	49 837	47 709	Créanciers publics
Multilateral	41 773	37 277	34 958	34 184	32 280	38 169	27 832	Mutilatéraux
IBRD	14 376	14 082	13 430	12 305	10 288	11 411	8 298	BIRD
IDA	5 556	5 397	5 219	6 092	6 768	6 378	6 347	IDA
Bilateral	21 857	23 318	19 018	17 155	13 998	11 669	19 877	Bilatéraux
Private creditors	95 037	82 164	83 862	68 196	66 509	74 413	110 495	Créanciers privés
Bonds	52 371	50 988	56 119	44 751	40 431	51 518	72 710	Obligations
Commercial banks	32 032	18 951	19 506	17 025	21 220	18 248	31 959	Banques commerciales
Other private	10 635	12 225	8 236	6 420	4 858	4 647	5 826	Autres institutions privés
Private non-guaranteed	122 675	116 841	109 757	124 737	135 909	175 699	135 890	Dette privé non garantie
Principal repayments	176 106	221 926	235 255	243 293	257 026	291 351	253 075	Remboursements du principal
Public and publicly guaranteed	104 251	110 298	122 141	120 117	122 265	143 614	125 045	Dette publique ou garantie par l'Etat
Official creditors	43 351	44 483	49 076	43 799	55 090	64 096	62 138	Créanciers publics
Multilateral	18 383	18 958	23 158	18 869	30 847	36 398	29 062	Multilatéraux
IBRD	10 487	9 834	9 827	9 806	16 022	17 628	14 465	BIRD
IDA	732	869	949	1 085	1 243	1 323	1 540	IDA
Bilateral	24 968	25 525	25 918	24 930	24 243	27 697	33 076	Bilatéraux
Private creditors	60 900	65 815	73 065	76 318	67 175	79 518	62 907	Créanciers privés
Bonds	22 848	23 201	35 322	34 505	28 339	38 732	30 356	Obligations
Commercial banks	22 261	28 919	25 232	28 842	27 511	29 835	21 040	Banques commerciales
Other private	15 791	13 695	12 511	12 972	11 325	10 951	11 511	Autres institutions privées
Private non-guaranteed	71 855	111 628	113 114	123 176	134 761	147 737	128 030	Dette privée non garantie

Total external and public/publicly guaranteed long-term debt of developing countries—Millions of US dollars (*continued*)

A.   Total external debt [+]

Total de la dette extérieure et dette publique extérieure à long terme garantie par l'Etat de pays en développement—Millions de dollars des E.-U. (*suite*)

A.   Total de la dette extérieure [+]

Developing economies	1998	1999	2000	2001	2002	2003	2004	Economies en développement
Net flows	105 236	37 674	12 340	979	−8 331	8 598	41 019	Apports nets
Public and publicly guaranteed	54 416	32 461	15 697	−582	−9 478	−19 364	33 159	Dette publique ou garantie par l'Etat
Official creditors	20 278	16 112	4 900	7 541	−8 813	−14 259	−14 429	Créanciers publics
Multilateral	23 390	18 319	11 800	15 315	1 433	1 770	−1 230	Multilatéraux
IBRD	3 889	4 248	3 603	2 500	−5 734	−6 217	−6 167	BIRD
IDA	4 824	4 528	4 271	5 007	5 525	5 056	4 808	IDA
Bilateral	−3 111	−2 207	−6 900	−7 775	−10 245	−16 029	−13 199	Bilatéraux
Private creditors	34 138	16 349	10 797	−8 122	−666	−5 105	47 588	Créanciers privés
Bonds	29 523	27 787	20 798	10 246	12 092	12 785	42 354	Obligations
Commercial banks	9 770	−9 968	−5 726	−11 816	−6 290	−11 586	10 919	Banques commerciales
Other private	−5 156	−1 470	−4 275	−6 552	−6 468	−6 304	−5 685	Autres institutions privées
Private non-guaranteed	50 820	5 214	−3 356	1 561	1 148	27 962	7 860	Dette privée non garantie
Interest payments	90 223	95 198	100 590	95 332	82 972	88 480	88 666	Paiements d'intérêts
Public and publicly guaranteed	61 590	63 015	67 522	64 546	57 768	61 352	58 779	Dette publique ou garantie par l'Etat
Official creditors	26 106	26 917	27 041	28 117	24 200	23 816	21 552	Créanciers publics
Multilateral	12 675	14 899	15 592	15 283	13 682	12 226	9 749	Multilatéraux
IBRD	6 612	7 267	7 682	7 469	6 392	5 133	3 917	BIRD
IDA	550	588	578	576	695	698	799	IDA
Bilateral	13 431	12 018	11 449	12 833	10 519	11 590	11 802	Bilatéraux
Private creditors	35 484	36 098	40 481	36 429	33 568	37 535	37 228	Créanciers privés
Bonds	19 677	23 177	26 791	23 241	22 700	25 880	27 449	Obligations
Commercial banks	10 739	8 622	9 899	9 696	8 502	9 318	7 405	Banques commerciales
Other private	5 069	4 299	3 791	3 492	2 366	2 338	2 374	Autres institutions privées
Private non-guaranteed	28 633	32 183	33 068	30 786	25 204	27 129	29 887	Dette privée non garantie
Net transfers	15 013	−57 524	−88 249	−94 353	−91 302	−79 882	−47 647	Transferts nets
Public and publicly guaranteed	−7 174	−30 555	−51 825	−65 127	−67 246	−80 716	−25 620	Dette publique ou garantie par l'Etat
Official creditors	−5 827	−10 806	−22 141	−20 576	−33 013	−38 075	−35 981	Créanciers publics
Multilateral	10 715	3 420	−3 792	32	−12 249	−10 456	−10 979	Multilatéraux
IBRD	−2 723	−3 019	−4 079	−4 970	−12 126	−11 350	−10 084	BIRD
IDA	4 274	3 940	3 693	4 430	4 830	4 358	4 009	IDA
Bilateral	−16 543	−14 225	−18 349	−20 608	−20 764	−27 619	−25 001	Bilatéraux
Private creditors	−1 347	−19 749	−29 684	−44 551	−34 233	−42 641	10 361	Créanciers privés
Bonds	9 847	4 610	−5 993	−12 995	−10 608	−13 094	14 905	Obligations
Commercial banks	−968	−18 590	−15 625	−21 512	−14 792	−20 905	3 514	Banques commerciales
Other private	−10 225	−5 769	−8 066	−10 044	−8 833	−8 642	−8 058	Autres institutions privées
Private non-guaranteed	22 187	−26 970	−36 424	−29 225	−24 056	833	−22 027	Dette privée non garantie
Total debt service	266 329	317 124	335 845	338 625	339 997	379 831	341 741	Total du service de la dette
Public and publicly guaranteed	165 841	173 313	189 663	184 663	180 032	204 965	183 824	Dette publique ou garantie par l'Etat
Official creditors	69 457	71 400	76 117	71 916	79 290	87 912	83 690	Créanciers publics
Multilateral	31 057	33 857	38 750	34 152	44 529	48 625	38 811	Multilatéraux
IBRD	17 099	17 101	17 510	17 275	22 414	22 761	18 381	BIRD
IDA	1 282	1 457	1 527	1 661	1 938	2 020	2 338	IDA
Bilateral	38 400	37 543	37 367	37 763	34 762	39 287	44 878	Bilatéraux
Private creditors	96 384	101 913	113 546	112 747	100 742	117 054	100 135	Créanciers publics
Bonds	42 524	46 378	62 113	57 746	51 039	64 612	57 805	Obligations
Commercial banks	33 000	37 541	35 131	38 537	36 013	39 153	28 445	Banques commerciales
Other private	20 860	17 994	16 302	16 464	13 691	13 289	13 884	Autres institutions privées
Private non-guaranteed	100 488	143 811	146 181	153 962	159 965	174 866	157 917	Dette privée non garantie

73

Total external and public/publicly guaranteed long-term debt of developing countries
Millions US dollars
B. Public and publicly guaranteed long-term debt

Total de la dette extérieure et dette publique extérieure à long terme garantie par l'Etat des pays en développement
Millions de dollars E.-U.
B. Dette publique extérieure à long terme garantie par l'Etat

Country or area — Pays ou zone	1995	1996	1997	1998	1999	2000	2001	2002	2003	2004
Albania Albanie	329.6	405.1	412.1	506.1	583.4	921.3	971.2	995.5	1 232.9	1 404.5
Algeria Algérie	31 303.0	31 285.5	28 712.0	28 481.6	25 895.6	23 331.6	20 870.2	21 336.3	21 881.2	20 249.3
Angola Angola	9 542.5	9 377.3	8 681.6	9 099.6	8 713.0	8 084.8	7 782.7	7 980.9	8 194.0	8 630.6
Argentina Argentine	54 930.2	62 226.7	66 888.7	77 147.7	84 444.4	88 122.1	88 441.9	91 981.9	99 192.0	103 850.2
Armenia Arménie	298.3	402.7	484.4	568.6	651.4	675.1	715.6	818.5	877.2	960.7
Azerbaijan Azerbaïdjan	206.1	247.9	237.3	314.2	528.4	761.3	805.6	1 065.2	1 307.2	1 409.4
Bangladesh Bangladesh	15 106.4	14 661.0	13 876.7	15 098.7	15 995.2	15 167.7	14 741.0	16 403.5	18 068.0	19 171.3
Barbados Barbade	371.5	383.0	366.9	387.8	443.9	548.2	700.7	712.2	721.2	702.5
Belarus Bélarus	1 301.1	728.9	681.4	796.4	709.1	688.9	664.3	748.6	710.0	743.5
Belize Belize	219.4	250.4	268.1	282.9	341.0	556.6	648.7	779.6	942.4	925.0
Benin Bénin	1 483.0	1 447.0	1 396.4	1 472.0	1 472.9	1 441.9	1 505.4	1 689.2	1 726.2	1 827.1
Bhutan Bhoutan	105.2	112.9	117.6	171.0	181.8	202.2	265.2	376.9	414.9	593.3
Bolivia Bolivie	4 458.6	4 256.6	4 130.3	4 293.0	4 243.0	4 133.7	3 121.2	3 511.6	4 249.2	4 644.8
Bosnia and Herzegovina Bosnie-Herzégovine	...	...	...	...	2 237.2	1 949.5	1 760.1	2 010.8	2 294.0	2 643.9
Botswana Botswana	707.0	620.5	534.7	524.7	484.5	437.8	378.9	472.4	484.6	488.3
Brazil Brésil	98 305.8	96 368.1	87 321.5	98 819.5	93 616.5	98 005.4	98 194.1	101 476.4	101 542.9	97 865.3
Bulgaria Bulgarie	8 807.9	8 223.0	7 736.8	7 972.8	7 777.6	7 671.3	7 386.6	7 479.9	7 749.1	7 433.7
Burkina Faso Burkina Faso	1 143.3	1 166.8	1 146.2	1 292.0	1 363.4	1 229.6	1 316.3	1 408.9	1 597.2	1 823.2
Burundi Burundi	1 099.3	1 084.9	1 025.6	1 082.1	1 053.1	1 036.0	985.6	1 104.3	1 251.9	1 324.9
Cambodia Cambodge	2 109.9	2 177.3	2 192.7	2 261.4	2 292.9	2 328.1	2 392.8	2 587.3	2 814.2	3 015.9
Cameroon Cameroun	8 050.0	7 990.3	7 763.6	8 228.2	7 650.6	7 440.8	6 971.1	7 289.8	8 045.0	7 924.3
Cape Verde Cap-Vert	185.0	196.0	199.5	240.9	308.0	314.6	341.3	385.0	441.4	463.0
Central African Rep. Rép. centrafricaine	853.9	850.4	801.5	841.0	826.1	795.7	756.8	980.0	900.4	926.2

Total external and public/publicly guaranteed long-term debt of developing countries — Millions US dollars (*continued*)

B.   Public and publicly guaranteed long term debt

Total de la dette extérieure et dette publique extérieure à long terme garantie par l'Etat de pays en développement — Millions de dollars E.-U. (*suite*)

B.   Dette publique extérieure à long terme garantie par l'Etat

Country or area — Pays ou zone	1995	1996	1997	1998	1999	2000	2001	2002	2003	2004
Chad Tchad	843.1	926.6	928.2	1 001.5	1 054.0	1 031.2	1 023.9	1 190.9	1 461.7	1 582.3
Chile Chili	7 178.3	4 883.3	4 367.1	5 004.8	5 654.6	5 255.2	5 581.2	6 799.5	8 046.3	9 426.0
China Chine	94 674.5	102 260.2	112 821.4	99 424.1	99 217.3	94 860.0	91 775.7	88 613.2	85 329.2	90 814.7
Colombia Colombie	13 949.6	14 854.1	15 436.5	16 749.4	20 220.1	20 803.2	21 776.5	20 668.8	22 783.5	23 372.4
Comoros Comores	202.1	214.7	211.9	220.7	214.8	207.9	223.1	245.4	265.3	275.2
Congo Congo	4 955.4	4 665.7	4 283.8	4 250.5	3 933.7	3 757.5	3 631.0	3 974.0	4 425.9	5 050.7
Costa Rica Costa Rica	3 133.4	2 923.2	2 768.7	3 032.5	3 194.8	3 264.0	3 272.8	3 139.1	3 621.9	3 858.8
Côte d'Ivoire Côte d'Ivoire	11 902.1	11 366.7	10 427.1	10 799.7	9 699.1	9 063.4	8 602.7	9 110.3	9 700.5	9 827.6
Croatia Croatie	1 860.4	3 337.1	4 273.8	4 924.8	5 523.2	6 111.3	6 424.5	7 679.3	10 062.1	11 668.3
Czech Republic République tchèque	9 760.4	12 232.3	12 939.7	11 596.4	7 684.5	6 557.0	5 708.4	7 090.3	8 735.3	12 020.1
Dem. Rep. of the Congo Rép. dém. du Congo	9 635.8	9 275.2	8 628.3	9 214.3	8 262.3	7 880.2	7 586.5	8 845.4	10 161.3	10 532.0
Djibouti Djibouti	268.9	279.3	253.0	263.8	248.4	237.9	235.7	305.2	366.5	393.9
Dominica Dominique	98.6	102.1	94.6	98.1	99.0	147.8	193.4	200.4	202.8	213.3
Dominican Republic Rép. dominicaine	3 652.6	3 523.4	3 461.1	3 482.4	3 584.0	3 311.3	3 790.3	4 029.9	5 080.6	5 815.2
Ecuador Equateur	12 067.7	12 443.8	12 876.2	13 089.0	13 555.8	11 337.3	11 251.0	11 243.6	11 371.8	10 628.6
Egypt Egypte	30 710.2	29 047.5	26 978.8	27 793.9	26 269.5	24 510.0	25 342.0	25 874.9	27 265.8	27 352.7
El Salvador El Salvador	2 079.8	2 316.6	2 396.3	2 441.6	2 647.0	2 772.0	3 250.0	4 712.2	5 212.5	5 383.8
Equatorial Guinea Guinée équatoriale	229.6	222.2	208.6	216.5	207.9	198.9	192.1	209.1	227.7	244.4
Eritrea Erythrée	36.7	44.3	75.5	146.1	252.6	298.0	394.8	489.2	605.1	666.4
Estonia Estonie	159.3	216.5	197.5	234.4	205.5	210.5	186.5	481.7	560.1	561.8
Ethiopia Ethiopie	9 773.6	9 483.8	9 424.8	9 613.8	5 361.9	5 326.9	5 561.4	6 318.8	6 943.1	6 351.4
Fiji Fidji	163.2	142.3	125.8	136.7	118.5	99.5	85.4	96.0	110.5	119.6
Gabon Gabon	3 976.4	3 971.6	3 664.8	3 835.4	3 293.0	3 453.5	3 041.3	3 240.9	3 394.8	3 800.1
Gambia Gambie	385.5	411.9	401.2	433.6	431.1	437.9	435.3	507.1	567.0	622.0
Georgia Géorgie	1 039.4	1 106.3	1 189.5	1 301.0	1 309.1	1 273.9	1 310.6	1 444.9	1 564.0	1 610.8

73

Total external and public/publicly guaranteed long-term debt of developing countries—Millions US dollars (*continued*)

B. Public and publicly guaranteed long term debt

Total de la dette extérieure et dette publique extérieure à long terme garantie par l'Etat de pays en développement—Millions de dollars E.-U. (*suite*)

B. Dette publique extérieure à long terme garantie par l'Etat

Country or area — Pays ou zone	1995	1996	1997	1998	1999	2000	2001	2002	2003	2004
Ghana Ghana	4 199.7	4 327.5	4 429.2	5 004.0	5 144.2	4 994.4	5 253.5	5 755.7	6 400.6	5 860.7
Grenada Grenade	112.4	118.8	107.7	107.2	112.1	179.8	183.9	294.1	300.1	347.1
Guatemala Guatemala	2 328.1	2 209.2	2 323.9	2 428.6	2 531.9	2 539.7	2 928.4	3 097.7	3 426.6	3 795.6
Guinea Guinée	2 987.1	2 980.6	3 008.7	3 126.4	3 061.0	2 940.4	2 843.8	2 972.5	3 154.0	3 187.7
Guinea-Bissau Guinée-Bissau	797.7	856.2	838.4	874.3	834.2	715.5	627.2	662.3	712.5	737.9
Guyana Guyana	1 794.4	1 351.6	1 328.9	1 197.9	1 129.8	1 123.8	1 095.4	1 145.4	1 217.1	1 140.1
Haiti Haïti	760.8	843.2	902.1	982.4	1 041.2	1 039.5	1 028.2	1 063.4	1 173.8	1 186.4
Honduras Honduras	4 187.4	4 020.9	4 058.5	4 042.9	4 311.5	4 420.6	3 994.7	4 187.7	4 570.6	5 124.1
Hungary Hongrie	23 974.4	18 724.5	15 128.7	15 904.3	16 869.3	14 354.5	12 696.5	13 551.3	16 342.8	20 725.4
India Inde	80 422.0	78 045.2	79 398.1	84 611.3	86 410.3	80 050.2	78 817.7	82 255.6	85 577.8	88 699.2
Indonesia Indonésie	65 308.8	60 011.9	55 856.7	67 304.7	73 678.4	69 784.8	68 738.7	70 519.8	73 976.1	72 916.7
Iran (Islamic Rep. of) Iran (Rép. islamique d')	15 115.6	11 710.6	8 285.1	7 712.0	5 731.9	4 706.6	5 291.5	6 604.0	8 933.4	9 984.9
Jamaica Jamaïque	3 712.1	3 192.6	2 774.5	2 975.5	2 883.9	3 759.5	4 308.4	4 598.9	4 501.0	5 170.5
Jordan Jordanie	6 624.2	6 448.1	6 143.4	6 498.3	6 714.2	6 182.8	6 632.3	7 071.7	7 172.6	7 233.6
Kazakhstan Kazakhstan	2 833.8	1 946.5	2 621.6	3 037.8	3 360.1	3 622.5	3 450.2	3 210.4	3 464.1	3 209.3
Kenya Kenya	5 856.8	5 573.7	5 093.1	5 513.2	5 344.1	5 045.5	4 745.1	5 267.5	5 797.3	5 978.4
Kyrgyzstan Kirghizistan	472.2	626.3	750.6	933.9	1 134.4	1 220.3	1 256.8	1 397.5	1 588.0	1 740.5
Lao People's Dem. Rep. Rép. dém. pop. lao	2 091.2	2 185.8	2 246.8	2 373.1	2 471.3	2 452.6	2 455.9	2 620.2	2 800.9	2 917.9
Latvia Lettonie	271.1	300.4	313.7	404.2	864.8	827.1	978.2	1 123.6	1 238.1	1 587.0
Lebanon Liban	1 550.5	1 933.4	2 349.1	4 047.8	5 332.4	6 579.4	8 952.4	13 829.1	14 778.2	17 459.9
Lesotho Lesotho	642.0	663.5	641.9	660.5	661.0	656.7	578.5	631.8	676.0	725.6
Liberia Libéria	1 161.4	1 110.0	1 061.3	1 092.3	1 062.2	1 040.1	1 011.8	1 064.6	1 126.8	1 167.7
Lithuania Lituanie	429.9	736.2	1 053.4	1 220.6	2 122.6	2 188.2	2 362.9	2 478.0	2 112.8	2 507.0
Madagascar Madagascar	3 687.3	3 535.7	3 865.1	4 096.1	4 358.2	4 285.8	3 786.7	4 130.1	4 615.8	3 232.0
Malawi Malawi	2 079.3	2 092.2	2 096.3	2 304.8	2 587.0	2 544.6	2 469.1	2 670.6	2 935.0	3 297.2

Total external and public/publicly guaranteed long-term debt of developing countries—Millions US dollars (*continued*)

B.   Public and publicly guaranteed long term debt

Total de la dette extérieure et dette publique extérieure à long terme garantie par l'Etat de pays en développement—Millions de dollars E.-U. (*suite*)

B.   Dette publique extérieure à long terme garantie par l'Etat

Country or area — Pays ou zone	1995	1996	1997	1998	1999	2000	2001	2002	2003	2004
Malaysia Malaisie	16 022.7	15 702.0	16 807.5	18 154.5	18 930.1	19 233.7	24 156.3	26 414.7	25 376.4	25 560.1
Maldives Maldives	151.9	163.5	164.3	183.4	194.1	184.7	180.7	223.0	255.1	304.4
Mali Mali	2 739.3	2 762.7	2 701.9	2 833.1	2 813.6	2 671.0	2 642.5	2 517.8	2 910.1	3 132.1
Mauritania Mauritanie	2 127.0	2 169.2	2 077.1	2 048.9	2 147.8	2 028.5	1 914.3	1 913.3	2 049.5	2 046.1
Mauritius Maurice	1 147.9	1 152.5	1 152.5	1 126.1	1 138.2	834.5	764.4	837.0	927.5	858.7
Mexico Mexique	93 901.6	92 797.6	83 302.2	87 044.7	87 910.7	81 488.2	77 026.8	76 326.0	77 511.0	77 193.0
Mongolia Mongolie	472.1	485.8	533.3	650.0	841.1	833.4	823.7	949.0	1 137.5	1 305.7
Morocco Maroc	23 190.0	22 393.3	20 413.9	20 730.7	18 850.9	17 277.9	15 722.6	14 783.9	15 164.3	14 862.8
Mozambique Mozambique	5 208.7	5 357.8	5 211.0	5 954.9	4 637.5	4 499.7	2 200.5	2 512.4	2 809.4	3 157.3
Myanmar Myanmar	5 377.7	4 803.5	5 068.7	5 052.7	5 337.1	5 241.6	5 006.5	5 390.8	5 857.4	5 646.6
Nepal Népal	2 346.5	2 345.7	2 332.3	2 590.6	2 932.9	2 804.9	2 654.3	2 928.5	3 175.6	3 332.0
Nicaragua Nicaragua	8 565.7	5 148.3	5 364.4	5 635.6	5 778.8	5 492.3	5 437.2	5 573.2	5 893.5	4 125.1
Niger Niger	1 314.4	1 315.4	1 308.1	1 436.7	1 451.3	1 459.3	1 408.4	1 603.9	1 897.9	1 772.1
Nigeria Nigéria	28 140.0	25 430.5	22 631.2	23 445.0	22 357.7	30 019.9	29 218.1	28 057.1	31 563.5	31 303.8
Oman Oman	2 637.3	2 645.8	2 567.1	2 235.0	2 595.8	2 970.0	2 687.5	2 048.7	1 558.1	1 209.1
Pakistan Pakistan	23 787.5	23 621.9	23 974.0	26 141.4	28 136.3	27 174.9	26 487.8	28 104.9	30 912.8	31 029.3
Panama Panama	3 784.0	5 138.4	5 077.2	5 423.0	5 681.0	5 708.1	6 329.6	6 406.1	6 565.5	7 305.2
Papua New Guinea Papouasie-Nouvelle-Guinée	1 667.7	1 544.9	1 338.4	1 430.0	1 517.1	1 490.3	1 397.0	1 479.3	1 504.5	1 445.1
Paraguay Paraguay	1 453.0	1 415.2	1 463.8	1 590.6	2 074.5	2 060.1	1 988.9	2 055.0	2 216.5	2 452.7
Peru Pérou	18 930.7	20 218.9	19 215.8	19 309.8	19 491.5	19 236.9	18 900.6	20 390.9	22 036.9	23 500.3
Philippines Philippines	28 525.3	27 072.0	26 394.8	29 172.9	34 765.4	33 739.2	29 210.4	32 323.7	36 033.0	35 564.0
Poland Pologne	41 073.4	39 208.4	34 177.5	35 136.2	33 150.6	30 784.5	25 709.2	29 374.0	34 964.0	36 594.9
Republic of Moldova République de Moldova	449.5	548.7	795.8	796.5	719.1	852.8	792.0	825.8	848.2	753.5
Romania Roumanie	3 957.0	5 631.7	6 346.5	6 646.4	5 640.6	6 589.2	7 034.3	9 034.4	11 729.4	13 667.1
Russian Federation Fédération de Russie	101 582.0	101 915.5	106 541.6	121 574.3	121 188.3	111 018.3	103 757.0	96 113.2	98 875.0	99 646.0

73

Total external and public/publicly guaranteed long-term debt of developing countries — Millions US dollars (*continued*)

B.   Public and publicly guaranteed long term debt

Total de la dette extérieure et dette publique extérieure à long terme garantie par l'Etat de pays en développement — Millions de dollars E.-U. (*suite*)

B.   Dette publique extérieure à long terme garantie par l'Etat

Country or area — Pays ou zone	1995	1996	1997	1998	1999	2000	2001	2002	2003	2004
Rwanda Rwanda	972.4	986.7	995.7	1 122.0	1 163.7	1 148.5	1 164.7	1 306.6	1 418.0	1 545.1
Saint Kitts and Nevis Saint-Kitts-et-Nevis	54.2	62.7	112.0	124.4	133.8	152.7	214.7	260.9	314.9	313.5
Saint Lucia Sainte-Lucie	111.3	121.4	119.9	133.6	140.9	167.6	166.0	210.7	235.0	256.7
St. Vincent-Grenadines St. Vincent-Grenadines	92.3	93.9	92.8	108.1	162.6	164.3	163.3	173.6	194.6	223.4
Samoa Samoa	168.1	162.8	148.3	154.3	156.6	147.3	143.3	156.8	169.3	177.1
Sao Tome and Principe Sao Tomé-et-Principe	231.0	225.7	226.0	244.5	294.4	300.4	301.6	317.2	337.8	349.7
Senegal Sénégal	3 244.3	3 219.9	3 228.8	3 482.1	3 349.9	3 192.5	3 163.0	3 541.3	4 001.1	3 553.4
Serbia and Montenegro Serbie-et-Monténégro	6 788.4	6 526.6	6 108.9	6 461.1	6 194.6	6 177.9	6 177.5	8 430.9	9 417.3	9 507.6
Seychelles Seychelles	186.5	177.1	170.6	202.3	213.2	310.9	401.7	427.2	439.0	513.5
Sierra Leone Sierra Leone	1 057.8	1 046.7	1 023.5	1 093.4	1 066.0	1 005.8	1 120.9	1 260.0	1 417.7	1 519.6
Slovakia Slovaquie	3 487.5	3 962.8	4 449.5	5 417.4	5 957.7	6 304.2	5 531.2	4 295.0	4 507.7	5 162.9
Solomon Islands Iles Salomon	100.3	100.5	96.5	113.7	125.3	120.7	130.9	150.2	151.3	155.3
Somalia Somalie	1 960.8	1 918.2	1 852.5	1 886.4	1 859.4	1 825.1	1 794.7	1 859.9	1 936.1	1 949.0
South Africa Afrique du Sud	9 836.7	10 347.5	11 516.9	10 667.8	8 173.3	9 087.7	7 941.0	9 427.1	9 120.1	9 793.4
Sri Lanka Sri Lanka	7 174.8	7 120.4	7 077.5	8 063.6	8 412.9	7 944.1	7 499.7	8 400.4	9 105.9	9 765.2
Sudan Soudan	9 779.4	9 369.2	8 998.2	9 225.9	8 852.0	10 431.1	10 625.0	10 922.1	11 374.6	11 724.2
Swaziland Swaziland	279.2	271.0	283.6	307.1	308.1	286.7	283.2	335.8	421.3	456.0
Syrian Arab Republic Rép. arabe syrienne	16 853.3	16 762.2	16 326.4	16 352.6	16 142.4	15 929.8	15 809.2	15 848.7	15 847.6	15 742.4
Tajikistan Tadjikistan	590.4	656.8	669.0	702.5	741.3	755.1	761.6	901.1	900.7	744.5
Thailand Thaïlande	16 826.4	16 887.1	22 292.0	28 087.6	31 305.8	29 452.5	26 208.0	22 523.8	17 701.6	15 322.6
TFYR of Macedonia L'ex-R.y. Macédoine	788.4	856.3	941.7	1 053.8	1 138.3	1 192.1	1 145.2	1 264.6	1 437.7	1 536.8
Togo Togo	1 286.2	1 310.2	1 214.1	1 325.3	1 286.6	1 230.4	1 204.3	1 337.1	1 497.3	1 597.2
Tonga Tonga	61.5	61.4	55.3	59.8	62.8	59.9	57.9	67.2	79.1	80.7
Trinidad and Tobago Trinité-et-Tobago	1 799.8	1 876.2	1 532.8	1 477.9	1 485.4	1 584.7	1 535.3	1 546.8	1 601.4	1 420.6
Tunisia Tunisie	9 022.4	9 376.8	9 333.2	9 494.3	9 474.5	8 884.3	9 069.4	10 929.9	13 227.7	14 573.8

73

Total external and public/publicly guaranteed long-term debt of developing countries—Millions US dollars (*continued*)

B. Public and publicly guaranteed long term debt

Total de la dette extérieure et dette publique extérieure à long terme garantie par l'Etat de pays en développement—Millions de dollars E.-U. (*suite*)

B. Dette publique extérieure à long terme garantie par l'Etat

Country or area—Pays ou zone	1995	1996	1997	1998	1999	2000	2001	2002	2003	2004
Turkey Turquie	50 317.0	48 403.8	47 513.3	50 197.3	50 755.3	56 418.8	54 236.7	60 220.4	64 506.9	68 212.1
Turkmenistan Turkménistan	384.9	464.2	1 242.4	1 731.2	...	...	...	...	...	...
Uganda Ouganda	3 071.9	3 160.8	3 375.9	3 385.2	2 994.2	3 051.3	3 304.9	3 576.7	4 170.3	4 497.5
Ukraine Ukraine	6 580.5	6 647.5	7 015.2	8 971.9	9 590.4	8 141.8	8 098.5	8 272.1	8 890.9	10 728.5
United Rep. of Tanzania Rép.-Unie de Tanzanie	6 216.9	6 104.3	5 775.6	6 086.9	6 316.3	5 732.0	5 276.3	5 679.5	5 722.4	6 225.0
Uruguay Uruguay	3 833.2	4 083.5	4 554.3	5 114.1	5 088.0	5 547.0	6 067.2	6 722.7	7 133.4	7 250.5
Uzbekistan Ouzbékistan	1 415.2	1 980.8	2 107.6	2 660.7	3 565.2	3 763.5	3 904.3	4 003.2	4 256.9	4 301.9
Vanuatu Vanuatu	43.9	42.9	39.7	55.2	64.5	73.1	70.2	76.5	79.8	81.2
Venezuela (Bolivarian Rep. of) Venezuela (Rép. bolivar. du)	28 222.5	27 745.9	27 368.4	28 349.9	27 968.9	27 747.5	25 230.3	23 378.8	24 470.6	25 851.6
Viet Nam Viet Nam	21 778.4	21 962.3	18 982.4	19 873.7	20 479.4	11 581.1	11 427.2	12 158.7	14 188.6	16 575.9
Yemen Yémen	5 527.9	5 622.0	3 433.8	5 231.8	5 372.3	4 059.2	4 276.8	4 497.4	4 744.5	4 799.3
Zambia Zambie	5 290.8	5 369.2	5 251.5	5 326.3	4 505.4	4 443.7	4 826.6	5 256.0	5 569.6	5 860.6
Zimbabwe Zimbabwe	3 460.8	3 317.2	3 066.9	3 191.3	2 982.5	2 774.0	2 678.8	3 020.7	3 388.3	3 558.0

Source

World Bank, Washington, D.C., *Global Development Finance 2005*, volumes 1 and 2.

Note

+ The following abbreviations have been used in the table:

IBRD: International Bank for Reconstruction and Development.

IDA: International Development Association.

Source

Banque mondiale, Washington, D.C., *Global Development Finance 2005*, volumes 1 et 2.

Note

+ Les abréviations ci-après ont été utilisées dans le tableau :

BIRD : Banque internationale pour la réconstruction et le développement.

IDA : Association internationale de développement.

Table 72: Foreign exchange rates are shown in units of national currency per US dollar. The exchange rates are classified into three broad categories, reflecting both the role of the authorities in the determination of the exchange and/or the multiplicity of exchange rates in a country. The *market rate* is used to describe exchange rates determined largely by market forces; the *official rate* is an exchange rate determined by the authorities, sometimes in a flexible manner. For countries maintaining multiple exchange arrangements, the rates are labelled *principal rate*, *secondary rate*, and *tertiary rate*. Unless otherwise stated, the table refers to end of period and period averages of market exchange rates or official exchange rates. For further information see *International Financial Statistics* [13] and www.imf.org.

Table 73: The data on external debt for developing countries were extracted from *Global Development Finance 2005* [32], published by the World Bank in April 2005 and do not reflect the World Bank 2006 fiscal year income classifications nor the November 2005 advance-release country data. In this table, developing countries are those in which 2003 GNI per capita was below $9,386.

The World Bank Debtor Reporting System (DRS) maintains statistics on the external debt of developing countries on a loan-by-loan basis. The estimated total external indebtedness of developing countries is a combination of DRS data and other information obtained from creditors through the debt data collection systems of other agencies such as the Bank for International Settlements (BIS) and the Organization for Economic Co-operation and Development (OECD), supplemented by market sources and estimates made by country economists of the World Bank and desk officers of the International Monetary Fund (IMF).

Long-term external debt is defined as debt that has an original or extended maturity of more than one year and that is owed to non-residents and is repayable in foreign currency, goods, or services. Long-term debt has three components: a) public debt, which is an external obligation of a public debtor, including the national government, a political subdivision (or an agency of either), and autonomous public bodies; b) publicly guaranteed debt, which is an external obligation of a private debtor that is guaranteed for repayment by a public entity; and c) private non-guaranteed external debt, which is an external obligation of a private debtor that is not guaranteed for repayment by a public entity. Public and publicly guaranteed long-term debt are aggregated.

All data related to public and publicly guaranteed debt are from debtors except for those on lending by some multilateral agencies, in which case the data are taken from the creditors' records. These creditors include the African Development

Tableau 72 : Les taux des changes sont exprimés par le nombre d'unités de monnaie nationale pour un dollar des Etats-Unis. Les taux de change sont classés en trois catégories, qui dénotent le rôle des autorités dans l'établissement des taux de change et/ou la multiplicité des taux de change dans un pays. Par *taux du marché*, on entend les taux de change déterminés essentiellement par les forces du marché; le *taux officiel* est un taux de change établi par les autorités, parfois selon des dispositions souples. Pour les pays qui continuent à mettre en œuvre des régimes de taux de change multiples, les taux sont désignés par les appellations suivantes : *"taux principal"*, *"taux secondaire"* et *"taux tertiaire"*. Sauf indication con-traire, le tableau indique des taux de fin de période et les moyennes sur la période, des taux de change du marché ou des taux de change officiels. Pour plus de renseignements, voir *Statistiques financières internationales* [13] et www.imf.org.

Tableau 73 : Les données concernant la dette extérieure des pays en développement sont tirées de *Global Development Finance 2005*, publié par la Banque mondiale en avril 2005, et ne correspondent donc pas au classement des revenus fixé par la Banque pour l'exercice 2006, ni aux données préliminaires publiées en novembre 2005. Les pays en développement sont dans ce tableau ceux où le RNB par habitant était en 2003 inférieur à 9.386 dollars.

Le Système de notification de la dette de la Banque mondiale sert à tenir à jour prêt par prêt les statistiques de la dette extérieure des pays en développement. Le total estimatif de la dette extérieure des pays en développement a été calculé en combinant les données du Système de notification avec d'autres informations obtenues auprès des créanciers par le biais des systèmes de collecte de données d'autres organismes, tels que la Banque des règlements internationaux (BRI) et l'Organisation de coopération et développement économiques, ou de sources du marché, et avec des estimations des économistes chargés des pays à la Banque mondiale et au Fonds monétaire international (FMI).

La dette extérieure à long terme s'entend de celle dont la maturité d'origine (ou la maturité après prorogation) est à plus d'un an, contractée auprès de non-résidents et remboursable en devises, en biens ou en services. La dette à long terme comporte trois éléments : a) la dette publique, dette (ou administration relevant de l'un ou de l'autre), et administrations publiques autonomes; b) la dette garantie par une administration publique, obligation extérieure d'un débiteur privé dont le remboursement est garanti par une entité publique; c) la dette extérieure privée non garantie, obligation extérieure d'un débiteur privé dont le remboursement n'est pas garanti par une entité publique. La dette extérieure publique et la dette extérieure garantie à long terme sont agrégées.

Bank, the Asian Development Bank, the Central Bank for Economic Integration, the Inter-American Development Bank, the International Bank for Reconstruction and Development (IBRD) and the International Development Association (IDA). (The IBRD and IDA are components of the World Bank.)

The data referring to public and publicly guaranteed debt do not include data for (a) transactions with the International Monetary Fund, (b) debt repayable in local currency, (c) direct investment and (d) short term debt (that is, debt with an original maturity of less than a year).

The data referring to private non guaranteed debt also exclude the above items but include contractual obligations on loans to direct investment enterprises by foreign parent companies or their affiliates.

Data are aggregated by type of creditor. The breakdown is as follows:

Official creditors

(a)   Loans from international organizations (multilateral loans), excluding loans from funds administered by an international organization on behalf of a single donor government. The latter are classified as loans from governments;

(b)   Loans from governments (bilateral loans) and from autonomous public bodies;

Private creditors

(a)   Suppliers: Credits from manufacturers, exporters, or other suppliers of goods;

(b)   Financial markets: Loans from private banks and other private financial institutions as well as publicly issued and privately placed bonds;

(c)   Other: External liabilities on account of nationalized properties and unclassified debts to private creditors.

A distinction is made between the following categories of external public debt:

- Debt outstanding (including undisbursed) is the sum of disbursed and undisbursed debt and represents the total outstanding external obligations of the borrower at year end;
- Debt outstanding (disbursed only) is total outstanding debt drawn by the borrower at year-end;
- Commitments are the total of loans for which contracts are signed in the year specified;
- Disbursements are drawings on outstanding loan commitments during the year specified;

Toutes les données concernant la dette publique et la dette garantie par une entité publique proviennent des débiteurs, sauf celles concernant les prêts consentis par certains organismes multilatéraux, pour lesquels les données proviennent des dossiers des créanciers : il s'agit notamment de la Banque africaine de développement, de la Banque asiatique de développement, de la Banque centrale d'intégration économique, de la Banque interaméricaine de développement, de la Banque internationale de reconstruction et de développement (BIRD) et de l'Association internationale de développement (IDA) (le BIRD et l'IDA font partie du groupe de la Banque mondiale).

Les statistiques relatives à la dette publique ou à la dette garantie par l'Etat ne comprennent pas les données concernant : a) les transactions avec le Fonds monétaire international; b) la dette remboursable en monnaie nationale; c) les investissements directs; et d) la dette à court terme (c'est-à-dire la dette dont l'échéance initiale est inférieure à un an).

Les statistiques relatives à la dette privée non garantie ne comprennent pas non plus les éléments précités, mais comprennent les obligations contractuelles au titre des prêts consentis par des sociétés mères étrangères ou leurs filiales à des entreprises créées dans le cadre d'investissements directs.

Les données sont groupées par type de créancier, comme suit :

Créanciers publics

a)   Les prêts obtenus auprès d'organisations internationales (prêts multilatéraux), à l'exclusion des prêts au titre de fonds administrés par une organisation internationale pour le compte d'un gouvernement donateur précis, qui sont classés comme prêts consentis par des gouvernements;

b)   Les prêts consentis par des gouvernements (prêts bilatéraux) et par des organisations publiques autonomes.

Créanciers privés

a)   Fournisseurs : Crédits consentis par des fabricants exportateurs et autres fournisseurs de biens;

b)   Marchés financiers : prêts consentis par des banques privées et autres institutions financières privées, et émissions publiques d'obligations placées auprès d'investisseurs privés;

c)   Autres créanciers : engagements vis-à-vis de l'extérieur au titre des biens nationalisés et dettes diverses à l'égard de créanciers privés.

On fait une distinction entre les catégories suivantes de dette publique extérieure :

- Service payments are actual repayments of principal amortization and interest payments made in foreign currencies, goods or services in the year specified;
- Net flows (or net lending) are disbursements minus principal repayments;
- Net transfers are net flows minus interest payments or disbursements minus total debt service payments.

The countries included in the table are those for which data are sufficiently reliable to provide a meaningful presentation of debt outstanding and future service payments.

- L'encours de la dette (y compris les fonds non décaissés) est la somme des fonds décaissés et non décaissés et représente le total des obligations extérieures en cours de l'emprunteur à la fin de l'année;
- L'encours de la dette (fonds décaissés seulement) est le montant total des tirages effectués par l'emprunteur sur sa dette en cours à la fin de l'année;
- Les engagements représentent le total des prêts dont les contrats ont été signés au cours de l'année considérée;
- Les décaissements sont les sommes tirées sur l'encours des prêts pendant l'année considérée;
- Les paiements au titre du service de la dette sont les remboursements effectifs du principal et les paiements d'intérêts effectués en devises, biens ou services pendant l'année considérée;
- Les flux nets (ou prêts nets) sont les décaissements moins les remboursements de principal;
- Les transferts nets désignent les flux nets moins les paiements d'intérêts, ou les décaissements moins le total des paiements au titre du service de la dette.

Les pays figurant sur ce tableau sont ceux pour lesquels les données sont suffisamment fiables pour permettre une présentation significative de l'encours de la dette et des paiements futurs au titre du service de la dette.

Disbursements of bilateral and multilateral official development
assistance and official aid to individual recipients

Versements d'aide publique au développement et d'aide publique
bilatérales et multilatérales aux bénéficiares

Country or area	Year	Net disbursements (US $) — Versements nets ($ E.-U.)			
Pays ou zone	Année	Bilateral (millions) Bilatérale (millions)	Multilateral (millions)[1] Multilatérale (millions)[1]	Total (millions)	Per capita Par habitant
World Monde	2000	40 947.1	16 377.7	57 324.8	...
	2001	38 755.7	18 916.6	57 672.3	...
	2002	45 224.6	19 330.7	64 555.3	...
	2003	53 616.8	21 063.9	74 680.7	...
	*2004	58 839.1	25 405.4	84 244.5	...
Afghanistan Afghanistan	2000	87.5	52.7	140.2	5.9
	2001	322.9	79.9	402.8	16.3
	2002	985.9	295.3	1 281.2	49.4
	2003	1 199.7	367.5	1 567.1	57.5
	2004	1 697.5	423.3	2 120.8	74.2
Albania Albanie	2000	141.9	176.5	318.4	104.0
	2001	149.8	117.9	267.7	87.3
	2002	177.2	123.8	301.0	97.8
	2003	230.3	110.3	340.6	110.1
	2004	228.4	121.9	350.3	112.6
Algeria Algérie	2000	65.7	64.1	129.7	4.3
	2001	63.4	106.6	170.1	5.5
	2002	122.8	63.0	185.8	5.9
	2003	168.8	68.3	237.1	7.4
	2004	234.6	78.2	312.8	9.7
Angola Angola	2000	189.1	111.5	300.6	21.7
	2001	179.4	110.1	289.5	20.4
	2002	286.4	136.4	422.8	28.9
	2003	372.2	126.0	498.2	33.1
	2004	1 015.0	131.4	1 146.4	74.0
Anguilla Anguilla	2000	3.8	−0.3	3.5	313.4
	2001	3.0	0.5	3.5	309.9
	2002	1.8	−1.1	0.7	62.8
	2003	1.8	2.1	3.9	333.4
	2004	1.4	1.3	2.7	223.9
Antigua and Barbuda Antigua-et-Barbuda	2000	3.7	1.1	4.8	63.1
	2001	6.0	1.8	7.8	100.7
	2002	11.1	4.1	15.2	192.8
	2003	3.0	2.0	5.0	63.2
	2004	1.2	1.4	2.6	32.4
Argentina Argentine	2000	43.5	25.3	68.8	1.9
	2001	10.1	137.9	148.0	4.0
	2002	51.9	−0.4	51.5	1.4
	2003	98.2	2.1	100.3	2.6
	2004	78.5	12.1	90.6	2.4
Armenia Arménie	2000	139.3	75.6	214.9	69.7
	2001	124.2	73.2	197.4	64.4
	2002	171.4	120.8	292.2	95.8
	2003	127.4	119.4	246.8	81.3
	2004	133.9	119.4	253.3	83.7
Aruba Aruba	2000	10.7	0.8	11.5	124.9
	2001	−1.5	−0.2	−1.7	−18.2
	2002	10.2	0.3	10.5	110.3
	2003	76.5	−0.2	76.2	788.2
	2004	−11.5	0.2	−11.3	−115.1
Azerbaijan Azerbaïdjan	2000	70.7	60.5	131.1	16.1
	2001	148.4	73.2	221.6	27.0
	2002	232.2	104.9	337.1	40.9
	2003	158.5	131.7	290.2	35.0
	2004	91.9	57.5	149.4	17.9

Country or area / Pays ou zone	Year / Année	Net disbursements (US $) — Versements nets ($ E.-U.)			
		Bilateral (millions) / Bilatérale (millions)	Multilateral (millions)[1] / Multilatérale (millions)[1]	Total (millions)	Per capita / Par habitant
Bahamas	2000	5.2	0.3	5.5	18.2
Bahamas	2001	7.3	1.2	8.5	27.6
	2002	6.9	−1.7	5.2	16.8
	2003	5.9	−2.0	3.9	12.4
	2004	6.3	−1.5	4.8	15.0
Bahrain	2000	1.6	0.0	1.6	2.4
Bahreïn	2001	1.2	−0.1	1.0	1.5
	2002	1.1	2.8	4.0	5.7
	2003	1.1	−0.1	1.1	1.5
	2004	1.4	−0.7	0.7	1.0
Bangladesh	2000	616.5	519.5	1 136.0	8.8
Bangladesh	2001	578.4	437.5	1 015.9	7.7
	2002	520.8	379.8	900.6	6.7
	2003	695.0	689.3	1 384.3	10.1
	2004	632.9	745.3	1 378.2	9.9
Barbados	2000	1.0	−0.8	0.2	0.9
Barbade	2001	2.8	−4.0	−1.2	−4.4
	2002	2.8	0.5	3.3	12.4
	2003	2.4	17.5	19.9	74.1
	2004	2.6	26.5	29.1	108.2
Belarus	2000	14.9	8.6	23.5	2.3
Bélarus	2001	22.1	5.9	28.0	2.8
	2002	26.0	3.4	29.4	3.0
	2003	20.1	3.7	23.8	2.4
	2004	31.4	3.7	35.1	3.6
Belize	2000	2.9	11.2	14.0	57.9
Belize	2001	10.2	10.9	21.1	85.1
	2002	9.0	9.3	18.3	72.1
	2003	4.2	7.8	12.0	46.2
	2004	3.8	4.2	8.0	30.2
Benin	2000	190.5	49.2	239.7	33.3
Bénin	2001	144.5	127.9	272.4	36.7
	2002	140.1	73.8	213.9	27.9
	2003	196.1	97.5	293.6	37.1
	2004	210.3	167.7	378.0	46.2
Bermuda	2000	0.1	0.0	0.1	1.0
Bermudes	2001	0.0	0.0	0.0	0.3
	2002	0.0	0.0	0.0	0.3
	2003	0.0	0.0	0.0	0.5
	2004	0.1	0.0	0.1	1.4
Bhutan	2000	33.7	20.0	53.7	27.7
Bhoutan	2001	42.5	19.3	61.8	31.2
	2002	42.9	31.8	74.7	36.8
	2003	52.1	24.8	76.9	37.1
	2004	53.1	25.6	78.7	37.2
Bolivia	2000	336.1	138.3	474.4	57.0
Bolivie	2001	535.8	198.9	734.7	86.6
	2002	482.2	198.2	680.4	78.6
	2003	552.9	376.1	929.0	105.1
	2004	557.4	208.5	765.8	85.0
Bosnia and Herzegovina	2000	452.2	266.4	718.6	186.8
Bosnie-Herzégovine	2001	376.7	242.1	618.9	158.7
	2002	292.3	250.6	543.0	138.5
	2003	331.2	202.0	533.3	136.1
	2004	301.0	351.4	652.4	166.9
Botswana	2000	23.5	8.1	31.6	18.0
Botswana	2001	24.2	3.5	27.7	15.7
	2002	36.7	2.6	39.3	22.2
	2003	27.4	2.7	30.1	17.0
	2004	32.6	8.2	40.8	23.1

Disbursements of bilateral and multilateral official development assistance and official aid to individual recipients (*continued*)
Versements d'aide publique au développement et d'aide publique bilatérales et multilatérales aux bénéficiares (*suite*)

Country or area Pays ou zone	Year Année	Net disbursements (US $) — Versements nets ($ E.-U.)			
		Bilateral (millions) Bilatérale (millions)	Multilateral (millions)[1] Multilatérale (millions)[1]	Total (millions)	Per capita Par habitant
Brazil Brésil	2000	222.5	98.4	320.9	1.8
	2001	156.8	191.1	347.9	2.0
	2002	197.6	131.0	328.6	1.8
	2003	184.3	110.2	294.4	1.6
	2004	147.3	136.3	283.6	1.5
British Virgin Islands Iles Vierges britanniques	2000	1.2	3.6	4.8	235.8
	2001	0.2	1.9	2.1	98.7
	2002	0.0	−0.1	−0.1	−3.8
	2003	0.1	−0.6	−0.5	−24.7
	2004	0.0	−1.2	−1.2	−54.7
Brunei Darussalam Brunéi Darussalam	2000	0.6	0.0	0.6	1.7
	2001	0.3	0.1	0.3	1.0
	2002	−1.9	0.1	−1.8	−5.0
	2003	0.4	0.0	0.4	1.2
	2004	0.7	0.0	0.7	1.9
Bulgaria Bulgarie	2000	207.0	101.8	308.8	38.6
	2001	173.4	169.6	343.0	43.2
	2002	189.2	135.5	324.7	41.2
	2003	226.1	185.7	411.8	52.6
	2004	246.0	361.1	607.0	78.0
Burkina Faso Burkina Faso	2000	227.8	104.5	332.3	29.4
	2001	220.9	157.8	378.7	32.5
	2002	229.9	198.1	428.0	35.6
	2003	265.7	238.0	503.7	40.6
	2004	331.3	278.1	609.4	47.5
Burundi Burundi	2000	40.9	51.7	92.6	14.3
	2001	54.7	82.6	137.3	20.7
	2002	84.7	87.4	172.0	25.2
	2003	121.2	103.7	224.9	32.0
	2004	184.3	166.4	350.7	48.2
Cambodia Cambodge	2000	248.0	149.7	397.7	31.2
	2001	264.8	153.9	418.7	32.2
	2002	272.8	191.3	464.1	35.0
	2003	319.2	179.3	498.5	36.8
	2004	297.8	156.0	453.8	32.9
Cameroon Cameroun	2000	213.5	169.1	382.6	25.8
	2001	356.7	132.4	489.1	32.3
	2002	436.2	220.4	656.6	42.5
	2003	755.8	143.5	899.3	57.1
	2004	572.0	188.6	760.6	47.4
Cape Verde Cap-Vert	2000	69.7	24.7	94.4	209.6
	2001	49.0	28.6	77.6	168.1
	2002	43.2	50.4	93.6	198.2
	2003	90.2	53.5	143.7	297.1
	2004	90.8	48.7	139.5	281.7
Cayman Islands Iles Caïmanes	2000	−3.2	−0.5	−3.6	−90.7
	2001	0.0	−0.8	−0.8	−19.1
	2002	0.0	−1.9	−1.9	−44.0
	2003	0.0	−1.4	−1.4	−33.2
	2004	0.4	0.0	0.4	8.8
Central African Rep. Rép. centrafricaine	2000	53.1	22.5	75.5	20.0
	2001	47.9	18.6	66.5	17.3
	2002	39.6	20.2	59.8	15.4
	2003	32.4	17.5	49.8	12.7
	2004	54.8	49.7	104.5	26.2
Chad Tchad	2000	53.3	76.7	130.0	15.8
	2001	72.8	113.8	186.6	21.9
	2002	67.0	160.0	227.0	25.8
	2003	95.5	151.4	246.9	27.0
	2004	162.2	153.6	315.8	33.4

Country or area / Pays ou zone	Year / Année	Net disbursements (US $) — Versements nets ($ E.-U.)			
		Bilateral (millions) / Bilatérale (millions)	Multilateral (millions)[1] / Multilatérale (millions)[1]	Total (millions)	Per capita / Par habitant
Chile / Chili	2000	41.0	7.7	48.7	3.2
	2001	39.6	17.4	57.0	3.7
	2002	−13.8	5.3	−8.5	−0.5
	2003	61.4	13.3	74.8	4.7
	2004	25.9	22.2	48.1	3.0
China[2] / Chine[2]	2000	1 256.2	460.4	1 716.5	1.3
	2001	1 079.8	345.8	1 425.6	1.1
	2002	1 211.5	231.3	1 442.9	1.1
	2003	1 139.5	162.3	1 301.7	1.0
	2004	1 585.4	38.5	1 623.9	1.2
China, Hong Kong SAR / Chine, Hong Kong RAS	2000	4.2	0.1	4.3	0.7
	2001	3.6	0.0	3.6	0.5
	2002	4.0	0.0	4.0	0.6
	2003	5.0	0.0	5.0	0.7
	2004	6.3	0.0	6.4	0.9
China, Macao SAR / Chine, Macao RAS	2000	0.2	0.5	0.7	1.5
	2001	0.4	0.1	0.5	1.2
	2002	0.4	0.7	1.0	2.3
	2003	0.1	0.1	0.2	0.5
	2004	0.1	13.6	13.7	30.0
Colombia / Colombie	2000	178.5	7.8	186.3	4.4
	2001	372.3	7.5	379.8	8.9
	2002	426.1	13.7	439.8	10.1
	2003	767.1	33.8	800.9	18.1
	2004	470.0	37.8	507.8	11.3
Comoros / Comores	2000	10.8	7.8	18.6	26.5
	2001	9.6	16.3	25.9	36.1
	2002	11.0	16.6	27.6	37.5
	2003	11.1	13.3	24.4	32.3
	2004	13.9	10.7	24.5	31.5
Congo / Congo	2000	23.0	10.2	33.2	9.6
	2001	29.6	45.6	75.3	21.2
	2002	41.4	15.9	57.3	15.7
	2003	33.9	35.9	69.8	18.5
	2004	47.5	68.3	115.8	29.8
Cook Islands / Iles Cook	2000	3.4	0.9	4.3	228.9
	2001	3.9	0.9	4.8	257.7
	2002	3.5	0.3	3.8	205.1
	2003	4.6	1.2	5.8	317.9
	2004	5.9	2.9	8.8	484.7
Costa Rica / Costa Rica	2000	17.2	−6.2	11.0	2.8
	2001	6.1	−4.6	1.5	0.4
	2002	4.5	−0.1	4.5	1.1
	2003	31.0	−3.7	27.2	6.5
	2004	11.2	1.4	12.7	3.0
Côte d'Ivoire / Côte d'Ivoire	2000	250.1	101.2	351.2	21.0
	2001	158.5	10.8	169.4	9.9
	2002	831.1	237.2	1 068.3	61.6
	2003	281.2	−29.3	251.9	14.3
	2004	196.0	−42.9	153.1	8.6
Croatia / Croatie	2000	42.5	22.8	65.3	14.5
	2001	74.4	24.5	98.9	22.0
	2002	82.1	29.8	111.9	24.8
	2003	80.3	36.9	117.2	25.9
	2004	87.3	32.4	119.7	26.4
Cuba / Cuba	2000	30.8	12.9	43.7	3.9
	2001	33.7	19.5	53.2	4.8
	2002	49.6	11.0	60.6	5.4
	2003	59.3	10.3	69.5	6.2
	2004	69.3	20.3	89.6	8.0

| Country or area / Pays ou zone | Year / Année | Net disbursements (US $) — Versements nets ($ E.-U.) | | | |
		Bilateral (millions) / Bilatérale (millions)	Multilateral (millions)[1] / Multilatérale (millions)[1]	Total (millions)	Per capita / Par habitant
Cyprus Chypre	2000	11.9	45.8	57.6	73.3
	2001	21.5	31.6	53.1	66.6
	2002	17.7	12.3	30.0	37.2
	2003	9.3	9.3	18.6	22.8
	2004	21.8	31.8	53.5	64.8
Czech Republic République tchèque	2000	25.3	411.9	437.2	42.6
	2001	29.7	283.4	313.1	30.5
	2002	48.5	109.3	157.8	15.4
	2003	43.2	219.1	262.3	25.6
	2004	42.8	236.8	279.6	27.3
Dem. Rep. of the Congo Rép. dém. du Congo	2000	102.7	80.7	183.4	3.7
	2001	143.4	119.1	262.4	5.1
	2002	351.0	836.5	1 187.5	22.5
	2003	5 009.5	411.2	5 420.7	100.0
	2004	1 164.4	650.4	1 814.8	32.5
Djibouti Djibouti	2000	42.1	19.7	61.8	86.5
	2001	28.1	29.7	57.8	78.8
	2002	36.9	38.8	75.7	101.0
	2003	37.0	39.5	76.5	100.0
	2004	39.4	27.3	66.7	85.6
Dominica Dominique	2000	5.9	6.5	12.4	159.4
	2001	5.0	13.9	18.9	241.9
	2002	14.0	15.9	29.9	382.3
	2003	3.4	7.5	10.8	138.3
	2004	10.7	18.3	29.0	368.8
Dominican Republic Rép. dominicaine	2000	44.6	17.8	62.4	7.6
	2001	101.9	5.6	107.4	12.8
	2002	138.2	7.0	145.2	17.1
	2003	60.4	8.4	68.8	8.0
	2004	84.4	2.4	86.8	9.9
Ecuador Equateur	2000	137.4	8.6	146.0	11.9
	2001	147.6	25.1	172.7	13.8
	2002	205.1	10.3	215.4	17.0
	2003	173.6	2.5	176.1	13.7
	2004	159.8	0.8	160.6	12.3
Egypt Egypte	2000	1 138.9	135.6	1 274.5	18.9
	2001	1 090.3	105.0	1 195.3	17.4
	2002	1 123.9	84.3	1 208.2	17.3
	2003	775.1	85.8	860.8	12.1
	2004	1 177.1	261.1	1 438.1	19.8
El Salvador El Salvador	2000	172.3	7.1	179.4	28.6
	2001	231.1	5.7	236.8	37.0
	2002	217.9	14.5	232.4	35.6
	2003	170.4	20.6	191.0	28.7
	2004	201.9	8.7	210.6	31.1
Equatorial Guinea Guinée équatoriale	2000	18.2	3.3	21.5	47.9
	2001	13.1	0.6	13.7	29.9
	2002	13.7	6.6	20.3	43.1
	2003	17.6	3.7	21.3	44.2
	2004	23.1	6.6	29.7	60.3
Eritrea Erythrée	2000	111.9	54.9	166.8	46.9
	2001	151.4	126.9	278.2	75.1
	2002	120.7	96.9	217.6	56.2
	2003	185.5	130.5	316.0	78.0
	2004	178.3	85.8	264.1	62.4
Estonia Estonie	2000	23.7	39.4	63.2	46.2
	2001	25.6	42.4	68.0	50.1
	2002	16.9	37.1	54.0	40.1
	2003	22.9	61.2	84.2	62.8
	2004	27.4	108.8	136.2	102.0

| Country or area
Pays ou zone | Year
Année | Net disbursements (US $) — Versements nets ($ E.-U.) | | | |
		Bilateral (millions) Bilatérale (millions)	Multilateral (millions)[1] Multilatérale (millions)[1]	Total (millions)	Per capita Par habitant
Ethiopia Ethiopie	2000	379.5	298.4	677.9	9.9
	2001	367.1	720.8	1 087.9	15.5
	2002	489.2	783.6	1 272.8	17.7
	2003	1 033.3	486.9	1 520.2	20.6
	2004	1 026.2	759.9	1 786.1	23.6
Falkland Is. (Malvinas) Iles Falkland (Malvinas)	2000	0.0	−0.2	−0.2	−80.5
	2001	0.0	−0.2	−0.2	−75.9
	2002	0.0	−0.3	−0.3	−82.0
	2003	0.0	−0.3	−0.3	−95.0
	2004	0.0	−0.3	−0.3	−108.0
Fiji Fidji	2000	28.7	0.2	28.8	35.6
	2001	24.0	1.8	25.7	31.4
	2002	31.3	2.5	33.8	40.9
	2003	42.9	7.9	50.8	60.9
	2004	36.4	27.1	63.5	75.5
French Polynesia Polynésie française	2000	400.2	2.4	402.6	1 705.0
	2001	383.7	4.6	388.3	1 616.1
	2002	417.4	1.0	418.4	1 711.4
	2003	510.1	8.5	518.5	2 085.6
	2004	574.9	4.9	579.8	2 294.3
Gabon Gabon	2000	−11.7	23.4	11.7	9.2
	2001	−8.0	16.7	8.7	6.7
	2002	49.5	22.4	71.8	54.4
	2003	−41.2	30.5	−10.7	−8.0
	2004	23.5	14.2	37.8	27.7
Gambia Gambie	2000	14.6	32.0	46.6	35.4
	2001	13.4	37.8	51.2	37.7
	2002	17.5	40.4	57.9	41.5
	2003	19.7	40.0	59.7	41.5
	2004	11.7	50.9	62.6	42.4
Georgia Géorgie	2000	120.3	43.1	163.4	34.6
	2001	151.6	142.0	293.6	62.9
	2002	209.6	92.4	302.0	65.4
	2003	163.9	52.2	216.2	47.4
	2004	210.3	95.0	305.4	67.6
Ghana Ghana	2000	376.0	222.1	598.1	30.1
	2001	386.7	253.9	640.7	31.5
	2002	406.2	238.3	644.4	31.0
	2003	478.8	462.0	940.8	44.4
	2004	896.9	451.5	1 348.4	62.2
Gibraltar Gibraltar	2000	0.0	0.0	0.0	1.4
	2001	0.7	0.0	0.7	26.3
	2002	0.0	0.0	0.0	0.4
	2003	0.0	0.0	0.0	0.7
	2004	0.2	0.0	0.2	6.8
Grenada Grenade	2000	9.9	3.2	13.1	129.1
	2001	3.3	4.1	7.5	73.3
	2002	2.2	9.1	11.3	110.8
	2003	8.3	3.4	11.7	114.6
	2004	10.5	5.3	15.8	154.6
Guatemala Guatemala	2000	230.3	32.8	263.1	23.6
	2001	201.2	25.0	226.1	19.8
	2002	199.6	48.6	248.3	21.2
	2003	216.0	29.6	245.6	20.5
	2004	203.4	14.0	217.3	17.7
Guinea Guinée	2000	92.8	57.6	150.4	17.8
	2001	122.1	160.3	282.4	32.8
	2002	125.6	118.1	243.6	27.7
	2003	134.6	105.0	239.5	26.6
	2004	178.4	100.9	279.2	30.3

| Country or area / Pays ou zone | Year / Année | Net disbursements (US $) — Versements nets ($ E.-U.) | | | |
		Bilateral (millions) / Bilatérale (millions)	Multilateral (millions)[1] / Multilatérale (millions)[1]	Total (millions)	Per capita / Par habitant
Guinea-Bissau Guinée-Bissau	2000	41.6	38.8	80.4	58.9
	2001	30.4	29.0	59.4	42.2
	2002	25.8	33.6	59.4	41.0
	2003	97.6	47.6	145.2	97.2
	2004	28.6	47.6	76.2	49.5
Guyana Guyana	2000	51.9	55.4	107.3	144.2
	2001	46.0	51.4	97.4	130.6
	2002	34.0	30.8	64.8	86.6
	2003	28.7	57.9	86.6	115.6
	2004	80.8	63.7	144.5	192.7
Haiti Haïti	2000	153.9	54.4	208.3	26.2
	2001	136.0	34.7	170.7	21.2
	2002	125.4	30.0	155.4	19.0
	2003	153.2	46.4	199.7	24.1
	2004	208.7	33.8	242.6	28.9
Honduras Honduras	2000	310.6	134.8	445.5	69.3
	2001	422.3	255.3	677.6	103.0
	2002	297.9	173.3	471.2	69.9
	2003	235.5	153.0	388.5	56.4
	2004	328.5	308.2	636.7	90.3
Hungary Hongrie	2000	53.5	197.1	250.5	24.5
	2001	54.5	362.1	416.6	40.8
	2002	40.3	119.5	159.8	15.7
	2003	54.5	193.4	247.8	24.4
	2004	61.0	241.1	302.1	29.8
India Inde	2000	650.3	846.5	1 496.9	1.5
	2001	904.5	823.8	1 728.3	1.7
	2002	785.3	680.3	1 465.7	1.4
	2003	384.3	554.7	939.1	0.9
	2004	20.9	667.2	688.1	0.6
Indonesia Indonésie	2000	1 544.0	109.5	1 653.5	7.9
	2001	1 345.2	100.7	1 445.9	6.8
	2002	1 162.0	130.7	1 292.7	6.0
	2003	1 550.7	162.6	1 713.3	7.9
	2004	−145.6	208.6	63.0	0.3
Iran (Islamic Rep. of) Iran (Rép. islamique d')	2000	112.8	17.2	129.9	2.0
	2001	90.8	25.3	116.1	1.7
	2002	81.5	32.5	114.0	1.7
	2003	102.1	29.2	131.3	1.9
	2004	140.2	34.7	174.9	2.5
Iraq Iraq	2000	84.1	16.6	100.7	4.0
	2001	100.8	21.3	122.1	4.7
	2002	85.1	30.3	115.4	4.3
	2003	2 095.0	85.6	2 180.6	79.9
	2004	4 392.1	151.3	4 543.4	161.9
Israel Israël	2000	800.4	−0.4	800.0	131.5
	2001	148.5	23.9	172.3	27.7
	2002	749.3	7.5	756.8	119.2
	2003	437.8	2.2	439.9	67.9
	2004	477.9	0.8	478.7	72.5
Jamaica Jamaïque	2000	−26.4	30.0	3.5	1.4
	2001	−1.0	44.2	43.2	16.6
	2002	−3.8	28.4	24.5	9.4
	2003	1.1	2.1	3.2	1.2
	2004	7.8	65.0	72.8	27.6
Jordan Jordanie	2000	385.3	168.0	553.3	111.3
	2001	302.1	133.1	435.2	85.1
	2002	370.9	148.8	519.7	98.8
	2003	1 092.2	134.5	1 226.6	226.6
	2004	432.9	146.2	579.1	104.1

| Country or area / Pays ou zone | Year / Année | Net disbursements (US $) — Versements nets ($ E.-U.) | | | |
		Bilateral (millions) / Bilatérale (millions)	Multilateral (millions)[1] / Multilatérale (millions)[1]	Total (millions)	Per capita / Par habitant
Kazakhstan	2000	159.3	14.8	174.1	11.6
Kazakhstan	2001	122.7	16.2	138.9	9.3
	2002	143.9	18.4	162.3	10.9
	2003	228.0	14.6	242.7	16.3
	2004	203.3	18.9	222.2	15.0
Kenya	2000	293.0	214.3	507.3	16.5
Kenya	2001	270.5	187.6	458.1	14.6
	2002	288.1	95.5	383.5	12.0
	2003	320.3	191.9	512.2	15.6
	2004	469.5	166.4	636.0	19.0
Kiribati	2000	14.8	3.1	17.9	199.1
Kiribati	2001	10.4	2.0	12.4	135.2
	2002	18.7	2.1	20.8	222.6
	2003	12.8	5.5	18.4	192.4
	2004	10.1	6.6	16.7	171.3
Korea, Dem. P. R.	2000	26.9	48.3	75.2	3.4
Corée, R. p. dém. de	2001	52.3	67.2	119.5	5.4
	2002	187.8	77.1	265.0	12.0
	2003	114.8	52.6	167.4	7.5
	2004	137.1	47.6	184.6	8.2
Korea, Republic of	2000	−196.6	−1.5	−198.0	−4.2
Corée, République de	2001	−108.6	−2.9	−111.4	−2.4
	2002	−79.8	−2.0	−81.8	−1.7
	2003	−459.8	2.0	−457.8	−9.6
	2004	−68.7	1.0	−67.7	−1.4
Kuwait	2000	2.0	0.9	2.9	1.3
Koweït	2001	2.9	0.8	3.6	1.6
	2002	3.0	1.6	4.6	1.9
	2003	1.7	2.7	4.4	1.7
	2004	2.2	0.4	2.6	1.0
Kyrgyzstan	2000	91.3	111.7	203.0	41.0
Kirghizistan	2001	71.3	113.3	184.6	36.8
	2002	95.2	83.4	178.6	35.1
	2003	112.6	80.9	193.5	37.6
	2004	108.8	112.4	221.2	42.5
Lao People's Dem. Rep.	2000	194.9	86.1	281.0	53.2
Rép. dém. pop. lao	2001	151.0	93.4	244.4	45.2
	2002	177.8	98.8	276.6	50.0
	2003	188.8	107.5	296.3	52.4
	2004	177.6	88.2	265.8	45.9
Latvia	2000	34.3	53.7	88.0	37.1
Lettonie	2001	49.6	54.9	104.5	44.3
	2002	26.2	49.9	76.1	32.5
	2003	34.8	77.5	112.3	48.2
	2004	29.1	134.9	163.9	70.7
Lebanon	2000	93.7	91.3	185.0	54.4
Liban	2001	103.7	60.3	164.0	47.8
	2002	102.4	78.1	180.5	52.0
	2003	118.8	111.7	230.5	65.8
	2004	128.2	139.6	267.7	75.6
Lesotho	2000	21.8	16.1	37.9	21.2
Lesotho	2001	29.5	27.9	57.4	32.0
	2002	29.7	47.9	77.6	43.1
	2003	32.9	46.1	78.9	43.9
	2004	35.1	68.0	103.0	57.3
Liberia	2000	23.8	44.0	67.8	22.1
Libéria	2001	15.6	23.6	39.2	12.4
	2002	27.0	25.5	52.5	16.4
	2003	70.3	36.6	106.9	33.2
	2004	161.9	48.4	210.3	64.9

Country or area / Pays ou zone	Year / Année	Net disbursements (US $) — Versements nets ($ E.-U.)			
		Bilateral (millions) / Bilatérale (millions)	Multilateral (millions)[1] / Multilatérale (millions)[1]	Total (millions)	Per capita / Par habitant
Libyan Arab Jamah. Jamah. arabe libyenne	2000	11.9	3.1	15.0	2.8
	2001	4.3	5.2	9.4	1.7
	2002	4.4	4.6	9.0	1.6
	2003	6.3	4.5	10.8	1.9
	2004	9.6	6.3	15.9	2.8
Lithuania Lituanie	2000	46.2	48.0	94.2	26.9
	2001	48.4	78.1	126.5	36.3
	2002	36.0	93.7	129.7	37.4
	2003	36.3	330.7	367.0	106.2
	2004	32.1	219.3	251.4	73.0
Madagascar Madagascar	2000	138.7	184.6	323.2	20.0
	2001	146.0	229.2	375.2	22.5
	2002	125.9	247.8	373.7	21.8
	2003	224.9	314.5	539.4	30.6
	2004	684.8	551.9	1 236.6	68.3
Malawi Malawi	2000	269.2	170.9	440.1	38.2
	2001	195.8	197.7	393.5	33.4
	2002	224.9	142.4	367.3	30.4
	2003	313.7	201.9	515.6	41.8
	2004	308.4	166.2	474.5	37.6
Malaysia Malaisie	2000	43.3	3.3	46.6	2.0
	2001	24.9	3.3	28.1	1.2
	2002	85.4	1.8	87.2	3.6
	2003	104.5	4.4	108.9	4.5
	2004	286.8	3.2	290.0	11.6
Maldives Maldives	2000	13.3	7.2	20.5	70.5
	2001	15.2	10.0	25.2	84.5
	2002	12.9	15.3	28.2	92.1
	2003	8.7	9.2	17.9	57.2
	2004	8.9	13.6	22.5	70.0
Mali Mali	2000	299.8	61.3	361.0	31.0
	2001	208.5	131.9	340.4	28.4
	2002	256.8	156.1	412.9	33.4
	2003	271.9	272.2	544.1	42.7
	2004	327.5	240.6	568.1	43.3
Malta Malte	2000	21.2	0.9	22.2	56.6
	2001	0.0	3.1	3.1	7.9
	2002	0.2	11.4	11.7	29.4
	2003	0.5	9.6	10.1	25.4
	2004	0.3	6.9	7.2	18.0
Marshall Islands Iles Marshall	2000	47.1	10.1	57.2	1 097.4
	2001	67.4	6.6	74.0	1 384.0
	2002	55.4	7.0	62.4	1 128.5
	2003	51.5	5.0	56.5	983.0
	2004	49.5	1.6	51.1	855.3
Mauritania Mauritanie	2000	82.5	129.3	211.8	80.1
	2001	81.3	187.7	269.0	98.8
	2002	146.6	200.2	346.8	123.6
	2003	136.1	105.7	241.8	83.6
	2004	82.6	96.4	178.9	60.0
Mauritius Maurice	2000	12.4	7.5	19.9	16.7
	2001	8.1	6.5	14.6	12.2
	2002	3.5	19.7	23.3	19.2
	2003	−17.7	2.5	−15.2	−12.4
	2004	14.7	25.5	40.2	32.6
Mayotte Mayotte	2000	103.0	0.2	103.2	...
	2001	119.3	0.9	120.2	...
	2002	125.2	−0.3	124.9	...
	2003	166.1	0.0	166.0	...
	2004	208.6	−0.2	208.5	...

| Country or area
Pays ou zone | Year
Année | Net disbursements (US $) — Versements nets ($ E.-U.) | | | |
		Bilateral (millions) Bilatérale (millions)	Multilateral (millions)[1] Multilatérale (millions)[1]	Total (millions) Total (millions)	Per capita Par habitant
Mexico Mexique	2000	−68.4	13.7	−54.7	−0.5
	2001	40.7	33.5	74.2	0.7
	2002	92.6	42.5	135.1	1.3
	2003	73.6	28.7	102.3	1.0
	2004	78.9	40.2	119.0	1.1
Micronesia (Fed. States of) Micronésie (Etats féd. de)	2000	96.6	5.0	101.6	948.7
	2001	134.6	2.9	137.6	1 280.7
	2002	110.1	1.6	111.6	1 033.6
	2003	109.3	3.0	112.4	1 032.5
	2004	85.2	1.1	86.3	786.8
Mongolia Mongolie	2000	150.8	60.6	211.4	84.6
	2001	141.1	64.3	205.4	81.4
	2002	141.3	45.1	186.4	73.0
	2003	148.0	85.8	233.8	90.5
	2004	154.7	94.8	249.5	95.4
Montserrat Montserrat	2000	30.9	0.1	30.9	7 935.4
	2001	32.7	0.3	33.0	9 480.3
	2002	45.3	−1.8	43.5	12 426.5
	2003	36.3	0.2	36.5	9 564.9
	2004	37.4	7.1	44.5	10 590.8
Morocco Maroc	2000	293.1	130.4	423.4	14.5
	2001	342.1	142.0	484.1	16.3
	2002	216.6	135.5	352.1	11.7
	2003	335.7	155.9	491.6	16.1
	2004	393.5	242.4	635.8	20.5
Mozambique Mozambique	2000	623.5	253.5	877.0	49.0
	2001	720.2	208.3	928.5	50.7
	2002	1 661.0	539.4	2 200.4	117.8
	2003	697.1	339.0	1 036.0	54.4
	2004	728.1	496.5	1 224.6	63.0
Myanmar Myanmar	2000	68.1	37.8	105.9	2.2
	2001	89.2	37.5	126.6	2.6
	2002	79.1	34.0	113.2	2.3
	2003	83.4	35.7	119.1	2.4
	2004	81.4	36.9	118.3	2.4
Namibia Namibie	2000	96.8	54.8	151.6	80.0
	2001	77.5	31.2	108.7	56.3
	2002	84.8	48.2	133.0	67.9
	2003	110.3	34.4	144.7	72.9
	2004	129.7	33.7	163.5	81.3
Nauru Nauru	2000	3.9	0.1	4.0	328.0
	2001	7.1	0.1	7.2	578.4
	2002	11.6	0.0	11.6	906.5
	2003	16.0	0.1	16.1	1 231.4
	2004	13.6	0.1	13.7	1 022.0
Nepal Népal	2000	231.2	154.9	386.1	15.8
	2001	270.2	118.0	388.2	15.5
	2002	279.4	65.3	344.7	13.5
	2003	320.4	144.6	464.9	17.8
	2004	318.5	105.8	424.3	16.0
Netherlands Antilles Antilles néerlandaises	2000	173.8	3.1	177.0	1 007.3
	2001	55.6	3.3	58.9	335.0
	2002	94.2	−1.6	92.6	523.4
	2003	33.6	1.2	34.8	194.4
	2004	18.7	2.8	21.5	119.0
New Caledonia Nouvelle-Calédonie	2000	348.7	1.4	350.2	1 626.5
	2001	295.0	−0.8	294.2	1 339.0
	2002	323.2	0.6	323.8	1 445.5
	2003	453.8	0.2	454.0	1 988.2
	2004	510.0	14.9	524.9	2 256.5

| Country or area / Pays ou zone | Year / Année | Net disbursements (US $) — Versements nets ($ E.-U.) | | | |
		Bilateral (millions) / Bilatérale (millions)	Multilateral (millions)[1] / Multilatérale (millions)[1]	Total (millions)	Per capita / Par habitant
Nicaragua Nicaragua	2000	325.9	235.3	561.1	113.2
	2001	714.7	215.5	930.1	183.8
	2002	287.2	227.9	515.2	99.8
	2003	521.8	306.8	828.5	157.3
	2004	858.0	373.0	1 231.0	229.0
Niger Niger	2000	105.8	105.1	210.9	17.9
	2001	113.6	142.3	255.9	21.0
	2002	114.5	180.8	295.3	23.4
	2003	244.5	212.8	457.3	35.0
	2004	305.7	230.3	536.0	39.7
Nigeria Nigéria	2000	84.3	100.2	184.5	1.6
	2001	107.5	78.6	186.1	1.5
	2002	215.0	100.5	315.5	2.6
	2003	199.8	118.3	318.1	2.5
	2004	314.2	259.6	573.8	4.5
Niue Nioué	2000	3.0	0.2	3.2	1 987.6
	2001	3.2	0.1	3.3	2 113.3
	2002	4.2	0.2	4.4	2 884.2
	2003	8.8	0.1	8.9	5 969.1
	2004	13.8	0.2	14.0	9 609.9
Northern Mariana Islands Iles Mariannes du Nord	2000	0.0	0.2	0.2	2.6
Occupied Palestinian Terr. Terr. palestinien occupé	2000	306.4	226.1	532.6	169.1
	2001	280.2	342.3	622.5	191.0
	2002	410.2	429.4	839.6	249.4
	2003	490.8	455.4	946.2	272.2
	2004	605.1	481.7	1 086.8	303.0
Oman Oman	2000	9.2	2.3	11.5	4.7
	2001	8.1	0.1	8.2	3.3
	2002	−0.4	1.0	0.6	0.3
	2003	10.5	1.8	12.2	4.9
	2004	2.0	0.1	2.1	0.8
Pakistan Pakistan	2000	475.1	226.7	701.8	4.9
	2001	1 110.1	823.5	1 933.6	13.3
	2002	702.5	1 391.5	2 094.0	14.1
	2003	536.3	531.0	1 067.2	7.0
	2004	382.7	1 024.6	1 407.3	9.1
Palau Palaos	2000	38.9	0.2	39.0	2 023.4
	2001	33.9	0.2	34.1	1 746.4
	2002	30.9	0.2	31.1	1 583.5
	2003	25.3	0.1	25.4	1 284.2
	2004	19.4	0.1	19.5	980.2
Panama Panama	2000	11.7	−3.3	8.4	2.8
	2001	17.1	0.3	17.4	5.8
	2002	23.3	−1.7	21.6	7.0
	2003	31.3	−1.2	30.2	9.7
	2004	25.3	11.9	37.2	11.7
Papua New Guinea Papouasie-Nouvelle-Guinée	2000	268.6	5.2	273.8	51.7
	2001	198.0	1.7	199.8	36.9
	2002	197.1	6.1	203.2	36.7
	2003	218.8	2.2	221.0	39.1
	2004	249.9	17.3	267.2	46.3
Paraguay Paraguay	2000	72.9	8.5	81.3	14.9
	2001	58.3	2.5	60.8	10.8
	2002	50.8	5.1	55.9	9.7
	2003	55.4	−5.7	49.8	8.5
	2004	5.4	−6.4	−1.0	−0.2
Peru Pérou	2000	372.7	26.0	398.7	15.4
	2001	425.6	25.8	451.4	17.1
	2002	463.0	30.7	493.7	18.4
	2003	447.7	49.4	497.0	18.3
	2004	460.2	23.2	483.4	17.5

		Net disbursements (US $) — Versements nets ($ E.-U.)			
Country or area Pays ou zone	Year Année	Bilateral (millions) Bilatérale (millions)	Multilateral (millions)[1] Multilatérale (millions)[1]	Total (millions)	Per capita Par habitant
Philippines	2000	502.1	72.2	574.2	7.6
Philippines	2001	501.8	68.5	570.3	7.4
	2002	509.1	36.2	545.3	6.9
	2003	703.8	26.5	730.3	9.1
	2004	433.4	17.4	450.8	5.5
Poland	2000	552.5	843.0	1 395.5	36.1
Pologne	2001	486.9	477.8	964.7	25.0
	2002	388.6	491.5	880.1	22.8
	2003	439.5	750.8	1 190.3	30.8
	2004	413.0	1 111.0	1 524.1	39.5
Qatar	2000	1.1	−0.6	0.5	0.8
Qatar	2001	0.8	0.2	1.0	1.6
	2002	2.0	0.2	2.2	3.2
	2003	1.2	0.8	2.0	2.7
	2004	2.0	0.2	2.2	2.8
Republic of Moldova	2000	61.5	51.2	112.7	26.4
République de Moldova	2001	78.8	37.6	116.4	27.3
	2002	86.3	50.5	136.9	32.2
	2003	80.4	31.8	112.2	26.5
	2004	76.9	35.1	112.0	26.6
Romania	2000	158.0	271.5	429.5	19.4
Roumanie	2001	142.1	504.7	646.8	29.4
	2002	176.6	229.7	406.4	18.5
	2003	239.9	342.0	581.9	26.6
	2004	209.3	705.1	914.4	42.0
Russian Federation	2000	1 344.5	121.4	1 465.9	10.0
Fédération de Russie	2001	906.6	153.4	1 059.9	7.3
	2002	1 109.3	152.5	1 261.8	8.7
	2003	993.9	214.2	1 208.1	8.4
	2004	1 075.2	189.1	1 264.3	8.8
Rwanda	2000	175.4	146.5	321.9	40.1
Rwanda	2001	148.9	149.5	298.4	35.6
	2002	199.1	155.8	354.9	41.2
	2003	213.4	119.8	333.3	38.1
	2004	217.2	250.3	467.4	52.6
Saint Helena	2000	18.4	0.3	18.7	3 785.5
Sainte-Hélène	2001	14.7	0.4	15.2	3 093.4
	2002	13.4	0.5	13.9	2 849.0
	2003	17.6	0.4	18.0	3 682.9
	2004	26.1	0.2	26.2	5 357.7
Saint Kitts and Nevis	2000	0.1	4.1	4.2	103.1
Saint-Kitts-et-Nevis	2001	1.3	7.7	8.9	219.3
	2002	6.1	20.1	26.2	635.9
	2003	−0.3	0.3	0.0	−0.2
	2004	−0.2	1.0	0.8	19.0
Saint Lucia	2000	7.1	4.4	11.5	74.6
Sainte-Lucie	2001	0.8	15.8	16.5	106.2
	2002	12.5	21.2	33.7	214.5
	2003	4.8	10.0	14.8	93.7
	2004	−23.7	2.4	−21.3	−133.8
St. Vincent-Grenadines	2000	3.8	1.1	5.0	42.8
St. Vincent-Grenadines	2001	0.7	7.8	8.5	72.8
	2002	1.1	4.3	5.3	45.2
	2003	3.7	2.6	6.3	53.3
	2004	7.3	3.8	11.1	93.5
Samoa	2000	18.1	9.2	27.3	153.8
Samoa	2001	27.3	15.7	43.0	239.9
	2002	30.8	6.4	37.2	205.6
	2003	27.0	6.0	33.0	180.7
	2004	24.6	6.0	30.6	166.8

Country or area Pays ou zone	Year Année	Net disbursements (US $) — Versements nets ($ E.-U.)			
		Bilateral (millions) Bilatérale (millions)	Multilateral (millions)[1] Multilatérale (millions)[1]	Total (millions)	Per capita Par habitant
Sao Tome and Principe Sao Tomé-et-Principe	2000	17.7	17.3	35.0	250.4
	2001	21.9	16.3	38.3	268.2
	2002	19.2	6.8	26.0	178.1
	2003	25.5	12.2	37.7	252.0
	2004	21.7	11.7	33.4	218.1
Saudi Arabia Arabie saoudite	2000	18.0	11.2	29.2	1.4
	2001	10.5	16.5	27.1	1.2
	2002	13.4	13.3	26.8	1.2
	2003	9.9	11.8	21.8	0.9
	2004	8.5	13.9	22.4	0.9
Senegal Sénégal	2000	288.4	139.7	428.2	41.4
	2001	223.7	189.4	413.1	39.0
	2002	242.8	191.8	434.6	40.0
	2003	314.4	134.6	449.1	40.4
	2004	755.4	295.7	1 051.0	92.3
Serbia and Montenegro Serbie-et-Monténégro	2000	592.9	541.3	1 134.3	107.6
	2001	631.1	671.4	1 302.5	123.6
	2002	1 921.3	4.8	1 926.1	183.0
	2003	853.0	443.9	1 296.9	123.3
	2004	585.3	563.3	1 148.6	109.3
Seychelles Seychelles	2000	3.3	8.4	11.7	151.3
	2001	8.2	5.2	13.5	173.0
	2002	3.7	4.2	7.9	100.7
	2003	4.9	3.2	8.1	102.6
	2004	6.1	2.9	9.1	113.3
Sierra Leone Sierra Leone	2000	115.6	66.8	182.4	40.4
	2001	166.8	176.0	342.8	73.2
	2002	225.3	125.5	350.8	71.7
	2003	208.3	91.6	299.9	58.6
	2004	163.1	195.6	358.7	67.2
Singapore Singapour	2000	0.7	0.4	1.1	0.3
	2001	0.7	0.2	1.0	0.2
	2002	7.1	0.3	7.4	1.8
	2003	7.0	0.1	7.1	1.7
	2004	9.1	0.1	9.2	2.1
Slovakia Slovaquie	2000	25.3	87.2	112.5	20.8
	2001	33.8	130.1	163.9	30.3
	2002	39.2	113.3	152.4	28.2
	2003	51.9	107.2	159.1	29.4
	2004	58.9	171.4	230.3	42.6
Slovenia Slovénie	2000	0.6	60.2	60.8	30.9
	2001	0.0	125.5	125.5	63.8
	2002	2.4	50.3	52.7	26.8
	2003	2.9	62.9	65.8	33.5
	2004	4.3	57.6	61.9	31.5
Solomon Islands Iles Salomon	2000	20.8	46.3	67.1	160.2
	2001	24.6	34.2	58.8	136.5
	2002	21.3	5.0	26.3	59.5
	2003	56.5	3.7	60.2	132.7
	2004	116.8	5.4	122.2	262.3
Somalia Somalie	2000	56.4	47.3	103.7	14.8
	2001	88.5	46.8	135.3	18.7
	2002	102.4	47.2	149.6	20.0
	2003	113.6	61.6	175.1	22.7
	2004	139.3	51.4	190.6	23.9
South Africa Afrique du Sud	2000	353.6	132.0	485.5	10.6
	2001	313.3	114.1	427.4	9.3
	2002	375.3	129.4	504.7	10.8
	2003	477.3	147.0	624.2	13.3
	2004	460.4	156.3	616.7	13.1

Country or area	Year	Net disbursements (US $) — Versements nets ($ E.-U.)			
		Bilateral (millions)	Multilateral (millions)[1]	Total (millions)	Per capita
Pays ou zone	Année	Bilatérale (millions)	Multilatérale (millions)[1]	Total (millions)	Par habitant
Sri Lanka	2000	240.2	25.2	265.4	13.4
Sri Lanka	2001	279.9	20.2	300.1	15.0
	2002	188.5	135.6	324.0	16.0
	2003	271.0	385.8	656.8	32.2
	2004	337.8	160.6	498.4	24.2
Sudan	2000	90.3	35.7	125.9	3.8
Soudan	2001	107.6	68.0	175.6	5.2
	2002	232.3	67.5	299.8	8.8
	2003	332.0	281.7	613.7	17.6
	2004	744.8	112.4	857.2	24.1
Suriname	2000	29.1	5.2	34.3	79.0
Suriname	2001	20.0	3.2	23.2	53.0
	2002	7.7	3.9	11.6	26.3
	2003	4.0	6.9	10.9	24.6
	2004	15.8	8.1	23.9	53.4
Swaziland	2000	2.8	10.3	13.0	12.7
Swaziland	2001	4.2	21.9	26.1	25.3
	2002	6.6	12.1	18.7	18.1
	2003	12.7	14.3	27.1	26.2
	2004	104.5	11.8	116.3	112.4
Syrian Arab Republic	2000	97.3	38.7	136.0	8.1
Rép. arabe syrienne	2001	92.3	36.7	129.0	7.5
	2002	25.0	51.7	76.6	4.3
	2003	28.8	127.4	156.2	8.6
	2004	14.9	115.4	130.3	7.0
Tajikistan	2000	38.1	86.0	124.1	20.1
Tadjikistan	2001	63.5	104.2	167.7	26.9
	2002	128.8	38.1	166.9	26.5
	2003	80.3	62.9	143.2	22.5
	2004	92.5	136.2	228.6	35.6
Thailand	2000	682.9	17.7	700.5	11.4
Thaïlande	2001	270.9	15.0	285.9	4.6
	2002	279.6	17.9	297.5	4.8
	2003	−984.4	16.3	−968.2	−15.3
	2004	−24.9	21.6	−3.3	−0.1
TFYR of Macedonia	2000	110.9	139.5	250.4	124.6
L'ex-R.y. Macédoine	2001	164.2	82.3	246.6	122.3
	2002	179.8	93.7	273.4	135.2
	2003	179.3	85.5	264.8	130.7
	2004	161.4	82.1	243.5	119.9
Timor-Leste	2000	212.3	20.6	232.9	322.5
Timor-Leste	2001	153.9	40.7	194.6	263.6
	2002	187.0	31.4	218.4	281.8
	2003	127.3	27.3	154.6	186.8
	2004	133.7	19.0	152.6	172.1
Togo	2000	51.9	16.4	68.3	12.7
Togo	2001	28.5	11.7	40.2	7.3
	2002	39.2	9.0	48.3	8.5
	2003	46.3	−1.5	44.8	7.7
	2004	52.3	8.9	61.3	10.2
Tokelau	2000	3.4	0.1	3.5	2 517.9
Tokélaou	2001	3.8	0.1	3.9	2 785.4
	2002	4.6	0.2	4.8	3 451.3
	2003	6.2	0.2	6.4	4 658.9
	2004	8.4	0.1	8.4	6 130.9
Tonga	2000	14.8	4.0	18.8	187.7
Tonga	2001	20.6	−0.4	20.2	200.9
	2002	16.7	5.5	22.2	219.5
	2003	15.0	10.8	25.8	254.0
	2004	14.9	4.3	19.2	188.1

| Country or area | Year | Net disbursements (US $) — Versements nets ($ E.-U.) | | | |
| | | Bilateral (millions) | Multilateral (millions)[1] | | Per capita |
Pays ou zone	Année	Bilatérale (millions)	Multilatérale (millions)[1]	Total (millions)	Par habitant
Trinidad and Tobago	2000	4.4	−5.9	−1.5	−1.2
Trinité-et-Tobago	2001	4.3	−6.1	−1.8	−1.4
	2002	5.7	−13.1	−7.4	−5.7
	2003	5.1	−7.4	−2.4	−1.8
	2004	7.2	−8.0	−0.8	−0.6
Tunisia	2000	150.3	71.9	222.1	23.2
Tunisie	2001	183.7	193.4	377.1	39.0
	2002	144.6	77.5	222.1	22.7
	2003	207.7	94.9	302.6	30.6
	2004	230.8	95.6	326.4	32.7
Turkey	2000	99.7	190.7	290.5	4.3
Turquie	2001	−29.0	143.3	114.2	1.6
	2002	99.0	161.3	260.3	3.7
	2003	19.5	146.0	165.5	2.3
	2004	−45.4	308.5	263.1	3.6
Turkmenistan	2000	9.9	5.7	15.6	3.5
Turkménistan	2001	33.1	7.2	40.4	8.8
	2002	26.0	5.7	31.7	6.9
	2003	16.7	6.7	23.5	5.0
	2004	11.3	7.2	18.4	3.9
Turks and Caicos Islands	2000	5.6	1.1	6.7	342.7
Iles Turques et Caïques	2001	5.1	1.6	6.7	321.9
	2002	2.6	1.5	4.1	184.5
	2003	1.2	1.0	2.2	92.1
	2004	1.2	1.9	3.2	125.1
Tuvalu	2000	3.8	0.2	4.0	395.7
Tuvalu	2001	6.9	2.6	9.5	926.3
	2002	11.2	0.6	11.7	1 137.0
	2003	5.5	0.4	5.8	564.3
	2004	5.4	2.6	8.0	770.5
Uganda	2000	578.2	235.6	813.8	33.5
Ouganda	2001	386.3	405.0	791.3	31.5
	2002	466.1	240.5	706.6	27.2
	2003	587.3	388.5	975.7	36.3
	2004	682.6	474.8	1 157.4	41.6
Ukraine	2000	352.3	79.4	431.7	8.8
Ukraine	2001	342.5	116.4	458.9	9.4
	2002	358.2	79.2	437.4	9.1
	2003	218.1	65.9	284.0	6.0
	2004	233.4	91.7	325.1	6.9
United Arab Emirates	2000	2.7	1.3	4.0	1.2
Emirats arabes unis	2001	2.5	0.5	3.0	0.9
	2002	3.7	0.5	4.2	1.1
	2003	4.9	0.3	5.2	1.3
	2004	5.2	0.4	5.6	1.3
United Rep. of Tanzania	2000	778.7	246.0	1 024.7	29.5
Rép.-Unie de Tanzanie	2001	943.8	332.9	1 276.7	36.0
	2002	902.8	333.5	1 236.3	34.1
	2003	965.6	737.5	1 703.2	46.1
	2004	1 029.5	713.8	1 743.2	46.3
Uruguay	2000	15.3	1.4	16.7	5.0
Uruguay	2001	10.7	3.9	14.7	4.4
	2002	6.8	3.2	9.9	2.9
	2003	7.7	6.3	14.1	4.1
	2004	9.4	11.8	21.2	6.2
Uzbekistan	2000	133.8	17.0	150.8	6.1
Ouzbékistan	2001	106.7	16.8	123.5	4.9
	2002	152.9	20.7	173.6	6.8
	2003	167.5	16.7	184.2	7.1
	2004	206.1	25.0	231.1	8.8

Country or area	Year	Net disbursements (US $) — Versements nets ($ E.-U.)			
Pays ou zone	Année	Bilateral (millions) / Bilatérale (millions)	Multilateral (millions)[1] / Multilatérale (millions)[1]	Total (millions)	Per capita / Par habitant
Vanuatu	2000	28.3	17.5	45.8	239.2
Vanuatu	2001	24.1	7.4	31.5	161.5
	2002	22.4	5.2	27.5	138.0
	2003	28.2	4.2	32.4	159.5
	2004	34.6	3.1	37.8	182.1
Venezuela (Bolivarian Republic of)	2000	61.3	14.6	75.9	3.1
Venezuela (Rép. bolivarienne du)	2001	33.5	10.9	44.4	1.8
	2002	42.0	14.6	56.7	2.2
	2003	64.2	17.4	81.5	3.2
	2004	28.3	19.6	47.9	1.8
Viet Nam	2000	1 246.2	419.5	1 665.7	21.2
Viet Nam	2001	819.5	594.2	1 413.7	17.7
	2002	746.0	511.0	1 257.0	15.5
	2003	967.7	785.2	1 752.9	21.4
	2004	1 181.5	611.2	1 792.7	21.6
Wallis and Futuna Islands	2000	52.1	0.0	52.1	3 479.7
Iles Wallis et Futuna	2001	50.3	0.0	50.3	3 338.2
	2002	52.7	0.1	52.7	3 479.4
	2003	53.6	1.9	55.5	3 643.6
	2004	71.5	1.3	72.8	4 747.0
Yemen	2000	159.6	104.0	263.6	14.7
Yémen	2001	99.8	243.3	343.1	18.5
	2002	119.4	107.2	226.6	11.9
	2003	126.6	109.6	236.2	12.0
	2004	152.6	98.7	251.4	12.4
Zambia	2000	486.2	308.6	794.8	74.3
Zambie	2001	274.1	74.1	348.2	31.9
	2002	359.5	278.9	638.4	57.5
	2003	591.9	−16.2	575.7	51.0
	2004	745.3	333.2	1 078.5	94.0
Zimbabwe	2000	192.6	−13.9	178.7	14.2
Zimbabwe	2001	148.6	18.9	167.5	13.2
	2002	177.8	22.5	200.3	15.7
	2003	160.7	25.3	186.0	14.5
	2004	165.4	20.8	186.2	14.4

Source

Organization for Economic Co-operation and Development (OECD), Paris, the OECD Development Assistance Committee database, last accessed February 2006. Per capita calculated by the United Nations Statistics Division from the World Population Prospects: The 2005 Revision, mid-year population data.

Notes

[1]   As reported by OECD/DAC, covers agencies of the United Nations family, the European Commission, IDA and the concessional lending facilities of regional development banks. Excludes non-concessional flows (i.e., less than 25% grant elements).

[2]   For statistical purposes, the data for China do not include those for the Hong Kong Special Administrative Region (Hong Kong SAR), Macao Special Administrative Region (Macao SAR) and Taiwan Province of China.

Source

Organisation de coopération et de développement économiques (OCDE), Paris, la base de données du comité d'aide au développement de l'OCDE, dernier accès février 2006. Les données par habitant ont été calculées par la Division de statistiques de l'ONU de *World Population Prospects: The 2005 Revision*, d'après les données de la population au milieu de l'année.

Notes

[1]   Communiqué par le Comité d'aide au développement de l'OCDE, comprend les institutions et organismes du système des Nations Unies, la commission européene, l'Association internationale de développement, et les mécanismes de prêt à des conditions privilégiées des banques régionales de développement. Les apports aux conditions du marché (élément de libéralité inférieur à 25) en sont exclus.

[2]   Pour la présentation des statistiques, les données pour Chine ne comprennent pas la Région Administrative Spéciale de Hong Kong (Hong Kong RAS), la Région Administrative Spéciale de Macao (Macao RAS) et la province de Taiwan.

Net official development assistance from DAC countries to developing countries and multilateral organizations

Net disbursements: millions of US dollars and as a percentage of gross national income (GNI)

Aide publique au développement nette des pays du CAD aux pays en développement et aux organisations multilatérales

Versements nets : millions de dollars E.-U. et en pourcentage du revenu national brut (RNB)

Country or area / Pays ou zone	1999 US $ $E.-U. (millions)	1999 As % of GNI En % du RNB	2000 US $ $E.-U. (millions)	2000 As % of GNI En % du RNB	2001 US $ $E.-U. (millions)	2001 As % of GNI En % du RNB	2002 US $ $E.-U. (millions)	2002 As % of GNI En % du RNB	2003 US $ $E.-U. (millions)	2003 As % of GNI En % du RNB	2004 US $ $E.-U. (millions)	2004 As % of GNI En % du RNB
Total **Total**	53 233	0.22	53 749	0.22	52 435	0.22	58 292	0.24	69 085	0.25	79 512	0.26
Australia Australie	982	0.26	987	0.27	873	0.25	989	0.26	1 219	0.25	1 460	0.25
Austria Autriche	492	0.24	440	0.23	633	0.34	520	0.26	505	0.20	678	0.23
Belgium Belgique	760	0.30	820	0.36	867	0.37	1 072	0.43	1 853	0.60	1 463	0.41
Canada Canada	1 706	0.28	1 744	0.25	1 533	0.22	2 004	0.28	2 031	0.24	2 599	0.27
Denmark Danemark	1 733	1.01	1 664	1.06	1 634	1.03	1 643	0.96	1 748	0.84	2 037	0.85
Finland Finlande	416	0.33	371	0.31	389	0.32	462	0.35	558	0.35	655	0.35
France France	5 639	0.38	4 105	0.30	4 198	0.31	5 486	0.37	7 253	0.40	8 473	0.41
Germany Allemagne	5 515	0.26	5 030	0.27	4 990	0.27	5 324	0.27	6 784	0.28	7 534	0.28
Greece Grèce	194	0.15	226	0.20	202	0.17	276	0.21	362	0.21	465	0.23
Ireland Irlande	245	0.31	234	0.29	287	0.33	398	0.40	504	0.39	607	0.39
Italy Italie	1 806	0.15	1 376	0.13	1 627	0.15	2 332	0.20	2 433	0.17	2 462	0.15
Japan Japon	12 163	0.27	13 508	0.28	9 847	0.23	9 283	0.23	8 880	0.20	8 906	0.19
Luxembourg Luxembourg	119	0.66	123	0.71	139	0.76	147	0.77	194	0.81	236	0.83
Netherlands Pays-Bas	3 134	0.79	3 135	0.84	3 172	0.82	3 338	0.81	3 972	0.80	4 204	0.73
New Zealand Nouvelle-Zélande	134	0.27	113	0.25	112	0.25	122	0.22	165	0.23	212	0.23
Norway Norvège	1 370	0.88	1 264	0.76	1 346	0.80	1 696	0.89	2 042	0.92	2 199	0.87
Portugal Portugal	276	0.26	271	0.26	268	0.25	323	0.27	320	0.22	1 031	0.63
Spain Espagne	1 363	0.23	1 195	0.22	1 737	0.30	1 712	0.26	1 961	0.23	2 437	0.24
Sweden Suède	1 630	0.70	1 799	0.80	1 666	0.77	2 012	0.84	2 400	0.79	2 722	0.78
Switzerland Suisse	984	0.35	890	0.34	908	0.34	939	0.32	1 299	0.39	1 545	0.41
United Kingdom Royaume-Uni	3 426	0.24	4 501	0.32	4 579	0.32	4 924	0.31	6 282	0.34	7 883	0.36
United States Etats-Unis	9 145	0.10	9 955	0.10	11 429	0.11	13 290	0.13	16 320	0.15	19 705	0.17

Source

Organisation for Economic Co-operation and Development (OECD), Paris, the OECD Development Assistance Committee database, last accessed February 2006, and the *Development Co-operation Report*.

Source

Organisation de Coopération et de Développement Economiques (OCDE), Paris, la base de données du Comité d'aide au développement de l'OCDE, dernier accès février 2006, et *Coopération pour le développement*.

76

Socio-economic development assistance through the United Nations system
Development grants: thousands of US dollars

Assistance en matière de développement socioéconomique fournie par le système des Nations Unies
Subventions au développement : en milliers de dollars des E.-U.

Region, country or area / Région, pays ou zone	Year / Année	UNDP / PNUD Central resources[a] / Ressources centrales[a]	UNDP / PNUD Admin. funds / Fonds gérés	UNFPA / FNUAP	UNICEF	WFP[b] / PAM[b]	Specialized agencies / Institutions spécialisées Regular budgets[c] / Budget ordinaire[c]	Specialized agencies / Institutions spécialisées Extra-budgetary[d] / Extra-budgétaire[d]	Total develop. grants / Total subventions au développ.
Total	2003	1 736 963	674 625	272 885	1 208 041	3 275 319	518 167	1 992 107	9 678 106
Total	2004	2 017 177	799 572	317 596	1 343 578	2 899 628	496 784	2 126 283	10 000 618
Total regional programmes	2003	100 652	114 969	56 087	74 520	62 125	215 110	1 106 806	1 730 269
Totaux régionaux	2004	26 435	5 468	68 205	67 115	4 502	222 337	1 282 154	1 676 216
Africa	2003	20 110	20 554	7 278	12 874	2 036	46 942	150 140	259 935
Afrique	2004	14 396	3 719	6 752	14 024	4 376	40 527	232 751	316 545
Asia and the Pacific	2003	8 815	11 476	5 631	6 733	10 363	29 388	54 919	127 325
Asie et le Pacifique	2004	2 514	0	11 328	5 293	96	27 114	70 517	116 862
Europe	2003	4 568	13 205	1 838	2 882	0	21 659	45 561	89 713
Europe	2004	93	1 059	112	3 142	0	21 928	51 808	78 142
Latin America	2003	13 340	9 342	2 461	2 657	0	29 072	31 439	88 311
Amérique latine	2004	3 746	833	3 157	2 391	30	23 932	32 908	66 997
Western Asia	2003	5 075	5 310	2 279	3 730	49 725	32 666	443 687	542 473
Asie occidentale	2004	5 686	−143	2 928	1 755	0	34 728	519 685	564 639
Interregional	2003	11 835	21 896	0	0	0	46 384	160 096	240 211
Interrégional	2004	0	0	43 928	0	0	28 733	173 287	245 948
Global	2003	36 909	33 186	36 599	45 645	0	8 999	220 963	382 301
Global	2004	0	0	0	40 510	0	45 375	201 198	287 083
Total all countries	2003	1 635 458	506 938	213 361	1 092 310	3 183 430	298 997	878 105	7 808 598
Total, tous pays	2004	1 986 741	794 104	243 803	1 261 727	2 866 355	272 384	840 234	8 265 349
Afghanistan	2003	30 001	60 945	6 015	78 292	140 750	4 093	39 274	359 371
Afghanistan	2004	150 864	162 292	3 265	57 186	130 676	3 916	30 698	538 897
Albania	2003	4 187	3 177	335	3 134	3 013	461	2 112	16 419
Albanie	2004	4 927	3 083	336	3 134	3 176	924	2 897	18 476
Algeria	2003	2 453	240	777	2 405	11 619	2 151	731	20 376
Algérie	2004	2 422	391	557	1 775	13 920	1 747	1 800	22 611
Angola	2003	5 567	3 665	1 974	32 109	148 551	3 416	16 669	211 951
Angola	2004	5 461	4 808	2 080	20 724	79 377	2 317	8 799	123 567
Anguilla	2003	39	0	0	0	0	0	0	39
Anguilla	2004	0	0	0	0	0	0	0	0
Antigua and Barbuda	2003	22	10	0	0	0	296	0	328
Antigua-et-Barbuda	2004	0	51	0	0	0	0	20	71
Argentina	2003	134 447	2 330	188	2 237	0	2 198	4 349	145 749
Argentine	2004	236 737	1 442	430	2 659	0	1 927	7 039	250 235
Aruba	2003	116	0	0	0	0	0	19	135
Aruba	2004	0	0	0	0	0	0	24	24
Azerbaijan	2003	4 116	2 225	572	1 108	6 599	539	114	15 272
Azerbaïdjan	2004	5 915	2 480	566	1 273	3 940	657	98	14 930
Bahamas	2003	0	0	0	0	0	536	2	538
Bahamas	2004	0	15	0	0	0	302	25	343
Bahrain	2003	1 091	−5	0	0	0	260	61	1 407
Bahreïn	2004	888	48	0	0	0	70	44	1 049
Bangladesh	2003	17 415	1 124	22 313	35 650	24 434	7 536	9 391	117 864
Bangladesh	2004	30 050	1 820	6 769	32 927	50 821	7 262	10 148	139 796
Barbados	2003	39	95	0	0	0	259	152	545
Barbade	2004	3 564	2 320	0	0	0	175	303	6 363

Socio-economic development assistance through the United Nations system— Development grants: thousands of US dollars (*continued*)

Assistance en matière de développement socioéconomique fournie par le système des Nations Unies— Subventions au développement : en milliers de dollars des E.-U. (*suite*)

Region, country or area / Région, pays ou zone	Year / Année	UNDP / PNUD Central resources[a] / Ressources centrales[a]	UNDP / PNUD Admin. funds / Fonds gérés	UNFPA / FNUAP	UNICEF	WFP[b] / PAM[b]	Specialized agencies / Institutions spécialisées Regular budgets[c] / Budget ordinaire[c]	Specialized agencies / Institutions spécialisées Extra–budgetary[d] / Extra–budgétaire[d]	Total develop. grants / Total subventions au développ.
Belize / Belize	2003	52	1 838	58	613	0	256	31	2 849
	2004	1 742	843	0	740	0	193	142	3 659
Benin / Bénin	2003	4 802	1 872	1 687	5 170	2 575	1 804	1 032	18 942
	2004	10 195	180	2 249	6 959	2 346	1 964	658	24 551
Bhutan / Bhoutan	2003	1 616	1 521	879	2 171	5 008	1 737	325	13 257
	2004	1 934	743	1 085	2 324	3 138	1 523	476	11 224
Bolivia / Bolivie	2003	44 753	1 690	2 213	5 933	7 263	1 990	4 835	68 677
	2004	15 488	1 789	2 565	8 767	4 262	2 059	3 868	38 799
Botswana / Botswana	2003	3 560	2 290	1 731	2 247	0	1 565	766	12 159
	2004	3 701	383	1 219	1 709	0	1 677	1 083	9 772
Brazil / Brésil	2003	127 418	5 854	650	14 046	0	3 891	106 363	258 223
	2004	129 271	8 121	921	10 540	0	4 134	136 137	289 123
British Virgin Islands / Iles Vierges britanniques	2003	0	0	0	0	0	77	0	77
	2004	0	0	0	0	0	0	27	27
Brunei Darussalam / Brunéi Darussalam	2003	0	0	0	0	0	11	0	11
	2004	0	0	0	0	0	27	0	27
Bulgaria / Bulgarie	2003	23 325	724	187	0	0	1 422	270	25 929
	2004	22 444	879	271	0	0	918	279	24 791
Burkina Faso / Burkina Faso	2003	6 591	3 773	1 715	10 129	5 054	2 937	3 186	33 385
	2004	10 320	939	2 695	12 535	6 876	3 115	4 074	40 555
Burundi / Burundi	2003	12 399	955	1 209	14 160	45 867	1 809	3 872	80 271
	2004	10 308	3 662	1 634	17 134	43 795	2 103	7 122	85 758
Cambodia / Cambodge	2003	16 118	15 196	3 789	14 942	17 605	2 557	11 410	81 617
	2004	10 219	14 028	2 778	14 988	15 205	2 066	10 360	69 644
Cameroon / Cameroun	2003	2 082	489	2 396	4 450	2 753	2 398	1 073	15 642
	2004	4 850	270	2 695	6 567	3 039	2 902	1 449	21 773
Cape Verde / Cap-Vert	2003	587	625	521	1 098	2 065	1 557	400	6 852
	2004	992	377	594	1 108	3 695	1 403	310	8 479
Cayman Islands / Iles Caïmanes	2003	41	0	0	0	0	0	0	41
	2004	0	0	0	0	0	532	0	532
Central African Rep. / Rép. centrafricaine	2003	2 964	−258	2 148	2 991	2 995	2 088	456	13 384
	2004	7 174	1 677	1 772	4 737	4 590	2 954	1 499	24 402
Chad / Tchad	2003	6 696	1 058	1 884	6 722	6 020	2 249	925	25 555
	2004	6 259	1 101	2 329	14 390	36 881	3 005	1 547	65 513
Chile / Chili	2003	24 406	2 454	91	871	0	1 693	1 184	30 700
	2004	28 982	1 391	203	691	0	1 559	951	33 777
China[1] / Chine[1]	2003	40 151	19 832	4 867	17 425	12 270	6 799	17 650	118 994
	2004	39 760	17 766	4 816	17 328	9 462	6 104	20 253	115 489
China, Hong Kong SAR / Chine, Hong Kong RAS	2003	101	0	0	0	0	1	0	102
	2004	0	0	0	0	0	39	26	65
China, Macao SAR / Chine, Macao RAS	2003	0	0	0	0	0	18	83	101
	2004	0	0	0	0	0	0	1	1
Colombia / Colombie	2003	145 679	1 806	416	4 158	2 163	2 065	3 355	159 642
	2004	147 821	2 976	1 881	4 716	6 727	2 055	3 542	169 718
Comoros / Comores	2003	569	1 431	907	911	0	1 696	186	5 700
	2004	925	1 597	393	930	0	1 904	190	5 938
Congo / Congo	2003	2 529	2 158	657	3 494	5 013	2 254	1 522	17 626
	2004	2 168	1 855	876	2 397	4 868	1 604	1 485	15 253
Cook Islands / Iles Cook	2003	74	45	0	0	0	349	0	468
	2004	0	0	0	0	0	312	14	326
Costa Rica / Costa Rica	2003	1 548	1 218	311	663	0	1 270	813	5 824
	2004	1 154	1 103	522	776	0	671	1 281	5 507

Socio-economic development assistance through the United Nations system — Development grants: thousands of US dollars (*continued*)

Assistance en matière de développement socioéconomique fournie par le système des Nations Unies — Subventions au développement : en milliers de dollars des E.-U. (*suite*)

Region, country or area / Région, pays ou zone	Year / Année	UNDP / PNUD Central resources[a] / Ressources centrales[a]	UNDP / PNUD Admin. funds / Fonds gérés	UNFPA / FNUAP	UNICEF	WFP[b] / PAM[b]	Specialized agencies / Institutions spécialisées Regular budgets[c] / Budget ordinaire[c]	Specialized agencies / Institutions spécialisées Extra-budgetary[d] / Extra-budgétaire[d]	Total develop. grants / Total subventions au développ.
Côte d'Ivoire	2003	4 858	994	1 067	7 904	17 954	1 931	1 553	36 261
Côte d'Ivoire	2004	14 624	1 049	1 376	18 094	23 753	1 368	2 770	63 034
Cuba	2003	7 003	3 918	507	1 468	2 734	1 896	630	18 157
Cuba	2004	9 145	2 261	850	1 461	3 638	1 266	741	19 362
Cyprus	2003	9 153	4 609	0	0	0	167	12	13 942
Chypre	2004	8 322	5 741	0	0	0	67	32	14 162
Czech Republic	2003	208	364	0	0	0	756	168	1 495
République tchèque	2004	0	0	0	0	0	378	1 244	1 621
Dem. Rep. of the Congo	2003	11 927	887	3 187	36 354	65 205	3 174	20 455	141 189
Rép. dém. du Congo	2004	19 976	7 207	4 761	52 354	42 656	2 991	11 576	141 521
Djibouti	2003	332	431	347	810	4 002	1 591	582	8 094
Djibouti	2004	777	1 144	299	2 207	2 900	1 359	1 002	9 689
Dominica	2003	61	193	0	0	0	221	62	538
Dominique	2004	140	88	0	0	0	82	189	499
Dominican Republic	2003	4 183	954	573	2 499	523	985	1 042	10 759
Rép. dominicaine	2004	7 025	382	798	1 971	182	1 267	4 667	16 293
Ecuador	2003	16 502	2 905	1 284	3 835	2 062	1 596	2 008	30 192
Equateur	2004	25 895	4 993	1 098	3 911	92	1 820	1 703	39 513
Egypt	2003	15 777	3 796	1 944	12 988	4 351	3 324	3 900	46 080
Egypte	2004	23 338	4 732	2 439	14 537	4 202	2 768	5 306	57 321
El Salvador	2003	27 940	1 627	856	2 019	3 963	1 408	1 793	39 605
El Salvador	2004	21 429	932	1 009	1 541	2 039	1 268	3 483	31 701
Equatorial Guinea	2003	752	225	489	1 020	0	1 244	415	4 145
Guinée équatoriale	2004	572	0	1 274	720	0	1 685	374	4 624
Eritrea	2003	6 454	4 113	1 588	10 817	67 674	2 802	2 425	95 873
Erythrée	2004	5 223	1 531	1 862	12 179	44 917	2 020	2 942	70 672
Ethiopia	2003	15 183	1 496	4 541	49 546	230 416	4 302	18 027	323 511
Ethiopie	2004	15 628	836	5 264	58 357	161 115	4 498	11 593	257 291
Fiji	2003	197	384	33	0	0	1 705	−175	2 143
Fidji	2004	5 617	1 674	0	0	0	1 774	329	9 393
French Guiana	2003	0	0	0	0	0	52	0	52
Guyane française	2004	0	0	0	0	0	28	0	28
French Polynesia	2003	0	0	0	0	0	27	0	27
Polynésie française	2004	0	0	0	0	0	32	0	32
Gabon	2003	402	127	198	981	1	1 420	707	3 835
Gabon	2004	753	53	222	1 435	0	1 940	753	5 156
Gambia	2003	2 653	558	475	1 423	3 416	1 937	1 099	11 561
Gambie	2004	2 264	68	723	1 873	1 485	2 001	981	9 393
Ghana	2003	6 091	678	3 981	9 562	4 292	2 541	3 294	30 439
Ghana	2004	4 805	2 580	4 180	13 911	2 873	1 760	3 361	33 470
Greece	2003	0	0	0	0	0	274	670	944
Grèce	2004	0	0	0	0	0	383	577	960
Grenada	2003	90	161	0	0	0	134	12	398
Grenade	2004	85	46	0	0	0	16	54	201
Guam	2003	0	0	0	0	0	6	0	6
Guam	2004	0	0	0	0	0	0	1 530	1 530
Guatemala	2003	42 780	5 042	10 273	4 012	6 797	1 073	6 586	76 563
Guatemala	2004	46 457	4 584	4 439	4 558	4 028	1 183	3 114	68 363
Guinea	2003	1 212	1 058	1 033	7 566	21 467	2 310	1 337	35 984
Guinée	2004	1 222	270	1 948	6 365	12 240	2 068	1 636	25 749
Guinea-Bissau	2003	2 977	1 767	437	2 332	4 246	2 055	128	13 943
Guinée-Bissau	2004	3 442	4 000	1 023	2 421	3 745	1 974	307	16 912

Region, country or area / Région, pays ou zone	Year / Année	UNDP / PNUD — Central resources[a] / Ressources centrales[a]	UNDP / PNUD — Admin. funds / Fonds gérés	UNFPA / FNUAP	UNICEF	WFP[b] / PAM[b]	Specialized agencies / Institutions spécialisées — Regular budgets[c] / Budget ordinaire[c]	Specialized agencies / Institutions spécialisées — Extra-budgetary[d] / Extra-budgétaire[d]	Total develop. grants / Total subventions au développ.
Guyana	2003	1 082	90	33	842	0	667	133	2 847
Guyana	2004	1 900	931	0	891	0	497	378	4 597
Haiti	2003	6 679	1 774	1 473	3 820	8 170	1 890	1 552	25 357
Haïti	2004	13 471	1 317	2 227	10 604	19 626	1 644	2 954	51 843
Honduras	2003	109 035	3 553	1 653	1 926	6 617	750	3 877	127 411
Honduras	2004	105 295	2 220	3 223	2 168	8 093	740	3 551	125 290
Hungary	2003	173	326	0	0	0	764	259	1 522
Hongrie	2004			0	0	0	352	256	608
India	2003	22 982	4 849	6 823	95 722	3 322	10 009	33 690	177 397
Inde	2004	25 489	11 081	11 883	81 370	8 690	9 906	51 772	200 191
Indonesia	2003	13 362	19 260	4 476	19 580	21 759	6 779	10 951	96 167
Indonésie	2004	13 653	43 847	5 298	12 281	20 911	6 876	7 494	110 360
Iran (Islamic Rep. of)	2003	1 635	2 103	2 255	4 491	11 174	3 562	5 767	30 987
Iran (Rép. islamique d')	2004	2 061	1 770	2 194	14 892	1 831	2 683	5 652	31 083
Iraq	2003	1 787	137 378	402	92 576	1 091 955	1 136	199 552	1 524 785
Iraq	2004	17 203	79 329	3 755	98 870	800 807	805	77 201	1 077 970
Jamaica	2003	971	301	58	1 658	0	1 474	410	4 872
Jamaïque	2004	802	521	0	2 097	0	1 335	479	5 234
Jordan	2003	2 191	1 235	337	1 419	15 959	1 780	1 576	24 498
Jordanie	2004	2 283	2 803	611	1 042	1 725	1 304	2 677	12 445
Kazakhstan	2003	1 001	1 572	514	1 368	0	814	326	5 595
Kazakhstan	2004	1 006	2 597	610	1 530	0	659	590	6 992
Kenya	2003	7 330	2 453	2 175	10 620	53 541	2 700	3 062	81 881
Kenya	2004	7 381	2 960	2 651	10 341	72 107	2 556	3 707	101 703
Kiribati	2003	30	54	0	0	0	472	55	611
Kiribati	2004	0	0	0	0	0	454	63	517
Korea, Dem. P. R.	2003	1 797	461	595	7 476	102 299	1 841	6 809	121 278
Corée, R. p. dém. de	2004	927	165	974	18 115	121 470	2 522	8 987	153 160
Korea, Republic of	2003	1 109	149	0	0	0	1 686	2 424	5 368
Corée, République de	2004	571	235	0	0	0	445	1 349	2 600
Kuwait	2003	4 992	0	0	0	0	238	106	5 336
Koweït	2004	4 989	0	0	126	0	374	198	5 687
Kyrgyzstan	2003	2 255	1 245	603	1 176	0	668	395	6 342
Kirghizistan	2004	3 627	2 200	700	1 264	0	295	1 443	9 529
Lao People's Dem. Rep.	2003	3 408	5 517	1 217	4 661	2 324	1 875	2 974	21 975
Rép. dém. pop. lao	2004	5 321	4 503	1 185	5 937	4 291	1 932	3 304	26 473
Lebanon	2003	7 969	1 731	517	1 335	0	1 515	2 313	15 380
Liban	2004	6 756	1 696	805	630	0	1 201	2 439	13 527
Lesotho	2003	1 648	1 470	397	3 342	23 292	1 454	630	32 233
Lesotho	2004	2 391	752	395	3 308	25 375	1 740	387	34 348
Liberia	2003	1 126	306	559	10 846	47 469	1 947	777	63 029
Libéria	2004	5 672	18 487	853	16 968	37 801	1 877	3 341	84 999
Libyan Arab Jamah.	2003	2 859	11	0	0	0	627	3 628	7 125
Jamah. arabe libyenne	2004	2 858	2	0	0	0	772	6 615	10 247
Madagascar	2003	5 976	2 048	2 133	6 401	10 467	2 266	6 687	35 978
Madagascar	2004	3 997	403	1 986	12 550	7 754	1 891	2 824	31 405
Malawi	2003	7 948	2 463	3 175	19 328	61 194	1 490	2 629	98 227
Malawi	2004	8 557	4 560	3 991	21 103	27 057	1 603	3 716	70 587
Malaysia	2003	1 875	2 770	222	449	0	1 224	48	6 587
Malaisie	2004	2 420	2 119	360	498	0	1 103	51	6 551
Maldives	2003	982	440	279	598	0	1 638	27	3 963
Maldives	2004	985	266	493	802	0	1 430	48	4 024

Assistance en matière de développement socioéconomique fournie par le système des Nations Unies — Subventions au développement : en milliers de dollars des E.-U. (*suite*)

Region, country or area / Région, pays ou zone	Year / Année	UNDP / PNUD Central resources[a] / Ressources centrales[a]	UNDP / PNUD Admin. funds / Fonds gérés	UNFPA / FNUAP	UNICEF	WFP[b] / PAM[b]	Specialized agencies / Institutions spécialisées Regular budgets[c] / Budget ordinaire[c]	Specialized agencies / Institutions spécialisées Extra– budgetary[d] / Extra– budgétaire[d]	Total develop. grants / Total subventions au développ.
Mali	2003	6 808	6 916	1 983	8 611	6 355	3 239	1 529	35 441
Mali	2004	9 537	1 968	2 290	12 437	7 648	3 175	2 303	39 358
Malta	2003	0	83	0	0	0	227	64	374
Malte	2004	0	0	0	0	0	364	6	370
Marshall Islands	2003	57	33	0	0	0	385	15	490
Iles Marshall	2004	0	0	0	0	0	250	25	275
Mauritania	2003	4 144	207	1 435	4 698	24 681	2 247	1 366	38 778
Mauritanie	2004	3 837	200	2 020	4 276	8 156	2 020	4 114	24 623
Mauritius	2003	289	366	66	474	0	1 183	12	2 389
Maurice	2004	118	658	61	0	0	989	132	1 958
Mexico	2003	12 739	4 470	2 542	1 557	0	1 968	10 804	34 080
Mexique	2004	8 021	4 872	2 095	2 493	0	1 961	18 180	37 622
Micronesia (Fed. States of)	2003	7	101	19	0	0	293	7	427
Micronésie (Etats féd. de)	2004	0	0	0	0	0	135	3	138
Mongolia	2003	2 770	2 277	1 488	1 523	0	2 737	1 128	11 922
Mongolie	2004	3 241	1 075	1 075	1 792	0	2 294	1 486	10 963
Montserrat	2003	155	50	0	0	0	0	0	205
Montserrat	2004	101	0	0	0	0	0	0	101
Morocco	2003	4 850	1 521	2 095	2 097	391	2 953	6 690	20 598
Maroc	2004	4 337	2 333	2 642	3 933	191	2 720	3 819	19 975
Mozambique	2003	20 696	4 433	9 044	18 340	67 055	2 883	6 810	129 261
Mozambique	2004	14 794	4 385	8 957	19 812	31 278	2 441	6 413	88 080
Myanmar	2003	9 471	1	1 732	15 167	1 989	4 681	2 143	35 183
Myanmar	2004	12 390	1 099	3 948	15 682	4 611	5 124	2 119	44 973
Namibia	2003	1 575	607	809	3 060	1 338	2 098	1 264	10 751
Namibie	2004	2 529	3 946	1 126	3 543	2 971	1 476	1 414	17 005
Nauru	2003	0	0	0	0	0	126	16	142
Nauru	2004	0	0	0	0	0	82	27	109
Nepal	2003	9 699	3 922	2 830	14 949	16 939	5 288	7 439	61 066
Népal	2004	11 480	1 612	5 752	12 088	20 500	5 305	7 325	64 062
Netherlands Antilles	2003	31	0	0	0	0	152	353	536
Antilles néerlandaises	2004	0	0	0	0	0	44	211	255
New Caledonia	2003	0	0	0	0	0	10	112	121
Nouvelle-Calédonie	2004	0	0	0	0	0	10	546	556
Nicaragua	2003	10 777	1 849	2 121	3 688	7 882	1 485	1 845	29 646
Nicaragua	2004	13 452	3 258	3 423	10 351	8 462	1 816	1 557	42 319
Niger	2003	6 453	3 797	3 105	11 589	2 590	3 247	2 102	32 883
Niger	2004	6 594	2 145	3 085	14 658	6 457	2 557	9 583	45 079
Nigeria	2003	6 758	8 352	6 596	31 590	0	4 020	23 932	81 247
Nigéria	2004	4 691	3 029	6 346	44 044	0	4 228	45 005	107 343
Niue	2003	17	39	0	0	0	58	0	114
Nioué	2004	0	0	0	0	0	197	0	197
Oman	2003	0	7	22	626	0	966	883	2 504
Oman	2004	0	0	2	496	0	705	986	2 189
Pakistan	2003	15 540	3 851	4 874	30 898	31 190	4 519	15 192	106 063
Pakistan	2004	13 906	1 881	5 041	38 834	17 310	4 005	29 704	110 681
Palau	2003	0	0	0	0	0	65	57	122
Palaos	2004	0	0	0	0	0	64	0	64
Panama	2003	126 357	65	422	890	0	1 018	13 294	142 046
Panama	2004	86 241	782	570	624	0	711	16 551	105 479
Papua New Guinea	2003	835	445	409	1 539	0	1 940	241	5 410
Papouasie-Nouvelle-Guinée	2004	3 125	1 211	841	2 211	0	2 148	584	10 120

Assistance en matière de développement socioéconomique fournie par le système des Nations Unies—Subventions au développement : en milliers de dollars des E.-U. (*suite*)

Region, country or area / Région, pays ou zone	Year / Année	UNDP / PNUD Central resources[a] / Ressources centrales[a]	UNDP / PNUD Admin. funds / Fonds gérés	UNFPA / FNUAP	UNICEF	WFP[b] / PAM[b]	Specialized agencies / Institutions spécialisées Regular budgets[c] / Budget ordinaire[c]	Specialized agencies / Institutions spécialisées Extra-budgetary[d] / Extra-budgétaire[d]	Total develop. grants / Total subventions au développ.
Paraguay	2003	15 115	1 818	668	1 146	0	689	27	19 464
Paraguay	2004	19 354	831	1 074	1 670	0	633	33	23 595
Peru	2003	98 385	3 352	1 555	4 589	3 546	2 542	9 123	123 093
Pérou	2004	80 457	1 911	9 369	3 726	2 145	2 380	4 714	104 702
Philippines	2003	5 615	3 555	3 723	6 274	0	2 691	3 785	25 643
Philippines	2004	6 104	6 239	4 508	6 045	0	2 377	5 246	30 519
Poland	2003	1 060	1 823	79	0	0	406	233	3 600
Pologne	2004	1 609	514	102	0	0	498	32	2 755
Portugal	2003	0	0	0	0	0	45	39	84
Portugal	2004	0	0	0	0	0	53	11	64
Qatar	2003	35	0	0	0	0	146	438	619
Qatar	2004	0	0	0	0	0	34	603	637
Réunion	2003	0	0	0	0	0	40	0	40
Réunion	2004	0	0	0	0	0	43	0	43
Romania	2003	1 710	488	481	2 989	0	950	653	7 271
Roumanie	2004	3 576	746	532	3 205	0	659	1 771	10 489
Rwanda	2003	6 001	11 806	1 953	5 532	17 381	2 187	1 753	46 612
Rwanda	2004	6 821	1 744	2 098	6 085	15 764	2 392	1 466	36 370
Saint Helena	2003	326	0	0	0	0	56	0	382
Sainte-Hélène	2004	0	0	0	0	0	53	0	53
Saint Kitts and Nevis	2003	90	59	0	0	0	65	27	240
Saint-Kitts-et-Nevis	2004	0	35	0	0	0	2	26	63
Saint Lucia	2003	88	31	58	0	0	91	26	294
Sainte-Lucie	2004	127	43	0	0	0	13	71	254
St. Vincent-Grenadines	2003	22	94	0	0	0	119	15	249
St. Vincent-Grenadines	2004	95	138	0	0	0	42	5	280
Samoa	2003	374	403	0	0	0	1 151	84	2 012
Samoa	2004	1 002	3 931	0	0	0	1 493	167	6 593
Sao Tome and Principe	2003	464	291	258	669	629	1 056	219	3 586
Sao Tomé-et-Principe	2004	529	234	324	769	446	877	205	3 384
Saudi Arabia	2003	6 642	52	−12	328	0	749	10 399	18 157
Arabie saoudite	2004	6 088	2 394	0	0	0	660	12 735	21 877
Senegal	2003	2 981	2 626	1 673	5 555	6 828	2 659	5 477	27 798
Sénégal	2004	7 313	2 079	2 153	7 054	6 785	2 302	2 338	30 024
Seychelles	2003	54	22	47	0	0	1 137	165	1 425
Seychelles	2004	0	0	17	0	0	893	177	1 087
Sierra Leone	2003	5 583	2 332	1 375	11 576	27 856	2 267	3 115	54 104
Sierra Leone	2004	10 000	2 341	1 792	10 142	13 787	1 737	3 661	43 460
Singapore	2003	0	0	0	0	0	36	71	108
Singapour	2004	0	0	0	0	0	12	71	83
Solomon Islands	2003	1 598	232	0	0	0	619	88	2 537
Iles Salomon	2004	0	0	0	0	0	1 148	882	2 030
Somalia	2003	9 937	2 555	551	24 670	9 741	3 536	6 436	57 426
Somalie	2004	10 623	3 264	440	22 766	18 147	3 086	7 588	65 914
South Africa	2003	6 618	771	640	3 545	0	3 396	2 242	17 212
Afrique du Sud	2004	8 014	2 824	413	4 539	0	3 024	1 866	20 680
Sri Lanka	2003	5 597	2 128	−172	14 136	7 909	4 943	3 936	38 477
Sri Lanka	2004	4 714	2 580	953	13 457	10 824	3 264	5 276	41 068
Sudan	2003	8 140	1 275	1 702	20 820	135 736	4 786	11 822	184 281
Soudan	2004	19 910	4 331	4 041	57 450	389 290	4 239	26 428	505 689
Suriname	2003	456	390	195	0	0	622	158	1 820
Suriname	2004	0	0	0	0	0	483	118	601

Assistance en matière de développement socioéconomique fournie par le système des Nations Unies — Subventions au développement : en milliers de dollars des E.-U. (*suite*)

Region, country or area Région, pays ou zone	Year Année	UNDP PNUD		UNFPA FNUAP	UNICEF	WFP[b] PAM[b]	Specialized agencies Institutions spécialisées		Total develop. grants Total subventions au développ.
		Central resources[a] Ressources centrales[a]	Admin. funds Fonds gérés				Regular budgets[c] Budget ordinaire[c]	Extra–budgetary[d] Extra–budgétaire[d]	
Swaziland Swaziland	2003	812	715	345	3 948	10 221	1 814	613	18 468
	2004	1 129	456	575	4 603	8 816	1 704	262	17 545
Syrian Arab Republic Rép. arabe syrienne	2003	2 882	3 770	1 646	1 340	8 351	3 174	37 533	58 696
	2004	1 858	1 438	2 395	1 068	2 903	1 451	5 801	16 914
Tajikistan Tadjikistan	2003	4 116	1 326	736	4 869	26 951	757	1 646	40 400
	2004	5 470	1 388	641	6 728	12 436	647	1 698	29 008
Thailand Thaïlande	2003	716	932	638	3 417	0	5 004	1 815	12 523
	2004	4 207	2 158	912	4 525	10	4 334	2 922	19 068
TFYR of Macedonia L'ex-R.y. Macédoine	2003	2 445	1 176	0	1 895	94	758	1 592	7 959
	2004	4 132	1 470	0	2 090	0	733	1 772	10 197
Timor-Leste Timor-Leste	2003	7 699	7 442	1 239	4 803	996	837	1 249	24 265
	2004	6 506	3 330	3 230	5 376	2 310	897	1 282	22 931
Togo Togo	2003	2 954	360	1 133	3 215	0	1 667	690	10 019
	2004	9 838	1	1 275	3 466	0	1 758	926	17 264
Tokelau Tokélaou	2003	169	0	0	0	0	55	0	224
	2004	0	0	0	0	0	52	0	52
Tonga Tonga	2003	20	−1	0	0	0	822	37	878
	2004	0	0	0	0	0	457	14	471
Trinidad and Tobago Trinité-et-Tobago	2003	1 641	611	21	0	0	631	797	3 700
	2004	6 009	3 542	0	0	0	569	1 294	11 414
Tunisia Tunisie	2003	600	999	481	865	0	1 570	2 832	7 347
	2004	808	1 957	811	1 724	0	1 871	3 404	10 575
Turkey Turquie	2003	3 123	1 229	935	2 586	0	856	1 024	9 753
	2004	4 254	2 322	1 120	2 670	0	853	1 292	12 511
Turkmenistan Turkménistan	2003	1 031	126	479	1 385	208	96	27	3 352
	2004	716	233	459	1 206	0	306	0	2 920
Turks and Caicos Islands Iles Turques et Caïques	2003	178	5	0	0	0	27	0	210
	2004	0	0	0	0	0	3	0	3
Tuvalu Tuvalu	2003	36	0	0	0	0	207	0	243
	2004	0	0	0	0	0	60	0	60
Uganda Ouganda	2003	6 144	4 160	6 221	16 914	88 584	4 313	3 828	130 164
	2004	6 198	501	5 313	20 295	87 741	2 878	5 100	128 026
United Arab Emirates Emirats arabes unis	2003	2 925	0	0	0	0	141	275	3 341
	2004	2 697	0	3	0	0	15	367	3 082
United Rep. of Tanzania Rép.-Unie de Tanzanie	2003	9 677	2 634	4 511	15 581	58 293	3 848	6 995	101 538
	2004	27 510	2 283	5 925	19 454	32 766	2 546	7 029	97 513
Uruguay Uruguay	2003	7 988	320	188	580	0	972	406	10 454
	2004	12 303	1 398	340	1 000	0	655	477	16 173
Uzbekistan Ouzbékistan	2003	5 019	455	605	2 407	0	739	773	9 998
	2004	4 331	521	684	2 066	0	811	951	9 364
Vanuatu Vanuatu	2003	56	8	0	0	0	985	50	1 099
	2004	0	0	0	0	0	1 033	398	1 431
Venezuela (Bolivarian Rep. of) Venezuela (Rép. Bolivar. du)	2003	24 498	1 143	740	1 347	0	1 840	2 249	31 816
	2004	24 026	939	974	1 188	0	1 595	4 721	33 443
Viet Nam Viet Nam	2003	9 288	2 324	5 298	8 825	0	4 915	4 544	35 194
	2004	11 746	1 299	7 737	10 734	0	4 566	10 201	46 283
Yemen Yémen	2003	6 888	1 366	2 243	5 388	9 584	3 643	1 386	30 497
	2004	8 083	1 253	4 056	4 988	7 521	3 155	1 258	30 314
Zambia Zambie	2003	3 278	356	1 500	12 548	55 877	2 401	4 991	80 951
	2004	4 560	322	1 478	9 260	23 054	2 946	3 083	44 703
Zimbabwe Zimbabwe	2003	3 791	3 768	1 061	12 524	163 269	2 256	7 890	194 559
	2004	4 875	4 181	1 348	12 287	73 017	2 094	3 996	101 798

Assistance en matière de développement socioéconomique fournie par le système des Nations Unies — Subventions au développement : en milliers de dollars des E.-U. (*suite*)

Region, country or area Région, pays ou zone	Year Année	UNDP PNUD		UNFPA FNUAP	UNICEF	WFP[b] PAM[b]	Specialized agencies Institutions spécialisées		Total develop. grants Total subventions au développ.
		Central resources[a] Ressources centrales[a]	Admin. funds Fonds gérés				Regular budgets[c] Budget ordinaire[c]	Extra– budgetary[d] Extra– budgétaire[d]	
Other countries Autres pays	2003	54 074	21 996	3 777	22 849	40 706	13 472	47 241	204 114
	2004	97 864	223 114	4 180	58 523	156 811	10 065	43 999	594 556
Not elsewhere classified Non-classé ailleurs	2003	853	52 718	3 438	41 211	29 764	4 060	7 196	139 239
	2004	4 001	0	5 588	14 736	28 771	2 063	3 894	59 053

Source

United Nations, "Operational activities of the United Nations for international development cooperation, Report of the Secretary-General, Addendum, Comprehensive statistical data on operational activities for development for the year 2003" (A/59/386) and "Operational activities of the United Nations for international development cooperation, Report of the Secretary-General, Addendum, Comprehensive statistical data on operational activities for development for the year 2004".

The following abbreviations have been used in the table:
* UNDP: United Nations Development Programme
* UNFPA: United Nations Population Fund
* UNICEF: United Nations Children's Fund
* WFP: World Food Programme.

Notes

[a] Including expenditures financed from government cost-sharing contributions.

[b] Includes extrabudgetary expenditures and WFP project expenditures for development activities and emergency operations. Of the latter, most was financed from the International Emergency Food Reserve and the remainder from WFP general resources.

[c] Grants financed by specialized agencies and other organizations; the major share of such expenditures is financed by WHO.

[d] Grants financed by specialized agencies and other organizations; i.e., from funds not elsewhere specified in the table. Starting in 1998 it includes UNEP extrabudgetary expenditures. Also included are expenditures financed from government "self-supporting" contributions.

[1] For statistical purposes, the data for China do not include those for the Hong Kong Special Administrative Region (Hong Kong SAR), Macao Special Administrative Region (Macao SAR) and Taiwan Province of China.

Source

Nations Unies, "Activités opérationnelles du système des Nations Unies au service de la coopération internationale pour le développement, Rapport du Secrétaire général, Additif, Données statistiques globales sur les activités opérationnelles au service du développement pour 2003" (A/59/386) et "Activités opérationnelles du système des Nations Unies au service de la coopération internationale pour le développement, Rapport du Secrétaire général, Additif, Données statistiques globales sur les activités opérationnelles au service du développement pour 2004".

Les abbréviations ci-après ont été utilisées dans le tableau :
* PNUD : Programme des Nations Unies pour le développement
* FNUAP : Fonds des Nations Unies pour la population
* UNICEF : Fonds des Nations Unies pour l'enfance
* PAM : Programme alimentaire mondial.

Notes

[a] Y compris les dépenses financées à l'aide des contributions versées par les gouvernements au titre de la participation aux coûts.

[b] Y compris les dépenses extrabudgétaires et celles afférentes aux projets du PAM rélatifs aux activités de développement et aux opérations de secours d'urgence. Les dépenses au titre des opérations de secours d'urgence ont été financées pour la plus grande partie au moyen de la réserve alimentaire internationale d'urgence, le reste étant imputé sur les ressources générales du PAM.

[c] Subventions financées par les institutions spécialisées et autres organisations sur les budgets ordinaires; la plus grande part est financée par l'OMS.

[d] Subventions financées par les institutions spécialisées et autres organisations sur les budgets ordinaires ; fonds ne figurant pas ailleurs dans le tableau, y compris les dépenses financées au moyen des contributions "d'auto-assistance" versées par les gouvernements, comme indiqué dans la rubrique explicative, et, à partir de 1998, les dépenses du PNUE financées à l'aide de fonds extrabudgétaires.

[1] Pour la présentation des statistiques, les données pour Chine ne comprennent pas la Région Administrative Spéciale de Hong Kong (Hong Kong RAS), la Région Administrative Spéciale de Macao (Macao RAS) et la province de Taiwan.

Table 74 presents estimates of flows of financial resources to individual recipients either directly (bilaterally) or through multilateral institutions (multilaterally).

The multilateral institutions include the World Bank Group, regional banks, financial institutions of the European Union and a number of United Nations institutions, programmes and trust funds.

The source of data is the Development Assistance Committee of OECD to which member countries reported data on their flow of resources to developing countries and territories and countries and territories in transition, and multilateral institutions.

Additional information on definitions, methods and sources can be found in OECD's *Geographical Distribution of Financial Flows to Aid Recipients* [20] and www.oecd.org.

Table 75 presents the development assistance expenditures of donor countries. This table includes donors' contributions to multilateral agencies, therefore, the overall totals differ from those in table 74, which include disbursements by multilateral agencies.

Table 76 includes data on expenditures on operational activities for development undertaken by the organizations of the United Nations system. Operational activities encompass, in general, those activities of a development cooperation character that seek to mobilize or increase the potential and capacity of countries to promote economic and social development and welfare, including the transfer of resources to developing countries or regions in a tangible or intangible form.

Expenditures on operational activities for development are financed from contributions from governments and other official and non official sources to a variety of funding channels in the United Nations system. These include United Nations funds and programmes such as contributions to the United Nations Development Programme, contributions to funds administered by the United Nations Development Programme, and regular (assessed) and other extrabudgetary contributions to specialized agencies.

Data are taken from the 2003 and 2004 reports of the Secretary-General to the General Assembly on operational activities for development [27].

Le *tableau 74* présente les estimations des flux de ressources financières mises à la disposition des pays soit directement (aide bilatérale) soit par l'intermédiaire d'institutions multilatérales (aide multilatérale).

Les institutions multilatérales comprennent le Groupe de la Banque mondiale, les banques régionales, les institutions financières de l'Union européenne et un certain nombre d'institutions, de programmes et de fonds d'affectation spéciale des Nations Unies.

La source de données est le Comité d'aide au développement de l'OCDE, auquel les pays membres ont communiqué des données sur les flux de ressources qu'ils mettent à la disposition des pays et territoires en développement et en transition et des institutions multilatérales.

Pour plus de renseignements sur les définitions, méthodes et sources, se reporter à la publication de l'OCDE, la *Répartition géographique des ressources financières de aux pays bénéficiaires de l'Aide* [20] et www.oecd.org.

Le *tableau 75* présente les dépenses que les pays donateurs consacrent à l'aide publique au développement (APD). Ces chiffres incluent les contributions des donateurs à des agences multilatérales, de sorte que les totaux diffèrent de ceux du tableau 74, qui incluent les dépenses des agences multilatérales.

Le *tableau 76* présente des données sur les dépenses consacrées à des activités opérationnelles pour le développement par les organisations du système des Nations Unies. Par "activités opérationnelles", on entend en général les activités ayant trait à la coopération au développement, qui visent à mobiliser ou à accroître les potentialités et aptitudes que présentent les pays pour promouvoir le développement et le bien-être économiques et sociaux, y compris les transferts de ressources vers les pays ou régions en développement sous forme tangible ou non.

Les dépenses consacrées aux activités opérationnelles pour le développement sont financées au moyen de contributions que les gouvernements et d'autres sources officielles et non officielles apportent à divers organes de financement, tels que fonds et programmes du système des Nations Unies. On peut citer notamment les contributions au Programme des Nations Unies pour le développement, les contributions aux fonds gérés par le Programme des Nations Unies pour le développement, les contributions régulières (budgétaires) et les contributions extrabudgétaires aux institutions spécialisées.

Les données sont extraites des rapports annuels de 2003 et de 2004 du Secrétaire général à la session de l'Assemblée générale sur les activités opérationnelles pour le développement [27].

Annex I

Country and area nomenclature, regional and other groupings

A. Changes in country or area names

In the periods covered by the statistics in the *Statistical Yearbook*, the following changes in designation have taken place:

Brunei Darussalam was formerly listed as Brunei;

Burkina Faso was formerly listed as Upper Volta;

Cambodia was formerly listed as Democratic Kampuchea;

Cameroon was formerly listed as United Republic of Cameroon;

Côte d'Ivoire was formerly listed as Ivory Coast;

Czech Republic, Slovakia: Since 1 January 1993, data for the Czech Republic and Slovakia, where available, are shown separately under the appropriate country name. For periods prior to 1 January 1993, where no separate data are available for the Czech Republic and Slovakia, unless otherwise indicated, data for the former Czechoslovakia are shown under the country name "former Czechoslovakia";

Democratic Republic of the Congo was formerly listed as Zaire;

Germany: Through the accession of the German Democratic Republic to the Federal Republic of Germany with effect from 3 October 1990, the two German States have united to form one sovereign State. As from the date of unification, the Federal Republic of Germany acts in the United Nations under the designation "Germany". All data shown which pertain to Germany prior to 3 October 1990 are indicated separately for the Federal Republic of Germany and the former German Democratic Republic based on their respective territories at the time indicated;

Hong Kong Special Administrative Region of China: Pursuant to a Joint Declaration signed on 19 December 1984, the United Kingdom restored Hong Kong to the People's Republic of China with effect from 1 July 1997; the People's Republic of China resumed the exercise of sovereignty over the territory with effect from that date;

Macao Special Administrative Region of China: Pursuant to the joint declaration signed on 13 April 1987, Portugal restored Macao to the People's Republic of China with effect from 20 December 1999; the People's Republic of China resumed the exercise of sovereignty over the territory with effect from that date;

Myanmar was formerly listed as Burma;

Annexe I

Nomenclature des pays ou zones, groupements régionaux et autres groupements

A. Changements dans le nom des pays ou zones

Au cours des périodes sur lesquelles portent les statistiques, dans l'*Annuaire Statistique* les changements de désignation suivants ont eu lieu :

Le *Brunéi Darussalam* apparaissait antérieurement sous le nom de Brunéi;

Le *Burkina Faso* apparaissait antérieurement sous le nom de la Haute-Volta;

Le *Cambodge* apparaissait antérieurement sous le nom de la Kampuchea démocratique;

Le *Cameroun* apparaissait antérieurement sous le nom de République-Unie du Cameroun;

République tchèque, Slovaquie : Depuis le 1er janvier 1993, les données relatives à la République tchèque, et à la Slovaquie, lorsqu'elles sont disponibles, sont présentées séparément sous le nom de chacun des pays. En ce qui concerne la période précédant le 1er janvier 1993, pour laquelle on ne possède pas de données séparées pour les deux Républiques, les données relatives à l'ex-Tchécoslovaquie sont, sauf indication contraire, présentées sous le titre "l'ex-Tchécoslovaquie";

La *République démocratique du Congo* apparaissait antérieurement sous le nom de Zaïre;

Allemagne : En vertu de l'adhésion de la République démocratique allemande à la République fédérale d'Allemagne, prenant effet le 3 octobre 1990, les deux Etats allemands se sont unis pour former un seul Etat souverain. A compter de la date de l'unification, la République fédérale d'Allemagne est désigné à l'ONU sous le nom d'"Allemagne". Toutes les données se rapportant à l'Allemagne avant le 3 octobre figurent dans deux rubriques séparées basées sur les territoires respectifs de la République fédérale d'Allemagne et l'ex-République démocratique allemande selon la période indiquée;

Hong Kong, région administrative spéciale de Chine : Conformément à une Déclaration commune signée le 19 décembre 1984, le Royaume-Uni a rétrocédé Hong Kong à la République populaire de Chine, avec effet au 1er juillet 1997; la souveraineté de la République populaire de Chine s'exerce à nouveau sur le territoire à compter de cette date;

Macao, région administrative spéciale de Chine : Conformément à une Déclaration commune signée le 13 avril 1987, le Portugal a rétrocédé Macao à la République populaire de Chine, avec effet au 20 décembre 1999; la souveraineté de la République populaire de Chine s'exerce à nouveau sur le territoire à compter de cette date;

Palau was formerly listed as Pacific Islands and includes data for Federated States of Micronesia, Marshall Islands and Northern Mariana Islands;

Saint Kitts and Nevis was formerly listed as Saint Christopher and Nevis;

Serbia and Montenegro: As of 4 February 2003, the official name of the "Federal Republic of Yugoslavia" has been changed to "Serbia and Montenegro". Unless otherwise indicated, data provided for Yugoslavia prior to 1 January 1992 refer to the Socialist Federal Republic of Yugoslavia which was composed of six republics. Data provided for Yugoslavia after that date refer to the Federal Republic of Yugoslavia which is composed of two republics (Serbia and Montenegro);

Timor-Leste: Formerly East Timor;

Former *USSR*: In 1991, the Union of Soviet Socialist Republics formally dissolved into fifteen independent countries (Armenia, Azerbaijan, Belarus, Estonia, Georgia, Kazakhstan, Kyrgyzstan, Latvia, Lithuania, Republic of Moldova, Russian Federation, Tajikistan, Turkmenistan, Ukraine and Uzbekistan). Whenever possible, data are shown for the individual countries. Otherwise, data are shown for the former USSR;

Yemen: On 22 May 1990 Democratic Yemen and Yemen merged to form a single State. Since that date they have been represented as one Member with the name 'Yemen'.

Data relating to the People's Republic of China generally include those for Taiwan Province in the field of statistics relating to population, area, land use, agriculture, natural resources and natural conditions such as climate. In other fields of statistics, they do not include Taiwan Province unless otherwise stated.

B. Regional groupings

The scheme of regional groupings given below presents seven regions based mainly on continents. Five of the seven continental regions are further subdivided into 21 regions that are so drawn as to obtain greater homogeneity in sizes of population, demographic circumstances and accuracy of demographic statistics. This nomenclature is widely used in international statistics and is followed to the greatest extent possible in the present *Yearbook* in order to promote consistency and facilitate comparability and analysis. However, it is by no means universal in international statistical compilation, even at the level of continental regions, and variations in international statistical sources and methods dictate many unavoidable differences in particular fields in the present *Yearbook*. General differences are indicated in the footnotes to the classification presented below. More detailed differences are given in the footnotes and technical notes to individual tables.

Le *Myanmar* apparaissait antérieurement sous le nom de Birmanie;

Les *Palaos* apparaissait antérieurement sous le nom de Iles du Pacifique y compris les données pour les Etats fédérés de Micronésie, les îles Marshall et îles Mariannes du Nord;

Saint-Kitts-et-Nevis apparaissait antérieurement sous le nom de Saint-Christophe-et-Nevis;

Serbie-et-Monténégro : A compter de février 2003, la "République fédérale de Yougoslavie" ayant changé de nom officiel, est devenue la "Serbie-et-Monténégro". Sauf indication contraire, les données fournies pour la Yougoslavie avant le 1er janvier 1992 se rapportent à la République fédérative socialiste de Yougoslavie, qui était composée de six républiques. Les données fournies pour la Yougoslavie après cette date se rapportent à la République fédérative de Yougoslavie, qui est composée de deux républiques (Serbie et Monténégro);

Timor-Leste : Ex Timor oriental;

L'ex-*URSS* : En 1991, l'Union des républiques socialistes soviétiques s'est séparé en 15 pays distincts (Arménie, Azerbaïdjan, Bélarus, Estonie, Géorgie, Kazakhstan, Kirghizistan, Lettonie, Lituanie, République de Moldova, Fédération de Russie, Tadjikistan, Turkménistan, Ukraine, Ouzbékistan). Les données sont présentées pour ces pays pris séparément quand cela est possible. Autrement, les données sont présentées pour l'ex-URSS;

Yémen : Le Yémen et le Yémen démocratique ont fusionné le 22 mai 1990 pour ne plus former qu'un seul Etat, qui est depuis lors représenté comme tel à l'Organisation, sous le nom Yémen.

Les données relatives à la République populaire de Chine comprennent en général les données relatives à la province de Taïwan lorsqu'il s'agit de statistiques concernant la population, la superficie, l'utilisation des terres, l'agriculture, les ressources naturelles, et les conditions naturelles telles que le climat, etc. Dans les statistiques relatives à d'autres domaines, la province de Taïwan n'est pas comprise, sauf indication contraire.

B. Groupements régionaux

Le système de groupements régionaux présenté ci-dessous comporte sept régions basés principalement sur les continents. Cinq des sept régions continentales sont elles-mêmes subdivisées, formant ainsi 21 régions délimitées de manière à obtenir une homogénéité accrue dans les effectifs de population, les situations démographiques et la précision des statistiques démographiques. Cette nomenclature est couramment utilisée aux fins des statistiques internationales et a été appliquée autant qu'il a été possible dans le présent *Annuaire* en vue de renforcer la cohérence et de faciliter la comparaison et l'analyse. Son utilisation pour l'établissement des statistiques internationales n'est cependant rien moins qu'universelle, même au

niveau des régions continentales, et les variations que présentent les sources et méthodes statistiques internationales entraînent inévitablement de nombreuses différences dans certains domaines de cet *Annuaire*. Les différences d'ordre général sont indiquées dans les notes figurant au bas de la classification présentée ci-dessous. Les différences plus spécifiques sont mentionnées dans les notes techniques et notes infrapaginales accompagnant les divers tableaux.

Africa

Eastern Africa

Burundi	Mozambique
Comoros	Réunion
Djibouti	Rwanda
Eritrea	Seychelles
Ethiopia	Somalia
Kenya	Uganda
Madagascar	United Republic of Tanzania
Malawi	Zambia
Mauritius	Zimbabwe

Middle Africa

Angola	Democratic Republic of the Congo
Cameroon	
Central African Republic	Equatorial Guinea
Chad	Gabon
Congo	Sao Tome and Principe

Northern Africa

Algeria	Morocco
Egypt	Sudan
Libyan Arab Jamahiriya	Tunisia
	Western Sahara

Southern Africa

Botswana	South Africa
Lesotho	Swaziland
Namibia	

Western Africa

Benin	Mali
Burkina Faso	Mauritania
Cape Verde	Niger
Côte d'Ivoire	Nigeria
Gambia	Saint Helena
Ghana	Senegal
Guinea	Sierra Leone
Guinea-Bissau	Togo
Liberia	

Afrique

Afrique orientale

Burundi	Mozambique
Comores	Ouganda
Djibouti	République-Unie de Tanzanie
Erythrée	Réunion
Ethiopie	Rwanda
Kenya	Seychelles
Madagascar	Somalie
Malawi	Zambie
Maurice	Zimbabwe

Afrique centrale

Angola	République centrafricaine
Cameroun	République démocratique du Congo
Congo	
Gabon	Sao Tomé-et-Principe
Guinée équatoriale	Tchad

Afrique septentrionale

Algérie	Maroc
Egypte	Sahara occidental
Jamahiriya arabe libyenne	Soudan
	Tunisie

Afrique australe

Afrique du Sud	Namibie
Botswana	Swaziland
Lesotho	

Afrique occidentale

Bénin	Mali
Burkina Faso	Mauritanie
Cap-Vert	Niger
Côte d'Ivoire	Nigéria
Gambie	Sainte-Hélène
Ghana	Sénégal
Guinée	Sierra Leone
Guinée-Bissau	Togo
Libéria	

Americas

Latin America and the Caribbean

Caribbean

Anguilla
Antigua and Barbuda
Aruba
Bahamas
Barbados
British Virgin Islands
Cayman Islands
Cuba
Dominica
Dominican Republic
Grenada
Guadeloupe
Haiti

Jamaica
Martinique
Montserrat
Netherlands Antilles
Puerto Rico
Saint Kitts and Nevis
Saint Lucia
Saint Vincent and the
    Grenadines
Trinidad and Tobago
Turks and Caicos Islands
United States Virgin
    Islands

Central America

Belize
Costa Rica
El Salvador
Guatemala

Honduras
Mexico
Nicaragua
Panama

South America

Argentina
Bolivia
Brazil
Chile
Colombia
Ecuador
Falkland Islands
    (Malvinas)

French Guiana
Guyana
Paraguay
Peru
Suriname
Uruguay
Venezuela (Bolivarian
    Republic of)

Northern America [a]

Bermuda
Canada
Greenland

Saint Pierre
    and Miquelon
United States of America

Asia

Eastern Asia

China
China, Hong Kong Special
    Administrative Region
China, Macao Special
    Administrative Region

Democratic People's
    Republic of Korea
Japan
Mongolia
Republic of Korea

Annexe I (*suite*)

Amériques

Amérique latine et Caraïbes

Caraïbes

Anguilla
Antigua-et-Barbuda
Antilles néerlandaises
Aruba
Bahamas
Barbade
Cuba
Dominique
Grenade
Guadeloupe
Haïti
Iles Caïmanes
Iles Turques et Caïques

Iles Vierges américaines
Iles Vierges britanniques
Jamaïque
Martinique
Montserrat
Porto Rico
République
    dominicaine
Sainte-Lucie
Saint-Kitts-et-Nevis
Saint-Vincent-et-les
    Grenadines
Trinité-et-Tobago

Amérique centrale

Belize
Costa Rica
El Salvador
Guatemala

Honduras
Mexique
Nicaragua
Panama

Amérique du Sud

Argentine
Bolivie
Brésil
Chili
Colombie
Equateur
Guyana
Guyane française

Iles Falkland
    (Malvinas)
Paraguay
Pérou
Suriname
Uruguay
Venezuela (République
    bolivarienne du)

Amérique septentrionale [a]

Bermudes
Canada
Etats-Unis d'Amérique

Groenland
Saint-Pierre
    et-Miquelon

Asie

Asie orientale

Chine
Chine, Hong Kong, région
    administrative spéciale
Chine, Macao, région
    administrative spéciale

Japon
Mongolie
République de Corée
République populaire
    démocratique de Corée

South-central Asia

Afghanistan	Maldives
Bangladesh	Nepal
Bhutan	Pakistan
India	Sri Lanka
Iran (Islamic	Tajikistan
Republic of)	Turkmenistan
Kazakhstan	Uzbekistan
Kyrgyzstan	

South-eastern Asia

Brunei Darussalam	Myanmar
Cambodia	Philippines
Indonesia	Singapore
Lao People's Democratic	Thailand
Republic	Timor-Leste
Malaysia	Viet Nam

Western Asia

Armenia	Occupied Palestinian
Azerbaijan	Territory
Bahrain	Oman
Cyprus	Qatar
Georgia	Saudi Arabia
Iraq	Syrian Arab Republic
Israel	Turkey
Jordan	United Arab Emirates
Kuwait	Yemen
Lebanon	

Europe

Eastern Europe

Belarus	Republic of Moldova
Bulgaria	Romania
Czech Republic	Russian Federation
Hungary	Slovakia
Poland	Ukraine

Northern Europe

Channel Islands	Latvia
Denmark	Lithuania
Estonia	Norway
Faeroe Islands	Svalbard and Jan Mayen
Finland	Islands
Iceland	Sweden
Ireland	United Kingdom
Isle of Man	

Asie centrale et du Sud

Afghanistan	Maldives
Bangladesh	Népal
Bhoutan	Ouzbékistan
Inde	Pakistan
Iran (République	Sri Lanka
islamique d')	Tadjikistan
Kazakhstan	Turkménistan
Kirghizistan	

Asie du Sud-Est

Brunéi Darussalam	République démocratique
Cambodge	populaire lao
Indonésie	Singapour
Malaisie	Thaïlande
Myanmar	Timor-Leste
Philippines	Viet Nam

Asie occidentale

Arabie saoudite	Koweït
Arménie	Liban
Azerbaïdjan	Oman
Bahreïn	Qatar
Chypre	République arabe syrienne
Emirats arabes unis	Territoire palestinien
Géorgie	occupé
Iraq	Turquie
Israël	Yémen
Jordanie	

Europe

Europe orientale

Bélarus	République de Moldova
Bulgarie	République tchèque
Fédération de Russie	Roumanie
Hongrie	Slovaquie
Pologne	Ukraine

Europe septentrionale

Danemark	Irlande
Estonie	Islande
Finlande	Lettonie
Ile de Man	Lituanie
Iles Anglo-Normandes	Norvège
Iles Féroé	Royaume-Uni
Iles Svalbard	Suède
et Jan Mayen	

Southern Europe

Albania	Malta
Andorra	Portugal
Bosnia and Herzegovina	San Marino
Croatia	Serbia and Montenegro
Gibraltar	Slovenia
Greece	Spain
Holy See	The former Yugoslav
Italy	Republic of Macedonia

Western Europe

Austria	Luxembourg
Belgium	Monaco
France	Netherlands
Germany	Switzerland
Liechtenstein	

Oceania

Australia and New Zealand

Australia	Norfolk Island
New Zealand	

Melanesia

Fiji	Solomon Islands
New Caledonia	Vanuatu
Papua New Guinea	

Micronesia-Polynesia

Micronesia

Guam	Nauru
Kiribati	Northern Mariana Islands
Marshall Islands	Palau
Micronesia (Federated States of)	

Polynesia

American Samoa	Samoa
Cook Islands	Tokelau
French Polynesia	Tonga
Niue	Tuvalu
Pitcairn	Wallis and Futuna Islands

C. Other groupings

Following is a list of other groupings and their compositions presented in the *Yearbook*. These groupings are organized mainly around economic and trade interests in regional associations.

Europe méridionale

Albanie	Grèce
Andorre	Italie
Bosnie-Herzégovine	Malte
Croatie	Portugal
Espagne	Saint-Marin
Ex-République yougoslave de Macédoine	Saint-Siège
Gibraltar	Serbie-et-Monténégro
	Slovénie

Europe occidentale

Allemagne	Luxembourg
Autriche	Monaco
Belgique	Pays-Bas
France	Suisse
Liechtenstein	

Océanie

Australie et Nouvelle-Zélande

Australie	Nouvelle-Zélande
Ile Norfolk	

Mélanésie

Fidji	Papouasie-Nouvelle-Guinée
Iles Salomon	Vanuatu
Nouvelle-Calédonie	

Micronésie-Polynésie

Micronésie

Guam	Kiribati
Iles Mariannes septentrionales	Micronésie (Etats fédérés de)
Iles Marshall	Nauru
	Palaos

Polynésie

Iles Cook	Samoa
Iles Wallis-et-Futuna	Samoa américaines
Nioué	Tokélaou
Pitcairn	Tonga
Polynésie française	Tuvalu

C. Autres groupements

On trouvera ci-après une liste des autres groupements et de leur composition, présentée dans l'*Annuaire*. Ces groupements correspondent essentiellement à des intérêts économiques et commerciaux d'après les associations régionales.

Andean Common Market (ANCOM)

Bolivia	Peru
Colombia	Venezuela (Bolivarian
Ecuador	Republic of)

Asia-Pacific Economic Cooperation (APEC)

Australia	New Zealand
Brunei Darussalam	Papua New Guinea
Canada	Peru
Chile	Philippines
China	Republic of Korea
China, Hong Kong Special	Russian Federation
Administrative Region	Singapore
Indonesia	Taiwan Province of China
Japan	Thailand
Malaysia	United States of America
Mexico	Viet Nam

Association of Southeast Asian Nations (ASEAN)

Brunei Darussalam	Myanmar
Cambodia	Philippines
Indonesia	Singapore
Lao People's Democratic	Thailand
Republic	Viet Nam
Malaysia	

Caribbean Community and Common Market (CARICOM)

Antigua and Barbuda	Jamaica
Bahamas (member of the	Montserrat
Community only)	Saint Kitts and Nevis
Barbados	Saint Lucia
Belize	Saint Vincent and the
Dominica	Grenadines
Grenada	Suriname
Guyana	Trinidad and Tobago
Haiti	

Central American Common Market (CACM)

Costa Rica	Honduras
El Salvador	Nicaragua
Guatemala	

Common Market for Eastern and Southern Africa (COMESA)

Angola	Madagascar
Burundi	Malawi
Comoros	Mauritius
Democratic Republic of the	Rwanda
Congo	Seychelles
Djibouti	Sudan
Egypt	Swaziland
Eritrea	Uganda

Marché commun andin (ANCOM)

Bolivie	Pérou
Colombie	Venezuela (République
Equateur	bolivarienne du)

Coopération économique Asie-Pacifique (CEAP)

Australie	Malaisie
Brunéi Darussalam	Mexique
Canada	Nouvelle-Zélande
Chili	Papouasie-Nouvelle-Guinée
Chine	Pérou
Chine, Hong Kong, région	Philippines
administrative spéciale	Province chinoise de Taiwan
Etats-Unis d'Amérique	République de Corée
Fédération de Russie	Singapour
Indonésie	Thaïlande
Japon	Viet Nam

Association des nations de l'Asie du Sud-Est (ANASE)

Brunéi Darussalam	République démocratique
Cambodge	populaire lao
Indonésie	Singapour
Malaisie	Thaïlande
Myanmar	Viet Nam
Philippines	

Communauté des Caraïbes et Marché commun des Caraïbes (CARICOM)

Antigua-et-Barbuda	Jamaïque
Bahamas (membre de la	Montserrat
communauté seulement)	Sainte-Lucie
Barbade	Saint-Kitts-et-Nevis
Belize	Saint-Vincent-et-les
Dominique	Grenadines
Grenade	Suriname
Guyana	Trinité-et-Tobago
Haïti	

Marché commun centraméricain (MCC)

Costa Rica	Honduras
El Salvador	Nicaragua
Guatemala	

Marché commun de l'Afrique de l'Est et de l'Afrique australe (COMESA)

Angola	Maurice
Burundi	Ouganda
Comores	République démocratique du
Djibouti	Congo
Egypte	Rwanda
Erythrée	Seychelles
Ethiopie	Soudan
Jamahiriya arabe libyenne	Swaziland

Ethiopia	Zambia
Kenya	Zimbabwe
Libyan Arab Jamahiriya	

Kenya	Zambie
Madagascar	Zimbabwe
Malawi	

Commonwealth of Independent States (CIS)

Armenia	Republic of Moldova
Azerbaijan	Russian Federation
Belarus	Tajikistan
Georgia	Turkmenistan
Kazakhstan	Ukraine
Kyrgyzstan	Uzbekistan

Communauté d'Etats indépendants (CEI)

Arménie	Kirghizistan
Azerbaïdjan	Ouzbékistan
Bélarus	République de Moldova
Fédération de Russie	Tadjikistan
Géorgie	Turkménistan
Kazakhstan	Ukraine

Economic and Monetary Community of Central Africa (EMCCA)

Cameroon	Congo
Central African Republic	Equatorial Guinea
Chad	Gabon

Communauté économique et monétaire de l'Afrique centrale (CEMAC)

Cameroun	Guinée équatoriale
Congo	République centrafricaine
Gabon	Tchad

Economic Community of West African States (ECOWAS)

Benin	Liberia
Burkina Faso	Mali
Cape Verde	Niger
Côte d'Ivoire	Nigeria
Gambia	Senegal
Ghana	Sierra Leone
Guinea	Togo
Guinea-Bissau	

Communauté économique des Etats de l'Afrique de l'Ouest (CEDEAO)

Bénin	Libéria
Burkina Faso	Mali
Cap-Vert	Niger
Côte d'Ivoire	Nigéria
Gambie	Sénégal
Ghana	Sierra Leone
Guinée	Togo
Guinée-Bissau	

European Free Trade Association (EFTA)

Iceland	Norway
Liechtenstein	Switzerland

Association européenne de libre-échange (AELE)

Islande	Norvège
Liechtenstein	Suisse

European Union (EU)

Austria	Latvia
Belgium	Lithuania
Cyprus	Luxembourg
Czech Republic	Malta
Denmark	Netherlands
Estonia	Poland
Finland	Portugal
France	Slovakia
Germany	Slovenia
Greece	Spain
Hungary	Sweden
Ireland	United Kingdom
Italy	

Union européenne (UE)

Allemagne	Lettonie
Autriche	Lithuanie
Belgique	Luxembourg
Chypre	Malte
Danemark	Pays-Bas
Espagne	Portugal
Estonie	Pologne
Finlande	République tchèque
France	Royaume-Uni
Grèce	Slovaquie
Hongrie	Slovénie
Irlande	Suède
Italie	

Latin American Integration Association (LAIA)

Argentina	Mexico
Bolivia	Paraguay
Brazil	Peru

Association latino-américaine pour l'intégration (ALAI)

Argentine	Mexique
Bolivie	Paraguay
Brésil	Pérou

Chile	Uruguay	Chili	Uruguay
Colombia	Venezuela (Bolivarian	Colombie	Venezuela (République
Cuba	Republic of)	Cuba	bolivarienne du)
Ecuador		Equateur	

Least developed countries (LDCs) [b]   *Pays les moins avancés (PMA)* [b]

Afghanistan	Liberia	Afghanistan	Mauritanie
Angola	Madagascar	Angola	Mozambique
Bangladesh	Malawi	Bangladesh	Myanmar
Benin	Maldives	Bénin	Népal
Bhutan	Mali	Bhoutan	Niger
Burkina Faso	Mauritania	Burkina Faso	Ouganda
Burundi	Mozambique	Burundi	République centrafricaine
Cambodia	Myanmar	Cambodge	République démocratique du
Cape Verde	Nepal	Cap-Vert	Congo
Central African Republic	Niger	Comores	République démocratique
Chad	Rwanda	Djibouti	populaire lao
Comoros	Samoa	Erythrée	République-Unie de Tanzanie
Democratic Republic	Sao Tome and Principe	Ethiopie	Rwanda
of the Congo	Senegal	Gambie	Samoa
Djibouti	Sierra Leone	Guinée	Sao Tomé-et-Principe
Equatorial Guinea	Solomon Islands	Guinée équatoriale	Sénégal
Eritrea	Somalia	Guinée-Bissau	Sierra Leone
Ethiopia	Sudan	Haïti	Somalie
Gambia	Timor-Leste	Iles Salomon	Soudan
Guinea	Togo	Kiribati	Tchad
Guinea-Bissau	Tuvalu	Lesotho	Timor-Leste
Haiti	Uganda	Libéria	Togo
Kiribati	United Republic of Tanzania	Madagascar	Tuvalu
Lao People's Democratic	Vanuatu	Malawi	Vanuatu
Republic	Yemen	Maldives	Yémen
Lesotho	Zambia	Mali	Zambie

Mercado Común Sudamericano (MERCOSUR)   *Marché commun sud-américain (Mercosur)*

Argentina	Paraguay	Argentine	Paraguay
Brazil	Uruguay	Brésil	Uruguay

North American Free Trade Agreement (NAFTA)   *Accord de libre-échange nord-américain (ALENA)*

Canada	United States of America	Canada	Mexique
Mexico		Etats-Unis d'Amérique	

Organisation for Economic Cooperation   *Organisation de coopération et de développement*
and Development (OECD)   *économiques (OCDE)*

Australia	Luxembourg	Allemagne	Japon
Austria	Mexico	Australie	Luxembourg
Belgium	Netherlands	Autriche	Mexique
Canada	New Zealand	Belgique	Norvège
Czech Republic	Norway	Canada	Nouvelle-Zélande
Denmark	Poland	Danemark	Pays-Bas
Finland	Portugal	Espagne	Pologne
France	Republic of Korea	Etats-Unis d'Amérique	Portugal

Germany	Slovakia
Greece	Spain
Hungary	Sweden
Iceland	Switzerland
Ireland	Turkey
Italy	United Kingdom
Japan	United States of America

Organization of Petroleum Exporting Countries (OPEC)

Algeria	Nigeria
Indonesia	Qatar
Iran (Islamic Republic of)	Saudi Arabia
Iraq	United Arab Emirates
Kuwait	Venezuela (Bolivarian
Libyan Arab Jamahiriya	Republic of)

Southern African Customs Union (SACU)

Botswana	South Africa
Lesotho	Swaziland
Namibia	

Notes

ᵃ The continent of North America comprises Northern America, Caribbean and Central America.

ᵇ As determined by the General Assembly in its resolution 58/112.

Finlande	République de Corée
France	République tchèque
Grèce	Royaume-Uni
Hongrie	Slovaquie
Irlande	Suède
Islande	Suisse
Italie	Turquie

Organisation des pays exportateurs de pétrole (OPEP)

Algérie	Jamahiriya arabe libyenne
Arabie saoudite	Koweït
Emirats arabes unis	Nigéria
Indonésie	Qatar
Iran (République islamique d')	Venezuela (République
Iraq	bolivarienne du)

Union douanière d'Afrique australe

Afrique du Sud	Namibie
Botswana	Swaziland
Lesotho	

Notes

ᵃ Le continent de l'Amérique du Nord comprend l'Amérique septentrionale, les Caraïbes et l'Amérique centrale.

ᵇ Comme déterminé par l'Assemblée générale dans sa résolution 58/112.

Annex II

Annexe II

Conversion coefficients and factors

The metric system of weights and measures is employed in the Statistical Yearbook. In this system, the relationship between units of volume and capacity is: 1 litre = 1 cubic decimetre (dm^3) exactly (as decided by the 12th International Conference of Weights and Measures, New Delhi, November 1964).

Section A shows the equivalents of the basic metric, British imperial and United States units of measurements. According to an agreement between the national standards institutions of English-speaking nations, the British and United States units of length, area and volume are now identical, and based on the yard = 0.9144 metre exactly. The weight measures in both systems are based on the pound = 0.45359237 kilogram exactly (*Weights and Measures Act 1963* (London), and *Federal Register Announcement of 1 July 1959: Refinement of Values for the Yard and Pound* (Washington D.C.)).

Section B shows various derived or conventional conversion coefficients and equivalents.

Section C shows other conversion coefficients or factors which have been utilized in the compilation of certain tables in the Statistical Yearbook. Some of these are only of an approximate character and have been employed solely to obtain a reasonable measure of international comparability in the tables.

For a comprehensive survey of international and national systems of weights and measures and of units weights for a large number of commodities in different countries, see *World Weights and Measures* [61].

Coefficients et facteurs de conversion

L'Annuaire statistique utilise le système métrique pour les poids et mesures. La relation entre unités métriques de volume et de capacité est: 1 litre = 1 décimètre cube (dm^3) exactement (comme fut décidé à la Conférence internationale des poids et mesures, New Delhi, novembre 1964).

La section A fournit les équivalents principaux des systèmes de mesure métrique, britannique et américain. Suivant un accord entre les institutions de normalisation nationales des pays de langue anglaise, les mesures britanniques et américaines de longueur, superficie et volume sont désormais identiques, et sont basées sur le yard = 0:9144 mètre exactement. Les mesures de poids se rapportent, dans les deux systèmes, à la livre (pound) = 0.45359237 kilogramme exactement (*Weights and Measures Act 1963* (Londres), et *Federal Register Announcement of 1 July 1959: Refinement of Values for the Yard and Pound* (Washington, D.C.)).

La section B fournit divers coefficients et facteurs de conversion conventionnels ou dérivés.

La section C fournit d'autres coefficients ou facteurs de conversion utilisés dans l'élaboration de certains tableaux de l'Annuaire statistique. D'aucuns ne sont que des approximations et n'ont été utilisés que pour obtenir un degré raisonnable de comparabilité sur le plan international.

Pour une étude d'ensemble des systèmes internationaux et nationaux de poids et mesures, et d'unités de poids pour un grand nombre de produits dans différents pays, voir *World Weights and Measures* [61].

A. Equivalents of metric, British imperial and United States units of measure

A. Equivalents des unités métriques, britanniques et des Etats-Unis

Metric units / Unités métriques	British imperial and US equivalents / Equivalents en mesures britanniques et des Etats-Unis		British imperial and US units / Unités britanniques et des Etats-Unis	Metric equivalents / Equivalents en mesures métriques	
Length — Longeur					
1 centimetre – centimètre (cm)	0.3937008	inch	1 inch	2.540	cm
1 metre – mètre (m)	3.280840	feet	1 foot	30.480	cm
	1.093613	yard	1 yard	0.9144	m
1 kilometre – kilomètre (km)	0.6213712	mile	1 mile	1609.344	m
	0.5399568	int. naut. mile	1 international nautical mile	1852.000	m
Area — Superficie					
1 square centimetre – (cm^2).	0.1550003	square inch	1 square inch	6.45160	cm^2
1 square metre – (m^2)	10.763910	square feet	1 square foot	9.290304	dm^2
	1.195990	square yards	1 square yard	0.83612736	m^2
1 hectare – (ha)	2.471054	acres	1 acre	0.4046856	ha
1 square kilometre – (km^2)	0.3861022	square mile	1 square mile	2.589988	km^2
Volume					
1 cubic centimetre – (cm^3)	0.06102374	cubic inch	1 cubic inch	16.38706	cm^3
1 cubic metre – (m^3)	35.31467	cubic feet	1 cubic foot	28.316847	dm^3
	1.307951	cubic yards	1 cubic yard	0.76455486	m^3

Metric units Unités métriques	British imperial and US equivalents Equivalents en mesures britanniques et des Etats-Unis		British imperial and US units Unités britanniques et des Etats-Unis	Metric equivalents Equivalents en mesures métriques	
Capacity — Capacité					
1 litre (l)	0.8798766	imp. quart	1 British imperial quart	1.136523	l
	1.056688	U.S. liq. quart	1 U.S. liquid quart	0.9463529	l
	0.908083	U.S. dry quart	1 U.S. dry quart	1.1012208	l
1 hectolitre (hl)	21.99692	imp. gallons	1 imperial gallon	4.546092	l
	26.417200	U.S. gallons	1 U.S. gallon	3.785412	l
	2.749614	imp. bushels	1 imperial bushel	36.368735	l
	2.837760	U.S. bushels	1 U.S. bushel	35.239067	l
Weight or mass — Poids					
1 kilogram (kg)	35.27396	av. ounces	1 av. ounce	28.349523	g
	32.15075	troy ounces	1 troy ounce	31.10348	g
	2.204623	av. pounds	1 av. pound	453.59237	g
			1 cental (100 lb.)	45.359237	kg
			1 hundredweight (112 lb.)	50.802345	kg
1 ton – tonne (t)	1.1023113	short tons	1 short ton (2 000 lb.)	0.9071847	t
	0.9842065	long tons	1 long ton (2 240 lb.)	1.0160469	t

B. Various conventional or derived coefficients

Railway and air transport

- 1 passenger-mile = 1.609344 voyageur (passager) - kilomètre
- 1 short ton-mile = 1.459972 tonne-kilomètre
- 1 long ton-mile = 1.635169 tonne kilomètre

Ship tonnage

- 1 register ton (100 cubic feet) – tonne de jauge = 2.83m³
- 1 British shipping ton (42 cubic feet) = 1.19m³
- 1 U.S. shipping ton (40 cubic feet) = 1.13m³
- 1 deadweight ton (dwt ton = long ton) = 1.016047 metric ton – tonne métrique

Electric energy

- 1 Kilowatt (kW) = 1.34102 British horsepower (hp)
1.35962 cheval vapeur (cv)

C. Other coefficients or conversion factors employed in *Statistical Yearbook* tables

Roundwood

- Equivalent in solid volume without bark

Sugar

- 1 metric ton raw sugar = 0.9 metric ton refined sugar

  For the United States and its possessions:

- 1 metric ton refined sugar = 1.07 metric tons raw sugar

B. Divers coefficients conventionnels ou dérivés

Transport ferroviaire et aérien

- 1 voyageur (passager) - kilomètre = 0.621371)
passenger-mile
- 1 tonne-kilomètre = 0.684945 short ton-mile
0.611558 long ton-mile

Tonnage de navire

- 1 cubic metre – m³ = 0.353 register ton - tonne de jauge
0.841 British shipping ton
0.885 US shipping ton
- 1 metric ton – tonne métrique = 0.984 dwt ton

Energie électrique

- 1 British horsepower (hp) = 0.7457 kW
- 1 cheval vapeur (cv) = 0.735499 kW

C. Autres coefficients ou facteurs de conversion utilisés dans les tableaux de l'*Annuaire statistique*

Bois rond

- Equivalences en volume solide sans écorce

Sucre

- 1 tonne métrique de sucre brut = 0.9 tonne métrique de sucre raffiné

  Pour les Etats-Unis et leurs possessions:

- 1 tonne métrique de sucre raffiné = 1.07 t.m. de sucre brut

Annex III

Annexe III

Tables added and omitted

A. *Tables added*

The present issue of the *Statistical Yearbook* includes the following two tables which were not presented in the previous issue:

- Table 12: Selected indicators of life expectancy, childbearing and mortality;

- Table 62: Ozone-depleting chlorofluorocarbons.

B. The following tables which were presented in previous issues are not presented in the present issue. They will be updated in future issues of the Yearbook when new data become available:

- Table 9: Population in urban and rural areas, rates of growth and largest urban agglomeration population (49th issue);

- Table 13: Book production: number of titles by the Universal Decimal Classification (47th issue);

- Table 14: Non-daily newspapers and periodicals (49th issue);

- Table 15: Cinemas: number, seating capacity and annual attendance (48th issue);

- Table 17: Television and radio receivers in use (46th issue);

- Table 28: Employment by industry (48th issue);

- Table 34: Livestock (49th issue);

- Table 37: Fertilizers (production and consumption) (49th issue);

- Table 65: Water supply and sanitation coverage (49th issue);

- Table 66: Threatened species (49th issue);

- Table 69: Patents (49th issue).

C. The following tables have been discontinued:

- Table 10: Illiterate population by sex (47th issue);

- Table 11: HIV/AIDS epidemic (47th issue).

Tableaux ajoutés et supprimés

A. *Tableaux ajoutés*

Dans ce numéro de l'*Annuaire statistique*, les deux tableaux suivants qui n'ont pas été présentés dans le numéro antérieur, ont été ajoutés :

- Tableau 12 : Choix d'indicateurs de l'espérance de vie, de la maternité et de la mortalité;

- Tableau 62 : Chlorofluorocarbones qui appauvrissent la couche d'ozone.

B. Les tableaux suivants qui ont été repris dans les éditions antérieures n'ont pas été repris dans la présente édition. Ils seront actualisés dans les futures livraisons de l'Annuaire à mesure que des données nouvelles deviendront disponibles :

- Tableau 9 : Population urbaine, population rurale, taux d'accroissement et population de l'agglomération urbaine la plus peuplée (49ème édition);

- Tableau 13 : Production de livres : nombre de titres classés d'après la Classification Décimale Universelle (47ème édition);

- Tableau 14 : Journaux non quotidiens et périodiques (49ème édition);

- Tableau 15 : Cinémas : nombre d'établissements, nombre de sièges et fréquentation annuelle (48ème édition);

- Tableau 17 : Récepteurs de télévision et de radiodiffusion sonore en circulation (46ème édition);

- Tableau 28 : Emploi par industrie (48ème édition);

- Tableau 34 : Cheptel (49ème édition);

- Tableau 37 : Engrais (production et consommation) (49ème édition);

- Tableau 65 : Accès à l'eau et à l'assainissement (49ème édition);

- Tableau 66 : Espèces menacées (49ème édition);

- Tableau 69 : Brevets (49ème édition).

C. Les tableaux suivants ont été discontinués :

- Tableau 10 : Population analphabète, selon le sexe (47ème édition);

- Tableau 11 : L'épidémie de VIH/SIDA (47ème édition).

Statistical sources and references

Sources statistiques et références

A. Statistical sources

1. American Automobile Manufacturers Association, *Motor Vehicle Facts and Figures* (Detroit, USA).
2. Carbon Dioxide Information Analysis Center, *Global, Regional, and National CO² Emissions Estimates from Fossil-Fuel Burning, Hydraulic Cement Production, and Gas Flaring* (Oak Ridge, Tennessee, USA); web site http://cdiac.esd.ornl.gov.
3. Food and Agriculture Organization of the United Nations, *FAO Fertilizer Yearbook* (Rome); web site http://faostat.fao.org.
4. _____, *FAO Food balance sheets* (Rome).
5. _____, *FAO Production Yearbook* (Rome).
6. _____, *FAO Yearbook of Fishery Statistics, Aquaculture production* (Rome).
7. _____, *FAO Yearbook of Fishery Statistics, Capture production* (Rome).
8. _____, *FAO Yearbook of Forest Products* (Rome).
9. _____, *Global Forest Resources Assessment 2005* (Rome); web site www.fao.org/forestry/fra2005.
10. International Civil Aviation Organization (Montreal); web site www.icao.int.
11. International Labour Office, *Yearbook of Labour Statistics* (Geneva); web site http://laborsta.ilo.org.
12. International Monetary Fund, *Balance of Payments Statistics Yearbook* (Washington, D.C.); web site www.imf.org.
13. _____, *International Financial Statistics* (Washington, D.C.).
14. International Sugar Organization, *Sugar Yearbook* (London).
15. International Telecommunication Union, *World Telecommunication Development Report* (Geneva); web site www.itu.int.
16. _____, *Yearbook of Statistics, Telecommunication Services, Chronological Time Series* (Geneva).
17. Lloyd's Register of Shipping, *World Fleet Statistics* (London); web site www.lrfairplay.com.
18. Motor and Equipment Manufacturers Association, *World Automotive Market Report* (Research Triangle Park, North Carolina, USA); web site www.mema.org.
19. Organisation for Economic Co-operation and Development, *Development Co-operation Report* (Paris); web site www.oecd.org.
20. _____, *Geographical Distribution of Financial Flows to Aid Recipients* (Paris).

A. Sources statistiques

1. American Automobile Manufacturers Association, *Motor Vehicle Facts and Figures* (Detroit, USA).
2. "Carbon Dioxide Information Analysis Center, *Global, Regional, and National CO² Emissions Estimates from Fossil-Fuel Burning, Hydraulic Cement Production, and Gas Flaring* (Oak Ridge, Tennessee, USA); site Web http://cdiac.esd.ornl.gov.
3. Organisation des Nations Unies pour l'alimen-tation et l'agriculture, *Annuaire FAO des engrais* (Rome); site Web http://faostat.fao.org.
4. _____, *Bilans alimentaires de la FAO* (Rome).
5. _____, *Annuaire FAO de la production* (Rome).
6. _____, *Annuaire statistique des pêches, production de l'aquaculture* (Rome).
7. _____, *Annuaire statistique des pêches, captures* (Rome).
8. _____, *Annuaire FAO des produits forestiers* (Rome); site Web www.fao.org/forestry/fra2005.
9. _____, *Evaluation des ressources forestières mondiales 2005* (Rome); site Web www.fao.org/forestry/fra2005.
10. Organisation de l'aviation civile internationale (Montreal); site Web www.icao.int.
11. Bureau international du Travail, *Annuaire des statistiques du Travail* (Genève); site Web http://laborsta.ilo.org.
12. Fonds monétaire international, *Balance of Payments Statistics Yearbook* (Washington, D.C.); site Web www.imf.org.
13. _____, *Statistiques financières internationales*, (Washington, D.C.).
14. Organisation internationale du sucre, *Annuaire du sucre* (Londres).
15. Union internationale des télécommunications, *World Telecommunication Development Report* (Genève); site Web www.itu.int.
16. _____, *Yearbook of Statistics, Telecommunication Services, Chronological Time Series* (Genève).
17. Lloyd's Register of Shipping, *World Fleet Statistics* (Londres); site Web www.lrfairplay.com.
18. Motor and Equipment Manufacturers Association, *World Automotive Market Report* (Research Triangle Park, North Carolina, USA); site Web http://www.mema.org.
19. Organisation de Coopération et de Développement Economiques, *Coopération pour le développement, Rapport* (Paris); site Web www.oecd.org.
20. _____, *Répartition géographique des ressources financières allouées aux pays bénéficiaires de l'aide,* (Paris).

21. United Nations, *Demographic Yearbook 2003* (United Nations publication, Sales No. E/F.06.XIII.1).

22. _____, *Energy Statistics Yearbook 2003* (United Nations publication, Sales No. E/F.06.XVII.2).

23. _____, *Industrial Commodity Statistics Yearbook 2003* (United Nations publications, Sales No. E/F. 05.XVII.9).

24. _____, *International Trade Statistics Yearbook 2004*, vols. I and II (United Nations publication, Sales No. E/F.06.XVII.4).

25. _____, *Monthly Bulletin of Statistics*, various issues up to January 2006 (United Nations publication, Series Q).

26. _____, *National Accounts Statistics: Main Aggregates and Detailed Tables, 2004* (United Nations publication, Sales No. E.05.XVII.8)

27. _____, *Operational activities of the United Nations for international development cooperation: Report of the Secretary-General, Comprehensive statistical data on operational activities for development for 2003* (A/59/386, A/60/74 - E/2005/57) and *Operational activities ... for* 2004 (A/61/77-E/2006/59).

28. _____, *World Population Prospects: The 2004 Revision* (United Nations publication, Sales No. E.05/XIII.6.

29. _____, *World Urbanization Prospects: The 2003 Revision, Data Tables and Highlights* (E.04.XIII.6.).

30. United Nations Educational, Scientific and Cultural Organization Institute for Statistics (Montreal); web site www.uis.unesco.org.

31. United Nations Environment Programme, World Conservation Monitoring Centre, *United Nations List of Protected Areas* (Nairobi); web site www.unep-wcmc.org.

32. World Bank, *Global Development Finance*, vols. I and II, (Washington, D.C.); web site www.worldbank.org.

33. World Conservation Union (IUCN) / Species Survival Commission (SSC), Gland, Switzerland and Cambridge, United Kingdom, "IUCN Red List of Threatened Species", 2002 and 2004; web site www.redlist.org.

34. World Health Organization, the United Nations Children's Fund and the United Nations Population Fund, "Maternal Mortality in 2000: Estimates developed by WHO, UNICEF, UNFPA".

35. World Intellectual Property Organization, *Industrial Property Statistics, Publication A* (Geneva); web site www.wipo.int/ipstats.

36. World Tourism Organization, *Compendium of Tourism Statistics, 2006 edition* (Madrid); web site www.world-tourism.org.

21. Nations Unies, *Annuaire démographique 2003* (publication des Nations Unies, No de vente E/F.06.XIII.1).

22. _____, *Annuaire des statistiques de l'énergie 2003* (publication des Nations Unies, No de vente E/F.05. XVII.2).

23. _____, *Annuaire des statistiques industrielles par produit 2003* (publications des Nations Unies, No de vente E/F.05.XVII.9).

24. _____, *Annuaire statistique du commerce international 2004*, Vols. I et II (publication des Nations Unies, No de vente E/F. 06.XVII.4).

25. _____, *Bulletin mensuel de statistique*, différentes éditions, jusqu'à janvier 2006 (publication des Nations Unies, Série Q).

26. _____, *National Accounts Statistics: Main Aggregates and Detailed Tables, 2004* (publication des Nations Unies, No de vente E.05.XVII.8.

27. _____, *Activités opérationnelles du système des Nations Unies au service de la coopération internationale pour le développement, Rapport du Secrétaire général, Additif, Données statistiques globales sur les activités opérationnelles au service du développement pour 2003* (A/59/386, A/60/74-E/2005/57) et *Activités ... pour 2004* (A/61/77-E/2006/59).

28. _____, *World Population Prospects: The 2004 Revision* (No de vente E.05/XIII.6.

29. _____, *World Urbanization Prospects: The 2003 Revision, Data Tables and Highlights* (E.04.XIII.6.).

30. Institut de statistique de l'Organisation des Nations Unies pour l'éducation, la science et la culture (Montreal); site Web www.uis.unesco.org.

31. Centre mondial de surveillance pour la conservation, "United Nations List of Protected Areas" (Nairobi); site Web www.unep-wcmc.org.

32. Banque mondiale, *Global Development Finance*, Vols. I et II, (Washington, D.C.).

33. Union mondiale pour la nature (UICN) / Commission de la sauvegarde des espèces, Gland, Suisse, et Cambridge, Royaume-Uni, "La liste rouge des espèces menacées de l'UICN", 2002 et 2004; site Web www. redlist.org.

34. Organisation mondiale de la santé, Fonds des Nations Unies pour l'enfance et Fonds des Nations Unies pour la population, "Maternal Mortality in 2000 : Estimates developed by WHO, UNICEF, UNFPA".

35. Organisation mondiale de la propriété intellectuelle, *Statistiques de propriété industrielle, Publication A* (Genève); site Web www.wipo.int/ipstats.

36. Organisation mondiale du tourisme, *Compendium des statistiques du tourisme, 2006* (Madrid); site Web www. world-tourism.org.

B. References

37. Food and Agriculture Organization of the United Nations, *The Fifth World Food Survey 1985* (Rome 1985.

38. International Labour Office, *International Standard Classification of Occupations, Revised Edition 1968* (Geneva, 1969); revised edition, 1988, *ISCO-88* (Geneva, 1990).

39. International Monetary Fund, *Balance of Payments Manual, Fifth Edition* (Washington, D.C., 1993).

40. United Nations, *Basic Methodological Principles Governing the Compilation of the System of Statistical Balances of the National Economy*, Studies in Methods, Series F, No. 17, Rev. 1, vols. 1 and 2 (United Nations publications, Sales No. E.89.XVII.5 and E.89.XVII.3).

41. _____, *Classifications of Expenditure According to Purpose: Classification of the Functions of Government (COFOG), Classification of Individual Consumption According to Purpose (COICOP), Classification of the Purposes of Non-Profit Institutions Serving Households (COPNI), Classification of the Outlays of Producers According to Purpose (COPP)*, Series M, No. 84 (United Nations publication, Sales No. E.00.XVII.6).

42. _____, *Energy Statistics: Definitions, Units of Measure and Conversion Factors*, Series F, No. 44 (United Nations publication, Sales No. E.86.XVII.21).

43. _____, *Energy Statistics: Manual for Developing Countries*, Series F, No. 56 (United Nations publication, Sales No. E.91.XVII.10).

44. _____, *Handbook of Vital Statistics Systems and Methods*, vol. I, *Legal, Organization and Technical Aspects*, Series F, No. 35, vol. I (United Nations publication, Sales No. E.91.XVII.5).

45. _____, *Handbook on Social Indicators*, Studies in Methods, Series F, No. 49 (United Nations publication, Sales No. E.89.XVII.6).

46. _____, *International Recommendations for Industrial Statistics*, Series M, No. 48, Rev. 1 (United Nations publication, Sales No. E.83.XVII.8).

47. _____, *International Standard Industrial Classification of All Economic Activities*, Statistical Papers, Series M, No. 4, Rev. 2 (United Nations publication, Sales No. E.68.XVII.8); Rev. 3 (United Nations publication, Sales No. E.90.XVII.11).

48. _____, *International Trade Statistics: Concepts and Definitions*, Series M, No. 52, Rev. 1 (United Nations publication, Sales No. E.82.XVII.14).

49. _____, *Methods Used in Compiling the United Nations Price Indexes for External Trade*, volume 1, Statistical Papers, Series M, No. 82 (United Nations Publication, Sales No. E.87.XVII.4).

B. Références

37. Organisation des Nations Unies pour l'alimentation et l'agriculture, *Cinquième enquête mondiale sur l'alimentation 1985* (Rome, 1985).

38. Organisation internationale du Travail, *Classification internationale type des professions, édition révisée* 1968 (Genève, 1969); édition révisée 1988, *CITP-88* (Genève, 1990).

39. Fonds monétaire international, *Manuel de la balance des paiements, cinquième édition* (Washington, D.C., 1993).

40. Organisation des Nations Unies, *Principes méthodologiques de base régissant l'établissement des balances statistiques de l'économie nationale*, Série F, No 17, Rev.1 Vol. 1 et Vol. 2 (publication des Nations Unies, No de vente F.89.XVII.5 et F.89.XVII.3).

41. _____, *Classifications of Expenditure According to Purpose: Classification of the Functions of Government (COFOG), Classification of Individual Consumption According to Purpose (COICOP), Classification of the Purposes of Non-Profit Institutions Serving Households (COPNI), Classification of the Outlays of Producers According to Purpose (COPP)*, Série M, No 84 (publication des Nations Unies, No de vente E. 00.XVII.6).

42. _____, *Statistiques de l'énergie: définitions, unités de mesures et facteurs de conversion*, Série F, No 44 (publication des Nations Unies, No de vente F.86.XVII.21).

43. _____, *Statistiques de l'énergie: Manuel pour les pays en développement*, Série F, No 56 (publication des Nations Unies, No de vente F.91.XVII.10).

44. _____, *Handbook of Vital Statistics System and Methods*, Vol. 1, *Legal, Organization and Technical Aspects*, Série F, No 35, Vol. 1 (publication des Nations Unies, No de vente E.91.XVII.5).

45. _____, *Manuel des indicateurs sociaux*, Série F, No 49 (publication des Nations Unies, No de vente F.89. XVII.6).

46. _____, *Recommandations internationales concernant les statistiques industrielles*, Série M, No 48, Rev. 1 (publication des Nations Unies, No de vente F.83. XVII.8).

47. _____, *Classification internationale type, par industrie, de toutes les branches d'activité économique*, Série M, No 4, Rev. 2 (publication des Nations Unies, No de vente F.68.XVII.8); Rev. 3 (publication des Nations Unies, No de vente F.90.XVII.11).

48. _____, *Statistiques du commerce international: Concepts et définitions*, Série M, No 52, Rev. 1 (publication des Nations Unies, No de vente F.82. XVII.14).

50. _____, *Principles and Recommendations for Population and Housing Censuses*, Statistical Papers, Series M, No. 67 (United Nations publication, Sales No. E.80.XVII.8).

51. _____, *Provisional Guidelines on Statistics of International Tourism*, Statistical Papers, Series M, No. 62 (United Nations publication, Sales No. E.78. XVII.6).

52. _____ and World Tourism Organization, *Recommendations on Tourism Statistics*, Statistical Papers, Series M, No. 83 (United Nations publication, Sales No. E.94.XVII.6).

53. _____, *Standard International Trade Classification, Revision 3*, Statistical Papers, Series M, No. 34, Rev. 3 (United Nations publication, Sales No. E.86.XVII.12), *Revision 2*, Series M, No. 34, Rev. 2 (United Nations publication), *Revision*, Series M, No. 34, Revision (United Nations publication, Sales No. E.61.XVII.6).

54. _____, *Supplement to the Statistical Yearbook and the Monthly Bulletin of Statistics, 1977*, Series S and Series Q, Supplement 2 (United Nations publication, Sales No. E.78.XVII.10).

55. _____, *System of National Accounts, Studies in Methods*, Series F, No. 2, Rev. 3 (United Nations publication, Sales No. E.69.XVII.3).

56. _____, *System of National Accounts 1993*, Studies in Methods, Series F, No. 2, Rev. 4 (United Nations publication, Sales No. E.94.XVII.4).

57. _____, *Towards a System of Social and Demographic Statistics, Studies in Methods*, Series F, No. 18 (United Nations publication, Sales No. E.74.XVII.8).

58. _____, *World Weights and Measures* (United Nations publication, Sales No. E.66.XVII.3).

59. World Health Organization, *Manual of the International Statistical Classification of Diseases, Injuries and Causes of Death*, vol. 1 (Geneva, 1977).

49. _____, *Méthodes utilisées par les Nations Unies pour établir les indices des prix des produits de base entrant dans le commerce international*, Série M, No 82, Vol. 1 (publication des Nations Unies, No de vente F.87. XVII.4).

50. _____, *Principes et recommandations concernant les recensements de la population et de l'habitation*, Série M, No 67 (publication des Nations Unies, No de vente F.80.XVII.8).

51. _____, *Directives provisoires pour l'établissement des statistiques du tourisme international*, Série M, No 62 (publication des Nations Unies, No de vente 78.XVII.6).

52. _____ et l'Organisation mondiale du tourisme, *Recommendations on Tourism Statistics*, Statistical Papers, Série M, No. 83 (publication des Nations Unies, No. de vente E.94.XVII.6).

53. _____, *Classification type pour le commerce international (troisième version révisée)*, Série M, No 34, Rev. 3 (publication des Nations Unies, No de vente F.86.XVII.12), *Révision 2*, Série M, No 34, Rev. 2 (publication des Nations Unies), *Révision*, Série M, No. 34, Révision (publication des Nations Unies, No de vente F.61.XVII.6).

54. _____, *Supplément à l'Annuaire statistique et au bulletin mensuel de statistique, 1977*, Série S et Série Q, supplément 2 (publication des Nations Unies, No de vente F.78.XVII.10).

55. _____, *Système de comptabilité nationale*, Série F, No 2, Rev. 3 (publication des Nations Unies, No de vente F.69.XVII.3).

56. _____, *Système de comptabilité nationale 1993*, Série F, No 2, Rev. 4 (publication des Nations Unies, No de vente F.94.XVII.4).

57. _____, *Vers un système de statistiques démographiques et sociales, Etudes méthodologiques*, Série F, No 18 (publication des Nations Unies, No. de vente F.74. XVII.8).

58. _____, *World Weights and Measures* (publication des Nations Unies, No. de vente E.66.XVII.3).

59. Organisation mondiale de la santé, *Manuel de la classification statistique internationale des maladies, traumatismes et causes de décès*, Vol. 1 (Genève, 1977).

Index

Note: References to tables are indicated by **boldface** type. For citations or organizations, see Index of Organizations.

communication industry. *See* transportation, storage and communication industries

communications, **99–133**. *See also* transportation and communications

Compendium of Tourism Statistics (UNWTO), 673, 698, 699, 700

compensation of employees to and from the rest of the world, as percentage of GDP, **181–193**

construction industry, value added by, **168–180**

consumer prices, **301–312**
    indexes of, **301–312**, 314

consumption. *See* government final consumption; household final consumption

conversion factors, currency, 154, 235–236

conversion tables
    for selected commodities, **802**
    for units of measure and weight, **801–802**

cotton fabrics
    defined, 450
    production, **392–396**

countries and areas
    boundaries and legal status of, not implied by this publication, ii
    coverage of, in *Statistical Yearbook*, 6
    economic and regional associations, **796–799**
    recent name changes, ix, **791–792**
    regional groupings for statistical purposes, **792–796**
    statistics reported for, 6, 642, 643
    surface area, **37–49**
    See also developed countries or areas; developing countries or areas

croplands, permanent, as percentage of total land area, **565–574**

crops
    production, **15**
    See also agricultural production

crude oil. *See* petroleum, crude

cultural indicators, **99–133**
    sources of information, 133

currency
    conversion factors, 154, 235–236
    exchange rates, 610, **737–752**
    method of calculating series, 154, 235–236, 643, 644

current transfers
    in balance of payments, **701–734**
    defined, 735

customs areas, 642

D

death, rate of, **18–19**, **86–95**

defence, national, expenditures, as percentage of government final consumption, 199

Demographic Yearbook (UN), 46, 50, 92

developed countries or areas
    defined, ii
    development assistance from, **781**

developing countries or areas
    development assistance to, **781**
    external debt of, **753–760**

development assistance, **765–790**
    bilateral and multilateral, to individuals, **765–780**
    to developing countries and multilateral organizations, **781**
    United Nations system, **782–789**, 790

Development Assistance Committee (DAC) countries, development assistance from, **781**

Development Cooperation Report (OECD), 781

discount rates, **239-244**
    defined, 255

domestic production, prices, **294–300**

domestic supply, prices, **294–300**

drilling and boring machines
    defined, 452
    production, 16, **441–445**

E

earnings. *See* wages

economic activity (industry), value added by kind of, **168–180**, 236

economic affairs, expenditures, as percentage of government final consumption, 199

economic associations, country lists, **796–799**

economic relations, international. *See* international economic relations

economic statistics, **135–610**

education
    definition of terms, 76
    expenditures, as percentage of government final consumption, 199
    expenditures, as percentage of household consumption, 205
    levels of, primary, secondary and tertiary, number of students, **51–69**
    method of calculating series, 77
    public expenditures on, **70–75**
    sources of information, 76–77
    See also recreation, education and entertainment

education sector, research and development expenditures by, **601–607**

electrical products. *See* office and related electrical products

electricity
    consumption, **28–29**, **518–546**
    defined, 564
    production, 16, **28–29**, **518–546**, **547–561**

electricity, gas, water utilities
    production, **22–27**, **206–234**
    value added by, **168–180**

national income, as percentage of GDP, **181–193**

natural gas
 defined, 564
 production, **15**, **22–27**, **547–561**

natural gas liquids (NGL)
 defined, 563
 production, **547–561**

net current transfers to and from the rest of the world, as percentage of GDP, **181–193**

net errors and omissions in balance of payments, **701–734**
 defined, 736

newspapers
 daily, numbers and circulation, **99–104**
 types of, defined, 133

nutrition. *See* food; health and nutrition

O

office and related electrical products, **22–27**

oil crops
 defined, 352–353
 production, **15**, **330–336**

oil tankers, tonnage registered, **482–491**

Operational activities of the United Nations for international development cooperation … (UN), 789, 790

ore and bulk carriers, tonnage registered, **482–491**

"other" economic activities, value added by, **168–180**

ozone-depleting chlorofluorocarbons (CFC), consumption, **583–589**

P

paper, printing, publishing, recorded media industries, production, **22–27**

paper and paperboard
 defined, 451
 production, **407–411**

passenger traffic
 air, **500–515**
 rail, **455–464**

peat
 defined, 562
 production, **547–561**

petroleum, crude
 defined, 562
 production, **15**, **22–27**, **547–561**

petroleum products
 defined, 562
 production, **547–561**

pig iron
 defined, 451
 production, **16**, **422–427**

population, **37–50**
 definition of terms, 32
 density, **18–19**, **37–49**

method of calculating series, 32
numbers, **15**, **18–19**, **37–49**
rate of increase, **18–19**, **37–49**
by sex, **37–49**
sources of information, 32

pork, production, **365–381**

power. *See* housing and utilities

prices
 consumer, **294–300**, **301–312**
 indexes of, **17**, **301–312**, 313
 method of calculating series, 313–314
 producer and wholesale, **294–300**
 types of, defined, 313

primary commodities (raw materials)
 price indexes, **17**
 prices, **294–300**

primary income, 237

printing industry. *See* paper, printing, publishing, recorded media industries

private consumption. *See* household final consumption

producer prices, **294–300**
 defined, 313
 indexes of, **206–234**

production, sources of information, 32

property income to and from the rest of the world
 in balance of payments, **701–734**
 defined, 735
 as percentage of GDP, **181–193**

protected lands
 categories of, 590
 as percentage of total land area, **565–574**

public order and safety, expenditures, as percentage of government final consumption, 199

public services, expenditures, as percentage of government final consumption, 199

publishing industry. *See* paper, printing, publishing, recorded media industries

purchasing power of exports, **629–635**, 644

Q

quarrying. *See* mining and quarrying

R

radio receivers, production, **431–433**

railway traffic
 definition of terms, 516
 passengers and freight carried, **455–464**

rates
 discount, **239–244**
 money market, **245–257**
 treasury bills, **245–257**

raw materials. *See* primary commodities

Index of Organizations

Carbon Dioxide Information Analysis Center (CDIAC) (Oak Ridge National Laboratory, USA), 582, 590

Development Assistance Committee (DAC) (OECD), 790

Food and Agriculture Organization of the United Nations (FAO), 17, 20, 21, 85, 96, 352, 590
    FAOSTAT data, 322, 329, 336, 342, 381, 406, 411, 574
    FISHSTAT database, 351

International Civil Aviation Organization (ICAO), 515, 517
International Labour Office (ILO), 280–281, 313
    labour statistics database, 277, 290, 311
International Monetary Fund (IMF), 17, 154, 235, 244, 644, 700, 735, 761
    database, 255, 734, 751
International Sugar Organization (ISO), 364
International Telecommunications Union (ITU), 113, 122, 131

Latin American Iron and Steel Institute, 451
Lloyd's Register of Shipping, 516

Organisation for Economic Cooperation and Development (OECD), 790
    DAC database, 780, 781

Statistics Division, UN. *See* United Nations Statistics Division

United Nations, development assistance programs, **782–789**, 790
United Nations Development Programme (UNDP), 790
United Nations Economic and Social Affairs Department, iii
United Nations Economic Commission for Europe (ECE), 451
United Nations Educational, Scientific, and Cultural Organization (UNESCO), Institute for Statistics, 69, 75, 76, 104, 133, 600, 606, 608, 609
United Nations Environment Programme (UNEP), 574, 590
    Ozone Secretariat, 589, 591
United Nations Framework Convention on Climate Change (UNFCCC), 582, 591

United Nations Population Division, 32, 96
United Nations Secretary General, 790
United Nations Statistics Division, 1, 235, 642, 644, 780
    Common Database (UNCDB), 8, 10
    demographic statistics database, 19, 46
    energy statistics database, 28, 546, 561
    how to contact, iv
    industrial statistics database, 27, 234, 386, 391, 396, 400, 417, 421, 427, 430, 433, 435, 438, 440, 445, 449
    national accounts database, 154, 166, 179, 193, 199, 205
    price statistics database, 300
    publications and databases of, 7–8
    staff, iv
    trade statistics database, 31, 627, 635, 641
    transport statistics database, 463, 479, 499
United Nations World Tourism Organization. *See* World Tourism Organization
United States of America, Bureau of Mines, 451, 591

World Bank, 761
World Conservation Monitoring Centre (WCMC), 590
    Protected Areas database, 574
World Conservation Union (IUCN), 590
World Tourism Organization (UNWTO), 698, 699, 700
    UNWTO statistics database, 673, 685, 698

Litho in United Nations, New York
05-63176—October 2006—4,460
ISBN 92-1-061220-5
ISSN 0082-8459

United Nations publication
Sales No. E/F.06.XVII.1
ST/ESA/STAT/SER.S/26